ISBN 978-0-282-98400-7
PIBN 10875685

FB &c Ltd, Dalton House, 60 Windsor Avenue, London, SW19 2RR.
Company number 08720141. Registered in England and Wales.

For support please visit www.forgottenbooks.com

OFFICIAL ROSTER

OF THE

SOLDIERS OF THE STATE OF OHIO

IN THE

WAR OF THE REBELLION,

1861–1866.

VOL. IX.

141st–184th Regiments—Infantry.

Compiled under Direction of the Roster Commission:

JOSEPH B. FORAKER, Governor, JAMES S. ROBINSON, Sec'y of State,
H. A. AXLINE, Adjutant-General.

Published by Authority of the General Assembly.

CINCINNATI.
The Ohio Valley Press.
1889.

OFFICIAL ROSTER

OF THE

SOLDIERS OF THE STATE OF OHIO

IN THE

WAR OF THE REBELLION,

1861–1866.

VOL. IX.

141st–184th Regiments—Infantry.

Compiled under Direction of the Roster Commission:

JOSEPH B. FORAKER, Governor, JAMES S. ROBINSON, Sec'y of State,
H. A. AXLINE, Adjutant-General.

PUBLISHED BY AUTHORITY OF THE GENERAL ASSEMBLY.

CINCINNATI.
The Ohio Valley Press.
1889.

OFFICIAL ROSTER

OF THE

SOLDIERS OF THE STATE OF OHIO

IN THE

WAR OF THE REBELLION,

1861—1866.

VOL. IX.

141st–184th Regiments—Infantry.

Compiled under Direction of the Roster Commission:

JOSEPH B. FORAKER, Governor, JAMES S. ROBINSON, Sec'y of State,
H. A. AXLINE, Adjutant-General.

Published by Authority of the General Assembly.

CINCINNATI.
The Ohio Valley Press.
1889.

Great care has been exercised to avoid errors in the preparation of this work, but should any be discovered, it is earnestly requested that information concerning them be promptly given to the Adjutant-General, that they may be corrected in the "Errata," which will appear in the last volume to be issued—to be known as "Volume I."

The Legislature, at its last session, passed on February 20, 1888, the following law (H. B. No. 67), to amend section two of an act entitled an act to provide for the publication and distribution of the Roster of Ohio Soldiers, passed May 12, 1886, and amended February 3, 1887, which reads as follows:

SECTION 1. *Be it enacted by the General Assembly of the State of Ohio,* That section two of the above-mentioned act be so amended as to read as follows:

SEC. 2. The distribution of said volumes shall be under the direction of the Adjutant-General, and shall be as follows:

To each Member of the Sixty-Seventh General Assembly, twenty copies of each volume, inclusive of copies already received, and each Member of the Sixty-Eighth General Assembly, twenty copies of each volume; but when any Member of the Sixty-Seventh General Assembly becomes a non-resident of the county, or district he represented, the said copies of each volume may be drawn by his successors.

To the Roster Commission, twenty-five copies of each volume.

To the Adjutant-General, for distribution to the Adjutant-General of each State and Territory, and proper officials of the War Department at Washington D. C., sixty copies of each volume.

To each of the State officers of Ohio, and to each of the various State departments and institutions, one copy of each volume.

To the State Library, fifty copies of each volume for exchanges, and ten copies of each volume to be retained permanently therein.

To each public library of an incorporated city or village of the State, one copy of each volume.

To each post of the Grand Army of the Republic, and to each command of the Union Veterans' Union, on condition that if the post, camp or command be disbanded at any time, the same shall be returned to the State Library, one copy of each volume; and to the Department of Ohio Grand Army of the Republic, and Loyal Legions, each one copy of each volume; and to each camp of the Sons of Veterans, on condition that if the camp be disbanded at any time, the same shall be returned to the State Library, one copy of each volume.

To each County Recorder, to be by him kept in his office and transferred to his successor as other public records, one copy of each volume.

To each Township Clerk, to be by him kept in his office and to be transferred to his successor, one copy of each volume.

To each Clerk in the Roster Department, one copy of each volume; *provided,* that any distribution herein provided for shall be inclusive of copies of volumes already distributed under former laws.

The remainder of said copies, after such distribution, shall be placed on sale by the Adjutant-General, at a price not exceeding one dollar per volume. He shall keep a record of such sales, and shall, at the end of each quarter of the fiscal year, pay into the State treasury the sum received, until all of said volumes are sold, unless otherwise directed by the General Assembly; *provided,* that he shall not sell more than one copy of each of said volumes to the same person.

SEC. 2. That section two of said act, passed May 12, 1886 (83 v. 146), as amended February 3, 1887, is hereby repealed.

SEC. 3. This act shall take effect and be in force from and after its passage.

Under provisions of law the Commissioners of Public Printing, together with the Adjutant-General, awarded the contract on May 25, 1888, for furnishing four volumes, 10,000 copies each, to the Ohio Valley Press, Cincinnati, O., at 84½ cents per volume. Much credit is due this company for the handsome manner in which the work has been executed, both in printing and binding.

J. B. FORAKER,
H. A. AXLINE,
J. S. ROBINSON,
Roster Commission.

ERRATA.

(RECEIVED FROM WAR DEPARTMENT SINCE PRINTING THIS VOLUME.)

Page 127. Remarks opposite name Hoback, John, should read Mustered out Oct. 18, 1864, at Cincinnati, O., to date Aug. 30, 1864.

Page 134. Donohoe, Alfred S., should read Donohoe, Alfred L.

Page 137. Harmell, Milton J., should read Hormell, Milton J.

Page 151. Wilson, Solan N., should read Wilson, Solon N.

Page 265. William E. Atwell, 1st Lieutenant, age 23, should read William Nevitt, age —.

Page 266. Kerte, Henry L., should read Korte, Henry L.

Page 322. Shafer, Benjamin, should read Shaffer, Benjamin; remarks opposite his name should read Mustered out with company Sept. 10, 1864.

Page 558. Sharen, David S., should read Sharer, David S.

Page 565. Wilder B. Dow, 2d Lieutenant, should read Promoted from Corporal Battery C, 1st Regiment O. L. A.; mustered out with company June 24, 1865.

Page 574. The following named unassigned recruits are found in Co. H, 179th O. V. I.: Bilsler, Joseph; Burkhalter, John; Green, Andrew J.; Green, James M.; Heudensfield, John; Houdensfield, Jacob; Martz, Jacob.

Page 632. Huffman, Elias, should read Mustered out June 16, 1865, at Wheeling, W. Va., by order of War Department.

ROSTER OF OHIO SOLDIERS.

WAR OF THE REBELLION.

141ST-184TH REGIMENTS--INFANTRY.

VOL. IX.

141st Regiment Ohio Volunteer Infantry.

ONE HUNDRED DAYS' SERVICE.

THIS Regiment was organized at Gallipolis, O., from the 11th to the 14th of May, 1864, to serve one hundred days. It was composed of the Thirty-sixth Battalion, Ohio National Guard, from Athens County; Sixteenth Battalion, Ohio National Guard, from Gallia County; a part of the Eighty-fourth Battalion, Ohio National Guard, from Adams County; and a part of the Twentieth Battalion, Ohio National Guard, from Scioto County. On the 21st of May the Regiment was ordered to report at Charleston, W. Va., to relieve the Thirteenth West Virginia Infantry. The One Hundred and Forty-first remained at this point, on guard duty, until the 25th of August, when it was ordered to Gallipolis, O., and mustered out September 3, 1864, on expiration of term of service.

141ST REGIMENT OHIO VOLUNTEER INFANTRY.

FIELD AND STAFF.

Mustered in May 11, 1864, at Gallipolis, O., by W. P. McCleery, 1st Lieutenant 18th Infantry, U. S. Army. Mustered out Sept. 3, 1864, at Gallipolis, O., by P. W. Horrigan, 2d Lieutenant 2d U. S. Cavalry.

Names.	Rank.	Age.	Date of Entering the Service.	Period of Service.	Remarks.
[illegible] D. Jaynes	Colonel.	36	May 2, 1864	100 dys.	Mustered out with regiment Sept. 3, 1864.
[illegible] W. Hampton	Lieut.Col	37	May 2, 1864	100 dys.	Mustered out with regiment Sept. 3, 1864.
[illegible] D. Brown	Major	32	May 2, 1864	100 dys.	Mustered out with regiment Sept. 3, 1864.
[illegible] L. Wilson	Surgeon.	32	May 2, 1864	100 dys.	Mustered out with regiment Sept. 3, 1864.
[illegible]	Asst. Sur.	30	May 2, 1864	100 dys.	Appointed May 18, 1864; mustered out with regiment Sept. 3, 1864.
[illegible] M. Goodspeed	Adjutant	29	May 2, 1864	100 dys.	Mustered out with regiment Sept. 3, 1864.
[illegible] T. Brown	R. Q. M.	30	May 2, 1864	100 dys.	Mustered out with regiment Sept. 3, 1864.
[illegible]	Chaplain	37	May 2, 1864	100 dys.	Promoted from private Co. D May 12, 1864; mustered out Aug. 30, 1864, at Gallipolis, O., by order of War Department.
Joseph W. Chase	Sergt.Maj	24	May 2, 1864	100 dys.	Promoted from private Co. D May 12, 1864; mustered out with regiment Sept. 3, 1864.
William J. Bawden	Q. M. S.	..	May 2, 1864	100 dys.	Apppointed May 12, 1864; mustered out with regiment Sept. 3, 1864
Cyrus Blazer	Com. Ser.	40	May 2, 1864	100 dys	Promoted from private Co. C May 2, 1864; mustered out with regiment Sept. 3, 1864.
[illegible] T. Bright	Hos. St'd	28	May 2, 1864	100 dys.	Promoted from Co. H May 12, 1864; mustered out with regiment Sept. 3, 1864.
[illegible] A. Taylor	Prin. Mus	30	May 2, 1864	100 dys.	Promoted from private Co. B May 11, 1864; mustered out with regiment Sept. 3, 1864.

COMPANY A.

Mustered in May 11, 1864, at Gallipolis, O., by W. P. McCleery, 1st Lieutenant 18th Infantry, U. S. Army. Mustered out Sept. 3, 1864, at Gallipolis, O., by P. W. Horrigan, 2d Lieutenant 2d U. S. Cavalry.

Names.	Rank.	Age.	Date of Entering the Service.	Period of Service.	Remarks.
....	Captain.	27	May 2, 1864	100 dys.	Mustered out with company Sept. 3, 1864.
....	1st Lieut.	30	May 2, 1864	100 dys.	Mustered out with company Sept. 3, 1864.
....	2d Lieut.	31	May 2, 1864	100 dys.	Mustered out with company Sept. 3, 1864.
....	1st Sergt.	44	May 2, 1864	100 dys.	Mustered out with company Sept. 3, 1864.
....	Sergeant.	44	May 2, 1864	100 dys.	Mustered out with company Sept. 3, 1864.
....	....do....	41	May 2, 1864	100 dys.	Mustered out with company Sept. 4, 1864.
....	....do....	35	May 2, 1864	100 dys.	Mustered out with company Sept. 3, 1864.
....	....do....	33	May 2, 1864	100 dys.	Mustered out with company Sept. 3, 1864.
....	Corporal	48	May 2, 1864	100 dys	Mustered out with company Sept. 3, 1864.
....	....do....	34	May 2, 1864	100 dys.	Appointed —; mustered out with company Sept. 3, 1864.
....	....do....	34	May 2, 1864	100 dys.	
....	....do....	29	May 2, 1864	100 dys.	Mustered out with company Sept. 3, 1864.
....	....do....	32	May 2, 1864	100 dys.	Mustered out with company Sept. 3, 1864.
....	....do....	23	May 2, 1864	100 dys.	Mustered out with company Sept. 3, 1864.
....	....do....	18	May 2, 1864	100 dys.	Mustered out with company Sept. 3, 1864.
....	....do....	26	May 2, 1864	100 dys.	Mustered out with company Sept. 3, 1864.
.....	Musician	19	May 2, 1864	100 dys.	Mustered out with company Sept. 3, 1864.
.....	....do....	16	May 2, 1864	100 dys.	Mustered out with company Sept. 3, 1864.
.....	Wagoner.	30	May 2, 1864	100 dys.	Mustered out Sept. 1, 1864, by order of War Department.
Bacheldoe, Daniel	Private..	31	May 2, 1864	100 dys.	Mustered out with company Sept. 3, 1864.
Barrows, George	....do....	26	May 2, 1864	100 dys.	Mustered out with company Sept. 3, 1864.
Blackwood, Harry L.	....do....	16	May 2, 1864	100 dys	Mustered out with company Sept. 3, 1864.
Blair, William	....do....	24	May 2, 1864	100 dys.	Mustered out with company Sept. 3, 1864.
Bower, Moses	....do....	42	May 2, 1864	100 dys.	Mustered out with company Sept. 3, 1864.
Brown, Charles	....do....	44	May 2, 1864	100 dys.	Mustered out with company Sept. 3, 1864.
Brown, Luther	....do....	[illegible]	May 2, 1864	100 dys.	
Carsey, James M.	....do....	22	May 2, 1864	100 dys.	Mustered out with company Sept. 3, 1864.
Carsey, Seldon	....do....	19	May 2, 1864	100 dys	Mustered out with company Sept. 3, 1864.
Clifford, Wellington	....do....	62	May 2, 1864	100 dys.	Mustered out with company Sept. 3, 1864.

Names.	Rank.	Age.	Date of Entering the Service.	Period of Service.	Remarks.
Cook, Harley A.	Private..	21	May 2, 1864	100 dys.	Mustered out with company Sept. 3, 1864.
Colvin, John D.	....do....	21	May 2, 1864	100 dys	Mustered out with company Sept. 3, 1864.
Copeland, Jonathan	....do....	36	May 2, 1864	100 dys.	Mustered out with company Sept. 3, 1864.
Copeland, Samuel	....do....	21	May 2, 1864	100 dys.	Mustered out with company Sept. 3, 1864.
Copeland, William C.	....do....	27	May 2, 1864	100 dys.	Mustered out with company Sept. 3, 1864.
Cowan, David	....do....	34	May 2, 1864	100 dys.	Mustered out with company Sept. 3, 1864.
Crawford, William N.	....do....	26	May 2, 1864	100 dys.	Mustered out with company Sept. 3, 1864.
Dewes, Greenberry W.	....do....	28	May 2, 1864	100 dys	
Douglas, Lindley	....do....	23	May 2, 1864	100 dys.	Mustered out with company Sept. 3, 1864.
Douglas, Melvin	....do....	18	May 2, 1864	100 dys.	Mustered out with company Sept. 3, 1864.
Eater, Ira	....do....	18	May 2, 1864	100 dys.	Mustered out with company Sept. 3, 1864.
Eastman, Samuel	....do....	20	May 2, 1864	100 dys.	Died July 11, 1864, at Barboursville, W. Va.
Evans, John R.	....do....	33	May 2, 1864	100 dys.	Mustered out with company Sept. 3, 1864.
Evans, Thomas W.	....do....	21	May 2, 1864	100 dys.	Mustered out with company Sept. 3, 1864.
Ferris, John D.	....do....	..	 1864	100 dys.	Detailed on U. S. service in Tennessee — No further record found.
Ferris, Thomas	....do....	..	 1864	100 dys.	Detailed on U. S. service in Tennessee — No further record found.
Fry, James C.	....do....	25	May 2, 1864	100 dys.	Mustered out with company Sept. 3, 1864.
Gaston, James	....do....	17	May 2, 1864	100 dys	Mustered out with company Sept. 3, 1864.
Gooden, John C.	....do....	30	May 2, 1864	100 dys	Mustered out with company Sept. 3, 1864.
Grandstaff, James	....do....	36	May 2, 1864	100 dys.	Mustered out with company Sept. 3, 1864.
Grandstaff, Madison	....do....	36	May 2, 1864	100 dys.	Mustered out with company Sept. 3, 1864.
Grandstaff, William	....do....	34	May 2, 1864	100 dys.	Mustered out with company Sept. 3, 1864.
Grim, George	....do...	32	May 2, 1864	100 dys	Mustered out with company Sept. 3, 1864.
Haines, Elisha C.	....do....	27	May 2, 1864	100 dys.	Mustered out with company Sept. 3, 1864.
Hawk, George	....do....	18	May 2, 1864	100 dys.	Mustered out with company Sept. 3, 1864.
Hawk, William	....do....	26	May 2, 1864	100 dys.	Mustered out with company Sept. 3, 1864.
Howard, McDonald	....do....	18	May 2, 1864	100 dys.	Mustered out with company Sept. 3, 1864.
Hull, Charles	....do....	..	May 2, 1864	100 dys.	
Jackson, David	....do....	39	May 2, 1864	100 dys	Mustered out with company Sept. 3, 1864.
Johnston, James	....do....	29	May 2, 1864	100 dys.	Mustered out with company Sept. 3, 1864.
Kinkade, George	....do....	26	May 2, 1864	100 dys.	Mustered out with company Sept. 3, 1864.
Ladd, Paul H.	....do....	33	May 2, 1864	100 dys.	Mustered out with company Sept. 3, 1864.
Lee, Jonathan R.	....do....	28	May 2, 1864	100 dys.	Mustered out with company Sept. 3, 1864.
Lorain, Lewis	....do....	18	May 2, 1864	100 dys.	Mustered out with company Sept. 3, 1864.
Madill, James	....do....	18	May 2, 1864	100 dys	Mustered out with company Sept. 3, 1864.
Manorter, Alexander	....do...	31	May 2, 1864	100 dys.	Mustered out with company Sept. 3, 1864.
Morrison, George	....do....	18	May 2, 1864	100 dys.	Mustered out with company Sept. 3, 1864.
Morrison, James	....do....	22	May 2, 1864	100 dys	Mustered out with company Sept. 3, 1864.
Muns, Warren	....do....	21	May 2, 1864	100 dys.	Mustered out with company Sept. 3, 1864.
Ong, George	....do....	34	May 2, 1864	100 dys.	Mustered out with company Sept. 3, 1864.
Patten, Oscar	....do....	19	May 2, 1864	100 dys.	Mustered out with company Sept. 3, 1864.
Patten, Preston	....do....	23	May 2, 1864	100 dys.	Mustered out with company Sept. 3, 1864.
Purcell, Theodore	....do....	18	May 2, 1864	100 dys	Mustered out with company Sept. 3, 1864.
Root, Perry	....do....	22	May 2, 1864	100 dys.	Mustered out with company Sept. 3, 1864.
Rowell, William W.	....do....	29	May 2, 1864	100 dys.	Mustered out with company Sept. 3, 1864.
Shetley, Peter	....do....	..	May 2, 1864	100 dys.	
Shotwell, Ezra M.	....do....	18	May 2, 1864	100 dys.	Mustered out with company Sept. 3, 1864.
Smith, James	....do....	21	May 2, 1864	100 dys.	Mustered out with company Sept. 3, 1864.
Starkey, John	....do....	36	May 2, 1864	100 dys.	Mustered out with company Sept. 3, 1864.
[illegible], David A.	....do....	20	May 2, 1864	100 dys.	Mustered out with company Sept. 3, 1864.
Terry, Thomas	....do....	36	May 2, 1864	100 dys.	Mustered out with company Sept. 3, 1864.
Totman, Nathan	....do....	19	May 2, 1864	100 dys.	Mustered out with company Sept. 3, 1864.
Watts, William	....do....	18	May 2, 1864	100 dys.	Mustered out with company Sept. 3, 1864.
Wilson, John	....do....	28	May 2, 1864	100 dys.	Mustered out with company Sept. 3, 1864.
Winter, Moses	....do....	28	May 2, 1864	100 dys	Mustered out with company Sept. 3, 1864.
Winter, William N.	....do....	30	May 2, 1864	100 dys.	Mustered out with company Sept. 3, 1864.
Wyatt, Frederick	....do....	40	May 2, 1864	100 dys.	Mustered out with company Sept. 3, 1864.
Wyatt, Joshua	....do....	38	May 2, 1864	100 dys.	Mustered out with company Sept. 3, 1864.
Yarnold, Jacob	....do....	43	May 2, 1864	100 dys.	
Yarnold, Thomas	....do....	21	May 2, 1864	100 dys.	Mustered out with company Sept. 3, 1864.
[illegible], Isaac	....do....	37	May 2, 1864	100 dys.	Mustered out with company Sept. 3, 1864.

COMPANY B.

Mustered in May 11, 1864, at Gallipolis, O., by W. P. McCleery, 1st Lieutenant 18th Infantry, U. S. Army. Mustered out Sept. 3, 1864, at Gallipolis, O., by P. W. Horrigan, 2d Lieutenant 2d U. S. Cavalry.

Names.	Rank.	Age.	Date of Entering the Service.	Period of Service.	Remarks.
[illegible] Stedman	Captain.	40	May 2, 1864	100 dys.	Mustered out with company Sept. 3, 1864.
Edward P. Smith	1st Lieut.	29	May 2, 1864	100 dys	Mustered out with company Sept. 3, 1864.
[illegible] P. Pruden	2d Lieut.	21	May 2, 1864	100 dys.	Mustered out with company Sept. 3, 1864.
[illegible] W. Hackman	1st Serg't.	23	May 2, 1864	100 dys.	Mustered out with company Sept. 3, 1864.
[illegible] Dunn	Sergeant.	18	May 2, 1864	100 dys	Appointed from private May 14, 1864; mustered out with company Sept. 3, 1864.
[illegible] W. Moore	....do....	34	May 2, 1864	100 dys.	Mustered out with company Sept. 3, 1864.
[illegible]	....do....	19	May 2, 1864	100 dys	Mustered out with company Sept. 3, 1864.
[illegible]	....do....	31	May 2, 1864	100 dys	Mustered out with company Sept. 3, 1864.
[illegible]	Corporal.	31	May 2, 1864	100 dys	Reduced from Sergeant May 14, 1864; mustered out with company Sept. 3, 1864.

	Rank.	Age.	Date of Entering the Service.	Period of Service.	Remarks.
Walker	Corporal.	29	May 2, 1864	100 dys.	Mustered out with company Sept. 3, 1864.
h	do.	27	May 2, 1864	100 dys.	Mustered out with company Sept. 3, 1864.
e	do.	24	May 2, 1864	100 dys.	Mustered out with company Sept. 3, 1864.
Smith	do.	18	May 2, 1864	100 dys.	Mustered out with company Sept. 3, 1864.
Rush	do.	20	May 2, 1864	100 dys.	Mustered out with company Sept. 3, 1864.
n	do.	19	May 2, 1864	100 dys.	Mustered out with company Sept. 3, 1864.
Wells	do.	22	May 2, 1864	100 dys.	Mustered out with company Sept. 3, 1864.
Maxwell	Musician	18	May 2, 1864	100 dys.	Mustered out with company Sept. 3, 1864.
I. Brown	do.	16	May 2, 1864	100 dys.	Mustered out with company Sept. 3, 1864.
Coats	Wagoner.	39	May 2, 1864	100 dys.	Appointed —; mustered out with company Sept. 3, 1864.
Emanuel	Private.	25	May 2, 1864	100 dys.	Mustered out with company Sept. 3, 1864.
ward P.	do.	20	May 2, 1864	100 dys.	Mustered out with company Sept. 3, 1864.
, James C.	do.	24	May 2, 1864	100 dys.	Mustered out with company Sept. 3, 1864.
William J.	do.	28	May 2, 1864	100 dys.	Promoted to Q. M. Sergeant May 11, 1864.
Nathan	do.	39	May 2, 1864	100 dys.	Mustered out with company Sept. 3, 1864.
Henry T.	do.	27	May 2, 1864	100 dys.	Mustered out with company Sept. 3, 1864.
rles M.	do.	19	May 2, 1864	100 dys.	Mustered out with company Sept. 3, 1864.
artin	do.	22	May 2, 1864	100 dys.	Mustered out with company Sept. 3, 1864.
ohn H.	do.	37	May 2, 1864	100 dys.	Mustered out with company Sept. 3, 1864.
lexander	do.	36	May 2, 1864	100 dys.	
enjamin C.	do.	19	May 2, 1864	100 dys.	Mustered out with company Sept. 3, 1864.
harles H.	do.	18	May 2, 1864	100 dys.	Mustered out with company Sept. 3, 1864.
ohn	do.	20	May 2, 1864	100 dys.	Mustered out with company Sept. 3, 1864.
David C	do.	19	May 2, 1864	100 dys.	Mustered out with company Sept. 3, 1864.
John C	do.	30	May 2, 1864	100 dys.	Mustered out with company Sept. 3, 1864.
ohn E.	do.	23	May 2, 1864	100 dys.	Reduced from Corporal May 14, 1864; mustered out with company Sept. 3, 1864.
omas E.	do.	24	May 2, 1864	100 dys.	Mustered out with company Sept. 3, 1864.
illiam E.	do.	18	May 2, 1864	100 dys.	Mustered out with company Sept. 3, 1864.
nry T.	do.	21	May 2, 1864	100 dys.	Mustered out with company Sept. 3, 1864.
les P.	do.	18	May 2, 1864	100 dys.	Mustered out with company Sept. 3, 1864.
illiam S.	do.	31	May 2, 1864	100 dys.	Mustered out with company Sept. 3, 1864.
ichael	do.	18	May 2, 1864	100 dys.	Mustered out with company Sept. 3, 1864.
atthew	do.	20	May 2, 1864	100 dys.	Mustered out with company Sept. 3, 1864.
ld, Jesse	do.	18	May 2, 1864	100 dys.	Mustered out with company Sept. 3, 1864.
illiam C.	do.	18	May 2, 1864	100 dys.	Mustered out with company Sept. 3, 1864.
William L.	do.	34	May 2, 1864	100 dys.	Mustered out with company Sept. 3, 1864.
ohn	do.	18	May 2, 1864	100 dys.	Mustered out with company Sept. 3, 1864.
es	do.	28	May 2, 1864	100 dys.	Mustered out with company Sept. 3, 1864.
St. C.	do.	18	May 2, 1864	100 dys.	Mustered out with company Sept. 3, 1864.
Elisha	do.	35	May 2, 1864	100 dys.	Mustered out with company Sept. 3, 1864.
ohn	do.	31	May 2, 1864	100 dys.	Mustered out with company Sept. 3, 1864.
efferson	do.	28	May 2, 1864	100 dys.	Mustered out with company Sept. 3, 1864.
acob	do.	25	May 2, 1864	100 dys.	Mustered out with company Sept. 3, 1864.
ohn	do.	37	May 2, 1864	100 dys.	Mustered out with company Sept. 3, 1864.
eorge W.	do.	33	May 2, 1864	100 dys.	Mustered out with company Sept. 3, 1864.
Able G.	do.	44	May 2, 1864	100 dys.	Rejected May 19, 1864, by Examining Physician.
us	do.	24	May 2, 1864	100 dys.	Mustered out with company Sept. 3, 1864.
Hugh	do.	19	May 2, 1864	100 dys.	Mustered out with company Sept. 3, 1864.
harles F.	do.	17	May 2, 1864	100 dys.	Mustered out with company Sept. 3, 1864.
ta	do.	20	May 2, 1864	100 dys.	Mustered out with company Sept. 3, 1864.
enry C.	do.	19	May 2, 1864	100 dys.	Mustered out with company Sept. 3, 1864.
ander	do.	36	May 2, 1864	100 dys.	Mustered out with company Sept. 3, 1864.
y, Robert	do.	38	May 2, 1864	100 dys.	Mustered out with company Sept. 3, 1864.
orris H.	do.	20	May 2, 1864	100 dys.	Mustered out with company Sept. 3, 1864.
ohn	do.	31	May 2, 1864	100 dys.	Mustered out with company Sept. 3, 1864.
Thomas	do.	18	May 2, 1864	100 dys.	Absent, sick, at Gallipolis, O., since Aug. 24, 1864. No further record found.
iah	do.	20	May 2, 1864	100 dys.	Mustered out with company Sept. 3, 1864.
ney	do.	24	May 2, 1864	100 dys.	Mustered out with company Sept. 3, 1864.
ter	do.	34	May 2, 1864	100 dys.	Mustered out with company Sept. 3, 1864.
ger, Alfred	do.	18	May 2, 1864	100 dys.	Mustered out with company Sept. 3, 1864.
Joseph L.	do.	18	May 2, 1864	100 dys.	Mustered out with company Sept. 3, 1864.
ge W.	do.	21	May 2, 1864	100 dys.	Mustered out with company Sept. 3, 1864.
illiam	do.	36	May 2, 1864	100 dys.	Mustered out with company Sept. 3, 1864.
n	do.	18	May 2, 1864	100 dys.	Mustered out with company Sept. 3, 1864.
lbert	do.	25	May 2, 1864	100 dys.	Mustered out with company Sept. 3, 1864.
n R.	do.	21	May 2, 1864	100 dys.	Mustered out with company Sept. 3, 1864.
iah W.	do.	40	May 2, 1864	100 dys.	Mustered out with company Sept. 3, 1864.
, James S.	do.	38	May 2, 1864	100 dys.	Mustered out with company Sept. 3, 1864.
rancis A.	do.	28	May 2, 1864	100 dys.	Mustered out with company Sept. 3, 1864.
quilla	do.	33	May 2, 1864	100 dys.	Mustered out with company Sept. 3, 1864.
illiam J.	do.	18	May 2, 1864	100 dys.	Mustered out with company Sept. 3, 1864.
Daniel	do.	29	May 2, 1864	100 dys.	Mustered out with company Sept. 3, 1864.
losco A.	do.	30	May 2, 1864	100 dys.	Promoted to Principal Musician May 11, 1864.
olomon	do.	25	May 2, 1864	100 dys.	Mustered out with company Sept. 1, 1864.
, William W.	do.	28	May 2, 1864	100 dys.	Died May 25, 1864, at Gallipolis, O.
, Henry	do.	17	May 2, 1864	100 dys.	Mustered out with company Sept. 3, 1864.
wis W.	do.	20	May 2, 1864	100 dys.	Mustered out with company Sept. 3, 1864.
John	do.	21	May 2, 1864	100 dys.	Mustered out with company Sept. 3, 1864.

COMPANY C.

Mustered in May 11, 1864, at Gallipolis, O., by W. P. McCleery, 1st Lieutenant 18th Infantry, U. S. Army. Mustered out Sept. 3, 1864, at Gallipolis, O., by P. W. Horrigan, 2d Lieutenant 2d U. S. Cavalry.

Names.	Rank.	Age.	Date of Entering the Service.	Period of Service.	Remarks.
Francis H. Gray	Captain.	23	May 2, 1864	100 dys.	Mustered out with company Sept. 3, 1864.
Thomas G. Angell	1st Lieut.	31	May 2, 1864	100 dys.	Mustered out with company Sept. 3, 1864.
Isaiah Bean	2d Lieut.	38	May 2, 1864	100 dys.	Mustered out with company Sept. 3, 1864.
George M. Miller	1st Sergt.	28	May 2, 1864	100 dys.	Mustered out with company Sept. 3, 1864.
John M. Chase	Sergeant.	21	May 2, 1864	100 dys.	Mustered out with company Sept. 3, 1864.
William H. Irwin	...do...	23	May 2, 1864	100 dys.	Mustered out with company Sept. 3, 1864.
Benjamin F Scott	...do...	22	May 2, 1864	100 dys.	Mustered out with company Sept. 3, 1864.
Edward Evans	...do...	28	May 2, 1864	100 dys.	Mustered out with company Sept. 3, 1864.
John J. Whaley	Corporal.	23	May 2, 1864	100 dys	Mustered out with company Sept. 3, 1864.
John B. Lash	...do...	23	May 2, 1864	100 dys.	Mustered out with company Sept. 3, 1864.
Thomas H. Gibson	...do...	21	May 2, 1864	100 dys.	Mustered out with company Sept. 3, 1864.
John Richey	...do...	31	May 2, 1864	100 dys.	Mustered out with company Sept. 3, 1864.
Wilson A. Phillips	...do...	23	May 2, 1864	100 dys.	Mustered out with company Sept. 3, 1864.
Josiah Long	...do...	19	May 2, 1864	100 dys	Mustered out with company Sept. 3, 1864.
Robert H. Six	...do...	20	May 2, 1864	100 dys.	Mustered out with company Sept. 3, 1864.
Archelaus Stanley	...do...	18	May 2, 1864	100 dys.	Mustered out with company Sept. 3, 1864.
Robert Axtell	Musician	19	May 2, 1864	100 dys.	Mustered out with company Sept. 3, 1864.
Edward B. Russ	...do...	25	May 2, 1864	100 dys.	Mustered out with company Sept 3, 1864.
Barnhill, Aaron	Private.	18	May 2, 1864	100 dys	Mustered out with company Sept. 3, 1864.
Bean, Elijah H	...do...	20	May 2, 1864	100 dys.	Mustered out with company Sept. 3, 1864.
Bean, Francis	...do...	19	May 2, 1864	100 dys	Mustered out with company Sept. 3, 1864.
Bean, John F	...do...	18	May 2, 1864	100 dys.	Mustered out with company Sept. 3, 1864.
Bean, Samuel	...do...	26	May 2, 1864	100 dys.	
Bean, Zebina	...do...	20	May 2, 1864	100 dys.	Mustered out with company Sept. 3, 1864.
Blakeway, Elser	...do...	19	May 2, 1864	100 dys.	Mustered out with company Sept. 3, 1864.
Blazer, Cyrus	...do...	40	May 2, 1864	100 dys.	Promoted to Com. Sergeant May 2, 1864.
Briggs Dallas	...do...	18	May 2, 1864	100 dys.	Mustered out with company Sept. 3, 1864.
Brooks, John	...do...	18	May 2, 1864	100 dys.	Mustered out with company Sept. 3, 1864.
Burley, Charles B	...do...	21	May 2, 1864	100 dys.	Mustered out with company Sept. 3, 1864.
Carsey, Ezra	...do...	26	May 2, 1864	100 dys.	Mustered out with company Sept. 3, 1864.
Carsey, Isaac J	...do...	55	May 2, 1864	100 dys.	Mustered out with company Sept. 3, 1864.
Condee, Harvey	...do...	38	May 2, 1864	100 dys.	Mustered out with company Sept. 3, 1864.
Dempsey, Joseph	...do...	18	May 2, 1864	100 dys	Mustered out with company Sept. 3, 1864.
Dickson, Marsha[illegible]	...do...	22	May 2, 1864	100 dys.	Mustered out with company Sept. 3, 1864.
Downy, James	...do...	37	May 2, 1864	100 dys.	Mustered out with company Sept. 3, 1864.
Fredline, Samuel	...do...	40	May 2, 1864	100 dys.	Mustered out with company Sept. 3, 1864.
Gibson, [illegible]mes	...do...	23	May 2, 1864	100 dys.	Mustered out with company Sept. 3, 1864.
Hanl[illegible]g, [illegible]mes	...do...	28	May 2, 1864	100 dys.	Mustered out with company Sept. 3, 1864.
Hanling, Emanuel	...do...	21	May 2, 1864	100 dys	Mustered out with company Sept. 3, 1864.
Haw[illegible], Charles	...do...	18	May 2, 1864	100 dys.	Mustered out with company Sept. 3, 1864.
Hooper, William	...do...	22	May 2, 1864	100 dys.	Mustered out with company Sept. 3, 1864.
Hoskinson, Elza B	...do...	21	May 2, 1864	100 dys.	Mustered out with company Sept. 3, 1864.
Hoskinson, Oscar E	...do...	18	May 2, 1864	100 dys.	Mustered out with company Sept. 3, 1864.
Kell[illegible], Ellis	...do...	31	May 2, 1864	100 dys.	Mustered out with company Sept. 3, 1864.
Kester, Stephen S	...do...	29	May 2, 1864	100 dys	Mustered out with company Sept. 3, 1864.
Laughlin, John	...do...	21	May 2, 1864	100 dys	Mustered out with company Sept. 3, 1864.
Leighty, Jacob	...do...	25	May 2, 1864	100 dys.	Mustered out with company Sept. 3, 1864.
Loiry, Samuel	...do...	36	May 2, 1864	100 dys.	Mustered out with company Sept. 3, 1864.
Louther, Granville	...do...	19	May 2, 1864	100 dys.	Mustered out with company Sept. 3, 1864.
Love, Isaiah	...do...	20	May 2, 1864	100 dys.	Mustered out with company Sept. 3, 1864.
Love, William	...do...	19	May 2, 1864	100 dys.	Absent, sick, since July 6, 1864. No further record found.
McVay, John G	...do...	21	May 2, 1864	100 dys.	Mustered out with company Sept. 3, 1864.
Masters, Henry	...do...	36	May 2, 1864	100 dys.	Mustered out with company Sept. 3, 1864.
Might, Samuel D	...do...	19	May 2, 1864	100 dys.	Mustered out with company Sept. 3, 1864.
Miles, Benjamin F	...do...	23	May 2, 1864	100 dys.	Mustered out with company Sept. 3, 1864.
Mitchell, James	...do...	37	May 2, 1864	100 dys.	Mustered out with company Sept. 3, 1864.
Moore, John J	...do...	36	May 2, 1864	100 dys.	Mustered out with company Sept. 3, 1864.
Parker, Andrew	...do...	20	May 2, 1864	100 dys.	Mustered out with company Sept. 3, 1864.
Patterson, John C	...do...	20	May 2, 1864	100 dys.	Mustered out with company Sept. 3, 1864.
Pittet, Daniel	...do...	19	May 2, 1864	100 dys.	Mustered out with company Sept. 3, 1864.
Richey, Peter	...do...	19	May 2, 1864	100 dys.	Mustered out with company Sept. 3, 1864.
Richey, William	...do...	26	May 2, 1864	100 dys.	Mustered out with company Sept. 3, 1864.
Robinson, Jesse	...do...	28	May 2, 1864	100 dys.	Mustered out with company Sept. 3, 1864.
Ryther, James F	...do...	20	May 2, 1864	100 dys.	Mustered out with company Sept. 3, 1864.
Saddler, Richard	...do...	22	May 2, 1864	100 dys	Mustered out with company Sept. 3, 1864.
Sams, Peter C	...do...	22	May 2, 1864	100 dys	Mustered out with company Sept. 3, 1864.
Scott, Milton	...do...	20	May 2, 1864	100 dys.	Mustered out with company Sept. 3, 1864.
Sewell, Andrew H	...do...	31	May 2, 1864	100 dys.	Mustered out with company Sept. 3, 1864.
Sewell, Henry	...do...	19	May 2, 1864	100 dys.	Mustered out with company Sept. 3, 1864.
Shafer, Robert	...do...	18	May 2, 1864	100 dys.	Mustered out with company Sept. 3, 1864.
Sharp, Granville	...do...	18	May 2, 1864	100 dys.	Mustered out with company Sept. 3, 1864.
Smith, John F	...do...	37	May 2, 1864	100 dys.	Mustered out with company Sept. 3, 1864.
Sylvus, George	...do...	19	May 2, 1864	100 dys.	Mustered out with company Sept. 3, 1864.
Tewksbury, Aaron	...do...	26	May 2, 1864	100 dys.	Mustered out with company Sept. 3, 1864.
Townsend, Charles	...do...	18	May 2, 1864	100 dys.	Mustered out with company Sept. 3, 1864.
Tribe, Henry	...do...	21	May 2, 1864	100 dys.	Mustered out with company Sept. 3, 1864.

Names.	Rank.	Age.	Date of Entering the Service.	Period of Service.	Remarks.
[illegible], Alexander J.	Private.	[illegible]	May 2, 1864	100 dys.	Mustered out with company Sept. 3, 1864.
[illegible]	...do...	[illegible]	May 2, 1864	100 dys.	Mustered out with company Sept. 3, 1864.
[illegible], James	...do...	[illegible]	May 2, 1864	100 dys.	Mustered out with company Sept. 3, 1864.
[illegible], Charles E.	...do...	[illegible]	May 2, 1864	100 dys.	Mustered out with company Sept. 3, 1864.
[illegible]	...do...	[illegible]	May 2, 1864	100 dys.	Mustered out with company Sept. 3, 1864.
[illegible], William H.	...do...	[illegible]	May 2, 1864	100 dys.	Mustered out with company Sept. 3, 1864.
[illegible], Clinton P.	...do...	19	May 2, 1864	100 dys.	Mustered out with company Sept. 3, 1864.
[illegible], William	...do...	[illegible]	May 2, 1864	100 dys.	Mustered out with company Sept. 3, 1864.
[illegible], John W.	...do...	20	May 2, 1864	100 dys.	Mustered out with company Sept. 3, 1864.
[illegible], Jesse	...do...	[illegible]	May 2, 1864	100 dys.	Mustered out with company Sept. 3, 1864.

COMPANY D.

Mustered in May 11, 1864, at Gallipolis, O., by W. P. McCleery, 1st Lieutenant 18th Infantry, U. S. Army. Mustered out Sept. 3, 1864, at Gallipolis, O., by P. W. Horrigan, 2d Lieutenant 2d U. S. Cavalry.

Names.	Rank.	Age.	Date of Entering the Service.	Period of Service.	Remarks.
Amos O. Mauck	Captain.	21	May 2, 1864	100 dys.	Mustered out with company Sept. 3, 1864.
Benjamin W. Rutherford	1st Lieut.	32	May 2, 1864	100 dys.	Mustered out with company Sept. 3, 1864.
Augustus P. Kerr	2d Lieut.	34	May 2, 1864	100 dys.	Mustered out with company Sept. 3, 1864.
Lewis W. Mauck	1st Sergt.	20	May 2, 1864	100 dys.	Promoted to 2d Lieutenant Aug. 1, 1864, but not mustered. No further record found.
Charles A. Guthrie	...do...	24	May 2, 1864	100 dys.	Appointed from Sergeant Aug. 1, 1864; mustered out with company Sept. 3, 1864.
David R. S. Schaffer	Sergeant.	26	May 2, 1864	100 dys.	Mustered out with company Sept. 3, 1864.
Alexander Davis	...do...	26	May 2, 1864	100 dys.	Mustered out with company Sept. 3, 1864.
Ellis Swisher	...do...	29	May 2, 1864	100 dys.	Mustered out with company Sept. 3, 1864.
Hugh [illegible]	Corporal.	42	May 2, 1864	100 dys.	Mustered out with company Sept. 3, 1864.
[illegible] M. Guthrie	...do...	37	May 2, 1864	100 dys.	Mustered out with company Sept. 3, 1864.
Robert Mauck	...do...	19	May 2, 1864	100 dys.	Mustered out with company Sept. 3, 1864.
John Grever	...do...	28	May 2, 1864	100 dys.	Mustered out with company Sept. 3, 1864.
Joseph Rausch	...do...	21	May 2, 1864	100 dys.	Mustered out with company Sept. 3, 1864.
Thomas Thompson	...do...	22	May 2, 1864	100 dys.	Mustered out with company Sept. 3, 1864.
James A. Grover	...do...	28	May 2, 1864	100 dys.	Mustered out with company Sept. 3, 1864.
George W. [illegible]	...do...	22	May 2, 1864	100 dys.	Mustered out with company Sept. 3, 1864.
Alonzo F. Mauck	Musician	18	May 2, 1864	100 dys.	Mustered out with company Sept. 3, 1864.
Athey, Thomas	Private.	39	May 2, 1864	100 dys.	Mustered out with company Sept. 3, 1864.
[illegible], Oscar E.	...do...	27	May 2, 1864	100 dys.	Promoted to Chaplain May 11, 1864.
[illegible], James C.	...do...	25	May 2, 1864	100 dys.	Mustered out with company Sept. 3, 1864.
[illegible], Andrew J.	...do...	19	May 2, 1864	100 dys.	Mustered out with company Sept. 3, 1864.
[illegible], Stephen H.	...do...	33	May 2, 1864	100 dys.	Died July 5, 1864, at Barboursville, W. Va.
[illegible], Henderson	...do...	26	May 2, 1864	100 dys.	Mustered out with company Sept. 3, 1864.
[illegible], R. Franklin	...do...	24	May 2, 1864	100 dys.	Mustered out with company Sept. 3, 1864.
[illegible], Horace R.	...do...	18	May 2, 1864	100 dys.	Mustered out with company Sept. 3, 1864.
[illegible], Perry	...do...	26	May 2, 1864	100 dys.	Mustered out with company Sept. 3, 1864.
[illegible], Thomas	...do...	28	May 2, 1864	100 dys.	Mustered out with company Sept. 3, 1864.
[illegible], William	...do...	25	May 2, 1864	100 dys.	Mustered out with company Sept. 3, 1864.
[illegible], Nimrod	...do...	35	May 2, 1864	100 dys.	Mustered out with company Sept. 3, 1864.
[illegible], Joseph W.	...do...	34	May 2, 1864	100 dys.	Promoted to Sergt. Major May 12, 1864.
[illegible], John	...do...	18	May 2, 1864	100 dys.	Mustered out with company Sept. 3, 1864.
[illegible], Franklin	...do...	20	May 2, 1864	100 dys.	Mustered out with company Sept. 3, 1864.
[illegible], Elias A.	...do...	28	May 2, 1864	100 dys.	Mustered out with company Sept. 3, 1864.
[illegible], William	...do...	28	May 2, 1864	100 dys.	Mustered out with company Sept. 3, 1864.
Edwards, Arthur E.	...do...	30	May 2, 1864	100 dys.	Mustered out with company Sept. 3, 1864.
[illegible], Cassius M.	...do...	19	May 2, 1864	100 dys.	Mustered out with company Sept. 3, 1864.
[illegible], Alexander	...do...	38	May 2, 1864	100 dys.	Mustered out with company Sept. 3, 1864.
[illegible], Henry B.	...do...	26	May 2, 1864	100 dys.	Mustered out with company Sept. 3, 1864.
[illegible], J. Wesley	...do...	28	May 2, 1864	100 dys.	Mustered out with company Sept. 3, 1864.
[illegible], John A.	...do...	28	May 2, 1864	100 dys.	Mustered out with company Sept. 3, 1864.
[illegible], Stephen H.	...do...	25	May 2, 1864	100 dys.	Mustered out with company Sept. 3, 1864.
[illegible], Jefferson	...do...	26	May 2, 1864	100 dys.	Mustered out with company Sept. 3, 1864.
[illegible], Benjamin	...do...	18	May 2, 1864	100 dys.	Mustered out with company Sept. 3, 1864.
[illegible], Franklin A.	...do...	22	May 2, 1864	100 dys.	Mustered out with company Sept. 3, 1864.
[illegible], Martin	...do...	18	May 2, 1864	100 dys.	Mustered out with company Sept. 3, 1864.
[illegible] W.	...do...	20	May 2, 1864	100 dys.	Mustered out with company Sept. 3, 1864.
[illegible], William	...do...	26	May 2, 1864	100 dys.	Mustered out with company Sept. 3, 1864.
[illegible], Charles	...do...	18	May 2, 1864	100 dys.	Mustered out with company Sept. 3, 1864.
[illegible], Charles A.	...do...	18	May 2, 1864	100 dys.	Mustered out with company Sept. 3, 1864.
[illegible], Jonas	...do...	24	May 2, 1864	100 dys.	Mustered out with company Sept. 3, 1864.
[illegible], Charles	...do...	18	May 2, 1864	100 dys.	Mustered out with company Sept. 3, 1864.
[illegible], Andrew	...do...	37	May 2, 1864	100 dys.	Mustered out with company Sept. 3, 1864.
[illegible]	...do...	21	May 2, 1864	100 dys.	Mustered out with company Sept. 3, 1864.
[illegible] Henry	...do...	28	May 2, 1864	100 dys.	Mustered out with company Sept. 3, 1864.
[illegible], Jacob	...do...	48	May 2, 1864	100 dys.	Mustered out with company Sept. 3, 1864.
[illegible] T.	...do...	19	May 2, 1864	100 dys.	Mustered out with company Sept. 3, 1864.
[illegible]	...do...	18	May 2, 1864	100 dys.	Mustered out with company Sept. 3, 1864; also borne on rolls as Park Reed.
Rife, Jacob, Sr.	...do...	25	May 2, 1864	100 dys.	Mustered out with company Sept. 3, 1864.
Rothgeb, John	...do...	29	May 2, 1864	100 dys.	Mustered out with company Sept. 3, 1864.
Roush, Philip	...do...	19	May 2, 1864	100 dys.	Mustered out with company Sept. 3, 1864.
Roush, Wilson	...do...	21	May 2, 1864	100 dys.	Mustered out with company Sept. 3, 1864.

Names.	Rank.	Age.	Date of Entering the Service.	Period of Service.	Remarks.
[illegible], Charles	Private	18	May 2, 1864	100 dys.	Mustered out with company Sept. 3, 1864.
[illegible], Daniel	do.	37	May 2, 1864	100 dys.	Mustered out with company Sept. 3, 1864.
Shaffer, Reese B.	do.	22	May 2, 1864	100 dys.	Mustered out with company Sept. 3, 1864.
[illegible], Jacob	do.	23	May 2, 1864	100 dys.	Mustered out with company Sept. 3, 1864.
[illegible], William M.	do.	21	May 2, 1864	100 dys.	Mustered out with company Sept. 3, 1864.
[illegible], Franklin	do.	19	May 2, 1864	100 dys.	Mustered out with company Sept. 3, 1864.
[illegible], William	do.	17	May 2, 1864	100 dys.	Mustered out with company Sept. 3, 1864.
[illegible], David	do.	38	May 2, 1864	100 dys.	Mustered out with company Sept. 3, 1864.
[illegible], George N.	do.	21	May 2, 1864	100 dys.	Mustered out with company Sept. 3, 1864.
[illegible], George W.	do.	26	May 2, 1864	100 dys.	Mustered out with company Sept. 3, 1864.
[illegible]	do.	20	May 2, 1864	100 dys.	Mustered out with company Sept. 3, 1864.
[illegible]	do.	29	May 2, 1864	100 dys.	Mustered out with company Sept. 3, 1864.
[illegible]	do.	29	May 2, 1864	100 dys.	Mustered out with company Sept. 3, 1864.
[illegible], Simeon	do.	31	May 2, 1864	100 dys.	Mustered out with company Sept. 3, 1864.
Thomas, William	do.	27	May 2, 1864	100 dys.	Mustered out with company Sept. 3, 1864.
[illegible], Jeremiah	do.	26	May 2, 1864	100 dys.	Mustered out with company Sept. 3, 1864.
[illegible], Samuel	do.	25	May 2, 1864	100 dys.	Mustered out with company Sept. 3, 1864.
[illegible]	do.	18	May 2, 1864	100 dys.	Mustered out with company Sept. 3, 1864.
[illegible]	do.	20	May 2, 1864	100 dys.	Mustered out with company Sept. 3, 1864.
[illegible], Nelson	do.	22	May 2, 1864	100 dys.	Mustered out with company Sept. 3, 1864.
[illegible], Augustus R.	do.	21	May 2, 1864	100 dys.	Mustered out with company Sept. 3, 1864.
[illegible], James W.	do.	32	May 2, 1864	100 dys.	Mustered out with company Sept. 3, 1864.
[illegible], Lambert L.	do.	19	May 2, 1864	100 dys.	Mustered out with company Sept. 3, 1864.

COMPANY E.

Mustered in May 11, 1864, at Gallipolis, O., by W. P. McCleery, 1st Lieutenant 18th Infantry, U. S. Army. Mustered out Sept. 3, 1864, at Gallipolis, O., by P. W. Horrigan, 2d Lieutenant 2d U. S. Cavalry.

Names.	Rank.	Age.	Date of Entering the Service.	Period of Service.	Remarks.
[illegible] Rothgeb	Captain.	38	May 2, 1864	100 dys.	Mustered out with company Sept. 3, 1864.
Charles Stuart	1st Lieut.	38	May 2, 1864	100 dys.	Mustered out with company Sept. 3, 1864.
[illegible] W. Berry	2d Lieut.	26	May 2, 1864	100 dys.	Mustered out with company Sept. 3, 1864.
[illegible] Pennington	1st Sergt.	32	May 2, 1864	100 dys.	Mustered out with company Sept. 3, 1864.
[illegible] Vanzant	Sergeant.	32	May 2, 1864	100 dys.	Mustered out with company Sept. 3, 1864.
[illegible] M. [illegible]land	do.	30	May 2, 1864	100 dys.	Mustered out with company Sept. 3, 1864.
[illegible] Kinkade	do.	23	May 2, 1864	100 dys.	Mustered out with company Sept. 3, 1864.
James Leonard	do.	31	May 2, 1864	100 dys.	Mustered out with company Sept. 3, 1864.
Elias Dickey	Corporal.	28	May 2, 1864	100 dys.	Mustered out with company Sept. 3, 1864.
[illegible] Clark	do.	26	May 2, 1864	100 dys.	Mustered out with company Sept. 3, 1864.
Thomas J. Coleman	do.	26	May 2, 1864	100 dys.	Mustered out with company Sept. 3, 1864.
John A. Martindale	do.	40	May 2, 1864	100 dys.	Mustered out with company Sept. 3, 1864.
Vincent A. Walker	do.	27	May 2, 1864	100 dys.	Mustered out with company Sept. 3, 1864.
Abram C. Shaver	do.	20	May 2, 1864	100 dys.	Mustered out with company Sept. 3, 1864.
Charles Watson	do.	19	May 2, 1864	100 dys.	Mustered out with company Sept. 3, 1864.
Jackson Brock	do.	31	May 2, 1864	100 dys.	Mustered out with company Sept. 3, 1864.
Alexander, William W.	Private.	28	May 2, 1864	100 dys.	Mustered out with company Sept. 3, 1864.
Baker, Andrew	do.	25	May 2, 1864	100 dys.	Mustered out with company Sept. 3, 1864.
Baker, Frederick	do.	41	May 2, 1864	100 dys.	Mustered out with company Sept. 3, 1864.
Beale, George H.	do.	30	May 2, 1864	100 dys.	Mustered out with company Sept. 3, 1864.
Boice, Lorenzo	do.	19	May 2, 1864	100 dys.	Mustered out with company Sept. 3, 1864.
Boster, Alexander	do.	27	May 2, 1864	100 dys.	Mustered out with company Sept. 3, 1864.
Boster, John R.	do.	18	May 2, 1864	100 dys.	Mustered out with company Sept. 3, 1864.
Brown, James E.	do.	29	May 2, 1864	100 dys.	Mustered out with company Sept. 3, 1864.
Bines, William	do.	..	May 2, 1864	100 dys.	Mustered out with company Sept. 3, 1864.
Cass, Lewis M.	do.	19	May 2, 1864	100 dys.	Mustered out with company Sept. 3, 1864.
Cales, William H.	do.	20	May 2, 1864	100 dys.	Mustered out with company Sept. 3, 1864.
Carns, Harry	do.	18	May 2, 1864	100 dys.	Mustered out with company Sept. 3, 1864.
[illegible]errington, Thomas J.	do.	19	May 2, 1864	100 dys.	Mustered out with company Sept. 3, 1864.
Clark, John H.	do.	30	May 2, 1864	100 dys.	Mustered out with company Sept. 3, 1864.
Clark, Samuel W.	do.	21	May 2, 1864	100 dys.	Mustered out with company Sept. 3, 1864.
Cowman, Richard	do.	35	May 2, 1864	100 dys.	Mustered out with company Sept. 3, 1864.
Craig, James S.	do.	21	May 2, 1864	100 dys.	Mustered out with company Sept. 3, 1864.
Drummond, Allen	do.	43	May 2, 1864	100 dys.	Mustered out with company Sept. 3, 1864.
Drummond, James T.	do.	26	May 2, 1864	100 dys.	Mustered out with company Sept. 3, 1864.
Essex, Everett	do.	[illegible]	May 2, 1864	100 dys.	Mustered out with company Sept. 3, 1864.
Everett, Henry	do.	26	May 2, 1864	100 dys.	Mustered out with company Sept. 3, 1864.
Fillinger, Isaac	do.	30	May 2, 1864	100 dys.	Mustered out with company Sept. 3, 1864.
Finley, John	do.	25	May 2, 1864	100 dys.	Mustered out with company Sept. 3, 1864.
Foden, Isaac	do.	32	May 2, 1864	100 dys.	Mustered out with company Sept. 3, 1864.
Foden, Robert	do.	[illegible]	May 2, 1864	100 dys.	Mustered out with company Sept. 3, 1864.
Fulton, David	do.	24	May 2, 1864	100 dys.	Mustered out with company Sept. 3, 1864.
Fulton, William H. H.	do.	34	May 2, 1864	100 dys.	Mustered out with company Sept. 3, 1864.
Gates, Lovell C.	do.	18	May 2, 1864	100 dys.	Mustered out with company Sept. 3, 1864.
Gates, Thomas J.	do.	18	May 2, 1864	100 dys.	Mustered out with company Sept. 3, 1864.
George, William	do.	18	May 2, 1864	100 dys.	Mustered out with company Sept. 3, 1864.
Grant, Julius A.	do.	19	May 2, 1864	100 dys.	Mustered out with company Sept. 3, 1864.
Grant, Thomas C.	do.	24	May 2, 1864	100 dys.	Mustered out with company Sept. 3, 1864.
Hall, William D.	do.	24	May 2, 1864	100 dys.	Mustered out with company Sept. 3, 1864.
Halfhill, Jacob	do.	31	May 2, 1864	100 dys.	Mustered out with company Sept. 3, 1864.
Harber, Perry	do.	18	May 2, 1864	100 dys.	Mustered out with company Sept. 3, 1864.

[illegible]	Rank.	Age.	Date of Entering the Service.		Period of Service.	Remarks.
[illegible]	Private..	[illegible]	May	2, 1864	100 dys.	Mustered out with company Sept. 3, 1864.
[illegible]	....do....	[illegible]	May	2, 1864	100 dys.	Mustered out with company Sept. 3, 1864.
[illegible] F.	....do....	19	May	2, 1864	100 dys.	Mustered out with company Sept. 3, 1864.
[illegible], William A.	....do....	20	May	2, 1864	100 dys.	Mustered out with company Sept. 3, 1864.
[illegible], Abel L.	....do....	25	May	2, 1864	100 dys.	Mustered out with company Sept. 3, 1864.
[illegible], James B.	....do....	21	May	2, 1864	100 dys.	Mustered out with company Sept. 3, 1864.
[illegible], Albert C.	....do....	19	May	2, 1864	100 dys.	Mustered out with company Sept. 3, 1864.
[illegible], Wilson M.	....do....	22	May	2, 1864	100 dys.	Mustered out with company Sept. 3, 1864.
[illegible], Joseph B.	....do....	22	May	2, 1864	100 dys.	Mustered out with company Sept. 3, 1864.
[illegible], Jeremiah C.	....do....	24	May	2, 1864	100 dys.	Mustered out with company Sept. 3, 1864.
[illegible], David	....do....	18	May	2, 1864	100 dys.	Mustered out with company Sept. 3, 1864.
[illegible], James W.	....do....	24	May	2, 1864	100 dys.	Mustered out with company Sept. 3, 1864.
[illegible] M.	....do....	18	May	2, 1864	100 dys.	Mustered out with company Sept. 3, 1864.
[illegible], Robert J.	....do....	18	May	2, 1864	100 dys.	Mustered out with company Sept. 3, 1864.
[illegible]	....do....	25	May	2, 1864	100 dys.	Mustered out with company Sept. 3, 1864.
[illegible] F.	....do....	27	May	2, 1864	100 dys.	Mustered out with company Sept. 3, 1864.
[illegible], Edmund	....do....	18	May	2, 1864	100 dys.	Mustered out with company Sept. 3, 1864.
[illegible], Stephen	....do....	18	May	2, 1864	100 dys.	Mustered out with company Sept. 3, 1864.
[illegible], Zachariah T.	....do....	18	May	2, 1864	100 dys.	Mustered out with company Sept. 3, 1864.
[illegible], James A.	....do....	30	May	2, 1864	100 dys.	Mustered out with company Sept. 3, 1864.
[illegible], Joseph	....do....	21	May	2, 1864	100 dys.	Mustered out with company Sept. 3, 1864.
[illegible], John	....do....	26	May	2, 1864	100 dys.	Mustered out with company Sept. 3, 1864.
[illegible], William T.	....do....	18	May	2, 1864	100 dys.	Mustered out with company Sept. 3, 1864.
[illegible], Alfred	....do....	18	May	2, 1864	100 dys.	Mustered out with company Sept. 3, 1864.
[illegible], Daniel W.	....do....	36	May	2, 1864	100 dys.	Mustered out with company Sept. 3, 1864.
[illegible], James W.	....do....	18	May	2, 1864	100 dys.	Mustered out with company Sept. 3, 1864.
Smith, Samuel B.	....do....	40	May	2, 1864	100 dys.	Mustered out with company Sept. 3, 1864.
[illegible], Edward	....do....	22	May	2, 1864	100 dys.	Mustered out with company Sept. 3, 1864.
[illegible], John J.	....do....	22	May	2, 1864	100 dys.	Mustered out with company Sept. 3, 1864.
[illegible], James	....do....	32	May	2, 1864	100 dys.	Mustered out with company Sept. 3, 1864.
[illegible], Elliot	....do....	21	May	2, 1864	100 dys.	Mustered out with company Sept. 3, 1864.
[illegible], James M.	....do....	18	May	2, 1864	100 dys.	Mustered out with company Sept. 3, 1864.
[illegible], Riley	....do....	20	May	2, 1864	100 dys.	Mustered out with company Sept. 3, 1864.
[illegible], Wilson	....do....	18	May	2, 1864	100 dys.	Mustered out with company Sept. 3, 1864.
[illegible], David	....do....	18	May	2, 1864	100 dys.	Mustered out with company Sept. 3, 1864.
Yeager, William H.	....do....	23	May	2, 1864	100 dys.	Mustered out with company Sept. 3, 1864.

COMPANY F.

Mustered in May 11, 1864, at Gallipolis, O., by W. P. McCleery, 1st Lieutenant 18th Infantry, U. S. Army. Mustered out Sept. 3, 1864, at Gallipolis, O., by P. W. Horrigan, 2d Lieutenant 2d U. S. Cavalry.

Amos Ripley	Captain.	61	May	2, 1864	100 dys.	Mustered out with company Sept. 3, 1864.
Nathan Waddell	1st Lieut.	38	May	2, 1864	100 dys.	Mustered out with company Sept. 3, 1864.
John W. Scott	2d Lieut.	24	May	2, 1864	100 dys.	Mustered out with company Sept. 3, 1864.
Stephen G. Keller	1st Sergt.	29	May	2, 1864	100 dys.	Mustered out with company Sept. 3, 1864.
Morgan D. Carter	Sergeant.	25	May	2, 1864	100 dys.	Mustered out with company Sept. 3, 1864.
William B. Allison	....do....	40	May	2, 1864	100 dys.	Mustered out with company Sept. 3, 1864.
George E. Johnson	....do....	20	May	2, 1864	100 dys.	Mustered out with company Sept. 3, 1864.
Henry J. Sharp	....do....	19	May	2, 1864	100 dys.	Mustered out with company Sept. 3, 1864.
Thomas M. [illegible]	Corporal.	29	May	2, 1864	100 dys.	Mustered out with company Sept. 3, 1864.
Josiah W. Williams	....do....	30	May	2, 1864	100 dys.	Mustered out with company Sept. 3, 1864.
George Wiseman	....do....	28	May	2, 1864	100 dys.	Mustered out with company Sept. 3, 1864.
Abraham Gilbert	....do....	36	May	2, 1864	100 dys.	Mustered out with company Sept. 3, 1864.
George F. Hixon	....do....	27	May	2, 1864	100 dys.	Mustered out with company Sept. 3, 1864.
David N. Jones	....do....	23	May	2, 1864	100 dys.	Mustered out with company Sept. 3, 1864.
Noah W. Wood	....do....	22	May	2, 1864	100 dys.	Mustered out with company Sept. 3, 1864.
John L. Ferrell	....do....	36	May	2, 1864	100 dys.	Mustered out with company Sept. 3, 1864.
Nathan Ripley	Musician	34	May	2, 1864	100 dys.	Mustered out with company Sept. 3, 1864.
Harvey Ripley	....do....	22	May	2, 1864	100 dys.	Mustered out with company Sept. 3, 1864.
Barkley Butler	Wagoner.	34	May	2, 1864	100 dys.	Mustered out with company Sept. 3, 1864.
Armintrout, Henry F.	Private.	28	May	2, 1864	100 dys.	Mustered out with company Sept. 3, 1864.
Armintrout, Thomas L.	....do....	30	May	2, 1864	100 dys.	Mustered out with company Sept. 3, 1864.
Biggs, Francis M.	....do....	25	May	2, 1864	100 dys.	Mustered out with company Sept. 3, 1864.
Biggs, James A.	....do....	19	May	2, 1864	100 dys.	Mustered out with company Sept. 3, 1864.
Bostic, Moses	....do....	31	May	2, 1864	100 dys.	Mustered out with company Sept. 3, 1864.
Bostic, Thomas	....do....	29	May	2, 1864	100 dys.	Mustered out with company Sept. 3, 1864.
Bostic, James K.	....do....	22	May	2, 1864	100 dys.	Mustered out with company Sept. 3, 1864.
Boyer, Samuel	....do....	36	May	2, 1864	100 dys.	Mustered out with company Sept. 3, 1864.
Campbell, George W.	....do....	24	May	2, 1864	100 dys.	Mustered out with company Sept. 3, 1864.
Campbell, John W.	....do....	20	May	2, 1864	100 dys.	Mustered out with company Sept. 3, 1864.
Carter, Amon J.	....do....	31	May	2, 1864	100 dys.	Mustered out with company Sept. 3, 1864.
Carter, Augustus J.	....do....	39	May	2, 1864	100 dys.	Mustered out with company Sept. 3, 1864.
Carter, Darius M.	....do....	27	May	2, 1864	100 dys.	Mustered out with company Sept. 3, 1864.
Carter, George M.	....do....	24	May	2, 1864	100 dys.	Mustered out with company Sept. 3, 1864.
Carter, William A.	....do....	28	May	2, 1864	100 dys.	Mustered out with company Sept. 3, 1864.
Chick, Charles J.	....do....	18	May	2, 1864	100 dys.	Mustered out with company Sept. 3, 1864.
Clark, Thomas J.	....do....	30	May	2, 1864	100 dys.	Mustered out with company Sept. 3, 1864.
Cochran, William H.	....do....	19	May	2, 1864	100 dys.	Mustered out with company Sept. 3, 1864.
Davis, William A.	....do....	18	May	2, 1864	100 dys.	Mustered out with company Sept. 3, 1864.

Names.	Rank.	Age.	Date of Entering the Service.	Period of Service.	Remarks.
Drummond, Thomas	Private	39	June 13, 1864	100 dys.	Mustered out with company Sept. 3, 1864.
Ecker, George W	do	42	June 4, 1864	100 dys.	Mustered out with company Sept. 3, 1864.
Erwin, Josiah	do	25	May 2, 1864	100 dys.	Mustered out with company Sept. 3, 1864.
Fry, Pinkney B	do	19	May 2, 1864	100 dys.	Mustered out with company Sept. 3, 1864.
Glen, George R	do	20	May 2, 1864	100 dys.	Mustered out with company Sept. 3, 1864.
Green, Isaac	do	35	May 2, 1864	100 dys.	Mustered out with company Sept. 3, 1864.
Green, Lemuel	do	37	May 2, 1864	100 dys.	Mustered out with company Sept. 3, 1864.
Hanlin, Moses	do	18	May 2, 1864	100 dys.	Mustered out with company Sept. 3, 1864.
Henshaw, Eli J	do	18	May 2, 1864	100 dys.	Mustered out with company Sept. 3, 1864.
Henshaw, Edward L	do	27	May 2, 1864	100 dys.	Mustered out with company Sept. 3, 1864.
Henshaw, James G	do	19	May 2, 1864	100 dys.	Mustered out with company Sept. 3, 1864.
Jones, Isaac	do	16	May 2, 1864	100 dys.	Mustered out with company Sept. 3, 1864.
Jones, Jenkin	do	21	May 2, 1864	100 dys.	Mustered out with company Sept. 3, 1864.
Keller, Robert N	do	34	May 2, 1864	100 dys.	Mustered out with company Sept. 3, 1864.
Kerns, Anthony W	do	17	May 2, 1864	100 dys.	Wounded twice June 20, 1864, in action wi bushwhackers, while guarding dispatc bearer, near Barboursville, W. Va.; mustered out with company Sept. 3, 1864.
McDaniel, Elemander	do	21	May 2, 1864	100 dys.	Mustered out with company Sept. 3, 1864.
McDaniel, Friend	do	29	May 2, 1864	100 dys.	Mustered out with company Sept. 3, 1864.
McDaniel, Henry	do	31	May 2, 1864	100 dys.	Mustered out with company Sept. 3, 1864.
McDaniel, Silas	do	36	May 2, 1864	100 dys.	Mustered out with company Sept. 3, 1864.
Minon, John	do	18	May 2, 1864	100 dys.	Mustered out with company Sept. 3, 1864.
Moodispaugh George	do	25	May 2, 1864	100 dys.	Mustered out with company Sept. 3, 1864.
Morgan, Joseph A	do	28	May 2, 1864	100 dys.	Mustered out with company Sept. 3, 1864.
Patterson Ansel A	do	43	May 2, 1864	100 dys.	Mustered out with company Sept. 3, 1864.
Patterson, Ephraim	do	39	May 2, 1864	100 dys.	Mustered out with company Sept. 3, 1864.
Prose, Alexander	do	18	May 2, 1864	100 dys.	Mustered out with company Sept. 3, 1864.
Prose, Jacob A	do	25	May 2, 1864	100 dys.	Mustered out with company Sept. 3, 1864.
Prose, John J	do	39	May 2, 1864	100 dys.	Mustered out with company Sept. 3, 1864.
Prose, William	do	43	May 2, 1864	100 dys.	Mustered out with company Sept. 3, 1864.
Ripley, James O	do	28	May 2, 1864	100 dys.	Mustered out with company Sept. 3, 1864.
Ripley, Philo	do	31	May 2, 1864	100 dys.	Mustered out with company Sept. 3, 1864.
Simmerman, Thomas J.	do	19	May 2, 1864	100 dys.	Mustered out with company Sept. 3, 1864.
Slagle, James W	do	42	May 2, 1864	100 dys.	Mustered out with company Sept. 3, 1864.
Smeltzer, Darius M	do	20	May 2, 1864	100 dys.	Mustered out with company Sept. 3, 1864.
Smeltzer, Joseph	do	28	May 2, 1864	100 dys.	Wounded twice June 20, 1864, by bu whackers, while guarding dispatch-bea near Barboursville, W. Va.; mustered with company Sept. 3, 1864.
Smeltzer, Peter	do	27	May 2, 1864	100 dys.	Mustered out with company Sept. 3, 1864.
Smith, James	do	46	May 2, 1864	100 dys.	Mustered out with company Sept. 3, 1864.
Taylor, Henry T	do	26	May 2, 1864	100 dys.	Mustered out with company Sept. 3, 1864.
Topping, Cincinnatus	do	19	May 2, 1864	100 dys.	Mustered out with company Sept. 3, 1864.
Watts, John W	do	20	May 2, 1864	100 dys.	Mustered out with company Sept. 3, 1864.
Wickline, Henry T	do	31	May 2, 1864	100 dys.	Mustered out with company Sept. 3, 1864.
Wigner, Daniel	do	36	May 2, 1864	100 dys.	Mustered out with company Sept. 3, 1864.
Wigner, John	do	39	May 2, 1864	100 dys.	Mustered out with company Sept. 3, 1864.
Williams, John H	do	28	May 2, 1864	100 dys.	Mustered out with company Sept. 3, 1864.
Williams, William H	do	21	May 2, 1864	100 dys.	Mustered out with company Sept. 3, 1864.
Wise, John H	do	27	May 2, 1864	100 dys.	Mustered out with company Sept. 3, 1864.
Wiseman, Andrew	do	35	May 2, 1864	100 dys.	Mustered out with company Sept. 3, 1864.
Wood, Charles	do	39	May 2, 1864	100 dys.	Mustered out with company Sept. 3, 1864.

COMPANY G.

Mustered in May 11, 1864, at Gallipolis, O., by W. P. McCleery, 1st Lieutenant 18th Infantry, U. S. Army. M tered out Sept. 3, 1864, at Gallipolis, O., by P. W. Horrigan, 2d Lieutenant 2d U. S. Cavalry.

Names.	Rank.	Age.	Date of Entering the Service.	Period of Service.	Remarks.
William W. Reilly	Captain.	38	May 2, 1864	100 dys.	Mustered out with company Sept. 3, 1864.
Thomas J. Pursell	1st Lieut.	34	May 2, 1864	100 dys.	Mustered out with company Sept. 3, 1864.
William H. Clark	2d Lieut.	36	May 2, 1864	100 dys.	Mustered out with company Sept. 3, 1864.
William A. Thomas	1st Sergt.	29	May 2, 1864	100 dys.	Mustered out with company Sept. 3, 1864.
John McCathron	Sergeant.	24	May 2, 1864	100 dys.	Mustered out with company Sept. 3, 1864.
James Matthers	do	34	May 2, 1864	100 dys.	Mustered out with company Sept. 3, 1864.
Thomas Dupler	do	18	May 2, 1864	100 dys.	Mustered out with company Sept. 3, 1864.
Alexander Ward	do	27	May 2, 1864	100 dys.	Mustered out with company Sept. 3, 1864.
Joel J. Allen	Corporal.	27	May 2, 1864	100 dys.	Mustered out with company Sept. 3, 1864.
James Brannen	do	24	May 2, 1864	100 dys.	Mustered out with company Sept. 3, 1864.
William H. McClellan	do	19	May 2, 1864	100 dys.	Mustered out with company Sept. 3, 1864.
Seth Shaner	do	26	May 2, 1864	100 dys.	Mustered out with company Sept. 3, 1864.
William J. McCathron	do	24	May 2, 1864	100 dys.	Mustered out with company Sept. 3, 1864.
Franklin D. Nide	do	23	May 2, 1864	100 dys.	Mustered out with company Sept. 3, 1864.
George Scott	do	34	May 2, 1864	100 dys.	Mustered out with company Sept. 3, 1864.
Joseph Walters	do	37	May 2, 1864	100 dys.	Mustered out with company Sept. 3, 1864.
William Fryer	Musician	16	May 2, 1864	100 dys.	Mustered out with company Sept. 3, 1864.
Frederick A. Stearns	do	19	May 2, 1864	100 dys.	Mustered out with company Sept. 3, 1864.
Alderman, Franklin T.	Private.	18	May 2, 1864	100 dys.	Mustered out with company Sept. 3, 1864.
Allen, Jehiel	do	28	May 2, 1864	100 dys.	Mustered out with company Sept. 3, 1864.
Anthony, Thomas R	do	42	May 2, 1864	100 dys.	Mustered out with company Sept. 3, 1864.

Names.	Rank.	Age.	Date of Entering the Service.	Period of Service.	Remarks.
[illegible], John	Private	27	May 2, 1864	100 dys.	Mustered out with company Sept. 3, 1864.
[illegible]	do.	26	May 2, 1864	100 dys.	Mustered out with company Sept. 3, 1864.
[illegible] K.	do.	23	May 2, 1864	100 dys.	Mustered out with company Sept. 3, 1864.
[illegible], [illegible] C.	do.	35	May 2, 1864	100 dys.	Mustered out with company Sept. 3, 1864.
[illegible]	do.	36	May 2, 1864	100 dys.	Mustered out with company Sept. 3, 1864.
[illegible]	do.	18	May 2, 1864	100 dys.	Mustered out with company Sept. 3, 1864.
[illegible]	do.	19	May 2, 1864	100 dys.	Mustered out with company Sept. 3, 1864.
[illegible], Samuel F.	do.	40	May 2, 1864	100 dys.	Mustered out with company Sept. 3, 1864.
[illegible], Henry	do.	21	May 2, 1864	100 dys.	Mustered out with company Sept. 3, 1864.
[illegible] F.	do.	18	May 2, 1864	100 dys.	Mustered out with company Sept. 3, 1864.
[illegible]	do.	18	May 2, 1864	100 dys.	Mustered out with company Sept. 3, 1864.
[illegible], James W.	do.	18	May 2, 1864	100 dys.	Mustered out with company Sept. 3, 1864.
[illegible], Horace	do.	18	May 2, 1864	100 dys.	Mustered out with company Sept. 3, 1864.
[illegible], Alexander	do.	18	May 2, 1864	100 dys.	Mustered out with company Sept. 3, 1864.
[illegible], Adam T.	do.	37	May 2, 1864	100 dys.	Mustered out with company Sept. 3, 1864.
[illegible], John M.	do.	26	May 2, 1864	100 dys.	Mustered out with company Sept. 3, 1864.
Harmon, King E.	do.	23	May 2, 1864	100 dys.	Mustered out with company Sept. 3, 1864.
[illegible], John J.	do.	29	May 2, 1864	100 dys.	Mustered out with company Sept. 3, 1864.
[illegible], Lewis	do.	28	May 2, 1864	100 dys.	Mustered out with company Sept. 3, 1864.
[illegible], Anderson	do.	26	May 2, 1864	100 dys.	Mustered out with company Sept. 3, 1864.
[illegible], Edward	do.	19	May 2, 1864	100 dys.	Mustered out with company Sept. 3, 1864.
[illegible], Leonidas W.	do.	21	May 2, 1864	100 dys.	Mustered out with company Sept. 3, 1864.
[illegible]ton, Stephen T.	do.	34	May 2, 1864	100 dys.	Mustered out with company Sept. 3, 1864.
[illegible], James	do.	22	May 2, 1864	100 dys.	Mustered out with company Sept. 3, 1864.
Lan[illegible], Joseph	do.	32	May 2, 1864	100 dys.	Mustered out with company Sept. 3, 1864.
[illegible], Joshua	do.	30	May 2, 1864	100 dys.	Mustered out with company Sept. 3, 1864.
[illegible], Alexander	do.	20	May 2, 1864	100 dys.	Mustered out with company Sept. 3, 1864.
Lombard, Alphonse E.	do.	27	May 2, 1864	100 dys.	Mustered out with company Sept. 3, 1864.
Love, James L.	do.	25	May 2, 1864	100 dys.	Mustered out with company Sept. 3, 1864.
Lowry, Jefferson	do.	20	May 2, 1864	100 dys.	Mustered out with company Sept. 3, 1864.
[illegible], James H. P.	do.	21	May 2, 1864	100 dys.	Mustered out with company Sept. 3, 1864.
McCutcheon, Hugh	do.	18	May 2, 1864	100 dys.	Mustered out with company Sept. 3, 1864.
McKee, Andrew	do.	24	May 2, 1864	100 dys.	Mustered out with company Sept. 3, 1864.
[illegible], George W.	do.	28	May 2, 1864	100 dys.	Mustered out with company Sept. 3, 1864.
Martin, James F.	do.	34	May 2, 1864	100 dys.	Mustered out with company Sept. 3, 1864.
Maxwell, John	do.	25	May 2, 1864	100 dys.	Mustered out with company Sept. 3, 1864.
Mills, Jacob F.	do.	20	May 2, 1864	100 dys.	Mustered out with company Sept. 3, 1864.
Morrison, William H.	do.	32	May 2, 1864	100 dys.	Mustered out with company Sept. 3, 1864.
Murphy, George	do.	26	May 2, 1864	100 dys.	Mustered out with company Sept. 3, 1864.
[illegible], Aaron	do.	21	May 2, 1864	100 dys.	Mustered out with company Sept. 3, 1864.
Myers, Adam C.	do.	22	May 2, 1864	100 dys.	Mustered out with company Sept. 3, 1864.
Myers, John W.	do.	24	May 2, 1864	100 dys.	Mustered out with company Sept. 3, 1864.
[illegible]ton, Clinton A.	do.	18	May 2, 1864	100 dys.	Mustered out with company Sept. 3, 1864.
[illegible], Matthew	do.	45	May 2, 1864	100 dys.	Mustered out with company Sept. 3, 1864.
Oliver, Elijah	do.	31	May 2, 1864	100 dys.	Mustered out with company Sept. 3, 1864.
Osborn, [illegible] H.	do.	26	May 2, 1864	100 dys.	Mustered out with company Sept. 3, 1864.
[illegible], Andrew	do.	27	May 2, 1864	100 dys.	Mustered out with company Sept. 3, 1864.
Peters, William	do.	30	May 2, 1864	100 dys.	Mustered out with company Sept. 3, 1864.
Powell, Alvey	do.	27	May 2, 1864	100 dys.	Mustered out with company Sept. 3, 1864.
[illegible], James	do.	34	May 2, 1864	100 dys.	Mustered out with company Sept. 3, 1864.
[illegible], Robert C.	do.	43	May 2, 1864	100 dys.	Mustered out with company Sept. 3, 1864.
[illegible], James S.	do.	28	May 2, 1864	100 dys.	Mustered out with company Sept. 3, 1864.
Smith, George W.	do.	19	May 2, 1864	100 dys.	Mustered out with company Sept. 3, 1864.
[illegible], George W.	do.	23	May 2, 1864	100 dys.	Mustered out with company Sept. 3, 1864.
[illegible], William P.	do.	29	May 2, 1864	100 dys.	Mustered out with company Sept. 3, 1864.
Thompson, James R.	do.	22	May 2, 1864	100 dys.	Mustered out with company Sept. 3, 1864.
[illegible], James V.	do.	45	May 2, 1864	100 dys.	Mustered out with company Sept. 3, 1864.
[illegible], Norman	do.	38	May 2, 1864	100 dys.	Mustered out with company Sept. 3, 1864.
[illegible], Henry C.	do.	19	May 2, 1864	100 dys.	Mustered out with company Sept. 3, 1864.
Wilson, Joseph	do.	20	May 2, 1864	100 dys.	Mustered out with company Sept. 3, 1864.
Wright, Thomas C.	do.	24	May 2, 1864	100 dys.	Mustered out with company Sept. 3, 1864.
[illegible], William	do.	19	May 2, 1864	100 dys.	Mustered out with company Sept. 3, 1864.
Young, Philip	do.	38	May 2, 1864	100 dys.	Mustered out with company Sept. 3, 1864.
[illegible], John P.	do.	35	May 2, 1864	100 dys.	Mustered out with company Sept. 3, 1864.

COMPANY H.

Mustered in May 11, 1864, at Gallipolis, O., by W. P. McCleery, 1st Lieutenant 18th Infantry, U. S. Army. Mustered out Sept. 3, 1864, at Gallipolis, O., by P. W. Horrigan, 2d Lieutenant 2d U. S. Cavalry.

Names.	Rank.	Age.	Date of Entering the Service.	Period of Service.	Remarks.
William W. Kurtz	Captain.	41	May 2, 1864	100 dys.	Mustered out with company Sept. 3, 1864.
Franklin Askins	1st Lieut.	41	May 2, 1864	100 dys.	Mustered out with company Sept. 3, 1864.
Warren R. Northrop	2d Lieut.	25	May 2, 1864	100 dys.	Mustered out with company Sept. 3, 1864.
Ira R. Fuller	1st Sergt.	26	May 2, 1864	100 dys.	Mustered out with company Sept. 3, 1864.
Josephus C. Robinet	Sergeant.	28	May 2, 1864	100 dys.	Mustered out with company Sept. 3, 1864.
David M. Cooper	do.	25	May 2, 1864	100 dys.	Mustered out with company Sept. 3, 1864.
Samuel V. Coe	do.	27	May 2, 1864	100 dys.	Mustered out with company Sept. 3, 1864.
Samuel R. Jennings	do.	28	May 2, 1864	100 dys.	Mustered out with company Sept. 3, 1864.
John Connor	Corporal.	25	May 2, 1864	100 dys.	Mustered out with company Sept. 3, 1864.
Daniel N. Brown	do.	20	May 2, 1864	100 dys.	Mustered out with company Sept. 3, 1864.
Asbury N. Fairley	do.	19	May 2, 1864	100 dys.	Mustered out with company Sept. 3, 1864.

Names.	Rank.	Age.	Date of Entering the Service.	Period of Service.	Remarks.
William W. Blake	Corporal.	22	May 2, 1864	100 dys.	Mustered out with company Sept. 3, 1864.
Frank P. Dell	...do....	29	May 2, 1864	100 dys.	Appointed June 18, 1864; mustered out with company Sept. 3, 1864.
Andrew Culver	...do....	18	May 2, 1864	100 dys.	Mustered out with company Sept. 3, 1864.
Henry Enlow	...do....	19	May 2, 1864	100 dys.	Mustered out with company Sept. 3, 1864.
Ezra Six	...do....	18	May 2, 1864	100 dys.	Mustered out with company Sept. 3, 1864.
James M. Adair	Musician	25	May 2, 1864	100 dys.	Mustered out with company Sept. 3, 1864.
George M. Gould	...do....	15	May 2, 1864	100 dys.	Mustered out with company Sept. 3, 1864.
Bean, George W	Private	36	May 2, 1864	100 dys.	Mustered out with company Sept. 3, 1864.
Bobo, Benson	...do....	18	May 2, 1864	100 dys.	Died July 26, 1864, at his home, in Athens County, O.
Bright, William I.	...do....	28	May 2, 1864	100 dys.	Promoted to Hospital Steward May 12, 1864.
Brown, James D.	...do....	18	May 2, 1864	100 dys.	Mustered out with company Sept. 3, 1864.
Campbell, Lowell M.	...do....	17	May 2, 1864	100 dys.	Mustered out with company Sept. 3, 1864.
Canny, William H.	...do....	23	May 2, 1864	100 dys.	Mustered out with company Sept. 3, 1864.
Carter, John H.	...do....	20	May 2, 1864	100 dys.	Mustered out with company Sept. 3, 1864.
Cass, Simeon W.	...do....	44	May 2, 1864	100 dys.	Mustered out with company Sept. 3, 1864.
Clements, Philip W.	...do....	17	May 2, 1864	100 dys.	Mustered out with company Sept. 3, 1864.
Cline, James	...do....	25	May 2, 1864	100 dys.	Mustered out with company Sept. 3, 1864.
Clouse, James W.	...do....	36	May 2, 1864	100 dys.	Appointed Corporal May 2, 1864; reduced June 18, 1864, at his own request; mustered out with company Sept. 3, 1864.
Crossan, David R.	...do....	37	May 2, 1864	100 dys.	Mustered out with company Sept. 3, 1864.
Crossan, Hiram	...do....	19	May 2, 1864	100 dys.	Mustered out with company Sept. 3, 1864.
Crossan, Israel	...do....	30	May 2, 1864	100 dys.	Mustered out with company Sept. 3, 1864.
Culver, Andrew M.	...do....	48	May 2, 1864	100 dys.	Mustered out with company Sept. 3, 1864.
Daily, Andrew	...do....	19	May 2, 1864	100 dys.	Mustered out with company Sept. 3, 1864.
Daily, James T.	...do....	18	May 2, 1864	100 dys.	Mustered out with company Sept. 3, 1864.
Davis, Orin W.	...do....	22	May 2, 1864	100 dys.	Mustered out with company Sept. 3, 1864.
DeWitt, Lewis C.	...do....	32	May 2, 1864	100 dys.	Mustered out with company Sept. 3, 1864.
Dickson, Jefferson	...do....	19	May 2, 1864	100 dys.	Mustered out with company Sept. 3, 1864.
Dickson, Marias	...do....	18	May 2, 1864	100 dys.	Mustered out with company Sept. 3, 1864.
Dickson, Robert	...do....	37	May 2, 1864	100 dys.	Mustered out with company Sept. 3, 1864.
Enlow, William	...do....	19	May 2, 1864	100 dys.	Mustered out with company Sept. 3, 1864.
Gabriel, Eber	...do....	18	May 2, 1864	100 dys.	Mustered out with company Sept. 3, 1864.
Graham, Elias	...do....	38	May 2, 1864	100 dys.	Mustered out with company Sept. 3, 1864.
Graham, Ira	...do....	22	May 2, 1864	100 dys.	Mustered out with company Sept. 3, 1864.
Graham, William	...do....	17	May 2, 1864	100 dys.	Mustered out with company Sept. 3, 1864.
Greathouse, George	...do....	42	May 2, 1864	100 dys.	Mustered out with company Sept. 3, 1864.
Harper, Homer C.	...do....	16	May 2, 1864	100 dys.	Mustered out with company Sept. 3, 1864.
Harvey, John	...do....	37	May 2, 1864	100 dys.	Mustered out with company Sept. 3, 1864.
Holmes, Albert G.	...do....	22	May 2, 1864	100 dys.	Mustered out with company Sept. 3, 1864.
Hummell, Joshua	...do....	39	May 2, 1864	100 dys.	Mustered out with company Sept. 3, 1864.
Irwin, William N.	...do....	39	May 2, 1864	100 dys.	Mustered out with company Sept. 3, 1864.
Keepers, John	...do....	24	May 2, 1864	100 dys.	Mustered out with company Sept. 3, 1864.
King, Silas D.	...do....	24	May 2, 1864	100 dys.	Mustered out with company Sept. 3, 1864.
Knight, Zalmon	...do....	19	May 2, 1864	100 dys.	Mustered out with company Sept. 3, 1864.
Knowlton, Levi	...do....	30	May 2, 1864	100 dys.	Mustered out with company Sept. 3, 1864.
Lindley, Lewis M.	...do....	18	May 2, 1864	100 dys.	Mustered out with company Sept. 3, 1864.
Lindley, Samuel S.	...do....	33	May 2, 1864	100 dys.	Mustered out with company Sept. 3, 1864.
Lindley, William C.	...do....	44	May 2, 1864	100 dys.	Mustered out with company Sept. 3, 1864.
Lynn, Torrence	...do....	27	May 2, 1864	100 dys.	Mustered out with company Sept. 3, 1864.
McCully, Joseph	...do....	26	May 2, 1864	100 dys.	Mustered out with company Sept. 3, 1864.
McCully, Vinton	...do....	22	May 2, 1864	100 dys.	Mustered out with company Sept. 3, 1864.
McLaughlin, Wyley	...do....	24	May 2, 1864	100 dys.	Mustered out with company Sept. 3, 1864.
Mahoney, James	...do....	36	May 2, 1864	100 dys.	Mustered out with company Sept. 3, 1864.
Martin, James T	...do....	44	May 2, 1864	100 dys.	Mustered out with company Sept. 3, 1864.
Martin, Samuel	...do....	18	May 2, 1864	100 dys.	Mustered out with company Sept. 3, 1864.
Matheny, Albert	...do....	21	May 2, 1864	100 dys.	Mustered out with company Sept. 3, 1864.
Matheny, James P.	...do....	37	May 2, 1864	100 dys.	Mustered out with company Sept. 3, 1864.
Nicholas, James	...do....	18	May 2, 1864	100 dys.	Mustered out with company Sept. 3, 1864.
Piles, Peter F.	...do....	23	May 2, 1864	100 dys.	Mustered out with company Sept. 3, 1864.
Pringy, Jonas	...do....	37	May 2, 1864	100 dys.	Mustered out with company Sept. 3, 1864.
Rickey, George W.	...do....	26	May 2, 1864	100 dys.	Mustered out with company Sept. 3, 1864.
Rigg, Parker	...do....	33	May 2, 1864	100 dys.	Mustered out with company Sept. 3, 1864.
Rigg, Josephus L.	...do....	18	May 2, 1864	100 dys.	Mustered out with company Sept. 3, 1864.
Schoonover, Jasper	...do....	27	May 2, 1864	100 dys.	Mustered out with company Sept. 3, 1864.
Scott, Francis T.	...do....	18	May 2, 1864	100 dys.	Mustered out with company Sept. 3, 1864.
Six, Moses	...do....	26	May 2, 1864	100 dys.	Mustered out with company Sept. 3, 1864.
Six, Oscar	...do....	25	May 2, 1864	100 dys.	Mustered out with company Sept. 3, 1864.
Stanley, Eugene	...do....	18	May 2, 1864	100 dys.	Mustered out with company Sept. 3, 1864.
Stemm, John M.	...do....	28	May 2, 1864	100 dys.	Mustered out with company Sept. 3, 1864.
Vorhes, John	...do....	29	May 2, 1864	100 dys.	Mustered out with company Sept. 3, 1864.
Warehime, George	...do....	21	May 2, 1864	100 dys.	Mustered out with company Sept. 3, 1864.
West, Mordecai	...do....	19	May 2, 1864	100 dys.	Mustered out with company Sept. 3, 1864.
Wilson, Alpheus	...do....	36	May 2, 1864	100 dys.	Mustered out with company Sept. 3, 1864.
Witham, Jedediah	...do....	37	May 2, 1864	100 dys.	Mustered out with company Sept. 3, 1864.
Wright, James O.	...do....	23	May 2, 1864	100 dys.	Mustered out with company Sept. 3, 1864.

COMPANY I.

Mustered in May 14, 1864, at Gallipolis, O., by W. P. McCleery, 1st Lieutenant 18th Infantry, U. S. Army. Mustered out Sept. 3, 1864, at Gallipolis, O., by P. W. Horrigan, 2d Lieutenant 2d U. S. Cavalry.

Names.	Rank.	Age.	Date of Entering the Service.	Period of Service.	Remarks.
George S. Kirker	Captain.	51	May 2, 1864	100 dys.	Mustered out with company Sept. 3, 1864.
John A. Morris	1st Lieut.	31	May 2, 1864	100 dys.	Mustered out with company Sept. 3, 1864.
Eli Washburn	2d Lieut.	32	May 2, 1864	100 dys.	Mustered out with company Sept. 3, 1864.
John L. Bussmann	1st Serg't.	37	May 2, 1864	100 dys.	Mustered out with company Sept. 3, 1864.
Fred E. Wilber	Sergeant.	40	May 2, 1864	100 dys.	Mustered out with company Sept. 3, 1864.
John E. Mahaffy	do.	40	May 2, 1864	100 dys.	Mustered out with company Sept. 3, 1864.
Oscar E. Sutton	do.	21	May 2, 1864	100 dys.	Mustered out with company Sept. 3, 1864.
Abraham H. Mahaffey	do.	47	May 2, 1864	100 dys.	Mustered out with company Sept. 3, 1864.
Casey Paxton	Corporal.	25	May 2, 1864	100 dys.	Mustered out with company Sept. 3, 1864.
George Gibbony	do.	29	May 2, 1864	100 dys.	Mustered out with company Sept. 3, 1864.
Daniel Riffle	do.	47	May 2, 1864	100 dys.	Mustered out with company Sept. 3, 1864.
William P. Hanna	do.	36	May 2, 1864	100 dys.	Mustered out with company Sept. 3, 1864.
Henry W. Teschner	do.	19	May 2, 1864	100 dys.	Mustered out with company Sept. 3, 1864.
Henry May	do.	41	May 2, 1864	100 dys.	Mustered out with company Sept. 3, 1864.
William E. F. M. Tener	do.	27	May 2, 1864	100 dys.	Mustered out with company Sept. 3, 1864.
John L. Baldridge	do.	18	May 2, 1864	100 dys.	Mustered out with company Sept. 3, 1864.
Simeon L. R. Morris	Musician	19	May 2, 1864	100 dys.	Mustered out with company Sept. 3, 1864.
Samuel Walker	do.	45	May 2, 1864	100 dys.	Mustered out with company Sept. 3, 1864.
William D. Kirkpatrick	Wagoner.	23	May 2, 1864	100 dys.	Mustered out with company Sept. 3, 1864.
Bayless, Calvin	Private.	19	May 2, 1864	100 dys.	Mustered out with company Sept. 3, 1864.
Bayless, Alonzo	do.	18	May 2, 1864	100 dys.	Mustered out with company Sept. 3, 1864.
Bloom, George	do.	21	May 2, 1864	100 dys.	Mustered out with company Sept. 3, 1864.
Campbell, John W.	do.	32	May 2, 1864	100 dys.	Mustered out with company Sept. 3, 1864.
Carrier, William H.	do.	23	May 2, 1864	100 dys.	Mustered out with company Sept. 3, 1864.
Copple, John E.	do.	30	May 2, 1864	100 dys.	Mustered out with company Sept. 3, 1864.
Copple, John	do.	..	May 2, 1864	100 dys.	Rejected by Examining Surgeon.
Curry, Freeborn G.	do.	42	May 2, 1864	100 dys.	Mustered out with company Sept. 3, 1864.
Ebrite, John W.	do.	18	May 2, 1864	100 dys.	Mustered out with company Sept. 3, 1864.
Ebrite, James M.	do.	18	May 2, 1864	100 dys.	Mustered out with company Sept. 3, 1864.
Ebrite, Andrew	do.	36	May 2, 1864	100 dys.	Mustered out with company Sept. 3, 1864.
Ellison, John	do.	25	May 2, 1864	100 dys.	Mustered out with company Sept. 3, 1864.
Elliott, Marion	do.	29	May 2, 1864	100 dys.	Mustered out with company Sept. 3, 1864.
Fitch, James F.	do.	36	May 2, 1864	100 dys.	Mustered out with company Sept. 3, 1864.
Frame, James W.	do.	15	May 2, 1864	100 dys.	Mustered out with company Sept. 3, 1864.
Frame, William K.	do.	48	May 2, 1864	100 dys.	Mustered out with company Sept. 3, 1864.
Frame, William P.	do.	17	May 2, 1864	100 dys.	Mustered out with company Sept. 3, 1864.
German, William T.	do.	21	May 2, 1864	100 dys.	Mustered out with company Sept. 3, 1864.
Gordon, John D.	do.	37	May 2, 1864	100 dys.	Mustered out with company Sept. 3, 1864.
Gordon, Francis M.	do.	18	May 2, 1864	100 dys.	Mustered out with company Sept. 3, 1864.
Holliday, James A.	do.	28	May 2, 1864	100 dys.	Mustered out with company Sept. 3, 1864.
Howland, David	do.	24	May 2, 1864	100 dys.	Mustered out with company Sept. 3, 1864.
Jackson, Winfield	do.	15	May 2, 1864	100 dys.	Mustered out with company Sept. 3, 1864.
Johnston, Adam M.	do.	38	May 2, 1864	100 dys.	Mustered out with company Sept. 3, 1864.
Kincaid, Andrew	do.	21	May 2, 1864	100 dys.	Mustered out with company Sept. 3, 1864.
Kirker, James A.	do.	42	May 2, 1864	100 dys.	Mustered out with company Sept. 3, 1864.
Kirkpatrick, John	do.	36	May 2, 1864	100 dys.	Mustered out with company Sept. 3, 1864.
Kirkpatrick, John E.	do.	35	May 2, 1864	100 dys.	Mustered out with company Sept. 3, 1864.
Kirkpatrick, John, Jr.	do.	18	May 2, 1864	100 dys.	Mustered out with company Sept. 3, 1864.
Kirkpatrick, Richard A.	do.	38	May 2, 1864	100 dys.	Mustered out with company Sept. 3, 1864.
Kirkpatrick, Samuel	do.	18	May 2, 1864	100 dys.	Mustered out with company Sept. 3, 1864.
Kirkpatrick, Thomas P.	do.	29	May 2, 1864	100 dys.	Mustered out with company Sept. 3, 1864.
[illegible], Jacob	do.	23	May 2, 1864	100 dys.	Mustered out with company Sept. 3, 1864.
Lepley, John	do.	37	May 2, 1864	100 dys.	Mustered out with company Sept. 3, 1864.
McClanahan, Samuel	do.	18	May 2, 1864	100 dys.	Mustered out with company Sept. 3, 1864.
Marshall, Samuel C.	do.	34	May 2, 1864	100 dys.	Mustered out with company Sept. 3, 1864.
May, Joseph S.	do.	35	May 2, 1864	100 dys.	Mustered out with company Sept. 3, 1864.
May, John D.	do.	18	May 2, 1864	100 dys.	Mustered out with company Sept. 3, 1864.
Miller, David R.	do.	27	May 2, 1864	100 dys.	Mustered out with company Sept. 3, 1864.
Moore, James	do.	41	May 2, 1864	100 dys.	Mustered out with company Sept. 3, 1864.
Moore, James P.	do.	19	May 2, 1864	100 dys.	Mustered out with company Sept. 3, 1864.
Moore, William L.	do.	20	May 2, 1864	100 dys.	Mustered out with company Sept. 3, 1864.
More, David	do.	..	May 2, 1864	100 dys.	Rejected by Examining Surgeon.
Morris, George W.	do.	25	May 2, 1864	100 dys.	Mustered out with company Sept. 3, 1864.
Morris, Joshua C.	do.	21	May 2, 1864	100 dys.	Mustered out with company Sept. 3, 1864.
Morris, Orange M.	do.	21	May 2, 1864	100 dys.	Mustered out with company Sept. 3, 1864.
Morris, Silas F.	do.	17	May 2, 1864	100 dys.	Mustered out with company Sept. 3, 1864.
Mosier, John	do.	40	May 2, 1864	100 dys.	Mustered out with company Sept. 3, 1864.
Mullen, Joseph	do.	22	May 2, 1864	100 dys.	Mustered out with company Sept. 3, 1864.
Patton, Cyrus	do.	31	May 2, 1864	100 dys.	Mustered out with company Sept. 3, 1864.
Perry, Needham B.	do.	18	May 2, 1864	100 dys.	Mustered out with company Sept. 3, 1864.
Pittenger, Jacob C.	do.	23	May 2, 1864	100 dys.	Mustered out with company Sept. 3, 1864.
Pittenger, Wilson M.	do.	19	May 2, 1864	100 dys.	Mustered out with company Sept. 3, 1864.
Platter, John D.	do.	18	May 2, 1864	100 dys.	Mustered out with company Sept. 3, 1864.
Porter, Powell B.	do.	26	May 2, 1864	100 dys.	Mustered out with company Sept. 3, 1864.
Purcell, Joseph B.	do.	..	May 2, 1864	100 dys.	Rejected by Examining Surgeon.
Riffle, Cyrus	do.	17	May 2, 1864	100 dys.	Mustered out with company Sept. 3, 1864.
Riffle, Thomas M.	do.	18	May 2, 1864	100 dys.	Mustered out with company Sept. 3, 1864.

Names.	Rank.	Age.	Date of Entering the Service.	Period of Service.	Remarks.
Robe, David	Private..	49	May 2, 1864	100 dys.	Mustered out with company Sept. 3, 1864.
Roebuck, Johnston	....do....	39	May 2, 1864	100 dys.	Mustered out with company Sept. 3, 1864.
Ryan, James L.	....do....	28	May 2, 1864	100 dys.	Mustered out with company Sept. 3, 1864.
Triebler, Daniel	....do....	36	May 2, 1864	100 dys.	Mustered out with company Sept. 3, 1864.
Walker, Charles	....do....	18	May 2, 1864	100 dys.	Mustered out with company Sept. 3, 1864.
Ward, Daniel A.	....do....	38	May 2, 1864	100 dys.	Mustered out with company Sept. 3, 1864.
Washburn, William	....do....	32	May 2, 1864	100 dys.	Mustered out with company Sept. 3, 1864.
Weeks, Risley	....do....	33	May 2, 1864	100 dys.	Mustered out with company Sept. 3, 1864.
West, George	....do....	18	May 2, 1864	100 dys.	Mustered out with company Sept. 3, 1864.
Werk, Samuel	....do....	22	May 2, 1864	100 dys.	Mustered out with company Sept. 3, 1864.
Wickerham, Peter M.	....do....	32	May 2, 1864	100 dys.	Mustered out with company Sept. 3, 1864.
Wright, Thomas J.	....do....	22	May 2, 1864	100 dys.	Mustered out with company Sept. 3, 1864.
Young, Thomas	....do....	43	May 2, 1864	100 dys.	Mustered out with company Sept. 3, 1864.
Zercher, William	....do....	16	May 2, 1864	100 dys.	Mustered out with company Sept. 3, 1864.

COMPANY K.

Mustered in May 11, 1861, at Gallipolis, O., by W. P. McCleery, 1st Lieutenant 18th Infantry, U. S. Army. Mustered out Sept. 3, 1864, at Gallipolis, O., by P. W. Horrigan, 2d Lieutenant 2d U. S. Cavalry.

Names.	Rank.	Age.	Date of Entering the Service.	Period of Service.	Remarks.
Simon M. Fields	Captain.	30	May 2, 1864	100 dys.	Mustered out with company Sept. 3, 1864.
Robert Parker	1st Lieut.	40	May 2, 1864	100 dys.	Mustered out with company Sept. 3, 1864.
Thomas Hayslip	2d Lieut.	29	May 2, 1864	100 dys.	Mustered out with company Sept. 3, 1864.
Thomas W. Gore	1st Sergt.	25	May 2, 1864	100 dys.	Mustered out with company Sept. 3, 1864.
Bartley Suttle	Sergeant.	39	May 2, 1864	100 dys.	Mustered out with company Sept. 3, 1864.
John B. Fields	....do....	26	May 2, 1864	100 dys.	Mustered out with company Sept. 3, 1864.
John E. McFarland	....do....	38	May 2, 1864	100 dys.	Mustered out with company Sept. 3, 1864.
John A. Bacon	....do....	22	May 2, 1864	100 dys.	Mustered out with company Sept. 3, 1864.
Willis L. Salesbury	Corporal.	41	May 2, 1864	100 dys.	Mustered out with company Sept. 3, 1864.
John F. Beck	....do....	19	May 2, 1864	100 dys.	Mustered out with company Sept. 3, 1864.
Joseph McFarland	....do....	35	May 2, 1864	100 dys.	Mustered out with company Sept. 3, 1864.
Jacob G. Porter	....do....	19	May 2, 1864	100 dys.	Mustered out with company Sept. 3, 1864.
Henry A. Newman	....do....	21	May 2, 1864	100 dys.	Mustered out with company Sept. 3, 1864.
Calvin R. Bradley	....do....	42	May 2, 1864	100 dys.	Mustered out with company Sept. 3, 1864.
Leonard Wolf	....do....	40	May 2, 1864	100 dys.	Mustered out with company Sept. 3, 1864.
John M. Fisher	....do....	43	May 2, 1864	100 dys.	Mustered out with company Sept. 3, 1864.
John M. Hayslip	Musician	18	May 2, 1864	100 dys.	Mustered out with company Sept. 3, 1864.
William J. Fields	....do....	19	May 2, 1864	100 dys.	Mustered out with company Sept. 3, 1864.
John N. Moore	Wagoner.	23	May 2, 1864	100 dys.	Mustered out with company Sept. 3, 1864.
Abbott, Amos	Private..	35	May 2, 1864	100 dys.	Mustered out with company Sept. 3, 1864.
Abbott, George	....do....	24	May 2, 1864	100 dys.	Mustered out with company Sept. 3, 1864.
Abbott, James	....do....	31	May 2, 1864	100 dys.	Mustered out with company Sept. 3, 1864.
Abbott, Reason	....do....	29	May 2, 1864	100 dys.	Mustered out with company Sept. 3, 1864.
Abbott, Richard	....do....	29	May 2, 1864	100 dys.	Mustered out with company Sept. 3, 1864.
Arnold, Mansfield	....do....	25	May 2, 1864	100 dys.	Mustered out with company Sept. 3, 1864.
Bashore, David	....do....	31	May 2, 1864	100 dys.	Mustered out with company Sept. 3, 1864.
Bashore, Thomas H. B.	....do....	19	May 2, 1864	100 dys.	Mustered out with company Sept. 3, 1864.
Beatman, Joseph	....do....	18	May 2, 1864	100 dys.	Mustered out with company Sept. 3, 1864.
Brewer, Henry B.	....do....	24	May 2, 1864	100 dys.	Mustered out with company Sept. 3, 1864.
Brooks, Robt. D.	....do....	18	May 2, 1864	100 dys.	Mustered out with company Sept. 3, 1864.
Brownlee, William T.	....do....	31	May 2, 1864	100 dys.	Mustered out with company Sept. 3, 1864.
Burbrage, [illegible] C.	....do....	18	May 2, 1864	100 dys.	Mustered out with company Sept. 3, 1864.
Burley, Nelson H.	....do....	18	May 2, 1864	100 dys.	Mustered out with company Sept. 3, 1864.
Campbell, James D.	....do....	28	May 2, 1864	100 dys.	Mustered out with company Sept. 3, 1864.
Citty, Josiah	....do....	31	May 2, 1864	100 dys.	Mustered out with company Sept. 3, 1864.
Clark, John S.	....do....	28	May 2, 1864	100 dys.	Mustered out with company Sept. 3, 1864.
Cline, Daniel A.	....do....	19	May 2, 1864	100 dys.	Mustered out with company Sept. 3, 1864.
Cobler, Isaac	....do....	18	May 2, 1864	100 dys.	Mustered out with company Sept. 3, 1864.
Cobler, Lewis	....do....	26	May 2, 1864	100 dys.	Mustered out with company Sept. 3, 1864.
Collins, Theodore S. F.	....do....	35	May 2, 1864	100 dys.	Mustered out with company Sept. 3, 1864.
Compton, Alexander G.	....do....	18	May 2, 1864	100 dys.	Mustered out with company Sept. 3, 1864.
Conaway, Leonidas	....do....	18	May 2, 1864	100 dys.	Mustered out with company Sept. 3, 1864.
Copas, James	....do....	33	May 2, 1864	100 dys.	Mustered out with company Sept. 3, 1864.
Copas, Jackson	....do....	19	May 2, 1864	100 dys.	Mustered out with company Sept. 3, 1864.
Downing, Josiah B.	....do....	42	May 2, 1864	100 dys.	Mustered out with company Sept. 3, 1864.
Elliott, Robert	....do....	25	May 2, 1864	100 dys.	Mustered out with company Sept. 3, 1864.
Ellis, James K. P.	....do....	19	May 2, 1864	100 dys.	Mustered out with company Sept. 3, 1864.
Evans, Elijah H.	....do....	28	May 2, 1864	100 dys.	Mustered out with company Sept. 3, 1864.
Evans, James	....do....	26	May 2, 1864	100 dys.	Mustered out with company Sept. 3, 1864.
Graham, James W.	....do....	28	May 2, 1864	100 dys.	Mustered out with company Sept. 3, 1864.
Grooms, Elias	....do....	39	May 2, 1864	100 dys.	Mustered out with company Sept. 3, 1864.
Hayslip, James	....do....	25	May 2, 1864	100 dys.	Mustered out with company Sept. 3, 1864.
Hardiner, William H.	....do....	21	May 2, 1864	100 dys.	Mustered out with company Sept. 3, 1864.
Humble, John	....do....	18	May 2, 1864	100 dys.	Mustered out with company Sept. 3, 1864.
Jones, Samuel	....do....	38	May 2, 1864	100 dys.	Mustered out with company Sept. 3, 1864.
Jones, John	....do....	36	May 2, 1864	100 dys.	Mustered out with company Sept. 3, 1864.
Kendall, Nelson	....do....	35	May 2, 1864	100 dys.	Mustered out with company Sept. 3, 1864.
McDaniel, John	....do....	19	May 2, 1864	100 dys.	Mustered out with company Sept. 3, 1864.
McMannis, Francis J.	....do....	21	May 2, 1864	100 dys.	Mustered out with company Sept. 3, 1864.
Manahan, William B.	....do....	22	May 2, 1864	100 dys.	Mustered out with company Sept. 3, 1864.

Names.	Rank.	Age.	Date of Entering the Service.	Period of Service.	Remarks.
Mires, Lewis	Private	26	May 2, 1864	100 dys.	Mustered out with company Sept. 3, 1864.
Moon, Samuel	...do...	42	May 2, 1864	100 dys.	Mustered out with company Sept. 3, 1864.
Moor, James C	...do...	18	May 2, 1864	100 dys.	Mustered out with company Sept. 3, 1864.
Newman, William G	...do...	28	May 2, 1864	100 dys.	Mustered out with company Sept. 3, 1864.
Parker, William	...do...	27	May 2, 1864	100 dys.	Mustered out with company Sept. 3, 1864.
Parks, Sylvester	...do...	28	May 2, 1864	100 dys.	Mustered out with company Sept. 3, 1864.
Peggs, Samuel	...do...	21	May 2, 1864	100 dys.	Mustered out with company Sept. 3, 1864.
Platt, John	...do...	31	May 2, 1864	100 dys.	Mustered out with company Sept. 3, 1864.
Porter, Sampson T	...do...	21	May 2, 1864	100 dys.	Mustered out with company Sept. 3, 1864.
Pursell, John M	...do...	23	May 2, 1864	100 dys.	Mustered out with company Sept. 3, 1864.
Pursell, Thomas A	...do...	27	May 2, 1864	100 dys.	Mustered out with company Sept. 3, 1864.
Rhodes, John W	...do...	20	May 2, 1864	100 dys.	Mustered out with company Sept. 3, 1864.
River, Adam	...do...	30	May 2, 1864	100 dys.	Mustered out with company Sept. 3, 1864.
Rothwell, John	...do...	27	May 2, 1864	100 dys.	Mustered out with company Sept. 3, 1864.
Rothwell, Jacob	...do...	37	May 2, 1864	100 dys.	Mustered out with company Sept. 3, 1864.
Rothwell, William G	...do...	31	May 2, 1864	100 dys.	Mustered out with company Sept. 3, 1864.
Smalley, Andrew	...do...	26	May 2, 1864	100 dys.	Mustered out with company Sept. 3, 1864.
Taylor, William	...do...	21	May 2, 1864	100 dys.	Mustered out with company Sept. 3, 1864.
Tenor, Daniel	...do...	20	May 2, 1864	100 dys.	Mustered out with company Sept. 3, 1864.
Thompson, George W	...do...	44	May 2, 1864	100 dys.	Mustered out with company Sept. 3, 1864.
Urton, Mahlon	...do...	39	May 2, 1864	100 dys.	Mustered out with company Sept. 3, 1864.
Walters, Truman	...do...	17	May 2, 1864	100 dys.	Mustered out with company Sept. 3, 1864.
Weaver, John W	...do...	31	May 2, 1864	100 dys.	Mustered out with company Sept. 3, 1864.
Whitmore, William	...do...	30	May 2, 1864	100 dys.	Mustered out with company Sept. 3, 1864.
Wilie, John E	...do...	20	May 2, 1864	100 dys.	Mustered out with company Sept. 3, 1864.
Wood, Isaac	...do...	29	May 2, 1864	100 dys.	Mustered out with company Sept. 3, 1864.
Yankee, Joseph T	...do...	19	May 2, 1864	100 dys.	Mustered out with company Sept. 3, 1864.
Zile, Edward A	...do...	19	May 2, 1864	100 dys.	Mustered out with company Sept. 3, 1864.

142nd Regiment Ohio Volunteer Infantry.

ONE HUNDRED DAYS' SERVICE.

This Regiment was organized at Camp Chase, O., May 13, 1864, to serv one hundred days. It was composed of the Twenty-second Battalion, Ohi National Guard, from Knox County; Sixty-eighth Battalion, Ohio Nation Guard, from Williams County; and a part of the Sixty-ninth Battalio Ohio National Guard, from Coshocton County. On the 14th of May th Regiment left Columbus, O., for Martinsburg, W. Va., where it remaine drilling, until the 19th of May, when it left for Washington City. Fro Washington it marched to Fort Lyon. The Regiment remained at Fort Lyo until the 5th of June, when orders were received to report to General Albe combie, at White House Landing. The Regiment took steamer at Alexandri on the 7th of June, and arrived at White House on the 9th, but was immed ately sent to guard a supply-train through the Wilderness to General Grant front, near Cold Harbor. The Regiment was then ordered to report at Bermud Hundred, but, without being permitted to land, it was conveyed, on transport to Point of Rocks. On the 19th of August the Regiment received orders t repair to Washington City, and thence to Camp Chase, O., where it was mustere out September 2, 1864, on expiration of term of service.

142ND REGIMENT OHIO VOLUNTEER INFANTRY.

FIELD AND STAFF.

[illegible]ered in May 13, 1864, at Camp Chase, O., by James P. W. Neill, 1st Lieutenant 18th Infantry, U. S. A. Mustered out Sept. 2, 1864, at Camp Chase, O., by Thomas H. Y. Bickham, 1st Lieutenant 19th Infantry, U. S. A.

	Rank.	Age.	Date of Entering the Service.	Period of Service.	Remarks.
...am C. Cooper	Colonel.	31	May 2, 1864	100 dys.	Mustered out with regiment Sept. 2, 1864.
...am Rogers	Lt. Col.	28	May 2, 1864	100 dys.	Mustered out with regiment Sept. 2, 1864.
...am M. Young	Major.	33	May 2, 1864	100 dys.	Mustered out with regiment Sept. 2, 1864.
...n N. King	Surgeon.	37	May 2, 1864	100 dys.	Mustered out with regiment Sept. 2, 1864.
... Stamp	Ast. Surg.	21	May 2, 1864	100 dys.	Mustered out with regiment Sept. 2, 1864.
...rick D. [illegible]	Adjutant	30	May 2, 1864	100 dys.	Mustered out with regiment Sept. 2, 1864.
...amlin H. Frieday	R. Q. M.	27	May 2, 1864	100 dys.	Mustered out with regiment Sept. 2, 1864.
...am J. Trimble	Chaplain	34	May 2, 1864	100 dys.	Promoted from private Co. I July 25, 1864; mustered out with regiment Sept. 2, 1864.
... C. Camp	Ser. Maj.	26	May 2, 1864	100 dys.	Mustered out with regiment Sept. 2, 1864.
...y L. Curtis	Q. M. S.	23	May 2, 1864	100 dys.	Promoted from private Co. K May 14, 1864; mustered out with regiment Sept. 2, 1864.
... W. Stanton	Com. Ser.	22	May 2, 1864	100 dys.	Promoted from private Co. G May 18, 1864; mustered out with regiment Sept. 2, 1864.
... Scribner	Hos. St'd.	20	May 2, 1864	100 dys.	Promoted from private Co. K May 18, 1864, mustered out with regiment Sept. 2, 1864.

COMPANY A.

[illegible]ered in May 13, 1864, at Camp Chase, O., by James P. W. Neill, 1st Lieutenant 18th Infantry, U. S. A. Mustered out Sept. 2, 1864, at Camp Chase, O., by Thomas H. Y. Bickham, 1st Lieutenant 19th Infantry, U. S. A.

	Rank.	Age.	Date of Entering the Service.	Period of Service.	Remarks.
... Davis	Captain.	52	May 2, 1864	100 dys.	Mustered out with company Sept. 2, 1864.
...n L. Mills	1st Lieut.	38	May 2, 1864	100 dys.	Mustered out with company Sept. 2, 1864.
...ander B. Tarr	2d Lieut.	26	May 2, 1864	100 dys.	Mustered out with company Sept. 2, 1864.
...er L. Hyatt	1st Sergt.	43	May 2, 1864	100 dys.	Mustered out with company Sept. 2, 1864.
...am H. Linn	Sergeant.	27	May 2, 1864	100 dys.	Mustered out with company Sept. 2, 1864.
...ord D. Bishop	...do...	26	May 2, 1864	100 dys.	Mustered out with company Sept. 2, 1864.
...am Frazier	...do...	28	May 2, 1864	100 dys.	Appointed from private May 24, 1864; mustered out with company Sept. 2, 1864.
...y Weller	...do...	27	May 2, 1864	100 dys.	Appointed from private May 24, 1864; mustered out with company Sept. 2, 1864.
... Cheshman	Corporal.	43	May 2, 1864	100 dys.	Mustered out with company Sept. 2, 1864.
... O. Shaw	...do...	21	May 2, 1864	100 dys.	Mustered out with company Sept. 2, 1864.
...e Scott	...do...	31	May 2, 1864	100 dys.	Mustered out with company Sept. 2, 1864.
...e Hollister	...do...	29	May 2, 1864	100 dys.	Mustered out with company Sept. 2, 1864.
... Weaver	...do...	32	May 2, 1864	100 dys.	Mustered out with company Sept. 2, 1864.
...min F. Hyatt	...do...	28	May 2, 1864	100 dys.	Mustered out with company Sept. 2, 1864.
...les Carey	...do...	27	May 2, 1864	100 dys.	Mustered out with company Sept. 2, 1864.
...n R. Lineweaver	...do...	39	May 2, 1864	100 dys.	Appointed May 25, 1864; mustered out with company Sept. 2, 1864.
...am Coffing	Musician	19	May 2, 1864	100 dys.	Mustered out with company Sept. 2, 1864.
...n H. Osborn.	...do...	18	May 2, 1864	100 dys.	Mustered out with company Sept. 2, 1864.
...l, John E.	Private.	26	May 2, 1864	100 dys.	Mustered out with company Sept. 2, 1864.
...l, Marshall	...do...	36	May 2, 1864	100 dys.	Mustered out with company Sept. 2, 1864.
...y, Henry	...do...	19	May 2, 1864	100 dys.	Mustered out with company Sept. 2, 1864.
...e, Allen J.	...do...	27	May 2, 1864	100 dys.	Mustered out with company Sept. 2, 1864.
...p, Daniel A.	...do...	19	May 2, 1864	100 dys.	Mustered out with company Sept. 2, 1864.
...p, George W.	...do...	19	May 2, 1864	100 dys.	Mustered out with company Sept. 2, 1864.
..., Abraham	...do...	45	May 2, 1864	100 dys.	Mustered out with company Sept. 2, 1864.
...enridge, David L.	...do...	43	May 2, 1864	100 dys.	Mustered out with company Sept. 2, 1864.
...w, William H.	...do...	18	May 2, 1864	100 dys.	Mustered out with company Sept. 2, 1864.
...n, Cassius	...do...	18	May 2, 1864	100 dys.	Mustered out with company Sept. 2, 1864.
...n, James	...do...	31	May 2, 1864	100 dys.	Died Aug. 10, 1864, in general hospital at Fortress Monroe, Va.
... John L.	...do...	18	May 2, 1864	100 dys.	Mustered out with company Sept. 2, 1864.

Names.	Rank.	Age.	Date of Entering the Service.	Period of Service.	Remarks.
[illegible]	Private..	26	May 2, 1864	100 dys.	Mustered out with company Sept. 2, 1864.
[illegible]	....do....	18	May 2, 1864	100 dys.	Mustered out with company Sept. 2, 1864; also borne on rolls as Joshua Celley.
[illegible]	....do....	20	May 2, 1864	100 dys.	Mustered out with company Sept. 2, 1864.
[illegible]	....do....	39	May 2, 1864	100 dys.	Mustered out with company Sept. 2, 1864.
[illegible]	....do....	25	May 2, 1864	100 dys.	Mustered out with company Sept. 2, 1864.
[illegible]	....do....	18	May 2, 1864	100 dys.	Mustered out with company Sept. 2, 1864.
[illegible]	....do....	18	May 2, 1864	100 dys.	Mustered out with company Sept. 2, 1864.
[illegible]	....do....	41	May 2, 1864	100 dys.	Mustered out with company Sept. 2, 1864.
[illegible]	....do....	44	May 2, 1864	100 dys.	Mustered out with company Sept. 2, 1864.
[illegible]	....do....	18	May 2, 1864	100 dys.	Mustered out with company Sept. 2, 1864.
[illegible]	....do....	22	May 2, 1864	100 dys.	Mustered out with company Sept. 2, 1864.
[illegible]	....do....	19	May 2, 1864	100 dys.	Mustered out with company Sept. 2, 1864.
[illegible]	....do....	19	May 2, 1864	100 dys.	Mustered out with company Sept. 2, 1864.
[illegible]	....do....	18	May 2, 1864	100 dys.	Mustered out with company Sept. 2, 1864.
[illegible]	....do....	43	May 2, 1864	100 dys.	Mustered out with company Sept. 2, 1864.
[illegible]	....do....	27	May 2, 1864	100 dys.	Mustered out with company Sept. 2, 1864.
[illegible]	....do....	33	May 2, 1864	100 dys.	Mustered out with company Sept. 2, 1864.
[illegible]	....do....	26	May 2, 1864	100 dys.	Mustered out with company Sept. 2, 1864.
[illegible]	....do....	21	May 2, 1864	100 dys.	Mustered out with company Sept. 2, 1864.
[illegible]	....do....	23	May 2, 1864	100 dys.	Mustered out with company Sept. 2, 1864.
[illegible] A.	....do....	21	May 2, 1864	100 dys.	Mustered out with company Sept. 2, 1864.
[illegible]	....do....	22	May 2, 1864	100 dys.	Mustered out with company Sept. 2, 1864.
[illegible] A.	....do....	18	May 2, 1864	100 dys.	Mustered out with company Sept. 2, 1864.
[illegible]	....do....	18	May 2, 1864	100 dys.	Mustered out with company Sept. 2, 1864.
[illegible]	....do....	21	May 2, 1864	100 dys.	Died July 3, 1864, in Douglas Hospital, Washington, D. C.
[illegible]	....do....	25	May 2, 1864	100 dys.	Mustered out with company Sept. 2, 1864.
[illegible]	....do....	35	May 2, 1864	100 dys.	Died Aug. 6, 1864, in hospital at Point of Rocks, Md.
[illegible]	....do....	18	May 2, 1864	100 dys.	Mustered out with company Sept. 2, 1864.
[illegible]	....do....	29	May 2, 1864	100 dys.	Mustered out with company Sept. 2, 1864.
[illegible]	....do....	18	May 2, 1864	100 dys.	Mustered out with company Sept. 2, 1864.
[illegible]	....do....	25	May 2, 1864	100 dys.	Mustered out with company Sept. 2, 1864.
[illegible]	....do....	18	May 2, 1864	100 dys.	Mustered out with company Sept. 2, 1864.
[illegible]	....do....	38	May 2, 1864	100 dys.	Mustered out with company Sept. 2, 1864.
[illegible]	....do....	22	May 2, 1864	100 dys.	Mustered out with company Sept. 2, 1864.
[illegible]	....do....	43	May 2, 1864	100 dys.	Mustered out with company Sept. 2, 1864.
[illegible]	....do....	19	May 2, 1864	100 dys.	Mustered out with company Sept. 2, 1864.
[illegible]	....do....	20	May 2, 1864	100 dys.	Mustered out with company Sept. 2, 1864.
[illegible] H.	....do....	21	May 2, 1864	100 dys.	Mustered out with company Sept. 2, 1864.
[illegible] T.	....do....	18	May 2, 1864	100 dys.	Mustered out with company Sept. 2, 1864.
[illegible]	....do....	23	May 2, 1864	100 dys.	Mustered out with company Sept. 2, 1864.
[illegible] F.	....do....	19	May 2, 1864	100 dys.	Mustered out with company Sept. 2, 1864.
[illegible] E.	....do....	20	May 2, 1864	100 dys.	Mustered out with company Sept. 2, 1864.
[illegible] T.	....do....	23	May 2, 1864	100 dys.	Mustered out with company Sept. 2, 1864.
[illegible]	....do....	43	May 2, 1864	100 dys.	Mustered out with company Sept. 2, 1864.
[illegible]	....do....	35	May 2, 1864	100 dys.	Mustered out with company Sept. 2, 1864.
[illegible]	....do....	25	May 2, 1864	100 dys.	Mustered out with company Sept. 2, 1864.
[illegible] B.	....do....	28	May 2, 1864	100 dys.	Mustered out with company Sept. 2, 1864.
[illegible]	....do....	21	May 2, 1864	100 dys.	Died July 17, 1864, in hospital at Fortress Monroe, Va.
[illegible] B.	....do....	19	May 2, 1864	100 dys.	Mustered out with company Sept. 2, 1864.
[illegible] P.	....do....	27	May 2, 1864	100 dys.	Mustered out with company Sept. 2, 1864.
[illegible]	....do....	45	May 2, 1864	100 dys.	Mustered out with company Sept. 2, 1864.
[illegible]	....do....	21	May 2, 1864	100 dys.	Mustered out with company Sept. 2, 1864.
[illegible]	....do....	24	May 2, 1864	100 dys.	Mustered out with company Sept. 2, 1864.
[illegible]	....do....	18	May 2, 1864	100 dys.	Mustered out with company Sept. 2, 1864.

COMPANY B.

[illegible] 1864, at Camp Chase, O., by James P. W. Neill, 1st Lieutenant 18th Infantry, U. S. A. Mustered out Sept. 2, 1864, at Camp Chase, O., by Thomas H. Y. Bickham, 1st Lieutenant 19th Infantry, U. S. A.

Names.	Rank.	Age.	Date of Entering the Service.	Period of Service.	Remarks.
[illegible]	Captain.	30	May 2, 1864	100 dys.	Mustered out with company Sept. 2, 1864.
[illegible]	1st Lieut.	28	May 2, 1864	100 dys.	Mustered out with company Sept. 2, 1864.
[illegible]	2d Lieut.	33	May 2, 1864	100 dys.	Mustered out with company Sept. 2, 1864.
[illegible]	1st Sergt.	35	May 2, 1864	100 dys.	Mustered out with company Sept. 2, 1864.
[illegible]	Sergeant.	29	May 2, 1864	100 dys.	Mustered out with company Sept. 2, 1864.
[illegible]	....do....	23	May 2, 1864	100 dys.	Mustered out with company Sept. 2, 1864.
[illegible]	....do....	18	May 2, 1864	100 dys.	Mustered out with company Sept. 2, 1864.
[illegible]	....do....	30	May 2, 1864	100 dys.	Mustered out with company Sept. 2, 1864.
[illegible]	Corporal.	19	May 2, 1864	100 dys.	Mustered out with company Sept. 2, 1864.
[illegible]	....do....	28	May 2, 1864	100 dys.	Mustered out with company Sept. 2, 1864.
[illegible]	....do....	22	May 2, 1864	100 dys.	Mustered out with company Sept. 2, 1864.
[illegible]	....do....	27	May 2, 1864	100 dys.	Mustered out with company Sept. 2, 1864.
[illegible]	....do....	26	May 2, 1864	100 dys.	Mustered out with company Sept. 2, 1864.
[illegible]	....do....	29	May 2, 1864	100 dys.	Mustered out with company Sept. 2, 1864.
[illegible]	....do....	18	May 2, 1864	100 dys.	Mustered out with company Sept. 2, 1864.

COMPANY C.

Mustered in May 13, 1864, at Camp Chase, O., by James P. W. Neill, 1st Lieutenant 18th Infantry, U. S. A. Mustered out Sept. 2, 1864, at Camp Chase, O., by Thomas H. Y. Bickham, 1st Lieutenant 19th Infantry, U. S. A.

Names.	Rank.	Age.	Date of Entering the Service.	Period of Service.	Remarks.
Henry C. Harris	Captain.	31	May 2, 1864	100 dys.	Mustered out with company Sept. 2, 1864.
Lucien B. Curtis	1st Lieut.	27	May 2, 1864	100 dys.	Mustered out with company Sept. 2, 1864.
Mills Harrod	2d Lieut.	35	May 2, 1864	100 dys.	Mustered out with company Sept. 2, 1864.
Ira Boyle	1st Sergt.	23	May 2, 1864	100 dys.	Mustered out with company Sept. 2, 1864.
George W. Davis	Sergeant.	28	May 2, 1864	100 dys.	Mustered out with company Sept. 2, 1864.
John Graham	do.	33	May 2, 1864	100 dys.	Mustered out with company Sept. 2, 1864.
Isaac Vance	do.	26	May 2, 1864	100 dys.	Mustered out with company Sept. 2, 1864.
Charles B. Gates	do.	24	May 2, 1864	100 dys.	Mustered out with company Sept. 2, 1864.
Edwin S. Miller	Color Ser.	22	May 2, 1864	100 dys.	Mustered out with company Sept. 2, 1864.
Aaron Boyle	Corporal.	[illegible]	May 2, 1864	100 dys.	Mustered out with company Sept. 2, 1864.
Henry J. Glaze	do.	31	May 2, 1864	100 dys.	Mustered out with company Sept. 2, 1864.
Stephen Stinger	do.	23	May 2, 1864	100 dys.	Mustered out with company Sept. 2, 1864.
Levi Winger	do.	36	May 2, 1864	100 dys.	Mustered out with company Sept. 2, 1864.
John Minor	do.	34	May 2, 1864	100 dys.	Mustered out with company Sept. 2, 1864.
Dana Miller	do.	21	May 2, 1864	100 dys.	Mustered out with company Sept. 2, 1864.
Matthew P. Smith	do.	41	May 2, 1864	100 dys.	Mustered out with company Sept. 2, 1864.
John B. Oldaker	do.	20	May 2, 1864	100 dys.	Mustered out with company Sept. 2, 1864.
Isaac C. Everette	Musician	18	May 2, 1864	100 dys.	Mustered out with company Sept. 2, 1864.
Alexander, Albert	Private.	18	May 2, 1864	100 dys.	Mustered out with company Sept. 2, 1864.
Alexander, Joseph H.	do.	18	May 2, 1864	100 dys.	Mustered out with company Sept. 2, 1864.
Babbs, Isaac N.	do.	21	May 2, 1864	100 dys.	Mustered out with company Sept. 2, 1864.
Babbs, John W.	do.	18	May 2, 1864	100 dys.	Died Aug. 27, 1864, in General hospital at Fortress Monroe, Va.
Babbs, Thomas	do.	21	May 2, 1864	100 dys.	Died Aug. 1, 1864, in hospital at Portsmouth, Virginia.
Baughman, Christopher	do.	[illegible]	May 2, 1864	100 dys.	Mustered out with company Sept. 2, 1864.
Bealmont, William	do.	2[illegible]	May 2, 1864	100 dys.	Died July 2[illegible], 1864, on hospital boat between Point of Rocks, Md. and Fortress Monroe, Virginia.
Peach, William A.	do.	2[illegible]	May 2, 1864	100 dys.	Mustered out with company Sept. 2, 1864.
Boyle, James S.	do.	1[illegible]	May 2, 1864	100 dys.	Mustered out with company Sept. 2, 1864.
Boyle, Joseph M.	do.	21	May 2, 1864	100 dys.	Mustered out with company Sept. 2, 1864.
Buxton, Francis A.	do.	[illegible]	May 2, 1864	100 dys.	Mustered out with company Sept. 2, 1864.
Buxton, Thomas	do.	[illegible]	May 2, 1864	100 dys.	Mustered out with company Sept. 2, 1864.
Cake, Howard	do.	23	May 2, 1864	100 dys.	Mustered out with company Sept. 2, 1864.
Conaway, Charles A.	do.	[illegible]	May 2, 1864	100 dys.	Mustered out with company Sept. 2, 1864.
Crawford, James	do.	[illegible]	May 2, 1864	100 dys.	Mustered out with company Sept. 2, 1864.
Dailey, Daniel M.	do.	[illegible]	May 2, 1864	100 dys.	Mustered out with company Sept. 2, 1864.
Dailey, George C.	do.	18	May 2, 1864	100 dys.	Mustered out with company Sept. 2, 1864.
Edmondson, Charles	do.	[illegible]	May 2, 1864	100 dys.	Sent to Field Hospital near Point of Rocks, Md. No further record found.
Evans, George F.	do.	[illegible]	May 2, 1864	100 dys.	Mustered out with company Sept. 2, 1864.
[illegible], James	do.	[illegible]	May 2, 1864	100 dys.	Mustered out with company Sept. 2, 1864.
[illegible], John	do.	[illegible]	May 2, 1864	100 dys.	Mustered out with company Sept. 2, 1864.
Fry, James R.	do.	[illegible]	May 2, 1864	100 dys.	Mustered out with company Sept. 2, 1864.
Fry, Jacob	do.	[illegible]	May 2, 1864	100 dys.	Mustered out with company Sept. 2, 1864.
[illegible], James W.	do.	44	May 2, 1864	100 dys.	Mustered out with company Sept. 2, 1864.
[illegible], Thomas	do.	[illegible]	May 2, 1864	100 dys.	Mustered out with company Sept. 2, 1864.
Graham, Robert F.	do.	[illegible]	May 2, 1864	100 dys.	Mustered out with company Sept. 2, 1864.
Groves, David	do.	27	May 2, 1864	100 dys.	Mustered out with company Sept. 2, 1864.
Groves, William	do.	18	May 2, 1864	100 dys.	Mustered out with company Sept. 2, 1864.
Hall, [illegible]	do.	4[illegible]	May 2, 1864	100 dys.	Mustered out with company Sept. 2, 1864.
Herod, Crawford	do.	4[illegible]	May 2, 1864	100 dys.	Mustered out with company Sept. 2, 1864.
[illegible], Henry	do.	[illegible]	May 2, 1864	100 dys.	Died July [illegible], 1864, in hospital near Point of Rocks, Md.
Hobbs, John W.	do.	[illegible]	May 2, 1864	100 dys.	Mustered out with company Sept. 2, 1864.
Hobbs, Samuel M.	do.	[illegible]	May 2, 1864	100 dys.	Mustered out with company Sept. 2, 1864.
Hunter, William A.	do.	[illegible]	May 2, 1864	100 dys.	Mustered out with company Sept. 2, 1864.
Hyatt, William [illegible]	do.	4[illegible]	May 2, 1864	100 dys.	Mustered out with company Sept. 2, 1864.
Jones, [illegible]	do.	[illegible]	May 2, 1864	100 dys.	Mustered out with company Sept. 2, 1864.
Lincoln, William H.	do.	[illegible]	May 2, 1864	100 dys.	Mustered out with company Sept. 2, 1864.
Lockwood, [illegible]	do.	[illegible]	May 2, 1864	100 dys.	Mustered out with company Sept. 2, 1864.
Lockwood, William M.	do.	[illegible]	May 2, 1864	100 dys.	Mustered out with company Sept. 2, 1864.
Miller, Harrison	do.	[illegible]	May 2, 1864	100 dys.	Mustered out with company Sept. 2, 1864.
[illegible], William H.	do.	[illegible]	May 2, 1864	100 dys.	Mustered out with company Sept. 2, 1864.
Morey, William	do.	[illegible]	May 2, 1864	100 dys.	Mustered out with company Sept. 2, 1864.
Murphy, [illegible] W.	do.	[illegible]	May 2, 1864	100 dys.	Mustered out with company Sept. 2, 1864.
Neal, George	do.	[illegible]	May 2, 1864	100 dys.	Mustered out with company Sept. 2, 1864.
Porter, Solomon	do.	[illegible]	May 2, 1864	100 dys.	Mustered out with company Sept. 2, 1864.
[illegible], Cyrus B.	do.	[illegible]	May 2, 1864	100 dys.	Mustered out with company Sept. 2, 1864.
Robinson, [illegible]	do.	[illegible]	May 2, 1864	100 dys.	Mustered out with company Sept. 2, 1864.
Robinson, George	do.	[illegible]	May 2, 1864	100 dys.	Mustered out with company Sept. 2, 1864.
Rowe, David	do.	[illegible]	May 2, 1864	100 dys.	Mustered out with company Sept. 2, 1864.
Shafer, James	do.	[illegible]	May 2, 1864	100 dys.	Mustered out with company Sept. 2, 1864.
Shanks, John	do.	[illegible]	May 2, 1864	100 dys.	Mustered out with company Sept. 2, 1864.
[illegible], Henry C.	do.	[illegible]	May 2, 1864	100 dys.	Mustered out with company Sept. 2, 1864.

	Rank.	Age.	Date of Entering the Service.	Period of Service.	Remarks.
....	Corporal.	18	May 2, 1864	100 dys.	Mustered out with company Sept. 2, 1864.
....	Private..	44	May 2, 1864	100 dys.	Mustered out with company Sept. 2, 1864.
....	....do....	21	May 2, 1864	100 dys.	Mustered out with company Sept. 2, 1864.
....	....do....	24	May 2, 1864	100 dys.	Mustered out with company Sept. 2, 1864.
....	....do....	18	May 2, 1864	100 dys.	Mustered out with company Sept. 2, 1864.
....	....do....	26	May 2, 1864	100 dys.	Mustered out with company Sept. 2, 1864.
....	....do....	21	May 2, 1864	100 dys.	Mustered out with company Sept. 2, 1864.
....	....do....	20	May 2, 1864	100 dys.	Mustered out with company Sept. 2, 1864.
....	....do....	18	May 2, 1864	100 dys.	Mustered out with company Sept. 2, 1864.
....	....do....	20	May 2, 1864	100 dys.	Mustered out with company Sept. 2, 1864.
....	....do....	31	May 2, 1864	100 dys.	Mustered out with company Sept. 2, 1864.
....	....do....	18	May 2, 1864	100 dys.	Mustered out with company Sept. 2, 1864.
....	....do....	18	May 2, 1864	100 dys.	Mustered out with company Sept. 2, 1864.
....	....do....	28	May 2, 1864	100 dys.	Mustered out with company Sept. 2, 1864.
....	....do....	25	May 2, 1864	100 dys.	Mustered out with company Sept. 2, 1864.
....	....do....	32	May 2, 1864	100 dys.	Mustered out with company Sept. 2, 1864.
....		19	May 2, 1864	100 dys.	Mustered out with company Sept. 2, 1864.
....		20	May 2, 1864	100 dys.	Mustered out with company Sept. 2, 1864.
....		19	May 2, 1864	100 dys.	In hospital at Fort Lyon, Va., June 6, 1864. No further record found.
....		18	May 2, 1864	100 dys.	Mustered out with company Sept. 2, 1864.
....		19	May 2, 1864	100 dys.	Mustered out with company Sept. 2, 1864.
....		21	May 2, 1864	100 dys.	Mustered out with company Sept. 2, 1864.
....		18	May 2, 1864	100 dys.	Mustered out with company Sept. 2, 1864.
....		31	May 2, 1864	100 dys.	Mustered out with company Sept. 2, 1864.
....		21	May 2, 1864	100 dys.	Died July 24, 1864, at Willett's Point, N. Y.
....		18	May 2, 1864	100 dys.	Mustered out with company Sept. 2, 1864.
....		18	May 2, 1864	100 dys.	Mustered out with company Sept. 2, 1864.
....		18	May 2, 1864	100 dys.	Mustered out with company Sept. 2, 1864.
....		18	May 2, 1864	100 dys.	Mustered out with company Sept. 2, 1864.
....		42	May 2, 1864	100 dys.	Mustered out with company Sept. 2, 1864.
....		19	May 2, 1864	100 dys.	Mustered out with company Sept. 2, 1864.
....		18	May 2, 1864	100 dys.	Mustered out with company Sept. 2, 1864.
....		43	May 2, 1864	100 dys.	Mustered out with company Sept. 2, 1864.
....		20	May 2, 1864	100 dys.	Mustered out with company Sept. 2, 1864.
....		18	May 2, 1864	100 dys.	Mustered out with company Sept. 2, 1864.
....		22	May 2, 1864	100 dys.	Sent to hospital near Point of Rocks, Md., — No further record found.
....	....do....	26	May 2, 1864	100 dys.	Mustered out with company Sept. 2, 1864.
....		21	May 2, 1864	100 dys.	Mustered out with company Sept. 2, 1864.
		20	May 2, 1864	100 dys.	Mustered out with company Sept. 2, 1864.
		42	May 2, 1864	100 dys.	Mustered out with company Sept. 2, 1864.
		23	May 2, 1864	100 dys.	Mustered out with company Sept. 2, 1864.
....		20	May 2, 1864	100 dys.	Mustered out with company Sept. 2, 1864.
....		18	May 2, 1864	100 dys.	Mustered out with company Sept. 2, 1864.
....		28	May 2, 1864	100 dys.	Mustered out with company Sept. 2, 1864.
....		22	May 2, 1864	100 dys.	Mustered out with company Sept. 2, 1864.
..	....do....	34	May 2, 1864	100 dys.	Mustered out with company Sept. 2, 1864.
..	....do....	22	May 2, 1864	100 dys.	Mustered out with company Sept. 2, 1864.
.	....do....	19	May 2, 1864	100 dys.	Mustered out with company Sept. 2, 1864.
....	....do....	21	May 2, 1864	100 dys.	Mustered out with company Sept. 2, 1864.
....	....do....	28	May 2, 1864	100 dys.	Mustered out with company Sept. 2, 1864.
....	....do....	19	May 2, 1864	100 dys.	Mustered out with company Sept. 2, 1864.
....	....do....	22	May 2, 1864	100 dys.	Died Aug. 1, 1864, in Regimental Hospital, near Point of Rocks, Md.
....	....do....	21	May 2, 1864	100 dys.	Mustered out with company Sept. 2, 1864.
....	....do....	24	May 2, 1864	100 dys.	Mustered out with company Sept. 2, 1864.
....	....do....	34	May 2, 1864	100 dys.	Mustered out with company Sept. 2, 1864.
....	....do....	18	May 2, 1864	100 dys.	Mustered out with company Sept. 2, 1864.
....	....do....	25	May 2, 1864	100 dys.	Mustered out with company Sept. 2, 1864.
....	....do....	22	May 2, 1864	100 dys.	Mustered out with company Sept. 2, 1864.
....	....do....	29	May 2, 1864	100 dys.	Mustered out with company Sept. 2, 1864.
....	....do....	32	May 2, 1864	100 dys.	Mustered out with company Sept. 2, 1864.
....	....do....	29	May 2, 1864	100 dys.	Mustered out with company Sept. 2, 1864.
....	....do....	18	May 2, 1864	100 dys.	Mustered out with company Sept. 2, 1864.
....	....do....	28	May 2, 1864	100 dys.	Mustered out with company Sept. 2, 1864.
....	....do....	18	May 2, 1864	100 dys.	Mustered out with company Sept. 2, 1864.
....	....do....	22	May 2, 1864	100 dys.	Mustered out with company Sept. 2, 1864.
....	....do....	29	May 2, 1864	100 dys.	Mustered out with company Sept. 2, 1864.
....	....do....	18	May 2, 1864	100 dys.	Mustered out with company Sept. 2, 1864.
....	....do....	31	May 2, 1864	100 dys.	Mustered out with company Sept. 2, 1864.
....	....do....	28	May 2, 1864	100 dys.	Mustered out with company Sept. 2, 1864.

Names.	Rank.	Age.	Date of Entering the Service.	Period of Service.	Remarks.
McConnell, John	Private	41	May 2, 1864	100 dys.	Mustered out with company Sept. 2, 1864.
Maple, Nelson	...do...	20	May 2, 1864	100 dys.	Mustered out with company Sept. 2, 1864.
Marshall, Da[illegible]	...do...	24	May 2, 1864	100 dys.	Mustered out with company Sept. 2, 1864.
Martin, William	...do...	20	May 2, 1864	100 dys.	Mustered out with company Sept. 2, 1864.
May, John	...do...	38	May 2, 1864	100 dys.	Mustered out with company Sept. 2, 1864.
Maynard, Harlem	...do...	19	May 2, 1864	100 dys.	Mustered out with company Sept. 2, 1864.
Moore, John W.	...do...	28	May 2, 1864	100 dys.	Mustered out with company Sept. 2, 1864.
Moore, William R.	...do...	18	May 2, 1864	100 dys.	Mustered out with company Sept. 2, 1864.
Pease, James W.	...do...	24	May 2, 1864	100 dys.	Mustered out with company Sept. 2, 1864.
Phelps, Thomas	...do...	19	May 2, 1864	100 dys.	Mustered out with company Sept. 2, 1864.
Porter, Samuel D.	...do...	22	May 2, 1864	100 dys.	Mustered out with company Sept. 2, 1864.
Pressler, Archibald B.	...do...	20	May 2, 1864	100 dys.	Mustered out with company Sept. 2, 1864.
Ritter, William	...do...	31	May 2, 1864	100 dys.	Mustered out with company Sept. 2, 1864.
Roshong, Josiah	...do...	28	May 2, 1864	100 dys.	Mustered out with company Sept. 2, 1864.
Sheppard, Lyman	...do...	42	May 2, 1864	100 dys.	Mustered out with company Sept. 2, 1864.
Shinebarger, John	...do...	34	May 2, 1864	100 dys.	Mustered out with company Sept. 2, 1864.
Shinebarger, Peter	...do...	26	May 2, 1864	100 dys.	Mustered out with company Sept. 2, 1864.
Shinebarger, William	...do...	20	May 2, 1864	100 dys.	Mustered out with company Sept. 2, 1864.
Silvernail, Richard	...do...	25	May 2, 1864	100 dys.	Mustered out with company Sept. 2, 1864.
Smethers, Theodore	...do...	22	May 2, 1864	100 dys.	Mustered out with company Sept. 2, 1864.
Smith, Guy	...do...	18	May 2, 1864	100 dys.	Mustered out with company Sept. 2, 1864.
Smith, Oscar D.	...do...	19	May 2, 1864	100 dys.	Mustered out with company Sept. 2, 1864.
Smoot, Daniel G.	...do...	22	May 2, 1864	100 dys.	Mustered out with company Sept. 2, 1864.
Smoot, William	...do...	20	May 2, 1864	100 dys.	Mustered out with company Sept. 2, 1864.
Speedy, James	...do...	30	May 2, 1864	100 dys.	Mustered out with company Sept. 2, 1864.
Stedn[illegible], Daniel K.	...do...	23	May 2, 1864	100 dys.	Mustered out with company Sept. 2, 1864.
Thompson, Wesley	...do...	19	May 2, 1864	100 dys.	Mustered out with company Sept. 2, 1864.
Tremains, Andrew J.	...do...	24	May 2, 1864	100 dys.	Mustered out with company Sept. 2, 1864.
Vandyke, David	...do...	20	May 2, 1864	100 dys.	Mustered out with company Sept. 2, 1864.
Weeks, Samuel T.	...do...	23	May 2, 1864	100 dys.	Mustered out with company Sept. 2, 1864.
Wilson, George	...do...	25	May 2, 1864	100 dys.	Mustered out with company Sept. 2, 1864.
Wilson, John W.	...do...	35	May 2, 1864	100 dys.	Mustered out with company Sept. 2, 1864.
Wiseman, John W.	...do...	30	May 2, 1864	100 dys.	Mustered out with company Sept. 2, 1864.
Zuver, Jacob	...do...	41	May 2, 1864	100 dys.	Mustered out with company Sept. 2, 1864.

COMPANY E.

Mustered in May 13, 1864, at Camp Chase, O., by James P. W. Neill, 1st Lieutenant 18th Infantry, U. S. A. Mustered out Sept. 2, 1864, at Camp Chase, O., by Thomas H. Y. Bickham, 1st Lieutenant 18th Infantry, U. S. A.

Names.	Rank.	Age.	Date of Entering the Service.	Period of Service.	Remarks.
Lambert B. Wolfe	Captain	29	May 2, 1864	100 dys.	Mustered out with company Sept. 2, 1864.
John A. Weatherwax	1st Lieut.	23	May 2, 1864	100 dys.	Mustered out with company Sept. 2, 1864.
Benjamin F. Leighninger	2d Lieut.	25	May 2, 1864	100 dys.	Mustered out with company Sept. 2, 1864.
Joseph Fletcher	1st Sergt.	34	May 2, 1864	100 dys.	Mustered out with company Sept. 2, 1864.
Ralph L. Bancroft	Sergeant	25	May 2, 1864	100 dys.	Mustered out with company Sept. 2, 1864.
Anderson Hedge	...do...	22	May 2, 1864	100 dys.	Mustered out with company Sept. 2, 1864.
William McGlaughlin	...do...	23	May 2, 1864	100 dys.	Mustered out with company Sept. 2, 1864.
Charles Conley	...do...	43	May 2, 1864	100 dys.	Mustered out with company Sept. 2, 1864.
Hiram Phillips	Corporal	[illegible]	May 2, 1864	100 dys.	Mustered out with company Sept. 2, 1864.
Asa H. Lou[illegible]	...do...	22	May 2, 1864	100 dys.	Mustered out with company Sept. 2, 1864.
Aaron G. Hedge	...do...	21	May 2, 1864	100 dys.	Mustered out with company Sept. 2, 1864.
George Leighninger	...do...	31	May 2, 1864	100 dys.	Died June [illegible], 1864, in Satterlee Hospital, Philadelphia, Pa.
Oren Jennings	...do...	30	May 2, 1864	100 dys.	Mustered out with company Sept. 2, 1864.
Milton Bressford	...do...	27	May 2, 1864	100 dys.	Mustered out with company Sept. 2, 1864.
Benjamin F. Chamberlain	...do...	26	May 2, 1864	100 dys.	Mustered out with company Sept. 2, 1864.
Thomas W. Culbertson	...do...	27	May 2, 1864	100 dys.	Mustered out with company Sept. 2, 1864.
Milton N. Wolfe	...do...	25	May 2, 1864	100 dys.	Appointed July 1, 1864; mustered out with company Sept. 2, 1864.
Joseph Love	Musician	28	May 2, 1864	100 dys.	Mustered out with company Sept. 2, 1864.
Alonzo Sibley	...do...	58	May 2, 1864	100 dys.	Mustered out with company Sept. 2, 1864.
Arnholt, Adam	Private	26	May 2, 1864	100 dys.	Mustered out with company Sept. 2, 1864.
Aunspaugh, Lewis F.	...do...	26	May 2, 1864	100 dys.	Mustered out with company Sept. 2, 1864.
Babcock, Tristram	...do...	32	May 2, 1864	100 dys.	Mustered out with company Sept. 2, 1864.
Baker, Esaias D.	...do...	23	May 2, 1864	100 dys.	Mustered out with company Sept. 2, 1864.
Barcroft, David	...do...	29	May 2, 1864	100 dys.	Mustered out with company Sept. 2, 1864.
Bible, Josiah	...do...	28	May 2, 1864	100 dys.	Mustered out with company Sept. 2, 1864.
Bowers, Chris.	...do...	36	May 2, 1864	100 dys.	Mustered out with company Sept. 2, 1864.
Brewer, Jacob	...do...	[illegible]	May 2, 1864	100 dys.	Mustered out with company Sept. 2, 1864.
Brillhart, Samuel	...do...	31	May 2, 1864	100 dys.	Mustered out with company Sept. 2, 1864.
Buck, Peter [illegible]	...do...	16	May 2, 1864	100 dys.	Mustered out with company Sept. 2, 1864.
Cashner, Isaac	...do...	20	May 2, 1864	100 dys.	Mustered out with company Sept. 2, 1864.
Chauvront, Samuel G.	...do...	31	May 2, 1864	100 dys.	Mustered out with company Sept. 2, 1864.
Duling, Hiram	...do...	35	May 2, 1864	100 dys.	Mustered out with company Sept. 2, 1864.
Duling, Martin	...do...	18	May 2, 1864	100 dys.	Mustered out with company Sept. 2, 1864.
Fowler, William H.	...do...	24	May 2, 1864	100 dys.	Died July 8, 1864, on board steamer Monitor.
Fox, Eli	...do...	37	May 2, 1864	100 dys.	Mustered out with company Sept. 2, 1864.
Frazee, James	...do...	22	May 2, 1864	100 dys.	Mustered out with company Sept. 2, 1864.
Fuller, Benjamin, Jr.	...do...	20	May 2, 1864	100 dys.	Mustered out with company Sept. 2, 1864.

Names.	Rank.	Age.	Date of Entering the Service.	Period of Service.	Remarks.
Smith, Harvey J	Private	18	May 2, 1864	100 dys.	Mustered out with company Sept. 2, 1864.
Smith, Robert H	...do...	31	May 2, 1864	100 dys.	Mustered out with company Sept. 2, 1864.
Smith, Willard	...do...	18	May 2, 1864	100 dys.	Mustered out with company Sept. 2, 1864.
Steinmates, Benjamin	...do...	31	May 2, 1864	100 dys.	Mustered out with company Sept. 2, 1864.
Steinmates, Jacob	...do...	23	May 2, 1864	100 dys.	Mustered out with company Sept. 2, 1864.
Steinmates, Upton	...do...	37	May 2, 1864	100 dys.	Mustered out with company Sept. 2, 1864.
Steinmates, John	...do...	31	May 2, 1864	100 dys.	Mustered out with company Sept. 2, 1864.
Tracey, James M	...do...	19	May 2, 1864	100 dys.	Mustered out with company Sept. 2, 1864.
Vernon, John	...do...	18	May 2, 1864	100 dys.	Mustered out with company Sept. 2, 1864.
Weaver, David H	...do...	33	May 2, 1864	100 dys.	Mustered out with company Sept. 2, 1864.
Webster, Glisner J	...do...	18	May 2, 1864	100 dys.	Mustered out with company Sept. 2, 1864.
Winn, John M	...do...	38	May 2, 1864	100 dys.	Mustered out with company Sept. 2, 1864.
Worman, Alfred	...do...	25	May 2, 1864	100 dys.	Mustered out with company Sept. 2, 1864.

COMPANY D.

Mustered in May 13, 1864, at Camp Chase, O., by James P. W. Neill, 1st Lieutenant 18th Infantry, U. S. A. Mustered out Sept. 2, 1864, at Camp Chase, O., by Thomas H. Y. Bickham, 1st Lieutenant 19th Infantry, U. S. A.

Names.	Rank.	Age.	Date of Entering the Service.	Period of Service.	Remarks.
Richard Gaudern	Captain.	33	May 2, 1864	100 dys.	Mustered out with company Sept. 2, 1864.
Andrew Irwin	1st Lieut.	33	May 2, 1864	100 dys.	Mustered out with company Sept. 2, 1864.
George Anderson	2d Lieut.	26	May 2, 1864	100 dys.	Mustered out with company Sept. 2, 1864.
John Oeiviler	1st Sergt.	37	May 2, 1864	100 dys.	Mustered out with company Sept. 2, 1864.
Joseph L. Haggerty	Sergeant.	27	May 2, 1864	100 dys.	Mustered out with company Sept. 2, 1864.
John Slater	...do...	41	May 2, 1864	100 dys.	Mustered out with company Sept. 2, 1864.
Alexander W. Crall	...do...	22	May 2, 1864	100 dys.	Mustered out with company Sept. 2, 1864.
Ethan A. Poole	...do...	27	May 2, 1864	100 dys.	Mustered out with company Sept. 2, 1864.
Jerome Follett	Corporal.	21	May 2, 1864	100 dys.	Died June 2?, 1864, at Alexandria, Va.
George Hodson	...do...	22	May 2, 1864	100 dys.	Mustered out with company Sept. 2, 1864.
John Weaver	...do...	34	May 2, 1864	100 dys.	Mustered out with company Sept. 2, 1864.
William McConnell	...do...	28	May 2, 1864	100 dys.	Mustered out with company Sept. 2, 1864.
John Greek	...do...	27	May 2, 1864	100 dys.	Mustered out with company Sept. 2, 1864.
John Q. Blair	...do...	30	May 2, 1864	100 dys.	Mustered out with company Sept. 2, 1864.
John Fulton	...do...	38	May 2, 1864	100 dys.	Mustered out with company Sept. 2, 1864.
Samuel Preston	...do...	36	May 2, 1864	100 dys.	Mustered out with company Sept. 2, 1864.
Daniel Cogswell	Musician	21	May 2, 1864	100 dys.	Mustered out to date Sept. 2, 1864.
Byron Brown	...do...	25	May 2, 1864	100 dys.	Mustered out with company Sept. 2, 1864.
Barnhart, John A	Private	21	May 2, 1864	100 dys.	Mustered out with company Sept. 2, 1864.
Baumont, Francis	...do...	18	May 2, 1864	100 dys.	Mustered out with company Sept. 2, 1864.
Best, Alexander	...do...	29	May 2, 1864	100 dys.	Sick, in Balfour General Hospital, at Portsmouth, Va.; transferred to Columbus, O., Aug. 30, 1864. No further record found.
Best, Josiah	...do...	24	May 2, 1864	100 dys.	Mustered out with company Sept. 2, 1864.
Boyd, Alexander	...do...	44	May 2, 1864	100 dys.	Mustered out with company Sept. 2, 1864.
Bradhurst, Thomas J	...do...	35	May 2, 1864	100 dys.	Mustered out with company Sept. 2, 1864.
Burns, William	...do...	21	May 2, 1864	100 dys.	Mustered out with company Sept. 2, 1864.
Close, Samuel L	...do...	18	May 2, 1864	100 dys.	Mustered out with company Sept. 2, 1864.
Cogswell, Hiram	...do...	18	May 2, 1864	100 dys.	Mustered out with company Sept. 2, 1864.
Cogswell, John	...do...	25	May 2, 1864	100 dys.	Died June 11, 1864, in hospital at Alexandria, Virginia.
DeHart, Seneca	...do...	18	May 2, 1864	100 dys.	Mustered out with company Sept. 2, 1864.
Dennis, John	...do...	24	May 2, 1864	100 dys.	Died Aug. 11, 1864, in Balfour General Hospital, at Portsmouth, Va.
DeWitt, Clark I	...do...	23	May 2, 1864	100 dys.	Mustered out with company Sept. 2, 1864.
Dohn, Samuel	...do...	38	May 2, 1864	100 dys.	Mustered out with company Sept. 2, 1864.
Durbin, William H	...do...	25	May 2, 1864	100 dys.	Mustered out with company Sept. 2, 1864.
Elliott, George W	...do...	19	May 2, 1864	100 dys.	Mustered out with company Sept. 2, 1864.
Elliott, John	...do...	18	May 2, 1864	100 dys.	Mustered out with company Sept. 2, 1864.
Ely, Samuel	...do...	34	May 2, 1864	100 dys.	Mustered out with company Sept. 2, 1864.
Franks, Conrad	...do...	26	May 2, 1864	100 dys.	Mustered out with company Sept. 2, 1864.
Frisbie, Edward G	...do...	19	May 2, 1864	100 dys.	Mustered out with company Sept. 2, 1864.
Frisbie, Francis E	...do...	22	May 2, 1864	100 dys.	Sent to Depot General Hospital near Point of Rocks, Md., July 13, 1864. No further record found.
Frisbie, Richard G	...do...	28	May 2, 1864	100 dys.	Mustered out with company Sept. 2, 1864.
Gifford, Hiram L	...do...	41	May 2, 1864	100 dys.	Mustered out with company Sept. 2, 1864.
Gorsach, Jesse H	...do...	20	May 2, 1864	100 dys.	Sent to Depot General Hospital, near Point of Rocks, Md., July 19, 1864. No further record found.
Hendricks, Levi	...do...	29	May 2, 1864	100 dys.	Mustered out with company Sept. 2, 1864.
Hershizer, Jacob H	...do...	37	May 2, 1864	100 dys.	Mustered out with company Sept. 2, 1864.
Householder, Calvin	...do...	23	May 2, 1864	100 dys.	Mustered out with company Sept. 2, 1864.
Householder, F	...do...	28	May 2, 1864	100 dys.	Mustered out with company Sept. 2, 1864.
Householder, John W	...do...	21	May 2, 1864	100 dys.	Mustered out with company Sept. 2, 1864.
Hunter, Aquilla	...do...	23	May 2, 1864	100 dys.	Died Aug. 5, 1864, in Depot General Hospital, at Point of Rocks, Md.
Kesler, Andrew J	...do...	27	May 2, 1864	100 dys.	Mustered out with company Sept. 2, 1864.
Laughlin, Joseph	...do...	21	May 2, 1864	100 dys.	Mustered out with company Sept. 2, 1864.
Lee, William	...do...	35	May 2, 1864	100 dys.	Mustered out with company Sept. 2, 1864.

Names.	Rank.	Age.	Date of Entering the Service.	Period of Service.	Remarks.
Barron, Randolph	Private	18	May 2, 1864	100 dys.	Mustered out with company Sept. 2, 1864.
Bevington, Levi	do	23	May 2, 1864	100 dys.	Mustered out with company Sept. 2, 1864.
Black, William	do	41	May 2, 1864	100 dys.	Mustered out with company Sept. 2, 1864.
Clark, Allen D.	do	32	May 2, 1864	100 dys.	Mustered out with company Sept. 2, 1864.
Clark, Amos	do	31	May 2, 1864	100 dys.	Mustered out with company Sept. 2, 1864.
Clements, Benjamin	do	18	May 2, 1864	100 dys.	Mustered out with company Sept. 2, 1864.
Condit, Winfield S.	do	22	May 2, 1864	100 dys.	Mustered out with company Sept. 2, 1864.
Craig, Clark N.	do	38	May 2, 1864	100 dys.	Mustered out with company Sept. 2, 1864.
Craig, Stephen	do	22	May 2, 1864	100 dys.	Mustered out with company Sept. 2, 1864.
Day, Jehiel F.	do	31	May 2, 1864	100 dys.	Mustered out with company Sept. 2, 1864.
Dazmude, John A.	do	18	May 2, 1864	100 dys.	Mustered out with company Sept. 2, 1864.
Dermody, John	do	21	May 2, 1864	100 dys.	Mustered out with company Sept. 2, 1864.
DeWitt, John F.	do	21	May 2, 1864	100 dys.	Mustered out with company Sept. 2, 1864.
Elliott, William	do	29	May 2, 1864	100 dys.	Mustered out with company Sept. 2, 1864.
Fletcher, Henry	do	26	May 2, 1864	100 dys.	Mustered out with company Sept. 2, 1864.
Goodale, Joseph	do	32	May 2, 1864	100 dys.	Mustered out with company Sept. 2, 1864.
Groer, Thomas E.	do	22	May 2, 1864	100 dys.	Mustered out with company Sept. 2, 1864.
Harsh, Levi	do	18	May 2, 1864	100 dys.	Mustered out with company Sept. 2, 1864.
Hagaman, John	do	29	May 2, 1864	100 dys.	Mustered out with company Sept. 2, 1864.
Hayes, Daniel	do	21	May 2, 1864	100 dys.	Mustered out with company Sept. 2, 1864.
Hess, Joseph	do	24	May 2, 1864	100 dys.	Mustered out with company Sept. 2, 1864.
Heston, John	do	37	May 2, 1864	100 dys.	Mustered out with company Sept. 2, 1864.
Heston, Nathan	do	42	May 2, 1864	100 dys.	Mustered out with company Sept. 2, 1864.
Hunt, Philip	do	28	May 2, 1864	100 dys.	Died Aug. 1, 1864, in hospital near Point of Rocks, Md.
Loback, Henry	do	33	May 2, 1864	100 dys.	Mustered out with company Sept. 2, 1864.
Long, William	do	27	May 2, 1864	100 dys.	Mustered out with company Sept. 2, 1864.
McCune, Robert	do	18	May 2, 1864	100 dys.	Mustered out with company Sept. 2, 1864.
McElroy, James	do	27	May 2, 1864	100 dys.	Mustered out with company Sept. 2, 1864.
Maish, Eber P.	do	57	May 2, 1864	100 dys.	Mustered out with company Sept. 2, 1864.
Majors, [illegible]man	do	26	May 2, 1864	100 dys.	Mustered out with company Sept. 2, 1864.
Mast, William I.	do	23	May 2, 1864	100 dys.	Mustered out with company Sept. 2, 1864.
Miller, Abel C.	do	23	May 2, 1864	100 dys.	Mustered out with company Sept. 2, 1864.
Miller, H. Wright	do	27	May 2, 1864	100 dys.	Mustered out with company Sept. 2, 1864.
Minard, Thomas G.	do	29	May 2, 1864	100 dys.	Mustered out with company Sept. 2, 1864.
Montis, Solomon	do	26	May 2, 1864	100 dys.	Mustered out with company Sept. 2, 1864.
Neal, Joseph	do	18	May 2, 1864	100 dys.	Mustered out with company Sept. 2, 1864.
Nichols, Jonas	do	22	May 2, 1864	100 dys.	Mustered out with company Sept. 2, 1864.
O'Brian, William E.	do	41	May 2, 1864	100 dys.	Mustered out with company Sept. 2, 1864.
Onry, Silas	do	23	May 2, 1864	100 dys.	Mustered out with company Sept. 2, 1864.
Pealer, Mahlon	do	33	May 2, 1864	100 dys.	Mustered out with company Sept. 2, 1864.
Phillips, Joshua	do	30	May 2, 1864	100 dys.	Mustered out with company Sept. 2, 1864.
Reed, J[illegible]	do	19	May 2, 1864	100 dys.	Died Aug. 13, 1864, in hospital near Point of Rocks, Md.
Reed, Samuel	do	47	May 2, 1864	100 dys.	Mustered out with company Sept. 2, 1864.
Rogers, William A.	do	31	May 2, 1864	100 dys.	Mustered out with company Sept. 2, 1864.
Rummel, James	do	27	May 2, 1864	100 dys.	Mustered out with company Sept. 2, 1864.
Scott, Thomas E.	do	41	May 2, 1864	100 dys.	Mustered out with company Sept. 2, 1864.
Serreis, Thomas	do	25	May 2, 1864	100 dys.	Mustered out with company Sept. 2, 1864.
Sharp, Wesley	do	18	May 2, 1864	100 dys.	Mustered out with company Sept. 2, 1864.
Shepard, Jeremiah	do	25	May 2, 1864	100 dys.	Died Aug. 15, 1864, in hospital near Point of Rocks, Md.
Shetler, Jacob	do	21	May 2, 1864	100 dys.	Mustered out with company Sept. 2, 1864.
Shetler, William	do	18	May 2, 1864	100 dys.	Mustered out with company Sept. 2, 1864.
Stonebrook, Mathias	do	35	May 2, 1864	100 dys.	Mustered out with company Sept. 2, 1864.
Stout, John	do	31	May 2, 1864	100 dys.	Mustered out with company Sept. 2, 1864.
Tilton, Asbury J.	do	23	May 2, 1864	100 dys.	Mustered out with company Sept. 2, 1864.
Tilton, Daniel M.	do	25	May 2, 1864	100 dys.	Mustered out with company Sept. 2, 1864.
Thompson, Samuel	do	29	May 2, 1864	100 dys.	Mustered out with company Sept. 2, 1864.
Vernon, James F.	do	30	May 2, 1864	100 dys.	Mustered out with company Sept. 2, 1864.
Waltz, Elias L.	do	26	May 2, 1864	100 dys.	Mustered out with company Sept. 2, 1864.
Whitney, Guerdon	do	25	May 2, 1864	100 dys.	Died Aug. 5, 1864, in hospital at Portsmouth, Virginia.
Wirick, James L.	do	22	May 2, 1864	100 dys.	Mustered out with company Sept. 2, 1864.
Wolfe, William	do	18	May 2, 1864	100 dys.	Mustered out with company Sept. 2, 1864.
Yarnall, John W.	do	19	May 2, 1864	100 dys.	Mustered out with company Sept. 2, 1864.

Names.	Rank.	Age.	Date of Entering the Service.	Period of Service.	Remarks.
Green, Josiah	Private	48	May 2, 1864	100 dys.	Mustered out with company Sept. 2, 1864.
Hedge, Porter	do	18	May 2, 1864	100 dys.	Mustered out with company Sept. 2, 1864.
Holser, Peter	do	28	May 2, 1864	100 dys.	Mustered out with company Sept. 2, 1864.
Jennings, Hiram W	do	31	May 2, 1864	100 dys.	Mustered out with company Sept. 2, 1864.
Johnson, James H	do	29	May 2, 1864	100 dys.	Mustered out with company Sept. 2, 1864.
Jones, Joseph	do	28	May 2, 1864	100 dys.	Mustered out with company Sept. 2, 1864.
Jones, Oliver P	do	35	May 2, 1864	100 dys.	Mustered out with company Sept. 2, 1864.
Jones, Samuel	do	22	May 2, 1864	100 dys.	Mustered out with company Sept. 2, 1864.
Kelley, Lewis	do	24	May 2, 1864	100 dys.	Mustered out with company Sept. 2, 1864.
Leighning, Levi	do	28	May 2, 1864	100 dys.	Mustered out with company Sept. 2, 1864.
Leingor, Levi	do	18	May 2, 1864	100 dys.	Mustered out with company Sept. 2, 1864.
Lewis, Abraham	do	22	May 2, 1864	100 dys.	Mustered out with company Sept. 2, 1864.
Loos, Adam	do	23	May 2, 1864	100 dys.	Mustered out with company Sept. 2, 1864.
McCoy, Andrew J	do	44	May 2, 1864	100 dys.	Mustered out with company Sept. 2, 1864.
McGuire, Francis	do	30	May 2, 1864	100 dys.	Died Aug. 21, 1864 on board steamer Andrew Harder.
McKee, Samuel	do	25	May 2, 1864	100 dys.	Mustered out with company Sept. 2, 1864.
McLain, James A	do	20	May 2, 1864	100 dys.	Mustered out with company Sept. 2, 1864.
Magness, Walter S.	do	18	May 2, 1864	100 dys.	Died July 15, 1864, near Camp Hatchers, Va.
Mathena, Charles H	do	20	May 2, 1864	100 dys.	Mustered out with company Sept. 2, 1864.
Mathena, John M	do	28	May 2, 1864	100 dys.	Mustered out with company Sept. 2, 1864.
Meeks, Sedorus	do	18	May 2, 1864	100 dys.	Mustered out with company Sept. 2, 1864.
Moffet, Asa W	do	18	May 2, 1864	100 dys.	Mustered out with company Sept. 2, 1864.
Morrison, John	do	18	May 2, 1864	100 dys.	Mustered out with company Sept. 2, 1864.
Mulvane, David B.	do	25	May 2, 1864	100 dys.	Mustered out with company Sept. 2, 1864.
Norman, [illegible]	do	28	May 2, 1864	100 dys.	Mustered out with company Sept. 2, 1864.
Owens, Richard	do	18	May 2, 1864	100 dys.	Mustered out with company Sept. 2, 1864.
Phillips, David B	do	22	May 2, 1864	100 dys.	Mustered out with company Sept. 2, 1864.
Phillips, John	do	21	May 2, 1864	100 dys.	Mustered out with company Sept. 2, 1864.
Phillips, Pinckney	do	34	May 2, 1864	100 dys.	Mustered out with company Sept. 2, 1864.
Poland, James A	do	26	May 2, 1864	100 dys.	Mustered out with company Sept. 2, 1864.
Potter, Adam	do	35	May 2, 1864	100 dys.	Mustered out with company Sept. 2, 1864.
Price, Washington J	do	18	May 2, 1864	100 dys.	Mustered out with company Sept. 2, 1864.
Rehard, Joe	do	28	May 2, 1864	100 dys.	Mustered out with company Sept. 2, 1864.
Rehard, Lemuel	do	34	May 2, 1864	100 dys.	Mustered out with company Sept. 2, 1864.
Richmond, James J	do	18	May 2, 1864	100 dys.	Mustered out with company Sept. 2, 1864.
Vanolinda, Henry	do	30	May 2, 1864	100 dys.	Mustered out with company Sept. 2, 1864.
Vanolinda, James	do	29	May 2, 1864	100 dys.	Mustered out with company Sept. 2, 1864.
Vansick, Levi	do	27	May 2, 1864	100 dys.	Mustered out with company Sept. 2, 1864.
Vansick, William	do	31	May 2, 1864	100 dys.	Mustered out with company Sept. 2, 1864.
Walton, Jasper L	do	18	May 2, 1864	100 dys.	Mustered out with company Sept. 2, 1864.
Weatherwax, James E	do	37	May 2, 1864	100 dys.	Mustered out with company Sept. 2, 1864.
Weiss, Elias	do	23	May 2, 1864	100 dys.	Mustered out with company Sept. 2, 1864.
West, Harrison	do	21	May 2, 1864	100 dys.	Died Aug. 1, 1864, in camp near Hatchers, Va.
Williams, William M	do	21	May 2, 1864	100 dys.	Died Aug. 26, 1864, in general hospital at Fortress Monroe, Va.
Williamson, Johnson	do	33	May 2, 1864	100 dys.	Mustered out with company Sept. 2, 1864.
Williamson, William	do	30	May 2, 1864	100 dys.	Mustered out with company Sept. 2, 1864.
Wolf, William	do	21	May 2, 1864	100 dys.	Mustered out with company Sept. 2, 1864.
Woodward, Stephen P	do	19	May 2, 1864	100 dys.	Mustered out with company Sept. 2, 1864.

COMPANY F.

Mustered in May 13, 1864, at Camp Chase, O., by James P. W. Neill, 1st Lieutenant 18th Infantry, U. S. A. Mustered out Sept. 2, 1864, at Camp Chase, O., by Thomas H. Y. Bickham 1st Lieutenant 19th Infantry, U. S. A.

Names.	Rank.	Age.	Date of Entering the Service.	Period of Service.	Remarks.
Anson B. Cummings	Captain	32	May 2, 1864	100 dys.	Mustered out with company Sept. 2, 1864.
William H. H. Miller	1st Lieut.	27	May 2, 1864	100 dys.	Mustered out with company Sept. 2, 1864.
Ira Pealer	2d Lieut	35	May 2, 1864	100 dys.	Died Aug. 11, 1864, in hospital at Fortress Monroe, Va.
Thomas H. Waltz	1st Sergt.	23	May 2, 1864	100 dys.	Mustered out with company Sept. 2, 1864.
Harmon Lybarger	Sergeant	30	May 2, 1864	100 dys.	Died Aug. 11, 1864, at Portsmouth, Va.
John Werick	do	30	May 2, 1864	100 dys.	Mustered out with company Sept. 2, 1864.
William S. Dowds	do	26	May 2, 1864	100 dys.	Mustered out with company Sept. 2, 1864.
John McElroy	do	29	May 2, 1864	100 dys.	Mustered out with company Sept. 2, 1864.
Jacob Nips	Corporal	21	May 2, 1864	100 dys.	Mustered out with company Sept. 2, 1864.
John Carter	do	22	May 2, 1864	100 dys.	Mustered out with company Sept. 2, 1864.
John Gilbert	do	25	May 2, 1864	100 dys.	Mustered out with company Sept. 2, 1864.
Richard Lybarger	do	26	May 2, 1864	100 dys.	Mustered out with company Sept. 2, 1864.
Alexander Gordon	do	22	May 2, 1864	100 dys.	Mustered out with company Sept. 2, 1864.
Alonzo Robinson	do	30	May 2, 1864	100 dys.	Mustered out with company Sept. 2, 1864.
John Worley	do	21	May 2, 1864	100 dys.	Mustered out with company Sept. 2, 1864.
John Rummel	do	21	May 2, 1864	100 dys.	Mustered out with company Sept. 2, 1864.
Smith Buchanan	Musician	32	May 2, 1864	100 dys.	Died Aug. 9, 1864, in hospital near Point of Rocks, Md.
Harvey Matheny	do	18	May 2, 1864	100 dys.	Mustered out with company Sept. 2, 1864.
Ball, George M. D.	Private	19	May 2, 1864	100 dys.	Mustered out with company Sept. 2, 1864.
Barker, George	do	22	May 2, 1864	100 dys.	Mustered out with company Sept. 2, 1864.
Barker, Lyman	do	18	May 2, 1864	100 dys.	Mustered out with company Sept. 2, 1864.

Names.	Rank.	Age.	Date of Entering the Service.	Period of Service.	Remarks.
Stewart, William	Private	19	May 2, 1864	100 dys.	Mustered out with company Sept. 2, 1864.
Stover, George W	do	19	May 2, 1864	100 dys.	Mustered out with company Sept. 2, 1864.
Taylor, John	do	38	May 2, 1864	100 dys.	Mustered out with company Sept. 2, 1864.
Terry, Hiram	do	36	May 2, 1864	100 dys.	Mustered out with company Sept. 2, 1864.
Thompson, Newton G	do	18	May 2, 1864	100 dys.	Mustered out with company Sept. 2, 1864.
Treadaway, Garrett S	do	20	May 2, 1864	100 dys.	Mustered out with company Sept. 2, 1864.
Treadaway, Joseph	do	26	May 2, 1864	100 dys.	Mustered out with company Sept. 2, 1864.
Ullman, Franklin	do	20	May 2, 1864	100 dys.	Mustered out with company Sept. 2, 1864.
Willis, Richard	do	21	May 2, 1864	100 dys.	Mustered out with company Sept. 2, 1864.
Willson, Charles W	do	22	May 2, 1864	100 dys.	Mustered out with company Sept. 2, 1864.
Wolford, Henry A	do	18	May 2, 1864	100 dys.	Mustered out with company Sept. 2, 1864.
Younker, John	do	35	May 2, 1864	100 dys.	Mustered out with company Sept. 2, 1864.

COMPANY H.

Mustered in May 12, 1864, at Camp Chase, O., by James P. W. Neill, 1st Lieutenant 18th Infantry, U. S. A. Mustered out Sept. 2, 1864, at Camp Chase, O., by Thomas H. Y. Bickham, 1st Lieutenant 19th Infantry, U. S. A.

Names.	Rank.	Age.	Date of Entering the Service.	Period of Service.	Remarks.
Josiah M. Cochran	Captain	43	May 2, 1864	100 dys.	Mustered out with company Sept. 2, 1864.
Alfred E. McIntire	1st Lieut.	23	May 2, 1864	100 dys.	Mustered out with company Sept. 2, 1864.
Columbus D. Hyler	2d Lieut.	35	May 2, 1864	100 dys.	Mustered out with company Sept. 2, 1864.
James F. Greenlee	1st Sergt.	24	May 2, 1864	100 dys.	Mustered out with company Sept. 2, 1864.
Artemus Rowley	Sergeant.	25	May 2, 1864	100 dys.	Mustered out with company Sept. 2, 1864.
Chauncey P. Hill	do	44	May 2, 1864	100 dys.	Mustered out with company Sept. 2, 1864.
Matthew Boner	do	22	May 2, 1864	100 dys.	Mustered out with company Sept. 2, 1864.
Harvey Devoe	do	35	May 2, 1864	100 dys.	Mustered out with company Sept. 2, 1864.
Joshua Durbin	Corporal.	25	May 2, 1864	100 dys.	Mustered out with company Sept. 2, 1864.
Abram Stephens	do	29	May 2, 1864	100 dys.	Mustered out with company Sept. 2, 1864.
David P. Wiltz	do	31	May 2, 1864	100 dys.	Mustered out with company Sept. 2, 1864.
James E. Ewers	do	23	May 2, 1864	100 dys.	Died Aug. 3, 1864, near Point of Rocks, Md.
A[illegible]ande Sylliman	do	25	May 2, 1864	100 dys.	Mustered out with company Sept. 2, 1864.
James C. McGrew	do	30	May 2, 1864	100 dys.	Mustered out with company Sept. 2, 1864.
John T. Cornell	do	26	May 2, 1864	100 dys.	Mustered out with company Sept. 2, 1864.
Leander Caywood	do	20	May 2, 1864	100 dys.	Mustered out with company Sept. 2, 1864.
Henan W. Strong	Musician	16	May 2, 1864	100 dys.	Mustered out with company Sept. 2, 1864.
Baxter, Porter	Private	23	May 2, 1864	100 dys.	Mustered out with company Sept. 2, 1864.
Bigbee, Royal	do	19	May 2, 1864	100 dys.	Mustered out with company Sept. 2, 1864.
Blackburn, David	do	18	May 2, 1864	100 dys.	Mustered out with company Sept. 2, 1864.
Blackburn, Moses	do	23	May 2, 1864	100 dys.	Mustered out with company Sept. 2, 1864.
Blackburn, Robert B	do	20	May 2, 1864	100 dys.	Mustered out with company Sept. 2, 1864.
Bricker, William	do	18	May 2, 1864	100 dys.	Mustered out with company Sept. 2, 1864.
Brown, John	do	19	May 2, 1864	100 dys.	Mustered out with company Sept. 2, 1864.
Bricker, William	do	18	May 2, 1864	100 dys.	Mustered out with company Sept. 2, 1864.
Bruce, E[illegible]m	do	24	May 2, 1864	100 dys.	Mustered out with company Sept. 2, 1864.
Buckwalter, Jehiel	do	20	May 2, 1864	100 dys.	Mustered out with company Sept. 2, 1864.
Case, Lew	do	[illegible]	May 2, 1864	100 dys.	Mustered out with company Sept. 2, 1864.
Caywood, Sylvester	do	19	May 2, 1864	100 dys.	Mustered out with company Sept. 2, 1864.
Chaney, James B	do	[illegible]	May 2, 1864	100 dys.	Mustered out with company Sept. 2, 1864.
Condon, David	do	32	May 2, 1864	100 dys.	Mustered out with company Sept. 2, 1864.
Condon, George W	do	32	May 2, 1864	100 dys.	Mustered out with company Sept. 2, 1864.
Condon, Jesse W	do	36	May 2, 1864	100 dys.	Mustered out with company Sept. 2, 1864.
Condon, William H	do	22	May 2, 1864	100 dys.	Mustered out with company Sept. 2, 1864.
Cullison, James	do	27	May 2, 1864	100 dys.	Mustered out with company Sept. 2, 1864.
Dehaven, Oliver F	do	18	May 2, 1864	100 dys.	Mustered out with company Sept. 2, 1864.
Dennis, Aaron	do	19	May 2, 1864	100 dys.	Mustered out with company Sept. 2, 1864.
Detwiler, George W	do	19	May 2, 1864	100 dys.	Mustered out with company Sept. 2, 1864.
Douglass, Abram L	do	21	May 2, 1864	100 dys.	Mustered out with company Sept. 2, 1864.
Durbin, Samuel	do	32	May 2, 1864	100 dys.	Mustered out with company Sept. 2, 1864.
Dunca[illegible], Ja[illegible]	do	18	May 2, 1864	100 dys.	Mustered out with company Sept. 2, 1864.
Ebersole, John	do	29	May 2, 1864	100 dys.	Mustered out with company Sept. 2, 1864.
Edwards, Charles W	do	23	May 2, 1864	100 dys.	Mustered out with company Sept. 2, 1864.
Elliott, Edwin	do	19	May 2, 1864	100 dys.	Died July 11, 1864, near Point of Rocks, Md.
Estile, Edwin H	do	27	May 2, 1864	100 dys.	Died Aug. 5, 1864, in hospital at Portsmouth, Virginia.
Fidler, Daniel	do	22	May 2, 1864	100 dys.	Mustered out with company Sept. 2, 1864.
Foot, Henry R	do	30	May 2, 1864	100 dys.	Mustered out with company Sept. 2, 1864.
Foot, Wilbur	do	21	May 2, 1864	100 dys.	Mustered out with company Sept. 2, 1864.
Gibson, Albert	do	21	May 2, 1864	100 dys.	Mustered out with company Sept. 2, 1864.
Gibson, Gideon	do	32	May 2, 1864	100 dys.	Mustered out with company Sept. 2, 1864.
Giffin, William C	do	22	May 2, 1864	100 dys.	Mustered out with company Sept. 2, 1864.
Gilbert, Samuel	do	22	May 2, 1864	100 dys.	Mustered out with company Sept. 2, 1864.
Gordon, Irvin	do	21	May 2, 1864	100 dys.	Mustered out with company Sept. 2, 1864.
Haines, Burgess	do	25	May 2, 1864	100 dys.	Mustered out with company Sept. 2, 1864.
Hall, Philip C	do	21	May 2, 1864	100 dys.	Mustered out with company Sept. 2, 1864.
Hollabaugh, John F	do	31	May 2, 1864	100 dys.	Mustered out with company Sept. 2, 1864.
Ireland, Lewis	do	21	May 2, 1864	100 dys.	Mustered out with company Sept. 2, 1864.
Jackson, John	do	20	May 2, 1864	100 dys.	Mustered out with company Sept. 2, 1864.
Knight, Fred W	do	22	May 2, 1864	100 dys.	Died Aug. 23, 1864, in hospital at Washington, D. C.

Names.	Rank.	Age.	Date of Entering the Service.	Period of Service.	Remarks.
Stewart, William	Private..	19	May 2, 1864	100 dys.	Mustered out with company Sept. 2,
Stover, George W.	...do...	19	May 2, 1864	100 dys.	Mustered out with company Sept. 2,
Taylor, John	...do...	38	May 2, 1864	100 dys.	Mustered out with company Sept. 2,
Terry, Hiram	...do...	26	May 2, 1864	100 dys.	Mustered out with company Sept. 2,
Thompson, Newton G.	...do...	18	May 2, 1864	100 dys.	Mustered out with company Sept. 2,
Treadway, Garrett S.	...do...	20	May 2, 1864	100 dys.	Mustered out with company Sept. 2,
Treadway, Joseph	...do...	26	May 2, 1864	100 dys.	Mustered out with company Sept. 2,
Ullman, Franklin	...do...	20	May 2, 1864	100 dys.	Mustered out with company Sept. 2,
Willis, Richard	...do...	21	May 2, 1864	100 dys.	Mustered out with company Sept. 2,
Willson, Charles W.	...do...	22	May 2, 1864	100 dys.	Mustered out with company Sept. 2,
Wolford, Henry A.	...do...	18	May 2, 1864	100 dys.	Mustered out with company Sept. 2,
Younker, John	...do...	35	May 2, 1864	100 dys.	Mustered out with company Sept. 2,

COMPANY H.

Mustered in May 2, 1864, at Camp Chase, O., by James P. W. Neill, 1st Lieutenant 18th Infantry. Mustered out Sept. 2, 1864, at Camp Chase, O., by Thomas H. Y. Bickham, 1st Lieutenant 19th Infantry U. S. A.

Names.	Rank.	Age.	Date of Entering the Service.	Period of Service.	Remarks.
Josiah M. Cochran	Captain..	43	May 2, 1864	100 dys.	Mustered out with company Sept. 2,
Alfred R. McIntire	1st Lieut.	23	May 2, 1864	100 dys.	Mustered out with company Sept. 2,
Columbus D. Hyler	2d Lieut.	3[illegible]	May 2, 1864	100 dys.	Mustered out with company Sept. 2,
James C. Greenlee	1st Sergt.	21	May 2, 1864	100 dys.	Mustered out with company Sept. 2,
Artemus C. Rowley	Sergeant.	25	May 2, 1864	100 dys.	Mustered out with company Sept. 2,
Chauncey P. Hill	...do...	14	May 2, 1864	100 dys.	Mustered out with company Sept. 2,
Matthew Bower	...do...	22	May 2, 1864	100 dys.	Mustered out with company Sept. 2,
Harvey Devoe	...do...	25	May 2, 1864	100 dys.	Mustered out with company Sept. 2,
Joshua Durbin	Corporal.	25	May 2, 1864	100 dys.	Mustered out with company Sept. 2,
Abram Stephens	...do...	29	May 2, 1864	100 dys.	Mustered out with company Sept. 2,
David P. Wiltz	...do...	31	May 2, 1864	100 dys.	Mustered out with company Sept. 2,
James E. Ewers	...do...	23	May 2, 1864	100 dys.	Died Aug. 3, 1864, near Point of Rock
Alexander Sv[illegible]man	...do...	25	May 2, 1864	100 dys.	Mustered out with company Sept. 2,
James C. McGrew	...do...	30	May 2, 1864	100 dys.	Mustered out with company Sept. 2,
John T. Cornell	...do...	26	May 2, 1864	100 dys.	Mustered out with company Sept. 2,
Leander Caywood	...do...	29	May 2, 1864	100 dys.	Mustered out with company Sept. 2,
Henan W. Strong	Musician	16	May 2, 1864	100 dys.	Mustered out with company Sept. 2,
Baxter, Porter	Private..	23	May 2, 1864	100 dys.	Mustered out with company Sept. 2,
Bigbee, Royal	...do...	19	May 2, 1864	100 dys.	Mustered out with company Sept. 2,
Blackburn, David	...do...	18	May 2, 1864	100 dys.	Mustered out with company Sept. 2,
Blackburn, Moses	...do...	23	May 2, 1864	100 dys.	Mustered out with company Sept. 2,
Blackburn, Robert R.	...do...	30	May 2, 1864	100 dys.	Mustered out with company Sept. 2,
Bricker, William	...do...	18	May 2, 1864	100 dys.	Mustered out with company Sept. 2,
Brown, John	...do...	33	May 2, 1864	100 dys.	Mustered out with company Sept. 2,
Bricker, William	...do...	18	May 2, 1864	100 dys.	Mustered out with company Sept. 2,
Bruce, Edson L.	...do...	21	May 2, 1864	100 dys.	Mustered out with company Sept. 2,
Buckwalter, Jehiel	...do...	20	May 2, 1864	100 dys.	Mustered out with company Sept. 2,
Case, Lew	...do...	[illegible]	May 2, 1864	100 dys.	Mustered out with company Sept. 2,
Caywood, Sylvester	...do...	19	May 2, 1864	100 dys.	Mustered out with company Sept. 2,
Chaney, James L.	...do...	23	May 2, 1864	100 dys.	Mustered out with company Sept. 2,
Condon, David	...do...	22	May 2, 1864	100 dys.	Mustered out with company Sept. 2,
Condon, George W.	...do...	32	May 2, 1864	100 dys.	Mustered out with company Sept. 2,
Condon, Jesse W.	...do...	36	May 2, 1864	100 dys.	Mustered out with company Sept. 2,
Condon, William H.	...do...	22	May 2, 1864	100 dys.	Mustered out with company Sept. 2,
Cullison, James	...do...	27	May 2, 1864	100 dys.	Mustered out with company Sept. 2,
Dehaven, Oliver F.	...do...	18	May 2, 1864	100 dys.	Mustered out with company Sept. 2, 1864
Dennis, Aaron	...do...	19	May 2, 1864	100 dys.	Mustered out with company Sept. 2, 1864
Detwiler, George W.	...do...	19	May 2, 1864	100 dys.	Mustered out with company Sept. 2, 1864
Douglass, Abram L.	...do...	21	May 2, 1864	100 dys.	Mustered out with company Sept. 2, 1864
Durbin, Samuel	...do...	32	May 2, 1864	100 dys.	Mustered out with company Sept. 2, 1864
Duncan, James	...do...	18	May 2, 1864	100 dys.	Mustered out with company Sept. 2, 1864
Ebersole, John	...do...	20	May 2, 1864	100 dys.	Mustered out with company Sept. 2, 1864
Edwards, Charles W.	...do...	23	May 2, 1864	100 dys.	Mustered out with company Sept. 2, 1864.
Elliott, Edwin	...do...	[illegible]	May 2, 1864	100 dys.	Died July [illegible], 1864, near Point of Rocks, M
Estle, Edwin H.	...do...	27	May 2, 1864	100 dys.	Died Aug. 5, 1864, in hospital at Portsmo Virginia.
Fidler, Daniel	...do...	22	May 2, 1864	100 dys.	Mustered out with company Sept. 2, 1864.
Foot, Henry R.	...do...	30	May 2, 1864	100 dys.	Mustered out with company Sept. 2, 1864.
Foot, Wilbur	...do...	21	May 2, 1864	100 dys.	Mustered out with company Sept. 2, 1864.
Gibson, Albert	...do...	21	May 2, 1864	100 dys.	Mustered out with company Sept. 2, 1864
Gibson, Gideon	...do...	32	May 2, 1864	100 dys.	Mustered out with company Sept. 2, 1864.
Giffin, William C.	...do...	22	May 2, 1864	100 dys.	Mustered out with company Sept. 2, 1864
Gilbert, Samuel	...do...	22	May 2, 1864	100 dys.	Mustered out with company Sept. 2, 1864
Gordon, Irvin	...do...	21	May 2, 1864	100 dys.	Mustered out with company Sept. 2, 1864
Haines, Burgess	...do...	26	May 2, 1864	100 dys.	Mustered out with company Sept. 2, 1864
Hall, Philip C.	...do...	21	May 2, 1864	100 dys.	Mustered out with company Sept. 2, 1864
Hollabaugh, John F.	...do...	31	May 2, 1864	100 dys.	Mustered out with company Sept. 2, 1864.
Ireland, Lewis	...do...	21	May 2, 1864	100 dys.	Mustered out with company Sept. 2, 1864.
Jackson, John	...do...	29	May 2, 1864	100 dys.	Mustered out with company Sept. 2, 1864.
Knight, Fred W.	...do...	22	May 2, 1864	100 dys.	Died Aug. 23, 1864, in hospital at Wash ton, D. C.

Names.	Rank.	Age.	Date of Entering the Service.	Period of Service.	Remarks.
Jones, George W	Private.	28	May 2, 1864	100 dys.	Died Aug. 14, 1864, in hospital at Fortress Monroe, Va.
Kerr, Alexander S	...do...	27	May 2, 1864	100 dys.	Mustered out with company Sept. 2, 1864.
Kerr, John	...do...	25	May 2, 1864	100 dys.	Mustered out with company Sept. 2, 1864.
Keys, Charles	...do...	19	May 2, 1864	100 dys.	Mustered out with company Sept. 2, 1864.
Larue, Henry	...do...	38	May 2, 1864	100 dys.	Mustered out with company Sept. 2, 1864.
Lewis, John	...do...	19	May 2, 1864	100 dys.	Mustered out with company Sept. 2, 1864.
McCamment, William	...do...	40	May 2, 1864	100 dys.	Mustered out with company Sept. 2, 1864.
McKay, William	...do...	19	May 2, 1864	100 dys.	Mustered out with company Sept. 2, 1864.
McMillen, Daniel	...do...	25	May 2, 1864	100 dys.	Mustered out with company Sept. 2, 1864.
McWilliam, Charles	...do...	18	May 2, 1864	100 dys.	Died Jul. 15, 1864, in hospital near Point of Rocks, Md.
Mahaffey, Milton	...do...	26	May 2, 1864	100 dys.	Mustered out with company Sept. 2, 1864.
Meek, Stephen S	...do...	18	May 2, 1864	100 dys.	Mustered out with company Sept. 2, 1864.
Murphy, Lewis M	...do...	18	May 2, 1864	100 dys.	Mustered out with company Sept. 2, 1864.
Murphy, Oliver F	...do...	23	May 2, 1864	100 dys.	Discharged Aug. 26, 1864.
Noffsinger, William	...do...	[illegible]	May 2, 1864	100 dys.	Mustered out with company Sept. 2, 1864.
P[illegible] m[illegible]hre[illegible], [illegible]osiah	...do...	[illegible]	May 2, 1864	100 dys.	Mustered out with company Sept. 2, 1864.
Reece, [illegible]us[illegible]	...do...	1[illegible]	May 2, 1864	100 dys.	Mustered out with company Sept. 2, 1864.
Rumsey, Ol[illegible]	...do...	18	May 2, 1864	100 dys.	Mustered out with company Sept. 2, 1864.
Russell, James	...do...	27	May 2, 1864	100 dys.	Mustered out with company Sept. 2, 1864.
Russell, William H	...do...	23	May 2, 1864	100 dys.	Mustered out with company Sept. 2, 1864.
Schooler, John	...do...	18	May 2, 1864	100 dys.	Died July 25, 1864, on board hospital boat on James River, Va.
Shaler, Elah H	...do...	19	May 2, 1864	100 dys.	Mustered out with company Sept. 2, 1864.
Shaw, Robert A	...do...	19	May 2, 1864	100 dys.	Mustered out with company Sept. 2, 1864.
Simpson, Josiah J	...do...	19	May 2, 1864	100 dys.	Mustered out with company Sept. 2, 1864.
Sims, John	...do...	[illegible]	May 2, 1864	100 dys.	Mustered out with company Sept. 2, 1864.
Sims, William	...do...	[illegible]	May 2, 1864	100 dys.	Mustered out with company Sept. 2, 1864.
Smith, William	...do...	2[illegible]	May 2, 1864	100 dys.	Mustered out with company Sept. 2, 1864.
Spry, John W	...do...	21	May 2, 1864	100 dys.	Mustered out with company Sept. 2, 1864.
Thompson, Samuel	...do...	30	May 2, 1864	100 dys.	Mustered out with company Sept. 2, 1864.
Thornhill, Amsard H	...do...	28	May 2, 1864	100 dys.	Mustered out with company Sept. 2, 1864.
Thornhill, William	...do...	26	May 2, 1864	100 dys.	Mustered out with company Sept. 2, 1864.
Trimble, William	...do...	24	May 2, 1864	100 dys.	Promoted to Chaplain June 2[illegible], 1864.
Van Voorhis, T[illegible]	...do...	29	May 2, 1864	100 dys.	Mustered out with company Sept. 2, 1864.
Walker, Alexander J	...do...	16	May 2, 1864	100 dys.	Mustered out with company Sept. 2, 1864.
Welch, Edward	...do...	19	May 2, 1864	100 dys.	Mustered out with company Sept. 2, 1864.
Welch, Robert M	...do...	28	May 2, 1864	100 dys.	Mustered out with company Sept. 2, 1864.
Wilson, William	...do...	27	May 2, 1864	100 dys.	Mustered out with company Sept. 2, 1864.
Wright, Amos	...do...	3[illegible]	May 2, 1864	100 dys.	Mustered out with company Sept. 2, 1864.
Wright, Phineas	...do...	18	May 2, 1864	100 dys.	Mustered out with company Sept. 2, 1864.
Wright, William	...do...	18	May 2, 1864	100 dys.	Mustered out with company Sept. 2, 1864.

COMPANY K.

Mustered in May 12, 1864, at Camp Chase, O., by James P. W. Neill, 1st Lieutenant 18th Infantry, U. S. A. Mustered out Sept. 2, 1864, at Camp Chase, O., by Thomas H. Y. Bickham, 1st Lieutenant 19th Infantry, U. S. A.

Names.	Rank.	Age.	Date of Entering the Service.	Period of Service.	Remarks.
Charles S. Pyle	Captain.	31	May 2, 1864	100 dys.	Mustered out with company Sept. 2, 1864.
John Eichelberger	1st Lieut.	42	May 2, 1864	100 dys.	Mustered out with company Sept. 2, 1864.
William B. Brown	2d Lieut.	32	May 2, 1864	100 dys.	Mustered out with company Sept. 2, 1864.
Erastus B. Coke	1st Sergt.	27	May 2, 1864	100 dys.	Mustered out with company Sept. 2, 1864.
John B. Twist	Sergeant.	28	May 2, 1864	100 dys.	Mustered out with company Sept. 2, 1864.
Amos Roberts	...do...	18	May 2, 1864	100 dys.	Mustered out with company Sept. 2, 1864.
Perlee C. Breckenridge	...do...	[illegible]	May 2, 1864	100 dys.	Mustered out with company Sept. 2, 1864.
Adam Adams	...do...	39	May 2, 1864	100 dys.	Mustered out with company Sept. 2, 1864.
George S. Bennett	Corporal.	[illegible]	May 2, 1864	100 dys.	Mustered out with company Sept. 2, 1864.
Campbell Errett	...do...	20	May 2, 1864	100 dys.	Died Aug. 9, 1864, near Point of Rocks, Md.
John M. Hildreth	...do...	[illegible]	May 2, 1864	100 dys.	Mustered out with company Sept. 2, 1864.
Arthur Adam	...do...	29	May 2, 1864	100 dys.	Mustered out with company Sept. 2, 1864.
John Magi	...do...	26	May 2, 1864	100 dys.	Mustered out with company Sept. 2, 1864.
Elias L. Cooper	...do...	21	May 2, 1864	100 dys.	Mustered out with company Sept. 2, 1864.
Robert M. George	...do...	20	May 2, 1864	100 dys.	Mustered out with company Sept. 2, 1864.
James L. Israel	...do...	20	May 2, 1864	100 dys.	Sick Aug. [illegible], 1864, in hospital near Point of Rocks, Md. No further record found.
Israel M. Mattison	Musician	19	May 2, 1864	100 dys.	Mustered out with company Sept. 2, 1864.
Baldwin, William F	Private.	19	May 2, 1864	100 dys.	Mustered out with company Sept. 2, 1864.
Bean, Isaac W	...do...	18	May 2, 1864	100 dys.	Mustered out with company Sept. 2, 18[illegible]; also borne on rolls as Isaac W. Beam.
Bean, John M	...do...	21	May 2, 1864	100 dys.	Mustered out with company Sept. 2, 18[illegible]; also borne on rolls as John M. Beam.
Beard, Oliver	...do...	18	May 2, 1864	100 dys.	Mustered out with company Sept. 2, 1864.
Blacher, De	...do...	20	May 2, 1864	100 dys.	Mustered out with company Sept. 2, 1864.
Bope, Charles A	...do...	19	May 2, 1864	100 dys.	Mustered out with company Sept. 2, 1864.
Bostwick, William M	...do...	18	May 2, 1864	100 dys.	Mustered out with company Sept. 2, 1864.
Burr, Jesse T	...do...	23	May 2, 1864	100 dys.	Mustered out with company Sept. 2, 1864.
Byrd, Sharpless	...do...	20	May 2, 1864	100 dys.	Mustered out with company Sept. 2, 1864.
Cooper, Charles G	...do...	18	May 2, 1864	100 dys.	Mustered out with company Sept. 2, 1864.

143rd Regiment Ohio Volunteer Infantry.

ONE HUNDRED DAYS' SERVICE.

This Regiment was organized at Camp Chase, O., May 12 and 13, 1864, to serve one hundred days. It was composed of the Eighteenth Battalion, Ohio National Guard, from Columbiana County, and a part of the Sixty-ninth Battalion, Ohio National Guard, from Coshocton County. On the 15th of May the Regiment left Camp Chase for Washington City, and was placed on garrison duty in Forts Slemmer, Totten, Slocum, and Stevens, north of the Potomac. On the 8th of June the Regiment embarked for White House, Va., but without debarking it was ordered to Bermuda Hundred. It was assigned to the Tenth Army Corps, and was placed in the intrenchments at City Point, where it remained until ordered to Fort Pocahontas. It was relieved from duty at Fort Pocahontas August 29th, and proceeded to Camp Chase, O., where it arrived on the 5th of September, and was mustered out September 13, 1864, on expiration of term of service.

Names	Rank.	Age.	Date of Entering the Service.	Period of Service.	Remarks.
Carpenter, Thomas W	....do....	23	May 2, 1864	100 dys.	Died Aug. 25, 1864, at Hampton, Va.
Chamberlain, Linton	....do....	19	May 2, 1864	100 dys.	Transferred from Co. C, 150th O. V. I., 21, 1864; mustered out with company 13, 1864.
Coburn, Robert	....do....	33	May 2, 1864	100 dys.	Mustered out with company Sept. 13, 1864
Cope, Thomas B	....do....	20	May 2, 1864	100 dys.	Mustered out with company Sept. 13, 1864
DeLair, Arthur	....do....	20	May 2, 1864	100 dys.	Transferred from Co. C, 150th O. V. I., 21, 1864; mustered out with company 13, 1864.
Dennis, David	....do....	36	May 2, 1864	100 dys.	Mustered out with company Sept. 13, 1864
Desellem, Jacob	....do....	37	May 2, 1864	100 dys.	Mustered out with company Sept. 13, 1864
Deveny, William	....do....	31	May 2, 1864	100 dys.	Mustered out with company Sept. 13, 1864
Douglass, Andrew A	....do....	41	May 2, 1864	100 dys.	Mustered out with company Sept. 13, 1864
Faloon, Samuel H	....do....	21	May 2, 1864	100 dys.	Mustered out with company Sept. 13, 1864
Farmer, George	....do....	35	May 2, 1864	100 dys.	Mustered out with company Sept. 13, 1864
Farmer, Henry A	....do....	32	May 2, 1864	100 dys.	Mustered out with company Sept. 13, 1864
Frazer, John	....do....	46	May 2, 1864	100 dys.	Mustered out with company Sept. 13, 1864
Galliher, Isaac	....do....	28	May 2, 1864	100 dys.	Mustered out with company Sept. 13, 1864
Galliher, James	....do....	26	May 2, 1864	100 dys.	Mustered out with company Sept. 13, 1864
Gilson, Richard E	....do....	20	May 2, 1864	100 dys.	Mustered out with company Sept. 13, 1864
Goddard, John	....do....	31	May 2, 1864	100 dys.	Died July 21, 1864, at Fort Pocahontas, Va
Green, Mathias	....do....	18	May 2, 1864	100 dys.	Mustered out with company Sept. 13, 1864
Griffith, John	....do....	27	May 2, 1864	100 dys.	Mustered out with company Sept. 13, 1864
Hart, Alexander	....do....	29	May 2, 1864	100 dys.	Mustered out with company Sept. 13, 1864
Hill, Thomas	....do....	35	May 2, 1864	100 dys.	Mustered out with company Sept. 13, 1864
Hunter, John W	....do....	18	May 2, 1864	100 dys.	Mustered out with company Sept. 13, 1864
Hyer, William	....do....	32	May 2, 1864	100 dys.	Mustered out with company Sept. 13, 1864
Johns, Levi	....do....	31	May 2, 1864	100 dys.	Mustered out with company Sept. 13, 1864
Kilgore, John D	....do....	31	May 2, 1864	100 dys.	Mustered out with company Sept. 13, 1864
McCracken, Andrew	....do....	23	May 2, 1864	100 dys.	Mustered out with company Sept. 13, 1864
McDanell, George W	....do....	19	May 2, 1864	100 dys.	Mustered out with company Sept. 13, 1864
McGaffick, George W	....do....	22	May 2, 1864	100 dys.	Mustered out with company Sept. 13, 1864
McGavern, Philip	....do....	20	May 2, 1864	100 dys.	Mustered out with company Sept. 13, 1864
McGillvry, Alexander	....do....	34	May 2, 1864	100 dys.	Mustered out with company Sept. 13, 1864
McGillvry, Michael	....do....	39	May 2, 1864	100 dys.	Mustered out with company Sept. 13, 1864
McGilvry, Peter	....do....	21	May 2, 1864	100 dys.	Mustered out with company Sept. 13, 1864.
McIntosh, William	....do....	19	May 2, 1864	100 dys.	Mustered out with company Sept. 13, 1864.
Maple, Albert G	....do....	28	May 2, 1864	100 dys.	Mustered out with company Sept. 13, 1864.
Maple, James	....do....	30	May 2, 1864	100 dys.	Mustered out with company Sept. 13, 1864.
Martin, Robert C	....do....	18	May 2, 1864	100 dys.	Mustered out with company Sept. 13, 1864.
Milner, John B	....do....	40	May 2, 1864	100 dys.	Mustered out with company Sept. 13, 1864.
Montgomery, Alexander	....do....	21	May 2, 1864	100 dys.	Mustered out with company Sept. 13, 1864.
Morrison, Washington	....do....	30	May 2, 1864	100 dys.	Mustered out with company Sept. 13, 1864.
Murphy, John	....do....	30	May 2, 1864	100 dys.	Mustered out with company Sept. 13, 1864.
Nile, William	....do....	18	May 2, 1864	100 dys.	Transferred to Co. D ——.
Norton, Herman G	....do....	22	May 2, 1864	100 dys.	Transferred from Co. C, 150th O. V. I., 21, 1864; mustered out with company 13, 1864.
Paisley, George	....do....	25	May 2, 1864	100 dys.	Mustered out with company Sept. 13, 1864.
Patterson, John	....do....	37	May 2, 1864	100 dys.	Mustered out with company Sept. 13, 1864.
Ray, Charles	....do....	35	May 2, 1864	100 dys.	Mustered out with company Sept. 13, 1864.
Ray, Thomas	....do....	32	May 2, 1864	100 dys.	Mustered out with company Sept. 13, 1864.
Saltsman, George W	....do....	22	May 2, 1864	100 dys.	Mustered out with company Sept. 13, 1864.
Sharp, Daniel B	....do....	18	May 2, 1864	100 dys.	Transferred to Co. D ——.
Sharp, Robert B	....do....	25	May 2, 1864	100 dys.	Mustered out with company Sept. 13, 1864.
Shoemaker, John	....do....	22	May 2, 1864	100 dys.	Discharged Sept. 7, 1864, on Surgeon's certificate of disability.
Solliday, Jacob T	....do....	28	May 2, 1864	100 dys.	Mustered out with company Sept. 13, 1864.
Starkey, William	....do....	18	May 2, 1864	100 dys.	Mustered out with company Sept. 13, 1864.
Stitt, William	....do....	21	May 2, 1864	100 dys.	Mustered out with company Sept. 13, 1864.
Thompson, John	....do....	18	May 2, 1864	100 dys.	Mustered out with company Sept. 13, 1864.
Thompson, John J	....do....	21	May 2, 1864	100 dys.	Mustered out with company Sept. 13, 1864.
Thorpe, Ira D	....do....	21	May 2, 1864	100 dys.	Transferred from Co. C, 150th O. V. I., 21, 1864; mustered out with company 13, 1864.
Walsh, Patrick	....do....	18	May 2, 1864	100 dys.	Transferred to Co. D ——.
Weaver, John	....do....	30	May 2, 1864	100 dys.	Mustered out with company Sept. 13, 1864.
Weaver, Lewis	....do....	32	May 2, 1864	100 dys.	Mustered out with company Sept. 13, 1864.
Wisebaugh, William P	....do....	23	May 2, 1864	100 dys.	Mustered out with company Sept. 13, 1864.
Wolcott, Henry R	....do....	19	May 2, 1864	100 dys.	Transferred from Co. C, 150th O. V. I., 21, 1864; mustered out with company 13, 1864.

COMPANY B.

...y 12, 1864, at Camp Chase, O., by John O. Cravens, Assistant Adjutant General and Commis... of Musters, Northern Department. Mustered out Sept. 13, 1864, at Camp Chase, O., by J. M. Kyster, Captain 18th Infantry, U. S. A.

	Rank.	Age.	Date of Entering the Service.	Period of Service.	Remarks.
ge......	Captain.	24	May 2, 1864	100 dys.	Mustered out with company Sept. 13, 1864.
...eron......	1st Lieut.	25	May 2, 1864	100 dys.	Mustered out with company Sept. 13, 1864.
...osh......	2d Lieut.	24	May 2, 1864	100 dys.	Mustered out with company Sept. 13, 1864.
...herson..	1st Sergt.	28	May 2, 1864	100 dys.	Mustered out with company Sept. 13, 1864.
......	Sergeant.	27	May 2, 1864	100 dys.	Mustered out with company Sept. 13, 1864.
...nan......	...do....	26	May 2, 1864	100 dys.	Mustered out with company Sept. 13, 1864.
...r......	...do....	21	May 2, 1864	100 dys.	Mustered out with company Sept. 13, 1864.
...r......	...do....	23	May 2, 1864	100 dys.	Mustered out with company Sept. 13, 1864.
...m......	Corporal.	25	May 2, 1864	100 dys.	Mustered out with company Sept. 13, 1864.
......	...do....	24	May 2, 1864	100 dys.	Mustered out with company Sept. 13, 1864.
...ias......	...do....	20	May 2, 1864	100 dys.	Mustered out with company Sept. 13, 1864.
...n......	...do....	20	May 2, 1864	100 dys.	Mustered out with company Sept. 13, 1864.
...oner......	...do....	20	May 2, 1864	100 dys.	Mustered out with company Sept. 13, 1864.
...uckle......	...do....	22	May 2, 1864	100 dys.	Mustered out with company Sept. 13, 1864.
...ee......	...do....	22	May 2, 1864	100 dys.	Mustered out with company Sept. 13, 1864.
	...do....	22	May 2, 1864	100 dys.	Mustered out with company Sept. 13, 1864.
	Musician	21	May 2, 1864	100 dys.	Mustered out with company Sept. 13, 1864.
	...do....	15	May 2, 1864	100 dys.	Mustered out with company Sept. 13, 1864.
	Wagoner.	28	May 2, 1864	100 dys.	Mustered out with company Sept. 13, 1864.
	Private..	21	May 2, 1864	100 dys.	Mustered out with company Sept. 13, 1864.
	...do....	18	May 2, 1864	100 dys.	Transferred from Co. D May 13, 1864; mustered out with company Sept. 13, 1864.
......	...do....	26	May 2, 1864	100 dys.	Mustered out with company Sept. 13, 1864.
..	...do....	20	May 2, 1864	100 dys.	Died July 19, 1864, at Wilson's Landing, Va.
..	...do....	24	May 2, 1864	100 dys.	Mustered out with company Sept. 13, 1864.
..	...do....	29	May 2, 1864	100 dys.	Mustered out with company Sept. 13, 1864.
..	...do....	23	May 2, 1864	100 dys.	Mustered out with company Sept. 13, 1864.
..	...do....	18	May 2, 1864	100 dys.	Mustered out with company Sept. 13, 1864.
..	...do....	22	May 2, 1864	100 dys.	Mustered out with company Sept. 13, 1864.
..	...do....	25	May 2, 1864	100 dys.	Mustered out with company Sept. 13, 1864.
..	...do....	23	May 2, 1864	100 dys.	Mustered out with company Sept. 13, 1864.
......	...do....	29	May 2, 1864	100 dys.	Mustered out with company Sept. 13, 1864.
......	...do....	24	May 2, 1864	100 dys.	Mustered out with company Sept. 13, 1864.
...ias......	...do....	43	May 2, 1864	100 dys.	Mustered out with company Sept. 13, 1864.
...drew....	...do....	18	May 2, 1864	100 dys.	Mustered out with company Sept. 13, 1864.
......	...do....	25	May 2, 1864	100 dys.	Mustered out with company Sept. 13, 1864.
......	...do....	24	May 2, 1864	100 dys.	Mustered out with company Sept. 13, 1864.
...us C....	...do....	26	May 2, 1864	100 dys.	Mustered out with company Sept. 13, 1864.
......	...do....	25	May 2, 1864	100 dys.	Mustered out with company Sept. 13, 1864.
......	...do....	20	May 2, 1864	100 dys.	Mustered out with company Sept. 13, 1864.
......	...do....	25	May 2, 1864	100 dys.	Mustered out with company Sept. 13, 1864.
...O......	...do....	30	May 2, 1864	100 dys.	Mustered out with company Sept. 13, 1864.
......	...do....	20	May 2, 1864	100 dys.	Mustered out with company Sept. 13, 1864.
...K......	...do....	20	May 2, 1864	100 dys.	Mustered out with company Sept. 13, 1864.
......	...do....	21	May 2, 1864	100 dys.	Mustered out with company Sept. 13, 1864.
......	...do....	21	May 2, 1864	100 dys.	Mustered out with company Sept. 13, 1864.
...nder....	...do....	44	May 2, 1864	100 dys.	Mustered out with company Sept. 13, 1864.
......	...do....	23	May 2, 1864	100 dys.	Mustered out with company Sept. 13, 1864.
......	...do....	22	May 2, 1864	100 dys.	Mustered out with company Sept. 13, 1864.
...H......	...do....	24	May 2, 1864	100 dys.	Mustered out with company Sept. 13, 1864.
...nder....	...do....	23	May 2, 1864	100 dys.	Mustered out with company Sept. 13, 1864.
......	...do....	36	May 2, 1864	100 dys.	Mustered out with company Sept. 13, 1864.
......	...do....	20	May 2, 1864	100 dys.	Mustered out with company Sept. 13, 1864.
...m......	...do....	24	May 2, 1864	100 dys.	Mustered out with company Sept. 13, 1864.
...orge....	...do....	34	May 2, 1864	100 dys.	Mustered out with company Sept. 13, 1864.
...n A....	...do....	19	May 2, 1864	100 dys.	Mustered out with company Sept. 13, 1864.
...s C....	...do....	20	May 2, 1864	100 dys.	Mustered out with company Sept. 13, 1864.
...s M....	...do....	22	May 2, 1864	100 dys.	Died Aug. 19, 1864, at Fortress Monroe, Va
...aniel....	...do....	30	May 2, 1864	100 dys.	Mustered out with company Sept. 13, 1864.
...ander ..	...do....	41	May 2, 1864	100 dys.	Mustered out with company Sept. 13, 1864.
...ander C.	...do....	44	May 2, 1864	100 dys.	Mustered out with company Sept. 13, 1864.
...ander S.	...do....	40	May 2, 1864	100 dys.	Mustered out with company Sept. 13, 1864.
...ol M....	...do....	18	May 2, 1864	100 dys.	Mustered out with company Sept. 13, 1864.
...nbar....	...do....	43	May 2, 1864	100 dys.	Mustered out with company Sept. 13, 1864.
...am F....	...do....	41	May 2, 1864	100 dys.	Mustered out with company Sept. 13, 1864.
...am T....	...do....	25	May 2, 1864	100 dys.	Mustered out with company Sept. 13, 1864.
......	...do....	43	May 2, 1864	100 dys.	Died July 18, 1864, at Balfour Hospital, Norfolk, Va.
...s C....	...do....	18	May 2, 1864	100 dys.	Mustered out with company Sept. 13, 1864.
...hlin....	...do....	22	May 2, 1864	100 dys.	Mustered out with company Sept. 13, 1864.
...as P....	...do....	23	May 2, 1864	100 dys.	Mustered out with company Sept. 13, 1864.
......	...do....	35	May 2, 1864	100 dys.	Mustered out with company Sept. 13, 1864.
...n......	...do....	20	May 2, 1864	100 dys.	Mustered out with company Sept. 13, 1864.
...rew....	...do....	23	May 2, 1864	100 dys.	Mustered out with company Sept. 13, 1864.
...rew....	...do....	19	May 2, 1864	100 dys.	Mustered out with company Sept. 13, 1864.
...n......	...do....	22	May 2, 1864	100 dys.	Mustered out with company Sept. 13, 1864.

Names.	Rank.	Age.	Date of Entering the Service.	Period of Service.	Remarks.
McQueen, Hugh	Private	44	May 2, 1864	100 dys	Mustered out with company Sept. 13, 1864.
Mays, John F	...do...	30	May 2, 1864	100 dys.	Mustered out with company Sept. 13, 1864.
Noble, Alexander	...do...	37	May 2, 1864	100 dys.	Died July 18, 1864, at Fortress Monroe, Va.
Noble, Donald	...do...	31	May 2, 1864	100 dys	Mustered out with company Sept. 13, 1864.
Noble, John	...do...	24	May 2, 1864	100 dys.	Mustered out with company Sept. 13, 1864.
Patterson, John	...do...	25	May 2, 1864	100 dys.	Mustered out with company Sept. 13, 1864.
Powers, William A	...do...	19	May 2, 1864	100 dys.	Mustered out with company Sept. 13, 1864.
Rose, John	...do...	23	May 2, 1864	100 dys.	Mustered out with company Sept. 13, 1864.
Sebring, Hugh, Jr	...do...	19	May 2, 1864	100 dys	Mustered out with company Sept. 13, 1864.
Smith, Daniel M	...do...	17	May 2, 1864	100 dys.	Transferred from Co. F May 15, 1864; mustered out with company Sept. 13, 1864.
Smith, Daniel S	...do...	24	May 2, 1864	100 dys.	Mustered out with company Sept. 13, 1864.
Smith, John L	...do...	28	May 2, 1864	100 dys.	Mustered out with company Sept. 13, 1864.
Smith, John M	...do...	19	May 2, 1864	100 dys.	Mustered out with company Sept. 13, 1864.
Smith, Laughlin	...do...	26	May 2, 1864	100 dys	Mustered out with company Sept. 13, 1864.
Smith, Philip	...do...	23	May 2, 1864	100 dys.	Mustered out with company Sept. 13, 1864.

COMPANY C.

Mustered in May 12, 1864, at Camp Chase, O., by John O. Cravens, Assistant Adjutant General and Commissary of Musters, Northern Department. Mustered out Sept. 13, 1864, at Camp Chase, O., by J. M. Eyster, Captain 18th Infantry, U. S. A.

Names.	Rank.	Age.	Date of Entering the Service.	Period of Service.	Remarks.
Albert R. Arter	Captain.	42	May 2, 1864	100 dys.	Mustered out with company Sept. 13, 1864.
David Burson	1st Lieut	42	May 2, 1864	100 dys.	Mustered out with company Sept. 13, 1864.
William H. Dressler	2d Lieut.	31	May 2, 1864	100 dys.	Promoted from private May 12, 1864; mustered out with company Sept. 13, 1864.
GreenburyT.Swearengen	1st Sergt.	27	May 2, 1864	100 dys.	Mustered out with company Sept. 13, 1864.
Reason Pritchard	Sergeant.	32	May 2, 1864	100 dys.	Mustered out with company Sept. 13, 1864.
John W. Fife	...do...	39	May 2, 1864	100 dys	Transferred from Co. D May 15, 1864; mustered out with company Sept. 13, 1864
William S. Johnson	...do...	23	May 2, 1864	100 dys	Mustered out with company Sept. 13, 1864.
Benjamin C. Battin	...do...	41	May 2, 1864	100 dys.	Mustered out with company Sept. 13, 1864.
Philip J. Voglesong	Corporal	30	May 2, 1864	100 dys.	Mustered out with company Sept. 13, 1864.
Franklin B. Marsh	...do...	29	May 2, 1864	100 dys.	Mustered out with company Sept. 13, 1864.
David Nigus	...do...	33	May 2, 1864	100 dys.	Mustered out with company Sept. 13, 1864.
Benjamin F. Wright	...do...	36	May 2, 1864	100 dys	Mustered out with company Sept. 13, 1864.
Robert Yates	...do...	25	May 2, 1864	100 dys.	Mustered out with company Sept. 13, 1864.
Josiah R. Fox	...do...	37	May 2, 1864	100 dys	Mustered out with company Sept. 13, 1864.
George F. Copeland	...do...	21	May 2, 1864	100 dys.	Mustered out with company Sept. 13, 1864.
John C. Anderson	...do...	19	May 2, 1864	100 dys.	Mustered out with company Sept. 13, 1864.
James McQuilkin	Musician	24	May 2, 1864	100 dys.	Mustered out with company Sept. 13, 1864.
Andrew Rish	...do...		May 2, 1864	100 dys.	Mustered out with company Sept. 13, 1864.
Adoniram J. Halderman	Wagoner	40	May 2, 1864	100 dys.	Mustered out with company Sept. 13, 1864.
Amon, Joshua	Private.	32	May 2, 1864	100 dys.	Mustered out with company Sept. 13, 1864.
Amon, William	...do...	33	May 2, 1864	100 dys	Died July 4, 1864, at Wilson's Landing, Va.
Andre, Jesse	...do...		May 2, 1864	100 dys.	Mustered out with company Sept. 13, 1864.
Arter, Leonard	...do...	18	May 2, 1864	100 dys.	Mustered out with company Sept. 13, 1864.
Baker, Hiram	...do...	29	May 2, 1864	100 dys.	Mustered out with company Sept. 13, 1864.
Breidenstein, Jonas	...do...	26	May 2, 1864	100 dys.	Mustered out with company Sept. 13, 1864.
Brown, Reason	...do...	26	May 2, 1864	100 dys.	Mustered out with company Sept. 13, 1864.
Burcaw, Joshua	...do...	26	May 2, 1864	100 dys.	Mustered out with company Sept. 13, 1864.
Bye, William	...do...	30	May 2, 1864	100 dys.	Mustered out with company Sept. 13, 1864.
Carruthers, Joseph G	...do...	36	May 2, 1864	100 dys	Mustered out with company Sept. 13, 1864.
Clempson, Isaac T	...do...	31	May 2, 1864	100 dys.	Mustered out with company Sept. 13, 1864.
Clempson, Joseph P	...do...		May 2, 1864	100 dys.	Died Aug. 28, 1864, at Wilson's Landing, Va.
Consor, Franklin B	...do...	20	May 2, 1864	100 dys.	Mustered out with company Sept. 13, 1864.
Davis, William	...do...	21	May 2, 1864	100 dys.	Mustered out with company Sept. 13, 1864.
Emmons, Elisha	...do...	34	May 2, 1864	100 dys.	Mustered out with company Sept. 13, 1864.
Finney, Robert	...do...	29	May 2, 1864	100 dys.	Mustered out with company Sept. 13, 1864.
Freed, George	...do...	42	May 2, 1864	100 dys.	Mustered out with company Sept. 13, 1864.
Grim, Isaac	...do...	25	May 2, 1864	100 dys.	Mustered out with company Sept. 13, 1864.
Halderman, Nathan A	...do...	19	May 2, 1864	100 dys.	Mustered out with company Sept. 13, 1864.
Halderman, Owen G	...do...	42	May 2, 1864	100 dys.	Mustered out with company Sept. 13, 1864.
Hamilton, John	...do...	26	May 2, 1864	100 dys.	Mustered out with company Sept. 13, 1864.
Haycock, Clarkson	...do...	21	May 2, 1864	100 dys.	Mustered out with company Sept. 13, 1864.
Heston, Joseph	...do...	25	May 2, 1864	100 dys.	Mustered out with company Sept. 13, 1864.
Holland, William J	...do...	26	May 2, 1864	100 dys.	Mustered out with company Sept. 13, 1864.
Houseman, Peter	...do...	34	May 2, 1864	100 dys.	Mustered out with company Sept. 13, 1864.
Hoover, Jacob P	...do...	22	May 2, 1864	100 dys.	Transferred from Co. D May 15, 1864, and there borne as James P. Hoover; mustered out with company Sept. 13, 1864
Horsefall, Jonas	...do...	35	May 2, 1864	100 dys.	Mustered out with company Sept. 13, 1864.
Jolly, Lorenzo D	...do...	19	May 2, 1864	100 dys.	Mustered out with company Sept. 13, 1864.
Keith, Stephen	...do...	27	May 2, 1864	100 dys.	Mustered out with company Sept. 13, 1864.
King, William F	...do...	37	May 2, 1864	100 dys.	Mustered out with company Sept. 13, 1864.
Laughlin, James H	...do...	25	May 2, 1864	100 dys.	Mustered out with company Sept. 13, 1864.
Lawson, Edward	...do...	29	May 2, 1864	100 dys	Mustered out with company Sept. 13, 1864.
McQuilkin, Jefferson	...do...	29	May 2, 1864	100 dys	Mustered out with company Sept. 13, 1864.
McQuilkin, Milton	...do...	26	May 2, 1864	100 dys.	Mustered out with company Sept. 13, 1864.

Name.	Rank.	Age.	Date of Entering the Service.	Period of Service.	Remarks.
[illegible]	Private..	26?	May 2, 1864	100 dys.	Mustered out with company Sept. 13, 1864.
[illegible]	....do....	35?	May 2, 1864	100 dys.	Mustered out with company Sept. 13, 1864.
[illegible]	....do....	46?	May 2, 1864	100 dys.	Mustered out with company Sept. 13, 1864.
[illegible]	....do....	19	May 2, 1864	100 dys.	Mustered out with company Sept. 13, 1864.
[illegible]	....do....	[illegible]	May 2, 1864	100 dys.	Mustered out with company Sept. 13, 1864.
[illegible]	....do....	26?	May 2, 1864	100 dys.	Mustered out with company Sept. 13, 1864.
[illegible]	....do....	30	May 2, 1864	100 dys.	Transferred from Co. D May 15, 1864; mustered out with company Sept. 13, 1864.
[illegible]	....do....	19	May 2, 1864	100 dys.	Mustered out with company Sept. 13, 1864.
[illegible]	....do....	21?	May 2, 1864	100 dys.	Mustered out with company Sept. 13, 1864.
[illegible]	....do....	[illegible]	May 2, 1864	100 dys.	Died Aug. 10, 1864, at Hampton, Va.
[illegible]	....do....	28?	May 2, 1864	100 dys.	Mustered out with company Sept. 13, 1864.
[illegible]	....do....	35?	May 2, 1864	100 dys.	Mustered out with company Sept. 13, 1864.
[illegible]	....do....	27	May 2, 1864	100 dys.	Mustered out with company Sept. 13, 1864.
[illegible]	....do....	30?	May 2, 1864	100 dys.	Mustered out with company Sept. 13, 1864.
[illegible]	....do....	35?	May 2, 1864	100 dys.	Mustered out with company Sept. 13, 1864.
[illegible]	....do....	24	May 2, 1864	100 dys.	Mustered out with company Sept. 13, 1864.
[illegible] M.	....do....	35?	May 2, 1864	100 dys.	Died July 23, 1864, at Wilson's Landing, Va.
[illegible]	....do....	[illegible]	May 2, 1864	100 dys.	Mustered out with company Sept. 13, 1864.
[illegible]	....do....	19	May 2, 1864	100 dys.	Mustered out with company Sept. 13, 1864.
[illegible]	....do....	34	May 2, 1864	100 dys.	Mustered out with company Sept. 13, 1864.
[illegible]	....do....	18	May 2, 1864	100 dys.	Mustered out with company Sept. 13, 1864.
[illegible]	....do....	40	May 2, 1864	100 dys.	Mustered out with company Sept. 13, 1864.
[illegible]	....do....	20	May 2, 1864	100 dys.	Mustered out with company Sept. 13, 1864.
[illegible]	....do....	24	May 2, 1864	100 dys.	Mustered out with company Sept. 13, 1864.
[illegible]	....do....	23	May 2, 1864	100 dys.	Mustered out with company Sept. 13, 1864.
[illegible]	....do....	22	May 2, 1864	100 dys.	Mustered out with company Sept. 13, 1864.
[illegible] L.	....do....	36	May 2, 1864	100 dys.	Mustered out with company Sept. 13, 1864.
[illegible]	....do....	19	May 2, 1864	100 dys.	Mustered out with company Sept. 13, 1864.
[illegible] E.	....do....	18	May 2, 1864	100 dys.	Mustered out with company Sept. 13, 1864.
[illegible]	....do....	19	May 2, 1864	100 dys.	Transferred from Co. D May 15, 1864; mustered out with company Sept. 13, 1864.
[illegible]		19	May 2, 1864	100 dys.	Mustered out with company Sept. 13, 1864.
[illegible] P.		42	May 2, 1864	100 dys.	Mustered out with company Sept. 13, 1864.
[illegible]		24	May 2, 1864	100 dys.	Mustered out with company Sept. 13, 1864.
[illegible]		18	May 2, 1864	100 dys.	Discharged Aug. 20, 1864, at New York City, on Surgeon's certificate of disability.

COMPANY D.

[illegible] May 12, 1864, at Camp Chase, O., by John O. Cravens, Assistant Adjutant General and Commissary of Musters, Northern Department. Mustered out Sept. 13, 1864, at Camp Chase, O., by J. M. Kyster, Captain 18th Infantry, U. S. A.

Name.	Rank.	Age.	Date of Entering the Service.	Period of Service.	Remarks.
[illegible]	Captain.	39	May 2, 1864	100 dys.	Mustered out with company Sept. 13, 1864.
[illegible]	1st Lieut.	33	May 14, 1864	100 dys.	Mustered out with company Sept. 13, 1864.
[illegible]	2d Lieut.	24	May 2, 1864	100 dys.	Promoted from private May 12, 1864; mustered out with company Sept. 13, 1864.
…annon	1st Sergt.	36	May 2, 1864	100 dys.	Mustered out with company Sept. 13, 1864.
…bridle	Sergeant.	23	May 2, 1864	100 dys.	Mustered out with company Sept. 13, 1864.
…xter	....do....	24	May 2, 1864	100 dys.	Mustered out with company Sept. 13, 1864.
…er	....do....	29	May 2, 1864	100 dys.	Mustered out with company Sept. 13, 1864.
[illegible]	....do....	23	May 2, 1864	100 dys.	Mustered out with company Sept. 13, 1864.
…wick	Corporal.	25	May 2, 1864	100 dys.	Mustered out with company Sept. 13, 1864.
…one	....do....	32	May 2, 1864	100 dys.	Mustered out with company Sept. 13, 1864.
…Ineman	....do....	25	May 2, 1864	100 dys.	Mustered out with company Sept. 13, 1864.
…iser	....do....	38	May 2, 1864	100 dys.	Mustered out with company Sept. 13, 1864.
…Gordon	....do....	23	May 2, 1864	100 dys.	Mustered out with company Sept. 13, 1864.
…Phillips	....do....	32?	May 2, 1864	100 dys.	Mustered out with company Sept. 13, 1864.
…well	....do....	27	May 2, 1864	100 dys.	Mustered out with company Sept. 13, 1864.
…Watson	....do....	38	May 2, 1864	100 dys.	Mustered out with company Sept. 13, 1864.
…gan	Musician	37	May 2, 1864	100 dys.	Mustered out with company Sept. 13, 1864.
…Ashball	....do....	18	May 2, 1864	100 dys.	Mustered out with company Sept. 13, 1864.
[illegible]	Wagoner.	27	May 2, 1864	100 dys.	Mustered out with company Sept. 13, 1864.
…P.	Private..	22	May 2, 1864	100 dys.	Mustered out with company Sept. 13, 1864.
…James	....do....	25?	May 2, 1864	100 dys.	Transferred to Co. B May 15, 1864.
…J.	....do....	23?	May 2, 1864	100 dys.	Mustered out with company Sept. 13, 1864.
…H.	....do....	19?	May 2, 1864	100 dys.	Mustered out with company Sept. 13, 1864.
…uel	....do....	44	May 2, 1864	100 dys.	Mustered out with company Sept. 13, 1864.
…M.	....do....	30	May 2, 1864	100 dys.	Mustered out with company Sept. 13, 1864.
…L.	....do....	19	May 2, 1864	100 dys.	Mustered out with company Sept. 13, 1864.
…orge L.	....do....	25	May 2, 1864	100 dys.	Promoted to Com. Sergeant May 12, 1864.
…avid H.	....do....	22	May 2, 1864	100 dys.	Mustered out with company Sept. 13, 1864.
…, William D.	....do....	31	May 2, 1864	100 dys.	Mustered out with company Sept. 13, 1864.
…amuel J.	....do....	[illegible]	May 2, 1864	100 dys.	Mustered out with company Sept. 13, 1864.
[illegible]	....do....	19	May 2, 1864	100 dys.	Mustered out with company Sept. 13, 1864.
…n H.	....do....	[illegible]	May 2, 1864	100 dys.	Mustered out with company Sept. 13, 1864.
…m	....do....	[illegible]	May 2, 1864	100 dys.	Mustered out with company Sept. 13, 1864.
…n	....do....	[illegible]	May 2, 1864	100 dys.	Mustered out with company Sept. 13, 1864.
…Lewellyn E.	....do....	[illegible]	May 2, 1864	100 dys.	Mustered out with company Sept. 13, 1864.

Names.	Rank.	Age.	Date of Entering the Service.	Period of Service.	Remarks.
Fawcett, Horace	Private	18	May 2, 1864	100 dys.	Mustered out with company Sept. 13, 1864.
Fawcett, Samuel	do.	19	May 2, 1864	100 dys.	Mustered out with company Sept. 13, 1864.
Fife, John W.	do.	29	May 2, 1864	100 dys.	Transferred to Co. C May 15, 1864.
[illegible], George L.	do.	20	May 2, 1864	100 dys.	Mustered out with company Sept. 13, 1864.
[illegible]macy, John W.	do.	40	May 2, 1864	100 dys.	Mustered out with company Sept. 13, 1864.
Ha[illegible], Jerry	do.	34	May 2, 1864	100 dys.	Absent since May 12, 1864. No further record found.
Hanes, William C.	do.	20	May 2, 1864	100 dys.	Mustered out with company Sept. 13, 1864.
Harris, Charles	do.	19	May 2, 1864	100 dys.	Mustered out with company Sept. 13, 1864.
Harris, James	do.	18	May 2, 1864	100 dys.	Mustered out with company Sept. 13, 1864.
Harwood, John	do.	28	May 2, 1864	100 dys.	Mustered out with company Sept. 13, 1864.
Holman, Jacob D.	do.	41	May 2, 1864	100 dys.	Mustered out with company Sept. 13, 1864.
Hoover, James P.	do.	22	May 2, 1864	100 dys.	Transferred to Co. C May 15, 1864.
[illegible], Samuel	do.	18	May 2, 1864	100 dys.	Mustered out with company Sept. 13, 1864.
Hyatt, William H.	do.	23	May 2, 1864	100 dys.	Mustered out with company Sept. 13, 1864.
[illegible], William C.	do.	21	May 2, 1864	100 dys.	Mustered out with company Sept. 13, 1864.
K[illegible], Frank	do.	18	May 2, 1864	100 dys.	Died Aug. 18, 1864, at Hampton Hospital, Va.
K[illegible], John	do.	18	May 2, 1864	100 dys.	Mustered out with company Sept. 13, 1864.
Knox, Robert C.	do.	36	May 2, 1864	100 dys.	Mustered out with company Sept. 13, 1864.
M[illegible], Fidler	do.	40	May 2, 1864	100 dys.	Mustered out with company Sept. 13, 1864.
Matthews, Charles	do.	18	May 2, 1864	100 dys.	Mustered out with company Sept. 13, 1864.
Newton, Orlando A.	do.	18	May 2, 1864	100 dys.	Mustered out with company Sept. 13, 1864.
N[illegible], William	do.	18	May 2, 1864	100 dys.	Transferred from Co. A —; mustered out with company Sept. 13, 1864.
[illegible], Lewis	do.	30	May 2, 1864	100 dys.	Transferred to Co. C May 15, 1864.
[illegible], Henry	do.	32	May 2, 1864	100 dys.	Mustered out with company Sept. 13, 1864.
[illegible], Reuben	do.	32	May 2, 1864	100 dys.	Mustered out with company Sept. 13, 1864.
[illegible], Frank	do.	19	May 2, 1864	100 dys.	Mustered out with company Sept. 13, 1864.
[illegible]	do.	31	May 2, 1864	100 dys.	Mustered out with company Sept. 13, 1864.
[illegible], Edwin A.	do.	27	May 2, 1864	100 dys.	Mustered out with company Sept. 13, 1864.
[illegible], William	do.	23	May 2, 1864	100 dys.	Mustered out with company Sept. 13, 1864.
[illegible], Samuel W.	do.	19	May 2, 1864	100 dys.	Mustered out with company Sept. 13, 1864.
[illegible], Patrick	do.	32	May 2, 1864	100 dys.	Mustered out with company Sept. 13, 1864.
[illegible] B.	do.	18	May 2, 1864	100 dys.	Transferred from Co. A —; mustered out with company Sept. 13, 1864.
[illegible], Kenner B.	do.	38	May 2, 1864	100 dys.	Absent since May 12, 1864. No further record found.
[illegible] A.	do.	19	May 2, 1864	100 dys.	Mustered out with company Sept. 13, 1864.
[illegible], William C.	do.	32	May 2, 1864	100 dys.	Mustered out with company Sept. 13, 1864.
[illegible] W.	do.	19	May 2, 1864	100 dys.	Mustered out with company Sept. 13, 1864.
[illegible] J.	do.	45	May 2, 1864	100 dys.	Mustered out with company Sept. 13, 1864.
[illegible], Harvey M.	do.	28	May 2, 1864	100 dys.	Mustered out with company Sept. 13, 1864.
[illegible]	do.	18	May 2, 1864	100 dys.	Transferred from Co. A —; mustered out with company Sept. 13, 1864.
[illegible] M.	do.	19	May 2, 1864	100 dys.	Transferred to Co. C May 15, 1864.
[illegible]	do.	15	May 2, 1864	100 dys.	Mustered out with company Sept. 13, 1864.
[illegible]	do.	18	May 2, 1864	100 dys.	Mustered out with company Sept. 13, 1864.
[illegible]	do.	19	May 2, 1864	100 dys.	Mustered out with company Sept. 13, 1864.
[illegible] J.	do.	22	May 2, 1864	100 dys.	Mustered out with company Sept. 13, 1864.
[illegible], Martin	do.	20	May 2, 1864	100 dys.	Mustered out with company Sept. 13, 1864.
[illegible]	do.	19	May 2, 1864	100 dys.	Mustered out with company Sept. 13, 1864.
[illegible]	do.	19	May 2, 1864	100 dys.	Mustered out with company Sept. 13, 1864.
[illegible]	do.	31	May 2, 1864	100 dys.	Mustered out with company Sept. 13, 1864.
[illegible]	do.	18	May 2, 1864	100 dys.	Mustered out with company Sept. 13, 1864.

COMPANY E.

[illegible] 1864, at Camp Chase, O., by John O. Cravens, Assistant Adjutant General and Commis[illegible]sters, Northern Department. Mustered out Sept. 13, 1864, at Camp Chase, O., by J. M. Eyster, Captain 18th Infantry, U. S. A.

Names.	Rank.	Age.	Date of Entering the Service.	Period of Service.	Remarks.
[illegible]	Captain.	27	May 2, 1864	100 dys.	Mustered out with company Sept. 13, 1864.
[illegible]	1st Lieut.	24	May 2, 1864	100 dys.	Mustered out with company Sept. 13, 1864.
[illegible]	2d Lieut.	22	May 2, 1864	100 dys.	Mustered out with company Sept. 13, 1864.
[illegible]	1st Sergt.	42	May 2, 1864	100 dys.	Mustered out with company Sept. 13, 1864.
[illegible]	Sergeant.	23	May 2, 1864	100 dys.	Mustered out with company Sept. 13, 1864.
[illegible]	do.	36	May 2, 1864	100 dys.	Mustered out with company Sept. 13, 1864.
[illegible]	do.	30	May 2, 1864	100 dys.	Died June 27, 1864, at Wilson's Landing, Va.
[illegible]	do.	28	May 2, 1864	100 dys.	Appointed from private June 2, 1864; mustered out with company Sept. 13, 1864.
[illegible]	do.	29	May 2, 1864	100 dys.	Appointed from Corporal June 28, 1864; mustered out with company Sept. 13, 1864.
[illegible]	Corporal.	22	May 2, 1864	100 dys.	Mustered out with company Sept. 13, 1864.
[illegible]	do.	33	May 2, 1864	100 dys.	Mustered out with company Sept. 13, 1864.
[illegible]	do.	19	May 2, 1864	100 dys.	Mustered out with company Sept. 13, 1864.
[illegible]	do.	25	May 2, 1864	100 dys.	Mustered out with company Sept. 13, 1864.
[illegible]	do.	25	May 2, 1864	100 dys.	Mustered out with company Sept. 13, 1864.
[illegible]	do.	26	May 2, 1864	100 dys.	Mustered out with company Sept. 13, 1864.
[illegible]	do.	18	May 2, 1864	100 dys.	Mustered out with company Sept. 13, 1864.
[illegible]	do.	25	May 2, 1864	100 dys.	Appointed June 28, 1864; mustered out with company Sept. 13, 1864.

	Rank.	Age.	Date of Entering the Service.	Period of Service.	Remarks.
	Musician	18	May 2, 1864	100 dys.	Mustered out with company Sept. 13, 1864.
...be.	...do...	28	May 2, 1864	100 dys.	Mustered out with company Sept. 13, 1864.
	Wagoner.	39	May 2, 1864	100 dys.	Mustered out with company Sept. 13, 1864.
...iel.	Private.	44	May 2, 1864	100 dys.	Mustered out with company Sept. 13, 1864.
...J.	...do...	18	May 2, 1864	100 dys.	Mustered out with company Sept. 13, 1864.
...E.	...do...	19	May 2, 1864	100 dys.	Died June 21, 1864, at Hampton Hospital, Va.
	...do...	18	May 2, 1864	100 dys.	Mustered out with company Sept. 13, 1864.
	...do...	25	May 2, 1864	100 dys.	Mustered out with company Sept. 13, 1864.
	...do...	18	May 2, 1864	100 dys.	Died June 25, 1864, at Wilson's Landing, Va.
...A.	...do...	35	May 2, 1864	100 dys.	Mustered out with company Sept. 13, 1864.
	...do...	24	May 2, 1864	100 dys.	Mustered out with company Sept. 13, 1864.
	...do...	35	May 2, 1864	100 dys.	Mustered out with company Sept. 13, 1864.
H.	...do...	20	May 2, 1864	100 dys.	Mustered out with company Sept. 13, 1864.
	...do...	30	May 2, 1864	100 dys.	Mustered out with company Sept. 13, 1864.
...W. H.	...do...	22	May 2, 1864	100 dys.	Mustered out with company Sept. 13, 1864.
...U.	...do...	29	May 2, 1864	100 dys.	Mustered out with company Sept. 13, 1864.
...W.	...do...	37	May 2, 1864	100 dys.	Mustered out with company Sept. 13, 1864.
	...do...	18	May 2, 1864	100 dys.	Died Aug. 28, 1864, at Fort Pocahontas, Va.
...ranklin.	...do...	43	May 2, 1864	100 dys.	Mustered out with company Sept. 13, 1864.
	...do...	19	May 2, 1864	100 dys.	Mustered out with company Sept. 13, 1864.
W.	...do...	19	May 2, 1864	100 dys.	Mustered out with company Sept. 13, 1864.
	...do...	19	May 2, 1864	100 dys.	Died July 4, 1864, at Hampton Hospital, Va.
	...do...	25	May 2, 1864	100 dys.	Mustered out with company Sept. 13, 1864.
...nder.	...do...	35	May 2, 1864	100 dys.	Mustered out with company Sept. 13, 1864.
	...do...	18	May 2, 1864	100 dys.	Mustered out with company Sept. 13, 1864.
L.	...do...	29	May 2, 1864	100 dys.	Mustered out with company Sept. 13, 1864.
	...do...	18	May 2, 1864	100 dys.	Mustered out with company Sept. 13, 1864.
	...do...	18	May 2, 1864	100 dys.	Mustered out with company Sept. 13, 1864.
	...do...	18	May 2, 1864	100 dys.	Mustered out with company Sept. 13, 1864.
...rard.	...do...	23	May 2, 1864	100 dys.	Died Aug. 19, 1864, at Hampton, Va.
	...do...	19	May 2, 1864	100 dys.	Mustered out with company Sept. 13, 1864.
	...do...	18	May 2, 1864	100 dys.	Mustered out with company Sept. 13, 1864.
	...do...	18	May 2, 1864	100 dys.	Reduced to the ranks from Sergeant June 2, 1864; mustered out with company Sept. 13, 1864.
...A.	...do...	18	May 2, 1864	100 dys.	Mustered out with company Sept. 13, 1864.
...M.	...do...	21	May 2, 1864	100 dys.	Mustered out with company Sept. 13, 1864.
	...do...	18	May 2, 1864	100 dys.	Mustered out with company Sept. 13, 1864.
...W.	...do...	21	May 2, 1864	100 dys.	Mustered out with company Sept. 13, 1864.
	...do...	30	May 2, 1864	100 dys.	Mustered out with company Sept. 13, 1864.
	...do...	44	May 2, 1864	100 dys.	Mustered out with company Sept. 13, 1864.
	...do...	20	May 2, 1864	100 dys.	Mustered out with company Sept. 13, 1864.
	...do...	18	May 2, 1864	100 dys.	Mustered out with company Sept. 13, 1864.
...nder.	...do...	29	May 2, 1864	100 dys.	Mustered out with company Sept. 13, 1864.
	...do...	31	May 2, 1864	100 dys.	Mustered out with company Sept. 14, 1864.
...L.	...do...	20	May 2, 1864	100 dys.	Mustered out with company Sept. 13, 1864.
...iel.	...do...	30	May 2, 1864	100 dys.	Mustered out with company Sept. 13, 1864.
	...do...	21	May 2, 1864	100 dys.	Mustered out with company Sept. 13, 1864.
	...do...	18	May 2, 1864	100 dys.	Died July 1, 1864, at Wilson's Landing, Va.
	...do...	18	May 2, 1864	100 dys.	Mustered out with company Sept. 13, 1864.
...W.	...do...	41	May 2, 1864	100 dys.	Mustered out with company Sept. 13, 1864.
	...do...	23	May 2, 1864	100 dys.	Mustered out with company Sept. 13, 1864.
...iel.	...do...	18	May 2, 1864	100 dys.	Mustered out with company Sept. 13, 1864.
	...do...	19	May 2, 1864	100 dys.	Mustered out with company Sept. 13, 1864.
	...do...	19	May 2, 1864	100 dys.	Mustered out with company Sept. 13, 1864.
...J.	...do...	24	May 2, 1864	100 dys.	Mustered out with company Sept. 13, 1864.
	...do...	18	May 2, 1864	100 dys.	Mustered out with company Sept. 13, 1864.
	...do...	33	May 2, 1864	100 dys.	Mustered out with company Sept. 13, 1864.
	...do...	22	May 2, 1864	100 dys.	Mustered out with company Sept. 13, 1864.
	...do...	18	May 2, 1864	100 dys.	Mustered out with company Sept. 13, 1864.
	...do...	26	May 2, 1864	100 dys.	Mustered out with company Sept. 13, 1864.
	...do...	33	May 2, 1864	100 dys.	Mustered out with company Sept. 13, 1864.
...son.	...do...	43	May 2, 1864	100 dys.	Mustered out with company Sept. 13, 1864.
	...do...	18	May 2, 1864	100 dys.	Mustered out with company Sept. 13, 1864.
	...do...	35	May 2, 1864	100 dys.	Mustered out with company Sept. 13, 1864.
	...do...	24	May 2, 1864	100 dys.	Mustered out with company Sept. 13, 1864.
	...do...	18	May 2, 1864	100 dys.	Mustered out with company Sept. 13, 1864.
	...do...	29	May 2, 1864	100 dys.	Died June 18, 1864, at Point of Rocks, Md.
...H.	...do...	20	May 2, 1864	100 dys.	Mustered out with company Sept. 13, 1864.
...A.	...do...	29	May 2, 1864	100 dys.	Mustered out with company Sept. 13, 1864.
...H.	...do...	19	May 2, 1864	100 dys.	Mustered out with company Sept. 13, 1864.

COMPANY F.

Mustered in May 12, 1864, at Camp Chase, O., by John O. Cravens, Assistant Adjutant General and Commissary of Musters, Northern Department. Mustered out Sept 13, 1864, at Camp Chase, O., by J. M. Eyster, Captain 18th Infantry, U. S. A.

Names.	Rank.	Age.	Date of Entering the Service.	Period of Service.	Remarks.
Benjamin S. Wright	Captain.	27	May 2, 1864	100 dys.	Mustered out with company Sept. 13, 1864.
Leonard D. Holloway	1st Lieut.	31	May 2, 1864	100 dys.	Mustered out with company Sept. 13, 1864.
John W. Detwiler	2d Lieut.	26	May 2, 1864	100 dys.	Mustered out with company Sept. 13, 1864.
Albert C. Shields	1st Sergt.	27	May 2, 1864	100 dys.	Mustered out with company Sept. 13, 1864.
Eli Sturgeon	Sergeant.	20	May 2, 1864	100 dys.	Mustered out with company Sept. 13, 1864.
John F. Woods	....do....	27	May 2, 1864	100 dys.	Mustered out with company Sept. 13, 1864.
Edmund Ferrall	....do....	28	May 2, 1864	100 dys.	Mustered out with company Sept. 13, 1864.
Joseph C. Wallace	....do....	19	May 2, 1864	100 dys.	Mustered out with company Sept. 13, 1864.
John J. Bushong	Corporal.	18	May 2, 1864	100 dys.	Mustered out with company Sept. 13, 1864.
Daniel Strickler	....do....	21	May 2, 1864	100 dys.	Mustered out with company Sept. 13, 1864.
George Heaton	....do....	18	May 2, 1864	100 dys.	Mustered out with company Sept. 13, 1864.
Albert W. Voglesong	....do....	34	May 2, 1864	100 dys.	Mustered out with company Sept. 13, 1864.
David Grim	....do....	26	May 2, 1864	100 dys.	Mustered out with company Sept. 13, 1864.
Jeremiah Groner	....do....	31	May 2, 1864	100 dys.	Mustered out with company Sept. 13, 1864.
Levi H. Esterly	....do....	20	May 2, 1864	100 dys.	Mustered out with company Sept. 13, 1864.
Israel H. Moredick	....do....	30	May 2, 1864	100 dys.	Mustered out with company Sept. 13, 1864.
Edwin McGregor	Musician	14	May 2, 1864	100 dys.	Mustered out with company Sept. 13, 1864.
Matthew McMichael	Wagoner.	24	May 2, 1864	100 dys.	Mustered out with company Sept. 13, 1864.
Arb, James	Private..	20	May 2, 1864	100 dys.	Transferred to Co. I May 15, 1864.
Augustine, Melancthon H	....do....	21	May 2, 1864	100 dys.	Mustered out with company Sept. 13, 1864.
Augustine, William	....do....	18	May 2, 1864	100 dys.	Mustered out with company Sept. 13, 1864.
Bailey, Oakley H	....do....	23	May 2, 1864	100 dys.	Mustered out with company Sept. 13, 1864.
Barclay, John T	....do....	30	May 2, 1864	100 dys.	
Bare, Jacob	....do....	23	May 2, 1864	100 dys.	Discharged May 14, 1864, on Surgeon's certificate of disability.
Barnhart, Franklin	....do....	18	May 2, 1864	100 dys.	Mustered out with company Sept. 13, 1864.
Biery, Theophilus E	....do....	20	May 2, 1864	100 dys.	Mustered out with company Sept. 13, 1864.
Brenner, Conrad M	....do....	36	May 2, 1864	100 dys.	
Bushong, Alexander B	....do....	24	May 2, 1864	100 dys.	Mustered out with company Sept. 13, 1864.
Bushong, Alpheus A	....do....	19	May 2, 1864	100 dys.	Mustered out with company Sept. 13, 1864.
Compton, John D	....do....	23	May 2, 1864	100 dys.	Mustered out with company Sept. 13, 1864.
Cope, Rufus	....do....	21	May 2, 1864	100 dys.	Mustered out with company Sept. 13, 1864.
Crawford, David	....do....	30	May 2, 1864	100 dys.	Mustered out with company Sept. 13, 1864.
Crow, Silas S	....do....	35	May 2, 1864	100 dys.	
Deemer, Jacob	....do....	18	May 2, 1864	100 dys.	Mustered out with company Sept. 13, 1864.
Deemer, John	....do....	37	May 2, 1864	100 dys.	Mustered out with company Sept. 13, 1864.
Engle, Hinchman	....do....	26	May 2, 1864	100 dys.	Mustered out with company Sept. 13, 1864.
Engle, Nathanie M	....do....	18	May 2, 1864	100 dys.	Mustered out with company Sept. 13, 1864.
Ferguson, Joseph	....do....	18	May 2, 1864	100 dys.	Mustered out with company Sept. 13, 1864.
Ferrall, Herennus H	....do....	24	May 2, 1864	100 dys.	
Ferrall, Samuel B	....do....	22	May 2, 1864	100 dys.	Mustered out with company Sept. 13, 1864.
Fesler, Henry	....do....	22	May 2, 1864	100 dys.	
Fitzpatrick, George W	....do....	28	May 2, 1864	100 dys.	Mustered out with company Sept. 13, 1864.
Forney, Sampson	....do....	35	May 2, 1864	100 dys.	Mustered out with company Sept. 13, 1864.
Gilbert, Jesse	....do....	29	May 2, 1864	100 dys.	Mustered out with company Sept. 13, 1864.
Gilbert, Joseph L	....do....	20	May 2, 1864	100 dys.	Mustered out with company Sept. 13, 1864.
Gleckner, Jonathan	....do....	23	May 2, 1864	100 dys.	Mustered out with company Sept. 13, 1864.
Grim, Michael	....do....	29	May 2, 1864	100 dys.	Mustered out with company Sept. 13, 1864.
Heacock, Alfred	....do....	23	May 2, 1864	100 dys.	Mustered out with company Sept. 13, 1864.
Hendricks, William B	....do....	36	May 2, 1864	100 dys.	Mustered out with company Sept. 13, 1864.
Hisey, Daniel	....do....	31	May 2, 1864	100 dys.	Mustered out with company Sept. 13, 1864.
Holloway, Samuel	....do....	20	May 2, 1864	100 dys.	Mustered out with company Sept. 13, 1864.
Holloway, Thomas F	....do....	35	May 2, 1864	100 dys.	
Houllett, Nicholas B	....do....	36	May 2, 1864	100 dys.	
Hum, Reuben	....do....	30	May 2, 1864	100 dys.	Discharged May 14, 1864, on Surgeon's certificate of disability.
Keyser, Franklin	....do....	25	May 2, 1864	100 dys.	
Kipp, George	....do....	29	May 2, 1864	100 dys.	
Lamb, William	....do....	29	May 2, 1864	100 dys.	
Lower, George	....do....	24	May 2, 1864	100 dys.	Absent, sick, Aug. 23, 1864. No further record found.
McGee, James	....do....	18	May 2, 1864	100 dys.	Transferred to Co. I May 15, 1864, and there borne as James McKee.
Mark, Conrad J	....do....	25	May 2, 1864	100 dys.	Mustered out with company Sept. 13, 1864.
Marlatt, Winfield	....do....	24	May 2, 1864	100 dys.	Mustered out with company Sept. 13, 1864.
Martin, Franklin B	....do....	30	May 2, 1864	100 dys.	Transferred to Co. I May 15, 1864.
Martin, Nathaniel	....do....	18	May 2, 1864	100 dys.	Transferred to Co. I May 15, 1864.
Miller, Henry S	....do....	25	May 2, 1864	100 dys.	Mustered out with company Sept. 13, 1864.
Miller, William W	....do....	24	May 2, 1864	100 dys.	Mustered out with company Sept. 13, 1864.
Moore, James H	....do....	20	May 2, 1864	100 dys.	Mustered out with company Sept. 13, 1864.
Nagle, Frederick	....do....	32	May 2, 1864	100 dys.	Transferred to Co. I May 15, 1864.
Scott, William B	....do....	18	May 2, 1864	100 dys.	Transferred to Co. I May 15, 1864.
Seacrist, David	....do....	28	May 2, 1864	100 dys.	Discharged May 14, 1864, on Surgeon's certificate of disability.
Shaffer, John	....do....	20	May 2, 1864	100 dys.	Mustered out with company Sept. 13, 1864.
Shenkle, Albert	....do....	18	May 2, 1864	100 dys.	Transferred to Co. I May 15, 1864.

Names.	Rank.	Age.	Date of Entering the Service.	Period of Service.	Remarks.
[illegible], John	Private.	28	May 2, 1864	100 dys.	Transferred to Co. I May 15, 1864.
[illegible], George	do.	42	May 2, 1864	100 dys.	Mustered out with company Sept. 13, 1864.
[illegible] M.	do.	19	May 2, 1864	100 dys.	Mustered out with company Sept. 13, 1864.
[illegible], Daniel M.	do.	17	May 2, 1864	100 dys.	Transferred to Co. B May 16, 1864.
[illegible], John	do.	35	May 2, 1864	100 dys.	Discharged May 14, 1864, on Surgeon's certificate of disability.
[illegible], George	do.	21	May 2, 1864	100 dys.	Discharged May 14, 1864, on Surgeon's certificate of disability.
[illegible], John	do.	28	May 2, 1864	100 dys.	Mustered out with company Sept. 13, 1864.
[illegible], Henry	do.	44	May 2, 1864	100 dys.	Mustered out with company Sept. 13, 1864.
[illegible], Andrew	do.	25	May 2, 1864	100 dys.	Discharged May 14, 1864, on Surgeon's certificate of disability.
[illegible] H.	do.	22	May 2, 1864	100 dys.	Mustered out with company Sept. 13, 1864.
[illegible], Wilson	do.	18	May 2, 1864	100 dys.	Transferred to Co. I May 15, 1864.
[illegible], John	do.	21	May 2, 1864	100 dys.	
[illegible], Frederick	do.	25	May 2, 1864	100 dys.	Mustered out with company Sept. 13, 1864.

COMPANY G.

Mustered in May 13, 1864, at Camp Chase, O., by John O. Cravens, Assistant Adjutant General and Commissary of Musters, Northern Department. Mustered out Sept. 13, 1864, at Camp Chase, O., by J. M. Kyster, Captain 18th Infantry, U. S. A.

Names.	Rank.	Age.	Date of Entering the Service.	Period of Service.	Remarks.
John [illegible] Dougherty	Captain.	36	May 2, 1864	100 dys.	Mustered out with company Sept. 13, 1864.
Andrew J. [illegible]	1st Lieut.	27	May 2, 1864	100 dys.	Mustered out with company Sept. 13, 1864.
[illegible]	2d Lieut.	33	May 2, 1864	100 dys.	Mustered out with company Sept. 13, 1864.
[illegible]	1st Sergt.	20	May 2, 1864	100 dys.	Mustered out with company Sept. 13, 1864.
Leander Bryant	Sergeant.	27	May 2, 1864	100 dys.	Appointed Color Sergeant May 14, 1864; mustered out with company Sept. 13, 1864.
[illegible] H. Shaw	do.	35	May 2, 1864	100 dys.	Promoted to Q. M. Sergeant May 14, 1864.
John W. Graves	do.	27	May 2, 1864	100 dys.	Mustered out with company Sept. 13, 1864.
[illegible] W. Reed	do.	34	May 2, 1864	100 dys.	Mustered out with company Sept. 13, 1864.
Thomas Le Rettiley	do.	33	May 2, 1864	100 dys.	Appointed from Corporal May 14, 1864; mustered out with company Sept. 13, 1864.
Alexander McCullough	Corporal.	28	May 2, 1864	100 dys.	Mustered out with company Sept. 13, 1864.
William [illegible]	do.	40	May 2, 1864	100 dys.	Mustered out with company Sept. 13, 1864.
William Austin	do.	30	May 2, 1864	100 dys.	Mustered out with company Sept. 13, 1864.
Albert Wright	do.	24	May 2, 1864	100 dys.	Mustered out with company Sept. 13, 1864.
[illegible]	do.	20	May 2, 1864	100 dys.	Mustered out with company Sept. 13, 1864.
[illegible]	do.	36	May 2, 1864	100 dys.	Mustered out with company Sept. 13, 1864.
[illegible]	do.	20	May 2, 1864	100 dys.	Mustered out with company Sept. 13, 1864.
[illegible]	do.	40	May 2, 1864	100 dys.	Appointed May 14, 1864; mustered out with company Sept. 13, 1864.
Lewis H. Reed	Musician	22	May 2, 1864	100 dys.	Mustered out with company Sept. 13, 1864.
Martin Hark	do.	16	May 2, 1864	100 dys.	Mustered out with company Sept. 13, 1864.
Samuel Squires	Wagoner.	29	May 2, 1864	100 dys.	Mustered out with company Sept. 13, 1864.
Akeroyd, Henry	Private.	19	May 2, 1864	100 dys.	Mustered out with company Sept. 13, 1864.
Allen, John	do.	27	May 2, 1864	100 dys.	Mustered out with company Sept. 13, 1864.
Barcroft, Jeremiah	do.	30	May 2, 1864	100 dys.	Mustered out with company Sept. 13, 1864.
Blackburn, Joseph	do.	19	May 2, 1864	100 dys.	Mustered out with company Sept. 13, 1864.
Bradfield, Henry	do.	24	May 2, 1864	100 dys.	Mustered out with company Sept. 13, 1864.
Bradfield, William	do.	19	May 2, 1864	100 dys.	Mustered out with company Sept. 13, 1864.
Brenneman, James	do.	26	May 2, 1864	100 dys.	Mustered out with company Sept. 13, 1864.
Cain, Lewis	do.	18	May 2, 1864	100 dys.	Mustered out with company Sept. 13, 1864.
Cantrell, Franklin	do.	24	May 2, 1864	100 dys.	Mustered out with company Sept. 13, 1864.
Chaney, Moses	do.	36	May 2, 1864	100 dys.	Mustered out with company Sept. 13, 1864.
Cook, Thomas	do.	30	May 2, 1864	100 dys.	Mustered out with company Sept. 13, 1864.
Cox, William H.	do.	21	May 2, 1864	100 dys.	Mustered out with company Sept. 13, 1864.
Cullison, William	do.	29	May 2, 1864	100 dys.	Mustered out with company Sept. 13, 1864.
Dawson, Jeremiah	do.	18	May 2, 1864	100 dys.	Mustered out with company Sept. 13, 1864.
Dawson, William	do.	30	May 2, 1864	100 dys.	Mustered out with company Sept. 13, 1864.
Dodd, William	do.	24	May 2, 1864	100 dys.	Died July 31, 1864, at Wilson's Landing, Va.
Doolittle, Jared	do.	38	May 2, 1864	100 dys.	Mustered out with company Sept. 13, 1864.
Dunfee, John	do.	23	May 2, 1864	100 dys.	Mustered out with company Sept. 13, 1864.
Dunfee, William	do.	18	May 2, 1864	100 dys.	Mustered out with company Sept. 13, 1864.
Edwards, Thomas J.	do.	24	May 2, 1864	100 dys.	Mustered out with company Sept. 13, 1864.
Finnell, Robert	do.	28	May 2, 1864	100 dys.	Mustered out with company Sept. 13, 1864.
Finnell, Thomas A.	do.	25	May 2, 1864	100 dys.	Mustered out with company Sept. 13, 1864.
Fortune, Jesse	do.	28	May 2, 1864	100 dys.	Mustered out with company Sept. 13, 1864.
Gooden, Samuel	do.	31	May 2, 1864	100 dys.	Mustered out with company Sept. 13, 1864.
Graham, James	do.	30	May 2, 1864	100 dys.	Mustered out with company Sept. 13, 1864.
Graves, Wesley	do.	37	May 2, 1864	100 dys.	Mustered out with company Sept. 13, 1864.
Hill, George	do.	24	May 2, 1864	100 dys.	Mustered out with company Sept. 13, 1864.
Hues, Samuel	do.	19	May 2, 1864	100 dys.	Mustered out with company Sept. 13, 1864.
Huffman, Joseph	do.	20	May 2, 1864	100 dys.	Died Aug. 15, 1864, at Fortress Monroe, Va.
Huffman, William	do.	36	May 2, 1864	100 dys.	Mustered out with company Sept. 13, 1864.
Hutton, John	do.	23	May 2, 1864	100 dys.	Mustered out with company Sept. 13, 1864.
Kern, Daniel	do.	41	May 2, 1864	100 dys.	Mustered out with company Sept. 13, 1864.
Keys, Samuel	do.	31	May 2, 1864	100 dys.	Mustered out with company Sept. 13, 1864.
Larr, Daniel R.	do.	34	May 2, 1864	100 dys.	Mustered out with company Sept. 13, 1864.

Names.	Rank.	Age.	Date of Entering the Service.	Period of Service.	Remarks.
Lowery, James	Private	36	May 2, 1864	100 dys.	Mustered out with company Sept. 13, 1864.
Lowery, Thomas	...do...	19	May 2, 1864	100 dys.	Mustered out with company Sept. 13, 1864.
Mc[illegible]ough, James	...do...	20	May 2, 1864	100 dys.	Mustered out with company Sept. 13, 1864.
Mc[illegible]ough, William	...do...	20	May 2, 1864	100 dys.	Mustered out with company Sept. 13, 1864.
[illegible], Franklin D	...do...	19	May 2, 1864	100 dys.	Mustered out with company Sept. 13, 1864.
[illegible], William J	...do...	26	May 2, 1864	100 dys.	Mustered out with company Sept. 13, 1864.
[illegible], Henry	...do...	44	May 2, 1864	100 dys.	Mustered out with company Sept. 13, 1864.
North, Joshua	...do...	38	May 2, 1864	100 dys.	Mustered out with company Sept. 13, 1864.
[illegible], Albert	...do...	20	May 2, 1864	100 dys.	Mustered out with company Sept. 13, 1864.
[illegible], Lamar	...do...	18	May 2, 1864	100 dys.	Mustered out with company Sept. 13, 1864.
[illegible], Joshua	...do...	18	May 2, 1864	100 dys.	Mustered out with company Sept. 13, 1864.
[illegible], William	...do...	18	May 2, 1864	100 dys.	Mustered out with company Sept. 13, 1864.
[illegible], Robert	...do...	18	May 2, 1864	100 dys.	Mustered out with company Sept. 13, 1864.
Pa[illegible], William H	...do...	18	May 2, 1864	100 dys.	Mustered out with company Sept. 13, 1864.
[illegible], Andrew J	...do...	26	May 2, 1864	100 dys.	Mustered out with company Sept. 13, 1864.
[illegible], John H	...do...	29	May 2, 1864	100 dys.	Mustered out with company Sept. 13, 1864.
[illegible], Josephus	...do...	20	May 2, 1864	100 dys.	Mustered out with company Sept. 13, 1864.
[illegible]son, George C	...do...	28	May 2, 1864	100 dys.	Mustered out with company Sept. 13, 1864.
Rosey, George	...do...	18	May 2, 1864	100 dys.	Mustered out with company Sept. 13, 1864.
Ross, William	...do...	18	May 2, 1864	100 dys.	Mustered out with company Sept. 13, 1864.
Seaman, George	...do...	29	May 2, 1864	100 dys.	Mustered out with company Sept. 13, 1864.
Shirley, James	...do...	44	May 2, 1864	100 dys.	Mustered out with company Sept. 13, 1864.
Smith, Thomas	...do...	18	May 2, 1864	100 dys.	Mustered out with company Sept. 13, 1864.
Squires, Stilwell	...do...	18	May 2, 1864	100 dys.	Mustered out with company Sept. 13, 1864.
Stephens, John	...do...	29	May 2, 1864	100 dys.	Mustered out with company Sept. 13, 1864.
[illegible], John	...do...	19	May 2, 1864	100 dys.	Mustered out with company Sept. 13, 1864.
Taylor, Joseph W	...do...	44	May 2, 1864	100 dys.	Mustered out with company Sept. 13, 1864.
Turner, James W	...do...	22	May 2, 1864	100 dys.	Mustered out with company Sept. 13, 1864.
Vaneman, Martin D	...do...	18	May 2, 1864	100 dys.	Mustered out with company Sept. 13, 1864.
Vansickle, Henry	...do...	44	May 2, 1864	100 dys.	Mustered out with company Sept. 13, 1864.
Vansickle, John W	...do...	21	May 2, 1864	100 dys.	Mustered out with company Sept. 13, 1864.
Wright, George W	...do...	21	May 2, 1864	100 dys.	Died Aug. 11, 1864, at Hampton, Va.
Wright, Henry	...do...	18	May 2, 1864	100 dys.	Mustered out with company Sept. 13, 1864.

COMPANY H.

Mustered in May 13, 1864, at Camp Chase, O., by John O. Cravens, Assistant Adjutant General and Com[missary] of Musters, Northern Department. Mustered out Sept. 13, 1864, at Camp Chase, O., by J. M. Eyster, Captain 18th Infantry, U. S. A.

Names.	Rank.	Age.	Date of Entering the Service.	Period of Service.	Remarks.
James R[illegible]	Captain.	22	May 2, 1864	100 dys.	Mustered out with company Sept. 13, 1864.
John T. Crawford	1st Lieut.	22	May 2, 1864	100 dys.	Mustered out with company Sept. 13, 1864.
Nathan Elliott	2d Lieut.	23	May 2, 1864	100 dys.	Mustered out with company Sept. 13, 1864.
William H. Park	1st Sergt.	27	May 2, 1864	100 dys.	Mustered out with company Sept. 13, 1864.
Eli Seward	Sergeant.	24	May 2, 1864	100 dys.	Died June 25, 1864, at Wilson's Landing, [illegible]
Nathan L. Glover	...do...	21	May 2, 1864	100 dys.	Mustered out with company Sept. 13, 1864.
Andrew Jack	...do...	24	May 2, 1864	100 dys.	Mustered out with company Sept. 13, 1864.
Thomas Love	...do...	28	May 2, 1864	100 dys.	Mustered out with company Sept. 13, 1864.
John Wier	...do...	33	May 2, 1864	100 dys.	Appointed from Corporal July 1, 1864; [mus]tered out with company Sept. 13, 1864.
John Darr	Corporal.	24	May 2, 1864	100 dys.	Appointed Aug. 10, 1864; mustered out [with] company Sept. 13, 1864.
John Waters	...do...	37	May 2, 1864	100 dys.	Died Aug. 5, 1864, at Balfour Hospital, [Ports]mouth, Va.
John E. Baker	...do...	27	May 2, 1864	100 dys.	Mustered out with company Sept. 13, 1864.
Hervey Ford	...do...	26	May 2, 1864	100 dys.	Mustered out with company Sept. 13, 1864.
Robert Magee	...do...	37	May 2, 1864	100 dys.	Mustered out with company Sept. 13, 1864.
John S. [illegible]unken	...do...	31	May 2, 1864	100 dys.	Mustered out with company Sept. 13, 1864.
Robert M. Karr	...do...	29	May 2, 1864	100 dys.	Mustered out with company Sept. 13, 1864.
Daniel Overholt	...do...	24	May 2, 1864	100 dys.	Died July 23, 1864, at Balfour Hospital, [Ports]mouth, Va.
William B. Finlay	...do...	25	May 2, 1864	100 dys.	Appointed July 1, 1864; mustered out [with] company Sept. 13, 1864.
Aaron Fitzwater	...do...	21	May 2, 1864	100 dys.	Appointed July 26, 1864; mustered out [with] company Sept. 13, 1864.
James P. Lanning	Musician	18	May 2, 1864	100 dys.	Mustered out with company Sept. 13, 1864.
William F. Sands	...do...	18	May 2, 1864	100 dys.	Mustered out with company Sept. 13, 1864.
Abram Shafer	Wagoner.	19	May 2, 1864	100 dys.	Mustered out with company Sept. 13, 1864.
Adams, John M	Private	18	May 2, 1864	100 dys.	Mustered out with company Sept. 13, 1864.
Andrews, Gabriel G	...do...	19	May 2, 1864	100 dys.	Mustered out with company Sept. 13, 1864.
Andrews, John	...do...	40	May 2, 1864	100 dys.	Mustered out with company Sept. 13, 1864.
Bechtol, Samuel E	...do...	19	May 2, 1864	100 dys.	Died July 17, 1864, at Hampton Hos[pital], Fortress Monroe, Va.
Bechtol, Samuel G	...do...	19	May 2, 1864	100 dys.	Mustered out with company Sept. 13, 1864.
Boyd, Henry B	...do...	23	May 2, 1864	100 dys.	Mustered out with company Sept. 13, 1864.
Boyd, James H	...do...	18	May 2, 1864	100 dys.	Mustered out with company Sept. 13, 1864.
Boyd, John C	...do...	25	May 2, 1864	100 dys.	Mustered out with company Sept. 13, 1864.
Boyd, Ramsey W	...do...	23	May 2, 1864	100 dys.	Mustered out with company Sept. 13, 1864.
Boyd, Robert D	...do...	18	May 2, 1864	100 dys.	Mustered out with company Sept. 13, 1864.
Buckalew, Francis M	...do...	24	May 2, 1864	100 dys.	Mustered out with company Sept. 13, 1864.

Names.	Rank.	Age.	Date of Entering the Service.	Period of Service.	Remarks.
[illegible]	Private.	21	May 2, 1864	100 dys.	Mustered out with company Sept. 13, 1864.
... Williams A.	...do...	19	May 2, 1864	100 dys.	Mustered out with company Sept. 13, 1864.
[illegible]	...do...	19	May 2, 1864	100 dys.	Mustered out with company Sept. 13, 1864.
[illegible]	...do...	21	May 2, 1864	100 dys.	Mustered out with company Sept. 13, 1864.
[illegible]	...do...	25	May 2, 1864	100 dys.	Mustered out with company Sept. 13, 1864.
[illegible]	...do...	37	May 2, 1864	100 dys.	Mustered out with company Sept. 13, 1864.
...H.	...do...	19	May 2, 1864	100 dys.	Mustered out with company Sept. 13, 1864.
...Joseph R.	...do...	19	May 2, 1864	100 dys.	Mustered out with company Sept. 13, 1864.
...George W.	...do...	22	May 2, 1864	100 dys.	Mustered out with company Sept. 13, 1864.
[illegible]	...do...	23	May 2, 1864	100 dys.	Mustered out with company Sept. 13, 1864.
...H.	...do...	46	May 2, 1864	100 dys.	Mustered out with company Sept. 13, 1864.
...Thomas L.	...do...	21	May 2, 1864	100 dys.	Mustered out with company Sept. 13, 1864.
...William A.	...do...	20	May 2, 1864	100 dys.	Mustered out with company Sept. 13, 1864.
...Washington	...do...	25	May 2, 1864	100 dys.	Mustered out with company Sept. 13, 1864.
...B.	...do...	21	May 2, 1864	100 dys.	Mustered out with company Sept. 13, 1864.
...G.	...do...	18	May 2, 1864	100 dys.	Mustered out with company Sept. 13, 1864.
[illegible]	...do...	21	May 2, 1864	100 dys.	Mustered out with company Sept. 13, 1864.
...W.	...do...	29	May 2, 1864	100 dys.	Mustered out with company Sept. 13, 1864.
...L.	...do...	30	May 2, 1864	100 dys.	Mustered out with company Sept. 13, 1864.
[illegible]	...do...	43	May 2, 1864	100 dys.	Mustered out with company Sept. 13, 1864.
...Milton A.	...do...	23	May 2, 1864	100 dys.	Mustered out with company Sept. 13, 1864.
[illegible]	...do...	26	May 2, 1864	100 dys.	Died July 14, 1864, at McDougall Hospital, David's Island, New York Harbor.
[illegible]	...do...	22	May 2, 1864	100 dys.	Mustered out with company Sept. 13, 1864.
[illegible]	...do...	32	May 2, 1864	100 dys.	Mustered out with company Sept. 13, 1864.
[illegible]	...do...	24	May 2, 1864	100 dys.	Mustered out with company Sept. 13, 1864.
...Benjamin J.	...do...	23	May 2, 1864	100 dys.	Mustered out with company Sept. 13, 1864.
..., Alexander	...do...	19	May 2, 1864	100 dys.	Mustered out with company Sept. 13, 1864.
..., James L.	...do...	20	May 2, 1864	100 dys.	Mustered out with company Sept. 13, 1864.
...James A.	...do...	19	May 2, 1864	100 dys.	Mustered out with company Sept. 13, 1864.
...E.	...do...	21	May 2, 1864	100 dys.	Mustered out with company Sept. 13, 1864.
[illegible]	...do...	18	May 2, 1864	100 dys.	Mustered out with company Sept. 13, 1864.
..., John J.	...do...	21	May 2, 1864	100 dys.	Mustered out with company Sept. 13, 1864.
...C.	...do...	18	May 2, 1864	100 dys.	Died June 22, 1864, at Hampton Hospital, Fortress Monroe, Va.
...Harvey S.	...do...	23	May 2, 1864	100 dys.	Mustered out with company Sept. 13, 1864.
...Thomas	...do...	31	May 2, 1864	100 dys.	Mustered out with company Sept. 13, 1864.
...William	...do...	26	May 2, 1864	100 dys.	Mustered out with company Sept. 13, 1864.
...M.	...do...	18	May 2, 1864	100 dys.	Mustered out with company Sept. 13, 1864.
...Emanuel	...do...	23	May 2, 1864	100 dys.	Mustered out with company Sept. 13, 1864.
[illegible]	...do...	27	May 2, 1864	100 dys.	Mustered out with company Sept. 13, 1864.
[illegible]	...do...	22	May 2, 1864	100 dys.	Mustered out with company Sept. 13, 1864.
[illegible]	...do...	18	May 2, 1864	100 dys.	Died Aug. 13, 1864, at Wilson's Landing, Va.
..., Joseph	...do...	18	May 2, 1864	100 dys.	Mustered out with company Sept. 13, 1864.
..., Samuel	...do...	42	May 2, 1864	100 dys.	Mustered out with company Sept. 13, 1864.
..., Robert W.	...do...	19	May 2, 1864	100 dys.	Mustered out with company Sept. 13, 1864.
...Robert G.	...do...	20	May 2, 1864	100 dys.	Mustered out with company Sept. 13, 1864.
...Richard	...do...	18	May 2, 1864	100 dys.	Mustered out with company Sept. 13, 1864.
..., John T.	...do...	23	May 2, 1864	100 dys.	Mustered out with company Sept. 13, 1864.
..., John A.	...do...	24	May 2, 1864	100 dys.	Mustered out with company Sept. 13, 1864.
..., [illegible]	...do...	21	May 2, 1864	100 dys.	Mustered out with company Sept. 13, 1864.
..., Emanuel	...do...	21	May 2, 1864	100 dys.	Mustered out with company Sept. 13, 1864.

COMPANY I.

...in May 12, 1864, at Camp Chase, O., by John O. Cravens, Assistant Adjutant General and Commissary of Musters, Northern Department. Mustered out Sept. 13, 1864, at Camp Chase, O., by J. M. Eyster, Captain 18th Infantry, U. S. A.

Names.	Rank.	Age.	Date of Entering the Service.	Period of Service.	Remarks.
..., Jr.	Captain.	32	May 2, 1864	100 dys.	Mustered out with company Sept. 13, 1864.
[illegible]	1st Lieut.	31	May 2, 1864	100 dys.	Promoted from private May 13, 1864; mustered out with company Sept. 13, 1864.
[illegible]	2d Lieut.	21	May 2, 1864	100 dys.	Mustered out with company Sept. 13, 1864.
[illegible]	1st Sergt.	21	May 2, 1864	100 dys.	Appointed from Corporal July 4, 1864; mustered out with company Sept. 13, 1864.
...B. Allen.	Sergeant.	21	May 2, 1864	100 dys.	Mustered out with company Sept. 13, 1864.
...imms	...do...	21	May 2, 1864	100 dys.	Mustered out with company Sept. 13, 1864.
...gh	...do...	35	May 2, 1864	100 dys.	Mustered out with company Sept. 13, 1864.
... Findley	...do...	21	May 2, 1864	100 dys.	Mustered out with company Sept. 13, 1864.
...rbuckle	Corporal.	23	May 2, 1864	100 dys.	Appointed July 4, 1864; mustered out with company Sept. 13, 1864.
...lmaker	...do...	31	May 2, 1864	100 dys.	Mustered out with company Sept. 13, 1864.
...baugh	...do...	43	May 2, 1864	100 dys.	Mustered out with company Sept. 13, 1864.
...nston	...do...	20	May 2, 1864	100 dys.	Mustered out with company Sept. 13, 1864.
...el	...do...	30	May 2, 1864	100 dys.	Mustered out with company Sept. 13, 1864.
...tteridge	...do...	44	May 2, 1864	100 dys.	Mustered out with company Sept. 13, 1864.
... Anderson	...do...	23	May 2, 1864	100 dys.	Mustered out with company Sept. 13, 1864.
...nson	...do...	23	May 2, 1864	100 dys.	Mustered out with company Sept. 13, 1864.
..., Betteridge	Musician	18	May 2, 1864	100 dys.	Mustered out with company Sept. 13, 1864.
...lour	...do...	18	May 2, 1864	100 dys.	Mustered out with company Sept. 13, 1864.
...dshaw	Wagoner.	41	May 2, 1864	100 dys.	Mustered out with company Sept. 13, 1864.

Names.	Rank.	Age.	Date of Entering the Service.	Period of Service.	Remarks.
Allison, Charles W	Private	31	May 2, 1864	100 dys.	Mustered out with company Sept. 13, 1864.
Anderson, John C	do	18	May 2, 1864	100 dys.	Mustered out with company Sept. 13, 1864.
Anderson, Thomas	do	27	May 2, 1864	100 dys.	Mustered out with company Sept. 13, 1864.
Anderson, William	do	28	May 2, 1864	100 dys.	Mustered out with company Sept. 13, 1864.
Arb, James	do	20	May 2, 1864	100 dys.	Transferred from Co. F May 15, 1864; mustered out with company Sept. 13, 1864.
Arb, Solomon	do	42	May 2, 1864	100 dys.	Mustered out with company Sept. 13, 1864.
Armstrong, James	do	38	May 2, 1864	100 dys.	Mustered out with company Sept. 13, 1864.
Ashbaugh, Samuel	do	38	May 2, 1864	100 dys.	Mustered out with company Sept. 13, 1864.
Barker, Joseph	do	38	May 2, 1864	100 dys.	Mustered out with company Sept. 13, 1864.
Baum, John	do	19	May 2, 1864	100 dys.	Mustered out with company Sept. 13, 1864.
Blythe, William	do	43	May 2, 1864	100 dys.	Mustered out with company Sept. 13, 1864.
Brunt, Henry	do	29	May 2, 1864	100 dys.	Mustered out with company Sept. 13, 1864.
Buckley, George	do	38	May 2, 1864	100 dys.	Mustered out with company Sept. 13, 1864.
Calvin, Luther	do	36	May 2, 1864	100 dys.	Promoted to Hospital Steward May 13, 1864.
Cartwright, Samuel	do	25	May 2, 1864	100 dys.	Mustered out with company Sept. 13, 1864.
Cartwright, William	do	28	May 2, 1864	100 dys.	Mustered out with company Sept. 13, 1864.
Cook, Joseph	do	18	May 2, 1864	100 dys.	Mustered out with company Sept. 13, 1864.
Cowen, James	do	18	May 2, 1864	100 dys.	Mustered out with company Sept. 13, 1864.
Crofts, Henry	do	40	May 2, 1864	100 dys.	Mustered out with company Sept. 13, 1864.
Davidson, Mitchell	do	34	May 2, 1864	100 dys.	Mustered out with company Sept. 13, 1864.
Douds, John	do	34	May 2, 1864	100 dys.	Mustered out with company Sept. 13, 1864.
Ellewell, William	do	43	May 2, 1864	100 dys.	Mustered out with company Sept. 13, 1864.
Farmer, Lycurgus	do	28	May 2, 1864	100 dys.	Mustered out with company Sept. 13, 1864.
Ferrell, Joseph D	do	24	May 2, 1864	100 dys.	Reduced to ranks from 1st Sergeant July 4, 1864; mustered out with company Sept. 13, 1864.
Findley, Richard	do	41	May 2, 1864	100 dys.	Mustered out with company Sept. 13, 1864.
Foster, James	do	37	May 2, 1864	100 dys.	Mustered out with company Sept. 13, 1864.
Fowler, Jacob	do	38	May 2, 1864	100 dys.	Mustered out with company Sept. 13, 1864.
Fresh, Jacob	do	21	May 2, 1864	100 dys.	Mustered out with company Sept. 13, 1864.
Fritz, Adolph	do	26	May 2, 1864	100 dys.	Mustered out with company Sept. 13, 1864.
Geddes, John	do	35	May 2, 1864	100 dys.	Mustered out with company Sept. 13, 1864.
Haines, Robert	do	29	May 2, 1864	100 dys.	Mustered out with company Sept. 13, 1864.
Hanley, Charles	do	35	May 2, 1864	100 dys.	Mustered out with company Sept. 13, 1864.
Harker, Benjamin	do	36	May 2, 1864	100 dys.	Mustered out with company Sept. 13, 1864.
Harvey, Isaac A	do	37	May 2, 1864	100 dys.	Mustered out with company Sept. 13, 1864.
Harsha, Haney M	do	18	May 2, 1864	100 dys.	Mustered out with company Sept. 13, 1864.
Hastings, William	do	37	May 2, 1864	100 dys.	Promoted to Chaplain May 3, 1864.
Hill, Harry	do	30	May 2, 1864	100 dys.	Mustered out with company Sept. 13, 1864.
Hull, Leonidas	do	24	May 2, 1864	100 dys.	Died July 10, 1864, at Wilson's Landing, Va.
Houser, John	do	26	May 2, 1864	100 dys.	Mustered out with company Sept. 13, 1864.
Hulin, William	do	37	May 2, 1864	100 dys.	Mustered out with company Sept. 13, 1864.
Jackson, Samuel P	do	20	May 2, 1864	100 dys.	Mustered out with company Sept. 13, 1864.
Kinsey, Sylvester	do	18	May 2, 1864	100 dys.	Mustered out with company Sept. 13, 1864.
Kinsey, Z[illegible] H	do	18	May 2, 1864	100 dys.	Mustered out with company Sept. 13, 1864.
Lake, John	do	27	May 2, 1864	100 dys.	Mustered out with company Sept. 13, 1864.
Logan, Robert	do	53	May 2, 1864	100 dys.	Promoted to Sergt. Major May 13, 1864.
McClure, Albert	do	[illegible]	May 2, 1864	100 dys.	Mustered out with company Sept. 13, 1864.
McKee, James	do	18	May 2, 1864	100 dys.	Transferred from Co. F May 15, 1864, and there borne as James McGee; mustered out with company Sept. 13, 1864.
Manl[illegible], A[illegible]	do	33	May 2, 1864	100 dys.	Mustered out with company Sept. 13, 1864.
[illegible], Jethro	do	30	May 2, 1864	100 dys.	Mustered out with company Sept. 13, 1864.
Marsh, Ralph	do	32	May 2, 1864	100 dys.	Mustered out with company Sept. 13, 1864.
Martin, Edward	do	35	May 2, 1864	100 dys.	Mustered out with company Sept. 13, 1864.
Martin, Franklin B	do	[illegible]	May 2, 1864	100 dys.	Transferred from Co. F May 15, 1864; mustered out with company Sept. 13, 1864.
Martin, Nathaniel	do	18	May 2, 1864	100 dys.	Transferred from Co. F May 15, 1864; mustered out with company Sept. 13, 1864.
Miller, Andrew	do	29	May 2, 1864	100 dys.	Mustered out with company Sept. 13, 1864.
[illegible], Frederick	do	42	May 2, 1864	100 dys.	Transferred from Co. F May 15, 1864; died Aug. 2, 1864, at Wilson's Landing, Va.
Orr, John M	do	19	May 2, 1864	100 dys.	Mustered out with company Sept. 13, 1864.
Patterson, Jonathan J	do	29	May 2, 1864	100 dys.	Mustered out with company Sept. 13, 1864.
Plunket, Edward	do	18	May 2, 1864	100 dys.	Mustered out with company Sept. 13, 1864.
Reed, [illegible]	do	27	May 2, 1864	100 dys.	Mustered out with company Sept. 13, 1864.
[illegible], Timothy	do	26	May 2, 1864	100 dys.	Mustered out with company Sept. 13, 1864.
[illegible], Basil	do	33	May 2, 1864	100 dys.	Mustered out with company Sept. 13, 1864.
[illegible], Philip	do	29	May 2, 1864	100 dys.	Mustered out with company Sept. 13, 1864.
Scott, William B	do	18	May 2, 1864	100 dys.	Transferred from Co. F May 15, 1864; mustered out with company Sept. 13, 1864.
[illegible], Ingram	do	32	May 2, 1864	100 dys.	Mustered out with company Sept. 13, 1864.
[illegible], Albert	do	18	May 2, 1864	100 dys.	Transferred from Co. F May 15, 1864; mustered out with company Sept. 13, 1864.
[illegible], Charles	do	21	May 2, 1864	100 dys.	Mustered out with company Sept. 13, 1864.
[illegible]wood, John	do	18	May 2, 1864	100 dys.	Transferred from Co. F May 15, 1864; mustered out with company Sept. 13, 1864.
[illegible], Daniel J	do	30	May 2, 1864	100 dys.	Mustered out with company Sept. 13, 1864.
[illegible], Jacob	do	26	May 2, 1864	100 dys.	Died Aug. 18, 1864, at U. S. General Hospital, Hampton, Va.
[illegible], Roland	do	35	May 2, 1864	100 dys.	Mustered out with company Sept. 13, 1864.
[illegible], Cassius C	do	18	May 2, 1864	100 dys.	Mustered out with company Sept. 13, 1864.
[illegible]	do	18	May 2, 1864	100 dys.	Transferred from Co. F May 15, 1864; mustered out with company Sept. 13, 1864.
[illegible], Albert	do	32	May 2, 1864	100 dys.	Mustered out with company Sept. 13, 1864.

COMPANY K.

12, 1864, at Camp Chase, O., by John O. Cravens, Assistant Adjutant General and Commis-Mustering, Northern Department. Mustered out Sept. 13, 1864, at Camp Chase, O., by J. M. Kyster, Captain 18th Infantry, U. S. A.

	Rank.	Age.	Date of Entering the Service.	Period of Service.	Remarks.
	Captain.	44	May 2, 1864	100 dys.	Mustered out with company Sept. 13, 1864.
	1st Lieut.	27	May 2, 1864	100 dys.	Mustered out with company Sept. 13, 1864.
......	2d Lieut.	23	May 2, 1864	100 dys.	Mustered out with company Sept. 13, 1864.
......	1st Sergt.	25	May 2, 1864	100 dys.	Mustered out with company Sept. 13, 1864.
......	Sergeant.	32	May 2, 1864	100 dys.	Mustered out with company Sept. 13, 1864.
......	....do....	23	May 2, 1864	100 dys.	Mustered out with company Sept. 13, 1864.
......	....do....	28	May 2, 1864	100 dys.	Mustered out with company Sept. 13, 1864.
......	....do....	35	May 2, 1864	100 dys.	Mustered out with company Sept. 13, 1864.
......	Corporal.	20	May 2, 1864	100 dys.	Mustered out with company Sept. 13, 1864.
	....do....	44	May 2, 1864	100 dys.	Mustered out with company Sept. 13, 1864.
	....do....	24	May 2, 1864	100 dys.	Mustered out with company Sept. 13, 1864.
	....do....	41	May 2, 1864	100 dys.	Mustered out with company Sept. 13, 1864.
	....do....	33	May 2, 1864	100 dys.	Mustered out with company Sept. 13, 1864.
......	....do....	22	May 2, 1864	100 dys.	Mustered out with company Sept. 13, 1864.
......	....do....	28	May 2, 1864	100 dys.	Mustered out with company Sept. 13, 1864.
......	....do....	44	May 2, 1864	100 dys.	Mustered out with company Sept. 13, 1864.
	Musician	18	May 2, 1864	100 dys.	Mustered out with company Sept. 13, 1864.
	....do....	25	May 2, 1864	100 dys.	Discharged May 18, 1864, on Surgeon's certificate of disability.
......	Wagoner.	44	May 2, 1864	100 dys.	Mustered out with company Sept. 13, 1864.
......	Private..	18	May 2, 1864	100 dys.	Mustered out with company Sept. 13, 1864.
	....do....	25	May 2, 1864	100 dys.	Mustered out with company Sept. 13, 1864.
	....do....	43	May 2, 1864	100 dys.	Mustered out with company Sept. 13, 1864.
ey	....do....	19	May 2, 1864	100 dys.	Mustered out with company Sept. 13, 1864.
	....do....	22	May 2, 1864	100 dys.	Mustered out with company Sept. 13, 1864.
	....do....	26	May 2, 1864	100 dys.	Mustered out with company Sept. 13, 1864.
	....do....	18	May 2, 1864	100 dys.	Mustered out with company Sept. 13, 1864.
	....do....	20	May 2, 1864	100 dys.	Mustered out with company Sept. 13, 1864.
	....do....	36	May 2, 1864	100 dys.	Mustered out with company Sept. 13, 1864.
......	....do....	37	May 2, 1864	100 dys.	Mustered out with company Sept. 13, 1864.
......	....do....	44	May 2, 1864	100 dys.	Mustered out with company Sept. 13, 1864.
......	....do....	34	May 2, 1864	100 dys.	Mustered out with company Sept. 13, 1864.
......	....do....	34	May 2, 1864	100 dys.	Mustered out with company Sept. 13, 1864.
......	....do....	23	May 2, 1864	100 dys.	Mustered out with company Sept. 13, 1864.
......	....do....	44	May 2, 1864	100 dys.	Mustered out with company Sept. 13, 1864.
......	....do....	27	May 2, 1864	100 dys.	Mustered out with company Sept. 13, 1864.
......	....do....	20	May 2, 1864	100 dys.	Mustered out with company Sept. 13, 1864.
......	....do....	27	May 2, 1864	100 dys.	Mustered out with company Sept. 13, 1864.
......	....do....	22	May 2, 1864	100 dys.	Mustered out with company Sept. 13, 1864.
......	....do....	28	May 2, 1864	100 dys.	Mustered out with company Sept. 13, 1864.
......	....do....	36	May 2, 1864	100 dys.	Mustered out with company Sept. 13, 1864.
......	....do....	43	May 2, 1864	100 dys.	Mustered out with company Sept. 13, 1864.
......	....do....	19	May 2, 1864	100 dys.	Mustered out with company Sept. 13, 1864.
......	....do....	31	May 2, 1864	100 dys.	Mustered out with company Sept. 13, 1864.
......	....do....	21	May 2, 1864	100 dys.	Mustered out with company Sept. 13, 1864.
......	....do....	29	May 2, 1864	100 dys.	Mustered out with company Sept. 13, 1864.
......	....do....	42	May 2, 1864	100 dys.	Mustered out with company Sept. 13, 1864.
I......	....do....	34	May 2, 1864	100 dys.	Mustered out with company Sept. 13, 1864.
......	....do....	19	May 2, 1864	100 dys.	Mustered out with company Sept. 13, 1864.
......	....do....	39	May 2, 1864	100 dys.	Mustered out with company Sept. 13, 1864.
......	....do....	37	May 2, 1864	100 dys.	Mustered out with company Sept. 13, 1864.
......	....do....	18	May 2, 1864	100 dys.	Mustered out with company Sept. 13, 1864.
......	....do....	18	May 2, 1864	100 dys.	Mustered out with company Sept. 13, 1864.
......	....do....	24	May 2, 1864	100 dys.	Mustered out with company Sept. 13, 1864.
......	....do....	23	May 2, 1864	100 dys.	Mustered out with company Sept. 13, 1864.
......	....do....	19	May 2, 1864	100 dys.	Mustered out with company Sept. 13, 1864.
......	....do....	18	May 2, 1864	100 dys.	Mustered out with company Sept. 13, 1864.
......	....do....	20	May 2, 1864	100 dys.	Promoted to Principal Musician May 12, 1864.
..	....do....	33	May 2, 1864	100 dys.	Mustered out with company Sept. 13, 1864.
..	....do....	19	May 2, 1864	100 dys.	Mustered out with company Sept. 13, 1864.
..	....do....	32	May 2, 1864	100 dys.	Mustered out with company Sept. 13, 1864.
......	....do....	24	May 2, 1864	100 dys.	Mustered out to date Sept. 13, 1864, at Columbus, O., by order of War Department.
......	....do....	37	May 2, 1864	100 dys.	Mustered out with company Sept. 13, 1864.
......	....do....	22	May 2, 1864	100 dys.	Mustered out with company Sept. 13, 1864.
......	....do....	19	May 2, 1864	100 dys.	Mustered out with company Sept. 13, 1864.
......	....do....	18	May 2, 1864	100 dys.	Mustered out with company Sept. 13, 1864.
......	....do....	21	May 2, 1864	100 dys.	Mustered out with company Sept. 13, 1864.
......	....do....	23	May 2, 1864	100 dys.	Mustered out with company Sept. 13, 1864.
......	....do....	35	May 2, 1864	100 dys.	Mustered out with company Sept. 13, 1864.
......	....do....	25	May 2, 1864	100 dys.	Mustered out with company Sept. 13, 1864.
......	....do....	20	May 2, 1864	100 dys.	Mustered out with company Sept. 13, 1864.
er W..	....do....	18	May 2, 1864	100 dys.	Mustered out with company Sept. 13, 1864.
l......	....do....	30	May 2, 1864	100 dys.	Mustered out with company Sept. 13, 1864.
......	....do....	18	May 2, 1864	100 dys.	Mustered out with company Sept. 13, 1864.
......	....do....	24	May 2, 1864	100 dys.	Mustered out with company Sept. 13, 1864.

144th Regiment Ohio Volunteer Infantry.

ONE HUNDRED DAYS' SERVICE.

This Regiment was organized at Camp Chase, O., May 11, 1864, to serve one hundred days. It was composed of the Sixty-fourth Battalion, Ohio National Guard, from Wood County, and the Nineteenth Battalion, Ohio National Guard, from Wyandot County. The Regiment was ordered to report, without delay, to General Wallace, at Baltimore. Upon its arrival in that city Companies G and K were detached for duty in the fortifications, and the remainder of the regiment reported to General Morris, at Fort McHenry, and from there Company E was ordered to Wilmington, Del.; Company B to Camp Parole, near Annapolis; and Company I to Fort Dix, at the Relay House. On the 18th of May the Regiment was relieved from duty at Fort McHenry, and ordered to the Relay House. Companies B, G, and I, were in the engagement at Monocacy Junction, losing in killed, wounded, and prisoners, about fifty men. On the 13th of July the Regiment was ordered to Washington, and from there moved toward Winchester. It halted at Snicker's Gap, and was moved back toward Washington, but it was soon again faced toward the Shenandoah Valley, moving via Harper's Ferry. On the 13th of August a portion of the One Hundred and Forty-fourth, while guarding a train near Berryville, Va., was attacked by Moseby's command with two pieces of artillery. The detachment lost five killed, six wounded, and sixty captured. The Regiment was mustered out Aug. 24 and 31, 1864, on expiration of term of service.

Names.	Rank.	Age.	Date of Entering the Service.	Period of Service.	Remarks.
Carnes, Arthur A.	Private.	18	May 2, 1864	100 dys.	Captured July 9, 1864, at battle of Monocacy, Md.; died Jan. 6, 1865, in Rebel Prison at Salisbury, N. C.
Clugston, Carlos	do.	18	May 2, 1864	100 dys.	Mustered out with company Aug. 31, 1864.
Cole, Leonard	do.	18	May 2, 1864	100 dys.	Mustered out with company Aug. 31, 1864.
Coppler, Charles	do.	18	May 2, 1864	100 dys.	Mustered out with company Aug. 31, 1864.
Cover, Erastus	do.	32	May 2, 1864	100 dys.	Mustered out with company Aug. 31, 1864.
Cover, Joshua	do.	30	May 2, 1864	100 dys.	Mustered out with company Aug. 31, 1864.
Craig, George E.	do.	18	May 2, 1864	100 dys.	Mustered out with company Aug. 31, 1864.
Crawford, Hubbard	do.	19	May 2, 1864	100 dys.	Mustered out with company Aug. 31, 1864.
Crawford, James	do.	28	May 2, 1864	100 dys.	Mustered out with company Aug. 31, 1864.
Cray, James	do.	23	May 2, 1864	100 dys.	Mustered out with company Aug. 31, 1864.
Duddleson, Albert	do.	36	May 2, 1864	100 dys.	Mustered out with company Aug. 31, 1864.
Ebersole, Harman	do.	40	May 2, 1864	100 dys.	Mustered out with company Aug. 31, 1864.
Everhart, Alfred	do.	26	May 2, 1864	100 dys.	Mustered out with company Aug. 31, 1864.
Gatchell, Henry T.	do.	19	May 2, 1864	100 dys.	Promoted to Hospital Steward May 12, 1864.
Gatchell, John S.	do.	18	May 2, 1864	100 dys.	Mustered out with company Aug. 31, 1864.
Gormly, Leander	do.	20	May 2, 1864	100 dys.	Mustered out with company Aug. 31, 1864.
Gravell, Rolandus	do.	18	May 2, 1864	100 dys.	Mustered out with company Aug. 31, 1864.
Gunder, George P.	do.	19	May 2, 1864	100 dys.	Mustered out with company Aug. 31, 1864.
Hale, David	do.	26	May 2, 1864	100 dys.	Mustered out with company Aug. 31, 1864.
Hale, Henry B	do.	22	May 2, 1864	100 dys.	Mustered out with company Aug. 31, 1864.
Hayman, George	do.	25	May 2, 1864	100 dys.	Mustered out with company Aug. 31, 1864.
Holdridge, William	do.	18	May 2, 1864	100 dys.	Mustered out with company Aug. 31, 1864.
Hunt, Abel R.	do.	18	May 2, 1864	100 dys.	Mustered out with company Aug. 31, 1864.
Hunt, Hiland	do.	18	May 2, 1864	100 dys.	Mustered out with company Aug. 31, 1864.
		28	May 2, 1864	100 dys.	Mustered out with company Aug. 31, 1864.
		28	May 2, 1864	100 dys.	Mustered out with company Aug. 31, 1864.
Konley, Frederick	do.	25	May 2, 1864	100 dys.	Mustered out with company Aug. 31, 1864.
McAninch, John H.	do.	19	May 2, 1864	100 dys.	Mustered out with company Aug. 31, 1864.
McClain, David P.	do.	18	May 2, 1864	100 dys.	Mustered out with company Aug. 31, 1864.
McClain, John G.	do.	29	May 2, 1864	100 dys.	Mustered out with company Aug. 31, 1864.
McCormick, Henry	do.	27	May 2, 1864	100 dys.	Wounded Aug. 13, 1864, in action near Berryville, Va.; mustered out with company Aug. 31, 1864.
Mack, William E.	do.	21	May 2, 1864	100 dys.	Mustered out with company Aug. 31, 1864.
Mason, Hugh C.	do.	30	May 2, 1864	100 dys.	Mustered out with company Aug. 31, 1864.
Mcilam, John E.	do.	29	May 2, 1864	100 dys.	Mustered out with company Aug. 31, 1864.
Miller, Orville K.	do.	30	May 2, 1864	100 dys.	Mustered out with company Aug. 31, 1864.
Mills, Jonathan	do.	19	May 2, 1864	100 dys.	Mustered out with company Aug. 31, 1864.
Moody, David	do.	23	May 2, 1864	100 dys.	Mustered out with company Aug. 31, 1864.
Moore, Milton M.	do.	33	May 2, 1864	100 dys.	Mustered out with company Aug. 31, 1864.
Morris, William	do.	34	May 2, 1864	100 dys.	Mustered out with company Aug. 31, 1864.
Myers, John F.	do.	19	May 2, 1864	100 dys.	Mustered out with company Aug. 31, 1864.
[illegible], William	do.	29	May 2, 1864	100 dys.	Mustered out with company Aug. 31, 1864.
[illegible], John S.	do.	35	May 2, 1864	100 dys.	Mustered out with company Aug. 31, 1864.
[illegible], Warner	do.	44	May 2, 1864	100 dys.	Killed Aug. 13, 1864, in action near Berryville, Virginia.
[illegible], George	do.	28	May 2, 1864	100 dys.	Mustered out with company Aug. 31, 1864.
[illegible], William	do.	25	May 2, 1864	100 dys.	Mustered out with company Aug. 31, 1864.
[illegible], William H.	do.	25	May 2, 1864	100 dys.	Mustered out with company Aug. 31, 1864.
[illegible], Robert	do.	30	May 2, 1864	100 dys.	Mustered out with company Aug. 31, 1864.
[illegible], Thomas	do.	37	May 2, 1864	100 dys.	Mustered out with company Aug. 31, 1864.
[illegible], James M.	do.	41	May 2, 1864	100 dys.	Mustered out with company Aug. 31, 1864.
[illegible]	do.	25	May 2, 1864	100 dys.	Mustered out with company Aug. 31, 1864.
[illegible], John	do.	24	May 2, 1864	100 dys.	Killed Aug. 13, 1864, in action near Berryville, Virginia.
[illegible]	do.	27	May 2, 1864	100 dys.	Mustered out with company Aug. 31, 1864.
[illegible]	do.	36	May 2, 1864	100 dys.	Mustered out with company Aug. 31, 1864.
[illegible], Albert	do.	18	May 2, 1864	100 dys.	Mustered out with company Aug. 31, 1864.
[illegible], Edward	do.	40	May 2, 1864	100 dys.	Captured Aug. 13, 1864, in action near Berryville, Va.; admitted to hospital at Belle Isle, Richmond, Va., Sept. 26, 1864. No further record found.
[illegible]	do.	19	May 2, 1864	100 dys.	Mustered out with company Aug. 31, 1864.
[illegible]	do.	19	May 2, 1864	100 dys.	Mustered out with company Aug. 31, 1864.
[illegible]	do.	18	May 2, 1864	100 dys.	Mustered out with company Aug. 31, 1864.
[illegible]	do.	24	May 2, 1864	100 dys.	Mustered out with company Aug. 31, 1864.
[illegible]	do.	41	May 2, 1864	100 dys.	Mustered out with company Aug. 31, 1864.
[illegible]	do.	18	May 2, 1864	100 dys.	Mustered out with company Aug. 31, 1864.

144TH REGIMENT OHIO VOLUNTEER INFANTRY.

FIELD AND STAFF.

Mustered in May 11, 1864, at Camp Chase, O., by James P. W. Neill, 1st Lieutenant 18th Infantry, U. S. A. Mustered out Aug. 31, 1864, at Camp Chase, O., by Thomas H. Y. Bickham, 1st Lieutenant 19th Infantry, U. S. A.

Names.	Rank.	Age.	Date of Entering the Service.	Period of Service.	Remarks.
Samuel H. Hunt	Colonel.	34	May 2, 1864	100 dys.	Mustered out with regiment Aug. 31, 1864.
Frederick R. Miller	Lieut.Col	36	May 2, 1864	100 dys	Mustered out with regiment Aug. 31, 1864.
Marquis D. L. Buell	Major.	31	May 2, 1864	100 dys.	Mustered out with regiment Aug. 31, 1864.
Jacob L. Mounts	Surgeon.	34	May 7, 1864	100 dys.	Mustered out with regiment Aug. 31, 1864.
Edward F. Baker	Asst. Sur.	21	May 2, 1864	100 dys.	Mustered out with regiment Aug. 31, 1864.
Granville M. White	....do....	24	May 10, 1864	100 dys.	Mustered out with regiment Aug. 31, 1864.
Jonathan Ayres	Adjutant	42	May 2, 1864	100 dys.	Mustered out with regiment Aug. 31, 1864.
John H. Reid	R. Q. M.	41	May 10, 1864	100 dys.	Mustered out with regiment Aug. 31, 1864.
Jacob G. Baughman	Chaplain	33	May 2, 1864	100 dys.	Promoted from private Co. D May 12, 1864; mustered out with regiment Aug. 31, 1864.
Benjamin F. Swartz	Ser. Maj.	26	May 2, 1864	100 dys.	Promoted from private Co. D May 12, 1864; mustered out with regiment Aug. 31, 1864
Addison E. Gibbs	Q. M. S.	33	May 2, 1864	100 dys.	Promoted from private Co. D May 12, 1864; mustered out with regiment Aug. 31, 1864.
Martin G. Snyder	Com. Ser.	29	May 2, 1864	100 dys.	Promoted from private Co. E May 11, 1864; mustered out with regiment Aug. 31, 1864.
Henry T. Gatchell	Hos. St'd.	19	May 2, 1864	100 dys.	Promoted from private Co. A May 12, 1864; mustered out with regiment Aug. 31, 1864.

COMPANY A.

Mustered in May 11, 1864, at Camp Chase, O., by James P. W. Neill, 1st Lieutenant 18th Infantry, U. S. A. Mustered out Aug. 31, 1864, at Camp Chase, O., by Thomas H. Y. Bickham, 1st Lieutenant 19th Infantry, U. S. A.

Names.	Rank.	Age.	Date of Entering the Service.	Period of Service.	Remarks.
Henry H. Ragon	Captain.	27	May 2, 1864	100 dys	Mustered out with company Aug. 31, 1864.
William McFee	1st Lieut.	29	May 2, 1864	100 dys.	Mustered out with company Aug. 31, 1864.
Eli R. Ragon	2d Lieut.	32	May 2, 1864	100 dys	Promoted from Sergeant May 17, 1864; mustered out with company Aug. 31, 1864.
David E. Hale	1st Sergt.	24	May 2, 1864	100 dys.	Mustered out with company Aug. 31, 1864.
Levi Schultz	Sergeant.	42	May 2, 1864	100 dys	Mustered out with company Aug. 31, 1864.
John McAfee	....do....	33	May 2, 1864	100 dys.	Mustered out with company Aug. 31, 1864.
Harvey J. Pool	....do....	23	May 2, 1864	100 dys.	Mustered out with company Aug. 31, 1864.
John S. Bowers	....do....	39	May 2, 1864	100 dys.	Appointed from Corporal May 17, 1864; mustered out with company Aug. 31, 1864.
John T. Stokes	Corporal.	30	May 2, 1864	100 dys	Mustered out with company Aug. 31, 1864.
Vincent V. Flack	....do....	22	May 2, 1864	100 dys.	Captured Aug. 13, 1864, in action near Berryville, Va.; enlisted in Rebel army Nov. 7, 1864, at Salisbury, N. C.
Elza Pool	....do....	30	May 2, 1864	100 dys.	Mustered out with company Aug. 31, 1864.
Matthew Moody	....do....	30	May 2, 1864	100 dys.	Mustered out with company Aug. 31, 1864.
David M. Bowers	....do....	33	May 2, 1864	100 dys.	Mustered out with company Aug. 31, 1864.
Edward Pancost	....do....	22	May 2, 1864	100 dys.	Mustered out with company Aug. 31, 1864.
Reed R. Cameron	....do....	32	May 2, 1864	100 dys.	Mustered out with company Aug. 31, 1864.
Benjamin Morris	....do....	41	May 2, 1864	100 dys.	Appointed May 17, 1864; mustered out with company Aug. 31, 1864.
Philip Oliver	Musician	18	May 2, 1864	100 dys.	Captured Aug. 13, 1864, in action near Berryville, Va.; mustered out March 20, 1865, at Columbus, O., by order of War Department.
Henry Berlean	....do....	25	May 2, 1864	100 dys.	Mustered out with company Aug. 31, 1864.
Solomon Hill	Wagoner.	40	May 2, 1864	100 dys.	Mustered out with company Aug. 31, 1864.
Ayers, Isaac	Private.	21	May 2, 1864	100 dys.	Mustered out with company Aug. 31, 1864.
Beistle, Joseph R.	....do....	19	May 2, 1864	100 dys	Died Aug. 9, 1864, at Frederick, Md.
Blackburn, Isaac	....do....	20	May 2, 1864	100 dys.	Mustered out with company Aug. 31, 1864.
Bowers, Harvey	....do....	18	May 2, 1864	100 dys.	Mustered out with company Aug. 31, 1864.
Brown, Henry	....do....	34	May 2, 1864	100 dys.	Mustered out with company Aug. 31, 1864.
Brown, Addison	....do....	19	May 2, 1864	100 dys.	Mustered out with company Aug. 31, 1864.

Names.	Rank.	Age.	Date of Entering the Service.	Period of Service.	Remarks.
Phillips, John	Private	26	May 2, 1864	100 dys.	Captured Aug. 13, 1864, in action near [illegible]ville, Va. No further record found.
Porrier, William	...do...	32	May 2, 1864	100 dys.	Mustered out with company Aug. 31, [illegible] also borne on rolls as William Poirier
Price, Isaac	...do...	27	May 2, 1864	100 dys.	Captured Aug. 13, 1864, in action near [illegible]ville, Va.; died Nov. 28, 1864, in Rebel [illegible] at Salisbury, N. C.
Reed, John C.	...do...	18	May 2, 1864	100 dys.	Mustered out with company Aug. 31, 18[illegible]
Reynolds, William	...do...	20	May 2, 1864	100 dys.	Mustered out with company Aug. 31, 18[illegible]
Russell, Jabez	...do...	37	May 2, 1864	100 dys.	Mustered out with company Aug. 31, 18[illegible]
Skinner, Sylvester	...do...	20	May 2, 1864	100 dys.	Mustered out with company Aug. 31, 18[illegible]
Sosh, John	...do...	28	May 2, 1864	100 dys.	Captured July 9, 1864, at battle of Mon[illegible] Md.; paroled Sept. 12, 1864; mustere[illegible] Oct. 3, 1864, at Columbus, O., by ord[illegible] War Department.
Stone, Thomas	...do...	33	May 2, 1864	100 dys.	Captured Aug. 13, 1864, in action near [illegible]ville, Va.; mustered out Dec. 1, 1864, [illegible]lumbus, O., by order of War Departm[illegible]
Tyler, Franklin	...do...	19	May 2, 1864	100 dys.	Mustered out with company Aug. 31, 18[illegible]
Van Tassel, Le Roy	...do...	20	May 2, 1864	100 dys.	Mustered out with company Aug. 31, 18[illegible]
Warner, Elliott M.	...do...	20	May 2, 1864	100 dys.	Mustered out with company Aug. 31, 18[illegible]
Warner, George L.	...do...	40	May 2, 1864	100 dys.	Mustered out with company Aug. 31, 18[illegible]
White, Hosea	...do...	23	May 2, 1864	100 dys.	
Williams, Emmett	...do...	18	May 2, 1864	100 dys.	Mustered out with company Aug. 31, 18[illegible]
Wood, Walter	...do...	18	May 2, 1864	100 dys.	Captured Aug. 13, 1864, in action near [illegible]ville, Va.; died Nov. 18, 1864, in [illegible] Prison at Salisbury, N. C.
W[illegible], Oscar N.	...do...	27	May 2, 1864	100 dys.	Mustered out with company Aug. 31, 18[illegible]

COMPANY C.

[illegible] May 11, 1864, at Camp Chase, O., by James P. W. Neill, 1st Lieutenant 18th Infantry, U. [illegible] Mustered out Aug. 31, 1864, at Camp Chase, O., by Thomas H. Y. Bickham, 1st Lieutenant 19th Infantry, U. S. A.

Names.	Rank.	Age.	Date of Entering the Service.	Period of Service.	Remarks.
[illegible]	Captain	43	May 2, 1864	100 dys.	Mustered out with company Aug. 31, 186[illegible]
[illegible]	1st Lieut.	28	May 2, 1864	100 dys.	Mustered out with company Aug. 31, 18[illegible]
[illegible]	2d Lieut.	27	May 2, 1864	100 dys.	Mustered out with company Aug. 31, 18[illegible]
[illegible]	1st Sergt.	23	May 2, 1864	100 dys.	Mustered out with company Aug. 31, 18[illegible]
[illegible]	Sergeant.	23	May 2, 1864	100 dys.	Mustered out with company Aug. 31, 18[illegible]
[illegible]	...do...	33	May 2, 1864	100 dys.	Mustered out with company Aug. 31, 18[illegible]
[illegible]	...do...	19	May 2, 1864	100 dys.	Captured Aug. 13, 1864, in action near [illegible]ville, Va.; mustered out March 20, 18[illegible] Columbus, O., by order of War Depart[illegible]
[illegible]	...do...	25	May 2, 1864	100 dys.	Captured Aug. 13, 1864, in action near B[illegible]ville, Va.; died Dec. 18, 1864, in [illegible] Prison at Salisbury, N. C.
[illegible]	Corporal.	29	May 2, 1864	100 dys.	Captured Aug. 13, 1864, in action near B[illegible]ville, Va.; mustered out March 20, 186[illegible] Columbus, O., by order of War Depart[illegible]
[illegible]	...do...	19	May 2, 1864	100 dys.	Mustered out with company Aug. 31, 186[illegible]
[illegible]	...do...	24	May 2, 1864	100 dys.	Mustered out with company Aug. 31, 18[illegible]
[illegible]	...do...	19	May 2, 1864	100 dys.	Mustered out with company Aug. 31, 1864
[illegible]	...do...	19	May 2, 1864	100 dys.	Mustered out with company Aug. 31, 1864
[illegible]	...do...	32	May 2, 1864	100 dys.	Mustered out with company Aug. 31, 1864
[illegible]	...do...	23	May 2, 1864	100 dys.	Mustered out with company Aug. 31, 1864
[illegible]	...do...	18	May 2, 1864	100 dys.	Mustered out with company Aug. 31, 1864
[illegible]	Musician	26	May 2, 1864	100 dys.	Mustered out with company Aug. 31, 1864
[illegible]	...do...	21	May 2, 1864	100 dys.	Mustered out with company Aug. 31, 1864
[illegible]	Private	2[illegible]	May 2, 1864	100 dys.	Mustered out with company Aug. 31, 1864
[illegible] W.	...do...	18	May 2, 1864	100 dys.	Mustered out with company Aug. 31, 1864
[illegible]	...do...	23	May 2, 1864	100 dys.	Mustered out with company Aug. 31, 1864
[illegible]	...do...	21	May 2, 1864	100 dys.	Mustered out with company Aug. 31, 1864
[illegible] W.	...do...	20	May 2, 1864	100 dys.	Mustered out with company Aug. 31, 1864
[illegible] P. C.	...do...	26	May 2, 1864	100 dys.	Mustered out with company Aug. 31, 1864
[illegible]	...do...	22	May 2, 1864	100 dys.	Mustered out with company Aug. 31, 1864
[illegible]	...do...	23	May 2, 1864	100 dys.	Mustered out with company Aug. 31, 1864
[illegible]	...do...	21	May 2, 1864	100 dys.	Mustered out with company Aug. 31, 1864
[illegible]	...do...	30	May 2, 1864	100 dys.	Mustered out with company Aug. 31, 1864
[illegible]	...do...	18	May 2, 1864	100 dys.	Mustered out with company Aug. 31, 1864
[illegible]	...do...	24	May 2, 1864	100 dys.	Mustered out with company Aug. 31, 1864
[illegible]	...do...	18	May 2, 1864	100 dys.	Mustered out with company Aug. 31, 1864
[illegible]	...do...	22	May 2, 1864	100 dys.	
[illegible]	...do...	25	May 2, 1864	100 dys.	Mustered out with company Aug. 31, 1864
[illegible]	...do...	24	May 2, 1864	100 dys.	Captured Aug. 13, 1864, in action near B[illegible]ville, Va.; mustered out Oct. 28, 1864, at [illegible]lumbus, O., by order of War Departme[illegible]
[illegible]	...do...	28	May 2, 1864	100 dys.	Mustered out with company Aug. 31, 1864
[illegible]	...do...	28	May 2, 1864	100 dys.	Mustered out with company Aug. 31, 1864
[illegible]	...do...	25	May 2, 1864	100 dys.	

COMPANY B.

11, 1864, at Camp Chase, O., by James P. W. Neill, 1st Lieutenant 18th Infantry, U. S. A. Mustered out Aug. 31, 1864, at Camp Chase, O., by Thomas H. Y. Bickham, 1st Lieutenant 19th Infantry, U. S. A.

	Rank.	Age.	Date of Entering the Service.	Period of Service.	Remarks.
[illegible]	Captain.	27	May 2, 1864	100 dys.	Promoted from 1st Lieutenant May 11, 1864; captured Aug. 13, 1864, in action near Berryville, Va.; mustered out Oct. 22, 1864, by order of War Department.
[illegible]	1st Sergt.	30	May 2, 1864	100 dys.	Mustered out with company Aug. 31, 1864.
[illegible]	Sergeant.	28	May 2, 1864	100 dys.	Mustered out with company Aug. 31, 1864.
[illegible]	...do...	27	May 2, 1864	100 dys.	Mustered out with company Aug. 31, 1864.
[illegible]	...do...	35	May 2, 1864	100 dys.	Mustered out with company Aug. 31, 1864.
[illegible]	...do...	43	May 2, 1864	100 dys.	Mustered out with company Aug. 31, 1864.
[illegible]	Corporal.	38	May 2, 1864	100 dys.	Mustered out with company Aug. 31, 1864.
[illegible]	...do...	38	May 2, 1864	100 dys.	Mustered out with company Aug. 31, 1864.
[illegible]	...do...	25	May 2, 1864	100 dys.	Mustered out with company Aug. 31, 1864.
[illegible]	...do...	31	May 2, 1864	100 dys.	Mustered out with company Aug. 31, 1864.
[illegible]	...do...	30	May 2, 1864	100 dys.	Mustered out with company Aug. 31, 1864.
[illegible]	...do...	28	May 2, 1864	100 dys.	Mustered out with company Aug. 31, 1864.
[illegible]	...do...	44	May 2, 1864	100 dys.	Mustered out with company Aug. 31, 1864.
[illegible]	...do...	38	May 2, 1864	100 dys.	Mustered out with company Aug. 31, 1864.
[illegible]	Musician	48	May 2, 1864	100 dys.	Mustered out with company Aug. 31, 1864.
[illegible]	...do...	18	May 2, 1864	100 dys.	Mustered out with company Aug. 31, 1864.
[illegible]	Private.	28	May 2, 1864	100 dys.	Captured July 9, 1864, at battle of Monocacy, Md.; paroled ——; mustered out April 5, 1865, at Columbus, O., by order of War Department.
[illegible]	...do...	19	May 2, 1864	100 dys.	Mustered out with company Aug. 31, 1864.
[illegible]	...do...	37	May 2, 1864	100 dys.	Mustered out with company Aug. 31, 1864.
[illegible]	...do...	32	May 2, 1864	100 dys.	Mustered out with company Aug. 31, 1864.
[illegible]	...do...	19	May 2, 1864	100 dys.	
[illegible]	...do...	31	May 2, 1864	100 dys.	Killed July 9, 1864, in battle of Monocacy, Md.
[illegible]	...do...	22	May 2, 1864	100 dys.	Mustered out with company Aug. 31, 1864.
[illegible]	...do...	21	May 2, 1864	100 dys.	Wounded July 9, 1864, in battle of Monocacy, Md.; mustered out with company Aug. 31, 1864.
[illegible]	...do...	18	May 2, 1864	100 dys.	Mustered out with company Aug. 31, 1864.
[illegible]	...do...	22	May 2, 1864	100 dys.	Captured July 9, 1864, at battle of Monocacy, Md.; paroled ——; mustered out April 6, 1865, at Columbus, O., by order of War Department.
[illegible]	...do...	29	May 2, 1864	100 dys.	Captured Aug. 13, 1864, in action near Berryville, Va.; died Nov. 1, 1864, in Rebel Prison at Salisbury, N. C.
[illegible]	...do...	18	May 2, 1864	100 dys.	Captured Aug. 13, 1864, in action near Berryville, Va.; died Oct. 28, 1864, in Rebel Prison at Salisbury, N. C.
[illegible]	...do...	28	May 2, 1864	100 dys.	Mustered out with company Aug. 31, 1864.
[illegible]	...do...	33	May 2, 1864	100 dys.	Mustered out with company Aug. 31, 1864.
[illegible]	...do...	27	May 2, 1864	100 dys.	Captured Aug. 13, 1864, in action near Berryville, Va.; confined Aug. 15, 1864, in Rebel Prison at Culpeper C. H., Va. No further record found.
[illegible]	...do...	36	May 2, 1864	100 dys.	Mustered out with company Aug. 31, 1864; also borne on rolls as William Jeffers.
[illegible]	...do...	21	May 2, 1864	100 dys.	Captured July 9, 1864, at battle of Monocacy, Md.; paroled ——; mustered out April 6, 1865, at Columbus, O., by order of War Department.
[illegible]	...do.	24	May 2, 1864	100 dys.	Mustered out with company Aug. 31, 1864.
[illegible]	...do.	19	May 2, 1864	100 dys.	Mustered out with company Aug. 31, 1864.
[illegible]	...do.	28	May 2, 1864	100 dys.	Mustered out with company Aug. 31, 1864.
[illegible]	...do.	29	May 2, 1864	100 dys.	Mustered out with company Aug. 31, 1864.
[illegible]	...do.	45	May 2, 1864	100 dys.	Captured Aug. 13, 1864, in action near Berryville, Va.; died Nov. 22, 1864, in Rebel Prison at Salisbury, N. C.
[illegible]	..	35	May 2, 1864	100 dys.	
[illegible]	..	19	May 2, 1864	100 dys.	Mustered out with company Aug. 31, 1864.
[illegible]	..	18	May 2, 1864	100 dys.	Captured Aug. 13, 1864, in action near Berryville, Va.; mustered out May 15, 1865, at Columbus, O., by order of War Department.
[illegible]	...do..	30	May 2, 1864	100 dys.	Mustered out with company Aug. 31, 1864.
[illegible]	...do..	31	May 2, 1864	100 dys.	Mustered out with company Aug. 31, 1864.
[illegible]	...do..	25	May 2, 1864	100 dys.	Mustered out with company Aug. 31, 1864.
[illegible]	...do..	36	May 2, 1864	100 dys.	Mustered out with company Aug. 31, 1864.
[illegible]	...do..	33	May 2, 1864	100 dys.	Captured July 9, 1864, at battle of Monocacy, Md.; paroled ——; mustered out April 6, 1865, at Columbus, O., by order of War Department.

Names.	Rank.	Age.	Date of Entering the Service.	Period of Service.	
Phillips, John	Private..	26	May 2, 1864	100 dys.	Captured Aug. 13, 1864, in action near ville, Va. No further record found.
Porrier, William	...do....	32	May 2, 1864	100 dys.	Mustered out with company Aug. 31, also borne on rolls as William Poirier
Price, Isaac	...do....	27	May 2, 1864	100 dys.	Captured Aug. 13, 1864, in action near ville, Va.; died Nov. 28, 1864, in Rebel at Salisbury, N. C.
Reed, John C.	...do....	18	May 2, 1864	100 dys.	Mustered out with company Aug. 31, 18
Reynolds, William	...do....	29	May 2, 1864	100 dys.	Mustered out with company Aug. 31, 18
Russell, Jabez	...do....	37	May 2, 1864	100 dys.	Mustered out with company Aug. 31, 18
Skinner, Sylvester	...do....	20	May 2, 1864	100 dys.	Mustered out with company Aug. 31, 18
Soash, John	...do....	28	May 2, 1864	100 dys.	Captured July 9, 1864, at battle of Mon Md.; paroled Sept. 12, 1864; mustere Oct. 8, 1864, at Columbus, O., by ord War Department.
Stone, Thomas	...do....	23	May 2, 1864	100 dys.	Captured Aug. 13, 1864, in action near ville, Va.; mustered out Dec. 1, 1864, lumbus, O., by order of War Departm
Tyler, Franklin	...do....	19	May 2, 1864	100 dys.	Mustered out with company Aug. 31, 18
Van Tassel, Le Roy	...do....	20	May 2, 1864	100 dys.	Mustered out with company Aug. 31, 18
Warner, Elliott M	...do....	20	May 2, 1864	100 dys.	Mustered out with company Aug. 31, 18
Warner, George L	...do....	40	May 2, 1864	100 dys.	Mustered out with company Aug. 31, 18
White, Hosea	...do....	23	May 2, 1864	100 dys.	
Williams, Emmett	...do....	18	May 2, 1864	100 dys.	Mustered out with company Aug. 31, 18
Wood, Walter	...do....	18	May 2, 1864	100 dys.	Captured Aug. 13, 1864, in action near ville, Va.; died Nov. 18, 1864, in Prison at Salisbury, N. C.
Worden, Oscar N.	...do....	27	May 2, 1864	100 dys.	Mustered out with company Aug. 31, 18

COMPANY C.

Mustered in May 11, 1864, at Camp Chase, O., by James P. W. Neill, 1st Lieutenant 18th Infantry, U. Mustered out Aug. 31, 1864, at Camp Chase, O., by Thomas H. Y. Bickham, 1st Lieutenant 19th Infantry, U. S. A.

Names.	Rank.	Age.	Date of Entering the Service.	Period of Service.	
Jeremiah Kitchen	Captain..	43	May 2, 1864	100 dys.	Mustered out with company Aug. 31, 18
Samuel J. Lamb	1st Lieut	28	May 2, 1864	100 dys.	Mustered out with company Aug. 31, 18
Thomas J. Avery	2d Lieut.	27	May 2, 1864	100 dys.	Mustered out with company Aug. 31, 18
Albert Froney	1st Sergt.	20	May 2, 1864	100 dys.	Mustered out with company Aug. 31, 18
Daniel W. Lowell	Sergeant.	23	May 2, 1864	100 dys.	Mustered out with company Aug. 31, 18
Joseph T. M. Reed	...do....	33	May 2, 1864	100 dys.	Mustered out with company Aug. 31, 18
Robert H. Barr	...do....	19	May 2, 1864	100 dys.	Captured Aug. 13, 1864, in action near ville, Va.; mustered out March 20, 18 Columbus, O., by order of War Departm
John J. Poe	...do....	25	May 2, 1864	100 dys.	Captured Aug. 13, 1864, in action near ville, Va.; died Dec. 18, 1864, in Prison at Salisbury, N. C.
Fitzland D. Noble	Corporal.	29	May 2, 1864	100 dys.	Captured Aug. 13, 1864, in action near ville, Va.; mustered out March 20, 18 Columbus, O., by order of War Departm
David H. Richards	...do....	19	May 2, 1864	100 dys.	Mustered out with company Aug. 31, 18
George Hyde	...do....	24	May 2, 1864	100 dys.	Mustered out with company Aug. 31, 18
George M. Brown	...do....	19	May 2, 1864	100 dys.	Mustered out with company Aug. 31, 18
George Bradley	...do....	19	May 2, 1864	100 dys.	Mustered out with company Aug. 31, 1864
Cyrus L. Brown	...do....	32	May 2, 1864	100 dys.	Mustered out with company Aug. 31, 1864
Abel F. Norris	...do....	33	May 2, 1864	100 dys.	Mustered out with company Aug. 31, 1864
Perry Thomas	...do....	18	May 2, 1864	100 dys.	Mustered out with company Aug. 31, 1864
Austin J. Stone	Musician	25	May 2, 1864	100 dys.	Mustered out with company Aug. 31, 1864
John W. Sargent	...do....	24	May 2, 1864	100 dys.	Mustered out with company Aug. 31, 1864
Abbott, Reuben	Private..	25	May 2, 1864	100 dys.	Mustered out with company Aug. 31, 1864
Avery, Ervin W	...do....	18	May 2, 1864	100 dys.	Mustered out with company Aug. 31, 1864
Bartels, William	...do....	23	May 2, 1864	100 dys.	Mustered out with company Aug. 31, 1864
Biddle, Henry	...do....	24	May 2, 1864	100 dys.	Mustered out with company Aug. 31, 1864
Boyce, Alexander W	...do....	20	May 2, 1864	100 dys.	Mustered out with company Aug. 31, 1864
Boyce, Alonzo P. C.	...do....	26	May 2, 1864	100 dys.	Mustered out with company Aug. 31, 1864
Brening, William	...do....	22	May 2, 1864	100 dys.	Mustered out with company Aug. 31, 1864
Brown, Simon R	...do....	23	May 2, 1864	100 dys.	Mustered out with company Aug. 31, 1864
Bullis, John	...do....	24	May 2, 1864	100 dys.	Mustered out with company Aug. 31, 1864
Cargo, David	...do....	30	May 2, 1864	100 dys.	Mustered out with company Aug. 31, 1864
Carter, David	...do....	18	May 2, 1864	100 dys.	Mustered out with company Aug. 31, 1864
Chadwick, George A	...do....	24	May 2, 1864	100 dys.	Mustered out with company Aug. 31, 1864
Chandler, Frederick	...do....	18	May 2, 1864	100 dys.	Mustered out with company Aug. 31, 1864
Chapman, Levi	...do....	22	May 2, 1864	100 dys.	
Cook, Allen	...do....	25	May 2, 1864	100 dys.	Mustered out with company Aug. 31, 1864
Crom, Joseph	...do....	24	May 2, 1864	100 dys.	Captured Aug. 13, 1864, in action near ville, Va.; mustered out Oct. 28, 1864, at lumbus, O., by order of War Departmen
Eldridge, John	...do....	28	May 2, 1864	100 dys.	Mustered out with company Aug. 31, 1864
Fay, Clinton	...do....	24	May 2, 1864	100 dys.	Mustered out with company Aug. 31, 1864
Finney, Roger	...do....	25	May 2, 1864	100 dys.	

COMPANY E.

...y 11, 1864, at Camp Chase, O., by James P. W. Neill, 1st Lieutenant 18th Infantry, U. S. A. Mustered out Aug. 24, 1864, at Camp Chase, O., by George H. McLaughlin, Captain 2d Infantry, U. S. A.

Names.	Rank.	Age.	Date of Entering the Service.	Period of Service.	Remarks.
	Captain	29	May 2, 1864	100 dys.	Mustered out with company Aug. 24, 1864.
	1st Lieut.	42	May 2, 1864	100 dys.	Mustered out with company Aug. 24, 1864.
	2d Lieut.	28	May 2, 1864	100 dys.	Mustered out with company Aug. 24, 1864.
	1st Sergt.	40	May 2, 1864	100 dys.	Mustered out with company Aug. 24, 1864.
...on	Sergeant	19	May 2, 1864	100 dys.	Mustered out with company Aug. 24, 1864.
	do	24	May 2, 1864	100 dys.	Mustered out with company Aug. 24, 1864.
	do	35	May 2, 1864	100 dys.	Mustered out with company Aug. 24, 1864.
	do	21	May 2, 1864	100 dys.	Mustered out with company Aug. 24, 1864.
	Corporal	26	May 2, 1864	100 dys.	Mustered out with company Aug. 24, 1864.
	do	33	May 2, 1864	100 dys.	Mustered out with company Aug. 24, 1864.
...smith	do	34	May 2, 1864	100 dys.	Mustered out with company Aug. 24, 1864.
	do	28	May 2, 1864	100 dys.	Mustered out with company Aug. 24, 1864.
	do	22	May 2, 1864	100 dys.	Mustered out with company Aug. 24, 1864.
	do	20	May 2, 1864	100 dys.	Mustered out with company Aug. 24, 1864.
	do	19	May 2, 1864	100 dys.	Mustered out with company Aug. 24, 1864.
	do	43	May 2, 1864	100 dys.	Mustered out with company Aug. 24, 1864.
...mbur	Musician	48	May 2, 1864	100 dys.	Granted furlough for one hundred days from Mar 11, 1864; mustered out with company Aug 24, 1864.
	do	16	May 2, 1864	100 dys.	Mustered out with company Aug. 24, 1864.
	Private	25	May 2, 1864	100 dys.	Mustered out with company Aug. 24, 1864.
	do	23	May 2, 1864	100 dys.	Mustered out with company Aug. 24, 1864.
	do	21	May 2, 1864	100 dys.	Mustered out with company Aug. 24, 1864.
	do	25	May 2, 1864	100 dys.	Mustered out with company Aug. 24, 1864.
	do	18	May 2, 1864	100 dys.	Mustered out with company Aug. 24, 1864.
...hn	do	29	May 2, 1864	100 dys.	Mustered out with company Aug. 24, 1864.
	do	30	May 2, 1864	100 dys.	Mustered out with company Aug. 24, 1864.
	do	20	May 2, 1864	100 dys.	Mustered out with company Aug. 24, 1864.
	do	18	May 2, 1864	100 dys.	Mustered out with company Aug. 24, 1864.
	do	37	May 2, 1864	100 dys.	Mustered out with company Aug. 24, 1864.
...e D.	do	25	May 2, 1864	100 dys.	Mustered out with company Aug. 24, 1864.
	do	23	May 2, 1864	100 dys.	Mustered out with company Aug. 24, 1864.
	do	30	May 2, 1864	100 dys.	Mustered out with company Aug. 24, 1864.
	do	24	May 2, 1864	100 dys.	Mustered out with company Aug. 24, 1864.
	do	42	May 2, 1864	100 dys.	Mustered out with company Aug. 24, 1864.
	do	37	May 2, 1864	100 dys.	Mustered out with company Aug. 24, 1864.
...F.	do	20	May 2, 1864	100 dys.	Mustered out with company Aug. 24, 1864.
	do	18	May 2, 1864	100 dys.	Mustered out with company Aug. 24, 1864.
	do	24	May 2, 1864	100 dys.	Mustered out with company Aug. 24, 1864.
	do	28	May 2, 1864	100 dys.	Mustered out with company Aug. 24, 1864.
	do	30	May 2, 1864	100 dys.	Mustered out with company Aug. 24, 1864.
	do	19	May 2, 1864	100 dys.	Mustered out with company Aug. 24, 1864.
	do	34	May 2, 1864	100 dys.	Mustered out with company Aug. 24, 1864.
	do	34	May 2, 1864	100 dys.	Mustered out with company Aug. 24, 1864.
	do	19	May 2, 1864	100 dys.	Mustered out with company Aug. 24, 1864.
	do	38	May 2, 1864	100 dys.	Mustered out with company Aug. 24, 1864.
	do	25	May 2, 1864	100 dys.	Mustered out with company Aug. 24, 1864.
...pher	do	24	May 2, 1864	100 dys.	Mustered out with company Aug. 24, 1864.
	do	22	May 2, 1864	100 dys.	Mustered out with company Aug. 24, 1864.
...uel	do	27	May 2, 1864	100 dys.	Mustered out with company Aug. 24, 1864.
	do	21	May 2, 1864	100 dys.	Mustered out with company Aug. 24, 1864.
	do	41	May 2, 1864	100 dys.	Mustered out with company Aug. 24, 1864.
	do	19	May 2, 1864	100 dys.	Mustered out with company Aug. 24, 1864.
...liam	do	39	May 2, 1864	100 dys.	Mustered out with company Aug. 24, 1864.
	do	32	May 2, 1864	100 dys.	Mustered out with company Aug. 24, 1864.
...D.	do	35	May 2, 1864	100 dys.	Mustered out with company Aug. 24, 1864.
	do	19	May 2, 1864	100 dys.	Mustered out with company Aug. 24, 1864.
...s H.	do	30	May 2, 1864	100 dys.	Mustered out with company Aug. 24, 1864.
	do	28	May 2, 1864	100 dys.	Mustered out with company Aug. 24, 1864.
	do	30	May 2, 1864	100 dys.	Mustered out with company Aug. 24, 1864.
	do	18	May 2, 1864	100 dys.	Mustered out with company Aug. 24, 1864.
	do	33	May 2, 1864	100 dys.	Mustered out with company Aug. 24, 1864.
	do	38	May 2, 1864	100 dys.	Mustered out with company Aug. 24, 1864.
...am H.	do	27	May 2, 1864	100 dys.	Mustered out with company Aug. 24, 1864.
	do	25	May 2, 1864	100 dys.	Mustered out with company Aug. 24, 1864.
	do	28	May 2, 1864	100 dys.	Mustered out with company Aug. 24, 1864.
	do	28	May 2, 1864	100 dys.	Mustered out with company Aug. 24, 1864.
	do	37	May 2, 1864	100 dys.	Mustered out with company Aug. 24, 1864.
	do	21	May 2, 1864	100 dys.	Mustered out with company Aug. 24, 1864.
	do	23	May 2, 1864	100 dys.	Mustered out with company Aug. 24, 1864.
	do	39	May 2, 1864	100 dys.	Promoted to Com. Sergeant May 11, 1864.
	do	34	May 2, 1864	100 dys.	Mustered out with company Aug. 24, 1864.
	do	26	May 2, 1864	100 dys.	Mustered out with company Aug. 24, 1864.
	do	21	May 2, 1864	100 dys.	Mustered out with company Aug. 24, 1864.
	do	21	May 2, 1864	100 dys.	Mustered out with company Aug. 24, 1864.
	do	30	May 2, 1864	100 dys.	Mustered out with company Aug. 24, 1864.

Names.	Rank.	Age.	Date of Entering the Service.	Period of Service.	Remarks.
Barnhizer, John	Private	20	May 2, 1864	100 dys.	Mustered out with company Aug 31, 1864.
Battenfield, John	...do...	27	May 2, 1864	100 dys.	Mustered out with company Aug. 31, 1864.
Baughman, Jacob G	...do...	32	May 2, 1864	100 dys.	Promoted to Chaplain May 12, 1864.
Berry, William	...do...	34	May 2, 1864	100 dys.	Mustered out with company Aug. 31, 1864.
Brining, Jacob J	...do...	29	May 2, 1864	100 dys.	Mustered out with company Aug. 31, 1864.
Bush, Gibson	...do...	35	May 2, 1864	100 dys.	Mustered out with company Aug. 31, 1864.
Carothers, Abraham A	...do...	19	May 2, 1864	100 dys.	Mustered out with company Aug. 31, 1864.
Clark, James B	...do...	33	May 2, 1864	100 dys.	Mustered out with company Aug. 31, 1864.
Clark, Marion A	...do...	37	May 2, 1864	100 dys.	Mustered out with company Aug. 31, 1864.
Conn, William C	...do...	31	May 2, 1864	100 dys	Mustered out with company Aug. 31, 1864.
Davis, William H	...do...	21	May 2, 1864	100 dys	Mustered out with company Aug. 31, 1864.
Deardorf, John	...do...	41	May 2, 1864	100 dys.	Mustered out with company Aug. 31, 1864.
Dudleson, Irvin	...do...	25	May 2, 1864	100 dys.	Mustered out with company Aug. 31, 1864.
Ellis[illegible], Alonzo	...do...	18	May 2, 1864	100 dys.	Mustered out with company Aug. 31, 1864.
Gear, Alvin S	...do...	18	May 2, 1864	100 dys.	Mustered out with company Aug. 31, 1864.
Gibbs, Addison E	...do...	32	May 2, 1864	100 dys.	Promoted to Q. M. Sergeant May 12, 1864.
Goodman, Erastus	...do...	34	May 2, 1864	100 dys.	Mustered out with company Aug. 31, 1864.
Harpster, Daniel	...do...	25	May 2, 1864	100 dys	Mustered out with company Aug. 31, 1864.
Harpster, John W	...do...	24	May 2, 1864	100 dys.	Mustered out with company Aug. 31, 1864.
Harpster, Solomon	...do...	40	May 2, 1864	100 dys.	Mustered out with company Aug. 31, 1864.
Harshbaugh, Abraham	...do...	30	May 2, 1864	100 dys	Mustered out with company Aug. 31, 1864.
Hibbins, James	...do...	40	May 2, 1864	100 dys.	Mustered out with company Aug. 31, 1864.
Hoisington, Albert	...do...	35	May 2, 1864	100 dys.	Captured Aug. 13, 1864, in action near Berryville, Va.; died Nov. 19, 1864, in Rebel Prison at Danville, Va.
Hoisington, Henry	...do...	38	May 2, 1864	100 dys.	Mustered out with company Aug 31, 1864
Humphrey, Charles	...do...	23	May 2, 1864	100 dys	Mustered out with company Aug. 31, 1864.
Hurd, William B	...do...	32	May 2, 1864	100 dys.	Captured Aug. 13, 1864, in action near Berryville, Va.; died Nov. 29, 1864, in Rebel Prison at Danville, Va.
Ish, John C	...do...	..	May 2, 1864	100 dys.	Mustered out with company Aug. 31, 1864.
Jones, John E	...do...	22	May 2, 1864	100 dys	Mustered out with company Aug. 31, 1864.
Karr, James P	...do...	28	May 2, 1864	100 dys.	Mustered out with company Aug. 31, 1864.
Karr, Lorenzo D	...do...	27	May 2, 1864	100 dys	Mustered out with company Aug. 31, 1864.
Karr, William H	...do...	21	May 2, 1864	100 dys	Mustered out with company Aug. 31, 1864.
Keeler, Samuel	...do...	28	May 2, 1864	100 dys.	Mustered out with company Aug. 31, 1864.
Kemely, John	...do...	28	May 2, 1864	100 dys	Mustered out with company Aug. 31, 1864.
Lang, John A	...do...	37	May 2, 1864	100 dys	Mustered out with company Aug. 31, 1864.
Lowery, William	...do...	18	May 2, 1864	100 dys	Mustered out with company Aug. 31, 1864.
McKinsey, Charles R	...do...	31	May 2, 1864	100 dys.	Mustered out with company Aug. 31, 1864.
Myers, James A	...do...	18	May 2, 1864	100 dys	Mustered out with company Aug. 31, 1864.
Nesbaum, Wellington	...do...	25	May 2, 1864	100 dys.	Mustered out with company Aug. 31, 1864.
Nye, George	...do...	34	May 2, 1864	100 dys.	Mustered out with company Aug. 31, 1864.
Nye, Samuel E	...do...	22	May 2, 1864	100 dys.	Mustered out with company Aug. 31, 1864.
Parks, Chauncey L	...do...	26	May 2, 1864	100 dys.	Mustered out with company Aug. 31, 1864.
Phillips, John	...do...	38	May 2, 1864	100 dys.	Mustered out with company Aug. 31, 1864.
Pla[illegible], William	...do...	21	May 2, 1864	100 dys.	Mustered out with company Aug. 31, 1864.
Ritchey, James M	...do...	27	May 2, 1864	100 dys.	Mustered out with company Aug. 31, 1864.
Robinson, Oliver	...do...	18	May 2, 1864	100 dys	Mustered out with company Aug. 31, 1864.
Sage, Egbert H	...do...	31	May 2, 1864	100 dys.	Wounded Aug. 13, 1864, in action near Berryville, Va.; mustered out with company Aug. 31, 1864.
Shain, Joseph	...do...	18	May 2, 1864	100 dys.	Mustered out with company Aug. 31, 1864.
Shellhouse, Edward S	...do...	30	May 2, 1864	100 dys.	Wounded Aug. 13, 1864, in action near Berryville, Va.; mustered out with company Aug. 31, 1864.
Shell, Daniel	...do...	18	May 2, 1864	100 dys.	Mustered out with company Aug. 31, 1864.
Sherman, Elkanah	...do...	39	May 2, 1864	100 dys.	Died June 27, 1864, at hospital, Relay House, Maryland.
Shireman, Jonathan	...do...	23	May 2, 1864	100 dys.	Mustered out with company Aug. 31, 1864.
Sipe, David	...do...	25	May 2, 1864	100 dys.	Mustered out with company Aug. 31, 1864
Smith, Landline	...do...	19	May 2, 1864	100 dys.	Mustered out with company Aug. 31, 1864.
Strahan, Harrison	...do...	23	May 2, 1864	100 dys.	Mustered out with company Aug. 31, 1864.
Straw, William H	...do...	22	May 2, 1864	100 dys.	Mustered out with company Aug. 31, 1864.
Swartz, Benjamin F	...do...	26	May 2, 1864	100 dys	Promoted to Sergt. Major May 12, 1864.
Trout, Anton	...do...	29	May 2, 1864	100 dys.	Mustered out with company Aug. 31, 1864.
Whipple, Oriel	...do...	23	May 2, 1864	100 dys.	Mustered out with company Aug. 31, 1864.
Williams, Saxton C	...do...	33	May 2, 1864	100 dys.	Mustered out with company Aug. 31, 1864.
Williams, Samuel Y	...do...	26	May 2, 1864	100 dys.	Mustered out with company Aug. 31, 1864.
Williams, William H	...do...	20	May 2, 1864	100 dys.	Mustered out with company Aug. 31, 1864.
Wisner, Asa	...do...	20	May 2, 1864	100 dys.	Absent, sick, Aug. 31, 1864, in Columbia Hospital, Washington, D. C. No further record found.
Wolgamuth, Solomon	...do...	22	May 2, 1864	100 dys.	Mustered out with company Aug. 31, 1864.
Wonder, Andrew J	...do...	33	May 2, 1864	100 dys	Mustered out with company Aug. 31, 1864.
Wonder, David H	...do...	18	May 2, 1864	100 dys.	Mustered out with company Aug. 31, 1864.
Wonder, Joseph F	...do...	21	May 2, 1864	100 dys.	Mustered out with company Aug. 31, 1864.

COMPANY E.

... at Camp Chase, O., by James P. W. Neill, 1st Lieutenant 18th Infantry, U. S. A.
... Aug. 24, 1864, at Camp Chase, O., by George H. McLaughlin, Captain 2d Infantry, U. S. A.

Rank.	Age.	Date of Entering the Service.	Period of Service.	Remarks.
Captain.	39	May 2, 1864	100 dys.	Mustered out with company Aug. 24, 1864.
1st Lieut.	42	May 2, 1864	100 dys.	Mustered out with company Aug. 24, 1864.
2d Lieut.	28	May 2, 1864	100 dys.	Mustered out with company Aug. 24, 1864.
1st Sergt.	40	May 2, 1864	100 dys.	Mustered out with company Aug. 24, 1864.
Sergeant.	[illegible]	May 2, 1864	100 dys.	Mustered out with company Aug. 24, 1864.
...do...	24	May 2, 1864	100 dys.	Mustered out with company Aug. 24, 1864.
...do...	35	May 2, 1864	100 dys.	Mustered out with company Aug. 24, 1864.
...do...	27	May 2, 1864	100 dys.	Mustered out with company Aug. 24, 1864.
Corporal.	26	May 2, 1864	100 dys.	Mustered out with company Aug. 24, 1864.
...do...	33	May 2, 1864	100 dys.	Mustered out with company Aug. 24, 1864.
...do...	28	May 2, 1864	100 dys.	Mustered out with company Aug. 24, 1864.
...do...	26	May 2, 1864	100 dys.	Mustered out with company Aug. 24, 1864.
...do...	22	May 2, 1864	100 dys.	Mustered out with company Aug. 24, 1864.
...do...	25	May 2, 1864	100 dys.	Mustered out with company Aug. 24, 1864.
...do...	19	May 2, 1864	100 dys.	Mustered out with company Aug. 24, 1864.
...do...	42	May 2, 1864	100 dys.	Mustered out with company Aug. 24, 1864.
Musician	48	May 2, 1864	100 dys.	Granted furlough for one hundred days from May 11, 1864; mustered out with company Aug. 24, 1864.
...do...	16	May 2, 1864	100 dys.	Mustered out with company Aug. 24, 1864.
Private.	25	May 2, 1864	100 dys.	Mustered out with company Aug. 24, 1864.
...do...	38	May 2, 1864	100 dys.	Mustered out with company Aug. 24, 1864.
...do...	21	May 2, 1864	100 dys.	Mustered out with company Aug. 24, 1864.
...do...	28	May 2, 1864	100 dys.	Mustered out with company Aug. 24, 1864.
...do...	18	May 2, 1864	100 dys.	Mustered out with company Aug. 24, 1864.
...do...	19	May 2, 1864	100 dys.	Mustered out with company Aug. 24, 1864.
...do...	39	May 2, 1864	100 dys.	Mustered out with company Aug. 24, 1864.
...do...	20	May 2, 1864	100 dys.	Mustered out with company Aug. 24, 1864.
...do...	18	May 2, 1864	100 dys.	Mustered out with company Aug. 24, 1864.
...do...	37	May 2, 1864	100 dys.	Mustered out with company Aug. 24, 1864.
...do...	25	May 2, 1864	100 dys.	Mustered out with company Aug. 24, 1864.
...do...	23	May 2, 1864	100 dys.	Mustered out with company Aug. 24, 1864.
...do...	30	May 2, 1864	100 dys.	Mustered out with company Aug. 24, 1864.
...do...	29	May 2, 1864	100 dys.	Mustered out with company Aug. 24, 1864.
...do...	42	May 2, 1864	100 dys.	Mustered out with company Aug. 24, 1864.
...do...	27	May 2, 1864	100 dys.	Mustered out with company Aug. 24, 1864.
...do...	20	May 2, 1864	100 dys.	Mustered out with company Aug. 24, 1864.
...do...	18	May 2, 1864	100 dys.	Mustered out with company Aug. 24, 1864.
...do...	21	May 2, 1864	100 dys.	Mustered out with company Aug. 24, 1864.
...do...	26	May 2, 1864	100 dys.	Mustered out with company Aug. 24, 1864.
...do...	40	May 2, 1864	100 dys.	Mustered out with company Aug. 24, 1864.
...do...	19	May 2, 1864	100 dys.	Mustered out with company Aug. 24, 1864.
...do...	34	May 2, 1864	100 dys.	Mustered out with company Aug. 24, 1864.
...do...	34	May 2, 1864	100 dys.	Mustered out with company Aug. 24, 1864.
...do...	19	May 2, 1864	100 dys.	Mustered out with company Aug. 24, 1864.
...do...	35	May 2, 1864	100 dys.	Mustered out with company Aug. 24, 1864.
...do...	38	May 2, 1864	100 dys.	Mustered out with company Aug. 24, 1864.
...do...	21	May 2, 1864	100 dys.	Mustered out with company Aug. 24, 1864.
...do...	22	May 2, 1864	100 dys.	Mustered out with company Aug. 24, 1864.
...do...	25	May 2, 1864	100 dys.	Mustered out with company Aug. 24, 1864.
...do...	21	May 2, 1864	100 dys.	Mustered out with company Aug. 24, 1864.
...do...	44	May 2, 1864	100 dys.	Mustered out with company Aug. 24, 1864.
...do...	19	May 2, 1864	100 dys.	Mustered out with company Aug. 24, 1864.
...do...	39	May 2, 1864	100 dys.	Mustered out with company Aug. 24, 1864.
...do...	22	May 2, 1864	100 dys.	Mustered out with company Aug. 24, 1864.
...do...	35	May 2, 1864	100 dys.	Mustered out with company Aug. 24, 1864.
...do...	19	May 2, 1864	100 dys.	Mustered out with company Aug. 24, 1864.
...do...	38	May 2, 1864	100 dys.	Mustered out with company Aug. 24, 1864.
...do...	29	May 2, 1864	100 dys.	Mustered out with company Aug. 24, 1864.
...do...	30	May 2, 1864	100 dys.	Mustered out with company Aug. 24, 1864.
...do...	18	May 2, 1864	100 dys.	Mustered out with company Aug. 24, 1864.
...do...	33	May 2, 1864	100 dys.	Mustered out with company Aug. 24, 1864.
...do...	38	May 2, 1864	100 dys.	Mustered out with company Aug. 24, 1864.
...do...	27	May 2, 1864	100 dys.	Mustered out with company Aug. 24, 1864.
...do...	24	May 2, 1864	100 dys.	Mustered out with company Aug. 24, 1864.
...do...	26	May 2, 1864	100 dys.	Mustered out with company Aug. 24, 1864.
...do...	26	May 2, 1864	100 dys.	Mustered out with company Aug. 24, 1864.
...do...	37	May 2, 1864	100 dys.	Mustered out with company Aug. 24, 1864.
...do...	21	May 2, 1864	100 dys.	Mustered out with company Aug. 24, 1864.
...do...	23	May 2, 1864	100 dys.	Mustered out with company Aug. 24, 1864.
...do...	29	May 2, 1864	100 dys.	Promoted to Com. Sergeant May 11, 1864.
...do...	34	May 2, 1864	100 dys.	Mustered out with company Aug. 24, 1864.
...do...	23	May 2, 1864	100 dys.	Mustered out with company Aug. 24, 1864.
...do...	21	May 2, 1864	100 dys.	Mustered out with company Aug. 24, 1864.
...do...	32	May 2, 1864	100 dys.	Mustered out with company Aug. 24, 1864.
...do...	30	May 2, 1864	100 dys.	Mustered out with company Aug. 24, 1864.

Names.	Rank.	Age.	Date of Entering the Service.	Period of Service.	Remarks.
Stonebrook, William	Private	43	May 2, 1864	100 dys.	Mustered out with company Aug. 24, 1864.
Stoor, John	do	34	May 2, 1864	100 dys.	Mustered out with company Aug. 24, 1864.
Stoor, Joseph	do	35	May 2, 1864	100 dys.	Mustered out with company Aug. 24, 1864.
Weaver, Joel	do	23	May 2, 1864	100 dys.	Mustered out with company Aug. 24, 1864.
Wiley, David	do	26	May 2, 1864	100 dys.	Mustered out with company Aug. 24, 1864.
Wilson, John	do	21	May 2, 1864	100 dys.	Mustered out with company Aug. 24, 1864.
Wimer, Moses	do	33	May 2, 1864	100 dys.	Mustered out with company Aug. 24, 1864.
Wineland, Valentine	do	38	May 2, 1864	100 dys.	Mustered out with company Aug. 24, 1864.
Yates, Lewis	do	19	May 2, 1864	100 dys.	Mustered out with company Aug. 24, 1864.
Zimmerman, Gabriel	do	37	May 2, 1864	100 dys.	Mustered out with company Aug. 24, 1864.

COMPANY F.

Mustered in May 11, 1864, at Camp Chase, O., by James P. W. Neill, 1st Lieutenant 18th Infantry, U. S. A. Mustered out Aug. 24, 1864, at Camp Chase, O., by George H. McLaughlin, Captain 2d Infantry, U. S. A.

Names.	Rank.	Age.	Date of Entering the Service.	Period of Service.	Remarks.
Asher Cook	Captain.	42	May 2, 1864	100 dys.	Mustered out with company Aug. 24, 1864.
Andrew Bloomfield	1st Lieut.	45	May 2, 1864	100 dys.	Mustered out with company Aug. 24, 1864.
Frank S. Tyler	2d Lieut.	23	May 2, 1864	100 dys.	Mustered out with company Aug. 24, 1864.
James P. Averill	1st Sergt.	22	May 2, 1864	100 dys.	Mustered out with company Aug. 24, 1864.
Charles C. Baird	Sergeant.	33	May 2, 1864	100 dys.	Mustered out with company Aug. 24, 1864.
Davis D. Bates	do	25	May 2, 1864	100 dys.	Mustered out with company Aug. 24, 1864.
David Main	do	27	May 2, 1864	100 dys.	Mustered out with company Aug. 24, 1864.
John Vannetten	do	27	May 2, 1864	100 dys.	Mustered out with company Aug. 24, 1864.
Simon Hartsing	Corporal.	37	May 2, 1864	100 dys.	Mustered out with company Aug. 24, 1864.
Alonzo L. Scott	do	21	May 2, 1864	100 dys.	Mustered out with company Aug. 24, 1864.
Christopher Sheets	do	19	May 2, 1864	100 dys.	Mustered out with company Aug. 24, 1864.
George Hoffman	do	24	May 2, 1864	100 dys.	
Jesse Bruce	do	24	May 2, 1864	100 dys.	Mustered out with company Aug. 24, 1864.
George W. Garner	do	32	May 2, 1864	100 dys.	Mustered out with company Aug. 24, 1864.
Lewis Householder	do	..	May 2, 1864	100 dys.	Mustered out with company Aug. 24, 1864.
John Barton	do	21	May 2, 1864	100 dys.	Mustered out with company Aug. 24, 1864.
Everett E. Smith	do	23	May 2, 1864	100 dys.	Appointed May 11, 1864; mustered out with company Aug. 24, 1864.
William F. Vetser	Musician	31	May 2, 1864	100 dys.	Mustered out with company Aug. 24, 1864.
Frederick Yager	do	29	May 2, 1864	100 dys.	Mustered out with company Aug. 24, 1864.
Algoner, Peter	Private	35	May 2, 1864	100 dys.	Mustered out with company Aug. 24, 1864.
Anderson, James D.	do	18	May 2, 1864	100 dys.	Mustered out with company Aug. 24, 1864.
Augustine, Charles	do	27	May 2, 1864	100 dys.	Mustered out with company Aug. 24, 1864.
Austin, [illegible]	do	19	May 2, 1864	100 dys.	Mustered out with company Aug. 24, 1864.
Austin, Rufus F.	do	47	May 2, 1864	100 dys.	Mustered out with company Aug. 24, 1864.
Baley, Charles	do	26	May 2, 1864	100 dys.	Mustered out with company Aug. 24, 1864.
Barton, William	do	25	May 2, 1864	100 dys.	Mustered out with company Aug. 24, 1864.
Beach, John	do	20	May 2, 1864	100 dys.	Mustered out with company Aug. 24, 1864.
Bender, George	do	28	May 2, 1864	100 dys.	Mustered out with company Aug. 24, 1864.
Bliss, Ira	do	25	May 2, 1864	100 dys.	
Bliss, James E.	do	20	May 2, 1864	100 dys.	Mustered out with company Aug. 24, 1864.
Bliss, Richard F.	do	23	May 2, 1864	100 dys.	Mustered out with company Aug. 24, 1864.
Bowers, George	do	43	May 2, 1864	100 dys.	Mustered out with company Aug. 24, 1864.
Brandeberry, Noah	do	21	May 2, 1864	100 dys.	Mustered out with company Aug. 24, 1864.
[illegible], Alexander B.	do	28	May 2, 1864	100 dys.	Mustered out with company Aug. 24, 1864.
[illegible], Jesse	do	26	May 2, 1864	100 dys.	Mustered out with company Aug. 24, 1864.
Burns, Andrew	do	25	May 2, 1864	100 dys.	Mustered out with company Aug. 24, 1864.
Bushnell, Alanson	do	41	May 2, 1864	100 dys.	Mustered out with company Aug. 24, 1864.
Caldwell, Beverly M.	do	24	May 2, 1864	100 dys.	Mustered out with company Aug. 24, 1864.
Champlin, Charles	do	26	May 2, 1864	100 dys.	Mustered out with company Aug. 24, 1864.
Chapel, [illegible] S.	do	29	May 2, 1864	100 dys.	Mustered out with company Aug. 24, 1864.
Charles, James M.	do	..	May 2, 1864	100 dys.	Mustered out with company Aug. 24, 1864.
Contine, Edward C.	do	28	May 2, 1864	100 dys.	Mustered out with company Aug. 24, 1864.
Cross, William	do	40	May 2, 1864	100 dys.	
[illegible], Wallace W.	do	40	May 2, 1864	100 dys.	Mustered out with company Aug. 24, 1864.
Davenport, William	do	22	May 2, 1864	100 dys.	Mustered out with company Aug. 24, 1864.
Davidson, Joel	do	33	May 2, 1864	100 dys.	Mustered out with company Aug. 24, 1864.
Dickerson, George W.	do	18	May 2, 1864	100 dys.	Mustered out with company Aug. 24, 1864.
Emmons, Robert	do	24	May 2, 1864	100 dys.	Mustered out with company Aug. 24, 1864.
Frasher, Thomas	do	28	May 2, 1864	100 dys.	Mustered out with company Aug. 24, 1864.
Goodman, Marion	do	30	May 2, 1864	100 dys.	Mustered out with company Aug. 24, 1864.
Graham, Walter	do	18	May 2, 1864	100 dys.	Mustered out with company Aug. 24, 1864.
Hickock, Cyrus	do	43	May 2, 1864	100 dys.	Mustered out with company Aug. 24, 1864.
Himmelman, John C.	do	36	May 2, 1864	100 dys.	Mustered out with company Aug. 24, 1864.
Hoffman, George G.	do	22	May 2, 1864	100 dys.	Mustered out with company Aug. 24, 1864.
Johnson, Freeman	do	37	May 2, 1864	100 dys.	Mustered out with company Aug. 24, 1864.
Jolley, Jesse S.	do	24	May 2, 1864	100 dys.	Mustered out with company Aug. 24, 1864.
Keebley, Matthias	do	22	May 2, 1864	100 dys.	Mustered out with company Aug. 24, 1864.
Kingfield, John	do	19	May 2, 1864	100 dys.	Mustered out with company Aug. 24, 1864.
Knoll, Aaron	do	18	May 2, 1864	100 dys.	Mustered out with company Aug. 24, 1864.
Kyes, Samuel	do	37	May 2, 1864	100 dys.	Mustered out with company Aug. 24, 1864.
Lafayette, Henry	do	18	May 2, 1864	100 dys.	Mustered out with company Aug. 24, 1864.
Mahr, Philip L.	do	28	May 2, 1864	100 dys.	Mustered out with company Aug. 24, 1864.

Name.	Rank.	Age.	Date of Entering the Service.	Period of Service.	Remarks.
[illegible]	Private..	45	May 2, 1864	100 dys.	Left, sick, at Relay House Barracks, near Baltimore, Md., June 5, 1864. No further record found.
[illegible], John A.	...do...	27	May 2, 1864	100 dys.	Mustered out with company Aug. 24, 1864.
[illegible], John L.	...do...	19	May 2, 1864	100 dys.	Mustered out with company Aug. 24, 1864.
[illegible]	...do...	28	May 2, 1864	100 dys.	Mustered out with company Aug. 24, 1864.
[illegible], Christopher	...do...	18	May 2, 1864	100 dys.	Mustered out with company Aug. 24, 1864.
[illegible]	...do...	26	May 2, 1864	100 dys.	Mustered out with company Aug. 24, 1864.
[illegible], James	...do...	39	May 2, 1864	100 dys.	Mustered out with company Aug. 24, 1864.
[illegible], Lewis	...do...	20	May 2, 1864	100 dys.	Mustered out with company Aug. 24, 1864.
[illegible], Raymond	...do...	28	May 2, 1864	100 dys.	Mustered out with company Aug. 24, 1864.
[illegible], Valentine	...do...	39	May 2, 1864	100 dys.	Mustered out with company Aug. 24, 1864.
[illegible], Andrew	...do...	38	May 2, 1864	100 dys.	Mustered out with company Aug. 24, 1864.
[illegible], Thomas	...do...	24	May 2, 1864	100 dys.	Mustered out with company Aug. 24, 1864.
[illegible], John	...do...	18	May 2, 1864	100 dys.	Mustered out with company Aug. 24, 1864.
[illegible]	...do...	36	May 2, 1864	100 dys.	Mustered out with company Aug. 24, 1864.
[illegible], Frederick	...do...	22	May 2, 1864	100 dys.	Mustered out with company Aug. 24, 1864.
[illegible], Leonard	...do...	31	May 2, 1864	100 dys.	Died June 14, 1864, at Annapolis Junction Maryland.
[illegible], William	...do...	20	May 2, 1864	100 dys.	Mustered out with company Aug. 24, 1864.
[illegible], John H.	...do...	22	May 2, 1864	100 dys.	Mustered out with company Aug. 24, 1864.
[illegible], Robert W.	...do...	18	May 2, 1864	100 dys.	Mustered out with company Aug. 24, 1864.
[illegible], Oliver	...do...	27	May 2, 1864	100 dys.	Mustered out with company Aug. 24, 1864.
[illegible], Robert	...do...	16	May 2, 1864	100 dys.	Mustered out with company Aug. 24, 1864.
[illegible], William D.	...do...	34	May 2, 1864	100 dys.	Mustered out with company Aug. 24, 1864.
Williams, James	...do...	36	May 2, 1864	100 dys.	Mustered out with company Aug. 24, 1864.
Wilson, James	...do...	19	May 2, 1864	100 dys.	Mustered out with company Aug. 24, 1864.
Wilson, Lewis	...do...	19	May 2, 1864	100 dys.	Mustered out with company Aug. 24, 1864.

COMPANY G.

Mustered in May 11, 1864, at Camp Chase, O., by James P. W. Neill, 1st Lieutenant 18th Infantry, U. S. A. Mustered out Aug. 31, 1864, at Camp Chase, O., by Thomas H. Y. Bickham, 1st Lieutenant 19th Infantry, U. S. A.

Name.	Rank.	Age.	Date of Entering the Service.	Period of Service.	Remarks.
William Frank	Captain.	28	May 2, 1864	100 dys.	Mustered out with company Aug. 31, 1864.
Howard Kennedy	1st Lieut.	28	May 2, 1864	100 dys.	Mustered out with company Aug. 31, 1864.
Samuel H. White	2d Lieut.	34	May 2, 1864	100 dys.	Captured Aug. 13, 1864, in action near Berryville, Va.; mustered out Sept. 27, 1864, at Columbus, O., by order of War Department.
Aaron Kennedy	1st Sergt.	30	May 2, 1864	100 dys.	Mustered out with company Aug. 31, 1864.
Marshall Custer	Sergeant.	35	May 2, 1864	100 dys.	Killed Aug. 13, 1864, in action near Berryville, Virginia.
Lucillus Hull	...do...	21	May 2, 1864	100 dys.	Mustered out with company Aug. 31, 1864.
Cornelius V. D. Worley	...do...	55	May 2, 1864	100 dys.	Captured July 0, 1864, at battle of Monocacy, Md., mustered out March 2, 1865, at Columbus, O., by order of War Department.
David J. Bower	...do...	28	May 2, 1864	100 dys.	Appointed from Corporal June 17, 1864; mustered out with company Aug. 31, 1864.
David Lindsey	Corporal	21	May 2, 1864	100 dys.	Died July 10, 1864, at Frederick, Md., of wounds received July 9, 1864, in battle of Monocacy, Md.
Allen Parker	...do...	20	May 2, 1864	100 dys.	Mustered out with company Aug. 31, 1864.
[illegible] Phelps	...do...	28	May 2, 1864	100 dys.	Mustered out with company Aug. 31, 1864.
John Rinehart	...do...	24	May 2, 1864	100 dys.	Mustered out with company Aug. 31, 1864.
Samuel [illegible]	...do...	22	May 2, 1864	100 dys.	Mustered out with company Aug. 31, 1864.
George Dill	...do...	27	May 2, 1864	100 dys.	Mustered out with company Aug. 31, 1864.
George W. Clark	...do...	25	May 2, 1864	100 dys.	Appointed June 17, 1864; mustered out with company Aug. 31, 1864.
[illegible]	...do...	30	May 2, 1864	100 dys.	Appointed June 17, 1864; mustered out with company Aug. 31, 1864.
[illegible]	Private.	28	May 2, 1864	100 dys.	Captured July 9, 1864, at battle of Monocacy, Md.; paroled ——; died Nov. 2, 1864, in hospital at Annapolis, Md.
[illegible], John	...do...	18	May 2, 1864	100 dys.	Mustered out with company Aug. 31, 1864.
[illegible], Andrew	...do...	21	May 2, 1864	100 dys.	Captured July 9, 1864, at battle of Monocacy, Md.; died Sept. 22, 1864, in Rebel Prison at Danville, Va.
[illegible], Jacob	...do...	20	May 2, 1864	100 dys.	Captured July 9, 1864, at battle of Monocacy, Md.; died Sept. 8, 1864, in Rebel Prison at Danville, Va.
Bibbler, William	...do...	18	May 2, 1864	100 dys.	Mustered out with company Aug. 31, 1864.
Blackburn, John	...do...	28	May 2, 1864	100 dys.	Mustered out with company Aug. 31, 1864.
Bliss, Thomas	...do...	18	May 2, 1864	100 dys.	Mustered out with company Aug. 31, 1864.
Blow, Edward	...do...	28	May 2, 1864	100 dys.	Mustered out with company Aug. 31, 1864.
Brown, John	...do...	28	May 2, 1864	100 dys.	Discharged May 12, 1864, on Surgeon's certificate of disability.
Butler, William	...do...	22	May 2, 1864	100 dys.	Mustered out with company Aug. 31, 1864.
Campbell, John	...do...	22	May 2, 1864	100 dys.	Captured July 9, 1864, at battle of Monocacy, Md., mustered out Sept. 21, 1864, at Camp Chase, O., by order of War Department.

Names.	Rank.	Age.	Date of Entering the Service.	Period of Service.	Remarks.
Clark, John	Private	20	May 2, 1864	100 dys.	Mustered out with company Aug. 31, 186
Clark, Noah C.	do.	26	May 2, 1864	100 dys.	Mustered out with company Aug. 31, 186
Cook, Simeon	do.	22	May 2, 1864	100 dys.	Mustered out with company Aug. 31, 186
Crabb, Daniel E.	do.	26	May 2, 1864	100 dys.	Mustered out with company Aug. 31, 186
Davis, Thomas	do.	30	May 2, 1864	100 dys.	Mustered out with company Aug. 31, 186
Dehart, William	do.	29	May 2, 1864	100 dys.	Mustered out with company Aug. 31, 186
Emmons, John	do.	30	May 2, 1864	100 dys.	Mustered out with company Aug. 31, 186
Emptage, James	do.	22	May 2, 1864	100 dys.	Mustered out with company Aug. 31, 186
Emptage, Thomas	do.	26	May 2, 1864	100 dys.	Mustered out with company Aug. 31, 186
Ferris, Randolph B.	do.	19	May 2, 1864	100 dys.	Discharged May 12, 1864, on Surgeon's certificate of disability.
Fisher, William	do.	21	May 2, 1864	100 dys.	Captured July 9, 1864, at battle of Monocacy, Md.; mustered out April [illegible], 1865, at Camp Chase, O., by order of War Department.
Haner, David	do.	33	May 2, 1864	100 dys.	Missing Aug. [illegible], 1864, in action near [illegible], Va. No further record found.
Hardin, Conrad	do.	18	May 2, 1864	100 dys.	Mustered out with company Aug. 31, 186
Hickman, Daniel	do.	22	May 2, 1864	100 dys.	Mustered out with company Aug. 31, 186
Hickman, William	do.	23	May 2, 1864	100 dys.	Mustered out with company Aug. 31, 186
Hildreth, Devin	do.	23	May 2, 1864	100 dys.	Mustered out with company Aug. 31, 186
Hildreth, William	do.	22	May 2, 1864	100 dys.	Mustered out with company Aug. 31, 186
Holland, Simon	do.	20	May 2, 1864	100 dys.	Mustered out with company Aug. 31, 186
Hullinger, Hiram	do.	21	May 2, 1864	100 dys.	Missing Aug. 13, 1864, in action near [illegible]ville, Va. No further record found.
Keckler, Josiah	do.	32	May 2, 1864	100 dys.	Missing Aug. 13, 1864, in action near [illegible]ville, Va. No further record found.
Kellogg, Theodore	do.	18	May 2, 1864	100 dys.	Mustered out with company Aug. 31, 186
Kennedy, Elijah	do.	18	May 2, 1864	100 dys.	Mustered out with company Aug. 31, 186
Krisher, Jeremiah	do.	22	May 2, 1864	100 dys.	Mustered out with company Aug. 31, 186
Laughlin, Frank	do.	18	May 2, 1864	100 dys.	Mustered out with company Aug. 31, 186
Lindsey, Robert	do.	19	May 2, 1864	100 dys.	Mustered out with company Aug. 31, 186
Long, Orrin	do.	18	May 2, 1864	100 dys.	Mustered out with company Aug. 31, 186
Longabaugh, Joseph	do.	2[illegible]	May 2, 1864	100 dys.	Mustered out with company Aug. 31, 186
Megahey, John	do.	[illegible]	May 2, 1864	100 dys.	Mustered out with company Aug. 31, 186
Mitchell, Robert H.	do.	[illegible]	May 2, 1864	100 dys.	Mustered out with company Aug. 31, 186
Montague, Cyrus	do.	18	May 2, 1864	100 dys.	Mustered out with company Aug. 31, 186
Mount, Henry	do.	25	May 2, 1864	100 dys.	Mustered out with company Aug. 31, 186
Mount, Thomas	do.	18	May 2, 1864	100 dys.	Mustered out with company Aug. 31, 186
Neal, Jerry C.	do.	21	May 2, 1864	100 dys.	Mustered out with company Aug. 31, 186
Norton, Hiram	do.	[illegible]	May 2, 1864	100 dys.	Mustered out with company Aug. 31, 186
Parker, Elias	do.	25	May 2, 1864	100 dys.	Mustered out with company Aug. 31, 186
Parks, Rose	do.	[illegible]	May 2, 1864	100 dys.	Mustered out with company Aug. 31, 186
Pentzer, David	do.	19	May 2, 1864	100 dys.	Mustered out with company Aug. 31, 186
Phillips, William O.	do.	18	May 2, 1864	100 dys.	Mustered out with company Aug. 31, 186
Reddick, John	do.	20	May 2, 1864	100 dys.	
Reynolds, John	do.	30	May 2, 1864	100 dys.	Mustered out with company Aug. 31, 186
Rose, George	do.	18	May 2, 1864	100 dys.	Mustered out with company Aug. 31, 186
Roseberry, Joseph	do.	26	May 2, 1864	100 dys.	Mustered out with company Aug. 31, 186
Robbins, Edward	do.	26	May 2, 1864	100 dys.	Discharged Aug. 24, 1864, at [illegible], on Surgeon's certificate of disability.
Rubins, Joseph	do.	19	May 2, 1864	100 dys.	Mustered out with company Aug. 31, 186
Sprague, Thomas	do.	28	May 2, 1864	100 dys.	Captured July 9, 1864, at battle of Monocacy, Md.; died [illegible] 11, 1864, in Rebel Prison, Danville, Va.
Stansbery, [illegible]	do.	30	May 2, 1864	100 dys.	Mustered out with company Aug. 31, 186
Straw, Irvin	do.	18	May 2, 1864	100 dys.	Accidentally killed May [illegible], 1864, near [illegible]burg, Pa.
Terry, James	do.	18	May 2, 1864	100 dys.	Mustered out with company Aug. 31, 186
Tyler, J. R.	do.	2[illegible]	May 2, 1864	100 dys.	No record subsequent to enlistment.
Umpleby, Theodore	do.	21	May 2, 1864	100 dys.	Captured July 9, 1864, at battle of Monocacy, Md.; mustered out April 13, 1865, at Camp Chase, O., by order of War Department.
Van Arsdal, Charles	do.	1[illegible]	May 2, 1864	100 dys.	Mustered out with company Aug. 31, 186
Walker, Dallas	do.	18	May 2, 1864	100 dys.	Mustered out with company Aug. 31, 186
Wessner, John	do.	20	May 2, 1864	100 dys.	Mustered out with company Aug. 31, 186
White, James A.	do.	11	May 2, 1864	100 dys.	Mustered out with company Aug. 31, 186
Willard, Reuben	do.	27	May 2, 1864	100 dys.	Captured July 9, 1864, at battle of Monocacy, Md.; paroled Sept. 1, 1864, sent to hospital; died Sept. 4, 1864, at Baltimore, Md. No further record found.
Williams, Jacob	do.	27	May 2, 1864	100 dys.	Mustered out with company Aug. 31, 186
Worthington, Joseph	do.	[illegible]	May 2, 1864	100 dys.	Mustered out with company Aug. 31, 186
Yeokam, Henry	do.	27	May 2, 1864	100 dys.	Missing Aug. 13, 1864, in action near B[illegible]ville, Va. No further record found.

COMPANY H.

...at Camp Chase, O., by James P. W. Neill, 1st Lieutenant 18th Infantry, U. S. A.
...Aug. 31, 1864, at Camp Chase, O., by Thomas H. Y. Bickham,
...Lieutenant 19th Infantry, U. S. A.

Rank.	Age.	Date of Entering the Service.	Period of Service.	Remarks.
Captain.	41	May 2, 1864	100 dys.	Mustered out with company Aug. 31, 1864.
1st Lieut.	25	May 2, 1864	100 dys.	Mustered out with company Aug. 31, 1864.
2d Lieut.	27	May 2, 1864	100 dys.	Mustered out with company Aug. 31, 1864.
1st Sergt.	24	May 2, 1864	100 dys.	Mustered out with company Aug. 31, 1864.
Sergeant.	26	May 2, 1864	100 dys.	Mustered out with company Aug. 31, 1864.
...do...	26	May 2, 1864	100 dys.	Absent, home, Aug. 31, 1864, on sick furlough. No further record found.
...do...	32	May 2, 1864	100 dys.	Mustered out with company Aug. 31, 1864.
...do...	35	May 2, 1864	100 dys.	Appointed from Corporal May [illegible], 1864; mustered out with company Aug. 31, 1864.
Corporal.	24	May 2, 1864	100 dys.	Mustered out with company Aug. 31, 1864.
...do...	23	May 2, 1864	100 dys.	Mustered out with company Aug. 31, 1864.
...do...	26	May 2, 1864	100 dys.	Mustered out with company Aug. 31, 1864.
...do...	20	May 2, 1864	100 dys.	Mustered out with company Aug. 31, 1864.
...do...	29	May 2, 1864	100 dys.	Mustered out with company Aug. 31, 1864.
...do...	19	May 2, 1864	100 dys.	Mustered out with company Aug. 31, 1864.
...do...	30	May 2, 1864	100 dys.	Captured Aug. 13, 1864, in action near Berryville, Va.; paroled ——; died Oct. 9, 1864, at Annapolis, Md.
Musician	27	May 2, 1864	100 dys.	Mustered out with company Aug. 31, 1864.
...do...	27	May 2, 1864	100 dys.	Mustered out with company Aug. 31, 1864.
Private..	24	May 2, 1864	100 dys.	Mustered out with company Aug. 31, 1864.
...do...	29	May 2, 1864	100 dys.	Mustered out with company Aug. 31, 1864.
...do...	21	May 2, 1864	100 dys.	Mustered out with company Aug. 31, 1864.
...do...	18	May 2, 1864	100 dys.	Mustered out with company Aug. 31, 1864.
...do...	19	May 2, 1864	100 dys.	Absent, home, Aug. 31, 1864, on sick furlough. No further record found.
...do...	18	May 2, 1864	100 dys.	Mustered out with company Aug. 31, 1864.
...do...	20	May 2, 1864	100 dys.	Mustered out with company Aug. 31, 1864.
...do...	22	May 2, 1864	100 dys.	Mustered out with company Aug. 31, 1864.
...do...	42	May 2, 1864	100 dys.	Mustered out with company Aug. 31, 1864.
...do...	21	May 2, 1864	100 dys.	Mustered out with company Aug. 31, 1864.
...do...	28	May 2, 1864	100 dys.	Mustered out with company Aug. 31, 1864.
...do...	24	May 2, 1864	100 dys.	Mustered out with company Aug. 31, 1864.
...do...	21	May 2, 1864	100 dys.	Mustered out with company Aug. 31, 1864.
...do...	25	May 2, 1864	100 dys.	Mustered out with company Aug. 31, 1864.
...do...	29	May 2, 1864	100 dys.	Mustered out with company Aug. 31, 1864.
...do...	25	May 2, 1864	100 dys.	Mustered out with company Aug. 31, 1864.
...do...	21	May 2, 1864	100 dys.	Mustered out with company Aug. 31, 1864.
...do...	21	May 2, 1864	100 dys.	Died July 28, 1864, at Relay House Barracks, Maryland.
...do...	29	May 2, 1864	100 dys.	Mustered out with company Aug. 31, 1864.
...do...	28	May 2, 1864	100 dys.	Mustered out with company Aug. 31, 1864.
...do...	20	May 2, 1864	100 dys.	Mustered out with company Aug. 31, 1864.
...do...	45	May 2, 1864	100 dys.	Mustered out with company Aug. 31, 1864.
...do...	20	May 2, 1864	100 dys.	Mustered out with company Aug. 31, 1864.
...do...	36	May 2, 1864	100 dys.	Mustered out with company Aug. 31, 1864.
...do...	22	May 2, 1864	100 dys.	Died Aug. 2, 1864, at Washington, D. C.
...do...	32	May 2, 1864	100 dys.	Mustered out with company Aug. 31, 1864.
...do...	24	May 2, 1864	100 dys.	Mustered out with company Aug. 31, 1864.
...do...	32	May 2, 1864	100 dys.	Discharged May 12, 1864, on Surgeon's certificate of disability.
...do...	36	May 2, 1864	100 dys.	Captured Aug. 13, 1864, in action near Berryville, Va.; died Nov. 21, 1864, in Rebel Prison at Salisbury, N. C.
...do...	24	May 2, 1864	100 dys.	Mustered out with company Aug. 31, 1864.
...do...	22	May 2, 1864	100 dys.	Mustered out with company Aug. 31, 1864.
...do...	31	May 2, 1864	100 dys.	Mustered out with company Aug. 31, 1864.
...do...	24	May 2, 1864	100 dys.	Mustered out with company Aug. 31, 1864.
...do...	27	May 2, 1864	100 dys.	Mustered out with company Aug. 31, 1864.
...do...	38	May 2, 1864	100 dys.	Mustered out with company Aug. 31, 1864.
...do...	24	May 2, 1864	100 dys.	Mustered out with company Aug. 31, 1864.
...do...	19	May 2, 1864	100 dys.	Mustered out with company Aug. 31, 1864.
...do...	18	May 2, 1864	100 dys.	Mustered out with company Aug. 31, 1864.
...do...	31	May 2, 1864	100 dys.	Mustered out with company Aug. 31, 1864.
...do...	28	May 2, 1864	100 dys.	Mustered out with company Aug. 31, 1864.
...do...	17	May 2, 1864	100 dys.	Mustered out with company Aug. 31, 1864; also borne on rolls as Matthew McKivy.
...do...	19	May 2, 1864	100 dys.	Mustered out with company Aug. 31, 1864.
...do...	29	May 2, 1864	100 dys.	Mustered out with company Aug. 31, 1864.
...do...	28	May 2, 1864	100 dys.	Mustered out with company Aug. 31, 1864.
...do...	35	May 2, 1864	100 dys.	Mustered out with company Aug. 31, 1864.
...do...	25	May 2, 1864	100 dys.	Mustered out with company Aug. 31, 1864.
...do...	25	May 2, 1864	100 dys.	Mustered out with company Aug. 31, 1864.
...do...	27	May 2, 1864	100 dys.	Mustered out with company Aug. 31, 1864.

Names.		Age.	Date of Entering the Service.	Period of Service.	
Price. Aaron R.	Private.	28	May 2, 1864	100 dys.	Captured Aug. 13, 1864, in action ne ville, Va.; died Sept. 19, 1864, at A Maryland.
Racy, William	...do...	28	May 2, 1864	100 dys.	Mustered out with company Aug. 31,
Reed, David H	...do...	44	May 2, 1864	100 dys.	Mustered out with company Aug. 31,
Robinson, Hunter	...do...	24	May 2, 1864	100 dys.	Mustered out with company Aug. 31,
Shafer, Jacob	...do...	18	May 2, 1864	100 dys.	Mustered out with company Aug. 31,
Shafer, John D	...do...	20	May 2, 1864	100 dys.	Mustered out with company Aug. 31,
Smith, Charles	...do...	39	May 2, 1864	100 dys.	Mustered out with company Aug. 31,
Stewart, Ezra	...do...	22	May 2, 1864	100 dys.	Mustered out with company Aug. 31,
Stinchcomb, John	...do...	38	May 2, 1864	100 dys.	Mustered out with company Aug. 31,
Stubbs, Theodore	...do...	18	May 2, 1864	100 dys.	Mustered out with company Aug. 31,
Swinehart, William H	...do...	29	May 2, 1864	100 dys.	Mustered out with company Aug. 31,
Vangundy, Enoch	...do...	18	May 2, 1864	100 dys.	Mustered out with company Aug. 31,
Vroman, Peter C	...do...	37	May 2, 1864	100 dys.	Mustered out with company Aug. 31,
Webb, Bowman	...do...	29	May 2, 1864	100 dys.	Mustered out with company Aug. 31,
Welty, Henry C	...do...	19	May 2, 1864	100 dys.	Mustered out with company Aug. 31,
Welty, James O	...do...	19	May 2, 1864	100 dys.	Mustered out with company Aug. 31,
Wilcox, Plimpton	...do...	18	May 2, 1864	100 dys.	Mustered out with company Aug. 31,
Wilcox, William J	...do...	26	May 2, 1864	100 dys.	Mustered out with company Aug. 31,
Wilsey, Maitland	...do...	44	May 2, 1864	100 dys.	Mustered out with company Aug. 31,
Wilson, George	...do...	21	May 2, 1864	100 dys.	Mustered out with company Aug. 31,
Wilson, Jehu	...do...	25	May 2, 1864	100 dys.	Mustered out with company Aug. 31,
Wilson, Zachariah S	...do...	21	May 2, 1864	100 dys.	Mustered out with company Aug. 31,
Young, Edward	...do...	20	May 2, 1864	100 dys.	Mustered out with company Aug. 31,
Young, Hezekiah	...do...	19	May 2, 1864	100 dys.	Mustered out with company Aug. 31,

COMPANY I.

Mustered in May 11, 1864, at Camp Chase, O., by James P. W. Neill, 1st Lieutenant 18th Infantry; Mustered out Aug. 31, 1864, at Camp Chase, O., by Thomas H. Y. Bickham, 1st Lieutenant 19th Infantry, U. S. A.

John McKee	Captain.	39	May 2, 1864	100 dys.	Mustered out with company Aug. 31,
George Weddell	1st Lieut.	27	May 2, 1864	100 dys.	Captured Aug. 13, 1864, in action ne ville, Va.; mustered out March 15 order of War Department.
George Kimberlin	2d Lieut.	39	May 2, 1864	100 dys.	Mustered out with company Aug. 31,
James Kerr	1st Sergt.	24	May 2, 1864	100 dys.	Mustered out with company Aug. 31,
William A. Benschoter	Sergeant.	22	May 2, 1864	100 dys.	Mustered out with company Aug. 31,
Morgan Brown	...do...	34	May 2, 1864	100 dys.	Mustered out with company Aug. 31,
Uriah S. Dewese	...do...	21	May 2, 1864	100 dys.	Mustered out with company Aug. 31,
Burnam L. Ashley	...do...	28	May 2, 1864	100 dys.	Mustered out with company Aug. 31,
George C. Gilmore	Corporal.	43	May 2, 1864	100 dys.	Mustered out with company Aug. 31,
Samuel R. Jenkins	...do...	31	May 2, 1864	100 dys.	Mustered out with company Aug. 31,
David Donaldson	...do...	34	May 2, 1864	100 dys.	Mustered out with company Aug. 31,
Joseph Gayer	...do...	41	May 2, 1864	100 dys.	Mustered out with company Aug. 31,
Jonathan Walters	...do...	30	May 2, 1864	100 dys.	Died July 19, 1864, of wounds receiv 1864, in battle of Monocacy, Md.
Joseph E. Barrett	...do...	28	May 2, 1864	100 dys.	Mustered out with company Aug. 31,
Jacob Kimberlin	...do...	37	May 2, 1864	100 dys.	Mustered out with company Aug. 31,
John Dunipace	...do...	18	May 2, 1864	100 dys.	Appointed May 11, 1864; captured 1864, in action near Berryville, V tered out Sept. 7, 1864, at Camp Cha order of War Department.
Findlay Barton	Musician	18	May 2 1864	100 dys.	Captured Aug. 13, 1864, in action ne ville, Va.; died Nov. 18, 1864, in Reb at Salisbury, N. C.
Samuel McLain	...do...	38	May 2, 1864	100 dys.	Captured Aug. 13, 1864, in action ne ville, Va.; died Dec. 19, 1864, in Reb at Salisbury, N. C.
Ash, Benjamin F	Private.	18	May 2, 1864	100 dys.	Mustered out Oct. 21, 1864, at Columb order of War Department.
Baker, Christ	...do...	32	May 2, 1864	100 dys.	Mustered out with company Aug. 31,
Baldwin, Edmund	...do...	20	May 2, 1864	100 dys.	Discharged May 12, 1864, at Columb Surgeon's certificate of disability.
Barket, Joseph	...do...	28	May 2, 1864	100 dys.	Captured July 9, 1864, at battle of M Md.; paroled ——; mustered out 1865, at Columbus, O., by order of partment.
Barton, Henry J	...do...	24	May 2, 1864	100 dys.	Mustered out with company Aug. 31,
Barton, William	...do...	18	May 2, 1864	100 dys.	Wounded July 9, 1864, in battle of M Md.; mustered out with company 1864.
Bassett, Austin D	...do...	19	May 2, 1864	100 dys.	Died June 28, 1864, at Annapolis, Md.
Bortle, Wesley	...do...	18	May 2, 1864	100 dys.	Mustered out with company Aug. 31,
Bowsprit, Edward	...do...	47	May 2, 1864	100 dys.	Rejected by examining Surgeon May
Brown, William	...do...	20	May 2, 1864	100 dys.	Captured Aug. 13, 1864, in action ne ville, Va.; died Dec. 7, 1864, in Reb at Salisbury, N. C.

E.	Age.	Date of Entering the Service.	Period of Service.	Remarks.
...	18	May 2, 1864	100 dys.	Captured July 9, 1864, at battle of Monocacy, Md.; died Nov. 10, 1864, in Rebel Prison at Salisbury, N. C.
...	[illegible]	May 2, 1864	100 dys.	Discharged May 12, 1864, at Columbus, O., on Surgeon's certificate of disability.
...	25	May 2, 1864	100 dys.	Mustered out with company Aug. 31, 1864.
...	18	May 2, 1861	100 dys.	Captured July 9, 1864, at battle of Monocacy, Md.; died Nov. 6, 1864, in Rebel Prison at Danville, Va.
...	18	May 2, 1864	100 dys.	Mustered out with company Aug. 31, 1864.
...	25	May 2, 1864	100 dys.	Discharged May 12, 1864, at Columbus, O., on Surgeon's certificate of disability.
...	18	May 2, 1864	100 dys.	Mustered out with company Aug. 31, 1864.
...	23	May 2, 1864	100 dys.	Captured Aug. 13, 1864, in action near Berryville, Va.; paroled ——; died March 24, 1865, at Baltimore, Md.
...	24	May 2, 1864	100 dys.	Mustered out with company Aug. 31, 1864.
...	28	May 2, 1864	100 dys.	Mustered out with company Aug. 31, 1864.
...	22	May 2, 1864	100 dys.	Mustered out with company Aug. 31, 1864.
...	25	May 2, 1864	100 dys.	Mustered out with company Aug. 31, 1864.
...	19	May 2, 1864	100 dys.	Killed July 9, 1864, in battle of Monocacy, Md
...	24	May 2, 1864	100 dys.	Mustered out with company Aug. 31, 1864.
...	[illegible]	May 2, 1864	100 dys.	Mustered out with company Aug. 31, 1864.
...	18	May 2, 1864	100 dys.	Mustered out with company Aug. 31, 1864.
...	29	May 2, 1864	100 dys.	Captured July 9, 1864, at battle of Monocacy, Md.; died Jan. 4, 1865, in Rebel Prison at Danville, Va.
...	18	May 2, 1864	100 dys.	Mustered out withcompany Aug. 31, 1864.
...	25	May 2, 1864	100 dys.	Mustered out with company Aug. 31, 1864.
...	41	May 2, 1864	100 dys.	Mustered out with company Aug. 31, 1864.
...	[illegible]	May 2, 1864	100 dys.	Captured July 9, 1864, at battle of Monocacy, Md.; died Feb. 16, 1865, in Rebel Prison at Danville, Va.
...	43	May 2, 1864	100 dys.	Mustered out with company Aug. 31, 1864.
...	40	May 2, 1864	100 dys.	Mustered out with company Aug. 31, 1864.
...	18	May 2, 1864	100 dys.	Mustered out with company Aug. 31, 1864.
...	34	May 2, 1864	100 dys.	Mustered out with company Aug. 31, 1864.
...	18	May 2, 1864	100 dys.	Captured July 9, 1864, at battle of Monocacy, Md.; mustered out Sept. 29, 1864, at Camp Chase, O., by order of War Department.
...	43	May 2, 1864	100 dys.	Mustered out with company Aug. 31, 1864.
...	19	May 2, 1864	100 dys.	Captured July 9, 1864, at battle of Monocacy, Md.; paroled ——; died April 8, 1865, at Gilead, O.
...	[illegible]	May 2, 1864	100 dys.	Discharged May 12, 1864, at Columbus, O., on Surgeon's certificate of disability.
...	33	May 2, 1864	100 dys.	Mustered out with company Aug. 31, 1864.
...	19	May 2, 1864	100 dys.	Mustered out with company Aug. 31, 1864.
...	19	May 2, 1864	100 dys.	Mustered out with company Aug. 31, 1864.
...	36	May 2, 1864	100 dys.	Mustered out with company Aug. 31, 1864.
...	22	May 2, 1864	100 dys.	Mustered out with company Aug. 31, 1864.
...	19	May 2, 1864	100 dys.	Mustered out with company Aug. 31, 1864.
...	27	May 2, 1861	100 dys.	Mustered out Oct. 8, 1864, at Columbus, O., by order of War Department.
...	..	May 2, 1864	100 dys.	Mustered out with company Aug. 31, 1864.
...	28	May 2, 1864	100 dys.	Reduced from Corporal May 11, 1864; mustered out with company Aug. 31, 1864.
...	19	May 2, 1864	100 dys.	Captured Aug. 13, 1864, in action near Berryville, Va.; died Jan. 1, 1865, in Rebel Prison at Salisbury, N. C.
...	42	May 2, 1864	100 dys.	Mustered out with company Aug. 31, 1864.
...	18	May 2, 1864	100 dys.	Mustered out with company Aug. 31, 1864.
...	37	May 2, 1864	100 dys.	Mustered out with company Aug. 31, 1864.
...	18	May 2, 1864	100 dys.	Mustered out with company Aug. 31, 1864.
...	26	May 2, 1864	100 dys.	Discharged May 12, 1864, at Columbus, O., on Surgeon's certificate of disability.
...	24	May 2, 1864	100 dys.	Captured Aug. 13, 1864, in action near Berryville, Va.; mustered out Sept. 7, 1864, at Camp Chase, O., by order of War Department.
...	18	May 2, 1864	100 dys.	Mustered out with company Aug. 31, 1864.
...	30	May 2, 1864	100 dys.	Mustered out with company Aug. 31, 1864.
...	22	May 2, 1864	100 dys	Prisoner of war ——; mustered out March 28, 1865, at Columbus, O., by order of War Department
...	19	May 2, 1864	100 dys.	Mustered out with company Aug. 31, 1864.
...	18	May 2, 1864	100 dys.	Mustered out with company Aug. 31, 1864.
...	22	May 2, 1864	100 dys.	Mustered out with company Aug. 31, 1864.
...	25	May 2, 1864	100 dys.	Mustered out with company Aug. 31, 1864.
...	18	May 2, 1864	100 dys.	Mustered out with company Aug. 31, 1864.
...	[illegible]	May 2, 1864	100 dys.	Mustered out with company Aug. 31, 1864.
...	18	May 2, 1864	100 dys.	Mustered out with company Aug. 31, 1864.
...	[illegible]	May 2, 1864	100 dys.	Mustered out with company Aug. 31, 1864.

COMPANY K.

Mustered in May 11, 1864, at Camp Chase, O., by James P. W. Neill, 1st Lieutenant 18th Infantry, U. S. A. Mustered out Aug. 31, 1864, at Camp Chase, O., by Thomas H. Y. Bickham, 1st Lieutenant 19th Infantry, U. S. A.

Names.	Rank.	Age.	Date of Entering the Service.	Period of Service.	Remarks.
Philo W. Hathaway	Captain.	42	May 2, 1864	100 dys.	Mustered out with company Aug. 31, 1864.
Benjamin Bacon	1st Lieut.	29	May 2, 1864	100 dys.	Mustered out with company Aug. 31, 1864.
Edwin R. Sage	2d Lieut.	39	May 2, 1864	100 dys.	Captured Aug. 13, 1864, in action near Berryville, Va.; discharged Sept. 27, 1864.
Daniel M. Palmer	1st Sergt.	29	May 2, 1864	100 dys.	Captured Aug. 13, 1864, in action near Berryville, Va.; confined in Rebel Prison at Richmond, Va., and sent to Rebel Prison at Salisbury, N. C., Oct. 9, 1864. No further record found.
Charles F. Stanton	Sergeant.	33	May 2, 1864	100 dys.	Mustered out with company Aug. 31, 1864.
Theodorus H. C. Frisbie	....do....	30	May 2, 1864	100 dys.	Captured Aug. 13, 1864, in action near Berryville, Va.; died Oct. 22, 1864, in Rebel Prison at Salisbury, N. C.
James Carter	....do....	25	May 2, 1864	100 dys.	Mustered out with company Aug. 31, 1864.
James S. Lincoln	....do....	39	May 2, 1864	100 dys.	Killed Aug. 13, 1864, in action near Berryville, Virginia.
Simon Edmonds	Corporal.	27	May 2, 1864	100 dys.	Captured Aug. 13, 1864, in action near Berryville, Va.; died Oct. 23, 1864, at Annapolis, Maryland.
Thomas A. Graham	....do....	21	May 2, 1864	100 dys.	Captured Aug. 13, 1864, in action near Berryville, Va.; paroled Oct. 7, 1864; mustered out Dec. 8, 1864, at Columbus, O., by order of War Department.
Joseph Lesher	....do....	25	May 2, 1864	100 dys.	Mustered out with company Aug. 31, 1864.
Timothy Gould	....do....	36	May 2, 1864	100 dys.	Mustered out with company Aug. 31, 1864.
James Martin	....do....	27	May 2, 1864	100 dys.	Captured Aug. 13, 1864, in action near Berryville, Va.; died Jan. 27, 1865, in Rebel Prison at Salisbury, N. C.
Nathaniel Sanderson	....do....	19	May 2, 1864	100 dys.	Prisoner of war ——; mustered out March 22, 1865, at Columbus, O., by order of War Department.
Henry B. Bearley	....do....	21	May 2, 1864	100 dys.	Mustered out with company Aug. 31, 1864.
Charles A. Bryant	....do....	24	May 2, 1864	100 dys.	Captured Aug. 13, 1864, in action near Berryville, Va.; died Nov. 14, 1864, in Rebel Prison at Salisbury, N. C.
Andrew Metcalf	Musician	27	May 2, 1864	100 dys.	Captured Aug. 13, 1864, in action near Berryville, Va.; mustered out March 23, 1865, at Columbus, O., by order of War Department.
Stephen Angus	....do....	18	May 2, 1864	100 dys.	Mustered out with company Aug. 31, 1864.
Adams, Robert W	Private..	22	May 2, 1864	100 dys.	Mustered out with company Aug. 31, 1864.
Angus, Frederick R	....do....	[illegible]	May 2, 1864	100 dys.	
Angus, Richard	....do....	[illegible]	May 2, 1864	100 dys.	Mustered out with company Aug. 31, 1864.
Baker, Adam H	....do....	27	May 2, 1864	100 dys.	Mustered out with company Aug. 31, 1864.
Baker, Samuel	....do....	37	May 2, 1864	100 dys.	
Bernard, William	....do....	18	May 2, 1864	100 dys.	Mustered out with company Aug. 31, 1864.
Billman, Daniel	....do....	38	May 2, 1864	100 dys.	Captured Aug. 13, 1864, in action near Berryville, Va.; mustered out April 28, 1865, at Columbus, O., by order of War Department.
Bovie, Adam	....do....	21	May 2, 1864	100 dys.	Captured Aug. 13, 1864, in action near Berryville, Va.; died Dec. 16, 1864, in Rebel Prison at Salisbury, N. C.
Bowen, John	....do....	42	May 2, 1864	100 dys.	Mustered out with company Aug. 31, 1864.
Bowsher, Miller	....do....	18	May 2, 1864	100 dys.	Missing Aug. 13, 1864, in action near Berryville, Va.; died Oct. 14, 1864, at Annapolis, Maryland.
Brooke, Alfred J	....do....	[illegible]	May 2, 1864	100 dys.	Mustered out with company Aug. 31, 1864.
Brosius, Joseph	....do....	39	May 2, 1864	100 dys.	Mustered out with company Aug. 31, 1864.
Burns, Israel	....do....	[illegible]	May 2, 1864	100 dys.	Captured Aug. 13, 1864, in action near Berryville, Va.; died Nov. 12, 1864, in Rebel Prison at Salisbury, N. C.
Buttolph, Harrison	....do....	18	May 2, 1864	100 dys.	Mustered out with company Aug. 31, 1864.
Cook, William B	....do....	20	May 2, 1864	100 dys.	Mustered out with company Aug. 31, 1864.
Cunningham, Hiram	....do....	37	May 2, 1864	100 dys.	Mustered out with company Aug. 31, 1864.
Edmonds, Sylvatus L	....do....	25	May 2, 1864	100 dys.	Captured Aug. 13, 1864, in action near Berryville, Va.; died March 25, 1865, at Wheeling, West Virginia.
Ensminger, Bramwell	....do....	20	May 2, 1864	100 dys.	Captured Aug. 13, 1864, in action near Berryville, Va.; died Nov. 12, 1864, in Rebel Prison at Salisbury, N. C.
Fairbanks, Oliver	....do....	18	May 2, 1864	100 dys.	
Faylor, John J	....do....	30	May 2, 1864	100 dys.	Mustered out with company Aug. 31, 1864.
Fulmer, Lyman	....do....	18	May 2, 1864	100 dys.	Captured Aug. 13, 1864, in action near Berryville, Va.; died Nov. 27, 1864, in Rebel Prison at Salisbury, N. C.
Furgurson, William H	....do....	35	May 2, 1864	100 dys.	Mustered out with company Aug. 31, 1864.
Harmon, John	....do....	16	May 2, 1864	100 dys.	Mustered out with company Aug. 31, 1864.

Names.	Rank.	Age.	Date of Entering the Service.	Period of Service.	Remarks.
Hastings, Charles	Private	22	May 2, 1864	100 dys.	Wounded Aug. 13, 1864, in action near Berryville, Va. No further record found.
Hemminger, David	do	18	May 2, 1864	100 dys.	Mustered out with company Aug. 31, 1864.
Hoffman, Aaron B.	do	19	May 2, 1864	100 dys.	Mustered out with company Aug. 31, 1864.
Holland, John J.	do	24	May 2, 1864	100 dys.	Mustered out with company Aug. 31, 1864.
Hoot, Henry	do	37	May 2, 1864	100 dys.	Mustered out with company Aug. 31, 1864.
Hoyles, Thomas	do	29	May 2, 1864	100 dys.	Mustered out with company Aug. 31, 1864; also borne on rolls as Thomas Hoils.
Hughey, Samuel	do	36	May 2, 1864	100 dys	Captured Aug. 13, 1864, in action near Berryville, Va.; mustered out May 19, 1865, at Columbus, O., by order of War Department.
Hughey, Thomas	do	35	May 2, 1864	100 dys.	Discharged May 12, 1864, at Tod Barracks, Columbus, O.
Hunt, Charles	do	32	May 2, 1864	100 dys.	Captured Aug. 13, 1864, in action near Berryville, Va.; mustered out Nov. 25, 1864, at Columbus, O., by order of War Department.
Hunt, Thomas	do	37	May 2, 1864	100 dys.	Mustered out with company Aug. 31, 1864.
Jackson, Thomas J	do	19	May 2, 1864	100 dys.	Captured Aug. 13, 1864, in action near Berryville, Va.; died Dec. 21, 1864, in Rebel Prison at Salisbury, N. C.
Keyzer, Samuel	do	29	May 2, 1864	100 dys.	Captured Aug. 13, 1864, in action near Berryville, Va.; died Oct. 20, 1864, at Annapolis, Maryland.
Kirts, Isaac	do	26	May 2, 1864	100 dys.	Wounded Aug. 13, 1864, in action near Berryville, Va.; mustered out with company Aug. 31, 1864; also borne on rolls as Isaac Kiets.
Lesher, Aaron	do	18	May 2, 1864	100 dys.	Mustered out with company Aug. 31, 1864.
Lloyd, Albert C	do	18	May 2, 1864	100 dys.	Mustered out with company Aug. 31, 1864.
Long, John W	do	37	May 2, 1864	100 dys.	Killed Aug. 13, 1864, in action near Berryville, Va.
Ludwig, David Park	do	18	May 2, 1864	100 dys.	Mustered out with company Aug. 31, 1864.
Lusk, David	do	29	May 2, 1864	100 dys.	Captured Aug. 13, 1864, in action near Berryville, Va., paroled Oct. 7, 1864; mustered out Dec. 8, 1864, at Columbus, O.
McLaughlin, Uriah T	do	42	May 2, 1864	100 dys.	Absent, sick, in hospital at Washington, D. C., Aug. 31, 1864. No further record found.
Mars, John	do	38	May 2, 1864	100 dys.	Captured Aug. 13, 1864, in action near Berryville, Va.; died Oct. 20, 1864, in Rebel Prison at Salisbury, N. C.
Mason, William	do	36	May 2, 1864	100 dys.	Mustered out with company Aug. 31, 1864.
Menz, John	do	31	May 2, 1864	100 dys.	Mustered out with company Aug. 31, 1864.
Morgan, John	do	26	May 2, 1864	100 dys.	Captured Aug. 13, 1864, in action near Berryville, Va.; died Oct. 24, 1864, in Rebel Prison at Salisbury, N. C.
Myers, Charles	do	18	May 2, 1864	100 dys.	Captured Aug. 13, 1864, in action near Berryville, Va.; died Jan. 10, 1865, in Rebel Prison at Salisbury, N. C.
Ostrander, Hiram	do	28	May 2, 1864	100 dys.	Mustered out with company Aug. 31, 1864.
Page, Allison	do	28	May 2, 1864	100 dys.	Mustered out with company Aug. 31, 1864.
Palmer, Randolph	do	44	May 2, 1864	100 dys.	Died July 14, 1864, in hospital at Relay Barracks, Maryland.
Peters, William S	do	22	May 2, 1864	100 dys.	Mustered out with company Aug. 31, 1864.
Phister, David	do	23	May 2, 1864	100 dys.	Mustered out with company Aug. 31, 1864.
Rainbow, Thomas	do	27	May 2, 1864	100 dys.	Captured Aug. 13, 1864, in action near Berryville, Va.; died Oct. 4, 1864, in Rebel Prison at Richmond, Va.
Ringer, John A	do	37	May 2, 1864	100 dys.	Missing Aug. 13, 1864, in action near Berryville, Va. No further record found.
Ripple, Joseph	do	28	May 2, 1864	100 dys.	Mustered out with company Aug. 31, 1864; also borne on rolls as Joseph Riffe.
Ruble, John	do	38	May 2, 1864	100 dys.	Captured Aug. 13, 1864, in action near Berryville, Va.; died Dec. 6, 1864, in Rebel Prison at Salisbury, N. C.
Sage, Orrin W	do	34	May 2, 1864	100 dys.	Captured Aug. 13, 1864, in action near Berryville, Va.; died Dec. 1, 1864, in Rebel Prison at Salisbury, N. C.
Sharp, Christopher	do	41	May 2, 1864	100 dys.	Mustered out with company Aug. 31, 1864.
Sheller, Conrad	do	37	May 2, 1864	100 dys.	Mustered out with company Aug. 31, 1864.
Shutt, William	do	37	May 2, 1864	100 dys.	Captured Aug. 15, 1864, in action near Berryville, Va.; died Oct. 4, 1864, in Rebel Prison at Richmond, Va.
Sigar, Joseph H	do	35	May 2, 1864	100 dys.	Mustered out with company Aug. 31, 1864.
Smith, Hiram S	do	18	May 2, 1864	100 dys.	Captured Aug. 13, 1864, in action near Berryville, Va.; paroled Feb. 27, 1865, at Northeast Ferry, N. C. No further record found.
Smith, Thomas	do	40	May 2, 1864	100 dys.	Mustered out with company Aug. 31, 1864.
Stephens, William L	do	34	May 2, 1864	100 dys.	Captured Aug. 13, 1864, in action near Berryville, Va.; died Nov. 13, 1864, at Annapolis, Maryland.
VanVoorhis, James M.	do	19	May 2, 1864	100 dys.	Mustered out with company Aug. 31, 1864.
Wideman, Joseph	do	41	May 2, 1864	100 dys.	Mustered out with company Aug. 31, 1864.

145th Regiment Ohio Volunteer Infantry.

ONE HUNDRED DAYS' SERVICE.

THIS Regiment was organized at Camp Chase, O., May 12, 1864, to se one hundred days. It was composed of the Twenty-first Battalion, O National Guard, from Delaware County, and the Thirteenth Battalion, O National Guard, from Erie County. The Regiment was immediately orde to Washington City, and, on its arrival, was assigned to General Augur as rison for Forts Whipple, Woodbury, Tillinghast, and Albany, comprising southern defenses of Washington on Arlington Heights. The service of Regiment consisted principally of garrison and fatigue duty. On the 20tl August, the time of its enlistment having expired, the Regiment was mov by the Baltimore and Ohio Railroad, to Baltimore, and thence by the North Central, Pennsylvania Central, etc., to Camp Chase, where, on the 24th August, it was mustered out on expiration of term of service.

145TH REGIMENT OHIO VOLUNTEER INFANTRY.

FIELD AND STAFF.

ed in May 12, 1864, at Camp Chase, O., by H. Douglas, Captain 18th Infantry, U. S. A. Mustered out Aug. 24, 1864, at Camp Chase, O., by John C. King, Captain 16th Infantry, U. S. A.

	Rank.	Age.	Date of Entering the Service.	Period of Service.	Remarks.
......	Colonel.	24	May 2, 1864	100 dys.	Mustered out with regiment Aug. 24, 1864.
......	Lt. Col.	41	May 2, 1864	100 dys.	Mustered out with regiment Aug. 24, 1864.
......	Major.	38	May 2, 1864	100 dys.	Mustered out with regiment Aug. 24, 1864.
......	Surgeon.	41	May 2, 1864	100 dys.	Mustered out with regiment Aug. 24, 1864.
......	Asst. Sur.	36	May 2, 1864	100 dys.	Mustered out with regiment Aug. 24, 1864.
......	....do....	32	May 2, 1864	100 dys.	Mustered out with regiment Aug. 24, 1864.
......	Adjutant	29	May 2, 1864	100 dys.	Mustered out with regiment Aug. 24, 1864.
..	R. Q. M.	37	May 2, 1864	100 dys.	Mustered out with regiment Aug. 24, 1864.
..	Chaplain	42	May 2, 1864	100 dys.	Mustered out with regiment Aug. 24, 1864.
..	Q. M. S.	26	May 2, 1864	100 dys.	Mustered out with regiment Aug. 24, 1864.
..	Com. Ser.	23	May 2, 1864	100 dys.	Promoted from private Co. E May 11, 1864; mustered out with regiment Aug. 24, 1864.
.	Hos. St'd.	18	May 2, 1864	100 dys.	Promoted from private Co. B May 11, 1864; mustered out with regiment Aug. 24, 1864.
J, Sherwood......	Prin. Mus.	24	May 2, 1864	100 dys.	Promoted from private Co. C May 11, 1864; mustered out with regiment Aug. 24, 1864.

COMPANY A.

ed in May 12, 1864, at Camp Chase, O., by H. Douglas, Captain 18th Infantry, U. S. A. Mustered out Aug. 24, 1864, at Camp Chase, O., by John C. King, Captain 16th Infantry, U. S. A.

1 M. Jones........	Captain.	24	May 2, 1864	100 dys.	Mustered out with company Aug. 24, 1864.
. Perry...........	1st Lieut.	28	May 2, 1864	100 dys.	Mustered out with company Aug. 24, 1864.
. Harmon.......	2d Lieut.	33	May 2, 1864	100 dys.	Mustered out with company Aug. 24, 1864.
Wolfley....	1st Sergt.	30	May 2, 1864	100 dys.	Mustered out with company Aug. 24, 1864.
bott..............	Sergeant.	25	May 2, 1864	100 dys.	Mustered out with company Aug. 24, 1864.
P. Adams........	....do....	25	May 2, 1864	100 dys.	Mustered out with company Aug. 24, 1864.
. Griffith...........	....do....	22	May 2, 1864	100 dys.	Mustered out with company Aug. 24, 1864.
. Kyle.....	....do....	21	May 2, 1864	100 dys.	Mustered out with company Aug. 24, 1864.
. Utz.....	Corporal.	25	May 2, 1864	100 dys.	Mustered out with company Aug. 24, 1864.
Powell.......	....do....	29	May 2, 1864	100 dys.	Mustered out with company Aug. 24, 1864.
eld................	....do....	24	May 2, 1864	100 dys.	Mustered out with company Aug. 24, 1864.
Thomas...........	....do....	23	May 2, 1864	100 dys.	Mustered out with company Aug. 24, 1864.
W. Jones.	....do....	38	May 2, 1864	100 dys.	Mustered out with company Aug. 24, 1864.
Burford...	....do....	22	May 2, 1864	100 dys.	Mustered out with company Aug. 24, 1864.
Curren..........	....do....	24	May 2, 1864	100 dys.	Mustered out with company Aug. 24, 1864.
Perry..........	....do....	23	May 2, 1864	100 dys.	Mustered out with company Aug. 24, 1864.
Baker......	Musician	18	May 2, 1864	100 dys.	Mustered out with company Aug. 24, 1864.
Lojard..........	....do....	18	May 2, 1864	100 dys.	Mustered out with company Aug. 24, 1864.
. Francis M.......	Private.	18	May 2, 1864	100 dys.	Mustered out with company Aug. 24, 1864.
. John S...........	....do....	23	May 2, 1864	100 dys.	Mustered out with company Aug. 24, 1864.
Benjamin..........	....do....	20	May 2, 1864	100 dys.	Mustered out with company Aug. 24, 1864.
Charles W.........	....do....	18	May 2, 1864	100 dys.	Mustered out with company Aug. 24, 1864.
., Cornelius.......	....do....	44	May 2, 1864	100 dys.	Mustered out with company Aug. 24, 1864.
homas P..........	....do....	21	May 2, 1864	100 dys.	Mustered out with company Aug. 24, 1864.
gham, James S. C	....do....	19	May 2, 1864	100 dys.	Mustered out with company Aug. 24, 1864.
. Henry W.........	....do....	20	May 2, 1864	100 dys.	Mustered out with company Aug. 24, 1864.
Benjamin F........	....do....	18	May 2, 1864	100 dys.	Mustered out with company Aug. 24, 1864.
Thomas F..........	....do....	37	May 2, 1864	100 dys.	Mustered out with company Aug. 24, 1864.
Albert..............	....do....	20	May 2, 1864	100 dys.	Mustered out with company Aug. 24, 1864.
or, George T.......	....do....	23	May 2, 1864	100 dys.	Mustered out with company Aug. 24, 1864.
., James W.....	....do....	36	May 2, 1864	100 dys.	Mustered out with company Aug. 24, 1864.
., Joseph..........	....do....	20	May 2, 1864	100 dys.	Mustered out with company Aug. 24, 1864.
Owen............	....do....	18	May 2, 1864	100 dys.	Mustered out with company Aug. 24, 1864.
Francis...........	....do....	23	May 2, 1864	100 dys.	Mustered out with company Aug. 24, 1864.
James............	....do....	22	May 2, 1864	100 dys.	Mustered out with company Aug. 24, 1864.
., Matthew C......	....do....	28	May 2, 1864	100 dys.	Mustered out with company Aug. 24, 1864.
., Moses H........	....do....	23	May 2, 1864	100 dys.	Mustered out with company Aug. 24, 1864.

Names.	Rank.	Age.	Date of Entering the Service.	Period of Service.	Remarks.
cob S. Miller	Corporal.	38	May 2, 1864	100 dys.	Mustered out with company Aug. 24, 1864.
hn M. Cole	....do....	23	May 2, 1864	100 dys.	Died Aug. 12, 1864, at Regimental Hospital, near Fort Woodbury, Va.
mes J. Sherwood	Musician	34	May 2, 1864	100 dys.	Promoted to Principal Musician May 11, 1864.
ban Jaycox	....do....	12	May 2, 1864	100 dys.	Mustered out with company Aug. 24, 1864.
hwell, Richard	Private..	31	May 2, 1864	100 dys.	Mustered out with company Aug. 24, 1864.
rtlett, George	....do....	21	May 2, 1864	100 dys.	Mustered out with company Aug. 24, 1864.
shop, Levi	....do....	33	May 2, 1864	100 dys.	Mustered out with company Aug. 24, 1864.
ack, Wilson	....do....	19	May 2, 1864	100 dys.	Mustered out with company Aug. 24, 1864.
rch, Adriel	....do....	20	May 2, 1864	100 dys.	Mustered out with company Aug. 24, 1864.
ers, Alfred G	....do....	25	May 2, 1864	100 dys.	Discharged May 11, 1864, at Camp Chase, O., on Surgeon's certificate of disability.
rter, William	....do....	30	May 2, 1864	100 dys.	Mustered out with company Aug. 24, 1864.
ark, Cicero V	....do....	19	May 2, 1864	100 dys.	Mustered out with company Aug. 24, 1864.
veland, S. Hall, Jr	....do....	18	May 2, 1864	100 dys.	Mustered out with company Aug. 24, 1864.
sart, Thomas	....do....	29	May 2, 1864	100 dys.	Mustered out with company Aug. 24, 1864.
ow, Joseph E	....do....	22	May 2, 1864	100 dys.	Mustered out with company Aug. 24, 1864.
nningham, John M	....do....	23	May 2, 1864	100 dys.	Mustered out with company Aug. 24, 1864.
rst, Milo J	....do....	23	May 2, 1864	100 dys.	Mustered out with company Aug. 24, 1864.
venport, John	....do....	39	May 2, 1864	100 dys.	Mustered out with company Aug. 24, 1864.
fany, Edward	....do....	37	May 2, 1864	100 dys.	Mustered out with company Aug. 24, 1864.
ummond, Lemuel	....do....	25	May 2, 1864	100 dys.	Mustered out with company Aug. 24, 1864.
maker, Frederick	....do....	33	May 2, 1864	100 dys.	Mustered out with company Aug. 24, 1864.
ulkner, J. Clark	....do....	24	May 2, 1864	100 dys.	Mustered out with company Aug. 24, 1864.
ster, George	....do....	39	May 2, 1864	100 dys.	Mustered out with company Aug. 24, 1864.
key, Jacob	....do....	23	May 2, 1864	100 dys.	Died June 30, 1864, at Regimental Hospital, near Ft. Woodbury, Va.
guson James	....do....	37	May 2, 1864	100 dys.	Mustered out with company Aug. 24, 1864.
Matthew W	....do....	18	May 2, 1864	100 dys.	Mustered out with company Aug. 24, 1864.
ett, Charles	....do....	23	May 2, 1864	100 dys.	Mustered out with company Aug. 24, 1864.
ett, Edward H	....do....	20	May 2, 1864	100 dys.	Mustered out with company Aug. 24, 1864.
ze, Adam C	....do....	27	May 2, 1864	100 dys.	Mustered out with company Aug. 24, 1864.
William W	....do....	23	May 2, 1864	100 dys.	Mustered out with company Aug. 24, 1864.
emiee John	....do....	29	May 2, 1864	100 dys.	Mustered out with company Aug. 24, 1864.
Albert F	....do....	23	May 2, 1864	100 dys.	Mustered out with company Aug. 24, 1864.
Nehemiah C	....do....	26	May 2, 1864	100 dys.	Mustered out with company Aug. 24, 1864.
Herman W	....do....	32	May 2, 1864	100 dys.	Mustered out with company Aug. 24, 1864.
William	....do....	20	May 2, 1864	100 dys.	Mustered out with company Aug. 24, 1864.
Gustavus	....do....	..	May 2, 1864	100 dys.	Discharged May 7, 1864, at Delaware, O.
John	....do....	30	May 2, 1864	100 dys.	Discharged to date June 17, 1864, at Fort Albany, Va.
Nicholas	....do....	20	May 2, 1864	100 dys.	Mustered out with company Aug. 24, 1864.
Winfield S	....do....	18	May 2, 1864	100 dys.	Mustered out with company Aug. 24, 1864.
Henry A	....do....	28	May 2, 1864	100 dys.	Mustered out with company Aug. 24, 1864.
Chauncey	....do....	30	May 2, 1864	100 dys.	Mustered out with company Aug. 24, 1864.
[illegible]	....do....	21	May 2, 1864	100 dys.	Mustered out with company Aug. 24, 1864.
[illegible] W	....do....	22	May 2, 1864	100 dys.	Mustered out with company Aug. 24, 1864.
Nehemiah	....do....	33	May 2, 1864	100 dys.	Mustered out with company Aug. 24, 1864.
[illegible]	....do....	28	May 2, 1864	100 dys.	Mustered out with company Aug. 24, 1864.
[illegible]	....do....	30	May 2, 1864	100 dys.	Mustered out with company Aug. 24, 1864.
[illegible]	....do....	27	May 2, 1864	100 dys.	Mustered out with company Aug. 24, 1864.
[illegible]	....do....	26	May 2, 1864	100 dys.	Mustered out with company Aug. 24, 1864.
[illegible]	....do....	34	May 2, 1864	100 dys.	Mustered out with company Aug. 24, 1864.
[illegible]	....do....	25	May 2, 1864	100 dys.	Mustered out with company Aug. 24, 1864.
[illegible]	....do....	23	May 2, 1864	100 dys.	Mustered out with company Aug. 24, 1864.
[illegible]	....do....	30	May 2, 1864	100 dys.	Mustered out with company Aug. 24, 1864.
[illegible] A	....do....	35	May 2, 1864	100 dys.	Mustered out with company Aug. 24, 1864.
[illegible] H	....do....	23	May 2, 1864	100 dys.	Mustered out with company Aug. 24, 1864.
[illegible]	....do....	33	May 2, 1864	100 dys.	Mustered out with company Aug. 24, 1864.
[illegible] D	....do....	20	May 2, 1864	100 dys.	Mustered out with company Aug. 24, 1864.
[illegible] A	....do....	18	May 2, 1864	100 dys.	Mustered out with company Aug. 24, 1864.
[illegible] A	....do....	29	May 2, 1864	100 dys.	Mustered out with company Aug. 24, 1864.
[illegible]	....do....	18	May 2, 1864	100 dys.	Mustered out with company Aug. 24, 1864.
[illegible]	....do....	21	May 2, 1864	100 dys.	Mustered out with company Aug. 24, 1864.
[illegible]	....do....	30	May 2, 1864	100 dys.	Mustered out with company Aug. 24, 1864.
[illegible]	....do....	36	May 2, 1864	100 dys.	Mustered out with company Aug. 24, 1864.
[illegible] A	....do....	18	May 2, 1864	100 dys.	Mustered out with company Aug. 24, 1864.
[illegible]	....do....	42	May 2, 1864	100 dys.	Mustered out with company Aug. 24, 1864.
[illegible]	....do....	23	May 2, 1864	100 dys.	Mustered out with company Aug. 24, 1864.
[illegible] W	....do....	23	May 2, 1864	100 dys.	Mustered out with company Aug. 24, 1864.
[illegible]	....do....	41	May 2, 1864	100 dys.	Mustered out with company Aug. 24, 1864.
[illegible]	....do....	20	May 2, 1864	100 dys.	Mustered out with company Aug. 24, 1864.
[illegible]	....do....	27	May 2, 1864	100 dys.	Mustered out with company Aug. 24, 1864.
[illegible]	....do....	43	May 2, 1864	100 dys.	Mustered out with company Aug. 24, 1864.
[illegible]	....do....	23	May 2, 1864	100 dys.	Mustered out with company Aug. 24, 1864.

COMPANY D.

[M]ay 12, 1864, at Camp Chase, O., by H. Douglas, Captain 18th Infantry, U. S. A. Mustered out Aug. 24, 1864, at Camp Chase, O., by John C. King, Captain 16th Infantry, U. S. A.

	Rank.	Age.	Date of Entering the Service.	Period of Service.	Remarks.
...wford	Captain.	39	May 2, 1864	100 dys.	Mustered out with company Aug. 24, 1864.
	1st Lieut.	25	May 2, 1864	100 dys.	Mustered out with company Aug. 24, 1864.
	2d Lieut.	23	May 2, 1864	100 dys.	Mustered out with company Aug. 24, 1864.
...y	1st Sergt.	24	May 2, 1864	100 dys.	Mustered out with company Aug. 24, 1864.
	Sergeant.	20	May 2, 1864	100 dys.	Mustered out with company Aug. 24, 1864.
...mond	do.	21	May 2, 1864	100 dys.	Mustered out with company Aug. 24, 1864.
	do.	23	May 2, 1864	100 dys.	Mustered out with company Aug. 24, 1864.
...lo	do.	34	May 2, 1864	100 dys.	Mustered out with company Aug. 24, 1864.
...n	Corporal.	18	May 2, 1864	100 dys.	Mustered out with company Aug. 24, 1864.
	do.	29	May 2, 1864	100 dys.	Mustered out with company Aug. 24, 1864.
	do.	28	May 2, 1864	100 dys.	Mustered out with company Aug. 24, 1864.
	do.	36	May 2, 1864	100 dys.	Mustered out with company Aug. 24, 1864.
...on	do.	25	May 2, 1864	100 dys.	Mustered out with company Aug. 24, 1864.
...way	do.	22	May 2, 1864	100 dys.	Mustered out with company Aug. 24, 1864.
	do.	32	May 2, 1864	100 dys.	Mustered out with company Aug. 24, 1864.
	do.	40	May 2, 1864	100 dys.	Mustered out with company Aug. 24, 1864.
	Private.	24	May 2, 1864	100 dys.	Mustered out with company Aug. 24, 1864.
	do.	19	May 2, 1864	100 dys.	Mustered out with company Aug. 24, 1864.
	do.	18	May 2, 1864	100 dys.	Mustered out with company Aug. 24, 1864.
	do.	21	May 2, 1864	100 dys.	Mustered out with company Aug. 24, 1864.
...n	do.	26	May 2, 1864	100 dys.	Mustered out with company Aug. 24, 1864.
...ob L.	do.	21	May 2, 1864	100 dys.	Mustered out with company Aug. 24, 1864.
	do.	25	May 2, 1864	100 dys.	Mustered out with company Aug. 24, 1864.
	do.	26	May 2, 1864	100 dys.	Mustered out with company Aug. 24, 1864.
	do.	29	May 2, 1864	100 dys.	Mustered out with company Aug. 24, 1864.
	do.	18	May 2, 1864	100 dys.	Mustered out with company Aug. 24, 1864.
	do.	19	May 2, 1864	100 dys.	Mustered out with company Aug. 24, 1864.
	do.	25	May 2, 1864	100 dys.	Mustered out with company Aug. 24, 1864.
...neser	do.	18	May 2, 1864	100 dys.	Mustered out with company Aug. 24, 1864.
	do.	24	May 2, 1864	100 dys.	Mustered out with company Aug. 24, 1864.
	do.	24	May 2, 1864	100 dys.	Mustered out with company Aug. 24, 1864.
	do.	18	May 2, 1864	100 dys.	Mustered out with company Aug. 24, 1864.
	do.	19	May 2, 1864	100 dys.	Mustered out with company Aug. 24, 1864.
	do.	25	May 2, 1864	100 dys.	Absent, sick, at Camp Chase O., Aug. 23, 1864. No further record found.
	do.	19	May 2, 1864	100 dys.	Mustered out with company Aug. 24, 1864.
	do.	18	May 2, 1864	100 dys.	Mustered out with company Aug. 24, 1864.
	do.	18	May 2, 1864	100 dys.	Mustered out with company Aug. 24, 1864.
	do.	23	May 2, 1864	100 dys.	Mustered out with company Aug. 24, 1864.
	do.	37	May 2, 1864	100 dys.	Mustered out with company Aug. 24, 1864.
	do.	22	May 2, 1864	100 dys.	Mustered out with company Aug. 24, 1864.
	do.	19	May 2, 1864	100 dys.	Mustered out with company Aug. 24, 1864.
	do.	24	May 2, 1864	100 dys.	Mustered out with company Aug. 24, 1864.
	do.	30	May 2, 1864	100 dys.	Mustered out with company Aug. 24, 1864.
	do.	30	May 2, 1864	100 dys.	Mustered out with company Aug. 24, 1864.
	do.	24	May 2, 1864	100 dys.	Mustered out with company Aug. 24, 1864.
	do.	20	May 2, 1864	100 dys.	Mustered out with company Aug. 24, 1864.
	do.	18	May 2, 1864	100 dys.	Mustered out with company Aug. 24, 1864.
	do.	21	May 2, 1864	100 dys.	Mustered out with company Aug. 24, 1864.
	do.	36	May 2, 1864	100 dys.	Mustered out with company Aug. 24, 1864.
	do.	18	May 2, 1864	100 dys.	Mustered out with company Aug. 24, 1864.
	do.	32	May 2, 1864	100 dys.	Mustered out with company Aug. 24, 1864.
	do.	43	May 2, 1864	100 dys.	Mustered out with company Aug. 24, 1864.
...njamin P.	do.	19	May 2, 1864	100 dys.	Mustered out with company Aug. 24, 1864.
...ezer U.	do.	26	May 2, 1864	100 dys.	Mustered out with company Aug. 24, 1864.
...nuel	do.	25	May 2, 1864	100 dys.	Mustered out with company Aug. 24, 1864.
...lexander	do.	20	May 2, 1864	100 dys.	On muster-in roll. No further record found.
...s	do.	22	May 2, 1864	100 dys.	Mustered out with company Aug. 24, 1864; also borne on rolls as Thomas Broyer.
...ard T.	do.	18	May 2, 1864	100 dys.	Mustered out with company Aug. 24, 1864.
...muel	do.	29	May 2, 1864	100 dys.	Mustered out with company Aug. 24, 1864.
...les	do.	18	May 2, 1864	100 dys.	Mustered out with company Aug. 24, 1864.
...A.	do.	21	May 2, 1864	100 dys.	Mustered out with company Aug. 24, 1864.
...er	do.	18	May 2, 1864	100 dys.	Mustered out with company Aug. 24, 1864.
...ool	do.	18	May 2, 1864	100 dys.	Mustered out with company Aug. 24, 1864.
...topher	do.	34	May 2, 1864	100 dys.	Mustered out with company Aug. 24, 1864.
	do.	33	May 2, 1864	100 dys.	Mustered out with company Aug. 24, 1864.
	do.	24	May 2, 1864	100 dys.	Mustered out with company Aug. 24, 1864.
...e F.	do.	39	May 2, 1864	100 dys.	Mustered out with company Aug. 24, 1864.
...y P.	do.	19	May 2, 1864	100 dys.	Mustered out with company Aug. 24, 1864.
...H.	do.	18	May 2, 1864	100 dys.	Mustered out with company Aug. 24, 1864.
...l	do.	23	May 2, 1864	100 dys.	Mustered out with company Aug. 24, 1864.
...n	do.	42	May 2, 1864	100 dys.	Mustered out with company Aug. 24, 1864.
...derick	do.	18	May 2, 1864	100 dys.	Mustered out with company Aug. 24, 1864.
...ard	do.	21	May 2, 1864	100 dys.	Mustered out with company Aug. 24, 1864.
...rles	do.	33	May 2, 1864	100 dys.	Mustered out with company Aug. 24, 1864.
	do.	16	May 2, 1864	100 dys.	Mustered out with company Aug. 24, 1864.

Names.	Rank.	Age.	Date of Entering the Service.	Period of Service.	Remarks.
Swope, Henry M	Private..	32	May 2, 1864	100 dys.	Mustered out with company Aug. 24, 186
Thomas, Wesley	....do....	30	May 2, 1864	100 dys.	Mustered out with company Aug. 24, 186
Trumbull, Oliver P	....do....	36	May 2, 1864	100 dys.	Mustered out with company Aug. 24, 186
Tuller, Irwin	....do....	34	May 2, 1864	100 dys.	Mustered out with company Aug. 24, 186
Van Horne, Girard G	....do....	24	May 2, 1864	100 dys.	Mustered out with company Aug. 24, 186
Vought, John F	....do....	18	May 2, 1864	100 dys.	Mustered out with company Aug. 24, 186
Wait, Addison	....do....	18	May 2, 1864	100 dys.	Mustered out with company Aug. 24, 186
Warner, Joseph	....do....	18	May 2, 1864	100 dys.	Mustered out with company Aug. 24, 186
Watkins, Nathaniel D	....do....	22	May 2, 1864	100 dys.	Mustered out with company Aug. 24, 186
Wise, Jacob	....do....	18	May 2, 1864	100 dys.	Mustered out with company Aug. 24, 186
Woltley, Silas D	....do....	18	May 2, 1864	100 dys.	Mustered out with company Aug. 24, 186

COMPANY E.

Mustered in May 12, 1864, at Camp Chase, O., by H. Douglas, Captain 18th Infantry, U. S. A. Mustere Aug. 24, 1864, at Camp Chase, O., by John C. King, Captain 16th Infantry, U. S. A.

Names.	Rank.	Age.	Date of Entering the Service.	Period of Service.	Remarks.
Richard W. Reynolds	Captain.	43	May 2, 1864	100 dys.	Mustered out with company Aug. 24, 186
John A. Cone	1st Lieut.	28	May 2, 1864	100 dys.	Mustered out with company Aug. 24, 186
John D. VanDeman	2d Lieut.	32	May 2, 1864	100 dys.	Mustered out with company Aug. 24, 186
John T. Evans	1st Sergt.	24	May 2, 1864	100 dys.	Mustered out with company Aug. 24, 186
Aaron Frantz	Sergeant.	29	May 2, 1864	100 dys.	Mustered out with company Aug. 24, 186
Samuel W. Torrence	....do....	34	May 2, 1864	100 dys.	Mustered out with company Aug. 24, 186
Thomas E. Powell	....do....	22	May 2, 1864	100 dys.	Mustered out with company Aug. 24, 186
Johnson C. Brecht	....do....	23	May 2, 1864	100 dys.	Mustered out with company Aug. 24, 186
Jackson Hipple	Corporal.	29	May 2, 1864	100 dys.	Mustered out with company Aug. 24, 186
L. Byron Welch	....do....	25	May 2, 1864	100 dys.	Mustered out with company Aug. 24, 186
Frederick M. Jaynes	....do....	26	May 2, 1864	100 dys.	Mustered out with company Aug. 24, 186
Alexander Mickle	....do....	38	May 2, 1864	100 dys.	Mustered out with company Aug. 24, 186
Iebe Allen	....do....	19	May 2, 1864	100 dys.	Mustered out with company Aug. 24, 186
Joseph G. Grove	....do....	34	May 2, 1864	100 dys.	Mustered out with company Aug. 24, 186
Orra Peasley	....do....	36	May 2, 1864	100 dys.	Mustered out with company Aug. 24, 186
John Carnahan	....do....	32	May 2, 1864	100 dys.	Appointed July 19, 1864; mustered out company Aug. 24, 1864.
Elias Nafus	Musician	18	May 2, 1864	100 dys.	Mustered out with company Aug. 24, 186
Jacob Drake	....do....	24	May 2, 1864	100 dys.	Mustered out with company Aug. 24, 186
Armstrong, John S	Private..	37	May 2, 1864	100 dys.	Mustered out with company Aug. 24, 186
Arthur, Francis T	....do....	23	May 2, 1864	100 dys.	Promoted to Com. Sergeant May 11, 1864.
Bentley, Edward E	....do....	20	May 2, 1864	100 dys.	Mustered out with company Aug. 24, 186
Bickle, David	....do....	18	May 2, 1864	100 dys.	Mustered out with company Aug. 24, 186
Blymeyer, Charles	....do....	20	May 2, 1864	100 dys.	Mustered out with company Aug. 24, 186
Bradley, Theodore	....do....	18	May 2, 1864	100 dys.	Mustered out with company Aug. 24, 186
Burroughs, Daniel	....do....	21	May 2, 1864	100 dys.	Mustered out with company Aug. 24, 186
Burroughs, Ebenezer	....do....	23	May 2, 1864	100 dys.	Mustered out with company Aug. 24, 186
Byers, T. Monroe	....do....	25	May 2, 1864	100 dys.	Mustered out with company Aug. 24, 186
Chandler, William	....do....	21	May 2, 1864	100 dys.	Mustered out with company Aug. 24, 186
Cochran, William M	....do....	18	May 2, 1864	100 dys.	Mustered out with company Aug. 24, 186
Cole, Charles W	....do....	21	May 2, 1864	100 dys.	Mustered out with company Aug. 24, 186
Commager, David H	....do....	18	May 2, 1864	100 dys.	Mustered out with company Aug. 24, 186
Cox, John S	....do....	39	May 2, 1864	100 dys.	Mustered out with company Aug. 24, 186
Crawford, Charles D	....do....	18	May 2, 1864	100 dys.	Mustered out with company Aug. 24, 186
Davis, Benjamin F	....do....	18	May 2, 1864	100 dys.	Mustered out with company Aug. 24, 186
Davis, Zachariah	....do....	22	May 2, 1864	100 dys.	Mustered out with company Aug. 24, 186
Dickinson, Abram R	....do....	21	May 2, 1864	100 dys.	Mustered out with company Aug. 24, 186
Dunham, James C	....do....	24	May 2, 1864	100 dys.	Mustered out with company Aug. 24, 186
Dunham, John B	....do....	21	May 2, 1864	100 dys.	Died Aug. 7, 1864, at hospital near Fort W bury, Va.
Havens, Robert	....do....	25	May 2, 1864	100 dys.	Mustered out with company Aug. 24, 186
Head, Merrick A	....do....	19	May 2, 1864	100 dys.	Mustered out with company Aug. 24, 186
Heck, John	....do....	27	May 2, 1864	100 dys.	Mustered out with company Aug. 24, 186
Hedges, William M	....do....	21	May 2, 1864	100 dys.	Mustered out with company Aug. 24, 186
Hendrickson, Hugh	....do....	30	May 2, 1864	100 dys.	Mustered out with company Aug. 24, 186
Hicks, John S	....do....	21	May 2, 1864	100 dys.	Mustered out with company Aug. 24, 186
Hills, Howell	....do....	20	May 2, 1864	100 dys.	Mustered out with company Aug. 24, 186
Hollenbaugh, William	....do....	31	May 2, 1864	100 dys.	Mustered out with company Aug. 24, 186
Houtz, Tobias E	....do....	19	May 2, 1864	100 dys.	Mustered out with company Aug. 24, 186
Houtz, David F	....do....	44	May 2, 1864	100 dys.	Mustered out with company Aug. 24, 186
Hults, Charles	....do....	21	May 2, 1864	100 dys.	Mustered out with company Aug. 24, 186
Hurlburt, Robert F	....do....	22	May 2, 1864	100 dys.	Mustered out with company Aug. 24, 186
Joy, Minick F	....do....	18	May 2, 1864	100 dys.	Mustered out with company Aug. 24, 186
Karr, Philip M	....do....	18	May 2, 1864	100 dys.	Mustered out with company Aug. 24, 186
Keller, George	....do....	38	May 2, 1864	100 dys.	Mustered out with company Aug. 24, 186
Loveless, Daniel	....do....	23	May 2, 1864	100 dys.	Mustered out with company Aug. 24, 186
Lumbert, Freelin C	....do....	20	May 2, 1864	100 dys.	Mustered out with company Aug. 24, 186
Lumbert, Silas	....do....	18	May 2, 1864	100 dys.	Mustered out with company Aug. 24, 186
Lumbert, Wesley		23	May 2, 1864	100 dys.	Mustered out with company Aug. 24, 186
McCullough, William P	....do....	22	May 2, 1864	100 dys.	Mustered out with company Aug. 24, 186
Manley, Marcellus	....do....	22	May 2, 1864	100 dys.	Mustered out with company Aug. 24, 186
Martin, Benjamin F	....do....	19	May 2, 1864	100 dys.	Mustered out with company Aug. 24, 186
Munson, Elisha	....do....	21	May 2, 1864	100 dys.	Mustered out with company Aug. 24, 186

Names.	Rank.	Age.	Date of Entering the Service.	Period of Service.	Remarks.
[illegible], William	Private.	18	May 2, 1864	100 dys.	Mustered out with company Aug. 24, 1864.
[illegible], Homer E.	...do...	21	May 2, 1864	100 dys.	Mustered out with company Aug. 24, 1864.
[illegible], Silas G.	...do...	45	May 2, 1864	100 dys.	Mustered out with company Aug. 24, 1864.
[illegible], Robert A.	...do...	23	May 2, 1864	100 dys.	Mustered out with company Aug. 24, 1864.
[illegible], Ward L.	...do...	36	May 2, 1864	100 dys.	Mustered out with company Aug. 24, 1864.
[illegible], Jonathan	...do...	26	May 2, 1864	100 dys.	Mustered out with company Aug. 24, 1864.
[illegible], Commodore P.	...do...	19	May 2, 1864	100 dys.	Mustered out with company Aug. 24, 1864.
[illegible], John	...do...	23	May 2, 1864	100 dys.	Mustered out with company Aug. 24, 1864.
[illegible], Benjamin F.	...do...	18	May 2, 1864	100 dys.	Mustered out with company Aug. 24, 1864.
[illegible], Luther	...do...	18	May 2, 1864	100 dys.	Mustered out with company Aug. 24, 1864.
[illegible], John	...do...	36	May 2, 1864	100 dys.	Mustered out with company Aug. 24, 1864.
[illegible], William	...do...	34	May 2, 1864	100 dys.	Mustered out with company Aug. 24, 1864.
[illegible], John A.	...do...	23	May 2, 1864	100 dys.	Mustered out with company Aug. 24, 1864.
[illegible], Homer L.	...do...	29	May 2, 1864	100 dys.	Mustered out with company Aug. 24, 1864.
[illegible], Alvin D.	...do...	19	May 2, 1864	100 dys.	Mustered out with company Aug. 24, 1864.
[illegible], John H.	...do...	30	May 2, 1864	100 dys.	Mustered out with company Aug. 24, 1864.
[illegible], Newman	...do...	24	May 2, 1864	100 dys.	Mustered out with company Aug. 24, 1864.
[illegible], Henry F.	...do...	18	May 2, 1864	100 dys.	Mustered out with company Aug. 24, 1864.
[illegible], Rufus	...do...	23	May 2, 1864	100 dys.	Mustered out with company Aug. 24, 1864.
[illegible], Greville	...do...	24	May 2, 1864	100 dys.	Mustered out with company Aug. 24, 1864.
[illegible], Silas D.	...do...	20	May 2, 1864	100 dys.	Mustered out with company Aug. 24, 1864.
[illegible], Philip	...do...	44	May 2, 1864	100 dys.	Mustered out with company Aug. 24, 1864.
[illegible], Oscar	...do...	20	May 2, 1864	100 dys.	Mustered out with company Aug. 24, 1864.

COMPANY F.

Mustered in May 12, 1864, at Camp Chase, O., by H. Douglas, Captain 18th Infantry, U. S. A. Mustered out Aug. 24, 1864, at Camp Chase, O., by John C. King, Captain 16th Infantry, U. S. A.

Names.	Rank.	Age.	Date of Entering the Service.	Period of Service.	Remarks.
John J. Penfield	Captain.	37	May 2, 1864	100 dys.	Mustered out with company Aug. 24, 1864.
William [illegible] Bates	1st Lieut.	28	May 2, 1864	100 dys.	Mustered out with company Aug. 24, 1864.
[illegible] Draper	2d Lieut.	34	May 2, 1864	100 dys.	Mustered out with company Aug. 24, 1864.
Nicholas [illegible] Merry	1st Sergt.	25	May 2, 1864	100 dys.	Mustered out with company Aug. 24, 1864.
[illegible] H. Oliver	Sergeant.	21	May 2, 1864	100 dys.	Mustered out with company Aug. 24, 1864.
Peter Williams	...do...	19	May 2, 1864	100 dys.	Mustered out with company Aug. 24, 1864.
[illegible] L. Stoddard	...do...	28	May 2, 1864	100 dys.	Mustered out with company Aug. 24, 1864.
[illegible]	...do...	19	May 2, 1864	100 dys.	Mustered out with company Aug. 24, 1864.
Warren H. [illegible]	Corporal.	28	May 2, 1864	100 dys.	Mustered out with company Aug. 24, 1864.
George C. Eddy	...do...	26	May 2, 1864	100 dys.	Mustered out with company Aug. 24, 1864.
Ira Walbridge	...do...	27	May 2, 1864	100 dys.	Mustered out with company Aug. 24, 1864.
Edward L. Story	...do...	19	May 2, 1864	100 dys.	Mustered out with company Aug. 24, 1864.
[illegible]	...do...	35	May 2, 1864	100 dys.	Mustered out with company Aug. 24, 1864.
John L. Minard	...do...	20	May 2, 1864	100 dys.	Mustered out with company Aug. 24, 1864; also borne on rolls as John M. Minard.
Philip S. Remlinger	...do...	25	May 2, 1864	100 dys.	Mustered out with company Aug. 24, 1864.
William H. Beemis	...do...	28	May 2, 1864	100 dys.	Mustered out with company Aug. 24, 1864.
Allen A. Barton	Musician	18	May 2, 1864	100 dys.	Mustered out with company Aug. 24, 1864.
David D. Bogert	...do...	58	May 2, 1864	100 dys.	Mustered out with company Aug. 24, 1864.
Abble, Henry A.	Private.	19	May 2, 1864	100 dys.	Mustered out with company Aug. 24, 1864.
Alexander, Ambrose	...do...	32	May 2, 1864	100 dys.	Mustered out with company Aug. 24, 1864.
Austin, George M.	...do...	19	May 2, 1864	100 dys.	Mustered out with company Aug. 24, 1864.
Balcom, John G.	...do...	21	May 2, 1864	100 dys.	Mustered out with company Aug. 24, 1864.
Bassett, Orlando	...do...	34	May 2, 1864	100 dys.	Mustered out with company Aug. 24, 1864.
Beers, William	...do...	44	May 2, 1864	100 dys.	Mustered out with company Aug. 24, 1864.
Blakesley, Edson M.	...do...	18	May 2, 1864	100 dys.	Mustered out with company Aug. 24, 1864.
Boehler, Joseph	...do...	34	May 2, 1864	100 dys.	Mustered out with company Aug. 24, 1864.
Breckenridge, Charles F.	...do...	27	May 2, 1864	100 dys.	Mustered out with company Aug. 24, 1864.
Bristol, Monroe E.	...do...	19	May 2, 1864	100 dys.	Mustered out with company Aug. 24, 1864.
Burns, Michael D.	...do...	24	May 2, 1864	100 dys.	Mustered out with company Aug. 24, 1864.
Burns, Nicholas	...do...	25	May 2, 1864	100 dys.	Mustered out with company Aug. 24, 1864.
Cherry, George	...do...	30	May 2, 1864	100 dys.	Mustered out with company Aug. 24, 1864.
Culley, Jay G.	...do...	27	May 2, 1864	100 dys.	Mustered out with company Aug. 24, 1864.
Cunningham, Patrick T.	...do...	20	May 2, 1864	100 dys.	Mustered out with company Aug. 24, 1864.
Danforth, Edward C.	...do...	18	May 2, 1864	100 dys.	Mustered out with company Aug. 24, 1864.
Eddy, William	...do...	20	May 2, 1864	100 dys.	Died Aug. 11, 1864, in Regimental Hospital at Fort Whipple, Va.
Emmons, Eugene	...do...	19	May 2, 1864	100 dys.	Mustered out with company Aug. 24, 1864.
Erion, Lewis	...do...	44	May 2, 1864	100 dys.	Mustered out with company Aug. 24, 1864.
Gardner, Charles R.	...do...	30	May 2, 1864	100 dys.	Mustered out with company Aug. 24, 1864.
Gardner, Elbert L.	...do...	18	May 2, 1864	100 dys.	Mustered out with company Aug. 24, 1864.
Gilbert, William	...do...	25	May 2, 1864	100 dys.	Mustered out with company Aug. 24, 1864.
Gwin, Truman	...do...	20	May 2, 1864	100 dys.	Mustered out with company Aug. 24, 1864.
Hadley, George C.	...do...	18	May 2, 1864	100 dys.	Mustered out with company Aug. 24, 1864.
Harris, John D.	...do...	37	May 2, 1864	100 dys.	Mustered out with company Aug. 24, 1864.
Harter, Martin	...do...	40	May 2, 1864	100 dys.	Mustered out with company Aug. 24, 1864.
Hastings, Sanford W.	...do...	25	May 2, 1864	100 dys.	Mustered out with company Aug. 24, 1864.
Himmell, John C.	...do...	29	May 2, 1864	100 dys.	Mustered out with company Aug. 24, 1864.
Hoffman, George	...do...	34	May 2, 1864	100 dys.	Mustered out with company Aug. 24, 1864.
Horning, Philip	...do...	24	May 2, 1864	100 dys.	Mustered out with company Aug. 24, 1864.
House, Alfred W.	...do...	25	May 2, 1864	100 dys.	Mustered out with company Aug. 24, 1864.

Names.	Rank.	Age.	Date of Entering the Service.	Period of Service	Remarks.
Howe, Frederick M	Private	18	May 2, 1864	100 dys.	Mustered out with company Aug. 24, 1864.
Keen, Emanuel	...do...	33	May 2, 1864	100 dys.	Mustered out with company Aug. 24, 1864.
Klapfer, Jacob	...do...	18	May 2, 1864	100 dys.	Mustered out with company Aug. 24, 1864.
Mann, William P	...do...	25	May 2, 1864	100 dys.	Mustered out with company Aug. 24, 1864.
Minard, George	...do...	18	May 2, 1864	100 dys.	Mustered out with company Aug. 24, 1864.
Minnse, Samuel S	...do...	19	May 2, 1864	100 dys.	Mustered out with company Aug. 24, 1864.
Nichols, Benjamin F	...do...	18	May 2, 1864	100 dys.	Mustered out with company Aug. 24, 1864.
Oldson, Eli	...do...	28	May 2, 1864	100 dys.	Mustered out with company Aug. 24, 1864.
O'Leary, Mark	...do...	22	May 2, 1864	100 dys.	Mustered out with company Aug. 24, 1864.
Palmer, James E	...do...	20	May 2, 1864	100 dys.	Mustered out with company Aug. 24, 1864.
Peak, Seth	...do...	21	May 2, 1864	100 dys.	Mustered out with company Aug. 24, 1864.
Potter, Ralph	...do...	18	May 2, 1864	100 dys.	Mustered out with company Aug. 24, 1864.
Rickard, Orange J	...do...	18	May 2, 1864	100 dys.	Mustered out with company Aug. 24, 1864.
Ritz, Henry	...do...	20	May 2, 1864	100 dys.	Mustered out with company Aug. 24, 1864.
Root, Eben	...do...	23	May 2, 1864	100 dys.	Mustered out with company Aug. 24, 1864.
Roscoe, Chauncey C	...do...	20	May 2, 1864	100 dys.	Mustered out with company Aug. 24, 1864.
Roscoe, Levi, Jr	...do...	25	May 2, 1864	100 dys.	Mustered out with company Aug. 24, 1864.
Sanders, Le Roy W	...do...	37	May 2, 1864	100 dys.	Mustered out with company Aug. 24, 1864.
Sands, George	...do...	..	May 2, 1864	100 dys.	Rejected by Examining Surgeon May 2…
Schaffer, Benjamin F	...do...	21	May 2, 1864	100 dys.	Mustered out with company Aug. 24, 1864.
Schaffer, George G	...do...	23	May 2, 1864	100 dys.	Mustered out with company Aug. 24, 1864.
Schaffer, John	...do...	19	May 2, 1864	100 dys.	Mustered out with company Aug. 24, 1864.
Schaffer, William H	...do...	22	May 2, 1864	100 dys.	Mustered out with company Aug. 24, 1864.
Schull, Frederick	...do...	39	May 2, 1864	100 dys.	Mustered out with company Aug. 24, 1864.
Sherong, Nick	...do...	20	May 2, 1864	100 dys.	Mustered out with company Aug. 24, 1864.
Shupe, Clarence E	...do...	20	May 2, 1864	100 dys.	Mustered out with company Aug. 24, 1864.
Soper, David	...do...	18	May 2, 1864	100 dys.	Mustered out with company Aug. 24, 1864.
Squires, Horati L	...do...	18	May 2, 1864	100 dys.	Mustered out with company Aug. 24, 1864.
Stoddard, Horace H	...do...	25	May 2, 1864	100 dys.	Mustered out with company Aug. 24, 1864.
Taylor, J. Woodhull	...do...	35	May 2, 1864	100 dys.	Mustered out with company Aug. 24, 1864.
Terrell, Harley S	...do...	19	May 2, 1864	100 dys.	Mustered out with company Aug. 24, 1864.
Terrell, John G	...do...	18	May 2, 1864	100 dys.	Mustered out with company Aug. 24, 1864.
Thompson, Frederick F	...do...	25	May 2, 1864	100 dys.	Mustered out with company Aug. 24, 1864.
Turner, Jam.s	...do...	18	May 2, 1864	100 dys.	Mustered out with company Aug. 24, 1864.
Washburn, Timothy	...do...	27	May 2, 1864	100 dys.	Mustered out with company Aug. 24, 1864.
Wilcoxon, David J	...do...	40	May 2, 1864	100 dys.	Mustered out with company Aug. 24, 1864.
Wood, Wade	...do...	28	May 2, 1864	100 dys.	Mustered out with company Aug. 24, 1864.

COMPANY G.

Mustered in May 12, 1864, at Camp Chase, O., by H. Dorglas, Captain 18th Infantry, U. S. A. Mustered Aug. 24, 1864, at Camp Chase, O., by John C. King, Captain 16th Infantry, U. S. A.

Names.	Rank.	Age.	Date of Entering the Service.	Period of Service	Remarks.
David H. James	Captain.	28	May 2, 1864	100 dys.	Mustered out to date Aug. 24, 1864.
George W. Flem ng	1st Lieut.	25	May 2, 1864	100 dys.	Mustered out with company Aug. 24, 1864.
Ienry B. Wood	2d Lieut.	28	May 2, 1864	100 dys.	Mustered out with company Aug. 24, 1864.
Samuel Magill	1st Sergt.	41	May 2, 1864	100 dys.	Mustered out with company Aug. 24, 1864.
William H. Byington	Sergeant.	25	May 2, 1864	100 dys.	Mustered out with company Aug. 24, 1864.
Charles Knauss	...do...	33	May 2, 1864	100 dys.	Mustered out with company Aug. 24, 1864.
Joseph H. Merriott	...do...	27	May 2, 1864	100 dys.	Mustered out with company Aug. 24, 1864.
Lionel E. Harrington	...do...	22	May 2, 1864	100 dys.	Mustered out with company Aug. 24, 1864.
George Brockway	Corporal.	30	May 2, 1864	100 dys.	Mustered out with company Aug. 24, 1864.
George W. Wheat	...do...	25	May 2, 1864	100 dys.	Mustered out with company Aug. 24, 1864.
James S. Howell	...do...	18	May 2, 1864	100 dys.	Mustered out with company Aug. 24, 1864.
George W. Fernald	...do...	18	May 2, 1864	100 dys.	Mustered out with company Aug. 24, 1864.
George D. Liles	...do...	21	May 2, 1864	100 dys.	Mustered out with company Aug. 24, 1864.
Charles M. Edwards	...do...	24	May 2, 1864	100 dys.	Mustered out with company Aug. 24, 1864.
William De Puy	...do...	36	May 2, 1864	100 dys.	Mustered out with company Aug. 24, 1864.
Alfred Magill	...do...	37	May 2, 1864	100 dys.	Appointed July 13, 1864; mustered out w… company Aug. 24, 1864.
John H. Harris	Musician	26	May 2, 1864	100 dys.	Mustered out with company Aug. 24, 1864.
Frank D. Carver	...do...	18	May 2, 1864	100 dys.	Mustered out with company Aug. 24, 1864.
Bardwell, Seth E	Private	18	May 2, 1864	100 dys.	Mustered out with company Aug. 24, 1864.
Barlow, Thomas	...do...	32	May 2, 1864	100 dys.	Mustered out with company Aug. 24, 1864.
Barnard, Asa N	...do...	26	May 2, 1864	100 dys.	Mustered out with company Aug. 24, 1864.
Barnard, Franklin	...do...	26	May 2, 1864	100 dys.	Mustered out with company Aug. 24, 1864.
Beard, Emery	...do...	33	May 2, 1864	100 dys.	Transferred from Co. H May 12, 1864; must… out with company Aug. 24, 1864.
Beard, Roswell	...do...	18	May 2, 1864	100 dys.	Transferred from Co. H May 12, 1864; m… tered out with company Aug. 24, 1864.
Bates, John	...do...	36	May 2, 1864	100 dys.	Mustered out with company Aug. 24, 1864
Beaver, John H	...do...	23	May 2, 1864	100 dys.	Mustered out with company Aug. 24, 1864
Bell, Joseph C	...do...	18	May 2, 1864	100 dys.	Died Aug. 18, 1864, in Lincoln Hospital, W… ington, D. C.
Boice, Henry	...do...	20	May 2, 1864	100 dys.	Mustered out with company Aug. 24, 1864
Boone, Lemuel D	...do...	20	May 2, 1864	100 dys.	Mustered out with company Aug. 24, 1864
Boop, Daniel K	...do...	26	May 2, 1864	100 dys.	Mustered out with company Aug. 24, 1864
Brockway, Frederick	...do...	23	May 2, 1864	100 dys.	Discharged Sept. 1, 1864, at Washington, I… on Surgeon's certificate of disability.
Chidester, Samuel	...do...	37	May 2, 1864	100 dys.	Mustered out with company Aug. 24, 1864

Names.	Rank.	Age.	Date of Entering the Service.	Period of Service.	Remarks.
Curtis, Alvin V.	Private	22	May 2, 1864	100 dys.	Mustered out with company Aug. 24, 1864.
[illegible], [illegible]	do	18	May 2, 1864	100 dys.	Mustered out with company Aug. 24, 1864.
[illegible], Leonard J.	do	18	May 2, 1864	100 dys.	Mustered out with company Aug. 24, 1864.
[illegible], [illegible]	do	21	May 2, 1864	100 dys.	Mustered out with company Aug. 24, 1864.
Dunham, [illegible]	do	18	May 2, 1864	100 dys.	Transferred from Co. H May 12, 1864; mustered out with company Aug. 24, 1864.
Dunham, Thomas H.	do	18	May 2, 1864	100 dys.	Transferred from Co. H May 12, 1864; mustered out with company Aug. 24, 1864.
Eggleston, Samuel L.	do	40	May 2, 1864	100 dys.	Mustered out with company Aug. 24, 1864.
[illegible], Henry	do	20	May 2, 1864	100 dys.	Mustered out with company Aug. 24, 1864; also borne on rolls as Henry Folsinger.
Ford, Andrew	do	22	May 2, 1864	100 dys.	Mustered out with company Aug. 24, 1864.
Fulkerson, Albert	do	18	May 2, 1864	100 dys.	Mustered out with company Aug. 24, 1864.
Germain, Silas	do	25	May 2, 1864	100 dys.	Mustered out with company Aug. 24, 1864.
Harper, Sanford B.	do	22	May 2, 1864	100 dys.	Mustered out with company Aug. 24, 1864.
Harrington, Noah S.	do	21	May 2, 1864	100 dys.	Mustered out with company Aug. 24, 1864.
[illegible], James F.	do	26	May 2, 1864	100 dys.	Mustered out with company Aug. 24, 1864.
[illegible], Daniel	do	41	May 2, 1864	100 dys.	Mustered out with company Aug. 24, 1864.
Hinkley, Stephen	do	45	May 2, 1864	100 dys.	Mustered out with company Aug. 24, 1864.
[illegible], William H.	do	18	May 2, 1864	100 dys.	Mustered out with company Aug. 24, 1864.
[illegible], Andrew	do	42	May 2, 1864	100 dys.	Mustered out with company Aug. 24, 1864.
James, Nathan	do	18	May 2, 1864	100 dys.	Mustered out with company Aug. 24, 1864.
Jones, Al	do	27	May 2, 1864	100 dys.	Mustered out with company Aug. 24, 1864.
Klepper, Christian	do	19	May 2, 1864	100 dys.	Mustered out with company Aug. 24, 1864.
[illegible], James	do	20	May 2, 1864	100 dys.	Mustered out with company Aug. 24, 1864.
Livengood, James	do	23	May 2, 1864	100 dys.	Mustered out with company Aug. 24, 1864.
Marks, Jacob	do	19	May 2, 1864	100 dys.	Mustered out with company Aug. 24, 1864.
Mitchell, Augustus	do	18	May 2, 1864	100 dys.	Mustered out with company Aug. 24, 1864.
Morehouse, Charles D.	do	24	May 2, 1864	100 dys.	Sick, in general hospital at Washington, D. C. No further record found.
Potter, James C.	do	40	May 2, 1864	100 dys.	On muster-in roll. No further record found.
[illegible], Solomon	do	20	May 2, 1864	100 dys.	Mustered out with company Aug. 24, 1864.
[illegible], Charles	do	39	May 2, 1864	100 dys.	Mustered out with company Aug. 24, 1864.
[illegible], William	do	19	May 2, 1864	100 dys.	Mustered out with company Aug. 24, 1864.
[illegible], Henry	do	26	May 2, 1864	100 dys.	Mustered out with company Aug. 24, 1864.
Smith, Charles H.	do	21	May 2, 1864	100 dys.	Mustered out with company Aug. 24, 1864.
Smith, John	do	18	May 2, 1864	100 dys.	Mustered out with company Aug. 24, 1864.
Sprow, George	do	34	May 2, 1864	100 dys.	On muster-in roll. No further record found.
Sprow, Jacob	do	30	May 2, 1864	100 dys.	Mustered out with company Aug. 24, 1864.
[illegible], John	do	29	May 2, 1864	100 dys.	Mustered out with company Aug. 24, 1864.
Stroh, Jacob	do	24	May 2, 1864	100 dys.	Mustered out with company Aug. 24, 1864.
Studer, Philip	do	21	May 2, 1864	100 dys.	Mustered out with company Aug. 24, 1864.
Sweet, Oscar B.	do	27	May 2, 1864	100 dys.	Mustered out with company Aug. 24, 1864.
[illegible], Henry M.	do	44	May 2, 1864	100 dys.	Mustered out with company Aug. 24, 1864.
Vernon, Enoch S.	do	19	May 2, 1864	100 dys.	Mustered out with company Aug. 24, 1864.
[illegible], Joseph	do	33	May 2, 1864	100 dys.	Mustered out with company Aug. 24, 1864.
Warren, John H.	do	41	May 2, 1864	100 dys.	Mustered out with company Aug. 24, 1864.
Webster, Phaon	do	25	May 2, 1864	100 dys.	Mustered out with company Aug. 24, 1864.
Weitz, Peter	do	21	May 2, 1864	100 dys.	Mustered out with company Aug. 24, 1864.
Wheeler, Chauncey B.	do	44	May 2, 1864	100 dys.	Mustered out with company Aug. 24, 1864.
[illegible], John T.	do	22	May 2, 1864	100 dys.	Mustered out with company Aug. 24, 1864.
[illegible], William A.	do	19	May 2, 1864	100 dys.	Mustered out with company Aug. 24, 1864.
Yarick, Holloway F.	do	18	May 2, 1864	100 dys.	Mustered out with company Aug. 24, 1864.
Yarick, James F.	do	21	May 2, 1864	100 dys.	Reduced from Corporal July 18, 1864; mustered out with company Aug. 24, 1864.
Yarick, John E.	do	19	May 2, 1864	100 dys.	Mustered out with company Aug. 24, 1864.

COMPANY H.

Mustered in May 12, 1864, at Camp Chase, O., by H. Douglas, Captain 18th Infantry, U. S. A. Mustered out Aug. 24, 1864, at Camp Chase, O., by John C. King, Captain 16th Infantry, U. S. A.

Names.	Rank.	Age.	Date of Entering the Service.	Period of Service.	Remarks.
Archibald Freshwater	Captain.	42	May 2, 1864	100 dys.	Mustered out with company Aug. 24, 1864.
Jackson J. Post	1st Lieut.	28	May 2, 1864	100 dys.	Mustered out with company Aug. 24, 1864.
Christopher R. Caulkins	2d Lieut.	41	May 2, 1864	100 dys.	Mustered out with company Aug. 24, 1864.
Samuel Davidson	1st Sergt.	51	May 2, 1864	100 dys.	Mustered out with company Aug. 24, 1864.
Frank Black	Sergeant.	30	May 2, 1864	100 dys.	Mustered out with company Aug. 24, 1864.
William Geary	do	21	May 2, 1864	100 dys.	Mustered out with company Aug. 24, 1864.
Mason J. Merrithew	do	22	May 2, 1864	100 dys.	Mustered out with company Aug. 24, 1864.
Orson N. Cummings	do	21	May 2, 1864	100 dys.	Mustered out with company Aug. 24, 1864.
George R. Staufer	Corporal.	39	May 2, 1864	100 dys.	Mustered out with company Aug. 24, 1864.
Job D. Ladd	do	48	May 2, 1864	100 dys.	Mustered out with company Aug. 24, 1864.
George Nelson	do	40	May 2, 1864	100 dys.	Mustered out with company Aug. 24, 1864.
Milo Patterson	do	28	May 2, 1864	100 dys.	Mustered out with company Aug. 24, 1864.
Asa D. Kelsey	do	21	May 2, 1864	100 dys.	Mustered out with company Aug. 24, 1864.
Russell C. Hall	do	41	May 2, 1864	100 dys.	Mustered out with company Aug. 24, 1864.
George Rooney	do	24	May 2, 1864	100 dys.	Mustered out with company Aug. 24, 1864.
Milton S. Thompson	do	27	May 2, 1864	100 dys.	Mustered out with company Aug. 24, 1864.
George C. Flagg	Musician	26	May 2, 1864	100 dys.	Mustered out with company Aug. 24, 1864.
Elmore Dunham	do	18	May 2, 1864	100 dys.	Mustered out with company Aug. 24, 1864.

Names.	Rank.	Age.	Date of Entering the Service.	Period of Service.	
Adams, Augustus	Private	[illegible]	May 2, 1864	100 dys.	Mustered out with
Allen, Frank	do	[illegible]	May 2, 1864	100 dys.	Mustered out with
Barnes, George	do	[illegible]	May 2, 1864	100 dys.	Mustered out with
Beard, Emery	do	[illegible]	May 2, 1864	100 dys.	Transferred to Co.
Beard, Roswell	do	18	May 2, 1864	100 dys.	Transferred to Co.
Caulkins, Albert J	do	30	May 2, 1864	100 dys.	Mustered out with
Cave, Grattan B	do	[illegible]	May 2, 1864	100 dys.	Mustered out with
Chambers, Cyrus	do	[illegible]	May 2, 1864	100 dys.	Mustered out with
Chambers, William	do	[illegible]	May 2, 1864	100 dys.	Mustered out with
Clark, John	do	33	May 2, 1864	100 dys.	Mustered out with
Cole, William	do	18	May 2, 1864	100 dys.	Mustered out with
Conklin, Martin	do	21	May 2, 1864	100 dys.	Mustered out with
Cowgill, Daniel	do	35	May 2, 1864	100 dys.	Mustered out with
Crumb, Sidney W	do	21	May 2, 1864	100 dys.	Mustered out with
Davidson, Samuel A	do	18	May 2, 1864	100 dys.	Mustered out with
DeWitt, George C	do	18	May 2, 1864	100 dys.	Mustered out with
Drake, Marcus	do	21	May 2, 1864	100 dys.	Mustered out with
Dunham, Ampudia	do	18	May 2, 1864	100 dys.	Transferred to
Dunham, Thomas H	do	18	May 2, 1864	100 dys.	Transferred to
Dutcher, John H	do	32	May 2, 1864	100 dys.	Mustered out with
Elsbree, Augustus	do	32	May 2, 1864	100 dys.	Mustered out with
Elsbree, George F	do	29	May 2, 1864	100 dys.	Mustered out with
Emerson, Asa	do	38	May 2, 1864	100 dys.	Mustered out with
Ferson, James	do	28	May 2, 1864	100 dys.	Mustered out with
Geary, Samuel	do	18	May 2, 1864	100 dys.	Mustered out with
Hardin, Erastus	do	39	May 2, 1864	100 dys.	Mustered out with
Havens, Alfred	do	28	May 2, 1864	100 dys.	Mustered out with
Havens, Andrew J	do	18	May 2, 1864	100 dys.	Mustered out with
Havens, John	do	22	May 2, 1864	100 dys.	Mustered out with
Hortenstein, Jacob	do	30	May 2, 1864	100 dys.	Mustered out with
Hills, Thomas J	do	28	May 2, 1864	100 dys.	Mustered out with
Hurlbut, Noah	do	38	May 2, 1864	100 dys.	Mustered out with
James, George L	do	19	May 2, 1864	100 dys.	Mustered out with
James, Hubert A	do	32	May 2, 1864	100 dys.	Mustered out with
James, Seymour	do	25	May 2, 1864	100 dys.	Mustered out with
Jaycox, Ephraim	do	42	May 2, 1864	100 dys.	Mustered out with
Jones, David	do	28	May 2, 1864	100 dys.	Mustered out with
Jones, Solomon	do	39	May 2, 1864	100 dys.	Died June 11, 1864,
Kelsey, Grover C	do	19	May 2, 1864	100 dys.	Mustered out with
Knight, William G	do	31	May 2, 1864	100 dys.	Mustered out with
Lewis, Charles F	do	23	May 2, 1864	100 dys.	Mustered out with
Lewis, John W	do	22	May 2, 1864	100 dys.	Died Aug. 20, 1864, ington, D. C.
Loop, James P	do	28	May 2, 1864	100 dys.	Mustered out with
McWilliams, Marshall S	do	18	May 2, 1864	100 dys.	Mustered out with
McWilliams, Smith	do	36	May 2, 1864	100 dys.	Mustered out with
May, Gabriel G	do	28	May 2, 1864	100 dys.	Mustered out with
May, Obed R	do	44	May 2, 1864	100 dys.	Mustered out with
Morton, Edward N	do	19	May 2, 1864	100 dys.	Mustered out with
Nettleton, Barron B	do	18	May 2, 1864	100 dys.	Mustered out with
Phinney, James F	do	19	May 2, 1864	100 dys.	Mustered out with
Phinney, Russell C	do	25	May 2, 1864	100 dys.	Mustered out with
Pixley, James	do	35	May 2, 1864	100 dys.	Mustered out with
Rains, James	do	23	May 2, 1864	100 dys.	Mustered out with
Reynolds, Horatio	do	34	May 2, 1864	100 dys.	Mustered out with
Robertson, William	do	31	May 2, 1864	100 dys.	Mustered out with
Rollison, William	do	..	May 2, 1864	100 dys.	Mustered out with
Roloson, DeWitt C	do	30	May 2, 1864	100 dys.	Mustered out with
Roloson, Utley	do	36	May 2, 1864	100 dys.	Mustered out with
Rust, Henry S	do	36	May 2, 1864	100 dys.	Mustered out with
Sacket, James F	do	33	May 2, 1864	100 dys.	Mustered out with
Saunders, Edwin P	do	33	May 2, 1864	100 dys.	Mustered out with
Schauck, Ephraim L	do	18	May 2, 1864	100 dys.	Mustered out with
Shade, Elijah	do	41	May 2, 1864	100 dys.	Mustered out with
Slack, Elijah H	do	42	May 2, 1864	100 dys.	Mustered out with
Slack, Lewis	do	39	May 2, 1864	100 dys.	Mustered out with
Slack, Pearson P	do	44	May 2, 1864	100 dys.	Mustered out with
Smith, Albert R	do	31	May 2, 1864	100 dys.	Mustered out with
Smith, Lucius D	do	29	May 4, 1864	100 dys.	Mustered out with
Sopher, Moses	do	40	May 2, 1864	100 dys.	Mustered out with
Spear, Anthony M	do	43	May 2, 1864	100 dys.	Mustered out with
Spear, George T	do	18	May 2, 1864	100 dys.	Died Aug. 8, 1864,
Steward, Wesley C	do	34	May 2, 1864	100 dys.	Mustered out with
Steward, William S	do	26	May 2, 1864	100 dys.	Mustered out with
Strimple, Francis L	do	25	May 2, 1864	100 dys.	Mustered out with
Vining, Benjamin	do	26	May 2, 1864	100 dys.	Mustered out with
Vining, Reuben D	do	20	May 2, 1864	100 dys.	Mustered out with
Ward, Philemon	do	24	May 2, 1864	100 dys.	Mustered out with
Whitman, George	do	22	May 2, 1864	100 dys.	Mustered out with
Wilcox, James H	do	21	May 2, 1864	100 dys.	Mustered out with
Wilcox, John	do	24	May 2, 1864	100 dys.	Mustered out with
Wilson, Thomas O	do	20	May 2, 1864	100 dys.	Mustered out with

Names.	Rank.	Age.	Date of Entering the Service.	Period of Service.	Remarks.
Starke, Isaac	Private.	39	May 2, 1864	100 dys.	Mustered out with company Aug.
Starks, James	....do....	19	May 2, 1864	100 dys.	Mustered out with company Aug.
Stevens, Charles	....do....	40	May 2, 1864	100 dys.	Mustered out with company Aug.
Switzer, LeRoy	....do....	19	May 2, 1864	100 dys.	Mustered out with company Aug.
Van Ness, Charles A	....do....	26	May 2, 1864	100 dys.	Mustered out with company Aug.
Wadsworth, Henry	....do....	19	May 2, 1864	100 dys.	Mustered out with company Aug.
Wall, Frederick	....do....	21	May 2, 1864	100 dys.	Mustered out with company Aug.
Wall, Jacob	....do....	25	May 2, 1864	100 dys.	Mustered out with company Aug.
Wheat, James	....do....	20	May 2, 1864	100 dys.	Mustered out with company Aug.
Whitmore, Uriah H	....do....	38	May 2, 1864	100 dys.	Mustered out with company Aug.
Wirt, John M	....do....	25	May 2, 1864	100 dys.	Mustered out with company Aug.
Yance, William	....do....	30	May 2, 1864	100 dys.	Mustered out with company Aug.

COMPANY K.

Mustered in May 12, 1864, at Camp Chase, O., by H. Douglas, Captain 18th Infantry, U. S. A. M
Aug. 24, 1864, at Camp Chase, O., by John C. King, Captain 16th Infantry, U. S. A.

Names.	Rank.	Age.	Date of Entering the Service.	Period of Service.	Remarks.
John Cellar	Captain.	44	May 2, 1864	100 dys.	Mustered out with company Aug.
Thomas S. Hall	1st Lieut.	21	May 2, 1864	100 dys.	Mustered out with company Aug.
Aaron M. Decker	2d Lieut.	21	May 2, 1864	100 dys.	Mustered out with company Aug.
Harvey A. Humphrey	1st Sergt.	22	May 2, 1864	100 dys.	Mustered out with company Aug.
Wilson S. Knapp	Sergeant.	28	May 2, 1864	100 dys.	Mustered out with company Aug.
Andrew J. Harter	....do....	27	May 2, 1864	100 dys.	Mustered out with company Aug.
Cicero T. Carson	....do....	28	May 2, 1864	100 dys.	Mustered out with company Aug.
Ezekiel Rodgers	....do....	31	May 2, 1864	100 dys.	Mustered out with company Aug.
Robert Anderson	....do....	..	May 2, 1864	100 dys.	Never reported to company.
James W. Kirkpatrick	Corporal.	30	May 2, 1864	100 dys.	Mustered out with company Aug.
Richard M. Long	....do....	34	May 2, 1864	100 dys.	Mustered out with company Aug.
David L. Dodds	....do....	30	May 2, 1864	100 dys.	Mustered out with company Aug.
Passwell Kauffman	....do....	29	May 2, 1864	100 dys.	Mustered out with company Aug.
John W. Clark	....do....	32	May 2, 1864	100 dys.	Mustered out with company Aug.
John H. Thomas	....do....	20	May 2, 1864	100 dys.	Mustered out with company Aug.
John Kirkpatrick	....do....	29	May 2, 1864	100 dys.	Mustered out with company Aug.
John H. Hardin	Musician	44	May 2, 1864	100 dys.	Mustered out with company Aug.
Charles W. Topliff	....do....	28	May 2, 1864	100 dys.	Mustered out with company Aug.
Samuel Anderson	....do....	..	May 2, 1864	100 dys.	Discharged May 18, 1864, on accou
Beiber, James	Private.	31	May 2, 1864	100 dys.	Mustered out with company Aug.
Bicket, Robert	....do....	43	May 2, 1864	100 dys.	Mustered out with company Aug.
Browning, Orin	....do....	37	May 2, 1864	100 dys.	Mustered out with company Aug.
Carpenter, Hiram R	....do....	48	May 2, 1864	100 dys.	Mustered out with company Aug.
Carr, Henry C	....do....	25	May 2, 1864	100 dys.	Mustered out with company Aug.
Carson, William W	....do....	..	May 2, 1864	100 dys.	Mustered out with company Aug.
Case, Cicero P	....do....	19	May 2, 1864	100 dys.	Mustered out with company Aug.
Case, John S	....do....	22	May 2, 1864	100 dys.	Mustered out with company Aug.
Case, Ralph	....do....	30	May 2, 1864	100 dys.	Mustered out with company Aug.
Cellar, John G. F	....do....	28	May 2, 1864	100 dys.	Mustered out with company Aug.
Cellar, Moses H	....do....	35	May 2, 1864	100 dys.	Mustered out with company Aug.
Cellar, Robert M	....do....	29	May 2, 1864	100 dys.	Mustered out with company Aug.
Cellar, Thomas J	....do....	36	May 2, 1864	100 dys.	Mustered out with company Aug.
Cherry, Burroughs	....do....	34	May 2, 1864	100 dys.	Mustered out with company Aug.
Clark, George	....do....	24	May 2, 1864	100 dys.	Mustered out with company Aug.
Clark, John	....do....	27	May 2, 1864	100 dys.	Mustered out with company Aug.
Crain, Reese N	....do....	38	May 2, 1864	100 dys.	Mustered out with company Aug.
Cronkleton, James	....do....	33	May 2, 1864	100 dys.	Mustered out with company Aug.
Decker, LeRoy	....do....	18	May 2, 1864	100 dys.	Mustered out with company Aug.
Dyarman, John P	....do....	37	May 2, 1864	100 dys.	Mustered out with company Aug.
Elsbree, Martin V	....do....	30	May 2, 1864	100 dys.	Mustered out with company Aug.
Farnsworth, Lorenzo D	....do....	36	May 2, 1864	100 dys.	Mustered out with company Aug.
Goodrich, Horace L	....do....	24	May 2, 1864	100 dys.	Discharged Sept. 1, 1864, at Washi on Surgeon's certificate of disabi
Gray, Ebenezer, S	....do....	24	May 2, 1864	100 dys.	Mustered out with company Aug.
Hall, Amos	....do....	36	May 2, 1864	100 dys.	Mustered out with company Aug.
Hall, Edwin J	....do....	39	May 2, 1864	100 dys.	Mustered out with company Aug.
Hall, George	....do....	36	May 2, 1864	100 dys.	Mustered out with company Aug.
Hardin, Nathan C	....do....	37	May 2, 1864	100 dys.	Mustered out with company Aug.
Harkness, John	....do....	25	May 2, 1864	100 dys.	Mustered out with company Aug.
Hinkle, James	....do....	37	May 2, 1864	100 dys.	Mustered out with company Aug.
Hinkle, Michael	....do....	19	May 2, 1864	100 dys.	Mustered out with company Aug.
Hughs, William	....do....	28	May 2, 1864	100 dys.	Mustered out with company Aug.
Johnston, Alexander	....do....	32	May 2, 1864	100 dys.	Mustered out with company Aug.
Kibby, John	....do....	18	May 2, 1864	100 dys.	Mustered out with company Aug.
Knight, Abner	....do....	32	May 2, 1864	100 dys.	Mustered out with company Aug.
Leady, John D	....do....	30	May 2, 1864	100 dys.	Mustered out with company Aug.
Leady, Joseph	....do....	32	May 2, 1864	100 dys.	Mustered out with company Aug.
Long, John P	....do....	29	May 2, 1864	100 dys.	Mustered out with company Aug.
Lowry, Andrew	....do....	42	May 2, 1864	100 dys.	Mustered out with company Aug.
McCollin, Andrew J	....do....	38	May 2, 1864	100 dys.	Mustered out with company Aug.
McCullough, John	....do....	21	May 2, 1864	100 dys.	Mustered out with company Aug.
McKinnie, Josiah	....do....	38	May 2, 1864	100 dys.	Mustered out with company Aug.

Names.	Rank.	Age.	Date of Entering the Service.	Period of Service.	Remarks.
Marks, Erastus B.	Private.	39	May 2, 1864	100 dys.	Mustered out with company Aug. 24, 1864.
Mercer, Washington Z.	do.	40	May 2, 1864	100 dys.	Mustered out with company Aug. 24, 1864.
Morehead, Alexander	do.	20	May 2, 1864	100 dys.	Mustered out with company Aug. 24, 1864.
Morey, Cyrus	do.	21	May 2, 1864	100 dys.	Mustered out with company Aug. 24, 1864.
Moyer, Thomas	do.	22	May 2, 1864	100 dys.	Mustered out with company Aug. 24, 1864.
Newhouse, Alexander	do.	23	May 2, 1864	100 dys.	Mustered out with company Aug. 24, 1864.
Pennell, William P.	do.	40	May 2, 1864	100 dys.	Mustered out with company Aug. 24, 1864.
Powers, Orrin	do.	29	May 2, 1864	100 dys.	Mustered out with company Aug. 24, 1864.
Richey, James	do.	22	May 2, 1864	100 dys.	Mustered out with company Aug. 24, 1864.
Rogers, Ezekiel	do.	43	May 2, 1864	100 dys.	Mustered out with company Aug. 24, 1864.
Roloson, Gustavus S.	do.	39	May 2, 1864	100 dys.	Mustered out with company Aug. 24, 1864.
Sanders, Cyrus	do.	19	May 2, 1864	100 dys.	Mustered out with company Aug. 24, 1864.
Seeley, Horace	do.	21	May 2, 1864	100 dys.	Mustered out with company Aug. 24, 1864.
Slane, Elias	do.	34	May 2, 1864	100 dys.	Mustered out with company Aug. 24, 1864.
Slane, Jacob	do.	44	May 2, 1864	100 dys.	Mustered out with company Aug. 24, 1864.
Smith, Jacob B.	do.	34	May 2, 1864	100 dys.	Mustered out Sept. 1, 1864, at Washington, D. C., by order of War Department.
Snodgrass, Samuel K.	do.	18	May 2, 1864	100 dys.	Mustered out with company Aug. 24, 1864.
Standish, Byron M	do.	19	May 2, 1864	100 dys.	Mustered out with company Aug. 24, 1864.
Standish, John M.	do.	..	May 2, 1864	100 dys.	Reduced from Corporal —; mustered out with company Aug. 24, 1864.
Thomas, Nasal	do.	32	May 2, 1864	100 dys.	Mustered out with company Aug. 24, 1864.
Thomas, Philo	do.	43	May 2, 1864	100 dys.	Mustered out with company Aug. 24, 1864.
Tone, Lafayette	do.	39	May 2, 1864	100 dys.	Mustered out with company Aug. 24, 1864.
Tuller, Edgar P	do.	20	May 2, 1864	100 dys.	Mustered out with company Aug. 24, 1864.
Vance, Edward J.	do.	22	May 2, 1864	100 dys.	Mustered out with company Aug. 24, 1864.
Whitcraft, John A.	do.	44	May 2, 1864	100 dys.	Mustered out with company Aug. 24, 1864.
Willis, Rollin	do.	20	May 2, 1864	100 dys.	Mustered out with company Aug. 24, 1864.
Zimmerman, Charles H.	do.	23	May 2, 1864	100 dys.	Mustered out with company Aug. 24, 1864.
Zimmerman, Volney B.	do.	26	May 2, 1864	100 dys.	Mustered out with company Aug. 24, 1864.

146th Regiment Ohio Volunteer Infantry.

ONE HUNDRED DAYS' SERVICE.

This Regiment was organized at Camp Dennison, O., from the 9th to the 12th of May, 1864, to serve one hundred days. It was composed of the Thirty-first Regiment, Ohio National Guard, from Warren County; Thirty-fifth Battalion, Ohio National Guard, from Clarke County; and the Twenty-fourth Battalion, Ohio National Guard, from Lawrence County. On the 17th of May the Regiment moved to Charleston, W.Va., when Companies A and H were detailed to guard Rebel prisoners at Camp Chase, O. On the 23d of May the One Hundred and Forty-sixth proceeded to Fayetteville, where it performed garrison duty. On the 27th of August the Regiment was ordered to report at Camp Piatt for transportation to Ohio. It was mustered out Sept. 7, 1864, on expiration of term of service.

Names	Rank.	Age.	Date of Entering the Service.	Period of Service.	Remarks.
Cretors, Albert	Private..	21	May 2, 1864	100 dys.	Mustered out with company Sept. 7, 1864.
Cretors, Huston	....do....	19	May 2, 1864	100 dys.	Mustered out with company Sept. 7, 1864.
Cretors, James	....do....	27	May 2, 1864	100 dys.	Mustered out with company Sept. 7, 1864.
Danbury, Jacob R.	....do....	27	May 2, 1864	100 dys.	Absent, sick, on furlough. No further record found.
Davis, Ellis	....do....	21	May 2, 1864	100 dys.	Mustered out with company Sept. 7, 1864.
Davis, Frank	....do....	17	May 2, 1864	100 dys.	Mustered out with company Sept. 7, 1864.
Decker, George H.	....do....	18	May 2, 1864	100 dys.	Mustered out with company Sept. 7, 1864.
Drake, Isaac L.	....do....	40	May 2, 1864	100 dys.	Promoted to Surgeon ——.
Drake, John	....do....	20	May 2, 1864	100 dys.	Mustered out with company Sept. 7, 1864.
Drake, Thomas	....do....	22	May 2, 1864	100 dys.	Mustered out with company Sept. 7, 1864.
Dunham, Peter B.	....do....	24	May 2, 1864	100 dys.	Mustered out with company Sept. 7, 1864.
Dyche, David T. D.	....do....	37	May 2, 1864	100 dys.	Mustered out with company Sept. 7, 1864.
Dynes, John H.	....do....	19	May 2, 1864	100 dys.	Mustered out with company Sept. 7, 1864.
Egbert, Marion D.	....do....	21	May 2, 1864	100 dys.	Appointed Ordnance Sergeant at Post Fayetteville, W. Va., May 28, 1864; returned to company Aug. 28, 1864; mustered out with company Sept. 7, 1864.
Elliott, Thomas C.	....do....	19	May 2, 1864	100 dys.	Mustered out with company Sept. 7, 1864.
Evans, Thomas M.	....do....	20	May 2, 1864	100 dys.	Mustered out with company Sept. 7, 1864.
Gleason, Frank	....do....	29	May 2, 1864	100 dys.	Mustered out with company Sept. 7, 1864.
Graftman, John	....do....	27	May 2, 1864	100 dys.	Mustered out with company Sept. 7, 1864; also borne on rolls as John Graffman.
Graham, Dallas	....do....	19	May 2, 1864	100 dys.	Mustered out with company Sept. 7, 1864.
Graham, John F.	....do....	22	May 2, 1864	100 dys.	Mustered out with company Sept. 7, 1864.
Hafer, Henry	....do....	26	May 2, 1864	100 dys.	Mustered out with company Sept. 7, 1864.
Hafer, Peter	....do....	29	May 2, 1864	100 dys.	Mustered out with company Sept. 7, 1864.
Hall, Charles L.	....do....	19	May 2, 1864	100 dys.	Mustered out with company Sept. 7, 1864.
Hardy, Charles A.	....do....	18	May 2, 1864	100 dys.	Reduced from Corporal, at his own request, June 25, 1864; mustered out with company Sept. 7, 1864.
Harris, Isaac	....do....	18	May 2, 1864	100 dys.	Mustered out with company Sept. 7, 1864.
Harris, John	....do....	33	May 2, 1864	100 dys.	Mustered out with company Sept. 7, 1864.
Hatfield, Ish	....do....	23	May 2, 1864	100 dys.	Mustered out with company Sept. 7, 1864.
Henry, John	....do....	20	May 2, 1864	100 dys.	Mustered out with company Sept. 7, 1864.
Hill, Thomas M.	....do....	28	May 2, 1864	100 dys.	Mustered out with company Sept. 7, 1864.
Howry, Wilber	....do....	18	May 2, 1864	100 dys.	Mustered out with company Sept. 7, 1864.
Irons, Charles C.	....do....	18	May 2, 1864	100 dys.	Mustered out with company Sept. 7, 1864.
Jameson, John	....do....	21	May 2, 1864	100 dys.	Mustered out with company Sept. 7, 1864.
Jeffery, Jacob	....do....	37	May 2, 1864	100 dys.	Mustered out with company Sept. 7, 1864.
Keever, George M.	....do....	20	May 2, 1864	100 dys.	Died Sept. 5, 1864, near Lebanon, O.
Lewis, George W.	....do....	30	May 2, 1864	100 dys.	Mustered out with company Sept. 7, 1864.
Ludlum, Walden	....do....	19	May 2, 1864	100 dys.	Mustered out with company Sept. 7, 1864.
McKinley, Horace D.	....do....	24	May 2, 1864	100 dys.	Mustered out with company Sept. 7, 1864.
Missildine, Benjamin	....do....	20	May 2, 1864	100 dys.	Mustered out with company Sept. 7, 1864.
Morris, John H.	....do....	20	May 2, 1864	100 dys.	Mustered out with company Sept. 7, 1864.
Mull, Benjamin	....do....	24	May 2, 1864	100 dys.	Mustered out with company Sept. 7, 1864.
Mull, Joseph	....do....	26	May 2, 1864	100 dys.	Mustered out with company Sept. 7, 1864.
Murphy, Joseph J.	....do....	44	May 2, 1864	100 dys.	Mustered out with company Sept. 7, 1864.
Murphy, Squire	....do....	17	May 2, 1864	100 dys.	Mustered out with company Sept. 7, 1864.
Osborn, Charles E.	....do....	27	May 2, 1864	100 dys.	Mustered out with company Sept. 7, 1864.
Pierson, Harry C.	....do....	17	May 2, 1864	100 dys.	Mustered out with company Sept. 7, 1864.
Probasco, Abram	....do....	18	May 2, 1864	100 dys.	Mustered out with company Sept. 7, 1864.
Reeder, Caleb T.	....do....	19	May 2, 1864	100 dys.	Mustered out with company Sept. 7, 1864.
Smith, Henry	....do....	18	May 2, 1864	100 dys.	Mustered out with company Sept. 7, 1864.
Smith, Samuel K.	....do....	26	May 2, 1864	100 dys.	Mustered out with company Sept. 7, 1864.
Stephenson, William R.	....do....	22	May 2, 1864	100 dys.	Mustered out with company Sept. 7, 1864.
Stewart, Flavius A.	....do....	20	May 2, 1864	100 dys.	Mustered out with company Sept. 7, 1864.
Stoddard, Grove	....do....	31	May 2, 1864	100 dys.	Absent, sick, on furlough. No further record found.
Stokes, Harry M.	....do....	18	May 2, 1864	100 dys.	Mustered out with company Sept. 7, 1864.
Thompson, Jefferson J.	....do....	21	May 2, 1864	100 dys.	Mustered out with company Sept. 7, 1864.
Thompson, John	....do....	19	May 2, 1864	100 dys.	Mustered out with company Sept. 7, 1864.
Thompson, William M.	....do....	31	May 2, 1864	100 dys.	Mustered out with company Sept. 7, 1864.
Tremble, John H.	....do....	37	May 2, 1864	100 dys.	Mustered out with company Sept. 7, 1864.
Whitacre, Caleb	....do....	18	May 2, 1864	100 dys.	Mustered out with company Sept. 7, 1864.

Names.	Rank.	Age.	Date of Entering the Service.	Period of Service.	Remarks.
Taylor, William	Private	23	May 2, 1864	100 dys.	Mustered out with company Sept. 7, 1864.
Thirkield, Eden B	...do...	18	May 2, 1864	100 dys.	Mustered out with company Sept. 7, 1864.
Thomas, Andrew E	...do...	19	May 2, 1864	100 dys.	Mustered out with company Sept. 7, 1864.
Thomas, Joseph W	...do...	18	May 2, 1864	100 dys.	Mustered out with company Sept. 7, 1864.
Tibbals, Joseph	...do...	30	May 2, 1864	100 dys.	Mustered out with company Sept. 7, 1864.
Townsend, Ethan	...do...	22	May 2, 1864	100 dys.	Mustered out with company Sept. 7, 1864.
Vail, John H	...do...	25	May 2, 1864	100 dys.	Mustered out with company Sept. 7, 1864.
Wear, James	...do...	18	May 2, 1864	100 dys.	Mustered out with company Sept. 7, 1864.
Weaver, John	...do...	18	May 2, 1864	100 dys.	Absent, sick ——. No further record found.
Welsh, James R	...do...	21	May 2, 1864	100 dys.	Mustered out with company Sept. 7, 1864.
Welsh, William D	...do...	27	May 2, 1864	100 dys.	Mustered out with company Sept. 7, 1864.
Wylie, Cyrus P	...do...	29	May 2, 1864	100 dys.	Mustered out with company Sept. 7, 1864.

COMPANY C.

Mustered in May 11, 1864, at Camp Dennison, O., by Robert S. Smith, Captain 2d Cavalry, U. S. A. Mustered out Sept. 7, 1864, at Camp Dennison, O., by William Stanley, 2d Lieutenant 10th Infantry, U. S. A.

Names.	Rank.	Age.	Date of Entering the Service.	Period of Service.	Remarks.
Robert H. Williason	Captain.	30	May 2, 1864	100 dys.	Mustered out with company Sept. 7, 1864.
Jonathan Sawyer	1st Lieut.	33	May 2, 1864	100 dys.	Mustered out with company Sept. 7, 1864.
John W. Foote	2d Lieut.	27	May 2, 1864	100 dys.	Mustered out with company Sept. 7, 1864.
Gustavus A. Spencer	1st Sergt.	27	May 2, 1864	100 dys.	Mustered out with company Sept. 7, 1864.
Jacob Emery	Sergeant.	20	May 2, 1864	100 dys.	Mustered out with company Sept. 7, 1864.
David Codington	...do...	37	May 2, 1864	100 dys.	Mustered out with company Sept. 7, 1864.
Samuel Bateman	...do...	30	May 2, 1864	100 dys.	Mustered out with company Sept. 7, 1864.
William H. H. Hitesman	...do...	23	May 2, 1864	100 dys.	Mustered out with company Sept. 7, 1864.
William P. Starkey	Corporal.	20	May 2, 1864	100 dys.	Mustered out with company Sept. 7, 1864.
James Thompson	...do...	35	May 2, 1864	100 dys.	Mustered out with company Sept. 7, 1864.
Thomas J. Hill	...do...	26	May 2, 1864	100 dys.	Mustered out with company Sept. 7, 1864.
John W. Carson	...do...	19	May 2, 1864	100 dys.	Mustered out with company Sept. 7, 1864.
Joel [illegible] Bird	...do...	19	May 2, 1864	100 dys.	Mustered out with company Sept. 7, 1864.
Albert [illegible]enger	...do...	23	May 2, 1864	100 dys.	Mustered out with company Sept. 7, 1864.
David Fox	...do...	23	May 2, 1864	100 dys.	Mustered out with company Sept. 7, 1864.
John Spence	...do...	29	May 2, 1864	100 dys.	Mustered out with company Sept. 7, 1864.
Beard, Joseph	Private.	21	May 2, 1864	100 dys.	Mustered out with company Sept. 7, 1864.
Bisher, Jacob	...do...	27	May 2, 1864	100 dys.	Mustered out with company Sept. 7, 1864.
Brown, John	...do...	23	May 2, 1864	100 dys.	Mustered out with company Sept. 7, 1864.
Cameron, James	...do...	46	May 2, 1864	100 dys.	Mustered out with company Sept. 7, 1864.
Carson, Peter	...do...	27	May 2, 1864	100 dys.	Mustered out with company Sept. 7, 1864.
Case, William	...do...	23	May 2, 1864	100 dys.	
Clark, John W	...do...	18	May 2, 1864	100 dys.	Mustered out with company Sept. 7, 1864.
Constable, Napthalia	...do...	24	May 2, 1864	100 dys.	Mustered out with company Sept. 7, 1864.
Cummins, Isaac T	...do...	18	May 2, 1864	100 dys.	Mustered out with company Sept. 7, 1864.
Doughman, Benjamin	...do...	42	May 2, 1864	100 dys.	Mustered out with company Sept. 7, 1864.
Fling, William S	...do...	21	May 2, 1864	100 dys.	Died July 12, 1864, in hospital at Fayetteville, West Virginia.
Flomerfelt, John	...do...	30	May 2, 1864	100 dys.	Mustered out with company Sept. 7, 1864.
Flomerfelt, Zachariah	...do...	24	May 2, 1864	100 dys.	Mustered out with company Sept. 7, 1864.
Foote, Amos B	...do...	21	May 2, 1864	100 dys.	Mustered out with company Sept. 7, 1864.
Fox, Charles	...do...	21	May 2, 1864	100 dys.	Mustered out with company Sept. 7, 1864.
Fox, John M	...do...	18	May 3, 1864	100 dys.	Mustered out with company Sept. 7, 1864.
Garrison, George W	...do...	20	May 2, 1864	100 dys.	Mustered out with company Sept. 7, 1864.
Garrison, Henry	...do...	29	May 2, 1864	100 dys.	Mustered out with company Sept. 7, 1864.
Goodpasture, William	...do...	19	May 2, 1864	100 dys.	Mustered out with company Sept. 7, 1864.
Grim, Herman	...do...	18	May 2, 1864	100 dys.	Mustered out with company Sept. 7, 1864.
Haines, Salathiel	...do...	20	May 2, 1864	100 dys.	Mustered out with company Sept. 7, 1864.
Haines, Zimri	...do...	27	May 2, 1864	100 dys.	Mustered out with company Sept. 7, 1864.
Hall, George W	...do...	17	May 2, 1864	100 dys.	Mustered out with company Sept. 7, 1864.
Hart, Joseph	...do...	37	May 2, 1864	100 dys.	No further record found.
Hitesman, George W., Sr	...do...	34	May 2, 1864	100 dys.	Promoted to Com. Sergeant May 12, 1864.
Hitesman, George W., Jr	...do...	18	May 2, 1864	100 dys.	Mustered out with company Sept. 7, 1864.
Hitesman, James C	...do...	39	May 2, 1864	100 dys.	Mustered out with company Sept. 7, 1864.
Hopewell, Joseph	...do...	17	May 2, 1864	100 dys.	Mustered out with company Sept. 7, 1864.
Hughes, James	...do...	36	May 2, 1864	100 dys.	Mustered out with company Sept. 7, 1864.
Hutchinson, William	...do...	18	May 2, 1864	100 dys.	Mustered out with company Sept. 7, 1864.
Ingersoll, Nelson G	...do...	26	May 2, 1864	100 dys.	Mustered out with company Sept. 7, 1864.
Jackson, Columbus	...do...	16	May 2, 1864	100 dys.	Mustered out with company Sept. 7, 1864.
Jackson, George	...do...	25	May 2, 1864	100 dys.	Mustered out with company Sept. 7, 1864.
Jones, George N	...do...	40	May 2, 1864	100 dys.	Mustered out with company Sept. 7, 1864.
Lawson, Courtland	...do...	22	May 2, 1864	100 dys.	Mustered out with company Sept. 7, 1864.
Laymon, John	...do...	28	May 2, 1864	100 dys.	Mustered out with company Sept. 7, 1864.
Laymon, William J	...do...	27	May 2, 1864	100 dys.	Mustered out with company Sept. 7, 1864.
Little, Theodore	...do...	17	May 2, 1864	100 dys.	Mustered out with company Sept. 7, 1864.
Lyle, Peachy	...do...	23	May 2, 1864	100 dys.	Mustered out with company Sept. 7, 1864.
McFe[illegible]ren, Samuel	...do...	19	May 2, 1864	100 dys.	Mustered out with company Sept. 7, 1864.
McMulen, William	...do...	18	May 2, 1864	100 dys.	Mustered out with company Sept. 7, 1864.
Mayer, Arjalon P	...do...	30	May 2, 1864	100 dys.	Mustered out with company Sept. 7, 1864.
Minick, John	...do...	26	May 2, 1864	100 dys.	Mustered out with company Sept. 7, 1864.
Minick, William	...do...	27	May 2, 1864	100 dys.	Mustered out with company Sept. 7, 1864.

Names.	Rank.	Age.	Date of Entering the Service.	Period of Service.	Remarks.
Morris, Osborn	Private..	30	May 2, 1864	100 dys.	Mustered out with company Sept. 7, 1864.
Morrison, Francis	....do....	36	May 2, 1864	100 dys.	Mustered out with company Sept. 7, 1864.
Morrison, Harris	....do....	18	May 2, 1864	100 dys.	Mustered out with company Sept. 7, 1864.
Morrison, William H	....do....	24	May 2, 1864	100 dys.	Mustered out with company Sept. 7, 1864.
Mosgrove, John	....do....	30	May 2, 1864	100 dys.	Mustered out with company Sept. 7, 1864
Myers, Zachariah	....do....	17	May 2, 1864	100 dys.	Mustered out with company Sept. 7, 1864.
Nixon, Allen	....do....	35	May 2, 1864	100 dys.	Mustered out with company Sept. 7, 1864.
Nixon, William	....do....	19	May 2, 1864	100 dys.	Mustered out with company Sept. 7, 1864.
Nossar, William	....do....	31	May 2, 1864	100 dys.	Mustered out with company Sept. 7, 1864.
Pouch, Adolph	....do....	38	May 2, 1864	100 dys.	Mustered out with company Sept. 7, 1864.
Renner, Samuel L	....do....	37	May 2, 1864	100 dys.	Mustered out with company Sept. 7, 1864.
Rogers, Spry H	....do....	47	May 2, 1864	100 dys.	Mustered out with company Sept. 7, 1864.
Roads, George	....do....	18	May 2, 1864	100 dys.	Mustered out with company Sept. 7, 1864.
Roads, Isaiah C	....do....	19	May 2, 1864	100 dys.	Mustered out with company Sept. 7, 1864.
Schooler, Levi	....do....	21	May 2, 1864	100 dys.	Mustered out with company Sept. 7, 1864.
Scott, Milton L	....do....	24	May 2, 1864	100 dys.	Mustered out with company Sept. 7, 1864.
Sears, Henry N	....do....	23	May 2, 1864	100 dys.	Mustered out with company Sept. 7, 1864.
Sellars, George W	....do....	35	May 2, 1864	100 dys.	Drowned May 12, 1864, in Ohio River; fell from boat nineteen miles above Cincinnati, Ohio.
Sly, George W	....do....	41	May 2, 1864	100 dys.	Mustered out with company Sept. 7, 1864.
Snyder, William H. H	....do....	20	May 2, 1864	100 dys.	Mustered out with company Sept. 7, 1864.
Soth, William P	....do....	17	May 2, 1864	100 dys.	Mustered out with company Sept. 7, 1864.
Stetson, George S	....do....	27	May 2, 1864	100 dys.	Promoted to Principal Musician May 12, 1864.
Spencer, Samuel A	....do....	24	May 2, 1864	100 dys.	Mustered out with company Sept. 7, 1864.
Spence, Theodore F	....do....	20	May 2, 1864	100 dys.	Mustered out with company Sept. 7, 1864.
Stowder, Ira	....do....	[illegible]	May 2, 1864	100 dys.	Mustered out with company Sept. 7, 1864.
Stuart, Elias R	....do....	25	May 2, 1864	100 dys.	Mustered out with company Sept. 7, 1864.
Taylor, Samuel M	....do....	[illegible]	May 2, 1864	100 dys.	Mustered out with company Sept. 7, 1864.
Wallace, William	....do....	[illegible]	May 2, 1864	100 dys.	Mustered out with company Sept. 7, 1864.
Wasson, Henry	....do....	[illegible]	May 2, 1864	100 dys.	Mustered out with company Sept. 7, 1864.
Weitman, Thomas E	....do....	[illegible]	May 2, 1864	100 dys.	Mustered out with company Sept. 7, 1864.
Whitmore, Lewis B	....do....	[illegible]	May 2, 1864	100 dys.	Mustered out with company Sept. 7, 1864.
Williams, John W	....do....	[illegible]	May 2, 1864	100 dys.	Mustered out with company Sept. 7, 1864.
Wilkins, David	....do....	[illegible]	May 2, 1864	100 dys.	Mustered out with company Sept. 7, 1864.

COMPANY D.

Mustered in May 11, 1864, at Camp Dennison, O., by Major [illegible], Mustering Officer. Mustered out Sept. 7, 1864, at Camp Dennison, O., by William Stanley, 1st Lieutenant [illegible] Infantry U. S. A.

Names.	Rank.	Age.	Date of Entering the Service.	Period of Service.	Remarks.
Alfred Miller	Captain.	[illegible]	May 2, 1864	100 dys.	Mustered out with company Sept. 7, 1864.
Thomas E. Stewart	1st Lieut.	[illegible]	May 2, 1864	100 dys.	Mustered out with company Sept. 7, 1864.
Harvey H. Tuttle	2d Lieut.	[illegible]	May 2, 1864	100 dys.	Mustered out with company Sept. 7, 1864.
John E. Stewart	1st Sergt.	[illegible]	May 2, 1864	100 dys.	Mustered out with company Sept. 7, 1864.
Webster Barrett	Sergeant.	[illegible]	May 2, 1864	100 dys.	Mustered out with company Sept. 7, 1864.
Francis M. Berry	[illegible]	[illegible]	May 2, 1864	100 dys.	Mustered out with company Sept. 7, 1864.
John S. Anderson	[illegible]	[illegible]	May 2, 1864	100 dys.	Mustered out with company Sept. 7, 1864.
William [illegible] Lafferty	[illegible]	[illegible]	May 2, 1864	[illegible]	[illegible]
David Tuttle	[illegible]	[illegible]	May 2, 1864	[illegible]	[illegible]
John Stafford	[illegible]	[illegible]	May 2, 1864	[illegible]	[illegible]
Francis M. Porter	[illegible]	[illegible]	[illegible]	[illegible]	[illegible]
[illegible] W. Wilson	[illegible]	[illegible]	[illegible]	[illegible]	[illegible]
[illegible] W. Baker	[illegible]	[illegible]	May [illegible]	[illegible]	[illegible]
[illegible]	[illegible]	[illegible]	[illegible]	[illegible]	[illegible]
[illegible]	[illegible]	[illegible]	[illegible]	[illegible]	[illegible]
[illegible] W. [illegible]	[illegible]	[illegible]	[illegible]	[illegible]	[illegible]
[illegible]	Private.	[illegible]	[illegible]	[illegible]	[illegible]
[illegible]	[illegible]	[illegible]	[illegible]	[illegible]	[illegible]
Baldwin, W[illegible]	[illegible]	[illegible]	May [illegible]	[illegible]	[illegible]
[illegible]	[illegible]	[illegible]	[illegible]	[illegible]	[illegible]
[illegible]	[illegible]	[illegible]	[illegible]	[illegible]	[illegible]
[illegible], Isaac	[illegible]	[illegible]	[illegible]	[illegible]	[illegible]
[illegible]	[illegible]	[illegible]	[illegible]	[illegible]	[illegible]
[illegible], Isaac T	[illegible]	[illegible]	[illegible]	[illegible]	[illegible]
[illegible] W	[illegible]	[illegible]	[illegible]	[illegible]	[illegible]
[illegible], William N	[illegible]	[illegible]	[illegible]	[illegible]	[illegible]
Cooper, [illegible]	[illegible]	[illegible]	[illegible]	[illegible]	[illegible]
[illegible]	[illegible]	[illegible]	May [illegible]	[illegible]	[illegible]
Cooper, John	[illegible]	[illegible]	May [illegible]	[illegible]	[illegible]
Dean, Aaron H	[illegible]	[illegible]	May [illegible]	[illegible]	[illegible]
Edes, Robert C	[illegible]	[illegible]	May [illegible]	[illegible]	[illegible]
Eder, Russel T	[illegible]	[illegible]	May [illegible]	[illegible]	[illegible]
Estle, Charles A	[illegible]	[illegible]	May [illegible]	[illegible]	[illegible]
Estle, William H	[illegible]	35	May [illegible]	[illegible]	[illegible]
Evans, Job	....do....	[illegible]	May [illegible]	[illegible]	Mustered out with company Sept. 7, 1864.
Evans, William E	....do....	[illegible]	May 2, 1864	100 dys.	Mustered out with company Sept. 7, 1864.
Forrest, William	....do....	28	May 2, 1864	100 dys.	Mustered out with company Sept. 7, 1864.
Frazier, William	....do....	32	May 2, 1864	100 dys.	Mustered out with company Sept. 7, 1864.

Names.	Rank.	Age.	Date of Entering the Service.	Period of Service.	Remarks.
Fry, Franklin S	Private	23	May 2, 1864	100 dys.	Mustered out with company Sept. 7, 1864.
Fry, Jacob R	do	19	May 2, 1864	100 dys.	Mustered out with company Sept. 7, 1864.
Hall, Nehemiah	do	29	May 2, 1864	100 dys.	Mustered out with company Sept. 7, 1864.
Harris, John F	do	34	May 2, 1864	100 dys.	Mustered out with company Sept. 7, 1864.
Hatfield, William H	do	18	May 2, 1864	100 dys.	Mustered out with company Sept. 7, 1864.
Hause, Abel	do	37	May 2, 1864	100 dys.	Mustered out with company Sept. 7, 1864.
Hess, Thomas M	do	22	May 2, 1864	100 dys.	Mustered out with company Sept. 7, 1864.
Highwood, James	do	37	May 2, 1864	100 dys.	Mustered out with company Sept. 7, 1864.
Hitchcock, Jesse D	do	18	May 2, 1864	100 dys.	Mustered out with company Sept. 7, 1864.
Huntington, Hugh K	do	18	May 2, 1864	100 dys.	Mustered out with company Sept. 7, 1864.
Hill, James B	do	25	May 2, 1864	100 dys.	Mustered out with company Sept. 7, 1864.
Kempton, William J	do	24	May 2, 1864	100 dys.	Mustered out with company Sept. 7, 1864.
Kiler, George W	do	19	May 2, 1864	100 dys.	Mustered out with company Sept. 7, 1864.
Knisley, David M. C	do	20	May 2, 1864	100 dys.	Mustered out with company Sept. 7, 1864.
Knisley, John W	do	21	May 2, 1864	100 dys.	Mustered out with company Sept. 7, 1864.
Knott, William A	do	19	May 2, 1864	100 dys.	Mustered out with company Sept. 7, 1864.
[illegible]bourne, Abel	do	35	May 2, 1864	100 dys.	Mustered out with company Sept. 7, 1864.
Laybourne, William H. H	do	22	May 2, 1864	100 dys.	Mustered out with company Sept. 7, 1864.
Leffe[illegible], Henry	do	42	May 2, 1864	100 dys.	Mustered out with company Sept. 7, 1864.
Little, William H	do	28	May 2, 1864	100 dys.	Mustered out with company Sept. 7, 1864.
McKuhan, James	do	21	May 2, 1864	100 dys.	Mustered out with company Sept. 7, 1864.
McMillen, George	do	19	May 2, 1864	100 dys.	Mustered out with company Sept. 7, 1864.
Miller, Benjamin	do	44	May 2, 1864	100 dys.	Mustered out with company Sept. 7, 1864.
Miller, Thomas P	do	35	May 2, 1864	100 dys.	Mustered out with company Sept. 7, 1864.
Mills, Jacob	do	39	May 2, 1864	100 dys.	Mustered out with company Sept. 7, 1864.
Morath, F. J	do	44	May 12, 1864	100 dys.	Mustered out with company Sept. 7, 1864.
Murray, John	do	22	May 2, 1864	100 dys.	Mustered out with company Sept. 7, 1864.
Nave, Enoch K	do	19	May 2, 1864	100 dys.	Mustered out with company Sept. 7, 1864.
Nave, John G	do	25	May 2, 1864	100 dys.	Mustered out with company Sept. 7, 1864.
Negley, Sampson W	do	25	May 2, 1864	100 dys.	Mustered out with company Sept. 7, 1864.
Negus, Albert	do	23	May 2, 1864	100 dys.	Mustered out with company Sept. 7, 1864.
Painter, Emanuel	do	23	May 2, 1864	100 dys.	Mustered out with company Sept. 7, 1864.
Porter, Robert	do	29	May 2, 1864	100 dys.	Mustered out with company Sept. 7, 1864.
Quinn, Henry	do	21	May 2, 1864	100 dys.	Mustered out with company Sept. 7, 1864.
Runyen, James M	do	22	May 2, 1864	100 dys.	Mustered out with company Sept. 7, 1864.
Sanders, Michael	do	18	May 2, 1864	100 dys.	Mustered out with company Sept. 7, 1864.
Sellers, Gustavus W	do	18	May 2, 1864	100 dys.	Mustered out with company Sept. 7, 1864.
Shafer, Michael H	do	19	May 2, 1864	100 dys.	Mustered out with company Sept. 7, 1864.
Snodgrass, Orrin	do	18	May 2, 1864	100 dys.	Mustered out with company Sept. 7, 1864.
Stewart, David	do	30	May 2, 1864	100 dys.	Mustered out with company Sept. 7, 1864.
Stewart, David W	do	18	May 2, 1864	100 dys.	Mustered out with company Sept. 7, 1864.
Stewart, Matthew S	do	18	May 2, 1864	100 dys.	Mustered out with company Sept. 7, 1864.
Taylor, Nathan K	do	19	May 2, 1864	100 dys.	Mustered out with company Sept. 7, 1864.
Todd, James J	do	16	May 2, 1864	100 dys.	Died June 1, 1864, in hospital at Fayetteville, W. Virginia.
Truesdal, James	do	25	May 2, 1864	100 dys.	Mustered out with company Sept. 7, 1864.
Turnbull, A. F	do	[illegible]	May 12, 1864	100 dys.	Mustered out with company Sept. 7, 1864.
Tuttle, Isaac	do	21	May 2, 1864	100 dys.	Mustered out with company Sept. 7, 1864.
Tyler, William H	do	24	May 2, 1864	100 dys.	Mustered out with company Sept. 7, 1864.
Vaivel, Richard D	do	32	May 2, 1864	100 dys.	Mustered out with company Sept. 7, 1864.
Warner, Simeon	do	[illegible]	May 2, 1864	100 dys.	Mustered out with company Sept. 7, 1864.
Weigle, Benjamin F	do	21	May 2, 1864	100 dys.	Mustered out with company Sept. 7, 1864.
Wheeler, Elliott D	do	18	May 2, 1864	100 dys.	Mustered out with company Sept. 7, 1864.
Wise, John	do	19	May 2, 1864	100 dys.	Mustered out with company Sept. 7, 1864.
Wolf, Amos	do	24	May 2, 1864	100 dys.	Mustered out with company Sept. 7, 1864.

COMPANY E.

[illegible] May 11, 1864, at Camp Dennison, O., by Robert S. Smith, Captain 2d Cavalry, U. S. A. Mustered out Sept. 7, 1864, at Camp Dennison, O., by William Stanley, 2d Lieutenant 10th Infantry, U. S. A.

Names.	Rank.	Age.	Date of Entering the Service.	Period of Service.	Remarks.
[illegible]	Captain	[illegible]	May 2, 1864	100 dys.	Mustered out with company Sept. 7, 1864.
[illegible]	1st Lieut.	[illegible]	May 2, 1864	100 dys.	Mustered out with company Sept. 7, 1864.
[illegible]	2d Lieut.	[illegible]	May 2, 1864	100 dys.	Mustered out with company Sept. 7, 1864.
[illegible]	1st Sergt.	30	May 2, 1864	100 dys.	Mustered out with company Sept. 7, 1864.
[illegible]	Sergeant	[illegible]	May 2, 1864	100 dys.	Mustered out with company Sept. 7, 1864.
[illegible]	do	[illegible]	May 2, 1864	100 dys.	Mustered out with company Sept. 7, 1864.
[illegible]	do	40	May 2, 1864	100 dys.	Mustered out with company Sept. 7, 1864.
[illegible]	do	[illegible]	May 2, 1864	100 dys.	Mustered out with company Sept. 7, 1864.
[illegible]	Corporal	[illegible]	May 2, 1864	100 dys.	Mustered out with company Sept. 7, 1864.
[illegible]	do	[illegible]	May 2, 1864	100 dys.	Mustered out with company Sept. 7, 1864.
[illegible]	do	[illegible]	May 2, 1864	100 dys.	Mustered out with company Sept. 7, 1864.
[illegible]	do	[illegible]	May 2, 1864	100 dys.	Mustered out with company Sept. 7, 1864.
[illegible]	do	[illegible]	May 2, 1864	100 dys.	Mustered out with company Sept. 7, 1864.
[illegible]	do	[illegible]	May 2, 1864	100 dys.	Mustered out with company Sept. 7, 1864.
[illegible]	do	[illegible]	May 2, 1864	100 dys.	Mustered out with company Sept. 7, 1864.
[illegible]	do	[illegible]	May 2, 1864	100 dys.	Mustered out with company Sept. 7, 1864.
[illegible]	Private	[illegible]	May 2, 1864	100 dys.	Mustered out with company Sept. 7, 1864.

Names.	Rank.	Age.	Date of Entering the Service.	Period of Service.	Remarks.
Williams, John	Private	18	May 2, 1864	100 dys.	Mustered out with company Sept. 7, 1864.
Williams, Samuel	....do....	45	May 2, 1864	100 dys.	Mustered out with company Sept. 7, 1864.
Woodward, George	....do....	22	May 2, 1864	100 dys.	Discharged May 12, 1864, at Camp Dennison, O., on Surgeon's certificate of disability.
Work, Samuel	....do....	33	May 2, 1864	100 dys.	Mustered out with company Sept. 7, 1864.

COMPANY F.

Mustered in May 11, 1864, at Camp Dennison, O., by Robert S. Smith, Captain 2d Cavalry, U. S. A. Mustered out Sept. 7, 1864, at Camp Dennison, O., by William Stanley, 2d Lieutenant 10th Infantry, U. S. A.

Names.	Rank.	Age.	Date of Entering the Service.	Period of Service.	Remarks.
Oliver H. Smith	Captain.	30	May 2, 1864	100 dys.	Mustered out with company Sept. 7, 1864.
Joseph R. Whitaker	1st Lieut.	22	May 2, 1864	100 dys.	Mustered out with company Sept. 7, 1864.
Stephen D. Varney	2d Lieut.	27	May 2, 1864	100 dys.	Mustered out with company Sept. 7, 1864.
Benjamin F. Wilson	1st Sergt.	33	May 2, 1864	100 dys.	Mustered out with company Sept. 7, 1864.
Thomas Thompson	Sergeant.	19	May 2, 1864	100 dys.	Mustered out with company Sept. 7, 1864.
William T. Whitmore	....do....	29	May 2, 1864	100 dys.	Mustered out with company Sept. 7, 1864.
Alfred N. Conden	....do....	20	May 2, 1864	100 dys.	Mustered out with company Sept. 7, 1864.
Joshua V. Taylor	....do....	23	May 2, 1864	100 dys.	Mustered out with company Sept. 7, 1864.
William D. Homan	Corporal.	29	May 2, 1864	100 dys.	Mustered out with company Sept. 7, 1864.
Enoch Kelley	....do....	20	May 2, 1864	100 dys.	Mustered out with company Sept. 7, 1864.
Matthew S. Shenard	....do....	32	May 2, 1864	100 dys.	Mustered out with company Sept. 7, 1864.
Mandly C. Hampton	....do....	17	May 2, 1864	100 dys.	Mustered out with company Sept. 7, 1864.
Peter C. Long	....do....	45	May 2, 1864	100 dys.	Mustered out with company Sept. 7, 1864.
James M. Henry	....do....	21	May 2, 1864	100 dys.	Mustered out with company Sept. 7, 1864.
William R Varney	....do....	24	May 2, 1864	100 dys.	Mustered out with company Sept. 7, 1864.
Ayers, John B. W	Private	20	May 2, 1864	100 dys.	Mustered out with company Sept. 7, 1864.
Ayers, Joseph	....do....	17	May 2, 1864	100 dys.	Mustered out with company Sept. 7, 1864.
Bailey, Andrew J	....do....	18	May 2, 1864	100 dys.	Mustered out with company Sept. 7, 1864.
Bailey, Scott	....do....	17	May 2, 1864	100 dys.	Mustered out with company Sept. 7, 1864.
Bailey, Thomas	....do....	28	May 2, 1864	100 dys.	Absent, on furlough ——. No further record found.
Baker, Andrew J	....do....	22	May 2, 1864	100 dys.	Mustered out with company Sept. 7, 1864.
Baker, James S	....do....	17	May 2, 1864	100 dys.	Mustered out with company Sept. 7, 1864.
Baker, John T	....do....	26	May 2, 1864	100 dys.	Mustered out with company Sept. 7, 1864.
Baker, Philip E	....do....	19	May 2, 1864	100 dys.	Mustered out with company Sept. 7, 1864.
Black, Joseph R	....do....	27	May 2, 1864	100 dys.	Mustered out with company Sept. 7, 1864.
Bowman, Elias	....do....	35	May 2, 1864	100 dys.	Mustered out with company Sept. 7, 1864.
Caton, Irwin L. M	....do....	28	May 2, 1864	100 dys.	Mustered out with company Sept. 7, 1864.
Clevenger, Hamilton W	....do....	40	May 2, 1864	100 dys.	Mustered out with company Sept. 7, 1864.
Clise, William G	....do....	18	May 2, 1864	100 dys.	Mustered out with company Sept. 7, 1864.
Coats, James	....do....	39	May 2, 1864	100 dys.	Mustered out with company Sept. 7, 1864.
Coddington, William E	....do....	19	May 2, 1864	100 dys.	Mustered out with company Sept. 7, 1864.
Conden, John W	....do....	20	May 2, 1864	100 dys.	Mustered out with company Sept. 7, 1864.
Corwin, James B	....do....	25	May 2, 1864	100 dys.	Mustered out with company Sept. 7, 1864.
Doughman, Peter	....do....	45	May 2, 1864	100 dys.	Mustered out with company Sept. 7, 1864.
Drake, Joseph H	....do....	23	May 2, 1864	100 dys.	Mustered out with company Sept. 7, 1864.
Dugal, George	....do....	44	May 2, 1864	100 dys.	Mustered out with company Sept. 7, 1864.
Dugan, John T	....do....	22	May 2, 1864	100 dys.	Mustered out with company Sept. 7, 1864.
Dunn, John	....do....	38	May 2, 1864	100 dys.	Mustered out with company Sept. 7, 1864.
Dynes, John M	....do....	27	May 2, 1864	100 dys.	Mustered out with company Sept. 7, 1864.
Eisenstedt, Isadore	....do....	21	May 2, 1864	100 dys.	Mustered out with company Sept. 7, 1864.
Farnham Marcellus	....do....	20	May 2, 1864	100 dys.	Transferred from Co. E ——; furloughed ——. No further record found.
Fetz, Michael	....do....	38	May 2, 1864	100 dys.	Mustered out with company Sept. 7, 1864.
Fite, William L	....do....	36	May 2, 1864	100 dys.	Mustered out with company Sept. 7, 1864.
Fitzer, John	....do....	23	May 2, 1864	100 dys.	Mustered out with company Sept. 7, 1864.
Gilliam, William	....do....	27	May 2, 1864	100 dys.	Mustered out with company Sept. 7, 1864.
Gruber, Philip S	....do....	36	May 2, 1864	100 dys.	Mustered out with company Sept. 7, 1864.
Hall, James	....do....	42	May 2, 1864	100 dys.	Mustered out with company Sept. 7, 1864.
Hampton, James T	....do....	29	May 2, 1864	100 dys.	Mustered out with company Sept. 7, 1864.
Harrell, Benjamin	....do....	40	May 2, 1864	100 dys.	Furloughed — . No further record found.
Hollingsworth, Abner	....do....	31	May 2, 1864	100 dys.	Mustered out with company Sept. 7, 1864.
Howard, Calvin R	....do....	36	May 2, 1864	100 dys.	Mustered out with company Sept. 7, 1864.
Kelley, Clarkson	....do....	26	May 2, 1864	100 dys.	Mustered out with company Sept. 7, 1864.
Koogle, Stephen	....do....	41	May 2, 1864	100 dys.	Mustered out with company Sept. 7, 1864.
Ledda, John	....do....	22	May 2, 1864	100 dys.	Mustered out with company Sept. 7, 1864.
Lemmon, Samuel	....do....	48	May 2, 1864	100 dys.	Mustered out with company Sept. 7, 1864.
Lemmon, William	....do....	19	May 2, 1864	100 dys.	Mustered out with company Sept. 7, 1864.
Lever, Benjamin	....do....	43	May 2, 1864	100 dys.	Mustered out with company Sept. 7, 1864.
Ludlum, Nathan R.	....do....	44	May 2, 1864	100 dys.	Mustered out with company Sept. 7, 1864.
Ludlum, Oscar	....do....	24	May 2, 1864	100 dys.	On muster-in roll. No further record found.
Lyons, Arthur	....do....	33	May 2, 1864	100 dys.	Mustered out with company Sept. 7, 1864.
McKinney, William H	....do....	37	May 2, 1864	100 dys.	Mustered out with company Sept. 7, 1864.
Marshall, George R	....do....	17	May 2, 1864	100 dys.	Reduced from Corporal May 26, 1864; mustered out with company Sept. 7, 1864.
Massive, Henry	....do....	18	May 2, 1864	100 dys.	Mustered out with company Sept. 7, 1864.
Miranda, James	....do....	35	May 2, 1864	100 dys.	Mustered out with company Sept. 7, 1864.
Mitchell, William	....do....	17	May 2, 1864	100 dys.	Mustered out with company Sept. 7, 1864.

[illegible]	Rank.	Age.	Date of Entering the Service.	Period of Service.	Remarks.
[illegible]	Private..	27	May 2, 1864	100 dys.	Mustered out with company Sept. 7, 1864.
[illegible]	...do...	33	May 2, 1864	100 dys.	Mustered out with company Sept. 7, 1864.
[illegible] D.	...do...	35	May 2, 1864	100 dys.	Mustered out with company Sept. 7, 1864.
[illegible]	...do...	38	May 2, 1864	100 dys.	Mustered out with company Sept. 7, 1864.
[illegible]	...do...	24	May 2, 1864	100 dys.	Mustered out with company Sept. 7, 1864.
[illegible]	...do...	28	May 2, 1864	100 dys.	Mustered out with company Sept. 7, 1864.
[illegible]	...do...	36	May 2, 1864	100 dys.	Mustered out with company Sept. 7, 1864.
[illegible]	...do...	27	May 2, 1864	100 dys.	
[illegible], John	...do...	31	May 2, 1864	100 dys.	Mustered out with company Sept. 7, 1864.
[illegible], Joseph H.	...do...	32	May 2, 1864	100 dys.	Absent since May 20, 1864. No further record found.
[illegible], Joseph	...do...	44	May 2, 1864	100 dys.	Mustered out with company Sept. 7, 1864.
[illegible], Joseph, Jr.	...do...	18	May 2, 1864	100 dys.	Mustered out with company Sept. 7, 1864.
[illegible]	...do...	43	May 2, 1864	100 dys.	Mustered out with company Sept. 7, 1864.
[illegible], Richard	...do...	32	May 2, 1864	100 dys.	Mustered out with company Sept. 7, 1864.
[illegible], Thomas	...do...	24	May 2, 1864	100 dys.	Mustered out with company Sept. 7, 1864.
[illegible]	...do...	28	May 2, 1864	100 dys.	Mustered out with company Sept. 7, 1864.
[illegible]	...do...	35	May 2, 1864	100 dys.	Mustered out with company Sept. 7, 1864.
[illegible]	...do...	36	May 2, 1864	100 dys.	Mustered out with company Sept. 7, 1864.
[illegible], William	...do...	33	May 2, 1864	100 dys.	Mustered out with company Sept. 7, 1864.
[illegible], George W.	...do...	47	May 2, 1864	100 dys.	Mustered out with company Sept. 7, 1864.
[illegible], Harvey	...do...	32	May 2, 1864	100 dys.	Mustered out with company Sept. 7, 1864.
[illegible]	...do...	30	May 2, 1864	100 dys.	Mustered out with company Sept. 7, 1864.
[illegible], John S.	...do...	20	May 2, 1864	100 dys.	Mustered out with company Sept. 7, 1864.
[illegible], Lorenzo	...do...	41	May 2, 1864	100 dys.	Mustered out with company Sept. 7, 1864.
[illegible], Christian	...do...	35	May 2, 1864	100 dys.	
[illegible]	...do...	38	May 2, 1864	100 dys.	
[illegible]	...do...	20	May 2, 1864	100 dys.	Died Aug. 7, 1864, at Fayetteville, W. Va.
[illegible], William W.	...do...	42	May 2, 1864	100 dys.	Mustered out with company Sept. 7, 1864.
[illegible], William	...do...	16	May 2, 1864	100 dys.	Mustered out with company Sept. 7, 1864.

COMPANY G.

[illegible] May 11, 1864, at Camp Dennison, O., by Robert S. Smith, Captain 2d Cavalry, U. S. A. Mustered out Sept. 7, 1864, at Camp Dennison, O., by William Stanley, 2d Lieutenant 10th Infantry, U. S. A.

Name	Rank.	Age.	Date of Entering the Service.	Period of Service.	Remarks.
[illegible]	Captain.	22	May 2, 1864	100 dys.	Mustered out with company Sept. 7, 1864.
[illegible]	1st Lieut.	24	May 2, 1864	100 dys.	Mustered out with company Sept. 7, 1864.
[illegible]	2d Lieut.	26	May 2, 1864	100 dys.	Mustered out with company Sept. 7, 1864.
[illegible]	1st Sergt.	32	May 2, 1864	100 dys.	Mustered out with company Sept. 7, 1864.
[illegible]	Sergeant	28	May 2, 1864	100 dys.	Mustered out with company Sept. 7, 1864.
[illegible]	...do...	21	May 2, 1864	100 dys.	Mustered out with company Sept. 7, 1864.
[illegible]	...do...	29	May 2, 1864	100 dys.	Mustered out with company Sept. 7, 1864.
[illegible]	...do...	20	May 2, 1864	100 dys.	Mustered out with company Sept. 7, 1864.
[illegible]	Corporal	24	May 2, 1864	100 dys.	Mustered out with company Sept. 7, 1864.
[illegible]	...do...	30	May 2, 1864	100 dys.	Mustered out with company Sept. 7, 1864.
[illegible]	...do...	27	May 2, 1864	100 dys.	Mustered out with company Sept. 7, 1864.
[illegible]	...do...	23	May 2, 1864	100 dys.	Mustered out with company Sept. 7, 1864.
[illegible]	...do...	29	May 2, 1864	100 dys.	Mustered out with company Sept. 7, 1864.
[illegible]	...do...	24	May 2, 1864	100 dys.	Mustered out with company Sept. 7, 1864.
[illegible]	...do...	30	May 2, 1864	100 dys.	Mustered out with company Sept. 7, 1864.
[illegible]	...do...	19	May 2, 1864	100 dys.	Mustered out with company Sept. 7, 1864.
[illegible]	Private..	27	May 2, 1864	100 dys.	Mustered out with company Sept. 7, 1864.
[illegible]	...do...	25	May 2, 1864	100 dys.	Discharged May 12, 1864, at Camp Dennison, O., on Surgeon's certificate of disability.
Chesnutt, Joseph	...do...	19	May 2, 1864	100 dys.	Mustered out with company Sept. 7, 1864.
Clark, Mark	...do...	20	May 2, 1864	100 dys.	Mustered out with company Sept. 7, 1864.
Clark, Thomas	...do...	28	May 2, 1864	100 dys.	Mustered out with company Sept. 7, 1864.
Cline, Frederick	...do...	27	May 2, 1864	100 dys.	Mustered out with company Sept. 7, 1864.
Clinton, John	...do...	21	May 2, 1864	100 dys.	Mustered out with company Sept. 7, 1864.
Clinton, Moses	...do...	19	May 2, 1864	100 dys.	Mustered out with company Sept. 7, 1864.
Collins, Emanuel	...do...	19	May 2, 1864	100 dys.	Mustered out with company Sept. 7, 1864.
Cook, Frederick	...do...	18	May 2, 1864	100 dys.	Mustered out with company Sept. 7, 1864.
Cook, Joseph	...do...	18	May 2, 1864	100 dys.	Mustered out with company Sept. 7, 1864.
Covert, John M.	...do...	37	May 2, 1864	100 dys.	Discharged May 12, 1864, at Camp Dennison, O., on Surgeon's certificate of disability.
Corkin, James	...do...	22	May 2, 1864	100 dys.	Mustered out with company Sept. 7, 1864.
Cullom, Edward H.	...do...	25	May 2, 1864	100 dys.	Mustered out with company Sept. 7, 1864.
Davis, Charles A.	...do...	19	May 2, 1864	100 dys.	On muster-in roll. No further record found.
Dennison, Alfred	...do...	19	May 2, 1864	100 dys.	Mustered out with company Sept. 7, 1864.
Dougherty, James M.	...do...	24	May 2, 1864	100 dys.	Mustered out with company Sept. 7, 1864.
Dunham, Asa	...do...	19	May 2, 1864	100 dys.	On muster-in roll. No further record found.
Eagle, George W.	...do...	18	May 2, 1864	100 dys.	Mustered out with company Sept. 7, 1864.
Eagle, John	...do...	20	May 2, 1864	100 dys.	Mustered out with company Sept. 7, 1864.
Ertler, Felix	...do...	19	May 2, 1864	100 dys.	Mustered out with company Sept. 7, 1864.
Ertler, William	...do...	20	May 2, 1864	100 dys.	Mustered out with company Sept. 7, 1864.
Freise, John F.	...do...	25	May 2, 1864	100 dys.	Drowned May 15, 1864, in Kanawha River, near Charleston, W. Va.
Friend, William T.	...do...	[illegible]	May 2, 1864	100 dys.	Mustered out with company Sept. 7, 1864.

Names.	Rank.	Age.	Date of Entering the Service.		Period of Service.	
Gilman, William	Private.	18	May	2, 1864	100 dys.	Mustered out company Sep
Goldsts, John C.	....do....	22	May	2, 1864	100 dys.	Discharged May 12, 1864, at Car O., on Surgeon's certificate of
Guttery, Benjamin C.	....do....	20	May	2, 1864	100 dys.	Discharged May 12, 1864, at Car O., on Surgeon's certificate of
Haney, John H.	....do....	25	May	2, 1864	100 dys.	Discharged May 12, 1864, at Can O., on Surgeon's certificate of
Haney, Theodore	....do....	18	May	2, 1864	100 dys.	Mustered out with company Sep
Hatfield, Morris	....do....	20	May	2, 1864	100 dys.	Mustered out with company Sep
Henry, William M.	....do....	18	May	2, 1864	100 dys.	Mustered out with company Sep
Hewitt, William	....do....	33	May	2, 1864	100 dys.	Mustered out with company Sep
Hilderbrant, Henry	....do....	18	May	2, 1864	100 dys.	Mustered out with company Sep
Hilderbrant, William	....do....	20	May	2, 1864	100 dys.	Mustered out with company Sep
Hill, Absalom	....do....	23	May	2, 1864	100 dys.	Mustered out with company Sep
Hill, Benjamin P.	....do....	25	May	2, 1864	100 dys.	Mustered out with company Sep
Hill, James B.	....do....	39	May	2, 1864	100 dys.	Mustered out with company Sep
Hill, John C.	....do....	28	May	2, 1864	100 dys.	Discharged May 12, 1864, at Car O., on Surgeon's certificate of
Hill, John C., Sr.	....do....	20	May	2, 1864	100 dys.	Mustered out with company Sep
Hill, Frank	....do....	31	May	2, 1864	100 dys.	Mustered out with company Sep
Hopkins, Huston	....do....	19	May	2, 1864	100 dys.	Mustered out with company Sep
Hopkins, Pliny D.	....do....	28	May	2, 1864	100 dys.	Mustered out with company Sep
Hopkinson, Marcellus	....do....	18	May	2, 1864	100 dys.	Discharged May 12, 1864, at Car O., on Surgeon's certificate of
Hughs, William B.	....do....	43	May	2, 1864	100 dys.	Discharged May 12, 1864, at Can O., on Surgeon's certificate of
Hyatt, Amariah	....do....	23	May	2, 1864	100 dys.	Mustered out with company Sep
Johnson, Joseph H.	....do....	35	May	2, 1864	100 dys.	Mustered out with company Sep
Keller, Henry	....do....	20	May	2, 1864	100 dys.	Mustered out with company Sep
Kibby, David S.	....do....	18	May	2, 1864	100 dys.	Mustered out with company Sep
Kirk, Eli	....do....	35	May	2, 1864	100 dys.	Discharged May 12, 1864, at Can O., on Surgeon's certificate of
Lambert, Harvey	....do....	30	May	2, 1864	100 dys.	Transferred to Co. K May 12, 186
Leller, Elias	....do....	40	May	2, 1864	100 dys.	Discharged May 12, 1864, at Can O., on Surgeon's certificate of
Leonard, Adolphus	....do....	25	May	2, 1864	100 dys.	Discharged May 12, 1864, at Can O., on Surgeon's certificate of
Lucks, William	....do....	28	May	2, 1864	100 dys.	Mustered out with company Sep
McGill, John	....do....	37	May	2, 1864	100 dys.	Mustered out with company Sep
McKibben, Joseph	....do....	27	May	2, 1864	100 dys.	On muster-in roll. No further
Madden, Cyrus	....do....	35	May	2, 1864	100 dys.	Discharged May 12, 1864, at Can O., on Surgeon's certificate of
Mart, Wesley	....do....		May	2, 1864	100 dys.	Mustered out with company Sep
Morrow, Emmett	....do....		May	2, 1864	100 dys.	Mustered out with company Sep
Morrow, Morris	....do....		May	2, 1864	100 dys.	Mustered out with company Sep
Moses, George	....do....	38	May	2, 1864	100 dys.	On muster-in roll. No further
Mulford, Jacob S.	....do....	[illegible]	May	2, 1864	100 dys.	Discharged May 12, 1864, at Can O., on Surgeon's certificate of
Perryman, Joseph W.	....do....	43	May	2, 1864	100 dys.	Mustered out with company Sep
Pierson, William	....do....	30	May	2, 1864	100 dys.	Discharged May 12, 1864, at Can O., on Surgeon's certificate of
Prall, James M.	....do....	22	May	2, 1864	100 dys.	Mustered out with company Sep
Riechel, John	....do....	36	May	2, 1864	100 dys.	Mustered out with company Sep
Ripley, Anthony	....do....	48	May	2, 1864	100 dys.	Mustered out with company Sep
Semon, Leander	....do....	20	May	2, 1864	100 dys.	Discharged May 12, 1864, at Can O., on Surgeon's certificate of
Semon, Thomas	....do....	18	May	2, 1864	100 dys.	Mustered out with company Sep
Shawhan, Lucius	....do....	18	May	2, 1864	100 dys.	Mustered out with company Sep
Smith, George	....do....	23	May	2, 1864	100 dys.	Mustered out with company Sep
Snell, John	....do....	18	May	2, 1864	100 dys.	Mustered out with company Sep
Snider, John	....do....	29	May	2, 1864	100 dys.	Mustered out with company Sep
Snyder, Jonathan J. J.	....do....	28	May	2, 1864	100 dys.	Mustered out with company Sep
Stephens, Scott E.	....do....	18	May	2, 1864	100 dys.	Mustered out with company Sep
Strader, George	....do....	48	May	2, 1864	100 dys.	Mustered out with company Sep
Taylor, Hugh	....do....	23	May	2, 1864	100 dys.	Discharged May 12, 1864, at Can O., on Surgeon's certificate of
Watkins, Richard	....do....	27	May	2, 1864	100 dys.	Mustered out with company Sep
Young, Lescom	....do....	33	May	2, 1864	100 dys.	Mustered out with company Sep

COMPANY H.

...11, 1864, at Camp Dennison, O., by Robert S. Smith, Captain 2d Cavalry, U. S. A. Mustered out Sept. 7, 1864, at Camp Dennison, O., by William Stanley, 2d Lieutenant 10th Infantry, U. S. A.

	Rank.	Age.	Date of Entering the Service.	Period of Service.	Remarks.
....	Captain.	30	May 2, 1864	100 dys.	Mustered out with company Sept. 7, 1864.
....	1st Lieut.	[illegible]	May 2, 1864	100 dys.	Mustered out with company Sept. 7, 1864.
...rson....	2d Lieut.	21	May 2, 1864	100 dys.	Mustered out with company Sept. 7, 1864.
....	1st Sergt.	27	May 2, 1864	100 dys.	Promoted to Asst. Surgeon May 13, 1864.
	....do....	25	May 2, 1864	100 dys.	Appointed from Sergeant ——; mustered out with company Sept. 7, 1864.
...e........	Sergeant.	24	May 2, 1864	100 dys.	Mustered out with company Sept. 7, 1864.
...hdeacon	....do....	26	May 2, 1864	100 dys.	Mustered out with company Sept. 7, 1864.
...Vheaton.	....do....	23	May 2, 1864	100 dys.	Mustered out with company Sept. 7, 1864.
....	....do....	24	May 2, 1864	100 dys.	Appointed from Corporal ——; mustered out with company Sept. 7, 1864.
		22	May 2, 1864	100 dys.	Mustered out with company Sept. 7, 1864.
		32	May 2, 1864	100 dys.	Mustered out with company Sept. 7, 1864.
....	....do....	24	May 2, 1864	100 dys.	Discharged May 12, 1864, on Surgeon's certificate of disability.
...phee....	....do....	26	May 2, 1864	100 dys.	Mustered out with company Sept. 7, 1864.
....	....do....	22	May 2, 1864	100 dys.	Mustered out with company Sept. 7, 1864.
	....do....	30	May 2, 1864	100 dys.	Mustered out with company Sept. 7, 1864.
	....do....	22	May 2, 1864	100 dys.	Mustered out with company Sept. 7, 1864.
....	....do....	25	May 2, 1864	100 dys.	Appointed ——; mustered out with company Sept. 7, 1864.
...as.......	....do....	22	May 2, 1864	100 dys.	Appointed ——; mustered out with company Sept. 7, 1864.
....	Musician	15	May 2, 1864	100 dys.	Mustered out with company Sept. 7, 1864.
...a B.....	Private..	23	May 2, 1864	100 dys.	Discharged May 12, 1864, on Surgeon's certificate of disability.
...orge....	....do....	32	May 2, 1864	100 dys.	Discharged May 9, 1864, on Surgeon's certificate of disability.
...les......	....do....	25	May 2, 1864	100 dys.	Discharged May 9, 1864, on Surgeon's certificate of disability.
... M.....	....do....	19	May 2, 1864	100 dys.	Mustered out with company Sept. 7, 1864.
....	....do....	20	May 2, 1864	100 dys.	Mustered out with company Sept. 7, 1864.
....	....do....	21	May 2, 1864	100 dys.	Discharged May 9, 1864, on Surgeon's certificate of disability.
...H........	....do....	20	May 2, 1864	100 dys.	Mustered out with company Sept. 7, 1864.
...ariah....	....do....	35	May 2, 1864	100 dys.	Mustered out with company Sept. 7, 1864.
....	....do....	19	May 2, 1864	100 dys.	Mustered out with company Sept. 7, 1864.
....	....do....	25	May 2, 1864	100 dys.	Mustered out with company Sept. 7, 1864.
....	....do....	24	May 2, 1864	100 dys.	Mustered out with company Sept. 7, 1864.
....	....do....	34	May 2, 1864	100 dys.	Mustered out with company Sept. 7, 1864.
....	....do....	27	May 2, 1864	100 dys.	Mustered out with company Sept. 7, 1864.
...ld.......	....do....	26	May 2, 1864	100 dys.	Mustered out with company Sept. 7, 1864.
....	....do....	21	May 2, 1864	100 dys.	Mustered out with company Sept. 7, 1864.
....	....do....	31	May 2, 1864	100 dys.	Mustered out with company Sept. 7, 1864.
....	....do....	47	May 2, 1864	100 dys.	Mustered out with company Sept. 7, 1864.
....	....do....	19	May 2, 1864	100 dys.	Mustered out with company Sept. 7, 1864.
....	....do....	17	May 2, 1864	100 dys.	Discharged ——; under age.
	....do....	20	May 2, 1864	100 dys.	Died July 10, 1864, at Fayetteville, W. Va.
	....do....	19	May 2, 1864	100 dys.	Mustered out with company Sept. 7, 1864.
	....do....	23	May 2, 1864	100 dys.	Mustered out with company Sept. 7, 1864.
....	....do....	17	May 2, 1864	100 dys.	Mustered out with company Sept. 7, 1864.
....	....do....	18	May 2, 1864	100 dys.	Mustered out with company Sept. 7, 1864.
....	....do....	29	May 2, 1864	100 dys.	Mustered out with company Sept. 7, 1864.
...S.......	....do....	28	May 2, 1864	100 dys.	Discharged May 12, 1864, on Surgeon's certificate of disability.
....	....do....	19	May 2, 1864	100 dys.	Discharged May 28, 1864, on Surgeon's certificate of disability.
...m.......	....do....	35	May 2, 1864	100 dys.	Mustered out with company Sept. 7, 1864.
....	....do....	30	May 2, 1864	100 dys.	Mustered out with company Sept. 7, 1864.
...s.......	....do....	35	May 2, 1864	100 dys.	Mustered out with company Sept. 7, 1864.
...K.......	....do....	30	May 2, 1864	100 dys.	Mustered out with company Sept. 7, 1864.
....	....do....	30	May 2, 1864	100 dys.	Mustered out with company Sept. 7, 1864.
	....do....	25	May 2, 1864	100 dys.	Mustered out with company Sept. 7, 1864.
...T	....do....	23	May 2, 1864	100 dys.	Mustered out with company Sept. 7, 1864.
..	....do....	19	May 2, 1864	100 dys.	Discharged May 12, 1864, on Surgeon's certificate of disability.
...W......	....do....	30	May 2, 1864	100 dys.	Mustered out with company Sept. 7, 1864.
....	....do....	[illegible]	May 2, 1864	100 dys.	Mustered out with company Sept. 7, 1864.
....	....do....	[illegible]	May 2, 1864	100 dys.	Mustered out with company Sept. 7, 1864.
....	....do....	21	May 2, 1864	100 dys.	Mustered out with company Sept. 7, 1864.
...s.......	....do....	[illegible]	May 2, 1864	100 dys.	Mustered out with company Sept. 7, 1864.
...F.......	....do....	[illegible]	May 2, 1864	100 dys.	No further record found.
....	....do....	[illegible]	May 2, 1864	100 dys.	Mustered out with company Sept. 7, 1864.
...am......	....do....	[illegible]	May 2, 1864	100 dys.	Mustered out with company Sept. 7, 1864.
....	....do....	[illegible]	May 2, 1864	100 dys.	Mustered out with company Sept. 7, 1864.
....	....do....	[illegible]	May 2, 1864	100 dys.	Mustered out with company Sept. 7, 1864.

Names.	Rank.	Age.	Date of Entering the Service.	Period of Service.	Remarks.
Suethen, William J.	Private.	21	May 2, 1864	100 dys.	Mustered
Somers, C. T.	....do....	27	May 2, 1864	100 dys.	No furthe
Suydam, Charles	....do....	19	May 2, 1864	100 dys.	Mustered out with company Sept. 7, 1864.
Sweney, Edmond	....do....	34	May 2, 1864	100 dys.	Discharged May 9, 1864, on Surgeon's certificate of disability.
Sweney, Franklin	....do....	21	May 2, 1864	100 dys.	Mustered out with company Sept. 7, 1864
Sweney, Monroe	....do....	30	May 2, 1864	100 dys.	Mustered out with company Sept. 7, 1864.
Symons, John	....do....	22	May 2, 1864	100 dys.	Mustered out with company Sept. 7, 1864.
Throckmorton, John	....do....	21	May 2, 1864	100 dys.	Mustered out with company Sept. 7, 1864.
Tresslar, Granville	....do....	23	May 2, 1864	100 dys.	Mustered out with company Sept. 7, 1864.
Tresslar, Hiram	....do....	19	May 2, 1864	100 dys.	Mustered out with company Sept. 7, 1864.
Unglebee, Charles	....do....	20	May 2, 1864	100 dys.	Mustered out with company Sept. 7, 1864.
Unglebee, Joseph	....do....	26	May 2, 1864	100 dys.	Mustered out with company Sept. 7, 1864.
Van Harlingen, Ferdinand S	....do....	[illegible]	May 2, 1864	100 dys.	Promoted to 1st Lieutenant and Adjutant May May 12, 1864.
Walters, Oliver P.	....do....	19	May 2, 1864	100 dys.	Mustered out with company Sept. 7, 1864.
Warrick, Daniel	....do....	24	May 2, 1864	100 dys.	Mustered out with company Sept. 7, 1864.
Warwick, William H.	....do....	26	May 2, 1864	100 dys.	Mustered out with company Sept. 7, 1864.
Watkinson, Joseph	....do....	20	May 2, 1864	100 dys.	Discharged May 9, 1864, on Surgeon's certificate of disability.
Wheaton, Henry C.	....do....	..	May 2, 1864	100 dys.	Discharged May 12, 1864, on Surgeon's certificate of disability.
White, Arthur W.	....do....	35	May 2, 1864	100 dys.	Mustered out with company Sept. 7, 1864.

COMPANY I.

Mustered in May 11, 1864, at Camp Dennison, O., by Major Granville E. Johnson, Mustering Officer. Mustered out Sept. 7, 1864, at Camp Dennison, O., by William Stanley, 2d Lieutenant 10th Infantry, U. S. A.

Names.	Rank.	Age.	Date of Entering the Service.	Period of Service.	Remarks.
Alfred Brown	Captain.	23	May 2, 1864	100 dys.	Mustered out with company Sept. 7, 1864.
Valentine Newman	1st Lieut.	30	May 2, 1864	100 dys.	Mustered out with company Sept. 7, 1864.
Elijah G. Coffin	2d Lieut.	35	May 2, 1864	100 dys.	Mustered out with company Sept. 7, 1864.
William E. R. Kemp	1st Sergt.	41	May 2, 1864	100 dys.	Mustered out with company Sept. 7, 1864.
John G. Warner	Sergeant.	22	May 2, 1864	100 dys.	Mustered out with company Sept. 7, 1864.
William H. Bird	....do....	28	May 2, 1864	100 dys.	Mustered out with company Sept. 7, 1864.
Charles H. Wentz	....do....	23	May 2, 1864	100 dys.	Mustered out with company Sept. 7, 1864.
Silas H. Curry	....do....	39	May 2, 1864	100 dys.	Mustered out with company Sept. 7, 1864.
Absalom M. Griffith	Corporal.	30	May 2, 1864	100 dys.	Mustered out with company Sept. 7, 1864.
James P. Sh[illegible]pton	....do....	30	May 2, 1864	100 dys.	Mustered out with company Sept. 7, 1864
Sa[illegible]uel Ra[illegible]	....do....	21	May 2, 1864	100 dys.	Mustered out with company Sept. 7, 1864.
Harrison Wigg[illegible]ns	....do....	35	May 2, 1864	100 dys.	Mustered out with company Sept. 7, 1864.
Gide[illegible] Landaker	....do....	38	May 2, 1864	100 dys.	Mustered out with company Sept. 7, 1864.
John Ghols[illegible]	....do....	20	May 2, 1864	100 dys.	Mustered out with company Sept. 7, 1864.
Hug[illegible] We[illegible]ter	....do....	24	May 2, 1864	100 dys.	Mustered out with company Sept. 7, 1864.
Alexand[illegible] [illegible]	Private.	30	May 2, 1864	100 dys.	Mustered out with company Sept. 7, 1864.
Andre, Darius	....do....	26	May 2, 1864	100 dys.	Mustered out with company Sept. 7, 1864.
Booth, Robert C.	....do....	30	May 2, 1864	100 dys.	Mustered out with company Sept. 7, 1864.
Boring, Zeller	....do....	20	May 2, 1864	100 dys.	Mustered out with company Sept. 7, 1864.
Botkin, Granville	....do....	24	May 2, 1864	100 dys.	Mustered out with company Sept. 7, 1864.
Bown, Stephen	....do....	18	May 2, 1864	100 dys.	Mustered out with company Sept. 7, 1864.
Breeden, James H.	....do....	28	May 2, 1864	100 dys.	Mustered out with company Sept. 7, 1864.
Breeden, William H.	....do....	20	May 2, 1864	100 dys.	Mustered out with company Sept. 7, 1864.
Bridwell, John	....do....	27	May 2, 1864	100 dys.	Mustered out with company Sept. 7, 1864.
Burke, Martin	....do....	24	May 2, 1864	100 dys.	Mustered out with company Sept. 7, 1864.
Bush, Corydon	....do....	19	May 2, 1864	100 dys.	Mustered out with company Sept. 7, 1864.
Campbell, Eli G.	....do....	23	May 2, 1864	100 dys.	Mustered out with company Sept. 7, 1864.
Carber, James	....do....	24	May 2, 1864	100 dys.	
Carten, Thomas C.	....do....	19	May 2, 1864	100 dys.	Mustered out with company Sept. 7, 1864.
Clarridge, Edward	....do....	21	May 2, 1864	100 dys.	
Cloninger, Philip	....do....	20	May 2, 1864	100 dys.	Mustered out with company Sept. 7, 1864.
Cole, Henry P.	....do....	18	May 2, 1864	100 dys.	Mustered out with company Sept. 7, 1864.
Corlon, Charles	....do....	22	May 2, 1864	100 dys.	Mustered out with company Sept. 7, 1864.
Davidson, McClain	....do....	19	May 2, 1864	100 dys.	Mustered out with company Sept. 7, 1864.
Davis, George B.	....do....	26	May 2, 1864	100 dys.	Mustered out with company Sept. 7, 1864.
Davis, John W.	....do....	20	May 2, 1864	100 dys.	Mustered out with company Sept. 7, 1864.
Dyer, Joshua	....do....	26	May 2, 1864	100 dys.	Mustered out with company Sept. 7, 1864.
Ellsworth, Wales A.	....do....	24	May 2, 1864	100 dys.	Mustered out with company Sept. 7, 1864; also borne on rolls as William W. Ellsworth.
Edwards, William	....do....	18	May 2, 1864	100 dys.	Mustered out with company Sept. 7, 1864.
Goetz, Jacob	....do....	23	May 2, 1864	100 dys.	Mustered out with company Sept. 7, 1864.
Hays, John	....do....	30	May 2, 1864	100 dys.	Mustered out with company Sept. 7, 1864.
Hedrick, Lewis	....do....	22	May 2, 1864	100 dys.	Mustered out with company Sept. 7, 1864.
Helskill, John	....do....	18	May 2, 1864	100 dys.	Mustered out with company Sept. 7, 1864.
Helman, Amos		19	May 2, 1864	100 dys.	Mustered out with company Sept. 7, 1864.
Henry, Elliot C.		20	May 2, 1864	100 dys.	Mustered out with company Sept. 7, 1864.
Henthorn, Henry C.		19	May 2, 1864	100 dys.	Mustered out with company Sept. 7, 1864.
Highwood, Edward	....do....	40	May 2, 1864	100 dys.	Mustered out with company Sept. 7, 1864.
Horshell, Edward	....do....	22	May 2, 1864	100 dys.	Mustered out with company Sept. 7, 1864.

Names.	Rank.	Age.	Date of Entering the Service.	Period of Service.	Remarks.
Caldwell, Joseph	Private	31	May 2, 1864	100 dys.	Mustered out with company Sept. 7, 1864.
Carter, Charles	...do...	19	May 2, 1864	100 dys.	Mustered out with company Sept. 7, 1864.
Carter, Francis	...do...	24	May 2, 1864	100 dys.	Discharged May 12, 1864, on Surgeon's certificate of disability.
Chance, Elijah	...do...	37	May 2, 1864	100 dys.	Mustered out with company Sept. 7, 1864.
Dilatush, William	...do...	23	May 2, 1864	100 dys.	Discharged May 12, 1864, on Surgeon's certificate of disability.
Drake, Addison	...do...	18	May 2, 1864	100 dys.	Mustered out with company Sept. 7, 1864.
Drake, John	...do...	46	May 2, 1864	100 dys.	Mustered out with company Sept. 7, 1864.
Drake, Peter	...do...	18	May 2, 1864	100 dys.	Mustered out with company Sept. 7, 1864.
Dudley, Adolphus S	...do...	29	May 2, 1864	100 dys.	Discharged May 12, 1864, on Surgeon's certificate of disability.
Dunham, Lewis	...do...	21	May 2, 1864	100 dys.	Mustered out with company Sept. 7, 1864.
Enfield, Francis	...do...	23	May 2, 1864	100 dys.	Mustered out with company Sept. 7, 1864.
Frazier, Peter	...do...	41	May 2, 1864	100 dys.	Mustered out with company Sept. 7, 1864.
Gilmor arles D.	...do...	30	May 2, 1864	100 dys.	Mustered out with company Sept. 7, 1864.
Harrell, Cyrenus	...do...	24	May 2, 1864	100 dys.	Mustered out with company Sept. 7, 1864.
Harrell, Nathan	...do...	30	May 2, 1864	100 dys.	Mustered out with company Sept. 7, 1864.
Hines, linton	...do...	19	May 2, 1864	100 dys.	Mustered out with company Sept. 7, 1864.
Hines, William	...do...	43	May 2, 1864	100 dys.	Mustered out with company Sept. 7, 1864.
Hiser, John	...do...	27	May 2, 1864	100 dys.	Mustered out with company Sept. 7, 1864.
Howard, Thomas	...do...	34	May 2, 1864	100 dys.	Mustered out with company Sept. 7, 1864.
Humphreys, Alfred	...do...	19	May 2, 1864	100 dys.	Mustered out with company Sept. 7, 1864.
Hutchinson, Charles	...do...	27	May 2, 1864	100 dys.	Discharged May 12, 1864, on Surgeon's certificate of disability.
Jack, James W	...do...	40	May 2, 1864	100 dys.	Mustered out with company Sept. 7, 1864.
Jennings, James	...do...	35	May 2, 1864	100 dys.	Mustered out with company Sept. 7, 1864.
Lambert, Harvey	...do...	21	May 2, 1864	100 dys.	Transferred from Co. G May 12, 1864; mustered out with company Sept. 7, 1864.
Lambert, Newton, J.	...do...	18	May 2, 1864	100 dys.	Mustered out with company Sept. 7, 1864.
Lucas, John	...do...	29	May 2, 1864	100 dys.	Mustered out with company Sept. 7, 1864.
Luce, Thompson W.	...do...	18	May 2, 1864	100 dys.	Mustered out with company Sept. 7, 1864.
ee, Sala iel	...do...	19	May 2, 1864	100 dys.	Mustered out with company Sept. 7, 1864.
evre, ohn	...do...	32	May 2, 1864	100 dys.	Mustered out with company Sept. 7, 1864.
McKillan, ewis	...do...	19	May 2, 1864	100 dys.	Mustered out with company Sept. 7, 1864.
Miller avi	...do...	23	May 2, 1864	100 dys.	Mustered out with company Sept. 7, 1864.
Murray, John	...do...	17	May 2, 1864	100 dys.	Mustered out with company Sept. 7, 1864.
Penquite, Burr F.	...do...	21	May 2, 1864	100 dys.	Discharged May 12, 1864, on Surgeon's certificate of disability.
Penquite, Joseph	...do...	28	May 2, 1864	100 dys.	Mustered out with company Sept. 7, 1864.
Phillips, Elisha	...do...	18	May 2, 1864	100 dys.	Mustered out with company Sept. 7, 1864.
Poppee, Gustav	...do...	28	May 2, 1864	100 dys.	Mustered out with company Sept. 7, 1864.
Reeder, Harrison	...do...	17	May 2, 1864	100 dys.	Mustered out with company Sept. 7, 1864.
Rhodes, Henry	...do...	41	May 2, 1864	100 dys.	Mustered out with company Sept. 7, 1864.
Roberts, William	...do...	22	May 2, 1864	100 dys.	Mustered out with company Sept. 7, 1864.
Roosa, George W.	...do...	38	May 2, 1864	100 dys.	Mustered out with company Sept. 7, 1864.
Roosa, Huston	...do...	19	May 2, 1864	100 dys.	Mustered out with company Sept. 7, 1864.
Rousch, John	...do...	35	May 2, 1864	100 dys.	Discharged May 12, 1864, on Surgeon's certificate of disability.
Schloss, Clemens	...do...	20	May 2, 1864	100 dys.	Mustered out with company Sept. 7, 1864.
Schloss, Joseph	...do...	18	May 2, 1864	100 dys.	Mustered out with company Sept. 7, 1864.
Shawhan, William	...do...	37	May 2, 1864	100 dys.	Mustered out with company Sept. 7, 1864.
Shepherd, Thomas	...do...	46	May 2, 1864	100 dys.	Mustered out with company Sept. 7, 1864.
Snider, Jacob	...do...	35	May 2, 1864	100 dys.	Mustered out with company Sept. 7, 1864.
Stephenson, James M.	...do...	23	May 2, 1864	100 dys.	Mustered out with company Sept. 7, 1864.
Stephenson, Samuel	...do...	35	May 2, 1864	100 dys.	Discharged May 12, 1864, on Surgeon's certificate of disability.
Steppich, Henry	...do...	35	May 2, 1864	100 dys.	Discharged May 12, 1864, on Surgeon's certificate of disability.
Stubbs, Samuel	...do...	19	May 2, 1864	100 dys.	Mustered out with company Sept. 7, 1864.
Thompson, Gilbert W.	...do...	26	May 2, 1864	100 dys.	Mustered out with company Sept. 7, 1864.
Thompson, Ransen	...do...	19	May 2, 1864	100 dys.	Mustered out with company Sept. 7, 1864.
Tindle, Lewis	...do...	36	May 2, 1864	100 dys.	Mustered out with company Sept. 7, 1864.
Urton, Charles	...do...	46	May 2, 1864	100 dys.	Mustered out with company Sept. 7, 1864.
Vandoren, Alfred	...do...	25	May 2, 1864	100 dys.	Mustered out with company Sept. 7, 1864.
Vandoren, Barkley	...do...	30	May 2, 1864	100 dys.	Mustered out with company Sept. 7, 1864.
Vanhorn, Andrew	...do...	43	May 2, 1864	100 dys.	Mustered out with company Sept. 7, 1864.
Vanriper, William	...do...	18	May 2, 1864	100 dys.	Mustered out with company Sept. 7, 1864.
Venard, James	...do...	22	May 2, 1864	100 dys.	Discharged May 12, 1864, on Surgeon's certificate of disability.
Voorhis, George	...do...	20	May 2, 1864	100 dys.	Mustered out with company Sept. 7, 1864.
Ward, Wilson	...do...	30	May 2, 1864	100 dys.	Discharged May 12, 1864, on Surgeon's certificate of disability.
Webb, William	...do...	28	May 2, 1864	100 dys.	Mustered out with company Sept. 7, 1864.
Wilkins, Samuel	...do...	43	May 2, 1864	100 dys.	
Wolfe, Michael	...do...	33	May 2, 1864	100 dys.	Mustered out with company Sept. 7, 1864.
Worley, John	...do...	32	May 2, 1864	100 dys.	Discharged May 12, 1864, on Surgeon's certificate of disability.

147th Regiment Ohio Volunteer Infantry.

ONE HUNDRED DAYS' SERVICE.

This Regiment was organized at Camp Dennison, O., May 16, 1864, to serve one hundred days. It was composed of the Twenty-fifth Regiment, and Eighty-seventh Battalion, Ohio National Guard, from Miami County. On the 20th of May the Regiment started for Washington City. Upon arrival it reported to General Augur, and was ordered on duty at Fort Ethan Allen. On the 27th of May four companies were ordered to Fort Marcy. On the 1st of June Company A was detailed to perform guard duty at Division Headquarters, and remained there during its term of service. At midnight on the 11th of June the Regiment was ordered to Fort Reno. Marching as far as Fort Stevens the One Hundred and Forty-seventh moved into the trenches as a support to the First Maine and First Ohio Batteries. In this position the Regiment remained until July 4th, when it returned to Fort Ethan Allen. On the 23d of August it was ordered to report at Camp Dennison, O., and was mustered out August 30, 1864, on expiration of term of service.

Names.	Rank.	Age.	Date of Entering the Service.	Period of Service.	Remarks.
[illegible] Perry	Private..	25	May 2, 1864	100 dys.	Mustered out with company Aug. 30, 1864.
[illegible], George	...do....	30	May 2, 1864	100 dys.	Mustered out with company Aug. 30, 1864.
[illegible]	...do....	39	May 2, 1864	100 dys.	Mustered out with company Aug. 30, 1864.
[illegible], Peter	...do....	43	May 2, 1864	100 dys.	Mustered out with company Aug. 30, 1864.
[illegible]an	...do....	29	May 2, 1864	100 dys.	Mustered out with company Aug. 30, 1864.
[illegible], David	...do....	35	May 2, 1864	100 dys.	Mustered out with company Aug. 30, 1864.
[illegible], Henry H	...do....	19	May 2, 1864	100 dys.	Mustered out with company Aug. 30, 1864.
[illegible], Nathaniel L	...do....	35	May 2, 1864	100 dys.	Mustered out with company Aug. 30, 1864.
[illegible], John	...do....	18	May 2, 1864	100 dys.	Mustered out with company Aug. 30, 1864.
[illegible], William R	...do....	19	May 2, 1864	100 dys.	Mustered out with company Aug. 30, 1864.
[illegible], Lewis	...do....	21	May 2, 1864	100 dys.	Mustered out with company Aug. 30, 1864.
[illegible], Levi	...do....	35	May 2, 1864	100 dys.	Mustered out with company Aug. 30, 1864.
[illegible], John	...do....	23	May 2, 1864	100 dys.	Mustered out with company Aug. 30, 1864.
[illegible], Simon	...do....	20	May 2, 1864	100 dys.	Mustered out with company Aug. 30, 1864.
[illegible]errance, Alexander	...do....	32	May 2, 1864	100 dys.	Mustered out with company Aug. 30, 1864.
[illegible]ough, William	...do....	34	May 2, 1864	100 dys.	Mustered out with company Aug. 30, 1864.
[illegible]essmer, Jasper	...do....	36	May 2, 1864	100 dys.	Mustered out with company Aug. 30, 1864.
[illegible]an, Thomas	...do....	33	May 2, 1864	100 dys.	Died Aug. 29, 1864, at Washington, D. C.
[illegible]erson, William F	...do....	19	May 2, 1864	100 dys.	Mustered out with company Aug. 30, 1864.
[illegible]rth, Washington	...do....	23	May 2, 1864	100 dys.	Mustered out with company Aug. 30, 1864.
[illegible]aks, William	...do....	40	May 2, 1864	100 dys.	Mustered out with company Aug. 30, 1864.
[illegible], Charles M	...do....	20	May 2, 1864	100 dys.	Mustered out with company Aug. 30, 1864.
[illegible]earson, Samuel	...do....	44	May 2, 1864	100 dys.	Mustered out with company Aug. 30, 1864.
[illegible]earson, James C	...do....	31	May 2, 1864	100 dys.	Mustered out with company Aug. 30, 1864.
[illegible]earson, Ephraim	...do....	29	May 2, 1864	100 dys.	Mustered out with company Aug. 30, 1864.
[illegible]earson, William H	...do....	22	May 2, 1864	100 dys.	Mustered out with company Aug. 30, 1864.
[illegible]ener, Abraham	...do....	37	May 2, 1864	100 dys.	Mustered out with company Aug. 30, 1864.
[illegible]idge, Charles W	...do....	25	May 2, 1864	100 dys.	Discharged June 18, 1864, on Surgeon's certificate of disability.
[illegible]edehammel, Henry	...do....	39	May 2, 1864	100 dys.	Mustered out with company Aug. 30, 1864.
[illegible]edehammel, Samuel	...do....	27	May 2, 1864	100 dys.	Mustered out with company Aug. 30, 1864.
[illegible]oyer, Louis	...do....	18	May 2, 1864	100 dys.	Mustered out with company Aug. 30, 1864.
[illegible]dy, Daniel J	...do....	34	May 2, 1864	100 dys.	Mustered out with company Aug. 30, 1864.
[illegible]haffer, Joseph L	...do....	26	May 2, 1864	100 dys.	Mustered out with company Aug. 30, 1864.
[illegible]haffer, William C	...do....	23	May 2, 1864	100 dys.	Mustered out with company Aug. 30, 1864.
[illegible]mith, Robert W	...do....	31	May 2, 1864	100 dys.	Mustered out with company Aug. 30, 1864.
[illegible]utherland, Alexander	...do....	34	May 2, 1864	100 dys.	Mustered out with company Aug. 30, 1864.
[illegible]wigart, Harrison	...do....	24	May 2, 1864	100 dys.	Mustered out with company Aug. 30, 1864.
[illegible]witzer, Levi	...do....	26	May 2, 1864	100 dys.	Mustered out with company Aug. 30, 1864.
[illegible]homas, David L	...do....	30	May 2, 1864	100 dys.	Mustered out with company Aug. 30, 1864.
[illegible]yrnan, James	...do....	25	May 2, 1864	100 dys.	Mustered out with company Aug. 30, 1864.
[illegible]son, John M	...do....	38	May 2, 1864	100 dys.	Mustered out with company Aug. 30, 1864.
[illegible]son, Joshua	...do....	35	May 2, 1864	100 dys.	Mustered out with company Aug. 30, 1864.
[illegible]ance, Charles	...do....	25	May 2, 1864	100 dys.	Mustered out with company Aug. 30, 1864.
[illegible]lson, Ephraim	...do....	30	May 2, 1864	100 dys.	Mustered out with company Aug. 30, 1864.
[illegible]kle, Henry	...do....	19	May 2, 1864	100 dys.	Mustered out with company Aug. 30, 1864.
[illegible]rigley, Irwin	...do....	33	May 2, 1864	100 dys.	Mustered out with company Aug. 30, 1864.
[illegible]oung, Benjamin F	...do....	19	May 2, 1864	100 dys.	Mustered out with company Aug. 30, 1864.

COMPANY B.

[illegible]tered in May 16, 1864, at Camp Dennison, O., by G. E. Johnson, Major and A. C. M. Mustered out Aug. 30, 1864, at Camp Dennison, O., by William Stanley, 2d Lieutenant 10th Infantry, U. S. A.

Names.	Rank.	Age.	Date of Entering the Service.	Period of Service.	Remarks.
[illegible] C. Mitchell	Captain.	36	May 2, 1864	100 dys.	Mustered out with company Aug. 30, 1864.
[illegible]ames S. Sayler	1st Lieut.	37	May 2, 1864	100 dys.	Mustered out with company Aug. 30, 1864.
[illegible] Scarff	2d Lieut.	39	May 2, 1864	100 dys.	Mustered out with company Aug. 30, 1864.
[illegible]an H. Albaugh	1st Sergt	30	May 2, 1864	100 dys.	Mustered out with company Aug. 30, 1864.
[illegible]am B. Ten Eyck	Sergeant.	29	May 2, 1864	100 dys.	Mustered out with company Aug. 30, 1864.
[illegible] Benham	...do....	34	May 2, 1864	100 dys.	Absent, sick ——, at home on furlough. No further record found.
[illegible] C. Shaffer	...do....	29	May 2, 1864	100 dys.	Mustered out with company Aug. 30, 1864.
[illegible] DeLong	...do....	26	May 2, 1864	100 dys.	Mustered out with company Aug. 30, 1864.
[illegible] Freeman	Corporal.	30	May 2, 1864	100 dys.	Mustered out with company Aug. 30, 1864.
[illegible]	...do....	28	May 2, 1864	100 dys.	Mustered out with company Aug. 30, 1864.
[illegible] L. Allen	...do....	35	May 2, 1864	100 dys.	Mustered out with company Aug. 30, 1864.
[illegible]	...do....	37	May 2, 1864	100 dys.	Mustered out with company Aug. 30, 1864.
[illegible]	...do....	25	May 2, 1864	100 dys.	Mustered out with company Aug. 30, 1864.
[illegible] Dinsmere	...do....	24	May 2, 1864	100 dys.	Mustered out with company Aug. 30, 1864.
[illegible]	...do....	30	May 2, 1864	100 dys.	Mustered out with company Aug. 30, 1864.
[illegible]	...do....	23	May 2, 1864	100 dys.	Mustered out with company Aug. 30, 1864.
[illegible] R	Private..	39	May 2, 1864	100 dys.	Mustered out with company Aug. 30, 1864.
[illegible] B	...do....	22	May 2, 1864	100 dys.	Absent, sick ——, at home on furlough. No further record found.
[illegible]	...do....	21	May 2, 1864	100 dys.	Mustered out with company Aug. 30, 1864.
[illegible] H	...do....	23	May 2, 1864	100 dys.	Mustered out with company Aug. 30, 1864.
[illegible]	...do....	18	May 2, 1864	100 dys.	Mustered out with company Aug. 30, 1864.
[illegible]	...do....	30	May 2, 1864	100 dys.	Died Aug. 4, 1864, in Regimental Hospital, Fort Ethan Allen, Va.
[illegible]	...do....	20	May 2, 1864	100 dys.	Mustered out with company Aug. 30, 1864.

Names.	Rank.	Age.	Date of Entering the Service.	Period of Service.	Remarks.
Demmitt, Andrew J.	Private.	24	May 2, 1864	100 dys.	Mustered out with company Aug. 30, 1864.
Demmitt, John R.	do.	39	May 2, 1864	100 dys.	Mustered out with company Aug. 30, 1864.
Dinsmore, Albert	do.	19	May 2, 1864	100 dys.	Mustered out with company Aug. 30, 1864.
Felter, David	do.	22	May 2, 1864	100 dys.	Mustered out with company Aug. 30, 1864.
Fergus, James C.	do.	18	May 2, 1864	100 dys.	Mustered out with company Aug. 30, 1864.
Fisher, David B.	do.	28	May 2, 1864	100 dys.	Mustered out with company Aug. 30, 1864.
Fisher, William C.	do.	39	May 2, 1864	100 dys.	Mustered out with company Aug. 30, 1864.
Freeman, George	do.	28	May 2, 1864	100 dys.	Mustered out with company Aug. 30, 1864.
Funderburg, Isaac	do.	27	May 2, 1864	100 dys.	Mustered out with company Aug. 30, 1864.
Funderburg, Solomon M. H.	do.	20	May 2, 1864	100 dys.	Mustered out with company Aug. 30, 1864.
Garrett, Elias W.	do.	24	May 2, 1864	100 dys.	Mustered out with company Aug. 30, 1864.
Garver, Harrison C.	do.	21	May 2, 1864	100 dys.	Mustered out with company Aug. 30, 1864.
Gearhart, Benjamin F.	do.	21	May 2, 1864	100 dys.	Mustered out with company Aug. 30, 1864.
Goudy, Boyd	do.	36	May 2, 1864	100 dys.	Mustered out with company Aug. 30, 1864.
Green, Wesley W.	do.	21	May 2, 1864	100 dys.	Mustered out with company Aug. 30, 1864.
Helmer, William J.	do.	38	May 2, 1864	100 dys.	Mustered out with company Aug. 30, 1864.
Helser, Andrew	do.	21	May 2, 1864	100 dys.	Mustered out with company Aug. 30, 1864.
Hughes, Stephen C.	do.	28	May 2, 1864	100 dys.	Mustered out with company Aug. 30, 1864.
Ingle, Samuel	do.	17	May 2, 1864	100 dys.	Mustered out with company Aug. 30, 1864.
Jacobs, Levi E.	do.	28	May 2, 1864	100 dys.	Mustered out with company Aug. 30, 1864.
Johnson, William	do.	38	May 2, 1864	100 dys.	Mustered out with company Aug. 30, 1864.
Jones, Jonathan	do.	28	May 2, 1864	100 dys.	Mustered out with company Aug. 30, 1864.
Kellenberger, Henry W.	do.	31	May 2, 1864	100 dys.	Mustered out with company Aug. 30, 1864.
Kuhl, Leonard	do.	28	May 2, 1864	100 dys.	Mustered out with company Aug. 30, 1864.
Latchford, John B.	do.	18	May 2, 1864	100 dys.	Mustered out with company Aug. 30, 1864.
Llewellyn, Oliver F.	do.	22	May 2, 1864	100 dys.	Mustered out with company Aug. 30, 1864.
Marsh, William	do.	24	May 2, 1864	100 dys.	Mustered out with company Aug. 30, 1864.
Maitland, Samuel B.	do.	45	May 2, 1864	100 dys.	Mustered out with company Aug. 30, 1864.
Mayall, George W.	do.	22	May 2, 1864	100 dys.	Died July 9, 1864, in Regimental Hospital, Fort Ethan Allen, Va.
Meredith, Thomas	do.	27	May 2, 1864	100 dys.	Mustered out with company Aug. 30, 1864.
Moore, William E.	do.	27	May 2, 1864	100 dys.	Mustered out with company Aug. 30, 1864.
Moore, James A.	do.	27	May 2, 1864	100 dys.	Mustered out with company Aug. 30, 1864.
Oliver, Abraham B.	do.	40	May 2, 1864	100 dys.	Mustered out with company Aug. 30, 1864.
Perrine, James F.	do.	20	May 2, 1864	100 dys.	Mustered out with company Aug. 30, 1864.
Porter, George M.	do.	37	May 2, 1864	100 dys.	Mustered out with company Aug. 30, 1864.
Putnam, Henry C.	do.	18	May 2, 1864	100 dys.	Mustered out with company Aug. 30, 1864.
Reeder, Daniel H.	do.	37	May 2, 1864	100 dys.	Mustered out with company Aug. 30, 1864.
Reddick, Lewis	do.	32	May 2, 1864	100 dys.	Mustered out with company Aug. 30, 1864.
Rench, David	do.	23	May 2, 1864	100 dys.	Mustered out with company Aug. 30, 1864.
Ross, Robert	do.	18	May 2, 1864	100 dys.	Mustered out with company Aug. 30, 1864.
Saylor, Elnathan C.	do.	38	May 2, 1864	100 dys.	Discharged June 26, 1864, on Surgeon's certificate of disability.
Seger, Frederick C.	do.	26	May 2, 1864	100 dys.	Mustered out with company Aug. 30, 1864.
Semler, Walter	do.	..	May 2, 1864	100 dys.	Mustered out with company Aug. 30, 1864.
Shaw, Erastus E.	do.	18	May 2, 1864	100 dys.	Mustered out with company Aug. 30, 1864.
Shaffer, George W.	do.	37	May 2, 1864	100 dys.	Mustered out with company Aug. 30, 1864.
Shaffer, Henry C.	do.	21	May 2, 1864	100 dys.	Died July 9, 1864, in Regimental Hospital, Fort Ethan Allen, Va.
Shaffer, Peter R.	do.	30	May 2, 1864	100 dys.	Mustered out with company Aug. 30, 1864.
Sipe, Henry W.	do.	27	May 2, 1864	100 dys.	Mustered out with company Aug. 30, 1864.
Smith, Nicholas J.	do.	43	May 2, 1864	100 dys.	Mustered out with company Aug. 30, 1864.
Smith, James M.	do.	35	May 2, 1864	100 dys.	Mustered out with company Aug. 30, 1864.
Snyder, Francis M.	do.	23	May 2, 1864	100 dys.	Mustered out with company Aug. 30, 1864.
Sullivan, Oliver	do.	18	May 2, 1864	100	Mustered out with company Aug. 30, 1864.
Sullivan, Thomas J.	do.	22	May 2, 1864	100 dys.	Mustered out with company Aug. 30, 1864.
Throckmorton, Joseph	do.	38	May 2, 1864	100 dys.	Mustered out with company Aug. 30, 1864.
Tuttle, Josiah L.	do.	40	May 2, 1864	100 dys.	Mustered out with company Aug. 30, 1864.
Ullery, John	do.	26	May 2, 1864	100 dys.	Mustered out with company Aug. 30, 1864.
Warfell, Philip	do.	21	May 2, 1864	100 dys.	Died June 9, 1864, at Fort Ethan Allen, Va.
Weaver, Daniel	do.	41	May 2, 1864	100 dys.	Mustered out with company Aug. 30, 1864.
Wild, Charles L.	do.	34	May 2, 1864	100 dys.	Mustered out with company Aug. 30, 1864.
Yetter, Abraham	do.	28	May 2, 1864	100 dys.	Mustered out with company Aug. 30, 1864.

COMPANY C.

Mustered in May 16, 1864, at Camp Dennison, O., by G. E. Johnson, Major and A. C. M. Mustered out Aug. 30, 1864, at Camp Dennison, O., by William Stanley, 2d Lieutenant 10th Infantry, U. S. A.

Names.	Rank.	Age.	Date of Entering the Service.	Period of Service.	Remarks.
[illegible] M. Reid	Captain	37	May 2, 1864	100 dys.	Mustered out with company Aug. 30, 1864.
[illegible] W. Statler	1st Lieut.	32	May 2, 1864	100 dys.	Mustered out with company Aug. 30, 1864.
[illegible] H. Park	2d Lieut.	27	May 2, 1864	100 dys.	Mustered out with company Aug. 30, 1864.
[illegible] Crozier	1st Sergt.	19	May 2, 1864	100 dys.	Mustered out with company Aug. 30, 1864.
A[illegible] Jackson	Sergeant.	19	May 2, 1864	100 dys.	Mustered out with company Aug. 30, 1864.
[illegible] Barnet	do.	22	May 2, 1864	100 dys.	Mustered out with company Aug. 30, 1864.
[illegible]	do.	21	May 2, 1864	100 dys.	Mustered out with company Aug. 30, 1864.
[illegible] Zellinger	do.	25	May 2, 1864	100 dys.	Mustered out with company Aug. 30, 1864.
[illegible] Anthony	Corporal.	23	May 2, 1864	100 dys.	Mustered out with company Aug. 30, 1864.
[illegible] Griggs	do.	22	May 2, 1864	100 dys.	Mustered out with company Aug. 30, 1864.
[illegible] R. Sowdle	do.	20	May 2, 1864	100 dys.	Mustered out with company Aug. 30, 1864.
[illegible] Elliott	do.	22	May 2, 1864	100 dys.	Mustered out with company Aug. 30, 1864.
[illegible] C. Johnston	do.	21	May 2, 1864	100 dys.	Mustered out with company Aug. 30, 1864.
[illegible] Graham	do.	29	May 2, 1864	100 dys.	Mustered out with company Aug. 30, 1864.
A[illegible] Houzer	do.	20	May 2, 1864	100 dys.	Mustered out with company Aug. 30, 1864.
[illegible] H. Alexander	do.	20	May 2, 1864	100 dys.	Mustered out with company Aug. 30, 1864.
[illegible] F. Weib	Musician	16	May 2, 1864	100 dys.	Mustered out with company Aug. 30, 1864.
[illegible] John Q.	Private.	37	May 2, 1864	100 dys.	Mustered out with company Aug. 30, 1864.
A[illegible] Clark	do.	..	May 2, 1864	100 dys.	Mustered out with company Aug. 30, 1864.
A[illegible] Daniel	do.	31	May 2, 1864	100 dys.	Mustered out with company Aug. 30, 1864.
[illegible]	do.	18	May 2, 1864	100 dys.	Mustered out with company Aug. 30, 1864.
[illegible] Thomas	do.	18	May 2, 1864	100 dys.	Mustered out with company Aug. 30, 1864.
[illegible] Benjamin E.	do.	19	May 2, 1864	100 dys.	Mustered out with company Aug. 30, 1864.
[illegible] Daniel	do.	11	May 2, 1864	100 dys.	Mustered out with company Aug. 30, 1864.
[illegible] Joseph	do.	18	May 2, 1864	100 dys.	Mustered out with company Aug. 30, 1864.
[illegible] William	do.	18	May 2, 1864	100 dys.	Mustered out with company Aug. 30, 1864.
[illegible] William B.	do.	21	May 2, 1864	100 dys.	Mustered out with company Aug. 30, 1864.
[illegible] Benjamin I.	do.	22	May 2, 1864	100 dys.	Mustered out with company Aug. 30, 1864.
F[illegible] William E.	do.	21	May 2, 1864	100 dys.	Mustered out with company Aug. 30, 1864.
F[illegible] John P.	do.	20	May 2, 1864	100 dys.	Mustered out with company Aug. 30, 1864.
F[illegible] Joseph	do.	19	May 2, 1864	100 dys.	Mustered out with company Aug. 30, 1864.
F[illegible] George	do.	18	May 2, 1864	100 dys.	Mustered out with company Aug. 30, 1864.
[illegible] William R.	do.	18	May 2, 1864	100 dys.	Mustered out with company Aug. 30, 1864.
[illegible]singer, Stephen	do.	33	May 2, 1864	100 dys.	Mustered out with company Aug. 30, 1864.
[illegible], Mahlon F.	do.	20	May 2, 1864	100 dys.	Discharged June 26, 1864, at Fort Ethan Allen, Va., by order of War Department.
[illegible] Solomon B.	do.	18	May 2, 1864	100 dys.	Mustered out with company Aug. 30, 1864.
[illegible] David	do.	19	May 2, 1864	100 dys.	Mustered out with company Aug. 30, 1864.
[illegible] John	do.	19	May 2, 1864	100 dys.	Mustered out with company Aug. 30, 1864.
[illegible], William	do.	21	May 2, 1864	100 dys.	Mustered out with company Aug. 30, 1864.
[illegible]ck, Luther M.	do.	57	May 2, 1864	100 dys.	Mustered out with company Aug. 30, 1864.
H[illegible] William P.	do.	21	May 2, 1864	100 dys.	Mustered out with company Aug. 30, 1864.
H[illegible] George	do.	20	May 2, 1864	100 dys.	Mustered out with company Aug. 30, 1864.
[illegible] Alexander	do.	30	May 2, 1864	100 dys.	Mustered out with company Aug. 30, 1864.
[illegible] Albert S.	do.	18	May 2, 1864	100 dys.	Mustered out with company Aug. 30, 1864.
K[illegible] Alexander	do.	19	May 2, 1864	100 dys.	Mustered out with company Aug. 30, 1864.
[illegible]	do.	36	May 2, 1864	100 dys.	Mustered out with company Aug. 30, 1864.
[illegible] Alfred	do.	25	May 2, 1864	100 dys.	Mustered out with company Aug. 30, 1864.
[illegible] P.	do.	22	May 2, 1864	100 dys.	Mustered out with company Aug. 30, 1864.
[illegible] E.	do.	18	May 2, 1864	100 dys.	Mustered out with company Aug. 30, 1864.
[illegible] James	do.	21	May 2, 1864	100 dys.	Discharged July 8, 1864, at Fort Ethan Allen, Va., by order of War Department.
[illegible] William C.	do.	21	May 2, 1864	100 dys.	Mustered out with company Aug. 30, 1864.
M[illegible] William	do.	23	May 2, 1864	100 dys.	Discharged July 4, 1864, at Fort Ethan Allen, Va., by order of War Department.
[illegible] William H.	do.	22	May 2, 1864	100 dys.	Mustered out with company Aug. 30, 1864.
[illegible] William H.	do.	28	May 2, 1864	100 dys.	Mustered out with company Aug. 30, 1864.
[illegible] M.	do.	18	May 2, 1864	100 dys.	Mustered out with company Aug. 30, 1864.
[illegible] Abel A.	do.	20	May 2, 1864	100 dys.	Mustered out with company Aug. 30, 1864.
[illegible] Daniel	do.	20	May 2, 1864	100 dys.	Mustered out with company Aug. 30, 1864.
[illegible] William B.	do.	22	May 2, 1864	100 dys.	Mustered out with company Aug. 30, 1864.
[illegible] Abraham Z.	do.	25	May 2, 1864	100 dys.	Mustered out with company Aug. 30, 1864.
[illegible] Daniel	do.	19	May 2, 1864	100 dys.	Mustered out with company Aug. 30, 1864.
[illegible] John W.	do.	32	May 2, 1864	100 dys.	Mustered out with company Aug. 30, 1864.
[illegible]	do.	[illegible]	May 2, 1864	100 dys.	Died July 28, 1864, in Regimental Hospital at Fort Ethan Allen, Va.
[illegible] William	do.	26	May 2, 1864	100 dys.	Mustered out with company Aug. 30, 1864.
[illegible]	do.	18	May 2, 1864	100 dys.	Mustered out with company Aug. 30, 1864.
[illegible] Smith	do.	18	May 2, 1864	100 dys.	Mustered out with company Aug. 30, 1864.
[illegible] John H.	do.	27	May 2, 1864	100 dys.	Promoted to Com. Sergeant May 16, 1864.
[illegible]	do.	18	May 2, 1864	100 dys.	Mustered out with company Aug. 30, 1864.
[illegible]	do.	19	May 2, 1864	100 dys.	Mustered out with company Aug. 30, 1864.
[illegible] Andrew	do.	18	May 2, 1864	100 dys.	Died July 2, 1864, in Regimental Hospital at Fort Ethan Allen, Va.
[illegible] Joshua W.	do.	20	May 2, 1864	100 dys.	Mustered out with company Aug. 30, 1864.
[illegible] George	do.	26	May 2, 1864	100 dys.	Mustered out with company Aug. 30, 1864.
[illegible] Francis	do.	21	May 2, 1864	100 dys.	Mustered out with company Aug. 30, 1864.

[illegible]	Rank.	Age.	Date of Entering the Service.	Period of Service.	Remarks.
[illegible], John W.	Private.	[illegible]	May 2, 1864	100 dys.	Mustered out with company Aug. 30, 1864.
[illegible], David	...do...	29	May 2, 1864	100 dys.	Mustered out with company Aug. 30, 1864.
[illegible]	...do...	19	May 2, 1864	100 dys.	Mustered out with company Aug. 30, 1864.
[illegible]	...do...	[illegible]	May 2, 1864	100 dys.	Discharged July 8, 1864, at Fort Ethan Allen, Va., by order of War Department.
[illegible]	...do...	21	May 2, 1864	100 dys.	Mustered out with company Aug. 30, 1864.
[illegible], John W.	...do...	[illegible]	May 2, 1864	100 dys.	Mustered out with company Aug. 30, 1864.
[illegible], Albert R.	...do...	[illegible]	May 2, 1864	100 dys.	Mustered out with company Aug. 30, 1864.
[illegible], Henry S.	...do...	21	May 2, 1864	100 dys.	Mustered out with company Aug. 30, 1864.
[illegible], John L.	...do...	18	May 2, 1864	100 dys.	Mustered out with company Aug. 30, 1864.
[illegible]	...do...	19	May 2, 1864	100 dys.	Mustered out with company Aug. 30, 1864.
[illegible], George W.	...do...	18	May 2, 1864	100 dys.	Mustered out with company Aug. 30, 1864.

COMPANY D.

Mustered in May 16, 1864, at Camp Dennison, O., by G. E. Johnson, Major and A. C. M. Mustered out Aug. 30, 1864, at Camp Dennison, O., by William Stanley, 2d Lieutenant 10th Infantry, U. S. A.

Name	Rank.	Age.	Date of Entering the Service.	Period of Service.	Remarks.
[illegible] R. Rendall	Captain.	42	May 2, 1864	100 dys.	Mustered out with company Aug. 30, 1864.
[illegible] R. [illegible]	1st Lieut.	35	May 2, 1864	100 dys.	Mustered out with company Aug. 30, 1864.
[illegible] A. Aldrich	2d Lieut.	37	May 2, 1864	100 dys.	Mustered out with company Aug. 30, 1864.
[illegible]	1st Sergt.	[illegible]	May 2, 1864	100 dys.	Mustered out with company Aug. 30, 1864.
[illegible]	Sergeant.	32	May 2, 1864	100 dys.	Mustered out with company Aug. 30, 1864.
[illegible]	...do...	34	May 2, 1864	100 dys.	Mustered out with company Aug. 30, 1864.
[illegible]	...do...	30	May 2, 1864	100 dys.	Mustered out with company Aug. 30, 1864.
[illegible]	...do...	30	May 2, 1864	100 dys.	Mustered out with company Aug. 30, 1864.
[illegible]	Corporal	26	May 2, 1864	100 dys.	Mustered out with company Aug. 30, 1864.
[illegible] A. [illegible]	...do...	31	May 2, 1864	100 dys.	Mustered out with company Aug. 30, 1864.
[illegible] Pickering	...do...	23	May 2, 1864	100 dys.	Mustered out with company Aug. 30, 1864.
[illegible]	...do...	38	May 2, 1864	100 dys.	Mustered out with company Aug. 30, 1864.
[illegible] D. [illegible]	...do...	25	May 2, 1864	100 dys.	Mustered out with company Aug. 30, 1864.
[illegible]	...do...	25	May 2, 1864	100 dys.	Mustered out with company Aug. 30, 1864.
[illegible] V. [illegible]	...do...	31	May 2, 1864	100 dys.	Mustered out with company Aug. 30, 1864.
[illegible]	...do...	19	May 2, 1864	100 dys.	Appointed July 17, 1864; mustered out with company Aug. 30, 1864.
[illegible], James M.	Private.	35	May 2, 1864	100 dys.	Mustered out with company Aug. 30, 1864.
[illegible], Edward	...do...	28	May 2, 1864	100 dys.	Died Aug. 28, 1864, in general hospital at Washington, D. C.
[illegible], John	...do...	42	May 2, 1864	100 dys.	Mustered out with company Aug. 30, 1864.
[illegible]	...do...	19	May 2, 1864	100 dys.	Mustered out with company Aug. 30, 1864.
[illegible]	...do...	23	May 2, 1864	100 dys.	Mustered out with company Aug. 30, 1864.
[illegible], David	...do...	22	May 2, 1864	100 dys.	Mustered out with company Aug. 30, 1864.
[illegible]	...do...	19	May 2, 1864	100 dys.	Mustered out with company Aug. 30, 1864.
[illegible]	...do...	35	May 2, 1864	100 dys.	Mustered out with company Aug. 30, 1864.
[illegible]	...do...	20	May 2, 1864	100 dys.	Mustered out with company Aug. 30, 1864.
[illegible]	...do...	19	May 2, 1864	100 dys.	Died July 17, 1864, in Regimental Hospital at Fort Ethan Allen, Va.
Crum, Hezekiah	...do...	31	May 2, 1864	100 dys.	Mustered out with company Aug. 30, 1864.
Curtis, Noah	...do...	20	May [illegible]	100 dys.	Mustered out with company Aug. 30, 1864.
Curtis, Lemuel	...do...	23	May [illegible]	100 dys.	Mustered out with company Aug. 30, 1864.
Daniels, Amos	...do...	19	May [illegible]	100 dys.	Mustered out with company Aug. 30, 1864.
Davis, Henry H.	...do...	20	May 2, 1864	100 dys.	Mustered out with company Aug. 30, 1864.
Davis, Adolphus A.	...do...	19	May 2, 1864	100 dys.	Mustered out with company Aug. 30, 1864.
Davis, John N.	...do...	[illegible]	May 2, 1864	100 dys.	Mustered out with company Aug. 30, 1864.
Divine, Michael	...do...	[illegible]	May 2, 1864	100 dys.	Mustered out with company Aug. 30, 1864.
Earhart, Henry H.	...do...	21	May 2, 1864	100 dys.	Mustered out with company Aug. 30, 1864.
Eiler, Enoch	...do...	[illegible]	May 2, 1864	100 dys.	Mustered out with company Aug. 30, 1864.
Flemery, William	...do...	18	May 2, 1864	100 dys.	Mustered out with company Aug. 30, 1864.
Filby, Oliver	...do...	[illegible]	May 2, 1864	100 dys.	Mustered out with company Aug. 30, 1864.
Foutz, Henry	...do...	[illegible]	May 2, 1864	100 dys.	Mustered out with company Aug. 30, 1864.
Gillams, William	...do...	37	May 2, 1864	100 dys.	Mustered out with company Aug. 30, 1864.
Glunt, Marion	...do...	19	May 2, 1864	100 dys.	Mustered out with company Aug. 30, 1864.
Goings, Michael	...do...	26	May 2, 1864	100 dys.	Mustered out with company Aug. 30, 1864.
Hahn, Jonathan	...do...	37	May 2, 1864	100 dys.	Discharged June 15, 1864, by order of War Department.
Hale, Thomas	..	[illegible]	May 2, 1864	100 dys.	Mustered out with company Aug. 30, 1864.
Hale, Henry H.	..	21	May 2, 1864	100 dys.	Mustered out with company Aug. 30, 1864.
Hale, John L.	..	[illegible]	May 2, 1864	100 dys.	Died July 23, 1864, in Regimental Hospital, at Fort Ethan Allen, Va.
Hart, Thomas C.	...do...	19	May 2, 1864	100 dys.	Mustered out with company Aug. 30, 1864.
Harris, Isaiah M.	...do...	[illegible]	May 2, 1864	100 dys.	Mustered out with company Aug. 30, 1864.
Haskell, Rees	...do...	21	May 2, 1864	100 dys.	Mustered out with company Aug. 30, 1864.
Houser, Isaac	...do...	[illegible]	May 2, 1864	100 dys.	Mustered out with company Aug. 30, 1864.
Jenkins, Robert	...do...	22	May 2, 1864	100 dys.	Mustered out with company Aug. 30, 1864.
Keating, Lawrence	...do...	[illegible]	May 2, 1864	100 dys.	Mustered out with company Aug. 30, 1864.
Kensinger, Lewis	...do...	[illegible]	May 2, 1864	100 dys.	Mustered out with company Aug. 30, 1864.
Kendall, Emanuel	...do...	[illegible]	May 2, 1864	100 dys.	Mustered out with company Aug. 30, 1864.
Kendall, Albert	...do...	[illegible]	May 2, 1864	100 dys.	Reduced from Corporal July 17, 1864; mustered out with company Aug. 30, 1864.
Kessler, John Q.	...do...	[illegible]	May 2, 1864	100 dys.	Mustered out with company Aug. 30, 1864.

Names.	Rank.	Age.	Date of Entering the Service.	Period of Service.	Remarks.
Kessler, Thomas J.	Private..	21	May 2, 1864	100 dys.	Mustered out with company Aug. 30, 1864.
Kessler, W. W.	...do....	30	May 2, 1864	100 dys.	No record subsequent to enlistment.
Kinsey, John	...do....	20	May 2, 1864	100 dys.	Mustered out with company Aug. 30, 1864.
Langston, H. C.	...do....	27	May 2, 1864	100 dys.	Mustered out with company Aug. 30, 1864.
Layer, John	...do....	32	May 2, 1864	100 dys.	Mustered out with company Aug. 30, 1864.
Macy, James	...do....	22	May 2, 1864	100 dys.	Mustered out with company Aug. 30, 1864.
Manning, J. W.	...do....	29	May 2, 1864	100 dys.	Mustered out with company Aug. 30, 1864.
Mendenhall, Thaddeus	...do....	18	May 2, 1864	100 dys.	Mustered out with company Aug. 30, 1864.
Miller, George W.	...do....	30	May 2, 1864	100 dys.	Mustered out with company Aug. 30, 1864.
Mote, David	...do....	19	May 2, 1864	100 dys.	Mustered out with company Aug. 30, 1864.
Patterson, John T. M.	...do....	29	May 2, 1864	100 dys.	Mustered out with company Aug. 30, 1864.
Pearson, Henry J.	...do....	22	May 2, 1864	100 dys.	Mustered out with company Aug. 30, 1864.
Pensle, C. D.	...do....	32	May 2, 1864	100 dys.	No record subsequent to enlistment.
Pierce, Moses C.	...do....	18	May 2, 1864	100 dys.	Mustered out with company Aug. 30, 1864.
Porter, Samuel A.	...do....	22	May 2, 1864	100 dys.	Mustered out with company Aug. 30, 1864.
Siler, George	...do....	41	May 2, 1864	100 dys.	Mustered out with company Aug. 30, 1864.
Swisher, John W.	...do....	32	May 2, 1864	100 dys.	Mustered out with company Aug. 30, 1864.
Swisher, Jacob M.	...do....	26	May 2, 1864	100 dys.	Mustered out with company Aug. 30, 1864.
Tenny, W. [illegible]	...do....	31	May 2, 1864	100 dys.	Mustered out with company Aug. 30, 1864.
Thayer, Erasmus	...do....	20	May 2, 1864	100 dys.	Mustered out with company Aug. 30, 1864.
Vore, Peter	...do....	40	May 2, 1864	100 dys.	Mustered out with company Aug. 30, 1864.
Vore, John	...do....	22	May 2, 1864	100 dys.	Mustered out with company Aug. 30, 1864.
Vore, Wesley W.	...do....	28	May 2, 1864	100 dys.	Mustered out with company Aug. 30, 1864.
Welbaum, Charles	...do....	27	May 2, 1864	100 dys.	Mustered out with company Aug. 30, 1864.
Werts, Benjamin F.	...do....	18	May 2, 1864	100 dys.	Mustered out with company Aug. 30, 1864.
Wesalle, Hiram	...do....	32	May 2, 1864	100 dys.	Discharged July 8, 1864, by order of War Department.
Wheelock, Davis	...do....	27	May 2, 1864	100 dys.	Mustered out with company Aug. 30, 1864.
Wheeler, Daniel	...do....	20	May 2, 1864	100 dys.	Mustered out with company Aug. 30, 1864.
Yountz, Jacob	...do....	38	May 2, 1864	100 dys.	Mustered out with company Aug. 30, 1864.
Yount, Hamilton	...do....	18	May 2, 1864	100 dys.	Mustered out with company Aug. 30, 1864.
[illegible], Theodore	...do....	32	May 2, 1864	100 dys.	Mustered out with company Aug. 30, 1864.

COMPANY E.

Mustered in May 16, 1864, at Camp Dennison, O., by G. E. Johnson, Major and A. C. M. Mustered out Aug. 30, 1864, at Camp Dennison, O., by William Stanley, 2d Lieutenant 10th Infantry, U. S. A.

Names.	Rank.	Age.	Date of Entering the Service.	Period of Service.	Remarks.
Frank E. Johnston	Captain.	30	May 2, 1864	100 dys.	Mustered out with company Aug. 30, 1864.
[illegible] Furrow	1st Lieut.	33	May 2, 1864	100 dys.	Mustered out with company Aug. 30, 1864.
James W. Robinson	2d Lieut.	31	May 2, 1864	100 dys.	Mustered out with company Aug. 30, 1864.
William Frost	1st Sergt.	30	May 2, 1864	100 dys.	Mustered out with company Aug. 30, 1864.
William [illegible] Wiley	Sergeant.	25	May 2, 1864	100 dys.	Mustered out with company Aug. 30, 1864.
James [illegible]	...do....	36	May 2, 1864	100 dys.	Discharged July 8, 1864, on Surgeon's certificate of disability.
John [illegible]	...do....	32	May 2, 1864	100 dys.	Mustered out with company Aug. 30, 1864.
[illegible] R. Bowden	...do....	38	May 2, 1864	100 dys.	Mustered out with company Aug. 30, 1864.
[illegible] Wiley	Corporal	21	May 2, 1864	100 dys.	Mustered out with company Aug. 30, 1864.
[illegible]	...do....	18	May 2, 1864	100 dys.	Discharged Sept. [illegible], 1864, at Washington, D. C., on Surgeon's certificate of disability.
Mathew Millhouse	...do....	20	May 2, 1864	100 dys.	Mustered out with company Aug. 30, 1864.
Lewis W[illegible]	...do....	23	May 2, 1864	100 dys.	Absent sick Aug. 20, 1864, in hospital at Washington, D. C. No further record found.
David Small	...do....	30	May 2, 1864	100 dys.	Absent, sick [illegible] in hospital at Washington, D. C. No further record found.
Thomas Maxwell	...do....	34	May 2, 1864	100 dys.	Mustered out with company Aug. 30, 1864.
[illegible] Patterson	...do....	22	May 2, 1864	100 dys.	Died Aug. 23, 1864, in Mt. Pleasant Hospital, Washington, D. C.
James E. Snodgrass	...do....	25	May 2, 1864	100 dys.	Discharged June 18, 1864, on Surgeon's certificate of disability.
Anderson, Newton	Private..	28	May 2, 1864	100 dys.	Mustered out with company Aug. 30, 1864.
Anderson, Robert S.	...do....	26	May 2, 1864	100 dys.	Mustered out with company Aug. 30, 1864.
Andrews, Thomas M.	...do....	19	May 2, 1864	100 dys.	Mustered out with company Aug. 30, 1864.
Baggs, Robert	...do....	26	May 2, 1864	100 dys.	Mustered out with company Aug. 30, 1864.
Bundy, William	...do....	25	May 2, 1864	100 dys.	Died July 25, 1864, in Regimental Hospital, at Fort Ethan Allen, Va.
Carr, David	...do....	25	May 2, 1864	100 dys.	Mustered out with company Aug. 30, 1864.
Cavin, George R.	...do....	26	May 2, 1864	100 dys.	Mustered out with company Aug. 30, 1864.
Coats, Harvey	...do....	18	May 2, 1864	100 dys.	Mustered out with company Aug. 30, 1864.
Conzatt, George	...do....	33	May 2, 1864	100 dys.	Mustered out with company Aug. 30, 1864.
Crozier, Theodore L.	...do....	38	May 2, 1864	100 dys.	Mustered out with company Aug. 30, 1864.
Cruise, Augustus	...do....	22	May 2, 1864	100 dys.	Mustered out with company Aug. 30, 1864.
Day, Stephen	...do....	22	May 2, 1864	100 dys.	Mustered out with company Aug. 30, 1864.
Deitman, Alexander	...do....	23	May 2, 1864	100 dys.	Mustered out with company Aug. 30, 1864.
Detric, John	...do....	21	May 2, 1864	100 dys.	Mustered out with company Aug. 30, 1864.
Deventy, Andrew	...do....	27	May 2, 1864	100 dys.	Mustered out with company Aug. 30, 1864.
Dillon, Richard	...do....	39	May 2, 1864	100 dys.	Mustered out with company Aug. 30, 1864.
Drake, John	...do....	19	May 2, 1864	100 dys.	Mustered out with company Aug. 30, 1864.
Edgar, John R.	...do....	19	May 2, 1864	100 dys.	Mustered out with company Aug. 30, 1864.
Edge, George	...do....	25	May 2, 1864	100 dys.	Mustered out with company Aug. 30, 1864.

Names.	Rank.	Age.	Date of Entering the Service.	Period of Service.	Remarks.
Carr, Cyrus	Private	19	May 2, 1864	100 dys.	Mustered out with company Aug. 30, 1864.
Coombs, William	do	28	May 2, 1864	100 dys.	Mustered out with company Aug. 30, 1864.
Cooper, Jesse	do	39	May 2, 1864	100 dys.	Mustered out with company Aug. 30, 1864.
Connelly, Patrick	do	42	May 2, 1864	100 dys.	Mustered out with company Aug. 30, 1864.
Cox, Paul V	do	20	May 2, 1864	100 dys.	Mustered out with company Aug. 30, 1864.
Dorsey, John L	do	18	May 2, 1864	100 dys.	Mustered out with company Aug. 30, 1864.
Dorsey, Charles W	do	36	May 2, 1864	100 dys.	Mustered out with company Aug. 30, 1864.
Dorsey, William M	do	31	May 2, 1864	100 dys.	Mustered out with company Aug. 30, 1864.
Duggan, Dennis	do	18	May 2, 1864	100 dys.	Mustered out with company Aug. 30, 1864.
Driver, G. S	do	31	May 2, 1864	100 dys.	Mustered out with company Aug. 30, 1864.
Eichelbarger, Edwin S	do	18	May 2, 1864	100 dys.	Mustered out with company Aug. 30, 1864.
Eshelman, Matthew	do	19	May 2, 1864	100 dys.	Mustered out with company Aug. 30, 1864.
Farrelley, Philip	do	26	May 2, 1864	100 dys.	Mustered out with company Aug. 30, 1864.
Fintrock, Martin	do	25	May 2, 1864	100 dys.	Mustered out with company Aug. 30, 1864.
Fuller, Thomas D	do	19	May 2, 1864	100 dys.	Mustered out with company Aug. 30, 1864.
Gaskill, Moses H	do	25	May 2, 1864	100 dys.	Mustered out with company Aug. 30, 1864.
Gibbs, John	do	34	May 2, 1864	100 dys.	Mustered out with company Aug. 30, 1864.
Grafton, Sampson	do	31	May 2, 1864	100 dys.	Died June 20, 1864, in Regimental Hospital at Fort Ethan Allen, Va.
Graham, Edward	do	24	May 2, 1864	100 dys.	Mustered out with company Aug. 26, 1864.
Gray, Joseph W	do	18	May 2, 1864	100 dys.	Mustered out with company Aug. 30, 1864.
Grubb, Joshua	do	19	May 2, 1864	100 dys.	Mustered out with company Aug. 30, 1864.
Harris, John	do	47	May 2, 1864	100 dys.	Absent, sick ——, in Columbus, O. No further record found.
Harner, John	do	45	May 2, 1864	100 dys.	Mustered out with company Aug. 30, 1864.
Howell, Morgan G	do	23	May 2, 1864	100 dys.	Mustered out with company Aug. 30, 1864.
Johnson, James	do	29	May 2, 1864	100 dys.	Mustered out with company Aug. 30, 1864.
Kneisley, Abraham	do	21	May 2, 1864	100 dys.	Mustered out with company Aug. 30, 1864.
Lane, Charles H	do	41	May 2, 1864	100 dys.	Mustered out with company Aug. 30, 1864.
Lane, William McK	do	23	May 2, 1864	100 dys.	Mustered out with company Aug. 30, 1864.
Layman, George W	do	28	May 2, 1864	100 dys.	Mustered out with company Aug. 30, 1864.
Lewis, Jonathan	do	18	May 2, 1864	100 dys.	Mustered out with company Aug. 30, 1864.
Liddy, Mike	do	28	May 2, 1864	100 dys.	Mustered out with company Aug. 30, 1864.
Long, John S	do	31	May 2, 1864	100 dys.	Mustered out with company Aug. 30, 1864.
Lukens, James A	do	19	May 2, 1864	100 dys.	Mustered out with company Aug. 30, 1864.
Lukemire, David A	do	18	May 2, 1864	100 dys.	Mustered out with company Aug. 30, 1864.
McClintock, Charles A	do	35	May 2, 1864	100 dys.	Mustered out with company Aug. 30, 1864.
Malosh, Joseph	do	22	May 2, 1864	100 dys.	Mustered out with company Aug. 30, 1864.
Marin, Oliver	do	20	May 2, 1864	100 dys.	Mustered out with company Aug. 30, 1864.
Merritt, Henry	do	19	May 2, 1864	100 dys.	Mustered out with company Aug. 30, 1864.
Miller, Moses	do	19	May 2, 1864	100 dys.	Mustered out with company Aug. 30, 1864.
Miller, Daniel	do	22	May 2, 1864	100 dys.	Mustered out with company Aug. 30, 1864.
Moore, T. Brooks	do	20	May 2, 1864	100 dys.	Mustered out with company Aug. 30, 1864.
Neff, Walter S	do	20	May 2, 1864	100 dys.	Mustered out with company Aug. 30, 1864.
Nicodemus, Samuel	do	31	May 2, 1864	100 dys.	Mustered out with company Aug. 30, 1864.
Nicodemus, Oliver	do	20	May 2, 1864	100 dys.	Mustered out with company Aug. 30, 1864.
O'Brien, William	do	18	May 2, 1864	100 dys.	Mustered out with company Aug. 30, 1864.
Reeder, Joseph	do	40	May 2, 1864	100 dys.	Mustered out with company Aug. 30, 1864.
Rees, Samuel	do	27	May 2, 1864	100 dys.	Mustered out with company Aug. 30, 1864.
Riley, E. W	do	25	May 2, 1864	100 dys.	Reduced from Corporal ——, mustered out with company Aug. 30, 1864.
Runyan, John M	do	22	May 2, 1864	100 dys.	Mustered out with company Aug. 30, 1864.
Shields, Clarkson	do	20	May 2, 1864	100 dys.	Mustered out with company Aug. 30, 1864.
Shoemaker, Josephus	do	30	May 2, 1864	100 dys.	Mustered out with company Aug. 30, 1864.
Shoup, Benjamin F	do	31	May 2, 1864	100 dys.	Mustered out with company Aug. 30, 1864.
Smith, Charles F	do	22	May 2, 1864	100 dys.	Mustered out with company Aug. 30, 1864.
Spittler, Henry	do	19	May 2, 1864	100 dys.	Mustered out with company Aug. 30, 1864.
Thomas, G. W	do	41	May 2, 1864	100 dys.	Mustered out with company Aug. 30, 1864.
Tomire, John W	do	29	May 2, 1864	100 dys.	Discharged June 18, 1864, by order of War Department.
Warner, E. M	do	18	May 2, 1864	100 dys.	Mustered out with company Aug. 30, 1864.
Warner, E. F	do	29	May 2, 1864	100 dys.	Mustered out with company Aug. 30, 1864.
White, G. M	do	26	May 2, 1864	100 dys.	Mustered out with company Aug. 30, 1864.
White, David A	do	24	May 2, 1864	100 dys.	Mustered out with company Aug. 30, 1864.
White, James W	do	22	May 2, 1864	100 dys.	Mustered out with company Aug. 30, 1864.
Wilson, Samuel	do	28	May 2, 1864	100 dys.	Mustered out with company Aug. 30, 1864.
Zeller, Samuel	do	18	May 2, 1864	100 dys.	Mustered out with company Aug. 30, 1864.

COMPANY G.

Mustered in May 1[illegible], 1864, at Camp Dennison, O., by G. [illegible] Johnson, Major and A. [illegible] M. Mustered out Aug. [illegible], 1864, at Camp Dennison, O., by William Stanley, [illegible] Lieutenant [illegible] Infantry, U. S. A.

Names.	Rank.	Age.	Date of Entering the Service.	Period of Service.	Remarks.
[illegible]	Captain.	[illegible]	May 2, 1864	100 dys.	[illegible]
[illegible]	1st Lieut.	[illegible]	May 2, 1864	100 dys.	[illegible]
[illegible]	2d Lieut.	[illegible]	May 2, 1864	100 dys.	[illegible]
[illegible]	1st Sergt.	[illegible]	May 2, 1864	100 dys.	[illegible]
Rowe, William	...do...	[illegible]	May 2, 1864	100 dys.	Mustered out with company Aug. 30, 1864.
[illegible] William	...do...	[illegible]	May 2, 1864	100 dys.	Mustered out with company Aug. 30, 1864.
[illegible] William	...do...	[illegible]	May 2, 1864	100 dys.	Mustered out with company Aug. 30, 1864.

Names.	Rank.	Age.	Date of Entering the Service.	Period of Service.	Remarks.
Shoe, Reuben	Private..	18	May 2, 1864	100 dys.	Mustered out with company Aug. 30, 1864.
Shoe, John	....do....	26	May 2, 1864	100 dys.	Mustered out with company Aug. 30, 1864.
Sinks, Jacob	....do....	32	May 2, 1864	100 dys.	Mustered out with company Aug. 30, 1864.
Skillen, William	....do....	19	May 2, 1864	100 dys.	Mustered out with company Aug. 30, 1864.
Sloan, William R	....do....	28	May 2, 1864	100 dys.	Mustered out with company Aug. 30, 1864.
Smith, John	....do....	31	May 2, 1864	100 dys.	Mustered out with company Aug. 30, 1864.
Stechter, William	....do....	18	May 2, 1864	100 dys.	Mustered out with company Aug. 30, 1864.
Ward, Eli	....do....	35	May 2, 1864	100 dys.	Mustered out with company Aug. 30, 1864.
Westlake, John B	....do....	20	May 2, 1864	100 dys.	Mustered out with company Aug. 30, 1864.
Williams, John M	....do....	24	May 2, 1864	100 dys.	Mustered out with company Aug. 30, 1864.
Zanglain, John	....do....	18	May 2, 1864	100 dys.	Mustered out with company Aug. 30, 1864.

COMPANY H.

Mustered in May 16, 1864, at Camp Dennison, O., by G. E. Johnson, Major and A. C. M. Mustered out Aug. 30, 1864, at Camp Dennison, O., by William Stanley, 2d Lieutenant 10th Infantry, U. S. A.

Names.	Rank.	Age.	Date of Entering the Service.	Period of Service.	Remarks.
David Kelly	Captain.	27	May 2, 1864	100 dys.	Mustered out with company Aug. 30, 1864.
Richard T. Sharp	1st Lieut.	43	May 2, 1864	100 dys.	Mustered out with company Aug. 30, 1864.
Samuel A. Cairns	2d Lieut.	33	May 2, 1864	100 dys.	Mustered out with company Aug. 30, 1864.
George Stockton	1st Sergt.	25	May 2, 1864	100 dys.	Mustered out with company Aug. 30, 1864.
Oliver M. Tullis	Sergeant.	40	May 2, 1864	100 dys.	Mustered out with company Aug. 30, 1864.
Thomas M. Biddle	....do....	23	May 2, 1864	100 dys.	Mustered out with company Aug. 30, 1864.
Horace Stockton	....do....	40	May 2, 1864	100 dys.	Mustered out with company Aug. 30, 1864.
Charles Reed	....do....		May 2, 1864	100 dys.	Mustered out with company Aug. 30, 1864.
Thomas O. McCain	Corporal.	22	May 2, 1864	100 dys.	Mustered out with company Aug. 30, 1864.
William Anderson	....do....	34	May 2, 1864	100 dys.	Mustered out with company Aug. 30, 1864.
Jacob Hartman	....do....	23	May 2, 1864	100 dys.	Mustered out with company Aug. 30, 1864.
George W. Fox	....do....	24	May 2, 1864	100 dys.	Mustered out with company Aug. 30, 1864.
Jacob Slagle	....do....		May 2, 1864	100 dys.	Mustered out with company Aug. 30, 1864.
John F. Adams	....do....	30	May 2, 1864	100 dys.	Mustered out with company Aug. 30, 1864.
Charles H. McCullough	....do....	29	May 2, 1864	100 dys.	Mustered out with company Aug. 30, 1864.
James W. Hickerson	....do....	28	May 2, 1864	100 dys.	Mustered out with company Aug. 30, 1864.
Baer, Harrison	Private..	25	May 2, 1864	100 dys.	Mustered out with company Aug. 30, 1864.
Barker, John	....do....		May 2, 1864	100 dys.	Mustered out with company Aug. 30, 1864.
Beedle, Asa F	....do....	32	May 2, 1864	100 dys.	Mustered out with company Aug. 30, 1864.
Brown, George M	....do....	18	May 2, 1864	100 dys.	Discharged June 17, 1864.
Brown, William E	....do....	18	May 2, 1864	100 dys.	Mustered out with company Aug. 30, 1864.
Carver, William H	....do....	18	May 2, 1864	100 dys.	Mustered out with company Aug. 30, 1864.
Clark, Franklin G	....do....	43	May 2, 1864	100 dys.	Mustered out with company Aug. 30, 1864.
Coleman, George E	....do....	30	May 2, 1864	100 dys.	Mustered out with company Aug. 30, 1864.
Conklin, George E	....do....	18	May 2, 1864	100 dys.	Mustered out with company Aug. 30, 1864.
Corse, Asa	....do....	19	May 2, 1864	100 dys.	Mustered out with company Aug. 30, 1864.
Croner, Gustav	....do....	34	May 2, 1864	100 dys.	Mustered out with company Aug. 30, 1864.
Dunning, Richard	....do....	18	May 2, 1864	100 dys.	Rejected by Mustering Officer.
Eaton, Artemus	....do....	40	May 2, 1864	100 dys.	Mustered out with company Aug. 30, 1864.
Eusey, Augustus W	....do....	27	May 2, 1864	100 dys.	Mustered out with company Aug. 30, 1864.
Fogel, Peter	....do....	23	May 2, 1864	100 dys.	Mustered out with company Aug. 30, 1864.
Fritz, John K	....do....	38	May 2, 1864	100 dys.	Mustered out with company Aug. 30, 1864.
Gerlach, William	....do....	19	May 2, 1864	100 dys.	Mustered out with company Aug. 30, 1864.
Green, Caleb E	....do....	19	May 2, 1864	100 dys.	Mustered out with company Aug. 30, 1864.
Grosvenor, Frederick C	....do....	19	May 2, 1864	100 dys.	Mustered out with company Aug. 30, 1864.
Hartsell, Emanuel	....do....	18	May 2, 1864	100 dys.	Mustered out with company Aug. 30, 1864.
Hensley, James T	....do....	20	May 2, 1864	100 dys.	Promoted to Principal Musician May 15, 1864.
Hubbard, Thomas	....do....	21	May 2, 1864	100 dys.	Mustered out with company Aug. 30, 1864.
Hustler, George E	....do....	37	May 2, 1864	100 dys.	Promoted to Hospital Steward May 16, 1864.
Iddings, Jackson	....do....	21	May 2, 1864	100 dys.	Mustered out with company Aug. 30, 1864.
Jackson, John M	....do....	44	May 2, 1864	100 dys.	Mustered out with company Aug. 30, 1864.
Johnson, Calvin	....do....	28	May 2, 1864	100 dys.	Mustered out with company Aug. 30, 1864.
Kelly, Leonidas	....do....	18	May 2, 1864	100 dys.	Mustered out with company Aug. 30, 1864.
Lambert, Edward	....do....	27	May 2, 1864	100 dys.	Mustered out with company Aug. 30, 1864
Landry, Aaron	....do....	21	May 2, 1864	100 dys.	Mustered out with company Aug. 30, 1864.
Latchford, John	....do....	16	May 2, 1864	100 dys.	Rejected by Mustering Officer on account of age.
Lever, Joseph	....do....	37	May 2, 1864	100 dys.	Mustered out with company Aug. 30, 1864.
McCain, William H	....do....	28	May 2, 1864	100 dys.	Mustered out with company Aug. 30, 1864.
McCain, James M	....do....	34	May 2, 1864	100 dys.	No record subsequent to muster-in.
McKinney, John	....do....	18	May 2, 1864	100 dys.	Mustered out with company Aug. 30, 1864.
Miller, David W	....do....	21	May 2, 1864	100 dys.	Mustered out with company Aug. 30, 1864.
Miller, John N	....do....	27	May 2, 1864	100 dys.	Mustered out with company Aug. 30, 1864.
Myers, Jamuel K	....do....	50	May 2, 1864	100 dys.	Mustered out with company Aug. 30, 1864.
Oblinger, John	....do....	20	May 2, 1864	100 dys.	Promoted to Principal Musician May 16, 1864.
Oblinger, Solomon	....do....	25	May 2, 1864	100 dys.	Mustered out with company Aug. 30, 1864.
Orbison, Stewart	....do....		May 2, 1864	100 dys.	Mustered out with company Aug. 30, 1864.
Peck, Oscar	....do....	19	May 2, 1864	100 dys.	Mustered out with company Aug. 30, 1864.
Peckham, George	....do....	28	May 2, 1864	100 dys.	Mustered out with company Aug. 30, 1864.
Perrin, James	....do....	25	May 2, 1864	100 dys.	Mustered out with company Aug. 30, 1864.
Rankin, Marion	....do....	16	May 2, 1864	100 dys.	Rejected by Examining Surgeon.
Rench, Jacob	....do....		May 2, 1864	100 dys.	Rejected by Mustering Officer.
Riddle, Joseph M	....do....	18	May 2, 1864	100 dys.	Mustered out with company Aug. 30, 1864.

Names.	Rank.	Age.	Date of Entering the Service.	Period of Service.	Remarks.
Lawhead, Philip S.	Private	26	May 2, 1864	100 dys.	Mustered out with company Aug. 30, 1864.
Lefever, Harrison	...do...	28	May 2, 1864	100 dys.	Died July 3, 1864, in hospital at Fort Ethan Allen, Va.
Lefettre, Robert E.	...do...	37	May 2, 1864	100 dys.	Mustered out with company Aug. 30, 1864.
Livingston, Thomas R.	...do...	19	May 2, 1864	100 dys.	Mustered out with company Aug. 30, 1864.
McKee, William R.	...do...	19	May 2, 1864	100 dys.	Mustered out with company Aug. 30, 1864.
Martin, Josiah W.	...do...	55	May 2, 1864	100 dys.	Mustered out with company Aug. 30, 1864.
Mikesel, Andrew F.	...do...	21	May 2, 1864	100 dys.	Mustered out with company Aug. 30, 1864.
Moore, George	...do...	26	May 2, 1864	100 dys.	Mustered out with company Aug. 30, 1864.
M[illegible], Edmund L.	...do...	19	May 2, 1864	100 dys.	Mustered out with company Aug. 30, 1864.
Nill, Conrad	...do...	23	May 2, 1864	100 dys.	Mustered out with company Aug. 30, 1864.
Nill, John	...do...	43	May 2, 1864	100 dys.	Mustered out with company Aug. 30, 1864.
Puterbaugh, Solomon	...do...	39	May 2, 1864	100 dys.	Mustered out with company Aug. 30, 1864.
Rankin, Marion F.	...do...	18	May 2, 1864	100 dys.	Mustered out with company Aug. 30, 1864.
Rench, Peter	...do...	19	May 2, 1864	100 dys.	Mustered out with company Aug. 30, 1864.
Rench, Jacob R.	...do...	18	May 2, 1864	100 dys.	Mustered out with company Aug. 30, 1864.
Robins, Sam[illegible]	...do...	34	May 2, 1864	100 dys.	Mustered out with company Aug. 30, 1864.
Rogers, John C.	...do...	19	May 2, 1864	100 dys.	Mustered out with company Aug. 30, 1864.
Routzahn, Joshua	...do...	31	May 2, 1864	100 dys.	Mustered out with company Aug. 30, 1864.
Routzahn, Josiah	...do...	28	May 2, 1864	100 dys.	Mustered out with company Aug. 30, 1864.
Sanders, [illegible] R.	...do...	22	May 2, 1864	100 dys.	Mustered out with company Aug. 30, 1864.
Sa[illegible]ers, Charles H.	...do...	31	May 2, 1864	100 dys.	Mustered out with company Aug. 30, 1864.
Shellen[illegible]rger, Angus K.	...do...	20	May 2, 1864	100 dys.	Mustered out with company Aug. 30, 1864.
Sheibach, Barnhart	...do...	30	May 2, 1864	100 dys.	Mustered out with company Aug. 30, 1864.
Sise, Gideon	...do...	20	May 2, 1864	100 dys.	Mustered out with company Aug. 30, 1864.
Simmons, John	...do...	20	May 2, 1864	100 dys.	Mustered out with company Aug. 30, 1864.
Smith, David M.	...do...	20	May 2, 1864	100 dys.	Mustered out with company Aug. 30, 1864.
Smith, James R.	...do...	23	May 2, 1864	100 dys.	Mustered out with company Aug. 30, 1864.
Stephenson, Giles	...do...	23	May 2, 1864	100 dys.	Mustered out with company Aug. 30, 1864.
Sterrett, Frank M.	...do...	19	May 2, 1864	100 dys.	Mustered out with company Aug. 30, 1864.
Stratton, DeWitt C.	...do...	28	May 2, 1864	100 dys.	Mustered out with company Aug. 30, 1864.
South, George H.	...do...	28	May 2, 1864	100 dys.	Mustered out with company Aug. 30, 1864.
Sowers, John T.	...do...	18	May 2, 1864	100 dys.	Mustered out with company Aug. 30, 1864.
Thackara, John C.	...do...	36	May 2, 1864	100 dys.	Mustered out with company Aug. 30, 1864.
Ulery, Frank	...do...	20	May 2, 1864	100 dys.	Mustered out with company Aug. 30, 1864.
Webb, James E.	...do...	18	May 2, 1864	100 dys.	Mustered out with company Aug. 30, 1864.
Webb, William K.	...do...	46	May 2, 1864	100 dys.	Mustered out with company Aug. 30, 1864.
Weatherhead, Rudolph	...do...	23	May 2, 1864	100 dys.	Mustered out with company Aug. 30, 1864.
Wray, Joseph	...do...	20	May 2, 1864	100 dys.	Mustered out with company Aug. 30, 1864.
Wright, Christopher C.	...do...	19	May 2, 1864	100 dys.	Mustered out with company Aug. 30, 1864.

COMPANY K.

Mustered in May 16, 1864, at Camp Dennison, O., by G. E. Johnson, Major and A. C. M. Mustered out Aug. 30, 1864, at Camp Dennison, O., by William Stanley, 2d Lieutenant 10th Infantry, U. S. A.

Names.	Rank.	Age.	Date of Entering the Service.	Period of Service.	Remarks.
Jeremiah F. Counts	Captain.	43	May 2, 1864	100 dys.	Mustered out with company Aug. 30, 1864.
Samuel A. Collins	1st Lieut.	24	May 2, 1864	100 dys.	Mustered out with company Aug. 30, 1864.
Eckert Shaffer	2d Lieut.	19	May 2, 1864	100 dys.	Mustered out with company Aug. 30, 1864.
M. B. Deweese	1st Sergt.	25	May 2, 1864	100 dys.	Mustered out with company Aug. 30, 1864.
David Deweese	Sergeant	31	May 2, 1864	100 dys.	Mustered out with company Aug. 30, 1864.
Jacob Peterson	...do...	29	May 2, 1864	100 dys.	Mustered out with company Aug. 30, 1864.
Horace J. Rollins	...do...	18	May 2, 1864	100 dys.	Mustered out with company Aug. 30, 1864.
Cornelius Bowers	...do...	25	May 2, 1864	100 dys.	Mustered out with company Aug. 30, 1864.
William B. Orbison	Corporal.	42	May 2, 1864	100 dys.	Mustered out with company Aug. 30, 1864.
George Buckles	...do...	35	May 2, 1864	100 dys.	Mustered out with company Aug. 30, 1864.
Daniel Stillwell	...do...	39	May 2, 1864	100 dys.	Mustered out with company Aug. 30, 1864.
Clemens Shaffer	...do...	33	May 2, 1864	100 dys.	Mustered out with company Aug. 30, 1864.
George W. Deweese	...do...	36	May 2, 1864	100 dys.	Mustered out with company Aug. 30, 1864.
Hiram Cushing	...do...	23	May 2, 1864	100 dys.	Mustered out with company Aug. 30, 1864.
George Skinner	...do...	41	May 2, 1864	100 dys.	Mustered out with company Aug. 30, 1864.
David D. Spencer	...do...	36	May 2, 1864	100 dys.	Mustered out with company Aug. 30, 1864.
Armstrong, Howard	Private	22	May 2, 1864	100 dys.	Mustered out with company Aug. 30, 1864.
Bercaw, Daniel	...do...	43	May 2, 1864	100 dys.	Mustered out with company Aug. 30, 1864.
Boyd, Nelson	...do...	41	May 2, 1864	100 dys.	No record subsequent to muster-in.
Brown, William M.	...do...	23	May 2, 1864	100 dys.	Mustered out with company Aug. 30, 1864.
Cecil, Ryan	...do...	19	May 2, 1864	100 dys.	No record subsequent to muster in.
Covault, Preston	...do...	18	May 2, 1864	100 dys.	No record subsequent to muster in.
Cox, Charles T.	...do...	21	May 2, 1864	100 dys.	Mustered out with company Aug. 30, 1864.
DeHaven, John	...do...	41	May 2, 1864	100 dys.	Mustered out with company Aug. 30, 1864.
DeHaven, Harrison D.	...do...	33	May 2, 1864	100 dys.	Mustered out with company Aug. 30, 1864.
Deputee, Oliver	...do...	18	May 2, 1864	100 dys.	Mustered out with company Aug. 30, 1864.
Deweese, Daniel B.	...do...	21	May 2, 1864	100 dys.	Mustered out with company Aug. 30, 1864.
Deweese, Lafayette	...do...	18	May 2, 1864	100 dys.	Absent, sick, July 27, 1864, in general hospital. No further record found.
Deweese, Samuel H.	...do...	34	May 2, 1864	100 dys.	Mustered out with company Aug. 30, 1864.
Deweese, Thomas W.	...do...	24	May 2, 1864	100 dys.	Mustered out with company Aug. 30, 1864.
Devol, Hiram	...do...	27	May 2, 1864	100 dys.	Mustered out with company Aug. 30, 1864.
Donahue, John	...do...	28	May 2, 1864	100 dys.	No record subsequent to muster-in.
Drawbaugh, Louis	...do...	29	May 2, 1864	100 dys.	Mustered out with company Aug. 30, 1864.

Names.	Rank.	Age.	Date of Entering the Service.	Period of Service.	Remarks.
Drake, Francis M.	Private.	33	May 2, 1864	100 dys.	Mustered out with company Aug. 30, 1864.
Dye, Nathan	...do...	41	May 2, 1864	100 dys.	Mustered out with company Aug. 30, 1864.
French, Orpheus	...do...	19	May 2, 1864	100 dys.	Mustered out with company Aug. 30, 1864.
Gearhart, William R.	...do...	27	May 2, 1864	100 dys.	Died July 11, 1864, at Fort Ethan Allen, Va.
Gearhart, Samuel M.	...do...	20	May 2, 1864	100 dys.	Mustered out with company Aug. 30, 1864.
Hart, Theodore R.	...do...	21	May 2, 1864	100 dys.	Mustered out with company Aug. 30, 1864.
Hardenbrook, John G.	...do...	58	May 2, 1864	100 dys.	Mustered out with company Aug. 30, 1864.
Harrett, Joshua	...do...	27	May 2, 1864	100 dys.	Mustered out with company Aug. 30, 1864.
Harrett, William	...do...	23	May 2, 1864	100 dys.	Mustered out with company Aug. 30, 1864.
Hilliard, Alpheus	...do...	14	May 2, 1864	100 dys.	Mustered out with company Aug. 30, 1864.
Hilliard, Stephen	...do...	23	May 2, 1864	100 dys.	Mustered out with company Aug. 30, 1864.
Inskeep, Angus	...do...	25	May 2, 1864	100 dys.	Mustered out with company Aug. 30, 1864.
Inskeep, Joseph	...do...	50	May 2, 1864	100 dys.	Mustered out with company Aug. 30, 1864.
Jones, Alvin	...do...	22	May 2, 1864	100 dys.	Mustered out with company Aug. 30, 1864.
Johnson, George W.	...do...	20	May 2, 1864	100 dys.	Mustered out with company Aug. 30, 1864.
Knoop, James M.	...do...	28	May 2, 1864	100 dys.	Mustered out with company Aug. 30, 1864.
Knoop, Henry	...do...	20	May 2, 1864	100 dys.	Mustered out with company Aug. 30, 1864.
Knoop, Sabin	...do...	19	May 2, 1864	100 dys.	No record subsequent to muster-in.
Kuhl, Leonard	...do...	28	May 2, 1864	100 dys.	No record subsequent to muster-in.
Lloyd, Henry	...do...	27	May 2, 1864	100 dys.	Mustered out with company Aug. 30, 1864.
Lower, Frederick	...do...	27	May 2, 1864	100 dys.	No record subsequent to muster in.
McGailliard, William H.	...do...	23	May 2, 1864	100 dys.	Mustered out with company Aug. 30, 1864.
Maxwell, Spofford W.	...do...	26	May 2, 1864	100 dys.	Mustered out with company Aug. 30, 1864.
Metcalf, Benjamin F.	...do...	31	May 2, 1864	100 dys.	Mustered out with company Aug. 30, 1864.
Miller, Jacob	...do...	21	May 2, 1864	100 dys.	Mustered out with company Aug. 30, 1864.
Moore, James	...do...	26	May 2, 1864	100 dys.	Mustered out with company Aug. 30, 1864.
Norris, John	...do...	24	May 2, 1864	100 dys.	No record subsequent to muster in.
Peterson, John G.	...do...	33	May 2, 1864	100 dys.	Mustered out with company Aug. 30, 1864.
Price, Mahlon	...do...	35	May 2, 1864	100 dys.	Mustered out with company Aug. 30, 1864.
Robins, Erastus	...do...	25	May 2, 1864	100 dys.	Mustered out with company Aug. 30, 1864.
Robins, Madison	...do...	29	May 2, 1864	100 dys.	Mustered out with company Aug. 30, 1864.
Rollins, Leander I.	...do...	28	May 2, 1864	100 dys.	Absent, sick, July 19, 1864, in general hospital. No further record found.
Rollins, Sylvester	...do...	22	May 2, 1864	100 dys.	Mustered out with company Aug. 30, 1864.
Russell, William R.	...do...	23	May 2, 1864	100 dys.	Mustered out with company Aug. 30, 1864.
Sch[illegible]man, John F.	...do...	34	May 2, 1864	100 dys.	Mustered out with company Aug. 30, 1864.
Sh[illegible]ll, Benjamin F.	...do...	30	May 2, 1864	100 dys.	Mustered out with company Aug. 30, 1864.
S[illegible], Leroy	...do...	18	May 2, 1864	100 dys.	No record subsequent to muster in.
[illegible], Francis M.	...do...	25	May 2, 1864	100 dys.	Mustered out with company Aug. 30, 1864.
Small, Louis C.	...do...	18	May 2, 1864	100 dys.	No record subsequent to muster in.
Smith, Thomas	...do...	38	May 2, 1864	100 dys.	Mustered out with company Aug. 30, 1864.
Smith, George W.	...do...	36	May 2, 1864	100 dys.	Mustered out with company Aug. 30, 1864.
Snyder, William H. H.	...do...	23	May 2, 1864	100 dys.	Mustered out with company Aug. 30, 1864.
Spencer, Daniel B.	...do...	31	May 2, 1864	100 dys.	Died July 31, 1864, at Fort Ethan Allen, Va.
St[illegible]ton, Daniel F.	...do...	31	May 2, 1864	100 dys.	No record subsequent to muster-in.
Thomas, John	...do...	23	May 2, 1864	100 dys.	Mustered out with company Aug. 30, 1864.
Thomas, John N.	...do...	22	May 2, 1864	100 dys.	Mustered out Sept. 8, 1864, at Washington, D. C., by order of War Department.
West, John L.	...do...	31	May 2, 1864	100 dys.	Mustered out with company Aug. 30, 1864.
Wright, William B.	...do...	45	May 2, 1864	100 dys.	No record subsequent to muster in.
Yates, Charles L.	...do...	33	May 2, 1864	100 dys.	Mustered out with company Aug. 30, 1864.
Yourt, Adam	...do...	33	May 2, 1864	100 dys.	Discharged by Surgeon, date and place not known.
Yourt, Andrew S.	...do...	29	May 2, 1864	100 dys.	Mustered out with company Aug. 30, 1864.

148th Regiment Ohio Volunteer Infantry.

ONE HUNDRED DAYS' SERVICE.

THIS Regiment was organized at Marietta, O., May 17 and 18, 1864, to serve one hundred days. It was composed of the Forty-sixth Regiment, Ohio National Guard, from Washington County, and the Twenty-sixth Battalion, Ohio National Guard, from Vinton County. On the 23d of May the Regiment left Marietta for the field. After remaining about ten days at Harper's Ferry the Regiment moved to Washington, and on the 9th of June left that city for White House. On the 11th it left White House, arrived at Bermuda Hundred on the 12th, and on the 13th went into General Butler's intrenchments at the front. On the 16th seven companies, under command of the Lieutenant Colonel, left Bermuda Hundred for City Point. The One Hundred and Forty-eighth left City Point on the 29th of August, and arrived at Marietta on the 5th of September, and was mustered out September 14, 1864, on expiration of term of service.

Names.	Rank.	Age.	Date of Entering the Service.	Period of Service.	Remarks.
Bosworth, Frank H	Private	21	May 2, 1864	100 dys.	Promoted to Q. M. Sergeant from private May 2, 1864; reduced to ranks July 24, 1864; mustered out with company Sept. 14, 1864.
Bratton, Anthony W	do	19	May 2, 1864	100 dys.	Transferred from Co. B ——; mustered out with company Sept. 14, 1864.
Braddock, Austin F	do	22	May 2, 1864	100 dys.	Mustered out with company Sept. 14, 1864.
Caywood, William	do	20	May 2, 1864	100 dys.	Mustered out with company Sept. 14, 1864.
Clark, Joseph D	do	18	May 2, 1864	100 dys.	Killed Aug. 9, 1864, at City Point, Va., by explosion of ordnance boat.
Clogston, Ansel W	do	23	May 2, 1864	100 dys.	Mustered out with company Sept. 14, 1864.
Coomes, Henry	do	18	May 2, 1864	100 dys.	Mustered out with company Sept. 14, 1864.
Dale, Theodore D	do	18	May 2, 1864	100 dys.	Mustered out with company Sept. 14, 1864.
Dana, Charles L	do	19	May 2, 1864	100 dys.	Mustered out with company Sept. 14, 1864.
Daybold, Jacob F	do	22	May 2, 1864	100 dys.	Mustered out with company Sept. 14, 1864.
Devol, Benjamin F	do	18	May 2, 1864	100 dys.	Mustered out with company Sept. 14, 1864.
Devol, John B	do	25	May 2, 1864	100 dys.	Mustered out with company Sept. 14, 1864.
Dice, Henry	do	18	May 2, 1864	100 dys.	Mustered out with company Sept. 14, 1864.
Dice, John	do	21	May 2, 1864	100 dys.	Mustered out with company Sept. 14, 1864.
Doane, William P	do	18	May 2, 1864	100 dys.	Mustered out with company Sept. 14, 1864.
Dye, Jacob	do	18	May 2, 1864	100 dys.	Mustered out with company Sept. 14, 1864.
Flanders, Enos J	do	21	May 2, 1864	100 dys.	Mustered out with company Sept. 14, 1864.
Grother, Peter	do	39	May 2, 1864	100 dys.	Mustered out with company Sept. 14, 1864.
Haberlian, Jacob	do	21	May 2, 1864	100 dys.	Mustered out with company Sept. 14, 1864.
Hartwig, Peter	do	22	May 2, 1864	100 dys.	Mustered out with company Sept. 14, 1864.
Henniger, Harmon	do	18	May 2, 1864	100 dys.	Mustered out with company Sept. 14, 1864.
[illegible], William W	do	52	May 2, 1864	100 dys.	Mustered out with company Sept. 14, 1864.
Hutchins, Charles	do	37	May 2, 1864	100 dys.	Mustered out with company Sept. 14, 1864.
Johnson, Worthy A	do	18	May 2, 1864	100 dys.	Mustered out with company Sept. 14, 1864.
Judd, Frank	do	19	May 2, 1864	100 dys.	Mustered out with company Sept. 14, 1864.
Kerbs, Leonard	do	19	May 2, 1864	100 dys.	Mustered out with company Sept. 14, 1864.
[illegible], Thomas	do	26	May 2, 1864	100 dys.	Mustered out with company Sept. 14, 1864.
Lapham, Luther	do	17	May 2, 1864	100 dys.	Mustered out with company Sept. 14, 1864.
[illegible], Owen	do	18	May 2, 1864	100 dys.	Mustered out with company Sept. 14, 1864.
Lewis, Samuel M	do	19	May 2, 1864	100 dys.	Mustered as Musician; mustered out with company Sept. 14, 1864.
[illegible], Frederick G	do	22	May 2, 1864	100 dys.	Mustered out with company Sept. 14, 1864.
Lower, Daniel	do	19	May 2, 1864	100 dys.	Mustered out with company Sept. 14, 1864.
[illegible], Joseph A	do	22	May 2, 1864	100 dys.	Mustered out with company Sept. 14, 1864.
[illegible], John	do	18	May 2, 1864	100 dys.	Mustered out with company Sept. 14, 1864.
Miller, Thomas J	do	28	May 2, 1864	100 dys.	Mustered out with company Sept. 14, 1864.
Morse, Winslow W	do	19	May 2, 1864	100 dys.	Mustered out with company Sept. 14, 1864.
O'[illegible], Philip F	do	17	May 2, 1864	100 dys.	Mustered out with company Sept. 14, 1864.
[illegible], George	do	19	May 2, 1864	100 dys.	Mustered out with company Sept. 14, 1864.
[illegible], Lewis	do	26	May 2, 1864	100 dys.	Mustered out with company Sept. 14, 1864.
[illegible], Frank	do	18	May 2, 1864	100 dys.	Mustered out with company Sept. 14, 1864.
[illegible], William P	do	19	May 2, 1864	100 dys.	Mustered out with company Sept. 14, 1864.
[illegible], John	do	35	May 2, 1864	100 dys.	Mustered out with company Sept. 14, 1864.
[illegible], William	do	30	May 2, 1864	100 dys.	Mustered out with company Sept. 14, 1864.
[illegible], William	do	18	May 2, 1864	100 dys.	Mustered out with company Sept. 14, 1864.
[illegible], John	do	19	May 2, 1864	100 dys.	Mustered out with company Sept. 14, 1864.
Shepard, Thomas R	do	19	May 2, 1864	100 dys.	Mustered out with company Sept. 14, 1864.
[illegible], Joseph	do	18	May 2, 1864	100 dys.	Mustered out with company Sept. 14, 1864.
[illegible], Edward	do	25	May 2, 1864	100 dys.	Mustered out with company Sept. 14, 1864.
[illegible], Albert	do	19	May 2, 1864	100 dys.	Mustered out with company Sept. 14, 1864.
Smith, Andrew	do	20	May 2, 1864	100 dys.	Mustered out with company Sept. 14, 1864.
Smith, John J	do	19	May 2, 1864	100 dys.	Mustered out with company Sept. 14, 1864.
Smith, Peter	do	18	May 2, 1864	100 dys.	
[illegible], Henry	do	19	May 2, 1864	100 dys.	Mustered out with company Sept. 14, 1864.
[illegible], Jeremiah	do	29	May 2, 1864	100 dys.	Killed May 23, 1864, near Marietta, O., by railroad accident.
Swallow, Washington W	do	19	May 2, 1864	100 dys.	Mustered out with company Sept. 14, 1864.
Swift, John	do	18	May 2, 1864	100 dys.	Mustered out with company Sept. 14, 1864.
Thayer, Edward	do	23	May 2, 1864	100 dys.	
[illegible], Christian	do	18	May 2, 1864	100 dys.	Mustered out with company Sept. 14, 1864.
[illegible], Albert	do	22	May 2, 1864	100 dys.	
[illegible], George H	do	18	May 2, 1864	100 dys.	Mustered out with company Sept. 14, 1864.
[illegible], Samuel R	do	35	May 2, 1864	100 dys.	Mustered out with company Sept. 14, 1864.
Will, Alfred H	do	21	May 2, 1864	100 dys.	Mustered out with company Sept. 14, 1864.
[illegible], Frederick	do	19	May 2, 1864	100 dys.	Mustered out with company Sept. 14, 1864.

Names.	Rank.	Age.	Date of Entering the Service.	Period of Service.	Remarks.
Bosworth, Frank H	Private	21	May 2, 1864	100 dys.	Promoted to Q. M. Sergeant from private May 2, 1864; reduced to ranks July 24, 1864; mustered out with company Sept. 14, 1864.
Bratton, Anthony W	...do...	19	May 2, 1864	100 dys.	Transferred from Co. B —; mustered out with company Sept. 14, 1864.
Braddock, Austin F	...do...	22	May 2, 1864	100 dys.	Mustered out with company Sept. 14, 1864.
Caywood, William	...do...	30	May 2, 1864	100 dys.	Mustered out with company Sept. 14, 1864.
Clark, Joseph D	...do...	18	May 2, 1864	100 dys.	Killed Aug. 9, 1864, at City Point, Va., by explosion of ordnance boat.
Clogston, Ansel W	...do...	23	May 2, 1864	100 dys.	Mustered out with company Sept. 14, 1864.
Coomes, Henry	...do...	18	May 2, 1864	100 dys.	Mustered out with company Sept. 14, 1864.
Dale, Theodore D	...do...	18	May 2, 1864	100 dys.	Mustered out with company Sept. 14, 1864.
Dana, Charles L	...do...	19	May 2, 1864	100 dys.	Mustered out with company Sept. 14, 1864.
Daybold, Jacob F	...do...	22	May 2, 1864	100 dys.	Mustered out with company Sept. 14, 1864.
Devol, Benjamin F	...do...	18	May 2, 1864	100 dys.	Mustered out with company Sept. 14, 1864.
Devol, John B	...do...	25	May 2, 1864	100 dys.	Mustered out with company Sept. 14, 1864.
Dice, Henry	...do...	18	May 2, 1864	100 dys.	Mustered out with company Sept. 14, 1864.
Dice, John	...do...	21	May 2, 1864	100 dys.	Mustered out with company Sept. 14, 1864.
Doane, William P	...do...	18	May 2, 1864	100 dys.	Mustered out with company Sept. 14, 1864.
Dye, Jacob	...do...	18	May 2, 1864	100 dys.	Mustered out with company Sept. 14, 1864.
Flanders, Enos J	...do...	21	May 2, 1864	100 dys.	Mustered out with company Sept. 14, 1864.
Grother, Peter	...do...	19	May 2, 1864	100 dys.	Mustered out with company Sept. 14, 1864.
Haberling, Jacob	...do...	21	May 2, 1864	100 dys.	Mustered out with company Sept. 14, 1864.
Hartwig, Peter	...do...	22	May 2, 1864	100 dys.	Mustered out with company Sept. 14, 1864.
Henniger, Harmon	...do...	18	May 2, 1864	100 dys.	Mustered out with company Sept. 14, 1864.
Hildebrand, William W	...do...	32	May 2, 1864	100 dys.	Mustered out with company Sept. 14, 1864.
Hutchins, Charles	...do...	37	May 2, 1864	100 dys.	Mustered out with company Sept. 14, 1864.
Hutchinson, Worthy A	...do...	18	May 2, 1864	100 dys.	Mustered out with company Sept. 14, 1864.
Judd, Frank	...do...	19	May 2, 1864	100 dys.	Mustered out with company Sept. 14, 1864.
Kerbs, Leonard	...do...	19	May 2, 1864	100 dys.	Mustered out with company Sept. 14, 1864.
Lane, Thomas	...do...	36	May 2, 1864	100 dys.	Mustered out with company Sept. 14, 1864.
Lapham, Luther	...do...	17	May 2, 1864	100 dys.	Mustered out with company Sept. 14, 1864.
Lapham, Owen	...do...	18	May 2, 1864	100 dys.	Mustered out with company Sept. 14, 1864.
Lewis, Samuel M	...do...	19	May 2, 1864	100 dys.	Mustered as Musician; mustered out with company Sept. 14, 1864.
Libran, Frederick G	...do...	22	May 2, 1864	100 dys.	Mustered out with company Sept. 14, 1864.
Lower, Daniel	...do...	19	May 2, 1864	100 dys.	Mustered out with company Sept. 14, 1864.
Luthering, Joseph A	...do...	22	May 2, 1864	100 dys.	Mustered out with company Sept. 14, 1864.
Mendall, John	...do...	18	May 2, 1864	100 dys.	Mustered out with company Sept. 14, 1864.
Miller, Thomas J	...do...	28	May 2, 1864	100 dys.	Mustered out with company Sept. 14, 1864.
Morse, Winslow W	...do...	19	May 2, 1864	100 dys.	Mustered out with company Sept. 14, 1864.
O'Heran, Philip F	...do...	17	May 2, 1864	100 dys.	Mustered out with company Sept. 14, 1864.
Page, George	...do...	19	May 2, 1864	100 dys.	Mustered out with company Sept. 14, 1864.
Phaff, Lewis	...do...	26	May 2, 1864	100 dys.	Mustered out with company Sept. 14, 1864.
Pixly, Frank	...do...	18	May 2, 1864	100 dys.	Mustered out with company Sept. 14, 1864.
Racer, William P	...do...	19	May 2, 1864	100 dys.	Mustered out with company Sept. 14, 1864.
Ratchin, John	...do...	35	May 2, 1864	100 dys.	Mustered out with company Sept. 14, 1864.
Robinson, William	...do...	30	May 2, 1864	100 dys.	Mustered out with company Sept. 14, 1864.
Roney, William	...do...	18	May 2, 1864	100 dys.	Mustered out with company Sept. 14, 1864.
Searle, John	...do...	19	May 2, 1864	100 dys.	Mustered out with company Sept. 14, 1864.
Sheppard, Thomas R	...do...	19	May 2, 1864	100 dys.	Mustered out with company Sept. 14, 1864.
Shilling, Joseph	...do...	18	May 2, 1864	100 dys.	Mustered out with company Sept. 14, 1864.
Skinnard, Edward	...do...	25	May 2, 1864	100 dys.	Mustered out with company Sept. 14, 1864.
Slocomb, Albert	...do...	19	May 2, 1864	100 dys.	Mustered out with company Sept. 14, 1864.
Smith, Andrew	...do...	20	May 2, 1864	100 dys.	Mustered out with company Sept. 14, 1864.
Smith, John J	...do...	19	May 2, 1864	100 dys.	Mustered out with company Sept. 14, 1864.
Smith, Peter	...do...	18	May 2, 1864	100 dys.	
Snyder, Henry	...do...	19	May 2, 1864	100 dys.	Mustered out with company Sept. 14, 1864.
Stuckey, Jeremiah	...do...	23	May 2, 1864	100 dys.	Killed May 23, 1864, near Marietta, O., by railroad accident.
Swallow, Washington W	...do...	19	May 2, 1864	100 dys.	Mustered out with company Sept. 14, 1864.
Sw[illegible], John	...do...	18	May 2, 1864	100 dys.	Mustered out with company Sept. 14, 1864.
Thayer, Edward	...do...	23	May 2, 1864	100 dys.	
Theis, Christian	...do...	18	May 2, 1864	100 dys.	Mustered out with company Sept. 14, 1864.
Tucker, Albert	...do...	22	May 2, 1864	100 dys.	
Vanbergen, George H	...do...	18	May 2, 1864	100 dys.	Mustered out with company Sept. 14, 1864.
Vandine, Samuel R	...do...	35	May 2, 1864	100 dys.	Mustered out with company Sept. 14, 1864.
Will, Alfred H	...do...	21	May 2, 1864	100 dys.	Mustered out with company Sept. 14, 1864.
Zollers, Frederick	...do...	19	May 2, 1864	100 dys.	Mustered out with company Sept. 14, 1864.

Names.	Rank.	Age.	Date of Entering the Service.	Period of Service.	Remarks.
...n, Abraham		37	May 2, 1864	100 dys.	Mustered out with company Sept. 14, 1864.
...line, Joseph		34	May 2, 1864	100 dys.	Mustered out with company Sept. 14, 1864.
... Joseph		25	May 2, 1864	100 dys.	Mustered out with company Sept. 14, 1864.
... George B.		22	May 2, 1864	100 dys.	Mustered out with company Sept. 14, 1864.
...son, William		20	May 2, 1864	100 dys.	Mustered out with company Sept. 14, 1864.
...barger, Henry		18	May 2, 1864	100 dys.	Mustered out with company Sept. 14, 1864.
...rson, John W.		21	May 2, 1864	100 dys.	Died July 5, 1864, at Bermuda Hundred, Va.
...rson, Fletcher		19	May 2, 1864	100 dys.	Mustered out with company Sept. 14, 1864.
...rson, William		23	May 2, 1864	100 dys.	Mustered out with company Sept. 14, 1864.
...r, Lafayette		41	May 2, 1864	100 dys.	Mustered out with company Sept. 14, 1864.
...rn, John		23	May 2, 1864	100 dys.	Mustered out with company Sept. 14, 1864.
...rn, Nelson		23	May 2, 1864	100 dys.	Mustered out with company Sept. 14, 1864.
..., James		36	May 2, 1864	100 dys.	Mustered out with company Sept. 14, 1864.
...r, Allison		27	May 2, 1864	100 dys.	Mustered out with company Sept. 14, 1864.
...n, [illegible] D.		18	May 2, 1864	100 dys.	Mustered out with company Sept. 14, 1864.
...ll, Benjamin F.		25	May 2, 1864	100 dys.	Died Aug. 2, 1864, at City Point, Va.
..., Henry A.		19	May 2, 1864	100 dys.	Mustered out with company Sept. 14, 1864.
..., Holden		38	May 2, 1864	100 dys.	Mustered out with company Sept. 14, 1864.
..., Stephen		23	May 2, 1864	100 dys.	Mustered out with company Sept. 14, 1864.
..., Theodore		21	May 2, 1864	100 dys.	Mustered out with company Sept. 14, 1864.
...oat, Henry		20	May 2, 1864	100 dys.	Mustered out with company Sept. 14, 1864.
...oat, John G.		38	May 2, 1864	100 dys.	Mustered out with company Sept. 14, 1864.
...ch, Elijah		41	May 2, 1864	100 dys.	Mustered out with company Sept. 14, 1864.
...McKendree		25	May 2, 1864	100 dys.	Mustered out with company Sept. 14, 1864.
..., Isaac		22	May 2, 1864	100 dys.	Mustered out with company Sept. 14, 1864.
...rn, Isaac		22	May 2, 1864	100 dys.	Mustered out with company Sept. 14, 1864.
...rn, Pharis B.		22	May 2, 1864	100 dys.	Mustered out with company Sept. 14, 1864.
...r, Sanford		19	May 2, 1864	100 dys.	Mustered out with company Sept. 14, 1864.
...off, James H.		31	May 2, 1864	100 dys.	Mustered out with company Sept. 14, 1864.

COMPANY D.

...red in May 17, 1864, at Marietta, O., by James P. W. Neill, 1st Lieutenant 18th Infantry, U. S. A. Mustered out Sept. 14, 1864, at Camp Marietta, O., by George M. Downey, 1st Lieutenant 14th Infantry, U. S. A.

Names.	Rank.	Age.	Date of Entering the Service.	Period of Service.	Remarks.
...n F. Dawson	Captain.	30	May 2, 1864	100 dys.	Mustered out with company Sept. 14, 1864.
... Randolph	1st Lieut.	30	May 2, 1864	100 dys.	Mustered out with company Sept. 14, 1864.
...min Arnold	2d Lieut.	28	May 2, 1864	100 dys.	Mustered out with company Sept. 14, 1864.
...l N. Hobson	1st Sergt.	31	May 2, 1864	100 dys.	Mustered out with company Sept. 14, 1864.
... Hildebrand	Sergeant.	44	May 2, 1864	100 dys.	Mustered out with company Sept. 14, 1864.
...Rotman	do.	22	May 2, 1864	100 dys.	Mustered out with company Sept. 14, 1864.
...r V. Smith	do.	30	May 2, 1864	100 dys.	Mustered out with company Sept. 14, 1864.
...n McMullen	do.	29	May 2, 1864	100 dys.	Mustered out with company Sept. 14, 1864.
...m F. Wilson	Corporal.	33	May 2, 1864	100 dys.	Mustered out with company Sept. 14, 1864.
...w Barton	do.	29	May 2, 1864	100 dys.	Mustered out with company Sept. 14, 1864.
...m H. Brill	do.	23	May 2, 1864	100 dys.	Mustered out with company Sept. 14, 1864.
...w Wilson	do.	28	May 2, 1864	100 dys.	Mustered out with company Sept. 14, 1864.
... Clayton	do.	28	May 2, 1864	100 dys.	Mustered out with company Sept. 14, 1864.
...l Lee	do.	34	May 2, 1864	100 dys.	Absent, sick, at home. No further record found.
...T. Haines	do.	28	May 2, 1864	100 dys.	Mustered out with company Sept. 14, 1864.
... Hueston	do.	24	May 2, 1864	100 dys.	Mustered out with company Sept. 14, 1864.
... L. King	Musician	18	May 2, 1864	100 dys.	Mustered out with company Sept. 14, 1864.
...W. Ellis	do.	18	May 2, 1864	100 dys.	Mustered out with company Sept. 14, 1864.
...m L. Ellis	Wagoner.	37	May 2, 1864	100 dys.	Mustered out with company Sept. 14, 1864.
...d, Philip A.	Private.	19	May 2, 1864	100 dys.	Mustered out with company Sept. 14, 1864.
...tt, Asa O.	do.	35	May 2, 1864	100 dys.	Absent, sick, at Point of Rocks, Md., June 12, 1864. No further record found.
..., George	do.	18	May 2, 1864	100 dys.	Mustered out with company Sept. 14, 1864.
...an, Henry	do.	18	May 2, 1864	100 dys.	Mustered out with company Sept. 14, 1864.
... Ezra	do.	35	May 2, 1864	100 dys.	Mustered out with company Sept. 14, 1864.
... John E.	do.	18	May 2, 1864	100 dys.	Mustered out with company Sept. 14, 1864.
..., Henry	do.	35	May 2, 1864	100 dys.	Mustered out with company Sept. 14, 1864.
...n, Isaac C.	do.	20	May 2, 1864	100 dys.	Mustered out with company Sept. 14, 1864.
... Felix W.	do.	26	May 2, 1864	100 dys.	Died Aug. 30, 1864, on board steamer John A. Warner, on Potomac River.
... George M.	do.	18	May 2, 1864	100 dys.	Died Aug. 20, 1864, in hospital at City Point, Virginia.
... John E.	do.	21	May 2, 1864	100 dys.	Mustered out with company Sept. 14, 1864.
...ston, Lewis	do.	24	May 2, 1864	100 dys.	Mustered out with company Sept. 14, 1864.
...y, Edward	do.	44	May 2, 1864	100 dys.	Mustered out with company Sept. 14, 1864.
... Robert J.	do.	22	May 2, 1864	100 dys.	Mustered out with company Sept. 14, 1864.
...ore, Lucius J.	do.	18	May 2, 1864	100 dys.	Absent, sick, at home. No further record found.
..., Otho B.	do.	18	May 2, 1864	100 dys.	Mustered out with company Sept. 14, 1864.
... Asbury	do.	26	May 2, 1864	100 dys.	Mustered out with company Sept. 14, 1864.
... Ira O.	do.	18	May 2, 1864	100 dys.	Mustered out with company Sept. 14, 1864.
... Lewis H.	do.	19	May 2, 1864	100 dys.	Mustered out with company Sept. 14, 1864.
...rt, George R.	do.	18	May 2, 1864	100 dys.	Mustered out with company Sept. 14, 1864.

Names.	Rank.	Age.	Date of Entering the Service.	Period of Service.	Remarks.
Graham, Findley	Private..	18	May 2, 1864	100 dys.	Mustered out with company Sept. 14, 1864.
Haines, Albert	....do....	18	May 2, 1864	100 dys.	Mustered out with company Sept. 14, 1864.
Haines, Isaac P	....do....	23	May 2, 1864	100 dys.	Mustered out with company Sept. 14, 1864.
Haines, Nathaniel	....do....	18	May 2, 1864	100 dys.	Drowned May 21, 1864, while bathing near Marietta, O.
Hildebrand, William R.	....do....	18	May 2, 1864	100 dys.	Mustered out with company Sept. 14, 1864.
Hull, Daniel	....do....	32	May 2, 1864	100 dys.	Mustered out with company Sept. 14, 1864.
Johnson, Corwin	....do....	18	May 2, 1864	100 dys.	Mustered out with company Sept. 14, 1864.
Johnson, William A.	....do....	18	May 2, 1864	100 dys.	Mustered out with company Sept. 14, 1864.
Jones, Stanton	....do....	18	May 2, 1864	100 dys.	Mustered out with company Sept. 14, 1864.
Jones, Wilders D.	....do....	42	May 2, 1864	100 dys.	Mustered out with company Sept. 14, 1864.
Keets, Francis A.	....do....	39	May 2, 1864	100 dys.	Mustered out with company Sept. 14, 1864.
Kelly, Monroe	....do....	19	May 2, 1864	100 dys.	Mustered out with company Sept. 14, 1864.
Lambert, Abner	....do....	18	May 2, 1864	100 dys.	Mustered out with company Sept. 14, 1864.
Lambert, Elwood	....do....	35	May 2, 1864	100 dys.	Mustered out with company Sept. 14, 1864.
Lee, Abdon	....do....	42	May 2, 1864	100 dys.	Mustered out with company Sept. 14, 1864.
McArthur, Daniel B.	....do....	18	May 2, 1864	100 dys.	Mustered out with company Sept. 14, 1864.
McKain, Franklin	....do....	20	May 2, 1864	100 dys.	Mustered out with company Sept. 14, 1864.
McKibben, William A.	....do....	22	May 2, 1864	100 dys.	Mustered out with company Sept. 14, 1864.
Majors, Wil[illegible]m C.	....do....	18	May 2, 1864	100 dys.	Mustered out with company Sept. 14, 1864.
Marshall, [illegible]aleb	....do....	85	May 2, 1864	100 dys.	Mustered out with company Sept. 14, 1864.
Marshall, Jesse B.	....do....	28	May 2, 1864	100 dys.	Mustered out with company Sept. 14, 1864.
Monroe, Isaac	....do....	24	May 2, 1864	100 dys.	Mustered out with company Sept. 14, 1864.
Monroe, Joseph	....do....	33	May 2, 1864	100 dys.	Mustered out with company Sept. 14, 1864.
Moore, William M.	....do....	26	May 2, 1864	100 dys.	Mustered out with company Sept. 14, 1864.
Morian, Jason E.	....do....	19	May 2, 1864	100 dys.	Mustered out with company Sept. 14, 1864.
Moran, Joshua	....do....	18	May 2, 1864	100 dys.	Died Sept. 12, 1864, at home, Wesley Township, Washington County, O.
Morrow, John	....do....	42	May 2, 1864	100 dys.	Mustered out with company Sept. 14, 1864.
Ormiston, William	....do....	39	May 2, 1864	100 dys.	Mustered out with company Sept. 14, 1864.
Pickering, Elwood E.	....do....	18	May 2, 1864	100 dys.	Mustered out with company Sept. 14, 1864.
Pickering, Evan R.	....do....	18	May 2, 1864	100 dys.	Mustered out with company Sept. 14, 1864.
Randolph, Stephens	....do....	31	May 2, 1864	100 dys.	Mustered out with company Sept. 14, 1864.
Sharp, Joel	....do....	20	May 2, 1864	100 dys.	Mustered out with company Sept. 14, 1864.
Sharp, Oliver	....do....	33	May 2, 1864	100 dys.	Mustered out with company Sept. 14, 1864.
Smith, Alexander F.	....do....	33	May 2, 1864	100 dys.	Mustered out with company Sept. 14, 1864.
Smith, Charles O.	....do....	18	May 2, 1864	100 dys.	Mustered out with company Sept. 14, 1864.
Smith, James H.	....do....	27	May 2, 1864	100 dys.	Killed Aug. 9, 1864, at City Point, Va., by explosion of ordnance boat.
Taylor, Wilson P.	....do....	18	May 2, 1864	100 dys.	Mustered out with company Sept. 14, 1864.
Vanway, Burris	....do....	21	May 2, 1864	100 dys.	Mustered out with company Sept. 14, 1864.
Wilson, Milo	....do....	29	May 2, 1864	100 dys.	Mustered out with company Sept. 14, 1864.
Wilson, Nathan	....do....	35	May 2, 1864	100 dys.	Mustered out with company Sept. 14, 1864.
Wisecarver, Isaac	....do....	44	May 2, 1864	100 dys.	Mustered out with company Sept. 14, 1864.
Witham, Nathan	....do....	41	May 2, 1864	100 dys.	Mustered out with company Sept. 14, 1864.
Wood, Elijah	....do....	29	May 2, 1864	100 dys.	Mustered out with company Sept. 14, 1864.
Wood, William	....do....	37	May 2, 1864	100 dys.	Mustered out with company Sept. 14, 1864.

COMPANY E.

[illegible] in May 17, 1864, at Marietta, O., by James P. W. Neill, 1st Lieutenant 18th Infantry, U. S. A. Mustered out Sept. 14, 1864, at Camp Marietta, O., by George M. Downey, 1st Lieutenant 14th Infantry, U. S. A.

Names.	Rank.	Age.	Date of Entering the Service.	Period of Service.	Remarks.
[illegible] H. McCormick	Captain..	27	May 2, 1864	100 dys.	Mustered out with company Sept. 14, 1864.
[illegible] Murphy	1st Lieut..	27	May 2, 1864	100 dys.	Mustered out with company Sept. 14, 1864.
[illegible]	2d Lieut..	43	May 2, 1864	100 dys.	Died July 12, 1864, at Bermuda Hundred, Va.
[illegible]son	1st Sergt.	85	May 2, 1864	100 dys.	Mustered out with company Sept. 14, 1864.
[illegible]	Sergeant.	36	May 2, 1864	100 dys.	Mustered out with company Sept. 14, 1864.
[illegible]	....do....	35	May 2, 1864	100 dys.	Mustered out with company Sept. 14, 1864.
[illegible] W. Brewster	....do....	36	May 2, 1864	100 dys.	Mustered out with company Sept. 14, 1864.
[illegible]	....do....	29	May 2, 1864	100 dys.	Mustered out with company Sept. 14, 1864.
[illegible]	Corporal.	41	May 2, 1864	100 dys.	Mustered out with company Sept. 14, 1864.
[illegible]	....do....	41	May 2, 1864	100 dys.	Mustered out with company Sept. 14, 1864.
[illegible]	....do....	36	May 2, 1864	100 dys.	Mustered out with company Sept. 14, 1864.
[illegible]	....do....	18	May 2, 1864	100 dys.	Mustered out with company Sept. 14, 1864.
[illegible] Dixon	....do....	18	May 2, 1864	100 dys.	Mustered out with company Sept. 14, 1864.
[illegible]	....do....	45	May 2, 1864	100 dys.	Appointed May 31, 1864; mustered out with company Sept. 14, 1864.
[illegible]	....do....	24	May 2, 1864	100 dys.	Mustered out with company Sept. 14, 1864.
[illegible]	....do....	23	May 2, 1864	100 dys.	Mustered out with company Sept. 14, 1864.
[illegible]	....do....	28	May 2, 1864	100 dys.	Appointed May 31, 1864; mustered out with company Sept. 14, 1864.
[illegible]	Musician	19	May 2, 1864	100 dys.	Mustered out with company Sept. 14, 1864.
[illegible] Forest	....do....	19	May 2, 1864	100 dys.	Mustered out with company Sept. 14, 1864.
[illegible] Anthony	Private..	32	May 2, 1864	100 dys.	Mustered out with company Sept. 14, 1864.
[illegible] M.	....do....	19	May 2, 1864	100 dys.	Mustered out with company Sept. 14, 1864.
[illegible] W.	....do....	18	May 2, 1864	100 dys.	Died Sept. 10, 1864, at home, while on furlough.
[illegible] M.	....do..	31	May 2, 1864	100 dys.	Mustered out with company Sept. 14, 1864.

Names.	Rank.	Age.	Date of Entering the Service.	Period of Service.	Remarks.
Bablet, Michael	Private	20	May 2, 1864	100 dys.	Mustered out with company Sept. 14, 1864.
Bamber, Sylvester	do	23	May 2, 1864	100 dys.	Mustered out with company Sept. 14, 1864.
Barnett, George	do	34	May 2, 1864	100 dys.	Mustered out with company Sept. 14, 1864.
Bates, James F	do	18	May 2, 1864	100 dys.	Mustered out with company Sept. 14, 1864.
Bay, John	do	21	May 2, 1864	100 dys.	Mustered out with company Sept. 14, 1864.
Blew, Noah	do	18	May 2, 1864	100 dys.	Mustered out with company Sept. 14, 1864.
Bull, Allen	do	20	May 2, 1864	100 dys.	Mustered out with company Sept. 14, 1864.
Carnes, William	do	37	May 2, 1864	100 dys.	Mustered out with company Sept. 14, 1864.
Carson, William W	do	18	May 2, 1864	100 dys.	Mustered out with company Sept. 14, 1864.
Castell, Joshua	do	33	May 2, 1864	100 dys.	Mustered out with company Sept. 14, 1864.
Clark, John F	do	41	May 2, 1864	100 dys.	Mustered out with company Sept. 14, 1864.
Coltrap, William	do	44	May 2, 1864	100 dys.	Mustered out with company Sept. 14, 1864.
Comer, Nathan	do	27	May 2, 1864	100 dys.	Mustered out with company Sept. 14, 1864.
Cowden, Robert G	do	38	May 2, 1864	100 dys.	Mustered out with company Sept. 14, 1864.
Crow, Conrad E	do	20	May 2, 1864	100 dys.	Mustered out with company Sept. 14, 1864.
Curry, Daniel	do	18	May 2, 1864	100 dys.	Mustered out with company Sept. 14, 1864.
Curry, Oliver	do	25	May 2, 1864	100 dys.	Mustered out with company Sept. 14, 1864.
Dearth, David	do	18	May 2, 1864	100 dys.	Mustered out with company Sept. 14, 1864.
Dillon, John S	do	30	May 2, 1864	100 dys.	Mustered out with company Sept. 14, 1864.
Dixon, Hiram	do	22	May 2, 1864	100 dys.	Mustered out with company Sept. 14, 1864.
Dunkle, Columbus S	do	18	May 2, 1864	100 dys.	Mustered out with company Sept. 14, 1864.
Forest, Joseph S	do	43	May 2, 1864	100 dys.	Mustered out with company Sept. 14, 1864.
George, Harrison	do	18	May 2, 1864	100 dys.	Mustered out with company Sept. 14, 1864.
Graves, Thomas	do	31	May 2, 1864	100 dys.	Mustered out with company Sept. 14, 1864.
Graves, Jacob	do	18	May 2, 1864	100 dys.	Mustered out with company Sept. 14, 1864.
Graves, William B	do	29	May 2, 1864	100 dys.	Mustered out with company Sept. 14, 1864.
Hasting, Thomas	do	18	May 2, 1864	100 dys.	Mustered out with company Sept. 14, 1864.
Hays, Robert	do	19	May 2, 1864	100 dys.	Mustered out with company Sept. 14, 1864.
Haws, Eli	do	29	May 2, 1864	100 dys.	Mustered out with company Sept. 14, 1864.
Heskett, William H	do	20	May 2, 1864	100 dys.	Mustered out with company Sept. 14, 1864.
Heskett, Thomas C	do	39	May 2, 1864	100 dys.	Died July 7, 1864, in hospital at Point of Rocks, Maryland.
Lacy, Isaiah C	do	18	May 2, 1864	100 dys.	Mustered out with company Sept. 14, 1864.
McNichols, George	do	28	May 2, 1864	100 dys.	Mustered out with company Sept. 14, 1864.
McNichols, Benjamin	do	20	May 2, 1864	100 dys.	Died Aug. 14, 1864, in hospital at Portsmouth, Virginia.
Nichols, David	do	18	May 2, 1864	100 dys.	Mustered out with company Sept. 14, 1864.
Nichols, James	do	25	May 2, 1864	100 dys.	Mustered out with company Sept. 14, 1864.
Randall, Jared B	do	45	May 2, 1864	100 dys.	Mustered out with company Sept. 14, 1864.
Randall, John C	do	28	May 2, 1864	100 dys.	Mustered out with company Sept. 14, 1864.
Ratcliff, Sylvester	do	27	May 2, 1864	100 dys.	Mustered out with company Sept. 14, 1864.
Riley, Hugh	do	22	May 2, 1864	100 dys.	Mustered out with company Sept. 14, 1864.
Riley, Smith	do	36	May 2, 1864	100 dys.	Mustered out with company Sept. 14, 1864.
Roach, James P	do	24	May 2, 1864	100 dys.	Mustered out with company Sept. 14, 1864.
Scott, Charles T	do	36	May 2, 1864	100 dys.	Mustered out with company Sept. 14, 1864.
Seitz, Jacob R	do	31	May 2, 1864	100 dys.	Mustered out with company Sept. 14, 1864.
Seitz, William A	do	27	May 2, 1864	100 dys.	Mustered out with company Sept. 14, 1864.
Shepherd, Jacob	do	18	May 2, 1864	100 dys.	Mustered out with company Sept. 14, 1864.
Shepherd, James H	do	19	May 2, 1864	100 dys.	Mustered out with company Sept. 14, 1864.
Shively, Isaac	do	38	May 2, 1864	100 dys.	Mustered out with company Sept. 14, 1864.
Sims, Lewis	do	44	May 2, 1864	100 dys.	Mustered out with company Sept. 14, 1864.
Sims, Simeon	do	40	May 2, 1864	100 dys.	Mustered out with company Sept. 14, 1864.
Smith, Henry	do	21	May 2, 1864	100 dys.	Mustered out with company Sept. 14, 1864.
Smith, Isaac M	do	19	May 2, 1864	100 dys.	Mustered out with company Sept. 14, 1864.
Tatman, George	do	27	May 2, 1864	100 dys.	Mustered out with company Sept. 14, 1864.
Tetirick, George	do	27	May 2, 1864	100 dys.	Mustered out with company Sept. 14, 1864.
Tilton, John	do	41	May 2, 1864	100 dys.	Mustered out with company Sept. 14, 1864.
Timmons, Isaac	do	23	May 2, 1864	100 dys.	Mustered out with company Sept. 14, 1864.
Vest, Andrew J	do	19	May 2, 1864	100 dys.	Mustered out with company Sept. 14, 1864.
Walker, William M	do	33	May 2, 1864	100 dys.	Mustered as Corporal; reduced to ranks ——; mustered out with company Sept. 14, 1864.
Westcoat, Isaac	do	29	May 2, 1864	100 dys.	Mustered out with company Sept. 14, 1864.
Wilcox, John M	do	18	May 2, 1864	100 dys.	Mustered out with company Sept. 14, 1864.

Names.	Rank.	Age.	Date of Entering the Service.	Period of Service.	Remarks.
Bablet, Michael	Private	20	May 2, 1864	100 dys.	Mustered out with company Sept. 14, 1864.
Bamber, Sylvester	do	23	May 2, 1864	100 dys.	Mustered out with company Sept. 14, 1864.
Barnett, George	do	34	May 2, 1864	100 dys.	Mustered out with company Sept. 14, 1864.
Bates, James F	do	18	May 2, 1864	100 dys.	Mustered out with company Sept. 14, 1864.
Bay, John	do	21	May 2, 1864	100 dys.	Mustered out with company Sept. 14, 1864.
Blew, Noah	do	18	May 2, 1864	100 dys.	Mustered out with company Sept. 14, 1864.
Bull, Allen	do	20	May 2, 1864	100 dys.	Mustered out with company Sept. 14, 1864.
Carnes, William	do	37	May 2, 1864	100 dys.	Mustered out with company Sept. 14, 1864.
Carson, William W	do	18	May 2, 1864	100 dys.	Mustered out with company Sept. 14, 1864.
Castell, Joshua	do	33	May 2, 1864	100 dys.	Mustered out with company Sept. 14, 1864.
Clark, John F	do	41	May 2, 1864	100 dys.	Mustered out with company Sept. 14, 1864.
Coltrap, William	do	44	May 2, 1864	100 dys.	Mustered out with company Sept. 14, 1864.
Comer, Nathan	do	27	May 2, 1864	100 dys.	Mustered out with company Sept. 14, 1864.
Cowden, Robert G	do	38	May 2, 1864	100 dys.	Mustered out with company Sept. 14, 1864.
Crow, Conrad E	do	20	May 2, 1864	100 dys.	Mustered out with company Sept. 14, 1864.
Curry, Daniel	do	18	May 2, 1864	100 dys.	Mustered out with company Sept. 14, 1864.
Curry, Oliver	do	25	May 2, 1864	100 dys.	Mustered out with company Sept. 14, 1864.
Dearth, David	do	18	May 2, 1864	100 dys.	Mustered out with company Sept. 14, 1864.
Dillon, John S	do	30	May 2, 1864	100 dys.	Mustered out with company Sept. 14, 1864.
Dixon, Hiram	do	22	May 2, 1864	100 dys.	Mustered out with company Sept. 14, 1864.
Dunkle, Columbus S	do	18	May 2, 1864	100 dys.	Mustered out with company Sept. 14, 1864.
Forest, Joseph S	do	43	May 2, 1864	100 dys.	Mustered out with company Sept. 14, 1864.
George, Harrison	do	18	May 2, 1864	100 dys.	Mustered out with company Sept. 14, 1864.
Graves, Thomas	do	31	May 2, 1864	100 dys.	Mustered out with company Sept. 14, 1864.
Graves, Jacob	do	18	May 2, 1864	100 dys.	Mustered out with company Sept. 14, 1864.
Graves, William B	do	29	May 2, 1864	100 dys.	Mustered out with company Sept. 14, 1864.
Hasting, Thomas	do	18	May 2, 1864	100 dys.	Mustered out with company Sept. 14, 1864.
Hays, Robert	do	19	May 2, 1864	100 dys.	Mustered out with company Sept. 14, 1864.
Haws, Eli	do	29	May 2, 1864	100 dys.	Mustered out with company Sept. 14, 1864.
Heskett, William H	do	20	May 2, 1864	100 dys.	Mustered out with company Sept. 14, 1864.
Heskett, Thomas C	do	39	May 2, 1864	100 dys.	Died July 7, 1864, in hospital at Point of Rocks, Maryland.
Lacy, Isaiah C	do	18	May 2, 1864	100 dys.	Mustered out with company Sept. 14, 1864.
McNichols, George	do	28	May 2, 1864	100 dys.	Mustered out with company Sept. 14, 1864.
McNichols, Benjamin	do	20	May 2, 1864	100 dys.	Died Aug. 14, 1864, in hospital at Portsmouth, Virginia.
Nichols, David	do	18	May 2, 1864	100 dys.	Mustered out with company Sept. 14, 1864.
Nichols, James	do	25	May 2, 1864	100 dys.	Mustered out with company Sept. 14, 1864.
Randall, Jared B	do	45	May 2, 1864	100 dys.	Mustered out with company Sept. 14, 1864.
Randall, John C	do	28	May 2, 1864	100 dys.	Mustered out with company Sept. 14, 1864.
Ratcliff, Sylvester	do	27	May 2, 1864	100 dys.	Mustered out with company Sept. 14, 1864.
Riley, Hugh	do	22	May 2, 1864	100 dys.	Mustered out with company Sept. 14, 1864.
Riley, Smith	do	36	May 2, 1864	100 dys.	Mustered out with company Sept. 14, 1864.
Roach, James P	do	24	May 2, 1864	100 dys.	Mustered out with company Sept. 14, 1864.
Scott, Charles T	do	36	May 2, 1864	100 dys.	Mustered out with company Sept. 14, 1864.
Seitz, Jacob R	do	31	May 2, 1864	100 dys.	Mustered out with company Sept. 14, 1864.
Seitz, William A	do	27	May 2, 1864	100 dys.	Mustered out with company Sept. 14, 1864.
Shepherd, Jacob	do	18	May 2, 1864	100 dys.	Mustered out with company Sept. 14, 1864.
Shepherd, James H	do	19	May 2, 1864	100 dys.	Mustered out with company Sept. 14, 1864.
Shively, Isaac	do	38	May 2, 1864	100 dys.	Mustered out with company Sept. 14, 1864.
Sims, Lewis	do	44	May 2, 1864	100 dys.	Mustered out with company Sept. 14, 1864.
Sims, Simeon	do	40	May 2, 1864	100 dys.	Mustered out with company Sept. 14, 1864.
Smith, Henry	do	21	May 2, 1864	100 dys.	Mustered out with company Sept. 14, 1864.
Smith, Isaac M	do	19	May 2, 1864	100 dys.	Mustered out with company Sept. 14, 1864.
Tatman, George	do	27	May 2, 1864	100 dys.	Mustered out with company Sept. 14, 1864.
Tetirick, George	do	27	May 2, 1864	100 dys.	Mustered out with company Sept. 14, 1864.
Tilton, John	do	41	May 2, 1864	100 dys.	Mustered out with company Sept. 14, 1864.
Timmons, Isaac	do	23	May 2, 1864	100 dys.	Mustered out with company Sept. 14, 1864.
Vest, Andrew J	do	19	May 2, 1864	100 dys.	Mustered out with company Sept. 14, 1864.
Walker, William M	do	33	May 2, 1864	100 dys.	Mustered as Corporal; reduced to ranks —; mustered out with company Sept. 14, 1864.
Westcoat, Isaac	do	29	May 2, 1864	100 dys.	Mustered out with company Sept. 14, 1864.
Wilcox, John M	do	18	May 2, 1864	100 dys.	Mustered out with company Sept. 14, 1864.

COMPANY F.

Mustered in May 17, 1864, at Marietta, O., by James P. W. Neill, 1st Lieutenant 18th Infantry, U. S. A. Mustered out Sept. 14 1864, at Camp Marietta, O., by George M. Downey, 1st Lieutenant 14th Infantry, U. S. A.

Names.	Rank.	Age.	Date of Entering the Service.	Period of Service.	Remarks.
George B. Turner	Captain.	31	May 2, 1864	100 dys.	Mustered out with company Sept. 14, 1864.
Leonidas P. Pond	1st Lieut.	38	May 2, 1864	100 dys.	Mustered out with company Sept. 14, 1864.
Benjamin F. Robinson	2d Lieut	41	May 2, 1864	100 dys.	Mustered out with company Sept. 14, 1864.
John C. Vincent	1st Sergt.	23	May 2, 1864	100 dys.	Mustered out with company Sept. 14, 1864.
William W. Hoffman	Sergeant.	27	May 2, 1864	100 dys.	Died Aug. 11, 1864, in Balfour U. S. General Hospital at Portsmouth, Va.
John Dustin	...do....	39	May 2, 1864	100 dys.	Mustered out with company Sept. 14, 1864.
Richard Trotter	...do....	38	May 2, 1864	100 dys.	Mustered out with company Sept. 14, 1864.
Isaiah F Palmer	...do....	20	May 2, 1864	100 dys.	Appointed May 28, 1864; mustered out with company Sept. 14, 1864.
Hiel Chapman	Corporal.	35	May 2, 1864	100 dys.	Mustered out with company Sept. 14, 1864.
Henry R. Deming	...do....	21	May 2, 1864	100 dys.	Mustered out with company Sept. 14, 1864.
James Bartlett	...do....	22	May 2, 1864	100 dys.	Mustered out with company Sept. 14, 1864.
Augustus W. Tompkins	...do....	19	May 2, 1864	100 dys.	Mustered out with company Sept. 14, 1864.
John L. Pugh	...do....	20	May 2, 1864	100 dys.	Mustered out with company Sept. 14, 1864.
Perley Dunsmore	...do....	19	May 2, 1864	100 dys.	Mustered out with company Sept. 14, 1864.
Harvey Campbell	...do....	33	May 2, 1864	100 dys.	Appointed May 28, 1864; mustered out with company Sept. 14, 1864.
William Thompson	...do....	56	May 2, 1864	100 dys.	Appointed May 28, 1864; mustered out with company Sept. 14, 1864.
George W. Towsley	Musician	14	June 25, 1864	100 dys.	Mustered out with company Sept. 14, 1864.
Again, William	Private..	35	May 2, 1864	100 dys.	Mustered out with company Sept. 14, 1864.
Ball, James W	...do....	26	May 2, 1864	100 dys.	Mustered out with company Sept. 14, 1864.
Ball, Ellis	...do....	44	May 2, 1864	100 dys.	Mustered out with company Sept. 14, 1864.
Breckenridge, Andrew	...do....	34	May 2, 1864	100 dys.	Mustered out with company Sept. 14, 1864.
Breckenridge, Hugh	...do....	27	May 2, 1864	100 dys.	Mustered out with company Sept. 14, 1864.
Call, Jacob	...do....	31	May 2, 1864	100 dys.	Mustered out with company Sept. 14, 1864.
Call, Joseph	...do....	35	May 2, 1864	100 dys.	Mustered out with company Sept. 14, 1864.
Cecil, Edward	...do....	24	May 2, 1864	100 dys.	Mustered out with company Sept. 14, 1864.
Croy, Nathan	...do....	20	May 2, 1864	100 dys.	Mustered out with company Sept. 14, 1864.
Croy, Calvin	...do....	18	May 2, 1864	100 dys.	Mustered out with company Sept. 14, 1864.
Cunningham, James	...do....	37	May 2, 1864	100 dys.	Mustered out with company Sept. 14, 1864.
Dilley, Joseph	...do....	18	May 2, 1864	100 dys.	Absent, sick, in hospital at New York Harbor. No further record found.
Dunsmore, Harvey	...do....	18	May 2, 1864	100 dys.	Mustered out with company Sept. 14, 1864.
Evans, Charles	...do....	18	May 2, 1864	100 dys.	Mustered out with company Sept. 14, 1864.
Fairbanks, Cornelius	...do....	31	May 2, 1864	100 dys.	Mustered out with company Sept. 14, 1864.
Ferguson, Andrew	...do....	18	May 2, 1864	100 dys.	Mustered out with company Sept. 14, 1864.
Ferguson, Henry J	...do....	18	May 2, 1864	100 dys.	Mustered out with company Sept. 14, 1864.
Gates, David	...do....	36	May 2, 1864	100 dys.	Mustered out with company Sept. 14, 1864.
Gooding, George W	...do....	18	May 2, 1864	100 dys.	Absent, sick, in hospital at Baltimore, Md. No further record found.
Gooding, Harvey	...do....	16	May 2, 1864	100 dys.	Mustered out with company Sept. 14, 1864.
Gould, James	...do....	28	May 2, 1864	100 dys.	Mustered out with company Sept. 14, 1864.
Greenlees, Andrew	...do....	25	May 2, 1864	100 dys.	Mustered out with company Sept. 14, 1864.
Hall, Justice W	...do....	18	May 2, 1864	100 dys.	Died Aug. 21, 1864, in general hospital at Fortress Monroe, Va.
Harvey, Andrew	...do....	18	May 2, 1864	100 dys.	Mustered out with company Sept. 14, 1864.
Harvey, Samuel F	...do....	18	May 2, 1864	100 dys.	Mustered out with company Sept. 14, 1864.
Henry, Julius A	...do....	28	May 2, 1864	100 dys.	Mustered out with company Sept. 14, 1864.
Henry, George O	...do....	27	May 2, 1864	100 dys.	Mustered out with company Sept. 14, 1864.
Hildebrand, Henry	...do....	19	May 2, 1864	100 dys.	Mustered out with company Sept. 14, 1864.
Hoffman, Francis A	...do....	18	May 2, 1864	100 dys.	Mustered out with company Sept. 14, 1864.
Ingraham, Thomas	...do....	18	May 2, 1864	100 dys.	Mustered out with company Sept. 14, 1864.
Jones, Jacob	...do....	19	May 2, 1864	100 dys.	Mustered out with company Sept. 14, 1864.
Jordon, Alva M	...do....	18	May 2, 1864	100 dys.	Mustered out with company Sept. 14, 1864.
Lamb, William F	...do....	19	May 2, 1864	100 dys.	Died July 31, 1864, in hospital at Bermuda Hundred, Va.
Lawton, Richard G	...do....	39	May 2, 1864	100 dys.	Mustered out with company Sept. 14, 1864.
Lightfritz, Samuel	...do....	37	May 2, 1864	100 dys.	Mustered out with company Sept. 14, 1864.
Little, William	...do....	35	May 2, 1864	100 dys.	Mustered out with company Sept. 14, 1864.
McKim, William	...do....	29	May 2, 1864	100 dys.	Mustered out with company Sept. 14, 1864.
Maxon, Edwin	...do....	18	May 2, 1864	100 dys.	Mustered out with company Sept. 14, 1864.
Morehead, John W	...do....	20	May 2, 1864	100 dys.	Mustered out with company Sept. 14, 1864.
Monroe, Geo. A	...do....	21	May 2, 1864	100 dys.	Mustered out with company Sept. 14, 1864.
Morris, George M	...do....	36	May 2, 1864	100 dys.	Mustered out with company Sept. 14, 1864.
Morris, Joseph	...do....	19	May 2, 1864	100 dys.	Mustered out with company Sept. 14, 1864.
Murchey, Daniel	...do....	44	May 2, 1864	100 dys.	Mustered out with company Sept. 14, 1864.
Murdough, Jesse G	...do....	29	May 2, 1864	100 dys.	Mustered out with company Sept. 14, 1864.
Nesselrode, Robert	...do....	21	May 2, 1864	100 dys.	Mustered out with company Sept. 14, 1864.
Norton, Charles E.	...do....	18	May 2, 1864	100 dys.	Mustered out with company Sept. 14, 1864.
Northrop, Henry	...do....	20	May 2, 1864	100 dys.	Mustered out with company Sept. 14, 1864.
Ormiston, Isaac A	...do....	26	May 2, 1864	100 dys.	Mustered out with company Sept. 14, 1864.
Ormiston, James F	...do....	20	May 2, 1864	100 dys.	Mustered out with company Sept. 14, 1864.
Page, Edward	...do....	23	May 2, 1864	100 dys.	Mustered out with company Sept. 14, 1864.
Pennoch, Jacob	...do....	18	May 2, 1864	100 dys.	Mustered out with company Sept. 14, 1864.

Names.	Rank.	Age.	Date of Entering the Service.	Period of Service.	Remarks.
Gitchell, Joseph	Private	22	May 2, 1864	100 dys.	Mustered out with company Sept. 14, 1864.
Greenwood, Frank	do	18	May 2, 1864	100 dys.	Mustered out with company Sept. 14, 1864.
Gregg, Levi L	do	33	May 2, 1864	100 dys.	Mustered as Corporal; reduced June 21, 1864; mustered out with company Sept. 14, 1864.
Hall, Eli W	do	18	May 2, 1864	100 dys.	Died July 9, 1864, in Regimental Hospital at Bermuda Hundred, Va.
Haynes, Alfred	do	18	May 2, 1864	100 dys.	Mustered out with company Sept. 14, 1864.
Hays, Preston G	do	18	May 2, 1864	100 dys.	Mustered as Corporal; reduced June 3, 1864; mustered out with company Sept. 14, 1864.
Hicks, John	do	32	May 2, 1864		with [illegible] y Sept. 14, 1864.
Higgins, Thomas N	do	23	May 2, 1864		Sept. 14, 1864.
Hull, Rolander	do	18	May 2, 1864	100 dys.	Mustered out with company Sept. 14, 1864.
Hupp, Silas	do	26	May 2, 1864	100 dys.	Mustered out with company Sept. 14, 1864.
Kinder, Erastus	do	20	May 2, 1864	100 dys.	Mustered out with company Sept. 14, 1864.
Kigans, Elijah	do	18	May 2, 1864	100 dys.	Mustered out with company Sept. 14, 1864.
Lang, Ebenezer	do	18	May 2, 1864	100 dys.	Mustered out with company Sept. 14, 1864.
Lighter, Edward	do	18	May 2, 1864	100 dys.	Mustered out with company Sept. 14, 1864.
McElfresh, Henry	do	28	May 2, 1864	100 dys.	Mustered out with company Sept. 14, 1864.
Newlen, David	do	32	May 2, 1864	100 dys.	Mustered out with company Sept. 14, 1864.
Noland, Augustus	do	26	May 2, 1864	100 dys.	Mustered out with company Sept. 14, 1864.
Noland, Johnston	do	21	May 2, 1864	100 dys.	Mustered out with company Sept. 14, 1864.
Noland, Stephen	do	23	May 2, 1864	100 dys.	Mustered out with company Sept. 14, 1864.
O'Bleness, Abram	do	20	May 2, 1864	100 dys.	Mustered out with company Sept. 14, 1864.
O'Neil, Gilbert	do	28	May 2, 1864	100 dys.	Mustered out with company Sept. 14, 1864.
Rea, Philip G	do	19	May 2, 1864	100 dys.	Mustered out with company Sept. 14, 1864.
Reese, Stephen	do	22	May 2, 1864	100 dys.	Mustered out with company Sept. 14, 1864.
Reynolds, Theodore M	do	18	May 2, 1864	100 dys.	Mustered out with company Sept. 14, 1864.
Riggs, David M	do	23	May 2, 1864	100 dys.	Mustered as Corporal; reduced June 3, 1864; mustered out with company Sept. 14, 1864.
Secord, David	do	22	May 2, 1864	100 dys.	Mustered out with company Sept. 14, 1864.
Seevers, Daniel D	do	41	May 2, 1864	100 dys.	Mustered out with company Sept. 14, 1864.
Scott, John	do	18	May 2, 1864	100 dys.	Mustered out with company Sept. 14, 1864.
Smith, George W	do	36	May 2, 1864	100 dys.	Mustered out with company Sept. 14, 1864.
Smith, James K	do	43	May 2, 1864	100 dys.	Mustered out with company Sept. 14, 1864.
Smith, Samuel T	do	35	May 2, 1864	100 dys.	Mustered out with company Sept. 14, 1864.
Smith, William P	do	18	May 2, 1864	100 dys.	Mustered out with company Sept. 14, 1864.
Tuttle, I. Cleveland	do	31	May 2, 1864	100 dys.	Promoted to Com. Sergeant May 20, 1864; reduced to ranks July 21, 1864; reappointed Aug. 28, 1864.
Wells, Lewis H	do	18	May 2, 1864	100 dys.	Mustered out with company Sept. 14, 1864.
Wetzel, Joseph D	do	41	May 2, 1864	100 dys.	Mustered as Corporal; reduced June 22, 1864; mustered out with company Sept. 14, 1864.
Wheeler, Jesse	do	41	May 2, 1864	100 dys.	Mustered out with company Sept. 14, 1864.
Wilgus, William M	do	18	May 2, 1864	100 dys.	Mustered out with company Sept. 14, 1864.
Williamson, Stephen	do	38	May 2, 1864	100 dys.	Mustered as Sergeant; reduced to ranks June 21, 1864; mustered out with company Sept. 14, 1864.
Wilson, William	do	29	May 2, 1864	100 dys.	Mustered out with company Sept. 14, 1864.
Wilson, John R	do	19	May 2, 1864	100 dys.	Mustered out with company Sept. 14, 1864.
Zies, John	do	44	May 2, 1864	100 dys.	Mustered out with company Sept. 14, 1864.

COMPANY I.

Mustered in May 17, 1864, at Marietta, O., by James P. W. Neill, 1st Lieutenant 18th Infantry, U. S. A. Mustered out Sept. 14, 1864, at Camp Marietta, O., by George M. Downey, 1st Lieutenant 11th Infantry, U. S. A.

Names.	Rank.	Age.	Date of Entering the Service.	Period of Service.	Remarks.
John Mitchell	Captain.	28	May 2, 1864	100 dys.	Mustered out with company Sept. 14, 1864.
Austin L. Curtis	1st Lieut.	35	May 2, 1864	100 dys.	Mustered out with company Sept. 14, 1864.
Alexander H. Browning	2d Lieut.	25	May 2, 1864	100 dys.	Mustered out with company Sept. 14, 1864.
John A. Brown	1st Sergt.	28	May 2, 1864	100 dys.	Mustered out with company Sept. 14, 1864.
Augustus D. Stone	Sergeant.	27	May 2, 1864	100 dys.	Mustered out with company Sept. 14, 1864.
Loring P. Allen	do	26	May 2, 1864	100 dys.	Mustered out with company Sept. 14, 1864.
John Drain	do	21	May 2, 1864	100 dys.	Mustered out with company Sept. 14, 1864.
Israel W. Putnam	do	28	May 2, 1864	100 dys.	Appointed from Corporal June 15, 1864; mustered out with company Sept. 14, 1864.
Columbus B. Curtis	Corporal.	29	May 2, 1864	100 dys.	Mustered out with company Sept. 14, 1864.
Charles H. Campbell	do	42	May 2, 1864	100 dys.	Mustered out with company Sept. 14, 1864.
Eli Davidson	do	33	May 2, 1864	100 dys.	Absent, sick Aug. 30, 1864, in hospital at Washington, D. C. No further record found.
John Drain	do	29	May 2, 1864	100 dys.	Mustered out with company Sept. 14, 1864.
Samuel E. Gorham	do	28	May 2, 1864	100 dys.	Killed by explosion of ordnance boat Aug. 9, 1864, at City Point, Va.
George A. Howe	do	21	May 2, 1864	100 dys.	Mustered out with company Sept. 14, 1864.
Robert A. Rouse	do	21	May 2, 1864	100 dys.	Mustered out with company Sept. 14, 1864.
[illegible] McGra	Musician	18	May 2, 1864	100 dys.	Mustered out with company Sept. 14, 1864.
Charles W. Barclay	do	18	May 2, 1864	100 dys.	Mustered out with company Sept. 14, 1864.
Allen, Harvey G	Private	20	May 2, 1864	100 dys.	Mustered out with company Sept. 14, 1864.
Anderson, George	do	41	May 2, 1864	100 dys.	Mustered out with company Sept. 14, 1864.
Ball, Jasper B	do	35	May 2, 1864	100 dys.	Mustered out with company Sept. 14, 1864.

	Rank.	Age.	Date of Entering the Service.	Period of Service.	Remarks.
...is M.	Private.	27	May 2, 1864	100 dys.	Mustered out with company Sept. 14, 1864.
...mes	do.	28	May 2, 1864	100 dys.	Mustered out with company Sept. 14, 1864.
...vid	do.	27	May 2, 1864	100 dys.	Mustered out with company Sept. 14, 1864.
...n B.	do.	28	May 2, 1864	100 dys.	Mustered out with company Sept. 14, 1864.
...iams	do.	28	May 2, 1864	100 dys.	Died July 6, 1864, at Hampton, Va.
...lge, Charles D.	do.	18	May 2, 1864	100 dys.	Mustered out with company Sept. 14, 1864.
...lge, Daniel M.	do.	27	May 2, 1864	100 dys.	Mustered out with company Sept. 14, 1864.
...Theodore W.	do.	18	May 2, 1864	100 dys.	Mustered out with company Sept. 14, 1864.
...acob	do.	28	May 2, 1864	100 dys.	Mustered out with company Sept. 14, 1864.
	do.	26	May 2, 1864	100 dys.	Mustered out with company Sept. 14, 1864.
	do.	28	May 2, 1864	100 dys.	Mustered out with company Sept. 14, 1864.
	do.	29	May 2, 1864	100 dys.	Mustered out with company Sept. 14, 1864.
	do.	18	May 2, 1864	100 dys.	Mustered out with company Sept. 14, 1864.
	do.	42	May 2, 1864	100 dys.	Mustered out with company Sept. 14, 1864.
	do.	26	May 2, 1864	100 dys.	Absent, sick Aug. 30, 1864, in hospital at Washington, D. C. No further record found.
	do.	29	May 2, 1864	100 dys.	Mustered out with company Sept. 14, 1864.
...on	do.	22	May 2, 1864	100 dys.	Mustered out with company Sept. 14, 1864.
	do.	37	May 2, 1864	100 dys.	Mustered out with company Sept. 14, 1864.
	do.	28	May 2, 1864	100 dys.	
	do.	18	May 2, 1864	100 dys.	Mustered out with company Sept. 14, 1864.
	do.	20	May 2, 1864	100 dys.	Mustered out with company Sept. 14, 1864.
	do.	26	May 2, 1864	100 dys.	Mustered out with company Sept. 14, 1864.
	do.	18	May 2, 1864	100 dys.	Mustered out with company Sept. 14, 1864.
	do.	28	May 2, 1864	100 dys.	Mustered out with company Sept. 14, 1864.
	do.	18	May 2, 1864	100 dys.	Mustered out with company Sept. 14, 1864.
	do.	19	May 2, 1864	100 dys.	Mustered out with company Sept. 14, 1864.
	do.	19	May 2, 1864	100 dys.	Mustered out with company Sept. 14, 1864.
	do.	28	May 2, 1864	100 dys.	Mustered out with company Sept. 14, 1864.
	do.	33	May 2, 1864	100 dys.	Mustered out with company Sept. 14, 1864.
	do.	21	May 2, 1864	100 dys.	Mustered out with company Sept. 14, 1864.
	do.	21	May 2, 1864	100 dys.	Died July 26, 1864, in U. S. General Hospital at Fortress Monroe, Va.
	do.	19	May 2, 1864	100 dys.	Died June 26, 1864, at Point of Rocks, Md.
	do.	34	May 2, 1864	100 dys.	Died Aug. 27, 1864, in U. S. General Hospital at Fortress Monroe, Va.
		41	May 2, 1864	100 dys.	Died July 2, 1864, in hospital.
		30	May 2, 1864	100 dys.	Mustered out with company Sept. 14, 1864.
		19	May 2, 1864	100 dys.	Mustered out with company Sept. 14, 1864.
		20	May 2, 1864	100 dys.	Mustered out with company Sept. 14, 1864.
		21	May 2, 1864	100 dys.	Mustered out with company Sept. 14, 1864.
		19	May 2, 1864	100 dys.	Mustered out with company Sept. 14, 1864.
		40	May 2, 1864	100 dys.	Mustered out with company Sept. 14, 1864.
	do.	18	May 2, 1864	100 dys.	Mustered out with company Sept. 14, 1864.
	do.	21	May 2, 1864	100 dys.	Mustered out with company Sept. 14, 1864.
		[illegible]	May 2, 1864	100 dys.	
		20	May 2, 1864	100 dys.	Mustered out with company Sept. 14, 1864.
		24	May 2, 1864	100 dys.	Mustered out with company Sept. 14, 1864.
		19	May 2, 1864	100 dys.	Mustered out with company Sept. 14, 1864.
		27	May 2, 1864	100 dys.	Mustered out with company Sept. 14, 1864.
		22	May 2, 1864	100 dys.	Mustered out with company Sept. 14, 1864.
...es		18	May 2, 1864	100 dys.	Mustered out with company Sept. 14, 1864.
...Isaac		18	May 2, 1864	100 dys.	Mustered out with company Sept. 14, 1864.
...l, John E.		42	May 2, 1864	100 dys.	Mustered out with company Sept. 14, 1864.
...homas		35	May 2, 1864	100 dys.	Mustered out with company Sept. 14, 1864.
...on B.		30	May 2, 1864	100 dys.	Died July 17, 1864, at Bermuda Hundred, Va.
...athan F.		25	May 2, 1864	100 dys.	Mustered out with company Sept. 14, 1864.
...drew J.	do.	18	May 2, 1864	100 dys.	Mustered out with company Sept. 14, 1864.
...Amos	do.	27	May 2, 1864	100 dys.	Mustered out with company Sept. 14, 1864.
...wis	do.	18	May 2, 1864	100 dys.	Mustered out with company Sept. 14, 1864.
...Isaac	do.	37	May 2, 1864	100 dys.	Died Oct. 22, 1864, in Judiciary Square Hospital, at Washington, D. C.
...enry M.	do.	29	May 2, 1864	100 dys.	Mustered out with company Sept. 14, 1864.
...alley	do.	21	May 2, 1864	100 dys.	Mustered out with company Sept. 14, 1864.
...ohn K.	do.	28	May 2, 1864	100 dys.	Mustered out with company Sept. 14, 1864.
...homas J.	do.	37	May 2, 1864	100 dys.	Mustered out with company Sept. 14, 1864.
...David	do.	21	May 2, 1864	100 dys.	Mustered out with company Sept. 14, 1864.
...George W.	do.	19	May 2, 1864	100 dys.	Mustered out with company Sept. 14, 1864.
...John	do.	28	May 2, 1864	100 dys.	Mustered out with company Sept. 14, 1864.

COMPANY I.

Mustered in May 17, 1864, at Marietta, O., by James P. W. Neill, 1st Lieutenant 18th Infantry, U. S. A. Mustered out Sept. 14, 1864, at Camp Marietta, O., by George M. Downey, 1st Lieutenant 14th Infantry, U. S. A.

Names.	Rank.	Age.	Date of Entering the Service.	Period of Service	Remarks.
David J. Richards	Captain.	30	May 2, 1864	100 dys.	Mustered out with company Sept. 14, 1864.
William L. Woodford	1st Lieut.	38	May 2, 1864	100 dys.	Mustered out with company Sept. 14, 1864.
Robert F. Alexander	2d Lieut.	30	May 2, 1864	100 dys.	Mustered out with company Sept. 14, 1864.
Charles E. Green	1st Sergt.	20	May 2, 1864	100 dys.	Mustered out with company Sept. 14, 1864.
Harley E. Danley	Sergeant.	21	May 2, 1864	100 dys.	Mustered out with company Sept. 14, 1864.
Thomas L. Sheppard	....do....	35	May 2, 1864	100 dys.	Mustered out with company Sept. 14, 1864.
Henry M. Deming	....do....	26	May 2, 1864	100 dys.	Mustered out with company Sept. 14, 1864.
William Breckenridge	....do....	27	May 2, 1864	100 dys.	Mustered out with company Sept. 14, 1864.
Charles Buchanan	Corporal.	22	May 2, 1864	100 dys.	Mustered out with company Sept. 14, 1864.
Robert V. King	....do....	28	May 2, 1864	100 dys.	Mustered out with company Sept. 14, 1864.
William Skipton	....do....	33	May 2, 1864	100 dys.	Mustered out with company Sept. 14, 1864.
Richard Bebee	....do....	24	May 2, 1864	100 dys.	Mustered out with company Sept. 14, 1864.
Orson Hemphill	....do....	19	May 2, 1864	100 dys.	Mustered out with company Sept. 14, 1864.
Francis M. Payne	....do....	20	May 2, 1864	100 dys.	Mustered out with company Sept. 14, 1864.
Cromwell Gilmore	....do....	35	May 2, 1864	100 dys.	Mustered out with company Sept. 14, 1864.
David Woodruff	....do....	18	May 2, 1864	100 dys.	Appointed ——; mustered out with company Sept. 14, 1864.
Andrews, Samuel	Private.	35	May 2, 1864	100 dys.	Mustered out with company Sept. 14, 1864.
Arnold, Joseph A	....do....	18	May 2, 1864	100 dys.	Mustered out with company Sept. 14, 1864.
Bebout, John	....do....	18	May 2, 1864	100 dys.	Mustered out with company Sept. 14, 1864.
Bebee, Franklin	....do....	22	May 2, 1864	100 dys.	Mustered out with company Sept. 14, 1864.
Bebee, Jeremiah R	....do....	27	May 2, 1864	100 dys.	Mustered out with company Sept. 14, 1864.
Bebee, John W	....do....	19	May 2, 1864	100 dys.	Mustered out with company Sept. 14, 1864.
Bebee, Lyman	....do....	26	May 2, 1864	100 dys.	Mustered out with company Sept. 14, 1864.
Berry, John T	....do....	18	May 2, 1864	100 dys.	Mustered out with company Sept. 14, 1864.
Breckenridge, James F	....do....	25	May 2, 1864	100 dys.	Mustered out with company Sept. 14, 1864.
Brown, Aseph E	....do....	21	May 2, 1864	100 dys.	Mustered out with company Sept. 14, 1864.
Brown, Silas A	....do....	21	May 2, 1864	100 dys.	Mustered out with company Sept. 14, 1864.
Chamberlain, John D	....do....	19	May 2, 1864	100 dys.	Mustered out with company Sept. 14, 1864.
Colerick, Nathaniel	....do....	24	May 2, 1864	100 dys.	Died Aug. 14, 1864, at Clark Station, Va.
Cornes, Jasper	....do....	22	May 2, 1864	100 dys.	Mustered out with company Sept. 14, 1864.
Cousins, Samuel	....do....	40	May 2, 1864	100 dys.	Mustered out with company Sept. 14, 1864.
Danley, Joseph W	....do....	44	May 2, 1864	100 dys.	Died June 28, 1864, at Bermuda Hundred, Va.
Darrow, John	....do....	18	May 2, 1864	100 dys.	Mustered out with company Sept. 14, 1864.
Deming, Lester C	....do....	19	May 2, 1864	100 dys.	Mustered out with company Sept. 14, 1864.
Donalson, Leroy	....do....	33	May 2, 1864	100 dys.	Mustered out with company Sept. 14, 1864.
Gossett, Ephraim	....do....	34	May 2, 1864	100 dys.	Mustered out with company Sept. 14, 1864.
Gossett, Jacob	....do....	42	May 2, 1864	100 dys.	Mustered out with company Sept. 14, 1864.
Green, Daniel P	....do....	26	May 2, 1864	100 dys.	Mustered out with company Sept. 14, 1864.
Hagerman, George W	....do....	32	May 2, 1864	100 dys.	Mustered out with company Sept. 14, 1864.
Hayward, Orloff	....do....	18	May 2, 1864	100 dys.	Died July 2, 1864, at Fortress Monroe, Va.
Henry, Benjamin F	....do....	37	May 2, 1864	100 dys.	Mustered out with company Sept. 14, 1864.
Henry, Calvin L	....do....	37	May 2, 1864	100 dys.	Mustered out with company Sept. 14, 1864.
Henry, George	....do....	35	May 2, 1864	100 dys.	Mustered out with company Sept. 14, 1864.
Hoon, James P	....do....	35	May 2, 1864	100 dys.	Mustered out with company Sept. 14, 1864.
Humiston, Charles	....do....	38	May 2, 1864	100 dys.	Died June 28, 1864, at Point of Rocks, Md.
Humiston, Miles	....do....	22	May 2, 1864	100 dys.	Mustered out with company Sept. 14, 1864.
Humphrey, Edwin O	....do....	18	May 2, 1864	100 dys.	Absent, sick ——. No further record found.
McGrew, Jesse	....do....	18	May 2, 1864	100 dys.	Mustered out with company Sept. 14, 1864.
McGuire, Patrick	....do....	18	May 2, 1864	100 dys.	Mustered out with company Sept. 14, 1864.
McNeal, Franklin	....do....	24	May 2, 1864	100 dys.	Mustered out with company Sept. 14, 1864.
Martin, Henry W	....do....	18	May 2, 1864	100 dys.	Mustered out with company Sept. 14, 1864.
Morris, Harvey	....do....	20	May 2, 1864	100 dys.	Mustered out with company Sept. 14, 1864.
Morris, John D	....do....	40	May 2, 1864	100 dys.	Mustered out with company Sept. 14, 1864.
Morris, William	....do....	31	May 2, 1864	100 dys.	Mustered out with company Sept. 14, 1864.
Myres, William	....do....	31	May 2, 1864	100 dys.	Mustered out with company Sept. 14, 1864.
Paine, Charles	....do....	31	May 2, 1864	100 dys.	Mustered out with company Sept. 14, 1864.
Patterson, James H	....do....	21	May 2, 1864	100 dys.	
Payne, Joseph D	....do....	24	May 2, 1864	100 dys.	Mustered out with company Sept. 14, 1864.
Power, Robert F	....do....	37	May 2, 1864	100 dys.	Mustered out with company Sept. 14, 1864.
Power, Tyranus	....do....	24	May 2, 1864	100 dys.	Mustered out with company Sept. 14, 1864.
Pratt, Charles W	....do....	18	May 2, 1864	100 dys.	Mustered out with company Sept. 14, 1864.
Price, William	....do....	33	May 2, 1864	100 dys.	Mustered as Corporal; mustered out with company Sept. 14, 1864.
Pryor, Smith	....do....	23	May 2, 1864	100 dys.	Mustered out with company Sept. 14, 1864.
Pugh, Austin	....do....	37	May 2, 1864	100 dys.	Mustered out with company Sept. 14, 1864.
Radaker, William	....do....	38	May 2, 1864	100 dys.	Mustered out with company Sept. 14, 1864.
Reed, George W	....do....	19	May 2, 1864	100 dys.	Mustered out with company Sept. 14, 1864.
Riley, Albert	....do....	19	May 2, 1864	100 dys.	Mustered out with company Sept. 14, 1864.
Shuster, William M	....do....	30	May 2, 1864	100 dys.	Mustered out with company Sept. 14, 1864.
Smith, Henry	....do....	24	May 2, 1864	100 dys.	Mustered out with company Sept. 14, 1864.
Snow, Commodore P	....do....	41	May 2, 1864	100 dys.	Mustered out with company Sept. 14, 1864.
Starlin, Stephen	....do....	30	May 2, 1864	100 dys.	Mustered out with company Sept. 14, 1864.
Stollar, Daniel	....do....	28	May 2, 1864	100 dys.	Mustered out with company Sept. 14, 1864.
Waterman, Charles	....do....	24	May 2, 1864	100 dys.	Died July 24, 1864, on board steamer [illegible] near Fortress Monroe, Va.

Names.	Rank.	Age.	Date of Entering the Service.	Period of Service.	Remarks.
[illegible]	Private.	[illegible]	May 2, 1864	100 dys.	Mustered out with company Sept. 14, 1864.
[illegible]	...do...	[illegible]	May 2, 1864	100 dys.	Mustered out with company Sept. 14, 1864.
[illegible]	...do...	[illegible]	May 2, 1864	100 dys.	Mustered out with company Sept. 14, 1864.
[illegible]	...do...	[illegible]	May 2, 1864	100 dys.	Mustered out with company Sept. 14, 1864.
[illegible]	...do...	[illegible]	May 2, 1864	100 dys.	Mustered out with company Sept. 14, 1864.
[illegible]	...do...	[illegible]	May 2, 1864	100 dys.	Mustered out with company Sept. 14, 1864.
[illegible]	...do...	[illegible]	May 2, 1864	100 dys.	Mustered out with company Sept. 14, 1864.
[illegible] O. [illegible]	...do...	[illegible]	May 2, 1864	100 dys.	Mustered out with company Sept. 14, 1864.
[illegible]	...do...	[illegible]	May 2, 1864	100 dys.	Mustered out with company Sept. 14, 1864.
[illegible]	...do...	[illegible]	May 2, 1864	100 dys.	Mustered out with company Sept. 14, 1864.

COMPANY K.

Mustered in May 18, 1864, at Marietta, O., by James P. W. Neill, 1st Lieutenant 18th Infantry, U. S. A. Mustered out Sept. 14, 1864, at Camp Marietta, O., by George M. Downey, 1st Lieutenant 14th Infantry, U. S. A.

Names.	Rank.	Age.	Date of Entering the Service.	Period of Service.	Remarks.
[illegible] Wolcott	1st Lieut.	29	May 2, 1864	100 dys.	Mustered out with company Sept. 14, 1864.
[illegible] H. Miller	1st Sergt.	37	May 2, 1864	100 dys.	Appointed June 2, 1864; transferred from Co. B June 3, 1864; mustered out with company Sept. 14, 1864
Austin Miller	Sergeant.	22	May 2, 1864	100 dys.	Mustered out with company Sept. 14, 1864.
Daniel Mankins	...do...	23	May 2, 1864	100 dys.	Mustered out with company Sept. 14, 1864.
James [illegible]	...do...	29	May 2, 1864	100 dys.	Mustered out with company Sept. 14, 1864.
Henry Coffman	...do...	21	May 2, 1864	100 dys.	Appointed June 2, 1864; transferred from Co. B June 3, 1864; mustered out with company Sept. 14, 1864.
Cornelius Boothby	Corporal.	26	May 2, 1864	100 dys.	Mustered out with company Sept. 14, 1864.
Clark Christopher	...do...	25	May 2, 1864	100 dys.	Mustered out with company Sept. 14, 1864.
Edward Anderson	...do...	25	May 2, 1864	100 dys.	Mustered out with company Sept. 14, 1864.
David Bowman	...do...	31	May 2, 1864	100 dys.	Mustered out with company Sept. 14, 1864.
[illegible] Huggins	...do...	33	May 2, 1864	100 dys.	Appointed June 2, 1864; transferred from Co. B June 3, 1864; mustered out with company Sept. 14, 1864.
Samuel M. Hart	...do...	34	May 2, 1864	100 dys.	Appointed June 2, 1864; transferred from Co. B June 3, 1864; mustered out with company Sept. 14, 1864.
William [illegible]	Musician	18	May 2, 1864	100 dys.	Mustered out with company Sept. 14, 1864.
Alexander, Henry	Private.	34	May 2, 1864	100 dys.	Mustered out with company Sept. 14, 1864.
[illegible], Spencer	...do...	35	May 2, 1864	100 dys.	Mustered out with company Sept. 14, 1864.
Armstrong, John W.	...do...	22	May 2, 1864	100 dys.	Mustered out with company Sept. 14, 1864.
[illegible], James W.	...do...	19	May 2, 1864	100 dys.	Mustered out with company Sept. 14, 1864.
[illegible], Seth	...do...	18	May 2, 1864	100 dys.	Mustered out with company Sept. 14, 1864.
Boothby, David	...do...	18	May 2, 1864	100 dys.	Transferred from Co. B June 2, 1864; mustered out with company Sept. 14, 1864.
Boothby, Joseph	...do...	23	May 2, 1864	100 dys.	Mustered out with company Sept. 14, 1864.
[illegible], John W.	...do...	26	May 2, 1864	100 dys.	Mustered out with company Sept. 14, 1864.
[illegible], Abraham	...do...	18	May 2, 1864	100 dys.	Mustered out with company Sept. 14, 1864.
[illegible], John	...do...	22	May 2, 1864	100 dys.	Mustered out with company Sept. 14, 1864.
[illegible], George	...do...	20	May 2, 1864	100 dys.	Mustered out with company Sept. 14, 1864.
[illegible], John	...do...	27	May 2, 1864	100 dys.	Transferred from Co. B June 2, 1864; mustered out with company Sept. 14, 1864.
[illegible], Charles	...do...	36	May 2, 1864	100 dys.	Mustered out with company Sept. 14, 1864.
Davis, James W.	...do...	24	May 2, 1864	100 dys.	Mustered out with company Sept. 14, 1864.
[illegible], Converse	...do...	22	May 2, 1864	100 dys.	Mustered out with company Sept. 14, 1864.
French, Columbus	...do...	20	May 2, 1864	100 dys.	Mustered out with company Sept. 14, 1864.
Gordon, Stephen	...do...	24	May 2, 1864	100 dys.	Died June 2, 1864, in Douglas Hospital, Washington, D. C.
[illegible], William	...do...	18	May 2, 1864	100 dys.	Mustered out with company Sept. 14, 1864.
Hart, [illegible]	...do...	18	May 2, 1864	100 dys.	Mustered out with company Sept. 14, 1864.
Hawkins, Thomas	...do...	18	May 2, 1864	100 dys.	Mustered out with company Sept. 14, 1864.
[illegible], Arthur W.	...do...	[illegible]	May 2, 1864	100 dys.	Mustered out with company Sept. 14, 1864.
[illegible], James	...do...	31	May 2, 1864	100 dys.	Mustered out with company Sept. 14, 1864.
[illegible], Austin	...do...	18	May 2, 1864	100 dys.	Mustered out with company Sept. 14, 1864.
[illegible], Richard	...do...	25	May 2, 1864	100 dys.	Mustered out with company Sept. 14, 1864.
[illegible], Joseph	...do...	28	May 2, 1864	100 dys.	Mustered out with company Sept. 14, 1864.
[illegible], John	...do...	27	May 2, 1864	100 dys.	Died July 12, 1864, in Regimental Hospital at Bermuda Hundred, Va.
Jobes, Peter	...do...	25	May 2, 1864	100 dys.	Mustered out with company Sept. 14, 1864.
Johnson, [illegible]	...do...	31	May 2, 1864	100 dys.	Mustered out with company Sept. 14, 1864.
Lynch, Thomas	...do...	27	May 2, 1864	100 dys.	Mustered out with company Sept. 14, 1864.
McCammon, James	...do...	25	May 2, 1864	100 dys.	Mustered out with company Sept. 14, 1864.
McClure, Alonzo	...do...	42	May 2, 1864	100 dys.	Mustered out with company Sept. 14, 1864.
Malcom, Horace	...do...	18	May 2, 1864	100 dys.	Mustered out with company Sept. 14, 1864.
Male, Solomon	...do...	18	May 2, 1864	100 dys.	Mustered out with company Sept. 14, 1864.
Mankins, Francis	...do...	23	May 2, 1864	100 dys.	Mustered out with company Sept. 14, 1864.
Mankins, Ezra	...do...	20	May 2, 1864	100 dys.	Mustered out with company Sept. 14, 1864.
Miller, Edward	...do...	25	May 2, 1864	100 dys.	Mustered out with company Sept. 14, 1864.

Names.	Rank.	Age.	Date of Entering the Service.	Period of Service.	Remarks.
Moore, Simpson	Private	24	May 2, 1864	100 dys.	Mustered out with company Sept. 14, 1864.
Mull, George W	....do....	20	May 2, 1864	100 dys.	Mustered out with company Sept. 14, 1864.
Petticord, James	....do....	31	May 2, 1864	100 dys.	Mustered as Corporal; reduced July 29, 1864; mustered out with company Sept. 14, 1864.
Reppert, Jacob	....do....	24	May 2, 1864	100 dys.	Mustered out with company Sept. 14, 1864.
Riley, George	....do....	27	May 2, 1864	100 dys.	Mustered out with company Sept. 14, 1864.
Roush, William	....do....	35	May 2, 1864	100 dys.	Mustered out with company Sept. 14, 1864.
Starlin, Simeon	....do....	21	May 2, 1864	100 dys.	Mustered out with company Sept. 14, 1864.
Stewart, George	....do....	36	May 2, 1864	100 dys.	Mustered out with company Sept. 14, 1864.
Wilson, William H	....do....	18	May 2, 1864	100 dys.	Mustered out with company Sept. 14, 1864.

149th Regiment Ohio Volunteer Infantry.

ONE HUNDRED DAYS' SERVICE.

THIS Regiment was organized at Camp Dennison, O., from the 8th to the 11th of May, 1864, to serve one hundred days. It was composed of the Twenty-seventh Regiment, Ohio National Guard, from Ross County, and the Fifty-fifth Battalion, Ohio National Guard, from Clinton County. On the 11th of May the Regiment left the State for Baltimore, Md. Upon arrival it was assigned to duty at various forts in and around the city, and remained there until the 29th of May, when it was ordered to the eastern shore of Maryland, and distributed at different points. About the 4th of July the Regiment was ordered to Monocacy Junction, and on the 9th took part in an engagement with the enemy. The Regiment lost in killed and wounded about thirty, and in prisoners over one hundred. After the battle of Monocacy it took part with the Sixth and Nineteenth Corps in the marches in Maryland and Virginia. Portions of the Regiment were with the One Hundred and Forty-fourth when it was attacked by Mosby's guerrillas, at Berryville, Va., Aug. 13. The Regiment returned to Ohio Aug. 20, 1864, and was mustered out on the 30th, on expiration of its term of service.

Names.	Rank.	Age.	Date of Entering the Service.	Period of Service.	Remarks.
Benner, Henry	Private..	20	May 2, 1864	100 dys.	Captured Aug. 13, 1864, in action near Berryville, Va.; died Nov. 1, 1864, in Rebel Prison at Salisbury, N. C.
Berry, Harwood	...do....	28	May 2, 1864	100 dys.	No further record found.
Bivins, John	...do....	34	May 2, 1864	100 dys.	Mustered out with company Aug. 30, 1864.
Bonner, Henry	...do....	18	May 2, 1864	100 dys.	Mustered out with company Aug. 30, 1864.
Bonner, Matthias	...do....	25	May 2, 1864	100 dys.	Mustered out with company Aug. 30, 1864.
Callendine, George	...do....	26	May 2, 1864	100 dys.	Mustered out with company Aug 30, 1864.
Campbell, Charles	...do....	29	May 2, 1864	100 dys.	Mustered out to date Aug. 30, 1864, at Camp Dennison, O., by order of War Department.
Campbell, Samuel	...do....	18	May 2, 1864	100 dys.	Mustered out with company Aug. 30, 1864.
Casad, Simeon D	...do....	19	May 2, 1864	100 dys.	Mustered out with company Aug. 30, 1864.
Clark, John M	...do....	21	May 2, 1864	100 dys.	Mustered out with company Aug. 30, 1864.
Cook, John F	...do....	25	May 2, 1864	100 dys.	Mustered out with company Aug. 30, 1864.
Decamp, Andrew	...do....	27	May 2, 1864	100 dys.	Mustered out with company Aug. 30, 1864.
Doyle, William E	...do....	19	May 2, 1864	100 dys.	Mustered out with company Aug. 30, 1864.
Evans, William E	...do....	18	May 2, 1864	100 dys.	Mustered out with company Aug. 30, 1864.
Fern[illegible]ld, John	...do....	21	May 2, 1864	100 dys.	Mustered out with company Aug. 30, 1864.
Frankli[illegible], James	...do....	18	May 2, 1864	100 dys.	Mustered out with company Aug. 30, 1864.
Gates, George B	...do....	21	May 2, 1864	100 dys.	On muster-in roll. No further record found.
Gerteisen, Augustus	...do....	18	May 2, 1864	100 dys.	Transferred from Co. D May 11, 1864; mustered out with company Aug. 30, 1864.
Gertelsen, Philip	...do....	21	May 2, 1864	100 dys.	Transferred from Co. C May 11, 1864; mustered out with company Aug. 30, 1864.
Ghormley, James	...do....	19	May 2, 1864	100 dys.	Captured Aug. 13, 1864, in action near Berryville, Va.; died Dec. 24, 1864, in Rebel Prison at Salisbury, N. C.
Gorsuch, Frank	...do....	17	May 2, 1864	100 dys.	Mustered out with company Aug. 30, 1864.
Gorsuch, James H	...do....	25	May 2, 1864	100 dys.	Mustered out with company Aug. 30, 1864.
Grow, John H	...do....	23	May 2, 1864	100 dys.	Mustered out with company Aug. 30, 1864.
Hamilton, Samuel A	...do....	18	May 2, 1864	100 dys.	Mustered out with company Aug. 30, 1864.
Hanley, William	...do....	..	May 2, 1864	100 dys.	Mustered out with company Aug. 30, 1864.
Harmon, Fletcher D	...do....	19	May 2, 1864	100 dys.	Mustered out with company Aug. 30, 1864.
Heskett, John M	...do....	18	May 2, 1864	100 dys.	Mustered out with company Aug. 30, 1864.
Higley, Charles	...do....	19	May 2, 1864	100 dys.	Mustered out with company Aug. 30, 1864.
Hill, Charles	...do....	18	May 2, 1864	100 dys.	Mustered out with company Aug. 30, 1864.
Iliss, Ferdinand	...do....	33	May 2, 1864	100 dys.	Mustered out with company Aug. 30, 1864.
Hunt, Jabez	...do....	28	May 2, 1864	100 dys.	Transferred from Co. D May 11, 1864; mustered out with company Aug. 30, 1864.
Hutchinson, William	...do....	36	May 2, 1864	100 dys.	Mustered out with company Aug. 30, 1864.
Kates, George B	...do....	21	May 2, 1864	100 dys.	Mustered out with company Aug. 30, 1864.
Keezer, George C	...do....	20	May 2, 1864	100 dys.	Mustered out with company Aug. 30, 1864.
Keller, Valentine	...do....	18	May 2, 1864	100 dys.	Mustered out with company Aug. 30, 1864.
Kellhofer, Jacob	...do....	19	May 2, 1864	100 dys.	Mustered out with company Aug. 30, 1864.
Kennedy, William W	...do....	19	May 2, 1864	100 dys.	Mustered out with company Aug. 30, 1864.
Lawhorn, John	...do....	18	May 2, 1864	100 dys.	Sick ——, in hospital. No further record found.
Limley, Henry	...do....	18	May 2, 1864	100 dys.	Mustered out with company Aug. 30, 1864.
Limley, John	...do....	28	May 2, 1864	100 dys.	Mustered out with company Aug. 30, 1864.
Lunbeck, William B	...do....	21	May 2, 1864	100 dys.	Mustered out with company Aug. 30, 1864.
McCommon, William	...do....	19	May 2, 1864	100 dys.	Transferred from Co. H ——; captured Aug. 13, 1864, in action near Berryville, Va.; mustered out May 15, 1865, at Cincinnati, O., by order of War Department.
McMasters, Hugh	...do....	18	May 2, 1864	100 dys.	Mustered out with company Aug. 30, 1864.
March, Joseph C	...do....	20	May 2, 1864	100 dys.	Transferred from Co. E May 11, 1864; mustered out with company Aug. 30, 1864.
Martin, Jefferson	...do....	18	May 2, 1864	100 dys.	Mustered out with company Aug. 30, 1864.
Mick, John E.	...do....	19	May 2, 1864		[illegible]h company Aug. [illegible], 1864.
Miessie, Benjamin F	...do....	22	May 2, 1864	100 dys	Absent ——. No further record found.
Miller, Moses	...do....	30	May 2, 1864	100 dys	Mustered out with company Aug. 30, 1864.
Mitchell, James	...do....	18	May 2, 1864	100 dys.	Mustered out with company Aug. 30, 1864.
Orr, Presley	...do....	31	May 2, 1864	100 dys	Mustered out with company Aug. 30, 1864.
Perkins, George	...do....	20	May 2, 1864	100 dys.	Mustered out with company Aug. 30, 1864.
Peterman, Jacob H	...do....	20	May 2, 1864	100 dys	Mustered out with company Aug. 30, 1864.
Phillips, Alonzo C	...do....	26	May 2, 1864	100 dys.	Mustered out with company Aug. 30, 1864.
Phillips, Charles	...do....	18	May 2, 1864	100 dys.	Mustered out with company Aug. 30, 1864.
Phillips, John	...do....	18	May 2, 1864	100 dys.	Mustered out with company Aug. 30, 1864.
Reid, Henry N	...do....	19	May 2, 1864	100 dys.	Absent, sick ——. No further record found.
Reis, Daniel	...do....	18	May 2, 1864	100 dys.	Mustered out with company Aug. 30, 1864.
Rittenour, George	...do....	21	May 2, 1864	100 dys.	Transferred from Co. E May 11, 1864; mustered out with company Aug. 30, 1864.
Rupel, Alfred A	...do....	19	May 2, 1864	100 dys.	Transferred from Co. D May 11, 1864; mustered out with company Aug. 30, 1864.
Schleyer, William	...do....	18	May 2, 1864	100 dys.	Mustered out with company Aug. 30, 1864.
Seeney, Warren L	...do....	18	May 2, 1864	100 dys.	Mustered out with company Aug. 30, 1864.
Selby, Thomas	...do....	28	May 2, 1864	100 dys.	Mustered out with company Aug. 30, 1864.
Shepherd, John H	...do....	27	May 2, 1864	100 dys.	Mustered out with company Aug. 30, 1864.
Spencer, Edward F	...do....	29	May 2, 1864	100 dys.	Mustered out with company Aug. 30, 1864.
Snyder, Henry	...do....	20	May 2, 1864	100 dys.	Mustered out with company Aug. 30, 1864.
Sosman, Joseph S	...do....	18	May 2, 1864	100 dys.	Transferred from Co. C May 11, 1864; mustered out with company Aug. 30, 1864.
Steel, James R	...do....	24	May 2, 1864	100 dys.	Mustered out with company Aug. 30, 1864.
Stout, Elijah B	...do....	39	May 2, 1864	100 dys.	Mustered out with company Aug. 30, 1864.
Straus, David	...do....	21	May 2, 1864	100 dys.	Mustered out with company Aug. 30, 1864.
Stricker, William	...do....	24	May 2, 1864	100 dys.	Mustered out with company Aug. 30, 1864.

Names.	Rank.	Age.	Date of Entering the Service.	Period of Service.	Remarks.
Hartley, Samuel	Private	21	May 2, 1864	100 dys.	Mustered out with company Aug. 30,
Henderson, James L	...do...	20	May 2, 1864	100 dys.	Mustered out with company Aug 30,
Henry, Cyrus	...do...	21	May 2, 1864	100 dys.	Mustered out with company Aug. 30,
Henry, Samuel	...do...	33	May 2, 1864	100 dys.	Killed July 9, 1864, in battle of Monoc
Hickman, Zachariah D	...do...	41	May 2, 1864	100 dys.	Transferred from Co. H —; captured 1864, at battle of Monocacy, Md.; m out with company Aug. 30, 1864.
Hill, A. A	...do...	47	May 2, 1864	100 dys.	On muster-in roll. No further record
Hodson, John H	...do...	27	May 2, 1864	100 dys.	On muster in roll. No further record
Holmes, Zachariah H	...do...	19	May 2, 1864	100 dys.	Mustered out with company Aug. 30,
Howe, Thomas D	...do...	..	May 2, 1864	100 dys.	On muster in roll. No further recor
Hubbard, James	...do...	16	May 2, 1864	100 dys.	Mustered out with company Aug. 30,
Hubble, Stineman	...do...	17	May 2, 1864	100 dys.	Mustered out with company Aug. 30,
Hurley, Creighton	...do...	32	May 2, 1864	100 dys.	Mustered out with company Aug. 30,
Hurley, Henry J	...do...	11	May 2, 1864	100 dys.	Discharged —, by Surgeon.
Hurley, Isaac H	...do...	18	May 2, 1864	100 dys.	Mustered out with company Aug. 30,
Hutchinson, Samuel	...do...	20	May 2, 1864	100 dys.	Absent —. No further record found
Jeffries, Jeremiah	...do...	25	May 2, 1864	100 dys.	On muster-in roll. No further record
Jordan, George W	...do...	33	May 2, 1864	100 dys.	Mustered out with company Aug. 30,
Kennedy, William	...do...	..	May 2, 1864	100 dys.	On muster-in roll. No further record
Lafetra, Albert	...do...	18	May 2, 1864	100 dys.	Mustered out with company Aug. 30,
Lamb, John	...do...	19	May 2, 1864	100 dys.	Captured July 9, 1864 at battle of Mo Md. mustered out March [illegible] 1865, at bus. O., by order of War Departmen
Lewis, Isaiah	...do...	21	May 2, 1864	100 dys.	Wounded July 9, 1864, in battle of M Md.; discharged Feb. 2, 1865, at U. S. Hospital, Frederick, Md., on Surgeo tificate of disability
Lindsey, Isaiah	...do...	19	May 2, 1864	100 dys.	Mustered out with company Aug. 30,
Madden, Moses G	...do...	26	May 2, 1864	100 dys.	Mustered out with company Aug 30,
Madden, Solomon	...do...	32	May 2, 1864	100 dys.	Mustered out with company Aug. 30,
Martin, Robert H	...do...	18	May 2, 1864	100 dys.	Mustered out with company Aug. 30,
Miller, Dickinson	...do...	11	May 2, 1864	100 dys.	Captured July 9, 1864, at battle of Mo Md.; mustered out March 29, 1865, at bus. O., by order of War Departmen
Mills, Daniel H	...do...	29	May 2, 1864	100 dys.	Mustered out with company Aug 30,
Mills, Richard H	...do...	31	May 2, 1864	100 dys.	Captured July 9, 1864, at battle of Mo Md.; died Sept. 19, 1864, in Rebel Pr Danville, Va.
Murrel, James	...do...	31	May 2, 1864	100 dys.	Mustered out with company Aug. 30,
O'Donnell, Peter	...do...	30	May 2, 1864	100 dys.	Absent —. No further record found
Oliver, Hezekiah	...do...	31	May 2, 1864	100 dys.	Mustered out with company Aug 30,
Oliver, Samuel	...do...	..	May 2, 1864	100 dys.	On muster-in roll. No further record
Parker, John K	...do...	50	May 2, 1864	100 dys.	Captured July 9, 1864, at battle of Mo Md.; died Feb. 17, 1865, in Rebel Pr Danville, Va.
Patterson, John	...do...	22	May 2, 1864	100 dys.	Mustered out with company Aug. 30,
Plymire, William	...do...	18	May 2, 1864	100 dys.	Mustered out with company Aug. 30,
Reed, David	...do...	19	May 2, 1864	100 dys.	Mustered out with company Aug. 30
Reynonds, David	...do...	41	May 2, 1864	100 dys.	Mustered out with comapny Aug 30,
Rockhi l, Jonathan	...do...	21	May 2, 1864	100 dys.	Transferred from Co. K — ; muste with company Aug. 30, 1864
Rooks, Amos	...do...	23	May 2, 1864	100 dys.	Mustered out with company Aug. 30,
Rowe, John	...do...	19	May 2, 1864	100 dys.	Died Aug. 17, 1864, in hospital at Bal Maryland.
Runnels, Isaac	...do...	20	May 2, 1864	100 dys.	Captured July 9, 1864, at battle of Mo Md.; mustered out April 6, 1865, at bus. O., by order of War Department
Smith, Isaac N	...do...	27	May 2, 1864	100 dys.	Mustered out with company Aug. 30,
States, Abraham H., Jr	...do...	19	May 2, 1864	100 dys.	Captured July 9, 1864, at battle of Mo Md.; mustered out April 6, 1865, bus. O., by order of War Departmen
States, Abraham H., Sr	...do...	30	May 2, 1864	100 dys.	Mustered out with company Aug. 30,
Surface, John S	...do...	26	May 2, 1864	100 dys.	Mustered out with company Aug. 30,
Sutton, Ja[illegible]es H	...do...	24	May 2, 1864	100 dys.	Mustered out with company Aug. 30,
Sutton, William G	...do...	29	May 2, 1864	100 dys.	Mustered out with company Aug 30,
Va[illegible]ress, Francis M	...do...	21	May 2, 1864	100 dys.	Mustered out with company Aug. 30,
Wade, George W	...do...	30	May 2, 1864	100 dys.	Mustered out with company Aug. 30,
Wall, Clarence	...do...	17	May 2, 1864	100 dys.	Killed July 9 1864, in battle of Monoc
Whitnery, Calvin	...do...	18	May 2, 1864	100 dys.	Mustered out with company Aug 30,
Whitson, Oliver	...do...	17	May 2, 1864	100 dys.	Mustered out with company Aug 30,
Wilson, Thomas C	...do...	27	May 2, 1864	100 dys.	Captured July 9, 1864, at battle of Mo Md.; mustered out April 6, 1865, at bus. O., by order of War Department
Woodmansee, Amos	...do...	27	May 2, 1864	100 dys.	Captured July 9, 1864, at battle of Mo Md.; died Jan. 15, 1865, in Rebel Pr Danville, Va.
Woodmansee, John M	...do...	26	May 2, 1864	100 dys.	Mustered out with company Aug. 30,
Woodmansee, Wilson S	...do...	24	May 2, 1864	100 dys.	Mustered out with company Aug. 30,

Names.	Rank.	Age.	Date of Entering the Service.	Period of Service.	Remarks.
Jones, John W.	Private.	18	May 2, 1864	100 dys.	Mustered out with company Aug. 30, 1864.
Jones, Thomas	...do...	37	May 2, 1864	100 dys.	Mustered out with company Aug. 30, 1864.
Kleine, Adam	...do...	20	May 2, 1864	100 dys.	Mustered out with company Aug. 30, 1864.
Krick, Jacob	...do...	34	May 2, 1864	100 dys.	Mustered out with company Aug. 30, 1864.
Liston, Ezra	...do...	18	May 2, 1864	100 dys.	Mustered out with company Aug. 30, 1864.
McGee, Jesse	...do...	19	May 2, 1864	100 dys.	Mustered out with company Aug. 30, 1864.
Masters, Leonard	...do...	26	May 2, 1864	100 dys.	Mustered out with company Aug. 30, 1864.
Masters, Moses	...do...	37	May 2, 1864	100 dys.	Mustered out with company Aug. 30, 1864
Minear, Adam C.	...do...	28	May 2, 1864	100 dys.	Mustered out with company Aug. 30, 1864.
Moats, James	...do...	27	May 2, 1864	100 dys.	Mustered out with company Aug. 30, 1864.
Orr, Presley	...do...	34	May 2, 1864	100 dys.	Mustered out with company Aug. 30, 1864.
Orr, Zebulon	...do...	18	May 2, 1864	100 dys.	Mustered out with company Aug. 30, 1864.
Phillips, Thomas	...do...	36	May 2, 1864	100 dys.	Captured July 9, 1864, at battle of Monocacy, Md.; mustered out March 16, 1865, at Columbus, O., by order of War Department.
Pyle, John	...do...	25	May 2, 1864	100 dys.	Mustered out with company Aug. 30, 1864.
Pyle, William H.	...do...	18	May 2, 1864	100 dys	Mustered out with company Aug. 30, 1864.
Quick, James	...do...	18	May 2, 1864	100 dys.	Mustered out with company Aug. 30, 1864.
Ray, James H.	...do...	26	May 2, 1864	100 dys.	Captured July 9, 1864, at battle of Monocacy, Md.; died Nov. 15, 1864, in Rebel Prison at Danville, Va.
Ross, Adam	...do...	28	May 8, 1864	100 dys.	Mustered out with company Aug. 30, 1864.
Ross, Conrad	...do...	18	May 2, 1864	100 dys.	Mustered out with company Aug. 30, 1864.
Ross, Jesse	...do...	19	May 2, 1864	100 dys.	Mustered out with company Aug. 30, 1864.
Ruple, Alfred A.	...do...	19	May 2, 1864	100 dys.	Transferred to Co. A May 11, 1864.
Sands, James	...do...	37	May 2, 1864	100 dys	Captured July 9, 1864, at battle of Monocacy, Md.; died March 5, 1865, in General Hospital No. 12, Richmond, Va., while a prisoner of war
Shepherd, Joseph	...do...	22	May 2, 1864	100 dys.	Captured July 9, 1864, at battle of Monocacy, Md.; mustered out to date Oct. 20, 1864, by order of War Department.
Smallwood, Truman	...do...	26	May 2, 1864	100 dys.	Mustered out with company Aug. 30, 1864.
Smith, Austin	...do...	19	May 2, 1864	100 dys.	Mustered out with company Aug. 30, 1864.
Smith, William W.	...do...	21	May 2, 1864	100 dys.	Mustered out with company Aug. 30, 1864.
Somers, John A.	...do...	17	May 2, 1864	100 dys	Mustered out with company Aug. 30, 1864.
Sowers, Laurence	...do...	27	May 2, 1864	100 dys.	Mustered out with company Aug. 30, 1864.
Stanhope, George	...do...	27	May 2, 1864	100 dys	Mustered out with company Aug. 30, 1864.
Stauffer, Henry	...do...	27	May 2, 1864	100 dys.	Mustered out with company Aug. 30, 1864.
Stauffer, Samuel	...do...	33	May 2, 1864	100 dys.	Captured July 9, 1864, at battle of Monocacy, Md.; mustered out to date Oct. 20, 1864, by order of War Department
Stauffer, Solomon	...do...	30	May 2, 1864	100 dys.	Mustered out with company Aug. 30, 1864.
Taylor, Charles	...do...	19	May 2, 1864	100 dys.	Mustered out with company Aug. 30, 1864.
Vangundy, Austin	...do...	18	May 2, 1864	100 dys.	Mustered out with company Aug. 30, 1864.
Vangundy, Charles M.	...do...	..	May 2, 1864	100 dys.	Mustered out with company Aug. 30, 1864.
Walker, Christian L.	...do...	18	May 2, 1864	100 dys.	Mustered out with company Aug. 30, 1864.
Woodrow, Robert	...do...	18	May 2, 1864	100 dys.	Mustered out with company Aug. 30, 1864.
Zimmerman, Antony	...do...	23	May 2, 1864	100 dys.	Captured July 9, 1864, at battle of Monocacy, Md., mustered out March 11, 1865, at Columbus, O., by order of War Department.

COMPANY E.

Mustered in May 8, 1864, at Camp Dennison, O., by Robert S. Smith, Captain 2d Cavalry, U. S. A. Mustered out Aug. 30, 1864, at Camp Dennison, O., by William Stanley, 2d Lieutenant 10th Infantry, U. S. A.

Names.	Rank.	Age.	Date of Entering the Service.	Period of Service.	Remarks.
Thomas B. Jenkins	Captain.	21	May 2, 1864	100 dys.	Mustered out with company Aug. 30, 1864.
Henry Grubb	1st Lieut.	28	May 2, 1864	100 dys.	Mustered out with company Aug. 30, 1864
Daniel M. Beard	2d Lieut.	25	May 2, 1864	100 dys.	Mustered out with company Aug. 30, 1864.
William H. Beard	1st Sergt.	29	May 2, 1864	100 dys.	Mustered out with company Aug. 30, 1864.
James Henness	Sergeant.	42	May 2, 1864	100 dys.	Mustered out with company Aug. 30, 1864.
William G. Stitt	...do...	30	May 2, 1864	100 dys.	Died Aug. 15, 1864, in U. S. Hospital at Washington, D. C.
Hamilton Robinson	...do...	36	May 2, 1864	100 dys.	Mustered out with company Aug. 30, 1864.
Robert W. Snyder	...do...	21	May 2, 1864	100 dys.	Mustered out with company Aug. 30, 1864.
Robert J. Banks	Corporal.	32	May 2, 1864	100 dys.	Mustered out with company Aug. 30, 1864.
Daniel Grubb	...do...	33	May 2, 1864	100 dys.	Mustered out with company Aug. 30, 1864.
John E. Mills	...do...	22	May 2, 1864	100 dys.	Mustered out with company Aug. 30, 1864.
Thomas W. McFarland	...do...	20	May 2, 1864	100 dys.	Mustered out with company Aug. 30, 1864.
Robert W. Earl	...do...	21	May 2, 1864	100 dys.	Mustered out with company Aug. 30, 1864.
Augustus Earl	...do...	31	May 2, 1864	100 dys.	Mustered out with company Aug. 30, 1864.
William H. Michael	...do...	24	May 2, 1864	100 dys.	Mustered out with company Aug. 30, 1864.
Samuel B. Egleson	...do...	29	May 2, 1864	100 dys.	Appointed ——; mustered out with company Aug. 30, 1864.
Acton, Lot	Private.	40	May 2, 1864	100 dys.	Died Aug. 11, 1864, in U. S. Hospital at Baltimore, Md.
Arnett, Jonathan P.	...do...	25	May 2, 1864	100 dys.	Mustered out with company Aug. 30, 1864.

Names.	Rank.	Age.	Date of Entering the Service.	Period of Service.	Remarks.
Augustus, John P.	Private.	23	May 2, 1864	100 dys.	Reduced from Corporal Aug. 25, 1864; mustered out with company Aug. 30, 1864.
Augustus, Presley T.	....do....	26	May 2, 1864	100 dys.	Mustered out with company Aug. 30, 1864.
Augustus, Thomas E.	....do....	28	May 2, 1864	100 dys.	Mustered out with company Aug. 30, 1864.
Barrett, Franklin.	....do....	20	May 2, 1864	100 dys.	Mustered out with company Aug. 30, 1864.
Binns, Charles	....do....	43	May 2, 1864	100 dys.	Mustered out with company Aug. 30, 1864.
Blozer, Noah	....do....	29	May 2, 1864	100 dys.	Mustered out with company Aug. 30, 1864.
Bostwick, Clinton W	....do....	18	May 2, 1864	100 dys.	Mustered out with company Aug. 30, 1864.
Bowdle, John W.	....do....	29	May 2, 1864	100 dys.	Mustered out with company Aug. 30, 1864.
Bowdle, William F.	....do....	33	May 2, 1864	100 dys.	Mustered out with company Aug. 30, 1864.
Bullock, George W.	....do....	25	May 2, 1864	100 dys.	Mustered out with company Aug. 30, 1864.
Butler, John D.	....do....	19	May 2, 1864	100 dys.	Mustered out with company Aug. 30, 1864.
Daniels, Abner W.	....do....	24	May 2, 1864	100 dys.	Mustered out with company Aug. 30, 1864.
Dorn, Peter	....do....	25	May 2, 1864	100 dys.	Absent, sick ——. No further record found.
Doty, William C.	....do....	36	May 2, 1864	100 dys.	Mustered out with company Aug. 30, 1864.
Earl, John	....do....	30	May 2, 1864	100 dys.	Mustered out with company Aug. 30, 1864.
Earl, Thomas	....do....	18	May 2, 1864	100 dys.	Mustered out with company Aug. 30, 1864.
Evans, John	....do....	25	May 2, 1864	100 dys.	Absent ——. No further record found.
Fenimore, Charles W.	....do....	26	May 2, 1864	100 dys.	Mustered out with company Aug. 30, 1864.
Fenimore, Ebenezer B.	....do....	36	May 2, 1864	100 dys.	Mustered out with company Aug. 30, 1864.
Fenimore, Henry W.	....do....	19	May 2, 1864	100 dys.	Mustered out with company Aug. 30, 1864.
Finly, Moses	....do....	18	May 2, 1864	100 dys.	Mustered out with company Aug. 30, 1864.
Freeman, Charles	....do....	18	May 2, 1864	100 dys.	Mustered out with company Aug. 30, 1864.
Freese, Isaac M.	....do....	31	May 2, 1864	100 dys.	Mustered out with company Aug. 30, 1864.
Gaib, John E.	....do....	18	May 2, 1864	100 dys.	Mustered out with company Aug. 30, 1864.
Gill, Lewis	....do....	21	May 2, 1864	100 dys.	Mustered out with company Aug. 30, 1864.
Glass, George W.	....do....	27	May 2, 1864	100 dys.	Mustered out with company Aug. 30, 1864.
Grubb, Andrew	....do....	27	May 2, 1864	100 dys.	Mustered out with company Aug. 30, 1864.
Grubb, Jacob.	....do....	18	May 2, 1864	100 dys.	Mustered out with company Aug. 30, 1864.
Hankins, Alexander	....do....	24	May 2, 1864	100 dys.	Mustered out with company Aug. 30, 1864.
Hankins, James W.	....do....	50	May 2, 1864	100 dys.	Mustered out with company Aug. 30, 1864.
Hardy, David A	....do....	20	May 2, 1864	100 dys.	Mustered out with company Aug. 30, 1864
Henness, George	....do....	20	May 2, 1864	100 dys.	Mustered out with company Aug. 30, 1864.
Henness, James A.	....do....	18	May 2, 1864	100 dys.	Mustered out with company Aug. 30, 1864.
Henness, James A., Sr.	....do....	38	May 2, 1864	100 dys.	Mustered out with company Aug. 30, 1864.
Hodsden, Alexander L.	....do....	38	May 2, 1864	100 dys.	Mustered out with company Aug. 30, 1864.
Hurt, Milton L.	....do....	18	May 2, 1864	100 dys.	Mustered out with company Aug. 30, 1864.
Jenkins, Roland Z.	....do....	18	May 2, 1864	100 dys.	Mustered out with company Aug. 30, 1864.
Johnson, Alexander	....do....	24	May 2, 1864	100 dys.	Mustered out with company Aug. 30, 1864.
Keller, Lucas C.	....do....	18	May 2, 1864	100 dys.	Mustered out with company Aug. 30, 1864.
Kilgore, George W.	....do....	18	May 2, 1864	100 dys.	Mustered out with company Aug. 30, 1864.
Kinnamon, George	....do....	25	May 2, 1864	100 dys.	Mustered out with company Aug. 30, 1864.
Kinnamon, Jeremiah	....do....	27	May 2, 1864	100 dys.	Captured July 9, 1864, at battle of Monocacy, Md.; died Sept. 25, 1864, in Rebel Prison at Danville, Va.
Lockwood, Henry C.	....do....	20	May 2, 1864	100 dys.	Mustered out with company Aug. 30, 1864.
Mallow, Owen T.	....do....	31	May 2, 1864	100 dys.	Mustered out with company Aug. 30, 1864.
Maren, Joseph C.	....do....	20	May 2, 1864	100 dys.	Transferred to Co. A May 11, 1864.
Michael, Albert J.	....do....	20	May 2, 1864	100 dys.	Mustered out with company Aug. 30, 1864.
Miller, Smith	....do....	22	May 2, 1864	100 dys.	Captured July 9, 1864, at battle of Monocacy, Md.; died March 21, 1865, at Annapolis, Md.
Ogden, Edward P.	....do....	22	May 2, 1864	100 dys.	Captured July 9, 1864, at battle of Monocacy, Md.; mustered out June 17, 1865, at Columbus, O., by order of War Department.
Ogden, Lewis	....do....	19	May 2, 1864	100 dys.	Mustered out with company Aug. 30, 1864.
Organ, Stephen S.	....do....	39	May 2, 1864	100 dys.	Mustered out with company Aug. 30, 1864.
Plyley, Leonidas T.	....do....	18	May 2, 1864	100 dys.	Mustered out with company Aug. 30, 1864.
Plyley, Morris J.	....do....	30	May 2, 1864	100 dys.	Mustered out with company Aug. 30, 1864.
Pursel, Oregon C.	....do....	20	May 2, 1864	100 dys.	Mustered out with company Aug. 30, 1864.
Pursel, Presley	....do....	38	May 2, 1864	100 dys.	Mustered out with company Aug. 30, 1864.
Rittenour, George	....do....	21	May 2, 1864	100 dys.	Transferred to Co. A May 11, 1864.
Rittenhouse, John G.	....do....	18	May 2, 1864	100 dys.	Mustered out with company Aug. 30, 1864.
Rodgers, John	....do....	30	May 2, 1864	100 dys.	Absent ——. No further record found.
Rose, Lewis L.	....do....	22	May 2, 1864	100 dys.	Mustered out with company Aug. 30, 1864.
Rout, Nathaniel W.	....do....	22	May 2, 1864	100 dys.	Mustered out with company Aug. 30, 1864.
Sanders, Milton	....do....	19	May 2, 1864	100 dys.	Mustered out with company Aug. 30, 1864.
Slay, James E.	....do....	39	May 2, 1864	100 dys.	Mustered out with company Aug. 30, 1864.
Thomas, Benjamin E.	....do....	18	May 2, 1864	100 dys.	Transferred to Co. A May 11, 1864.
Uhn, Edward	....do....	43	May 2, 1864	100 dys.	Mustered out with company Aug. 30, 1864.
Whitten, Solomon I.	....do....	26	May 2, 1864	100 dys.	Captured July 9, 1864, at battle of Monocacy, Md.; mustered out March 27, 1865, at Columbus, O., by order of War Department.
Wilkins, John	....do....	31	May 2, 1864	100 dys.	Mustered out with company Aug. 30, 1864.
Withgott, Jesse L.	....do....	33	May 2, 1864	100 dys.	Mustered out with company Aug. 30, 1864.
Withgott, Thomas M.	....do....	22	May 2, 1864	100 dys.	Mustered out with company Aug. 30, 1864.
Young, Frederick	....do....	20	May 2, 1864	100 dys.	Transferred to Co. A May 11, 1864.

Names.	Rank.	Age.	Date of Entering the Service.	Period of Service.	Remarks.
Augustus, John P.	Private..	23	May 2, 1864	100 dys.	Reduced from Corporal Aug. 25, 1864; mustered out with company Aug. 30, 1864.
Augustus, Presley T.	...do...	26	May 2, 1864	100 dys.	Mustered out with company Aug. 30, 1864.
Augustus, Thomas E.	...do...	28	May 2, 1864	100 dys.	Mustered out with company Aug. 30, 1864.
Barrett, Franklin	...do...	20	May 2, 1864	100 dys.	Mustered out with company Aug. 30, 1864.
Binns, Charles	...do...	43	May 2, 1864	100 dys.	Mustered out with company Aug. 30, 1864.
Bloser,		29	May 2, 1864	100 dys.	Mustered out with company Aug. 30, 1864.
Bostwick, Clinton W	...do...	18	May 2, 1864	100 dys.	Mustered out with company Aug. 30, 1864.
Bowdle, John W.	...do...	29	May 2, 1864	100 dys.	Mustered out with company Aug. 30, 1864.
Bowdle, William F.	...do...	33	May 2, 1864	100 dys.	Mustered out with company Aug. 30, 1864.
Bullock, George W.	...do...	25	May 2, 1864	100 dys.	Mustered out with company Aug. 30, 1864.
Butler, John D.	...do...	19	May 2, 1864	100 dys.	Mustered out with company Aug. 30, 1864.
Daniels, Abner W.	...do...	24	May 2, 1864	100 dys.	Mustered out with company Aug. 30, 1864.
Dorn, Peter	...do...	25	May 2, 1864	100 dys.	Absent, sick ——. No further record found.
Doty, William C.	...do...	36	May 2, 1864	100 dys.	Mustered out with company Aug. 30, 1864.
Earl, John	...do...	30	May 2, 1864	100 dys.	Mustered out with company Aug. 30, 1864.
Earl, Thomas	...do...	18	May 2, 1864	100 dys.	Mustered out with company Aug. 30, 1864.
Evans, John	...do...	25	May 2, 1864	100 dys.	Absent ——. No further record found.
Fenimore, Charles W.	...do...	26	May 2, 1864	100 dys.	Mustered out with company Aug. 30, 1864.
Fenimore, Ebenezer B.	...do...	[illegible]	May 2, 1864	100 dys.	Mustered out with company Aug. 30, 1864.
Fenimore, Henry W.	...do...	[illegible]	May 2, 1864	100 dys.	Mustered out with company Aug. 30, 1864.
Finly, Moses	...do...	18	May 2, 1864	100 dys.	Mustered out with company Aug. 30, 1864.
Freeman, Charles	...do...	18	May 2, 1864	100 dys.	Mustered out with company Aug. 30, 1864.
Fr[illegible]se, Isaac M.	...do...	31	May 2, 1864	100 dys.	Mustered out with company Aug. 30, 1864.
Gaib, John E.	...do...	18	May 2, 1864	100 dys.	Mustered out with company Aug. 30, 1864.
Gill, Lewis	...do...	21	May 2, 1864	100 dys.	Mustered out with company Aug. 30, 1864.
Glass, George W.	...do...	27	May 2, 1864	100 dys.	Mustered out with company Aug. 30, 1864.
Grubb, Andrew	...do...	27	May 2, 1864	100 dys.	Mustered out with company Aug. 30, 1864.
Grubb, Jacob	...do...	18	May 2, 1864	100 dys.	Mustered out with company Aug. 30, 1864.
Hankins, Alexander	...do...	21	May 2, 1864	100 dys.	Mustered out with company Aug. 30, 1864.
Hankins, James W.	...do...	[illegible]	May 2, 1864	100 dys.	Mustered out with company Aug. 30, 1864.
Hardy, David A.	...do...	20	May 2, 1864	100 dys.	Mustered out with company Aug. 30, 1864.
H[illegible]ness, George	...do...	20	May 2, 1864	100 dys.	Mustered out with company Aug. 30, 1864.
H[illegible]ness, James A.	...do...	18	May 2, 1864	100 dys.	Mustered out with company Aug. 30, 1864.
H[illegible]ness, James A. Sr.	...do...	58	May 2, 1864	100 dys.	Mustered out with company Aug. 30, 1864.
H[illegible]sley, Alexander L.	...do...	58	May 2, 1864	100 dys.	Mustered out with company Aug. 30, 1864.
H[illegible], Milton L.	...do...	18	May 2, 1864	100 dys.	Mustered out with company Aug. 30, 1864.
Jenkins, Roland Z.	...do...	18	May 2, 1864	100 dys.	Mustered out with company Aug. 30, 1864.
[illegible]son, Alexander	...do...	21	May 2, 1864	100 dys.	Mustered out with company Aug. 30, 1864.
Keller, Lucas C.	...do...	18	May 2, 1864	100 dys.	Mustered out with company Aug. 30, 1864.
Kilgore, George W.	...do...	18	May 2, 1864	100 dys.	Mustered out with company Aug. 30, 1864.
Kinnamon, George	...do...	25	May 2, 1864	100 dys.	Mustered out with company Aug. 30, 1864.
Kinnamon, Jeremiah	...do...	27	May 2, 1864	100 dys.	Captured July 9, 1864, at battle of Monocacy, Md.; died Sept. 25, 1864, in Rebel Prison at Danville, Va.
L[illegible]wood, Henry C.	...do...	20	May 2, 1864	100 dys.	Mustered out with company Aug. 30, 1864.
[illegible], Owen T.	...do...	21	May 2, 1864	100 dys.	Mustered out with company Aug. 30, 1864.
Ma[illegible], Joseph C.	...do...	20	May 2, 1864	100 dys.	Transferred to Co. A May 11, 1864.
[illegible], Albert L.	...do...	20	May 2, 1864	100 dys.	Mustered out with company Aug. 30, 1864.
M[illegible], Smith	...do...	22	May 2, 1864	100 dys.	Captured July 9, 1864, at battle of Monocacy, Md.; died March 21, 1865, at Annapolis, Md.
[illegible], Edward P.	...do...	22	May 2, 1864	100 dys.	Captured July 9, 1864, at battle of Monocacy, Md.; mustered out June 17, 1865, at Columbus, O., by order of War Department.
[illegible], Lewis	...do...	19	May 2, 1864	100 dys.	Mustered out with company Aug. 30, 1864.
[illegible], Stephen S.	...do...	[illegible]	May 2, 1864	100 dys.	Mustered out with company Aug. 30, 1864.
[illegible], Thomas T.	...do...	18	May 2, 1864	100 dys.	Mustered out with company Aug. 30, 1864.
[illegible], George J.	...do...	[illegible]	May 2, 1864	100 dys.	Mustered out with company Aug. 30, 1864.
[illegible], Gideon C.	...do...	20	May 2, 1864	100 dys.	Mustered out with company Aug. 30, 1864.
[illegible]	...do...	[illegible]	May 2, 1864	100 dys.	Mustered out with company Aug. 30, 1864.
P[illegible], George	...do...	21	May 2, 1864	100 dys.	Transferred to Co. A May 11, 1864.
[illegible], John G.	...do...	18	May 2, 1864	100 dys.	Mustered out with company Aug. 30, 1864.
[illegible], John	...do...	30	May 2, 1864	100 dys.	Absent ——. No further record found.
[illegible], Lewis L.	...do...	22	May 2, 1864	100 dys.	Mustered out with company Aug. 30, 1864.
[illegible], Edward W.	...do...	22	May 2, 1864	100 dys.	Mustered out with company Aug. 30, 1864.
[illegible], Milton	...do...	19	May 2, 1864	100 dys.	Mustered out with company Aug. 30, 1864.
[illegible], James L.	...do...	39	May 2, 1864	100 dys.	Mustered out with company Aug. 30, 1864.
[illegible], Benjamin E.	...do...	18	May 2, 1864	100 dys.	Transferred to Co. A May 11, 1864.
[illegible]	...do...	43	May 2, 1864	100 dys.	Mustered out with company Aug. 30, 1864.
[illegible], Solomon L.	...do...	26	May 2, 1864	100 dys.	Captured July 9, 1864, at battle of Monocacy, Md.; mustered out March 27, 1865, at Columbus, O., by order of War Department.
[illegible], John	...do...	31	May 2, 1864	100 dys.	Mustered out with company Aug. 30, 1864.
[illegible], Jesse L.	...do...	33	May 2, 1864	100 dys.	Mustered out with company Aug. 30, 1864.
[illegible], Thomas M.	...do...	22	May 2, 1864	100 dys.	Mustered out with company Aug. 30, 1864.
[illegible], Frederick	...do...	20	May 2, 1864	100 dys.	Transferred to Co. A May 11, 1864.

Names.	Rank.	Age.	Date of Entering the Service.	Period of Service.	Remarks.
Rinehart, David G	Private	38	May 2, 1864	100 dys.	Mustered out with company Aug. 30, 1864.
Rinehart, Silas	do	21	May 2, 1864	100 dys.	Mustered out with company Aug. 30, 1864.
Rood, Stephen C	do	35	May 2, 1864	100 dys.	Mustered out with company Aug. 30, 1864.
Ruley, Samuel	do	20	May 2, 1864	100 dys.	Mustered out with company Aug. 30, 1864.
Sayre, Preston H	do	21	May 2, 1861	100 dys.	Captured July 9, 1864, at battle of Monocacy, Md.; died Dec. 2, 1864, in Rebel Prison at Salisbury, N. C.
Scholl, Nicholas	do	19	May 2, 1864	100 dys.	Mustered out with company Aug. 30, 1864.
Sproat, James F	do	32	May 2, 1864	100 dys.	Promoted to Hospital Steward May 11, 1864.
Stadler, John	do	18	May 2, 1864	100 dys.	Died July 1, 1864, at McKims' Hospital, Baltimore, Md.
Stall, Wilson	do	18	May 2, 1864	100 dys.	Mustered out with company Aug. 30, 1864.
Stickroth, Conrad	do	33	May 2, 1864	100 dys.	Mustered out with company Aug. 30, 1864.
Thoma, Sebastian	do	39	May 2, 1864	100 dys.	Mustered out with company Aug. 30, 1864.
Thompson, James	do	47	May 2, 1864	100 dys.	Mustered out with company Aug. 30, 1864.
Toops, Henry	do	39	May 2, 1864	100 dys.	Mustered out with company Aug. 30, 1864.
Toops, James W	do	23	May 2, 1864	100 dys.	Mustered out with company Aug. 30, 1864.
Trochler, George	do	29	May 2, 1864	100 dys.	Died Aug. 6, 1864, at Sandy Hook Hospital, Maryland.
Troubb, George	do	24	May 2, 1864	100 dys.	Mustered out with company Aug. 30, 1864.
Vanscoy, George	do	44	May 2, 1864	100 dys.	Mustered out with company Aug. 30, 1864.
Vanscoy, Noah	do	18	May 2, 1864	100 dys.	Mustered out with company Aug. 30, 1864.
Wentworth, Benning	do	43	May 2, 1864	100 dys.	Mustered out with company Aug. 30, 1864.
Wilt, George	do	31	May 2, 1864	100 dys.	Mustered out with company Aug. 30, 1864.
Wilt, Samuel	do	36	May 2, 1864	100 dys.	Mustered out with company Aug. 30, 1864.
Wilson, Martin	do	18	May 2, 1864	100 dys.	Mustered out with company Aug. 30, 1864.
Wilson, William	do	25	May 2, 1864	100 dys.	Mustered out with company Aug. 30, 1864.
Wyatt, Augustus	do	20	May 2, 1864	100 dys.	Mustered out with company Aug. 30, 1864.

COMPANY G.

Mustered in May 8, 1864, at Camp Dennison, O., by Robert S. Smith, Captain 2d Cavalry, U. S. A. Mustered out Aug. 30, 1864, at Camp Dennison, O., by William Stanley, 2d Lieutenant 10th Infantry, U. S. A.

Names.	Rank.	Age.	Date of Entering the Service.	Period of Service.	Remarks.
Joshua Hussey	Captain	31	May 2, 1864	100 dys.	Mustered out with company Aug. 30, 1864.
George F. Bowers	1st Lieut.	..	May 2, 1864	100 dys.	Mustered out with company Aug. 30, 1864.
Sinclair L. Pitzer	2d Lieut.	34	May 2, 1864	100 dys.	Mustered out with company Aug. 30, 1864.
Amos B. Beard	1st Sergt.	33	May 2, 1864	100 dys.	Mustered out with company Aug. 30, 1864.
Charles S. Drake	Sergeant	22	May 2, 1864	100 dys.	Mustered out with company Aug. 30, 1864.
John W. Cline	do	26	May 2, 1864	100 dys.	Mustered out with company Aug. 30, 1864.
John C. Routh	do	28	May 2, 1864	100 dys.	Mustered out with company Aug. 30, 1864.
Calvin R. Vantress	do	21	May 2, 1864	100 dys.	Mustered out with company Aug. 30, 1864.
Samuel Mower	Corporal	30	May 2, 1864	100 dys.	Mustered out with company Aug. 30, 1864.
John Newby	do	21	May 2, 1864	100 dys.	Captured July 9, 1864, at battle of Monocacy, Md.; mustered out April 5, 1865, at Columbus, O., by order of War Department.
Cornelis Robison	do	33	May 2, 1864	100 dys.	Mustered out with company Aug. 30, 1864.
Benjamin Stout	do	32	May 2, 1864	100 dys.	Mustered out with company Aug. 30, 1864.
Savetus Swartz	do	28	May 2, 1864	100 dys.	Mustered out with company Aug. 30, 1864.
Christopher Underwood	do	29	May 2, 1864	100 dys.	Mustered out with company Aug. 30, 1864.
Edward Williams	do	26	May 2, 1864	100 dys.	Mustered out with company Aug. 30, 1864.
John Hodson	do	36	May 2, 1864	100 dys.	Mustered out with company Aug. 30, 1864.
Austin, George W	Private	18	May 2, 1864	100 dys.	Mustered out with company Aug. 30, 1864.
Austin, James A	do	20	May 2, 1864	100 dys.	Mustered out with company Aug. 30, 1864.
Barnes, George D	do	43	May 2, 1864	100 dys.	Mustered out with company Aug. 30, 1864.
Barnes, John W	do	18	May 2, 1864	100 dys.	Mustered out with company Aug. 30, 1864.
Belford, Jonathan	do	28	May 2, 1864	100 dys.	Captured July 9, 1864, at battle of Monocacy, Md.; mustered out April 5, 1865, at Columbus, O., by order of War Department.
Bohar, David	do	28	May 2, 1864	100 dys.	Mustered out with company Aug. 30, 1864.
Brewer, Joel	do	42	May 2, 1864	100 dys.	Mustered out with company Aug. 30, 1864.
Brown, William A	do	36	May 2, 1864	100 dys.	No record subsequent to muster-in.
Burnes, Robert	do	19	May 2, 1864	100 dys.	Captured July 9, 1864, at battle of Monocacy, Md.; died Nov. 23, 1864, in Rebel Prison at Danville, Va.
Chamberlain, William	do	18	May 2, 1864	100 dys.	Mustered out with company Aug. 30, 1864.
Clabaugh, M. F	do	29	May 2, 1864	100 dys.	Captured July 9, 1864, at battle of Monocacy, Md.; mustered out April 6, 1865, at Columbus, O., by order of War Department.
Clark, William	do	26	May 2, 1864	100 dys.	Captured July 9, 1864, at battle of Monocacy, Md.; mustered out April 5, 1865, at Columbus, O., by order of War Department.
Cline, Samuel	do	21	May 2, 1864	100 dys.	Mustered out with company Aug. 30, 1864.
Cluxton, Catey	do	18	May 2, 1864	100 dys.	Mustered out with company Aug. 30, 1864.
Cox, David	do	18	May 2, 1864	100 dys.	Mustered out with company Aug. 30, 1864.
Davis, Thomas L	do	18	May 2, 1864	100 dys.	Wounded July 9, 1864, in battle of Monocacy, Md.; mustered out with company Aug. 30, 1864.
Devore, Levi	do	18	May 2, 1861	100 dys.	Mustered out with company Aug. 30, 1864.

COMPANY H.

Mustered in May 8, 1864, at Camp Dennison, O., by Robert S. Smith, Captain 2d Cavalry, U. S. A. Mustered out Aug. 30, 1864, at Camp Dennison, O., by William Stanley, 2d Lieutenant 10th Infantry, U. S. A.

Names.	Rank.	Age.	Date of Entering the Service.	Period of Service.	Remarks.
William R. Farlow	Captain.	21	May 2, 1864	100 dys.	Mustered out with company Aug. 30, 1864.
James Brown	1st Lieut.	37	May 2, 1864	100 dys.	Mustered out with company Aug. 30, 1864.
John F. Burris	2d Lieut.	32	May 2, 1864	100 dys.	Mustered out with company Aug. 30, 1864.
William F. Smith	1st Sergt.	21	May 2, 1864	100 dys.	Mustered out with company Aug. 30, 1864.
William H. Smith	Sergeant.	33	May 2, 1864	100 dys.	Mustered out with company Aug. 30, 1864.
Joseph Carnean	....do....	28	May 2, 1864	100 dys.	Mustered out with company Aug. 30, 1864.
William Jones	....do....	31	May 2, 1864	100 dys.	Mustered out with company Aug. 30, 1864.
Charles D. Parker	....do....	30	May 2, 1864	100 dys.	Mustered out with company Aug. 30, 1864.
Thomas M. Junk	Corporal.	26	May 2, 1864	100 dys.	Mustered out with company Aug. 30, 1864.
John G. W. Donohoe	....do....	33	May 2, 1864	100 dys.	Mustered out with company Aug. 30, 1864.
John N. Timmons	....do....	25	May 2, 1864	100 dys.	Mustered out with company Aug. 30, 1864.
Nelson L. Hurtt	....do....	19	May 2, 1864	100 dys.	Mustered out with company Aug. 30, 1864.
William Darby	....do....	39	May 2, 1864	100 dys.	Mustered out with company Aug. 30, 1864.
Anson H. Mallow	....do....	27	May 2, 1864	100 dys.	Mustered out with company Aug. 30, 1864.
Strawder G. Nier	....do....	25	May 2, 1864	100 dys.	Mustered out with company Aug. 30, 1864.
Ewing W. Templin	....do....	22	May 2, 1864	100 dys.	Mustered out with company Aug. 30, 1864.
Adams, Samuel	Private..	24	May 2, 1864	100 dys.	Mustered out with company Aug. 30, 1864.
Ayers, Elkena	....do....	33	May 2, 1864	100 dys.	Transferred to Co. B May 11, 1864.
Barton, George L.	....do....	18	May 2, 1864	100 dys.	Mustered out with company Aug. 30, 1864.
Bowers, George A.	....do....	19	May 2, 1864	100 dys.	Mustered out with company Aug. 30, 1864.
Campbell, Michael	....do....	32	May 2, 1864	100 dys.	Mustered out with company Aug. 30, 1864.
Castle, William R.	....do....	25	May 2, 1864	100 dys.	Mustered out with company Aug. 30, 1864.
Collins, Elias	....do....	19	May 2, 1864	100 dys.	Mustered out with company Aug. 30, 1864.
Collins, Jonas	....do....	21	May 2, 1864	100 dys.	Mustered out with company Aug. 30, 1864.
Crabb, George D.	....do....	19	May 2, 1864	100 dys.	Mustered out with company Aug. 30, 1864.
Cupp, John H.	....do....	22	May 2, 1864	100 dys.	Mustered out with company Aug. 30, 1864.
Deerexson, Henry A.	....do....	30	May 2, 1864	100 dys.	Mustered out with company Aug. 30, 1864.
Dennis, Daniel	....do....	31	May 2, 1864	100 dys.	Mustered out with company Aug. 30, 1864.
Dennis, George	....do....	27	May 2, 1864	100 dys.	Mustered out with company Aug. 30, 1864.
Dennis, Henry	....do....	35	May 2, 1864	100 dys.	Mustered out with company Aug. 30, 1864.
Dennis, William	....do....	35	May 2, 1864	100 dys.	No record subsequent to muster-in.
Donohoe, Alfred S.	....do....	19	May 2, 1864	100 dys.	Mustered out with company Aug. 30, 1864.
Donohoe, Owen	....do....	31	May 2, 1864	100 dys.	Mustered out with company Aug. 30, 1864.
Donohoe, William	....do....	26	May 2, 1864	100 dys.	Mustered out with company Aug. 30, 1864.
Downing, Melvin	....do....	28	May 2, 1864	100 dys.	Mustered out with company Aug. 30, 1864.
Downing, William	....do....	34	May 2, 1864	100 dys.	Mustered out with company Aug. 30, 1864.
Fix, Andrew	....do....	28	May 2, 1864	100 dys.	Died Feb. 13, 1865, in Rebel Prison at Salisbury, N. C.
Grove, William	....do....	21	May 2, 1864	100 dys.	Mustered out with company Aug. 30, 1864.
Handeher, George W.	....do....	22	May 2, 1864	100 dys.	Mustered out with company Aug. 30, 1864.
Handeher, Andrew J.	....do....	18	May 2, 1864	100 dys.	Mustered out with company Aug. 30, 1864.
Harmount, Robert S.	....do....	28	May 2, 1864	100 dys.	Mustered out with company Aug. 30, 1864.
Hickman, Zachariah D.	....do....	41	May 2, 1864	100 dys.	Transferred to Co. B ——.
Hill, Benjamin A.	....do....	27	May 2, 1864	100 dys.	Mustered out with company Aug. 30, 1864.
Hill, John C.	....do....	33	May 2, 1864	100 dys.	Mustered out with company Aug. 30, 1864.
Hitch, Clement	....do....	38	May 2, 1864	100 dys.	Mustered out with company Aug. 30, 1864.
Holloway, Joseph	....do....	36	May 2, 1864	100 dys.	Mustered out with company Aug. 30, 1864.
Horsey, Stephen G.	....do....	40	May 2, 1864	100 dys.	Mustered out with company Aug. 30, 1864.
Hughes, Charles	....do....	27	May 2, 1864	100 dys.	Mustered out with company Aug. 30, 1864.
Junk, John C.	....do....	28	May 2, 1864	100 dys.	Mustered out with company Aug. 30, 1864.
Junk, Robert W.	....do....	21	May 2, 1864	100 dys.	Mustered out with company Aug. 30, 1864.
Kearney, William	....do....	21	May 2, 1864	100 dys.	Mustered out with company Aug. 30, 1864.
Kimmey, Solomon	....do....	40	May 2, 1864	100 dys.	Mustered out with company Aug. 30, 1864.
Kiser, Eli	....do....	38	May 2, 1864	100 dys.	Mustered out with company Aug. 30, 1864.
Lambert, Zachariah	....do....	38	May 2, 1864	100 dys.	Mustered out with company Aug. 30, 1864.
McCammon, William	....do....	19	May 2, 1864	100 dys.	Transferred to Co. A ——, as William McCommon.
McCollister, James	....do....	33	May 2, 1864	100 dys.	Mustered out with company Aug. 30, 1864.
McKee, Harry	....do....	18	May 2, 1864	100 dys.	Mustered out with company Aug. 30, 1864.
Maddox, John H.	....do....	27	May 2, 1864	100 dys.	Mustered out with company Aug. 30, 1864.
Miller, William	....do....	43	May 2, 1864	100 dys.	Mustered out with company Aug. 30, 1864.
Nier, John	....do....	22	May 2, 1864	100 dys.	Mustered out with company Aug. 30, 1864.
Norris, David	....do....	20	May 2, 1864	100 dys.	Mustered out with company Aug. 30, 1864.
Richards, Benjamin	....do....	28	May 2, 1864	100 dys.	Mustered out with company Aug. 30, 1864.
Severs, Israel T.	....do....	41	May 2, 1864	100 dys.	Transferred to Co. G ——.
Timmons, Jason L.	....do....	21	May 2, 1864	100 dys.	Mustered out with company Aug. 30, 1864.
Timmons, John W.	....do....	19	May 2, 1864	100 dys.	Mustered out with company Aug. 30, 1864.
Timmons, William	....do....	28	May 2, 1864	100 dys.	Mustered out with company Aug. 30, 1864.
Tomlinson, M.	....do....	19	May 2, 1864	100 dys.	Mustered out with company Aug. 30, 1864.
Tootle, Owen R.	....do....	20	May 2, 1864	100 dys.	Mustered out with company Aug. 30, 1864.
Waggaman, Thomas H.	....do....	27	May 2, 1864	100 dys.	Mustered out with company Aug. 30, 1864.
Watt, Cyrus A.	....do....	23	May 2, 1864	100 dys.	Mustered out with company Aug. 30, 1864.
Whitten, John	....do....	28	May 2, 1864	100 dys.	Mustered out with company Aug. 30, 1864.
Whitten, Ranson	....do....	19	May 2, 1864	100 dys.	Mustered out with company Aug. 30, 1864.

Names.	Rank.	Age.	Date of Entering the Service.	Period of Service.	Remarks.
Haynes, Monroe	Private.	16	May 2, 1864	100 dys.	Transferred to Co. K May 11, 1864.
Hays, George W	...do...	17	May 2, 1864	100 dys.	Mustered out with company Aug. 30, 1864.
Hays, Josiah	...do...	33	May 2, 1864	100 dys.	Mustered out with company Aug. 30, 1864.
Hays, Samuel	...do...	34	May 2, 1864	100 dys.	Mustered out with company Aug. 30, 1864.
Hester, Jackson	...do...	21	May 2, 1864	100 dys.	Mustered out with company Aug. 30, 1864.
Hollis, Thomas B.	...do...	18	May 2, 1864	100 dys.	Mustered out with company Aug. 30, 1864.
Howser, William	...do...	26	May 2, 1864	100 dys.	Captured July 9, 1864, at battle of Monocacy, Md. died Jan, 27, 1865, in Rebel Prison at
Hunt, Harvey	...do...	16	May 2, 1864	100 dys.	Transferred to Co. K May 11, 1864.
Hunt, Uriah W	...do...	36	May 2, 1864	100 dys.	Transferred to Co. K May 11, 1864.
Jeffries, Jeremiah	...do...	25	May 2, 1864	100 dys.	Transferred to Co. K May 11, 1864.
Jump, George	...do...	19	May 2, 1864	100 dys.	Mustered out with company Aug. 30, 1864.
Kammerar, Joseph	...do...	29	May 2, 1864	100 dys.	Mustered out with company Aug. 30, 1864.
Kanish, Conrad	...do...	25	May 2, 1864	100 dys.	Mustered out with company Aug. 30, 1864.
Kirk, Jesse	...do...	27	May 2, 1864	100 dys.	Transferred to Co. K May 11, 1864.
Lightle, James	...do...	23	May 2, 1864	100 dys.	Mustered out with company Aug. 30, 1864.
Long, Samuel T	...do...	19	May 2, 1864	100 dys.	Mustered out with company Aug. 30, 1864.
Mc[illegible], William W	...do...	21	May 2, 1864	100 dys.	Captured July 9, 1864, at battle of Monocacy, Md.; mustered out March 29, 1865, at Columbus, O., by order of War Department.
Mc[illegible], Samuel	...do...	24	May 2, 1864	100 dys.	Mustered out with company Aug. 30, 1864.
McKenzie, William H	...do...	23	May 2, 1864	100 dys.	Discharged Sept. 2, 1864, at U. S. General Hospital at Baltimore, Md., on Surgeon's certificate of disability.
M[illegible], John	...do...	39	May 2, 1864	100 dys.	Mustered out with company Aug. 30, 1864.
M[illegible], William I	...do...	24	May 2, 1864	100 dys.	Mustered out with company Aug. 30, 1864.
N[illegible], John W	...do...	20	May 2, 1864	100 dys.	Mustered out with company Aug. 30, 1864.
[illegible], John L	...do...	35	May 2, 1864	100 dys.	Mustered out with company Aug. 30, 1864.
P[illegible], John W	...do...	26	May 2, 1864	100 dys.	Mustered out with company Aug. 30, 1864.
R[illegible], George	...do...	39	May 2, 1864	100 dys.	Mustered out with company Aug. 30, 1864.
R[illegible], Moses D	...do...	43	May 2, 1864	100 dys.	Mustered out with company Aug. 30, 1864.
Rowe, George	...do...	25	May 2, 1864	100 dys.	Mustered out with company Aug. 30, 1864.
Rowe, James F	...do...	37	May 2, 1864	100 dys.	Sick, in hospital at Baltimore, Md., since July —, 1864. No further record found.
Sailer, William H	...do...	18	May 2, 1864	100 dys.	Mustered out with company Aug. 30, 1864.
S[illegible], David I	...do...	35	May 2, 1864	100 dys.	Mustered out with company Aug. 30, 1864.
Sealock, Robert W	...do...	38	May 2, 1864	100 dys.	Mustered out with company Aug. 30, 1864.
Shela, Alfred	...do...	30	May 2, 1864	100 dys.	Mustered out with company Aug. 30, 1864.
Smart, Joshua E.	...do...	19	May 2, 1864	100 dys.	Mustered out with company Aug. 30, 1864.
Sturgess, William H	...do...	18	May 2, 1864	100 dys.	Mustered out with company Aug. 30, 1864.
Tovell, James B.	...do...	18	May 2, 1864	100 dys.	Mustered out with company Aug. 30, 1864.
Vanderburg, Paul D.	...do...	24	May 2, 1864	100 dys.	Transferred to Co. K May 11, 1864.
Watson, Marion	...do...	19	May 2, 1864	100 dys.	Mustered out with company Aug. 30, 1864.
Weath[illegible], William A.	...do...	24	May 2, 1864	100 dys.	Mustered out with company Aug. 30, 1864.
Wilcox, Isaac N	...do...	18	May 2, 1864	100 dys.	Mustered out with company Aug. 30, 1864.
Wilcox, Robert	...do...	46	May 2, 1864	100 dys.	Mustered out with company Aug. 30, 1864.
Wood, William	...do...	18	May 2, 1864	100 dys.	Mustered out with company Aug. 30, 1864.

COMPANY K.

Mustered in May 8, 1864, at Camp Dennison, O., by Robert S. Smith, Captain 2d Cavalry, U. S. A. Mustered out Aug. 30, 1864, at Camp Dennison, O., by William Stanley, 2d Lieutenant 10th Infantry, U. S. A.

Names.	Rank.	Age.	Date of Entering the Service.	Period of Service.	Remarks.
William C. Wilson	Captain.	42	May 2, 1864	100 dys.	Mustered out with company Aug. 30, 1864.
James V. Rannels	1st Lieut.	29	May 2, 1864	100 dys.	Mustered out with company Aug. 30, 1864.
Newton Shoemaker	2d Lieut.	28	May 2, 1864	100 dys.	Mustered out with company Aug. 30, 1864.
[illegible] Shockley	1st Sergt.	27	May 2, 1864	100 dys.	Mustered out with company Aug. 30, 1864.
[illegible] M Johnson	Sergeant.	30	May 2, 1864	100 dys.	Mustered out with company Aug. 30, 1864.
James J Gregory	...do...	41	May 2, 1864	100 dys.	Mustered out with company Aug. 30, 1864.
Edward P Bond	...do...	21	May 2, 1864	100 dys.	Mustered out with company Aug. 30, 1864.
George [illegible]	Corporal.	26	May 2, 1864	100 dys.	Mustered out with company Aug. 30, 1864.
Henry [illegible]	...do...	21	May 2, 1864	100 dys.	Mustered out with company Aug. 30, 1864.
[illegible]	...do...	21	May 2, 1864	100 dys.	Mustered out to date Aug. 30, 1864, by order of War Department.
[illegible]	...do...	21	May 2, 1864	100 dys.	Mustered out with company Aug. 30, 1864.
[illegible]	...do...	19	May 2, 1864	100 dys.	Mustered out with company Aug. 30, 1864.
[illegible]	...do...	25	May 2, 1864	100 dys.	Mustered out with company Aug. 30, 1864.
[illegible]	...do...	23	May 2, 1864	100 dys.	Mustered out with company Aug. 30, 1864.
[illegible]	...do...	22	May 2, 1864	100 dys.	Mustered out with company Aug. 30, 1864.
[illegible]	Private.	35	May 2, 1864	100 dys.	Discharged —. No further record found.
[illegible]	...do...	30	May 2, 1864	100 dys.	Mustered out with company Aug. 30, 1864.
[illegible]	...do...	31	May 2, 1864	100 dys.	Mustered out with company Aug. 30, 1864.
[illegible]	...do...	18	May 2, 1864	100 dys.	Mustered out with company Aug. 30, 1864.
[illegible]	...do...	20	May 2, 1864	100 dys.	Mustered out with company Aug. 30, 1864.
[illegible]	...do...	..	May 2, 1864	100 dys.	Mustered out with company Aug. 30, 1864.

Rank.	Age.	Date of Entering the Service.	Period of Service.	Remarks.
[illegible]	[illegible]	May 2, 1864	100 dys.	Mustered out with company Aug. 30, 1864.
..do....	[illegible]	May 2, 1864	100 dys.	Mustered out with company Aug. 30, 1864.
..do....	[illegible]	May 2, 1864	100 dys.	Mustered out with company Aug. 30, 1864.
..do....	[illegible]	May 2, 1864	100 dys.	Mustered out with company Aug. 30, 1864.
..do....	[illegible]	May 2, 1864	100 dys.	Mustered out with company Aug. 30, 1864.
..do....	25	May 2, 1864	100 dys.	Mustered out with company Aug. 30, 1864.
..do....	43	May 2, 1864	100 dys.	Mustered out with company Aug. 30, 1864.
..do....	[illegible]	May 2, 1864	100 dys.	Killed July 9, 1864, in battle of Monocacy, Md.
..do....	[illegible]	May 2, 1864	100 dys.	No further record found.
..do....	[illegible]	May 2, 1864	100 dys.	Mustered out with company Aug. 30, 1864.
..do....	[illegible]	May 2, 1864	100 dys.	Mustered out with company Aug. 30, 1864.
..do....	18	May 2, 1864	100 dys.	Captured July 9, 1864, at battle of Monocacy, Md.; mustered out April 6, 1865, at Columbus, O., by order of War Department.
..do....	27	May 2, 1864	100 dys.	Mustered out with company Aug. 30, 1864.
..do....	30	May 2, 1864	100 dys.	Mustered out with company Aug. 30, 1864.
..do....	19	May 2, 1864	100 dys.	Captured July 9, 1864, at battle of Monocacy, Md.; died July 14, 1865, at Wilmington, O.
..do....	18	May 2, 1864	100 dys.	Mustered out with company Aug. 30, 1864.
..do....	37	May 2, 1864	100 dys.	Transferred from Co. I May 11, 1864; mustered out with company Aug. 30, 1864.
..do....	38	May 2, 1864	100 dys.	Mustered out with company Aug. 30, 1864.
..do....	24	May 2, 1864	100 dys.	Mustered out with company Aug. 30, 1864.
..do....	28	May 2, 1864	100 dys.	Mustered out with company Aug. 30, 1864.
..do....	35	May 2, 1864	100 dys.	Mustered out with company Aug. 30, 1864.
..do....	42	May 2, 1864	100 dys.	Mustered out with company Aug. 30, 1864.
..do....	20	May 2, 1864	100 dys.	Mustered out with company Aug. 30, 1864.
..do....	45	May 2, 1864	100 dys.	Mustered out with company Aug. 30, 1864.
..do....	16	May 2, 1864	100 dys.	Transferred from Co. I May 11, 1864; mustered out with company Aug. 30, 1864.
..do....	30	May 2, 1864	100 dys.	Mustered out with company Aug. 30, 1864.
..do....	18	May 2, 1864	100 dys.	Transferred from Co. I May 11, 1864; mustered out with company Aug. 30, 1864.
..do....	28	May 2, 1864	100 dys.	Mustered out with company Aug. 30, 1864.
..do....	25	May 2, 1864	100 dys.	Mustered out with company Aug. 30, 1864.
..do....	24	May 2, 1864	100 dys.	Mustered out with company Aug. 30, 1864.
..do....	19	May 2, 1864	100 dys.	Transferred from Co. I May 11, 1864; mustered out with company Aug. 30, 1864.
..do....	35	May 2, 1864	100 dys.	Transferred from Co. I May 11, 1864; mustered out with company Aug. 30, 1864.
..do....	27	May 2, 1864	100 dys.	Mustered out with company Aug. 30, 1864.
..do....	27	May 2, 1864	100 dys.	On muster-in roll. No further record found.
..do....	18	May 2, 1864	100 dys.	Mustered out with company Aug. 30, 1864.
..do....	29	May 2, 1864	100 dys.	Captured July 9, 1864, at battle of Monocacy, Md.; died March 10, 1865, in hospital at Annapolis, Md.
..do....	24	May 2, 1864	100 dys.	Mustered out with company Aug. 30, 1864.
..do....	16	May 2, 1864	100 dys.	Transferred from Co. I May 11, 1864; died June June 4, 1864, at Easton, Md.
..do....	36	May 2, 1864	100 dys.	Transferred from Co. I May 11, 1864; mustered out with company Aug. 30, 1864.
..do....	25	May 2, 1864	100 dys.	Transferred from Co. I May 11, 1864; mustered out with company Aug. 30, 1864.
..do....	21	May 2, 1864	100 dys.	Mustered out with company Aug. 30, 1864.
..do....	27	May 2, 1864	100 dys.	Transferred from Co. I May 11, 1864; mustered out with company Aug. 30, 1864.
..do....	24	May 2, 1864	100 dys.	Mustered out with company Aug. 30, 1864.
..do....	30	May 2, 1864	100 dys.	On muster-in roll. No further record found.
..do....	27	May 2, 1864	100 dys.	Mustered out with company Aug. 30, 1864.
..do....	26	May 2, 1864	100 dys.	Mustered out with company Aug. 30, 1864.
..do....	28	May 2, 1864	100 dys.	On muster-in roll. No further record found.
..do....	30	May 2, 1864	100 dys.	Mustered out with company Aug. 30, 1864.
..do....	30	May 2, 1864	100 dys.	Mustered out with company Aug. 30, 1864.
..do....	26	May 2, 1864	100 dys.	Absent ——. No further record found.
..do....	20	May 2, 1864	100 dys.	Mustered out with company Aug. 30, 1864.
..do....	28	May 2, 1864	100 dys.	Mustered out with company Aug. 30, 1864.
..do....	25	May 2, 1864	100 dys.	Absent ——. No further record found.
..do....	34	May 2, 1864	100 dys.	Mustered out with company Aug. 30, 1864.
..do....	33	May 2, 1864	100 dys.	Mustered out with company Aug. 30, 1864.
..do....	28	May 2, 1864	100 dys.	Mustered out with company Aug. 30, 1864.
..do....	25	May 2, 1864	100 dys.	Mustered out with company Aug. 30, 1864.
..do....	21	May 2, 1864	100 dys.	Mustered out with company Aug. 30, 1864.
..do....	22	May 2, 1864	100 dys.	Mustered out with company Aug. 30, 1864.
..do....	46	May 2, 1864	100 dys.	Mustered out with company Aug. 30, 1864.
..do....	37	May 2, 1864	100 dys.	Mustered out with company Aug. 30, 1864.
..do....	27	May 2, 1864	100 dys.	Mustered out with company Aug. 30, 1864.
..do....	28	May 2, 1864	100 dys.	Discharged ——. No further record found.
..do....	31	May 2, 1864	100 dys.	Absent ——. No further record found.
..do....	28	May 2, 1864	100 dys.	Captured July 9, 1864, at battle of Monocacy, Md.; mustered out May 3, 1865, at Columbus, O., by order of War Department.
..do....	24	May 2, 1864	100 dys.	Mustered out with company Aug. 30, 1864.
..do....	18	May 2, 1864	100 dys.	Mustered out with company Aug. 30, 1864.
..do....	24	May 2, 1864	100 dys.	Transferred to Co. B ——.
..do....	18	May 2, 1864	100 dys.	Mustered out with company Aug. 30, 1864.

Names.	Rank.	Age.	Date of Entering the Service.	Period of Service.	Remarks.
Sherbick, Samuel........	Private..	30	May 2, 1864	100 dys.	Mustered out with company Aug. 30, 1864.
Slate, Daniel P...........	....do....	22	May 2, 1864	100 dys.	Mustered out with company Aug. 30, 1864.
Smith, Isaac N...........	....do....	27	May 2, 1864	100 dys.	Transferred to Co. B ——.
Spencer, Alfred...........	....do....	22	May 2, 1864	100 dys.	Absent ——. No further record found.
Spencer, Harvey..........	....do....	25	May 2, 1864	100 dys.	Mustered out with company Aug. 30, 1864.
Stackhouse, Albert......	....do....	18	May 2, 1864	100 dys.	Mustered out with company Aug. 30, 1864.
Stackhouse, Jesse.......	....do....	21	May 2, 1864	100 dys.	Mustered out with company Aug. 30, 1864.
Stackhouse, Joshua......	....do....	20	May 2, 1864	100 dys.	Mustered out with company Aug. 30, 1864.
Thorn, Elbert............	....do....	30	May 2, 1864	100 dys.	Mustered out with company Aug. 30, 1864.
Tupes, William............	....do....	40	May 2, 1864	100 dys.	Absent ——. No further record found.
Vanderburg, Paul D......	....do....	24	May 2, 1864	100 dys.	Transferred from Co. I May 11, 1864; mustered out with company Aug. 30, 1864.
Walker, Asa............	....do....	18	May 2, 1864	100 dys.	Mustered out with company Aug. 30, 1864.
Walker, Elijah T.........	....do....	20	May 2, 1864	100 dys.	Mustered out with company Aug. 30, 1864.
Walker, Robert B.........	....do....	25	May 2, 1864	100 dys.	Mustered out with company Aug. 30, 1864.
Wilson, Henry H.........	....do....	19	May 2, 1864	100 dys.	Mustered out with company Aug. 30, 1864.

150th Regiment Ohio Volunteer Infantry.

ONE HUNDRED DAYS' SERVICE.

THIS Regiment was organized at Cleveland, O., May 5, 1864, to serve one hundred days. It was composed of the Twenty-ninth Regiment, Ohio National Guard, from Cuyahoga County; one Company of the Thirtieth Battalion, Ohio National Guard, from Cuyahoga County; and one Company of the Thirty-seventh Regiment, Ohio National Guard, from Lorain County. The Regiment immediately started for Washington City. On arrival it was ordered to garrison Forts Lincoln, Saratoga, Thayer, Bunker Hill, Slocum, Totten, and Stevens, forming part of the chain of fortifications surrounding the National Capital. The One Hundred and Fiftieth remained in these forts during the whole term of its service, and participated in the fight before Washington, with a part of Early's Corps, July 10 and 11, 1864. The Regiment returned to Ohio, and was mustered out August 23, 1864, on expiration of term of service.

[illegible]TH REGIMENT OHIO VOLUNTEER INFANTRY.

FIELD AND STAFF.

[illegible] in May 5, 1864, at Cleveland, O., by W. L. Kellogg, Lieutenant 10th Infantry, U. S. A. Mustered out Aug. 28, 1864, at Cleveland, O., by Thomas Drummond, Captain 5th Cavalry, U. S. A.

Names.	Rank.	Age.	Date of Entering the Service.	Period of Service.	Remarks.
H. Hayward....		..	May 5, 1864	100 dys.	Commanded 1st Brigade, Hoskin's Division, from May 19, 1864, to Aug. 23, 1864; mustered out with regiment Aug. 28, 1864.
[illegible]........		..	May 5, 1864	100 dys.	Mustered out with regiment Aug. 28, 1864.
[illegible]........		..	May 5, 1864	100 dys.	Mustered out with regiment Aug. 28, 1864.
[illegible]........		..	May 5, 1864	100 dys.	Was Brigade Surgeon from June 4, 1864, to Aug. 28, 1864; mustered out with regiment Aug. 28, 1864.
[illegible].......	Asst. Sur.	32	May 5, 1864	100 dys.	Promoted from private Co. G May 5, 1864; mustered out with regiment Aug. 28, 1864.
[illegible]....	....do....	..	May 5, 1864	100 dys.	Mustered out with regiment Aug. 28, 1864.
[illegible].....	Adjutant	..	May 5, 1864	100 dys.	Act. Asst. Adj. General from May 19, 1864, to Aug. 28, 1864; mustered out with regiment Aug. 28, 1864.
M. Chapin	R. Q. M.	..	May 5, 1864	100 dys.	Act. Asst. Quartermaster from May 19, 1864, to Aug. 28, 1864; mustered out with regiment Aug. 28, 1864.
Burton	Sergt. Maj.	21	May 5, 1864	100 dys.	Promoted from Sergeant Co. G May 6, 1864; mustered out with regiment Aug. 28, 1864.
[illegible].........	Q. M. S.	23	May 2, 1864	100 dys.	Promoted from private Co. F May 5, 1864; mustered out with regiment Aug. 28, 1864.
Severance.	Com. Ser.	25	May 2, 1864	100 dys.	Promoted from private Co. F May 5, 1864; mustered out with regiment Aug. 28, 1864.
Gardner.	Hos. St'd.	31	May 2, 1864	100 dys.	Promoted from private Co. D May 9, 1864; mustered out with regiment Aug. 28, 1864.
M. Leland.	Prin. Mus	46	May 2, 1864	100 dys.	Promoted from private Co. D ——; mustered out with regiment Aug. 28, 1864.

COMPANY A.

[illegible] May 2, 1864, at Cleveland, O., by W. L. Kellogg, Lieutenant 10th Infantry, U. S. A. Mustered out Aug. 28, 1864, at Cleveland, O., by Thomas Drummond, Captain 5th Cavalry, U. S. A.

Names.	Rank.	Age.	Date of Entering the Service.	Period of Service.	Remarks.
Paddock.........	Captain.	50	May 2, 1864	100 dys.	Mustered out with company Aug. 28, 1864.
A. Richards.....	1st Lieut.	40	May 2, 1864	100 dys.	Mustered out with company Aug. 28, 1864.
N. Tibbetts.....	2d Lieut.	34	May 2, 1864	100 dys.	Mustered out with company Aug. 28, 1864.
. Parsons.......	1st Sergt.	29	May 2, 1864	100 dys.	Mustered out with company Aug. 28, 1864.
Morgan.........	Sergeant.	24	May 2, 1864	100 dys.	Mustered out with company Aug. 28, 1864.
C. Baldwin......	....do....	26	May 2, 1864	100 dys.	Mustered out with company Aug. 28, 1864.
....	....do....	36	May 2, 1864	100 dys.	Mustered out with company Aug. 28, 1864.
Wilkinson.......	....do....	30	May 2, 1864	100 dys.	Mustered out with company Aug. 28, 1864.
E. Daken........	Corporal.	22	May 2, 1864	100 dys.	Mustered out with company Aug. 28, 1864.
Potter...	....do....	31	May 2, 1864	100 dys.	Mustered out with company Aug. 28, 1864.
n W. Smith.....	....do....	27	May 2, 1864	100 dys.	Mustered out with company Aug. 28, 1864.
L. Allen........	....do....	20	May 2, 1864	100 dys.	Mustered out with company Aug. 28, 1864.
D. Briggs.......	....do....	21	May 2, 1864	100 dys.	Mustered out with company Aug. 28, 1864.
. Thomas	....do....	27	May 2, 1864	100 dys.	Mustered out with company Aug. 28, 1864.
J. Moulton	....do....	35	May 2, 1864	100 dys.	Mustered out with company Aug. 28, 1864.
O. Rawson.......	....do....	25	May 2, 1864	100 dys.	Mustered out with company Aug. 28, 1864.
E. Danton.......	Musician	28	May 2, 1864	100 dys.	Mustered out with company Aug. 28, 1864.
North	....do....	21	May 2, 1864	100 dys.	Mustered out with company Aug. 28, 1864.
ames M..... ...	Private..	22	May 2, 1864	100 dys.	Mustered out with company Aug. 28, 1864.
ictor J.........	....do....	28	May 2, 1864	100 dys.	Mustered out with company Aug. 28, 1864.
William M.......	....do....	18	May 2, 1864	100 dys.	Mustered out with company Aug. 28, 1864.
, John A........	....do....	35	May 2, 1864	100 dys.	Mustered out with company Aug. 28, 1864.
eorge D.........	....do....	32	May 2, 1864	100 dys.	Mustered out with company Aug. 28, 1864.
s, Charles E....	....do....	18	May 2, 1864	100 dys.	Mustered out with company Aug. 28, 1864.
s, Flavil J.....	....do....	22	May 2, 1864	100 dys.	Mustered out with company Aug. 28, 1864.
ewis.....	....do....	22	May 2, 1864	100 dys.	Mustered out with company Aug. 28, 1864.

Names.	Rank.	Age.	Date of Entering the Service.	Period of Service.	Remarks.
Bradner, John (2d)	Private	28	May 2, 1864	100 dys.	Mustered out with company Aug. 23, 1864.
Brown, Byron M.	do.	25	May 2, 1864	100 dys.	Mustered out with company Aug. 23, 1864.
Brown, Charles E.	do.	29	May 2, 1864	100 dys.	Mustered out with company Aug. 23, 1864.
Brown, Judson A.	do.	28	May 2, 1864	100 dys.	Mustered out with company Aug. 23, 1864.
Bruner, John	do.	19	May 2, 1864	100 dys.	Mustered out with company Aug. 23, 1864.
Carroll, Michael	do.	22	May 2, 1864	100 dys.	Mustered out with company Aug. 23, 1864.
Clark, Jerome H.	do.	21	May 2, 1864	100 dys.	Returned to 122d Regiment, New York Volunteers, Aug. 7, 1864, where he had previously enlisted.
Curtis, Aberdeen G.	do.	21	May 2, 1864	100 dys.	Mustered out with company Aug. 23, 1864.
Curtis, James	do.	22	May 2, 1864	100 dys.	Mustered out with company Aug. 23, 1864.
Davis, John J.	do.	26	May 2, 1864	100 dys.	Mustered out with company Aug. 23, 1864.
Dickinson, Albert	do.	29	May 2, 1864	100 dys.	Mustered out with company Aug. 23, 1864.
Doolittle, Charles L. O.	do.	40	May 2, 1864	100 dys.	Mustered out with company Aug. 23, 1864.
Fairchilds, Charles S.	do.	25	May 2, 1864	100 dys.	Mustered out with company Aug. 23, 1864.
Fields, Reuben A.	do.	28	May 2, 1864	100 dys.	Mustered out with company Aug. 23, 1864.
Finch, Lucas E.	do.	20	May 2, 1864	100 dys.	Mustered out with company Aug. 23, 1864.
Fowler, Edward D.	do.	22	May 2, 1864	100 dys.	Mustered out with company Aug. 23, 1864.
Francis, Henry	do.	30	May 2, 1864	100 dys.	Mustered out with company Aug. 23, 1864.
Gardner, Orlando S.	do.	24	May 2, 1864	100 dys.	Mustered out with company Aug. 23, 1864.
Good, Charles W.	do.	19	May 2, 1864	100 dys.	Mustered out with company Aug. 23, 1864.
Goodale, Samuel N.	do.	19	May 2, 1864	100 dys.	Mustered out with company Aug. 23, 1864.
Goodman, Alfred T.	do.	18	May 2, 1864	100 dys.	Mustered out with company Aug. 23, 1864.
Guy, Thomas	do.	21	May 2, 1864	100 dys.	Mustered out with company Aug. 23, 1864.
Hitchcock, Frederick	do.	35	May 2, 1864	100 dys.	Mustered out with company Aug. 23, 1864.
Hoyt, George	do.	25	May 2, 1864	100 dys.	Mustered out with company Aug. 23, 1864.
Keeler, Charles D.	do.	19	May 2, 1864	100 dys.	Mustered out with company Aug. 23, 1864.
Kidd, William	do.	55	May 2, 1864	100 dys.	Mustered out with company Aug. 23, 1864.
Kyser, Erwin J.	do.	20	May 2, 1864	100 dys.	Mustered out with company Aug. 23, 1864.
Lenner, Henry E.	do.	19	May 2, 1864	100 dys.	Mustered out with company Aug. 23, 1864.
L[illegible]h, James H.	do.	22	May 2, 1864	100 dys.	Mustered out with company Aug. 23, 1864.
Lyman, Charles M.	do.	24	May 2, 1864	100 dys.	Mustered out with company Aug. 23, 1864.
McLeod, Hiram N.	do.	28	May 2, 1864	100 dys.	Mustered out with company Aug. 23, 1864.
McNary, William J.	do.	27	May 2, 1864	100 dys.	Mustered out with company Aug. 23, 1864.
Mann, Thomas D.	do.	25	May 2, 1864	100 dys.	Mustered out with company Aug. 23, 1864.
Mears, L. Byron	do.	22	May 2, 1864	100 dys.	Mustered out with company Aug. 23, 1864.
Medsker, William	do.	23	May 2, 1864	100 dys.	Mustered out with company Aug. 23, 1864.
Nickels, Benjamin J.	do.	19	May 2, 1864	100 dys.	Mustered out with company Aug. 23, 1864.
Noble, [illegible] W.	do.	21	May 2, 1864	100 dys.	Mustered out with company Aug. 23, 1864.
Ormsby, Henry	do.	39	May 2, 1864	100 dys.	Mustered out with company Aug. 23, 1864.
Orth, Jacob G.	do.	18	May 2, 1864	100 dys.	Mustered out with company Aug. 23, 1864.
Orton, Samuel C.	do.	21	May 2, 1864	100 dys.	Mustered out with company Aug. 23, 1864.
Payne, George S.	do.	22	May 2, 1864	100 dys.	Mustered out with company Aug. 23, 1864.
Perkins, Jerome T.	do.	27	May 2, 1864	100 dys.	Mustered out with company Aug. 23, 1864.
Pratt, Norman D.	do.	25	May 2, 1864	100 dys.	Discharged June 27, 1864, on Surgeon's certificate of disability.
Prentiss, Mendon L.	do.	25	May 2, 1864	100 dys.	Mustered out with company Aug. 23, 1864.
[illegible] Arthur	do.	24	May 2, 1864	100 dys.	Mustered out with company Aug. 23, 1864.
[illegible] George W.	do.	22	May 2, 1864	100 dys.	Mustered out with company Aug. 23, 1864.
[illegible] John H.	do.	20	May 2, 1864	100 dys.	Mustered out with company Aug. 23, 1864.
[illegible] Joseph W.	do.	23	May 2, 1864	100 dys.	Mustered out with company Aug. 23, 1864.
[illegible] William H.	do.	21	May 2, 1864	100 dys.	Mustered out with company Aug. 23, 1864.
[illegible] Charles W.	do.	21	May 2, 1864	100 dys.	Mustered out with company Aug. 23, 1864.
[illegible] Edward D.	do.	21	May 2, 1864	100 dys.	Mustered out with company Aug. 23, 1864.
[illegible] Sanford D.	do.	19	May 2, 1864	100 dys.	Mustered out with company Aug. 23, 1864.
[illegible] Spencer	do.	26	May 2, 1864	100 dys.	Mustered out with company Aug. 23, 1864.
[illegible] Albert A.	do.	20	May 2, 1864	100 dys.	Mustered out with company Aug. 23, 1864.
[illegible] Alfred E.	do.	21	May 2, 1864	100 dys.	Mustered out with company Aug. 23, 1864.
[illegible] George	do.	18	May 2, 1864	100 dys.	Mustered out with company Aug. 23, 1864.
[illegible] P.	do.	27	May 2, 1864	100 dys.	Mustered out with company Aug. 23, 1864.
[illegible] Edwin	do.	26	May 2, 1864	100 dys.	Mustered out with company Aug. 23, 1864.
[illegible] William H.	do.	25	May 2, 1864	100 dys.	Mustered out with company Aug. 23, 1864.
[illegible] Austin	do.	19	May 2, 1864	100 dys.	Mustered out with company Aug. 23, 1864.
[illegible] Peter G.	do.	18	May 2, 1864	100 dys.	Mustered out with company Aug. 23, 1864.
[illegible] Charles W.	do.	28	May 2, 1864	100 dys.	Mustered out with company Aug. 23, 1864.
[illegible] Frank	do.	18	May 2, 1864	100 dys.	Mustered out with company Aug. 23, 1864.
[illegible] Theodore L.	do.	26	May 2, 1864	100 dys.	Mustered out with company Aug. 23, 1864.
[illegible] George	do.	21	May 2, 1864	100 dys.	Mustered out with company Aug. 23, 1864.
[illegible] R.	do.	18	May 2, 1864	100 dys.	Mustered out with company Aug. 23, 1864.
[illegible] Henry	do.	36	May 2, 1864	100 dys.	Mustered out with company Aug. 23, 1864.
[illegible]	do.	22	May 2, 1864	100 dys.	Mustered out with company Aug. 23, 1864.
[illegible] David S.	do.	23	May 2, 1864	100 dys.	Mustered out with company Aug. 23, 1864.
[illegible] Matthew	do.	18	May 2, 1864	100 dys.	Mustered out with company Aug. 23, 1864.
[illegible] L.	do.	20	May 2, 1864	100 dys.	Mustered out with company Aug. 23, 1864.
[illegible] H.	do.	19	May 2, 1864	100 dys.	Mustered out with company Aug. 23, 1864.

COMPANY B.

Cleveland, O., by W. L. Kellogg, Lieutenant 10th Infantry, U. S. A. Mustered at Cleveland, O., by Thomas Drummond, Captain 5th Cavalry, U. S. A.

...nk.	Age.	Date of Entering the Service.	Period of Service.	Remarks.
...ptain.	37	May 2, 1864	100 dys.	Mustered out with company Aug. 23, 1864.
...Lieut.	22	May 2, 1864	100 dys.	Mustered out with company Aug. 23, 1864.
...Lieut.	19	May 2, 1864	100 dys.	Mustered out with company Aug. 23, 1864.
...Sergt.	24	May 2, 1864	100 dys.	Mustered out with company Aug. 23, 1864.
...rgeant.	26	May 2, 1864	100 dys.	Mustered out with company Aug. 23, 1864.
.do....	22	May 2, 1864	100 dys.	Mustered out with company Aug. 23, 1864.
.do....	28	May 2, 1864	100 dys.	Mustered out with company Aug. 23, 1864.
.do....	21	May 2, 1864	100 dys.	Mustered out with company Aug. 23, 1864.
...rporal.	19	May 2, 1864	100 dys.	Mustered out with company Aug. 23, 1864.
.do....	19	May 2, 1864	100 dys.	Mustered out with company Aug. 23, 1864.
.do....	19	May 2, 1864	100 dys.	Mustered out with company Aug. 23, 1864.
.do....	18	May 2, 1864	100 dys.	Mustered out with company Aug. 23, 1864.
.do....	25	May 2, 1864	100 dys.	Mustered out with company Aug. 23, 1864.
.do....	18	May 2, 1864	100 dys.	Mustered out with company Aug. 23, 1864.
.do....	23	May 2, 1864	100 dys.	Mustered out with company Aug. 23, 1864.
.do....	19	May 2, 1864	100 dys.	Mustered out with company Aug. 23, 1864.
...sician	18	May 2, 1864	100 dys.	Mustered out with company Aug. 23, 1864.
...rivate..	18	May 2, 1864	100 dys.	Mustered out with company Aug. 23, 1864.
.do....	18	May 2, 1864	100 dys.	Mustered out with company Aug. 23, 1864.
.do....	18	May 2, 1864	100 dys.	Mustered out with company Aug. 23, 1864.
.do....	19	May 2, 1864	100 dys.	Mustered out with company Aug. 23, 1864.
.do....	25	May 2, 1864	100 dys.	Mustered out with company Aug. 23, 1864.
.do....	24	May 2, 1864	100 dys.	Mustered out with company Aug. 23, 1864.
.do....	16	May 2, 1864	100 dys.	Mustered out with company Aug. 23, 1864.
.do....	21	May 2, 1864	100 dys.	Mustered out with company Aug. 23, 1864.
.do....	20	May 2, 1864	100 dys.	Mustered out with company Aug. 23, 1864.
.do....	19	May 2, 1864	100 dys.	Mustered out with company Aug. 23, 1864.
.do....	19	May 2, 1864	100 dys.	Mustered out with company Aug. 23, 1864.
.do....	27	May 2, 1864	100 dys.	Discharged Aug. 21, 1864, at Washington, D. C., on Surgeon's certificate of disability.
.do....	24	May 2, 1864	100 dys.	Mustered out with company Aug. 23, 1864.
.do....	22	May 2, 1864	100 dys.	Mustered out with company Aug. 23, 1864.
.do....	42	May 2, 1864	100 dys.	Mustered out with company Aug. 23, 1864.
.do....	18	May 2, 1864	100 dys.	Mustered out with company Aug. 23, 1864.
.do....	31	May 2, 1864	100 dys.	Mustered out with company Aug. 23, 1864.
.do....	18	May 2, 1864	100 dys.	Mustered out with company Aug. 23, 1864.
.do....	19	May 2, 1864	100 dys.	Mustered out with company Aug. 23, 1864.
.do....	32	May 2, 1864	100 dys.	Mustered out with company Aug. 23, 1864.
.do....	42	May 2, 1864	100 dys.	Mustered out with company Aug. 23, 1864.
.do....	18	May 2, 1864	100 dys.	Mustered out with company Aug. 23, 1864.
.do....	20	May 2, 1864	100 dys.	Mustered out with company Aug. 23, 1864.
.do....	18	May 2, 1864	100 dys.	Mustered out with company Aug. 23, 1864.
.do....	21	May 2, 1864	100 dys.	Mustered out with company Aug. 23, 1864.
.do....	18	May 2, 1864	100 dys.	Mustered out with company Aug. 23, 1864.
.do....	20	May 2, 1864	100 dys.	Mustered out with company Aug. 23, 1864.
.do....	19	May 2, 1864	100 dys.	Mustered out with company Aug. 23, 1864.
.do....	22	May 2, 1864	100 dys.	Mustered out with company Aug. 23, 1864.
.do....	22	May 2, 1864	100 dys.	Mustered out with company Aug. 23, 1864.
.do....	19	May 2, 1864	100 dys.	Mustered out with company Aug. 23, 1864.
.do....	19	May 2, 1864	100 dys.	Mustered out with company Aug. 23, 1864.
.do....	18	May 2, 1864	100 dys.	Mustered out with company Aug. 23, 1864.
.do....	25	May 2, 1864	100 dys.	Mustered out with company Aug. 23, 1864.
.do....	22	May 2, 1864	100 dys.	Mustered out with company Aug. 23, 1864.
.do....	33	May 2, 1864	100 dys.	Mustered out with company Aug. 23, 1864.
.do....	23	May 2, 1864	100 dys.	Mustered out with company Aug. 23, 1864.
.do....	18	May 2, 1864	100 dys.	Mustered out with company Aug. 23, 1864.
.do....	18	May 2, 1864	100 dys.	Mustered out with company Aug. 23, 1864.
.do....	19	May 2, 1864	100 dys.	Mustered out with company Aug. 23, 1864.
.do....	18	May 2, 1864	100 dys.	Mustered out with company Aug. 23, 1864.
.do....	21	May 2, 1864	100 dys.	Mustered out with company Aug. 23, 1864.
.do....	37	May 2, 1864	100 dys.	Mustered out with company Aug. 23, 1864.
.do....	18	May 2, 1864	100 dys.	Mustered out with company Aug. 23, 1864.
.do....	23	May 2, 1864	100 dys.	Mustered out with company Aug. 23, 1864.
	18	May 2, 1864	100 dys.	Mustered out with company Aug. 23, 1864.
.do....	36	May 2, 1864	100 dys.	Mustered out with company Aug. 23, 1864.
.do....	23	May 2, 1864	100 dys.	Mustered out with company Aug. 23, 1864.
.do....	19	May 2, 1864	100 dys.	Mustered out with company Aug. 23, 1864.
.do....	18	May 2, 1864	100 dys.	Mustered out with company Aug. 23, 1864.
.do....	32	May 2, 1864	100 dys.	Mustered out with company Aug. 23, 1864.
.do....	42	May 2, 1864	100 dys.	Mustered out with company Aug. 23, 1864.
.do....	21	May 2, 1864	100 dys.	Mustered out with company Aug. 23, 1864.
.do....	23	May 2, 1864	100 dys.	Mustered out with company Aug. 23, 1864.
.do....	25	May 2, 1864	100 dys.	Mustered out with company Aug. 23, 1864.
.do....	23	May 2, 1864	100 dys.	Mustered out with company Aug. 23, 1864.
.do....	18	May 2, 1864	100 dys.	Mustered out with company Aug. 23, 1864.
.do....	21	May 2, 1864	100 dys.	Mustered out with company Aug. 23, 1864.
.do....	20	May 2, 1864	100 dys.	Mustered out with company Aug. 23, 1864.

Names.	Rank.	Age.	Date of Entering the Service.	Period of Service.	Remarks.
Richardson, Henry H.	Private.	18	May 2, 1864	100 dys.	Discharged June 27, 1864, at Fort Bunker Hill D. C., on Surgeon's certificate of disability.
Riskemier, John H.	do.	26	May 2, 1864	100 dys.	Mustered out with company Aug. 23, 1864.
Robbins William	do.	21	May 2, 1864	100 dys.	Mustered out with company Aug. 23, 1864.
Rosenkrans, David	do.	23	May 2, 1864	100 dys.	Mustered out with company Aug. 23, 1864.
Sackett, Homer W.	do.	27	May 2, 1864	100 dys.	Mustered out with company Aug. 23, 1864.
Schott, Adam	do.	21	May 2, 1864	100 dys.	Mustered out with company Aug. 24, 1864.
Skinner, Henry	do.	32	May 2, 1864	100 dys.	Mustered out with company Aug. 23, 1864.
Spencer, Charles F.	do.	22	May 2, 1864	100 dys.	Mustered out with company Aug. 23, 1864.
Stephens, John K.	do.	31	May 2, 1864	100 dys.	Mustered out with company Aug. 24, 1864.
Taylor, George	do.	19	May 2, 1864	100 dys.	Mustered out with company Aug. 23, 1864.
Tamblin, Charles	do.	19	May 2, 1864	100 dys.	Mustered out with company Aug. 23, 1864.
Thomas, William S.	do.	31	May 2, 1864	100 dys.	Mustered out with company Aug. 23, 1864.
Updike, John B.	do.	18	May 2, 1864	100 dys.	Mustered out with company Aug. 23, 1864.
Van Druver David	do.	19	May 2, 1864	100 dys.	Mustered out with company Aug. 23, 1864.
Vickers, Thomas	do.	19	May 2, 1864	100 dys.	Mustered out with company Aug. 23, 1864.
Wilcox, Andrew R.	do.	32	May 2, 1864	100 dys.	Mustered out with company Aug. 23, 1864.
Williams, Charles H.	do.	22	May 2, 1864	100 dys.	Mustered out with company Aug. 23, 1864.
Wilson, Hiram V.	do.	26	May 2, 1864	100 dys.	Mustered out with company Aug. 23, 1864.

COMPANY C.

Mustered in May 5, 1864, at Cleveland, O., by W. L. Kellogg, Lieutenant 10th Infantry, U. S. A. Mustered out Aug. 23, 1864, at Cleveland, O., by Thomas Drummond, Captain 5th Cavalry, U. S. A.

Names.	Rank.	Age.	Date of Entering the Service.	Period of Service.	Remarks.
Louis G. DeForest	Captain.	26	May 2, 1864	100 dys.	Mustered out with company Aug. 23, 1864.
Marcus A. Hanna	2d Lieut.	[illegible]	May 2, 1864	100 dys.	Mustered out with company Aug. 23, 1864.
Ebenezer B. Thomas	1st Sergt.	25	May 2, 1864	100 dys.	Mustered out with company Aug. 23, 1864.
Henry A. Harvey	Sergeant.	21	May 2, 1864	100 dys.	Mustered out with company Aug. 23, 1864.
Jay [illegible] Morse	do.	25	May 2, 1864	100 dys.	Mustered out with company Aug. 23, 1864.
George W. Chapin	do.	27	May 2, 1864	100 dys.	Mustered out with company Aug. 23, 1864.
Charles H. Tucker	do.	25	May 2, 1864	100 dys.	Mustered out with company Aug. 23, 1864.
Perry Prentiss	Corporal.	30	May 2, 1864	100 dys.	Mustered out with company Aug. 23, 1864.
John J. Wighman	do.	24	May 2, 1864	100 dys.	Mustered out with company Aug. 23, 1864.
Edward S. Page	do.	21	May 2, 1864	100 dys.	Mustered out with company Aug. 23, 1864.
Henry T. Fenton	do.	26	May 2, 1864	100 dys.	Mustered out with company Aug. 23, 1864.
Levi A. Sack [illegible]	do.	21	May 2, 1864	100 dys.	Mustered out with company Aug. 23, 1864.
William H. Wyman	do.	21	May 2, 1864	100 dys.	Accidentally killed July 4, 1864, near Washington, D. C.
Alexander I. McIntosh	do.	19	May 2, 1864	100 dys.	Mustered out with company Aug. 23, 1864.
George A. Brown	do.	22	May 2, 1864	100 dys.	Mustered out with company Aug. 23, 1864.
George E. Stewart	do.	19	May 2, 1864	100 dys.	Appointed —; mustered out with company Aug. 23, 1864.
[illegible] Brockway	Musician	29	May 2, 1864	100 dys.	Mustered out with company Aug. 24, 1864.
[illegible]	Private.	19	May 2, 1864	100 dys.	Mustered out with company Aug. 23, 1864.
[illegible]	do.	20	May 2, 1864	100 dys.	Mustered out with company Aug. 23, 1864.
[illegible] Daniel M.	do.	18	May 2, 1864	100 dys.	Mustered out with company Aug. 23, 1864.
[illegible] George W.	do.	26	May 2, 1864	100 dys.	Mustered out Aug. 13, 1864, at Washington D. C., on expiration of term of service.
[illegible]	do.	21	May 2, 1864	100 dys.	Mustered out with company Aug. 23, 1864.
[illegible] Edward F.	do.	21	May 2, 1864	100 dys.	Discharged May 12, 1864, by order of War Department.
[illegible] A.	do.	27	May 2, 1864	100 dys.	Mustered out with company Aug. 23, 1864.
[illegible] George F.	do.	20	May 2, 1864	100 dys.	Mustered out with company Aug. 23, 1864.
[illegible] Charles S.	do.	22	May 2, 1864	100 dys.	Mustered out with company Aug. 23, 1864.
[illegible] M.	do.	31	May 2, 1864	100 dys.	Mustered out with company Aug. 23, 1864.
[illegible]	do.	22	May 2, 1864	100 dys.	Mustered out with company Aug. 23, 1864.
[illegible] H.	do.	31	May 2, 1864	100 dys.	Mustered out with company Aug. 23, 1864.
[illegible]	do.	20	May 2, 1864	100 dys.	Mustered out with company Aug. 23, 1864.
[illegible] C.	do.	25	May 2, 1864	100 dys.	Mustered out with company Aug. 23, 1864.
[illegible] Lanton	do.	19	May 2, 1864	100 dys.	Transferred to Co. A, 143d O. V. I., June 2, 1864.
[illegible] M.	do.	20	May 2, 1864	100 dys.	Mustered out with company Aug. 23, 1864.
[illegible] K.	do.	23	May 2, 1864	100 dys.	Mustered out with company Aug. 23, 1864.
[illegible]	do.	20	May 2, 1864	100 dys.	Mustered out with company Aug. 23, 1864.
[illegible] M.	do.	26	May 2, 1864	100 dys.	Mustered out with company Aug. 23, 1864.
[illegible] H.	do.	28	May 2, 1864	100 dys.	Mustered out with company Aug. 23, 1864.
[illegible] Adam	do.	21	May 2, 1864	100 dys.	Mustered out with company Aug. 23, 1864.
[illegible]	do.	20	May 2, 1864	100 dys.	Transferred to Co. A, 143d O. V. I., June 2, 1864.
[illegible] H.	do.	28	May 2, 1864	100 dys.	Mustered out with company Aug. 23, 1864.
[illegible] A.	do.	20	May 2, 1864	100 dys.	Mustered out with company Aug. 23, 1864.
[illegible] Charles J.	do.	25	May 2, 1864	100 dys.	Mustered out with company Aug. 23, 1864.
[illegible]	do.	23	May 2, 1864	100 dys.	Mustered out with company Aug. 23, 1864.
[illegible] William	do.	27	May 2, 1864	100 dys.	Mustered out with company Aug. 23, 1864.
[illegible]	do.	21	May 2, 1864	100 dys.	Mustered out with company Aug. 23, 1864.
[illegible] Charles	do.	26	May 2, 1864	100 dys.	Mustered out with company Aug. 23, 1864.
[illegible] J.	do.	29	May 2, 1864	100 dys.	Mustered out with company Aug. 24, 1864.
[illegible] W.	do.	24	May 2, 1864	100 dys.	Mustered out with company Aug. 23, 1864.
[illegible]	do.	19	May 2, 1864	100 dys.	Mustered out with company Aug. 23, 1864.

Names.	Rank.	Age.	Date of Entering the service.	Period of Service.	Remarks.
Goodwin, Charles T	Private	19	May 2, 1864	100 dys.	Mustered out with company Aug. 23, 1864.
Guy, Thomas	do	19	May 2, 1864	100 dys.	Mustered out with company Aug. 23, 1864.
Hanscomb, Edward B	do	21	May 2, 1864	100 dys.	Mustered out with company Aug. 23, 1864.
Harrington, Martin	do	31	May 2, 1864	100 dys.	Mustered out with company Aug. 23, 1864.
Harvey, Edward H	do	19	May 2, 1864	100 dys.	Mustered out with company Aug. 23, 1864.
Henricle, Daniel	do	20	May 2, 1864	100 dys.	Mustered out with company Aug. 23, 1864.
Hill, Augustus F	do	28	May 2, 1864	100 dys.	Mustered out with company Aug. 23, 1864.
Hoyt, Frank W	do	21	May 2, 1864	100 dys.	Mustered out with company Aug. 23, 1864.
Hubby, Frank W	do	22	May 2, 1864	100 dys.	Mustered out with company Aug. 23, 1864.
Hunt, Edward P	do	25	May 2, 1864	100 dys.	Mustered out with company Aug. 23, 1864.
Iddings, Richard M	do	20	May 2, 1864	100 dys.	Mustered out with company Aug. 23, 1864.
Kelly, William H	do	23	May 2, 1864	100 dys.	Mustered out with company Aug. 23, 1864.
Kimball, William W	do	19	May 2, 1864	100 dys.	Mustered out with company Aug. 23, 1864.
Lang, George H	do	27	May 2, 1864	100 dys.	Mustered out with company Aug. 23, 1864.
Lang, James	do	23	May 2, 1864	100 dys.	Mustered out with company Aug. 23, 1864.
Lang, Robert	do	20	May 2, 1864	100 dys.	Mustered out with company Aug. 23, 1864.
Latch, William F	do	22	May 2, 1864	100 dys.	Mustered out with company Aug. 23, 1864.
Lyman, George C	do	24	May 2, 1864	100 dys.	Mustered out with company Aug. 23, 1864.
McMillen, George W	do	33	May 2, 1864	100 dys.	Mustered out with company Aug. 23, 1864.
Morrison, Henry E	do	20	May 2, 1864	100 dys.	Mustered out with company Aug. 23, 1864.
Morris, William	do	22	May 2, 1864	100 dys.	Mustered out with company Aug. 23, 1864.
Morse, Charles D	do	19	May 2, 1864	100 dys.	Mustered out with company Aug. 23, 1864.
Myer, Henry E	do	26	May 2, 1864	100 dys.	Mustered out with company Aug. 23, 1864.
Norton, Elijah H	do	20	May 2, 1864	100 dys.	Mustered out with company Aug. 23, 1864.
Norton, Herman	do	22	May 2, 1864	100 dys.	Transferred to Co. A, [illegible] O. V. I., June 21, 1864.
Papworth, Robert R	do	35	May 2, 1864	100 dys.	Mustered out with company Aug. 23, 1864.
Payne, Nathan P	do	27	May 2, 1864	100 dys.	Mustered out with company Aug. 23, 1864.
Pease, Luther M	do	20	May 2, 1864	100 dys.	Mustered out with company Aug. 23, 1864.
Perkins, Charles	do	20	May 2, 1864	100 dys.	Died Aug. 18, 1864, at Cleveland, O.
Porter, Andrew	do	22	May 2, 1864	100 dys.	Mustered out with company Aug. 23, 1864.
Prentis, Chauncey	do	23	May 2, 1864	100 dys.	Mustered out with company Aug. 23, 1864.
Price, Charles J	do	[illegible]	May 2, 1864	100 dys.	Mustered out with company Aug. 23, 1864.
Reid, William R	do	21	May 2, 1864	100 dys.	Mustered out with company Aug. 23, 1864.
Scott, Ashley D	do	23	May 2, 1864	100 dys.	Mustered out with company Aug. 23, 1864.
Segar, George W	do	20	May 2, 1864	100 dys.	Mustered out with company Aug. 23, 1864.
Segar, Henry G	do	[illegible]	May 2, 1864	100 dys.	Mustered out with company Aug. 23, 1864.
Sheppard, [illegible]	do	26	May 2, 1864	100 dys.	
Steadman, Frank B	do	22	May 2, 1864	100 dys.	Mustered out with company Aug. 23, 1864.
Stillman, William H	do	19	May 2, 1864	100 dys.	Mustered out with company Aug. 23, 1864.
Strong, Lorenzo A	do	22	May 2, 1864	100 dys.	Mustered out with company Aug. 23, 1864.
Tennis, John S	do	21	May 2, 1864	100 dys.	Mustered out with company Aug. 23, 1864.
Thorpe, Ira D	do	21	May 2, 1864	100 dys.	Transferred to Co. A, [illegible] O. V. I., June 21, 1864.
Vaillant, Edmund	do	21	May 2, 1864	100 dys.	Mustered out with company Aug. 23, 1864.
Virgil, Henry J	do	28	May 2, 1864	100 dys.	Mustered out with company Aug. 23, 1864.
Wall, Thomas	do	22	May 2, 1864	100 dys.	Mustered out with company Aug. 23, 1864.
Wall, William R	do	23	May 2, 1864	100 dys.	Mustered out with company Aug. 23, 1864.
Ward, William	do	20	May 2, 1864	100 dys.	Mustered out with company Aug. 23, 1864.
Wheeler, John W	do	20	May 2, 1864	100 dys.	Mustered out with company Aug. 23, 1864.
Whitmore, Augustus W	do	19	May 2, 1864	100 dys.	Mustered out with company Aug. 23, 1864.
Wightman, Louis	do	18	May 2, 1864	100 dys.	Mustered out with company Aug. 23, 1864.
Walcutt, Henry R	do	19	May 2, 1864	100 dys.	Transferred to Co. A, [illegible] O. V. I., June 21, 1864.

COMPANY D.

Mustered in May 5, 1864, at Cleveland, O., by W. L. Kellogg, Lieutenant [illegible] Infantry, U. S. A. Mustered out Aug. 23, 1864, at Cleveland, O., by Thomas Drummond, Captain 5th Cavalry, U. S. A.

Names.	Rank.	Age.	Date of Entering the service.	Period of Service.	Remarks.
John J. Wizeman	Captain.	40	May 2, 1864	100 dys.	Mustered out with company Aug. 23, 1864.
Jason Canfield	1st Lieut.	34	May 2, 1864	100 dys.	Mustered out with company Aug. 23, 1864.
George W. Whitehead	2d Lieut.	21	May 2, 1864	100 dys.	Mustered out with company Aug. 23, 1864.
Alexander W. Davies	1st Sergt.	29	May 2, 1864	100 dys.	Mustered out with company Aug. 23, 1864.
William Towner	Sergeant.	43	May 2, 1864	100 dys.	Mustered out with company Aug. 23, 1864.
Albert B. Smith	do	21	May 2, 1864	100 dys.	Mustered out with company Aug. 23, 1864.
Horace [illegible] Pettingill	do	29	May 2, 1864	100 dys.	Mustered out with company Aug. 23, 1864.
[illegible] Howard Meriam	do	23	May 2, 1864	100 dys.	Mustered out with company Aug. 23, 1864.
Jacob P. [illegible]	Corporal	25	May 2, 1864	100 dys.	Mustered out with company Aug. 23, 1864.
Newell S. Cozad	do	33	May 2, 1864	100 dys.	Mustered out with company Aug. 23, 1864.
Staymaker M. Davis	do	[illegible]	May 2, 1864	100 dys.	Mustered out with company Aug. 23, 1864.
James A. Gribben	do	19	May 2, 1864	100 dys.	Mustered out with company Aug. 23, 1864.
Octave L. Goyette	do	35	May 2, 1864	100 dys.	Mustered out with company Aug. 23, 1864.
John W. Gibbons	do	39	May 2, 1864	100 dys.	Mustered out with company Aug. 23, 1864.
Carlos M. Sturtevant	do	22	May 2, 1864	100 dys.	Mustered out with company Aug. 23, 1864.
John L. McIntosh	do	22	May 2, 1864	100 dys.	Appointed June [illegible], 1864; mustered out with company Aug. 23, 1864.
Ansley, George W	Private	20	May 2, 1864	100 dys.	Mustered out with company Aug. 23, 1864.
Baker, Samuel J	do	18	May 2, 1864	100 dys.	Mustered out with company Aug. 23, 1864.
Bell, George	do	34	May 2, 1864	100 dys.	Mustered out with company Aug. 23, 1864.

Names.	Rank.	Age.	Date of Entering the Service.	Period of Service.	Remarks.
[illegible] Frederick H.	Private	28	May 2, 1864	100 dys.	Mustered out with company Aug. 23, 1864.
[illegible] William E.	do	33	May 2, 1864	100 dys.	Mustered out with company Aug. 23, 1864.
[illegible] Joseph E.	do	24	May 2, 1864	100 dys.	Mustered out with company Aug. 23, 1864.
[illegible] H. Gilbert	do	17	May 2, 1864	100 dys.	Mustered out with company Aug. 23, 1864.
[illegible] Charles C.	do	19	May 2, 1864	100 dys.	Mustered out with company Aug. 23, 1864.
[illegible] Henry S.	do	25	May 2, 1864	100 dys.	Mustered out with company Aug. 23, 1864.
[illegible] J. Eugene	do	17	May 2, 1864	100 dys.	
[illegible] Richard	do	22	May 2, 1864	100 dys.	Mustered out with company Aug. 23, 1864.
[illegible] William P.	do	17	May 2, 1864	100 dys.	Mustered out with company Aug. 23, 1864.
[illegible] Lewis H.	do	18	May 2, 1864	100 dys.	Mustered out with company Aug. 23, 1864.
[illegible] Burton K.	do	17	May 2, 1864	100 dys.	Mustered out with company Aug. 23, 1864.
[illegible] Frederick	do	18	May 2, 1864	100 dys.	Mustered out with company Aug. 23, 1864.
[illegible] R.	do	17	May 2, 1864	100 dys.	Mustered out with company Aug. 23, 1864.
[illegible]	do	19	May 2, 1864	100 dys.	Mustered out with company Aug. 23, 1864.
[illegible] Charles H.	do	18	May 2, 1864	100 dys.	Mustered out with company Aug. 23, 1864.
[illegible] George E.	do	17	May 2, 1864	100 dys.	Mustered out with company Aug. 23, 1864.
[illegible] Richard M.	do	45	May 2, 1864	100 dys.	Mustered out with company Aug. 23, 1864.
[illegible] Winfield S.	do	[illegible]	May 2, 1864	100 dys.	Mustered out with company Aug. 23, 1864.
[illegible] William D.	do	26	May 2, 1864	100 dys.	Mustered out with company Aug. 23, 1864.
[illegible] William H.	do	19	May 2, 1864	100 dys.	Mustered out with company Aug. 23, 1864.
[illegible] Thomas	do	18	May 2, 1864	100 dys.	Mustered out with company Aug. 23, 1864.
[illegible]	do	[illegible]	May 2, 1864	100 dys.	Mustered out with company Aug. 23, 1864.
[illegible]	do	[illegible]	May 2, 1864	100 dys.	Mustered out with company Aug. 23, 1864.
[illegible] James P.	do	[illegible]	May 2, 1864	100 dys.	Promoted to Hospital Steward May 9, 1864.
[illegible] Edward F.	do	20	May 2, 1864	100 dys.	Mustered out with company Aug. 23, 1864.
[illegible] Frederick C.	do	21	May 2, 1864	100 dys.	Mustered out with company Aug. 23, 1864.
[illegible] L.	do	[illegible]	May 2, 1864	100 dys.	Mustered out with company Aug. 23, 1864.
[illegible] George	do	[illegible]	May 2, 1864	100 dys.	Mustered out with company Aug. 23, 1864.
[illegible] James B.	do	[illegible]	May 2, 1864	100 dys.	Mustered out with company Aug. 23, 1864.
[illegible] Charles L.	do	19	May 2, 1864	100 dys.	Mustered out with company Aug. 23, 1864.
[illegible]	do	[illegible]	May 2, 1864	100 dys.	Mustered out with company Aug. 23, 1864.
[illegible]	do	27	May 2, 1864	100 dys.	[illegible] June 10, 1864, [illegible]
[illegible]	do	[illegible]	May 2, 1864	100 dys.	Mustered out with company Aug. 23, 1864.
[illegible] W.	do	18	May 2, 1864	100 dys.	Mustered out with company Aug. 23, 1864.
[illegible] John, Jr.	do	[illegible]	May 2, 1864	100 dys.	Mustered out with company Aug. 23, 1864.
[illegible] M.	do	16	May 2, 1864	100 dys.	Promoted to Principal Musician —.
[illegible]	do	22	May 2, 1864	100 dys.	Mustered out with company Aug. 23, 1864.
[illegible] B.	do	18	May 2, 1864	100 dys.	Mustered out with company Aug. 23, 1864.
[illegible] A.	do	20	May 2, 1864	100 dys.	Mustered out with company Aug. 23, 1864.
[illegible] Robert M.	do	22	May 2, 1864	100 dys.	Mustered out with company Aug. 23, 1864.
[illegible] Jesse	do	37	May 2, 1864	100 dys.	Mustered out with company Aug. 23, 1864.
[illegible] William	do	31	May 2, 1864	100 dys.	Mustered out with company Aug. 23, 1864.
[illegible] A.	do	19	May 2, 1864	100 dys.	Mustered out with company Aug. 23, 1864.
[illegible] P.	do	27	May 2, 1864	100 dys.	Mustered out with company Aug. 23, 1864.
[illegible]	do	19	May 2, 1864	100 dys.	Mustered out with company Aug. 23, 1864.
[illegible] W.	do	20	May 2, 1864	100 dys.	Mustered out with company Aug. 23, 1864.
[illegible] H.	do	21	May 2, 1864	100 dys.	Mustered out with company Aug. 23, 1864.
[illegible]	do	[illegible]	May 2, 1864	100 dys.	Mustered out with company Aug. 23, 1864.
[illegible] D.	do	17	May 2, 1864	100 dys.	Mustered out with company Aug. 23, 1864.
[illegible]	do	20	May 2, 1864	100 dys.	Mustered out with company Aug. 23, 1864.
[illegible] Francis	do	[illegible]	May 2, 1864	100 dys.	Mustered out with company Aug. 23, 1864.
[illegible]	do	18	May 2, 1864	100 dys.	Mustered out with company Aug. 23, 1864.
[illegible] George	do	[illegible]	May 2, 1864	100 dys.	
[illegible]	do	[illegible]	May 2, 1864	100 dys.	Mustered out with company Aug. 23, 1864.
[illegible] W.	do	20	May 2, 1864	100 dys.	Mustered out with company Aug. 23, 1864.
[illegible] B.	do	18	May 2, 1864	100 dys.	Mustered out with company Aug. 23, 1864.
[illegible]	do	19	May 2, 1864	100 dys.	Mustered out with company Aug. 23, 1864.
[illegible] L.	do	43	May 2, 1864	100 dys.	Mustered out with company Aug. 23, 1864.
[illegible] A.	do	[illegible]	May 2, 1864	100 dys.	Mustered out with company Aug. 23, 1864.
[illegible] P.	do	18	May 2, 1864	100 dys.	Mustered out with company Aug. 23, 1864.
[illegible] L.	do	[illegible]	May 2, 1864	100 dys.	Reduced from Corporal May 31, 1864; mustered out with company Aug. 23, 1864.
[illegible] R.	do	[illegible]	May 2, 1864	100 dys.	Mustered out with company Aug. 23, 1864.
[illegible] M.	do	[illegible]	May 2, 1864	100 dys.	Mustered out with company Aug. 23, 1864.
[illegible] G.	do	[illegible]	May 2, 1864	100 dys.	Mustered out with company Aug. 23, 1864.
[illegible] T.	do	22	May 2, 1864	100 dys.	Mustered out with company Aug. 23, 1864.
[illegible]	do	[illegible]	May 2, 1864	100 dys.	Mustered out with company Aug. 23, 1864.
[illegible] J.	do	[illegible]	May 2, 1864	100 dys.	Mustered out with company Aug. 23, 1864.
[illegible] B.	do	17	May 2, 1864	100 dys.	Mustered out with company Aug. 23, 1864.
[illegible] B.	do	21	May 2, 1864	100 dys.	Mustered out with company Aug. 23, 1864.
[illegible] J.	do	21	May 2, 1864	100 dys.	Mustered out with company Aug. 23, 1864.
[illegible] L.	do	19	May 2, 1864	100 dys.	Mustered out with company Aug. 23, 1864.
[illegible]	do	[illegible]	May 2, 1864	100 dys.	Mustered out with company Aug. 23, 1864.
[illegible]	do	[illegible]	May 2, 1864	100 dys.	Mustered out with company Aug. 23, 1864.

COMPANY E.

at Cleveland, O., by W. L. Kellogg, Lieutenant 10th Infantry, U. S. A. Mustered at Cleveland, O., by Thomas Drummond, Captain 5th Cavalry, U. S. A.

Rank.	Age.	Date of Entering the Service.	Period of Service.	Remarks.
ptain.	24	May 2, 1864	100 dys.	Mustered out with company Aug. 23, 1864.
Lieut.	21	May 2, 1864	100 dys.	Mustered out with company Aug. 23, 1864.
Lieut.	25	May 2, 1864	100 dys.	Mustered out with company Aug. 23, 1864.
Sergt.	25	May 2, 1864	100 dys.	Mustered out with company Aug. 23, 1864.
rgeant.	21	May 2, 1864	100 dys.	Mustered out with company Aug. 23, 1864.
..do...	20	May 2, 1864	100 dys.	Mustered out with company Aug. 23, 1864.
..do...	22	May 2, 1864	100 dys.	Mustered out with company Aug. 23, 1864.
..do...	25	May 2, 1864	100 dys.	Mustered out with company Aug. 23, 1864.
rporal.	21	May 2, 1864	100 dys.	Mustered out with company Aug. 23, 1864.
..do...	22	May 2, 1864	100 dys.	Mustered out with company Aug. 23, 1864.
..do...	22	May 2, 1864	100 dys.	Mustered out with company Aug. 23, 1864.
..do...	27	May 2, 1864	100 dys.	Mustered out with company Aug. 23, 1864.
..do...	20	May 2, 1864	100 dys.	Mustered out with company Aug. 23, 1864.
..do...	18	May 2, 1864	100 dys.	Mustered out with company Aug. 23, 1864.
..do...	24	May 2, 1864	100 dys.	Mustered out with company Aug. 23, 1864.
..do...	18	May 2, 1864	100 dys.	Mustered out with company Aug. 23, 1864.
rivate..	25	May 2, 1864	100 dys.	Mustered out with company Aug. 23, 1864.
..do...	21	May 2, 1864	100 dys.	Mustered out with company Aug. 23, 1864.
..do...	23	May 2, 1864	100 dys.	Mustered out with company Aug. 23, 1864.
..do...	25	May 2, 1864	100 dys.	Mustered out with company Aug. 23, 1864.
..do...	20	May 2, 1864	100 dys.	Mustered out with company Aug. 23, 1864.
..do...	20	May 2, 1864	100 dys.	Mustered out with company Aug. 23, 1864.
..do...	19	May 2, 1864	100 dys.	Mustered out with company Aug. 23, 1864.
..do...	18	May 2, 1864	100 dys.	Mustered out with company Aug. 23, 1864.
..do...	19	May 2, 1864	100 dys.	Mustered out with company Aug. 23, 1864.
..do...	18	May 2, 1864	100 dys.	Mustered out with company Aug. 23, 1864.
..do...	19	May 2, 1864	100 dys.	Mustered out with company Aug. 23, 1864.
..do...	18	May 2, 1864	100 dys.	Mustered out with company Aug. 23, 1864.
..do...	21	May 2, 1864	100 dys.	Mustered out with company Aug. 23, 1864.
..do...	27	May 2, 1864	100 dys.	Mustered out with company Aug. 23, 1864.
..do...	22	May 2, 1864	100 dys.	Mustered out with company Aug. 23, 1864.
..do...	19	May 2, 1864	100 dys.	Mustered out with company Aug. 23, 1864.
..do...	25	May 2, 1864	100 dys.	Mustered out with company Aug. 23, 1864.
..do...	18	May 2, 1864	100 dys.	Mustered out with company Aug. 23, 1864.
..do...	18	May 2, 1864	100 dys.	Mustered out with company Aug. 23, 1864.
..do...	18	May 2, 1864	100 dys.	Mustered out with company Aug. 23, 1864.
..do...	21	May 2, 1864	100 dys.	Mustered out with company Aug. 23, 1864.
..do...	18	May 2, 1864	100 dys.	Mustered out with company Aug. 23, 1864.
..do...	19	May 2, 1864	100 dys.	Mustered out with company Aug. 23, 1864.
..do...	18	May 2, 1864	100 dys.	Mustered out with company Aug. 23, 1864.
..do...	19	May 2, 1864	100 dys.	Mustered out with company Aug. 23, 1864.
..do..	18	May 2, 1864	100 dys.	Mustered out with company Aug. 23, 1864.
..do...	19	May 2, 1864	100 dys.	Mustered out with company Aug. 23, 1864.
..do...	16	May 2, 1864	100 dys.	Mustered out with company Aug. 23, 1864.
..do...	18	May 2, 1864	100 dys.	Mustered out with company Aug. 23, 1864.
..do...	20	May 2, 1864	100 dys.	Mustered out with company Aug. 23, 1864.
..do...	32	May 2, 1864	100 dys.	Mustered out with company Aug. 23, 1864.
..do...	22	May 2, 1864	100 dys.	Mustered out with company Aug. 23, 1864.
..do...	19	May 2, 1864	100 dys.	Transferred to Co. F ——.
..do...	18	May 2, 1864	100 dys.	Mustered out with company Aug. 23, 1864.
..do...	18	May 2, 1864	100 dys.	Mustered out with company Aug. 23, 1864.
..do...	18	May 2, 1864	100 dys.	Mustered out with company Aug. 23, 1864.
..do...	19	May 2, 1864	100 dys.	Mustered out with company Aug. 23, 1864.
..do...	18	May 2, 1864	100 dys.	Mustered out with company Aug. 23, 1864.
..do...	19	May 2, 1864	100 dys.	Mustered out with company Aug. 23, 1864.
..do...	20	May 2, 1864	100 dys.	Mustered out with company Aug. 23, 1864.
..do...	21	May 2, 1864	100 dys.	Mustered out with company Aug. 23, 1864.
..do...	19	May 2, 1864	100 dys.	Mustered out with company Aug. 23, 1864.
..do...	20	May 2, 1864	100 dys.	Mustered out with company Aug. 23, 1864.
..do...	18	May 2, 1864	100 dys.	Mustered out with company Aug. 23, 1864.
..do...	18	May 2, 1864	100 dys.	Mustered out with company Aug. 23, 1864.
..do...	19	May 2, 1864	100 dys.	Mustered out with company Aug. 23, 1864.
..do...	19	May 2, 1864	100 dys.	Mustered out with company Aug. 23, 1864.
..do...	18	May 2, 1864	100 dys.	Transferred to Co. F ——.
..do...	18	May 2, 1864	100 dys.	Mustered out with company Aug. 23, 1864.
..do...	24	May 2, 1864	100 dys.	Mustered out with company Aug. 23, 1864.
..do...	22	May 2, 1864	100 dys.	Mustered out with company Aug. 23, 1864.
..do...	26	May 2, 1864	100 dys.	Mustered out with company Aug. 23, 1864.
..do...	20	May 2, 1864	100 dys.	Mustered out with company Aug. 23, 1864.
..do...	19	May 2, 1864	100 dys.	Mustered out with company Aug. 23, 1864.
..do...	19	May 2, 1864	100 dys.	Mustered out with company Aug. 23, 1864.
..do...	18	May 2, 1864	100 dys.	Mustered out with company Aug. 23, 1864.
..do...	19	May 2, 1864	100 dys.	Mustered out with company Aug. 23, 1864.
..do...	19	May 2, 1864	100 dys.	Mustered out with company Aug. 23, 1864.
..do...	27	May 2, 1864	100 dys.	Mustered out with company Aug. 23, 1864.
..do...	22	May 2, 1864	100 dys.	Mustered out with company Aug. 23, 1864.

Names.	Rank.	Age.	Date of Entering the Service.	Period of Service.	Remarks.
Wadsworth, Charles M.	Private.	24	May 2, 1864	100 dys.	Mustered out with company Aug. 23, 1864.
Wadsworth, William H.	....do....	19	May 2, 1864	100 dys.	Mustered out with company Aug. 23, 1864.
Walsh, Alexander S.	....do....	22	May 2, 1864	100 dys.	Mustered out with company Aug. 23, 1864.
Walther, Henry	....do....	22	May 2, 1864	100 dys.	Mustered out with company Aug. 23, 1864.
White, Samuel	....do....	30	May 2, 1864	100 dys.	Mustered out with company Aug. 23, 1864.
Wilson, William	....do....	24	May 2, 1864	100 dys.	Mustered out with company Aug. 23, 1864.
Woodward, Edward J.	....do....	19	May 2, 1864	100 dys.	Mustered out with company Aug. 23, 1864.
Woolridge, John	....do....	20	May 2, 1864	100 dys.	Mustered out with company Aug. 23, 1864.
Worden, George	....do....	29	May 2, 1864	100 dys.	Mustered out with company Aug. 23, 1864.
Yarhouse, John	....do....	20	May 2, 1864	100 dys.	Mustered out with company Aug. 23, 1864.

COMPANY F.

Mustered in May 5, 1864, at Cleveland, O., by W. L. Kellogg, Lieutenant 10th Infantry, U. S. A. Mustered out Aug. 23, 1864, at Cleveland, O., by Thomas Drummond, Captain 5th Cavalry, U. S. A.

Names.	Rank.	Age.	Date of Entering the Service.	Period of Service.	Remarks.
Jeremiah Ensworth	Captain.	45	May 2, 1864	100 dys.	Mustered out with company Aug. 23, 1864.
Edwin C. Rouse	1st Lieut.	36	May 2, 1864	100 dys.	Mustered out with company Aug. 23, 1864.
Charles J. McDowell	2d Lieut.	27	May 2, 1864	100 dys.	Mustered out with company Aug. 23, 1864.
Frederick P. Farrand	1st Sergt.	30	May 2, 1864	100 dys.	Mustered out with company Aug. 23, 1864.
Joshua B. Glenn	Sergeant.	31	May 2, 1864	100 dys.	Mustered out with company Aug. 23, 1864.
George Spangler	....do....	21	May 2, 1864	100 dys.	Mustered out with company Aug. 23, 1864.
Charles B. Fargo	....do....	2[illegible]	May 2, 1864	100 dys.	Mustered out with company Aug. 23, 1864.
Frederick Weidenkopf	....do....	17	May 2, 1864	100 dys.	Mustered out with company Aug. 23, 1864.
Peter Diemer	Corporal.	19	May 2, 1864	100 dys.	Mustered out with company Aug. 23, 1864.
Henry W. Herwig	....do....	20	May 2, 1864	100 dys.	Mustered out with company Aug. 23, 1864.
Samuel P. Fox	....do....	21	May 2, 1864	100 dys.	Mustered out with company Aug. 23, 1864.
Sidney F. Dickerman	....do....	28	May 2, 1864	100 dys.	Mustered out with company Aug. 23, 1864.
George Pollyblank	....do....	18	May 2, 1864	100 dys.	Mustered out with company Aug. 23, 1864.
Charles P. Vanpel	....do....	22	May 2, 1864	100 dys.	Mustered out with company Aug. 23, 1864.
John Hart	....do....	21	May 2, 1864	100 dys.	Mustered out with company Aug. 23, 1864.
Nicholas Weidenkopf	....do....	20	May 2, 1864	100 dys.	Mustered out with company Aug. 23, 1864.
John N. Stewart	Musician	17	May 2, 1864	100 dys.	Mustered out with company Aug. 23, 1864.
Otto Decker	....do....	16	May 2, 1864	100 dys.	Mustered out with company Aug. 23, 1864.
Adams, Augustus	Private.	19	May 2, 1864	100 dys.	Mustered out with company Aug. 23, 1864.
Atherton, Joseph	....do....	18	May 2, 1864	100 dys.	Mustered out with company Aug. 23, 1864.
Barrett, Patrick	....do....	20	May 2, 1864	100 dys.	Mustered out with company Aug. 23, 1864.
Bentley, Thomas C.	....do....	18	May 2, 1864	100 dys.	Mustered out with company Aug. 23, 1864.
Bloom, Addison M.	....do....	27	May 2, 1864	100 dys.	Mustered out with company Aug. 23, 1864.
Boddy, John	....do....	20	May 2, 1864	100 dys.	Mustered out with company Aug. 23, 1864.
Bowles, James H.	....do....	25	May 2, 1864	100 dys.	Mustered out with company Aug. 23, 1864.
Brewer, John William	....do....	21	May 2, 1864	100 dys.	Mustered out with company Aug. 23, 1864.
Britton, Benjamin	....do....	32	May 2, 1864	100 dys.	Mustered out with company Aug. 23, 1864.
Buhne, Frederick	....do....	36	May 2, 1864	100 dys.	Mustered out with company Aug. 23, 1864.
Burrows, Johnson	....do....	17	May 2, 1864	100 dys.	Mustered out with company Aug. 23, 1864.
Campbell, Charles H.	....do....	27	May 2, 1864	100 dys.	Mustered out with company Aug. 23, 1864.
Carman, William	....do....	38	May 2, 1864	100 dys.	Mustered out with company Aug. 23, 1864.
Chipman, William	....do....	19	May 2, 1864	100 dys.	
Christian, George B.	....do....	17	May 2, 1864	100 dys.	Mustered out with company Aug. 23, 1864.
Clark, Louis D.	....do....	19	May 2, 1864	100 dys.	Mustered out with company Aug. 23, 1864.
Conkey, Joseph	....do....	18	May 2, 1864	100 dys.	Mustered out with company Aug. 23, 1864.
Creighton, Wilfred	....do....	17	May 2, 1864	100 dys.	Mustered out with company Aug. 23, 1864.
Curtis, William	....do....	18	May 2, 1864	100 dys.	Mustered out with company Aug. 23, 1864.
Dakin, Henry M.	....do....	28	May 2, 1864	100 dys.	Mustered out with company Aug. 23, 1864.
Davis, Henry	....do....	25	May 2, 1864	100 dys.	Mustered out with company Aug. 23, 1864.
Dickey, John H.	....do....	29	May 2, 1864	100 dys.	Mustered out with company Aug. 23, 1864.
Dodge, Wilson S.	....do....	25	May 2, 1864	100 dys.	Promoted to Q. M. Sergeant May 5, 1864.
Doren, Myron C.	....do....	19	May 2, 1864	100 dys.	Mustered out with company Aug. 23, 1864.
Fairbanks, Franklin	....do....	18	May 2, 1864	100 dys.	Mustered out with company Aug. 23, 1864.
Fhe[illegible], Alfred W.	....do....	20	May 2, 1864	100 dys.	Mustered out with company Aug. 23, 1864.
Frank, Edward H.	....do....	22	May 2, 1864	100 dys.	Mustered out with company Aug. 23, 1864.
Gray, Edward C.	....do....	23	May 2, 1864	100 dys.	Mustered out with company Aug. 23, 1864.
Griffen, Samuel R.	....do....	21	May 2, 1864	100 dys.	Mustered out with company Aug. 23, 1864.
Guilford, Edwin R.	....do....	32	May 2, 1864	100 dys.	Mustered out with company Aug. 23, 1864.
Guy, William S.	....do....	18	May 2, 1864	100 dys.	Mustered out with company Aug. 23, 1864.
Hales, Ansel	....do....	18	May 2, 1864	100 dys.	Mustered out with company Aug. 23, 1864.
Henry, Albert	....do....	18	May 2, 1864	100 dys.	Mustered out with company Aug. 23, 1864.
Henry, Daniel	....do....	31	May 2, 1864	100 dys.	Mustered out with company Aug. 23, 1864.
Henricle, Christian L.	....do....	19	May 2, 1864	100 dys.	Mustered out with company Aug. 23, 1864.
Higlen, Joseph	....do....	23	May 2, 1864	100 dys.	Mustered out with company Aug. 23, 1864.
Hobbs, George W.	....do....	27	May 2, 1864	100 dys.	Mustered out with company Aug. 23, 1864.
Holderman, George	....do....	21	May 2, 1864	100 dys.	Mustered out with company Aug. 23, 1864.
Hopkins, William A.	....do....	21	May 2, 1864	100 dys.	Mustered out with company Aug. 23, 1864.
Janke, Gustavus	....do....	18	May 2, 1864	100 dys.	Mustered out with company Aug. 23, 1864.
Johnson, George J.	....do....	19	May 2, 1864	100 dys.	Transferred from Co. E ——; mustered out with company Aug. 23, 1864.
Joyce, William	....do....	21	May 2, 1864	100 dys.	Mustered out with company Aug. 23, 1864.
Keller, William C.	....do....	17	May 2, 1864	100 dys.	Mustered out with company Aug. 23, 1864.
Kellogg, Charles E.	....do....	17	May 2, 1864	100 dys.	Mustered out with company Aug. 23, 1864.
Koch, Moses	....do....	19	May 2, 1864	100 dys.	Mustered out with company Aug. 23, 1864.

Names.	Rank.	Age.	Date of Entering the Service.	Period of Service.	Remarks.
Leffler, Henry		22	May 2, 1864	100 dys.	Mustered out with company Aug. 23, 1864.
Lockwood, Samuel		24	May 2, 1864	100 dys.	Mustered out with company Aug. 23, 1864.
Lowrie, Hugh		17	May 2, 1864	100 dys.	Mustered out with company Aug. 23, 1864.
McComber, Elbridge J.		18	May 2, 1864	100 dys.	Mustered out with company Aug. 23, 1864.
McKenzie, James		25	May 2, 1864	100 dys.	Mustered out with company Aug. 23, 1864.
McReynolds, William		34	May 2, 1864	100 dys.	Mustered out with company Aug. 23, 1864.
Monteverdi, Samuel		28	May 2, 1864	100 dys.	Mustered out with company Aug. 23, 1864.
Newton, James L.		17	May 2, 1864	100 dys.	Mustered out with company Aug. 24, 1864.
Norton, John A.		18	May 2, 1864	100 dys.	Transferred from Co. E —; mustered out with company Aug. 23, 1864.
[illegible], John	do.	..	May 2, 1864	100 dys.	Mustered out with company Aug. 23, 1864.
[illegible] B.	do.	28	May 2, 1864	100 dys.	Mustered out with company Aug. 23, 1864.
[illegible], Robert	do.	31	May 2, 1864	100 dys.	Mustered out with company Aug. 23, 1864.
[illegible]	do.	42	May 2, 1864	100 dys.	Mustered out with company Aug. 23, 1864.
[illegible], John T.	do.	23	May 2, 1864	100 dys.	Mustered out with company Aug. 23, 1864.
[illegible], J. Porter	do.	37	May 2, 1864	100 dys.	Mustered out with company Aug. 23, 1864.
[illegible], J. John	do.	23	May 2, 1864	100 dys.	Mustered out with company Aug. 23, 1864.
[illegible]son, William	do.	22	May 2, 1864	100 dys.	Mustered out with company Aug. 23, 1864.
[illegible], [illegible] B.	do.	18	May 2, 1864	100 dys.	Mustered out with company Aug. 23, 1864.
[illegible], Louis H.	do.	23	May 2, 1864	100 dys.	Promoted to Com. Sergeant May 5, 1864.
[illegible], Frederick J.	do.	18	May 2, 1864	100 dys.	Mustered out with company Aug. 23, 1864.
[illegible], Albert T.	do.	30	May 2, 1864	100 dys.	Mustered out with company Aug. 23, 1864.
[illegible], William	do.	18	May 2, 1864	100 dys.	Mustered out with company Aug. 23, 1864.
[illegible], Floyd E.	do.	22	May 2, 1864	100 dys.	Mustered out with company Aug. 23, 1864.
[illegible], Caleb	do.	44	May 2, 1864	100 dys.	Mustered out with company Aug. 23, 1864.
[illegible], Moses G.	do.	28	May 2, 1864	100 dys.	Mustered out with company Aug. 23, 1864.
[illegible], Michael	do.	19	May 2, 1864	100 dys.	Mustered out with company Aug. 23, 1864.
[illegible], William	do.	45	May 2, 1864	100 dys.	Discharged July 28, 1864, on Surgeon's certificate of disability.
[illegible], August	...	19	May 2, 1864	100 dys.	Mustered out with company Aug. 23, 1864.
[illegible], John	...	20	May 2, 1864	100 dys.	Mustered out with company Aug. 23, 1864.
[illegible], Martin L.	...	17	May 2, 1864	100 dys.	Mustered out with company Aug. 23, 1864.
[illegible], John W.	...	22	May 2, 1864	100 dys.	Mustered out with company Aug. 23, 1864.

COMPANY G.

Mustered in May 5, 1864, at Cleveland, O., by W. L. Kellogg, Lieutenant 10th Infantry, U. S. A. Mustered out Aug. 23, 1864, at Cleveland, O., by Thomas Drummond, Captain 5th Cavalry, U. S. A.

Names.	Rank.	Age.	Date of Entering the Service.	Period of Service.	Remarks.
[illegible] Nevins	Captain.	35	May 2, 1864	100 dys.	Mustered out with company Aug. 23, 1864.
[illegible] C. Hall	1st Lieut.	26	May 2, 1864	100 dys.	Mustered out with company Aug. 23, 1864.
[illegible] M. Burrett	2d Lieut.	26	May 2, 1864	100 dys.	Mustered out with company Aug. 23, 1864.
John [illegible]	1st Sergt.	28	May 2, 1864	100 dys.	Mustered out with company Aug. 23, 1864.
John P. McMahon	Sergeant.	27	May 2, 1864	100 dys.	Mustered out with company Aug. 23, 1864.
William R. Quayle	do.	24	May 2, 1864	100 dys.	Mustered out with company Aug. 23, 1864.
[illegible] E. Burton	do.	21	May 2, 1864	100 dys.	Promoted to Sergt. Major May 6, 1864.
[illegible] G. White	do.	41	May 2, 1864	100 dys.	Mustered out with company Aug. 23, 1864.
Benjamin F. Dexter	do.	35	May 2, 1864	100 dys.	Appointed —; mustered out with company Aug. 23, 1864.
Louis L. Davis	Corporal.	19	May 2, 1864	100 dys.	Mustered out with company Aug. 23, 1864.
[illegible] M. Turner	do.	22	May 2, 1864	100 dys.	Mustered out with company Aug. 23, 1864.
[illegible] J. Schwind	do.	25	May 2, 1864	100 dys.	Mustered out with company Aug. 23, 1864.
[illegible] A. Bryan	do.	21	May 2, 1864	100 dys.	Mustered out with company Aug. 23, 1864.
William Sims	do.	20	May 2, 1864	100 dys.	Mustered out with company Aug. 23, 1864.
[illegible] A. [illegible]	do.	19	May 2, 1864	100 dys.	Mustered out with company Aug. 23, 1864.
[illegible] W. McMahon	do.	18	May 2, 1864	100 dys.	Mustered out with company Aug. 23, 1864.
William H. Merrick	do.	33	May 2, 1864	100 dys.	Appointed —; mustered out with company Aug. 23, 1864.
Isaac A. Tiffany	Musician	18	May 2, 1864	100 dys.	Mustered out with company Aug. 23, 1864.
Allen, [illegible] G.	Private.	44	May 2, 1864	100 dys.	Mustered out with company Aug. 23, 1864.
Ball, John Warren	do.	18	May 2, 1864	100 dys.	Mustered out with company Aug. 23, 1864.
Bennett, A. C. W.	do.	20	May 2, 1864	100 dys.	Mustered out with company Aug. 23, 1864.
Blake, James G.	do.	38	May 2, 1864	100 dys.	Mustered out with company Aug. 23, 1864.
Blake, John W.	do.	24	May 2, 1864	100 dys.	Mustered out with company Aug. 23, 1864.
Boehringer, Peter J.	do.	22	May 2, 1864	100 dys.	Mustered out with company Aug. 23, 1864.
Brelsford, William H.	do.	32	May 2, 1864	100 dys.	Mustered out with company Aug. 23, 1864.
Brown, Albert	do.	19	May 2, 1864	100 dys.	Mustered out with company Aug. 23, 1864.
Brown, James	do.	20	May 2, 1864	100 dys.	Mustered out with company Aug. 23, 1864.
Carr, Richard	do.	20	May 2, 1864	100 dys.	Mustered out with company Aug. 23, 1864.
Carter, Lewis	do.	22	May 2, 1864	100 dys.	Mustered out with company Aug. 23, 1864.
Cowell, John	do.	33	May 2, 1864	100 dys.	Mustered out with company Aug. 23, 1864.
Crowl, William H.	do.	31	May 2, 1864	100 dys.	Mustered out with company Aug. 23, 1864.
Daily, Charles R.	do.	32	May 2, 1864	100 dys.	Mustered out with company Aug. 23, 1864.
Douglas, George W.	do.	28	May 2, 1864	100 dys.	Mustered out with company Aug. 23, 1864.
Douglass, John	do.	41	May 2, 1864	100 dys.	Mustered out with company Aug. 23, 1864.
Dutton, Charles F.	do.	32	May 2, 1864	100 dys.	Promoted to Asst. Surgeon May 5, 1864.
Farrand, Andrew	do.	34	May 2, 1864	100 dys.	Mustered out with company Aug. 23, 1864.
Fey, Frederick, Jr.	do.	20	May 2, 1864	100 dys.	Mustered out with company Aug. 23, 1864.
Foote, Charles D.	do.	37	May 2, 1864	100 dys.	Mustered out with company Aug. 23, 1864.
Foote, Henry C.	do.	18	May 2, 1864	100 dys.	Mustered out with company Aug. 23, 1864.

Names.	Rank.	Age.	Date of Entering the Service.	Period of Service.	Remarks.
Granger, Frank	Private.	18	May 2, 1864	100 dys.	Mustered out with company Aug. 23, 1864.
Grannis, Joseph S	...do...	34	May 2, 1864	100 dys	Mustered out with company Aug. 23, 1864.
Grotenrath, Philip	...do...	31	May 2, 1864	100 dys	Mustered out with company Aug. 23, 1864.
Hartzell, Albert	...do...	28	May 2, 1864	100 dys	Mustered out with company Aug. 23, 1864.
Haserot, John G	...do...	32	May 2, 1864	100 dys.	Mustered out with company Aug. 23, 1864.
Hayward, George B	...do...	18	May 2, 1864	100 dys.	Mustered out with company Aug. 23, 1864.
Hertzog, John	...do...	21	May 2, 1864	100 dys.	Mustered out with company Aug. 23, 1864.
Hoag, James E	...do...	37	May 2, 1864	100 dys.	Mustered out with company Aug. 23, 1864.
Huffman, Frederick	...do...	30	May 2, 1864	100 dys.	Mustered out with company Aug. 23, 1864.
Ingle, Charles	...do...	39	May 2, 1864	100 dys	Mustered out with company Aug. 23, 1864.
Jones, Carlos	...do...	18	May 2, 1864	100 dys.	Mustered out with company Aug. 23, 1864.
King, Jacob	...do...	33	May 2, 1864	100 dys.	Mustered out with company Aug. 23, 1864.
Kintz, Frederick	...do...	25	May 2, 1864	100 dys.	Mustered out with company Aug. 23, 1864.
Langell, Benjamin	...do...	18	May 2, 1864	100 dys.	Mustered out with company Aug. 23, 1864.
Lindsley, Edward	...do...	30	May 2, 1864	100 dys.	Mustered out with company Aug. 23, 1864.
Logan, John	...do...	32	May 2, 1864	100 dys.	Mustered out with company Aug. 23, 1864.
Lynch, John	...do...	28	May 2, 1864	100 dys.	Mustered out with company Aug. 23, 1864.
McClure, Louis	...do...	18	May 2, 1864	100 dys	Mustered out with company Aug. 23, 1864.
McGinnis, Frederick H	...do...	31	May 2, 1864	100 dys.	Mustered out with company Aug. 23, 1864.
Martin, Jacob	...do...	28	May 2, 1864	100 dys.	Left, sick, at Cleveland, O., May 12, 1864. No further record found.
Mathias, Henry H	...do...	26	May 2, 1864	100 dys.	Mustered out with company Aug. 23, 1864.
Miller, Frank	...do...	20	May 2, 1864	100 dys	Mustered out with company Aug. 23, 1864.
Miller, Julius	...do...	18	May 2, 1864	100 dys.	Mustered out with company Aug. 23, 1864.
Neal, Thomas	...do...	25	May 2, 1864	100 dys	Mustered out with company Aug. 23, 1864.
Norton, Erastus M	...do...	31	May 2, 1864	100 dys	Mustered out with company Aug. 23, 1864.
Palmer, Charles W	...do...	26	May 2, 1864	100 dys	Mustered out with company Aug. 23, 1864.
Peck, Edmund	...do...	23	May 2, 1864	100 dys.	Mustered out with company Aug. 23, 1864.
Perkins, Riall	...do...	31	May 2, 1864	100 dys.	Discharged May 27, 1864, at Fort Lincoln, D. C., on Surgeon's certificate of disability.
Perrin, Henry	...do...	30	May 2, 1864	100 dys	Mustered out with company Aug. 23, 1864.
Peterson, Joseph C	...do...	19	May 2, 1864	100 dys.	Mustered out with company Aug. 23, 1864.
Phelps, William H	...do...	19	May 2, 1864	100 dys.	Mustered out with company Aug. 23, 1864.
Porter, Albert	...do...	25	May 2, 1864	100 dys	Mustered out with company Aug. 23, 1864.
Powell, Joshua	...do...	29	May 2, 1864	100 dys.	Mustered out with company Aug. 23, 1864.
Proufont, John P	...do...	27	May 2, 1864	100 dys.	Mustered out with company Aug. 23, 1864.
Radcliff, William H	...do...	37	May 2, 1864	100 dys.	Mustered out with company Aug. 23, 1864.
Russell, Charles W	...do...	19	May 2, 1864	100 dys.	Mustered out with company Aug. 23, 1864.
Russell, Cornelius L	...do...	17	May 2, 1864	100 dys.	Mustered out with company Aug. 23, 1864.
Sanford, Benjamin	...do...	18	May 2, 1864	100 dys.	Mustered out with company Aug. 23, 1864.
Schenk, Theodore C	...do...	[illegible]	May 2, 1864	100 dys.	Mustered out with company Aug. 23, 1864.
Schriber, Charles	...do...	29	May 2, 1864	100 dys	
Scott, Clarence F	...do...	18	May 2, 1864	100 dys.	Mustered out with company Aug. 23, 1864.
Sloan, Wilson F	...do...	22	May 2, 1864	100 dys.	Mustered out with company Aug. 23, 1864.
Smith, Michael	...do...	22	May 2, 1864	100 dys	Mustered out with company Aug. 23, 1864.
Spies, Joseph	...do...	24	May 2, 1864	100 dys	Mustered out with company Aug. 23, 1864.
Stevens, William H	...do...	18	May 2, 1864	100 dys.	Mustered out with company Aug. 23, 1864.
Stevens, William N	...do...	26	May 2, 1864	100 dys.	Mustered out with company Aug. 23, 1864.
Thompson, John	...do...	39	May 2, 1864	100 dys.	Mustered out with company Aug. 2 , 1864.
Townsend, Frank	...do...	18	May 2, 1864	100 dys	Mustered out with company Aug. 23, 1864.
Tyler, Samuel	...do...	18	May 2, 1864	100 dys.	Mustered out with company Aug. 23, 1864.
Waltner, John W	...do...	19	May 2, 1864	100 dys	Mustered out with company Aug. 23, 1864.
Walters, David H	...do...	18	May 2, 1864	100 dys	Mustered out with company Aug. 23, 1864.
Wheeler, Sanford	...do...	28	May 2, 1864	100 dys.	Mustered out with company Aug. 23, 1864.
Williams, Thomas J	...do...	36	May 2, 1864	100 dys.	Mustered out with company Aug. 23, 1864.
Wilson, George	...do...	18	May 2, 1864	100 dys.	Mustered out with company Aug. 23, 1864.
Wright, Arthur	...do...	19	May 2, 1864	100 dys	Discharged Aug. 21, 1864, at Findley Hospital, Washington, D. C.; died Aug. 29, 1864, at same place.

COMPANY H.

Mustered in May 5, 1864, at Cleveland, O., by W. L. Kellogg, Lieutenant 10th Infantry, U. S. A. Mustered out Aug. 23, 1864, at Cleveland, O., by Thomas Drummond, Captain 5th Cavalry, U. S. A.

Names.	Rank.	Age.	Date of Entering the Service.	Period of Service.	Remarks.
Samuel H. Baird	Captain.	36	May 2, 1864	100 dys.	Mustered out with company Aug. 23, 1864.
Frank Dutton	1st Lieut.	26	May 2, 1864	100 dys	Mustered out with company Aug. 23, 1864.
Edwin Denison	2d Lieut.	27	May 2, 1864	100 dys	Mustered out with company Aug. 23, 1864.
James M. Gates	1st Sergt.	27	May 2, 1864	100 dys.	Mustered out with company Aug. 23, 1864.
Matthew J. Lowman	Sergeant.	21	May 2, 1864	100 dys.	Mustered out with company Aug. 23, 1864.
Charles G. A[illegible]ood	...do...	28	May 2, 1864	100 dys	Mustered out with company Aug. 23, 1864.
William G. McNally	...do...	21	May 2, 1864	100 dys.	Mustered out with company Aug. 23, 1864.
David T. Carpenter	...do...	36	May 2, 1864	100 dys.	Mustered out with company Aug. 23, 1864.
Charles Loth[illegible]	Corporal.	24	May 2, 1864	100 dys.	Mustered out with company Aug. 23, 1864.
David B. Andrews	...do...	18	May 2, 1864	100 dys.	Mustered out with company Aug. 23, 1864.
Israel B. Heller	...do...	23	May 2, 1864	100 dys.	Mustered out with company Aug. 23, 1864.
Wilford H. [illegible]inker	...do...	23	May 2, 1864	100 dys.	Mustered out with company Aug. 23, 1864.
Stillman S. Scott	...do...	24	May 2, 1864	100 dys.	Mustered out with company Aug. 23, 1864.
Ephraim Klock	...do...	36	May 2, 1864	100 dys.	Mustered out with company Aug. 23, 1864.
William Dutton	...do...	29	May 2, 1864	100 dys.	Mustered out with company Aug. 23, 1864.

Names.	Rank.	Age.	Date of Entering the Service.	Period of Service.	Remarks.
Oliver K. Brooks	Corporal.	18	May 2, 1864	100 dys.	Mustered out with company Aug. 23, 1864.
Abbott, Jonathan	Private..	24	May 2, 1864	100 dys.	Mustered out with company Aug. 23, 1864.
Allen, George D.	...do..	18	May 2, 1864	100 dys.	Mustered out with company Aug. 23, 1864.
Armstrong, John	...do....	29	May 2, 1864	100 dys.	Mustered out with company Aug. 23, 1864.
Baldwin, Wallace	...do....	18	May 2, 1864	100 dys.	Mustered out with company Aug. 23, 1864.
Barber, William P.	...do....	20	May 2, 1864	100 dys.	Mustered out with company Aug. 23, 1864.
Bohn, Henry	...do....	23	May 2, 1864	100 dys.	Mustered out with company Aug. 23, 1864.
Borger, Christopher	...do....	23	May 2, 1864	100 dys.	Mustered out with company Aug. 23, 1864.
Bowles, Darius S.	...do....	30	May 2, 1864	100 dys.	Mustered out with company Aug. 23, 1864.
Brinesmade, Allan T.	...do....	27	May 2, 1864	100 dys.	Mustered out with company Aug. 23, 1864.
Bull, Henry C.	...do....	28	May 2, 1864	100 dys.	Mustered out with company Aug. 23, 1864.
Butler, Charles K.	...do....	33	May 2, 1864	100 dys.	Mustered out with company Aug. 23, 1864.
Carlile, Robert	...do....	18	May 2, 1864	100 dys.	Mustered out with company Aug. 23, 1864.
Chamberlain, Asa H.	...do...	17	May 2, 1864	100 dys.	Mustered out with company Aug. 23, 1864.
Chapman, Hiram	...do....	36	May 2, 1864	100 dys.	Mustered out with company Aug. 23, 1864.
Church, Austin	...do....	25	May 2, 1864	100 dys.	Mustered out with company Aug. 23, 1864.
Cones, John	...do....	23	May 2, 1864	100 dys.	Mustered out with company Aug. 23, 1864.
Deeser, Charles	...do....	18	May 2, 1864	100 dys.	Mustered out with company Aug. 23, 1864.
Dewey, Almon	...do....	18	May 2, 1864	100 dys.	Mustered out with company Aug. 23, 1864.
Dunham, Frederick H.	...do....	18	May 2, 1864	100 dys.	Mustered out with company Aug. 23, 1864.
Dunwell, Henry J.	...do....	18	May 2, 1864	100 dys.	Mustered out with company Aug. 23, 1864.
Edwards, John R.	...do....	21	May 2, 1864	100 dys.	Mustered out with company Aug. 23, 1864.
Ehrlich, Myer	...do...	17	May 2, 1864	100 dys.	Mustered out with company Aug. 23, 1864.
Ehrlich, William	...do....	16	May 2, 1864	100 dys.	Mustered out with company Aug. 23, 1864.
Ellis, James C.	...do...	23	May 2, 1864	100 dys.	Mustered out with company Aug. 23, 1864.
Emerson, Alvin L.	...do....	20	May 2, 1864	100 dys.	Mustered out with company Aug. 23, 1864.
Evans, Andrew E.	...do....	19	May 2, 1864	100 dys.	Mustered out with company Aug. 23, 1864.
Ferris, William H.	...do....	22	May 2, 1864	100 dys.	Mustered out with company Aug. 23, 1864.
Foot, John H.	...do....	20	May 2, 1864	100 dys.	Mustered out with company Aug. 23, 1864.
Fergue, Daniel	...do....	18	May 2, 1864	100 dys.	Mustered out with company Aug. 23, 1864.
Fuller, George	...do....	17	May 2, 1864	100 dys.	Mustered out with company Aug. 23, 1864.
Gale, George R.	...do....	18	May 2, 1864	100 dys.	Mustered out with company Aug. 23, 1864.
Gifford, Harvey C.	...do....	22	May 2, 1864	100 dys.	Mustered out with company Aug. 23, 1864.
Gleason, Solomon H.	...do....	19	May 2, 1864	100 dys.	Mustered out with company Aug. 23, 1864.
Hall, James C.	...do....	17	May 2, 1864	100 dys.	Mustered out with company Aug. 23, 1864.
Hanford, John R.	...do....	30	May 2, 1864	100 dys.	Mustered out with company Aug. 23, 1864.
Handyside, John G.	...do....	23	May 2, 1864	100 dys.	Mustered out with company Aug. 23, 1864.
Harris, Lorenzo D.	...do....	32	May 2, 1864	100 dys.	Mustered out with company Aug. 23, 1864.
Hart, Edward S.	...do....	16	May 2, 1864	100 dys.	Mustered out with company Aug. 23, 1864.
Higby, William B.	...do....	17	May 2, 1864	100 dys.	Mustered out with company Aug. 23, 1864.
Hill, Chester	...do...	20	May 2, 1864	100 dys.	Mustered out with company Aug. 23, 1864.
Hoffmeyer, John H.	...do....	18	May 2, 1864	100 dys.	Mustered out with company Aug. 23, 1864.
Horner, Richard	...do....	18	May 2, 1864	100 dys.	Mustered out with company Aug. 23, 1864.
Huston, N. Kelly	...do....	18	May 2, 1864	100 dys.	Mustered out with company Aug. 23, 1864.
Ingraham, Frank	...do...	18	May 2, 1864	100 dys.	Mustered out with company Aug. 23, 1864.
Kahoe, Thomas J.	...do....	19	May 2, 1864	100 dys.	Mustered out with company Aug. 23, 1864.
Kuhn, Frank	...do....	19	May 2, 1864	100 dys.	Mustered out with company Aug. 23, 1864.
Lester, Sanford W.	...do....	29	May 2, 1864	100 dys.	Mustered out with company Aug. 23, 1864.
McConnaughey, William J.	...do....	36	May 2, 1864	100 dys.	Mustered out with company Aug. 23, 1864.
McGrath, John H.	...do...	21	May 2, 1864	100 dys.	Mustered out with company Aug. 23, 1864.
Marks, Edward N.	...do....	18	May 2, 1864	100 dys.	Mustered out with company Aug. 23, 1864.
Marks, Moses	...do....	20	May 2, 1864	100 dys.	Mustered out with company Aug. 23, 1864.
Meredith, James L. M.	...do....	24	May 2, 1864	100 dys.	Mustered out with company Aug. 23, 1864.
Merrill, Robin R. K.	...do....	18	May 2, 1864	100 dys.	Mustered out with company Aug. 23, 1864.
Merritt, Charles E.	...do....	18	May 2, 1864	100 dys.	Mustered out with company Aug. 23, 1864.
Messer, John	...do....	42	May 2, 1864	100 dys.	Mustered out with company Aug. 23, 1864.
Mills, Orin	...do....	23	May 2, 1864	100 dys.	Mustered out with company Aug. 23, 1864.
Mitchell, Charles H.	...do....	23	May 2, 1864	100 dys.	Mustered out with company Aug. 23, 1864.
Parker, Albert M.	...do....	20	May 2, 1864	100 dys.	Died Aug. 7, 1864, at Washington, D. C.
Richards, Frank O.	...do....	18	May 2, 1864	100 dys.	Mustered out with company Aug. 23, 1864.
Richards, Moses J.	...do....	25	May 2, 1864	100 dys.	Mustered out with company Aug. 23, 1864.
Rogers, Charles, Jr.	...do....	18	May 2, 1864	100 dys.	Mustered out with company Aug. 23, 1864.
Sanders, Charles H.	...do....	20	May 2, 1864	100 dys.	
Sawyer, Abel W.	...do....	37	May 2, 1864	100 dys.	Mustered out with company Aug. 23, 1864.
Schnarline, Jacob	...do...	22	May 2, 1864	100 dys.	Mustered out with company Aug. 23, 1864.
Sessions, Samuel A.	...do....	26	May 2, 1864	100 dys.	Mustered out with company Aug. 23, 1864.
Sloss, Jonas	...do....	18	May 2, 1864	100 dys.	Mustered out with company Aug. 23, 1864.
Smith, Albert M.	...do....	32	May 2, 1864	100 dys.	Mustered out with company Aug. 23, 1864.
Smith, George R.	...do....	19	May 2, 1864	100 dys.	Mustered out with company Aug. 23, 1864.
Smith, Warner E.	...do....	18	May 2, 1864	100 dys.	Mustered out with company Aug. 23, 1864.
Souter, Elijah	...do....	18	May 2, 1864	100 dys.	Mustered out with company Aug. 23, 1864.
Stevens, Alfred	...do....	38	May 2, 1864	100 dys.	Mustered out with company Aug. 23, 1864.
Stockwell, Brutus E.	...do....	18	May 2, 1864	100 dys.	Mustered out with company Aug. 23, 1864.
Stone, Carlos M.	...do....	18	May 2, 1864	100 dys.	Mustered out with company Aug. 23, 1864.
Strong, George	...do....	18	May 2, 1864	100 dys.	Mustered out with company Aug. 23, 1864.
Taylor, Vincent A.	...do....	19	May 2, 1864	100 dys.	Mustered out with company Aug. 23, 1864.
Thompson, John F.	...do....	21	May 2, 1864	100 dys.	Mustered out with company Aug. 23, 1864.
Thompson, Robert	...do....	18	May 2, 1864	100 dys.	Mustered out with company Aug. 23, 1864.
Tinker, Edward R.	...do....	20	May 2, 1864	100 dys.	Mustered out with company Aug. 23, 1864.
Turner, Lucien	...do....	20	May 2, 1864	100 dys.	Mustered out with company Aug. 23, 1864.
Weismann, Robert	...do....	36	May 2, 1864	100 dys.	Mustered out with company Aug. 23, 1864.
Wiener, Michael M.	...do....	19	May 2, 1864	100 dys.	Mustered out with company Aug. 23, 1864.
Wilcox, Sherwood	...do....	19	May 2, 1864	100 dys.	Mustered out with company Aug. 23, 1864.
Wilson, Solan N.	...do...	20	May 2, 1864	100 dys.	Mustered out with company Aug. 23, 1864.
Young, Elijah F.	...do....	37	May 2, 1864	100 dys.	Mustered out with company Aug. 23, 1864.
Zann, George	...do....	18	May 2, 1864	100 dys.	Mustered out with company Aug. 23, 1864.

COMPANY I.

Mustered in May 5, 1864, at Cleveland, O., by W. L. Kellogg, Lieutenant 10th Infantry, U. S. A. Mustered out Aug. 23, 1864, at Cleveland, O., by Thomas Drummond, Captain 5th Cavalry, U. S. A.

Names.	Rank.	Age	Date of Entering the Service.	Period of Service.	Remarks.
Edwin Farr	Captain.	42	May 2, 1864	100 dys.	Mustered out with company Aug. 23, 1864.
Jonas F. Rice	1st Lieut.	38	May 2, 1864	100 dys.	Mustered out with company Aug. 23, 1864.
John G. Fitch	2d Lieut.	25	May 2, 1864	100 dys.	Mustered out with company Aug. 23, 1864.
James P. Rice	1st Sergt.	43	May 2, 1864	100 dys.	Mustered out with company Aug. 23, 1864.
James A. Potter	Sergeant.	31	May 2, 1864	100 dys.	Mustered out with company Aug. 23, 1864.
Junid Sperry	do.	41	May 2, 1864	100 dys.	Mustered out with company Aug. 23, 1864.
Daniel A. Brown	do.	32	May 2, 1864	100 dys.	Mustered out with company Aug. 23, 1864.
Marvin O. Taylor	do.	31	May 2, 1864	100 dys.	Mustered out with company Aug. 23, 1864.
Harvey Richardson	Corporal.	45	May 2, 1864	100 dys.	Mustered out with company Aug. 23, 1864.
Herbert O. Kennedy	do.	25	May 2, 1864	100 dys.	Mustered out with company Aug. 23, 1864.
Eli S. Martick	do.	32	May 2, 1864	100 dys.	Mustered out with company Aug. 23, 1864.
Charles Dow	do.	27	May 2, 1864	100 dys.	Mustered out with company Aug. 23, 1864.
Richard Carpenter	do.	18	May 2, 1864	100 dys.	Mustered out with company Aug. 23, 1864.
Edwin Martles	do.	19	May 2, 1864	100 dys.	Mustered out with company Aug. 23, 1864.
James E. Parker	do.	33	May 2, 1864	100 dys.	Mustered out with company Aug. 23, 1864.
Charles D. Knapp	do.	33	May 2, 1864	100 dys.	Mustered out with company Aug. 23, 1864.
Alexander, Chauncey	Private.	22	May 2, 1864	100 dys.	Mustered out with company Aug. 23, 1864.
Alexander, Lester	do.	25	May 2, 1864	100 dys.	Mustered out with company Aug. 23, 1864.
Andrews, William	do.	18	May 2, 1864	100 dys.	Mustered out with company Aug. 23, 1864.
Atwell, Charles [illegible]	do.	18	May 2, 1864	100 dys.	Mustered out with company Aug. 23, 1864.
Barker, John S	do.	38	May 2, 1864	100 dys.	Mustered out with company Aug. 23, 1864.
Bell, Charles C	do.	37	May 2, 1864	100 dys.	Mustered out with company Aug. 23, 1864.
Berry, Matthew	do.	19	May 2, 1864	100 dys.	Mustered out with company Aug. 23, 1864.
Bommer, Joseph	do.	29	May 2, 1864	100 dys.	Mustered out with company Aug. 23, 1864.
Carpenter, George W	do.	33	May 2, 1864	100 dys.	Mustered out with company Aug. 23, 1864.
Chappell, Benjamin	do.	35	May 2, 1864	100 dys.	Mustered out with company Aug. 23, 1864.
Clague, Thomas	do.	20	May 2, 1864	100 dys.	Mustered out with company Aug. 23, 1864.
Colton, Hiram W	do.	25	May 2, 1864	100 dys.	Mustered out with company Aug. 23, 1864.
Cooly, John M	do.	23	May 2, 1864	100 dys.	Mustered out with company Aug. 23, 1864.
Coolahan, John	do.	23	May 2, 1864	100 dys.	
Daily, Hezekiah	do.	37	May 2, 1864	100 dys.	Mustered out with company Aug. 23, 1864.
Finley, Philip	do.	20	May 2, 1864	100 dys.	Mustered out with company Aug. 23, 1864.
Fitch, Herbert O	do.	19	May 2, 1864	100 dys.	Mustered out with company Aug. 23, 1864.
Ford, Newell	do.	31	May 2, 1864	100 dys.	Mustered out with company Aug. 23, 1864.
Frost, Lorenzo E	do.	19	May 2, 1864	100 dys.	Mustered out with company Aug. 23, 1864.
Hall, Reuben	do.	37	May 2, 1864	100 dys.	Mustered out with company Aug. 23, 1864.
Hall, Zibia S	do.	[illegible]	May 2, 1864	100 dys.	Mustered out with company Aug. 23, 1864.
Howkins, John	do.	[illegible]	May 2, 1864	100 dys.	Mustered out with company Aug. 23, 1864.
Kellogg, Myron	do.	30	May 2, 1864	100 dys.	Mustered out with company Aug. 23, 1864.
Kennedy, George W	do.	31	May 2, 1864	100 dys.	Mustered out with company Aug. 23, 1864.
Kirk, [illegible]	do.	38	May 2, 1864	100 dys.	Mustered out with company Aug. 23, 1864.
Knapp, Harvey	do.	22	May 2, 1864	100 dys.	Mustered out with company Aug. 23, 1864.
Lattimer, Robert	do.	27	May 2, 1864	100 dys.	Mustered out with company Aug. 23, 1864.
Lewis, David	do.	18	May 2, 1864	100 dys.	Mustered out with company Aug. 23, 1864.
Lilley, Erastus	do.	23	May 2, 1864	100 dys.	Mustered out with company Aug. 23, 1864.
McCarty, Edson K	do.	25	May 2, 1864	100 dys.	Mustered out with company Aug. 23, 1864.
McKenzie, Roswell	do.	19	May 2, 1864	100 dys.	Mustered out with company Aug. 23, 1864.
Nelson, Curtis S	do.	19	May 2, 1864	100 dys.	Discharged July 6, 1864, at Washington, D. C.
Noble, William	do.	18	May 2, 1864	100 dys.	Mustered out with company Aug. 23, 1864.
Parsons, Oscar N	do.	26	May 2, 1864	100 dys.	Mustered out with company Aug. 23, 1864.
Perkins, John, Jr.	do.	26	May 2, 1864	100 dys.	Mustered out with company Aug. 23, 1864.
Phillips, Philip	do.	31	May 2, 1864	100 dys.	Mustered out with company Aug. 23, 1864.
Porter, James C.	do.	[illegible]	May 2, 1864	100 dys.	Mustered out with company Aug. 23, 1864.
Osborn, Jerome	do.	21	May 2, 1864	100 dys.	Mustered out with company Aug. 23, 1864.
Reed, James P	do.	23	May 2, 1864	100 dys.	Mustered out with company Aug. 23, 1864.
Ross, Henry A	do.	21	May 2, 1864	100 dys.	Mustered out with company Aug. 23, 1864.
Saxer, Martin	do.	19	May 2, 1864	100 dys.	Mustered out with company Aug. 23, 1864.
Schindler, Joseph	do.	23	May 2, 1864	100 dys.	Mustered out with company Aug. 23, 1864.
Smith, Hiram, Jr.	do.	[illegible]	May 2, 1864	100 dys.	Mustered out with company Aug. 23, 1864.
Smith, Orleans	do.	25	May 2, 1864	100 dys.	Mustered out with company Aug. 23, 1864.
Sorter, Alexander	do.	29	May 2, 1864	100 dys.	Mustered out with company Aug. 23, 1864.
Southworth, Henry Y.	do.	28	May 2, 1864	100 dys.	Mustered out with company Aug. 23, 1864.
Sperry, Amos	do.	31	May 2, 1864	100 dys.	Mustered out with company Aug. 23, 1864.
Sprague, William T.	do.	22	May 2, 1864	100 dys.	Mustered out with company Aug. 23, 1864.
Stauder, George	do.	52	May 2, 1864	100 dys.	Mustered out with company Aug. 23, 1864.
Stearns, Asher	do.	28	May 2, 1864	100 dys.	Mustered out with company Aug. 23, 1864.
Stearns, Cassius	do.	20	May 2, 1864	100 dys.	Mustered out with company Aug. 23, 1864.
Stearns, Henry E.	do.	18	May 2, 1864	100 dys.	Mustered out with company Aug. 23, 1864.
Stearns, Oscar D	do.	30	May 2, 1864	100 dys.	Mustered out with company Aug. 23, 1864.
Steele, Henry	do.	24	May 2, 1864	100 dys.	Mustered out with company Aug. 23, 1864.
Stocking, Joseph, Jr	do.	38	May 2, 1864	100 dys.	Mustered out with company Aug. 23, 1864.
Strope, Carroll C	do.	21	May 2, 1864	100 dys.	Mustered out with company Aug. 23, 1864.
Taylor, Conant B	do.	44	May 2, 1864	100 dys.	Mustered out with company Aug. 23, 1864.
Townsend, George	do.	28	May 2, 1864	100 dys.	Mustered out with company Aug. 23, 1864.
Tuttle, Frederick	do.	19	May 2, 1864	100 dys.	Mustered out with company Aug. 23, 1864.
Underhill, Bloomer D.	do.	29	May 2, 1864	100 dys.	Mustered out with company Aug. 23, 1864.

Names.	Rank.	Age.	Date of Entering the Service.		Period of Service.	Remarks.
Underhill, Charles L	Private	39	May	2, 1864	100 dys.	Mustered out with company Aug. 23, 1864.
Upham, William R	do	27	May	2, 1864	100 dys.	Mustered out with company Aug. 23, 1864.
White, Joseph	do	20	May	2, 1864	100 dys.	Mustered out with company Aug. 23, 1864.
Williams, Clark	do	37	May	2, 1864	100 dys.	Mustered out with company Aug. 23, 1864.
Williams, Thomas	do	44	May	2, 1864	100 dys.	Mustered out with company Aug. 23, 1864.
Winslow, Daniel	do	24	May	2, 1864	100 dys.	Mustered out with company Aug. 23, 1864.
Wolf, Alfred	do	36	May	2, 1864	100 dys.	Mustered out with company Aug. 23, 1864.
Wright, Albert	do	18	May	2, 1864	100 dys.	Mustered out with company Aug. 23, 1864.

COMPANY K.

Mustered in May 5, 1864, at Cleveland, O., by W. L. Kellogg, Lieutenant 10th Infantry, U. S. A. Mustered out Aug. 23, 1864, at Cleveland, O., by Thomas Drummond, Captain 5th Cavalry, U. S. A.

Names.	Rank.	Age.	Date of Entering the Service.		Period of Service.	Remarks.
Albert A. Safford	Captain.	24	May	2, 1864	100 dys.	Mustered out with company Aug. 23, 1864.
Henry L. Turner	1st Lieut.	19	May	2, 1864	100 dys.	Mustered out with company Aug. 23, 1864.
George W. Phinney	2d Lieut.	30	May	2, 1864	100 dys.	Mustered out with company Aug. 23, 1864.
James H. Laird	1st Sergt.	31	May	2, 1864	100 dys.	Mustered out with company Aug. 23, 1864.
Russel T. Hall	Sergeant.	19	May	2, 1864	100 dys.	Mustered out with company Aug. 23, 1864.
George W. Facklen	do	22	May	2, 1864	100 dys.	Mustered out with company Aug. 23, 1864.
George W. Keys	do	25	May	2, 1864	100 dys.	Mustered out with company Aug. 23, 1864.
Anson H. Robbins	do	26	May	2, 1864	100 dys.	Mustered out with company Aug. 23, 1864.
Lucian C. Warner	Corporal.	22	May	2, 1864	100 dys.	Mustered out with company Aug. 23, 1864.
William H. Ryder	do	21	May	2, 1864	100 dys.	Mustered out with company Aug. 23, 1864.
ames T Hudso	do	18	May	2, 1864	100 dys.	Mustered out with company Aug. 23, 1864.
R. Dwight Burrell	do	21	May	2, 1864	100 dys.	Mustered out with company Aug. 23, 1864.
Theodore W. Otis	do	28	May	2, 1864	100 dys.	Mustered out with company Aug. 23, 1864.
Edward A. Ells	do	18	May	2, 1864	100 dys.	Died Aug. 4, 1864, at Washington, D. C.
Elihu C. Barnard	do	28	May	2, 1864	100 dys.	Mustered out with company Aug. 23, 1864.
W. Irving Squire	do	20	May	2, 1864	100 dys.	Mustered out with company Aug. 23, 1864.
Beech, Edgar L	Private	18	May	2, 1864	100 dys.	Died Aug. 1, 1864, at Washington, D. C.
Bedient, John A	do	25	May	2, 1864	100 dys.	Mustered out with company Aug. 23, 1864.
Bennett, Henry S	do	26	May	2, 1864	100 dys.	Mustered out with company Aug. 23, 1864.
Boise, Eugene P	do	17	May	2, 1864	100 dys.	Mustered out with company Aug. 23, 1864.
Burns, Franklin M	do	20	May	2, 1864	100 dys.	Mustered out with company Aug. 23, 1864.
Call, Frank J	do	20	May	2, 1864	100 dys.	Mustered out with company Aug. 23, 1864.
annon ames	do	22	May	2, 1864	100 dys.	Mustered out with company Aug. 23, 1864.
Chapman, Edgar A	do	17	May	2, 1864	100 dys.	Mustered out with company Aug. 23, 1864.
Chidester, Buel	do	21	May	2, 1864	100 dys.	Mustered out with company Aug. 23, 1864.
Church, Edward P	do	28	May	2, 1864	100 dys.	Mustered out with company Aug. 23, 1864.
Clark, William T	do	21	May	2, 1864	100 dys.	Mustered out with company Aug. 23, 1864.
Cleveland, Findley	do	18	May	2, 1864	100 dys.	Mustered out with company Aug. 23, 1864.
Copeland, William E	do	18	May	2, 1864	100 dys.	Mustered out with company Aug. 23, 1864.
Cowles, Henry A	do	18	May	2, 1864	100 dys.	Died July 15, 1864, at Washington, D. C.
Dean, Charles F	do	20	May	2, 1864	100 dys.	Mustered out with company Aug. 23, 1864.
Devells, Albert	do	20	May	2, 1864	100 dys.	Mustered out with company Aug. 23, 1864.
Doughty, John C	do	17	May	2, 1864	100 dys.	Mustered out with company Aug. 23, 1864.
Eccles, Joseph	do	20	May	2, 1864	100 dys.	Mustered out with company Aug. 23, 1864.
Fillmore, John C	do	21	May	2, 1864	100 dys.	Mustered out with company Aug. 23, 1864.
Frazer, Thomas J	do	22	May	2, 1864	100 dys.	Mustered out with company Aug. 23, 1864.
Fuller, William	do	19	May	2, 1864	100 dys.	Mustered out with company Aug. 23, 1864.
Gates, Henry W	do	19	May	2, 1864	100 dys.	Mustered out with company Aug. 23, 1864.
Goss, James	do	17	May	2, 1864	100 dys.	Mustered out with company Aug. 23, 1864.
Hall, Charles F	do	18	May	2, 1864	100 dys.	Mustered out with company Aug. 23, 1864.
Hammond, Chalmers	do	20	May	2, 1864	100 dys.	Mustered out with company Aug. 23, 1864.
Hathaway, Daniel E	do	27	May	2, 1864	100 dys.	Mustered out with company Aug. 23, 1864.
Hawley, Arthur E	do	18	May	2, 1864	100 dys.	Mustered out with company Aug. 23, 1864.
Hawley, Edward K	do	20	May	2, 1864	100 dys.	Mustered out with company Aug. 23, 1864.
Holland, Richard	do	17	May	2, 1864	100 dys.	Mustered out with company Aug. 23, 1864.
Hotchkiss, Lucius C	do	31	May	2, 1864	100 dys.	Mustered out with company Aug. 23, 1864.
Hudson, Lemon	do	16	May	2, 1864	100 dys.	Mustered out with company Aug. 23, 1864.
Hughes, Nicholas P	do	17	May	2, 1864	100 dys.	Mustered out with company Aug. 23, 1864.
Hulbert, Theodore	do	18	May	2, 1864	100 dys.	Mustered out with company Aug. 23, 1864.
Hunman, Edgar	do	17	May	2, 1864	100 dys.	Mustered out with company Aug. 23, 1864.
Jackson, Harlan P	do	18	May	2, 1864	100 dys.	Mustered out with company Aug. 23, 1864.
Jeffers, John	do	21	May	2, 1864	100 dys.	Mustered out with company Aug. 23, 1864.
Johnson, Cyrus M	do	20	May	2, 1864	100 dys.	Mustered out with company Aug. 23, 1864.
Judd, Jay L	do	18	May	2, 1864	100 dys.	Mustered out with company Aug. 23, 1864.
Kellogg, Amos A	do	18	May	2, 1864	100 dys.	Mustered out with company Aug. 23, 1864.
Kingsley, Eugene P	do	19	May	2, 1864	100 dys.	Mustered out with company Aug. 23, 1864.
Kiser, Peter B	do	23	May	2, 1864	100 dys.	Mustered out with company Aug. 23, 1864.
Kreinel, Charles T	do	19	May	2, 1864	100 dys.	Mustered out with company Aug. 23, 1864.
Leach, William E	do	20	May	2, 1864	100 dys.	Died July 13, 1864, at Slocum Hospital, near Washington, D. C., of wounds received in action.
Lincoln, Marcus M	do	20	May	2, 1864	100 dys.	Mustered out with company Aug. 23, 1864.
McWade, Frederick J	do	17	May	2, 1864	100 dys.	Mustered out with company Aug. 23, 1864.

Names.	Rank.	Age.	Date of Entering the Service.	Period of Service.	Remarks.
Marietta, J. Henry	Private..	17	May 2, 1864	100 dys.	Mustered out with company Aug. 23, 1864.
Miner, William A.	....do....	24	May 2, 1864	100 dys.	Mustered out with company Aug. 23, 1864.
Monroe, John	....do....	22	May 2, 1864	100 dys.	Died Aug. 8, 1864, at Washington, D. C.
Morgan, George R.	....do....	21	May 2, 1864	100 dys.	Mustered out with company Aug. 23, 1864.
Nash, George K.	....do....	21	May 2, 1864	100 dys.	Mustered out with company Aug. 23, 1864.
Nept, Chapman C.	....do....	22	May 2, 1864	100 dys.	Mustered out with company Aug. 23, 1864.
Orton, Thomas	....do....	19	May 2, 1864	100 dys.	Mustered out with company Aug. 23, 1864.
Partridge, Joel M.	....do....	28	May 2, 1864	100 dys.	Mustered out with company Aug. 23, 1864.
Plympton, Edward L.	....do....	20	May 2, 1864	100 dys.	Mustered out with company Aug. 23, 1864.
Reed, Albert P.	....do....	18	May 2, 1864	100 dys.	Mustered out with company Aug. 23, 1864.
[illegible], Josiah	....do....	22	May 2, 1864	100 dys.	Mustered out with company Aug. 23, 1864.
Stickle, Edwin	....do....	18	May 2, 1864	100 dys.	Mustered out with company Aug. 23, 1864.
Straight, Henry H.	....do....	19	May 2, 1864	100 dys.	Mustered out with company Aug. 23, 1864.
Street, Horace, Jr.	....do....	18	May 2, 1864	100 dys.	Mustered out with company Aug. 23, 1864.
Strong, John	....do....	25	May 2, 1864	100 dys.	Mustered out with company Aug. 23, 1864.
Todd, James E.	....do....	18	May 2, 1864	100 dys.	Mustered out with company Aug. 23, 1864.
Van Antwerp, Carter	....do....	17	May 2, 1864	100 dys.	Mustered out with company Aug. 23, 1864.
Van Fossen, Levi	....do....	23	May 2, 1864	100 dys.	Mustered out with company Aug. 23, 1864.
Warren, Alanson B.	....do....	16	May 2, 1864	100 dys.	Mustered out with company Aug. 23, 1864.
Warren, Henry L.	....do....	18	May 2, 1864	100 dys.	Mustered out with company Aug. 23, 1864.
Wells, Calvin M.	....do....	20	May 2, 1864	100 dys.	Mustered out with company Aug. 23, 1864.
Wildman, Alfred R.	....do....	19	May 2, 1864	100 dys.	Mustered out with company Aug. 23, 1864.
Wilson, Lewis E.	....do....	18	May 2, 1864	100 dys.	Mustered out with company Aug. 23, 1864.
Wright, Albert A.	....do....	18	May 2, 1864	100 dys.	Mustered out with company Aug. 23, 1864.
Wright, Walter E. C.	....do....	20	May 2, 1864	100 dys.	Mustered out with company Aug. 23, 1864.

151st Regiment Ohio Volunteer Infantry.

ONE HUNDRED DAYS' SERVICE.

THIS Regiment was organized at Camp Chase, O., May 13, 1864, to serve one hundred days. It was composed of the Thirty-third Regiment, Ohio National Guard, from Allen County, and the Fifty-seventh Battalion, Ohio National Guard, from Hocking County. On the 14th of May the Regiment left Camp Chase for Washington City, via Ohio Central and Baltimore Railroads. It reached Washington on the 21st of May, and reported to General Augur. The Regiment was first stationed at Forts Sumner, Mansfield, and Simmons. During the active operations of the Rebels against Washington, on the 11th and 12th of July, the larger part of the Regiment was under fire. Several of the companies were in the forts which were engaged in the battle. Companies C and G were at Fort Stevens, Company I at Battery Smeade, and Company K at Fort Kearney. On the 17th of August orders were received to concentrate the Regiment at Fort Simmons. From this place the Regiment moved, via Baltimore and Pittsburg, to Camp Chase, where it arrived on the 23d. It was mustered out August 27, 1864, on expiration of its term of service.

151st REGIMENT OHIO VOLUNTEER INFANTRY.

FIELD AND STAFF.

Mustered in May 13, 1864, at Camp Chase, O., by H. Douglas, Captain 18th Infantry, U. S. A. Mustered out Aug. 27, 1864, at Camp Chase, O.

Names	Rank.	Age.	Date of Entering the Service.	Period of Service.	Remarks.
John M. C. Marble	Colonel.	31	May 2, 1864	100 dys.	Mustered out with regiment Aug. 27, 1864.
Richard T. Hughes	Lt. Col.	35	May 2, 1864	100 dys.	Mustered out with regiment Aug. 27, 1864.
John L. Williams	Major.	44	May 2, 1864	100 dys.	Mustered out with regiment Aug. 27, 1864.
William H. Harper	Surgeon.	45	May 2, 1864	100 dys.	Mustered out with regiment Aug. 27, 1864.
Augustus G. Holloway	Ast. Surg.	34	May 2, 1864	100 dys.	Mustered out with regiment Aug. 27, 1864.
James R. Kelch	....do....	30	May 2, 1864	100 dys.	Mustered out with regiment Aug. 27, 1864.
John A. Collins	Adjutant	26	May 2, 1864	100 dys.	Mustered out with regiment Aug. 27, 1864.
Samuel D. Chambers	R. Q. M.	28	May 2, 1864	100 dys.	Mustered out with regiment Aug. 27, 1864.
Francis Plum	Chaplain	..	May 2, 1864	100 dys.	Promoted from private Co. D May 13, 1864; mustered out with regiment Aug. 27, 1864.
George Shotwell	Ser. Maj.	33	May 2, 1864	100 dys.	Mustered out with regiment Aug. 27, 1864.
Hollis Tucker	Q. M. S.	34	May 2, 1864	100 dys.	Mustered out with regiment Aug. 27, 1864.
Alfred B. Crall	Com. Ser.	30	May 2, 1864	100 dys.	Mustered out with regiment Aug. 27, 1864.
DeWitt Webb	Hos. St'd.	25	May 2, 1864	100 dys.	Promoted from private Co. K May 13, 1864; mustered out with regiment Aug. 27, 1864.
John T. Sanderson	Prin. Mus	19	May 2, 1864	100 dys.	Promoted from Musician Co. K May 13, 1864; mustered out with regiment Aug. 27, 1864.

COMPANY A.

Mustered in May 13, 1864, at Camp Chase, O., by H. Douglas, Captain 18th Infantry, U. S. A. Mustered out Aug. 27, 1864, at Camp Chase, O.

Names	Rank.	Age.	Date of Entering the Service.	Period of Service.	Remarks.
Edward King	Captain.	39	May 2, 1864	100 dys.	Mustered out with company Aug. 27, 1864.
Enos Foster	1st Lieut.	34	May 2, 1864	100 dys.	Mustered out with company Aug. 27, 1864.
William Deming	2d Lieut.	36	May 2, 1864	100 dys.	Mustered out with company Aug. 27, 1864.
Augustus L. Teubner	1st Sergt.	21	May 2, 1864	100 dys.	Mustered out with company Aug. 27, 1864.
Oliver P. Darling	Sergeant.	33	May 2, 1864	100 dys.	Mustered out with company Aug. 27, 1864.
Evan A. Evans	....do....	23	May 2, 1864	100 dys.	Mustered out with company Aug. 27, 1864.
George W. Rhodes	....do....	32	May 2, 1864	100 dys.	Died July 31, 1864, at Fort Reno, D. C.
Charles E. Ross	....do....	28	May 2, 1864	100 dys.	Mustered out with company Aug. 27, 1864.
George O. Waterbury	Corporal.	42	May 2, 1864	100 dys.	Mustered out with company Aug. 27, 1864.
Theodore B. Moore	....do....	29	May 2, 1864	100 dys.	Mustered out with company Aug. 27, 1864.
Noah Chamberlin	....do....	35	May 2, 1864	100 dys.	Mustered out with company Aug. 27, 1864.
David Stemple	....do....	30	May 2, 1864	100 dys.	Mustered out with company Aug. 27, 1864.
Lemuel Eversole	....do....	38	May 2, 1864	100 dys.	Mustered out with company Aug. 27, 1864.
Henry F. Dabler	....do....	31	May 2, 1864	100 dys.	Mustered out with company Aug. 27, 1864.
Jacob Custer	....do....	25	May 2, 1864	100 dys.	Mustered out with company Aug. 27, 1864.
Josiah Walters	....do....	41	May 2, 1864	100 dys.	Died Aug. 21, 1864, at Fort Reno, D. C.
Columbus Bowers	Musician	18	May 2, 1864	100 dys.	Mustered out with company Aug. 27, 1864.
Oscar E. Moore	....do....	16	May 2, 1864	100 dys.	Mustered out with company Aug. 27, 1864.
Hiram Runyan	Wagoner.	24	May 2, 1864	100 dys.	Mustered out with company Aug. 27, 1864.
Alexander, William	Private..	37	May 2, 1864	100 dys.	Mustered out with company Aug. 27, 1864.
Allen, Albert	....do....	18	May 2, 1864	100 dys.	Mustered out with company Aug. 27, 1864.
Bentley, Gould W	....do....	35	May 2, 1864	100 dys.	Discharged June 23, 1864, on Surgeon's certificate of disability.
Berryman, Allen B	....do....	24	May 2, 1864	100 dys.	Mustered out with company Aug. 27, 1864.
Binkley, Richard	....do....	21	May 2, 1864	100 dys.	Died May 18, 1864, at New Creek, W. Va.
Bisickommer, Adam C.	....do....	28	May 2, 1864	100 dys.	Transferred to Co. I —.
Bliss, Legrand L	....do....	18	May 2, 1864	100 dys.	Mustered out with company Aug. 27, 1864.
Boop, Michael	....do....	25	May 2, 1864	100 dys.	Mustered out with company Aug. 27, 1864.
Bowman, Martin	....do....	18	May 2, 1864	100 dys.	Mustered out with company Aug. 27, 1864.
Breese, William	....do....	27	May 2, 1864	100 dys.	Mustered out with company Aug. 27, 1864.
Bryan, James M	....do....	18	May 2, 1864	100 dys.	Mustered out with company Aug. 27, 1864.
Chamberlin, Henry	....do....	32	May 2, 1864	100 dys.	Mustered out with company Aug. 27, 1864.

Names.	Rank.	Age.	Date of Entering the Service.	Period of Service.	Remarks.
Chamberlin, William	Private	43	May 2, 1864	100 dys.	Discharged June 14, 1864, on Surgeon's certificate of disability.
Clawson, Aaron	...do...	20	May 2, 1864	100 dys.	Mustered out with company Aug. 27, 1864.
Cline, James H	...do...	24	May 2, 1864	100 dys.	Mustered out with company Aug. 27, 1864.
Cook, Samuel B	...do...	19	May 2, 1864	100 dys.	Mustered out with company Aug. 27, 1864.
Crothers, George D	...do...	28	May 2, 1864	100 dys.	Mustered out with company Aug. 27, 1864.
Deal, William	...do...	27	May 2, 1864	100 dys.	Mustered out with company Aug. 27, 1864.
Enslin, William	...do...	19	May 2, 1864	100 dys.	Mustered out with company Aug. 27, 1864.
Eysenbach, Henry P	...do...	20	May 2, 1864	100 dys.	Mustered out with company Aug. 27, 1864.
Eysenbach, William	...do...	18	May 2, 1864	100 dys.	Mustered out with company Aug. 27, 1864.
Fettig, William	...do...	38	May 2, 1864	100 dys.	Mustered out with company Aug. 27, 1864.
Fritz, Alfred	...do...	42	May 2, 1864	100 dys.	Mustered out with company Aug. 27, 1864.
Fritz, Eli	...do...	41	May 2, 1864	100 dys.	Mustered out with company Aug. 27, 1864.
Goliver Benjamin W	...do...	27	May 2, 1864	100 dys.	Mustered out with company Aug. 27, 1864.
Harkins, Augustus A	...do...	19	May 2, 1864	100 dys.	Mustered out with company Aug. 27, 1864.
Harsh, Abraham	...do...	40	May 2, 1864	100 dys.	Mustered out with company Aug. 27, 1864.
Harsh, Daniel	...do...	34	May 2, 1864	100 dys.	Mustered out with company Aug. 27, 1864.
Harshe, James R	...do...	21	May 2, 1864	100 dys.	Mustered out with company Aug. 27, 1864.
Helt, Daniel	...do...	25	May 2, 1864	100 dys.	Mustered out with company Aug. 27, 1864.
Hetrick, Jacob	...do...	18	May 2, 1864	100 dys.	Mustered out with company Aug. 27, 1864.
Hockenberry, David	...do...	34	May 2, 1864	100 dys.	Mustered out with company Aug. 27, 1864.
Hoffrichter, John	...do...	44	May 2, 1864	100 dys.	Mustered out with company Aug. 27, 1864.
Hudkins, John	...do...	18	May 2, 1864	100 dys.	Mustered out with company Aug. 27, 1864.
Jamison, Adam	...do...	18	May 2, 1864	100 dys.	Mustered out with company Aug. 27, 1864.
Jamison, Francis	...do...	20	May 2, 1864	100 dys.	Mustered out with company Aug. 27, 1864.
Klinger, Joseph	...do...	45	May 2, 1864	100 dys.	Mustered out with company Aug. 27, 1864.
Krutsch, David O	...do...	33	May 2, 1864	100 dys.	Mustered out with company Aug. 27, 1864.
Lasuer, Newton	...do...	34	May 2, 1864	100 dys.	Mustered out with company Aug. 27, 1864.
Lloyd, Edward	...do...	21	May 2, 1864	100 dys.	Mustered out with company Aug. 27, 1864.
Ludwig, George W	...do...	44	May 2, 1864	100 dys.	Mustered out with company Aug. 27, 1864.
McEower, John	...do...	20	May 2, 1864	100 dys.	Mustered out with company Aug. 27, 1864.
Martin, Wellington	...do...	25	May 2, 1864	100 dys.	Mustered out with company Aug. 27, 1864.
Miller, Henry	...do...	18	May 2, 1864	100 dys.	Mustered out with company Aug. 27, 1864.
Nay Eli	...do...	18	May 2, 1864	100 dys.	Mustered out with company Aug. 27, 1864.
Oatman Samuel	...do...	35	May 2, 1864	100 dys.	Mustered out with company Aug. 27, 1864.
Osborne, Samuel W	...do...	27	May 2, 1864	100 dys.	Mustered out with company Aug. 27, 1864.
Pangle, John	...do...	19	May 2, 1864	100 dys.	Mustered out with company Aug. 27, 1864.
Parrott, John	...do...	41	May 2, 1864	100 dys.	Transferred to Co. I —.
Price, Frederick	...do...	18	May 2, 1864	100 dys.	Mustered out with company Aug. 27, 1864.
Rider, Phares	...do...	18	May 2, 1864	100 dys.	Mustered out with company Aug. 27, 1864.
Rigdon, John	...do...	31	May 2, 1864	100 dys.	Mustered out with company Aug. 27, 1864.
Rigdon, Newton W	...do...	20	May 2, 1864	100 dys.	Mustered out with company Aug. 27, 1864.
Riggle, Jacob	...do...	33	May 2, 1864	100 dys.	Mustered out with company Aug. 27, 1864.
Seiser, Matthias	...do...	30	May 2, 1864	100 dys.	Mustered out with company Aug. 27, 1864.
Shenk, Constantine	...do...	25	May 2, 1864	100 dys.	Mustered out with company Aug. 27, 1864.
Stemple, Jacob	...do...	38	May 2, 1864	100 dys.	Mustered out with company Aug. 27, 1864.
Stevens, Nathan	...do...	27	May 2, 1864	100 dys.	Mustered out with company Aug. 27, 1864.
Stophlet, John W	...do...	19	May 2, 1864	100 dys.	Mustered out with company Aug. 27, 1864.
Styppich, Paul	...do...	43	May 2, 1864	100 dys.	Mustered out with company Aug. 27, 1864.
Tollan, William	...do...	30	May 2, 1864	100 dys.	Mustered out with company Aug. 27, 1864.
Tong, Amos	...do...	20	May 2, 1864	100 dys.	Mustered out with company Aug. 27, 1864.
Tong, Thomas	...do...	30	May 2, 1864	100 dys.	Mustered out with company Aug. 27, 1864.
Utter, Abraham	...do...	32	May 2, 1864	100 dys.	Mustered out with company Aug. 27, 1864.
Walls, Jesse	...do...	37	May 2, 1864	100 dys.	Mustered out with company Aug. 27, 1864.
Waterbury, Charles	...do...	18	May 2, 1864	100 dys.	Mustered out with company Aug. 27, 1864.
Webster, Daniel	...do...	24	May 2, 1864	100 dys.	Mustered out with company Aug. 27, 1864.
Wegesin, Henry	...do...	27	May 2, 1864	100 dys.	Mustered out with company Aug. 27, 1864.
Wells, Simeon	...do...	19	May 2, 1864	100 dys.	Mustered out with company Aug. 27, 1864.
Wilson, William	...do...	30	May 2, 1864	100 dys.	Mustered out with company Aug. 27, 1864.
Workman, Absalom	...do...	44	May 2, 1864	100 dys.	Discharged June 27, 1864, on Surgeon's certificate of disability.

COMPANY B.

Mustered in May 13, 1864, at Camp Chase, O., by H. Douglas, Captain 18th Infantry, U. S. A. Mustered out Aug. 27, 1864, at Camp Chase, O.

Names.	Rank.	Age.	Date of Entering the Service.	Period of Service.	Remarks.
William Huston	Captain.	36	May 2, 1864	100 dys.	Mustered out with company Aug. 27, 1864.
George K. Truesdale	1st Lieut.	23	May 2, 1864	100 dys.	Mustered out with company Aug. 27, 1864.
William Hall	2d Lieut.	36	May 2, 1864	100 dys.	Mustered out with company Aug. 27, 1864.
Henry C. Adgate	1st Sergt.	29	May 2, 1864	100 dys.	Mustered out with company Aug. 27, 1864.
Samuel H. Ward	Sergeant.	37	May 2, 1864	100 dys.	Mustered out with company Aug. 27, 1864.
Warren F. Reed	...do...	24	May 2, 1864	100 dys.	Mustered out with company Aug. 27, 1864.
John McKean	...do...	22	May 2, 1864	100 dys.	Mustered out with company Aug. 27, 1864.
Jesse Hall	...do...	40	May 2, 1864	100 dys.	Discharged June 22, 1864, on Surgeon's certificate of disability.
David M. Breese	...do...	39	May 2, 1864	100 dys.	Appointed June 23, 1864; mustered out with company Aug. 27, 1864.
Jacob Vohris	Corporal.	24	May 2, 1864	100 dys.	Mustered out with company Aug. 27, 1864.
Andrew J. Chapman	...do...	29	May 2, 1864	100 dys.	Mustered out with company Aug. 27, 1864.

Names.	Rank.	Age.	Date of Entering the Service.	Period of Service.	Remarks.
Lyman W. McMillen	Corporal.	33	May 2, 1864	100 dys.	Mustered out with company Aug. 27, 1864.
Joshua Pillars	...do...	28	May 2, 1864	100 dys.	Mustered out with company Aug. 27, 1864.
James R. Cunningham	...do...	27	May 2, 1864	100 dys.	Mustered out with company Aug. 27, 1864.
William H. Evans	...do...	45	May 2, 1864	100 dys.	Mustered out with company Aug. 27, 1864.
Joseph H. Cowden	...do...	28	May 2, 1864	100 dys.	Mustered out with company Aug. 27, 1864.
Joseph Dixon	...do...	37	May 2, 1864	100 dys.	Mustered out with company Aug. 27, 1864.
John W. Heisler	Musician	24	May 2, 1864	100 dys.	Mustered out with company Aug. 27, 1864.
James S. Armor	...do...	46	May 2, 1864	100 dys.	Mustered out with company Aug. 27, 1864.
Adams, John T	Private.	32	May 2, 1864	100 dys.	Mustered out with company Aug. 27, 1864.
Allen, Joseph D	...do...	25	May 2, 1864	100 dys.	Mustered out with company Aug. 27, 1864.
Babcock, Lyman	...do...	35	May 2, 1864	100 dys.	Mustered out with company Aug. 27, 1864.
Ballard, William W	...do...	22	May 2, 1864	100 dys.	Mustered out with company Aug. 27, 1864.
Beatty, Wilson A	...do...	23	May 2, 1864	100 dys.	Mustered out with company Aug. 27, 1864.
Bedford, Milton T	...do...	19	May 2, 1864	100 dys.	Mustered out with company Aug. 27, 1864.
Beiler, John	...do...	45	May 2, 1864	100 dys.	Mustered out with company Aug. 27, 1864.
Bird, Abram L	...do...	35	May 2, 1864	100 dys.	Mustered out with company Aug. 27, 1864.
Blythe, John	...do...	29	May 2, 1864	100 dys.	Mustered out with company Aug. 27, 1864.
Breese, John	...do...	44	May 2, 1864	100 dys.	Mustered out with company Aug. 27, 1864.
Buck, Uriah H	...do...	29	May 2, 1864	100 dys.	Mustered out with company Aug. 27, 1864.
Burns, Valentine	...do...	19	May 2, 1864	100 dys.	Mustered out with company Aug. 27, 1864.
Carlisle, David	...do...	23	May 2, 1864	100 dys.	Mustered out with company Aug. 27, 1864.
Carr, Solomon	...do...	28	May 2, 1864	100 dys.	Mustered out with company Aug. 27, 1864.
Chapman, Henry B	...do...	30	May 2, 1864	100 dys.	Mustered out with company Aug. 27, 1864.
Conkle, Adam	...do...	21	May 2, 1864	100 dys.	Mustered out with company Aug. 27, 1864.
Coon, John	...do...	37	May 2, 1864	100 dys.	Mustered out with company Aug. 27, 1864.
Cowen, John	...do...	28	May 2, 1864	100 dys.	Mustered out with company Aug. 27, 1864.
Culver, David	...do...	20	May 2, 1864	100 dys.	Mustered out with company Aug. 27, 1864.
Daniels, John C	...do...	35	May 2, 1864	100 dys.	Discharged July 9, 1864, on Surgeon's certificate of disability.
Dennis, Elijah G	...do...	32	May 2, 1864	100 dys.	Mustered out with company Aug. 27, 1864.
Dishinger, Valentine	...do...	42	May 2, 1864	100 dys.	Mustered out with company Aug. 27, 1864.
Douglass, John	...do...	40	May 2, 1864	100 dys.	Mustered out with company Aug. 27, 1864.
Edman, Elijah	...do...	37	May 2, 1864	100 dys.	Mustered out with company Aug. 27, 1864.
Edman, Oliver P	...do...	32	May 2, 1864	100 dys.	Discharged June 22, 1864, on Surgeon's certificate of disability.
Foster, Barnett	...do...	27	May 2, 1864	100 dys.	Mustered out with company Aug. 27, 1864.
Furry, Franklin	...do...	44	May 2, 1864	100 dys.	Mustered out with company Aug. 27, 1864.
Gardner, William	...do...	44	May 2, 1864	100 dys.	Mustered out with company Aug. 27, 1864.
Grubb, Jacob	...do...	38	May 2, 1864	100 dys.	Mustered out with company Aug. 27, 1864.
Haines, Henry	...do...	28	May 2, 1864	100 dys.	Mustered out with company Aug. 27, 1864.
Hanson, Joseph B	...do...	18	May 2, 1864	100 dys.	Mustered out with company Aug. 27, 1864.
Harper, Thomas	...do...	18	May 2, 1864	100 dys.	Mustered out with company Aug. 27, 1864.
Hoak, Cyrus	...do...	43	May 2, 1864	100 dys.	Mustered out with company Aug. 27, 1864.
Holmes, William	...do...	19	May 2, 1864	100 dys.	Mustered out with company Aug. 27, 1864.
Huston, Philip B	...do...	44	May 2, 1864	100 dys.	Mustered out with company Aug. 27, 1864.
Johnson, Thomas P	...do...	23	May 2, 1864	100 dys.	Mustered out with company Aug. 27, 1864.
Kemp, John W	...do...	37	May 2, 1864	100 dys.	Mustered out with company Aug. 27, 1864.
Madden, Alexander	...do...	31	May 2, 1864	100 dys.	Mustered out with company Aug. 27, 1864.
Medsker, John J	...do...	35	May 2, 1864	100 dys.	Mustered out with company Aug. 27, 1864.
Miller, Curtis	...do...	38	May 2, 1864	100 dys.	Mustered out with company Aug. 27, 1864.
Miller, Fielding L	...do...	41	May 2, 1864	100 dys.	Mustered out with company Aug. 27, 1864.
Miller, James A	...do...	33	May 2, 1864	100 dys.	Mustered out with company Aug. 27, 1864.
Miller, Joseph	...do...	33	May 2, 1864	100 dys.	Mustered out with company Aug. 27, 1864.
Mowen, Carson L	...do...	31	May 2, 1864	100 dys.	Mustered out with company Aug. 27, 1864.
Orsborn, John	...do...	20	May 2, 1864	100 dys.	Mustered out with company Aug. 27, 1864.
Reed, Isaac	...do...	19	May 2, 1864	100 dys.	Mustered out with company Aug. 27, 1864.
Robbins, John	...do...	22	May 2, 1864	100 dys.	Mustered out with company Aug. 27, 1864.
Rose, Ezekiel S	...do...	48	May 2, 1864	100 dys.	Discharged June 5, 1864, on Surgeon's certificate of disability.
Sawmiller, Daniel	...do...	41	May 2, 1864	100 dys.	Mustered out with company Aug. 27, 1864.
Schofield, Lemuel	...do...	41	May 2, 1864	100 dys.	Mustered out with company Aug. 27, 1864.
Schwab, Frank	...do...	23	May 2, 1864	100 dys.	Mustered out with company Aug. 27, 1864.
Sharp, Joshua	...do...	38	May 2, 1864	100 dys.	Mustered out with company Aug. 27, 1864.
Spiker, Henry	...do...	18	May 2, 1864	100 dys.	Mustered out with company Aug. 27, 1864.
Sprague, Henry	...do...	43	May 2, 1864	100 dys.	Mustered out with company Aug. 27, 1864.
Stewart, Jerome V	...do...	21	May 2, 1864	100 dys.	Mustered out with company Aug. 27, 1864.
Stuckey, Cornelius	...do...	29	May 2, 1864	100 dys.	Mustered out with company Aug. 27, 1864.
Turner, John A	...do...	45	May 2, 1864	100 dys.	Mustered out with company Aug. 27, 1864.
Underwood, Isaac L	...do...	34	May 2, 1864	100 dys.	Mustered out with company Aug. 27, 1864.
Vanschoyk, Francis	...do...	24	May 2, 1864	100 dys.	Mustered out with company Aug. 27, 1864.
Wamsley, Hicks	...do...	18	May 2, 1864	100 dys.	Discharged June 7, 1864, on Surgeon's certificate of disability.
Ward, Joseph	...do...	36	May 2, 1864	100 dys.	Mustered out with company Aug. 27, 1864.
Welker, Frederick N	...do...	18	May 2, 1864	100 dys.	Mustered out with company Aug. 27, 1864.
West, Jonathan H	...do...	33	May 2, 1864	100 dys.	Mustered out with company Aug. 27, 1864.
Wilson, David H	...do...	45	May 2, 1864	100 dys.	Mustered out with company Aug. 27, 1864.
Wollet, George	...do...	18	May 2, 1864	100 dys.	Mustered out with company Aug. 27, 1864.
Wonnel, Edward	...do...	23	May 2, 1864	100 dys.	Mustered out with company Aug. 27, 1864.

COMPANY C.

Mustered in May 13, 1864, at Camp Chase, O., by H. Douglas, Captain 18th Infantry, U. S. A. Mustered out Aug. 27, 1864, at Camp Chase, O.

Names.	Rank.	Age.	Date of Entering the Service.	Period of Service.	Remarks.
James L. Booth	Captain.	29	May 2, 1864	100 dys.	Mustered out with company Aug. 27, 1864.
Thomas J. Snodgrass	1st Lieut.	33	May 2, 1864	100 dys.	Mustered out with company Aug. 27, 1864.
Lewis Mumaugh	2d Lieut.	29	May 2, 1864	100 dys.	Mustered out with company Aug. 27, 1864.
Gregory Jennings	1st Sergt.	27	May 2, 1864	100 dys.	Mustered out with company Aug. 27, 1864.
John Brown	Sergeant.	28	May 2, 1864	100 dys.	Mustered out with company Aug. 27, 1864.
James Downing	do.	39	May 2, 1864	100 dys.	Mustered out with company Aug. 27, 1864.
Christian Dolph	do.	38	May 2, 1864	100 dys.	Mustered out with company Aug. 27, 1864.
Peter M[illegible]	do.	27	May 2, 1864	100 dys.	Mustered out with company Aug. 27, 1864.
George Cowden	Corporal.	27	May 2, 1864	100 dys.	Mustered out with company Aug. 27, 1864.
Emanuel G. Waltz	do.	25	May 2, 1864	100 dys.	Mustered out with company Aug. 27, 1864.
William G. Fowler	do.	30	May 2, 1864	100 dys.	Mustered out with company Aug. 27, 1864.
Leonard E[illegible]	do.	19	May 2, 1864	100 dys.	Mustered out with company Aug. 27, 1864.
Abraham Hall	do.	39	May 2, 1864	100 dys.	Mustered out with company Aug. 27, 1864.
Robert N. Rockhill	do.	23	May 2, 1864	100 dys.	Mustered out with company Aug. 27, 1864.
Christian Hook	do.	22	May 2, 1864	100 dys.	Mustered out with company Aug. 27, 1864.
James Jennings	do.	26	May 2, 1864	100 dys.	Mustered out with company Aug. 27, 1864.
George Harpster	Musician	44	May 2, 1864	100 dys.	Mustered out with company Aug. 27, 1864.
Isaac N. [illegible]straw	do.	27	May 2, 1864	100 dys.	Mustered out with company Aug. 27, 1864.
Thomas [illegible]	do.	34	May 2, 1864	100 dys.	Mustered out with company Aug. 27, 1864.
Charles J. States	Wagoner.	37	May 2, 1864	100 dys.	Mustered out with company Aug. 27, 1864.
Barnes, Robert S.	Private.	24	May 2, 1864	100 dys.	Mustered out with company Aug. 27, 1864.
Bear, John	do.	32	May 2, 1864	100 dys.	Mustered out with company Aug. 27, 1864.
B[illegible], Nathaniel D.	do.	18	May 2, 1864	100 dys.	Mustered out with company Aug. 27, 1864.
B[illegible], Jonathan C.	do.	21	May 2, 1864	100 dys.	Mustered out with company Aug. 27, 1864.
B[illegible], Nathaniel	do.	28	May 2, 1864	100 dys.	Mustered out with company Aug. 27, 1864.
B[illegible], Lewis	do.	29	May 2, 1864	100 dys.	Mustered out with company Aug. 27, 1864.
[illegible], William	do.	[illegible]	May 2, 1864	100 dys.	Mustered out with company Aug. 27, 1864.
B[illegible], William H.	do.	25	May 2, 1864	100 dys.	Mustered out with company Aug. 27, 1864.
Bow[illegible], James	do.	19	May 2, 1864	100 dys.	Mustered out with company Aug. 27, 1864.
B[illegible], Isaac [illegible]	do.	42	May 2, 1864	100 dys.	Mustered out with company Aug. 27, 1864.
Brougan, Charles	do.	41	May 2, 1864	100 dys.	Mustered out with company Aug. 27, 1864.
Brown, Nathaniel M.	do.	24	May 2, 1864	100 dys.	Mustered out with company Aug. 27, 1864.
Bryan, [illegible]	do.	21	May 2, 1864	100 dys.	Mustered out with company Aug. 27, 1864.
Conklin, Moses W.	do.	23	May 2, 1864	100 dys.	Mustered out with company Aug. 27, 1864.
Cook, Elza J.	do.	25	May 2, 1864	100 dys.	Mustered out with company Aug. 27, 1864.
C[illegible], Henry	do.	21	May 2, 1864	100 dys.	Mustered out with company Aug. 27, 1864.
D[illegible], Hugh	do.	34	May 2, 1864	100 dys.	Mustered out with company Aug. 27, 1864.
D[illegible], Samuel S.	do.	42	May 2, 1864	100 dys.	Mustered out with company Aug. 27, 1864.
[illegible], Samuel	do.	18	May 2, 1864	100 dys.	Transferred to Co. I May 13, 1864, and there borne as Samuel Allison.
E[illegible], Abraham	do.	30	May 2, 1864	100 dys.	Mustered out with company Aug. 27, 1864.
[illegible], John	do.	40	May 2, 1864	100 dys.	Mustered out with company Aug. 27, 1864.
[illegible], John W.	do.	21	May 2, 1864	100 dys.	Mustered out with company Aug. 27, 1864.
[illegible], Samuel A.	do.	19	May 2, 1864	100 dys.	Mustered out with company Aug. 27, 1864.
[illegible], Samuel S.	do.	21	May 2, 1864	100 dys.	Mustered out with company Aug. 27, 1864.
F[illegible], Jonathan	do.	26	May 2, 1864	100 dys.	Mustered out with company Aug. 27, 1864.
[illegible], Moses	do.	21	May 2, 1864	100 dys.	Mustered out with company Aug. 27, 1864.
[illegible], Edwin	do.	28	May 2, 1864	100 dys.	Transferred to Co. I May 13, 1864.
[illegible], William H.	do.	22	May 2, 1864	100 dys.	Mustered out with company Aug. 27, 1864.
[illegible], Levi	do.	24	May 2, 1864	100 dys.	Mustered out with company Aug. 27, 1864.
[illegible], John	do.	24	May 2, 1864	100 dys.	Mustered out with company Aug. 27, 1864.
[illegible], Philip C.	do.	[illegible]	May 2, 1864	100 dys.	Mustered out with company Aug. 27, 1864.
[illegible], Amos	do.	21	May 2, 1864	100 dys.	Mustered out with company Aug. 27, 1864.
[illegible], Alexander	do.	[illegible]	May 2, 1864	100 dys.	Mustered out with company Aug. 27, 1864.
[illegible], Charles W.	do.	21	May 2, 1864	100 dys.	Mustered out with company Aug. 27, 1864.
[illegible]	do.	27	May 2, 1864	100 dys.	Mustered out with company Aug. 27, 1864.
[illegible], David E.	do.	21	May 2, 1864	100 dys.	Mustered out with company Aug. 27, 1864.
[illegible]	do.	40	May 2, 1864	100 dys.	Mustered out with company Aug. 27, 1864.
[illegible], Samuel A.	do.	30	May 2, 1864	100 dys.	Mustered out with company Aug. 27, 1864.
[illegible], George	do.	[illegible]	May 2, 1864	100 dys.	Mustered out with company Aug. 27, 1864.
[illegible]	do.	25	May 2, 1864	100 dys.	Mustered out with company Aug. 27, 1864.
[illegible]	do.	[illegible]	May 2, 1864	100 dys.	Mustered out with company Aug. 27, 1864.
[illegible]	do.	23	May 2, 1864	100 dys.	Mustered out with company Aug. 27, 1864.
[illegible], Philip	do.	18	May 2, 1864	100 dys.	Mustered out with company Aug. 27, 1864.
[illegible]	do.	[illegible]	May 2, 1864	100 dys.	Mustered out with company Aug. 27, 1864.
[illegible]	do.	35	May 2, 1864	100 dys.	Mustered out with company Aug. 27, 1864.
[illegible]	do.	22	May 2, 1864	100 dys.	Mustered out with company Aug. 27, 1864.
[illegible]	do.	30	May 2, 1864	100 dys.	Mustered out with company Aug. 27, 1864.
[illegible]	do.	18	May 2, 1864	100 dys.	Mustered out with company Aug. 27, 1864.
[illegible]	do.	28	May 2, 1864	100 dys.	Mustered out with company Aug. 27, 1864.
[illegible]	do.	[illegible]	May 2, 1864	100 dys.	Mustered out with company Aug. 27, 1864.
[illegible]	do.	25	May 2, 1864	100 dys.	Discharged June 27, 1864, on Surgeon's certificate of disability.
[illegible]	do.	18	May 2, 1864	100 dys.	Mustered out with company Aug. 27, 1864.
[illegible]	do.	38	May 2, 1864	100 dys.	Mustered out with company Aug. 27, 1864.
[illegible]	do.	40	May 2, 1864	100 dys.	Discharged June 26, 1864, on Surgeon's certificate of disability.

Names.	Rank.	Age.	Date of Entering the Service.	Period of Service.	Remarks.
	Private.	40	May 2, 1864	100 dys.	Mustered out with company Aug. 27, 1864.
	...do...	20	May 2, 1864	100 dys.	Mustered out with company Aug. 27, 1864.
	...do...	31	May 2, 1864	100 dys.	Mustered out with company Aug. 27, 1864.
	...do...	23	May 2, 1864	100 dys.	Mustered out with company Aug. 27, 1864.
	...do...	19	May 2, 1864	100 dys.	Mustered out with company Aug. 27, 1864.
	...do...	18	May 2, 1864	100 dys.	Mustered out with company Aug. 27, 1864.
	...do...	22	May 2, 1864	100 dys.	Mustered out with company Aug. 27, 1864.
	...do...	21	May 2, 1864	100 dys.	Mustered out with company Aug. 27, 1864.
	...do...	18	May 2, 1864	100 dys.	Mustered out with company Aug. 27, 1864.
	...do...	25	May 2, 1864	100 dys.	Mustered out with company Aug. 27, 1864.
	...do...	38	May 2, 1864	100 dys.	Mustered out with company Aug. 27, 1864.
	...do...	19	May 3, 1864	100 dys.	Mustered out with company Aug. 27, 1864.
	...do...	28	May 2, 1864	100 dys.	Mustered out with company Aug. 27, 1864.
	...do...	26	May 2, 1864	100 dys.	Mustered out with company Aug. 27, 1864.
	...do...	22	May 4, 1864	100 dys.	Mustered out with company Aug. 27, 1864.
	...do...	25	May 2, 1864	100 dys.	Mustered out with company Aug. 27, 1864.
	...do...	34	May 2, 1864	100 dys.	Discharged June 20, 1864, on surgeon's certificate of disability.

COMPANY D.

d in May 13, 1864, at Camp Chase, O., by H. Douglas, Captain 18th Infantry, U. S. A. Mustered out Aug. 27, 1864, at Camp Chase, O.

Names.	Rank.	Age.	Date of Entering the Service.	Period of Service.	Remarks.
. Smith	Captain.	37	May 2, 1864	100 dys.	Mustered out with company Aug. 27, 1864.
cGinnis	1st Lieut.	21	May 2, 1864	100 dys.	Mustered out with company Aug. 27, 1864.
Ward	2d Lieut.	34	May 2, 1864	100 dys.	Mustered out with company Aug. 27, 1864.
r A. Creps	1st Sergt.	20	May 2, 1864	100 dys.	Mustered out with company Aug. 27, 1864.
n D. Creps	Sergeant.	24	May 2, 1864	100 dys.	Mustered out with company Aug. 27, 1864.
McCoy	...do...	26	May 2, 1864	100 dys.	Mustered out with company Aug. 27, 1864.
. McClain	...do...	38	May 2, 1864	100 dys.	Mustered out with company Aug. 27, 1864.
. Bond	...do...	28	May 2, 1864	100 dys.	Mustered out with company Aug. 27, 1864.
M. McCoy	Corporal.	23	May 2, 1864	100 dys.	Mustered out with company Aug. 27, 1864.
y Walters	...do...	25	May 2, 1864	100 dys.	Mustered out with company Aug. 27, 1864.
C. Ford	...do...	38	May 2, 1864	100 dys.	Mustered out with company Aug. 27, 1864.
Hillinger	...do...	29	May 2, 1864	100 dys.	Mustered out with company Aug. 27, 1864.
R. Bailey	...do...	26	May 2, 1864	100 dys.	Mustered out with company Aug. 27, 1864.
. Baily	...do...	23	May 2, 1864	100 dys.	Mustered out with company Aug. 27, 1864.
evenson	...do...	25	May 2, 1864	100 dys.	Mustered out with company Aug. 27, 1864.
s Foster	Musician	14	May 2, 1864	100 dys.	Mustered out with company Aug. 27, 1864.
M. McGinnis	...do...	34	May 2, 1864	100 dys.	Mustered out with company Aug. 27, 1864.
m Smith	Wagoner.	26	May 2, 1864	100 dys.	Mustered out with company Aug. 27, 1864.
, James R.	Private.	35	May 2, 1864	100 dys.	Mustered out with company Aug. 27, 1864.
John	...do...	19	May 2, 1864	100 dys.	Mustered out with company Aug. 27, 1864.
Israel	...do...	18	May 2, 1864	100 dys.	Mustered out with company Aug. 27, 1864.
William	...do...	28	May 2, 1864	100 dys.	Mustered out with company Aug. 27, 1864.
nathan	...do...	22	May 2, 1864	100 dys.	Mustered out with company Aug. 27, 1864.
n, Charles H.	...do...	25	May 2, 1864	100 dys.	Mustered out with company Aug. 27, 1864.
n, James H.	...do...	28	May 2, 1864	100 dys.	Mustered out with company Aug. 27, 1864.
athan	...do...	21	May 2, 1864	100 dys.	Mustered out with company Aug. 27, 1864.
Hiram	...do...	18	May 2, 1864	100 dys.	Mustered out with company Aug. 27, 1864.
William R.	...do...	29	May 2, 1864	100 dys.	Mustered out with company Aug. 27, 1864.
er, James	...do...	29	May 2, 1864	100 dys.	Mustered out with company Aug. 27, 1864.
William H.	...do...	29	May 2, 1864	100 dys.	Mustered out with company Aug. 27, 1864.
William	...do...	22	May 2, 1864	100 dys.	Mustered out with company Aug. 27, 1864.
Downs	...do...	27	May 2, 1864	100 dys.	Mustered out with company Aug. 27, 1864.
David	...do...	38	May 2, 1864	100 dys.	Mustered out with company Aug. 27, 1864.
o, Daniel	...do...	31	May 2, 1864	100 dys.	Mustered out with company Aug. 27, 1864.
ger, Abraham	...do...	29	May 2, 1864	100 dys.	Mustered out with company Aug. 27, 1864.
ln, George W.	...do...	19	May 2, 1864	100 dys.	Mustered out with company Aug. 27, 1864.
ln, James	...do...	31	May 2, 1864	100 dys.	Mustered out with company Aug. 27, 1864.
, David	...do...	22	May 2, 1864	100 dys.	Mustered out with company Aug. 27, 1864.
n, Brice W.	...do...	40	May 2, 1864	100 dys.	Mustered out with company Aug. 27, 1864.
y, Joshua	...do...	20	May 2, 1864	100 dys.	Mustered out with company Aug. 27, 1864.
Henry H.	...do...	22	May 2, 1864	100 dys.	Mustered out with company Aug. 27, 1864.
Benton	...do...	22	May 2, 1864	100 dys.	Mustered out with company Aug. 27, 1864.
saac	...do...	31	May 2, 1864	100 dys.	Mustered out with company Aug. 27, 1864.
er, Charles	...do...	18	May 2, 1864	100 dys.	Mustered out with company Aug. 27, 1864.
er, Henry H.	...do...	18	May 2, 1864	100 dys.	Mustered out with company Aug. 27, 1864.
er, Stephen	...do...	18	May 2, 1864	100 dys.	Mustered out with company Aug. 27, 1864.
. Joshua	...do...	25	May 2, 1864	100 dys.	Mustered out with company Aug. 27, 1864.
. David	...do...	30	May 2, 1864	100 dys.	Mustered out with company Aug. 27, 1864.
ott, William	...do...	29	May 2, 1864	100 dys.	Died Aug. 7, 1864, at Fort Reno, D. C.
d, Robert G.	...do...	21	May 2, 1864	100 dys.	Mustered out with company Aug. 27, 1864.
, John	...do...	18	May 2, 1864	100 dys.	Mustered out with company Aug. 27, 1864.
ick, John	...do...	21	May 2, 1864	100 dys.	Mustered out with company Aug. 27, 1864.
Adam F.	...do...	18	May 2, 1864	100 dys.	Mustered out with company Aug. 27, 1864.
David	...do...	35	May 2, 1864	100 dys.	Mustered out with company Aug. 27, 1864.
n, Erasmus	...do...	20	May 2, 1864	100 dys.	Mustered out with company Aug. 27, 1864.
John D.	...do...	32	May 2, 1864	100 dys.	Mustered out with company Aug. 27, 1864.

Names.	Rank.	Age.	Date of Entering the Service.	Period of Service.	Remarks.
Marsh, Peter	Private	27	May 2, 1864	100 dys.	Mustered out with company Aug. 27, 1864.
Marsh, William H.	do	31	May 2, 1864	100 dys.	Mustered out with company Aug. 27, 1864.
Marshall, Henry M.	do	18	May 2, 1864	100 dys.	Mustered out with company Aug. 27, 1864.
May, Francis	do	18	May 2, 1864	100 dys.	Mustered out with company Aug. 27, 1864.
Meeks, George W.	do	22	May 2, 1864	100 dys.	Mustered out with company Aug. 27, 1864.
Musser, Isaac	do	18	May 2, 1864	100 dys.	Mustered out with company Aug. 27, 1864.
O'Neal, Samuel	do	41	May 2, 1864	100 dys.	Mustered out with company Aug. 27, 1864.
Parker, Silas	do	36	May 2, 1864	100 dys.	Mustered out with company Aug. 27, 1864.
Patterson, John	do	24	May 2, 1864	100 dys.	Mustered out with company Aug. 27, 1864.
Phillips, William	do	32	May 2, 1864	100 dys.	Mustered out with company Aug. 27, 1864.
Plum, Francis	do	41	May 2, 1864	100 dys.	Promoted to Chaplain May 13, 1864.
Plummer, William M.	do	27	May 2, 1864	100 dys.	Mustered out with company Aug. 27, 1864.
Ramagen, Peter	do	43	May 2, 1864	100 dys.	Mustered out with company Aug. 27, 1864.
Russell, Wi[illegible]lar	do	27	May 2, 1864	100 dys.	Mustered out with company Aug. 27, 1864.
Sh[illegible]llenbarger, Shepard	do	18	May 2, 1864	100 dys.	Mustered out with company Aug. 27, 1864.
Shockey, Samuel A.	do	34	May 2, 1864	100 dys.	Mustered out with company Aug. 27, 1864.
Shockey, William C.	do	31	May 2, 1864	100 dys.	Discharged June 18, 1864, on Surgeon's certificate of disability.
Shriner, Uriah	do	[illegible]	May 2, 1864	100 dys.	Mustered out with company Aug. 27, 1864.
Smith, Isaac N.	do	[illegible]	May 2, 1864	100 dys.	Mustered out with company Aug. 27, 1864.
Sproul, Robert	do	[illegible]	May 2, 1864	100 dys.	Mustered out with company Aug. 27, 1864.
Staley, John F.	do	[illegible]	May 2, 1864	100 dys.	Mustered out with company Aug. 27, 1864.
Stevenson, Nelson	do	24	May 2, 1864	100 dys.	Mustered out with company Aug. 27, 1864.
Strawser, Samuel	do	23	May 2, 1864	100 dys.	Mustered out with company Aug. 27, 1864.
Sulliven, James	do	18	May 2, 1864	100 dys.	Mustered out with company Aug. 27, 1864.
Taylor, Isaiah	do	20	May 2, 1864	100 dys.	Mustered out with company Aug. 27, 1864.
Thomas, Griffith	do	[illegible]	May 2, 1864	100 dys.	Mustered out with company Aug. 27, 1864.
Thrailkill, Enos	do	42	May 2, 1864	100 dys.	Mustered out with company Aug. 27, 1864.
Williams, James P.	do	[illegible]	May 2, 1864	100 dys.	Mustered out with company Aug. 27, 1864.
Wonnell, James	do	25	May 2, 1864	100 dys.	Mustered out with company Aug. 27, 1864.

COMPANY E.

Mustered in May 13, 1864, at Camp Chase, O., by H. Douglas, Captain 18th Infantry, U. S. A. Mustered out Aug. 27, 1864, at Camp Chase, O.

Names.	Rank.	Age.	Date of Entering the Service.	Period of Service.	Remarks.
Samuel D. McKee	Captain	[illegible]	May 2, 1864	100 dys.	Mustered out with company Aug. 27, 1864.
John Jennings	1st Lieut.	[illegible]	May 2, 1864	100 dys.	Mustered out with company Aug. 27, 1864.
Amos Critley	2d Lieut.	[illegible]	May 2, 1864	100 dys.	Mustered out with company Aug. 27, 1864.
Alfred J. McKee	1st Sergt.	[illegible]	May 2, 1864	100 dys.	Mustered out with company Aug. 27, 1864.
Andrew L. Rice	Sergeant	[illegible]	May 2, 1864	100 dys.	Mustered out with company Aug. 27, 1864.
Stephen Olmsted	do	[illegible]	May 2, 1864	100 dys.	Mustered out with company Aug. 27, 1864.
Isaac E. Thayer	do	[illegible]	May 2, 1864	100 dys.	Mustered out with company Aug. 27, 1864.
Jesse P. Olmsted	do	[illegible]	May 2, 1864	100 dys.	Mustered out with company Aug. 27, 1864.
Simon W. Cramer	Corporal	[illegible]	May 2, 1864	100 dys.	Mustered out with company Aug. 27, 1864.
Theophilus R. Mayberry	do	[illegible]	May 2, 1864	100 dys.	Mustered out with company Aug. 27, 1864.
Abel Jennings	do	[illegible]	May 2, 1864	100 dys.	Mustered out with company Aug. 27, 1864.
John A. Ruggles	do	[illegible]	May 2, 1864	100 dys.	Mustered out with company Aug. 27, 1864.
Robert W. McKee	do	[illegible]	May 2, 1864	100 dys.	Mustered out with company Aug. 27, 1864.
David P. Wade	do	[illegible]	May 2, 1864	100 dys.	Mustered out with company Aug. 27, 1864.
Lewis Roberts	do	[illegible]	May 2, 1864	100 dys.	Mustered out with company Aug. 27, 1864.
Julius Curtis	do	[illegible]	May 2, 1864	100 dys.	Mustered out with company Aug. 27, 1864.
Benjamin W. Shay	Musician	[illegible]	May 2, 1864	100 dys.	Mustered out with company Aug. 27, 1864.
[illegible] Tippen	do	17	May 2, 1864	100 dys.	Mustered out with company Aug. 27, 1864.
Allison [illegible]	Private	[illegible]	May 2, 1864	100 dys.	Mustered out with company Aug. 27, 1864.
Arnold, Joseph [illegible]	do	18	May 2, 1864	100 dys.	Mustered out with company Aug. 27, 1864.
Barnhard, Leonidas Q.	do	[illegible]	May 2, 1864	100 dys.	Mustered out with company Aug. 27, 1864.
[illegible] M.	do	[illegible]	May 2, 1864	100 dys.	
[illegible] George F.	do	18	May 2, 1864	100 dys.	Mustered out with company Aug. 27, 1864.
Binkley, William	do	[illegible]	May 2, 1864	100 dys.	Mustered out with company Aug. 27, 1864.
Blair, Clement	do	[illegible]	May 2, 1864	100 dys.	Mustered out with company Aug. 27, 1864.
[illegible], Samuel B.	do	[illegible]	May 2, 1864	100 dys.	Discharged June 22, 1864, at Fort Reno, D. C., on Surgeon's certificate of disability.
[illegible], John	do	[illegible]	May 2, 1864	100 dys.	Mustered out with company Aug. 27, 1864.
Campbell, Isaac	do	21	May 2, 1864	100 dys.	Mustered out with company Aug. 27, 1864.
[illegible]	do	[illegible]	May 2, 1864	100 dys.	Mustered out with company Aug. 27, 1864.
[illegible]	do	18	May 2, 1864	100 dys.	Mustered out with company Aug. 27, 1864.
[illegible], Nathaniel	do	[illegible]	May 2, 1864	100 dys.	Mustered out with company Aug. 27, 1864.
[illegible]	do	[illegible]	May 2, 1864	100 dys.	Mustered out with company Aug. 27, 1864.
[illegible]	do	[illegible]	May 2, 1864	100 dys.	Mustered out with company Aug. 27, 1864.
[illegible]	do	[illegible]	May 2, 1864	100 dys.	Mustered out with company Aug. 27, 1864.
[illegible], John S.	do	[illegible]	May 2, 1864	100 dys.	Mustered out with company Aug. 27, 1864.
[illegible]	do	20	May 2, 1864	100 dys.	Mustered out with company Aug. 27, 1864.
[illegible], John R.	do	18	May 2, 1864	100 dys.	Mustered out with company Aug. 27, 1864.
[illegible], George W.	do	24	May 2, 1864	100 dys.	Mustered out with company Aug. 27, 1864.
[illegible]	do	43	May 2, 1864	100 dys.	Mustered out with company Aug. 27, 1864.
[illegible], Samuel	do	21	May 2, 1864	100 dys.	Mustered out with company Aug. 27, 1864.
[illegible], Samuel P.	do	27	May 2, 1864	100 dys.	Mustered out with company Aug. 27, 1864.
[illegible], J.	do	26	May 2, 1864	100 dys.	Mustered out with company Aug. 27, 1864.
[illegible]	do	28	May 2, 1864	100 dys.	Mustered out with company Aug. 27, 1864.

Names.	Rank.	Age.	Date of Entering the Service.	Period of Service.	Remarks.
Eberman, Joseph B.	Private.	18	May 2, 1864	100 dys.	Mustered out with company Aug. 27, 1864.
Elwell, Hiram S.	...do...	30	May 2, 1864	100 dys.	Mustered out with company Aug. 27, 1864.
Evans, Evan	...do...	19	May 2, 1864	100 dys.	Mustered out with company Aug. 27, 1864.
Evans, John E.	...do...	18	May 2, 1864	100 dys.	Discharged June 22, 1864, at Fort Reno, D. C., on Surgeon's certificate of disability.
Evans, Meredith	...do...	34	May 2, 1864	100 dys.	Mustered out with company Aug. 27, 1864.
Ferlel, William	...do...	25	May 2, 1864	100 dys.	Mustered out with company Aug. 27, 1864.
Foster, David H.	...do...	37	May 2, 1864	100 dys.	Mustered out with company Aug. 27, 1864.
Funk, Abraham	...do...	18	May 2, 1864	100 dys.	Mustered out with company Aug. 27, 1864.
Funk, David	...do...	19	May 2, 1864	100 dys.	Mustered out with company Aug. 27, 1864.
Funk, John	...do...	23	May 2, 1864	100 dys.	Mustered out with company Aug. 27, 1864.
Griffith, John H.	...do...	36	May 2, 1864	100 dys.	Mustered out with company Aug. 27, 1864.
Hardesty, Rufus F.	...do...	26	May 2, 1864	100 dys.	Mustered out with company Aug. 27, 1864.
Hughes, John M.	...do...	31	May 2, 1864	100 dys.	Mustered out with company Aug. 27, 1864.
Humphreys, Thomas W.	...do...	27	May 2, 1864	100 dys.	Mustered out with company Aug. 27, 1864.
Jones, Evan W.	...do...	36	May 2, 1864	100 dys.	Mustered out with company Aug. 27, 1864.
Jones, Thomas R.	...do...	37	May 2, 1864	100 dys.	Mustered out with company Aug. 27, 1864.
Jones, William A.	...do...	25	May 2, 1864	100 dys.	Mustered out with company Aug. 27, 1864.
Keith, William	...do...	34	May 2, 1864	100 dys.	Discharged June 22, 1864, at Fort Reno, D. C., on Surgeon's certificate of disability.
Laman, Levi L.	...do...	42	May 2, 1864	100 dys.	Mustered out with company Aug. 27, 1864.
Lones, Theodore H.	...do...	20	May 2, 1864	100 dys.	Mustered out with company Aug. 27, 1864.
McKinney, Daniel	...do...	27	May 2, 1864	100 dys.	Mustered out with company Aug. 27, 1864.
Martin, Jared A.	...do...	42	May 2, 1864	100 dys.	Mustered out with company Aug. 27, 1864.
Miller, Isaac	...do...	30	May 2, 1864	100 dys.	Mustered out with company Aug. 27, 1864.
Morgan, David T.	...do...	18	May 2, 1864	100 dys.	Mustered out with company Aug. 27, 1864.
Morgan, Evan D.	...do...	24	May 2, 1864	100 dys.	Mustered out with company Aug. 27, 1864.
Osman, Aaron J.	...do...	20	May 2, 1864	100 dys.	Mustered out with company Aug. 27, 1864.
Owens, Owen R.	...do...	39	May 2, 1864	100 dys.	Mustered out with company Aug. 27, 1864.
Owens, Richard R.	...do...	27	May 2, 1864	100 dys.	Mustered out with company Aug. 27, 1864.
Paul, Richard	...do...	37	May 2, 1864	100 dys.	Mustered out with company Aug. 27, 1864.
Plumb, Henry L.	...do...	30	May 2, 1864	100 dys.	Mustered out with company Aug. 27, 1864.
Purtill, Patrick	...do...	37	May 2, 1864	100 dys.	Discharged May 13, 1864, at Camp Chase, O., on Surgeon's certificate of disability.
Rees, David	...do...	31	May 2, 1864	100 dys.	Mustered out with company Aug. 27, 1864.
Rees, Thomas	...do...	22	May 2, 1864	100 dys.	Mustered out with company Aug. 27, 1864.
Richards, Thomas	...do...	40	May 2, 1864	100 dys.	Mustered out with company Aug. 27, 1864.
Roberts, David J.	...do...	26	May 2, 1864	100 dys.	Mustered out with company Aug. 27, 1864.
Roberts, Oliver C.	...do...	20	May 2, 1864	100 dys.	Mustered out with company Aug. 27, 1864.
Rumbaugh, William N.	...do...	18	May 2, 1864	100 dys.	Mustered out with company Aug. 27, 1864.
Sheets, Jesse	...do...	25	May 2, 1864	100 dys.	Mustered out with company Aug. 27, 1864.
Sherick, Henry J.	...do...	30	May 2, 1864	100 dys.	Mustered out with company Aug. 27, 1864.
Stevens, William	...do...	18	May 2, 1864	100 dys.	Mustered out with company Aug. 27, 1864.
Stukey, Harvey	...do...	26	May 2, 1864	100 dys.	Mustered out with company Aug. 27, 1864.
Stukey, Levi	...do...	22	May 2, 1864	100 dys.	Mustered out with company Aug. 27, 1864.
Thomas, David	...do...	19	May 2, 1864	100 dys.	Mustered out with company Aug. 27, 1864.
Thomas, John W.	...do...	30	May 2, 1864	100 dys.	Mustered out with company Aug. 27, 1864.
Thomas, Morris	...do...	26	May 2, 1864	100 dys.	Mustered out with company Aug. 27, 1864.
Thomas, William A.	...do...	21	May 2, 1864	100 dys.	Mustered out with company Aug. 27, 1864.
Tunget, Thomas H.	...do...	31	May 2, 1864	100 dys.	Mustered out with company Aug. 27, 1864.
Watkins, Joseph	...do...	33	May 2, 1864	100 dys.	Mustered out with company Aug. 27, 1864.
Weyer, William B.	...do...	19	May 2, 1864	100 dys.	Discharged May 13, 1864, at Camp Chase, O., on Surgeon's certificate of disability.
White, James	...do...	18	May 2, 1864	100 dys.	Mustered out with company Aug. 27, 1864.
Williams, John M.	...do...	20	May 2, 1864	100 dys.	Mustered out with company Aug. 27, 1864.
Williams, Reuben B.	...do...	44	May 2, 1864	100 dys.	Discharged May 13, 1864, at Camp Chase, O., on Surgeon's certificate of disability.
Wilson, Henry	...do...	24	May 2, 1864	100 dys.	Mustered out with company Aug. 27, 1864.
Wollet, Jacob	...do...	20	May 2, 1864	100 dys.	Mustered out with company Aug. 27, 1864.

COMPANY G.

Mustered in May 13, 1864, at Camp Chase, O., by H. Douglas, Captain 18th Infantry, U. S. A. Mustered out Aug. 27, 1864, at Camp Chase, O.

Names.	Rank.	Age.	Date of Entering the Service.	Period of Service.	Remarks.
Uriah Guess	Captain.	28	May 2, 1864	100 dys.	Mustered out with company Aug. 27, 1864.
Manchester H. Devol	1st Lieut.	26	May 2, 1864	100 dys.	Mustered out with company Aug. 27, 1864.
George G. Moore	2d Lieut.	23	May 2, 1864	100 dys.	Mustered out with company Aug. 27, 1864.
Zephaniah S. Drake	1st Sergt.	28	May 2, 1864	100 dys.	Discharged June 14, 1864, at Fort De Russey, D. C., on Surgeon's certificate of disability.
George W. Smith	Sergeant.	30	May 2, 1864	100 dys.	Mustered out with company Aug. 27, 1864.
James Jones	...do...	24	May 2, 1864	100 dys.	Mustered out with company Aug. 27, 1864.
Eaton Smith	...do...	25	May 2, 1864	100 dys.	Mustered out with company Aug. 27, 1864.
Hezekiah T. Sanders	...do...	37	May 2, 1864	100 dys.	Mustered out with company Aug. 27, 1864.
Carrison B. Elsminger	Corporal.	36	May 2, 1864	100 dys.	Mustered out with company Aug. 27, 1864.
Isaac Botts	...do...	33	May 2, 1864	100 dys.	Mustered out with company Aug. 27, 1864.
John Maneoff	...do...	37	May 2, 1864	100 dys.	Mustered out with company Aug. 27, 1864.
Thomas Price	...do...	32	May 2, 1864	100 dys.	Mustered out with company Aug. 27, 1864.
Abram Cook	...do...	28	May 2, 1864	100 dys.	Mustered out with company Aug. 27, 1864.
Ferdinand E. Linn	...do...	37	May 2, 1864	100 dys.	Mustered out with company Aug. 27, 1864.

Names.	Rank.	Age.	Date of entering the service.	Period of service.	Remarks.
[illegible]	Corporal.	23	May 2, 1864	100 dys.	Mustered out with company Aug. 27, 1864.
[illegible]	...do...	22	May 2, 1864	100 dys.	Mustered out with company Aug. 27, 1864.
[illegible]	Wagoner.	41	May 2, 1864	100 dys.	Discharged June 20, 1864, at Fort De Russey, D. C., on Surgeon's certificate of disability.
[illegible]	Private..	27	May 2, 1864	100 dys.	Mustered out with company Aug. 27, 1864.
[illegible]	...do...	20	May 2, 1864	100 dys.	Mustered out with company Aug. 27, 1864.
[illegible] L.	...do...	20	May 2, 1864	100 dys.	Mustered out with company Aug. 27, 1864.
[illegible]	...do...	20	May 2, 1864	100 dys.	Discharged June 20, 1864, at Fort De Russey, D. C., on Surgeon's certificate of disability.
[illegible]	.. ..	18	May 2, 1864	100 dys.	Mustered out with company Aug. 27, 1864.
[illegible]	.. ..	31	May 2, 1864	100 dys.	Mustered out with company Aug. 27, 1864.
[illegible]	.. ..	37	May 2, 1864	100 dys.	Mustered out with company Aug. 27, 1864.
[illegible]	.. ..	44	May 2, 1864	100 dys.	Mustered out with company Aug. 27, 1864.
[illegible]	.. ..	28	May 2, 1864	100 dys.	Mustered out with company Aug. 27, 1864.
[illegible]	.. ..	35	May 2, 1864	100 dys.	Mustered out with company Aug. 27, 1864.
[illegible]	.. ..	26	May 2, 1864	100 dys.	Mustered out with company Aug. 27, 1864.
[illegible]	.. ..	31	May 2, 1864	100 dys.	Mustered out with company Aug. 27, 1864.
[illegible]	.. ..	26	May 2, 1864	100 dys.	Discharged June 14, 1864, at Fort De Russey, D. C., on Surgeon's certificate of disability.
[illegible]		23	May 2, 1864	100 dys.	Mustered out with company Aug. 27, 1864.
[illegible]		28	May 2, 1864	100 dys.	Mustered out with company Aug. 27, 1864.
[illegible]		35	May 2, 1864	100 dys.	Discharged June 14, 1864, at Fort De Russey, D. C., on Surgeon's certificate of disability.
[illegible]vy	...do...	21	May 2, 1864	100 dys.	Mustered out with company Aug. 27, 1864.
[illegible]	...do...	18	May 2, 1864	100 dys.	Mustered out with company Aug. 27, 1864.
[illegible]h S.	...do...	28	May 2, 1864	100 dys.	Mustered out with company Aug. 27, 1864.
[illegible]er	...do...	19	May 2, 1864	100 dys.	Died Aug. 19, 1864, at Fort Simmons, D. C.
[illegible]illiam S.	...do...	20	May 2, 1864	100 dys.	Mustered out with company Aug. 27, 1864.
[illegible]	...do...	21	May 2, 1864	100 dys.	Mustered out with company Aug. 27, 1864.
[illegible]orge	...do...	25	May 2, 1864	100 dys.	Mustered out with company Aug. 27, 1864.
[illegible]	...do...	25	May 2, 1864	100 dys.	Mustered out with company Aug. 27, 1864.
[illegible]	...do...	18	May 2, 1864	100 dys.	Mustered out with company Aug. 27, 1864.
[illegible], Austin	...do...	19	May 2, 1864	100 dys.	Mustered out with company Aug. 27, 1864.
[illegible]	...do...	28	May 2, 1864	100 dys.	Mustered out with company Aug. 27, 1864.
[illegible], Isaac P.	...do...	29	May 2, 1864	100 dys.	Mustered out with company Aug. 27, 1864.
[illegible]amuel	...do...	20	May 2, 1864	100 dys.	Mustered out with company Aug. 27, 1864.
[illegible], Simon	...do...	30	May 2, 1864	100 dys.	On muster-in roll. No further record found.
[illegible]amuel	...do...	38	May 2, 1864	100 dys.	Mustered out with company Aug. 27, 1864.
[illegible]	...do...	24	May 2, 1864	100 dys.	Mustered out with company Aug. 27, 1864.
[illegible]ohn	...do...	20	May 2, 1864	100 dys.	Discharged June 14, 1864, at Fort De Russey, D. C., on Surgeon's certificate of disability.
[illegible], Calvin	...do...	28	May 2, 1864	100 dys.	Mustered out with company Aug. 27, 1864.
[illegible] Joshua	...do...	43	May 2, 1864	100 dys.	Mustered out with company Aug. 27, 1864.
[illegible]emuel	...do...	37	May 2, 1864	100 dys.	Mustered out with company Aug. 27, 1864.
[illegible]siah	...do...	29	May 2, 1864	100 dys.	Mustered out with company Aug. 27, 1864.
[illegible] David	...do...	26	May 2, 1864	100 dys.	Mustered out with company Aug. 27, 1864.
[illegible]bner	...do...	34	May 2, 1864	100 dys.	On muster-in roll. No further record found.
[illegible]orace M.	...do...	38	May 2, 1864	100 dys.	Mustered out with company Aug. 27, 1864.
[illegible], William	...do...	29	May 2, 1864	100 dys.	Mustered out with company Aug. 27, 1864.
[illegible] Joshua	...do...	24	May 2, 1864	100 dys.	Mustered out with company Aug. 27, 1864.
[illegible]illiam	...do...	25	May 2, 1864	100 dys.	Mustered out with company Aug. 27, 1864.
[illegible]d, George	...do...	28	May 2, 1864	100 dys.	Mustered out with company Aug. 27, 1864.
[illegible] Elijah	...do...	18	May 2, 1864	100 dys.	Mustered out with company Aug. 27, 1864.
[illegible] Henry	...do...	39	May 2, 1864	100 dys.	Mustered out with company Aug. 27, 1864.
[illegible] Peter	...do...	30	May 2, 1864	100 dys.	Mustered out with company Aug. 27, 1864.
[illegible] Kingsley	...do...	18	May 2, 1864	100 dys.	Mustered out with company Aug. 27, 1864.
[illegible]ohn	...do...	41	May 2, 1864	100 dys.	Mustered out with company Aug. 27, 1864.
[illegible] John	...do...	29	May 2, 1864	100 dys.	Mustered out with company Aug. 27, 1864.
[illegible] Lorenzo D.	...do...	27	May 2, 1864	100 dys.	Mustered out with company Aug. 27, 1864.
[illegible] John H.	...do...	18	May 2, 1864	100 dys.	On muster in roll. No further record found.
[illegible], Josiah	...do...	38	May 2, 1864	100 dys.	Mustered out with company Aug. 27, 1864.
[illegible], Nathan	...do...	30	May 2, 1864	100 dys.	On muster-in roll. No further record found.
[illegible]h, Cromwell	...do...	21	May 2, 1864	100 dys.	Mustered out with company Aug. 27, 1864.
[illegible]h, David O.	...do...	39	May 2, 1864	100 dys.	Mustered out with company Aug. 27, 1864.
[illegible]timson	...do...	20	May 2, 1864	100 dys.	Mustered out with company Aug. 27, 1864.
[illegible] Marion	...do...	18	May 2, 1864	100 dys.	Mustered out with company Aug. 27, 1864.
[illegible]h, Gilbert	...do...	20	May 2, 1864	100 dys.	Mustered out with company Aug. 27, 1864.
[illegible]h, Samuel	...do...	22	May 2, 1864	100 dys.	Mustered out with company Aug. 27, 1864.
[illegible]cob W.	...do...	19	May 2, 1864	100 dys.	Mustered out with company Aug. 27, 1864.
[illegible]arrison	...do...	23	May 2, 1864	100 dys.	Mustered out with company Aug. 27, 1864.
[illegible] John	...do...	24	May 2, 1864	100 dys.	Mustered out with company Aug. 27, 1864.
[illegible], Obadiah	...do...	18	May 2, 1864	100 dys.	Mustered out with company Aug. 27, 1864.
[illegible]J, George	...do...	18	May 2, 1864	100 dys.	Mustered out with company Aug. 27, 1864.
[illegible] Aaron C.	...do...	37	May 2, 1864	100 dys.	Mustered out with company Aug. 27, 1864.

COMPANY H.

Mustered in May 13, 1864, at Camp Chase, O., by H. Douglas, Captain 18th Infantry, U. S. A. Mustered out Aug. 27, 1864, at Camp Chase, O.

Names.	Rank.	Age.	Date of Entering the Service.	Period of Service.	Remarks.
John Oaks	Captain.	37	May 2, 1864	100 dys.	Mustered out with company Aug. 27, 1864.
James Johnston	1st Lieut.	35	May 2, 1864	100 dys.	Mustered out with company Aug. 27, 1864.
Joshua Chilcote	2d Lieut.	35	May 2, 1864	100 dys.	Mustered out with company Aug. 27, 1864.
John M. Herron	1st Sergt.	38	May 2, 1864	100 dys.	Mustered out with company Aug. 27, 1864.
Jesse C. Allen	Sergeant.	33	May 2, 1864	100 dys.	Mustered out with company Aug. 27, 1864.
Samuel Davidson	....do....	22	May 2, 1864	100 dys.	Mustered out with company Aug. 27, 1864.
Silas Allison	....do....	33	May 2, 1864	100 dys.	Mustered out with company Aug. 27, 1864.
Oliver Oaks	Corporal.	32	May 2, 1864	100 dys.	Appointed June 27, 1864; mustered out with company Aug. 27, 1864.
Samuel Gardner	....do....	27	May 2, 1864	100 dys.	Mustered out with company Aug. 27, 1864.
Aaron Davis	....do....	25	May 2, 1864	100 dys.	Mustered out with company Aug. 27, 1864.
Augustus Floyd	....do....	28	May 2, 1864	100 dys.	Mustered out with company Aug. 27, 1864.
James Hone	....do....	42	May 2, 1864	100 dys.	Discharged June 9, 1864, at Fort Reno, D. C., on Surgeon's certificate of disability.
Bernard Moody	....do....	40	May 2, 1864	100 dys.	Mustered out with company Aug. 27, 1864.
William Stone	....do....	41	May 2, 1864	100 dys.	Discharged May [illegible], 1864, at Camp Chase, O., on Surgeon's certificate of disability.
Samuel Appleman	....do....	25	May 2, 1864	100 dys.	Mustered out with company Aug. 27, 1864.
William H. Everett	....do....	23	May 2, 1864	100 dys.	Appointed ——; mustered out with company Aug. 27, 1864.
Franklin Ramoo	Musician.	17	May 2, 1864	100 dys.	Mustered out with company Aug. 27, 1864.
Bruce F. Green	....do....	20	May 2, 1864	100 dys.	Mustered out with company Aug. 27, 1864.
Albert Pettit	Wagoner.	[illegible]	May 2, 1864	100 dys.	Mustered out with company Aug. 27, 1864.
Allen, Benjamin	Private.	19	May 2, 1864	100 dys.	Mustered out with company Aug. 27, 1864.
Amrine, Harvey	....do....	19	May 2, 1864	100 dys.	Mustered out with company Aug. 27, 1864.
Barran, James	....do....	[illegible]	May 2, 1864	100 dys.	
Bennett, William	....do....	21	May 2, 1864	100 dys.	Mustered out with company Aug. 27, 1864.
Black, James	....do....	[illegible]	May 2, 1864	100 dys.	Mustered out with company Aug. 27, 1864.
Black, Thomas	....do....	37	May 2, 1864	100 dys.	Mustered out with company Aug. 27, 1864.
Blackstone, James	....do....	[illegible]	May 2, 1864	100 dys.	Mustered out with company Aug. 27, 1864.
Bowenos, Samuel J.	....do....	[illegible]	May 2, 1864	100 dys.	Mustered out with company Aug. 27, 1864.
Bowls, Isaac	....do....	25	May 2, 1864	100 dys.	Mustered out with company Aug. 27, 1864.
Brown, Horatio	....do....	18	May 2, 1864	100 dys.	Mustered out with company Aug. 27, 1864.
Camp, Robert	....do....	34	May 2, 1864	100 dys.	Mustered out with company Aug. 27, 1864.
Campbell, John	....do....	22	May 2, 1864	100 dys.	Mustered out with company Aug. 27, 1864.
Crawford, William	....do....	28	May 2, 1864	100 dys.	Died Aug. 17, 1864, at Fort Reno, D. C.
Daley, Jesse W.	....do....	[illegible]	May 2, 1864	100 dys.	Mustered out with company Aug. 27, 1864.
Dalton, William	....do....	42	May 2, 1864	100 dys.	Mustered out with company Aug. 27, 1864.
Darman, John	....do....	[illegible]	May 2, 1864	100 dys.	Mustered out with company Aug. 27, 1864.
Davidson, Richard	....do....	[illegible]	May 2, 1864	100 dys.	Mustered out with company Aug. 27, 1864.
Davis, Sylvester	....do....	[illegible]	May 2, 1864	100 dys.	Mustered out with company Aug. 27, 1864.
Englehardt, William	....do....	[illegible]	May 2, 1864	100 dys.	Mustered out with company Aug. 27, 1864.
Eveland, Samuel	....do....	41	May 2, 1864	100 dys.	Mustered out with company Aug. 27, 1864.
Everett, A[illegible]	....do....	[illegible]	May 2, 1864	100 dys.	Mustered out with company Aug. 27, 1864.
Ford, Francis D.	....do....	27	May 2, 1864	100 dys.	Mustered out with company Aug. 27, 1864.
Galligher, John	....do....	[illegible]	May 2, 1864	100 dys.	Mustered out with company Aug. 27, 1864.
Gardner, Thomas W.	....do....	[illegible]	May 2, 1864	100 dys.	Mustered out with company Aug. 27, 1864.
Glass, James R.	....do....	[illegible]	May 2, 1864	100 dys.	Mustered out with company Aug. 27, 1864.
Gray, Aaron	....do....	27	May 2, 1864	100 dys.	Mustered out with company Aug. 27, 1864.
Griffith, Joshua	....do....	21	May 2, 1864	100 dys.	Discharged June 19, 1864, at Fort Reno, D. C., on Surgeon's certificate of disability.
Hadden, William	....do....	43	May 2, 1864	100 dys.	Mustered out with company Aug. 27, 1864.
Hampshire, John	....do....	33	May 2, 1864	100 dys.	Mustered out with company Aug. 27, 1864.
Higgins, Augustus	....do....	27	May 2, 1864	100 dys.	Mustered out with company Aug. 27, 1864.
Hurl, Samuel	....do....	31	May 2, 1864	100 dys.	Mustered out with company Aug. 27, 1864.
Hutton, George	....do....	27	May 2, 1864	100 dys.	Mustered out with company Aug. 27, 1864.
Hutton, Peter	....do....	21	May 2, 1864	100 dys.	Mustered out with company Aug. 27, 1864.
Johnston, Andrew	....do....	40	May 2, 1864	100 dys.	Mustered out with company Aug. 27, 1864.
Kennedy, John O.	....do....	[illegible]	May 2, 1864	100 dys.	Mustered out with company Aug. 27, 1864; also borne on rolls as John O. [illegible].
Kilbecker, David	....do....	[illegible]	May 2, 1864	100 dys.	Mustered out with company Aug. 27, 1864.
Lehman, Thomas	....do....	20	May 2, 1864	100 dys.	Mustered out with company Aug. 27, 1864.
Lehman, William	....do....	22	May 2, 1864	100 dys.	Mustered out with company Aug. 27, 1864.
Lindsey, James	....do....	[illegible]	May 2, 1864	100 dys.	Mustered out with company Aug. 27, 1864.
Lindsey, Jesse	....do....	[illegible]	May 2, 1864	100 dys.	Mustered out with company Aug. 27, 1864.
Lowery, George	....do....	28	May 2, 1864	100 dys.	Mustered out with company Aug. 27, 1864.
McArthur, John	....do....	[illegible]	May 2, 1864	100 dys.	Mustered out with company Aug. 27, 1864.
Moore, Leonard	....do....	18	May 2, 1864	100 dys.	Mustered out with company Aug. 27, 1864.
Mulett, Thomas	....do....	38	May 2, 1864	100 dys.	Mustered out with company Aug. 27, 1864.
Palmer, John	....do....	28	May 2, 1864	100 dys.	Mustered out with company Aug. 27, 1864.
Parish, Alfred	....do....	25	May 2, 1864	100 dys.	Mustered out with company Aug. 27, 1864.
Pettit, Daniel	....do....	27	May 2, 1864	100 dys.	Mustered out with company Aug. 27, 1864.
Poling, Silas	....do....	40	May 2, 1864	100 dys.	Mustered out with company Aug. 27, 1864.
Price, Franklin	....do....	18	May 2, 1864	100 dys.	Mustered out with company Aug. 27, 1864.
Price, Isaac	....do....	32	May 2, 1864	100 dys.	Mustered out with company Aug. 27, 1864.
Price, John L.	....do....	37	May 2, 1864	100 dys.	Mustered out with company Aug. 27, 1864.

..mes.	Rank.	Age.	Date of Entering the Service.	Period of Service.	Remarks.
..oses	Private..	45	May 2, 1864	100 dys.	Discharged July 30, 1864, at Fort Reno, D. C., on Surgeon's certificate of disability.
..renzo D.	....do....	19	May 2, 1864	100 dys.	Mustered out with company Aug. 27, 1864.
..jamin	....do....	30	May 2, 1864	100 dys.	Reduced from Corporal Aug. 11, 1864; mustered out with company Aug. 27, 1864.
..ther M.	....do....	22	May 2, 1864	100 dys.	Mustered out with company Aug. 27, 1864.
..n A.	....do....	35	May 2, 1864	100 dys.	Reduced from Sergeant Aug. 11, 1864; mustered out with company Aug. 27, 1864.
..mos	....do....	19	May 2, 1864	100 dys.	Mustered out with company Aug. 27, 1864.
..ury	....do....	26	May 2, 1864	100 dys.	Mustered out with company Aug. 27, 1864.
..nard	....do....	22	May 2, 1864	100 dys.	Mustered out with company Aug. 27, 1864.
..aniel	....do....	45	May 2, 1864	100 dys.	Mustered out with company Aug. 27, 1864.
..cob	....do....	42	May 2, 1864	100 dys.	Mustered out with company Aug. 27, 1864.
..er	....do....	21	May 2, 1864	100 dys.	Mustered out with company Aug. 27, 1864.
..annes	....do....	44	May 2, 1864	100 dys.	Discharged June 21, 1864, at Fort Reno, D. C., on Surgeon's certificate of disability.
..obert	....do....	41	May 2, 1864	100 dys.	Mustered out with company Aug. 27, 1864.
.. John	....do....	38	May 2, 1864	100 dys.	Mustered out with company Aug. 27, 1864.
..erick	....do....	20	May 2, 1864	100 dys.	Mustered out with company Aug. 27, 1864.
..iel	....do....	18	May 2, 1864	100 dys.	Mustered out with company Aug. 27, 1864.
..niel	....do....	44	May 2, 1864	100 dys.	Mustered out with company Aug. 27, 1864.

COMPANY I.

..n May 13, 1864, at Camp Chase, O., by H. Douglas, Captain 18th Infantry, U. S. A. Mustered out Aug. 27, 1864, at Camp Chase, O.

Names.	Rank.	Age.	Date of Entering the Service.	Period of Service.	Remarks.
..ney	Captain.	27	May 2, 1864	100 dys.	Mustered out with company Aug. 27, 1864.
.. Wiggins	1st Lieut.	28	May 2, 1864	100 dys.	Mustered out with company Aug. 27, 1864.
..owe	2d Lieut.	29	May 2, 1864	100 dys.	Mustered out with company Aug. 27, 1864.
..d	1st Sergt.	28	May 2, 1864	100 dys.	Mustered out with company Aug. 27, 1864.
.. Lowe	Sergeant.	25	May 2, 1864	100 dys.	Mustered out with company Aug. 27, 1864.
..y	....do....	32	May 2, 1864	100 dys.	Mustered out with company Aug. 27, 1864.
..s	....do....	26	May 2, 1864	100 dys.	Mustered out with company Aug. 27, 1864.
..Eggleston	....do....	20	May 2, 1864	100 dys.	Mustered out with company Aug. 27, 1864.
..mos	Corporal.	44	May 2, 1864	100 dys.	Mustered out with company Aug. 27, 1864.
..r	....do....	31	May 2, 1864	100 dys.	Mustered out with company Aug. 27, 1864.
..	....do....	42	May 2, 1864	100 dys.	Mustered out with company Aug. 27, 1864.
..ins	....do....	25	May 2, 1864	100 dys.	Mustered out with company Aug. 27, 1864.
..er	....do....	39	May 2, 1864	100 dys.	Mustered out with company Aug. 27, 1864.
..y	....do....	36	May 2, 1864	100 dys.	Mustered out with company Aug. 27, 1864.
..mes	....do....	25	May 2, 1864	100 dys.	Mustered out with company Aug. 27, 1864.
..iger	....do....	21	May 2, 1864	100 dys.	Mustered out with company Aug. 27, 1864.
.. Campbell	Musician	21	May 2, 1864	100 dys.	Mustered out with company Aug. 27, 1864.
..s	....do....	27	May 2, 1864	100 dys.	Mustered out with company Aug. 27, 1864.
..mael	Private..	18	May 2, 1864	100 dys.	Transferred from Co. C May 13, 1864; mustered out with company Aug. 27, 1864.
..	....do....	21	May 2, 1864	100 dys.	Mustered out with company Aug. 27, 1864.
..h	....do....	[illegible]	May 2, 1864	100 dys.	Mustered out with company Aug. 27, 1864.
..ner, Adam C.	....do....	28	May 2, 1864	100 dys.	Transferred from Co. A —; mustered out with company Aug. 27, 1864.
.. Warren	....do....	44	May 2, 1864	100 dys.	Mustered out with company Aug. 27, 1864.
..as S.	....do....	24	May 2, 1864	100 dys.	Mustered out with company Aug. 27, 1864.
..ussell	....do....	24	May 2, 1864	100 dys.	Mustered out with company Aug. 27, 1864.
.. K.	....do....	27	May 2, 1864	100 dys.	Mustered out with company Aug. 27, 1864.
.. L. C.	....do....	27	May 2, 1864	100 dys.	Mustered out with company Aug. 27, 1864.
..n	....do....	18	May 2, 1864	100 dys.	Mustered out with company Aug. 27, 1864.
.. Peter	....do....	38	May 2, 1864	100 dys.	Mustered out with company Aug. 27, 1864.
.. M.	....do....	31	May 2, 1864	100 dys.	Mustered out with company Aug. 27, 1864.
..id	....do....	18	May 2, 1864	100 dys.	Mustered out with company Aug. 27, 1864.
..ms	....do....	40	May 2, 1864	100 dys.	Mustered out with company Aug. 27, 1864.
..jamin	....do....	21	May 2, 1864	100 dys.	Mustered out with company Aug. 27, 1864.
..h	....do....	29	May 2, 1864	100 dys.	Mustered out with company Aug. 27, 1864.
..ry	....do....	25	May 2, 1864	100 dys.	Mustered out with company Aug. 27, 1864.
..mos D.	....do....	34	May 2, 1864	100 dys.	Mustered out with company Aug. 27, 1864.
..mes	....do....	38	May 2, 1864	100 dys.	Mustered out with company Aug. 27, 1864.
.. M.	....do....	24	May 2, 1864	100 dys.	Mustered out with company Aug. 27, 1864.
..ry	....do....	32	May 2, 1864	100 dys.	Mustered out with company Aug. 27, 1864.
..nzo C.	....do....	19	May 2, 1864	100 dys.	Mustered out with company Aug. 27, 1864.
..Samuel	....do....	18	May 2, 1864	100 dys.	Mustered out with company Aug. 27, 1864.
..William C.	....do....	21	May 2, 1864	100 dys.	Mustered out with company Aug. 27, 1864.
..Stephen	....do....	42	May 2, 1864	100 dys.	Mustered out with company Aug. 27, 1864.
..win	....do....	28	May 2, 1864	100 dys.	Transferred from Co. C May 13, 1864. No further record found.
..cob	....do....	42	May 2, 1864	100 dys.	Mustered out with company Aug. 27, 1864.
..seph	....do....	28	May 2, 1864	100 dys.	Mustered out with company Aug. 27, 1864.
..y	....do....	..	May 2, 1864	100 dys.	Mustered out with company Aug. 27, 1864.
..	....do....	44	May 2, 1864	100 dys.	Died July 7, 1864, at Fort De Russey, D. C.
..land Q.	....do....	19	May 2, 1864	100 dys.	Mustered out with company Aug. 27, 1864.
.. F.	....do....	20	May 2, 1864	100 dys.	Mustered out with company Aug. 27, 1864.

Names.	Rank.	Age.	Date of Entering the Service.	Period of Service.	Remarks.
Huffines, Joseph	Private..	37	May 2, 1864	100 dys.	Mustered out with company Aug. 27, 1864.
Hunter, Curtis	...do....	20	May 2, 1864	100 dys.	Mustered out with company Aug. 27, 1864.
Ingmire, Franklin	...do....	29	May 2, 1864	100 dys.	Mustered out with company Aug. 27, 1864.
Ingmire, Robert L	...do....	32	May 2, 1864	100 dys.	Mustered out with company Aug. 27, 1864.
Kelen, Horatio G	...do....	27	May 2, 1864	100 dys.	Mustered out with company Aug. 27, 1864.
Krion, Daniel	...do....	21	May 2, 1864	100 dys.	Mustered out with company Aug. 27, 1864.
McKean, Alfred	...do....	33	May 2, 1864	100 dys.	Mustered out with company Aug. 27, 1864.
Miets, Isaac	...do....	28	May 2, 1864	100 dys.	Discharged June 22, 1864, on Surgeon's certificate of disability.
Miller, Jonathan	...do....	27	May 2, 1864	100 dys.	Mustered out with company Aug. 27, 1864.
Mitchell, Basil	...do....	34	May 2, 1864	100 dys.	Mustered out with company Aug. 27, 1864.
Mitchell, Charles	...do....	18	May 2, 1864	100 dys.	Mustered out with company Aug. 27, 1864.
Mitchell, Elisha	...do....	18	May 2, 1864	100 dys.	Mustered out with company Aug. 27, 1864.
Mitchell, William	...do....	46	May 2, 1864	100 dys.	Mustered out with company Aug. 27, 1864.
Moore, Michael	...do....	46	May 2, 1864	100 dys.	Mustered out with company Aug. 27, 1864.
Morse, James	...do....	19	May 2, 1864	100 dys.	Mustered out with company Aug. 27, 1864.
Morse, Seth	...do....	26	May 2, 1864	100 dys.	Mustered out with company Aug. 27, 1864.
Neise, Harvey	...do....	18	May 2, 1864	100 dys.	Mustered out with company Aug. 27, 1864.
Odell, William W.	...do....	42	May 2, 1864	100 dys.	Discharged June 19, 1864, on Surgeon's certificate of disability.
Parrott, John	...do....	41	May 2, 1864	100 dys.	Transferred from Co. A ——; mustered out with company Aug. 27, 1864.
Peddycoart, John S	...do....	32	May 2, 1864	100 dys.	Mustered out with company Aug. 27, 1864.
Poland, Robert H	...do....	18	May 2, 1864	100 dys.	Mustered out with company Aug. 27, 1864.
Primmer, Abraham	...do....	42	May 2, 1864	100 dys.	Mustered out with company Aug. 27, 1864.
Reynolds, John W	...do....	23	May 2, 1864	100 dys.	Mustered out with company Aug. 27, 1864.
Robinson, Joseph	...do....	20	May 2, 1864	100 dys.	Mustered out with company Aug. 27, 1864.
Rouse, Benjamin	...do....	22	May 2, 1864	100 dys.	Mustered out with company Aug. 27, 1864.
Smyers, James K	...do....	18	May 2, 1864	100 dys.	Mustered out with company Aug. 27, 1864.
Smyers, John	...do....	37	May 2, 1864	100 dys.	Mustered out with company Aug. 27, 1864.
Snider, Jacob	...do....	23	May 2, 1864	100 dys.	Mustered out with company Aug. 27, 1864.
Springer, John M	...do....	34	May 2, 1864	100 dys.	Mustered out with company Aug. 27, 1864.
Stockdale, Robert	...do....	41	May 2, 1864	100 dys.	Mustered out with company Aug. 27, 1864.
Tombleson, John	...do....	35	May 2, 1864	100 dys.	Mustered out with company Aug. 27, 1864.
Traut, Jacob	...do....	40	May 2, 1864	100 dys.	Mustered out with company Aug. 27, 1864.
Whitcraft, George D	...do....	22	May 2, 1864	100 dys.	Mustered out with company Aug. 27, 1864.
Whitcraft, Isaac	...do....	30	May 2, 1864	100 dys.	Died Aug. 15, 1864, at Fort De Russey, D. C.
Whitcraft, John L	...do....	27	May 2, 1864	100 dys.	Mustered out with company Aug. 27, 1864.
Wiggins, George	...do....	43	May 2, 1864	100 dys.	Mustered out with company Aug. 27, 1864.
Williams, Lafayette	...do....	20	May 2, 1864	100 dys.	Mustered out with company Aug. 27, 1864.
Wolf, Edmond	...do....	24	May 2, 1864	100 dys.	Mustered out with company Aug. 27, 1864.
Yoas, Earnes	...do....	36	May 2, 1864	100 dys.	Mustered out with company Aug. 27, 1864.

COMPANY K.

Mustered in May 13, 1864, at Camp Chase, O., by H. Douglas, Captain 18th Infantry, U. S. A. Mustered out Aug. 27, 1864, at Camp Chase, O.

Names.	Rank.	Age.	Date of Entering the Service.	Period of Service.	Remarks.
Gilruth M. Webb	Captain.	53	May 2, 1864	100 dys.	Mustered out with company Aug. 27, 1864.
Anthony G. Walker	1st Lieut.	38	May 2, 1864	100 dys.	Mustered out with company Aug. 27, 1864.
Edward P. Strong	2d Lieut.	24	May 2, 1864	100 dys.	Mustered out with company Aug. 27, 1864.
Charles W. James, Jr.	1st Sergt.	26	May 2, 1864	100 dys.	Mustered out with company Aug. 27, 1864.
Thomas J. Cline	Sergeant.	25	May 2, 1864	100 dys.	Mustered out with company Aug. 27, 1864.
Nathaniel Troy	...do....	30	May 2, 1864	100 dys.	Mustered out with company Aug. 27, 1864.
James Meldrim	...do....	31	May 2, 1864	100 dys.	Mustered out with company Aug. 27, 1864.
James Pleukharp	...do....	30	May 2, 1864	100 dys.	Mustered out with company Aug. 27, 1864.
Ephraim Sigman	Corporal.	31	May 2, 1864	100 dys.	Mustered out with company Aug. 27, 1864.
Otho Kanode	...do....	38	May 2, 1864	100 dys.	Mustered out with company Aug. 27, 1864.
Wesley C. Fickle	...do....	19	May 2, 1864	100 dys.	Mustered out with company Aug. 27, 1864.
Peter Kittsmiller	...do....	40	May 2, 1864	100 dys.	Mustered out with company Aug. 27, 1864.
William M. Oaks	...do....	28	May 2, 1864	100 dys.	Mustered out with company Aug. 27, 1864.
John Funk	...do....	28	May 2, 1864	100 dys.	Mustered out with company Aug. 27, 1864.
John Deffenbaugh	...do....	28	May 2, 1864	100 dys.	Mustered out with company Aug. 27, 1864.
John J. Webb	...do....	21	May 2, 1864	100 dys.	Mustered out with company Aug. 27, 1864.
John T. Sangerson	Musician.	19	May 2, 1864	100 dys.	Promoted to Principal Musician May 13, 1864
Joseph A. Nail	...do....	18	May 2, 1864	100 dys.	Mustered out with company Aug. 27, 1864.
Jackson Mosure	Wagoner.	23	May 2, 1864	100 dys.	Mustered out with company Aug. 27, 1864.
Allen, Isaac	Private..	18	May 2, 1864	100 dys.	Mustered out with company Aug. 27, 1864.
Allen, James W	...do....	27	May 2, 1864	100 dys.	Mustered out with company Aug. 27, 1864.
Austin, James	...do....	20	May 2, 1864	100 dys.	Mustered out with company Aug. 27, 1864.
Baker, John	...do....	18	May 2, 1864	100 dys.	Mustered out with company Aug. 27, 1864.
Banks, Benjamin	...do....	44	May 2, 1864	100 dys.	Mustered out with company Aug. 27, 1864.
Bennett, Clinton	...do....	39	May 2, 1864	100 dys.	Mustered out with company Aug. 27, 1864.
Bennett, Leroy	...do....	18	May 2, 1864	100 dys.	Mustered out with company Aug. 27, 1864.
Blosse, Lewis	...do....	34	May 2, 1864	100 dys.	Mustered out with company Aug. 27, 1864.
Brown, Thomas H	...do....	39	May 2, 1864	100 dys.	Mustered out with company Aug. 27, 1864.
Butin, Jesse B	...do....	18	May 2, 1864	100 dys.	Mustered out with company Aug. 27,
Cline, Daniel W	...do....	28	May 2, 1864	100 dys.	Mustered out with company Aug. 27,
Collins, Isaac	...do....	18	May 2, 1864	100 dys.	Mustered out with company Aug. 27,
Collins, William	...do....	22	May 2, 1864	100 dys.	Died Aug. 4, 1864, at Washington, D

Names.	Rank.	Age.	Date of Entering the Service.	Period of Service.	Remarks.
Crawford, James	Private	19	May 2, 1864	100 dys.	Mustered out with company Aug. 27, 1864.
Crawford, John W	do	24	May 2, 1864	100 dys.	Mustered out with company Aug. 27, 1864.
Crosby,		40	May 2, 1864	100 dys.	Mustered out with company Aug. 27, 1864.
Crosby,		33	May 2, 1864	100 dys.	Mustered out with company Aug. 27, 1864.
Croy, Richard	do	31	May 2, 1864	100 dys.	Mustered out with company Aug. 27, 1864.
Davis, John R.	do	31	May 2, 1864	100 dys.	Mustered out with company Aug. 27, 1864.
Dewar, John	do	21	May 2, 1864	100 dys.	Mustered out with company Aug. 27, 1864.
Donaldson, Gilbert A	do	30	May 2, 1864	100 dys.	Mustered out with company Aug. 27, 1864.
Eby, Henry	do	18	May 2, 1864	100 dys.	Mustered out with company Aug. 27, 1864.
Friesner, John	do	18	May 2, 1864	100 dys.	Mustered out with company Aug. 27, 1864.
Funk, Adam	do	23	May 2, 1864	100 dys.	Mustered out with company Aug. 27, 1864.
Gage, George G	do	19	May 2, 1864	100 dys.	Mustered out with company Aug. 27, 1864.
Gibson, Isaiah	do	32	May 2, 1864	100 dys.	Mustered out with company Aug. 27, 1864.
Goodwin, Lyman	do	30	May 2, 1864	100 dys.	Mustered out with company Aug. 27, 1864.
	do	32	May 2, 1864	100 dys.	Mustered out with company Aug. 27, 1864.
	do	26	May 2, 1864	100 dys.	Mustered out with company Aug. 27, 1864.
	do	35	May 2, 1864	100 dys.	Mustered out with company Aug. 27, 1864.
Harris, Daniel	do	26	May 2, 1864	100 dys.	Mustered out with company Aug. 27, 1864.
Henderson, John C	do	31	May 2, 1864	100 dys.	Mustered out with company Aug. 27, 1864.
James, Henry	do	18	May 2, 1864	100 dys.	Mustered out with company Aug. 27, 1864.
James, Thomas E	do	20	May 2, 1864	100 dys.	Mustered out with company Aug. 27, 1864.
Judkins, Joel	do	40	May 2, 1864	100 dys.	Mustered out with company Aug. 27, 1864.
Kittsmiller, Benjamin F	do	32	May 2, 1864	100 dys.	Mustered out with company Aug. 27, 1864.
Linton, William F	do	25	May 2, 1864	100 dys.	Mustered out with company Aug. 27, 1864.
Lytle, Peter	do	24	May 2, 1864	100 dys.	Mustered out with company Aug. 27, 1864.
McFadden, Isaac G	do	25	May 2, 1864	100 dys.	Mustered out with company Aug. 27, 1864.
McGravey, James	do	23	May 2, 1864	100 dys.	Mustered out with company Aug. 27, 1864.
McKinley, Edward	do	33	May 2, 1864	100 dys.	Mustered out with company Aug. 27, 1864.
McKinley, James	do	21	May 2, 1864	100 dys.	Mustered out with company Aug. 27, 1864.
McKinley, William	do	29	May 2, 1864	100 dys.	Mustered out with company Aug. 27, 1864.
Montgomery, William M	do	28	May 2, 1864	100 dys.	Mustered out with company Aug. 27, 1864.
Moore, Eli James	do	20	May 2, 1864	100 dys.	Mustered out with company Aug. 27, 1864.
Myers, Jacob J	do	18	May 2, 1864	100 dys.	Mustered out with company Aug. 27, 1864.
Orr, William C	do	23	May 2, 1864	100 dys.	Mustered out with company Aug. 27, 1864.
Palmer, James	do	31	May 2, 1864	100 dys.	Mustered out with company Aug. 27, 1864.
Palmer, William	do	26	May 2, 1864	100 dys.	Mustered out with company Aug. 27, 1864.
Polling, John	do	18	May 2, 1864	100 dys.	Mustered out with company Aug. 27, 1864.
Polling, William	do	26	May 2, 1864	100 dys.	Mustered out with company Aug. 27, 1864.
Rathburn, Elliott	do	18	May 2, 1864	100 dys.	Mustered out with company Aug. 27, 1864.
Rochester, John C	do	36	May 2, 1864	100 dys.	Mustered out with company Aug. 27, 1864.
Rodman, Isaac	do	18	May 2, 1864	100 dys.	Mustered out with company Aug. 27, 1864.
Ross, James	do	31	May 2, 1864	100 dys.	Discharged June 25, 1864, at Fort Reno, D. C., on Surgeon's certificate of disability.
Rowe, Francis M	do	26	May 2, 1864	100 dys.	Mustered out with company Aug. 27, 1864.
Sanderson, Richard C	do	18	May 2, 1864	100 dys.	Mustered out with company Aug. 27, 1864.
Sheets, John	do	38	May 2, 1864	100 dys.	Mustered out with company Aug. 27, 1864.
Smith, John L.	do	33	May 2, 1864	100 dys.	Mustered out with company Aug. 27, 1864.
Sudlow, Jesse	do	30	May 2, 1864	100 dys.	Mustered out with company Aug. 27, 1864.
Tannyhill, John	do	39	May 2, 1864	100 dys.	Mustered out with company Aug. 27, 1864.
Webb, Charles T	do	21	May 2, 1864	100 dys.	Mustered out with company Aug. 27, 1864.
Webb, DeWitt	do	25	May 2, 1864	100 dys.	Promoted to Hospital Steward May 13, 1864.
Webby, William	do	30	May 2, 1864	100 dys.	Mustered out with company Aug. 27, 1864.
Westenhaver, William	do	32	May 2, 1864	100 dys.	Mustered out with company Aug. 27, 1864.
Woodard, John	do	29	May 2, 1864	100 dys.	Mustered out with company Aug. 27, 1864.
Work, Robert R	do	31	May 2, 1864	100 dys.	Mustered out with company Aug. 27, 1864.

152nd Regiment Ohio Volunteer Infantry.

ONE HUNDRED DAYS' SERVICE.

This Regiment was organized at Camp Dennison, O., from the 8th to the 11th of May, 1864, to serve one hundred days. It was composed of the Twenty-eighth Regiment, Ohio National Guard, from Darke County, and two companies of the Thirty-fifth Regiment, Ohio National Guard, from Clarke County. The One Hundred and Fifty-second left Camp Dennison about the middle of May, 1864, and on its arrival at New Creek, W. Va., went into camp, where it performed guard and picket duty. From New Creek the Regiment marched to Martinsburg, and on the 4th of June started for the front. It reached Beverly, Va., on the 27th of June. During this march the Regiment was twice attacked by the Rebels. After resting a couple of days at Beverly the Regiment started for Cumberland, Md., where it arrived on the 2d of July. From here detachments were sent to various points. They returned to Cumberland about the last of July, where they remained until the Regiment received orders to return home. On the 25th of August the One Hundred and Fifty-second left Cumberland for Camp Dennison, where it arrived on the morning of the 28th. It was mustered out Sept. 2, 1864, on expiration of its term of service.

152ND REGIMENT OHIO VOLUNTEER INFANTRY.

FIELD AND STAFF.

Mustered in May 11, 1864, at Camp Dennison, O., by Robert S. Smith, Captain 2d Cavalry, U. S. A. Mustered out Sept. 2, 1864, at Camp Dennison, O., by L. H. Warner, 1st Lieutenant 17th Infantry, U. S. A.

Names.	Rank.	Age.	Date of Entering the service.	Period of Service.	Remarks.
David Putman	Colonel.	43	May 2, 1864	100 dys.	Mustered out with regiment Sept. 2, 1864.
Edward M. Doty	Lt. Col.	45	May 2, 1864	100 dys.	Mustered out with regiment Sept. 2, 1864.
John H. Hunter	Major.	[illegible]	May 2, 1864	100 dys.	Mustered out with regiment Sept. 2, 1864.
John C. Williamson	Surgeon	37	May 2, 1864	100 dys.	Mustered out with regiment Sept. 2, 1864.
John A. Jobes	Ast. Surg.	27	May 2, 1864	100 dys.	Mustered out with regiment Sept. 2, 1864.
Edwin B. Putman	Adjutant	[illegible]	May 2, 1864	100 dys.	Mustered out with regiment Sept. 2, 1864.
Jacob W. Shively	R. Q. M.	40	May 2, 1864	100 dys.	Mustered out with regiment Sept. 2, 1864.
Thomas S. Guthrie	Chaplain	33	May 2, 1864	100 dys.	Promoted from private Co. B May [illegible], 1864; mustered out with regiment Sept. 2, 1864.
John Beers	Ser. Maj.	[illegible]	May 2, 1864	100 dys.	Mustered out with regiment Sept. 2, 1864.
William H. McGuire	Q. M. S.	[illegible]	May 2, 1864	100 dys.	Mustered out with regiment Sept. 2, 1864.
James Werts	Com. Ser.	[illegible]	May 2, 1864	100 dys.	Mustered out with regiment Sept. 2, 1864.
Paul H. Larsh	Hos. Std.	[illegible]	May 2, 1864	100 dys.	[illegible] May [illegible], 1864; mustered out with regiment Sept. 2, 1864.
[illegible] L. Elliott	Prin. Mus.	[illegible]	May 2, 1864	100 dys.	[illegible] May [illegible], 1864; mustered out with regiment Sept. 2, 1864.

COMPANY A.

Mustered in May [illegible], 1864, at Camp Dennison, O., by [illegible] U. S. A. Mustered out Sept. [illegible], 1864, at Camp Dennison, O., by L. H. Warner, 1st Lieutenant 17th Infantry, U. S. A.

Names.	Rank.	Age.	Date of Entering the service.	Period of Service.	Remarks.
Amos L. [illegible]	[illegible]	[illegible]	[illegible]	[illegible]	[illegible] 1864.
James [illegible]	[illegible]	[illegible]	[illegible]	[illegible]	[illegible]
Jesse [illegible]	[illegible]	[illegible]	[illegible]	[illegible]	[illegible]
George W. [illegible]	[illegible]	[illegible]	[illegible]	[illegible]	[illegible]
[illegible]	[illegible]	[illegible]	[illegible]	[illegible]	[illegible]
James A. [illegible]	[illegible]	[illegible]	[illegible]	[illegible]	[illegible]
Peter [illegible] Van [illegible]	[illegible]	[illegible]	[illegible]	[illegible]	[illegible]
William H. [illegible]	[illegible]	[illegible]	[illegible]	[illegible]	[illegible]
[illegible] L. Wills	Corporal	[illegible]	[illegible]	[illegible]	[illegible]
Levi Sharp	[illegible]	[illegible]	[illegible]	[illegible]	[illegible]
Daniel P. Albright	[illegible]	[illegible]	[illegible]	[illegible]	[illegible]
Andrew Stevenson	[illegible]	[illegible]	[illegible]	[illegible]	[illegible]
James H. [illegible]	[illegible]	[illegible]	[illegible]	[illegible]	[illegible]
David Bennett	do.	[illegible]	[illegible]	[illegible]	[illegible]
Solomon [illegible]	[illegible]	[illegible]	[illegible]	[illegible]	[illegible]
Cornelius W. Van [illegible]	do.	[illegible]	May [illegible]	[illegible]	[illegible]
Baker [illegible]	Musician	[illegible]	May 2, 1864	[illegible]	[illegible]
Daniel [illegible]	[illegible]	[illegible]	May 2, 1864	[illegible]	[illegible]
Addington, Isaac H.	Private	[illegible]	[illegible]	[illegible]	[illegible]
Albright, Allen	do.	[illegible]	[illegible]	[illegible]	[illegible]
Albright, Henderson L.	do.	[illegible]	[illegible]	[illegible]	[illegible]
Albright, Henry M.	do.	[illegible]	[illegible]	[illegible]	[illegible]
Albright, Johnson K.	do.	[illegible]	[illegible]	[illegible]	[illegible]
Anderson, Benjamin F.	do.	[illegible]	[illegible]	[illegible]	[illegible]
[illegible], William	do.	[illegible]	[illegible]	[illegible]	[illegible]
[illegible], James L.	do.	[illegible]	[illegible]	[illegible]	Mustered out with [illegible]
Bennett, Joseph S.	do.	[illegible]	[illegible]	[illegible]	Mustered out with [illegible]
[illegible], David W.	do.	[illegible]	May [illegible]	[illegible]	[illegible]
[illegible], Reuben B.	do.	[illegible]	May [illegible]	[illegible]	[illegible]
Brock, Allen	do.	[illegible]	[illegible]	100 dys.	[illegible]
Brock, Daniel	do.	[illegible]	[illegible]	[illegible]	Mustered out with company Sept. 2, 1864.
Caywood, William	do.	37	May 2, 1864	100 dys.	Mustered out with company Sept. 2, 1864.

Names.	Rank.	Age.	Date of Entering the Service.	Period of Service.	Remarks.
Clark, Andrew	Private	34	May 2, 1864	100 dys.	Reduced from Corporal May 15, 1864; mustered out with company Sept. 2, 1864.
Colvill, James H.	do.	19	May 2, 1864	100 dys.	Mustered out with company Sept. 2, 1864.
Colvill, John S.	do.	40	May 2, 1864	100 dys.	Mustered out with company Sept. 2, 1864.
Colvill, Martin J.	do.	34	May 2, 1864	100 dys.	Mustered out with company Sept. 2, 1864.
Colvill, Vivian	do.	22	May 2, 1864	100 dys.	Mustered out with company Sept. 2, 1864.
Condon, John	do.	36	May 2, 1864	100 dys.	Mustered out with company Sept. 2, 1864.
Cooper, William	do.	45	May 2, 1864	100 dys.	Mustered out with company Sept. 2, 1864.
Creeger, George	do.	29	May 2, 1864	100 dys.	Mustered out with company Sept. 2, 1864.
Cromwell, William W.	do.	26	May 2, 1864	100 dys.	Mustered out with company Sept. 2, 1864.
Davis, William	do.	42	May 2, 1864	100 dys.	Mustered out with company Sept. 2, 1864.
Eichelbarger, John	do.	24	May 2, 1864	100 dys.	Mustered out with company Sept. 2, 1864.
Engle, Peter	do.	18	May 2, 1864	100 dys.	Mustered out with company Sept. 2, 1864.
Fellers, Harvey	do.	20	May 2, 1864	100 dys.	Mustered out with company Sept. 2, 1864.
Fellers, William H.	do.	23	May 2, 1864	100 dys.	Left sick in hospital at Camp Dennison, O., May 12, 1864. No further record found.
Fisher, Isaiah	do.	18	May 2, 1864	100 dys.	Mustered out with company Sept. 2, 1864.
Foreman, George W.	do.	22	May 2, 1864	100 dys.	Mustered out with company Sept. 2, 1864.
Galbreath, Perry	do.	20	May 2, 1864	100 dys.	Mustered out with company Sept. 2, 1864.
Garland, Daniel	do.	34	May 2, 1864	100 dys.	Mustered out with company Sept. 2, 1864.
Graum, Adam	do.	18	May 2, 1864	100 dys.	Died May 29, 1864, at New Creek, W. Va.
Gunder, Daniel	do.	18	May 2, 1864	100 dys.	Mustered out with company Sept. 2, 1864.
Hefleinger, Cyrus J.	do.	31	May 2, 1864	100 dys.	Mustered out with company Sept. 2, 1864.
House, John	do.	55	May 2, 1864	100 dys.	Mustered out with company Sept. 2, 1864.
Huffer, Francis M.	do.	26	May 2, 1864	100 dys.	Mustered out with company Sept. 2, 1864.
Huffer, Simon S.	do.	28	May 2, 1864	100 dys.	Mustered out with company Sept. 2, 1864.
Jones, Alonzo	do.	19	May 2, 1864	100 dys.	Mustered out with company Sept. 2, 1864.
Keys, John	do.	38	May 2, 1864	100 dys.	Mustered out with company Sept. 2, 1864.
Kilby, Horatio S.	do.	31	May 2, 1864	100 dys.	Mustered out with company Sept. 2, 1864.
Lansdown, James M.	do.	18	May 2, 1864	100 dys.	Mustered out with company Sept. 2, 1864.
Meats, Levi	do.	20	May 2, 1864	100 dys.	Mustered out with company Sept. 2, 1864.
Perkins, Elias S.	do.	33	May 2, 1864	100 dys.	Mustered out with company Sept. 2, 1864.
Price, John G.	do.	43	May 2, 1864	100 dys.	Mustered out with company Sept. 2, 1864.
Ratcliff, Joseph M.	do.	18	May 2, 1864	100 dys.	Mustered out with company Sept. 2, 1864.
Read, John, Jr.	do.	18	May 2, 1864	100 dys.	Mustered out with company Sept. 2, 1864.
Reed, John, Sr.	do.	35	May 2, 1864	100 dys.	Mustered out with company Sept. 2, 1864.
Ridenour, William	do.	19	May 2, 1864	100 dys.	Mustered out with company Sept. 2, 1864.
Roser, William H.	do.	26	May 2, 1864	100 dys.	Mustered out with company Sept. 2, 1864.
Rynearson, Stroud	do.	20	May 2, 1864	100 dys.	Mustered out with company Sept. 2, 1864.
Sharp, John	do.	58	May 2, 1864	100 dys.	Mustered out with company Sept. 2, 1864.
Snodderly, William H.	do.	18	May 2, 1864	100 dys.	Mustered out with company Sept. 2, 1864.
Sprecher, Benjamin F.	do.	18	May 2, 1864	100 dys.	Mustered out with company Sept. 2, 1864.
Stevenson, William	do.	39	May 2, 1864	100 dys.	Mustered out with company Sept. 2, 1864.
Studebaker, David	do.	30	May 2, 1864	100 dys.	Mustered out with company Sept. 2, 1864.
Swank, Jabez	do.	25	May 2, 1864	100 dys.	Mustered out with company Sept. 2, 1864.
Thatcher, Elijah	do.	25	May 2, 1864	100 dys.	Mustered out with company Sept. 2, 1864.
Thatcher, George	do.	32	May 2, 1864	100 dys.	Mustered out with company Sept. 2, 1864.
Trump, Uriah	do.	27	May 2, 1864	100 dys.	Mustered out with company Sept. 2, 1864.
Trump, William H.	do.	26	May 2, 1864	100 dys.	Mustered out with company Sept. 2, 1864.
Warner, Samuel	do.	18	May 2, 1864	100 dys.	Mustered out with company Sept. 2, 1864.
Weaver, Daniel	do.	39	May 2, 1864	100 dys.	Mustered out with company Sept. 2, 1864.
Weaver, William	do.	19	May 2, 1864	100 dys.	Mustered out with company Sept. 2, 1864.
Wooten, Moses	do.	19	May 2, 1864	100 dys.	Mustered out with company Sept. 2, 1864.

COMPANY B.

Mustered in May 8, 1864, at Camp Dennison, O., by Robert S. Smith, Captain 2d Cavalry, U. S. A. Mustered out Sept. 2, 1864, at Camp Dennison, O., by L. H. Warner, 1st Lieutenant 17th Infantry, U. S. A.

Names.	Rank.	Age.	Date of Entering the Service.	Period of Service.	Remarks.
Elias Harter	Captain.	42	May 2, 1864	100 dys.	Mustered out with company Sept. 2, 1864.
Charles B. Northrop	1st Lieut.	26	May 2, 1864	100 dys.	Mustered out with company Sept. 2, 1864.
Guy B. L. Northrop	2d Lieut.	22	May 2, 1864	100 dys.	Mustered out with company Sept. 2, 1864.
William P. Brodrick	1st Sergt.	36	May 2, 1864	100 dys.	Mustered out with company Sept. 2, 1864.
William J. Biddle	Sergeant.	31	May 2, 1864	100 dys.	Mustered out with company Sept. 2, 1864.
Alexander L. Augbee	do.	32	May 2, 1864	100 dys.	Mustered out with company Sept. 2, 1864.
Nehemiah Townsend	do.	35	May 2, 1864	100 dys.	Mustered out with company Sept. 2, 1864.
William P. Espy	do.	30	May 2, 1864	100 dys.	Mustered out with company Sept. 2, 1864.
Henry L. Hyde	Corporal	44	May 2, 1864	100 dys.	Mustered out with company Sept. 2, 1864.
Howard, Laurence	do.	34	May 2, 1864	100 dys.	Mustered out with company Sept. 2, 1864.
James Eubank	do.	27	May 2, 1864	100 dys.	Mustered out with company Sept. 2, 1864.
Samuel Sparklin	do.	40	May 2, 1864	100 dys.	Mustered out with company Sept. 2, 1864.
George Hossafons	do.	41	May 2, 1864	100 dys.	Mustered out with company Sept. 2, 1864.
Sidney Middleton	do.	33	May 2, 1864	100 dys.	Mustered out with company Sept. 2, 1864.
A. F. Knight	do.	28	May 2, 1864	100 dys.	Mustered out with company Sept. 2, 1864.
James W. Yours	do.	33	May 2, 1864	100 dys.	Accidentally wounded June 19, 1864, near Fincastle, Va.; mustered out with company Sept. 2, 1864.
Robert L. Porter	Musician	18	May 2, 1864	100 dys.	Mustered out with company Sept. 2, 1864.
William Marlatt	do.	18	May 2, 1864	100 dys.	Mustered out with company Sept. 2, 1864.

Names.	Rank.	Age.	Date of Entering the Service.	Period of Service.	Remarks.
Alexander, Joseph	Private..	23	May 2, 1864	100 dys.	Mustered out with company Sept. 2, 1864.
Ault, David	...do....	34	May 2, 1864	100 dys.	Mustered out with company Sept. 2, 1864.
Bates, William	...do....	29	May 2, 1864	100 dys.	Mustered out with company Sept. 2, 1864.
Benson, James M	...do....	22	May 2, 1864	100 dys.	Mustered out with company Sept. 2, 1864.
Berry, Nathaniel	...do....	23	May 2, 1864	100 dys.	Mustered out with company Sept. 2, 1864.
Billman, Henry	...do....	27	May 2, 1864	100 dys.	Mustered out with company Sept. 2, 1864.
Billman, Jacob L	...do....	25	May 2, 1864	100 dys.	Mustered out with company Sept. 2, 1864.
Bowersox, David C	...do....	19	May 2, 1864	100 dys.	Mustered out with company Sept. 2, 1864.
Brandeburg, Anthony	...do....	[illegible]	May 2, 1864	100 dys.	Mustered out with company Sept. 2, 1864.
Brown, Alexander	...do....	23	May 2, 1864	100 dys.	Mustered out with company Sept. 2, 1864.
Brown, John	...do....	31	May 2, 1864	100 dys.	Mustered out with company Sept. 2, 1864.
Butt, J. [illegible]	...do....	[illegible]	May 2, 1864	100 dys.	Mustered out with company Sept. 2, 1864.
Butt, William	...do....	25	May 2, 1864	100 dys.	Mustered out with company Sept. 2, 1864.
Carter, Ephraim M	...do....	19	May 2, 1864	100 dys.	Mustered out with company Sept. 2, 1864.
Chenoweth, Charles W	...do....	[illegible]	May 2, 1864	100 dys.	Mustered out with company Sept. 2, 1864.
Coblentz, Lewis H	...do....	31	May 2, 1864	100 dys.	Mustered out with company Sept. 2, 1864.
Cook, John	...do....	[illegible]	May 2, 1864	100 dys.	Mustered out with company Sept. 2, 1864.
Daugherty, John W	...do....	19	May 2, 1864	100 dys.	Mustered out with company Sept. 2, 1864.
Dowler, Evan	...do....	18	May 2, 1864	100 dys.	Mustered out with company Sept. 2, 1864.
Dowler, George W	...do....	22	May 2, 1864	100 dys.	Mustered out with company Sept. 2, 1864.
Garrett, John M	...do....	19	May 2, 1864	100 dys.	Mustered out with company Sept. 2, 1864.
Gist, Hosea F	...do....	21	May 2, 1864	100 dys.	Mustered out with company Sept. 2, 1864.
Greer, John W	...do....	18	May 2, 1864	100 dys.	Mustered out with company Sept. 2, 1864.
Guthrie, Thomas S	...do....	[illegible]	May 2, 1864	100 dys.	Promoted to Chaplain May 11, 1864.
Hahn, Joseph W	...do....	21	May 2, 1864	100 dys.	Mustered out with company Sept. 2, 1864.
Harter, Mark K	...do....	21	May 2, 1864	100 dys.	Mustered out with company Sept. 2, 1864.
Hetzler, John	...do....	[illegible]	May 2, 1864	100 dys.	Mustered out with company Sept. 2, 1864.
Hinsley, David D	...do....	[illegible]	May 2, 1864	100 dys.	Mustered out with company Sept. 2, 1864.
Hughes, William M	...do....	[illegible]	May 2, 1864	100 dys.	Mustered out with company Sept. 2, 1864.
Jaqua, Cassius M	...do....	[illegible]	May 2, 1864	100 dys.	Mustered out with company Sept. 2, 1864.
Jones, Wallace	...do....	18	May 2, 1864	100 dys.	Mustered out with company Sept. 2, 1864.
Juday, Emanuel	...do....	19	May 2, 1864	100 dys.	Mustered out with company Sept. 2, 1864.
Kunkle, David	...do....	[illegible]	May 2, 1864	100 dys.	Mustered out with company Sept. 2, 1864.
Lawrence, [illegible]	...do....	[illegible]	May 2, 1864	100 dys.	Mustered out with company Sept. 2, 1864.
Livingood, William W	...do....	24	May 2, 1864	100 dys.	Mustered out with company Sept. 2, 1864.
McIntire, Nathaniel B	...do....	[illegible]	May 2, 1864	100 dys.	Mustered out with company Sept. 2, 1864.
[illegible], Mark	...do....	22	May 2, 1864	100 dys.	Mustered out with company Sept. 2, 1864.
Mackey, Wesley	...do....	[illegible]	May 2, 1864	100 dys.	Mustered out with company Sept. 2, 1864.
[illegible], John	...do....	18	May 2, 1864	100 dys.	Mustered out with company Sept. 2, 1864.
[illegible], George	...do....	[illegible]	May 2, 1864	100 dys.	Mustered out with company Sept. 2, 1864.
Miller, George	...do....	18	May 2, 1864	100 dys.	Mustered out with company Sept. 2, 1864.
Mitchell, Isaac P	...do....	[illegible]	May 2, 1864	100 dys.	Mustered out with company Sept. 2, 1864.
Moore, Andrew J	...do....	[illegible]	May 2, 1864	100 dys.	Mustered out with company Sept. 2, 1864.
[illegible], Andrew	...do....	[illegible]	May 2, 1864	100 dys.	Mustered out with company Sept. 2, 1864.
Parks, John	...do....	[illegible]	May 2, 1864	100 dys.	Mustered out with company Sept. 2, 1864.
Polly, E[illegible]	...do....	[illegible]	May 2, 1864	100 dys.	Mustered out with company Sept. 2, 1864.
Polly, Henry V	...do....	[illegible]	May 2, 1864	100 dys.	Mustered out with company Sept. 2, 1864.
Powell, David D	...do....	[illegible]	May 2, 1864	100 dys.	Mustered out with company Sept. 2, 1864.
Reinhart, George	...do....	[illegible]	May 2, 1864	100 dys.	Mustered out with company Sept. 2, 1864.
Roberts, Conrad	...do....	[illegible]	May 2, 1864	100 dys.	Mustered out with company Sept. 2, 1864.
Roberts, John	...do....	34	May 2, 1864	100 dys.	Mustered out with company Sept. 2, 1864.
Roberts, Samuel E	...do....	24	May 2, 1864	100 dys.	Mustered out with company Sept. 2, 1864.
Roberts, Thomas	...do....	44	May 2, 1864	100 dys.	Mustered out with company Sept. 2, 1864.
Ryan, William H	...do....	[illegible]	May 2, 1864	100 dys.	Died May [illegible], 1864, at New Creek, W. Va.
Spencer, John F	...do....	[illegible]	May 2, 1864	100 dys.	Mustered out with company Sept. 2, 1864.
Spencer, [illegible]	...do....	[illegible]	May 2, 1864	100 dys.	Mustered out with company Sept. 2, 1864.
Thomas, David [illegible]	...do....	18	May 2, 1864	100 dys.	Mustered out with company Sept. 2, 1864.
Thomas, Matthew	...do....	[illegible]	May 2, 1864	100 dys.	Mustered out with company Sept. 2, 1864.
Tilson, Enos	...do....	[illegible]	May 2, 1864	100 dys.	Mustered out with company Sept. 2, 1864.
Ulom, William	...do....	[illegible]	May 2, 1864	100 dys.	Mustered out with company Sept. 2, 1864.
Vore, Clark [illegible]	...do....	[illegible]	May 2, 1864	100 dys.	Mustered out with company Sept. 2, 1864.
Woolverton, Charles W	...do....	[illegible]	May 2, 1864	100 dys.	Mustered out with company Sept. 2, 1864.
Wooten, George W	...do....	29	May 2, 1864	100 dys.	Mustered out with company Sept. 2, 1864.
Worden, Oren	...do....	4[illegible]	May 2, 1864	100 dys.	Mustered out with company Sept. 2, 1864.

COMPANY C.

Mustered in May 8, 1864, at Camp Dennison, O., by Robert S. Smith, Captain 2d Cavalry, U. S. A. Mustered out Sept. 2, 1864, at Camp Dennison, O., by L. H. Warner, 1st Lieutenant 17th Infantry, U. S. A.

Names.	Rank.	Age.	Date of Entering the Service.	Period of Service.	Remarks.
William P. Orr	Captain.	30	May 2, 1864	100 dys.	Mustered out with company Sept. 2, 1864.
Alexander McHorner	1st Lieut.	39	May 2, 1864	100 dys.	Mustered out with company Sept. 2, 1864.
Henry Gilbert	2d Lieut.	33	May 2, 1864	100 dys.	Mustered out with company Sept. 2, 1864.
James C. Hartzell	1st Sergt.	30	May 2, 1864	100 dys.	Died Aug. 16, 1864, in hospital at Camp Dennison, O.
Martin V. Long	Sergeant.	23	May 2, 1864	100 dys.	Mustered out with company Sept. 2, 1864.
William L. Reck	do.	29	May 2, 1864	100 dys.	Mustered out with company Sept. 2, 1864.
Jacob Gutshal	do.	33	May 2, 1864	100 dys.	Mustered out with company Sept. 2, 1864.
Wilkins Reck	do.	22	May 2, 1864	100 dys.	Mustered out with company Sept. 2, 1864.
Solomon Stoltz	Corporal.	30	May 2, 1864	100 dys.	Mustered out with company Sept. 2, 1864.
William H. McCune	do.	38	May 2, 1864	100 dys.	Mustered out with company Sept. 2, 1864.
Isaac Hershey	do.	25	May 2, 1864	100 dys.	Mustered out with company Sept. 2, 1864.
Henry A. Moore	do.	44	May 2, 1864	100 dys.	Mustered out with company Sept. 2, 1864.
Charles Naylor	do.	33	May 2, 1864	100 dys.	Mustered out with company Sept. 2, 1864.
Davis Shearer	do.	35	May 2, 1864	100 dys.	Mustered out with company Sept. 2, 1864.
Samuel F. Reed	do.	40	May 2, 1864	100 dys.	Mustered out with company Sept. 2, 1864.
William Reck	do.	29	May 2, 1864	100 dys.	Mustered out with company Sept. 2, 1864.
Arnett, Noah	Private.	20	May 2, 1864	100 dys.	Mustered out with company Sept. 2, 1864.
Babylon, Andrew	do.	37	May 2, 1864	100 dys.	Mustered out with company Sept. 2, 1864.
Beard, Emanuel J	do.	39	May 2, 1864	100 dys.	Mustered out with company Sept. 2, 1864.
Beam, George K	do.	23	May 2, 1864	100 dys.	Mustered out with company Sept. 2, 1864.
Bidlack, Calvin	do.	19	May 2, 1864	100 dys.	Mustered out with company Sept. 2, 1864.
Bookwalter, Franklin	do.	22	May 2, 1864	100 dys.	Died July 26, 1864, in hospital at Cumberland, Maryland.
Brandon, James	do.	27	May 2, 1864	100 dys.	Died July 28, 1864, in hospital at Cumberland, Maryland.
Brandon, John T	do.	18	May 2, 1864	100 dys.	Died Aug. 22, 1864, in hospital at Cumberland, Maryland.
Brown, Daniel	do.	23	May 2, 1864	100 dys.	Mustered out with company Sept. 2, 1864.
Brown, William	do.	34	May 2, 1864	100 dys.	Mustered out with company Sept. 2, 1864.
Cain, Benjamin	do.	23	May 2, 1864	100 dys.	Mustered out with company Sept. 2, 1864.
Clark, John	do.	21	May 2, 1864	100 dys.	Mustered out with company Sept. 2, 1864.
Cromer, George H	do.	29	May 2, 1864	100 dys.	Mustered out with company Sept. 2, 1864.
Cromer, John A	do.	24	May 2, 1864	100 dys.	Mustered out with company Sept. 2, 1864.
Dershem, David	do.	21	May 2, 1864	100 dys.	Mustered out with company Sept. 2, 1864.
Dye, Christian	do.	19	May 2, 1864	100 dys.	Mustered out with company Sept. 2, 1864.
Ernest, David W	do.	35	May 2, 1864	100 dys.	Mustered out with company Sept. 2, 1864.
Froek, Philip H	do.	35	May 2, 1864	100 dys.	Mustered out with company Sept. 2, 1864.
Frybarger, John	do.	27	May 2, 1864	100 dys.	Mustered out with company Sept. 2, 1864.
Garner, Samuel	do.	26	May 2, 1864	100 dys.	Mustered out with company Sept. 2, 1864.
Gilbert, Levi S	do.	28	May 2, 1864	100 dys.	Mustered out with company Sept. 2, 1864.
Hahn, Jeremiah	do.	18	May 2, 1864	100 dys.	Mustered out with company Sept. 2, 1864.
Hahn, William	do.	22	May 2, 1864	100 dys.	Mustered out with company Sept. 2, 1864.
Haines, George	do.	42	May 2, 1864	100 dys.	Died May 28, 1864, at New Creek, W. Va.
Harmon, John	do.	41	May 2, 1864	100 dys.	Mustered out with company Sept. 2, 1864.
Harmon, Anson	do.	18	May 2, 1864	100 dys.	Mustered out with company Sept. 2, 1864.
Hartzell, Philip J	do.	28	May 2, 1864	100 dys.	Mustered out with company Sept. 2, 1864.
Heckman, Daniel	do.	28	May 2, 1864	100 dys.	Mustered out with company Sept. 2, 1864.
Hersbey, David	do.	23	May 2, 1864	100 dys.	Mustered out with company Sept. 2, 1864.
Hill, Samuel	do.	38	May 2, 1864	100 dys.	Mustered out with company Sept. 2, 1864.
Hoffman, John S	do.	18	May 2, 1864	100 dys.	Mustered out with company Sept. 2, 1864.
Horner, George W	do.	18	May 2, 1864	100 dys.	Mustered out with company Sept. 2, 1864.
Horner, John N	do.	23	May 2, 1864	100 dys.	Mustered out with company Sept. 2, 1864.
Hornet, Robert C	do.	26	May 2, 1864	100 dys.	Mustered out with company Sept. 2, 1864.
Hullinger, John F	do.	36	May 2, 1864	100 dys.	Mustered out with company Sept. 2, 1864.
Johnson, William W	do.	30	May 2, 1864	100 dys.	Mustered out with company Sept. 2, 1864.
Ketshner, Daniel	do.	38	May 2, 1864	100 dys.	Mustered out with company Sept. 2, 1864.
Miller, George W	do.	36	May 2, 1864	100 dys.	Mustered out with company Sept. 2, 1864.
Miller, George Y	do.	19	May 2, 1864	100 dys.	Mustered out with company Sept. 2, 1864.
Mullen, Jason E	do.	38	May 2, 1864	100 dys.	Mustered out with company Sept. 2, 1864.
Myers, Jacob	do.	37	May 2, 1864	100 dys.	Mustered out with company Sept. 2, 1864.
Newton, Edmond	do.	33	May 2, 1864	100 dys.	Mustered out with company Sept. 2, 1864.
Noler, Frederick	do.	39	May 2, 1864	100 dys.	Mustered out with company Sept. 2, 1864.
Palmer, George	do.	20	May 2, 1864	100 dys.	Mustered out with company Sept. 2, 1864.
Patty, Clark	do.	19	May 2, 1864	100 dys.	Died June 5, 1864, at New Creek, W. Va.
Pfeffer, [illegible]	do.	18	May 2, 1864	100 dys.	Mustered out with company Sept. 2, 1864.
Peiffer, M[illegible]nuel	do.	22	May 2, 1864	100 dys.	Mustered out with company Sept. 2, 1864.
Reck, Amos	do.	23	May 2, 1864	100 dys.	Mustered out with company Sept. 2, 1864.
Reck, Franklin	do.	22	May 2, 1864	100 dys.	Mustered out with company Sept. 2, 1864.
Reck, Isaac	do.	25	May 2, 1864	100 dys.	Mustered out with company Sept. 2, 1864.
Reck, John	do.	19	May 2, 1864	100 dys.	Mustered out with company Sept. 2, 1864.
Rudy, Samuel	do.	21	May 2, 1864	100 dys.	Mustered out with company Sept. 2, 1864.
Runkle, Benjamin F	do.	21	May 2, 1864	100 dys.	Mustered out with company Sept. 2, 1864.
Seaman, Samuel H	do.	21	May 2, 1864	100 dys.	Mustered out with company Sept. 2, 1864.
Smith, Joseph	do.	18	May 2, 1864	100 dys.	Mustered out with company Sept. 2, 1864.
Stahl, Samuel	do.	36	May 2, 1864	100 dys.	Mustered out with company Sept. 2, 1864.

Names.	Rank.	Age.	Date of Entering the Service.	Period of Service.	Remarks.
Neff, Hiram D.	Private.	24	May 2, 1864	100 dys.	Mustered out with company Sept. 2, 1864.
Nichols, George W.	do.	18	May 2, 1864	100 dys.	Mustered out with company Sept. 2, 1864.
Paramore, Cassius S.	do.	22	May 2, 1864	100 dys.	Mustered out with company Sept. 2, 1864.
Paxson, Heston	do.	44	May 2, 1864	100 dys.	Mustered out with company Sept. 2, 1864.
Porter, John A.	do.	23	May 2, 1864	100 dys.	Mustered out with company Sept. 2, 1864.
Rice, Leslie	do.	27	May 2, 1864	100 dys.	Mustered out with company Sept. 2, 1864.
Rife, Obed C.	do.	21	May 2, 1864	100 dys.	Mustered out with company Sept. 2, 1864.
Roe, Joel	do.	24	May 2, 1864	100 dys.	Mustered out with company Sept. 2, 1864.
Ross, George W.	do.	23	May 2, 1864	100 dys.	Mustered out with company Sept. 2, 1864.
Seibert, John	do.	26	May 2, 1864	100 dys.	Mustered out with company Sept. 2, 1864.
States, Charles	do.	17	May 2, 1864	100 dys.	Mustered out with company Sept. 2, 1864.
Stone, Edwin N.	do.	18	May 2, 1864	100 dys.	Mustered out with company Sept. 2, 1864.
Stover, Philip	do.	25	May 2, 1864	100 dys.	Mustered out with company Sept. 2, 1864.
Thomas, George	do.	19	May 2, 1864	100 dys.	Mustered out with company Sept. 2, 1864.
Thomas, Johnson F.	do.	18	May 2, 1864	100 dys.	Mustered out with company Sept. 2, 1864.
Thomas, William	do.	21	May 2, 1864	100 dys.	Mustered out with company Sept. 2, 1864.
Vandon, William R.	do.	27	May 2, 1864	100 dys.	Mustered out with company Sept. 2, 1864.
Vinso, Jacob A.	do.	18	May 2, 1864	100 dys.	Mustered out with company Sept. 2, 1864.
Whitacre, [illegible] R.	do.	26	May 2, 1864	100 dys.	Mustered out with company Sept. 2, 1864.
White, John H.	do.	21	May 2, 1864	100 dys.	Mustered out with company Sept. 2, 1864.
Wickersham, George W.	do.	29	May 2, 1864	100 dys.	Mustered out with company Sept. 2, 1864.
Zumbrum, Henry	do.	29	May 2, 1864	100 dys.	Mustered out with company Sept. 2, 1864.

COMPANY E.

Mustered in May 10, 1864, at Camp Dennison, O., by Robert S. Smith, Captain 2d Cavalry, U. S. A. Mustered out Sept. 2, 1864, at Camp Dennison, O., by L. H. Warner, 1st Lieutenant 17th Infantry, U. S. A.

Names.	Rank.	Age.	Date of Entering the Service.	Period of Service.	Remarks.
Asa S. Bushnell	Captain	29	May 2, 1864	100 dys.	Mustered out with company Sept. 2, 1864.
Richard L. Parker	1st Lieut.	32	May 2, 1864	100 dys.	Mustered out with company Sept. 2, 1864.
Asa W. Hatch	2d Lieut.	25	May 2, 1864	100 dys.	Mustered out with company Sept. 2, 1864.
Madison C. Powell	1st Sergt.	24	May 2, 1864	100 dys.	Mustered out with company Sept. 2, 1864.
George Driscoll	Sergeant	20	May 2, 1864	100 dys.	Mustered out with company Sept. 2, 1864.
Joseph Harrison	do.	22	May 2, 1864	100 dys.	Mustered out with company Sept. 2, 1864.
Isaac B. Trimmer	do.	19	May 2, 1864	100 dys.	Mustered out with company Sept. 2, 1864.
James Cooper	do.	27	May 2, 1864	100 dys.	Mustered out with company Sept. 2, 1864.
Bushrod Spencer	Corporal	18	May 2, 1864	100 dys.	Mustered out with company Sept. 2, 1864.
Percy B. S. Dyer	do.	19	May 2, 1864	100 dys.	Mustered out with company Sept. 2, 1864.
Clement T. Seyes	do.	19	May 2, 1864	100 dys.	Mustered out with company Sept. 2, 1864.
Rodney Shain	do.	23	May 2, 1864	100 dys.	Mustered out with company Sept. 2, 1864.
John Johnson	do.	25	May 2, 1864	100 dys.	Mustered out with company Sept. 2, 1864.
John H. Littler	do.	44	May 2, 1864	100 dys.	Discharged May 25, 1864, by order of War Department.
A. P. Linn Cochran	do.	27	May 2, 1864	100 dys.	Mustered out with company Sept. 2, 1864.
John C. Miller	do.	30	May 2, 1864	100 dys.	Mustered out with company Sept. 2, 1864.
Clifton M. Nichols	do.	33	May 2, 1864	100 dys.	Appointed July 3, 1864; mustered out with company Sept. 2, 1864.
Albert B. Lewis	Musician	19	May 2, 1864	100 dys.	Mustered out with company Sept. 2, 1864.
Richard Rayner	do.	18	May 2, 1864	100 dys.	Mustered out with company Sept. 2, 1864.
Albin, Cyrus	Private.	38	May 2, 1864	100 dys.	Mustered out with company Sept. 2, 1864.
Albin, Joseph P.	do.	18	May 2, 1864	100 dys.	Mustered out with company Sept. 2, 1864.
Baker, Henry	do.	19	May 2, 1864	100 dys.	Mustered out with company Sept. 2, 1864.
Best, Benjamin F.	do.	32	May 2, 1864	100 dys.	Mustered out with company Sept. 2, 1864.
Blair, Joseph	do.	21	May 2, 1864	100 dys.	Mustered out with company Sept. 2, 1864.
Bretney, Edwin V.	do.	22	May 2, 1864	100 dys.	Mustered out with company Sept. 2, 1864.
Bretney, John [illegible]	do.	47	May 2, 1864	100 dys.	Mustered out with company Sept. 2, 1864.
Brown, Thomas	do.	23	May 2, 1864	100 dys.	Mustered out with company Sept. 2, 1864.
Brown, William L.	do.	21	May 2, 1864	100 dys.	Mustered out with company Sept. 2, 1864.
Bruce, George D.	do.	19	May 2, 1864	100 dys.	Mustered out with company Sept. 2, 1864.
Burnett, Theodore	do.	18	May 10, 1864	100 dys.	Mustered out with company Sept. 2, 1864.
Cartwell, Thomas	do.	19	May 2, 1864	100 dys.	Mustered out with company Sept. 2, 1864.
Clapp, Chester H.	do.	18	May 2, 1864	100 dys.	Mustered out with company Sept. 2, 1864.
Clokey, Josiah M.	do.	19	May 2, 1864	100 dys.	Mustered out with company Sept. 2, 1864.
Crocker, Frank N.	do.	18	May 2, 1864	100 dys.	Mustered out with company Sept. 2, 1864.
Cross, Nathaniel	do.	30	May 2, 1864	100 dys.	Mustered out with company Sept. 2, 1864.
Davidson, James	do.	21	May 2, 1864	100 dys.	Mustered out with company Sept. 2, 1864.
Deihl, Wallace	do.	18	May 2, 1864	100 dys.	Mustered out with company Sept. 2, 1864.
Drury, Jones	do.	24	May 2, 1864	100 dys.	Mustered out with company Sept. 2, 1864.
Dudly, John	do.	21	May 2, 1864	100 dys.	Mustered out with company Sept. 2, 1864.
Fitzpatrick, John	do.	19	May 2, 1864	100 dys.	Died July 10, 1864, in hospital at Clarysville, Maryland.
Floyd, George	do.	22	May 2, 1864	100 dys.	Mustered out with company Sept. 2, 1864.
Folger, Charles E.	do.	20	May 2, 1864	100 dys.	Mustered out with company Sept. 2, 1864.
Grant, William H.	do.	27	May 2, 1864	100 dys.	Mustered out with company Sept. 2, 1864.
Grimes, William	do.	25	May 2, 1864	100 dys.	Mustered out with company Sept. 2, 1864.
Hamilton, William W.	do.	23	May 2, 1864	100 dys.	Mustered out with company Sept. 2, 1864.
Hill, George A.	do.	18	May 2, 1864	100 dys.	Mustered out with company Sept. 2, 1864.
Hindes, James M.	do.	26	May 2, 1864	100 dys.	Mustered out with company Sept. 2, 1864.
Huben, Daniel J.	do.	24	May 2, 1864	100 dys.	Mustered out with company Sept. 2, 1864.

Names.	Rank.	Age.	Date of Entering the Service.	Period of Service.	Remarks.
Dunwoody, James	Private	27	May 2, 1864	100 dys.	Mustered out with company Sept. 2, 1864.
English, Porter	do	22	May 2, 1864	100 dys.	Mustered out with company Sept. 2, 1864.
English, Stephen N.	do	18	May 2, 1864	100 dys.	Mustered out with company Sept. 2, 1864.
English, Samuel H	do	21	May 2, 1864	100 dys.	Mustered out with company Sept. 2, 1864.
English, William	do	33	May 2, 1864	100 dys.	Mustered out with company Sept. 2, 1864.
Elson, William	do	22	May 2, 1864	100 dys.	Transferred to Co. K May 10, 1864.
Evans, Russell	do	20	May 2, 1864	100 dys.	Mustered out with company Sept. 2, 1864.
Frobe, Frederick	do	33	May 2, 1864	100 dys.	Mustered out with company Sept. 2, 1864.
Greer, S. A	do	47	May 2, 1864	100 dys.	Mustered out with company Sept. 2, 1864.
Hole, Jay	do	31	May 2, 1864	100 dys.	Mustered out with company Sept. 2, 1864.
Hole, John B.	do	22	May 2, 1864	100 dys.	Mustered out with company Sept. 2, 1864.
Hole, Xury	do	23	May 2, 1864	100 dys.	Mustered out with company Sept. 2, 1864.
Hoover, Benjamin F	do	18	May 2, 1864	100 dys.	Mustered out with company Sept. 2, 1864.
Kirshner, D. B.	do	39	May 2, 1864	100 dys.	Mustered out with company Sept. 2, 1864.
Kirshner, Jonathan	do	44	May 2, 1864	100 dys.	Mustered out with company Sept. 2, 1864.
Loeper, C. M	do	29	May 2, 1864	100 dys.	Mustered out with company Sept. 2, 1864.
Lehman, John	do	22	May 2, 1864	100 dys.	Mustered out with company Sept. 2, 1864.
Lehman, Peter	do	28	May 2, 1864	100 dys.	Mustered out with company Sept. 2, 1864.
Lime, Christopher	do	31	May 2, 1864	100 dys.	Mustered out with company Sept. 2, 1864.
Lime, Michael	do	26	May 2, 1864	100 dys.	Mustered out with company Sept. 2, 1864.
Lime, Samuel	do	23	May 2, 1864	100 dys.	Mustered out with company Sept. 2, 1864.
Lodge, James N.	do	30	May 2, 1864	100 dys.	Mustered out with company Sept. 2, 1864.
Lyons, Jacob	do	25	May 2, 1864	100 dys.	Mustered out with company Sept. 2, 1864.
McDorman, J	do	[illegible]	May 2, 1864	100 dys.	Mustered out with company Sept. 2, 1864.
McVity, Thomas	do	24	May 2, 1864	100 dys.	Mustered out with company Sept. 2, 1864.
Medford, Aaron N.	do	22	May 2, 1864	100 dys.	Mustered out with company Sept. 2, 1864.
Medford, Isaac N.	do	18	May 2, 1864	100 dys.	Mustered out with company Sept. 2, 1864.
Meed, H. E.	do	20	May 2, 1864	100 dys.	Mustered out with company Sept. 2, 1864.
Mendinhall, Benjamin.	do	19	May 2, 1864	100 dys.	Mustered out with company Sept. 2, 1864.
Mendinhall, C. E.	do	25	May 2, 1864	100 dys.	Mustered out with company Sept. 2, 1864.
Mendinhall, William	do	39	May 2, 1864	100 dys.	Mustered out with company Sept. 2, 1864.
Metzcar, Jonathan	do	29	May 2, 1864	100 dys.	Mustered out with company Sept. 2, 1864.
Miller, Hiram.	do	27	May 2, 1864	100 dys.	Mustered out with company Sept. 2, 1864.
Miller, John	do	18	May 2, 1864	100 dys.	Mustered out with company Sept. 2, 1864.
Pitsenbarger, Francis	do	20	May 2, 1864	100 dys.	Mustered out with company Sept. 2, 1864.
Pitsenbarger, Isaiah	do	22	May 2, 1864	100 dys.	Mustered out with company Sept. 2, 1864.
Siford, Charles	do	33	May 2, 1864	100 dys.	Mustered out with company Sept. 2, 1864.
Simon, August	do	26	May 2, 1864	100 dys.	Mustered out with company Sept. 2, 1864.
Shontz, Leonard	do	21	May 2, 1864	100 dys.	Mustered out with company Sept. 2, 1864.
Straker Henry	do	37	May 2, 1864	100 dys.	Mustered out with company Sept. 2, 1864.
Swallow, Harrison.	do	29	May 2, 1864	100 dys.	Mustered out with company Sept. 2, 1864.
Swisher, B. L.	do	38	May 2, 1864	100 dys.	Mustered out with company Sept. 2, 1864.
Swisher, Henry	do	18	May 2, 1864	100 dys.	Died Aug 19, 1864, at Cumberland, Md.
Taylor, Salem	do	23	May 2, 1864	100 dys.	Mustered out with company Sept. 2, 1864.
Yoder, Christopher	do	27	May 2, 1864	100 dys.	Mustered out with company Sept. 2, 1864.

COMPANY G.

Mustered in May 8, 1864, at Camp Dennison, O., by Robert S. Smith, Captain 2d Cavalry, U. S. A. Mustered out Sept. 2, 1864, at Camp Dennison, O., by L. H. Warner, 1st Lieutenant 17th Infantry, U. S. A.

Names.	Rank.	Age.	Date of Entering the Service.	Period of Service.	Remarks.
William A. Bonner	Captain.	44	May 2, 1864	100 dys.	Mustered out with company Sept. 2, 1864.
Joshua S. Miller	1st Lieut	26	May 2, 1864	100 dys.	Mustered out with company Sept. 2, 1864.
Solomon Beam	2d Lieut.	41	May 2, 1864	100 dys.	Mustered out with company Sept. 2, 1864.
Lewis Nowlin	1st Sergt.	20	May 2, 1864	100 dys.	Mustered out with company Sept. 2, 1864.
Francis M. Harless	Sergeant.	24	May 2, 1864	100 dys.	Mustered out with company Sept. 2, 1864.
William Wassan	do	22	May 2, 1864	100 dys.	Mustered out with company Sept. 2, 1864.
Jacob B. Chenoworth	do	39	May 2, 1864	100 dys.	Mustered out with company Sept. 2, 1864.
Nathan S. Warvel	do	25	May 2, 1864	100 dys.	Mustered out with company Sept. 2, 1864.
Franklin Rank	Corporal	27	May 2, 1864	100 dys.	Mustered out with company Sept. 2, 1864.
Isaiah S. Wanger	do	25	May 2, 1864	100 dys.	Mustered out with company Sept. 2, 1864.
Louis C. Williams	do	26	May 2, 1864	100 dys.	Died May 29, 1864, at New Creek, W. Va.
Abraham H[illegible]arless	do	22	May 2, 1864	100 dys.	Mustered out with company Sept. 2, 1864.
Isaac Elston	do	34	May 2, 1864	100 dys.	Mustered out with company Sept. 2, 1864.
Jahne McNeil	do	33	May 2, 1864	100 dys.	Mustered out with company Sept. 2, 1864.
John Hiller	do	25	May 2, 1864	100 dys.	Mustered out with company Sept. 2, 1864.
Andrew D. Kersner	do	26	May 2, 1864	100 dys.	Mustered out with company Sept. 2, 1864.
William C. Shepherd	do	33	May 2, 1864	100 dys.	Appointed May 30, 1864; mustered out with company Sept. 2, 1864.
Agen, Michael	Private	26	May 2, 1864	100 dys.	Mustered out with company Sept. 2, 1864.
Beam, Daniel C.	do	19	May 2, 1864	100 dys.	Mustered out with company Sept. 2, 1864.
Beentol, Joseph	do	18	May 2, 1864	100 dys.	Mustered out with company Sept. 2, 1864.
Britt, Daniel	do	19	May 2, 1864	100 dys.	Mustered out with company Sept. 2, 1864.
Cole, David	do	31	May 2, 1864	100 dys.	Died July 17, 1864, in hospital at Cumberland, Maryland.
Cole, Henry	do	19	May 2, 1864	100 dys.	Mustered out with company Sept. 2, [illegible]
Countryman, Michael	do	33	May 2, 1864	100 dys.	Mustered out with company Sept. 2, [illegible]
Crowel, Joseph E.	do	26	May 2, 1864	100 dys.	Mustered out with company Sept. 2, [illegible]
Crumrine, Benjamin F.	do	19	May 2, 1864	100 dys.	Mustered out with company Sept. 2, [illegible]

Names.	Rank.	Age.	Date of Entering the Service.	Period of Service.	Remarks.
[illegible] William C.	Private.	30	May 2, 1864	100 dys.	Mustered out with company Sept. 2, 1864.
[illegible]	do.	21	May 2, 1864	100 dys.	Mustered out with company Sept. 2, 1864.
[illegible] Alpen	do.	35	May 2, 1864	100 dys.	Mustered out with company Sept. 2, 1864.
[illegible] W.	do.	25	May 2, 1864	100 dys.	Mustered out with company Sept. 2, 1864.
[illegible]	do.	30	May 2, 1864	100 dys.	Mustered out with company Sept. 2, 1864.
[illegible]	do.	18	May 2, 1864	100 dys.	Mustered out with company Sept. 2, 1864.
[illegible]	do.	43	May 2, 1864	100 dys.	Mustered out with company Sept. 2, 1864.
[illegible] H.	do.	21	May 2, 1864	100 dys.	Mustered out with company Sept. 2, 1864.
[illegible]	do.	44	May 2, 1864	100 dys.	Mustered out with company Sept. 2, 1864.
[illegible] P.	do.	21	May 2, 1864	100 dys.	Mustered out with company Sept. 2, 1864.
[illegible], Francis M.	do.	28	May 2, 1864	100 dys.	Mustered out with company Sept. 2, 1864.
[illegible]	do.	23	May 2, 1864	100 dys.	Mustered out with company Sept. 2, 1864.
[illegible]	do.	26	May 2, 1864	100 dys.	Mustered out with company Sept. 2, 1864.
[illegible]	do.	21	May 2, 1864	100 dys.	Mustered out with company Sept. 2, 1864.
[illegible]	do.	30	May 2, 1864	100 dys.	Mustered out with company Sept. 2, 1864.
[illegible] W.	do.	22	May 2, 1864	100 dys.	Captured June 22, 1864, in action near White Sulphur Springs, W. Va.; mustered out Feb. 21, 1865, at Columbus, O., by order of War Department.
[illegible] D.	do.	28	May 2, 1864	100 dys.	Mustered out with company Sept. 2, 1864.
[illegible]	do.	24	May 2, 1864	100 dys.	Mustered out with company Sept. 2, 1864.
[illegible]	do.	23	May 2, 1864	100 dys.	Mustered out with company Sept. 2, 1864.
[illegible]	do.	19	May 2, 1864	100 dys.	Mustered out with company Sept. 2, 1864.
[illegible] Abraham	do.	35	May 2, 1864	100 dys.	Mustered out with company Sept. 2, 1864.
[illegible] E.	do.	19	May 2, 1864	100 dys.	Mustered out with company Sept. 2, 1864.
[illegible]	do.	18	May 2, 1864	100 dys.	Mustered out with company Sept. 2, 1864.
[illegible]	do.	34	May 2, 1864	100 dys.	Mustered out with company Sept. 2, 1864.
[illegible]	do.	27	May 2, 1864	100 dys.	Mustered out with company Sept. 2, 1864.
[illegible] S.	do.	34	May 2, 1864	100 dys.	Mustered out with company Sept. 2, 1864.
[illegible]	do.	37	May 2, 1864	100 dys.	Mustered out with company Sept. 2, 1864.
[illegible]	do.	24	May 2, 1864	100 dys.	Mustered out with company Sept. 2, 1864.
[illegible] W	do.	18	May 2, 1864	100 dys.	Mustered out with company Sept. 2, 1864.
[illegible] E.	do.	22	May 2, 1864	100 dys.	Mustered out with company Sept. 2, 1864.
[illegible]	do.	31	May 2, 1864	100 dys.	Mustered out with company Sept. 2, 1864.
[illegible]	do.	20	May 2, 1864	100 dys.	Mustered out with company Sept. 2, 1864.
[illegible]	do.	24	May 2, 1864	100 dys.	Mustered out with company Sept. 2, 1864.
[illegible] Andrew	do.	40	May 2, 1864	100 dys.	Mustered out with company Sept. 2, 1864.
[illegible]	do.	34	May 2, 1864	100 dys.	Mustered out with company Sept. 2, 1864.
[illegible] Franklin	do.	19	May 2, 1864	100 dys.	Mustered out with company Sept. 2, 1864.
[illegible]	do.	18	May 2, 1864	100 dys.	Mustered out with company Sept. 2, 1864.
[illegible]	do.	34	May 2, 1864	100 dys.	Mustered out with company Sept. 2, 1864.
[illegible]	do.	26	May 2, 1864	100 dys.	Mustered out with company Sept. 2, 1864.
[illegible]	do.	18	May 2, 1864	100 dys.	Mustered out with company Sept. 2, 1864.
[illegible] L.	do.	20	May 2, 1864	100 dys.	Mustered out with company Sept. 2, 1864.
[illegible]	do.	17	May 2, 1864	100 dys.	Mustered out with company Sept. 2, 1864.
[illegible] L.	do.	41	May 2, 1864	100 dys.	Mustered out with company Sept. 2, 1864.
[illegible] K.	do.	24	May 2, 1864	100 dys.	Mustered out with company Sept. 2, 1864.
[illegible]	do.	23	May 2, 1864	100 dys.	Mustered out with company Sept. 2, 1864.
[illegible]	do.	40	May 2, 1864	100 dys.	Mustered out with company Sept. 2, 1864.
[illegible] F.	do.	31	May 2, 1864	100 dys.	Mustered out with company Sept. 2, 1864.
[illegible]	do.	34	May 2, 1864	100 dys.	Mustered out with company Sept. 2, 1864.
[illegible] W.	do.	18	May 2, 1864	100 dys.	Mustered out with company Sept. 2, 1864.
[illegible] E.	do.	18	May 2, 1864	100 dys.	Mustered out with company Sept. 2, 1864.
[illegible] W.	do.	30	May 2, 1864	100 dys.	Mustered out with company Sept. 2, 1864.
[illegible]	do.	42	May 2, 1864	100 dys.	Mustered out with company Sept. 2, 1864.
[illegible] F.	do.	21	May 2, 1864	100 dys.	Mustered out with company Sept. 2, 1864.
[illegible]	do.	28	May 2, 1864	100 dys.	Mustered out with company Sept. 2, 1864.
[illegible]	do.	23	May 2, 1864	100 dys.	Mustered out with company Sept. 2, 1864.
[illegible] George W.	do.	24	May 2, 1864	100 dys.	Mustered out with company Sept. 2, 1864.
[illegible] E.	do.	34	May 2, 1864	100 dys.	Mustered out with company Sept. 2, 1864.
[illegible] E.	do.	33	May 2, 1864	100 dys.	Mustered out with company Sept. 2, 1864.

COMPANY H.

[illegible] 8, 1864, at Camp Dennison, O., by Robert S. Smith, Captain 2d Cavalry, U. S. A. Mustered out Sept. 2, 1864, at Camp Dennison, O., L. H. by Warner, 1st Lieutenant 17th Infantry, U. S. A.

Names.	Rank.	Age.	Date of Entering the Service.	Period of Service.	Remarks.
[illegible]ruy	Captain.	45	May 2, 1864	100 dys.	Mustered out with company Sept. 2, 1864.
[illegible] Hyde	1st Lieut.	29	May 2, 1864	100 dys.	Mustered out with company Sept. 2, 1864.
[illegible]lls	2d Lieut.	48	May 2, 1864	100 dys.	Mustered out with company Sept. 2, 1864.
[illegible] Rodgers	1st Sergt.	37	May 2, 1864	100 dys.	Mustered out with company Sept. 2, 1864.
[illegible] Keater	Sergeant.	24	May 2, 1864	100 dys.	Mustered out with company Sept. 2, 1864.
[illegible]ale	do.	36	May 2, 1864	100 dys.	Mustered out with company Sept. 2, 1864.
[illegible]ter	do.	36	May 2, 1864	100 dys.	Mustered out with company Sept. 2, 1864.
[illegible]oodbury	do.	32	May 2, 1864	100 dys.	Mustered out with company Sept. 2, 1864.
[illegible]stick	Corporal.	43	May 2, 1864	100 dys.	Died Aug. 4, 1864, in hospital at Cumberland, Maryland.
[illegible] Black	do.	36	May 2, 1864	100 dys.	Mustered out with company Sept. 2, 1864.
[illegible]con	do.	31	May 2, 1864	100 dys.	Mustered out with company Sept. 2, 1864.

Names.	Rank.	Age.	Date of Entering the Service.	Period of Service.	Remarks.
John Stowers	Corporal.	33	May 2, 1864	100 dys.	Mustered out with company Sept. 2, 1864.
William M. Argubright	....do....	31	May 2, 1864	100 dys.	Mustered out with company Sept. 2, 1864.
Frederick Aukerman	....do..	22	May 2, 1864	100 dys.	Mustered out with company Sept. 2, 1864.
John F. Judy	....do....	20	May 2, 1864	100 dys.	Mustered out with company Sept. 2, 1864.
Nathan Hiller	....do....	20	May 2, 1864	100 dys.	Mustered out with company Sept. 2, 1864.
Anderson, C. Alexander	Private..	18	May 2, 1864	100 dys.	Mustered out with company Sept. 2, 1864.
Anderson, Joseph	....do....	35	May 2, 1864	100 dys.	Died Aug. 28, 1864, in hospital at Camp Dennison, O.
Balser, Henry	....do....	31	May 2, 1864	100 dys.	Mustered out with company Sept. 2, 1864.
Bishop, Peter W	....do....	32	May 2, 1864	100 dys.	Mustered out with company Sept. 2, 1864.
Bishop, Thompson L	....do....	24	May 2, 1864	100 dys.	Mustered out with company Sept. 2, 1864.
Burch, John F	....do....	18	May 2, 1864	100 dys.	Mustered out with company Sept. 2, 1864.
Cable, Samuel	....do....	38	May 2, 1864	100 dys.	Mustered out with company Sept. 2, 1864.
Carter, William	....do....	27	May 2, 1864	100 dys.	
Clark, Rufus	....do....	20	May 2, 1864	100 dys.	Mustered out with company Sept. 2, 1864.
Corbit, Wiley A	....do....	24	May 2, 1864	100 dys.	Mustered out with company Sept. 2, 1864.
Crandell, Adelbert	....do....	20	May 2, 1864	100 dys.	Mustered out with company Sept. 2, 1864.
Crandell, William	....do....	41	May 2, 1864	100 dys.	Mustered out with company Sept. 2, 1864.
Darkus, Absalom	....do....	38	May 2, 1864	100 dys.	Mustered out with company Sept. 2, 1864.
Davidson, Edward J	....do....	18	May 2, 1864	100 dys.	Mustered out with company Sept. 2, 1864.
Dye, Robert S	....do....	20	May 2, 1864	100 dys.	Mustered out with company Sept. 2, 1864.
Elliott, Samuel	....do....	22	May 2, 1864	100 dys.	Mustered out with company Sept. 2, 1864.
Finfrock, Samuel	....do....	18	May 2, 1864	100 dys.	Mustered out with company Sept. 2, 1864.
Fitzgerald, Ezekiel	....do....	31	May 2, 1864	100 dys.	Mustered out with company Sept. 2, 1864.
Fryar, Clark	....do....	21	May 2, 1864	100 dys.	Mustered out with company Sept. 2, 1864.
Gillum, Matthias	....do....	35	May 2, 1864	100 dys.	Mustered out with company Sept. 2, 1864.
Harding, James	....do....	38	May 2, 1864	100 dys.	Mustered out with company Sept. 2, 1864.
Harding, Samuel	....do....	45	May 2, 1864	100 dys.	Mustered out with company Sept. 2, 1864.
Haines, Abel	....do....	25	May 2, 1864	100 dys.	Mustered out with company Sept. 2, 1864.
Harnish, Samuel	....do....	23	May 2, 1864	100 dys.	Mustered out with company Sept. 2, 1864.
		20	May 2, 1864	100 dys.	Mustered out with company Sept. 2, 1864.
Harrington, Thomas	....do....	34	May 2, 1864	100 dys.	Mustered out with company Sept. 2, 1864.
Harrison, Joseph G	....do....	18	May 2, 1864	100 dys.	Mustered out with company Sept. 2, 1864.
Harrison, William T	....do..	41	May 2, 1864	100 dys.	Mustered out with company Sept. 2, 1864.
Harter, Josiah	....do....	39	May 2, 1864	100 dys.	Mustered out with company Sept. 2, 1864.
Hartzell, William	....do....	20	May 2, 1864	100 dys.	Mustered out with company Sept. 2, 1864.
Hill, Rufus	....do....	19	May 2, 1864	100 dys.	Mustered out with company Sept. 2, 1864.
House, Elijah	....do....	20	May 2, 1864	100 dys.	Mustered out with company Sept. 2, 1864.
Hunter, John A	....do....	19	May 2, 1864	100 dys.	Mustered out with company Sept. 2, 1864.
Jefferis, Joshua	....do....	25	May 2, 1864	100 dys.	Mustered out with company Sept. 2, 1864.
Keener, Milton	....do....	20	May 2, 1864	100 dys.	Mustered out with company Sept. 2, 1864.
Kenard, Leonard	....do....	20	May 2, 1864	100 dys.	Mustered out with company Sept. 2, 1864.
Larsh, George W	....do....	38	May 2, 1864	100 dys.	Mustered out with company Sept. 2, 1864.
Larsh, Paul H	....do....	38	May 2, 1864	100 dys.	Promoted to Hospital Steward May 11, 1864.
Lynch, William	....do..	20	May 2, 1864	100 dys.	Mustered out with company Sept. 2, 1864.
Maynor, Benjamin F	....do....	23	May 2, 1864	100 dys.	Mustered out with company Sept. 2, 1864.
Michael, Joseph	....do....	21	May 2, 1864	100 dys.	Mustered out with company Sept. 2, 1864.
Midlam, William	....do....	41	May 2, 1864	100 dys.	Mustered out with company Sept. 2, 1864.
Mills, William H	....do....	19	May 2, 1864	100 dys.	Mustered out with company Sept. 2, 1864.
Morningstar, William H.	....do..	44	May 2, 1864	100 dys.	Mustered out with company Sept. 2, 1864.
Parent, Gordon	....do....	25	May 2, 1864	100 dys.	Mustered out with company Sept. 2, 1864.
Pember, Willard	....do....	35	May 2, 1864	100 dys.	Mustered out with company Sept. 2, 1864.
Phipps, William	....do....	19	May 2, 1864	100 dys.	Mustered out with company Sept. 2, 1864.
Puterbaugh, John	....do..	20	May 2, 1864	100 dys.	Mustered out with company Sept. 2, 1864.
Ratliff, Elijah	....do....	19	May 2, 1864	100 dys.	Mustered out with company Sept. 2, 1864.
Ratliff, Jacob	....do....	34	May 2, 1864	100 dys.	Mustered out with company Sept. 2, 1864.
Reusler, George	....do....	29	May 2, 1864	100 dys.	Mustered out with company Sept. 2, 1864.
Roberts, Samuel	....do....	35	May 2, 1864	100 dys.	Mustered out with company Sept. 2, 1864.
Rodgers, Adam S	....do....	20	May 2, 1864	100 dys.	Mustered out with company Sept. 2, 1864.
Roland, William	....do....	37	May 2, 1864	100 dys.	Mustered out with company Sept. 2, 1864.
Ross, Josiah	....do....	24	May 2, 1864	100 dys.	Died Aug. 24, 1864, in hospital at Camp Dennison, O
Rupe, William	....do....	44	May 2, 1864	100 dys.	Mustered out with company Sept. 2, 1864.
Shaible, John	....do....	28	May 2, 1864	100 dys.	Mustered out with company Sept. 2, 1864.
Sharp, James	....do....	24	May 2, 1864	100 dys.	Mustered out with company Sept. 2, 1864.
Smith, Perry P	....do....	42	May 2, 1864	100 dys.	Mustered out with company Sept. 2, 1864.
Sparks, Isaac	....do....	24	May 2, 1864	100 dys.	Mustered out with company Sept. 2, 1864.
Spencer, Irwin	....do....	19	May 2, 1864	100 dys.	Mustered out with company Sept. 2, 1864.
Stowers, Joseph	....do....	..	May 2, 1864	100 dys.	Absent ——, on sick furlough, at muster-in of company. No further record found.
Thomas, Daniel	....do....	34	May 2, 1864	100 dys.	Killed June [illegible]4, 1864, in action at Greenbrier Gap, W. Va.
Thompson, Jacob W	....do....	18	May 2, 1864	100 dys.	Mustered out with company Sept. 2, 1864.
Trimble, John	....do....	25	May 2, 1864	100 dys.	Mustered out with company Sept. 2, 1864.
Vail, Aaron	....do....	40	May 2, 1864	100 dys.	Mustered out with company Sept. 2, 1864.
Wade, David	....do...	38	May 2, 1864	100 dys.	Mustered out with company Sept. 2, 1864.
Wenger, Ezra	....do...	30	May 2, 1864	100 dys.	Mustered out with company Sept. 2, 1864.
Willcox, Charles	....do....	43	May 2, 1864	100 dys.	Mustered out with company Sept. 2, 1864.
Wise, Jacob	....do....	15	May 2, 1864	100 dys.	Mustered out with company Sept. 2, 1864.

Names.	Rank.	Age.	Date of Entering the Service.	Period of Service.	Remarks.
Turner, William P.	Private.	19	May 2, 1864	100 dys.	Mustered out with company Sept. 2, 1864.
Vanati, Isaac I	....do....	43	May 2, 1864	100 dys.	Mustered out with company Sept. 2, 1864.
Vance, James H.	....do....	19	May 2, 1864	100 dys.	Mustered out with company Sept. 2, 1864.
Viets, Charles	....do....	31	May 2, 1864	100 dys.	Mustered out with company Sept. 2, 1864.
Viets, John W.	....do....	29	May 2, 1864	100 dys.	Mustered out with company Sept. 2, 1864.
Ward, Thomas	....do....	37	May 2, 1864	100 dys.	Mustered out with company Sept. 2, 1864.
Warvel, Irvin	....do....	19	May 2, 1864	100 dys.	Mustered out with company Sept. 2, 1864.
Weller, Louis H.	....do....	38	May 2, 1864	100 dys.	Mustered out with company Sept. 2, 1864.
Whitman, Amos T.	....do....	24	May 2, 1864	100 dys.	Mustered out with company Sept. 2, 1864.
Williams, David	....do....	45	May 2, 1864	100 dys.	Mustered out with company Sept. 2, 1864.
Wolf, Emanuel	....do....	44	May 2, 1864	100 dys.	Mustered out with company Sept. 2, 1864.
Yost, Peter	....do....	19	May 2, 1864	100 dys.	Mustered out with company Sept. 2, 1864.

COMPANY K.

Mustered in May 10, 1864, at Camp Dennison, O., by Robert S. Smith, Captain 2d Cavalry, U. S. A. Mustered out Sept. 2, 1864, at Camp Dennison, O., by L. H. Warner, 1st Lieutenant 17th Infantry, U. S. A.

Names.	Rank.	Age.	Date of Entering the Service.	Period of Service.	Remarks.
Charles A. Welsh	Captain.	31	May 2, 1864	100 dys.	Mustered out with company Sept. 2, 1864.
Benjamin H. Warder	1st Lieut.	38	May 2, 1864	100 dys.	Mustered out with company Sept. 2, 1864.
Martin L. Frantz	2d Lieut.	23	May 2, 1864	100 dys.	Mustered out with company Sept. 2, 1864.
Joel Funk	1st Sergt.	34	May 2, 1864	100 dys.	Mustered out with company Sept. 2, 1864.
Deluna Lawrence	Sergeant.	24	May 2, 1864	100 dys.	Mustered out with company Sept. 2, 1864.
William W. Neal	....do....	37	May 2, 1864	100 dys.	Mustered out with company Sept. 2, 1864.
Andrew R. Benson	....do....	38	May 2, 1864	100 dys.	Mustered out with company Sept. 2, 1864.
Jacob L. McClellan	....do....	43	May 2, 1864	100 dys.	Mustered out with company Sept. 2, 1864.
John Pennell	Corporal.	26	May 2, 1864	100 dys.	Mustered out with company Sept. 2, 1864.
John Shinn	....do....	23	May 2, 1864	100 dys.	Mustered out with company Sept. 2, 1864.
William Locke	....do....	29	May 2, 1864	100 dys.	Mustered out with company Sept. 2, 1864.
Miner Tuttle	....do....	28	May 2, 1864	100 dys.	Mustered out with company Sept. 2, 1864.
[illegible]ny Whiteley	....do....	23	May 2, 1864	100 dys.	Mustered out with company Sept. 2, 1864.
James A. Bird	....do....	21	May 2, 1864	100 dys.	Mustered out with company Sept. 2, 1864.
Charles E. Gillen	....do....	33	May 2, 1864	100 dys.	Mustered out with company Sept. 2, 1864.
Walter, Henchman	....do....	19	May 2, 1864	100 dys.	Mustered out with company Sept. 2, 1864.
Allen, Albert	Private.	22	May 2, 1864	100 dys.	Mustered out with company Sept. 2, 1864.
Anderson, Samuel	....do....	27	May 2, 1864	100 dys.	Mustered out with company Sept. 2, 1864.
Arbogast, Isaac A.	....do....	21	May 2, 1864	100 dys.	Mustered out with company Sept. 2, 1864.
Arbogast, John A.	....do....	23	May 2, 1864	100 dys.	Mustered out with company Sept. 2, 1864.
Beard, Willis H.	....do....	29	May 2, 1864	100 dys.	Mustered out with company Sept. 2, 1864.
Bird, Flavius	....do....	20	May 2, 1864	100 dys.	Mustered out with company Sept. 2, 1864.
Bird, John A.	....do....	24	May 2, 1864	100 dys.	Mustered out with company Sept. 2, 1864.
Butler, James	....do....	28	May 2, 1864	100 dys.	Mustered out with company Sept. 2, 1864.
Cornell, John W.	....do....	37	May 2, 1864	100 dys.	Mustered out with company Sept. 2, 1864.
Dennis, John H.	....do....	29	May 2, 1864	100 dys.	Mustered out with company Sept. 2, 1864.
Doty, Levi	....do....	21	May 2, 1864	100 dys.	Mustered out with company Sept. 2, 1864.
Dyson, Joseph G.	....do....	18	May 2, 1864	100 dys.	Mustered out with company Sept. 2, 1864.
Elston, William	....do....	22	May 2, 1864	100 dys.	Transferred from Co. F May 10, 1864, as William Elson; mustered out with company Sept. 2, 1864.
Fox, Richard	....do....	19	May 2, 1864	100 dys.	Mustered out with company Sept. 2, 1864.
Frey, Frank F.	....do....	18	May 2, 1864	100 dys.	Mustered out with company Sept. 2, 1864.
Gadd, John B.	....do....	23	May 28, 1864	100 dys.	Mustered out with company Sept. 2, 1864.
Gallagher, Michael	....do....	19	May 2, 1864	100 dys.	Mustered out with company Sept. 2, 1864.
Gates, Henry	....do....	20	May 2, 1864	100 dys.	Mustered out with company Sept. 2, 1864.
Gedling, Samuel	....do....	22	May 2, 1864	100 dys.	Mustered out with company Sept. 2, 1864.
Gedling, William	....do....	20	May 2, 1864	100 dys.	Mustered out with company Sept. 2, 1864.
Gillett, Alden H.	....do....	20	May 2, 1864	100 dys.	Absent, sick, at Springfield, O., at muster out of company. No further record found.
Graham, Timothy	....do....	18	May 2, 1864	100 dys.	Mustered out with company Sept. 2, 1864.
Greenwood, Thomas	....do....	18	May 2, 1864	100 dys.	Mustered out with company Sept. 2, 1864.
Hardacre, Jonas	....do....	41	May 2, 1864	100 dys.	Mustered out with company Sept. 2, 1864.
Hartle, Abraham	....do....	37	May 2, 1864	100 dys.	Mustered out with company Sept. 2, 1864.
Hays, Allen	....do....	18	May 2, 1864	100 dys.	Mustered out with company Sept. 2, 1864.
Hendrickson, David	....do....	28	May 2, 1864	100 dys.	Mustered out with company Sept. 2, 1864.
Huffman, James D.	....do....	21	May 2, 1864	100 dys.	Mustered out with company Sept. 2, 1864.
Huffman, Reuben	....do....	19	May 2, 1864	100 dys.	Mustered out with company Sept. 2, 1864.
England, Isaac	....do....	33	May 2, 1864	100 dys.	Mustered out with company Sept. 2, 1864.
Ireland, George W.	....do....	22	May 2, 1864	100 dys.	Mustered out with company Sept. 2, 1864.
Jacobs, Cyrus	....do....	19	May 2, 1864	100 dys.	Mustered out with company Sept. 2, 1864.
Kershner, Benjamin F.	....do....	22	May 2, 1864	100 dys.	Mustered out with company Sept. 2, 1864.
Kershner, Daniel	....do....	18	May 2, 1864	100 dys.	Mustered out with company Sept. 2, 1864.
Kimball, William H.	....do....	19	May 2, 1864	100 dys.	Died Aug. 24, 1864, in hospital at Camp Dennison, O.
Laney, Cephas F.	....do....	20	May 28, 1864	100 dys.	Mustered out with company Sept. 2, 1864.
Laner, Henry	....do....	42	May 2, 1864	100 dys.	Mustered out with company Sept. 2, 1864.
McMann, James	....do....	21	May 2, 1864	100 dys.	Mustered out with company Sept. 2, 1864.
Markwood, Thomas J.	....do....	22	May 2, 1864	100 dys.	Mustered out with company Sept. 2, 1864.
Maxwell, Harry	....do....	18	May 28, 1864	100 dys.	Mustered out with company Sept. 2, 1864.
Meenach, Joseph	....do....	19	May 2, 1864	100 dys.	Mustered out with company Sept. 2, 1864.

Names.	Rank.	Age.	Date of Entering the Service.	Period of Service.	Remarks.
Elias	Private..	43	May 2, 1864	100 dys.	Mustered out with company Sept. 2, 1864.
., Richard C.	....do....	28	May 2, 1864	100 dys.	Mustered out with company Sept. 2, 1864.
, Charles	....do....	18	May 2, 1864	100 dys.	Mustered out with company Sept. 2, 1864.
m, John C.	....do....	18	May 2, 1864	100 dys.	Mustered out with company Sept. 2, 1864.
nd, Martin L.	....do....	31	May 2, 1864	100 dys.	Mustered out with company Sept. 2, 1864.
r, Edward	....do....	23	May 2, 1864	100 dys.	Mustered out with company Sept. 2, 1864.
James	....do....	40	May 2, 1864	100 dys.	Mustered out with company Sept. 2, 1864.
ner, Fountain D.	....do....	18	May 2, 1864	100 dys.	Mustered out with company Sept. 2, 1864.
Edward	....do....	53	May 2, 1864	100 dys	Mustered out with company Sept. 2, 1864.
rs, Robert	....do....	19	May 2, 1864	100 dys.	Mustered out with company Sept. 2, 1864.
rs, David	....do....	32	May 2, 1864	100 dys.	Mustered out with company Sept. 2, 1864.
nan, Samuel B.	....do....	26	May 2, 1864	100 dys.	Mustered out with company Sept. 2, 1864.
ch, Eldred	....do....	21	May 2, 1864	100 dys.	Mustered out with company Sept. 2, 1864.
, William G.	....do....	24	May 2, 1864	100 dys.	Mustered out with company Sept. 2, 1864.
enson, Eston M.	....do....	30	May 2, 1864	100 dys.	Mustered out with company Sept. 2, 1864.
enson, Henry	....do....	26	May 2, 1864	100 dys.	Mustered out with company Sept. 2, 1864.
ns, John H.	....do....	22	May 2, 1864	100 dys.	Mustered out with company Sept. 2, 1864.
r, Algernon	....do....	42	May 2, 1864	100 dys.	Mustered out with company Sept. 2, 1864.
ner, Isaac	....do....	19	May 2, 1864	100 dys.	Mustered out with company Sept. 2, 1864.
, Albert	....do....	22	May 2, 1864	100 dys.	Mustered out with company Sept. 2, 1864.
, William H.	....do....	24	May 2, 1864	100 dys.	Mustered out with company Sept. 2, 1864.
, John W.	....do....	18	May 2, 1864	100 dys.	Mustered out with company Sept. 2, 1864.
er, John	....do....	30	May 2, 1864	100 dys.	Mustered out with company Sept. 2, 1864.
James E.	....do....	37	May 2, 1864	100 dys.	Mustered out with company Sept. 2, 1864.
el, George H.	....do....	35	May 2, 1864	100 dys.	Mustered out with company Sept. 2, 1864.
Aaron.	....do...	22	May 2, 1864	100 dys.	Mustered out with company Sept. 2, 1864.
, William	....do....	19	May 2, 1864	100 dys.	Mustered out with company Sept. 2, 1864.
ey, Joel	....do....	34	May 2, 1864	100 dys.	Mustered out with company Sept. 2, 1864.
, William H.	....do....	26	May 2, 1864	100 dys	Mustered out with company Sept. 2, 1864.

153rd Regiment Ohio Volunteer Infantry.

ONE HUNDRED DAYS' SERVICE.

This Regiment was organized at Camp Dennison, O., May 10, 1864, to serve one hundred days. It was composed of the Forty-first Regiment, Ohio National Guard, from Clermont County, and a part of the Thirty-fifth Regiment, Ohio National Guard, from Clarke County. The Regiment immediately started for Harper's Ferry, W. Va. The greater part of May and June was consumed by the Regiment in performing guard duty at Harper's Ferry and along the line of the Baltimore and Ohio Railroad. In the latter part of June it was ordered to join General Butler's forces, at Bermuda Hundred, and hold itself subject to his orders. A detachment of the Regiment was engaged with the enemy at Hammack's Mills, North River, W. Va., on July 3, 1864, and lost several officers and men, killed and wounded. It was mustered out September 9, 1864, on expiration of its term of service.

153RD REGIMENT OHIO VOLUNTEER INFANTRY.

FIELD AND STAFF.

Mustered in May 10, 1864, at Camp Dennison, O., by Robert S. Smith, Captain 2d Cavalry, U. S. A. Mustered out Sept. 9, 1864, at Camp Dennison, O.

Names.	Rank.	Age.	Date of Entering the Service.	Period of Service.	Remarks.
Israel Stough	Colonel.	..	May 2, 1864	100 dys.	Mustered out with regiment Sept. 9, 1864.
[illegible] A. Leeds	Lt. Col.	..	May 2, 1864	100 dys.	Captured July 3, 1864, at battle of Hammack's Mills, W. Va.; mustered out March 12, 1865, by order of War Department.
[illegible] South	Major.	..	May 2, 1864	100 dys.	Mustered out with regiment Sept. 9, 1864.
John S. Coombs	Surgeon.	..	May 2, 1864	100 dys.	Mustered out with regiment Sept. 9, 1864.
John O. Marsh	Ass't Surg.	..	May 2, 1864	100 dys.	Mustered out with regiment Sept. 9, 1864.
[illegible] A. Farmer	Adjutant	..	May 2, 1864	100 dys.	Mustered out with regiment Sept. 9, 1864.
Charles A. Browning	R. Q. M.	22	May 2, 1864	100 dys.	Promoted from private Co. D May 18, 1864; mustered out with regiment Sept. 9, 1864.
[illegible] Clark	Chaplain	..	May 2, 1864	100 dys.	Mustered out with regiment Sept. 9, 1864.
[illegible] Green	Sergt. Maj	27	May 2, 1864	100 dys.	Promoted from private Co. G May 10, 1864; mustered out with regiment Sept. 9, 1864.
Samuel G. Monce	Q. M. S.	19	May 2, 1864	100 dys.	Promoted from Corporal Co. B May 10, 1864; mustered out with regiment Sept. 9, 1864.
[illegible] D. Wood	Com. Ser.	..	May 2, 1864	100 dys.	Mustered out with regiment Sept. 9, 1864.
L. W. Brown	Hos. St'd	24	May 2, 1864	100 dys.	Promoted from Corporal Co. D June 2, 1864; mustered out with regiment Sept. 9, 1864.
Alfred Squire	Prin. Mus	24	May 2, 1864	100 dys.	Promoted from Sergeant Co. H May 11, 1864; mustered out with regiment Sept. 9, 1864.

COMPANY A.

Mustered in May 10, 1864, at Camp Dennison, O., by Robert S. Smith, Captain 2d Cavalry, U. S. A. Mustered out Sept. 9, 1864, at Camp Dennison, O.

Names.	Rank.	Age.	Date of Entering the Service.	Period of Service.	Remarks.
Thomas W. Rathbone	Captain..	20	May 2, 1864	100 dys.	Captured July 3, 1864, at battle of Hammack's Mills, W. Va.; escaped from Rebel prison, near Columbia, S. C., Nov. 1, 1864; discharged to date Nov. 18, 1864, by order of War Department.
John W. [illegible]	1st Lieut.	26	May 2, 1864	100 dys.	Mustered out with company Sept. 9, 1864.
[illegible]	2d Lieut.	20	May 2, 1864	100 dys.	Mustered out with company Sept. 9, 1864.
William W. [illegible]	1st Sergt.	31	May 2, 1864	100 dys.	Captured July 3, 1864, at battle of Hammack's Mills, W. Va.; mustered out Jan. 27, 1865, at Columbus, O., by order of War Department.
William R. Thomas	Sergeant.	35	May 2, 1864	100 dys.	Mustered out with company Sept. 9, 1864.
[illegible]	....do....	33	May 2, 1864	100 dys.	Mustered out with company Sept. 9, 1864.
William [illegible]	....do....	44	May 2, 1864	100 dys.	Mustered out with company Sept. 9, 1864.
[illegible]	....do....	22	May 2, 1864	100 dys.	Appointed from Corporal May 22, 1864; captured July 3, 1864, at battle of Hammack's Mills, W. Va.; mustered out June 7, 1865, at Columbus, O., by order of War Department.
Henry M. Hancock	Corporal.	24	May 2, 1864	100 dys.	Mustered out with company Sept. 9, 1864.
Jerome Bellymer	....do....	26	May 2, 1864	100 dys.	Mustered out with company Sept. 9, 1864.
John W. Strawbewer	....do....	23	May 2, 1864	100 dys.	Mustered out with company Sept. 9, 1864.
William W. Hopkins	....do....	22	May 2, 1864	100 dys.	Mustered out with company Sept. 9, 1864.
Garrett O. Van Saun	....do....	28	May 2, 1864	100 dys.	Mustered out with company Sept. 9, 1864.
Oliver P. Bellymer	....do....	29	May 2, 1864	100 dys.	Mustered out with company Sept. 9, 1864.
Aaron S. DeHymer	....do....	31	May 2, 1864	100 dys.	Appointed ——; mustered out with company Sept. 9, 1864.
...	Private..	22	May 2, 1864	100 dys.	Mustered out with company Sept. 9, 1864.
...	....do....	19	May 2, 1864	100 dys.	Mustered as Musician; mustered out with company Sept. 9, 1864.
Barton, Theodore J.	....do....	24	May 2, 1864	100 dys.	No record subsequent to muster-in.
Beiler, Andrew	....do....	21	May 2, 1864	100 dys.	Captured July 3, 1864, at battle of Hammack's Mills, W. Va.; mustered out June 3, 1865, at Columbus, O., by order of War Department.

Names.	Rank.	Age.	Date of Entering the Service.	Period of Service.	Remarks.
Moler, Matthias	Private	28	May 2, 1864		Mustered
Morgan, James	...do...	27	May 2, 1864		Mustered
Meyer, Kilby H	...do...	23	May 2, 1864		Mustered
Needham, Thomas	...do...	19	May 2, 1864		Mustered
Needham, John	...do...	33	May 2, 1864		Mustered as company Se
Nell, Robert	...do...	..	May 2, 1864		Mustered out
Nichols, Nathan	...do...	42	May 2, 1864		Mustered as company Se
Nicolas, Victor	...do...	22	May 2, 1864		Mustered out
Orebaugh, Alfred	...do...	23	May 2, 1864		Mustered out
Orebaugh, Eli	...do...	28	May 2, 1864		Mustered out
Orr, Barton	...do...	25	May 2, 1864		Mustered as company Se
Patterson, Alexander	...do...	40	May 2, 1864		Mustered out
Patterson, Milton	...do...	35	May 2, 1864		Mustered out
Prickett, Alfred	...do...	21	May 2, 1864		Mustered
Rapp, Jacob	...do...	30	May 2, 1864		Mustered out
Reynolds, H. S	...do...	38	May 2, 1864		Mustered out
Roye, John	...do...	22	May 2, 1864		Mustered out
Runyan, Henry J	...do...	24	May 2, 1864		Mustered out
Runyan, Elias C	...do...	30	May 2, 1864		Mustered out
Runyan, Samuel	...do...	35	May 2, 1864		Mustered out
Sattler, James	...do...	28	May 2, 1864		Mustered
Shumard, Peter	...do...	25	May 2, 1864		Mustered
Shumard, Richard	...do...	27	May 2, 1864		Mustered out
Smith, Louis H	...do...	35	May 2, 1864		Mustered out
South, Andred J	...do...	28	May 2, 1864		Mustered
Stymets, James	...do...	21	May 2, 1864		Mustered out
Tice, Elias	...do...	30	May 2, 1864		Mustered out
Turner, James	...do...	34	May 2, 1864		No record subs
Turner, William	...do...	32	May 2, 1864		Mustered out
Van Camp, Thomas	...do...	19	May 2, 1864		See Co. K.
Van Horn, Jonah	...do...	19	May 2, 1864		Mustered out
Waite, Francis A	...do...	24	May 2, 1864		Mustered out
Whitaker, Thomas	...do...	27	May 2, 1864		Mustered out
White, Ansel	...do...	30	May 2, 1864		Mustered out
White, Francis M	...do...	23	May 2, 1864		Mustered out
White, Thomas	...do...	28	May 2, 1864		Mustered out
Willis, William H	...do...	25	May 2, 1864		Mustered out

COMPANY C.

Mustered in May 10, 1864, at Camp Dennison, O., by Robert S. Smith, Captain
out Sept. 9, 1864, at Camp Dennison, O.

Names.	Rank.	Age.	Date of Entering the Service.	Period of Service.	Remarks.
John McNeill	Captain.	33	May 2, 1864	100 dys.	Mustered out
Leonidas W. Frasier	1st Lieut.	35	May 2, 1864	100 dys.	Killed July 3, Mills, W. Va
William A. Frambers	2d Lieut.	27	May 2, 1864	100 dys.	Mustered out
William F. Landon	1st Sergt.	27	May 2, 1864	100 dys.	Mustered
E. R. Salt	Sergeant.	24	May 2, 1864	100 dys.	Mustered out
L. W. Pemberton	...do...	34	May 2, 1864	100 dys.	Mustered out
W. F. Crane	...do...	28	May 2, 1864	100 dys.	Mustered out
Michael Altman	...do...	30	May 2, 1864	100 dys.	Mustered out
John McMurchy	Corporal.	27	May 2, 1864	100 dys.	Mustered out
Robert McNair	...do...	23	May 2, 1864	100 dys.	Mustered out
G. W. Pemberton	...do...	27	May 2, 1864	100 dys.	Mustered out
Perry S. Mace	...do...	25	May 2, 1864	100 dys.	Mustered out
Archibald McNair	...do...	30	May 2, 1864	100 dys.	Mustered out
James McMurchy	...do...	25	May 2, 1864	100 dys.	Appointed — tle of Hamn out March order of War
Altman, John R	Private.	21	May 2, 1864	100 dys.	Mustered as company Se
Altman, Philip	...do...	21	May 2, 1864	100 dys.	Mustered out
Altman, W. A	...do...	18	May 2, 1864	100 dys.	Mustered out
Anderson, G. W	...do...	19	May 2, 1864	100 dys.	Mustered out
Anderson, W. B	...do...	22	May 2, 1864	100 dys.	Mustered out
Armacost, Aaron	...do...	24	May 2, 1864	100 dys.	Mustered out
Austin, Edward	...do...	18	May 2, 1864	100 dys.	Captured July Mills, W. V.; Columbus, O
Bess, A. E. L	...do...	41	May 2, 1864	100 dys.	Mustered out
Boggess, Jordon	...do...	25	May 2, 1864	100 dys.	Mustered out
Boggess, Randolph	...do...	22	May 2, 1864	100 dys.	Mustered out
Bowlare, James	...do...	30	May 2, 1864	100 dys.	Mustered as company Se
Brooks, Pat	...do...	41	May 2, 1864		No record subs

COMPANY D.

Mustered in May 10, 1864, at Camp Dennison, O., by Robert S. Smith, Capt
out Sept. 8, 1864, at Camp Dennison, O.

Names.	Rank.	Age.	Date of Entering the Service.		Period of Service.	
Archibald McNair, Jr.	Captain.	35	May	2, 1864	100 dys.	Mustered o
William E. Nichols	1st Lieut.	28	May	2, 1864	100 dys.	Mustered o
James R. Scott	2d Lieut.	23	May	2, 1864	100 dys.	Mustered o
James H. Brannon	1st Sergt.	40	May	2, 1864	100 dys.	Mustered o
John M. Flannagan	Sergeant.	21	May	2, 1864	100 dys.	Mustered
B. L. Winans	....do....	28	May	2, 1864	100 dys.	Mustered
Joseph Ernst	....do....	34	May	2, 1864	100 dys.	Mustered
Thomas Sargent	....do....	28	May	2, 1864	100 dys.	Mustered
J. Wesley Simmons	Corporal.	21	May	2, 1864	100 dys.	Mustered
Charles Hancock	....do....	22	May	2, 1864	100 dys.	Mustered
G. W. Lakin	....do....	28	May	2, 1864	100 dys.	Mustered
Hugh McNair	....do....	31	May	2, 1864	100 dys.	Mustered
John L. Barkley	....do....	21	May	2, 1864	100 dys.	Mustered
I. N. Brown	....do....	24	May	2, 1864	100 dys.	Promoted t
W. H. Altman	....do....	24	May	2, 1864	100 dys.	Mustered o
Josephus Donley	....do....	34	May	2, 1864	100 dys.	Appointed Sept. 9, 1
James F. Prather	....do....	33	May	2, 1864	100 dys.	Appointed Sept. 9, 1
Benjamin Packard	Musician	21	May	2, 1864	100 dys.	Mustered o
John McLane	....do....	..	May	2, 1864	100 dys.	No record s
Altman, William R.	Private.	34	May	2, 1864	100 dys.	Mustered o
Archard, J. B.	....do....	20	May	2, 1864	100 dys.	No record s
Armacost, George F.	....do....	28	May	2, 1864	100 dys.	Mustered o
Ashley, T. J.	....do....	26	May	2, 1864	100 dys.	Mustered o
Balnum, Isaac	....do....	30	May	2, 1864	100 dys.	Mustered o
Balnum, J. C.	....do....	40	May	2, 1864	100 dys.	Mustered o
Baker, Hyman	....do....	30	May	2, 1864	100 dys.	No record s
Bettle, F. E.	....do....	27	May	2, 1864	100 dys.	Mustered o
Browning, Charles N.	....do....	32	May	2, 1864	100 dys.	Promoted t master M
Cook, George W.	....do....	20	May	2, 1864	100 dys.	No record s
Cooper, Alexander	....do....	19	May	2, 1864	100 dys.	Mustered o
Creamer, Andrew J.	....do....	20	May	2, 1864	100 dys.	Mustered o
Creamer, George D.	....do....	30	May	2, 1864	100 dys.	Transferre tered out
Davis, Owen W.	....do....	48	May	2, 1864	100 dys.	Mustered o
Day, Elisha W.	....do....	37	May	2, 1864	100 dys.	Mustered o
Day, Wilson	....do....	38	May	2, 1864	100 dys.	Mustered o
Donley, Edward F.	....do....	27	May	2, 1864	100 dys.	Mustered o
Dunn, Alexander	....do....	29	May	2, 1864	100 dys.	Mustered o
Florer, Robert	....do....	36	May	2, 1864	100 dys.	Mustered o
Gelvin, Lewis	....do....	35	May	2, 1864	100 dys.	Mustered o
Gustin, Benijah	....do....	23	May	2, 1864	100 dys.	Transferre tered out
Hancock, William R.	....do....	24	May	2, 1864	100 dys.	No record s
Hewitt, William F.	....do....	29	May	2, 1864	100 dys.	Mustered company
Hillis, William	....do....	26	May	2, 1864	100 dys.	Mustered o
Husted, Thomas D.	....do....	30	May	2, 1864	100 dys.	Mustered o
Jones, Christopher	....do....	32	May	2, 1864	100 dys.	Mustered o
Knowles, John	....do....	19	May	2, 1864	100 dys.	Mustered o
Lakin, Benjamin D.	....do....	21	May	2, 1864	100 dys.	Mustered o
Lakin, John R.	....do....	29	May	2, 1864	100 dys.	Mustered o
Laney, John H.	....do....	38	May	2, 1864	100 dys.	Mustered o
Leeds, Samuel	....do....	31	May	2, 1864	100 dys.	Mustered o
Light, Samuel	....do....	21	May	2, 1864	100 dys.	Mustered o
Littleton, Darius	....do....	43	May	2, 1864	100 dys.	Mustered o
McKee, Emory	....do....	23	May	2, 1864	100 dys.	Mustered o
McLane, John	....do....	33	May	2, 1864	100 dys.	Mustered o
McMurchy, Archie	....do....	35	May	2, 1864	100 dys.	Mustered o
McNair, William	....do....	26	May	2, 1864	100 dys.	Mustered o
Means, John	....do....	33	May	2, 1864	100 dys.	Mustered o
Miller, Jacob D.	....do....	18	May	2, 1864	100 dys.	Transferre out with
Nichols, John P.	....do....	21	May	2, 1864	100 dys.	No record s
Nichols, William M.	....do....	20	May	2, 1864	100 dys.	Mustered o
Paltz, Julius	....do....	30	May	2, 1864	100 dys.	Mustered o
Peddicord, Wesley	....do....	21	May	2, 1864	100 dys.	Mustered o
Peppers, Sampson	....do....	36	May	2, 1864	100 dys.	Mustered o
Placard, John	....do....	29	May	2, 1864	100 dys.	No record s
Placard, Marion	....do....	27	May	2, 1864	100 dys.	Mustered o
Placard, Thomson L.	....do....	31	May	2, 1864	100 dys.	Mustered o
Porter, William	....do....	42	May	2, 1864	100 dys.	Mustered o
Porter, William, Jr.	....do....	42	May	2, 1864	100 dys.	Mustered o
Purkhiser, Wesley	....do....	35	May	2, 1864	100 dys.	Mustered o
Riley, Michael C.	....do....	30	May	2, 1864	100 dys.	Mustered o

	Rank.	Age.	Date of Entering the Service.	Period of Service.	Remarks.
	Private..	23	May 2, 1864	100 dys.	Mustered out with company Sept. 9, 1864.
	....do....	27	May 2, 1864	100 dys.	Mustered out with company Sept. 9, 1864.
	....do....	27	May 2, 1864	100 dys.	Mustered out with company Sept. 9, 1864.
	....do....	18	May 2, 1864	100 dys.	Mustered out with company Sept. 9, 1864.
	... .	18	May 2, 1864	100 dys.	Died May 30, 1864, at Paw Paw, W. Va.
	... .	19	May 2, 1864	100 dys.	Mustered out with company Sept. 9, 1864.
	... .	26	May 2, 1864	100 dys.	Mustered out with company Sept. 9, 1864.
	... .	24	May 2, 1864	100 dys.	Mustered out with company Sept. 9, 1864.
	... .	21	May 2, 1864	100 dys.	Mustered out with company Sept. 9, 1864.
	... .	24	May 2, 1864	100 dys.	Mustered out with company Sept. 9, 1864.
	... .	26	May 2, 1864	100 dys.	Mustered out with company Sept. 9, 1864.
	... .	28	May 2, 1864	100 dys.	No record subsequent to muster-in.
	... .	18	May 2, 1864	100 dys.	Mustered out with company Sept. 9, 1864.
	... .	20	May 2, 1864	100 dys.	Mustered out with company Sept. 9, 1864.
	... .	29	May 2, 1864	100 dys.	Mustered out with company Sept. 9, 1864.
	... .	23	May 2, 1864	100 dys.	Mustered out with company Sept. 9, 1864.
	... .	22	May 2, 1864	100 dys.	No record subsequent to muster-in.
	... .	24	May 2, 1864	100 dys.	Mustered out with company Sept. 9, 1864.

COMPANY E.

Mustered in May 10, 1864, at Camp Dennison, O., by Robert S. Smith, Captain 2d Cavalry, U. S. A. Mustered out Sept. 9, 1864, at Camp Dennison, O.

Name	Rank	Age	Date of Entering the Service	Period of Service	Remarks
James L. McKinney	Captain.	25	May 2, 1864	100 dys.	Mustered out with company Sept. 9, 1864.
Ira H. Miller	1st Lieut.	21	May 2, 1864	100 dys.	Mustered out with company Sept. 9, 1864.
John E. Layton	2d Lieut.	..	May 2, 1864	100 dys.	Mustered out with company Sept. 9, 1864.
Henry Harnish	1st Sergt.	31	May 2, 1864	100 dys.	Mustered out with company Sept. 9, 1864.
Abraham Martin	Sergeant.	32	May 2, 1864	100 dys.	Mustered out with company Sept. 9, 1864.
Andrew H. Miller	....do....	26	May 2, 1864	100 dys.	Mustered out with company Sept. 9, 1864.
George Grimm	....do....	25	May 2, 1864	100 dys.	No record subsequent to muster in.
John Jenkins	....do....	21	May 2, 1864	100 dys.	Mustered out with company Sept. 9, 1864.
John C. DeGroot	....do....	28	May 2, 1864	100 dys.	Appointed from private Co. F ——; mustered out with company Sept. 9, 1864.
J. A. Miller	Corporal.	26	May 2, 1864	100 dys.	Mustered out with company Sept. 9, 1864.
Levi Kaufman	....do....	26	May 2, 1864	100 dys.	Mustered out with company Sept. 9, 1864.
DeWitt C. Minick	....do....	22	May 2, 1864	100 dys.	Mustered out with company Sept. 9, 1864.
Jacob Hershey	....do....	36	May 2, 1864	100 dys.	Mustered out with company Sept. 9, 1864.
Michael Garst	....do....	33	May 2, 1864	100 dys.	Mustered out with company Sept. 9, 1864.
James Allen	....do....	41	May 2, 1864	100 dys.	Mustered out with company Sept. 9, 1864.
Joel T. Forry	....do....	37	May 2, 1864	100 dys.	Mustered out with company Sept. 9, 1864.
Henry Martin	....do....	43	May 2, 1864	100 dys.	Appointed ——; mustered out with company Sept. 9, 1864.
Albin, Gabriel	Private..	30	May 2, 1864	100 dys.	Mustered out with company Sept. 9, 1864.
Alspaugh, John	....do....	35	May 2, 1864	100 dys.	Mustered out with company Sept. 9, 1864; also borne on rolls as Elias Alspaugh.
Aston, Joseph	....do....	30	May 2, 1864	100 dys.	Mustered out with company Sept. 9, 1864.
Atkinson, John F	....do....	19	May 2, 1864	100 dys.	Mustered out with company Sept. 9, 1864.
Bair, Solomon	....do....	20	May 2, 1864	100 dys.	Mustered out with company Sept. 9, 1864.
Baker, Alonzo	....do....	24	May 2, 1864	100 dys.	No record subsequent to muster-in.
Baker, Ambrose	....do....	34	May 2, 1864	100 dys.	Mustered out with company Sept. 9, 1864.
Barkman, Jesse	....do....	38	May 2, 1864	100 dys.	No record subsequent to muster-in.
Bean, William H	....do....	19	May 2, 1864	100 dys.	No record subsequent to muster-in.
Boyd, William W	....do....	22	May 2, 1864	100 dys.	Mustered out with company Sept. 9, 1864.
Brehm, Philip	....do....	30	May 2, 1864	100 dys.	Mustered out with company Sept. 9, 1864.
Bromley, Isaac	....do....	32	May 2, 1864	100 dys.	Mustered out with company Sept. 9, 1864.
Brown, Samuel	....do....	27	May 2, 1864	100 dys.	Mustered out with company Sept. 9, 1864.
Burns, Isaac	....do....	23	May 2, 1864	100 dys.	No record subsequent to muster-in.
Burns, Jacob G	....do....	41	May 2, 1864	100 dys.	Mustered out with company Sept. 9, 1864.
Burns, James	....do....	35	May 2, 1864	100 dys.	Mustered out with company Sept. 9, 1864.
Campbell, James P	....do....	36	May 2, 1864	100 dys.	Mustered out with company Sept. 9, 1864.
Crail, George	....do....	18	May 2, 1864	100 dys.	Mustered out with company Sept. 9, 1864.
Crane, John B	....do....	18	May 2, 1864	100 dys.	No record subsequent to muster-in.
Creevy, John D	....do....	24	May 2, 1864	100 dys.	Mustered out with company Sept. 9, 1864.
Dean, Joseph S	....do....	22	May 2, 1864	100 dys.	Transferred from Co. F ——; captured ——; paroled ——; died Dec. 10, 1864, at Annapolis, Maryland.
Deaton, Nathan	....do....	22	May 2, 1864	100 dys.	Mustered out with company Sept. 9, 1864.
Dille, George L	....do....	24	May 2, 1864	100 dys.	Mustered out with company Sept. 9, 1864.
Dingess, William	....do....	25	May 2, 1864	100 dys.	Mustered out with company Sept. 9, 1864.
Ellis, Benjamin	....do....	26	May 2, 1864	100 dys.	Mustered out with company Sept. 9, 1864.
Forbes, Henry G	....do....	18	May 2, 1864	100 dys.	Mustered out with company Sept. 9, 1864.
Frantz, George	....do....	18	May 2, 1864	100 dys.	Transferred from Co. F ——; mustered out with company Sept. 9, 1864.
Frantz, Israel	....do....	20	May 2, 1864	100 dys.	Mustered out with company Sept. 9, 1864.
Franz, Daniel	....do....	24	May 2, 1864	100 dys.	Mustered out with company Sept. 9, 1864.
Fruck, Peter	....do....	35	May 2, 1864	100 dys.	No record subsequent to muster in.
Garst, Elias	....do....	28	May 2, 1864	100 dys.	Mustered out with company Sept. 9, 1864.
Garver, Ezra	....do....	27	May 2, 1864	100 dys.	Mustered out with company Sept. 9, 1864.
Gordon, Henry	....do....	27	May 2, 1864	100 dys.	Transferred to Co. F ——.

Names.	Rank.	Age.	Date of Entering the Service.	Period of Service.	Remarks.
Harnish, Amos B.	Private.	18	May 2, 1864	100 dys.	Mustered out with company Sept. 9, 1864.
Harnish, Christ	...do...	26	May 2, 1864	100 dys.	Mustered out with company Sept. 9, 1864.
Harnish, John S.	...do...	20	May 2, 1864	100 dys.	Mustered out with company Sept. 9, 1864.
Heck, David S.	...do...	19	May 2, 1864	100 dys.	Mustered out with company Sept. 9, 1864.
Herr, Jacob	...do...	39	May 2, 1864	100 dys.	Mustered out with company Sept. 9, 1864.
Hershey, Jefferson	...do...	20	May 2, 1864	100 dys.	Mustered out with company Sept. 9, 1864.
Hill, Robert B.	...do...	19	May 2, 1864	100 dys.	Transferred from Co. F —; mustered out with company Sept. 9, 1864.
Hill, Littleton W. T.	...do...	22	May 2, 1864	100 dys.	Transferred from Co. F —; mustered out with company Sept. 9, 1864.
Howard, Peter	...do...	23	May 2, 1864	100 dys.	Mustered out with company Sept. 9, 1864.
Hughs, Albert	...do...	18	May 2, 1864	100 dys.	Transferred from Co. F —; mustered out with company Sept. 9, 1864.
Jenkins, David	...do...	29	May 2, 1864	100 dys.	Mustered out with
Johnson, William F.	...do...	24	May 2, 1864	ys	out with 9, 1864.
Jones, Amos	...do...	26	May 2, 1864	ys	out with 9, 1864.
Kauffman, John	...do...	30	May 2, 1864	100 dys.	Mustered out with 9, 1864.
Kleinfelter, Alexander	...do...	36	May 2, 1864	100 dys.	Mustered out with company Sept. 9, 1864.
Kline, Tobias	...do...	24	May 2, 1864	100 dys.	Mustered out with company Sept. 9, 1864.
Kongore, James A.	...do...	40	May 2, 1864	100 dys.	Absent, sick —. No further record found.
Lafferty, Samuel	...do...	22	May 2, 1864	100 dys.	Mustered out with company Sept. 9, 1864.
Lamme, James G.	...do...	34	May 2, 1864	100 dys.	Mustered out with company Sept. 9, 1864.
Lamme, John W.	...do...	25	May 2, 1864	100 dys.	Mustered out with company Sept. 9, 1864.
Latourette, Robert	...do...	30	May 2, 1864	100 dys.	Mustered out with company Sept. 9, 1864.
Layton, Ezra	...do...	18	May 2, 1864	100 dys.	Mustered out with company Sept. 9, 1864.
Layton, Orin	...do...	18	May 2, 1864	100 dys.	Mustered out with company Sept. 9, 1864.
Layton, Thomas E.	...do...	19	May 2, 1864	100 dys.	Mustered out with company Sept. 9, 1864.
Leffel, Henry	...do...	25	May 2, 1864	100 dys.	Mustered out with company Sept. 9, 1864.
Leffel, Joseph	...do...	22	May 2, 1864	100 dys.	Mustered out with company Sept. 9, 1864.
Lough, John	...do...	23	May 2, 1864	100 dys.	Mustered out with company Sept. 9, 1864.
Lyle, William	...do...	21	May 2, 1864	100 dys.	Absent, sick —. No further record found.
McLaren, Duncan	...do...	20	May 2, 1864	100 dys.	Mustered out with company Sept. 9, 1864.
Miller, A. S.	...do...	35	May 2, 1864	100 dys.	Mustered out with company Sept. 9, 1864.
Miller, John P.	...do...	18	May 2, 1864	100 dys.	Transferred to Co. F —.
Musselman, Michael	...do...	47	May 2, 1864	100 dys.	Transferred to Co. F —.
Myers, Daniel O.	...do...	27	May 2, 1864	100 dys.	Mustered out with company Sept. 9, 1864.
Neff, Warren	...do...	29	May 2, 1864	100 dys.	Mustered out with company Sept. 9, 1864.
Omert, Jacob	...do...	38	May 2, 1864	100 dys.	Mustered out with company Sept. 9, 1864.
Plants, Robert	...do...	28	May 2, 1864	100 dys.	Mustered out with company Sept. 9, 1864.
Prince, Henry	...do...	36	May 2, 1864	100 dys.	No record subsequent to muster-in.
Scorce, William	...do...	30	May 2, 1864	100 dys.	Captured —; paroled —; died Dec. 8, 1864 at Annapolis, Md.
Serfece, J. A.	...do...	22	May 2, 1864	100 dys.	Mustered out with company Sept. 9, 1864.
Shepard, Jacob	...do...	39	May 2, 1864	100 dys.	Mustered out with company Sept. 9, 1864.
Spidel, John	...do...	35	May 2, 1864	100 dys.	Mustered out with company Sept. 9, 1864.
Stetsel, Lewis	...do...	22	May 2, 1864	100 dys.	Mustered out with company Sept. 9, 1864.
Stonebarger, William L.	...do...	22	May 2, 1864	100 dys.	Mustered out with company Sept. 9, 1864.
Stroup, John E.	...do...	40	May 2, 1864	100 dys.	Mustered out with company Sept. 9, 1864.
Trousdale, Joseph A.	...do...	22	May 2, 1864	100 dys.	Transferred from Co. F —; mustered out with company Sept. 9, 1864.
Trout, John	...do...	42	May 2, 1864	100 dys.	Mustered out with company Sept. 9, 1864.
Trowbridge, James W.	...do...	34	May 2, 1864	100 dys.	Mustered out with company Sept. 9, 1864.
Trumbo, William	...do...	22	May 2, 1864	100 dys.	Mustered out with company Sept. 9, 1864.
Vay, Michael	...do...	40	May 2, 1864	100 dys.	Mustered out with company Sept. 9, 1864.
Wallace, Benjamin F.	...do...	41	May 2, 1864	100 dys.	No record subsequent to muster in.
Wallace, James H.	...do...	35	May 2, 1864	100 dys.	Mustered out with company Sept. 9, 1864.
Weingand, William	...do...	20	May 2, 1864	100 dys.	Mustered out with company Sept. 9, 1864.
Wilson, John	...do...	28	May 2, 1864	100 dys.	Mustered out with company Sept. 9, 1864.
Wilson, Timothy	...do...	24	May 2, 1864	100 dys.	Mustered out with company Sept. 9, 1864.
Wise, George	...do...	21	May 2, 1864	100 dys.	Mustered out with company Sept. 9, 1864.
Youler, Philip D. R.	...do...	23	May 2, 1864	100 dys.	Mustered out with company Sept. 9, 1864.
Zellers, John W.	...do...	32	May 2, 1864	100 dys.	No record subsequent to muster in.

COMPANY F.

Mustered in May 10, 1864, at Camp Dennison, O., by Robert S. Smith, Captain 2d Cavalry, U. S. A. Mustered out Sept. 9, 1864, at Camp Dennison, O.

Names.	Rank.	Age.	Date of Entering the Service.	Period of Service.	Remarks.
Harrison C. Cross	Captain.	29	May 2, 1864	100 dys.	Mustered out with company Sept. 9, 1864.
Jacob Hanes	1st Lieut.	26	May 2, 1864	100 dys.	Mustered out with company Sept. 9, 1864.
Samuel Esterline	2d Lieut.	34	May 2, 1864	100 dys.	Mustered out with company Sept. 9, 1864.
Aaron W. Hampleman	1st Sergt.	29	May 2, 1864	100 dys.	Mustered out with company Sept. 9, 1864.
Samuel S. Taylor	Sergeant.	27	May 2, 1864	100 dys.	Mustered out with company Sept. 9, 1864.
Josiah W. S. Reed	...do...	41	May 2, 1864	100 dys.	Captured July 8, 1864, in action near Buffalo Gap, W. Va., and confined in Rebel Prison at Andersonville, Ga.; sent to Rebel Prison at Millen, Ga., Oct. 31, 1864. No further record found.
Mark Drummond	...do...	23	May 2, 1864	100 dys.	Mustered out with company Sept. 9, 1864.
James T. Akin	...do...	41	May 2, 1864	100 dys.	Mustered out with company Sept. 9, 1864.
Joseph Myers	Corporal.	38	May 2, 1864	100 dys.	No record subsequent to muster in.

Names.	Rank.	Age.	Date of Entering the Service.	Period of Service.	Remarks.
[illegible]	Private..	29	May 2, 1864	100 dys.	Mustered out with company Sept. 9, 1864.
[illegible]	...do....	41	May 2, 1864	100 dys.	Mustered out with company Sept. 9, 1864.
[illegible]	...do....	41	May 2, 1864	100 dys.	Mustered out with company Sept. 9, 1864.
[illegible]	...do....	34	May 2, 1864	100 dys.	Mustered out with company Sept. 9, 1864.
[illegible]	...do....	30	May 2, 1864	100 dys.	Mustered out with company Sept. 9, 1864.
[illegible], Thomas	...do....	23	May 2, 1864	100 dys.	Transferred to Co. I May 19, 1864.
[illegible], John D.	...do....	27	May 2, 1864	100 dys.	Mustered out with company Sept. 9, 1864.
[illegible]	...do....	15	May 2, 1864	100 dys.	Mustered as Corporal; mustered out with company Sept. 9, 1864.
[illegible], William L.	...do....	20	May 2, 1864	100 dys.	Died July 11, 1864, at Batavia, O.
[illegible], Jefferson M.	...do....	20	May 2, 1864	100 dys.	Mustered out with company Sept. 9, 1864.
[illegible], Alexander B.	...do....	30	May 2, 1864	100 dys.	Mustered out with company Sept. 9, 1864.
[illegible], Randolph	...do....	20	May 2, 1864	100 dys.	Mustered out with company Sept. 9, 1864.
[illegible], Charles W.	...do....	18	May 2, 1864	100 dys.	Mustered out with company Sept. 9, 1864.
[illegible], Henry C.	...do....	24	May 2, 1864	100 dys.	Mustered out with company Sept. 9, 1864.
[illegible], Oliver R.	...do....	25	May 2, 1864	100 dys.	Mustered out with company Sept. 9, 1864.
[illegible], Robert	...do....	26	May 2, 1864	100 dys.	Mustered out with company Sept. 9, 1864.

COMPANY H.

Mustered in May 10, 1864, at Camp Dennison, O., by Robert S. Smith, Captain 2d Cavalry, U. S. A. Mustered out Sept. 9, 1864, at Camp Dennison, O.

Names.	Rank.	Age.	Date of Entering the Service.	Period of Service.	Remarks.
[illegible] W. [illegible]		42	May 2, 1864	100 dys.	Mustered out with company Sept. 9, 1864.
[illegible]		38	May 2, 1864	100 dys.	Mustered out with company Sept. 9, 1864.
[illegible]		32	May 2, 1864	100 dys.	Mustered out with company Sept. 9, 1864.
William T. [illegible]		28	May 2, 1864	100 dys.	Appointed May 11, 1864; mustered out with company Sept. 9, 1864.
William J. [illegible]		31	May 2, 1864	100 dys.	Mustered out with company Sept. 9, 1864.
[illegible] H. Allen		41	May 2, 1864	100 dys.	Mustered out with company Sept. 9, 1864.
William S. [illegible]		25	May 2, 1864	100 dys.	Captured July 3, 1864, at battle of Hammack's Mills, W. Va.; died Jan. 15, 1865, in Rebel Prison at Florence, S. C.
[illegible]		34	May 2, 1864	100 dys.	Promoted to Principal Musician May 11, 1864.
[illegible]		18	May 2, 1864	100 dys.	Appointed from Corporal May 24, 1864; mustered out with company Sept. 9, 1864.
[illegible]		23	May 2, 1864	100 dys.	Appointed from Corporal July 1, 1864; mustered out with company Sept. 9, 1864.
[illegible]		25	May 2, 1864	100 dys.	Mustered out with company Sept. 9, 1864.
[illegible]		37	May 2, 1864	100 dys.	Mustered out with company Sept. 9, 1864.
[illegible]		20	May 2, 1864	100 dys.	Mustered out with company Sept. 9, 1864.
[illegible]		43	May 2, 1864	100 dys.	Mustered out with company Sept. 9, 1864.
[illegible]		41	May 2, 1864	100 dys.	Appointed May 11, 1864; mustered out with company Sept. 9, 1864.
John W. Saunders	...do....	31	May 2, 1864	100 dys.	Appointed May 24, 1864; mustered out with company Sept. 9, 1864.
[illegible]	...do....	18	May 2, 1864	100 dys.	Appointed July 1, 1864; mustered out with company Sept. 9, 1864.
[illegible]	...do....	20	May 2, 1864	100 dys.	Appointed July 20, 1864; mustered out with company Sept. 9, 1864.
[illegible] W.	Private..	25	May 2, 1864	100 dys.	Mustered out with company Sept. 9, 1864.
[illegible]	...do....	24	May 2, 1864	100 dys.	Mustered as Corporal; mustered out with company Sept. 9, 1864.
[illegible]	...do....	33	May 2, 1864	100 dys.	Mustered out with company Sept. 9, 1864.
[illegible], Charles H.	...do....	22	May 2, 1864	100 dys.	Mustered out with company Sept. 9, 1864.
[illegible] A.	..	35	May 2, 1864	100 dys.	Mustered out with company Sept. 9, 1864.
[illegible]	..	25	May 2, 1864	100 dys.	Mustered out with company Sept. 9, 1864.
[illegible] D.	..	44	May 2, 1864	100 dys.	Mustered out with company Sept. 9, 1864.
[illegible]	..	20	May 2, 1864	100 dys.	Mustered out with company Sept. 9, 1864.
[illegible] C.	..	29	May 2, 1864	100 dys.	Mustered as Corporal; mustered out with company Sept. 9, 1864.
Cramer, James	...do....	32	May 2, 1864	100 dys.	Transferred from Co. G May 19, 1864; mustered out with company Sept. 9, 1864.
[illegible]		34	May 2, 1864	100 dys.	Mustered out with company Sept. 9, 1864.
[illegible]		33	May 2, 1864	100 dys.	Mustered out with company Sept. 9, 1864.
[illegible]		35	May 2, 1864	100 dys.	Mustered out with company Sept. 9, 1864.
[illegible]	..	31	May 2, 1864	100 dys.	Died March 12, 1865, at Martinsburg, W. Va.
[illegible]	..	18	May 2, 1864	100 dys.	Mustered out with company Sept. 9, 1864.
[illegible]	..	23	May 2, 1864	100 dys.	Mustered out with company Sept. 9, 1864.
[illegible]	..	27	May 2, 1864	100 dys.	Mustered out with company Sept. 9, 1864.
[illegible]	..	21	May 2, 1864	100 dys.	Mustered out with company Sept. 9, 1864.
[illegible]	..	44	May 2, 1864	100 dys.	Mustered out with company Sept. 9, 1864.
[illegible]	..	19	May 2, 1864	100 dys.	Mustered out with company Sept. 9, 1864.
[illegible]	..	19	May 2, 1864	100 dys.	Transferred from Co. G May 19, 1864; captured July 3, 1864, at battle of Hammack's Mills, W. Va.; died Dec. 9, 1864, in Rebel Prison at Andersonville, Ga.
[illegible]		32	May 2, 1864	100 dys.	Mustered out with company Sept. 9, 1864.
[illegible]		21	May 2, 1864	100 dys.	Mustered out with company Sept. 9, 1864.
[illegible]		27	May 2, 1864	100 dys.	Mustered out with company Sept. 9, 1864.

Names.	Rank.	Age.	Date of Entering the Service	Period of Service.	Remarks.
Hill, Thomas	Private..	23	May 2, 1864	100 dys.	Mustered out with company Sept.
Hoffman, George F	....do....	38	May 2, 1864	100 dys.	Mustered out with company Sept.
Holt, Samuel	....do....	37	May 2, 1864	100 dys.	Mustered out with company Sept.
Hopkins, William O	....do....	26	May 2, 1864	100 dys.	Mustered out with company Sept.
Hudleston, James	....do....	35	May 2, 1864	100 dys.	Died June 5, 1864, in hospital a West Virginia.
Hunt, Washington W	....do....	26	May 2, 1864	100 dys.	Mustered out with company Sept.
Hutchinson, Job	....do....	28	May 2, 1864	100 dys.	Mustered out with company Sept.
Jones, Albert	....do....	18	May 2, 1864	100 dys.	Captured July 3, 1864, at battle of Mills, W. Va.; died Nov. 28, 18 Prison at Florence, S. C.
Jordon, Jacob S	....do....	18	May 2, 1864	100 dys.	Mustered out with company Sept.
Kautz, Louis P	....do....	19	May 2, 1864	100 dys.	Mustered out with company Sept.
Knott, Isaac	....do....	42	May 2, 1864	100 dys.	Transferred from Co. K May 21, 18 July 3, 1864, at battle of Hamm W. Va.; died Oct. 15, 1864, in at Andersonville, Ga.
Kyle, Stephen R	....do....	35	May 2, 1864	100 dys.	Captured July 3, 1864, at battle of Mills, W. Va.; mustered out Ju Columbus, O., by order of War
Leming, George W	....do....	18	May 2, 1864	00 dys.	Mustered out with company Sept.
Leming, Hiram	....do....	18	May 2, 1864	00 dys.	Mustered out with company Sept.
Leming, Randall B	....do....	40	May 2, 1864	00 dys.	Mustered out with company Sept.
Leming, Randolph H	....do....	40	May 2, 1864	0 ys.	Mustered out with company Sept.
Long, Isaac N	....do....	21	May 2, 1864	00 dys.	Mustered out with company Sept.
Longworth, Arch	....do....	19	May 2, 1864	0 dys.	Mustered out with company Sept.
Longworth, Joseph N	....do....	25	May 2, 1864	00 dys.	Mustered out with company Sept.
McLaughlin, James M	....do....	18	May 2, 1864	00 dys.	Mustered out with company Sept.
McNutt, Samuel	....do....	35	May 2, 1864	00 dys.	Captured July 3, 1864, at battle of Mills, W. Va.; mustered out Mar Columbus, O., by order of War
Matson, Aaron D	....do....	19	May 2, 1864	100 dys.	Mustered out with company Sept.
Meek, James D	....do....	25	May 2, 1864	100 dys.	Transferred from Co. K May 21, tered out with company Sept. 9,
Mitchell, Matthias C	....do....	23	May 2, 1864	100 dys.	Transferred from Co. K May 21, tered out with company Sept. 9,
Peters, Henry	....do....	20	May 2, 1864	100 dys.	Captured July 3, 1864, at battle of Mills, W. Va.; mustered out Ju Columbus, O., by order of War
Porter, John P	....do....	18	May 2, 1864	100 dys.	Mustered out with company Sept.
Queal, Albert F	....do....	35	May 2, 1864	100 dys.	Mustered out with company Sept.
Queal, George W	....do....	23	May 2, 1864	100 dys.	Mustered out with company Sept.
Rybolt, Charles R	....do....	23	May 2, 1864	100 dys.	Captured July 3, 1864, at battle of Mills, W. Va.; died May 11, 1865 ville, Fla.
Rybolt, Thomas D	....do....	23	May 2, 1864	100 dys.	Mustered out with company Sept.
Shaw, Achilles B	....do....	22	May 2, 1864	100 dys.	Mustered out with company Sept.
Shaw, James M	....do....		May 2, 1864	0 dys.	Mustered out with company Sept.
Shumard, Thomas	....do....		May 2, 1864	00 dys.	Mustered out with company Sept.
Shumard, Warren	....do....	33	May 2, 1864	00 dys.	Mustered out with company Sept.
Sills, Philip	....do....	32	May 2, 1864	00 dys.	Mustered out with company Sept.
Simkins, Ezra	....do....	27	May 2, 1864	00 dys.	Mustered out with company Sept.
Sparks, David G	....do....	37	May 2, 1864	00 dys.	Mustered out with company Sept.
Smith, Lewis W	....do....	21	May 2, 1864	00 d s.	Captured July 3, 1864, at battle of Mills, W. Va.; died Sept. 20, 18 Prison at Andersonville, Ga.
Smizer, Henry P	....do....	31	May 2, 1864	100 dys.	Captured July 3, 1864, at battle of Mills, W. Va.; mustered out Mar Columbus, O., by order of War
South, Thomas	....do....	27	May 2, 1864	100 dys.	Mustered out with company Sept.
Stewart, William	....do....	18	May 2, 1864	100 dys.	Mustered out with company Sept.
Teal, Oliver F	....do....	33	May 2, 1864	100 dys.	Mustered out with company Sept.
Tudor, Amos	....do....	18	May 2, 1864	100 dys.	Mustered out with company Sept.
Waits, William	....do....	18	May 2, 1864	100 dys.	Mustered out with company Sept.
Whittaker, Henry	....do....	34	May 2, 1864	100 dys.	Mustered out with company Sept.
Woods, Stephen	....do....	38	May 2, 1864	100 dys.	Mustered out with company Sept.

Names.	Rank.	Age.	Date of Entering the Service		Period of Service.	Remarks.
Pattison, John N.	Private.	38	May	2, 1864	100 dys.	Mustered out with company Sept. 9, 1864.
Patterson, Thomas	...do...	33	May	2, 1864	100 dys.	Transferred from Co. G May 19, 1864; mustered out with company Sept. 9, 1864.
Rapp, Joseph B.	...do...	33	May	2, 1864	100 dys.	Mustered out with company Sept. 9, 1864.
Redding, Albert	...do...	38	May	2, 1864	100 dys.	Mustered out with company Sept. 9, 1864.
Robinson, Zach	...do...	18	May	2, 1864	100 dys.	Mustered out with company Sept. 9, 1864.
Rust, E. E.	...do...	30	May	2, 1864	100 dys.	No record subsequent to muster in.
Smith, Samuel	...do...	36	May	2, 1864	100 dys.	Mustered out with company Sept. 9, 1864.
South, Albert G.	...do...	19	May	2, 1864	100 dys.	Mustered out with company Sept. 9, 1864.
South, Darius	...do...	31	May	2, 1864	100 dys.	Mustered out with company Sept. 9, 1864.
South, Isaac	...do...	44	May	2, 1864	100 dys.	Mustered out with company Sept. 9, 1864.
South, John M.	...do...	19	May	2, 1864	100 dys.	Mustered out with company Sept. 9, 1864.
South, Thomas	...do...	29	May	2, 1864	100 dys.	Mustered out with company Sept. 9, 1864.
South, W. E.	...do...	18	May	2, 1864	100 dys.	No record subsequent to muster in.
Swift, John	...do...	30	May	2, 1864	100 dys.	No record subsequent to muster-in.
Thompson, Cuthbert L.	...do...	38	May	2, 1864	100 dys.	Mustered out with company Sept. 9, 1864.
Ulrey, Addison E.	...do...	19	May	2, 1864	100 dys.	Mustered out with company Sept. 9, 1864.
Van Camp, David	...do...	30	May	2, 1864	100 dys.	Mustered out with company Sept. 9, 1864.
Wayne, Elias B.	...do...	22	May	2, 1864	100 dys.	Substitute for Jeremiah Cavalt, and supposed to have served under his name; mustered out with company Sept. 9, 1864.
Whittaker, Jonathan	...do...	32	May	2, 1864	100 dys.	Mustered out with company Sept. 9, 1864.
Worthington, Silas	...do...	36	May	2, 1864	100 dys.	Mustered out with company Sept. 9, 1864.
Williams, Wright	...do...	20	May	2, 1864	100 dys.	Transferred from Co. K May 21, 1864; mustered out with company Sept. 9, 1864.

COMPANY K.

Mustered in May 10, 1864, at Camp Dennison, O., by Robert S. Smith, Captain 2d Cavalry, U. S. A. Mustered out Sept. 9, 1864, at Camp Dennison, O.

Names.	Rank.	Age.	Date of Entering the Service		Period of Service.	Remarks.
James W. Deem	Captain.	30	May	2, 1864	100 dys.	Mustered out with company Sept. 9, 1864.
Edwin D. Titus	1st Lieut.	37	May	2, 1864	100 dys.	Mustered out with company Sept. 9, 1864.
Daniel Kidd	2d Lieut.	31	May	2, 1864	100 dys.	Mustered out with company Sept. 9, 1864.
William H. Standish	1st Sergt.	22	May	2, 1864	100 dys.	Mustered out with company Sept. 9, 1864.
[illegible] N. Ku[illegible]er	Sergeant.	35	May	2, 1864	100 dys.	Mustered out with company Sept. 9, 1864.
Wesley T. Swee[illegible]	...do...	31	May	2, 1864	100 dys.	Mustered out with company Sept. 9, 1864.
Thomas F. Brown	...do...	33	May	2, 1864	100 dys.	Mustered out with company Sept. 9, 1864.
Nathan J. Troy	...do...	22	May	2, 1864	100 dys.	Mustered out with company Sept. 9, 1864.
Daniel Brunk	Corporal.	24	May	2, 1864	100 dys.	Mustered out with company Sept. 9, 1864.
Albert Henriel	...do...	24	May	2, 1864	100 dys.	Mustered out with company Sept. 9, 1864.
Andrew J. Applegate	...do...	30	May	2, 1864	100 dys.	Mustered out with company Sept. 9, 1864.
William H. Mead	...do...	33	May	2, 1864	100 dys.	Mustered out with company Sept. 9, 1864.
James L. Brown	...do...	25	May	2, 1864	100 dys.	Mustered out with company Sept. 9, 1864.
Robert L. Gest	...do...	22	May	2, 1864	100 dys.	Mustered out with company Sept. 9, 1864.
James N. Lytle	...do...	36	May	2, 1864	100 dys.	Mustered out with company Sept. 9, 1864.
John Bricker	...do...	19	May	2, 1864	100 dys.	Mustered out with company Sept. 9, 1864.
Applegate, William E.	Private.	16	May	2, 1864	100 dys.	Mustered out with company Sept. 9, 1864.
Ashburn, Allen W.	...do...	17	May	2, 1864	100 dys.	Mustered out with company Sept. 9, 1864.
Avy, Joseph J.	...do...	18	May	2, 1864	100 dys.	Mustered out with company Sept. 9, 1864.
Avy, John M.	...do...	17	May	2, 1864	100 dys.	Mustered out with company Sept. 9, 1864.
Brown, James A.	...do...	28	May	2, 1864	100 dys.	Mustered out with company Sept. 9, 1864.
Cade, William T.	...do...	18	May	2, 1864	100 dys.	Mustered out with company Sept. 9, 1864.
Crane, Charles B.	...do...	36	May	2, 1864	100 dys.	Mustered out with company Sept. 9, 1864.
Crowshaw, D. S.	...do...	37	May	2, 1864	100 dys.	Mustered out with company Sept. 9, 1864.
Davis, James A.	...do...	34	May	2, 1864	100 dys.	Mustered out with company Sept. 9, 1864.
Dimmitt, William A.	...do...	20	May	2, 1864	100 dys.	Mustered out with company Sept. 9, 1864.
Glancey, Elias M.	...do...	18	May	2, 1864	100 dys.	Mustered out with company Sept. 9, 1864.
Grant, John	...do...	39	May	2, 1864	100 dys.	Mustered out with company Sept. 9, 1864.
Groves, George	...do...	19	May	2, 1864	100 dys.	Mustered out with company Sept. 9, 1864.
Groves, John W.	...do...	26	May	2, 1864	100 dys.	Mustered out with company Sept. 9, 1864.
Holter, Hanson	...do...	16	May	2, 1864	100 dys.	Mustered out with company Sept. 9, 1864.
Homan, Joseph W.	...do...	23	May	2, 1864	100 dys.	Mustered out with company Sept. 9, 1864.
Hutton, George W.	...do...	33	May	2, 1864	100 dys.	Mustered out with company Sept. 9, 1864.
Jeffreys, Thomas H.	...do...	16	May	2, 1864	100 dys.	Mustered out with company Sept. 9, 1864.
Jones, Albert	...do...	18	May	2, 1864	100 dys.	Transferred to Co. H May 21, 1864.
Kain, Charles	...do...	28	May	2, 1864	100 dys.	Mustered out with company Sept. 9, 1864.
Kain, John M.	...do...	15	May	2, 1864	100 dys.	Mustered out with company Sept. 9, 1864.
Kidd, Thomas	...do...	27	May	2, 1864	100 dys.	Mustered out with company Sept. 9, 1864.
Kugler, Matthias M.	...do...	15	May	2, 1864	100 dys.	Mustered out with company Sept. 9, 1864.
Leonard, James P.	...do...	..	May	2, 1864	100 dys.	Mustered out with company Sept. 9, 1864.
McGuire, Thomas	...do...	43	May	2, 1864	100 dys.	Mustered out with company Sept. 9, 1864.
McGuire, William W.	...do...	16	May	2, 1864	100 dys.	Mustered out with company Sept. 9, 1864.
Meek, James D.	...do...	25	May	2, 1864	100 dys.	Transferred to Co. H May 21, 1864.
Mitchell, Matthias C.	...do...	23	May	2, 1864	100 dys.	Transferred to Co. H May 21, 1864.
Moore, Charles A.	...do...	40	May	2, 1864	100 dys.	Mustered out with company Sept. 9, 1864.
Mount, John R.	...do...	24	May	2, 1864	100 dys.	Mustered out with company Sept. 9, 1864.
Mover, W. C.	...do...	19	May	2, 1864	100 dys.	Mustered out with company Sept. 9, 1864.
Needham, David	...do...	27	May	2, 1864	100 dys.	Mustered out with company Sept. 9, 1864.
Needham, Robert	...do...	28	May	2, 1864	100 dys.	Mustered out with company Sept. 9, 1864.

Names.	Rank.	Age.	Date of Entering the Service.	Period of Service.	Remarks.
Needham, Thomas M....	Private..	19	May 2, 1864	100 dys.	Mustered out with company Sept. 9, 1864.
Newberry, Samuel......	....do....	38	May 2, 1864	100 dys.	Mustered out with company Sept. 9, 1864.
Orebaugh, Ephraim.....	....do....	18	May 2, 1864	100 dys.	Mustered out with company Sept. 9, 1864.
Rhodes, Oliver W.......	....do....	19	May 2, 1864	100 dys.	Mustered out with company Sept. 9, 1864.
Robinson, Charles.......	....do....	27	May 2, 1864	100 dys.	Mustered out with company Sept. 9, 1864.
Robinson, James........	....do....	21	May 2, 1864	100 dys.	Mustered out with company Sept. 9, 1864.
Slack, James L..........	....do....	16	May 2, 1864	100 dys.	Mustered out with company Sept. 9, 1864.
Smith, Thomas L.........	....do....	22	May 2, 1864	100 dys.	Mustered out with company Sept. 9, 1864.
Snyder, Anthony	....do....	19	May 2, 1864	100 dys.	Mustered out with company Sept. 9, 1864.
Strimple, Josiah	....do....	44	May 2, 1864	100 dys.	Mustered out with company Sept. 9, 1864.
Tate, Daniel..............	....do....	22	May 2, 1864	100 dys.	Mustered out with company Sept. 9, 1864.
Teal, George W	....do....	25	May 2, 1864	100 dys.	Mustered out with company Sept. 9, 1864.
Thompson, David F......	....do....	18	May 2, 1864	100 dys.	Mustered out with company Sept. 9, 1864.
VanCamp, Thomas.......	....do....	19	May 2, 1864	100 dys.	Mustered out with company Sept. 9, 1864.
Wallace, David...........	....do....	26	May 2, 1864	100 dys.	Mustered out with company Sept. 9, 1864.
Watts, Jared..............	....do....	41	May 2, 1864	100 dys.	Mustered out with company Sept. 9, 1864.
Weaver, Jeremiah C.....	....do....	34	May 2, 1864	100 dys.	Mustered out with company Sept. 9, 1864.
Williams, Wright	....do....	20	May 2, 1864	100 dys.	Transferred to Co. I May 21, 1864.
Wills, Charles B.........	....do....	29	May 2, 1864	100 dys.	Mustered out with company Sept. 9, 1864.
Wood, Arthur............	....do....	16	May 2, 1864	100 dys.	Mustered out with company Sept. 9, 1864.

154th Regiment Ohio Volunteer Infantry.

ONE HUNDRED DAYS' SERVICE.

THIS Regiment was organized at Camp Dennison, O., May 9, 1864, to serve one hundred days. It was composed of the Twenty-third Battalion, Ohio National Guard, from Madison County, and the Sixtieth Regiment, Ohio National Guard, from Green County. On the 12th of May the Regiment proceeded, via Columbus and Bellaire, to New Creek, W. Va., arriving on the evening of the 14th. On the 22d, Company F was ordered to Piedmont, W. Va., where it remained until the Regiment started to Ohio for muster-out.

The One Hundred and Fifty-fourth performed guard, picket, and escort duty until the 29th of May, when one company moved to Youghiogheny Bridge, and the remaining eight companies to Greenland Gap. On the 4th of June a detachment of the Regiment had a skirmish with McNeil's Battalion, near Moorfield. Detachments of the Regiment were sent out on various scouting expeditions from the 12th of June to the 4th of July. On the 25th of July the Regiment again fell back to New Creek. An attack was made by the Rebels on the forces at New Creek on the 4th of August. On the evening of the 22d the Regiment started for Ohio, arriving at Camp Dennison on the 27th, and was mustered out Sept. 1, 1864, on expiration of its term of service.

154TH REGIMENT OHIO VOLUNTEER INFANTRY.

FIELD AND STAFF.

Mustered in May 9, 1864, at Camp Dennison, O., by Captain R. S. Smith. Mustered out Sept. 1, 1864, at Camp Dennison, O., by Lyman H. Warren, 1st Lieutenant 17th Infantry, U. S. A.

Names.	Rank.	Age.	Date of Entering the Service.	Period of Service.	Remarks.
Robert Stevenson	Colonel.	..	May 2, 1864	100 dys.	Mustered out with regiment Sept. 1, 1864.
Joseph E. Wilson	Lieut.Col	..	May 2, 1864	100 dys.	Mustered out with regiment Sept. 1, 1864.
William A. Neil	Major.	..	May 2, 1864	100 dys.	Mustered out with regiment Sept. 1, 1864.
George Watt	Surgeon.	..	May 2, 1864	100 dys.	Mustered out with regiment Sept. 1, 1864.
Leigh McClung	Asst. Sur.	..	May 2, 1864	100 dys.	Mustered out with regiment Sept. 1, 1864.
John B. Hagan	Adjutant	..	May 2, 1864	100 dys.	Mustered out with regiment Sept. 1, 1864.
A. L. Trader	R. Q. M.	..	May 2, 1864	100 dys.	Mustered out with regiment Sept. 1, 1864.
Robert McCaslin	Chaplain	..	May 2, 1864	100 dys.	Mustered out with regiment Sept. 1, 1864.
Linus P. Bonner	Ser. Maj.	34	May 2, 1864	100 dys.	Promoted from private Co. F May 9, 1864; mustered out with regiment Sept. 1, 1864.
James H. Miller	Q. M. S.	21	May 2, 1864	100 dys.	Promoted from private Co. B May 9, 1864; mustered out with regiment Sept. 1, 1864.
George L. Paine	Com. Ser.	42	May 2, 1864	100 dys.	Promoted from private Co. B May 9, 1864; mustered out with regiment Sept. 1, 1864.
John E. Martin	Hos. St'd.	21	May 2, 1864	100 dys.	Promoted from private Co. B May 9, 1864; mustered out with regiment Sept. 1, 1864.
Julius Cone	Prin. Mus	37	May 2, 1864	100 dys.	Promoted from private Co. A May 9, 1864; mustered out with regiment Sept. 1, 1864.
Newton T. Guthridge	....do....	44	May 2, 1864	100 dys.	Promoted from private Co. K May 12, 1864; mustered out with regiment Sept. 1, 1864.

COMPANY A.

Mustered in May 9, 1864, at Camp Dennison, O., by Captain R. S. Smith. Mustered out Sept. 1, 1864, at Camp Dennison, O., by Lyman H. Warren, 1st Lieutenant 17th Infantry, U. S. A.

Names.	Rank.	Age.	Date of Entering the Service.	Period of Service.	Remarks.
James B. Corry	Captain.	40	May 2, 1864	100 dys.	Mustered out with company Sept. 1, 1864.
John J. Hering	1st Lieut.	21	May 2, 1864	100 dys.	Mustered out with company Sept. 1, 1864.
Jasper W. Reed	2d Lieut.	30	May 2, 1864	100 dys.	Mustered out with company Sept. 1, 1864.
Pierce Folkerth	1st Sergt.	20	May 2, 1864	100 dys.	Mustered out with company Sept. 1, 1864.
Samuel W. Cox, Jr.	Sergeant.	30	May 2, 1864	100 dys.	Mustered out with company Sept. 1, 1864.
Charles Shaw	....do....	27	May 2, 1864	100 dys.	Mustered out with company Sept. 1, 1864.
John Hume	....do....	21	May 2, 1864	100 dys.	Mustered out with company Sept. 1, 1864.
Joseph K. Bull	....do....	28	May 2, 1864	100 dys.	Mustered out with company Sept. 1, 1864.
Isaac A. Ferguson	Corporal.	22	May 2, 1864	100 dys.	Mustered out with company Sept. 1, 1864.
Henry Corry	....do....	35	May 2, 1864	100 dys.	Mustered out with company Sept. 1, 1864.
George K. Hyde	....do....	28	May 2, 1864	100 dys.	Mustered out with company Sept. 1, 1864.
Martin Musselman	....do....	22	May 2, 1864	100 dys.	Mustered out with company Sept. 1, 1864.
Charles B. Lewis	....do....	24	May 2, 1864	100 dys.	Mustered out with company Sept. 1, 1864.
Seymour J. Ward	....do....	30	May 2, 1864	100 dys.	Mustered out with company Sept. 1, 1864.
Benjamin R. Glass	....do....	27	May 2, 1864	100 dys.	Mustered out with company Sept. 1, 1864.
James E. Gregg	....do....	26	May 2, 1864	100 dys.	Mustered out with company Sept. 1, 1864.
Armstrong, Andrew	Private.	31	May 2, 1864	100 dys.	Mustered out with company Sept. 1, 1864.
Armstrong, Robert	....do....	21	May 2, 1864	100 dys.	Mustered out with company Sept. 1, 1864.
Baker, George	....do....	32	May 2, 1864	100 dys.	Mustered out with company Sept. 1, 1864.
Baker, James M	....do....	22	May 2, 1864	100 dys.	Mustered out with company Sept. 1, 1864.
Baker, William	....do....	27	May 2, 1864	100 dys.	Mustered out with company Sept. 1, 1864.
Baldwin, Joseph	....do....	45	May 2, 1864	100 dys.	Died Aug. 5, 1864, of wounds received Aug. 4, 1864, in battle of New Creek, W. Va.
[illegible], John H	....do....	20	May 2, 1864	100 dys.	Mustered out with company Sept. 1, 1864.
[illegible], John	....do....	21	May 2, 1864	100 dys.	Mustered out with company Sept. 1, 1864.
[illegible], Walter	....do....	16	May 2, 1864	100 dys.	Mustered out with company Sept. 1, 1864.
[illegible], Sylvester B.	....do....	30	May 2, 1864	100 dys.	Mustered out with company Sept. 1, 1864.
[illegible], David B.	....do....	18	May 2, 1864	100 dys.	Mustered out with company Sept. 1, 1864.
[illegible], William	....do....	24	May 2, 1864	100 dys.	Mustered out with company Sept. 1, 1864.
[illegible], A. Newton	....do....	30	May 2, 1864	100 dys.	Mustered out with company Sept. 1, 1864.
[illegible], George	....do....	28	May 2, 1864	100 dys.	Captured Aug. 4, 1864, at New Creek, W. Va., while on picket duty; recaptured Aug. 7, 1864, at Moorfield, W. Va.; mustered out with company Sept. 1, 1864.

Names.	Rank.	Age.	Date of Entering the Service.	Period of Service.	
Cleveland, William	Private	[illegible]	May 2, 1864	100 dys.	Mustered out with comp
Collier, Ira	...do...	28	May 2, 1864	100 dys.	Mustered out with comp
Cone, Julius	...do...	37	May 2, 1864	100 dys.	Promoted to Principal
Cornwell, William B.	...do...	24	May 2, 1864	100 dys.	Mustered out with comp
Corry, William R.	...do...	37	May 2, 1864	100 dys.	Mustered out comp
Crist, Cornelius	...do...	20	May 2, 1864	100 dys.	Mustered out comp
Crowell, Isaac M.	...do...	25	May 2, 1864	100 dys.	Mustered out comp
Currie, James D	...do...	20	May 2, 1864	100 dys.	Mustered out comp
Deming, Chauncey W.	...do...	26	May 2, 1864	100 dys.	Mustered out comp
Deming, William H. H.	...do...	22	May 2, 1864	100 dys.	Mustered out comp
Dodds, Andrew	...do...	36	May 2, 1864	100 dys.	Mustered out comp
Farmer, Kimball	...do...	21	May 2, 1864	100 dys.	Mustered out comp
Fogarty, Patrick	...do...	26	May 2, 1864	100 dys.	Mustered out comp
Folck, Jonathan	...do...	29	May 2, 1864	100 dys.	Mustered out comp
Hafner, William	...do...	20	May 2, 1864	100 dys.	Mustered out comp
Harlan, Charles	...do...	18	May 2, 1864	100 dys.	Mustered out comp
Harris, James	...do...	36	May 2, 1864	100 dys.	Mustered out comp
Hopkins, Alburton F.	...do...	17	May 2, 1864	100 dys.	Mustered out with comp
Hopkins, Elmer B	...do...	18	May 2, 1864	100 dys.	Mustered out with comp
Hopkins, Wilson A.	...do...	19	May 2, 1864	100 dys.	Mustered out with comp
Hopping, Moses	...do...	19	May 2, 1864	100 dys.	Mustered out with comp
Hopping, Silas	...do...	21	May 2, 1864	100 dys.	Mustered out with comp
Jobe, Daniel	...do...	48	May 2, 1864	100 dys.	Mustered out with comp
Jones, Augustus H.	...do...	41	May 2, 1864	100 dys.	Mustered out with comp
Jones, Baker	...do...	18	May 2, 1864	100 dys.	Mustered out with comp
Kennedy, Philip	...do...	19	May 2, 1864	100 dys.	Mustered out with comp
Kershner, David	...do...	34	May 2, 1864	100 dys.	Mustered out with comp
King, Nathaniel	...do...	20	May 2, 1864	100 dys.	Mustered out with comp
Knott, Charles	...do...	28	May 2, 1864	100 dys.	Mustered out with comp
LeFevre, Edgar	...do...	16	May 2, 1864	100 dys.	Mustered out with comp
Leonard, Theodore	...do...	18	May 2, 1864	100 dys.	Mustered out with comp
McCulloch, Samuel	...do...	39	May 2, 1864	100 dys.	Mustered out with comp
McNeal, James	...do...	34	May 2, 1864	100 dys.	Mustered out with comp
Marr, Frederick	...do...	20	May 2, 1864	100 dys.	Mustered out with comp
Miller, James C.	...do...	21	May 2, 1864	100 dys.	Mustered out with comp
Nevis, James	...do...	25	May 2, 1864	100 dys.	Mustered out with comp
Nichols, John	...do...	18	May 2, 1864	100 dys.	Mustered out with comp
Records, Joel B.	...do...	41	May 2, 1864	100 dys.	Mustered out with comp
Smith, Andrew J.	...do...	31	May 2, 1864	100 dys.	Mustered out with comp
Tulleys, Russell	...do...	16	May 2, 1864	100 dys.	Mustered out with comp
Wilder, Frank	...do...	31	May 2, 1864	100 dys.	Mustered out with comp
Wilson, Daniel	...do...	44	May 2, 1864	100 dys.	Mustered out with comp
Wilson, Joseph M. C.	...do...	32	May 2, 1864	100 dys.	Mustered out with comp
Wilson, William L.	...do...	28	May 2, 1864	100 dys.	Mustered out with comp

COMPANY B.

Mustered in May 9, 1864, at Camp Dennison, O., by Captain R. S. Smith. Mustered out Dennison, O., by Lyman H. Warren, 1st Lieutenant 17th Infantry, U. S

Names.	Rank.	Age.	Date of Entering the Service.	Period of Service.	
Andrew C. Miller	Captain.	32	May 2, 1864	100 dys.	Mustered out with comp
James H. Matthews	1st Lieut.	30	May 2, 1864	100 dys.	Mustered out with comp
Oscar Poole	2d Lieut.	22	May 2, 1864	100 dys.	Mustered out with comp
William B. Smith	1st Sergt.	33	May 2, 1864	100 dys.	Mustered out with comp
Philip L. McDowell	Sergeant.	33	May 2, 1864	100 dys.	Mustered out with comp
Charles W. Taylor	...do...	30	May 2, 1864	100 dys.	Mustered out with comp
Robert F. Marshall	...do...	19	May 2, 1864	100 dys.	Mustered out with comp
James P. Polland	...do...	19	May 2, 1864	100 dys.	Mustered out with comp
Mark F. Anderson	Corporal.	23	May 2, 1864	100 dys.	Mustered out with comp
Luther King	...do...	18	May 2, 1864	100 dys.	Mustered out with comp
Philip L. Davis	...do...	37	May 2, 1864	100 dys.	Mustered out with comp
William M. Beveridge	...do...	28	May 2, 1864	100 dys.	Mustered out with comp
Edgar C. Hamilton	...do...	28	May 2, 1864	100 dys.	Mustered out with comp
George Lauman	...do...	19	May 2, 1864	100 dys.	Mustered out with comp
Charles J. Nesbitt	...do...	19	May 2, 1864	100 dys.	Mustered out with comp
George R. Gibney	...do...	20	May 2, 1864	100 dys.	Mustered out with comp
Alberger, William	Private.	19	May 2, 1864	100 dys.	Mustered out with comp
Alexander, John S.	...do...	19	May 2, 1864	100 dys.	Mustered out with comp
Anderson, William B	...do...	19	May 2, 1864	100 dys.	Mustered out with comp
Barlow, Henry E.	...do...	19	May 2, 1864	100 dys.	Mustered out with comp
Beall, George	...do...	18	May 2, 1864	100 dys.	Mustered out with comp
Berry, Barclay Y.	...do...	32	May 2, 1864	100 dys.	Mustered out with comp
Blessing, John	...do...	18	May 2, 1864	100 dys.	Mustered out with comp
Boyce, Robert	...do...	19	May 2, 1864	100 dys.	Mustered out with comp
Boyd, Gavin M.	...do...	27	May 2, 1864	100 dys.	Mustered out with comp
Brown, William	...do...	18	May 2, 1864	100 dys.	Mustered out with comp
Buckels, Robert F.	...do...	32	May 2, 1864	100 dys.	Mustered out with comp
Case, Charles E	...do...	21	May 2, 1864	100 dys.	Mustered out with comp
Collins, Nathaniel	...do...	19	May 2, 1864	100 dys.	Mustered out with comp
Crabb, George H.	...do...	23	May 2, 1864	100 dys.	Mustered out with comp

Names.	Rank.	Age.	Date of Entering the Service.	Period of Service.	Remarks.
Blair, Oscar		16	May 2, 1864		Mustered out
Boswell, George		44	May 2, 1864		Mustered out
Boswell, John		36	May 2, 1864		Mustered out
Boyd, William		37	May 2, 1864		Mustered out
Bradfield, George M.		23	May 2, 1864		Mustered out
Burnham, George		20	May 2, 1864		Mustered out
Carter, Jasper N.	do.	20	May 2, 1864		Mustered out
Carter, Joseph H.		22	May 2, 1864		Mustered out with co
Clark, Baty K.		33	May 2, 1864		Mustered out with co
Clifton, Peter		25	May 2, 1864		Mustered out with co
Cromwell, George		30	May 2, 1864		Mustered out with co
Furry, James		28	May 2, 1864		Mustered out with co
Grabill, Isaac		22	May 2, 1864		Mustered out with co
Grabill, Joseph		24	May 2, 1864		Mustered out with co
Green, David		31	May 2, 1864		Mustered out with co
Hann, William		21	May 2, 1864		Mustered out with co
Hanson, Elias	do.	28	May 2, 1864		Mustered out with co
Haynes, Emery		27	May 2, 1864		Mustered out with co
Haynes, Martin	do.	21	May 2, 1864		Mustered out with co
Hume, Roswell	do.	19	May 2, 1864		Mustered out with co
Irwin, Goodwin	do.	14	May 2, 1864		Mustered out with co
Johnson, Lewis	do.	27	May 2, 1864		Mustered out with co
Jones, Samuel R.		35	May 2, 1864		Mustered out with co
Jones, Wilson		15	May 2, 1864		Absent, sick, at West … 27, 1864. No furth…
Kepler, Andrew J.		23	May 2, 1864	100 dys.	Mustered out with c
Lambert, William H.		24	May 2, 1864	100 dys.	Mustered out with c
Loder, James		39	May 2, 1864	100 dys.	Mustered out with c
Loyd, John M.		26	May 2, 1864	100 dys.	
Lucas, Alexander		31	May 2, 1864	100 dys.	Mustered out with co
McClusky, Patrick		25	May 2, 1864	100 dys.	Mustered out with co
Mason, James		18	May 2, 1864	100 dys.	Mustered out with co
Mattes, Alfred		18	May 2, 1864	100 dys.	Mustered out with co
Miller, Andrew		41	May 2, 1864	100 dys.	Mustered out with co
Mowell, Emanuel		33	May 2, 1864	100 dys.	Mustered out with co
Oakley, David		43	May 2, 1864	100 dys.	Mustered out with co
Plymell, Christopher		23	May 2, 1864	100 dys.	Mustered out with co
Potes, Claudius		23	May 2, 1864	100 dys.	Mustered out with c
Powell, Richard	do.	27	May 2, 1864	100 dys.	Mustered out with co
Randall, Jeremiah	do.	23	May 2, 1864	100 dys.	Mustered out with co
Roberson, Hiram	do.	22	May 2, 1864	100 dys.	Mustered out with co
Severn, Jacob		37	May 2, 1864	100 dys.	Mustered out with co
Sidner, David M.	do.	21	May 2, 1864	100 dys.	Mustered out with co
Sidner, Philip	do.	33	May 2, 1864	100 dys.	Absent, sick, since A… ferson, O. No furt…
Silver, John	do.	15	May 2, 1864	100 dys.	Mustered out with co
Snider, Charles	do.	18	May 2, 1864	100 dys.	Mustered out with co
Spohn, William	do.	18	May 2, 1864	100 dys.	Mustered out with co
Stickley, John	do.	17	May 2, 1864	100 dys.	Absent, sick, since … ferson, O. No furt…
Stickley, Samuel M.	do.	21	May 2, 1864	100 dys.	Mustered out with
Stoner, Labynetus	do.	21	May 2, 1864	100 dys.	Mustered out with
Stutson, Charles	do.	27	May 2, 1864	100 dys.	Mustered out with
Swager, Sylvester	do.	28	May 2, 1864	100 dys.	Mustered out with
Tilman, John H.	do.	30	May 2, 1864	100 dys.	Mustered out with
Timmons, Isaac	do.	18	May 2, 1864	100 dys.	Mustered out with
Walker, Alphonso B.	do.	27	May 2, 1864	100 dys.	See Co. I.
Weber, Christian	do.	28	May 2, 1864	100 dys.	Mustered out with
Whorton, Fletcher	do.	17	May 2, 1864	100 dys.	Mustered out with
Whorton, John	do.	21	May 2, 1864	100 dys.	Mustered out with

COMPANY D.

Mustered in May 9, 1864, at Camp Dennison, O., by Captain R. S. Smith. Mustered … Dennison, O., by Lyman H. Warren, 1st Lieutenant 17th Infantry,

Names.	Rank.	Age.	Date of Entering the Service.	Period of Service.	Remarks.
Henry B. Guthrie	Captain.	28	May 2, 1864	100 dys.	Mustered out with c
George C. Canfield	1st Lieut.	25	May 2, 1864	100 dys.	Mustered out with c
Benjamin F. Darst	2d Lieut.	26	May 2, 1864	100 dys.	Mustered out with c
Silas B. Shaner	1st Sergt.	27	May 2, 1864	100 dys.	Mustered out with c
John R. Ridenour	Sergeant.	28	May 2, 1864	100 dys.	Mustered out with c
Thomas Haverstick	do.	27	May 2, 1864	100 dys.	Mustered out with c
Abram B. Cosler	do.	25	May 2, 1864	100 dys.	Prisoner of war — … 1865, at Columbus, … partment.
George A. Harner	do.	40	May 2, 1864	100 dys.	Mustered out with c
Joseph Swaynie	Corporal.	20	May 2, 1864	100 dys.	Absent, sick, since … record found.
Henry C. Glotfeller	do.	21	May 2, 1864	100 dys.	Mustered out with c
Albert Swadner	do.	19	May 2, 1864	100 dys.	Mustered out with c

Date of Entering the Service.	Period of Service.	Remarks.
May 2, 1864	100 dys.	Mustered out with company Sept. 1, 1864.
May 2, 1864	100 dys.	Mustered out with company Sept. 1, 1864.
May 2, 1864	100 dys.	Mustered out with company Sept. 1, 1864.
May 2, 1864	100 dys.	Mustered out with company Sept. 1, 1864.
May 2, 1864	100 dys.	Mustered out with company Sept. 1, 1864.
May 2, 1864	100 dys.	Mustered out with company Sept. 1, 1864.
May 2, 1864	100 dys.	Mustered out with company Sept. 1, 1864.
May 2, 1864	100 dys.	Mustered out with company Sept. 1, 1864.
May 2, 1864	100 dys.	Mustered out with company Sept. 1, 1864.
May 2, 1864	100 dys.	Mustered out with company Sept. 1, 1864.
May 2, 1864	100 dys.	Mustered out with company Sept. 1, 1864.
May 2, 1864	100 dys.	Mustered out with company Sept. 1, 1864.
May 2, 1864	100 dys.	Mustered out with company Sept. 1, 1864.
May 2, 1864	100 dys.	Mustered out with company Sept. 1, 1864.
May 2, 1864	100 dys.	Mustered out with company Sept. 1, 1864.
May 2, 1864	100 dys.	Mustered out with company Sept. 1, 1864.
May 2, 1864	100 dys.	Mustered out with company Sept. 1, 1864.
May 2, 1864	100 dys	Mustered out with company Sept. 1, 1864.
May 2, 1864	100 dys.	Mustered out with company Sept. 1, 1864.
May 2, 1864	100 dys.	Mustered out with company Sept. 1, 1864.
May 2, 1864	100 dys.	Mustered out with company Sept. 1, 1864.
May 2, 1864	100 dys.	Mustered out with company Sept. 1, 1864.
May 2, 1864	100 dys.	Mustered out with company Sept. 1, 1864.
May 2, 1864	100 dys.	Mustered out with company Sept. 1, 1864.
May 2, 1864	100 dys.	Mustered out with company Sept. 1, 1864.
May 2, 1864	100 dys.	Mustered out with company Sept. 1, 1864.
May 2, 1864	100 dys.	Mustered out with company Sept. 1, 1864.
May 2, 1864	100 dys.	Mustered out with company Sept. 1, 1864.
May 2, 1864	100 dys.	Mustered out with company Sept. 1, 1864.
May 2, 1864	100 dys.	Prisoner of war ——; mustered out Nov. 23, 1864, at Columbus, O., by order of War Department.
May 2, 1864	100 dys.	Mustered out with company Sept. 1, 1864.
May 2, 1864	100 dys.	Transferred from Co. E ——; mustered out with company Sept. 1, 1864.
May 2, 1864	100 dys.	Died Feb. 5, 1865, in Rebel Prison at Salisbury, N. C.
May 2, 1864	100 dys.	Mustered out with company Sept. 1, 1864.
May 2, 1864	100 dys.	Absent, sick, since Aug. 26, 1864. No further record found.
May 2, 1864	100 dys.	Mustered out with company Sept. 1, 1864.
May 2, 1864	100 dys.	Mustered out with company Sept. 1, 1864.
May 2, 1864	100 dys.	Prisoner of war ——; mustered out Nov. 23, 1864, at Columbus, O., by order of War Department.
May 2, 1864	100 dys.	Absent, sick, since Aug. 26, 1864. No further record found.
May 2, 1864	100 dys.	Mustered out with company Sept. 1, 1864.
May 2, 1864	100 dys.	Mustered out with company Sept. 1, 1864.
May 2, 1864	100 dys.	Mustered out with company Sept. 1, 1864.
May 2, 1864	100 dys.	Mustered out with company Sept. 1, 1864.
May 2, 1864	100 dys.	Mustered out with company Sept. 1, 1864.
May 2, 1864	100 dys.	Mustered out with company Sept. 1, 1864.
May 2, 1864	100 dys.	Mustered out with company Sept. 1, 1864.
May 2, 1864	100 dys.	Mustered out with company Sept. 1, 1864.
May 2, 1864	100 dys.	Mustered out with company Sept. 1, 1864.
May 2, 1864	100 dys.	Mustered out with company Sept. 1, 1864.
May 2, 1864	100 dys.	Mustered out with company Sept. 1, 1864.
May 2, 1864	100 dys.	Mustered out with company Sept. 1, 1864.
May 2, 1864	100 dys.	Absent, sick, since Aug. 26, 1864. No further record found.
May 2, 1864	100 dys.	Mustered out with company Sept. 1, 1864.
May 2, 1864	100 dys.	Transferred from Co. E ——; mustered out with company Sept. 1, 1864.
May 2, 1864	100 dys.	Mustered out with company Sept. 1, 1864.
May 2, 1864	100 dys.	Mustered out with company Sept. 1, 1864.
May 2, 1864	100 dys.	Mustered out with company Sept. 1, 1864.
May 2, 1864	100 dys.	Mustered out with company Sept. 1, 1864.
May 2, 1864	100 dys.	Mustered out with company Sept. 1, 1864.
May 2, 1864	100 dys.	Absent, sick, since Aug. 26, 1864. No further record found.
May 2, 1864	100 dys.	Mustered out with company Sept. 1, 1864.
May 2, 1864	100 dys.	Mustered out with company Sept. 1, 1864.
May 2, 1864	100 dys.	Mustered out with company Sept. 1, 1864.
May 2, 1864	100 dys.	Mustered out with company Sept. 1, 1864.
May 2, 1864	100 dys.	Mustered out with company Sept. 1, 1864.

COMPANY E.

Mustered in May 9, 1864, at Camp Dennison, O., by Captain R. S. Smith. Must
Dennison, O., by Lyman H. Warren, 1st Lieutenant 17th Infa

Names.	Rank.	Age.	Date of Entering the Service.		Period of Service.	
Joseph F. Boock	Captain.	31	May	2, 1864	100 dys.	Mustered out
Benjamin H. Barney	1st Lieut.	28	May	2, 1864	100 dys.	Mustered out
John W. Tobias	2d Lieut.	32	May	2, 1864	100 dys.	Mustered out
John K. Felton	1st Sergt.	31	May	2, 1864	100 dys.	Mustered out
Oliver H. P. Moler	Sergeant.	23	May	2, 1864	100 dys.	Mustered out
Mark Newland	....do....	37	May	2, 1864	100 dys.	Mustered out
Jacob L. Lantz	....do....	26	May	2, 1864	100 dys.	Mustered out
Cornelius Zimmerman	....do....	19	May	2, 1864	100 dys.	Mustered out
Levi T. Nagle	Corporal.	18	May	2, 1864	100 dys.	Discharged on
Samuel H. Prather	....do....	23	May	2, 1864	100 dys.	Transferred to
William Haverstick	....do....	24	May	2, 1864	100 dys.	Mustered out
Clark M. Galloway	....do....	21	May	2, 1864	100 dys.	Transferred to
Sampson Conrad	....do....	23	May	2, 1864	100 dys.	Mustered out
Paris R. Peterson	....do....	24	May	2, 1864	100 dys.	Mustered out
Samuel H. Harshman	....do....	21	May	2, 1864	100 dys.	Mustered out
Simon Garst	....do....	31	May	2, 1864	100 dys.	Mustered out
David Sherman	Musician	14	May	2, 1864	100 dys.	Mustered out
Aley, Noah	Private.	24	May	2, 1864	100 dys.	Mustered out
Baker, David H	....do....	45	May	2, 1864	100 dys.	Mustered out
Blessing, Wesley	....do....	24	May	2, 1864	100 dys.	Mustered out
Broadstone, Jacob L	....do....	19	May	2, 1864	100 dys.	Mustered out
Bush, Albert F	....do....	18	May	2, 1864	100 dys.	Mustered out
Carson, Thomas W	....do....	18	May	2, 1864	100 dys.	Mustered out
Carter, John	....do....	37	May	2, 1864	100 dys.	Mustered out
Chany, William S	....do....	18	May	2, 1864	100 dys.	Mustered out
Cover, Joseph	....do....	44	May	2, 1864	100 dys.	Mustered out
Coy, Aaron	....do....	18	May	2, 1864	100 dys.	Absent, sick, further recor
Coy, Benjamin F	....do....	21	May	2, 1864	100 dys.	Discharged M cate of disab
Coy, Henry J	....do....	42	May	2, 1864	100 dys.	Mustered out
Coy, Valentine	....do....	20	May	2, 1864	100 dys.	Mustered out
Davison, Ezra	....do....	17	May	2, 1864	100 dys.	Mustered out
Dinwiddie, James	....do....	27	May	2, 1864	100 dys.	Mustered out
Engle, William H	....do....	34	May	2, 1864	100 dys.	Discharged M cate of disab
Fookes, Milton	....do....	19	May	2, 1864	100 dys.	Mustered out
Garst, Jacob	....do....	30	May	2, 1864	100 dys.	Mustered out
Gordon, John W	....do....	18	May	2, 1864	100 dys.	Mustered out
Harmon, John O	....do....	18	May	2, 1864	100 dys.	Mustered out
Harshman, Montgomery	....do....	18	May	2, 1864	100 dys.	Mustered out
Haus, John	....do....	18	May	2, 1864	100 dys.	Mustered out
Haus, Sylvester	....do....	18	May	2, 1864	100 dys.	Rejected by M
Helmer, Jacob	....do....	28	May	2, 1864	100 dys.	Mustered out
Hook, John J	....do....	19	May	2, 1864	100 dys.	Mustered out
John, William	....do....	42	May	2, 1864	100 dys.	Mustered out
Kelley, Samuel B	....do....	28	May	2, 1864	100 dys.	Mustered out
King, Douglass E	....do....	27	May	2, 1864	100 dys.	Mustered out
Kolbe, Joseph H	....do....	22	May	2, 1864	100 dys.	Mustered out
Koogler, George W	....do....	21	May	2, 1864	100 dys.	Mustered out
Lentz, John	....do....	25	May	2, 1864	100 dys.	Mustered out
Lesher, David K	....do....	34	May	2, 1864	100 dys.	Mustered out
Lesher, William	....do....	21	May	2, 1864	100 dys.	Absent, sick, further reco
Lindsy, David	....do....	38	May	2, 1864	100 dys.	Discharged M cate of disab
Mallon, John	....do....	43	May	2, 1864	100 dys.	Mustered out
Miller, John	....do....	37	May	2, 1864	100 dys.	Mustered out
Peterson, John L	....do....	..	May	2, 1864	100 dys.	Mustered out
Quinn, Elias	....do....	36	May	2, 1864	100 dys.	Mustered out
Reeker, John	....do....	38	May	2, 1864	100 dys.	Mustered out
Richeson, Robert	....do....	41	May	2, 1864	100 dys.	Mustered out
Robins, John	....do....	41	May	2, 1864	100 dys.	Mustered out
Shingledecker, Aaron	....do....	30	May	2, 1864	100 dys.	Mustered out
Smith, William	....do....	30	May	2, 1864	100 dys.	Mustered out
Snyder, Emanuel	....do....	37	May	2, 1864	100 dys.	Mustered out
Steward, John A	....do....	20	May	2, 1864	100 dys.	Mustered out
Stewart, James M. C	....do....	18	May	2, 1864	100 dys.	Mustered out
Stine, Edward	....do....	42	May	2, 1864	100 dys.	Discharged M cate of disab
Strickle, Samuel H	....do....	29	May	2, 1864	100 dys.	Mustered out
Stull, Francis P	....do....	19	May	2, 1864	100 dys.	Mustered out
Suebel, John	....do....	40	May	2, 1864	100 dys.	Mustered out
Trubee, Harrison	....do....	23	May	2, 1864	100 dys.	Rejected by E
Yates, John	....do....	25	May	2, 1864	100 dys.	
Yingling, John D	....do....	21	May	2, 1864	100 dys.	

Names.	Rank.	Age.	Date of Entering the Service.	Period of Service.	Remarks.
Wead, Alexander J C	Private	21	May 2, 1864	100 dys.	Mustered out with company Sept. 1, 1864.
Wead, James C. F	do	18	May 2, 1864	100 dys.	Mustered out with company Sept. 1, 1864.
Whiteman, Jackson	do	18	May 2, 1864	100 dys.	Mustered out with company Sept. 1, 1864.
Wilson, William H	do	31	May 2, 1864	100 dys.	Mustered out with company Sept. 1, 1864.
Winter, William C	do	39	May 2, 1864	100 dys.	Mustered out with company Sept. 1, 1864.

COMPANY G.

Mustered in May 9, 1864, at Camp Dennison, O., by Captain R. S. Smith. Mustered out Sept. 1, 1864, at Camp Dennison, O., by Lyman H. Warren, 1st Lieutenant 17th Infantry, U. S. A.

Names.	Rank.	Age.	Date of Entering the Service.	Period of Service.	Remarks.
John A. Seiss	Captain	35	May 2, 1864	100 dys.	Mustered out with company Sept. 1, 1864.
Walker D. Williamson	1st Lieut.	24	May 2, 1864	100 dys.	Mustered out with company Sept. 1, 1864.
John F. Dougherty	2d Lieut.	28	May 2, 1864	100 dys.	Mustered out with company Sept. 1, 1864.
George Truman	1st Sergt.	31	May 2, 1864	100 dys.	Mustered out with company Sept. 1, 1864.
William Kirkpatrick	Sergeant.	38	May 2, 1864	100 dys.	Mustered out with company Sept. 1, 1864.
Charles Gage	do	40	May 2, 1864	100 dys.	Mustered out with company Sept. 1, 1864.
Levi Riddell	do	28	May 2, 1864	100 dys.	Mustered out with company Sept. 1, 1864.
Christopher Bingamon	do	36	May 2, 1864	100 dys.	Mustered out with company Sept. 1, 1864.
Frederick Spellbring	Corporal.	37	May 2, 1864	100 dys.	Mustered out with company Sept. 1, 1864.
Jerry H. Gest	do	24	May 2, 1864	100 dys.	Mustered out with company Sept. 1, 1864.
Michael Daugherty, Jr	do	33	May 2, 1864	100 dys.	Mustered out with company Sept. 1, 1864.
William Anderson	do	25	May 2, 1864	100 dys.	Mustered out with company Sept. 1, 1864.
James Stanfield	do	40	May 2, 1864	100 dys.	Mustered out with company Sept. 1, 1864.
Robert Hamilton	do	41	May 2, 1864	100 dys.	Mustered out with company Sept. 1, 1864.
James R. Anderson	do	31	May 2, 1864	100 dys.	Mustered out with company Sept. 1, 1864.
John B. Mason	Musician	33	May 2, 1864	100 dys.	Mustered out with company Sept. 1, 1864.
Joseph Day	do	45	May 2, 1864	100 dys.	
Anderson, Abijah	Private	18	May 2, 1864	100 dys.	Mustered out with company Sept. 1, 1864.
Anderson, Philip P	do	19	May 2, 1864	100 dys.	Mustered out with company Sept. 1, 1864.
Austin, Charles	do	20	May 2, 1864	100 dys.	Mustered out with company Sept. 1, 1864.
Bingamon, Abner	do	37	May 2, 1864	100 dys.	Mustered out with company Sept. 1, 1864.
Broadstone, James	do	27	May 2, 1864	100 dys.	Mustered out with company Sept. 1, 1864.
Chambers, Benjamin F	do	34	May 2, 1864	100 dys.	Mustered out with company Sept. 1, 1864.
Cullum, George	do	37	May 2, 1864	100 dys.	
Disbro, Samuel L	do	29	May 2, 1864	100 dys.	Mustered out with company Sept. 1, 1864.
Dunevant, Peter	do	26	May 2, 1864	100 dys.	Mustered out with company Sept. 1, 1864.
Elam, William	do	22	May 2, 1864	100 dys.	Mustered out with company Sept. 1, 1864.
Evans, Joseph C	do	19	May 2, 1864	100 dys.	Mustered out with company Sept. 1, 1864.
Fowler, William D	do	35	May 2, 1864	100 dys.	Mustered out with company Sept. 1, 1864.
Frazier, William S	do	29	May 2, 1864	100 dys.	Mustered out with company Sept. 1, 1864.
Gest, Albert	do	19	May 2, 1864	100 dys.	Mustered out with company Sept. 1, 1864.
Griswold, Leonard	do	20	May 2, 1864	100 dys.	Mustered out with company Sept. 1, 1864.
Harper, Hugh W	do	35	May 2, 1864	100 dys.	Mustered out with company Sept. 1, 1864.
Holland, Thad	do	28	May 2, 1864	100 dys.	Mustered out with company Sept. 1, 1864.
Kenedy, James	do	18	May 2, 1864	100 dys.	Mustered out with company Sept. 1, 1864.
McClelland, William H., Jr	do	20	May 2, 1864	100 dys.	Mustered out with company Sept. 1, 1864.
McClelland, William H., Sr	do	30	May 2, 1864	100 dys.	Mustered out with company Sept. 1, 1864.
McFerren, Frank	do	20	May 2, 1864	100 dys.	Mustered out with company Sept. 1, 1864.
Macoubrie, George	do	20	May 2, 1864	100 dys.	Mustered out with company Sept. 1, 1864.
Mendenhall, John	do	27	May 2, 1864	100 dys.	Mustered out with company Sept. 1, 1864.
Mendenhall, Thomas P	do	20	May 2, 1864	100 dys.	Mustered out with company Sept. 1, 1864.
Moffitt, Francis M	do	29	May 2, 1864	100 dys.	Mustered out with company Sept. 1, 1864.
Morris, Orin	do	19	May 2, 1864	100 dys.	Mustered out with company Sept. 1, 1864.
Norman, Benjamin F	do	23	May 2, 1864	100 dys.	
Perrine, William H	do	26	May 2, 1864	100 dys.	Mustered out with company Sept. 1, 1864.
Powers, John	do	27	May 2, 1864	100 dys.	Mustered out with company Sept. 1, 1864.
Riddell, Robert W	do	27	May 2, 1864	100 dys.	Mustered out with company Sept. 1, 1864.
Salisberry, Daniel	do	39	May 2, 1864	100 dys.	Mustered out with company Sept. 1, 1864.
Salisberry, Ryan	do	30	May 2, 1864	100 dys.	Mustered out with company Sept. 1, 1864.
Sanders, John M	do	43	May 2, 1864	100 dys.	Mustered out with company Sept. 1, 1864.
Sims, Joseph C	do	24	May 2, 1864	100 dys.	Mustered out with company Sept. 1, 1864.
Stanfield, Samuel	do	17	May 2, 1864	100 dys.	Mustered out with company Sept. 1, 1864.
Stanfield, William	do	45	May 2, 1864	100 dys.	Mustered out with company Sept. 1, 1864.
Stiles, George R	do	48	May 2, 1864	100 dys.	Mustered out with company Sept. 1, 1864.
Stiles, Isaac	do	44	May 2, 1864	100 dys.	Mustered out with company Sept. 1, 1864.
Stump, Daniel S	do	24	May 2, 1864	100 dys.	Mustered out with company Sept. 1, 1864.
Stump, William J	do	21	May 2, 1864	100 dys.	Mustered out with company Sept. 1, 1864.
Taylor, John	do	21	May 2, 1864	100 dys.	Mustered out with company Sept. 1, 1864.
Tolbert, George B	do	26	May 2, 1864	100 dys.	Mustered out with company Sept. 1, 1864.
Tolbert, James S	do	19	May 2, 1864	100 dys.	Mustered out with company Sept. 1, 1864.
Wild, Joseph	do	18	May 2, 1864	100 dys.	Mustered out with company Sept. 1, 1864.

COMPANY I.

Mustered in May 9, 1864, at Camp Dennison, O., by Captain R. S. Smith. Mustered out Sept. 1, 1864, at Camp Dennison, O., by Lyman H. Warren, 1st Lieutenant 17th Infantry, U. S. A.

Names.	Rank.	Age.	Date of Entering the Service.	Period of Service.	Remarks.
David Watson	Captain.	33	May 2, 1864	100 dys.	Mustered out with company Sept. 1, 1864.
Harford Toland	1st Lieut.	26	May 2, 1864	100 dys.	Mustered out with company Sept. 1, 1864.
Levin Willoughby	2d Lieut.	35	May 2, 1864	100 dys.	Mustered out with company Sept. 1, 1864.
Patrick Kennelly	1st Sergt.	19	May 2, 1864	100 dys.	Mustered out with company Sept. 1, 1864.
George W. Bodkin	Sergeant.	41	May 2, 1864	100 dys.	Mustered out with company Sept. 1, 1864.
Auburn Smith	....do....	24	May 2, 1864	100 dys.	Mustered out with company Sept. 1, 1864.
Samuel Souve	....do....	23	May 2, 1864	100 dys.	Mustered out with company Sept. 1, 1864.
James Dungan	....do....	22	May 2, 1864	100 dys.	Mustered out with company Sept. 1, 1864.
Julius W. Curd	Corporal.	32	May 2, 1864	100 dys.	Mustered out with company Sept. 1, 1864.
John Hull	....do....	31	May 2, 1864	100 dys.	Mustered out with company Sept. 1, 1864.
James McCann	....do....	33	May 2, 1864	100 dys.	Mustered out with company Sept. 1, 1864.
William Withrow	....do....	26	May 2, 1864	100 dys.	Mustered out with company Sept. 1, 1864.
Samuel Coberly	....do....	34	May 2, 1864	100 dys.	Mustered out with company Sept. 1, 1864.
Matthew Hixson	....do....	34	May 2, 1864	100 dys.	Mustered out with company Sept. 1, 1864.
Albert Stutson	....do....	28	May 2, 1864	100 dys.	Mustered out with company Sept. 1, 1864.
Burdine Blake	....do....	41	May 2, 1864	100 dys.	Mustered out with company Sept. 1, 1864.
Armstrong, John	Private.	20	May 2, 1864	100 dys.	Mustered out with company Sept. 1, 1864.
Armstrong, John T	....do....	25	May 2, 1864	100 dys.	Mustered out with company Sept. 1, 1864.
Armstrong, William H	....do....	22	May 2, 1864	100 dys.	Mustered out with company Sept. 1, 1864.
Atchison, Charles	....do....	18	May 2, 1864	100 dys.	Mustered out with company Sept. 1, 1864.
Bales, Thomas M	....do....	19	May 2, 1864	100 dys.	Mustered out with company Sept. 1, 1864.
Baskerville, Madison	....do....	22	May 2, 1864	100 dys.	Mustered out with company Sept. 1, 1864.
Berry, John W	....do....	19	May 2, 1864	100 dys.	Mustered out with company Sept. 1, 1864.
Betts, Thomas B	....do....	20	May 2, 1864	100 dys.	Mustered out with company Sept. 1, 1864.
Bird, Dennis S	....do....	41	May 2, 1864	100 dys.	Mustered out with company Sept. 1, 1864.
Blake, William	....do....	18	May 2, 1864	100 dys.	Mustered out with company Sept. 1, 1864.
Bogenrife, John H	....do....	28	May 2, 1864	100 dys.	Mustered out with company Sept. 1, 1864.
Brown, John F	....do....	19	May 2, 1864	100 dys.	Mustered out with company Sept. 1, 1864.
Burnham, James S	....do....	25	May 2, 1864	100 dys.	Mustered out with company Sept. 1, 1864.
Carnes, Marsh ville	....do....	18	May 2, 1864	100 dys.	Mustered out with company Sept. 1, 1864.
Carter, Joseph J.	....do....	27	May 2, 1864	100 dys.	Mustered out with company Sept. 1, 1864.
Chenowith, John F	....do....	19	May 2, 1864	100 dys.	Mustered out with company Sept. 1, 1864.
Christman, Addison	....do....	23	May 2, 1864	100 dys.	Mustered out with company Sept. 1, 1864.
Coberly, Andrew J	....do....	36	May 2, 1864	100 dys.	Mustered out with company Sept. 1, 1864.
Coberly, Thomas	....do....	31	May 2, 1864	100 dys.	Mustered out with company Sept. 1, 1864.
Coberly, William W	....do....	21	May 2, 1864	100 dys.	Mustered out with company Sept. 1, 1864.
Corey Marshall	....do....	19	May 2, 1864	100 dys.	Mustered out with company Sept. 1, 1864.
Cox, William	....do....	18	May 2, 1864	100 dys.	Mustered out with company Sept. 1, 1864.
Crawford, James	....do....	25	May 2, 1864	100 dys.	Mustered out with company Sept. 1, 1864.
Creath, George W	....do....	26	May 2, 1864	100 dys.	Mustered out with company Sept. 1, 1864.
Devault, Henry	....do....	28	May 2, 1864	100 dys.	Mustered out with company Sept. 1, 1864.
Douglass, Charles A	....do....	19	May 2, 1864	100 dys.	Mustered out with company Sept. 1, 1864.
Eply, William H	....do....	19	May 2, 1864	100 dys.	Mustered out with company Sept. 1, 1864.
Evans, Charles	....do....	18	May 2, 1864	100 dys.	Mustered out with company Sept. 1, 1864.
Forbus, Angus	....do....	21	May 2, 1864	100 dys.	Mustered out with company Sept. 1, 1864.
Gyton, John	....do....	18	May 2, 1864	100 dys.	Mustered out with company Sept. 1, 1864.
Hardin, Winfield S	....do....	19	May 2, 1864	100 dys.	Mustered out with company Sept. 1, 1864.
Helphenstine, Hannibal	....do....	22	May 2, 1864	100 dys.	Mustered out with company Sept. 1, 1864.
Helphenstine, James O. K	....do....	34	May 2, 1864	100 dys.	Mustered out with company Sept. 1, 1864.
Helphenstine, Jasper P	....do....	19	May 2, 1864	100 dys.	Mustered out with company Sept. 1, 1864.
Horn, Elijah	....do....	32	May 2, 1864	100 dys.	Mustered out with company Sept. 1, 1864.
Hussey, Frank	....do....	19	May 2, 1864	100 dys.	Mustered out with company Sept. 1, 1864.
Hussey, Uriah S	....do....	29	May 2, 1864	100 dys.	Mustered out with company Sept. 1, 1864.
Johnson, William	....do....	22	May 2, 1864	100 dys.	Mustered out with company Sept. 1, 1864.
Jones, Benjamin	....do....	18	May 2, 1864	100 dys.	Mustered out with company Sept. 1, 1864.
Jones, Lucien	....do....	19	May 2, 1864	100 dys.	Mustered out with company Sept. 1, 1864.
Jones, William	....do....	20	May 2, 1864	100 dys.	Mustered out with company Sept. 1, 1864.
Kilgore, Henry	....do....	31	May 2, 1864	100 dys.	Mustered out with company Sept. 1, 1864.
King, Isaac	....do....	37	May 2, 1864	100 dys.	Mustered out with company Sept. 1, 1864.
Minshall, Isaac	....do....	38	May 2, 1864	100 dys.	Mustered out with company Sept. 1, 1864.
Minter Reuben	....do....	22	May 2, 1864	100 dys.	Mustered out with company Sept. 1, 1864.
Newbolt, Thomas	....do....	34	May 2, 1864	100 dys.	Mustered out with company Sept. 1, 1864.
O'Brian, Richard	....do....	22	May 2, 1864	100 dys.	Mustered out with company Sept. 1, 1864.
O'Brian, William	....do....	21	May 2, 1864	100 dys.	Mustered out with company Sept. 1, 1864.
Pain, Bushrod	....do....	24	May 2, 1864	100 dys.	Mustered out with company Sept. 1, 1864.
Pain, George	....do....	18	May 2, 1864	100 dys.	Mustered out with company Sept. 1, 1864.
Pemberton, William H	....do....	25	May 2, 1864	100 dys.	Mustered out with company Sept. 1, 1864.
Phifer, George	....do....	20	May 2, 1864	100 dys.	Mustered out with company Sept. 1, 1864.
Preston, Thomas	....do....	23	May 2, 1864	100 dys.	Mustered out with company Sept. 1, 1864.
Rafferty, Ferguson	....do....	23	May 2, 1864	100 dys.	Mustered out with company Sept. 1, 1864.
Rayborn, Crayton M	....do....	44	May 2, 1864	100 dys.	Mustered out with company Sept. 1, 1864.
Rouse, William A	....do....	23	May 2, 1864	100 dys.	Mustered out with company Sept. 1, 1864.
Rush, John A	....do....	21	May 2, 1864	100 dys.	Mustered out with company Sept. 1, 1864.
Sales, David	....do....	25	May 2, 1864	100 dys.	Mustered out with company Sept. 1, 1864.
Seinan, William	....do....	22	May 2, 1864	100 dys.	Mustered out with company Sept. 1, 1864.
Slagle, Oliver	....do....	22	May 2, 1864	100 dys.	Mustered out with company Sept. 1, 1864.
Smith, Joseph C.	....do....	19	May 2, 1864	100 dys.	Mustered out with company Sept. 1, 1864.

Names.	Rank.	Age.	Date of Entering the Service.	Period of Service.	Remarks.
Martin, David G	Private..	20	May 2, 1864	100 dys.	Mustered out with company Sept. 1, 1864.
Mays, Henry B.	....do....	22	May 2, 1864	100 dys.	Mustered out with company Sept. 1, 1864.
Miller, Henry	....do....	21	May 2, 1864	100 dys.	Absent, sick ——. No further record found.
Miller, Oliver J.	....do....	18	May 2, 1864	100 dys.	Mustered out with company Sept. 1, 1864.
Miller, William K.	....do....	44	May 2, 1864	100 dys.	Mustered out to date Sept. 1, 1864, by order of War Department.
Moody, John J.	....do....	19	May 2, 1864	100 dys.	Mustered out with company Sept. 1, 1864.
North, George W.	....do....	33	May 2, 1864	100 dys.	Mustered out with company Sept. 1, 1864.
Palmer, Charles	....do....	21	May 2, 1864	100 dys.	Mustered out with company Sept. 1, 1864.
Parsons, James	....do....	30	May 2, 1864	100 dys.	Mustered out with company Sept. 1, 1864.
Rockafield, Henry H.	....do....	27	May 2, 1864	100 dys.	Mustered out with company Sept. 1, 1864.
Rupert, John	....do....	33	May 2, 1864	100 dys.	Mustered out with company Sept. 1, 1864.
Smith, William	....do....	21	May 2, 1864	100 dys.	Mustered out with company Sept. 1, 1864.
Stine, Henry	....do....	37	May 2, 1864	100 dys.	Mustered out with company Sept. 1, 1864.
Stine, Jacob	....do....	20	May 2, 1864	100 dys.	Mustered out with company Sept. 1, 1864.
Swadener, David	....do....	23	May 2, 1864	100 dys.	Mustered out with company Sept. 1, 1864.
Swigart, Abraham	....do....	26	May 2, 1864	100 dys.	Mustered out with company Sept. 1, 1864.
Swigart, Isaac	....do....	26	May 2, 1864	100 dys.	Mustered out with company Sept. 1, 1864.
Swisher, Michael	....do....	31	May 2, 1864	100 dys.	Mustered out with company Sept. 1, 1864.
Tingley, Henry	....do....	21	May 2, 1864	100 dys.	Mustered out with company Sept. 1, 1864.
Tobias, Samuel	....do....	21	May 2, 1864	100 dys.	Mustered out with company Sept. 1, 1864.
Truby, Elias	....do....	18	May 2, 1864	100 dys.	Mustered out with company Sept. 1, 1864.
Truby, Emanuel	....do....	21	May 2, 1864	100 dys.	Mustered out with company Sept. 1, 1864.
Vancuren, Charles	....do....	20	May 2, 1864	100 dys.	Mustered out with company Sept. 1, 1864.
Wilson, William R.	....do....	33	May 2, 1864	100 dys.	Mustered out with company Sept. 1, 1864.
Wolf, Benjamin	....do....	21	May 2, 1864	100 dys.	Mustered out with company Sept. 1, 1864.
Wolf, Daniel H.	....do....	33	May 2, 1864	100 dys.	Mustered out with company Sept. 1, 1864.

155th Regiment Ohio Volunteer Infantry.

ONE HUNDRED DAYS' SERVICE.

:IS Regiment was organized at Camp Dennison, O., May 8, 1864, to ne hundred days. It was composed of the Ninety-second Battalion, ational Guard, from Pickaway County, and the Forty-fourth Battalion, ational Guard, from Mahoning County. Immediately after muster-in :giment was ordered to New Creek, W. Va., and upon arrival was Martinsburg, where it performed garrison and escort duty until the June, when it was ordered to Washington City. From there it led to White House, thence to Bermuda Hundred and City Point, it remained until the 29th, when it was ordered to Norfolk. The :nt was placed on duty in an intrenched camp near Norfolk. On th of July five hundred men of the One Hundred and Fifth-fifth, ›ther troops, marched to Elizabeth City, N. C. The expedition d to Norfolk, where the Regiment remained until the 19th of , when it was ordered to Ohio for muster-out. It arrived at Camp on on the 24th, and was mustered out August 27, 1864, on expiration .erm of service.

Names.	Rank.	Age.	Date of Entering the Service.	Period of Service.	Remarks.
Clark, E. B.	Private.	19	May 2, 1864	100 dys.	Mustered out with company Aug. 27, 1864.
Cook, Amos	do.	39	May 2, 1864	100 dys.	Mustered out with company Aug. 27, 1864.
Crist, Henry	do.	19	May 2, 1864	100 dys.	Mustered out with company Aug. 27, 1864.
Croakham, G. L.	do.	18	May 2, 1864	100 dys.	Mustered out with company Aug. 27, 1864.
Crouse, W. S.	do.	18	May 2, 1864	100 dys.	Mustered out with company Aug. 27, 1864.
[illegible]rrey, Henry	do.	18	May 2, 1864	100 dys.	Mustered out with company Aug. 27, 1864.
Davenport, J. W.	do.	18	May 2, 1864	100 dys.	Discharged May 9, 1864, at Camp Dennison, O., on Surgeon's certificate of disability.
Dodd, Charles N.	do.	26	May 2, 1864	100 dys.	Promoted to Sergt. Major May 8, 1864.
Downey, Harvey	do.	27	May 2, 1864	100 dys.	Mustered out with company Aug. 27, 1864.
Downs, G. W.	do.	36	May 2, 1864	100 dys.	Mustered out with company Aug. 27, 1864.
Dreisbach, M. E.	do.	37	May 2, 1864	100 dys.	Mustered out with company Aug. 27, 1864.
Dunlap, Joseph B.	do.	33	May 2, 1864	100 dys.	Promoted to Com. Sergeant May 8, 1864.
Ernheart, A. W.	do.	19	May 2, 1864	100 dys.	Mustered out with company Aug. 27, 1864.
Eskridge, William	do.	18	May 2, 1864	100 dys.	Mustered out with company Aug. 27, 1864.
Foresman, A.	do.	45	May 2, 1864	100 dys.	Mustered out with company Aug. 27, 1864.
Fitzpatrick, Ed.	do.	18	May 2, 1864	100 dys.	Mustered out with company Aug. 27, 1864.
Gotschall, John	do.	19	May 2, 1864	100 dys.	Discharged May 9, 1864, at Camp Dennison, O., on Surgeon's certificate of disability.
Hall, James H.	do.	18	May 2, 1864	100 dys.	Mustered out with company Aug. 27, 1864.
Hanis, John	do.	27	May 2, 1864	100 dys.	Mustered out with company Aug. 27, 1864.
Harmount, George	do.	25	May 2, 1864	100 dys.	Mustered out with company Aug. 27, 1864.
Harris, Henry	do.	29	May 2, 1864	100 dys.	Mustered out with company Aug. 27, 1864.
Harris, J. N.	do.	20	May 2, 1864	100 dys.	Mustered out with company Aug. 27, 1864.
Hank, Henry	do.	37	May 2, 1864	100 dys.	Mustered out with company Aug. 27, 1864.
Hood, Fred	do.	19	May 2, 1864	100 dys.	Mustered out with company Aug. 27, 1864.
Hopleton, J. K. P.	do.	..	May 2, 1864	100 dys.	Mustered out with company Aug. 27, 1864.
Hott, William	do.	54	May 2, 1864	100 dys.	Mustered out with company Aug. 27, 1864.
Householder, P. M.	do.	26	May 2, 1864	100 dys.	Mustered out with company Aug. 27, 1864.
Howard, William	do.	25	May 2, 1864	100 dys.	Mustered out with company Aug. 27, 1864.
Hunsicker, Jerome	do.	20	May 2, 1864	100 dys.	Mustered out with company Aug. 27, 1864.
Irwin, G. A.	do.	25	May 2, 1864	100 dys.	Mustered out with company Aug. 27, 1864.
Kent, James	do.	19	May 2, 1864	100 dys.	Mustered out with company Aug. 27, 1864.
Kuhn, Adam	do.	18	May 2, 1864	100 dys.	Mustered out with company Aug. 27, 1864.
Lee, Joshua	do.	28	May 2, 1864	100 dys.	Mustered out with company Aug. 27, 1864.
McAllister, W. S.	do.	18	May 2, 1864	100 dys.	Mustered out with company Aug. 27, 1864.
Maderia, James K.	do.	27	May 2, 1864	100 dys.	Mustered out with company Aug. 27, 1864.
Mertz, A. J.	do.	..	May 2, 1864	100 dys.	Mustered out with company Aug. 27, 1864.
Metzger, Jacob	do.	38	May 2, 1864	100 dys.	Mustered out with company Aug. 27, 1864.
Metzger, Jonas	do.	23	May 2, 1864	100 dys.	Mustered out with company Aug. 27, 1864.
Moore, J. L.	do.	21	May 2, 1864	100 dys.	Mustered out with company Aug. 27, 1864.
Moore, R. H.	do.	25	May 2, 1864	100 dys.	Mustered out with company Aug. 27, 1864.
Morris, A.	do.	33	May 2, 1864	100 dys.	Mustered out with company Aug. 27, 1864.
Morris, Charles	do.	21	May 2, 1864	100 dys.	Mustered out with company Aug. 27, 1864.
Needham, John	do.	23	May 2, 1864	100 dys.	Mustered out with company Aug. 27, 1864.
Orpwood, Thomas	do.	41	May 2, 1864	100 dys.	Mustered out with company Aug. 27, 1864.
Palmer, Theodore	do.	52	May 2, 1864	100 dys.	Mustered out with company Aug. 27, 1864.
Prugh, A. A.	do.	21	May 2, 1864	100 dys.	Mustered out with company Aug. 27, 1864.
Rabstock, C.	do.	28	May 2, 1864	100 dys.	Mustered out with company Aug. 27, 1864.
Rayburn, John	do.	36	May 2, 1864	100 dys.	Mustered out with company Aug. 27, 1864.
Richardson, J. P.	do.	20	May 2, 1864	100 dys.	Mustered out with company Aug. 27, 1864.
Rose, George	do.	18	May 2, 1864	100 dys.	Mustered out with company Aug. 27, 1864.
Rowland, Samuel	do.	41	May 2, 1864	100 dys.	Mustered out with company Aug. 27, 1864.
Rudy, Fred	do.	32	May 2, 1864	100 dys.	Mustered out with company Aug. 27, 1864.
Schwin, John	do.	19	May 2, 1864	100 dys.	Mustered out with company Aug. 27, 1864.
Stetson, William	do.	25	May 2, 1864	100 dys.	Mustered out with company Aug. 27, 1864.
Supinard, William	do.	29	May 2, 1864	100 dys.	Discharged May 9, 1864, at Camp Dennison, O., on Surgeon's certificate of disability.
Taylor, James	do.	19	May 2, 1864	100 dys.	Mustered out with company Aug. 27, 1864.
Vincent, Fred	do.	3[illegible]	May 2, 1864	100 dys.	Mustered out with company Aug. 27, 1864.
Wilder, Jerome	do.	20	May 2, 1864	100 dys.	Discharged May 9, 1864, at Camp Dennison, O., on Surgeon's certificate of disability.
Williams, Henry	do.	27	May 2, 1864	100 dys.	
Woltly, John	do.	29	May 2, 1864	100 dys.	Mustered out with company Aug. 27, 1864.
Wright, J. D.	do.	32	May 2, 1864	100 dys.	

Names.	Rank.	Age.	Date of Entering the Service.	Period of Service.	Remarks.
Welsh, Randolph J.	Private.	18	May 2, 1864	100 dys.	Mustered out with company Aug. 27, 1864.
Welsh, William	do.	16	May 2, 1864	100 dys.	Discharged Aug. 29, 1864, at Portsmouth, Va., on Surgeon's certificate of disability.
White, Henry B.	do.	30	May 2, 1864	100 dys.	Mustered out with company Aug. 27, 1864.
Wilder, Milton A.	do.	18	May 2, 1864	100 dys.	Mustered out with company Aug. 27, 1864.
Wilhelmn, Benjamin	do.	30	May 2, 1864	100 dys.	Mustered out with company Aug. 27, 1864.
Williams, Frank	do.	25	May 2, 1864	100 dys.	Mustered out with company Aug. 27, 1864.
Williams, Thomas W.	do.	36	May 2, 1864	100 dys.	Mustered out with company Aug. 27, 1864.
Wilson, Thomas	do.	19	May 2, 1864	100 dys.	Mustered out with company Aug. 27, 1864.
Wiseman, Andrew	do.	28	May 2, 1864	100 dys.	Mustered out with company Aug. 27, 1864.
Wood, Thomas	do.	36	May 2, 1864	100 dys.	Mustered out with company Aug. 27, 1864.

COMPANY C.

Mustered in May 8, 1864, at Camp Dennison, O., by Robert S. Smith, Captain 2d U. S. Cavalry. Mustered out Aug. 27, 1864, at Camp Dennison, O.

Names.	Rank.	Age.	Date of Entering the Service.	Period of Service.	Remarks.
Henry W. Peters	Captain.	21	May 2, 1864	100 dys.	Mustered out with company Aug. 27, 1864.
John B. Smith	1st Lieut.	28	May 2, 1864	100 dys.	Mustered out with company Aug. 27, 1864.
Van B. Pritchet	2d Lieut.	27	May 2, 1864	100 dys.	Mustered out with company Aug. 27, 1864.
Emanuel Westenhaver	1st Sergt.	38	May 2, 1864	100 dys.	Appointed from private May 8, 1864; mustered out with company Aug. 27, 1864.
Levi Shawhn	Sergeant.	28	May 2, 1864	100 dys.	Mustered out with company Aug. 27, 1864.
Frank B. Scothorn	do.	27	May 2, 1864	100 dys.	Mustered out with company Aug. 27, 1864.
John J. Cookson	do.	21	May 2, 1864	100 dys.	Rejected by Mustering Officer.
Josiah Ward	do.	33	May 2, 1864	100 dys.	Mustered out with company Aug. 27, 1864.
James M. Long	do.	30	May 2, 1864	100 dys.	Appointed from Corporal May 8, 1864; mustered out with company Aug. 27, 1864.
James Ward	Corporal.	19	May 2, 1864	100 dys.	Mustered out with company Aug. 27, 1864.
James Reno	do.	26	May 2, 1864	100 dys.	Mustered out with company Aug. 27, 1864.
McElvaine, Graphis	do.	29	May 2, 1864	100 dys.	Mustered out with company Aug. 27, 1864.
Leonard Widoe	do.	32	May 2, 1864	100 dys.	Mustered out with company Aug. 27, 1864.
Joash M. Long	do.	20	May 2, 1864	100 dys.	
Joseph Pressett	do.	30	May 2, 1864	100 dys.	
Flavius Allen	do.	22	May 2, 1864	100 dys.	Appointed May 8, 1864; mustered out with company Aug. 27, 1864.
Henry W. Reber	do.	28	May 2, 1864	100 dys.	Appointed May 8, 1864; mustered out with company Aug. 27, 1864.
James Wanamaker	do.	19	May 2, 1864	100 dys.	Appointed May 8, 1864; mustered out with company Aug. 27, 1864.
Appil, Andrew	Private.	24	May 2, 1864	100 dys.	Mustered out with company Aug. 27, 1864.
Augustine, Cyrus	do.	29	May 2, 1864	100 dys.	Mustered out with company Aug. 27, 1864.
Barcus, Sylvester	do.	23	May 2, 1864	100 dys.	Mustered out with company Aug. 27, 1864.
Bashford, Isaac	do.	58	May 2, 1864	100 dys.	Rejected by Mustering Officer.
Battelle, Levelle	do.	23	May 2, 1864	100 dys.	Reduced from 1st Sergeant May 8, 1864; mustered out with company Aug. 27, 1864.
Bell, Joseph	do.	19	May 2, 1864	100 dys.	Mustered out with company Aug. 27, 1864.
Blue, Absalom	do.	41	May 2, 1864	100 dys.	Mustered out with company Aug. 27, 1864.
Bonnell, William S.	do.	22	May 2, 1864	100 dys.	Mustered out with company Aug. 27, 1864.
Booth, John R.	do.	20	May 2, 1864	100 dys.	Mustered out with company Aug. 27, 1864.
Broomhall, Eli	do.	25	May 2, 1864	100 dys.	Mustered out with company Aug. 27, 1864.
Broomhall, Isaac N.	do.	28	May 2, 1864	100 dys.	Mustered out with company Aug. 27, 1864.
Broomhall, Lindlay N.	do.	33	May 2, 1864	100 dys.	Mustered out with company Aug. 27, 1864.
Brown, George	do.	21	May 2, 1864	100 dys.	
Brown, Joseph	do.	27	May 2, 1864	100 dys.	
Burnett, William	do.	24	May 2, 1864	100 dys.	Mustered out with company Aug. 27, 1864.
Burwell, John P.	do.	41	May 2, 1864	100 dys.	Mustered out with company Aug. 27, 1864.
Bushnell, John H.	do.	22	May 2, 1864	100 dys.	Mustered out with company Aug. 27, 1864.
Caldwell, Henry	do.	23	May 2, 1864	100 dys.	Mustered out with company Aug. 27, 1864.
Cole, Joseph	do.	18	May 2, 1864	100 dys.	Mustered out with company Aug. 27, 1864.
Cramer, John	do.	27	May 2, 1864	100 dys.	Mustered out with company Aug. 27, 1864.
Davis, John R.	do.	23	May 2, 1864	100 dys.	Mustered out with company Aug. 27, 1864.
Etherington, George	do.	21	May 2, 1864	100 dys.	Mustered out with company Aug. 27, 1864.
Etherington, Parkhurst	do.	42	May 2, 1864	100 dys.	Furloughed July 25, 1864. No further record found.
Fausnaugh, Andrew	do.	35	May 2, 1864	100 dys.	Rejected by Mustering Officer.
Fausnaugh, Ferris	do.	19	May 2, 1864	100 dys.	Mustered out with company Aug. 27, 1864.
Fellows, Henry C.	do.	26	May 2, 1864	100 dys.	
Fields, Thomas N.	do.	25	May 2, 1864	100 dys.	Mustered out with company Aug. 27, 1864.
Founes, Benjamin H.	do.	19	May 2, 1864	100 dys.	Mustered out with company Aug. 27, 1864.
Gavin, Wilmot	do.	18	May 2, 1864	100 dys.	Mustered out with company Aug. 27, 1864.
Gilman, Charles	do.	21	May 2, 1864	100 dys.	Mustered out with company Aug. 27, 1864.
Hankison, George	do.	26	May 2, 1864	100 dys.	Mustered out with company Aug. 27, 1864.
Hedges, John	do.	18	May 2, 1864	100 dys.	Mustered out with company Aug. 27, 1864.
Hedges, Obed N.	do.	23	May 2, 1864	100 dys.	Mustered out with company Aug. 27, 1864.
Helvering, William	do.	18	May 2, 1864	100 dys.	Mustered out with company Aug. 27, 1864.
Hott, John H.	do.	35	May 2, 1864	100 dys.	Mustered out with company Aug. 27, 1864.
Hunter, William H.	do.	18	May 2, 1864	100 dys.	Died July 19, 1864, at City Point, Va.
Johnson, James W.	do.	30	May 2, 1864	100 dys.	Mustered out with company Aug. 27, 1864.

Names.	Rank.	Age.	Date of Entering the Service.	Period of Service.	Remarks.
Freeman, Job	Private	19	May 2, 1864	100 dys.	Mustered out with company Aug. 27, 1864.
Fusselman, James	do	18	May 2, 1864	100 dys.	Mustered out with company Aug. 27, 1864.
Gerloh, Augustus	do	20	May 2, 1864	100 dys.	Mustered out with company Aug. 27, 1864.
Grute, George B.	do	28	May 2, 1864	100 dys.	Mustered out with company Aug. 27, 1864.
Hamilton, Jesse	do	37	May 2, 1864	100 dys.	Mustered out with company Aug. 27, 1864.
Hoffman, Frederick	do	23	May 2, 1864	100 dys.	Mustered out with company Aug. 27, 1864.
Hoffman, Virgil	do	32	May 2, 1864	100 dys.	Mustered out with company Aug. 27, 1864.
Jewell, Samuel W.	do	19	May 2, 1864	100 dys.	Absent, sick ——. No further record found.
Johns, Richard	do	20	May 2, 1864	100 dys.	Mustered out with company Aug. 27, 1864.
Johnston, Thomas W.	do	42	May 2, 1864	100 dys.	Absent, sick ——. No further record found.
Kennedy, Henderson G.	do	27	May 2, 1864	100 dys.	Died Aug. 25, 1864, at Washington, D. C.
Kennedy, Joseph C.	do	35	May 2, 1864	100 dys.	Mustered out with company Aug. 27, 1864.
Kennedy, William H.	do	36	May 2, 1864	100 dys.	Mustered out with company Aug. 27, 1864.
Kyle, Edward	do	19	May 2, 1864	100 dys.	Discharged Aug. 29, 1864, at Portsmouth, Va., on surgeon's certificate of disability.
Lauterman, George	do	27	May 2, 1864	100 dys.	Mustered out with company Aug. 27, 1864.
Leopard, Manuel	do	22	May 2, 1864	100 dys.	Died Aug. 1, 1864, at Portsmouth, Va.
Logan, William O.	do	18	May 2, 1864	100 dys.	Mustered out with company Aug. 27, 1864.
Lyons, William D.	do	29	May 2, 1864	100 dys.	Mustered out with company Aug. 27, 1864.
McClure, John	do	29	May 2, 1864	100 dys.	Mustered out with company Aug. 27, 1864.
McClure, William	do	27	May 2, 1864	100 dys.	Mustered out with company Aug. 27, 1864.
McCollom, Joel	do	19	May 2, 1864	100 dys.	Died July 20, 1864, on board transport Atlantic, en route from Norfolk, Va., to New York.
McCollom, Thompson	do	27	May 2, 1864	100 dys.	Mustered out with company Aug. 27, 1864.
McCombs, James H.	do	19	May 2, 1864	100 dys.	Mustered out with company Aug. 27, 1864.
McGowan, James P.	do	20	May 2, 1864	100 dys.	Mustered out with company Aug. 27, 1864.
McKay, John	do	[illegible]	May 2, 1864	100 dys.	Mustered out with company Aug. 27, 1864.
McNabb, Darius	do	19	May 2, 1864	100 dys.	Mustered out with company Aug. 27, 1864.
Mansell, James	do	31	May 2, 1864	100 dys.	Mustered out with company Aug. 27, 1864.
Maxwell, Samuel	do	26	May 2, 1864	100 dys.	Mustered out with company Aug. 27, 1864.
Miller, James	do	43	May 2, 1864	100 dys.	Mustered out with company Aug. 27, 1864.
Miller, James C.	do	42	May 2, 1864	100 dys.	Died July 31, 1864, at Portsmouth, Va.
Murray, James	do	41	May 2, 1864	100 dys.	Mustered out with company Aug. 27, 1864.
Osborne, [illegible]	do	23	May 2, 1864	100 dys.	Mustered out with company Aug. 27, 1864.
Park, John J.	do	19	May 2, 1864	100 dys.	Mustered out with company Aug. 27, 1864.
Pollock, Lewis N.	do	22	May 2, 1864	100 dys.	Mustered out with company Aug. 27, 1864.
Porter, George W.	do	21	May 2, 1864	100 dys.	Mustered out with company Aug. 27, 1864.
Robinson, Leander D.	do	[illegible]	May 2, 1864	100 dys.	Mustered out with company Aug. 27, 1864.
Shaffer, Enoch	do	21	May 2, 1864	100 dys.	Mustered out with company Aug. 27, 1864.
Shely, Robert	do	32	May 2, 1864	100 dys.	Mustered out with company Aug. 27, 1864.
Simpkins, David N.	do	30	May 2, 1864	100 dys.	Mustered out with company Aug. 27, 1864.
Simonton, Levi J.	do	23	May 2, 1864	100 dys.	Mustered out with company Aug. 27, 1864.
Stuart, John G.	do	29	May 2, 1864	100 dys.	Mustered out with company Aug. 27, 1864.
Stuart, William	do	19	May 2, 1864	100 dys.	Mustered out with company Aug. 27, 1864.
Thomas, Isaac	do	28	May 2, 1864	100 dys.	Mustered out with company Aug. 27, 1864.
Viall, Charles D.	do	36	May 2, 1864	100 dys.	Mustered out with company Aug. 27, 1864.
Wehr, Perry	do	29	May 2, 1864	100 dys.	Mustered out with company Aug. 27, 1864.
Wilson, Robert	do	22	May 2, 1864	100 dys.	Discharged Aug. 29, 1864, at Portsmouth, Va., on surgeon's certificate of disability.
Zedaker, Solomon	do	19	May 2, 1864	100 dys.	Mustered out with company Aug. 27, 1864.

COMPANY E.

Mustered in May 8, 1864, at Camp Dennison, O., by Robert S. Smith, Captain 2d U. S. Cavalry. Mustered out Aug. 27, 1864, at Camp Dennison, O.

Names.	Rank.	Age.	Date of Entering the Service.	Period of Service.	Remarks.
Will Scott	Captain	23	May 2, 1864	100 dys.	Mustered out with company Aug. 27, 1864.
William Graham	1st Lieut.	22	May 2, 1864	100 dys.	Mustered out with company Aug. 27, 1864.
William H. Magill	2d Lieut.	[illegible]	May 2, 1864	100 dys.	Mustered out with company Aug. 27, 1864.
Levi B. Kelso	1st Sergt.	33	May 2, 1864	100 dys.	Mustered out with company Aug. 27, 1864.
Robert Gilbreath	Sergeant	36	May 2, 1864	100 dys.	Mustered out with company Aug. 27, 1864.
F. M. Snyder	do	37	May 2, 1864	100 dys.	Discharged May 9, 1864, on Surgeon's certificate of disability.
Joseph H. Pritchard	do	29	May 2, 1864	100 dys.	Mustered out with company Aug. 27, 1864.
David R. Baird	do	21	May 2, 1864	100 dys.	Mustered out with company Aug. 27, 1864.
Samuel Whitesel	Corporal.	33	May 2, 1864	100 dys.	Mustered out with company Aug. 27, 1864.
Ezra F. Rowe	do	18	May 2, 1864	100 dys.	Discharged Aug. 30, 1864, at Portsmouth, Va., on surgeon's certificate of disability.
James W. Elliott	do	36	May 2, 1864	100 dys.	Mustered out with company Aug. 27, 1864.
James W. Swank	do	38	May 2, 1864	100 dys.	Mustered out with company Aug. 27, 1864.
Jackson Fullen	do	38	May 2, 1864	100 dys.	Mustered out with company Aug. 27, 1864.
W. T. Hewitt	do	23	May 2, 1864	100 dys.	Discharged Aug. 30, 1864, at Portsmouth, Va., on Surgeon's certificate of disability.
John Bolin	do	24	May 2, 1864	100 dys.	Mustered out with company Aug. 27, 1864.
William McKinlay	do	22	May 2, 1864	100 dys.	Mustered out with company Aug. 27, 1864.
Baggs, William	Private	23	May 2, 1864	100 dys.	Mustered out with company Aug. 27, 1864.
Ball, George W.	do	30	May 2, 1864	100 dys.	Mustered out to date Aug. 27, 1864, at Columbus, O., by order of War Department.
Beathard, Joseph H.	do	20	May 2, 1864	100 dys.	Mustered out with company Aug. 27, 1864.

COMPANY F.

Mustered in May 8, 1864, at Camp Dennison, O., by Robert S. Smith, Captain 2d U. S. Cavalry. Mustered out Aug. 27, 1864, at Camp Dennison, O.

Names.	Rank.	Age.	Date of Entering the Service.	Period of Service.	Remarks.
Philip Warner	Captain.	24	May 2, 1864	100 dys.	Mustered out with company Aug. 27, 1864.
Chauncey Scutt	1st Lieut.	28	May 2, 1864	100 dys.	Mustered out with company Aug. 27, 1864.
Charles F. Silliman	2d Lieut.	21	May 2, 1864	100 dys.	Mustered out with company Aug. 27, 1864.
Matthias Chittum	1st Sergt.	24	May 2, 1864	100 dys.	Appointed from private May 9, 1864; mustered out with company Aug. 27, 1864.
W. P. Thompson	Sergeant.	21	May 2, 1864	100 dys.	Mustered out with company Aug. 27, 1864.
R. A. Forseman	....do....	18	May 2, 1864	100 dys.	Mustered out with company Aug. 27, 1864.
Frank Woolington	....do....	22	May 2, 1864	100 dys.	Mustered out with company Aug. 27, 1864.
R. A. Pollock	....do....	28	May 2, 1864	100 dys.	Mustered out with company Aug. 27, 1864.
George Cook	Corporal.	38	May 2, 1864	100 dys.	
George Moore	....do....	32	May 2, 1864	100 dys.	Mustered out with company Aug. 27, 1864.
Perry Hunaway	....do....	27	May 2, 1864	100 dys.	Mustered out with company Aug. 27, 1864.
Thomas Dolby	....do....	23	May 2, 1864	100 dys.	Mustered out with company Aug. 27, 1864.
Thomas Sharon	....do....	29	May 2, 1864	100 dys.	Mustered out with company Aug. 27, 1864.
Joseph R. Finney	....do....	24	May 2, 1864	100 dys.	Mustered out with company Aug. 27, 1864.
James McNeal	....do....	28	May 2, 1864	100 dys.	Mustered out with company Aug. 27, 1864.
A. G. Jones	....do....	42	May 2, 1864	100 dys.	Appointed July 26, 1864; mustered out with company Aug. 27, 1864.
Beaver, Reuben E	Private..	29	May 2, 1864	100 dys.	Mustered out with company Aug. 27, 1864.
Beers, John	....do....	22	May 2, 1864	100 dys.	
Borden, Frank	....do....	21	May 2, 1864	100 dys.	Mustered out with company Aug. 27, 1864.
Borland, Theodore	....do....	18	May 2, 1864	100 dys.	
Campbell, George	....do....	43	May 2, 1864	100 dys.	Mustered out with company Aug. 27, 1864.
Clark, Frank	....do....	19	May 2, 1864	100 dys.	Mustered out with company Aug. 27, 1864.
Clark, Isaac	....do....	23	May 2, 1864	100 dys.	Mustered out with company Aug. 27, 1864.
Cline, David	....do....	30	May 2, 1864	100 dys.	Mustered out with company Aug. 27, 1864.
Crabill, Jacob	....do....	38	May 2, 1864	100 dys.	Mustered out with company Aug. 27, 1864.
Croman, Michael	....do....	34	May 2, 1864	100 dys.	Mustered out with company Aug. 27, 1864.
Davis, Frank	....do....	18	May 2, 1864	100 dys.	Mustered out with company Aug. 27, 1864.
Davis, William	....do....	26	May 2, 1864	100 dys.	Mustered out with company Aug. 27, 1864.
Demerest, E. L	....do....	18	May 2, 1864	100 dys.	Mustered out with company Aug. 27, 1864.
Dowler, John	....do....	18	May 2, 1864	100 dys.	Mustered out with company Aug. 27, 1864.
Evans, John	....do....	20	May 2, 1864	100 dys.	Mustered out with company Aug. 27, 1864.
Fisher, Michael	....do....	26	May 2, 1864	100 dys.	Mustered out with company Aug. 27, 1864.
Galleson, Dudley	....do....	18	May 2, 1864	100 dys.	Mustered out with company Aug. 27, 1864.
Gibson, James	....do....	20	May 2, 1864	100 dys.	Mustered out with company Aug. 27, 1864.
Gibson, James D	....do....	19	May 2, 1864	100 dys.	Sick May 12, 1864, at Camp Dennison, O. No further record found.
Gibson, James L	....do....	18	May 2, 1864	100 dys.	Mustered out with company Aug. 27, 1864.
Guseman, A. J	....do....	18	May 2, 1864	100 dys.	Mustered out with company Aug. 27, 1864.
Hall, Charles F	....do....	18	May 2, 1864	100 dys.	
Harrison, George	....do....	30	May 2, 1864	100 dys.	
Harris, Alexander	....do....	18	May 2, 1864	100 dys.	Mustered out with company Aug. 27, 1864.
Heman, Henry H	....do....	18	May 2, 1864	100 dys.	Mustered out with company Aug. 27, 1864.
Hollowood, Thomas	....do....	31	May 2, 1864	100 dys.	Mustered out with company Aug. 27, 1864.
Hoover, Emanuel	....do....	21	May 2, 1864	100 dys.	Mustered out with company Aug. 27, 1864.
Hoover, John	....do....	18	May 2, 1864	100 dys.	
Hott, Adam	....do....	34	May 2, 1864	100 dys.	Mustered out with company Aug. 27, 1864.
Howells, Howell E	....do....	18	May 2, 1864	100 dys.	Discharged Aug. 23, 1864, at Portsmouth, Va., on Surgeon's certificate of disability.
Irwin, William W	....do....	19	May 2, 1864	100 dys.	Mustered out with company Aug. 27, 1864.
Johns, Archibald	....do....	35	May 2, 1864	100 dys.	Mustered out with company Aug. 27, 1864.
Jones, Henry	....do....	20	May 2, 1864	100 dys.	Mustered out with company Aug. 27, 1864.
Jones, John N	....do....	25	May 2, 1864	100 dys.	
Justice, G. A	....do....	20	May 2, 1864	100 dys.	Died July 17, 1864, at City Point, Va.
Kahn, Samuel	....do....	18	May 2, 1864	100 dys.	Mustered out with company Aug. 27, 1864.
Leslie, Henry G	....do....	21	May 2, 1864	100 dys.	Sick June 13, 1864, at White House, Va. No further record found.
Lewis, Thomas J	....do....	24	May 2, 1864	100 dys.	Mustered out with company Aug. 27, 1864.
McClelland, E. W	....do....	21	May 2, 1864	100 dys.	Mustered out with company Aug. 27, 1864.
McKinley, Abner O	....do....	18	May 2, 1864	100 dys.	Mustered out with company Aug. 27, 1864.
McKinnie, David K	....do....	28	May 2, 1864	100 dys.	Mustered out with company Aug. 27, 1864.
McKinnie, Jerry T	....do....	18	May 2, 1864	100 dys.	Mustered out with company Aug. 27, 1864.
McNabb, Charles W	....do....	18	May 2, 1864	100 dys.	Mustered out with company Aug. 27, 1864.
Mack, Jacob	....do....	51	May 2, 1864	100 dys.	Mustered out with company Aug. 27, 1864.
Mack, Levi	....do....	41	May 2, 1864	100 dys.	Mustered out with company Aug. 27, 1864.
Mack, Philip	....do....	23	May 2, 1864	100 dys.	Mustered out with company Aug. 27, 1864.
Mahan, William A	....do....	27	May 2, 1864	100 dys.	Mustered out with company Aug. 27, 1864.
Mash, Wayne	....do....	24	May 2, 1864	100 dys.	
Montgomery, Lewis W	....do....	24	May 2, 1864	100 dys.	Mustered out with company Aug. 27, 1864.
Niven, John	....do....	21	May 2, 1864	100 dys.	Mustered out with company Aug. 27, 1864.
Orr, James K	....do....	18	May 2, 1864	100 dys.	Mustered out with company Aug. 27, 1864.
Ott, John	....do....	30	May 2, 1864	100 dys.	Mustered out with company Aug. 27, 1864.
Painter, Ephraim	....do....	20	May 2, 1864	100 dys.	Mustered out with company Aug. 27, 1864.
Penell, Samuel	....do....	20	May 2, 1864	100 dys.	Mustered out with company Aug. 27, 1864.
Poindexter, Edward	....do....	27	May 2, 1864	100 dys.	Mustered out with company Aug. 27, 1864.
Ryan, Thomas	....do....	29	May 2, 1864	100 dys.	

Names.	Rank.	Age.	Date of Entering the Service.	Period of Service.	Remarks.
[illegible]	Private..	18	May 2, 1864	100 dys.	Mustered out with company Aug. 27, 1864.
[illegible]	....do....	45	May 2, 1864	100 dys.	Mustered out with company Aug. 27, 1864.
[illegible]	....do....	21	May 2, 1864	100 dys.	Reduced from Corporal July 15, 1864; mustered out with company Aug. 27, 1864.
[illegible]	[illegible]	23	May 2, 1864	100 dys.	Mustered out with company Aug. 27, 1864.
[illegible]	[illegible]	25	May 2, 1864	100 dys.	Mustered out with company Aug. 27, 1864.
[illegible]	[illegible]	18	May 2, 1864	100 dys.	Mustered out with company Aug. 27, 1864.
[illegible]	[illegible]	22	May 2, 1864	100 dys.	Mustered out with company Aug. 27, 1864.
[illegible]	[illegible]	22	May 2, 1864	100 dys.	Mustered out with company Aug. 27, 1864.
[illegible]	[illegible]	18	May 2, 1864	100 dys.	Mustered out with company Aug. 27, 1864.
[illegible]	[illegible]	18	May 2, 1864	100 dys.	Mustered out with company Aug. 27, 1864.
[illegible]	[illegible]	23	May 2, 1864	100 dys.	
[illegible]	[illegible]	37	May 2, 1864	100 dys.	Discharged Aug. 30, 1864, at Portsmouth, Va., on Surgeon' certificate of disability.
[illegible]	....do....	44	May 2, 1864	100 dys.	Mustered out with company Aug. 27, 1864.

COMPANY G.

Mustered in May 8, 1864, at Camp Dennison, O., by Robert S. Smith, Captain 2d U. S. Cavalry. Mustered out Aug. 27, 1864, at Camp Dennison, O.

Names.	Rank.	Age.	Date of Entering the Service.	Period of Service.	Remarks.
[illegible] E. Nagle	Captain.	[illegible]	May 2, 1864	100 dys.	Mustered out with company Aug. 27, 1864.
[illegible]	1st Lieut.	[illegible]	May 2, 1864	100 dys.	Mustered out with company Aug. 27, 1864.
[illegible]	2d Lieut.	27	May 2, 1864	100 dys.	Mustered out with company Aug. 27, 1864.
[illegible]	1st Sergt.	[illegible]	May 2, 1864	100 dys.	Discharged Aug. 30, 1864, at Portsmouth, Va., on Surgeon's certificate of disability.
Alexander Baker	Sergeant.	[illegible]	May 2, 1864	100 dys.	Mustered out with company Aug. 27, 1864.
Benjamin F. Baldwin	....do....	29	May 2, 1864	100 dys.	Discharged May 8, 1864, at Camp Dennison, O., on Surgeon's certificate of disability.
[illegible]	....do....	29	May 2, 1864	100 dys.	Mustered out with company Aug. 27, 1864.
[illegible]	....do....	20	May 2, 1864	100 dys.	Mustered out with company Aug. 27, 1864.
[illegible]	Corporal.	[illegible]	May 2, 1864	100 dys.	Mustered out with company Aug. 27, 1864.
William F. Lancaster	....do....	31	May 2, 1864	100 dys.	Mustered out with company Aug. 27, 1864.
[illegible]	....do....	40	May 2, 1864	100 dys.	Mustered out with company Aug. 27, 1864.
[illegible]	....do....	18	May 2, 1864	100 dys.	Mustered out with company Aug. 27, 1864.
[illegible] Wilson	....do....	35	May 2, 1864	100 dys.	Mustered out with company Aug. 27, 1864.
[illegible] Wilson	....do....	20	May 2, 1864	100 dys.	Mustered out with company Aug. 27, 1864.
[illegible] H. Chamberlain	....do....	18	May 2, 1864	100 dys.	Mustered out with company Aug. 27, 1864.
[illegible] Cummins	....do....	33	May 2, 1864	100 dys.	Mustered out with company Aug. 27, 1864.
[illegible], Silas	Private..	19	May 2, 1864	100 dys.	Discharged Aug. 24, 1864, at Portsmouth, Va., on Surgeon's certificate of disability.
[illegible]	....do....	18	May 2, 1864	100 dys.	Mustered out with company Aug. 27, 1864.
[illegible] Johnson	....do....	18	May 2, 1864	100 dys.	Mustered out with company Aug. 27, 1864.
[illegible]	....do....	20	May 2, 1864	100 dys.	Mustered out with company Aug. 27, 1864.
[illegible]	....do....	20	May 2, 1864	100 dys.	Mustered out with company Aug. 27, 1864.
[illegible]	....do....	20	May 2, 1864	100 dys.	Mustered out with company Aug. 27, 1864.
[illegible] M.	....do....	20	May 2, 1864	100 dys.	Mustered out with company Aug. 27, 1864.
[illegible], Abraham	....do....	20	May 2, 1864	100 dys.	Mustered out with company Aug. 27, 1864.
[illegible]	....do....	22	May 2, 1864	100 dys.	Mustered out with company Aug. 27, 1864.
[illegible]	....do....	20	May 2, 1864	100 dys.	Discharged May 8, 1864, at Camp Dennison, O., on Surgeon's certificate of disability.
[illegible]	....do....	27	May 2, 1864	100 dys.	Mustered out with company Aug. 27, 1864.
[illegible]	....do....	26	May 2, 1864	100 dys.	Mustered out with company Aug. 27, 1864.
[illegible]	....do....	21	May 2, 1864	100 dys.	Mustered out with company Aug. 27, 1864.
[illegible]	....do....	29	May 2, 1864	100 dys.	Mustered out with company Aug. 27, 1864.
[illegible]	....do....	19	May 2, 1864	100 dys.	Died Aug. 14, 1864, in Balfour Hospital, Portsmouth, Va.
Fogg, Josiah	....do....	42	May 2, 1864	100 dys.	Mustered out with company Aug. 27, 1864.
Gault, James G.	....do....	21	May 2, 1864	100 dys.	Mustered out with company Aug. 27, 1864.
Gee, Francis	....do....	19	May 2, 1864	100 dys.	Mustered out with company Aug. 27, 1864.
Greenamyre, Solomon E.	....do....	[illegible]	May 2, 1864	100 dys.	Mustered out with company Aug. 27, 1864.
Greenamyre, Tobias	....do....	[illegible]	May 2, 1864	100 dys.	Mustered out with company Aug. 27, 1864.
Hahn, Samuel	....do....	[illegible]	May 2, 1864	100 dys.	Mustered out with company Aug. 27, 1864.
Hammond, Oscar E.	....do....	19	May 2, 1864	100 dys.	Mustered out with company Aug. 27, 1864.
Hartzel, Joshua	....do....	23	May 2, 1864	100 dys.	Mustered out with company Aug. 27, 1864.
Haskins, Jacob B.	....do....	[illegible]	May 2, 1864	100 dys.	Mustered out with company Aug. 27, 1864.
Hawkins, William	....do....	19	May 2, 1864	100 dys.	Discharged Aug. 23, 1864, at Portsmouth, Va., on Surgeon's certificate of disability.
Heisel, Jacob	....do....	[illegible]	May 2, 1864	100 dys.	Mustered out with company Aug. 27, 1864.
Holman, Uriah	....do....	22	May 2, 1864	100 dys.	Mustered out with company Aug. 27, 1864.
Howard, Cowden	....do....	[illegible]	May 2, 1864	100 dys.	Died July 14, 1864, in hospital at Norfolk, Va.
Hoyle, Comfort	....do....	[illegible]	May 2, 1864	100 dys.	Mustered out with company Aug. 27, 1864.
Hull, Hiram	....do....	[illegible]	May 2, 1864	100 dys.	Mustered out with company Aug. 27, 1864.
Kale, Andrew	....do....	[illegible]	May 2, 1864	100 dys.	Discharged Aug. 30, 1864, at Portsmouth, Va., on Surgeon's certificate of disability.
King, Joseph	....do....	[illegible]	May 2, 1864	100 dys.	Mustered out with company Aug. 27, 1864.
Kirkbride, Mahlon	....do....	[illegible]	May 2, 1864	100 dys.	Mustered out with company Aug. 27, 1864.
Kump, John	....do....	[illegible]	May 2, 1864	100 dys.	Mustered out with company Aug. 27, 1864.
McNutt, Sampson	....do....	[illegible]	May 2, 1864	100 dys.	Mustered out with company Aug. 27, 1864.
Martin, George W.	....do....	[illegible]	May 2, 1864	100 dys.	Mustered out with company Aug. 27, 1864.

Names.	Rank.	Age.	Date of Entering the Service.	Period of Service.	Remarks.
Martz, Elias	Private	30	May 2, 1864	100 dys.	Mustered out with company Aug. 27, 1864.
Martz, Solomon	...do...	36	May 2, 1864	100 dys.	Died Aug. 1, 1864, in Balfour Hospital, Portsmouth, Va.
Mellinger, John B.	...do...	28	May 2, 1864	100 dys.	Mustered out with company Aug. 27, 1864.
Middleton, Evan	...do...	18	May 2, 1864	100 dys.	Mustered out with company Aug. 27, 1864.
Middleton, Joel	...do...	30	May 2, 1864	100 dys.	Mustered out with company Aug. 27, 1864.
Mitchell, Thomas	...do...	31	May 2, 1864	100 dys.	Mustered out with company Aug. 27, 1864.
Mock, David	...do...	26	May 2, 1864	100 dys.	Mustered out with company Aug. 27, 1864.
Mock, Eli	...do...	19	May 2, 1864	100 dys.	Mustered out with company Aug. 27, 1864.
Mock, John	...do...	37	May 2, 1864	100 dys.	Mustered out with company Aug. 27, 1864.
Naylor Samuel	...do...	20	May 2, 1864	100 dys.	Mustered out with company Aug. 27, 1864.
Phillips, Samuel T	...do...	25	May 2, 1864	100 dys.	Discharged Aug. 24, 1864, at Portsmouth, Va. on Surgeon's certificate of
Powell, Thomas	...do...	33	May 2, 1864	100 dys.	Mustered out with company Aug. 27, 1864.
Reed, Jared P	...do...	..	May 2, 1864	100 dys.	Discharged May 8, 1864, at Camp Dennison, O., on Surgeon's certificate of disability.
Ripley, Edgar	...do...	18	May 2, 1864	100 dys.	Mustered out with company Aug. 27, 1864.
Ripley, John	...do...	19	May 2, 1864	100 dys.	Mustered out with company Aug. 27, 1864.
Rummel, Henry	...do...	33	May 2, 1864	100 dys.	Discharged Aug. 24, 1864, at Portsmouth, Va. on Surgeon's certificate of disability.
Rummel, John (No. 1)	...do...	29	May 2, 1864	100 dys.	Mustered out with company Aug. 27, 1864.
Rummel, John (No. 2)	...do...	27	May 2, 1864	100 dys.	Mustered out with company Aug. 27, 1864.
Scott, Thomas	...do...	18	May 2, 1864	100 dys.	Mustered out with company Aug. 27, 1864.
Sell, Jonathan	...do...	31	May 2, 1864	100 dys.	Mustered out with company Aug. 27, 1864.
Shafer, David	...do...	18	May 2, 1864	100 dys.	Died Aug. 16, 1864, in hospital near Norfolk, Virginia.
Smyth, William	...do...	18	May 2, 1864	100 dys.	Mustered out with company Aug. 27, 1864.
Steel, Samuel M	...do...	24	May 2, 1864	100 dys.	Discharged Aug. 25, 1864, at Portsmouth, Va. on Surgeon's certificate of disability.
Swartz, Hugh	...do...	29	May 2, 1864	100 dys.	Mustered out with company Aug. 27, 1864.
Toot, John	...do...	18	May 2, 1864	100 dys.	Mustered out with company Aug. 27, 1864.
Trail, Madison	...do...	32	May 2, 1864	100 dys.	Mustered out with company Aug. 27, 1864.
Vatau, Lindley G	...do...	19	May 2, 1864	100 dys.	Mustered out with company Aug. 27, 1864.
Warton, Samuel D	...do...	18	May 2, 1864	100 dys.	Discharged Aug. 24, 1864, at Portsmouth, Va. on Surgeon's certificate of disability.
Warton, William	...do...	18	May 2, 1864	100 dys.	Mustered out with company Aug. 27, 1864.
Weldy, Alva	...do...	36	May 2, 1864	100 dys.	Mustered out with company Aug. 27, 1864.
Weldy, William Q	...do...	32	May 2, 1864	100 dys.	Mustered out with company Aug. 27, 1864.
Wise, John M	...do...	18	May 2, 1864	100 dys.	Mustered out with company Aug. 27, 1864.
Yancy, Joseph	...do...	24	May 2, 1864	100 dys.	

COMPANY H.

Mustered in May 8, 1864, at Camp Dennison, O., by Robert S. Smith, Captain 2d U. S. Cavalry. Mustered out Aug. 27, 1864, at Camp Dennison, O.

Names.	Rank.	Age.	Date of Entering the Service.	Period of Service.	Remarks.
John D. Mundell	Captain.	35	May 2, 1864	100 dys.	Mustered out with company Aug. 27, 1864.
Jesse M. Clarke	1st Lieut.	39	May 2, 1864	100 dys.	Mustered out with company Aug. 27, 1864.
Isaac Carfrey	2d Lieut.	31	May 2, 1864	100 dys.	Mustered out with company Aug. 27, 1864.
H. B. O'Harra	1st Sergt.	33	May 2, 1864	100 dys.	Mustered out with company Aug. 27, 1864.
Edward Rayen	Sergeant.	32	May 2, 1864	100 dys.	Mustered out with company Aug. 27, 1864.
J. L. Miller	...do...	44	May 2, 1864	100 dys.	Mustered out with company Aug. 27, 1864.
J. G. Mundell	...do...	28	May 2, 1864	100 dys.	Mustered out with company Aug. 27, 1864.
Robert Humphrey	...do...	27	May 2, 1864	100 dys.	Appointed from private July 1, 1864; mustered out with company Aug. 27, 1864.
William R. Bunch	Corporal.	26	May 2, 1864	100 dys.	Mustered out with company Aug. 27, 1864.
J. W. Durrett	...do...	21	May 2, 1864	100 dys.	Mustered out with company Aug. 27, 1864.
H. M. Harlor	...do...	37	May 2, 1864	100 dys.	Mustered out with company Aug. 27, 1864.
George C. McKee	...do...	20	May 2, 1864	100 dys.	Mustered out with company Aug. 27, 1864.
Matthias Hott	...do...	26	May 2, 1864	100 dys.	Mustered out with company Aug. 27, 1864.
John Grove	...do...	33	May 2, 1864	100 dys.	Mustered out with company Aug. 27, 1864.
S. C. Holland	...do...	20	May 2, 1864	100 dys.	Mustered out with company Aug. 27, 1864.
I. N. Green	...do...	32	May 2, 1864	100 dys.	Mustered out with company Aug. 27, 1864.
R. A. Satch	Musician.	15	May 2, 1864	100 dys.	Mustered out with company Aug. 27, 1864.
Beckett, Thomas J	Private.	29	May 2, 1864	100 dys.	Mustered out with company Aug. 27, 1864.
Beers, John	...do...	22	May 2, 1864	100 dys.	Mustered out with company Aug. 27, 1864.
Bensil, H. C	...do...	18	May 2, 1864	100 dys.	Mustered out with company Aug. 27, 1864.
Berkhead, Thomas	...do...	20	May 2, 1864	100 dys.	Mustered out with company Aug. 27, 1864.
Bethards, Matthias	...do...	20	May 2, 1864	100 dys.	Mustered out with company Aug. 27, 1864.
Cherry, R. D	...do...	18	May 2, 1864	100 dys.	Mustered out with company Aug. 27, 1864.
Crabb, Joseph	...do...	20	May 2, 1864	100 dys.	Mustered out with company Aug. 27, 1864.
Duffield, Thomas	...do...	40	May 2, 1864	100 dys.	Mustered out with company Aug. 27, 1864.
Durrett, William W	...do...	19	May 2, 1864	100 dys.	Mustered out with company Aug. 27, 1864.
Fairbanks, John	...do...	25	May 2, 1864	100 dys.	Mustered out with company Aug. 27, 1864.
Fling, John	...do...	37	May 2, 1864	100 dys.	
French, Henry	...do...	19	May 2, 1864	100 dys.	Mustered out with company Aug. 27, 1864.
Fulcher, B. F	...do...	32	May 2, 1864	100 dys.	Mustered out with company Aug. 27, 1864.
Gibson, John	...do...	24	May 2, 1864	100 dys.	Mustered out with company Aug. 27, 1864.
Gibson, Oliver	...do...	27	May 2, 1864	100 dys.	Mustered out with company Aug. 27, 1864.
Gochenour, Henry	...do...	21	May 2, 1864	100 dys.	Mustered out with company Aug. 27, 1864.

Names.	Rank.	Age.	Date of Entering the Service.	Period of Service.	Remarks.
Green, Isaiah	Private..	31	May 2, 1864	100 dys.	Mustered out with company Aug. 27, 1864.
Groves, Adam	...do....	26	May 2, 1864	100 dys.	Mustered out with company Aug. 27, 1864.
Harbor, T. J	...do....	19	May 2, 1864	100 dys.	Reduced to ranks from Sergeant June 22, 1864; mustered out with company Aug. 27, 1864.
Harlor, Thomas	...do....	41	May 2, 1864	100 dys.	Mustered out with company Aug. 27, 1864.
Hathaway, A	...do....	28	May 2, 1864	100 dys.	Discharged Aug. 24, 1864, at Portsmouth, Va., on Surgeon's certificate of disability.
Hewitt, A. P	...do....	21	May 2, 1864	100 dys.	Mustered out with company Aug. 27, 1864.
Hill, Hiram	...do....	29	May 2, 1864	100 dys.	Mustered out to date Aug. 27, 1864, at Camp Dennison, O., by order of War Department.
Hudson, R. D	...do....	26	May 2, 1864	100 dys.	Mustered out with company Aug. 27, 1864.
Johnston, John	...do....	40	May 2, 1864	100 dys.	Mustered out with company Aug. 27, 1864.
Johnston, S. A	...do....	27	May 2, 1864	100 dys.	Mustered out with company Aug. 27, 1864
Kees, John	...do....	36	May 2, 1864	100 dys.	Mustered out with company Aug. 27, 1864.
Kingery, J. M	...do....	32	May 2, 1864	100 dys.	Mustered out with company Aug. 27, 1864.
Lerch, William	...do....	19	May 2, 1864	100 dys.	Mustered out with company Aug. 27, 1864
McClain, John	...do....	28	May 2, 1864	100 dys.	Died Aug. 15, 1864, in Balfour Hospital, at Portsmouth, Va.
McElery, F	...do....	18	May 2, 1864	100 dys.	Mustered out with company Aug. 27, 1864.
McKinney, Jonathan	...do....	31	May 2, 1864	100 dys.	Mustered out with company Aug. 27, 1864.
McMillen, J. H	...do....	40	May 2, 1864	100 dys.	Mustered out with company Aug. 27, 1864.
Martin, O. S	...do....	18	May 2, 1864	100 dys.	Mustered out with company Aug. 27, 1864.
Miller, R. N	...do....	20	May 2, 1864	100 dys.	Mustered out with company Aug. 27, 1864.
Powell, John	...do....	35	May 2, 1864	100 dys.	Mustered out with company Aug. 27, 1864.
Propeck, H	...do....	36	May 2, 1864	100 dys	Mustered out with company Aug. 27, 1864.
Pursell, Lauson	...do....	18	May 2, 1864	100 dys	Mustered out with company Aug. 27, 1864.
Reesman, J. T	...do....	20	May 2, 1864	100 dys.	Mustered out with company Aug. 27, 1864.
Reesman, Samuel	...do....	21	May 2, 1864	100 dys.	Mustered out with company Aug. 27, 1864.
Rigby, George C	...do....	20	May 2, 1864	100 dys.	Mustered out with company Aug. 27, 1864.
Sample, Thomas	...do....	41	May 2, 1864	100 dys.	Mustered out with company Aug. 27, 1864.
Simpson, George	...do....	26	May 2, 1864	100 dys.	Mustered out with company Aug. 27, 1864.
Sines, John	...do....	19	May 2, 1864	100 dys.	Mustered out with company Aug. 27, 1864.
Sines, Samuel	...do....	28	May 2, 1864	100 dys.	Mustered out with company Aug. 27, 1864.
Smith, A	...do....	19	May 2, 1864	100 dys	Mustered out with company Aug. 27, 1864.
Spencer, Elihu	...do....	25	May 2, 1864	100 dys.	Mustered out with company Aug. 27, 1864.
Strader, D. W	...do....	21	May 2, 1864	100 dys.	Mustered out with company Aug. 27, 1864.
Strader, J. M	...do....	23	May 2, 1864	100 dys.	Mustered out with company Aug. 27, 1864.
Terry, J. R	...do....	36	May 2, 1864	100 dys.	Mustered out with company Aug. 27, 1864.
Thorn, J. H	...do....	27	May 2, 1864	100 dys.	Mustered out with company Aug. 27, 1864.
Van Fleet, J. D	...do....	21	May 2, 1864	100 dys.	Mustered out with company Aug. 27, 1864.
Van Houten, A. A	...do....	21	May 2, 1864	100 dys.	Never mustered.
Ward, J. C	...do....	29	May 2, 1864	100 dys.	Mustered out with company Aug. 27, 1864.
Webb, R. S	...do....	21	May 2, 1864	100 dys.	Mustered out with company Aug. 27, 1864.
Welch, Davenport	...do....	19	May 2, 1864	100 dys.	Mustered out with company Aug. 27, 1864.
Welch, J. C	...do....	23	May 2, 1864	100 dys.	Mustered out with company Aug. 27, 1864.
Welch, Marcus	...do....	25	May 2, 1864	100 dys.	Mustered out with company Aug. 27, 1864
Welsh, Franklin	...do....	18	May 2, 1864	100 dys.	Mustered out with company Aug. 27, 1864.
Wheaton, Allen	...do....	24	May 2, 1864	100 dys.	
Wheaton, Emen	...do....	20	May 2, 1864	100 dys.	Mustered out with company Aug. 27, 1864.
Wick, W. H	...do....	20	May 2, 1864	100 dys.	Never mustered.
Wilkins, Alfred	...do....	27	May 2, 1864	100 dys	Mustered out with company Aug. 27, 1864.
Wilkins, Elisha	...do....	33	May 2, 1864	100 dys.	Mustered out with company Aug. 27, 1864.
Wilson, T. H	...do....	23	May 2, 1864	100 dys.	Discharged May 9, 1864, at Camp Dennison, O., on Surgeon's certificate of disability
Wood, J. A	...do....	35	May 2, 1864	100 dys.	Mustered out with company Aug. 27, 1864.

COMPANY I.

Mustered in May 8, 1864, at Camp Dennison, O., by Robert S. Smith, Captain 2d U. S. Cavalry. Mustered out Aug. 27, 1864, at Camp Dennison, O.

Names.	Rank.	Age.	Date of Entering the Service.	Period of Service.	Remarks.
William J. Cochran	Captain.	38	May 2, 1864	100 dys.	Mustered out with company Aug. 27, 1864.
Charles C. Evans	1st Lieut.	28	May 2, 1864	100 dys.	Mustered out with company Aug. 27, 1864.
James M. Lewis	2d Lieut.	28	May 2, 1864	100 dys.	Mustered out with company Aug. 27, 1864.
Joseph W. Kirkpatrick	1st Sergt.	26	May 2, 1864	100 dys.	Mustered out with company Aug. 27, 1864.
Henry D. Seymour	Sergeant.	21	May 2, 1864	100 dys.	Mustered out with company Aug. 27, 1864.
David Wadkins	do.	28	May 2, 1864	100 dys.	Mustered out with company Aug. 27, 1864.
Deming Hoskins	do.	29	May 2, 1864	100 dys.	Mustered out with company Aug. 27, 1864.
Ausmous Rowe	do.	26	May 2, 1864	100 dys.	Mustered out with company Aug. 27, 1864.
William J. Bonner	Corporal.	30	May 2, 1864	100 dys.	Mustered out with company Aug. 27, 1864.
Thomas Garrison	do.	19	May 2, 1864	100 dys.	Mustered out with company Aug. 27, 1864.
Abraham Anderson	do.	24	May 2, 1864	100 dys.	Mustered out with company Aug. 27, 1864.
Isaac Powers	do.	22	May 2, 1864	100 dys.	Mustered out with company Aug. 27, 1864.
Robert McCurdy, Jr.	do.	22	May 2, 1864	100 dys.	Mustered out with company Aug. 27, 1864.
Warren, Timmins	do.	21	May 2, 1864	100 dys.	Mustered out with company Aug. 27, 1864.
Isaac Snyder	do.	21	May 2, 1864	100 dys.	Mustered out with company Aug. 27, 1864.
Joseph H. Gooley	do.	18	May 2, 1864	100 dys.	Mustered out with company Aug. 27, 1864.
Adams, Albert W.	Private.	18	May 2, 1864	100 dys.	Mustered out with company Aug. 27, 1864.
Aid, Joseph	do.	30	May 2, 1864	100 dys.	Mustered out with company Aug. 27, 1864.
Asher, James	do.	33	May 2, 1864	100 dys.	Mustered out with company Aug. 27, 1864.
Berry, Martin	do.	18	May 2, 1864	100 dys.	Rejected by Mustering Officer.
Bennett, Hiram M.	do.	44	May 2, 1864	100 dys.	Mustered out with company Aug. 27, 1864.
Black, James W.	do.	35	May 2, 1864	100 dys.	Mustered out with company Aug. 27, 1864.
Britton, Jesse	do.	48	May 2, 1864	100 dys.	Discharged May 9, 1864, at Camp Dennison, O., on Surgeon's certificate of disability.
Brown, Harrison	do.	18	May 2, 1864	100 dys.	Mustered out with company Aug. 27, 1864.
Bruce, William	do.	26	May 2, 1864	100 dys.	Mustered out with company Aug. 27, 1864.
Carder, Samuel	do.	23	May 2, 1864	100 dys.	Mustered out with company Aug. 27, 1864.
Champlin, Ezra B.	do.	26	May 2, 1864	100 dys.	Mustered out with company Aug. 27, 1864.
[illegible], James S.	do.	44	May 2, 1864	100 dys.	Mustered out with company Aug. 27, 1864.
[illegible]rkwell, Benjamin	do.	32	May 2, 1864	100 dys.	Mustered out with company Aug. 27, 1864.
Dale, Timothy	do.	18	May 2, 1864	100 dys.	Mustered out with company Aug. 27, 1864.
Duncan, Daniel L.	do.	40	May 2, 1864	100 dys.	Mustered out with company Aug. 27, 1864.
Elliott, Jacob	do.	41	May 2, 1864	100 dys.	Mustered out with company Aug. 27, 1864.
Erskine, John	do.	23	May 2, 1864	100 dys.	Mustered out with company Aug. 27, 1864.
Everett, Jacob	do.	37	May 2, 1864	100 dys.	Mustered out with company Aug. 27, 1864.
Funk, John A.	do.	30	May 2, 1864	100 dys.	Mustered out with company Aug. 27, 1864.
Girten, William	do.	18	May 2, 1864	100 dys.	Absent, sick ——, at Camp Dennison, O. No further record found.
Glaze, Thomas	do.	22	May 2, 1864	100 dys.	Mustered out with company Aug. 27, 1864.
Godwin, George W.	do.	18	May 2, 1864	100 dys.	Mustered out with company Aug. 27, 1864.
Gooley, Henry T.	do.	21	May 2, 1864	100 dys.	Mustered out with company Aug. 27, 1864.
Gordon, Ransom S.	do.	42	May 2, 1864	100 dys.	Mustered out with company Aug. 27, 1864.
Grandstaff, John	do.	19	May 2, 1864	100 dys.	Mustered out with company Aug. 27, 1864.
Grimes, Jefferson	do.	19	May 2, 1864	100 dys.	Mustered out with company Aug. 27, 1864.
Grimes, William	do.	19	May 2, 1864	100 dys.	Mustered out with company Aug. 27, 1864.
Haggard, Thomas C.	do.	19	May 2, 1864	100 dys.	Died Aug. 21, 1864, at Portsmouth, Va.
Haynes, Carey T.	do.	18	May 2, 1864	100 dys.	Mustered out with company Aug. 27, 1864.
Heiserman, Christopher	do.	36	May 2, 1864	100 dys.	Mustered out with company Aug. 27, 1864.
Hoagland, Monroe	do.	19	May 2, 1864	100 dys.	Mustered out with company Aug. 27, 1864.
Houser, Parley C.	do.	18	May 2, 1864	100 dys.	Mustered out with company Aug. 27, 1864.
Jester, Henry	do.	26	May 2, 1864	100 dys.	Mustered out with company Aug. 27, 1864.
Johnson, William	do.	25	May 2, 1864	100 dys.	Discharged May 9, 1864, at Camp Dennison, O., on Surgeon's certificate of disability.
Lewis, Andrew J.	do.	34	May 2, 1864	100 dys.	Mustered out with company Aug. 27, 1864.
Lewis, William R.	do.	23	May 2, 1864	100 dys.	Discharged May 9, 1864, at Camp Dennison, O., on Surgeon's certificate of disability.
Loyd, John A.	do.	18	May 2, 1864	100 dys.	Mustered out with company Aug. 27, 1864.
McCrea, Charles C.	do.	18	May 2, 1864	100 dys.	Mustered out with company Aug. 27, 1864.
Maughmer, George W.	do.	18	May 2, 1864	100 dys.	Mustered out with company Aug. 27, 1864.
Miller, James A.	do.	19	May 2, 1864	100 dys.	Mustered out with company Aug. 27, 1864.
Miller, Samuel	do.	41	May 2, 1864	100 dys.	Mustered out with company Aug. 27, 1864.
Moberry, William	do.	32	May 2, 1864	100 dys.	Mustered out with company Aug. 27, 1864.
Mongold, Jacob	do.	37	May 2, 1864	100 dys.	Mustered out with company Aug. 27, 1864.
Nichols, William R.	do.	31	May 2, 1864	100 dys.	Mustered out with company Aug. 27, 1864.
O'Laughlin, Anthony	do.	44	May 2, 1864	100 dys.	Mustered out with company Aug. 27, 1864.
Park, Charles K.	do.	19	May 2, 1864	100 dys.	Mustered out with company Aug. 27, 1864.
Parker, Andrew J.	do.	32	May 2, 1864	100 dys.	Mustered out with company Aug. 27, 1864.
Parker, George W.	do.	24	May 2, 1864	100 dys.	Mustered out with company Aug. 27, 1864.
Parker, William	do.	27	May 2, 1864	100 dys.	Mustered out with company Aug. 27, 1864.
Patterson, C. L.	do.	22	May 2, 1864	100 dys.	Mustered out with company Aug. 27, 1864.
Phelps, Vespacian	do.	22	May 2, 1864	100 dys.	Mustered out with company Aug. 27, 1864.
Porter, Charles W.	do.	18	May 2, 1864	100 dys.	Mustered out with company Aug. 27, 1864.
Probert, Frederick R.	do.	19	May 2, 1864	100 dys.	Rejected by Mustering Officer.
Ramy, James A.	do.	20	May 2, 1864	100 dys.	Mustered out with company Aug. 27, 1864.
Reed, William A.	do.	18	May 2, 1864	100 dys.	Mustered out with company Aug. 27, 1864.

Names.	Rank.	Age.	Date of Entering the Service.	Period of Service.	Remarks.
[illegible], James	Private..	20	May 2, 1864	100 dys.	Discharged Aug. 30, 1864, at Portsmouth, Va., on Surgeon's certificate of disability.
[illegible], Thomas	....do....	29	May 2, 1864	100 dys.	Discharged May 9, 1864, at Camp Dennison, O., on Surgeon's certificate of disability.
[illegible], David	....do....	29	May 2, 1864	100 dys.	Mustered out with company Aug. 27, 1864.
[illegible], John	....do....	23	May 2, 1864	100 dys.	Mustered out with company Aug. 27, 1864.
[illegible]	....do....	18	May 2, 1864	100 dys.	Mustered out with company Aug. 27, 1864.
[illegible]	....do....	18	May 2, 1864	100 dys.	Mustered out with company Aug. 27, 1864.
[illegible], William	....do....	18	May 2, 1864	100 dys.	Mustered out with company Aug. 27, 1864.
[illegible], Nathaniel	....do....	19	May 2, 1864	100 dys.	Mustered out with company Aug. 27, 1864.
[illegible], Owen	....do....	28	May 2, 1864	100 dys.	Mustered out with company Aug. 27, 1864.
[illegible], Andrew	....do....	34	May 2, 1864	100 dys.	Mustered out with company Aug. 27, 1864.
[illegible]	....do....	19	May 2, 1864	100 dys.	Mustered out with company Aug. 27, 1864.
[illegible], William	....do....	19	May 2, 1864	100 dys.	Mustered out with company Aug. 27, 1864.
[illegible], Wesley	....do....	22	May 2, 1864	100 dys.	Mustered out with company Aug. 27, 1864.
[illegible], Lewis T.	....do....	40	May 2, 1864	100 dys.	Mustered out with company Aug. 27, 1864.

COMPANY K.

Mustered in May 8, 1864, at Camp Dennison, O., by Robert S. Smith, Captain 2d U. S. Cavalry. Mustered out Aug. 27, 1864, at Camp Dennison, O.

Names.	Rank.	Age.	Date of Entering the Service.	Period of Service.	Remarks.
A. J. [illegible]	Captain.	37	May 2, 1864	100 dys.	Mustered out with company Aug. 27, 1864.
[illegible]	1st Lieut.	[illegible]	May 2, 1864	100 dys.	Mustered out with company Aug. 27, 1864.
James Williams	2d Lieut.	[illegible]	May 2, 1864	100 dys.	Mustered out with company Aug. 27, 1864.
[illegible] D. [illegible]	1st Sergt.	21	May 2, 1864	100 dys.	Mustered out with company Aug. 27, 1864.
[illegible]	Sergeant.	[illegible]	May 2, 1864	100 dys.	Mustered out with company Aug. 27, 1864.
[illegible]	....do....	[illegible]	May 2, 1864	100 dys.	Mustered out with company Aug. 27, 1864.
[illegible]	....do....	44	May 2, 1864	100 dys.	Mustered out with company Aug. 27, 1864.
[illegible]	....do....	20	May 2, 1864	100 dys.	Mustered out with company Aug. 27, 1864.
[illegible] Miller	Corporal.	[illegible]	May 2, 1864	100 dys.	Mustered out with company Aug. 27, 1864.
[illegible]	....do....	[illegible]	May 2, 1864	100 dys.	Mustered out with company Aug. 27, 1864.
James [illegible]	....do....	22	May 2, 1864	100 dys.	Mustered out with company Aug. 27, 1864.
[illegible] Miller	....do....	[illegible]	May 2, 1864	100 dys.	Mustered out with company Aug. 27, 1864.
[illegible]	....do....	30	May 2, 1864	100 dys.	Mustered out with company Aug. 27, 1864.
[illegible]	....do....	28	May 2, 1864	100 dys.	Mustered out with company Aug. 27, 1864.
[illegible] Gardner	....do....	[illegible]	May 2, 1864	100 dys.	Mustered out with company Aug. 27, 1864.
[illegible] W. Hall	....do....	22	May 2, 1864	100 dys.	Mustered out with company Aug. 27, 1864.
[illegible], Hiram	Private..	27	May 2, 1864	100 dys.	Mustered out with company Aug. 27, 1864.
Brown, Amos	....do....	19	May 2, 1864	100 dys.	Mustered out with company Aug. 27, 1864.
[illegible], J. P	....do....	[illegible]	May 2, 1864	100 dys.	Mustered out with company Aug. 27, 1864.
Campbell, James S	....do....	[illegible]	May 2, 1864	100 dys.	Mustered out with company Aug. 27, 1864.
[illegible], Alonzo	....do....	18	May 2, 1864	100 dys.	Mustered out with company Aug. 27, 1864.
Clark, Samuel	....do....	43	May 2, 1864	100 dys.	Mustered out with company Aug. 27, 1864.
[illegible], Winfield S.	....do....	18	May 2, 1864	100 dys.	Mustered out with company Aug. 27, 1864.
[illegible], P. W	....do....	25	May 2, 1864	100 dys.	Mustered out with company Aug. 27, 1864.
[illegible], Harvey	....do....	18	May 2, 1864	100 dys.	Mustered out with company Aug. 27, 1864.
[illegible], Peter	....do....	18	May 2, 1864	100 dys.	Mustered out with company Aug. 27, 1864.
[illegible], Lewis	....do....	17	May 2, 1864	100 dys.	Mustered out with company Aug. 27, 1864.
[illegible], S	....do....	18	May 2, 1864	100 dys.	Mustered out with company Aug. 27, 1864.
[illegible], Richard B	....do....	18	May 2, 1864	100 dys.	Mustered out with company Aug. 27, 1864.
[illegible], David	....do....	19	May 2, 1864	100 dys.	Mustered out with company Aug. 27, 1864.
[illegible], Jacob S	....do....	17	May 2, 1864	100 dys.	Mustered out with company Aug. 27, 1864.
[illegible], Jacob H	....do....	19	May 2, 1864	100 dys.	Mustered out with company Aug. 27, 1864.
[illegible], Christian	....do....	27	May 2, 1864	100 dys.	Discharged Aug. [illegible]4, 1864, at Portsmouth, Va., on Surgeon's certificate of disability.
[illegible], Frederick	....do....	34	May 2, 1864	100 dys.	Mustered out with company Aug. 27, 1864.
[illegible], John	....do....	19	May 2, 1864	100 dys.	Mustered out with company Aug. 27, 1864.
[illegible], G. W	....do....	[illegible]	May 2, 1864	100 dys.	Discharged May 9, 1864, at Camp Dennison, O., on Surgeon's certificate of disability.
[illegible], Charles	....do....	20	May 2, 1864	100 dys.	Discharged May 8, 1864, at Camp Dennison, O., on Surgeon's certificate of disability.
Igo, Sylvester	....do....	18	May 2, 1864	100 dys.	Mustered out with company Aug. 27, 1864.
Jones, Burgess	....do....	18	May 2, 1864	100 dys.	Mustered out with company Aug. 27, 1864.
Kidnocker, Robert	....do....	[illegible]	May 2, 1864	100 dys.	
Kitchen, Isaac	....do....	[illegible]	May 2, 1864	100 dys.	
Kitzmiller, Upton	....do....	30	May 2, 1864	100 dys.	Mustered out with company Aug. 27, 1864.
Kuhn, Ferguson	....do....	18	May 2, 1864	100 dys.	Mustered out with company Aug. 27, 1864.
Long, Otis	....do....	25	May 2, 1864	100 dys.	Mustered out with company Aug. 27, 1864.
Markel, Nelson	....do....	21	May 2, 1864	100 dys.	Mustered out with company Aug. 27, 1864.
Miller, James	....do....	19	May 2, 1864	100 dys.	Mustered out with company Aug. 27, 1864.
Miller, Joseph	....do....	18	May 2, 1864	100 dys.	Mustered out with company Aug. 27, 1864.
Miner, Henry	....do....	..	May 2, 1864	100 dys.	
Moyer, Henry	....do....	21	May 2, 1864	100 dys.	Mustered out with company Aug. 27, 1864.
Parker, Samuel	....do....	24	May 2, 1864	100 dys.	Mustered out with company Aug. 27, 1864.
Patterson, W. H	....do....	24	May 2, 1864	100 dys.	Discharged Aug. 24, 1864, at Portsmouth, Va., on Surgeon's certificate of disability.
Penn, Abraham	....do....	[illegible]	May 2, 1864	100 dys.	Mustered out with company Aug. 27, 1864.
Rhymer, Michael	....do....	30	May 2, 1864	100 dys.	Mustered out with company Aug. 27, 1864.
Rife, Joel R	....do....	[illegible]	May 2, 1864	100 dys.	Mustered out with company Aug. 27, 1864.

Names.	Rank.	Age.	Date of Entering the Service.	Period of Service.	Remarks.
Ringhizer, Ferdinand	Private	30	May 2, 1864	100 dys.	Mustered out with company Aug. 27, 1864.
Roberts, Archibald	do	21	May 2, 1864	100 dys.	Mustered out with company Aug. 27, 1864.
Rogers, Nelson	do	21	May 2, 1864	100 dys.	Mustered out with company Aug. 27, 1864.
Rogers, Salmon C	do	30	May 2, 1864	100 dys.	Discharged Aug. 30, 1864, at Portsmouth, Va., on Surgeon's certificate of disability.
Ross, James N	do	14	May 2, 1864	100 dys.	Mustered out with company Aug. 27, 1864.
Ross, Lemuel	do	19	May 2, 1864	100 dys.	Mustered out with company Aug. 27, 1864.
Rush, William	do	45	May 2, 1864	100 dys.	Mustered out with company Aug. 27, 1864.
Russell, Daniel	do	26	May 2, 1864	100 dys.	Mustered out with company Aug 27, 1864.
Sands, Jacob	do	17	May 2, 1864	100 dys.	Mustered out with company Aug 27, 1864.
Sands, William	do	27	May 2, 1864	100 dys.	Discharged June 6, 1864, at Circleville, O., on Surgeon's certificate of disability.
Shain, Cornelius	do	18	May 2, 1864	100 dys.	Mustered out with company Aug. 27, 1864.
Smith, Bernard G	do	32	May 2, 1864	100 dys.	Mustered out with company Aug. 27, 1864.
Snively, Oliver	do	19	May 2, 1864	100 dys.	Mustered out with company Aug. 27, 1864.
Snyder, Byron	do	18	May 2, 1864	100 dys.	Mustered out with company Aug. 27, 1864.
Spencer, Nelson	do	22	May 2, 1864	100 dys.	Mustered out with company Aug. 27, 1864.
Stephens, Edward	do	27	May 2, 1864	100 dys.	
Taffe, Matthew	do	21	May 2, 1864	100 dys.	Mustered out with company Aug. 27, 1864.
Tammany, John	do	22	May 2, 1864	100 dys.	Mustered out with company Aug. 27, 1864.
Todd, Samuel	do	19	May 2, 1864	100 dys.	Mustered out with company Aug. 27, 1864.
Trimmer, Isaac	do	39	May 2, 1864	100 dys.	Mustered out with company Aug. 27, 1864.
Wallace, George S	do	29	May 2, 1864	100 dys.	Mustered out with company Aug. 27, 1864.
Wetherby, Jason	do	44	May 2, 1864	100 dys.	Mustered out with company Aug. 27, 1864.
Whisler, John	do	21	May 2, 1864	100 dys.	Mustered out with company Aug. 27, 1864.
Whisler, Jonathan	do	29	May 2, 1864	100 dys.	Mustered out with company Aug. 27, 1864.
White, J	do	20	May 2, 1864	100 dys.	
Widner, Peter	do	27	May 2, 1864	100 dys.	Mustered out with company Aug. 27, 1864.
Wilson, Thomas	do	18	May 2, 1864	100 dys.	Mustered out with company Aug. 27, 1864.
Wolf, George A	do	29	May 2, 1864	100 dys.	Mustered out with company Aug. 27, 1864.
Wolf, John D	do	27	May 2, 1864	100 dys.	Discharged May 8, 1864, at Camp Dennison, O., on Surgeon's certificate of disability.
Woolington, George	do	19	May 2, 1864	100 dys.	Mustered out with company Aug. 27, 1864.
Young, Jacob	do	19	May 2, 1864	100 dys.	Mustered out with company Aug. 27, 1864.

156th Regiment Ohio Volunteer Infantry.

ONE HUNDRED DAYS' SERVICE.

THIS Regiment was organized May 15, 16 and 17, 1864, at Camp Dennison, O., to serve one hundred days. It was composed of the Thirty-fourth Battalion, Ohio National Guard, from Preble County; Eightieth Battalion, Ohio National Guard, from Mercer County; and the Eighty-first Battalion, Ohio National Guard, from Auglaize County. On the 20th of May Companies A, B, C, D, E, F, and H, proceeded to Cincinnati, where they performed guard duty. Companies G, I, and K, remained at Camp Dennison, on guard and patrol duty, until Morgan appeared in the vicinity of Cynthiana, Ky., when they were sent to Falmouth, Ky. The seven Companies remained on duty at Cincinnati until July 18th, when the entire Regiment was brought together at Covington and moved to Paris, Ky. The Regiment was soon ordered to Cumberland, Md., arriving on the 31st of July, and went into camp near that city. On the 1st of August the Regiment had an engagement with the enemy near Folck's Mills, with slight loss. After this engagement the Regiment remained on duty at and near Cumberland until the 26th of August, when it was ordered to Ohio for muster-out. It was mustered out September 1, 1864, on expiration of its term of service.

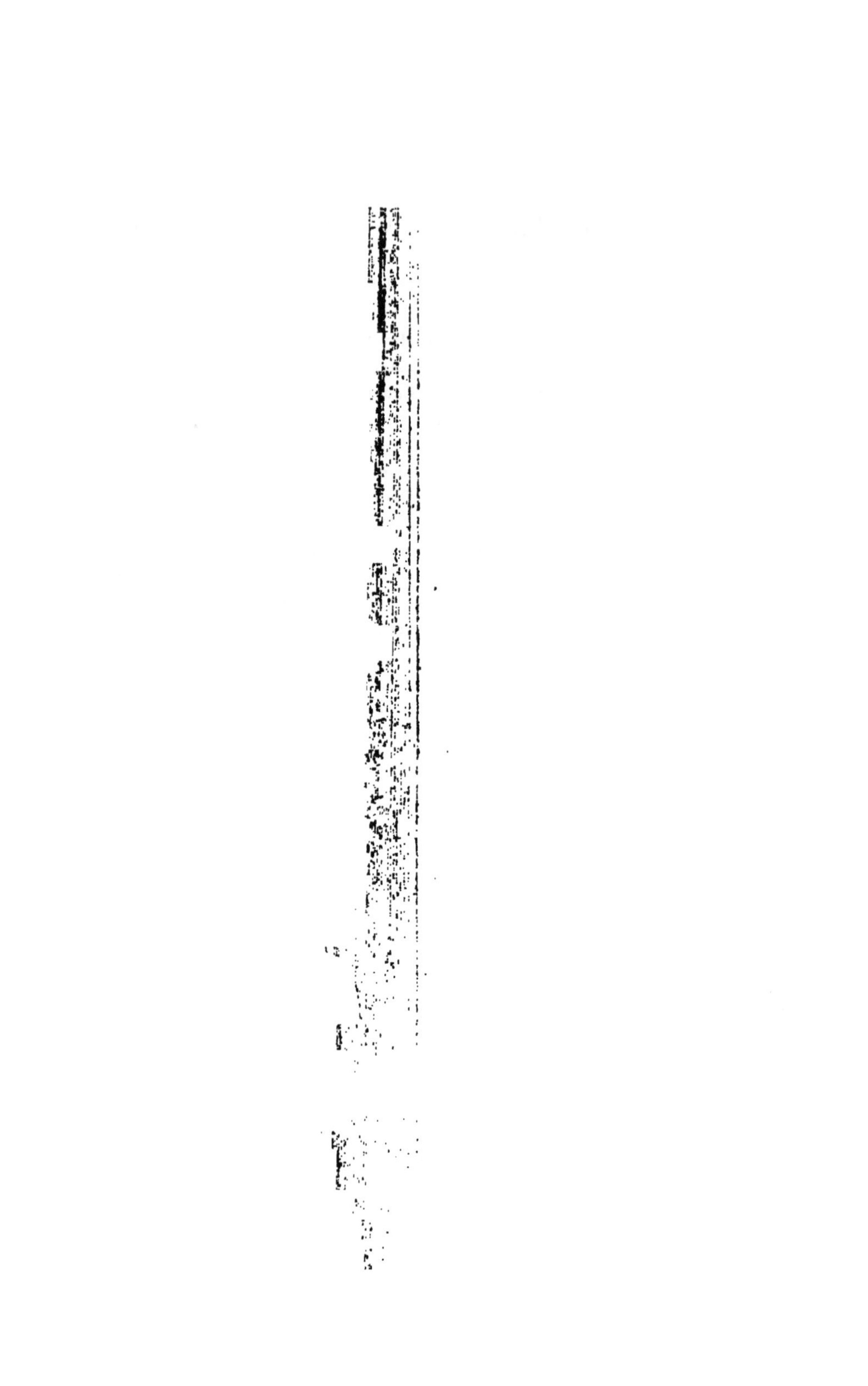

[illegible] Troops

Promoted / [illegible]	Remarks
	[illegible] company Sept. [illegible]
	[illegible] company Sept. [illegible]
	[illegible] company Sept. [illegible]
	[illegible] company Sept. [illegible]
	[illegible] company Sept. [illegible]
	[illegible] company Sept. [illegible]
	[illegible] company Sept. [illegible]
	[illegible] company Sept. [illegible]
	[illegible] company Sept. [illegible]
	[illegible] company Sept. [illegible]
	[illegible] company Sept. [illegible]
	[illegible] with [illegible] Sept. [illegible]
	[illegible] company Sept. [illegible]
	[illegible] with company Sept. 1, 186[illegible]
	[illegible] with company Sept. 1, 186[illegible]
	[illegible] with company Sept. [illegible]
	[illegible] with company Sept. [illegible]
	[illegible] with company Sept. [illegible]
	[illegible] with company Sept. [illegible]
	[illegible] with company Sept. [illegible]
	[illegible] with company Sept. [illegible]
	[illegible] with company Sept. [illegible]
	[illegible] with company Sept. 1, 186[illegible]
	[illegible] with company Sept. [illegible]
	[illegible] with company Sept. [illegible]
	[illegible] with company Sept. [illegible]
	[illegible] with company Sept. [illegible]
	[illegible] with company Sept. [illegible]
	[illegible] with company Sept. [illegible]
	[illegible] out with company Sept. [illegible]
	[illegible] out with company Sept. 1, 186[illegible]
	Mustered out with company Sept. [illegible]
	[illegible] out with company Sept. 1, 186[illegible]
	[illegible] out with company Sept. 1, 186[illegible]
	[illegible] out with company Sept. [illegible]
	[illegible] out with company Sept. [illegible]
	[illegible] out with company Sept. [illegible]
	[illegible] out with company Sept. 1, 186[illegible]
	[illegible] out with company Sept. 1, 186[illegible]
	[illegible] out with company Sept. [illegible]
	[illegible] out with company Sept. 1, 186[illegible]
	[illegible] out with company Sept. [illegible]
	[illegible] out with company Sept. 1, 186[illegible]
	[illegible] out with company Sept. [illegible]
	[illegible] out with company Sept. [illegible]
	[illegible] out with company Sept. 1, 186[illegible]
	[illegible] 22, 186[illegible], in hospital at [illegible]
	[illegible] out with company Sept. [illegible]
	[illegible] out with company Sept. [illegible]
	[illegible] out with company [illegible]
	[illegible] out with company Sept. [illegible]
	Mustered out with company [illegible]
	[illegible] out with company [illegible]
	Mustered out with company Sept. [illegible]
	Mustered out with company Sept. [illegible]
	[illegible] of discharge.
	Mustered out with company Sept. [illegible]
	Mustered out with company Sept. [illegible]
	Promoted to Asst. Surgeon [illegible]
	Mustered out with company Sept. [illegible]
	Mustered out with company Sept. [illegible]
	Mustered out with company Sept. [illegible]
	Mustered out with company Sept. [illegible]
	Mustered out with company Sept. [illegible]
	Mustered out with company Sept. [illegible]

Names.	Rank.	Age.	Date of Entering the Service.	Period of Service.	Remarks.
Shelley, William	Private.	27	May 2, 1864	100 dys.	Mustered out with company Sept. 1, 1864.
Shewman, Allen	....do....	19	May 2, 1864	100 dys.	Mustered out with company Sept. 1, 1864.
Shewman, Christian	....do....	22	May 2, 1864	100 dys.	Mustered out with company Sept. 1, 1864.
Shewman, Monroe	....do....	18	May 2, 1864	100 dys.	Mustered out with company Sept. 1, 1864.
Simpson, Matthew	....do....	39	May 2, 1864	100 dys.	Reduced from Corporal ——; absent, sick ——. No further record found.
Slifer, William C.	....do....	32	May 2, 1864	100 dys.	Mustered out with company Sept. 1, 1864.
Smith, Levi	....do....	30	May 2, 1864	100 dys.	Reduced from Corporal ——; mustered out with company Sept. 1, 1864.
Sterling, McMin	....do....	17	May 2, 1864	100 dys.	Mustered out with company Sept. 1, 1864.
Stevens, James B.	....do....	30	May 2, 1864	100 dys.	Mustered out with company Sept. 1, 1864.
Studebaker, Hiram	....do....	23	May 2, 1864	100 dys.	Mustered out with company Sept. 1, 1864.
Surface, Noah	....do....	19	May 2, 1864	100 dys.	Mustered out with company Sept. 1, 1864.
Swain, Peter	....do....	21	May 2, 1864	100 dys.	Mustered out with company Sept. 1, 1864.
Ullom, Marcus	....do....	29	May 2, 1864	100 dys.	Mustered out with company Sept. 1, 1864.
Wehrly, Eli	....do....	28	May 2, 1864	100 dys.	Mustered out with company Sept. 1, 1864.
Wehrly, Nelson	....do....	26	May 2, 1864	100 dys.	Mustered out with company Sept. 1, 1864.
Wehrly, Wesley	....do....	18	May 2, 1864	100 dys.	Mustered out with company Sept. 1, 1864.
Wyrick, Frederick	....do....	25	May 2, 1864	100 dys.	Mustered out with company Sept. 1, 1864.
Young, Jacob	....do....	39	May 2, 1864	100 dys.	Mustered out with company Sept. 1, 1864.

COMPANY C.

Mustered in May 17, 1864, at Camp Dennison, O., by G. E. Johnston, Major and A. D. C. Mustered out Sept. 1, 1864, at Camp Dennison, O., by William Stanley, 2d Lieutenant 10th Infantry, U. S. A.

Names.	Rank.	Age.	Date of Entering the Service.	Period of Service.	Remarks.
Ephraim Sheller	Captain.	31	May 2, 1864	100 dys.	Mustered out with company Sept. 1, 1864.
George A. Ellis	1st Lieut.	35	May 2, 1864	100 dys.	Mustered out with company Sept. 1, 1864.
Joseph S. Brown	2d Lieut.	35	May 2, 1864	100 dys.	Mustered out with company Sept. 1, 1864.
Thomas J. Brower	1st Sergt.	22	May 2, 1864	100 dys.	Mustered out with company Sept. 1, 1864.
William Cox	Sergeant.	22	May 2, 1864	100 dys.	Mustered out with company Sept. 1, 1864.
Abraham Cosler	....do....	34	May 2, 1864	100 dys.	Mustered out with company Sept. 1, 1864.
Michael L. Brown	....do....	35	May 2, 1864	100 dys.	Mustered out with company Sept. 1, 1864.
William Tice	....do....	33	May 2, 1864	100 dys.	Mustered out with company Sept. 1, 1864.
David G. Achey	Corporal.	29	May 2, 1864	100 dys.	Mustered out with company Sept. 1, 1864.
Robert H. Wilson	....do....	40	May 2, 1864	100 dys.	Mustered out with company Sept. 1, 1864.
James D. Smock	....do....	24	May 2, 1864	100 dys.	Mustered out with company Sept. 1, 1864.
Perry D. Hapner	....do....	35	May 2, 1864	100 dys.	Mustered out with company Sept. 1, 1864.
William J. Ellis	....do....	25	May 2, 1864	100 dys.	Mustered out with company Sept. 1, 1864.
Abraham E. Sheller	....do....	21	May 2, 1864	100 dys.	Mustered out with company Sept. 1, 1864.
Calvin L. Hiens	....do....	21	May 2, 1864	100 dys.	Mustered out with company Sept. 1, 1864.
William H. Brower	....do....	25	May 2, 1864	100 dys.	Appointed ——; mustered out with company Sept. 1, 1864.
William F. Chance	Musician	23	May 2, 1864	100 dys.	Mustered out with company Sept. 1, 1864.
John W. Chance	....do....	19	May 2, 1864	100 dys.	Mustered out with company Sept. 1, 1864.
Aikman, William F.	Private.	36	May 2, 1864	100 dys.	Mustered out with company Sept. 1, 1864.
Anderson, George W.	....do....	27	May 2, 1864	100 dys.	Mustered out with company Sept. 1, 1864.
Aydelott, Benjamin	....do....	18	May 2, 1864	100 dys.	Mustered out with company Sept. 1, 1864.
Aydelott, William H.	....do....	30	May 2, 1864	100 dys.	Mustered out with company Sept. 1, 1864.
Banker, John P.	....do....	18	May 2, 1864	100 dys.	Mustered out with company Sept. 1, 1864.
Besecker, Noah	....do....	25	May 2, 1864	100 dys.	Mustered out with company Sept. 1, 1864.
Bish, Jacob	....do....	40	May 2, 1864	100 dys.	Mustered out with company Sept. 1, 1864.
Bowman, Benjamin F.	....do....	17	May 2, 1864	100 dys.	Mustered out with company Sept. 1, 1864.
Brown, Abraham	....do....	34	May 2, 1864	100 dys.	Mustered out with company Sept. 1, 1864.
Brown, David L.	....do....	32	May 2, 1864	100 dys.	Died June 27, 1864, in hospital at Cincinnati, Ohio.
Brown, Eli	....do....	25	May 2, 1864	100 dys.	Mustered out with company Sept. 1, 1864.
Bulger, James	....do....	21	May 2, 1864	100 dys.	Mustered out with company Sept. 1, 1864.
Bunger, William	....do....	28	May 2, 1864	100 dys.	Mustered out with company Sept. 1, 1864.
Clevenger, William H.	....do....	24	May 2, 1864	100 dys.	Mustered out with company Sept. 1, 1864.
Clevenger, William H. H.	....do....	26	May 2, 1864	100 dys.	Mustered out with company Sept. 1, 1864.
Corwin, Joseph W.	....do....	33	May 2, 1864	100 dys.	Mustered out with company Sept. 1, 1864.
Crisler, Allen	....do....	23	May 2, 1864	100 dys.	Mustered out with company Sept. 1, 1864.
Davis, Benjamin F.	....do....	18	May 2, 1864	100 dys.	Mustered out with company Sept. 1, 1864.
Davis, Elihu	....do....	36	May 2, 1864	100 dys.	Mustered out with company Sept. 1, 1864.
Detamore, David A.	....do....	18	May 2, 1864	100 dys.	Mustered out with company Sept. 1, 1864.
Emmons, George W.	....do....	25	May 2, 1864	100 dys.	Mustered out with company Sept. 1, 1864.
Fleagle, John A.	....do....	25	May 2, 1864	100 dys.	Mustered out with company Sept. 1, 1864.
Fowble, John W.	....do....	21	May 2, 1864	100 dys.	Mustered out with company Sept. 1, 1864.
Freel, William	....do....	27	May 2, 1864	100 dys.	Mustered out with company Sept. 1, 1864.
Francisco, John A.	....do....	25	May 2, 1864	100 dys.	Mustered out with company Sept. 1, 1864.
Griffith, William	....do....	38	May 2, 1864	100 dys.	Mustered out with company Sept. 1, 1864.
Grimes, Cornelius H.	....do....	34	May 2, 1864	100 dys.	Mustered out with company Sept. 1, 1864.
Hall, George	....do....	21	May 2, 1864	100 dys.	Mustered out with company Sept. 1, 1864.
Hapner, James B.	....do....	33	May 2, 1864	100 dys.	Mustered out with company Sept. 1, 1864.
Hapner, Nathan	....do....	21	May 2, 1864	100 dys.	Died July 10, 1864, in hospital at Cincinnati, Ohio.
Hapner, William A.	....do....	23	May 2, 1864	100 dys.	Mustered out with company Sept. 1, 1864.
Hart, Adam	....do....	26	May 2, 1864	100 dys.	Mustered out with company Sept. 1, 1864.

Names.	Rank.	Age.	Date of Entering the Service.		Period of Service.	Remarks.
[illegible]man, Elias	Private	41	May	2, 1864	100 dys.	Mustered out with company Sept. 1, 1864.
[illegible] Martin	do	26	May	2, 1864	100 dys.	Mustered out with company Sept. 1, 1864.
[illegible]son, Benjamin F.	do	18	May	2, 1864	100 dys.	Mustered out with company Sept. 1, 1864.
[illegible]ger, Francis M.	do	18	May	2, 1864	100 dys.	Mustered out with company Sept. 1, 1864.
[illegible]ler, Charles J. S.	do	19	May	2, 1864	100 dys.	Promoted to Sergt. Major —.
[illegible]er, Robert	do	38	May	2, 1864	100 dys.	Mustered out with company Sept. 1, 1864.
[illegible]swood, Edward P.	do	45	May	2, 1864	100 dys.	Promoted to Principal Musician —.
[illegible]ckwood, John L.	do	38	May	2, 1864	100 dys.	Mustered out with company Sept. 1, 1864.
[illegible]y, Oliver	do	32	May	2, 1864	100 dys.	Mustered out with company Sept. 1, 1864.
McCabe, Reeder	do	18	May	2, 1864	100 dys.	Mustered out with company Sept. 1, 1864.
McCright, Joseph	do	20	May	2, 1864	100 dys.	Mustered out with company Sept. 1, 1864.
Menaffey, George W.	do	18	May	2, 1864	100 dys.	Mustered out with company Sept. 1, 1864.
Minshall, Albert	do	18	May	2, 1864	100 dys.	Mustered out with company Sept. 1, 1864.
Morris, Henry	do	25	May	2, 1864	100 dys.	Mustered out with company Sept. 1, 1864.
Morris, John	do	28	May	2, 1864	100 dys.	Mustered out with company Sept. 1, 1864.
Morris, Samuel	do	19	May	2, 1864	100 dys.	Mustered out with company Sept. 1, 1864.
Morton, William	do	26	May	2, 1864	100 dys.	Mustered out with company Sept. 1, 1864.
Neal, Benjamin	do	20	May	2, 1864	100 dys.	Mustered out with company Sept. 1, 1864.
Neal, John P.	do	20	May	2, 1864	100 dys.	Mustered out with company Sept. 1, 1864.
Neal, William	do	20	May	2, 1864	100 dys.	Mustered out with company Sept. 1, 1864.
Plummer, James	do	21	May	2, 1864	100 dys.	Mustered out with company Sept. 1, 1864.
Plummer, Lewis B.	do	19	May	2, 1864	100 dys.	Mustered out with company Sept. 1, 1864.
Pugh, William W.	do	18	May	2, 1864	100 dys.	Mustered out with company Sept. 1, 1864.
Quinn, James L.	do	22	May	2, 1864	100 dys.	Mustered out with company Sept. 1, 1864.
Quinn, Samuel	do	20	May	2, 1864	100 dys.	Mustered out with company Sept. 1, 1864.
Railsback, William M.	do	19	May	2, 1864	100 dys.	Mustered out with company Sept. 1, 1864.
Richardson, Benjamin C.	do	18	May	2, 1864	100 dys.	Mustered out with company Sept. 1, 1864.
Richardson, John	do	26	May	2, 1864	100 dys.	Mustered out with company Sept. 1, 1864.
Rogers, Isaac	do	25	May	2, 1864	100 dys.	Mustered out with company Sept. 1, 1864.
Rogers, Samuel S.	do	35	May	2, 1864	100 dys.	Mustered out with company Sept. 1, 1864.
Shealer, William W.	do	19	May	2, 1864	100 dys.	On detached duty at Lytle Barracks, O. —. No further record found.
Shinn, Jacob	do	18	May	2, 1864	100 dys.	Mustered out with company Sept. 1, 1864.
Shinn, William	do	22	May	2, 1864	100 dys.	Mustered out with company Sept. 1, 1864.
Show, John L.	do	23	May	2, 1864	100 dys.	Mustered out with company Sept. 1, 1864.
Smith, George	do	31	May	2, 1864	100 dys.	Mustered out with company Sept. 1, 1864.
Stephen, John B.	do	44	May	2, 1864	100 dys.	Mustered out with company Sept. 1, 1864.
Stroud, Thomas T.	do	23	May	2, 1864	100 dys.	Mustered out with company Sept. 1, 1864.
Sturr, Jacob	do	27	May	2, 1864	100 dys.	Mustered out with company Sept. 1, 1864.
Tracy, Joseph D.	do	30	May	2, 1864	100 dys.	Mustered out with company Sept. 1, 1864.
Truitt, George H.	do	24	May	2, 1864	100 dys.	Mustered out with company Sept. 1, 1864.
[illegible]ham, John	do	24	May	2, 1864	100 dys.	Mustered out with company Sept. 1, 1864.
[illegible]la, Benjamin F.	do	29	May	2, 1864	100 dys.	Mustered out with company Sept. 1, 1864.
Walters, Joseph	do	32	May	2, 1864	100 dys.	Mustered out with company Sept. 1, 1864.
Weaver, Frank H.	do	20	May	2, 1864	100 dys.	Mustered out with company Sept. 1, 1864.
Wilkinson, David	do	20	May	2, 1864	100 dys.	Mustered out with company Sept. 1, 1864.

COMPANY E.

Mustered in May 15, 1864, at Camp Dennison, O., by G. E. Johnston, Major and A. D. C. Mustered out Sept. 1, 1864, at Camp Dennison, O., by William Stanley, 2d Lieutenant 10th Infantry, U. S. A.

Names.	Rank.	Age.	Date of Entering the Service.		Period of Service.	Remarks.
William A. Swihart	Captain.	31	May	2, 1864	100 dys.	Mustered out with company Sept. 1, 1864.
James Gabel	1st Lieut.	30	May	2, 1864	100 dys.	Mustered out with company Sept. 1, 1864.
Eli A. Patty	2d Lieut.	29	May	2, 1864	100 dys.	Mustered out with company Sept. 1, 1864.
James W. Pottenger	1st Sergt.	21	May	2, 1864	100 dys.	Mustered out with company Sept. 1, 1864.
Joel Simpson	Sergeant.	42	May	2, 1864	100 dys.	Mustered out with company Sept. 1, 1864.
James Gard	do	21	May	2, 1864	100 dys.	Mustered out with company Sept. 1, 1864.
Dennis Lewellyn	do	38	May	2, 1864	100 dys.	Mustered out with company Sept. 1, 1864.
John Q. Pottenger	do	30	May	2, 1864	100 dys.	Mustered out with company Sept. 1, 1864.
William Barnet	Corporal.	30	May	2, 1864	100 dys.	Mustered out with company Sept. 1, 1864.
John W. Reed	do	36	May	2, 1864	100 dys.	Mustered out with company Sept. 1, 1864.
John W. Tucker	do	27	May	2, 1864	100 dys.	Mustered out with company Sept. 1, 1864.
Thomas Griffin	do	41	May	2, 1864	100 dys.	Mustered out with company Sept. 1, 1864.
James Campbell	do	32	May	2, 1864	100 dys.	Mustered out with company Sept. 1, 1864.
[illegible] M. Fornshell	do	28	May	2, 1864	100 dys.	Mustered out with company Sept. 1, 1864.
[illegible] C. Burns	do	38	May	2, 1864	100 dys.	Mustered out with company Sept. 1, 1864.
H[illegible]	do	40	May	2, 1864	100 dys.	Mustered out with company Sept. 1, 1864.
[illegible], John P.	Private.	36	May	2, 1864	100 dys.	Mustered out with company Sept. 1, 1864.
[illegible] Theodore C.	do	35	May	2, 1864	100 dys.	Died Aug. 12, 1864, at Camden, Preble County, Ohio.
[illegible]	do	38	May	2, 1864	100 dys.	Mustered out with company Sept. 1, 1864.
[illegible]	do	20	May	2, 1864	100 dys.	Mustered out with company Sept. 1, 1864.
[illegible] John	do	21	May	2, 1864	100 dys.	Mustered out with company Sept. 1, 1864.
[illegible]	do	27	May	2, 1864	100 dys.	Mustered out with company Sept. 1, 1864.
[illegible]	do	26	May	2, 1864	100 dys.	Mustered out with company Sept. 1, 1864.
[illegible]	do	22	May	2, 1864	100 dys.	Mustered out with company Sept. 1, 1864.
[illegible] W.	do	38	May	2, 1864	100 dys.	Mustered out with company Sept. 1, 1864.
[illegible]	do	21	May	2, 1864	100 dys.	Mustered out with company Sept. 1, 1864.

Names.	Rank.	Age.	Date of Entering the Service.	Period of Service.	Remarks.
John A. Bridge	Corporal.	23	May 2, 1864	100 dys.	Mustered out with company Sept. 1, 1864.
William H. Garretson	do.	18	May 2, 1864	100 dys.	Mustered out with company Sept. 1, 1864.
John Mills	do.	40	May 2, 1864	100 dys.	Mustered out with company Sept. 1, 1864.
Charles W. Bloom	do.	18	May 2, 1864	100 dys.	Appointed —— ; mustered out with company Sept. 1, 1864.
Oliver Y. Sackman	do.	21	May 2, 1864	100 dys.	Mustered out with company Sept. 1, 1864.
William C. Street	Musician	22	May 2, 1864	100 dys.	Mustered out with company Sept. 1, 1864.
Adams, James H	Private	21	May 2, 1864	100 dys.	Mustered out with company Sept. 1, 1864.
Aker, James W	do.	22	May 2, 1864	100 dys.	Mustered out with company Sept. 1, 1864.
Austin, William	do.	45	May 2, 1864	100 dys.	Mustered out with company Sept. 1, 1864.
Barnett, John W	do.	19	May 2, 1864	100 dys.	Mustered out with company Sept. 1, 1864.
Bell, William H	do.	25	May 2, 1864	100 dys.	Mustered out with company Sept. 1, 1864.
Berman, John M	do.	32	May 2, 1864	100 dys.	Mustered out with company Sept. 1, 1864.
Berman, Nathan W	do.	21	May 2, 1864	100 dys.	Mustered out with company Sept. 1, 1864.
Bilbee, Joseph	do.	19	May 2, 1864	100 dys.	Mustered out with company Sept. 1, 1864.
Bradstreet, Theodore L.	do.	20	May 2, 1864	100 dys.	Mustered out with company Sept. 1, 1864.
Brawley, Hiram C.	do.	23	May 2, 1864	100 dys.	Mustered out with company Sept. 1, 1864.
Brawley, Theodore C	do.	19	May 2, 1864	100 dys.	Mustered out with company Sept. 1, 1864.
Brown, Clinton	do.	20	May 2, 1864	100 dys.	Mustered out with company Sept. 1, 1864.
Brown, James D	do.	22	May 2, 1864	100 dys.	Mustered out with company Sept. 1, 1864.
Brown, Lucas V	do.	18	May 2, 1864	100 dys.	Mustered out with company Sept. 1, 1864.
Brown, Robert F	do.	25	May 2, 1864	100 dys.	Mustered out with company Sept. 1, 1864.
Burgoyne, Joseph	do.	32	May 2, 1864	100 dys.	Mustered out with company Sept. 1, 1864.
Burtch, George L	do.	24	May 2, 1864	100 dys.	Mustered out with company Sept. 1, 1864.
Cooper, Isaac	do.	38	May 2, 1864	100 dys.	Mustered out with company Sept. 1, 1864.
Cooper, Newton	do.	19	May 2, 1864	100 dys.	Mustered out with company Sept. 1, 1864.
Dix, Samuel S.	do.	30	May 2, 1864	100 dys.	Mustered out with company Sept. 1, 1864.
Edwards, Dallas P	do.	19	May 2, 1864	100 dys.	Mustered out with company Sept. 1, 1864.
Emerick, David	do.	20	May 2, 1864	100 dys.	Mustered out with company Sept. 1, 1864.
Ervin, Thomas N	do.	18	May 2, 1864	100 dys.	Mustered out with company Sept. 1, 1864.
Fisher, Andrew	do.	42	May 2, 1864	100 dys.	Mustered out with company Sept. 1, 1864.
Fudge, Samuel	do.	38	May 2, 1864	100 dys.	Mustered out with company Sept. 1, 1864.
Hallar, William	do.	37	May 2, 1864	100 dys.	Mustered out with company Sept. 1, 1864.
Harvey, Abner D	do.	28	May 2, 1864	100 dys.	Mustered out with company Sept. 1, 1864.
Herman, Jacob J	do.	25	May 2, 1864	100 dys.	Mustered out with company Sept. 1, 1864.
Huffman, Eli	do.	19	May 2, 1864	100 dys.	Mustered out with company Sept. 1, 1864.
Hutton, Cornelius	do.	38	May 2, 1864	100 dys.	Mustered out with company Sept. 1, 1864.
Ireland, Clement C. H	do.	33	May 2, 1864	100 dys.	Reduced from Corporal —— ; mustered out with company Sept. 1, 1864.
James, Fleming	do.	44	May 2, 1864	100 dys.	Mustered out with company Sept. 1, 1864.
Jaqua, John R	do.	19	May 2, 1864	100 dys.	Mustered out with company Sept. 1, 1864.
Johnson, Hiram	do.	37	May 2, 1864	100 dys.	Mustered out with company Sept. 1, 1864.
Judy, John W	do.	21	May 2, 1864	100 dys.	Mustered out with company Sept. 1, 1864.
Kessler, James H	do.	18	May 2, 1864	100 dys.	Mustered out with company Sept. 1, 1864.
King, Clinton	do.	19	May 2, 1864	100 dys.	Mustered out with company Sept. 1, 1864.
King, Samuel	do.	33	May 2, 1864	100 dys.	Mustered out with company Sept. 1, 1864.
Leitwick, Charles R.	do.	18	May 2, 1864	100 dys.	Mustered out with company Sept. 1, 1864.
Longman, Henry	do.	22	May 2, 1864	100 dys.	Mustered out with company Sept. 1, 1864.
McClellan, Theodore	do.	18	May 2, 1864	100 dys.	Mustered out with company Sept. 1, 1864.
McDonald, William A	do.	19	May 2, 1864	100 dys.	Mustered out with company Sept. 1, 1864.
Mackey, John A	do.	18	May 2, 1864	100 dys.	Mustered out with company Sept. 1, 1864.
Mackey, Lewis	do.	38	May 2, 1864	100 dys.	Promoted to Q. M. Sergeant May 15, 1864.
Mikesell, Osmond	do.	19	May 2, 1864	100 dys.	Mustered out with company Sept. 1, 1864.
Mikesell, Peter	do.	20	May 2, 1864	100 dys.	Mustered out with company Sept. 1, 1864.
Miller, John	do.	18	May 2, 1864	100 dys.	Mustered out with company Sept. 1, 1864.
Mitchell, William V	do.	19	May 2, 1864	100 dys.	Mustered out with company Sept. 1, 1864.
Morrison, James D	do.	38	May 2, 1864	100 dys.	Mustered out with company Sept. 1, 1864.
Morse, Asbury	do.	18	May 2, 1864	100 dys.	Mustered out with company Sept. 1, 1864.
Murry, James	do.	21	May 2, 1864	100 dys.	Mustered out with company Sept. 1, 1864.
Murry, Joseph	do.	32	May 2, 1864	100 dys.	Mustered out with company Sept. 1, 1864.
Nicodemus, Jacob	do.	26	May 2, 1864	100 dys.	Mustered out with company Sept. 1, 1864.
Paul, James H	do.	22	May 2, 1864	100 dys.	Mustered out with company Sept. 1, 1864.
Porterfield, Thomas L.	do.	18	May 2, 1864	100 dys.	Mustered out with company Sept. 1, 1864.
Rayburn, James	do.	28	May 2, 1864	100 dys.	Mustered out with company Sept. 1, 1864.
Reinhe[illegible]r, George W	do.	18	May 2, 1864	100 dys.	Mustered out with company Sept. 1, 1864.
Skiles, Samuel	do.	29	May 2, 1864	100 dys.	Mustered out with company Sept. 1, 1864.
Snyder, Jeremiah	do.	28	May 2, 1864	100 dys.	Mustered out with company Sept. 1, 1864.
Sparklin, William	do.	37	May 2, 1864	100 dys.	Mustered out with company Sept. 1, 1864.
Stakebeck, John	do.	27	May 2, 1864	100 dys.	Mustered out with company Sept. 1, 1864.
Stubbs, John M	do.	33	May 2, 1864	100 dys.	Mustered out with company Sept. 1, 1864.
Thomas, John G	do.	30	May 2, 1864	100 dys.	Mustered out with company Sept. 1, 1864.
Thompson, George W	do.	18	May 2, 1864	100 dys.	Mustered out with company Sept. 1, 1864.
Whitaker, Edward	do.	18	May 2, 1864	100 dys.	Mustered out with company Sept. 1, 1864.
Whitridge, William F	do.	28	May 2, 1864	100 dys.	Mustered out with company Sept. 1, 1864.
Woodering, Peter	do.	18	May 2, 1864	100 dys.	Mustered out with company Sept. 1, 1864.
Young, Cyrus	do.	28	May 2, 1864	100 dys.	Mustered out with company Sept. 1, 1864.

Names.	Rank.	Age.	Date of Entering the Service.		Period of Service.	
Walters, Adam	Private	23	May	2, 1864	100 dys.	Mustered
Watt, William H	....do....	21	May	2, 1864	100 dys.	Mustered
Watson, George W	....do....	18	May	2, 1864	100 dys.	Mustered
Wheeler, M. B	....do....	23	May	2, 1864	100 dys.	Mustered
Williams, Oscar B	....do....	19	May	2, 1864	100 dys.	Mustered
Young, James P	....do....	24	May	2, 1864	100 dys.	Mustered
Young, Job	....do....	20	May	2, 1864	100 dys.	Mustered
Young, William	....do....	29	May	2, 1864	100 dys.	Mustered
Zerkel, Jacob	....do....	20	May	2, 1864	100 dys.	Mustered
Zerkel, William	....do....	18	May	2, 1864	100 dys.	Mustered

COMPANY H.

Mustered in May 15, 1864, at Camp Dennison, O., by G. E. Johnston, Major a
1, 1864, at Camp Dennison, O., by William Stanley, 2d
10th Infantry, U. S. A.

Names.	Rank.	Age.	Date of Entering the Service.		Period of Service.	
Isaac R. McDivitt	Captain.	20	May	2, 1864	100 dys.	Mustered out
James Skinner	1st Lieut.	40	May	2, 1864	100 dys.	Mustered out
Philip Dils	2d Lieut.	26	May	2, 1864	100 dys.	Mustered
John G. Larah	1st Sergt.	30	May	2, 1864	100 dys.	Mustered
David D. Murray	Sergeant.	27	May	2, 1864	100 dys.	Mustered
Charles H. McManus	....do....	26	May	2, 1864	100 dys.	Mustered
Barnett W. Huffman	....do....	22	May	2, 1864	100 dys.	Mustered
William H. Marshall	....do....	27	May	2, 1864	100 dys.	Mustered
Clark Gray	Corporal.	29	May	2, 1864	100 dys.	Mustered
John G. Oxier	....do....	25	May	2, 1864	100 dys.	Mustered
Cornelius McDivitt	....do....	26	May	2, 1864	100 dys.	Mustered
William A. Davenport	....do....	31	May	2, 1864	100 dys.	Mustered
Levi P. Harris	....do....	32	May	2, 1864	100 dys.	Mustered
John R. Burson	....do....	25	May	2, 1864	100 dys.	Mustered
Jesse Runyan	....do....	20	May	2, 1864	100 dys.	Mustered out
John W. Lincoln	....do....	20	May	2, 1864	100 dys.	Mustered out
Aker, Empress B	Private.	18	May	2, 1864	100 dys.	Mustered out
Ammerman, David	....do....	44	May	2, 1864	100 dys.	Mustered out
Ammerman, William	....do....	18	May	2, 1864	100 dys.	Mustered
Bailor, William A	....do....	32	May	2, 1864	100 dys.	Mustered
Bougher, John	....do....	42	May	2, 1864	100 dys.	Mustered
Brower, John	....do....	21	May	2, 1864	100 dys.	Mustered
Brown, Wesley	....do....	17	May	2, 1864	100 dys.	Mustered
Cline, Philip	....do....	19	May	2, 1864	100 dys.	Mustered
Daily, J. K	....do....	22	May	2, 1864	100 dys.	Mustered
Daily, J. K	....do....	16	May	2, 1864	100 dys.	Mustered
Daily, Joseph W	....do....	25	May	2, 1864	100 dys.	Mustered
Elliott, J. H	....do....	27	May	2, 1864	100 dys.	Mustered
Friend, Theodore	....do....	20	May	2, 1864	100 dys.	Mustered out
Gaus, Philip T	....do....	48	May	2, 1864	100 dys.	Mustered out
Gooding, Jacob F	....do....	19	May	2, 1864	100 dys.	Mustered out
Greenfield, William	....do....	31	May	2, 1864	100 dys.	Mustered out
Gregg, Israel	....do....	19	May	2, 1864	100 dys.	Mustered out
Hambidge, William	....do....	17	May	2, 1864	100 dys.	Mustered out
Harris, David W	....do....	24	May	2, 1864	100 dys.	Mustered out
Hilderbolt, Andrew	....do....	38	May	2, 1864	100 dys.	Mustered out
Hornady, Nelson	....do....	37	May	2, 1864	100 dys.	Mustered out
Huffman, Harvey	....do....	23	May	2, 1864	100 dys.	Mustered out
Huffman, Joseph G	....do....	21	May	2, 1864	100 dys.	Mustered out
Jellison, William	....do....	18	May	2, 1864	100 dys.	Mustered out
Kelley, Joseph	....do....	24	May	2, 1864	100 dys.	Mustered out
Larah, John K	....do....	44	May	2, 1864	100 dys.	Mustered out
Larah, Louis A	....do....	32	May	2, 1864	100 dys.	Mustered out
Larah, Newton S	....do....	29	May	2, 1864	100 dys.	Mustered out
Lewellyn, Isaac	....do....	32	May	2, 1864	100 dys.	Mustered out
McClellan, Newton	....do....	31	May	2, 1864	100 dys.	Mustered out
McComas, Joseph M	....do....	21	May	2, 1864	100 dys.	Mustered out
McWhinney, Benjamin T	....do....	21	May	2, 1864	100 dys.	Died Aug. 19,
McWhinney, John	....do....	19	May	2, 1864	100 dys.	Mustered out
Miles, Henry	....do....	19	May	2, 1864	100 dys.	Mustered out
Miles, John S	....do....	25	May	2, 1864	100 dys.	Mustered out
Morris, Samuel	....do....	23	May	2, 1864	100 dys.	Mustered out
Morrow, John	....do....	40	May	2, 1864	100 dys.	Mustered out
Murray, Henry C	....do....	18	May	2, 1864	100 dys.	Mustered out
Newton, Thomas	....do....	18	May	2, 1864	100 dys.	Mustered out
Norris, Francis M	....do....	18	May	2, 1864	100 dys.	Mustered out
Parker, John B	....do....	18	May	2, 1864	100 dys.	Mustered out
Patterson, John C	....do....	43	May	2, 1864	100 dys.	Died Aug. 10,
Penny, Isaac	....do....	37	May	2, 1864	100 dys.	Mustered out
Pottenger, Henry	....do....	23	May	2, 1864	100 dys.	Mustered out
Rhea, John C	....do....	27	May	2, 1864	100 dys.	Mustered out
Runyan, George W	....do....	30	May	2, 1864	100 dys.	Mustered out
Shaw, John S	....do....	35	May	2, 1864	100 dys.	Mustered out

Names.	Rank.	Age.	Date of Entering the Service.	Period of Service.	Remarks.
, Elias	Private.	28	May 2, 1864	100 dys.	Mustered out with company Sept. 1, 1864.
, William	....do....	30	May 2, 1864	100 dys.	Died Aug. 10, 1864, at Cumberland, Md.
, Jesse	....do....	41	May 2, 1864	100 dys.	Mustered out with company Sept. 1, 1864.
, John	....do....	41	May 2, 1864	100 dys.	Mustered out with company Sept. 1, 1864.
l, Lester	....do....	18	May 2, 1864	100 dys.	Mustered out with company Sept. 1, 1864.
James C	....do....	36	May 2, 1864	100 dys.	Mustered out with company Sept. 1, 1864.
Justus B	....do....	39	May 2, 1864	100 dys.	Mustered out with company Sept. 1, 1864.
ngs, Samuel	....do....	27	May 2, 1864	100 dys.	Mustered out with company Sept. 1, 1864.
, William L	....do....	33	May 2, 1864	100 dys.	Mustered out with company Sept. 1, 1864.
, George W	....do....	21	May 2, 1864	100 dys.	Mustered out with company Sept. 1, 1864.
, William	....do....	23	May 2, 1864	100 dys.	Mustered out with company Sept. 1, 1864.
Andrew J	....do....	34	May 2, 1864	100 dys.	Mustered out with company Sept. 1, 1864.
, John M	....do....	26	May 2, 1864	100 dys.	Mustered out with company Sept. 1, 1864.
an, Andrew J	....do....	..	May 2, 1864	100 dys.	Mustered out with company Sept. 1, 1864.
r, Erastus D	....do....	40	May 2, 1864	100 dys.	Mustered out with company Sept. 1, 1864.
r, Jacob D	....do....	18	May 2, 1864	100 dys.	Mustered out with company Sept. 1, 1864.
, Daniel	....do....	25	May 2, 1864	100 dys.	Mustered out with company Sept. 1, 1864.
William H	....do....	24	May 2, 1864	100 dys.	Mustered out with company Sept. 1, 1864.
, William	....do....	38	May 2, 1864	100 dys.	Mustered out with company Sept. 1, 1864.
Jacob	....do....	18	May 2, 1864	100 dys.	Mustered out with company Sept. 1, 1864.
, Jonas	....do....	44	May 2, 1864	100 dys.	Mustered out with company Sept. 1, 1864.
Curtis	....do....	39	May 2, 1864	100 dys.	Mustered out with company Sept. 1, 1864.
ns, Timothy J. R.	....do....	20	May 2, 1864	100 dys.	Mustered out with company Sept. 1, 1864.
r, Benjamin	....do....	40	May 2, 1864	100 dys.	Mustered out with company Sept. 1, 1864.
ens, Jacob C	....do....	19	May 2, 1864	100 dys.	Mustered out with company Sept. 1, 1864.
, John E	....do....	30	May 2, 1864	100 dys.	Mustered out with company Sept. 1, 1864.
id, Peregrine D	....do....	20	May 2, 1864	100 dys.	Mustered out with company Sept. 1, 1864.
an, John	....do....	32	May 2, 1864	100 dys.	Mustered out with company Sept. 1, 1864.
an, John B	....do....	31	May 2, 1864	100 dys.	Mustered out with company Sept. 1, 1864.
Joel I	....do....	25	May 2, 1864	100 dys.	Mustered out with company Sept. 1, 1864.
h, William	....do....	19	May 2, 1864	100 dys.	Mustered out with company Sept. 1, 1864.
ley, Albert W	....do....	27	May 2, 1864	100 dys.	Mustered out with company Sept. 1, 1864.
mitt, John T	....do....	23	May 2, 1864	100 dys.	Mustered out with company Sept. 1, 1864.
g, Jay F	....do....	21	May 2, 1864	100 dys.	Mustered out with company Sept. 1, 1864.
ng, Jesse	....do....	22	May 2, 1864	100 dys.	Mustered out with company Sept. 1, 1864.
ng, William R	....do....	29	May 2, 1864	100 dys.	Mustered out to date Sept. 1, 1864.
, Joseph	....do....	21	May 2, 1864	100 dys.	Mustered out with company Sept. 1, 1864.
, Daniel A	....do....	34	May 2, 1864	100 dys.	Mustered out with company Sept. 1, 1864.
, John H	....do....	35	May 2, 1864	100 dys.	Mustered out with company Sept. 1, 1864.
r, Joseph	....do....	45	May 2, 1864	100 dys.	Mustered out with company Sept. 1, 1864.
, George G	....do....	35	May 2, 1864	100 dys.	Mustered out with company Sept. 1, 1864.
, Jacob H	....do....	23	May 2, 1864	100 dys.	Mustered out with company Sept. 1, 1864.
, Jasper	....do....	21	May 2, 1864	100 dys.	Mustered out with company Sept. 1, 1864.
, Charles M	....do....	30	May 2, 1864	100 dys.	Mustered out with company Sept. 1, 1864.
, John W	....do....	30	May 2, 1864	100 dys.	Mustered out with company Sept. 1, 1864.
s, Miner B	....do....	30	May 2, 1864	100 dys.	Mustered out with company Sept. 1, 1864.
ts, George	....do....	29	May 2, 1864	100 dys.	Mustered out with company Sept. 1, 1864.
augh, Benjamin F.	....do....	38	May 2, 1864	100 dys.	Died Aug. 7, 1864, in hospital at Cincinnati, O.
lin, James M	....do....	18	May 2, 1864	100 dys.	Mustered out with company Sept. 1, 1864.
, John	....do....	35	May 2, 1864	100 dys.	Mustered out with company Sept. 1, 1864.
John	....do....	27	May 2, 1864	100 dys.	Mustered out with company Sept. 1, 1864.
nson, Benjamin F.	....do....	32	May 2, 1864	100 dys.	Mustered out with company Sept. 1, 1864.
nson, Peter A	....do....	27	May 2, 1864	100 dys.	Mustered out with company Sept. 1, 1864.
end, Smith	....do....	39	May 2, 1864	100 dys.	Mustered out with company Sept. 1, 1864.
Vesley A	....do....	34	May 2, 1864	100 dys.	Mustered out with company Sept. 1, 1864.
Elihu C	....do....	24	May 2, 1864	100 dys.	Mustered out with company Sept. 1, 1864.
an, James V	....do....	22	May 2, 1864	100 dys.	Mustered out with company Sept. 1, 1864.
t, Edward	....do....	38	May 2, 1864	100 dys.	Mustered out with company Sept. 1, 1864.
, Calvin	....do....	39	May 2, 1864	100 dys.	Mustered out with company Sept. 1, 1864.
t, Isaac	....do....	18	May 2, 1864	100 dys.	Mustered out with company Sept. 1, 1864.

157th Regiment Ohio Volunteer Infantry.

ONE HUNDRED DAYS' SERVICE.

This Regiment was organized at Camp Chase, O., May 15, 1864, to serve one hundred days. It was composed of the Thirty-ninth Battalion, Ohio National Guard, from Jefferson County, and the Eighty-eighth Battalion, Ohio National Guard, from Carroll County. On the 17th of May the Regiment was ordered to report to General Wallace, at Baltimore. It was assigned to General Tyler's command, and, after remaining in camp a few weeks, was ordered by the War Department to Fort Delaware. During the remainder of its term of service the Regiment performed guard duty over from twelve to fourteen thousand prisoners. At the expiration of its term of enlistment the Regiment reported at Camp Chase, and was mustered out September 2, 1864, on expiration of term of service, except Company C, which was on detached duty, and mustered out September 10.

Names.	Rank.	Age.	Date of Entering the Service.	Period of Service.	Remarks.
Crawford, Edward	Private	27	May 2, 1864	100 dys.	Mustered out with company Sept. 2, 1864.
Curtman, John	do	28	May 2, 1864	100 dys.	Mustered out with company Sept. 2, 1864.
Davidson, James	do	38	May 2, 1864	100 dys.	Mustered out with company Sept. 2, 1864.
Donnelly, Arthur	do	33	May 2, 1864	100 dys.	Mustered out with company Sept. 2, 1864.
Dunn, Edward	do	31	May 2, 1864	100 dys.	Mustered out with company Sept. 2, 1864.
Duvall, Jackson	do	25	May 2, 1864	100 dys.	Mustered out with company Sept. 2, 1864.
Duvall, Thomas	do	23	May 2, 1864	100 dys.	Mustered out with company Sept. 2, 1864.
Duvall, William W	do	32	May 2, 1864	100 dys.	Mustered out with company Sept. 2, 1864.
Elliott, Alfred	do	31	May 2, 1864	100 dys.	Mustered out with company Sept. 2, 1864.
Elliott, Joseph B	do	27	May 2, 1864	100 dys.	Mustered out with company Sept. 2, 1864.
Ellison, Edward	do	31	May 2, 1864	100 dys.	Mustered out with company Sept. 2, 1864.
Ferguson, Cyrus	do	25	May 2, 1864	100 dys.	Mustered out with company Sept. 2, 1864.
Ferguson, George	do	26	May 2, 1864	100 dys.	Mustered out with company Sept. 2, 1864.
Fieldman, Richard	do	28	May 2, 1864	100 dys.	Mustered out with company Sept. 2, 1864.
Flanagan, John	do	19	May 2, 1864	100 dys.	Mustered out with company Sept. 2, 1864.
Flora, George	do	21	May 2, 1864	100 dys.	Mustered out with company Sept. 2, 1864.
Gamble, Andrew	do	29	May 2, 1864	100 dys.	Mustered out with company Sept. 2, 1864.
Greer, William	do	30	May 2, 1864	100 dys.	Mustered out with company Sept. 2, 1864.
Hamilton, John	do	28	May 2, 1864	100 dys.	Mustered out with company Sept. 2, 1864.
Hicks, David B	do	25	May 2, 1864	100 dys.	Mustered out with company Sept. 2, 1864.
Hinds, Elisha	do	20	May 2, 1864	100 dys.	Mustered out with company Sept. 2, 1864.
Horner, John	do	25	May 2, 1864	100 dys.	Mustered out with company Sept. 2, 1864.
Ingler, George M	do	33	May 2, 1864	100 dys.	Mustered out with company Sept. 2, 1864.
Jones, William	do	29	May 2, 1864	100 dys.	Mustered out with company Sept. 2, 1864.
Kerr, John	do	27	May 2, 1864	100 dys.	Mustered out with company Sept. 2, 1864.
Lee, John	do	26	May 2, 1864	100 dys.	Mustered out with company Sept. 2, 1864.
Lee, Richard	do	21	May 2, 1864	100 dys.	Mustered out with company Sept. 2, 1864.
Lenhart, Edward	do	18	May 2, 1864	100 dys.	Mustered out with company Sept. 2, 1864.
Leonard, Lemuel	do	38	May 2, 1864	100 dys.	Mustered out with company Sept. 2, 1864.
McCoy, James	do	39	May 2, 1864	100 dys.	Mustered out with company Sept. 2, 1864.
McElhinny, Henry H	do	31	May 2, 1864	100 dys.	Mustered out with company Sept. 2, 1864.
Moncreith, Alexander	do	35	May 2, 1864	100 dys.	Mustered out with company Sept. 2, 1864.
Nelson, James	do	39	May 2, 1864	100 dys.	Mustered out with company Sept. 2, 1864.
North, William	do	31	May 2, 1864	100 dys.	Mustered out with company Sept. 2, 1864.
Odbert, David	do	36	May 2, 1864	100 dys.	Mustered out with company Sept. 2, 1864.
Owens, David	do	35	May 2, 1864	100 dys.	Mustered out with company Sept. 2, 1864.
Owesney, Frank	do	33	May 2, 1864	100 dys.	Mustered out with company Sept. 2, 1864.
Patterson, James	do	29	May 2, 1864	100 dys.	Mustered out with company Sept. 2, 1864.
Pearce, Edward	do	30	May 2, 1864	100 dys.	Mustered out with company Sept. 2, 1864.
Permar, Henry	do	28	May 2, 1864	100 dys.	Promoted to Sergt. Major May 17, 1864.
Robertshaw, Edward	do	24	May 2, 1864	100 dys.	Mustered out with company Sept. 2, 1864.
Shaup, William	do	19	May 2, 1864	100 dys.	Mustered out with company Sept. 2, 1864.
Van Ostrand, William	do	29	May 2, 1864	100 dys.	Mustered out with company Sept. 2, 1864.
Walters, William	do	32	May 2, 1864	100 dys.	Mustered out with company Sept. 2, 1864.
Wilcoxon, John	do	32	May 2, 1864	100 dys.	Mustered out with company Sept. 2, 1864.
Wilcoxon, Stephen	do	34	May 2, 1864	100 dys.	Mustered out with company Sept. 2, 1864.
Wilson, John	do	22	May 2, 1864	100 dys.	Mustered out with company Sept. 2, 1864.
Workman, Gordon	do	23	May 2, 1864	100 dys.	Mustered out with company Sept. 2, 1864.

COMPANY B.

Mustered in May 15, 1864, at Camp Chase, O., by H. Douglas, Captain 18th Infantry, U. S. A. Mustered out Sept. 2, 1864, at Camp Chase, O., by G. E. Johnson, Major and A. D. C.

Names.	Rank.	Age.	Date of Entering the Service.	Period of Service.	Remarks.
William A. Walden	Captain.	30	May 2, 1864	100 dys.	Mustered out with company Sept. 2, 1864.
John McLeish	1st Lieut.	30	May 2, 1864	100 dys.	Mustered out with company Sept. 2, 1864.
James A. Cloman	2d Lieut.	42	May 2, 1864	100 dys.	Mustered out with company Sept. 2, 1864.
Nathaniel A. Jepson	1st Sergt.	29	May 2, 1864	100 dys.	Mustered out with company Sept. 2, 1864.
Abram M. Blackburn	Sergeant.	22	May 2, 1864	100 dys.	Mustered out with company Sept. 2, 1864.
John H. Lindsay	do	37	May 2, 1864	100 dys.	Mustered out with company Sept. 2, 1864.
George M. Gault	do	38	May 2, 1864	100 dys.	Mustered out with company Sept. 2, 1864.
John W. Evans	do	24	May 2, 1864	100 dys.	Mustered out with company Sept. 2, 1864.
Samuel R. Zinn	Corporal.	33	May 2, 1864	100 dys.	Mustered out with company Sept. 2, 1864.
George W. Weaver	do	35	May 2, 1864	100 dys.	Mustered out with company Sept. 2, 1864.
James A. McCurdy	do	25	May 2, 1864	100 dys.	Mustered out with company Sept. 2, 1864.
James D. Maxwell	do	32	May 2, 1864	100 dys.	Mustered out with company Sept. 2, 1864.
Joseph Mellor	do	25	May 2, 1864	100 dys.	Mustered out with company Sept. 2, 1864.
John J. Riley	do	41	May 2, 1864	100 dys.	Mustered out with company Sept. 2, 1864.
Ross Kells	do	24	May 2, 1864	100 dys.	Mustered out with company Sept. 2, 1864.
Daniel P. Copeland	do	20	May 2, 1864	100 dys.	Mustered out with company Sept. 2, 1864.
Erskine M. Hamilton	Musician	25	May 2, 1864	100 dys.	Mustered out with company Sept. 2, 1864.
Richard Huff	do	18	May 2, 1864	100 dys.	Mustered out with company Sept. 2, 1864.
Busey Cahill	Wagoner	34	May 2, 1864	100 dys.	Mustered out with company Sept. 2, 1864.
Barr, Edward	Private	22	May 2, 1864	100 dys.	Mustered out with company Sept. 2, 1864.
Beck, William	do	27	May 2, 1864	100 dys.	Mustered out with company Sept. 2, 1864.
Betz, McCourtney	do	38	May 2, 1864	100 dys.	Mustered out with company Sept. 2, 1864.
Blinn, James B	do	27	May 2, 1864	100 dys.	Mustered out with company Sept. 2, 1864.
Brandenburgh, Lemuel	do	27	May 2, 1864	100 dys.	Mustered out with company Sept. 2, 1864.
Cahill, Frank	do	23	May 2, 1864	100 dys.	Mustered out with company Sept. 2, 1864.
Caldwell, William H	do	21	May 2, 1864	100 dys.	Mustered out with company Sept. 2, 1864.

Names.	Rank.	Age.	Date of Entering the Service.	Period of Service.	
Charles Quimby	Musician	18	May 2, 1864	100 dys.	Mustered out with
Joseph Zahn	...do...	25	May 2, 1864	100 dys.	Mustered out with
Samuel McMillien	Wagoner.	35	May 2, 1864	100 dys.	Mustered out with
Alban, George	Private..	21	May 2, 1864	100 dys.	Mustered out with
Anderson, Henry	...do...	18	May 2, 1864	100 dys.	Mustered out with
Barthold, George	...do...	20	May 2, 1864	100 dys.	Mustered out with
Basler, Joseph	...do...	18	May 2, 1864	100 dys.	Mustered out with
Beans, James	...do...	18	May 2, 1864	100 dys.	Mustered out with
Berry, George L	...do...	18	May 2, 1864	100 dys.	Mustered out with
Blackburn, David E	...do...	19	May 2, 1864	100 dys.	Mustered out with
Blackburn, Henry	...do...	21	May 2, 1864	100 dys.	Mustered out with
Bond, Leonidas	...do...	18	May 2, 1864	100 dys.	Mustered out with
Boyd, Thomas	...do...	18	May 2, 1864	100 dys.	Mustered out with
Bruney, Mitchell	...do...	21	May 2, 1864	100 dys.	Mustered out with
Buchanan, William	...do...	18	May 2, 1864	100 dys.	Mustered out with
Burchard, William	...do...	22	May 2, 1864	100 dys.	Mustered out with
Burns, Andrew R	...do...	18	May 2, 1864	100 dys.	Mustered out with
Bynon, Edmund	...do...	19	May 2, 1864	100 dys.	Mustered out with
Cahill, Almanus	...do...	19	May 17, 1864	100 dys.	Mustered out with
Caldwell, John C	...do...	18	May 2, 1864	100 dys.	Mustered out with
Campbell, John B	...do...	19	May 14, 1864	100 dys.	Mustered out with
Campbell, Samuel H	...do...	18	May 2, 1864	100 dys.	Mustered out with
Coleman, Thomas	...do...	18	May 2, 1864	100 dys.	Mustered out with
Coleman, William	...do...	18	May 2, 1864	100 dys.	Mustered out with
Curry, James	...do...	19	May 2, 1864	100 dys.	Mustered out with
Davidson, Norton	...do...	22	May 11, 1864	100 dys.	Mustered out with
Devinny, Edward	...do...	19	May 10, 1864	100 dys.	Mustered out with
Dillon, George H	...do...	21	May 2, 1864	100 dys.	Mustered out with
Downs, John M	...do...	18	May 2, 1864	100 dys.	Mustered out with
Douglass, William G	...do...	18	May 18, 1864	100 dys.	Mustered out with
Dunbar, Oliver P	...do...	19	May 2, 1864	100 dys.	Mustered out with
Dunn, Thomas	...do...	22	May 11, 1864	100 dys.	Mustered out with
Edgar, John	...do...	18	May 2, 1864	100 dys.	Mustered out with
Eping, Frederick	...do...	21	May 10, 1864	100 dys.	Mustered out with
Frazier, James	...do...	18	May 2, 1864	100 dys.	Mustered out with
Frye, James	...do...	18	May 2, 1864	100 dys.	Mustered out with
Fulton, Thomas J	...do...	30	May 2, 1864	100 dys.	Mustered out with
Hamilton, Samuel	...do...	20	May 14, 1864	100 dys.	Mustered out with
Hanna, Rush	...do...	18	May 17, 1864	100 dys.	Mustered out with
Hinds, James H	...do...	20	May 2, 1864	100 dys.	Mustered out with
Hunter, William B	...do...	19	May 14, 1864	100 dys.	Mustered out with
Huntsman, Edmund	...do...	18	May 2, 1864	100 dys.	Mustered out with
Huscroft, William	...do...	18	May 2, 1864	100 dys.	Mustered out with
Jackman, Winfield	...do...	18	May 14, 1864	100 dys.	Mustered out with
Johnson, Guy	...do...	20	May 2, 1864	100 dys.	Mustered out with
Johnson, William	...do...	39	May 2, 1864	100 dys.	Mustered out with
Klages, Augustus	...do...	18	May 2, 1864	100 dys.	Mustered out with
Lavery, Washington	...do...	19	May 2, 1864	100 dys.	Mustered out with
Lee, George	...do...	22	May 2, 1864	100 dys.	Mustered out with
Leetch, William	...do...	18	May 14, 1864	100 dys.	Mustered out with
McCarty, Richard	...do...	20	May 2, 1864	100 dys.	Mustered out with
McCay, Frank	...do...	26	May 2, 1864	100 dys.	Mustered out with
McCord, Robert	...do...	18	May 2, 1864	100 dys.	Mustered out with
McCoy, Edwin	...do...	19	May 2, 1864	100 dys.	Mustered out with
McKinney, Frank	...do...	18	May 2, 1864	100 dys.	Mustered out with
McMullen, Matthew	...do...	18	May 17, 1864	100 dys.	Mustered out with
Manley, James S	...do...	18	May 2, 1864	100 dys.	Mustered out with
Mellor, James I	...do...	30	May 2, 1864	100 dys.	Mustered out with
Miller, George E	...do...	19	May 2, 1864	100 dys.	Mustered out with
Norton, Alexander	...do...	18	May 16, 1864	100 dys.	Mustered out with
Odbert, Archibald	...do...	30	May 2, 1864	100 dys.	Mustered out with
O'Hara, Bernard	...do...	18	May 17, 1864	100 dys.	Mustered out with
Ridgley, Joseph G	...do...	21	May 2, 1864	100 dys.	Mustered out with
Robinson, William	...do...	18	May 2, 1864	100 dys.	Mustered out with
Rogers, John	...do...	18	May 15, 1864	100 dys.	Mustered out with
Sharp, Henry	...do...	23	May 2, 1864	100 dys.	Mustered out with
Solomon, Cornelius R	...do...	18	May 2, 1864	100 dys.	Mustered out with
Stafford, Thomas	...do...	20	May 12, 1864	100 dys.	Mustered out with
Stark, James	...do...	18	May 2, 1864	100 dys.	Mustered out with
Stephens, Frank	...do...	18	May 17, 1864	100 dys.	Mustered out with
Stewart, Henry B	...do...	23	May 2, 1864	100 dys.	Mustered out with
Stewart, John	...do...	18	May 17, 1864	100 dys.	Mustered out with
Sutcliff, Richard	...do...	18	May 17, 1864	100 dys.	Mustered out with
Sweeney, Edward	...do...	18	May 2, 1864	100 dys.	Mustered out with
Viers, Brice	...do...	18	May 2, 1864	100 dys.	Mustered out with
Warren, Robert A	...do...	21	May 14, 1864	100 dys.	Mustered out with
Wigginton, George	...do...	18	May 2, 1864	100 dys.	Mustered out with
Winters, George H	...do...	27	May 2, 1864	100 dys.	Mustered out with

Names.	Rank.	Age.	Date of Entering the Service.		Period of Service.	Remarks.
Walters, James	Private..	25	May	2, 1864	100 dys.	Died July 21, 1864, at Fort Delaware, Del.
Watt, John W	....do....	18	May	2, 1864	100 dys.	Mustered out with company Sept. 2, 1864.
Welch, Nathaniel C	....do....	18	May	2, 1864	100 dys.	Mustered out with company Sept. 2, 1864.
White, Addison J	....do....	22	May	2, 1864	100 dys.	Mustered out with company Sept. 2, 1864.
White, Almon G	....do....	25	May	2, 1864	100 dys.	Mustered out with company Sept. 2, 1864.
Wilson, John	....do....	19	May	2, 1864	100 dys.	Mustered out with company Sept. 2, 1864.
Zink, George L	....do....	25	May	2, 1864	100 dys.	Mustered out with company Sept. 2, 1864.

COMPANY E.

Mustered in May 15, 1864, at Camp Chase, O., by H. Douglas, Captain 18th Infantry, U. S. A. Mustered out Sept. 2, 1864, at Camp Chase, O., by G. E. Johnson, Major and A. D. C.

Names.	Rank.	Age.	Date of Entering the Service.		Period of Service.	Remarks.
Thomas A. Gamble	Captain.	32	May	2, 1864	100 dys.	Mustered out with company Sept. 2, 1864.
Charles M. Jones	1st Lieut.	30	May	2, 1864	100 dys.	Mustered out with company Sept. 2, 1864.
Nicholas Winters	2d Lieut.	30	May	2, 1864	100 dys.	Mustered out with company Sept. 2, 1864.
Thomas S. Markle	1st Sergt.	32	May	2, 1864	100 dys.	Mustered out with company Sept. 2, 1864.
Thomas C. Davis	Sergeant.	22	May	2, 1864	100 dys.	Mustered out with company Sept. 2, 1864.
Alexander O. Scott	....do....	33	May	2, 1864	100 dys.	Mustered out with company Sept. 2, 1864.
William Stone	....do....	31	May	2, 1864	100 dys.	Mustered out with company Sept. 2, 1864.
William T. Leech	....do....	21	May	2, 1864	100 dys.	Mustered out with company Sept. 2, 1864.
William Stark	Corporal.	44	May	2, 1864	100 dys.	Mustered out with company Sept. 2, 1864.
Solomon Hipsley	....do....	39	May	2, 1864	100 dys.	Mustered out with company Sept. 2, 1864.
George Plummer	....do....	36	May	2, 1864	100 dys.	Mustered out with company Sept. 2, 1864.
Eli Kir	....do....	28	May	2, 1864	100 dys.	Mustered out with company Sept. 2, 1864.
Jacob Bickerstaff	....do....	36	May	2, 1864	100 dys.	Mustered out with company Sept. 2, 1864.
David Hall	....do....	36	May	2, 1864	100 dys.	Mustered out with company Sept. 2, 1864.
James Lindsey	....do....	33	May	2, 1864	100 dys.	Mustered out with company Sept. 2, 1864.
James R. Cunningham	....do....	28	May	2, 1864	100 dys.	Mustered out with company Sept. 2, 1864.
Aloysius Feist	Musician	34	May	2, 1864	100 dys.	Mustered out with company Sept. 2, 1864.
Marshall R. Hobbs	....do....	32	May	2, 1864	100 dys.	Mustered out with company Sept. 2, 1864.
Alexander, James	Private..	21	May	2, 1864	100 dys.	Mustered out with company Sept. 2, 1864.
Allensworth, Samuel	....do..	26	May	2, 1864	100 dys.	Mustered out with company Sept. 2, 1864.
Armstrong, Lewis	....do....	28	May	2, 1864	100 dys.	Mustered out with company Sept. 2, 1864.
Barrett, Charles	....do....	36	May	2, 1864	100 dys.	Mustered out with company Sept. 2, 1864.
Bowers, Joseph C	....do....	19	May	2, 1864	100 dys.	Mustered out with company Sept. 2, 1864.
Butcher, Isaac	....do....	43	May	2, 1864	100 dys.	Mustered out with company Sept. 2, 1864.
Call, David	....do....	37	May	2, 1864	100 dys.	Mustered out with company Sept. 2, 1864.
Castner Michael C	....do....	28	May	2, 1864	100 dys.	Mustered out with company Sept. 2, 1864.
Coe, Andrew H	....do....	26	May	2, 1864	100 dys.	Mustered out with company Sept. 2, 1864.
Cunningham, Alex. H	....do....	38	May	2, 1864	100 dys.	Mustered out with company Sept. 2, 1864.
Cunningham, Baxter	....do....	22	May	2, 1864	100 dys.	Mustered out with company Sept. 2, 1864.
Dance, Benjam n R	....do....	21	May	2, 1864	100 dys.	Mustered out with company Sept. 2, 1864.
Dobbins, Henry	....do....	22	May	2, 1864	100 dys.	Mustered out with company Sept. 2, 1864.
Doughert ohn	....do....	44	May	2, 1864	100 dys.	Mustered out with company Sept. 2, 1864.
Ekey Rez n B	....do....	19	May	2, 1864	100 dys.	Mustered out with company Sept. 2, 1864.
Elliott, Andrew	....do....	19	May	2, 1864	100 dys.	Mustered out with company Sept. 2, 1864.
Fisher, Samuel D	....do....	37	May	2, 1864	100 dys.	Mustered out with company Sept. 2, 1864.
Grafton, George W	....do....	32	May	2, 1864	100 dys.	Mustered out with company Sept. 2, 1864.
Grieves, Frederick	....do....	25	May	2, 1864	100 dys.	Mustered out with company Sept. 2, 1864.
Gunkle, Joseph	....do....	23	May	2, 1864	100 dys.	Mustered out with company Sept. 2, 1864.
Hale, Charles W	....do....	19	May	2, 1864	100 dys.	Mustered out with company Sept. 2, 1864.
Hanna, George P.	....do....	19	May	2, 1864	100 dys.	Mustered out with company Sept. 2, 1864.
Hart, Philip	....do....	19	May	2, 1864	100 dys.	Mustered out with company Sept. 2, 1864.
Hipsley, William	....do....	18	May	2, 1864	100 dys.	Mustered out with company Sept. 2, 1864.
Holmes, Allen	....do....	22	May	2, 1864	100 dys.	Mustered out with company Sept. 2, 1864.
Irons Samuel W	....do....	21	May	2, 1864	100 dys.	Mustered out with company Sept. 2, 1864.
Jones, Thomas	....do....	21	May	2, 1864	100 dys.	Mustered out with company Sept. 2, 1864.
Kirk, Benjamin F	....do....	22	May	2, 1864	100 dys.	Mustered out with company Sept. 2, 1864.
Kirk, William H	....do....	36	May	2, 1864	100 dys.	Mustered out with company Sept. 2, 1864.
Kirkpatrick, James	....do....	26	May	2, 1864	100 dys.	Mustered out with company Sept. 2, 1864.
Kirkpatrick, Robinson D	....do....	30	May	2, 1864	100 dys.	Mustered out with company Sept. 2, 1864.
Lenhart Thomas	....do....	18	May	2, 1864	100 dys.	Mustered out with company Sept. 2, 1864.
Lindaff, Benjamin N	....do....	20	May	2, 1864	100 dys.	Mustered out with company Sept. 2, 1864.
Liston, Albert	....do....	20	May	2, 1864	100 dys.	Mustered out with company Sept. 2, 1864.
Long, John	....do....	36	May	2, 1864	100 dys.	Mustered out with company Sept. 2, 1864.
Lowry, Elijah	....do....	37	May	2, 1864	100 dys.	Mustered out with company Sept. 2, 1864.
McCullough, John A	....do....	19	May	2, 1864	100 dys.	Died Aug. 28, 1864, at Steubenville, O.
McCullough, William H	....do....	25	May	2, 1864	100 dys.	Mustered out with company Sept. 2, 1864.
McKee, Grier	....do....	36	May	2, 1864	100 dys.	Mustered out with company Sept. 2, 1864.
McManus, ugh	....do....	18	May	2, 1864	100 dys.	Mustered out with company Sept. 2, 1864.
Mansfield, Thomas	....do....	22	May	2, 1864	100 dys.	Mustered out with company Sept. 2, 1864.
Maxwel Thomas	....do....	44	May	2, 1864	100 dys.	Mustered out with company Sept. 2, 1864.
Mille John H	....do....	33	May	2, 1864	100 dys.	Mustered out with company Sept. 2, 1864.
Myers Ebenezer	....do....	38	May	2, 1864	100 dys.	Mustered out with company Sept. 2, 1864.
Powel Thomas C	....do....	23	May	2, 1864	100 dys.	Mustered out with company Sept. 2, 1864.
Ramsay, William	....do....	32	May	2, 1864	100 dys.	Mustered out with company Sept. 2, 1864.
Robinson, Thomas	....do....	33	May	2, 1864	100 dys.	Mustered out with company Sept. 2, 1864.
Ross, David	....do....	25	May	2, 1864	100 dys.	Mustered out with company Sept. 2, 1864.
Rutledge, Thomas	....do....	37	May	2, 1864	100 dys.	Mustered out with company Sept. 2, 1864.

Names.	Rank.	Age.	Date of Entering the Service.	Period of Service.	Remarks.
Negus, William	Private	40	May 2, 1864	100 dys.	Died Aug. 1, 1864, at Fort Delaware, Del.
Newbern, John	do.	18	May 2, 1864	100 dys.	Mustered out with company Sept. 2, 1864.
Oliver, Henry	do.	37	May 2, 1864	100 dys.	Mustered out with company Sept. 2, 1864.
Purviance, George R.	do.	18	May 2, 1864	100 dys.	Mustered out with company Sept. 2, 1864.
Ralston, Ephraim	do.	19	May 2, 1864	100 dys.	Mustered out with company Sept. 2, 1864.
Rideour, David	do.	18	May 2, 1864	100 dys.	Mustered out with company Sept. 2, 1864.
Rine, Oliver H.	do.	26	May 2, 1864	100 dys.	Mustered out with company Sept. 2, 1864.
Rine, Rudolph	do.	18	May 2, 1864	100 dys.	Mustered out with company Sept. 2, 1864.
Rush, Amos	do.	38	May 2, 1864	100 dys.	Mustered out with company Sept. 2, 1864.
Rouse, Levi	do.	27	May 2, 1864	100 dys.	
Scott, James	do.	20	May 2, 1864	100 dys.	Mustered out with company Sept. 2, 1864.
Scott, Thomas H.	do.	41	May 2, 1864	100 dys.	Mustered out with company Sept. 2, 1864.
Taylor, Henry	do.	19	May 2, 1864	100 dys.	Mustered out with company Sept. 2, 1864.
Thomas, William	do.	18	May 2, 1864	100 dys.	Mustered out with company Sept. 2, 1864.
Thompson, John	do.	19	May 2, 1864	100 dys.	Mustered out with company Sept. 2, 1864.
Timmerman, James	do.	18	May 2, 1864	100 dys.	Mustered out with company Sept. 2, 1864.
Timmerman, William	do.	21	May 2, 1864	100 dys.	Mustered out with company Sept. 2, 1864.
Tonley, Martin	do.	28	May 2, 1864	100 dys.	Mustered out with company Sept. 2, 1864.
Tubble, Isaac	do.	18	May 2, 1864	100 dys.	Mustered out with company Sept. 2, 1864.
Underwood, James	do.	15	May 2, 1864	100 dys.	Mustered out with company Sept. 2, 1864.
We[illegible], Alexander	do.	28	May 2, 1864	100 dys.	Mustered out with company Sept. 2, 1864.
Welt, William	do.	18	May 2, 1864	100 dys.	Mustered out with company Sept. 2, 1864.
Wilburn, Thomas	do.	55	May 2, 1864	100 dys.	Mustered out with company Sept. 2, 1864.
Woos[illegible], An[illegible]	do.	36	May 2, 1864	100 dys.	Mustered out with company Sept. 2, 1864.
Wood, Thomas	do.	21	May 2, 1864	100 dys.	Mustered out with company Sept. 2, 1864.
Zink, John	do.	37	May 2, 1864	100 dys.	Mustered out with company Sept. 2, 1864.

COMPANY G.

Mustered in May 15, 1864, at Camp Chase, O., by H. Douglas, Captain 18th Infantry, U. S. A. Mustered out Sept. 2, 1864, at Camp Chase, O., by G. E. Johnson, Major and A. D. C.

Names.	Rank.	Age.	Date of Entering the Service.	Period of Service.	Remarks.
Hiram H. Cope	Captain.	26	May 2, 1864	100 dys.	Mustered out with company Sept. 2, 1864.
Thomas B. Coulter	1st Lieut.	20	May 2, 1864	100 dys.	Mustered out with company Sept. 2, 1864.
James M. Sineral	2d Lieut.	29	May 2, 1864	100 dys.	Mustered out with company Sept. 2, 1864.
George Potts	1st Sergt.	31	May 2, 1864	100 dys.	Mustered out with company Sept. 2, 1864.
George E. Megrail	Sergeant.	31	May 2, 1864	100 dys.	Mustered out with company Sept. 2, 1864.
Thomas M. Reed	do.	23	May 2, 1864	100 dys.	Mustered out with company Sept. 2, 1864.
James R. Ritterhouse	do.	23	May 2, 1864	100 dys.	Mustered out with company Sept. 2, 1864.
Joseph H. Hammond	do.	22	May 2, 1864	100 dys.	Mustered out with company Sept. 2, 1864.
Lindley H. Megrail	Corporal.	22	May 2, 1864	100 dys.	Mustered out with company Sept. 2, 1864.
John S. Parsons	do.	25	May 2, 1864	100 dys.	Mustered out with company Sept. 2, 1864.
Albert B. Paul	do.	30	May 2, 1864	100 dys.	Mustered out with company Sept. 2, 1864.
Joshua W. Cole	do.	2[illegible]	May 2, 1864	100 dys.	Mustered out with company Sept. 2, 1864.
Edwin M. Crawford	do.	29	May 2, 1864	100 dys.	Mustered out with company Sept. 2, 1864.
Jonas Anspoker	do.	41	May 2, 1864	100 dys.	Mustered out with company Sept. 2, 1864.
Elijah P. Mansfield	do.	36	May 2, 1864	100 dys.	Mustered out with company Sept. 2, 1864.
William E. Cookson	do.	25	May 2, 1864	100 dys.	Mustered out with company Sept. 2, 1864.
Almeran Matlack	Musician	16	May 2, 1864	100 dys.	Mustered out with company Sept. 2, 1864.
Robertson Day	Wagoner.	29	May 2, 1864	100 dys.	Mustered out with company Sept. 2, 1864.
Adrian, Robert C.	Private.	20	May 2, 1864	100 dys.	Mustered out with company Sept. 2, 1864.
Allen, Aaron C.	do.	[illegible]	May 2, 1864	100 dys.	Mustered out with company Sept. 2, 1864.
Black, Alexander	do.	35	May 2, 1864	100 dys.	Mustered out with company Sept. 2, 1864.
Blackburn, John W. L.	do.	19	May 2, 1864	100 dys.	Mustered out with company Sept. 2, 1864.
Carman, Samuel	do.	[illegible]	May 2, 1864	100 dys.	Mustered out with company Sept. 2, 1864.
Collin, Thomas	do.	18	May 2, 1864	100 dys.	Mustered out with company Sept. 2, 1864.
Cole, Fartin B.	do.	38	May 2, 1864	100 dys.	Mustered out with company Sept. 2, 1864.
Cole, Joshua W.	do.	22	May 2, 1864	100 dys.	Mustered out with company Sept. 2, 1864.
Cole, William B.	do.	20	May 2, 1864	100 dys.	Mustered out with company Sept. 2, 1864.
Crawford, John M.	do.	21	May 2, 1864	100 dys.	Died July 31, 1864, at Fort Delaware, Del.
Creal, Alexander	do.	30	May 2, 1864	100 dys.	Mustered out with company Sept. 2, 1864.
Davis, George W.	do.	18	May 2, 1864	100 dys.	Mustered out with company Sept. 2, 1864.
Day, John M.	do.	[illegible]	May 2, 1864	100 dys.	Mustered out with company Sept. 2, 1864.
Ewing, James	do.	24	May 2, 1864	100 dys.	Mustered out with company Sept. 2, 1864.
Ferguson, Robert	do.	19	May 2, 1864	100 dys.	Mustered out with company Sept. 2, 1864.
Ferguson, Robert J.	do.	18	May 2, 1864	100 dys.	Mustered out with company Sept. 2, 1864.
Ford, John	do.	21	May 2, 1864	100 dys.	Mustered out with company Sept. 2, 1864.
Forester, Edwin O.	do.	23	May 2, 1864	100 dys.	Mustered out with company Sept. 2, 1864.
Goodlin, John J. S.	do.	2[illegible]	May 2, 1864	100 dys.	Mustered out with company Sept. 2, 1864.
Hammond, Hugh	do.	26	May 2, 1864	100 dys.	Mustered out with company Sept. 2, 1864.
Hammond, John C.	do.	19	May 2, 1864	100 dys.	Mustered out with company Sept. 2, 1864.
Hammond, John G.	do.	19	May 2, 1864	100 dys.	Mustered out with company Sept. 2, 1864.
Hammond, Lewis	do.	18	May 2, 1864	100 dys.	Mustered out with company Sept. 2, 1864.
Hastings, James D.	do.	22	May 2, 1864	100 dys.	Mustered out with company Sept. 2, 1864.
Hastings, Stephen B.	do.	30	May 2, 1864	100 dys.	Died Aug. 23, 1864, at his home, Jefferson County, O.
Hench, Samuel B.	do.	23	May 2, 1864	100 dys.	Mustered out with company Sept. 2, 1864.
Hervey, James R.	do.	27	May 2, 1864	100 dys.	Mustered out with company Sept. 2, 1864.
Hicks, Isaac	do.	22	May 2, 1864	100 dys.	Mustered out with company Sept. 2, 1864.
Johnston, George	do.	43	May 2, 1864	100 dys.	Mustered out with company Sept. 2, 1864.

Names.	Rank.	Age.	Date of Entering the Service.	Period of Service.	Remarks.
Irwin W. Thompson	Corporal.	28	May 2, 1864	100 dys.	Mustered out with company Sept. 2, 1864.
William Porter	....do....	19	May 2, 1864	100 dys.	Mustered out with company Sept. 2, 1864.
Josiah Morehead	....do....	27	May 2, 1864	100 dys.	Mustered out with company Sept. 2, 1864.
Jacob M. Westfall	....do....	24	May 2, 1864	100 dys.	Mustered out with company Sept. 2, 1864.
Enoch C. Ross	Musician	18	May 2, 1864	100 dys.	Mustered out with company Sept. 2, 1864.
William A. Hardesty	....do....	16	May 2, 1864	100 dys.	Mustered out with company Sept. 2, 1864.
Valentine M. Thomas	Wagoner	40	May 2, 1864	100 dys.	Mustered out with company Sept. 2, 1864.
Ackey, Henry W	Private..	41	May 2, 1864	100 dys.	Mustered out with company Sept. 2, 1864.
Amos, William R	....do....	18	May 2, 1864	100 dys.	Mustered out with company Sept. 2, 1864.
Barton, Joseph	....do....	22	May 2, 1864	100 dys.	Mustered out with company Sept. 2, 1864.
Baughman, Obediah	....do....	30	May 2, 1864	100 dys.	Mustered out with company Sept. 2, 1864.
Bell, Joseph C	....do....	35	May 2, 1864	100 dys.	Mustered out with company Sept. 2, 1864.
Bliss, John	....do....	22	May 2, 1864	100 dys.	Mustered out with company Sept. 2, 1864.
Bower, Cletus	....do....	30	May 2, 1864	100 dys.	Mustered out with company Sept. 2, 1864.
Brady, John R	....do....	18	May 2, 1864	100 dys.	Mustered out with company Sept. 2, 1864.
Bushong, John	....do....	20	May 2, 1864	100 dys.	Died —, at his home, Carroll County, O.
Buss, Franklin A	....do....	18	May 2, 1864	100 dys.	Mustered out with company Sept. 2, 1864.
Byers, Jeremiah R	....do....	23	May 2, 1864	100 dys.	Mustered out with company Sept. 2, 1864.
Close, John A	....do....	35	May 2, 1864	100 dys.	Mustered out with company Sept. 2, 1864.
Cooper, William	....do....	35	May 2, 1864	100 dys.	Mustered out with company Sept. 2, 1864.
Crissinger, Simon P	....do....	18	May 2, 1864	100 dys.	Mustered out with company Sept. 2, 1864.
Crowl, Daniel	....do....	24	May 2, 1864	100 dys.	Mustered out with company Sept. 2, 1864; borne on muster out roll as David Crowel
Davis, James L	....do....	20	May 2, 1864	100 dys.	Mustered out with company Sept. 2, 1864.
Deckman, George	....do....	31	May 2, 1864	100 dys.	Mustered out with company Sept. 2, 1864.
Downes, Franklin	....do....	32	May 2, 1864	100 dys.	Mustered out with company Sept. 2, 1864.
Denny, James	....do....	18	May 2, 1864	100 dys.	Mustered out with company Sept. 2, 1864.
Eachy, James	....do....	30	May 2, 1864	100 dys.	Mustered out with company Sept. 2, 1864.
Eakin, James D	....do....	30	May 2, 1864	100 dys.	Mustered out with company Sept. 2, 1864.
Goodlin, Joshua	....do....	37	May 2, 1864	100 dys.	Mustered out with company Sept. 2, 1864.
Gregory, Thomas J	....do....	18	May 2, 1864	100 dys.	Mustered out with company Sept. 2, 1864.
Grossman, Jacob	....do....	19	May 2, 1864	100 dys.	Mustered out with company Sept. 2, 1864.
Grunder, Jacob	....do....	32	May 2, 1864	100 dys.	Mustered out with company Sept. 2, 1864.
Grunder, John	....do....	22	May 2, 1864	100 dys.	Mustered out with company Sept. 2, 1864.
Gutekoontz, William	....do....	18	May 2, 1864	100 dys.	Mustered out with company Sept. 2, 1864.
Hardesty, George	....do....	19	May 2, 1864	100 dys.	Mustered out with company Sept. 2, 1864.
Harsh, Benjamin	....do....	39	May 2, 1864	100 dys.	Mustered out with company Sept. 2, 1864.
Haughton, Francis M	....do....	36	May 2, 1864	100 dys.	Mustered out with company Sept. 2, 1864.
Hoon, Oliver H	....do....	40	May 2, 1864	100 dys.	Mustered out with company Sept. 2, 1864.
Howes, Jonathan	....do....	25	May 2, 1864	100 dys.	Mustered out with company Sept. 2, 1864.
Jerome, John F	....do....	18	May 2, 1864	100 dys.	Mustered out with company Sept. 2, 1864.
Lautzenheizer, Amos	....do....	18	May 2, 1864	100 dys.	Mustered out with company Sept. 2, 1864.
McDonald, Duncan S	....do....	29	May 2, 1864	100 dys.	Mustered out with company Sept. 2, 1864.
McLane, James L	....do....	30	May 2, 1864	100 dys.	Mustered out with company Sept. 2, 1864.
McLane, Josiah	....do....	26	May 2, 1864	100 dys.	Mustered out with company Sept. 2, 1864.
McLane, William	....do....	31	May 2, 1864	100 dys.	Mustered out with company Sept. 2, 1864.
Marshall, Daniel	....do....	40	May 2, 1864	100 dys.	Mustered out with company Sept. 2, 1864.
Marshall, Silas B	....do....	27	May 2, 1864	100 dys.	Mustered out with company Sept. 2, 1864.
Martin, John D	....do....	25	May 2, 1864	100 dys.	Mustered out with company Sept. 2, 1864
Miller, Elanson B	....do....	19	May 2, 1864	100 dys.	Mustered out with company Sept. 2, 1864.
Moore, Joseph	....do....	19	May 2, 1864	100 dys.	Mustered out with company Sept. 2, 1864.
Moore, William J	....do....	18	May 2, 1864	100 dys.	Mustered out with company Sept. 2, 1864.
Nichol, Thomas T	....do....	27	May 2, 1864	100 dys.	Mustered out with company Sept. 2, 1864.
Peopler, Otto H	....do....	18	May 2, 1864	100 dys.	Mustered out with company Sept. 2, 1864.
Peters, Marion O	....do....	27	May 2, 1864	100 dys.	Mustered out with company Sept. 2, 1864.
Reed, David	....do....	22	May 2, 1864	100 dys.	Mustered out with company Sept. 2, 1864.
Reed, John R	....do....	37	May 2, 1864	100 dys.	Mustered out with company Sept. 2, 1864.
Richardson, David	....do....	31	May 2, 1864	100 dys.	Mustered out with company Sept. 2, 1864.
Roudebush, George M	....do....	28	May 2, 1864	100 dys.	Mustered out with company Sept. 2, 1864.
Roudebush, Henry	....do....	30	May 2, 1864	100 dys.	Mustered out with company Sept. 2, 1864.
Saltzman, William B	....do....	30	May 2, 1864	100 dys.	Mustered out with company Sept. 2, 1864.
Shaw, Mahlon	....do....	19	May 2, 1864	100 dys.	Mustered out with company Sept. 2, 1864.
Speedy, John	....do....	37	May 2, 1864	100 dys.	Died July 2, 1864, at Fort Delaware, Del.
Stackhouse, Levi	....do....	19	May 2, 1864	100 dys.	Mustered out with company Sept. 2, 1864.
Stokes, John	....do....	43	May 2, 1864	100 dys.	Mustered out with company Sept. 2, 1864.
Sweipheim, Joseph M	....do....	25	May 2, 1864	100 dys.	Mustered out with company Sept. 2, 1864.
Taggart, William	....do....	28	May 2, 1864	100 dys.	Mustered out with company Sept. 2, 1864.
Ware, Benjamin F	....do....	37	May 2, 1864	100 dys.	Mustered out with company Sept. 2, 1864.
Wasmer, George	....do....	19	May 2, 1864	100 dys.	Mustered out with company Sept. 2, 1864.
Wasmer, John	....do....	18	May 2, 1864	100 dys.	Mustered out with company Sept. 2, 1864
Willington, John	....do....	27	May 2, 1864	100 dys.	Mustered out with company Sept. 2, 1864.
Worley, Jacob H	....do....	20	May 2, 1864	100 dys.	Mustered out with company Sept. 2, 1864.
Young, John W	....do....	44	May 2, 1864	100 dys.	Mustered out with company Sept. 2, 1864.

159TH REGIMENT OHIO VOLUNTEER INFANTRY.

FIELD AND STAFF.

red in May 10, 1864, at Zanesville, O., by H. E. Hasen, 2d Lieutenant 8th Infantry, U. S. A. Mustered out Aug. 24, 1864, at Zanesville, O., by J. S. Small, 2d Lieutenant 1st U. S. Cavalry.

		Age.	Date of Entering the Service.	Period of Service.	Remarks.
		..	May 2, 1864	100 dys.	Mustered out with regiment Aug. 24, 1864.
	Lt. Col.	..	May 2, 1864	100 dys.	Mustered out with regiment Aug. 24, 1864.
	Major.	..	May 2, 1864	100 dys.	Mustered out with regiment Aug. 24, 1864.
.....	Surgeon.	..	May 2, 1864	100 dys.	Mustered out with regiment Aug. 24, 1864.
.....	Ast. Surg.	37	May 19, 1864	100 dys.	Mustered out with regiment Aug. 24, 1864.
.....	Adjutant	..	May 2, 1864	100 dys.	Mustered out with regiment Aug. 24, 1864.
.....	R. Q. M.	29	May 2, 1864	100 dys.	Mustered out Sept. 8, 1864, at Zanesville, O.
.....	Chaplain	33	May 2, 1864	100 dys.	Promoted from private Co. H July 7, 1864; died Aug. 18, 1864, at Baltimore, Md.
A. Guthrie........	Ser. Maj.	..	May 2, 1864	100 dys.	Absent, sick Aug. 17, 1864. No further record found.
M. Brown........		..	May 2, 1864	100 dys.	Mustered out with regiment Aug. 24, 1864.
E. Chapman.....		..	May 2, 1864	100 dys.	Mustered out with regiment Aug. 24, 1864.
Lynn............		19	May 2, 1864	100 dys.	Promoted from private Co. A June 1, 1864; mustered out with regiment Aug. 24, 1864.
W. Lilienthal......	Prin. Mus	25	May 2, 1864	100 dys.	Promoted from private Co. A June 1, 1864; mustered out with regiment Aug. 24, 1864.
m H. McKinney...	....do....	23	May 2, 1864	100 dys.	Promoted from Musician Co. C July 1, 1864; mustered out with regiment Aug. 24, 1864.

COMPANY A.

red in May 9, 1864, at Zanesville, O., by H. E. Hasen, 2d Lieutenant 8th Infantry, U. S. A. Mustered out Aug. 22, 1864, at Zanesville, O., by J. S. Small, 2d Lieutenant 1st U. S. Cavalry.

		Age.	Date of Entering the Service.	Period of Service.	Remarks.
P. Marsh.........	Captain.	41	May 2, 1864	100 dys.	
W. Potwin.......	1st Lieut.	44	May 2, 1864	100 dys.	Mustered out with company Aug. 22, 1864.
ck Geiger.........	2d Lieut.	21	May 2, 1864	100 dys.	Mustered out with company Aug. 22, 1864.
Ellis..............	1st Sergt.	27	May 2, 1864	100 dys.	Mustered out with company Aug. 22, 1864.
Randal...........	Sergeant.	23	May 2, 1864	100 dys.	Absent, sick Aug. 17, 1864, at home. No further record found.
n E. Guthrie.......	....do....	21	May 2, 1864	100 dys.	Absent, sick Aug. 17, 1864, at home. No further record found.
in Wheeler, Jr....	....do....	24	May 2, 1864	100 dys.	Mustered out with company Aug. 22, 1864.
n G. Stark.........	....do....	36	May 2, 1864	100 dys.	Mustered out with company Aug. 22, 1864.
J. J. Harkins.....	Corporal.	25	May 2, 1864	100 dys.	Mustered out with company Aug. 22, 1864.
Palmer...........	....do....	22	May 2, 1864	100 dys.	Mustered out with company Aug. 22, 1864.
Hull...............	....do....	19	May 2, 1864	100 dys.	Mustered out with company Aug. 22, 1864.
C. Lee.............	....do....	36	May 2, 1864	100 dys.	Absent, sick Aug. 17, 1864, at home. No further record found.
R. Moore.........	....do....	27	May 2, 1864	100 dys.	Mustered out with company Aug. 22, 1864.
Howard, Jr.......	....do....	22	May 2, 1864	100 dys.	Mustered out with company Aug. 22, 1864.
y Frame..........	....do....	45	May 2, 1864	100 dys.	Mustered out with company Aug. 22, 1864.
Applegate........	....do....	28	May 2, 1864	100 dys.	Mustered out with company Aug. 22, 1864.
Harvey............	Private..	22	May 2, 1864	100 dys.	Mustered out with company Aug. 22, 1864.
y, Alexander W..	....do....	19	May 2, 1864	100 dys.	Mustered out with company Aug. 22, 1864.
Joel	....do....	20	May 2, 1864	100 dys.	Mustered out with company Aug. 22, 1864.
William...........	....do....	26	May 2, 1864	100 dys.	Mustered out with company Aug. 22, 1864.
lius.................	....do....	22	May 2, 1864	100 dys.	Mustered out with company Aug. 22, 1864.
ames A...........	....do....	19	May 2, 1864	100 dys.	Mustered out with company Aug. 22, 1864.
p, Samuel C.......	....do....	25	May 2, 1864	100 dys.	Mustered out with company Aug. 22, 1864.
eorge B...........	....do....	19	May 2, 1864	100 dys.	Mustered out with company Aug. 22, 1864.
, Jacob N	....do....	19	May 2, 1864	100 dys.	Mustered out with company Aug. 22, 1864.
n, William........	....do....	23	May 2, 1864	100 dys.	Mustered out with company Aug. 22, 1864.
William...........	....do....	35	May 2, 1864	100 dys.	Admitted to hospital at Annapolis, Md., July 12, 1864; transferred to Camp Parole, Md., July 13, 1864. No further record found.
gham, James......	....do....	32	May 2, 1864	100 dys.	Mustered out with company Aug. 22, 1864.

Names.	Rank.	Age.	Date of Entering the Service.	Period of Service.	Remarks.
Butler, Lewis	Private.	19	May 2, 1864	100 dys.	Mustered out with company Aug. 22, 1864.
Cherry, Robert M	...do...	34	May 2, 1864	100 dys.	Mustered out with company Aug. 22, 1864.
Convers, Charles G	...do...	19	May 2, 1864	100 dys.	Absent, sick Aug. 17, 1864, at home. No further record found.
Cordes, Herman	...do...	18	May 2, 1864	100 dys.	Mustered out with company Aug. 22, 1864.
Cox, Augustus C	...do...	21	May 2, 1864	100 dys.	Mustered out with company Aug. 22, 1864.
Emmet, John	...do...	24	May 2, 1864	100 dys.	Mustered out with company Aug. 22, 1864.
Erwin, George W	...do...	19	May 2, 1864	100 dys.	Mustered out with company Aug. 22, 1864.
Feasley, Gutliep	...do...	19	May 2, 1864	100 dys.	Mustered out with company Aug. 22, 1864.
Fell, Benjamin	...do...	21	May 2, 1864	100 dys.	Mustered out with company Aug. 22, 1864.
Fillmore, Alfred E	...do...	26	May 2, 1864	100 dys.	Mustered out with company Aug. 22, 1864.
Fox, Theodore	...do...	19	May 2, 1864	100 dys.	Absent, sick Aug. 17, 1864, at home. No further record found.
Gitter, Henry	...do...	43	May 2, 1864	100 dys.	Mustered out with company Aug. 22, 1864.
Guard, William A	...do...	21	May 2, 1864	100 dys.	Mustered out with company Aug. 22, 1864.
Hahn, Charles	...do...	18	May 2, 1864	100 dys.	Mustered out with company Aug. 22, 1864.
Hahn, William	...do...	23	May 2, 1864	100 dys.	Mustered out with company Aug. 22, 1864.
Harris, John	...do...	20	May 2, 1864	100 dys.	Left sick Aug. —, 1864, at Baltimore, Md. No further record found.
Hollister, Frank M	...do...	40	May 2, 1864	100 dys.	Mustered out with company Aug. 22, 1864.
Hurley, John	...do...	20	May 2, 1864	100 dys.	Mustered out with company Aug. 22, 1864.
Hurst, Henry C	...do...	19	May 2, 1864	100 dys.	Mustered out with company Aug. 22, 1864.
Kappes, Charles	...do...	19	May 2, 1864	100 dys.	Mustered out with company Aug. 22, 1864.
Kintz, Albert J	...do...	20	May 2, 1864	100 dys.	Mustered out with company Aug. 22, 1864.
Knight, Llewellyn	...do...	21	May 2, 1864	100 dys.	Mustered out with company Aug. 22, 1864.
Lilienthal, Peter W	...do...	35	May 2, 1864	100 dys.	Promoted to Principal Musician June 1, 1864.
Lynn, George	...do...	19	May 2, 1864	100 dys.	Promoted to Hospital Steward June 1, 1864.
McCleary, James A	...do...	19	May 2, 1864	100 dys.	Mustered out with company Aug. 22, 1864.
Mast, Frederick	...do...	29	May 2, 1864	100 dys.	Mustered out with company Aug. 22, 1864.
Merhman, Jacob F	...do...	25	May 2, 1864	100 dys.	Mustered out with company Aug. 22, 1864.
Mitchell, David E	...do...	41	May 2, 1864	100 dys.	Mustered out with company Aug. 22, 1864.
Mitchell, James H	...do...	18	May 2, 1864	100 dys.	Mustered out with company Aug. 22, 1864.
Moore, Charles E	...do...	38	May 2, 1864	100 dys.	Mustered out with company Aug. 22, 1864.
Moore, Cyrus F	...do...	18	May 2, 1864	100 dys.	Mustered out with company Aug. 22, 1864.
Neet, James	...do...	19	May 2, 1864	100 dys.	Mustered out with company Aug. 22, 1864.
Ordrey, Robert W	...do...	21	May 2, 1864	100 dys.	Absent, sick Aug. 17, 1864, at home. No further record found.
Osmond, Richard B	...do...	43	May 2, 1864	100 dys.	Absent, sick Aug. 17, 1864, at home. No further record found.
Palmer, Isaac	...do...	24	May 2, 1864	100 dys.	Mustered out with company Aug. 22, 1864.
Peabody, Arthur J	...do...	28	May 2, 1864	100 dys.	Mustered out with company Aug. 22, 1864.
Peters, Henry C	...do...	39	May 2, 1864	100 dys.	Mustered out with company Aug. 22, 1864.
Peters, James L	...do...	29	May 2, 1864	100 dys.	Mustered out with company Aug. 22, 1864.
Pierce, Andrew	...do...	26	May 2, 1864	100 dys.	Mustered out with company Aug. 22, 1864.
Pollock, John W	...do...	31	May 2, 1864	100 dys.	Mustered out with company Aug. 22, 1864.
Porter, John A	...do...	25	May 2, 1864	100 dys.	Mustered out with company Aug. 22, 1864.
Prosser, James	...do...	20	May 2, 1864	100 dys.	Mustered out with company Aug. 22, 1864.
Roberts, George	...do...	35	May 2, 1864	100 dys.	Absent, sick at muster-in. No further record found.
Ross, Albert	...do...	18	May 2, 1864	100 dys.	Mustered out with company Aug. 22, 1864.
Sauer, Joseph	...do...	18	May 2, 1864	100 dys.	Mustered out with company Aug. 22, 1864.
Shirer, James M	...do...	44	May 2, 1864	100 dys.	Mustered out with company Aug. 22, 1864.
Shirer, Winfield S	...do...	18	May 2, 1864	100 dys.	Mustered out with company Aug. 22, 1864.
Sloan, William	...do...	24	May 2, 1864	100 dys.	Absent, sick Aug. 17, 1864, at home. No further record found.
Smith, Alexander C	...do...	33	May 2, 1864	100 dys.	Mustered out with company Aug. 22, 1864.
Smith, Edward	...do...	29	May 2, 1864	100 dys.	Mustered out with company Aug. 22, 1864.
Smith, Henry	...do...	26	May 2, 1864	100 dys.	Mustered out with company Aug. 22, 1864.
Smith, Henry H	...do...	29	May 2, 1864	100 dys.	Mustered out with company Aug. 22, 1864.
Stulz, Ferd	...do...	20	May 2, 1864	100 dys.	Mustered out with company Aug. 22, 1864.
Tanner, John	...do...	39	May 2, 1864	100 dys.	Aug. 22, 1864.
Taylor, William A	...do...	30	May 2, 1864	100 dys.	Mustered out with company Aug. 22, 1864.
Twaddle, William A	...do...	39	May 2, 1864	100 dys.	Mustered out with company Aug. 22, 1864.
Vanllamm, Clarence	...do...	20	May 2, 1864	100 dys.	Absent Aug. —, 1864, on detached duty at Baltimore, Md. No further record found.
Walker, William	...do...	28	May 2, 1864	100 dys.	Mustered out with company Aug. 22, 1864.
Wall, Lewis	...do...	27	May 2, 1864	100 dys.	Absent, sick Aug. 17, 1864, at home. No further record found.
Wilson, Edward	...do...	18	May 2, 1864	100 dys.	Mustered out with company Aug. 22, 1864.
Wollard, William S	...do...	18	May 2, 1864	100 dys.	Mustered out with company Aug. 22, 1864.
Woodworth, John	...do...	31	May 2, 1864	100 dys.	Mustered out with company Aug. 22, 1864.

Names.	Rank.	Age.	Date of Entering the Service.	Period of Service.	Remarks.
Terry, David	Private	35	May 2, 1864	100 dys.	Mustered out with company Aug. 24, 1864.
Terry, James W	do	20	May 2, 1864	100 dys.	Absent, sick July 24, 1864, at Baltimore, Md. No further record found.
Terry, John	do	18	May 2, 1864	100 dys.	Mustered out with company Aug. 24, 1864.
Terry, Joseph	do	39	May 2, 1864	100 dys.	Mustered out with company Aug. 24, 1864.
Thomas, Stephen R	do	23	May 2, 1864	100 dys.	Mustered out with company Aug. 24, 1864.
Thompson, Robert M	do	34	May 2, 1864	100 dys.	Mustered out with company Aug. 24, 1864.
Tomlinson, John	do	42	May 2, 1864	100 dys.	Mustered out with company Aug. 24, 1864.
Valentine, John	do	18	May 2, 1864	100 dys.	Mustered out with company Aug. 24, 1864.
Webster, Thomas	do	31	May 2, 1864	100 dys.	Mustered out with company Aug. 24, 1864.
White, John H	do	22	May 2, 1864	100 dys.	Mustered out with company Aug. 24, 1864.
Wymer, Daniel	do	30	May 2, 1864	100 dys.	Mustered out with company Aug. 24, 1864.

COMPANY C.

Mustered in May 9, 1864, at Zanesville, O., by H. E. Hazen, 2d Lieutenant 8th Infantry, U. S. A. Mustered out Aug. 22, 1864, at Zanesville, O., by J. S. Small, 2d Lieutenant 1st U. S. Cavalry.

Names.	Rank.	Age.	Date of Entering the Service.	Period of Service.	Remarks.
Jacob M. Robinson	Captain.	34	May 2, 1864	100 dys.	Mustered out with company Aug. 22, 1864.
Noah Forsythe	1st Lieut.	39	May 2, 1864	100 dys.	Mustered out with company Aug. 22, 1864.
Thomas Stewart	2d Lieut.	34	May 2, 1864	100 dys.	Mustered out with company Aug. 22, 1864.
Edwin A. Wilhelm	1st Sergt.	21	May 2, 1864	100 dys.	Mustered out with company Aug. 22, 1864.
William T. Allen	Sergeant.	22	May 2, 1864	100 dys.	Mustered out with company Aug. 22, 1864.
Hugh McVey	do	33	May 2, 1864	100 dys.	Mustered out with company Aug. 22, 1864.
Abraham Cox	do	44	May 2, 1864	100 dys.	Mustered out with company Aug. 22, 1864.
Robert L. Evans	do	21	May 2, 1864	100 dys.	Mustered out with company Aug. 22, 1864.
Hugh Morehead	Corporal.	22	May 2, 1864	100 dys.	Mustered out with company Aug. 22, 1864.
Alexander P. Morehead	do	37	May 2, 1864	100 dys.	Mustered out with company Aug. 22, 1864.
Henry Ludman	do	37	May 2, 1864	100 dys.	Mustered out with company Aug. 22, 1864.
John Melone	do	40	May 2, 1864	100 dys.	Mustered out with company Aug. 22, 1864.
Henry C. Sniff	do	37	May 2, 1864	100 dys.	Mustered out with company Aug. 22, 1864.
David M. Watson	do	34	May 2, 1864	100 dys.	Mustered out with company Aug. 22, 1864.
Robert W. Walker	do	21	May 2, 1864	100 dys.	Mustered out with company Aug. 22, 1864.
Reuben C. Storer	do	37	May 2, 1864	100 dys.	Mustered out with company Aug. 22, 1864.
William H. McKinney	Musician	23	May 2, 1864	100 dys.	Promoted to Principal Musician July 1, 1864.
William Reynolds	do	31	May 2, 1864	100 dys.	Mustered out with company Aug. 22, 1864.
Alexander, Hugh H	Private	20	May 2, 1864	100 dys.	Mustered out with company Aug. 22, 1864.
Ardrey, James	do	22	May 2, 1864	100 dys.	Mustered out with company Aug. 22, 1864.
Atchinson, Alanson W	do	25	May 2, 1864	100 dys.	Mustered out with company Aug. 22, 1864.
Barnett, John N	do	18	May 2, 1864	100 dys.	Mustered out with company Aug. 22, 1864.
Barnett, John S	do	36	May 2, 1864	100 dys.	Mustered out with company Aug. 22, 1864.
Barnett, William W	do	23	May 2, 1864	100 dys.	Mustered out with company Aug. 22, 1864.
Bearry, Benoni	do	25	May 2, 1864	100 dys.	Mustered out with company Aug. 22, 1864.
Bell, Edward A	do	40	May 2, 1864	100 dys.	Mustered out with company Aug. 22, 1864.
Blackstone, William	do	39	May 2, 1864	100 dys.	Mustered out with company Aug. 22, 1864.
Blosser, Samuel	do	31	May 2, 1864	100 dys.	Mustered out with company Aug. 22, 1864.
Bohrer, George J	do	25	May 2, 1864	100 dys.	Mustered out with company Aug. 22, 1864.
Boyer, Alexander	do	21	May 2, 1864	100 dys.	Mustered out with company Aug. 22, 1864.
Boyer, Thomas W	do	21	May 2, 1864	100 dys.	Mustered out with company Aug. 22, 1864.
Cabeen, Robert	do	38	May 2, 1864	100 dys.	Mustered out with company Aug. 22, 1864.
Campbell, David	do	23	May 2, 1864	100 dys.	Mustered out with company Aug. 22, 1864.
Campbell, David J	do	21	May 2, 1864	100 dys.	Mustered out with company Aug. 22, 1864.
Carmichael, James	do	29	May 2, 1864	100 dys.	Absent, sick Aug. 17, 1864, at home. No further record found.
Cox, James W	do	21	May 2, 1864	100 dys.	Mustered out with company Aug. 22, 1864.
Crawford, Edward	do	20	May 2, 1864	100 dys.	Mustered out with company Aug. 22, 1864.
Crawford, William G	do	31	May 2, 1864	100 dys.	Mustered out with company Aug. 22, 1864.
Davis, Spencer	do	21	May 2, 1864	100 dys.	Absent, sick Aug. 17, 1864, at home. No further record found.
Elliott, Simon W	do	26	May 2, 1864	100 dys.	Mustered out with company Aug. 22, 1864.
Frazier, William	do	42	May 2, 1864	100 dys.	Mustered out with company Aug. 22, 1864.
Forsythe, David P	do	28	May 2, 1864	100 dys.	Mustered out with company Aug. 22, 1864.
Forsythe, James W	do	36	May 2, 1864	100 dys.	Mustered out with company Aug. 22, 1864.
Given, David S	do	20	May 2, 1864	100 dys.	Mustered out with company Aug. 22, 1864.
Given, James D	do	19	May 2, 1864	100 dys.	Mustered out with company Aug. 22, 1864.
Gregory, William D	do	19	May 2, 1864	100 dys.	Absent, sick Aug. 17, 1864, at home. No further record found.
Hardesty, Hugh E	do	31	May 2, 1864	100 dys.	Mustered out with company Aug. 22, 1864.
Hardesty, William H	do	20	May 2, 1864	100 dys.	Mustered out with company Aug. 22, 1864.
Hendershot, William M	do	19	May 2, 1864	100 dys.	Mustered out with company Aug. 22, 1864.
Heron, Henry	do	22	May 2, 1864	100 dys.	Mustered out with company Aug. 22, 1864.
Hines, John	do	35	May 2, 1864	100 dys.	Mustered out with company Aug. 22, 1864.
Howell, John L	do	18	May 2, 1864	100 dys.	Mustered out with company Aug. 22, 1864.
Humphrey, Abner	do	41	May 2, 1864	100 dys.	Absent, sick at home, Aug. 17, 1864. No further record found.
Hutchinson, John	do	30	May 2, 1864	100 dys.	Mustered out with company Aug. 22, 1864.
Johnson, Watson A	do	38	May 2, 1864	100 dys.	Mustered out with company Aug. 22, 1864.
Larimer, James A	do	24	May 2, 1864	100 dys.	Mustered out with company Aug. 22, 1864.
Ledman, Frederick L	do	18	May 2, 1864	100 dys.	Mustered out with company Aug. 22, 1864.

Names.	Rank.	Age.	Date of Entering the Service.	Period of Service.	Remarks.
[illegible], William H.	Private.	28	May 2, 1864	100 dys.	Mustered out with company Aug. 22, 1864.
[illegible], John	do.	28	May 2, 1864	100 dys.	Mustered out with company Aug. 22, 1864.
[illegible], William	do.	20	May 2, 1864	100 dys.	Mustered out with company Aug. 22, 1864.
[illegible]	do.	[illegible]	May 2, 1864	100 dys.	Mustered out with company Aug. 22, 1864.
[illegible], James	do.	23	May 2, 1864	100 dys.	Mustered out with company Aug. 22, 1864.
[illegible], Smith G.	do.	28	May 2, 1864	100 dys.	Mustered out with company Aug. 22, 1864.
[illegible], Alex	do.	27	May 2, 1864	100 dys.	Absent, sick Aug. 17, 1864, at home. No further record found.
[illegible], Charles W.	do.	19	May 2, 1864	100 dys.	Mustered out with company Aug. 22, 1864.
[illegible], James S.	do.	34	May 2, 1864	100 dys.	Mustered out with company Aug. 22, 1864.
[illegible], John	do.	24	May 2, 1864	100 dys.	Mustered out with company Aug. 22, 1864.
[illegible], Richard C.	do.	33	May 2, 1864	100 dys.	Mustered out with company Aug. 22, 1864.
[illegible], William W.	do.	21	May 2, 1864	100 dys.	Mustered out with company Aug. 22, 1864.
[illegible], Wylie	do.	22	May 2, 1864	100 dys.	Mustered out with company Aug. 22, 1864.
[illegible], George	do.	25	May 2, 1864	100 dys.	Mustered out with company Aug. 22, 1864.
[illegible], John	do.	24	May 2, 1864	100 dys.	Mustered out with company Aug. 22, 1864.
[illegible]	do.	22	May 2, 1864	100 dys.	Mustered out with company Aug. 22, 1864.
[illegible], William W.	do.	21	May 2, 1864	100 dys.	Mustered out with company Aug. 22, 1864.
[illegible], Robert M.	do.	20	May 2, 1864	100 dys.	Mustered out with company Aug. 22, 1864.
[illegible], Esmond F.	do.	20	May 2, 1864	100 dys.	Mustered out with company Aug. 22, 1864.
[illegible], Finley E.	do.	20	May 2, 1864	100 dys.	Mustered out with company Aug. 22, 1864.
[illegible], John E.	do.	24	May 2, 1864	100 dys.	Mustered out with company Aug. 22, 1864.
[illegible], William O.	do.	20	May 2, 1864	100 dys.	Mustered out with company Aug. 22, 1864.
[illegible], Richard	do.	40	May 2, 1864	100 dys.	Mustered out with company Aug. 22, 1864.
[illegible], Samuel	do.	22	May 2, 1864	100 dys.	Mustered out with company Aug. 22, 1864.
[illegible], Jacob G.	do.	42	May 2, 1864	100 dys.	Mustered out with company Aug. 22, 1864.
[illegible], Thomas	do.	36	May 2, 1864	100 dys.	Mustered out with company Aug. 22, 1864.
[illegible], Seth C.	do.	20	May 2, 1864	100 dys.	Mustered out with company Aug. 22, 1864.
[illegible], William F.	do.	21	May 2, 1864	100 dys.	Mustered out with company Aug. 22, 1864.

COMPANY D.

Mustered in May 9, 1864, at Zanesville, O., by H. E. Hasen, 2d Lieutenant 8th Infantry, U. S. A. Mustered out Aug. 22, 1864, at Zanesville, O., by J. S. Small, 2d Lieutenant 1st U. S. Cavalry.

Names.	Rank.	Age.	Date of Entering the Service.	Period of Service.	Remarks.
John W. [illegible]	Captain.	21	May 2, 1864	100 dys.	Mustered out with company Aug. 22, 1864.
Thomas J. Newman	1st Lieut.	22	May 2, 1864	100 dys.	Mustered out with company Aug. 22, 1864.
William Newman	2d Lieut.	34	May 2, 1864	100 dys.	Mustered out with company Aug. 22, 1864.
Horatio R. Bodine	1st Sergt.	40	May 2, 1864	100 dys.	Mustered out with company Aug. 22, 1864.
Jesse Lee	Sergeant	42	May 2, 1864	100 dys.	Mustered out with company Aug. 22, 1864.
William H. Fountain	do.	22	May 2, 1864	100 dys.	Mustered out with company Aug. 22, 1864.
John H. Richey	do.	25	May 2, 1864	100 dys.	Mustered out with company Aug. 22, 1864.
Charles M. Vandenbark	do.	20	May 2, 1864	100 dys.	Mustered out with company Aug. 22, 1864.
Thomas Caldwell	Corporal	41	May 2, 1864	100 dys.	Mustered out with company Aug. 22, 1864.
Elijah Ray	do.	28	May 2, 1864	100 dys.	Mustered out with company Aug. 22, 1864.
Henry D. Butler	do.	21	May 2, 1864	100 dys.	Mustered out with company Aug. 22, 1864.
Benjamin Crabbin	do.	22	May 2, 1864	100 dys.	Mustered out with company Aug. 22, 1864.
Elijah H. Moore	do.	19	May 2, 1864	100 dys.	Mustered out with company Aug. 22, 1864.
Lloyd Varner	do.	28	May 2, 1864	100 dys.	Mustered out with company Aug. 22, 1864.
Byron Crabtree	do.	30	May 2, 1864	100 dys.	Mustered out with company Aug. 22, 1864.
Samuel M. Bell	do.	25	May 2, 1864	100 dys.	Mustered out with company Aug. 22, 1864.
Adams, Morris S.	Private.	20	May 2, 1864	100 dys.	Mustered out with company Aug. 22, 1864.
Allen, Seth	do.	18	May 2, 1864	100 dys.	Mustered out with company Aug. 22, 1864.
Baird, Jacob	do.	20	May 2, 1864	100 dys.	Mustered out with company Aug. 22, 1864.
Berry, James	do.	19	May 2, 1864	100 dys.	Mustered out with company Aug. 22, 1864.
Bowers, John	do.	42	May 2, 1864	100 dys.	Mustered out with company Aug. 22, 1864.
Burlingame, George.	do.	19	May 2, 1864	100 dys.	Mustered out with company Aug. 22, 1864.
Carmichael, George.	do.	27	May 2, 1864	100 dys.	Mustered out with company Aug. 22, 1864.
Carter, Thomas	do.	30	May 2, 1864	100 dys.	Mustered out with company Aug. 22, 1864.
Carl, James	do.	20	May 2, 1864	100 dys.	Mustered out with company Aug. 22, 1864.
Caw, James	do.	37	May 2, 1864	100 dys.	Mustered out with company Aug. 22, 1864.
Clest, George		19	May 2, 1864	100 dys.	Mustered out with company Aug. 22, 1864.
Conn, John W		18	May 2, 1864	100 dys.	Mustered out with company Aug. 22, 1864.
Cook, Joseph A		28	May 2, 1864	100 dys.	Absent, sick Aug. 17, 1864, at home. No further record found.
Crabtree, William J	do.	40	May 2, 1864	100 dys.	Mustered out with company Aug. 22, 1864.
Crabtree, Julius	do.	[illegible]	May 2, 1864	100 dys.	Mustered out with company Aug. 22, 1864.
Craig, James	do.	[illegible]	May 2, 1864	100 dys.	Mustered out with company Aug. 22, 1864.
Craig, Nathaniel	do.	[illegible]	May 2, 1864	100 dys.	Mustered out with company Aug. 22, 1864.
Dowell, James M	do.	[illegible]	May 2, 1864	100 dys.	Mustered out with company Aug. 22, 1864.
Dowell, Lorenzo J	do.	[illegible]	May 2, 1864	100 dys.	Mustered out with company Aug. 22, 1864.
Dowell, Thomas J	do.	[illegible]	May 2, 1864	100 dys.	Mustered out with company Aug. 22, 1864.
Eaton, James R	do.	[illegible]	May 2, 1864	100 dys.	Mustered out with company Aug. 22, 1864.
Evans, John H	do.	[illegible]	May 2, 1864	100 dys.	Mustered out with company Aug. 22, 1864.
Everbark, Henry	do.	[illegible]	May 2, 1864	100 dys.	
Flanigan, William	do.	[illegible]	May 2, 1864	100 dys.	Mustered out with company Aug. 22, 1864.
Flesher, George W	do.	[illegible]	May 2, 1864	100 dys.	Mustered out with company Aug. 22, 1864.
Flesher, John	do.	[illegible]	May 2, 1864	100 dys.	Mustered out with company Aug. 22, 1864.
Forsythe, William	do.	[illegible]	May 2, 1864	100 dys.	Mustered out with company Aug. 22, 1864.

Names.	Rank.	Age.	Date of Entering the Service	Period of Service.	Remarks.
Fountain, John	Private..	18	May 2, 1864	100 dys.	Mustered out with company Aug. 22, 1864.
Fowler, Marion	...do...	26	May 2, 1864	100 dys.	Mustered out with company Aug. 22, 1864.
Fowler, Wilson	...do...	38	May 2, 1864	100 dys.	Mustered out with company Aug. 22, 1864.
George, Thomas	...do...	18	May 2, 1864	100 dys.	Mustered out with company Aug. 22, 1864.
Grubb, Decatur	...do...	38	May 2, 1864	100 dys.	Mustered out with company Aug. 22, 1864.
Haines, Henry	...do...	26	May 2, 1864	100 dys.	Mustered out with company Aug. 22, 1864.
Harris, Thomas	...do...	38	May 2, 1864	100 dys.	Mustered out with company Aug. 22, 1864.
Hillier, Isaac	...do...	37	May 2, 1864	100 dys.	Mustered out with company Aug. 22, 1864.
Koos, Louis	...do...	..	May 2, 1864	100 dys.	Died July 20, 1864, at Baltimore, Md.
Laird, Robert	...do...	23	May 2, 1864	100 dys.	Mustered out with company Aug. 22, 1864.
McCullough, Robert	...do...	19	May 2, 1864	100 dys.	Mustered out with company Aug. 22, 1864.
Mercer, James A	...do...	27	May 2, 1864	100 dys.	Mustered out with company Aug. 22, 1864.
Mohler, Wellington	...do...	18	May 2, 1864	100 dys.	Mustered out with company Aug. 22, 1864.
Mukzingo, Woodford	...do...	19	May 2, 1864	100 dys.	Mustered out with company Aug. 22, 1864; also borne on rolls as Woodford Makzirgo.
Myers, Joseph	...do...	22	May 2, 1864	100 dys.	Mustered out with company Aug. 22, 1864.
Norman, David	...do...	28	May 2, 1864	100 dys.	Mustered out with company Aug. 22, 1864.
Northover, William	...do...	32	May 2, 1864	100 dys.	Mustered out with company Aug. 22, 1864.
Osborn, Alvin	...do...	39	May 2, 1864	100 dys.	Mustered out with company Aug. 22, 1864.
Overbark, Henry	...do...	37	May 2, 1864	100 dys.	Mustered out with company Aug. 22, 1864.
Pake, Perry W	...do...	29	May 2, 1864	100 dys.	Mustered out with company Aug. 22, 1864.
Pansler, John B	...do...	24	May 2, 1864	100 dys.	Mustered out with company Aug. 22, 1864.
Pansler, William	...do...	41	May 2, 1864	100 dys.	Mustered out with company Aug. 22, 1864.
Ramey, Sanford W	...do...	37	May 2, 1864	100 dys.	Mustered out with company Aug. 22, 1864.
Roberts, Henry C	...do...	35	May 2, 1864	100 dys.	Mustered out with company Aug. 22, 1864.
Rudy, Samuel	...do...	50	May 2, 1864	100 dys.	Mustered out with company Aug. 22, 1864.
Saup, Michael	...do...	18	May 2, 1864	100 dys.	Mustered out with company Aug. 22, 1864.
Sherman, George	...do...	21	May 2, 1864	100 dys.	Mustered out with company Aug. 22, 1864.
Sidle, Cornelius F	...do...	22	May 2, 1864	100 dys.	Mustered out with company Aug. 22, 1864.
Simpson, Thomas H	...do...	21	May 2, 1864	100 dys.	Mustered out with company Aug. 22, 1864.
Smith, Timothy R	...do...	18	May 2, 1864	100 dys.	Mustered out with company Aug. 22, 1864.
Starkey, Harrison	...do...	28	May 2, 1864	100 dys.	Mustered out with company Aug. 22, 1864.
Tanner, David	...do...	38	May 2, 1864	100 dys.	Mustered out with company Aug. 22, 1864.
Tanner, Thomas	...do...	42	May 2, 1864	100 dys.	Mustered out with company Aug. 22, 1864.
Toben, William F	...do...	24	May 2, 1864	100 dys.	Mustered out with company Aug. 22, 1864.
Van Winkle, James	...do...	39	May 2, 1864	100 dys.	Mustered out with company Aug. 22, 1864.
Varner, Mahlon	...do...	20	May 2, 1864	100 dys.	Mustered out with company Aug. 22, 1864.
Waddle, Thomas	...do...	30	May 2, 1864	100 dys.	Mustered out with company Aug. 22, 1864.
Wagner, George	...do...	23	May 2, 1864	100 dys.	Mustered out with company Aug. 22, 1864.
Wilkinson, David	...do...	21	May 2, 1864	100 dys.	Mustered out with company Aug. 22, 1864.
Wise, Francis N	...do...	34	May 2, 1864	100 dys.	Mustered out with company Aug. 22, 1864.
Woods, John	...do...	24	May 2, 1864	100 dys.	Mustered out with company Aug. 22, 1864.
Wortman, William	...do...	27	May 2, 1864	100 dys.	Mustered out with company Aug. 22, 1864.

COMPANY E.

Mustered in May 9, 1864, at Zanesville, O., by H. E. Hazen, 2d Lieutenant 8th Infantry, U. S. A. Mustered out Aug. 22, 1864, at Zanesville, O., by J. S. Small, 2d Lieutenant 1st U. S. Cavalry.

Names.	Rank.	Age.	Date of Entering the Service	Period of Service.	Remarks.
Charles H. Fox	Captain.	27	May 2, 1864	100 dys.	Mustered out with company Aug. 22, 1864.
William E. Atwell	1st Lieut.	23	May 2, 1864	100 dys.	Mustered out with company Aug. 22, 1864.
Milton H. Carter	2d Lieut.	55	May 2, 1864	100 dys.	Mustered out with company Aug. 22, 1864.
Richard H. Galigher	1st Sergt.	23	May 2, 1864	100 dys.	Mustered out with company Aug. 22, 1864.
James E. Scarvell	Sergeant.	26	May 2, 1864	100 dys.	Mustered out with company Aug. 22, 1864.
Samuel Cochrell	...do...	40	May 2, 1864	100 dys.	Mustered out with company Aug. 22, 1864.
Lafayette Story	...do...	21	May 2, 1864	100 dys.	Mustered out with company Aug. 22, 1864.
Joseph Purcell	...do...	22	May 2, 1864	100 dys.	Mustered out with company Aug. 22, 1864.
Newton Brookover	Corporal	22	May 2, 1864	100 dys.	Mustered out with company Aug. 22, 1864.
Peter [illegible]ashbaugh	...do...	19	May 2, 1864	100 dys.	Mustered out with company Aug. 22, 1864.
Harvey Corbin	...do...	22	May 2, 1864	100 dys.	Mustered out with company Aug. 22, 1864.
William Roll	...do...	19	May 2, 1864	100 dys.	Mustered out with company Aug. 22, 1864.
John Mears	...do...	27	May 2, 1864	100 dys.	Mustered out with company Aug. 22, 1864.
Washington Brookover	...do...	31	May 2, 1864	100 dys.	Absent, sick Aug. 17, 1864, at home. No further record found.
John Barnell	...do...	37	May 2, 1864	100 dys.	Mustered out with company Aug. 22, 1864.
Joseph Mihlfelt	...do...	19	May 2, 1864	100 dys.	Mustered out with company Aug. 22, 1864.
Acheson, David	Private..	19	May 2, 1864	100 dys.	Mustered out with company Aug. 22, 1864.
Acheson, James	...do...	27	May 2, 1864	100 dys.	Mustered out with company Aug. 22, 1864.
Anderson, Charles G	...do...	30	May 2, 1864	100 dys.	Mustered out with company Aug. 22, 1864.
Anderson, Charles H	...do...	22	May 2, 1864	100 dys.	Absent, sick Aug. 17, 1864, at home. No further record found.
Anderson, John W	...do...	19	May 2, 1864	100 dys.	Mustered out with company Aug. 22, 1864.
Arnold, Andrew	...do...	22	May 2, 1864	100 dys.	Mustered out with company Aug. 22, 1864.
Arter, Alva	...do...	36	May 2, 1864	100 dys.	Mustered out with company Aug. 22, 1864.
Baker, John	...do...	18	May 2, 1864	100 dys.	Mustered out with company Aug. 22, 1864.
Bowman, George	...do...	22	May 2, 1864	100 dys.	Mustered out with company Aug. 22, 1864.
Border, Charles	...do...	21	May 2, 1864	100 dys.	Mustered out with company Aug. 22, 1864.
Brookover, Charles	...do...	18	May 2, 1864	100 dys.	Mustered out with company Aug. 22, 1864.
Brookover, Davis	...do...	18	May 2, 1864	100 dys.	Mustered out with company Aug. 22, 1864.

Names.	Rank.	Age.	Date of Entering the Service.	Period of Service.	Remarks.
Jesse S. Arter	Corporal.	24	May 2, 1864	100 dys.	Mustered out with company Aug. 22, 1864.
James Bellinger	Musician	..	May 2, 1864	100 dys.	Mustered out with company Aug. 22, 1864.
Alexander, Samuel	Private..	25	May 2, 1864	100 dys.	Mustered out with company Aug. 22, 1864.
Arter, Charles	....do....	18	May 2, 1864	100 dys.	Mustered out with company Aug. 22, 1864.
Baldwin, Austin	....do....	31	May 2, 1864	100 dys.	Mustered out with company Aug. 22, 1864.
Balsley, William	....do....	18	May 2, 1864	100 dys.	Mustered out with company Aug. 22, 1864.
Bean, Perry V	....do....	21	May 2, 1864	100 dys.	Mustered out with company Aug. 22, 1864.
Blosser Noah	....do....	24	May 2, 1864	100 dys.	Sick Aug. 17, 1864. No further record found.
Bowm n, John	....do....	29	May 2, 1864	100 dys.	Mustered out with company Aug. 22, 1864.
Boyd James	....do....	18	May 2, 1864	100 dys.	Mustered out with company Aug. 22, 1864.
Burton, Williard	....do....	21	May 2, 1864	100 dys.	Mustered out with company Aug. 22, 1864.
Butler Willia C	....do....	18	May 2, 1864	100 dys.	Mustered out with company Aug. 22, 1864.
Courtn Edward	....do....	18	May 2, 1864	100 dys.	Mustered out with company Aug. 22, 1864.
DeYarm tt, Edward B	....do....	18	May 2, 1864	100 dys.	Mustered out with company Aug. 22, 1864.
Dugan, Peter	....do....	29	May 2, 1864	100 dys.	Mustered out with company Aug. 22, 1864.
Dunn, Jacob T.	....do....	25	May 2, 1864	100 dys.	Mustered out with company Aug. 22, 1864.
Emery, James	....do....	21	May 2, 1864	100 dys.	Mustered out with company Aug. 22, 1864.
Friesner Samuel	....do....	29	May 2, 1864	100 dys.	Mustered out with company Aug. 22, 1864.
Flowers, George	....do....	18	May 2, 1864	100 dys.	Mustered out with company Aug. 22, 1864.
Ford, Will n	....do....	18	May 2, 1864	100 dys.	Mustered out with company Aug. 22, 1864.
Geeson Charles	....do....	31	May 2, 1864	100 dys.	Mustered out with company Aug. 22, 1864.
Gigax, Frederick	....do....	20	May 2, 1864	100 dys.	Mustered out with company Aug. 22, 1864.
Good, William	....do....	20	May 2, 1864	100 dys.	Mustered out with company Aug. 22, 1864.
Greives, Peter	....do....	18	May 2, 1864	100 dys.	Mustered out with company Aug. 22, 1864.
Griffith, George	....do....	21	May 2, 1864	100 dys.	Mustered out with company Aug. 22, 1864.
Griffith, William	....do....	20	May 2, 1864	100 dys.	Mustered out with company Aug. 22, 1864.
Groves, David	....do....	19	May 2, 1864	100 dys.	Mustered out with company Aug. 22, 1864.
Hamonth, Adolph	....do....	19	May 2, 1864	100 dys.	Mustered out with company Aug. 22, 1864.
Henry, Peter	....do....	44	May 2, 1864	100 dys.	Mustered out with company Aug. 22, 1864.
Hirst, John	....do....	18	May 2, 1864	100 dys.	Mustered out with company Aug. 22, 1864.
Kerker, Adam A	....do....	19	May 2, 1864	100 dys.	Mustered out with company Aug. 22, 1864.
Kimberly, Fuller	....do....	18	May 2, 1864	100 dys.	Mustered out with company Aug. 22, 1864.
Kerte, Henry L	....do....	21	May 2, 1864	100 dys.	Mustered out with company Aug. 22, 1864.
Lenhart, James H	....do....	20	May 2, 1864	100 dys.	Mustered out with company Aug. 22, 1864.
Leslie, Charles	....do....	18	May 2, 1864	100 dys.	Mustered out with company Aug. 22, 1864.
Longshore, Henry C	....do....	..	May 2, 1864	100 dys.	Mustered out with company Aug. 22, 1864.
McCall, Alonzo	....do....	18	May 2, 1864	100 dys.	Mustered out with company Aug. 22, 1864.
	....do....	19	May 2, 1864	100 dys.	Mustered out with company Aug. 22, 1864.
	....do....	18	May 2, 1864	100 dys.	Mustered out with company Aug. 22, 1864.
	....do....	20	May 2, 1864	100 dys.	Mustered out with company Aug. 22, 1864.
McKee, Samuel	....do....	18	May 2, 1864	100 dys.	Mustered out with company Aug. 22, 1864.
Matthews, Byron	....do....	20	May 2, 1864	100 dys.	Mustered out with company Aug. 22, 1864.
Mercer, Jesse	....do....	19	May 2, 1864	100 dys.	Mustered out with company Aug. 22, 1864.
Miles, George W	....do....	22	May 2, 1864	100 dys.	Mustered out with company Aug. 22, 1864.
Mitchell, Edward	....do....	18	May 2, 1864	100 dys.	Mustered out with company Aug. 22, 1864.
Mohler, George H	....do....	28	May 2, 1864	100 dys.	Mustered out with company Aug. 22, 1864.
Mosier, Robert	....do....	21	May 2, 1864	100 dys.	Mustered out with company Aug. 22, 1864.
Myers, Jacob	....do....	20	May 2, 1864	100 dys.	Mustered out with company Aug. 22, 1864.
Nevin, Benjamin	....do....	18	May 2, 1864	100 dys.	Mustered out with company Aug. 22, 1864.
Nevitt, James C	....do....	18	May 2, 1864	100 dys.	Absent, sick Aug. 17, 1864, at home. No further record found.
Nosker, Edwin L	....do....	21	May 2, 1864	100 dys.	Mustered out with company Aug. 22, 1864.
Nutt, William	....do....	21	May 2, 1864	100 dys.	Mustered out with company Aug. 22, 1864.
Palmer, Charles	....do....	18	May 2, 1864	100 dys.	Mustered out with company Aug. 22, 1864.
Pelton, Theodore R	....do....	18	May 2, 1864	100 dys.	Mustered out with company Aug. 22, 1864.
Rhodes, Henry S	....do....	44	May 2, 1864	100 dys.	Mustered out with company Aug. 22, 1864.
Rowles, James A	....do....	19	May 2, 1864	100 dys.	Mustered out with company Aug. 22, 1864.
Rusk, John W	....do....	19	May 2, 1864	100 dys.	Mustered out with company Aug. 22, 1864.
Shaffer, William	....do....	18	May 2, 1864	100 dys.	Mustered out with company Aug. 22, 1864.
Shellhammer Milton B.	....do....	20	May 2, 1864	100 dys.	Mustered out with company Aug. 22, 1864.
Smith, George	....do....	18	May 2, 1864	100 dys.	Mustered out with company Aug. 22, 1864.
Smith, William	....do....	19	May 2, 1864	100 dys.	Mustered out with company Aug. 22, 1864.
Stausberry, George	....do....	18	May 2, 1864	100 dys.	Mustered out with company Aug. 22, 1864.
Steiz, George	....do....	22	May 2, 1864	100 dys.	Mustered out with company Aug. 22, 1864.
Steinhaur, Michael	....do....	19	May 2, 1864	100 dys.	
Strow, Henry	....do....	26	May 2, 1864	100 dys.	Mustered out with company Aug. 22, 1864.
Van Horn, Jacob	....do....	41	May 2, 1864	100 dys.	Mustered out with company Aug. 22, 1864.
Weagley, Jacob	....do....	35	May 2, 1864	100 dys.	Mustered out with company Aug. 22, 1864.
Webb, Robert	....do....	20	May 2, 1864	100 dys.	Mustered out with company Aug. 22, 1864.
Weldy, Henry	....do....	27	May 2, 1864	100 dys.	Mustered out with company Aug. 22, 1864.
Willey, Robert S	....do....	22	May 2, 1864	100 dys.	Mustered out with company Aug. 22, 1864.
Wilson, Dempsey	....do....	42	May 2, 1864	100 dys.	Mustered out with company Aug. 22, 1864.
Wolf, Peter	....do....	40	May 2, 1864	100 dys.	Mustered out with company Aug. 22, 1864.

Names.	Rank.	Age.	Date of Entering the Service.	Period of Service.	Remarks.
Frasier, James W.	Private.	26	May 2, 1864	100 dys.	Absent, sick Aug. 15, 1864, at Baltimore, Md. No further record found.
Frasier, John R.	...do...	20	May 2, 1864	100 dys.	Mustered out with company Aug. 22, 1864.
Frasier, William H.	...do...	18	May 2, 1864	100 dys.	Mustered out with company Aug. 22, 1864.
Gray, John	...do...	21	May 2, 1864	100 dys.	Mustered out with company Aug. 22, 1864.
Gray, Thomas	...do...	25	May 2, 1864	100 dys.	Mustered out with company Aug. 22, 1864.
Graham, Robert	...do...	26	May 2, 1864	100 dys.	Mustered out with company Aug. 22, 1864.
Graham, Thomas	...do...	24	May 2, 1864	100 dys.	Mustered out with company Aug. 22, 1864.
Graham, Robert	...do...	26	May 2, 1864	100 dys.	Mustered out with company Aug. 22, 1864.
Horn, James S.	...do...	44	May 2, 1864	100 dys.	Mustered out with company Aug. 22, 1864.
Horner, John	...do...	36	May 2, 1864	100 dys.	Mustered out with company Aug. 22, 1864.
Jackson, John C.	...do...	18	May 2, 1864	100 dys.	Mustered out with company Aug. 22, 1864.
Jewett, Henry	...do...	27	May 2, 1864	100 dys.	Discharged July 1, 1864, at Baltimore, Md., by order of War Department.
James, Franklin R.	...do...	39	May 2, 1864	100 dys.	Mustered out with company Aug. 22, 1864.
Kugon, Christian	...do...	37	May 2, 1864	100 dys.	Discharged July 1, 1864, at Baltimore, Md., by order of War Department.
Lanahan, Ennis M.	...do...	28	May 2, 1864	100 dys.	Mustered out with company Aug. 22, 1864.
McCandlish, John	...do...	22	May 2, 1864	100 dys.	Mustered out with company Aug. 22, 1864.
McClenahan, John L.	...do...	36	May 2, 1864	100 dys.	Mustered out with company Aug. 22, 1864.
McQuiston, Robert	...do...	38	May 2, 1864	100 dys.	Mustered out with company Aug. 22, 1864.
Madden, John	...do...	37	May 2, 1864	100 dys.	
Miller, Adam	...do...	33	May 2, 1864	100 dys.	Mustered out with company Aug. 22, 1864.
Minor, John O.	...do...	22	May 2, 1864	100 dys.	Mustered out with company Aug. 22, 1864.
Moore, Joseph G.	...do...	33	May 2, 1864	100 dys.	Promoted to Chaplain July 7, 1864.
Morrison, Robert	...do...	18	May 2, 1864	100 dys.	Mustered out with company Aug. 22, 1864.
Morrow, David B.	...do...	24	May 2, 1864	100 dys.	Mustered out with company Aug. 22, 1864.
Neely, David	...do...	26	May 2, 1864	100 dys.	Mustered out with company Aug. 22, 1864.
Neff, Oladdis	...do...	20	May 2, 1864	100 dys.	Mustered out with company Aug. 22, 1864.
Neible, Christian	...do...	33	May 2, 1864	100 dys.	Mustered out with company Aug. 22, 1864.
Osborn, Abraham	...do...	36	May 2, 1864	100 dys.	Mustered out with company Aug. 22, 1864.
Parks, James	...do...	32	May 2, 1864	100 dys.	Died July 18, 1864, at Baltimore, Md.
Phillips, Levi	...do...	19	May 2, 1864	100 dys.	Mustered out with company Aug. 22, 1864.
Shacklett, John D.	...do...	36	May 2, 1864	100 dys.	Mustered out with company Aug. 22, 1864.
Shacklett, Lavellen C.	...do...	22	May 2, 1864	100 dys.	Rejected by Examining Surgeon after muster-in.
Shacklett, Lucius D.	...do...	29	May 2, 1864	100 dys.	Mustered out with company Aug. 22, 1864.
Shaffer, John C.	...do...	34	May 2, 1864	100 dys.	Mustered out with company Aug. 22, 1864.
Sherward, Curtis G	...do...	39	May 2, 1864	100 dys.	Mustered out with company Aug. 22, 1864.
Smith, Hiland B.	...do...	27	May 2, 1864	100 dys.	Discharged July 1, 1864, at Baltimore, Md., by order of War Department.
Simpson, Thomas C.	...do...	28	May 2, 1864	100 dys.	Mustered out with company Aug. 22, 1864.
Sucrett, George P.	...do...	34	May 2, 1864	100 dys.	Mustered out with company Aug. 22, 1864.
Stockdale, Amos	...do...	19	May 2, 1864	100 dys.	Mustered out with company Aug. 22, 1864.
Thumwood, Edward J.	...do...	30	May 2, 1864	100 dys.	Mustered out with company Aug. 22, 1864.
Tracy, Abner L.	...do...	18	May 2, 1864	100 dys.	Mustered out with company Aug. 22, 1864.
Voris, Nelson	...do...	40	May 2, 1864	100 dys.	Discharged July 1, 1864, at Baltimore, Md., by order of War Department.
Walcott, James	...do...	24	May 2, 1864	100 dys.	Died July 31, 1864, at Baltimore, Md.
Wallis, Fenton	...do...	34	May 2, 1864	100 dys.	Mustered out with company Aug. 22, 1864.
Westenberger, Noah	...do...	31	May 2, 1864	100 dys.	Mustered out with company Aug. 22, 1864.
Williams, Campbell	...do...	44	May 2, 1864	100 dys.	
Woodard, David H.	...do...	20	May 2, 1864	100 dys.	Mustered out with company Aug. 22, 1864.

COMPANY I.

Mustered in May 10, 1864, at Zanesville, O., by H. E. Hasen, 2d Lieutenant 8th Infantry, U. S. A. Mustered out Aug. 22, 1864, at Zanesville, O., by J. S. Small, 2d Lieutenant 1st U. S. Cavalry.

Names.	Rank.	Age.	Date of Entering the Service.	Period of Service.	Remarks.
Elliott Griffith	Captain.	32	May 2, 1864	100 dys.	Mustered out with company Aug. 22, 1864.
Jasper J. Barnet	1st Lieut.	32	May 2, 1864	100 dys.	Mustered out with company Aug. 22, 1864.
Thomas Griffith	2d Lieut.	26	May 2, 1864	100 dys.	Mustered out with company Aug. 22, 1864.
George W. Ashbrook	1st Sergt.	28	May 2, 1864	100 dys.	Mustered out with company Aug. 22, 1864.
Henry Conrad	Sergeant.	22	May 2, 1864	100 dys.	Mustered out with company Aug. 22, 1864.
Jeremiah Williams	...do...	28	May 2, 1864	100 dys.	Mustered out with company Aug. 22, 1864.
Wesley Lawrence	...do...	27	May 2, 1864	100 dys.	Mustered out with company Aug. 22, 1864.
Daniel L. Conrad	...do...	21	May 2, 1864	100 dys.	Mustered out with company Aug. 22, 1864.
Zeno Glick	Corporal.	22	May 2, 1864	100 dys.	Mustered out with company Aug. 22, 1864.
Henry Pontius	...do...	32	May 2, 1864	100 dys.	Mustered out with company Aug. 22, 1864.
Levy Lutz	...do...	33	May 2, 1864	100 dys.	Mustered out with company Aug. 22, 1864.
Joseph Bachtel	...do...	34	May 2, 1864	100 dys.	Mustered out with company Aug. 22, 1864.
Jacob Ernst	...do...	38	May 2, 1864	100 dys.	Mustered out with company Aug. 22, 1864.
David Bogle	...do...	38	May 2, 1864	100 dys.	Mustered out with company Aug. 22, 1864.
Thomas J. Swope	...do...	25	May 2, 1864	100 dys.	Mustered out with company Aug. 22, 1864.
James Ingman	...do...	34	May 2, 1864	100 dys.	Mustered out with company Aug. 22, 1864.
William Stine	Musician	29	May 2, 1864	100 dys.	Mustered out with company Aug. 22, 1864.
Daniel Stine	...do...	31	May 2, 1864	100 dys.	Mustered out with company Aug. 22, 1864.
Allen, Jesse	Private.	25	May 2, 1864	100 dys.	Mustered out with company Aug. 22, 1864.
Ashbrook, Benjamin F.	...do...	26	May 2, 1864	100 dys.	Mustered out with company Aug. 22, 1864.

Names.	Rank.	Age.	Date of Entering the Service.	Period of Service.	Remarks.
Ashbrook, James R.	Private.	21	May 2, 1864	100 dys.	Mustered out with company Aug. 22, 1864.
Barnett, Lewis	do.	23	May 2, 1864	100 dys.	Mustered out with company Aug. 22, 1864.
Barnett, Robert	do.	26	May 2, 1864	100 dys.	Mustered out with company Aug. 22, 1864.
Bradagan, Nathan	do.	41	May 2, 1864	100 dys.	Mustered out with company Aug. 22, 1864.
Bussard, Salem	do.	28	May 2, 1864	100 dys.	Mustered out with company Aug. 22, 1864.
Carpenter, David	do.	32	May 2, 1864	100 dys.	Mustered out with company Aug. 22, 1864.
Chatman, Wells W	do.	37	May 2, 1864	100 dys.	Mustered out with company Aug. 22, 1864.
Christy, Samuel F	do.	25	May 2, 1864	100 dys.	Mustered out with company Aug. 22, 1864.
Clark, Jefferson L	do.	28	May 2, 1864	100 dys.	Mustered out with company Aug. 22, 1864.
Cole, Joseph R	do.	21	May 2, 1864	100 dys.	Mustered out with company Aug. 22, 1864.
Conrad, John L	do.	25	May 2, 1864	100 dys.	Mustered out with company Aug. 22, 1864.
Conrad, Jonas	do.	33	May 2, 1864	100 dys.	Mustered out with company A 22, 1864.
Conrad, Martin D	do.	19	May 2, 1864	100 dys.	Mustered out with company Aug. 22, 1864.
Conrad, William L	do.	37	May 2, 1864	100 dys.	Mustered out with company Aug. 22, 1864.
Cross, Abraham	do.	20	May 2, 1864	100 dys.	Mustered out with company Aug. 22, 1864.
Cross, Edward	do.	31	May 2, 1864	100 dys.	Mustered out with company Aug. 22, 1864.
Dorring, John	do.	27	May 2, 1864	100 dys.	Mustered out with company Aug. 22, 1864.
Fisher, William	do.	39	May 2, 1864	100 dys.	Mustered out with company Aug. 22, 1864.
Fleming, John W	do.	23	May 2, 1864	100 dys.	Mustered out with company Aug. 22, 1864.
Frizzie, Samuel	do.	39	May 2, 1864	100 dys.	Mustered out with company Aug. 22, 1864.
Gift, Charles W	do.	25	May 2, 1864	100 dys.	Mustered out with company Aug. 22, 1864.
Griner, William	do.	20	May 2, 1864	100 dys.	Mustered out with company Aug. 22, 1864.
Haines, Michael H	do.	29	May 2, 1864	100 dys.	Mustered out with company Aug. 22, 1864.
Hanaway, Francis M	do.	30	May 2, 1864	100 dys.	Mustered out with company Aug. 22, 1864.
Heckman, John	do.	31	May 2, 1864	100 dys.	Mustered out with company Aug. 22, 1864.
Hedges, Jonas	do.	34	May 2, 1864	100 dys.	Mustered out with company Aug. 22, 1864.
Holtzman, William R	do.	27	May 2, 1864	100 dys.	Mustered out with company Aug. 22, 1864.
House, Ezra	do.	26	May 2, 1864	100 dys.	Mustered out with company Aug. 22, 1864.
House, William	do.	28	May 2, 1864	100 dys.	Mustered out with company Aug. 22, 1864.
Huffman, Jacob A	do.	30	May 2, 1864	100 dys.	Mustered out with company Aug. 22, 1864.
Hunter, Solomon	do.	27	May 2, 1864	100 dys.	Mustered out with company Aug. 22, 1864.
Jackson, Larkin F	do.	30	May 2, 1864	100 dys.	Mustered out with company Aug. 22, 1864.
Kunkle, Lawrence	do.	18	May 2, 1864	100 dys.	Mustered out with company Aug. 22, 1864.
Lawrence, James	do.	21	May 2, 1864	100 dys.	Mustered out with company Aug. 22, 1864.
Lytle, James	do.	23	May 2, 1864	100 dys.	Mustered out with company Aug. 22, 1864.
McCabe, John	do.	37	May 2, 1864	100 dys.	Mustered out with company Aug. 22, 1864.
McChristian, Edward	do.	18	May 2, 1864	100 dys.	Mustered out with company Aug. 22, 1864.
Markle, George S	do.	18	May 2, 1864	100 dys.	Mustered out with company Aug. 22, 1864.
Markle, James W	do.	32	May 2, 1864	100 dys.	Mustered out with company Aug. 22, 1864.
Marsvy, John	do.	36	May 2, 1864	100 dys.	Mustered out with company Aug. 22, 1864.
Marsvy, William	do.	38	May 2, 1864	100 dys.	Mustered out with company Aug. 22, 1864.
Markwood, Jacob	do.	18	May 2, 1864	100 dys.	Mustered out with company Aug. 22, 1864.
Markwood, James W	do.	18	May 2, 1864	100 dys.	Mustered out with company Aug. 22, 1864.
Moore, Jeremiah	do.	37	May 2, 1864	100 dys.	Mustered out with company Aug. 22, 1864.
Murphy, Henry	do.	19	May 2, 1864	100 dys.	Mustered out with company Aug. 22, 1864.
Murry, Lewis	do.	24	May 2, 1864	100 dys.	Mustered out with company Aug. 22, 1864.
Reber, Thornton	do.	22	May 2, 1864	100 dys.	Mustered out with company Aug. 22, 1864.
Rice, Aquilla	do.	21	May 2, 1864	100 dys.	Mustered out with company Aug. 22, 1864.
Rockey, Scott	do.	34	May 2, 1864	100 dys.	Mustered out with company Aug. 22, 1864.
Shupe, Ferdinand	do.	18	May 2, 1864	100 dys.	Mustered out with company Aug. 22, 1864.
Sidner, Frederick	do.	36	May 2, 1864	100 dys.	Mustered out with company Aug. 22, 1864.
Smith Peter	do.	23	May 2, 1864	100 dys.	Mustered out with company Aug. 22, 1864.
Swope, Abner R	do.	23	May 2, 1864	100 dys.	Mustered out with company Aug. 22, 1864.
Tartman Joshua	do.	33	May 2, 1864	100 dys.	Mustered out with company Aug. 22, 1864.
Valentine, Levi	do.	23	May 2, 1864	100 dys.	Mustered out with company Aug. 22, 1864.
Valentine, Nash, Jr	do.	32	May 2, 1864	100 dys.	Mustered out with company Aug. 22, 1864.
Valentine, Wesley	do.	28	May 2, 1864	100 dys.	Mustered out with company Aug. 22, 1864.
Walter Samu	do.	18	May 2, 1864	100 dys.	Mustered out with company Aug. 22, 1864.
Welsh, Silas	do.	18	May 2, 1864	100 dys.	Mustered out with company Aug. 22, 1864.
Welty, Joseph	do.	28	May 2, 1864	100 dys.	Mustered out with company Aug. 22, 1864.
White, William H	do.	18	May 2, 1864	100 dys.	Mustered out with company Aug. 22, 1864.
Williams, Charles W	do.	19	May 2, 1864	100 dys.	Mustered out with company Aug. 22, 1864.
Wolf, William A	do.	24	May 2, 1864	100 dys.	Mustered out witd company Aug. 22, 1864.
Young, William	do.	24	May 2, 1864	100 dys.	Mustered out with company Aug. 22, 1864.

Names.	Rank.	Age.	Date of Entering the Service.	Period of Service.	Remarks.
Swingle, Franklin	Private	32	May 2, 1864	100 dys.	Mustered out with company Aug. 22, 1864.
Swingle, Isaac C	do	22	May 2, 1864	100 dys.	Mustered out with company Aug. 22, 1864.
Stultz, Nathaniel	do	34	May 2, 1864	100 dys.	Mustered out with company Aug. 22, 1864.
Tompson, Samuel	do	36	May 2, 1864	100 dys.	Mustered out with company Aug. 22, 1864.
Troyman, William	do	44	May 2, 1864	100 dys.	Mustered out with company Aug. 22, 1864.
Turner, George	do	20	May 2, 1864	100 dys.	Mustered out with company Aug. 22, 1864.
White, Alexander	do	43	May 2, 1864	100 dys.	Mustered out with company Aug. 22, 1864.
Willison, Jasper	do	34	May 2, 1864	100 dys.	Mustered out with company Aug. 22, 1864.
Wilson, Alexander	do	43	May 2, 1864	100 dys.	Mustered out with company Aug. 22, 1864.
Wilson, Zeddoc	do	18	May 2, 1864	100 dys.	Mustered out with company Aug. 22, 1864.

160th Regiment Ohio Volunteer Infantry.

ONE HUNDRED DAYS' SERVICE.

THIS Regiment was organized at Zanesville, O., May 12, 13, and 14, 1864, to › one hundred days. It was composed of the Fifty-third Battalion, Ohio onal Guard, from Perry County; Ninety-first Battalion, Ohio National -d, from Muskingum County; a part of the Fortieth Battalion, Ohio onal Guard, from Brown County; and a part of the Seventy-third Bat- n, Ohio National Guard, from Fairfield County. The Regiment was ediately placed *en-route* to Harper's Ferry. Its first duty was to guard pply train to Martinsburg. On its return it was placed in the First ade, First Division, of General Hunter's Army, and on the morning of 25th of May moved with it to Woodstock, W. Va. It then marched with ral Hunter toward the front, but was again detached and sent back to .insburg in charge of a supply train. Reaching the vicinity of Middle- ι the Regiment was engaged in a skirmish with Moseby's Guerrillas. a this time until the muster-out of the Regiment it was subjected to st continual marching and counter-marching through the Shenandoah ey, during which time the Regiment was engaged in a number of skir- ιes. On the 25th of August the Regiment started for Ohio, and arrived anesville on the 29th. It was mustered out September 7, 1864, on expi- n of its term of service.

Rank.	Age.	Date of Entering the Service.	Period of Service.	Remarks.
Private	26	May 2, 1864	100 dys.	Mustered out with company Sept. 7, 1864.
....do....	34	May 2, 1864	100 dys.	Mustered out with company Sept. 7, 1864.
....do....	24	May 2, 1864	100 dys.	Mustered out with company Sept. 7, 1864.
....do....	20	May 2, 1864	100 dys.	Mustered out with company Sept. 7, 1864.
....do....	18	May 2, 1864	100 dys.	Mustered out with company Sept. 7, 1864.
....do....	44	May 2, 1864	100 dys.	Mustered out with company Sept. 7, 1864.
....do....	19	May 2, 1864	100 dys.	Mustered out with company Sept. 7, 1864.
....do....	23	May 2, 1864	100 dys.	Mustered out with company Sept. 7, 1864.
....do....	20	May 2, 1864	100 dys.	Mustered out with company Sept. 7, 1864.
....do....	18	May 2, 1864	100 dys.	Mustered out with company Sept. 7, 1864.
....do....	31	May 2, 1864	100 dys.	Mustered out with company Sept. 7, 1864.
....do....	19	May 2, 1864	100 dys.	Mustered out with company Sept. 7, 1864.
....do....	18	May 2, 1864	100 dys.	Mustered out with company Sept. 7, 1864.
....do....	38	May 2, 1864	100 dys.	Mustered out with company Sept. 7, 1864.
....do....	39	May 2, 1864	100 dys.	Mustered out with company Sept. 7, 1864.
....do....	40	May 2, 1864	100 dys.	Mustered out with company Sept. 7, 1864.
....do....	18	May 2, 1864	100 dys.	Mustered out with company Sept. 7, 1864.
....do....	19	May 2, 1864	100 dys.	Mustered out with company Sept. 7, 1864.
....do....	20	May 2, 1864	100 dys.	Mustered out with company Sept. 7, 1864.
....do....	19	May 2, 1864	100 dys.	Mustered out with company Sept. 7, 1864.
....do....	35	May 2, 1864	100 dys.	Mustered out with company Sept. 7, 1864.
....do....	38	May 2, 1864	100 dys.	Mustered out with company Sept. 7, 1864.
....do....	34	May 2, 1864	100 dys.	Mustered out with company Sept. 7, 1864.
....do....	39	May 2, 1864	100 dys.	Mustered out with company Sept. 7, 1864.
....do....	40	May 2, 1864	100 dys.	Mustered out with company Sept. 7, 1864.
....do....	41	May 2, 1864	100 dys.	Mustered out with company Sept. 7, 1864.
....do....	22	May 2, 1864	100 dys.	Mustered out with company Sept. 7, 1864.
....do....	26	May 2, 1864	100 dys.	Mustered out with company Sept. 7, 1864.
....do....	22	May 2, 1864	100 dys.	Mustered out with company Sept. 7, 1864.
....do....	18	May 2, 1864	100 dys.	Mustered out with company Sept. 7, 1864.
....do....	33	May 2, 1864	100 dys.	Mustered out with company Sept. 7, 1864.
....do....	30	May 2, 1864	100 dys.	Mustered out with company Sept. 7, 1864.
....do....	42	May 2, 1864	100 dys.	Mustered out with company Sept. 7, 1864.
....do....	18	May 2, 1864	100 dys.	Mustered out with company Sept. 7, 1864.
....do....	19	May 2, 1864	100 dys.	Mustered out with company Sept. 7, 1864.
....do....	18	May 2, 1864	100 dys.	Mustered out with company Sept. 7, 1864.
....do....	27	May 2, 1864	100 dys.	Mustered out with company Sept. 7, 1864.
....do....	18	May 2, 1864	100 dys.	Mustered out with company Sept. 7, 1864.
....do....	27	May 2, 1864	100 dys.	Mustered out with company Sept. 7, 1864.
....do....	20	May 2, 1864	100 dys.	Mustered out with company Sept. 7, 1864.
....do....	32	May 2, 1864	100 dys.	Mustered out with company Sept. 7, 1864.
....do....	33	May 2, 1864	100 dys.	Mustered out with company Sept. 7, 1864.
....do....	21	May 2, 1864	100 dys.	Mustered out with company Sept. 7, 1864.
....do....	26	May 2, 1864	100 dys.	Mustered out with company Sept. 7, 1864.
....do....	25	May 2, 1864	100 dys.	Mustered out with company Sept. 7, 1864.
....do....	32	May 2, 1864	100 dys.	Mustered out with company Sept. 7, 1864.
....do....	42	May 2, 1864	100 dys.	Mustered out with company Sept. 7, 1864.
....do....	18	May 2, 1864	100 dys.	Mustered out with company Sept. 7, 1864.
....do....	20	May 2, 1864	100 dys.	Mustered out with company Sept. 7, 1864.
....do....	31	May 2, 1864	100 dys.	Mustered out with company Sept. 7, 1864.
....do....	19	May 2, 1864	100 dys.	Mustered out with company Sept. 7, 1864.
....do....	43	May 2, 1864	100 dys.	Mustered out with company Sept. 7, 1864.
....do....	30	May 2, 1864	100 dys.	Mustered out with company Sept. 7, 1864.
....do....	27	May 2, 1864	100 dys.	Mustered out with company Sept. 7, 1864.
....do....	24	May 2, 1864	100 dys.	Mustered out with company Sept. 7, 1864.
....do....	29	May 2, 1864	100 dys.	Mustered out with company Sept. 7, 1864.
....do....	41	May 2, 1864	100 dys.	Mustered out with company Sept. 7, 1864.
....do....	41	May 2, 1864	100 dys.	Mustered out with company Sept. 7, 1864.
....do....	26	May 2, 1864	100 dys.	Mustered out with company Sept. 7, 1864.
....do....	30	May 2, 1864	100 dys.	Mustered out with company Sept. 7, 1864.
....do....	39	May 2, 1864	100 dys.	Mustered out with company Sept. 7, 1864.
....do....	22	May 2, 1864	100 dys.	Mustered out with company Sept. 7, 1864.
....do....	21	May 2, 1864	100 dys.	Mustered out with company Sept. 7, 1864.
....do....	27	May 2, 1864	100 dys.	Mustered out with company Sept. 7, 1864.
....do....	18	May 2, 1864	100 dys.	Mustered out with company Sept. 7, 1864.

COMPANY C

[illegible]

Names.	Rank.	Age.	Date of Entering the Service.	Period of Service.	Remarks.
[illegible], Daniel	Private	24	May 2, 1864	100 dys.	Mustered out with company Sept. 7, 1864.
[illegible], Carl	do	44	May 2, 1864	100 dys.	Mustered out with company Sept. 7, 1864.
[illegible], John	do	19	May 2, 1864	100 dys.	Mustered out with company Sept. 7, 1864.
[illegible], Orin	do	18	May 2, 1864	100 dys.	Mustered out with company Sept. 7, 1864.
[illegible], James W	do	20	May 2, 1864	100 dys.	Mustered out with company Sept. 7, 1864.
[illegible], John B.	do	18	May 2, 1864	100 dys.	Mustered out with company Sept. 7, 1864.
[illegible], George	do	22	May 2, 1864	100 dys.	Mustered out with company Sept. 7, 1864.
[illegible], Henry C.	do	[illegible]	May 2, 1864	100 dys.	Mustered out with company Sept. 7, 1864.
[illegible], [illegible] J	do	19	May 2, 1864	100 dys.	Mustered out with company Sept. 7, 1864.
[illegible]	do	18	May 2, 1864	100 dys.	Mustered out with company Sept. 7, 1864.
[illegible], William B	do	29	May 2, 1864	100 dys.	Mustered out with company Sept. 7, 1864.
[illegible], Jacob A.	do	35	May 2, 1864	100 dys.	Mustered out with company Sept. 7, 1864.
[illegible], William	do	29	May 2, 1864	100 dys.	Mustered out with company Sept. 7, 1864.
[illegible], Washington	do	[illegible]	May 2, 1864	100 dys.	Mustered out with company Sept. 7, 1864.
[illegible], David H	do	25	May 2, 1864	100 dys.	Mustered out with company Sept. 7, 1864.
[illegible], Isaac N.	do	18	May 2, 1864	100 dys.	Died July 31, 1864, at Frederick, Md.
[illegible], John J	do	25	May 2, 1864	100 dys.	Killed July 4, 1864, on march between Sharpsburg and Sandy Hook, Md., by accidental discharge of his gun.
[illegible], Isaac N.	do	19	May 2, 1864	100 dys.	Mustered out with company Sept. 7, 1864.
[illegible], Adam C	do	20	May 2, 1864	100 dys.	Mustered out with company Sept. 7, 1864.
[illegible], Jacob L	do	21	May 2, 1864	100 dys.	Mustered out with company Sept. 7, 1864.
[illegible], Solomon D.	do	31	May 2, 1864	100 dys.	Mustered out with company Sept. 7, 1864.
[illegible], George	do	30	May 2, 1864	100 dys.	Mustered out with company Sept. 7, 1864.
[illegible], Jacob T.	do	18	May 2, 1864	100 dys.	Mustered out with company Sept. 7, 1864.
[illegible], Clinton C	do	22	May 2, 1864	100 dys.	Mustered out with company Sept. 7, 1864.
Taylor, John C.	do	27	May 2, 1864	100 dys.	Mustered out with company Sept. 7, 1864.
[illegible], George	do	27	May 2, 1864	100 dys.	Mustered out with company Sept. 7, 1864.
[illegible], Oliver M.	do	22	May 2, 1864	100 dys.	Mustered out with company Sept. 7, 1864.
[illegible], Jacob	do	[illegible]	May 2, 1864	100 dys.	Mustered out with company Sept. 7, 1864.
[illegible], John	do	19	May 2, 1864	100 dys.	Mustered out with company Sept. 7, 1864.
[illegible], Thomas V	do	27	May 2, 1864	100 dys.	Mustered out with company Sept. 7, 1864.
[illegible], William	do	29	May 2, 1864	100 dys.	Mustered out with company Sept. 7, 1864.
[illegible], Franklin	do	18	May 2, 1864	100 dys.	Mustered out with company Sept. 7, 1864.
Williams, Harrison H	do	22	May 2, 1864	100 dys.	Mustered out with company Sept. 7, 1864.
[illegible], Armstead M	do	18	May 2, 1864	100 dys.	Mustered out with company Sept. 7, 1864.
[illegible], Michael	do	28	May 2, 1864	100 dys.	Mustered out with company Sept. 7, 1864.

COMPANY F.

Mustered in May 12, 1864, at Zanesville, O., by H. B. Hazen, 2d Lieutenant 8th Infantry, U. S. A. Mustered out Sept. 7, 1864, at Zanesville, O., by J. P. Small, 2d Lieutenant 1st Cavalry, U. S. A.

Names.	Rank.	Age.	Date of Entering the Service.	Period of Service.	Remarks.
[illegible] O. Fowler	Captain		May 2, 1864	100 dys.	Mustered out with company Sept. 7, 1864.
[illegible] M. Wright	1st Lieut.		May 2, 1864	100 dys.	Mustered out with company Sept. 7, 1864.
[illegible]	2d Lieut.		May 2, 1864	100 dys.	Mustered out with company Sept. 7, 1864.
[illegible]	1st Sergt.		May 2, 1864	100 dys.	Mustered out with company Sept. 7, 1864.
[illegible] W. [illegible]low	Sergeant		May 2, 1864	100 dys.	Captured Aug. 5, 1864, at Brown's Crossing, Va.; died Feb. 1, 1865, in Rebel Prison at Richmond, Va.
George Conwell	do		May 2, 1864	100 dys.	Mustered out with company Sept. 7, 1864.
Samuel Diller	do		May 2, 1864	100 dys.	Mustered out with company Sept. 7, 1864.
Andrew J. Wright	do		May 2, 1864	100 dys.	Died Aug. 18, 1864, at Maryland Heights, Md.
George L. Hays	Corporal.		May 2, 1864	100 dys.	Mustered out with company Sept. 7, 1864.
Samuel Puterbaugh	do		May 2, 1864	100 dys.	Mustered out with company Sept. 7, 1864.
Franklin McKeever	do		May 2, 1864	100 dys.	Mustered out with company Sept. 7, 1864.
James Ashbaugh	do		May 2, 1864	100 dys.	Mustered out with company Sept. 7, 1864.
Isaac Kennard	do		May 2, 1864	100 dys.	Mustered out with company Sept. 7, 1864.
Jacob Carey	do		May 2, 1864	100 dys.	Mustered out with company Sept. 7, 1864.
William Wilson	do		May 2, 1864	100 dys.	Mustered out with company Sept. 7, 1864.
Samuel Zarley	do		May 2, 1864	100 dys.	Mustered out with company Sept. 7, 1864.
John Vanroye	Musician		May 2, 1864	100 dys.	Mustered out with company Sept. 7, 1864.
David U. Alwine	do		May 2, 1864	100 dys.	Mustered out with company Sept. 7, 1864.
Adams, Charles	Private.		May 2, 1864	100 dys.	Mustered out with company Sept. 7, 1864.
Adams, Joseph	do		May 2, 1864	dys.	Mustered out with company Sept. 7, 1864.
Adcock, George W	do		May 2, 1864	dys.	Mustered out with company Sept. 7, 1864.
Baily, William A	do		May 2, 1864	dys.	Mustered out with company Sept. 7, 1864.
Barns, Arza	do		May 2, 1864	100 dys.	Mustered out with company Sept. 7, 1864.
Barns, James	do		May 2, 1864	100 dys.	Mustered out with company Sept. 7, 1864.
Barns, John	do		May 2, 1864	100 dys.	Mustered out with company Sept. 7, 1864.
Beery, David	do		May 2, 1864	100 dys.	Discharged May 12, 1864.
Beery, Jacob	do		May 2, 1864	100 dys.	Mustered out with company Sept. 7, 1864.
Blair, Austin	do		May 2, 1864	100 dys.	Mustered out with company Sept. 7, 1864.
Blair, Seldon W	do		May 2, 1864	100 dys.	Mustered out with company Sept. 7, 1864.
Brooks, Jonathan	do		May 2, 1864	100 dys.	Mustered out with company Sept. 7, 1864.
Chappellaer, John W	do		May 2, 1864	100 dys.	Mustered out with company Sept. 7, 1864.
Colborn, Alfred	do		May 2, 1864	100 dys.	Mustered out with company Sept. 7, 1864.
Conwell, Charles	do		May 2, 1864	100 dys.	Mustered out with company Sept. 7, 1864.
Conrad, Christopher	do		May 2, 1861	100 dys.	Mustered out with company Sept. 7, 1864.
Daniher, William A	do		May 2, 1864	100 dys.	Discharged May 12, 1864.

COMPANY C.

Mustered in May 12, 1864, at Zanesville, O., by H. E. Hazen, 2d Lieutenant 8th Infantry, U. S. A. Mustered out Sept. 7, 1864, at Zanesville, O., by J. F. Small, 2d Lieutenant 1st Cavalry, U. S. A.

Names.	Rank.	Age.	Date of Entering the Service.	Period of Service	Remarks.
William H. Spencer	Captain.	33	May 2, 1864	100 dys.	Mustered out with company Sept. 7, 1864.
Levi Bowman	1st Lieut.	27	May 2, 1864	100 dys.	Mustered out with company Sept. 7, 1864.
Andrew Whips	2d Lieut.	25	May 2, 1864	100 dys.	Mustered out with company Sept. 7, 1864.
John Middagh	1st Sergt.	41	May 2, 1864	100 dys.	Mustered out with company Sept. 7, 1864.
Asbury Elder	Sergeant.	37	May 2, 1864	100 dys.	Mustered out with company Sept. 7, 1864.
Henry H. Heck	do.	27	May 2, 1864	100 dys.	Mustered out with company Sept. 7, 1864.
William M. Ream	do.	29	May 2, 1864	100 dys.	Mustered out with company Sept. 7, 1864.
John Petty	do.	28	May 2, 1864	100 dys.	Mustered out with company Sept. 7, 1864.
Josiah Petty	Corporal.	30	May 2, 1864	100 dys.	Wounded July 7, 1864, in battle of Maryland Heights, Md.; mustered out with company Sept. 7, 1864.
David Brookhart	do.	44	May 2, 1864	100 dys.	Mustered out with company Sept. 7, 1864.
George Caywood	do.	23	May 2, 1864	100 dys.	Mustered out with company Sept. 7, 1864.
Ezra Thomas	do.	25	May 2, 1864	100 dys.	Mustered out with company Sept. 7, 1864.
Elias Vannatta	do.	26	May 2, 1864	100 dys.	Mustered out with company Sept. 7, 1864.
John W. Westall	do.	31	May 2, 1864	100 dys.	Mustered out with company Sept. 7, 1864.
Daniel Griggs	do.	42	May 2, 1864	100 dys.	Mustered out with company Sept. 7, 1864.
Isaac Haine	do.	24	May 2, 1864	100 dys.	Mustered out with company Sept. 7, 1864.
James W. Dollison	Musician	31	May 2, 1864	100 dys.	Mustered out with company Sept. 7, 1864.
Anderson, Samuel	Private.	41	May 2, 1864	100 dys.	Died Aug. 28, 1864, at Crestline, O.
Angle, George	do.	18	May 2, 1864	100 dys.	Mustered out with company Sept. 7, 1864.
Auspach, Adam	do.	37	May 2, 1864	100 dys.	Mustered out with company Sept. 7, 1864.
Auspach, Jonathan	do.	36	May 2, 1864	100 dys.	Mustered out with company Sept. 7, 1864.
Barnes, Jacob	do.	18	May 2, 1864	100 dys.	Mustered out with company Sept. 7, 1864.
Bowman, Amos	do.	18	May 2, 1864	100 dys.	Mustered out with company Sept. 7, 1864.
Brehm, Joel	do.	30	May 2, 1864	100 dys.	Mustered out with company Sept. 7, 1864.
Brehm, Joseph	do.	23	May 2, 1864	100 dys.	Mustered out with company Sept. 7, 1864.
Brehm, Samuel	do.	31	May 2, 1864	100 dys.	Mustered out with company Sept. 7, 1864.
Burton, David S.	do.	28	May 2, 1864	100 dys.	Mustered out with company Sept. 7, 1864.
Combs, John	do.	20	May 2, 1864	100 dys.	Mustered out with company Sept. 7, 1864.
Dickson, James H.	do.	31	May 2, 1864	100 dys.	Promoted to Principal Musician May 13, 1864; returned to company —; mustered out with company Sept. 7, 1864.
Dickson, Samuel A.	do.	34	May 2, 1864	100 dys.	Mustered out with company Sept. 7, 1864.
Eidet, Charles	do.	23	May 2, 1864	100 dys.	Mustered out with company Sept. 7, 1864.
Elder, Levi	do.	39	May 2, 1864	100 dys.	Mustered out with company Sept. 7, 1864.
Elder, Simeon	do.	28	May 2, 1864	100 dys.	Mustered out with company Sept. 7, 1864.
Fink, Thomas J.	do.	20	May 2, 1864	100 dys.	Mustered out with company Sept. 7, 1864.
Fisher, George	do.	34	May 2, 1864	100 dys.	Mustered out with company Sept. 7, 1864.
Folk, Daniel	do.	26	May 2, 1864	100 dys.	Mustered out with company Sept. 7, 1864.
Folk, Joshua	do.	27	May 2, 1864	100 dys.	Mustered out with company Sept. 7, 1864.
Forsythe, John	do.	28	May 2, 1864	100 dys.	Mustered out with company Sept. 7, 1864.
Forsythe, William	do.	24	May 2, 1864	100 dys.	Mustered out with company Sept. 7, 1864.
Furgeson, Judson	do.	18	May 2, 1864	100 dys.	Mustered out with company Sept. 7, 1864.
Goble, Jeremiah	do.	28	May 2, 1864	100 dys.	Mustered out with company Sept. 7, 1864.
Griggs, Adam	do.	37	May 2, 1864	100 dys.	Mustered out with company Sept. 7, 1864.
Griggs, George H.	do.	22	May 2, 1864	100 dys.	Mustered out with company Sept. 7, 1864.
Griggs, Levi D.	do.	18	May 2, 1864	100 dys.	Mustered out with company Sept. 7, 1864.
Griggs, Levi	do.	38	May 2, 1864	100 dys.	Mustered out with company Sept. 7, 1864.
Griggs, William	do.	24	May 2, 1864	100 dys.	Mustered out with company Sept. 7, 1864.
Gorton, John	do.	23	May 2, 1864	100 dys.	Mustered out with company Sept. 7, 1864.
Haines, John W.	do.	21	May 2, 1864	100 dys.	Mustered out with company Sept. 7, 1864.
H[illegible], William H.	do.	29	May 2, 1864	100 dys.	Mustered out with company Sept. 7, 1864.
Hodge, Andrew V.	do.	31	May 2, 1864	100 dys.	Mustered out with company Sept. 7, 1864.
Householder, John	do.	18	May 2, 1864	100 dys.	Mustered out with company Sept. 7, 1864.
Householder, Thomas L.	do.	21	May 2, 1864	100 dys.	Mustered out with company Sept. 7, 1864.
Johnson, Jacob R.	do.	31	May 2, 1864	100 dys.	Mustered out with company Sept. 7, [illegible]
Kingler, David	do.	28	May 2, 1864	100 dys.	Mustered out with company Sept. 7
Kingler, George W.	do.	21	May 2, 1864	100 dys.	Mustered out with company Sept.
Klinger, Joseph	do.	40	May 2, 1864	100 dys.	Mustered out with company Sep[illegible]
Leach, Andrew B.	do.	28	May 2, 1864	100 dys.	Mustered out with company Se[illegible]
Leckrone, James	do.	33	May 2, 1864	100 dys.	Mustered out with company Se[illegible]
Lehman, Adam	do.	18	May 2, 1864	100 dys.	Mustered out with company Se[illegible]
Lehman, Louis B.	do.	42	May 2, 1864	100 dys.	Mustered out with company [illegible]
Loveberry, George W.	do.	26	May 2, 1864	100 dys.	Mustered out with company [illegible]
Maffit, James A.	do.	22	May 2, 1864	100 dys.	Mustered out with company [illegible]
McPitt, William T.	do.	33	May 2, 1864	100 dys.	Mustered out with company [illegible]
Middagh, David	do.	40	May 2, 1864	100 dys.	Mustered out with company [illegible]
Miller, John L.	do.	23	May 2, 1864	100 dys.	Mustered out with company [illegible]
Moldet, Owen T.	do.	28	May 2, 1864	100 dys.	Mustered out with compa[illegible]
[illegible], Arthur	do.	21	May 2, 1864	100 dys.	Mustered out with compa[illegible]
[illegible], Benoni F.	do.	37	May 2, 1864	100 dys.	Mustered out with compa[illegible]
[illegible], James C.	do.	18	May 2, 1864	100 dys.	Mustered out with compa[illegible]
[illegible], Peter	do.	42	May 2, 1864	100 dys.	Mustered out with comp[illegible]
[illegible], William	do.	24	May 2, 1864	100 dys.	Mustered out with com[illegible]
[illegible], Samuel	do.	27	May 2, 1864	100 dys.	Mustered out with com[illegible]
Spatzer, Samuel	do.	27	May 2, 1864	100 dys.	Mustered out with com[illegible]

Names.	Rank.	Age.	Date of Entering the Service.	Period of Service.	Remarks.
Ritter, John H	Private	23	May 2, 1864	100 dys.	Mustered out with company Sept. 7, 1864.
Scott, John B	...do...	28	May 2, 1864	100 dys.	Mustered out with company Sept. 7, 1864.
Scott, James M	...do...	38	May 2, 1864	100 dys.	Mustered out with company Sept. 7, 1864.
Scott, Robert H	...do...	18	May 2, 1864	100 dys.	Mustered out with company Sept. 7, 1864.
Shaw, Thomas F	...do...	22	May 2, 1864	100 dys.	Mustered out with company Sept. 7, 1864.
Simpson, Jacob	...do...	42	May 2, 1864	100 dys.	Mustered out with company Sept. 7, 1864.
Smith, James McC	...do...	32	May 2, 1864	100 dys.	Mustered out with company Sept. 7, 1864.
Smith, William C	...do...	21	May 2, 1864	100 dys.	Mustered out with company Sept. 7, 1864.
Spitler, Simon P	...do...	31	May 2, 1864	100 dys.	Mustered out with company Sept. 7, 1864.
Starrett, Austin J	...do...	30	May 2, 1864	100 dys.	Mustered out with company Sept. 7, 1864.
Stonder, Joseph	...do...	34	May 2, 1864	100 dys.	Mustered out with company Sept. 7, 1864.
Thompson, David G	...do...	41	May 2, 1864	100 dys.	Mustered out with company Sept. 7, 1864.
Trace, Daniel	...do...	24	May 2, 1864	100 dys.	Mustered out with company Sept. 7, 1864.
Vickers, Thomas	...do...	40	May 2, 1864	100 dys.	Mustered out with company Sept. 7, 1864.
White, Benjamin B	...do...	35	May 2, 1864	100 dys.	Mustered out with company Sept. 7, 1864.
White, Joseph	...do...	21	May 2, 1864	100 dys.	Mustered out with company Sept. 7, 1864.
Wilson, James	...do...	26	May 2, 1864	100 dys.	Mustered out with company Sept. 7, 1864.
Wilson, Thomas H	...do...	19	May 2, 1864	100 dys.	Mustered out with company Sept. 7, 1864.
Wortman, Samuel	...do...	40	May 2, 1864	100 dys.	Mustered out with company Sept. 7, 1864.
Wylie, William	...do...	18	May 2, 1864	100 dys.	Mustered out with company Sept. 7, 1864.

COMPANY E.

Mustered in May 12, 1864, at Zanesville, O., by H. E. Hazen, 2d Lieutenant 8th Infantry, U. S. A. Mustered out Sept. 7, 1864, at Zanesville, O., by J. F. Small, 2d Lieutenant 1st Cavalry, U. S. A.

Names.	Rank.	Age.	Date of Entering the Service.	Period of Service.	Remarks.
Simeon Siegfried, Jr	Captain.	36	May 2, 1864	100 dys.	Mustered out with company Sept. 7, 1864.
Solomon H. Shroyer	1st Lieut.	28	May 2, 1864	100 dys.	Mustered out with company Sept. 7, 1864.
John H. Smoots	2d Lieut.	33	May 2, 1864	100 dys.	Mustered out with company Sept. 7, 1864.
William B. Livingston	1st Sergt.	28	May 2, 1864	100 dys.	Mustered out with company Sept. 7, 1864.
William Armstrong	Sergeant.	44	May 2, 1864	100 dys.	Mustered out with company Sept. 7, 1864.
Samuel H. Honnold	...do...	30	May 2, 1864	100 dys.	Mustered out with company Sept. 7, 1864.
Nixon Stewart	...do...	21	May 2, 1864	100 dys.	Mustered out with company Sept. 7, 1864.
Barton Cone	...do...	39	May 2, 1864	100 dys.	Mustered out with company Sept. 7, 1864.
George Wagoner	Corporal.	38	May 2, 1864	100 dys.	Mustered out with company Sept. 7, 1864.
John Fitz	...do...	42	May 2, 1864	100 dys.	Mustered out with company Sept. 7, 1864.
Julius C. Taylor	...do...	36	May 2, 1864	100 dys.	Mustered out with company Sept. 7, 1864.
Oliver H. Ross	...do...	19	May 2, 1864	100 dys.	Mustered out with company Sept. 7, 1864.
James R. Shirer	...do...	40	May 2, 1864	100 dys.	Mustered out with company Sept. 7, 1864.
Joseph Brown	...do...	34	May 2, 1864	100 dys.	Mustered out with company Sept. 7, 1864.
Martin R. Palmer	...do...	28	May 2, 1864	100 dys.	Mustered out with company Sept. 7, 1864.
Samuel W. Sutton	...do...	19	May 2, 1864	100 dys.	Mustered out with company Sept. 7, 1864.
John V. Zimmer	Musician	19	May 2, 1864	100 dys.	Mustered out with company Sept. 7, 1864.
Aler, Christian F	Private	32	May 2, 1864	100 dys.	Mustered out with company Sept. 7, 1864.
Aler, Christopher F	...do...	24	May 2, 1864	100 dys.	Mustered out with company Sept. 7, 1864.
Armstrong, Alexander	...do...	36	May 2, 1864	100 dys.	Mustered out with company Sept. 7, 1864.
Bagen, William	...do...	26	May 2, 1864	100 dys.	Mustered out with company Sept. 7, 1864.
Baker, Samuel L	...do...	23	May 2, 1864	100 dys.	Mustered out with company Sept. 7, 1864.
Bell, William H	...do...	28	May 2, 1864	100 dys.	Mustered out with company Sept. 7, 1864.
Bell, Wilson S	...do...	25	May 2, 1864	100 dys.	Mustered out with company Sept. 7, 1864.
Bowden, Edwin	...do...	27	May 2, 1864	100 dys.	Mustered out with company Sept. 7, 1864.
Bowden, John	...do...	38	May 2, 1864	100 dys.	Mustered out with company Sept. 7, 1864.
Bowden, Timothy	...do...	23	May 2, 1864	100 dys.	Mustered out with company Sept. 7, 1864.
Bowden, William	...do...	21	May 2, 1864	100 dys.	Mustered out with company Sept. 7, 1864.
Bowman, William W	...do...	21	May 2, 1864	100 dys.	Mustered out with company Sept. 7, 1864.
Brock, Edwin	...do...	23	May 2, 1864	100 dys.	Mustered out with company Sept. 7, 1864.
Crane, Jacob H	...do...	28	May 2, 1864	100 dys.	Mustered out with company Sept. 7, 1864.
Dailey, Samuel H	...do...	37	May 2, 1864	100 dys.	Mustered out with company Sept. 7, 1864.
Davis, Benjamin F	...do...	22	May 2, 1864	100 dys.	Mustered out with company Sept. 7, 1864.
Edwards, William	...do...	24	May 2, 1864	100 dys.	Mustered out with company Sept. 7, 1864.
Ferris, Charles W	...do...	24	May 2, 1864	100 dys.	Mustered out with company Sept. 7, 1864.
Garrett, Andrew	...do...	30	May 2, 1864	100 dys.	Died Aug. 19, 1864, at Maryland Heights, Md.
Gardner, Henry	...do...	19	May 2, 1864	100 dys.	Mustered out with company Sept. 7, 1864.
Geyer, James W	...do...	30	May 2, 1864	100 dys.	Mustered out with company Sept. 7, 1864.
Geyer, Samuel H	...do...	34	May 2, 1864	100 dys.	Mustered out with company Sept. 7, 1864.
Hammond, Samuel S	...do...	36	May 2, 1864	100 dys.	Mustered out with company Sept. 7, 1864.
Hammond, John	...do...	20	May 2, 1864	100 dys.	Mustered out with company Sept. 7, 1864.
Hanks, Jacob H	...do...	20	May 2, 1864	100 dys.	Mustered out with company Sept. 7, 1864.
Hanks, Jeremiah J	...do...	40	May 2, 1864	100 dys.	Mustered out with company Sept. 7, 1864.
Hardy, Washington	...do...	28	May 2, 1864	100 dys.	Mustered out with company Sept. 7, 1864.
Hommond, George E	...do...	18	May 2, 1864	100 dys.	Mustered out with company Sept. 7, 1864.
Hommond, George P	...do...	18	May 2, 1864	100 dys.	Mustered out with company Sept. 7, 1864.
Ijams, William W	...do...	35	May 2, 1864	100 dys.	Mustered out with company Sept. 7, 1864.
Jackson, George B	...do...	27	May 2, 1864	100 dys.	Mustered out with company Sept. 7, 1864.
Jenkins, Francis M	...do...	31	May 2, 1864	100 dys.	Mustered out with company Sept.
Joy, Stephen	...do...	22	May 2, 1864	100 dys.	Mustered out with company Sept.
Kinney, Daniel F	...do...	28	May 2, 1864	100 dys.	Mustered out with company Sept
Kneeley, Isaac	...do...	21	May 2, 1864	100 dys.	Mustered out with company Se
Lane, Abraham	...do...	22	May 2, 1864	100 dys.	Mustered out with company Se

Names.	Rank.	Age.	Date of Entering the Service.	Period of Service.	Remarks.
Samuel Hamitt	Corporal.	40	May 2, 1864	100 dys.	Appointed May 20, 1864; mustered out with company Sept. 7, 1864.
Ardrey, Edward H	Private.	18	May 2, 1864	100 dys.	Mustered out with company Sept. 7, 1864.
Baird, Archibald H	...do...	23	May 2, 1864	100 dys.	Mustered out with company Sept. 7, 1864.
Baker, Silas G N	...do...	20	May 2, 1864	100 dys.	Mustered out with company Sept. 7, 1864.
Barner, Peter	...do...	36	May 2, 1864	100 dys.	Mustered out with company Sept. 7, 1864.
Barnett, James I	...do...	23	May 2, 1864	100 dys.	Mustered out with company Sept. 7, 1864.
Barnett, William H	...do...	19	May 2, 1864	100 dys.	Mustered out with company Sept. 7, 1864.
Beard, Thomas A	...do...	20	May 2, 1864	100 dys.	Mustered out with company Sept. 7, 1864.
Berry, George W	...do...	29	May 2, 1864	100 dys.	Discharged Sept. 5, 1864, at Columbus, O., Surgeon's certificate of disability.
Beth, Daniel	...do...	22	May 2, 1864	100 dys.	Mustered out with company Sept. 7, 1864.
Beth, Peter	...do...	24	May 2, 1864	100 dys.	Killed Aug. 13, 1864, in action at Maryland Heights, Md.
Bogle, Joseph S	...do...	22	May 2, 1864	100 dys.	Mustered out with company Sept. 7, 1864.
Bright, Enoch	...do...	34	May 2, 1864	100 dys.	Mustered out with company Sept. 7, 1864.
Bright, John	...do...	37	May 2, 1864	100 dys.	Mustered out with company Sept. 7, 1864.
Brown, Wesley J	...do...	38	May 2, 1864	100 dys.	Mustered out with company Sept. 7, 1864.
Burley, William N	...do...	18	May 2, 1864	100 dys.	Mustered out with company Sept. 7, 1864.
Campbell, James G	...do...	21	May 2, 1864	100 dys.	Mustered out with company Sept. 7, 1864.
Cannon, David	...do...	19	May 2, 1864	100 dys.	Mustered out with company Sept. 7, 1864.
Cannon, Isaac J	...do...	27	May 2, 1864	100 dys.	Mustered out with company Sept. 7, 1864.
Coun, Isaac F	...do...	20	May 2, 1864	100 dys.	Mustered out with company Sept. 7, 1864.
Croskey, Robert	...do...	41	May 2, 1864	100 dys.	Mustered out with company Sept. 7, 1864.
Crossen, William H	...do...	30	May 2, 1864	100 dys.	Mustered out with company Sept. 7, 1864.
Curren, Charles W	...do...	19	May 2, 1864	100 dys.	Mustered out with company Sept. 7, 1864.
Danison, Joel	...do...	33	May 2, 1864	100 dys.	Mustered out with company Sept. 7, 1864.
Dean, Alford D	...do...	20	May 2, 1864	100 dys.	Mustered out with company Sept. 7, 1864.
Deselm, Robert I	...do...	19	May 2, 1864	100 dys.	Mustered out with company Sept. 7, 1864.
Hazlett, James W	...do...	18	May 2, 1864	100 dys.	Mustered out with company Sept. 7, 1864.
Hazlett, William R	...do...	19	May 2, 1864	100 dys.	Mustered out with company Sept. 7, 1864.
Hightshoe, Christian	...do...	33	May 2, 1864	100 dys.	Mustered out with company Sept. 7, 1864.
Hitts, Joseph I	...do...	22	May 2, 1864	100 dys.	Mustered out with company Sept. 7, 1864.
Kelly, Isaac	...do...	29	May 2, 1864	100 dys.	Killed Aug. 13, 1864, in action at Maryland Heights, Md.
Keohler, George	...do...	26	May 2, 1864	100 dys.	Mustered out with company Sept. 7, 1864.
Keohler, Joseph	...do...	24	May 2, 1864	100 dys.	Mustered out with company Sept. 7, 1864.
Knepper, Aaron	...do...	23	May 2, 1864	100 dys.	Mustered out with company Sept. 7, 1864.
Laizlier, George W	...do...	26	May 2, 1864	100 dys.	Mustered out with company Sept. 7, 1864.
Lefler, Jacob	...do...	24	May 2, 1864	100 dys.	Mustered out with company Sept. 7, 1864.
Lewis, John W	...do...	20	May 2, 1864	100 dys.	Mustered out with company Sept. 7, 1864.
Lyle, John W	...do...	22	May 2, 1864	100 dys.	Mustered out with company Sept. 7, 1864.
Lyle, Robert	...do...	28	May 2, 1864	100 dys.	Mustered out with company Sept. 7, 1864.
McCortney, William	...do...	34	May 2, 1864	100 dys.	Mustered out with company Sept. 7, 1864; also borne on rolls as William McCormer.
McLain, Lawson H	...do...	18	May 2, 1864	100 dys.	Mustered out with company Sept. 7, 1864.
May, Daniel	...do...	25	May 2, 1864	100 dys.	Mustered out with company Sept. 7, 1864.
Miller, Enoch F	...do...	20	May 2, 1864	100 dys.	Discharged Sept. 5, 1864, at Columbus, O., Surgeon's certificate of disability.
Miller, Peter	...do...	21	May 2, 1864	100 dys.	Mustered out with company Sept. 7, 1864.
Miller, William H	...do...	29	May 2, 1864	100 dys.	Mustered out with company Sept. 7, 1864.
Moore, James W	...do...	22	May 2, 1864	100 dys.	Mustered out with company Sept. 7, 1864.
Myers, John	...do...	19	May 2, 1864	100 dys.	Mustered out with company Sept. 7, 1864.
Pembarton, William	...do...	35	May 2, 1864	100 dys.	Mustered out with company Sept. 7, 1864.
Reachum, John W	...do...	18	May 2, 1864	100 dys.	Mustered out with company Sept. 7, 1864.
Rockhold, Elisha J	...do...	36	May 2, 1864	100 dys.	Mustered out with company Sept. 7, 1864.
Shaw, Stephen	...do...	42	May 2, 1864	100 dys.	Mustered out with company Sept. 7, 1864.
Shearer, Elias S	...do...	29	May 2, 1864	100 dys.	Mustered out with company Sept. 7, 1864.
Shearer, Lewis	...do...	20	May 2, 1864	100 dys.	Mustered out with company Sept. 7, 1864.
Shriver, William I	...do...	18	May 2, 1864	100 dys.	Mustered out with company Sept. 7, 1864.
Skinner, George G	...do...	28	May 2, 1864	100 dys.	Mustered out with company Sept. 7, 1864.
Smith, Alexander	...do...	18	May 2, 1864	100 dys.	Mustered out with company Sept. 7, 1864.
State, George	...do...	27	May 2, 1864	100 dys.	Killed Aug. 13, 1864, in action at Maryland Heights, Md.
Stoneburner, Noah	...do...	21	May 2, 1864	100 dys.	Mustered out with company Sept. 7, 1864.
Sturts, Valentine	...do...	27	May 2, 1864	100 dys.	Mustered out with company Sept. 7, 1864.
Taylor, William	...do...	19	May 2, 1864	100 dys.	Mustered out with company Sept. 7, 1864.
Turner, William	...do...	27	May 2, 1864	100 dys.	Mustered out with company Sept. 7, 1864.
Vanarsdalen, William	...do...	25	May 2, 1864	100 dys.	Mustered out with company Sept. 7, 1864.
Virts, Richard H	...do...	25	May 2, 1864	100 dys.	Mustered out with company Sept. 7, 1864.
Wallace, William	...do...	18	May 2, 1864	100 dys.	Mustered out with company Sept. 7, 1864.
W tts, William H	...do...	22	May 2, 1864	100 dys.	Mustered out with company Sept. 7, 1864.
Williams, Isaac	...do...	21	May 2, 1864	100 dys.	Reduced from Corporal May 19, 1864; mustered out with company Sept. 7, 1864.
Williams, Simeon	...do...	20	May 2, 1864	100 dys.	Mustered out with company Sept. 7, 1864.
Yager, Daniel	...do...	25	May 2, 1864	100 dys.	Mustered out with company Sept. 7, 1864.

...nes.	Rank.	Age.	Date of Entering the Service.	Period of Service.	Remarks.
...ary	Private	24	May 2, 1864	100 dys.	Mustered out with company Sept. 7, 1864.
...cob B.	...do...	18	May 2, 1864	100 dys.	Mustered out with company Sept. 7, 1864.
...hn	...do...	28	May 2, 1864	100 dys.	Mustered out with company Sept. 7, 1864.
...noch	...do...	27	May 2, 1864	100 dys.	Mustered out with company Sept. 7, 1864.
...aac	...do...	36	May 2, 1864	100 dys.	Mustered out with company Sept. 7, 1864.
...mith	...do...	39	May 2, 1864	100 dys.	Mustered out with company Sept. 7, 1864.
...B.	...do...	35	May 2, 1864	100 dys.	Mustered out with company Sept. 7, 1864.
...r.	...do...	19	May 2, 1864	100 dys.	Mustered out with company Sept. 7, 1864.
...ph	...do...	23	May 2, 1864	100 dys.	Mustered out with company Sept. 7, 1864.
...es J.	...do...	25	May 2, 1864	100 dys.	Mustered out with company Sept. 7, 1864.
...er.	...do...	19	May 2, 1864	100 dys.	Mustered out with company Sept. 7, 1864.
...eodore	...do...	18	May 2, 1864	100 dys.	Mustered out with company Sept. 7, 1864.
...am H.	...do...	20	May 2, 1864	100 dys.	Mustered out with company Sept. 7, 1864.
...nes.	...do...	19	May 2, 1864	100 dys.	Mustered out with company Sept. 7, 1864.
...han.	...do...	37	May 2, 1864	100 dys.	Mustered out with company Sept. 7, 1864.
...niel	...do...	20	May 2, 1864	100 dys.	Mustered out with company Sept. 7, 1864.
...liam	...do...	19	May 2, 1864	100 dys.	Mustered out with company Sept. 7, 1864.
...cis.	...do...	23	May 2, 1864	100 dys.	Mustered out with company Sept. 7, 1864.
...el H.	...do...	31	May 2, 1864	100 dys.	Mustered out with company Sept. 7, 1864.

161st Regiment Ohio Volunteer Infantry.

ONE HUNDRED DAYS' SERVICE.

THIS Regiment was organized at Camp Chase, O., May 9, 1864, to serve one hundred days. It was composed of the Seventieth Battalion, Ohio National Guard, from Tuscarawas County; Forty-third Battalion, Ohio National Guard, from Noble County; and one company of the Fifty-eight Battalion, Ohio National Guard, from Hancock County. The Regiment was immediately ordered to Cumberland, Md., where it arrived at noon on the 12th. On the 28th the Regiment moved to Martinsburg, W. Va., and on the 4th of June Companies A, B, D, F, and H, with other troops, were sent up the Shenandoah Valley with a supply-train for Hunter's Army, then supposed to be near Staunton. On reaching that place it was found that General Hunter had advanced, but they finally overtook him, at Lexington, on the 11th. They remained with the Regiment until it arrived at Lynchburg, when, having turned over the supplies, they were ordered back to Martinsburg. After considerable marching and guard-duty the Regiment fell back to Maryland Heights. Early on the morning of the 6th of July skirmishing commenced, and continued for two days, the One Hundred and Sixty-first taking an active part. On the 25th of August it was ordered to Ohio, and mustered out September 2, 1864, on expiration of its term of service.

Names.	Rank.	Age.	Date of Entering the Service.	Period of Service.	Remarks.
Fawcett, John T.	Private.	26	May 2, 1864	100 dys.	Mustered out with company Sept. 2, 1864.
Fromm, Josiah T.	....do....	32	May 2, 1864	100 dys.	Mustered out with company Sept. 2, 1864.
Glidden, James	....do....	36	May 2, 1864	100 dys.	Wounded July 6, 1864, in acton at Maryland Heights, Md.; mustered out with company Sept. 2, 1864.
Glidden, Leonard	....do....	18	May 2, 1864	100 dys.	Wounded July 6, 1864, in action at Maryland Heights, Md.; mustered out with company Sept. 2, 1864.
Gram, John T.	....do....	18	May 2, 1864	100 dys.	Mustered out with company Sept. 2, 1864.
Harding, John B.	....do....	18	May 2, 1864	100 dys.	Mustered out with company Sept. 2, 1864.
Hebner, Lawrence L.	....do....	22	May 2, 1864	100 dys.	Mustered out with company Sept. 2, 1864.
Herrick, John	....do....	32	May 2, 1864	100 dys.	Mustered out with company Sept. 2, 1864.
Hudson, Jesse A.	....do....	23	May 2, 1864	100 dys.	Mustered out with company Sept. 2, 1864.
Johnston, John	....do....	41	May 2, 1864	100 dys.	Mustered out with company Sept. 2, 1864.
Kail, John	....do....	25	May 2, 1864	100 dys.	Mustered out with company Sept. 2, 1864.
Keyser, Jacob	....do....	28	May 2, 1864	100 dys.	Mustered out with company Sept. 2, 1864.
Kuhn, Daniel G.	....do....	23	May 2, 1864	100 dys.	Mustered out with company Sept. 2, 1864.
McGarry, David	....do....	39	May 2, 1864	100 dys.	Mustered out with company Sept. 2, 1864.
Markee, James	....do....	19	May 2, 1864	100 dys.	Mustered out with company Sept. 2, 1864.
Messerly, Charles	....do....	28	May 2, 1864	100 dys.	Mustered out with company Sept. 2, 1864.
Metzger, John J.	....do....	26	May 2, 1864	100 dys.	Mustered out with company Sept. 2, 1864.
Miksch, Frederick I.	....do....	28	May 2, 1864	100 dys.	Mustered out with company Sept. 2, 1864.
Miller, Joseph L.	....do....	25	May 2, 1864	100 dys.	Mustered out with company Sept. 2, 1864.
Mohn, Henry L.	....do....	29	May 2, 1864	100 dys.	Mustered out with company Sept. 2, 1864.
Mohn, Reuben T.	....do....	37	May 2, 1864	100 dys.	Mustered out with company Sept. 2, 1864.
Norney, Benjamin	....do....	19	May 2, 1864	100 dys.	Mustered out with company Sept. 2, 1864.
Parrish, Eliza	....do....	40	May 2, 1864	100 dys.	Mustered out with company Sept. 2, 1864.
Parrish, James R.	....do....	18	May 2, 1864	100 dys.	Mustered out with company Sept. 2, 1864.
Peter, Amadeus	....do....	18	May 2, 1864	100 dys.	Mustered out with company Sept. 2, 1864.
Pickup, Edmund	....do....	32	May 2, 1864	100 dys.	Mustered out with company Sept. 2, 1864.
Pickens, John	....do....	28	May 2, 1864	100 dys.	Mustered out with company Sept. 2, 1864.
Rauck, Edward	....do....	32	May 2, 1864	100 dys.	Mustered out with company Sept. 2, 1864.
Rehnel, Tobias E.	....do....	22	May 2, 1864	100 dys.	Promoted to Principal Musician May 17, 1864.
Robertson, Anthony	....do....	19	May 2, 1864	100 dys.	Mustered out with company Sept. 2, 1864.
Rosenbaugh, Peter A.	....do....	20	May 2, 1864	100 dys.	Mustered out with company Sept. 2, 1864.
Rousa, Philip G.	....do....	37	May 2, 1864	100 dys.	Mustered out with company Sept. 2, 1864.
Sanders, John	....do....	26	May 2, 1864	100 dys.	Mustered out with company Sept. 2, 1864.
Schneider, Jacob	....do....	18	May 2, 1864	100 dys.	Mustered out with company Sept. 2, 1864.
Scholes, Hiram	....do....	32	May 2, 1864	100 dys.	Mustered out with company Sept. 2, 1864.
Schweitzer, Samuel	....do....	18	May 2, 1864	100 dys.	Died July 7, 1864, of wounds received July 6, 1864, in action at Maryland Heights, Md.
Shull, John	....do....	28	May 2, 1864	100 dys.	Mustered out with company Sept. 2, 1864.
Simmers, James M.	....do....	18	May 2, 1864	100 dys.	Mustered out with company Sept. 2, 1864.
Stocker, Cyrus S.	....do....	28	May 2, 1864	100 dys.	Wounded July 6, 1864, in action at Maryland Heights, Md.; mustered out with company Sept. 2, 1864.
Taylor, Daniel	....do....	31	May 2, 1864	100 dys.	Mustered out with company Sept. 2, 1864.
Tschudy, Edward B.	....do....	38	May 2, 1864	100 dys.	Mustered out with company Sept. 2, 1864.
Wenz, John	....do....	37	May 2, 1864	100 dys.	Mustered out with company Sept. 2, 1864.
Wheland, Benjamin P.	....do....	20	May 2, 1864	100 dys.	Accidentally wounded in shoulder Aug. 2, 1864; mustered out with company Sept. 2, 1864.
Wheland, Peter S.	....do....	35	May 2, 1864	100 dys.	Mustered out with company Sept. 2, 1864.
Wilson, Barney	....do....	37	May 2, 1864	100 dys.	Mustered out with company Sept. 2, 1864.
Wolf, Casimir	....do....	20	May 2, 1864	100 dys.	Mustered out with company Sept. 2, 1864.
Woodford, Allen	....do....	18	May 2, 1864	100 dys.	Mustered out with company Sept. 2, 1864.
Woodford, Joseph A.	....do....	29	May 2, 1864	100 dys.	Mustered out with company Sept. 2, 1864.
Woodford, William	....do....	42	May 2, 1864	100 dys.	Mustered out with company Sept. 2, 1864.
Wright, John W.	....do....	34	May 2, 1864	100 dys.	Mustered out with company Sept. 2, 1864.

COMPANY B.

Mustered in May 9, 1864, at Camp Chase, O., by H. Douglas, Captain 18th Infantry, U. S. A. Mustered out Sept. 2, 1864, at Camp Chase, O., by D. M. Vance, 1st Lieutenant 11th Infantry, U. S. A.

Names.	Rank.	Age.	Date of Entering the Service.	Period of Service.	Remarks.
Robert Lutton	Captain.	36	May 2, 1864	100 dys.	Mustered out with company Sept. 2, 1864.
Samuel Price	1st Lieut.	25	May 2, 1864	100 dys.	Mustered out with company Sept. 2, 1864.
Fenton L. Daniels	2d Lieut.	37	May 2, 1864	100 dys.	Mustered out with company Sept. 2, 1864.
Frank Manley	1st Sergt.	24	May 2, 1864	100 dys.	Mustered out with company Sept. 2, 1864.
Solomon S. Beckwith	Sergeant.	27	May 2, 1864	100 dys.	Mustered out with company Sept. 2, 1864.
Hanson Spurrier	....do....	31	May 2, 1864	100 dys.	Mustered out with company Sept. 2, 1864.
Perly I. Stanberry	....do....	33	May 2, 1864	100 dys.	Mustered out with company Sept. 2, 1864.
Isaac Stubbs	....do....	35	May 2, 1864	100 dys.	Captured June 19, 1864; paroled ——; mustered out with company Sept. 2, 1864.
John Bailey	Corporal.	32	May 2, 1864	100 dys.	Absent, sick ——. No further record found.
Jacob Golden	....do....	43	May 2, 1864	100 dys.	Mustered out with company Sept. 2, 1864.
William H. Weitzell	....do....	19	May 2, 1864	100 dys.	Mustered out with company Sept. 2, 1864.
Joel Walker	....do....	32	May 2, 1864	100 dys.	Died Sept. 3, 1864, after muster-out of company.
David C. Ray	....do....	22	May 2, 1864	100 dys.	Mustered out with company Sept. 2, 1864.

Names.	Rank.	Age.	Date of Entering the Service.	Period of Service.	Remarks.
Benjamin Severance	Corporal.	41	May 2, 1864	100 dys.	Mustered out with company Sept. 2, 1864.
Jesse W. Baumgardner	...do...	[illegible]	May 2, 1864	100 dys.	Mustered out with company Sept. 2, 1864.
Joseph Lenz	...do...	[illegible]	May 2, 1864	100 dys.	Mustered out with company Sept. 2, 1864.
John R. Kirby	Musician.	[illegible]	May 2, 1864	100 dys.	Mustered out with company Sept. 2, 1864.
William [illegible]	...do...	[illegible]	May 2, 1864	100 dys.	Mustered out with company Sept. 2, 1864.
Anderson Jesse	Private.	[illegible]	May 2, 1864	100 dys.	Mustered out with company Sept. 2, 1864.
Bailey James D.	...do...	[illegible]	May 2, 1864	100 dys.	Absent, sick —. No further record found.
Beckwith Laban	...do...	[illegible]	May 2, 1864	100 dys.	Mustered out with company Sept. 2, 1864.
Benjamin James	...do...	[illegible]	May 2, 1864	100 dys.	[illegible]
Berry Joseph T.	...do...	[illegible]	May 2, 1864	100 dys.	[illegible]
Berry Reese W.	...do...	[illegible]	May 2, 1864	100 dys.	[illegible]
Bricker James H.	...do...	[illegible]	May 2, 1864	100 dys.	[illegible]
Briggs [illegible]	...do...	[illegible]	May 2, 1864	100 dys.	[illegible]
Browning Samuel	...do...	[illegible]	May 2, 1864	100 dys.	[illegible]
Clements John R.	...do...	[illegible]	May 2, 1864	100 dys.	Absent, sick —. No further record found.
Cook P[illegible]	...do...	[illegible]	May 2, 1864	100 dys.	[illegible]
Core Ja[illegible]	...do...	[illegible]	May 2, 1864	100 dys.	[illegible]
Cornelius A[illegible]	...do...	[illegible]	May 2, 1864	100 dys.	[illegible]
Corner Warren L.	...do...	[illegible]	May 2, 1864	100 dys.	[illegible]
Corner William [illegible]	...do...	[illegible]	May 2, 1864	100 dys.	[illegible]
[illegible]	...do...	[illegible]	May 2, 1864	[illegible]	[illegible]
[illegible] Manasseh	...do...	[illegible]	[illegible]	[illegible]	[illegible]
[illegible] H.	...do...	[illegible]	[illegible]	[illegible]	[illegible]
[illegible] Henry	...do...	[illegible]	[illegible]	[illegible]	[illegible]
[illegible] William	...do...	[illegible]	[illegible]	[illegible]	[illegible]
E[illegible] Benjamin	...do...	[illegible]	[illegible]	[illegible]	[illegible]
Fox [illegible]	...do...	[illegible]	[illegible]	[illegible]	[illegible]
Ham[illegible] K.	...do...	[illegible]	[illegible]	[illegible]	[illegible]
Harris [illegible] W.	...do...	[illegible]	[illegible]	[illegible]	[illegible]
Henry [illegible]	...do...	[illegible]	[illegible]	[illegible]	[illegible]
H[illegible]	...do...	[illegible]	[illegible]	[illegible]	[illegible]
Ho[illegible]	...do...	[illegible]	[illegible]	[illegible]	[illegible]
H[illegible] Henry	...do...	[illegible]	[illegible]	[illegible]	[illegible]
H[illegible] Benjamin	...do...	[illegible]	[illegible]	[illegible]	[illegible]
[illegible]	...do...	[illegible]	[illegible]	[illegible]	[illegible]
M[illegible]	...do...	[illegible]	[illegible]	[illegible]	[illegible]
M[illegible]	...do...	[illegible]	[illegible]	[illegible]	[illegible]
M[illegible] E.	...do...	[illegible]	[illegible]	[illegible]	[illegible]
M[illegible]	...do...	[illegible]	[illegible]	[illegible]	[illegible]
Mart[illegible]	...do...	[illegible]	[illegible]	[illegible]	[illegible]
Martin [illegible]	...do...	[illegible]	[illegible]	[illegible]	[illegible]
M[illegible]	...do...	[illegible]	[illegible]	[illegible]	[illegible]
Newman [illegible]	...do...	[illegible]	[illegible]	[illegible]	[illegible]
[illegible]	...do...	[illegible]	[illegible]	[illegible]	[illegible]
Palmer [illegible]	...do...	[illegible]	[illegible]	[illegible]	[illegible]
Palmer W[illegible]	...do...	[illegible]	[illegible]	[illegible]	[illegible]
Patters[illegible]	...do...	[illegible]	[illegible]	[illegible]	[illegible]
[illegible]	...do...	[illegible]	[illegible]	[illegible]	[illegible]
P[illegible]	...do...	[illegible]	[illegible]	[illegible]	[illegible]
P[illegible]	...do...	[illegible]	[illegible]	[illegible]	[illegible]
Pr[illegible]	...do...	[illegible]	[illegible]	[illegible]	[illegible]
R[illegible] W.	...do...	[illegible]	[illegible]	[illegible]	[illegible]
R[illegible]	...do...	[illegible]	[illegible]	[illegible]	[illegible]
R[illegible]	...do...	[illegible]	[illegible]	[illegible]	[illegible]
[illegible]	...do...	[illegible]	[illegible]	[illegible]	[illegible]
Scott Andrew	...do...	[illegible]	[illegible]	[illegible]	[illegible]
[illegible] William	...do...	[illegible]	[illegible]	[illegible]	[illegible]
Smith Daniel	...do...	[illegible]	[illegible]	[illegible]	[illegible]
Smith Francis	...do...	[illegible]	[illegible]	[illegible]	[illegible]
Smith William B.	...do...	[illegible]	[illegible]	[illegible]	[illegible]
Taylor [illegible]	...do...	[illegible]	[illegible]	[illegible]	[illegible]
Timmons Henry	...do...	[illegible]	[illegible]	[illegible]	[illegible]
Timmons James	...do...	[illegible]	[illegible]	[illegible]	[illegible]
Townsend [illegible]	...do...	[illegible]	[illegible]	[illegible]	[illegible]
Updike [illegible]	...do...	[illegible]	[illegible]	[illegible]	[illegible]
Walker [illegible]	...do...	[illegible]	[illegible]	[illegible]	[illegible]
Wetherell Edwin	...do...	[illegible]	[illegible]	[illegible]	[illegible]
Weston William	...do...	[illegible]	[illegible]	[illegible]	[illegible]
Whitaker Lyman	...do...	[illegible]	[illegible]	[illegible]	[illegible]
Wilde Samuel	...do...	[illegible]	[illegible]	[illegible]	[illegible]
Wiseman Patrick	...do...	[illegible]	[illegible]	[illegible]	[illegible]

COMPANY C.

Mustered in May 9, 1864, at Camp Chase, O., by H. Douglas, Captain 18th Infantry, U. S. A. Mustered out Sept. 2, 1864, at Camp Chase, O., by D. M. Vance, 1st Lieutenant 11th Infantry, U. S. A.

Names.	Rank.	Age.	Date of Entering the Service.	Period of Service.	Remarks.
William A. Allen	Captain	27	May 2, 1864	100 dys.	Mustered out with company Sept. 2, 1864.
Carolus J. Barnes	1st Lieut.	39	May 2, 1864	100 dys.	Accidentally drowned July 28, 1864, in Monocacy Creek, at Frederick Junction, Md.
Isaac Philpot	2d Lieut.	38	May 2, 1864	100 dys.	Mustered out with company Sept. 2, 1864.
James M. Shankland	1st Sergt.	32	May 2, 1864	100 dys.	Mustered out with company Sept. 2, 1864.
James R. H. Smith	Sergeant.	32	May 2, 1864	100 dys.	Mustered out with company Sept. 2, 1864.
William H. Wharton	....do....	24	May 2, 1864	100 dys.	Mustered out with company Sept. 2, 1864.
James W. Robinson	....do....	26	May 2, 1864	100 dys.	Mustered out with company Sept. 2, 1864.
James S. Rownd	....do....	21	May 2, 1864	100 dys.	Mustered out with company Sept. 2, 1864.
William C. Calland	Corporal.	20	May 2, 1864	100 dys.	Mustered out with company Sept. 2, 1864.
William M. Nowell	....do....	20	May 2, 1864	100 dys.	Mustered out with company Sept. 2, 1864.
William Dailey	....do....	33	May 2, 1864	100 dys.	Mustered out with company Sept. 2, 1864.
William H. Piggott	....do....	23	May 2, 1864	100 dys.	Mustered out with company Sept. 2, 1864.
Nathan Wharton	....do....	20	May 2, 1864	100 dys.	Mustered out with company Sept. 2, 1864.
William H. Wilson	....do....	36	May 2, 1864	100 dys.	Mustered out with company Sept. 2, 1864.
George Farley	....do....	27	May 2, 1864	100 dys.	Mustered out with company Sept. 2, 1864.
Charles W. Philpot	....do....	18	May 2, 1864	100 dys.	Mustered out with company Sept. 2, 1864.
James S. Drake	Musician	18	May 2, 1864	100 dys.	Mustered out with company Sept. 2, 1864.
John R. McGinnis	....do....	18	May 2, 1864	100 dys.	Mustered out with company Sept. 2, 1864.
Arthur Dunn	Wagoner.	18	May 2, 1864	100 dys.	Mustered out with company Sept. 2, 1864.
Amos, Benjamin W	Private	19	May 2, 1864	100 dys.	Mustered out with company Sept. 2, 1864.
Baldwin, Francis R	....do....	22	May 2, 1864	100 dys.	Mustered out with company Sept. 2, 1864.
Barnes, Jesse R	....do....	43	May 2, 1864	100 dys.	Mustered out with company Sept. 2, 1864.
Barnes, Otho	....do....	42	May 2, 1864	100 dys.	Mustered out with company Sept. 2, 1864.
Bell, Joseph	....do....	19	May 2, 1864	100 dys.	Mustered out with company Sept. 2, 1864.
Bishop, John	....do....	24	May 2, 1864	100 dys.	Died ——, at Post Hospital, near Cumberland, Maryland.
Brown, John	....do....	18	May 2, 1864	100 dys.	Mustered out with company Sept. 2, 1864.
Brock, Nathaniel D	....do....	18	May 2, 1864	100 dys.	Mustered out with company Sept. 2, 1864.
Calland, Charles	....do....	18	May 2, 1864	100 dys.	Mustered out with company Sept. 2, 1864.
Carmichael, James	....do....	18	May 2, 1864	100 dys.	Mustered out with company Sept. 2, 1864.
Courtney, Lauthony	....do....	23	May 2, 1864	100 dys.	Mustered out with company Sept. 2, 1864.
Cunningham, James S	....do....	20	May 2, 1864	100 dys.	Mustered out with company Sept. 2, 1864.
Curtis, John	....do....	18	May 2, 1864	00 dys.	Mustered out with company Sept. 2, 1864.
Dailey, John H	....do....	25	May 2, 1864	100 dys.	Mustered out with company Sept. 2, 1864.
Davis, Joseph G	....do....	18	May 2, 1864	100 dys.	Mustered out with company Sept. 2, 1864.
Delaney, James	....do....	20	May 2, 1864	100 dys.	Mustered out with company Sept. 2, 1864.
Dotson, George	....do....	26	May 2, 1864	100 dys.	Mustered out with company Sept. 2, 1864.
Dunn, Henry	....do....	25	May 2, 1864	100 dys.	Mustered out with company Sept. 2, 1864.
Dunn, William	....do....	37	May 2, 1864	100 dys.	Mustered out with company Sept. 2, 1864.
Farley, Joseph	....do....	19	May 2, 1864	100 dys.	Mustered out with company Sept. 2, 1864.
Forshey, John	....do....	27	May 2, 1864	100 dys.	Mustered out with company Sept. 2, 1864.
Forshey, Thomas A	....do....	24	May 2, 1864	100 dys.	Mustered out with company Sept. 2, 1864.
Fowler, William H	....do....	18	May 2, 1864	100 dys.	Mustered out with company Sept. 2, 1864.
Gant, Joel	....do....	20	May 2, 1864	100 dys.	Mustered out with company Sept. 2, 1864.
Gant, Samuel C	....do....	30	May 2, 1864	100 dys.	Mustered out with company Sept. 2, 1864.
Gessell, David	....do....	37	May 2, 1864	100 dys.	Mustered out with company Sept. 2, 1864.
Gessell, John	....do....	40	May 2, 1864	100 dys.	Mustered out with company Sept. 2, 1864.
Gessell, Samuel	....do....	38	May 2, 1864	100 dys.	Mustered out with company Sept. 2, 1864.
Giller, Henry	....do....	18	May 2, 1864	100 dys.	Mustered out with company Sept. 2, 1864.
Haines, Hiram	....do....	32	May 2, 1864	100 dys.	Mustered out with company Sept. 2, 1864.
Hindman, Richard	....do....	30	May 2, 1864	100 dys.	Mustered out with company Sept. 2, 1864.
Hineman, Jesse	....do....	35	May 2, 1864	100 dys.	Mustered out with company Sept. 2, 1864.
Kent, George	....do....	22	May 10, 1864	100 dys.	Mustered out with company Sept. 2, 1864.
McBride, William	....do....	21	May 2, 1864	100 dys.	Mustered out to date Sept. 2, 1864, by order of War Department.
McClintock, William	....do....	27	May 2, 1864	100 dys.	Mustered out with company Sept. 2, 1864.
McGirk, Andrew	....do....	27	May 2, 1864	100 dys.	Mustered out with company Sept. 2, 1864.
McGuire, Josiah	....do....	36	May 2, 1864	100 dys.	Mustered out with company Sept. 2, 1864.
Master, Thomas	....do....	36	May 2, 1864	100 dys.	Mustered out with company Sept. 2, 1864.
Merrill, Wesley	....do....	18	May 2, 1864	100 dys.	Wounded July 7, 1864, in battle of Maryland Heights, Md.; mustered out Nov. 2, 1864, at Philadelphia, Pa., by order of War Department.
Niswonger, William D	....do....	23	May 2, 1864	100 dys.	Mustered out with company Sept. 2, 1864.
Ogg, John D	....do....	35	May 2, 1864	100 dys.	Mustered out with company Sept. 2, 1864.
Okey, Richard	....do....	18	May 2, 1864	100 dys.	Mustered out with company Sept. 2, 1864.
O'Neil, Thomas	....do....	22	May 2, 1864	100 dys.	Mustered out with company Sept. 2, 1864.
Osborn, Samuel	....do....	30	May 2, 1864	100 dys.	Mustered out with company Sept. 2, 1864.
Parcell, William	....do....	28	May 2, 1864	100 dys.	Mustered out with company Sept. 2, 1864.
Phillips, Frank W	....do....	18	May 2, 1864	100 dys.	Never mustered; died May —, 1864, at Camp Chase, O.
Phillips, John H	....do....	21	May 2, 1864	100 dys.	Mustered out with company Sept. 2, 1864.
Phillips, Lewis	....do....	41	May 2, 1864	100 dys.	Mustered out with company Sept. 2, 1864.
Prettyman, James S	....do....	18	May 2, 1864	100 dys.	Mustered out with company Sept. 2, 1864.
Reed, Edward	....do....	21	May 2, 1864	100 dys.	Mustered out with company Sept. 2, 1864.
Reed, Wesley W	....do....	39	May 2, 1864	100 dys.	Mustered out with company Sept. 2, 1864.

Names.	Rank.	Age.	Date of Entering the Service.	Period of Service.	Remarks.
Keplinger, John H.	Private	18	May 2, 1864	100 dys.	Mustered out with company Sept. 2, 1864.
Korns, Charles F.	do.	18	May 2, 1864	100 dys.	Mustered out with company Sept. 2, 1864.
Lehn, George W.	do.	25	May 2, 1864	100 dys.	Mustered out with company Sept. 2, 1864.
Loyd, Horace	do.	35	May 2, 1864	100 dys.	Mustered out with company Sept. 2, 1864.
McLean, William	do.	22	May 2, 1864	100 dys.	Promoted to Sergt. Major May 9, 1864.
Newton, John	do.	22	May 2, 1864	100 dys.	Mustered out with company Sept. 2, 1864.
Ort, George	do.	41	May 2, 1864	100 dys.	Mustered out with company Sept. 2, 1864.
Permick, Samuel	do.	29	May 2, 1864	100 dys.	Mustered out with company Sept. 2, 1864.
Rogers, John	do.	18	May 2, 1864	100 dys.	Mustered out with company Sept. 2, 1864.
Schnertzer, Alexander	do.	18	May 2, 1864	100 dys.	Mustered out with company Sept. 2, 1864.
Shull, Peter	do.	21	May 2, 1864	100 dys.	Mustered out with company Sept. 2, 1864.
Shull, Samuel	do.	26	May 2, 1864	100 dys.	Mustered out with company Sept. 2, 1864.
Still, Lodwell	do.	23	May 2, 1864	100 dys.	Mustered out with company Sept. 2, 1864.
Tabor, John M.	do.	32	May 2, 1864	100 dys.	Mustered out with company Sept. 2, 1864.
Tiechman, Frederick C.	do.	31	May 2, 1864	100 dys.	Mustered out with company Sept. 2, 1864.
Thompson, James C.	do.	41	May 2, 1864	100 dys.	Mustered out with company Sept. 2, 1864.
Thompson, John	do.	23	May 2, 1864	100 dys.	Mustered out with company Sept. 2, 1864.
Toland, John W.	do.	18	May 2, 1864	100 dys.	Mustered out with company Sept. 2, 1864.
Vesy, Silas	do.	19	May 2, 1864	100 dys.	Mustered out with company Sept. 2, 1864.
Wagoner, Jefferson	do.	25	May 2, 1864	100 dys.	Mustered out with company Sept. 2, 1864.
Walker, William	do.	26	May 2, 1864	100 dys.	Mustered out with company Sept. 2, 1864.
Walters, Henry	do.	30	May 2, 1864	100 dys.	Mustered out with company Sept. 2, 1864.
Waltz, Aires	do.	34	May 2, 1864	100 dys.	Mustered out with company Sept. 2, 1864.
Weber, Frederick	do.	21	May 2, 1864	100 dys.	Mustered out with company Sept. 2, 1864.
Weber, Gottlieb	do.	18	May 2, 1864	100 dys.	Mustered out with company Sept. 2, 1864.
Weltz, Charles	do.	20	May 2, 1864	100 dys.	Mustered out with company Sept. 2, 1864.
Williams, Thomas	do.	18	May 2, 1864	100 dys.	Mustered out with company Sept. 2, 1864.

COMPANY E.

Mustered in May 9, 1864, at Camp Chase, O., by H. Douglas, Captain 18th Infantry, U. S. A. Mustered out Sept. 2, 1864, at Camp Chase, O., by D. M. Vance, 1st Lieutenant 11th Infantry, U. S. A.

Names.	Rank.	Age.	Date of Entering the Service.	Period of Service.	Remarks.
Laffer Caples	Captain.	39	May 2, 1864	100 dys.	Mustered out with company Sept. 2, 1864.
William McCollam	1st Lieut.	33	May 2, 1864	100 dys.	Mustered out with company Sept. 2, 1864.
Josiah Welch	2d Lieut.	23	May 2, 1864	100 dys.	Mustered out with company Sept. 2, 1864.
George M. Warfel	1st Sergt.	34	May 2, 1864	100 dys.	Mustered out with company Sept. 2, 1864.
Theodore A. Packer	Sergeant.	42	May 2, 1864	100 dys.	Mustered out with company Sept. 2, 1864.
Elias Johnson	do.	44	May 2, 1864	100 dys.	Mustered out with company Sept. 2, 1864.
Samuel B. Price	do.	22	May 2, 1864	100 dys.	Mustered out with company Sept. 2, 1864.
John B. Jones	do.	20	May 2, 1864	100 dys.	Mustered out with company Sept. 2, 1864.
Caldwell Sproull	Corporal.	27	May 2, 1864	100 dys.	Mustered out with company Sept. 2, 1864.
Andrew Latta	do.	20	May 2, 1864	100 dys.	Mustered out with company Sept. 2, 1864.
Horace Riker	do.	21	May 2, 1864	100 dys.	Mustered out with company Sept. 2, 1864.
William Dempster	do.	18	May 2, 1864	100 dys.	Mustered out with company Sept. 2, 1864.
Edward Westnafer	do.	20	May 2, 1864	100 dys.	Mustered out with company Sept. 2, 1864.
Daniel Lenheart	do.	31	May 2, 1864	100 dys.	Appointed Aug. 12, 1864; mustered out with company Sept. 2, 1864.
Stephen Gatchell	do.	20	May 2, 1864	100 dys.	Appointed Aug. 12, 1864; mustered out with company Sept. 2, 1864.
Isaac Haskins	Musician	14	May 2, 1864	100 dys.	Mustered out with company Sept. 2, 1864.
Armstrong, Milton	Private	38	May 2, 1864	100 dys.	Mustered out with company Sept. 2, 1864.
Beitz, James A.	do.	18	May 2, 1864	100 dys.	Mustered out with company Sept. 2, 1864.
Buffington, George	do.	42	May 2, 1864	100 dys.	Mustered out with company Sept. 2, 1864.
Conwell, Thomas	do.	29	May 2, 1864	100 dys.	
Cox, Joshua	do.	18	May 2, 1864	100 dys.	Mustered out with company Sept. 2, 1864.
Cummings, Robert	do.	43	May 2, 1864	100 dys.	Absent, sick since Aug. 14, 1864, in hospital at Frederick, Md. No further record found.
Delong, Esple	do.	31	May 2, 1864	100 dys.	Mustered out with company Sept. 2, 1864.
Delong, Jesse W.	do.	20	May 2, 1864	100 dys.	Mustered out with company Sept. 2, 1864.
Delong, Obediah G.	do.	21	May 2, 1864	100 dys.	Mustered out with company Sept. 2, 1864.
Delong, Lemuel	do.	18	May 2, 1864	100 dys.	Mustered out with company Sept. 2, 1864.
Dempster, Jesse S.	do.	19	May 2, 1864	100 dys.	Mustered out with company Sept. 2, 1864.
Edie, William A.	do.	22	May 2, 1864	100 dys.	Mustered out with company Sept. 2, 1864.
Ewart, John	do.	18	May 2, 1864	100 dys.	Mustered out with company Sept. 2, 1864.
Foster, Henry	do.	38	May 2, 1864	100 dys.	Mustered out with company Sept. 2, 1864.
Fowler, Benjamin	do.	42	May 2, 1864	100 dys.	Mustered out with company Sept. 2, 1864.
Foy, Vincent	do.	18	May 2, 1864	100 dys.	Mustered out with company Sept. 2, 1864.
Gatchell, David	do.	25	May 2, 1864	100 dys.	Mustered out with company Sept. 2, 1864.
Gatchell, Frank	do.	18	May 2, 1864	100 dys.	Mustered out with company Sept. 2, 1864.
Gatchell, Kersey	do.	19	May 2, 1864	100 dys.	Mustered out with company Sept. 2, 1864.
Goings, Joel	do.	18	May 2, 1864	100 dys.	Mustered out with company Sept. 2, 1864.
Goings, John	do.	18	May 2, 1864	100 dys.	Mustered out with company Sept. 2, 1864.
Grafton, Robert	do.	37	May 2, 1864	100 dys.	Reduced from Corporal Aug. 12, 1864; mustered out with company Sept. 2, 1864.
Grim, Joshua P.	do.	25	May 2, 1864	100 dys.	Mustered out with company Sept. 2, 1864.
Grimes, Oliver C.	do.	40	May 2, 1864	100 dys.	Reduced from Corporal Aug. 12, 1864; mustered out with company Sept. 2, 1864.
Grimes, William B.	do.	18	May 2, 1864	100 dys.	Mustered out with company Sept. 2, 1864.
Harmon, John	do.	24	May 2, 1864	100 dys.	Mustered out with company Sept. 2, 1864.

Names.	Rank.	Age.	Date of Entering the Service.	Period of Service.	Remarks.
Dyer, Hebron	Private	32	May 2, 1864	100 dys.	Mustered out with company Sept. 2, 1864.
Eckman, John	...do...	21	May 2, 1864	100 dys.	Mustered out with company Sept. 2, 1864.
Fry, Martin L.	...do...	20	May 2, 1864	100 dys.	Mustered out with company Sept. 2, 1864.
Fenner, Matthias B.	...do...	26	May 2, 1864	100 dys.	Mustered out with company Sept. 2, 1864.
Glidden, Sydney J.	...do...	26	May 2, 1864	100 dys.	Promoted to Com. Sergeant May 14, 1864.
Gram, Eli H.	...do...	19	May 2, 1864	100 dys.	Mustered out with company Sept. 2, 1864.
Hamra, Henry	...do...	18	May 2, 1864	100 dys.	Mustered out with company Sept. 2, 1864.
Hardin, Absalom	...do...	18	May 2, 1864	100 dys.	Mustered out with company Sept. 2, 1864.
Harman, Jacob	...do...	21	May 2, 1864	100 dys.	Mustered out with company Sept. 2, 1864.
Headley, Francis R.	...do...	27	May 2, 1864	100 dys.	Mustered out with company Sept. 2, 1864.
Hert, Nicholas	...do...	18	May 2, 1864	100 dys.	Mustered out with company Sept. 2, 1864.
Hodel, Christian, Jr.	...do...	23	May 2, 1864	100 dys.	Mustered out with company Sept. 2, 1864.
Houk, Ferdinand	...do...	30	May 2, 1864	100 dys.	Mustered out with company Sept. 2, 1864.
Huether, John F.	...do...	25	May 2, 1864	100 dys.	Mustered out with company Sept. 2, 1864.
Hutchins, Aurelius	...do...	41	May 2, 1864	100 dys.	Mustered out with company Sept. 2, 1864.
Keller, Emanuel	...do...	23	May 2, 1864	100 dys.	Mustered out with company Sept. 2, 1864.
Krammer, George	...do...	27	May 2, 1864	100 dys.	Mustered out with company Sept. 2, 1864.
Laporte, John	...do...	19	May 2, 1864	100 dys.	Mustered out with company Sept. 2, 1864.
Laubaugh, Charles F.	...do...	19	May 2, 1864	100 dys.	Mustered out with company Sept. 2, 1864.
Lehn, John N.	...do...	18	May 2, 1864	100 dys.	Mustered out with company Sept. 2, 1864.
Lehr, Martin L.	...do...	26	May 2, 1864	100 dys.	Mustered out with company Sept. 2, 1864.
Lichte, Abraham	...do...	21	May 2, 1864	100 dys.	Mustered out with company Sept. 2, 1864.
Lowe, Chester P.	...do...	23	May 2, 1864	100 dys.	Captured June 18, 1864, near Liberty, Va.; mustered out June 2, 1865, at Columbus, O., by order of War Department.
McCreary, William	...do...	22	May 2, 1864	100 dys.	Mustered out with company Sept. 2, 1864.
McKee, Andrew	...do...	21	May 2, 1864	100 dys.	Mustered out with company Sept. 2, 1864.
Marti, John	...do...	20	May 2, 1864	100 dys.	Mustered out with company Sept. 2, 1864.
Minnich, Henry C.	...do...	19	May 2, 1864	100 dys.	Captured June 18, 1864, near Fincastle, Va.; mustered out Feb. 18, 1865, at Columbus, O., by order of War Department.
Moore, David	...do...	20	May 2, 1864	100 dys.	Mustered out with company Sept. 2, 1864.
Myers, Philip	...do...	26	May 2, 1864	100 dys.	Mustered out with company Sept. 2, 1864.
Narney, Jacob W.	...do...	18	May 2, 1864	100 dys.	Died Oct. 4, 1864, at Patterson Park Hospital, Baltimore, Md.
Parker, Welcome	...do...	22	May 2, 1864	100 dys.	Mustered out with company Sept. 2, 1864.
Romig, Henry, Jr.	...do...	19	May 2, 1864	100 dys.	Mustered out with company Sept. 2, 1864.
Romig, Isaiah	...do...	19	May 2, 1864	100 dys.	Mustered out with company Sept. 2, 1864.
Romig, Orrin T.	...do...	18	May 2, 1864	100 dys.	Mustered out with company Sept. 2, 1864.
Schindler, Daniel	...do...	20	May 2, 1864	100 dys.	Mustered out with company Sept. 2, 1864.
Schindler, Jacob	...do...	25	May 2, 1864	100 dys.	Mustered out with company Sept. 2, 1864.
Schneider, Philip	...do...	40	May 2, 1864	100 dys.	Mustered out with company Sept. 2, 1864.
Shamel, Samuel	...do...	34	May 2, 1864	100 dys.	Mustered out with company Sept. 2, 1864.
Simpkins, Lewis W.	...do...	21	May 2, 1864	100 dys.	Mustered out with company Sept. 2, 1864.
Sponsler, Michael	...do...	[illegible]	May 2, 1864	100 dys.	Mustered out with company Sept. 2, 1864.
Stuber, Jacob	...do...	21	May 2, 1864	100 dys.	Mustered out with company Sept. 2, 1864.
Struchen, Gottlieb	...do...	31	May 2, 1864	100 dys.	Mustered out with company Sept. 2, 1864.
Taylor, John	...do...	[illegible]	May 2, 1864	100 dys.	Mustered out with company Sept. 2, 1864.
Underhill, Joseph	...do...	31	May 2, 1864	100 dys.	Mustered out with company Sept. 2, 1864.
Wardell, Joseph H.	...do...	[illegible]	May 2, 1864	100 dys.	Mustered out with company Sept. 2, 1864.
Warner, Elias	...do...	38	May 2, 1864	100 dys.	Mustered out with company Sept. 2, 1864.
Weber, Enoch F.	...do...	23	May 2, 1864	100 dys.	Mustered out with company Sept. 2, 1864.
Weber, James W.	...do...	28	May 2, 1864	100 dys.	Mustered out with company Sept. 2, 1864.
Wheeler, Allen	...do...	[illegible]	May 2, 1864	100 dys.	Mustered out with company Sept. 2, 1864.
Wheeler, Jonathan	...do...	22	May 2, 1864	100 dys.	Mustered out with company Sept. 2, 1864.
Wheeler, Luther	...do...	21	May 2, 1864	100 dys.	Mustered out with company Sept. 2, 1864.
Wiley, Daniel W.	...do...	20	May 2, 1864	100 dys.	Mustered out with company Sept. 2, 1864.
Wood, Henry P.	...do...	28	May 2, 1864	100 dys.	Mustered out with company Sept. 2, 1864.

COMPANY G.

Mustered in May 9, 1864, at Camp Chase, O., by H. Douglas, Captain 18th Infantry, U. S. A. Mustered out Sept. 2, 1864, at Camp Chase, O., by D. M. Vance, 1st Lieutenant 11th Infantry, U. S. A.

Names.	Rank.	Age.	Date of Entering the Service.	Period of Service.	Remarks.
Eli G. Coulson	Captain.	42	May 2, 1864	100 dys.	Mustered out with company Sept. 2, 1864.
James J. Lewis	1st Lieut.	31	May 2, 1864	100 dys.	Lost left eye May 30, 1864, at Martinsburg, W. Va., from accidental injuries received while erecting a tent; mustered out with company Sept. 2, 1864.
George M. Matson	2d Lieut.	30	May 2, 1864	100 dys.	Mustered out with company Sept. 2, 1864.
Dennis M. Bingman	1st Sergt.	23	May 2, 1864	100 dys.	Mustered out with company Sept. 2, 1864.
John M. Hitchcock	Sergeant.	44	May 2, 1864	100 dys.	Mustered out with company Sept. 2, 1864.
William H. Scott	...do...	21	May 2, 1864	100 dys.	Mustered out with company Sept. 2, 1864.
William S. Wade	...do...	41	May 2, 1864	100 dys.	Mustered out with company Sept. 2, 1864.
John T. L. Naylor	...do...	32	May 2, 1864	100 dys.	Mustered out with company Sept. 2, 1864.
Alexander Bailey	Corporal.	33	May 2, 1864	100 dys.	Mustered out with company Sept. 2, 1864.
Lewis Tompkins	...do...	26	May 2, 1864	100 dys.	Mustered out with company Sept. 2, 1864.
George Thompson	...do...	26	May 2, 1864	100 dys.	Mustered out with company Sept. 2, 1864.
Jonathan Naylor	...do...	34	May 2, 1864	100 dys.	Mustered out with company Sept. 2, 1864.
Jerome D. Bann	...do...	24	May 2, 1864	100 dys.	Mustered out with company Sept. 2, 1864.

	Rank.	Age.	Date of Entering the Service.	Period of Service.	Remarks.
. Maun	Corporal.	21	May 2, 1864	100 dys.	Mustered out with company Sept. 2, 1864.
W. Cain	....do....	40	May 2, 1864	100 dys.	Mustered out with company Sept. 2, 1864.
ooper	....do....	32	May 2, 1864	100 dys.	Mustered out with company Sept. 2, 1864.
ilson	Musician	17	May 2, 1864	100 dys.	Mustered out with company Sept. 2, 1864.
. Moore	....do....	18	May 2, 1864	100 dys.	Mustered out with company Sept. 2, 1864.
Samuel	Private..	29	May 2, 1864	100 dys.	Mustered out with company Sept. 2, 1864.
ibson	....do....	20	May 2, 1864	100 dys.	Mustered out with company Sept. 2, 1864.
t, Charles V.	....do....	18	May 2, 1864	100 dys.	Mustered out with company Sept. 2, 1864.
, Elias	....do....	30	May 2, 1864	100 dys.	Died July 27, 1864, at Cumberland, Md.
, Matthias	....do....	18	May 2, 1864	100 dys.	Mustered out with company Sept. 2, 1864.
Stewart	....do....	19	May 2, 1864	100 dys.	Mustered out with company Sept. 2, 1864.
dmond	....do....	28	May 2, 1864	100 dys.	Mustered out with company Sept. 2, 1864.
William	....do....	21	May 2, 1864	100 dys.	Mustered out with company Sept. 2, 1864.
illiam	....do....	48	May 2, 1864	100 dys.	Mustered out with company Sept. 2, 1864.
Jacob	....do....	28	May 2, 1864	100 dys.	Mustered out with company Sept. 2, 1864.
William P.	....do....	38	May 2, 1864	100 dys.	Mustered out with company Sept. 2, 1864.
obert S.	....do....	30	May 2, 1864	100 dys.	Mustered out with company Sept. 2, 1864.
l	....do....	24	May 2, 1864	100 dys.	Mustered out with company Sept. 2, 1864.
William	....do....	26	May 2, 1864	100 dys.	Mustered out with company Sept. 2, 1864.
ames W	....do....	28	May 2, 1864	100 dys.	Mustered out with company Sept. 2, 1864.
. Levi	....do....	28	May 2, 1864	100 dys.	Mustered out with company Sept. 2, 1864.
Reason P.	....do....	22	May 2, 1864	100 dys.	Mustered out with company Sept. 2, 1864.
Andrew S.	....do....	18	May 2, 1864	100 dys.	Mustered out with company Sept. 2, 1864.
, Amos	....do....	18	May 2, 1864	100 dys.	Mustered out with company Sept. 2, 1864.
William	....do....	19	May 2, 1864	100 dys.	Mustered out with company Sept. 2, 1864.
aleb	....do....	24	May 2, 1864	100 dys.	Mustered out with company Sept. 2, 1864.
George	....do....	18	May 2, 1864	100 dys.	Mustered out with company Sept. 2, 1864.
, Enos	....do....	18	May 2, 1864	100 dys.	Mustered out with company Sept. 2, 1864.
cob	....do....	39	May 2, 1864	100 dys.	Mustered out with company Sept. 2, 1864.
James R.	....do....	32	May 2, 1864	100 dys.	Mustered out with company Sept. 2, 1864.
ohn	....do....	20	May 2, 1864	100 dys.	Mustered out with company Sept. 2, 1864.
William	....do....	18	May 2, 1864	100 dys.	Mustered out with company Sept. 2, 1864.
, George W.	....do....	20	May 2, 1864	100 dys.	Mustered out with company Sept. 2, 1864.
, John	....do....	18	May 2, 1864	100 dys.	Mustered out with company Sept. 2, 1864.
Thomas P.	....do....	28	May 2, 1864	100 dys.	Mustered out with company Sept. 2, 1864.
, Daniel	....do....	19	May 2, 1864	100 dys.	Mustered out with company Sept. 2, 1864.
David	....do....	21	May 2, 1864	100 dys.	Mustered out with company Sept. 2, 1864.
Alvertus H.	....do....	18	May 2, 1864	100 dys.	Mustered out with company Sept. 2, 1864.
all, Benjamin F	....do....	18	May 2, 1864	100 dys.	Mustered out with company Sept. 2, 1864.
William	....do....	32	May 2, 1864	100 dys.	Mustered out with company Sept. 2, 1864.
James	....do....	18	May 2, 1864	100 dys.	Mustered out with company Sept. 2, 1864.
ohn F.	....do....	24	May 2, 1864	100 dys.	Mustered out with company Sept. 2, 1864.
Daniel	....do....	29	May 2, 1864	100 dys.	Mustered out with company Sept. 2, 1864.
John	....do....	18	May 2, 1864	100 dys.	Mustered out with company Sept. 2, 1864.
George W.	....do....	23	May 2, 1864	100 dys.	Mustered out with company Sept. 2, 1864.
. William	....do....	28	May 2, 1864	100 dys.	Mustered out with company Sept. 2, 1864.
homas	....do....	18	May 2, 1864	100 dys.	Mustered out with company Sept. 2, 1864.
David	....do....	36	May 2, 1864	100 dys.	Mustered out with company Sept. 2, 1864.
arvey	....do....	44	May 2, 1864	100 dys.	Mustered out with company Sept. 2, 1864.
, Israel	....do....	29	May 2, 1864	100 dys.	Mustered out with company Sept. 2, 1864.
Washington V. D	....do....	32	May 2, 1864	100 dys.	Mustered out with company Sept. 2, 1864.
eo H.	....do....	19	May 2, 1864	100 dys.	Mustered out with company Sept. 2, 1864.
Warren	....do....	38	May 2, 1864	100 dys.	Mustered out with company Sept. 2, 1864.
Marion	....do....	29	May 2, 1864	100 dys.	Mustered out with company Sept. 2, 1864.
, William S.	....do....	18	May 2, 1864	100 dys.	Mustered out with company Sept. 2, 1864.
Plummer	....do....	36	May 2, 1864	100 dys.	Mustered out with company Sept. 2, 1864.
, Luther B.	....do....	19	May 2, 1864	100 dys.	Mustered out with company Sept. 2, 1864.
n, Eli	....do....	29	May 2, 1864	100 dys.	Mustered out with company Sept. 2, 1864.
n, Josiah R.	....do....	42	May 2, 1864	100 dys.	Mustered out with company Sept. 2, 1864.
n, William G.	....do....	29	May 2, 1864	100 dys.	Mustered out with company Sept. 2, 1864.
n, George	....do....	18	May 2, 1864	100 dys.	Mustered out with company Sept. 2, 1864.
, Martin	....do....	18	May 2, 1864	100 dys.	Mustered out with company Sept. 2, 1864.
David	....do....	35	May 2, 1864	100 dys.	Mustered out with company Sept. 2, 1864.
ames	....do....	24	May 2, 1864	100 dys.	Mustered out with company Sept. 2, 1864.
William	....do....	25	May 2, 1864	100 dys.	Mustered out with company Sept. 2, 1864.
ne, Jesse	....do....	19	May 2, 1864	100 dys.	Mustered out with company Sept. 2, 1864.

COMPANY H.

Mustered in May 9, 1864, at Camp Chase, O., by H. Douglas, Captain 18th Infantry, U. S. A. Mustered out Sept. 2, 1864, at Camp Chase, O., by D. M. Vance, 1st Lieutenant 11th Infantry, U. S. A.

Names.	Rank.	Age.	Date of Entering the Service.	Period of Service.	Remarks.
William Fowler	Captain.	26	May 2, 1864	100 dys.	Mustered out with company Sept. 2, 1864.
Benjamin Clouser	1st Lieut.	37	May 2, 1864	100 dys.	Mustered out with company Sept. 2, 1864.
Frederick Secrest	2d Lieut.	40	May 2, 1864	100 dys.	Mustered out with company Sept. 2, 1864.
Lewis Fowler	1st Sergt.	57	May 2, 1864	100 dys.	Mustered out with company Sept. 2, 1864.
Isaac N. Hickle	Sergeant.	25	May 2, 1864	100 dys.	Mustered out with company Sept. 2, 1864.
William McCandless	....do....	32	May 2, 1864	100 dys.	Mustered out with company Sept. 2, 1864.
Thomas N. Newton	....do....	41	May 2, 1864	100 dys.	Mustered out with company Sept. 2, 1864.
George H. McCandless	....do....	34	May 2, 1864	100 dys.	Mustered out with company Sept. 2, 1864.
John Halley	Corporal.	25	May 2, 1864	100 dys.	Mustered out with company Sept. 2, 1864.
Elihu Lippett	....do....	34	May 2, 1864	100 dys.	Died June 22, 1864, at Martinsburg, W. Va.
Joseph Davis	....do....	30	May 2, 1864	100 dys.	Mustered out with company Sept. 2, 1864.
William McLaughlin	....do....	24	May 2, 1864	100 dys.	Mustered out with company Sept. 2, 1864.
Abraham Vernon	....do....	41	May 2, 1864	100 dys.	Mustered out with company Sept. 2, 1864.
Virgil M. Bratton	....do....	22	May 2, 1864	100 dys.	Mustered out with company Sept. 2, 1864.
Charles Arndt	....do....	28	May 2, 1864	100 dys.	Absent since Aug. 3, 1864, in hospital at Annapolis, Md. No further record found.
Lewis Westcott	....do....	44	May 2, 1864	100 dys.	Mustered out with company Sept. 2, 1864.
Matthew McClary	Musician	40	May 2, 1864	100 dys.	Mustered out with company Sept. 2, 1864.
Aduddle, George	Private.	37	May 2, 1864	100 dys.	Mustered out with company Sept. 2, 1864.
Ayres, David	....do....	18	May 2, 1864	100 dys.	Mustered out with company Sept. 2, 1864.
Bond, Isaac	....do....	18	May 2, 1864	100 dys.	Mustered out with company Sept. 2, 1864.
Booher, Alexander	....do....	41	May 2, 1864	100 dys.	Mustered out with company Sept. 2, 1864.
Brown, James	....do....	41	May 2, 1864	100 dys.	Mustered out with company Sept. 2, 1864.
Browning, Hiram	....do....	18	May 2, 1864	100 dys.	Mustered out with company Sept. 2, 1864.
Buckey, J[illegible]n	....do....	30	May 2, 1864	100 dys.	Mustered out with company Sept. 2, 1864.
Buckey, Samuel	....do....	19	May 2, 1864	100 dys.	Mustered out with company Sept. 2, 1864.
Clark, Benjamin	....do....	20	May 2, 1864	100 dys.	Mustered out with company Sept. 2, 1864.
Clark, Lawrence	....do....	26	May 2, 1864	100 dys.	Absent since Aug. 3, 1864, in hospital at Annapolis, Md. No further record found.
Coffield, Charles	....do....	19	May 2, 1864	100 dys.	Mustered out with company Sept. 2, 1864.
Coffman, Elijah	....do....	18	May 2, 1864	100 dys.	Mustered out with company Sept. 2, 1864.
Cope, Jacob	....do....	18	May 2, 1864	100 dys.	Mustered out with company Sept. 2, 1864.
Courtney, Robert	....do....	20	May 2, 1864	100 dys.	Mustered out with company Sept. 2, 1864.
David, Gillespie	....do....	26	May 2, 1864	100 dys.	Mustered out with company Sept. 2, 1864.
Davis, Eli	....do....	18	May 2, 1864	100 dys.	Mustered out with company Sept. 2, 1864.
Devold, William	....do....	19	May 2, 1864	100 dys.	Mustered out with company Sept. 2, 1864.
Downey, Merriman	....do....	28	May 2, 1864	100 dys.	Mustered out with company Sept. 2, 1864.
Downey, Thomas	....do....	31	May 2, 1864	100 dys.	Mustered out with company Sept. 2, 1864.
Fogg, Rufus	....do....	18	May 2, 1864	100 dys.	Mustered out with company Sept. 2, 1864.
Fowler, John R.	....do....	18	May 2, 1864	100 dys.	Mustered out with company Sept. 2, 1864.
Fowler, William	....do....	33	May 2, 1864	100 dys.	Mustered out with company Sept. 2, 1864.
Fry, Isaac	....do....	29	May 2, 1864	100 dys.	Mustered out with company Sept. 2, 1864.
Fry, George	....do....	37	May 2, 1864	100 dys.	Mustered out with company Sept. 2, 1864.
F[illegible], John	....do....	22	May 2, 1864	100 dys.	Mustered out with company Sept. 2, 1864.
G[illegible], George W.	....do....	28	May 2, 1864	100 dys.	Mustered out with company Sept. 2, 1864.
G[illegible], Alfred	....do....	24	May 2, 1864	100 dys.	Mustered out with company Sept. 2, 1864.
G[illegible], William	....do....	22	May 2, 1864	100 dys.	Mustered out with company Sept. 2, 1864.
Gregg, James M.	....do....	19	May 2, 1864	100 dys.	Absent since Aug. 3, 1864, in hospital at Annapolis, Md. No further record found.
Groves, David	....do....	20	May 2, 1864	100 dys.	Mustered out with company Sept. 2, 1864.
Hamilton, Abraham	....do....	18	May 2, 1864	100 dys.	Mustered out with company Sept. 2, 1864.
Hamilton, Walker	....do....	30	May 2, 1864	100 dys.	Mustered out with company Sept. 2, 1864.
J[illegible], Eiza	....do....	18	May 2, 1864	100 dys.	Mustered out with company Sept. 2, 1864.
Johnson, John	....do....	33	May 2, 1864	100 dys.	Mustered out with company Sept. 2, 1864.
Johnson, Uriah	....do....	38	May 2, 1864	100 dys.	Mustered out with company Sept. 2, 1864.
K[illegible], Noah	....do....	23	May 2, 1864	100 dys.	Mustered out with company Sept. 2, 1864.
K[illegible], James	....do....	18	May 2, 1864	100 dys.	Mustered out with company Sept. 2, 1864.
King, Abraham	....do....	20	May 2, 1864	100 dys.	Mustered out with company Sept. 2, 1864.
Knight, Hiram	....do....	18	May 2, 1864	100 dys.	Mustered out with company Sept. 2, 1864.
Laughlin, James	....do....	19	May 2, 1864	100 dys.	Mustered out with company Sept. 2, 1864.
Lippet, Christopher	....do....	36	May 2, 1864	100 dys.	Mustered out with company Sept. 2, 1864.
Lyons, Alexander	....do....	36	May 2, 1864	100 dys.	Mustered out with company Sept. 2, 1864.
McElroy, William	....do....	27	May 2, 1864	100 dys.	Mustered out with company Sept. 2, 1864.
McGeary, Findley	....do....	18	May 2, 1864	100 dys.	Mustered out with company Sept. 2, 1864.
McIntyre, Benjamin F.	....do....	23	May 2, 1864	100 dys.	Mustered out with company Sept. 2, 1864.
McLaughlin, Joseph	....do....	27	May 2, 1864	100 dys.	Mustered out with company Sept. 2, 1864.
Mathena, Scot	....do....	18	May 2, 1864	100 dys.	Mustered out with company Sept. 2, 1864.
Nickelson, Levi	....do....	19	May 2, 1864	100 dys.	Mustered out with company Sept. 2, 1864.
Norman, Nathan	....do....	22	May 2, 1864	100 dys.	Mustered out with company Sept. 2, 1864.
Piper, Elisha	....do....	22	May 2, 1864	100 dys.	Mustered out with company Sept. 2, 1864.
Piper, Jonathan	....do....	18	May 2, 1864	100 dys.	Mustered out with company Sept. 2, 1864.
Rhinehart, James	....do....	27	May 2, 1864	100 dys.	Mustered out with company Sept. 2, 1864.
Roberts, Steward	....do....	30	May 2, 1864	100 dys.	Mustered out with company Sept. 2, 1864.
Rowland, James	....do....	19	May 2, 1864	100 dys.	Mustered out with company Sept. 2, 1864.
Russell, Ezra	....do....	21	May 2, 1864	100 dys.	Mustered out with company Sept. 2, 1864.
Russell, John	....do....	18	May 2, 1864	100 dys.	Mustered out with company Sept. 2, 1864.
Simons, James	....do....	29	May 2, 1864	100 dys.	Mustered out with company Sept. 2, 1864.

Names.	Rank.	Age.	Date of Entering the Service.	Period of Service.	Remarks.
Pitcock, David	Private..	38	May 2, 1864	100 dys.	Mustered out with company Sept. 2, 1864.
Ray, Albert W	....do....	18	May 2, 1864	100 dys.	Mustered out with company Sept. 2, 1864.
Rennond, Adam	....do....	19	May 2, 1864	100 dys.	Mustered out with company Sept. 2, 1864.
Robinson, Otis	....do....	18	May 2, 1864	100 dys.	Mustered out with company Sept. 2, 1864.
Robinson, Sydner	....do....	35	May 2, 1864	100 dys.	Mustered out with company Sept. 2, 1864.
Rogers, William	....do....	21	May 2, 1864	100 dys.	Mustered out with company Sept. 2, 1864.
Sayler, McChias	....do....	18	May 2, 1864	100 dys.	Mustered out with company Sept. 2, 1864.
Scott, Robert F	....do....	18	May 2, 1864	100 dys.	Mustered out with company Sept. 2, 1864.
Smith, Jehiel	....do....	21	May 2, 1864	100 dys.	Mustered out with company Sept. 2, 1864.
Snyder, Daniel J	....do....	23	May 2, 1864	100 dys.	Mustered out with company Sept. 2, 1864.
Stackhouse, Thomas J	....do....	29	May 2, 1864	100 dys.	Mustered out with company Sept. 2, 1864.
Sterner, Emanuel P	....do....	28	May 2, 1864	100 dys.	Mustered out with company Sept. 2, 1864.
Strother Absalom H	....do....	20	May 2, 1864	100 dys.	Mustered out with company Sept. 2, 1864.
Swingle, Lyman	....do....	22	May 2, 1864	100 dys.	Mustered out with company Sept. 2, 1864.
Taylor Thomas W	....do....	26	May 2, 1864	100 dys.	Absent, sick ——, at Frederick, Md. No further record found.
Thomas, Paul	....do....	11	May 2, 1864	100 dys.	Mustered out with company Sept. 2, 1864.
Thomas, Samuel S	....do....	33	May 2, 1864	100 dys.	Mustered out with company Sept. 2, 1864.
Tilton, Theodore	....do....	27	May 2, 1864	100 dys.	
Walker, Eli D	....do....	20	May 2, 1864	100 dys.	Mustered out with company Sept. 2, 1864.
Wallace, Daniel	....do....	18	May 2, 1864	100 dys.	Mustered out with company Sept. 2, 1864.
Warner, William	....do....	19	May 2, 1864	100 dys.	Mustered out with company Sept. 2, 1864.
Williams, John	....do....	34	May 2, 1864	100 dys.	Mustered out with company Sept. 2, 1864.

COMPANY K.

Mustered in May 9, 1864, at Camp Chase, O., by H. Douglas, Captain 18th Infantry, U. S. A. Mustered out Sept. 2, 1864, at Camp Chase, O., by D. M. Vance, 1st Lieutenant 11th Infantry, U. S. A.

Names.	Rank.	Age.	Date of Entering the Service.	Period of Service.	Remarks.
Asa Vincent	Captain.	37	May 2, 1864	100 dys.	Mustered out with company Sept. 2, 1864.
John Galbreath	1st. Lieut.	25	May 2, 1864	100 dys.	Mustered out with company Sept. 2, 1864.
William J. Weller	2d Lieut.	21	May 2, 1864	100 dys.	Mustered out with company Sept. 2, 1864.
Elijah G. Lees	1st Sergt.	22	May 2, 1864	100 dys.	Mustered out with company Sept. 2, 1864.
Otho Elliot	Sergeant.	29	May 2, 1864	100 dys.	Mustered out with company Sept. 2, 1864.
William A. Rogers	....do....	19	May 2, 1864	100 dys.	Mustered out with company Sept. 2, 1864.
Dexter G. Croy	....do....	26	May 2, 1864	100 dys.	Mustered out with company Sept. 2, 1864.
Robert C. McMichael	....do....	23	May 2, 1864	100 dys.	Mustered out with company Sept. 2, 1864.
Andrew Ralston	Corporal.	32	May 2, 1864	100 dys.	Mustered out with company Sept. 2, 1864.
Elijah Williams	....do....	25	May 2, 1864	100 dys.	Died July 5, 1864, at Cumberland, Md.
Lewis Andrews	....do....	27	May 2, 1864	100 dys.	Mustered out with company Sept. 2, 1864.
Ebeneze E. Law	....do....	35	May 2, 1864	100 dys.	Mustered out with company Sept. 2, 1864.
ohn Tibbles	....do....	19	May 2, 1864	100 dys.	Mustered out with company Sept. 2, 1864.
William Johnson	....do....	19	May 2, 1864	100 dys.	Mustered out with company Sept. 2, 1864.
Wallace Woodyard	....do....	21	May 2, 1864	100 dys.	Mustered out with company Sept. 2, 1864.
Isaac T. Simmers	....do....	34	May 2, 1864	100 dys.	Mustered out with company Sept. 2, 1864.
Bates, Alfred	Private..	43	May 2, 1864	100 dys.	Mustered out with company Sept. 2, 1864.
Beasley, Sargeant	....do....	27	May 2, 1864	100 dys.	Mustered out with company Sept. 2, 1864.
Beatty, Addison	....do....	18	May 2, 1864	100 dys.	Mustered out with company Sept. 2, 1864.
Broderick, William	....do....	43	May 2, 1864	100 dys.	Mustered out with company Sept. 2, 1864.
Brown, William	....do....	44	May 2, 1864	100 dys.	Mustered out with company Sept. 2, 1864.
Clark, George W	....do....	21	May 2, 1864	100 dys.	Mustered out with company Sept. 2, 1864.
Cope, Nathan P	....do....	43	May 2, 1864	100 dys.	Mustered out with company Sept. 2, 1864.
Danford, Robert R	....do....	35	May 2, 1864	100 dys.	Mustered out with company Sept. 2, 1864.
Daugherty, Harrison	....do....	18	May 2, 1864	100 dys.	Died Aug. 14, 1864, at Camp Distribution, Va.
Daugherty, James I	....do....	19	May 2, 1864	100 dys.	Mustered out with company Sept. 2, 1864.
Daugherty, William H	....do....	18	May 2, 1864	100 dys.	Mustered out with company Sept. 2, 1864.
Daugherty, Thomas	....do....	29	May 2, 1864	100 dys.	Mustered out with company Sept. 2, 1864.
Done, Joseph	....do....	39	May 2, 1864	100 dys.	Mustered out with company Sept. 2, 1864.
Elliott, Isaac	....do....	20	May 2, 1864	100 dys.	Mustered out with company Sept. 2, 1864.
Falconer, John A	....do....	26	May 2, 1864	100 dys.	Mustered out with company Sept. 2, 1864.
Fell, William	....do....	25	May 2, 1864	100 dys.	Mustered out with company Sept. 2, 1864.
Gardner, Joseph	....do....	22	May 2, 1864	100 dys.	Mustered out with company Sept. 2, 1864.
Gray, Edgar W	....do....	18	May 2, 1864	100 dys.	Mustered out with company Sept. 2, 1864.
Gray, Samuel C	....do....	26	May 2, 1864	100 dys.	Mustered out with company Sept. 2, 1864.
Hale, William	....do....	24	May 2, 1864	100 dys.	Mustered out with company Sept. 2, 1864.
Hammond Mordecai	....do....	19	May 2, 1864	100 dys.	Mustered out with company Sept. 2, 1864.
Hazen, George A	....do....	24	May 2, 1864	100 dys.	Mustered out with company Sept. 2, 1864.
Hivener Joseph	....do....	16	May 2, 1864	100 dys.	Mustered out with company Sept. 2, 1864.
Hutton, Jesse	....do....	18	May 2, 1864	100 dys.	Mustered out with company Sept. 2, 1864.
James, Austin	....do....	27	May 2, 1864	100 dys.	Mustered out with company Sept. 2, 1864.
Joy, Harrison	....do....	27	May 2, 1864	100 dys.	Mustered out with company Sept. 2, 1864.
Lazarus, William	....do....	32	May 2, 1864	100 dys.	Mustered out with company Sept. 2, 1864.
Lansford, Benjamin	....do....	35	May 2, 1864	100 dys.	Mustered out with company Sept. 2, 1864.
Law, John W	....do....	32	May 2, 1864	100 dys.	Mustered out with company Sept. 2, 1864.
Lewis, George I	....do....	26	May 2, 1864	100 dys.	Mustered out with company Sept. 2, 1864.
Lewis, Walter J	....do....	19	May 2, 1864	100 dys.	Mustered out with company Sept. 2, 1864.
Longstreth, Thomas	....do....	18	May 2, 1864	100 dys.	Mustered out with company Sept. 2, 1864.
Mathews, Charles W	....do....	21	May 2, 1864	100 dys.	Mustered out with company Sept. 2, 1864.
Mathews, John E	....do....	32	May 2, 1864	100 dys.	Mustered out with company Sept. 2, 1864.
Miller Hiel	....do....	16	May 2, 1864	100 dys.	Mustered out with company Sept. 2, 1864.

Names.	Rank.	Age.	Date of Entering the Service.	Period of Service.	Remarks.
, Francis	Private	18	May 2, 1864	100 dys.	Mustered out with company Sept. 2, 1864.
, Ely W	...do...	44	May 2, 1864	100 dys.	Mustered out with company Sept. 2, 1864.
, James W	...do...	18	May 2, 1864	100 dys.	Mustered out with company Sept. 2, 1864.
, Moses W	...do...	22	May 2, 1864	100 dys.	Mustered out with company Sept. 2, 1864.
n, Joseph	...do...	20	May 2, 1864	100 dys.	Mustered out with company Sept. 2, 1864.
scar B	...do...	25	May 2, 1864	100 dys.	Mustered out with company Sept. 2, 1864.
s, Francis M	...do...	18	May 2, 1864	100 dys.	Mustered out with company Sept. 2, 1864.
er, Chester	...do...	21	May 2, 1864	100 dys.	Mustered out with company Sept. 2, 1864.
er, Hiram	...do...	19	May 2, 1864	100 dys.	Mustered out with company Sept. 2, 1864.
er, Michael	...do...	19	May 2, 1864	100 dys.	Mustered out with company Sept. 2, 1864.
er, Wesley A	...do...	36	May 2, 1864	100 dys.	Mustered out with company Sept. 2, 1864.
er, William W	...do...	20	May 2, 1864	100 dys.	Mustered out with company Sept. 2, 1864.
Harrison	...do...	23	May 2, 1864	100 dys.	Mustered out with company Sept. 2, 1864.
ll, John	...do...	21	May 2, 1864	100 dys.	Mustered out with company Sept. 2, 1864.
n, John	...do...	33	May 2, 1864	100 dys.	Mustered out with company Sept. 2, 1864.
rs, Jacob	...do...	30	May 2, 1864	100 dys.	Mustered out with company Sept. 2, 1864
rs, Washington	...do...	27	May 2, 1864	100 dys.	Mustered out with company Sept. 2, 1864
, Francis	...do...	29	May 2, 1864	100 dys.	Mustered out with company Sept. 2, 1864
rd, Erastus M	...do...	18	May 2, 1864	100 dys.	Mustered out with company Sept. 2, 1864.
erry, Jacob M	...do...	18	May 2, 1864	100 dys.	Mustered out with company Sept. 2, 1864.
, Hiram	...do...	37	May 2, 1864	100 dys.	Mustered out with company Sept. 2, 1864.
, John	...do...	20	May 2, 1864	100 dys.	Mustered out with company Sept. 2, 1864.
, Samuel	...do...	32	May 2, 1864	100 dys.	Mustered out with company Sept. 2, 1864.
, Isaac	...do...	38	May 2, 1864	100 dys.	Mustered out with company Sept. 2, 1864.
, Ephraim	...do...	40	May 2, 1864	100 dys.	Mustered out with company Sept. 2, 1864.
, Theodore S	...do...	33	May 2, 1864	100 dys.	Mustered out with company Sept. 2, 1864.
, William E	...do...	44	May 2, 1864	100 dys.	Mustered out with company Sept. 2, 1864.
Thomas N	...do...	21	May 2, 1864	100 dys.	Mustered out with company Sept. 2, 1864.
er, John	...do...	23	May 2, 1864	100 dys.	Mustered out with company Sept. 2, 1864.
, Joseph	...do...	18	May 2, 1864	100 dys.	Mustered out with company Sept. 2, 1864.
Morris D	...do...	28	May 2, 1864	100 dys.	Mustered out with company Sept. 2, 1864.
ward, Cary P	...do...	16	May 2, 1864	100 dys.	Mustered out with company Sept. 2, 1864.

162nd Regiment Ohio Volunteer Infantry.

ONE HUNDRED DAYS' SERVICE.

THIS Regiment was organized at Camp Chase, O., May 20, 1864, to serve one hundred days. It was composed of the Forty-fifth Regiment, Ohio National Guard, from Stark County, and one Company of the Fortieth Battalion, Ohio National Guard, from Brown County. Companies A, C, F, and K, were assigned to duty at Tod Barracks, near Columbus, O., and the remaining Companies were assigned to duty at Camp Chase, where they remained until they were ordered into Kentucky, to assist in repelling John Morgan. Several of the Companies were placed on duty in and around Covington, and the remainder of the Regiment moved down the river to Carrollton. After remaining at Carrollton a few days the Companies returned to Covington and performed post-duty. They recruited the One Hundred and Seventeenth Regiment, United States Colored Infantry. This Regiment was mustered out Sept. 4, 1864, on expiration of its term of service.

Names.	Rank.	Age.	Date of Entering the Service.	Period of Service.	Remarks.
Boenar, Andrew	Private..	19	May 2, 1864	100 dys.	Mustered out with company Sept. 4, 1864.
Bumberger, Anton	....do....	19	May 2, 1864	100 dys.	Mustered out with company Sept. 4, 1864.
Butler, Samuel S	....do....	23	May 2, 1864	100 dys.	Mustered out with company Sept. 4, 1864.
Carr, Oaro	....do....	18	May 2, 1864	100 dys.	Mustered out with company Sept. 4, 1864.
Colemen, David M	....do....	37	May 2, 1864	100 dys.	Mustered out with company Sept. 4, 1864.
Corl, Henry	....do....	27	May 2, 1864	100 dys.	Mustered out with company Sept. 4, 1864.
Cramer, Frank J	....do....	20	May 2, 1864	100 dys.	Mustered out with company Sept. 4, 1864.
Creighton, James K. P.	....do....	19	May 2, 1864	100 dys.	Mustered out with company Sept. 4, 1864.
Crone, Anton	....do....	27	May 2, 1864	100 dys.	Mustered out with company Sept. 4, 1864.
Dangler, Frank I	....do....	19	May 2, 1864	100 dys.	Mustered out with company Sept. 4, 1864.
Dawley, Elisha	....do....	28	May 2, 1864	100 dys.	Mustered out with company Sept. 4, 1864.
Dawson, William	....do....	28	May 2, 1864	100 dys.	Mustered out with company Sept. 4, 1864.
Dickey, Hiram W	....do....	19	May 2, 1864	100 dys.	Mustered out with company Sept. 4, 1864.
Dumont, Henry	....do....	28	May 2, 1864	100 dys.	Mustered out with company Sept. 4, 1864.
Earl, George W	....do....	21	May 2, 1864	100 dys.	Mustered out with company Sept. 4, 1864.
Fogel, Adam	....do....	19	May 2, 1864	100 dys.	Mustered out with company Sept. 4, 1864.
Gibler, William	....do....	40	May 2, 1864	100 dys.	Mustered out with company Sept. 4, 1864.
Gonder, Joseph	....do....	36	May 2, 1864	100 dys.	Mustered out with company Sept. 4, 1864.
Hardgrove, Bennett E	....do....	35	May 24, 1864	100 dys.	Mustered out with company Sept. 4, 1864.
Hinderer, Louis	....do....	20	May 2, 1864	100 dys.	Mustered out with company Sept. 4, 1864.
Hoover, Collins M	....do....	22	May 2, 1864	100 dys.	Mustered out with company Sept. 4, 1864.
Hose, Jacob	....do....	19	May 2, 1864	100 dys.	Mustered out with company Sept. 4, 1864.
Huffman, Charles V	....do....	37	May 2, 1864	100 dys.	Mustered out with company Sept. 4, 1864.
Jeffers, Pardon	....do....	18	May 2, 1864	100 dys.	Mustered out with company Sept. 4, 1864.
Kackler, Charles	....do....	19	May 2, 1864	100 dys.	Discharged Aug. 20, 1864, at Camp Chase, O. on Surgeon's certificate of disability.
Karr, Lemuel	....do....	19	May 2, 1864	100 dys.	Mustered out with company Sept. 4, 1864.
Killinger, Henry E	....do....	27	May 2, 1864	100 dys.	Died Aug. 19, 1864, at Columbus, O.
Lehman, Samuel H	....do....	36	May 2, 1864	100 dys.	Mustered out with company Sept. 4, 1864.
Long, Charles W	....do....	27	May 2, 1864	100 dys.	
Madder, John, Jr	....do....	24	May 2, 1864	100 dys.	Died Aug. 19, 1864, at Covington, Ky.
Martin, Christopher C	....do....	20	May 2, 1864	100 dys.	Mustered out with company Sept. 4, 1864.
Mauger, Henry	....do....	23	May 23, 1864	100 dys.	Mustered out with company Sept. 4, 1864.
Mauger, Samuel	....do....	18	May 2, 1864	100 dys.	Died Aug. 25, 1864, at Columbus, O.
Merrill, Duparry M	....do....	25	May 2, 1864	100 dys.	Mustered out with company Sept. 4, 1864.
Miller, Jonathan D	....do....	31	May 2, 1864	100 dys.	Reduced from Corporal May 25, 1864; mustered out with company Sept. 4, 1864.
Moles, George M	....do....	19	May 2, 1864	100 dys.	Mustered out with company Sept. 4, 1864.
Morgenthaler, Henry	....do....	20	May 2, 1864	100 dys.	Mustered out with company Sept. 4, 1864.
Myers, Jacob W	....do....	38	May 2, 1864	100 dys.	Mustered out with company Sept. 4, 1864.
Ogden, John H	....do....	32	May 2, 1864	100 dys.	Mustered out with company Sept. 4, 1864.
Pease, A. Per Lee	....do....	18	May 2, 1864	100 dys.	Mustered out with company Sept. 4, 1864.
Pease, Theodore P	....do....	19	May 2, 1864	100 dys.	Mustered out with company Sept. 4, 1864.
Poorman, John F	....do....	28	May 2, 1864	100 dys.	Mustered out with company Sept. 4, 1864.
Porter, Thomas J	....do....	20	May 2, 1864	100 dys.	Discharged Aug. 10, 1864, at Columbus, O., on Surgeon's certificate of disability.
Rank, Henry	....do....	27	May 2, 1864	100 dys.	Mustered out with company Sept. 4, 1864.
Ritter, Jacob	....do....	37	May 2, 1864	100 dys.	Mustered out with company Sept. 4, 1864.
Rodenberger, George	....do....	19	May 2, 1864	100 dys.	Mustered out with company Sept. 4, 1864.
Rogers, William	....do....	40	May 2, 1864	100 dys.	Mustered out with company Sept. 4, 1864.
Rohr, Michael	....do....	20	May 24, 1864	100 dys.	Mustered out with company Sept. 4, 1864.
Ross, Samuel	....do....	37	May 2, 1864	100 dys.	Mustered out with company Sept. 4, 1864.
Ryder, Joseph M	....do....	26	May 2, 1864	100 dys.	Mustered out with company Sept. 4, 1864.
Sabin, Eugene E	....do....	25	May 2, 1864	100 dys.	Mustered out with company Sept. 4, 1864.
Seabold, Louis G	....do....	21	May 2, 1864	100 dys.	Mustered out with company Sept. 4, 1864.
Shoemaker, George	....do....	22	May 2, 1864	100 dys.	Mustered out with company Sept. 4, 1864.
Shouf, Peter	....do....	33	May 2, 1864	100 dys.	Mustered out with company Sept. 4, 1864.
Smith, John	....do....	42	May 2, 1864	100 dys.	Mustered out with company Sept. 4, 1864.
Smith, Samuel	....do....	18	May 2, 1864	100 dys.	Mustered out with company Sept. 4, 1864.
Smith, William	....do....	22	May 21, 1864	100 dys.	Mustered out with company Sept. 4, 1864.
Snyder, Andy	....do....	20	May 2, 1864	100 dys.	Mustered out with company Sept. 4, 1864.
Snyder, George	....do....	20	May 2, 1864	100 dys.	Mustered out with company Sept. 4, 1864.
Stevens, Ansel	....do....	21	May 2, 1864	100 dys.	Mustered out with company Sept. 4, 1864.
Thorp, Moses	....do....	24	May 2, 1864	100 dys.	Mustered out with company Sept. 4, 1864.
Volkmar, Adam	....do....	22	May 2, 1864	100 dys.	Reduced from Corporal June 29, 1864; mustered out with company Sept. 4, 1864.
Wagoner, Lehman	....do....	24	May 2, 1864	100 dys.	Mustered out with company Sept. 4, 1864.
Wagoner, Milo	....do....	20	May 2, 1864	100 dys.	Mustered out with company Sept. 4, 1864.
Williams, James G	....do....	18	May 2, 1864	100 dys.	Mustered out with company Sept. 4, 1864.
Wurtz, Thomas J	....do....	19	May 2, 1864	100 dys.	Mustered out with company Sept. 4, 1864.
Zieiley, Richard	....do....	31	May 2, 1864	100 dys.	Mustered out with company Sept. 4, 1864.

Names.	Rank.	Age.	Date of Entering the Service.	Period of Service.	Remarks.
Venable, Joel	Private	28	May 2, 1864	100 dys.	Mustered out with company Sept. 4, 1864.
Wagner, John S	....do....	20	May 2, 1864	100 dys.	Mustered out with company Sept. 4, 1864.
Walcutt, Lewis H	....do....	20	May 2, 1864	100 dys.	Mustered out with company Sept. 4, 1864.
West, Andrew	....do....	38	May 2, 1864	100 dys.	Mustered out with company Sept. 4, 1864.
Whitacre, Lewis	....do....	18	May 2, 1864	100 dys.	Mustered out with company Sept. 4, 1864.
Wielandt, George A	....do....	18	May 2, 1864	100 dys.	Mustered out with company Sept. 4, 1864.
Wise, Henry A	....do....	18	May 2, 1864	100 dys.	Mustered out with company Sept. 4, 1864.
Wolf, George H	....do....	18	May 2, 1864	100 dys.	Mustered out with company Sept. 4, 1864.
Zollars, Lewis	....do....	18	May 2, 1864	100 dys.	Mustered out with company Sept. 4, 1864.

COMPANY C.

Mustered in May 20, 1864, at Camp Chase, O., by James P. W. Neill, 1st Lieutenant 18th Infantry, U. S. A. Mustered out Sept. 4, 1864, at Camp Chase, O., by D. M. Vance, 1st Lieutenant 11th Infantry, U. S. A.

Names.	Rank.	Age.	Date of Entering the Service.	Period of Service.	Remarks.
Homer J. Ball	Captain.	22	May 2, 1864	100 dys.	Mustered out with company Sept. 4, 1864.
Seraphine Shively	1st Lieut.	25	May 2, 1864	100 dys.	Mustered out with company Sept. 4, 1864.
William Kingsnorth	2d Lieut.	25	May 2, 1864	100 dys.	Mustered out with company Sept. 4, 1864.
Joshua Raynolds	1st Sergt.	18	May 2, 1864	100 dys.	Appointed from Sergeant May 20, 1864; mustered out with company Sept. 4, 1864.
Griffith Dishart	Sergeant.	23	May 2, 1864	100 dys.	Mustered out with company Sept. 4, 1864.
Arthur Underhill	....do....	19	May 2, 1864	100 dys.	Absent sick Aug. 15, 1864, at Canton, O. No further record found.
Isaac Ruhman	....do....	22	May 2, 1864	100 dys.	Mustered out with company Sept. 4, 1864.
Isaac S. Stone	....do....	31	May 2, 1864	100 dys.	Reduced to ranks from 1st Sergeant and appointed Sergeant May 20, 1864; mustered out with company on Sept. 4, 1864.
William Ball	Corporal.	18	May 2, 1864	100 dys.	Mustered out with company Sept. 4, 1864.
Andrew Price	....do....	21	May 2, 1864	100 dys.	Mustered out with company Sept. 4, 1864.
Thomas Lautzenheiser	....do....	26	May 2, 1864	100 dys.	Mustered out with company Sept. 4, 1864.
Henry Cook	....do....	19	May 2, 1864	100 dys.	Mustered out with company Sept. 4, 1864.
Franklin S. Patton	....do....	18	May 2, 1864	100 dys.	Mustered out with company Sept. 4, 1864.
David Miller	....do....	25	May 2, 1864	100 dys.	Mustered out with company Sept. 4, 1864.
Benjamin J. Frymeyer	....do....	22	May 2, 1864	100 dys.	Appointed June 10, 1864; mustered out with company Sept. 4, 1864.
George Awe	....do....	18	May 2, 1864	100 dys.	Appointed June 18, 1864; mustered out with company Sept. 4, 1864.
Warren Douds	Musician	20	May 2, 1864	100 dys.	Mustered out Sept. 4, 1864, by order of War Department.
Henry Shearer	....do....	42	May 2, 1864	100 dys.	Mustered out with company Sept. 4, 1864.
Marshall Barbee	Wagoner.	18	May 2, 1864	100 dys.	Mustered out with company Sept. 4, 1864.
Barger, Harmon	Private	19	May 2, 1864	100 dys.	Mustered out with company Sept. 4, 1864.
Barnett, James	....do....	37	May 2, 1864	100 dys.	Mustered out with company Sept. 4, 1864.
Beardsley, Lyman I	....do....	23	May 2, 1864	100 dys.	Mustered out with company Sept. 4, 1864.
Beardsley, Price W	....do....	25	May 2, 1864	100 dys.	Mustered out with company Sept. 4, 1864.
Birchfield, Charles	....do....	19	May 2, 1864	100 dys.	Mustered out with company Sept. 4, 1864.
Blackford, John H	....do....	18	May 2, 1864	100 dys.	Mustered out with company Sept. 4, 1864.
Bliss, Henry	....do....	21	May 2, 1864	100 dys.	Mustered out with company Sept. 4, 1864.
Bott, Benjamin	....do....	25	May 2, 1864	100 dys.	Mustered out with company Sept. 4, 1864.
Clinton, James M	....do....	18	May 2, 1864	100 dys.	Mustered out with company Sept. 4, 1864.
Crowl, Theodore	....do....	19	May 2, 1864	100 dys.	Furloughed July 30, 1864, for twenty days, to accept recruiting commission. See 2d Lieutenant Co. I, 178th O. V. I.
Drabenstot, Henry	....do....	39	May 2, 1864	100 dys.	Reduced from Corporal June 18, 1864; mustered out with company Sept. 4, 1864.
Feagen, Silas J	....do....	27	May 2, 1864	100 dys.	Mustered out with company Sept. 4, 1864.
Fogle, Alva	....do....	18	May 2, 1864	100 dys.	Mustered out with company Sept. 4, 1864.
Ford, Homer J	....do....	18	May 2, 1864	100 dys.	Mustered out with company Sept. 4, 1864.
Fringer, Herman J	....do....	18	May 2, 1864	100 dys.	Mustered out with company Sept. 4, 1864.
Fulton, Rufus	....do....	21	May 2, 1864	100 dys.	Mustered out with company Sept. 4, 1864.
Green, William	....do....	19	May 2, 1864	100 dys.	Mustered out with company Sept. 4, 1864.
Hane, Charles F	....do....	18	May 2, 1864	100 dys.	Discharged Aug. 15, 1864, at Columbus, O., on surgeon's certificate of disability.
Hensel, John	....do....	26	May 2, 1864	100 dys.	Mustered out with company Sept. 4, 1864.
Honek, John	....do....	18	May 2, 1864	100 dys.	Mustered out with company Sept. 4, 1864.
Hullinger, Samuel	....do....	44	May 2, 1864	100 dys.	Mustered out with company Sept. 4, 1864.
Karns, Michael	....do....	43	May 2, 1864	100 dys.	Died July 27, 1864, at Seminary Hospital, Columbus, O.
Kimball, George	....do....	18	May 2, 1864	100 dys.	Mustered out with company Sept. 4, 1864.
Kreiter, James	....do....	18	May 2, 1864	100 dys.	Mustered out with company Sept. 4, 1864.
Krumlauf, Lewis	....do....	18	May 2, 1864	100 dys.	Mustered out with company Sept. 4, 1864.
Kyle, John	....do....	21	May 2, 1864	100 dys.	Mustered out with company Sept. 4, 1864.
Laird, John	....do....	19	May 2, 1864	100 dys.	Mustered out Sept. 1, 1864, by order of War Department.
Lefevre, James	....do....	18	May 2, 1864	100 dys.	Mustered out with company Sept. 4, 1864.
Leighth-iser, Samuel	....do....	21	May 2, 1864	100 dys.	Mustered out with company Sept. 4, 1864.
Leiter, Charles A	....do....	21	May 2, 1864	100 dys.	Promoted to 1st Lieutenant and Adjutant May 7, 1864.
Marburger, John	....do....	27	May 2, 1864	100 dys.	Mustered out with company Sept. 4, 1864.

Names.	Rank.	Age.	Date of Entering the Service.	Period of Service.	Remarks.
Ferguson, William M.	Private.	24	May 2, 1864	100 dys.	Mustered out with company Sept. 4, 1864.
Fox, Jesse W.	do.	18	May 2, 1864	100 dys.	Mustered out with company Sept. 4, 1864.
Harsh, Henry	do.	18	May 2, 1864	100 dys.	Mustered out with company Sept. 4, 1864.
Harsh, Philip	do.	21	May 2, 1864	100 dys.	Mustered out with company Sept. 4, 1864.
Hart, John M.	do.	18	May 2, 1864	100 dys.	Mustered out with company Sept. 4, 1864.
Haynam, Emanuel	do.	18	May 2, 1864	100 dys.	Mustered out with company Sept. 4, 1864.
Hostetter, Hillary	do.	18	May 2, 1864	100 dys.	Absent, sick ——. No further record found.
Hostetter, Lewis C.	do.	21	May 2, 1864	100 dys.	Mustered out with company Sept. 4, 1864.
Jackson, Frank	do.	21	May 2, 1864	100 dys.	Mustered out with company Sept. 4, 1864.
Keith, Smith	do.	20	May 2, 1864	100 dys.	Mustered out with company Sept. 4, 1864.
Kitzmiller, Albertus A.	do.	18	May 2, 1864	100 dys.	Mustered out with company Sept. 4, 1864.
Kryder, George	do.	31	May 2, 1864	100 dys.	Mustered out with company Sept. 4, 1864.
Kurtz, Francis	do.	18	May 2, 1864	100 dys.	Absent, sick ——, at home. No further record found.
Logan, Isaac	do.	33	May 2, 1864	100 dys.	Furloughed June 10, 1864, for five days. No further record found.
Lowrey, William M.	do.	36	May 2, 1864	100 dys.	Mustered out with company Sept. 4, 1864.
Markham, Joseph	do.	18	May 2, 1864	100 dys.	Mustered out with company Sept. 4, 1864.
Miller, David H.	do.	29	May 2, 1864	ys	Surgeon May 10, 1864.
Morckle, John	do.	33	May 2, 1864	ys	company Sept. 4, 1864.
Morrow, Obediah	do.	30	May 2, 1864	100 dys.	Mustered out with company Sept. 4, 1864.
Murray, John	do.	19	May 2, 1864	100 dys.	Mustered out with company Sept. 4, 1864.
Neidig, Jonas	do.	37	May 2, 1864	100 dys.	Mustered out with company Sept. 4, 1864.
Neiman, John	do.	25	May 2, 1864	100 dys.	Promoted to Sergt. Major May 10, 1864.
Oyer, John E.	do.	20	May 2, 1864	100 dys.	Mustered out with company Sept. 4, 1864.
Oyster, Solomon	do.	18	May 2, 1864	100 dys.	Mustered out with company Sept. 4, 1864.
Perdue, Samuel K.	do.	18	May 2, 1864	100 dys.	Mustered out with company Sept. 4, 1864.
Permar, Joshua	do.	31	May 2, 1864	100 dys.	Mustered out with company Sept. 4, 1864.
Prince, Edwin	do.	18	May 2, 1864	100 dys.	Mustered out with company Sept. 4, 1864.
Richard, Rudolph	do.	19	May 2, 1864	100 dys.	Mustered out with company Sept. 4, 1864.
Ringle, Albert	do.	20	May 2, 1864	100 dys.	Mustered out with company Sept. 4, 1864.
Roach, Thomas J.	do.	36	May 2, 1864	100 dys.	Mustered out with company Sept. 4, 1864.
Roarer, Martin	do.	20	May 2, 1864	100 dys.	Mustered out with company Sept. 4, 1864.
Scott, Samuel	do.	42	May 2, 1864	100 dys.	Mustered out with company Sept. 4, 1864.
Sefert, Washington	do.	18	May 2, 1864	100 dys.	Mustered out with company Sept. 4, 1864.
Shaw, Wilson	do.	39	May 2, 1864	100 dys.	Mustered out with company Sept. 4, 1864.
Sheppard, John B.	do.	19	May 2, 1864	100 dys.	Mustered out with company Sept. 4, 1864.
Slagle, Henry	do.	18	May 2, 1864	100 dys.	Mustered out with company Sept. 4, 1864.
Speakman, Joseph	do.	24	May 2, 1864	100 dys.	Mustered out with company Sept. 4, 1864.
Spore, Cornelius	do.	38	May 2, 1864	100 dys.	Mustered out with company Sept. 4, 1864.
Taylor, Elmer	do.	18	May 2, 1864	100 dys.	Mustered out with company Sept. 4, 1864.
Taylor, Harrison P.	do.	23	May 2, 1864	100 dys.	Mustered out with company Sept. 4, 1864.
Thomas, Pinm	do.	18	May 2, 1864	100 dys.	Mustered out with company Sept. 4, 1864.
Treap, John	do.	19	May 2, 1864	100 dys.	Mustered out with company Sept. 4, 1864.
Ulman, Adam	do.	18	May 2, 1864	100 dys.	Mustered out with company Sept. 4, 1864.
Unkefer, Alvin	do.	18	May 2, 1864	100 dys.	Mustered out with company Sept. 4, 1864.
Walker, George	do.	24	May 2, 1864	100 dys.	Mustered out with company Sept. 4, 1864.
Walker, Isaac P.	do.	19	May 2, 1864	100 dys.	Mustered out with company Sept. 4, 1864.
Walker, Jacob	do.	21	May 2, 1864	100 dys.	Mustered out with company Sept. 4, 1864.
Walker, Lewis	do.	18	May 2, 1864	100 dys.	Mustered out with company Sept. 4, 1864.
Wallace, William D.	do.	21	May 2, 1864	100 dys.	Mustered out with company Sept. 4, 1864.
Watson, Andrew	do.	38	May 2, 1864	100 dys.	Mustered out with company Sept. 4, 1864.
Weatherspoon, John	do.	28	May 2, 1864	100 dys.	Mustered out with company Sept. 4, 1864.
Whitacre, Jonathan	do.	19	May 2, 1864	100 dys.	Mustered out with company Sept. 4, 1864.
Widener, Benjamin	do.	20	May 2, 1864	100 dys.	Absent, sick ——. No further record found.
Wier, James J.	do.	25	May 2, 1864	100 dys.	Mustered out with company Sept. 4, 1864.
Wier, John J.	do.	29	May 2, 1864	100 dys.	Mustered out with company Sept. 4, 1864.

COMPANY E.

Mustered in May 20, 1864, at Camp Chase, O., by James P. W. Neill, 1st Lieutenant 18th Infantry, U. S. A. Mustered out Sept. 4, 1864, at Camp Chase, O., by D. M. Vance, 1st Lieutenant 11th Infantry, U. S. A.

Names.	Rank.	Age.	Date of Entering the Service.	Period of Service.	Remarks.
Hiram H. Housel	Captain.	23	May 2, 1864	100 dys.	Mustered out with company Sept. 4, 1864.
George Machemer	1st Lieut.	40	May 2, 1864	100 dys.	Mustered out with company Sept. 4, 1864.
Reuben Senick	2d Lieut.	26	May 2, 1864	100 dys.	Mustered out with company Sept. 4, 1864.
Reuben Z. Wise	1st Sergt.	27	May 2, 1864	100 dys.	Mustered out with company Sept. 4, 1864.
Henry L. Schlott	Sergeant.	29	May 2, 1864	100 dys.	Mustered out with company Sept. 4, 1864.
Andrew M. Wise	do.	21	May 2, 1864	100 dys.	Mustered out with company Sept. 4, 1864.
Joshua Lautz	do.	19	May 2, 1864	100 dys.	Mustered out with company Sept. 4, 1864.
John D. Firestone	do.	21	May 2, 1864	100 dys.	Mustered out with company Sept. 4, 1864.
James K. McDowel	Corporal.	22	May 2, 1864	100 dys.	Mustered out with company Sept. 4, 1864.
George Spangler	do.	19	May 2, 1864	100 dys.	Mustered out with company Sept. 4, 1864.
Henry S. Stone	do.	21	May 2, 1864	100 dys.	Mustered out with company Sept. 4, 1864.
W[illegible] W. Conell	do.	20	May 2, 1864	100 dys.	Mustered out with company Sept. 4, 1864.
Jacob Holl	do.	39	May 2, 1864	100 dys.	Mustered out with company Sept. 4, 1864.
Nerias L. Schlott	do.	22	May 2, 1864	100 dys.	Mustered out with company Sept. 4, 1864.
Daniel Lichty	do.	18	May 2, 1864	100 dys.	Mustered out with company Sept. 4, 1864.
Lewis Lind	do.	19	May 2, 1864	100 dys.	Mustered out with company Sept. 4, 1864.

Names.	Rank.	Age.	Date of Entering the Service.	Period of Service.	Remarks.
Ritz, Charles	Private	38	May 2, 1864	100 dys.	Mustered out with company Sept. 4, 1864.
Rosenberry, George W.	...do...	34	May 2, 1864	100 dys.	Mustered out with company Sept. 4, 1864.
Roush, Daniel F.	...do...	18	May 2, 1864	100 dys.	Died Sept. 4, 1864, in hospital at Covington, Kentucky.
Seil, Daniel	...do...	19	May 2, 1864	100 dys.	Mustered out with company Sept. 4, 1864.
Shadley, John	...do...	18	May 2, 1864	100 dys.	Mustered out with company Sept. 4, 1864.
Shankleton, Samuel	...do...	18	May 2, 1864	100 dys.	Mustered out with company Sept. 4, 1864.
Shearer, Henry	...do...	18	May 2, 1864	100 dys.	Mustered out with company Sept. 4, 1864.
Shearer, Hezekiah	...do...	18	May 2, 1864	100 dys.	Mustered out with company Sept. 4, 1864.
Sigle, Henry	...do...	40	May 2, 1864	100 dys.	Mustered out with company Sept. 4, 1864.
Silvers, Samuel B.	...do...	18	May 2, 1864	100 dys.	Mustered out with company Sept. 4, 1864.
Snyder, Hiram	...do...	20	May 2, 1864	100 dys.	Mustered out with company Sept. 4, 1864.
Spangle, Franklin	...do...	21	May 2, 1864	100 dys.	Mustered out with company Sept. 4, 1864.
Stahl, Cyrus	...do...	19	May 2, 1864	100 dys.	Mustered out with company Sept. 4, 1864.
Strouse, Jacob	...do...	18	May 2, 1864	100 dys.	Mustered out with company Sept. 4, 1864.
Sullivan, Benjamin F.	...do...	18	May 2, 1864	100 dys.	Mustered out with company Sept. 4, 1864.
Virtue, George	...do...	24	May 2, 1864	100 dys.	Mustered out with company Sept. 4, 1864.
Williamson, Obed	...do...	24	May 2, 1864	100 dys.	Mustered out with company Sept. 4, 1864.
Wilson, John	...do...	39	May 2, 1864	100 dys.	Mustered out with company Sept. 4, 1864.
Wise, Franklin	...do...	19	May 2, 1864	100 dys.	Died July 19, 1864, at Covington, Ky.

COMPANY H.

Mustered in May 20, 1864, at Camp Chase, O., by James P. W. Neill, 1st Lieutenant 18th Infantry, U. S. A. Mustered out Sept. 4, 1864, at Camp Chase, O., by D. M. Vance, 1st Lieutenant 11th Infantry, U. S. A.

Names.	Rank.	Age.	Date of Entering the Service.	Period of Service.	Remarks.
James B. Michener	Captain.	25	May 2, 1864	100 dys.	Mustered out with company Sept. 4, 1864.
Henry R. Bennett	1st Lieut.	28	May 2, 1864	100 dys.	Mustered out with company Sept. 4, 1864.
Alpheus Hamilton	2d Lieut.	36	May 2, 1864	100 dys.	Mustered out with company Sept. 4, 1864.
Harvey D. Smalley	1st Sergt.	39	May 2, 1864	100 dys.	Mustered out with company Sept. 4, 1864.
James Morgan	Sergeant.	31	May 2, 1864	100 dys.	Mustered out with company Sept. 4, 1864.
John F. Grossklaus	...do...	37	May 2, 1864	100 dys.	Promoted to Hospital Steward June 27, 1864.
Abram Holabaugh	...do...	22	May 2, 1864	100 dys.	Appointed from Corporal ——; mustered out with company Sept. 4, 1864.
William F. Holabaugh	...do...	21	May 2, 1864	100 dys.	Mustered out with company Sept. 4, 1864.
Hiram W. Britton	...do...	20	May 2, 1864	100 dys.	Mustered out with company Sept. 4, 1864.
Franklin M. Henderson	Corporal.	24	May 2, 1864	100 dys.	Mustered out with company Sept. 4, 1864.
Alfred Brooke	...do...	27	May 2, 1864	100 dys.	Mustered out with company Sept. 4, 1864.
Samuel Ren[illegible]	...do...	28	May 2, 1864	100 dys.	Mustered out with company Sept. 4, 1864.
Henry W. Lyon	...do...	30	May 2, 1864	100 dys.	Mustered out with company Sept. 4, 1864.
Joseph L. Wickersham	...do...	31	May 2, 1864	100 dys.	Mustered out with company Sept. 4, 1864.
John L. Watsh[illegible]	...do...	27	May 2, 1864	100 dys.	Mustered out with company Sept. 4, 1864.
David Ho[illegible]	...do...	[illegible]	May 2, 1864	100 dys.	Mustered out with company Sept. 4, 1864.
Edwin D. M[illegible]	...do...	28	May 2, 1864	100 dys.	Mustered out with company Sept. 4, 1864.
Simeon [illegible]	Musician.	19	May 2, 1864	100 dys.	Mustered out with company Sept. 4, 1864.
Franklin Lew[illegible]	...do...	18	May 2, 1864	100 dys.	Mustered out with company Sept. 4, 1864.
Allman, James P.	Private.	18	May 2, 1864	100 dys.	Mustered out with company Sept. 4, 1864.
Aller, [illegible]	...do...	18	May 2, 1864	100 dys.	Mustered out with company Sept. 4, 1864.
Barnes, John S.	...do...	[illegible]	May 2, 1864	100 dys.	Mustered out with company Sept. 4, 1864.
Bartholomew, Crossman	...do...	[illegible]	May 2, 1864	100 dys.	Mustered out with company Sept. 4, 1864.
Bowers, Samuel	...do...	30	May 2, 1864	100 dys.	Mustered out with company Sept. 4, 1864.
Brooks, [illegible]	...do...	18	May 2, 1864	100 dys.	Mustered out with company Sept. 4, 1864.
Brown, [illegible]	...do...	[illegible]	May 2, 1864	100 dys.	Mustered out with company Sept. 4, 1864.
Capsaddle, Lawrence	...do...	[illegible]	May 2, 1864	100 dys.	Mustered out with company Sept. 4, 1864.
[illegible], Robert	...do...	[illegible]	May 2, 1864	100 dys.	Mustered out with company Sept. 4, 1864.
Cole, Reason	...do...	[illegible]	May 2, 1864	100 dys.	Mustered out with company Sept. 4, 1864.
Cox[illegible]	...do...	[illegible]	May 2, 1864	100 dys.	Mustered out with company Sept. 4, 1864.
Cross, Joseph	...do...	18	May 2, 1864	100 dys.	Mustered out with company Sept. 4, 1864.
D[illegible], W[illegible]	...do...	[illegible]	May 2, 1864	100 dys.	Mustered out with company Sept. 4, 1864.
D[illegible], David	...do...	[illegible]	May 2, 1864	100 dys.	Mustered out with company Sept. 4, 1864.
D[illegible], James L.	...do...	[illegible]	May 2, 1864	100 dys.	Mustered out with company Sept. 4, 1864.
[illegible], Dempsey	...do...	[illegible]	May 2, 1864	100 dys.	Mustered out with company Sept. 4, 1864.
Farrington, Jesse	...do...	[illegible]	May 2, 1864	100 dys.	Mustered out with company Sept. 4, 1864.
Finch, Samuel	...do...	[illegible]	May 2, 1864	100 dys.	Mustered out with company Sept. 4, 1864.
F[illegible]	...do...	[illegible]	May 2, 1864	100 dys.	Mustered out with company Sept. 4, 1864.
Fore[illegible]	...do...	[illegible]	May 2, 1864	100 dys.	Mustered out with company Sept. 4, 1864.
Garver, [illegible]	...do...	[illegible]	May 2, 1864	100 dys.	Mustered out with company Sept. 4, 1864.
Hart, [illegible]	...do...	[illegible]	May 2, 1864	100 dys.	Mustered out with company Sept. 4, 1864.
Haw[illegible]	...do...	[illegible]	May 2, 1864	100 dys.	Mustered out with company Sept. 4, 1864.
H[illegible]	...do...	[illegible]	May 2, 1864	100 dys.	Mustered out with company Sept. 4, 1864.
Holabaugh, [illegible]	...do...	[illegible]	May 2, 1864	100 dys.	Mustered out with company Sept. 4, 1864.
Holabaugh, Edward	...do...	[illegible]	May 2, 1864	100 dys.	Mustered out with company Sept. 4, 1864.
[illegible]	...do...	[illegible]	May 2, 1864	100 dys.	Mustered out with company Sept. 4, 1864.
Kee[illegible]	...do...	[illegible]	May 2, 1864	100 dys.	Mustered out with company Sept. 4, 1864.
Keller, [illegible]	...do...	[illegible]	May 2, 1864	100 dys.	Mustered out with company Sept. 4, 1864.
Mc[illegible], William W.	...do...	[illegible]	May 2, 1864	100 dys.	Mustered out with company Sept. 4, 1864.
Mc[illegible], W[illegible]	...do...	[illegible]	May 2, 1864	100 dys.	Mustered out with company Sept. 4, 1864.
Mas[illegible]	...do...	[illegible]	May 2, 1864	100 dys.	Mustered out with company Sept. 4, 1864.
Mas[illegible]	...do...	[illegible]	May 2, 1864	100 dys.	Mustered out with company Sept. 4, 1864.

Names.	Rank.	Age.	Date of Entering the Service.	Period of Service.	Remarks.
Hamilton, George W	Private	21	May 2, 1864	100 dys.	Mustered out with company Sept. 4, 1864.
Hissem, Samuel	do	35	May 2, 1864	100 dys.	Mustered out with company Sept. 4, 1864.
Huffman, David	do	19	May 2, 1864	100 dys.	Mustered out with company Sept. 4, 1864.
Keagle, Levi S.	do	28	May 2, 1864	100 dys.	Promoted to Chaplain May 20, 1864.
Kimmel, Sands	do	20	May 2, 1864	100 dys.	Mustered out with company Sept. 4, 1864.
Klingler, Henry	do	21	May 2, 1864	100 dys.	Mustered out with company Sept. 4, 1864.
Long, Christian	do	19	May 2, 1864	100 dys.	Mustered out with company Sept. 4, 1864.
Long, Jacob	do	18	May 2, 1864	100 dys.	Mustered out with company Sept. 4, 1864.
McDaniel, Alexander H	do	18	May 2, 1864	100 dys.	Mustered out with company Sept. 4, 1864.
McLean, Oscar	do	18	May 2, 1864	100 dys.	Mustered out with company Sept. 4, 1864.
Mays, Wilton D	do	19	May 2, 1864	100 dys.	Mustered out with company Sept. 4, 1864.
Mottice, James W	do	29	May 2, 1864	100 dys.	Mustered out with company Sept. 4, 1864.
Mottice, John	do	21	May 2, 1864	100 dys.	Mustered out with company Sept. 4, 1864.
Mottice, Kinsley	do	18	May 2, 1864	100 dys.	Mustered out with company Sept. 4, 1864.
Mottice, Milton	do	19	May 2, 1864	100 dys.	Mustered out with company Sept. 4, 1864.
Muckley, John	do	27	May 2, 1864	100 dys.	Died Aug. 24, 1864, at his home, Ohio
Prouse, John	do	18	May 2, 1864	100 dys.	Mustered out with company Sept. 4, 1864.
Reed, Edward	do	25	May 2, 1864	100 dys.	Died July 26, 1864, at Fort McLean, Ky.
Reed, John L	do	30	May 2, 1864	100 dys.	Mustered out with company Sept. 4, 1864.
Reed, John W	do	43	May 2, 1864	100 dys.	Mustered out with company Sept. 4, 1864.
Rhinehart, George M	do	18	May 2, 1864	100 dys.	Mustered out with company Sept. 4, 1864.
Rhoades, George W	do	21	May 2, 1864	100 dys.	Mustered out with company Sept. 4, 1864.
Rice, Benjamin F.	do	23	May 2, 1864	100 dys.	Mustered out with company Sept. 4, 1864.
Robertson, John L	do	23	May 2, 1864	100 dys.	Mustered out with company Sept. 4, 1864.
Ross, Thomas H	do	18	May 2, 1864	100 dys.	Mustered out with company Sept. 4, 1864.
Shaeffer, Milton	do	18	May 2, 1864	100 dys.	Mustered out with company Sept. 4, 1864.
Shaeffer, Peter	do	29	May 2, 1864	100 dys.	Mustered out with company Sept. 4, 1864.
Shanebruck, Anthony J	do	19	May 2, 1864	100 dys.	Mustered out with company Sept. 4, 1864.
Shank, Matthew F	do	18	May 2, 1864	100 dys.	Mustered out with company Sept. 4, 1864.
Sherer, Peter	do	36	May 2, 1864	100 dys.	Mustered out with company Sept. 4, 1864.
Shine, Henry W	do	39	May 2, 1864	100 dys.	Absent, sick ——. No further record found.
Simmons, George	do	30	May 2, 1864	100 dys.	Mustered out with company Sept. 4, 1864.
Smith, George F	do	24	May 2, 1864	100 dys.	Mustered out with company Sept. 4, 1864.
Spruce, Abel S.	do	18	May 2, 1864	100 dys.	Mustered out with company Sept. 4, 1864.
VanMeter, John	do	24	May 2, 1864	100 dys.	Mustered out with company Sept. 4, 1864.
Weaver, John D	do	20	May 2, 1864	100 dys.	Mustered out with company Sept. 4, 1864.
Weedling, William	do	23	May 2, 1864	100 dys.	Mustered out with company Sept. 4, 1864.
Welker, George W	do	28	May 2, 1864	100 dys.	Absent, sick ——. No further record found.
Welker, James J	do	22	May 2, 1864	100 dys.	Mustered out with company Sept. 4, 1864.
Welker, John L	do	18	May 2, 1864	100 dys.	Mustered out with company Sept. 4, 1864.
Wenning, Barnhart	do	23	May 2, 1864	100 dys.	Mustered out with company Sept. 4, 1864.
Wheadon, John F	do	21	May 2, 1864	100 dys.	Mustered out with company Sept. 4, 1864.
Whetstone, Absalom	do	27	May 2, 1864	100 dys.	Mustered out with company Sept. 4, 1864.
Whitacre, Thomas H	do	41	May 2, 1864	100 dys.	Promoted to Asst. Surgeon May 20, 1864.
Wilson, Harper W	do	18	May 2, 1864	100 dys.	Mustered out with company Sept. 4, 1864.

COMPANY K.

Mustered in May 14, 1864, at Gallipolis, O., by W. P. McCleery, 1st Lieutenant 18th Infantry, U. S. A. Mustered out Sept. 4, 1864, at Camp Chase, O., by D. M. Vance, 1st Lieutenant 11th Infantry, U. S. A.

Names.	Rank.	Age.	Date of Entering the Service.	Period of Service.	Remarks.
William N. Ramey	Captain.	41	May 2, 1864	100 dys.	Mustered out with company Sept. 4, 1864.
William A. Work	1st Lieut.	25	May 2, 1864	100 dys.	Mustered out with company Sept. 4, 1864.
Thomas D. Saunders	2d Lieut.	38	May 2, 1864	100 dys.	Mustered out with company Sept. 4, 1864.
William Kerr	1st Sergt.	38	May 2, 1864	100 dys.	Mustered out with company Sept. 4, 1864.
James B. Norton	Sergeant.	27	May 2, 1864	100 dys.	Mustered out with company Sept. 4, 1864.
Hiram W. Kindle	do	22	May 2, 1864	100 dys.	Mustered out with company Sept. 4, 1864.
Wilson M. McKnight	do	21	May 2, 1864	100 dys.	Mustered out with company Sept. 4, 1864.
Alexander N. Martin	do	39	May 2, 1864	100 dys.	Mustered out with company Sept. 4, 1864.
Samuel D. Carson	Corporal.	28	May 2, 1864	100 dys.	Mustered out with company Sept. 4, 1864.
Edward Burbage	do	27	May 2, 1864	100 dys.	Discharged May 26, 1864, at Camp Chase, O., on Surgeon's certificate of disability.
Thomas W. Mooney	do	24	May 2, 1864	100 dys.	Mustered out with company Sept. 4, 1864.
William W. Francis	do	41	May 2, 1864	100 dys.	Mustered out with company Sept. 4, 1864.
Russell West	do	33	May 2, 1864	100 dys.	Mustered out with company Sept. 4, 1864.
James Alexander	do	28	May 2, 1864	100 dys.	Mustered out with company Sept. 4, 1864.
George E. Kirkpatrick	do	28	May 2, 1864	100 dys.	Mustered out with company Sept. 4, 1864.
Lawrence McLaughlin	do	28	May 2, 1864	100 dys.	Discharged Aug. 10, 1864, at Columbus, O., on Surgeon's certificate of disability
Alexander, Joshua P	Private	25	May 2, 1864	100 dys.	Mustered out with company Sept. 4, 1864.
Anderson, Elbert H	do	38	May 2, 1864	100 dys.	Mustered out with company Sept. 4, 1864.
Baird, William W	do	37	May 2, 1864	100 dys.	Mustered out with company Sept. 4, 1864.
Bell, William	do	44	May 2, 1864	100 dys.	Mustered out with company Sept. 4, 1864.
Boggs, Charles	do	44	May 2, 1864	100 dys.	Mustered out with company Sept. 4, 1864.
Brooks, Thomas C	do	22	May 2, 1864	100 dys.	Mustered out with company Sept. 4, 1864.
Brown, William C	do	19	May 2, 1864	100 dys.	Mustered out with company Sept. 4, 1864.
Burbage, John	do	32	May 2, 1864	100 dys.	Mustered out with company Sept. 4, 1864.
Burns, William	do	32	May 2, 1864	100 dys.	Mustered out with company Sept. 4, 1864.
Carey, Joshua R	do	33	May 2, 1864	100 dys.	Mustered out with company Sept. 4, 1864.

Names.	Rank.	Age.	Date of Entering the Service.	Period of Service.	Remarks.
Carson, Finley K	Private	19	May 2, 1864	100 dys.	Mustered out with company Sept. 4, 1864.
Claxton, Samuel P	...do...	23	May 2, 1864	100 dys.	Mustered out with company Sept. 4, 1864.
Cole, Lee P	...do...	18	May 2, 1864	100 dys.	Mustered out with company Sept. 4, 1864.
Collins, Samuel A	...do...	26	May 2, 1864	100 dys.	Mustered out with company Sept. 4, 1864.
Collins, Aid	...do...	21	May 2, 1864	100 dys.	Mustered out with company Sept. 4, 1864.
Conn, Albert	...do...	20	May 2, 1864	100 dys.	Mustered out with company Sept. 4, 1864.
Cornelius, George W	...do...	35	May 2, 1864	100 dys.	Mustered out with company Sept. 4, 1864.
Cowen, Richard M	...do...	28	May 2, 1864	100 dys.	Mustered out with company Sept. 4, 1864.
Cox, John T	...do...	37	May 2, 1864	100 dys.	Mustered out with company Sept. 4, 1864.
Davidson, Amos F	...do...	19	May 2, 1864	100 dys.	Mustered out with company Sept. 4, 1864.
Dillinger, George W	...do...	23	May 2, 1864	100 dys.	Mustered out with company Sept. 4, 1864.
Drake, William J	...do...	25	May 2, 1864	100 dys.	Mustered out with company Sept. 4, 1864.
Draper, John	...do...	20	May 2, 1864	100 dys.	Mustered out with company Sept. 4, 1864.
Finney, Jonathan	...do...	36	May 2, 1864	100 dys.	Mustered out with company Sept. 4, 1864.
Gayly, Joseph	...do...	27	May 2, 1864	100 dys.	Mustered out with company Sept. 4, 1864.
Hamilton, Samuel Y	...do...	25	May 2, 1864	100 dys.	Mustered out with company Sept. 4, 1864.
Henry, Alvin L	...do...	19	May 2, 1864	100 dys.	Mustered out with company Sept. 4, 1864.
Howland, Thomas	...do...	21	May 2, 1864	100 dys.	Mustered out with company Sept. 4, 1864.
Inskeep, James P	...do...	18	May 2, 1864	100 dys.	Discharged Aug. 10, 1864, at Columbus, O., on Surgeon's certificate of disability.
Johnson, Norval	...do...	18	May 2, 1864	100 dys.	Mustered out with company Sept. 4, 1864.
Johnson, Oliver M	...do...	32	May 2, 1864	100 dys.	Mustered out with company Sept. 4, 1864.
Jones, Alvin	...do...	18	May 2, 1864	100 dys.	Mustered out with company Sept. 4, 1864.
Jones, John W	...do...	20	May 2, 1864	100 dys.	Mustered out with company Sept. 4, 1864.
Kane, William T	...do...	22	May 2, 1864	100 dys.	Mustered out with company Sept. 4, 1864.
Kirkpatrick, Newton	...do...	32	May 2, 1864	100 dys.	Mustered out with company Sept. 4, 1864.
Liggett, Albert F	...do...	22	May 2, 1864	100 dys.	Mustered out with company Sept. 4, 1864.
McElfresh, James	...do...	18	May 2, 1864	100 dys.	Mustered out with company Sept. 4, 1864.
McFerson, Adam H	...do...	30	May 2, 1864	100 dys.	Mustered out with company Sept. 4, 1864.
McNoun, Scott	...do...	16	May 2, 1864	100 dys.	Mustered out with company Sept. 4, 1864.
McNoun, Thomas	...do...	19	May 2, 1864	100 dys.	Mustered out with company Sept. 4, 1864.
Mannon, Samuel B	...do...	20	May 2, 1864	100 dys.	Mustered out with company Sept. 4, 1864.
Mannon, William R	...do...	27	May 2, 1864	100 dys.	Mustered out with company Sept. 4, 1864.
Melford, John D	...do...	21	May 2, 1864	100 dys.	Mustered out with company Sept. 4, 1864.
Montgomery, George T	...do...	24	May 2, 1864	100 dys.	Discharged Aug. 15, 1864, at Camp Chase, O., on Surgeon's certificate of disability.
Moore, George T	...do...	26	May 2, 1864	100 dys.	Mustered out with company Sept. 4, 1864.
Morris, Henry	...do...	18	May 2, 1864	100 dys.	Mustered out with company Sept. 4, 1864.
Morris, Silas T	...do...	23	May 2, 1864	100 dys.	Mustered out with company Sept. 4, 1864.
Mulligan, Jacob C	...do...	24	May 2, 1864	100 dys.	Mustered out with company Sept. 4, 1864.
Naylor, William R	...do...	25	May 2, 1864	100 dys.	Mustered out with company Sept. 4, 1864.
Pickerel, John F	...do...	22	May 2, 1864	100 dys.	Mustered out with company Sept. 4, 1864.
Pickerel, Samuel W	...do...	23	May 2, 1864	100 dys.	Mustered out with company Sept. 4, 1864.
Pickerel Thomas L	...do...	29	May 2, 1864	100 dys.	Mustered out with company Sept. 4, 1864.
Pilson, Samuel	...do...	21	May 2, 1864	100 dys.	Discharged Aug. 20, 1864, at Columbus, O., on Surgeon's certificate of disability.
Porter, John B	...do...	20	May 2, 1864	100 dys.	Mustered out with company Sept. 4, 1864.
Potts, Andrew P	...do...	24	May 2, 1864	100 dys.	Mustered out with company Sept. 4, 1864.
Ramsey, Martin B	...do...	42	May 2, 1864	100 dys.	Mustered out with company Sept. 4, 1864.
Ramsey, William A	...do...	20	May 2, 1864	100 dys.	Mustered out with company Sept. 4, 1864.
Reed, Absalom	...do...	36	May 2, 1864	100 dys.	Mustered out with company Sept. 4, 1864.
Reed, Albert	...do...	18	May 2, 1864	100 dys.	Mustered out with company Sept. 4, 1864.
Robinson, Samuel	...do...	31	May 2, 1864	100 dys.	Mustered out with company Sept. 4, 1864.
Seipe, Jacob	...do...	22	May 2, 1864	100 dys.	Died June 21, 1864, at Seminary Hospital, Columbus, O.
Stevenson, Robert	...do...	32	May 2, 1864	100 dys.	Mustered out with company Sept. 4, 1864.
Stivers, William	...do...	18	May 2, 1864	100 dys.	Mustered out with company Sept. 4, 1864.
Taggart, William	...do...	32	May 2, 1864	100 dys.	Died Aug. 21 1864, at Seminary Hospital, Columbus, O.
Thompson, Alexander B.	...do...	18	May 2, 1864	100 dys.	Mustered out with company Sept. 4, 1864.
Warner, George	...do...	18	May 2, 1864	100 dys.	Mustered out with company Sept. 4, 1864.
Williams, John H	...do...	22	May 2, 1864	100 dys.	Mustered out with company Sept. 4, 1864.
Winters, Marshall L	...do...	21	May 2, 1864	100 dys.	Mustered out with company Sept. 4, 1864.
Wright, Robert A	...do...	25	May 2, 1864	100 dys.	Mustered out with company Sept. 4, 1864.

163rd Regiment Ohio Volunteer Infantry.

ONE HUNDRED DAYS' SERVICE.

THIS Regiment was organized at Camp Chase, O., May 12, 1864, to serve one hundred days. It was composed of the Forty-eighth Regiment, Ohio National Guard, from Richland County; Seventy-second Battalion, Ohio National Guard, from Henry County; Ninety-sixth Battalion, Ohio National Guard, from Ashland County; and the Ninety-ninth Battalion, Ohio National Guard, from Stark County. On the 13th of May the Regiment proceeded to Washington City, under orders from General Heintzelman, commanding the Department of Ohio. It was assigned to duty with headquarters at Fort Reno, D. C., where it remained until the 8th of June, when it was ordered to the front, and proceeded in transports to White House, Va., and thence to Bermuda Hundred. It reported to General Butler, at Point of Rocks, on the 12th of June, and on the 14th took part in a reconnaissance on the Petersburg and Richmond Railroad. Two hundred and fifty men of the One Hundred and Sixty-third were engaged in a severe skirmish on the 15th, and on the 16th it proceeded to Wilson's Landing, and from that point made several reconnaissances to the west side of the James. On the 29th of August the Regiment was relieved from duty, and proceeded to Columbus, O., and was mustered out September 10, 1864, on expiration of term of service.

COMPANY C.

Mustered in May 12, 1864, at Camp Chase, O., by James P. W. Neill, 1st Lieutenant 18th Infantry, U. S. A. Mustered out Sept. 10, 1864, at Camp Chase, O., by George R. Vernon. 1st Lieutenant 14th Infantry, U. S. A.

Names.	Rank.	Age.	Date of Entering the Service.	Period of Service.	Remarks.
William W. Cockley	Captain.	28	May 2, 1864	100 dys.	Mustered out with company Sept. 10, 1864.
Wesley Cashell	1st Lieut.	24	May 2, 1864	100 dys.	Mustered out with company Sept. 10, 1864.
John Spayd	2d Lieut.	36	May 2, 1864	100 dys.	Mustered out with company Sept. 10, 1864.
Robert S. McFarland	1st Sergt.	29	May 2, 1864	100 dys.	Mustered out with company Sept. 10, 1864.
Simon P. Armstrong	Sergeant.	36	May 2, 1864	100 dys.	Mustered out with company Sept. 10, 1864.
Wesley W. Sparks	....do....	24	May 2, 1864	100 dys.	Mustered out with company Sept. 10, 1864.
Samuel W. McFarland	....do....	32	May 2, 1864	100 dys.	Mustered out with company Sept. 10, 1864.
Andrew J. Enlow	....do....	36	May 2, 1864	100 dys.	Mustered out with company Sept. 10, 1864.
John Williams	Corporal.	33	May 2, 1864	100 dys.	Absent, sick ——. No further record found.
Jonah Clever	....do....	28	May 2, 1864	100 dys.	Mustered out with company Sept. 10, 1864.
John A. McJunkin	....do....	21	May 2, 1864	100 dys.	Mustered out with company Sept. 10, 1864.
John Hirst	....do....	25	May 2, 1864	100 dys.	Mustered out with company Sept. 10, 1864.
James Thompson	....do....	36	May 2, 1864	100 dys.	Mustered out with company Sept. 10, 1864.
William McFarland	....do....	27	May 2, 1864	100 dys.	Mustered out with company Sept. 10, 1864.
Hiram Baker	....do....	35	May 2, 1864	100 dys.	Mustered out with company Sept. 10, 1864.
Samuel Leiter	....do....	18	May 2, 1864	100 dys.	Mustered out with company Sept. 10, 1864.
Henry Behlich	Musician	18	May 2, 1864	100 dys.	Mustered out with company Sept. 10, 1864.
James Cease	....do....	30	May 2, 1864	100 dys.	Mustered out with company Sept. 10, 1864.
Altgeld, John Peter	Private..	20	May 2, 1864	100 dys.	Mustered out with company Sept. 10, 1864.
Andrews, Jacob	....do....	24	May 2, 1864	100 dys.	Mustered out with company Sept. 10, 1864.
Berry, Philip	....do....	18	May 2, 1864	100 dys.	Died Sept. 10, 1864, en-route home.
Bierly, Jeremiah	....do....	26	May 2, 1864	100 dys.	Mustered out with company Sept. 10, 1864.
Bowden, John W	....do....	18	May 2, 1864	100 dys.	Mustered out with company Sept. 10, 1864.
Cainan, Edward	....do....	22	May 2, 1864	100 dys.	
Carnahan, James C	....do....	40	May 2, 1864	100 dys.	Mustered out with company Sept. 10, 1864.
Cashell, Chester	....do....	19	May 2, 1864	100 dys.	Mustered out with company Sept. 10, 1864.
Cate, William	....do....	18	May 2, 1864	100 dys.	Died Sept. 13, 1864, at home, Washington Township, Richland County, O.
Clever, Daniel	....do....	18	May 2, 1864	100 dys.	Mustered out with company Sept. 10, 1864.
Clever, Henry	....do....	24	May 2, 1864	100 dys.	Mustered out with company Sept. 10, 1864.
Cottelllious, William	....do....	19	May 2, 1864	100 dys.	Mustered out with company Sept. 10, 1864.
Culver, Thomas J	....do....	29	May 2, 1864	100 dys.	Absent, sick ——. No further record found.
Day, Joseph	....do....	19	May 2, 1864	100 dys.	Mustered out with company Sept. 10, 1864.
Deems, William	....do....	28	May 2, 1864	100 dys.	Mustered out with company Sept. 10, 1864.
Farmer, John S	....do....	19	May 2, 1864	100 dys.	Mustered out with company Sept. 10, 1864.
Fleming, Charles	....do....	47	May 2, 1864	100 dys.	Mustered out with company Sept. 10, 1864.
Ford, Howard	....do....	18	May 2, 1864	100 dys.	Mustered out with company Sept. 10, 1864.
Ford, Samuel N	....do....	18	May 2, 1864	100 dys.	Mustered out with company Sept. 10, 1864.
Fry, George B	....do....	37	May 2, 1864	100 dys.	Mustered out with company Sept. 10, 1864.
Grubaugh, Andrew	....do....	19	May 2, 1864	100 dys.	Mustered out with company Sept. 10, 1864.
Hamilton, Alexander	....do....	18	May 2, 1864	100 dys.	Mustered out with company Sept. 10, 1864.
Hesseldon, Henry	....do....	33	May 2, 1864	100 dys.	Mustered out with company Sept. 10, 1864.
Hill, William F	....do....	30	May 2, 1864	100 dys.	Mustered out with company Sept. 10, 1864.
Hull, John C	....do....	18	May 2, 1864	100 dys.	Mustered out with company Sept. 10, 1864.
Keller, Thomas J	....do....	18	May 2, 1864	100 dys.	Mustered out with company Sept. 10, 1864.
Kenton, Thomas H	....do....	18	May 2, 1864	100 dys.	Mustered out with company Sept. 10, 1864.
Lash, Aaron T	....do....	19	May 2, 1864	100 dys.	Mustered out with company Sept. 10, 1864.
Leech, Robert J	....do....	22	May 2, 1864	100 dys.	Mustered out with company Sept. 10, 1864.
[illegible], John	....do....	28	May 2, 1864	100 dys.	
Lindsey, Charles W	....do....	22	May 2, 1864	100 dys.	Mustered out with company Sept. 10, 1864.
McCready, David	....do....	21	May 2, 1864	100 dys.	Mustered out with company Sept. 10, 1864.
McFarland, Andrew	....do....	29	May 2, 1864	100 dys.	Mustered out with company Sept. 10, 1864.
McFarland, Mark	....do....	18	May 2, 1864	100 dys.	Mustered out with company Sept. 10, 1864.
Marlow, Moses	....do....	29	May 2, 1864	100 dys.	
Martin, John	....do....	20	May 2, 1864	100 dys.	Mustered out with company Sept. 10, 1864.
Pearce, John	....do....	18	May 2, 1864	100 dys.	Mustered out with company Sept. 10, 1864.
Pollock, Joseph	....do....	30	May 2, 1864	100 dys.	Mustered out with company Sept. 10, 1864.
Pollock, Thomas M	....do....	18	May 2, 1864	100 dys.	Mustered out with company Sept. 10, 1864.
Potter, Isaac [illegible]	....do....	18	May 2, 1864	100 dys.	Mustered out with company Sept. 10, 1864.
Ridenour, Benjamin	....do....	29	May 2, 1864	100 dys.	Mustered out with company Sept. 10, 1864.
Ridenour, George W	....do....	31	May 2, 1864	100 dys.	Mustered out with company Sept. 10, 1864.
Ridenour, William C	....do....	19	May 2, 1864	100 dys.	Absent, sick ——. No further record found.
Roach, Daniel	....do....	29	May 2, 1864	100 dys.	Mustered out with company Sept. 10, 1864.
[illegible], John	....do....	22	May 2, 1864	100 dys.	Mustered out with company Sept. 10, 1864.
[illegible], Alonzo	....do....	18	May 2, 1864	100 dys.	Mustered out with company Sept. 10, 1864.
[illegible], Andrew	....do....	21	May 2, 1864	100 dys.	Mustered out with company Sept. 10, 1864.
[illegible], Jacob	....do....	29	May 2, 1864	100 dys.	Mustered out with company Sept. 10, 1864.
[illegible], George	....do....	20	May 2, 1864	100 dys.	Mustered out with company Sept. 10, 1864.
[illegible], Henry	....do....	45	May 2, 1864	100 dys.	Mustered out with company Sept. 10, 1864.
Sheap, William	....do....	21	May 2, 1864	100 dys.	Mustered out with company Sept. 10, 1864.
Smith, [illegible]	....do....	34	May 2, 1864	100 dys.	Died Aug. 13, 1864, at Hampton Hospital, [illegible]
Sparks, George W	....do....	18	May 2, 1864	100 dys.	Mustered out with company Sept. 10, 1864.
Stoler, [illegible]	....do....	20	May 2, 1864	100 dys.	Mustered out with company Sept. 10, 1864.
Stone, Charles W	....do....	18	May 2, 1864	100 dys.	Mustered out with company Sept. 10, 1864.
Stone, John	....do....	23	May 2, 1864	100 dys.	Mustered out with company Sept. 10, 1864.
Stone, William	....do....	29	May 2, 1864	100 dys.	Mustered out with company Sept. 10, 1864.

Names.	Rank.	Age.	Date of Entering the Service.	Period of Service.	Remarks.
Painter, John	Private..	20	May 2, 1864	100 dys.	Died Aug. 31, 1864, on steamer City of Albany, en route from Fort Pocahontas, Va. to Washington, D. C.
Parr, Robert	...do...	31	May 2, 1864	100 dys.	Mustered out with company Sept. 10, 1864.
Plank, Elam	...do...	22	May 2, 1864	100 dys.	Mustered out with company Sept. 10, 1864.
Richards, David	...do...	26	May 2, 1864	100 dys.	Mustered out with company Sept. 10, 1864.
Richards, William	...do...	28	May 2, 1864	100 dys.	Mustered out with company Sept. 10, 1864.
Ridenour, John	...do...	18	May 2, 1864	100 dys.	Mustered out with company Sept. 10, 1864.
Rinehart, David	...do...	19	May 2, 1864	100 dys.	Mustered out with company Sept. 10, 1864.
Rinehart, James H	...do...	18	May 2, 1864	100 dys.	Mustered out with company Sept. 10, 1864.
Riggs, Harrison	...do...	23	May 2, 1864	100 dys.	Mustered out with company Sept. 10, 1864.
Sanders, Joseph L	...do...	31	May 2, 1864	100 dys.	Mustered out with company Sept. 10, 1864.
Sargent, Columbus D.	...do...	18	May 2, 1864	100 dys.	Mustered out with company Sept. 10, 1864.
Secrist, Elah	...do...	19	May 2, 1864	100 dys.	Mustered out with company Sept. 10, 1864.
Shafer, Benjamin	...do...	37	May 2, 1864	100 dys.	Absent, sick ——. No further record found.
Smith, Aaron	...do...	24	May 2, 1864	100 dys.	Mustered out with company Sept. 10, 1864.
Smith, John	...do...	32	May 2, 1864	100 dys.	Mustered out with company Sept. 10, 1864.
Smith, Joseph	...do...	29	May 2, 1864	100 dys.	Mustered out with company Sept. 10, 1864.
Spohn, John	...do...	18	May 2, 1864	100 dys.	Mustered out with company Sept. 10, 1864.
Stoner, Dennis	...do...	19	May 2, 1864	100 dys.	
Sweet, Archibald S.	...do...	24	May 2, 1864	100 dys.	Mustered out with company Sept. 10, 1864.
Traxler, James	...do...	31	May 2, 1864	100 dys.	Mustered out with company Sept. 10, 1864.
White, Sanford D.	...do...	18	May 2, 1864	100 dys.	Mustered out with company Sept. 10, 1864.
Wilen, Jacob	...do...	45	May 2, 1864	100 dys.	Mustered out with company Sept. 10, 1864.
Yarger, Samuel	...do...	18	May 2, 1864	100 dys.	Mustered out with company Sept. 10, 1864.

COMPANY E.

Mustered in May 12, 1864, at Camp Chase, O., by James P. W. Neill, 1st Lieutenant 18th Infantry, U. S. A. Mustered out Sept. 10, 1864, at Camp Chase, O., by George R. Vernon, 1st Lieutenant 11th Infantry, U. S. A.

Names.	Rank.	Age.	Date of Entering the Service.	Period of Service.	Remarks.
William F. Curtis	Captain.	34	May 2, 1864	100 dys.	Mustered out with company Sept. 10, 1864.
Joseph H. Brown	1st Lieut.	20	May 2, 1864	100 dys.	Mustered out with company Sept. 10, 1864.
Peter Starret	2d Lieut.	25	May 2, 1864	100 dys.	Mustered out with company Sept. 10, 1864.
Jacob H. Re[illegible]er	1st Sergt.	26	May 2, 1864	100 dys.	Mustered out with company Sept. 10, 1864.
Amos O. Jump	Sergeant.	29	May 2, 1864	100 dys.	Mustered out with company Sept. 10, 1864.
Joseph [illegible] F. Balderson	...do...	25	May 2, 1864	100 dys.	Mustered out with company Sept. 10, 1864.
James Hughes	...do...	41	May 2, 1864	100 dys.	Mustered out with company Sept. 10, 1864.
Isaac [illegible]nnelly	...do...	44	May 2, 1864	100 dys.	Mustered out with company Sept. 10, 1864.
George W. Ewalt	Corporal.	43	May 2, 1864	100 dys.	Mustered out with company Sept. 10, 1864.
Melvin Osburn	...do...	19	May 2, 1864	100 dys.	Mustered out with company Sept. 10, 1864.
Joshua Bradley	...do...	22	May 2, 1864	100 dys.	Mustered out with company Sept. 10, 1864.
William Hay[illegible]eld	...do...	24	May 2, 1864	100 dys.	Mustered out with company Sept. 10, 1864.
William W Patterson	...do...	24	May 2, 1864	100 dys.	Mustered out with company Sept. 10, 1864.
David Berry	...do...	37	May 2, 1864	100 dys.	Mustered out with company Sept. 10, 1864.
George W. Parr	...do...	23	May 2, 1864	100 dys.	Mustered out with company Sept. 10, 1864.
William Applegate	...do...	21	May 2, 1864	100 dys.	Mustered out with company Sept. 10, 1864.
Benjamin H Egner	Musician	30	May 2, 1864	100 dys.	Mustered out with company Sept. 10, 1864.
Milton Saylers	...do...	28	May 2, 1864	100 dys.	Mustered out with company Sept. 10, 1864.
Andrews, Edward	Private..	19	May 2, 1864	100 dys.	Mustered out with company Sept. 10, 1864.
Bennett, Alexander	...do...	18	May 2, 1864	100 dys.	Mustered out with company Sept. 10, 1864.
Black, James	...do...	32	May 2, 1864	100 dys.	Mustered out with company Sept. 10, 1864.
Brown, George W.	...do...	18	May 2, 1864	100 dys.	Mustered out with company Sept. 10, 1864.
Brown, Wesley	...do...	18	May 2, 1864	100 dys.	Died Aug. 6, 1864, at Fort Pocahontas, Va.
Brubaker, David	...do...	22	May 2, 1864	100 dys.	Mustered out with company Sept. 10, 1864.
Brubaker, Samuel	...do...	18	May 2, 1864	100 dys.	Mustered out with company Sept. 10, 1864.
Carnahan, Scott	...do...	18	May 2, 1864	100 dys.	Mustered out with company Sept. 10, 1864.
Carey, Thomas	...do...	18	May 2, 1864	100 dys.	Mustered out with company Sept. 10, 1864.
Chamberlain, Washington	...do...	26	May 2, 1864	100 dys.	Mustered out with company Sept. 10, 1864.
Cline, George	...do...	22	May 2, 1864	100 dys.	Mustered out with company Sept. 10, 1864.
Cotner, John	...do...	23	May 2, 1864	100 dys.	Absent, sick ——. No further record found.
Crabb, Benjamin	...do...	26	May 2, 1864	100 dys.	Mustered out with company Sept. 10, 1864.
Cosgrove, Stephen H.	...do...	18	May 2, 1864	100 dys.	Mustered out with company Sept. 10, 1864.
Daniels, Henry	...do...	44	May 2, 1864	100 dys.	Mustered out with company Sept. 10, 1864.
Daniels, John F.	...do...	18	May 2, 1864	100 dys.	Mustered out with company Sept. 10, 1864.
Dinner, Sylvester	...do...	20	May 2, 1864	100 dys.	Mustered out with company Sept. 10, 1864.
Ebert, Henry	...do...	18	May 2, 1864	100 dys.	Mustered out with company Sept. 10, 1864.
Ferguson, James	...do...	20	May 2, 1864	100 dys.	Mustered out with company Sept. 10, 1864.
Ferree, Samuel	...do...	18	May 2, 1864	100 dys.	Mustered out with company Sept. 10, 1864.
Guyseman, Ezra	...do...	18	May 2, 1864	100 dys.	Mustered out with company Sept. 10, 1864.
Hagerman, Oliver S.	...do...	18	May 2, 1864	100 dys.	Mustered out with company Sept. 10, 1864.
Hatfield, Allen	...do...	38	May 2, 1864	100 dys.	Absent, sick ——. No further record found.
Hilton, Albert M	...do...	18	May 2, 1864	100 dys.	Mustered out with company Sept. 10, 1864.
Holmes, Gilbert	...do...	35	May 2, 1864	100 dys.	Mustered out with company Sept. 10, 1864.
Houston, William	...do...	19	May 2, 1864	100 dys.	Mustered out with company Sept. 10, 1864.
Houston, Winfield	...do...	18	May 2, 1864	100 dys.	Mustered out with company Sept. 10, 1864.
Holmes, Thomas	...do...	42	May 2, 1864	100 dys.	Died Aug. 27, 1864, at Hampton Hospital, Va.
Hummel, Aaron B.	...do...	19	May 2, 1864	100 dys.	Mustered out with company Sept. 10, 1864.
Kendal, Samuel	...do...	23	May 2, 1864	100 dys.	Mustered out with company Sept. 10, 1864.

	Rank.	Age.	Date of Entering the Service.	Period of Service.	Remarks.
...od, Lewis	Private.	[illegible]	May 2, 1864	100 dys.	Mustered out with company Sept. 10, 1864.
...nan, William	...do...	42	May 2, 1864	100 dys.	Mustered out with company Sept. 10, 1864.
...efer, Ezra	...do...	[illegible]	May 2, 1864	100 dys.	Mustered out with company Sept. 10, 1864.
...cker, Benton	...do...	18	May 2, 1864	100 dys.	Mustered out with company Sept. 10, 1864.
...ly, Milton	...do...	18	May 2, 1864	100 dys.	Mustered out with company Sept. 10, 1864.
...Henry	...do...	24	May 2, 1864	100 dys.	Mustered out with company Sept. 10, 1864.
..., Levi	...do...	29	May 2, 1864	100 dys.	Mustered out with company Sept. 10, 1864.
..., Franklin	...do...	40	May 2, 1864	100 dys.	Mustered out with company Sept. 10, 1864.
...Melvin	...do...	19	May 2, 1864	100 dys.	Mustered out with company Sept. 10, 1864.
..., William A.	...do...	18	May 2, 1864	100 dys.	Mustered out with company Sept. 10, 1864.
...Robert	...do...	18	May 2, 1864	100 dys.	Mustered out with company Sept. 10, 1864.
..., Joseph	...do...	28	May 2, 1864	100 dys.	Mustered out with company Sept. 10, 1864.
..., William C.	...do...	18	May 2, 1864	100 dys.	Mustered out with company Sept. 10, 1864.
...ohn	...do...	24	May 2, 1864	100 dys.	Mustered out with company Sept. 10, 1864.
...on, Samuel A.	...do...	[illegible]	May 2, 1864	100 dys.	Mustered out with company Sept. 10, 1864.
...William	...do...	19	May 2, 1864	100 dys.	Mustered out with company Sept. 10, 1864.
...Edgar	...do...	30	May 2, 1864	100 dys.	Mustered out with company Sept. 10, 1864.
...er, Abiram	...do...	42	May 2, 1864	100 dys.	Absent, sick ——. No further record found.
...er, Rowland	...do...	18	May 2, 1864	100 dys.	Mustered out with company Sept. 10, 1864.
..., Washington C.	...do...	18	May 2, 1864	100 dys.	Mustered out with company Sept. 10, 1864.
..., Henry	...do...	24	May 2, 1864	100 dys.	Died Aug. 20, 1864, at Hampton Hospital, Va.
...l, William	...do...	18	May 2, 1864	100 dys.	Died Aug. 27, 1864, at Hampton Hospital, Va.
..., Jacob	...do...	21	May 2, 1864	100 dys.	Mustered out with company Sept. 10, 1864.
..., Marvin	...do...	18	May 2, 1864	100 dys.	Mustered out with company Sept. 10, 1864.
...William A.	...do...	21	May 2, 1864	100 dys.	Mustered out with company Sept. 10, 1864.
...nson, Levi	...do...	22	May 2, 1864	100 dys.	Mustered out with company Sept. 10, 1864.
...nson, William	...do...	20	May 2, 1864	100 dys.	Mustered out with company Sept. 10, 1864.
...d, Calvin	...do...	20	May 2, 1864	100 dys.	Mustered out with company Sept. 10, 1864.
...d, Philo	...do...	18	May 2, 1864	100 dys.	Mustered out with company Sept. 10, 1864.
..., William	...do...	18	May 2, 1864	100 dys.	Mustered out with company Sept. 10, 1864.
..., Obadiah	...do...	23	May 2, 1864	100 dys.	Mustered out with company Sept. 10, 1864.
..., Rod D.	...do...	28	May 2, 1864	100 dys.	Promoted to Q. M. Sergeant May 13, 1864.
..., John N.	...do...	21	May 2, 1864	100 dys.	Mustered out with company Sept. 10, 1864.
...Alfred	...do...	25	May 2, 1864	100 dys.	Mustered out with company Sept. 10, 1864.
...e, William A.	...do...	18	May 2, 1864	100 dys.	Mustered out with company Sept. 10, 1864.

COMPANY F.

...red in May 12, 1864, at Camp Chase, O., by James P. W. Neill, 1st Lieutenant 18th Infantry, U. S. A. Mustered out Sept. 10, 1864, at Camp Chase, O., by George R. Vernon, 1st Lieutenant 14th Infantry, U. S. A.

	Rank.	Age.	Date of Entering the Service.	Period of Service.	Remarks.
...nitzgaber	Captain	30	May 2, 1864	100 dys.	Mustered out with company Sept. 10, 1864.
... W. Bilbow	1st Lieut.	27	May 2, 1864	100 dys.	Mustered out with company Sept. 10, 1864.
...ck Dennis	2d Lieut.	30	May 2, 1864	100 dys.	Mustered out with company Sept. 10, 1864.
...n H. Brown	1st Sergt.	26	May 2, 1864	100 dys.	Mustered out with company Sept. 10, 1864.
...Snider	Sergeant	22	May 2, 1864	100 dys.	Mustered out with company Sept. 10, 1864.
...Wilson	...do...	23	May 2, 1864	100 dys.	Mustered out with company Sept. 10, 1864.
...Selters	...do...	27	May 2, 1864	100 dys.	Mustered out with company Sept. 10, 1864.
...E. Kingsborough	...do...	18	May 2, 1864	100 dys.	Mustered out with company Sept. 10, 1864.
...ngton Gernhart	Corporal.	22	May 2, 1864	100 dys.	Mustered out with company Sept. 10, 1864.
...V. Welser	...do...	29	May 2, 1864	100 dys.	Mustered out with company Sept. 10, 1864.
...D. Sigs	...do...	19	May 2, 1864	100 dys.	Mustered out with company Sept. 10, 1864.
...Gamble	...do...	37	May 2, 1864	100 dys.	Mustered out with company Sept. 10, 1864.
...W. [illegible]	...do...	26	May 2, 1864	100 dys.	Mustered out with company Sept. 10, 1864.
...Bowman	...do...	29	May 2, 1864	100 dys.	Mustered out with company Sept. 10, 1864.
...ro Anderson	...do...	24	May 2, 1864	100 dys.	Mustered out with company Sept. 10, 1864.
...n Hedges	...do...	25	May 2, 1864	100 dys.	Mustered out with company Sept. 10, 1864.
...tine Saber	Musician	18	May 2, 1864	100 dys.	Mustered out with company Sept. 10, 1864.
...Moore	...do...	18	May 2, 1864	100 dys.	Mustered out with company Sept. 10, 1864.
...uster, John	Private.	28	May 2, 1864	100 dys.	Mustered out with company Sept. 10, 1864.
...James W.	...do...	18	May 2, 1864	100 dys.	Mustered out with company Sept. 10, 1864.
..., James H.	...do...	20	May 2, 1864	100 dys.	Mustered out with company Sept. 10, 1864.
...n, George S.	...do...	28	May 2, 1864	100 dys.	Died July 26, 1864, at Fortress Monroe, Va.
...iser, Jacob H.	...do...	31	May 2, 1864	100 dys.	Mustered out with company Sept. 10, 1864.
...lber, Lewis O.	...do...	25	May 2, 1864	100 dys.	Mustered out with company Sept. 10, 1864.
..., Samuel R.	...do...	19	May 2, 1864	100 dys.	Mustered out with company Sept. 10, 1864.
..., Solomon	...do...	24	May 2, 1864	100 dys.	Mustered out with company Sept. 10, 1864.
...rd, Jacob	.	28	May 2, 1864	100 dys.	Mustered out with company Sept. 10, 1864.
...ill, Henry	.	18	May 2, 1864	100 dys.	Discharged June 20, 1864, at Fort Reno, D. C., on Surgeon's certificate of disability.
...hill, William	...do...	28	May 2, 1864	100 dys.	Mustered out with company Sept. 10, 1864.
..., George	...do...	20	May 2, 1864	100 dys.	Mustered out with company Sept. 10, 1864.
...ghan, Sylvester M.	...do...	24	May 2, 1864	100 dys.	Died July 27, 1864, at Fortress Monroe, Va.
...John	...do...	27	May 2, 1864	100 dys.	Mustered out with company Sept. 10, 1864.
...nau, John	...do...	[illegible]	May 2, 1864	100 dys.	Mustered out with company Sept. 10, 1864.
...y, Elijah	...do...	19	May 2, 1864	100 dys.	Mustered out with company Sept. 10, 1864.
...Jacob	...do...	42	May 2, 1864	100 dys.	Mustered out with company Sept. 10, 1864.
...Cassius L.	...do...	19	May 2, 1864	100 dys.	Mustered out with company Sept. 10, 1864.
...r, William S.	...do...	25	May 2, 1864	100 dys.	Mustered out with company Sept. 10, 1864.

Names.	Rank.	Age.	Date of Entering the Service.	Period of Service.	Remarks.
Cox, Otho	Private	19	May 2, 1864	100 dys.	Mustered out with company Sept. 10, 1864.
Cruthers, Martin M.	do.	19	May 2, 1864	100 dys.	Mustered out with company Sept. 10, 1864.
Cunningham, James M.	do.	20	May 2, 1864	100 dys.	Mustered out with company Sept. 10, 1864.
Douglas, William	do.	20	May 2, 1864	100 dys.	Mustered out with company Sept. 10, 1864.
Dull, Wesley	do.	22	May 2, 1864	100 dys.	Mustered out with company Sept. 10, 1864.
Eckis, Samuel	do.	18	May 2, 1864	100 dys.	Absent, sick ——. No further record found.
Falkner, Daniel S.	do.	18	May 2, 1864	100 dys.	Mustered out with company Sept. 10, 1864.
Fasnacht, Philip	do.	30	May 2, 1864	100 dys.	Mustered out with company Sept. 10, 1864.
Foglea[illegible]g, William	do.	24	May 2, 1864	100 dys.	Mustered out with company Sept. 10, 1864.
[illegible]lkison, Aaron R.	do.	20	May 2, 1864	100 dys.	Mustered out with company Sept. 10, 1864.
Haines, Jac[illegible] F.	do.	28	May 2, 1864	100 dys.	Mustered out with company Sept. 10, 1864.
Hamm[illegible] [illegible]enman J.	do.	29	May 2, 1864	100 dys.	Mustered out with company Sept. 10, 1864.
Hoadley, Orson	do.	20	May 2, 1864	100 dys.	Mustered out with company Sept. 10, 1864.
Holenbaugh, Isaac	do.	2[illegible]	May 2, 1864	100 dys.	Mustered out with company Sept. 10, 1864.
Holenbaugh, William	do.	27	May 2, 1864	100 dys.	Mustered out with company Sept. 10, 1864.
Kennel, Paul	do.	19	May 2, 1864	100 dys.	Mustered out with company Sept. 10, 1864.
Leach, Monroe S.	do.	18	May 2, 1864	100 dys.	Mustered out with company Sept. 10, 1864.
Latter, John H.	do.	25	May 2, 1864	100 dys.	Mustered out with company Sept. 10, 1864.
Leyman, Bartley H.	do.	18	May 2, 1864	100 dys.	Mustered out with company Sept. 10, 1864.
Long, Doran H.	do.	27	May 2, 1864	100 dys.	Mustered out with company Sept. 10, 1864.
McConnell, Charles	do.	22	May 2, 1864	100 dys.	Mustered out with company Sept. 10, 1864.
McMillen, John A.	do.	24	May 2, 1864	100 dys.	Mustered out with company Sept. 10, 1864.
Mey[illegible]lo, John A.	do.	19	May 2, 1864	100 dys.	Mustered out with company Sept. 10, 1864.
M[illegible]cley, Charles W.	do.	25	May 2, 1864	100 dys.	Mustered out with company Sept. 10, 1864.
Mickey, Herbert C.	do.	18	May 2, 1864	100 dys.	Mustered out with company Sept. 10, 1864.
Mickey, Jefferson T.	do.	18	May 2, 1864	100 dys.	Mustered out with company Sept. 10, 1864.
Morehead, James	do.	18	May 2, 1864	100 dys.	Mustered out with company Sept. 10, 1864.
Myers, Conrad	do.	41	May 2, 1864	100 dys.	Discharged May 13, 1864, at Camp Chase, O., on surgeon's certificate of disability.
Ott, Frederick B.	do.	30	May 2, 1864	100 dys.	Mustered out with company Sept. 10, 1864.
Plank, John J.	do.	29	May 2, 1864	100 dys.	Mustered out with company Sept. 10, 1864.
Prickett, John W.	do.	28	May 2, 1864	100 dys.	Mustered out with company Sept. 10, 1864.
Ra[illegible]bo, Aaron	do.	21	May 2, 1864	100 dys.	Mustered out with company Sept. 10, 1864.
Reyn[illegible]ls, Shadrach	do.	33	May 2, 1864	100 dys.	Mustered out with company Sept. 10, 1864.
R[illegible]odes, Jer[illegible]iah	do.	41	May 2, 1864	100 dys.	Mustered out with company Sept. 10, 1864.
R[illegible]wel[illegible], Albert	do.	21	May 2, 1864	100 dys.	Mustered out with company Sept. 10, 1864.
Simons, Theo[illegible]ore	do.	28	May 2, 1864	100 dys.	Mustered out with company Sept. 10, 1864.
Slaybaugh, Br[illegible]ce	do.	18	May 2, 1864	100 dys.	Mustered out with company Sept. 10, 1864.
Slaybaug[illegible], Frank	do.	21	May 2, 1864	100 dys.	Mustered out with company Sept. 10, 1864.
Smiley, John J.	do.	25	May 2, 1864	100 dys.	Mustered out with company Sept. 10, 1864.
Snider, John W.	do.	27	May 2, 1864	100 dys.	Mustered out with company Sept. 10, 1864.
Stiock, John B.	do.	20	May 2, 1864	100 dys.	Mustered out with company Sept. 10, 1864.
Tucker, Sylvester	do.	23	May 2, 1864	100 dys.	Mustered out with company Sept. 10, 1864.
Turb[illegible], [illegible]hn S.	do.	21	May 2, 1864	100 dys.	Mustered out with company Sept. 10, 1864.
Th[illegible]mas, Alfred	do.	41	May 2, 1864	100 dys.	Mustered out with company Sept. 10, 1864.
Ward, John B.	do.	29	May 2, 1864	100 dys.	Mustered out with company Sept. 10, 1864.
Young, Gabriel M.	do.	23	May 2, 1864	100 dys.	Mustered out with company Sept. 10, 1864.

COMPANY G.

Mustered in May 12, 1864, at Camp Chase, O., by James P. W. Neill, 1st Lieutenant 18th Infantry, U. S. A. Mustered out Sept. 10, 1864, at Camp Chase, O., by George R. Vernon, 1st Lieutenant 14th Infantry, U. S. A.

Names.	Rank.	Age.	Date of Entering the Service.	Period of Service.	Remarks.
R. P. [illegible]sborn	Captain.	29	May 2, 1864	100 dys.	Mustered out with company Sept. 10, 1864.
[illegible]harles W. Kahlo	1st Lieut.	24	May 2, 1864	100 dys.	Mustered out with company Sept. 10, 1864.
[illegible]ry E. Carey	2d Lieut.	26	May 2, 1864	100 dys.	Mustered out with company Sept. 10, 1864.
Thomas [illegible]arrol	1st Sergt.	22	May 2, 1864	100 dys.	Mustered out with company Sept. 10, 1864.
John Gardner	Sergeant.	35	May 2, 1864	100 dys.	Mustered out with company Sept. 10, 1864.
Wellington D. Golding	do.	26	May 2, 1864	100 dys.	Mustered out with company Sept. 10, 1864.
Henry Yeager	do.	23	May 2, 1864	100 dys.	Mustered out with company Sept. 10, 1864.
John Waterman	do.	30	May 2, 1864	100 dys.	Mustered out with company Sept. 10, 1864.
Jabez Dennis	Corporal.	28	May 2, 1864	100 dys.	Mustered out with company Sept. 10, 1864.
David Foulk	do.	28	May 2, 1864	100 dys.	Mustered out with company Sept. 10, 1864.
Cyrus Gunn	do.	24	May 2, 1864	100 dys.	Died Aug. 14, 1864, on steamer Wyoming, near Wilson's Landing, Va.
Hampton Harrison	do.	32	May 2, 1864	100 dys.	Mustered out with company Sept. 10, 1864.
Locke Lemert	do.	19	May 2, 1864	100 dys.	Mustered out with company Sept. 10, 1864.
Nathaniel H. Hartman	do.	29	May 2, 1864	100 dys.	Discharged June 18, 1864, by order of War Department.
Thomas Williams	do.	18	May 2, 1864	100 dys.	Mustered out with company Sept. 10, 1864.
Wallace Blair	do.	22	May 2, 1864	100 dys.	Appointed June 1, 1864; mustered out with company Sept. 10, 1864.
Milton E. Heller	do.	21	May 2, 1864	100 dys.	Appointed June 19, 1864; mustered out with company Sept. 10, 1864.
John M. Bolmer	Musician	18	May 2, 1864	100 dys.	Mustered out with company Sept. 10, 1864.
Jonah Adams	do.	18	May 2, 1864	100 dys.	Mustered out with company Sept. 10, 1864.
Aller, Frederick	Private.	29	May 2, 1864	100 dys.	Mustered out with company Sept. 10, 1864.
Banks, George	do.	21	May 2, 1864	100 dys.	Mustered out with company Sept. 10, 1864.
Barnes, Wheaton P.	do.	19	May 2, 1864	100 dys.	Mustered out with company Sept. 10, 1864.

Names.	Rank.	Age.	Date of Entering the Service.	Period of Service.	Remarks.
Bascome, Daniel	Private..	22	May 2, 1864	100 dys.	Mustered out with company Sept. 10, 1864.
Battenfelt, John	..do....	23	May 2, 1864	100 dys.	Mustered out with company Sept. 10, 1864.
Battles, John T	....do....	27	May 2, 1864	100 dys.	Absent, sick ——. No further record found.
Brickhisen, Jacob	....do....	21	May 2, 1864	100 dys.	Mustered out with company Sept. 10, 1864.
Brooks, Fenton	....do....	36	May 2, 1864	100 dys.	Mustered out with company Sept. 10, 1864.
Burger, Baxter	....do....	25	May 2, 1864	100 dys.	Mustered out with company Sept. 10, 1864.
Campbell, William	....do....	18	May 2, 1864	100 dys.	Mustered out with company Sept. 10, 1864.
Corbin, Ja[illegible]es	....do....	22	May 2, 1864	100 dys.	Mustered out with company Sept. 10, 1864.
Davis, George	....do....	22	May 2, 1864	100 dys.	Mustered out with company Sept. 10, 1864.
Delong, Charles	....do....	32	May 2, 1864	100 dys.	Transferred to Co. K May 12, 1864.
Dicus, Benjamin F	....do....	32	May 2, 1864	100 dys.	Mustered out with company Sept. 10, 1864.
Dodd, Edward	....do....	18	May 2, 1864	100 dys.	Mustered out with company Sept. 10, 1864.
Dota, William	....do....	18	May 2, 1864	100 dys.	Mustered out with company Sept. 10, 1864.
Ellenwood, Gifford D	....do....	20	May 2, 1864	100 dys.	Mustered out with company Sept. 10, 1864.
Gillson, Hiram	....do....	23	May 2, 1864	100 dys.	Mustered out with company Sept. 10, 1864.
Gillson, Rease	....do....	20	May 2, 1864	100 dys.	Mustered out with company Sept. 10, 1864.
Hess, Stillwell	....do....	22	May 2, 1864	100 dys.	Mustered out with company Sept. 10, 1864.
Henry, James	....do....	27	May 2, 1864	100 dys.	Absent, sick ——. No further record found.
Howard, Henry	....do....	22	May 2, 1864	100 dys.	Mustered out with company Sept. 10, 1864.
Ireland, Thomas	....do....	27	May 2, 1864	100 dys.	Mustered out with company Sept. 10, 1864.
Jacobs, Stephen H	....do....	33	May 2, 1864	100 dys.	Mustered out with company Sept. 10, 1864.
Kegler, Charles	....do....	18	May 2, 1864	100 dys.	Mustered out with company Sept. 10, 1864.
Killitts, Morris	....do....	19	May 2, 1864	100 dys.	Absent, sick ——. No further record found.
Leiter, John	....do....	19	May 2, 1864	100 dys.	Mustered out with company Sept. 10, 1864.
Leiter, Samuel	....do....	21	May 2, 1864	100 dys.	Absent, sick ——. No further record found.
Lighthizer, William	....do....	22	May 2, 1864	100 dys.	Mustered out with company Sept. 10, 1864.
Long, Miller	....do....	21	May 2, 1864	100 dys.	Mustered out with company Sept. 10, 1864.
Lowery, William	....do....	28	May 2, 1864	100 dys.	Absent, sick ——. No further record found.
McCombs, William	....do....	20	May 2, 1864	100 dys.	Mustered out with company Sept. 10, 1864.
Margrat, Samuel	....do....	..	May 2, 1864	100 dys.	Mustered out with company Sept. 10, 1864.
Martin, Elton F	....do....	23	May 2, 1864	100 dys.	Mustered out with company Sept. 10, 1864.
Masden, Isaac	....do....	24	May 2, 1864	100 dys.	Mustered out with company Sept. 10, 1864.
Mason, Frank	....do....	20	May 2, 1864	100 dys.	Mustered out with company Sept. 10, 1864.
Mealy, Maxwell F	....do....	25	May 2, 1864	100 dys.	Mustered out with company Sept. 10, 1864.
Merriman, Philetus	....do....	25	May 2, 1864	100 dys.	Mustered out with company Sept. 10, 1864.
Moffitt, David	....do....	18	May 2, 1864	100 dys.	Mustered out with company Sept. 10, 1864.
Ohler, Martin	....do....	25	May 2, 1864	100 dys.	Mustered out with company Sept. 10, 1864.
Paul, John	....do....	24	May 2, 1864	100 dys.	Absent, sick ——. No further record found.
Pearce, Lewis	....do....	21	May 2, 1864	100 dys.	Mustered out with company Sept. 10, 1864.
Powell, George	....do....	19	May 2, 1864	100 dys.	Mustered out with company Sept. 16, 1864.
Powell, Volney	....do....	24	May 2, 1864	100 dys.	Mustered out with company Sept. 10, 1864.
Radle, Washington	....do....	19	May 2, 1864	100 dys.	Mustered out with company Sept. 10, 1864.
Raff, George W	....do....	28	May 2, 1864	100 dys.	Absent, sick ——. No further record found.
Raff, Landon	....do....	25	May 2, 1864	100 dys.	Mustered out with company Sept. 10, 1864.
Randall, Winfield	....do....	19	May 2, 1864	100 dys.	Mustered out with company Sept. 10, 1864.
Ritter, Joseph N	....do....	19	May 2, 1864	100 dys.	Mustered out with company Sept. 10, 1864.
Senter, Asa C	....do....	25	May 2, 1864	100 dys.	Mustered out with company Sept. 10, 1864.
Shasteen, James	....do....	18	May 2, 1864	100 dys.	Mustered out with company Sept. 10, 1864.
Shoemaker, Hiram S	....do....	27	May 2, 1864	100 dys.	Mustered out with company Sept. 10, 1864.
Smeed, Robert B	....do....	25	May 2, 1864	100 dys.	Mustered out with company Sept. 10, 1864.
Smith, Achilles	....do....	18	May 2, 1864	100 dys.	Mustered out with company Sept. 10, 1864.
Smith, George	....do....	18	May 2, 1864	100 dys.	Mustered out with company Sept. 10, 1864.
Smith, Israel	....do....	36	May 2, 1864	100 dys.	Mustered out with company Sept. 10, 1864.
Spangler, Joseph M	....do....	19	May 2, 1864	100 dys.	Mustered out with company Sept. 10, 1864.
Travis, Joseph	....do....	48	May 2, 1864	100 dys.	Absent, sick ——. No further record found.
Tyler, Romin	....do....	18	May 2, 1864	100 dys.	Mustered out with company Sept. 10, 1864.
Volentine, George	....do....	25	May 2, 1864	100 dys.	Mustered out with company Sept. 10, 1864.
Williams, Isaac	....do....	23	May 2, 1864	100 dys.	Absent, sick ——. No further record found.
Worthington, Archibald B	....do....	..	May 2, 1864	100 dys.	
Yeager, John	....do....	18	May 2, 1864	100 dys.	Mustered out with company Sept. 10, 1864.
Zallner, George W	....do....	23	May 2, 1864	100 dys.	Mustered out with company Sept. 10, 1864.
Zedeker, Solomon	....do....	19	May 2, 1864	100 dys.	Mustered out with company Sept. 10, 1864.

COMPANY H.

Mustered in May 12, 1864, at Camp Chase, O., by James P. W. Neill, 1st Lieutenant 18th Infantry, U. S. A. Mustered out Sept. 10, 1864, at Camp Chase, O., by George R. Vernon, 1st Lieutenant 14th Infantry, U. S. A.

Names.	Rank.	Age.	Date of Entering the service.	Period of Service.	Remarks.
Wells Rogers	Captain.	34	May 2, 1864	100 dys.	Mustered out with company Sept. 10, 1864.
Andrew Thompson	1st Lieut.	34	May 2, 1864	100 dys.	Mustered out with company Sept. 10, 1864.
James M. Hirst	2d Lieut.	32	May 2, 1864	100 dys.	Mustered out with company Sept. 10, 1864.
Michael W. Williams	1st Sergt.	27	May 2, 1864	100 dys.	Mustered out with company Sept. 10, 1864.
Albert Gettings	Sergeant.	29	May 2, 1864	100 dys.	Mustered out with company Sept. 10, 1864.
Peter Cornell	...do...	22	May 2, 1864	100 dys.	Mustered out with company Sept. 10, 1864.
George W. Koerber	...do...	28	May 2, 1864	100 dys.	Mustered out with company Sept. 10, 1864.
Albert Runyan	...do...	20	May 2, 1864	100 dys.	Mustered out with company Sept. 10, 1864.
Henry Beelman	Corporal.	24	May 2, 1864	100 dys.	Mustered out with company Sept. 10, 1864.
John Preston	...do...	24	May 2, 1864	100 dys.	Mustered out with company Sept. 10, 1864.
John B. Keeler	...do...	28	May 2, 1864	100 dys.	Mustered out with company Sept. 10, 1864.
Elijah J. Mitchell	...do...	21	May 2, 1864	100 dys.	Mustered out with company Sept. 10, 1864.
Samuel K. Kaler	...do...	33	May 2, 1864	100 dys.	Mustered out with company Sept. 10, 1864.
David Long	...do...	23	May 2, 1864	100 dys.	Mustered out with company Sept. 10, 1864.
David B. King	...do...	20	May 2, 1864	100 dys.	Mustered out with company Sept. 10, 1864.
John Waite	...do...	26	May 2, 1864	100 dys.	Mustered out with company Sept. 10, 1864.
John W. Laser	Musician	27	May 2, 1864	100 dys.	Mustered out with company Sept. 10, 1864.
Michael McQuillen	...do...	..	May 2, 1864	100 dys.	Mustered out with company Sept. 10, 1864.
William R. Teeson	Wagoner.	25	May 2, 1864	100 dys.	Mustered out with company Sept. 10, 1864.
Applegate, James M.	Private.	33	May 2, 1864	100 dys.	Mustered out with company Sept. 10, 1864.
Baldwin, William	...do...	25	May 2, 1864	100 dys.	Mustered out with company Sept. 10, 1864.
Catlocth, Augustus	...do...	18	May 2, 1864	100 dys.	Mustered out with company Sept. 10, 1864.
Lell, Peter S.	...do...	27	May 2, 1864	100 dys.	Mustered out with company Sept. 10, 1864.
Iverson, John	...do...	26	May 2, 1864	100 dys.	Mustered out with company Sept. 10, 1864.
Bever, James	...do...	29	May 2, 1864	100 dys.	Discharged June 18, 1864, at Fort Reno, D. C., on Surgeon's certificate of disability.
Bliss, George	...do...	18	May 2, 1864	100 dys.	Mustered out with company Sept. 10, 1864.
Carmichael, John	...do...	26	May 2, 1864	100 dys.	Mustered out with company Sept. 10, 1864.
Case, Frank	...do...	21	May 2, 1864	100 dys.	Mustered out with company Sept. 10, 1864.
Charity, Thomas	...do...	29	May 2, 1864	100 dys.	Mustered out with company Sept. 10, 1864.
Clinesmith, John A.	...do...	19	May 2, 1864	100 dys.	Mustered out with company Sept. 10, 1864.
Conklin, Artemus K.	...do...	20	May 2, 1864	100 dys.	Mustered out with company Sept. 10, 1864.
Cornell, James S.	...do...	18	May 2, 1864	100 dys.	Mustered out with company Sept. 10, 1864.
Colwell, James C.	...do...	30	May 2, 1864	100 dys.	Mustered out with company Sept. 10, 1864.
Cutler, Robert E.	...do...	18	May 2, 1864	100 dys.	Mustered out with company Sept. 10, 1864.
Delaney, James	...do...	18	May 2, 1864	100 dys.	Mustered out with company Sept. 10, 1864.
Deviney, Benjamin F.	...do...	24	May 2, 1864	100 dys.	Mustered out with company Sept. 10, 1864.
Deviney, John	...do...	30	May 2, 1864	100 dys.	Mustered out with company Sept. 10, 1864.
Dewitt, Thomas	...do...	28	May 2, 1864	100 dys.	Mustered out with company Sept. 10, 1864.
Dieg, Michael	...do...	19	May 2, 1864	100 dys.	Transferred to Co. K —.
Fleming, George B.	...do...	19	May 2, 1864	100 dys.	Mustered out with company Sept. 10, 1864.
Flickinger, George W.	...do...	18	May 2, 1864	100 dys.	Mustered out with company Sept. 10, 1864.
Force, Oscar	...do...	19	May 2, 1864	100 dys.	Mustered out with company Sept. 10, 1864.
Forsythe, Robert	...do...	35	May 2, 1864	100 dys.	Mustered out with company Sept. 10, 1864.
Forsythe, Samuel	...do...	32	May 2, 1864	100 dys.	Mustered out with company Sept. 10, 1864.
Garrison, James	...do...	32	May 2, 1864	100 dys.	Mustered out with company Sept. 10, 1864.
Heath, Homer	...do...	23	May 2, 1864	100 dys.	Mustered out with company Sept. 10, 1864.
Hodges, Horace T.	...do...	22	May 2, 1864	100 dys.	Absent, sick —. No further record found.
Hall, William	...do...	21	May 2, 1864	100 dys.	Mustered out with company Sept. 10, 1864.
Hunt, John D.	...do...	26	May 2, 1864	100 dys.	Mustered out with company Sept. 10, 1864.
Jennings, John S.	...do...	20	May 2, 1864	100 dys.	Mustered out with company Sept. 10, 1864.
King, Robert	...do...	2[illegible]	May 2, 1864	100 dys.	Mustered out with company Sept. 10, 1864.
Koerber, Jacob	...do...	33	May 2, 1864	100 dys.	Mustered out with company Sept. 10, 1864.
Lacir, Levi	...do...	18	May 2, 1864	100 dys.	Mustered out with company Sept. 10, 1864.
Mattison, Mahlon	...do...	18	May 2, 1864	100 dys.	Mustered out with company Sept. 10, 1864.
Menck, J. Jefferson	...do...	20	May 2, 1864	100 dys.	Died Sept. 3, 1864, at Baltimore, Md.
Mishinger, Jesse	...do...	29	May 2, 1864	100 dys.	Mustered out with company Sept. 10, 1864.
Morton, Jacob	...do...	19	May 2, 1864	100 dys.	Mustered out with company Sept. 10, 1864.
Opdyke, John S.	...do...	19	May 2, 1864	100 dys.	Mustered out with company Sept. 10, 1864.
Oswalt, Benjamin	...do...	30	May 2, 1864	100 dys.	Mustered out with company Sept. 10, 1864.
Pettit, Thomas	...do...	35	May 2, 1864	100 dys.	Mustered out with company Sept. 10, 1864.
Preston, George	...do...	22	May 2, 1864	100 dys.	Mustered out with company Sept. 10, 1864.
Rhea, John	...do...	36	May 2, 1864	100 dys.	Mustered out with company Sept. 10, 1864.
Rhone, John	...do...	33	May 2, 1864	100 dys.	Mustered out with company Sept. 10, 1864.
Rose, Elmore	...do...	19	May 2, 1864	100 dys.	Mustered out with company Sept. 10, 1864.
Roessman, Peter	...do...	..	May 2, 1864	100 dys.	
Seiler, Simon	...do...	18	May 2, 1864	100 dys.	Mustered out with company Sept. 10, 1864.
Shoup, Austin	...do...	19	May 2, 1864	100 dys.	Mustered out with company Sept. 10, 1864.
Shonts, Cyrus H.	...do...	22	May 2, 1864	100 dys.	Mustered out with company Sept. 10, 1864.
Spencer, John H.	...do...	19	May 2, 1864	100 dys.	Mustered out with company Sept. 10, 1864.
Steffy, Lewis	...do...	20	May 2, 1864	100 dys.	Mustered out with company Sept. 10, 1864.
Swaley, David	...do...	20	May 2, 1864	100 dys.	Mustered out with company Sept. 10, 1864.
Swain, George	...do...	30	May 2, 1864	100 dys.	Mustered out with company Sept. 10, 1864.
Swope, Abram	...do...	19	May 2, 1864	100 dys.	Mustered out with company Sept. 10, 1864.
Vanderl, Joseph	...do...	40	May 2, 1864	100 dys.	Mustered out with company Sept. 10, 1864.
Wagner, Josiah	...do...	26	May 2, 1864	100 dys.	Mustered out with company Sept. 10, 1864.

Names	Rank.	Age.	Date of Entering the Service	Period of Service.	Remarks.
Palmer, George W.	Private.	31	May 2, 1864	100 dys.	Mustered out with company Sept. 10, 1864.
Parr, Robert	...do...	27	May 2, 1864	100 dys.	
Patterson, James	...do...	40	May 2, 1864	100 dys.	Absent, sick ——. No further record found.
Pocock, Finley	...do...	21	May 2, 1864	100 dys.	Mustered out with company Sept. 10, 1864.
Ray, Samuel W.	...do...	38	May 2, 1864	100 dys.	Mustered out with company Sept. 10, 1864.
Rennie, James	...do...	18	May 2, 1864	100 dys.	Mustered out with company Sept. 10, 1864.
Robb, Valentine D.	...do...	37	May 2, 1864	100 dys.	Mustered out with company Sept. 10, 1864.
Royer, William	...do...	18	May 2, 1864	100 dys.	Mustered out with company Sept. 10, 1864.
Ryland, William	...do...	20	May 2, 1864	100 dys.	Absent, sick ——. No further record found.
Selby, Enoch G.	...do...	19	May 2, 1864	100 dys.	Mustered out with company Sept. 10, 1864.
Selby, Milton H.	...do...	25	May 2, 1864	100 dys.	Mustered out with company Sept. 10, 1864.
Seibert, Michael K.	...do...	32	May 2, 1864	100 dys.	Mustered out with company Sept. 10, 1864.
Smalley, Henry C.	...do...	22	May 2, 1864	100 dys.	Mustered out with company Sept. 10, 1864.
Smalley, John W.	...do...	22	May 2, 1864	100 dys.	Mustered out with company Sept. 10, 1864.
Snyder, John W.	...do...	51	May 2, 1864	100 dys.	Mustered out with company Sept. 10, 1864.
Springer, James	...do...	28	May 2, 1864	100 dys.	Mustered out with company Sept. 10, 1864.
Springer, John	...do...	21	May 2, 1864	100 dys.	Mustered out with company Sept. 10, 1864.
Stauffer, Michael W.	...do...	37	May 2, 1864	100 dys.	Mustered out with company Sept. 10, 1864.
Stauffer, William	...do...	21	May 2, 1864	100 dys.	Mustered out with company Sept. 10, 1864.
Troxel, John	...do...	32	May 2, 1864	100 dys.	Mustered out with company Sept. 10, 1864.
Wiler, David	...do...	39	May 2, 1864	100 dys.	Mustered out with company Sept. 10, 1864.

COMPANY K.

Mustered in May 13, 1864, at Camp Chase, O., by James P. W. Neill, 1st Lieutenant 18th Infantry, U. S. A. Mustered out Sept. 10, 1864, at Camp Chase, O., by George R. Vernon, 1st Lieutenant 14th Infantry, U. S. A.

Names	Rank.	Age.	Date of Entering the Service	Period of Service.	Remarks.
William M. Johnston	Captain.	30	May 2, 1864	100 dys.	Mustered out with company Sept. 10, 1864.
John H. Hammaker	1st Lieut.	33	May 2, 1864	100 dys.	Mustered out with company Sept. 10, 1864.
Timothy C. Putman	2d Lieut.	36	May 2, 1864	100 dys.	Mustered out with company Sept. 10, 1864.
Robert Rowland	1st Sergt.	35	May 2, 1864	100 dys.	Mustered out with company Sept. 10, 1864.
James Ellis	Sergeant.	42	May 2, 1864	100 dys.	Mustered out with company Sept. 10, 1864.
Truman Palmer	...do...	23	May 2, 1864	100 dys.	Mustered out with company Sept. 10, 1864.
John W. Ulrich	...do...	25	May 2, 1864	100 dys.	Mustered out with company Sept. 10, 1864.
Eli B. Flexer	...do...	28	May 2, 1864	100 dys.	Killed Aug. 18, 1864, by the accidental discharge of a gun.
Daniel Bose	Corporal.	26	May 2, 1864	100 dys.	Mustered out with company Sept. 10, 1864.
Josiah Bash	...do...	28	May 2, 1864	100 dys.	Mustered out with company Sept. 10, 1864.
Jesse C. Ward	...do...	23	May 2, 1864	100 dys.	Mustered out with company Sept. 10, 1864.
John Meese	...do...	29	May 2, 1864	100 dys.	Mustered out with company Sept. 10, 1864.
Jeremiah Egler	...do...	31	May 2, 1864	100 dys.	Mustered out with company Sept. 10, 1864.
John Soidle	...do...	26	May 2, 1864	100 dys.	Mustered out with company Sept. 10, 1864.
Julius Gleitsman	...do...	25	May 2, 1864	100 dys.	Mustered out with company Sept. 10, 1864.
Enos Kanaga	...do...	19	May 2, 1864	100 dys.	Mustered out with company Sept. 10, 1864.
Aukerman, Andrew	Private.	27	May 2, 1864	100 dys.	Mustered out with company Sept. 10, 1864.
Aukerman, John	...do...	32	May 2, 1864	100 dys.	Mustered out with company Sept. 10, 1864.
Bash, Philip	...do...	19	May 2, 1864	100 dys.	Mustered out with company Sept. 10, 1864.
Bash, Samuel	...do...	33	May 2, 1864	100 dys.	Mustered out with company Sept. 10, 1864.
Bell, William H.	...do...	36	May 2, 1864	100 dys.	Mustered out with company Sept. 10, 1864.
Bent, Joseph	...do...	31	May 2, 1864	100 dys.	
Bergen, Adam	...do...	39	May 2, 1864	100 dys.	Mustered out with company Sept. 10, 1864.
Bowers, John	...do...	18	May 2, 1864	100 dys.	Mustered out with company Sept. 10, 1864.
Bradley, Stokes	...do...	38	May 2, 1864	100 dys.	Mustered out with company Sept. 10, 1864.
Chamberlain, Albert	...do...	22	May 2, 1864	100 dys.	Mustered out with company Sept. 10, 1864.
Davey, William W.	...do...	21	May 2, 1864	100 dys.	Transferred from Co. D ——; mustered out with company Sept. 10, 1864.
Deal, John	...do...	21	May 2, 1864	100 dys.	Mustered out with company Sept. 10, 1864.
Delong, Charles	...do...	32	May 2, 1864	100 dys.	Transferred from Co. G May 12, 1864; mustered out with company Sept. 10, 1864.
Dick, Michael	...do...	19	May 2, 1864	100 dys.	Transferred from Co. H ——; mustered out with company Sept. 10, 1864.
Duck, George W.	...do...	20	May 2, 1864	100 dys.	Mustered out with company Sept. 10, 1864.
Fisher, David	...do...	35	May 2, 1864	100 dys.	Mustered out with company Sept. 10, 1864.
Fleming, George W.	...do...	18	May 2, 1864	100 dys.	Transferred from Co. B May 13, 1864.
Flickinger, Christian	...do...	30	May 2, 1864	100 dys.	Mustered out with company Sept. 10, 1864.
Frey, Frederick	...do...	58	May 2, 1864	100 dys.	Mustered out with company Sept. 10, 1864.
Friedline, Samuel	...do...	37	May 2, 1864	100 dys.	Transferred from Co. I May 13, 1864; mustered out with company Sept. 10, 1864.
Gleitsman, Frederick	...do...	43	May 2, 1864	100 dys.	Mustered out with company Sept. 10, 1864.
Gleitsman, Julius J.	...do...	18	May 2, 1864	100 dys.	Mustered out with company Sept. 10, 1864.
Gotchen, Adam	...do...	32	May 2, 1864	100 dys.	Mustered out with company Sept. 10, 1864.
Grant, Bayliss	...do...	25	May 2, 1864	100 dys.	Mustered out with company Sept. 10, 1864.
Greger, Isaiah	...do...	19	May 2, 1864	100 dys.	Mustered out with company Sept. 10, 1864.
Hipsher, Adam	...do...	20	May 2, 1864	100 dys.	Mustered out with company Sept. 10, 1864.
Hipsher, Thomas	...do...	27	May 2, 1864	100 dys.	Mustered out with company Sept. 10, 1864.
Hobbs, George W.	...do...	31	May 2, 1864	100 dys.	Discharged June 18, 1864, at Fort Reno, D. C.
Hunley, Thomas P.	...do...	22	May 2, 1864	100 dys.	
Huntsman, Amariah C.	...do...	33	May 2, 1864	100 dys.	Transferred from Co. B May 13, 1864; mustered out Sept. —, 1864, at Columbus, O., by order of War Department.

Names.	Rank.	Age.	Date of Entering the Service.	Period of Service.	Remarks.
Keeter, Jeremiah	Private..	38	May 2, 1864	100 dys.	Mustered out with company Sept. 10, 1864.
Kelso, Samuel	....do....	40	May 2, 1864	100 dys.	Transferred from Co. B May 13, 1864; absent, sick ——. No further record found.
Kiel, Daniel	....do....	45	May 2, 1864	100 dys.	Mustered out with company Sept. 10, 1864.
Kilgore, Jerome	....do....	25	May 2, 1864	100 dys.	Mustered out with company Sept. 10, 1864.
King, Daniel	....do....	26	May 2, 1864	100 dys.	Mustered out with company Sept. 10, 1864.
King, Wilson	....do....	19	May 2, 1864	100 dys.	Mustered out with company Sept. 10, 1864.
Koons, Solomon B	....do....	30	May 2, 1864	100 dys.	Mustered out with company Sept. 10, 1864.
Lentz, Christian	....do....	22	May 2, 1864	100 dys.	Mustered out with company Sept. 10, 1864.
Longlicker, Joseph	....do....	22	May 2, 1864	100 dys.	Mustered out with company Sept. 10, 1864.
Meese, William	....do....	19	May 2, 1864	100 dys.	Mustered out with company Sept. 10, 1864.
Meese, Joseph	....do....	28	May 2, 1864	100 dys.	Mustered out with company Sept. 10, 1864.
Miller, Sebastian	....do....	23	May 2, 1864	100 dys.	Mustered out with company Sept. 10, 1864.
Mowrier, Samuel	....do....	26	May 2, 1864	100 dys.	
Ohlts, Frederick	....do....	23	May 2, 1864	100 dys.	Mustered out with company Sept. 10, 1864.
Ruff, George W	....do....	19	May 2, 1864	100 dys.	
Rash, Daniel	....do....	29	May 2, 1864	100 dys.	Mustered out with company Sept. 10, 1864.
Reed, Franklin	....do....	18	May 2, 1864	100 dys.	Mustered out with company Sept. 10, 1864.
Reed, John P	....do....	34	May 2, 1864	100 dys.	Mustered out with company Sept. 10, 1864.
Seager, George	....do....	45	May 2, 1864	100 dys.	Mustered out with company Sept. 10, 1864.
Shultz, Herman	....do....	26	May 2, 1864	100 dys.	Mustered out with company Sept. 10, 1864.
Shunk, Joseph	....do....	19	May 2, 1864	100 dys.	Mustered out with company Sept. 10, 1864.
Sibbetts, Frank	....do....	19	May 2, 1864	100 dys.	Transferred from Co. A May 12, 1864; mustered out with company Sept. 10, 1864.
Sprangkle, George W	....do....	18	May 2, 1864	100 dys.	Mustered out with company Sept. 10, 1864.
Steel, Isaiah	....do....	28	May 2, 1864	100 dys.	Mustered out with company Sept. 10, 1864
Thompson, William	....do....	28	May 2, 1864	100 dys.	Mustered out with company Sept. 10, 1864.
Ulrick, Jacob	....do....	25	May 2, 1864	100 dys.	Mustered out with company Sept. 10, 1864.
Vannkennel, Abraham	....do....	28	May 2, 1864	100 dys.	Mustered out with company Sept. 10, 1864.
Walters, Martin	....do....	28	May 2, 1864	100 dys.	Mustered out with company Sept. 10, 1864.
Wanel, John B	....do....	29	May 2, 1864	100 dys.	
Weimer, Henry C	....do....	29	May 2, 1864	100 dys.	Mustered out with company Sept. 10, 1864.
Weimer, Josiah W	....do....	19	May 2, 1864	100 dys.	Absent, sick ——. No further record found.
Weimer, Oliver H	....do....	21	May 2, 1864	100 dys.	Mustered out with company Sept. 10, 1864.
Weimer, Uriah	....do....	18	May 2, 1864	100 dys.	Mustered out with company Sept. 10, 1864.
Wilhelm, George W	....do....	18	May 2, 1864	100 dys.	Mustered out with company Sept. 10, 1864.
Will, Peter	....do....	31	May 2, 1864	100 dys.	Mustered out with company Sept. 10, 1864.
Wyand, Daniel F	....do....	21	May 2, 1864	100 dys.	Died Aug. 1, 1864, in Hampton Hospital, Virginia.

164th Regiment Ohio Volunteer Infantry.

ONE HUNDRED DAYS' SERVICE.

THIS Regiment was organized at Camp Cleveland, O., May 11, 1864, to serve one hundred days. It was composed of the Forty-ninth Regiment, Ohio National Guard, from Seneca County, and the Fifty-fourth Battalion, Ohio National Guard, from Summit County. On the 14th of May the Regiment left Cleveland, and proceeding via Dunkirk, Elmira, Harrisburg, and Baltimore, reached Washington City on the 17th. It took position in the defenses on the south side of the Potomac, and during its one hundred days' service garrisoned Forts Smith, Strong, Bennett, Haggarty, and other forts. At the expiration of its term of enlistment the Regiment returned to Cleveland, via Baltimore, Harrisburg, and Pittsburgh, and was mustered out August 27, 1864, on expiration of term of service.

Names.	Rank.	Age.	Date of Entering the Service.	Period of Service.	Remarks.
Daldine, Dallas	Private	19	May 2, 1864	100 dys.	Mustered out with company Aug. 27, 1864.
Davis, John S.	do.	31	May 2, 1864	100 dys.	Mustered out with company Aug. 27, 1864.
Davis, Isaac	do.	19	May 2, 1864	100 dys.	Mustered out with company Aug. 27, 1864.
D[illegible]ffield William H.	do.	18	May 2, 1864	100 dys.	Mustered out with company Aug. 27, 1864.
Eckis, Jacob B.	do.	19	May 2, 1864	100 dys.	Mustered out with company Aug. 27, 1864.
Flahiff, Michael	do.	20	May 2, 1864	100 dys.	Mustered out with company Aug. 27, 1864.
Foncannon, Hiram I.	do.	18	May 2, 1864	100 dys.	Mustered out with company Aug. 27, 1864.
Fox, Oscar E.	do.	19	May 2, 1864	100 dys.	Mustered out with company Aug. 27, 1864.
German, David F.	do.	23	May 2, 1864	100 dys.	Mustered out with company Aug. 27, 1864.
Gilmer, John W.	do.	19	May 2, 1864	100 dys.	Mustered out with company Aug. 27, 1864.
Graham, John [illegible]	do.	45	May 2, 1864	100 dys.	Mustered out with company Aug. 27, 1864.
Haas, Melanchthon	do.	30	May 2, 1864	100 dys.	Mustered out with company Aug. 27, 1864.
Harrison Joseph D.	do.	21	May 2, 1864	100 dys.	Mustered out with company Aug. 27, 1864.
Hartman Lewis	do.	20	May 2, 1864	100 dys.	Mustered out with company Aug. 27, 1864.
Hawk, Mandos	do.	18	May 2, 1864	100 dys.	Mustered out with company Aug. 27, 1864.
Hittle, Edwin M.	do.	22	May 2, 1864	100 dys.	Mustered out with company Aug. 27, 1864.
Holt, William	do.	42	May 2, 1864	100 dys.	Promoted to Com. Sergeant May 11, 1864.
Hotz, John J.	do.	19	May 2, 1864	100 dys.	Mustered out with company Aug. 27, 1864.
Hunt, Jonathan	do.	44	May 2, 1864	100 dys.	Mustered out with company Aug. 27, 1864.
Keller, Alfred O.	do.	29	May 2, 1864	100 dys.	Mustered out with company Aug. 27, 1864.
Keller, William H.	do.	30	May 2, 1864	100 dys.	Mustered out with company Aug. 27, 1864.
Keller, Amos	do.	24	May 2, 1864	100 dys.	Mustered out with company Aug. 27, 1864.
Kuder, David	do.	18	May 2, 1864	100 dys.	Mustered out with company Aug. 27, 1864.
Kuder, John W.	do.	19	May 2, 1864	100 dys.	Mustered out with company Aug. 27, 1864.
Lautzenhiser, John B.	do.	28	May 2, 1864	100 dys.	Mustered out with company Aug. 27, 1864.
Lindsley, Silas B.	do.	34	May 2, 1864	100 dys.	Mustered out with company Aug. 27, 1864.
McIntire, Orson	do.	25	May 2, 1864	100 dys.	Mustered out with company Aug. 27, 1864.
Martin, Charles	do.	27	May 2, 1864	100 dys.	Mustered out with company Aug. 27, 1864.
Michaels, Leroy J.	do.	18	May 2, 1864	100 dys.	Mustered out with company Aug. 27, 1864.
Moorehouse, Charles L.	do.	22	May 2, 1864	100 dys.	Mustered out with company Aug. 27, 1864.
Myers, David K.	do.	20	May 2, 1864	100 dys.	Mustered out with company Aug. 27, 1864.
Myers, Albert J.	do.	27	May 2, 1864	100 dys.	Mustered out with company Aug. 27, 1864.
Park, John	do.	32	May 2, 1864	100 dys.	Mustered out with company Aug. 27, 1864.
Poorman, George S.	do.	18	May 2, 1864	100 dys.	Mustered out with company Aug. 27, 1864.
Reynolds, Walter	do.	19	May 2, 1864	100 dys.	Mustered out with company Aug. 27, 1864.
Robinson, William	do.	18	May 2, 1864	100 dys.	Mustered out with company Aug. 27, 1864.
Robinson, Elias W.	do.	42	May 2, 1864	100 dys.	Mustered out with company Aug. 27, 1864.
Ruess, Anthony J.	do.	25	May 2, 1864	100 dys.	Mustered out with company Aug. 27, 1864.
Seeholtz, Daniel	do.	32	May 2, 1864	100 dys.	Mustered out with company Aug. 27, 1864.
Sell, Enos	do.	35	May 2, 1864	100 dys.	Died June 1, 1864, in hospital at Fort [illegible], Virginia.
Scannell, Michael	do.	19	May 2, 1864	100 dys.	Mustered out with company Aug. 27, 1864.
Schaull, Dennis	do.	30	May 2, 1864	100 dys.	Mustered out with company Aug. 27, 1864.
Schaull, George I.	do.	25	May 2, 1864	100 dys.	Mustered out with company Aug. 27, 1864.
Sheetenhelm, Thomas M.	do.	18	May 2, 1864	100 dys.	Mustered out with company Aug. 27, 1864.
Six, Hiram S.	do.	18	May 2, 1864	100 dys.	Mustered out with company Aug. 27, 1864.
Spindler, Henry C.	do.	39	May 2, 1864	100 dys.	Mustered out with company Aug. 27, 1864.
Stone, Uriah	do.	42	May 2, 1864	100 dys.	Mustered out with company Aug. 27, 1864.
Swing, Laboid	do.	29	May 2, 1864	100 dys.	Mustered out with company Aug. 27, 1864.
Vetter Orlando M.	do.	37	May 2, 1864	100 dys.	Mustered out with company Aug. 27, 1864.
Walters, John W.	do.	40	May 2, 1864	100 dys.	Mustered out with company Aug. 27, 1864.
Whitmore, Frederick	do.	25	May 2, 1864	100 dys.	Mustered out with company Aug. 27, 1864.
Wisebecker, John J.	do.	20	May 2, 1864	100 dys.	Mustered out with company Aug. 27, 1864.
Yerk William L.	do.	18	May 2, 1864	100 dys.	Mustered out with company Aug. 27, 1864.
Yost, Henry	do.	19	May 2, 1864	100 dys.	Mustered out with company Aug. 27, 1864.
Zint, George W.	do.	19	May 2, 1864	100 dys.	Mustered out with company Aug. 27, 1864.

COMPANY B.

Mustered in May 11, 1864, at Camp Cleveland, O., by C. B. Throckmorton, 1st Lieutenant 4th Artillery, U. S. A. Mustered out Aug. 27, 1864, at Cleveland, O., by C. B. Throckmorton, 1st Lieutenant 4th Artillery, U. S. A.

Names.	Rank.	Age.	Date of Entering the Service.	Period of Service.	Remarks.
Benjamin M. Gibson	Captain.	46	May 2, 1864	100 dys.	Mustered out with company Aug. 27, 1864.
Edward Andre	1st Lieut.	29	May 2, 1864	100 dys.	Mustered out with company Aug. 27, 1864.
Samuel Baker	2d Lieut.	26	May 2, 1864	100 dys.	Mustered out with company Aug. 27, 1864.
William B. Conger	1st Sergt.	29	May 2, 1864	100 dys.	Mustered out with company Aug. 27, 1864.
Henry Gray	Sergeant.	23	May 2, 1864	100 dys.	Mustered out with company Aug. 27, 1864.
Ralph W. Tittle	do.	32	May 2, 1864	100 dys.	Mustered out with company Aug. 27, 1864.
William A. Watson	do.	34	May 2, 1864	100 dys.	Mustered out with company Aug. 27, 1864.
Edward Wing	do.	33	May 2, 1864	100 dys.	Appointed May 11, 1864; mustered out with company Aug. 27, 1864.
Harrison Thornburgh	Corporal.	28	May 2, 1864	100 dys.	Mustered out with company Aug. 27, 1864.
Samuel Bretz	do.	28	May 2, 1864	100 dys.	Appointed May 11, 1864; mustered out with company Aug. 27, 1864.
Madison Finch	do.	40	May 2, 1864	100 dys.	Mustered out with company Aug. 27, 1864.
David K. Holmes	do.	32	May 2, 1864	100 dys.	Mustered out with company Aug. 27, 1864.
Jonathan A. Tittle	do.	26	May 2, 1864	100 dys.	Mustered out with company Aug. 27, 1864.
Daniel G. Heck	do.	33	May 2, 1864	100 dys.	Appointed May 11, 1864; mustered out with company Aug. 27, 1864.

COMPANY C.

Mustered in May 11, 1864, at Camp Cleveland, O., by C. B. Throckmorton, 1st Lieutenant 4th Artillery, U. S. A. Mustered out Aug. 27, 1864, at Cleveland, O., by C. B. Throckmorton, 1st Lieutenant 4th Artillery, U. S. A.

Names.	Rank.	Age.	Date of Entering the Service.	Period of Service.	Remarks.
William M. Miller	Captain.	28	May 2, 1864	100 dys.	Mustered out with company Aug. 27, 1864.
John Foster	1st Lieut.	33	May 2, 1864	100 dys.	Mustered out with company Aug. 27, 1864.
Hugh McKibben	2d Lieut.	38	May 2, 1864	100 dys.	Mustered out with company Aug. 27, 1864.
Simon A. Bougle	1st Sergt.	33	May 2, 1864	100 dys.	Mustered out with company Aug. 27, 1864; also borne on rolls as Simon A. B[illegible].
George W. Carson	Sergeant.	56	May 2, 1864	100 dys.	Mustered out with company Aug. 27, 1864.
Christian Sheely	...do...	37	May 2, 1864	100 dys.	Mustered out with company Aug. 27, 1864.
James W. Brown	...do...	33	May 2, 1864	100 dys.	Mustered out with company Aug. 27, 1864.
Ichabod A. Spencer	...do...	36	May 2, 1864	100 dys.	Mustered out with company Aug. 27, 1864.
William Spencer	Corporal.	31	May 2, 1864	100 dys.	Mustered out with company Aug. 27, 1864.
James Ford	...do...	34	May 2, 1864	100 dys.	Mustered out with company Aug. 27, 1864.
Hiram Royce	...do...	36	May 2, 1864	100 dys.	Mustered out with company Aug. 27, 1864.
Thomas Webster	...do...	18	May 2, 1864	100 dys.	Mustered out with company Aug. 27, 1864.
Hiram Leonard	...do...	33	May 2, 1864	100 dys.	Mustered out with company Aug. 27, 1864.
Samuel Leddick	...do...	32	May 2, 1864	100 dys.	Mustered out with company Aug. 27, 1864.
Walter Robinson	...do...	23	May 2, 1864	100 dys.	Mustered out with company Aug. 27, 1864.
George [illegible]way	...do...	19	May 2, 1864	100 dys.	Mustered out with company Aug. 27, 1864.
Garrison Reed	Musician	15	May 2, 1864	100 dys.	Mustered out with company Aug. 27, 1864.
Alberger, Albert	Private.	20	May 2, 1864	100 dys.	Mustered out with company Aug. 27, 1864.
Alger, Nathaniel	...do...	46	May 2, 1864	100 dys.	Mustered out with company Aug. 27, 1864.
Begman, James	...do...	25	May 2, 1864	100 dys.	Mustered out with company Aug. 27, 1864.
Bonnel, James P.	...do...	25	May 2, 1864	100 dys.	Mustered out with company Aug. 27, 1864.
Bonnel, Jacob F.	...do...	26	May 2, 1864	100 dys.	Mustered out with company Aug. 27, 1864.
Carpenter, David S.	...do...	30	May 2, 1864	100 dys.	Mustered out with company Aug. 27, 1864.
Coltster, Daniel	...do...	27	May 2, 1864	100 dys.	Mustered out with company Aug. 27, 1864.
Cook, Morton M.	...do...	26	May 2, 1864	100 dys.	Mustered out with company Aug. 27, 1864.
Cridler, Elmer	...do...	18	May 2, 1864	100 dys.	Mustered out with company Aug. 27, 1864.
Crouninger, Lorenzo	...do...	20	May 2, 1864	100 dys.	Mustered out with company Aug. 27, 1864; also borne on rolls as Lorenzo Croning.
Culver, Thornton W.	...do...	[illegible]	May 2, 1864	100 dys.	Mustered out with company Aug. 27, 1864.
Decker, Jacob	...do...	40	May 2, 1864	100 dys.	Mustered out with company Aug. 27, 1864.
Feagles, William H.	...do...	18	May 2, 1864	100 dys.	Mustered out with company Aug. 27, 1864.
Foster, Daniel	...do...	21	May 2, 1864	100 dys.	Mustered out with company Aug. 27, 1864.
Geddis, John H.	...do...	[illegible]	May 2, 1864	100 dys.	Mustered out with company Aug. 27, 1864.
Galbreath, John R.	...do...	28	May 2, 1864	100 dys.	Mustered out with company Aug. 27, 1864.
Gibbons, Jacob	...do...	26	May 2, 1864	100 dys.	Mustered out with company Aug. 27, 1864.
Grimes, William	...do...	36	May 2, 1864	100 dys.	Died July 31, 1864, in hospital at Fort [illegible], Virginia.
Hall, Albert	...do...	18	May 2, 1864	100 dys.	Mustered out with company Aug. 27, 1864.
Hapler, Joseph	...do...	18	May 2, 1864	100 dys.	Mustered out with company Aug. 27, 1864; also borne on rolls as Joseph Hase[illegible].
Harsh, Joseph W.	...do...	[illegible]	May 2, 1864	100 dys.	Mustered out with company Aug. 27, 1864.
Heabler, Henry	...do...	31	May 2, 1864	100 dys.	Mustered out with company Aug. 27, 1864.
Heabler, David	...do...	25	May 2, 1864	100 dys.	Mustered out with company Aug. 27, 1864.
Heabler, George	...do...	35	May 2, 1864	100 dys.	Mustered out with company Aug. 27, 1864.
Heabler, Christian	...do...	18	May 2, 1864	100 dys.	Mustered out with company Aug. 27, 1864.
Hosben, Henry F.	...do...	22	May 2, 1864	100 dys.	Mustered out with company Aug. 27, 1864.
Hershiser, David	...do...	28	May 2, 1864	100 dys.	Mustered out with company Aug. 27, 1864.
Hillis, Taylor	...do...	18	May 2, 1864	100 dys.	Mustered out with company Aug. 27, 1864.
Hime, John L.	...do...	30	May 2, 1864	100 dys.	Discharged Sept. 1, 1864, at Washington, D. C., on Surgeon's certificate of disability.
Hoffman, Josiah W.	...do...	23	May 2, 1864	100 dys.	Mustered out with company Aug. 27, 1864.
Hoffman, John	...do...	19	May 2, 1864	100 dys.	Mustered out with company Aug. 27, 1864.
Hull, George F.	...do...	22	May 2, 1864	100 dys.	Mustered out with company Aug. 27, 1864.
Keasel, George	...do...	19	May 2, 1864	100 dys.	Mustered out with company Aug. 27, 1864.
Kimble, John	...do...	32	May 2, 1864	100 dys.	Mustered out with company Aug. 27, 1864.
King, Leeil Lewis	...do...	18	May 2, 1864	100 dys.	Mustered out with company Aug. 27, 1864.
Lapham, John M.	...do...	20	May 2, 1864	100 dys.	Mustered out with company Aug. 27, 1864.
Larmer, Marquis	...do...	30	May 2, 1864	100 dys.	Mustered out with company Aug. 27, 1864.
Lebold, Christian	...do...	32	May 2, 1864	100 dys.	Mustered out with company Aug. 27, 1864.
Lebold, Conrad	...do...	25	May 2, 1864	100 dys.	Mustered out with company Aug. 27, 1864.
Leonard, William F.	...do...	38	May 2, 1864	100 dys.	Mustered out with company Aug. 27, 1864.
Lindley, Erastus	...do...	29	May 2, 1864	100 dys.	Mustered out with company Aug. 27, 1864.
Lozier, John	...do...	18	May 2, 1864	100 dys.	Mustered out with company Aug. 27, 1864.
Lombard, William A.	...do...	18	May 2, 1864	100 dys.	Mustered out with company Aug. 27, 1864.
Lux, Jacob	...do...	18	May 2, 1864	100 dys.	Mustered out with company Aug. 27, 1864.
McKee, Samuel	...do...	38	May 2, 1864	100 dys.	Mustered out with company Aug. 27, 1864.
Michener, Adam D.	...do...	20	May 2, 1864	100 dys.	Mustered out with company Aug. 27, 1864.
Michener, William	...do...	41	May 2, 1864	100 dys.	Mustered out with company Aug. 27, 1864.
Miller, John J.	...do...	32	May 2, 1864	100 dys.	Mustered out with company Aug. 27, 1864.
Molts, Charles H.	...do...	19	May 2, 1864	100 dys.	Mustered out with company Aug. 27, 1864.
Moore, Theodore R.	...do...	18	May 2, 1864	100 dys.	Mustered out with company Aug. 27, 1864.
Moore, Franklin B.	...do...	21	May 2, 1864	100 dys.	Mustered out with company Aug. 27, 1864.
Myers, George W.	...do...	28	May 2, 1864	100 dys.	Mustered out with company Aug. 27, 1864.
Omler, Joseph S.	...do...	31	May 2, 1864	100 dys.	Mustered out with company Aug. 27, 1864.

Names.	Rank.	Age.	Date of Entering the Service.	Period of Service.	Remarks.
McNeal, John	Private.	31	May 2, 1864	100 dys.	Mustered out with company Aug. 27, 1864.
Means, Andrew F	...do...	21	May 2, 1864	100 dys.	Mustered out with company Aug. 27, 1864.
Miller, William H	...do...	18	May 2, 1864	100 dys.	Mustered out with company Aug. 27, 1864.
Ogle, Atkin	...do...	21	May 2, 1864	100 dys.	Mustered out with company Aug. 27, 1864.
Owen, John	...do...	20	May 2, 1864	100 dys.	Mustered out with company Aug. 27, 1864.
Owen, William T	...do...	27	May 2, 1864	100 dys.	Mustered out with company Aug. 27, 1864.
Palmer, John	...do...	18	May 2, 1864	100 dys.	Mustered out with company Aug. 27, 1864.
Peck, Leonard B	...do...	44	May 2, 1864	100 dys.	Mustered out with company Aug. 27, 1864.
Pettibone, Sherman B	...do...	20	May 2, 1864	100 dys.	Mustered out with company Aug. 27, 1864.
Pierce, Lawrence B	...do...	24	May 2, 1864	100 dys.	Mustered out with company Aug. 27, 1864.
Pittinger, Robert M	...do...	18	May 2, 1864	100 dys.	Mustered out with company Aug. 27, 1864.
Rice, George W	...do...	18	May 2, 1864	100 dys.	Mustered out with company Aug. 27, 1864.
Rickard, Levi	...do...	26	May 2, 1864	100 dys.	Mustered out with company Aug. 27, 1864.
Ripley, William	...do...	19	May 2, 1864	100 dys.	Mustered out with company Aug. 27, 1864.
Rowdabush, John	...do...	23	May 2, 1864	100 dys.	Mustered out with company Aug. 27, 1864; also borne on rolls as John Roundbush.
Rowinsky, John	...do...	18	May 2, 1864	100 dys.	Mustered out with company Aug. 27, 1864.
Sackett, Clark A	...do...	27	May 2, 1864	100 dys.	Mustered out with company Aug. 27, 1864.
Shenkenberger, Fred'k C	...do...	25	May 2, 1864	100 dys.	Mustered out with company Aug. 27, 1864.
Shoemaker, Edmund	...do...	18	May 2, 1864	100 dys.	Mustered out with company Aug. 27, 1864.
Skinner, Bradford W	...do...	29	May 2, 1864	100 dys.	Mustered out with company Aug. 27, 1864.
Sperry, Francis W	...do...	18	May 2, 1864	100 dys.	Mustered out with company Aug. 27, 1864.
Sprague, Oliver	...do...	18	May 2, 1864	100 dys.	Mustered out with company Aug. 27, 1864.
Stone, Lyman	...do...	18	May 2, 1864	100 dys.	Mustered out with company Aug. 27, 1864.
Stouffer, Franklin L	...do...	19	May 2, 1864	100 dys.	Mustered out with company Aug. 27, 1864.
Strohl, Benjamin	...do...	19	May 2, 1864	100 dys.	Mustered out with company Aug. 27, 1864.
Thomas, William L	...do...	26	May 2, 1864	100 dys.	Mustered out with company Aug. 27, 1864.
Treat, Orange S	...do...	25	May 2, 1864	100 dys.	Mustered out with company Aug. 27, 1864.
Treat, John C	...do...	31	May 2, 1864	100 dys.	Mustered out with company Aug. 27, 1864.
Umsted, Jesse R	...do...	18	May 2, 1864	100 dys.	Mustered out with company Aug. 27, 1864.
Upson, Daniel A	...do...	43	May 2, 1864	100 dys.	Mustered out with company Aug. 27, 1864.
Upson, Henry C	...do...	18	May 2, 1864	100 dys.	Mustered out with company Aug. 27, 1864.
Upson, Joseph E	...do...	22	May 2, 1864	100 dys.	Mustered out with company Aug. 27, 1864.
Upson, Norton L	...do...	18	May 2, 1864	100 dys.	Mustered out with company Aug. 27, 1864.
Voght, Daniel	...do...	27	May 2, 1864	100 dys.	Mustered out with company Aug. 27, 1864.
Wetmore, Willard W	...do...	21	May 2, 1864	100 dys.	Mustered out with company Aug. 27, 1864.
Westover, Harry	...do...	22	May 2, 1864	100 dys.	Mustered out with company Aug. 27, 1864.
Young, George	...do...	21	May 2, 1864	100 dys.	Mustered out with company Aug. 27, 1864.

COMPANY E.

Mustered in May 11, 1864, at Camp Cleveland, O., by C. B. Throckmorton, 1st Lieutenant 4th Artillery, U. S. A. Mustered out Aug. 27, 1864, at Cleveland, O., by C. B. Throckmorton, 1st Lieutenant 4th Artillery, U. S. A.

Names.	Rank.	Age.	Date of Entering the Service.	Period of Service.	Remarks.
Abraham Ash	Captain.	40	May 2, 1864	100 dys.	Mustered out with company Aug. 27, 1864.
Martin P. Klotz	1st Lieut.	22	May 2, 1864	100 dys.	Mustered out with company Aug. 27, 1864.
George W. Hartsock	2d Lieut.	24	May 2, 1864	100 dys.	Mustered out with company Aug. 27, 1864.
Andrew J. Feasel	1st Sergt.	24	May 2, 1864	100 dys.	Mustered out with company Aug. 27, 1864.
Moses F. Hosler	Sergeant.	33	May 2, 1864	100 dys.	Mustered out with company Aug. 27, 1864.
George E. Cessna	...do...	25	May 2, 1864	100 dys.	Mustered out with company Aug. 27, 1864.
Isaac N. Wyant	...do...	40	May 2, 1864	100 dys.	Mustered out with company Aug. 27, 1864.
David A. Long	...do...	43	May 2, 1864	100 dys.	Mustered out with company Aug. 27, 1864.
Samuel P. Bowers	Corporal.	28	May 2, 1864	100 dys.	Mustered out with company Aug. 27, 1864.
John R. Dicken	...do...	30	May 2, 1864	100 dys.	Mustered out with company Aug. 27, 1864.
Edmund R. Ash	...do...	19	May 2, 1864	100 dys.	Mustered out with company Aug. 27, 1864.
James P. Seagraves	...do...	19	May 2, 1864	100 dys.	Mustered out with company Aug. 27, 1864.
Reuben V. Lott	...do...	24	May 2, 1864	100 dys.	Mustered out with company Aug. 27, 1864.
John D. Cessna	...do...	19	May 2, 1864	100 dys.	Mustered out with company Aug. 27, 1864.
George Halter	...do...	21	May 2, 1864	100 dys.	Mustered out with company Aug. 27, 1864.
Henry Borough	...do...	23	May 2, 1864	100 dys.	Mustered out with company Aug. 27, 1864.
Jacob Ash	Musician	28	May 2, 1864	100 dys.	Mustered out with company Aug. 27, 1864.
Isaac Craun	...do...	21	May 2, 1864	100 dys.	Mustered out with company Aug. 27, 1864.
Ash, George W	Private.	21	May 2, 1864	100 dys.	Mustered out with company Aug. 27, 1864.
Ash, Manuel	...do...	26	May 2, 1864	100 dys.	Mustered out with company Aug. 27, 1864.
Basom, Daniel F	...do...	40	May 2, 1864	100 dys.	Mustered out with company Aug. 27, 1864.
Bastion, Hiram	...do...	19	May 2, 1864	100 dys.	Mustered out with company Aug. 27, 1864.
Bear, Loammi C	...do...	18	May 2, 1864	100 dys.	Mustered out with company Aug. 27, 1864.
Berger, William H	...do...	18	May 2, 1864	100 dys.	Died Aug. 13, 1864, in Lincoln Hospital, Washington, D. C.
Blackford, Joseph	...do...	20	May 2, 1864	100 dys.	Mustered out with company Aug. 27, 1864.
Borough, John	...do...	32	May 2, 1864	100 dys.	Mustered out with company Aug. 27, 1864.
Boyd, Hugh W. A	...do...		May 2, 1864	100 dys.	Mustered out with company Aug. 27, 1864.
Bunn, Oliver P	...do...	29	May 2, 1864	100 dys.	Mustered out with company Aug. 27, 1864.
Celpher, Jacob	...do...	23	May 2, 1864	100 dys.	Mustered out with company Aug. 27, 1864.
Condon, Daniel	...do...	18	May 2, 1864	100 dys.	Mustered out with company Aug. 27, 1864.
Cromer, Hiram	...do...	20	May 2, 1864	100 dys.	Mustered out with company Aug. 27, 1864.
Cromer, John	...do...	21	May 2, 1864	100 dys.	Mustered out with company Aug. 27, 1864.
Flack, William, Jr	...do...	23	May 2, 1864	100 dys.	Mustered out with company Aug. 27, 1864.
Frankhouser, Solomon	...do...	21	May 2, 1864	100 dys.	Mustered out with company Aug. 27, 1864.

Name	Rank.	Age.	Date of Entering the Service.	Period of Service.	Remarks.
	Private..	27	May 2, 1864	100 dys.	Discharged Sept. 1, 1864, at Washington, D. C., on Surgeon's certificate of disability.
Henry..........	..do....	20	May 2, 1864	100 dys.	Mustered out with company Aug. 27, 1864; also borne on rolls as Henry Robison.
	....do....	27	May 2, 1864	100 dys.	Mustered out with company Aug. 27, 1864.
....	....do....	19	May 2, 1864	100 dys.	Mustered out with company Aug. 27, 1864.
....	....do....	21	May 2, 1864	100 dys.	Mustered out with company Aug. 27, 1864.
....	....do....	22	May 2, 1864	100 dys.	Mustered out with company Aug. 27, 1864.
	....do....	18	May 2, 1864	100 dys.	Mustered out with company Aug. 27, 1864.
	....do....	18	May 2, 1864	100 dys.	Mustered out with company Aug. 27, 1864.
....	....do....	20	May 2, 1864	100 dys.	Mustered out with company Aug. 27, 1864.
....	....do....	25	May 2, 1864	100 dys.	Mustered out with company Aug. 27, 1864.
....	....do....	28	May 2, 1864	100 dys.	Mustered out with company Aug. 27, 1864.
....	....do....	18	May 2, 1864	100 dys.	Mustered out with company Aug. 27, 1864.
....	....do....	23	May 2, 1864	100 dys.	Mustered out with company Aug. 27, 1864.
	....do....	24	May 2, 1864	100 dys.	Mustered out with company Aug. 27, 1864.

COMPANY D.

d in May 11, 1864, at Camp Cleveland, O., by C. B. Throckmorton, 1st Lieutenant 4th Artillery, U. S. A. Mustered out Aug. 27, 1864, at Cleveland, O., by C. B. Throckmorton, 1st Lieutenant 4th Artillery, U. S. A.

Name	Rank.	Age.	Date of Entering the Service.	Period of Service.	Remarks.
....	Captain.		May 2, 1864	100 dys.	Mustered out with company Aug. 27, 1864.
....	1st Lieut.		May 2, 1864	100 dys.	Mustered out with company Aug. 27, 1864.
....	2d Lieut.		May 2, 1864	100 dys.	Mustered out with company Aug. 27, 1864.
....	1st Sergt.		May 2, 1864	100 dys.	Mustered out with company Aug. 27, 1864.
	Sergeant.		May 2, 1864	100 dys.	Mustered out with company Aug. 27, 1864.
	...do....		May 2, 1864	100 dys.	Mustered out with company Aug. 27, 1864.
....	...do....		May 2, 1864	100 dys.	Mustered out with company Aug. 27, 1864.
....	...do....		May 2, 1864	100 dys.	Appointed May 11, 1864; mustered out with company Aug. 27, 1864.
....			May 2, 1864	100 dys.	Mustered out with company Aug. 27, 1864.
....			May 2, 1864	100 dys.	Mustered out with company Aug. 27, 1864.
			May 2, 1864	100 dys.	Mustered out with company Aug. 27, 1864.
			May 2, 1864	100 dys.	Mustered out with company Aug. 27, 1864.
......			May 2, 1864	100 dys.	Mustered out with company Aug. 27, 1864.
......			May 2, 1864	100 dys.	Mustered out with company Aug. 27, 1864.
......			May 2, 1864	100 dys.	Mustered out with company Aug. 27, 1864.
......			May 2, 1864	100 dys.	Appointed May 11, 1864; mustered out with company Aug. 27, 1864.
H. Crane			May 2, 1864	100 dys.	Mustered out with company Aug. 27, 1864.
, Louis H			May 2, 1864	100 dys.	Mustered out with company Aug. 27, 1864.
. Bruce..........			May 2, 1864	100 dys.	Mustered out with company Aug. 27, 1864.
Francis N.......			May 2, 1864	100 dys.	Mustered out with company Aug. 27, 1864.
Clark E....			May 2, 1864	100 dys.	Mustered out with company Aug. 27, 1864.
, Peter..........	...	..	May 2, 1864	100 dys.	Mustered out with company Aug. 27, 1864.
James	...	..	May 2, 1864	100 dys.	Mustered out with company Aug. 27, 1864.
, William H ...	...	..	May 2, 1864	100 dys.	Mustered out with company Aug. 27, 1864.
n, Christopher..	...	..	May 2, 1864	100 dys.	Died June 6, 1864, at Fort Cochran, Va.
Henry M.... ..	...	..	May 2, 1864	100 dys.	Mustered out with company Aug. 27, 1864.
Leroy W....	...	..	May 2, 1864	100 dys.	Mustered out with company Aug. 27, 1864.
Albert W.	...	..	May 2, 1864	100 dys.	Mustered out with company Aug. 27, 1864.
Franklin A	...	..	May 2, 1864	100 dys.	Mustered out with company Aug. 27, 1864.
, Henry C.	...	..	May 2, 1864	100 dys.	Mustered out with company Aug. 27, 1864.
Upton F	..	..	May 2, 1864	100 dys.	Mustered out with company Aug. 27, 1864.
. A. Dallas......	..	..	May 2, 1864	100 dys.	Mustered out with company Aug. 27, 1864.
homas	..	..	May 2, 1864	100 dys.	Mustered out with company Aug. 27, 1864.
t, William......	..	..	May 2, 1864	100 dys.	Mustered out with company Aug. 27, 1864.
hn	..	..	May 2, 1864	100 dys.	Mustered out with company Aug. 27, 1864.
illiam..........	..	..	May 2, 1864	100 dys.	Mustered out with company Aug. 27, 1864.
ames...........	..	..	May 2, 1864	100 dys.	Mustered out with company Aug. 27, 1864.
William.........	..	..	May 2, 1864	100 dys.	Mustered out with company Aug. 27, 1864.
avid	..	..	May 2, 1864	100 dys.	Mustered out with company Aug. 27, 1864.
ames	..	..	May 2, 1864	100 dys.	Mustered out with company Aug. 27, 1864.
braham F.......	..	..	May 2, 1864	100 dys.	Discharged June 11, 1864, at Fort Woodbury, Virginia.
rederick B	...do....		May 2, 1864	100 dys.	Mustered out with company Aug. 27, 1864.
riah D..........	...do....		May 2, 1864	100 dys.	Mustered out with company Aug. 27, 1864.
r, Robert H.....	...do....		May 2, 1864	100 dys.	Mustered out with company Aug. 27, 1864.
h, Joseph	...do....		May 2, 1864	100 dys.	Died Aug. 4, 1864, at Fort Strong, Va.
ury L..........	...do....		May 2, 1864	100 dys.	Died May 25, 1864, at Fort Strong, Va.
Henry..........	...do....		May 2, 1864	100 dys.	Mustered out with company Aug. 27, 1864.
arles D.........	...do....		May 2, 1864	100 dys.	Mustered out with company Aug. 27, 1864.
r, George E.....	...do....		May 2, 1864		Mustered out with company Aug. 27, 1864.
ward	...do....		May 2, 1864		Discharged July 19, 1864, at Fort Woodbury, Virginia.
Josiah..........	...do....		May 2, 1864		Mustered out with company Aug. 27, 1864.
Jefferson.......	...do....		May 2, 1864		Mustered out with company Aug. 27, 1864.
Charles A	...do....		May 2, 1864		Mustered out with company Aug. 27, 1864.

Names.	Rank.	Age.	Date of Entering the Service.	Period of Service.	Remarks.
Abbey, Henry E.	Private.	18	May 2, 1864	100 dys.	Mustered out with company Aug. 27, 1864.
Ackley, Frank C	...do...	22	May 2, 1864	100 dys.	Mustered out with company Aug. 27, 1864.
Allen, William E.	...do...	19	May 2, 1864	100 dys.	Mustered out with company Aug. 27, 1864.
Alexander, Joseph H	...do...	32	May 2, 1864	100 dys.	Mustered out with company Aug. 27, 1864.
Atwood, Watson C	...do...	18	May 2, 1864	100 dys.	Mustered out with company Aug. 27, 1864.
Atwood, William J.	...do...	28	May 2, 1864	100 dys.	Mustered out with company Aug. 27, 1864.
Babcock Williams	...do...	28	May 2, 1864	100 dys.	Mustered out with company Aug. 27, 1864.
Baldwin, James N	...do...	25	May 2, 1864	100 dys.	Mustered out with company Aug. 27, 1864.
Baughman, David	...do...	22	May 2, 1864	100 dys.	Mustered out with company Aug. 27, 1864.
Beardsley, Mills H	...do...	28	May 2, 1864	100 dys.	Mustered out with company Aug. 27, 1864.
Benjamin, Clarence L	...do...	18	May 2, 1864	100 dys.	Mustered out with company Aug. 27, 1864.
Bernard, Charles B.	...do...	35	May 2, 1864	100 dys.	Promoted to 1st Lieutenant and Adjutant May 13, 1864.
Berry, George C	...do...	27	May 2, 1864	100 dys.	Mustered out with company Aug. 27, 1864.
Bien, George H	...do...	27	May 2, 1864	100 dys.	Mustered out with company Aug. 27, 1864.
Bisbee George A	...do...	20	May 2, 1864	100 dys.	Mustered out with company Aug. 27, 1864.
Britton, Wilson G	...do...	25	May 2, 1864	100 dys.	Mustered out with company Aug. 27, 1864.
Brouse, Cornelius A	...do...	26	May 2, 1864	100 dys.	Mustered out with company Aug. 27, 1864.
Burlison, James	...do...	38	May 2, 1864	100 dys.	Mustered out with company Aug. 27, 1864.
Butler, James K	...do...	30	May 2, 1864	100 dys.	Mustered out with company Aug. 27, 1864.
Canfield, Horace G	...do...	34	May 2, 1864	100 dys.	Mustered out with company Aug. 27, 1864.
Carter, William H	...do...	19	May 2, 1864	100 dys.	Mustered out with company Aug. 27, 1864.
Christy, John H	...do...	33	May 2, 1864	100 dys.	Mustered out with company Aug. 27, 1864.
Cross, Amos G	...do...	19	May 2, 1864	100 dys.	Mustered out with company Aug. 27, 1864.
Cutler, Morrell T	...do...	36	May 2, 1864	100 dys.	Mustered out with company Aug. 27, 1864.
[illegible]	...do...	27	May 2, 1864	100 dys.	Mustered out with company Aug. 27, 1864.
Gardner, George D	...do...	23	May 2, 1864	100 dys.	Mustered out with company Aug. 27, 1864.
Grubb, Henry A	...do...	25	May 2, 1864	100 dys.	Mustered out with company Aug. 27, 1864.
Guyer, Gottleib	...do...	23	May 2, 1864	100 dys.	Mustered out July 6, 1864, by order of War Department.
Hanscom, Asa S	...do...	19	May 2, 1864	100 dys.	Mustered out with company Aug. 27, 1864.
Harper, Lecky R	...do...	21	May 2, 1864	100 dys.	Mustered out with company Aug. 27, 1864.
Hastings, Lorenzo A	...do...	27	May 2, 1864	100 dys.	Mustered out with company Aug. 27, 1864.
Hawkins, Horace W	...do...	23	May 2, 1864	100 dys.	Mustered out with company Aug. 27, 1864.
Hibbard, Dwight A	...do...	20	May 2, 1864	100 dys.	Mustered out with company Aug. 27, 1864.
Helfer, Clinton E	...do...	19	May 2, 1864	100 dys.	Mustered out with company Aug. 27, 1864.
Hine, Henry D	...do...	31	May 2, 1864	100 dys.	Mustered out with company Aug. 27, 1864.
Howard, Henry C	...do...	24	May 2, 1864	100 dys.	Mustered out with company Aug. 27, 1864.
Hutton, John W	...do...	25	May 2, 1864	100 dys.	Mustered out with company Aug. 27, 1864.
Jones, William H	...do...	26	May 2, 1864	100 dys.	Mustered out with company Aug. 27, 1864.
King, Henry C	...do...	20	May 2, 1864	100 dys.	Died Aug. 11, 1864, at Fort Strong, Va.
Kock, Jacob	...do...	24	May 2, 1864	100 dys.	Mustered out with company Aug. 27, 1864.
Koehler, Robert	...do...	17	May 2, 1864	100 dys.	Mustered out with company Aug. 27, 1864.
McNeal, Andrew	...do...	38	May 2, 1864	100 dys.	Mustered out with company Aug. 27, 1864.
Merrill, Henry E.	...do...	24	May 2, 1864	100 dys.	Mustered out with company Aug. 27, 1864.
Moore, John R	...do...	25	May 2, 1864	100 dys.	Mustered out with company Aug. 27, 1864.
Noble, John L	...do...	32	May 2, 1864	100 dys.	Mustered out with company Aug. 27, 1864.
Oberholser, Jacob	...do...	36	May 2, 1864	100 dys.	Discharged Sept. 1, 1864, at Washington, D.C. on Surgeon's certificate of disability.
Oviatt, Edward	...do...	41	May 2, 1864	100 dys.	Mustered out with company Aug. 27, 1864.
Purdy, Daniel W	...do...	27	May 2, 1864	100 dys.	Mustered out with company Aug. 27, 1864.
Raymond, John G	...do...	18	May 2, 1864	100 dys.	Mustered out with company Aug. 27, 1864.
Rhinehart James	...do...	19	May 2, 1864	100 dys.	Mustered out with company Aug. 27, 1864.
Robertson, Orville A	...do...	18	May 2, 1864	100 dys.	Mustered out with company Aug. 27, 1864.
Sanford, Henry M	...do...	34	May 2, 1864	100 dys.	Mustered out with company Aug. 27, 1864.
Sickle William	...do...	21	May 2, 1864	100 dys.	Mustered out with company Aug. 27, 1864.
Somers Edgar L	...do...	18	May 2, 1864	100 dys.	Mustered out with company Aug. 27, 1864.
Snyder, David	...do...	35	May 2, 1864	100 dys.	Mustered out with company Aug. 27, 1864.
Steese, Dallas G	...do...	19	May 2, 1864	100 dys.	Mustered out with company Aug. 27, 1864.
Taplin, John L	...do...	20	May 2, 1864	100 dys.	Mustered out with company Aug. 27, 1864.
Viele, Henry C	...do...	22	May 2, 1864	100 dys.	Mustered out with company Aug. 27, 1864.
Voght, George	...do...	21	May 2, 1864	100 dys.	Mustered out with company Aug. 27, 1864.
Washburn, Able, A	...do...	25	May 2, 1864	100 dys.	Mustered out with company Aug. 27, 1864.
Weimer, George C	...do...	22	May 2, 1864	100 dys.	Mustered out with company Aug. 27, 1864.
Wellhouse, George	...do...	37	May 2, 1864	100 dys.	Mustered out with company Aug. 27, 1864.
Wetmore, Henry W.	...do...	38	May 2, 1864	100 dys.	Mustered out with company Aug. 27, 1864.
Weygandt, Jacob K	...do...	26	May 2, 1864	100 dys.	Mustered out with company Aug. 27, 1864.
Wilson, Andrew T.	...do...	24	May 2, 1864	100 dys.	Mustered out with company Aug. 27, 1864.
Wolf, John	...do...	27	May 2, 1864	100 dys.	Mustered out with company Aug. 27, 1864.
Zeisloft, Daniel	...do...	38	May 2, 1864	100 dys.	Mustered out with company Aug. 27, 1864.

Names.	Rank.	Age.	Date of Entering the Service.	Period of Service.	Remarks.
...hum	Private.	22	May 2, 1864	100 dys.	Mustered out with company Aug. 27, 1864.
... Daniel	do.	41	May 2, 1864	100 dys.	Died July 17, 1864, in Fort Strong Hospital, Virginia.
... Jacob	do.	22	May 2, 1864	100 dys.	Mustered out with company Aug. 27, 1864.
...S. H.	do.	18	May 2, 1864	100 dys.	Mustered out with company Aug. 27, 1864.
[illegible]	do.	39	May 2, 1864	100 dys.	Mustered out with company Aug. 27, 1864.
...rles S.	do.	20	May 2, 1864	100 dys.	Mustered out with company Aug. 27, 1864.
...erick	do.	40	May 2, 1864	100 dys.	Mustered out with company Aug. 27, 1864.
...ateman	do.	28	May 2, 1864	100 dys.	Mustered out with company Aug. 27, 1864.
... William	do.	26	May 2, 1864	100 dys.	Mustered out with company Aug. 27, 1864.
... Charles	do.	18	May 2, 1864	100 dys.	Mustered out with company Aug. 27, 1864.
[illegible]	do.	27	May 2, 1864	100 dys.	Mustered out with company Aug. 27, 1864.
...vid H.	do.	26	May 2, 1864	100 dys.	Mustered out with company Aug. 27, 1864.
...ry T.	do.	21	May 2, 1864	100 dys.	Mustered out with company Aug. 27, 1864.
...H.	do.	25	May 2, 1864	100 dys.	Mustered out with company Aug. 27, 1864.
...hn T.	do.	37	May 2, 1864	100 dys.	Mustered out with company Aug. 27, 1864.
... William	do.	32	May 2, 1864	100 dys.	Mustered out with company Aug. 27, 1864.
[illegible]	do.	24	May 2, 1864	100 dys.	Mustered out with company Aug. 27, 1864.
...rick	do.	18	May 2, 1864	100 dys.	Mustered out with company Aug. 27, 1864.
... Rufus N.	do.	18	May 2, 1864	100 dys.	Mustered out with company Aug. 27, 1864.
...m A.	do.	17	May 2, 1864	100 dys.	Mustered out with company Aug. 27, 1864.
... John W.	do.	15	May 2, 1864	100 dys.	Mustered out with company Aug. 27, 1864.
...ohn	do.	19	May 2, 1864	100 dys.	Mustered out with company Aug. 27, 1864.
...	do.	18	May 2, 1864	100 dys.	Mustered out with company Aug. 27, 1864.
...	do.	37	May 2, 1864	100 dys.	Mustered out with company Aug. 27, 1864.
...am	do.	32	May 2, 1864	100 dys.	Mustered out with company Aug. 27, 1864.
... Jacob	do.	20	May 2, 1864	100 dys.	Mustered out with company Aug. 27, 1864; also borne on rolls as Jacob Nighswander.
...n W.	do.	18	May 2, 1864	100 dys.	Mustered out with company Aug. 27, 1864.
...illiam	do.	41	May 2, 1864	100 dys.	Mustered out with company Aug. 27, 1864.
...rick	do.	19	May 2, 1864	100 dys.	Mustered out with company Aug. 27, 1864.
...	do.	29	May 2, 1864	100 dys.	Mustered out with company Aug. 27, 1864.
..., John	do.	30	May 2, 1864	100 dys.	Mustered out with company Aug. 27, 1864.
...	do.	21	May 2, 1864	100 dys.	Mustered out with company Aug. 27, 1864.
...	do.	19	May 2, 1864	100 dys.	Mustered out with company Aug. 27, 1864.
...illiam	do.	42	May 2, 1864	100 dys.	Mustered out with company Aug. 27, 1864.
...	do.	21	May 2, 1864	100 dys.	Mustered out with company Aug. 27, 1864.
...	do.	19	May 2, 1864	100 dys.	Mustered out with company Aug. 27, 1864.
...niel	do.	19	May 2, 1864	100 dys.	Mustered out with company Aug. 27, 1864.
..., John	do.	24	May 2, 1864	100 dys.	Mustered out with company Aug. 27, 1864.
...	do.	35	May 2, 1864	100 dys.	Mustered out with company Aug. 27, 1864.
...	do.	27	May 2, 1864	100 dys.	Mustered out with company Aug. 27, 1864.
...	do.	18	May 2, 1864	100 dys.	Mustered out with company Aug. 27, 1864.
..., Noah	do.	30	May 2, 1864	100 dys.	Mustered out with company Aug. 27, 1864.
... George	do.	43	May 2, 1864	100 dys.	Mustered out with company Aug. 27, 1864.
...	do.	45	May 2, 1864	100 dys.	Mustered out with company Aug. 27, 1864.
...	do.	42	May 2, 1864	100 dys.	Mustered out with company Aug. 27, 1864.
...rtin	do.	29	May 2, 1864	100 dys.	Mustered out with company Aug. 27, 1864.
...	do.	21	May 2, 1864	100 dys.	Mustered out with company Aug. 27, 1864.
...	do.	39	May 2, 1864	100 dys.	Mustered out with company Aug. 27, 1864.
...	do.	23	May 2, 1864	100 dys.	Mustered out with company Aug. 27, 1864.
... H.	do.	35	May 2, 1864	100 dys.	Mustered out with company Aug. 27, 1864.

COMPANY F.

... May 11, 1864, at Camp Cleveland, O., by C. B. Throckmorton, 1st Lieutenant 4th Artillery, U. S. A. Mustered out Aug. 27, 1864, at Cleveland, O., by C. B. Throckmorton, 1st Lieutenant 4th Artillery, U. S. A.

Names.	Rank.	Age.	Date of Entering the Service.	Period of Service.	Remarks.
...	Captain.	37	May 2, 1864	100 dys.	Mustered out with company Aug. 27, 1864.
...ter	1st Lieut.	35	May 2, 1864	100 dys.	Mustered out with company Aug. 27, 1864.
...	2d Lieut.	22	May 2, 1864	100 dys.	Mustered out with company Aug. 27, 1864.
... Raymond	1st Sergt.	23	May 2, 1864	100 dys.	Appointed from Sergeant May 27, 1864; mustered out with company Aug. 27, 1864.
...	Sergeant.	30	May 2, 1864	100 dys.	Reduced from 1st Sergeant May 27, 1864; mustered out with company Aug. 27, 1864.
...illiam	do.	27	May 2, 1864	100 dys.	Mustered out with company Aug. 27, 1864.
...illiam	do.	30	May 2, 1864	100 dys.	Mustered out with company Aug. 27, 1864.
...omas	do.	22	May 2, 1864	100 dys.	Mustered out with company Aug. 27, 1864.
...mond	Corporal.	29	May 2, 1864	100 dys.	Mustered out with company Aug. 27, 1864.
...	do.	31	May 2, 1864	100 dys.	Mustered out with company Aug. 27, 1864.
...yder	do.	23	May 2, 1864	100 dys.	Mustered out with company Aug. 27, 1864.
...	do.	20	May 2, 1864	100 dys.	Mustered out with company Aug. 27, 1864.
...	do.	36	May 2, 1864	100 dys.	Mustered out with company Aug. 27, 1864.
...	do.	41	May 2, 1864	100 dys.	Mustered out with company Aug. 27, 1864.
...	do.	20	May 2, 1864	100 dys.	Mustered out with company Aug. 27, 1864.
...	do.	23	May 2, 1864	100 dys.	Appointed May 11, 1864; mustered out with company Aug. 27, 1864.
...	Musician	25	May 2, 1864	100 dys.	Mustered out with company Aug. 27, 1864.
..., John	do.	18	May 2, 1864	100 dys.	Mustered out with company Aug. 27, 1864.

Names.	Rank.	Age.	Date of Entering the Service.	Period of Service.	
Sowards, Thomas J	Private.	20	May 2, 1864		ustered
Tabor, William	do	19	May 2, 1864		ustered
Teel, Hiram	do	34	May 2, 1864		ustered
Thorn, George B	do	19	May 2, 1864		
Wall, George	do	27	May 2, 1864		
Williams, John B	do	22	May 2, 1864		
Williams, Isaac V	do	23	May 2, 1864		
Williams, Joseph L	do	21	May 2, 1864		
Wilson, William	do	18	May 2, 1864		Died June 19,
Zeppernick, Ira	do	22	May 2, 1864		Mustered out

COMPANY H.

Mustered in May 11, 1864, at Camp Cleveland, O., by C. B. Throckmorton, 1st I
Mustered out Aug. 27, 1864, at Cleveland, O., by C. B. Thr
1st Lieutenant 4th Artillery, U. S. A.

Names.	Rank.	Age.	Date of Entering the Service.	Period of Service.	
Darius F. Hunsberger	Captain.	29	May 2, 1864		Mustered out
Norman D. Egbert	1st Lieut.	21	May 2, 1864		Mustered out
Daniel J. Mottinger	2d Lieut.	28	May 2, 1864		Mustered out
Noah N. Leohner	1st Sergt.	30	May 2, 1864		Mustered out
Cyrus W. Harris	Sergeant.	28	May 2, 1864		Mustered out
William Buchtel	do	41	May 2, 1864		Appointed fr tered out wi
Balser Shriver	do	24	May 2, 1864	100	Mustered out
Samuel C. Marsh	do	28	May 2, 1864	100	Mustered out
Thomas Wright, Jr	Corporal.	44	May 2, 1864	100	Reduced fro tered out w
Aaron Swartz	do	31	May 2, 1864	100 dys.	Mustered out
Franklin G. Stipe	do	19	May 2, 1864	100 dys.	Mustered out
Samuel Breckenridge	do	30	May 2, 1864	100 dys.	Mustered out
Jacob Long	do	19	May 2, 1864	100 dys.	Mustered out
Robert Thompson	do	31	May 2, 1864	100 dys.	Mustered out
Daniel G. Shutt	do	28	May 2, 1864	100 dys.	Mustered out
Jacob Weaver	do	23	May 2, 1864	100 dys.	Mustered out
Jonathan B. Krieghbaum	Musician	38	May 2, 1864	100 dys.	Mustered out
Acker, John B	Private.	21	May 2, 1864	100 dys.	Mustered out
Beymer, Merritt C	do	24	May 2, 1864	100 dys.	Mustered
Brumbaugh, Henry	do	37	May 2, 1864	100 dys.	Mustered out
Chamberlin, John W	do	19	May 2, 1864	100 dys.	Mustered out
Chisnell, Benjamin	do	36	May 2, 1864	100 dys.	Mustered out
Courtney, William	do	41	May 2, 1864	100 dys.	Mustered out
Cramer, William	do	34	May 2, 1864	100 dys.	Mustered out
Cramer, Elias	do	28	May 2, 1864	100 dys.	Mustered out
Drown, Joseph R	do	28	May 2, 1864	100 dys.	Mustered out
Egbert, Newton C	do	19	May 2, 1864	100 dys.	Mustered out
Egbert, Uriah S	do	23	May 2, 1864	100 dys.	Mustered out
Egbert, Edward G	do	19	May 2, 1864	100 dys.	Mustered out
Fasnacht, George H	do	30	May 2, 1864	100 dys.	Mustered out
Fasnacht, Levi	do	37	May 2, 1864	100 dys.	Mustered out
Finkle, William	do	30	May 2, 1864	100 dys.	Mustered out
Foster, Sewell	do	30	May 2, 1864	100 dys.	Mustered out
Foster, Jonathan	do	36	May 2, 1864	100 dys.	Mustered out
Foust, Daniel S	do	21	May 2, 1864	100 dys.	Mustered out
Foust, Hiram	do	18	May 2, 1864	100 dys.	Mustered out
Fry, John	do	33	May 2, 1864	100 dys.	Mustered out
Goss, Benjamin	do	37	May 2, 1864	100 dys.	Mustered out
Grable, Alexander	do	25	May 2, 1864	100 dys.	Mustered out
Grable, Jacob, Jr	do	27	May 2, 1864	100 dys.	Mustered out
Harris, Ezra	do	34	May 2, 1864	100 dys.	Mustered out
Harris, William L	do	36	May 2, 1864	100 dys.	Mustered out
Harris, James W	do	38	May 2, 1864	100 dys.	Mustered out
Hart, George W	do	31	May 2, 1864	100 dys.	Mustered out
Hartong, Levi J	do	19	May 2, 1864	100 dys.	Mustered out
Hartong, Lewis	do	22	May 2, 1864	100 dys.	Mustered out
Henderson, Hamel A	do	19	May 2, 1864	100 dys.	Mustered out
Holtz, Jacob S	do	22	May 2, 1864	100 dys.	Died July 1, I Virginia.
Jarret, Henry	do	20	May 2, 1864	100 dys.	Mustered out
Kepler, John P	do	19	May 2, 1864	100 dys.	Mustered out
Kline, David	do	20	May 2, 1864	100 dys.	Mustered out
Kline, Martin	do	38	May 2, 1864	100 dys.	Mustered out
Koons, Alchia	do	18	May 2, 1864	100 dys.	Mustered out
Kryder, Ira F	do	24	May 2, 1864	100 dys.	Mustered out
Long, Ishmael	do	35	May 2, 1864	100 dys.	Mustered out
Long, Obed	do	30	May 2, 1864	100 dys.	Mustered out
May, Emory W	do	32	May 2, 1864	100 dys.	Mustered out
Marsh, John J	do	50	May 2, 1864	100 dys.	Mustered out
Miller, William	do	28	May 2, 1864	100 dys.	Mustered out
Miller, Isaac S	do	20	May 2, 1864	100 dys.	Mustered out

Names.	Rank.	Age.	Date of Entering the Service.	Period of Service.	Remarks.
Sowards, Thomas J	Private	20	May 2, 1864	100 dys.	Mustered out with
Tabor, William		19	May 2, 1864	100 dys.	Mustered out with
Teel, Hiram		34	May 2, 1864	100 dys.	Mustered out with
Thorn, George S	...do...	19	May 2, 1864	100 dys.	Died Aug. 7, 1864, a
Wall, George	...do...	27	May 2, 1864	100 dys.	Mustered out with
Williams, John B	...do...	22	May 2, 1864	100 dys.	Mustered out with
Williams, Isaac V	...do...	23	May 2, 1864	100 dys.	Mustered out with
Williams, Joseph L	...do...	21	May 2, 1864	100 dys.	Mustered out with
Wilson, William		18	May 2, 1864	100 dys.	Died June 19, 1864.
Zepperuick, Ira		22	May 2, 1864	100 dys.	Mustered out with

COMPANY H.

Mustered in May 11, 1864, at Camp Cleveland, O., by C. B. Throckmorton, 1st Lieute
Mustered out Aug. 27, 1864, at Cleveland, O., by C. B. Throckm
1st Lieutenant 4th Artillery, U. S. A.

Names.	Rank.	Age.	Date of Entering the Service.	Period of Service.	Remarks.
Darius F. Hunsberger	Captain.	29	May 2, 1864	100 dys	Mustered out with
Norman D. Egbert	1st Lieut.	21	May 2, 1864	100 dys.	Mustered out with
Daniel J. Mottinger	2d Lieut.	28	May 2, 1864	100 dys	Mustered out with
Noah N. Leohner	1st Sergt.	20	May 2, 1864	100 dys	Mustered out with
Cyrus W. Harris	Sergeant.	28	May 2, 1864	100 dys.	Mustered out with
William Buchtel	...do...	41	May 2, 1864	100 dys	Appointed from C… tered out with co…
Balser Shriver	...do...	24	May 2, 1864	100 dys	Mustered out with
Samuel C. Marsh	...do...	24	May 2, 1864	100 dys.	Mustered out with
Thomas Wright, Jr	Corporal.	34	May 2, 1864	100 dys.	Reduced from Ser… tered out with c…
Aaron Swartz	...do...	31	May 2, 1864	100 dys	Mustered out with
Franklin G. Stipe	...do...	19	May 2, 1864	100 dys.	Mustered out with
Samuel Breckenridge	...do...	30	May 2, 1864	100 dys.	Mustered out with
Jacob Long	...do...	19	May 2, 1864	100 dys.	Mustered out with
Robert Thompson	...do...	31	May 2, 1864	100 dys.	Mustered out with
Daniel G. Shutt	...do...	28	May 2, 1864	100 dys.	Mustered out with
Jacob Weaver	...do...	23	May 2, 1864	100 dys	Mustered out with
Jonathan B. Krieghbaum	Musician	38	May 2, 1864	100 dys.	Mustered out with
Acker, John B	Private.	21	May 2, 1864	100 dys.	Mustered out with
Beymer, Merritt C	...do...	24	May 2, 1864	100 dys	Mustered out with
Brumbaugh, Henry	...do...	37	May 2, 1864	100 dys.	Mustered out with
Chamberlin, John W	...do...	19	May 2, 1864	100 dys.	Mustered out with
Chisnell, Benjamin	...do...	36	May 2, 1864	100 dys.	Mustered out with
Courtney, William	...do...	41	May 2, 1864	100 dys.	Mustered out with
Cramer, William	...do...	34	May 2, 1864	100 dys.	Mustered out with
Cramer, Elias	...do...	28	May 2, 1864	100 dys.	Mustered out with
Drown, Joseph R	...do...	28	May 2, 1864	100 dys.	Mustered out with
Egbert, Newton U	...do...	19	May 2, 1864	100 dys.	Mustered out with
Egbert, Uriah S	...do...	22	May 2, 1864	100 dys.	Mustered out with
Egbert, Edward G	...do...	19	May 2, 1864	100 dys	Mustered out with
Fasnacht, George H	...do...	36	May 2, 1864	100 dys	Mustered out with
Fasnacht, Levi	...do...	37	May 2, 1864	100 dys.	Mustered out with
Finkle, William	...do...	30	May 2, 1864	100 dys.	Mustered out with
Foster, Sewell	...do...	30	May 2, 1864	100 dys.	Mustered out with
Foster, Jonathan	...do...	36	May 2, 1864	100 dys	Mustered out with
Foust, Daniel S	...do...	21	May 2, 1864	100 dys.	Mustered out with
Foust, Hiram	...do...	18	May 2, 1864	100 dys.	Mustered out with
Fry, John	...do...	23	May 2, 1864	100 dys.	Mustered out with
Goss, Benjamin	...do...	37	May 2, 1864	100 dys.	Mustered out with
Grable, Alexander	...do...	25	May 2, 1864	100 dys.	Mustered out with
Grable, Jacob, Jr	...do...	27	May 2, 1864	100 dys.	Mustered out with
Harris, Ezra	...do...	34	May 2, 1864	100 dys.	Mustered out with
Harris, William L	...do...	36	May 2, 1864	100 dys.	Mustered out with
Harris, James W	...do...	38	May 2, 1864	100 dys.	Mustered out with
Hart, George W	...do...	31	May 2, 1864	100 dys.	Mustered out with
Hartong, Levi J	...do...	19	May 2, 1864	100 dys.	Mustered out with
Hartong, Lewis	...do...	22	May 2, 1864	100 dys	Mustered out with
Henderson, Hamel A	...do...	19	May 2, 1864	100 dys.	Mustered out with
Holtz, Jacob S	...do...	22	May 2, 1864	100 dys.	Died July 1, 1864, i… Virginia.
Jarret, Henry	...do...	20	May 2, 1864	100 dys.	Mustered out with
Kepler, John F	...do...	19	May 2, 1864	100 dys.	Mustered out with
Kline, David	...do...	20	May 2, 1864	100 dys.	Mustered out with
Kline, Martin	...do...	38	May 2, 1864	100 dys	Mustered out with
Koons, Alchia	...do...	18	May 2, 1864	100 dys.	Mustered out with
Krytser, Ira F	...do...	24	May 2, 1864	100 dys.	Mustered out with
Long, Ishmael	...do...	35	May 2, 1864	100 dys.	Mustered out with
Long, Obed	...do...	30	May 2, 1864	100 dys.	Mustered out with
May, Emory W	...do...	32	May 2, 1864	100 dys.	Mustered out with
Marsh, John J	...do...	30	May 2, 1864	100 dys.	Mustered out with
Miller, William	...do...	23	May 2, 1864	100 dys.	Mustered out with
Miller, Isaac S	...do...	30	May 2, 1864	100 dys.	Mustered out with

Names.	Rank.	Age.	Date of Entering the Service.	Period of Service.	Remarks.
[illegible], William D.	Private.	19	May 2, 1864	100 dys.	Mustered out with company Aug. 27, 1864.
[illegible], Thomas L.	...do...	20	May 2, 1864	100 dys.	Mustered out with company Aug. 27, 1864.
[illegible], Nicholas	...do...	22	May 2, 1864	100 dys.	Mustered out with company Aug. 27, 1864.
[illegible], Daniel	...do...	28	May 2, 1864	100 dys.	Mustered out with company Aug. 27, 1864.
[illegible], William J.	...do...	21	May 2, 1864	100 dys.	Mustered out with company Aug. 27, 1864.
[illegible], Lewis	...do...	23	May 2, 1864	100 dys.	Mustered out with company Aug. 27, 1864.
[illegible], William H.	...do...	21	May 2, 1864	100 dys.	Mustered out with company Aug. 27, 1864.
[illegible], Hiram	...do...	19	May 2, 1864	100 dys.	Mustered out with company Aug. 27, 1864.
[illegible], Cyrus F.	...do...	19	May 2, 1864	100 dys.	Mustered out with company Aug. 27, 1864.
[illegible], Henry	...do...	27	May 2, 1864	100 dys.	Mustered out with company Aug. 27, 1864.
Smith, [illegible] B.	...do...	27	May 2, 1864	100 dys.	Died July 24, 1864, in hospital at Fort Strong, Virginia.
[illegible], Ira	...do...	21	May 2, 1864	100 dys.	Mustered out with company Aug. 27, 1864.
[illegible], Daniel	...do...	34	May 2, 1864	100 dys.	Mustered out with company Aug. 27, 1864.
[illegible], Joel	...do...	28	May 2, 1864	100 dys.	Mustered out with company Aug. 27, 1864.
[illegible], William	...do...	27	May 2, 1864	100 dys.	Mustered out with company Aug. 27, 1864.
[illegible], Royal S.	...do...	20	May 2, 1864	100 dys.	Mustered out with company Aug. 27, 1864.
[illegible], Philetus H.	...do...	18	May 2, 1864	100 dys.	Mustered out with company Aug. 27, 1864.
[illegible], George	...do...	40	May 2, 1864	100 dys.	Mustered out with company Aug. 27, 1864.
[illegible], Joel T.	...do...	17	May 2, 1864	100 dys.	Mustered out with company Aug. 27, 1864.
[illegible], Solomon N.	...do...	37	May 2, 1864	100 dys.	Mustered out with company Aug. 27, 1864.
[illegible], Franklin	...do...	19	May 2, 1864	100 dys.	Mustered out with company Aug. 27, 1864.
[illegible], Hiram	...do...	21	May 2, 1864	100 dys.	Mustered out with company Aug. 27, 1864.
[illegible], Andrew	...do...	22	May 2, 1864	100 dys.	Mustered out with company Aug. 27, 1864.
[illegible], Alfred	...do...	22	May 2, 1864	100 dys.	Mustered out with company Aug. 27, 1864.

COMPANY I.

Mustered in May 11, 1864, at Camp Cleveland, O., by C. B. Throckmorton, 1st Lieutenant 4th Artillery, U. S. A. Mustered out Aug. 27, 1864, at Cleveland, O., by C. B. Throckmorton, 1st Lieutenant 4th Artillery, U. S. A.

Names.	Rank.	Age.	Date of Entering the Service.	Period of Service.	Remarks.
[illegible] Alcott	Captain.	27	May 2, 1864	100 dys.	Mustered out with company Aug. 27, 1864.
Charles Olmstead	1st Lieut.	34	May 2, 1864	100 dys.	Mustered out with company Aug. 27, 1864.
John Noble	2d Lieut.	30	May 2, 1864	100 dys.	Mustered out with company Aug. 27, 1864.
Allen Hale	1st Sergt.	20	May 2, 1864	100 dys.	Mustered out with company Aug. 27, 1864.
[illegible] P. Robbins	Sergeant	30	May 2, 1864	100 dys.	Mustered out with company Aug. 27, 1864.
Oliver G. Leach	...do...	26	May 2, 1864	100 dys.	Mustered out with company Aug. 27, 1864.
[illegible]	...do...	23	May 2, 1864	100 dys.	Mustered out with company Aug. 27, 1864.
[illegible]	...do...	27	May 2, 1864	100 dys.	Mustered out with company Aug. 27, 1864.
[illegible] H. Howenstein	Corporal.	25	May 2, 1864	100 dys.	Mustered out with company Aug. 27, 1864.
[illegible]	...do...	27	May 2, 1864	100 dys.	Mustered out with company Aug. 27, 1864.
[illegible] W. Young	...do...	23	May 2, 1864	100 dys.	Mustered out with company Aug. 27, 1864.
[illegible]	...do...	18	May 2, 1864	100 dys.	Mustered out with company Aug. 27, 1864.
[illegible]	...do...	36	May 2, 1864	100 dys.	Mustered out with company Aug. 27, 1864.
[illegible]	...do...	28	May 2, 1864	100 dys.	Mustered out with company Aug. 27, 1864.
[illegible]	...do...	28	May 2, 1864	100 dys.	Mustered out with company Aug. 27, 1864.
[illegible] C. Thomas	...do...	31	May 2, 1864	100 dys.	Died July 24, 1864, in hospital at Fort Strong, Virginia.
Bair, Jehiel	Private.	24	May 2, 1864	100 dys.	Mustered out with company Aug. 27, 1864.
Baker, Milton S.	...do...	32	May 2, 1864	100 dys.	Mustered out with company Aug. 27, 1864.
Beller, George	...do...	32	May 2, 1864	100 dys.	Mustered out with company Aug. 27, 1864.
Benham, Warren L.	...do...	19	May 2, 1864	100 dys.	Mustered out with company Aug. 27, 1864.
Billyard, Thomas	...do...	34	May 2, 1864	100 dys.	Mustered out with company Aug. 27, 1864.
Bonnell, Christian	...do...	42	May 2, 1864	100 dys.	Mustered out with company Aug. 27, 1864.
Brown, James W.	...do...	[illegible]	May 2, 1864	100 dys.	Mustered out with company Aug. 27, 1864.
Byers, Philip	...do...	46	May 2, 1864	100 dys.	Mustered out with company Aug. 27, 1864.
Bucher, Frederick	...do...	28	May 2, 1864	100 dys.	Mustered out with company Aug. 27, 1864.
Campbell, Samuel S.	...do...	23	May 2, 1864	100 dys.	Mustered out with company Aug. 27, 1864.
Carl, John	...do...	22	May 2, 1864	100 dys.	Mustered out with company Aug. 27, 1864.
Cuthberson, Walter	...do...	30	May 2, 1864	100 dys.	Mustered out with company Aug. 27, 1864.
Cuthberson, Brewster	...do...	19	May 2, 1864	100 dys.	Mustered out with company Aug. 27, 1864.
DeWolf, Clarence	...do...	19	May 2, 1864	100 dys.	Mustered out with company Aug. 27, 1864.
Diddine, Henry A.	...do...	19	May 2, 1864	100 dys.	Mustered out with company Aug. 27, 1864.
Doe, Volney H.	...do...	19	May 2, 1864	100 dys.	Mustered out with company Aug. 27, 1864.
Elder, David S.		21	May 2, 1864	100 dys.	Mustered out with company Aug. 27, 1864.
England, Joseph	...do...	40	May 2, 1864	100 dys.	Mustered out with company Aug. 27, 1864.
Flahiff, John	...do...	28	May 2, 1864	100 dys.	Mustered out with company Aug. 27, 1864.
Grapes, Frank M.	...do...	18	May 2, 1864	100 dys.	Mustered out with company Aug. 27, 1864.
Harsh, Leonard	...do...	24	May 2, 1864	100 dys.	Mustered out with company Aug. 27, 1864.
Helfer, William	...do...	21	May 2, 1864	100 dys.	Mustered out with company Aug. 27, 1864.
Henderson, Willis D.	...do...	19	May 2, 1864	100 dys.	Mustered out with company Aug. 27, 1864.
Hofmaster, Gideon	...do...	21	May 2, 1864	100 dys.	Mustered out with company Aug. 27, 1864.
Kaup, John T.	...do...	25	May 2, 1864	100 dys.	Promoted to Sergt. Major May 11, 1864.
King, William	...do...	24	May 2, 1864	100 dys.	Mustered out with company Aug. 27, 1864.
Lemp, George	...do...	18	May 2, 1864	100 dys.	Mustered out with company Aug. 27, 1864.
Longley, Samuel	...do...	18	May 2, 1864	100 dys.	Mustered out with company Aug. 27, 1864.
McDougal, James W.	...do...	20	May 2, 1864	100 dys.	Mustered out with company Aug. 27, 1864.
McKee, Matthew	...do...	25	May 2, 1864	100 dys.	Mustered out with company Aug. 27, 1864.
McKean, John M.	...do...	19	May 2, 1864	100 dys.	Mustered out with company Aug. 27, 1864.

Names.	Rank.	Age.	Date of Entering the Service.	Period of Service.	Remarks.
Mickey, William E.	Private	[illegible]	May 2, 1864	[illegible] dys	Died July 22, 1864, in hospital at [illegible], Virginia.
M[illegible], John L.	do	24	May 2, 1864	100 dys	Mustered out with company Aug. 27, 1864.
Miller, Daniel F.	do	27	May 2, 1864	[illegible] dys	Died Aug. [illegible], 1864, at Washington, D. C.
Miller, Wesley W.	do	24	May 2, 1864	100 dys	Mustered out with company Aug. 27, 1864.
Miller, Chesselden	do	18	May 2, 1864	[illegible] dys	Died Aug. 7, 1864, in hospital at [illegible], Virginia.
Myers, Philip	do	[illegible]	May 2, 1864	[illegible] dys	Mustered out with company Aug. 27, 1864.
N[illegible], Henry B.	do	[illegible]	May 2, 1864	[illegible] dys	Mustered out with company Aug. 27, 1864.
N[illegible], Reuben	do	[illegible]	May 2, 1864	[illegible] dys	Mustered out with company Aug. 27, 1864.
Norton, Rufus	do	[illegible]	May 2, 1864	[illegible] dys	Mustered out with company Aug. 27, 1864.
[illegible], Jacob	do	24	May 2, 1864	[illegible]	Mustered out with company Aug. 27, 1864.
P[illegible], Barney	do	[illegible]	May 2, 1864	[illegible]	Mustered out with company Aug. 27, 1864.
[illegible], Jacob	do	19	May 2, 1864	[illegible]	Mustered out with company Aug. 27, 1864.
R[illegible], John	do	[illegible]	May 2, 1864	[illegible]	Mustered out with company Aug. 27, 1864.
S[illegible], Irving W.	do	[illegible]	May 2, 1864	[illegible]	Mustered out with company Aug. 27, 1864.
S[illegible], Jacob	do	[illegible]	May 2, 1864	[illegible]	Mustered out with company Aug. 27, 1864.
S[illegible], Benjamin	do	[illegible]	May 2, 1864	[illegible]	Mustered out with company Aug. 27, 1864.
S[illegible], Hiram	do	18	May 2, 1864	[illegible]	Mustered out with company Aug. 27, 1864.
S[illegible], James A.	do	42	May 2, 1864	[illegible]	Mustered out with company Aug. 27, 1864.
S[illegible], George	do	[illegible]	May 2, 1864	[illegible]	Mustered out with company Aug. 27, 1864.
S[illegible], Joseph	do	[illegible]	May 2, 1864	[illegible]	Mustered out with company Aug. 27, 1864.
[illegible], Joseph	do	[illegible]	May 2, 1864	[illegible]	Mustered out with company Aug. 27, 1864.
S[illegible], David S.	do	19	May 2, 1864	[illegible]	Mustered out with company Aug. 27, 1864.
T[illegible], John	do	46	May 2, 1864	[illegible]	Mustered out with company Aug. 27, 1864.
T[illegible], Benjamin F.	do	[illegible]	May 2, 1864	[illegible]	Mustered out with company Aug. 27, 1864.
T[illegible], Robert	do	24	May 2, 1864	[illegible]	Mustered out with company Aug. 27, 1864.
U[illegible], William	do	18	May 2, 1864	[illegible]	Mustered out with company Aug. 27, 1864.
V[illegible], Jacob	do	[illegible]	May 2, 1864	[illegible]	Mustered out with company Aug. 27, 1864.
V[illegible], William A.	do	18	May 2, 1864	[illegible]	Mustered out with company Aug. 27, 1864.
Weaver, William	do	38	May 2, 1864	[illegible]	Mustered out with company Aug. 27, 1864.
Weaver, Henry	do	18	May 2, 1864	[illegible]	Mustered out with company Aug. 27, 1864.
[illegible], William H.	do	[illegible]	May 2, 1864	[illegible]	Mustered out with company Aug. 27, 1864.
W[illegible], [illegible] H.	do	18	May 2, 1864	[illegible]	Mustered out with company Aug. 27, 1864.
W[illegible], Samuel [illegible]	do	[illegible]	May 2, 1864	[illegible]	[illegible] to Hospital [illegible] May [illegible]
W[illegible], Robert	do	[illegible]	May 2, 1864	[illegible]	Mustered out with company Aug. 27, 1864.
W[illegible], Lewis	do	18	May 2, 1864	[illegible]	Mustered out with company Aug. 27, 1864.
[illegible], John H.	do	[illegible]	May 2, 1864	[illegible]	Mustered out with company Aug. 27, 1864.
Young, David H.	do	32	May 2, 1864	[illegible]	Mustered out with company Aug. 27, 1864.

COMPANY K.

Mustered in May [illegible], 1864, at Camp Cleveland, O., by [illegible], 1st Lieutenant 4th Artillery U. S. A. Mustered out Aug. 27, 1864, at [illegible], O., by [illegible], 1st Lieutenant [illegible].

Names.	Rank.	Age.	Date of Entering the Service.	Period of Service.	Remarks.
[illegible]	Captain	[illegible]	May 2, 1864	[illegible]	Mustered out with company Aug. 27, 1864.
[illegible]	1st Lieut.	[illegible]	May 2, 1864	[illegible]	Mustered out with company Aug. 27, 1864.
[illegible]	2d Lieut.	[illegible]	May 2, 1864	[illegible]	Mustered out with company Aug. 27, 1864.
[illegible]	1st Sergt.	[illegible]	May 2, 1864	[illegible]	Mustered out with company Aug. 27, 1864.
[illegible] W. Stewart	Sergeant	[illegible]	May 2, 1864	[illegible]	Mustered out with company Aug. 27, 1864.
[illegible]	do	42	May 2, 1864	[illegible]	Mustered out with company Aug. 27, 1864.
[illegible]	do	27	May 2, 1864	[illegible]	Mustered out with company [illegible]
[illegible]	do	[illegible]	May 2, 1864	[illegible]	[illegible] May [illegible], 1864; mustered out with company Aug. 27, 1864.
[illegible]	Corporal	[illegible]	May 2, 1864	[illegible]	Mustered out with company Aug. 27, 1864.
W[illegible]	do	[illegible]	May 2, 1864	[illegible]	Mustered out with company Aug. 27, 1864.
W[illegible] H. [illegible]	do	[illegible]	May 2, 1864	[illegible]	Mustered out with company Aug. 27, 1864.
[illegible]	do	[illegible]	May 2, 1864	[illegible]	Mustered out with company Aug. 27, 1864.
[illegible] W. [illegible]	do	[illegible]	May 2, 1864	[illegible]	Mustered out with company Aug. 27, 1864.
A[illegible] K[illegible]	do	[illegible]	May 2, 1864	[illegible]	Mustered out with company Aug. 27, 1864.
[illegible]	do	[illegible]	May 2, 1864	[illegible]	Mustered out with company Aug. 27, 1864.
[illegible]	do	[illegible]	May 2, 1864	[illegible]	Mustered out with company Aug. 27, 1864.
William [illegible]	Musician	[illegible]	May 2, 1864	[illegible]	Mustered out with company Aug. 27, 1864.
A[illegible]	Private	[illegible]	May 2, 1864	[illegible]	Mustered out with company Aug. 27, 1864.
A[illegible], Joseph [illegible]	do	[illegible]	May 2, 1864	[illegible]	Mustered out with company Aug. 27, 1864.
A[illegible]	do	[illegible]	May 2, 1864	[illegible]	Mustered out with company Aug. 27, 1864.
A[illegible]	do	[illegible]	May 2, 1864	[illegible]	Mustered out [illegible]
B[illegible], David	do	[illegible]	May 2, 1864	[illegible]	Mustered out [illegible]
B[illegible]	do	[illegible]	May 2, 1864	[illegible]	Mustered out [illegible]
B[illegible], William	do	[illegible]	May 2, 1864	[illegible]	Mustered out [illegible]
[illegible]	do	[illegible]	May 2, 1864	[illegible]	Mustered out [illegible]
[illegible]	do	[illegible]	May 2, 1864	[illegible]	Mustered out [illegible]
B[illegible]	do	[illegible]	May 2, 1864	[illegible]	Mustered out [illegible]
B[illegible]	do	[illegible]	May 2, 1864	[illegible]	Mustered out [illegible]
[illegible] W[illegible] T.	do	[illegible]	May 2, 1864	[illegible]	Died June [illegible], 1864, in [illegible], Virginia.
C[illegible], Edward	do	[illegible]	May 2, 1864	100 dys	Mustered out [illegible]
C[illegible]	do	[illegible]	May 2, 1864	100 dys	Mustered out [illegible]

Names.	Rank.	Age.	Date of Entering the Service.	Period of Service.	Remarks.
Cooley, William A.	Private..	18	May 2, 1864	100 dys.	Mustered out with company Aug. 27, 1864.
Cooley, William H.	....do....	38	May 2, 1864	100 dys.	Mustered out with company Aug. 27, 1864.
Cooper, Frederick	....do....	27	May 2, 1864	100 dys.	Died July 30, 1864, in hospital at Fort Strong, Virginia.
Consadine, Henry M.	....do....	22	May 2, 1864	100 dys.	Mustered out with company Aug. 27, 1864.
Coup, John	....do....	21	May 2, 1864	100 dys.	Mustered out with company Aug. 27, 1864.
Dildine, Shannon	....do....	18	May 2, 1864	100 dys.	Mustered out with company Aug. 27, 1864.
Drew, Horace	....do....	38	May 2, 1864	100 dys.	Mustered out with company Aug. 27, 1864.
Eckleberry, John P.	....do....	19	June 10, 1864	100 dys.	Mustered out with company Aug. 27, 1864.
Gasser, Frederick	....do....	37	May 2, 1864	100 dys.	Mustered out with company Aug. 27, 1864.
Grey, Edson	....do....	19	May 2, 1864	100 dys.	Mustered out with company Aug. 27, 1864.
Griffin, Sheldon H.	....do....	20	May 2, 1864	100 dys.	Mustered out with company Aug. 27, 1864.
Hall, Rufus B.	....do....	21	May 2, 1864	100 dys.	Mustered out with company Aug. 27, 1864.
Hall, William H.	....do....	27	May 2, 1864	100 dys.	Mustered out with company Aug. 27, 1864.
Hartsill, John	....do....	44	May 2, 1864	100 dys.	Mustered out with company Aug. 27, 1864.
Hawk, Aaron	....do....	34	May 2, 1864	100 dys.	Mustered out with company Aug. 27, 1864.
Hawblitz, Henry	....do....	27	May 2, 1864	100 dys.	Mustered out with company Aug. 27, 1864.
Heaton, John L.	....do....	26	May 2, 1864	100 dys.	Mustered out with company Aug. 27, 1864.
Huddle, Jacob K.	....do....	18	May 2, 1864	100 dys.	Mustered out with company Aug. 27, 1864.
Hunsicker, Garret C.	....do....	29	May 2, 1864	100 dys.	Mustered out with company Aug. 27, 1864.
Jones, James	....do....	41	May 2, 1864	100 dys.	Mustered out with company Aug. 27, 1864.
Kershner, Levi	....do....	28	May 2, 1864	100 dys.	Mustered out with company Aug. 27, 1864.
Lapham, Stephen	....do....	42	May 2, 1864	100 dys.	Mustered out with company Aug. 27, 1864.
Lehman, Samuel	....do....	22	May 2, 1864	100 dys.	Mustered out with company Aug. 27, 1864.
Lamber, Jason P.	....do....	31	May 2, 1864	100 dys.	Mustered out with company Aug. 27, 1864.
Martin, Albert S.	....do....	21	May 2, 1864	100 dys.	Mustered out with company Aug. 27, 1864.
Martin, George M.	....do....	24	May 2, 1864	100 dys.	Mustered out with company Aug. 27, 1864.
Muckley, Michael	....do....	25	June 10, 1864	100 dys.	Mustered out with company Aug. 27, 1864.
Newkirk, William	....do....	22	May 2, 1864	100 dys.	Mustered out with company Aug. 27, 1864.
Niles, Albert G.	....do....	26	May 2, 1864	100 dys.	Mustered out with company Aug. 27, 1864.
Norris, Basil	....do....	18	May 2, 1864	100 dys.	Mustered out with company Aug. 27, 1864.
Nutt, Elias	....do....	31	May 2, 1864	100 dys.	Mustered out with company Aug. 27, 1864.
Ogden, Erwin A.	....do....	18	May 2, 1864	100 dys.	Discharged July 23, 1864, on Surgeon's certificate of disability.
Orner, John	....do....	20	May 2, 1864	100 dys.	Mustered out with company Aug. 27, 1864.
Petty, Hubert	....do....	18	May 2, 1864	100 dys.	Mustered out with company Aug. 27, 1864.
Reed, William L.	....do....	24	May 2, 1864	100 dys.	Mustered out with company Aug. 27, 1864.
Robinson, John	....do....	22	May 2, 1864	100 dys.	Mustered out with company Aug. 27, 1864.
Robinson, Joseph	....do....	19	May 2, 1864	100 dys.	Mustered out with company Aug. 27, 1864.
Ruck, David	....do....	21	May 2, 1864	100 dys.	Mustered out with company Aug. 27, 1864.
Shafer, William	....do....	41	May 2, 1864	100 dys.	Mustered out with company Aug. 27, 1864.
Shetterly, Oscar	....do....	18	May 2, 1864	100 dys.	Mustered out with company Aug. 27, 1864.
Smith, Elroy C.	....do....	23	May 2, 1864	100 dys.	Mustered out with company Aug. 27, 1864.
Stearnes, George W.	....do....	37	May 2, 1864	100 dys.	Mustered out with company Aug. 27, 1864.
Strong, Charles R.	....do....	44	May 2, 1864	100 dys.	Mustered out with company Aug. 27, 1864.
Strouse, John	....do....	33	May 2, 1864	100 dys.	Mustered out with company Aug. 27, 1864.
Turner, Edward J.	....do....	34	May 2, 1864	100 dys.	Mustered out with company Aug. 27, 1864.
Valentine, Charles V.	....do....	29	May 2, 1864	100 dys.	Mustered out with company Aug. 27, 1864.
Valentine, James	....do....	26	May 2, 1864	100 dys.	Mustered out with company Aug. 27, 1864.
Wall, Abijah R.	....do....	27	May 2, 1864	100 dys.	Mustered out with company Aug. 27, 1864.
Wales, John (2d)	....do....	19	May 2, 1864	100 dys.	Mustered out with company Aug. 27, 1864.
Welker, Isaac	....do....	21	May 2, 1864	100 dys.	
Weller, Luke	....do....	42	May 2, 1864	100 dys.	Mustered out with company Aug. 27, 1864.
West, Fernando	....do....	19	May 2, 1864	100 dys.	Mustered out with company Aug. 27, 1864.
West, Sylvester D.	....do....	27	May 2, 1864	100 dys.	Mustered out with company Aug. 27, 1864.
Wheeler, David	....do....	18	May 2, 1864	100 dys.	Mustered out with company Aug. 27, 1864.
Wyant, David	....do....	[illegible]	May 2, 1864	100 dys.	Mustered out with company Aug. 27, 1864.
Wyant, Samuel	....do....	19	May 2, 1864	100 dys.	Mustered out [illegible] at Washington, D. C., by order of War Department.
Zimmerman, Frank	....do....	18	May 2, 1864	100 dys.	Mustered out with company Aug. 27, 1864.

165th Battalion Ohio Volunteer Infantry.

ONE HUNDRED DAYS' SERVICE.

THIS Battalion, consisting of seven companies, was organized a Dennison, O., May 14 and 19, 1864, to serve one hundred days. It w posed of the Tenth Regiment, Ohio National Guard, from Cincinnat Battalion remained on duty at Camp Dennison until the 20th of May, was transferred to Johnson's Island, O., to guard Rebel prisoners. On t of June it was ordered to Kentucky, and remained there until August and was then ordered to Cumberland, Maryland. It remained in Ma and Virginia until the 27th of August, 1864, and then returned to Camp nison, where it was mustered out August 31, 1864, on expiration of te service.

165TH BATTALION OHIO VOLUNTEER INFANTRY.

FIELD AND STAFF.

Mustered in May 19, 1864, at Camp Dennison, O., by Robert S. Smith, Captain 2d Cavalry, U. S. A. Mustered out Aug. 31, 1864, at Camp Dennison, O., by A. J. Bellows, 1st Lieutenant 14th Infantry, U. S. A.

Names.	Rank.	Age.	Date of Entering the Service.	Period of Service.	Remarks.
Alexander Bohlender	Lt. Col.	41	May 2, 1864	100 dys.	Mustered out with battalion Aug. 31, 1864.
Matthew Reiching	Major.	49	May 2, 1864	100 dys.	Mustered out with battalion Aug. 31, 1864.
Henry Mallory	Surgeon.	42	June 7, 1864	100 dys.	Mustered out with battalion Aug. 31, 1864.
Solomon Wolff	Asst. Sur.	24	June 14, 1864	100 dys.	Mustered out with battalion Aug. 31, 1864.
Frank A. Walz	Adjutant	31	May 2, 1864	100 dys.	Mustered out with battalion Aug. 31, 1864.
William Kleinoehle	R. Q. M.	..	May 2, 1864	100 dys.	Mustered out with battalion Aug. 31, 1864.
Emil Koch	Sergt. Maj	25	May 2, 1864	100 dys.	Promoted from private Co. B May 14, 1864; mustered out with battalion Aug. 31, 1864.
Louis Weihlert	Q. M. S.	31	May 2, 1864	100 dys.	Promoted from private Co. B May 14, 1864; mustered out with battalion Aug. 31, 1864.
Louis Knipping	Com. Ser.	..	May 2, 1864	100 dys.	Mustered out with battalion Aug. 31, 1864.
Henry [illegible]	Hos. St'd.	21	May 2, 1864	100 dys.	Promoted from private Co. H May 26, 1864; mustered out with battalion Aug. 31, 1864.
Richard Meinhardt	Prin. Mus	22	May 2, 1864	100 dys.	Promoted from private Co. B May 14, 1864; mustered out with battalion Aug. 31, 1864.

COMPANY A.

Mustered in May 14, 1864, at Camp Dennison, O., by Robert S. Smith, Captain 2d Cavalry, U. S. A. Mustered out Aug. 31, 1864, at Camp Dennison, O., by A. J. Bellows, 1st Lieutenant 14th Infantry, U. S. A.

Names.	Rank.	Age.	Date of Entering the Service.	Period of Service.	Remarks.
William Raine	Captain.	42	May 2, 1864	100 dys.	Mustered out with company Aug. 31, 1864.
[illegible]	1st Lieut.	34	May 2, 1864	100 dys.	Mustered out with company Aug. 31, 1864.
Frederick Stockhove	2d Lieut.	22	May 2, 1864	100 dys.	Mustered out with company Aug. 31, 1864.
Henry [illegible]	1st Sergt.	30	May 2, 1864	100 dys.	Mustered out with company Aug. 31, 1864.
Frederick Nordman	Sergeant.	26	May 2, 1864	100 dys.	Mustered out with company Aug. 31, 1864.
William Falk	do.	30	May 2, 1864	100 dys.	Mustered out with company Aug. 31, 1864.
Charles Piepenbrink	do.	40	May 2, 1864	100 dys.	Mustered out with company Aug. 31, 1864.
George Schwab	do.	20	May 2, 1864	100 dys.	Mustered out with company Aug. 31, 1864.
[illegible]	Corporal.	25	May 2, 1864	100 dys.	Appointed ——; mustered out with company Aug. 31, 1864.
John [illegible]	do.	21	May 2, 1864	100 dys.	Mustered out with company Aug. 31, 1864.
Henry Smith	do.	18	May 2, 1864	100 dys.	Mustered out with company Aug. 31, 1864.
Louis [illegible]	do.	26	May 2, 1864	100 dys.	Mustered out with company Aug. 31, 1864.
Joseph [illegible]	do.	32	May 2, 1864	100 dys.	Appointed ——; mustered out with company Aug. 31, 1864.
Henry Lindeman	do.	38	May 2, 1864	100 dys.	Discharged May 16, 1864, by order of War Department.
Frederick H. Nordman	do.	26	May 2, 1864	100 dys.	Appointed ——; mustered out with company Aug. 31, 1864.
Henry Rohenkamp	do.	30	May 2, 1864	100 dys.	Appointed ——; mustered out with company Aug. 31, 1864.
	do.	38	May 2, 1864	100 dys.	Mustered out with company Aug. 31, 1864.
	Private.	42	May 2, 1864	100 dys.	Mustered out with company Aug. 31, 1864.
	do.	37	May 2, 1864	100 dys.	Mustered out with company Aug. 31, 1864.
....	do.	43	May 2, 1864	100 dys.	Mustered out with company Aug. 31, 1864.
......	do.	35	May 2, 1864	100 dys.	No record subsequent to muster in.
......	do.	23	May 2, 1864	100 dys.	Mustered as Corporal; reduced ——; mustered out with company Aug. 31, 1864.
Bruns, Frederick	do.	28	May 2, 1864	100 dys.	Mustered out with company Aug. 31, 1864
Buck, Henry	do.	46	May 2, 1864	100 dys.	Mustered out with company Aug. 31, 1864.
Cummings, Louis	do.	23	May 2, 1864	100 dys.	No record subsequent to muster-in.
Dellendahl, Henry	do.	23	May 2, 1864	100 dys.	Mustered out with company Aug. 31, 1864.
Derue, Jacob	do.	34	May 2, 1864	100 dys.	Discharged Aug. 31, 1864, by order of War Department.
Dierkers, John	do.	17	May 2, 1864	100 dys.	Mustered out with company Aug. 31, 1864.

Names.	Rank.	Age.	Date of Entering the Service.	Period of Service.	
Pickle, Max	Private	30	May 2, 1864	100 dys.	Mustered out
Reif, Frank	....do....	25	May 2, 1864	100 dys.	Mustered out
Roller, Charles	....do....	27	May 2, 1864		
Schiess, L. Jacob	....do....	24	May 2, 1864		
Schmidt, Carl	....do....	40	May 2, 1864		
Schmidt, Franz	....do....	31	May 2, 1864		
Schwarm, Carl	....do....	29	May 2, 1864		
Sieber, Carl A	....do....	44	May 2, 1864		
Siemon, Adolph	....do....	41	May 2, 1864		
Stehle, Conrad	....do....	34	May 2, 1864		
Vogel, Carl	....do....	20	May 2, 1864		
Werner, A. Frederick	....do....	25	May 2, 1864		
Wielert, Louis	....do....	21	May 2, 1864		
Woehrle, John T	....do....	34	May 2, 1864		
Wolf, George	....do....	40	May 2, 1864		

COMPANY D.

Mustered in May 14, 1864, at Camp Dennison, O., by Robert S. Smith, Captain ... out Aug. 31, 1864, at Camp Dennison, O., by A. J. Be... Lieutenant 14th Infantry, U. S. A.

Names.	Rank.	Age.	Date of Entering the Service.	Period of Service.	
Joseph Haider	Captain.	35	May 2, 1864	100 dys.	Mustered out
Louis Neubacher	1st Lieut.	28	May 2, 1864	100 dys.	Mustered out
William Mayer	2d Lieut.	24	May 2, 1864	100 dys.	Mustered out
Jacob Korn	1st Sergt.	39	May 2, 1864	100 dys.	Mustered out
Theodore Brunner	Sergeant.	37	May 2, 1864	100 dys.	Mustered out
Lew Rheinwardt	....do....	44	May 2, 1864	100 dys.	Mustered out
Chr. Schentt	....do....	36	May 2, 1864	100 dys.	Mustered out
John G. Arnold	....do....	39	May 2, 1864	100 dys.	Mustered out
Henry Munder	Corporal.	41	May 2, 1864	100 dys.	Mustered out
Joseph Gerhard	....do....	36	May 2, 1864	100 dys.	Mustered out
Conrad Menzel	....do....	44	May 2, 1864	100 dys.	Mustered out
Christ. Frohmann	....do....	27	May 2, 1864	100 dys.	Mustered out
John Hammelbacher	....do....	30	May 2, 1864	100 dys.	Mustered out
R. Jungkind	....do....	34	May 2, 1864	100 dys.	Mustered out
William Voeste	....do....	24	May 2, 1864	100 dys.	Mustered out
John Fries	....do....	22	May 2, 1864	100 dys.	Appointed Aug. 31, 186
Althammer, William	Private.	39	May 2, 1864	100 dys.	Mustered out
Bachmann, Charles	....do....	35	May 2, 1864	100 dys.	Mustered out
Becker, Julius	....do....	18	May 2, 1864	100 dys.	Mustered
Bendel, Henry	....do....	20	May 2, 1864	100 dys.	Mustered
Bindhammer, Paul	....do....	46	May 2, 1864	100 dys.	Mustered
Bleyle, Romann	....do....	35	May 2, 1864	100 dys.	Mustered
Boebinger, Lew	....do....	30	May 2, 1864	100 dys.	Mustered
Brodbeck, Conrad	....do....	37	May 2, 1864	100 dys.	Mustered
Brunst, Peter	....do....	41	May 2, 1864	100 dys.	Mustered
Buehler, Lew	....do....	20	May 2, 1864	100 dys.	Mustered
Butscha, Frederick	....do....	40	May 2, 1864	100 dys.	Mustered out
Butz, Christ	....do....	39	May 2, 1864	100 dys.	Died Aug. 2, 1
Doell, Henry	....do....	27	May 2, 1864	100 dys.	Mustered out
Drautz, Fritz H	....do....	30	May 2, 1864	100 dys.	Mustered out
Dohme, Henry	....do....	24	May 2, 1864	100 dys.	Mustered out
Ebbers, Henry	....do....	29	May 2, 1864	100 dys.	Mustered out
Eppens, Henry	....do....	28	May 2, 1864	100 dys.	Mustered out
Finkler, Henry	....do....	23	May 2, 1864	100 dys.	Mustered out
Fortmann, Frederick	....do....	19	May 2, 1864	100 dys.	Mustered out
Fries, Joseph	....do....	22	May 2, 1864	100 dys.	Mustered out
Gast, Sebastian	....do....	21	May 2, 1864	100 dys.	Mustered out
Geheffer, Cornelius	....do....	34	May 2, 1864	100 dys.	Mustered out
Gelder, August	....do....	20	May 2, 1864	100 dys.	Mustered out
Gerhard, Lew	....do....	33	May 2, 1864	100 dys.	Mustered out
Glaser, Jacob	....do....	38	May 2, 1864	100 dys.	Mustered out
Haidmann, William	....do....	24	May 2, 1864	100 dys.	Mustered out
Helm, Conrad	....do....	19	May 2, 1864	100 dys.	Mustered as company Au
Kaiser, Christ	....do....	18	May 2, 1864	100 dys.	Mustered out
Kiess, Thomas	....do....	18	May 2, 1864	100 dys.	Mustered out
Klein, Michael	....do....	36	May 2, 1864	100 dys.	Mustered out
Koob, Paul	....do....	29	May 2, 1864	100 dys.	
Kraus, Christopher	....do....	40	May 2, 1864	100 dys.	Mustered out
Kreutzer, Christ.	....do....	39	May 2, 1864	100 dys.	
Lague, Peter	....do....	25	May 2, 1864	100 dys.	Mustered out
Lehmann, Frederick	....do....	30	May 2, 1864	100 dys.	Mustered as company Au
Lehmann, John	....do....	35	May 2, 1864	100 dys.	Mustered out
Lindemann, Herman	....do....	20	May 2, 1864	100 dys.	Mustered out

	Rank.	Age.	Date of Entering the Service.	Period of Service.	Remarks.
Mann, John	Private	[illegible]	May 2, 1864	100 dys.	Mustered out with company Aug. 31, 1864.
Manger, Guston	do	18	May 2, 1864	100 dys.	Mustered out with company Aug. 31, 1864.
Mansberger, Christ	do	..	May 2, 1864	100 dys.	No record subsequent to enlistment.
Marten, Fridolin	do	26	May 2, 1864	100 dys.	Mustered out with company Aug. 31, 1864.
Menzler, George	do	24	May 2, 1864	100 dys.	No record subsequent to muster-in.
Messner, Gottfried	do	21	May 2, 1864	100 dys.	Mustered out with company Aug. 31, 1864.
Meyer, Charles	do	35	May 2, 1864	100 dys.	Mustered out with company Aug. 31, 1864.
Mohlenhoff, John	do	..	May 2, 1864	100 dys.	Promoted to Com. Sergeant, but not borne on rolls of Field and Staff. No further record found.
Mueller, Herman	do	30	May 2, 1864	100 dys.	
Mueller, Peter	do	30	May 2, 1864	100 dys.	Mustered out with company Aug. 31, 1864.
Neubacher, Joseph	do	44	May 2, 1864	100 dys.	Mustered out with company Aug. 31, 1864.
Neubacher, William	do	14	May 2, 1864	100 dys.	Mustered as Musician; mustered out with company Aug. 31, 1864.
[illegible], Henry	do	[illegible]	May 2, 1864	100 dys.	Mustered out with company Aug. 31, 1864.
[illegible], Henry	do	[illegible]	May 2, 1864	100 dys.	Mustered out with company Aug. 31, 1864.
[illegible], John	do	37	May 2, 1864	100 dys.	Mustered out with company Aug. 31, 1864.
[illegible], Adam	do	35	May 2, 1864	100 dys.	Mustered out with company Aug. 31, 1864.
[illegible], Jacob	do	20	May 2, 1864	100 dys.	Absent, sick ——, at Cincinnati, O. No further record found.
Rapp, Lew	do	27	May 2, 1864	100 dys.	Mustered out with company Aug. 31, 1864.
Reis, Alexander	do	24	May 2, 1864	100 dys.	Mustered out with company Aug. 31, 1864.
Rickert, Alexander	do	28	May 2, 1864	100 dys.	Mustered out with company Aug. 31, 1864.
Sander, Theodore	do	20	May 2, 1864	100 dys.	Mustered out with company Aug. 31, 1864.
Sandhammer, John	do	25	May 2, 1864	100 dys.	Mustered out with company Aug. 31, 1864.
Sass, Lew	do	19	May 2, 1864	100 dys.	Mustered out with company Aug. 31, 1864.
Schaefer, Lew	do	26	May 2, 1864	100 dys.	Mustered out with company Aug. 31, 1864.
Schlotterbeck, Gottlieb	do	25	May 2, 1864	100 dys.	Mustered out with company Aug. 31, 1864.
Schmalz, John	do	34	May 2, 1864	100 dys.	Mustered out with company Aug. 31, 1864.
Schmidt, John	do	24	May 2, 1864	100 dys.	Mustered out with company Aug. 31, 1864.
Scultetus, Charles	do	[illegible]	May 2, 1864	100 dys.	Mustered out with company Aug. 31, 1864.
Spraimly, John	do	18	May 2, 1864	100 dys.	Mustered out with company Aug. 31, 1864.
Spraimly, Philip	do	21	May 2, 1864	100 dys.	Mustered out with company Aug. 31, 1864.
Stengel, Theodore	do	29	May 2, 1864	100 dys.	Mustered out with company Aug. 31, 1864.
Stuemer, Charles	do	18	May 2, 1864	100 dys.	Mustered out with company Aug. 31, 1864.
Tow, Lew	do	24	May 2, 1864	100 dys.	Mustered as Musician; mustered out with company Aug. 31, 1864.
[illegible], Frederick	do	24	May 2, 1864	100 dys.	Mustered out with company Aug. 31, 1864.
[illegible], John	do	[illegible]	May 2, 1864	100 dys.	No record subsequent to muster-in.
[illegible], Fred	do	29	May 2, 1864	100 dys.	Mustered out with company Aug. 31, 1864.
[illegible], Leopold	do	32	May 2, 1864	100 dys.	No record subsequent to muster-in.
[illegible], Gustave	do	28	May 2, 1864	100 dys.	No record subsequent to muster-in.
Wuerthwein, John	do	44	May 2, 1864	100 dys.	Mustered out with company Aug. 31, 1864.

COMPANY E.

Mustered in May 14, 1864, at Camp Dennison, O., by Robert S. Smith, Captain 2d Cavalry, U. S. A. Mustered out Aug. 31, 1864, at Camp Dennison, O., by A. J. Bellows, 1st Lieutenant 14th Infantry, U. S. A.

	Rank.	Age.	Date of Entering the Service.	Period of Service.	Remarks.
William Ohmann	Captain.	32	May 2, 1864	100 dys.	Mustered out with company Aug. 31, 1864.
Adolph Frey	1st Lieut.	26	May 2, 1864	100 dys.	Mustered out with company Aug. 31, 1864.
Adam Fauth	2d Lieut.	30	May 2, 1864	100 dys.	Mustered out with company Aug. 31, 1864.
Louis Pochat	1st Sergt.	[illegible]	May 2, 1864	100 dys.	Mustered out with company Aug. 31, 1864.
Theodore Brueck	Sergeant.	35	May 2, 1864	100 dys.	Mustered out with company Aug. 31, 1864.
Peter Rath	do	26	May 2, 1864	100 dys.	Mustered out with company Aug. 31, 1864.
Carl Heidenreich	do	29	May 2, 1864	100 dys.	Mustered out with company Aug. 31, 1864.
Otto Zell	do	18	May 2, 1864	100 dys.	Mustered out with company Aug. 31, 1864.
David Abbihl	Corporal.	22	May 2, 1864	100 dys.	Mustered out with company Aug. 31, 1864.
Adolph Werchan	do	40	May 2, 1864	100 dys.	Mustered out with company Aug. 31, 1864.
John Hatzig	do	32	May 2, 1864	100 dys.	Mustered out with company Aug. 31, 1864.
Carl Kuenemund	do	37	May 2, 1864	100 dys.	Mustered out with company Aug. 31, 1864.
Henry Reis	do	33	May 2, 1864	100 dys.	Mustered out with company Aug. 31, 1864.
John Zimpelmann	do	25	May 2, 1864	100 dys.	Mustered out with company Aug. 31, 1864.
Ernst Giesler	do	25	May 2, 1864	100 dys.	Appointed May 27, 1864; mustered out with company Aug. 31, 1864.
John Becker	do	18	May 2, 1864	100 dys.	Appointed July 21, 1864; mustered out with company Aug. 31, 1864.
Daniel Koch	Musician	18	May 2, 1864	100 dys.	Mustered out with company Aug. 31, 1864.
Frank Gulde	do	18	May 2, 1864	100 dys.	Mustered out with company Aug. 31, 1864.
Henry Jacob	Wagoner.	26	May 2, 1864	100 dys.	Mustered out with company Aug. 31, 1864.
Adam, Valentine	Private.	42	May 2, 1864	100 dys.	Mustered out with company Aug. 31, 1864.
Armstroff, Gustav	do	35	May 2, 1864	100 dys.	Mustered out with company Aug. 31, 1864.
Aspenleiter, Sebastian	do	40	May 2, 1864	100 dys.	Mustered out with company Aug. 31, 1864.
Baumann, Henry	do	18	May 2, 1864	100 dys.	Mustered out with company Aug. 31, 1864.
Blum, Louis	do	37	May 2, 1864	100 dys.	Mustered out with company Aug. 31, 1864.
Conradi, Christian	do	[illegible]	May 2, 1864	100 dys.	
Dalber, Henry	do	[illegible]	May 2, 1864	100 dys.	Mustered out with company Aug. 31, 1864.
Deicke, Louis	do	[illegible]	May 2, 1864	100 dys.	Mustered out with company Aug. 31, 1864.

Names.	Rank.	Age.	Date of Entering the Service.	Period of Service.	
Denk, Henry	Private	28	May 2, 1864	100 dys.	Mustered out with compa
Detert, Henry	...do...	28	May 2, 1864	100 dys.	Mustered out with compa
Dietz, Henry	...do...	18	May 2, 1864	100 dys.	Mustered out with
Doebring, Joseph	...do...	26	May 2, 1864	100 dys.	Mustered out with
Dorst, Valentine	...do...	31	May 2, 1864	100 dys.	Mustered out with
Fachmann, H. Friederich	...do...	21	May 2, 1864	100 dys.	Mustered out with compa
Frommel, Friederich	...do...	37	May 2, 1864	100 dys.	Mustered out with com
Gieske, Hermann	...do...	31	May 2, 1864	100 dys.	Mustered out with comp
Goerig, Charles	...do...	25	May 2, 1864	100 dys.	Transferred and deliver shall, 12th District, Pe having been drafted.
Goldstein, Anton	...do...	40	May 2, 1864	100 dys.	
Gulde, Franz	...do...	..	May 2, 1864	100 dys.	No record subsequent to
Heiter, Joseph	...do...	30	May 2, 1864	100 dys.	Mustered out with
Herfurth, H. Moritz	...do...	32	May 2, 1864	100 dys.	Mustered out with
Heyl, Henry	...do...	34	May 2, 1864	100 dys.	Mustered out with
Hoffmann, George	...do...	29	May 2, 1864	100 dys.	Mustered out with
Jaeger, Henry	...do...	18	May 2, 1864	100 dys.	Mustered out with
Johnson, John	...do...	38	May 2, 1864	100 dys.	Mustered out with
Keck, Gustav	...do...	28	May 2, 1864	100 dys.	Mustered out with
Keck, John G	...do...	42	May 2, 1864	100 dys.	Mustered out with compa
Kernen, Rudolph	...do...	18	May 2, 1864	100 dys.	Mustered out with compa
Knickel, Jacob	...do...	38	May 2, 1864	100 dys.	Mustered out with compa
Kress, Michael	...do...	41	May 2, 1864	100 dys.	Mustered out with compa
Kurz, Louis	...do...	27	May 2, 1864	100 dys.	
Leive, Henry	...do...	19	May 2, 1864	100 dys.	Mustered out with compa
Ludewig, Carl	...do...	36	May 2, 1864	100 dys.	Mustered out with compa
Mansch, Albert	...do...	19	May 2, 1864	100 dys.	
Meyer, Frank	...do...	31	May 2, 1864	100 dys.	Mustered out with compa
Meyer, Michael	...do...	37	May 2, 1864	100 dys.	Mustered out with compa
Niemann, Henry	...do...	20	May 2, 1864	100 dys.	Mustered out with compa
Oeser, Frank	...do...	25	May 2, 1864	100 dys.	
Pfaff, Jacob	...do...	36	May 2, 1864	100 dys.	Mustered out with
Polster, August	...do...	39	May 2, 1864	100 dys.	Mustered out with
Renner, George	...do...	23	May 2, 1864	100 dys.	Mustered out with
Roerig, August	...do...	30	May 2, 1864	100 dys.	Mustered out with
Rothfuss, Louis	...do...	31	May 2, 1864	100 dys.	Mustered out with
Rothfuss, Paul	...do...	21	May 2, 1864	100 dys.	Mustered out with
Ruehl, Charles	...do...	37	May 2, 1864	100 dys.	Mustered out with compa
Schmidt, Henry	...do...	36	May 2, 1864	100 dys.	Mustered out with compa
Schmidt, Jacob	...do...	19	May 2, 1864	100 dys.	Mustered out with compa
Schroer, Henry	...do...	36	May 2, 1864	100 dys.	Mustered out with compa
Schumacher, Henry	...do...	27	May 2, 1864	100 dys.	Mustered as Corporal; r mustered out with com
Stern, Simon	...do...	37	May 2, 1864	100 dys.	Mustered out with compa
Stubenrauch, Joseph	...do...	21	May 2, 1864	100 dys.	
Suhr, Frank	...do...	36	May 2, 1864	100 dys.	Mustered out with compa
Tempel, Carl	...do...	36	May 2, 1864	100 dys.	Mustered out with compa
Uhl, Jacob	...do...	38	May 2, 1864	100 dys.	Mustered out with compa
Weinmann, Jacob	...do...	34	May 2, 1864	100 dys.	Mustered out with compa
Weisse, Friederich	...do...	29	May 2, 1864	100 dys.	Mustered out with compa
Wells, John	...do...	18	May 2, 1864	100 dys.	Mustered out with compa
Weusler, George	...do...	29	May 2, 1864	100 dys.	Mustered out with compa
Wernz, Matthew	...do...	31	May 2, 1864	100 dys.	Mustered out with compa
Wieger, Adolph	...do...	25	May 2, 1864	100 dys.	
Wiegmann, Joseph	...do...	18	May 2, 1864	100 dys.	Mustered out with compa
Wild, John G.	...do...	32	May 2, 1864	100 dys.	Mustered out with compa
Wocher, Leopold	...do...	32	May 2, 1864	100 dys.	Mustered out with compa
Wolf, Frank	...do...	22	May 2, 1864	100 dys.	Mustered out with compa
Zimpelmann, Peter	...do...	28	May 2, 1864	100 dys.	Mustered as Corporal; r mustered out with com

COMPANY F.

Mustered in May 14, 1864, at Camp Dennison, O., by Robert S. Smith, Captain 2d Cavalry out Aug. 31, 1864, at Camp Dennison, O., by A. J. Bellows, 1st Lieutenant 14th Infantry, U. S. A.

Names.	Rank.	Age.	Date of Entering the Service.	Period of Service.	
Martin Hauser	Captain.	48	May 2, 1864	100	Mustered out with comp
Frederick W. Rau	1st Lieut.	32	May 2, 1864	100	Mustered out with comp
John Pfisterer	2d Lieut.	25	May 2, 1864	100	Mustered out with comp
Matthias Weusler	1st Sergt.	27	May 2, 1864	100	Mustered out with comp
George Rebholz	Sergeant.	36	May 2, 1864	100	Mustered out with comp
Anthony Schleich	...do...	39	May 2, 1864	100	Mustered out with comp
George Heilman	...do...	38	May 2, 1864	100	Mustered out with comp
Henry Weil	...do...	37	May 2, 1864	100	Mustered out with comp
John Wahl	Corporal.	33	May 2, 1864	100	Mustered out with comp
Christian Nienouse	...do...	27	May 2, 1864	100	Mustered out with comp
Henry Scheutse	...do...	36	May 2, 1864	100	Mustered out with comp
Christian Gaibel	...do...	42	May 2, 1864	100	Mustered out with comp

Names.		Age.	Date of Entering the Service.	Period of Service.	
Schaefer, Nicholaus		39	May 2, 1864	100 dys.	Discharged May 15, 1 O., on Surgeon's cer
Scherer, Henry		43	May 2, 1864	100 dys.	Mustered out with co
Scheurer, Adam		48	May 2, 1864	100 dys.	Mustered out with co
Schwab, Peter		28	May 2, 1864	100 dys.	Mustered out with co
Sprimeweber, Peter		30	May 2, 1864	100 dys.	Mustered out with co
Tassler, Daniel		23	May 2, 1864	100 dys.	Absent June 30, 18 as Daniel Fossler.
Traerich, Clements		37	May 2, 1864	100 dys.	Absent June 30, 18 found.
Trarbach, Nicolaus		27	May 2, 1864	100 dys.	Mustered out with co
Weisgerber, August		29	May 2, 1864	100 dys	Mustered out with co
Winter, Henry		40	May 2, 1864	100 dys.	Discharged May 15, 1 cate of disability.
Yeager, Frank	....do....	25	May 2, 1864	100 dys.	Absent June 30, 18 found.

COMPANY G.

Mustered in May 14, 1864, at Camp Dennison, O., by Robert S. Smith, Captain 2d Cav out Aug. 31, 1864, at Camp Dennison, O., by A. J. Bellows, Lieutenant 14th Infantry, U. S. A.

Names.	Rank.	Age.	Date of Entering the Service.	Period of Service.	Remarks.
Julius Hoffmann	Captain.	29	May 2, 1864	100 dys.	Mustered out with
John Zimmermann	1st Lieut.	37	May 2, 1864	100 dys.	Mustered out with
Conrad Nickel	2d Lieut.	39	May 2, 1864	100 dys.	Mustered out with
Charles Bode	1st Sergt.	26	May 2, 1864	100 dys	Mustered out with
Peter Wolf	Sergeant.	28	May 2, 1864	100 dys.	Mustered out with
David Ringold	....do....	32	May 2, 1864	100 dys.	Mustered out with
Peter Johannes	....do....	31	May 2, 1864	100 dys.	Mustered out with
Mathias Mader	....do....	27	May 2, 1864	100 dys.	Mustered out with
Jacob Hills	Corporal.	31	May 2, 1864	100 dys.	Mustered out with co
John Frick	....do....	26	May 2, 1864	100 dys.	Mustered out with
August Stahle	....do....	33	May 2, 1864	100 dys.	Mustered out with co
Charles Wentzel	....do....	32	May 2, 1864	100 dys.	Mustered out with
Xavier Reiss	....do....	32	May 2, 1864	100 dys	Mustered out with
Ignatz Speck	....do....	34	May 2, 1864	100 dys.	Mustered out with
Heinrich Lehmann	....do....	34	May 2, 1864	100 dys.	Mustered out with co
Wilhelm Fricke	....do....	37	May 2, 1864	100 dys.	Mustered out with co
Louis Sturow	Musician	29	May 2, 1864	100 dys.	Mustered out with co
Bach, Mathias	Private..	32	May 2, 1864	100 dys	
Baumgarten, William	....do....	27	May 2, 1864	100 dys.	Mustered out with co
Benz, Edward	....do....	35	May 2, 1864	100 dys.	Mustered in as Erns with company Aug.
Boas, August	....do....	32	May 2, 1864	100 dys.	Absent, sick May 15. No further record f
Boehner, Adam	....do...	32	May 2, 1864	100 dys	Mustered out with co
Bollar, Charles	....do....	38	May 2, 1864	100 dys.	
Brichel, Sebast	....do....	29	May 2, 1864	100 dys	Mustered out with co
Buch, Mathias	....do....	34	May 2, 1864	100 dys.	
Demmer, Frantz	....do....	27	May 2, 1864	100 dys.	Mustered out with co
Dewald, Louis	....do....	39	May 2, 1864	100 dys.	No record subsequent
Diepold, Louis	....do....	29	May 2, 1864	100 dys.	Mustered out with co
Dorn, Conrad	....do....	33	May 2, 1864	100 dys.	Absent, sick May 15 No further record
Ecker, Matthias	....do....	28	May 2, 1864	100 dys.	Absent, sick ——, at ther record found.
Elf, Adam	....do....	38	May 2, 1864	100 dys.	Absent, sick May 16, No further record
Espenleider, William	....do....	37	May 2, 1864	100 dys.	Mustered out with co
Friedrich, William	....do....	32	May 2, 1864	100 dys	
Fuchs, Adam	....do...	39	May 2, 1864	100 dys	Absent, sick May 17, No further record
Georg, Wilhelm	....do....	42	May 2, 1864	100 dys.	
Gerber, Peter	....do....	40	May 2, 1864	100 dys.	Mustered out with co
Geschwind, Friedrich F.	....do....	36	May 2, 1864	100 dys.	Mustered out with co
Gundrum, Peter	....do....	39	May 2, 1864	100 dys.	Mustered out with co
Haymuth, A.	....do....	27	May 2, 1864	100 dys.	No record subsequent
Hahnemann, Christian	....do....	24	May 2, 1864	100 dys.	Mustered out with co
Hempfling, George	....do....	28	May 2, 1864	100 dys.	
Henke, Christian	....do....	30	May 2, 1864	100 dys.	Absent, sick May 17, No further record
Hochstuhl, Matthias	....do....	32	May 2, 1864	100 dys.	Mustered out with co
Hoffmann, Christian	....do....	37	May 2, 1864	100 dys.	Mustered out with co
Ider, Heinrich	....do....	37	May 2, 1864	100 dys.	
Kaeser, Valentine	....do....	29	May 2, 1864	100 dys.	Mustered out with co
Kautz, Philip	....do....	43	May 2, 1864	100 dys.	Absent, sick May 14. No further record
Knupfer, Henry	....do....	27	May 2, 1864	100 dys.	Mustered out with co
Koehler, John	....do....	19	May 2, 1864	100 dys.	Mustered out with co

Names.	Rank.	Age.	Date of Entering the Service.	Period of Service.	Remarks.
Bloonar, George	Private	26	May 2, 1864	100 dys.	Mustered out with company Aug 31, 1864.
B[illegible]echle, Frederick	...do...	33	May 2, 1864	100 dys.	Discharged May 18, 1864, on account of having been drafted.
Bratfisch, Edward	...do...	18	May 2, 1864	100 dys.	Mustered out with company Aug. 31, 1864.
Bre[illegible]sen, Henry	...do...	21	May 2, 1864	100 dys.	Mustered out with company Aug. 31, 1864.
Brown, Charles	...do...	44	May 2, 1864	100 dys.	Mustered out with company Aug. 31, 1864.
[illegible]ruch, John	...do...	37	May 2, 1864	100 dys.	Discharged May 16, 1864, at Cincinnati, O., on Surgeon's certificate of disability.
Deckwitz, August	...do...	35	May 2, 1864	100 dys.	Discharged May 18, 1864, on account of having been drafted.
Dettmering, Frederick	...do...	36	May 2, 1864	100 dys.	Mustered out with company Aug. 31, 1864.
Eichenlaub, John	...do...	27	May 2, 1864	100 dys.	Mustered out with company Aug. 31, 1864.
Eichenlaub, Valentine	...do...	41	May 2, 1864	100 dys.	Mustered out with company Aug. 31, 1864.
Geisler, Samuel	...do...	35	May 2, 1864	100 dys.	Mustered out with company Aug. 31, 1864.
Gross, Peter	...do...	19	May 2, 1864	100 dys.	Mustered out with company Aug. 31, 1864.
Guntner, Nicholas	...do...	36	May 2, 1864	100 dys.	
Hagebrook, Bernard	...do...	32	May 2, 1864	100 dys.	Mustered out with company Aug. 31, 1864.
Helmig, Henry	...do...	44	May 2, 1864	100 dys.	Absent, ——. No further record found.
Helmig, William	...do...	29	May 2, 1864	100 dys.	Discharged May 18, 1864, on account of having been drafted.
Hochstuhl, Martin	...do...	36	May 2, 1864	100 dys.	Absent, ——. No further record found.
Herwig, Frederick	...do...	38	May 2, 1864	100 dys.	Mustered out with company Aug. 31, 1864.
Josterand, Herman	...do...	22	May 2, 1864	100 dys.	Mustered out with company Aug. 31, 1864.
Joung, Philip	...do...	35	May 2, 1864	100 dys.	Mustered out with company Aug. 31, 1864.
Kauffman, John	...do...	25	May 2, 1864	100 dys.	Mustered out with company Aug. 31, 1864.
Kimmel, Charles	...do...	36	May 2, 1864	100 dys.	Mustered out with company Aug. 31, 1864.
Klaus, Christian	...do...	28	May 2, 1864	100 dys.	Mustered out with company Aug. 31, 1864.
Klingler, August	...do...	20	May 2, 1864	100 dys.	Mustered out with company Aug. 31, 1864.
Klingler, Joseph	...do...	..	May 2, 1864	100 dys.	No record subsequent to muster-in, June 8, 1864.
Koch, Balthasar	...do...	37	May 2, 1864	100 dys.	Mustered out with company Aug. 31, 1864.
Korn, Joseph	...do...	27	May 2, 1864	100 dys.	
Krabel, John	...do...	28	May 2, 1864	100 dys.	
Laue, F. William	...do...	30	May 2, 1864	100 dys.	Mustered out with company Aug. 31, 1864.
Leonard, George	...do...	30	May 2, 1864	100 dys.	Mustered out with company Aug. 31, 1864.
Martin, Charles	...do...	34	May 2, 1864	100 dys.	Mustered as Charles Martens; mustered out with company Aug. 31, 1864.
Miller, Frederick	...do...	38	May 2, 1864	00 dys.	Mustered out with company Aug. 31, 1864.
Moter, Anton	...do...	34	May 2, 1864	100 dys.	Mustered out with company Aug. 31, 1864.
Nay, Lewis	...do...	[illegible]3	May 2, 1864	100 dys.	Mustered out with company Aug. 31, 1864.
Niemeyer, Henry	...do...	36	May 2, 1864	100 dys.	Mustered out with company Aug. 31, 1864.
Pell, Bassillius	...do...	34	May 2, 1864	100 dys.	Mustered out with company Aug. 31, 1864.
Rahke, Lewis	...do...	28	May 2, 1864	100 dys.	Mustered out with company Aug. 31, 1864.
Rakel, John H.	...do...	32	May 2, 1864	100 dys.	Mustered out with company Aug. 31, 1864.
Richard, Adolph	...do...	24	May 2, 1864	100 dys.	Mustered out with company Aug. 31, 1864.
Roller, Charles	...do...	27	May 2, 1864	100 dys.	Transferred from Co. B May 25, 1864; mustered out with company Aug. 31, 1864.
Rossel, Martin	...do...	22	May 2, 1864	100 dys.	Mustered out with company Aug. 31, 1864.
Salzman, George	...do...	30	May 2, 1864	100 dys.	Mustered out with company Aug. 31, 1864.
Schneeberger, Anton	...do...	..	May 2, 1864	100 dys.	No record subsequent to June 30, 1864.
Simon, Michael	...do...	40	May 2, 1864	100 dys.	Mustered out with company Aug. 31, 1864.
Stallkamp, Henry	...do...	25	May 2, 1864	100 dys.	Mustered out with company Aug. 31, 1864.
Steigewald, Adam	...do...	43	May 2, 1864	100 dys.	Mustered out with company Aug. 31, 1864.
Steinborn, Jacob	...do...	32	May 2, 1864	100 dys.	Mustered out with company Aug. 31, 1864.
Steinke, Henry	...do...	21	May 2, 1864	100 dys.	Promoted to Hospital Steward May 2[illegible], 1864.
Stern, Edward	...do...	38	May 2, 1864	100 dys.	Mustered out with company Aug. 31, 1864.
Stock, David	...do...	21	May 2, 1864	100 dys.	Mustered out with company Aug. 31, 1864.
Trometer, George	...do...	19	May 2, 1864	100 dys.	Mustered out with company Aug. 31, 1864.
Volz, David	...do...	19	May 2, 1864	100 dys.	
Walter, Jacob	...do...	30	May 2, 1864	100 dys.	Mustered out with company Aug. 31, 1864.
Weibel, Henry	...do...	38	May 2, 1864	100 dys.	Discharged May 18, 1864, on account of having been drafted.
Wickert, William	...do...	32	May 2, 1864	100 dys.	Mustered out with company Aug. 31, 1864.
Wingerberg, George	...do...	26	May 2, 1864	100 dys.	Mustered out with company Aug. 31, 1864.
Woell, Anton	...do...	34	May 2, 1864	100 dys.	Mustered out with company Aug. 31, 1864.

166th Regiment Ohio Volunteer Infantry.

ONE HUNDRED DAYS' SERVICE.

This Regiment was organized at Camp Cleveland, O., May 13 and 15, 1864, to serve one hundred days. It was composed of the Fifty-ninth Battalion, Ohio National Guard, from Holmes County; Sixty-third Regiment, Ohio National Guard, from Huron County; Seventy-ninth Battalion, Ohio National Guard, from Medina County; and one company of the Fifty-second Battalion, Ohio National Guard, from Wayne County. Immediately after muster-in the Regiment proceeded to Virginia, and was placed on duty in Forts Richardson, Barnard, Reynolds, Ward, and Worth, with headquarters at Fort Richardson. The Regiment returned to Ohio, and was mustered out September 9, 1864, on expiration of its term of service.

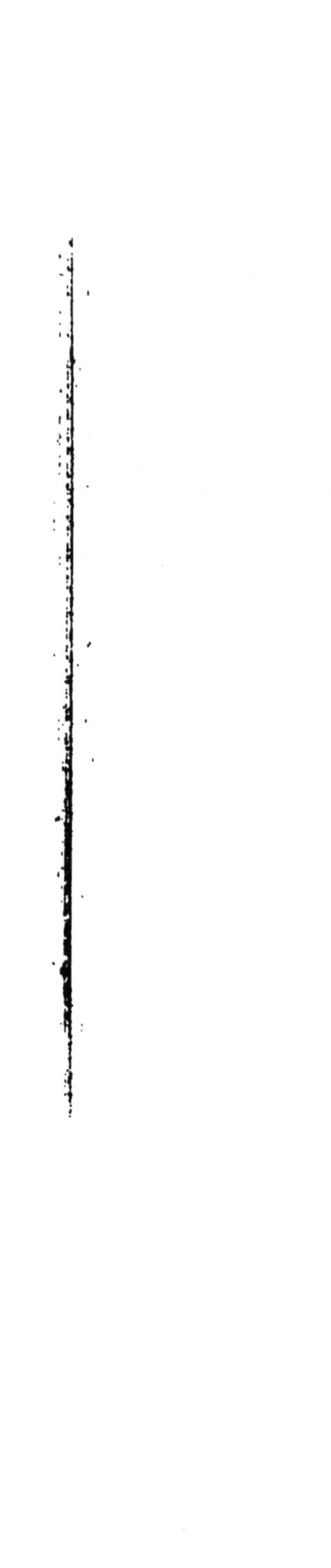

Names.	Rank.	Age.	Date of Entering the Service.	Period of Service.	Remarks.
Crawford, John M	Private	19	May 2, 1864	100 dys.	Mustered out with company Sept. 9, 1864.
Crawford, Morris	do	18	May 2, 1864	100 dys.	Mustered out with company Sept. 9, 1864.
Crawford, Lewis H	do	20	May 2, 1864	100 dys.	Mustered out with company Sept. 9, 1864.
Darnel, Henry L	do	28	May 2, 1864	100 dys.	Mustered out with company Sept. 9, 1864.
Dobbins, Nicholas S	do	34	May 2, 1864	100 dys.	Mustered out with company Sept. 9, 1864.
Donley, James	do	24	May 2, 1864	100 dys.	Mustered out with company Sept. 9, 1864.
Fleming, James	do	32	May 2, 1864	100 dys.	Mustered out with company Sept. 9, 1864.
Fleming, Robert	do	36	May 2, 1864	100 dys.	Mustered out with company Sept. 9, 1864.
Fleming, William	do	27	May 2, 1864	100 dys.	Mustered out with company Sept. 9, 1864.
Gilmore, Charles W	do	25	May 2, 1864	100 dys.	Mustered out with company Sept. 9, 1864.
Gorrell, Wilson	do	42	May 2, 1864	100 dys.	Mustered out with company Sept. 8, 1864.
Graven, Clark	do	19	May 2, 1864	100 dys.	Mustered out with company Sept. 9, 1864.
Hague, Aaron	do	34	May 2, 1864	100 dys.	Mustered out with company Sept. 9, 1864.
Harper, John	do	19	May 2, 1864	100 dys.	Mustered out with company Sept. 9, 1864.
Hill, William	do	28	May 2, 1864	100 dys.	Mustered out with company Sept. 9, 1864.
Johnston, Andrew	do	29	May 2, 1864	100 dys.	Mustered out with company Sept. 9, 1864.
K[illegible] Holmes	do	19	May 2, 1864	100 dys.	Mustered out with company Sept. 9, 1864.
Kester, Joseph	do	44	May 2, 1864	100 dys.	Mustered out with company Sept. 9, 1864.
Korns, Charles W	do	27	May 2, 1864	100 dys.	Mustered out with company Sept. 9, 1864.
Lee, Thomas W	do	37	May 2, 1864	100 dys.	Mustered out with company Sept. 9, 1864.
Leyenberger, Lawrence	do	21	May 2, 1864	100 dys.	Mustered out with company Sept. 9, 1864.
Lightcap, Martin V	do	18	May 2, 1864	100 dys.	Mustered out with company Sept. 9, 1864.
Lisle, James	do	30	May 2, 1864	100 dys.	Mustered out with company Sept. 9, 1864.
Livingston, Henry	do	21	May 2, 1864	100 dys.	Mustered out with company Sept. 9, 1864.
Lockhart, Albert	do	41	May 2, 1864	100 dys.	Mustered out with company Sept. 9, 1864.
Law, Milton J	do	22	May 2, 1864	100 dys.	Mustered out with company Sept. 9, 1864.
Low, Newton H	do	19	May 2, 1864	100 dys.	Mustered out with company Sept. 9, 1864.
McClaran, John	do	35	May 2, 1864	100 dys.	Mustered out with company Sept. 9, 1864.
McClelland, Thomas L	do	25	May 2, 1864	100 dys.	Died Sept. 5, 1864, in general hospital at Cleveland, O.
McClure, Samuel	do	34	May 2, 1864	100 dys.	Mustered out with company Sept. 9, 1864.
McCullough, John	do	29	May 2, 1864	100 dys.	Mustered out with company Sept. 9, 1864.
McNulty, James	do	30	May 2, 1864	100 dys.	Mustered out with company Sept. 9, 1864.
Marquis, Charles K	do	28	May 2, 1864	100 dys.	Mustered out with company Sept. 9, 1864.
Marquis, Hiram	do	36	May 2, 1864	100 dys.	Mustered out with company Sept. 9, 1864.
Martin, Franklin	do	27	May 2, 1864	100 dys.	Mustered out with company Sept. 9, 1864.
Martin, John H	do	25	May 2, 1864	100 dys.	Mustered out with company Sept. 9, 1864.
Martin, William*	do	21	May 2, 1864	100 dys.	Died Aug. 15, 1864, in general hospital at Fairfax Seminary, Va.
Maxwell, William A	do	17	May 2, 1864	100 dys.	Mustered out with company Sept. 9, 1864.
Moreland, James	do	20	May 2, 1864	100 dys.	Mustered out with company Sept. 9, 1864.
Moreland, Samuel	do	32	May 2, 1864	100 dys.	Mustered out with company Sept. 9, 1864.
Moore, Abraham J	do	19	May 2, 1864	100 dys.	Mustered out with company Sept. 9, 1864.
Moore, Brison	do	30	May 2, 1864	100 dys.	Mustered out with company Sept. 9, 1864.
Murry, Perry	do	39	May 2, 1864	100 dys.	Mustered out with company Sept. 9, 1864.
Parker, George G	do	18	May 2, 1864	100 dys.	Mustered out with company Sept. 9, 1864.
Peckham, Joseph R	do	37	May 2, 1864	100 dys.	Mustered out with company Sept. 9, 1864.
Price, Joseph D	do	17	May 2, 1864	100 dys.	Mustered out with company Sept. 9, 1864.
Price, Madison	do	19	May 2, 1864	100 dys.	Mustered out with company Sept. 9, 1864.
Pyers, Hiram	do	20	May 2, 1864	100 dys.	Mustered out with company Sept. 9, 1864.
Ray, Jeremiah	do	25	May 2, 1864	100 dys.	Mustered out with company Sept. 9, 1864.
Richards, Smith	do	22	May 2, 1864	100 dys.	Mustered out with company Sept. 9, 1864.
Sadd[illegible], Rufus B	do	18	May 2, 1864	100 dys.	Mustered out with company Sept. 9, 1864.
Schaaf, Adam	do	32	May 2, 1864	100 dys.	Mustered out with company Sept. 9, 1864.
Schamp, Peter	do	25	May 2, 1864	100 dys.	Mustered out with company Sept. 9, 1864.
Scott, Edward B	do	19	May 2, 1864	100 dys.	Mustered out with company Sept. 9, 1864.
Shadle, William A	do	18	May 2, 1864	100 dys.	Mustered out with company Sept. 9, 1864.
Shrimplin, James	do	19	May 2, 1864	100 dys.	Died Aug. 18, 1864, in general hospital at Fairfax Seminary, Va.
Smith, Oliver N	do	33	May 2, 1864	100 dys.	Mustered out with company Sept. 9, 1864.
Snyder, Isaac	do	22	May 2, 1864	100 dys.	Mustered out with company Sept. 9, 1864.
St[illegible]lfire, Francis	do	18	May 2, 1864	100 dys.	Mustered out with company Sept. 9, 1864.
Taylor, Thomas B	do	30	May 2, 1864	100 dys.	Mustered out with company Sept. 9, 1864.
Todd, John	do	44	May 2, 1864	100 dys.	Mustered out with company Sept. 9, 1864.
Todd, William	do	39	May 2, 1864	100 dys.	Mustered out with company Sept. 9, 1864.
Torbet, David	do	19	May 2, 1864	100 dys.	Mustered out with company Sept. 9, 1864.
Torbet, John L	do	23	May 2, 1864	100 dys.	Mustered out with company Sept. 9, 1864.
Trent, Darius	do	25	May 2, 1864	100 dys.	Mustered out with company Sept. 9, 1864.
Vorhes, Thomas O	do	29	May 2, 1864	100 dys.	Mustered out with company Sept. 9, 1864.
Way, Joseph C	do	19	May 2, 1864	100 dys.	Mustered out with company Sept. 9, 1864.
Williams, McCarty	do	20	May 2, 1864	100 dys.	Mustered out with company Sept. 9, 1864.
Williams, Thomas	do	24	May 2, 1864	100 dys.	Mustered out with company Sept. 9, 1864.
Young, Hiram W	do	41	May 2, 1864	100 dys.	Mustered out with company Sept. 9, 1864.

Names.	Rank.	Age.	Date of Entering the Service.	Period of Service.	Remarks.
Palmer, Harvey	Private	41	May 2, 1864	100 dys.	Mustered out with company Sept. 9, 1864.
Perkins, John B.	...do...	30	May 2, 1864	100 dys.	Mustered out with company Sept. 9, 1864.
Pinney, John	...do...	24	May 2, 1864	100 dys.	Died Aug. 19, 1864, in Fairfax Seminary Hospital, Virginia.
Plue, Cornelius S.	...do...	39	May 15, 1864	100 dys.	Died Sept. 2, 1864.
Rice, William	...do...	28	May 2, 1864	100 dys.	Mustered out with company Sept. 9, 1864.
Sayers, Henry	...do...	34	May 2, 1864	100 dys.	Mustered out with company Sept. 9, 1864.
Sloat, Hiram	...do...	27	May 2, 1864	100 dys.	Mustered out with company Sept. 9, 1864.
Sly, John R.	...do...	29	May 2, 1864	100 dys.	Mustered out with company Sept. 9, 1864.
Smith, William S.	...do...	22	May 15, 1864	100 dys.	Mustered out with company Sept. 9, 1864.
Soules, Elijah	...do...	36	May 2, 1864	100 dys.	Mustered out with company Sept. 9, 1864.
Sowers, John	...do...	18	May 2, 1864	100 dys.	Mustered out with company Sept. 9, 1864.
States, Marcus M.	...do...	18	May 2, 1864	100 dys.	Mustered out with company Sept. 9, 1864.
Swift, Vanrensselaer	...do...	34	May 2, 1864	100 dys.	Mustered out with company Sept. 9, 1864.
Tietsworth, Ezra	...do...	31	May 2, 1864	100 dys.	Mustered out with company Sept. 9, 1864.
Tietsworth, Jared C.	...do...	19	May 2, 1864	100 dys.	Absent, sick ——. No further record found.
Waldron, Wilbur	...do...	21	May 2, 1864	100 dys.	Mustered out with company Sept. 9, 1864.
Winchester, Steadman	...do...	26	May 2, 1864	100 dys.	Mustered out with company Sept. 9, 1864.
Worthington, Benjamin	...do...	21	May 2, 1864	100 dys.	Mustered out with company Sept. 9, 1864.
Yaples, Giles	...do...	29	May 2, 1864	100 dys.	Mustered out with company Sept. 9, 1864.

COMPANY C.

Mustered in May 15, 1864, at Camp Cleveland, O., by W. L. Kellogg, 1st Lieutenant 10th Infantry, U. S. A. Mustered out Sept. 9, 1864, at Camp Cleveland, O., by C. B. Throckmorton, 1st Lieutenant 4th Artillery, U. S. A.

Names.	Rank.	Age.	Date of Entering the Service.	Period of Service.	Remarks.
Joseph Sutton	Captain.	42	May 2, 1864	100 dys.	Mustered out with company Sept. 9, 1864.
John M. Terry	1st Lieut.	28	May 2, 1864	100 dys.	Detailed as Post Adjutant July 16, 1864; mustered out with company Sept. 9, 1864.
Henry W. Buckman	2d Lieut.	30	May 2, 1864	100 dys.	Mustered out with company Sept. 9, 1864.
Charles W. Manahan, Jr.	1st Sergt.	20	May 15, 1864	100 dys.	Mustered out with company Sept. 9, 1864.
Philip Hauxhurst	Sergeant.	34	May 2, 1864	100 dys.	Mustered out with company Sept. 9, 1864.
James Dickson	...do...	27	May 2, 1864	100 dys.	Mustered out with company Sept. 9, 1864.
Rufus W. Reynolds	...do...	25	May 2, 1864	100 dys.	Mustered out with company Sept. 9, 1864.
Ransom . Hackett	...do...	26	May 2, 1864	100 dys.	Mustered out with company Sept. 9, 1864.
John Clarkson	Corporal.	38	May 2, 1864	100 dys.	Mustered out with company Sept. 9, 1864.
Silas Crawford	...do...	21	May 2, 1864	100 dys.	Mustered out with company Sept. 9, 1864.
John Q. Heck	...do...	32	May 2, 1864	100 dys.	Mustered out with company Sept. 9, 1864.
Freeman Morrill	...do...	27	May 2, 1864	100 dys.	Mustered out with company Sept. 9, 1864.
Emery J. Benson	...do...	3[illegible]	May 2, 1864	100 dys.	Mustered out with company Sept. 9, 1864.
Allen Purdy	...do...	22	May 2, 1864	100 dys.	Mustered out with company Sept. 9, 1864.
Calvert G. Green	...do...	19	May 2, 1864	100 dys.	Mustered out with company Sept. 9, 1864.
Robert Metcher	...do...	22	May 2, 1864	100 dys.	Mustered out with company Sept. 9, 1864.
Allen, Harvey V.	Private.	29	May 2, 1864	100 dys.	Mustered out with company Sept. 9, 1864.
Allison, Gardner W.	...do...	19	May 2, 1864	100 dys.	Mustered out with company Sept. 9, 1864.
Anderson, Robert	...do...	42	May 2, 1864	100 dys.	Mustered out with company Sept. 9, 1864.
Baker, William M.	...do...	22	May 2, 1864	100 dys.	Mustered out with company Sept. 9, 1864.
Bare, Corvis	...do...	18	May 2, 1864	100 dys.	Mustered out with company Sept. 9, 1864.
Bare, Henry W.	...do...	26	May 2, 1864	100 dys.	Mustered out with company Sept. 9, 1864.
Barber, Albert	...do...	18	May 2, 1864	100 dys.	Mustered out with company Sept. 9, 1864.
Barnes, Sumner E.	...do...	18	May 2, 1864	100 dys.	Mustered out with company Sept. 9, 1864.
Barnes, William C.	...do...	18	May 2, 1864	100 dys.	Mustered out with company Sept. 9, 1864.
Beach, William R.	...do...	19	May 2, 1864	100 dys.	Mustered out with company Sept. 9, 1864.
Carpenter, John W.	...do...	39	May 2, 1864	100 dys.	Mustered out with company Sept. 9, 1864.
Clark, Azel	...do...	24	May 2, 1864	100 dys.	Mustered out with company Sept. 9, 1864.
Conklin, Henry S.	...do...	39	May 2, 1864	100 dys.	Mustered out with company Sept. 9, 1864.
Conner, John	...do...	21	May 2, 1864	100 dys.	Mustered out with company Sept. 9, 1864.
Crawford, William	...do...	19	May 2, 1864	100 dys.	Mustered out with company Sept. 9, 1864.
Crist, William	...do...	23	May 2, 1864	100 dys.	Mustered out with company Sept. 9, 1864.
Crittenden, Immer	...do...	27	May 2, 1864	100 dys.	Died July 12, 1864, in Regimental Hospital.
Fleisinger, Charles B.	...do...	27	May 2, 1864	100 dys.	Mustered out with company Sept. 9, 1864.
Fisher, Alonzo B.	...do...	19	May 2, 1864	100 dys.	Mustered out with company Sept. 9, 1864.
Foot, Bronson H.	...do...	26	May 2, 1864	100 dys.	Mustered out with company Sept. 9, 1864.
Freeman, Albert	...do...	28	May 2, 1864	100 dys.	Mustered out with company Sept. 9, 1864.
Geer, William E.	...do...	19	May 2, 1864	100 dys.	Mustered out with company Sept. 9, 1864.
Gibson, Isaac S.	...do...	20	May 2, 1864	100 dys.	Mustered out with company Sept. 9, 1864.
Green, Mason	...do...	42	May 2, 1864	100 dys.	Mustered out with company Sept. 9, 1864.
Griffin, Corwin G.	...do...	19	May 2, 1864	100 dys.	Mustered out with company Sept. 9, 1864.
Hakes, James H.	...do...	19	May 2, 1864	100 dys.	Mustered out with company Sept. 9, 1864.
Hale, Charles W.	...do...	22	May 2, 1864	100 dys.	Mustered out with company Sept. 9, 1864.
Hammond, Isaac	...do...	..	May 2, 1864	100 dys.	Died July 24, 1864, in Regimental Hospital.
Hartman, John W.	...do...	20	May 2, 1864	100 dys.	Mustered out with company Sept. 9, 1864.
Hartman, Samuel E.	...do...	19	May 2, 1864	100 dys.	Mustered out with company Sept. 9, 1864.
Hawkins, Frank E.	...do...	19	May 2, 1864	100 dys.	Mustered out with company Sept. 9, 1864.
Hewitt, Fran	...do...	18	May 2, 1864	100 dys.	Mustered out with company Sept. 9, 1864.
Hibberd, John L.	...do...	21	May 2, 1864	100 dys.	Mustered out with company Sept. 9, 1864.
Howe, Charles L.	...do...	21	May 2, 1864	100 dys.	Mustered out with company Sept. 9
Hurd, David	...do...	43	May 2, 1864	100 dys.	Mustered out with company Sept. 9
Jenney, George D.	...do...	19	May 2, 1864	100 dys.	Mustered out with company Sept. 9

Names.	Rank.	Age.	Date of Entering the Service.	Period of Service.	Remarks.
Eaken, Abram	Private.	24	May 2, 1864	100 dys.	Mustered out with company Sept. 9, 1864.
Eaken, Abram H	...do....	22	May 2, 1864	100 dys.	Mustered out with company Sept. 9, 1864.
Eaken, George	...do....	28	May 2, 1864	100 dys.	Mustered out with company Sept. 9, 1864.
Ellis, Sylvester T	...do....	37	May 2, 1864	100 dys.	No record subsequent to enlistment.
Everhart, John H	...do....	18	May 2, 1864	100 dys.	Mustered out with company Sept. 9, 1864.
Gardner, Darwin	...do....	18	May 2, 1864	100 dys.	Mustered out with company Sept. 9, 1864.
Hanelspaugh, Henry	...do....	18	May 2, 1864	100 dys.	Mustered out with company Sept. 9, 1864.
Hanshue, Samuel	...do....	18	May 2, 1864	100 dys.	Mustered out with company Sept. 9, 1864.
Heckart, George W	...do....	28	May 2, 1864	100 dys.	Mustered out with company Sept. 9, 1864.
Hollowell, Chauncey C	...do....	18	May 2, 1864	100 dys.	Mustered out with company Sept. 9, 1864.
Homer, James I	...do....	30	May 2, 1864	100 dys.	Mustered out with company Sept. 9, 1864.
Horner, John	...do....	38	May 2, 1864	100 dys.	Mustered out with company Sept. 9, 1864.
Houser, Adam M	...do....	28	May 2, 1864	100 dys.	Mustered out with company Sept. 9, 1864.
Jefferson, Albert C	...do....	19	May 2, 1864	100 dys.	Mustered out with company Sept. 9, 1864.
Judson, Knapp	...do....	27	May 2, 1864	100 dys.	Mustered out with company Sept. 9, 1864; also borne on rolls as Judson Knapp.
Kennedy, David P	...do....	35	May 2, 1864	100 dys.	Mustered out with company Sept. 9, 1864.
Lauce, Ezra H	...do....	22	May 2, 1864	100 dys.	Mustered out with company Sept. 9, 1864.
Lebeau, McCurdy C	...do....	18	May 15, 1864	100 dys.	Mustered out with company Sept. 9, 1864.
Lewis, Amnah J	...do....	32	May 2, 1864	100 dys.	Mustered out with company Sept. 9, 1864.
Lowe, George H	...do....	19	May 15, 1864	100 dys.	Mustered out with company Sept. 9, 1864.
Lutz, Sylvester H	...do....	20	May 15, 1864	100 dys.	Mustered out with company Sept. 9, 1864.
Mack, Henry	...do....	32	May 2, 1864	100 dys.	Mustered out with company Sept. 9, 1864.
Melrose, Thomas	...do....	30	May 2, 1864	100 dys.	Mustered out with company Sept. 9, 1864.
Merritt, Alphon	...do....	18	May 2, 1864	100 dys.	Mustered out with company Sept. 9, 1864.
Merritt, Sylvester	...do....	36	May 2, 1864	100 dys.	Mustered out with company Sept. 9, 1864.
Miller, George E	...do....	36	May 2, 1864	100 dys.	Mustered out with company Sept. 9, 1864.
Miller, Jacob	...do....	32	May 2, 1864	100 dys.	Died July 10, 1864, in Regimental Hospital, Virginia.
Miller, Levi	...do....	18	May 2, 1864	100 dys.	Died July 20, 1864, in Regimental Hospital, Virginia.
Moulton, William E	...do....	35	May 2, 1864	100 dys.	Mustered out with company Sept. 9, 1864.
Nash, Henry	...do....	19	May 2, 1864	100 dys.	Mustered out with company Sept. 9, 1864.
Overdorf, Abram A	...do....	22	May 2, 1864	100 dys.	Mustered out with company Sept. 9, 1864.
Phillips, Dewece	...do....	19	May 2, 1864	100 dys.	Mustered out with company Sept. 9, 1864.
Pond, Henry	...do....	18	May 2, 1864	100 dys.	Died Aug. 11, 1864, in Regimental Hospital, Virginia.
Presley, Alfred L	...do....	18	May 2, 1864	100 dys.	Mustered out with company Sept. 9, 1864.
Randall, Austin	...do....	18	May 2, 1864	100 dys.	Died Aug. 19, 1864, in Regimental Hospital, Virginia.
Randall, Thomas	...do....	20	May 2, 1864	100 dys.	Mustered out with company Sept. 9, 1864.
Reed, George R	...do....	19	May 2, 1864	100 dys.	Mustered out with company Sept. 9, 1864.
Reynolds, Albert A	...do....	19	May 2, 1864	100 dys.	Mustered out with company Sept. 9, 1864.
Schamp, David	...do....	32	May 2, 1864	100 dys.	Mustered out with company Sept. 9, 1864.
Schamp, Jacob	...do....	23	May 2, 1864	100 dys.	Mustered out with company Sept. 9, 1864.
Shaw, Millard F	...do....	18	May 2, 1864	100 dys.	Mustered out with company Sept. 9, 1864.
Shepard, Blair	...do....	18	May 2, 1864	100 dys.	Died Aug. 13, 1864, in Regimental Hospital, Virginia.
Sinclair, William	...do....	20	May 2, 1864	100 dys.	Mustered out with company Sept. 9, 1864.
Smith, Charles	...do....	23	May 2, 1864	100 dys.	Mustered out with company Sept. 9, 1864.
Smith, Henry	...do....	28	May 2, 1864	100 dys.	Mustered out with company Sept. 9, 1864.
Stewart, James L	...do....	20	May 2, 1864	100 dys.	Mustered out with company Sept. 9, 1864.
Stinson, Robert	...do....	21	May 2, 1864	100 dys.	Mustered out with company Sept. 9, 1864.
St. John, Albert	...do....	18	May 2, 1864	100 dys.	Mustered out with company Sept. 9, 1864.
Thomas, Charles W	...do....	33	May 2, 1864	100 dys.	Mustered out with company Sept. 9, 1864.
Todd, Edgar M	...do....	28	May 2, 1864	100 dys.	Mustered out with company Sept. 9, 1864.
Tyler, Franklin	...do....	35	May 2, 1864	100 dys.	Mustered out with company Sept. 9, 1864.
Ware, Henry	...do....	19	May 2, 1864	100 dys.	Mustered out with company Sept. 9, 1864.
Welch, Nehemiah H	...do....	29	May 2, 1864	100 dys.	Mustered out with company Sept. 9, 1864.
Wepner, Addison G	...do....	21	May 2, 1864	100 dys.	Mustered out with company Sept. 9, 1864.
Wheeler, William	...do....	40	May 2, 1864	100 dys.	Mustered out with company Sept. 9, 1864.
Wilber, William F	...do....	31	May 2, 1864	100 dys.	Mustered out with company Sept. 9, 1864.

Names.	Rank.	Age.	Date of Entering the Service.	Period of Service.	Remarks.
Overhoult, Joseph A	Private	19	May 2, 1864	100 dys.	Mustered out with company Sept. 9, 1864.
Overhoult, Martin	do	20	May 2, 1864	100 dys.	Mustered out with company Sept. 9, 1864.
Page, Jirah P	do	17	May 2, 1864	100 dys.	Mustered out with company Sept. 9, 1864.
Peck, Adelbert E	do	21	May 2, 1864	100 dys.	Mustered out with company Sept. 9, 1864.
Piper, Benjamin E	do	19	May 2, 1864	100 dys.	Mustered out with company Sept. 9, 1864.
Rasor, Charles J	do	18	May 2, 1864	100 dys.	Mustered out with company Sept. 9, 1864.
Rettig, Romeo R	do	18	May 2, 1864	100 dys.	Mustered out with company Sept. 9, 1864.
Rounds, Frank A	do	18	May 2, 1864	100 dys.	Mustered out with company Sept. 9, 1864.
Sanford, Gordon F	do	18	May 2, 1864	100 dys.	Mustered out with company Sept. 9, 1864.
Shane, James B	do	23	May 2, 1864	100 dys.	Mustered out with company Sept. 9, 1864.
Smolk, Hiram	do	28	May 2, 1864	100 dys.	Mustered out with company Sept. 9, 1864.
Squire, Julius	do	28	May 15, 1864	100 dys.	Mustered out with company Sept. 9, 1864.
Stone, Henry A	do	26	May 2, 1864	100 dys.	Mustered out with company Sept. 9, 1864.
Tyler, Nathan	do	18	May 2, 1864	100 dys.	Mustered out with company Sept. 9, 1864.
Vaughn, John J. S	do	24	May 2, 1864	100 dys.	Mustered out with company Sept. 9, 1864.
Vaugh, Joshua R	do	33	May 2, 1864	100 dys.	Mustered out with company Sept. 9, 1864.
Vonwie, Anthony	do	31	May 2, 1864	100 dys.	Mustered out with company Sept. 9, 1864.
Whitney, Herman W	do	38	May 2, 1864	100 dys.	Mustered out with company Sept. 9, 1864.
Whitney, Theodore B	do	24	May 2, 1864	100 dys.	Mustered out with company Sept. 9, 1864.
Wilson, Orange B	do	31	May 2, 1864	100 dys.	Mustered out with company Sept. 9, 1864.
Wolcott, Chester J	do	20	May 2, 1864	100 dys.	Mustered out with company Sept. 9, 1864.
Zimmerman, Daniel	do	29	May 2, 1864	100 dys.	Mustered out with company Sept. 9, 1864.

COMPANY F.

Mustered in May 15, 1864, at Camp Cleveland, O., by W. L. Kellogg, 1st Lieutenant 10th Infantry, U. S. A. Mustered out Sept. 9, 1864, at Camp Cleveland, O., by C. B. Throckmorton, 1st Lieutenant 4th Artillery, U. S. A.

Names.	Rank.	Age.	Date of Entering the Service.	Period of Service.	Remarks.
William Bigham	Captain	29	May 2, 1864	100 dys.	Mustered out with company Sept. 9, 1864.
Daniel Shaw	1st Lieut.	30	May 2, 1864	100 dys.	Mustered out with company Sept. 9, 1864.
Stiles A. Hosmer	2d Lieut.	35	May 2, 1864	100 dys.	Mustered out with company Sept. 9, 1864.
J. D. Ross	1st Sergt.	26	May 2, 1864	100 dys.	Mustered out with company Sept. 9, 1864.
Levett K. Hosmer	Sergeant.	23	May 2, 1864	100 dys.	Mustered out with company Sept. 9, 1864.
Eli J. Kelder	do	23	May 2, 1864	100 dys.	Mustered out with company Sept. 9, 1864.
O. Strong	do	20	May 2, 1864	100 dys.	Mustered out with company Sept. 9, 1864.
Herbert S. Ross	do	19	May 2, 1864	100 dys.	Mustered out with company Sept. 9, 1864.
Ervin Bartholomew	Corporal.	19	May 2, 1864	100 dys.	Mustered out with company Sept. 9, 1864.
William Cotton	do	38	May 2, 1864	100 dys.	Mustered out with company Sept. 9, 1864.
Charles H. Dix	do	17	May 2, 1864	100 dys.	Mustered out with company Sept. 9, 1864.
Orelmus Graves	do	31	May 2, 1864	100 dys.	Mustered out with company Sept. 9, 1864.
Charles Leland	do	18	May 2, 1864	100 dys.	Mustered out with company Sept. 9, 1864.
George D. McDonald	do	28	May 2, 1864	100 dys.	Mustered out with company Sept. 9, 1864.
I. J. Rickard	do	39	May 2, 1864	100 dys.	Mustered out with company Sept. 9, 1864.
W. Crawford	do	19	May 2, 1864	100 dys.	Mustered out with company Sept. 9, 1864.
Agness, Thomas	Private	44	May 2, 1864	100 dys.	Mustered out with company Sept. 9, 1864.
Ainsworth, Danforth	do	18	May 2, 1864	100 dys.	Mustered out with company Sept. 9, 1864.
Andrews, Edwin E	do	34	May 15, 1864	100 dys.	Mustered out with company Sept. 9, 1864.
Arnett, Cyrus	do	18	May 2, 1864	100 dys.	
Bergy, Joseph K	do	32	May 2, 1864	100 dys.	Mustered out with company Sept. 9, 1864.
Blakeman, J. H	do	29	May 2, 1864	100 dys.	Mustered out with company Sept. 9, 1864.
Bull, Frank D	do	15	May 15, 1864	100 dys.	Mustered out with company Sept. 9, 1864.
Cannon Perry	do	18	May 2, 1864	100 dys.	Mustered out with company Sept. 9, 1864.
Caughey, James H	do	23	May 2, 1864	100 dys.	Mustered out with company Sept. 9, 1864.
Caughey, I. H. Rollin	do	13	May 2, 1864	100 dys.	Mustered out with company Sept. 9, 1864.
Chapin, Roswell	do	..	May 2, 1864	100 dys.	Mustered out with company Sept. 9, 1864.
Cook, Elisha B	do	18	May 2, 1864	100 dys.	Mustered out with company Sept. 9, 1864.
Cotton Gilbert L	do	18	May 2, 1864	100 dys.	Mustered out with company Sept. 9, 1864.
Cotton [illegible]	do	40	May 2, 1864	100 dys.	Mustered out with company Sept. 9, 1864.
Coulborn, Marion J	do	18	May 2, 1864	100 dys.	Mustered out with company Sept. 9, 1864.
Dix, Julius B	do	30	May 2, 1864	100 dys.	Mustered out with company Sept. 9, 1864.
Easton, Giles H	do	30	May 2, 1864	100 dys.	Mustered out with company Sept. 9, 1864.
Easton, Lucius A	do	39	May 2, 1864	100 dys.	Mustered out with company Sept. 9, 1864.
Fisher, Spencer	do	19	May 2, 1864	100 dys.	Mustered out with company Sept. 9, 1864.
Foster, Melvin E	do	22	May 2, 1864	100 dys.	Mustered out with company Sept. 9, 1864.
Fox, Alexander	do	32	May 2, 1864	100 dys.	Mustered out with company Sept. 9, 1864.
Fritz, Allen P	do	24	May 2, 1864	100 dys.	Mustered out with company Sept. 9, 1864.
Fritz, David J	do	29	May 2, 1864	100 dys.	Mustered out with company Sept. 9, 1864.
Graves, John T	do	26	May 2, 1864	100 dys.	Mustered out with company Sept. 9, 1864.
Grey, Isaac J	do	19	May 2, 1864	100 dys.	Mustered out with company Sept. 9, 1864.
Hay, George H	do	20	May 2, 1864	100 dys.	Mustered out with company Sept. 9, 1864.
Hill, Frank	do	18	May 2, 1864	100 dys.	Mustered out with company Sept. 9, 1864.
Hoisington, George	do	18	May 2, 1864	100 dys.	Mustered out with company Sept. 9, 1864.
Hosmer, Hom[illegible] I	do	33	May 2, 1864	100 dys.	Mustered out with company Sept. 9, 1864.
James, Thomas	do	44	May 2, 1864	100 dys.	Mustered out with company Sept. 9, 1864.
Johnson, Stephen K	do	32	May 2, 1864	100 dys.	Mustered out with company Sept. 9, 1864.
Kidd, William K	do	20	May 2, 1864	100 dys.	Mustered out with company Sept. 9, 1864.
Kindig, John H	do	35	May 2, 1864	100 dys.	Mustered out with company Sept. 9, 1864.
Koppes, David	do	23	May 2, 1864	100 dys.	Mustered out with company Sept. 9, 1864.
Lancaster, Joseph	do	38	May 2, 1864	100 dys.	Mustered out with company Sept. 9, 1864.
McDonald, Andrew L	do	18	May 2, 1864	100 dys.	Mustered out with company Sept. 9, 1864.

Names.	Rank.	Age.	Date of Entering the Service.	Period of Service.	Remarks.
Devoignes, Julius	Private.	28	May 2, 1864	100 dys.	Mustered out with company Sept. 9, 1864.
Dobbins, James M	...do...	25	May 2, 1864	100 dys.	Mustered out with company Sept. 9, 1864.
Dobbins, Samuel	...do...	19	May 2, 1864	100 dys.	Mustered out with company Sept. 9, 1864.
Dunham George D.	...do...	19	May 2, 1864	100 dys.	Mustered out with company Sept. 9, 1864.
Firestone, Eugene	...do...	16	May 2, 1864	100 dys.	Mustered out with company Sept. 9, 1864.
First, Samuel	...do...	31	May 2, 1864	100 dys.	Mustered out with company Sept. 9, 1864.
Foltz, Samuel	...do...	30	May 2, 1864	100 dys.	Mustered out with company Sept. 9, 1864.
Foltz, William H	...do...	24	May 2, 1864	100 dys.	Mustered out with company Sept. 9, 1864.
Freeze, George	...do...	23	May 2, 1864	100 dys.	Mustered out with company Sept. 9, 1864.
Fry, Henry	...do...	18	May 2, 1864	100 dys.	Mustered out with company Sept. 9, 1864.
Greene, Joshua	...do...	28	May 2, 1864	100 dys.	Mustered out with company Sept. 9, 1864.
Grow, Samuel	...do...	18	May 2, 1864	100 dys.	Mustered out with company Sept. 9, 1864.
Hackett, George	...do...	31	May 2, 1864	100 dys.	Mustered out with company Sept. 9, 1864.
Hackett, William H	...do...	19	May 2, 1864	100 dys.	Mustered out with company Sept. 9, 1864.
Hanna, Alexander	...do...	26	May 2, 1864	100 dys.	Mustered out with company Sept. 9, 1864.
Hayes, Levi	...do...	19	May 2, 1864	100 dys.	Mustered out with company Sept. 9, 1864.
Keys, Thomas C	...do...	18	May 2, 1864	100 dys.	Mustered out with company Sept. 9, 1864.
Kilgore, Philo	...do...	18	May 2, 1864	100 dys.	Mustered out with company Sept. 9, 1864.
Knox, William M.	...do...	39	May 2, 1864	100 dys.	Mustered out with company Sept. 9, 1864.
Lennix, John.	...do...	18	May 2, 1864	100 dys.	Mustered out with company Sept. 9, 1864.
Lisle, George R	...do...	22	May 2, 1864	100 dys.	Mustered out with company Sept. 9, 1864.
Lisle, Thomas.	...do...	28	May 2, 1864	100 dys.	Mustered out with company Sept. 9, 1864.
McCay, William F	...do...	24	May 2, 1864	100 dys.	Mustered out with company Sept. 9, 1864.
McMillan, James P	...do...	42	May 2, 1864	100 dys.	Mustered out with company Sept. 9, 1864.
Maize, Horace A	...do...	19	May 2, 1864	100 dys.	Mustered out with company Sept. 9, 1864.
Mauk, John F.	...do...	18	May 2, 1864	100 dys.	Mustered out with company Sept. 9, 1864.
Melong, Samuel	...do...	26	May 2, 1864	100 dys.	Mustered out with company Sept. 9, 1864.
Miller, Amos	...do...	19	May 2, 1864	100 dys.	Mustered out with company Sept. 9, 1864.
Mirinez, Adolphus	...do...	16	May 2, 1864	100 dys.	Mustered out with company Sept. 9, 1864.
Newman, David W	...do...	25	May 2, 1864	100 dys.	Mustered out with company Sept. 9, 1864.
Nixon, Solomon	...do...	18	May 2, 1864	100 dys.	Mustered out with company Sept. 9, 1864.
Ott, John A	...do...	18	May 2, 1864	100 dys.	Mustered out with company Sept. 9, 1864.
Patrick, Samuel K	...do...	17	May 2, 1864	100 dys.	Mustered out with company Sept. 9, 1864.
Peppards, Franklin W	...do...	42	May 2, 1864	100 dys.	Discharged Sept. 12, 1864, at Newton U. S. General Hospital, Baltimore, Md., on surgeon's certificate of disability.
Pocock, Eli	...do...	18	May 2, 1864	100 dys.	Mustered out with company Sept. 9, 1864.
Pocock, John F	...do...	18	May 2, 1864	100 dys.	Mustered out with company Sept. 9, 1864.
Porter, William S.	...do...	16	May 2, 1864	100 dys.	Mustered out with company Sept. 9, 1864.
Richards Samuel A	...do...	24	May 2, 1864	100 dys.	Mustered out with company Sept. 9, 1864.
Robertson, James W	...do...	22	May 2, 1864	100 dys.	Mustered out with company Sept. 9, 1864.
Seward John W	...do...	37	May 2, 1864	100 dys.	Mustered out with company Sept. 9, 1864.
Shriber, Henry	...do...	32	May 2, 1864	100 dys.	Mustered out with company Sept. 9, 1864.
Shoup, James H	...do...	20	May 2, 1864	100 dys.	Mustered out with company Sept. 9, 1864.
Stoner, David	...do...	33	May 2, 1864	100 dys.	Mustered out with company Sept. 9, 1864.
Swartz, Ira A	...do...	19	May 2, 1864	100 dys.	Mustered out with company Sept. 9, 1864.
Thompson, Cyrus	...do...	26	May 2, 1864	100 dys.	Mustered out with company Sept. 9, 1864.
Throckmartin, Allen	...do...	35	May 2, 1864	100 dys.	Mustered out with company Sept. 9, 1864.
Tidball, Abraham	...do...	36	May 2, 1864	100 dys.	Mustered out with company Sept. 9, 1864.
Tracy, Jacob	...do...	25	May 2, 1864	100 dys.	Mustered out with company Sept. 9, 1864.
Tracy, John W	...do...	18	May 2, 1864	100 dys.	Mustered out with company Sept. 9, 1864.
Truesdale, David P	...do...	39	May 2, 1864	100 dys.	Mustered out with company Sept. 9, 1864.
Truesdale, Eli	...do...	25	May 2, 1864	100 dys.	Mustered out with company Sept. 9, 1864.
Warner, John	...do...	18	May 2, 1864	100 dys.	Mustered out with company Sept. 9, 1864.
Wells, Benjamin	...do...	39	May 2, 1864	100 dys.	Mustered out with company Sept. 9, 1864.
White, John C	...do...	18	May 2, 1864	100 dys.	Mustered out with company Sept. 9, 1864.
Yocum, Charles M	...do...	22	May 2, 1864	100 dys.	Mustered out with company Sept. 9, 1864.

COMPANY H.

Mustered in May 15, 1864, at Camp Cleveland, O., by W. L. Kellogg, 1st Lieutenant 10th Infantry, U. S. A. Mustered out Sept. 9, 1864, at Camp Cleveland, O., by C. B. Throckmorton, 1st Lieutenant 4th Artillery, U. S. A.

Names.	Rank.	Age.	Date of Entering the Service.	Period of Service.	Remarks.
Benjamin F. McCormick	Captain.	44	May 2, 1864	100 dys.	Mustered out with company Sept. 9, 1864.
Sidney M. Owen	1st Lieut.	25	May 2, 1864	100 dys.	Mustered out with company Sept. 9, 1864.
John E. LaBarre	2d Lieut.	35	May 2, 1864	100 dys.	Mustered out with company Sept. 9, 1864.
Albert Gage	1st Sergt.	35	May 15, 1864	100 dys.	Mustered out with company Sept. 9, 1864.
Doctor F. Brown	Sergeant.	38	May 2, 1864	100 dys.	Mustered out with company Sept. 9, 1864.
John Heffner	...do...	44	May 2, 1864	100 dys.	Mustered out with company Sept. 9, 1864.
Henry L. Moore	...do...	43	May 2, 1864	100 dys.	Mustered out with company Sept. 9, 1864.
William F Smith	...do...	32	May 2, 1864	100 dys.	Mustered out with company Sept. 9, 1864.
Joseph Briggs	Corporal.	39	May 2, 1864	100 dys.	Mustered out with company Sept. 9, 1864.
Albert L. Crosby	...do...	23	May 2, 1864	100 dys.	Mustered out with company Sept. 9, 1864.
Leonard R. Fornwald	...do...	22	May 2, 1864	100 dys.	Mustered out with company Sept. 9, 1864.
Marcus S. Miles	...do...	21	May 2, 1864	100 dys.	Mustered out with company Sept. 9, 1864.
David Simmerlin	...do...	21	May 2, 1864	100 dys.	Mustered out with company Sept. 9, 1864.
Thomas C. Trimmer	...do...	28	May 15, 1864	100 dys.	Mustered out with company Sept. 9, 1864; borne on rolls as Thomas Simson.

Names.	Rank.	Age.	Date of Entering the Service.	Period of Service.	Remarks.
Vogle, William H.	Private.	18	May 2, 1864	100 dys.	Mustered out with company Sept. 9, 1864.
Watrous, Daniel S.	....do....	20	May 2, 1864	100 dys.	Mustered out with company Sept. 9, 1864.
Wheaton, William	....do....	23	May 2, 1864	100 dys.	Mustered out with company Sept. 9, 1864.
Winslow, Humphrey	....do....	19	May 2, 1864	100 dys.	
Woodruff, Peter V.	....do....	37	May 2, 1864	100 dys.	Mustered out with company Sept. 9, 1864.

COMPANY I.

Mustered in May 13, 1864, at Camp Cleveland, O., by Thomas Drummond, Captain 5th Cavalry, U. S. A. Mustered out Sept. 9, 1864, at Camp Cleveland, O., by C. B. Throckmorton, 1st Lieutenant 4th Artillery, U. S. A.

Names.	Rank.	Age.	Date of Entering the Service.	Period of Service.	Remarks.
Abraham B. Rudy	Captain.	34	May 2, 1864	100 dys.	Mustered out with company Sept. 9, 1864.
James G. Carr	1st Lieut.	..	May 2, 1864	100 dys.	Mustered out with company Sept. 9, 1864.
John G. Frizell	2d Lieut.	30	May 2, 1864	100 dys.	Mustered out with company Sept. 9, 1864.
Edward H. Hull	1st Sergt.	43	May 2, 1864	100 dys.	Mustered out with company Sept. 9, 1864.
John M. Snyder	Sergeant.	21	May 2, 1864	100 dys.	Mustered out with company Sept. 9, 1864.
John C. Donahey	....do....	31	May 2, 1864	100 dys.	Mustered out with company Sept. 9, 1864.
Leonard Harrison	....do....	19	May 2, 1864	100 dys.	Mustered out with company Sept. 9, 1864.
Jacob E. Hoyman	....do....	20	May 2, 1864	100 dys.	Died Aug. 2, 1864, at Fort Ward Hospital, Va.
James J. Bell	Corporal.	40	May 2, 1864	100 dys.	Mustered out with company Sept. 9, 1864.
David T. Simpson	....do....	32	May 2, 1864	100 dys.	Mustered out with company Sept. 9, 1864.
William Miller	....do....	20	May 2, 1864	100 dys.	Mustered out with company Sept. 9, 1864.
Sanford Harrison	....do....	19	May 2, 1864	100 dys.	Mustered out with company Sept. 9, 1864.
Isaac [illegible]yers	....do....	38	May 2, 1864	100 dys.	Mustered out with company Sept. 9, 1864.
Henry Johnson	....do....	40	May 2, 1864	100 dys.	Mustered out with company Sept. 9, 1864.
William C. McCaughey	....do....	25	May 2, 1864	100 dys.	Mustered out with company Sept. 9, 1864.
Alexander Mitchell	....do....	27	May 2, 1864	100 dys.	Mustered out with company Sept. 9, 1864.
Edward H. McKee	Musician	18	May 2, 1864	100 dys.	Mustered out with company Sept. 9, 1864.
Barnthouse, Thomas	Private.	18	May 2, 1864	100 dys.	Mustered out with company Sept. 9, 1864.
Beaty, Marshall	....do....	32	May 2, 1864	100 dys.	Mustered out with company Sept. 9, 1864.
Beeson, Isaac	....do....	30	May 2, 1864	100 dys.	Mustered out with company Sept. 9, 1864.
Brooks, William	....do....	20	May 2, 1864	100 dys.	Mustered out with company Sept. 9, 1864.
Buchanan, Thomas	....do....	21	May 2, 1864	100 dys.	Mustered out with company Sept. 9, 1864.
Butler, Allen	....do....	50	May 2, 1864	100 dys.	Mustered out with company Sept. 9, 1864.
Close, Jacob	....do....	36	May 2, 1864	100 dys.	Died Aug. 8, 1864, at Camp Chase, O.
Close, Solomon	....do....	38	May 2, 1864	100 dys.	Mustered out with company Sept. 9, 1864.
Corbus, Josephus R.	....do....	21	May 2, 1864	100 dys.	Promoted to Hospital Steward May 25, 1864.
Dellinger, Jacob	....do....	40	May 2, 1864	100 dys.	Mustered out with company Sept. 9, 1864.
Douglas, Andrew	....do....	18	May 2, 1864	100 dys.	Mustered out with company Sept. 9, 1864.
Druhaut, John	....do....	18	May 2, 1864	100 dys.	Mustered out with company Sept. 9, 1864.
Duncan, James E.	....do....	18	May 2, 1864	100 dys.	Mustered out with company Sept. 9, 1864.
Durler, Alexander	....do....	22	May 2, 1864	100 dys.	Mustered out with company Sept. 9, 1864.
Ensly, James C.	....do....	33	May 2, 1864	100 dys.	Mustered out with company Sept. 9, 1864.
Foust, Charles	....do....	19	May 2, 1864	100 dys.	Mustered out with company Sept. 9, 1864.
Freshwater, Isaac	....do....	37	May 2, 1864	100 dys.	Mustered out with company Sept. 9, 1864.
Gard, William H.	....do....	27	May 2, 1864	100 dys.	Mustered out with company Sept. 9, 1864.
Gephart, Philip	....do....	18	May 2, 1864	100 dys.	Mustered out with company Sept. 9, 1864.
Graham, John F.	....do....	26	May 2, 1864	100 dys.	Mustered out with company Sept. 9, 1864.
Graham, William G.	....do....	21	May 2, 1864	100 dys.	Mustered out with company Sept. 9, 1864.
Green, David H.	....do....	18	May 2, 1864	100 dys.	Mustered out with company Sept. 9, 1864.
Hall, Edward L.	....do....	27	May 2, 1864	100 dys.	Discharged July 6, 1864, on Surgeon's certificate of disability.
Hall, Samuel	....do....	21	May 2, 1864	100 dys.	Mustered out with company Sept. 9, 1864.
Hammond, Livingston	....do....	19	May 2, 1864	100 dys.	Died Aug. 9, 1864, at Camp Chase, O.
Hand, Albert	....do....	18	May 2, 1864	100 dys.	Mustered out with company Sept. 9, 1864.
Hites, John	....do....	44	May 2, 1864	100 dys.	Mustered out with company Sept. 9, 1864.
Hochstetler, Samuel C.	....do....	19	May 2, 1864	100 dys.	Mustered out with company Sept. 9, 1864.
Hochstetler, William	....do....	18	May 2, 1864	100 dys.	Mustered out with company Sept. 9, 1864.
Holser, Christian	....do....	18	May 2, 1864	100 dys.	Mustered out with company Sept. 9, 1864.
Howard, Robert	....do....	21	May 2, 1864	100 dys.	Mustered out with company Sept. 9, 1864.
Huffman, Rudolph	....do....	21	May 2, 1864	100 dys.	Mustered out with company Sept. 9, 1864.
Huston, John	....do....	26	May 2, 1864	100 dys.	Mustered out with company Sept. 9, 1864.
Huston, Robert	....do....	18	May 2, 1864	100 dys.	Mustered out with company Sept. 9, 1864.
Hutchinson, Samuel L.	....do....	40	May 2, 1864	100 dys.	Mustered out with company Sept. 9, 1864.
Ing[illegible]s, Andrew	....do....	44	May 2, 1864	100 dys.	Mustered out with company Sept. 9, 1864.
Johnston, Andrew	....do....	29	May 2, 1864	100 dys.	Mustered out with company Sept. 9, 1864.
Lee, David	....do....	18	May 2, 1864	100 dys.	Mustered out with company Sept. 9, 1864.
Lee, Howard	....do....	18	May 2, 1864	100 dys.	Mustered out with company Sept. 9, 1864.
Lemmon, Samuel	....do....	40	May 2, 1864	100 dys.	Mustered out with company Sept. 9, 1864.
Ling, Josiah	....do....	44	May 2, 1864	100 dys.	Mustered out with company Sept. 9, 1864.
Linn, Isaiah B.	....do....	42	May 2, 1864	100 dys.	Mustered out with company Sept. 9, 1864.
Linn, John F.	....do....	19	May 2, 1864	100 dys.	Mustered out with company Sept. 9, 1864.
McCartney, William P.	....do....	21	May 2, 1864	100 dys.	Mustered out with company Sept. 9, 1864.
McCaughey, James L.	....do....	23	May 2, 1864	100 dys.	Mustered out with company Sept. 9, 1864.
McKenzie, James	....do....	38	May 2, 1864	100 dys.	Mustered out with company Sept. 9, 1864.
McKenzie, Samuel	....do....	29	May 2, 1864	100 dys.	Mustered out with company Sept. 9, 1864.
McKenzie, William A.	....do....	31	May 2, 1864	100 dys.	Mustered out with company Sept. 9, 1864.
McLaughlin, George	....do....	19	May 2, 1864	100 dys.	Mustered out with company Sept. 9, 1864.
McLaughlin, James	....do....	19	May 2, 1864	100 dys.	Mustered out with company Sept. 9, 1864.

Names.	Rank.	Age.	Date of Entering the Service.	Period of Service.	
Grant, Parkinson	Private	[illegible]	May 2, 1864	100 dys.	Mustered out
Guenther, Jacob	do	27	May 2, 1864	100 dys.	Mustered out
Guenther, Philip	do	25	May 2, 1864	100 dys.	Mustered
Harbaugh, David	do	18	May 2, 1864	100 dys.	Mustered out
Harding, Daniel	do	25	May 2, 1864	100 dys.	Mustered out
Harris, Ellis J	do	[illegible]	May 2, 1864	100 dys.	Mustered out
Harris, Henry B	do	27	May 2, 1864	100 dys.	Mustered out
Harris, Nelson	do	[illegible]	May 2, 1864	100 dys.	Mustered out
Heath, Martin W	do	[illegible]	May 2, 1864	100 dys.	Mustered out
Hishew, William	do	30	May 2, 1864	100 dys.	Mustered out
Homer, John	do	20	May 2, 1864	100 dys.	Mustered out
Homer, Peter	do	34	May 2, 1864	100 dys.	Mustered out
Hough, Abraham	do	34	May 2, 1864	100 dys.	Mustered out
Hudson, John	do	[illegible]	May 2, 1864	100 dys.	Mustered out
Hudson, Thomas P	do	18	May 2, 1864	100 dys.	Mustered out
Hull, Abraham	do	19	May 2, 1864	100 dys.	Mustered out
Jones, Aaron	do	24	May 2, 1864	100 dys.	Mustered out
Jones, George	do	19	May 2, 1864	100 dys.	Mustered out
Jones, Nathan	do	28	May 2, 1864	100 dys.	Mustered out
Keiser, Louis	do	29	May 2, 1864	100 dys.	Mustered out
Kline, Abraham	do	25	May 2, 1864	100 dys.	Mustered out
Knox, Thomas	do	18	May 2, 1864	100 dys.	Mustered out
Koms, John	do	19	May 2, 1864	100 dys.	Mustered out
Leach, Benjamin	do	18	May 2, 1864	100 dys.	Mustered out
Lee, Stephen	do	20	May 2, 1864	100 dys.	Died Aug. 22,
Lentzy, William L	do	20	May 2, 1864	100 dys.	Mustered out
Liggett, Cyrus S	do	30	May 2, 1864	100 dys.	Mustered out
Liggett, James	do	25	May 2, 1864	100 dys.	Mustered out
Liggett, James T	do	25	May 2, 1864	100 dys.	Mustered out
Liggett, Robert R	do	20	May 2, 1864	100 dys.	Mustered out
Longshore, Mahlon	do	43	May 2, 1864	100 dys.	Mustered out
Lozier, Eli J	do	21	May 2, 1864	100 dys.	Mustered out
Lozier, George P	do	40	May 2, 1864	100 dys.	Mustered out
McClaran, Clark	do	18	May 2, 1864	100 dys.	Mustered out
McIntire, James W	do	40	May 2, 1864	100 dys.	Mustered out
McIntire, Hiram	do	18	May 2, 1864	100 dys.	Mustered out
Mattock, David	do	24	May 2, 1864	100 dys.	Mustered out
Mattock, Samuel	do	18	May 2, 1864	100 dys.	Mustered out
Moore, James W	do	30	May 2, 1864	100 dys.	Mustered out
Moore, John J	do	18	May 2, 1864	100 dys.	Mustered out
Newton, La Fayette	do	40	May 2, 1864	100 dys.	Mustered out
Nouse, Henry	do	41	May 2, 1864	100 dys.	Mustered out
Orr, Josiah	do	44	May 2, 1864	100 dys.	Mustered out
Painter, Alfred S. C	do	20	May 2, 1864	100 dys.	Mustered out
Perdue, George	do	21	May 2, 1864	100 dys.	Mustered out
Peters, Joseph D	do	19	May 2, 1864	100 dys.	Mustered out
Platz, William	do	41	May 2, 1864	100 dys.	Mustered out
Robison, Jonas W	do	20	May 2, 1864	100 dys.	Mustered out
Rowland, James H	do	28	May 2, 1864	100 dys.	Mustered out
Seibert, John C	do	18	May 2, 1864	100 dys.	Mustered out
Shank, James	do	21	May 2, 1864	100 dys.	Mustered out
Sleggel, William	do	19	May 2, 1864	100 dys.	Mustered out
Smith, Gilbert A	do	19	May 2, 1864	100 dys.	Mustered out
Smith, James	do	19	May 2, 1864	100 dys.	Mustered out
Stout, William	do	25	May 2, 1864	100 dys.	Mustered out
Swaggard, John L	do	21	May 2, 1864	100 dys.	Mustered out
Taylor, Samuel S	do	29	May 2, 1864	100 dys.	Mustered out
Taylor, William L	do	19	May 2, 1864	100 dys.	Mustered out
Thomas, Ebenezer	do	28	May 2, 1864	100 dys.	Mustered out
Thomas, Louis D	do	18	May 2, 1864	100 dys.	Mustered out
Thompson, Robert R	do	31	May 2, 1864	100 dys.	Mustered out
Turney, Amos	do	30	May 2, 1864	100 dys.	Mustered out
Wachtel, Abraham	do	34	May 2, 1864	100 dys.	Mustered out
Weatherbee, John	do	28	May 2, 1864	100 dys.	Mustered out
Wiggins, Harrison	do	28	May 2, 1864	100 dys.	Mustered out
Wiggins, Isaac	do	38	May 2, 1864	100 dys.	Mustered out
Wright, Joseph	do	48	May 2, 1864	100 dys.	Mustered out
Zollers, John	do	43	May 2, 1864	100 dys.	Mustered out

167th Regiment Ohio Volunteer Infantry.

ONE HUNDRED DAYS' SERVICE.

THIS Regiment was organized at Hamilton, O., May 14, 16 and 17, 1864, to serve one hundred days. It was composed of the Sixty-first and Sixty-fifth Battalions, Ohio National Guard, from Butler County. Two days after muster-in the Regiment received orders to proceed to Charleston, W. Va., which place it reached on the 21st of May, and reported to Colonel Ewart, commanding the post. Six companies were immediately sent to Camp Piatt, and four to Gauley Bridge, relieving the Second, Third, and Seventh Regiments Virginia Cavalry. The points named were posts of supply, and the only duty the Regiment was called upon to perform was guarding Government stores and accompanying trains to and from the main bodies of the National forces in that part of Western Virginia. It was mustered out September 8, 1864, on expiration of its term of service.

Names.		Age.	Date of Entering the Service.		
Cone, William H........		20	May 2, 1864	100 dys.	Reduced from Cor with company Se
Davis, William R........	.do.	19	May 2, 1864	100 dys.	Mustered out with
Douglass, John H........	.do.	18	May 2, 1864	100 dys.	Mustered out with
Douglass, William C....	.do.	19	May 2, 1864	100 dys.	Mustered out with
Everett, C. Edward.....		28	May 2, 1864	100 dys.	Mustered out with
Farr, William L.........		20	May 2, 1864	100 dys.	Mustered out with
Ferguson, William M. .		19	May 2, 1864	100 dys	Mustered out with
Fisher, Samuel.........		56	May 2, 1864	100 dys	Promoted to Princi
Garrod, Orby F.........	....do....	22	May 2, 1864	100 dys.	Mustered out with
Garrod, Walter J.......		24	May 2, 1864	100 dys.	Mustered out with
Gill, Heber...............		21	May 2, 1864	100 dys.	Mustered out with
Graham, Harvey W......	....do....	18	May 2, 1864	100 dys.	Mustered out with
Harmon, George O......	....do....	19	May 2, 1864	100 dys	Mustered out with
Hatton, Lemuel C......		18	May 2, 1864	100 dys	Mustered out with
Haus, Jacob.............		23	May 2, 1864	100 dys	
Haseltine, William T...		25	May 2, 1864	100 dys.	Mustered out with
Herman, Frank.........		24	May 2, 1864	100 dys.	Mustered out with
Houren, Abner L........	....do....	38	May 2, 1864	100 dys.	Reduced from Co tered out with co
Mouston, Robert M. L...		19	May 2, 1864		Mustered out with
Howe, Francis M........		26	May 2, 1864		Mustered out with
Keely, George W........		41	May 2, 1864		Mustered out with
Kerwood, John W.		19	May 2, 1864		Mustered out with
Kingsley, George B......		46	May 2, 1864		Mustered out with
Kumler, William F.....		24	May 2, 1864		Mustered out with
Kyler, Henry L.........		37	May 2, 1864		Mustered out with
Lee, Harvey.............		18	May 2, 1864		Mustered out with
Lyons, James D.........		20	May 2, 1864		Mustered out with
Lyons, Robert L.........		18	May 2, 1864		Mustered out with
McArthur, John D......		32	May 2, 1864		Mustered out with
McClung, William C...		18	May 2, 1864		Mustered out with
McMillen, Duncan.......	. .	20	May 2, 1864		Mustered out with
Markle, Joseph B.........	. .	21	May 2, 1864		Mustered out with
Miller, Alexander,.......	. .	21	May 2, 1864		Mustered out with
Miller, John W...........	. .	23	May 2, 1864		Mustered out with
Mitchell, James M.....		21	May 2, 1864	dys.	Mustered out with
Mollyneaux, Joseph....		23	May 2, 1864	dys.	Mustered out with
Moore, Henry M.........		18	May 2, 1864	dys.	Mustered out with
Muller, Frederick W....	...do....	31	May 2, 1864	100	Mustered out with
Naggle, Frederick W....	...do....	22	May 2, 1864	100	Mustered out with
Parrish, Oakey V.........	...do....	19	May 2, 1864	100	Mustered out with
Rickey, Mortimer F.....		22	May 2, 1864	100	Mustered out with
Rollins, Edwin P.........		19	May 2, 1864	100	Mustered out with
Saunders, James M......		24	May 2, 1864	100	Mustered out with
Shears, Charles..........		20	May 2, 1864	100	Mustered out with
Sheppard, Samuel C....		20	May 2, 1864	100	Mustered out with
Shuey, Alfred............		18	May 2, 1864	100	Mustered out with
Skinner, Sidney M......		46	May 2, 1864	100	Mustered out with
Smith, George T.........		19	May 2, 1864	100	Died Aug. 14, 1864.
Smith, Palmer W........		18	May 2, 1864	100	Mustered out with
Stevick, George H.......		26	May 2, 1864	100	Mustered out with
Stork, Adam H...........		30	May 2, 1864	100	Mustered out with
Warner, Silas W.........		43	May 2, 1864	100	Mustered out with
White, Joseph B.........		24	May 2, 1864	100	Mustered out with

COMPANY B.

Mustered in May 17, 1864, at Hamilton, O., by T. D. Urmston, 1st Lieutenant 12th In out Sept. 8, 1864, at Hamilton, O., by C. P. Horton, Captain and

Edward T. Jones........	Captain.	30	May 2, 1864	100 dys.	Mustered out with
Samuel W. Woodruff...	1st Lieut.	24	May 2, 1864	100 dys.	Mustered out with
Crosby Vaughn	2d Lieut.	29	May 2, 1864	100 dys.	Mustered out with
David Mercer............	1st Sergt.	29	May 2, 1864	100 dys.	Mustered out with
James Scott..............	Sergeant.	34	May 2, 1864	100 dys.	Mustered out with
Isaac Erven..............	....do....	37	May 2, 1864	100 dys.	Mustered out with
James Dearmond.......	....do....	20	May 2, 1864	100 dys.	Mustered out with
Leonard G. Farr	....do....	21	May 2, 1864	100 dys.	Mustered out with
Levi Nease...............	Corporal.	31	May 2, 1864	100 dys.	Mustered out with
Maurice Jones...........	....do....	41	May 2, 1864	100 dys.	Mustered out with
Cornelius Stoughton....	....do....	36	May 2, 1864	100 dys.	Mustered out with
Thomas G. Caldwell....	....do....	34	May 2, 1864	100 dys.	Mustered out with
Alonzo Buell.............	....do....	32	May 2, 1864	100 dys.	Mustered out with
James E. Rebb...........	....do....	19	May 2, 1864	100 dys.	Mustered out with
Theodore Fields.........	....do....	33	May 2, 1864	100 dys.	Mustered out with
Evan B. Jones	....do....	24	May 2, 1864	100 dys.	Mustered out with
Appleton, Abel	Private..	26	May 2, 1864	100 dys	Mustered out with
Ashton, Richard.........	....do....	21	May 2, 1864	100 dys.	Mustered out with
Bebb, Thomas............	....do....	49	May 2, 1864	100 dys.	Mustered out with

Names.	Rank.	Age.	Date of Entering the Service.		
George Baumann	Corporal.	31	May 2, 1864	100 dys	Appointed
George Dilg	..do...	31	May 2, 1864		
Bender, Ernst	Private.	21	May 2, 1864	dys.	
Benzing, John	...do...	30	May 2, 1864	dys.	
Biehlman, John	...do...	28	May 2, 1864	dys.	
Blum, Ernst	...do...	38	May 2, 1864	100 dys.	
Boebel, Thomas	...do...	38	May 2, 1864	100 dys.	
Bonney, Robert	...do...	19	May 2, 1864	100 dys.	
Brinkman, J. H.	...do...	34	May 2, 1864	100 dys.	
Brinkman, William	...do...	22	May 2, 1864	100 dys.	
Brock, George	...do...	33	May 2, 1864	100 dys.	
Diefenbach, George	...do...	..	May 2, 1864	100 dys.	
Dilg, Frederick	...do...	18	May 2, 1864	100 dys.	
Dillman, Gabriel	...do...	35	May 2, 1864	100 dys.	
Donges, John	...do...	33	May 2, 1864	100 dys.	
Faist, Godfried	...do...	27	May 2, 1864	100 dys.	
Friedricks, August	...do...	35	May 2, 1864	100 dys.	Mustered
Fritz, Adolph	...do...	18	May 2, 1864	100 dys.	Mustered
Fritz, August	...do...	28	May 2, 1864	100 dys.	Mustered
Garver, John	...do...	40	May 2, 1864	100 dys.	Mustered
Gresde, Matthias	...do...	20	May 2, 1864	100 dys.	Mustered
Gromlsch, Michael	...do...	30	May 2, 1864	100 dys.	Mustered
Haferiepen, Anton	...do...	20	May 2, 1864	100 dys.	Mustered
Haller, Martin	...do...	38	May 2, 1864	100 dys.	Mustered
Heger, Nic	...do...	42	May 2, 1864	100 dys.	Mustered
Held, Philip	...do...	..	May 2, 1864	100 dys.	
Henes, Louis	...do...	36	May 2, 1864	100 dys.	Mustered
Herzog, Andreas	...do...	39	May 2, 1864	100 dys.	Mustered
Hess, Nathan	...do...	30	May 2, 1864		Mustered
Heuser, William	...do...	36	May 2, 1864		Mustered
Hoehle, Philip	...do...	38	May 2, 1864		Mustered
Huenker, George	...do...	28	May 2, 1864		Mustered
Iwig, John	...do...	24	May 2, 1864		Mustered
Jackson, Isaac	...do...	35	May 2, 1864		
Kappler, Mathias	...do...	35	May 2, 1864		
Keller, Ernst	...do...	32	May 2, 1864		
Lorenz, Jacob	...do...	26	May 2, 1864		
Meuche, Balthasar	...do...	38	May 2, 1864		
Moorman, Ernst	...do...	42	May 2, 1864		
Muller, John	...do...	34	May 2, 1864		
Murray, James	...do...	31	May 2, 1864		Mustered
Niederauer, Henry	...do...	27	May 2, 1864		Mustered
Papst, J. J.	...do...	35	May 2, 1864		Mustered
Pfeil, Valentine	...do...	30	May 2, 1864		Mustered
Reuter, Conrad	...do...	29	May 2, 1864		Mustered
Ross, C. D.	...do...	24	May 2, 1864		Mustered
Ruder, Charles	...do...	37	May 2, 1864		Mustered
Ruehl, George	...do...	40	May 2, 1864		Transferred ... tered ou
Schwarz, Joseph	...do...	27	May 2, 1864	dys.	Mustered
Severs, Henry	...do...	30	May 2, 1864	dys.	Mustered
Shaviel, Frank	...do...	35	May 2, 1864	dys.	
Symmes, Timothy	...do...	24	May 2, 1864	dys.	Mustered
Theis, Jacob	...do...	28	May 2, 1864	dys.	Mustered
Turner, Leonard	...do...	42	May 2, 1864	dys.	Mustered

COMPANY D.

Mustered in May 14, 1864, at Hamilton, O., by T. D. Urmston, 1st Lieutena... out Sept. 8, 1864, at Hamilton, O., by C. P. Horton, Cap...

Benjamin F. Bookwalter	Captain.	44	May 2, 1864	100 dys.	
Augustus W. Eckert	1st Lieut.	32	May 2, 1864	100 dys.	
Alexander P. Richardson	2d Lieut.	42	May 2, 1864	100 dys.	
James Ray	1st Sergt.	25	May 2, 1864	100 dys.	Mustered
William F. Wilson	Sergeant.	33	May 2, 1864	100 dys.	Mustered
Martin O. Beam	...do...	22	May 2, 1864	100 dys.	Mustered
Job S. Inman	...do...	20	May 2, 1864	100 dys.	Mustered
John Jacobs	...do...	20	May 2, 1864	100 dys.	Mustered
Amos D. Kumler	Corporal.	33	May 2, 1864	100 dys.	Mustered
John Smith	...do...	21	May 2, 1864	100 dys.	Mustered
Samuel C. Rose	...do...	35	May 2, 1864	100 dys.	Mustered
Brown, Wilson	...do...	22	May 2, 1864	100 dys.	Mustered
William F. Jacobs	...do...	41	May 2, 1864	100 dys.	Mustered
Elliott Huffman	...do...	27	May 2, 1864	100 dys.	Mustered
John Fellers	...do...	26	May 2, 1864	100 dys.	Appointed ... compan

	Rank.	Age.	Date of Entering the Service.	Period of Service.	Remarks.
Eli Beam	Corporal.	26	May 2, 1864	100 dys.	Appointed June 20, 1864; mustered out with company Sept. 8, 1864.
Baird, James H		23	May 2, 1864	100 dys.	Mustered out with company Sept. 8, 1864.
Beam, Jacob F		19	May 2, 1864	100 dys.	Mustered out with company Sept. 8, 1864.
Blane, John		38	May 2, 1864	100 dys.	Mustered out with company Sept. 8, 1864.
Boyer, George		31	May 2, 1864	100 dys.	Mustered out with company Sept. 8, 1864.
Bosh, Frederick		35	May 2, 1864	100 dys.	Mustered out with company Sept. 8, 1864.
Braden, George W		21	May 2, 1864	100 dys.	Mustered out with company Sept. 8, 1864.
Campbell, Hezekiah		24	May 2, 1864	100 dys.	Mustered out with company Sept. 8, 1864.
Carr, Charles		39	May 2, 1864	100 dys.	Mustered out with company Sept. 8, 1864.
Conger, David N		38	May 2, 1864	100 dys.	Mustered out with company Sept. 8, 1864.
Crist, Allison R		38	May 2, 1864	100 dys.	Reduced from Corporal June 20, 1864; mustered out with company Sept. 8, 1864.
Crosby, James N	...do...	26	May 2, 1864	100 dys.	Mustered out with company Sept. 8, 1864.
Curtis, Joseph	...do...	17	May 2, 1864	100 dys.	Mustered out with company Sept. 8, 1864.
Emrick, Charles	...do...	18	May 2, 1864	100 dys.	Mustered out with company Sept. 8, 1864.
Fellers, David	...do...	32	May 2, 1864	100 dys.	Mustered out with company Sept. 8, 1864.
Graft, Abraham	...do...	43	May 2, 1864	100 dys.	Mustered out with company Sept. 8, 1864.
High, Nathaniel	...do...	41	May 2, 1864	100 dys.	Mustered out with company Sept. 8, 1864.
Hoel, Firman	...do...	24	May 2, 1864	100 dys.	Mustered out with company Sept. 8, 1864.
Huffman, William	...do...	29	May 2, 1864	100 dys.	Mustered out with company Sept. 8, 1864.
Hunsicker, John		..	May 2, 1864	100 dys.	Reduced from Corporal June 20, 1864; mustered out with company Sept. 8, 1864.
Jenkins, James		43	May 2, 1864	100 dys.	Mustered out with company Sept. 8, 1864.
Kumler, Jacob H		25	May 2, 1864	100 dys.	Mustered out with company Sept. 8, 1864.
Kumler, William E		36	May 2, 1864	100 dys.	Mustered out with company Sept. 8, 1864.
Louthan, William H		18	May 2, 1864	100 dys.	Mustered out with company Sept. 8, 1864.
McCain, William		19	May 2, 1864	100 dys.	Mustered out with company Sept. 8, 1864.
McKee, George		22	May 2, 1864	100 dys.	Mustered out with company Sept. 8, 1864.
Martin, Potter		19	May 2, 1864	100 dys.	Mustered out with company Sept. 8, 1864.
Mikesell, Andrew		19	May 2, 1864	100 dys.	Mustered out with company Sept. 8, 1864.
Myers, William		18	May 2, 1864	100 dys.	Mustered out with company Sept. 8, 1864.
Myers, William H		18	May 2, 1864	100 dys.	Mustered out with company Sept. 8, 1864.
Parker, Samuel E		52	May 2, 1864	100 dys.	Mustered out with company Sept. 8, 1864.
Patten, William H		43	May 2, 1864	100 dys.	Mustered out with company Sept. 8, 1864.
Phares, George		27	May 2, 1864	100 dys.	Mustered out with company Sept. 8, 1864.
Phares, William C		37	May 2, 1864	100 dys.	Mustered out with company Sept. 8, 1864.
Phares, Winfield S		34	May 2, 1864	100 dys.	Mustered out with company Sept. 8, 1864.
Potts, John M		23	May 2, 1864	100 dys.	Mustered out with company Sept. 8, 1864.
Price, Abraham		30	May 2, 1864	100 dys.	Mustered out with company Sept. 8, 1864.
Price, Thomas D		18	May 2, 1864	100 dys.	Mustered out with company Sept. 8, 1864.
Ray, Joseph		25	May 2, 1864	100 dys.	Mustered out with company Sept. 8, 1864.
Richardson, John C		40	May 2, 1864	100 dys.	Mustered out with company Sept. 8, 1864.
Richley, Andrew		39	May 2, 1864	100 dys.	Mustered out with company Sept. 8, 1864.
Rolff, Taylor		17	May 2, 1864	100 dys.	Mustered out with company Sept. 8, 1864.
Samuels, Ezekiel		44	May 2, 1864	100 dys.	Mustered out with company Sept. 8, 1864.
Smith, Francis M		22	May 2, 1864	100 dys.	Mustered out with company Sept. 8, 1864.
Smith, Wilson B		20	May 2, 1864	100 dys.	Mustered out with company Sept. 8, 1864.
Speers, George W		41	May 2, 1864	100 dys.	Mustered out with company Sept. 8, 1864.
Sterrett, John B. W		20	May 2, 1864	100 dys.	Mustered out with company Sept. 8, 1864.
Thomas, James L		40	May 2, 1864	100 dys.	Mustered out with company Sept. 8, 1864.
Watt, John B		33	May 2, 1864	100 dys.	Mustered out with company Sept. 8, 1864.
Wesco, John H		25	May 2, 1864	100 dys.	Mustered out with company Sept. 8, 1864.
Wilson, Henry C		25	May 2, 1864	100 dys.	Mustered out with company Sept. 8, 1864.
Yergan, John A	...do...	37	May 2, 1864	100 dys.	Mustered out with company Sept. 8, 1864.
Yingling, John H		24	May 2, 1864	100 dys.	Mustered out with company Sept. 8, 1864.

COMPANY E.

Mustered in May 17, 1864, at Hamilton, O., by T. D. Urmston, 1st Lieutenant 12th Infantry, U. S. A. Mustered out Sept. 8, 1864, at Hamilton, O., by C. P. Horton, Captain and A. D. C.

	Rank.	Age.	Date of Entering the Service.	Period of Service.	Remarks.
George C. Warvel	Captain.	38	May 2, 1864	100 dys.	Mustered out with company Sept. 8, 1864.
Benjamin F. Banker	1st Lieut.	35	May 2, 1864	100 dys.	Mustered out with company Sept. 8, 1864.
John Busenbark	2d Lieut.	32	May 2, 1864	100 dys.	Mustered out with company Sept. 8, 1864.
D. D. Evans	1st Sergt.	35	May 2, 1864	100 dys.	Mustered out with company Sept. 8, 1864.
Amos Potter	Sergeant.	34	May 2, 1864	100 dys.	Mustered out with company Sept. 8, 1864.
Hampton H. Long	...do...	21	May 2, 1864	100 dys.	Mustered out with company Sept. 8, 1864.
Isaac Gelbart	...do...	37	May 2, 1864	100 dys.	Mustered out with company Sept. 8, 1864.
Frank Cornthwait	...do...	23	May 2, 1864	100 dys.	Mustered out with company Sept. 8, 1864.
Henry V. Williamson	Corporal.	26	May 2, 1864	100 dys.	Mustered out with company Sept. 8, 1864.
Nelson Lucas	...do...	20	May 2, 1864	100 dys.	Mustered out with company Sept. 8, 1864.
Philip H. Kumler	...do...	26	May 2, 1864	100 dys.	Mustered out with company Sept. 8, 1864.
Austin L. Kumler	...do...	20	May 2, 1864	100 dys.	Mustered out with company Sept. 8, 1864.
Henry Carney	...do...	32	May 2, 1864	100 dys.	Mustered out with company Sept. 8, 1864.
Samuel D. Weaver	...do...	22	May 2, 1864	100 dys.	Mustered out with company Sept. 8, 1864.
Albert Potter	...do...	21	May 2, 1864	100 dys.	Mustered out with company Sept. 8, 1864.
Augustus Cornthwait	...do...	19	May 2, 1864	100 dys.	Mustered out with company Sept. 8, 1864.
Henry Good	Wagoner.	23	May 2, 1864	100 dys.	Mustered out with company Sept. 8, 1864.

Names.	Rank.	Age.	Date of Entering the Service.		
Ackley, Hezekiah H	Private.	45	May 2, 1864	100 dys.	Mustered out with
Aldridge, Andrew J	....do....	28	May 2, 1864	100 dys.	Mustered out with
Bancroft, John N	....do....	23	May 2, 1864	100 dys.	Mustered out
Banker, Christopher	....do....	[illegible]	May 2, 1864	100 dys.	Mustered out
Bloom, Thomas C	....do....	22	May 2, 1864	100 dys.	Mustered out
Bonner, Absalom	....do....	43	May 2, 1864	100 dys.	Absent, sick —
Boner, Wesley	....do....	28	May 2, 1864	100 dys.	Mustered out with
Carney, Jacob	....do....	27	May 2, 1864	100 dys.	Mustered out with
Carney, Joseph D	....do....	20	May 2, 1864	100 dys.	Mustered out with
Chaney, George C	....do....	19	May 2, 1864	100 dys.	Mustered out with
Clark, Frank	....do....	23	May 2, 1864	100 dys.	Mustered out with
Cornthwait, William H	....do....	26	May 2, 1864	100 dys.	Mustered out with
Craig, Thomas	....do....	18	May 2, 1864	100 dys.	Mustered out with
DeGroat, Isaac B	....do....	38	May 2, 1864	100 dys.	Mustered out with
DeGroat, John G	....do....	21	May 2, 1864	100 dys.	Mustered out with
Dunham, John	....do....	20	May 2, 1864	100 dys.	Mustered out with
Eckert, David	....do....	25	May 2, 1864	100 dys.	Mustered out with
Emrick, Henry	....do....	19	May 2, 1864	100 dys.	Mustered out with
Evans, Robert	....do....	21	May 2, 1864	100 dys.	Mustered out with
Farr, Henry	....do....	20	May 2, 1864	100 dys.	Mustered out with
Garrison, Israel	....do....	33	May 2, 1864	100 dys.	Mustered out with
Gebhart, Andrew J	....do....	35	May 2, 1864	100 dys.	Mustered out with
Gill, Patrick	....do....	18	May 2, 1864	100 dys.	Mustered out with
Golliday, Edward	....do....	19	May 2, 1864	100 dys.	Mustered out with
Good, John V	....do....	22	May 2, 1864	100 dys.	Mustered out with
Harrison, William	....do....	22	May 2, 1864	100 dys.	Mustered out with
Heartfelter, William	....do....	20	May 2, 1864	100 dys.	Mustered out with
Hubbell, John A	....do....	31	May 2, 1864	100 dys.	Mustered out with
Johns, William	....do....	19	May 2, 1864	100 dys.	Mustered out with
Jones, Ed.	....do....	25	May 2, 1864	100 dys.	Alias William E. D
Jones, John W	....do....	28	May 2, 1864	100 dys.	Mustered out with
Kern, John W	....do....	22	May 2, 1864	100 dys.	Mustered out with
Law, Ferdinand	....do....	18	May 2, 1864	100 dys.	Mustered out with
Lee, James	....do....	19	May 2, 1864	100 dys.	Mustered out with
Long, John W	....do....	20	May 2, 1864	100 dys.	Mustered out with
Lucas, William H	....do....	24	May 2, 1864	100 dys.	Mustered out with
Marston, Shobal V	....do....	20	May 2, 1864	100 dys.	Mustered out with
Paullin, Henry C	....do....	25	May 2, 1864	100 dys.	Mustered out with
Paullin, Jacob	....do....	27	May 2, 1864	100 dys.	Mustered out with
Perham, Harrison	....do....	49	May 2, 1864	100 dys.	Mustered out with
Phillips, Homer	....do....	36	May 2, 1864	100 dys.	Mustered out with
Ruehl, George	....do....	40	May 2, 1864	100 dys.	Transferred to Co.
Sarver, Thomas	....do....	23	May 2, 1864	100 dys.	Mustered out with
Sayler, Jacob	....do....	26	May 2, 1864	100 dys.	Mustered out with
Selby, Isaac	....do....	28	May 2, 1864	100 dys.	Mustered out with
Shafer, H. Lee	....do....	28	May 2, 1864	100 dys.	Mustered out with
Sherman, Asher D	....do....	22	May 2, 1864	100 dys.	Mustered out with
Spidle, Conrad	....do....	37	May 2, 1864	100 dys.	Mustered out with
Thomas, Gabriel	....do....	23	May 2, 1864	100 dys.	Mustered out with
Thomas, Peter	....do....	20	May 2, 1864	100 dys.	Mustered out with
Vance, Van Buren	....do....	25	May 2, 1864	100 dys.	
Vannatta, Sanford K	....do....	18	May 2, 1864	100 dys.	Mustered out with
Vanness, Daniel P	....do....	21	May 2, 1864	100 dys.	Mustered out with
Vanscoyk, David	....do....	34	May 2, 1864	100 dys.	Mustered out with
Weinland, Augustus J	....do....	18	May 2, 1864	100 dys.	Mustered out with
White, Harrison L	....do....	18	May 2, 1864	100 dys.	Mustered out with
Wolford, Daniel	....do....	32	May 2, 1864	100 dys.	Mustered out with
Wolford, Joseph	....do....	..	May 2, 1864	100 dys.	Absent, sick —
Wolford, Samuel	....do....	30	May 2, 1864	100 dys.	Mustered out with

COMPANY F.

Mustered in May 14, 1864, at Hamilton, O., by T. D. Urmston, 1st Lieutenant 12th In out Sept. 8, 1864, at Hamilton, O., by C. P. Horton, Captain and

John C. Lewis	Captain.	28	May 2, 1864	100 dys.	Mustered out with
James T. Imlay	1st Lieut.	38	May 2, 1864	100 dys.	Mustered out with
Samuel S. Garver	2d Lieut.	26	May 2, 1864	100 dys.	Mustered out with
John S. Chapman	1st Sergt.	34	May 2, 1864	100 dys.	Mustered out with
Adam C. Brewer	Sergeant.	32	May 2, 1864	100 dys.	Mustered out with
George W. Anderson	....do....	21	May 2, 1864	100 dys.	Mustered out with
Archibald Laurie	....do....	26	May 2, 1864	100 dys.	Mustered out with
Luther P. Huston	....do....	22	May 2, 1864	100 dys.	Mustered out with
Harry Bobemyer	Corporal.	34	May 2, 1864	100 dys.	Mustered out with
John T. Stone	....do....	21	May 2, 1864	100 dys.	Mustered out with
Leonard W. O'Brien	....do....	35	May 2, 1864	100 dys.	Mustered out with
Benjamin S. Randolph	....do....	19	May 2, 1864	100 dys.	Mustered out with
Timothy E. Scobey	....do....	18	May 2, 1864	100 dys.	Mustered out with
Hiram G. O'Dair	....do....	30	May 2, 1864	100 dys.	Mustered out with
George B. Watson	....do....	19	May 2, 1864	100 dys.	Mustered out with
Daniel W. Fitton	....do....	22	May 2, 1864	100 dys.	Mustered out with

Names.	Rank.	Age.	Date of Entering the Service.	Period of Service.	
Waldon, David	Private.	29	May 2, 1864	100 dys.	Mustered out with
Webb, Henry R.	....do....	24	May 2, 1864	100 dys.	Reduced from Se own request; mu Sept. 8, 1864.
Wingler, James	....do....	32	May 2, 1864	100 dys.	Mustered out with
Woodside, John P.	....do....	43	May 2, 1864	100 dys.	Promoted to Q. M.
Wright, William H.	....do....	28	May 2, 1864	100 dys.	Mustered out with
Yeargin, James	....do....	17	May 2, 1864	100 dys.	Mustered out with
Young, Franklin E.	....do....	19	May 2, 1864	100 dys.	Mustered out with
Young, John	....do....	18	May 2, 1864	100 dys.	Mustered out with
Young, Samuel E.	....do....	26	May 2, 1864	100 dys.	Mustered out with
Young, William E.	....do....	19	May 2, 1864	100 dys.	Mustered out with

COMPANY I.

Mustered in May 14, 1864, at Hamilton, O., by T. D. Urmston, 1st Lieutenant 12th I
out Sept. 8, 1864, at Hamilton, O., by C. P. Horton, Captain and

Names.	Rank.	Age.	Date of Entering the Service.	Period of Service.	
Samuel K. Wickard	Captain.	29	May 2, 1864	100 dys.	Mustered out
Philip H. Welty	1st Lieut.	23	May 2, 1864	100 dys.	Mustered out
Henry C. Gray	2d Lieut.	21	May 2, 1864	100 dys.	Mustered out
Clayton T. Rees	1st Sergt.	19	May 2, 1864	100 dys.	Mustered out
James P. Martindale	Sergeant.	19	May 2, 1864	100 dys.	Mustered out
Miles J. Spoor	....do....	28	May 2, 1864	100 dys.	Mustered out
Freeman P. Applegate	....do....	30	May 2, 1864	100 dys.	Mustered out
Theodore F. Gray	....do....	19	May 2, 1864	100 dys.	Mustered out
William B. Wallace	Corporal.	22	May 2, 1864	100 dys.	Mustered out
Thomas J. Woodruff	....do....	28	May 2, 1864	100 dys.	Mustered out
Samuel J. Dunwoody	....do....	24	May 2, 1864	100 dys.	Mustered out
John D. Scott	....do....	22	May 2, 1864	100 dys.	Mustered out
Joseph F. Welty	....do....	17	May 2, 1864	100 dys.	Mustered out
Rufus Cone	....do....	26	May 2, 1864	100 dys.	Mustered out
John W. St. Clair	....do....	21	May 2, 1864	100 dys.	Mustered out
Richard Colo	....do....	39	May 2, 1864	100 dys.	Mustered out
Andrews, Charles W.	Private.	21	May 2, 1864	100 dys.	Mustered out
Applegate, Isaac N.	....do....	18	May 2, 1864	100 dys.	Mustered out
Applegate, Richard S.	....do....	24	May 2, 1864	100 dys.	Mustered out
Barnard, Eugene	....do....	19	May 2, 1864	100 dys.	Mustered out
Barnard, William C.	....do....	18	May 2, 1864	100 dys.	Mustered out
Beaton, William M.	....do....	18	May 2, 1864	100 dys.	Mustered out
Bell, Cyrus, W.	....do....	21	May 2, 1864	100 dys.	Mustered out
Boyd, Alfred D.	....do....	20	May 2, 1864	100 dys.	Mustered out
Boyd, Benjamin	....do....	24	May 2, 1864	100 dys.	Mustered out
Brown, William H. H.	....do....	28	May 2, 1864	100 dys.	Mustered out
Callahan, Thomas	....do....	39	May 2, 1864	100 dys.	Mustered out
Carl, Samuel B.	....do....	40	May 2, 1864	100 dys.	Mustered out
Clark, Edwin A.	....do....	18	May 2, 1864	100 dys.	Mustered out
Clark, James H.	....do....	20	May 2, 1864	100 dys.	Mustered out
Cooper, Granville M.	....do....	19	May 2, 1864	100 dys.	Mustered out
Cooper, James M.	....do....	18	May 2, 1864	100 dys.	Mustered out
Crawford, James J.	....do....	27	May 2, 1864	100 dys.	Mustered out
Cubberly, William G.	....do....	27	May 2, 1864	100 dys.	Mustered out
Decker, James	....do....	19	May 2, 1864	100 dys.	Mustered out
Decker, Richard	....do....	26	May 2, 1864	100 dys.	Mustered out
Deneen, Calvin E.	....do....	18	May 2, 1864	100 dys.	Absent, sick ——.
Doty, Hiram B.	....do....	18	May 2, 1864	100 dys.	Mustered out with
Dodge, John H.	....do....	20	May 2, 1864	100 dys.	Mustered out with
Dunham, Edwin	....do....	24	May 2, 1864	100 dys.	Mustered out with
Dunham, Eleazer	....do....	18	May 2, 1864	100 dys.	Mustered out with
Duval, Randolph C.	....do....	28	May 2, 1864	100 dys.	Mustered out with
Dye, George W.	....do....	26	May 2, 1864	100 dys.	
Eichler, Charles	....do....	36	May 2, 1864	100 dys.	Mustered out with
Faber, James	....do....	18	May 2, 1864	100 dys.	Mustered out with
Forman, Alexander	....do....	21	May 2, 1864	100 dys.	Mustered out with
Garner, George W.	....do....	24	May 2, 1864	100 dys.	Mustered out with
Garner, Jackson	....do....	21	May 2, 1864	100 dys.	Mustered out with
Garner, John	....do....	38	May 2, 1864	100 dys.	Mustered wit
Garner, Samuel	....do....	35	May 2, 1864	100 dys.	Mustered with
Garner, William	....do....	42	May 2, 1864	100 dys.	Mustered with
Gardner, Warner	....do....	18	May 2, 1864	100 dys.	Mustered out with
Gates, William N.	....do....	20	May 2, 1864	100 dys.	Mustered out with
Geer, Horace W.	....do....	18	May 2, 1864	100 dys.	Mustered out with
Gilmore, John	....do....	30	May 2, 1864	100 dys.	Mustered with
Goff, James B.	....do....	28	May 2, 1864	100 dys.	Mustered out with
Graham, Frank	....do....	18	May 2, 1864	100 dys.	Mustered out with
Gregg, John C.	....do....	20	May 2, 1864	100 dys.	Mustered out with
Griffin, David	....do....	43	May 2, 1864	100 dys.	Mustered out wit
Haggerty, Patrick	....do....	39	May 2, 1864	100 dys.	Mustered out wit
Hamilton, William	....do....	21	May 2, 1864	100 dys.	Mustered out wit
Harter, Charles W.	....do....	18	May 2, 1864	100 dys.	Mustered out wit

	Rank.	Age.	Date of Entering the Service.		Period of Service.	Remarks.
en, Christopher.		38	May	2, 1864	100 dys.	Mustered out with company Sept. 8, 1864.
ricks, Zadok H..		20	May	2, 1864	100 dys.	Mustered out with company Sept. 8, 1864.
on, Bennett C.....		22	May	2, 1864	100 dys.	Mustered out with company Sept. 8, 1864.
William..........		18	May	2, 1864	100 dys.	Mustered out with company Sept. 8, 1864.
ertson, Nelson....		25	May	2, 1864	100 dys.	Mustered out with company Sept. 8, 1864.
, Wesley A..		24	May	2, 1864	100 dys.	Mustered out with company Sept. 8, 1864.
n, Smith C.........	..do...	19	May	2, 1864	100 dys.	Mustered out with company Sept. 8, 1864.
, Joseph A.........	...	43	May	2, 1864	100 dys.	Mustered out with company Sept. 8, 1864.
eil, John H.........	...	18	May	2, 1864	100 dys.	Mustered out with company Sept. 8, 1864.
ell, William H....	...	21	May	2, 1864	100 dys.	Mustered out with company Sept. 8, 1864.
. Milton..........	...	23	May	2, 1864	100 dys.	Mustered out with company Sept. 8, 1864.
, William H.........	...	28	May	2, 1864	100 dys.	Mustered out with company Sept. 8, 1864.
s, Samuel W.........	...	18	May	2, 1864	100 dys.	Mustered out with company Sept. 8, 1864.
s, Avon H..........	...	18	May	2, 1864	100 dys.	Mustered out with company Sept. 8, 1864.
s, George C.........	...	20	May	2, 1864	100 dys.	Mustered out with company Sept. 8, 1864.
ick, Seth............	...	23	May	2, 1864	100 dys.	Mustered out with company Sept. 8, 1864.
Ephraim............	...	19	May	2, 1864	100 dys.	Absent, sick ——. No further record found.
William............	...	26	May	2, 1864	100 dys.	Mustered out with company Sept. 8, 1864.
William L.........	...	37	May	2, 1864	100 dys.	Mustered out with company Sept. 8, 1864.
r, Otto.............	...	21	May	2, 1864	100 dys.	Mustered out with company Sept. 8, 1864.
n, Joseph..........	...	18	May	2, 1864	100 dys.	Mustered out with company Sept. 8, 1864.
r, Thomas.........	....do...	44	May	2, 1864	100 dys.	Mustered out with company Sept. 8, 1864.
f, George M.........	....do...	19	May	2, 1864	100 dys.	Mustered out with company Sept. 8, 1864.
Morton J..........	....do...	27	May	2, 1864	100 dys.	Mustered out with company Sept. 8, 1864.
, Amos.............	....do...	31	May	2, 1864	100 dys.	Mustered out with company Sept. 8, 1864.
, Silas R..........	....do...	20	May	2, 1864	100 dys.	Mustered out with company Sept. 8, 1864.
r, William V.......	....do...	20	May	2, 1864	100 dys.	Mustered out with company Sept. 8, 1864.
ns, Lorenzo D.......	....do...	19	May	2, 1864	100 dys.	Mustered out with company Sept. 8, 1864.
James..............	....do...	18	May	2, 1864	100 dys.	Mustered out with company Sept. 8, 1864.
Joseph M..........	....do...	25	May	2, 1864	100 dys.	Mustered out with company Sept. 8, 1864.
pson, Augustus G.	....do...	31	May	2, 1864	100 dys.	Mustered out with company Sept. 8, 1864.
ndall, William ...	....do...	28	May	2, 1864	100 dys.	Mustered out with company Sept. 8, 1864.
o, Francis M......	....do...	26	May	2, 1864	100 dys.	Mustered out with company Sept. 8, 1864.
, Levi E........	....do...	26	May	2, 1864	100 dys.	Mustered out with company Sept. 8, 1864.
n, David........	....do...	20	May	2, 1864	100 dys.	Mustered out with company Sept. 8, 1864.
, Martin S......	....do...	20	May	2, 1864	100 dys.	Mustered out with company Sept. 8, 1864.

COMPANY K.

ered in May 16, 1864, at Hamilton, O., by T. D. Urmston, 1st Lieutenant 12th Infantry, U. S. A. Mustered out Sept. 8, 1864, at Hamilton, O., by C. P. Horton, Captain and A. D. C.

	Rank.	Age.	Date of Entering the Service.		Period of Service.	Remarks.
l K. Zeller..........	Captain.	41	May	2, 1864	100 dys.	Mustered out with company Sept. 8, 1864.
ington B. Davis....	1st Lieut.	34	May	2, 1864	100 dys.	Mustered out with company Sept. 8, 1864.
ew T. Whipple....	2d Lieut.	24	May	2, 1864	100 dys.	Mustered out with company Sept. 8, 1864.
nder B. Emrick....	1st Sergt.	25	May	2, 1864	100 dys.	Absent, sick ——. No further record found.
iam C. Kumler....	Sergeant	30	May	2, 1864	100 dys.	Mustered out with company Sept. 8, 1864.
n W. Bailey.......	....do....	34	May	2, 1864	100 dys.	Mustered out with company Sept. 8, 1864.
m T. Hall..........	....do....	25	May	2, 1864	100 dys.	Mustered out with company Sept. 8, 1864.
nder H. Miller....	....do....	31	May	2, 1864	100 dys.	Mustered out with company Sept. 8, 1864.
in Cochran.. ..	Corporal.	27	May	2, 1864	100 dys.	Mustered out with company Sept. 8, 1864.
l D. Beal...........	....do....	22	May	2, 1864	100 dys.	Mustered out with company Sept. 8, 1864.
K. Wickard.........	....do....	22	May	2, 1864	100 dys.	Mustered out with company Sept. 8, 1864.
iam Rumple.........	....do....	34	May	2, 1864	100 dys.	Mustered out with company Sept. 8, 1864.
G. Knox............	....do....	21	May	2, 1864	100 dys.	Mustered out with company Sept. 8, 1864.
McCaskey..........	....do....	35	May	2, 1864	100 dys.	Appointed ——; mustered out with company Sept. 8, 1864.
is M. Kumler.......	....do....	18	May	2, 1864	100 dys.	Appointed ——; mustered out with company Sept. 8, 1864.
Ross...............	....do....	28	May	2, 1864	100 dys.	Died Aug. 7, 1864.
ws, William.......	Private..	18	May	2, 1864	100 dys.	Mustered out with company Sept. 8, 1864.
, Michael..........	....do....	24	May	2, 1864	100 dys.	Mustered out with company Sept. 8, 1864.
s, William C.......	....do....	40	May	2, 1864	100 dys.	Mustered out with company Sept. 8, 1864.
han, James.........	....do....	17	May	2, 1864	100 dys.	Mustered out with company Sept. 8, 1864.
James A...........	....do....	27	May	2, 1864	100 dys.	Mustered out with company Sept. 8, 1864.
r, Isaac............	....do....	31	May	2, 1864	100 dys.	Mustered out with company Sept. 8, 1864.
it, James	....do....	19	May	2, 1864	100 dys.	Mustered out with company Sept. 8, 1864.
. Henry...........	....do....	22	May	2, 1864	100 dys.	Mustered out with company Sept. 8, 1864.
, John W...........	....do....	19	May	2, 1864	100 dys.	Mustered out with company Sept. 8, 1864.
ker, St. Clair......	....do....	20	May	2, 1864	100 dys.	Mustered out with company Sept. 8, 1864.
ck, George M.......	....do....	18	May	2, 1864	100 dys.	Absent, sick ——. No further record found.
nstein, Jacob.......	....do....	25	May	2, 1864	100 dys.	Mustered out with company Sept. 8, 1864.
, Joseph...........	....do....	18	May	2, 1864	100 dys.	Mustered out with company Sept. 8, 1864.
nger, Titus........	....do....	17	May	2, 1864	100 dys.	Mustered out with company Sept. 8, 1864.
Stephen E.........	....do....	20	May	2, 1864	100 dys.	Mustered out with company Sept. 8, 1864.
, John P...........	....do....	26	May	2, 1864	100 dys.	Mustered out with company Sept. 8, 1864.
Alexander.........	....do....	19	May	2, 1864	100 dys.	Mustered out with company Sept. 8, 1864.
y, Fenton.........	....do....	18	May	2, 1864	100 dys.	Mustered out with company Sept. 8, 1864.
rn, Hugh D.........	....do....	34	May	2, 1864	100 dys.	Reduced from Corporal ——; mustered out with company Sept. 8, 1864.

Names.	Rank.	Age.	Date of Entering the Service.	Period of Service.	Remarks.
Goshorn, Silas R.	Private.	23	May 2, 1864	100 dys.	Mustered out with company Sept. 8, 1864.
Hawk, Alfred T.	...do...	17	May 2, 1864	100 dys.	Mustered out with company Sept. 8, 1864.
Hill, William	...do...	17	May 2, 1864	100 dys.	Mustered out with company Sept. 8, 1864.
Kahler, Jacob	...do...	21	May 2, 1864	100 dys.	Mustered out with company Sept. 8, 1864.
Kemple, David	...do...	27	May 2, 1864	100 dys.	Mustered out with company Sept. 8, 1864.
Lane, George	...do...	16	May 2, 1864	100 dys.	Mustered out with company Sept. 8, 1864.
Leffler, Samuel P.	...do...	25	May 2, 1864	100 dys.	Mustered out with company Sept. 8, 1864.
Lewis, Robert	...do...	40	May 2, 1864	100 dys.	Mustered out with company Sept. 8, 1864.
Long, Henry	...do...	18	May 2, 1864	100 dys.	Mustered out with company Sept. 8, 1864.
Miller, James B.	...do...	18	May 2, 1864	100 dys.	Mustered out with company Sept. 8, 1864.
Minton, William	...do...	20	May 2, 1864	100 dys.	Absent, sick ——. No further record found.
Nelson, William H.	...do...	21	May 2, 1864	100 dys.	Mustered out with company Sept. 8, 1864.
Oswalt, Daniel	...do...	19	May 2, 1864	100 dys.	Mustered out with company Sept. 8, 1864.
Popst, Christian	...do...	35	May 2, 1864	100 dys.	Mustered out with company Sept. 8, 1864.
Powell, John M.	...do...	39	May 2, 1864	100 dys.	Mustered out with company Sept. 8, 1864.
Riley, Alexander	...do...	22	May 2, 1864	100 dys.	Mustered out with company Sept. 8, 1864.
Robinson, George W.	...do...	41	May 2, 1864	100 dys.	Mustered out with company Sept. 8, 1864.
Roll, Elias	...do...	22	May 2, 1864	100 dys.	Mustered out with company Sept. 8, 1864.
Roll, Nicholas	...do...	23	May 2, 1864	100 dys.	Mustered out with company Sept. 8, 1864.
Roll, William W.	...do...	25	May 2, 1864	100 dys.	Mustered out with company Sept. 8, 1864.
Ross, Pierson M.	...do...	19	May 2, 1864	100 dys.	Mustered out with company Sept. 8, 1864.
Sayers, Alexander C.	...do...	18	May 2, 1864	100 dys.	Mustered out with company Sept. 8, 1864.
Shipley, James	...do...	18	May 2, 1864	100 dys.	Mustered out with company Sept. 8, 1864.
Simons, John	...do...	34	May 2, 1864	100 dys.	Mustered out with company Sept. 8, 1864.
Sipe, Isaac	...do...	20	May 2, 1864	100 dys.	Mustered out with company Sept. 8, 1864.
Skinner, Charles	...do...	17	May 2, 1864	100 dys.	Mustered out with company Sept. 8, 1864.
Soehner, Charles	...do...	20	May 2, 1864	100 dys.	Mustered out with company Sept. 8, 1864.
Stephenson, James	...do...	18	May 2, 1864	100 dys.	Mustered out with company Sept. 8, 1864.
Sterrett, William	...do...	22	May 2, 1864	100 dys.	Died Aug. 15, 1864.
Umston, Nelson	...do...	42	May 2, 1864	100 dys.	Mustered out with company Sept. 8, 1864.
Wickard, John	...do...	18	May 2, 1864	100 dys.	Mustered out with company Sept. 8, 1864.
Wickard, Samuel	...do...	20	May 2, 1864	100 dys.	Mustered out with company Sept. 8, 1864.
Williams, William J.	...do...	18	May 2, 1864	100 dys.	Died Aug. 14, 1864.
Zeller, Elias R.	...do...	20	May 2, 1864	100 dys.	Mustered out with company Sept. 8, 1864.

168th Regiment Ohio Volunteer Infantry.

ONE HUNDRED DAYS' SERVICE.

Ƭhis Regiment was organized at Camp Dennison, O., from the 12th to the of May, 1864, to serve one hundred days. It was composed of the Sixty- Battalion, Ohio National Guard, from Highland County; Sixty-seventh ılion, Ohio National Guard, from Fayette County; and one Company of 'hirty-fifth Battalion, Ohio National Guard, from Clarke County. On the f June the Regiment proceeded to Covington, Ky., and embarked on the ıgton and Lexington Railroad. Company B, with twenty men from Com- G, was detached at Falmouth to guard the railroad bridge, and at other ts Companies were stationed to protect the road. On the 10th of June a hment of three hundred occupied Cynthiana. At six o'clock on the morn- f the 11th of June a large force of Rebel Cavalry moved against the town, ıich engagement the One Hundred and Sixty-eighth lost seven men killed, een wounded, and two hundred and eighty captured. That portion of the ment under command of Major Newton remained in Kentucky until the of July, when it was ordered to Camp Dennison, to join the paroled pris- ı. The Regiment was then sent to Cincinnati, where it performed guard . It was mustered out Sept. 8, 1864, on expiration of term of service.

Names.	Rank.	Age.	Date of Entering the Service.		Period of Service.	
Campbell, Mahlon	Private..	32	May	2, 1864	100 dys.	
Carr, Byron	..do....	22	May	2, 1864	100 dys.	
Cornetet, John	....do....	18	May	2, 1864	100 dys.	
Davidson, Joseph	....do....	36	May	2, 1864	100 dys.	
Davidson, W. K	....do....	25	May	2, 1864	100 dys.	
Davidson, W. S.	....do....	30	May	2, 1864	100 dys.	Must
Donohoe, David	....do....	23	May	2, 1864	100 dys.	Must
Easter, Carey	....do....	22	May	2, 1864	100 dys.	Must
Easter, Milton	....do....	19	May	2, 1864	100 dys.	Must
Edgington, John	....do....	18	May	2, 1864	100 dys.	Died
Edingfield, Cornelius	....do....	21	May	2, 1864	100 dys.	Must
Emery, G. C.	....do....	22	May	2, 1864	100 dys.	Must
Harris, Charles E	....do....	18	May	2, 1864	100 dys.	Must
Harris, H. K.	....do....	22	May	2, 1864	100 dys.	Must
Harshbarger, David	....do....	19	May	2, 1864	100 dys.	
Heisley, Henry	....do....	45	May	2, 1864	100 dys.	
Henderson, James	....do....	28	May	2, 1864	100 dys.	
Hetherington, H. E.	....do....	40	May	2, 1864	100 dys.	Must
Huston, Matthew	....do....	27	May	2, 1864	100 dys.	Must
Huston, William	....do....	20	May	2, 1864	100 dys.	
Laforge, J. K.	....do....	20	May	2, 1864	100 dys.	
Lemon, Mark	....do....	18	May	2, 1864	100 dys.	
Lindsey, Christa	....do....	40	May	2, 1864	100 dys.	
Lyons, Samuel	....do....	22	May	2, 1864	100 dys.	
Matthews, D. W.	....do....	21	May	2, 1864	100 dys.	
Matthews, Oscar	....do....	18	May	2, 1864	100 dys.	
Miller, W. C.	....do....	23	May	2, 1864	100 dys.	
Moore, Henry	....do....	36	May	2, 1864	100 dys.	
Morrow, J. K.	....do....	47	May	2, 1864	100 dys.	
Morrow, R. A.	....do....	25	May	2, 1864	100 dys.	
Mowery, George	....do....	35	May	2, 1864	100 dys.	
Nace, J. H.	....do....	27	May	2, 1864	100 dys.	
Nailor, M	....do....	18	May	2, 1864	100 dys.	
Pence, David	....do....	21	May	2, 1864	100 dys.	
Phibbs, David	....do....	27	May	2, 1864	100 dys.	
Robison, G. W.	....do....	19	May	2, 1864	100 dys.	
Robison, John	....do....	23	May	2, 1864	100 dys.	
Robison, John H	....do....	23	May	2, 1864	100 dys.	
Robison, W. P.	....do....	21	May	2, 1864	100 dys.	
Shaw, Marion	....do....	18	May	2, 1864	100 dys.	
Shaw, Wesley	....do....	18	May	2, 1864	100 dys.	
Soner, Simon	....do....	18	May	2, 1864	100 dys.	
Stout, W. D.	....do....	18	May	2, 1864	100 dys.	
Strode, J. S.	....do....	35	May	2, 1864	100 dys.	
Taylor, John	....do....	29	May	2, 1864	100 dys.	
Taylor, Josephus	....do....	20	May	2, 1864	100 dys.	
Turner Hugh	....do....	38	May	2, 1864	100 dys.	
Turner, James	....do....	27	May	2, 1864	100 dys.	
Turner, Samuel	....do....	36	May	2, 1864	100 dys.	Must
Vance, Henry	....do....	22	May	2, 1864	100 dys.	Must
Walker, G. K.	....do....	23	May	2, 1864	100 dys.	Must
White, L. C.	....do....	18	May	2, 1864	100 dys.	Must
Wood, Daniel	....do....	25	May	2, 1864	100 dys.	Must
Wood, Samuel	....do....	30	May	2, 1864	100 dys.	Kille Ke
Zink, Allen	....do....	34	May	2, 1864	100 dys.	

COMPANY B.

Mustered in May 13, 1864, at Camp Dennison, O., by G. E. Johnson, out Sept. 8, 1864, at Camp Dennison, O., by William 10th Infantry, U. S. A.

Names.	Rank.	Age.	Date of Entering the Service.		Period of Service.	
Joseph H. Mullenix	Captain.	47	May	2, 1864	100 dys.	Must
Jonah Britton	1st Lieut.	36	May	2, 1864	100 dys.	Must
Lemuel B. Morris	2d Lieut.	30	May	2, 1864	100 dys.	Must
Anderson Murray	1st Sergt.	35	May	2, 1864	100 dys.	Must
William Morris	Sergeant.	27	May	2, 1864	100 dys.	Must
James B. Gibson	....do....	32	May	2, 1864	100 dys.	Must
James Nevin	....do....	21	May	2, 1864	100 dys.	Must
James C. Love	....do....	38	May	2, 1864	100 dys.	Must
James Lynn	Corporal.	31	May	2, 1864	100 dys.	Must
Benjamin Jones	....do....	42	May	2, 1864	100 dys.	Must
Fenner St. Clair	....do....	31	May	2, 1864	100 dys.	Must
Robert B. Nevin	....do....	33	May	2, 1864	100 dys.	Must
George Shepherd	....do....	26	May	2, 1864	100 dys.	Must
Samuel Shoemaker	....do....	25	May	2, 1864	100 dys.	Must
Newton Thomas	....do....	20	May	2, 1864	100 dys.	Must

COMPANY C.

Mustered in May 12, 1864, at Camp Dennison, O., by Robert S. Sm
out Sept. 8, 1864, at Camp Dennison, O., by Willi
10th Infantry, U. S. A

Names.	Rank.	Age.	Date of Entering the Service.	
William H. Hogue	Captain.	35	May 2, 1864	100
Samuel Ayres	1st Lieut.	44	May 2, 1864	100
John L. Barnes	2d Lieut.	20	May 2, 1864	100
Daniel L. Robey	1st Sergt.	36	May 2, 1864	100
Henry C. Wimer	Sergeant.	20	May 2, 1864	100
William F. Hill	...do...	29	May 2, 1864	100
John M. Smith	...do...	28	May 2, 1864	100
Thomas Riley	...do...	33	May 2, 1864	100
James R. Stewart	...do...	23	May 2, 1864	100
Jackson Powell	Corporal.	36	May 2, 1864	100
Russell B. Dobbins	...do...	35	May 2, 1864	100
Charles P. Smith	...do...	25	May 2, 1864	
Alfred H. Mark	...do...	27	May 2, 1864	
William H. Steele	...do...	28	May 2, 1864	dys.
Allen Latham	...do...	31	May 2, 1864	dys.
Isaac Teter	...do...	19	May 2, 1864	dys.
Jacob Smith	...do...	19	May 2, 1864	
Bennett, Isaac W	Private	18	May 2, 1864	
Blair, John J	...do...	23	May 2, 1864	
Blair, Robert H	...do...	19	May 2, 1864	
Blas r, Joseph	...do...	28	May 2, 1864	
Bush, Walter	...do...	21	May 2, 1864	100 dys. R
Coll, Thomas, Jr	...do...	19	May 2, 1864	100
Coll, Thomas, Sr	...do...	40	May 2, 1864	100
Constant, Isaac	...do...	26	May 2, 1864	100
Davis, John W	...do...	28	May 2, 1864	100
Devolt, George	...do...	25	May 2, 1864	100
Downe, John	...do...	40	May 2, 1864	100
Duff, Harvey T	...do...	18	May 2, 1864	100
Duff, Hiram G	...do...	21	May 2, 1864	100
Eastlack, Isaac	...do...	20	May 2, 1864	
Eibe, George W	...do...	37	May 2, 1864	
Fannon, Andrew	...do...	21	May 2, 1864	
Fannon, Jacob	...do...	18	May 2, 1864	
Fuel, Bartholomew L	...do...	25	May 2, 1864	
Ginkins, Andrew J	...do...	30	May 2, 1864	
Gray, Jacob M	...do...	28	May 2, 1864	
Haines, Joshua	...do...	22	May 2, 1864	
Hartman, Allen	...do...	44	May 2, 1864	
Henderson, Robert B	...do...	30	May 2, 1864	
Hixon, James	...do...	25	May 2, 1864	
Horney, John J	...do...	36	May 2, 1864	
Jacks, David H	...do...	20	May 2, 1864	
Jacks, Har nan	...do...	24	May 2, 1864	
Jacks, Harvey	...do...	28	May 2, 1864	
Johnson, Henry C	...do...	28	May 2, 1864	
Johnson, Robert	...do...	44	May 2, 1864	
Keller, John	...do...	36	May 2, 1864	
Kotteman, John	...do...	25	May 2, 1864	
Kittle, Elam	...do...	26	May 2, 1864	
Kittle, John	...do...	36	May 2, 1864	
Lambert, Smith	...do...	25	May 2, 1864	
Lambert, Thomas	...do...	19	May 2, 1864	
Latham, Bela	...do...	36	May 2, 1864	
Meade, Ichabod	...do...	39	May 2, 1864	
Mees, Jacob	...do...	17	May 2, 1864	
Peggs, William	...do...	21	May 2, 1864	
Perdam, John	...do...	17	May 2, 1864	
Rankin, William A	...do...	21	May 2, 1864	
Rupert, George	...do...	30	May 2, 1864	
Rupert, William H	...do...	20	May 2, 1864	
Shockey, Isaac	...do...	33	May 2, 1864	
Smith, William A	...do...	34	May 2, 1864	
Sellers, Wells B	...do...	18	May 2, 1864	
Spurlock, Robert C	...do...	34	May 2, 1864	
Tobin, Henry	...do...	18	May 2, 1864	
Tobin, Jacob	...do...	19	May 2, 1864	
Tobin, Joseph	...do...	19	May 2, 1864	

Names.	Rank.	Date of Entering the Service.	
Rogers, Alexander	Private	May 2, 1864	
Rotruck, Isaiah	do	May 2, 1864	
Sanders, Austin	do	May 2, 1864	
Seaton, J. F	do	May 2, 1864	
Shely, John W	do	May 2, 1864	
Shoemaker, Henry	do	May 2, 1864	Mustered out
Shoemaker, Jasper	do	May 2, 1864	
Shoemaker, John	do	May 2, 1864	
Smith, William	do	May 2, 1864	
Stoughton, William	do	May 2, 1864	
Taylor, David	do	May 2, 1864	
Taylor, F. B.	do	May 2, 1864	
Taylor, George	do	May 2, 1864	
Thomas, Moses	do	May 2, 1864	
Thompson, Joseph	do	May 2, 1864	
Ulmer, Jacob	do	May 2, 1864	
Ulmer, John	do	May 2, 1861	
Wallace, R. A	do	May 2, 1864	
Weimer, Daniel	do	May 2, 1864	
Whitcomb, J. S	do	May 2, 1864	
White, Lycurgus	do	May 2, 1864	

COMPANY E.

Mustered in May 13, 1864, at Camp Dennison, O., by G. E. Johnson, Major out Sept. 8, 1864, at Camp Dennison, O., by William Stanley 10th Infantry, U. S. A.

Joseph Smith	Captain	34	May 2, 1864	Mustered out
Timothy S. Ream	1st Lieut.	24	May 2, 1864	Mustered out
David Troutwine	2d Lieut	31	May 2, 1864	Mustered out
J. H. Deniston	1st Sergt.	32	May 2, 1864	Mustered out
A. J. Swain	Sergeant.	30	May 2, 1864	Mustered out
I. J. Smith	do	25	May 2, 1864	Appointed fr July 31, 18[illegible] Ohio.
Hugh Murphy	do	31	May 2, 1864	Appointed fr tered out w
Richard McClelland	do	30	May 2, 1864	Appointed fr tered out w
F. M. Murphy	Corporal.	27	May 2, 1864	Mustered out
G. W. Davidson	do	34	May 2, 1864	Mustered out
Andrew Bishir	do	35	May 2, 1864	Mustered out
Robert King	do	22	May 2, 1864	Mustered out
Joseph Belford	do	30	May 2, 1864	Appointed Ju company Se
J. M. Bartley	do	19	May 2, 1864	Appointed Ju company Se
Levi Faris	do	33	May 2, 1864	Appointed A company Se
S. M. Smith	do	19	May 2, 1864	Appointed Ju his home, H
John M. Smith	do	40	May 2, 1864	Appointed Ju company Se
Ashmore, J. R.	Private	33	May 2, 1864	Mustered out
Baker, P. L	do	31	May 2, 1864	Mustered out
Barnes, Samuel	do	29	May 2, 1864	Mustered out
Barr, Matthias	do	40	May 2, 1864	Mustered out
Bell, William E	do	24	May 2, 1864	Mustered out
Carpenter, Daniel	do	35	May 2, 1864	Mustered out
Chaney, J. C	do	23	May 2, 1864	Mustered out
Clark, Abraham	do	20	May 2, 1864	Discharged J
Colvin, Edward	do	19	May 2, 1864	Mustered out
Colvin, N. J	do	31	May 2, 1864	Mustered out
[illegible]	do	29	May 2, 1864	Reduced fro tered out w
Daugherty, J. N	do	43	May 2, 1864	Mustered out
Davidson, P. S	do	28	May 2, 1864	Mustered out
Deniston, John D	do	28	May 2, 1864	Mustered out
Eaglin, Alfred	do	30	May 2, 1864	Reduced fro tered out wi
Faris, J. B.	do	26	May 2, 1864	Reduced fro tered out wi
Faris, Josephus	do	35	May 2, 1864	Mustered out
Fenner, Erastus	do	35	May 2, 1864	Mustered out
Floyd, Henry	do	20	May 2, 1864	Mustered out
Foster, Isaac	do	25	May 2, 1864	Mustered out
Foust, John M	do	25	May 2, 1864	Reduced fro tered out wi

Names.	Rank.	Age.	Date of Entering the Service.		
Burnett, Jesse H	Private	24	May 2, 1864		Mustered
Bush, Austin	do	19	May 2, 1864		Mustered
Bush, Benjamin F	do	19	May 2, 1864		Mustered
Bush, Henry L	do	24	May 2, 1864		Mustered
Bush, John S	do	29	May 2, 1864		Mustered
Bush, Martin P	do	24	May 2, 1864		Mustered
Carr, Philip	do	41	May 2, 1864		Mustered
Credit, John W	do	31	May 2, 1864		Mustered out
Curtis, Fielding	do	33	May 2, 1864		
Draper, Richard	do	22	May 2, 1864		Mustered out
Dye, Wesley	do	22	May 2, 1864		Mustered out
Faushier, Henry	do	37	May 2, 1864		Mustered out
Fanshier, James	do	18	May 2, 1864		
Freeman, Granville	do	37	May 2, 1864		Mustered out
Gordon, Richard	do	39	May 2, 1864		Mustered out
Gordon, Sampson	do	35	May 2, 1864		Mustered out
Harrison, Andrew	do	42	May 2, 1864		Mustered out
Henderson, George W	do	28	May 2, 1864		Mustered out
Henderson, Samuel	do	23	May 2, 1864		
Henkle, Simeon W	do	19	May 2, 1864		Died Aug. 13, 1
Hiser, Abraham	do	33	May 2, 1864		
Hyer, Anderson	do	29	May 2, 1864		Mustered out
Hyer, Charles W	do	24	May 2, 1864		Mustered out
Hyer, Milton	do	23	May 2, 1864		Mustered out
Lacy, Thomas A	do	27	May 2, 1864		Mustered out
Mark, John W	do	30	May 2, 1864		Mustered out
Mason, John	do	29	May 2, 1864		Mustered out
Millburn, John W	do	33	May 2, 1864		Mustered out
Moon, Henry H	do	30	May 2, 1864		Mustered out
Moore, Peter	do	18	May 2, 1864		Mustered out
Newland, John W	do	21	May 2, 1864		
Parkinson, Henry	do	21	May 2, 1864		Mustered out
Parkinson, Robert	do	19	May 2, 1864		Mustered out
Parrott, Jacob	do	36	May 2, 1864		Mustered out
Patton, Charles	do	30	May 2, 1864		Mustered out
Paugh, Enoch G	do	30	May 2, 1864		Mustered out
Paul Henderson	do	28	May 2, 1864		Mustered out
Peterson, Daniel	do	41	May 2, 1864		Mustered out
Peterson, Jesse	do	27	May 2, 1864		Mustered out
Pummill, Andrew	do	30	May 2, 1864		
Pummill, John W	do	28	May 2, 1864		
Rowe, Franklin	do	19	May 2, 1864		Mustered out
Schmidt, William C	do	27	May 2, 1864		Mustered out
Sever, George W	do	19	May 2, 1864		Mustered out
Shelton, William T	do	27	May 2, 1864		Mustered out
Shoop, Walter W	do	18	May 2, 1864		Mustered out
Shoop, William H	do	26	May 2, 1864		Mustered out
Smith, George	do	18	May 2, 1864		
Smith, John M	do	21	May 2, 1864		Mustered out
Taylor, John T	do	37	May 2, 1864		Mustered out
Tudor, John	do	33	May 2, 1864		Mustered out
Tudor, Robert	do	21	May 2, 1864		Mustered out
Tupes, Daniel	do	18	May 2, 1864		Mustered out
Tupes, David	do	20	May 2, 1864		Mustered out
Upp, N. G	do	23	May 2, 1864		
Upp, William	do	23	May 2, 1864		
Webb, Benjamin	do	22	May 2, 1864		No record sub
Williams, Charles R	do	21	May 2, 1864		
Williams, Jacob	do	18	May 2, 1864		Mustered out
Williamson, Howard	do	25	May 2, 1864		Mustered out
Wood, Jeremiah	do	24	May 2, 1864		Mustered out

COMPANY G.

Mustered in May 13, 1864, at Camp Dennison, O., by Robert S. Smith, Captain out Sept. 6, 1864, at Camp Dennison, O., by William Stanley, 10th Infantry, U. S. A.

Names.	Rank.	Age.	Date of Entering the Service.		
Thomas Rankin	Captain.	35	May 2, 1864	100 dys.	Mustered out
William J. Horney	1st Lieut.	33	May 2, 1864	100 dys.	Mustered out
Samuel B. Straley	2d Lieut.	41	May 2, 1864	100 dys.	Mustered out
James Straley	1st Sergt.	34	May 2, 1864	100 dys.	Mustered out
Copsy D. Martin	Sergeant.	25	May 2, 1864	100 dys.	Mustered out
Joseph Turner	do	26	May 2, 1864	100 dys.	Mustered out
Henry Huffman	do	44	May 2, 1864	100 dys.	Mustered out
Joseph Straley	do	28	May 2, 1864	100 dys.	Mustered out
John W. Wimer	Corporal.	40	May 2, 1864	100 dys.	Mustered out
John Cole	do	35	May 2, 1864	100 dys.	Mustered out
John V. B. Martin	do	27	May 2, 1864	100 dys.	Mustered out
Horace Ballard	do	42	May 2, 1864	100 dys.	Mustered out

Names.	Rank.	Age.	Date of Entering the Service.	Period of Service.	Remarks.
James W. King	Corporal.	22	May 2, 1864	100 dys.	Mustered out with company Sept. 8, 1864.
Washington West	....do....	23	May 2, 1864	100 dys.	Mustered out with company Sept. 8, 1864.
Jones, Cosmo	....do....	19	May 2, 1864	100 dys.	Mustered out with company Sept. 8, 1864.
Jacob Mills	....do....	34	May 2, 1864	100 dys.	Mustered out with company Sept. 8, 1864.
Allen, Charles W	Private.	20	May 2, 1864	100 dys.	Mustered out with company Sept. 8, 1864.
Allen, George	....do....	18	May 2, 1864	100 dys.	Mustered out with company Sept. 8, 1864.
Baker, John	....do....	27	May 2, 1864	100 dys.	Mustered out with company Sept. 8, 1864.
Carnes, William	....do....	21	May 2, 1864	100 dys.	Mustered out with company Sept. 8, 1864.
Carr, Oliver S	....do....	18	May 2, 1864	100 dys.	Mustered out with company Sept. 8, 1864.
Chaney, J. W	....do....	28	May 2, 1864	100 dys.	Mustered out with company Sept. 8, 1864.
Giddings, John D	....do....	32	May 2, 1864	100 dys.	Mustered out with company Sept. 8, 1864.
Clopaine, Henry	....do....	28	May 2, 1864	100 dys.	Mustered out with company Sept. 8, 1864.
Coffee, Joseph A	....do....	32	May 2, 1864	100 dys.	Transferred to Co. K ——.
Conger, John S	....do....	37	May 2, 1864	100 dys.	Mustered out with company Sept. 8, 1864.
Conner, John	....do....	44	May 2, 1864	100 dys.	Mustered out with company Sept. 8, 1864.
Cranmer, William H	....do....	20	May 2, 1864	100 dys.	Mustered out with company Sept. 8, 1864.
Edgar, Samuel	....do....	18	May 2, 1864	100 dys.	Mustered out with company Sept. 8, 1864.
Filer, John C	....do....	23	May 2, 1864	100 dys.	Mustered out with company Sept. 8, 1864.
Flax, Matthias	....do....	25	May 2, 1864	100 dys.	Mustered out with company Sept. 8, 1864.
Grant, John M	....do....	35	May 2, 1864	100 dys.	Mustered out with company Sept. 8, 1864.
Gray, Franklin	....do....	27	May 2, 1864	100 dys.	Mustered out with company Sept. 8, 1864.
Gray, Jacob M	....do....	28	May 2, 1864	100 dys.	Transferred to Co. C ——.
Griffith, Elijah C	....do....	18	May 2, 1864	100 dys.	Mustered out with company Sept. 8, 1864.
Griffith, Nathan L	....do....	35	May 2, 1864	100 dys.	Mustered out with company Sept. 8, 1864.
Harper, George W	....do....	19	May 2, 1864	100 dys.	Mustered out with company Sept. 8, 1864.
Harper, Thomas	....do....	26	May 2, 1864	100 dys.	Mustered out with company Sept. 8, 1864.
Hart, James W	....do....	22	May 2, 1864	100 dys.	Mustered out with company Sept. 8, 1864.
Hatfield, Elias	....do....	18	May 2, 1864	100 dys.	Mustered out with company Sept. 8, 1864.
Hawk, Moses I	....do....	23	May 2, 1864	100 dys.	Mustered out with company Sept. 8, 1864.
Hidy, Solomon	....do....	25	May 2, 1864	100 dys.	Mustered out with company Sept. 8, 1864.
Hosler, Murrel	....do....	36	May 2, 1864	100 dys.	Mustered out with company Sept. 8, 1864.
Langan, Francis	....do....	20	May 2, 1864	100 dys.	Mustered out with company Sept. 8, 1864.
Lemon, Alexander S	....do....	27	May 2, 1864	100 dys.	Mustered out with company Sept. 8, 1864.
Martin, Charles L	....do....	21	May 2, 1864	100 dys.	Mustered out with company Sept. 8, 1864.
Miller, Jacob	....do....	38	May 2, 1864	100 dys.	Mustered out with company Sept. 8, 1864.
Mills, Owen D	....do....	18	May 2, 1864	100 dys.	Mustered out with company Sept. 8, 1864.
Murry, Patrick	....do....	36	May 2, 1864	100 dys.	Mustered out with company Sept. 8, 1864.
Patton, John A	....do....	18	May 2, 1864	100 dys.	Mustered out with company Sept. 8, 1864.
Powell, Philip	....do....	26	May 2, 1864	100 dys.	Absent, sick ——. No further record found.
Rankin, James	....do....	38	May 2, 1864	100 dys.	Mustered out with company Sept. 8, 1864.
Rankin, Smith	....do....	43	May 2, 1864	100 dys.	Mustered out with company Sept. 8, 1864.
Redding, William	....do....	35	May 2, 1864	100 dys.	Mustered out with company Sept. 8, 1864.
Roebuck, David	....do....	42	May 2, 1864	100 dys.	Mustered out with company Sept. 8, 1864.
Sanderson, John B	....do....	41	May 2, 1864	100 dys.	Mustered out with company Sept. 8, 1864.
Sanderson, Samuel N	....do....	35	May 2, 1864	100 dys.	Mustered out with company Sept. 8, 1864.
Shafer, Samuel	....do....	43	May 2, 1864	100 dys.	Mustered out with company Sept. 8, 1864.
Shakelford, John A	....do....	22	May 2, 1864	100 dys.	Mustered out with company Sept. 8, 1864.
Sheley, John A	....do....	28	May 2, 1864	100 dys.	
Sodders, Andrew J	....do....	32	May 2, 1864	100 dys.	Mustered out with company Sept. 8, 1864.
Sodders, Jefferson J	....do....	29	May 2, 1864	100 dys.	Mustered out with company Sept. 8, 1864.
Smith, Nathan W	....do....	29	May 2, 1864	100 dys.	Mustered out with company Sept. 8, 1864.
Snider, William	....do....	18	May 2, 1864	100 dys.	Mustered out with company Sept. 8, 1864.
Taylor, Andrew J	....do....	19	May 2, 1864	100 dys.	Mustered out with company Sept. 8, 1864.
Thayer, Barnabas B	....do....	45	May 2, 1864	100 dys.	Mustered out with company Sept. 8, 1864.
Thomas, Samuel	....do....	20	May 2, 1864	100 dys.	Mustered out with company Sept. 8, 1864.
Tobin, Samuel D	....do....	20	May 2, 1864	100 dys.	Absent, sick ——, at home. No further record found.
Tossett, William	....do....	22	May 2, 1864	100 dys.	Mustered out with company Sept. 8, 1864.
Turner, Charles	....do....	38	May 2, 1864	100 dys.	Transferred to Co. I ——.
West, Edmund	....do....	44	May 2, 1864	100 dys.	Mustered out with company Sept. 8, 1864.
West, Moses	....do....	20	May 2, 1864	100 dys.	Mustered out with company Sept. 8, 1864.
West, William	....do....	36	May 2, 1864	100 dys.	Mustered out with company Sept. 8, 1864.
Whitehead, Amos	....do....	33	May 2, 1864	100 dys.	Mustered out with company Sept. 8, 1864.
Williams, Henry B	....do....	27	May 2, 1864	100 dys.	Mustered out with company Sept. 8, 1864.
Williams, John W	....do....	19	May 2, 1864	100 dys.	Mustered out with company Sept. 8, 1864.

Names	Rank	Age.	Date of Entering the Service.	Period of Service.	Remarks
Limes, William H.		18	May 2, 1864	100 dys.	Mustered out with co
Loyd, John		37	May 2, 1864	100 dys.	Mustered out with c
McDaniel, Samuel		18	May 2, 1864	100 dys.	Mustered out with
Merchant, Isaac		40	May 2, 1864	100 dys.	Mustered out with
Murry, James N.		18	May 2, 1864	100 dys.	Mustered out with
Painter, Charles		31	May 2, 1864	100 dys.	Mustered out with
Pernell, Hugh		21	May 2, 1864	100 dys.	Mustered out with
Phillips, N. L.		37	May 2, 1864	100 dys.	Mustered out with
Pine, John A.		18	May 2, 1864	100 dys.	Wounded June 11 ana, Ky.; dischar ington, Ky., on Su bility.
Post, Nelson	do.	20	May 2, 1864	100 dys.	Mustered out with c
Priddy, Strawder	do.	30	May 2, 1864	100 dys.	Mustered out with c
Smith, Jabez	do.	30	May 2, 1864	100 dys.	Mustered out with c
Smith, James W.	do.	19	May 2, 1864	100 dys.	Mustered out with c
Smith, Josephus	do.	36	May 2, 1864	100 dys.	Mustered out with c
Smith, John J.	do.	36	May 2, 1864	100 dys.	Transferred to Co. B
Smith, Leander C.	do.	18	May 2, 1864	100 dys.	Mustered out with c
Smith, Levi	do.	35	May 2, 1864	100 dys.	Killed June 11, 1864 Kentucky.
Smith, Peter W.	do.	38	May 2, 1864	100 dys.	Mustered out with c
Smith, Watson D.	do.	20	May 2, 1864	100 dys.	Mustered out with c
Sollars, Samuel	do.	26	May 2, 1864	100 dys.	Wounded June 11, ana, Ky.; died Se Kentucky.
Sollars, Wells B.	do.	18	May 2, 1864	100 dys.	See Co. C.
Spruance, Henry	do.	30	May 2, 1864	100 dys.	Mustered out with c
Templeton, James C.	do.	25	May 2, 1864	100 dys.	Mustered out with c
Templeton, John B.	do.	31	May 2, 1864	100 dys.	Mustered out with c
Turner, Charles	do.	38	May 2, 1864	100 dys.	Transferred from C with company Sep
Waters, Bernard	do.	28	May 2, 1864	100 dys.	Mustered out with c
Wells, Marmaduke	do.	30	May 2, 1864	100 dys.	Mustered out with c

COMPANY K.

Mustered in May 18, 1864, at Camp Dennison, O., by G. E. Johnson, Major and A. out Sept. 8, 1864, at Camp Dennison, O., by William Stanley, 2d Li 10th Infantry, U. S. A.

Names	Rank	Age	Date of Entering the Service	Period of Service	Remarks
Edwin K. Retter	Captain.	29	May 2, 1864	100 dys.	Mustered out with
Lewis H. Mark	1st Lieut.	25	May 2, 1864	100 dys.	Mustered out with
William Reid	2d Lieut.	42	May 2, 1864	100 dys.	Mustered out with
Edwin O. Kershner	1st Sergt.	21	May 2, 1864	100 dys.	Mustered out with
John Kruft	Sergeant.	31	May 2, 1864	100 dys.	Mustered out with
William P. Dick	do.	24	May 2, 1864	100 dys.	Mustered out with
Joseph Horseman	do.	29	May 2, 1864	100 dys.	Mustered out with
George W. Conner	do.	20	May 2, 1864	100 dys.	Mustered out with
Henry S. Adams	Corporal.	33	May 2, 1864	100 dys.	Mustered out with
William L. Werts	do.	28	May 2, 1864	100 dys.	Mustered out with
John H. Ferguson	do.	40	May 2, 1864	100 dys.	Mustered out with
Cornelius Wou	do.	22	May 2, 1864	100 dys.	Mustered out with
George Niroud	do.	34	May 2, 1864	100 dys.	Mustered out with
Jacob Coble	do.	27	May 2, 1864	100 dys.	Appointed July 20, company Sept. 8, 1
Harman A. Rowe	do.	33	May 2, 1864	100 dys.	Appointed July 20, company Sept. 8, 1
William C. Worthington	do.	20	May 2, 1864	100 dys.	Appointed July 20, company Sept. 8, 1
Alfred Mead	Musician	16	May 2, 1864	100 dys.	Mustered out with
John H. Stahesel	do.	30	May 2, 1864	100 dys.	Mustered out with
Affleck, Henry	Private.	18	May 2, 1864	100 dys.	Mustered out with
Affleck, William	do.	18	May 2, 1864	100 dys.	Mustered out with
Allen, Clement	do.	36	May 2, 1864	100 dys.	
Allen, Frank	do.	18	May 2, 1864	100 dys.	Mustered out with
Barnshof, Ezra	do.	19	May 2, 1864	100 dys.	Mustered out with
Beebe, Walter	do.	18	May 2, 1864	100 dys.	Mustered out with
Bilew, Pat	do.	35	May 2, 1864	100 dys.	On muster-in roll.
Bonecutter, George W.	do.	40	May 2, 1864	100 dys.	Mustered out with
Bought, John H.	do.	23	May 2, 1864	100 dys.	Mustered out with
Bowman, Frederick	do.	28	May 2, 1864	100 dys.	Mustered out with
Boy, William V.	do.	34	May 2, 1864	100 dys.	Mustered out with
Brinkman, Adam	do.	50	May 2, 1864	100 dys.	Mustered out with
Cannon, James W.	do.	26	May 2, 1864	100 dys.	Mustered out with
Cary, Cyrus	do.	27	May 2, 1864	100 dys.	Mustered out with
Chalfant, William	do.	19	May 2, 1864	100 dys.	Transferred to Co.
Clark, William	do.	36	May 2, 1864	100 dys.	Mustered out with
Coffee, Joseph A.	do.	32	May 2, 1864	100 dys.	Transferred from with company Se

169th Regiment Ohio Volunteer Infantry.

ONE HUNDRED DAY'S SERVICE.

This Regiment was organized at Camp Cleveland, O., from the 13th to the 15th of May, 1864, to serve one hundred days. It was composed of the Fiftieth Battalion, Ohio National Guard, from Sandusky County, and the Fifty-second Battalion, Ohio National Guard, from Wayne County. On the 19th of May the Regiment proceeded to Washington City, and upon its arrival was ordered on garrison duty in Fort Ethan Allen, where it remained during its term of service. It participated in the defeat of Early's attack on Washington City. The One Hundred and Sixty-ninth returned to Ohio, and was mustered out Sept. 4, 1864, on expiration of term of service.

Names.	Rank.	Age.	Date of Entering the Service.	Period of Service.	Remarks.
Easterday, William H	Private	21	May 2, 1864	100 dys.	Mustered out with company Sept. 4, 1864.
Eberly, John S	do	22	May 2, 1864	100 dys.	Mustered out with company Sept. 4, 1864.
Eberly, Peter	do	25	May 2, 1864	100 dys.	Died July 17, 1864, at Fort Ethan Allen, Va.
Eberly, Samuel	do	21	May 2, 1864	100 dys.	Mustered out with company Sept. 4, 1864.
Elliott, John	do	33	May 2, 1864	100 dys.	Mustered out with company Sept. 4, 1864.
Farner, Henry C	do	22	May 2, 1864	100 dys.	Mustered out with company Sept. 4, 1864.
Fetter, Samuel	do	33	May 2, 1864	100 dys.	Mustered out with company Sept. 4, 1864.
Forney, Samuel S	do	22	May 2, 1864	100 dys.	Mustered out with company Sept. 4, 1864.
Garver, David	do	29	May 2, 1864	100 dys.	Mustered out with company Sept. 4, 1864.
Glass, James	do	87	May 2, 1864	100 dys.	Mustered out with company Sept. 4, 1864.
Griffith, Oliver K	do	32	May 2, 1864	100 dys.	Mustered out with company Sept. 4, 1864.
Hardy, Neal	do	18	May 2, 1864	100 dys.	Mustered out with company Sept. 4, 1864.
Hoff, Andrew	do	18	May 2, 1864	100 dys.	Mustered out with company Sept. 4, 1864.
Hooly, Daniel	do	24	May 2, 1864	100 dys.	
Hoover, Samuel	do	19	May 2, 1864	100 dys.	Mustered out with company Sept. 4, 1864.
Hough, William D	do	32	May 2, 1864	100 dys.	Mustered out with company Sept. 4, 1864.
Hoverstock, Conrad	do	19	May 2, 1864	100 dys.	Mustered out with company Sept. 4, 1864.
Hoverstock, Henry	do	23	May 2, 1864	100 dys.	Mustered out with company Sept. 4, 1864.
Hutchison, Ezra P	do	18	May 2, 1864	100 dys.	Mustered out with company Sept. 4, 1864.
Johnson, George	do	23	May 2, 1864	100 dys.	Mustered out with company Sept. 4, 1864.
Jolliff, Andrew J	do	35	May 2, 1864	100 dys.	Mustered out with company Sept. 4, 1864.
Keifer, Henry M	do	20	May 2, 1864	100 dys.	Mustered out with company Sept. 4, 1864.
Keifer, Isaiah N	do	20	May 2, 1864	100 dys.	Mustered out with company Sept. 4, 1864.
Keifer, Josiah M	do	23	May 2, 1864	100 dys.	Absent, sick ——. No further record found.
Keister, Jacob A. H	do	25	May 2, 1864	100 dys.	Mustered out with company Sept. 4, 1864.
Keister, Thomas P	do	20	May 2, 1864	100 dys.	Mustered out with company Sept. 4, 1864.
Kintner, Jacob	do	29	May 2, 1864	100 dys.	
Lehr, Abraham	do	38	May 2, 1864	100 dys.	Mustered out with company Sept. 4, 1864.
Lightner, William B	do	18	May 2, 1864	100 dys.	Mustered out with company Sept. 4, 1864.
Limberger, Simon	do	20	May 2, 1864	100 dys.	Mustered out with company Sept. 4, 1864.
Long, John	do	41	May 2, 1864	100 dys.	Mustered out with company Sept. 4, 1864.
Lowry, John H	do	27	May 2, 1864	100 dys.	Mustered out with company Sept. 4, 1864.
McConahay, Hugh	do	27	May 2, 1864	100 dys.	Mustered out with company Sept. 4, 1864.
McMillen, Wilson S	do	26	May 2, 1864	100 dys.	Mustered out with company Sept. 4, 1864.
McNeal, Augusta	do	18	May 2, 1864	100 dys.	Mustered out with company Sept. 4, 1864.
McNeal, Edwin W	do	21	May 2, 1864	100 dys.	Mustered out with company Sept. 4, 1864.
Miller, Augustus B	do	20	May 2, 1864	100 dys.	Mustered out with company Sept. 4, 1864.
Miller, Otho	do	27	May 2, 1864	100 dys.	Mustered out with company Sept. 4, 1864.
Monasmith, Cyrus A	do	19	May 2, 1864	100 dys.	Mustered out with company Sept. 4, 1864.
Myers, Ross	do	23	May 2, 1864	100 dys.	Died July 27, 1864, at Fort Ethan Allen, Va.
Myler, John T	do	22	May 2, 1864	100 dys.	Mustered out with company Sept. 4, 1864.
Painter, John	do	19	May 2, 1864	100 dys.	Mustered out with company Sept. 4, 1864.
Perine, William M	do	30	May 2, 1864	100 dys.	Mustered out with company Sept. 4, 1864.
Plymesser, Amos	do	42	May 2, 1864	100 dys.	
Porter, George	do	18	May 2, 1864	100 dys.	Mustered out with company Sept. 4, 1864.
Redrick, John	do	19	May 2, 1864	100 dys.	Mustered out with company Sept. 4, 1864.
Reed, William	do	26	May 2, 1864	100 dys.	Mustered out with company Sept. 4, 1864.
Rider, James	do	23	May 2, 1864	100 dys.	Mustered out with company Sept. 4, 1864.
Sandos, Charles	do	18	May 2, 1864	100 dys.	Mustered out with company Sept. 4, 1864.
Sanford, Josiah B	do	25	May 2, 1864	100 dys.	Mustered out with company Sept. 4, 1864.
Schwamm, Francis M	do	20	May 2, 1864	100 dys.	Mustered out with company Sept. 4, 1864.
Sharp, Philip W	do	41	May 2, 1864	100 dys.	Mustered out with company Sept. 4, 1864.
Shoemaker, Samuel	do	39	May 2, 1864	100 dys.	Absent, sick ——. No further record found.
Smith, Henry L	do	36	May 2, 1864	100 dys.	Mustered out with company Sept. 4, 1864.
Smith, James P	do	34	May 2, 1864	100 dys.	Mustered out with company Sept. 4, 1864.
Smith, Richard H	do	31	May 2, 1864	100 dys.	Mustered out with company Sept. 4, 1864.
Steele, George W	do	41	May 2, 1864	100 dys.	Transferred to Co. F May 31, 1864.
Stuckey, Jacob	do	20	May 2, 1864	100 dys.	
Stutzman, Aaron	do	23	May 2, 1864	100 dys.	Mustered out with company Sept. 4, 1864.
Wagon, [illegible] George	do	41	May 2, 1864	100 dys.	Mustered out with company Sept. 4, 1864.
Willour, [illegible]homas	do	18	May 2, 1864	100 dys.	Absent, sick ——. No further record found.
Win[illegible]ler, [illegible]av[illegible]d	do	18	May 2, 1864	100 dys.	Mustered out with company Sept. 4, 1864.
W[illegible] [illegible]evi	do	18	May 2, 1864	100 dys.	Mustered out with company Sept. 4, 1864.
Yoder, Jac[illegible] D	do	21	May 2, 1864	100 dys.	Mustered out with company Sept. 4, 1864.
Zaring, Daniel	do	40	May 2, 1864	100 dys.	Mustered out with company Sept. 4, 1864.
Zimmerman, Emanuel	do	34	May 2, 1864	100 dys.	Mustered out with company Sept. 4, 1864.

Names.	Rank.	Age.	Date of Entering the Service.	Period of Service.	Remarks.
Terry, Charles	Private.	32	May 2, 1864	100 dys.	Mustered out with company Sept. 4, 1864.
Terry, Francis	....do...	28	May 2, 1864	100 dys.	Mustered out with company Sept. 4, 1864.
Terry, Sanford	....do...	25	May 2, 1864	100 dys.	Mustered out with company Sept. 4, 1864.
Thacker, John B	....do...	40	May 2, 1864	100 dys.	Mustered out with company Sept. 4, 1864.
Thomas, Scott	....do...	18	May 2, 1864	100 dys.	Mustered out with company Sept. 4, 1864.
Thomas, Theodore	....do...	22	May 2, 1864	100 dys.	Mustered out with company Sept. 4, 1864.
Thorp, John	....do...	21	May 2, 1864	100 dys.	Mustered out with company Sept. 4, 1864.
Tibbells, Samuel H	....do...	36	May 2, 1864	100 dys.	Mustered out with company Sept. 4, 1864.
Tuttle, Bradford	....do...	20	May 2, 1864	100 dys.	Mustered out with company Sept. 4, 1864.
Walters, Aseph	....do...	23	May 2, 1864	100 dys.	Mustered out with company Sept. 4, 1864.
Watson, Tobias	....do...	19	May 2, 1864	100 dys.	Mustered out with company Sept. 4, 1864.
Weeks, Milton	....do...	18	May 2, 1864	100 dys.	Mustered out with company Sept. 4, 1864.
West, Elijah	....do...	32	May 2, 1864	100 dys.	Died Aug. 31, 1864, at Clyde, O.
Whitehead, William	....do...	22	May 2, 1864	100 dys.	Died July 18, 1864, at Fort Ethan Allen, Va.
Wise, William	....do...	34	May 2, 1864	100 dys.	Mustered out with company Sept. 4, 1864.
Wykoff, Samuel D	....do...	28	May 2, 1864	100 dys.	Mustered out with company Sept. 4, 1864.
Zuel, Robert	....do...	31	May 2, 1864	100 dys.	Mustered out with company Sept. 4, 1864.

COMPANY C.

Mustered in May 13, 1864, at Camp Cleveland, O., by Thomas Drummond, Captain 5th Cavalry, U. S. A. Mustered out Sept. 4, 1864, at Camp Cleveland, O.

Names.	Rank.	Age.	Date of Entering the Service.	Period of Service.	Remarks.
Harry C Shirk	Captain.	24	May 2, 1864	100 dys.	Mustered out with company Sept. 4, 1864.
Thomas Robison	1st Lieut.	..	May 2, 1864	100 dys.	Mustered out with company Sept. 4, 1864.
Samuel B. Hughes	2d Lieut.	21	May 2, 1864	100 dys.	Mustered out with company Sept. 4, 1864.
Fenelon F. H. Pope	1st Sergt.	19	May 2, 1864	100 dys.	Mustered out with company Sept. 4, 1864.
James T. Stitt	Sergeant.	25	May 2, 1864	100 dys.	Mustered out with company Sept. 4, 1864.
Jacob Snyder	....do...	32	May 2, 1864	100 dys.	Mustered out with company Sept. 4, 1864.
Abram Saybolt, Jr	....do...	19	May 2, 1864	100 dys.	Mustered out with company Sept. 4, 1864.
George Reaser	....do...	22	May 2, 1864	100 dys.	Mustered out with company Sept. 4, 1864.
John W. Taggart	Corporal.	22	May 2, 1864	100 dys.	Mustered out with company Sept. 4, 1864.
George W. Weltmore	....do...	30	May 2, 1864	100 dys.	Mustered out with company Sept. 4, 1864.
Henry Markwalter	....do...	18	May 2, 1864	100 dys.	Mustered out with company Sept. 4, 1864.
Finley L. Parsons	....do...	20	May 2, 1864	100 dys.	Mustered out with company Sept. 4, 1864.
John E. Woodbridge	....do...	24	May 2, 1864	100 dys.	Mustered out with company Sept. 4, 1864.
Abraham Soliday, Jr	....do...	37	May 2, 1864	100 dys.	Mustered out with company Sept. 4, 1864.
Ross Chaffin	....do...	27	May 2, 1864	100 dys.	Mustered out with company Sept. 4, 1864.
William Shaner	....do...	19	May 2, 1864	100 dys.	Mustered out with company Sept. 4, 1864.
George N. Her	Musician	18	May 2, 1864	100 dys.	Mustered out with company Sept. 4, 1864.
William F Dee	Wagoner.	20	May 2, 1864	100 dys.	Mustered out with company Sept. 4, 1864.
Adleblue, Wilson	Private.	33	May 2, 1864	100 dys.	Mustered out with company Sept. 4, 1864.
Ames, Samuel	....do...	20	May 2, 1864	100 dys.	Mustered out with company Sept. 4, 1864.
Anderson, Samuel D	....do...	18	May 2, 1864	100 dys.	Mustered out with company Sept. 4, 1864.
Arnold, Jacob P	....do...	38	May 2, 1864	100 dys.	Mustered out with company Sept. 4, 1864.
Baker, Daniel C	....do...	18	May 2, 1864	100 dys.	Mustered out with company Sept. 4, 1864.
Bartoe, Stephen	....do...	19	May 2, 1864	100 dys.	Mustered out with company Sept. 4, 1864.
Beistle, Edson	....do...	18	May 2, 1864	100 dys.	Died July 21, 1864, at Fort Ethan Allen, Va.
Berry, John	....do...	42	May 2, 1864	100 dys.	Mustered out with company Sept. 4, 1864.
Bowers, Samuel	....do...	33	May 2, 1864	100 dys.	Mustered out with company Sept. 4, 1864.
Bowlas, John	....do...	19	May 2, 1864	100 dys.	Mustered out with company Sept. 4, 1864; also borne on rolls as John Bolous.
Bowman, Harrison	....do...	26	May 2, 1864	100 dys.	Mustered out with company Sept. 4, 1864.
Burnett, James C	....do...	18	May 2, 1864	100 dys.	Mustered out with company Sept. 4, 1864.
Chaffin, Hiram W	....do...	20	May 2, 1864	100 dys.	Mustered out with company Sept. 4, 1864.
Chaffin, William H	....do...	18	May 2, 1864	100 dys.	
Cumberland, Thomas W	....do...	18	May 2, 1864	100 dys.	Mustered out with company Sept. 4, 1864.
Cutler, Charles	....do...	30	May 2, 1864	100 dys.	Mustered out with company Sept. 4, 1864.
Daniels, Isaac	....do...	25	May 2, 1864	100 dys.	Mustered out with company Sept. 4, 1864.
Deitrich, Benjamin G	....do...	34	May 2, 1864	100 dys.	Mustered out with company Sept. 4, 1864.
Dillon, Robert	....do...	18	May 2, 1864	100 dys.	Mustered out with company Sept. 4, 1864.
Eppy, Reynolds	....do...	36	May 2, 1864	100 dys.	Mustered out with company Sept. 4, 1864.
Fishburn, William	....do...	31	May 2, 1864	100 dys.	Mustered out with company Sept. 4, 1864.
Funk, David B	....do...	37	May 2, 1864	100 dys.	Mustered out with company Sept. 4, 1864.
Hall, Robert	....do...	19	May 2, 1864	100 dys.	Mustered out with company Sept. 4, 1864.
Hanna, Carrington	....do...	19	May 2, 1864	100 dys.	Mustered out with company Sept. 4, 1864.
Hawk, David	....do...	19	May 2, 1864	100 dys.	Mustered out with company Sept. 4, 1864.
Hellmeer, Frank	....do...	18	May 2, 1864	100 dys.	Mustered out with company Sept. 4, 1864.
He[illegible], John P	....do...	34	May 2, 1864	100 dys.	Mustered out with company Sept. 4, 1864.
Hirschy, John F	....do...	19	May 2, 1864	100 dys.	Mustered out with company Sept. 4, 1864.
Hunter, Jefferson	....do...	17	May 2, 1864	100 dys.	Mustered out with company Sept. 4, 1864.
Hunter, Thomas	....do...	21	May 2, 1864	100 dys.	Mustered out with company Sept. 4, 1864.
Kramer, John	....do...	20	May 2, 1864	100 dys.	Mustered out with company Sept. 4, 1864.
Loch, William	....do...	22	May 2, 1864	100 dys.	Mustered out with company Sept. 4, 1864.
McAdams, Charles	....do...	18	May 2, 1864	100 dys.	Mustered out with company Sept. 4, 1864.
McCulloch, Wilton R	....do...	18	May 2, 1864	100 dys.	Mustered out with company Sept. 4, 1864.
McClure, James	....do...	19	May 2, 1864	100 dys.	Mustered out with company Sept. 4, 1864.
McKee, Thomas	....do...	19	May 2, 1864	100 dys.	Mustered out with company Sept. 4, 1864.
Mars, Wesley	....do...	18	May 2, 1864	100 dys.	Mustered out with company Sept. 4, 1864.
Marshall, William V	....do...	18	May 2, 1864	100 dys.	Mustered out with company Sept. 4, 1864.

Names.	Rank.	Age.	Date of Entering the Service.	Period of Service.	Remarks.
Ellet, Austin	Private	18	May 2, 1864	100 dys.	Mustered out with company Sept. 4, 1864.
Eyman, Benjamin	do	23	May 2, 1864	100 dys.	Mustered out with company Sept. 4, 1864.
Eyman, John	do	20	May 2, 1864	100 dys.	Mustered out with company Sept. 4, 1864.
Forbes, William A	do	18	May 2, 1864	100 dys.	Mustered out with company Sept. 4, 1864.
Forrer, Henry	do	21	May 2, 1864	100 dys.	Mustered out with company Sept. 4, 1864.
Fraise, Benjamin F	do	18	May 2, 1864	100 dys.	Mustered out with company Sept. 4, 1864.
Gardner, Elias K	do	20	May 2, 1864	100 dys.	Mustered out with company Sept. 4, 1864.
Hamilton, William	do	18	May 2, 1864	100 dys.	Mustered out with company Sept. 4, 1864.
Hamlin, William G	do	18	May 2, 1864	100 dys.	Mustered out with company Sept. 4, 1864.
Hazen, Wilson	do	18	May 2, 1864	100 dys.	Mustered out with company Sept. 4, 1864.
Heller, William	do	18	May 2, 1864	100 dys.	Mustered out with company Sept. 4, 1864.
Huntsberger, Jacob	do	18	May 2, 1864	100 dys.	Mustered out with company Sept. 4, 1864.
Ingram, Arnold A	do	20	May 2, 1864	100 dys.	Mustered out with company Sept. 4, 1864.
Joliff, Emanuel	do	24	May 2, 1864	100 dys.	Mustered out with company Sept. 4, 1864.
Kahn, Augustus	do	24	May 2, 1864	100 dys.	Mustered out with company Sept. 4, 1864.
Kimber, Emmos	do	28	May 2, 1864	100 dys.	Mustered out with company Sept. 4, 1864.
Knox, John B	do	35	May 2, 1864	100 dys.	Mustered out with company Sept. 4, 1864.
Kope, James H	do	26	May 2, 1864	100 dys.	Mustered out with company Sept. 4, 1864.
Landis, Amos	do	19	May 2, 1864	100 dys.	Mustered out with company Sept. 4, 1864.
Lash, William H	do	18	May 2, 1864	100 dys.	Mustered out with company Sept. 4, 1864.
Lichty, David	do	24	May 2, 1864	100 dys.	Died Aug. 9, 1864, at Fort Ethan Allen, Va.
Lichty, William	do	27	May 2, 1864	100 dys.	Mustered out with company Sept. 4, 1864.
Lefever, John	do	35	May 2, 1864	100 dys.	Mustered out with company Sept. 4, 1864.
Lefever, Martin	do	28	May 2, 1864	100 dys.	Mustered out with company Sept. 4, 1864.
McDonough, James	do	18	May 2, 1864	100 dys.	Mustered out with company Sept. 4, 1864.
McGiffin, Samuel	do	20	May 2, 1864	100 dys.	Mustered out with company Sept. 4, 1864.
Markle, Augustus	do	35	May 2, 1864	100 dys.	Mustered out with company Sept. 4, 1864.
Martin, Emanuel	do	20	May 2, 1864	100 dys.	Mustered out with company Sept. 4, 1864.
Martin, John	do	22	May 2, 1864	100 dys.	Mustered out with company Sept. 4, 1864.
Martin, Joseph	do	19	May 2, 1864	100 dys.	Mustered out with company Sept. 4, 1864.
Mower, George	do	18	May 2, 1864	100 dys.	Mustered out with company Sept. 4, 1864.
Murry, William	do	30	May 2, 1864	100 dys.	Mustered out with company Sept. 4, 1864.
Musselman, Zachariah	do	18	May 2, 1864	100 dys.	Mustered out with company Sept. 4, 1864.
Myers, Stephen	do	21	May 2, 1864	100 dys.	Mustered out with company Sept. 4, 1864.
Oldroyd, Wilbur F	do	20	May 2, 1864	100 dys.	Mustered out with company Sept. 4, 1864.
Orr, Smith	do	18	May 2, 1864	100 dys.	Mustered out with company Sept. 4, 1864.
Orr, William M	do	25	May 2, 1864	100 dys.	Mustered out with company Sept. 4, 1864.
Postlewait, [illegible]	do	20	May 2, 1864	100 dys.	Mustered out with company Sept. 4, 1864.
Priest, Richard	do	27	May 2, 1864	100 dys.	Mustered out with company Sept. 4, 1864.
Rizer, Martin	do	26	May 2, 1864	100 dys.	Mustered out with company Sept. 4, 1864.
Romick, Andrew	do	37	May 2, 1864	100 dys.	Mustered out with company Sept. 4, 1864.
Roach, George H	do	26	May 2, 1864	100 dys.	Mustered out with company Sept. 4, 1864.
Rouch, Philip A	do	27	May 2, 1864	100 dys.	Mustered out with company Sept. 4, 1864.
Schmuck, William H	do	21	May 2, 1864	100 dys.	Mustered out with company Sept. 4, 1864.
Shaff, David A	do	19	May 2, 1864	100 dys.	Mustered out with company Sept. 4, 1864.
Shultz, David D	do	28	May 2, 1864	100 dys.	Mustered out with company Sept. 4, 1864.
Simkins, Lewis	do	18	May 2, 1864	100 dys.	Mustered out with company Sept. 4, 1864.
Simmons, John	do	18	May 2, 1864	100 dys.	Mustered out with company Sept. 4, 1864.
Snyder, Alexander H	do	34	May 2, 1864	100 dys.	Mustered out with company Sept. 4, 1864.
Snyder, George H	do	19	May 2, 1864	100 dys.	Died July 29, 1864, at Fort Ethan Allen, Va.
Snyder, Jacob H	do	24	May 2, 1864	100 dys.	Mustered out with company Sept. 4, 1864.
Springer, Joseph L	do	25	May 2, 1864	100 dys.	Mustered out with company Sept. 4, 1864.
Starner, John	do	34	May 2, 1864	100 dys.	Mustered out with company Sept. 4, 1864.
Swartz, Samuel T	do	22	May 2, 1864	100 dys.	Mustered out with company Sept. 4, 1864.
Taggart, William	do	37	May 2, 1864	100 dys.	Mustered out with company Sept. 4, 1864.
Van [illegible], David	do	18	May 2, 1864	100 dys.	Mustered out with company Sept. 4, 1864.
Warner, David E	do	18	May 2, 1864	100 dys.	Mustered out with company Sept. 4, 1864.
Willford, Henry B.	do	18	May 2, 1864	100 dys.	Mustered out with company Sept. 4, 1864.
Williams, Joseph	do	18	May 2, 1864	100 dys.	Mustered out with company Sept. 4, 1864.
Woolbauch, William H.	do	18	May 2, 1864	100 dys.	Mustered out with company Sept. 4, 1864.

COMPANY E.

Mustered in May 13, 1864, at Camp Cleveland, O., by Thomas Drummond, Captain 5th Cavalry, U. S. A. Mustered out Sept. 4, 1864, at Camp Cleveland, O., by Thomas Drummond, Captain 5th Cavalry, U. S. A.

Names.	Rank.	Age.	Date of Entering the Service.	Period of Service.	Remarks.
William K. Boone	Captain.	29	May 2, 1864	100 dys.	Mustered out with company Sept. 4, 1864.
William H. Fleck	1st Lieut.	23	May 2, 1864	100 dys.	Mustered out with company Sept. 4, 1864.
Benjamin F. Baltzby	2d Lieut.	28	May 2, 1864	100 dys.	Mustered out with company Sept. 4, 1864.
George Jameson	1st Sergt.	25	May 2, 1864	100 dys.	Mustered out with company Sept. 4, 1864.
Jacob Eckard	Sergeant.	27	May 2, 1864	100 dys.	Mustered out with company Sept. 4, 1864.
Martin Buchwalter	do	28	May 2, 1864	100 dys.	Mustered out with company Sept. 4, 1864.
Jacob G. Dague	do	22	May 2, 1864	100 dys.	Mustered out with company Sept. 4, 1864.
Eber Homan	do	27	May 2, 1864	100 dys.	Mustered out with company Sept. 4, 1864.
George H. Kountz	Corporal.	27	May 2, 1864	100 dys.	Mustered out with company Sept. 4, 1864.
Reason B. Wertz	do	23	May 2, 1864	100 dys.	Mustered out with company Sept. 4, 1864.
B. Frank Barclay	do	24	May 2, 1864	100 dys.	Absent on furlough since Aug. 2, 1864, at Dalton, O. No further record found.
Webster Groff	do	18	May 2, 1864	100 dys.	Mustered out with company Sept. 4, 1864.
William C. Lyon	do	27	May 2, 1864	100 dys.	Mustered out with company Sept. 4, 1864.

COMPANY F.

Mustered in May 15, 1864, at Camp Cleveland, O., by C. B. Throckmorton, 1st L
Mustered out Sept. 4, 1864, at Camp Cleveland, O., by Thom
Captain 5th Cavalry, U. S. A.

Names.	Rank.	Age.	Date of Entering the Service.	Period of Service.	
Charles Thompson	Captain.	28	May 2, 1864	100 dys.	Mustered
Charles A. Baldwin	1st Lieut.	41	May 2, 1864	100 dys.	Mustered
George J. Krebs	2d Lieut.	26	May 2, 1864	100 dys.	Mustered
Peter Kessler	1st Sergt.	20	May 2, 1864	100 dys.	Mustered
Harvey H. Axlin	Sergeant.	24	May 2, 1864	100 dys.	Mustered out
Joseph H. Parkhurst	do.	35	May 2, 1864	100 dys.	Mustered out
Henry C. Stacy	do.	44	May 2, 1864	100 dys.	Mustered out
Joseph H. Mawrer	do.	35	May 2, 1864	100 dys.	Mustered out
Austin Whitaker	Corporal.	18	May 2, 1864	100 dys.	Mustered out
Selah K. Anderson	do.	36	May 2, 1864	100 dys.	Mustered out
Washington Younkman	do.	21	May 2, 1864	100 dys.	Mustered out
Lewis Bolan	do.	34	May 2, 1864	100 dys.	Mustered out
Thomas Fowler	do.	25	May 2, 1864	100 dys.	Mustered out
Gilbert Williams	do.	18	May 2, 1864	100 dys.	Died Aug. 4, 1
Henry Ernest	do.	21	May 2, 1864	100 dys.	Mustered out
Isaac Joseph	do.	29	May 2, 1864	100 dys.	Mustered out
Henry Honsinger	Musician	18	May 2, 1864	100 dys.	Mustered out
Abram R. Hall	do.	32	May 2, 1864	100 dys.	Mustered out
Henry W. Imler	Wagoner.	35	May 2, 1864	100 dys.	Appointed — Sept. 4, 1864.
Alexander, Henry P.	Private.	38	May 2, 1864	100 dys.	Mustered out
Barkheimer, George	do.	44	May 2, 1864	100 dys.	Mustered out
Bixler, Forrest	do.	22	May 2, 1864	100 dys.	Reduced from with compa
Blood, Hiram W	do.	36	May 2, 1864	100 dys.	Mustered out
Briggs, James	do.	18	May 2, 1864	100 dys.	Mustered out
Burg, John	do.	17	May 2, 1864	100 dys.	Mustered out
Burgoon, Isadore	do.	25	May 2, 1864	100 dys.	Promoted to S
Claghorn, Harrison	do.	27	May 2, 1864	100 dys.	Mustered out
Clark, Darvin	do.	34	May 2, 1864	100 dys.	Mustered out
Cochran, Henry	do.	17	May 2, 1864	100 dys.	Mustered out
Deal, John P	do.	30	May 2, 1864	100 dys.	Mustered out
Downs, Flavel W	do.	16	May 2, 1864	100 dys.	Mustered out
Durfee, Thomas	do.	16	May 2, 1864	100 dys.	Mustered out
England, Theodore	do.	22	May 2, 1864	100 dys.	Promoted to C
Frederick, Andrew J	do.	35	May 2, 1864	100 dys.	Mustered out
Freeman, Calvin	do.	19	May 2, 1864	100 dys.	Mustered out
Garvin, John	do.	16	May 2, 1864	100 dys.	Mustered out
Gilmore, Thomas E.	do.	43	May 2, 1864	100 dys.	Mustered out
Golden, Daniel	do.	29	May 2, 1864	100 dys.	Mustered out
Green, Stephen	do.	27	May 2, 1864	100 dys.	Mustered out
Hall, Benjamin I.	do.	38	May 2, 1864	100 dys.	Mustered out
Hall, Edward J	do.	20	May 2, 1864	100 dys.	Mustered out
Halter, David	do.	20	May 2, 1864	100 dys.	Died July 24, 1
Helt, William	do.	21	May 2, 1864	100 dys.	Mustered out
Hilt, Frederick	do.	20	May 2, 1864	100 dys.	Mustered out
Hooke, Otto	do.	21	May 2, 1864	100 dys.	Mustered out
Holbrook, Erastus	do.	39	May 2, 1864	100 dys.	Mustered out
Holcomb, Edwin	do.	33	May 2, 1864	100 dys.	Died July 31, 1
Hughes, James W	do.	32	May 2, 1864	100 dys.	Mustered out
Hunter, William	do.	30	May 2, 1864	100 dys.	Mustered out
Huss, Burr	do.	18	May 2, 1864	100 dys.	Mustered out
Ice, John	do.	32	May 2, 1864	100 dys.	Mustered out
Ice, Samuel	do.	37	May 2, 1864	100 dys.	Mustered out
Ice, William	do.	41	May 2, 1864	100 dys.	Mustered out
Jenks, Oliver P.	do.	18	May 2, 1864	100 dys.	Mustered out
King, John	do.	26	May 2, 1864	100 dys.	Mustered out
Leppelman, David	do.	19	May 2, 1864	100 dys.	Mustered out
Lockwood, Sardis S.	do.	21	May 2, 1864	100 dys.	Mustered out
Lott, John B	do.	31	May 2, 1864	100 dys.	Mustered out
Maggrum, Joseph	do.	29	May 2, 1864	100 dys.	Mustered out
Manning, Wilbur F.	do.	27	May 2, 1864	100 dys.	Mustered out
Meek, William C.	do.	25	May 2, 1864	100 dys.	Mustered out
Mellen, Joshua E	do.	39	May 2, 1864	100 dys.	Mustered out
Mock, Hiram	do.	22	May 2, 1864	100 dys.	Mustered out
Mooney, Benjamin	do.	26	May 2, 1864	100 dys.	Mustered out
Mourer, Eli	do.	19	May 2, 1864	100 dys.	Mustered out
Myers, Joseph	do.	..	May 2, 1864	100 dys.	
Myers, Leander	do.	21	May 2, 1864	100 dys.	Mustered out
Ott, William	do.	21	May 2, 1864	100 dys.	Mustered out
Parker, Sylvanus P	do.	44	May 2, 1864	100 dys.	Mustered out
Patterson, John	do.	19	May 2, 1864	100 dys.	Mustered out
Pease, John	do.	18	May 2, 1864	100 dys.	Mustered out
Pelton, Eugene	do.	18	May 2, 1864	100 dys.	Mustered out
Purcell, John	do.	27	May 2, 1864	100 dys.	Mustered out
Quinn, John	do.	17	May 2, 1864	100 dys.	Mustered out
Rathbone, Chaplain	do.	18	May 2, 1864	100 dys.	Mustered out

Names.	Rank.	Age.	Date of Entering the Service.	Period of Service.	Remarks.
Geiger, Jacob	Private.	22	May 2, 1864	100 dys.	Mustered out with company Sept. 4, 1864.
Golden, Rodney	...do...	27	May 2, 1864	100 dys.	Mustered out with company Sept. 4, 1864.
Grivel, George	...do...	37	May 2, 1864	100 dys.	Mustered out with company Sept. 4, 1864.
Harley, Isaac	...do...	25	May 2, 1864	100 dys.	Mustered out with company Sept. 4, 1864.
Harley, Samuel	...do...	24	May 2, 1864	100 dys.	Mustered out with company Sept. 4, 1864.
Herrick, Jerome	...do...	30	May 2, 1864	100 dys.	Mustered out with company Sept. 4, 1864.
Holbrook, Henry C	...do...	25	May 2, 1864	100 dys.	Mustered out with company Sept. 4, 1864.
Holcomb, Grant	...do...	27	May 2, 1864	100 dys.	Died May 30, 1864, at Fort Ethan Allen, Va.
Hoff, Samuel	...do...	33	May 2, 1864	100 dys.	Mustered out with company Sept. 4, 1864.
Huffman, Oliver P	...do...	26	May 2, 1864	100 dys.	Discharged June 27, 1864, by order of War Department.
Huffman, Stanton	...do...	25	May 2, 1864	100 dys.	Mustered out with company Sept. 4, 1864.
Huffman, Victor J	...do...	18	May 2, 1864	100 dys.	Mustered out with company Sept. 4, 1864.
Hurdick, George	...do...	18	May 2, 1864	100 dys.	Mustered as Wagoner; mustered out with company Sept. 4, 1864.
Hutchinson, John W	...do...	32	May 2, 1864	100 dys.	Mustered out with company Sept. 4, 1864.
Immel, Solomon	...do...	34	May 2, 1864	100 dys.	Mustered out with company Sept. 4, 1864.
Jones, James	...do...	24	May 2, 1864	100 dys.	Mustered out with company Sept. 4, 1864.
Jones, John W.	...do...	27	May 2, 1864	100 dys.	Mustered out with company Sept. 4, 1864.
Karbler, George	...do...	28	May 2, 1864	100 dys.	Died July 6, 1864, at Fort Ethan Allen, Va.
Keller, Andrew J	...do...	39	May 2, 1864	100 dys.	Mustered out with company Sept. 4, 1864.
Klutz, Samuel	...do...	32	May 2, 1864	100 dys.	Mustered out with company Sept. 4, 1864.
Krieger, John	...do...	38	May 2, 1864	100 dys.	Mustered out with company Sept. 4, 1864.
Lemon, William	...do...	18	May 2, 1864	100 dys.	Mustered out with company Sept. 4, 1864.
Lemon, William H	...do...	26	May 2, 1864	100 dys.	Mustered out with company Sept. 4, 1864.
Madden, Thomas	...do...	18	May 2, 1864	100 dys.	Mustered out with company Sept. 4, 1864.
Manning, Joh n W	...do...	27	May 2, 1864	100 dys.	Mustered out with company Sept. 4, 1864.
Miller, Adam	...do...	19	May 2, 1864	100 dys.	Mustered out with company Sept. 4, 1864.
Miller, Calvin	...do...	18	May 2, 1864	100 dys.	Mustered out with company Sept. 4, 1864.
Nachtrieb, John	...do...	18	May 2, 1864	100 dys.	Mustered out with company Sept. 4, 1864.
Plants, Peter	...do...	27	May 2, 1864	100 dys.	Mustered out with company Sept. 4, 1864.
Rahm, Henry	...do...	35	May 2, 1864	100 dys.	Mustered out with company Sept. 4, 1864.
Ream onathan	...do...	27	May 2, 1864	100 dys.	Mustered out with company Sept. 4, 1864.
Reinhart, Theodore	...do...	22	May 2, 1864	100 dys.	Mustered out with company Sept. 4, 1864.
Risley, Charles	...do...	18	May 2, 1864	100 dys.	Died July 4, 1864, at Fort Ethan Allen, Va.
Root Edmund	...do...	39	May 2, 1864	100 dys.	Mustered out with company Sept. 4, 1864.
Rutherford, Robert	...do...	21	May 2, 1864	100 dys.	Mustered out with company Sept. 4, 1864.
Sanders, Isaac	...do...	29	May 2, 1864	100 dys.	Mustered out with company Sept. 4, 1864.
Shesely, Solomon	...do...	21	May 2, 1864	100 dys.	Mustered out with company Sept. 4, 1864.
Smith, Philander H	...do...	18	May 2, 1864	100 dys.	Mustered out with company Sept. 4, 1864.
Sting, William	...do...	18	May 2, 1864	100 dys.	Mustered out with company Sept. 4, 1864.
Taylor Adam N	...do...	18	May 2, 1864	100 dys.	Mustered out with company Sept. 4, 1864.
Thomas, Herbert	...do...	41	May 2, 1864	100 dys.	Mustered out with company Sept. 4, 1864.
Thompson, Charles F	...do...	19	May 2, 1864	100 dys.	Mustered out with company Sept. 4, 1864.
Thompson, William	...do...	21	May 2, 1864	100 dys.	Mustered out with company Sept. 4, 1864.
Totton, William	...do...	18	May 2, 1864	100 dys.	Mustered out with company Sept. 4, 1864.
Tyler, Charles J	...do...	18	May 2, 1864	100 dys.	Mustered out with company Sept. 4, 1864.
Yearling, Jacob	...do...	19	May 2, 1864	100 dys.	Mustered out with company Sept. 4, 1864.
Zimmerman, Philip	...do...	18	May 2, 1864	100 dys.	Mustered out with company Sept. 4, 1864.

COMPANY H.

Mustered in May 15, 1864, at Camp Cleveland, O., by C. B. Throckmorton, 1st Lieutenant 4th Artillery, U. S. A. Mustered out Sept. 4, 1864, at Camp Cleveland, O., by Thomas Drummond, Captain 5th Cavalry, U. S. A.

Names.	Rank.	Age.	Date of Entering the Service.	Period of Service.	Remarks.
Jacob D. Thomas	Captain.	23	May 2, 1864	100 dys.	Mustered out with company Sept. 4, 1864.
William J. Havens	1st Lieut.	30	May 2, 1864	100 dys.	Mustered out with company Sept. 4, 1864.
Solomon Warner	2d Lieut.	32	May 2, 1864	100 dys.	Mustered out with company Sept. 4, 1864.
Thomas El dge	1st Sergt.	29	May 2, 1864	100 dys.	Mustered out with company Sept. 4, 1864.
Valentine Shade	Sergeant.	25	May 2, 1864	100 dys.	Mustered out with company Sept. 4, 1864.
Peter C Smith	...do...	27	May 2, 1864	100 dys.	Mustered out with company Sept. 4, 1864.
Samuel Doll	...do...	29	May 2, 1864	100 dys.	Mustered out with company Sept. 4, 1864.
Henry Lance	...do...	21	May 2, 1864	100 dys.	Died July 23, 1864, at Fort Ethan Allen, Va.
Isaac Bruner	Corporal.	31	May 2, 1864	100 dys.	Mustered out with company Sept. 4, 1864.
ristian F M ller	...do...	29	May 2, 1864	100 dys.	Mustered out with company Sept. 4, 1864.
W liam I. Lee	...do...	26	May 2, 1864	100 dys.	Mustered out with company Sept. 4, 1864.
Isaac W Krotzer	...do...	22	May 2, 1864	100 dys.	Mustered out with company Sept. 4, 1864.
Robert Kessler	...do...	32	May 2, 1864	100 dys.	Mustered out with company Sept. 4, 1864.
ucien Hull	...do...	26	May 2, 1864	100 dys.	Mustered out with company Sept. 4, 1864.
Hubbard H. Hill	...do...	35	May 2, 1864	100 dys.	Mustered out with company Sept. 4, 1864.
Amos T. add	...do...	30	May 2, 1864	100 dys.	Mustered out with company Sept. 4, 1864.
John Fa ings	Musician	39	May 2, 1864	100 dys.	Mustered out with company Sept. 4, 1864.
Thomas J. Keenan	...do...	35	May 2, 1864	100 dys.	Mustered out with company Sept. 4, 1864.
Abel, Piers	Private.	39	May 2, 1864	100 dys.	Mustered out with company Sept. 4, 1864.
Babb, Danie F	...do...	20	May 2, 1864	100 dys.	Mustered out with company Sept. 4, 1864.
Batesole, Christopher	...do...	30	May 2, 1864	100 dys.	Mustered out with company Sept. 4, 1864.
Bee man, Henry	...do...	32	May 2, 1864	100 dys.	Mustered out with company Sept. 4, 1864.
Bement, Dwight	...do...	18	May 2, 1864	100 dys.	Mustered out with company Sept. 4, 1864.
Boor, William C	...do...	31	May 2, 1864	100 dys.	Mustered out with company Sept. 4, 1864.

Names.	Rank.	Age.	Date of Entering the Service.	Period of Service.	Remarks.
Bowlus, William	Private.	21	May 2, 1864	100 dys.	Discharged June 24, 1864, at Fort Ethan Allen, Va., on surgeon's certificate of disability.
Brannon, William	....do....	21	May 2, 1864	100 dys.	Mustered out with company Sept. 4, 1864.
Bruner, Abraham	....do....	[illegible]	May 2, 1864	100 dys.	Mustered out with company Sept. 4, 1864.
Bruner, Martin	....do....	[illegible]	May 2, 1864	100 dys.	Mustered out with company Sept. 4, 1864.
Burner, Jacob	....do....	[illegible]	May 2, 1864	100 dys.	Mustered out with company Sept. 4, 1864.
Burket, Joseph	....do....	[illegible]	May 2, 1864	100 dys.	Mustered out with company Sept. 4, 1864.
Campbell, James	....do....	[illegible]	May 2, 1864	100 dys.	Mustered out with company Sept. 4, 1864.
Chira, Jacob	....do....	[illegible]	May 2, 1864	100 dys.	Mustered out with company Sept. 4, 1864.
Cobb, Alfred	....do....	[illegible]	May 2, 1864	100 dys.	
Cole, Philip	....do....	25	May 2, 1864	100 dys.	Mustered out with company Sept. 4, 1864.
Daniels, George	....do....	4[illegible]	May 2, 1864	100 dys.	Mustered out with company Sept. 4, 1864.
Derlem, Franklin	....do....	[illegible]	May 2, 1864	100 dys.	Mustered out with company Sept. 4, 1864.
Dell, Daniel	....do....	[illegible]	May 2, 1864	100 dys.	
Dell, John	....do....	[illegible]	May 2, 1864	100 dys.	Mustered out with company Sept. 4, 1864.
Donnels, John L.	....do....	22	May 2, 1864	100 dys.	Mustered out with company Sept. 4, 1864.
Drake, Darius	....do....	[illegible]	May 2, 1864	100 dys.	
Drittmore, Henry	....do....	18	May 2, 1864	100 dys.	Mustered out with company Sept. 4, 1864.
Elliott, Samuel W.	....do....	18	May 2, 1864	100 dys.	Mustered out with company Sept. 4, 1864.
Freese, Lewis	....do....	[illegible]	May 2, 1864	100 dys.	Mustered out with company Sept. 4, 1864.
Fuller, James	....do....	[illegible]	May 2, 1864	100 dys.	Mustered out with company Sept. 4, 1864.
Gilmore, Phineas	....do....	22	May 2, 1864	100 dys.	Mustered out with company Sept. 4, 1864.
Gray, [illegible]	....do....	18	May 2, 1864	100 dys.	
Harvey, David	....do....	18	May 2, 1864	100 dys.	Mustered out with company Sept. 4, 1864.
Havens, Hugh	....do....	[illegible]	May 2, 1864	100 dys.	Mustered out with company Sept. 4, 1864.
Henderson, John	....do....	28	May 2, 1864	100 dys.	Mustered out with company Sept. 4, 1864.
Holcomb, Lester L.	....do....	[illegible]	May 2, 1864	100 dys.	Mustered out with company Sept. 4, 1864.
Howard, Emmett	....do....	[illegible]	May 2, 1864	100 dys.	Mustered out with company Sept. 4, 1864.
H[illegible]	....do....	18	May 2, 1864	100 dys.	Mustered out with company Sept. 4, 1864.
Jones, James	....do....	[illegible]	May 2, 1864	100 dys.	Mustered out with company Sept. 4, 1864.
Keenan, Peter	....do....	[illegible]	May 2, 1864	100 dys.	[illegible]
K[illegible]	....do....	[illegible]	May 2, 1864	100 dys.	[illegible]
L[illegible]	....do....	[illegible]	May 2, 1864	100 dys.	[illegible]
Long, Newton	....do....	[illegible]	May 2, 1864	100 dys.	[illegible]
[illegible], William	....do....	[illegible]	May 2, 1864	100 dys.	[illegible]
M[illegible]	....do....	[illegible]	May 2, 1864	100 dys.	[illegible]
McIntyre, W[illegible]	....do....	[illegible]	May 2, 1864	100 dys.	[illegible]; mustered out with company Sept. 4, 1864.
Maurer, Martin	....do....	[illegible]	May 2, 1864	100 dys.	Mustered out with company Sept. 4, 1864.
Miller, John	....do....	[illegible]	May 2, 1864	100 dys.	Mustered out with company Sept. 4, 1864.
Miller, William	....do....	24	May 2, 1864	100 dys.	Mustered out with company Sept. 4, 1864.
Mills, James A.	....do....	18	May 2, 1864	100 dys.	Mustered out with company Sept. 4, 1864.
Mitchell, Irvin	....do....	18	May 2, 1864	100 dys.	Mustered out with company Sept. 4, 1864.
Mowry, Henry	....do....	[illegible]	May 2, 1864	100 dys.	Died [illegible] 1864, at Fort Ethan Allen, Va.
Mowry, Jacob L.	....do....	18	May 2, 1864	100 dys.	Mustered out with company Sept. 4, 1864.
Myers, Joseph	....do....	[illegible]	May 2, 1864	100 dys.	Mustered out with company Sept. 4, 1864.
Myers, Samuel	....do....	[illegible]	May 2, 1864	100 dys.	Mustered out with company Sept. 4, 1864.
Overmire, Jacob I.	....do....	20	May 2, 1864	100 dys.	Mustered out with company Sept. 4, 1864.
P[illegible], Joseph	....do....	[illegible]	May 2, 1864	100 dys.	Mustered out with company Sept. 4, 1864.
Price, Thomas	....do....	41	May 2, 1864	100 dys.	Mustered out with company Sept. 4, 1864.
Robinson, John	....do....	18	May 2, 1864	100 dys.	Mustered out with company Sept. 4, 1864.
Roach, John	....do....	22	May 2, 1864	100 dys.	Mustered out with company Sept. 4, 1864.
Satersel, Jacob	....do....	19	May 2, 1864	100 dys.	Mustered out with company Sept. 4, 1864.
Shaie, Jacob	....do....	21	May 2, 1864	100 dys.	Mustered out with company Sept. 4, 1864.
Shasteen, Beriah	....do....	27	May 2, 1864	100 dys.	Died [illegible] 1864, at Fort Ethan Allen, Va.
Stoner, Jacob	....do....	19	May 2, 1864	100 dys.	Died June 2[illegible], 1864, at Fort Ethan Allen, Va.
Shoup, Adam	....do....	[illegible]	May 2, 1864	100 dys.	Mustered out with company Sept. 4, 1864.
Shoup, Steward	....do....	32	May 2, 1864	100 dys.	Mustered out with company Sept. 4, 1864.
Shrants, John	....do....	27	May 2, 1864	100 dys.	Mustered out with company Sept. 4, 1864.
Small, Leonard	....do....	[illegible]	May 2, 1864	100 dys.	Mustered out with company Sept. 4, 1864.
Speece, Daniel	....do....	37	May 2, 1864	100 dys.	Mustered out with company Sept. 4, 1864.
Stahl, John M.	....do....	28	May 2, 1864	100 dys.	Died [illegible] 2[illegible], 1864, at Fort Ethan Allen, Va.
Vanderson, Isaac	....do....	2[illegible]	May 2, 1864	100 dys.	Mustered out with company Sept. 4, 1864.
Vanderson, Isaiah	....do....	28	May 2, 1864	100 dys.	Mustered out with company Sept. 4, 1864.
Ver Wanoter, Miller	....do....	26	May 2, 1864	100 dys.	Mustered out with company Sept. 4, 1864.
Walters, Henry	....do....	[illegible]	May 2, 1864	100 dys.	Mustered out with company Sept. 4, 1864.
Warner, Daniel	....do....	[illegible]	May 2, 1864	100 dys.	Mustered out with company Sept. 4, 1864.
Warner, Samuel	....do....	[illegible]	May 2, 1864	100 dys.	Mustered out with company Sept. 4, 1864.
Weigelsam, Taylor G.	....do....	[illegible]	May 2, 1864	100 dys.	Mustered out with company Sept. 4, 1864.
Whitmore, Andrew	....do....	2[illegible]	May 2, 1864	100 dys.	Mustered out with company Sept. 4, 1864.
Whitehead, Joseph	....do....	2[illegible]	May 2, 1864	100 dys.	Mustered out with company Sept. 4, 1864.
Williamson, George	....do....	28	May 2, 1864	100 dys.	Mustered out with company Sept. 4, 1864.
Winters, Francis	....do....	[illegible]	May 2, 1864	100 dys.	Mustered out with company Sept. 4, 1864.
Winters, Nelson	....do....	3[illegible]	May 2, 1864	100 dys.	Discharged July [illegible], 1864, at Fort Ethan Allen, Va., on surgeon's certificate of disability.
Wise, Cyrus	....do....	19	May 2, 1864	100 dys.	Mustered out with company Sept. 4, 1864.
Wolfe, Levi	....do....	27	May 2, 1864	100 dys.	Mustered out with company Sept. 4, 1864.
Wright, Benjamin	....do....	20	May 2, 1864	100 dys.	Mustered out with company Sept. 4, 1864.
Wright, Lafayette	....do....	25	May 2, 1864	100 dys.	Mustered out with company Sept. 4, 1864.
Young, Gustavus	....do....	20	May 2, 1864	100 dys.	Mustered out with company Sept. 4, 1864.

Mustered in May 15, 1864, at Camp Cleveland, O., by C. B. Throckmorton, 1st Lieutenant 4th Artillery, U. S. A.
Mustered out Sept. 4, 1864, at Camp Cleveland O., by Thomas Drummond,
Captain 5th Cavalry U. S. A.

Names.	Rank.	Age.	Date of Entering the Service.	Period of Service.	Remarks.
Abram C. Anderson	Captain.	34	May 2, 1864	100 dys.	Mustered out with company Sept. 4, 1864.
William H. Goodson	1st Lieut.	23	May 2, 1864	100 dys.	Mustered out with company Sept. 4, 1864.
Sidney F. Sinclair	2d Lieut.	31	May 2, 1864	100 dys.	Promoted from Sergeant to date May 15, 1864; mustered out with company Sept. 4, 1864.
William D. Gilpin	1st Sergt.	25	May 2, 1864	100 dys.	Mustered out with company Sept. 4, 1864.
James Brady	Sergeant.	21	May 2, 1864	100 dys.	Mustered out with company Sept. 4, 1864.
William Travis	...do...	32	May 2, 1864	100 dys.	Mustered out with company Sept. 4, 1864.
David Marion	...do...	31	May 2, 1864	100 dys.	Died July 5, 1864, at Fort Ethan Allen, Va.
Francis P. Gale	...do...	19	May 2, 1864	100 dys.	Appointed from Corporal July 13, 1864; mustered out with company Sept. 4, 1864.
Walton, E. Long	...do...	19	May 2, 1864	100 dys.	Appointed from Corporal July 6, 1864; mustered out with company Sept. 4, 1864.
William E. Sheffield	Corporal.	24	May 2, 1864	100 dys.	Mustered out with company Sept. 4, 1864.
Thomas Warren	...do...	20	May 2, 1864	100 dys.	Mustered out with company Sept. 4, 1864.
Jay A. Higbee	...do...	19	May 2, 1864	100 dys.	Mustered out with company Sept. 4, 1864.
Samuel Frederick	...do...	23	May 2, 1864	100 dys.	Mustered out with company Sept. 4, 1864.
William T. Parkhurst	...do...	30	May 2, 1864	100 dys.	Mustered out with company Sept. 4, 1864.
Michael Phelan	...do...	27	May 2, 1864	100 dys.	Mustered out with company Sept. 4, 1864.
Lewis T. Kirk	...do...	18	May 2, 1864	100 dys.	Appointed July 13, 1864; mustered out with company Sept. 4, 1864.
John Scullen	...do...	20	May 2, 1864	100 dys.	Appointed July 13, 1864; mustered out with company Sept. 4, 1864.
Columbus M. Coulter	Musician	25	May 2, 1864	100 dys.	Promoted to Principal Musician May 2, 1864.
Edwin Vandoran	...do...	34	May 2, 1864	100 dys.	Mustered out with company Sept. 4, 1864.
William Sizer	Wagoner.	28	May 2, 1864	100 dys.	Mustered out with company Sept. 4, 1864.
Aigler, Isaac	Private.	22	May 2, 1864	100 dys.	Mustered out with company Sept. 4, 1864.
Aigler, James	...do...	19	May 2, 1864	100 dys.	Mustered out with company Sept. 4, 1864.
Aves, Frederick	...do...	18	May 2, 1864	100 dys.	Mustered out with company Sept. 4, 1864.
Barber, Arthur	...do...	20	May 2, 1864	100 dys.	Mustered out with company Sept. 4, 1864.
Bowman, Conrad	...do...	18	May 2, 1864	100 dys.	Mustered out with company Sept. 4, 1864.
Britton, David T	...do...	22	May 2, 1864	100 dys.	Mustered out with company Sept. 4, 1864.
Bulger, John K	...do...	21	May 2, 1864	100 dys.	Mustered out with company Sept. 4, 1864.
Carroll, James	...do...	22	May 2, 1864	100 dys.	Mustered out with company Sept. 4, 1864.
Catherman, William	...do...	28	May 2, 1864	100 dys.	Mustered out with company Sept. 4, 1864.
Catlin, Seymour	...do...	18	May 2, 1864	100 dys.	Mustered out with company Sept. 4, 1864.
Charvill, George	...do...	22	May 2, 1864	100 dys.	Mustered out with company Sept. 4, 1864.
Clarke, Theodore E	...do...	21	May 2, 1864	100 dys.	Mustered out with company Sept. 4, 1864.
Cook, James D.	...do...	20	May 2, 1864	100 dys.	Absent, sick ——. No further record found.
Davison, John	...do...	21	May 2, 1864	100 dys.	Mustered out with company Sept. 4, 1864.
Davison, Lewellyn C.	...do...	19	May 2, 1864	100 dys.	Mustered out with company Sept. 4, 1864.
Drake, Dyer	...do...	20	May 2, 1864	100 dys.	Mustered out with company Sept. 4, 1864.
Dumont, Frank P.	...do...	25	May 2, 1864	100 dys.	Mustered out with company Sept. 4, 1864.
Eckhart, Joseph F.	...do...	24	May 2, 1864	100 dys.	Mustered out with company Sept. 4, 1864.
Ensign, John	...do...	21	May 2, 1864	100 dys.	Mustered out with company Sept. 4, 1864.
Flubeck, John.	...do...	20	May 2, 1864	100 dys.	Mustered out with company Sept. 4, 1864.
Frederick, Henry	...do...	19	May 2, 1864	100 dys.	Mustered out with company Sept. 4, 1864.
Gamberling, Edward	...do...	23	May 2, 1864	100 dys.	Mustered out with company Sept. 4, 1864.
Gamberling, William	...do...	22	May 2, 1864	100 dys.	Mustered out with company Sept. 4, 1864.
Gamble, John L.	...do...	22	May 2, 1864	100 dys.	Mustered out with company Sept. 4, 1864.
Gardiner, Dyer C.	...do...	18	May 2, 1864	100 dys.	Mustered out with company Sept. 4, 1864.
Greene, Furgason	...do...	22	May 2, 1864	100 dys.	Promoted to Q. M. Sergeant May 2, 1864.
Grill, Frank	...do...	19	May 2, 1864	100 dys.	Mustered out with company Sept. 4, 1864.
Grover, Sylvester	...do...	18	May 2, 1864	100 dys.	Mustered out with company Sept. 4, 1864.
Harting, John	...do...	26	May 2, 1864	100 dys.	Mustered out with company Sept. 4, 1864.
Hollingshead, Samuel W.	...do...	18	May 2, 1864	100 dys.	Died Aug. 12, 1864, at Fort Ethan Allen, Va.
Huber, Frank	...do...	18	May 2, 1864	100 dys.	Mustered out with company Sept. 4, 1864.
Jacobs, Barney H	...do...	20	May 2, 1864	100 dys.	Mustered out with company Sept. 4, 1864.
Kaser, Samuel	...do...	26	May 2, 1864	100 dys.	Mustered out with company Sept. 4, 1864.
Kemp, Orrin D.	...do...	18	May 2, 1864	100 dys.	Mustered out with company Sept. 4, 1864.
King, James C.	...do...	18	May 2, 1864	100 dys.	Mustered out with company Sept. 4, 1864.
Kingham, Joseph	...do...	24	May 2, 1864	100 dys.	Mustered out with company Sept. 4, 1864.
Kingsley, Richard	...do...	31	May 2, 1864	100 dys.	Mustered out with company Sept. 4, 1864.
Kinney, William	...do...	20	May 2, 1864	100 dys.	Mustered out with company Sept. 4, 1864.
Lindsley, James M.	...do...	29	May 2, 1864	100 dys.	Mustered out with company Sept. 4, 1864.
Lutz, Samuel	...do...	23	May 2, 1864	100 dys.	Mustered out with company Sept. 4, 1864.
McCormick, Samuel	...do...	36	May 2, 1864	100 dys.	Mustered out with company Sept. 4, 1864.
McKim, Frank C.	...do...	19	May 2, 1864	100 dys.	Mustered out with company Sept. 4, 1864.
Marcellus, Peter	...do...	19	May 2, 1864	100 dys.	Mustered out with company Sept. 4, 1864.
Meek, John	...do...	19	May 2, 1864	100 dys.	Mustered out with company Sept. 4, 1864.
Miller, John C.	...do...	25	May 2, 1864	100 dys.	Mustered out with company Sept. 4, 1864.
Moore, Benjamin	...do...	19	May 2, 1864	100 dys.	Mustered out with company Sept. 4, 1864.
Morey, Giles	...do...	21	May 2, 1864	100 dys.	Mustered out with company Sept. 4, 1864.
Moyer, John C.	...do...	19	May 2, 1864	100 dys.	Mustered out with company Sept. 4, 1864.
Myers, William	...do...	19	May 2, 1864	100 dys.	Mustered out with company Sept. 4, 1864.
Pierson, Milan	...do...	18	May 2, 1864	100 dys.	Mustered out with company Sept. 4, 1864.
Poly, Amos W.	...do...	19	May 2, 1864	100 dys.	Mustered out with company Sept. 4, 1864.
Pontious, Edward	...do...	20	May 2, 1864	100 dys.	Mustered out with company Sept. 4, 1864.

	Rank.	Age.	Date of Entering the Service.	Period of Service.	Remarks.
ll, John......	Private..	20	May 2, 1864	100 dys.	Mustered out with company Sept. 4, 1864.
lspocher, Jacob....	....do....	21	May 2, 1864	100 dys.	Mustered out with company Sept. 4, 1864.
rds, Charles M.....	....do....	20	May 2, 1864	100 dys.	Mustered out with company Sept. 4, 1864.
nson, Sylvester.....	....do....	32	May 2, 1864	100 dys.	Mustered out with company Sept. 4, 1864.
rs, George F........	....do....	32	May 2, 1864	100 dys.	Mustered out with company Sept. 4, 1864.
el, Andrew J......	....do....	30	May 2, 1864	100 dys.	
r, Charles A........	....do....	19	May 2, 1864	100 dys.	Mustered out with company Sept. 4, 1864.
, Andrew J.........	....do....	18	May 2, 1864	100 dys.	Mustered out with company Sept. 4, 1864.
, Henry M..........	....do....	18	May 2, 1864	100 dys.	Mustered out with company Sept. 4, 1864.
, John....	....do....	..	May 2, 1864	100 dys.	
n, Charles A........	....do....	19	May 2, 1864	100 dys.	Mustered out with company Sept. 4, 1864.
, Edwin...........	....do....	18	May 2, 1864	100 dys.	Mustered out with company Sept. 4, 1864.
an, Daniel..........	....do....	37	May 2, 1864	100 dys.	Mustered out with company Sept. 4, 1864.
Richard.............	....do....	35	May 2, 1864	100 dys.	Mustered out with company Sept. 4, 1864.
, Patrick O.	....do....	18	May 2, 1864	100 dys.	Mustered out with company Sept. 4, 1864.
	....do....	18	May 2, 1864	100 dys.	Mustered out with company Sept. 4, 1864.
	....do....	19	May 2, 1864	100 dys.	Mustered out with company Sept. 4, 1864.
	....do....	25	May 2, 1864	100 dys.	Mustered out with company Sept. 4, 1864.
	....do....	24	May 2, 1864	100 dys.	Mustered out with company Sept. 4, 1864.
	....do....	23	May 2, 1864	100 dys.	Mustered out with company Sept. 4, 1864.

COMPANY K.

ered in May 15, 1864, at Camp Cleveland, O., by C. B. Throckmorton, 1st Lieutenant 4th Artillery, U. S. A.
Mustered out Sept. 4, 1864, at Camp Cleveland, O., by Thomas Drummond,
Captain 5th Cavalry, U. S. A.

	Rank.	Age.	Date of Entering the Service.	Period of Service.	Remarks.
on R. Bowlus......	Captain..	25	May 2, 1864	100 dys.	Mustered out with company Sept. 4, 1864.
han Loveberry....	1st Lieut.	32	May 2, 1864	100 dys.	Mustered out with company Sept. 4, 1864.
A. Overmoyer....	2d Lieut.	40	May 2, 1864	100 dys.	Mustered out with company Sept. 4, 1864.
e W. Seibert......	1st Sergt.	21	May 2, 1864	100 dys.	Mustered out with company Sept. 4, 1864.
us Hendricks......	Sergeant.	24	May 2, 1864	100 dys.	Mustered out with company Sept. 4, 1864.
ew J. Wolfe........	....do....	21	May 2, 1864	100 dys.	Mustered out with company Sept. 4, 1864.
m H. Benner........	....do....	24	May 2, 1864	100 dys.	Mustered out with company Sept. 4, 1864.
S. Fisher..........	....do....	22	May 2, 1864	100 dys.	Mustered out with company Sept. 4, 1864.
nand Willson......	Corporal.	22	May 2, 1864	100 dys.	Died Aug. 5, 1864, at Fort Ethan Allen, Va.
uel Bowersox......	....do....	28	May 2, 1864	100 dys.	Mustered out with company Sept. 4, 1864.
Stults.............	....do....	22	May 2, 1864	100 dys.	Mustered out with company Sept. 4, 1864.
e Ohlinger.........	....do....	25	May 2, 1864	100 dys.	Mustered out with company Sept. 4, 1864.
rd Overmoyer......	....do....	21	May 2, 1864	100 dys.	Mustered out with company Sept. 4, 1864.
h Kearick..........	....do....	22	May 2, 1864	100 dys.	Mustered out with company Sept. 4, 1864.
Kooms..........	....do....	28	May 2, 1864	100 dys.	Mustered out with company Sept. 4, 1864.
es June............	....do....	24	May 2, 1864	100 dys.	Mustered out with company Sept. 4, 1864.
klin Rideout.......	Musician	20	May 2, 1864	100 dys.	Mustered out with company Sept. 4, 1864.
ette Rideout.......	....do....	19	May 2, 1864	100 dys.	Died July 25, 1864, at Fort Ethan Allen, Va.
t, Melanchthon ...	Private..	18	May 2, 1864	100 dys.	Mustered out with company Sept. 4, 1864.
ews, John Q.........	....do....	36	May 2, 1864	100 dys.	Mustered out with company Sept. 4, 1864.
r, James..........	....do....	28	May 2, 1864	100 dys.	Mustered out with company Sept. 4, 1864.
ley, Romanus	....do....	18	May 2, 1864	100 dys.	Mustered out with company Sept. 4, 1864.
rsox, Edward.......	....do....	37	May 2, 1864	100 dys.	Mustered out with company Sept. 4, 1864.
rsox, Levi.........	....do....	25	May 2, 1864	100 dys.	Mustered out with company Sept. 4, 1864.
rsox, Simon	....do....	29	May 2, 1864	100 dys.	Mustered out with company Sept. 4, 1864.
ns, Silas..........	....do....	19	May 2, 1864	100 dys.	Died July 8, 1864, at Fort Ethan Allen, Va.
r, Amos	....do....	20	May 2, 1864	100 dys.	Mustered out with company Sept. 4, 1864.
r, William.........	....do....	23	May 2, 1864	100 dys.	Mustered out with company Sept. 4, 1864.
icom, Amos.........	....do....	19	May 2, 1864	100 dys.	Mustered out with company Sept. 4, 1864.
fan, John..........	....do....	18	May 2, 1864	100 dys.	Mustered out with company Sept. 4, 1864.
, George...........	....do....	18	May 2, 1864	100 dys.	Mustered out with company Sept. 4, 1864.
, David...........	....do....	18	May 2, 1864	100 dys.	Mustered out with company Sept. 4, 1864.
er, Edward........	....do....	27	May 2, 1864	100 dys.	Mustered out with company Sept. 4, 1864.
er, William........	....do....	36	May 2, 1864	100 dys.	Mustered out with company Sept. 4, 1864.
ling, John	....do....	40	May 2, 1864	100 dys.	Died Sept. 6, 1864, in Mt. Pleasant Hospital, Washington, D. C.
tmiller, Joseph....	....do....	18	May 2, 1864	100 dys.	Mustered out with company Sept. 4, 1864.
r, Abraham.........	....do....	35	May 2, 1864	100 dys.	Mustered out with company Sept. 4, 1864.
ole, Noah..........	....do....	18	May 2, 1864	100 dys.	Mustered out with company Sept. 4, 1864.
rman, Solomon.	....do....	21	May 2, 1864	100 dys.	Mustered out with company Sept. 4, 1864.
r, Peter	....do....	18	May 2, 1864	100 dys.	Mustered out with company Sept. 4, 1864.
. Frederic..........	....do....	18	May 2, 1864	100 dys.	Mustered out with company Sept. 4, 1864.
. Daniel...........	....do....	27	May 2, 1864	100 dys.	Mustered out with company Sept. 4, 1864.
man, David.........	....do....	37	May 2, 1864	100 dys.	Mustered out with company Sept. 4, 1864.
per, Ernst.........	....do....	40	May 2, 1864	100 dys.	Mustered out with company Sept. 4, 1864.
berger, Jacob	....do....	20	May 2, 1864	100 dys.	Died July 21, 1864, at Fort Ethan Allen, Va.
grove, Daniel......	....do....	26	May 2, 1864	100 dys.	Mustered out with company Sept. 4, 1864.
grove, James	....do....	23	May 2, 1864	100 dys.	Mustered out with company Sept. 4, 1864.
n, Charles.........	....do....	18	May 2, 1864	100 dys.	Died Aug. 28, 1864, at Washington, D. C.
nger, Wesley......	....do....	48	May 2, 1864	100 dys.	Mustered out with company Sept. 4, 1864.
. Adam.	....do....	34	May 2, 1864	100 dys.	Mustered out with company Sept. 4, 1864.
, Albert...........	....do....	28	May 2, 1864	100 dys.	Mustered out with company Sept. 4, 1864.

Names.	Rank.	Age.	Date of Entering the Service.	Period of Service.	Remarks.
Karns, John	Private	35	May 2, 1864	100 dys.	Died Aug. 12, 1864, at Defiance, O., while at home on furlough.
Linton, Samuel	do	24	May 2, 1864	100 dys.	Mustered out with company Sept. 4, 1864.
Lomalla, William	do	19	May 2, 1864	100 dys.	Mustered out with company Sept. 4, 1864.
McAllister, John	do	23	May 2, 1864	100 dys.	Mustered out with company Sept. 4, 1864.
Mapes, Joseph	do	44	May 2, 1864	100 dys.	Mustered out with company Sept. 4, 1864.
Miller, Daniel	do	30	May 2, 1864	100 dys.	Mustered out with company Sept. 4, 1864.
Mowery, Aaron	do	20	May 2, 1864	100 dys.	Mustered out with company Sept. 4, 1864.
Mowery, Harrison	do	20	May 2, 1864	100 dys.	Died Aug. 23, 1864, at general hospital, Washington, D. C.
Moyer, John	do	18	May 2, 1864	100 dys.	Mustered out with company Sept. 4, 1864.
Munch, Solomon	do	18	May 2, 1864	100 dys.	Mustered out with company Sept. 4, 1864.
Newton Lester	do	18	May 2, 1864	100 dys.	Mustered out with company Sept. 4, 1864.
Overmoyer, Amos	do	20	May 2, 1864	100 dys.	Mustered out with company Sept. 4, 1864.
Overmoyer, Henry	do	21	May 2, 1864	100 dys.	Mustered out with company Sept. 4, 1864.
Overmoyer, Homer	do	19	May 2, 1864	100 dys.	Mustered out with company Sept. 4, 1864.
Overmoyer, Isaiah	do	21	May 2, 1864	100 dys.	Mustered out with company Sept. 4, 1864.
Overmoyer, Michael	do	32	May 2, 1864	100 dys.	Mustered out with company Sept. 4, 1864.
Rearick, George	do	28	May 2, 1864	100 dys.	Mustered out with company Sept. 4, 1864.
Reed, Daniel	do	21	May 2, 1864	100 dys.	Mustered out with company Sept. 4, 1864.
Reed, Samuel	do	27	May 2, 1864	100 dys.	Mustered out with company Sept. 4, 1864.
Remsburg, John	do	18	May 2, 1864	100 dys.	Mustered out with company Sept. 4, 1864.
Rickel, Park	do	18	May 2, 1864	100 dys.	Mustered out with company Sept. 4, 1864.
Rikerd, William	do	25	May 2, 1864	100 dys.	Died Aug. 1, 1864, at Fort Ethan Allen, Va.
Scherf, Gustave	do	19	May 2, 1864	100 dys.	Mustered out with company Sept. 4, 1864.
Seibert, Jerome	do	19	May 2, 1864	100 dys.	Died July 17, 1864, at Fort Ethan Allen, Va.
Shively Henry	do	35	May 2, 1864	100 dys.	Mustered out with company Sept. 4, 1864.
Skinner, George	do	29	May 2, 1864	100 dys.	Mustered out with company Sept. 4, 1864.
Smith, Levi	do	31	May 2, 1864	100 dys.	Mustered out with company Sept. 4, 1864.
Stauffer, John H	do	25	May 2, 1864	100 dys.	Mustered out with company Sept. 4, 1864.
Stiffler, Aaron	do	20	May 2, 1864	100 dys.	Mustered out with company Sept. 4, 1864.
Stults, Daniel	do	24	May 2, 1864	100 dys.	Mustered out with company Sept. 4, 1864.
Ulch, Moses	do	20	May 2, 1864	100 dys.	Mustered out with company Sept. 4, 1864.
Walborn, Israel	do	21	May 2, 1864	100 dys.	Mustered out with company Sept. 4, 1864.
Walters, Emanuel	do	28	May 2, 1864	100 dys.	Mustered out with company Sept. 4, 1864.
Walters, Joshua	do	20	May 2, 1864	100 dys.	Mustered out with company Sept. 4, 1864.
Wolfe, Josiah	do	23	May 2, 1864	100 dys.	Mustered out with company Sept. 4, 1864.
Woolcott, Peter	do	18	May 2, 1864	100 dys.	Mustered out with company Sept. 4, 1864.
Zickgraf, Charles	do	21	May 2, 1864	100 dys.	Mustered out with company Sept. 4, 1864; also borne on rolls as Charles Zickraft.

170th Regiment Ohio Volunteer Infantry.

ONE HUNDRED DAYS' SERVICE.

THIS Regiment was organized at Bellaire, O., May 13 and 14, 1864, to serve ne hundred days. It was composed of the Seventy-fourth Battalion, Ohio ational Guard, from Belmont County, and the Seventy-eighth Battalion, hio National Guard, from Harrison County. The Regiment immediately roceeded to Washington City, and upon its arrival, May 22d, was assigned duty in Forts Simmons, Mansfield, Bayard, Gaines, and Battery Vermont. n the night of the 4th of July it left the defenses at Washington and roceeded to Sandy Hook, Md., to join the forces assembled in the defense of aryland Heights. The Regiment remained in the vicinity of Maryland eights until the 15th of July, when it was attached to the Second rigade, First Division, Army of West Virginia, and participated, during e remainder of its term of service, in the movements and engagements of at army. While lying at Cedar Creek the Regiment was detached and rdered to Harper's Ferry as escort to a supply-train. It remained at arper's Ferry until the 24th of August, when transportation to Ohio was urnished. The Regiment arrived at Columbus, O., on the 27th of August, nd was mustered out September 10, 1864, on expiration of its term of ervice.

Names.	Rank.	Age.	Date of Entering the Service.	Period of Service.	Remarks.
Waters, Harvey	Private	24	May 2, 1864	100 dys.	Mustered out with company Sept. 10, 1864.
Webster, John L	do	18	May 2, 1864	100 dys.	Wounded July 18, 1864, in battle of Snicker's Ferry, Va.; absent, sick ——, in hospital at Camp Chase, O. No further record found.
Willet, Lewis M	do	18	May 2, 1864	100 dys.	Mustered out with company Sept. 10, 1864.

COMPANY C.

Mustered in May 13, 1864, at Bellaire, O., by C. P. Horton, Captain and A. D. C. Mustered out Sept. 10, 1864, at Camp Chase, O., by William B. Lowe, Captain 11th Infantry, U. S. A.

Names.	Rank.	Age.	Date of Entering the Service.	Period of Service.	Remarks.
Samuel Glover	Captain.	23	May 2, 1864	100 dys.	Mustered out with company Sept. 10, 1864.
George C. Gordon	1st Lieut.	33	May 2, 1864	100 dys.	Mustered out with company Sept. 10, 1864.
George W. Green	2d Lieut.	28	May 2, 1864	100 dys.	Mustered out with company Sept. 10, 1864.
John Boger	1st Sergt.	18	May 2, 1864	100 dys.	Mustered out with company Sept. 10, 1864.
George Crozier	Sergeant.	34	May 2, 1864	100 dys.	Mustered out with company Sept. 10, 1864.
Ferdinand Dorsey	do	23	May 2, 1864	100 dys.	Absent, sick since July 19, 1864, in hospital at Sandy Hook, Md. No further record found.
William Dent	do	21	May 2, 1864	100 dys.	Mustered out with company Sept. 10, 1864.
William Beabout	do	36	May 2, 1864	100 dys.	Mustered out with company Sept. 10, 1864.
Frederick Boetticher	Corporal.	28	May 2, 1864	100 dys.	Mustered out with company Sept. 10, 1864.
Joseph L. Gordon	do	26	May 2, 1864	100 dys.	Mustered out with company Sept. 10, 1864.
William H. Gibson	do	18	May 2, 1864	100 dys.	Mustered out with company Sept. 10, 1864.
Orloff Dorsey	do	21	May 2, 1864	100 dys.	Mustered out with company Sept. 10, 1864.
Madison Scott	do	25	May 2, 1864	100 dys.	Mustered out with company Sept. 10, 1864.
John Wright	do	22	May 2, 1864	100 dys.	Appointed June 13, 1864; mustered out with company Sept. 10, 1864.
Daniel Steiner	do	22	May 2, 1864	100 dys.	Mustered out with company Sept. 10, 1864.
Davis P. Woodburn	do	39	May 2, 1864	100 dys.	Mustered out with company Sept. 10, 1864.
John Wade	Musician	35	May 2, 1864	100 dys.	Mustered out with company Sept. 10, 1864.
David C. Bergandthal	do	18	May 2, 1864	100 dys.	Absent, sick since Aug. 8, 1864, in hospital at Sandy Hook, Md. No further record found.
Abrigg, Samuel	Private	22	May 2, 1864	100 dys.	Absent, sick since Sept. 6, 1864, at home. No further record found.
Anthony, William	do	19	May 2, 1864	100 dys.	Absent, sick since Aug. 13, 1864, in hospital at Bolivar Heights, Md. No further record found.
Baker, Alfred	do	23	May 2, 1864	100 dys.	Mustered out with company Sept. 10, 1864.
Baker, Daniel	do	19	May 2, 1864	100 dys.	Mustered out with company Sept. 10, 1864.
Barnes, Leander	do	37	May 2, 1864	100 dys.	Mustered out with company Sept. 10, 1864.
Boston, John	do	25	May 2, 1864	100 dys.	Mustered out with company Sept. 10, 1864.
Brock, George	do	21	May 2, 1864	100 dys.	Mustered out with company Sept. 10, 1864.
Brown, John	do	28	May 2, 1864	100 dys.	Mustered out with company Sept. 10, 1864.
Burgy, John	do	11	May 2, 1864	100 dys.	Mustered out with company Sept. 10, 1864.
Burkhart, Arnold	do	19	May 2, 1864	100 dys.	Mustered out with company Sept. 10, 1864.
Carpenter, George	do	33	May 2, 1864	100 dys.	Died Aug. 19, 1864, at Sandy Hook, Md.
Carpenter, Robert	do	23	May 2, 1864	100 dys.	Mustered out with company Sept. 10, 1864.
Cline, Andrew	do	18	May 2, 1864	100 dys.	Mustered out with company Sept. 10, 1864.
Gross, Joseph	do	36	May 2, 1864	100 dys.	Mustered out with company Sept. 10, 1864.
Dennis [illegible]usen	do	21	May 2, 1864	100 dys.	Mustered out with company Sept. 10, 1864.
Dillon, Josiah	do	22	May 2, 1864	100 dys.	Mustered out with company Sept. 10, 1864.
Eggers, Lewis	do	18	May 2, 1864	100 dys.	Absent, sick since Sept. 6, 1864, at home. No further record found.
Ewers, Amer	do	27	May 2, 1864	100 dys.	Mustered out with company Sept. 10, 1864.
Fort, George	do	26	May 2, 1864	100 dys.	
George, Bently T	do	18	May 2, 1864	100 dys.	Mustered out with company Sept. 10, 1864.
Gordon, Samuel	do	18	May 2, 1864	100 dys.	Mustered out with company Sept. 10, 1864.
Gordon, Thomas	do	18	May 2, 1864	100 dys.	Mustered out with company Sept. 10, 1864.
Green, Sylvester	do	31	May 2, 1864	100 dys.	Mustered out with company Sept. 10, 1864.
Grimes, Noah J	do	18	May 2, 1864	100 dys.	Mustered out with company Sept. 10, 1864.
Harriott, William	do	[illegible]	May 2, 1864	100 dys.	Mustered out with company Sept. 10, 1864.
Helmes, Isaiah	do	11	May 2, 1864	100 dys.	Mustered out with company Sept. 10, 1864.
Hess, Michael	do	[illegible]	May 2, 1864	100 dys.	Mustered out with company Sept. 10, 1864.
Hoffman, Henry	do	18	May 2, 1864	100 dys.	Mustered out with company Sept. 10, 1864.
Kelch, George	do	28	May 2, 1864	100 dys.	Mustered out with company Sept. 10, 1864.
Kelch, William	do	23	May 2, 1864	100 dys.	Mustered out with company Sept. 10, 1864.
Kocher, Samuel	do	31	May 2, 1864	100 dys.	Mustered out with company Sept. 10, 1864.
Kornet, Gustavus A	do	18	May 2, 1864	100 dys.	Mustered out with company Sept. 10, 1864.
Leudon, John H	do	19	May 2, 1864	100 dys.	Wounded and captured July 18, 1864, at battle of Snicker's Ferry, Va.; mustered out Sept. 10, 1864, at Columbus, O., by order of War Department.
Lockwood, Sylvanus	do	22	May 2, 1864	100 dys.	Mustered out with company Sept. 10, 1864.
Mead, Alonzo	do	18	May 2, 1864	100 dys.	Mustered out with company Sept. 10, 1864.
Miller, Francis	do	39	May 2, 1864	100 dys.	Mustered out with company Sept. 10, 1864.
Moore, Joseph	do	41	May 2, 1864	100 dys.	Mustered out with company Sept. 10, 1864.
Moore, Thomas L	do	18	May 2, 1864	100 dys.	Mustered out with company Sept. 10, 1864.
Morrison, Caleb	do	11	May 2, 1864	100 dys.	Mustered out with company Sept. 10, 1864.

Names.	Rank.	Age.	Date of Entering the Service.	Period of Service.	Remarks.
Crim, William R.	Private.	21	May 2, 1864	100 dys.	Mustered out with company Sept. 10, 1864.
Crowl, John N.	...do...	34	May 2, 1864	100 dys.	
Ervin, James P.	...do...	24	May 2, 1864	100 dys.	Absent, sick since May 17, 1864, at home. No further record found.
Erwin, Robert W.	...do...	21	May 2, 1864	100 dys.	Reduced from Corporal May 20, 1864; mustered out with company Sept. 10, 1864.
Fowler, John E.	...do...	38	May 2, 1864	100 dys.	Mustered out with company Sept. 10, 1864.
Gallaher, Samuel F.	...do...	19	May 2, 1864	100 dys.	Mustered out with company Sept. 10, 1864.
Gladman, John	...do...	19	May 2, 1864	100 dys.	Mustered out with company Sept. 10, 1864.
Hammel, Watson	...do...	26	May 2, 1864	100 dys.	Mustered out with company Sept. 10, 1864.
Hammond, George W.	...do...	16	May 2, 1864	100 dys.	Mustered out with company Sept. 10, 1864.
Hillyer, Henry	...do...	22	May 2, 1864	100 dys.	Mustered out with company Sept. 10, 1864.
Hillyer, Thomas	...do...	27	May 2, 1864	100 dys.	Mustered out with company Sept. 10, 1864.
Hillyer, William	...do...	19	May 2, 1864	ys.	
Hilton, John H. T.	...do...	45	May 2, 1864	100 dys.	Mustered out with company Sept. 10, 1864.
Hitchcock, Samuel	...do...	21	May 2, 1864	100 dys.	Mustered out with company Sept. 10, 1864.
Hix, Guyan M.	...do...	18	May 2, 1864	100 dys.	Mustered out with company Sept. 10, 1864.
Hoagland, Isaiah	...do...	25	May 2, 1864	100 dys.	Mustered out with company Sept. 10, 1864.
Horn, John D.	...do...	19	May 2, 1864	100 dys.	Mustered out with company Sept. 10, 1864.
Host, Homer W.	...do...	18	May 2, 1864	100 dys.	Mustered out with company Sept. 10, 1864.
House, James F.	...do...	19	May 2, 1864	100 dys.	Mustered out with company Sept. 10, 1864.
Hurless, John H.	...do...	37	May 2, 1864	100 dys.	Died Aug. 15, 1864, at Annapolis, Md.
Johnson, Joseph R.	...do...	40	May 2, 1864	100 dys.	Mustered out with company Sept. 10, 1864.
Johnson, William L.	...do...	18	May 2, 1864	100 dys.	Mustered out with company Sept. 10, 1864.
Jones, Alfred P.	...do...	18	May 2, 1864	100 dys.	Mustered out with company Sept. 10, 1864.
Kennedy, Citizen J.	...do...	31	May 2, 1864	100 dys.	Reduced from Sergeant May 20, 1864; mustered out with company Sept. 10, 1864.
Lukens, Daniel A.	...do...	26	May 2, 1864	100 dys.	
Lukens, Thomas	...do...	21	May 2, 1864	100 dys.	Mustered out with company Sept. 10, 1864.
McClintock, Thomas	...do...	19	May 2, 1864	100 dys.	Mustered out with company Sept. 10, 1864.
McRa Fauquiber	...do...	42	May 2, 1864	100 dys.	
Mahew, David	...do...	19	May 2, 1864	100 dys.	Mustered out with company Sept. 10, 1864.
Martin, Lafayette	...do...	18	May 2, 1864	100 dys.	Mustered out with company Sept. 10, 1864.
Merryman, James R.	...do...	19	May 2, 1864	100 dys.	
Moor, John S.	...do...	23	May 2, 1864	100 dys.	
Moore, Joseph D.	...do...	19	May 2, 1864	100 dys.	Mustered out with company Sept. 10, 1864.
Patterson, Isaac	...do...	18	May 2, 1864	100 dys.	Mustered out with company Sept. 10, 1864.
Pittis, John A.	...do...	18	May 2, 1864	100 dys.	Mustered out with company Sept. 10, 1864.
Poulson, John M.	...do...	22	May 2, 1864	100 dys.	Mustered out with company Sept. 10, 1864.
Reynard, William	...do...	21	May 2, 1864	100 dys.	Mustered out with company Sept. 10, 1864.
Richardson, Jesse	...do...	34	May 2, 1864	100 dys.	
Robinson, Joseph	...do...	24	May 2, 1864	100 dys.	Mustered out with company Sept. 10, 1864.
Rose, William J.	...do...	22	May 2, 1864	100 dys.	Mustered out with company Sept. 10, 1864.
Rowland, William	...do...	20	May 2, 1864	100 dys.	Mustered out with company Sept. 10, 1864.
Simpson, Matthew W.	...do...	18	May 2, 1864	100 dys.	Mustered out with company Sept. 10, 1864.
Stine, John R.	...do...	31	May 2, 1864	100 dys.	Mustered out with company Sept. 10, 1864.
Straus, Samuel	...do...	42	May 2, 1864	100 dys.	Mustered out with company Sept. 10, 1864.
Underhill, Archibald	...do...	19	May 2, 1864	100 dys.	Mustered out with company Sept. 10, 1864.
Underhill, Jacob	...do...	26	May 2, 1864	100 dys.	Mustered out with company Sept. 10, 1864.
Utterback, Samuel	...do...	19	May 2, 1864	100 dys.	Mustered out with company Sept. 10, 1864.
White, Warren R.	...do...	26	May 2, 1864	100 dys.	Mustered out with company Sept. 10, 1864.
Wilson, Henry W.	...do...	18	May 2, 1864	100 dys.	Mustered out with company Sept. 10, 1864.
Wood, John D.	...do...	18	May 2, 1864	100 dys.	Died Aug. 27, 1864, near Pittsburgh, Pa.

COMPANY E.

Mustered in May 11, 1864, at Bellaire, O., by C. P. Horton, Captain and A. D. C. Mustered out Sept. 10, 1864, at Camp Chase, O., by William B. Lowe, Captain 11th Infantry, U. S. A.

Names.	Rank.	Age.	Date of Entering the Service.	Period of Service.	Remarks.
Albert W. Lee	Captain.	24	May 2, 1864	100 dys.	Mustered out with company Sept. 10, 1864.
Alexander C. Patton	1st Lieut.	21	May 2, 1864	100 dys.	Mustered out with company Sept. 10, 1864.
Matthew N. Henderson	2d Lieut.	21	May 2, 1864	100 dys.	Mustered out with company Sept. 10, 1864.
Marcus Howell	1st Sergt.	22	May 2, 1864	100 dys.	Mustered out with company Sept. 10, 1864.
William A. Frater	Sergeant.	21	May 2, 1864	100 dys.	Mustered out with company Sept. 10, 1864.
Samuel B. Ward	...do...	19	May 2, 1864	100 dys.	Appointed from Corporal May 17, 1864; mustered out with company Sept. 10, 1864.
David A. Duff	...do...	18	May 2, 1864	100 dys.	Mustered out with company Sept. 10, 1864.
Landen Grimes	...do...	21	May 2, 1864	100 dys.	Mustered out with company Sept. 10, 1864.
Alexander Hammond	Corporal.	26	May 2, 1864	100 dys.	Appointed May 17, 1864; mustered out with company Sept. 10, 1864.
Charles Lee	...do...	18	May 2, 1864	100 dys.	Appointed July 21, 1864; mustered out with company Sept. 10 1864.
Eli Sebirt	...do...	37	May 2, 1864	100 dys.	Mustered out with company Sept. 10, 1864.
Abram Loper	...do...	19	May 2, 1864	100 dys.	Mustered out with company Sept. 10, 18[illegible]
John E. Stewart	...do...	29	May 2, 1864	100 dys.	Mustered out with company Sept. 10, [illegible]
Robert W. Palmer	...do...	22	May 2, 1864	100 dys.	Mustered out with company Sept. 10, [illegible]
Robert A. Todd	...do...	28	May 2, 1864	100 dys.	Mustered out with company Sept. 10, [illegible]
John L. Grimes	...do...	27	May 2, 1864	100 dys.	Wounded July 18, 1864, in battle of [illegible] Ferry, Va.; mustered out with [illegible] Sept. 10, 1864.

COMPANY F.

Mustered in May 14, 1864, at Bellaire, O., by C. P. Horton, Captain and A. D. C. Mustered out Sept. 10, 1864, at Camp Chase, O., by William B. Lowe, Captain 11th Infantry, U. S. A.

Names.	Rank.	Age.	Date of Entering the Service.	Period of Service.	Remarks.
Leonard B. Peck	Captain.	25	May 2, 1864	100 dys.	Mustered out with company Sept. 10, 1864.
James H. Graham	1st Lieut.	27	May 2, 1864	100 dys.	Died Aug. 11, 1864, at Sandy Hook, Md.
John H. Hammond	2d Lieut.	43	May 2, 1864	100 dys.	Mustered out with company Sept. 10, 1864.
Junius H. Lewis	1st Sergt.	21	May 2, 1864	100 dys.	Mustered out with company Sept. 10, 1864.
Lewis W. Furbay	Sergeant.	38	May 2, 1864	100 dys.	Mustered out with company Sept. 10, 1864.
Isaac Booth	do.	26	May 2, 1864	100 dys.	Mustered out with company Sept. 10, 1864.
Elisha Moore	do.	41	May 2, 1864	100 dys.	Mustered out with company Sept. 10, 1864.
James M. Adams	do.	22	May 2, 1864	100 dys.	Mustered out with company Sept. 10, 1864.
James M. Howerth	Corporal.	27	May 2, 1864	100 dys.	Mustered out with company Sept. 10, 1864.
Ezra Thompson	do.	45	May 2, 1864	100 dys.	Mustered out with company Sept. 10, 1864.
John Hanna	do.	36	May 2, 1864	100 dys.	Mustered out with company Sept. 10, 1864.
James Coulter	do.	23	May 2, 1864	100 dys.	Mustered out with company Sept. 10, 1864.
John E. Dutton	do.	19	May 2, 1864	100 dys.	Mustered out with company Sept. 10, 1864.
ohn E. K ser	do.	30	May 2, 1864	100 dys.	Mustered out with company Sept. 10, 1864.
George Holmes	do.	19	May 2, 1864	100 dys.	Mustered out with company Sept. 10, 1864.
Edward Regan	do.	21	May 2, 1864	100 dys.	Mustered out with company Sept. 10, 1864.
Franklin Anderson	Musician	16	May 2, 1864	100 dys.	Mustered out with company Sept. 10, 1864.
Israel Waterman	do.	16	May 2, 1864	100 dys.	Mustered out with company Sept. 10, 1864.
William Harriman	Wagoner.	24	May 2, 1864	100 dys.	Discharged June 3, 1864.
Anderson, Owen	Private.	24	May 2, 1864	100 dys.	Mustered out with company Sept. 10, 1864.
Atkinson, George	do.	16	May 2, 1864	100 dys.	Mustered out with company Sept. 10, 1864.
Baldwin, George	do.	24	May 2, 1864	100 dys.	Mustered out with company Sept. 10, 1864.
Barkhurst, William	do.	38	May 2, 1864	100 dys.	Mustered out with company Sept. 10, 1864.
Beck, John B	do.	26	May 2, 1864	100 dys.	Mustered out with company Sept. 10, 1864.
Blackburn, Abner R	do.	34	May 2, 1864	100 dys.	Mustered out with company Sept. 10, 1864.
Brown, Henry	do.	16	May 2, 1864	100 dys.	Mustered out with company Sept. 10, 1864.
Butler, John	do.	44	May 2, 1864	100 dys.	Mustered out with company Sept. 10, 1864.
Carrick, Ezra L	do.	19	May 2, 1864	100 dys.	Mustered out with company Sept. 10, 1864.
Carter, Edward	do.	28	May 2, 1864	100 dys.	Mustered out with company Sept. 10, 1864
Carter, Isaac	do.	26	May 2, 1864	100 dys.	Mustered out with company Sept. 10, 1864.
Clark, John	do.	39	May 2, 1864	100 dys.	Mustered out with company Sept. 10, 1864.
Coulter, John	do.	17	May 2, 1864	100 dys.	Mustered out with company Sept. 10, 1864.
Custered, William	do.	41	May 2, 1864	100 dys.	Mustered out with company Sept. 10, 1864.
Darmour, John	do.	37	May 2, 1864	100 dys.	Mustered out with company Sept. 10, 1864.
Dickerson, Theodore	do.	19	May 2, 1864	100 dys.	Mustered out with company Sept. 10, 1864.
Ely, George	do.	33	May 2, 1864	100 dys.	Mustered out with company Sept. 10, 1864.
Fields, Isaiah	do.	21	May 2, 1864	100 dys.	Mustered out with company Sept. 10, 1864.
Frater, George	do.	36	May 2, 1864	100 dys.	Mustered out with company Sept. 10, 1864.
Goodling, Samuel	do.	19	May 2, 1864	100 dys.	Mustered out with company Sept. 10, 1864.
Griffith, Benj in B.	do.	28	May 2, 1864	100 dys.	Mustered out with company Sept. 10, 1864.
Hammond, Archibald	do.	28	May 2, 1864	100 dys.	Mustered out with company Sept. 10, 1864.
Hargrave, Joseph M	do.	25	May 2, 1864	100 dys.	Mustered out with company Sept. 10, 1864.
Harrison, Joseph	do.	16	May 2, 1864	100 dys.	Mustered out with company Sept. 10, 1864.
Haw rn Francis	do.	18	May 2, 1864	100 dys.	Mustered out with company Sept. 10, 1864.
H wther hn R.	do.	21	May 2, 1864	100 dys.	Mustered out with company Sept. 10, 1864.
Hollilay n	do.	21	May 2, 1864	100 dys.	Mustered out with company Sept. 10, 1864.
Jamieson Andrew	do.	39	May 2, 1864	100 dys.	Mustered out with company Sept. 10, 1864.
K rr, seph L.	do.	19	May 2, 1864	100 dys.	Mustered out with company Sept. 20, 1864.
Kerr R ert	do.	30	May 2, 1864	100 dys.	Mustered out with company Sept. 10, 1864.
Lam , Sylvanus	do.	33	May 2, 1864	100 dys.	Mustered out with company Sept. 10, 1864.
Lawrence, William	do.	40	May 2, 1864	100 dys.	Mustered out with company Sept. 10, 1864.
Lemmon, John A	do.	17	May 2, 1864	100 dys.	Mustered out with company Sept. 10, 1864.
Lynn, Estep	do.	21	May 2, 1864	100 dys.	
McCombs, Charles	do.	35	May 2, 1864	100 dys.	Mustered out with company Sept. 10, 1864.
McCombs, William	do.	24	May 2, 1864	100 dys.	
McGrew Samuel	do.	28	May 2, 1864	100 dys.	Mustered out with company Sept. 10, 1864.
Mercer William H.	do.	20	May 2, 1864	100 dys.	Died Aug. 24, 1864, at Sandy Hook, Md.
Mintier James	do.	35	May 2, 1864	100 dys.	Mustered out with company Sept. 10, 1864.
Moore, Jo	do.	16	May 2, 1864	100 dys.	Mustered out with company Sept. 10, 1864.
Perry W liam	do.	40	May 2, 1864	100 dys.	Mustered out with company Sept. 10, 1864.
Peterman, col	do.	39	May 2, 1864	100 dys.	Mustered out with company Sept. 10, 1864.
Pollard, W liam	do.	49	May 2, 1864	100 dys.	Mustered out with company Sept. 10, 1864.
Shepherd, Joseph	do.	22	May 2, 1864	100 dys.	Mustered out with company Sept. 10, 1864.
Shields, Eli	do.	32	May 2, 1864	100 dys.	Mustered out with company Sept. 10, 1864.
Singer, John	do.	21	May 2, 1864	100 dys.	Mustered out with company Sept. 10, 1864.
Smallwood, James	do.	27	May 2, 1864	100 dys.	Mustered out with company Sept. 10, 1864.
Smallwood, Robert	do.	19	May 2, 1864	100 dys.	Mustered out with company Sept. 10, 1864.
Speer harles E.	do.	39	May 2, 1864	100 dys.	Mustered out with company Sept. 10, 1864.
Stevens, bert B.	do.	37	May 2, 1864	100 dys.	Mustered out with company Sept. 10, 1864.
Stevens, S las	do.	22	May 2, 1864	100 dys.	Mustered out with company Sept. 10, 1864.
Stone J mes	do.	28	May 2, 1864	100 dys.	Mustered out with company Sept. 10, 1864.
Thompson, Joseph	do.	33	May 2, 1864	100 dys.	Mustered out with company Sept. 10, 1864.
Toland, Michael H	do.	42	May 2, 1864	100 dys.	Mustered out with company Sept. 10, 1864.
Townse hn W.	do.	21	May 2, 1864	100 dys.	Mustered out with company Sept. 10, 1864.
Wallace, William A.	do.	19	May 2, 1864	100 dys.	Mustered out with company Sept. 10, 1864.
Walker Samuel	do.	28	May 2, 1864	100 dys.	Mustered out with company Sept. 10, 1864.

Names.	Rank.	Age.	Date of Entering the Service.	Period of Service.	Remarks.
Lewis, Elisha W.	Private.	26	May 2, 1864	100 dys.	Mustered out with company Sept. 10, 1864.
Loper, Isaiah	...do...	43	May 2, 1864	100 dys.	Mustered out with company Sept. 10, 1864.
McCall, Charles H.	...do...	19	May 2, 1864	100 dys.	Mustered out with company Sept. 10, 1864.
Mead, Charles	...do...	18	May 2, 1864	100 dys.	Mustered out with company Sept. 10, 1864.
Nelan, Gilbert	...do...	24	May 2, 1864	100 dys.	Mustered out with company Sept. 10, 1864.
Nichols, Jesse	...do...	17	May 2, 1864	100 dys.	Mustered out with company Sept. 10, 1864.
Nichols, Mortimore	...do...	22	May 2, 1864	100 dys.	Mustered out with company Sept. 10, 1864.
Oxley, Elisha	...do...	33	May 2, 1864	100 dys.	Mustered out with company Sept. 10, 1864.
Palmer, William	...do...	19	May 2, 1864	100 dys.	Mustered out with company Sept. 10, 1864.
Perry, Charles W.	...do...	18	May 2, 1864	100 dys.	Mustered out with company Sept. 10, 1864.
Perry, Thomas H.	...do...	2[illegible]	May 2, 1864	100 dys.	Died June 8, 1864.
Porterfield, Alonzo	...do...	22	May 2, 1864	100 dys.	Mustered out with company Sept. 10, 1864.
Pratt, Jesse	...do...	20	May 2, 1864	100 dys.	Mustered out with company Sept. 10, 1864.
Rennard, Benjamin	...do...	19	May 2, 1864	100 dys.	Mustered out with company Sept. 10, 1864.
Roberts, Harrison	...do...	21	May 2, 1864	100 dys.	Mustered out with company Sept. 10, 1864.
Roberts, Samuel	...do...	23	May 2, 1864	100 dys.	Mustered out with company Sept. 10, 1864.
Seals, Thomas	...do...	18	May 2, 1864	100 dys.	Mustered out with company Sept. 10, 1864.
Shively, George	...do...	19	May 2, 1864	100 dys.	Mustered out with company Sept. 10, 1864.
Sloan, William	...do...	18	May 2, 1864	100 dys.	Mustered out with company Sept. 10, 1864.
Smith, Nathan	...do...	27	May 2, 1864	100 dys.	Mustered out with company Sept. 10, 1864.
Steele, Wesley A.	...do...	29	May 2, 1864	100 dys.	Mustered out with company Sept 10, 1864.
Stillwell, David D.	...do...	28	May 2, 1864	100 dys.	Mustered out with company Sept. 10, 1864.
Tarbert, William	...do...	20	May 2, 1864	100 dys.	Mustered out with company Sept. 10, 1864.
Thornton, James	...do...	19	May 2, 1864	100 dys.	
Vickers, Leander	...do...	20	May 2, 1864	100 dys.	Mustered out with company Sept. 10, 1864.
Walker, Joel	...do...	26	May 2, 1864	100 dys.	Mustered out with company Sept. 10, 1864.
Wear, James	...do...	31	May 2, 1864	100 dys.	Wounded July 24, 1864, in battle of Winchester, Va; mustered out with company Sept. 10, 1864.
Wells, David	...do...	26	May 2, 1864	100 dys.	Discharged June 22, 1864.
Westlake, Benjamin	...do...	45	May 2, 1864	100 dys.	Captured July 25, 1864, in action at Martinsburg, W. Va.; escaped and returned to company July 29, 1864; mustered out with company Sept. 10, 1864.
Woodward, William	...do...	31	May 2, 1864	100 dys.	

COMPANY H.

Mustered in May 14, 1864, at Bellaire, O., by C. P. Horton, Captain and A. D. C. Mustered out Sept. 10, 1864, at Camp Chase, O., by William B. Lowe, Captain 11th Infantry ' S. A.

Names.	Rank.	Age.	Date of Entering the Service.	Period of Service.	Remarks.
Edwin Regal	Captain.	35	May 2, 1864	100 dys.	Mustered out with company Sept. 10, 1864.
John E. Cannon	1st Lieut.	38	May 2, 1864	100 dys.	Mustered out with company Sept. 10, 1864.
Robert P. Hanna	2d Lieut.	38	May 2, 1864	100 dys.	Mustered out with company Sept. 10, 1864.
George A. Crew	1st Sergt.	25	May 2, 1864	100 dys.	Mustered out with company Sept. 10, 1864.
George Lanning	Sergeant.	32	May 2, 1864	100 dys.	Died Sept. 1, 1864, at Sandy Hook, Md.
Thomas Dawson	...do...	31	May 2, 1864	100 dys.	Mustered out with company Sept. 10, 1864.
James McWatty	...do...	43	May 2, 1864	100 dys.	Furloughed for 100 days from May 15, 1864. No further record found.
Daniel L. Parrish	...do...	27	May 2, 1864	100 dys.	Mustered out with company Sept. 10, 1864.
Thomas A. Jobes	Corporal.	21	May 2, 1864	100 dys.	Mustered out with company Sept. 10, 1864.
William Peregoy	...do...	24	May 2, 1864	100 dys.	Mustered out with company Sept. 10, 1864.
William McCullough	...do...	24	May 2, 1864	100 dys.	Mustered out with company Sept. 10, 1864.
Thomas H. Baldwin	...do...	32	May 2, 1864	100 dys.	Mustered out with company Sept. 10, 1864.
James H. Culbertson	...do...	29	May 2, 1864	100 dys.	Absent, sick ——, at New Athens, O. No further record found.
W. Wesley Mansfield	...do...	18	May 2, 1864	100 dys.	Mustered out with company Sept. 10, 1864.
John C. Dickerson	...do...	20	May 2, 1864	100 dys.	Absent, sick ——, at New Athens, O. No further record found.
John W. P. Gallaher	...do...	19	May 2, 1864	100 dys.	Mustered out with company Sept. 10, 1864.
George W. Rife	Musician	28	May 2, 1864	100 dys.	Mustered out with company Sept. 10, 1864.
Jonathan Copeland	...do...	48	May 2, 1864	100 dys.	Mustered out with company Sept. 10, 1864.
Jonathan McGuire	Wagoner.	30	May 2, 1864	100 dys.	Furloughed for 100 days from May 15, 1864. No further record found.
Beatty, David R.	Private.	23	May 2, 1864	100 dys.	Mustered out with company Sept. 10, 1864.
Beatty, John	...do...	[illegible]	May 2, 1864	100 dys.	Mustered out with company Sept. 10, 1864.
Beck, Anthony	...do...	21	May 2, 1864	100 dys.	Mustered out with company Sept. 10, 1864.
Bouls, David	...do...	47	May 2, 1864	100 dys.	Mustered out with company Sept. 10, 1864.
Bogardus, Benjamin	...do...	18	May 2, 1864	100 dys.	Mustered out with company Sept. 10, 1864.
Brown, John C.	...do...	18	May 2, 1864	100 dys.	Mustered out with company Sept. 10, 1864.
Brown, Samuel H.	...do...	23	May 2, 1864	100 dys.	Mustered out with company Sept. 10, 1864.
Bruner, Samuel	...do...	41	May 2, 1864	100 dys.	Mustered out with company Sept. 10, 1864.
Calderhead, John	...do...	18	May 2, 1864	100 dys.	Died Aug. 3, 1864, at Camp Parole, near Annapolis, Md.
Cannon, Moses W.	...do...	28	May 2, 1864	100 dys.	Mustered ou[illegible] company Sept. 10, 1864.
Cassell, John W.	...do...	43	May 2, 1864	100 dys.	Promoted to Principal Musician June 1, 1864.
Chandler, John A.	...do...	26	May 2, 1864	100 dys.	Mustered out with company Sept. 10, 1864.
Clark, Silas	...do...	29	May 2, 1864	100 dys.	Mustered out with company Sept. 10, 1864.
Cramblet, John P.	...do...	21	May 2, 1864	100 dys.	Mustered out with company Sept. 10, 1864.

COMPANY I.

Mustered in May 13, 1864, at Bellaire, O., by C. P. Horton, Captain and A. D. C. Mustered out Sept. 10, 1864, at Camp Chase, O., by William B. Lowe, Captain 11th Infantry, U. S. A.

Names.	Rank.	Age.	Date of Entering the Service.	Period of Service.	Remarks.
Nathan H. Rowles	Captain.	35	May 2, 1864	100 dys.	Mustered out with company Sept. 10, 1864.
Elias B. Lowman	1st Lieut.	43	May 2, 1864	100 dys.	Mustered out with company Sept. 10, 1864.
Daniel Westlake	2d Lieut.	34	May 2, 1864	100 dys.	Mustered out with company Sept. 10, 1864.
William Rankin	1st Sergt.	36	May 2, 1864	100 dys.	Died Aug. 11, 1864, at Baltimore, Md.
Samuel S. Martin	....do....	30	May 2, 1864	100 dys.	Appointed from Sergeant Aug. 11, 1864; mustered out with company Sept. 10, 1864.
Cyrus H. Strahl	Sergeant.	25	May 2, 1864	100 dys.	Mustered out with company Sept. 10, 1864.
John F. Wortman	....do....	35	May 2, 1864	100 dys.	Mustered out with company Sept. 10, 1864.
James F. Anderson	....do....	23	May 2, 1864	100 dys.	Mustered out with company Sept. 10, 1864.
William McFarland	....do....	25	May 2, 1864	100 dys.	Appointed from Corporal Aug. 11, 1864; mustered out with company Sept. 10, 1864.
Mord Nelson	Corporal.	20	May 2, 1864	100 dys.	Captured July 25, 1864, in action at Martinsburg, W. Va.; escaped and returned to company Aug. 4, 1864; mustered out with company Sept. 10, 1864.
Thomas K. Crozier	....do....	21	May 2, 1864	100 dys.	Mustered out with company Sept. 10, 1864.
Joseph H. Heatherington	....do....	21	May 2, 1864	100 dys.	Captured July 25, 1864, in action at Martinsburg, W. Va.; paroled ——; died March 21, 1865, at Annapolis, Md.
Charles W. Hall	....do....	36	May 2, 1864	100 dys.	Mustered out with company Sept. 10, 1864.
Leander Greenlee	....do....	26	May 2, 1864	100 dys.	Mustered out with company Sept. 10, 1864.
John Dunfee	....do....	37	May 2, 1864	100 dys.	Mustered out with company Sept. 10, 1864.
James McGregor	....do....	23	May 2, 1864	100 dys.	Mustered out with company Sept. 10, 1864.
Robert McLellan	....do....	30	May 2, 1864	100 dys.	Mustered out with company Sept. 10, 1864.
Abel, John C.	Private.	34	May 2, 1864	100 dys.	Mustered out with company Sept. 10, 1864.
Anderson, Isaac	....do....	43	May 2, 1864	100 dys.	Mustered out with company Sept. 10, 1864.
Archer, Daniel W.	....do....	18	May 2, 1864	100 dys.	Mustered out with company Sept. 10, 1864.
Austin, Lafayette	....do....	37	May 2, 1864	100 dys.	Mustered out with company Sept. 10, 1864.
Austin, Lycurgus	....do....	42	May 2, 1864	100 dys.	Mustered out with company Sept. 10, 1864.
Bair, John	....do....	37	May 2, 1864	100 dys.	Mustered out with company Sept. 10, 1864.
Bickel, Frederick	....do....	18	May 2, 1864	100 dys.	Mustered out with company Sept. 10, 1864.
Boyd, Samuel	....do....	23	May 2, 1864	100 dys.	Mustered out with company Sept. 10, 1864.
Clark, Robert	....do....	30	May 2, 1864	100 dys.	Died July 27, 1864, at Sandy Hook, Md.
Cunningham, John W.	....do....	35	May 2, 1864	100 dys.	Died Sept. 8, 1864, at Jarvis Hospital, Baltimore, Md.
Davis, James	....do....	19	May 2, 1864	100 dys.	Mustered out with company Sept. 10, 1864.
Dean, Alfred	....do....	18	May 2, 1864	100 dys.	Mustered out with company Sept. 10, 1864.
Dunfee, Jacob	....do....	27	May 2, 1864	100 dys.	Mustered out with company Sept. 10, 1864.
Ferry, William H.	....do....	22	May 2, 1864	100 dys.	Mustered out with company Sept. 10, 1864.
Forbes, William J.	....do....	37	May 2, 1864	100 dys.	Mustered out with company Sept. 10, 1864.
Foster, Joshua	....do....	18	May 2, 1864	100 dys.	Mustered out with company Sept. 10, 1864.
Fry, William	....do....	26	May 2, 1864	100 dys.	Mustered out with company Sept. 10, 1864.
Fuller, Charles A.	....do....	37	May 2, 1864	100 dys.	Mustered out with company Sept. 10, 1864.
Garloen, Frederick	....do....	31	May 2, 1864	100 dys.	Mustered out with company Sept. 10, 1864.
Gibler, Patrick	....do....	30	May 2, 1864	100 dys.	
Goldsworthy, John	....do....	33	May 2, 1864	100 dys.	Captured July 25, 1864, in action at Martinsburg, W. Va.; mustered out March 15, 1865, at Columbus, O., by order of War Department.
Greenlee, William H.	....do....	21	May 2, 1864	100 dys.	Mustered out with company Sept. 10, 1864.
Groff, Melvin	....do....	33	May 2, 1864	100 dys.	Mustered out with company Sept. 10, 1864.
Grubb, Edward	....do....	53	May 2, 1864	100 dys.	Mustered out with company Sept. 10, 1864.
Hall, William	....do....	41	May 2, 1864	100 dys.	Mustered out with company Sept. 10, 1864.
Hammond, Alexander	....do....	43	May 2, 1864	100 dys.	
Heatherington, John E.	....do....	28	May 2, 1864	100 dys.	Mustered out with company Sept. 10, 1864.
Hend[illegible] H.	....do....	25	May 2, 1864	100 dys.	Mustered out with company Sept. 10, 1864.
Hines, Samuel	....do....	44	May 2, 1864	100 dys.	Mustered out with company Sept. 10, 1864.
Hipkins, Stephen	....do....	23	May 2, 1864	100 dys.	Mustered out with company Sept. 10, 1864.
Ing, [illegible]ram	....do....	35	May 2, 1864	100 dys.	Mustered out with company Sept. 10, 1864.
Jones, William W.	....do....	18	May 2, 1864	100 dys.	Mustered out with company Sept. 10, 1864.
Keyser, Isaac A.	....do....	39	May 2, 1864	100 dys.	Mustered out with company Sept. 10, 1864.
Keyser, Jacob P.	....do....	51	May 2, 1864	100 dys.	Mustered out with company Sept. 10, 1864.
Keyser, Jacob T.	....do....	22	May 2, 1864	100 dys.	Mustered out with company Sept. 10, 1864.
Keyser, Jesse B.	....do....	36	May 2, 1864	100 dys.	Mustered out with company Sept. 10, 1864.
Keyser, William A.	....do....	37	May 2, 1864	100 dys.	Mustered out with company Sept. 10, 1864.
King, George	....do....	16	May 2, 1864	100 dys.	Mustered out with company Sept. 10, 1864.
Long, John H.	....do....	22	May 2, 1864	100 dys.	Mustered out with company Sept. 10, 1864.
Lyal, Alexander	....do....	38	May 2, 1864	100 dys.	Mustered out with company Sept. 10, 1864.
McMahon, James	....do....	19	May 2, 1864	100 dys.	Mustered out with company Sept. 10, 1864.
McMahon, Thomas	....do....	20	May 2, 1864	100 dys.	Mustered out with company Sept. 10, 1864.
McMillen, Samuel	....do....	21	May 2, 1864	100 dys.	Mustered out with company Sept. 10, 1864.
Mertz, Henry	....do....	18	May 2, 1864	100 dys.	Mustered out with company Sept. 10, 1864.
Nelson, Joseph C.	....do....	26	May 2, 1864	100 dys.	Mustered out with company Sept. 10, 1864.
Nesbit, John	....do....	23	May 2, 1864	100 dys.	Mustered out with company Sept. 10, 1864.
Norman, Albert	....do....	19	May 2, 1864	100 dys.	Mustered out with company Sept. 10, 1864.
Patterson, John M.	....do....	18	May 2, 1864	100 dys.	Mustered out with company Sept. 10, 1864.

Names.	Rank.	Age.	Date of Entering the Service.	Period of Service.	Remarks.
Howard, George W	Private..	18	May 2, 1864	100 dys.	Mustered out with company Sept. 10, 1864.
Johnston, Joseph L	....do....	22	May 2, 1864	100 dys.	Mustered out with company Sept. 10, 1864.
Johnson, Thomas	....do....	18	May 2, 1864	100 dys.	Died Aug. 11, 1864, at Pleasant Valley Hospital, Sandy Hook, Md.
Kerr, Alexander B	....do....	36	May 2, 1864	100 dys.	Discharged June 22, 1864, on Surgeon's certificate of disability.
Laizure, William C	....do....	19	May 2, 1864	100 dys.	Mustered out with company Sept. 10, 1864.
Layport, Addison	....do....	26	May 2, 1864	100 dys.	Mustered out with company Sept. 10, 1864.
Lee, William	....do....	28	May 2, 1864	100 dys.	Mustered out with company Sept. 10, 1864.
Leeper, Archibald	....do....	22	May 2, 1864	100 dys.	Died Aug. 12, 1864, at Pleasant Valley Hospital, Sandy Hook, Md.
Leeper, Samuel	....do....	22	May 2, 1864	100 dys.	Mustered out with company Sept. 10, 1864.
McAfee, John A	....do....	18	May 2, 1864	100 dys.	Mustered out with company Sept. 10, 1864.
McBride, John	....do....	42	May 2, 1864	100 dys.	Mustered out with company Sept. 10, 1864.
McConnell, Samuel B	....do....	25	May 2, 1864	100 dys.	Mustered out with company Sept. 10, 1864.
McKee, Henry	....do....	21	May 2, 1864	100 dys.	Mustered out with company Sept. 10, 1864.
Magee, Stephen B	....do....	43	May 2, 1864	100 dys.	Promoted to Q. M. Sergeant May 13, 1864.
Mansfield, Nathan H	....do....	18	May 2, 1864	100 dys.	Mustered out with company Sept. 10, 1864.
Marsh, James K	....do....	19	May 2, 1864	100 dys.	Mustered out with company Sept. 10, 1864.
Marshall, John B	....do....	18	May 2, 1864	100 dys.	Mustered out with company Sept. 10, 1864.
Mattern, Henry	....do....	22	May 2, 1864	100 dys.	Mustered out with company Sept. 10, 1864.
Mollett, William	....do....	18	May 2, 1864	100 dys.	Mustered out with company Sept. 10, 1864.
Moorehead, Morrison	....do....	25	May 2, 1864	100 dys.	Reduced from Corporal July 18, 1864; mustered out with company Sept. 10, 1864.
Nichols, John H	....do....	25	May 2, 1864	100 dys.	Discharged June 18, 1864, on Surgeon's certificate of disability.
Penn, James A	....do....	18	May 2, 1864	100 dys.	Mustered out with company Sept. 10, 1864.
Penn, John A	....do....	20	May 2, 1864	100 dys.	Mustered out with company Sept. 10, 1864.
Phillips, Thomas	....do....	18	May 2, 1864	100 dys.	Mustered out with company Sept. 10, 1864.
Phillips, William	....do....	21	May 2, 1864	100 dys.	Reduced from Sergeant July 18, 1864; mustered out with company Sept. 10, 1864.
Ramsey, William T	....do....	26	May 2, 1864	100 dys.	Mustered out with company Sept. 10, 1864.
Richey, Thomas J	....do....	18	May 2, 1864	100 dys.	Mustered out with company Sept. 10, 1864.
Roberts, Griffith	....do....	25	May 2, 1864	100 dys.	Mustered out with company Sept. 10, 1864.
Selby, Thomas	....do....	23	May 2, 1864	100 dys.	Mustered out with company Sept. 10, 1864.
Sheets, Robert M	....do....	23	May 2, 1864	100 dys.	Mustered out with company Sept. 10, 1864.
Shivers, George	....do....	37	May 2, 1864	100 dys.	Mustered out with company Sept. 10, 1864.
Shivers, Samuel	....do....	35	May 2, 1864	100 dys.	Mustered out with company Sept. 10, 1864.
Thompson, Thomas W	....do....	31	May 2, 1864	100 dys.	Mustered out with company Sept. 10, 1864.
Tipton, Albert R	....do....	38	May 2, 1864	100 dys.	Mustered out with company Sept. 10, 1864.
Tipton, Randolph	....do....	18	May 2, 1864	100 dys.	Mustered out with company Sept. 10, 1864.
West, Lafayette	....do....	19	May 2, 1864	100 dys.	Mustered out with company Sept. 10, 1864.

171st Regiment Ohio Volunteer Infantry.

ONE HUNDRED DAYS' SERVICE.

THIS Regiment was organized at Sandusky, O., May 7, 1864, to serve one hundred days. It was composed of the Fifty-first Battalion, Ohio National Guard, from Trumbull County; Fourteenth Battalion, Ohio National Guard, from Portage County; Eighty-fifth Battalion, Ohio National Guard, from Lake County; and the Eighty-sixth Battalion, Ohio National Guard, from Geauga County. The Regiment was ordered to Johnson's Island, O., where it was engaged in guard- and fatigue-duty. On the 9th of June the One Hundred and Seventy-first was ordered to Covington, Ky., reporting on arrival to General Hobson. It was then placed on cars and ordered to Cynthiana, but upon arriving at Keller's Bridge the Regiment debarked, where it was attacked by a force of Morgan's Cavalry, on the 11th of June, in which engagement the Regiment lost thirteen killed and fifty-four wounded. Soon after the fight at Keller's Bridge, Morgan was pressed so closely that he was compelled to parole his prisoners, who made their way to Augusta; from there they were taken on boats to Covington, and then transferred to Camp Dennison, where they joined the Regiment. The Regiment moved from Camp Dennison to Johnson's Island, where it remained until the 20th of August, 1864, when it was mustered out on expiration of term of service.

Names.	Rank.	Age.	Date of Entering the Service.	Period of Service.	
Stevenson, Jacob	Private.	31	April 27, 1864	100 dys.	Killed June Bridge, Ky.
Stein, Henry	....do....	46	April 27, 1864	100 dys.	Mustered out
Stone, John	....do....	24	April 27, 1864	100 dys.	Mustered out
Swindler, Peter	....do....	22	April 27, 1864	100 dys.	Mustered out
Thomson, Mortimer C.	....do....	19	April 27, 1864	100 dys.	Killed June 11, 1 Bridge, Ky.
Turnbull, Thomas	....do....	30	April 27, 1864	100 dys.	Mustered out
Tyler, John M	....do....	23	April 27, 1864	100 dys.	Mustered out
Wallace, Samuel	....do....	32	April 27, 1864	100 dys.	Mustered out
Whipple, Jackson	....do....	27	April 27, 1864	100 dys.	Mustered out
White, Lemuel	....do....	25	April 27, 1864	100 dys.	Mustered out
Wilson, James G	....do....	28	April 27, 1864	100 dys.	Mustered out

COMPANY C.

Mustered in May 5, 1864, at Sandusky, O., by C. P. Horton, Captain and A. D. C. at Johnson's Island, O., by J. M. Eyster, Captain 18th Infantry.

Names.	Rank.	Age.	Date of Entering the Service.	Period of Service.	
Joseph M. Jackson	Captain.	35	April 27, 1864	100 dys.	Mustered out with
Milton Matthews	1st Lieut.	21	April 27, 1864	100 dys.	Mustered out with
Benjamin Veach	2d Lieut.	22	April 27, 1864	100 dys.	Mustered out with
Mahlon B. White	1st Sergt.	26	April 27, 1864	100 dys.	Mustered out with
Alfred W. Hume	Sergeant.	28	April 27, 1864	100 dys.	Mustered out with
Andrew R. Bailey	....do....	22	April 27, 1864	100 dys.	Mustered out with
John Randall	....do....	30	April 27, 1864	100 dys.	Mustered as Corp May 5, 1864; mu Aug. 20, 1864.
John Applegate	....do....	21	April 27, 1864	100 dys.	Mustered as Corp May 5, 1864; mu Aug. 20, 1864.
Samuel Kennedy	Corporal.	24	April 27, 1864	100 dys.	Died July 29, 18 County, O.
John Mitchletree	....do....	29	April 27, 1864	100 dys.	Mustered out with
John Kimmel	....do....	29	April 27, 1864	100 dys.	Mustered out with
James Treester	....do....	25	April 27, 1864	100 dys.	Mustered out with
Hiram L. Stephens	....do....	27	April 27, 1864	100 dys.	Mustered out with
Cyrus B. Leyde	....do....	28	April 27, 1864	100 dys.	Mustered out with
William C. Hall	....do....	19	April 27, 1864	100 dys.	Appointed May 5 company Aug. 2
Lewis G. Campbell	....do....	18	April 27, 1864	100 dys.	Appointed May 5 company Aug. 2
Ephraim Blackburn	....do....	27	April 27, 1864	100 dys.	Appointed July 2 company Aug. 2
Hugh Veach	Wagoner.	32	April 27, 1864	100 dys.	Mustered out with
Barringer, John	Private.	18	April 27, 1864	100 dys.	Mustered out with
Bently, Martin	....do....	19	April 27, 1864	100 dys.	Mustered out with
Brumstetter, Samuel	....do....	19	April 27, 1864	100 dys.	Mustered out with
Buck, John V	....do....	28	April 27, 1864	100 dys.	Mustered out with
Burnett, Leander W	....do....	21	April 27, 1864	100 dys.	Mustered out with
Calhoun, Wesley	....do....	18	April 27, 1864	100 dys.	Mustered out with
Clark, Byron	....do....	22	April 27, 1864	100 dys.	Mustered out with
Clingman, Hewett	....do....	20	April 27, 1864	100 dys.	Mustered out with
Clingman, Lorenzo	....do....	24	April 27, 1864	100 dys.	Mustered out with
Crawford, Milo	....do....	26	April 27, 1864	100 dys.	Mustered out with
Crawford, William W	....do....	18	April 27, 1864	100 dys.	Mustered out with
Davidson, James H	....do....	37	April 27, 1864	100 dys.	Mustered out with
Dilley, James	....do....	21	April 27, 1864	100 dys.	Discharged Aug. 2 on Surgeon's cer
Dilley, Jonathan	....do....	20	April 27, 1864	100 dys.	Died June 25, 1864,
Dixon, Thomas	....do....	20	April 27, 1864	100 dys.	Mustered out with
Everett, Solomon	....do....	40	April 27, 1864	100 dys.	
Everhart, Joseph	....do....	29	April 27, 1864	100 dys.	Mustered out with
Fusselman, Edward	....do....	18	April 27, 1864	100 dys.	Mustered out with
Gregory, Harvey	....do....	37	April 27, 1864	100 dys.	Mustered out with
Herrington, Enos L	....do....	29	April 27, 1864	100 dys.	Mustered out with
Holenbeck, Vincent	....do....	40	April 27, 1864	100 dys.	Mustered out with
Hoover, Jesse	....do....	28	April 27, 1864	100 dys.	Mustered as Serge 5, 1864.
Hoover, James S	....do....	20	April 27, 1864	100 dys.	Mustered out with
Hoover, William H	....do....	27	April 27, 1864	100 dys.	Discharged Aug. on Surgeon's cer
Housel, Eno M	....do....	19	April 27, 1864	100 dys.	Mustered out with
Huff, John G	....do....	19	April 27, 1864	100 dys.	Mustered out with
Hultz, Howard W	....do....	18	April 27, 1864	100 dys.	Mustered out with
Jackson, John G	....do....	36	April 27, 1864	100 dys.	Mustered out with
Jackson, William J	....do....	31	April 27, 1864	100 dys.	Mustered out with
Jewell, Robert H	....do....	35	April 27, 1864	100 dys.	Mustered out with
Kimmel, Smith	....do....	34	April 27, 1864	100 dys.	Mustered out with
Kashner, Daniel	....do....	19	April 27, 1864	100 dys.	Mustered out with

Names.	Rank.	Age.	Date of Entering the Service.	Period of Service.	Remarks.
Stevenson, Jacob	Private..	34	April 27, 1864	100 dys.	Killed June 11, 1864, in action at Keller's Bridge, Ky.
Stein, Henry	....do....	46	April 27, 1864	100 dys.	Mustered out with company Aug. 20, 1864.
Stone, John	....do....	24	April 27, 1864	100 dys.	Mustered out with company Aug. 20, 1864.
Swindler, Peter	....do....	22	April 27, 1864	100 dys.	Mustered out with company Aug. 20, 1864.
Thomson, Mortimer C.	....do....	19	April 27, 1864	100 dys.	Killed June 11, 1864, in action at Keller's Bridge, Ky.
Turnbull, Thomas	....do....	30	April 27, 1864	100 dys.	Mustered out with company Aug. 20, 1864.
Tyler, John M.	....do....	23	April 27, 1864	100 dys.	Mustered out with company Aug. 20, 1864.
Wallace, Samuel	....do....	32	April 27, 1864	100 dys.	Mustered out with company Aug. 20, 1864.
Whipple, Jackson	....do....	27	April 27, 1864	100 dys.	Mustered out with company Aug. 20, 1864.
White, Lemuel	....do....	25	April 27, 1864	100 dys.	Mustered out with company Aug. 20, 1864.
Wilson, James G	....do....	38	April 27, 1864	100 dys.	Mustered out with company Aug. 20, 1864.

COMPANY C.

Mustered in May 5, 1864, at Sandusky, O., by C. P. Horton, Captain and A. D. C. Mustered out Aug. 20, 1864, at Johnson's Island, O., by M. Eyster, Captain 18th Infantry, U. S. A.

Names.	Rank.	Age.	Date of Entering the Service.	Period of Service.	Remarks.
Joseph M. Jackson	Captain.	35	April 27, 1864	100 dys.	Mustered out with company Aug. 20, 1864.
Milton Matthews	1st Lieut.	21	April 27, 1864	100 dys.	Mustered out with company Aug. 20, 1864.
Benjamin Veach	2d Lieut.	22	April 27, 1864	100 dys.	Mustered out with company Aug. 20, 1864.
Mahlon B. White	1st Sergt.	28	April 27, 1864	100 dys.	Mustered out with company Aug. 20, 1864.
Alfred W. Hume	Sergeant.	23	April 27, 1864	100 dys.	Mustered out with company Aug. 20, 1864.
Andrew R. Bailey	....do....	22	April 27, 1864	100 dys.	Mustered out with company Aug. 20, 1864.
John Randall	....do....	30	April 27, 1864	100 dys.	Mustered as Corporal; appointed Sergeant May 5, 1864; mustered out with company Aug. 20, 1864.
John Applegate	....do....	21	April 27, 1864	100 dys.	Mustered as Corporal; appointed Sergeant May 5, 1864; mustered out with company Aug. 20, 1864.
Samuel Kennedy	Corporal.	24	April 27, 1864	100 dys.	Died July 20, 1864, at Hubbard, Trumbull County, O.
John Mitchletree	....do....	29	April 27, 1864	100 dys.	Mustered out with company Aug. 20, 1864.
John Kimmel	....do....	29	April 27, 1864	100 dys.	Mustered out with company Aug. 20, 1864.
James Treester	....do....	25	April 27, 1864	100 dys.	Mustered out with company Aug. 20, 1864.
Hiram L. Stephens	....do....	27	April 27, 1864	100 dys.	Mustered out with company Aug. 20, 1864.
Cyrus B. Leyde	....do....	28	April 27, 1864	100 dys.	Mustered out with company Aug. 20, 1864.
William C. Hall	....do....	19	April 27, 1864	100 dys.	Appointed May 5, 1864; mustered out with company Aug. 20, 1864.
Lewis G. Campbell	....do....	18	April 27, 1864	100 dys.	Appointed May 5, 1864; mustered out with company Aug. 20, 1864.
Ephraim Blackburn	....do....	27	April 27, 1864	100 dys.	Appointed July 21, 1861; mustered out with company Aug. 20, 1864.
Hugh Veach	Wagoner.	32	April 27, 1864	100 dys.	Mustered out with company Aug. 20, 1864.
Barringer, John	Private..	18	April 27, 1864	100 dys.	Mustered out with company Aug. 20, 1864.
Bently, Martin	....do....	19	April 27, 1864	100 dys.	Mustered out with company Aug. 20, 1864.
Brumstetter, Samuel	....do....	19	April 27, 1864	100 dys.	Mustered out with company Aug. 20, 1864.
Buck, John V.	....do....	23	April 27, 1864	100 dys.	Mustered out with company Aug. 20, 1864.
Burnett, Leander W.	....do....	21	April 27, 1864	100 dys.	Mustered out with company Aug. 20, 1864.
Calhoun, Wesley	....do....	18	April 27, 1864	100 dys.	Mustered out with company Aug. 20, 1864.
Clark, Byron	....do....	22	April 27, 1864	100 dys.	Mustered out with company Aug. 20, 1864.
Clingman, Hewett	....do....	20	April 27, 1864	100 dys.	Mustered out with company Aug. 20, 1864.
Clingman, Lorenzo	....do....	24	April 27, 1864	100 dys.	Mustered out with company Aug. 20, 1864.
Crawford, Milo	....do....	26	April 27, 1864	100 dys.	Mustered out with company Aug. 20, 1864.
Crawford, William W.	....do....	18	April 27, 1864	100 dys.	Mustered out with company Aug. 20, 1864.
Davidson, James H.	....do....	37	April 27, 1864	100 dys.	Mustered out with company Aug. 20, 1864.
Dilley, James	....do....	21	April 27, 1864	100 dys.	Discharged Aug. 20, 1864, at Covington, Ky., on Surgeon's certificate of disability.
Dilley, Jonathan	....do....	20	April 27, 1864	100 dys.	Died June 26, 1864, at Camp Dennison, O.
Dixon, Thomas	....do....	20	April 27, 1864	100 dys.	Mustered out with company Aug. 20, 1864.
Everet, Solomon	....do....	40	April 27, 1864	100 dys.	
Everhart, Joseph	....do....	29	April 27, 1864	100 dys.	Mustered out with company Aug. 20, 1864.
Fusselman, Edward	....do....	18	April 27, 1864	100 dys.	Mustered out with company Aug. 20, 1864.
Gregory, Harvey	....do....	37	April 27, 1864	100 dys.	Mustered out with company Aug. 20, 1864.
Herrington, Enos L.	....do....	29	April 27, 1864	100 dys.	Mustered out with company Aug. 20, 1864.
Holenbeck, Vincent	....do....	40	April 27, 1864	100 dys.	Mustered out with company Aug. 20, 1864.
Hoover, Jesse	....do....	36	April 27, 1864	100 dys.	Mustered as Sergeant; reduced to ranks May 5, 1864.
Hoover, James S.	....do....	20	April 27, 1864	100 dys.	Mustered out with company Aug. 20, 1864.
Hoover, William H.	....do....	27	April 27, 1864	100 dys.	Discharged Aug. 20, 1864, at Covington, Ky., on Surgeon's certificate of disability.
Housel, Eno M.	....do....	19	April 27, 1864	100 dys.	Mustered out with company Aug. 20, 1864.
Huff, John G.	....do....	19	April 27, 1864	100 dys.	Mustered out with company Aug. 20, 1864.
Hultz, Howard W.	....do....	18	April 27, 1864	100 dys.	Mustered out with company Aug. 20, 1864.
Jackson, ohn G.	....do....	36	April 27, 1864	100 dys.	Mustered out with company Aug. 20, 1864.
Jackson, William J.	....do....	31	April 27, 1864	100 dys.	Mustered out with company Aug. 20, 1864.
Jewell, Ro ert H.	....do....	35	April 27, 1864	100 dys.	Mustered out with company Aug. 20, 1864.
Kimmel, Smith	....do....	31	April 27, 1864	106 dys.	Mustered out with company Aug. 20, 1864.
Kashner, Daniel	....do....	19	April 27, 1864	100 dys.	Mustered out with company Aug. 20, 1864.

Names.	Rank.	Age.	Date of Entering the Service.	Period of Service.	Remarks.
Davis, Benjamin	Private	33	April 27, 1864	100 dys.	Mustered out with company Aug. 20, 1864.
Davis, Edward	do	18	April 27, 1864	100 dys.	Mustered out with company Aug. 20, 1864.
Davis, Jacob	do	24	April 27, 1864	100 dys.	Mustered out with company Aug. 20, 1864.
Davis, Rosser	do	24	April 27, 1864	100 dys.	Mustered out with company Aug. 20, 1864.
Davis, William E	do	25	April 27, 1864	100 dys.	Mustered out with company Aug. 20, 1864.
Eckman, Ambrose	do	19	April 27, 1864	100 dys.	Mustered out with company Aug. 20, 1864.
Evans, Edward	do	21	April 27, 1864	100 dys.	
Evans, Evan J	do	26	April 27, 1864	100 dys.	Mustered out with company Aug. 20, 1864.
Evans, Zenith	do	20	April 27, 1864	100 dys.	
Fatchell, Frederick	do	38	April 27, 1864	100 dys.	Mustered out with company Aug. 20, 1864.
Frack, George M	do	18	April 27, 1864	100 dys.	Mustered out with company Aug. 20, 1864.
Frazer, George B	do	20	April 27, 1864	100 dys.	Mustered out with company Aug. 20, 1864.
Gilbert, Harry R	do	18	April 27, 1864	100 dys.	Mustered out with company Aug. 20, 1864.
Goist, Hiram K	do	26	April 27, 1864	100 dys.	Died June 2, 1864, in hospital at Johnson's Island, O.
Green, Nicholas H	do	30	April 27, 1864	100 dys.	Mustered out with company Aug. 20, 1864.
Gridley, Talbot	do	30	April 27, 1864	100 dys.	Mustered out with company Aug. 20, 1864.
Griffith, David	do	19	April 27, 1864	100 dys.	Mustered out with company Aug. 20, 1864.
Harper, George	do	19	April 27, 1864	100 dys.	Mustered out with company Aug. 20, 1864.
Harris, John	do	19	April 27, 1864	100 dys.	Mustered out with company Aug. 20, 1864.
Hood, Amos L	do	26	April 27, 1864	100 dys.	Mustered out with company Aug. 20, 1864.
Hull, Benjamin F	do	29	April 27, 1864	100 dys.	Mustered out with company Aug. 20, 1864.
Jeffreys, John	do	40	April 27, 1864	100 dys.	Mustered out with company Aug. 20, 1864.
Jones, Thomas D	do	18	April 27, 1864	100 dys.	Mustered out with company Aug. 20, 1864.
Jones, William G	do	21	April 27, 1864	100 dys.	Mustered out with company Aug. 20, 1864.
Keefer, Jonathan	do	31	April 27, 1864	100 dys.	Mustered out with company Aug. 20, 1864.
Lewis, John B	do	20	April 27, 1864	100 dys.	Mustered out with company Aug. 20, 1864.
Lewis, John E	do	45	April 27, 1864	100 dys.	Mustered out with company Aug. 20, 1864.
Lewis, Lewis D	do	22	April 27, 1864	100 dys.	Mustered out with company Aug. 20, 1864.
McCartney, Andrew	do	18	April 27, 1864	100 dys.	Mustered out with company Aug. 20, 1864.
Mansell, Samuel	do	31	April 27, 1864	100 dys.	Mustered out with company Aug. 20, 1864.
Miller, Charles S	do	28	April 27, 1864	100 dys.	Mustered out with company Aug. 20, 1864.
Miller, Ezra B	do	19	April 27, 1864	100 dys.	Mustered out with company Aug. 20, 1864.
Miller, William W	do	27	April 27, 1864	100 dys.	Mustered out with company Aug. 20, 1864.
Morgan, Evan W	do	40	April 27, 1864	100 dys.	Mustered out with company Aug. 20, 1864.
Morris, Isaiah	do	22	April 27, 1864	100 dys.	Mustered out with company Aug. 20, 1864.
Morris, James D	do	19	April 27, 1864	100 dys.	Mustered out with company Aug. 20, 1864.
Neal, Augustus	do	37	April 27, 1864	100 dys.	Mustered out with company Aug. 20, 1864.
Nelson, John C	do	34	April 27, 1864	100 dys.	Mustered out with company Aug. 20, 1864.
Parker, James	do	32	April 27, 1864	100 dys.	Mustered out with company Aug. 20, 1864.
Perkins, William	do	21	April 27, 1864	100 dys.	Mustered out with company Aug. 20, 1864.
Rayen, Joseph	do	26	April 27, 1864	100 dys.	Mustered out with company Aug. 20, 1864.
Reynolds, Thomas	do	29	April 27, 1864	100 dys.	Mustered out with company Aug. 20, 1864.
Richmond, Theodore	do	23	April 27, 1864	100 dys.	Mustered out with company Aug. 20, 1864.
Roberts, Robert	do	38	April 27, 1864	100 dys.	Mustered out with company Aug. 20, 1864.
Rodgers, George N	do	30	April 27, 1864	100 dys.	Mustered out with company Aug. 20, 1864.
Schropp, Simon	do	27	April 27, 1864	100 dys.	
Shults, [illegible]	do	40	April 27, 1864	100 dys.	Mustered out with company Aug. 20, 1864.
Taylor, Robert	do	39	April 27, 1864	100 dys.	Mustered out with company Aug. 20, 1864.
Williams, David	do	19	April 27, 1864	100 dys.	Died Aug. 7, 1864, in hospital at Johnson's Island, O.
Williams, Thomas	do	18	April 27, 1864	100 dys.	
Wooldridge, John	do	25	April 27, 1864	100 dys.	Mustered out with company Aug. 20, 1864.

COMPANY E.

Mustered in May 7, 1864, at Sandusky, O., by C. P. Horton, Captain and A. D. C. Mustered out Aug. 20, 1864 at Johnson's Island, O., by J. M. Eyster, Captain 18th Infantry, U. S. A.

Names.	Rank.	Age.	Date of Entering the Service.	Period of Service.	Remarks.
William D. Shepherd	Captain.	25	May 2, 1864	100 dys.	Discharged July 1, 1864, to accept appointment of Captain and C. S., U. S. Volunteers, received May 18, 1864; mustered out Oct. 4, 1865.
James L. Parmly	1st Lieut.	30	May 2, 1864	100 dys.	Mustered out with company Aug. 20, 1864.
Stephen N. Ford	2d Lieut.	30	May 2, 1864	100 dys.	Mustered out with company Aug. 20, 1864.
Newton S. Watts	1st Sergt.	33	May 2, 1864	100 dys.	Mustered out with company Aug. 20, 1864.
Philander P. Race	Sergeant.	25	May 2, 1864	100 dys.	Mustered out with company Aug. 20, 1864.
Thomas C. Hickock	do	22	May 2, 1864	100 dys.	Mustered out with company Aug. 20, 1864.
Thomas Perry	do	23	May 2, 1864	100 dys.	Mustered out with company Aug. 20, 1864.
Alvin O. Shepard	do	25	May 2, 1864	100 dys.	Mustered out with company Aug. 20, 1864.
William A. Davis	Corporal.	43	May 2, 1864	100 dys.	Mustered out with company Aug. 20, 1864.
Philip Lockwood	do	36	May 2, 1864	100 dys.	
Hiram Owen	do	40	May 2, 1864	100 dys.	Mustered out with company Aug. 20, 1864.
Lucius Green	do	34	May 2, 1864	100 dys.	Mustered out with company Aug. 20, 1864.
Alonzo A. Wheeler	do	33	May 2, 1864	100 dys.	Discharged July 9, 1864, from hospital at Cleveland, O.
Charles M. Thompson	do	37	May 2, 1864	100 dys.	Mustered out with company Aug. 20, 1864.
Joel B. Vrooman	do	19	May 2, 1864	100 dys.	Mustered out with company Aug. 20, 1864.
Andrew J. Whiting	do	42	May 2, 1864	100 dys.	Mustered out with company Aug. 20, 1864.
Henry Sinclair	do	25	May 2, 1864	100 dys.	Appointed —; mustered out with company Aug. 20, 1864.

COMPANY F.

Mustered in May 5, 1864, at Sandusky, O., by C. P. Horton, Captain and A. D. C. Mustered out Aug. 20, 1864, at Johnson's Island, O., by J. M. Eyster, Captain 18th Infantry, U. S. A.

Names.	Rank.	Age.	Date of Entering the Service.	Period of Service.	Remarks.
Manning A. Fowler	Captain.	33	April 27, 1864	100 dys.	Promoted to Major May 10, 1864.
Lyman T. Soule	...do...	30	April 27, 1864	100 dys.	Promoted from 1st Sergeant June 3, 1864; mustered out with company Aug. 20, 1864.
Newton Sutherland	1st. Lieut.	39	April 27, 1864	100 dys.	Mustered out with company Aug. 20, 1864.
William W. Herbert	2d Lieut.	27	April 27, 1864	100 dys.	Mustered out with company Aug. 20, 1864.
Albert Briscol	1st Sergt.	18	April 27, 1864	100 dys.	Appointed from Corporal July 14, 1864; mustered out with company Aug. 20, 1864.
William H. Tew	Sergeant.	31	April 27, 1864	100 dys.	Mustered out with company Aug. 20, 1864.
Milo M. Smith	...do...	21	April 27, 1864	100 dys.	Mustered out with company Aug. 20, 1864.
Abraham D. Bailey	...do...	24	April 27, 1864	100 dys.	Mustered out with company Aug. 20, 1864.
Hiram H. Porter	...do...	18	April 27, 1864	100 dys.	Appointed from Corporal July 14, 1864; mustered out with company Aug. 20, 1864.
Ellis Ensign	Corporal.	19	April 27, 1864	100 dys.	Mustered out with company Aug. 20, 1864.
Randall Simmons	...do...	22	April 27, 1864	100 dys.	Mustered out with company Aug. 20, 1864.
Ira A. Hine	...do...	33	April 27, 1864	100 dys.	Mustered out with company Aug. 20, 1864.
David D. Jones	...do...	34	April 27, 1864	100 dys.	Mustered out with company Aug. 20, 1864.
Jacob M. Dickerson	...do...	34	April 27, 1864	100 dys.	Appointed July 14, 1864; mustered out with company Aug. 20, 1864.
Zelotus Hillman	...do...	33	April 27, 1864	100 dys.	Appointed July 14, 1864; mustered out with company Aug. 20, 1864.
William Small-reed	...do...	28	April 27, 1864	100 dys.	Appointed July 14, 1864; mustered out with company Aug. 20, 1864.
Ansel S. Wood	...do...	20	April 27, 1864	100 dys.	Mustered out with company Aug. 20, 1864.
Sylvanus Oviatt	Musician	27	April 27, 1864	100 dys.	Promoted to Principal Musician May [illegible], 1864.
Conkling Prescott	...do...	35	April 27, 1864	100 dys.	Mustered out with company Aug. 20, 1864.
Baily, Levi	Private.	18	April 27, 1864	100 dys.	Mustered out with company Aug. 20, 1864.
Barber, Charles	...do...	18	April 27, 1864	100 dys.	Mustered out with company Aug. 20, 1864.
Barger, John	...do...	40	April 27, 1864	100 dys.	Mustered out with company Aug. 20, 1864.
Barnum, Henry T	...do...	27	April 27, 1864	100 dys.	Mustered out with company Aug. 20, 1864.
Brown, George W	...do...	30	May 23, 1864	100 dys.	Mustered out with company Aug. 20, 1864.
Callendar, James M	...do...	21	April 27, 1864	100 dys.	Reduced from Corporal July 14, 1864; mustered out with company Aug. 20, 1864.
Chapman, Arel	...do...	31	April 27, 1864	100 dys.	Mustered out with company Aug. 20, 1864.
Chapman, Sanford	...do...	38	April 27, 1864	100 dys.	Died July 1, 1864, at Johnson's Island, O.
Clark, Andrew	...do...	30	April 27, 1864	100 dys.	Mustered out with company Aug. 20, 1864.
Cline, Levi	...do...	22	April 27, 1864	100 dys.	Mustered out with company Aug. 20, 1864.
Dally, Henry H	...do...	32	April 27, 1864	100 dys.	Mustered out with company Aug. 20, 1864.
Edwards, Thomas H	...do...	29	April 27, 1864	100 dys.	Mustered out with company Aug. 20, 1864.
Elkins, Franklin	...do...	27	April 27, 1864	100 dys.	Mustered out with company Aug. 20, 1864.
Folsom, James G	...do...	18	April 27, 1864	100 dys.	Mustered out with company Aug. 20, 1864.
Frister, Albert M	...do...	18	April 27, 1864	100 dys.	Mustered out with company Aug. 20, 1864.
Geddes, James	...do...	28	April 27, 1864	100 dys.	Mustered out with company Aug. 20, 1864.
Gentner, Martin L	...do...	18	April 27, 1864	100 dys.	Mustered out with company Aug. 20, 1864.
Gillet, John	...do...	18	April 27, 1864	100 dys.	Mustered out with company Aug. 20, 1864.
Gilmer, James	...do...	25	April 27, 1864	100 dys.	Mustered out with company Aug. 20, 1864.
Goodrich, William P	...do...	27	April 27, 1864	100 dys.	Mustered out with company Aug. 20, 1864.
Haines, George F	...do...	[illegible]	April 27, 1864	100 dys.	Mustered out with company Aug. 20, 1864.
Hallock, Erdly D	...do...	20	April 27, 1864	100 dys.	Mustered out with company Aug. 20, 1864.
Hewit, George	...do...	26	April 27, 1864	100 dys.	Mustered out with company Aug. 20, 1864.
Hipple, Sidney	...do...	18	April 27, 1864	100 dys.	Mustered out with company Aug. 20, 1864.
Hoed, Henry	...do...	36	April 27, 1864	100 dys.	Mustered out with company Aug. 20, 1864.
Hudson, Samuel	...do...	31	April 27, 1864	100 dys.	Mustered out with company Aug. 20, 1864.
Heff, Joshua	...do...	23	April 27, 1864	100 dys.	Mustered out with company Aug. 20, 1864.
Ingraham, Harvey R	...do...	18	April 27, 1864	100 dys.	Mustered out with company Aug. 20, 1864.
Jones, Isaac	...do...	26	April 27, 1864	100 dys.	Mustered out with company Aug. 20, 1864.
Jones, John	...do...	22	April 27, 1864	100 dys.	Mustered out with company Aug. 20, 1864.
Jones, Owen R	...do...	18	April 27, 1864	100 dys.	Mustered out with company Aug. 20, 1864.
Kelly, Seymour	...do...	18	April 27, 1864	100 dys.	Mustered out with company Aug. 20, 1864.
Kistler, Charles	...do...	43	April 27, 1864	100 dys.	Mustered out with company Aug. 20, 1864.
Kistler, Stephen	...do...	32	April 27, 1864	100 dys.	Mustered out with company Aug. 20, 1864.
Ladd, Ira	...do...	18	April 27, 1864	100 dys.	Mustered out with company Aug. 20, 1864.
Lee, Austin	...do...	22	April 27, 1864	100 dys.	Mustered out with company Aug. 20, 1864.
Lentz, Benjamin	...do...	20	April 27, 1864	100 dys.	Mustered out with company Aug. 20, 1864.
Lewis, Andrew	...do...	27	April 27, 1864	100 dys.	Mustered out with company Aug. 20, 1864.
Lewis, Jonathan	...do...	22	April 27, 1864	100 dys.	Mustered out with company Aug. 20, 1864.
Little, Warren J	...do...	27	April 27, 1864	100 dys.	Mustered out with company Aug. 20, 1864.
McCready James A	...do...	18	April 27, 1864	100 dys.	Mustered out with company Aug. 20, 1864.
Monnasmith, Levi	...do...	32	April 27, 1864	100 dys.	Killed June 11, 1864, in action at Keller's Bridge, Ky.
Osborn, LaFayette	...do...	18	April 27, 1864	100 dys.	Mustered out with company Aug. 20, 1864.
Parker, Anson	...do...	28	April 27, 1864	100 dys.	Reduced from Sergeant July 14, 1864; mustered out with company Aug. 20, 1864.
Platt, William P	...do...	23	April 27, 1864	100 dys.	Mustered out with company Aug. 20, 1864.
Porter, Charles	...do...	26	April 27, 1864	100 dys.	Mustered out with company Aug. 20, 1864.
Porter, Colwell T	...do...	19	April 27, 1864	100 dys.	Died July 2, 1864, at Soldiers' Home, Cleveland, O.
Ramalia, Joshua	...do...	24	April 27, 1864	100 dys.	Mustered out with company Aug. 20, 1864.

Names.	Rank.	Age.	Date of Entering the Service.	Period of Service	Remarks.
Eatinger, Oscar F	Private	25	April 27, 1864	100 dys.	Mustered out with company Aug. 20, 1864.
Fletcher, Walter	do	21	May 10, 1864	100 dys.	Mustered out with company Aug. 20, 1864.
Fobes, Ethelbert	do	27	April 27, 1864	100 dys.	Sick June 12, 1864, at home. No further record found.
Fobes, Joseph	do	18	April 27, 1864	100 dys.	Died June 23, 1864, in hospital at Camp Dennison, Ohio.
Fobes, Loren B	do	33	April 27, 1864	100 dys.	Mustered out with company Aug. 20, 1864.
Gilder, Henry	do	33	April 27, 1864	100 dys.	Mustered out with company Aug. 20, 1864.
Gilder, Miles	do	23	April 27, 1864	100 dys.	Mustered out with company Aug. 20, 1864.
Haynes, Fayette M	do	18	April 27, 1864	100 dys.	Mustered out with company Aug. 20, 1864.
Heeter, Charles	do	20	April 27, 1864	100 dys.	Absent, sick July 3, 1864, at Ravenna, O. No further record found.
Heeter, Henry	do	18	April 27, 1864	100 dys.	Mustered out with company Aug. 20, 1864.
Higbee, George H	do	18	April 27, 1864	100 dys.	Mustered out with company Aug. 20, 1864.
Hobart, Clinton H	do	21	April 27, 1864	100 dys.	Mustered out with company Aug. 20, 1864.
Hobart, Corwin T	do	20	April 27, 1864	100 dys.	Mustered out with company Aug. 20, 1864.
Hobart, Oscar F	do	23	April 27, 1864	100 dys.	Mustered out with company Aug. 20, 1864.
Howe, William H	do	18	April 27, 1864	100 dys.	Mustered out with company Aug. 20, 1864.
Hudson, Herbert	do	19	May 10, 1864	100 dys.	Mustered out with company Aug. 20, 1864.
Hull, Riley N	do	20	April 27, 1864	100 dys.	Mustered out with company Aug. 20, 1864.
Jackson, William	do	28	April 27, 1864	100 dys.	Wounded June 11, 1864, in action at Keller's Bridge, Ky.; mustered out with company Aug. 20, 1864.
Jewell, Andrew	do	19	April 27, 1864	100 dys.	Mustered out with company Aug. 20, 1864.
Jones, Linus B	do	20	April 27, 1864	100 dys.	Mustered out with company Aug. 20, 1864.
King, Norris	do	23	April 27, 1864	100 dys.	Mustered out with company Aug. 20, 1864.
Kinnie, Alfred	do	23	April 27, 1864	100 dys.	Wounded June 11, 1864, in action at Keller's Bridge, Ky.; mustered out with company Aug. 20, 1864.
Kulp, Jacob	do	41	April 27, 1864	100 dys.	Mustered out with company Aug. 20, 1864.
Kyle, George W	do	28	April 27, 1864	100 dys.	Mustered out with company Aug. 20, 1864.
Leffingwill, Frederick J	do	19	April 27, 1864	100 dys.	Mustered out with company Aug. 20, 1864.
Lewis Wiley	do	27	April 27, 1864	100 dys.	Mustered out with company Aug. 20, 1864.
Linsley, Leander	do	33	April 27, 1864	100 dys.	Mustered out with company Aug. 20, 1864.
Loutzenhisar, Jacob	do	44	April 27, 1864	100 dys.	Mustered out with company Aug. 20, 1864.
McCormic David R	do	23	April 27, 1864	100 dys.	Mustered out with company Aug. 20, 1864.
McElroy George W C	do	22	April 27, 1864	100 dys.	Mustered out with company Aug. 20, 1864.
McGahan Jesse W	do	31	April 27, 1864	100 dys.	Mustered out with company Aug. 20, 1864.
McKey, George W	do	21	April 27, 1864	100 dys.	Mustered out with company Aug. 20, 1864.
Many, Joseph	do	20	April 27, 1864	100 dys.	Mustered out with company Aug. 20, 1864.
Matthews, Zalmon T	do	38	May 20, 1864	100 dys.	Mustered out with company Aug. 20, 1864.
Meacham, Philo	do	29	April 27, 1864	100 dys.	Mustered out with company Aug. 20, 1864.
Meister, Edward L	do	21	April 27, 1864	100 dys.	Mustered out with company Aug. 20, 1864.
Miller, Isaac J	do	20	April 27, 1864	100 dys.	Mustered out with company Aug. 20, 1864.
Morris [illegible] M	do	18	April 27, 1864	100 dys.	Mustered out with company Aug. 20, 1864.
Mossman [illegible]mes A	do	22	April 27, 1864	100 dys.	Mustered out with company Aug. 20, 1864.
Mullin, Cyrus	do	27	April 27, 1864	100 dys.	Mustered out with company Aug. 20, 1864.
Newton, Isaac M	do	39	April 27, 1864	100 dys.	Mustered out with company Aug. 20, 1864.
Niece, Seymour C	do	44	April 27, 1864	100 dys.	Mustered out with company Aug. 20, 1864.
Par[illegible], Almon	do	33	April 27, 1864	100 dys.	Mustered out with company Aug. 20, 1864.
Pease, Charles	do	21	April 27, 1864	100 dys.	Mustered out with company Aug. 20, 1864.
Peck, Theron B	do	19	April 27, 1864	100 dys.	Mustered out with company Aug. 20, 1864.
Peer, George W	do	39	April 27, 1864	100 dys.	Mustered out with company Aug. 20, 1864.
Porter, Alonzo H	do	42	April 27, 1864	100 dys.	Mustered out with company Aug. 20, 1864.
Ripley Elias S	do	25	April 27, 1864	100 dys.	Died June 20, 1864, at Camp Dennison, O.
Runyan, James	do	21	April 27, 1864	100 dys.	Mustered out with company Aug. 20, 1864.
Smith, Stephen J	do	26	April 27, 1864	100 dys.	Mustered out with company Aug. 20, 1864.
Snyder, William P	do	18	April 27, 1864	100 dys.	Mustered out with company Aug. 20, 1864.
Spencer, Robert	do	23	April 27, 1864	100 dys.	Mustered out with company Aug. 20, 1864.
Spencer, Malcolm	do	31	April 27, 1864	100 dys.	Wounded June 11, 1864, in action at Keller's Bridge, Ky.; mustered out with company Aug. 20, 1864.
Stoner, John	do	18	April 27, 1864	100 dys.	Killed June [illegible], 1864, in action at Keller's Bridge, Ky.
Tidd, Ebenezer	do	19	April 27, 1864	100 dys.	Abs[illegible], sick July 28, 1864. No further record fou[illegible]d.
Tidd, John W	do	22	April 27, 1864	100 dys.	Must[illegible]red out with company Aug. 20, 1864.
Tracy, George C	do	19	April 27, 1864	100 dys.	Wounded [illegible]une 11, 1864, in action at Keller's Bridge, Ky.; discharged Aug. 20, 1864, at Covington, Ky., on Surgeon's certificate of disability.
Wallace, John	do	24	April 27, 1864	100 dys.	Mustered out with company Aug. 20, 1864.
Wallace, Robert	do	27	April 27, 1864	100 dys.	Mustered out with company Aug. 20, 1864.
Webber, Thomas	do	40	April 27, 1864	100 dys.	Mustered out with company Aug. 20, 1864.
Williard, Edwin C	do	19	April 27, 1864	100 dys.	Wounded June 11, 1864, in action at Keller's Bridge, Ky.; mustered out with company Aug. 20, 1864.
Wilson, James E	do	18	April 27, 1864	100 dys.	Mustered out with company Aug. 20, 1864.
Wool, John O	do	36	April 27, 1864	100 dys.	Mustered out with company Aug. 20, 1864.

Names.	Rank.	Age.	Date of Entering the Service.	Period of Service.	Remarks.
Spitler, Abraham W.	Private.	26	April 27, 1864	100 dys.	Mustered out with company Aug. 20, 1864.
Steel, Chester	...do...	30	April 27, 1864	100 dys.	Mustered out with company Aug. 20, 1864.
Strickland, Wilbur	...do...	18	April 27, 1864	100 dys.	Died Aug. 16, 1864, at Johnson's Island, O.
Strohm, Jacob	...do...	40	April 27, 1864	100 dys.	Mustered out with company Aug. 20, 1864.
Taylor, William	...do...	28	April 27, 1864	100 dys.	Discharged July 30, 1864, at Johnson's Island, Ohio.
Travis, Chauncy	...do...	25	April 27, 1864	100 dys.	Mustered out with company Aug. 20, 1864.
Waters, George A	...do...	25	May 17, 1864	100 dys.	Mustered out with company Aug. 20, 1864.
Waters, James A	...do...	24	May 17, 1864	100 dys.	Mustered out with company Aug. 20, 1864.
Wildman, Benson E	...do...	18	April 27, 1864	100 dys.	Mustered out with company Aug. 20, 1864.
Wildman, Ezra G	...do...	40	April 27, 1864	100 dys.	Mustered out with company Aug. 20, 1864.
Williams, Isaac	...do...	18	April 27, 1864	100 dys.	Mustered out with company Aug. 20, 1864.
Wilson, Albert	...do...	26	April 27, 1864	100 dys.	Mustered out with company Aug. 20, 1864.
Wilson, Joseph	...do...	37	April 27, 1864	100 dys.	Wounded June 11, 1864, in action at Keller's Bridge, Ky.; mustered out with company Aug. 20, 1864.
Wolcott, Addison L	...do...	19	April 27, 1864	100 dys.	Mustered out with company Aug. 20, 1864.
Wolcott, Darwin B	...do...	18	April 27, 1864	100 dys.	Mustered out with company Aug. 20, 1864.
Wolcott, Leander H	...do...	18	April 27, 1864	100 dys.	Killed June 11, 1864, in action at Keller's Bridge, Ky.
Wolcott, Lyman B	...do...	38	April 27, 1864	100 dys.	Mustered out with company Aug. 20, 1864.
Worrell, George B	...do...	25	April 27, 1864	100 dys.	Mustered out with company Aug. 20, 1864.

COMPANY I.

Mustered in May 5, 1864, at Sandusky, O., by C. P. Horton, Captain and A. D. C. Mustered out Aug. 20, 1864, at Johnson's Island, O., by J. M. Eyster, Captain 18th Infantry, U. S. A.

Names.	Rank.	Age.	Date of Entering the Service.	Period of Service.	Remarks.
Cyrus A. Mason	Captain.	48	April 27, 1864	100 dys.	Mustered out with company Aug. 20, 1864.
William H. Earl	1st Lieut.	30	April 27, 1864	100 dys.	Mustered out with company Aug. 20, 1864.
Frank H. Snow	2d Lieut.	34	April 27, 1864	100 dys.	Mustered out with company Aug. 20, 1864.
William R. Little	1st Sergt.	47	April 27, 1864	100 dys.	Mustered out with company Aug. 20, 1864.
Sheldon F. Higley	Sergeant.	30	April 27, 1864	100 dys.	Mustered out with company Aug. 20, 1864.
Wilson S. Messenger	...do...	40	April 27, 1864	100 dys.	Mustered out with company Aug. 20, 1864.
Alvan Smith	...do...	38	April 27, 1864	100 dys.	Mustered out with company Aug. 20, 1864.
Edward W. Williams	...do...	36	April 27, 1864	100 dys.	Mustered out with company Aug. 20, 1864.
Edwin D. Earl	Corporal.	22	April 27, 1864	100 dys.	Killed June 11, 1864, in action at Keller's Bridge, Ky.
Jason B. Johnson	...do...	27	April 27, 1864	100 dys.	Mustered out with company Aug. 20, 1864.
Francis D. Snow	...do...	26	April 27, 1864	100 dys.	Mustered out with company Aug. 20, 1864.
Henry B. Walden	...do...	32	April 27, 1864	100 dys.	Mustered out with company Aug. 20, 1864.
Alfred M. Higley	...do...	41	April 27, 1864	100 dys.	Mustered out with company Aug. 20, 1864.
Spencer G. Frary	...do...	20	April 27, 1864	100 dys.	Mustered out with company Aug. 20, 1864.
Charles W. Goodsell	...do...	26	April 27, 1864	100 dys.	Mustered out with company Aug. 20, 1864.
Henry J. Noble	...do...	30	April 27, 1864	100 dys.	Mustered out with company Aug. 20, 1864.
Philander R. Higley	...do...	21	April 27, 1864	100 dys.	Appointed July 1, 1864; mustered out with company Aug. 20, 1864.
Samuel M. Sharp	Musician.	10	April 27, 1864	100 dys.	Mustered out with company Aug. 20, 1864.
James A. Snow	...do...	21	April 27, 1864	100 dys.	Mustered out with company Aug. 20, 1864.
Wolcott Chaffee, Jr	Wagoner.	37	April 27, 1864	100 dys.	Mustered out with company Aug. 20, 1864.
Alderman, Francis R	Private.	31	April 27, 1864	100 dys.	Mustered out with company Aug. 20, 1864.
Alford, Charles E	...do...	20	April 27, 1864	100 dys.	Mustered out with company Aug. 20, 1864.
Alford, Elijah	...do...	25	April 27, 1864	100 dys.	Mustered out with company Aug. 20, 1864.
Allen, Hiram G	...do...	37	April 27, 1864	100 dys.	Discharged June 30, 1864.
Angel, Thomas O	...do...	28	April 27, 1864	100 dys.	Mustered out with company Aug. 20, 1864.
Barber, Warren L	...do...	26	April 27, 1864	100 dys.	Mustered out with company Aug. 20, 1864.
Beckwith, Perry E	...do...	21	April 27, 1864	100 dys.	Mustered out with company Aug. 20, 1864.
Birchard, Nathan E	...do...	21	April 27, 1864	100 dys.	Mustered out with company Aug. 20, 1864.
Bond, Oscar	...do...	18	April 27, 1864	100 dys.	Mustered out with company Aug. 20, 1864.
Bostwick, Gideon C	...do...	20	April 27, 1864	100 dys.	Mustered out with company Aug. 20, 1864.
Bowers, William C	...do...	45	April 27, 1864	100 dys.	Mustered out with company Aug. 20, 1864.
Bow, Charles J	...do...	18	April 27, 1864	100 dys.	Died July 8, 1864, in hospital at Covington, Kentucky.
Bradley, Henry W	...do...	18	April 27, 1864	100 dys.	Mustered out with company Aug. 20, 1864.
Bristol, Frederick	...do...	28	April 27, 1864	100 dys.	Mustered out with company Aug. 20, 1864.
Brooks, James C	...do...	18	April 27, 1864	100 dys.	Mustered out with company Aug. 20, 1864.
Buck, Harvey M	...do...	23	April 27, 1864	100 dys.	Mustered out with company Aug. 20, 1864.
Bush, Levi	...do...	39	April 27, 1864	100 dys.	Mustered out with company Aug. 20, 1864.
Clark, Myron S	...do...	23	April 27, 1864	100 dys.	Promoted to Hospital Steward May [illegible], 1864.
Cline, William B	...do...	18	April 27, 1864	100 dys.	Mustered out with company Aug. 20, 1864.
Curtiss, Elizer A	...do...	10	April 27, 1864	100 dys.	Mustered out with company Aug. 20, 1864.
Ensign, Isaac H	...do...	36	April 27, 1864	100 dys.	Mustered out with company Aug. 20, 1864.
Fay, George B	...do...	34	April 27, 1864	100 dys.	Mustered out with company Aug. 20, 1864.
Freeman, Oscar D	...do...	28	April 27, 1864	100 dys.	Mustered out with company Aug. 20, 1864.
Goldie, George G	...do...	22	April 27, 1864	100 dys.	Died June 26, 1864, in hospital at Camp Dennison, O.
Harmon, Francis B	...do...	19	April 27, 1864	100 dys.	Mustered out with company Aug. 20, 1864.
Higley, William A	...do...	21	April 27, 1864	100 dys.	Mustered out with company Aug. 20, 1864.
Hilderhof, George	...do...	25	April 27, 1864	100 dys.	Mustered out with company Aug. 20, 1864.
Humiston, Ransom F	...do...	21	April 27, 1864	100 dys.	Mustered out with company Aug. 20, 1864.

Names.	Rank.	Age.	Date of Entering the Service.	Period of Service.	Remarks.
Bosworth, Lyman F.	Private	39	May 2, 1864	100 dys.	Mustered out with company Aug. 20, 1864.
Bosworth, Stephen	do	28	May 2, 1864	100 dys.	Mustered out with company Aug. 20, 1864.
Bower, John A.	do	35	May 2, 1864	100 dys.	Mustered out with company Aug. 20, 1864.
Brown, Murray	do	19	May 2, 1864	100 dys.	Mustered out with company Aug. 20, 1864.
Buck, John	do	18	May 2, 1864	100 dys.	Mustered out with company Aug. 20, 1864.
Clark, Henry	do	19	May 2, 1864	100 dys.	Mustered out with company Aug. 20, 1864.
Davis, Henry	do	18	May 2, 1864	100 dys.	Mustered out with company Aug. 20, 1864.
Dickerman, John	do	37	May 2, 1864	100 dys.	Mustered out with company Aug. 20, 1864.
Doolittle, James C.	do	18	May 2, 1864	100 dys.	Mustered out with company Aug. 20, 1864.
Doty, Wesley	do	21	May 2, 1864	100 dys.	Mustered out with company Aug. 20, 1864.
Ferris, Francis	do	27	May 2, 1864	100 dys.	Mustered out with company Aug. 20, 1864.
Forrow, Asher	do	40	May 2, 1864	100 dys.	Mustered out with company Aug. 20, 1864.
Fowler, Andrew L.	do	43	May 2, 1864	100 dys.	Mustered out with company Aug. 20, 1864.
Fowler, Timothy H.	do	36	May 2, 1864	100 dys.	Mustered out with company Aug. 20, 1864.
Fowler, Wheeler W.	do	28	May 2, 1864	100 dys.	Mustered out with company Aug. 20, 1864.
Granger, James S.	do	22	May 2, 1864	100 dys.	Died Aug. 9, 1864, at Mantua, Portage County, Ohio.
Grant, Amos E.	do	26	May 2, 1864	100 dys.	Mustered out with company Aug. 20, 1864.
Green, Anson	do	29	May 2, 1864	100 dys.	Mustered out with company Aug. 20, 1864.
Greenfield, Augustus	do	23	May 2, 1864	100 dys.	Mustered out with company Aug. 20, 1864.
Hale, Horace S.	do	22	May 22, 1864	100 dys.	Mustered out with company Aug. 20, 1864.
Hawes, Addison	do	26	May 2, 1864	100 dys.	Mustered out with company Aug. 20, 1864.
Hayden, Clifford	do	18	May 2, 1864	100 dys.	Mustered out with company Aug. 20, 1864.
Hitchcock, Reuben A.	do	22	May 2, 1864	100 dys.	Mustered out with company Aug. 20, 1864.
Hoard, Harrison	do	43	May 2, 1864	100 dys.	Mustered out with company Aug. 20, 1864.
Hodges, Henry	do	28	May 2, 1864	100 dys.	Mustered out with company Aug. 20, 1864.
Hodges, Waterman S.	do	33	May 2, 1864	100 dys.	Mustered out with company Aug. 20, 1864.
Humiston, James	do	21	May 22, 1864	100 dys.	Mustered out with company Aug. 20, 1864.
Johnson, Madison J.	do	28	May 2, 1864	100 dys.	Mustered out with company Aug. 20, 1864.
Johnson, Warren S.	do	20	May 2, 1864	100 dys.	Mustered out with company Aug. 20, 1864.
Lampson, Adelbert	do	20	May 2, 1864	100 dys.	Mustered out with company Aug. 20, 1864.
Lampson, Byron	do	19	May 2, 1864	100 dys.	Died July 31, 1864, at Johnson's Island, O.
Latham, Newell P.	do	31	May 2, 1864	100 dys.	Mustered out with company Aug. 20, 1864.
Luther, Benjamin F.	do	33	May 2, 1864	100 dys.	Mustered out with company Aug. 20, 1864.
Merriman, David J.	do	29	May 2, 1864	100 dys.	Mustered out with company Aug. 20, 1864.
Merriman, Henry L.	do	24	May 2, 1864	100 dys.	Discharged July 13, 1864, at Cleveland, O., on Surgeon's certificate of disability.
Millard, Quincy D.	do	25	May 2, 1864	100 dys.	Mustered out with company Aug. 20, 1864.
Moffet, Augustus	do	37	May 2, 1864	100 dys.	Mustered out with company Aug. 20, 1864.
Moor, James M.	do	43	May 2, 1864	100 dys.	Mustered out with company Aug. 20, 1864.
Morton, Charles	do	38	May 2, 1864	100 dys.	Discharged July 13, 1864, at Cleveland, O., on Surgeon's certificate of disability.
Morton, Stephen H.	do	34	May 2, 1864	100 dys.	Mustered out with company Aug. 20, 1864.
Osborn, Dwight H.	do	19	May 2, 1864	100 dys.	Mustered out with company Aug. 20, 1864.
Pierce, John A.	do	26	May 2, 1864	100 dys.	Mustered out with company Aug. 20, 1864.
Pierce, Lorin G.	do	21	May 2, 1864	100 dys.	Mustered out with company Aug. 20, 1864.
Pulsipher, Edwin K.	do	39	May 2, 1864	100 dys.	Mustered out with company Aug. 20, 1864.
Rhoads, Abraham	do	30	May 2, 1864	100 dys.	Mustered out with company Aug. 20, 1864.
Riddle, Roswell	do	41	May 2, 1864	100 dys.	Mustered out with company Aug. 20, 1864.
Russell, Norton T.	do	25	May 2, 1864	100 dys.	Mustered out with company Aug. 20, 1864.
Siltor, James	do	24	May 2, 1864	100 dys.	Mustered out with company Aug. 20, 1864.
Smith, Burt L.	do	22	May 2, 1864	100 dys.	Mustered out with company Aug. 20, 1864.
Smith, Julius J.	do	28	May 2, 1864	100 dys.	Mustered out with company Aug. 20, 1864.
Smith, Orin P.	do	22	May 2, 1864	100 dys.	Mustered out with company Aug. 20, 1864.
Smith, Reuben Z.	do	39	May 2, 1864	100 dys.	Mustered out with company Aug. 20, 1864.
Spring, L[illegible]en	do	20	May 2, 1864	100 dys.	Mustered out with company Aug. 20, 1864.
Stone, Wallace	do	25	May 2, 1864	100 dys.	Mustered out with company Aug. 20, 1864.
Stricklan, Wesley	do	32	May 2, 1864	100 dys.	Mustered out with company Aug. 20, 1864.
Thayer, Franklin	do	42	May 2, 1864	100 dys.	Mustered out with company Aug. 20, 1864.
Tracy, DeWitt C.	do	37	May 2, 1864	100 dys.	Mustered out with company Aug. 20, 1864.
Tuttle, Albert J.	do	23	May 2, 1864	100 dys.	Mustered out with company Aug. 20, 1864.
Welton, Lewis	do	21	May 2, 1864	100 dys.	Mustered out with company Aug. 20, 1864.
Whitney, Jona B.	do	20	May 2, 1864	100 dys.	Mustered out with company Aug. 20, 1864.
Williams, Aaron	do	41	May 2, 1864	100 dys.	Mustered out with company Aug. 20, 1864.
Wilson, Lyman C.	do	33	May 2, 1864	100 dys.	Mustered out with company Aug. 20, 1864.

172nd Regiment Ohio Volunteer Infantry.

ONE HUNDRED DAYS' SERVICE.

THIS Regiment was organized at Gallipolis, O., May 14, 1864, to serve one hundred days. It was composed of the Forty-seventh Battalion, Ohio National Guard, from Guernsey County; a part of the Fortieth Battalion, Ohio National Guard, from Brown County; the Eighty-fourth Battalion, Ohio National Guard, from Adams County; and the Seventy-seventh Battalion, Ohio National Guard, from Jackson County. The One Hundred and Seventy-second performed guard-duty at Gallipolis, O., during its whole term of service. It was mustered out Sept. 3, 1864, on expiration of term of service.

[illegible]D REGIMENT OHIO VOLUNTEER INFANTRY.

FIELD AND STAFF.

[illegible]y 1, 1864, at Cambridge, O., by John O. Cravens, A. A. G. and C. M. N. D. Mustered out Sept [illegible] 1864, at Gallipolis, O., by George H. McLaughlin, Captain 2d Infantry, [illegible] A

Names.	Rank.	Age.	Date of Entering the Service.	Period of Service.	Remarks.
[illegible]	Colonel.	[illegible]	April 27, 1864	100 dys.	Mustered out with regiment Sept. [illegible], 1864.
[illegible]	Lt. Col.	[illegible]	April 27, 1864	100 dys.	Mustered out with regiment Sept. [illegible], 1864.
[illegible]	Major.	[illegible]	April 27, 1864	100 dys.	Mustered out with regiment Sept. [illegible], 1864.
[illegible]	Surgeon.	[illegible]	May [illegible], 1864	100 dys.	Promoted from Asst. Surgeon [illegible], 1864; mustered out with regiment Sept. [illegible], 1864.
[illegible]	Ast. Surg.	[illegible]	June [illegible], 1864	100 dys.	Mustered out with regiment Sept. [illegible], 1864.
[illegible]	[illegible]	[illegible]	June 11, 1864	100 dys.	Mustered out with regiment Sept. [illegible], 1864.
[illegible]	Adjutant	[illegible]	April 27, 1864	100 dys.	Mustered out with regiment Sept. [illegible], 1864.
[illegible]	R. Q. M.	[illegible]	April 27, 1864	100 dys.	Mustered out with regiment Sept. [illegible], 1864.
[illegible]	Chaplain.	[illegible]	April 27, 1864	100 dys.	[illegible], 1864; [illegible], 1864.
[illegible]	Sergt. Maj.	[illegible]	April 27, 1864	100 dys.	Promoted [illegible] Co. A May [illegible], 1864; [illegible], 1864.
[illegible]	Q. M. S.	[illegible]	April 27, 1864	100 dys.	Promoted [illegible] Co. A May [illegible], 1864; [illegible], 1864.
[illegible]	[illegible]	[illegible]	April 27, 1864	100 dys.	Promoted [illegible] May [illegible], 1864; [illegible], 1864.
[illegible]	[illegible]	[illegible]	April 27, 1864	100 dys.	Promoted [illegible] Co. A May [illegible], 1864; [illegible], 1864.

COMPANY A.

[illegible]

[illegible]

Names.	Rank.	Age.	Date of Entering the Service.	Period of Service.	
Dunifer, Wesley	Private	18	April 27, 1864	100 dys.	Mustered out with
Dyer, Hugh	....do....	29	April 27, 1864	100 dys.	Mustered out with
Ferbrache, David	....do....	21	April 27, 1864	100 dys.	Mustered out
Finley, David	....do....	43	April 27, 1864	100 dys.	Mustered out
Furney, Josephus W	....do....	39	April 27, 1864	100 dys.	Mustered
Gibson, George W	....do....	30	April 27, 1864	100 dys.	Mustered out with
Gibson, Harrison	....do....	22	April 27, 1864	100 dys.	Mustered out with
Gibson, James B	....do....	23	April 27, 1864	100 dys.	Mustered out with
Gibson, William P	....do....	24	April 27, 1864	100 dys.	Mustered out with
Graham, John	....do....	38	April 27, 1864	100 dys.	Mustered out with
Gunther, Charles H	....do....	31	April 27, 1864	100 dys.	Mustered out with
Hanna, George	....do....	23	April 27, 1864	100 dys.	Mustered out with
Hawthorn, Thomas	....do....	27	April 27, 1864	100 dys.	Mustered out with
Hetherington, John W	....do....	24	April 27, 1864	100 dys.	Mustered out with
Hill, John	....do....	35	April 27, 1864	100 dys.	Mustered out with
Hyatt, Thomas	....do....	18	April 27, 1864	100 dys.	Mustered out with
Imley, Isaac	....do....	36	April 27, 1864	100 dys.	Mustered out with
Klingman, Henry	....do....	18	April 27, 1864	100 dys.	Mustered out with
Lepage, Thomas, Jr	....do....	33	April 27, 1864	100 dys.	Mustered out with
McCathern, Hugh	....do....	46	April 27, 1864	100 dys.	Reduced from Cor tered out with co
McCathern, William	....do....	18	April 27, 1864	100	Mustered out with
McDonald, William	....do....	18	April 27, 1864	100	Mustered out with
Maffett, Robert	....do....	25	April 27, 1864	100	Mustered out with
Magness, Hiram	....do....	19	April 27, 1864	100	Mustered out with
Marsh, Abraham	....do....	38	April 27, 1864	100	Mustered out with
Marsh, Dillon	....do....	36	April 27, 1864	100	Reduced from Cor tered out with co
Mehaffy, John P	....do....	19	April 27, 1864	100 dys.	Mustered out with
Monroe, Leonidas F	....do....	18	April 27, 1864	100 dys.	Mustered out with
Motte, Henry C	....do....	32	April 27, 1864	100 dys.	Mustered out with
Nicholson, Benjamin	....do....	19	April 27, 1864	100 dys.	Mustered out with
Oldham, William F	....do....	20	April 27, 1864	100 dys.	Mustered out with
Piper, Edward	....do....	22	April 27, 1864	100 dys.	Mustered out with
Rake, William	....do....	18	April 27, 1864	100 dys.	Mustered out with
Ratliff, Joseph	....do....	19	April 27, 1864	100 dys.	Mustered out with
Ross, James	....do....	28	April 27, 1864	100 dys.	Mustered out with
Ross, John A	....do....	20	April 27, 1864	100 dys.	Mustered out with
Salmon, Milton	....do....	20	April 27, 1864	100 dys.	Mustered out with
Sarchet, Simon P	....do....	20	April 27, 1864	100 dys.	Mustered out with
Sills, Jonathan	....do....	18	April 27, 1864	100 dys.	Mustered out with
Sines, Leonard	....do....	25	April 27, 1864	100 dys.	Mustered out with
Stottlemeir, Nathan	....do....	18	April 27, 1864	100 dys.	Mustered out with
Stewart, John	....do....	23	April 27, 1864	100 dys.	Mustered out with
Thompson, John W	....do....	18	April 27, 1864	100 dys.	Mustered out with
Turner, Elza	....do....	41	April 27, 1864	100 dys.	Promoted to Sergt.
Turner, George	....do....	18	April 27, 1864	100 dys.	Mustered out with
Vanpelt, Leander	....do....	36	April 27, 1864	100 dys.	Mustered out with
Vansickle, George	....do....	22	April 27, 1864	100 dys.	Mustered out with
Vansickle, Levi	....do....	18	April 27, 1864	100 dys.	Mustered out with
Veitch, Henry	....do....	18	April 27, 1864	100 dys.	Mustered out with
Walters, William	....do....	21	April 27, 1864	100 dys.	Mustered out with
Wharton, Smith	....do....	27	April 27, 1864	100 dys.	Mustered out with
Whites, Samuel R	....do....	18	April 27, 1864	100 dys.	Mustered out with
Williams, Frederick	....do....	18	April 27, 1864	100 dys.	Mustered out with
Williams, Truman	....do....	18	April 27, 1864	100 dys.	Mustered out with
Wishard, George D	....do....	30	April 27, 1864	100 dys.	Mustered out with
Worthing, John E	....do....	18	April 27, 1864	100 dys.	Mustered out with
Zahniser, Mathias	....do....	42	April 27, 1864	100 dys.	Promoted to Q. M.

COMPANY B.

Mustered in May 14, 1864, at Gallipolis, O., by William P. McCleery, 1st Lieuten
Mustered out Sept. 8, 1864, at Gallipolis, O., by George H. McLa
Captain 2d Infantry, U. S. A.

Names.	Rank.	Age.	Date of Entering the Service.	Period of Service.	
John T. McCormick	Captain.	32	May 2, 1864	100 dys.	Mustered out with
Samuel W. Wright	1st Lieut.	27	May 2, 1864	100 dys.	Mustered out with
William G. Kinkead	2d Lieut.	30	May 2, 1864	100 dys.	Mustered out with
Milton Cutler	1st Sergt.	26	May 2, 1864	100 dys.	Mustered out with
Benjamin Tweed	Sergeant.	39	May 2, 1864	100 dys.	Mustered out with
Julius Lane	....do....	28	May 2, 1864	100 dys.	Mustered out with
Orange Sutton	....do....	32	May 2, 1864	100 dys.	Mustered out with
Thomas W. Kirkpatrick	....do....	33	May 2, 1864	100 dys.	Mustered out with
Marion Tweed	Corporal.	25	May 2, 1864	100 dys.	Mustered out with
Christopher White	....do....	37	May 2, 1864	100 dys.	Mustered out with
John P. Kinkead	....do....	22	May 2, 1864	100 dys.	Mustered out with
Samuel Martin	....do....	29	May 2, 1864	100 dys.	Mustered out with
Gilbert H. Smitson	....do....	26	May 2, 1864	100 dys.	Mustered out with
William H. Snedaker	....do....	28	May 2, 1864	100 dys.	Mustered out with

COMPANY C.

Mustered in May 1, 1864, at Cambridge, O., by John O. Cravens, A. A. G. a
3, 1864, at Gallipolis, O., by George H. McLa
Captain 2d Infantry, U. S. A.

Names.	Rank.	Age.	Date of Entering the Service.
James A. Coleman	Captain.	32	April 27, 1864
John S. Smock	1st Lieut.	29	April 27, 1864
Barkley B. Scott	2d Lieut.	..	....
Joseph V. Harris	1st Sergt.	24	April 27, 1864
James L. Cooper	Sergeant.	21	April 27, 1864
Alexander Cockins	....do....	21	April 27, 1864
Daniel P. Ferbrache	....do....	28	April 27, 1864
David A. Lemmon	....do....	25	April 27, 1864
Jonathan S. Gander	Corporal.	26	April 27, 1864
Smith George	....do....	21	April 27, 1864
George Hickel	....do....	35	April 27, 1864
William Huhn	....do....	45	April 27, 1864
William Kerr	....do....	45	April 27, 1864
John C. Moore	....do....	27	April 27, 1864
Marshall Stone	....do....	37	April 27, 1864
James L. Starr	....do....	24	April 27, 1864
Levi Conner	Musician	18	April 27, 1864
William Forsythe	....do....	21	April 27, 1864
Barton, Benjamin	Private.	25	April 27, 1864
Ray, Harvey	....do....	22	April 27, 1864
Beach, Lysander	....do....	39	April 27, 1864
Beckett, John	....do....	29	April 27, 1864
Berry, Jackson	....do....	45	April 27, 1864
Bird, Absalom	....do....	29	April 27, 1864
Blackstone, Ebon	....do....	21	April 27, 1864
Blackstone, Isaac	....do....	19	April 27, 1864
Blackstone, Michael B.	....do....	25	April 27, 1864
Bugher, George	....do....	40	April 27, 1864
Bugher, Henry	....do....	38	April 27, 1864
Burlingame, Horace	....do....	51	April 27, 1864
Carnes, Samuel	....do....	30	April 27, 1864
Cowgill, James W	....do....	38	April 27, 1864
Conkle, Henry	....do....	30	April 27, 1864
Cooper, Abraham	....do....	28	April 27, 1864
Cooper, Henry	....do....	19	April 27, 1864
Cubbison, James	....do....	35	April 27, 1864
Cubbison, William B.	....do....	29	April 27, 1864
Culver, James F.	....do....	28	April 27, 1864
Deeren, Alexander M	....do....	25	April 27, 1864
Deeren, William	....do....	35	April 27, 1864
Finley, Ezra	....do....	22	April 27, 1864
Finley, Joseph	....do....	32	April 27, 1864
Finley, William	....do....	38	April 27, 1864
Forsythe, Andrew E.	....do....	18	April 27, 1864
Galbreath, Potter H.	....do....	41	April 27, 1864
Gander, David C.	....do....	19	April 27, 1864
Hammond, Ezekiel A.	....do....	19	April 27, 1864
Hickle, Isaac	....do....	30	April 27, 1864
Hinton, Thomas	....do....	41	April 27, 1864
Jeffrey, William M. C.	....do....	21	April 27, 1864
Jordan, Lewis	....do....	44	April 27, 1864
Jordan, Nathan E.	....do....	35	April 27, 1864
Lyons, Levi W.	....do....	26	April 27, 1864
McCort, Thomas	....do....	24	April 27, 1864
Marshall, Kella A.	....do....	32	April 27, 1864
Moore, Alpheus C.	....do....	18	April 27, 1864
Moore, Lile	....do....	18	April 27, 1864
Moore, Thomas I.	....do....	31	April 27, 1864
Moore, Peter	....do....	21	April 27, 1864
Morton, Cooper E.	....do....	19	April 27, 1864
Morton, Hamilton	....do....	19	April 27, 1864
Nelson, Robert	....do....	38	April 27, 1864
Ogan, Ephraim	....do....	44	April 27, 1864
Scofield, Joseph	....do....	43	April 27, 1864
Shepler, John I.	....do....	19	April 27, 1864
Shepler, Peter I	....do....	31	April 27, 1864
Shipley, Henry H.	....do....	23	April 27, 1864
Shively, Peter R.	....do....	29	April 27, 1864
Spencer, David	....do....	37	April 27, 1864
Spencer, John Q	....do....	26	April 27, 1864
Spencer, William	....do....	18	April 27, 1864
Steele, Andrew J	....do....	29	April 27, 1864
Stevens, Richard	....do....	24	April 27, 1864

Names.	Rank.	Age.	Date of Entering the Service.	Period of Service.	Remarks.
Neel, Asbury	Private	20	April 27, 1864	100 dys.	Mustered out with company Sept. 3, 1864.
Neel, John	....do....	20	April 27, 1864	100 dys.	
Orr, John	....do....	32	April 27, 1864	100 dys.	Mustered out with company Sept. 3, 1864.
Orr, Perry	....do....	30	April 27, 1864	100 dys.	Mustered out with company Sept. 3, 1864.
Owen, Jacob G. W.	....do....	28	April 27, 1864	100 dys.	Mustered out with company Sept. 3, 1864.
Oxley, John H.	....do....	19	April 27, 1864	100 dys.	Mustered out with company Sept. 3, 1864.
Pack, Charles W.	....do....	28	April 27, 1864	100 dys.	Mustered out with company Sept. 3, 1864.
Pack, Thomas K.	....do....	30	April 27, 1864	100 dys.	Mustered out with company Sept. 3, 1864.
Saviers, Jacob	....do....	26	April 27, 1864	100 dys.	Mustered out with company Sept. 3, 1864.
Sheridan, John C.	....do....	18	April 27, 1864	100 dys.	Mustered out with company Sept. 3, 1864.
Smith, Wesley Y.	....do....	23	April 27, 1864	100 dys.	Mustered out with company Sept. 3, 1864.
Soverns, Oscar	....do....	18	April 27, 1864	100 dys.	Mustered out with company Sept. 3, 1864.
Sperier, John	....do....	20	April 27, 1864	100 dys.	Mustered out with company Sept. 3, 1864.
Stevens, Owen C.	....do....	29	April 27, 1864	100 dys.	Mustered out with company Sept. 3, 1864.
Stewart, William H.	....do....	18	April 27, 1864	100 dys.	Mustered out with company Sept. 3, 1864.
Taylor, James	....do....	26	April 27, 1864	100 dys.	Mustered out with company Sept. 3, 1864.
Thompson, Rankin	....do....	20	April 27, 1864	100 dys.	Mustered out with company Sept. 3, 1864.
Vance, William	....do....	18	April 27, 1864	100 dys.	Mustered out with company Sept. 3, 1864.
Vanscyoc, Dennis P.	....do....	38	April 27, 1864	100 dys.	Mustered out with company Sept. 3, 1864.
Wallace, David H.	....do....	18	April 27, 1864	100 dys.	Mustered out with company Sept. 3, 1864.
Wallace, William T.	....do....	18	April 27, 1864	100 dys.	Mustered out with company Sept. 3, 1864.
Warnock, Lawrence D.	....do....	25	April 27, 1864	100 dys.	Mustered out with company Sept. 3, 1864.
White, Benjamin	....do....	44	April 27, 1864	100 dys.	Mustered out with company Sept. 3, 1864.

COMPANY E.

Mustered in May 1, 1864, at Cambridge, O., by John O. Cravens, A. A. G. and C. M. N. D. Mustered out Sept. 3, 1864, at Gallipolis, O., by George H. McLaughlin, Captain 2d Infantry, U. S. A.

Names.	Rank.	Age.	Date of Entering the Service.	Period of Service.	Remarks.
David W. Nicholson	Captain.	42	April 27, 1864	100 dys.	Mustered out with company Sept. 3, 1864.
Robert S. Forbes	1st Lieut.	29	April 27, 1864	100 dys.	
John Fry	2d Lieut.	36	April 27, 1864	100 dys.	Mustered out with company Sept. 3, 1864.
James Rainey	1st Sergt.	35	April 27, 1864	100 dys.	Mustered out with company Sept. 3, 1864.
Alexander W. Holladay	Sergeant.	32	April 27, 1864	100 dys.	Mustered out with company Sept. 3, 1864.
Joseph Meek	....do....	27	April 27, 1864	100 dys.	Mustered out with company Sept. 3, 1864.
David McConaha	....do....	18	April 27, 1864	100 dys.	Mustered out with company Sept. 3, 1864.
Solomon Peters	....do....	23	April 27, 1864	100 dys.	Absent Aug. 1, 1864, at Columbus, O. No further record found
Jerome H. Britton	Corporal.	27	April 27, 1864	100 dys.	Mustered out with company Sept. 3, 1864.
Jacob Collins	....do....	42	April 27, 1864	100 dys.	Mustered out with company Sept. 3, 1864.
James McClure	....do....	36	April 27, 1864	100 dys.	Mustered out with company Sept. 3, 1864.
David S. McClutcheon	....do....	45	April 27, 1864	100 dys.	Mustered out with company Sept. 3, 1864.
Asbury J. Miller	....do....	25	April 27, 1864	100 dys.	Died June 11, 1864, at Gallipolis, O.
Mark G. Shriver	....do....	32	April 27, 1864	100 dys.	Mustered out with company Sept. 3, 1864.
Francis M. Shriver	....do....	19	April 27, 1864	100 dys.	Mustered out with company Sept. 3, 1864.
Robert N. Williams	....do....	38	April 27, 1864	100 dys.	Mustered out with company Sept. 3, 1864.
John W. Ferguson	Musician	18	April 27, 1864	100 dys.	Mustered out with company Sept. 3, 1864.
Abels, James	Private.	30	April 27, 1864	100 dys.	Mustered out with company Sept. 3, 1864.
Alaway, William	....do....	30	April 27, 1864	100 dys.	Mustered out with company Sept. 3, 1864.
Anderson, William P.	....do....	18	April 27, 1864	100 dys.	Mustered out with company Sept. 3, 1864.
Bevis, Alva	....do....	26	April 27, 1864	100 dys.	Mustered out with company Sept. 3, 1864.
Bishard, Daniel M.	....do....	34	April 27, 1864	100 dys.	Mustered out with company Sept. 3, 1864.
Bishard, Thomas	....do....	41	April 27, 1864	100 dys.	Mustered out with company Sept. 3, 1864.
Boyd, Samuel A.	....do....	18	April 27, 1864	100 dys.	Mustered out with company Sept. 3, 1864.
Burt, Cyrus D.	....do....	19	April 27, 1864	100 dys.	Mustered out with company Sept. 3, 1864.
Burt, John P.	....do....	18	April 27, 1864	100 dys.	Died May 29, 1864, at Gallipolis, O.
Burt, Zepaniah E.	....do....	42	April 27, 1864	100 dys.	Mustered out with company Sept. 3, 1864.
Burton, James	....do....	28	April 27, 1864	100 dys.	Mustered out with company Sept. 3, 1864.
Campbell, David E.	....do....	26	April 27, 1864	100 dys.	Mustered out with company Sept. 3, 1864.
Collins, Monterville	....do....	21	April 27, 1864	100 dys.	Mustered out with company Sept. 3, 1864.
Collins, Nathan	....do....	25	April 27, 1864	100 dys.	Mustered out with company Sept. 3, 1864.
Dawson, James	....do....	34	April 27, 1864	100 dys.	Mustered out with company Sept. 3, 1864.
Dawson, Hillery	....do....	53	April 27, 1864	100 dys.	Mustered out with company Sept. 3, 1864.
Dennis, Hiram	....do....	38	April 27, 1864	100 dys.	Mustered out with company Sept. 3, 1864.
Dickinson, Richard	....do....	32	April 27, 1864	100 dys.	Mustered out with company Sept. 3, 1864.
Dickinson, William	....do....	32	April 27, 1864	100 dys.	Mustered out to date Sept. 3, 1864, by order of War Department.
Endley, John W.	....do....	18	April 27, 1864	100 dys.	Mustered out with company Sept. 3, 1864.
Enos, William	....do....	28	April 27, 1864	100 dys.	Mustered out with company Sept. 3, 1864.
Fox, Henry	....do....	32	April 27, 1864	100 dys.	Mustered out with company Sept. 3, 1864.
Gallager, George	....do....	21	April 27, 1864	100 dys.	Mustered out with company Sept. 3, 1864.
Green, Obadiah	....do....	30	April 27, 1864	100 dys.	Mustered out with company Sept. 3, 1864.
Hare, John P.	....do....	38	April 27, 1864	100 dys.	Mustered out with company Sept. 3, 1864.
Hazlett, Isaac	....do....	31	April 27, 1864	100 dys.	Mustered out with company Sept. 3, 1864.
Hickle, Elias	....do....	26	April 27, 1864	100 dys.	Died June 30, 1864, at Gallipolis, O.
Hinton, Joseph	....do....	18	April 27, 1864	100 dys.	Mustered out with company Sept. 3, 1864.
Hudson, Thomas	....do....	42	April 27, 1864	100 dys.	Mustered out with company Sept. 3, 1864.
Jarvis, James	....do....	28	April 27, 1864	100 dys.	Mustered out with company Sept. 3, 1864.
Lanning, James	....do....	43	April 27, 1864	100 dys.	Mustered out with company Sept. 3, 1864.

Names.	Rank.	Age.	Date of Entering the Service.	Period of Service.	Rem
Kerr, Robert M	Private	19	April 27, 1864	100 dys.	Mustered out with con
Lewis, Ephraim	....do....	19	April 27, 1864	100 dys.	Mustered out with con
Little, Reuben	....do....	26	April 27, 1864	100 dys.	Mustered out with con
Lucas, Andrew	....do....	22	April 27, 1864	100 dys.	Died July 27, 1864, at (
McCulley, James A	....do....	18	April 27, 1864	100 dys.	Mustered out with con
McCullough, William B.	....do....	36	April 27, 1864	100 dys.	Mustered out with con
McFee, Joseph J	....do....	25	April 27, 1864	100 dys.	Mustered out with con
McGill, John M	....do....	22	April 27, 1864	100 dys.	Mustered out with con
McKee, Thomas N	....do....	35	April 27, 1864	100 dys.	Mustered out with con
McMurry, Robert	....do....	20	April 27, 1864	100 dys.	Mustered out with con
McNutt, James C	....do....	22	April 27, 1864	100 dys.	Mustered out with con
McPeek, John	....do....	43	April 27, 1864	100 dys.	Mustered out with con
McPeek, Robert	....do....	43	April 27, 1864	100 dys.	Mustered out with con
Mackey, Richard V	....do....	18	April 27, 1864	100 dys.	Mustered out with con
Mason, William	....do....	24	April 27, 1864	100 dys.	Mustered out with con
Metcalf, Eli	....do....	38	April 27, 1864	100 dys.	Mustered out with con
Milner, Milton	....do....	18	April 27, 1864	00 dys.	Mustered out with con
Mitchell, David	....do....	25	April 27, 1864	100 dys.	Mustered out with con
Montgomery, George M.	....do....	18	April 27, 1864	100 dys.	Mustered out with con
Ohaver, William	....do....	19	April 27, 1864	100 dys.	Mustered out with con
Oldham, William J	....do....	21	April 27, 1864	100 dys.	Mustered out with con
Parker, William J	....do....	18	April 27, 1864	100 dys.	Mustered out with con
Phillips, George S	....do....	19	April 27, 1864	100 dys.	Mustered out with con
Priaulx, John T	....do....	25	April 27, 1864	100 dys.	Mustered out with con
Priaulx, William H	....do....	23	April 27, 1864	100 dys.	Mustered out with con
Purcell, Francis H	....do....	18	April 27, 1864	100 dys.	Mustered out with con
Rankin, Thomas G	....do....	29	April 27, 1864	100 dys.	Mustered out with con
Reasoner, William	....do....	23	April 27, 1864	100 dys.	Mustered out with con
Schwyhart, Joseph Z	....do....	38	April 27, 1864	100 dys.	Mustered out with con
Sherrard, James H	....do....	22	April 27, 1864	100 dys.	Mustered out with con
Simpson, Valentine F.	....do....	32	April 27, 1864	100 dys.	Mustered out with con
Stewart, James T	....do....	19	April 27, 1864	100 dys.	Mustered out with con
Thompson, David G	....do....	18	April 27, 1864	100 dys.	Mustered out with con
Thompson, James	....do....	18	April 27, 1864	100 dys.	Mustered out with con
Thompson, John G	....do....	32	April 27, 1864	100 dys.	Mustered out with con
Umstot, Jacob	....do....	38	April 27, 1864	100 dys.	Mustered out with con
Waddle, David	....do....	23	April 27, 1864	100 dys.	Mustered out with con
Wallace, Thomas	....do....	50	April 27, 1864	100 dys.	Mustered out with con
Wilson, James	....do....	32	April 27, 1864	100 dys.	Mustered out with con
Young, James	....do....	24	April 27, 1864	100 dys.	Mustered out with con
Young, William A	....do....	39	April 27, 1864	100 dys.	Mustered out with con
Young, William, J	....do....	24	April 27, 1864	100 dys.	Mustered out with con
Young, William, Sr	....do....	47	April 27, 1864	100 dys.	Mustered out with con

COMPANY G.

Mustered in May 11, 1864, at Gallipolis, O., by William P. McCleery, 1st Lieutenant
Mustered out Sept. 3, 1864, at Gallipolis, O., by George H. McLaug
Captain 2d Infantry, U. S. A.

Names.	Rank.	Age.	Date of Entering the Service.	Period of Service.	Rem
Samuel Laird	Captain.	37	May 2, 1864	100 dys.	Mustered out with con
Robert P. McClure	1st Lieut.	46	May 2, 1864	100 dys.	Mustered out with co
William A. Blair	2d Lieut.	35	May 2, 1864	100 dys.	Mustered out with con
William N. Vance	1st Sergt.	28	May 2, 1864	100 dys.	Mustered out with con
William C. Gustin	Sergeant.	36	May 2, 1864	100 dys.	Mustered out with con
William H. Jones	....do....	36	May 2, 1864	100 dys.	Mustered out with con
Joshua Shenkle	....do....	25	May 2, 1864	100 dys.	Mustered out with con
William P. Breckenridge	....do....	33	May 2, 1864	100 dys.	Mustered out with con
Joseph Batson	Corporal.	23	May 2, 1864	100 dys.	Mustered out with con
William H. Queery	....do....	20	May 2, 1864	100 dys.	Mustered out with con
Matthew M. Smiley	....do....	37	May 2, 1864	100 dys.	Mustered out with con
Robert W. Thompson	....do....	25	May 2, 1864	100 dys.	Mustered out with con
Joseph H. McCreight	....do....	22	May 2, 1864	100 dys.	Mustered out with con
Joseph H. McAdoo	....do....	35	May 2, 1864	100 dys.	Mustered out with con
Hugh, McCasland	....do....	29	May 2, 1864	100 dys.	Mustered out with con
Nathaniel J. Whiterow	....do....	34	May 2, 1864	100 dys.	Mustered out with con
Adams, John M	Private.	33	May 2, 1864	100 dys.	Mustered out with con
Batson, John W.	....do....	18	May 2, 1864	100 dys.	Mustered out with con
Bayless, William J	....do....	18	May 2, 1864	100 dys.	Mustered out with con
Bierley, James	....do....	33	May 2, 1864	100 dys.	Mustered out with con
Bohnam, Joseph	....do....	26	May 2, 1864	100 dys.	Mustered out with con
Brown, Henly	....do....	39	May 2, 1864	100 dys.	Mustered out with con
Bryan, Henry C	....do....	39	May 2, 1864	100 dys.	Mustered out with con
Burlin, John N. H	....do....	18	May 2, 1864	100 dys.	Mustered out with con
Campbell, William A	....do....	19	May 2, 1864	100 dys.	Mustered out with con
Collins, Charles O.	....do....	28	May 2, 1864	100 dys.	Mustered out with con
Compton, Joseph	....do....	20	May 2, 1864	100 dys.	Mustered out with con
Cornelius, Robert	....do....	42	May 2, 1864	100 dys.	Mustered out with con
Couser, James B	....do....	18	May 2, 1864	100 dys.	Mustered out with con

Names.	Rank.	Age.	Date of Entering the Service.	Period of Service.	Remarks.
Joseph Armstrong	Musician	18	April 27, 1864	100 dys.	Mustered out with company Sept. 3, 1864.
Curtis Parker	...do...	18	April 27, 1864	100 dys.	Mustered out with company Sept. 3, 1864.
Adair, Henry C	Private..	39	April 27, 1864	100 dys.	Mustered out with company Sept. 3, 1864.
Archer, Andrew	...do...	39	April 27, 1864	100 dys.	Mustered out with company Sept. 3, 1864.
Barnett, Ephraim	...do...	44	April 27, 1864	100 dys.	Mustered out with company Sept. 3, 1864.
Barnett, James K	...do...	34	April 27, 1864	100 dys.	Mustered out with company Sept. 3, 1864.
Barnett, Joseph A	...do...	25	April 27, 1864	100 dys.	Mustered out with company Sept. 3, 1864.
Barnett, William W	...do...	18	April 27, 1864	100 dys.	Mustered out with company Sept. 3, 1864.
Benson, William	...do...	18	April 27, 1864	100 dys.	Mustered out with company Sept. 3, 1864.
Bond, Thomas E	...do...	19	April 27, 1864	100 dys.	Mustered out with company Sept. 3, 1864.
Burnsworth, William	...do...	33	April 27, 1864	100 dys.	Mustered out with company Sept. 3, 1864.
Charnock, Joseph	...do...	20	April 27, 1864	100 dys.	Mustered out with company Sept. 3, 1864.
Conner, Nathan	...do...	18	April 27, 1864	100 dys.	Mustered out with company Sept. 3, 1864.
Conner, Samuel H	...do...	19	April 27, 1864	100 dys.	Mustered out with company Sept. 3, 1864.
Crawford, Samuel	...do...	18	April 27, 1864	100 dys.	Mustered out with company Sept. 3, 1864.
Culbertson, Gillespie	...do...	20	April 27, 1864	100 dys.	Mustered out with company Sept. 3, 1864.
Darling, James T.	...do...	18	April 27, 1864	100 dys.	Mustered out with company Sept. 3, 1864.
Farrar, James G	...do...	18	April 27, 1864	100 dys.	Mustered out with company Sept. 3, 1864.
Freeman, William	...do...	22	April 27, 1864	100 dys.	Mustered out with company Sept. 3, 1864.
Fulton, Alexander	...do...	18	April 27, 1864	100 dys	Mustered out with company Sept. 3, 1864.
[illegible]	...do...	40	April 27, 1864	100 dys.	Mustered out with company Sept. 3, 1864.
[illegible] P.	...do...	20	April 27, 1864	100 dys.	Mustered out with company Sept. 3, 1864.
[illegible]	...do...	18	April 27, 1864	100 dys	Mustered out with company Sept. 3, 1864.
Giffin, Thomas	...do...	35	April 27, 1864	100 dys.	Reduced from Corporal June 20, 1864; mustered out with comany Sept. 3, 1864.
Hall, James	...do...	24	April 27, 1864	100 dys.	Mustered out with company Sept. 3, 1864.
Harting, Daniel T	...do...	26	April 27, 1864	100 dys.	Mustered out with company Sept. 3, 1864.
Hodges, John W	...do...	38	April 27, 1864	100 dys.	Mustered out with company Sept. 3, 1864.
Hunter, Cassius	...do...	19	April 27, 1864	100 dys.	Mustered out with company Sept. 3, 1864.
Hyatt, Hezekiah	...do...	25	April 27, 1864	100 dys.	Mustered out with company Sept. 3, 1864.
Layman, William	...do...	20	April 27, 1864	100 dys.	Mustered out with company Sept. 3, 1864.
Lynn, David	...do...	20	April 27, 1864	100 dys.	Mustered out with company Sept. 3, 1864.
Lynn, Nathan J	...do...	24	April 27, 1864	100 dys.	Mustered out with company Sept. 3, 1864.
McCreary, George	...do...	38	April 27, 1864	100 dys.	Mustered out with company Sept. 3, 1864.
McFarland, John A	...do...	20	April 27, 1864	100 dys.	Mustered out with company Sept. 3, 1864.
McGiffin, Thomas	...do...	21	April 27, 1864	100 dys.	Mustered out with company Sept. 3, 1864.
Mahary, Alexander	...do...	25	April 27, 1864	100 dys.	Mustered out with company Sept. 3, 1864.
Marshall, Andrew H	...do...	34	April 27, 1864	100 dys.	Mustered out with company Sept. 3, 1864.
Matthews, Zephaniah	...do...	25	April 27, 1864	100 dys.	Mustered out with company Sept. 3, 1864.
Mercer, John	...do...	18	April 27, 1864	100 dys.	Mustered out with company Sept. 3, 1864.
Miller, William T	...do...	20	April 27, 1864	100 dys.	Mustered out with company Sept. 3, 1864.
Moore, William Mc	...do...	18	April 27, 1864	100 dys.	Mustered out with company Sept. 3, 1864.
Morgan, Charles P	...do...	22	April 27, 1864	100 dys.	Mustered out with company Sept. 3, 1864.
Murphy, Judson J	...do...	22	April 27, 1864	100 dys.	Mustered out with company Sept. 3, 1864.
Nace, Samuel	...do...	23	April 27, 1864	100 dys.	Mustered out with company Sept. 3, 1864.
Neeland, Andrew	...do...	20	April 27, 1864	100 dys.	Mustered out with company Sept. 3, 1864.
Nelson, Thomas	...do...	18	April 27, 1864	100 dys.	Mustered out with company Sept. 3, 1864.
Nesbit, James	...do...	37	April 27, 1864	100 dys.	Mustered out with company Sept. 3, 1864.
Newland, Elza	...do...	18	April 27, 1864	100 dys.	Mustered out with company Sept. 3, 1864.
Perry, Jesse A	...do...	18	April 27, 1864	100 dys.	Mustered out with company Sept. 3, 1864.
Proctor, Joseph	...do...	20	April 27, 1864	100 dys.	Mustered out with company Sept. 3, 1864.
Proudfit, David	...do...	21	April 27, 1864	100 dys.	Mustered out with company Sept. 3, 1864.
Proudfit, James B	...do...	19	April 27, 1864	100 dys.	Mustered out with company Sept. 3, 1864.
Rodgers, Si[illegible]	...do...	20	April 27, 1864	100 dys.	Mustered out with company Sept. 3, 1864.
Sherrard, William	...do...	18	April 27, 1864	100 dys.	Mustered out with company Sept. 3, 1864.
Smith, John	...do...	19	April 27, 1864	100 dys.	Mustered out with company Sept. 3, 1864.
Smith, William	...do...	[illegible]4	April 27, 1864	100 dys.	Mustered out with company Sept. 3, 1864.
Taylor, Jacob	...do...	21	April 27, 1864	100 dys.	Mustered out with company Sept. 3, 1864.
Tinsman, Andrew J	...do...	20	April 27, 1864	100 dys	Mustered out with company Sept. 3, 1864.
Vessels, John	...do...	19	April 27, 1864	100 dys.	Mustered out with company Sept. 3, 1864.
Waller, Ephraim	...do...	28	April 27, 1864	100 dys	Mustered out with company Sept. 3, 1864.
White, John	...do...	19	April 27, 1864	100 dys.	Mustered out with company Sept. 3, 1864.
White, Joseph	...do...	32	April 27, 1864	100 dys.	Mustered out with company Sept. 3, 1864.
White, Samuel	...do...	33	April 27, 1864	100 dys.	Mustered out with company Sept. 3, 1864.
Wilson, Elijah	...do..	18	April 27, 1864	100 dys.	Mustered out with company Sept. 3, 1864.
Wilson, Hamberry	...do...	20	April 27, 1864	100 dys.	Mustered out with company Sept. 3, 1864.
Wilson, Joshua, Jr	...do...	18	April 27, 1864	100 dys.	Mustered out with company Sept. 3, 1864.
Winters, Meredith	...do...	18	April 27, 1864	100 dys.	Mustered out with company Sept. 3, 1864.

COMPANY I.

Mustered in May 14, 1864, at Gallipolis, O., by William P. McCleery, 1st Lieutenant 18th Infantry, U. S. A.
Mustered out Sept. 3, 1864, at Gallipolis, O., by George H. McLaughlin, Captain 2d Infantry, U. S. A.

Names.	Rank.	Age.	Date of Entering the Service.	Period of Service.	Remarks.
Timothy J. Evans	Captain	21	May 2, 1864	100 dys.	Mustered out with company Sept. 3, 1864.
James W. Vaughn	1st Lieut.	37	May 2, 1864	100 dys.	Mustered out with company Sept. 3, 1864.
William Claar	2d Lieut.	26	May 2, 1864	100 dys.	Mustered out with company Sept. 3, 1864.
William Schellenger	1st Sergt.	27	May 2, 1864	100 dys.	Mustered out with company Sept. 3, 1864.
James Barlow	Sergeant	31	May 2, 1864	100 dys.	Mustered out with company Sept. 3, 1864.
Simeon E. Evans	do	20	May 2, 1864	100 dys.	Mustered out with company Sept. 3, 1864.
Jonathan McCoy	do	23	May 2, 1864	100 dys.	Mustered out with company Sept. 3, 1864.
Oscar Weed	do	20	May 2, 1864	100 dys.	Mustered out with company Sept. 3, 1864.
Samuel G. Stephenson	Corporal	24	May 2, 1864	100 dys.	Mustered out with company Sept. 3, 1864.
John Claar	do	24	May 2, 1864	100 dys.	Mustered out with company Sept. 3, 1864.
John Twaddle	do	25	May 2, 1864	100 dys.	Mustered out with company Sept. 3, 1864.
Armstead Spurlock	do	35	May 2, 1864	100 dys.	Mustered out with company Sept. 3, 1864.
Allen Stockham	do	34	May 2, 1864	100 dys.	Mustered out with company Sept. 3, 1864.
John Pierce	do	37	May 2, 1864	100 dys.	Mustered out with company Sept. 3, 1864.
Henry Burnsides	do	29	May 2, 1864	100 dys.	Mustered out with company Sept. 3, 1864.
Vinton Spriggs	do	23	May 2, 1864	100 dys.	Mustered out with company Sept. 3, 1864.
Charles H. Johnson	Musician	18	May 2, 1864	100 dys.	Mustered out with company Sept. 3, 1864.
Owen Weed	do	18	May 2, 1864	100 dys.	Mustered out with company Sept. 3, 1864.
Barton, Reed	Private	18	May 2, 1864	100 dys.	Mustered out with company Sept. 3, 1864.
Bishop, William	do	37	May 2, 1864	100 dys.	Mustered out with company Sept. 3, 1864.
Brown, Samuel	do	22	May 2, 1864	100 dys.	Mustered out with company Sept. 3, 1864.
Brunton, Jacob	do	34	May 2, 1864	100 dys.	Mustered out with company Sept. 3, 1864.
Brunton, Joseph	do	35	May 2, 1864	100 dys.	Mustered out with company Sept. 3, 1864.
Bunn, Harmon	do	17	May 2, 1864	100 dys.	Mustered out with company Sept. 3, 1864.
Burnsides, James	do	30	May 2, 1864	100 dys.	Mustered out with company Sept. 3, 1864.
Burnsides, John	do	34	May 2, 1864	100 dys.	Mustered out with company Sept. 3, 1864.
Carrick, Henry C	do	25	May 13, 1864	100 dys.	Mustered out with company Sept. 3, 1864.
Chamberlain, William	do	27	May 2, 1864	100 dys.	Mustered out with company Sept. 3, 1864.
Cheatham, William A	do	37	May 2, 1864	100 dys.	Mustered out with company Sept. 3, 1864.
Cherington, Leander	do	32	May 2, 1864	100 dys.	Mustered out with company Sept. 3, 1864.
Cherington, Stewart	do	17	May 2, 1864	100 dys.	Mustered out with company Sept. 3, 1864.
Claar, Robert	do	42	May 2, 1864	100 dys.	Mustered out with company Sept. 3, 1864.
Clark, Picket M	do	23	May 2, 1864	100 dys.	Mustered out with company Sept. 3, 1864.
Cline, Samuel	do	26	May 2, 1864	100 dys.	Mustered out with company Sept. 3, 1864.
Cummons, William	do	18	May 2, 1864	100 dys.	Mustered out with company Sept. 3, 1864.
Davis, John D	do	44	May 2, 1864	100 dys.	Mustered out with company Sept. 3, 1864.
Davis, William	do	17	May 2, 1864	100 dys.	Mustered out with company Sept. 3, 1864.
Dougherty, Ezra	do	17	May 2, 1864	100 dys.	Mustered out with company Sept. 3, 1864.
Downs, George H	do	26	May 2, 1864	100 dys.	Mustered out with company Sept. 3, 1864.
Gilliland, George	do	20	May 2, 1864	100 dys.	Mustered out with company Sept. 3, 1864.
Gilliland, John	do	18	May 2, 1864	100 dys.	Mustered out with company Sept. 3, 1864.
Gilliland, William	do	25	May 2, 1864	100 dys.	Mustered out with company Sept. 3, 1864.
Harmon, Edward F	do	24	May 2, 1864	100 dys.	Mustered out with company Sept. 3, 1864.
Horton, Harrison	do	18	May 2, 1864	100 dys.	Mustered out with company Sept. 3, 1864.
Horton, Henry	do	44	May 2, 1864	100 dys.	Mustered out with company Sept. 3, 1864.
Horton, William H	do	18	May 2, 1864	100 dys.	Mustered out with company Sept. 3, 1864.
Jenkins, Francis	do	18	May 2, 1864	100 dys.	Mustered out with company Sept. 3, 1864.
Jenkins, James	do	18	May 2, 1864	100 dys.	Mustered out with company Sept. 3, 1864.
Jenkins, John	do	20	May 2, 1864	100 dys.	Mustered out with company Sept. 3, 1864.
Johnson, Alexander	do	42	May 2, 1864	100 dys.	Mustered out with company Sept. 3, 1864.
Jones, Evan	do	44	May 2, 1864	100 dys.	Mustered out with company Sept. 3, 1864.
Kinnison, Lorenzo W	do	29	May 2, 1864	100 dys.	Mustered out with company Sept. 3, 1864.
Lockard, Henry	do	23	May 2, 1864	100 dys.	Mustered out with company Sept. 3, 1864.
McCain, Benjamin	do	31	May 2, 1864	100 dys.	Mustered out with company Sept. 3, 1864.
McCoy, Levi	do	39	May 2, 1864	100 dys.	Mustered out with company Sept. 3, 1864.
McCoy, William C	do	26	May 2, 1864	100 dys.	Mustered out with company Sept. 3, 1864.
Mayhew, James	do	25	May 2, 1864	100 dys.	Mustered out with company Sept. 3, 1864.
Mayhew, Joseph W	do	22	May 2, 1864	100 dys.	Mustered out with company Sept. 3, 1864.
Mercer, John	do	18	May 2, 1864	100 dys.	Mustered out with company Sept. 3, 1864.
Miller, Andrew H	do	27	May 2, 1864	100 dys.	Mustered out with company Sept. 3, 1864.
Mitchell, David	do	25	May 2, 1864	100 dys.	Mustered out with company Sept. 3, 1864.
Moore, William	do	26	May 2, 1864	100 dys.	Mustered out with company Sept. 3, 1864.
Patton, Erastus	do	30	May 2, 1864	100 dys.	Mustered out with company Sept. 3, 1864.
Poor, Andrew J	do	27	May 2, 1864	100 dys.	Mustered out with company Sept. 3, 1864.
Poor, Lewis	do	25	May 2, 1864	100 dys.	Mustered out with company Sept. 3, 1864.
Riegel, George W	do	20	May 2, 1864	100 dys.	Mustered out with company Sept. 3, 1864.
Schellenger, George W	do	20	May 2, 1864	100 dys.	Mustered out with company Sept. 3, 1864.
Schellenger, Harrison	do	24	May 2, 1864	100 dys.	Mustered out with company Sept. 3, 1864.
Sheward, David	do	18	May 2, 1864	100 dys.	Mustered out with company Sept. 3, 1864.
Sheward, Isaac V	do	20	May 2, 1864	100 dys.	Mustered out with company Sept. 3, 1864.
Spriggs, William	do	29	May 2, 1864	100 dys.	Mustered out with company Sept. 3, 1864.
Stiffler, Gaston	do	19	May 2, 1864	100 dys.	Mustered out with company Sept. 3, 1864.
Stiffler, Samuel	do	17	May 2, 1864	100 dys.	Mustered out with company Sept. 3, 1864.
Stephenson, John	do	18	May 2, 1864	100 dys.	Mustered out with company Sept. 3, 1864.
Stephenson, Richard	do	25	May 2, 1864	100 dys.	Mustered out with company Sept. 3, 1864.
Stephenson, Samuel	do	[illegible]	May 2, 1864	100 dys.	Mustered out with company Sept. 3, 1864.

Names.		Age.	Date of Entering the Service.	Period of Service.	
Stewart, Hamilton	.	22	May 2, 1864	100 dys.	
Stropes, Henry C	.	36	May 2, 1864	100 dys.	
Thompson, Clark	.	23	May 2, 1864	100 dys.	
Titus, Elza C	.	30	May 2, 1864	100 dys.	
Weed, Judson	.	18	May 2, 1864	100 dys.	
Wilson, Joseph	.	22	May 2, 1864	100 dys.	
Yeager, Andrew	.	44	May 2, 1864	100 dys.	Mustered
Yeager, James A	.	18	May 2, 1864	100 dys.	Mustered

COMPANY K.

Mustered in May 14, 1864, at Gallipolis, O., by William P. McCleery, 1st Lie
Mustered out Sept. 3, 1864, at Gallipolis, O., by George H.
Captain 2d Infantry, U. S. A.

Samuel White	Captain.	31	May 2, 1864	100 dys.	Mustered out
Willis M. Boyer	1st Lieut.	28	May 2, 1864	100 dys.	Mustered out
VanBuren B. Johnson	2d Lieut.	31	May 2, 1864	100 dys.	Mustered out
Johnson Wade	1st Sergt.	27	May 2, 1864	100 dys.	Mustered out
Milton A. Conley	Sergeant.	26	May 2, 1864	100 dys.	Mustered out
William M. Smith	....do....	23	May 2, 1864	100 dys.	Mustered out
William C. Lewis	....do....	18	May 2, 1864	100 dys.	Mustered out
John W. Boyer	....do....	24	May 2, 1864	100 dys.	Mustered out
William Yerian	Corporal.	29	May 2, 1864	100 dys.	Mustered out
Jordan Crabtree	....do....	25	May 2, 1864	100 dys.	Mustered out
Robert A. Thompson	....do....	23	May 2, 1864	100 dys.	Mustered out
David Kilpatrick	....do....	32	May 2, 1864	100 dys.	Mustered out
John Garrett	....do....	33	May 2, 1864	100 dys.	Mustered out
Joseph Harper	....do....	37	May 2, 1864	100 dys.	Mustered out
Tilman H. Culp	....do....	48	May 2, 1864	100 dys.	Mustered out
Nathaniel Brafford	....do....	27	May 2, 1864	100 dys.	Mustered out
William D. Edwards	Musician	20	May 2, 1864	100 dys.	Mustered out
William H. Gibson	....do....	24	May 2, 1864	100 dys.	Mustered out
Allen, Joseph	Private.	32	May 2, 1864	100 dys.	On muster-in
Barton, William A	....do....	27	May 2, 1864	100 dys.	Mustered out
Baxter, John M	....do....	25	May 2, 1864	100 dys.	Mustered out
Behem, Gilbert L	....do....	19	May 2, 1864	100 dys.	Mustered out
Behem, Jerome	....do....	18	May 2, 1864	100 dys.	Mustered out
Brafford, Thomas	....do....	29	May 2, 1864	100 dys.	Mustered out
Brooks, Thomas J	....do....	33	May 2, 1864	100 dys.	Mustered out
Brown, Reason	....do....	28	May 2, 1864	100 dys.	Mustered out
Butcher, George	....do....	30	May 2, 1864	100 dys.	Mustered out
Byron, Perry	....do....	31	May 2, 1864	100 dys.	Mustered out
Claar, Samuel	....do....	39	May 2, 1864	100 dys.	Mustered out
Clark, Abram	....do....	44	May 2, 1864	100 dys.	Mustered out
Coles, Samuel	....do....	28	May 2, 1864	100 dys.	Mustered out
Crabtree, Edward E	....do....	38	May 2, 1864	100 dys.	Mustered out
Crabtree, Enoch	....do....	39	May 2, 1864	100 dys.	Mustered out
Crabtree, John L	....do....	42	May 2, 1864	100 dys.	Mustered out
Crabtree, Lewis	....do....	18	May 2, 1864	100 dys.	Mustered out
Crabtree, Madison	....do....	30	May 2, 1864	100 dys.	Mustered out
Crabtree, Samuel W	....do....	36	May 2, 1864	100 dys.	Mustered out
Creekbaum, Charles C	....do....	18	May 2, 1864	100 dys.	Mustered out
Daniels, Alexander	....do....	25	May 2, 1864	100 dys.	Mustered out
Delay, Greenberry	....do....	41	May 2, 1864	100 dys.	Mustered out
Dixon, Griffe	....do....	20	May 2, 1864	100 dys.	Mustered out
Dixon, John	....do....	18	May 2, 1864	100 dys.	Mustered out
Dixon, Samuel	....do....	18	May 2, 1864	100 dys.	Mustered out
Downey, Francis	....do....	44	May 2, 1864	100 dys.	Mustered out
Dyson, Lawrence G	....do....	45	May 2, 1864	100 dys.	Mustered out
Elliott, Thomas	....do....	23	May 2, 1864	100 dys.	Mustered out
Esterby, Richard	....do....	28	May 2, 1864	100 dys.	Mustered out
Fields, John	....do....	41	May 2, 1864	100 dys.	Mustered out
Fout, Francis	....do....	18	May 2, 1864	100 dys.	Mustered out
Garrett, Benjamin	....do....	28	May 2, 1864	100 dys.	Mustered out
Green, David	....do....	31	May 2, 1864	100 dys.	Mustered out
Green, William	....do....	36	May 2, 1864	100 dys.	Mustered out
Gregory, David	....do....	37	May 2, 1864	100 dys.	Mustered out
Halterman, Christian	....do....	25	May 2, 1864	100 dys.	Mustered out
Halterman, Daniel	....do....	45	May 2, 1864	100 dys.	Mustered out
Helms, Hiram	....do....	33	May 2, 1864	100 dys.	Mustered out
Hill, Nathan	....do....	38	May 2, 1864	100 dys.	Died July 30,
Jones, Byron A	....do....	20	May 2, 1864	100 dys.	Mustered out
Karn, Simon P	....do....	37	May 2, 1864	100 dys.	Mustered out
Kellar, Francis M	....do....	29	May 2, 1864	100 dys.	Mustered out
Kessinger, George W	....do....	20	May 2, 1864	100 dys.	Mustered out
Kessinger, Marion	....do....	18	May 2, 1864	100 dys.	Mustered out
Landrum, Lewis	....do....	18	May 2, 1864	100 dys.	Mustered out
Lemon, Campbell	....do....	17	May 2, 1864	100 dys.	Transferred f out with co

Names.	Rank.	Age.	Date of Entering the Service.	Period of Service.	Remarks.
Lindsey, Albert W......	Private..	20	May 2, 1864	100 dys.	Mustered out with company Sept. 3, 1864.
McCartney, John.........	....do....	25	May 2, 1864	100 dys.	Mustered out with company Sept. 3, 1864.
Malone, Samuel M.........	....do....	33	May 2, 1864	100 dys.	Mustered out with company Sept. 3, 1864.
Mercer, William..........	....do....	45	May 2, 1864	100 dys.	Mustered out with company Sept. 3, 1864.
Metcalf, Alexander......	....do....	19	May 2, 1864	100 dys.	Mustered out with company Sept. 3, 1864.
Ross, Ferdinand.........	....do....	23	May 2, 1864	100 dys.	Mustered out with company Sept. 3, 1864.
Rose, Sylvester..........	....do....	24	May 2, 1864	100 dys.	Mustered out with company Sept. 3, 1864.
Ross, Stephen D.........	....do....	39	May 2, 1864	100 dys.	Mustered out with company Sept 3, 1864.
Scurlock, Hiram	....do....	28	May 2, 1864	100 dys.	Mustered out with company Sept. 3, 1864.
Sellers, John M..........	....do....	44	May 2, 1864	100 dys.	Mustered out with company Sept. 3, 1864.
Sexton, John W.........	....do....	18	May 2, 1864	100 dys.	Mustered out with company Sept. 3, 1864.
Shaw, Ira H	....do....	45	May 2, 1864	100 dys.	Mustered out with company Sept. 3, 1864.
Shaw, Salem.............	....do....	29	May 2, 1864	100 dys.	Mustered out with company Sept. 3, 1864.
Sheward, David..........	....do....	37	May 2, 1864	100 dys.	Mustered out with company Sept. 3, 1864.
Smith, Milton............	....do....	42	May 2, 1864	100 dys.	Mustered out with company Sept. 3, 1864.
Stevens, Thomas J.......	....do....	41	May 2, 1864	100 dys.	Mustered out with company Sept. 3, 1864.
Sturm, Charles A.........	....do....	18	May 2, 1864	100 dys.	Mustered out with company Sept. 3, 1864.
Swisher, Aelas...........	....do....	30	May 2, 1864	100 dys.	Mustered out with company Sept. 3, 1864.
Thompson, James H....	....do....	18	May 2, 1864	100 dys.	Mustered out with company Sept. 3, 1864.
Thompson, Thomas M..	....do....	18	May 2, 1864	100 dys.	Mustered out with company Sept. 3, 1864.
Throckmorton, Thomas.	....do....	45	May 2, 1864	100 dys.	Mustered out with company Sept. 3, 1864.
Vandavoort, Isaac.......	....do....	22	May 2, 1864	100 dys.	Mustered out with company Sept. 3, 1864.
Vorhes, Isaac S..........	....do....	44	May 2, 1864	100 dys.	Mustered out with company Sept. 3, 1864.
Wade, William..........	....do....	18	May 2, 1864	100 dys.	Mustered out with company Sept. 3, 1864.
Walker, Henry...........	....do....	18	May 2, 1864	100 dys.	Mustered out with company Sept. 3, 1864.
White, Alexander L.....	....do....	18	May 2, 1864	100 dys.	Mustered out with company Sept. 3, 1864.
White, James J..........	....do....	29	May 2, 1864	100 dys.	Mustered out with company Sept. 3, 1864.
Williams, Abraham.....	....do....	23	May 2, 1864	100 dys.	Mustered out with company Sept. 3, 1864.

173d Regiment Ohio Volunteer Infantry.

ONE YEAR'S SERVICE.

This Regiment was organized at Gallipolis, O., in September, 1864, to serve one year. Immediately after muster-in the Regiment was ordered to Nashville, Tenn., where it arrived about the 1st of October, and was assigned to duty in the city. Early on the morning of the 15th of December the Regiment took position on the Murfreesboro Pike. After daylight the Regiment was moved to the left of Fort Negley, and in the afternoon it moved to the right of the fort, and remained there during the battle. After the battle the Regiment was employed in guarding prisoners at Nashville and in their transit from Nashville to Louisville. On the 15th of February, 1865, the One Hundred and Seventy-third was ordered to Columbia, and, after remaining there a few days, was directed to proceed to Johnsonville. On the 20th of June the Regiment was ordered to Nashville, where it was mustered out June 26, 1865, by order of the War Department.

Names.	Rank.	Age.	Date of Entering the Service.	Period of Service.	Remarks.
Thomas C. Barber	Corporal.	32	Aug. 29, 1864	1 year.	Mustered out with company June 26, 1865.
Alfred Dearmy	....do....	22	Aug. 16, 1864	1 year.	Mustered out with company June 26, 1865.
Claborn C. Turley	....do....	32	Aug. 16, 1864	1 year.	Mustered out with company June 26, 1865.
John H. Sutton	....do....	23	Aug. 8, 1864	1 year.	Mustered out with company June 26, 1865.
Jonathan T. Hughes	....do....	24	Aug. 8, 1864	1 year.	Mustered out with company June 26, 1865.
James M. Allen	....do....	26	Aug. 8, 1864	1 year.	Mustered out with company June 26, 1865.
William C. Langdon	....do....	20	Aug. 20, 1864	1 year.	Appointed Nov. 9, 1864; mustered out with company June 26, 1865.
John Allen	....do....	39	Aug. 8, 1864	1 year.	Appointed Dec. 24, 1864; mustered out with company June 26, 1865.
Frank Coles	Musician	16	Aug. 31, 1864	1 year.	Mustered out with company June 26, 1865.
George W. Hunt	....do....	16	Aug. 29, 1864	1 year.	Mustered out with company June 26, 1865.
Andrew J. Partlow	Wagoner.	39	Aug. 16, 1864	1 year.	Died Feb. 8, 1865, at Nashville, Tenn.
Adams, Simon	Private..	27	Aug. 15, 1864	1 year	Mustered out with company June 26, 1865.
Allis, Christopher C.	....do....	40	Aug. 10, 1864	1 year.	Mustered out with company June 26, 1865.
Angel, Henry	....do....	25	Aug. 24, 1864	1 year.	Mustered out with company June 26, 1865.
Baise, Abednego	....do....	23	Aug. 6, 1864	1 year.	Mustered out with company June 26, 1865.
Bickford, Oscar C.	....do....	19	Aug. 16, 1864	1 year.	Mustered out with company June 26, 1865.
Boyer, Henry	....do....	37	Aug. 16, 1864	1 year.	Mustered out with company June 26, 1865.
Branaham, Isaac C.	....do....	22	Aug. 10, 1864	1 year.	Mustered out with company June 26, 1865.
Britton, Abraham	....do....	19	Aug. 18, 1864	1 year.	Mustered out with company June 26, 1865.
Bruce, Amaziah C.	....do....	19	Aug. 15, 1864	1 year.	Mustered out with company June 26, 1865.
Bruce, Cyrus C.	....do....	18	Aug. 17, 1864	1 year.	Mustered out with company June 26, 1865.
Bruce, James	....do....	21	Aug. 8, 1864	1 year.	Mustered out with company June 26, 1865.
Bruce, Linzy	....do....	18	Aug. 18, 1864	1 year.	Mustered out with company June 26, 1865.
Bruce, William L.	....do....	18	Aug. 16, 1864	1 year.	Mustered out with company June 26, 1865.
Cline, Michael	....do....	22	Aug. 15, 1864	1 year.	Mustered out with company June 26, 1865.
Corban, Serd[illegible]ne	....do....	23	Aug. 9, 1864	1 year.	Mustered out with company June 26, 1865.
Crawford, Samuel	....do....	18	Aug. 6, 1864	1 year.	Mustered out with company June 26, 1865.
Davidson, Jeremiah	....do....	19	Aug. 8, 1864	1 year.	Mustered out with company June 26, 1865.
Davis, William	....do....	18	Aug. 17, 1864	1 year.	Died Feb 8, 1865, at Nashville, Tenn.
Ellis, James	....do....	18	Aug. 29, 1864	1 year.	Mustered out with company June 26, 1865.
Faris, John	....do....	30	Aug. 6, 1864	1 year.	Mustered out with company June 26, 1865.
Farmer, Edward	....do....	18	Aug. 18, 1864	1 year.	Mustered out with company June 26, 1865.
Fodge, William	....do....	27	Aug. 6, 1864	1 year.	Mustered out with company June 26, 1865.
Glover, Samuel	....do....	18	Aug. 8, 1864	1 year.	Mustered out with company June 26, 1865.
Gray, John P.	....do....	18	Aug. 9, 1864	1 year.	Mustered out with company June 26, 1865.
Hastings, Samuel	....do....	18	Aug. 8, 1864	1 year.	Mustered out with company June 26, 1865.
Hess, James H.	....do....	28	Aug. 26, 1864	1 year.	Mustered out with company June 26, 1865.
Holliday, Homer B.	....do....	18	Aug. 20, 1864	1 year.	Mustered out with company June 26, 1865.
Hughes, Charles B.	....do....	19	Aug. 10, 1864	1 year.	Mustered out with company June 26, 1865.
Hughes, Joseph C.	....do....	18	Aug. 10, 1864	1 year.	Died April 4, 1865, at Post Hospital, Johnsonville, Tenn.
Justice, Riley	....do....	28	Aug. 13, 1864	1 year.	Mustered out with company June 26, 1865.
Keys, William H.	....do....	18	Aug. 18, 1864	1 year.	Mustered out with company June 26, 1865.
Kramer, Frederick	....do....	18	Aug. 11, 1864	1 year.	Mustered out with company June 26, 1865.
Kramer, Stephen	....do....	18	Aug. 16, 1864	1 year.	Mustered out with company June 26, 1865.
Langdon, Enoch	....do....	22	Aug. 9, 1864	1 year.	Mustered out with company June 26, 1865.
Littrel, George	....do....	18	Aug. 10, 1864	1 year.	Mustered out with company June 26, 1865.
Lynd, Jacob J.	....do....	20	Aug. 17, 1864	1 year.	Mustered out with company June 26, 1865.
McCurdy, John T.	....do....	22	Aug. 16, 1864	1 year.	Mustered out with company June 26, 1865.
McNight, Daniel, Jr.	....do....	36	Aug. 18, 1864	1 year.	Mustered out with company June 26, 1865.
McNight, James	....do....	42	Aug. 22, 1864	1 year.	Mustered out with company June 26, 1865.
McNight, William	....do....	38	Aug. 27, 1864	1 year.	Mustered out with company June 26, 1865.
Mann, James W.	....do....	23	Aug. 6, 1864	1 year.	Mustered out with company June 26, 1865.
Markins, Thomas	....do....	35	Aug. 15, 1864	1 year.	Mustered out with company June 26, 1865.
Moore, Amos L.	....do....	28	Aug. 6, 1864	1 year.	Discharged May 21, 1865, at Johnsonville, Tenn., on Surgeon's certificate of disability.
Moore, Asberry	....do....	27	Aug. 9, 1864	1 year.	Mustered out with company June 26, 1865.
Moore, John	....do....	29	Aug. 6, 1864	1 year.	Mustered out with company June 26, 1865.
Moore, Miles	....do....	39	Aug. 6, 1864	1 year.	Mustered out June 1, 1865, at Nashville, Tenn., by order of War Department.
Morris, James M.	....do....	39	Aug. 11, 1864	1 year.	Mustered out with company June 26, 1865.
Nelson, Absalom	....do....	30	Aug. 19, 1864	1 year.	Mustered out with company June 26, 1865.
Noble, James	....do....	19	Aug. 15, 1864	1 year.	Died March 21, 1865, at Post Hospital, Johnsonville, Tenn.
Patrick, Andrew	....do....	30	Aug. 13, 1864	1 year.	Mustered out with company June 26, 1865.
Pemberton, James C.	....do....	25	Aug. 16, 1864	1 year.	Mustered out with company June 26, 1865.
Pemberton, Moses	....do....	19	Aug. 9, 1864	1 year.	Mustered out with company June 26, 1865.
Pierce, George W.	....do....	27	Aug. 8, 1864	1 year.	Mustered out with company June 26, 1865.
Pine, James	....do....	35	Aug. 6, 1864	1 year.	Mustered out with company June 26, 1865.
Pine, Perry O.	....do....	19	Aug. 6, 1864	1 year.	Mustered out with company June 26, 1865.
Platt, William	....do....	21	Aug. 15, 1864	1 year.	Mustered out with company June 26, 1865.
Powers, Cyrus H.	....do....	19	Aug. 17, 1864	1 year.	Mustered out with company June 26, 1865.
Ransbottom, Hiram	....do....	31	Aug. 9, 1864	1 year.	Mustered out with company June 26, 1865.
Ransbottom, George W.	....do....	29	Aug. 9, 1864	1 year.	Mustered out with company June 26, 1865.
Reynolds, William A.	....do....	33	Aug. 14, 1864	1 year.	Mustered out with company June 26, 1865.
Riel, William	....do....	20	Aug. 8, 1864	1 year.	Mustered out with company June 26, 1865.
Rigg, David	....do....	36	Aug. 10, 1864	1 year.	Mustered out with company June 26, 1865.
Robinson, James	....do....	25	Aug. 8, 1864	1 year.	Mustered out with company June 26, 1865.
Ross, John	....do....	38	Aug. 18, 1864	1 year.	Mustered out with company June 26, 1865.
Ryan, Merriman B.	....do....	18	Aug. 10, 1864	1 year.	Mustered out with company June 26, 1865.
Smith, Calvin	....do....	30	Aug. 16, 1864	1 year.	Mustered out with company June 26, 1865.
Snell, Albert L.	....do....	18	Aug. 17, 1864	1 year.	Mustered out with company June 26, 1865.
Stonebraker, William M.	....do....	27	Aug. 17, 1864	1 year.	Mustered out with company June 26, 1865.
Sutton, James H.	....do....	21	Aug. 8, 1864	1 year.	Rejected by Examining Surgeon.

	Rank.	Age.	Date of Entering the Service.	Period of Service.	Remarks.
..	Private..	44	Aug. 6, 1864	1 year.	Mustered out with company June 26, 1865.
..	....do....	23	Aug. 9, 1864	1 year.	Mustered out with company June 26, 1865.
..	....do....	19	Aug. 10, 1864	1 year.	
..	....do....	18	Sept. 2, 1864	1 year.	Mustered out with company June 26, 1865.
....	....do....	29	Aug. 9, 1864	1 year.	Mustered out with company June 26, 1865.
	....do....	30	Aug. 9, 1864	1 year.	Mustered out with company June 26, 1865.
....	....do....	33	Aug. 16, 1864	1 year.	Mustered out with company June 26, 1865.
....	....do....	25	Aug. 16, 1864	1 year.	Died Feb. 27, 1865, at Nashville, Tenn.
....	....do....	41	Aug. 20, 1864	1 year.	Mustered out with company June 26, 1865.
....	....do....	30	Sept. 2, 1864	1 year.	Discharged April 29, 1865, at Nashville, Tenn on Surgeon's certificate of disability.
	....do....	33	Aug. 28, 1864	1 year.	Mustered out with company June 26, 1865.
	....do....	18	Aug. 6, 1864	1 year.	Reduced from Corporal Nov. 8, 1864; mustered out with company June 26, 1865.
	....do....	23	Aug. 16, 1864	1 year.	Discharged May 22, 1865, at Murfreesboro, Tenn., on Surgeon's certificate of disability.
rthington, James K.P.	....do....	18	Aug. 16, 1864	1 year.	Mustered out with company June 26, 1865.

COMPANY B.

stered in Sept. 16, 1864, at Gallipolis, O., by George H. McLaughlin, Captain 2d Infantry, U. S. A. Mustered out June 26, 1865, at Nashville, Tenn., by John W. Chickering, Captain 88th Illinois V. I., and A. C. M. 2d Division, 4th A. C.

r W. Saunders.......	Captain.	25	July 30, 1864	1 year.	Appointed Sept. 17, 1864; resigned Dec. 3, 1864.
ses N. Hanna.........	....do....	27	July 30, 1864	1 year.	Promoted from 1st Lieutenant Co. F Nov. 26, 1864; resigned April 1, 1865.
id F. Hover..........	....do....	28	July 29, 1864	1 year.	Appointed 1st Lieutenant Sept. 17, 1864; promoted to Captain April 10, 1865; mustered out with company June 26, 1865.
orge G. Menely.......	1st Lieut.	26	Aug. 31, 1864	1 year.	Promoted from 2d Lieutenant Co. H April 10, 1865; mustered out with company June 26, 1865.
n H. Saunders.......	2d Lieut.	39	Aug. 11, 1864	1 year.	Appointed Sept. 17, 1864; resigned Nov. 10, 1864.
omas M. Smith.......	....do....	29	Aug. 31, 1864	1 year.	Promoted from Q. M. Sergeant Nov. 26, 1864; mustered out with company June 26, 1865.
uel D. Wells........	1st Sergt.	25	Sept. 3, 1864	1 year.	Appointed Sept. 16, 1864; mustered out with company June 26, 1865.
shington M. Sydenstricker...............	Sergeant.	22	Aug. 1, 1864	1 year.	Appointed Sept. 16, 1864; mustered out with company June 26, 1865.
ney G. Haskins.......	....do....	25	Aug. 20, 1864	1 year.	Appointed Sept. 16, 1864; mustered out with company June 26, 1865.
rge E. Chapman......	....do....	29	Aug. 20, 1864	1 year.	Appointed Sept. 16, 1864; mustered out with company June 26, 1865.
m T. Huston..........	....do....	21	Aug. 11, 1864	1 year.	Appointed Corporal Sept. 16, 1864; Sergeant Oct. 15, 1864; mustered out with company June 26, 1865.
n T. Wooten.........	Corporal.	27	Aug. 3, 1864	1 year.	
dy L. Fowler.........	....do....	22	Aug. 26, 1864	1 year.	Appointed Sept. 16, 1864; died Jan. 29, 1865, at U. S. General Hospital, Nashville, Tenn.
liam H. Waugh.......	....do....	32	Aug. 20, 1864	1 year.	Appointed Sept. 16, 1864; died Jan. 30, 1865, at U. S. General Hospital, Nashville, Tenn.
nuel H. Sydenstricker	....do....	18	Aug. 6, 1864	1 year.	Appointed ——; died Jan. 3, 1865, at U. S. General Hospital, Louisville, Ky.
vid W. North.........	....do....	18	Aug. 8, 1864	1 year.	Appointed Sept. 16, 1864; mustered out with company June 26, 1865.
rge W. Sheets	....do....	34	Sept. 14, 1864	1 year.	Appointed Sept. 16, 1864; mustered out with company June 26, 1865.
ert E. Channell......	....do....	37	Sept. 7, 1864	1 year.	Appointed Oct. 10, 1864; mustered out with company June 26, 1865.
phen A. Massie......	....do....	25	Sept. 3, 1864	1 year.	Appointed Oct. 10, 1864; mustered out with company June 26, 1865.
nry Pope.............	....do....	20	Sept. 2, 1864	1 year.	Appointed Jan. 5, 1865; mustered out with company June 26, 1865.
ward McLaughlin......	....do....	18	Aug. 1, 1864	1 year.	Appointed Nov. 21, 1864; mustered out with company June 26, 1865.
nes M. Defender......	....do....	24	Aug. 29, 1864	1 year.	Appointed Dec. 20, 1864; mustered out with company June 26, 1865.
eph G. Fox...........	....do....	38	Sept. 3, 1864	1 year.	Appointed Feb. 25, 1865; mustered out with company June 26, 1865.
ob J. Saunders......	Musician	16	Aug. 11, 1864	1 year.	Mustered out with company June 26, 1865.
lerick Klages........	....do....	18	Sept. 2, 1864	1 year.	Mustered out with company June 26, 1865.
ney Boatman.........	Wagoner.	44	Sept. 4, 1864	1 year.	Mustered out with company June 26, 1865.
ott, James W........	Private.	18	Sept. 14, 1864	1 year.	Died April 8, 1865, at Post Hospital, Johnsonville, Tenn.
ins, Luke............	....do....	42	Aug. 27, 1864	1 year.	Mustered out with company June 26, 1865.

Names.	Rank.	Age.	Date of Entering the Service.	Period of Service.	Remarks.
Adkins, Nathaniel	Private.	19	Aug. 23, 1864	1 year.	Mustered out with company June 26, 1865.
Alburn, Charles	...do...	41	Sept. 2, 1864	1 year.	Mustered out with company June 26, 1865.
Backman, Cortland	...do...	21	Aug. 15, 1864	1 year.	Mustered out with company June 26, 1865.
Baustick, Andrew A	...do...	44	Sept. 2, 1864	1 year.	Mustered out with company June 26, 1865.
Beeden, William	...do...	24	Feb. 10, 1865	1 year.	Transferred to Co. C, 18th O. V. I., July 8, 1865.
Blankenship, Stephen V.	...do...	27	Aug. 27, 1864	1 year.	Mustered out with company June 26, 1865.
Bocock, Joel F	...do...	40	Aug. 19, 1864	1 year.	Mustered out July 27, 1865, at Columbus, O., by order of War Department.
Bollen, William T	...do...	21	Aug. 27, 1864	1 year.	Appointed Corporal Sept. 16, 1864; reduced Oct. —, 1864; mustered out with company June 26, 1865.
Boren, Samuel S	...do...	18	Aug. 4, 1864	1 year.	Mustered out with company June 26, 1865.
Brannan, Thomas	...do...	28	Aug. 27, 1864	1 year.	Mustered out with company June 26, 1865.
Breedlove, James L	...do...	18	Sept. 10, 1864	1 year.	Mustered out with company June 26, 1865.
Brown, Martin	...do...	32	Aug. 29, 1864	1 year.	Mustered out to date June 26, 1865, at Columbus, O., by order of War Department.
Brumfield James A	...do...	28	Aug. 11, 1864	1 year.	Mustered out with company June 26, 1865.
Carter John	...do...	34	Sept. 2, 1864	1 year.	Mustered out May 19, 1865, at Louisville, Ky., by order of War Department.
Chapman, Isaac Floyd	...do...	18	Aug. 23, 1864	1 year.	Mustered out with company June 26, 1865.
Clark, Bartlett B	...do...	32	Sept. 2, 1864	1 year.	Mustered out with company June 26, 1865.
Clice, James A	...do...	21	Sept. 2, 1864	1 year.	Mustered out with company June 26, 1865.
Clinger, Eli	...do...	19	Aug. 5, 1864	1 year.	Mustered out with company June 26, 1865.
Cook, Lewis	...do...	38	Sept. 2, 1864	1 year.	Mustered out with company June 26, 1865.
Cook, William H	...do...	18	Aug. 3, 1864	1 year.	Mustered out with company June 26, 1865.
Cornell, George W	...do...	22	Sept. 12, 1864	1 year.	Discharged July 10, 1865, at Gallipolis, O., on Surgeon's certificate of disability.
Cornell, Harrison	...do...	18	Aug. 10, 1864	1 year.	Died Jan. 7, 1865, at U. S. General Hospital, Nashville, Tenn.
Doughty, Isaac W	...do...	36	Aug. 19, 1864	1 year.	Discharged May 31, 1865, at Johnsonville, Tenn., on Surgeon's certificate of disability.
Davis, Evan	...do...	18	Sept. 9, 1864	1 year.	Mustered out with company June 26, 1865.
Elkins, William	...do...	33	Aug. 19, 1864	1 year.	Died Jan. 2, 1865, at U. S. General Hospital, Nashville, Tenn.
Fullerton, Isaac	...do...	21	Aug. 29, 1864	1 year.	Mustered out with company June 26, 1865.
Gates, James R	...do...	18	Sept. 3, 1864	1 year.	Mustered out with company June 26, 1865.
Gruby, August	...do...	26	Sept. 2, 1864	1 year.	Mustered out with company June 26, 1865.
Gruby, Henry	...do...	21	Sept. 2, 1864	1 year.	Mustered out with company June 26, 1865.
Hager, Russell	...do...	30	Aug. 27, 1864	1 year.	Mustered out with company June 26, 1865.
Halley, William R	...do...	43	Aug. 15, 1864	1 year.	Mustered out with company June 26, 1865.
Hamlin, Robert	...do...	18	Aug. 1, 1864	1 year.	Mustered out with company June 26, 1865.
Haner, Noah	...do...	19	Aug. 16, 1864	1 year.	Mustered out with company June 26, 1865.
Henry, John	...do...	30	Aug. 15, 1864	1 year.	Mustered out with company June 26, 1865.
Henson, Jacob	...do...	19	Aug. 29, 1864	1 year.	Mustered out with company June 26, 1865.
Hively, David J	...do...	18	Aug. 21, 1864	1 year.	Mustered out with company June 26, 1865.
Hively, Jonathan	...do...	43	Sept. 2, 1864	1 year.	Died Jan. 21, 1865, at U. S. General Hospital, Nashville, Tenn.
Huggins, Thomas	...do...	42	Aug. 14, 1864	1 year.	Died April 26, 1865, at Johnsonville, Tenn.
Lear, Henry	...do...	25	Aug. 2, 1864	1 year.	Mustered out with company June 26, 1865.
Mabe, Martin	...do...	18	Aug. 11, 1864	1 year.	Mustered out with company June 26, 1865.
Mahan, Andrew B	...do...	19	Aug. 18, 1864	1 year.	Died Jan. 1, 1865, at U. S. General Hospital, Nashville, Tenn.
Mahan, Joseph S	...do...	25	Aug. 20, 1864	1 year.	Mustered out with company June 26, 1865.
Martt, Isaac M	...do...	41	Aug. 29, 1864	1 year.	Died Dec. 8, 1864, at U. S. General Hospital, Nashville, Tenn.
Martt, James H	...do...	27	Aug. 27, 1864	1 year.	Mustered out with company June 26, 1865.
Mase, Elza	...do...	27	Aug. 20, 1864	1 year.	Mustered out with company June 26, 1865.
Massie, George	...do...	21	Aug. 13, 1864	1 year.	Died Feb. 13, 1865, at U. S. General Hospital, Nashville, Tenn.
Massie, Peter	...do...	25	Sept. 14, 1864	1 year.	Mustered out to date June 26, 1865, by order of War Department.
Massie, William	...do...	18	Aug. 13, 1864	1 year.	Mustered out with company June 26, 1865.
Noland, David	...do...	19	Aug. 27, 1864	1 year.	Mustered out with company June 26, 1865.
Nul[illegible] James M	...do...	22	Aug. 29, 1864	1 year.	Mustered out with company Ju[illegible]
Nul[illegible], W[illegible] W	...do...	21	Sept. 2, 1864	1 year.	Died Aug. 3, 1865, at Louisville, Ky.
Pritchet, [illegible]ames	...do...	42	Sept. 9, 1864	1 year.	Returned to 2d West Virginia Cavalry Sept. 16, 1864, where he had previously enlisted.
Raigan, Josep[illegible]	...do...	19	Aug. 1, 1864	1 year.	
Reynolds, John M	...do...	20	Sept. 10, 1864	1 year.	Appointed Sergeant Sept. 16, 1864; reduced Oct. —, 1864; mustered out with company June 26, 1865.
Rockwell, John	...do...	18	Aug. 26, 1864	1 year.	Died Jan. 14, 1865, in U. S. General Hospital, Nashville, Tenn.
Root, Frederick	...do...	38	Sept. 2, 1864	1 year.	Mustered out with company June 26, 1865.
Ropeter, Frederick	...do...	36	Sept. 2, 1864	1 year.	Mustered out with company June 26, 1865.
Roup, John J	...do...	35	Aug. 11, 1864	1 year.	Mustered out with company June 26, 1865.
Roush, Richard M	...do...	18	Sept. 14, 1864	1 year.	Died Dec. 28, 1864, at Post Hospital, Nashville, Tenn.
Saunders, Hezekiah H	...do...	24	Aug. 15, 1864	1 year.	Mustered out with company June 26, 1865.
Sheets, Henry W	...do...	32	Aug. 21, 1864	1 year.	Mustered out with company June 26, 1865.
Sheets, Samuel M	...do...	22	Sept. 4, 1864	1 year.	Appointed Corporal Sept. 16, 1864; reduced Sept. 18, 1864, at his own request; mustered out with company June 26, 1865.
Sheets, William F	...do...	18	Aug. 11, 1864	1 year.	Mustered out with company June 26, 1865.
Shumaker, John L	...do...	28	Sept. 4, 1864	1 year.	Mustered out with company June 26, 1865.

Names.	Rank.	Age.	Date of Entering the Service.	Period of Service.	Remarks.
Crabtree, Edward	Private	18	Sept. 1, 1864	1 year.	Discharged May 23, 1865, at Johnsonville, Tenn., on Surgeon's certificate of disability.
Crabtree, Elisha	...do...	30	Sept. 1, 1864	1 year.	Mustered out with company June 26, 1865.
Crabtree, Kendall	...do...	27	Aug. 20, 1864	1 year.	Mustered out with company June 26, 1865.
Crabtree, Thomas	...do...	24	Aug. 20, 1864	1 year.	Mustered out with company June 26, 1865.
Cummings, Joseph	...do...	40	Aug. 29, 1864	1 year.	Mustered out with company June 26, 1865.
Daniels, Christopher	...do...	30	Sept. 1, 1864	1 year.	Mustered out with company June 26, 1865.
Dauner, James H	...do...	28	Aug. 15, 1864	1 year.	Died Dec. 23, 1864, at Post Hospital, Nashville, Tenn.
Dean, Wesley	...do...	18	Aug. 27, 1864	1 year.	Mustered out with company June 26, 1865.
Doss, Nicholas	...do...	19	Aug. 27, 1864	1 year.	Died Jan. 25, 1865, at Post Hospital, Nashville, Tenn.
Evans, David T	...do...	19	Aug. 29, 1864	1 year.	Mustered out May 15, 1865, at Nashville, Tenn., by order of War Department.
Evans, John	...do...	18	Aug. 10, 1864	1 year.	Mustered out with company June 26, 1865.
Evans, John D	...do...	18	Aug. 27, 1864	1 year.	Mustered out with company June 26, 1865.
Ferrel, William S	...do...	32	Aug. 27, 1864	1 year.	Mustered out with company June 26, 1865.
Foster, Francis M	...do...	21	Aug. 19, 1864	1 year.	Died May 6, 1865, at Post Hospital, Johnsonville, Tenn.
Foster, Marcus L	...do...	18	Aug. 27, 1864	1 year.	Mustered out with company June 26, 1865.
Fox, Jacob	...do...	19	Sept. 5, 1864	1 year.	Died March 4, 1865, at Johnsonville, Tenn.
Frame, Marcellus	...do...	19	Aug. 1, 1864	1 year.	Mustered out with company June 26, 1865.
Gaskins, Reuben	...do...	18	Aug. 22, 1864	1 year.	Mustered out with company June 26, 1865.
Gauze, Henry F	...do...	18	Aug. 6, 1864	1 year.	Mustered out with company June 26, 1865.
Gillilan, James	...do...	22	Aug. 25, 1864	1 year.	Mustered out with company June 26, 1865.
Groves, Jacob	...do...	33	Aug. 3, 1864	1 year.	Mustered out with company June 26, 1865.
Ham, David F	...do...	20	Aug. 26, 1864	1 year.	Appointed Corporal Sept. 17, 1864; reduced Oct. 20, 1864; mustered out with company June 26, 1865.
Ham, George A	...do...	18	Sept. 1, 1864	1 year.	Died Dec. 23, 1864, at Post Hospital, Nashville, Tennessee.
Hamilton, Robert	...do...	18	Aug. 6, 1864	1 year.	Mustered out with company June 26, 1865.
Henry, Charles	...do...	40	Sept. 5, 1864	1 year.	Mustered out with company June 26, 1865.
Henry, Hugh	...do...	19	Sept. 4, 1864	1 year.	Mustered out with company June 26, 1865.
Hunt, James	...do...	18	Aug. 12, 1864	1 year.	Mustered out with company June 26, 1865.
Irion, Jerome B	...do...	18	Aug. 9, 1864	1 year.	Discharged Feb. 4, 1865, at on Surgeon's certificate of
Jenks, Lawrence	...do...	33	Aug. 15, 1864	1 year.	Mustered out with company
Jones, John B.	...do...	20	Aug. 10, 1864	1 year.	Appointed Corporal Sept. 17, 1864; reduced Oct. 31, 1864; mustered out June 26, 1865.
Kessinger, Ward W	...do...	35	Aug. 15, 1864	1 year.	Died March 12, 1865, at Post Hospital, Nashville, Tenn.
Kinder, William F	...do...	18	Sept. 10, 1864	1 year.	Mustered out with company June 26, 1865.
Kyre, Joseph N	...do...	19	Aug. 18, 1864	1 year.	Died March 8, 1865, at Post Hospital, Johnsonville, Tenn.
Lloyd, Evan, Sr	...do...	19	Sept. 10, 1864	1 year.	Mustered out with company June 26, 1865.
Lloyd, Evan, Jr	...do...	18	Aug. 3, 1864	1 year.	Mustered out with company June 26, 1865.
Love, Parker	...do...	35	Aug. 29, 1864	1 year.	Mustered out with company June 26, 1865.
McCarley, Franklin	...do...	22	Sept. 12, 1864	1 year.	Mustered out with company June 26, 1865.
McCarley, John D	...do...	26	Sept. 12, 1864	1 year.	Died Feb. 19, 1865, at Post Hospital, Nashville, Tennessee.
McKean, Hiram F	...do...	22	Sept. 4, 1864	1 year.	Died Feb. 18, 1865, at Post Hospital, Nashville, Tennessee.
McNeal, Joseph J	...do...	37	Sept. 10, 1864	1 year.	Mustered out with company June 26, 1865.
Massie, Benjamin	...do...	19	Aug. 29, 1864	1 year.	Mustered out with company June 26, 1865.
Massie, William N	...do...	29	Aug. 29, 1864	1 year.	Mustered out with company June 26, 1865.
Morrow, Henry C	...do...	19	Aug. 5, 1864	1 year.	Mustered out with company June 26, 1865.
Nelson, Nathaniel	...do...	36	Sept. 5, 1864	1 year.	Mustered out with company June 26, 1865.
Oney, Hiram	...do...	37	Sept. 1, 1864	1 year.	Mustered out with company June 26, 1865.
Oshman, John	...do...	36	Aug. 8, 1864	1 year.	Mustered out with company June 26, 1865.
Phillips, Milton	...do...	24	Mch. 22, 1865	1 year.	Transferred to Co. C, 18th O. V. I., July [illegible], 1865.
Polly, William	...do...	20	Aug. 7, 1864	1 year.	Mustered out with company June 26, 1865.
Price, Christian B	...do...	20	Aug. 17, 1864	1 year.	Mustered out with company June 26, 1865.
Price, George P	...do...	27	Aug. 12, 1864	1 year.	Died Jan. 17, 1865, at Post Hospital, Nashville, Tennessee.
Price, James	...do...	28	Sept. 10, 1864	1 year.	Mustered out with company June 26, 1865.
Reese, Reese	...do...	19	Aug. 15, 1864	1 year.	Mustered out with company June 26, 1865.
Roberts, Robert	...do...	23	Sept. 10, 1864	1 year.	Mustered out with company June 26, 1865.
Rose, Pleasant	...do...	43	Aug. 23, 1864	1 year.	Mustered out with company June 26, 1865.
Saunders, Jacob J	...do...	27	Sept. 4, 1864	1 year.	Mustered out with company June 26, 1865.
Seel, William	...do...	32	Aug. 20, 1864	1 year.	Mustered out with company June 26, 1865.
Shafer, William D	...do...	18	Aug. 19, 1864	1 year.	Mustered out with company June 26, 1865.
Shiltz, Absalom	...do...	30	Aug. 25, 1864	1 year.	Mustered out with company June 26, 1865.
Smith, Andrew	...do...	18	Aug. 8, 1864	1 year.	Mustered out with company June 26, 1865.
Stratton, Jeremiah	...do...	36	Aug. 23, 1864	1 year.	Mustered out with company June 26, 1865.
Sumpter, Andrew J	...do...	42	Aug. 29, 1864	1 year.	Mustered out with company June 26, 1865.
Swingle, Lewis	...do...	39	Aug. 27, 1864	1 year.	Mustered out with company June 26, 1865.
Taylor, Andrew J	...do...	22	Aug. 23, 1864	1 year.	Died April 26, 1865, at Post Hospital, Johnsonville, Tenn.
Thomas, Morgan	...do...	32	Sept. 10, 1864	1 year.	Died April 18, 1865, at Post Hospital, Nashville, Tenn.
Thompson, Jackson P	...do...	25	Aug. 29, 1864	1 year.	Mustered out with company June 26, 1865.
Warrell, Granville	...do...	27	Aug. 3, 1864	1 year.	Promoted to Principal Musician Jan. [illegible]
Wheelbarger, Moses M	...do...	22	Sept. 5, 1864	1 year.	Mustered out with company June 26, 1865.

Rank.	Age.	Date of Entering the Service.	Period of Service.	Remarks.
Private..	41	Aug. 29, 1864	1 year.	Mustered out with company June 26, 1865.
....do....	20	Aug. 10, 1864	1 year.	Discharged April 6, 1865, at Nashville, Tenn., on Surgeon's certificate of disability.
....do....	18	Aug. 18, 1864	1 year.	Mustered out with company June 26, 1865.

COMPANY D.

stered in Sept. 16, 1864, at Gallipolis, O., by George H. McLaughlin, Captain 2d Infantry, U. S. A. Mustered out June 26, 1865, at Nashville, Tenn., by John W. Chickering, Captain 88th Illinois V. I., and A. C. M. 2d Division, 4th A. C.

Name	Rank	Age	Date of Entering the Service	Period of Service	Remarks
n C. Malone	Captain.	31	Aug. 8, 1864	1 year.	Appointed Sept. 17, 1864; mustered out with company June 26, 1865.
rge W. Helfsinstein.	1st Lieut.	27	Aug. 10, 1864	1 year.	Appointed Sept. 17, 1864; Adjutant Dec. 21, 1864.
ert E. Morrison	....do....	18	Aug. 25, 1864	1 year.	Appointed 2d Lieutenant Sept. 17, 1864; promoted to 1st Lieutenant Dec. 14, 1864; mustered out with company June 26, 1865.
R. O. Thomas	2d Lieut.	26	Aug. 13, 1864	1 year.	Promoted from 1st Sergeant Co. F Dec. 30, 1864; mustered out with company June 26, 1865.
a K. Finton	1st Sergt.	22	Aug. 29, 1864	1 year.	Appointed Sept. 16, 1864; mustered out with company June 26, 1865.
ry C. Gilruth	Sergeant.	19	Aug. 25, 1864	1 year.	Appointed Sept. 16, 1864; died Jan. 28, 1865, at Nashville, Tenn.
liam H. Swatswalter.	....do....	37	Aug. 26, 1864	1 year.	Appointed Sept. 16, 1864; mustered out with company June 26, 1865.
n W. Devoss	....do....	21	Aug. 25, 1864	1 year.	Appointed Sept. 16, 1864; mustered out with company June 26, 1865.
ourn Smith	....do....	31	Aug. 15, 1864	1 year.	Appointed Sept. 16, 1864; mustered out with company June 26, 1865.
mas Cashier	....do....	29	Aug. 20, 1864	1 year.	Appointed Corporal Nov. 1, 1864; Sergeant Feb. 1, 1865; mustered out with company June 26, 1865.
ding B. Ham	Corporal.	37	Aug. 30, 1864	1 year.	Mustered out May 25, 1865, at Louisville, Ky., by order of War Department.
ld Fisher	....do....	36	Aug. 29, 1864	1 year.	Appointed Sept. 16, 1864; mustered out with company June 26, 1865.
on Hollingshead	....do....	44	Aug. 23, 1864	1 year.	Appointed Sept. 16, 1864; mustered out with company June 26, 1865.
nel Warren	....do....	21	Aug. 23, 1864	1 year.	Appointed Sept. 16, 1864; mustered out with company June 26, 1865.
W. Buckley	....do....	19	Aug. 25, 1864	1 year.	Appointed Sept. 16, 1864; mustered out with company June 26, 1865.
ard Masters	....do....	18	Aug. 13, 1864	1 year.	Appointed Sept. 16, 1864; mustered out with company June 26, 1865.
mas Deaver	....do....	22	Aug. 16, 1864	1 year.	Appointed Nov. 1, 1864; mustered out with company June 26, 1865.
ld C. Brock	....do....	22	Aug. 8, 1864	1 year.	Appointed March 1, 1865; mustered out with company June 26, 1865.
rles Hood	Musician	17	Aug. 12, 1864	1 year.	Mustered out with company June 26, 1865.
es Metz	....do....	18	Sept. 1, 1864	1 year.	Mustered as Corporal; appointed Musician ——; mustered out with company June 26, 1865.
mas Hedges	Wagoner.	30	Aug. 15, 1864	1 year.	Mustered out with company June 26, 1865.
ire, Jonathan	Private..	18	Aug. 23, 1864	1 year.	Mustered out with company June 26, 1865.
er, Levi	....do....	24	Sept. 1, 1864	1 year.	Mustered out with company June 26, 1865.
ker, Esquire	....do....	27	Aug. 23, 1864	1 year.	Mustered out with company June 26, 1865.
linger, Adam	....do....	18	Aug. 23, 1864	1 year.	Mustered out with company June 26, 1865.
man, Joseph W	....do....	19	Aug. 22, 1864	1 year.	Mustered out with company June 26, 1865.
ich, John	....do....	21	Feb. 13, 1865	1 year.	Transferred to Co. C, 18th O. V. I., July 9, 1865.
ey, Joseph	....do....	18	Sept. 15, 1864	1 year.	Mustered out with company June 26, 1865.
ter, Elijah E	....do....	21	Aug. 23, 1864	1 year.	Mustered out with company June 26, 1865.
ter, James V	....do....	18	Aug. 23, 1864	1 year.	Mustered out with company June 26, 1865.
ter, Lorenzo D	....do....	30	Aug. 17, 1864	1 year.	Mustered out with company June 26, 1865.
ter, Warren	....do....	21	Aug. 13, 1864	1 year.	Mustered out with company June 26, 1865.
er, Andrew	....do....	39	Aug. 29, 1864	1 year.	
er, Alexander	....do....	41	Aug. 29, 1864	1 year.	Mustered out with company June 26, 1865.
er, Fleming T	....do....	19	Aug. 19, 1864	1 year.	Mustered out with company June 26, 1865.
mberlin, Lucas	....do....	18	Aug. 27, 1864	1 year.	Died April 8, 1865, at Nashville, Tenn.
k, John J	....do....	20	Aug. 11, 1864	1 year.	Mustered out with company June 26, 1865.
k, Richard	....do....	29	Aug. 25, 1864	1 year.	Mustered out with company June 26, 1865.
man, Michael C	....do....	28	Aug. 29, 1864	1 year.	
ler, John	....do....	22	Aug. 29, 1864	1 year.	Mustered out with company June 26, 1865.
Smith	....do....	25	Aug. 26, 1864	1 year.	Mustered out with company June 26, 1865.
tree, William J	....do....	38	Aug. 26, 1864	1 year.	Mustered out with company June 26, 1865.
r, Lewis	....do....	[illegible]	Aug. 29, 1864	1 year.	Mustered out with company June 26, 1865.

Names.	Rank.	Age.	Date of Entering the Service.	Period of Service	Remarks.
Deaver, John W	Private	28	Aug. 16, 1864	1 year.	Muster-out roll reports him absent, sick —.
Deaver, William	do	19	Aug. 13, 1864	1 year.	Mustered out with company June 26, 1865.
Essman, William	do	18	Aug. 31, 1864	1 year.	Mustered out with company June 26, 1865.
Friley, James K. P	do	18	Aug. 26, 1864	1 year.	Mustered out with company June 26, 1865.
Friley, Timothy	do	19	Aug. 26, 1864	1 year.	Mustered out May 24, 1865, at Nashville, Tenn., by order of War Department.
Goins, Absalom	do	18	Aug. 23, 1864	1 year.	Mustered out with company June 26, 1865.
Graney, John	do	35	Aug. 29, 1864	1 year.	
Halterman, William	do	28	Aug. 27, 1864	1 year.	Mustered out with company June 26, 1865.
Hanning, Jacob	do	26	Aug. 20, 1864	1 year.	Mustered out with company June 26, 1865.
Havens, William	do	18	Aug. 15, 1864	1 year.	Mustered out with company June 26, 1865.
Hedges, George W	do	18	Aug. 31, 1864	1 year.	Mustered out with company June 26, 1865.
Hilt, Oliver N	do	23	Sept. 1, 1864	1 year.	Mustered out with company June 26, 1865.
Hiner, Lafayette	do	19	Aug. 29, 1864	1 year.	Mustered out with company June 26, 1865.
Hollangsworth, Joseph A	do	18	Aug. 24, 1864	1 year.	Mustered out June 8, 1865, at Nashville, Tenn. by order of War Department.
Homire, Henry	do	18	Aug. 22, 1864	1 year.	Mustered out with company June 26, 1865.
Hudson, Charles W	do	21	Aug. 25, 1864	1 year.	Mustered out with company June 26, 1865.
Irwin, Jacob	do	34	Aug. 20, 1864	1 year.	Mustered out with company June 26, 1865.
Israel, Foster	do	22	Aug. 17, 1864	1 year.	Mustered out with company June 26, 1865.
Johnson, Abraham	do	18	Aug. 16, 1864	1 year.	Mustered out with company June 26, 1865.
Kealrns, Thomas	do	18	Aug. 17, 1864	1 year.	Mustered out with company June 26, 1865.
Keeny, David	do	19	Aug. 27, 1864	1 year.	Mutsered out with company June 26, 1865.
Lamb, Willard	do	19	Aug. 23, 1864	1 year.	Mustered out with company June 26, 1865.
Lewis, Samuel	do	23	Feb. 13, 1865	1 year.	Transferred to Co. C, 18th O. V. L. July 8, 1865.
Lindsey, Horace T	do	19	Aug. 16, 1864	1 year.	Appointed Corporal Sept. 17, 1864; reduced Oct. 17, 1864; mustered out with company June 26, 1865.
Lynd, Samuel B	do	17	Oct. 17, 1864	1 year.	Transferred to Co. C, 18th O. V. L. July 8, 1865.
McCall, William K	do	20	Aug. 25, 1864	1 year.	Mustered out with company June 26, 1865.
McChesney, Aaron L	do	28	Aug. 22, 1864	1 year.	Mustered out with company June 26, 1865.
McCreary, William H	do	18	Aug. 29, 1864	1 year.	Mustered out with company June 26, 1865.
McGath, Jesse S	do	18	Aug. 23, 1864	1 year.	Mustered out with company June 26, 1865.
McNeel, Archibald	do	40	Aug. 23, 1864	1 year.	Mustered out with company June 26, 1865.
Mabis, Peter	do	28	Oct. 21, 1864	1 year.	Transferred to Co. C, 18th O. V. L., July 8, 1865.
Minard, James D	do	18	Aug. 16, 1864	1 year.	Mustered out with company June 26, 1865.
Morris, Lyman T	do	20	Aug. 27, 1864	1 year.	Mustered out with company June 26, 1865.
Munyan, William	do	19	Aug. 29, 1864	1 year.	Mustered out with company June 26, 1865.
Murphy, John R	do	19	Aug. 23, 1864	1 year.	Mustered out with company June 26, 1865.
Neff, Leonard	do	14	Aug. 17, 1864	1 year.	Mustered out with company June 26, 1865.
Palmer, William S	do	19	Sept. 10, 1864	1 year.	Mustered out with company June 26, 1865.
Parr, Henry M	do	22	Aug. 24, 1864	1 year.	Mustered out with company June 26, 1865.
Petitt, Henry	do	19	Aug. 25, 1864	1 year.	Mustered out with company June 26, 1865.
Reed, George	do	23	Aug. 23, 1864	1 year.	Mustered out with company June 26, 1865.
Russell, Washington	do	18	Aug. 18, 1864	1 year.	Mustered as Musician; mustered out with company June 26, 1865.
Shepard, Joseph	do	30	Aug. 24, 1864	1 year.	Died Dec. 11, 1864, at Post Hospital, Nashville, Tennessee.
Shuff, James	do	18	Aug. 23, 1864	1 year.	Mustered out with company June 26, 1865.
Shuman, Joshua	do	20	Aug. 27, 1864	1 year.	Died April 3, 1865, at Post Hospital Johnsonville, Tenn.
Simmering, Henry	do	19	Aug. 21, 1864	1 year.	Mustered out with company June 26, 1865.
Smith, Eleazer W	do	31	Aug. 12, 1864	1 year.	Mustered out with company June 26, 1865.
Stall, Christian	do	18	Aug. 29, 1864	1 year.	Mustered out with company June 26, 1865.
Staton, William W	do	21	Aug. 23, 1864	1 year.	Mustered out with company June 26, 1865.
Strickland, Jonathan	do	28	Aug. 17, 1864	1 year.	Mustered out with company June 26, 1865.
Sudbrook, Henry	do	21	Aug. 17, 1864	1 year.	Mustered out with company June 26, 1865.
Sullivan, Owen	do	39	Aug. 19, 1864	1 year.	Mustered out with company June 26, 1865.
Teters, Joseph J	do	42	Aug. 29, 1864	1 year.	Mustered out with company June 26, 1865.
Triggs, Eli	do	18	Aug. 9, 1864	1 year.	Died June 16, 1865, at Johnsonville, Tenn.
Walk, George W	do	23	Aug. 23, 1864	1 year.	Mustered out with company June 26, 1865.
Walker, Charles W	do	18	Aug. 26, 1864	1 year.	Mustered out with company June 26, 1865.
Walker, William W	do	51	Aug. 29, 1864	1 year.	Mustered out with company June 26, 1865.
Wells, Andrew C	do	31	Aug. 13, 1864	1 year.	Mustered out with company June 26, 1865.
Winkler, James O	do	21	Aug. 23, 1864	1 year.	Mustered out with company June 26, 1865.
Witherow, William	do	30	Aug. 13, 1864	1 year.	Mustered out with company June 26, 1865.
Wolf, Jonathan	do	35	Aug. 17, 1864	1 year.	Mustered out with company June 26, 1865.
Woodworth, William D	do	20	Aug. 25, 1864	1 year.	Mustered out with company June 26, 1865.
Young, Oliver	do	18	Aug. 15, 1864	1 year.	Mustered out with company June 26, 1865.
Zornes, John	do	40	Aug. 29, 1864	1 year.	Mustered out with company June 26, 1865.

COMPANY E.

ered in Sept. 18, 1864, at Gallipolis, O., by George H. McLaughlin, Captain 2d Infantry, U. S. A. Mustered out June 26, 1865, at Nashville, Tenn., by John W. Chickering, Captain 88th Illinois V. I., and A. C. M. 2d Division, 4th A. C.

	Rank.	Age.	Date of Entering the Service.	Period of Service.	Remarks.
ony W. Bowen	Captain	34	Aug. 5, 1864	1 year.	Appointed Sept. 18, 1864; mustered out with company June 26, 1865.
O. Wall	1st Lieut.	20	Aug. 15, 1864	1 year.	Appointed Sept. 18, 1864; mustered out with company June 26, 1865.
n Martin	2d Lieut.	26	Aug. 23, 1864	1 year.	Appointed Sept. 18, 1864; discharged May 15, 1865, on Surgeon's certificate of disability.
bury T. Shirkey	1st Sergt.	38	Aug. 26, 1864	1 year.	Mustered out with company June 26, 1865.
H. Truesdell	Sergeant	27	Aug. 13, 1864	1 year.	Mustered out with company June 26, 1865.
iam Zimmerman	....do....	24	Aug. 26, 1864	1 year.	Mustered out with company June 26, 1865.
m H. Lemley	....do....	18	Aug. 18, 1864	1 year.	Mustered out with company June 26, 1865.
H. Burcham	....do....	22	Aug. 13, 1864	1 year.	Mustered out with company June 26, 1865.
m G. Mount	Corporal	25	Aug. 26, 1864	1 year.	Died Dec. 6, 1864, at Nashville, Tenn.
Briggs	....do....	24	Aug. 16, 1864	1 year.	Mustered out with company June 26, 1865.
W. Lewis	....do....	29	Aug. 8, 1864	1 year.	Mustered out with company June 26, 1865.
m F. Burcham	....do....	44	Aug. 16, 1864	1 year.	Mustered out with company June 26, 1865.
Lunsford	....do....	26	Aug. 21, 1864	1 year.	Mustered out with company June 26, 1865.
rd J. Bowen	....do....	24	Aug. 10, 1864	1 year.	Mustered out with company June 26, 1865.
m H. Pinkerman	....do....	26	Aug. 26, 1864	1 year.	Mustered out with company June 26, 1865.
iah Blackburn	....do....	22	Aug. 12, 1864	1 year.	Mustered out with company June 26, 1865.
n Millup	....do....	37	Aug. 26, 1864	1 year.	Appointed Dec. 24, 1864; mustered out with company June 26, 1865.
E. Foster	Musician	16	Aug. 26, 1864	1 year.	Mustered out with company June 26, 1865.
Scott	....do....	16	Sept. 1, 1864	1 year.	Mustered out with company June 26, 1865.
el Lemley	Wagoner	39	Aug. 14, 1864	1 year.	Mustered out with company June 26, 1865.
s, Jacob	Private	35	Aug. 16, 1864	1 year.	Mustered out with company June 26, 1865.
, Ephraim	....do....	32	Aug. 21, 1864	1 year.	Died Dec. 4, 1864, at Nashville, Tenn.
Joseph	....do....	34	Aug. 26, 1864	1 year.	Mustered out with company June 26, 1865.
, Anderson	....do....	18	Aug. 18, 1864	1 year.	Mustered out with company June 26, 1865.
, William	....do....	31	Sept. 4, 1864	1 year.	
, Asbury G	....do....	20	Aug. 13, 1864	1 year.	Mustered out with company June 26, 1865.
am, William F	....do....	34	Aug. 18, 1864	1 year.	Mustered out with company June 26, 1865.
ans, Joseph	....do....	18	Aug. 13, 1864	1 year.	Mustered out with company June 26, 1865.
, Joseph J.	....do....	39	Aug. 18, 1864	1 year.	Died March 6, 1865, at Nashville, Tenn.
Samuel F	....do....	26	Sept. 18, 1864	1 year.	Mustered out with company June 26, 1865.
s, Hezekiah	....do....	18	Aug. 21, 1864	1 year.	Mustered out with company June 26, 1865.
Jesse	....do....	20	Aug. 12, 1864	1 year.	Mustered out with company June 26, 1865.
, John	....do....	31	Aug. 18, 1864	1 year.	Mustered out with company June 26, 1865.
, John C	....do....	24	Aug. 13, 1864	1 year.	Mustered out with company June 26, 1865.
, Cyrus	....do....	21	Aug. 26, 1864	1 year.	Mustered out with company June 26, 1865.
, John W	....do....	25	Aug. 13, 1864	1 year.	Mustered out with company June 26, 1865.
, Welcome	....do....	18	Aug. 18, 1864	1 year.	Died Dec. 30, 1864, at Nashville, Tenn.
, William H.	....do....	23	Aug. 26, 1864	1 year.	Mustered out with company June 26, 1865.
Martin S	....do....	27	Aug. 26, 1864	1 year.	Mustered out with company June 26, 1865.
, Robert	....do....	18	Sept. 8, 1864	1 year.	Mustered out with company June 26, 1865.
, William	....do....	41	Sept. 8, 1864	1 year.	Mustered out with company June 26, 1865.
er, Harrison	....do....	24	Aug. 18, 1864	1 year.	Mustered out with company June 26, 1865.
, Jedediah	....do....	26	Sept. 10, 1864	1 year.	Mustered out with company June 26, 1865.
, John	....do....	27	Aug. 13, 1864	1 year.	Died Jan. 27, 1865, at Nashville, Tenn.
h, Peter	....do....	44	Aug. 25, 1864	1 year.	Mustered out July 5, 1865, at Columbus, O., by order of War Department.
tt, Mathias	....do....	23	Aug. 13, 1864	1 year.	Mustered out with company June 26, 1865.
h, Benjamin	....do....	20	Aug. 18, 1864	1 year.	Mustered out with company June 26, 1865.
ns, William McD	....do....	24	Aug. 26, 1864	1 year.	Promoted to Principal Musician Oct. 10, 1864.
David H	....do....	18	Sept. 1, 1864	1 year.	Mustered out with company June 26, 1865.
William S	....do....	18	Aug. 17, 1864	1 year.	Mustered out with company June 26, 1865.
, Joseph	....do....	21	Sept. 11, 1864	1 year.	Mustered out with company June 26, 1865.
ger, Marion	....do....	19	Sept. 5, 1864	1 year.	Mustered out with company June 26, 1865.
ger, Newton J	....do....	19	Sept. 5, 1864	1 year.	Mustered out with company June 26, 1865.
ry, Amos H	....do....	18	Aug. 26, 1864	1 year.	Mustered out with company June 26, 1865.
ry, Henry F	....do....	18	Aug. 18, 1864	1 year.	Mustered out with company June 26, 1865.
ry, John P	..do.	20	Aug. 18, 1864	1 year.	Mustered out with company June 26, 1865.
, Henley J	..do.	24	Aug. 26, 1864	1 year.	Mustered out with company June 26, 1865.
y, Slater	..do.	30	Sept. 11, 1864	1 year.	Mustered out with company June 26, 1865.
de, Solomon	..do.	44	Aug. 26, 1864	1 year.	Mustered out May 15, 1865, at Nashville, Tenn., by order of War Department.
han, Micager	....do....	20	Aug. 13, 1864	1 year.	Mustered out with company June 26, 1865.
han, Montraville	....do....	25	Aug. 13, 1864	1 year.	Mustered out May 19, 1865, by order of War Department.
on, Andrew	....do....	20	Aug. 13, 1864	1 year.	Mustered out with company June 26, 1865.
on, Anthony	....do....	40	Aug. 18, 1864	1 year.	Mustered out with company June 26, 1865.
on, Henry	....do....	22	Aug. 13, 1864	1 year.	Mustered out with company June 26, 1865.
rty, Patrick	....do....	30	Aug. 26, 1864	1 year.	Mustered out with company June 26, 1865.
, William L	....do....	24	Aug. 13, 1864	1 year.	Mustered out with company June 26, 1865.
, William H.	....do....	22	Aug. 20, 1864	1 year.	Mustered out with company June 26, 1865.
, David	....do....	[illegible]	Aug. 13, 1864	1 year.	Mustered out with company June 26, 1865.

Names.	Rank.	Age.	Date of Entering the Service.	Period of Service.	Remarks.
Nance, Moses	Private.	38	Aug. 18, 1864	1 year.	Mustered out with company June 26, 1865.
Nance, Solomon	....do....	25	Aug. 18, 1864	1 year.	Mustered out with company June 26, 1865.
Nesbit, Alexander	....do....	30	Sept. 4, 1864	1 year.	Mustered out with company June 26, 1865.
Null, William H.	....do....	26	Aug. 20, 1864	1 year.	Mustered out with company June 26, 1865.
Paul, Joshua	....do....	25	Aug. 26, 1864	1 year.	Mustered out with company June 26, 1865.
Paul, Sardine	....do....	37	Aug. 26, 1864	1 year.	Mustered out with company June 26, 1865.
Paxton, Alfred	....do....	29	Aug. 18, 1864	1 year.	Mustered out with company June 26, 1865.
Peck, Alfred	....do....	29	Aug. 22, 1864	1 year.	Died Feb. 15, 1865, at Nashville, Tenn.
Pemberton, Elijah	....do....	24	Aug. 26, 1864	1 year.	Mustered out with company June 26, 1865.
Pemberton, Elisha	....do....	23	Aug. 21, 1864	1 year.	Died Feb. 14, 1865, at Nashville, Tenn.
Pemberton, Elliott	....do....	32	Aug. 26, 1864	1 year.	Mustered out with company June 26, 1865.
Pemberton, Jasper N.	....do....	18	Aug. 26, 1864	1 year.	Mustered out with company June 26, 1865.
Perkins, Andrew J.	....do....	34	Aug. 13, 1864	1 year.	Mustered out with company June 26, 1865.
Petry, Jacob	....do....	24	Aug. 26, 1864	1 year.	Died May 6, 1865, at Johnsonville, Tenn.
Petry, James	....do....	30	Aug. 10, 1864	1 year.	Mustered out with company June 26, 1865.
Petry, Marion	....do....	21	Aug. 13, 1864	1 year.	Died June 16, 1865, at Johnsonville, Tenn.
Petry, William T.	....do....	19	Aug. 18, 1864	1 year.	Mustered out with company June 26, 1865.
Pinkerman, James M.	....do....	23	Aug. 26, 1864	1 year.	Mustered out with company June 26, 1865.
Platt, Albert	....do....	20	Aug. 18, 1864	1 year.	Mustered out with company June 26, 1865.
Pratt, Andrew	....do....	25	Aug. 26, 1864	1 year.	Mustered out with company June 26, 1865.
Rice, James	....do....	32	Aug. 18, 1864	1 year.	Mustered out with company June 26, 1865.
Roach, James	....do....	32	Aug. 18, 1864	1 year.	Mustered out with company June 26, 1865.
Runyan, Adam	....do....	39	Aug. 26, 1864	1 year.	Mustered out with company June 26, 1865.
Short, Daniel	....do....	35	Aug. 13, 1864	1 year.	Mustered out with company June 26, 1865.
Short, James	....do....	40	Aug. 13, 1864	1 year.	Mustered out with company June 26, 1865.
Speers, Robinson	....do....	38	Aug. 13, 1864	1 year.	Mustered out with company June 26, 1865.
Speers, William	....do....	18	Aug. 13, 1864	1 year.	Mustered out with company June 26, 1865.
Suthers, James	....do....		Aug. 13, 1864	1 year.	Died Jan. 6, 1865, at Nashville, Tenn.
Taylor, Nathaniel	....do....	30	Aug. 26, 1864	1 year.	Died Feb. 9, 1865, at Nashville, Tenn.
Walls, Cyrus K.	....do....	25	Aug. 4, 1864	1 year.	Mustered out with company June 26, 1865.
Watson, James R.	....do....	21	Aug. 18, 1864	1 year.	Died Feb. 10, 1865, at Nashville, Tenn.
Wells, James	....do....	39	Aug. 13, 1864	1 year.	Mustered out with company June 26, 1865.
White, William B.	....do....	19	Aug. 26, 1864	1 year.	Mustered out with company June 26, 1865.

COMPANY F.

Mustered in Sept. 15, 1864, at Gallipolis, O., by George H. McLaughlin, Captain 2d Infantry, U. S. A. Mustered out June 26, 1865, at Nashville, Tenn., by John W. Chickering, Captain 88th Illinois V. I., and A. C. M. 2d Division, 4th A. C.

Names.	Rank.	Age.	Date of Entering the Service.	Period of Service.	Remarks.
Miles L. Blake	Captain.	23	Aug. 8, 1864	1 year.	Appointed Sept. 16, 1864; mustered out with company June 26, 1865.
James N. Hanna	1st Lieut.	27	July 30, 1864	1 year.	Appointed Sept. 16, 1864; promoted to Captain Co. B Nov. 26, 1864.
John N. Thomas	....do....	35	Aug. 13, 1864	1 year.	Appointed 2d Lieutenant Sept. 16, 1864; promoted to 1st Lieutenant Nov. 26, 1864; mustered out with company June 26, 1865.
Charles S. Edwards	2d Lieut.	40	Aug. 10, 1864	1 year.	Promoted from 1st Sergeant Co. A Dec. [illegible], 1864; mustered out with company June 26, 1865.
Asa R. O. Thomas	1st Sergt.	26	Aug. 13, 1864	1 year.	Promoted to 2d Lieutenant Co D Dec. 30, 1864.
Milton C. Keenan	....do....	21	Aug. 11, 1864	1 year.	Appointed Sergeant Sept 15, 1864; 1st Sergeant March 12, 1865; mustered out with company June 26, 1865.
John T. Higgins	Sergeant.	33	Sept. 5, 1864	1 year.	Appointed Sept. 15, 1864; mustered out with company June 26, 1865.
John C. McLean	....do....	27	Aug. 13, 1864	1 year.	Appointed Sept. 15, 1864; mustered out with company June 26, 1865.
Thomas W. Swan	....do....	41	Aug. 22, 1864	1 year.	Appointed Sept. 15, 1864; mustered out with company June 26, 1865.
John B. Burton	....do..	25	Aug. 13, 1864	1 year.	Appointed Corporal Sept. 15, 1864; 1st Sergeant Jan. 19, 1865; reduced to Sergeant March [illegible], 1865; mustered out with company June 26, 1865.
William F. Wymer	Corporal.	24	Aug. 13, 1864	1 year.	Appointed Sept. 15, 1864; died Nov. 26, 1864, at Nashville, Tenn.
Israel S. Sayre	....do....	37	Aug. 13, 1864	1 year.	Appointed Sept 15, 1864; died March 7, 1865, at Johnsonville, Tenn.
William Starkey	....do....	27	Aug. 13, 1864	1 year.	Appointed Sept. 15, 1864; mustered out with company June 26, 1865.
Uriah Payne	....do....	40	Aug. 20, 1864	1 year.	Appointed Sept. 15, 1864; mustered out with company June 26, 1865.
Amos A. Tope	....do....	36	Aug. 22, 1864	1 year.	Appointed Sept. 15, 1864; mustered out with company June 26, 1865.
Charles C. Keenan	....do....	24	Aug. 16, 1864	1 year.	Appointed Sept. 15, 1864; mustered out with company June 26, 1865.
James Shafer	....do....	32	Aug. 13, 1864	1 year.	Appointed Sept. 15, 1864; mustered out with company June 26, 1865.
Robert L. Massie	....do....	34	Sept. 2, 1864	1 year.	Appointed Feb. 12, 1865; mustered out with company June 26, 1865.

Names.	Rank.	Age.	Date of Entering the Service.	Period of Service.	Remarks.
Tucker, James	Private	44	Aug. 18, 1864	1 year.	Mustered out with company June 26, 1865.
Umpleby, Charles	...do...	22	Aug. 26, 1864	1 year.	Mustered out with company June 26, 1865.
Umpleby, Samuel L	...do...	[illegible]	Aug. 29, 1864	1 year.	Mustered out with company June 26, 1865.
Waugh, William	...do...	22	Aug. 19, 1864	1 year.	Mustered out with company June 26, 1865.
Wells, Zaccheus	...do...	32	Aug. 13, 1864	1 year.	Mustered out with company June 26, 1865.
West, Joseph C	...do...	40	Aug. 24, 1864	1 year.	Mustered out with company June 26, 1865.
Wilson, Quincy	...do...	35	Aug. 20, 1861	1 year.	Died Feb. 6, 1865, at Nashville, Tenn.
Wollam, Jacob	...do...	23	Aug. 24, 1864	1 year	Mustered out with company June 26, 1865.
Wollam, Raymond	...do...	25	Aug. 24, 1864	1 year.	Mustered out with company June 26, 1865.
Woods, George	...do...	41	Aug. 25, 1864	1 year.	Mustered out with company June 26, 1865.

COMPANY G.

Mustered in Sept. 18, 1864, at Gallipolis, O., by George H. McLaughlin, Captain 2d Infantry, U. S. A. Mustered out June 26, 1865, at Nashville, Tenn., by John W. Chickering, Captain 88th Illinois V. I., and A. C. M. 2d Division, 4th A. C.

Names.	Rank.	Age.	Date of Entering the Service.	Period of Service.	Remarks.
Charles Slavens	Captain.	22	Aug. 12, 1864	1 year.	Appointed Sept. 18, 1864; mustered out with company June 26, 1865.
John T. Brady	1st Lieut.	23	Aug. 11, 1864	1 year.	Appointed Sept. 18, 1864; mustered out with company June 26, 1865.
William T. Shades	2d Lieut.	20	July 26, 1864	1 year.	Appointed Sept. 18, 1864; mustered out with company June 26, 1865.
Louis E. Booth	1st Sergt.	21	Aug. 22, 1864	1 year.	Mustered out with company June 26, 1865.
Elias V. Samson	Sergeant.	20	Aug. 22, 1864	1 year.	Mustered out with company June 26, 1865.
John J. Baldwin	...do...	18	Aug. 1, 1864	1 year.	Mustered out with company June 26, 1865.
John W. Chamberlin	...do...	21	Aug. 22, 1864	1 year.	Mustered out with company June 26, 1865.
Benjamin F. Bennett	...do...	20	Aug. 10, 1864	1 year.	Mustered out with company June 26, 1865.
Isaac Donohoo	Corporal.	38	Aug. 9, 1864	1 year.	Mustered out with company June 26, 1865.
Israel J. Dewey	...do...	35	Aug. 26, 1864	1 year.	Mustered out with company June 26, 1865.
Jonathan Pyles	...do...	28	Aug. 23, 1864	1 year.	Mustered out with company June 26, 1865.
William J. Samson	...do...	33	Aug. 22, 1864	1 year.	Mustered out with company June 26, 1865.
August Nichtewitz	...do...	39	Aug. 15, 1864	1 year.	Mustered out with company June 26, 1865.
David Shoop	...do...	22	Aug. 22, 1864	1 year.	Mustered out with company June 26, 1865.
John M. Colvin	...do...	30	Aug. 1, 1864	1 year.	Appointed Jan. 20, 1865; mustered out with company June 26, 1865.
Andrew Powell	...do...	36	Aug. 21, 1864	1 year.	Appointed Jan. 20, 1865; mustered out with company June 26, 1865.
Benjamin F. Allen	Musician	18	Sept. 7, 1864	1 year	Mustered out with company June 26, 1865.
James Hoover	...do...	31	Aug. 30, 1864	1 year.	Appointed ——; mustered out with company June 26, 1865.
James Musgrave	Wagoner.	18	Aug. 26, 1864	1 year.	Mustered out with company June 26, 1865.
Balsiger, Christopher	Private	30	Aug. 22, 1864	1 year.	Died April 29, 1865, at Murfreesboro, Tenn.
Bennett, Lafayette	...do...	18	Aug. 20, 1864	1 year.	Mustered out with company June 26, 1865.
Bilyne, John M	...do...	32	Aug. 27, 1864	1 year.	Mustered out with company June 26, 1865.
Boyer, Charles H	...do...	39	Aug. 29, 1864	1 year.	Mustered out with company June 26, 1865.
Brewer, Elijah	...do...	39	Aug. 27, 1864	1 year.	Mustered out with company June 26, 1865.
Brown, James N	...do...	22	Aug. 22, 1864	1 year.	Mustered out with company June 26, 1865.
Burnett, William	...do...	44	Aug. 3, 1864	1 year.	Mustered out with company June 26, 1865.
Burnett, William M	...do...	18	Aug. 3, 1864	1 year.	Mustered out with company June 26, 1865.
Call, Charles	...do...	20	Aug. 31, 1864	1 year.	
Canter, Joseph	...do...	21	Aug. 15, 1864	1 year.	Mustered out with company June 26, 1865.
Carter, Daniel	...do...	35	Aug. 16, 1864	1 year.	Mustered out with company June 26, 1865.
Clayton, Willis S	...do...	29	Sept. 2, 1864	1 year.	Mustered out with company June 26, 1865.
Cline, Henry	...do...	24	Aug. 27, 1864	1 year.	Mustered out with company June 26, 1865.
Cox, Allen T	...do...	32	Aug. 18, 1864	1 year.	Mustered out with company June 26, 1865.
Dalrymple, Charles	...do...	18	Aug. 6, 1864	1 year.	Mustered out with company June 26, 1865.
Daniels, Samuel	...do...	21	Aug. 31, 1864	1 year.	Mustered out with company June 26, 1865.
Davis, William	...do...	28	Aug. 27, 1864	1 year.	Mustered out with company June 26, 1865.
Deamer, Lewis	...do...	27	Aug. 26, 1864	1 year.	Mustered out with company June 26, 1865.
Downey, John	...do...	30	Aug. 27, 1864	1 year.	Mustered out with company June 26, 1865.
Dunkle, Lawson	...do...	30	Aug. 15, 1864	1 year.	Mustered as Corporal; reduced Jan. 20, 1865; mustered out with company June 26, 1865.
Evans, James H	...do...	37	Aug. 21, 1864	1 year.	
Farley, David	...do...	26	Sept. 1, 1864	1 year.	Mustered as Musician; mustered out with company June 26, 1865.
Fife, Joseph	...do...	23	Aug. 22, 1864	1 year.	Mustered out with company June 26, 1865.
Fitch, Hiram	...do...	22	Aug. 22, 1864	1 year.	Mustered out with company June 26, 1865.
Franze, Henry	...do...	25	Aug. 27, 1864	1 year.	Mustered out with company June 26, 1865.
Friday, Frederick	...do...	18	Sept. 7, 1864	1 year.	Mustered out with company June 26, 1865.
Garey, Jesse	...do...	39	Sept. 3, 1864	1 year.	Mustered out with company June 26, 1865.
Glover, John	...do...	17	Aug. 27, 1864	1 year.	Mustered out with company June 26, 1865.
Hass, Abraham	...do...	25	Aug. 13, 1864	1 year.	Mustered out with company June 26, 1865.
Hawk, John F	...do...	31	Aug. 27, 1864	1 year.	Mustered out with company June 26, 1865.
Hunter, Henry J	...do...	21	Aug. 27, 1864	1 year.	Mustered out with company June 26, 1865.
Ish, George	...do...	18	Aug. 4, 1864	1 year.	Mustered out with company June 26, 1865.
Jackson, Stephen F	...do...	19	Aug. 23, 1864	1 year.	Mustered out with company June 26, 1865.
Jarvis, William V	...do...	24	Aug. 12, 1864	1 year.	Mustered out with company June 26, 1865.
Jaynes, George W	...do...	18	Aug. 30, 1864	1 year.	Mustered out with company June 26, 1865.

Names.	Rank.	Age.	Date of Entering the Service.	Period of Service.	
Joseph S. Foster	Sergeant.	21	Aug. 25, 1864	1 year.	Appointe Dec. [illegible] June [illegible]
James A. Stout	Corporal.	20	Aug. 17, 1864	1 year.	Appointe compan
George T. Goldsberry	....do....	30	Aug. 30, 1864	1 year.	Appointe compan
William Caskey	....do....	19	Aug. 27, 1864	1 year.	Appointe compan
Marion F. Crissman	....do....	22	Aug. 31, 1864	1 year.	Appointe compan
Samuel Thatcher	....do....	32	Aug. 18, 1864	1 year.	Appointe compan
James N. Vance	....do....	20	Aug. 25, 1864	1 year.	Appointe compan
Eli F. Rhodes	....do....	22	Sept. 5, 1864	1 year.	Appointe compan
William J. B. Downing	....do....	18	Sept. 6, 1864	1 year.	Appointe compan
Cary B. Bradley	Musician	16	Aug. 30, 1864	1 year.	Mustered
George W. Wheat	....do....	16	Sept. 13, 1864	1 year.	Mustered
Arnett, William	Private..	18	Sept. 5, 1864	1 year.	Mustered
Bayless, Daniel	....do....	37	Aug. 31, 1864	1 year.	Mustered
Bogue, Elias	....do....	44	Sept. 5, 1864	1 year.	Died Marc
Bradford, Charles H	....do....	29	Sept. 4, 1864	1 year.	Mustered
Burbage, Joseph W	....do....	22	Aug. 24, 1864	1 year.	Mustered
Burbage, Theodore C	....do....	18	Sept. 4, 1864	1 year.	Mustered
Calvert, Eli	....do....	20	Sept. 1, 1864	1 year.	Died Feb.
Cameron, William H	....do....	25	Sept. 13, 1864	1 year.	Died Jan.
Chambers, George	....do....	39	Aug. 15, 1864	1 year.	Mustered
Clark, Edward G	....do....	28	Aug. 31, 1864	1 year.	Mustered
Collings, James L	....do....	25	Sept. 10, 1864	1 year.	Died Feb.
Davis, Samuel T. S	....do....	28	Sept. 13, 1864	1 year.	Died Feb.
Destley, Nicholas	....do....	19	Aug. 18, 1864	1 year.	Mustered
Dixson, William W	....do....	22	Aug. 24, 1864	1 year.	Died Feb.
Downing, Isaac T	....do....	26	Sept. 6, 1864	1 year.	Mustered
Duffey, William C	....do....	24	Aug. 23, 1864	1 year.	Mustered
Dunlap, Albert M	....do....	22	Aug. 22, 1864	1 year.	Mustered
Edgington, Amos D	....do....	18	Aug. 23, 1864	1 year.	Mustered
Edgington, Azariah	....do....	32	Sept. 3, 1864	1 year.	Mustered
Edgington, Franklin	....do....	21	Sept. 3, 1864	1 year.	Mustered
Edgington, Thomas S	....do....	20	Aug. 20, 1864	1 year.	Mustered
Elliott, Franklin	....do....	18	Sept. 16, 1864	1 year.	Mustered
Elliott, John W	....do....	20	Sept. 5, 1864	1 year.	Mustered
Fenton, George	....do....	31	Aug. 31, 1864	1 year.	Mustered
Fenton, James	....do....	30	Aug. 31, 1864	1 year.	Mustered
Foster, Nathaniel G	....do....	18	Sept. 8, 1864	1 year.	Mustered
Foster, Thomas P	....do....	21	Aug. 30, 1864	1 year.	Mustered
Freeland, George	....do....	30	Aug. 31, 1864	1 year.	Mustered
Graham, William B	....do....	33	Aug. 25, 1864	1 year.	Mustered by order
Harrison, George W	....do....	43	Sept. 5, 1864	1 year.	Mustered
Harsha, Walter	....do....	41	Aug. 31, 1864	1 year.	Mustered
Howland, John L	....do....	20	Sept. 3, 1864	1 year.	Mustered
Hughes, John W	....do....	20	Sept. 5, 1864	1 year.	Died Feb.
Hurd, John W	....do....	30	Sept. 4, 1864	1 year.	Mustered
Keach, Joseph M	....do....	21	Aug. 24, 1864	1 year.	Mustered
Kirk, David A	....do....	22	Aug. 31, 1864	1 year.	Mustered compan
Kirker, John H	....do....	30	Sept. 5, 1864	1 year.	Mustered
Lawell, John W	....do....	19	Aug. 31, 1864	1 year.	Promoted
Leach, James A	....do....	22	Aug. 29, 1864	1 year.	Mustered
Leedom, Alexander Mc	....do....	20	Aug. 30, 1864	1 year.	Mustered
McClure, James A	....do....	18	Aug. 22, 1864	1 year.	Mustered
McCutchen, David	....do....	23	Aug. 26, 1864	1 year.	Mustered
McCutchen, James	....do....	31	Aug. 26, 1864	1 year.	Mustered
McLean, Samuel W. K	....do....	28	Sept. 8, 1864	1 year.	Died Marc
McNown, John J	....do....	19	Sept. 13, 1864	1 year.	Mustered
McNulty, Asahel B	....do....	30	Aug. 30, 1864	1 year.	Mustered
Mahaffey, James H	....do....	44	Aug. 29, 1864	1 year.	Discharge
Morehouse, James S	....do....	31	Sept. 3, 1864	1 year.	Mustered
Morris, Francis M	....do....	25	Sept. 5, 1864	1 year.	Mustered
Mowrar, Francis M	....do....	20	Aug. 31, 1864	1 year.	Mustered
Mulvey, John	....do....	35	Sept. 6, 1864	1 year.	Mustered
Pence, George	....do....	21	Aug. 30, 1864	1 year.	Mustered War Dep
Pence, Jacob	....do....	24	Sept. 4, 1864	1 year.	Mustered
Pence, Peter	....do....	23	Sept. 4, 1864	1 year.	Mustered
Perdon, Jason	....do....	19	Aug. 20, 1864	1 year.	Mustered
Perkins, John	....do....	21	Aug. 4, 1864	1 year.	Mustered
Reid, Leander	....do....	20	Aug. 20, 1864	1 year.	Mustered
Reynolds, Henry J	....do....	21	Aug. 31, 1864	1 year.	Mustered
Riggs, Noah	....do....	24	Aug. 19, 1864	1 year.	Mustered
Robinson, Robert H	....do....	24	Aug. 30, 1864	1 year.	Mustered
Roush, Allen	....do....	21	Aug. 30, 1864	1 year.	Mustered
Russell, John M	....do....	43	Aug. 30, 1864	1 year.	Died Feb.

Names.	Rank.	Age.	Date of Entering the Service.	Period of Service.	Remarks.
[illegible], Samuel	Private..	36	Aug. 19, 1864	1 year.	Mustered out May 19, 1865, at Nashville, Tenn., by order of War Department.
[illegible], Duncan G	....do....	41	Sept. 3, 1864	1 year.	Died July 1, 1865, at Nashville, Tenn.
[illegible], John	....do....	26	Sept. 3, 1864	1 year.	Died May 20, 1865, at Ash Ridge, O.
[illegible], Martin	....do....	29	Sept. 3, 1864	1 year.	Mustered out with company June 26, 1865.
[illegible], Charles	....do....	18	Aug. 31, 1864	1 year.	Mustered out with company June 26, 1865.
[illegible], George L.	....do....	25	Aug. 30, 1864	1 year.	Mustered out with company June 26, 1865.
[illegible], John P.	....do....	18	Aug. 20, 1864	1 year.	Mustered out with company June 26, 1865.
Swearingen, James	....do....	21	Sept. 5, 1864	1 year.	Mustered out with company June 26, 1865.
Swearingen, Nelson	....do....	21	Aug. 31, 1864	1 year.	Mustered out with company June 26, 1865.
[illegible], Sylvester	....do....	28	Aug. 29, 1864	1 year.	Mustered out with company June 26, 1865.
[illegible], Nathaniel	....do....	25	Sept. 6, 1864	1 year.	Mustered out May 20, 1865, at Nashville, Tenn., by order of War Department.
[illegible], Elijah	....do....	23	Sept. 5, 1864	1 year.	Mustered out with company June 26, 1865.
W[illegible], William F.	....do....	18	Aug. 22, 1864	1 year.	Absent, sick at Jeffersonville, Ind., since June 3, 1865. No further record found.
West, Napoleon B.	....do....	18	Aug. 31, 1864	1 year.	Mustered out with company June 26, 1865.
Williamson, Samuel H.	....do....	25	Sept. 13, 1864	1 year.	Mustered out with company June 26, 1865.
Wilson, William M.	....do....	42	Aug. 18, 1864	1 year.	Mustered out with company June 26, 1865.
Woodruff, John K.	....do....	18	Sept. 5, 1864	1 year.	Mustered out with company June 26, 1865.
Young, James A.	....do....	20	Aug. 20, 1864	1 year.	Appointed Corporal Sept. 18, 1864; reduced Sept. 24, 1864, at his own request; mustered out with company June 26, 1865.
Young, James D.	....do....	20	Aug. 31, 1864	1 year.	Mustered out with company June 26, 1865.
Young, Samuel P.	....do....	26	Aug. 31, 1864	1 year.	Mustered out with company June 26, 1865.
Young, William M.	....do....	25	Sept. 1, 1864	1 year.	Appointed Corporal Sept. 18, 1864; reduced Sept. 30, 1864, at his own request; mustered out with company June 26, 1865.

COMPANY I.

Mustered in Sept. 16, 1864, at Gallipolis, O., By George H. McLaughlin, Captain 2d Infantry, U. S. A. Mustered out June 26, 1865, at Nashville, Tenn., by John W. Chickering, Captain 88th Illinois V. I., and A. C. M. 2d Division, 4th A. C.

Names.	Rank.	Age.	Date of Entering the Service.	Period of Service.	Remarks.
Samuel Walker	Captain.	45	Aug. 5, 1864	1 year.	Appointed Sept. 18, 1864; mustered out with company June 26, 1865.
James M. Edmonston	1st Lieut.	22	July 27, 1864	1 year.	Appointed Sept. 17, 1864; resigned Nov. 18, 1864.
John H. Parker	....do....	30	Aug. 16, 1864	1 year.	Promoted from 2d Lieutenant Co. K Nov. 26, 1864; mustered out with company June 26, 1865.
Hiram E. Grove	2d Lieut.	21	Aug. 23, 1864	1 year.	Appointed Sept. 17, 1864; mustered out with company June 26, 1865.
Martin Swick	1st Sergt.	36	Aug. 8, 1864	1 year.	Died Feb. 4, 1865, at Nashville, Tenn.
Benjamin W. Simon	....do....	18	Aug. 20, 1864	1 year.	Appointed Sergeant Sept. 16, 1864; 1st Sergeant April 16, 1865; mustered out with company June 26, 1865.
Israel Williams	Sergeant.	36	Aug. 28, 1864	1 year.	Appointed Sept. 16, 1864; mustered out with company June 26, 1865.
William B. Cherington	....do....	18	Aug. 24, 1864	1 year.	Appointed Sept. 16, 1864; mustered out with company June 26, 1865.
Isaac Walker	....do....	37	Sept. 12, 1864	1 year.	Appointed Sept. 16, 1864; mustered out with company June 26, 1865.
Richard D. Edwards	....do....	28	Sept. 13, 1864	1 year.	Appointed Corporal Sept. 16, 1864; 1st Sergeant Feb. 5, 1865; reduced to Sergeant April 16, 1865; mustered out with company June 26, 1865.
Ira E. Cherington	Corporal.	18	Aug. 31, 1864	1 year.	Appointed Sept. 16, 1864; mustered out with company June 26, 1865.
[illegible] E. Walker	....do....	44	Aug. 10, 1864	1 year.	Appointed Sept. 16, 1864; mustered out with company June 26, 1865.
Isaac Hill	....do....	30	Aug. 10, 1864	1 year.	Appointed Sept. 16, 1864; mustered out with company June 26, 1865.
George C. Hartsook	....do....	22	Aug. 5, 1864	1 year.	Appointed Sept. 16, 1864; mustered out with company June 26, 1865.
John W. Fillmore	....do....	19	Sept. 4, 1864	1 year.	Appointed Sept. 16, 1864; mustered out with company June 26, 1865.
[illegible] L. [illegible]	....do....	28	Aug. 20, 1864	1 year.	Appointed Nov. 17, 1864; mustered out with company June 26, 1865.
[illegible] Cherington	....do....	29	Sept. 4, 1864	1 year.	Appointed Nov. 17, 1864; mustered out with company June 26, 1865.
Charles [illegible]	....do....	21	Aug. 19, 1864	1 year.	Appointed Feb. 13, 1865; mustered out with company June 26, 1865.
Richard Hartsook	Musician	18	Sept. 7, 1864	1 year.	Appointed ——; mustered out with company June 26, 1865.
Charles Wilson	....do....	25	Sept. 5, 1864	1 year.	Appointed ——; mustered out with company June 26, 1865.
Addis, Barton D.	Private..	18	Aug. 9, 1864	1 year.	Died March 7, 1865, at Nashville, Tenn.
Addis, Thomas B.	....do....	23	Aug. 29, 1864	1 year.	Mustered out with company June 26, 1865.

Names.	Rank.	Age.	Date of Entering the Service.	Period of Service.	Remarks.
Adkins, Albert	Private	18	Sept. 5, 1864	1 year.	Mustered out with company June 26, 1865.
Angle, Zachariah	...do...	18	Aug. 29, 1864	1 year.	Mustered out with company June 26, 1865.
Ballard, Charles H	...do...	18	Aug. 29, 1864	1 year.	Mustered out with company June 26, 1865.
Barrett, Isaac	...do...	42	Sept. 4, 1864	1 year.	Mustered out with company June 26, 1865.
Beazer, Christopher	...do...	18	Sept. 10, 1864	1 year.	Mustered as Musician; mustered out with company June 26, 1865.
Cade, Thomas	...do...	23	Aug. 29, 1864	1 year.	Mustered out with company June 26, 1865.
Calhoon, William K	...do...	24	Aug. 8, 1864	1 year.	Mustered out with company June 26, 1865.
Carter, James	...do...	36	July 29, 1864	1 year.	Mustered as Wagoner; mustered out with company June 26, 1865.
Colwell, Jacob	...do...	27	Sept. 4, 1864	1 year.	Mustered out with company June 26, 1865.
Colwell, William R	...do...	24	Aug. 13, 1864	1 year.	Mustered out with company June 26, 1865.
Corn, George W	...do...	38	Sept. 2, 1864	1 year.	Died Feb. 5, 1865, at Nashville, Tenn.
Cotrell, John	...do...	18	Sept. 12, 1864	1 year.	Mustered out with company June 26, 1865.
Daniels, Abraham H	...do...	37	Sept. 1, 1864	1 year.	Mustered out with company June 26, 1865.
Daniels, Madison	...do...	25	Sept. 1, 1864	1 year.	Mustered out with company June 26, 1865.
Darst, Charles	...do...	36	Aug. 4, 1864	1 year.	Mustered out with company June 26, 1865.
Deckard, Campbell	...do...	22	Aug. 5, 1864	1 year.	Died Jan. 21, 1865, at Nashville, Tenn.
Denney, Isariah	...do...	41	Aug. 16, 1864	1 year.	Mustered out with company June 26, 1865.
Denney, Samuel	...do...	30	Aug. 28, 1864	1 year.	Mustered out with company June 26, 1865.
Detlante, George	...do...	18	Aug. 10, 1864	1 year.	Mustered out with company June 26, 1865.
Ewing, George B	...do...	35	Aug. 20, 1864	1 year.	Died Jan. 12, 1865, at Nashville, Tenn.
Fisher, George C	...do...	18	Aug. 25, 1864	1 year.	Mustered out with company June 26, 1865.
George, Benjamin P	...do...	31	Aug. 10, 1864	1 year.	Mustered out with company June 26, 1865.
George, John P	...do...	22	Aug. 16, 1864	1 year.	Mustered out with company June 26, 1865.
George, Richard S	...do...	24	Aug. 10, 1864	1 year.	Mustered out with company June 26, 1865.
Gleason, Hiram	...do...	19	Aug. 13, 1864	1 year.	Died Dec. 7, 1864, near Nashville, Tenn.
Gleason, Riel	...do...	32	Aug. 9, 1864	1 year.	Mustered out with company June 26, 1865.
Gould, Andrew	...do...	40	Sept. 1, 1864	1 year.	Mustered out with company June 26, 1865.
Gould, Joseph	...do...	18	Sept. 4, 1864	1 year.	Mustered out with company June 26, 1865.
Grady, James H	...do...	18	Aug. 15, 1864	1 year.	Mustered out with company June 26, 1865.
Grover, John W	...do...	21	Nov. 12, 1864	1 year.	Transferred to Co. C, 18th O. V. I., July [illegible]
Grover, Levi	...do...	38	Aug. 11, 1864	1 year.	Mustered out with company June 26, 1865.
Hartsook, Joseph	...do...	33	Aug. 5, 1864	1 year.	Mustered out with company June 26, 1865.
Heckar, Wilders J	...do...	20	Aug. 14, 1864	1 year.	Mustered out with company June 26, 1865.
Holcomb, Anselm T	...do...	26	Aug. 5, 1864	1 year.	Mustered out with company June 26, 1865.
Huffman, William	...do...	18	Sept. 5, 1864	1 year.	Mustered out with company June 26, 1865.
Hughes, Calvin	...do...	34	Aug. 12, 1864	1 year.	Mustered out with company June 26, 1865.
Hull, John	...do...	22	Aug. 5, 1864	1 year.	Mustered out with company June 26, 1865.
Kimball, Solomon	...do...	18	Aug. 27, 1864	1 year.	Mustered out with company June 26, 1865.
Kingery, Peter	...do...	31	Aug. 29, 1864	1 year.	Mustered out with company June 26, 1865.
Lambert, Lafayette	...do...	35	Aug. 29, 1864	1 year.	Transferred to Co. I, 17th Regiment, Veteran Reserve Corps, March 24, 1865, from which mustered out June 30, 1865, at Indianapolis, Ind., by order of War Department.
Lanham, Jesse	...do...	44	Sept. 12, 1864	1 year.	Mustered out with company June 26, 1865.
Lewis, David T	...do...	37	Aug. 10, 1864	1 year.	Mustered out with company June 26, 1865.
Long, Charles	...do...	18	Aug. 15, 1864	1 year.	Mustered out with company June 26, 1865.
McClain, William	...do...	21	Sept. 12, 1864	1 year.	Transferred to Co. C, 18th O. V. I., July [illegible]
McCullough, John B	...do...	25	Aug. 11, 1864	1 year.	Mustered out with company June 26, 1865.
McQuiston, William	...do...	22	Aug. 11, 1864	1 year.	Mustered out with company June 26, 1865.
Massie, Alexander	...do...	22	Aug. 8, 1864	1 year.	Mustered out with company June 26, 1865.
Miller, Richard S. A. B.	...do...	35	Aug. 11, 1864	1 year.	Discharged June 2, 1865, for wounds received in action.
Moler, Thomas	...do...	26	Sept. 1, 1864	1 year.	Appointed Corporal Sept. 16, 1864; reduced Nov. 16, 1864; mustered out with company June 26, 1865.
Moreland, John H	...do...	20	Aug. 11, 1864	1 year.	Mustered out with company June 26, 1865.
Mossman, John	...do...	25	Sept. 4, 1864	1 year.	Mustered out with company June 26, 1865.
Murray, Robert	...do...	30	Aug. 27, 1864	1 year.	Mustered out with company June 26, 1865.
Needham, Alfred	...do...	26	Aug. 13, 1864	1 year.	Mustered out with company June 26, 1865.
Neighborgall, John L	...do...	20	Sept. 12, 1864	1 year.	Died Dec. 15, 1864, at Nashville, Tenn.
Oiler, John	...do...	18	Aug. 27, 1864	1 year.	Mustered out with company June 26, 1865.
Peden, Thomas E	...do...	31	Aug. 28, 1864	1 year.	Mustered out with company June 26, 1865.
Poteet, William	...do...	20	Sept. 1, 1864	1 year.	Mustered out with company June 26, 1865.
Ralston, David	...do...	44	Aug. 27, 1864	1 year.	Mustered out with company June 26, 1865.
Reeves, Thomas	...do...	21	Aug. 29, 1864	1 year.	Mustered out with company June 26, 1865.
Rice, Richard N	...do...	35	Sept. 1, 1864	1 year.	Mustered out with company June 26, 1865.
Rowe, Stephen	...do...	20	Aug. 28, 1864	1 year.	Mustered out with company June 26, 1865.
Rowland, Enoch	...do...	39	Sept. 4, 1864	1 year.	Mustered out with company June 26, 1865.
Russell, Alvin	...do...	37	Sept. 4, 1864	1 year.	Mustered out to date June 26, 1865, by order of War Department.
Russell, Andrew J	...do...	23	Aug. 27, 1864	1 year.	Died March 19, 1865, at Nashville, Tenn.
Russell, Harvey H	...do...	22	Sept. 2, 1864	1 year.	Mustered out with company June 26, 1865.
Russell, Isaac	...do...	35	Sept. 15, 1864	1 year.	Mustered out with company June 26, 1865.
Russell, Sylvester	...do...	27	Sept. 3, 1864	1 year.	Mustered out with company June 26, 1865.
Shields, William	...do...	18	Sept. 2, 1864	1 year.	Mustered out with company June 26, 1865.
Slusher, Lafayette	...do...	21	Aug. 16, 1864	1 year.	Mustered out with company June 26, 1865.
Smith, George W (1st)	...do...	18	Aug. 12, 1864	1 year.	Mustered out with company June 26, 1865.
Smith, George W (2d)	...do...	18	Aug. 12, 1864	1 year.	Mustered out with company June 26, 1865.
Smith, Joseph	...do...	18	Aug. 12, 1864	1 year.	Mustered out with company June 26, 1865.
Smith, Thomas V	...do...	23	Aug. 12, 1864	1 year.	Appointed Corporal Sept. 16, 1864; reduced Nov. 16, 1864; mustered out with company June 26, 1865.
Swick, John	...do...	21	Aug. 11, 1864	1 year.	Died Jan. 30, 1865, at Nashville, Tenn.

Names.	Rank.	Age.	Date of Entering the Service.	Period of Enlistment.	
Handley, Samuel B.	Private.	26	Aug. 19, 1864	1 year.	Died
Hanshaw, George W	...do...	24	Aug. 25, 1864	1 year.	Died
Harrison, Greenville	...do...	25	Aug. 17, 1864	1 year.	Died
Harrison, Lewis	...do...	33	Aug. 17, 1864	1 year.	Mustered
Herron, Henderson	...do...	43	Aug. 9, 1864	1 year.	Mustered
Higgins, Thomas	...do...	19	Aug. 29, 1864	1 year.	Mustered
Hisel, Jonathan	...do...	30	Aug. 19, 1864	1 year.	Mustered
Howard, David	...do...	33	Aug. 25, 1864	1 year.	Mustered out
Hudson, John	...do...	18	Aug. 17, 1864	1 year.	Mustered out wit
Hunt, Andrew	...do...	21	Aug. 27, 1864	1 year.	Mustered out
Hunt, Hanley	...do...	26	Aug. 22, 1864	1 year.	Mustered out
Hunt, William	...do...	19	Aug. 18, 1864	1 year.	Mustered out
James, David J	...do...	24	Sept. 17, 1864	1 year.	Mustered out
Jarvis, John E	...do...	25	Aug. 25, 1864	1 year.	Mustered out
Jenkins, Henry	...do...	27	Aug. 18, 1864	1 year.	Mustered out
Justice, Amos	...do...	21	Aug. 19, 1864	1 year.	Mustered out
Logan, Meredith C	...do...	36	Aug. 24, 1864	1 year.	Mustered out
Lowe, William H	...do...	18	Aug 29, 1864	1 year.	Mustered out
McDaniel, John L.	...do...	20	Sept. 8, 1864	1 year.	Mustered out
McDowell, Henderson	...do...	27	Aug. 18, 1864	1 year.	Mustered out
McLellon, James	...do...	20	Aug. 18, 1864	1 year.	Mustered out
McNight, Daniel	...do...	26	Aug. 18, 1864	1 year.	Mustered out wit
Mackley, Morrison	...do...	31	Aug. 20, 1864	1 year.	Mustered out wit
Miller, George	...do...	22	Aug. 18, 1864	1 year.	Mustered out wit
Miller, Henry	...do...	28	Aug. 18, 1864	1 year.	Mustered out wit
Miller, Thomas	...do...	25	Aug. 18, 1864	1 year.	Mustered out wit
Miller, Walter	...do...	28	Aug. 18, 1864	1 year.	Mustered out wit
O'Keefe, John	...do...	24	Aug. 24, 1864	1 year.	Transferred to Co
Price, William	...do...	41	Aug. 24, 1864	1 year.	Mustered out wit
Pyle, Henry H	...do...	39	Aug. 13, 1864	1 year.	Mustered out wit
Ramsey, William E.	...do...	18	Aug. 13, 1864	1 year.	Died March 31, 18
Rice, Thomas J	...do...	28	Aug. 18, 1864	1 year.	Mustered out wit
Richards, John	...do...	18	Aug. 20, 1864	1 year.	Mustered out wit
Rockford, William	...do...	37	Oct. 17, 1864	1 year.	Transferred to Co
Scott, David	...do...	43	Aug. [illegible]0, 1864	1 year.	Mustered out wit
Selix, Joseph	...do...	31	Sept. 15, 1864	1 year.	Mustered out wit
Shaffer, David	...do...	41	Aug. 24, 1864	1 year.	Mustered out wit
Shuff, James	...do...	21	Aug. 18, 1864	1 year.	Died Jan. 17, 1865.
Sipher, James W	...do...	20	Aug. 22, 1864	1 year.	Died Jan. 18, 1865.
Sisson, John	...do...	18	Aug. 19, 1864	1 year.	Mustered out wit
Slavens, Henry	...do...	26	Aug. 16, 1864	1 year.	Mustered out wit
Slavens, John	...do...	32	Aug. 26, 1864	1 year.	Mustered out wit
Slimp, William	...do...	24	Aug. 18, 1864	1 year.	Mustered out wit
Smith, William	...do...	22	Aug. 18, 1864	1 year.	Mustered out wit
Spencer, Thomas	...do...	21	Aug. 6, 1864	1 year.	Died March 27, 18
Stewart, Absalom N	...do...	33	Sept. 6, 1864	1 year.	Mustered out wit
Tasker, John	...do...	31	Aug. 26, 1864	1 year.	Mustered out wit
Toland, John	...do...	37	Sept. 1, 1864	1 year.	Mustered out wit
Trist, Robert	...do...	39	Aug. 31, 1864	1 year.	Mustered out wit
Vermillion, Green	...do...	38	Aug. 31, 1864	1 year.	Mustered out Ju by order of War
Vermillion, Jesse	...do...	35	Aug. 31, 1864	1 year.	Absent, on sick f No further reco
Ward, Jacob	...do...	30	Aug. 23, 1864	1 year.	Mustered out wit
Ward, Robert	...do...	30	Aug. 23, 1864	1 year.	Mustered out wit
Williams, Ballard P.	...do...	34	Aug. 15, 1864	1 year.	Died Feb. 28, 1865.
Wiseman, Abner	...do...	38	Aug. 25, 1864	1 year.	Mustered out wit
Woods, Jack	...do...	33	Aug. 29, 1864	1 year.	Mustered out wit
York, Glacus	...do...	20	Aug. 9, 1864	1 year.	Mustered out wit

UNASSIGNED RECRUITS.

NOTE.—The following list of recruits is found on muster and descriptive rol not borne on any of the company rolls of the regiment:

Names.	Rank.	Age.	Date of Entering the Service.	Period of Enlistment.	
Arnout, George	Private.	19	Sept. 20, 1864	1 year.	
Barbee, Isadore L.	...do...	18	Sept. 16, 1864	1 year.	
Barker, Elacha	...do...	24	Sept. 20, 1864	1 year.	
Barry, William	...do...	22	Sept. 19, 1864	1 year.	
Bowman, John	...do...	25	Sept. 27, 1864	1 year.	
Breen, Hugh	...do...	38	Sept. 14, 1864	1 year.	Died Nov. 7, 1864.
Brown, William L.	...do...	26	Sept. 19, 1864	1 year.	
Burke, James	...do...	31	Sept. 6, 1864	1 year.	
Craig, Robert	...do...	22	Sept. 19, 1864	1 year.	
Davis, John	...do...	28	Sept. 14, 1864	1 year.	
Davis, William	...do...	26	Sept. 16, 1864	1 year.	
Fisher, August	...do...	34	Sept. 27, 1864	1 year.	
Foster, Charles	...do...	22	Sept. 12, 1864	1 year.	
Green, Matthew M.	...do...	28	Sept. 5, 1864	1 year.	
Golden, George W	...do...	24	Sept. 15, 1864	1 year.	

Names.	Rank.	Age.	Date of Entering the Service.	Period of Service.	Remarks.
Half, John A	Private	28	Sept. 29, 1864	1 year.	
Hartman, John	do	20	Sept. 28, 1864	1 year.	
Hase, Michael	do	18	Sept. 14, 1864	1 year.	
Henry, James	do	23	Sept. 16, 1864	1 year.	
Herron, Alonzo	do	18	Sept. 21, 1864	1 year.	
Heshian, Patrick	do	22	Sept. 15, 1864	1 year.	
Hill, William M	do	21	Sept. 6, 1864	1 year.	
Ivens, James M	do	43	Sept. 12, 1864	1 year.	
James, John	do	42	Sept. 24, 1864	1 year.	
Johnson, William D	do	22	Sept. 14, 1864	1 year.	
Jones, Nathaniel L	do	27	Sept. 28, 1864	1 year.	
Jordan, John B	do	25	Sept. 30, 1864	1 year.	
Kaufman, David K	do	19	Sept. 13, 1864	1 year.	
King, Charles	do	26	Sept. 26, 1864	1 year.	
King, James	do	25	Sept. 20, 1864	1 year.	
Lagrange, Amma D	do	25	Sept. 16, 1864	1 year.	
Lewis, Franklin	do	25	Sept. 15, 1864	1 year.	
Lyon, William	do	18	Sept. 8, 1864	1 year.	
McDevitt, Frank	do	19	Sept. 12, 1864	1 year.	
McMahon, John	do	29	Sept. 30, 1864	1 year.	
Malone, Jerry	do	18	Sept. 20, 1864	1 year.	
Martin, William	do	27	Sept. 28, 1864	1 year.	
Morrison, William T	do	26	Sept. 12, 1864	1 year.	
Moss, Andrew	do	27	Sept. 13, 1864	1 year.	
Murray, William F	do	18	Sept. 13, 1864	1 year.	Discharged Dec. 3, 1864, at Camp Dennison, O., on Surgeon's certificate of disability.
Musgrave, Andrew	do	25	Sept. 22, 1864	1 year.	
Nebaeer, John	do	18	Sept. 13, 1864	1 year.	Discharged Dec. 3, 1864, at Camp Dennison, O., on Surgeon's certificate of disability.
O'Harron, John	do	32	Sept. 21, 1864	1 year.	
Olson, John	do	32	Sept. 21, 1864	1 year.	
Pinnow, Robert	do	28	Sept. 20, 1864	1 year.	
Pierce, Richard	do	26	Sept. 16, 1864	1 year.	
Plumber, Thomas	do	43	Sept. 13, 1864	1 year.	
Potts, Noah	do	31	Sept. 21, 1864	1 year.	
Ray, John	do	18	Sept. 23, 1864	1 year.	
Reeves, John	do	30	Sept. 13, 1864	1 year.	
Robinson, Horace	do	24	Sept. 21, 1864	1 year.	Discharged Dec. 3, 1864, at Camp Dennison, O., on Surgeon's certificate of disability.
Serth, Joseph	do	18	Sept. 12, 1864	1 year.	
Stewart, George	do	25	Sept. 20, 1864	1 year.	
Sullivan, James	do	25	Sept. 23, 1864	1 year.	
Tieman, Edward P	do	21	Sept. 10, 1864	1 year.	
Turner, John	do	30	Sept. 20, 1864	1 year.	
Whitesides, Charles	do	21	Sept. 19, 1864	1 year.	
Winderstine, Christian	do	22	Sept. 20, 1864	1 year.	

174th Regiment Ohio Volunteer Infantry.

ONE YEAR'S SERVICE.

THIS Regiment was organized at Camp Chase, O., from August 18 to September 21, 1864, to serve one year. It was ordered to proceed to Nashville, Tenn., and to report to Gen. W. T. Sherman. The Regiment reached Nashville Sept. 26, and was immediately ordered to proceed to Murfreesboro. It remained at Murfreesboro until the 27th of October, when it was ordered to report to the commanding officer at Decatur, Ala. It was then moved to the mouth of Elk River, leaving, on the way, four companies as a garrison for Athens, Ala. The Regiment soon returned to Decatur, where it remained until the 26th of November, when the town was evacuated. It then returned to Murfreesboro, where it remained during the siege (Dec. 4), and participated in the battle of Overall's Creek. On the 7th of December the Regiment was engaged in the battle of the Cedars. On the 17th of January it moved down the Tennessee and up the Ohio River to Cincinnati. It was then ordered to Washington City, which place it reached on the 29th of January, 1865. The Regiment remained in camp at Washington City until the 21st of February, when it started for North Carolina, reaching Fort Fisher on the 23d. It marched to Morehead City, reaching there on the 24th, and Newbern on the 25th. It took part in the battle of Wise's Fork, at Kinston, N. C.

Under the order mustering out volunteers whose term of service expired previous to the 1st of October, the One Hundred and Seventy-Fourth was mustered out June 28, 1865.

COMPANY A.

Mustered in August 18, 1864, at Camp Chase, O., by W. P. Richardson,
June 28, 1865, at Charlotte, N. C., by E. A. Folsom, Cap
Department of North Carolina.

Names.	Rank.	Age.	Date of Entering the Service.	Period of Service.	
William G. Beatty	Captain.	25	Aug. 16, 1864	1 year.	Promoted
Henry Rigby	....do....	42	Aug. 16, 1864	1 year.	Promoted discha
John B. White	1st Lieut.	25	July 27, 1864	1 year.	Mustered ant Au 1864; d
William F. Wallace	2d Lieut.	27	July 25, 1864	1 year.	Mustered Aug. 1 Dec. 3 June 2
Noah A. Stewart	1st Sergt.	28	Aug. 8, 1864	1 year.	Mustered 11, 1864 tered
James M. Watson	Sergeant.	23	July 25, 1864	1 year.	Mustered
Clayton N. Willits	....do....	19	July 25, 1864	1 year.	Mustered
Cicero H. Breniser	....do....	21	Aug. 3, 1864	1 year.	Appointe muster
Lewis L. Barge	....do....	21	July 27, 1864	1 year.	Appointe tered o
Theodore Purvis	Corporal.	19	July 25, 1864	1 year.	Mustered
Marvin Burt	....do....	18	July 25, 1864	1 year.	Mustered
Samuel L. Milligan	....do....	19	July 25, 1864	1 year.	Died Ma
John P. Demuth	....do....	18	July 26, 1864	1 year.	Died Feb
Benjamin Everett	....do....	27	July 26, 1864	1 year.	Mustered
Samuel R. Cratty	....do....	23	Aug. 2, 1864	1 year.	Appoint compa
Isaac Doty	....do....	20	Aug. 17, 1864	1 year.	Appointe compa
William Morey	....do....	21	July 28, 1864	1 year.	Appointe compa
Marcellus Edgell	....do....	18	Sept. 8, 1864	1 year.	Appointe compa
Thomas Z. Pierce	....do....	20	July 25, 1864	1 year.	Appointe compa
Asher E. Campbell	Musician	44	Sept. 1, 1864	1 year.	Mustered
Davis McCreary	....do....	19	Aug. 17, 1864	1 year.	Promoted
Aldrich, Lafayette	Private..	20	Aug. 9, 1864	1 year.	Died Jan.
Anderson, Albert	....do....	18	Aug. 10, 1864	1 year.	Mustered
Aurand, Balera J	....do....	25	Aug. 1, 1864	1 year.	Promoted
Bendle, Lewis W	....do....	18	July 25, 1864	1 year.	Mustered
Bennett, Isaac M	....do....	18	July 28, 1864	1 year.	Mustered by orde
Beven, James	....do....	24	Aug. 15, 1864	1 year.	
Bitzer, Christian	....do....	30	July 28, 1864	1 year.	Mustered
Blue, David S	....do....	18	July 26, 1864	1 year.	Mustered
Breniser, William H	....do....	19	July 26, 1864	1 year.	Mustered
Brown, Eben	....do....	27	July 28, 1864	1 year.	Appointe Oct. 11, June 2
Brown, Gilbert M	....do...	18	July 28, 1864	1 year.	Mustered
Brown, William A	....do....	24	July 30, 1864	1 year.	Mustered
Buck, Wesley	....do....	21	Feb. 28, 1865	1 year.	Transfer 1865.
Bunker, Elwood	....do...	19	July 25, 1864	1 year.	Mustered
Casey, John B	....do....	32	July 25, 1864	1 year.	Mustered
Clancey, Charles L	....do....	18	Aug. 1, 1864	1 year.	Mustered
Clark, William C. P	....do....	18	July 31, 1864	1 year.	Mustered D. C., b
Core, Andrew	....do....	19	July 26, 1864	1 year.	Mustered by ord
Creiglow, Samuel	....do....	19	Aug. 3, 1864	1 year.	Mustered
Dipert, William W	....do....	26	Aug. 8, 1864	1 year.	Mustered
Dixon, Lincoln B	....do....	18	July 26, 1864	1 year.	Mustered
Dodge, Peleg S	....do....	18	July 23, 1864	1 year.	Mustered
Fairchild, Henry	....do....	19	Aug. 4, 1864	1 year.	Died Jan
Fields, John	....do....	23	Aug. 18, 1864	1 year.	Mustered
Furer, Louis	....do....	18	Aug. 15, 1864	1 year.	
Garberson, Job	....do....	22	July 27, 1864	1 year.	Appointe Nov. 17, June 2
Gardner, John	....do....	20	Aug. 8, 1864	1 year.	
Groves, James W	....do....	18	Aug. 9, 1864	1 year.	
Hannaman, John W	....do....	40	July 24, 1864	1 year.	Mustered
Henry, William A	....do....	19	Sept. 14, 1864	1 year.	Died Ju 2d Ar
Holland, John	....do....	26	Aug. 8, 1864	1 year.	

Names.	Rank.	Age.	Date of Entering the Service.	Period of Service.	Remarks.
Hymes, George M. D.	Private..	19	July 24, 1864	1 year.	Mustered out with company June 28, 1865.
Ingmier, David	....do....	18	Aug. 17, 1864	1 year.	Mustered out June 9, 1865, at Louisville, Ky., by order of War Department.
James, Thomas W.	....do....	18	July 25, 1864	1 year.	Mustered out with company June 28, 1865.
Jaynes, James J.	....do....	20	Aug. 4, 1864	3 yrs.	Transferred to Co. G, 181st O. V. I., June 15, 1865.
Jones, James M.	....do....	19	July 27, 1864	1 year.	Mustered out with company June 28, 1865.
Kern, Michael	....do....	23	July 25, 1864	1 year.	
Kirk, Edmund C	....do....	27	July 24, 1864	1 year.	Mustered out with company June 28, 1865.
Koch, William	....do....	18	July 30, 1864	1 year.	Mustered out June 15, 1865, at Philadelphia, Pa., by order of War Department.
Ludwich, John L.	....do....	18	Aug. 20, 1864	1 year.	Mustered out with company June 28, 1865.
McCullough, John E.	....do....	18	Dec. 23, 1864	1 year.	Transferred to Co. G, 181st O. V. I., June 15, 1865.
McManis, Levi	....do....	23	July 30, 1864	1 year.	Mustered out with company June 28, 1865.
McQuiston, Peter	....do....	18	July 23, 1864	1 year.	Mustered out with company June 28, 1865.
Mann, Jasper	....do....	21	July 26, 1864	1 year.	Reduced from Sergeant June 17, 1865; mustered out with company June 28, 1865.
Matthews, Albert	....do....	17	July 25, 1864	1 year.	Died Feb. 27, 1865, at Cumberland, Md.
Maxwell, Winfield S.	....do....	18	July 23, 1864	1 year.	Mustered out July 3, 1865, at Chester U. S. A. Hospital, Chester, Pa.
Merrill, Charles	....do....	18	July 24, 1864	1 year.	Mustered out with company June 28, 1865.
Mowry, Cyrus	....do....	18	July 30, 1864	1 year.	Died Jan. 22, 1865, at Nashville, Tenn.
Myers, Warner	....do....	18	July 25, 1864	1 year.	Mustered out June 2, 1865, at Columbus, O., by order of War Department.
Newville, James E	....do....	18	July 26, 1864	1 year.	Mustered out June 15, 1865, at Beaufort, N. C., by order of War Department.
Nichols, Melville W	....do....	18	July 25, 1864	1 year.	Died Feb. 12, 1865, at Nashville, Tenn.
Nicholas, Joseph W.	....do....	19	July 22, 1864	1 year.	Mustered out with company June 28, 1865.
Nolk, Henry	....do....	40	Aug. 3, 1864	1 year.	Mustered out June [illegible], 1865, at Madison, Ind., by order of War Department.
Olds, Walter	....do....	18	Aug. 1, 1864	1 year.	Mustered out May [illegible], 1865, at Beaufort, N. C., by order of War Department.
Opper, George	....do....	44	July 25, 1864	1 year.	Mustered out with company June 28, 1865.
Patterson, John D.	....do....	37	July 25, 1864	1 year.	Mustered out to date June 28, 1865, by order of War Department.
Peak, Wesley H.	....do....	[illegible]	July 23, 1864	1 year.	Died April [illegible], 1865, at Raleigh, N. C.
Perkins, Isaac	....do....	[illegible]	July 27, 1864	1 year.	Died Feb. [illegible], 1865, at Louisville, Ky.
Perkins, Japtha	....do....	18	Aug. 6, 1864	1 year.	Mustered out May [illegible], 1865, at Columbus, O., by order of War Department.
Pierce, John L.	....do....	18	July 22, 1864	1 year.	Mustered out with company June 28, 1865.
Purvis, Martin B.	....do....	18	July [illegible], 1864	1 year.	Mustered out with company June 28, 1865.
Reed, Bryant	....do....	18	Aug. [illegible], 1864	1 year.	Mustered out with company June 28, 1865.
Reed, Joseph	....do....	19	July 30, 1864	1 year.	Died Jan. 12, 1865, at [illegible]
Rhoades, Walter W.	....do....	[illegible]	Sept. 17, 1864	1 year.	Mustered out July [illegible], 1865, at Columbus, O., by order of War Department.
Roach, John A.	....do....	[illegible]	July [illegible], 1864	1 year.	Mustered out with company June 28, 1865.
Rose, John W.	....do....	[illegible]	Aug. 6, 1864	[illegible]	Mustered out May [illegible], 1865, at Columbus, O., by order of War Department.
Sage, [illegible]	....do....	[illegible]	July 30, 1864	1 year.	[illegible]
[illegible]	....do....	[illegible]	Aug. [illegible], 1864	1 year.	Mustered out with company June 28, 1865; [illegible]
Sherman, William H.	....do....	[illegible]	Sept. 17, 1864	1 year.	Mustered out with company June 28, 1865.
Smith, Franklin T.	....do....	[illegible]	July 23, 1864	1 year.	[illegible]
[illegible]	....do....	[illegible]	[illegible]	1 year.	Mustered out with company June 28, 1865.
[illegible]	....do....	[illegible]	[illegible]	1 year.	Mustered out with company June 28, 1865.
[illegible]	....do....	[illegible]	[illegible]	1 year.	Mustered out with company June 28, 1865.
[illegible]	....do....	[illegible]	Aug. [illegible], 1864	1 year.	Mustered out May [illegible], 1865, [illegible], by order of War Department.
Underwood, George W.	....do....	21	Aug. [illegible], 1864	1 year.	Mustered out with company June 28, 1865.
[illegible]	....do....	[illegible]	July 28, 1864	1 year.	Mustered out with company June 28, 1865.
Wall, Thomas	....do....	24	Aug. 28, 1864	1 year.	
Williams, William [illegible]	....do....	[illegible]	July [illegible], 1864	1 year.	Mustered out [illegible], 1865, at [illegible], by order of War Department.
Wood, James M.	....do....	21	Aug. [illegible], 1864	1 year.	Mustered out with company June 28, 1865.
[illegible]	....do....	[illegible]	Aug. [illegible], 1864	1 year.	Mustered out with company June 28, 1865.

COMPANY [illegible]

Mustered in August 18, 1864, at Camp Chase, O., by W. P. Ri[illegible]
June 28, 1865, at Charlotte, N. C., by E. A. F[illegible]
Department of North C[illegible]

Names.	Rank.	Age.	Date of Entering the Service.	Period of Service.
Ulysses D. Cole	Captain.	23	Sept. 1, 1864	1 year.
Peter Hill	1st Lieut.	31	Sept. 1, 1864	1 year.
George Harriman	2d Lieut.	27	Sept. 24, 1864	1 year.
Richard T. Field	1st Sergt.	22	Aug. 5, 1864	1 year.
Andrew N. McGinnis	Sergeant.	22	Aug. 16, 1864	1 year.
George W. Snodgrass	....do....	24	Aug. 20, 1864	1 year.
Solomon Heasly	....do....	22	Aug. 20, 1864	1 year.
Franklin Welsh	....do....	21	Aug. 20, 1864	1 year.
David Wood	....do....	24	Aug. 29, 1864	1 year.
John A. Roach	Corporal.	44	Aug. 16, 1864	1 year.
John Lister	....do....	34	Aug. 16, 1864	1 year.
Jeremiah Cole	....do....	21	Aug. 20, 1864	1 year.
Alexander S. Hornback	....do....	18	July 25, 1864	1 year.
John Harris	....do....	35	Aug. 29, 1864	1 year.
Henry C. Moffitt	....do....	20	Sept. 1, 1864	1 year.
Robert E. Benson	....do....	29	Aug. 29, 1864	1 year.
Andrew J. Sellers	....do....	19	Aug. 20, 1864	1 year.
Thomas J. Cartmell	Musician	20	Sept. 20, 1864	1 year.
Adamson, Charles W	Private	20	Aug. 9, 1864	1 year.
Allen, Homer	....do....	18	Sept. 1, 1864	1 year.
Aller, Hiram	....do....	26	Sept. 1, 1864	1 year.
Atha, Washington	....do....	28	Aug. 20, 1864	1 year.
Bash, Thomas	....do....	18	Aug. 8, 1864	1 year.
Beck, Amos	....do....	18	Aug. 16, 1864	1 year.
Benson, John	....do....	18	Aug. 29, 1864	1 year.
Benson, William	....do....	30	Aug. 29, 1864	1 year.
Berry, John L	....do....	35	Aug. 15, 1864	1 year.
Berry, Josiah	....do....	19	Aug. 16, 1864	1 year.
Brown, John	....do....	25	Aug. 30, 1864	1 year.
Brown, Maxon M	....do....	21	Aug. 30, 1864	1 year.
Brown, Silas	....do....	26	Aug. 30, 1864	1 year.
Brown, Vincent	....do....	46	Aug. 30, 1864	1 year.
Brown, William	....do....	31	Aug. 30, 1864	1 year.
Bushong, John	....do....	18	Aug. 3, 1864	1 year.
Bushong, Milton	....do....	18	Sept. 1, 1864	1 year.
Cassiday, George	....do....	20	Aug. 8, 1864	1 year.
Clark, James	....do....	18	Sept. 18, 1864	1 year.
Crabtree, Matthew	....do....	39	Aug. 15, 1864	1 year.
Crawford, Edward	....do....	35	Aug. 16, 1864	1 year.
Debolt, Meeker	....do....	22	Sept. 8, 1864	1 year.
Dickison, Thomas	....do....	21	Aug. 16, 1864	1 year.

COMPANY C.

Mustered in August 18, 1864, at Camp Chase, O., by W. P. Richardson, Colonel [...] June 28, 1865, at Charlotte, N. C., by E. A. Folsom, Captain an[d] [...] Department of North Carolina.

Names.	Rank.	Age.	Date of Entering the Service.	Period of Service.	
William H. Robb	Captain.	38	Sept. 6, 1864	1 year.	Wounded Dec. 7, [...] Tenn.; dischar[...] ton, D. C.
William B. Brown	1st Lieut.	42	Aug. 15, 1864	1 year.	Appointed Sept. [...] 1865, in battle [...] moted to Capta[...] tered; mustere[...] 1865.
Joseph Swartz	2d Lieut.	26	Aug. 20, 1864	1 year.	Appointed Sept. [...] company June
Jacob S. Newcomb	1st Sergt.	36	Sept. 13, 1864	1 year.	Mustered out Ma[...] by order of Wa[...]
Charles W. Webster	....do....	26	Aug. 20, 1864	1 year.	Appointed from [...] mustered out w[...]
James C. Marshall	Sergeant.	22	Aug. 11, 1864	1 year.	Appointed Sept. [...] company June
Adam Sherwood	....do....	22	Aug. 29, 1864	1 year.	Appointed Sept. [...] company June
Vachtel F. Collins	....do....	30	Aug. 20, 1864	1 year.	Appointed Sept. [...] date May 18, 18[...] of War Departr[...]
Charles J. Sayre	....do....	23	Aug. 2, 1864	1 year.	Appointed from [...] tered out with
Warren C. Winget	....do....	28	Aug. 3, 1864	1 year.	Mustered as priv[...] 21, 1865; muste[...] 28, 1865.
Charles M. Adams	Corporal.	38	Aug. 30, 1864	1 year.	Appointed Sept. [...] company June
John Hudson	....do....	28	Aug. 20, 1864	1 year.	Appointed Sept. [...] 6, 1865, at Tripl[...] bus, O., by ord[...]
George C. Woodruff	....do....	34	Aug. 20, 1864	1 year.	Appointed Sept. [...] in battle of Wi[...]
Greenberry Shipley	....do....	38	Aug. 4, 1864	1 year.	Appointed Sept. [...] company June
William J. Browning	....do....	35	Aug. 3, 1864	1 year.	Appointed Jan. [...] company June
John M. Dollison	....do....	44	Aug. 3, 1864	1 year.	Appointed Jan. [...] company June
Conroy M. Ingman	....do....	18	Sept. 3, 1864	1 year.	Appointed March [...] company June
Elijah Smith	....do....	19	Sept. 1, 1864	1 year.	Appointed May [...] company June
Daniel B. Hagan	....do....	39	Aug. 22, 1864	1 year.	Appointed May [...] company June
Zachariah T. Alexander	Musician	16	Aug. 29, 1864	1 year.	Mustered out wit[...]
Bradley Tucker	....do....	17	Aug. 20, 1864	1 year.	Mustered out wit[...]
Argo, Andrew	Private.	18	Aug. 11, 1864	1 year.	Died June 17, 186[...]
Bell, Eugene B.	....do....	29	Aug. 22, 1864	1 year.	Mustered out Jun[...] by order of War
Bowie, Benson C.	....do....	40	Sept. 1, 1864	1 year.	Mustered out Ma[...] O., by order of
Burrows, William F.	....do....	28	Aug. 8, 1864	1 year.	Mustered out Ju[...] New York Har[...] ment.
Caryl, Andrew L.	....do....	18	Aug. 5, 1864	1 year.	Mustered out wit[...]
Coffenberger, Samuel B.	....do....	29	Sept. 5, 1864	1 year.	Mustered out May [...] O., by order of
Crofford, John	....do....	28	Aug. 22, 1864	1 year.	Mustered out Jun[...] by order of War
Danforth, Hiram	....do....	44	Aug. 2, 1864	1 year.	Mustered out wit[...]
Everts, Henry E.	....do....	19	Aug. 20, 1864	1 year.	Mustered out wit[...]
Gill, Lewis F.	....do....	18	Aug. 30, 1864	1 year.	Mustered out wit[...]
Hamler, Isaac	....do....	18	Aug. 24, 1864	1 year.	Died Dec. 26, 1864, [...] Tennessee
Hamler, John	....do....	44	Aug. 24, 1864	1 year.	Died May 27, 18[...] North Carolina.
Hodgeden, Henry	....do....	20	Aug. 20, 1864	1 year.	Mustered out Jun[...] New York Har[...] ment.
Hornbeck, Claris H.	....do....	34	Aug. 17, 1864	1 year.	Mustered out Ma[...] Hospital, Phila[...] Department.
Isaac, John	....do....	40	Sept. 14, 1864	1 year.	Mustered out wit[...]
Knachel, Joseph	....do....	23	Sept. 20, 1864	1 year.	Mustered out wit[...]

Names.	Rank.	Age.	Date of Entering the Service.	Period of Service.	Remarks.
Wurtsbaugh, David H..	Private..	45	Aug. 24, 1864	1 year.	Mustered out June 17, 1865, at Mower General Hospital, Philadelphia, Pa., by order of War Department.
Wurtsbaugh, John........	....do....	21	Aug. 14, 1864	1 year.	Mustered out with company June 28, 1865.
Wurtsbaugh, Thomas.....	....do....	19	Aug. 24, 1864	1 year.	Mustered out May 29, 1865, at Camp Dennison, O., by order of War Department.
Zuck, William H........	....do....	20	Aug. 20, 1864	1 year.	Mustered out with company June 28, 1865.

COMPANY D.

Mustered in August 18, 1864, at Camp Chase, O., by W. P. Richardson, Colonel 25th O. V. I. Mustered out June 28, 1865, at Charlotte, N. C., by E. A. Folsom, Captain and A. C. M., Department of North Carolina.

Names.	Rank.	Age.	Date of Entering the Service.	Period of Service.	Remarks.
James W. Combs........	Captain.	30	July 26, 1864	1 year.	Appointed Sept. 10, 1864; mustered out with company June 28, 1865.
David J. Hussey.........	1st Lieut.	21	Aug. 5, 1864	1 year.	Appointed Sept. 10, 1864; promoted to Captain June 16, 1865, but not mustered; mustered out with company June 28, 1865.
George D. Coe...........	2d Lieut.	26	Aug. 12, 1864	1 year.	Appointed Sept. 10, 1864; promoted to 1st Lieutenant June 16, 1865, but not mustered; mustered out with company June 28, 1865.
John F. Hubler..........	1st Sergt.	21	Aug. 1, 1864	1 year.	Promoted to 2d Lieutenant June 16, 1865, but not mustered; mustered out with company June 28, 1865.
Cartwright C. Davis.....	Sergeant.	20	Aug. 8, 1864	1 year.	Mustered out with company June 28, 1865.
William Bell	....do....	19	Aug. 25, 1864	1 year.	Mustered out with company June 28, 1865.
George Jeffries	....do....	21	Aug. 31, 1864	1 year.	Mustered out with company June 28, 1865.
Armstead T. Mace.......	....do....	18	Aug. 1, 1864	1 year.	Mustered as private; appointed Sergeant March 1, 1865; mustered out with company June 28, 1865.
Nathan J. Smith	Corporal.	18	Aug. 23, 1864	1 year.	Killed Dec. 7, 1864, in battle of the Cedars, Tennessee.
John P. McGill..........	....do....	28	Sept. 6, 1864	1 year.	Mustered out with company June 28, 1865.
Ernest D. Davis.........	....do....	18	Aug. 5, 1864	1 year.	Mustered out with company June 28, 1865.
Edward DeLackso.......	....do....	33	Aug. 12, 1864	1 year.	Mustered out June 8, 1865, at Columbus, O., by order of War Department.
Theodore M. Pickering..	....do....	19	Sept. 6, 1864	1 year.	Appointed ——; mustered out with company June 28, 1865.
Jacob Moore.............	....do....	21	Aug. 12, 1864	1 year.	Appointed ——; mustered out with company June 28, 1865.
George M. Matthews	....do....	18	Aug. 1, 1864	1 year.	Appointed March 1, 1865; mustered out with company June 28, 1865.
Samuel Maxwell..........	....do....	19	July 30, 1864	1 year.	Appointed March 1, 1865; mustered out with company June 28, 1865.
John F. McHugh...	....do....	19	Sept. 2, 1864	1 year.	Appointed March 1, 1865; mustered out with company June 28, 1865.
Charles Heuigar..........	....do....	18	Aug. 8, 1864	1 year.	Appointed March 1, 1865; mustered out with company June 28, 1865.
Christopher C. McCurdy	Musician	17	Aug. 15, 1864	1 year.	Mustered out with company June 28, 1865.
Andrew J. South........	....do....	18	July 30, 1864	1 year.	Wounded March 10, 1865, in battle of Wise's Fork, N. C.; mustered out June 15, 1865, at Beaufort, N. C., by order of War Department.
John Baker..............	Wagoner.	35	July 23, 1864	1 year.	Mustered out with company June 28, 1865.
Angel, William	Private..	18	Aug. 8, 1864	1 year.	Mustered out with company June 28, 1865.
Archer, Stephen..........	....do....	35	Aug. 17, 1864	1 year.	Mustered out with company June 28, 1865.
Augenstine, Matthew...	....do....	20	Feb. 21, 1865	1 year.	Transferred to Co. G, 181st O. V. I., June 5, 1865.
Bailey, George W.........	....do....	26	Aug. 26, 1864	1 year.	Died Feb. 15, 1865, at Washington, D. C.
Baker, Francis M.........	....do....	21	Aug. 13, 1864	1 year.	Mustered out with company June 28, 1865.
Barnhart, Jasper.........	....do....	19	Sept. 5, 1864	1 year.	Mustered out with company June 28, 1865.
Barnhart, William.......	....do....	19	Sept. 5, 1864	1 year.	Mustered out with company June 28, 1865.
Bean, Rufus.............	....do....	18	Aug. 5, 1864	1 year.	Mustered out with company June 28, 1865.
Bennett, Lewis..........	....do....	20	Aug. 20, 1864	1 year.	Mustered out with company June 28, 1865.
Bobo, Curtis.............	....do....	34	Aug. 6, 1864	1 year.	Mustered out June 7, 1865, at Washington, D. C., by order of War Department.
Briggs, James F..........	....do....	25	Sept. 5, 1864	1 year.	Reduced from Corporal ——; mustered out with company June 28, 1865.
Brown, Jacob............	....do....	20	Aug. 15, 1864	1 year.	Mustered out with company June 28, 1865.
Burchfield, Charles......	....do....	18	Aug. 15, 1864	1 year.	Died Jan. 2, 1865, at Murfreesboro, Tenn.; also borne on rolls as Charles Butterfield.
Burchfield, Thomas.....	....do....	19	Aug. 15, 1864	1 year.	Mustered out with company June 28, 1865.
Carpenter, William H...	....do....	30	Aug. 15, 1864	1 year.	Mustered out with company June 28, 1865.
Carsey, Jasper N.........	....do....	28	Sept. 3, 1864	1 year.	Mustered out with company June 28, 1865.
Chandler, Isaiah.........	....do....	18	Aug. 15, 1864	1 year.	Mustered out with company June 28, 1865.
Clark, William...........	....do....	18	Aug. 6, 1864	1 year.	Died Jan. 24, 1865, at Louisville, Ky.
Cooley, Henry A	....do....	18	Sept. 6, 1864	1 year.	Mustered out with company June 28, 1865.
Cross, Eli D..............	....do....	21	Sept. 12, 1864	1 year.	Mustered out with company June 28, 1865.
Delong, Charles F.......	....do....	17	Aug. 18, 1864	1 year.	Mustered out with company June 28, 1865.

Names.	Rank.	Age.	Date of Entering the Service.	Period of Service.	Remarks.
[illegible], Joseph C.	Private.	18	Aug. 10, 1864	1 year.	Mustered out with company June 28, 1865.
[illegible], William H	...do...	19	Aug. 18, 1864	1 year.	Mustered out with company June 28, 1865.
[illegible], Peter A.	...do...	34	Aug. 12, 1864	1 year.	Mustered out with company June 28, 1865.
[illegible], Daniel M.	...do...	25	Feb. 21, 1865	1 year.	Transferred to Co. G, 181st O. V. I., June 15, 1865.
Driskill, George B.	...do...	30	Feb. 21, 1865	1 year.	Transferred to Co. G, 181st O. V. I., June 15, 1865.
[illegible], John	...do...	29	Aug. 29, 1864	1 year.	Mustered out with company June 28, 1865.
[illegible], John.	...do...	18	Aug. 26, 1864	1 year.	Mustered out with company June 28, 1865.
[illegible], John.	...do...	18	Aug. 6, 1864	1 year.	Mustered out with company June 28, 1865.
[illegible], Sabina.	...do...	18	Aug. 6, 1864	1 year.	Mustered out with company June 28, 1865.
[illegible], William J.	...do...	17	Aug. 3, 1864	1 year.	Died Dec. 26, 1864, at Murfreesboro, Tenn.
[illegible], William.	...do...	23	Aug. 21, 1864	1 year.	
[illegible], John T.	...do...	18	Aug. 16, 1864	1 year.	Mustered out with company June 28, 1865.
[illegible], George.	...do...	25	Aug. 21, 1864	1 year.	Mustered out with company June 28, 1865.
[illegible], William.	...do...	19	Aug. 22, 1864	1 year.	Mustered out with company June 28, 1865.
[illegible], James.	...do...	26	Aug. 15, 1864	1 year.	
[illegible], James M.	...do...	27	Sept. 6, 1864	1 year.	Mustered out with company June 28, 1865.
[illegible], Jackson.	...do...	18	Aug. 23, 1864	1 year.	Mustered out with company June 28, 1865.
[illegible], Jesse.	...do...	17	Sept. 3, 1864	1 year.	Mustered out with company June 28, 1865.
[illegible], William H.	...do...	18	Aug. 3, 1864	1 year.	Mustered out with company June 28, 1865.
[illegible], [illegible].	...do...	18	Aug. 6, 1864	1 year.	Mustered out with company June 28, 1865.
[illegible], Orin.	...do...	18	Aug. 21, 1864	1 year.	Wounded Dec. 7, 1864, in battle of the Cedars, Tenn.; mustered out July 31, 1865, at Columbus, O., by order of War Department.
Love, Jonas.	...do...	19	Aug. 1, 1864	1 year.	Transferred to Co. G, 181st O. V. I., June 15, 1865.
[illegible], Michael.	...do...	18	Aug. 3, 1864	1 year.	Mustered out with company June 28, 1865.
[illegible], Henry.	...do...	44	Sept. 2, 1864	1 year.	Died Feb. 12, 1865, at Nashville, Tenn.
[illegible], Joseph.	...do...	18	July 30, 1864	1 year.	Mustered out with company June 28, 1865.
[illegible], William H.	...do...	18	Aug. 18, 1864	1 year.	Mustered out with company June 28, 1865.
[illegible], Marcus L.	...do...	40	Sept. 7, 1864	1 year.	Died Feb. 9, 1865, at Washington, D. C.
[illegible], Jefferson.	...do...	18	Sept. 6, 1864	1 year.	Mustered out with company June 28, 1865.
[illegible]Whorter, Joseph D.	...do...	20	Aug. 1, 1864	1 year.	Mustered out with company June 28, 1865.
[illegible], Eber L.	...do...	18	Aug. 1, 1864	1 year.	Mustered out with company June 28, 1865.
[illegible], James G.	...do...	18	Aug. 15, 1864	1 year.	Reduced from Corporal ——; mustered out with company June 28, 1865.
Matthews, John W.	...do...	21	July 30, 1864	1 year.	Reduced from Sergeant March 1, 1865; mustered out with company June 28, 1865.
[illegible], George.	...do...	18	Aug. 26, 1864	1 year.	Mustered out with company June 28, 1865.
[illegible], Henry.	...do...	17	Sept. 5, 1864	1 year.	Mustered out with company June 28, 1865.
[illegible], William B.	...do...	18	Aug. 26, 1864	1 year.	Mustered out July 22, 1865, at Cumberland, Md., by order of War Department.
[illegible], Robert T.	...do...	18	Aug. 26, 1864	1 year.	Mustered out with company June 28, 1865.
[illegible], Caleb A.	...do...	18	Aug. 8, 1864	1 year.	Died Feb. 10, 1865, at Louisville, Ky.
[illegible], James W.	...do...	19	Sept. 15, 1864	1 year.	Mustered out with company June 28, 1865.
[illegible], Frederick.	...do...	18	Aug. 8, 1864	1 year.	Mustered out with company June 28, 1865.
[illegible], John S.	...do...	31	Aug. 31, 1864	1 year.	Killed Dec. 4, 1864, in battle of Overall's Creek, Tenn.
[illegible], Culbert M.	...do...	18	Aug. 31, 1864	1 year.	Mustered out with company June 28, 1865.
[illegible], Franklin.	...do...	18	Aug. 15, 1864	1 year.	Mustered out with company June 28, 1865.
[illegible], [illegible] W.	...do...	19	Aug. 6, 1864	1 year.	Mustered out with company June 28, 1865.
[illegible], Franklin.	...do...	19	Sept. 5, 1864	1 year.	Mustered out with company June 28, 1865.
[illegible], William M.	...do...	18	Aug. 16, 1864	1 year.	Died Feb. 16, 1865, at Washington, D. C.
[illegible], Augustus.	...do...	18	Aug. 15, 1864	1 year.	Mustered out with company June 28, 1865.
[illegible], William R.	...do...	[illegible]	Aug. 13, 1864	1 year.	Reduced from Corporal March 1, 1865; mustered out with company June 28, 1865.
[illegible], James E.	...do...	19	Aug. 4, 1864	1 year.	Mustered out with company June 28, 1865.
St. Clair, William.	...do...	18	Aug. 1, 1864	1 year.	Died March 8, 1865, at Nashville, Tenn.
[illegible], James P.	...do...	22	Aug. 15, 1864	1 year.	Mustered out June 19, 1865, at Annapolis, Md., by order of War Department.
[illegible], William W.	...do...	18	Aug. 8, 1864	1 year.	Mustered out with company June 28, 1865.
[illegible], James M.	...do...	24	Sept. 1, 1864	1 year.	Killed Dec. 7, 1864, in battle of the Cedars, Tennessee.
[illegible], Aaron I.	...do...	22	Aug. 15, 1864	1 year.	Mustered out with company June 28, 1865.
[illegible], George M.	...do...	16	Aug. 23, 1864	1 year.	Mustered out with company June 28, 1865.
[illegible], [illegible].	...do...	22	Aug. 3, 1864	1 year.	Wounded Dec. 7, 1864, in battle of the Cedars, Tenn.; mustered out July 24, 1865, at Camp Dennison, O., by order of War Department.
Tucker, Masham.	...do...	34	Aug. 6, 1864	1 year.	Died Feb. 1, 1865, at Murfreesboro, Tenn.
Tucker, Zachariah.	...do...	18	Aug. 21, 1864	1 year.	Mustered out with company June 28, 1865.
Tully, Richard M.	...do...	30	Sept. 1, 1864	1 year.	Mustered out with company June 28, 1865.
Waller, Lewis.	...do...	19	Aug. 18, 1864	1 year.	Mustered out July 14, 1865, at Camp Dennison, O., by order of War Department.
White, Josiah.	...do...	18	Aug. 21, 1864	1 year.	Killed Dec. 4, 1864, in battle of Overall's Creek, Tenn.
Winters, William R.	...do...	22	Aug. 4, 1864	1 year.	Mustered out with company June 28, 1865.
Wise, William H.	...do...	18	Aug. 18, 1864	1 year.	Mustered out with company June 28, 1865.
Wolfe, John.	...do...	23	Aug. 15, 1864	1 year.	Mustered out May 23, 1865, at Camp Dennison, O., by order of War Department.

COMPANY E.

Mustered in August 18, 1864, at Camp Chase, O., by W. P. Richardson, Colonel 25th O. V. I. Mustered out June 28, 1865, at Charlotte, N. C., by E. A. Folsom, Captain and A. C. M., Department of North Carolina.

Names.	Rank.	Age.	Date of Entering the Service.	Period of Service.	Remarks.
George Campbell	Captain.	30	Aug. 1, 1864	1 year.	Appointed Sept. 10, 1864; mustered out with company June 28, 1865.
James Clements	1st Lieut.	48	Sept. 10, 1864	1 year.	Mustered out with company June 28, 1865
Alfred D. Henry	2d Lieut.	36	Aug. 17, 1864	1 year.	Appointed Sept. 10, 1864; promoted to 1st Lieutenant June 16, 1865, but not mustered; mustered out with company June 28, 1865.
Lybrand Maxwell	1st Sergt.	41	Aug. 17, 1864	1 year.	Appointed Sept. 13, 1864; promoted to 2d Lieutenant June 16, 1865, but not mustered; mustered out with company June 28, 1865.
John A. Cuscaden	Sergeant.	25	Aug. 27, 1864	1 year.	Appointed Sept. 13, 1864; mustered out with company June 28, 1865.
James W. Clements	....do....	19	Aug. 9, 1864	1 year.	Appointed Sept. 13, 1864; mustered out with company June 28, 1865.
Hiram C. Frost	....do....	36	Aug. 29, 1864	1 year.	Appointed from Corporal March 12, 1865; mustered out with company June 28, 1865.
John P. Harris	....do....	20	Aug. 6, 1864	1 year.	Appointed from Corporal March 12, 1865; mustered out with company June 28, 1865.
Ithamar B. Brookins	Corporal.	18	Aug. 20, 1864	1 year.	Appointed Sept. 13, 1864; mustered out with company June 28, 1865.
Samuel S. Newton	....do....	18	Aug. 20, 1864	1 year.	Appointed Sept. 13, 1864; mustered out with company June 28, 1865.
John W. Lawrence	....do....	32	Aug. 27, 1864	1 year.	Died March 15, 1865, at Newbern, N. C., of wounds received March 10, 1865, in battle of Wise's Fork, N. C.
David Graham	....do....	38	Sept. 2, 1864	1 year.	Appointed March 12, 1865; mustered out with company June 28, 1865.
James B. Spicer	....do....	23	Aug. 10, 1864	1 year.	Reduced to ranks from Sergeant —; appointed Corporal March 21, 1865; mustered out with company June 28, 1865.
Hiram Blazer	....do....	31	Aug. 29, 1864	1 year.	Appointed March 21, 1865; mustered out with company June 28, 1865.
Kosciusko Elliott	....do....	20	Aug. 27, 1864	1 year.	Appointed March 21, 1865; mustered out with company June 28, 1865.
Jared C. Ross	....do....	19	Aug. 2, 1864	1 year.	Appointed March 21, 1865; mustered out with company June 28, 1865.
Dillon I. Haining	....do....	18	Oct. 13, 1864	1 year.	Transferred to Co. G, 181st O. V. I., June 15, 1865, as private.
James Decker	Musician.	16	Aug. 5, 1864	1 year.	Mustered out May 29, 1865, at Columbus, O., by order of War Department.
James L. Norris	....do....	18	Aug. 20, 1864	1 year.	Discharged May 1, 1865, at Murfreesboro, Tenn., on Surgeon's certificate of disability.
Samuel Calaway	Wagoner.	40	Aug. 29, 1864	1 year.	Mustered out May 25, 1865, at Mower General Hospital, Philadelphia, Pa., by order of War Department.
Atkinson, William H	Private..	33	July 26, 1864	1 year.	Died Jan. 14, 1865, on board steamer Swallow on Tennessee River.
Banks, Charles W	....do....	35	Aug. 20, 1864	1 year.	Mustered out with company June 28, 1865.
Biddeson, Thomas	....do....	27	Aug. 17, 1864	1 year.	Mustered out May 29, 1865, at Camp Dennison, O., by order of War Department.
Black, Hiram D	....do....	24	Sept. 2, 1864	1 year.	Died Dec. 28, 1864, at Murfreesboro, Tenn
Boyles, William H	....do....	16	Aug. 29, 1864	1 year.	Mustered out with company June 28, 1865.
Bryson, Joseph W	....do....	19	Aug. 20, 1864	1 year.	Mustered out with company June 28, 1865
Burrows, John L	....do....	27	Sept. 1, 1864	1 year.	Mustered out with company June 28, 1865.
Burton, William	....do....	41	Aug. 16, 1864	1 year.	Mustered out June 27, 1865, at White Hall Hospital, Philadelphia, Pa., by order of War Department.
Butler, William	....do....	44	Aug. 25, 1864	1 year.	Reduced from Corporal March 21, 1865; mustered out with company June 28, 1865.
Carder, Champ C	....do....	25	Aug. 4, 1864	1 year.	Mustered out June 22, 1865, at General Hospital, Division No. 2, Annapolis, Md., by order of War Department.
Carmichael, David L	....do....	21	Sept. 2, 1864	1 year.	Mustered out with company June 28, 1865
Chalker, Hiram C	....do....	19	Aug. 29, 1864	1 year.	Died Feb. 7, 1865, at Grafton, W. Va.
Cottrill, Henry	....do....	18	Aug. 21, 1864	1 year.	Mustered out with company June 28, 1865.
Creppin, Worthy S	....do....	16	Sept. 1, 1864	1 year.	Mustered out June 13, 1865, at general hospital, Gallipolis, O., by order of War Department.
Daft, George W	....do....	38	Sept. 2, 1864	1 year.	Mustered out with company June 28, 1865.
Day, William	....do....	26	Aug. 27, 1864	1 year.	Mustered out with company June 28, 1865.
Dew, Henry C	....do....	27	Aug. 17, 1864	1 year.	Mustered out with company June 28, 1865.
Dew, James C.	....do....	38	Aug. 17, 1864	1 year.	Mustered out with company June 28, 1865.
Dixon, William W	....do....	21	Aug. 4, 1864	1 year.	Mustered out with company June 28, 1865.
Dunlevy, David	....do....	27	Aug. 22, 1864	1 year.	Mustered out with company June 28, 1865.
Dunlevy, Joshua	....do....	23	Aug. 22, 1864	1 year.	Died Jan. 15, 1865, at Murfreesboro, Tenn.
Dugan, Henry H	....do....	23	Aug. 30, 1864	1 year.	Mustered out with company June 28, 1865.
Dye, Reuben	....do....		Aug. 16, 1864	1 year.	Died Jan. 12, 1865, at Jeffersonville, Ind.

k.	Age.	Date of Entering the Service.	Period of Service.	Remarks.
	18	Aug. [illegible], 1864	1 year.	Mustered out with company June 28, 1865.
....	19	Aug. 12, 1864	1 year.	Mustered out May 24, 1865, at Philadelphia, Pa., by order of War Department.
	18	Aug. 30, 1864	1 year.	Mustered out with company June 28, 1865.
	18	Aug. 14, 1864	1 year.	Mustered out with company June 28, 1865.
	16	Aug. 18, 1864	1 year.	Drowned Jan. 13, 1865, in railroad accident.
	18	Aug. 20, 1864	1 year.	Mustered out with company June 28, 1865.
	17	Aug. 27, 1864	1 year.	Mustered out with company June 28, 1865.
	22	Aug. 29, 1864	1 year.	Mustered out with company June 28, 1865.
....	18	Sept. 1, 1864	1 year.	Mustered out with company June 28, 1865.
....	35	Aug. 6, 1864	1 year.	Discharged June 5, 1865, on Surgeon's certificate of disability.
	19	Aug. 10, 1864	1 year.	Mustered out June 19, 1865, at Beaufort, N. C., by order of War Department.
....	35	Aug. 27, 1864	1 year.	Transferred to Co. C, 22d Regiment, Veteran Reserve Corps, ——; mustered out July 1, 1865, at Camp Cleveland, O., by order of War Department.
....	18	Aug. 13, 1864	1 year.	Mustered out May 29, 1865, at Camp Dennison, O., by order of War Department.
	41	Aug. 17, 1864	1 year.	Mustered out June 26, 1865, at Columbus, O., by order of War Department.
	17	Sept. 2, 1864	1 year.	Discharged June 14, 1865, at DeCamp General Hospital, Philadelphia, Pa., on surgeon's certificate of disability.
	18	Aug. 9, 1864	1 year.	Mustered out with company June 28, 1865.
	18	Sept. 1, 1864	1 year.	Mustered out July 9, 1865, at general hospital, Grafton, W. Va., by order of War Department.
	18	Aug. 18, 1864	1 year.	Mustered out May 22, 1865, at Murfreesboro, Tenn., by order of War Department.
	18	Aug. 11, 1864	1 year.	Mustered out with company June 28, 1865.
	18	Aug. 10, 1864	1 year.	Mustered out May 26, 1865, at Washington, D. C., by order of War Department.
	18	Aug. 13, 1864	1 year.	Mustered out with company June 28, 1865.
	18	Sept. 1, 1864	1 year.	Mustered out with company June 28, 1865.
	18	Sept. 1, 1864	1 year.	Mustered out with company June 28, 1865.
	17	Aug. 23, 1864	1 year.	Died March 29, 1865, at Murfreesboro, Tenn.
	20	Aug. 17, 1864	1 year.	Mustered out with company June 28, 1865.
	17	Sept. 12, 1864	1 year.	Died Oct. 6, 1864, at Columbus, O.
	39	Aug. 29, 1864	1 year.	Mustered out June 27, 1865, at White Hall Hospital, Philadelphia, Pa., by order of War Department.
		Aug. 17, 1864	1 year.	Reduced from Corporal March 21, 1865; mustered out with company June 28, 1865.
		Aug. 17, 1864	1 year.	Mustered out with company June 28, 1865.
		Aug. 30, 1864	1 year.	Mustered out with company June 28, 1865.
		Aug. 26, 1864	1 year.	Died Dec. 27, 1864, at Jeffersonville, Ind.
		Sept. 2, 1864	1 year.	Mustered out with company June 28, 1865.
		Aug. 17, 1864	1 year.	Died June 8, 1865, at Newark, N. J.
		Aug. 16, 1864	1 year.	Mustered out with company June 28, 1865.
		Aug. 27, 1864	1 year.	Mustered out with company June 28, 1865.
		Aug. 19, 1864	1 year.	Mustered out with company June 28, 1865.
		Aug. 31, 1864	1 year.	Mustered out June 27, 1865, at Columbus, O., by order of War Department.
		Aug. 25, 1864	1 year.	Mustered out with company June 28, 1865.
		Aug. 30, 1864	1 year.	Died March 2, 1865, at Grafton, W. Va.
		Aug. 25, 1864	1 year.	Mustered out with company June 28, 1865.
		Aug. 25, 1864	1 year.	Mustered out May 29, 1865, at Camp Dennison, O., by order of War Department.
		Aug. 31, 1864	1 year.	Mustered out July 1, 1865, at Washington, D. C., by order of War Department.
		Aug. 11, 1864	1 year.	Mustered out to date May 11, 1865, at Detroit, Mich., by order of War Department.
		Aug. 10, 1864	1 year.	Mustered out with company June 28, 1865.
		Aug. 27, 1864	1 year.	Mustered out with company June 28, 1865.
		Aug. 11, 1864	1 year.	Wounded Dec. 7, 1864, in battle of the Cedars, Tenn.; mustered out May 28, 1865, at Murfreesboro, Tenn., by order of War Department.
		Sept. 2, 1864	1 year.	Mustered out with company June 28, 1865.
		Aug. 20, 1864	1 year.	Mustered out with company June 28, 1865.
		Aug. 20, 1864	1 year.	Mustered out with company June 28, 1865.
		Aug. 31, 1864	1 year.	Mustered out with company June 28, 1865.
		Sept. 2, 1864	1 year.	Mustered out with company June 28, 1865.
		Aug. 22, 1864	1 year.	Mustered out with company June 28, 1865.
		Aug. 22, 1864	1 year.	Mustered out with company June 28, 1865.
		Aug. 29, 1864	1 year.	Mustered out with company June 28, 1865; also borne on rolls as John Wayne.
		Aug. 17, 1864		Mustered out with company June 28, 1865.
		Sept. 2, 1864		Mustered out with company June 28, 1865.
		Sept. 2, 1864		Reduced from Corporal March 21, 1865; mustered out with company June 28, 1865.
		Sept. 2, 1864		Mustered out with company June 28, 1865.
		Aug. 27, 1864		Reduced from Sergeant March 12, 1865; mustered out with company June 28, 1865.

Mustered in August 18, 1864, at Camp Chase, O., by W. P. Richardson, Colonel 25th O. V. I. Mustered out June 28, 1865, at Charlotte, N. C., by E. A. Folsom, Captain and A. C. M., Department of North Carolina.

Names.	Rank.	Age.	Date of Entering the Service.	Period of Service.	Remarks.
Ephraim C. Carson......	Captain.	30	Aug. 4, 1864	1 year.	Appointed Sept. 14, 1864; detailed and assigned to duty on staff of Gen. Milroy Oct. 13, 1864; mustered out with company June 28, 1865.
Thornton B. Myers......	1st Lieut.	22	Sept. 1, 1864	1 year.	Appointed Sept. 14, 1864; mustered out with company June 28, 1865.
Samuel A. Price..	2d Lieut.	29	Aug. 11, 1864	1 year.	Appointed Sept. 14, 1864; promoted to 1st Lieutenant June 16, 1865, but not mustered; mustered out with company June 28, 1865.
Isaac L. Cowfer..........	1st Sergt.	25	Aug. 26, 1864	1 year.	Appointed March 28, 1865; mustered out with company June 28, 1865.
Thomas W. Wilcoxen...	Sergeant.	22	Aug. 18, 1864	1 year.	Mustered out with company June 28, 1865.
James M. Weldon........	....do....	18	Aug. 30, 1864	1 year.	Mustered out with company June 28, 1865.
Mortimer Cunningham.	....do....	28	Aug. 17, 1864	1 year.	Appointed March 28, 1865; mustered out with company June 28. 1865.
Sylvester Bigley.........	....do....	18	Aug. 25, 1864	1 year.	Appointed May 21, 1865; mustered out with company June 28, 1865.
David B. Carson.........	....do....	26	Aug. 26, 1864	1 year.	Mustered out May 20, 1865, at Newbern, N. C., by order of War Department.
John A. Rhodes.........	Corporal.	25	Sept. 2, 1864	1 year.	Mustered out with company June 28, 1865.
David B. Cross..........	....do....	26	Aug. 30, 1864	1 year.	Mustered out with company June 28, 1865.
John Ruffcorn............	....do....	26	Aug. 22, 1864	1 year.	Mustered out with company June 28, 1865.
Samuel Taylor	....do....	16	Aug. 16, 1864	1 year.	Mustered out June 27, 1865, at Tripler Hospital, Columbus, O., by order of War Department.
Benjamin Ollom	....do....	43	Aug. 23, 1864	1 year.	Mustered out with company June 28, 1865.
Devol J. Sarber..........	....do....	27	Aug. 18, 1864	1 year.	Appointed June 5, 1865; mustered out with company June 28, 1865.
James H. Schwegman...	....do....	18	Sept. 2, 1864	1 year.	Appointed March 21, 1865; mustered out with company June 28, 1865.
Robert C. White.........	....do....	18	Aug. 16, 1864	1 year.	Appointed June 9, 1865; mustered out with company June 28, 1865.
John W. Miles............	....do....	20	Aug. 30, 1864	1 year.	Mustered out June 9, 1865, at Newbern, N. C., by order of War Department.
Levi L. Daugherty.......	....do....	20	Aug. 16, 1864	1 year.	Died Dec. 5, 1864, at Nashville, Tenn.
Allen, Augustus A......	Private..	18	Aug. 26, 1864	1 year.	Wounded Dec. 7, 1864, in battle of the Cedars, Tenn.; mustered out July 4, 1865, at Murfreesboro, Tenn., by order of War Department.
Alexander, David......	....do....	20	Aug. 29, 1864	1 year.	Discharged June 14, 1865, at Gallipolis, O., for wounds received Dec. 4, 1864, in battle of Overall's Creek, Tenn.
Applegate, William H ..	....do....	40	Aug. 23, 1864	1 year.	Mustered out with company June 28, 1865.
Arnold, Andrew J........	....do....	18	Sept. 3, 1864	1 year.	Mustered out with company June 28, 1865.
Batey, David.............	....do....	30	Sept. 3, 1864	1 year.	Mustered out July 11, 1865, at Washington, D. C., by order of War Department.
Bell, John................	....do....	18	Aug. 25, 1864	1 year.	Mustered out with company June 28, 1865.
Birchfield, Lewis.........	....do....	17	Aug. 15, 1864	1 year	Died Dec. 4, 1864, at Nashville, Tenn.
Black, William H.........	....do....	18	Sept. 9, 1864	1 year.	Mustered out with company June 28, 1865.
Blackamore, Lewis......	....do....	18	Aug. 30, 1864	1 year.	Mustered out with company June 28, 1865.
Campbell, Robert	....do....	18	Aug. 30, 1864	1 year.	Mustered out with company June 28, 1865.
Cochran, Andrew........	....do....	23	Aug. 16, 1864	1 year.	Mustered out May 26, 1865, at New York City, N. Y., by order of War Department.
Congrove, Isaac..	....do....	24	Aug. 29, 1864	1 year.	Mustered out with company June 28, 1865.
Cooper, William R......	....do....	18	Sept. 1, 1864	1 year.	Mustered out June 1, 1865, at Louisville, Ky., by order of War Department.
Coulter, Amos............	....do....	21	Sept. 3, 1864	1 year.	Mustered out July 5, 1865, at Camp Dennison, O., by order of War Department.
Coulter, Harvey..........	....do....	23	Sept. 2, 1864	1 year.	Mustered out June 17, 1865, at Mower General Hospital, Philadelphia, Pa., by order of War Department.
Cross, Timothy S.........	....do....	30	Aug. 26, 1864	1 year.	Reduced from 1st Sergeant, at his own request, March 26, 1865; mustered out with company June 28, 1865.
Dailey, Charles K........	....do....	24	Sept. 5, 1864	1 year.	Also borne on rolls as Charles K. Driley.
Daniels, Thomas.........	....do....	18	Aug. 13, 1864	1 year.	Mustered out July 28, 1865, at Washington, D. C., by order of War Department.
Daugherty, Ferree	....do....	18	Aug. 16, 1864	1 year.	Died March 21, 1865, in hospital at Newbern, North Carolina.
Dewees, Elijah S	....do....	18	Aug. 29, 1864	1 year.	Mustered out with company June 28, 1865.
Duff, David A............	....do....	18	Sept. 2, 1864	1 year.	Died Jan. 24, 1865, at home, while on furlough.
Egan, James E	....do....	23	Aug. 30, 1864	1 year.	Mustered out with company June 28, 1865.
Ewing, Cassius...........	....do....	18	Aug. 30, 1864	1 year.	Mustered out with company June 28, 1865.
Fletcher, William M....	....do....	32	Aug. 29, 1864	1 year	Mustered out with company June 28, 1865.
Gandee, Jesse....... ...	....do....	18	Aug. 16, 1864	1 year.	Mustered out with company June 28, 1865.
Geary, Truman A........	....do....	18	Aug. 9, 1864	1 year.	Mustered out with company June 28, 1865.

COMPANY G.

Mustered in August 18, 1864, at Camp Chase, O., by W. P. Richardson, Colonel 25th O. V. I. Mustered out June 28, 1865, at Charlotte, N. C., by E. A. Folsom, Captain and A. C. M., Department of North Carolina.

Names.	Rank.	Age.	Date of Entering the Service.	Period of Service.	Remarks.
Alfred H. Evans	Captain.	25	July 25, 1864	1 year.	Appointed Sept. 16, 1864; Discharged March 25, 1865, at Washington, D. C., for physical disability.
John S. Nace	1st Lieut.	32	July 27, 1864	1 year.	Appointed Sept. 16, 1864; mustered out with company June 28, 1865.
William N. Robinson	2d Lieut.	23	Aug. 1, 1864	1 year.	Appointed Sept. 16, 1864; discharged Sept. [illegible], 1864, for physical disability.
John R. Rosemond	1st Sergt.	18	July 27, 1864	1 year.	Appointed from Sergeant March 24, 1865; mustered out with company June 28, 1865.
Elisha Patterson	Sergeant.	32	Aug. 25, 1864	1 year.	Mustered out with company June 28, 1865.
Darwin S. Curtis	....do....	18	July 27, 1864	1 year.	Mustered out July 11, 1865, at Columbus, O., by order of War Department.
James W. Coultrap	....do....	19	July 27, 1864	1 year.	Wounded Dec. 7, 1864, in battle of the Cedars, Tenn.; discharged June 22, 1865, at Harewood General Hospital, Washington, D. C., on Surgeon's certificate of disability.
David Paugle	....do....	25	Sept. 3, 1864	1 year.	Appointed from Corporal March 24, 1865; mustered out with company June 28, 1865.
Abraham B. Stroup	Corporal.	20	Aug. 3, 1864	1 year.	Died Feb. 16, 1865, in hospital at Nashville, Tennessee.
Reuben M. Powell	....do....	18	Aug. 1, 1864	1 year.	Mustered out with company June 28, 1865.
Linley Hoge	....do....	20	Sept. 3, 1864	1 year.	Mustered out with company June 28, 1865.
Richard H. Rose	....do....	25	Sept. 2, 1864	1 year.	Mustered out with company June 28, 1865.
William P. Thompson	....do....	19	Aug. 27, 1864	1 year.	Mustered out with company June 28, 1865.
Edmond Bailey	....do....	24	Aug. 25, 1864	1 year.	Mustered out with company June 28, 1865.
Marion Beaty	....do....	25	Sept. 3, 1864	1 year.	Mustered out with company June 28, 1865.
William H. Gleave	....do....	22	Sept. 3, 1864	1 year.	Appointed ——; mustered out with company June 28, 1865.
Clinton C. Haney	....do....	18	Sept. 3, 1864	1 year.	Appointed ——; mustered out with company June 28, 1865.
Vachel A. Williams	Musician	16	Aug. 23, 1864	1 year.	Mustered out with company June 28, 1865.
Edward Stephens	Wagoner	29	Sept. 16, 1864	1 year.	Mustered out July 15, 1865, at Portsmouth Grove, R. I., by order of War Department.
Armstrong, George W	Private	39	Sept. 5, 1864	1 year.	Mustered out May 30, 1865, at Columbus, O., by order of War Department.
Barr, Joseph H	....do....	44	Sept. 3, 1864	1 year.	Mustered out with company June 28, 1865.
Beall, William B	....do....	18	Aug. 18, 1864	1 year.	Mustered out with company June 28, 1865.
Bridge, James W	....do....	41	Sept. 3, 1864	1 year.	Mustered out with company June 28, 1865.
Brown, Entwistle	....do....	20	Sept. 3, 1864	1 year.	Died Feb. 25, 1865, in hospital at Nashville, Tennessee.
Brown, James T	....do....	18	Aug. 12, 1864	1 year.	Mustered out with company June 28, 1865.
Burson, Cyrus H	....do....	22	Sept. 12, 1864	1 year.	Re[illegible]ed from Corporal ——; mustered out Oct [illegible] 1865, at Camp Dennison, O., by order of War Department.
Carpenter, Edward S	....do....	23	July 27, 1864	1 year.	Transferred to Co. G, 181st O. V. I., June 15, 1865.
Carpenter, William E	....do....	28	Sept. 16, 1864	1 year.	Mustered out May 29, 1865, at Camp Dennison, O., by order of War Department.
Carter, Ephraim T	....do....	18	Sept. 5, 1864	1 year.	
Carter, Hector	....do....	32	Sept. 3, 1864	1 year.	Mustered out with company June 28, 1865.
Case, Johnson	....do....	36	Aug. 30, 1864	1 year.	Mustered out July 6, 1865, at David's Island, New York Harbor, by order of War Department.
Clipner, John C	....do....	18	Aug. 18, 1864	1 year.	Mustered out June 24, 1865, at Fortress Monroe, Va., by order of War Department.
Coultrap, Morgan V	....do....	32	Sept. 3, 1864	1 year.	Died Feb. 14, 1865, at Columbus, O.
Davis, George W	....do....	21	Sept. 8, 1864	1 year.	Mustered out with company June 28, 1865.
Davis, Henry M	....do....	18	Aug. 17, 1864	1 year.	Mustered out with company June 28, 1865.
Donlen, Thomas	....do....	31	Aug. 23, 1864	1 year.	Mustered out with company June 28, 1865.
Edwards, Walter	....do....	18	Aug. 18, 1864	1 year.	Captured March 24, 1865, near Goldsboro, N. C.; sent to Guards' Hospital [illegible] No further record found.
Foreman, Josephus	....do....	24	Sept. 10, 1864	1 year.	Mustered out May 29, 1865, at Camp Dennison, O., by order of War Department.
Flager, Jacob	....do....	30	Aug. 19, 1864	1 year.	Mustered out June 15, 1865, at Beaufort, N. C., by order of War Department.
Galligher, Elza	....do....	40	Sept. 3, 1864	1 year.	Died April 4, 1865, at Murfreesboro, Tenn., of wounds received Dec. 7, 1864, in battle of the Cedars, Tenn.
Galligher, Oliver	....do....	18	Aug. 27, 1864	1 year.	Mustered out with company June 28, 1865.
Givens, Benjamin F	....do....	25	Sept. 8, 1864	1 year.	Mustered out with company June 28, 1865.
Givens, James H	....do....	26	Sept. 8, 1864	1 year.	Accidentally wounded ——; mustered out May 25, 1865, at Columbus, O., by order of War Department.
Gleave, Josiah	....do....	36	Sept. 3, 1864	1 year.	Mustered out with company June 28, 1865.
Graham, Abner	....do....	22	Aug. 18, 1864	1 year.	Mustered out with company June 28, 1865.

Names.	Rank.	Age.	Date of Entering the Service.	Period of Service.	Remarks.
...ith, John W.	Private.	18	Aug. 8, 1864	1 year.	Mustered out June 20, 1865, at Louisville, Ky., by order of War Department.
...th, Reese L.	...do...	27	Sept. 8, 1864	1 year.	Mustered out with company June 28, 1865.
..., William	...do...	44	Aug. 20, 1864	1 year.	Mustered out May 30, 1865, at Columbus, O., by order of War Department.
...dison, Joseph W.	...do...	18	Aug. 17, 1864	1 year.	Mustered out with company June 28, 1865.
...is, Joseph V.	...do...	24	Sept. 22, 1864	1 year.	Reduced from Hospital Steward, at his own request, Nov. 10, 1864; mustered out May 14, 1865, at Huntsville, Ala., by order of War Department.
...ter, David H.	...do...	18	Aug. 3, 1864	1 year.	Mustered out with company June 28, 1865.
..., John E.	...do...	18	Sept. 9, 1864	1 year.	Mustered out with company June 28, 1865.
...son, Francis	...do...	28	Aug. 13, 1864	1 year.	
...son, James C.	...do...	18	Sept. 9, 1864	1 year.	Mustered out with company June 28, 1865.
..., John A.	...do...	24	Sept. 8, 1864	1 year.	Transferred to Co. G, 181st O. V. I., June 15, 1865.
...ew, Armstead M.	...do...	23	Sept. 2, 1864	1 year.	Mustered out with company June 28, 1865.
..., John A.	...do...	18	Sept. 15, 1864	1 year.	Mustered out with company June 28, 1865.
...rmick, Michael	...do...	18	Sept. 2, 1864	1 year.	Mustered out with company June 28, 1865.
...illen, Samuel B.	...do...	18	Aug. 15, 1864	1 year.	Mustered out with company June 28, 1865.
...ire, Alexander	...do...	19	Sept. 28, 1864	1 year.	Mustered out with company June 28, 1865.
...r, Francis	...do...	18	Aug. 18, 1864	1 year.	
...r, Samuel	...do...	26	Aug. 30, 1864	1 year.	Mustered out with company June 28, 1865.
..., Luther S.	...do...	18	Aug. 22, 1864	1 year.	Accidentally wounded ——; mustered out June 26, 1865, at Washington, D. C., by order of War Department.
...at, Israel	...do...	18	Aug. 8, 1864	1 year.	Mustered out with company June 28, 1865.
...at, John W.	...do...	24	Aug. 8, 1864	1 year.	Mustered out with company June 28, 1865.
...comb, Nathan L.	...do...	31	Aug. 16, 1864	1 year.	Sent to hospital at Greensboro, N. C., June 14, 1865; R. R. amputation right arm; mustered out with company June 28, 1865.
...el, David	...do...	21	Aug. 20, 1864	1 year.	Mustered out with company June 28, 1865.
...el, Thomas M.	...do...	20	Sept. 21, 1864	1 year.	Mustered out with company June 28, 1865.
...rn, George C.	...do...	19	Aug. 22, 1864	1 year.	Mustered out with company June 28, 1865.
...rn, John	...do...	18	Aug. 22, 1864	1 year.	Mustered out with company June 28, 1865.
..., Shelton	...do...	32	Aug. 13, 1864	1 year.	Mustered out with company June 28, 1865.
..., Thomas R.	...do...	44	Aug. 18, 1864	1 year.	Mustered out May 29, 1865, at Nashville, Tenn., by order of War Department.
..., John	...do...	34	Aug. 26, 1864	3 yrs.	Mustered out June 29, 1865, at Washington, D. C., by order of War Department.
...lips, Henderson	...do...	27	Sept. 18, 1864	1 year.	Mustered out with company June 28, 1865.
...son, Henry	...do...	43	Aug. 25, 1864	1 year.	Died April 30, 1865, in hospital.
...rts, James	...do...	19	Aug. 15, 1864	1 year.	
...son, Thomas	...do...	18	Aug. 23, 1864	1 year.	Mustered out with company June 28, 1865.
...son, William H.	...do...	18	Aug. 12, 1864	1 year.	Died Oct. 4, 1864, at Camp Chase, O.
..., John E.	...do...	18	Aug. 15, 1864	1 year.	Mustered out June 19, 1865, at Camp Chase, O. by order of War Department.
..., William B.	...do...	18	Aug. 15, 1864	1 year.	Mustered out May 24, 1865, at Philadelphia, Pa., by order of War Department.
..., Noble V.	...do...	19	Aug. 8, 1864	1 year.	Mustered out with company June 28, 1865.
...ll, James	...do...	40	Sept. 5, 1864	1 year.	Mustered out June 22, 1865, at Philadelphia, Pa., by order of War Department.
..., David S.	...do...	36	Aug. 25, 1864	1 year.	Mustered out with company June 28, 1865.
..., Eli	...do...	19	Aug. 10, 1864	1 year.	Mustered out with company June 28, 1865.
...man, Joseph	...do...	18	Aug. 25, 1864	1 year.	Mustered out with company June 28, 1865.
...re, Joseph	...do...	20	Aug. 20, 1864	1 year.	Mustered out to date June 28, 1865, at Charlotte, N. C., by order of War Department.
...al, Alexander C.	...do...	20	Sept. 8, 1864	1 year.	Mustered out with company June 28, 1865.
..., Emery	...do...	38	Sept. 8, 1864	1 year.	Mustered out with company June 28, 1865.
..., Elbert F.	...do...	25	Sept. 15, 1864	1 year.	Mustered out with company June 28, 1865.
...up, Thomas	...do...	23	Sept. 3, 1864	1 year.	Mustered out with company June 28, 1865.
...mpson, Moses	...do...	36	Aug. 27, 1864	1 year.	Mustered out with company June 28, 1865.
...man, Andrew J.	...do...	18	Sept. 3, 1864	1 year.	Accidentally killed Oct. 24, 1864, at Duck River Bridge, Tenn.
...man, William R.	...do...	20	July 27, 1864	1 year.	Captured March 24, 1865, near Goldsboro, N.C., and reduced from 1st Sergeant the same day; mustered out June 21, 1865, at Camp Chase, O., by order of War Department; also borne on rolls as Riley Tinsman.
...well, David F.	...do...	18	Aug. 30, 1864	1 year.	Mustered out June 13, 1865, at Washington, D. C., by order of War Department.
...ll, David	...do...	42	Aug. 19, 1864	1 year.	Mustered out June 17, 1865, at Washington, D. C., by order of War Department.
...ers, Amos	...do...	18	Sept. 8, 1864	1 year.	Mustered out May 29, 1865, at Nashville, Tenn., by order of War Department.
..., Alfred	...do...	30	Sept. 2, 1864	1 year.	Died Oct. 12, 1864, in hospital.
...ll, William	...do...	24	Aug. 16, 1864	1 year.	Mustered out with company June 28, 1865.
..., Seth	...do...	28	Sept. 12, 1864	1 year.	Mustered out with company June 28, 1865.
..., Jacob	...do...	18	Aug. 15, 1864	1 year.	Mustered out with company June 28, 1865.

COMPANY H.

Mustered in August 18, 1864, at Camp Chase, O., by W. P. Richardso
June 28, 1865, at Charlotte, N. C., by E. A. Folsom,
Department of North Carolina

Names.	Rank.	Age.	Date of Entering the Service.	Period of Service.	
John R. Basiger	Captain.	22	Sept. 16, 1864	1 year.	Must
David M. Howe	1st Lieut.	20	Sept. 16, 1864	1 year.	Detail [illegible] [illegible] [illegible] 28, 1
William E. Webber	2d Lieut.	21	Sept. 16, 1864	1 year.	Promo not June
John Alexander	1st Sergt.	21	Sept. 5, 1864	1 year.	Appoi Lieu mus
John Bacon	Sergeant.	26	Aug. 31, 1864	1 year.	Appoi 16, 1 Dep
Fletcher L. Brown	do.	19	Aug. 6, 1864	1 year.	Appoi tere
Charles Bockover	do.	21	Sept. 10, 1864	1 year.	Appoi tere
Monroe Marsh	do.	18	Aug. 22, 1864	1 year.	Appoi tere
Stanley Bell	do.	21	Aug. 5, 1864	1 year.	Promo
Judson Nettleton	do.	26	Sept. 1, 1864	1 year.	Died wou Over
Joseph Brownmiller	Corporal.	20	Aug. 18, 1864	1 year.	Appoi com
John Whery	do.	26	Aug. 17, 1864	1 year.	Appoi com
Warner Marquard	do.	34	Aug. 27, 1864	1 year.	Appoi com
George W. Williamson	do.	18	Sept. 9, 1864	1 year.	Appoi com
Charles W. Main	do.	22	Aug. 13, 1864	1 year.	Appoi com
Joseph Gibbart	do.	19	Sept. 9, 1864	1 year.	Appoi com
Patrick Griffin	do.	20	Aug. 22, 1864	1 year.	Appoi com
George Dill	do.	22	Sept. 5, 1864	1 year.	Muste by o
Samuel Weiser	Musician	18	Sept. 5, 1864	1 year.	Muste
Daniel Patterson	do.	42	Sept. 5, 1864	1 year.	Reduc requ 1865; Dep
Alexander, Edward	Private.	22	Sept. 2, 1864	1 year.	Muste
Anway, Nicholas	do.	35	Aug. 31, 1864	1 year.	Muste
Barton, Ebenezer	do.	31	Aug. 27, 1864	1 year.	Muste
Battenfield, Milton B.	do.	20	Aug. 10, 1864	1 year.	Muste
Beaty, Joseph	do.	18	Aug. 10, 1864	1 year.	Muste
Bell, James A.	do.	19	Aug. 10, 1864	1 year.	Muste by o
Binder, Dolph	do.	37	Sept. 21, 1864	1 year.	Muste
Bolton, Thomas M.	do.	31	Sept. 5, 1864	1 year.	Muste C., b
Brainard, George	do.	18	Sept. 12, 1864	1 year.	Died fres Char
Brown, James	do.	18	Sept. 13, 1864	1 year.	Muste
Brown, Leonard	do.	21	Sept. 13, 1864	1 year.	Muste
Browning, Oliver D.	do.	20	Sept. 8, 1864	1 year.	Muste
Brum, Michael	do.	18	Aug. 4, 1864	1 year.	Muste
Carnes, Charles	do.	18	Aug. 10, 1864	1 year.	
Case, Andrew	do.	18	Sept. 12, 1864	1 year.	Woun Cree June
Chappel, John A.	do.	22	Aug. 12, 1864	1 year.	Muste
Clark, Asbury	do.	18	Aug. 13, 1864	1 year.	Muste
Clark, Charles W.	do.	18	Aug. 31, 1864	1 year.	Muste
Coy, Columbus C.	do.	22	Sept. 5, 1864	1 year.	Muste
Crook, James	do.	19	Aug. 6, 1864	1 year.	Muste
Cunningham, James S.	do.	22	Aug. 10, 1864	1 year.	Died
Dean, Marvin	do.	19	Sept. 9, 1864	1 year.	Muste by o
Debolt, Jackson	do.	24	Sept. 2, 1864	1 year.	Muste

Names.	Rank.	Age.	Date of Entering the Service.	Period of Service.	
Williams, Morris........	Private..	45	Aug. 15, 1864	1 year.	Mustered out Jun by order of War
Williamson, Alonzo.....	....do....	21	Sept. 10, 1864	1 year.	Mustered out with
Williamson, Eli.........	....do....	18	Sept. 10, 1864	1 year.	Mustered out with
Wilson, John............	....do....	44	Sept. 2, 1864	1 year.	Mustered out with
Wood, Perry.............	....do....	18	Sept. 10, 1864	1 year.	Mustered out to da War Departmen

COMPANY I.

Mustered in August 18, 1864, at Camp Chase, O., by W. P. Richardson, Colonel 2 June 28, 1865, at Charlotte, N. C., by E. A. Folsom, Captain and Department of North Carolina.

Names.	Rank.	Age.	Date of Entering the Service.	Period of Service.	
William H. Garrett......	Captain.	26	Sept. 16, 1864	1 year.	Mustered out with
Harry L. Boyd.....	1st Lieut.	26	Sept. 16, 1864	1 year.	Appointed Act. I 1865; mustered 1865.
James S. Armstrong.....	2d Lieut.	32	Sept. 16, 1864	1 year.	Discharged May 15
Sanford W. Devore......	1st Sergt.	21	Aug. 28, 1864	1 year.	Appointed from S moted to 2d Lie not mustered; r June 28, 1865.
James S. Elliott..........	Sergeant.	28	Aug. 28, 1864	1 year.	Appointed Sept. 1 Major Sept. 29, 1.
William H. Patton......	....do....	24	Aug. 28, 1864	1 year.	Appointed Sept. 1 company June 2
Joseph E. Crow..........	....do....	22	Aug. 28, 1864	1 year.	Appointed Sept. 1 Sergeant Oct. 6, 1 in battle of the C to date June 28, partment.
William S. Drake........	....do....	20	Aug. 10, 1864	1 year.	Appointed from C tered out with c
Joshua A. Francis.......	....do....	25	Aug. 18, 1864	1 year.	Reduced from 1st tered out May 3 order of War De
James B. Strawbridge...	Corporal.	18	Aug. 6, 1864	1 year.	Appointed Sept. 1 company June 2
Henry Stratton..........	....do....	36	Aug. 18, 1864	1 year.	Appointed Sept. 1 27, 1865, at McDo York Harbor, by
Christopher B. Vanfleet.	....do....	39	Aug. 22, 1864	1 year.	Appointed Sept. 1 18, 1865, at Davi bor, by order of
Thaddeus S. Selanders..	....do....	24	Sept. 10, 1864	1 year.	Appointed Sept. 1 company June 2
Samuel H. Kemper......	....do....	21	Aug. 27, 1864	1 year.	Appointed Sept. 1 17, 1865, at Davi bor, by order of
Abraham Boyer.........	....do....	19	Aug. 22, 1864	1 year.	Appointed Sept. 1 company June 2
John B. Corbin..........	....do....	27	Aug. 29, 1864	1 year.	Appointed Sept. 1 company June 2
James M. Francis........	....do....	23	Aug. 29, 1864	1 year.	Appointed Sept. 2 company June 2
Arkison B. Owen........	Musician	19	Aug. 27, 1864	1 year.	Mustered out with
John H. Eversoll........	....do....	20	Sept. 1, 1864	1 year.	Mustered out May by order of War
Armstrong, John........	Private..	24	Sept. 2, 1864	1 year.	Mustered out with
Baker, Mahlon...........	....do....	18	Aug. 27, 1864	1 year.	Mustered out with
Barnhart, David M......	....do....	20	Sept. 1, 1864	1 year.	Mustered out June C., by order of W
Bishop, William H......	....do....	21	Aug. 13, 1864	1 year.	Died Sept. 20, 1864,
Blue, Adam..............	....do....	43	Sept. 12, 1864	1 year.	Mustered out with
Boyer, Adam............	....do....	18	Aug. 22, 1864	1 year.	Mustered out with
Brady, David J..........	....do....	21	Aug. 15, 1864	1 year.	Mustered out with
Brady, Jonathan S......	....do....	24	Aug. 29, 1864	1 year.	Mustered out with
Carr, Newton M.........	....do....	18	Sept. 10, 1864	1 year.	Mustered out with
Carmine, James.........	....do....	19	Sept. 10, 1864	1 year.	Mustered out with
Carter, James M.........	....do....	18	Sept. 10, 1864	1 year.	Mustered out with
Clay, Wesley P.....	....do....	19	Aug. 8, 1864	1 year.	Died Jan. 31, 1865,
Cole, Ira B...............	....do....	18	Aug. 18, 1864	1 year.	Mustered out Jun by order of War
Coleman, William S.....	....do....	21	Aug. 28, 1864	1 year.	Mustered out wit also borne on ro
Collins, Elijah...........	....do....	36	Sept. 13, 1864	1 year.	Mustered out with
Coonrod, Howard W....	....do....	18	Aug. 22, 1864	1 year.	Mustered out with
Cratty, David............	....do....	35	Aug. 18, 1864	1 year.	Mustered out with

Names.	Rank.	Age.	Date of Entering the Service.	Period of Service.	Remarks.
Cratty, Hiram	Private..	33	Aug. 8, 1864	1 year.	Killed Dec. 4, 1864, in battle of Overall's Creek, Tennessee.
Crawford, George W.	...do...	24	Sept. 13, 1864	1 year.	Mustered out with company June 28, 1865.
Culp, John R.	...do...	26	Aug. 30, 1864	1 year.	Mustered out May 29, 1865, at Camp Dennison, O., by order of War Department.
Curren, Eli W	...do...	28	Aug. 29, 1864	1 year.	Mustered out with company June 28, 1865.
Daniels, Paul	...do...	25	Sept. 6, 1864	1 year.	Mustered out June 6, 1865, at Columbus, O., by order of War Department.
Davids, Judson N.	...do...	18	Aug. 8, 1864	1 year.	Mustered out with company June 28, 1865.
Davis, Justin C.	...do...	32	Sept. 6, 1864	1 year.	Mustered out with company June 28, 1865.
Davis, Lewis W.	...do...	31	Sept. 12, 1864	1 year.	Mustered out with company June 28, 1865.
De Turk, John	...do...	18	Aug. 8, 1864	1 year.	Mustered out with company June 28, 1865.
Essex, Lemuel J	...do...	24	Sept. 10, 1864	1 year.	Mustered out with company June 28, 1865.
Essex, Samuel A	...do...	23	Aug. 20, 1864	1 year.	Mustered out with company June 28, 1865.
Ferguson, William	...do...	30	Sept. 10, 1864	1 year.	Mustered out with company June 28, 1865.
Fox, Jacob F	...do...	22	Aug. 15, 1864	1 year.	Mustered out with company June 28, 1865.
Francisco, George	...do...	19	Aug. 26, 1864	1 year.	Transferred to 180th O. V. I.; name not borne on any record of that organization. No further record found.
George, Benjamin J	...do...	28	Aug. 15, 1864	1 year.	Promoted to Chaplain Nov. 22, 1864.
Gillett, Andrew A	...do...	34	Aug. 28, 1864	1 year.	Mustered out with company June 28, 1865.
Harshberger, Leonard D.	...do...	18	Aug. 8, 1864	1 year.	Mustered out with company June 28, 1865.
Hawkins, Augustus Z.	...do...	20	Sept. 12, 1864	1 year.	Mustered out with company June 28, 1865.
Hecker, Frederick	...do...	19	Aug. 22, 1864	1 year.	Died Dec. 24, 1864, at Murfreesboro, Tenn., of wounds received Dec. 7, 1864, in battle of the Cedars, Tenn.
Hurd, John N	...do...	20	Aug. 26, 1864	1 year.	Mustered out with company June 28, 1865.
Knachel, Emanuel	...do...	34	Aug. 30, 1864	1 year.	Mustered out with company June 28, 1865.
Landon, Samuel M	...do...	20	Aug. 16, 1864	1 year.	Mustered out with company June 28, 1865.
Martin, Samuel	...do...	20	Sept. 13, 1864	1 year.	
Mattox, Simon	...do...	18	Aug. 17, 1864	1 year.	Mustered out with company June 28, 1865.
Messenger, Henry N.	...do...	26	Sept. 4, 1864	1 year.	Mustered out June 17, 1865, at Mower General Hospital, Philadelphia, Pa., by order of War Department.
Messenger, Norman	...do...	25	Aug. 13, 1864	1 year.	Mustered out with company June 28, 1865.
Messenger, Rufus	...do...	33	Sept. 4, 1864	1 year.	Mustered out with company June 28, 1865.
Miller, Silas H.	...do...	18	Aug. 15, 1864	1 year.	Died March 9, 1865, at Newbern, N. C.
Minnich, David	...do...	38	Sept. 13, 1864	1 year.	Mustered out with company June 28, 1865.
Morgan, William H	...do...	33	Aug. 22, 1864	1 year.	Mustered out June 6, 1865, at David's Island, New York Harbor, by order of War Department.
Mounts, Samuel C.	...do...	44	Aug. 15, 1864	1 year.	Mustered out June 16, 1865, at Newbern, N. C., by order of War Department.
Owen, George W	...do...	19	Aug. 25, 1864	1 year.	Mustered out with company June 28, 1865.
Olmstead, Van R.	...do...	18	Jan. 23, 1865	1 year.	Transferred to Co. G, 181st O. V. I., June 15, 1865.
Palmer, Reed S.	...do...	41	Sept. 3, 1864	1 year.	Mustered out June 2, 1865, at Albany, N. Y., by order of War Department.
Parker, Jeremiah	...do...	30	Sept. 12, 1864	1 year.	Mustered out with company June 28, 1865.
Patton, Asa L.	...do...	24	Aug. 24, 1864	1 year.	Died Feb. 9, 1865, at Washington, D. C.
Patton, William H	...do...	19	Aug. 6, 1864	1 year.	Mustered out with company June 28, 1865.
Payne, David J	...do...	28	Aug. 31, 1864	1 year.	Killed Dec. 7, 1864, in battle of the Cedars, Tennessee.
Pitney, Robert H	...do...	18	Aug. 8, 1864	1 year.	Mustered out with company June 28, 1865.
Price, John	...do...	26	Sept. 12, 1864	1 year.	Mustered out with company June 28, 1865.
Redding, Isaac	...do...	30	Sept. 4, 1864	1 year.	Died Feb. 10, 1865, at Camp Stoneman, D. C.
Ransenberger, John	...do...	29	Aug. 29, 1864	1 year.	Mustered out with company June 28, 1865.
Rogers, Napoleon B.	...do...	23	Aug. 25, 1864	1 year.	Mustered out with company June 28, 1865.
Ross, Martianus	...do...	18	Sept. 13, 1864	1 year.	Wounded Dec. 8, 1864, in battle of the Cedars, Tenn.; mustered out June 24, 1865, at Louisville, Ky., by order of War Department.
Rupp, John	...do...	32	Sept. 13, 1864	1 year.	Mustered out May 27, 1865, at Washington, D. C., by order of War Department.
Rutter, Orsamus	...do...	30	Aug. 13, 1864	1 year.	Mustered out with company June 28, 1865.
Self, William H.	...do...	39	Sept. 13, 1864	1 year.	Mustered out with company June 28, 1865.
Shaffer, James	...do...	39	Aug. 29, 1864	1 year.	Discharged March 4, 1865, at Columbus, O., by order of War Department.
Shannon, Henry	...do...	29	Aug. 13, 1864	1 year.	Mustered out with company June 28, 1865.
[illegible], Samuel	...do...	33	Sept. 5, 1864	1 year.	Mustered out with company June 28, 1865.
[illegible], Jacob	...do...	22	Sept. 13, 1864	1 year.	Wounded Dec. 7, 1864, in battle of the Cedars, Tenn.; mustered out June 2, 1865, at Columbus, O., by order of War Department.
[illegible], William	...do...	23	Aug. 27, 1864	1 year.	Mustered out with company June 28, 1865.
[illegible], Jacob S	...do...	34	Aug. 29, 1864	1 year.	Mustered out with company June 28, 1865.
[illegible], Henry	...do...	18	Aug. 23, 1864	1 year.	Mustered out with company June 28, 1865.
[illegible], William H.	...do...	32	Aug. 25, 1864	1 year.	Mustered out June 22, 1865, at Washington, D. C., by order of War Department.
[illegible], Samuel	...do...	42	Sept. 5, 1864	1 year.	Wounded Dec. 4, 1864, in battle of Overall's Creek, Tenn.; mustered out May 24, 1865, at Columbus, O., by order of War Department.
Southwick, Corydon C.	...do...	[illegible]	Sept. 12, 1864	1 year.	Died Jan. 22, 1865, at Murfreesboro, Tenn.
Southwick, Lemuel	...do...	21	Aug. 12, 1864	1 year.	Mustered out with company June 28, 1865.
Sprague, William	...do...	22	Sept. 13, 1864	1 year.	Mustered out with company June 28, 1865.
Squibb, Thomas J.	...do...	18	Aug. 27, 1864	1 year.	Mustered out with company June 28, 1865.
Stockwell, Chandler M.	...do...	[illegible]	Sept. 1, 1864	1 year.	Mustered out with company June 28, 1865.
Stockwell, Willard	...do...	[illegible]	Sept. 1, 1864	1 year.	Mustered out with company June 28, 1865.

Names.	Rank.	Age.	Date of Entering the Service.	Period of Service.	
Straw, William	Private.	26	Sept. 13, 1864	1 year.	Died March 2, 186
Sutley, George	....do....	43	Aug. 31, 1864	1 year.	Mustered out wit
Swart, John	....do....	44	Aug. 11, 1864	1 year.	Mustered out Ma C., by order of
Taylor, James V	....do....	26	Aug. 15, 1864	1 year.	Mustered out with
Thomas, John	....do....	20	Sept. 13, 1864	1 year.	
Tyler, Enoch H	....do....	20	Aug. 11, 1864	1 year.	Mustered out with
Vestal, Marshall	....do....	30	Sept. 7, 1864	1 year.	Mustered out with
Wyatt, David H	....do....	40	Aug. 29, 1864	1 year.	Died Oct. 11, 1864,

COMPANY K.

Mustered in August 18, 1864, at Camp Chase, O., by W. P. Richardson, Colonel June 28, 1865, at Charlotte, N. C., by E. A. Folsom, Captain and Department of North Carolina.

Names.	Rank.	Age.	Date of Entering the Service.	Period of Service.	
Henry McPeek	Captain.	29	Sept. 21, 1864	1 year.	Mustered out wit
Benjamin B. McGowan	1st Lieut.	31	Sept. 21, 1864	1 year.	Mustered out wit
Thomas J. Weatherby	2d Lieut.	22	Sept. 21, 1864	1 year.	Promoted to 1st I not mustered; June 28, 1865.
William W. McCracken	1st Sergt.	26	Sept. 14, 1864	1 year.	Appointed Sept. 2 1865, by order of
Thomas Mitchell	....do....	28	Sept. 17, 1864	1 year.	Appointed from S tered out with c
John H. Morrison	Sergeant.	19	Sept. 10, 1864	1 year.	Appointed Sept. 2 company June 2
Leander E. Parsons	....do....	37	Sept. 10, 1864	1 year.	Appointed Sept. 2 company June 2
John S. Reasoner	....do....	22	Sept. 13, 1864	1 year.	Appointed Sept. 2 company June 2
Boyd M. Bowlsud	....do....	35	Sept. 12, 1864	1 year.	Appointed from C tered out with co
John M. Dawson	Corporal.	27	Sept. 13, 1864	1 year.	Appointed Sept. 2 14, 1865, at Covin Department.
Alexander M. Proctor	....do....	39	Sept. 12, 1864	1 year.	Appointed Sept. 2 company June 2
Edwin Armstrong	....do....	22	Sept. 6, 1864	1 year.	Appointed Sept. 2 company June 2
Byram E. James	....do....	21	Sept. 14, 1864	1 year.	Appointed Sept. 2 company June 2
George W. Bovard	....do....	42	Sept. 12, 1864	1 year.	Appointed Sept. 21
Immer Robinson	....do....	21	Sept. 13, 1864	1 year.	Appointed Sept. 2 9, 1865, at Newb Department.
Samuel Hindman	....do....	20	Sept. 16, 1864	1 year.	Appointed April 1 company June 2
John Heffelfinger	....do....	23	Sept. 10, 1864	1 year.	Appointed May 1 company June 2
George Glauner	....do....	32	Sept. 12, 1864	1 year.	Appointed May 1 company June 2
Henry H. Marshall	....do....	24	Sept. 13, 1864	1 year.	Appointed June 1 company June 2
Adams, James	Private.	37	Sept. 9, 1864	1 year.	Mustered out June eral Hospital, N of War Departm
Adams, John	....do....	30	Sept. 9, 1864	1 year.	Mustered out with
Albright, Silas	....do....	18	Sept. 14, 1864	1 year.	Mustered out with
Andrews, Samuel	....do....	17	Sept. 15, 1864	1 year.	Mustered out with
Armstrong, John J	....do....	27	Sept. 12, 1864	1 year.	Mustered out with
Arthur, Benjamin	....do....	31	Sept. 14, 1864	1 year.	Mustered out with
Arthur, Joseph A	....do....	18	Sept. 13, 1864	1 year.	Mustered out with
Auld, Levi	....do....	17	Sept. 17, 1864	1 year.	Mustered out May by order of War
Austin, Alexander	....do....	37	Sept. 9, 1864	1 year.	Reduced from Co tered out July 1 O., by order of
Bauldauf, Andrew	....do....	36	Sept. 13, 1864	1 year.	Mustered out with
Blake, William H.	....do....	18	Oct. 13, 1864	1 year.	Transferred to Co 1865.
Book, Israel	....do....	19	Sept. 13, 1864	1 year.	Mustered out with
Breese, Henry W	....do....	44	Sept. 11, 1864	1 year.	Mustered out with
Casey, William	....do....	38	Sept. 2, 1864	1 year.	Mustered out with
Clink, John	....do....	44	Sept. 14, 1864	1 year.	Mustered out with
Conger, John	....do....	27	Oct. 6, 1864	1 year.	Transferred to Co 1865.
Conklin, Gilbert J	....do....	20	Sept. 12, 1864	1 year.	Wounded —; mu Camp Dennison partment.

	Rank.	Age.	Date of Entering the Service.	Period of Service.	Remarks.
klin, James E........	Private..	44	Sept. 13, 1864	1 year.	Mustered out June 9, 1865, at Camp Dennison, O., by order of War Department.
in, Alexander........	....do....	28	Aug. 20, 1864	1 year.	Mustered out with company June 28, 1865.
well, Robert J........	....do....	21	Sept. 12, 1864	1 year.	Mustered out with company June 28, 1865.
ningham, Warren K.	....do....	20	Sept. 14, 1864	1 year.	Mustered out with company June 28, 1865.
man, Isaac...........	....do....	35	Sept. 9, 1864	1 year.	Discharged March 14, 1865, by order of War Department.
ert, Jacob...........	....do....	17	Sept. 14, 1864	1 year.	Mustered out with company June 28, 1865.
y, Ira B.............	....do....	16	Sept. 12, 1864	1 year.	Mustered out with company June 28, 1865.
t, Joel...............	....do....	43	Sept. 14, 1864	1 year.	Died Jan. 6, 1865, at Camp Dennison, O.; also borne on rolls as Joel Fint.
ls, Edward...........	....do....	35	Sept. 9, 1864	1 year.	No record subsequent to enlistment.
re, Robert E..........	....do....	20	Sept. 14, 1864	1 year.	Mustered out July 11, 1865, at Columbus, O., by order of War Department
son, Joseph..........	....do....	28	Sept. 14, 1864	1 year.	Mustered out with company June 28, 1865.
ith, Gilman T........	....do....	19	Sept. 14, 1864	1 year.	Mustered out with company June 28, 1865.
inger, Mathias......	....do....	29	Sept. 12, 1864	1 year.	Mustered out with company June 28, 1865.
ilton, David.........	....do....	27	Sept. 13, 1864	1 year.	
uff, Henry...........	....do....	44	Sept. 13, 1864	1 year.	Mustered out with company June 28, 1865.
uff, James P.........	....do....	20	Sept. 12, 1864	1 year.	Mustered out with company June 28, 1865.
ellinger, Hibbert....	....do....	21	Sept. 14, 1864	1 year.	Mustered out with company June 28, 1865.
lershot, Lorenso.....	....do....	18	Sept. 13, 1864	1 year.	Mustered out with company June 28, 1865.
lershot, Nathan S..	....do....	40	Sept. 13, 1864	1 year.	Mustered out with company June 28, 1865.
, William L..........	....do....	24	Sept. 13, 1864	1 year.	Mustered out July 11, 1865, at Columbus, O., by order of War Department.
ard, William M.......	....do....	18	Sept. 15, 1864	1 year.	Mustered out with company June 28, 1865.
Jeremiah S...........	....do....	33	Sept. 12, 1864	1 year.	Mustered out with company June 28, 1865.
s, George W..........	....do....	19	Sept. 14, 1864	1 year.	Mustered out with company June 28, 1865.
s, John...............	....do....	29	Sept. 12, 1864	1 year.	Mustered out with company June 28, 1865.
m, George............	....do....	18	Sept. 14, 1864	1 year.	Mustered out with company June 28, 1865.
eicelter, Henry.......	....do....	29	Sept. 12, 1864	1 year.	Mustered out with company June 28, 1865.
gel, Adam............	....do....	20	Sept. 13, 1864	1 year.	Mustered out with company June 28, 1865.
isey, Elli M..........	....do....	18	Sept. 14, 1864	1 year.	Mustered out May 22, 1865, at Murfreesboro, Tenn., by order of War Department.
, William............	....do....	22	Sept. 14, 1864	1 year.	No record subsequent to enlistment.
, Benjamin...........	....do....	25	Sept. 10, 1864	1 year.	Mustered out with company June 28, 1865.
in, Christian.........	....do....	28	Sept. 12, 1864	1 year.	Mustered out with company June 28, 1865.
r, James..............	....do....	22	Sept. 9, 1864	1 year.	Mustered out with company June 28, 1865.
hell, Albert..........	....do....	33	Sept. 9, 1864	1 year.	Mustered out with company June 28, 1865.
hell, George N.......	....do....	18	Sept. 9, 1864	1 year.	Mustered out with company June 28, 1865.
ly, Joseph G.........	....do....	19	Sept. 6, 1864	1 year.	Mustered out with company June 28, 1865.
ser, George..........	....do....	18	Sept. 9, 1864	1 year.	Mustered out with company June 28, 1865.
er, Peter P...........	....do....	39	Sept. 24, 1864	1 year.	Mustered out with company June 28, 1865.
er, William M........	....do....	25	Sept. 9, 1864	1 year.	Died March 30, 1865.
s, Alexander M......	....do....	44	Sept. 13, 1864	1 year.	Died March 7, 1865.
s, Clarkson C.........	....do....	21	Sept. 13, 1864	1 year.	Died Jan. 14, 1865.
l, James..............	....do....	23	Sept. 12, 1864	1 year.	Mustered out with company June 28, 1865.
nd, George W. C.....	....do....	16	Sept. 12, 1864	1 year.	Mustered out May 29, 1865, at New York City, by order of War Department.
nd, Samuel T.........	....do....	28	Sept. 12, 1864	1 year.	Mustered out with company June 28, 1865.
h, Jacob..............	....do....	18	Sept. 13, 1864	1 year.	Mustered out June 22, 1865, at Washington, D. C., by order of War Department.
, John................	....do....	36	Sept. 13, 1864	1 year.	Mustered out with company June 28, 1865; also borne on rolls as John Rush.
bury, Adin W.........	....do....	19	Sept. 13, 1864	1 year.	Discharged June 1, 1865, for wounds received in action.
er, William S.........	....do....	18	Sept. 13, 1864	1 year.	Mustered out with company June 28, 1865.
ock, William..........	....do....	41	Sept. 10, 1864	1 year.	Mustered out with company June 28, 1865.
er, Israel.............	....do....	42	Sept. 12, 1864	1 year.	Died March 29, 1865.
maker, Christian.....	....do....	18	Sept. 14, 1864	1 year.	No record subsequent to enlistment.
k, Adam..............	....do....	21	Sept. 9, 1864	1 year.	Mustered out with company June 28, 1865.
h, William S.........	....do....	38	Sept. 9, 1864	1 year.	Mustered out June 22, 1865, at Washington, D. C., by order of War Department.
ob, Lewis.............	....do....	18	Sept. 9, 1864	1 year.	Mustered out with company June 28, 1865.
r, William............	....do....	20	Sept. 14, 1864	1 year.	Mustered out with company June 28, 1865.
dell, Charles H......	....do....	18	Sept. 14, 1864	1 year.	No record subsequent to enlistment.
rwood, Andrew......	....do....	20	Aug. 20, 1864	1 year.	Mustered out with company June 28, 1865.
rwood, Jesse.........	....do....	21	Sept. 9, 1864	1 year.	Mustered out with company June 28, 1865.
er, David.............	....do....	22	Sept. 13, 1864	1 year.	Mustered out with company June 28, 1865.
rman, George........	....do....	18	Aug. 13, 1864	1 year.	Mustered out with company June 28, 1865.
er, Henry.............	....do....	..	....	1 year.	Assigned to company Oct. 23, 1864.
h, Dewitt C...........	....do....	44	Sept. 12, 1864	1 year.	Mustered out with company June 28, 1865.
on, Jonathan P.......	....do....	30	Sept. 14, 1864	1 year.	Mustered out June 9, 1865, at Newbern, N. C., by order of War Department.
sford, Julius M.......	....do....	30	Aug. 9, 1864	1 year.	Died Dec. 8, 1864, of wounds received Dec. 7, 1864, in battle of the Cedars, Tenn.
ord, David E.........	....do....	25	Sept. 13, 1864	1 year.	Promoted to Principal Musician Oct. 4, 1864.
ord, John A..........	....do....	18	Sept. 13, 1864	1 year.	Mustered out with company June 28, 1865.
ord, William E.......	....do....	20	Sept. 13, 1864	1 year.	Mustered out with company June 28, 1865.

UNASSIGNED RECRUITS.

The following list of recruits is found on muster and descriptive rolls for this organization, bu borne on any of the company rolls of this Regiment.

Names.	Rank.	Age.	Date of Entering the Service.	Period of Service.	Remarks.
Haning, Daniel	Private..	18	April 3, 1865	1 year.	Mustered out May 15, 1865, on detached r at Hart Island, New York Harbor, by o of War Department.
Hanley, Charles A.	....do....	19	Mch. 27, 1865	year.	
Heid, Jacob I.	....do....	33	Aug. 25, 1864	year.	
Herst, William	....do....	19	Oct. 3, 1864	year.	
Hetter, John	....do....	35	Oct. 17, 1864	year.	
Hoesch, Sigmund	....do....	34	Oct. 14, 864	year.	
Hug, Mathias	....do....	40	Sept. 28, 1864	year.	
Matthews, Millard F.	....do....	18	Feb. 16, 1865	year.	
Nichol, Thomas M.	....do....	20	Sept. 21, 1864	year.	
Quigly, Simon	....do....	21	Aug. 23, 1864	year.	
Schmidberger, Christopher	....do....	28	Sept. 6, 1864	1 year.	
Schmidt, Jacob	....do....	27	Oct. 6, 1864	1 year.	
Schmidt, John	....do....	32	Oct. 13, 1864	1 year.	
Seitz, John	....do....	33	Sept. 6, 1864	1 year.	
Slevin, Michael	....do....	19	Aug. 23, 1864	1 year.	

175th Regiment Ohio Volunteer Infantry.

ONE YEAR'S SERVICE.

This Regiment was organized at Camp Dennison, O., in October, 1864, to serve one year. It was ordered to Columbia, Tenn., where it performed post and garrison duty in the town, and was also engaged in guarding the Tennessee and Alabama Railroad. In the advance of Hood one of the Regiment's outposts was captured, south of Columbia, while the remainder of the Regiment fell back to Franklin, and took part in the battle at that place on the 30th of November. The Regiment then fell back to Nashville, and took position in Fort Negley, where it remained during the battle, and on the 25th of December was again ordered to Columbia, and engaged in the usual garrison duties, and in guarding the railroad bridges. It was mustered out June 27, 1865, in accordance with orders from the War Department.

175TH REGIMENT OHIO VOLUNTEER INFANTRY.

FIELD AND STAFF.

Mustered in October 10, 1864, at Camp Dennison, O. Mustered out June 27, 1865, at Nashville, Tenn., by Philip Reefy, Captain 19th O. V. I., and A. C. M., 3d Division, 4th Army Corps.

Names.	Rank.	Age.	Date of Entering the Service.	Period of Service.	Remarks.
Wesley R. Adams	Colonel.	28	July 26, 1862	3 yrs.	Resigned as Captain Co. K, 89th O. V. I., Nov. 16, 1864, to accept commission as Colonel of this regiment, but not mustered; commission returned.
Daniel McCoy	Lt. Col.	24	Sept. 14, 1864	1 year.	Promoted to Colonel June 6, 1865, but not mustered; mustered out with regiment June 27, 1865.
Edward E. Mullenix	Major.	28	Oct. 8, 1864	1 year.	Promoted to Lieut. Colonel June 6, 1865, but not mustered; mustered out with regiment June 27, 1865.
Rufus A. Dwyre	Surgeon.	37	Sept. 20, 1864	1 year.	Mustered out with regiment June 27, 1865.
Benjamin D. Granger	Ast. Surg.	29	Sept. 20, 1864	1 year.	Mustered out with regiment June 27, 1865.
William F. Hani	....do....	22	Sept. 29, 1864	1 year.	Resigned May 11, 1865.
John E. Carpenter	Adjutant	28	Sept. 30, 1864	1 year.	Promoted to Captain June 6, 1865, but not mustered; mustered out with regiment June 27, 1865.
Francis M. Possgate	R. Q. M.	26	Sept. 16, 1864	1 year.	Appointed 1st Lieutenant and Regt. Quartermaster Oct. 10, 1864; mustered out with regiment June 27, 1865. See Co. E.
James P. Shultz	Chaplain	30	Sept. 20, 1864	1 year.	Promoted from private Co. F Sept. 30, 1864; mustered out with regiment June 27, 1865.
Dossey A. Lennin	Ser. Maj.	20	July 30, 1864	1 year.	Promoted from private Co. A Oct. 11, 1864; to 2d Lieutenant Co. A March 18, 1865.
William A. Quarterman	Q. M. S.	31	Oct. 11, 1864	1 year.	Promoted from private Co. H Oct. 11, 1864; mustered out with regiment June 27, 1865.
Lycurgus Duncanson	Com. Ser.	21	Sept. 1, 1864	1 year.	Promoted from private Co. B Oct. 11, 1864; mustered out May 25, 1865, at Camp Dennison, O., by order of War Department.
John W. Hill	....do....	28	Sept. 1, 1864	1 year.	Promoted from Corporal Co. B May 28, 1865; mustered out with regiment June 27, 1865.
Alexander Leadbetter	Hos. St'd.	27	Aug. 29, 1864	1 year.	Promoted from Corporal Co. A Oct. 11, 1864; mustered out with regiment June 27, 1865.

COMPANY A.

Mustered in September 10, 1864, at Camp Dennison, O., by Wm. Von Doehn, Captain and A. A. G. Mustered out June 27, 1865, at Nashville, Tenn., by Philip Reefy, Captain 19th O. V. I., and A. C. M., 3d Division, 4th Army Corps.

Names.	Rank.	Age.	Date of Entering the Service.	Period of Service.	Remarks.
Robert A. Johnston	Captain.	25	Sept. 10, 1864	1 year.	Promoted to Major June 6, 1865, but not mustered; mustered out with company June 27, 1865.
[illegible] M. Dennis	1st Lieut.	47	Sept. 10, 1864	1 year.	Resigned Dec. 17, 1864.
Stephen E. Lemon	....do....	20	Sept. 10, 1864	1 year.	Promoted from 2d Lieutenant Jan. 6, 1865; mustered out with company June 27, 1865.
Dossey A. Lennin	2d Lieut.	20	July 30, 1864	1 year.	Promoted to Sergt. Major from private Oct. 11, 1864; 2d Lieutenant March 18, 1865; mustered out with company June 27, 1865.
Thomas Elliott	1st Sergt.	38	Aug. 2, 1864	1 year.	Killed Nov. 30, 1864, in battle of Franklin, Tennessee.
John Boswell	....do....	21	Aug. 29, 1864	1 year.	Appointed from Sergeant April 1, 1865; mustered out with company June 27, 1865.
Hugh A. [illegible]	Sergeant.	31	Aug. 15, 1864	1 year.	Died Jan. 7, 1865, at St. Louis, Mo.
John E. [illegible]	....do....	22	Aug. 29, 1864	1 year.	Mustered out with company June 27, 1865.
William [illegible]	....do....	23	Sept. 4, 1864	1 year.	Appointed from private Nov. 30, 1864; mustered out with company June 27, 1865.
Condy Campbell	....do....	21	Aug. 1, 1864	1 year.	Appointed from Corporal April 1, 1865; mustered out with company June 27, 1865.

Names.	Rank.	Age.	Date of Entering the Service.	Period of Service.	Remarks.
Wesley R. Patterson	Sergeant.	42	Aug. 29, 1864	1 year.	Appointed from Corporal April 1, 1865; mustered out with company June 27, 1865.
Joseph B. McCollum	Corporal.	30	Sept. 4, 1864	1 year.	Died Feb. 11, 1865, at Columbia, Tenn.
Alexander Leadbetter	...do...	27	Aug. 29, 1864	1 year.	Promoted to Hospital Steward Oct. 11, 1864.
David Pierson	...do...	36	Sept. 2, 1864	1 year.	Mustered out with company June 27, 1865.
Oliver A. Hall	...do...	43	Aug. 29, 1864	1 year.	Mustered out with company June 27, 1865.
Samuel R. Easter	...do...	31	Aug. 1, 1864	1 year.	Mustered out with company June 27, 1865.
Wilson P. Lucas	...do...	34	Aug. 1, 1864	1 year.	Mustered out June 10, 1865, at Jeffersonville, Ind., by order of War Department.
James Waddle	...do...	37	Sept. 4, 1864	1 year.	Appointed April 1, 1865; mustered out with company June 27, 1865.
Philip Elliott	...do...	29	Aug. 1, 1864	1 year.	Appointed April 1, 1865; mustered out with company June 27, 1865.
William Pierson	...do...	31	Sept. 2, 1864	1 year.	Appointed April 1, 1865; mustered out with company June 27, 1865.
Samuel S. Brooks	...do...	26	Sept. 4, 1864	1 year.	Appointed April 1, 1865; mustered out with company June 27, 1865.
George R. Wolf	Musician	20	Aug. 29, 1864	1 year.	Mustered out with company June 27, 1865.
James Stewart	...do...	22	Sept. 2, 1864	1 year.	
Willard J. Edgington	Wagoner	28	Aug. 13, 1864	1 year.	Mustered out with company June 27, 1865.
Barclay, Alonzo	Private	22	Sept. 2, 1864	1 year.	Mustered out with company June 27, 1865.
Barr, James A	...do...	18	Aug. 29, 1864	1 year.	Mustered out with company June 27, 1865.
Barrow, John W	...do...	19	Aug. 29, 1864	1 year.	Mustered out with company June 27, 1865.
Beard, Asa G	...do...	18	Aug. 29, 1864	1 year.	Mustered out with company June 27, 1865.
Beard, David H	...do...	18	Aug. 6, 1864	1 year.	Mustered out with company June 27, 1865.
Bogan, Benjamin M	...do...	18	Sept. 5, 1864	1 year.	Mustered out with company June 27, 1865.
Bogan, Moses	...do...	21	Sept. 2, 1864	1 year.	Mustered out with company June 27, 1865.
Bogan, William	...do...	44	Sept. 5, 1864	1 year.	Killed Nov. 30, 1864, in battle of Franklin, Tennessee.
Boyd, Erasmus D	...do...	42	Sept. 1, 1864	1 year.	Mustered out with company June 27, 1865.
Boyle, William H	...do...	19	Aug. 20, 1864	1 year.	Mustered out with company June 27, 1865.
Brooks, Jordan	...do...	34	Sept. 4, 1864	1 year.	Mustered out with company June 27, 1865.
Brown, Edward	...do...	18	Aug. 24, 1864	1 year.	Mustered out with company June 27, 1865.
Burns, Robert	...do...	20	Sept. 6, 1864	1 year.	Mustered out with company June 27, 1865.
Butters, George W	...do...	18	Aug. 6, 1864	1 year.	Mustered out May 16, 1865, at Cincinnati, O., by order of War Department.
Buzzard, Francis M	...do...	18	Aug. 30, 1864	1 year.	Mustered out with company June 27, 1865.
Cashatt, William R	...do...	33	Aug. 29, 1864	1 year.	Mustered out with company June 27, 1865.
Colvin, Richard	...do...	18	Aug. 16, 1864	1 year.	Captured Nov. 30, 1864, at battle of Franklin, Tenn. No further record found.
Coons, Abraham G. W	...do...	31	Sept. 5, 1864	1 year.	Mustered out with company June 27, 1865.
Cordery, William H	...do...	43	Sept. 4, 1864	1 year.	Died March 23, 1865, at Nashville, Tenn.
Crawford, Alexander R	...do...	26	Aug. 15, 1864	1 year.	Mustered out with company June 27, 1865.
Crew, Eli	...do...	25	Aug. 30, 1864	1 year.	Mustered out with company June 27, 1865.
Culter, William M	...do...	43	Sept. 2, 1864	1 year.	Mustered out with company June 27, 1865.
Curry, John W	...do...	22	Sept. 4, 1864	1 year.	Mustered out with company June 27, 1865.
Donley, James W	...do...	39	Sept. 3, 1864	1 year.	Mustered out with company June 27, 1865.
Duncanson, James	...do...	25	Sept. 3, 1864	1 year.	Discharged March 28, 1865, at St. Louis, Mo., on Surgeon's certificate of disability.
Duncanson, Robert H	...do...	38	Sept. 4, 1864	1 year.	Mustered out with company June 27, 1865.
Garner, Joseph T	...do...	22	Sept. 1, 1864	1 year.	Mustered out with company June 27, 1865.
Garrett, Michael O	...do...	18	Aug. 29, 1864	1 year.	Mustered out with company June 27, 1865.
Gizzleman, George W	...do...	18	Aug. 13, 1864	1 year.	Mustered out with company June 27, 1865.
Glass, Crawford	...do...	20	Sept. 2, 1864	1 year.	Mustered out with company June 27, 1865.
Gleadell, Edward	...do...	22	Aug. 8, 1864	1 year.	Mustered out with company June 27, 1865.
Grady, William M	...do...	18	Aug. 19, 1864	1 year.	Mustered out with company June 27, 1865.
Hall, John B	...do...	28	Aug. 22, 1864	1 year.	Died March 7, 1865, at Jeffersonville, Ind.
Hart, William R	...do...	18	Aug. 29, 1864	1 year.	Mustered out with company June 27, 1865.
Henderson, John	...do...	44	Sept. 3, 1864	1 year.	Mustered out with company June 27, 1865.
Himes, James M	...do...	39	Sept. 3, 1864	1 year.	Mustered out with company June 27, 1865.
Hiser, Daniel F	...do...	18	Sept. 4, 1864	1 year.	Died April 7, 1865, at Vicksburg, Miss.
Hunter, James W	...do...	18	Feb. 21, 1865	1 year.	Transferred to Co. C, 189th O. V. I., July 12, 1865.
Kiskaden, Laban J	...do...	43	Sept. 2, 1864	1 year.	Mustered out with company June 27, 1865.
Knisely, Richard	...do...	35	Sept. 2, 1864	1 year.	Mustered out with company June 27, 1865.
Knisely, Samuel	...do...	25	Sept. 1, 1864	1 year.	Mustered out with company June 27, 1865.
Lindsey, John B	...do...	32	Aug. 28, 1864	1 year.	Mustered out with company June 27, 1865.
Ludwig, Jackson	...do...	18	Aug. 29, 1864	1 year.	Mustered out with company June 27, 1865.
Ludwig, Louis P	...do...	18	Aug. 31, 1864	1 year.	Mustered out with company June 27, 1865.
Ludwig, William H	...do...	18	Aug. 29, 1864	1 year.	Mustered out with company June 27, 1865.
Lyle, Robert M	...do...	18	Aug. 29, 1864	1 year.	Mustered out with company June 27, 1865.
McCoppin, Ambrose	...do...	34	Aug. 1, 1864	1 year.	Mustered out with company June 27, 1865.
McCoy, William A	...do...	27	Aug. 23, 1864	1 year.	Killed Nov. 30, 1864, in battle of Franklin, Tennessee.
McCully, John M	...do...	18	Feb. 25, 1865	1 year.	Transferred to Co. C, 189th O. V. I., July 12, 1865, and there borne as John M. [illegible]
Madden, John	...do...	20	Aug. 2, 1864	1 year.	Mustered out with company June 27, 1865.
Madden, Thomas	...do...	23	Aug. 2, 1864	1 year.	Mustered out with company June 27, 1865.
Milner, James D	...do...	23	Sept. 3, 1864	1 year.	Mustered out with company June 27, 1865.
Moore, James	...do...	24	Aug. 10, 1864	1 year.	Captured Nov. 30, 1864, at battle of Franklin, Tenn.; mustered out May 20, 1865, at Camp Chase, O., by order of War Department.
Mull, William	...do...	19	Aug. 29, 1864	1 year.	Mustered out with company June 27, 1865.
Neal, John	...do...	36	Sept. 3, 1864	1 year.	Mustered out with company June 27, 1865.
O'Connell, John	...do...	18	Aug. 24, 1864	1 year.	Captured Nov. 30, 1864, at battle of Franklin, Tenn.; mustered out June 17, 1865, at Camp Chase, O., by order of War Department.

Names.	Rank.	Age.	Date of Entering the Service.	Period of Service.	Remarks.
Enoch P. Erskine	Musician	18	Aug. 18, 1864	1 year.	Died Feb. 16, 1865, while prisoner of war.
John W. Hite	....do....	18	Aug. 20, 1864	1 year.	Mustered out with company June 27, 1865.
Reuben Simpson	Wagoner.	39	Sept. 1, 1864	1 year.	Mustered out with company June 27, 1865.
Argo, James	Private..	27	Aug. 23, 1864	1 year.	Died March 4, 1865, at Sinking Springs, Highland County, O.
Barker, George W	....do....	44	Aug. 2, 1864	1 year.	Mustered out May 25, 1865, at Camp Dennison, O., by order of War Department.
Beekman, Snowden H	....do....	34	Sept. 2, 1864	1 year.	Discharged May 31, 1865, at St. Louis, Mo., on Surgeon's certificate of disability.
Bobb, Isaac	....do....	20	Aug. 25, 1864	1 year.	Captured Nov. 30, 1864, at battle of Franklin, Tenn.; died May 18, 1865, at New Orleans, La.
Brock, Daniel	....do....	25	Jan. 23, 1865	1 year.	Transferred to Co. D, 189th O. V. I., July 12, 1865.
Brock, Samuel	....do....	20	Aug. 23, 1864	1 year.	Mustered out with company June 27, 1865.
Broomhall, John C	....do....	25	Sept. 2, 1864	1 year.	Wounded Nov. 30, 1864, in battle of Franklin, Tenn.; transferred to Co. D, 6th Regiment Veteran Reserve Corps, April 5, 1865; mustered out July 5, 1865, at Cleveland, O., by order of War Department.
Butler, Henry	....do....	20	Aug. 19, 1864	1 year.	Captured Nov. 24, 1864, in action at Bridge No. 15, Tennessee and Alabama Railroad; mustered out June 17, 1865, at Camp Chase, O., by order of War Department.
Butler, Jacob	....do....	19	Aug. 22, 1864	1 year.	Mustered out with company June 27, 1865.
Butler, Josiah M	....do....	32	Aug. 23, 1864	1 year.	Mustered out with company June 27, 1865.
Carter, Henry	....do....	36	Sept. 4, 1864	1 year.	Mustered out with company June 27, 1865.
Chaney, Henry O	....do....	18	Sept. 3, 1864	1 year.	Died Oct. 8, 1864, at Camp Dennison, O.
Chestnut, Samuel	....do....	21	Sept. 4, 1864	1 year.	Mustered out with company June 27, 1865.
Chrisman, Jonathan C	....do....	26	Aug. 31, 1864	1 year.	Mustered out with company June 27, 1865.
Chrisman, John	....do....	36	Sept. 5, 1864	1 year.	Mustered out with company June 27, 1865.
Conover, George W	....do....	34	Aug. 30, 1864	1 year.	Captured Nov. 24, 1864, in action at Bridge No. 15, Tennessee and Alabama Railroad; mustered out June 22, 1865, at Camp Chase, O., by order of War Department.
Conover, Sommers	....do....	38	Sept. 1, 1864	1 year.	Captured Nov. 24, 1864, in action at Bridge No. 15, Tennessee and Alabama Railroad; died Jan. 19, 1865, in Rebel Prison at Andersonville, Ga.
Cropper, George W	....do....	33	Sept. 4, 1864	1 year.	Mustered out with company June 27, 1865.
Crosier, Samuel B	....do....	24	Sept. 3, 1864	1 year.	Mustered out with company June 27, 1865.
Crum, Elijah L	....do....	31	Sept. 1, 1864	1 year.	Mustered out May 1[illegible], 1865, at Columbia, Tenn., by order of War Department.
Cummings, Daniel	....do....	32	Sept. 4, 1864	1 year.	Mustered out with company June 27, 1865.
Day, Aaron E	....do....	19	Sept. 3, 1864	1 year.	Reduced to ranks from 1st Sergeant Dec. [illegible], 1864; detailed at headquarters Department of the Cumberland, May 28, 1865; mustered out with company June 27, 1865.
Dick, Quinton	....do....	25	Sept. 2, 1864	1 year.	Mustered out with company June 27, 1865.
Duncanson, Lycurgus	....do....	21	Sept. 1, 1864	1 year.	Promoted to Cor. Sergeant Oct. 11, 1864.
Earhart, William D	....do....	19	Sept. 2, 1864	1 year.	Captured Nov. 24, 1864, in action at Bridge No. 15, Tennessee and Alabama Railroad; died March 31, 1865, at Vicksburg, Miss.
Eubanks, James M	....do....	20	Aug. 16, 1864	1 year.	Captured Nov. 29, 1864, in action at Thompson's Station, Tennessee and Alabama Railroad; mustered out June 15, 1865, at Camp Chase, O., by order of War Department.
Eubanks, Josephus	....do....	19	Aug. 18, 1864	1 year.	Captured Nov. 29, 1864, in action at Thompson's Station, Tennessee and Alabama Railroad; mustered out June 8, 1865, at Columbus, O., by order of War Department.
Fite, Samuel W	....do....	18	Aug. 30, 1864	1 year.	Captured Nov. 30, 1864, at battle of Franklin, Tenn.; died Apr. 16, 1865, at Mound City, Ill.
Foreman, George S	....do....	18	Aug. 30, 1864	1 year.	Mustered out with company June 27, 1865.
Foulk, Jacob	....do....	38	Sept. 4, 1864	1 year.	Killed Nov. 30, 1864, in battle of Franklin, Tennessee.
Frump, Joel	....do....	21	Sept. 2, 1864	1 year.	Captured Nov. 24, 1864, in action at Bridge No. 15, Tennessee and Alabama Railroad; exchanged ——; died March 30, 1865, at Big Black River Bridge, Miss.
Frump, John	....do....	22	Sept. 5, 1864	1 year.	Mustered out with company June 27, 1865.
Frump, John W	....do....	22	Sept. 5, 1864	1 year.	Mustered out with company June 27, 1865.
Fry, Lewis A	....do....	28	Sept. 1, 1864	1 year.	Captured Nov. 24, 1864, in action at Bridge No. 15, Tennessee and Alabama Railroad; mustered out June 22, 1865, at Camp Chase, O., by order of War Department.
Garman, Cyrenus G	....do....	21	Aug. 15, 1864	1 year.	Mustered out with company June 27, 1865.
Garman, Daniel H	....do....	18	Aug. 17, 1864	1 year.	Mustered out with company June 27, 1865.
Garman, Esaias P	....do....	25	Sept. 2, 1864	1 year.	Discharged Dec. 3, 1864, at Camp Dennison, O., on Surgeon's certificate of disability.
Greenfield, Joseph	....do....	39	Jan. 23, 1865	1 year.	Transferred to Co. D, 189th O. V. I., July 12, 1865.
Hall, William R	....do....	26	Aug. 30, 1864	1 year.	Mustered out with company June 27, 1865.
Harshbarger, William H	....do....	23	Aug. 30, 1864	1 year.	Mustered out with company June 27, 1865.
Jenkins, Daniel	....do....	35	Sept. 5, 1864	1 year.	Mustered out with company June 27, 1865.
Jenkins, Jesse	....do....	28	Sept. 5, 1864	1 year.	Mustered out June 19, 1865, at Columbia, Tenn., by order of War Department.

Names.	Rank.	Age.	Date of Entering the Service.	Period of Service.	Remarks.
Oliver, John	Private.	28	Sept. 3, 1864	1 year.	Mustered out June 19, 1865, at Columbia, Tenn., by order of War Department.
Patton, James	....do....	37	Sept. 6, 1864	1 year.	Mustered out May 25, 1865, at Camp Dennison, O., by order of War Department.
Phillips, Francis M.	....do....	29	Sept. 3, 1864	1 year.	Mustered out with company June 27, 1865.
[illegible], John	....do....	34	Aug. 26, 1864	1 year.	Mustered out June 19, 1865, at Columbia, Tenn., by order of War Department.
[illegible], Robert M.	....do....	18	Aug. 24, 1864	1 year.	Mustered out May 11, 1865, at Columbia, Tenn., by order of War Department.
Porter, Calvin W.	....do....	21	Aug. 24, 1864	1 year.	Mustered out with company June 27, 1865.
Rhodes, John	....do....	23	Sept. 3, 1864	1 year.	Mustered out July 2, 1865, at Louisville, Ky., by order of War Department.
[illegible], David	....do....	48	Aug. 30, 1864	1 year.	Mustered out with company June 27, 1865.
[illegible], Robert	....do....	18	Sept. 9, 1864	1 year.	Mustered out with company June 27, 1865.
Shaw, James	....do....	44	Sept. 2, 1864	1 year.	Transferred to Co. I, 6th Regiment, Veteran Reserve Corps, June 12, 1865, from which mustered out July 13, 1865, at Indianapolis, Ind., by order of War Department.
Shields, George W.	....do....	23	Aug. 29, 1864	1 year.	Mustered out with company June 27, 1865.
Shull, Joseph W.	....do....	21	Sept. 3, 1864	1 year.	Mustered out with company June 27, 1865.
Snowhill, Charles	....do....	29	Aug. 26, 1864	1 year.	Mustered out June 19, 1865, at Columbia, Tenn., by order of War Department.
Stevens, George B.	....do....	19	Aug. 29, 1864	1 year.	Mustered out May 25, 1865, at Camp Dennison, O., by order of War Department.
Stevens, Joseph N.	....do....	30	Sept. 5, 1864	1 year.	Wounded Nov. 30, 1864, in battle of Franklin, Tenn.; discharged June 13, 1865, at Camp Dennison, O., on Surgeon's certificate of disability.
[illegible], Jacob	....do....	22	Sept. 3, 1864	1 year.	Mustered out with company June 27, 1865.
Thornhill, William H.	....do....	28	Aug. 30, 1864	1 year.	Mustered out with company June 27, 1865.
[illegible], William	....do....	21	Sept. 3, 1864	1 year.	Mustered out with company June 27, 1865.
Vandervort, John	....do....	25	Sept. 3, 1864	1 year.	Mustered out with company June 27, 1865.
[illegible], Levi	....do....	26	Sept. 6, 1864	1 year.	Mustered out with company June 27, 1865.
Williams, Francis S.	....do....	19	Sept. 6, 1864	1 year.	Mustered out with company June 27, 1865.
Williams, Thomas W.	....do....	21	Sept. 2, 1864	1 year.	Mustered out with company June 27, 1865.
Wolf, Benjamin F.	....do....	18	Aug. 29, 1864	1 year.	Mustered out with company June 27, 1865.
Workman, Noah L.	....do....	18	Sept. 7, 1864	1 year.	
Young, William F.	....do....	32	Sept. 3, 1864	1 year.	Mustered out with company June 27, 1865.

COMPANY D.

Mustered in September 18, 1864, at Camp Dennison, O., by Wm. Von Doehn, Captain and A. A. G. Mustered out June 27, 1865, at Nashville, Tenn., by Philip Reefy, Captain 19th O. V. I., and A. C. M., 3d Division, 4th Army Corps.

Names.	Rank.	Age.	Date of Entering the Service.	Period of Service.	Remarks.
Wilson B. Logan	Captain.	34	Sept. 13, 1864	1 year.	Killed Nov. 30, 1864, in battle of Franklin, Tennessee.
Charles W. Apley	....do....	21	Sept. 10, 1864	1 year.	Promoted from 1st Lieutenant Co. B March 29, 1865; mustered out with company June 27, 1865.
Francis M. Harover	1st Lieut.	22	Sept. 13, 1864	1 year.	Prisoner of war ——; promoted to Captain Jan. 6, 1865, but not mustered; resigned May 23, 1865.
[illegible] Tyler	2d Lieut.	21	Sept. 13, 1864	1 year.	Promoted to 1st Lieutenant Jan. 6, 1865, but not mustered; resigned June 11, 1865.
William R. Van Winkle	....do....	43	Sept. 3, 1864	1 year.	Promoted from 1st Sergeant Co. C March 29, 1865; mustered out with company June 27, 1865.
David S. Flaugher	1st Sergt.	21	Sept. 4, 1864	1 year.	Captured Nov. 24, 1864, in action at Bridge No. 16, Tennessee and Alabama Railroad; mustered out June 15, 1865, at Camp Chase, O., by order of War Department.
[illegible] McKinley	Sergeant.	21	Aug. 30, 1864	1 year.	Mustered out with company June 27, 1865.
[illegible]	....do....	24	Aug. 20, 1864	1 year.	Mustered out with company June 27, 1865.
[illegible] H. C. Graham	....do....	25	Aug. 24, 1864	1 year.	Captured Nov. 24, 1864, in action at Bridge No. 16, Tennessee and Alabama Railroad; mustered out with company June 27, 1865.
[illegible] C. Taylor	....do....	30	Aug. 20, 1864	1 year.	Appointed from Corporal Oct. 20, 1864; mustered out with company June 27, 1865.
[illegible]	Corporal.	22	Sept. 4, 1864	1 year.	Died Jan. 17, 1865, at Camp Dennison, O., of wounds received in action.
David [illegible]	...	27	Aug. 10, 1864	1 year.	Mustered out with company June 27, 1865.
Jesse Day	...	34	Sept. 8, 1864	1 year.	Mustered out with company June 27, 1865.
Alcinus Bruner	...	[illegible]	Sept. 4, 1864	1 year.	Mustered out with company June 27, 1865.
Jeremiah R. Paul	...	[illegible]	Sept. 4, 1864	1 year.	Captured Nov. 24, 1864, in action at Bridge No. 16, Tennessee and Alabama Railroad; mustered out June 15, 1865, at Camp Chase, O., by order of War Department.
Joab Carr	....do....	19	Aug. 6, 1864	1 year.	Mustered out with company June 27, 1865.

Names.	Rank.	Age.	Date of Entering the Service.
Daniel Bailey	Corporal.	44	Aug. 30, 1864
John H. Clelland	....do....	20	Sept. 2, 1864
David Montgomery	....do....	30	Sept. 2, 1864
George Hudson	....do....	36	Aug. 30, 1864
Joseph McChesney	....do....	38	Sept. 8, 1864
Fergus Carnahan	Musician	34	Sept. 5, 1864
George O. Easton	....do....	18	Sept. 7, 1864
Henry Lee	Wagoner	27	Aug. 24, 1864
Anderson, John W	Private..	18	Aug. 24, 1864
Baker, Benjamin J	....do....	43	Aug. 24, 1864
Barnett, James	....do....	31	Aug. 26, 1864
Beck, Alfred L	....do....	30	Aug. 24, 1864
Biggs, George	....do....	40	Sept. 3, 1864
Boatwright, William B.	....do....	26	Aug. 27, 1864
Bosorth, William	....do....	43	Sept. 10, 1864
Carnahan, Aaron E.	....do....	26	Sept. 3, 1864
Cassady, James P	....do....	21	Sept. 3, 1864
Charles, John D	....do....	18	Sept. 7, 1864
Charlton, Charles W	....do....	18	Sept. 6, 1864
Clark, James J	....do....	23	Aug. 20, 1864
Clark, Sales G.	....do....	28	Sept. 8, 1864
Constable, Cortland	....do....	18	Sept. 3, 1864
Cowman, Henry W	....do....	18	Aug. 24, 1864
Darby, Samuel	....do....	33	Aug. 30, 1864
Darby, William A	....do....	44	Aug. 30, 1864
Durbin, William J	....do....	36	Sept. 3, 1864
Engle, Oliver	....do....	18	Sept. 9, 1864
Ewan, Levi	....do....	22	Sept. 3, 1864
Farquer, James H	....do....	41	Sept. 3, 1864
Fisher, William B	....do....	31	Aug. 26, 1864
Garrison, Calvin L	....do....	18	Sept. 9, 1864
Girton, William	....do....	18	Sept. 3, 1864
Grim, Joseph	....do....	38	Sept. 3, 1864
Hahn, Philip	....do...	18	Sept. 9, 1864
Hahn, William	....do....	18	Sept. 9, 1864
Haines, Mordecai M	....do....	32	Sept. 3, 1864
Haines, William	....do....	28	Sept. 9, 1864
Hammer, Peter	....do....	32	Sept. 3, 1864
Horr, Jacob W	....do....	25	Sept. 3, 1864
Hinshaw, Garner	....do....	33	Aug. 30, 1864
Hockett, Asa	....do....	24	Aug. 24, 1864
Hockett, Isaac J	....do....	36	Sept. 3, 1864
Hockett, Levi	....do....	44	Aug. 29, 1864
Hockett, William	....do....	21	Aug. 24, 1864
Hodson, George W	....do....	26	Sept. 8, 1864
Hodson, George W., Sr.	....do....	37	Sept. 3, 1864
Holaday, Charles	....do....	18	Sept. 3, 1864
Hunt, Josiah L	....do....	28	Aug. 29, 1864
Hunt, William H	....do....	21	Aug. 24, 1864
Jackson, William M	....do....	44	Aug. 29, 1864
Johnson, Francis M	....do....	23	Sept. 3, 1864
Kenny, Levi	....do....	27	Sept. 3, 1864
Layman, Joseph	....do....	29	Sept. 3, 1864
Liming, Isaac	....do....	23	Sept. 2, 1864
Liming, John P	....do....	29	Sept. 2, 1864
McChesney, Jasper	....do....	26	Sept. 8, 1864
McFeeters, Marion	....do....	23	Sept. 3, 1864
McHenry, Alexander	....do....	20	Sept. 3, 1864
Maltbie, Milo B.	....do....	26	Sept. 3, 1864
Monce, George M	....do....	18	Sept. 3, 1864
Moon, Wilkerson T	....do....	31	Aug. 26, 1864
Newton, Edward P	....do....	19	Sept. 8, 1864

Names.	Rank.	Age.	Date of Entering the Service.	Period of Service.	
Samuel N. Bradford	Corporal.	18	Aug. 30, 1864		Appoi com
Timothy Pancoast	...do...	18	Aug. 13, 1864		Appoi 1864, and Rebe
Joshua G. Davidson	...do...	23	Sept. 3, 1864		Appoi com
James C. Stewart	Musician	19	Aug. 6, 1864	1	Muster
Eli Bereman	...do...	19	Aug. 6, 1864	1	Muster
George Logan	Wagoner.	24	Sept. 9, 1864	1	Muster
Askew, Nicholas	Private.	37	Sept. 3, 1864	1	Muster
Baird, Smith H	...do...	25	Sept. 2, 1864	1	Died F Alab
Bayne, James	...do...	19	Sept. 1, 1864		Captur No. 1
Black, John W	...do...	20	Sept. 1, 1864		
Blair, James	...do...	20	Aug. 29, 1864		
Botts, Benjamin F	...do...	27	Sept. 4, 1864		Captur No. 1
Bower, Daniel	...do...	19	Aug. 20, 1864		
Burns, Robert	...do...	20	Sept. 6, 1864		
Bybee, Wesley	...do...	39	Aug. 9, 1864		
Campbell, John A	...do...	28	Sept. 4, 1864		
Campbell, William J	...do...	36	Sept. 4, 1864		
Carroll, William	...do...	18	Aug. 24, 1864		
					perisl on M April
Clark, David	...do...	18	Sept. 2, 1864	1	Muster
Clutter, William	...do...	18	Aug. 20, 1864	1	Muster
Colan, Abraham	...do...	18	Aug. 10, 1864	1	Muster
Courts, Andrew J	...do...	18	Aug. 22, 1864	1	Muster
Crabtree, William	...do...	38	Sept. 4, 1864		
Davis, Alfred	...do...	40	Sept. 4, 1864	1	
Dillinger, Thomas	...do...	19	Sept. 2, 1864	1	
Dixon, Thomas J	...do...	20	Sept. 1, 1864	1	
Dunn, Aaron W	...do...	18	Aug. 20, 1864	1	
Fluharty, Eli	...do...	21	Sept. 10, 1864	1	
Gray, Noah	...do...	19	Sept. 19, 1864	1	
Gray, Thomas M	...do...	20	Sept. 4, 1864	1	
Hall, Alexander	...do...	27	Sept. 4, 1864	1	
Hall, Thomas P	...do...	17	Aug. 30, 1864	1	
Hanson, Samuel	...do...	42	Aug. 31, 1864	1	
Hare, Daniel	...do...	27	Sept. 4, 1864	1	
Hayes, Bailey P	...do...	18	Aug. 20, 1864	1	
Herbert, John	...do...	32	Sept. 1, 1864	1 year.	
Hetherman, John	...do...	43	Sept. 1, 1864	1	
					O., by
Hizer, John P	...do...	17	Aug. 30, 1864	1 year.	Muster
Holmes, Samuel A	...do...	28	Aug. 24, 1864	1 year.	Captur No. 1
Howard, Francis	...do...	28	Aug. 31, 1864		
Howard, James D	...do...	27	Sept. 4, 1864		
Jennings, Israel F	...do...	42	Sept. 2, 1864		
Jones, Martin	...do...	18	Sept. 3, 1864		Muster
King, William	...do...	18	Sept. 5, 1864		Muster
Kirk, Joseph	...do...	40	Aug. 30, 1864		Muster O., by
Lawderback, Uriah	...do...	41	Sept. 1, 1864		Muster
Little, William	...do...	20	Sept. 4, 1864		Captur No. 1 died sonvi
McDaniel, Jesse	...do...	18	Sept. 4, 1864		Muster

COMPANY E.

*Mustered in September 16, 1864, at Camp Dennison, O., by Wm. V
out June 27, 1865, at Nashville, Tenn., by Philip F
and A. C. M., 3d Division, 4th Ar

Names.	Rank.	Age.	Date of Entering the Service.	Period of Service.	
Francis M. Posegate.....	Captain.	26	Sept. 16, 1864	1 year.	
Robert F. Watson	....do....	28	Sept. 16, 1864	1 year.	
William H. Langstaff....	....do....	24	Sept. 16, 1864	1 year.	
Andrew J. Hodson......	1st Lieut.	24	Sept. 13, 1864	1 year.	
Samuel S. Jolly..........	2d Lieut.	21	Oct. 10, 1864	1 year.	Ap
William B. McKee.......	1st Sergt.	38	Aug. 16, 1864	1 year.	Mu
Jonathan L. Sanders....	Sergeant.	34	Aug. 5, 1864	1 year.	Mu
Elias H. Way............	....do....	36	Aug. 27, 1864	1 year.	Mu
Isaac F. Phillips..........	....do....	30	Sept. 8, 1864	1 year.	Mu
William N. Hendrixon..	....do....	26	Aug. 28, 1864	1 year.	Mu
James T. Davis..........	Corporal.	19	Aug. 11, 1864	1 year.	
Francis M. Earhart......	....do....	34	Sept. 3, 1864	1 year.	
James W. Massey........	....do....	24	July 29, 1864	1 year.	M
Robert McLachlan.......	....do....	34	Sept. 3, 1864	1 year.	M
John H. Daughters......	....do....	22	Aug. 15, 1864	1 year.	
William M. Wells........	....do....	31	Aug. 11, 1864	1 year.	
William Thompson	....do....	26	Sept. 3, 1864	1 year.	
James Ackley	....do....	41	Sept. 3, 1864	1 year.	
William Glover..........	Musician	18	Sept. 13, 1864	1 year.	
Paine Mullen............	....do....	33	Aug. 15, 1864	1 year.	
Elijah McGohan.........	Wagoner.	34	Sept. 3, 1864	1 year.	
Barnes, John............	Private..	19	Sept. 13, 1864	1 year.	
Bernard, William H.....	....do....	24	Aug. 1, 1864	1 year.	
Brooks, Asher E..........	....do....	30	Sept. 3, 1864	1 year.	
Bryan, David.............	....do....	28	Aug. 12, 1864	1 year.	
Camery, James C.........	....do....	18	Aug. 11, 1864	1 year.	
Carey, Joseph...........	....do....	23	Sept. 2, 1864	1 year.	
Cole, Warren E..........	....do....	22	Aug. 8, 1864	1 year.	
Conard, William.........	....do....	19	July 30, 1864	1 year.	
Conoyer, William.........	....do....	44	Sept. 3, 1864	1 year.	
Conway, James W........	....do....	36	Aug. 15, 1864	1 year.	
Cook, Perry L...........	....do....	21	Sept. 2, 1864	1 year.	
Culter, Maffett...........	....do....	43	Aug. 24, 1864	1 year.	
Day, William A	....do....	21	Sept. 3, 1864	1 year.	
Dunley, Lee C............	....do....	28	Sept. 6, 1864	1 year.	
Douley, Zeno............	....do....	34	Aug. 30, 1864	1 year.	
Duffey, Michael A........	....do....	36	Sept. 2, 1864	1 year.	
Elwood, Ashford B.......	....do....	19	Sept. 8, 1864	1 year.	
Farmer, Eli...............	....do....	29	Aug. 26, 1864	1 year.	
Furry, Elijah.............	....do....	21	Aug. 26, 1864	1 year.	
Galvin, Washington......	....do....	18	Aug. 16, 1864	1 year.	
Good, Ellis...............	....do....	18	Aug. 30, 1864	1 year.	
Gray, Thomas J..........	....do....	18	Aug. 11, 1864	1 year.	
Gwynn, William..........	....do....	21	Aug. 11, 1864	1 year.	M
Hall, William H..........	....do....	18	Aug. 15, 1864	1 year.	M
Hancock, Joseph H.......	....do....	30	Sept. 3, 1864	1 year.	M
Hancock, William........	....do....	34	Sept. 3, 1864	1 year.	M
Harbour, Abner J........	....do....	25	April 6, 1865	1 year.	T
Hare, John M	....do....	29	Sept. 1, 1864	1 year.	M
Hatch, Hiram............	....do....	26	Sept. 10, 1864	1 year.	Di

Names.	Rank.	Age.	Date of Entering the Service.	Period of Service.	Remarks.
Hemmings, Thomas	Private	26	Aug. 16, 1864	1 year.	Captured Nov. 24, 1864, in action near Columbia, Tenn.; died on or about Jan. 1, 1865, in Rebel Prison at Meridian, Miss.
Hendrixon, George W.	do	24	Aug. 26, 1864	1 year.	Captured Nov. 30, 1864, at battle of Franklin, Tenn.; perished by explosion of steamer Sultana, on Mississippi River, near Memphis, Tenn., April 27, 1865.
Henning, Alexander P.	do	44	Sept. 3, 1864	1 year.	Mustered out with company June 27, 1865.
Hockman, Benjamin	do	38	Sept. 3, 1864	1 year.	Mustered out with company June 27, 1865.
Hough, George W.	do	22	Aug. 15, 1864	1 year.	Reduced from Corporal Oct. 31, 1864, at his own request; mustered out with company June 27, 1865.
Howard, William	do	27	Sept. 1, 1864	1 year.	
Jones, Dent W.	do	21	Aug. 29, 1864	1 year.	Mustered out May 26, 1865, at Camp Dennison, O., by order of War Department.
Judkins, Eugene S.	do	18	Aug. 8, 1864	1 year.	Mustered out with company June 27, 1865.
Lafery, Jacob	do	24	Sept. 13, 1864	1 year.	Absent ——, in hospital at Jeffersonville, Ind. No further record found.
Little, Simpson	do	22	Aug. 5, 1864	1 year.	Mustered out with company June 27, 1865.
Long, Nelson	do	2[illegible]	Sept. 1, 1864	1 year.	Mustered out with company June 27, 1865.
McFadden, Charles	do	44	Aug. 16, 1864	1 year.	Mustered out with company June 27, 1865.
McFarland, Edward T.	do	19	Aug. 11, 1864	1 year.	Mustered out with company June 27, 1865.
McHugh, Michael	do	27	Sept. 13, 1864	1 year.	
McIntire, James T.	do	29	Aug. 11, 1864	1 year.	Mustered out with company June 27, 1865.
McKnight, William W.	do	27	Sept. 1, 1864	1 year.	Mustered out with company June 27, 1865.
Mascoutes, John	do	24	Sept. 6, 1864	1 year.	Captured Nov. 24, 1864, in action near Columbia, Tenn; mustered out June 17, 1865, at Camp Chase, O., by order of War Department.
Meeker, Timothy	do	42	Sept. 3, 1864	1 year.	Captured Nov. 29, 1864, in action near Columbia, Tenn.; perished by explosion of steamer Sultana, on Mississippi River, near Memphis, Tenn., April 27, 1865.
Mercer, Jason	do	21	Aug. 15, 1864	1 year.	Mustered out with company June 27, 1865.
Michael, Carey	do	22	Sept. 2, 1864	1 year.	Mustered out with company June 27, 1865.
Milmer, William G.	do	28	Sept. 2, 1864	1 year.	Mustered out with company June 27, 1865.
Montgomery, William T.	do	18	Sept. 3, 1864	1 year.	Captured Nov. 29, 1864, in action near Columbia, Tenn.; discharged July 31, 1865, at Camp Dennison, O., on Surgeon's certificate of disability.
Moore, John	do	23	Aug. 3, 1864	1 year.	Died March 3, 1865.
Morgan, Edward	do	21	Aug. 11, 1864	1 year.	Mustered out with company June 27, 1865.
Moss, William P.	do	21	Sept. 2, 1864	1 year.	Mustered out June 19, 1865, at Columbia, Tenn., by order of War Department.
Myers, Abraham	do	23	Sept. 13, 1864	1 year.	Captured Nov. 29, 1864, in action near Columbia, Tenn.; mustered out June 21, 1865, at Camp Chase, O., by order of War Department.
Newland, Allen C.	do	19	Aug. 5, 1864	1 year.	Mustered out with company June 27, 1865.
Ogden, Dean	do	26	Sept. 3, 1864	1 year.	Mustered out June 19, 1865, at Columbia, Tenn., by order of War Department.
Osborn, Ralph	do	37	Aug. 21, 1864	1 year.	Mustered out with company June 27, 1865.
Overacker, William J.	do	29	Sept. 5, 1864	1 year.	Mustered out with company June 27, 1865.
Penn, Daniel	do	29	Aug. 5, 1864	1 year.	Mustered out with company June 27, 1865.
Pennyl, George R.	do	16	Aug. 5, 1864	1 year.	Mustered out with company June 27, 1865.
Pfeffer, Andrew J.	do	44	Aug. 11, 1864	1 year.	Mustered out with company June 27, 1865.
Phillips, William H.	do	18	Aug. 23, 1864	1 year.	Mustered out with company June 27, 1865.
Plummer, Ignatius	do	38	Aug. 11, 1864	1 year.	Mustered out with company June 27, 1865.
Reed, Ralph B.	do	36	Aug. 21, 1864	1 year.	Mustered out May 25, 1865, at Camp Dennison, O., by order of War Department.
Russell, Louis	do	42	Sept. 3, 1864	1 year.	Mustered out with company June 27, 1865.
Scott, Milton S.	do	34	Sept. 5, 1864	1 year.	Mustered out with company June 27, 1865.
Sexton, Willard	do	37	Sept. 24, 1864	1 year.	Mustered out May 18, 1865, at Covington, Ky., by order of War Department.
Smith, Ordway	do	31	Aug. 27, 1864	1 year.	Mustered out with company June 27, 1865.
Smith, Sala M.	do	26	Aug. 15, 1864	1 year.	Mustered out with company June 27, 1865.
Stevens, George W.	do	21	Sept. 10, 1864	1 year.	Captured Nov. 29, 1864, in action near Columbia, Tenn.; perished by explosion of steamer Sultana, on Mississippi River, near Memphis, Tenn., April 27, 1865.
Tivis, Hudson	do	23	Aug. 11, 1864	1 year.	See Co. C, 178th O. V. I.
Vanpelt, William	do	18	Sept. 12, 1864	1 year.	Captured Nov. 30, 1864, at battle of Franklin, Tenn.; mustered out June 15, 1865, at Camp Chase, O., by order of War Department.
Vickroy, Francis M.	do	25	Aug. 13, 1864	1 year.	Mustered out with company June 27, 1865.
Ware, Eliphas L.	do	26	Aug. 24, 1864	1 year.	Captured Nov. 30, 1864, at battle of Franklin, Tenn.; mustered out June 16, 1865, at Camp Chase, O., by order of War Department.
Washburn, George H.	do	35	Aug. 25, 1864	1 year.	Captured Nov. 24, 1864, in action near Columbia, Tenn.; mustered out June 16, 1865, at Camp Chase, O., by order of War Department.
White, David E.	do	30	Aug. 23, 1864	1 year.	Mustered out with company June 27, 1865.
Williams, James A.	do	19	Sept. 3, 1864	1 year.	Mustered out with company June 27, 1865.
Wilson, Reuben	do	24	Sept. 3, 1864	1 year.	Mustered out with company June 27, 1865.

Names.	Rank.	Date of Entering the Service.	
Woodmansee, David S..	Private..	Aug. 8, 1864	1 year.
Wrestler, John	....do....	Sept. 12, 1864	1 year.

COMPANY F.

Mustered in September 28, 1864, at Camp Dennison, O., by Wm. Von Doehn
out June 27, 1865, at Nashville, Tenn., by Philip Reefy, Cap
and A. C. M., 3d Division, 4th Army Corp

William H. McCoy	Captain.	22	Sept. 28, 1864	1 year.	
					road: per tana, on Tenn., Ap
George W. Henderson...	1st Lieut.	24	Sept. 28, 1864	1 year.	Resigned J
Josiah H. Deniston......	....do....	31	Sept. 28, 1864	1 year.	Promoted f mustered
Charles M. Hughes......	1st Sergt.	27	Sept. 15, 1864	1 year.	Mustered May 9, 18 June 27, 1
Thomas J. Colvin.......	Sergeant.	28	Sept. 17, 1864	1 year.	Mustered o
William H. Rhine.......	....do....	25	Sept. 20, 1864	1 year.	Mustered o
James Conover.........	....do....	42	Sept. 17, 1864	1 year.	Captured N son's Stati road; die while pri
Edward A. Zile..........	....do....	20	Sept. 17, 1864	1 year.	Wounded a of Frankl 1865, at Ca permanent.
James H. Matthews.....	Corporal.	19	Sept. 6, 1864	1 year.	Died March
James Tullis	....do....	35	Sept. 20, 1864	1 year.	Mustered Tenn., by
Enoch W. Overman......	....do....	30	Sept. 14, 1864	1 year.	Mustered o O., by ord
Joseph Belford..........	....do....	34	Sept. 16, 1864	1 year.	Mustered o
John W. Rhodes........	....do....	20	Sept. 12, 1864	1 year.	Mustered o
Nathan Brock.......	....do....	27	Sept. 19, 1864	1 year.	Mustered o
Enos Malott.............	....do....	41	Sept. 17, 1864	1 year.	Mustered o
Lancelott B. Cass........	....do....	20	Sept. 20, 1864	1 year.	Appointed company
Christian Hatch..........	....do....	22	Sept. 20, 1864	1 year.	Appointed company
Edward Barnes..........	Musician	18	Sept. 14, 1864	1 year.	Captured N son's Stat road; per tana, on Tenn., Ap
Andrew J. McConnahay	Wagoner	32	Sept. 14, 1864	1 year.	Mustered o
Baker, Charles...........	Private..	19	Sept. 19, 1864	1 year.	
Barrow, Charles N.......	....do....	18	Sept. 16, 1864	1 year.	
Barry, James.....	....do....	22	Sept. 17, 1864	1 year.	
Brace, Francis..........	....do....	27	Sept. 20, 1864	1 year.	
Brace, William..........	....do....	25	Sept. 20, 1864	1 year.	
Breman, Porter..........	....do....	23	Sept. 9, 1864	1 year.	
Buckner, James E........	....do....	24	Sept. 8, 1864	1 year.	
Buckner, William T.....	....do....	18	Sept. 9, 1864	1 year.	
Butler, Joseph B.........	....do....	20	Sept. 17, 1864	1 year.	
Charlton, John A.........	....do....	17	Sept. 15, 1864	1 year.	
Clark, Frank	....do...	23	Sept. 16, 1864	1 year.	
Conklin, Peter...........	....do....	22	Sept. 20, 1864	1 year.	
Davis, Moses.............	....do....	28	Sept. 17, 1864	1 year.	
Drake, Ambrose.........	....do....	21	Sept. 15, 1864	1 year.	
Garretson, John E........	....do....	31	Sept. 15, 1864	1 year.	
Good, John	....do....	18	Sept. 21, 1864	1 year.	
Hadley, William H......	....do....	28	Sept. 20, 1864	1 year.	Mustered o O., by ord
Haines, George W.......	....do....	18	Sept. 8, 1864	1 year.	Absent — No furthe
Hancock, David..........	....do....	27	Sept. 11, 1864	1 year.	Mustered o
Hancock, Henry J	....do....	26	Sept. 11, 1864	1 year.	Mustered o

	Rank.	Age.	Date of Entering the Service.	Period of Service.	
[illegible]		18	Sept. 12, 1864	1 year.	Mustered out with company June 27, 1865.
George		20	Sept. 20, 1864	1 year.	Mustered out with company June 27, 1865.
George A.		23	Sept. 21, 1864	1 year.	
John W.		23	Sept. 11, 1864	1 year.	
on, John M.		27	Sept. 17, 1864	1 year.	Mustered out with company June 27, 1865.
dus, John		37	Sept. 14, 1864	1 year.	Killed Nov. 30, 1864, in battle of Franklin, Tennessee.
nd, Randolph	do.	44	Sept. 15, 1864	1 year.	Mustered out May 23, 1865, at Covington, Ky., by order of War Department.
Alfred	do.	21	Sept. 20, 1864	1 year.	Mustered out with company June 27, 1865.
ble, Newton	do.	21	Nov. 3, 1864	1 year.	Transferred to Co. D, 18th O. V. I., July 12, 1865.
r, Isaac		18	Sept. 13, 1864	1 year.	Died Nov. 9, 1864, at Columbia, Tenn.
Charles		22	Sept. 21, 1864	1 year.	
er, Joseph T.		21	Sept. 21, 1864	1 year.	Reduced from 1st Sergeant May 4, 1865, at his own request; promoted to 2d Lieutenant June 6, 1865, but not mustered; mustered out with company June 27, 1865.
er, Noah	do.	27	Sept. 19, 1864	1 year.	Mustered out with company June 27, 1865.
r, John		20	Sept. 14, 1864	1 year.	
Charles H		23	Sept. 20, 1864	1 year.	
, John		27	Sept. 20, 1864	1 year.	Mustered out with company June 27, 1865.
hart, John		24	Sept. 16, 1864	1 year.	
John		27	Sept. 21, 1864	1 year.	
er, Sanford		22	Sept. 16, 1864	1 year.	Captured Nov. 29, 1864, in action at Thompson's Station, Tennessee and Alabama Railroad; mustered out June 16, 1865, at Camp Chase, O., by order of War Department.
ell, George		19	Sept. 20, 1864	1 year.	
el, George W.		37	Sept. 20, 1864	1 year.	Mustered out with company June 27, 1865.
r, Daniel M		24	Sept. 17, 1864	1 year.	Died May 3, 1865, at Columbia, Tenn.
Charles		21	Sept. 16, 1864	1 year.	
William	...	23	Sept. 15, 1864	1 year.	
n, George R.	...	21	Sept. 16, 1864	1 year.	
ntz, Henry H.	...	17	Sept. 16, 1864	1 year.	Mustered out with company June 27, 1865.
y, Patrick	...	23	Sept. 20, 1864	1 year.	
, John M	do.	20	Sept. 20, 1864	1 year.	
r, Benjamin F.	do.	30	Sept. 18, 1864	1 year.	Mustered out with company June 27, 1865.
n, John M.	do.	34	Sept. 21, 1864	1 year.	Died Dec. 30, 1864, at Nashville, Tenn.
Isaac M.	do.	18	Sept. 13, 1864	1 year.	Mustered out with company June 27, 1865.
n, Jacob	do.	20	Sept. 11, 1864	1 year.	
Samuel J.	do.	34	Sept. 20, 1864	1 year.	
, James	do.	28	Sept. 14, 1864	1 year.	
n, Henry	do.	22	Sept. 20, 1864	1 year.	Died Dec. 18, 1864, at Nashville, Tenn.
r, Alfred	do.	20	Sept. 17, 1864	1 year.	Mustered out with company June 27, 1865.
r, Ira	do.	18	Sept. 15, 1864	1 year.	Mustered out with company June 27, 1865.
in, Horatio P.	do.	18	Sept. 19, 1864	1 year.	Mustered out with company June 27, 1865.
z, James P.	do.	30	Sept. 20, 1864	1 year.	Promoted to Chaplain Sept. 30, 1864.
er, Marshall	do.	19	Sept. 13, 1864	1 year.	
, Henry	do.	18	Sept. 20, 1864	1 year.	
, James	do.	26	Sept. 17, 1864	1 year.	Mustered out with company June 27, 1865.
, Jeremiah	do.	38	Sept. 14, 1864	1 year.	
, Sylvester	do.	40	Sept. 17, 1864	1 year.	Died June 17, 1865, at Jeffersonville, Ind.
, William	do.	18	Sept. 16, 1864	1 year.	
berry, John F.	do.	28	Sept. 12, 1864	1 year.	Mustered out with company June 27, 1865.
Ralph A	do.	29	Sept. 21, 1864	1 year.	Mustered out with company June 27, 1865.
y, John	do.	20	Sept. 21, 1864	1 year.	
, John	do.	18	Sept. 8, 1864	1 year.	Mustered out with company June 27, 1865.
pson, George D. H.	do.	18	Sept 13, 1864	1 year.	Mustered out May 15, 1865, at Columbia, Tenn., by order of War Department.
nt, Allen	do.	19	Sept. 13, 1864	1 year.	
Enoch B.	do.	40	Sept. 19, 1864	1 year.	
n, Carmichael	do.	35	Sept. 17, 1864	1 year.	Mustered out with company June 27, 1865.

COMPANY G

Mustered in September 29, 1864, at Camp Dennison, O., by Wm.
out June 27, 1865, at Nashville, Tenn., by Philip
and A. C. M., 3d Division, 4th A

Names.	Rank.	Age.	Date of Entering the Service.	
William P. Wolf	Captain	35	Aug. 26, 1864	1 year. F
Isaac N. Bundy	1st Lieut.	20	Sept. 29, 1864	
William Barrere	2d Lieut.	25	Sept. 29, 1864	
John D. Deniston	1st Sergt.	23	Sept. 24, 1864	
John R. Ashmore	do	38	Sept. 21, 1864	
Matthew T. Van Eman	Sergeant.	22	Sept. 17, 1864	
Samuel W. Wright	do	27	Sept. 26, 1864	1 year.
James M. Gustin	do	38	Sept. 24, 1864	1 year.
John Means	do	34	Sept. 24, 1864	1 year.
John C. Glover	do	27	Sept. 28, 1864	1 year.
Daniel Coffman	do	39	Sept. 23, 1864	1 year.
Francis Jacobs	do	39	Sept. 22, 1864	1 year.
Martin Guthbridge	Corporal.	28	Sept. 20, 1864	1
Samuel Howland	do	27	Sept. 25, 1864	1 year.
Ebenezer D. Leonard	do	33	Sept. 17, 1864	1 year.
Robert McKinney	do	29	Sept. 24, 1864	1 year.
Philip N. Shell	do	37	Sept. 24, 1864	1 year.
Thomas Young	do	37	Sept. 27, 1864	1 year.
Jeremiah M. Spence	do	36	Sept. 27, 1864	1 year.
Joseph E. Winters	do	44	Sept. 22, 1864	1 year.
Perry Haas	do	28	Sept. 24, 1864	1 year.
Joel C. Gabriel	Musician	34	Sept. 22, 1864	1 year.
James Nicely	do	35	Sept. 26, 1864	1 year.
Courtland C. Cusick	Wagoner.	19	Sept. 22, 1864	
Applegate, Milton	Private	34	Sept. 24, 1864	
Badgly, Benton	do	30	Sept. 25, 1864	
Baldwin, Thomas B.	do	21	Sept 24, 1864	
Ballard, William E.	do	25	Sept. 28, 1864	
Bercaw, Norman	do	24	Sept. 22, 1864	

...ames.	Rank.	Age.	Date of Entering the Service.	Period of Service.	Remarks.
...James	Private.	[illegible]	Sept. 24, 1864	1 year.	Captured Nov. 25, 1864, in action at Block House No. 14, Tennessee and Alabama Railroad; died April 14, 1865, at Vicksburg, Miss.
...ge W	...do...	19	Sept. 28, 1864	1 year.	Captured Nov. 25, 1864, in action at Block House No. 14, Tennessee and Alabama Railroad; perished by explosion of steamer Sultana, on Mississippi River, near Memphis, Tenn., April 27, 1865.
...illiam H	...do...	26	Sept. 28, 1864	1 year.	Mustered out with company June 27, 1865.
...es M	...do...	19	Sept. 27, 1864	1 year.	Captured Nov. 25, 1864, in action at Block House No. 14, Tennessee and Alabama Railroad; mustered out June 21, 1865, at Camp Chase, O., by order of War Department.
...dward	...do...	21	Sept. 24, 1864	1 year.	Captured Nov. 25, 1864, in action at Block House No. 14, Tennessee and Alabama Railroad; died May 1, 1865, at St. Louis, Mo.
...George A	...do...	22	Sept. 28, 1864	1 year.	Mustered out May 11, 1865, at Columbia, Tenn., by order of War Department.
...orge W	...do...	27	Sept. 29, 1864	1 year.	Captured Nov. 25, 1864, in action at Block House No. 14, Tennessee and Alabama Railroad; mustered out June 17, 1865, at Camp Chase, O., by order of War Department.
...hn W	...do...	21	Sept. 21, 1864	1 year.	Captured Nov. 25, 1864, in action at Block House No. 14, Tennessee and Alabama Railroad; mustered out June 24, 1865, at Camp Chase, O., by order of War Department.
...ey	...do...	22	Sept. 24, 1864	1 year.	Captured Nov. 25, 1864, in action at Block House No. 14, Tennessee and Alabama Railroad; died on or about March 20, 1865, in Rebel Prison at Cahaba, Ala.
...Allen	...do...	36	Oct. 1, 1864	1 year.	Transferred to Co. D, 189th O. V. I., July 12, 1865.
...am	...do...	18	Oct. 3, 1864	1 year.	Transferred to Co. D, 189th O. V. I., July 12, 1865.
...exander	...do...	42	Oct. 1, 1864	1 year.	Transferred to Co. D, 189th O. V. I., July 12, 1865.
...amuel	...do...	26	Sept. 21, 1864	1 year.	Mustered out with company June 27, 1865.
...William W	...do...	32	Sept. 17, 1864	1 year.	Mustered out with company June 27, 1865.
...rris	...do...	25	Sept. 24, 1864	1 year.	Captured Nov. 25, 1864, in action at Block House No. 14, Tennessee and Alabama Railroad; died Feb. —, 1865, in Rebel Prison at Cahaba, Ala.
...nes G	...do...	22	Sept. 25, 1864	1 year.	Mustered out May 15, 1865, at Columbia, Tenn., by order of War Department.
...homas S	...do...	41	Sept. 23, 1864	1 year.	Mustered out May 25, 1865, at Camp Dennison, O., by order of War Department.
...e W	...do...	29	Sept. 22, 1864	1 year.	Mustered out with company June 27, 1865.
...Thomas	...do...	21	Sept. 22, 1864	1 year.	Mustered out with company June 27, 1865.
...William O	...do...	20	Sept. 25, 1864	1 year.	Died April 1, 1865, at Columbia, Tenn.
...William P	...do...	17	Sept. 25, 1864	1 year.	Mustered out with company June 27, 1865.
...enry	...do...	22	Sept. 26, 1864	1 year.	Mustered out May 10, 1865, at St. Louis, Mo., by order of War Department.
...ames	...do...	23	Sept. 26, 1864	1 year.	Captured Nov. 25, 1864, in action at Block House No. 14, Tennessee and Alabama Railroad; perished by explosion of steamer Sultana, on Mississippi River, near Memphis, Tenn., April 27, 1865.
...red	...do...	36	Sept. 24, 1864	1 year.	Mustered out with company June 27, 1865.
...linton	...do...	22	Sept. 26, 1864	1 year.	Mustered out with company June 27, 1865.
...Wilson	...do...	39	Sept. 22, 1864	1 year.	Mustered out with company June 27, 1865.
...lvey	...do...	43	Sept. 23, 1864	1 year.	Captured Nov. 25, 1864, in action at Block House No. 14, Tennessee and Alabama Railroad; mustered out June 27, 1865, at Camp Chase, O., by order of War Department.
...ris	...do...	28	Sept. 28, 1864	1 year.	Mustered out with company June 27, 1865.
...athan	...do...	19	Sept. 22, 1864	1 year.	Mustered out May 20, 1865, at Camp Chase, O., by order of War Department.
...mes H	...do...	43	Sept. 29, 1864	1 year.	Mustered out with company June 27, 1865.
..., Henry H	...do...	26	Sept. 24, 1864	1 year.	Mustered out with company June 27, 1865.
...njamin	...do...	[illegible]	Sept. 26, 1864	1 year.	Captured Nov. 25, 1864, in action at Block House No. 14, Tennessee and Alabama Railroad; mustered out July 12, 1865, at Camp Chase, O., by order of War Department.
...ha	...do...	29	Sept. 26, 1864	1 year.	Mustered out with company June 27, 1865.
...ey	...do...	34	Sept. 26, 1864	1 year.	Captured Nov. 25, 1864, in action at Block House No. 14, Tennessee and Alabama Railroad; perished by explosion of steamer Sultana, on Mississippi River, near Memphis, Tenn., April 27, 1865.
...illiam	...do...	26	Dec. 5, 1864	1 year.	Died Jan. 31, 1865, at Columbia, Tenn.
...n F	...do...	17	Oct. 5, 1864	1 year.	Transferred to Co. D, 189th O.V.I., July 12, 1865.
...William	...do...	18	Sept. 22, 1864	1 year.	
...liam H	...do...	30	Sept. 25, 1864	1 year.	Captured Nov. 25, 1864, in action at Block House No. 14, Tennessee and Alabama Railroad; mustered out June 28, 1865, at Camp Chase, O., by order of War Department.

Names.	Rank.	Age.	Date of Entering the Service.	Period of Service	Remarks.
Phillips, Marion P	Private	34	Sept. 29, 1864	1 year.	Mustered out with company June 27, 1865.
Priest, Thomas E	...do...	18	Sept. 24, 1864	1 year.	Mustered out with company June 27, 1865.
Reddick, Richard P	...do...	26	Sept. 27, 1864	1 year.	Mustered out with company June 27, 1865.
Rickey, Brice	...do...	23	Sept. 24, 1864	1 year.	Mustered out June 19, 1865, at Columbia, Tenn., by order of War Department.
Robbins Vincent	...do...	26	Sept. 24, 1864	1 year.	Discharged Feb. 25, 1865, at Columbia, Tenn., for wounds received in action.
Rude, William	...do...	28	Sept. 26, 1864	1 year.	Mustered out with company June 27, 1865.
Shank, James H	...do...	34	Sept. 24, 1864	1 year.	Captured Nov. 25, 1864, in action at Red House No. 14, Tennessee and Alabama Railroad; died Jan. 21, 1865, in Rebel Prison at Cahaba, Ala.
Shaw, David Q	...do...	30	Sept. 30, 1864	1 year.	Mustered out with company June 27, 1865.
Sidles, Israel	...do...	23	Sept. 24, 1864	1 year.	Captured Nov. 25, 1864, in action at Red House No. 14, Tennessee and Alabama Railroad; died March 3, 1865, in Rebel Prison at Cahaba, Ala.
Simpson, Wilford	...do...	21	Sept. 26, 1864	1 year.	Mustered out with company June 27, 1865.
Smith, John G	...do...	25	Sept. 24, 1864	1 year.	Mustered out May 25, 1865, at Camp Dennison, O., by order of War Department.
Stewart, John P	...do...	32	Sept. 24, 1864	1 year.	Mustered out with company June 27, 1865.
Strain, David M	...do...	39	Sept. 28, 1864	1 year.	Mustered out with company June 27, 1865.
Strain, Trimble	...do...	18	Sept. 19, 1864	1 year.	Captured Nov. 25, 1864, in action at Red House No. 14, Tennessee and Alabama Railroad; mustered out to date June 27, 1865, by order of War Department.
Templin, Thomas	...do...	44	Sept. 24, 1864	1 year.	Mustered out with company June 27, 1865.
Tumbleson, John	...do...	30	Sept. 23, 1864	1 year.	Mustered out with company June 27, 1865.
Walker, Joseph E	...do...	38	Sept. 20, 1864	1 year.	Mustered out with company June 27, 1865.
Wardlow, Jacob	...do...	26	Sept. 26, 1864	1 year.	Mustered out May 11, 1865, at Columbia, Tenn., by order of War Department.
Wardlow, Silas A	...do...	29	Sept. 29, 1864	1 year.	Mustered out with company June 27, 1865.
Welch, Andrew	...do...	39	Sept. 27, 1864	1 year.	Mustered out with company June 27, 1865.
Whistler, Abraham	...do...	23	Sept. 29, 1864	1 year.	Mustered out with company June 27, 1865.
White, Zachariah J	...do...	36	Sept. 21, 1864	1 year.	Mustered out with company June 27, 1865.
Wiley, William	...do...	37	Sept. 26, 1864	1 year.	
Williams, John A	...do...	33	Sept. 28, 1864	1 year.	Died June 25, 1865, at Columbia, Tenn.
Williams, John S	...do...	33	Sept. 19, 1864	1 year.	Mustered out with company June 27, 1865.
Wisby, Thompson	...do...	36	Sept. 27, 1864	1 year.	Mustered out May 25, 1865, at Camp Dennison, O., by order of War Department.
Wright, Thomas J	...do...	23	Sept. 22, 1864	1 year.	Mustered out with company June 27, 1865.
Wright, William	...do...	44	Oct. 1, 1864	1 year.	Mustered out Aug. 2, 1865, at Camp Dennison, O., by order of War Department.
Yarger, John W	...do...	18	Sept. 29, 1864	1 year.	Mustered out with company June 27, 1865.
Yarger, William	...do...	14	Oct. 1, 1864	1 year.	Transferred to Co. D, 189th O. V. I., July 12, 1865.

COMPANY H.

Mustered in October 8, 1864, at Camp Dennison, O., by William Von Doehn, Captain and A. A. G. Mustered out June 27, 1865, at Nashville, Tenn., by Philip Reefy, Captain 19th O. V. I., and A. C. M., 3d Division, 4th Army Corps.

Names.	Rank.	Age.	Date of Entering the Service.	Period of Service	Remarks.
John F. Hill	Captain	29	Oct. 8, 1864	1 year.	Mustered out with company June 27, 1865.
Joseph L. Harman	1st Lieut.	24	Oct. 8, 1864	1 year.	Transferred to Co. B April 3, 1865.
Joseph M. Ellis	2d Lieut.	20	Oct. 8, 1864	1 year.	Promoted to 1st Lieutenant June 6, 1865, but not mustered; mustered out with company June 27, 1865.
George Saylor	1st Sergt.	35	Sept. 28, 1864	1 year.	Promoted to 2d Lieutenant June 6, 1865, but not mustered; mustered out with company June 27, 1865.
Cornelius W. Edenfield	Sergeant.	21	Sept. 29, 1864	1 year.	Mustered out with company June 27, 1865.
John Winegardner	...do...	26	Sept. 29, 1864	1 year.	Mustered out with company June 27, 1865.
Alexander Quitter	...do...	36	Sept. 28, 1864	1 year.	Mustered out with company June 27, 1865.
Philip T. South	...do...	19	Oct. 5, 1864	1 year.	Promoted to 2d Lieutenant June 6, 1865, but not mustered; mustered out July 5, 1865, at Nashville, Tenn., by order of War Department.
John Hatch	Corporal.	24	Sept. 26, 1864	1 year.	
William N. Hill	...do...	32	Sept. 22, 1864	1 year.	
George J. Perrine	...do...	18	Oct. 5, 1864	1 year.	Mustered out July 28, 1865, at Nashville, Tenn., by order of War Department.
Oren S. Hadley	...do...	23	Oct. 4, 1864	1 year.	Mustered out July 12, 1865, at Huntsville, Ala., by order of War Department.
Zachariah F. Riley	...do...	29	Oct. 5, 1864	1 year.	Mustered out July 12, 1865, at Huntsville, Ala., by order of War Department.
John Shoemaker	...do...	38	Oct. 5, 1864	1 year.	Mustered out July 12, 1865, at Huntsville, Ala., by order of War Department.
Michael Shultz	...do...	23	Oct. 8, 1864	1 year.	Mustered out July 12, 1865, at Huntsville, Ala., by order of War Department.

Names.	Rank.	Age.	Date of Entering the Service.	Period of Service.	Remarks.
[illegible]	Corporal.	[illegible]	Sept. [illegible], 1864	1 year.	Mustered out with company June 27, 1865.
[illegible] Mulcher	...do...	[illegible]	Sept. 29, 1864	1 year.	Mustered out with company June 27, 1865.
[illegible]	...do...	[illegible]	Sept. [illegible], 1864	1 year.	Mustered out with company June 27, 1865.
[illegible]	Musician.	44	Oct. 11, 1864	1 year.	Transferred to Co. F, 189th O. V. I., July 12, 1865.
[illegible]lph Ellis	...do...	18	Oct. 11, 1864	1 year.	Transferred to Co. F, 189th O. V. I., July 12, 1865.
[illegible]	Wagoner.	[illegible]	Sept. 27, 1864	1 year.	Mustered out with company June 27, 1865
[illegible], George	Private.	[illegible]	Oct. 4, 1864	1 year.	
[illegible], John	...do...	[illegible]	Oct. 4, 1864	1 year.	
[illegible], William E.	...do...	[illegible]	Sept. 28, 1864	1 year.	Mustered out with company June 27, 1865.
[illegible], James	...do...	[illegible]	Sept. 29, 1864	1 year.	Mustered out with company June 27, 1865.
[illegible]an, Allen H	...do...	[illegible]	Sept. 28, 1864	1 year.	Killed Nov. 30, 1864, in battle of Franklin, Tennessee.
[illegible]an, Joseph	...do...	28	Sept. 30, 1864	1 year.	Mustered out with company June 27, 1865.
[illegible], [illegible]	...do...	21	Sept. 30, 1864	1 year.	Died Dec. 24, 1864, at Jeffersonville, Ind.
[illegible], Francis X	...do...	40	Sept. 29, 1864	1 year.	Mustered out with company June 27, 1865.
[illegible], Ambrose	...do...	18	Sept. 24, 1864	1 year.	Mustered out with company June 27, 1865.
[illegible]man, Henry	...do...	28	Sept. 29, 1864	1 year.	
[illegible] John	...do...	22	Sept. 28, 1864	1 year.	
[illegible], Washington D.	...do...	19	Oct. 7, 1864	1 year.	Transferred to Co. F, 189th O. V. I., July 12, 1865.
[illegible], Madison	...do...	18	Oct. 5, 1864	1 year.	Transferred to Co. F, 189th O. V. I., July 12, 1865.
[illegible]yron	...do...	22	Oct. 7, 1864	1 year.	Transferred to Co. F, 189th O. V. I., July 12, 1865.
[illegible], William	...do...	22	Sept. 24, 1864	1 year.	
[illegible]an, Silas	...do...	22	Sept. 29, 1864	1 year.	Mustered out June 19, 1865, at Columbia, Tenn., by order of War Department.
[illegible]nis, James	...do...	29	Oct. 8, 1864	1 year.	Mustered out June 19, 1865, at Columbia, Tenn., by order of War Department.
[illegible]n, Robert M	...do...	28	Sept. 27, 1864	1 year.	Mustered out with company June 27, 1865.
[illegible]r, John M	...do...	42	Oct. 7, 1864	1 year.	Transferred to Co. F, 189th O. V. I., July 12, 1865.
[illegible]ay, John T.	...do...	34	Oct. 3, 1864	1 year.	Transferred to Co. F, 189th O. V. I., July 12, 1865.
[illegible]r, Samuel	...do...	33	Sept. 30, 1864	1 year.	Mustered out June 19, 1865, at Columbia, Tenn., by order of War Department.
[illegible] Amos B.	...do...	19	Sept. 30, 1864	1 year.	Mustered out with company June 27, 1865.
[illegible]r, Byron	...do...	18	Oct. 3, 1864	1 year.	Transferred to Co. F, 189th O. V. I., July 12, 1865.
[illegible]amuel	...do...	18	Oct. 11, 1864	1 year.	Transferred to 124th Co., 2d Battalion, Veteran Reserve Corps, April 2, 1865.
[illegible]oo, Thomas	...do...	22	Sept. 24, 1864	1 year.	
[illegible]nl, Daniel	...do...	44	Sept. 29, 1864	1 year.	Died Dec. 30, 1864, at Nashville, Tenn.
[illegible], Granville C.	...do...	22	Sept. 29, 1864	1 year.	Mustered out with company June 27, 1865.
[illegible]r, William	...do...	27	Sept. 26, 1864	1 year.	
[illegible]n, Joseph D.	...do...	19	Oct. 1, 1864	1 year.	Transferred to Co. F, 189th O. V. I., July 12, 1865.
[illegible], William	...do...	18	Sept. 13, 1864	1 year.	
[illegible], William H	...do...	24	Sept. 26, 1864	1 year.	
[illegible] Thomas J.	...do...	26	Sept. 29, 1864	1 year.	Mustered out with company June 27, 1865.
[illegible]orn, Francis	...do...	31	Sept. 29, 1864	1 year.	Mustered out with company June 27, 1865.
[illegible], Josiah	...do...	39	Sept. 29, 1864	1 year.	Died March 14, 1865, at Columbia, Tenn.
[illegible]n, Samuel	...do...	28	Sept. 27, 1864	1 year.	Mustered out with company June 27, 1865.
[illegible]r, George	...do...	34	Oct. 3, 1864	1 year.	Transferred to Co. F, 189th O. V. I., July 12, 1865.
[illegible]ell, Joseph J.	...do...	18	Oct. 3, 1864	1 year.	Transferred to Co. F, 189th O. V. I., July 12, 1865.
[illegible]m, Williamson B.	...do...	20	Sept. 27, 1864	1 year.	Mustered out with company June 27, 1865.
[illegible]ger, Isaac W	...do...	22	Oct. 7, 1864	1 year.	Died March 26, 1865, at Columbia, Tenn.
[illegible] William H	...do...	20	Sept. 24, 1864	1 year.	
[illegible]s, Jacob	...do...	29	Sept. 29, 1864	1 year.	Mustered out with company June 27, 1865.
[illegible]n, Peter C.	...do...	33	Oct. 7, 1864	1 year.	Transferred to Co. F, 189th O. V. I., July 12, 1865.
[illegible], George	...do...	21	Sept. 24, 1864	1 year.	
[illegible], William A	...do...	24	Sept. 30, 1864	1 year.	Mustered out with company June 27, 1865.
[illegible], Paul J.	...do...	18	Sept. 27, 1864	1 year.	Mustered out May 15, 1865, at Columbia, Tenn., by order of War Department.
[illegible] Job S.	...do...	21	Sept. 27, 1864	1 year.	Mustered out May 11, 1865, at Columbia, Tenn., by order of War Department.
[illegible], David J.	...do...	19	Sept. 30, 1864	1 year.	Mustered out with company June 27, 1865.
[illegible] David	...do...	23	Sept. 22, 1864	1 year.	
[illegible] Joseph	...do...	41	Oct. 4, 1864	1 year.	Transferred to Co. F, 189th O. V. I., July 12, 1865.
[illegible], Isaac	...do...	23	Sept. 30, 1864	1 year.	Mustered out with company June 27, 1865.
[illegible]eil, Patrick	...do...	22	Sept. 30, 1864	1 year.	
[illegible], John	...do...	28	Oct. 8, 1864	1 year.	Transferred to Co. F, 189th O. V. I., July 12, 1865.
[illegible]s, John B.	...do...	16	Oct. 8, 1864	1 year.	Transferred to Co. A, 189th O. V. I., July 12, 1865.
[illegible], Eben H.	...do...	36	Sept. 29, 1864	1 year.	Mustered out with company June 27, 1865.
[illegible] W	...do...	30	Oct. 6, 1864	1 year.	Mustered out May 25, 1865, at Camp Dennison, O., by order of War Department.
[illegible], William A.	...do...	33	Oct. 11, 1864	1 year.	Promoted to Q. M. Sergeant Oct. 11, 1864.

Names.	Rank.	Age.	Date of Entering the Service.	Period of Service.	Remarks.
Rice, James	Private..	26	Sept. 24, 1864	1 year.	
Sailing, Michael	....do....	36	Sept. 27, 1864	1 year.	Died April 6, 1865, at Nashville, Tenn.
Sloane, Francis M	....do....	30	Sept. 29, 1864	1 year.	Mustered out with company June 27, 1865.
Smith, John	....do....	23	Sept. 29, 1864	1 year.	Mustered out with company June 27, 1865.
Sowers, Joseph	....do....	25	Sept. 28, 1864	1 year.	Mustered out May 25, 1865, at Camp Dennison, O., by order of War Department.
Spence, Thompson D	....do....	18	Oct. 10, 1864	1 year.	Transferred to Co. F, 189th O. V. I., July 12, 1865.
Spets, Anthony	....do....	29	Sept. 29, 1864	1 year.	Mustered out with company June 27, 1865.
Strawbridge, Samuel	....do....	24	Sept. 22, 1864	1 year.	
Stree[illegible], Henry	....do....	18	Oct. 7, 1864	1 year.	Transferred to Co. F, 189th O. V. I., July 12, 1865.
Sweeney, John	....do....	22	Sept. 24, 1864	1 year.	
Thompson, Edward	....do....	27	Sept. 22, 1864	1 year.	
Thompson, Sylvester	....do....	18	Oct. 10, 1864	1 year.	Mustered out May 11, 1865, at [illegible], Tenn., by order of War Department.
Titus, Jasper H	....do....	22	Sept. 27, 1864	1 year.	
Vanpelt, Thomas B	....do....	27	Sept. 26, 1864	1 year.	Mustered out with company June 27, 1865.
Weimer, John W	....do....	40	Sept. 29, 1864	1 year.	Mustered out with company June 27, 1865.
Wheeler, Joseph	....do....	19	Sept. 24, 1864	1 year.	
Williams, George J	....do....	20	Sept. 30, 1864	1 year.	Discharged July 31, 1865, at Jeffersonville, Ind., on Surgeon's certificate of disability.
Williams, James	....do....	18	Sept. 30, 1864	1 year.	Mustered out May 25, 1865, at Camp Dennison, O., by order of War Department.
Williamson, James	....do....	21	Oct. 5, 1864	1 year.	Transferred to Co. F, 189th O. V. I., July 12, 1865.
Wilson, George	....do....	36	Sept. 29, 1864	1 year.	Mustered out with company June 27, 1865.
Woods, James	....do....	25	Sept. 24, 1864	1 year.	

COMPANY I.

Mustered in October 8, 1864, at Camp Chase, O., by W. P. Richardson, Colonel 25th O. V. I. Mustered out June 27, 1865, at Nashville, Tenn., by Philip Reefy, Captain 19th O. V. I., and A. C. M., 3d Division, 4th Army Corps.

Names.	Rank.	Age.	Date of Entering the Service.	Period of Service.	Remarks.
Abram Houghland	Captain.	34	Oct. 8, 1864	1 year.	Detailed as Acting Commissary of Subsistence Nov. 16, 1864; returned to company April 26, 1865; mustered out with company June 27, 1865.
Isaiah Larkin	1st Lieut.	29	Oct. 8, 1864	1 year.	Detailed as Acting Assistant Commissary of Subsistence Nov. 24, 1864; appointed [illegible] Inspector at Columbia, Tenn., Feb. 17, 1865; mustered out with company June [illegible] 1865.
William Rummell	2d Lieut.	29	Oct. 8, 1864	1 year.	In command of company from Nov. 17, 1864, to June [illegible] 1865; promoted to [illegible] Lieutenant June [illegible] 1865, but not mustered; mustered out with company June 27, 1865.
David Case	1st Sergt.	32	Sept. 29, 1864	1 year.	Promoted to 2d Lieutenant June 6, 1865, but not mustered; mustered out with company June 27, 1865.
Asher Rice	Sergeant.	22	Sept. 20, 1864	1 year.	Killed Nov. 30, 1864, in battle of Franklin, Tennessee.
George H. Reubens	....do....	21	Sept. 23, 1864	1 year.	Mustered out with company June 27, 1865.
Francis Wood	....do....	21	Sept. 19, 1864	1 year.	Mustered out with company June 27, 1865.
John W. Plott	....do....	21	Sept. 29, 1864	1 year.	Mustered out with company June 27, 1865.
Gustavus S. Grate	....do....	23	Sept. 21, 1864	1 year.	Appointed from Corporal Dec. 17, 1864; mustered out with company June 27, 1865.
Andrew J. Kridler	Corporal.	29	Aug. 21, 1864	1 year.	Died Dec. 31, 1864, in hospital at Nashville, Tennessee.
Isaac Griner	....do....	32	Sept. 17, 1864	1 year.	Discharged Feb. 21, 1864, at Camp Dennison, O., on Surgeon's certificate of disability.
George Wood	....do....	25	Sept. 29, 1864	1 year.	Mustered out with company June 27, 1865.
Henry Crown	....do....	27	Sept. 27, 1864	1 year.	Mustered out with company June 27, 1865.
James G. Sterling	....do....	25	Sept. 29, 1864	1 year.	Mustered out with company June 27, 1865.
George W. Jones	....do....	29	Sept. 5, 1864	1 year.	Mustered out with company June 27, 1865.
Lewis S. Wagoner	....do....	36	Sept. 3, 1864	1 year.	Mustered out June 28, 1865, at Louisville, Ky., by order of War Department.
Nathaniel G. Case	....do....	23	Sept. 29, 1864	1 year.	Mustered out with company June 27, 1865.
William Baker	....do....	23	Sept. 29, 1864	1 year.	Appointed April 1, 1865; mustered out with company June 27, 1865.
Isaac Hughey	....do....	23	Oct. 5, 1864	1 year.	Appointed April 1, 1865; mustered out with company June 27, 1865.
Barnhart, David M	Private..	20	Sept. 1, 1864	1 year.	
Bechtel, Samuel	....do....	37	Sept. 29, 1864	1 year.	
Bishop, Chauncey	....do....	18	Sept. 30, 1864	1 year.	Mustered out with company June 27, 1865.
Bishop, Percival C	....do....	21	Sept. 27, 1864	1 year.	Mustered out June 19, 1865, at Columbia, Tenn., by order of War Department.
Butnworth, George W	....do....	30	Aug. 21, 1864	1 year.	Mustered out with company June 27, 1865.
Callahan, William H	....do....	18	Sept. 19, 1864	1 year.	Mustered out May 14, 1865, at Columbia, Tenn., by order of War Department.

	Rank.	Age.	Date of Entering the Service.	Period of Service.	Remarks.
, George H.	Private.	21	Sept. 28, 1864	1 year.	Mustered out June 14, 1865, at Louisville, Ky., by order of War Department.
ly, Ira.		38	Sept. 6, 1864	1 year.	Mustered out with company June 27, 1865.
, Daniel.		37	Sept. 13, 1864	1 year.	Mustered out with company June 27, 1865.
, Jesse.		37	Sept. 22, 1864	1 year.	Mustered out June 30, 1865, at St. Louis, Mo., by order of War Department.
erman, Jacob C.	do.	20	Oct. 4, 1864	1 year.	Transferred to Co. D, 189th O. V. I., July 12, 1865.
George.	do.	18	Sept. 16, 1864	1 year.	Mustered out with company June 27, 1865.
Lewis A.	do.	25	Sept. 29, 1864	1 year.	Mustered out June 2, 1865, at Camp Dennison, O., by order of War Department.
le, William H.	do.	28	Oct. 3, 1864	1 year.	Mustered out with company June 27, 1865.
nins, James.	do.	25	Sept. 23, 1864	1 year.	
, William.	do.	18	Oct. 3, 1864	1 year.	Transferred to Co. D, 189th O. V. I., July 12, 1865.
ds, William H.		32	Aug. 27, 1864	1 year.	Died Dec. 17, 1864, in hospital at Jeffersonville, Indiana.
sing, Charles.	do.	41	Oct. 7, 1864	1 year.	Mustered out May 11, 1865, at Columbia, Tenn., by order of War Department.
ton, James.	do.	19	Oct. 3, 1864	1 year.	Mustered out with company June 27, 1865.
, Franklin.	do.	23	Aug. 27, 1864	1 year.	
ey, David.	do.	28	Sept. 23, 1864	1 year.	
st, Owen.	do.	17	Sept. 27, 1864	1 year.	Mustered out with company June 27, 1865.
nis, Charles.	do.	36	Sept. 29, 1864	1 year.	
, Gilbert.	do.	34	Sept. 2, 1864	1 year.	Mustered out with company June 27, 1865.
, James.		21	Sept. 8, 1864	1 year.	
es, George W.		31	Sept. 23, 1864	1 year.	Mustered out with company June 27, 1865.
, John.		22	Sept. 15, 1864	1 year.	
, Michael.		41	Oct. 5, 1864	1 year.	
n, Miles.		18	Oct. 3, 1864	1 year.	Mustered out with company June 27, 1865.
s, Eli.		31	Oct. 3, 1864	1 year.	
nell, David.	do.	21	Sept. 29, 1864	1 year.	Died April 5, 1865, in hospital at Columbia, Tennessee.
nell, William.		19	Oct. 5, 1864	1 year.	Died March 7, 1865, in hospital at Columbia, Tennessee.
ann, Charles.		19	Oct. 3, 1864	1 year.	Mustered out with company June 27, 1865.
n, Americus.		20	Oct. 5, 1864	1 year.	Transferred to Co. D, 189th O. V. I., July 12, 1865.
, John W.		21	Sept. 29, 1864	1 year.	Mustered out with company June 27, 1865.
r, George W.	do.	29	Sept. 2, 1864	1 year.	Died Nov. 20, 1864, in hospital at Columbia, Tennessee.
, James.		18	Sept. 29, 1864	1 year.	
lde, Carlisle.		36	Aug. 31, 1864	1 year.	Mustered out with company June 27, 1865.
rland, Isaac.		18	Oct. 3, 1864	1 year.	
hall, John.		23	Sept. 29, 1864	1 year.	Mustered out with company June 27, 1865.
tt, Benjamin.		19	Sept. 29, 1864	1 year.	
e, Albert.		27	Oct. 4, 1864	1 year.	
s, James H.		42	Sept. 20, 1864	1 year.	Mustered out with company June 27, 1865.
ls, John.		19	Oct. 3, 1864	1 year.	Mustered out with company June 27, 1865.
up, John E.		29	Sept. 3, 1864	1 year.	Mustered out with company June 27, 1865.
er, David.		23	Oct. 7, 1864	1 year.	
ippi, Henry.		18	Sept. 29, 1864	1 year.	Mustered out with company June 27, 1865.
mell, Wesley J.		25	Sept. 29, 1864	1 year.	
nell, William L.		28	Sept. 29, 1864	1 year.	On muster-in roll. No further record found.
house, Albert J.	do.	27	Sept. 19, 1864	1 year.	Mustered out with company June 27, 1865.
, Daniel.	do.	42	Oct. 3, 1864	1 year.	Mustered out with company June 27, 1865.
, Charles.	do.	26	Sept. 2, 1864	1 year.	Mustered out with company June 27, 1865.
, Henry.	do.	19	Sept. 27, 1864	1 year.	Captured Nov. 30, 1864, at battle of Franklin, Tenn.; perished by explosion of steamer Sultana, on Mississippi River, near Memphis, Tenn., April 27, 1865.
h, Patterson.	do.	18	Sept. 19, 1864	1 year.	
ward, John S.	do.	40	Sept. 29, 1864	1 year.	
n, Daniel.	do.	40	Sept. 29, 1864	1 year.	Mustered out with company June 27, 1865.
n, David.	do.	30	Sept. 29, 1864	1 year.	Mustered out with company June 27, 1865.
ner, Christopher.	do.	23	Oct. 3, 1864	1 year.	Mustered out with company June 27, 1865.
r, Jacob.	do.	30	Sept. 28, 1864	1 year.	Mustered out with company June 27, 1865.
rwood, Benjamin L.	do.	37	Sept. 8, 1864	1 year.	
cholk, Sherman.	do.	..	Oct. 5, 1864	1 year.	Mustered out with company June 27, 1865.
herell, Thomas.	do.	20	Sept. 18, 1864	1 year.	
er, John A.	do.	32	Sept. 29, 1864	1 year.	On muster-in roll as John A. Wenner; mustered out May 25, 1865, at Camp Dennison, O., by order of War Department.
rty, Mathias.	do.	33	Sept. 2, 1864	1 year.	Mustered out with company June 27, 1865.
tzer, John D.	do.	21	Sept. 29, 1864	1 year.	Mustered out with company June 27, 1865.
ling, Elias.	do.	23	Sept. 29, 1864	1 year.	Mustered out with company June 27, 1865.

COMPANY K.

Mustered in October 8, 1864, at Camp Chase, O., by W. P. Richards
June 27, 1865, at Nashville, Tenn., by Philip Reefy
and A. C. M., 3d Division, 4th Army

Names.	Rank.	Age.	Date of Entering the Service.	Period of Service.	
George C. Sedwick	Captain.	43	Oct. 8, 1864		
Isaac S. McCowan	1st. Lieut.	21	Oct. 8, 1864		
Leroy C. Sedwick	2d Lieut.	20	Oct. 8, 1864		
William H. Bendell	1st Sergt.	23	Sept. 2, 1864		
Andrew J. Downer	Sergeant.	21	Oct. 4, 1864		by
James McBerney	....do....	27	Sept. 26, 1864		Died
Thomas C. Rice	....do....	19	Sept. 5, 1864		Must
Edwin D. Reyner	....do....	22	Sept. 3, 1864		
William Nicholson	....do....	26	Aug. 30, 1864		
Ebenezer Myers	Corporal.	18	Oct. 5, 1864		
Ralph W. Cuthbert	....do....	19	Aug. 11, 1864		
Thomas H. Mackinson	....do....	42	Sept. 2, 1864		
Richard Edwards	....do....	20	Aug. 24, 1864		by
Hiram Snodgrass	....do....	19	Sept. 7, 1864	1	Must
James S. Lewis	....do....	31	Sept. 26, 1864	1	
Isaac Imlay	....do....	26	Sept. 21, 1864	1	
Alexander McCollum	....do....	32	Sept. 18, 1864	1	
James S. Groves	....do....	20	Aug. 16, 1864	1 year.	
Minor M. Dye	....do....	20	Sept. 6, 1864		
Thomas Amons	Musician	18	Aug. 31, 1864	1	
Oliver Porter	....do....	19	Aug. 30, 1864	1	
Allison, Samuel	Private..	19	Aug. 30, 1864	1	
Barnett, Alvertus	....do....	21	Aug. 31, 1864	1	
Bowers, Valentine	....do....	30	Aug. 31, 1864	1	
Boyd, James S	....do....	27	Oct. 4, 1864	1	
Britton, William H	....do....	21	Aug. 18, 1864	1 year.	
Brown, William	....do....	20	Oct. 4, 1864	1	
Burris, Henry C	....do....	20	Aug. 17, 1864		
Callaghan, Oliver	....do....	24	Sept. 17, 1864		
Cameron, Andrew	....do....	18	Sept. 15, 1864		
Carr, William	....do....	18	Oct. 5, 1864	1	
Cavanah, Franklin	....do....	18	Sept. 7, 1864	1	
Coby, Thomas	....do....	25	Oct. 6, 1864	1	
Coker, David	....do....	18	Sept. 2, 1864	1	
Congleton, William	....do....	33	Sept. 7, 1864	1	
Covey, Morgan	....do....	23	Sept. 2, 1864	1	
Cranston, William	....do....	30	Sept. 5, 1864	1	
Cutshaw, Shannon	....do....	18	Sept. 14, 1864	1	
Dupill, Franklin	....do....	29	Aug. 25, 1864	1	
Edwards, William	....do....	18	Sept. 21, 1864	1	
Fairman, George W	....do....	18	Oct. 5, 1864	1	
Ford, John M	....do....	30	Oct. 3, 1864		Trans 186
Gearheart, George T	....do....	20	Aug. 30, 1864	1	
Gillespie, Cornelius	....do....	18	Sept. 30, 1864	1	
Gorrell, James M	....do....	23	Sept. 20, 1864	1	
Gramlich, Christian	....do....	18	Sept. 15, 1864	1	
Hardy, Samuel	....do....	29	Aug. 22, 1864	1	
Heslop, George	....do....	25	Sept. 7, 1864	1	
Higgins, John W	....do....	18	Oct. 8, 1864	1	
Hobaugh, Charles B	....do....	18	Sept. 15, 1864		
Huffman, Michael	....do....	28	Aug. 29, 1864		
Jones, Edward	....do....	18	Oct. 4, 1864		
King, Jesse	....do....	26	Aug. 31, 1864		
King, William W	....do....	20	Aug. 10, 1864	1	Must
Lewis, William H	....do....	26	Aug. 26, 1864	1	Must
Love, Hugh	....do....	28	Aug. 31, 1864	1	Must
McCandless, Samuel D	....do....	18	Aug. 29, 1864	1	Died
McConn, Thomas	....do....	25	Sept. 18, 1864	1	Must
McKinley, William M	....do....	25	Aug. 26, 1864		Must O.

	Rank.	Age.	Date of Entering the Service.	Period of Service.	Remarks.
W	Private..	26	Sept. 21, 1864	1 year.	Mustered out with company June 27, 1865.
....	....do....	22	Oct. 5, 1864	1 year.	Transferred to Co. I, 189th O. V. I., July 12, 1865.
y..........	....do....	31	Oct. 4, 1864	1 year.	
....	....do....	24	Sept. 19, 1864	1 year.	Mustered out with company June 27, 1865.
H..........	....do....	19	Oct. 6, 1864	1 year.	Died Dec. 31, 1864, at Nashville, Tenn.
l..........	....do....	29	Oct. 4, 1864	1 year.	Mustered out June 12, 1865, at Columbia, Tenn., by order of War Department.
am E....	....do....	20	Sept. 19, 1864	1 year.	Mustered out with company June 27, 1865.
....	....do....	28	Sept. 27, 1864	1 year.	
es J......	....do....	18	Sept. 15, 1864	1 year.	Mustered out with company June 27, 1865.
....	....do....	26	Oct. 3, 1864	1 year.	
am.......	....do....	18	Oct. 6, 1864	1 year.	
....	....do....	43	Aug. 18, 1864	1 year.	Mustered out with company June 27, 1865.
am B....	....do....	19	Oct. 3, 1864	1 year.	Mustered out June 7, 1865, at Nashville, Tenn., by order of War Department.
W..........	....do....	22	Oct. 10, 1864	1 year.	Transferred to Co. I, 189th O. V. I., July 12, 1865.
....	....do....	21	Aug. 21, 1864	1 year.	Mustered out with company June 27, 1865.
H..........	....do....	17	Sept. 22, 1864	1 year.	Mustered out with company June 27, 1865.
G..........	....do....	19	Sept. 3, 1864	1 year.	Mustered out with company June 27, 1865.
R..........	....do....	25	Sept. 2, 1864	1 year.	Mustered out with company June 27, 1865.
n H	....do....	20	Oct. 5, 1864	1 year.	Died March 2, 1865, at Columbia, Tenn.
R..........	....do....	28	Oct. 5, 1864	1 year.	
d..........	....do....	33	Sept. 24, 1864	1 year.	
....	....do....	20	Oct. 5, 1864	1 year.	Transferred to Co. F, 189th O. V. I., July 12, 1865.
....	....do....	22	Oct. 1, 1864	1 year.	Mustered out June 19, 1865, at Columbia, Tenn., by order of War Department.
....	....do....	18	Oct. 4, 1864	1 year.	Transferred to Co. I, 189th O. V. I., July 12, 1865.
....	....do....	41	Sept. 17, 1864	1 year.	Died May 29, 1865, at Camp Dennison, O.
re	....do....	20	Aug. 16, 1864	1 year.	Mustered out May 11, 1865, at Columbia, Tenn., by order of War Department.
....	....do....	22	Oct. 3, 1864	1 year.	
h..........	....do....	18	Sept. 7, 1864	1 year.	Mustered out with company June 27, 1865.
rge	....do....	18	Sept. 5, 1864	1 year.	Mustered out with company June 27, 1865.
W..........	....do....	25	Sept. 18, 1864	1 year.	Mustered out with company June 27, 1865.
rick......	....do....	20	Aug. 11, 1864	1 year.	Discharged June 3, 1865, at Jeffersonville, Ind., on Surgeon's certificate of disability.
....	....do....	33	Sept. 6, 1864	1 year.	
l..........	....do....	32	Oct. 4, 1864	1 year.	Transferred to Co. I, 189th O. V. I., July 12, 1865.
b..........	....do....	19	Oct. 3, 1864	1 year.	Transferred to Co. I, 189th O. V. I., July 12, 1865.

UNASSIGNED RECRUITS.

following list of recruits is found on muster and descriptive rolls for this organization, but y of the company rolls of the regiment

....	Private..	26	Aug. 19, 1864	1 year.	
an... ...	....do....	37	Sept. 3, 1864	1 year.	
....	....do....	18	Sept. 20, 1864	1 year.	
n..........	....do....	22	Sept. 3, 1864	1 year.	
....	....do....	18	Sept. 13, 1864	1 year.	
er L.....	....do....	20	Sept. 29, 1864	1 year.	
....	....do....	33	Aug. 25, 1864	1 year.	
l..........	....do....	26	Aug. 19, 1864	1 year.	
rge......	....do....	27	Oct. 17, 1864	1 year.	Mustered out May 17, 1865, at Cincinnati, O., by order of War Department.
....	....do....	19	Sept. 27, 1864	1 year.	
....	....do....	25	Oct. 24, 1864	1 year.	
....	....do....	21	Aug. 29, 1864	1 year.	
....	....do....	20	Sept. 27, 1864	1 year.	
....	....do....	23	Aug. 31, 1864	1 year.	
....	....do....	40	Sept. 1, 1864	1 year.	
s..........	....do....	21	Aug. 31, 1864	1 year.	
h..........	....do....	21	Oct. 7, 1864	1 year.	
....	....do....	23	Aug. 19, 1864	1 year.	
....	....do....	17	Aug. 19, 1864	1 year.	
as..........	....do....	28	Sept. 15, 1864	1 year.	
C..........	....do....	20	Aug. 29, 1864	1 year.	
....	....do....	21	Sept. 15, 1864	1 year.	
....	....do....	22	Aug. 31, 1864	1 year.	
ust......	....do....	22	Oct. 1, 1864	1 year.	
....	....do....	41	Sept. 3, 1864	1 year.	
ck........	....do....	26	Sept. 9, 1864	1 year.	
....	....do....	20	Sept. 6, 1864	1 year.	
....	....do....	18	Sept. 30, 1864	1 year.	

Names.	Rank.	Age.	Date of Entering the Service.	Period of Service.	Remarks.
Myers, Charles	Private.	28	Sept. 16, 1864	1 year.	
Myers, John F.	...do...	17	Oct. 5, 1864	1 year.	
Niceley, George W	...do...	37	Sept. 21, 1864	1 year.	
Niceley, James M.	...do...	17	Sept. 21, 1864	1 year.	
Pember, De Loss	...do...	21	Sept. 2, 1864	1 year.	
Pickard, Joseph	...do...	18	Oct. 5, 1864	1 year.	
Raw, John	...do...	21	Aug. 30, 1864	1 year.	
Rice, John W	...do...	18	Feb. 14, 1865	1 year.	
Rider, Josiah	...do...	35	Sept. 21, 1864	1 year.	
Riley, Samuel B.	...do...	41	Jan. 23, 1865	1 year.	Mustered out June 15, 1865, at Camp by order of War Department.
Routsaw, Conrad	...do...	36	Sept. 21, 1864	1 year.	
Schoup, George	...do...	21	Sept. 29, 1864	1 year.	
Shaffer, Henry P	...do...	38	Sept. 1, 1864	1 year.	
Shockey, Isaac	...do...	36	Sept. 14, 1864	1 year.	
Smith, William M	...do...	42	Sept. 26, 1864	1 year.	
Thomson, John	...do...	30	Oct. 24, 1864	1 year.	
Thresher, Gilbert	...do...	34	Sept. 17, 1864	1 year.	
Turner, Joseph	...do...	27	Oct. 24, 1864	1 year.	
Wacker, John	...do...	31	Sept. 26, 1864	1 year.	
Weatherby, Henry	...do...	26	Sept. 28, 1864	1 year.	
Webber, Matthew	...do...	18	Sept. 28, 1864	1 year.	
Wilson, Henry	...do...	23	Oct. 24, 1864	1 year.	
Worley, Jonathan	...do...	18	Aug. 31, 1864	1 year.	
Wright, William R.	...do...	44	Oct. 10, 1864	1 year.	

176th Regiment Ohio Volunteer Infantry.

ONE YEAR'S SERVICE.

THIS Regiment was organized at Columbus, Sandusky, Wooster, Alliance Camp Chase, and Circleville, O., from August 10 to September 21, 1864, to serve one year. As soon as the organization was completed the Regiment was ordered to Nashville, Tenn., and assigned to the Second Brigade, Fourth Division, Twentieth Army Corps. Soon after its arrival it was detailed to perform provost-guard duty at Nashville, and during the battle of Nashville it was in the works; but, with the exception of a few companies under Major Cummings, the Regiment was not engaged. It was mustered out June 14, 1865, in accordance with orders from the War Department.

Names.	Rank.	Age.	Date of Entering the Service.	Period of Service.	Remarks.
Zephaniah P. Thompson	Sergeant.	26	Aug. 15, 1864	1 year.	Died Jan. 10, 1865, in general hospital at Louisville, Ky.
Jacob F. Mehrman	....do....	25	Aug. 29, 1864	1 year.	Appointed Sept. 12, 1864; mustered out with company June 14, 1865.
Thomas Rein	....do....	25	Aug. 22, 1864	1 year.	Appointed from Corporal Jan. 1, 1865; mustered out with company June 14, 1865; also borne on rolls as Thomas Ryan.
Horace P. Thompson	....do....	23	Aug. 16, 1864	1 year.	Appointed from Corporal March 3, 1865; mustered out with company June 14, 1865.
Levi Weiser	....do....	28	Aug. 29, 1864	1 year.	Appointed from Corporal April 10, 1865; mustered out with company June 14, 1865.
William C. Huddleson	Corporal.	20	Aug. 28, 1864	1 year.	Died April 5, 1865, while at home on furlough.
William Lauer	....do....	25	Aug. 29, 1864	1 year.	Appointed Sept. 12, 1864; mustered out with company June 14, 1865.
John Nonemaker	....do....	22	Aug. 15, 1864	1 year.	Appointed Dec. 17, 1864; mustered out with company June 14, 1865.
George Hunter	....do....	30	Aug. 31, 1864	1 year.	Appointed Jan. 18, 1865; mustered out with company June 14, 1865.
Joseph Thum	....do....	35	Aug. 15, 1864	1 year.	Appointed Jan. 18, 1865; mustered out with company June 14, 1865.
Alonzo Hiday	....do....	18	Sept. 16, 1864	1 year.	Appointed March 8, 1865; mustered out with company June 14, 1865.
John Reisdorf	....do....	39	Aug. 23, 1864	1 year.	Appointed March 8, 1865; mustered out with company June 14, 1865.
George Blesch	....do....	18	Aug. 12, 1864	1 year.	Appointed April 10, 1865; mustered out with company June 14, 1865.
Frank Wagner	....do....	18	Aug. 22, 1864	1 year.	Appointed May 2, 1865; mustered out with company June 14, 1865.
Ransom Fritter	....do....	30	Aug. 29, 1864	1 year.	Died April 21, 1865, at Post Hospital, Nashville, Tenn.
Henry M. Brown	Musician	22	Aug. 31, 1864	1 year.	Promoted to Principal Musician Sept. 30, 1864.
Lewis Juergens	....do....	18	Aug. 25, 1864	1 year.	Mustered out with company June 14, 1865.
Adam, Anthony	Private..	32	Aug. 8, 1864	1 year.	Mustered out with company June 14, 1865.
Airny, John	....do....	39	Aug. 17, 1864	1 year.	
Akison, William	....do....	38	Aug. 30, 1864	1 year.	Mustered out with company June 14, 1865.
Angle, Joseph	....do....	18	Aug. 27, 1864	1 year.	Mustered out with company June 14, 1865.
Armentrout, Marion	....do....	25	Aug. 27, 1864	1 year.	Mustered out June 21, 1865, at Nashville, Tenn., by order of War Department.
Arnold, George	....do....	37	Aug. 25, 1864	1 year.	
Bailey, James	....do....	33	Aug. 31, 1864	1 year.	Mustered out with company June 14, 1865.
Baker, David	....do....	18	July 29, 1864	1 year.	Reduced from Corporal —; mustered out with company June 14, 1865.
Brandt, Henry	....do....	39	Aug. 25, 1864	1 year.	Mustered out with company June 14, 1865.
Bare, Peter	....do....	23	Aug. 12, 1864	1 year.	Mustered out with company June 14, 1865.
Bennett, Ephraim	....do....	43	Aug. 30, 1864	1 year.	Died March 7, 1865, in hospital at Nashville, Tennessee.
Blake, George C.	....do....	18	Aug. 31, 1864	1 year	Mustered out with company June 14, 1865.
Blesch, Michael	....do....	31	Aug. 31, 1864	1 year.	Mustered out with company June 14, 1865.
Bohlander Charles	....do....	44	Aug. 29, 1864	1 year.	Mustered out with company June 14, 1865.
Booth John A.	....do....	18	Aug. 30, 1864	1 year.	Mustered out with company June 14, 1865.
Bowers, Jacob	....do....	19	Aug. 13, 1864	1 year.	Mustered as Musician; mustered out with company June 14, 1865.
Boyd, John F.	....do....	35	Aug. 15, 1864	1 year.	
Bumbarger, George	....do....	39	Aug. 31, 1864	1 year.	Mustered out with company June 14, 1865.
Bunn, Rees H.	....do....	41	Aug. 29, 1864	1 year.	Mustered out with company June 14, 1865; also borne on rolls as Rees H. Baner.
Burns, John	....do....	43	Aug. 12, 1864	1 year.	
Chase, Barak	....do....	20	Sept. 2, 1864	1 year.	Mustered out with company June 14, 1865.
Church, Joseph	....do....	18	Aug. 29, 1864	1 year.	Mustered out with company June 14, 1865.
Cober, William G.	....do....	23	Aug. 29, 1864	1 year.	
Cummings, James	....do....	23	Aug. 23, 1864	1 year.	Appointed Corporal Sept. 12, 1864; reduced April 10, 1865; mustered out with company June 14, 1865.
Dartmunt, Charles	....do....	31	Sept. 2, 1864	1 year.	Mustered out with company June 14, 1865.
Daum, Adam	....do....	41	Aug. 16, 1864	1 year.	Mustered out May 23, 1865, at Nashville, Tenn., by order of War Department.
Davis, Perry	....do....	19	Aug. 15, 1864	1 year.	
Dixon, Joseph	....do....	32	Aug. 31, 1864	1 year.	Mustered out with company June 14, 1865.
Donovan William C.	....do....	18	Aug. 15, 1864	1 year.	Mustered out with company June 14, 1865.
Dreisichicker, Jacob	....do....	26	Aug. 29, 1864	1 year.	Mustered out with company June 14, 1865.
Drummer, John W.	....do....	25	Aug. 29, 1864	1 year.	
Dudgeon, Joseph W.	....do....	18	Aug. 22, 1864	1 year.	Mustered out with company June 14, 1865.
Eireman, Lewis	....do....	21	Aug. 22, 1864	1 year.	Mustered out with company June 14, 1865.
Elsessor, Lorenzo	....do....	43	Aug. 19, 1864	1 year.	Mustered out May 20, 1865, at Nashville, Tenn., by order of War Department.
Engle, George	....do....	41	Aug. 22, 1864	1 year.	
Fisher, John	....do....	31	Aug. 10, 1864	1 year.	
Fleck, Alpheus B.	....do....	35	Aug. 6, 1864	1 year.	
Fletcher, Thomas	....do....	29	Aug. 17, 1864	1 year.	Reduced from Sergeant March 3, 1865; mustered out with company June 14, 1865.
Folz, Jacob	....do....	37	Aug. 23, 1864	1 year.	Mustered out with company June 14, 1865.
Foreman, Gordon	....do....	36	Aug. 12, 1864	1 year.	Mustered out with company June 14, 1865.
Freidchen, John	....do....	23	Sept. 3, 1864	1 year.	Mustered out with company June 14, 1865.
Freidchen, William	....do....	24	Aug. 31, 1864	1 year.	Mustered out with company June 14, 1865.
Fullwiler, John	....do....	27	Aug. 25, 1864	1 year.	Mustered out with company June 14, 1865.
Graham, John	....do....	22	Aug. 25, 1864	1 year.	

Names.	Rank.	Age.	Date of Entering the Service.	Period of Service.	Remarks.
Huff, Frank K.	Private.	21	Aug. 21, 1864	1 year.	Mustered out with company June 14, 1865.
Henderson, Matthew	...do...	27	Aug. 25, 1864	1 year.	Mustered out with company June 14, 1865.
Henry, Theron	...do...	35	Aug. 21, 1864	1 year.	Sick ——, in hospital. No further record found.
Higgins, John H.	...do...	42	Aug. 30, 1864	1 year.	
Hunnesell, Carl	...do...	38	Aug. 22, 1864	1 year.	Mustered out May 20, 1865, at Nashville, Tenn., by order of War Department.
Hunter, Swan	...do...	19	Sept. 6, 1864	1 year.	
Jones, Thomas	...do...	18	Aug. 21, 1864	1 year.	Mustered out with company June 14, 1865.
Jones, Thomas B.	...do...	27	Aug. 15, 1864	1 year.	
Keller, Henry	...do...	35	Aug. 31, 1864	1 year.	Mustered out with company June 14, 1865.
Kibbel, Xavier	...do...	30	Feb. 1, 1865	1 year.	Mustered out June 8, 1865, at Nashville, Tenn., by order of War Department.
Kirn, Philip	...do...	38	Aug. 22, 1864	1 year.	Mustered out with company June 14, 1865.
Lenderbaugh, Frank	...do...	18	Sept. 1, 1864	1 year.	Mustered out with company June 14, 1865.
Lindner, Frederick	...do...	27	Aug. 29, 1864	1 year.	Died Oct. 19, 1864, in hospital at Nashville, Tennessee.
McCann, John N.	...do...	29	Aug. 27, 1864	1 year.	Mustered out with company June 14, 1865.
McIntire, Erastus	...do...	22	Aug. 23, 1864	1 year.	Mustered out with company June 14, 1865.
Magley, John M.	...do...	35	Aug. 16, 1864	1 year.	Mustered out with company June 14, 1865.
Miller, Albert	...do...	29	Aug. 18, 1864	1 year.	Mustered out with company June 14, 1865.
Miller, Augustus	...do...	18	Aug. 10, 1864	1 year.	Mustered out with company June 14, 1865.
Miller, John	...do...	18	Aug. 16, 1864	1 year.	Mustered out with company June 14, 1865.
Morningstar, Joseph	...do...	31	Sept. 1, 1864	1 year.	Mustered out with company June 14, 1865.
Neighbor, George	...do...	37	Aug. 26, 1864	1 year.	Mustered out with company June 14, 1865.
Newcomb, Rudolph	...do...	28	Sept. 1, 1864	1 year.	Died Feb. 4, 1865, in hospital at Nashville, Tennessee.
Patterson, Charles C.	...do...	22	Aug. 16, 1864	1 year.	Reduced from Sergeant Dec. 31, 1864; mustered out with company June 14, 1865.
Patton, Gustavus	...do...	26	Aug. 31, 1864	1 year.	Mustered out with company June 14, 1865.
Pock, Hermon	...do...	39	Aug. 11, 1864	1 year.	
Pobley, Charles	...do...	19	Aug. 23, 1864	1 year.	Mustered out with company June 14, 1865.
Reitze, John	...do...	37	Aug. 31, 1864	1 year.	Mustered out June 22, 1865, at Nashville, Tenn., by order of War Department.
Sawyer, Jacob	...do...	25	Aug. 26, 1864	1 year.	
Schneider, Henry	...do...	54	Aug. 27, 1864	1 year.	Mustered out with company June 14, 1865.
Shrom, William P.	...do...	23	Aug. 25, 1864	1 year.	Promoted to 2d Lieutenant Co. B, 178th O. V. I., Sept. 23, 1864.
Spohr, Conrad	...do...	29	Aug. 8, 1864	1 year.	
Steinmetz, Henry	...do...	19	Sept. 2, 1864	1 year.	Mustered out with company June 14, 1865.
Steuche, Herman	...do...	32	Aug. 30, 1864	1 year.	Mustered out June 19, 1865, at Tripler Hospital, Columbus, O., by order of War Department.
Stutz, Charles	...do...	32	Aug. 24, 1864	1 year.	Mustered out with company June 14, 1865.
Sypherd, Henry G.	...do...	22	Feb. 28, 1865	1 year.	Mustered out June 8, 1865, at Nashville, Tenn., by order of War Department.
Tussing, David E.	...do...	26	Aug. 29, 1864	1 year.	Reduced from Corporal Jan. 28, 1865; mustered out with company June 14, 1865.
Wagner, Mart	...do...	18	Aug. 27, 1864	1 year.	Mustered out with company June 14, 1865.
Weist, Michael	...do...	34	Aug. 31, 1864	1 year.	Mustered out with company June 14, 1865.
Widman, Joseph	...do...	29	Aug. 22, 1864	1 year.	Mustered out with company June 14, 1865.
Wilhelm, Adam	...do...	30	Aug. 15, 1864	1 year.	Mustered out with company June 14, 1865.
Williams, William H.	...do...	23	Aug. 30, 1864	1 year.	Mustered out May 29, 1865, at Columbus, O., by order of War Department.
Wire, Alfred D.	...do...	22	Aug. 15, 1864	1 year.	Appointed Corporal Jan. 5, 1865; reduced March 8, 1865; mustered out with company June 14, 1865.
Wise, Benjamin	...do...	20	Aug. 22, 1864	1 year.	Mustered out with company June 14, 1865.

COMPANY B.

Mustered in Sept. 21, 1864, at Camp Chase, O., by W. P. Richardson, Colonel 25th O. V. I. Mustered out June 14, 1865, at Nashville, Tenn., by W. S. Wilson, Captain 71st O. V. I.

Names.	Rank.	Age.	Date of Entering the Service.	Period of Service.	Remarks.
Ira B. Wambaugh	Captain.	30	Sept. 8, 1864	1 year.	Mustered out with company June 14, 1865.
Henry H. Crane	1st Lieut.	21	Sept. 8, 1864	1 year.	Promoted to Captain Co. G March 18, 1865.
Perry T. Nichols	...do...	23	Sept. 21, 1864	1 year.	Promoted from 2d Lieutenant Co. I March 29, 1865; mustered out with company June 14, 1865.
Joseph P. Owen	2d Lieut.	26	Sept. 8, 1864	1 year.	Promoted to 1st Lieutenant Co. E Jan. 18, 1865.
Joel Funk	...do...	34	Sept. 20, 1864	1 year.	Promoted from 1st Sergeant Co. E Jan. 18, 1865; mustered out with company June 14, 1865.
[illegible]	1st Sergt.	25	Sept. 8, 1864	1 year.	Died Dec. 19, 1864, at Nashville, Tenn.
[illegible]	...do...	23	Sept. 7, 1864	1 year.	Mustered as Corporal; appointed 1st Sergeant ——; promoted to 2d Lieutenant Co. C March 18, 1865.
[illegible]	...do...	21	Sept. 3, 1864	1 year.	Appointed Sergeant from Corporal Dec. 26, 1864; 1st Sergeant March 30, 1865; mustered out with company June 14, 1865.
William Wright	Sergeant.	28	Aug. 18, 1864	1 year.	Appointed from Corporal Sept. 8, 1864; mustered out with company June 14, 1865.

Names.	Rank.	Age.	Date of Entering the Service.	Period of Service.
Edgar H. Bowen	Sergeant.	30	Sept. 2, 1864	1 year.
Willie Hague	...do...	18	Sept. 3, 1864	1 year.
John Snyder	...do...	20	Aug. 26, 1864	1 year.
John J. Lowery	Corporal.	30	Aug. 25, 1864	1 year.
Theodore J. Young	...do...	22	Aug. 29, 1864	1 year.
John Keller	...do...	37	Aug. 29, 1864	1 year.
Leonard Delamater	...do...	22	Aug. 30, 1864	1 year.
Cyrus Hinkley	...do...	18	Aug. 28, 1864	1 year.
John E. Pattison	...do...	31	Sept. 3, 1864	1 year.
William S. McGowan	...do...	26	Aug. 29, 1864	1 year.
George B. Powers	...do...	23	Aug. 30, 1864	1 year.
Orin E. Harris	...do...	29	Sept. 3, 1864	1 year.
George Schneider	Musician	16	Aug. 17, 1864	1 year.
Charles McKelvey	...do...	18	Aug. 23, 1864	1 year.
Bard, James C.	Private.	18	Aug. 20, 1864	1 year.
Barkdull, Thomas H	...do...	20	Feb. 1, 1865	1 year.
Barkdull, Watson H	...do...	23	Feb. 1, 1865	1 year.
Berns, Anthony	...do...	24	Sept. 3, 1864	1 year.
Brayton, William	...do...	30	Sept. 2, 1864	1 year.
Brooks, Ira H	...do...	21	Feb. 18, 1865	1 year.
Burkett, Stephen	...do...	27	Sept. 2, 1864	1 year.
Bushshawn, Eli	...do...	18	Aug. 26, 1864	1 year.
Butcher, Edward	...do...	19	Sept. 4, 1864	1 year.
Byron, John M	...do...	37	Feb. 13, 1865	1 year.
Carl, James P	...do...	18	Sept. 1, 1864	1 year.
Carpenter, Frederick W.	...do...	26	Feb. 13, 1865	1 year.
Chamberlain, Cornelius	...do...	36	Sept 4, 1864	1 year.
Chamberlain, Jeremiah.	...do...	25	Sept. 4, 1864	1 year.
Childs, Frederick M.	...do...	27	Sept. 4, 1864	1 year.
Collins, Charles	...do...	38	Aug. 26, 1864	1 year.
Cooper, Joseph	...do...	22	Sept. 3, 1864	1 year.
Couples, William	...do...	26	Aug. 29, 1864	1 year.
Darby, Charles	...do...	43	Sept. 3, 1864	1 year.
Darr, Jacob	...do...	42	Sept. 2, 1864	1 year.
Davis, John	...do...	22	Aug. 30, 1864	1 year.
Dieble, Lewis	...do...	20	Sept. 1, 1864	1 year.
Doleson, Frederick M	...do...	27	Aug. 28, 1864	1 year.
Eckle, William	...do...	18	Aug. 30, 1864	1 year.
Engleby, Henry	...do...	31	Aug. 29, 1864	1 year.
Evans, Thomas	...do...	29	Sept. 3, 1864	1 year.
Fiser, Charles M	...do...	24	Aug. 29, 1864	1 year.
Fleming, Sylvester B.	...do...	24	Sept. 2, 1864	1 year.
Fletcher, Charles H.	...do...	23	Feb. 13, 1865	1 year.
Fletcher, William H	...do...	28	Feb. 13, 1865	1 year.
Fowler, Benjamin F	...do...	43	Sept. 3, 1864	1 year.
Gossman, John G.	...do...	32	Aug. 27, 1864	1 year.
Gray, James	...do...	19	Feb. 18, 1865	1 year.
Grubb, Simon	...do...	37	Sept. 3, 1864	1 year.
Gunn, Nelson P.	...do...	39	Sept. 2, 1864	1 year.
Hall, Calvin	...do...	31	Sept. 4, 1864	1 year.
Hall, Charles	...do...	21	Aug. 24, 1864	1 year.
Hatch, Erastus	...do...	42	Aug. 24, 1864	1 year.
Heath, Charles A.	...do...	23	Sept. 3, 1864	1 year.
Hendrixon, Isaac L.	...do...	36	Sept. 7, 1864	1 year.
Highland, Nelson P.	...do...	35	Aug. 24, 1864	1 year.

	Rank.	Age.	Date of Entering the Service.	Period of Service.	Remarks.
	Private	25	Aug. 26, 1864	1 year.	Mustered out with company June 14, 1865.
B.	....do....	22	Sept. 7, 1864	1 year.	Mustered out with company June 14, 1865.
S.	....do....	25	Sept. 7, 1864	1 year.	Mustered out with company June 14, 1865.
ah.	....do....	25	Sept. 5, 1864	1 year.	Mustered out with company June 14, 1865.
	....do....	42	Sept. 3, 1864	1 year.	Died March 18, 1865, at Nashville, Tenn.
ain F.	....do....	29	Sept. 4, 1864	1 year.	Mustered out with company June 14, 1865.
d	....do....	36	Aug. 25, 1864	1 year.	Mustered out with company June 14, 1865.
	....do....	24	Sept. 3, 1864	1 year.	Mustered out with company June 14, 1865.
h E.	....do....	27	Feb. 22, 1865	1 year.	Transferred to Co. G, 18th O. V. I., June 28, 1865.
n A	....do....	22	Aug. 26, 1864	1 year.	Mustered out to date June 14, 1865, by order of War Department.
	....do....	18	Aug. 31, 1864	1 year.	Mustered as Musician; died Jan. 4, 1865, at Nashville, Tenn.
	....do....	42	Aug. 15, 1864	1 year.	Mustered out July 15, 1865, at Nashville, Tenn., by order of War Department.
	....do....	18	Sept. 2, 1864	1 year.	Mustered out June 14, 1865, at Columbus, O., by order of War Department.
	....do....	37	Sept. 2, 1864	1 year.	Died Jan. 6, 1865, at Nashville, Tenn.
E	....do....	18	Aug. 26, 1864	1 year.	Mustered out with company June 14, 1865.
K.	....do....	38	Sept. 2, 1864	1 year.	Died Dec. 5, 1864, at Nashville, Tenn.
	....do....	18	Aug. 18, 1864	1 year.	Mustered out May 20, 1865, at Nashville, Tenn., by order of War Department.
E.	....do....	43	Feb. 1, 1865	1 year.	Promoted to Principal Musician March 28, 1865.
	....do....	23	Aug. 30, 1864	1 year.	Mustered out with company June 14, 1865.
ob	....do....	36	Sept. 3, 1864	1 year.	Mustered out with company June 14, 1865.
	....do....	38	Sept. 3, 1864	1 year.	Reduced from Sergeant ——; mustered out with company June 14, 1865.
s	....do....	18	Sept. 3, 1864	1 year.	Mustered out with company June 14, 1865.
	....do....	28	Sept. 3, 1864	1 year.	Mustered out with company June 14, 1865.
	....do....	38	Aug. 30, 1864	1 year.	
a.	....do....	28	Sept. 4, 1864	1 year.	Mustered out with company June 14, 1865.
	....do....	18	Aug. 22, 1864	1 year.	Mustered out with company June 14, 1865.
	....do....	30	Aug. 8, 1864	1 year.	Reduced from Corporal ——; mustered out April 12, 1865, at New Albany, Ind., by order of War Department.
n	....do....	37	Sept. 3, 1864	1 year.	Mustered out with company June 14, 1865.
	....do....	18	Sept. 3, 1864	1 year.	Mustered out with company June 14, 1865.
	....do....	36	Sept. 8, 1864	1 year.	Mustered out with company June 14, 1865.
	....do....	28	Aug. 28, 1864	1 year.	Mustered out with company June 14, 1865.
ohn	....do....	34	Aug. 18, 1864	1 year.	Mustered out with company June 14, 1865.
	....do....	22	Aug. 23, 1864	1 year.	Mustered out May 28, 1865, at Nashville, Tenn., by order of War Department.
	....do....	36	Aug. 28, 1864	1 year.	Mustered out with company June 14, 1865.
l	....do....	39	Aug. 27, 1864	1 year.	Mustered out with company June 14, 1865.
o	....do....	27	Sept. 3, 1864	1 year.	Mustered out June 7, 1865, at Nashville, Tenn., by order of War Department.
r.	....do....	18	Aug. 22, 1864	1 year.	Mustered out June 22, 1865, at Nashville, Tenn., by order of War Department.
	....do....	28	Sept. 3, 1864	1 year.	Mustered out with company June 14, 1865.
L.	....do....	19	Sept. 3, 1864	1 year.	Mustered out with company June 14, 1865.
	....do....	26	Sept. 3, 1864	1 year.	Died Jan. 18, 1865, at Nashville, Tenn.
T	....do....	19	Aug. 30, 1864	1 year.	Mustered out May 23, 1865, at Nashville, Tenn., by order of War Department.
	....do....	27	Aug. 31, 1864	1 year.	Mustered out with company June 14, 1865.
H.	....do....	29	Aug. 23, 1864	1 year.	Reduced from Sergeant Dec. 28, 1864; died Jan. 6, 1865, at Cleveland, O.
	....do....	34	Aug. 19, 1864	1 year.	Mustered out with company June 14, 1865.
al	....do....	19	Sept. 4, 1864	1 year.	Mustered out with company June 14, 1865; also borne on rolls as Gabriel Sultzer.
	....do....	23	Sept. 4, 1864	1 year.	Appointed Corporal Dec. 26, 1864; reduced April 20, 1865; mustered out with company June 14, 1865.
n	....do....	28	Sept. 2, 1864	1 year.	Mustered out with company June 14, 1865.
	....do....	35	Sept. 2, 1864	1 year.	Mustered out with company June 14, 1865.
O.	....do....	41	Aug. 29, 1864	1 year.	Mustered out with company June 14, 1865.
anklin	....do....	18	Aug. 27, 1864	1 year.	Mustered out with company June 14, 1865.
n L.	....do....	35	Sept. 2, 1864	1 year.	Mustered out with company June 14, 1865.
se	....do....	37	Sept. 4, 1864	1 year.	Died Feb. 10, 1865, at Nashville, Tenn.
H	....do....	25	Sept. 2, 1864	1 year.	Mustered out with company June 14, 1865.
	....do....	18	Sept. 4, 1864	1 year.	Died Jan. 26, 1865, at Nashville, Tenn.
	....do....	37	Sept. 4, 1864	1 year.	Died Feb. 3, 1865, at Nashville, Tenn.
	....do....	18	Sept. 4, 1864	1 year.	Mustered out with company June 14, 1865.
	....do....	32	Sept. 3, 1864	1 year.	Mustered out with company June 14, 1865.
	....do....	18	Aug. 23, 1864	1 year.	Mustered out with company June 14, 1865.
D	....do....	31	Sept. 5, 1864	1 year.	Mustered out with company June 14, 1865.
	....do....	21	Sept. 1, 1864	1 year.	
	....do....	24	Aug. 29, 1864	1 year.	Mustered out May 29, 1865, at Camp Dennison, O., by order of War Department.

COMPANY G.

Mustered in Sept. 21, 1864, at Camp Chase, O., by W. P. Richardso
14, 1865, at Nashville, Tenn., by W. S. Wilso

Names.	Rank.	Age.	Date of Entering the Service.	Period of Service.	
Aaron K. Lindsley	Captain.	47	Sept. 8, 1864	1 year.	M
Joseph A. Lovejoy	1st Lieut.	46	Sept. 8, 1864	1 year.	Pr
Marcena M. Murphy	....do....	26	Aug. 12, 1864	1 year.	Pr
Ransom Peabody	2d Lieut.	37	Sept. 8, 1864	1 year.	Pr
Lafayette L. Trask	....do....	23	Sept. 7, 1864	1 year.	Pr
Henry W. Houghton	1st Sergt.	20	Sept. 8, 1864	1 year.	Pr
Henry S. Viets	....do....	25	Sept. 1, 1864	1 year.	Ap
Ezekiel Jones	Sergeant.	26	Aug. 8, 1864	1 year.	Ap
Henry Bennett	....do....	28	Aug. 11, 1864	1 year.	Ap
Leonard G. Perry	....do....	36	Aug. 22, 1864	1 year.	Ap
Luther W. Clark	....do....	31	Aug. 9, 1864	1 year.	Ap
Grantham Grundy	Corporal.	36	Aug. 9, 1864	1 year.	Ap
Henry J. Rossiter	....do....	26	Aug. 29, 1864	1 year.	Ap
Carolus Hickok	....do....	21	Aug. 30, 1864	1 year.	Ap
Robert N. Blair	....do....	23	Aug. 30, 1864	1 year.	Ap
George W. Sutliff	....do....	18	Aug. 28, 1864	1 year.	Ap
Edgar C. Jeffries	....do....	21	Aug. 25, 1864	1 year.	Ap
William Jickles	....do....	34	Aug. 31, 1864	1 year.	Ap
Thomas W. Dougherty	....do....	24	Sept. 3, 1864	1 year.	Ap
Charles Hays	Musician	17	Aug. 22, 1864	1 year.	Mu
Adam Miller	....do....	18	Aug. 25, 1864	1 year.	Mu
Allen, William D. W	Private.	20	Jan. 31, 1865	1 year.	Mu
Avery, Lewis B	....do....	36	Aug. 22, 1864	1 year.	Mu
Battle, Joseph H	....do....	18	Aug. 26, 1864	1 year.	Mu
Battle, Wesley S	....do....	22	Aug. 8, 1864	1 year.	Mu
Bemis, Francis	....do....	31	Mch. 7, 1865	1 year.	Mu
Bennett, Frank W	....do....	22	Feb. 1, 1865	1 year.	Mu
Bodman, Christopher F.	....do....	28	Mch. 7, 1865	1 year.	
Braman, Jonathan W	....do....	34	Aug. 29, 1864	1 year.	Mu
Brown, Luther S	....do....	18	Sept. 3, 1864	1 year.	
Bruce, Almond G	....do....	18	July 27, 1864	1 year.	Mu
Canfield, Walter	....do....	18	Sept. 3, 1864	1 year.	Mu
Clark, George F	....do....	25	Aug. 19, 1864	1 year.	Mu
Clifford, Herman V	....do....	18	Feb. 1, 1865	1 year.	Tr
Crotzer, John	....do....	18	Sept. 1, 1864	1 year.	Mu
Daly, James R	....do....	22	Aug. 29, 1864	1 year.	Mu
Dougherty, James H	....do....	34	Sept. 3, 1864	1 year.	Mu
Dudley, William G	....do....	39	Aug. 8, 1864	1 year.	Mu
Everlee, DeWitt C	....do....	18	Aug. 30, 1864	1 year.	Mu
Foote, James	....do....	35	Aug. 11, 1864	1 year.	Die
Forbes, Albert	....do....	18	Aug. 28, 1864	1 year.	Die
Forbes, Washington	....do....	24	Aug. 21, 1864	1 year.	Mu
Gibbs, Robert P	....do....	26	Aug. 15, 1864	1 year.	Mu
Gilson, Eli D	....do....	40	Aug. 16, 1864	1 year.	Mu
Grey, Joseph	....do....	31	Aug. 31, 1864	1 year.	Mu
Grey, Nathan	....do....	24	Aug. 24, 1864	1 year.	Die

Names.	Rank.	Age.	Date of Entering the Service.	Period of Service.	Remarks.
Grimm, Addison W.	Private.	20	Aug. 8, 1864	1 year.	Mustered out with company June 14, 1865.
Griggs, George W.	do.	18	Sept. 1, 1864	1 year.	Mustered out with company June 14, 1865.
Gwynn, Lewis	do.	22	Sept. 5, 1864	1 year.	Mustered out with company June 14, 1865.
Hamilton, Linville E.	do.	20	Aug. 12, 1864	1 year.	Reduced from Corporal Dec. 31, 1864; mustered out with company June 14, 1865.
Hanna, George C.	do.	20	Aug. 29, 1864	1 year.	Mustered out with company June 14, 1865.
Harpster, Hiram	do.	34	Aug. 9, 1864	1 year.	Mustered out with company June 14, 1865.
Huston, Daniel	do.	19	Sept. 3, 1864	1 year.	Died March 6, 1865, in hospital at Nashville, Tennessee.
Hinds, Richard S.	do.	34	Aug. 24, 1864	1 year.	Mustered out with company June 14, 1865.
Inman, Orle M.	do.	18	July 27, 1864	1 year.	Mustered out with company June 14, 1865.
King, Joseph E.	do.	18	Aug. 19, 1864	1 year.	Mustered out with company June 14, 1865.
Lewis, Benjamin J	do.	38	Aug. 28, 1864	1 year.	Mustered out to date June 14, 1865, at Nashville, Tenn., by order of War Department.
Lewis, James	do.	41	Aug. 10, 1864	1 year.	Mustered out with company June 14, 1865.
Little, William T.	do.	17	Aug. 22, 1864	1 year.	Mustered out with company June 14, 1865.
Main, Nelson L.	do.	19	July 25, 1864	1 year.	Mustered out with company June 14, 1865.
Mallery, Hiram W.	do.	22	July 25, 1864	1 year.	Reduced from Corporal Dec. 31, 1864; mustered out with company June 14, 1865.
Mandeville, David N	do.	19	July 27, 1864	1 year.	Mustered out with company June 14, 1865.
Mandeville, William J.	do.	18	July 27, 1864	1 year.	Mustered out June 8, 1865, at Nashville, Tenn., by order of War Department.
Marcy, Eugene R.	do.	18	Aug. 15, 1864	1 year.	Mustered out with company June 14, 1865.
Mence, Peter	do.	36	Mch. 7, 1865	1 year.	Mustered out July 12, 1865, at Nashville, Tenn., by order of War Department.
Minard, Linus	do.	18	Aug. 19, 1864	1 year.	Mustered out with company June 14, 1865.
Moon, Henry E	do.	28	Aug. 18, 1864	1 year.	
Moon, John W.	do.	28	Aug. 24, 1864	1 year.	Mustered out with company June 14, 1865.
Munsinger, Edward	do.	19	Aug. 6, 1864	1 year.	Mustered out with company June 14, 1865.
Munsinger, George	do.	22	Aug. 6, 1864	1 year.	Mustered out with company June 14, 1865.
Nickles, Benjamin J.	do.	18	Jan. 27, 1865	1 year.	Mustered out Aug. 4, 1865, at Nashville, Tenn., by order of War Department.
Ogden, Charles H.	do.	18	Aug. 15, 1864	1 year.	Mustered out with company June 14, 1865.
Palmer, Henry D.	do.	25	Aug. 22, 1864	1 year.	Mustered out with company June 14, 1865.
Payne, John	do.	29	Aug. 24, 1864	1 year.	Mustered out with company June 14, 1865.
Peabody, Alvah	do.	30	Aug. 6, 1864	1 year.	Mustered out with company June 14, 1865.
Pelton, Eugene	do.	18	Sept. 14, 1864	1 year.	Mustered out with company June 14, 1865.
Pelton, Russell	do.	20	Sept. 1, 1864	1 year.	Mustered out with company June 14, 1865.
Plumber, James	do.	34	Aug. 29, 1864	1 year.	Mustered out with company June 14, 1865.
Plain, Morris W.	do.	24	Aug. 9, 1864	1 year.	Died April 14, 1865, in hospital at Nashville, Tennessee.
Pomeroy, Henry W	do.	29	Feb. 1, 1865	1 year.	Transferred to Co. E, 18th O. V. I., June 28, 1865.
Reynolds, Albert S.	do.	18	July 25, 1864	1 year.	Died Dec. 21, 1864, in hospital at Nashville, Tennessee.
Robins, Nicholas	do.	32	Aug. 29, 1864	1 year.	Mustered out with company June 14, 1865.
Rock, Lewis	do.	18	Sept. 8, 1864	1 year.	Mustered out with company June 14, 1865.
Sackett, William R.	do.	31	Aug. 12, 1864	1 year.	Mustered out May 26, 1865, at Nashville, Tenn by order of War Department.
Scheele, Frederick	do.	38	Mch. 7, 1865	1 year.	Mustered out June 7, 1865, at Nashville, Tenn., by order of War Department.
Scrogg, John	do.	21	Aug. 11, 1864	1 year.	Mustered out with company June 14, 1865.
Smith, John G.	do.	18	Aug. 26, 1864	1 year.	Mustered out with company June 14, 1865.
Smith, Sidney A.	do.	38	Sept. 2, 1864	1 year.	Mustered out with company June 14, 1865.
Smith, William N.	do.	40	Aug. 30, 1864	1 year.	Died June 8, 1865, in hospital at Nashville, Tennessee.
Soles, Walter	do.	37	Aug. 28, 1864	1 year.	Mustered out with company June 14, 1865.
Starr, Charles E.	do.	20	Aug. 29, 1864	1 year.	Reduced from Corporal Dec. 31, 1864; mustered out with company June 14, 1865.
Swain, Charles	do.	19	Aug. 15, 1864	1 year.	Mustered out with company June 14, 1865.
Swain, Thomas	do.	21	Aug. 24, 1864	1 year.	Mustered out with company June 14, 1865.
Sweet, Lucien B.	do.	18	Sept. 5, 1864	1 year.	Transferred from Co. F —; mustered out with company June 14, 1865.
Upson, George W	do.	28	Aug. 31, 1864	1 year.	Mustered out with company June 14, 1865.
Voorhees, Albert	do.	21	Aug. 22, 1864	1 year.	Mustered out with company June 14, 1865.
Ward, Hazelton	do.	18	Sept. 3, 1864	1 year.	Mustered out with company June 14, 1865; also borne on rolls as Hazelton Ware.
Warner, Edgar A.	do.	18	Aug. 18, 1864	1 year.	Mustered out June 8, 1865, at Nashville, Tenn., by order of War Department.
Wilcox, Stanley E.	do.	20	Feb. 1, 1865	1 year.	Mustered out June 8, 1865, at Nashville, Tenn., by order of War Department.
Woodbury, Roland C.	do.	26	Aug. 18, 1864	1 year.	Mustered out with company June 14, 1865.

COMPANY G

Mustered in Sept. 21, 1864, at Camp Chase, O., by W. P. Richardso[n] ... 14, 1865, at Nashville, Tenn., by W. S. Wilso[n]

Names.	Rank.	Age.	Date of Entering the Service.	Period of Service.	
Aaron K. Lindsley	Captain.	47	Sept. 8, 1864	1 year.	Mu
Joseph A. Lovejoy	1st Lieut.	45	Sept. 8, 1864	1 year.	Pr
Marcena M. Murphy	...do...	25	Aug. 12, 1864	1 year.	Pr
Ransom Peabody	2d Lieut.	37	Sept. 8, 1864	1 year.	Pr
Lafayette L. Trask	...do...	23	Sept. 7, 1864	1 year.	Pr
Henry W. Houghton	1st Sergt.	30	Sept. 8, 1864	1 year.	Pr
Henry S. Viets	...do...	25	Sept. 1, 1864	1 year.	Ap
Ezekiel Jones	Sergeant.	28	Aug. 8, 1864	1 year.	Ap
Henry Bennett	...do...	28	Aug. 11, 1864	1 year.	Ap
Leonard G. Perry	...do...	30	Aug. 22, 1864	1 year.	Ap
Luther W. Clark	...do...	31	Aug. 9, 1864	1 year.	Ap
Grantham Grundy	Corporal.	36	Aug. 9, 1864	1 year.	Ap
Henry J. Rossiter	...do...	26	Aug. 29, 1864	1 year.	Ap
Carolus Hickok	...do...	21	Aug. 30, 1864	1 year.	Ap
Robert N. Blair	...do...	28	Aug. 30, 1864	1 year.	Ap
George W. Sutliff	...do...	18	Aug. 23, 1864	1 year.	Ap
Edgar C. Jeffries	...do...	21	Aug. 25, 1864	1 year.	Ap
William Jickles	...do...	34	Aug. 31, 1864	1 year.	Ap
Thomas W. Dougherty	...do...	24	Sept. 3, 1864	1 year.	Ap
Charles Hays	Musician	17	Aug. 22, 1864	1 year.	Mu
Adam Miller	...do...	18	Aug. 25, 1864	1 year.	Mu
Allen, William D. W	Private.	20	Jan. 31, 1865	1 year.	Mu
Avery, Lewis H	...do...	36	Aug. 22, 1864	1 year.	Mu
Battle, Joseph H	...do...	18	Aug. 26, 1864	1 year.	Mu
Battle, Wesley S	...do...	22	Aug. 8, 1864	1 year.	Mu
Bemis, Francis	...do...	31	Mch. 7, 1865	1 year.	Mu
Bennett, Frank W	...do...	22	Feb. 1, 1865	1 year.	Mu
Bodman, Christopher F.	...do...	28	Mch. 7, 1865	1 year.	Tr
Braman, Jonathan W	...do...	34	Aug. 29, 1864	1 year.	Mu
Brown, Luther S	...do...	18	Sept. 3, 1864	1 year.	Dis
Bruce, Almond G	...do...	18	July 27, 1864	1 year.	Mu
Canfield, Walter	...do...	18	Sept. 3, 1864	1 year.	Mu
Clark, George F	...do...	25	Aug. 19, 1864	1 year.	Mu
Clifford, Herman V	...do...	18	Feb. 1, 1865	1 year.	Tr
Crotzer, John	...do...	18	Sept. 1, 1864	1 year.	Mu
Daly, James R	...do...	22	Aug. 29, 1864	1 year.	Mu
Dougherty, James H	...do...	34	Sept. 3, 1864	1 year.	Mu
Dudley, William G	...do...	39	Aug. 8, 1864	1 year.	Mu
Everlee, DeWitt C	...do...	18	Aug. 30, 1864	1 year.	Mu
Foote, James	...do...	35	Aug. 11, 1864	1 year.	Dis
Forbes, Albert	...do...	18	Aug. 26, 1864	1 year.	Dis
Forbes, Washington	...do...	24	Aug. 21, 1864	1 year.	Mu
Gibbs, Robert P	...do...	26	Aug. 15, 1864	1 year.	Mu
Gilson, Eli D	...do...	40	Aug. 16, 1864	1 year.	Mu
Grey, Joseph	...do...	31	Aug. 31, 1864	1 year.	Mu
Grey, Nathan	...do...	24	Aug. 24, 1864	1 year.	Dis

Names.	Rank.	Age.	Date of Entering the Service.	Period of Service.	Remarks.
Griggs, Addison W	Private	20	Aug. 8, 1864	1 year.	Mustered out with company June 14, 1865.
Griggs, George W	do	18	Sept. 1, 1864	1 year.	Mustered out with company June 14, 1865.
Gwynn, Lewis	do	23	Sept. 5, 1864	1 year.	Mustered out with company June 14, 1865.
Hamilton, Linville E	do	20	Aug. 12, 1864	1 year.	Reduced from Corporal Dec. 31, 1864; mustered out with company June 14, 1865.
Hanes, George C	do	29	Aug. 29, 1864	1 year.	Mustered out with company June 14, 1865.
Harpster, Hiram	do	34	Aug. 9, 1864	1 year.	Mustered out with company June 14, 1865.
Huston, Ezekiel	do	19	Sept. 3, 1864	1 year.	Died March 6, 1865, in hospital at Nashville, Tennessee.
Himes, Richard S	do	24	Aug. 24, 1864	1 year.	Mustered out with company June 14, 1865.
Inman, Orie M	do	18	July 27, 1864	1 year.	Mustered out with company June 14, 1865.
King, Joseph E	do	18	Aug. 19, 1864	1 year.	Mustered out with company June 14, 1865.
Lewis, Benjamin J	do	28	Aug. 23, 1864	1 year.	Mustered out to date June 14, 1865, at Nashville, Tenn., by order of War Department.
Lewis, James	do	41	Aug. 10, 1864	1 year.	Mustered out with company June 14, 1865.
Little, William T	do	17	Aug. 22, 1864	1 year.	Mustered out with company June 14, 1865.
Main, Nelson L	do	19	July 25, 1864	1 year.	Mustered out with company June 14, 1865.
Mallory, Hiram W	do	22	July 25, 1864	1 year.	Reduced from Corporal Dec. 31, 1864; mustered out with company June 14, 1865.
Mandeville, David N	do	19	July 27, 1864	1 year.	Mustered out with company June 14, 1865.
Mandeville, William J	do	18	July 27, 1864	1 year.	Mustered out June 8, 1865, at Nashville, Tenn., by order of War Department.
Marcy, Eugene R	do	18	Aug. 15, 1864	1 year.	Mustered out with company June 14, 1865.
Mence, Peter	do	36	Mch. 7, 1865	1 year.	Mustered out July 12, 1865, at Nashville, Tenn., by order of War Department.
Minard, Linza	do	18	Aug. 19, 1864	1 year.	Mustered out with company June 14, 1865.
Moon, Henry E	do	28	Aug. 18, 1864	1 year.	
Moon, John W	do	23	Aug. 24, 1864	1 year.	Mustered out with company June 14, 1865.
Munsinger, Edward	do	19	Aug. 6, 1864	1 year.	Mustered out with company June 14, 1865.
Munsinger, George	do	22	Aug. 6, 1864	1 year.	Mustered out with company June 14, 1865.
Nickles, Benjamin J	do	18	Jan. 27, 1865	1 year.	Mustered out Aug. 4, 1865, at Nashville, Tenn., by order of War Department.
Ogden, Charles R	do	18	Aug. 15, 1864	1 year.	Mustered out with company June 14, 1865.
Palmer, Henry D	do	25	Aug. 22, 1864	1 year.	Mustered out with company June 14, 1865.
Payne, John	do	29	Aug. 24, 1864	1 year.	Mustered out with company June 14, 1865.
Peabody, Alvah	do	20	Aug. 6, 1864	1 year.	Mustered out with company June 14, 1865.
Pelton, Eugene	do	18	Sept. 14, 1864	1 year.	Mustered out with company June 14, 1865.
Pelton, Russell	do	20	Sept. 1, 1864	1 year.	Mustered out with company June 14, 1865.
Pember, James	do	34	Aug. 29, 1864	1 year.	Mustered out with company June 14, 1865.
Plain, Morris W	do	24	Aug. 9, 1864	1 year.	Died April 14, 1865, in hospital at Nashville, Tennessee.
Pomeroy, Henry W	do	29	Feb. 1, 1865	1 year.	Transferred to Co. E, 18th O. V. I., June 28, 1865.
Reynolds, Albert S	do	18	July 25, 1864	1 year.	Died Dec. 24, 1864, in hospital at Nashville, Tennessee.
Robins, Nicholas	do	32	Aug. 29, 1864	1 year.	Mustered out with company June 14, 1865.
Rock, Lewis	do	18	Sept. 3, 1864	1 year.	Mustered out with company June 14, 1865.
Sackett, William R	do	31	Aug. 12, 1864	1 year.	Mustered out May 29, 1865, at Nashville, Tenn., by order of War Department.
Scheele, Frederick	do	33	Mch. 7, 1865	1 year.	Mustered out June 7, 1865, at Nashville, Tenn., by order of War Department.
Scruggs, John	do	21	Aug. 11, 1864	1 year.	Mustered out with company June 14, 1865.
Smith, John G	do	18	Aug. 26, 1864	1 year.	Mustered out with company June 14, 1865.
Smith, Sidney A	do	28	Sept. 2, 1864	1 year.	Mustered out with company June 14, 1865.
Smith, William N	do	40	Aug. 30, 1864	1 year.	Died June 8, 1865, in hospital at Nashville, Tennessee.
Soles, Walter	do	37	Aug. 23, 1864	1 year.	Mustered out with company June 14, 1865.
Starr, Charles E	do	30	Aug. 29, 1864	1 year.	Reduced from Corporal Dec. 31, 1864; mustered out with company June 14, 1865.
Swain, Charles	do	19	Aug. 15, 1864	1 year.	Mustered out with company June 14, 1865.
Swain, Thomas	do	21	Aug. 24, 1864	1 year.	Mustered out with company June 14, 1865.
Sweet, Lucius B	do	18	Sept. 5, 1864	1 year.	Transferred from Co. F —; mustered out with company June 14, 1865.
Upson, George W	do	28	Aug. 31, 1864	1 year.	Mustered out with company June 14, 1865.
Voorhees, Albert	do	21	Aug. 22, 1864	1 year.	Mustered out with company June 14, 1865.
Ward, Hazelton	do	18	Sept. 3, 1864	1 year.	Mustered out with company June 14, 1865; also borne on rolls as Hazelton Ware.
Warner, Edgar A	do	18	Aug. 18, 1864	1 year.	Mustered out June 8, 1865, at Nashville, Tenn., by order of War Department.
Wilcox, Stanley E	do	20	Feb. 1, 1865	1 year.	Mustered out June 8, 1865, at Nashville, Tenn., by order of War Department.
Woodbury, Roland C	do	36	Aug. 18, 1864	1 year.	Mustered out with company June 14, 1865.

COMPANY B.

Mustered in Sept. 21, 1864, at Camp Chase, O., by W. P. Richardson, Colonel 2
14, 1865, at Nashville, Tenn., by W. S. Wilson, Captain 7

Names.	Rank.	Age.	Date of Entering the Service.	Period of Service.	
John A. Myers	Captain.	25	Sept. 12, 1864	1 year.	Mustered out
George W. Beck	1st Lieut.	21	Sept. 12, 1864	1 year.	Resigned Feb.
Peter J. Medick	....do....	25	Sept. 15, 1864	1 year.	Transferred as 20, 1865; pro March 15, 18 June 14, 186
Randolph T. Douglas	2d Lieut.	19	Sept. 12, 1864	1 year.	Resigned Dec.
Marcena M. Murphy	....do....	25	Aug. 18, 1864	1 year.	Promoted from to 1st Lieute
James A. Carson	....do....	20	Sept. 17, 1864	1 year.	Promoted fro 1865; muste 1865
Harvey H. Campbell	1st Sergt.	21	Aug. 20, 1864	1 year.	Appointed Se Lieutenant (
William J. Swearinger	....do....	24	Sept. 5, 1864	1 year.	Appointed fro tered out wi
Thomas B. Crook	Sergeant.	20	Aug. 22, 1864	1 year.	Appointed Se company Ju
Tobias Cole	....do....	21	Aug. 22, 1864	1 year.	Appointed Se company Ju
Robert Morrow	....do....	30	Aug. 27, 1864	1 year.	Appointed fro tered out wi
Aaron B. Arter	....do....	28	Sept. 4, 1864	1 year.	Appointed fro tered out wi
Andrew Allabaugh	Corporal.	44	Sept. 2, 1864	1 year.	Appointed Ja company Ju
Dallas G. Morrison	....do....	21	Sept. 18, 1864	1 year.	Appointed Se company Ju
James Campbell	....do....	19	Sept. 8, 1864	1 year.	Appointed Ma company Ju
John S. Atterholt	....do....	29	Sept. 5, 1864	1 year.	Appointed Ma company Ju
James Howell	....do....	28	Aug. 27, 1864	1 year.	Appointed Ma company Ju
James L. Daugherty	....do....	22	Feb. 8, 1865	1 year.	Appointed Nashville ment.
William Menough	....do....	21	Sept. 2, 1864	1 year.	Appointed Nashville ment.
John Gallagher	....do....	31	Sept. 2, 1864	1 year.	Appointed Nashville, T ment.
Edwin F. McClain	Musician	43	Sept. 1, 1864	1 year.	Mustered out
John Painter	....do....	19	Sept. 1, 1864	1 year.	Mustered out
Ash, Elias	Private.	18	Aug. 26, 1864	1 year.	Died Sept. 24, Ohio.
Atterholt, Jason	....do....	26	Aug. 28, 1864	1 year.	Mustered out
Atterholt, Wilson H	....do....	22	Aug. 22, 1864	1 year.	Mustered out
Baker, Leonard	....do....	18	Aug. 26, 1864	1 year.	Mustered out
Batchelor, Robert C	....do....	28	Sept. 5, 1864	1 year.	Mustered out
Bell, Morris S	....do....	30	Aug. 31, 1864	1 year.	
Biglow, Seth G	....do....	38	Sept. 1, 1864	1 year.	Mustered out by order of
Bones, Robert	....do....	35	Sept. 2, 1864	1 year.	Mustered out
Brainard, Franklin A	....do....	20	Feb. 8, 1865	1 year.	Transferred t 1865.
Brecht, John	....do....	32	Aug. 29, 1864	1 year.	Mustered out
Burns, Nathaniel	....do....	21	Aug. 20, 1864	1 year.	Mustered out by order of
Butler, Thomas	....do....	22	Sept. 3, 1864	1 year.	
Clark, William	....do....	23	Sept. 2, 1864	1 year.	
Cooper, Henry	....do....	22	Sept. 2, 1864	1 year.	Reduced from tered out wi
Cooper, William P	....do....	21	Sept. 3, 1864	1 year.	Mustered out
Craig, Archibald	....do....	24	Sept. 6, 1864	1 year.	Mustered out
Crawford, John Y	....do....	40	Aug. 31, 1864	1 year.	Mustered out O., by order
Croscup, Samuel	....do....	32	Aug. 29, 1864	1 year.	Mustered out
Crosser, James H	....do....	22	Sept. 5, 1864	1 year.	Mustered out
Culbertson, Martin	....do....	36	Sept. 7, 1864	1 year.	Died April 21 Tennessee.
Daugherty, Andrew	....do....	18	Sept. 6, 1864	1 year.	Mustered out
Douglas, John W	....do....	18	Aug. 20, 1864	1 year	Mustered out
Downard, George W	....do....	29	Aug. 29, 1864	1 year.	Mustered out
Downard, William	....do....	25	Sept. 2, 1864	1 year.	Mustered out by order of

Date of Entering the Service.	Period of Service.	Remarks.
Aug. 27, 1864		Mustered out with company June 14, 1865.
Aug. 25, 1864		Died Jan. 17, 1865, in hospital at Nashville, Tennessee.
Sept. 2, 1864		Reduced from Corporal ——; mustered out with company June 14, 1865.
Sept. 6, 1864	1 year.	Mustered out with company June 14, 1865.
Aug. 30, 1864	1 year.	Mustered out July 6, 1865, at Columbus, O., by order of War Department.
Sept. 2, 1864		Mustered out with company June 14, 1865.
Sept. 6, 1864		Mustered out with company June 14, 1865.
Sept. 2, 1864		Mustered out May 29, 1865, at Camp Dennison, O., by order of War Department.
Sept. 3, 1864		Mustered out with company June 14, 1865.
Sept. 2, 1864		Appointed Corporal Oct. 27, 1864; reduced March 17, 1865; mustered out with company June 14, 1865.
Feb. 10, 1865	1 year.	Transferred to Co. E, 18th O. V. I., June 28, 1865.
Sept. 5, 1864	1 year.	Mustered out with company June 14, 1865.
Feb. 10, 1865	1	Transferred to Co. E, 18th O. V. I., June 28, 1865.
Sept. 2, 1864	1 year.	Mustered out with company June 14, 1865.
Sept. 1, 1864	1	Mustered out June 12, 1865, at Nashville, Tenn., by order of War Department.
Aug. 31, 1864	1 year.	Mustered out with company June 14, 1865.
Aug. 26, 1864	1	Reduced from Corporal Nov. 6, 1864; mustered out with company June 14, 1865.
Sept. 1, 1864		Mustered out with company June 14, 1865.
Aug. 15, 1864		Mustered out with company June 14, 1865.
Sept. 6, 1864		Died Feb. 18, 1865, in hospital at Nashville, Tennessee.
Sept. 3, 1864	1	Mustered out with company June 14, 1865.
Aug. 27, 1864	1	Mustered out with company June 14, 1865.
Sept. 10, 1864	1	
Sept. 6, 1864	1 year.	Mustered out with company June 14, 1865.
Aug. 18, 1864	1 year.	Mustered out with company June 14, 1865.
Sept. 5, 1864	1	Mustered out with company June 14, 1865.
Sept. 9, 1864	1	Mustered out with company June 14, 1865.
Sept. 7, 1864	1	Mustered out with company June 14, 1865.
Sept. 1, 1864	1 year.	Mustered out with company June 14, 1865.
Sept. 5, 1864	1	Appointed Corporal Dec. 28, 1864; reduced March 17, 1865; mustered out with company June 14, 1865.
Aug. 28, 1864	1 year.	Mustered out with company June 14, 1865.
Feb. 23, 1865	1 year.	Transferred to Co. B, 18th O. V. I., June 28, 1865.
Jan. 27, 1865	1 year.	Mustered out June 12, 1865, at Nashville, Tenn., by order of War Department.
Jan. 24, 1865		Mustered out June 12, 1865, at Nashville, Tenn., by order of War Department.
Sept. 10, 1864	1 year.	Mustered out with company June 14, 1865.
Sept. 2, 1864	1 year.	Mustered out with company June 14, 1865.
Aug. 15, 1864	1 year.	Mustered out with company June 14, 1865.
Aug. 22, 1864	1	Mustered out May 24, 1865, at New Albany, Ind., by order of War Department.
Sept. 9, 1864		Mustered out with company June 14, 1865.
Sept. 2, 1864		Mustered out May 30, 1865, at Nashville, Tenn., by order of War Department.
Sept. 2, 1864		Mustered out June 21, 1865, at Nashville, Tenn., by order of War Department.
Sept. 1, 1864	1	
Sept. 3, 1864	1	Mustered out with company June 14, 1865.
Aug. 24, 1864	1	
Aug. 20, 1864	1	Discharged June 26, 1865, on Surgeon's certificate of disability.
Aug. 22, 1864	1	Mustered out with company June 14, 1865.
Sept. 1, 1864	1	Mustered out with company June 14, 1865.
Aug. 10, 1864	1	Mustered out with company June 14, 1865.
Aug. 26, 1864	1	
Sept. 2, 1864	1	Mustered out with company June 14, 1865.
Sept. 1, 1864	1	Reduced from Corporal Nov. 10, 1864; mustered out with company June 14, 1865.
Feb. 23, 1865		Transferred to Co. B, 18th O. V. I., June 28, 1865.
Aug. 29, 1864		Reduced from Corporal Nov. 10, 1864; mustered out with company June 14, 1865.
Sept. 2, 1864		Mustered out with company June 14, 1865.
Aug. 31, 1864		Mustered out with company June 14, 1865.
Sept. 2, 1864		Mustered out with company June 14, 1865.
Aug. 23, 1864		Mustered out with company June 14, 1865.
Aug. 27, 1864		Mustered out with company June 14, 1865.
Aug. 25, 1864		Mustered out with company June 14, 1865.
Aug. 27, 1864		
Sept. 2, 1864		Mustered out with company June 14, 1865.

Names.	Rank.	Age.	Date of Entering the Service.	Period of Service.	Remarks.
Nick, Christopher	Private	21	Sept. 7, 1864	1 year.	Reduced from 1st Sergeant ——; died Feb. 9 1865, in hospital at Nashville, Tenn.
O'Riley, William	....do....	18	Sept. 9, 1864	1 year.	Mustered out with company June 14, 1865.
Palen, James O	....do....	15	Aug. 15, 1864	1 year.	Mustered out May 30, 1865, at Nashville, Tenn., by order of War Department.
Peeples, William	....do....	39	Aug. 25, 1864	1 year.	Mustered out with company June 14, 1865.
Reed, Nathan W	....do....	28	Sept. 26, 1864	1 year.	Mustered out with company June 14, 1865.
Ridenour, David A	....do....	40	Sept. 6, 1864	1 year.	Mustered out May 27, 1865, at Nashville, Tenn., by order of War Department.
Ritter, George H	....do....	20	Sept. 2, 1864	1 year.	Mustered out with company June 14, 1865.
Ruff, John	....do....	27	Sept. 3, 1864	1 year.	Mustered out June 7, 1865, at Nashville, Tenn., by order of War Department.
Scanland, John W	....do....	18	Sept. 23, 1864	1 year.	Promoted to Q. M. Sergeant Oct. 20, 1864.
Shay, Patrick	....do....	30	Feb. 23, 1865	1 year.	Mustered out June 14, 1865, at Nashville, Tenn., by order of War Department.
Shepard, Henry W	....do....	28	Sept. 1, 1864	1 year.	Died Jan. 13, 1865, in hospital at Nashville, Tennessee.
Shepard, James	....do....	29	Aug. 10, 1864	1 year.	
Sinclair, Francis M	....do....	26	Aug. 6, 1864	1 year.	Also borne on rolls as Francis M. St. Clair
Smith, Andrew	....do....	43	Aug. 29, 1864	1 year.	
Smith, Howard	....do....	25	Sept. 6, 1864	1 year.	Mustered out with company June 14, 1865.
Smith, John C	....do....	39	Sept. 3, 1864	1 year.	Reduced from Corporal Nov. 22, 1864; mustered out with company June 14, 1865.
Smith, John W	....do....	39	Aug. 20, 1864	1 year.	
Smith, Thomas	....do....	28	Sept. 7, 1864	1 year.	Mustered out with company June 14, 1865.
Stiles, Robert	....do....	20	Sept. 2, 1864	1 year.	Mustered out with company June 14, 1865.
Swinehart, Adam	....do....	43	Aug. 29, 1864	1 year.	Mustered out with company June 14, 1865.
Sullivan, Daniel	....do....	33	Feb. 23, 1865	1 year.	Mustered out June 12, 1865, at Nashville, Tenn., by order of War Department.
Taylor, Thomas	....do....	26	Aug. 6, 1864	1 year.	Mustered out with company June 14, 1865.
Thomas, Cyrus	....do....	42	Sept. 14, 1864	1 year.	Mustered out May 27, 1865, at Nashville, Tenn., by order of War Department.
Thompson, David S	....do....	18	Aug. 3, 1864	1 year.	Mustered out with company June 14, 1865.
Thrasher Fred	....do....	21	Sept. 1, 1864	1 year.	Mustered out with company June 14, 1865.
Tobin, John R	....do....	22	Sept. 3, 1864	1 year.	Mustered out with company June 14, 1865.
Vestal, George W	....do....	41	Sept. 1, 1864	1 year.	Mustered out with company June 14, 1865.
Wagner, Abraham	....do....	23	Aug. 20, 1864	1 year.	Died March —, 1865, at Columbus, O.
Wagner, George W	....do....	44	Aug. 25, 1864	1 year.	Mustered out May 23, 1865, at Nashville, Tenn., by order of War Department.
Walker, Anthony P	....do....	39	Sept. 7, 1864	1 year.	Mustered out May 30, 1865, at Nashville, Tenn., by order of War Department.
Ward, Robert G	....do....	32	Sept. 10, 1864	1 year.	
Watters, Samuel	....do....	42	Aug. 23, 1864	1 year.	Died May 5, 1865, at Nashville, Tenn.
Wood, Joseph D	....do....	44	Sept. 23, 1864	1 year.	Promoted to Com. Sergeant Oct. 20, 1864.
Worthington, James C	....do....	24	Aug. 2, 1864	1 year.	Mustered out June 2, 1865, at Nashville, Tenn., by order of War Department.

COMPANY F.

Mustered in Sept. 21, 1864, at Camp Chase, O., by W. P. Richardson, Colonel 25th O. V. I. Mustered out June 14, 1865, at Nashville, Tenn., by W. S. Wilson, Captain 71st O. V. I.

Names.	Rank.	Age.	Date of Entering the Service.	Period of Service.	Remarks.
George W. Streby	Captain.	38	Sept. 15, 1864	1 year.	Mustered out with company June 14, 1865.
Henry M. Goldsmith	1st Lieut	41	Sept. 14, 1864	1 year.	Appointed Sept. 15, 1864; Regt. Quartermaster Feb. 22, 1865; transferred from 1st Lieutenant and Regt. Quartermaster May [illegible] 1865; mustered out with company June 14, 1865.
William J. Drumheller	....do....	23	Sept. 15, 1864	1 year.	Promoted from 2d Lieutenant March 18, 1865; resigned April 24, 1865.
William M. Eberly	2d Lieut.	22	Aug. 18, 1864	1 year.	Appointed 1st Sergeant from private Aug. [illegible] 1864; promoted to 2d Lieutenant March [illegible] 1865; mustered out with company June 14, 1865.
Joseph Cameron	1st Sergt.	20	Sept. 2, 1864	1 year.	Appointed Sergeant from Corporal Jan. 5, 1865; 1st Sergeant April 8, 1865; mustered out with company June 14, 1865.
Reason Eberhardt	Sergeant.	19	Aug. 16, 1864	1 year.	Appointed Sept. 15, 1864; mustered out with company June 14, 1865.
Joseph Dennis	....do....	38	Sept. 5, 1864	1 year.	Appointed Sept. 15, 1864; mustered out with company June 14, 1865.
Zurah Colekglazer	....do....	36	Sept. 2, 1864	1 year.	Appointed Sept. 15, 1864; promoted to Q. M. Sergeant April 20, 1865.
John Watters	....do....	36	Sept. 2, 1864	1 year.	Appointed from Corporal March 23, 1865; mustered out with company June 14, 1865.
Jonathan Bevington	....do....	18	Aug. 16, 1864	1 year.	Appointed from Corporal April 2, 1865; mustered out with company June 14, 1865.
Peter H. Wilson	Corporal.	38	Sept. 2, 1864	1 year.	Appointed Sept. 15, 1864; mustered out with company June 14, 1865.
Calvin Hines	....do....	19	Aug. 27, 1864	1 year.	Appointed Sept. 15, 1864; mustered out with company June 14, 1865.

Names.	Rank.	Age.	Date of Entering the Service.	Period of Service.	Remarks.
B. Helman	Corporal.	25	Sept. 2, 1864	1 year.	Appointed Sept. 15, 1864; mustered out with company June 14, 1865.
rd Welker	...do...	30	Sept. 2, 1864	1 year.	Died Jan. 5, 1865, in hospital at Nashville, Tennessee.
Johnson	...do...	30	Sept. 2, 1864	1 year.	Appointed March 28, 1865; mustered out with company June 14, 1865.
Reed	...do...	20	Sept. 5, 1864	1 year.	Appointed March 28, 1865; mustered out with company June 14, 1865.
om Hines	...do...	31	Aug. 25, 1864	1 year.	Appointed March 28, 1865; mustered out with company June 14, 1865.
l Kush	...do...	25	Sept. 2, 1864	1 year.	Appointed March 23, 1865; mustered out with company June 14, 1865.
E. Miller	...do...	22	Sept. 5, 1864	1 year.	Appointed April 22, 1865; mustered out with company June 14, 1865.
ght, Daniel	Private.	19	Sept. 2, 1864	1 year.	Died Jan. 25, 1865, in hospital at Nashville, Tennessee.
nder, Joseph B.	...do...	38	Sept. 2, 1864	1 year.	Mustered out with company June 14, 1865.
bee, George O.	...do...	18	Sept. 1, 1864	1 year.	
, John	...do...	31	Sept. 7, 1864	1 year.	Mustered out with company June 14, 1865.
l, John	...do...	27	Aug. 30, 1864	1 year.	Mustered out with company June 14, 1865.
lt, Henry	...do...	32	Mch. 14, 1865	1 year.	Mustered out June 8, 1865, at Nashville, Tenn., by order of War Department.
l, Frederick	...do...	18	Sept. 5, 1864	1 year.	Mustered out with company June 14, 1865.
Solomon	...do...	29	Sept. 2, 1864	1 year.	Mustered out with company June 14, 1865.
, George	...do...	28	Mch. 14, 1865	1 year.	Transferred to Co. F, 18th O. V. I., June 28, 1865.
George	...do...	40	Mch. 14, 1865	1 year.	Mustered out June 12, 1865, at Nashville, Tenn., by order of War Department.
erd, William S	...do...	26	Sept. 2, 1864	1 year.	Mustered out with company June 14, 1865.
t, John	...do...	34	Sept. 1, 1864	1 year.	Mustered out May 16, 1865, at Nashville, Tenn., by order of War Department.
nbacher, Henry	...do...	31	Mch. 14, 1865	1 year.	Transferred to Co. D, 18th O. V. I., June 28, 1865.
, James	...do...	27	Sept. 7, 1864	1 year.	Mustered out with company June 14, 1865.
r, William H.	...do...	21	Aug. 30, 1864	1 year.	Promoted to Sergt. Major Oct. 1, 1864.
berlain, Thomas	...do...	18	Aug. 31, 1864	1 year.	Mustered out to date June 14, 1865, by order of War Department.
Samuel L.	...do...	18	Mch. 7, 1865	1 year.	Transferred to Co. B, 18th O. V. I. June 28, 1865.
lins, David	...do...	21	Aug. 25, 1864	1 year.	Mustered out with company June 14, 1865.
, Israel	...do...	31	Aug. 25, 1864	1 year.	Mustered out May 22, 1865, at Columbus, O., by order of War Department.
n, Matthew	...do...	28	Sept. 5, 1864	1 year.	Mustered out with company June 14, 1865.
Jacob	...do...	18	Sept. 5, 1864	1 year.	Mustered out with company June 14, 1865.
ns, Gibson	...do...	26	Sept. 5, 1864	1 year.	
ing, Hugh	...do...	20	Sept 2, 1864	1 year.	Mustered out with company June 14, 1865.
heller, David C	...do...	21	Mch. 6, 1865	1 year.	Mustered out May 12, 1865, at Nashville, Tenn., by order of War Department.
, Elijah G. W	...do...	18	Sept. 5, 1864	1 year.	Mustered out with company June 14, 1865.
, George	...do...	37	Sept. 8, 1864	1 year.	Mustered out with company June 14, 1865.
Samuel	...do...	18	Sept. 1, 1864	1 year.	Mustered out with company June 14, 1865.
er, Loammi	...do...	28	Sept. 3, 1864	1 year.	Mustered out with company June 14, 1865.
berger, Peter	...do...	43	Sept. 2, 1864	1 year.	Mustered out with company June 14, 1865.
r, Patrick	...do...	38	Sept. 15, 1864	1 year.	Mustered out with company June 14, 1865.
urn, Jacob	...do...	20	Aug. 25, 1864	1 year.	Accidentally shot Feb. 19, 1865, and died same day.
ng, William H.	...do...	22	Sept. 5, 1864	1 year.	Mustered out with company June 14, 1865.
ere, William H.	...do...	24	Sept. 1, 1864	1 year.	Died April 4, 1865, in hospital at Nashville, Tennessee.
ther, William	...do...	28	Aug. 25, 1864	1 year.	Mustered out with company June 14, 1865.
er, John H	...do...	24	Sept. 8, 1864	1 year.	Mustered out with company June 14, 1865.
er, Godfred	...do...	40	Sept. 3, 1864	1 year.	Died Sept. 25, 1864, at Cincinnati, O.; also borne on rolls as Godfred Grachen.
land, John H	...do...	18	Sept. 3, 1864	1 year.	Died Jan. 3, 1865, in hospital at Louisville, Kentucky.
enger, Charles	...do...	20	Mch. 6, 1865	1 year.	Mustered out May 16, 1865, at Nashville, Tenn., by order of War Department.
y, Elijah	...do...	22	Sept. 5, 1864	1 year.	Mustered out with company June 14, 1865.
n, Michael	...do...	27	Mch. 14, 1865	1 year.	Mustered out with company June 14, 1865.
nan, John	...do...	36	Sept. 1, 1864	1 year.	Mustered out with company June 14, 1865.
augh, Daniel R.	...do...	33	Sept. 2, 1864	1 year.	Mustered out June 8, 1865, at Nashville, Tenn., by order of War Department.
ey, William	...do...	28	Sept. 5, 1864	1 year.	Died April 18, 1865, in hospital at Nashville, Tennessee.
, William	...do...	22	Aug. 29, 1864	1 year.	Mustered out May 17, 1865, at Nashville, Tenn., by order of War Department.
, Charles P	...do...	26	Sept. 6, 1864	1 year.	Mustered out with company June 14, 1865.
, David Y.	...do...	35	Aug. 29, 1864	1 year.	Mustered out with company June 14, 1865.
Herman	...do...	33	Aug. 29, 1864	1 year.	Mustered out with company June 14, 1865.
r, Franklin	...do...	21	Aug. 25, 1864	1 year.	Mustered out with company June 14, 1865.
, William H.	...do...	30	Sept. 5, 1864	1 year.	Mustered out May 16, 1865, at Nashville, Tenn., by order of War Department.
gs, Alvah T	...do...	22	Jan. 27, 1865	1 year.	Mustered out June 8, 1865, at Nashville, Tenn., by order of War Department.
n, Sylvester	...do...	25	Sept. 2, 1864	1 year.	Mustered out with company June 14, 1865.

Names.	Rank.	Age.	Date of Entering the Service.	Period of Service.	
Nick, Christopher	Private	21	Sept. 7, 1864		Reduced from 1st Ser 1865, in hospital at
O'Riley, William	....do....	18	Sept. 9, 1864		Mustered out with co
Palen, James O	....do....	15	Aug. 15, 1864		Mustered out May 20, 1 by order of War Dep
Peeples, William	....do....	39	Aug. 25, 1864		Mustered out with co
Reed, Nathan W	....do....	28	Sept. 26, 1864		Mustered out with co
Ridenour, David A	....do....	40	Sept. 6, 1864		Mustered out May 27, 1 by order of War Dep
Ritter, George H	....do....	20	Sept. 2, 1864		Mustered out with co
Ruff, John	....do....	27	Sept. 3, 1864		Mustered out June 7, 1 by order of War De
Scanland, John W	....do....	18	Sept. 28, 1864		Promoted to Q. M. Ser
Shay, Patrick	....do....	30	Feb. 28, 1865		Mustered out June 14, 1 by order of War Dep
Shepard, Henry W	....do....	28	Sept. 1, 1864		Died Jan. 18, 1865, in Tennessee.
Shepard, James	....do....	29	Aug. 10, 1864	1	
Sinclair, Francis M	....do....	26	Aug. 6, 1864	1	Also borne on rolls as
Smith, Andrew	....do....	43	Aug. 29, 1864	1	
Smith, Howard	....do....	25	Sept. 6, 1864	1	Mustered out with com
Smith, John C	....do....	39	Sept. 3, 1864	1	Reduced from Corpor tered out with comp
Smith, John W	....do....	39	Aug. 20, 1864	1	
Smith, Thomas	....do....	28	Sept. 7, 1864	1	Mustered out with con
Stiles, Robert	....do....	20	Sept. 2, 1864	1	Mustered out with con
Swinehart, Adam	....do....	48	Aug. 29, 1864	1	Mustered out with con
Sullivan, Daniel	....do....	23	Feb. 28, 1865	1	Mustered out June 12, 1 by order of War Dep
Taylor, Thomas	....do....	26	Aug. 6, 1864	1 year.	Mustered out with con
Thomas, Cyrus	....do....	42	Sept. 14, 1864	1 year.	Mustered out May 27, 1 by order of War Dep
Thompson, David S	....do....	18	Aug. 3, 1864	1 year.	Mustered out with con
Thrasher Fred	....do....	21	Sept. 1, 1864	1 year.	Mustered out with con
Tobin, John R	....do....	23	Sept. 3, 1864	1 year.	Mustered out with con
Vestal, George W	....do....	44	Sept. 1, 1864	1 year.	Mustered out with con
Wagner, Abraham	....do....	23	Aug. 20, 1864	1 year.	Died March —, 1865, at
Wagner, George W	....do....	44	Aug. 25, 1864	1 year.	Mustered out May 23, 1 by order of War Dep
Walker, Anthony P	....do....	39	Sept. 7, 1864	1 year.	Mustered out May 30, 1 by order of War Dep
Ward, Robert G	....do....	32	Sept. 10, 1864	1 year.	
Watters, Samuel	....do....	42	Aug. 23, 1864	1 year.	Died May 5, 1865, at N
Wood, Joseph D	....do....	44	Sept. 23, 1864	1 year.	Promoted to Com. Ser
Worthington, James C	....do....	24	Aug. 2, 1864	1 year.	Mustered out June 2, 1 by order of War Dep

COMPANY F.

Mustered in Sept. 21, 1864, at Camp Chase, O., by W. P. Richardson, Colonel 25th O. V.
14, 1865, at Nashville, Tenn., by W. S. Wilson, Captain 71st O. V.

Names.	Rank.	Age.	Date of Entering the Service.	Period of Service.	
George W. Streby	Captain.	38	Sept. 15, 1864	1 year.	Mustered out with com
Henry M. Goldsmith	1st Lieut.	41	Sept. 14, 1864	1 year.	Appointed Sept. 15, 18 Feb. 22, 1865; transfe ant and Regt. Quar mustered out with co
William J. Drumheller	....do....	23	Sept. 15, 1864	1 year.	Promoted from 2d Lieu resigned April 21, 18
William M. Eberly	2d Lieut.	22	Aug. 18, 1864	1 year.	Appointed 1st Sergean 1864; promoted to 2 1865; mustered out v 1865.
Joseph Cameron	1st Sergt.	20	Sept. 2, 1864	1 year.	Appointed Sergeant f 1865; 1st Sergeant A out with company J
Reason Eberhardt	Sergeant.	19	Aug. 16, 1864	1 year.	Appointed Sept. 15, 18 company June 14, 18
Joseph Dennis	....do....	38	Sept. 5, 1864	1 year.	Appointed Sept. 15, 1 company June 14, 18
Zurah Colckglazer	....do....	36	Sept. 2, 1864	1 year.	Appointed Sept. 15, 1 Sergeant April 20, 18
John Watters	....do....	36	Sept. 2, 1864	1 year.	Appointed from Corp mustered out with co
Jonathan Bevington	....do....	18	Aug. 16, 1864	1 year.	Appointed from Cor mustered out with co
Peter H. Wilson	Corporal.	38	Sept. 2, 1864	1 year.	Appointed Sept. 15, 18 company June 14, 18
Calvin Hines	....do....	19	Aug. 27, 1864	1 year.	Appointed Sept. 15, 1 company June 14, 18

Date of Entering the Service.	Period of Service.	Remarks.
Sept. 2, 1864	1 year.	Appointed Sept. 15, 1864; mustered out with company June 14, 1865.
Sept. 2, 1864	1 year.	Died Jan. 5, 1865, in hospital at Nashville, Tennessee.
Sept. 2, 1864	1 year.	Appointed March 28, 1865; mustered out with company June 14, 1865.
Sept. 5, 1864	1 year.	Appointed March 23, 1865; mustered out with company June 14, 1865.
Aug. 25, 1864	1 year.	Appointed March 23, 1865; mustered out with company June 14, 1865.
Sept. 2, 1864	1 year.	Appointed March 23, 1865; mustered out with company June 14, 1865.
Sept. 8, 1864	1 year.	Appointed April 22, 1865; mustered out with company June 14, 1865.
Sept. 2, 1864	1 year.	Died Jan. 25, 1865, in hospital at Nashville, Tennessee.
Sept. 2, 1864	1 year.	Mustered out with company June 14, 1865.
Sept. 1, 1864	1 year.	
Sept. 7, 1864	1 year.	Mustered out with company June 14, 1865.
Aug. 30, 1864	1 year.	Mustered out with company June 14, 1865.
Mch. 14, 1865	1 year.	Mustered out June 8, 1865, at Nashville, Tenn., by order of War Department.
Sept. 5, 1864	1 year.	Mustered out with company June 14, 1865.
Sept. 2, 1864	1 year.	Mustered out with company June 14, 1865.
Mch. 14, 1865	1 year.	Transferred to Co. F, 18th O. V. I., June 28, 1865.
Mch. 14, 1865	1 year.	Mustered out June 12, 1865, at Nashville, Tenn., by order of War Department.
Sept. 2, 1864	1 year.	Mustered out with company June 14, 1865.
Sept. 1, 1864	1 year.	Mustered out May 16, 1865, at Nashville, Tenn., by order of War Department.
Mch. 14, 1865	1 year.	Transferred to Co. D, 18th O. V. I., June 28, 1865.
Sept. 7, 1864	1 year.	Mustered out with company June 14, 1865.
Aug. 30, 1864	1 year.	Promoted to Sergt. Major Oct. 1, 1864.
Aug. 31, 1864	1 year.	Mustered out to date June 14, 1865, by order of War Department.
Mch. 7, 1865	1 year.	Transferred to Co. B, 18th O. V. I, June 28, 1865.
Aug. 25, 1864	1 year.	Mustered out with company June 14, 1865.
Aug. 25, 1864	1 year.	Mustered out May 22, 1865, at Columbus, O., by order of War Department.
Sept. 5, 1864	1 year.	Mustered out with company June 14, 1865.
Sept. 5, 1864	1 year.	Mustered out with company June 14, 1865.
Sept. 5, 1864	1 year.	
Sept 2, 1864	1 year.	Mustered out with company June 14, 1865.
Mch. 6, 1865	1 year.	Mustered out May 12, 1865, at Nashville, Tenn., by order of War Department.
Sept. 5, 1864	1 year.	Mustered out with company June 14, 1865.
Sept. 8, 1864	1 year.	Mustered out with company June 14, 1865.
Sept. 1, 1864	1 year.	Mustered out with company June 14, 1865.
Sept. 3, 1864	1 year.	Mustered out with company June 14, 1865.
Sept. 2, 1864	1 year.	Mustered out with company June 14, 1865.
Sept. 15, 1864	1 year.	Mustered out with company June 14, 1865.
Aug. 25, 1864	1 year.	Accidentally shot Feb. 19, 1865, and died same day.
Sept. 5, 1864	1 year.	Mustered out with company June 14, 1865.
Sept. 1, 1864	1 year.	Died April 4, 1865, in hospital at Nashville, Tennessee.
Aug. 25, 1864	1 year.	Mustered out with company June 14, 1865.
Sept. 3, 1864	1 year.	Mustered out with company June 14, 1865.
Sept. 3, 1864	1 year.	Died Sept. 25, 1864, at Cincinnati, O.; also borne on rolls as Godfred Grachen.
Sept. 3, 1864	1 year.	Died Jan. 3, 1865, in hospital at Louisville, Kentucky.
Mch. 6, 1865	1 year.	Mustered out May 16, 1865, at Nashville, Tenn., by order of War Department.
Sept. 5, 1864	1 year.	Mustered out with company June 14, 1865.
Mch. 14, 1865	1 year.	Mustered out with company June 14, 1865.
Sept. 1, 1864	1 year.	Mustered out with company June 14, 1865.
Sept. 2, 1864	1 year.	Mustered out June 8, 1865, at Nashville, Tenn., by order of War Department.
Sept. 5, 1864	1 year.	Died April 18, 1865, in hospital at Nashville, Tennessee.
Aug. 29, 1864	1 year.	Mustered out May 17, 1865, at Nashville, Tenn., by order of War Department.
Sept. 6, 1864	1 year.	Mustered out with company June 14, 1865.
Aug. 29, 1864	1 year.	Mustered out with company June 14, 1865.
Aug. 29, 1864	1 year.	Mustered out with company June 14, 1865.
Aug. 25, 1864	1 year.	Mustered out with company June 14, 1865.
Sept. 5, 1864	1 year.	Mustered out May 16, 1865, at Nashville, Tenn., by order of War Department.
Jan. 27, 1865	1 year.	Mustered out June 8, 1865, at Nashville, Tenn., by order of War Department.
Sept. 2, 1864	1 year.	Mustered out with company June 14, 1865.

Names.	Rank.	Age.	Date of Entering the Service.	Period of Service.	Remarks.
Luke, Thomas	Private	20	Aug. 30, 1864	1 year.	Mustered out with company June 14, 1865.
McConnell, Thomas	...do...	18	Sept. 3, 1864	1 year.	Mustered out with company June 14, 1865.
Merry, Andrew J	...do...	18	Sept. 16, 1864	1 year.	Mustered out with company June 14, 1865.
Mitchell, David	...do...	19	Aug. 30, 1864	1 year.	Mustered out with company June 14, 1865.
Moore, Nathan	...do...	17	Aug. 21, 1864	1 year.	Mustered out with company June 14, 1865.
Moran, Robert	...do...	24	Aug. 10, 1864	1 year.	Mustered out May 23, 1865, at Nashville, Tenn., by order of War Department.
Mossburg, Christian A	...do...	19	Sept. 9, 1864	1 year.	Mustered out with company June 14, 1865.
Odell, Joseph H	...do...	18	Aug. 29, 1864	1 year.	Mustered out with company June 14, 1865.
Osborn, Theodore	...do...	18	Sept. 14, 1864	1 year.	Mustered out with company June 14, 1865.
Palmer, Harrison	...do...	23	Aug. 17, 1864	1 year.	Mustered out with company June 14, 1865.
Palmer, Jacob	...do...	18	Sept. 1, 1864	1 year.	Died Feb. 22, 1865, in hospital at Nashville
Peters, Henley E	...do...	18	Aug. 17, 1864	1 year.	Mustered out May 31, 1865, at Cleveland, O., by order of War Department.
Poulton, John Washington	...do...	18	Sept. 9, 1864	1 year.	Mustered out with company June 14, 1865.
Poulton, John William	...do...	18	Aug. 20, 1864	1 year.	Mustered out with company June 14, 1865.
Powell, John	...do...	18	Aug. 29, 1864	1 year.	Mustered out with company June 14, 1865.
Right, Joseph	...do...	22	Aug. 22, 1864	1 year.	Mustered out with company June 14, 1865.
Rinehart, William	...do...	18	Sept. 8, 1864	1 year.	Mustered out with company June 14, 1865.
Robinson, John A	...do...	22	Aug. 22, 1864	1 year.	Mustered out with company June 14, 1865.
Robinson, Sylvanus L	...do...	18	Aug. 31, 1864	1 year.	Died Feb. 6, 1865, in hospital at Nashville, Tennessee.
Rock, Samuel F	...do...	39	Aug. 27, 1864	1 year.	Reduced from 1st Sergeant Oct. 1, 1864; mustered out with company June 14, 1865.
Ross, Henry	...do...	44	Aug. 30, 1864	1 year.	Discharged April 11, 1865, at general hospital, Columbus, O., by order of War Department.
Rucker, George	...do...	18	Feb. 15, 1865	1 year.	Transferred to Co. E, 18th O. V. I., June 3, 1865, and there mustered out with company Oct. 9, 1865.
Rucker, Peter	...do...	18	Sept. 1, 1864	1 year.	Mustered out with company June 14, 1865.
Shanks, Philip	...do...	22	Aug. 31, 1864	1 year	Mustered out with company June 14, 1865.
Shilling, Thomas	...do...	21	Sept. 2, 1864	1 year.	Mustered out with company June 14, 1865.
Shipley, William	...do...	35	Sept. 4, 1864	1 year.	Mustered out with company June 14, 1865.
Shirk, John W	...do...	18	Sept. 3, 1864	1 year.	Mustered out with company June 14, 1865.
Smith, John	...do...	19	Aug. 27, 1864	1 year.	Mustered out with company June 14, 1865.
Spicer, Charles A	...do...	41	Feb. 1, 1865	1 year.	Mustered out June 8, 1865, at Nashville, Tenn., by order of War Department.
Stephens, Benjamin	...do...	34	Sept. 1, 1864	1 year.	Mustered out with company June 14, 1865.
Stoddard, Henry E	...do...	18	Feb. 1, 1865	1 year.	Mustered out June 12, 1865, at Nashville, Tenn., by order of War Department.
Thomas, John	...do...	19	Aug. 27, 1864	1 year.	Mustered out with company June 14, 1865.
Tuttle, Uriah	...do...	21	Sept. 2, 1864	1 year.	Mustered out May 27, 1865, at Nashville, Tenn., by order of War Department.
Voore, Ellis	...do...	25	Aug. 24, 1864	1 year.	Mustered out with company June 14, 1865.
Waller, Thomas J	...do...	21	Aug. 28, 1864	1 year.	Reduced from Corporal March 12, 1865; mustered out with company June 14, 1865.
West, Joshua W	...do...	19	Sept. 19, 1864	1 year.	Mustered out with company June 14, 1865.
West, William M	...do...	18	Sept. 19, 1864	1 year.	Mustered out with company June 14, 1865.
White, John	...do...	18	Aug. 31, 1864	1 year.	Mustered out with company June 14, 1865.
Wickham, Alexander	...do...	21	Aug. 12, 1864	1 year.	Mustered out with company June 14, 1865.
Wickham, Jacob	...do...	18	Sept. 13, 1864	1 year	Mustered out with company June 14, 1865.
Wickham, Nathan	...do...	24	Aug. 22, 1864	1 year.	Died Jan. 7, 1865, in hospital at Nashville, Tennessee.
Wickham, Rouse	...do...	31	Aug. 22, 1864	1 year.	Mustered out with company June 14, 1865.
Wilson, David	...do...	19	Aug. 29, 1864	1 year.	Mustered out with company June 14, 1865.
Woolford, Alfred	...do...	19	Sept. 19, 1864	1 year.	Mustered out with company June 14, 1865.

COMPANY H.

Mustered in Sept. 21, 1864, at Camp Chase, O., by W. P. Richardson, Colonel 25th O. V. I. Mustered out June 14, 1865, at Nashville, Tenn., by W. S. Wilson, Captain 71st O. V. I.

Names.	Rank.	Age.	Date of Entering the Service.	Period of Service.	Remarks.
Robert A. Scott	Captain.	38	Sept. 21, 1864	1 year.	Resigned March 15, 1865.
Joseph A. Lovejoy	...do...	45	Sept. 8, 1864	1 year.	Promoted from 1st Lieutenant Co. C March 3, 1865; mustered out with company June 14, 1865.
James Houstin	1st Lieut.	20	Sept. 21, 1864	1 year.	Mustered out with company June 14, 1865.
Franklin Barger	2d Lieut.	35	Sept. 21, 1864	1 year.	Resigned Jan. 16, 1865.
William H. Bucher	...do...	21	Aug. 30, 1864	1 year.	Promoted from Sergt. Major Jan. 16, 1865; to 1st Lieutenant Co. I May 2, 1865.
Thomas M. Stevens	...do...	28	Aug. 29, 1864	1 year.	Promoted from 1st Sergeant Co. K May 2, 1865; mustered out with company June 14, 1865.
Alexander Pricer	1st Sergt.	33	Aug. 8, 1864	1 year.	Promoted to 2d Lieutenant Co. I March 3, 1865.
William D. James	...do...	33	Aug. 22, 1864	1 year.	Appointed from Sergeant April 3, 1865; mustered out with company June 14, 1865.
William W. Mowbray	Sergeant.	28	Aug. 10, 1864	1 year.	Appointed Sept. 23, 1864; mustered out with company June 14, 1865.
James McScurlock	...do...	21	Aug. 11, 1864	1 year.	Appointed Sept. 23, 1864; mustered out [illegible] June 14, 1865, by order of War Department.

Age.	Date of Entering the Service.	Period of Service.	Remarks.
45	Aug. 4, 1864		Appointed Sept. 21, 1864; mustered out with company June 14, 1865.
10	Aug. 30, 1864		Appointed Sept. 21, 1864; mustered out with company June 14, 1865.
22	Sept. 15, 1864		Appointed from Corporal March 12, 1865; mustered out with company June 14, 1865.
30	Oct. 6, 1864		Mustered as private; appointed Sergeant April 2, 1865; mustered out June 12, 1865, at Nashville, Tenn., by order of the War Department.
27	Sept. 2, 1864		Appointed Sept. 21, 1864; mustered out with company June 14, 1865.
26	Aug. 23, 1864		Appointed Sept. 21, 1864; mustered out with company June 14, 1865.
20	Aug. 29, 1864		Appointed Sept. 21, 1864; mustered out with company June 14, 1865.
26	Aug. 27, 1864		Appointed Sept. 21, 1864; mustered out with company June 14, 1865.
20	Sept. 12, 1864		Appointed Sept. 21, 1864; mustered out with company June 14, 1865.
20	Aug. 4, 1864		Appointed Jan. 25, 1865; mustered out with company June 14, 1865.
18	Aug. 22, 1864	1 year.	Appointed Jan. 25, 1865; mustered out with company June 14, 1865.
19	Sept. 4, 1864		Appointed April 3, 1865; mustered out with company June 14, 1865.
18	Sept. 4, 1864		Mustered out with company June 14, 1865.
17	Sept. 13, 1864		Mustered out with company June 14, 1865.
18	Aug. 30, 1864		Mustered out to date June 14, 1865, by order of War Department.
22	Sept. 16, 1864		Mustered out May 31, 1865, at Camp Dennison, O., by order of War Department.
21	Aug. 23, 1864		Mustered out to date June 14, 1865, by order of War Department.
24	Aug. 27, 1864		Mustered out with company June 14, 1865.
35	Aug. 23, 1864		Mustered out with company June 14, 1865.
26	Aug. 23, 1864		Mustered out May 20, 1865, at Nashville, Tenn., by order of War Department.
25	Feb. 1, 1865		Mustered out June 8, 1865, at Nashville, Tenn., by order of War Department.
23	Jan. 24, 1865		Mustered out June 8, 1865, at Nashville, Tenn., by order of War Department.
18	Aug. 27, 1864		Mustered out with company June 14, 1865.
18	Aug. 29, 1864	1	Mustered out with company June 14, 1865.
24	Aug. 10, 1864	1	Mustered out with company June 14, 1865.
23	Aug. 30, 1864	1	Mustered out with company June 14, 1865.
17	Sept. 1, 1864	1	Mustered out with company June 14, 1865.
31	Aug. 23, 1864		Mustered out May 20, 1865, at Nashville, Tenn., by order of War Department.
22	Aug. 25, 1864		Mustered out June 6, 1865, at Madison, Ind., by order of War Department.
18	Aug. 27, 1864	1 year.	Mustered out with company June 14, 1865.
23	Aug. 27, 1864	1 year.	Mustered out with company June 14, 1865.
41	Aug. 27, 1864	1 year.	Mustered out with company June 14, 1865.
19	Aug. 27, 1864	1 year.	Mustered out with company June 14, 1865.
23	Aug. 24, 1864	1 year	Mustered out with company June 14, 1865.
18	Sept. 12, 1864	1 year.	Mustered out with company June 14, 1865.
19	Aug. 27, 1864	1 year.	Mustered out with company June 14, 1865.
18	Sept. 4, 1864	1 year.	Mustered out with company June 14, 1865.
18	Sept. 16, 1864	1 year.	Mustered out with company June 14, 1865.
20	Aug. 27, 1864	1 year	Mustered out with company June 14, 1865.
18	Aug. 27, 1864	1 year.	Mustered out with company June 14, 1865.
28	Aug. 27, 1864	1 year.	Died Jan. 22, 1865, in hospital at Nashville, Tennessee
20	Aug. 23, 1864	1 year.	Mustered out with company June 14, 1865.
18	Sept. 9, 1864	1 year.	Mustered out with company June 14, 1865.
25	Aug. 27, 1864	1 year.	Mustered out with company June 14, 1865.
18	Sept. 14, 1864	1 year.	Mustered out with company June 14, 1865.
25	Sept. 11, 1864	1 year.	Mustered out with company June 14, 1865.
23	Aug. 27, 1864	1 year.	Discharged Feb. 11, 1865, at hospital in St. Louis, Mo., on Surgeon's certificate of disability.
21	Aug. 27, 1864	1 year.	Mustered out with company June 14, 1865.
18	Sept. 16, 1864	1 year.	Mustered out with company June 14, 1865.
20	Aug. 27, 1864	1 year.	Died Jan. 30, 1865, in hospital at Nashville, Tennessee.
18	Sept. 15, 1864	1 year.	Died Dec. 17, 1864, in hospital at Jeffersonville, Ind.
21	Aug. 29, 1864	1 year.	Mustered out with company June 14, 1865.
17	Sept. 1, 1864	1 year.	Mustered out with company June 14, 1865.
22	Sept. 4, 1864	1 year.	Mustered out with company June 14, 1865.
[illegible]	Aug. 27, 1864	1 year.	Mustered out with company June 14, 1865.
[illegible]	Sept. 12, 1864	1 year.	Mustered out with company June 14, 1865.
24	Aug. 23, 1864	1 year.	Reduced from Corporal Feb. 12, 1865; mustered out with company June 14, 1865.
[illegible]	Aug. 27, 1864	1 year.	Mustered out with company June 14, 1865.

Names.	Rank.	Age.	Date of Entering the Service.	Period of Service.	Remarks.
Kerr, John H	Private	42	Aug. 9, 1864	1 year.	Reduced from Corporal Nov. 10, 1864; mustered out with company June 14, 1865.
Kibby, John R. W	...do...	18	Aug. 4, 1864	1 year.	Mustered out with company June 14, 1865.
Kime, John	...do...	30	Aug. 27, 1864	1 year.	Mustered out with company June 14, 1865.
Kirk, George	...do...	43	Sept. 12, 1864	1 year.	See Co. C, 178th O. V. I.
Kormlun, Charles	...do...	28	Sept. 15, 1864	1 year.	See Co. C, 178th O. V. I.
Larkins, John	...do...	22	Aug. 13, 1864	1 year.	Mustered out with company June 14, 1865.
Lawson, James	...do...	18	Aug. 23, 1864	1 year.	Mustered out with company June 14, 1865.
Leffler, Samuel	...do...	44	Aug. 22, 1864	1 year.	Died March 10, 1865, in hospital at Nashville, Tennessee.
Leohner, William	...do...	25	Sept. 14, 1864	1 year.	See Co. C, 178th O. V. I.
Linn, Ervin D	...do...	36	Sept. 9, 1864	1 year.	See Co. C, 178th O. V. I.
Ludwick, John F	...do...	19	Aug. 30, 1864	1 year.	Mustered out with company June 14, 1865.
Luzader, Joseph	...do...	25	Sept. 10, 1864	1 year.	Mustered out with company June 14, 1865.
McCutcheon, Isaac T	...do...	19	Aug. 3, 1864	1 year.	Mustered out with com June 14, 1865.
McCutcheon, William	...do...	18	Dec. 20, 1864	1 year.	
McDole, John W	...do...	27	Aug. 6, 1864	1 year	Reduced from Corporal Jan. 25, 1865; mustered out with company June 14, 1865
Merritt, John T	...do...	23	Aug. 30, 1864	1 year.	Mustered out with company June 14, 1865.
Middleton, John F	...do...	19	Sept. 15, 1865	1 year.	Mustered out with company June 14, 1865.
Miles, James W	...do...	32	Aug. 12, 1864	1 year.	Died March 8, 1865, in hospital at Nashville, Tennessee.
Miller, Michael T	...do...	27	Aug. 31, 1864	1 year.	Died April 5, 1865, in hospital at Nashville, Tennessee.
Newland, Allen	...do...	25	Sept. 11, 1864	1 year.	Mustered out June 7, 1865, at Nashville, Tenn., by order of War Department.
Nickerson, Charles	...do...	23	Aug. 3, 1864	1 year.	Mustered out with company June 14, 1865.
Noel, James P	...do...	28	Aug. 30, 1864	1 year.	Mustered out with company June 14, 1865.
Osmun, Zibia	...do...	26	Sept. 6, 1864	1 year.	Mustered out with company June 14, 1865.
Parker, Thomas G	...do...	41	Aug. 29, 1864	1 year.	Mustered out with company June 14, 1865.
Pearce, William H	...do...	33	Aug. 5, 1864	1 year.	Appointed Corporal Nov. 14, 1864; reduced April 30, 1865; mustered out with company June 14, 1865.
Pepple, John M	...do...	23	Aug. 29, 1864	1 year.	Mustered out June 13, 1865, at St. Louis, Mo., by order of War Department.
Pummell, William	...do...	18	Aug. 20, 1864	1 year.	Mustered out with company June 14, 1865.
Russell, John S	...do...	19	Aug. 30, 1864	1 year.	Died Jan. 23, 1865, in hospital at Nashville, Tennessee.
Sailor, Jesse	...do...	24	Aug. 13, 1864	1 year.	Died Jan. 16, 1865, in hospital at Nashville, Tennessee.
Sheline, Amos W	...do...	25	Aug. 24, 1864	1 year.	Mustered out with company June 14, 1865.
Sherwood, Levi	...do...	19	Aug. 16, 1864	1 year.	Mustered out with company June 14, 1865.
Shingle, Madison	...do...	24	Aug. 29, 1864	1 year.	Transferred to Co. B, 18th O. V. I., June 2, 1865.
Smith, Daniel D	...do...	22	Aug. 6, 1864	1 year.	Mustered out with company June 14, 1865.
Stewart, John	...do...	39	Sept. 15, 1864	1 year.	See John Swartz, Co. C, 178th O. V. I.
Taylor, John	...do...	23	Aug. 30, 1864	1 year.	Mustered out with company June 14, 1865.
Taylor, Levi	...do...	21	Aug. 30, 1864	1 year.	Mustered out with company June 14, 1865.
Tipton, Charles	...do...	26	Sept. 5, 1864	1 year	Mustered out with company June 14, 1865.
Tweed, Harvey W	...do...	18	Aug. 13, 1864	1 year.	Mustered out with company June 14, 1865.
Vanmeter, James H	...do...	27	Sept. 13, 1864	1 year.	Mustered out with company June 14, 1865.
Watkins, David M	...do...	18	Aug. 19, 1864	1 year.	Discharged Feb. 14, 1865, at Tripler U. S. General Hospital, Columbus, O., on Surgeon's certificate of disability.
Ward, Nathan	...do...	19	Aug. 31, 1864	1 year.	Mustered out with company June 14, 1865.
Watson, Marion	...do...	19	Sept. 2, 1864	1 year.	Mustered out with company June 14, 1865.
Watson, Samuel	...do...	18	Sept. 2, 1864	1 year.	Died Jan 17, 1865, in hospital at Nashville, Tennessee.
Weaver, Henry	...do...	21	Aug. 23, 1864	1 year.	On muster-in roll. No further record found.
Wesson, Thomas	...do...	26	Aug. 23, 1864	1 year.	
Westfall, Joel	...do...	25	Sept. 4, 1864	1 year.	Died June 4, 1865, in hospital at Nashville, Tennessee.
White, John W	...do...	37	Sept. 13, 1864	1 year.	Transferred to Co. I, 18th O. V. I., June 2, 1865.
Wilson, George	...do...	18	Sept. 16, 1864	1 year.	See Co. C, 178th O. V. I.
Wilson, Jacob M	...do...	43	Aug. 16, 1864	1 year.	Mustered out May 19, 1865, at Nashville, Tenn., by order of War Department.
Wilson, John	...do...	34	Aug. 22, 1864	1 year.	Mustered out with company June 14, 1865.
Woodruff, Henry	...do...	24	Aug. 29, 1864	1 year.	Died Jan. 28, 1865, in hospital at Nashville, Tennessee.

COMPANY I.

tered in Sept. 21, 1864, at Camp Chase, O., by W. P. Richardson, Colonel 25th O. V. I. Mustered out June 14, 1865, at Nashville, Tenn., by W. S. Wilson, Captain 71st O. V. I.

	Rank.	Age.	Date of Entering the Service.	Period of Service.	Remarks.
iam McMackin	Captain.	27	Sept. 21, 1864	1 year.	Mustered out with company June 14, 1865.
Holland	1st Lieut.	42	Sept. 21, 1864	1 year.	Appointed Regt. Quartermaster May 3, 1865.
iam H. Bucher	....do....	21	Aug. 30, 1864	1 year.	Promoted from 2d Lieutenant Co. H May 2, 1865; appointed Acting Adjutant May 12, 1865; mustered out with company June 14, 1865.
y T. Nichols	2d Lieut.	23	Sept. 21, 1864	1 year.	Promoted to 1st Lieutenant Co. B March 29, 1865.
tander Pricer	....do....	33	Aug. 8, 1864	1 year.	Promoted from 1st Sergeant Co. H March 29, 1865; mustered out with company June 14, 1865.
ert W. Hamilton	1st Sergt.	19	Aug. 7, 1864	1 year.	Appointed from Sergeant ——; promoted to 2d Lieutenant Co. A March 18, 1865.
s A. Carson	....do....	20	Sept. 17, 1864	1 year.	Appointed from Sergeant April 3, 1865; promoted to 2d Lieutenant Co. D March 31, 1865.
mas W. Osbel	Sergeant.	23	Sept. 1, 1864	1 year.	Appointed Sept. 23, 1864; mustered out with company June 14, 1865.
ph P. Graham	....do....	18	Sept. 13, 1864	1 year.	Appointed ——; promoted to Sergt. Major April 3, 1865.
ry G. Parker	....do....	21	Sept. 13, 1864	1 year.	Appointed from Corporal Nov. 25, 1864; mustered out with company June 14, 1865.
iam Rhodes	....do....	31	Aug. 25, 1864	1 year.	Appointed from Corporal April 3, 1865; mustered out with company June 14, 1865.
es K. Gregory	....do....	18	Aug. 31, 1864	1 year.	Appointed from Corporal April 3, 1865; mustered out with company June 14, 1865.
iam H. Hanna	Corporal.	44	Sept. 16, 1864	1 year.	Appointed Sept. 23, 1864; mustered out with company June 14, 1865.
es Williams	....do....	30	Sept. 2, 1864	1 year.	Appointed Sept. 23, 1864; mustered out with company June 14, 1865.
net S. Bennett	....do....	37	Sept. 20, 1864	1 year.	Appointed Sept. 23, 1864; mustered out with company June 14, 1865.
ld Wilson	....do....	25	Sept. 12, 1864	1 year.	Appointed ——; died Dec. 29, 1864, in hospital at Cincinnati, O.
h Sayers	....do....	37	Sept. 17, 1864	1 year.	Appointed Nov. 14, 1864; mustered out with company June 14, 1865.
mas B. Tarleton	....do....	28	Aug. 25, 1864	1 year.	Appointed Dec. 1, 1864; mustered out with company June 14, 1865.
iam Tripp	....do....	20	Sept. 2, 1864	1 year.	Appointed April —, 1865; mustered out with company June 14, 1865.
uel Hesson	....do....	23	Sept. 19, 1864	1 year.	Appointed April —, 1865; mustered out with company June 14, 1865.
than Cash	....do....	16	Aug. 25, 1864	1 year.	Appointed May 30, 1865; mustered out with company June 14, 1865.
L. Weirick	....do....	24	Sept. 6, 1864	1 year.	Appointed ——; mustered out May 23, 1865, at Nashville, Tenn., by order of War Department.
mas E. Matthews	Musician	26	Aug. 27, 1864	1 year.	Appointed ——; mustered out with company June 14, 1865.
es A. Cook	....do....	21	Sept. 16, 1864	1 year.	Appointed ——; mustered out with company June 14, 1865.
ier, James	Private.	27	Aug. 25, 1864	1 year.	Mustered out with company June 14, 1865.
ier, William	....do....	23	Sept. 6, 1864	1 year.	Mustered out with company June 14, 1865.
s, Nathaniel	....do....	16	Aug. 23, 1864	1 year.	Mustered out with company June 14, 1865.
, James	....do....	25	Sept. 17, 1864	1 year.	Mustered out with company June 14, 1865.
nell, Thomas C	....do....	23	Sept. 4, 1864	1 year.	Mustered out with company June 14, 1865.
nell, William A	....do....	37	Sept. 16, 1864	1 year.	Mustered out May 16, 1865, at Nashville, Tenn., by order of War Department.
nell, William H. H.	....do....	27	Mch. 7, 1865	1 year.	Mustered out to date June 14, 1865, at Nashville, Tenn., by order of War Department.
h, Josephus B	....do....	41	Sept. 4, 1864	1 year.	Mustered out with company June 14, 1865.
ers, Alexander J	....do....	23	Sept. 15, 1864	1 year.	Mustered out with company June 14, 1865.
l, Thomas	....do....	22	Sept. 6, 1864	1 year.	Mustered out with company June 14, 1865.
ert, John D	....do....	26	Feb. 27, 1865	1 year.	Transferred to Co. A, 18th O. V. I., June 28, 1865.
ert, William T	....do....	37	Sept. 4, 1864	1 year.	Mustered out with company June 14, 1865.
, Orleno	....do....	29	Sept. 2, 1864	1 year.	Mustered out with company June 14, 1865.
, Simpson	....do....	31	Sept. 13, 1864	1 year.	Died May 9, 1865, in hospital at Nashville, Tennessee.
nling, Frank	....do....	21	Feb. 1, 1865	1 year.	Mustered out June 8, 1865, at Nashville, Tenn., by order of War Department.
mings, William	....do....	17	Sept. 2, 1864	1 year.	Mustered out with company June 14, 1865.
dson, Richardson J	....do....	27	Sept. 13, 1864	1 year.	
glas, Samuel	....do....	21	Sept. 17, 1864	1 year	Mustered out with company June 14, 1865.
John	....do....	17	Aug. 25, 1864	1 year.	Mustered out with company June 14, 1865.
ish, Hugh	....do....	42	Sept. 16, 1864	1 year.	Mustered out May 20, 1865, at Nashville, Tenn., by order of War Department.

Names.	Rank.	Age.	Date of Entering the Service.	Period of Service.	Remarks.
Farly, James S	Private	28	Aug. 27, 1864	1 year.	Reduced from Corporal Nov. 19, 1864; mustered out with company June 14, 1865.
Gallagher John	....do....	31	Sept. 13, 1864	1 year.	Mustered out with company June 14, 1865.
Gardner George	....do....	27	Mch. 8, 1865	1 year.	Transferred to Co. A, 18th O. V. I., June 3, 1865.
Gray, Jesse M	....do....	18	Sept. 10, 1864	1 year.	Mustered out with company June 14, 1865.
Hagerman, James	....do....	19	Mch. 2, 1865	1 year.	Transferred to Co. A, 18th O. V. I., June 3, 1865.
Hanna, Robert W	....do....	18	Sept. 7, 1864	1 year.	Mustered out with company June 14, 1865.
Harding, Hiram	....do....	43	Sept. 16, 1864	1 year.	Mustered out to date June 14, 1865, by order of War Department.
Hawkins, John	....do....	18	Mch. 2, 1865	1 year.	Transferred to Co. A, 18th O. V. I., June 3, 1865.
Henry, James	....do....	22	Sept. 4, 1864	1 year.	Mustered out with company June 14, 1865.
Henry, James G	....do....	37	Sept. 6, 1864	1 year.	Mustered out June 7, 1865, at Nashville, Tenn., by order of War Department.
Hessen, Aaron	....do....	38	Aug. 5, 1864	1 year	Reduced from 1st Sergeant Nov. 19, 1864; mustered out with company June 14, 1865.
Hill, James A	....do....	18	Sept. 14, 1864	1 year.	Died Jan. 14, 1865, in hospital at Nashville, Tennessee.
Hill, Edmund W	....do....	19	Sept. 19, 1864	1 year.	Mustered out May 28, 1865, at Nashville, Tenn., by order of War Department.
Hixon, John B	....do....	43	Sept. 16, 1864	1 year.	Mustered out May 3, 1865, at Camp Dennison, O., by order of War Department.
James, Demas	....do....	39	Sept. 16, 1864	1 year.	Mustered out with company June 14, 1865.
Johnston, William P	....do....	18	Sept. 15, 1864	1 year	Mustered out with company June 14, 1865.
Keepers, Israel J	....do....	35	Sept. 15, 1864	1 year.	Mustered out with company June 14, 1865.
Kirkman George W	....do....	20	Sept. 1, 1864	1 year.	Mustered out with company June 14, 1865.
Lawrence, Alexander J	....do....	31	Sept. 16, 1864	1 year.	Mustered out with company June 14, 1865.
Layman, William T	....do....	17	Sept. 17, 1864	1 year.	Mustered out with company June 14, 1865.
Lindsey, William	....do....	43	Sept. 12, 1864	1 year.	Mustered out with company June 14, 1865.
McBride, John	....do....	31	Sept. 12, 1864	1 year.	Mustered out with company June 14, 1865.
McDowell, Luke	....do....	35	Sept. 16, 1864	1 year.	Died Jan. 13, 1865, in hospital at Nashville, Tennessee.
McFarland, William	....do....	22	Sept. 12, 1864	1 year.	Transferred to Co. D, 6th Regiment, Veteran Reserve Corps, Dec. 22, 1864; discharged June 1, 1865, at Post Hospital, Johnson's Island, O.
McGlaughlin, James	....do....	20	Aug. 26, 1864	1 year.	Mustered as Musician; mustered out with company June 14, 1865.
McKitrick, John	....do....	22	Aug. 27, 1864	1 year.	Appointed Corporal Sept. 23, 1864; reduced Nov. 10, 1864; mustered out with company June 14, 1865.
McPeak, George	....do....	24	Sept. 4, 1864	1 year.	Died Feb. 15, 1865, in hospital at Nashville, Tennessee.
Mantle, Joseph	....do....	30	Sept. 2, 1864	1 year	Mustered out with company June 14, 1865.
Matthews, Levi	....do....	43	Sept. 16, 1864	1 year.	Mustered out May 15, 1865, at Nashville, Tenn., by order of War Department.
Melton, Marion	....do....	18	Aug. 19, 1864	1 year	Mustered out May 23, 1865, at Nashville, Tenn., by order of War Department.
Miles, William H	....do....	27	Aug. 29, 1864	1 year.	Mustered out with company June 14, 1865.
Miller, Robert B	....do....	39	Aug. 27, 1864	1 year.	Mustered out with company June 14, 1865.
Milliner, Absalom	....do....	19	Sept. 5, 1864	1 year.	Mustered out with company June 14, 1865.
Mimzoner Joseph	....do....	18	Sept. 5, 1864	1 year	Mustered out with company June 14, 1865.
Nichols, George S	....do....	27	Sept. 4, 1864	1 year	Mustered out June 2, 1865, at Nashville, Tenn., by order of War Department.
Nichols, Jerome T	....do....	22	Sept. 4, 1864	1 year.	Mustered out with company June 14, 1865.
Orr, William	....do....	26	Mch. 7, 1865	1 year.	Transferred to Co. I, 18th O. V. I., June 3, 1865, and there mustered out with company.
Parlet, John W	....do....	25	Sept. 16, 1864	1 year	Mustered out May 27, 1865, at Louisville, Ky., by order of War Department.
Patterson, Sylvester	....do....	25	Sept. 13, 1864	1 year.	Mustered out June 19, 1865, at Camp Chase, O., by order of War Department.
Potter, Thaddeus S	....do....	26	Feb. 1, 1865	1 year.	Mustered out June 8, 1865, at Nashville, Tenn., by order of War Department.
Pritchard, Jacob	....do....	25	Aug. 26, 1864	1 year.	Mustered out with company June 14, 1865.
Saviers, John W	....do....	19	Sept. 17, 1864	1 year.	Mustered out with company June 14, 1865.
Stockdale, Sylvanus W	....do....	32	Sept. 16, 1864	1 year	Mustered out with company June 14, 1865.
Stone, James F	....do....	36	Sept. 19, 1864	1 year.	Mustered out with company June 14, 1865.
Stull, Noble	....do....	18	Aug. 19, 1864	1 year.	Mustered out with company June 14, 1865.
Taylor, Philander C	....do....	18	Sept. 20, 1864	1 year.	Died Jan. 5, 1865, at Clay U. S. General Hospital, Louisville, Ky.
Teterick, Charles	....do....	34	Sept. 18, 1864	1 year	Mustered out with company June 14, 1865.
Teterick, Eli	....do....	44	Sept. 18, 1864	1 year	Mustered out with company June 14, 1865.
Teterick, James	....do....	33	Sept. 6, 1864	1 year.	Mustered out May 30, 1865, at Nashville, Tenn., by order of War Department.
Tipton, Aquilla	....do....	23	Sept. 16, 1864	1 year.	Mustered out with company June 14, 1865.
Tople, Hoco H	....do....	18	Sept. 12, 1864	1 year.	Mustered out with company June 14, 1865.
Vance, Isaac A	....do....	18	Aug. 24, 1864	1 year.	Died Dec. 8, 1864, at Jefferson Barracks, Mo.
Watt, Joseph A	....do....	18	Sept. 5, 1864	1 year.	Mustered out with company June 14, 1865.
Wheeler, Jacob	....do....	18	Mch. 2, 1865	1 year.	Transferred to Co. B, 18th O. V. I., June 3, 1865.
Widdoes, David A	....do....	18	Sept. 14, 1864	1 year.	Mustered out with company June 14, 1865.
Wiley, Daniel	....do....	24	Sept. 12, 1864	1 year.	Mustered out with company June 14, 1865.
Williams, Anthony	....do....	18	Sept. 2, 1864	1 year	Mustered out with company June 14, 1865.

Names.	Rank.	Age.	Date of Entering the Service.	Period of Service.
Farly, James S	Private	23	Aug. 27, 1864	
Gallagher, John	...do...	31	Sept. 12, 1864	
Gardner, George	...do...	27	Mch. 8, 1865	
Gray, Jesse M	...do...	18	Sept. 10, 1864	
Hagerman, James	...do...	19	Mch. 2, 1865	
Hanna, Robert W	...do...	18	Sept. 7, 1864	1 year.
Harding, Hiram	...do...	43	Sept. 16, 1864	1 year.
Hawkins, John	...do...	18	Mch. 2, 1865	
Henry, James	...do...	22	Sept. 4, 1864	1 year.
Henry, James G	...do...	37	Sept. 6, 1864	1 year.
Hessen, Aaron	...do...	36	Aug. 5, 1864	
Hill, James A	...do...	18	Sept. 14, 1864	
Hill, Edmund W	...do...	19	Sept. 19, 1864	1 year.
Hixon, John B	...do...	43	Sept. 16, 1864	
James, Demas	...do...	39	Sept. 16, 1864	1
Johnston, William P	...do...	18	Sept. 15, 1864	1
Keepers, Israel J	...do...	33	Sept. 15, 1864	1
Kirkman, George W	...do...	30	Sept. 1, 1864	1 year.
Lawrence, Alexander J	...do...	31	Sept 16, 1864	1
Layman, William T	...do...	17	Sept. 17, 1864	1
Lindsey, William	...do...	43	Sept. 12, 1864	
McBride, John	...do...	31	Sept. 12, 1864	
McDowell, Luke	...do...	35	Sept. 16, 1864	
McFarland, William	...do...	22	Sept. 12, 1864	
McGlaughlin, James	...do...	20	Aug. 26, 1864	
McKitrick, John	...do...	22	Aug. 27, 1864	
McPeak, George	...do...	24	Sept. 4, 1864	
Mantle, Joseph	...do...	30	Sept. 2, 1864	
Matthews, Levi	...do...	43	Sept. 16, 1864	
Melton, Marion	...do...	18	Aug. 19, 1864	1 year.
Miles, William H	...do...	27	Aug 29, 1864	1 year.
Miller, Robert B	...do...	39	Aug. 27, 1864	1
Millner, Absalom	...do...	19	Sept. 5, 1864	1
Mimzoner, Joseph	...do...	18	Sept. 5, 1864	1
Nichols, George S	...do...	27	Sept. 4, 1864	1
Nichols, Jerome T	...do...	22	Sept. 4, 1861	
Orr, William	...do...	26	Mch. 7, 1865	
Pariet, John W	...do...	25	Sept. 16, 1864	
Patterson, Sylvester	...do...	25	Sept. 13, 1861	
Potter, Thaddeus S	...do...	26	Feb. 1, 1865	
Pritchard, Jacob	...do...	25	Aug. 26, 1864	
Saviers, John W	...do...	19	Sept. 17, 1864	
Stockdale, Sylvanus W	...do...	32	Sept. 16, 1864	
Stone, James F	...do...	36	Sept. 19, 1864	
Stull, Noble	...do...	18	Aug. 19, 1864	
Taylor, Philander C	...do...	18	Sept. 20, 1864	
Teterick, Charles	...do...	34	Sept. 18, 1864	
Teterick, Eli	...do...	44	Sept. 18, 1864	
Teterick, James	...do...	33	Sept. 6, 1864	
Tipton, Aquilla	...do...	23	Sept. 16, 1864	
Topie, Hoco H	...do...	18	Sept. 12, 1864	1
Vance, Isaac A	...do...	18	Aug. 24, 1864	1
Watt, Joseph A	...do...	18	Sept. 5, 1864	1
Wheeler, Jacob	...do...	18	Mch. 2, 1865	1
Widdoes, David A	...do...	18	Sept. 14, 1864	
Wiley, Daniel	...do...	24	Sept. 12, 1864	
Williams, Anthony	...do...	18	Sept. 2, 1864	

Names.	Rank.	Age.	Date of Entering the Service.	Period of Service.	Remarks.
Chester, John	Private.	23	Aug. 6, 1864	1 year.	Died Dec. 20, 1864, in hospital at Nashville, Tennessee.
Collins, John	...do...	18	Aug. 8, 1864	1 year.	Mustered out with company June 14, 1865.
Corder, James	...do...	18	Aug. 15, 1864	1 year.	Died Jan. 14, 1865, in hospital at Nashville, Tennessee.
Cottrill, Charles H	...do...	31	Aug. 31, 1864	1 year.	Mustered out with company June 14, 1865.
Cottrill, Samuel	...do...	27	Aug. 28, 1864	1 year.	Mustered out with company June 14, 1865.
Davis, Noah	...do...	18	Aug. 18, 1864	1 year	Mustered out with company June 14, 1865.
Davis, Thomas	...do...	18	Aug. 14, 1864	1 year.	Mustered out with company June 14, 1865
Dennis, Owen	...do...	18	Aug. 4, 1864	1 year.	Discharged Jan. 3, 1865, at Camp Chase, O., on Surgeon's certificate of disability.
Dollen, Frank	...do...	27	Mch. 1, 1865	1 year.	Transferred to Co. I, 18th O. V. I., June 24, 1865.
Dowdle, Charles	...do...	31	Aug. 31, 1864	1 year.	Mustered out with company June 14, 1865.
Downing, James	...do...	25	Aug. 29, 1864	1 year.	Mustered out with company June 14, 1865
Egleson, Francis M	...do...	19	Aug. 8, 1864	1 year.	Mustered out May 12, 1865, at Nashville, Tenn., by order of War Department
Ewing, Clark	...do...	30	Sept. 13, 1864	1 year.	Mustered out June 18, 1865, at Nashville, Tenn., by order of War Department.
Forest, Daniel	...do...	29	Aug. 1, 1864	1 year.	Mustered out with company June 14, 1865.
Gill, John	...do...	22	Aug. 20, 1864	1 year.	Mustered out with company June 14, 1865.
Graham, Thomas L	...do...	23	Aug. 3, 1864	1 year.	Mustered out with company June 14, 1865.
Graham, William M	...do...	19	Aug. 5, 1864	1 year	Mustered out May 12, 1865, at Nashville, Tenn., by order of War Department.
Hatfield, Henry	...do...	37	Sept. 3, 1864	1 year	Died March 11, 1865, in hospital at Nashville, Tennessee
Hatfield, Joseph C	...do...	21	Sept 3, 1864	1 year.	Mustered out with company June 14, 1865.
Hill, Francis	...do...	32	Aug. 20, 1864	1 year.	Mustered out with company June 14, 1865.
Huddleson, Abel	...do...	44	Sept. 13, 1864	1 year.	Mustered out with company June 14, 1865.
Jones, John	...do...	19	Aug. 13, 1864	1 year.	Died Jan. 4, 1865, in hospital at Nashville, Tennessee.
Jones, Joseph	...do...	18	Sept. 9, 1864	1 year.	Mustered out with company June 14, 1865
Jones, William	...do...	44	Aug. 8, 1864	1 year.	Died May 18, 1865, in hospital at Nashville, Tennessee.
Longberry, Harrison	...do...	18	Aug. 23, 1864	1 year.	Mustered out with company June 14, 1865.
Lucas, David H	...do...	34	Sept. 7, 1864	1 year.	Mustered out with company June 14, 1865.
Martin Riley	...do...	37	Aug. 22, 1864	1 year.	Mustered out with company June 14, 1865
Miller, Samuel	...do...	22	Aug. 1, 1864	1 year.	Mustered out May 20, 1865, at Nashville, Tenn., by order of War Department.
Moats, Alfred	...do...	36	Aug. 29, 1864	1 year.	Mustered out June 21, 1865, at Nashville, Tenn., by order of War Department
Moats, Allen	...do...	41	Aug. 31, 1864	1 year.	Died April 29, 1865, in hospital at Nashville, Tennessee.
Mowser, Joseph	...do...	21	Aug. 20, 1864	1 year	Mustered out May 30, 1865, at Nashville, Tenn., by order of War Department.
Norris, James H P	...do...	18	Aug. 4, 1864	1 year	Mustered out with company June 14, 1865.
O'Harra, M. M	...do...	22	Sept. 7, 1864	1 year	
Osenbaugh, Lafayette	...do...	22	Aug. 10, 1864	1 year.	Mustered out June 22, 1865, at Nashville, Tenn., by order of War Department.
Paully, Joseph	...do...	34	Aug. 31, 1864	1 year.	Mustered out with company June 14, 1865
Prescoat, John H	...do...	18	Sept. 6, 1864	1 year.	Mustered out with company June 14, 1865; also borne on rolls as John H Prescott
Packet, John W	...do...	18	Sept. 1, 1864	1 year.	Mustered out with company June 14, 1865
Redding Daniel N	...do...	20	July 30, 1864	1 year.	Mustered out June 22, 1865, at Nashville, Tenn., by order of War Department
Robinson, Henry B	...do...	37	Aug. 29, 1864	1 year.	Mustered out May 20, 1865, at Nashville, Tenn., by order of War Department.
Russel Henry R	...do...	18	Sept. 12, 1864	1 year.	Mustered out with company June 14, 1865
Sa[illegible]ty, Joseph	...do...	26	Aug. 14, 1864	1 year.	Mustered out with company June 14, 1865.
Shockley, Theodore	...do...	18	Aug. 1, 1864	1 year	Mustered out with company June 14, 1865
Smith, Elijah R	...do...	18	Aug. 4, 1864	1 year.	Mustered out with company June 14, 1865
Smith, James L	...do...	38	Sept. 15, 1864	1 year.	Reduced from Sergean[illegible]; mustered out with company June 14, 1865.
Stickel, John J	...do...	20	Sept. 14, 1864	1 year.	Mustered out with company June 14, 1865.
Tanner, William	...do...	23	Sept. 8, 1864	1 year.	Also borne on rolls as Wilson Tanner.
Taylor, Seymour	...do...	19	July 31, 1864	1 year.	Reduced from Sergeant [illegible] mustered out with company June 1[illegible], 1865.
Thomas, George	...do...	18	Sept. 10, 1864	1 year.	Died Jan. 21, 1865, at Jeffersonville Ind.
Ward, John	...do...	43	Aug. 26, 1864	1 year	Mustered out May 26, 1865, at Columbus O., by order of War Department.
Weaver, John T	...do...	18	Aug. 26, 1864	1 year.	Mustered out June 5, 1865, at Louisville Ky., by order of War Department
Wheeler, David B	...do...	18	Sept. 12, 1864	1 year.	Mustered out with company June 14, 1865.
Wilkins, Henry	...do...	26	Aug. 31, 1864	1 year.	Mustered out with company June 14, 1865
Willis, James	...do...	31	Aug. 31, 1864	1 year.	Mustered out May 16, 1865, at Nashville, Tenn., by order of War Department.
Wilson, Robert	...do...	27	Aug. 23, 1864	1 year.	
Wimer, Enos	...do...	35	Aug. 4, 1864	1 year.	Mustered out with company June 14 1865.
Wood, Genel M	...do...	18	Jan. 25, 1865	1 year.	Mustered out June 12, 1865, at Nashville, Tenn., by order of War Department
Worrick, Jacob	...do...	21	Aug. 8, 1864	1 year.	Reduced from Corporal March 16, 1865; mustered out with company June 14, 1865

UNASSIGNED RECRUITS.

NOTE.—The following list of recruits is found on muster and descriptive rolls for this organization, but ot borne on any of the company rolls of the Regiment:

Names.	Rank.	Age.	Date of Entering the Service.	Period of Service.	Remarks.
own, Thomas	Private..	21	Sept. 30, 1864	1 year.	
rey, Andrew J.......	...do. ..	18	Sept. 12, 1864	1 year.	
rk, Rufus H.	....do....	34	Oct. 10, 1864	1 year.	
eltzer, Michael R....	....do....	24	April 12, 1865	1 year.	Mustered out May 15, 1865, at Tod Barracks, O., by order of War Department,
ilson, Robert	....do....	29	Sept. 24, 1864	1 year.	
atts, Franklin A.......	....do...	25	Oct. 3, 1861	1 year.	

177th Regiment Ohio Volunteer Infantry.

ONE YEAR'S SERVICE.

THIS Regiment was organized at Camp Cleveland, O., from September 23 to October 4, 1864, to serve one year. Immediately after its organization the Regiment proceeded to Nashville, Tenn., via Indianapolis and Louisville. The day after its arrival it was ordered to Tullahoma, and constituted a part of the garrison at that place under General Milroy. The Regiment remained at Tullahoma until Hood's invasion, when it was ordered to Murfreesboro, where it arrived on the 2d day of December. On the 7th of December, Milroy's command, including the One Hundred and Seventy-seventh, charged the works, drove the Rebels back, and captured two pieces of artillery and over two hundred prisoners. A few days after this, while on a foraging expedition, the Regiment had an engagement with the enemy, in which it lost several wounded. After Hood had been driven from Tennessee the Regiment was ordered to Clifton. About the middle of January, 1865, the Regiment embarked at Clifton, proceeded down the Tennessee, and up the Ohio to Cincinnati, where it took the cars for Washington City. From there it moved to Annapolis, Md., and embarked on a vessel for North Carolina, arriving at Fort Fisher on the 7th of February.

The Regiment was engaged in two attacks on the enemy's works from the Cape Fear River to the coast, and crossed the river and participated in the flank movement which compelled the Rebels to evacuate Fort Anderson. It next engaged the enemy at Town Creek, charged them in the rear, and captured the entire command. The next morning the Regiment arrived opposite Wilmington, where it remained about a week, and then joined General Cox, at Kinston, and proceeded to Goldsboro, where it joined Sherman's army. After the surrender of Johnston's army the Regiment was sent to Greensboro, N. C., where it was mustered out June 24, 1865, in accordance with orders from the War Department.

177TH REGIMENT OHIO VOLUNTEER INFANTRY.

FIELD AND STAFF.

Mustered in from September 23, 1864, to October 4, 1864, at Camp Cleveland, O., by Thomas Drummond, Captain 5th Cavalry, U. S. A. Mustered out June 24, 1865, at Greensboro, N. C., by A. B. Smith, Captain 100th O. V. I., and C. M. 23d Army Corps.

Names.	Rank.	Age.	Date of Entering the Service.	Period of Service.	Remarks.
Arthur T. Wilcox	Colonel.	29	Sept. 23, 1864	1 year.	Mustered out with regiment June 24, 1865.
William H. Zimmerman.	Lt. Col.	28	Sept. 23, 1864	1 year.	Mustered out with regiment June 24, 1865.
Ernst J. Kreiger	Major.	31	Sept. 23, 1864	1 year.	Mustered out with regiment June 24, 1865.
Sylvester S. Burrows	Surgeon.	37	Sept. 20, 1864	1 year.	Mustered out with regiment June 24, 1865.
Richard Edwards	Ast. Surg	36	Sept. 20, 1864	1 year.	Mustered out with regiment June 24, 1865.
W. A. Sivans	....do....	34	Sept. 20, 1864	1 year.	Resigned Nov. 20, 1864.
Harvey N. Rogers	....do....	[illegible]	April 8, 1865	1 year.	Mustered out with regiment June 24, 1865.
George C. Ketchum	Adjutant	28	Sept. 27, 1864	1 year.	Resigned May 20, 1865.
George B. Huston	....do....	22	Sept. 7, 1864	1 year.	Appointed from 1st Lieutenant Co. C May 21, 1865; mustered out with regiment June 24, 1865.
James W. Raymond	R. Q. M.	24	Sept. 20, 1864	1 year.	Detached on General Milroy's staff as Act. Asst. Quartermaster since Dec. 19, 1864; mustered out with regiment June 24, 1865.
Henry V. Hitchcock	Chaplain	36	Oct. 6, 1864	1 year.	Promoted from private Co. G Oct. 6, 1864; mustered out with regiment June 24, 1865.
Jere G. Claflin	Ser. Maj.	33	Sept. 13, 1864	1 year.	Promoted from Sergeant Co. H ——; to 2d Lieutenant Co. B Jan. 24, 1865.
Herman G. Norton	....do....	23	Sept. 21, 1864	1 year.	Promoted from 1st Sergeant Co. F Feb. 1, 1865; mustered out with regiment June 24, 1865.
James W. Wheelock	Q. M. S.	21	Aug. 26, 1864	1 year.	Promoted from 1st Sergeant Co. H Oct. 1, 1864; mustered out with regiment June 24, 1865.
John T. Cramor	Com. Ser.	28	Sept. 17, 1864	1 year.	Promoted from private Co. G Oct. 5, 1864; to 2d Lieutenant Co. C Jan. 24, 1865.
William E. Edwards	....do....	25	Aug. 19, 1864	1 year.	Promoted from Sergeant Co. A March 1, 1865; mustered out with regiment June 24, 1865.
Alexander Leslie	Hos. St'd.	22	Aug. 6, 1864	1 year.	Promoted from Corporal Co. C ——; reduced to ranks and returned to Co. C March 31, 1865.
Erasmus Abt	....do....	18	Aug. 18, 1864	1 year.	Promoted from private Co. B April 1, 1865; mustered out with regiment June 24, 1865.
Jacob Markt	Prin. Mus	39	Sept. 2, 1864	1 year.	Promoted from Musician Co. B Oct. 27, 1864; mustered out with regiment June 24, 1865.
Joshua L. Woodard	....do....	22	Sept. 2, 1864	1 year.	Promoted from private Co. G Oct. 4, 1864; mustered out with regiment June 24, 1865.

COMPANY A.

Mustered in September 23, 1864, at Camp Cleveland, O., by Thomas Drummond, Captain 5th Cavalry, U. S. A. Mustered out June 24, 1865, at Greensboro, N. C., by A. B. Smith, Captain 100th O. V. I., and C. M. 23d Army Corps.

Names.	Rank.	Age.	Date of Entering the Service.	Period of Service.	Remarks.
William C. Turner	Captain.	33	Sept. 7, 1864	1 year.	On detached duty at Murfreesboro, Tenn., Nov. 9, 1864; mustered out with company June 24, 1865.
Henry J. Virgil	1st Lieut.	28	Aug. 19, 1864	1 year.	Appointed Sept. 7, 1864; mustered out with company June 24, 1865.
Albert J. [illegible]	2d Lieut.	31	Aug. 19, 1864	1 year.	Appointed Sept. 7, 1864; mustered out with company June 24, 1865.
George E. Needham	1st Sergt.	31	Aug. 19, 1864	1 year.	Appointed Sept. 8, 1864; mustered out with company June 24, 1865.
George E. Dunbar	Sergeant.	31	Aug. 19, 1864	1 year.	Appointed Sept. 8, 1864; mustered out with company June 24, 1865.
William E. Edwards	....do....	25	Aug. 19, 1864	1 year.	Promoted to Com. Sergeant March 1, 1865.
Arthur DeLair	....do....	20	Sept. 16, 1864	1 year.	Appointed Sept. 28, 1864; mustered out with company June 24, 1865.

Names.	Rank.	Age.	Date of Entering the Service.	Period of Service.	
George J. Duncan	Sergeant.	23	Aug. 19, 1864	1 year	Appointed Sept. 8, 1864; mustered out with company June 24, 1865.
Daniel Vose	....do....	23	Aug. 19, 1864	1 year.	Appointed from private March 1, 1865; mustered out with company June 24, 1865.
Newton N. Cooley	Corporal.	28	Aug. 31, 1864	1 year.	Appointed Sept. 8, 1864; mustered out with company June 24, 1865.
Charles S. Ruggles	....do....	32	Aug. 19, 1864	1 year.	Appointed Sept. 8, 1864; mustered out with company June 24, 1865.
Horace D. Austin	....do....	35	Aug. 19, 1864	1 year	Appointed Sept. 8, 1864; mustered out with company June 24, 1865.
Samuel E. Gordon	....do....	23	Aug. 19, 1864	1 year	Appointed Sept. 8, 1864; mustered out with company June 24, 1865
Leonard H. Cochran	....do....	27	Aug. 19, 1864	1 year.	Killed Jan. 23, 1865, by cars.
Josiah Browning	....do....	29	Sept. 2, 1864	1 year	Appointed Sept. 8, 1864; mustered out with company June 24, 1865.
Hugh A. Bowland	....do....	29	Aug. 31, 1864	1 year	Appointed Sept. 8, 1864; mustered out with company June 24, 1865.
Torbert P. Taylor	....do....	37	Aug. 31, 1864	1 year.	Appointed Oct. 9, 1864; mustered out with company June 24, 1865
Thomas G. Rowell	Musician	20	Aug. 19, 1864	1 year.	Mustered out with company June 24, 1865.
Frank M. Audrus	....do....	19	Aug. 19, 1864	1 year.	Mustered out with company June 24, 1865.
Adams, George	Private..	33	Sept. 15, 1864	1 year.	Mustered out with company June 24, 1865.
Ames, Freeland H	....do...	19	Aug. 19, 1864	1 year.	Mustered out June 6, 1865, at David's Island, New York Harbor, by order of War Department.
Baldwin, Thomas J	....do....	32	Aug. 31, 1864	1 year	Mustered out with company June 24, 1865.
Beakle, Philo S	....do....	21	Aug. 19, 1864	1 year.	Mustered out with company June 24, 1865.
Bingham, John	....do....	31	Oct. 4, 1864	1 year	Transferred to Co. A, 181st O. V. I., [illegible] 1865
Bisnett, James	....do....	24	Sept. 5, 1864	1 year.	Mustered out with company June 24, 1865.
Brainard, George	....do..	41	Aug. 19, 1864	1 year.	Died Jan. 19, 1865, on hospital boat, on the Ohio River.
Brainard, Joseph L	....do....	36	Aug. 19, 1864	1 year	Mustered out with company June 24, 1865.
Briggs, Oscar	....do....	28	Aug. 19, 1864	1 year	Mustered out with company June 24, 1865.
Brock, Edward F	....do....	18	Aug. 19, 1864	1 year.	Mustered out with company June 24, 1865.
Brooks, Freeman	....do..	44	Aug. 19, 1864	1 year.	Mustered out with company June 24, 1865.
Brooks, Samuel E	....do....	20	Aug. 19, 1864	1 year.	Wounded Dec. 7, 1864, in action near Murfreesboro, Tenn.; mustered out June [illegible], at Cleveland, O., by order of War Department.
Burroughs, Dorsey W	....do....	33	Aug. 19, 1864	1 year.	Mustered out with company June 24, 1865.
Butler, William D	....do....	18	Aug. 19, 1864	1 year.	Mustered out with company June 24, 1865.
Cannell, Emory G	....do..	19	Oct. 20, 1864	1 year.	Mustered out with company June 24, 1865.
Chandler, John	....do....	50	Aug. 30, 1864	1 year.	Mustered out with company June 24, 1865.
Chase, Theodore G	....do....	20	Sept. 5, 1864	1 year.	Mustered out with company June 24, 1865.
Chambers, Joseph	....do....	42	Aug. 31, 1864	1 year.	Discharged June 27, 1865, at Tripler Hospital, Columbus, O., on Surgeon's certificate of disability
Cheney, Edmund	....do..	26	Aug. 31, 1864	1 year.	Wounded Dec 14, 1864, in action near Murfreesboro, Tenn.; mustered out with company June 24, 1865.
Coe, Daniel L	....do....	39	Sept. 5, 1864	1 year.	Wounded Dec 14, 1864, in action near Murfreesboro, Tenn.; mustered out with company June 24, 1865
Cochran, Francis M	....do....	23	Aug. 19, 1864	1 year.	Mustered out with company June 24, 1865.
Cold, John F. G	....do....	23	Aug. 19, 1864	1 year.	Mustered out with company June 24, 1865.
Cooley, George W	....do..	22	Feb. 14, 1865	1 year	Transferred to Co. A, 181st O. V. I., June [illegible], 1865.
Cowin, Edward	....do....	18	Aug. 19, 1864	1 year	Mustered out with company June 24, 1865.
Croll, Nicholas	....do....	22	Sept. 5, 1864	1 year.	Mustered out with company June 24, 1865.
Deasy, Patrick	....do....	19	Aug. 19, 1864	1 year	Mustered out with company June 24, 1865.
Faier, Jonathan	....do....	43	Sept. 5, 1864	1 year	Mustered out with company June 24, 1865.
Fickes, Silas G	....do..	40	Sept. 2, 1864	1 year	Mustered out with company June 24, 1865.
Fletcher, James	....do....	31	Aug. 31, 1864	1 year.	Mustered out with company June 24, 1865.
Flick, Daniel	....do....	[illegible]	Aug. 19, 1864	1 year.	Died May 9, 1865, in hospital at Salisbury, North Carolina.
Flick, Warren	....do....	20	Aug. 19, 1864	1 year.	Mustered out with company June 24, 1865.
Gannon, William	....do....	30	Aug. 31, 1864	1 year.	Mustered out with company June 24, 1865.
Gasser, John	....do....	43	Sept. 15, 1864	1 year.	Died Feb. 16, 1865, in hospital near [illegible], North Carolina.
Geiger, Conrad	....do....	31	Aug. 31, 1864	1 year.	Mustered out with company June 24, 1865.
Geiger, John J	....do....	22	Sept. 1, 1864	1 year	Mustered out with company June 24, 1865.
Gould, Henry M	....do....	38	Aug. 19, 1864	1 year.	Mustered out with company June 24, 1865.
Graves, James	....do....	22	Sept. 13, 1864	1 year	
Harley, Russell B	....do....	21	Aug. 19, 1864	1 year.	Wounded Dec. 7, 1864, in action near Murfreesboro, Tenn.; mustered out with company June 24, 1865.
Hays, William	....do....	18	Aug. 19, 1864	1 year.	Mustered out with company June 24, 1865.
Helm, Henry	....do....	30	Sept. 1, 1864	1 year.	Mustered out with company June 24, 1865.
Hewitt, William	....do....	18	Aug. 19, 1864	1 year	Mustered out with company June 24, 1865.
[illegible]brook, Eugene	....do....	18	Aug. 19, 1864	1 year.	Mustered out with company June 24, 1865.
Hoyt, Daniel W	....do....	20	Sept. 2, 1864	1 year.	Mustered out with company June 24, 1865.
Irenhart, Isaac J	....do....	40	Aug. 31, 1864	1 year.	Mustered out June 28, 1865, at Columbus, O., by order of War Department.
Jackson, Philip C	....do....	27	Aug. 31, 1864	1 year.	Mustered out with company June 24, 1865.

Names.	Rank.	Age.	Date of Entering the Service.	Period of Service.	Remarks.
Jones, Samuel	Private..	44	Aug. 19, 1864	1 year.	Mustered out June 7, 1865, at David's Island, New York Harbor, by order of War Department.
Jones, William	...do...	21	Aug. 19, 1864	1 year.	Mustered out with company June 21, 1865.
Jones, William D	...do...	20	Aug. 19, 1864	1 year.	Mustered out with company June 24, 1865.
Karr, Elisb	...do..	43	Sept. 15, 1864	1 year.	Mustered out with company June 24, 1865.
Keegan, Richard	...do...	19	Aug. 19, 1864	1 year.	Mustered out May 29, 1865, at Camp Dennison, O., by order of War Department.
Kellogg, Leslie H	...do...	20	Sept. 5, 1864	1 year.	Mustered out June 2, 1865, at David's Island, New York Harbor, by order of War Department.
Kittridge, James R	...do...	22	Aug. 29, 1864	1 year.	Mustered out with company June 24, 1865.
Long, Samuel K	...do...	29	Sept. 13, 1864	1 year.	Mustered out with company June 24, 1865.
Long, Jacob L	...do...	21	Aug. 19, 1864	1 year.	Mustered out with company June 24, 1865.
McDowell, James	...do...	8	Aug. 19, 1864	1 year.	Mustered out May 31, 1865, at Camp Dennison, O., by order of War Department.
McLean, William	...do...	19	Sept. 2, 1864	1 year.	Mustered out with company June 24, 1865.
McMillen, Jefferson J	...do...	19	Aug. 19, 1864	1 year.	Mustered out with company June 24, 1865.
Mendell, George H	...do..	26	Aug. 31, 1864	1 year.	Mustered out May 31, 1865, at McDougall General Hospital, New York Harbor, by order of War Department.
Morse, James M	...do...	19	Aug. 19, 1864	1 year.	Mustered out with company June 24, 1865.
North, Charles	...do...	22	Aug. 19, 1864	1 year.	Mustered out June 15, 1865, at David's Island, New York Harbor, by order of War Department.
Palmiter, Allen	...do...	42	Sept. 5, 1864	1 year.	Died April 11, 1865, on board hospital transport J. K. Barnes.
Pease, Osceola R	...do...	21	Aug. 19, 1864	1 year.	Mustered out with company June 24, 1865.
Perkins, Lafayette	...do...	20	Aug. 19, 1864	1 year.	Discharged May 11, 1865, on Surgeon's certificate of disability.
Richards, Simeon	...do...	31	Oct. 3, 1864	1 year.	Transferred to Co. A, 181st O. V. I., June 15, 1865.
Rock, Henry A	...do...	22	Aug. 19, 1864	1 year.	Mustered out with company June 24, 1865.
Rose, Henry	...do...	2[illegible]	Aug. 19, 1864	1 year.	Mustered out with company June 24, 1865.
Roush, Thomas	...do...	43	Aug. 19, 1864	1 year.	Mustered out with company June 24, 1865.
Ruggles, Oscar B	...do...	25	Aug. 19, 1864	1 year.	Discharged June 12, 1865, at McDougall General Hospital, New York Harbor, on Surgeon's certificate of disability.
Selby, John	...do...	44	Aug. 19, 1864	1 year.	Mustered out with company June 24, 1865.
Seymour, William	...do...	19	Aug. 19, 1864	1 year.	Mustered out with company June 24, 1865.
Shauer, Russell M.	...do...	37	Sept. 5, 1864	1 year.	Mustered out May 29, 1865, at Trenton, N. J., by order of War Department.
Shattuck, Francis R	...do...	18	Aug. 19, 1864	1 year.	Mustered out with company June 24, 1865.
Shiffert, Amos	...do...	[illegible]5	Aug. 31, 1864	1 year.	Mustered out with company June 24, 1865.
Shiffert, Allen	...do..	40	Aug. 31, 1864	1 year.	Mustered out with company June 24, 1865.
Shoemaker, Jacob	...do..	41	Aug. 19, 1864	1 year.	Mustered out with company June 24, 1865.
Short, James	...do...	18	Sept. 5, 1864	1 year.	
Smith, Samuel S	...do...	26	Aug. 22, 1864	1 year.	Mustered out July 3, 1865, at Columbus, O., by order of War Department.
Thomas, Daniel W	...do...	41	Aug. 19, 1864	1 year.	Mustered out with company June 24, 1865.
Tullzein, Charles	...do...	19	Sept. 1, 1864	1 year.	Mustered out with company June 24, 1865.
Tyler, Lagrange	...do...	34	Aug. 19, 1864	1 year.	Mustered out with company June 24, 1865.
Waldick, John L	...do...	19	Aug. 19, 1864	1 year.	Discharged June 5, 1865, by order of War Department.
Wilcox, Eugene A	...do...	18	Aug. 27, 1864	1 year.	Mustered out with company June 24, 1865.
Wiggins, Charles B	...do...	19	Aug. 19, 1864	1 year.	Mustered out with company June 24, 1865.
Wilson, William	...do...	27	Sept. 15, 1864	1 year	
Wire, Theodore B	...do...	38	Sept. 30, 1864	1 year.	Promoted to 1st Lieutenant Co. I Sept. 30, 1864.
Witter, Henry C	...do..	26	Sept. 2, 1864	1 year.	Mustered out June 5, 1865, at David's Island, New York Harbor, by order of War Department.
Wright, William J	...do...	32	Aug. 19, 1864	1 year.	Mustered out June 2, 1865, at David's Island, New York Harbor, by order of War Department.

COMPANY B.

Mustered in September 23, 1864, at Camp Cleveland, O., by Thomas Drummond, Captain 5th Cavalry, U.S.A. Mustered out June 24, 1865, at Greensboro, N. C., by A. B. Smith, Captain 100th O. V. I., and C. M. 23d Army Corps.

Names.	Rank.	Age.	Date of Entering the Service.	Period of Service.	Remarks.
Isaac N. Rogers	Captain.	22	Sept. 7, 1864	1 year.	Mustered out with company June 24, 1865.
Julian H. Gates	1st Lieut.	28	Sept. 7, 1864	1 year.	Promoted from Sergeant Co. F, 10th O. V. C. Sept. 7, 1864; discharged May 12, 1865.
George B. Huston	2d Lieut.	21	Sept. 7, 1864	1 year.	Promoted to 1st Lieutenant Co. C. Jan. 2, 1865.
Jere G. Claflin	...do...	33	Sept. 13, 1864	1 year.	Promoted to Sergt. Major from Sergeant —; 2d Lieutenant Jan. 24, 1865; mustered out with company June 24, 1865.
James W. Wheelock	1st Sergt.	21	Aug. 26, 1864	1 year.	Promoted to Q. M. Sergeant Oct. 1, 1864.
Frederick W. Hoffman	...do...	27	Sept. 13, 1864	1 year.	Appointed from Sergeant Jan. 8, 1865; mustered out with company June 24, 1865.
Eben Mellen	Sergeant.	28	Aug. 26, 1864	1 year.	Mustered out July 7, 1865, at Portsmouth Grove, R. I., by order of War Department.
Thomas C. Bester	...do...	20	Aug. 17, 1864	1 year.	Appointed from private Oct. 31, 1864; mustered out with company June 24, 1865.
Parley Sheldon, Jr.	...do...	20	Aug. 27, 1864	1 year.	Appointed from Corporal —; mustered out with company June 24, 1865.
Charles H. Halsey	...do...	26	Sept. 5, 1864	1 year.	Appointed from Corporal Jan. 8, 1865; mustered out with company June 24, 1865.
John R. Sheets	Corporal.	29	Sept. 1, 1864	1 year.	Mustered out with company June 24, 1865.
George Lewis	...do...	22	Aug. 26, 1864	1 year.	Mustered out with company June 24, 1865.
Roswell Jackson	...do...	26	Sept. 1, 1864	1 year.	Mustered out with company June 24, 1865.
James W. Derthick	...do...	26	Aug. 29, 1864	1 year.	Mustered out with company June 24, 1865.
Clarence M. Peck	...do...	19	Sept. 20, 1864	1 year.	Mustered out with company June 24, 1865.
Ephraim Clemens	...do...	23	Sept. 13, 1864	1 year.	Appointed Jan. 8, 1865; mustered out with company June 24, 1865.
John W. Towl	...do...	23	Aug. 30, 1864	1 year.	Appointed Feb. 1, 1865; mustered out with company June 24, 1865.
Joseph G. Kestler	...do...	18	Sept. 6, 1864	1 year.	Appointed May 1, 1865; mustered out with company June 24, 1865.
Horace Upson	Musician	18	Aug. 12, 1864	1 year.	Transferred to Co. A, 181st O. V. I., June 8, 1865.
Jacob Markt	...do...	39	Sept. 2, 1864	1 year.	Promoted to Principal Musician Oct. 27, 1864.
Allen, Frank A.	Private.	22	Sept. 8, 1864	1 year.	Reduced from 1st Sergeant Jan. 8, 1865; mustered out with company June 24, 1865.
Abt, Erasmus	...do...	18	Aug. 18, 1864	1 year.	Promoted to Hospital Steward April 1, 1865.
Baker, Ira D.	...do...	27	Sept. 1, 1864	1 year.	Mustered out June 26, 1865, at Pittsburgh, Pa., by order of War Department.
Bartholomew, Harvey	...do...	23	Aug. 12, 1864	1 year.	Mustered out June 7, 1865, at David's Island, N. Y., by order of War Department.
Baughman, David	...do...	32	Sept. 15, 1864	1 year.	
Beebe, Hiram	...do...	23	Sept. 12, 1864	1 year.	Mustered out with company June 24, 1865.
Belcore, Andrew	...do...	38	Aug. 25, 1864	1 year.	Mustered out with company June 24, 1865.
Bryant, Lyman	...do...	19	Aug. 26, 1864	1 year.	Mustered out with company June 24, 1865.
Burt, Irving H.	...do...	18	Aug. 30, 1864	1 year.	Mustered out with company June 24, 1865.
Burtis, Charles	...do...	18	Aug. 27, 1864	1 year	Mustered out with company June 24, 1865.
Bushor, Henry	...do...	21	Sept. 17, 1864	1 year	
Chadwick, Benjamin B.	...do...	44	Sept. 2, 1864	1 year.	Mustered out with company June 24, 1865.
Clark, Rowley	...do...	38	Aug. 26, 1864	1 year.	Mustered out with company June 24, 1865.
Cogswell, Marion	...do...	18	Sept. 5, 1864	1 year.	Died Jan. 27, 1865, in hospital at Camp Dennison, O.
Cottrell, Deverly	...do...	31	Sept. 3, 1864	1 year.	Mustered out with company June 24, 1865.
Daily, Isaac D.	...do...	22	Aug. 30, 1864	1 year.	Mustered out with company June 24, 1865.
Decker, Clark	...do...	28	Aug. 26, 1864	1 year.	Mustered out Aug. 7, 1865, at Washington, D. C., by order of War Department.
Depuy, Harvey	...do...	38	Aug. 31, 1864	1 year	Mustered out June 26, 1865, at Camp Dennison, O., by order of War Department.
Dodge, Francis M.	...do...	21	Aug. 31, 1864	1 year.	Mustered out with company June 24, 1865.
Durian, James	...do...	28	Aug. 29, 1864	1 year	Mustered out with company June 24, 1865.
Durian, John C.	...do...	25	Aug. 24, 1864	1 year.	Mustered out with company June 24, 1865.
Elliott, Andrew	...do...	22	Sept. 12, 1864	1 year.	Mustered out May 31, 1865, at David's Island, New York Harbor, by order of War Department.
Ford, William E.	...do...	27	Aug. 29, 1864	1 year	Reduced from Corporal Feb. 1, 1865; mustered out with company June 24, 1865.
Foster, Joseph B.	...do...	35	Sept. 6, 1864	1 year	Mustered out with company June 24, 1865.
Francis, John C.	...do...	39	Aug. 21, 1864	1 year.	Mustered out with company June 24, 1865.
Fuller, Sylvanus H.	...do...	33	Aug. 31, 1864	1 year.	Mustered out June 5, 1865, at Davenport, Iowa, by order of War Department.
Gillett, Lewis W.	...do...	23	Sept. 14, 1864	1 year.	Mustered out with company June 24, 1865.
Hadlock, Aaron	...do...	29	Sept. 1, 1864	1 year.	Died Feb. 6, 1865, in Judiciary Square Hospital, Washington, D. C.
Hall, Henry	...do...	19	Aug. 30, 1864	1 year.	Mustered out with company June 24, 1865.
Hamlin, William B.	...do...	19	Aug. 29, 1864	1 year.	Mustered out with company June 24, 1865.
Hawkins, Albert	...do...	33	Aug. 23, 1864	1 year.	Discharged April 4, 1865, on Surgeon's certificate of disability.

Names.	Rank.	Age.	Date of Entering the Service.	Period of Service.	Remarks.
er, Charles F	Private..	44	Aug. 31, 1864	1 year.	Discharged June 2, 1865, at Camp Dennison, O., on Surgeon's certificate of disability.
ar, George		18	Sept. 6, 1864	1 year.	Mustered out with company June 24, 1865.
fins, Elisha		20	Feb. 15, 1865	1 year.	Transferred to Co. A, 181st O. V. I., June 15, 1865.
r, Wilbur S		19	Aug. 19, 1864	1 year.	Mustered out June 7, 1865, at Columbus, O., by order of War Department.
day, John		22	Sept. 2, 1864	1 year.	Mustered out with company June 24, 1865.
ker, James W		36	Aug. 15, 1864	1 year.	Reduced from Corporal Feb. 1, 1865; mustered out with company June 24, 1865.
, David D	.. ..	20	Aug. 29, 1864	1 year.	Mustered out with company June 24, 1865.
, Isaac	.. ..	19	Aug. 30, 1864	1 year.	Mustered out with company June 24, 1865.
bell, Robert S	.. ..	34	Aug. 27, 1864	1 year.	Mustered out with company June 24, 1865.
er, Joseph	.. ..	28	Sept. 16, 1864	1 year.	Mustered out with company June 24, 1865.
chings, Newton	.. ..	27	Sept. 2, 1864	1 year.	Mustered out June 10, 1865, at Louisville, Ky., by order of War Department.
ins, William	..	43	Oct. 4, 1864	1 year.	Transferred to Co. A, 181st O.V.I., June 15, 1865.
, Hiram	..	23	Sept. 6, 1864	1 year.	Mustered out with company June 24, 1865.
, Joseph	..	18	Oct. 1, 1864	1 year.	Mustered out with company June 24, 1865.
m, Myron L	..	18	Sept. 3, 1864	1 year.	Mustered out with company June 24, 1865.
, William C	..	27	Sept. 12, 1864	1 year.	Mustered out with company June 24, 1865.
pan, Parmer J	..	18	Sept. 5, 1864	1 year.	
e, Alden	..	22	Sept. 2, 1864	1 year.	Mustered out with company June 24, 1865.
ls, Mark		31	Sept. 1, 1864	1 year.	Mustered out with company June 24, 1865.
n, Horace H		34	Sept. 1, 1864	1 year.	Mustered out with company June 24, 1865.
y, Charles P	....do....	28	Sept. 3, 1864	1 year.	Mustered out with company June 24, 1865.
sey, John W	....do....	20	Sept. 5, 1864	1 year.	Mustered out with company June 24, 1865.
ert, Henry		22	Sept. 1, 1864	1 year.	Mustered out with company June 24, 1865.
oney, William H		25	Aug. 16, 1864	1 year.	Mustered out with company June 24, 1865.
, Charles F	....do....	22	Sept. 6, 1864	1 year.	Mustered out July 1, 1865, at Columbus, O., by order of War Department.
, Jacob G		18	Oct. 4, 1864	1 year.	Transferred to Co. A, 181st O.V.I., June 15, 1865.
, Jefferson		28	Sept. 1, 1864	1 year.	Mustered out June 26, 1865, at Camp Dennison, O., by order of War Department.
ner, Jonathan	....do....	37	Sept. 2, 1864	1 year.	Died Feb. 23, 1865, at Washington, D. C.
ey, John		18	Sept. 2, 1864	1 year.	Mustered out June 3, 1865, at Washington, D. C., by order of War Department.
r, Ansil		18	Sept. 2, 1864	1 year.	Mustered out with company June 24, 1865.
rts, William R	....do....	18	Aug. 25, 1864	1 year.	Mustered out with company June 24, 1865.
s, James	....do....	22	Sept. 17, 1864	1 year.	
nd, John J	....do....	29	Aug. 30, 1864	1 year.	Mustered out with company June 24, 1865.
, George W	....do....	18	Aug. 29, 1864	1 year.	Reduced from Corporal Dec. 10, 1864, at his own request; mustered out with company June 24, 1865.
son, Daniel	....do....	18	Sept. 2, 1864	1 year.	Transferred to Co. A, 181st O. V. I., June 15, 1865.
man, Martin V. B	....do....	27	Sept. 2, 1864	1 year.	
erman, Joseph L	....do....	18	Sept. 6, 1864	1 year.	Mustered out with company June 24, 1865.
bert, Daniel	....do....	18	Sept. 3, 1864	1 year.	Mustered out with company June 24, 1865.
ds, William B	....do....	32	Aug. 31, 1864	1 year.	Mustered out June 2, 1865, at Washington, D. C., by order of War Department.
h, John	....do....	22	Sept. 14, 1864	1 year.	
h, Jeremiah	....do....	19	Sept. 16, 1864	1 year.	Mustered out July 7, 1865, at Portsmouth Grove, R. I., by order of War Department.
h, Thomas	....do....	24	Aug. 26, 1864	1 year.	Discharged May 11, 1865, on Surgeon's certificate of disability.
s, Emanuel	....do....	21	Sept. 8, 1864	1 year.	Mustered out with company June 24, 1865.
, George	....do....	18	Sept. 14, 1864	1 year.	
ell, James W	....do....	22	Aug. 31, 1864	1 year	Mustered out with company June 24, 1865.
pson, John	....do....	18	Sept. 7, 1864	1 year.	
pson, Hiram H	....do....	24	Aug. 30, 1864	1 year.	Mustered out with company June 24, 1865.
, Joshua P	....do....	22	Aug. 7, 1864	1 year.	Discharged June 12, 1865, on Surgeon's certificate of disability.
pkins, Jabez S	....do....	40	Sept. 2, 1864	1 year.	Mustered out June 20, 1865, at David's Island, New York Harbor, by order of War Department.
, Christopher C	....do....	20	Aug. 29, 1864	1 year.	Reduced from Corporal May 1, 1865; mustered out May 11, 1865, by order of War Department.
, Conrad	....do....	20	Aug. 22, 1864	1 year.	Mustered out with company June 24, 1865.
, Joseph	....do....	37	Aug. 22, 1864	1 year.	Mustered out with company June 24, 1865.
, Thomas	....do....	22	Sept. 8, 1864	1 year.	
[illegible], Benjamin	....do....	21	Sept. 14, 1864	1 year.	
[illegible], Henry	....do....	27	Sept. 7, 1864	1 year.	
mmet, Henry	....do....	18	Sept. 9, 1864	1 year.	Mustered out with company June 24, 1865.
[illegible]	....do....	30	Aug. 30, 1864	1 year.	Mustered out with company June 24, 1865.

COMPANY C.

Mustered in September 23, 1864, at Camp Cleveland, O., by Thomas Drummond, Captain 5th Cavalry, U.S.A. Mustered out June 24, 1865, at Greensboro, N. C., by A. B. Smith, Captain 100th O. V. I., and C. M. 23d Army Corps.

Names.	Rank.	Age.	Date of Entering the Service.	Period of Service.	Remarks.
Leander C. Reeve	Captain.	36	Aug. 2, 1864	1 year.	Appointed Sept. 7, 1864; mustered out with company June 24, 1865
Fennemore E. Peck	1st Lieut.	32	Sept. 7, 1864	1 year.	Resigned Jan. 8, 1865.
George B. Huston	...do...	21	Sept. 7, 1864	1 year.	Promoted from 2d Lieutenant Co. B Jan. [illegible], 1865; appointed Adjutant May 21, 1865.
Earle N. Jayne	2d Lieut.	22	Aug. 5, 1864	1 year.	Resigned March 1, 1865.
John T. Cramer	...do...	26	Sept. 17, 1864	1 year.	Promoted from Com. Sergeant Jan. [illegible], 1865; transferred to Co. A, 181st O. V. I., June [illegible], 1865.
Silas R. Reeve	1st Sergt.	19	Aug. 9, 1864	1 year.	Mustered out with company June 24, 1865.
Emory J. Adams	Sergeant.	25	Aug. 31, 1864	1 year.	Mustered out with company June 24, 1865.
James E. Stevens	...do...	26	Aug. 24, 1864	1 year.	Mustered out with company June 24, 1865.
Ezra A. Hoskins	...do...	29	Aug. 22, 1864	1 year.	Mustered out with company June 24, 1865.
Edwin C. French	...do...	29	Aug. 23, 1864	1 year.	Mustered out with company June 24, 1865.
George A. Winslow	Corporal.	22	Aug. 31, 1864	1 year.	Mustered out with company June 24, 1865.
Reuben W. Alderman	...do...	35	Aug. 15, 1864	1 year.	Mustered out with company June 24, 1865.
Albert H. Brainard	...do...	22	Aug. 24, 1864	1 year.	Mustered out June 13, 1865, at David's Island, New York Harbor, by order of War Department.
Herbert D. Adams	...do...	32	Aug. 25, 1864	1 year.	Mustered out with company June 24, 1865.
William C. Means	...do...	25	Sept. 29, 1864	1 year.	Mustered out July 4, 1865, at Nashville, Tenn., by order of War Department.
Joseph McIntosh	...do...	37	Sept. 3, 1864	1 year.	Mustered out with company June 24, 1865.
Milton Black	...do...	33	Aug. 18, 1864	1 year.	Mustered out to date June 24, 1865, by order of War Department.
Noah Day	...do...	30	Aug. 5, 1864	1 year.	Appointed Feb. 14, 1865; mustered out with company June 24, 1865.
Edwin C. Piper	...do...	21	Aug. 24, 1864	1 year.	Appointed ——; died Feb. 16, 1865, in hospital at Louisville, Ky.
Demetrius F. Alderman.	Musician	19	Aug. 29, 1864	1 year	Died Feb. 12, 1865, in hospital at Louisville, Kentucky.
John O. Knowles	Wagoner.	28	Sept. 5, 1864	1 year.	Died April 6, 1865, in Marine Hospital, Wilmington, N. C.
Andrus, States	Private.	18	Sept. 4, 1864	1 year.	Mustered out with company June 24, 1865; also borne on rolls as Streeter Andrews.
Bacon, Augustus H	...do...	20	Aug. 24, 1864	1 year.	Mustered out June 26, 1865, at Camp Dennison, O., by order of War Department.
Ball, David W	...do...	18	Aug. 6, 1864	1 year	Mustered out with company June 24, 1865.
Barrett, John A	...do...	23	Aug. 19, 1864	1 year	Mustered out with company June 24, 1865.
Baur, Peter	...do...	19	Aug. 6, 1864	1 year.	Mustered out June 7, 1865, at David's Island, New York Harbor, by order of War Department.
Beach, Samuel	...do...	19	Aug. 24, 1864	1 year.	Mustered out with company June 24, 1865.
Bennett, Edward	...do...	18	Oct. 4, 1864	1 year.	
Blanchard, Perry W	...do...	18	Aug. 25, 1864	1 year.	Mustered out with company June 24, 1865.
Bowker, Thomas	...do...	22	Sept. 30, 1864	1 year	
Brown, Charles	...do...	24	Sept. 30, 1864	1 year.	
Burns, Thomas	...do...	25	Sept. 30, 1864	1 year	
Carey, Plummer D	...do...	19	Aug. 16, 1864	1 year.	Mustered out with company June 24, 1865.
Chaffee, Simon U	...do...	40	Aug. 25, 1864	1 year.	Mustered out June 24, 1865, at Tullahoma, Tenn., by order of War Department.
Clark, Russell R	...do...	28	Aug. 31, 1864	1 year.	Died March 7, 1865, at Ladies' Hospital, New York City.
Clark, Oren	...do...	41	Sept. 2, 1864	1 year.	Mustered out with company June 24, 1865.
Cole, David	...do...	26	Oct. 1, 1864	1 year	Mustered out with company June 24, 1865.
Cook, William W	...do...	28	Aug. 18, 1864	1 year.	Mustered out to date June 24, 1865, by order of War Department.
Curtis, Drayton D	...do...	20	Aug. 19, 1864	1 year.	Mustered out with company June 24, 1865.
Criddle, Robert F	...do...	29	Aug. 11, 1864	1 year.	Transferred to Co. A, 181st O. V. I., June [illegible], 1865.
Day, Cyrus W	...do...	22	Aug. 5, 1864	1 year.	Mustered out with company June 24, 1865.
Dodge, Levant	...do...	26	Aug. 16, 1864	1 year.	Mustered out with company June 24, 1865.
Edson, Sidney	...do...	19	Aug. 9, 1864	1 year	Reduced from Corporal ——; mustered out with company June 24, 1865.
Ellsworth, Alonzo H	...do...	28	Sept. 23, 1864	1 year.	Mustered out with company June 24, 1865.
Ellsworth, George M	...do...	18	Aug. 24, 1864	1 year	Mustered out July 15, 1865, at Portsmouth Grove, R. I., by order of War Department.
Evans, Daniel	...do...	39	Aug. 17, 1864	1 year.	Died May 17, 1865, in hospital at [illegible], North Carolina.
Evans, Hiram	...do...	44	Aug. 17, 1864	1 year.	Reduced from Corporal ——; mustered out with company June 24, 1865.
Farr, Lyman M	...do...	32	Aug. 17, 1864	1 year.	Mustered out with company June 24, 1865.
Foster, James A	...do...	18	Aug. 25, 1864	1 year.	Died Sept. 29, 1864, in hospital at [illegible], Ohio.
Fowler, John W	...do...	18	Aug. 10, 1864	1 year.	Mustered out with company June 24, 1865.
Gardner, David N	...do...	29	Aug. 9, 1864	1 year.	Died Feb. 11, 1865, in hospital at Fort [illegible], North Carolina.

Names.	Rank.	Age.	Date of Entering the Service.	Period of Service.	Remarks.
Gardner, Orlando J	Private	21	Aug. 23, 1864	1 year.	Mustered out to date June 24, 1865, by order of War Department.
Grover, Leonard	...do...	43	Aug. 26, 1864	1 year.	Died July 3, 1865, at home.
Hartsock, William	...do...	22	Oct. 1, 1864	1 year.	
Hepburn, Orville	...do...	21	Aug. 9, 1864	1 year.	Mustered out with company June 24, 1865.
Hilands, Franklin	...do...	19	Aug. 6, 1864	1 year.	Mustered out with company June 24, 1865.
Higley, Lewis	...do...	27	Aug. 23, 1864	1 year.	Mustered out to date June 24, 1865, by order of War Department.
Holcomb, Alvin	...do...	18	Aug. 13, 1864	1 year.	Mustered out with company June 24, 1865.
Hopkins, James W	...do...	19	Aug. 13, 1864	1 year.	Mustered out with company June 24, 1865.
Hoskins, Rodimer	...do...	25	Aug. 31, 1864	1 year.	Mustered out with company June 24, 1865.
Howard, William H.	...do...	18	Sept. 2, 1864	1 year.	Mustered out with company June 24, 1865.
Hubbard, Robert B. A.	...do...	31	Aug. 24, 1864	1 year.	Mustered out with company June 24, 1865.
Hubbard, Nathan	...do...	25	Aug. 25, 1864	1 year.	Mustered out May 24, 1865, at West Philadelphia, Pa., by order of War Department.
Hubbard, Selah B.	...do...	21	Aug. 13, 1864	1 year.	Died April 28, 1865, in hospital at Wilmington, North Carolina.
Humphrey, Henry S.	...do...	25	Sept. 2, 1864	1 year.	Mustered out with company June 24, 1865.
Jenkins, Chauncey	...do...	18	Aug. 15, 1864	1 year.	Died March 1, 1865, in hospital at Wilmington, North Carolina.
Knapp, Elliott M	...do...	18	Aug. 31, 1864	1 year.	Mustered out with company June 24, 1865.
Knowles, Andrew A.	...do...	18	Aug. 5, 1864	1 year.	
Leslie, Alexander	...do...	22	Aug. 6, 1864	1 year.	Promoted to Hospital Steward ——; reduced to ranks March 31, 1865, and returned to company; mustered out May 30, 1865, at Cleveland, O., by order of War Department.
Longworthy, Irving J.	...do...	21	Aug. 23, 1864	1 year.	Died Dec. 22, 1864, at Murfreesboro, Tenn., of wounds received Dec. 14, 1864, in action near Murfreesboro, Tenn.
Lucas, Jonathan P.	...do...	43	Sept. 2, 1864	1 year.	Mustered out to date June 24, 1865, by order of War Department.
McArthur, Clayton	...do...	19	Aug. 31, 1864	1 year.	Mustered out with company June 24, 1865.
McCright, George	...do...	15	Aug. 21, 1864	1 year.	Mustered out with company June 24, 1865.
Matthews, Daniel	...do...	42	Sept. 23, 1864	1 year.	Mustered out with company June 24, 1865.
Mills, Henry M	...do...	28	Aug. 24, 1864	1 year.	Mustered out June 27, 1865, at Columbus, O., by order of War Department.
Morrison, John	...do...	18	Aug. 22, 1864	1 year.	Mustered out June 22, 1865, at Chester, Pa., by order of War Department.
Moorehouse, Eugene O.	...do...	18	Aug. 15, 1864	1 year.	Mustered out with company June 24, 1865.
Munger, David	...do...	27	Aug. 26, 1864	1 year.	Mustered out with company June 24, 1865.
Murphy, George A.	...do...	20	Aug. 19, 1864	1 year.	Mustered out with company June 24, 1865.
Nelson, Walter J.	...do...	19	Sept. 22, 1864	1 year.	Mustered out with company June 24, 1865.
Norris, Monroe J	...do...	24	Aug. 25, 1864	1 year.	Died Jan. 28, 1865, in hospital at Tullahoma, Tennessee.
Norris, George G.	...do...	35	Aug. 15, 1864	1 year.	Mustered out with company June 24, 1865.
Orr, John J.	...do...	28	Aug. 25, 1864	1 year.	Died Feb. 18, 1865, in hospital at Washington, District of Columbia.
Partridge, Milo L.	...do...	18	Aug. 17, 1864	1 year.	Died Feb. 22, 1865, in hospital at Smithville, North Carolina.
Peck, Amos A.	...do...	29	Aug. 23, 1864	1 year.	Reduced from Corporal ——; mustered out with company June 24, 1865.
Proctor, William	...do...	38	Aug. 20, 1864	1 year.	Mustered out May 24, 1865, at New York, by order of War Department.
Rich, Alonzo	...do...	18	Aug. 23, 1864	1 year.	Mustered out with company June 24, 1865.
Reed, Fayette C.	...do...	19	Aug. 26, 1864	1 year.	Mustered out with company June 24, 1865.
Shannon, Philip	...do...	28	Sept. 5, 1864	1 year.	
Spellman, Luther A	...do...	18	Oct. 1, 1864	1 year.	Mustered out with company June 24, 1865.
Stevens, Elias A.	...do...	35	Aug. 24, 1864	1 year.	Mustered out with company June 24, 1865.
Stockwell, Austin F	...do...	29	Aug. 17, 1864	1 year.	Mustered out July 28, 1865, at Washington, D. C., by order of War Department.
Stocking, Albion M	...do...	18	Aug. 30, 1864	1 year.	Mustered out June 2, 1865, at Albany, N. Y., by order of War Department.
Stone, Emmons M	...do...	30	Aug. 12, 1864	1 year.	Mustered out with company June 24, 1865.
Stoughton, Rexford	...do...	27	Aug. 25, 1864	1 year.	Mustered out with company June 24, 1865.
Thompson, Theodore	...do...	31	Aug. 15, 1864	1 year.	
Tompkins, Levi	...do...	16	Aug. 5, 1864	1 year.	Mustered out May 30, 1865, at Cleveland, O., by order of War Department.
Townsley, Daniel	...do...	38	Aug. 24, 1864	1 year.	Mustered out with company June 24, 1865.
Townsend, Henry	...do...	40	Aug. 20, 1864	1 year.	Mustered out with company June 24, 1865.
Washburn, John H	...do...	28	Aug. 10, 1864	1 year.	
Wyatt, Erastus J	...do...	29	Sept. 22, 1864	1 year.	Died Feb. 16, 1865, while on furlough, at his home, New Lyme, O.
Wilder, Leonard	...do...	37	Aug. 23, 1864	1 year.	Died June 1, 1865, in hospital at David's Island, New York Harbor.
Williams, Richard	...do...	22	Sept. 1, 1864	1 year.	Mustered out with company June 24, 1865.
Williams, William W.	...do...	32	Aug. 24, 1864	1 year.	Mustered out June 13, 1865, at David's Island, New York Harbor, by order of War Department.
Woodworth, Augustus	...do...	29	Aug. 17, 1864	1 year.	Mustered out with company June 24, 1865.

COMPANY D.

Mustered in September 23, 1864, at Camp Cleveland, O., by Thomas Drummond, Captain 5th Cavalry, U.S.A. Mustered out June 24, 1865, at Greensboro, N. C., by A. B. Smith, Captain 100th O. V. I., and C. M. 23d Army Corps.

Names.	Rank.	Age.	Date of Entering the Service.	Period of Service.	Remarks.
Rufus H. Burr	Captain.	23	Sept. 7, 1864	1 year.	Mustered out with company June 24, 1865.
George C. Gilbert	1st Lieut.	35	Sept. 7, 1864	1 year.	Mustered out with company June 24, 1865.
Abner Loomis	2d Lieut.	20	Sept. 7, 1864	1 year.	Mustered out with company June 24, 1865.
Joseph M. Waldorf	1st Sergt.	22	Sept. 2, 1864	1 year.	Appointed from Sergeant Jan. 14, 1865; mustered out with company June 24, 1865.
George F. Waters	Sergeant.	24	Aug. 16, 1864	1 year.	Appointed Sept. 20, 1864; mustered out with company June 24, 1865.
I. Dana Morse	....do....	20	Aug. 12, 1864	1 year.	Reduced from 1st Sergeant Jan. 14, 1865; mustered out with company June 24, 1865.
James T. Kyle	....do....	30	Sept. 3, 1864	1 year.	Mustered out June 7, 1865, at David's Island, New York Harbor, by order of War Department.
John A. Blanchard	....do....	29	Aug. 27, 1864	1 year.	Mustered out with company June 24, 1865.
Vandorn Root	Corporal.	30	Aug. 27, 1864	1 year.	Mustered out with company June 24, 1865.
Orlo G. F. Marvin	....do....	20	Aug. 13, 1864	1 year.	Appointed Sept. 20, 1864; mustered out June 21, 1865, at Beaufort, N. C., by order of War Department.
William McCartney	....do....	18	Aug. 20, 1864	1 year.	Mustered out with company June 24, 1865.
William H. Anderson	....do....	18	Aug. 27, 1864	1 year.	Appointed Sept. 20, 1864; mustered out with company June 24, 1865.
Hiram D. Holcomb	....do....	30	Sept. 2, 1864	1 year.	Mustered out to date June 24, 1865, by order of War Department.
Edwin Gibbs	....do....	36	Aug. 16, 1864	1 year.	Appointed March 10, 1865; mustered out with company June 24, 1865.
Henry D. Johnson	....do....	37	Aug. 30, 1864	1 year.	Mustered out with company June 24, 1865.
John Paul	....do....	31	Sept. 29, 1864	1 year.	Appointed Jan. 14, 1865; mustered out with company June 24, 1865.
James M. Henry	....do....	25	Aug. 27, 1864	1 year.	Appointed Sept. 20, 1864; died March [illegible]
George N. Jackson	Musician	27	Aug. 30, 1864	1 year.	Mustered out with company June 24, 1865.
Cornelius M. Turner	....do....	38	Oct. 4, 1864	1 year.	Mustered out July 17, 1865, at Cleveland, O., by order of War Department.
Allen, Riley	Private.	18	Aug. 27, 1864	1 year.	Mustered out May 29, 1865, at Camp Dennison, O., by order of War Department.
Boyd, Edwin	....do....	20	Aug. 23, 1864	1 year.	Mustered out June 9, 1865, at Washington, D. C., by order of War Department.
Bridges, Alonzo W	....do....	27	Sept. 2, 1864	1 year.	Mustered out with company June 24, 1865.
Brockway, Clarence	....do....	18	Aug. 30, 1864	1 year.	Mustered out with company June 24, 1865.
Brown, James	....do....	20	Sept. 5, 1864	1 year.	Mustered out with company June 24, 1865.
Brown, Edwin B	....do....	35	Sept. 3, 1864	1 year.	Reduced from Corporal Jan. 14, 1865; mustered out with company June 24, 1865.
Burlingham, Curtis	....do....	41	Aug. 30, 1864	1 year.	Mustered out with company June 24, 1865.
Burlingham, Arthur D	....do....	36	Aug. 30, 1864	1 year.	Mustered out with company June 24, 1865.
Case, Thomas	....do....	34	Feb. 21, 1865	1 year.	Transferred to Co. A, 181st O. V. I. June [illegible], 1865.
Creesy, Lyman T	....do....	20	Aug. 27, 1864	1 year.	Mustered out with company June 24, 1865.
Crosby, Joseph B	....do....	32	Aug. 27, 1864	1 year.	
Demo, George W	....do....	27	Aug. 27, 1864	1 year.	Died Jan. 17, 1865, of wounds received in line of duty.
Dewoolver, James	....do....	23	Sept. 29, 1864	1 year.	
Dunbar, Barnabas	....do....	33	Aug. 30, 1864	1 year.	Mustered out with company June 24, 1865.
Eversole, Simeon	....do....	40	Sept. 21, 1864	1 year.	Died May 3, 1865, at Washington, D. C.
Fenn, George	....do....	19	Aug. 29, 1864	1 year.	
Fitzgerald, Michael	....do....	26	Aug. 31, 1864	1 year.	Mustered out with company June 24, 1865.
Foote, Curtis	....do....	18	Sept. 9, 1864	1 year.	Died Feb. 27, 1865, at Nashville, Tenn.
Giddings, Elisha E	....do....	18	Aug. 27, 1864	1 year.	Mustered out June 16, 1865, at Chester, Pa., by order of War Department.
Goulding, Stephen M	....do....	27	Aug. 26, 1864	1 year.	
Grokenbarger John D	....do....	18	Aug. 27, 1864	1 year.	Mustered out with company June 24, 1865.
Hall, Aaron G	....do....	35	Sept. 1, 1864	1 year.	Died March 20, 1865, at Wilmington, N. C.
Hall, David A	....do....	24	Aug. 29, 1864	1 year.	Mustered out with company June 24, 1865.
Hamilton, James	....do....	36	Aug. 18, 1864	1 year.	Mustered out with company June 24, 1865.
Hamilton, William	....do....	25	Sept. 13, 1864	1 year.	
Hays, Lucien I	....do....	20	Aug. 27, 1864	1 year.	Mustered out with company June 24, 1865.
Heath, James	....do....	36	Sept. 3, 1864	1 year.	Mustered out July 3, 1865, at Columbus, O., by order of War Department.
Heath, Luther F	....do....	24	Sept. 3, 1864	1 year.	Mustered out with company June 24, 1865.
Hill, John W	....do....	39	Sept. 5, 1864	1 year.	Mustered out with company June 24, 1865.
Holcomb, Richard	....do....	22	Aug. 29, 1864	1 year.	Mustered out with company June 24, 1865.
Hoogs, Willis F	....do....	18	Sept. 7, 1864	1 year.	Died Feb. 7, 1865, at Fort Fisher, N. C.
Hogan, Daniel	....do....	23	Sept. 2, 1864	1 year.	
Hull, Benjamin F	....do....	27	Aug. 26, 1864	1 year.	
Johnson, Fayette N	....do....	19	Aug. 30, 1864	1 year.	Mustered out with company June 24, 1865.
Karr, Franklin H	....do....	29	Sept. 2, 1864	1 year.	Mustered out with company June 24, 1865.
Labounty, William H	....do....	33	Aug. 29, 1864	1 year.	Mustered out with company June 24, 1865.
Lamont, David	....do....	44	Aug. 23, 1864	1 year.	Died April 30, 1865, at Beaufort, N. C.
Lasky, John W	....do....	18	Aug. 10, 1864	1 year.	Mustered out May 29, 1865, at Camp Dennison, O., by order of War Department.

Names.	Rank.	Age.	Date of Entering the Service.	Period of Service.	Remarks.
Loughlin, Dalzell	Private.	18	Aug. 26, 1864	1 year.	Mustered out with company June 24, 1865.
Law, John	...do...	37	Sept. 2, 1864	1 year.	Mustered out June 8, 1865, at Newbern, N. C., by order of War Department.
Lewis, Abel	...do...	18	Sept. 5, 1864	1 year.	
Loomis, Elmer	...do...	30	Aug. 27, 1864	1 year.	Mustered out with company June 24, 1865.
Loomis, Wickliff	...do...	18	Sept. 9, 1864	1 year.	Mustered out with company June 24, 1865.
Mann, Selwyn	...do...	18	Sept. 1, 1864	1 year.	Mustered out with company June 24, 1865.
Mead, Thomas B.	...do...	18	Aug. 27, 1864	1 year.	Mustered out June 14, 1865, at Wheeling, W. Va., by order of War Department.
Morse, George R.	...do...	18	Aug. 24, 1864	1 year.	Died Jan. 20, 1865, at Louisville, Ky.
Moulton, Jeremiah C.	...do...	42	Sept. 15, 1864	1 year.	Mustered out with company June 24, 1865.
Mowen, William M.	...do...	22	Aug. 17, 1864	1 year.	Mustered out July 6, 1865, at Columbus, O., by order of War Department.
Morse, Fortis A.	...do...	18	Aug. 16, 1864	1 year.	Mustered out May 30, 1865, at Cleveland, O., by order of War Department.
Newton, Isaac M.	...do...	40	Sept. 1, 1864	1 year.	Mustered out with company June 24, 1865.
Oatman, Andrew	...do...	25	Aug. 15, 1864	1 year.	
Ogram, William	...do...	39	Aug. 20, 1864	1 year.	Mustered out July 7, 1865, at Portsmouth Grove, R. I., by order of War Department.
Patch, Jackson D.	...do...	37	Sept. 6, 1864	1 year.	Mustered out June 9, 1865, at Louisville, Ky., by order of War Department.
Phelps, Orville M.	...do...	26	Aug. 27, 1864	1 year.	Mustered out with company June 24, 1865.
Pierce, Charles	...do...	29	Aug. 27, 1864	1 year.	Mustered out with company June 24, 1865.
Piper, Ralph R.	...do...	21	Aug. 12, 1864	1 year.	Mustered out with company June 24, 1865.
Rhodes, Seneca S.	...do...	30	Aug. 24, 1864	1 year.	Discharged June 21, 1865, at Cleveland, O., on Surgeon's certificate of disability.
Rider, Eleazer	...do...	36	Sept. 3, 1864	1 year.	Mustered as Musician; mustered out with company June 24, 1865.
Roberts, Charles H.	...do...	22	Aug. 30, 1864	1 year.	Mustered out with company June 24, 1865.
Root, James D.	...do...	19	Aug. 8, 1864	1 year.	Died Jan. 29, 1865, at Nashville, Tenn.
Rose, Henry	...do...	28	Aug. 6, 1864	1 year.	Mustered out with company June 24, 1865.
Ross, Alva C.	...do...	43	Oct. 4, 1864	1 year.	Transferred to Co. A, 181st O. V. I., June 15, 1865.
Rogers, Adolphus	...do...	42	Oct. 4, 1864	1 year.	Transferred to Co. A, 181st O. V. I., June 15, 1865.
Rowland, Matthew	...do...	19	Oct. 4, 1864	1 year.	Transferred to Co. A, 181st O. V. I., June 15, 1865.
Ryan, Peter	...do...	23	Sept. 13, 1864	1 year.	Discharged April 4, 1865, at St. Louis, Mo., on Surgeon's certificate of disability.
Scoville, Lucius H.	...do...	21	Aug. 23, 1864	1 year.	Mustered out with company June 24, 1865.
Sessions, Russell M.	...do...	32	Aug. 27, 1864	1 year.	Mustered out with company June 24, 1865.
Sloat, Edgar	...do...	18	Aug. 30, 1864	1 year.	Mustered out with company June 24, 1865.
Sloat, Edmond	...do...	18	Aug. 22, 1864	1 year.	Mustered out with company June 24, 1865.
Smith, Valentine	...do...	33	Aug. 18, 1864	1 year.	Mustered out with company June 24, 1865.
Strickland, Willis	...do...	18	Aug. 18, 1864	1 year.	Mustered out with company June 24, 1865.
Spellman, Freeman F.	...do...	18	Sept. 5, 1864	1 year.	Mustered out May 30, 1865, at Cleveland, O., by order of War Department.
Spellman, Darwin R.	...do...	21	Sept. 1, 1864	1 year.	Reduced from Corporal ——; discharged Feb. 27, 1865, at Cleveland, O., on Surgeon's certificate of disability.
Tinkham, Isaac V.	...do...	22	Sept. 5, 1864	1 year.	Mustered out with company June 24, 1865.
Turner, Harrison	...do...	20	Aug. 18, 1864	1 year.	Mustered out with company June 24, 1865.
Wass, John	...do...	30	Sept. 5, 1864	1 year.	Mustered out with company June 24, 1865.
Weir, James	...do...	35	Sept. 5, 1864	1 year.	Mustered out with company June 24, 1865.
Williams, Jerome E.	...do...	17	Sept. 12, 1864	1 year.	Mustered out with company June 24, 1865.
Willey, Francis H.	...do...	18	Aug. 18, 1864	1 year.	Mustered out with company June 24, 1865.
Winch, Samuel	...do...	36	Aug. 30, 1864	1 year.	Mustered out with company June 24, 1865.
Winch, David, Jr.	...do...	39	Aug. 30, 1864	1 year.	Mustered out with company June 24, 1865.
Winans, Roderick M.	...do...	31	Sept. 29, 1864	1 year.	Mustered out with company June 24, 1865.
Wilsonbury, Adolphus B.	...do...	22	Aug. 18, 1864	1 year.	Mustered out with company June 24, 1865.

COMPANY E.

Mustered in September 28, 1864, at Camp Cleveland, O., by Thomas Drummond, Captain 5th Cavalry, U. S. A. Mustered out June 24, 1865, at Greensboro, N. C., by A. B. Smith, Captain 100th O. V. I., and C. M. 23d Army Corps.

Names.	Rank.	Age.	Date of Entering the Service.	Period of Service.	Remarks.
Osmer C. Chase	Captain.	26	Sept. 26, 1864	1 year.	Mustered out with company June 24, 1865.
John Peterson	1st Lieut.	35	Sept. 26, 1864	1 year.	Mustered out with company June 24, 1865.
Squire S. Brown	2d Lieut.	33	Sept. 26, 1864	1 year.	Mustered out with company June 24, 1865.
Joseph G. Durfee	1st Sergt.	30	Aug. 23, 1864	1 year.	Mustered out with company June 24, 1865.
Sherwood Wilcox	Sergeant.	19	Aug. 29, 1864	1 year.	Mustered out with company June 24, 1865.
Henderson Smith	...do...	22	Aug. 12, 1864	1 year.	Mustered out with company June 24, 1865.
William H. Kibble	...do...	23	Sept. 1, 1864	1 year.	Mustered out with company June 24, 1865.
Andrew J. Jewell	...do...	20	Aug. 30, 1864	1 year.	Mustered out May 7, 1865, at Columbus, O., by order of War Department.
Charles E. Crowe	...do...	19	Aug. 30, 1864	1 year.	Appointed from Corporal May 31, 1865; mustered out with company June 24, 1865.
Joseph Q. Oviatt	Corporal.	24	Aug. 29, 1864	1 year.	Appointed September 28, 1864; mustered out May 29, 1865, at Albany, N. Y., by order of War Department.

Names.	Rank.	Age.	Date of Entering the Service.	Period of Service	Remarks.
Dudley R. Travis	Corporal.	44	Aug. 24, 1864	1 year.	Wounded Dec. 14, 1864, in action near Murfreesboro, Tenn.; discharged June [illegible] at Louisville, Ky., on Surgeon's certificate of disability.
Daniel Lodwick	...do...	25	Aug. 30, 1864	1 year.	Mustered out with company June 24, 1865.
Horton H. Faulk	...do...	29	Aug. 13, 1864	1 year.	Mustered out with company June 24, 1865.
Farrington Case	...do...	22	Sept. 13, 1864	1 year.	Mustered out with company June 24, 1865.
Levi O. Billington	...do...	24	Sept. 3, 1864	1 year.	Appointed March 1, 1865; mustered out with company June 24, 1865.
William T. Corlett	...do...	22	Aug. 26, 1864	1 year.	Appointed March 1, 1865; mustered out with company June 24, 1865.
Albert E. Thayer	...do...	18	Sept. 8, 1864	1 year.	Appointed May 31, 1865; mustered out with company June 24, 1865.
Newton Leggett	...do...	19	Aug. 29, 1864	1 year.	Died Feb. 22, 1865, in hospital at [illegible] North Carolina.
Henry King	Musician	18	Aug. 16, 1864	1 year.	Mustered out with company June 24, 1865.
George B. Patterson	Wagoner	22	Sept 1, 1864	1 year.	Mustered out with company June 24, 1865.
Ackley, James H	Private	22	Sept. 13, 1865	1 year.	Died Feb. 25, 1865, in hospital at [illegible] North Carolina.
Allen, George	...do...	23	Sept. 8, 1864	1 year.	
Alexander, David	...do...	21	Sept. 3, 1864	1 year.	Mustered out June 26, 1865, at David's Island, New York Harbor, by order of War Department.
Andrews, George L	...do...	19	Aug. 29, 1864	1 year.	Mustered out with company June 24, 1865.
Andrews, Andrew A	...do...	18	Aug. 31, 1864	1 year.	Mustered out with company June 24, 1865.
Austin, William H	...do...	18	Aug. 31, 1864	1 year.	Mustered out with company June 24, 1865.
Auringer, Daniel	...do...	44	Aug. 30, 1864	1 year.	Mustered out with company June 24, 1865.
Bailey, Frank D	...do...	18	Aug. 31, 1864	1 year.	Mustered out with company June 24, 1865.
Barrett, John	...do...	21	Aug. 31, 1864	1 year.	Mustered out with company June 24, 1865.
Basquin, Oliver	...do...	18	Aug. 29, 1864	1 year.	Mustered out June 19, 1865, at Columbus, O., by order of War Department.
Bell, Charles	...do...	27	Sept. 13, 1864	1 year.	
Blodgett, Morris	...do...	42	Aug. 29, 1864	1 year.	Mustered out July 3, 1865, at Columbus, O., by order of War Department.
Brown, Beaufort	...do...	18	Aug. 27, 1864	1 year.	Mustered out with company June 24, 1865.
Burns, James	...do...	24	Aug. 24, 1864	1 year.	Mustered out with company June 24, 1865.
Case, Emery	...do...	21	Sept. 7, 1864	1 year.	Mustered out with company June 24, 1865.
Dangler, Andrew	...do...	33	Aug. 29, 1864	1 year.	Mustered out with company June 24, 1865.
Dangler, Carl A	...do...	31	Aug. 20, 1864	1 year.	Mustered out with company June 24, 1865.
Dankleman, James	...do...	22	Sept. 24, 1864	1 year.	
Day, Charles S	...do...	44	Aug. 29, 1864	1 year.	Mustered out with company June 24, 1865.
Davidson, Elwood	...do...	19	Sept. 2, 1864	1 year.	Mustered as Musician; mustered out with company June 24, 1865.
Devoe, Chauncey A	...do...	24	Aug. 31, 1864	1 year.	
Dewey, Oliver E	...do...	20	Sept. 5, 1864	1 year.	Mustered out with company June 24, 1865.
Diehl, John M	...do...	19	Sept. 19, 1864	1 year.	Mustered out with company June 24, 1865.
Eastman, Judah O	...do...	29	Aug. 17, 1864	1 year.	Mustered out with company June 24, 1865.
Eaton, William H	...do...	20	Aug. 13, 1864	1 year.	Mustered out with company June 24, 1865.
Elliott, Randolph S	...do...	28	Aug. 29, 1864	1 year.	Mustered out with company June 24, 1865.
Exceen, Abraham	...do...	31	Aug. 24, 1864	1 year.	Mustered out with company June 24, 1865.
Fenstermaker, Peter	...do...	19	Aug. 20, 1864	1 year.	Mustered out June 20, 1865, at Washington, D. C., by order of War Department.
Flohr, John	...do...	23	Aug. 29, 1864	1 year.	Mustered out with company June 24, 1865.
Flohr, Henry	...do...	19	Aug. 29, 1864	1 year.	Mustered out with company June 24, 1865.
Freeman, Monroe	...do...	26	Sept. 1, 1864	1 year.	Mustered out June 22, 1865, at [illegible] by order of War Department.
Grant, Charles W	...do...	18	Oct. 12, 1864	1 year.	Transferred to Co. A, [illegible] O. V. I., [illegible] 1865.
Griswold, Robert W	...do...	32	Aug. 24, 1864	1 year.	
Grove, Merryman Y	...do...	23	Aug. 31, 1864	1 year.	Mustered out May 31, 1865, at Camp Dennison, O., by order of War Department.
Hamilton, James	...do...	23	Sept. 10, 1864	1 year.	
Harlow, Charles H	...do...	21	Aug. 29, 1864	1 year.	Mustered out with company June 24, 1865.
Hazen, Roswell	...do...	18	Aug. 17, 1864	1 year.	Mustered out with company June 24, 1865.
Heather, Clinton B	...do...	18	Sept. 12, 1864	1 year.	Mustered out with company June 24, 1865.
Heather, Spofford	...do...	18	Sept. 5, 1864	1 year.	Mustered out with company June 24, 1865.
Hoffman, Franklin L.	...do...	21	Aug. 29, 1864	1 year.	Wounded Dec. 14, 1864, in action near Murfreesboro, Tenn.; mustered out June [illegible] at Cleveland, O., by order of War Department.
Holcomb, Henry	...do...	20	Aug. 29, 1864	1 year.	Reduced from Corporal Feb. [illegible] 1865, at his own request; mustered out with company June 24, 1865.
Hosmer, Newall A	...do...	38	Aug. 27, 1864	1 year.	Died May 1, 1865, in DeCamp Hospital, David's Island, New York Harbor.
Howell, William	...do...	21	Sept. 16, 1864	1 year.	
Hull, Ferris C	...do...	21	Aug. 29, 1864	1 year.	Mustered out with company June 24, 1865.
Jones, Frank	...do...	35	Sept. 5, 1864	1 year.	Reduced from Corporal —; mustered out with company June 24, 1865.
Kelley, John	...do...	28	Sept. 9, 1864	1 year.	
King, John	...do...	33	Aug. 29, 1864	1 year.	Detached at Post Headquarters, Tullahoma, Tenn.; mustered out June 19, 1865, at Tullahoma, Tenn., by order of War Department.
Latimore, Robert	...do...	18	Aug. 20, 1864	1 year.	Mustered out with company June [illegible]
Livingston, Henry	...do...	34	Aug. 29, 1864	1 year.	Mustered out with company June [illegible]

Names.	Rank.	Age.	Date of Entering the Service.	Period of Service.	Remarks.
Long, Samuel W.	Private	[illegible]	Sept. 1, 1864	1 year.	Died Jan. 18, 1865, in hospital at Nashville, Tennessee.
McFadden, Carlisle	...do...	22	Aug. 25, 1864	1 year.	Discharged Feb. 18, 1865, at Jefferson Barracks, Mo., on Surgeon's certificate of disability.
McNamara, Patrick	...do...	42	Sept. 9, 1864	1 year.	Mustered out with company June 24, 1865.
Martin, James	...do...	18	Sept. 7, 1864	1 year.	Mustered out with company June 24, 1865.
Moore, George M.	...do...	21	Aug. 31, 1864	1 year.	
Montgomery, Thomas	...do...	19	Aug. 19, 1864	1 year.	Mustered out with company June 24, 1865.
Nash, James M.	...do...	22	Aug. 26, 1864	1 year.	Died Feb. 25, 1865, in hospital at Louisville, Kentucky.
Ovlatt, Lyman	...do...	20	Aug. 29, 1864	1 year.	Mustered out with company June 24, 1865.
Parks, William	...do...	17	Sept. 18, 1864	1 year.	Mustered out with company June 24, 1865.
Parker, George W.	...do...	19	Aug. 31, 1864	1 year.	Mustered out with company June 24, 1865.
Parker, Ashley	...do...	18	Aug. 13, 1864	1 year.	Mustered as Musician; mustered out with company June 24, 1865.
Purrieville, Martin	...do...	42	Sept. 21, 1864	1 year.	Mustered out with company June 24, 1865.
Powers, Edwin	...do...	18	Aug. 29, 1864	1 year.	Mustered out with company June 24, 1865.
Ransom, Giles T.	...do...	34	Aug. 31, 1864	1 year.	Mustered out with company June 24, 1865.
Reed, Delos A.	...do...	26	Aug. 24, 1864	1 year.	Mustered out with company June 24, 1865.
Reed, Ethan A.	...do...	28	Aug. 31, 1864	1 year.	
Rouller, William H.	...do...	21	Sept. 1, 1864	1 year.	Died April 29, 1865, in hospital at Camp Dennison, O.
Riley, John	...do...	19	Sept. 9, 1864	1 year.	
Roark, Milton	...do...	19	Sept. 8, 1864	1 year.	Died March 9, 1865, in hospital at Wilmington, North Carolina.
Sanner, Reuben	...do...	31	Sept. 1, 1864	1 year.	Mustered out with company June 24, 1865.
Searle, Ambrose	...do...	19	Aug. 16, 1864	1 year.	Mustered out with company June 24, 1865.
Smith, George W.	...do...	43	Sept. 12, 1864	1 year.	
Starkweather, Thomas L.	...do...	31	Sept. 3, 1864	1 year.	Reduced from Corporal ——; mustered out with company June 24, 1865.
Staley, William H.	...do...	18	Aug. 19, 1864	1 year.	Died Feb. 7, 1865, in hospital at Louisville, Kentucky.
Stevens, Frank	...do...	18	Aug. 30, 1864	1 year.	Mustered out with company June 24, 1865.
Stevens, James	...do...	19	Aug. 28, 1864	1 year.	Died March 10, 1865, in hospital at Wilmington, North Carolina.
Swayne, John	...do...	34	Aug. 17, 1864	1 year.	
Tinkham, Reuben	...do...	27	Aug. 27, 1864	1 year	
Wade, Stanley	...do...	18	Aug. 18, 1864	1 year.	Mustered out April 10, 1865, at New Albany, Ind., by order of War Department.
Watts, Elbert	...do...	18	Aug. 31, 1864	1 year.	Mustered out June 2, 1865, at Cleveland, O., by order of War Department.
Williams, John E.	...do...	19	Sept. 12, 1864	1 year.	
Winnagle, Charles H.	...do...	31	Aug. 26, 1864	1 year	
Wooden, George L.	...do...	19	Sept. 4, 1864	1 year.	Mustered out with company June 24, 1865.

COMPANY F.

Mustered in September 28, 1864, at Camp Cleveland, O., by Thomas Drummond, Captain 5th Cavalry, U. S. A. Mustered out June 24, 1865, at Greensboro, N. C., by A. B. Smith, Captain 100th O. V. I., and C. M. 23d Army Corps.

Names.	Rank.	Age.	Date of Entering the Service.	Period of Service.	Remarks.
Charles J. McDowell	Captain.	28	Sept. 26, 1864	1 year.	Mustered out with company June 24, 1865.
Henry J. Rice	1st Lieut.	31	Sept. 26, 1864	1 year.	Mustered out with company June 24, 1865.
Walter B. Dow	2d Lieut.	26	Sept. 26, 1864	1 year.	Discharged Jan. 15, 1865, by order of War Department.
Herman O. Norton	1st Sergt.	23	Sept. 21, 1864	1 year.	Promoted to Sergt. Major Feb. 1, 1865.
Delos Elliott	...do...	21	Sept. 3, 1864	1 year.	Appointed from Sergeant Feb. 1, 1865; mustered out with company June 24, 1865.
Francis O. Richards	Sergeant.	18	Sept. 7, 1864	1 year.	Mustered out with company June 24, 1865.
Henry A. Hollister	...do...	24	Aug. 27, 1864	1 year.	Mustered out June 9, 1865, at Portsmouth Grove, R. I., by order of War Department.
Henry C. Eckert	...do...	21	Sept. 3, 1864	1 year.	Mustered out with company June 24, 1865.
Addison A. Root	...do...	24	Sept. 5, 1864	1 year.	Appointed from Corporal Feb. 1, 1865; mustered out with company June 24, 1865.
Roderick McCormick	Corporal.	30	Sept. 17, 1864	1 year.	Mustered out with company June 24, 1865.
William D. Miner	...do...	30	Sept. 13, 1864	1 year.	Mustered out with company June 24, 1865.
Thomas C. Bentley	...do...	18	Sept. 10, 1864	1 year.	Appointed Feb. 1, 1865; mustered out with company June 24, 1865.
Asahel Chamberlin	...do...	18	Sept. 10, 1864	1 year.	Mustered out with company June 24, 1865.
Edward T. Hayes	...do...	19	Sept. 18, 1864	1 year.	Mustered out with company June 24, 1865.
Isaac T. Ralph	...do...	26	Sept. 22, 1864	1 year.	Mustered out with company June 24, 1865.
Luther M. Holloway	...do...	19	Sept. 13, 1864	1 year.	Mustered out with company June 24, 1865.
Emmons J. Godfrey	...do...	26	Sept. 3, 1864	1 year.	Appointed June 1, 1865; mustered out with company June 24, 1865.
William Walters	Musician.	19	Sept. 8, 1864	1 year.	
Frank H. Dean	...do...	19	Sept. 2, 1864	1 year.	Mustered out with company June 24, 1865.
Adair, Robert	Private.	[illegible]	Sept. 19, 1864	1 year.	
Ault, Michael	...do...	[illegible]	Sept. 14, 1864	1 year.	
Barker, Charles	...do...	[illegible]	Sept. 14, 1864	1 year.	
Becker, Alvin E.	...do...	[illegible]	[illegible] 16, 1864	1 year.	Mustered out with company June 24, 1865.

Names.	Rank.	Age.	Date of Entering the Service.	Period of Service.	Remarks.
Bennett, James F	Private	23	Sept. 8, 1864	1 year.	Mustered out May 20, 1865, at [illegible] Tenn., by order of War Department.
Blackwell, William	...do...	26	Sept. 30, 1864	1 year.	
Brock, Alphonzo	...do...	19	Sept. 9, 1864	1 year.	Mustered out with company June 2[illegible], 18[illegible].
Bryan, James	...do...	36	Sept. 15, 1864	1 year.	Mustered out with company June 2[illegible], 18[illegible].
Burns, Patrick	...do...	35	Sept. 15, 1864	1 year.	
Chapman George F	...do...	18	Sept. 15, 1864	1 year.	Mustered out May 24, 1865, at Wilmington, N. C., by order of War Department.
Collins, Jerry	...do...	19	Sept. 16, 1864	1 year.	
Cole, Henry	...do...	21	Sept. 8, 1864	1 year.	
Dancer, George W	...do...	20	Sept. 22, 1864	1 year.	Mustered out with company June 24, 18[illegible].
Dayton, Morris	...do...	25	Sept. 12, 1864	1 year.	
Dillory, Joseph	...do...	42	Sept. 15, 1864	1 year.	Mustered out with company June 24, 18[illegible].
Dwyer, John H	...do...	24	Sept. 16, 1864	1 year.	
Earle, William	...do...	33	Sept. 22, 1864	1 year.	Mustered out with company June 24, 18[illegible].
Edwards, John	...do...	44	Sept. 15, 1864	1 year.	
Fadden, James	...do...	22	Sept. 21, 1864	1 year.	
Fairfax, Sidney	...do...	28	Sept. 22, 1864	1 year.	
Fay, Romanzo	...do...	18	Sept. 9, 1864	1 year.	Died March 4, 1865, in general hospital at [illegible]ville, Tenn.
Fisher, Lewis	...do...	23	Sept. 28, 1864	1 year.	Mustered out with company June 24, 18[illegible].
Funk, David	...do...	33	Sept. 26, 1864	1 year.	Mustered out June 19, 1865, at Camp Chase, O., by order of War Department.
Gill, Henry C	...do...	26	Aug. 25, 1864	1 year.	Mustered out with company June 24, 18[illegible].
Glasser, Theophilus	...do...	18	Sept. 10, 1864	1 year.	Reduced from Corporal —.
[illegible]ray, Hugh	...do...	36	Sept. 5, 1864	1 year.	Mustered out with company June 24, 18[illegible].
[illegible]reen, Simon	...do...	18	Sept. 12, 1864	1 year.	Mustered out with company June 24, 18[illegible].
Griffin, Clark C	...do...	18	Sept. 7, 1864	1 year.	Reduced from Corporal —, mustered out with company June 24, 1865.
Griswold, Russell E	...do...	19	Sept. 13, 1864	1 year.	Mustered out July 15, 1865, at Portsmouth Grove, R. I., by order of War Department.
Grogan, James	...do...	21	Sept. 16, 1864	1 year.	Mustered out June 12, 1865, at Portsmouth Grove, R. I., by order of War Department.
Grubb, Henry A.	...do...	27	Sept. 16, 1864	1 year.	Mustered out May 29, 1865, at Camp Dennison, O., by order of War Department.
Hackney, Joseph M	...do...	18	Sept. 2, 1864	1 year.	Mustered out March 17, 1865, by order of War Department.
Harris, Joseph K	...do...	34	Sept. 16, 1864	1 year.	Mustered out with company June 24, 18[illegible].
Harrington, Michael	...do...	19	Sept. 21, 1864	1 year.	
Hanvey, Robert E	...do...	22	Sept. 16, 1864	1 year.	
Hellmer, Hammond	...do...	21	Sept. 21, 1864	1 year.	Mustered out with company June 24, 18[illegible].
[illegible]		18	Sept. 19, 1864	1 year.	
[illegible]		25	Sept. 21, 1864	1 year.	Mustered out with company June 24, 18[illegible].
Hoskins, Julius	...do...	18	Aug. 25, 1864	1 year.	Mustered out June 7, 1865, at Washington, D. C., by order of War Department.
Hudson, John	...do...	27	Sept. 16, 1864	1 year.	Mustered out with company June 24, 18[illegible].
Huntington, Charles D	...do...	23	Sept. 22, 1864	1 year	
Jetts, Harris L	...do...	22	Sept. 23, 1864	1 year.	Mustered out to date June 24, 1865, by order of War Department.
Jones, Charles H	...do...	21	Sept. 9, 1864	1 year.	
Kelley, James	...do...	21	Sept. 16, 1864	1 year.	
Kelley, Francis	...do...	21	Sept. 21, 1864	1 year.	
Kihr, August	...do...	19	Sept. 17, 1864	1 year.	Died Dec. 12, 1864, in general hospital at Murfreesboro, Tenn.
Knight, James F	...do...	36	Sept. 22, 1864	1 year.	Discharged July 20, 1865, at [illegible] on Surgeon's certificate of disability.
Ludick, Charles A	...do...	38	Aug. 26, 1864	1 year.	Mustered out with company June 2[illegible]
McCurdy, Robert	...do...	26	Sept. 14, 1864	1 year.	
McClarin, Alfred H	...do...	19	Sept. 10, 1864	1 year.	Absent, sick in hospital, June [illegible], 1865, at Greensboro, N. C. No further record.
McLaughlin, John	...do...	21	Sept. 16, 1864	1 year.	Mustered out with company June 2[illegible]
McMichael, Samuel W	...do...	23	Sept. 2[illegible], 1864	1 year.	
Marsh, Shubael S	...do...	31	Sept. 2, 1864	1 year.	Mustered out with company June 2[illegible]
Martin, Robert	...do...	29	Sept. 21, 1864	1 year.	
Maxwell, Robert	...do...	18	Aug. 31, 1864	1 year.	Mustered out June 1, 1865, at Cleveland, O., by order of War Department.
Multer, John E	...do...	23	Aug. 25, 1864	1 year.	Died July 7, 1865, in hospital at [illegible], North Carolina.
O'Connor, Daniel	...do...	20	Oct. 12, 1864	1 year.	Transferred to Co. A, 181st O. V. I., [illegible] 1865.
Olcott, Abraham	...do...	21	Sept. 2, 1864	1 year.	Mustered out June 19, 1865, at David's Island, New York Harbor, by order of War Department.
Olcott, George H	...do...	26	Aug. 30, 1864	1 year.	Died April 19, 1865, in general hospital at David's Island, New York Harbor.
Onterkirk, Isaac	...do...	19	Aug. 31, 1864	1 year.	Mustered out with company June 2[illegible]
Packer, Arthur	...do...	26	Sept. 9, 1864	1 year.	
Peters, David	...do...	29	Sept. 16, 1864	1 year.	Mustered out June 10, 1865, at Washington, D. C., by order of War Department.
Ranney, Charles H	...do...	28	Sept. 21, 1864	1 year.	Reduced from Corporal [illegible]; mustered out with company June 24, 1865.
Reber, Jacob G	...do...	19	Sept. 22, 1864	1 year.	Died Feb. 15, 1865, in field hospital at Cape Fear River, N. C.
Riley, John	...do...	20	Sept. 15, 1864	1 year.	Mustered out with company June [illegible]
Root, Lemuel	...do...	40	Sept. 12, 1864	1 year.	Mustered out June 1, 1865, at Cleveland, O., by order of War Department.

Names.	Rank.	Age.	Date of Entering the Service.	Period of Service.	Remarks.
Roggen, Edward P.	Private.	18	Sept. 10, 1864	1 year.	Mustered out July 7, 1865, at Washington, D. C., by order of War Department.
Romara, Michael	do.	28	Sept. 22, 1864	1 year.	Mustered out with company June 21, 1865.
Rowley, Patrick	do.	34	Sept. 12, 1864	1 year.	Mustered out May 31, 1865, at David's Island, New York Harbor, by order of War Department.
Rymers, Henry W.	do.	24	Sept. 16, 1864	1 year.	Mustered out June 23, 1865, at Wilmington, N. C., by order of War Department.
Schneider, Jacob	do.	29	Sept. 23, 1864	1 year.	Mustered out with company June 21, 1865.
Scrivens, James	do.	20	Sept. 16, 1864	1 year.	Mustered out June 10, 1865, at Washington, D. C., by order of War Department.
Scott, James	do.	21	Sept. 21, 1864	1 year.	
Smith, Orsamus B.	do.	22	Sept. 16, 1864	1 year.	
Stearnes, Charles W.	do.	18	Sept. 21, 1864	1 year.	Died Feb. 7, 1865, in general hospital at Louisville, Ky.
Terry, Henry	do.	18	Sept. 7, 1864	1 year.	Mustered out with company June 21, 1865.
Throne, David	do.	19	Sept. 11, 1864	1 year.	Mustered out with company June 21, 1865.
Treep, Samuel	do.	34	Sept. 13, 1864	1 year.	Mustered out with company June 21, 1865.
Treep, Albert	do.	21	Sept. 17, 1864	1 year.	Transferred to Co. A, 181st O. V. I. June 15, 1865.
VanHolt, George	do.	21	Sept. 12, 1864	1 year.	
Waldo, James H.	do.	21	Sept. 12, 1864	1 year.	Mustered out with company June 21, 1865.
Warner, Hiram	do.	38	Aug. 25, 1864	1 year.	Mustered out with company June 21, 1865.
Williams, Henry W.	do.	22	Sept. 13, 1864	1 year.	
Wilson, William	do.	31	Sept. 13, 1864	1 year.	
Winn, Powhattan	do.	18	Sept. 9, 1864	1 year.	Mustered out July 2, 1865, at Troy, N. Y., by order of War Department.
Woodworth, Marcus M.	do.	21	Aug. 25, 1864	1 year.	Died March 4, 1865, in general hospital at Louisville, Ky.

COMPANY G.

Mustered in September [illegible] 1864, at Camp Cleveland, O., by [illegible] U. S. A. Mustered out June 2[illegible], 1865, at [illegible], N. C., by A. B. [illegible], Captain [illegible] O. V. I. and [illegible] Army Corps.

Names.	Rank.	Age.	Date of Entering the Service.	Period of Service.	Remarks.
William Vesy[illegible]	Captain	[illegible]	Sept. 27, 1864	1 year.	Transferred to Co. [illegible] June 22 [illegible]
[illegible]	[illegible]	[illegible]	[illegible]	[illegible]	[illegible]
Betz, John B.	[illegible]	[illegible]	[illegible]	[illegible]	[illegible] War Department.
[illegible]	[illegible]	[illegible]	[illegible]	[illegible]	[illegible]
Clark, Charles	do.	[illegible]	Aug. 2[illegible], 1864	1 year.	Mustered out with company June 2[illegible], 1865.
Clark, William	do.	[illegible]	Aug. 2[illegible], 1864	1 year.	
Cochran, Robert	do.	2[illegible]	Sept. [illegible], 1864	1 year.	Mustered out May [illegible], 1865, at Newbern, N. C., by order of War Department.
Cole, Amos H.	do.	[illegible]	Sept. [illegible], 1864	1 year.	Reduced from Corporal [illegible]; mustered out with company June 2[illegible], 1865.

Names.	Rank.		Date of Entering the Service.	Period of Service.
Conant, Elbert R	Private	31	Sept. 20, 1864	
Cowan, John C	...do...	18	July [illegible], 1864	1
Cramer, John T	...do...	23	Sept. 17, 1864	1
Dent, Henry	...do...	27	Aug. 30, 1864	1
Doyle, John	...do...	30	Sept. 5, 1864	1
Durose, James W	...do...	21	Sept. 6, 1864	1
Earue, Hiram F	...do...	19	Aug. 30, 1864	1
Farrington, John E	...do...	18	Aug. 31, 1864	1
Fish, Charles H	...do...	30	Sept. 27, 1864	1
Ford, Harvey	...do...	26	Sept. 3, 1864	1
Gaskill, Benjamin	...do...	43	Aug. 27, 1864	
Graham, William	...do...	21	Sept. 2, 1864	1 year.
Hadley, Andrew J	...do...	25	Aug. 27, 1864	1 year.
Harrison, Sylvester	...do...	22	Aug. 16, 1864	1 year.
Hatch, Amerious A	...do...	22	Aug. 29, 1864	1 year.
Hatch, Augustus J	...do...	19	Aug. 29, 1864	1 year.
Henning, John	...do...	23	Sept. 10, 1864	1 year.
Hitchcock, Henry V	...do...	25	Aug. 30, 1864	1 year.
Hoadly, John B	...do...	33	Sept. 10, 1864	1 year.
Hopkins, David H	...do...	26	Sept. 9, 1864	1 year.
Howard, Charles	...do...	23	Sept. 8, 1864	1 year.
Howes, James	...do...	28	Sept. 8, 1864	1 year.
Hutton, Mordecai Y	...do...	33	Aug. 24, 1864	1 year.
Johnston, Samuel G	...do...	21	Aug. 18, 1864	1 year.
Kennedy, Patrick	...do...	22	Sept. 15, 1864	1 year.
Lobdell, Dennis	...do...	18	Aug. 24, 1864	1 year.
McCoy, Amasa	...do...	18	Sept. 2, 1864	1 year.
McCreary, Edward D	...do...	20	Aug. 15, 1864	1 year.
Mason, James	...do...	21	Sept. 27, 1864	1 year.
Mason, Theodore R	...do...	28	Sept. 3, 1864	1 year.
Morrison, Charles J	...do.*	37	Aug. 16, 1864	1 year.
Mountain, Austin	...do...	19	Aug. 11, 1864	1 year.
Mountain, Hubbard	...do...	25	Aug. 11, 1864	1 year.
Mountain, Monroe	...do...	21	Aug. 11, 1864	1 year.
Mountain, Sylvester	...do...	27	Aug. 11, 1864	1 year.
Nettorfield, Joseph	...do...	18	July 26, 1864	1 year.
Newberry, Thomas	...do...	22	Sept. 2, 1864	1 year.
Nims, Julius K	...do...	18	Aug. 22, 1864	1 year.
Oak, Henry	...do...	22	Sept. 8, 1864	1 year.
O'Conner, James	...do...	22	Sept. 27, 1864	1 year.
Patterson, Robert D	...do...	37	Sept. 12, 1864	1 year.
Pelton, William S	...do...	20	Aug. 22, 1864	1 year.
Phelps, Ambrose	...do...	19	Sept. 11, 1864	1 year.
Queale, James	...do...	30	Aug. 23, 1864	1 year.
Rouse, Sylvester J	...do...	18	Aug. 16, 1864	1 year.
Russell, John	...do...	23	Sept. 11, 1864	1 year.
Sharen, David S	...do...	22	Aug. 26, 1864	1 year.
Sharp, John R	...do...	18	Aug. 20, 1864	1 year.
Shinn, Samuel A	...do...	38	Aug. 20, 1864	1 year.
Shumaker, Alford	...do...	19	Aug. 30, 1864	1 year.
Skinner, Edwin E	...do...	27	Sept. 10, 1864	1 year.
Smith, Albert C	...do...	29	Aug. 30, 1864	1 year.
Smith, Lyman F	...do...	18	Sept. 18, 1864	1 year.
Snyder, George	...do...	37	Sept. 5, 1864	1 year.
St. John, Clayton	...do...	27	Aug. 24, 1864	1 year.
Stow, Henry	...do...	20	Aug. 26, 1864	1 year.
Taft, Benjamin F	...do...	28	Aug. 25, 1864	1 year.
Taylor, Thomas J	...do...	23	Aug. 30, 1864	1 year.
Taylor, Walter C	...do...	33	Aug. 31, 1864	1 year.
Truman, Charles W	...do...	18	Sept. 5, 1864	1 year.
Vance, Wilson J.	...do...	19	Sept. 27, 1864	1 year.

Names.	Rank.	Age.	Date of Entering the Service.	Period of Service.	Remarks.
Wakefield, Burrett E.	Private	18	Aug. 25, 1864	1 year.	Mustered out to date June 24, 1865, by order of War Department.
Walker, Robert A.	do.	22	Sept. 5, 1864	1 year.	Mustered out June 3, 1865, at Trenton, N. J., by order of War Department.
Warren, Lafayette	do.	20	Aug. 24, 1864	1 year.	Reduced from Corporal Dec. 31, 1864; mustered out with company June 24, 1865.
Washington, John	do.	22	Aug. 20, 1864	1 year.	
Washington, Washington	do.	21	Aug. 20, 1864	1 year.	
Wilbirt, John D.	do.	24	Aug. 25, 1864	1 year.	Mustered out with company June 24, 1865.
Williams, John W.	do.	44	Aug. 19, 1864	1 year.	
Winchel, Edward	do.	22	Aug. 20, 1864	1 year.	Mustered out with company June 24, 1865.
Woodard, Joshua L.	do.	22	Sept. 2, 1864	1 year.	Promoted to Principal Musician Oct. 4, 1864.
Worley, Valentine	do.	20	Aug. 31, 1864	1 year.	Mustered out with company June 24, 1865.

COMPANY H.

Mustered in September 30, 1864, at Camp Cleveland, O., by Thomas Drummond, Captain 5th Cavalry, U. S. A. Mustered out June 24, 1865, at Greensboro, N. C., by A. B. Smith, Captain 100th O. V. I., and C. M. 23d Army Corps.

Names.	Rank.	Age.	Date of Entering the Service.	Period of Service.	Remarks.
Samuel J. Tracy	Captain.	29	July 27, 1864	1 year.	Mustered out with company June 24, 1865.
Edwin W. Poole	1st Lieut.	22	Aug. 27, 1864	1 year.	Mustered out with company June 24, 1865.
Balthaser R. Tremelin	2d Lieut.	31	Aug. 27, 1864	1 year.	Promoted from 1st Sergeant Sept. 24, 1864; mustered out June 28, 1865, at Columbus, O., by order of War Department.
Charles P. Townsend	1st Sergt.	32	Aug. 29, 1864	1 year.	Appointed from Sergeant Oct. 8, 1864; mustered out with company June 24, 1865.
Jarvin M. Holcomb	Sergeant.	22	Aug. 24, 1864	1 year.	Mustered out with company June 24, 1865.
Nathan S. Brittan	do.	33	Aug. 28, 1864	1 year.	Mustered out with company June 24, 1865.
Robert L. Andrew	do.	21	Aug. 25, 1864	1 year.	Mustered out with company June 24, 1865.
Evelyn A. Parmlee	do.	21	Aug. 23, 1864	1 year.	Appointed from Corporal Oct. 8, 1864; mustered out June 3, 1865, at Washington, D. C., by order of War Department.
Henry H. Scott	Corporal.	23	Aug. 23, 1864	1 year.	Mustered out with company June 24, 1865.
Orson H. Buck	do.	24	Aug. 29, 1864	1 year.	Died April 29, 1865, in hospital.
Andrew J. Lamb	do.	22	Sept. 1, 1864	1 year.	Mustered out with company June 24, 1865.
John H. Best	do.	21	Aug. 25, 1864	1 year.	Mustered out with company June 24, 1865.
Wilber F. Upson	do.	20	Aug. 26, 1864	1 year.	Mustered out May 31, 1865, at Camp Dennison, O., by order of War Department.
Chauncey B. Lane	do.	20	Aug. 23, 1864	1 year.	Mustered out with company June 24, 1865.
Ebenezer J. Baird	do.	23	Sept. 3, 1864	1 year.	Appointed Oct. 8, 1864; mustered out with company June 24, 1865.
John R. Moore	do.	27	Sept. 26, 1864	1 year.	Wounded in head by shell Dec. 7, 1864, and appointed Corporal same day; mustered out with company June 24, 1865.
Kenneth F. Davidson	do.	31	Aug. 31, 1864	1 year.	Appointed April 30, 1865; mustered out with company June 24, 1865.
William H. Avery	do.	19	Sept. 3, 1864	1 year.	Appointed June 1, 1865; mustered out with company June 24, 1865.
Jeremiah V. Crall	Musician	35	Aug. 30, 1864	1 year.	Mustered out with company June 24, 1865.
Richard R. Redfield	do.	28	Aug. 23, 1864	1 year.	Mustered out with company June 24, 1865.
Andrew, Angelo	Private	18	Aug. 26, 1864	1 year.	Mustered out with company June 24, 1865.
Barnett, Jacob T.	do.	18	Aug. 28, 1864	1 year.	Mustered out with company June 24, 1865.
Barr, James E.	do.	44	Aug. 31, 1864	1 year.	Died May 16, 1865, at Jacksonville, Fla.
Barrett, George W.	do.	18	Aug. 29, 1864	1 year.	Died March 22, 1865, at Wilmington, N. C.
Beckley, Charles S.	do.	25	Aug. 27, 1864	1 year.	Mustered out with company June 24, 1865.
Beldin, Frederick E.	do.	24	Aug. 25, 1864	1 year.	Mustered out with company June 24, 1865.
Bently, Martin C.	do.	20	Aug. 29, 1864	1 year.	Mustered out with company June 24, 1865.
Bissell, Henry A.	do.	19	Aug. 24, 1864	1 year.	Mustered out with company June 24, 1865.
Blackwood, George C.	do.	23	Oct. 7, 1864	1 year.	Mustered out May 26, 1865, at Columbus, O., by order of War Department.
Bolles, William	do.	18	Sept. 1, 1864	1 year.	Mustered out with company June 24, 1865.
[illegible], David	do.	36	Sept. 6, 1864	1 year.	Died April 10, 1865, on board hospital transport Ben Deford, en-route from Morehead City, N. C., to New York City.
Boothe, John H.	do.	18	Aug. 24, 1864	1 year.	Mustered out with company June 24, 1865.
[illegible], John	do.	18	Sept. 1, 1864	1 year.	Mustered out with company June 24, 1865.
[illegible], Reynolds	do.	19	Oct. 3, 1864	1 year.	Transferred to Co. A, 181st O. V. I., June 15, 1865.
[illegible], Andrew H.	do.	22	Aug. 22, 1864	1 year.	Mustered out with company June 24, 1865.
[illegible]	do.	23	Aug. 30, 1864	1 year.	
[illegible]	do.	21	Sept. 3, 1864	1 year.	Mustered out June 17, 1865, at David's Island, New York Harbor, by order of War Department.
Carter, John E.	do.	20	Aug. 26, 1864	1 year.	Died March 15, 1865, in hospital at Wilmington, N. C.
Chamberlin, Walter G.	do.	18	Sept. 2, 1864	1 year.	Died Feb. 15, 1865, at Federal Point, N. C.
Chart, George	do.	23	Aug. 27, 1864	1 year.	Mustered out with company June 24, 1865.
Chart, John	do.	35	Aug. 29, 1864	1 year.	Mustered out June 5, 1865, at David's Island, New York Harbor, by order of War Department.

Names.	Rank.	Age.	Date of Entering the Service.	Period of Service.	Remarks.
Chase, Increase	Private	24	Aug. 29, 1864	1 year.	Mustered out with company June 24, 1865.
Chase, George	...do...	19	Aug. 29, 1864	1 year.	Mustered out with company June 24, 1865.
Churchill, Charles A	...do...	20	Sept. 3, 1864	1 year.	Mustered out with company June 24, 1865.
Clark, John	...do...	35	Sept. 7, 1864	3 yrs.	
Clark, Louis B	...do...	18	Sept. 3, 1864	1 year.	Mustered out June 16, 1865, at Albany, N. Y., by order of War Department.
Colvin, Almer H	...do...	37	Sept. 10, 1864	1 year.	Mustered out with company June 24, 1865.
Coy, Simon	...do...	42	Sept. 5, 1864	1 year.	Mustered out with company June 24, 1865.
Dalton, Richard	...do...	20	Sept. 1, 1864	1 year.	
Dotts, George H	...do...	28	Sept. 1, 1864	1 year.	Mustered out with company June 24, 1865.
Dustin, Harvey E	...do...	18	Aug. 29, 1864	1 year.	Mustered out with company June 24, 1865.
Faze, Charles N	...do...	21	Aug. 28, 1864	1 year.	Mustered out with company June 24, 1865.
Flohrs, William	...do...	24	Aug. 30, 1864	1 year.	Mustered out with company June 24, 1865.
Gallaspie, Louis	...do...	30	Sept. 9, 1864	1 year.	Mustered out with company June 24, 1865.
Garrett, James B	...do...	18	Aug. 27, 1864	1 year.	Mustered out with company June 24, 1865.
Gilbert, Thomas	...do...	18	Sept. 12, 1864	1 year.	Mustered out with company June 24, 1865.
Hall, Andrew J	...do...	27	Sept. 5, 1864	1 year.	Died Jan. 22, 1865, in hospital at Louisville, Kentucky.
Hall, John D	...do...	20	Aug. 27, 1864	1 year.	Mustered out with company June 24, 1865.
Halliwill, Absalom O	...do...	34	Aug. 29, 1864	1 year.	Mustered out with company June 24, 1865.
Harris, Julian C	...do...	18	Aug. 24, 1864	[illegible]	[illegible] company June 24, 1865.
Hewitt, Albert R	...do...	31	Aug. 27, 1864	[illegible]	[illegible] company June [illegible] 1865.
Hogue, Robert	...do...	38	Aug. 29, 1864	[illegible]	[illegible] e 20, 1865, at Philadelphia, Pa., by order of War Department.
Horton, Charles	...do...	27	Aug. 30, 1864	1 year.	
Jenkins, Edmund S	...do...	18	Sept. 3, 1864	1 year.	Mustered out with company June 24, 1865.
Johnson, Chipman R	...do...	23	Sept. 3, 1864	1 year.	Mustered out June 17, 1865, at Chester, Pa., by order of War Department.
Johnson, John W	...do...	27	Sept. 3, 1864	1 year.	Died Feb. 25, 1865, in hospital.
Johnson, Joseph P	...do...	43	Sept. 3, 1864	1 year.	Mustered out with company June 24, 1865.
Jones, William H	...do...	31	Oct. 5, 1864	1 year.	
Kirkham, Orville A	...do...	25	Aug. 30, 1864	1 year.	Reduced from Corporal Oct. 8, 1864; mustered out with company June 24, 1865.
Lamb, Orris P	...do...	28	Sept. 1, 1864	1 year.	Mustered out with company June 24, 1865.
Lapping, Windsor	...do...	18	Aug. 29, 1864	1 year.	Mustered out June 28, 1865, at Smithville, N. C., by order of War Department.
Lee, John S	...do...	18	Aug. 29, 1864	1 year.	Mustered out with company June 24, 1865.
Lockert, Lorain H	...do...	24	Aug. 29, 1864	1 year.	Mustered out June 15, 1865, at David's Island, New York Harbor, by order of War Department.
McCoy, Marcus H	...do...	26	Sept. 7, 1864	1 year.	Mustered out with company June 24, 1865.
McLoney, Luke	...do...	36	Sept. 3, 1864	1 year.	Mustered out July 12, 1865, at Columbus, O., by order of War Department.
Mann, George	...do...	19	Sept. 28, 1864	1 year.	Mustered out with company June 24, 1865.
Markham, Orin	...do...	29	Sept. 5, 1864	1 year.	Mustered out with company June 24, 1865.
Mead, John	...do...	18	Aug. 24, 1864	1 year.	Mustered out with company June 24, 1865.
Miller, James H	...do...	18	Jan. 31, 1865	1 year.	Transferred to Co. A, 181st O. V. I., [illegible] 1865.
Napp, Augustus	...do...	19	Aug. 29, 1864	1 year.	Died April 7, 1865, in hospital.
Palmer, Lewis L	...do...	21	Sept. 2, 1864	1 year.	Mustered out with company June 24, 1865.
Palmer, Emmet A	...do...	19	Jan. 31, 1865	1 year.	Transferred to Co. A, 181st O. V. I., [illegible] 1865.
Payne, Silas	...do...	25	Aug. 29, 1864	1 year.	Appointed Corporal Oct. 4, 1864; reduced [illegible] 6, 1864; mustered out with company June 24, 1865.
Peck, Hubert C	...do...	38	Aug. 27, 1864	1 year.	Mustered out with company June 24, 1865.
Peeples, Charles	...do...	23	Sept. 3, 1864	1 year.	Mustered out June 16, 1865, at Albany, N. Y., by order of War Department.
Reed, Oscar F	...do...	19	Aug. 29, 1864	1 year.	Mustered out with company June 24, 1865.
Robinson, Lester	...do...	18	Sept. 30, 1864	1 year.	Mustered out with company June 24, 1865.
Rourke, John	...do...	20	Sept. 8, 1864	1 year.	Mustered out with company June 24, 1865.
Shall, Eugene	...do...	19	Aug. 29, 1864	1 year.	Mustered out with company June 24, 1865.
Sherbondy, Nelson	...do...	19	Oct. 7, 1864	1 year.	Mustered out May 25, 1865, at Albany, N. Y., by order of War Department.
Sherman, William H	...do...	20	Sept. 3, 1864	1 year.	Mustered out with company June 24, 1865.
Stofer, Milton H	...do...	22	Sept. 3, 1864	1 year.	Mustered out with company June 24, 1865.
Strong, Nathan G	...do...	21	Sept. 10, 1864	1 year.	Mustered out with company June 24, 1865.
Taylor, [illegible] A	...do...	18	Sept. 29, 1864	1 year.	Mustered out with company June 24, 1865.
Thompson, Orlow	...do...	27	Aug. 29, 1864	1 year.	Mustered out with company June 24, 1865.
Treap, Christian	...do...	28	Sept. 6, 1864	1 year.	Mustered out July 6, 1865, at [illegible], by order of War Department.
Tucker, Aurelius	...do...	22	Aug. 25, 1864	1 year.	Mustered out June 3, 1865, at Washington, D. C., by order of War Department.
Turner, George L	...do...	33	Aug. 27, 1864	1 year.	Mustered out with company June 24, 1865.
Upson, Orville	...do...	21	Aug. 29, 1864	1 year.	Mustered out with company June 24, 1865.
Wait, Henry C	...do...	18	Aug. 23, 1864	1 year.	Mustered out with company June 24, 1865.
Waite, Seth A	...do...	38	Sept. 3, 1864	1 year.	Mustered out with company June 24, 1865.
Wallace, Joseph T	...do...	44	Sept. 2, 1864	1 year.	Mustered out with company June 24, 1865.
Wetmore, Edward	...do...	37	Sept. 1, 1864	1 year.	Mustered out with company June 24, 1865.
Wilson, John H	...do...	27	Sept. 1, 1864	1 year.	
Wright, Nelson	...do...	18	Aug. 23, 1864	1 year.	Mustered out with company June 24, 1865.

COMPANY I.

Mustered in October 3, 1864, at Camp Cleveland, O., by Thomas Drummond, Captain 5th Cavalry, U. S. A. Mustered out June 24, 1865, at Greensboro, N. C., by A. B. Smith, Captain 100th O. V. I., and C. M. 23d Army Corps.

Names.	Rank.	Age.	Date of Entering the Service.	Period of Service.	Remarks.
George B. Squire	Captain.	24	Sept. 27, 1862	3 yrs.	Promoted from Sergeant Co. C, 88th O. V. I., Sept. 30, 1864; mustered out with company June 24, 1865.
Theodore B. Wire	1st Lieut.	28	Sept. 30, 1864	1 year.	Promoted from private Co. A Sept. 30, 1864; mustered out with company June 24, 1865.
Silas H. Kent	2d Lieut.	32	Sept. 30, 1864	1 year.	Mustered out with company June 24, 1865.
George W. Bailey	1st Sergt.	30	Sept. 21, 1864	1 year.	Appointed from Sergeant ——; mustered out with company June 24, 1865.
Israel S. Mack	Sergeant.	38	Aug. 3, 1864	1 year.	Mustered out June 26, 1865, at Camp Dennison, O., by order of War Department.
Marcus E. Gregory	....do....	28	Sept. 4, 1864	1 year.	Mustered out with company June 24, 1865.
Ransom S. Krahl	....do....	22	Aug. 22, 1864	1 year.	Mustered out with company June 24, 1865.
Henry Strachle	....do....	27	Sept. 28, 1864	1 year.	Mustered as private; appointed Sergeant ——; mustered out with company June 24, 1865.
Abijah Cone	Corporal.	20	Aug. 13, 1864	1 year.	Mustered out June 7, 1865, at David's Island, New York Harbor, by order of War Department.
Edward H. Jones	....do....	28	Aug. 30, 1864	1 year.	Mustered out with company June 24, 1865.
Edwin H. Richmond	....do....	22	Sept. 12, 1864	1 year.	Mustered out with company June 24, 1865.
Charles Owen	....do....	29	Sept. 4, 1864	1 year.	Mustered out with company June 24, 1865.
Alfred W. Barnes	....do....	23	Sept. 6, 1864	1 year.	Mustered out July 11, 1865, at Portsmouth Grove, R. I., by order of War Department.
Romans Binkley	....do....	18	Sept. 15, 1864	1 year.	Appointed ——; mustered out with company June 24, 1865.
Jonathan W. Williams	....do....	28	Sept. 19, 1864	1 year.	Appointed ——; mustered out July 11, 1865, at Portsmouth Grove, R. I., by order of War Department.
Luther Morton	....do....	20	Oct. 3, 1864	1 year.	Appointed ——; transferred to Co. A, 181st O. V. I., June 15, 1865.
George Perkins	Musician	18	Sept. 6, 1864	1 year.	Mustered out with company June 24, 1865.
Emerson E. Brainard	....do....	26	Sept. 1, 1864	1 year.	Mustered out with company June 24, 1865.
Atkins, John	Private.	44	Sept. 3, 1864	1 year.	Mustered out May 31, 1865, at Camp Dennison, O., by order of War Department.
Baker, John R.	....do....	31	Aug. 25, 1864	1 year.	Mustered out June 30, 1865, at Baltimore, Md., by order of War Department.
Ball, George	....do....	24	Oct. 3, 1864	1 year.	
Binkley, Melanchthon	....do....	19	Sept. 15, 1864	1 year.	Mustered out with company June 24, 1865.
Birch, Jefferson	....do....	43	Sept. 13, 1864	1 year.	Mustered out June 2, 1865, at Washington, D. C., by order of War Department.
Black, Robert	....do....	18	Sept. 2, 1864	1 year.	Mustered out with company June 24, 1865.
Boday, Julius	....do....	24	Sept. 21, 1864	1 year.	Mustered out with company June 24, 1865.
Boday, Peter	....do....	19	Sept. 15, 1864	1 year.	Mustered out with company June 24, 1865.
Boyd, Hugh	....do....	33	Sept. 12, 1864	1 year.	Appointed Corporal ——; reduced Jan. 27, 1865; mustered out with company June 24, 1865.
Brown, Adelbert M	....do....	18	Aug. 27, 1864	1 year.	Mustered out with company June 24, 1865.
Brown, John T.	....do....	18	Sept. 21, 1864	1 year.	Mustered out with company June 24, 1865.
Brown, William R.	....do....	31	Sept. 16, 1864	1 year.	
Butler, Warren D	....do....	24	Sept. 3, 1864	1 year.	Mustered out with company June 24, 1865.
Byrnes, John	....do....	23	Sept. 17, 1864	1 year.	
Champlain, Lewis	....do....	18	Aug. 27, 1864	1 year.	Died April 4, 1865, at Willett's Point, N. Y.
Cochenspagger, David	....do....	32	Sept. 27, 1864	1 year.	Mustered out with company June 24, 1865.
Colwell, Albert	....do....	22	Sept. 12, 1864	1 year.	Reduced from Corporal Dec. 15, 1864; mustered out with company June 24, 1865.
Colwell, Lamar	....do....	18	Aug. 30, 1864	1 year.	Mustered out with company June 24, 1865.
Davis, William W.	....do....	25	Sept. 21, 1864	1 year.	
Donovan, John	....do....	20	Oct. 3, 1864	1 year.	
Falkner, William H	....do....	28	Sept. 27, 1864	1 year.	Mustered out with company June 24, 1865.
Fairchild, John	....do....	31	Sept. 2, 1864	1 year.	Mustered out May 17, 1865, at Washington, D. C., by order of War Department.
Ferrell, William	....do....	18	Sept. 13, 1864	1 year.	
Fenn, Martin V	....do....	32	Oct. 4, 1864	1 year.	Transferred to Co. A, 181st O. V. I., June 15, 1865.
Franklin, Daniel T	....do....	23	Sept. 3, 1864	1 year.	Mustered out with company June 24, 1865.
Groat, Simon	....do....	40	Oct. 1, 1864	1 year.	Mustered out with company June 24, 1865.
Grover, Justin L.	....do....	35	Sept. 1, 1864	1 year.	Died March 31, 1865, at Kinston, N. C.
Hardy, Edward	....do....	24	Aug. 30, 1864	1 year.	Mustered out with company June 24, 1865.
Hartnett, John	....do....	18	Sept. 2, 1864	1 year.	Mustered out with company June 24, 1865.
Harvey, George W	....do....	18	Sept. 5, 1864	1 year.	Died March 20, 1865, at Wilmington, N. C.
Hays, Charles N.	....do....	33	Sept. 13, 1864	1 year	Mustered out with company June 24, 1865.
Helmer, William H	....do....	19	Nov. 11, 1864	1 year.	
Higley, George G.	....do....	27	Sept. 19, 1864	1 year.	Died March 19, 1865, at Wilmington, N. C.
Huffman, Washington	....do....	30	Sept. 14, 1864	1 year.	Mustered out June 5, 1865, at David's Island, New York Harbor, by order of War Department.

Names.	Rank.	Age.	Date of Entering the Service.	Period of Service.	Remarks.
Irish, Chauncey	Private..	22	Sept. 27, 1864	1 year.	Mustered out May 29, 1865, at Camp Dennison, O., by order of War Department.
Irwin, John	....do....	48	Sept. 19, 1864	1 year.	Mustered out May 31, 1865, at David's Island, New York Harbor, by order of War Department.
Johnson, Myron	....do....	39	Sept. 4, 1864	1 year.	
Jones, Nelson A	....do....	18	Sept. 2, 1864	1 year.	Mustered out with company June 24, 1865.
Jordon, Maurice	....do....	39	Sept. 16, 1864	1 year.	
Kerby, Thomas	....do....	18	Sept. 6, 1864	1 year.	Mustered out with company June 24, 1865.
Keveny, Martin	....do....	44	Sept. 5, 1864	1 year.	Mustered out June 19, 1865, at Washington, D. C., by order of War Department.
Knox, Alanson	....do....	25	Aug. 25, 1864	1 year.	Transferred to Co. A, 181st O. V. I., June 5, 1865.
Lamunion, Charles A	....do....	34	Sept. 1, 1864	1 year.	Mustered out with company June 24, 1865.
Lane, Charles D	....do....	30	Sept. 19, 1864	1 year.	Reduced from Corporal ——; mustered out with company June 24, 1865.
Lane, John	....do....	26	Sept. 3, 1864	1 year.	
Lee, Julius A	....do....	23	Sept. 2, 1864	1 year.	Mustered out with company June 24, 1865.
Loomis, Charles F	....do....	18	Sept. 10, 1864	1 year.	Reduced to ranks from 1st Sergeant Dec. 8, 1864, at his own request; mustered out May 19, 1865, at Wilmington, N. C., by order of War Department.
Lott, George	....do....	18	Sept. 13, 1864	1 year.	Mustered out with company June 24, 1865.
Louden, Almon	....do....	18	Sept. 13, 1864	1 year.	Mustered out with company June 24, 1865.
Lutes, Samuel M	....do....	23	Sept. 13, 1864	1 year.	Mustered out May 30, 1865, at Camp Chase, O., by order of War Department.
Lyons, William	....do....	24	Sept. 16, 1864	1 year.	
Matthews, Lewis	....do....	16	Sept. 13, 1864	1 year.	Died Oct. 4, 1864, at Louisville, Ky.
Meek, John F	....do....	19	Sept. 19, 1864	1 year.	Mustered out with company June 24, 1865.
Mellin, Elial T	....do....	39	Sept. 13, 1864	1 year.	Mustered out with company June 24, 1865.
Miller, Charles	....do....	22	Sept. 13, 1864	1 year.	
Miller, Thadford	....do....	17	Sept. 3, 1864	1 year.	Mustered out with company June 24, 1865.
North, George W	....do....	18	Aug. 23, 1864	1 year.	Mustered out with company June 24, 1865.
Northrop, George W	....do....	20	Aug. 30, 1864	1 year.	Died Dec. 31, 1864, at Nashville, Tenn.
Osmond, Herbert	....do....	19	Sept. 1, 1864	1 year.	Mustered out with company June 24, 1865.
Overmire, Homer	....do....	19	Sept. 15, 1864	1 year.	Mustered out with company June 24, 1865.
Owen, Eugene	....do....	18	Aug. 29, 1864	1 year.	Mustered out June 6, 1865, at Louisville, Ky., by order of War Department.
Palmer, William H	....do....	38	Aug. 21, 1864	1 year.	Mustered out with company June 24, 1865.
Pomeroy, Ansel	....do....	30	Sept. 24, 1864	1 year.	Mustered out with company June 24, 1865.
Renny, John	....do....	28	Sept. 16, 1864	1 year.	
Riley, Michael	....do....	21	Sept. 2, 1864	1 year.	
Scott, Frederick T	....do....	26	Sept. 19, 1864	1 year.	
Sharp, Andrew L	....do....	22	Aug. 16, 1864	1 year.	Mustered out with company June 24, 1865.
Shorer, Frederick	....do....	18	Sept. 15, 1864	1 year.	Mustered out with company June 24, 1865.
Smith, Alexander F	....do....	18	Sept. 16, 1864	1 year.	Mustered out with company June 24, 1865.
Spring, Orville W	....do....	25	Sept. 19, 1864	1 year.	Mustered out with company June 24, 1865.
Stevenson, Clayton	....do....	18	Aug. 29, 1864	1 year.	Mustered out Aug. 7, 1865, at Cleveland, O., by order of War Department.
Stone, Warren S	....do....	29	Sept. 19, 1864	1 year.	
Talcott, Edwin M	....do....	24	Sept. 2, 1864	1 year.	Mustered out June 26, 1865, at Camp Dennison, O., by order of War Department.
Tatro, George	....do....	25	Sept. 10, 1864	1 year.	Died Jan. 10, 1865, at Murfreesboro, Tenn.
Thompson, Cyrus	....do....	21	Aug. 23, 1864	1 year.	Mustered out May 17, 1865, at Washington, D. C., by order of War Department.
Turner, Michael	....do....	21	Sept. 15, 1864	1 year.	
Tuttle, Austin	....do....	32	Sept. 10, 1864	1 year.	Mustered out with company June 24, 1865.
Van Gordet, John B	....do....	28	Sept. 3, 1864	1 year.	Mustered out with company June 24, 1865.
Wallace, George H	....do....	18	Aug. 18, 1864	1 year.	Mustered out May 17, 1865, at Washington, D. C., by order of War Department.
Ward, Henry	....do....	22	Sept. 12, 1865	1 year.	Reduced from Corporal March 18, 1865; mustered out with company June 24, 1865.
White, Thomas	....do....	28	Sept. 13, 1864	1 year.	
Wilder, Milton	....do....	30	Sept. 2, 1864	1 year.	Mustered out May 17, 1865, at Washington, D. C., by order of War Department.
Williams, James C	....do....	23	Sept. 13, 1864	1 year.	
Willison, Frederick	....do....	18	Sept. 21, 1864	1 year.	Mustered out with company June 24, 1865.
Wood, William T	....do....	20	Nov. 11, 1864	1 year.	Transferred to Co. A, 181st O. V. I., June 5, 1865.

COMPANY K.

[illegible]ered in October 4, 1864, at Camp Cleveland, O., by Charles C. Smith, Colonel 10th O. V. C. Mustered out June 24, 1865, at Greensboro, N. C., by A. B. Smith, Captain 100th O. V. I., and C. M. 23d Army Corps.

Names.	Rank.	Age.	Date of Entering the Service.	Period of Service.	Remarks.
...ow N. Spencer	Captain.	[illegible]	Oct. 3, 1864	1 year.	Mustered out with company June 24, 1865.
...el H. H. Wheaton	1st Lieut.	28	Oct. 3, 1864	1 year.	Mustered out with company June 24, 1865.
... Schramling	2d Lieut.	[illegible]	Oct. 3, 1864	1 year.	Mustered out with company June 24, 1865.
... Wintersteen	1st Sergt.	19	Aug. 29, 1864	1 year.	Mustered out with company June 24, 1865.
...d G. Sturgis	Sergeant.	19	Sept. 6, 1864	1 year.	Mustered out with company June 24, 1865.
...n C. Mastic	...do...	28	Sept. 8, 1864	1 year.	Mustered out with company June 24, 1865.
...um J. Slitor	...do...	26	Sept. 15, 1864	1 year.	Appointed from Corporal Feb. 1, 1865; mustered out with company June 24, 1865.
...b Van Slyke	...do...	27	Aug. 23, 1864	1 year.	Appointed from Corporal May 1, 1865; mustered out with company June 24, 1865.
...am N. Coleman	...do...	21	Sept. 6, 1864	1 year.	Died Dec. 1, 1864, at Nashville, Tenn.
...ert B. Fisher	...do...	24	Aug. 30, 1864	1 year.	Died April 28, 1865, at Louisville, Ky.
...m J. Brayman	Corporal.	37	Aug. 26, 1864	1 year.	Mustered out with company June 24, 1865.
...r T. Allen	...do...	21	Aug. 14, 1864	1 year.	Mustered out with company June 24, 1865.
... W. Sanford	...do...	22	Aug. 29, 1864	1 year.	Mustered out with company June 24, 1865.
...ncey W. Hopkins	...do...	22	Aug. 24, 1864	1 year.	Appointed ——; mustered out with company June 24, 1865.
... Pugsley	...do...	22	Aug. 7, 1864	1 year.	Appointed ——; mustered out with company June 24, 1865.
...ius M. Hurlburt	...do...	19	Aug. 24, 1864	1 year.	Appointed Feb. 1, 1865; mustered out with company June 24, 1865.
...llis Little	...do...	22	Aug. 27, 1864	1 year.	Appointed Feb. 28, 1865; mustered out with company June 24, 1865.
...ard M. Alden	...do...	21	Sept. 16, 1864	1 year.	Mustered out with company June 24, 1865.
...iam C. Hodges	Musician	33	Aug. 27, 1864	1 year.	Mustered out with company June 24, 1865.
...itt F. Witherell	...do...	21	Aug. 27, 1864	1 year.	Mustered out with company June 24, 1865.
..., Daniel	Private.	18	Sept. 26, 1864	1 year.	
...rre, Peter	...do...	18	Aug. 6, 1864	1 year.	Mustered out with company June 24, 1865.
...le, John	...do...	20	Sept. 20, 1864	1 year.	
...r, Newell	...do...	28	Sept. 7, 1864	1 year.	Died June 17, 1865, at Greensboro, N. C.
...holder, Charles W.	...do...	27	Sept. 21, 1864	1 year.	Mustered out with company June 24, 1865.
...her, Jerry	...do...	37	Aug. 29, 1864	1 year.	Mustered out with company June 24, 1865.
...ett, James H.	...do...	44	Aug. 25, 1864	1 year.	Mustered out with company June 24, 1865.
...h, Jacob	...do...	36	Aug. 24, 1864	1 year.	Mustered out with company June 24, 1865.
...ford, John J.	...do...	44	Sept. 20, 1864	1 year.	Mustered out with company June 24, 1865.
...h, Edwin S.	...do...	18	Aug. 23, 1864	1 year.	Mustered out with company June 24, 1865.
...er, George W.	...do...	28	Aug. 15, 1864	1 year.	Mustered out June 9, 1865, at Wheeling, W. Va., by order of War Department.
...ee, Peter, Jr.	...do...	18	Sept. 8, 1864	1 year.	Died March 21, 1865, at Wilmington, N. C.
...kett, Justus J.	...do...	27	Sept. 22, 1864	1 year.	Mustered out with company June 24, 1865.
...sley, Daniel	...do...	22	Sept. 5, 1864	1 year.	
...eld, Asa G.	...do...	18	Aug. 31, 1864	1 year.	Mustered out with company June 24, 1865.
...e, Emery A.	...do...	18	Sept. 16, 1864	1 year.	Mustered out with company June 24, 1865.
...e, Jacob	...do...	34	Aug. 23, 1864	1 year.	Mustered out June 14, 1865, at Columbus, O., by order of War Department.
...don, Michael	...do...	30	Aug. 29, 1864	1 year.	
...ow, George W.	...do...	18	Aug. 23, 1864	1 year.	
..., William H.	...do...	21	Aug. 24, 1864	1 year.	Reduced from Corporal ——; died June 20, 1865, in hospital at David's Island, New York Harbor.
...aite, Daniel H.	...do...	24	Aug. 29, 1864	1 year.	Reduced from Corporal ——; mustered out July 4, 1865, at Murfreesboro, Tenn., by order of War Department.
...ry, Cyrus	...do...	32	Aug. 23, 1864	1 year.	Mustered out June 20, 1865, at Washington, D. C., by order of War Department.
...t, Daniel G.	...do...	16	Sept. 20, 1864	1 year.	Died Dec. 13, 1864, at Murfreesboro, Tenn.
...s, George N.	...do...	33	Aug. 19, 1864	1 year.	Mustered out June 17, 1865, at David's Island, New York Harbor, by order of War Department.
...s, John	...do...	36	Aug. 19, 1864	1 year.	Died April 21, 1865, at Wilmington, N. C.
...s, Joseph H.	...do...	22	Aug. 25, 1864	1 year.	Mustered out with company June 24, 1865.
...er, Charles	...do...	27	Sept. 21, 1864	1 year.	
...immons, Charles	...do...	21	Sept. 21, 1864	1 year.	
...ow, Henry	...do...	25	Sept. 5, 1864	1 year.	
...er, Joel K.	...do...	34	Sept. 1, 1864	1 year.	Mustered out May 11, 1865, at Cincinnati, O., by order of War Department.
...ison, Franklin	...do...	23	Aug. 27, 1864	1 year.	Mustered out with company June 24, 1865.
...nore, Joseph	...do...	20	Sept. 1, 1864	1 year.	Died March 7, 1865, at Wilmington, N. C.
...rich, Cyrus	...do...	35	Sept. 5, 1864	1 year.	Mustered out with company June 24, 1865.
..., Nathan	...do...	36	Aug. 24, 1864	1 year.	Died Dec. 31, 1864, at Nashville, Tenn.
...s, Melvin J.	...do...	20	Aug. 29, 1864	1 year.	Mustered out with company June 24, 1865.
...son, Alfred C.	...do...	18	Sept. 19, 1864	1 year.	Died Jan. 31, 1865, at Nashville, Tenn.
...h, Amos	...do...	27	Aug. 22, 1864	1 year.	Mustered out with company June 24, 1865.
...deen, Monroe L.	...do...	[illegible]	Sept. 5, 1864	1 year.	Mustered out May 22, 1865, at Washington, D. C., by order of War Department.

Names.	Rank.	Age.	Date of Entering the Service.	Period of Service.	Remarks.
Hines, John	Private..	27	Aug. 25, 1864	1 year.	Mustered out July 15, 1865, at Portsmouth Grove, R. I., by order of War Department.
Hubbard, Truman J	....do....	37	Sept. 5, 1864	1 year.	Mustered out June 9, 1865, at Philadelphia, Pa., by order of War Department.
Hull, Cloud	....do....	22	Sept. 25, 1864	1 year.	Mustered out with company June 24, 1865.
Landon, Salmon J	....do....	42	Aug. 30, 1864	1 year.	Mustered out with company June 24, 1865.
Lillie, Albert G	....do....	18	Sept. 17, 1864	1 year.	Mustered out with company June 24, 1865.
Lisk, James S	....do....	25	Sept. 16, 1864	1 year.	
Luce, Benjamin M	....do....	31	Sept. 5, 1864	1 year.	Mustered out with company June 24, 1865.
McKee, Robert	....do....	43	Aug. 15, 1864	1 year.	Mustered out with company June 24, 1865.
Mathews, Charles W	....do....	20	Aug. 26, 1864	1 year.	Mustered out with company June 24, 1865.
Mattocks, James	....do....	18	Sept. 6, 1864	1 year.	Mustered out with company June 24, 1865.
Morse, Esquire	....do....	28	Aug. 30, 1864	1 year.	Mustered out with company June 24, 1865.
Morse, Lowell R	....do....	22	Aug. 26, 1864	1 year.	Mustered out with company June 24, 1865.
Murray, Alexander	....do....	36	Sept. 6, 1864	1 year.	Mustered out with company June 24, 1865.
Murray, Ephraim B	....do....	31	Aug. 24, 1864	1 year.	Mustered out June 14, 1865, at Columbus, O., by order of War Department.
Myers, John	....do....	39	Aug. 30, 1864	1 year.	Mustered out with company June 24, 1865.
Newell, Edgar F	....do....	18	Aug. 30, 1864	1 year.	Mustered out June 2, 1865, at Washington, D. C., by order of War Department; also borne on rolls as Elza F. Newell.
Parsons, Orrin H	....do....	18	Aug. 30, 1864	1 year.	Mustered out with company June 24, 1865.
Pelton, Harlow C	....do....	27	Aug. 30, 1864	1 year.	Mustered out Aug. 16, 1865, at Washington, D. C., by order of War Department.
Perkins, Zethan	....do....	18	Aug. 15, 1864	1 year.	Died Jan. 15, 1865, at Clifton, Tenn.
Pugsley, Samuel	....do....	18	Aug. 18, 1864	1 year.	Died March 13, 1865, at Wilmington, N. C.
Rasey, Charles W	....do....	25	Sept. 1, 1864	1 year.	Mustered out with company June 24, 1865.
Rockwell, Horace	....do....	31	Sept. 2, 1864	1 year.	Mustered out with company June 24, 1865.
Rood, George G	....do....	25	Aug. 31, 1864	1 year.	Mustered out with company June 24, 1865.
Rowans, Reuben	....do....	40	Sept. 5, 1864	1 year.	Mustered out with company June 24, 1865.
Russell, Almon P	....do....	26	Aug. 19, 1864	1 year.	Mustered out with company June 24, 1865.
Searles, Gilman	....do....	28	Aug. 23, 1864	1 year.	Mustered out with company June 24, 1865.
Sell, Michael	....do....	20	Aug. 30, 1864	1 year.	Died March 18, 1865, at Wilmington, N. C.
Shannon, James	....do....	22	Sept. 26, 1864	1 year.	
Shears, Adelbert D	....do....	18	Sept. 7, 1864	1 year.	Mustered out with company June 24, 1865.
Shears, Minard C	....do....	22	Aug. 23, 1864	1 year.	Died Jan. 6, 1865, at Murfreesboro, Tenn.
Sherman, James	....do....	22	Sept. 26, 1864	1 year.	
Simpson, Samuel	....do....	28	Sept. 3, 1864	1 year.	Mustered out with company June 24, 1865.
Smith, Warren	....do....	44	Sept. 19, 1864	1 year.	Mustered out with company June 24, 1865.
Sours, John	....do....	18	Aug. 15, 1864	1 year.	Died Feb. 27, 1865, at Smithville, N. C.
Taylor, Robert	....do....	22	Sept. 21, 1864	1 year.	
Warren, Cassius	....do....	20	Aug. 26, 1864	1 year.	Mustered out with company June 24, 1865.
West, Andrew	....do....	25	Sept. 21, 1864	1 year.	
Wiley, John J	....do....	26	Sept. 5, 1864	1 year.	
Williams, George (No. 1)	....do....	25	Sept. 21, 1864	1 year.	
Williams, George (No. 2)	....do....	21	Sept. 25, 1864	1 year.	
Williams, Solomon M	....do....	22	Aug. 30, 1864	1 year.	Mustered out with company June 24, 1865.
Williams, Thomas	....do....	25	Sept. 3, 1864	1 year.	Died Feb. 4, 1865, at Wheeling, W. Va.
Wintersteen, Charles H	....do....	18	Aug. 28, 1864	1 year.	Mustered out with company June 24, 1865.
Wright, Francis	....do....	26	Aug. 26, 1864	1 year.	Mustered out with company June 24, 1865.
Wright, Lampson	....do....	21	Sept. 3, 1864	1 year.	Mustered out with company June 24, 1865.

UNASSIGNED RECRUITS.

NOTE.—The following list of recruits is found on muster and descriptive rolls for this organization, but not borne on any of the company rolls of this Regiment:

Names.	Rank.	Age.	Date of Entering the Service.	Period of Service.	Remarks.
Barson, John D	Private..	22	Sept. 22, 1864	1 year.	
Bates, Isaac	....do....	27	Sept. 26, 1864	1 year.	
Bennett, Simon	....do....	26	Oct. 12, 1864	1 year.	Mustered out June 27, 1865, at Louisville, Ky., by order of War Department.
Bilsler, Joseph	....do....	38	Sept. 7, 1864	1 year.	
Blavis, Edwin C	....do....	35	Sept. 28, 1864	1 year.	
Boyle, Francis	....do....	21	Sept. 27, 1864	1 year.	
Burkhalter, John	....do....	23	Sept. 5, 1864	1 year.	
Caverly, Ira	....do....	36	Sept. 6, 1864	1 year.	
Chaney, James	....do....	28	Oct. 3, 1864	1 year.	
Cox, John C	....do....	19	Sept. 29, 1864	1 year.	
Crawford, Charles R	....do....	19	Sept. 29, 1864	1 year.	
Dempsey, Martin	....do....	25	Oct. 4, 1864	1 year.	
Frost, John	....do....	19	Sept. 27, 1864	1 year.	
Fuller, James F	....do....	38	Sept. 28, 1864	1 year.	
Green, Andrew J	....do....	20	Sept. 28, 1864	1 year.	
Green, James M	....do....	26	Sept. 28, 1864	1 year.	
Houdensfield, John	....do....	40	Sept. 5, 1864	1 year.	
Houdensfield, Jacob	....do....	32	Sept. 5, 1864	1 year.	
Hughes, Thomas	....do....	29	Sept. 27, 1864	1 year.	
Irwin, John	....do....	22	Sept. 27, 1864	1 year.	
Irwin, Edmond G	....do....	20	Oct. 4, 1864	1 year.	

Names.	Rank.	Age.	Date of Entering the Service.	Period of Service.	Remarks.
Jones, James A.	Private.	20	Sept. 21, 1864	1 year.	
Krause, Franklin	....do....	23	Sept. 26, 1864	1 year.	
Martz, Jacob	....do....	29	Sept. 5, 1864	1 year.	
Miller, James	....do....	39	Sept. 28, 1864	1 year.	
Murphy, Thomas	....do....	30	Sept. 29, 1864	1 year.	
Newcomb, Frederick	....do...	24	Sept. 3, 1864	1 year.	
O'Donnell, Robert	....do....	24	Sept. 29, 1864	1 year.	
Pier, Arthur H.	....do....	18	Feb. 16, 1865	1 year.	Mustered out June 17, 1865, at David's Island, New York Harbor, by order of War Department.
Poland, Nathaniel	....do....	18	Feb. 16, 1865	1 year.	Mustered out March 17, 1866, at Columbus, O., by order of War Department.
Reck, Clarence M.	....do....	19	Sept. 27, 1864	1 year.	
Rector, James C.	....do....	21	Sept. 21, 1864	1 year.	
Riley, James	....do....	19	Sept. 29, 1864	1 year.	
Shannon, William	....do....	30	Sept. 27, 1864	1 year.	
Smith, Dewitt C.	....do....	..	Feb. 16, 1865	1 year.	Mustered out July 5, 1865, at Washington, D. C., by order of War Department.
Smith, Peter	....do....	19	Sept. 29, 1864	1 year.	
Spencer, Louis	....do....	22	Sept. 26, 1864	1 year.	
Stephenson, Charles	....do....	20	Sept. 5, 1864	1 year.	
Sullivan, John	....do....	23	Sept. 29, 1864	1 year.	
Thurlow, James H.	....do....	29	Oct. 1, 1864	1 year.	
Waber, John W.	....do....	35	Sept. 5, 1864	1 year.	
Wright, Joseph J.	....do....	34	Oct. 7, 1864	1 year.	

178th Regiment Ohio Volunteer Infantry.

ONE YEAR'S SERVICE.

THIS Regiment was organized at Camp Chase, O., September 26, 1864, to serve one year, and was at once dispatched, by rail and river, to Nashville, with orders to report to Major General George H. Thomas for duty. The Regiment remained in Nashville some two weeks, performing guard duty, when it was sent to Tullahoma, Tenn., where it composed part of the post command. The post at Tullahoma was evacuated in the winter of 1864, and the One Hundred and Seventy-eighth was sent to Murfreesboro, where it remained during the siege. After the defeat of General Hood's army, at Nashville, the One Hundred and Seventy-eighth was ordered to North Carolina. It landed at Morehead City, N. C., with the Twenty-third Army Corps, and a few days thereafter participated in a skirmish with the enemy at Wise's Fork. After the surrender of Johnston's army, the Regiment was ordered to Charlotte, N. C., where it performed garrison duty, until mustered out of service June 29, 1865, in accordance with orders from the War Department.

178TH REGIMENT OHIO VOLUNTEER INFANTRY.

FIELD AND STAFF.

Mustered in September 26, 1864, at Camp Chase, O., by Lieutenant Small. Mustered out June 29, 1865, at Charlotte, N. C., by E. A. Folsom, Captain and A. C. M., Department of North Carolina.

Names.	Rank.	Age.	Date of Entering the Service.	Period of Service.	Remarks.
Joab A. Stafford	Colonel.	34	Sept. 26, 1864	1 year.	Mustered out with regiment June 29, 1865.
Aaron C. Johnson	Lt. Col.	43	Sept. 26, 1864	1 year.	Mustered out with regiment June 29, 1865.
John C. Hamilton	Major.	27	Sept. 26, 1864	1 year.	Mustered out with regiment June 29, 1865.
John Campbell	Surgeon.	39	Sept. 26, 1864	1 year.	Mustered out with regiment June 29, 1865.
Edwin Booth	Ast.Surg.	34	Sept. 26, 1864	1 year.	Mustered out with regiment June 29, 1865.
Robert Taylor	....do....	34	Sept. 27, 1864	1 year.	Mustered out with regiment June 29, 1865.
James L. Richardson	Adjutant	..	Sept. 27, 1864	1 year.	Resigned Nov. 29, 1864.
Joseph T. Jacobs	....do....	25	Sept. 21, 1864	1 year.	Appointed from 1st Lieutenant Co. A Jan. 1, 1865; mustered out with regiment June 29, 1865.
Henry C. Lillibridge	R. Q. M.	29	Sept. 26, 1864	1 year.	Mustered out with regiment June 29, 1865.
James Mitchell	Chaplain	43	Oct. 6, 1864	1 year.	Mustered out with regiment June 29, 1865.
John A. Boly	Sergt.Maj	22	Aug. 25, 1864	1 year.	Promoted from Sergeant Co. G Oct. 1, 1864; to 2d Lieutenant Co. A Feb. 10, 1865.
John McKinley	....do....	45	Sept. 7, 1864	1 year.	Promoted from Sergeant Co. B March 1, 1865; mustered out with regiment June 29, 1865.
John V. Morrison	Q. M. S.	28	Sept. 3, 1864	1 year.	Promoted from Sergeant Co. B Sept. 29, 1864; to 2d Lieutenant Co. C May 11, 1865.
John M. Todd	Com. Ser.	36	Sept. 10, 1864	1 year.	Promoted from private Co. H Oct. 4, 1864; mustered out June 17, 1865, at Columbus, O., by order of War Department.
William E. McDivitt	Hos. St'd.	28	Sept. 18, 1864	1 year.	Promoted from private Co. H Oct. 3, 1864; mustered out with regiment June 29, 1865.
Edward Plant	Prin.Mus	19	Aug. 9, 1864	1 year.	Promoted from private Co. C Oct. 7, 1864; reduced to Musician and returned to Co. C Feb. 16, 1865.
Frank Shepley	....do....	20	Aug. 13, 1864	1 year.	Promoted from private Co. D Jan. 1, 1865; mustered out with regiment June 29, 1865.
William Bauer	....do....	32	Sept. 12, 1864	1 year.	Promoted from Musician Co. F Jan. 1, 1865; mustered out with regiment June 29, 1865.

COMPANY A.

Mustered in September 26, 1864, at Camp Chase, O., by W. P. Richardson, Colonel 25th O. V. I. Mustered out June 29, 1865, at Charlotte, N. C., by E. A. Folsom, Captain and A. C. M., Department of North Carolina.

Names.	Rank.	Age.	Date of Entering the Service.	Period of Service.	Remarks.
George L. Wells	Captain.	28	Sept. 21, 1864	1 year.	Mustered out with company June 29, 1865.
Joseph T. Jacobs	1st Lieut.	25	Sept. 21, 1864	1 year.	Appointed Adjutant Jan. 1, 1865.
William E. Atwell	....do....	24	Sept. 21, 1864	1 year.	Promoted from 2d Lieutenant Feb. 10, 1865; mustered out with company June 29, 1865.
John A. Boly	2d Lieut.	22	Aug. 25, 1864	1 year.	Promoted from Sergt. Major Feb. 10, 1865; mustered out with company June 29, 1865.
Martin Suetser	1st Sergt.	20	Sept. 3, 1864	1 year.	Appointed from Sergeant Feb. 4, 1865; mustered out with company June 29, 1865.
Martin Pendergast	Sergeant.	27	Sept. 10, 1864	1 year.	Reduced from 1st Sergeant Feb. 4, 1865; mustered out with company June 29, 1865.
Francis Mulvany	....do....	18	Sept. 3, 1864	1 year.	Appointed from private Feb. 4, 1865; mustered out with company June 29, 1865.
Calvin W. Dush	....do....	22	Aug. 4, 1864	1 year.	Appointed from Corporal Feb. 4, 1865; mustered out with company June 29, 1865.
Henry H. Spence	....do....	25	Sept. 12, 1864	1 year.	Appointed from Corporal Feb. 4, 1865; mustered out with company June 29, 1865.
Gilman P. Woodworth	Corporal.	22	Sept. 9, 1864	1 year.	Appointed Sept. 22, 1864; mustered out June 19, 1865, at Camp Chase, O., by order of War Department.
George S. Wilson	....do....	19	Sept. 5, 1864	1 year.	Appointed Feb. 4, 1865; mustered out June 20, 1865, at Columbus, O., by order of War Department.

Names.	Rank.	Age.	Date of Entering the Service.	Period of Service.	Remarks.
John Barnell	Corporal.	36	Sept. 19, 1864	1 year.	Appointed Oct. 10, 1864; mustered out with company June 29, 1865.
William Seacord	...do...	22	Aug. 29, 1864	1 year.	Appointed Feb. 4, 1865; mustered out with company June 29, 1865.
Hugh V. Hughes	...do...	37	Sept. 9, 1864	1 year.	Appointed Feb. 4, 1865; mustered out June 20, 1865, at Columbus, O., by order of War Department.
Sanford Smith	...do...	23	Sept. 19, 1864	1 year.	Appointed Feb. 4, 1865; mustered out with company June 29, 1865.
Robert J. Magill	...do...	19	Sept. 12, 1864	1 year.	Appointed April 2, 1865; mustered out with company June 29, 1865.
John McCrary	...do...	20	Sept. 6, 1864	1 year.	Appointed Feb. 4, company June 29,
John F. Heely	...do...	38	Sept. 3, 1864	1 year.	Mustered out May 26, 1865, at Columbus, O., by order of War Department.
Palm Amick	Musician	16	Sept. 13, 1864	1 year.	Mustered ith company June 29, 1865.
John P. Laird	...do...	24	Sept. 3, 1864	1 year.	Mustered out with company June 29, 1865.
Albright, Thomas	Private..	27	Sept. 20, 1864	1 year.	
Anders, Charles J.	...do...	17	Aug. 31, 1864	1 year.	Mustered out with company June 29, 1865.
Anders, James E.	...do...	28	Aug. 31, 1864	1 year.	Mustered out with company June 29, 1865.
Armstrong, George	...do...	42	Sept. 1, 1864	1 year.	Mustered out with company June 29, 1865.
Arter, Alva B.	...do...	38	Sept. 3, 1864	1 year.	Reduced from Corporal Feb. 4, 1865; mustered out with company June 29, 1865.
Atwell, Eden	...do...	21	Sept. 5, 1864	1 year.	Reduced from Sergeant Feb. 4, 1865; mustered out with company June 29, 1865.
Backus, Joseph	...do...	24	Sept. 8, 1864	1 year.	Mustered out with company June 29, 1865.
Bernard, Henry	...do...	25	Sept. 27, 1864	1 year.	
Bond James	...do...	23	Sept. 27, 1864	1 year.	
Bowen, Andrew	...do...	26	Sept. 27, 1864	1 year.	
Boyer, Percival S.	...do...	38	Sept. 3, 1864	1 year.	Mustered out with company June 29, 1865.
Brooks, Cyrus	...do...	19	Sept. 9, 1864	1 year.	Mustered out with company June 29, 1865.
Brownscombe WilliamH	...do...	22	Sept. 6, 1864	1 year.	Mustered out with company June 29, 1865.
Buskirk Rufus V.	...do...	33	Sept. 6, 1864	1 year.	
Davis, Robert	...do...	22	Sept. 9, 1864	1 year.	
Dorr, Amos W.	...do...	22	Aug. 11, 1864	1 year.	Mustered out with company June 29, 1865.
Erow, Jacob	...do...	24	Aug. 23, 1864	1 year.	Mustered out with company June 29, 1865.
Grandstaff, Joseph M.	...do...	18	Sept. 19, 1864	1 year.	Mustered out with company June 29, 1865.
Grice, John N.	...do...	30	Aug. 18, 1864	1 year.	Mustered out with company June 29, 1865.
Griffin Charles	...do...	22	Sept. 3, 1864	1 year.	Mustered out with company June 29, 1865.
Hall, Ace	...do...	25	Aug. 26, 1864	1 year.	Mustered out with company June 29, 1865.
Harris, John	...do...	19	Sept. 27, 1864	1 year.	
Harrington, Dayton	...do...	23	Sept. 5, 1864	1 year.	Mustered out with company June 29, 1865.
Harding, Charles	...do...	18	Sept. 28, 1864	1 year.	Died Jan. 13, 1865, at Columbia, Tenn.
Heamington, Murray B.	...do...	25	Sept. 6, 1864	1 year.	Reduced from Corporal Oct. 10, 1864; mustered out June 14, 1865, at Columbus, O., by order of War Department.
Hofferd, John	...do...	22	Aug. 30, 1864	1 year.	Mustered out with company June 29, 1865.
Hobar, David R.	...do...	18	Sept. 10, 1864	1 year.	Died Dec. 1, 1864, at Murfreesboro, Tenn.
Jefferson, Thomas	...do...	22	Sept. 20, 1864	1 year.	
Johnson, William	...do...	26	Aug. 31, 1864	1 year.	
Kent, David H.	...do...	18	Sept. 5, 1864	1 year.	Mustered out May 25, 1865, at Louisville, Ky., by order of War Department.
King, Samuel	...do...	18	Aug. 3, 1864	1 year.	Mustered out with company June 29, 1865.
Kingston, Christopher	...do...	26	Aug. 31, 1864	1 year.	Mustered out June 2, 1865, at Camp Dennison, O., by order of War Department.
Lantz, Henry R.	...do...	26	Sept. 19, 1864	1 year.	Mustered out with company June 29, 1865.
Lantz, Benjamin F.	...do...	25	Aug. 12, 1864	1 year.	Reduced from Sergeant Feb. 4, 1865; mustered out with company June 29, 1865.
Lane, Charles G.	...do...	22	Sept. 9, 1864	1 year.	Mustered out with company June 29, 1865.
Larson, John	...do...	19	Sept. 21, 1864	1 year.	Mustered out with company June 29, 1865.
Laughery Edward B.	...do...	25	Aug. 24, 1864	1 year.	Mustered out with company June 29, 1865.
Lee, William W.	...do...	18	Sept. 9, 1864	1 year.	Mustered out with company June 29, 1865.
Leonard, Benjamin F.	...do...	38	Sept. 5, 1864	1 year.	
McDaniel, James L.	...do...	23	Sept. 8, 1864	1 year.	Mustered out June 2, 1865, at Camp Dennison, O., by order of War Department.
McNeal, James	...do...	19	Sept. 21, 1864	1 year.	Mustered out with company June 29, 1865.
Martin, James M.	...do...	27	Sept. 12, 1864	1 year.	On muster-in roll. No further record found.
Mitchell, James H.	...do...	38	Sept. 6, 1864	1 year.	Mustered out with company June 29, 1865.
Mitchell, Mack	...do...	23	Aug. 18, 1864	1 year.	Mustered out with company June 29, 1865.
Monkler, Edward	...do...	37	Sept. 9, 1864	1 year.	Killed May 1, 1865, at Raleigh, N. C., by musket shot.
Moore, Scott E.	...do...	28	Sept. 7, 1864	1 year.	Mustered out with company June 29, 1865.
Norton, James	...do...	21	Sept. 1, 1864	1 year.	Mustered out May 27, 1865, at McDougall Hospital, New York Harbor, by order of War Department.
Orndoff, John W.	...do...	21	Aug. 22, 1864	1 year.	Reduced from Corporal Feb. 4, 1865; transferred to Co. E, 181st O. V. I., June 15, 1865.
Peck, Almerin	...do...	21	Sept. 5, 1864	1 year.	Mustered out with company June 29, 1865.
Peck, Henry H.	...do...	22	Sept. 2, 1864	1 year.	Mustered out with company June 29, 1865.
Perry, John W.	...do...	21	Sept. 17, 1864	1 year.	Mustered out with company June 29, 1865.
Pickard, Lafayette	...do...	22	Sept. 3, 1864	1 year.	Appointed Corporal ——; reduced Feb. 4, 1865; mustered out with company June 29, 1865.
Pontzer, George	...do...	25	Sept. 7, 1864	1 year.	Mustered out with company June 29, 1865.
Proctor, Ethelbert	...do...	18	Sept. 17, 1864	1 year.	Mustered out with company June 29, 1865.

Names.	Rank.	Age.	Date of Entering the Service.	Period of Service.	Remarks.
Pursell, Joseph W	Private	22	Sept. 12, 1864	1 year.	Reduced from Sergeant Feb. 4, 1865; mustered out with company June 29, 1865.
Rankin, Abraham J	...do...	22	Sept. 1, 1864	1 year.	Mustered out with company June 29, 1865.
[illegible], William P	...do...	19	Sept. 7, 1864	1 year.	Mustered out with company June 29, 1865.
[illegible], John	...do...	18	Sept. 8, 1864	1 year.	Transferred to Co. E, 181st O. V. I., June 15, 1865.
Richards, John	...do...	22	Aug. 22, 1864	1 year.	Mustered out with company June 29, 1865.
Richards, Wesley	...do...	36	Sept. 6, 1864	1 year.	Mustered out with company June 29, 1865.
[illegible], Elijah	...do...	29	Aug. 22, 1864	1 year.	Discharged May 26, 1865, at Louisville, Ky., on Surgeon's certificate of disability.
Scott, Alexander	...do...	26	Aug. 17, 1864	1 year.	Died Jan. 31, 1865, in hospital at Camp Dennison, O.
[illegible], John	...do...	40	Sept. 29, 1864	1 year.	Mustered out with company June 29, 1865.
Swartz, Charles	...do...	22	Sept. 30, 1864	1 year.	Mustered out with company June 29, 1865.
[illegible], George W	...do...	23	Sept. 6, 1864	1 year.	Mustered out with company June 29, 1865.
Smith Charles	...do...	19	Aug. 30, 1864	1 year.	
Spaulding, James W	...do...	32	Sept. 10, 1864	1 year.	
[illegible], William H	...do...	20	Sept. 20, 1864	1 year.	Mustered out June 2, 1865, at Washington, D. C., by order of War Department.
Story, Lafayette	...do...	22	Sept. 1, 1864	1 year.	Mustered as Corporal; mustered out June 2, 1865, at Camp Dennison, O., by order of War Department.
Sweeny, Charles	...do...	26	Sept. 27, 1864	1 year.	
Tharp, William	...do...	30	Sept. 25, 1864	1 year.	Mustered out July 26, 1865, at Newark, N. J., by order of War Department.
Thuma, William H	...do...	18	Sept. 6, 1864	1 year.	Mustered out with company June 29, 1865.
[illegible], John	...do...	23	Aug. 23, 1864	1 year.	Mustered out with company June 29, 1865.
Upbold, William	...do...	37	Sept. 3, 1864	1 year.	Mustered out with company June 29, 1865.
Valentine, Charles	...do...	18	Sept. 5, 1864	1 year.	Mustered out with company June 29, 1865.
Wagner, Louis	...do...	28	Aug. 23, 1864	1 year.	Mustered out May 24, 1865, at McDougall Hospital, New York Harbor, by order of War Department.
Wald, Richard A	...do...	22	Aug. 18, 1864	1 year.	Mustered out with company June 29, 1865.
Wald, Zephaniah	...do...	29	Aug. 18, 1864	1 year.	Mustered out with company June 29, 1865.
Wallis, Sweeney L	...do...	22	Sept. 12, 1864	1 year.	
Walker, Solomon	...do...	31	Aug. 22, 1864	1 year.	Reduced from Corporal April 2, 1865; mustered out with company June 29, 1865.
Williams, Charles	...do...	22	Sept. 5, 1864	1 year.	Mustered out with company June 29, 1865.
Williamson, Marquis	...do...	40	Sept. 6, 1864	1 year.	Reduced from Corporal Feb. 4, 1865; mustered out with company June 29, 1865.
Zippery, William H	...do...	24	Sept. 3, 1864	1 year.	

COMPANY B.

Mustered in September 22, 1864, at Camp Chase, O., by W. P. Richardson, Colonel 25th O. V. I. Mustered out June 29, 1865, at Charlotte, N. C., by E. A. Folsom Captain and A. C. M., Department of North Carolina.

Names.	Rank.	Age.	Date of Entering the Service.	Period of Service.	Remarks.
John B. Slade	Captain.	..	Sept. 23, 1864	1 year.	Mustered out with company June 29, 1865.
Charles A. Poland	1st Lieut.	..	Sept. 2, 1864	1 year.	Promoted from private Sept. 23, 1864; Act. Regt. Quartermaster since Dec. 24, 1864; mustered out with company June 29, 1865.
William P. Shrom	2d Lieut.	..	Aug. 26, 1864	1 year.	Promoted from private Sept. 23, 1864; mustered out with company June 29, 1865.
Thomas W. Hedges	1st Sergt.	28	Sept. 3, 1864	1 year.	Appointed Sept. 23, 1864; died Feb. 1, 1865, in hospital at Camp Dennison, O.
Thomas A. Fritter	...do...	36	Sept. 13, 1864	1 year.	Appointed Sergeant Sept. 23, 1864; 1st Sergeant Feb. 1, 1865; mustered out with company June 29, 1865.
Marsden H. Sammis	Sergeant.	20	Aug. 26, 1864	1 year.	Appointed Sept. 23, 1864; mustered out with company June 29, 1865.
William McCaffrey	...do...	44	Sept. 19, 1864	1 year.	Appointed Corporal Oct. 31, 1864; Sergeant Jan. 23, 1865; mustered out with company June 29, 1865.
John R. [illegible]	...do...	23	Sept. 7, 1864	1 year.	
Thomas W. Griffith	...do...	24	Sept. 3, 1864	1 year.	Appointed Sept. 23, 1864; Sergeant Sept. 29, 1864; died Jan. 23, 1865, at Louisville, Ky.
John V. Morrison	...do...	28	Sept. 3, 1864	1 year.	Appointed Sept. 23, 1864; promoted to Q. M. Sergeant Sept. 29, 1864.
John Herdline	...do...	20	Sept. 3, 1864	1 year.	Appointed Corporal Sept. 23, 1864; Sergeant March 1, 1865; mustered out with company June 29, 1865.
....	...do...	45	Sept. 7, 1864	1 year.	Appointed Sept. 26, 1864; promoted to Sergt. Major March 1, 1865.
....	...do...	[illegible]	Sept. 6, 1864	1 year.	Appointed Corporal Sept. 23, 1864; Sergeant Jan. 23, 1865; mustered out June 5, 1865, at Columbus, O., by order of War Department.
Thaddeus A. Scheffler	Corporal.	[illegible]	Sept. 9, 1864	1 year.	Appointed Jan. 23, 1865; mustered out June 19, 1865, at Columbus, O., by order of War Department.

Names.	Rank.	Age.	Date of Entering the Service.	Period of Service.	
Thomas Jones	Corporal.	42	Sept. 17, 1864	1 year.	
Charles Steinmetz	...do...	20	Sept. 8, 1864	1 year.	App co
Jacob Bowers	...do...	21	Sept. 13, 1864	1 year.	App '7 W
Ervin Foltz	...do...	22	Sept. 17, 1864	1 year.	App ho
Francis M. Stanfield	...do...	23	Sept. 13, 1864	1 year.	App 18 De
John H. Smith	...do...	23	Sept. 8, 1864	year.	App co
Lewis D. Spangler	...do...	32	Sept. 15, 1864	year.	App co
John Beitle	...do...	21	Sept. 7, 1864		App co
Solomon S. Lehman	...do...	22	Sept. 17, 1864		App co
Adams, James O	Private.	18	Sept. 13, 1864		Mus da
Adams, George W	...do...	18	Sept. 13, 1864		Mus
Allen, Mitchell S	...do...	18	Sept. 12, 1864		Mus
Bailey, Rufus W	...do...	42	Sept. 12, 1864		Mus by
Barkman, David	...do...	25	Sept. 14, 1864	1	
Baughman, John	...do...	25	Sept. 15, 1864	1	
Bishop, John W.	...do...	21	Sept. 13, 1864	1	Mus
Bishop, Isaac H	...do...	18	Sept. 17, 1864	1	Mus
Bolen, John H	...do...	24	Aug. 31, 1864	1	Died
Botkin, Lycurgus	...do...	20	Sept. 5, 1864	1	Mus C.,
Bowers, John W	...do...	23	Sept. 13, 1864	1	Mus
Brown, James H	...do...	29	Sept. 17, 1864	1	
Brown, Frederick W	...do...	18	Sept. 28, 1864	1	
Brown, John	...do...	23	Sept. 15, 1864	1	
Byram, Algernon T	...do...	32	Sept. 17, 1864	1	
Casey, John B.	...do...	33	Sept. 21, 1864	1	
Cheeseman, William	...do...	20	Sept. 8, 1864	1	
Connell, Dennis	...do...	22	Sept. 5, 1864	1	
Collins, Robert	...do...	22	Sept. 13, 1864	1	
Cramsey, Harry	...do...	19	Sept. 15, 1864	1	
Croft, George	...do...	22	Sept. 9, 1864	1	
Cunningham, John T	...do...	21	Sept. 15, 1864	1	
Cutmore, William	...do...	19	Sept. 18, 1864	1	
Davis, Robert	...do...	22	Sept. 13, 1864	1	
De Largey, John	...do...	22	July 30, 1864	1	
Dunn, Charles	...do...	32	Sept. 10, 1864	1 year.	
Dunlap, Peter.	...do...	23	Sept. 14, 1864	1 year.	
Edwards, William H	...do...	41	Sept. 12, 1864	1 year.	
Ellis, George R	...do...	27	Sept. 10, 1864	1	
Evans, John	...do...	43	Sept. 12, 1864	1	
Flynn, James	...do...	23	Sept. 15, 1864	1	
Graham, John	...do...	22	Aug. 26, 1864	1	
Green, Ira	...do...	45	Sept. 16, 1864		
Hacket, David	...do...	25	Sept. 16, 1864	1 year.	
Hangs, John D	...do...	35	Sept. 19, 1864		
Harwood, Henry	...do...	21	Sept. 12, 1864		
Harrison, Charles E	...do...	18	Sept. 13, 1864		Mus O.,
Harris, James E	...do...	19	Sept. 5, 1864	1 year.	Mus by
Harpet, William	...do...	35	Sept. 16, 1864		Mus
Hoskins, Ebenezer	...do...	28	Sept. 16, 1864		
Huston, Leonard	...do...	25	Sept. 17, 1864		
Huggett, Robert	...do...	20	Sept. 8, 1864		
Hyatt, Hervey B	...do...	18	Sept. 26, 1864		
Jerman, Thomas	...do...	20	Sept. 3, 1864	1	
Johnson, William	...do...	23	Sept. 12, 1864	1	
Kelley, Edward	...do...	23	Sept. 8, 1864	1	
Leach, William N.	...do...	18	Sept. 3, 1864	1	Mus
Lester, Stephen A	...do...	18	Sept. 10, 1864	1	Mus
McCarty, Eugene	...do...	19	Sept. 5, 1864	1	Mus by
Matthews, Garrett	...do...	18	Sept. 8, 1864		Mus
Mayhew, George	...do...	38	Sept. 17, 1864		Mus
Miller, Jackson	...do...	20	Sept. 13, 1864		

Names.	Rank.	Age.	Date of Entering the Service.	Period of Service.	Remarks.
Miller, Stephen J.	Private.	18	Sept. 13, 1864	1 year.	Mustered out June 20, 1865, at Annapolis, Md., by order of War Department.
Monroe, James	...do...	27	Sept. 7, 1864	1 year.	
Morrison, Thomas E.	...do...	44	Sept. 27, 1864	1 year.	Mustered out to date June 29, 1865, by order of War Department.
O'Donnell, Morris	...do...	28	Sept. 24, 1864	1 year.	Mustered out with company June 29, 1865.
O'Neil, John H.	...do...	18	Sept. 22, 1864	1 year.	Mustered out with company June 29, 1865.
Pangborn, Charles E.	...do...	28	Sept. 13, 1864	1 year.	Died March 21, 1865, in hospital at Camp Chase, Ohio.
Powell, George	...do...	18	Sept. 9, 1864	1 year.	Died Oct. 15, 1864, in hospital at Camp Chase, Ohio.
Ramsey, William W.	...do...	21	Sept. 8, 1864	1 year.	Died Jan. 16, 1865, in hospital at Columbia, Tennessee.
Riley, John E.	...do...	22	Sept. 16, 1864	1 year.	
Ryan, John	...do...	20	Sept. 18, 1864	1 year.	Sent to hospital at Camp Dennison, O., Jan. 26, 1865. No further record found.
Roberts, William H.	...do...	18	Sept. 1, 1864	1 year.	Mustered out with company June 29, 1865.
Schultz, William H.	...do...	24	Sept. 8, 1864	1 year.	Mustered out with company June 29, 1865.
Sherman, Vincent M.	...do...	23	Sept. 22, 1864	1 year.	Admitted to hospital at Camp Dennison, O., Jan 24, 1865; furloughed Feb. 13, 1865. No further record found.
Simmons, Wilson	...do...	24	Sept. 17, 1864	1 year.	Mustered out with company June 29, 1865.
Smith, Stephen	...do...	19	Sept. 19, 1864	1 year.	Mustered out by order of War Department, dated May 3, 1865.
Smith, Daniel	...do...	24	Sept. 22, 1864	1 year.	Mustered out May 31, 1865, at Camp Dennison, O., by order of War Department.
Smith, John	...do...	24	Sept. 15, 1864	1 year.	
Spencer, George	...do...	26	Sept. 14, 1864	1 year.	
Sullivant, Timothy	...do...	46	Sept. 14, 1864	1 year.	Mustered out with company June 29, 1865.
Tallman, William H.	...do...	18	Sept. 16, 1864	1 year.	Mustered out with company June 29, 1865.
Taylor, Samuel J.	...do...	23	Sept. 6, 1864	1 year.	
Valentine, Jeremiah	...do...	28	Sept. 19, 1864	1 year.	Mustered out with company June 29, 1865.
Vernon, George H	...do...	26	Sept. 7, 1864	1 year.	
Vermillion, George H.	...do...	29	Sept. 18, 1864	1 year.	Mustered out with company June 29, 1865.
Ward, Robert G.	...do...	32	Sept. 13, 1864	1 year.	
Warner, William	...do...	19	Sept. 12, 1864	1 year.	
West, Samuel	...do...	19	Sept. 5, 1864	1 year.	Mustered out to date June 29, 1865, by order of War Department.
Williams, John T.	...do...	24	Sept. 27, 1864	1 year.	Mustered out with company June 29, 1865.
Wiles, John	...do...	19	Sept. 12, 1864	1 year.	
Williams, Samuel	...do...	31	Sept. 7, 1864	1 year.	Reduced from Corporal Oct. 1, 1864; mustered out June 19, 1865, at David's Island, New York Harbor, by order of War Department.
Wilson, Edward	...do...	22	Sept. 13, 1864	1 year.	
Wilson, George P.	...do...	19	Sept. 2, 1864	1 year.	Reduced from Corporal Dec. 10, 1864; mustered out with company June 29, 1865.
Wood, Amos A	...do...	18	Sept. 2, 1864	1 year.	Erroneously taken up, and dropped from rolls Oct. 31, 1864.

COMPANY C.

Mustered in September 23, 1864, at Camp Chase, O., by W. P. Richardson, Colonel 25th O. V. I. Mustered out June 29, 1865, at Charlotte, N. C., by E. A. Folsom, Captain and A. C. M., Department of North Carolina.

Names.	Rank.	Age.	Date of Entering the Service.	Period of Service.	Remarks.
Charles Cavener	Captain.	22	Sept. 23, 1864	1 year.	Mustered out with company June 29, 1865.
Patrick H. McGrew	1st Lieut.	23	Sept. 23, 1864	1 year.	
John A. Sears	2d Lieut.	38	Sept. 23, 1864	1 year.	Discharged April 4, 1865, at Camp Wheat Swamp Church, N. C., on Surgeon's certificate of disability.
John V. Morrison	...do...	28	Sept. 3, 1864	1 year.	Promoted from Q. M. Sergeant May 11, 1865; mustered out with company June 29, 1865.
Daniel Crumley	1st Sergt.	24	Sept. 21, 1864	1 year.	Mustered out with company June 29, 1865.
Joseph W. Gorrell	Sergeant.	25	Sept. 16, 1864	1 year.	Mustered out with company June 29, 1865.
[illegible] Finley	...do...	18	Aug. 16, 1864	1 year.	Mustered out with company June 29, 1865.
Irvin B. Linn	...do...	36	Sept. 9, 1864	1 year.	Discharged June 8, 1865, at Columbus O., on Surgeon's certificate of disability.
James Lockard	...do...	39	Aug. 11, 1864	1 year.	Appointed Corporal Sept. 28, 1864; Sergeant Oct. 31, 1864; mustered out May 19, 1865, at Louisville, Ky., by order of War Department; also borne on rolls as James Lochlard.
George W. Crumley	Corporal.	19	Aug. 20, 1864	1 year.	Appointed Sept. 28, 1864; wounded Dec. 14, 1864, in action near Murfreesboro, Tenn; mustered out June 21, 1865, at Camp Dennison, O., by order of War Department.
Thomas Ray	...do...	44	Aug. 22, 1864	1 year.	Mustered out with company June 29, 1865.
Stacy Smith	...do...	23	Aug. 8, 1864	1 year.	Appointed Sept. 28, 1864; mustered out July 3, 1865, at Annapolis, Md., by order of War Department.
John M. Kinney	...do...	[illegible]	Aug. 11, 1864	1 year.	Mustered out to date June 29, 1865, by order of War Department.

Names.	Rank.	Age.	Date of Entering the Service.	Period of Service.	Remarks.
Thomas Jones	Corporal.	42	Sept. 17, 1864	1 year.	
Charles Steinmetz	....do....	20	Sept. 3, 1864	1 year.	Appointed Dec. 10, 1864; mustered out with company June 29, 1865.
Jacob Bowers	....do....	21	Sept. 13, 1864	1 year.	Appointed Sept. 23, 1864; mustered out [illegible] 27, 1865, at Washington, D. C., by order of War Department.
Ervin Foltz	....do....	22	Sept. 17, 1864	1 year.	Appointed Sept. 23, 1864; died Dec. [illegible] in hospital at Nashville, Tenn.
Francis M. Stanfield	....do....	23	Sept. 13, 1864	1 year.	Appointed Oct. 1, 1864; mustered out [illegible] 1865, at Washington, D. C., by order of War Department.
John H. Smith	....do....	33	Sept. 3, 1864	1 year.	Appointed Feb. 4, 1865; mustered out with company June 29, 1865.
Lewis D. Spangler	....do....	32	Sept. 15, 1864	1 year.	Appointed Jan. 28, 1865; mustered out with company June 29, 1865.
John Beitle	....do....	21	Sept. 7, 1864	1 year.	Appointed March 1, 1865; mustered out with company June 29, 1865.
Solomon S. Lehman	....do....	22	Sept. 17, 1864	1 year.	Appointed April 1, 1865; mustered out with company June 29, 1865.
Adams, James O	Private..	18	Sept. 13, 1864	1 year.	Mustered out by order of War Department dated Oct. 3, 1865.
Adams, George W	....do....	18	Sept. 13, 1864	1 year.	Mustered out with company June 29, 18[illegible]
Allen, Mitchell S	....do....	18	Sept. 12, 1864	1 year.	Mustered out with company June 29, 18[illegible]
Bailey, Rufus W	....do....	42	Sept. 12, 1864	1 year.	Mustered out June 27, 1865, at Louisville, [illegible] by order of War Department.
Barkman, David	....do....	25	Sept. 14, 1864	1 year.	
Baughman, John	....do....	25	Sept. 15, 1864	1 year.	
Bishop, John W.	....do....	21	Sept. 13, 1864	1 year.	Mustered out with company June 29, 18[illegible]
Bishop, Isaac H	....do....	18	Sept. 17, 1864	1 year.	Mustered out with company June 29, 18[illegible]
Bolen, John H	....do....	23	Aug. 31, 1864	1 year.	Died Jan. 30, 1865, at Lockbourne, O.
Botkin, Lycurgus	....do....	20	Sept. 5, 1864	1 year.	Mustered out July 3, 1865, at Washington, D. C., by order of War Department.
Bowers, John W	....do....	23	Sept. 13, 1864	1 year.	Mustered out with company June 29, 18[illegible]
Brown, James H	....do....	29	Sept. 17, 1864	1 year.	
Brown, Frederick W	....do....	18	Sept. 28, 1864	1 year.	Mustered out with company June 29, 18[illegible]
Brown, John	....do....	23	Sept. 15, 1864	1 year.	
Byram, Algernon T	....do....	32	Sept. 17, 1864	1 year.	Mustered out May 25, 1865, at Columbus, [illegible] by order of War Department.
Casey, John B.	....do....	33	Sept. 21, 1864	1 year.	
Cheeseman, William	....do....	20	Sept. 8, 1864	1 year.	Mustered out with company June 29, 18[illegible]
Connell, Dennis	....do....	22	Sept. 5, 1864	1 year.	Mustered out with company June 29, 18[illegible]
Collins, Robert	....do....	22	Sept. 13, 1864	1 year.	
Cramsey, Harry	....do....	19	Sept. 15, 1864	1 year.	
Croft, George	....do....	22	Sept. 9, 1864	1 year.	
Cunningham, John T	....do....	21	Sept. 15, 1864	1 year	
Cutmore, William	....do....	19	Sept. 13, 1864	1 year.	
Davis, Robert	....do....	22	Sept. 13, 1864	1 year.	
De Largey, John	....do....	22	July 30, 1864	1 year.	Mustered out by order of War Department dated May 3, 1865; also borne [illegible] Delanger.
Dunn, Charles	....do....	32	Sept. 10, 1864	1 year.	
Dunlap, Peter.	....do....	23	Sept. 14, 1864	1 year.	Mustered out with company June 2[illegible]
Edwards, William H	....do....	44	Sept. 12, 1864	1 year.	Mustered out June 19, 1865, at [illegible] by order of War Department.
Ellis, George R	....do....	27	Sept. 10, 1864	1 year.	
Evans, John	....do....	43	Sept. 12, 1864	1 year.	Mustered out with company June 2[illegible]
Flynn, James	....do....	23	Sept. 15, 1864	1 year.	
Graham, John	....do....	22	Aug. 26, 1864	1 year.	
Green, Ira	....do....	45	Sept. 16, 1864	1 year.	Mustered out June 6, 1865, at Beaufort, [illegible] by order of War Department.
Hacket, David	....do....	25	Sept. 16, 1864	1 year.	Mustered out with company June 2[illegible]
Hangs, John D	....do....	35	Sept. 19, 1864	1 year.	Mustered out with company June 2[illegible]
Harwood, Henry	....do....	21	Sept. 12, 1864	1 year.	
Harrison, Charles E	....do....	18	Sept. 13, 1864	1 year.	Mustered out May 31, 1865, at Camp De[illegible] O., by order of War Department.
Harris, James E	....do....	19	Sept. 5, 1864	1 year.	Mustered out June 14, 1865, at Louisville, [illegible] by order of War Department.
Harpet, William	....do....	35	Sept. 16, 1864	1 year.	Mustered out with company June 2[illegible]
Hoskins, Ebenezer	....do....	28	Sept. 16, 1864	1 year.	Mustered out June 1, 1865, at David's [illegible] New York Harbor, by order of War [illegible]ment.
Huston, Leonard	....do....	25	Sept. 17, 1864	1 year.	
Huggett, Robert	....do....	20	Sept. 3, 1864	1 year.	Died March 30, 1865, at Washington, [illegible]
Hyatt, Hervey B	....do....	18	Sept. 26, 1864	1 year.	Mustered out May 31, 1865, at Camp D[illegible] O., by order of War Department.
Jerman, Thomas	....do....	20	Sept. 3, 1864	1 year.	Mustered out with company
Johnson, William	....do....	23	Sept. 12, 1864	1 year.	
Kelley, Edward	....do....	23	Sept. 8, 1864	1 year.	
Leach, William N.	....do....	18	Sept. 3, 1864	1 year.	Mustered out with company June 2[illegible]
Lester, Stephen A	....do....	18	Sept. 10, 1864	1 year.	Mustered out with company June 2[illegible]
McCarty, Eugene	....do....	19	Sept. 5, 1864	1 year.	Mustered out June 22, 1865, at Columbus, [illegible] by order of War Department.
Matthews, Garrett	....do....	18	Sept. 8, 1864	1 year.	Mustered out with company June 2[illegible]
Mayhew, George	....do....	38	Sept. 17, 1864	1 year.	Mustered out with company June 2[illegible]
Miller, Jackson	....do....	20	Sept. 13, 1864	1 year.	

Names.	Rank.	Age.	Date of Entering the Service.	Period of Service.	Remarks.
Nisewonger, Jasper	Private..	20	Aug. 16, 1864	1 year.	Mustered out with company June 29, 1865; also borne on rolls as Joseph Nisewonger.
O'Nail, James	....do....	41	Sept. 21, 1864	1 year.	Mustered out with company June 29, 1865.
Olderman, Francis M	....do....	21	Aug. 18, 1864	1 year.	
Prother, Jeremiah	....do....	29	Sept. 23, 1864	1 year.	Mustered out to date June 29, 1865, by order of War Department.
Ringer, Jacob	....do....	34	Sept. 3, 1864	1 year.	Died Jan. 15, 1865, at Pittsburgh, Pa.
Roach, John T	....do....	19	Aug. 11, 1864	1 year.	Mustered out June 14, 1865, at Beaufort, N. C., by order of War Department.
Robnet, Amos	....do....	25	Aug. 6, 1864	1 year.	
Schreckengaust, Jacob	....do....	33	Sept. 2, 1864	1 year.	Mustered out with company June 29, 1865.
Schoch, William H	....do....	26	Sept. 3, 1864	1 year.	
Scott, John	....do....	25	Aug. 11, 1864	1 year.	Mustered out with company June 29, 1865.
Shears, Isaac	....do....	24	Aug. 31, 1864	1 year.	Mustered out with company June 29, 1865.
Smith, Jackson	....do....	30	Aug. 17, 1864	1 year.	
Smith, William	....do....	33	Aug. 29, 1864	1 year.	Mustered out June 17, 1865, at Columbus, O., by order of War Department.
Swank, James	....do....	17	Sept. 21, 1864	1 year.	
Swartz, John	....do....	39	Sept. 15, 1864	1 year.	Mustered out with company June 29, 1865.
Taylor, Wesley A	....do....	19	Sept. 7, 1864	1 year.	Mustered out with company June 29, 1865.
Thorne, Henry	....do....	18	Aug. 17, 1864	1 year.	
Tivis, Hutson	....do....	23	Aug. 6, 1864	1 year.	Mustered out with company June 29, 1865.
Vanbuskirk, James	....do....	21	Sept. 2, 1864	1 year.	Mustered out with company June 29, 1865.
Vaught, Hugh L	....do....	22	Aug. 11, 1864	1 year.	Mustered out with company June 29, 1865.
Watson, John W	....do....	26	Aug. 22, 1864	1 year.	Mustered out June 10, 1865, at Beaufort, N. C., by order of War Department.
Welch, Edward	....do....	18	Sept. 10, 1864	1 year.	
White, James H	....do....	18	Sept. 8, 1864	1 year.	Died March 25, 1865, at Newbern, N. C.
Widner, Frederick	....do....	20	Aug. 11, 1864	1 year.	
Wilson, George	....do....	18	Sept. 16, 1864	1 year.	
Wilcox, Nathaniel C	....do....	19	Aug. 16, 1864	1 year.	Mustered out with company June 29, 1865.
Wilcox, Robert S	....do....	25	Aug. 16, 1864	1 year.	Mustered out with company June 29, 1865.
Wilkins, Wesley H	....do....	32	Sept. 15, 1864	1 year.	
Wolf Joseph H	....do....	18	Sept. 1, 1864	1 year.	Mustered out with company June 29, 1865.
Woodgar, George W	....do....	22	Aug. 16, 1864	1 year.	
Ziegler, David B	....do....	32	Aug. 13, 1864	1 year.	Reduced from 1st Sergeant Nov. 26, 1864; mustered out with company June 29, 1865.

COMPANY D.

Mustered in September 23, 1864, at Camp Chase, O., by W. P. Richardson, Colonel 25th O. V. I. Mustered out June 29, 1865, at Charlotte, N. C., by E. A. Folsom, Captain and A. C. M., Department of North Carolina.

Names.	Rank.	Age.	Date of Entering the Service.	Period of Service.	Remarks.
Edwin R Rickey	Captain.	23	July 25, 1864	1 year.	Appointed Sept 23, 1864; mustered out with company June 29, 1865.
David B. Russell	1st Lieut.	25	Aug. 9, 1864	1 year.	Appointed Sept. 23, 1864; mustered out with company June 29, 1865
Merrick A. Mihills	2d Lieut.	23	Aug. 15, 1864	1 year.	Appointed Sept. 23, 1864; mustered out with company June 29, 1865
Wallace W. Hitchcock	1st Sergt.	22	Sept. 2, 1864	1 year.	Appointed Sept. 23, 1864; mustered out with company June 29, 1865.
Richmond C. Vanaman	Sergeant.	35	Aug. 24, 1864	1 year.	Appointed Sept. 23, 1864; mustered out with company June 29, 1865.
John W. Preston	....do....	24	Aug. 17, 1864	1 year.	Appointed Sept 23, 1864; mustered out June 19, 1865, at Columbus, O., by order of War Department.
Erwin McRoberts	....do....	20	Aug. 2, 1864	1 year.	Appointed Sept. 23, 1864; mustered out with company June 29, 1865.
Edward B. Lowe	....do....	42	Aug. 26, 1864	1 year.	Appointed from Corporal April 3, 1865; mustered out with company June 29, 1865.
William Morris	Corporal.	22	Sept. 3, 1864	1 year.	Appointed Sept. 23, 1864; mustered out with company June 29, 1865.
Robert Meek	....do....	19	Aug. 31, 1864	1 year.	Appointed Sept. 23, 1864; mustered out with company June 29, 1865.
Elnathan Peabody	....do....	32	Aug. 25, 1864	1 year.	Appointed Sept. 23, 1864; mustered out with company June 29, 1865.
Albert Adams	....do....	32	Aug. 29, 1864	1 year.	Appointed Dec. 23, 1864; mustered out with company June 29, 1865.
William Henson	....do....	24	Aug. 20, 1864	1 year.	Appointed April 3, 1865; mustered out with company June 29, 1865.
Delancy Holley	....do....	19	Sept. 5, 1864	1 year.	Appointed April 3, 1865; mustered out with company June 29, 1865.
Philemon Knapp	....do....	38	Aug. 31, 1864	1 year.	Appointed April 3, 1865; mustered out June 21, 1865, at Columbus, O., by order of War Department.
Hezekiah Chrisman	....do....	34	Aug. 30, 1864	1 year.	Appointed April 3, 1865; mustered out with company June 29, 1865.
Allen, Cineas	Private..	18	Sept. 5, 1864	1 year.	Died Feb. 20, 1865, at Washington, D. C.

Names.	Rank.	Age	Date of Entering the Service.		
Aldrich, Edward	Private	20	Aug. 2, 1864		
Andrews, Robert	do	25	Sept. 6, 1864	1	
Appleby, George O	do	18	Sept. 20, 1864	1	
Beaver, Benjamin F	do	38	Aug. 17, 1864	1	
Bellows, Nathaniel	do	20	Sept. 5, 1864	1	
Benham, Thomas A	do	21	Sept. 5, 1864	1	
Buswell, John	do	33	Aug. 26, 1864	1	
Cady, Jerome P	do	40	Aug. 26, 1864	1	
Carpenter, James G	do	20	Aug. 31, 1864	1	
Casbern, Jesse	do	19	Sept. 13, 1864	1	
Chapin, Harlow	do	21	Sept. 2, 1864	1	
Chrisman, Judson	do	18	Sept. 2, 1864	1 year.	
Cobb, Melvin G	do	18	Aug. 30, 1864	1	
Coughlan, John	do	22	Aug. 31, 1864	1	
Colley, Watson	do	33	Aug. 29, 1864	1	
Cunningham, George W.	do	29	Sept. 12, 1864	1	
Danforth, Charles	do	20	Aug. 18, 1864	1	
Decker, Jacob	do	26	Sept. 2, 1864	1	
Decker, Frederick	do	21	Aug. 30, 1864	1	
Dopp, Addison	do	25	Sept. 8, 1864	1	
Douglass, Gibson	do	26	Sept. 8, 1864		
Duntley, Hasen O	do	22	Aug. 25, 1864		
Earl, Warren	do	20	Aug. 30, 1864		
Easterwood, Charles	do	18	Sept. 13, 1864	1	
Emmons, Harley	do	19	Aug. 29, 1864	1	
Emmons, Melvin	do	21	Aug. 25, 1864	1 year.	
Evans, Wilson B.	do	40	Aug. 30, 1864	1 year.	
Geddy, William H	do	40	Aug. 31, 1864	1	
Henges, Mathias	do	38	Aug. 31, 1864	1	Must
Hill, Walter F	do	21	Aug. 30, 1864	1	Must
Hickox, James G	do	36	Aug. 30, 1864	1 year.	by Must
Hicks, Samuel	do	30	Sept. 8, 1864	1 year.	
Holland, Richard	do	18	Sept. 2, 1864	1 year.	
Jennings, Charles	do	27	Aug. 29, 1864	1 year.	
Kellegg, Edwin	do	20	Sept. 5, 1864		
Loynes, Ira	do	18	Aug. 29, 1864		
Matteson, Abner L	do	38	Aug. 31, 1864		
Matteson, Archibald E.	do	18	Sept. 5, 1864	year.	Must
Morris, New Year B.	do	24	Aug. 30, 1864		Died
Mumford, Thomas	do	24	Aug. 30, 1864	1 year.	
Musser, Daniel O	do	20	Sept. 4, 1864	1 year.	
Myers, Albert	do	23	Sept. 1, 1864	1 year.	
Myers, Cornelius	do	18	Aug. 24, 1864	1 year.	
Nugent, Patrick	do	34	Aug. 29, 1864		
Null, Andrew	do	18	Aug. 31, 1864	1 year.	
O'Harra, Patrick	do	20	Aug. 30, 1864	1 year.	
Parsons, George E.	do	28	Aug. 17, 1864		
Porter, Sidney	do	18	Aug. 29, 1864		
Peabody, Moses	do	18	Aug. 23, 1864		
Perrin, Orrin	do	23	Sept. 4, 1864		
Petty, Thomas	do	26	Aug. 25, 1864	1 year.	
Preston, Robert	do	19	Aug. 2, 1864	1 year.	
Rawson, Andrew	do	21	Aug. 17, 1864	1 year.	
Rickey, Edgar D.	do	25	Aug. 29, 1864	1 year.	
Robinson, Levi S.	do	23	July 29, 1864	1 year.	
Robinson, William D.	do	44	Sept. 15, 1864		
Ross, Milo	do	31	Aug. 29, 1864	1 year.	
Ross, William	do	29	Aug. 31, 1864	1	
Ruddy, Michael	do	44	Aug. 30, 1864	1	
Ryan, James	do	20	Sept. 1, 1864	1	
Schriber, Michael	do	18	Sept. 5, 1864	1	
Sens, Jacob	do	22	Aug. 21, 1864	1	
Shacelton, Robert	do	26	Aug. 26, 1864	1	
Shepley, Frank	do	20	Aug. 12, 1864	1	
Short, Frederick	do	18	Sept. 5, 1864	1	
Stineman, Peter	do	27	Aug. 23, 1864	1	
Stockings, Samuel S.	do	21	Aug. 23, 1864	1	
Taylor, Lewis P.	do	19	Aug. 25, 1864	1	
Terrill, Edgar H.	do	33	Sept. 4, 1864	1	
Thompson, Samuel	do	20	Sept. 1, 1864	1	
Trumbull, William	do	44	Aug. 26, 1864		
Udall, Luther	do	18	Aug. 26, 1864		

Names.	Rank.	Age.	Date of Entering the Service.	Period of Service.	Remarks.
Vaughn, William C.	Private	28	Sept. 1, 1864	1 year.	Mustered out July 6, 1865, at Philadelphia, Pa., by order of War Department.
Wait, Thomas A.	do.	28	Aug. 26, 1864	1 year.	Mustered out with company June 29, 1865.
Walsh, John	do.	35	Aug. 26, 1864	1 year.	Mustered out with company June 29, 1865.
Walde, Anson	do.	22	Sept. 5, 1864	1 year.	Mustered out to date June 29, 1865, by order of War Department.
Welton, Melanchthon	do.	18	Sept. 3, 1864	1 year.	Mustered out with company June 29, 1865.
Wheeler, Daniel G.	do.	37	Sept. 2, 1864	1 year.	Mustered out with company June 29, 1865.
Williams, Hessor	do.	26	Aug. 13, 1864	1 year.	
Williamson, William H.	do.	28	Aug. 27, 1864	1 year.	Mustered out June 8, 1865, at Chester, Pa., by order of War Department.
Williamson, Henry C.	do.	37	Aug. 26, 1864	1 year.	Died May 22, 1865, in hospital.
Wyse, Washington W.	do.	20	Sept. 12, 1864	1 year.	Mustered out with company June 29, 1865.

COMPANY E.

Mustered in September 23, 1864, at Camp Chase, O., by W. P. Richardson, Colonel 25th O. V. I. Mustered out June 29, 1865, at Charlotte, N. C., by E. A. Folsom, Captain and A. C. M., Department of North Carolina.

Names.	Rank.	Age.	Date of Entering the Service.	Period of Service.	Remarks.
Isaac N. C. Mellinger	Captain.	..	Sept. 28, 1864	1 year.	Mustered out with company June 29, 1865.
James Mauger	1st Lieut.	..	Sept. 23, 1864	1 year.	Mustered out May 18, 1865, by order of War Department.
Ashbury Gardner	2d Lieut.	..	Sept. 23, 1864	1 year.	Mustered out with company June 29, 1865.
Thomas J. Porter	1st Sergt.	20	Sept. 3, 1864	1 year.	Appointed from Sergeant May 18, 1865; mustered out with company June 29, 1865.
Christopher Young	Sergeant.	43	Sept. 1, 1864	1 year.	Appointed Sept. 23, 1864; mustered out with company June 29, 1865.
William H. Harding	do.	19	Sept. 12, 1864	1 year.	Appointed Sept. 23, 1864; mustered out with company June 29, 1865.
Rollin B. Shower	do.	23	Sept. 1, 1864	1 year.	Appointed Sept. 23, 1864; mustered out with company June 29, 1865.
Solomon Crider	do.	36	Sept. 4, 1864	1 year.	Appointed from Corporal May 18, 1865; mustered out with company June 29, 1865.
Jacob Baird	Corporal.	20	Aug. 28, 1864	1 year.	Appointed Sept. 23, 1864; mustered out with company June 29, 1865.
William H. Gardner	do.	35	Sept. 5, 1864	1 year.	Appointed Sept. 23, 1864; mustered out June 18, 1865, at Columbus, O., by order of War Department.
Sylvanus A. Peters	do.	19	Sept. 3, 1864	1 year.	Appointed Sept. 23, 1864; mustered out with company June 29, 1865.
Amos Sriver	do.	18	Sept. 12, 1864	1 year.	Appointed Sept. 23, 1864; mustered out with company June 29, 1865.
John Salts	do.	22	Aug. 31, 1864	1 year.	Appointed Sept. 23, 1864; mustered out with company June 29, 1865.
David Owens	do.	38	Sept. 10, 1864	1 year.	Discharged May 30, 1865, at Camp Dennison, O., for wounds received Dec. 14, 1864, in action near Murfreesboro, Tenn.
William S. Sherman	do.	30	Sept. 19, 1864	1 year.	Appointed May 18, 1865; mustered out with company June 29, 1865.
George W. Alwood	do.	18	Sept. 18, 1864	1 year.	Appointed May 18, 1865; mustered out with company June 29, 1865.
Zachariah Search	do.	19	Sept. 5, 1864	1 year.	Appointed June 11, 1865; transferred to Co. K, 181st O. V. I., June 15, 1865.
Arts, William R.	Private.	22	Sept. 3, 1864	1 year.	Transferred to Co. E, 181st O. V. I., June 15, 1865.
Alwood, William	do.	18	Sept. 15, 1864	1 year.	Mustered out with company June 29, 1865.
Barrick, William H.	do.	24	Sept. 5, 1864	1 year.	Mustered out with company June 29, 1865.
Beck, William	do.	25	Sept. 21, 1864	1 year.	Mustered out with company June 29, 1865.
Benkler, Baptist	do.	42	Sept. 4, 1864	1 year.	Mustered out with company June 29, 1865.
Boyle, Peter	do.	30	Sept. 19, 1864	1 year.	
Bradbury, Gershaw	do.	22	Sept. 14, 1864	1 year.	Mustered out with company June 29, 1865.
Carr, Peter	do.	23	Sept. 5, 1864	1 year.	Mustered out with company June 29, 1865.
Cunningham, John	do.	44	Aug. 31, 1864	1 year.	
Davis, Thomas	do.	22	Aug. 31, 1864	1 year.	Mustered out with company June 29, 1865.
Davenport, Lewis	do.	25	Sept. 5, 1864	1 year.	Mustered out with company June 29, 1865.
Donovan, Henry	do.	18	Aug. 18, 1864	1 year.	Transferred to Co. K, 22d Regiment, Veteran Reserve Corps, April 21, 1865; mustered out July 1, 1865, at Columbus, O., by order of War Department.
Dunlap, John W.	do.	19	Sept. 3, 1864	1 year.	Mustered out May 31, 1865, at McDougall Hospital, New York Harbor, by order of War Department.
Estill, Alanson C.	do.	24	Sept. 8, 1864	1 year.	
Ester, Peter	do.	[illegible]	Sept. 3, 1864	1 year.	Mustered out with company June 29, 1865.
Fast, Abraham	do.	[illegible]	Sept. 5, 1864	1 year.	Mustered out with company June 29, 1865.
Flanegan, Archibald	do.	19	Sept. 14, 1864	1 year.	Died Dec. 6, 1864, at Chattanooga, Tenn.
Forsythe, Robert W.	do.	[illegible]	Aug. 27, 1864	1 year.	Reduced from 1st Sergeant May 18, 1865; mustered out with company June 29, 1865.
Ferrins, Marion	do.	20	Sept. 16, 1864	1 year.	Also borne on rolls as Marion Furris.

Names.	Rank.	Age.	Date of Entering the Service	Period of Service.	Remarks.
Aldrich, Edward	Private	20	Aug. 2, 1864	1 year.	Reduced from Sergeant Jan. 24, 1865; transferred to Co. E, 181st O. V. I., June 15, 1865.
Andrews, Robert	...do...	25	Sept. 5, 1864	1 year.	Died Dec. 16, 1864, at Louisville, Ky.
Appleby, George O	...do...	18	Sept. 30, 1864	1 year.	Mustered out with company June 29, 1865.
Beaver, Benjamin F.	...do...	38	Aug. 17, 1864	1 year.	Mustered out with company June 29, 1865.
Bellows, Nathaniel	...do...	20	Sept. 5, 1864	1 year.	Died May 12, 1865, at Newbern, N. C.
Benham, Thomas A.	...do...	21	Sept. 5, 1864	1 year.	Mustered out May 12, 1865, at Philadelphia, Pa., by order of War Department.
Buswell, John	...do...	33	Aug. 25, 1864	1 year.	Mustered out with company June 29, 1865.
Cady, Jerome P.	...do...	40	Aug. 25, 1864	1 year.	Mustered out with company June 29, 1865.
Carpenter, James G.	...do...	20	Aug. 31, 1864	1 year.	Mustered out with company June 29, 1865.
Casbern, Jesse	...do...	19	Sept. 13, 1864	1 year.	Mustered out with company June 29, 1865.
Chapin, Harlow	...do...	21	Sept. 2, 1864	1 year.	Mustered out with company June 29, 1865.
Chrisman, Judson	...do...	18	Sept. 2, 1864	1 year.	Mustered out with company June 29, 1865.
Cobb, Mel[illegible]n	...do...	18	Aug. 30, 1864	1 year.	Mustered out with company June 29, 1865.
Coughlan, J[illegible]n	...do...	22	Aug. 31, 1864	1 year.	
Colley, Watson	...do...	33	Aug. 29, 1864	1 year.	Mustered out with company June 29, 1865.
Cunningham, George W.	...do...	29	Sept. 12, 1864	1 year.	Mustered out with company June 29, 1865.
Danforth, Charles	...do...	20	Aug. 18, 1864	1 year.	Mustered out with company June 29, 1865.
Decker, Jacob	...do...	26	Sept. 3, 1864	1 year.	Mustered out with company June 29, 1865.
Decker, Frederick	...do...	21	Aug. 30, 1864	1 year.	Died Jan. 11, 1865, at Jefferson Barracks, Mo.
Dopp, Addison	...do...	25	Sept. 3, 1864	1 year.	Mustered out with company June 29, 1865.
Douglass, Gibson	...do...	26	Sept. 3, 1864	1 year.	Mustered out May 22, 1865, at Nashville, Tenn., by order of War Department.
Duntley, Hazen G.	...do...	22	Aug. 25, 1864	1 year.	Mustered out with company June 29, 1865.
Earl, Warren	...do...	20	Aug. 30, 1864	1 year.	Mustered out May 19, 1865, at Philadelphia, Pa., by order of War Department.
Easterwood, Charles	...do...	18	Sept. 13, 1864	1 year.	Mustered out with company June 29, 1865.
Emmons, Harley	...do...	19	Aug. 29, 1864	1 year.	Died Jan. 31, 1865, at Murfreesboro, Tenn.
Emmons, Melvin	...do...	21	Aug. 25, 1864	1 year.	Mustered out with company June 29, 1865.
Evans, Wilson B.	...do...	40	Aug. 30, 1864	1 year.	Mustered out with company June 29, 1865.
Geddy, William I.	...do...	40	Aug. 31, 1864	1 year.	Mustered out with company June 29, 1865.
Henges, Mathias	...do...	28	Aug. 31, 1864	1 year.	Mustered out with company June 29, 1865.
Hill, Walter F.	...do...	21	Aug. 30, 1864	1 year.	Mustered out May 18, 1865, at Nashville, Tenn., by order of War Department.
Hickox, James G.	...do...	36	Aug. 30, 1864	1 year.	Mustered out with company June 29, 1865.
Hicks, Samuel	...do...	30	Sept. 3, 1864	1 year.	Mustered out with company June 29, 1865.
Holland, Richard	...do...	18	Sept. 2, 1864	1 year.	Mustered out with company June 29, 1865.
Jennings, Charles	...do...	27	Aug. 29, 1864	1 year.	Mustered out July 12, 1865, at Columbus, O., by order of War Department.
Kellogg, Edwin	...do...	20	Sept. 5, 1864	1 year.	Mustered out June 10, 1865, at McDougall Hospital, New York Harbor, by order of War Department.
Loynes, Ira	...do...	18	Aug. 29, 1864	1 year.	Mustered out with company June 29, 1865.
Matteson, Abner I.	...do...	38	Aug. 31, 1864	1 year.	Mustered out with company June 29, 1865.
Matteson, Archibald E.	...do...	18	Sept. 5, 1864	1 year.	Mustered out with company June 29, 1865.
Mor[illegible], New Year B.	...do...	21	Aug. 30, 1864	1 year.	Died Feb. 16, 1865, at Camp Chase, O.
Mumford, Thomas	...do...	24	Aug. 30, 1864	1 year.	Mustered out with company June 29, 1865.
Musser, Daniel O.	...do...	2[illegible]	Sept. 4, 1864	1 year.	Mustered out with company June 29, 1865.
Myers, Albert	...do...	23	Sept. 1, 1864	1 year.	Mustered out with company June 29, 1865.
Myers, Cornelius	...do...	18	Aug. 21, 1864	1 year.	Mustered out with company June 29, 1865.
Nugent, Patrick	...do...	31	Aug. 20, 1864	1 year.	Mustered out with company June 29, 1865.
Null, Andrew	...do...	18	Aug. 31, 1864	1 year.	Mustered out with company June 29, 1865.
O'Harra, Patrick	...do...	20	Aug. 30, 1864	1 year.	Mustered out May 15, 1865, at Wilmington, N. C., by order of War Department.
Parsons, George E.	...do...	28	Aug. 17, 1864	1 year.	Mustered out with company June 29, 1865.
Porter, Sidney	...do...	18	Aug. 20, 1864	1 year.	Mustered out with company June 29, 1865.
Peabody, Moses	...do...	18	Aug. 23, 1864	1 year.	Mustered out with company June 29, 1865.
Perrin, Orrin	...do...	23	Sept. 4, 1864	1 year.	Mustered out to date June 29, 1865, by order of War Department.
Petty, Thomas	...do...	26	Aug. 25, 1864	1 year.	Mustered out with company June 29, 1865.
Preston, Robert	...do...	19	Aug. 2, 1864	1 year.	Mustered out with company June 29, 1865.
Rawson, Andrew	...do...	21	Aug. 17, 1864	1 year.	Died Feb. 2, 1865, at Jefferson Barracks, Mo.
Rickey, Edgar D.	...do...	25	Aug. 29, 1864	1 year.	Mustered out with company June 29, 1865.
Robinson, Levi S.	...do...	23	July 29, 1864	1 year.	Mustered out June 6, 1865, at Beaufort, N. C., by order of War Department.
Robinson, William D.	...do...	41	Sept. 15, 1864	1 year.	Mustered out with company June 29, 1865.
Ross, Milo	...do...	31	Aug. 29, 1864	1 year.	Killed Dec. 7, 1864, in action at Wilkinson's Pike, Tenn.
Ross, William	...do...	29	Aug. 31, 1864	1 year.	Mustered out with company June 29, 1865.
Ruddy, Michael	...do...	41	Aug. 30, 1864	1 year.	Mustered out with company June 29, 1865.
Ryan, James	...do...	20	Sept. 1, 1864	1 year.	
Schriber, Michael	...do...	18	Sept. 5, 1864	1 year.	Mustered out with company June 29, 1865.
Sens, Jacob	...do...	22	Aug. 21, 1864	1 year.	Mustered out with company June 29, 1865.
Shacelton, Robert	...do...	26	Aug. 26, 1864	1 year.	Mustered out with company June 29, 1865.
Shepley, Frank	...do...	20	Aug. 13, 1864	1 year.	Promoted to Principal Musician Jan. [illegible] 1865.
Short, Frederick	...do...	18	Sept. 5, 1864	1 year.	Mustered out with company June 29, 1865.
Stineman, Peter	...do...	27	Aug. 23, 1864	1 year.	Mustered out with company June 29, 1865.
Stockings, Samuel S.	...do...	21	Aug. 23, 1864	1 year.	Mustered out with company June 29, 1865.
Taylor, Lewis P.	...do...	19	Aug. 25, 1864	1 year.	Died May 8, 1865, in hospital at —.
Terrill, Edgar H.	...do...	33	Sept. 4, 1864	1 year.	Mustered out with company June 29, 1865.
Thompson, Samuel	...do...	20	Sept. 1, 1864	1 year.	Transferred to Co. E, 181st O. V. I., June 15, 1865.
Trumbull, William	...do...	41	Aug. 25, 1864	1 year.	Mustered out July 4, 1865, at Murfreesboro, Tenn., by order of War Department.
Udall, Luther	...do...	18	Aug. 25, 1864	1 year.	Died Feb. 8, 1865, in hospital.

Names.	Rank.	Age.	Date of Entering the Service.	Period of Service.	Remarks.
...gton, William C.	Private.	[illegible]	Sept. 1, 1864	1 year.	Mustered out July 6, 1865, at Philadelphia, Pa., by order of War Department.
...tt, Thomas A.	...do...	[illegible]	Aug. 26, 1864	1 year.	Mustered out with company June 29, 1865.
...le, John	...do...	[illegible]	Aug. 26, 1864	1 year.	Mustered out with company June 29, 1865.
...ble, Anson	...do...	[illegible]	Sept. 5, 1864	1 year.	Mustered out to date June 29, 1865, by order of War Department.
...ton, Melanchthon	...do...	18	Sept. 3, 1864	1 year.	Mustered out with company June 29, 1865.
...ler, Daniel G.	...do...	37	Sept. 3, 1864	1 year.	Mustered out with company June 29, 1865.
...ams, Hector	...do...	[illegible]	Aug. 18, 1864	1 year.	
...mson, William H.	...do...	[illegible]	Aug. 27, 1864	1 year.	Mustered out June 8, 1865, at Chester, Pa., by order of War Department.
...mson, Henry C.	...do...	37	Aug. 26, 1864	1 year.	Died May 22, 1865, in hospital.
...e, Washington W.	...do...	[illegible]	Sept. 12, 1864	1 year.	Mustered out with company June 29, 1865.

COMPANY E.

...stered in September 23, 1864, at Camp Chase, O., by W. P. Richardson, Colonel 25th O. V. I. Mustered out June 29, 1865, at Charlotte, N. C., by E. A. Folsom, Captain and A. C. M., Department of North Carolina.

Names.	Rank.	Age.	Date of Entering the Service.	Period of Service.	Remarks.
...N. C. Mellinger	Captain.	..	Sept. 23, 1864	1 year.	Mustered out with company June 29, 1865.
...lin Mauger	1st Lieut.	..	Sept. 23, 1864	1 year.	Mustered out May 15, 1865, by order of War Department.
...bury Gardiner	2d Lieut.	..	Sept. 23, 1864	1 year.	Mustered out with company June 29, 1865.
...in J. Porter	1st Sergt.	20	Sept. 3, 1864	1 year.	Appointed from Sergeant May 18, 1865; mustered out with company June 29, 1865.
...stopher Young	Sergeant.	43	Sept. 1, 1864	1 year.	Appointed Sept. 23, 1864; mustered out with company June 29, 1865.
...liam H. Harding	...do...	19	Sept. 18, 1864	1 year.	Appointed Sept. 23, 1864; mustered out with company June 29, 1865.
...lin B. Shower	...do...	23	Sept. 1, 1864	1 year.	Appointed Sept. 23, 1864; mustered out with company June 29, 1865.
...mon Crider	...do...	36	Sept. 4, 1864	1 year.	Appointed from Corporal May 18, 1865; mustered out with company June 29, 1865.
...ob Baird	Corporal.	20	Aug. 28, 1864	1 year.	Appointed Sept. 23, 1864; mustered out with company June 29, 1865.
...liam H. Gardner	...do...	35	Sept. 5, 1864	1 year.	Appointed Sept. 23, 1864; mustered out June 13, 1865, at Columbus, O., by order of War Department.
...vanus A. Peters	...do...	19	Sept. 3, 1864	1 year.	Appointed Sept. 23, 1864; mustered out with company June 29, 1865.
...ac Sriver	...do...	18	Sept. 12, 1864	1 year.	Appointed Sept. 23, 1864; mustered out with company June 29, 1865.
...n Saltz	...do...	22	Aug. 31, 1864	1 year.	Appointed Sept. 23, 1864; mustered out with company June 29, 1865.
...vid Owens	...do...	38	Sept. 10, 1864	1 year.	Discharged May 30, 1865, at Camp Dennison, O., for wounds received Dec. 14, 1864, in action near Murfreesboro, Tenn.
...liam S. Sherman	...do...	30	Sept. 19, 1864	1 year.	Appointed May 18, 1865; mustered out with company June 29, 1865.
...rge W. Alwood	...do...	43	Sept. 18, 1864	1 year.	Appointed May 18, 1865; mustered out with company June 29, 1865.
...bariah Search	...do...	19	Sept. 5, 1864	1 year.	Appointed June 11, 1865; transferred to Co. K, 181st O. V. I., June 15, 1865.
...s, William R.	Private.	22	Sept. 3, 1864	1 year.	Transferred to Co. E, 181st O. V. I., June 15, 1865.
...ood, William	...do...	18	Sept. 15, 1864	1 year.	Mustered out with company June 29, 1865.
...ick, William H.	...do...	24	Sept. 5, 1864	1 year.	Mustered out with company June 29, 1865.
..., William	...do...	25	Sept. 21, 1864	1 year.	Mustered out with company June 29, 1865.
...ler, Baptist	...do...	42	Sept. 4, 1864	1 year.	Mustered out with company June 29, 1865.
..., Peter	...do...	39	Sept. 19, 1864	1 year.	
...s, Gershaw	...do...	22	Sept. 14, 1864	1 year.	Mustered out with company June 29, 1865.
..., Peter	...do...	23	Sept. 5, 1864	1 year.	Mustered out with company June 29, 1865.
...ngham, John	...do...	44	Aug. 31, 1864	1 year.	
..., Thomas	...do...	22	Aug. 31, 1864	1 year.	Mustered out with company June 29, 1865.
...pert, Lewis	...do...	25	Sept. 5, 1864	1 year.	Mustered out with company June 29, 1865.
...van, Henry	...do...	18	Aug. 18, 1864	1 year.	Transferred to Co. K, 22d Regiment, Veteran Reserve Corps, April 21, 1865; mustered out July 1, 1865, at Columbus, O., by order of War Department.
..., John W.	...do...	19	Sept. 3, 1864	1 year.	Mustered out May 31, 1865, at McDougall Hospital, New York Harbor, by order of War Department.
...ill, Alanson C.	...do...	24	Sept. 8, 1864	1 year.	
...er, Peter	...do...	[illegible]	Sept. 3, 1864	1 year.	Mustered out with company June 29, 1865.
...t, Abraham	...do...	[illegible]	Sept. 5, 1864	1 year.	Mustered out with company June 29, 1865.
...negan, Archibald	...do...	19	Sept. 14, 1864	1 year.	Died Dec. 6, 1864, at Chattanooga, Tenn.
...sythe, Robert W.	...do...	28	Aug. 27, 1864	1 year.	Reduced from 1st Sergeant May 18, 1865; mustered out with company June 29, 1865.
...vins, Marion	...do...	20	Sept. 18, 1864	1 year.	Also borne on rolls as Marion Purdie.

Names.	Rank.	Age.	Date of Entering the Service.	Period of Service.	Remarks.
Francis, Eli	Private	19	Sept. 13, 1864	1 year.	Mustered out with company June 29, 1865.
Groff, Zachariah A	...do...	19	Sept. 4, 1864	1 year.	Died January 22, 1865, at Louisville, Ky.
Groff, Franklin	...do...	23	Sept. 10, 1864	1 year.	Mustered out with company June 29, 1865.
Gommere, Alonzo E	...do...	18	Sept. 13, 1864	1 year.	Mustered out with company June 29, 1865.
Harding, Winfield S	...do...	18	Sept. 14, 1864	1 year.	Mustered out with company June 29, 1865.
Havens, George	...do...	39	Sept. 1, 1864	1 year.	
Heinberger, Daniel	...do...	21	Sept. 5, 1864	1 year.	Died May 16, 1865, at Columbus, O.
Hill, James W	...do...	37	Sept. 13, 1864	1 year.	Mustered out with company June 29, 1865.
Hoffer, John	...do...	35	Sept. 6, 1864	1 year.	Transferred to Co. E, 181st O. V. I., June 3, 1865.
Hollinger, John G	...do...	29	Sept. 4, 1864	1 year.	Mustered out May 23, 1865, at Murfreesboro, Tenn., by order of War Department.
Huber, Matthias	...do...	40	Aug. 31, 1864	1 year.	Mustered out with company June 29, 1865.
Kaylor, Samuel	...do...	31	Sept. 3, 1864	1 year.	Mustered out with company June 29, 1865.
Keller, Daniel	...do...	43	Aug. 22, 1864	1 year.	Died Oct. 10, 1864, at Columbus, O.
Keller, John	...do...	26	Sept. 6, 1864	1 year.	Mustered out with company June 29, 1865.
King, George W	...do...	18	Aug. 31, 1864	1 year.	Mustered out with company June 29, 1865.
King, William	...do...	29	Aug. 31, 1864	1 year.	Mustered out with company June 29, 1865.
Kittinger, Abraham	...do...	19	Sept. 3, 1864	1 year.	Mustered out with company June 29, 1865.
Kittinger, Abraham R	...do...	20	Sept. 3, 1864	1 year.	Mustered out with company June 29, 1865.
Kline, John	...do...	19	Sept. 4, 1864	1 year.	Mustered out with company June 29, 1865.
Kunkle, George O	...do...	18	Sept. 14, 1864	1 year.	Mustered out with company June 29, 1865.
Kurtz, John R	...do...	25	Sept. 4, 1864	1 year.	Wounded Dec. 7, 1864, in action at Murfreesboro, Tenn.; mustered out with company June 29, 1865.
Landford, George W	...do...	18	Sept. 13, 1864	1 year.	Mustered out June 2, 1865, at Camp [illegible], O., by order of War Department.
Lester, David C	...do...	18	Sept. 4, 1864	1 year.	Mustered out with company June 29, 1865.
Levers, William	...do...	18	Sept. 3, 1864	1 year.	Mustered out with company June 29, 1865.
Lindzly, James E	...do...	18	Sept. 19, 1864	1 year.	Died January 14, 1865, in hospital; also borne on rolls as James E. Lindzsey.
Lyttle, Francis M	...do...	18	Sept. 19, 1864	1 year.	Transferred to Co. E, 181st O. V. I., June 6, 1865.
McGlennen, Michael	...do...	43	Aug. 26, 1864	1 year.	Mustered out with company June 29, 1865.
Mason, Lafayette	...do...	20	Sept. 1, 1864	1 year.	Mustered out with company June 29, 1865.
Miller, Frederick	...do...	24	Sept. 5, 1864	1 year.	Mustered out with company June 29, 1865.
Miller, Andrew	...do...	18	Sept. 17, 1864	1 year.	Mustered out with company June 29, 1865.
Miller, Samuel	...do...	35	Sept. 3, 1864	1 year.	Mustered out June 17, 1865, at Columbus, O., by order of War Department.
Miller, Israel	...do...	18	Sept. 3, 1864	1 year.	Mustered out with company June 29, 1865.
Moles, Winfield S	...do...	18	Sept. 3, 1864	1 year.	Mustered out June 7, 1865, at Columbus, O., by order of War Department.
Mullvain, William	...do...	39	Aug. 25, 1864	1 year.	Mustered out with company June 29, 1865.
Myers, Jacob F	...do...	23	Sept. 3, 1864	1 year.	Mustered out with company June 29, 1865.
Packer, John	...do...	21	Sept. 4, 1864	1 year.	Mustered out with company June 29, 1865.
Phister, Samuel	...do...	18	Sept. 1, 1864	1 year.	Mustered out with company June 29, 1865.
Raber, Oswald	...do...	37	Sept. 3, 1864	1 year.	Mustered out with company June 29, 1865.
Rodenberger, David	...do...	23	Sept. 1, 1864	1 year.	Mustered out with company June 29, 1865.
Salts, Hugh	...do...	37	Aug. 31, 1864	1 year.	Mustered out with company June 29, 1865.
Sharp, Joseph	...do...	43	Aug. 28, 1864	1 year.	Mustered out with company June 29, 1865.
Showd, Jacob	...do...	20	Sept. 13, 1864	1 year.	Mustered out with company June 29, 1865.
Shower, John H	...do...	20	Aug. 31, 1864	1 year.	Mustered out July 6, 1865, at Columbus, O., by order of War Department.
Shlup, John	...do...	21	Sept. 14, 1864	1 year.	Mustered out with company June 29, 1865.
Shlup, Stephen	...do...	18	Sept. 14, 1864	1 year.	Mustered out July 7, 1865, at David's Island, New York Harbor, by order of War Department.
Simpson, Edward	...do...	24	Sept. 8, 1864	1 year.	
Smith, Hiram J	...do...	23	Sept. 3, 1864	1 year.	Mustered out with company June 29, 1865.
Smyser, John A	...do...	29	Sept. 14, 1864	1 year.	
Smoodz, Josiah	...do...	28	Sept. 6, 1864	1 year.	Mustered out June 27, 1865, at David's Island, New York Harbor, by order of War Department.
Snyder, Gotlieb	...do...	18	Sept. 3, 1864	1 year.	Mustered out with company June 29, 1865.
Stinehilber, Emil G	...do...	28	Sept. 1, 1864	1 year.	Mustered out with company June 29, 1865.
Stover, George	...do...	18	Aug. 31, 1864	1 year.	Mustered out with company June 29, 1865.
Sutter, Frederick	...do...	18	Sept. 5, 1864	1 year.	Mustered out with company June 29, 1865.
Todd, George W	...do...	19	Sept. 19, 1864	1 year.	Mustered out June 28, 1865, at Louisville, Ky., by order of War Department.
Trigg, John W	...do...	18	Sept. 5, 1864	1 year.	
Uhler, William S	...do...	25	Sept. 3, 1864	1 year.	Mustered out with company June 29, 1865.
Waisner, George W	...do...	20	Aug. 28, 1864	1 year.	Mustered out May 23, 1865, at New York City, by order of War Department.
Washington, George D	...do...	18	Sept. 14, 1864	1 year.	Mustered out June 10, 1865, at Camp [illegible], by order of War Department.
Wells, John E	...do...	35	Aug. 31, 1864	1 year.	Mustered out with company June 29, 1865.
Wingert, Henry	...do...	30	Sept. 3, 1864	1 year.	Mustered out with company June 29, 1865.
Worley, John Q	...do...	31	Sept. 5, 1864	1 year.	Mustered out with company June 29, 1865.

COMPANY G.

Mustered in September 23, 1864, at Camp Chase, O., by W. P. Richardson, Colonel 25th O. V. I. Mustered out June 29, 1865, at Charlotte, N. C., by R. A. Folsom, Captain and A. C. M., Department of North Carolina.

Names.	Rank.	Age.	Date of Entering the Service.	Period of Service.	Remarks.
Mungo D. Miller	Captain	37	Aug. 12, 1864	1 year.	Appointed Sept. 24, 1864; mustered out with company June 29, 1865.
William D. Matthews	1st Lieut.	21	July 27, 1864	1 year.	Appointed Sept. 24, 1864; mustered out with company June 29, 1865.
William H. Weagley	2d Lieut.	36	Aug. 16, 1864	1 year.	Appointed Sept. 24, 1864; mustered out with company June 29, 1865.
Jacob C. Hasen	1st Sergt.	26	Aug. 25, 1864	1 year.	Appointed Sept. 23, 1864; mustered out with company June 29, 1865.
John Boly	Sergeant.	22	Aug. 25, 1864	1 year.	Promoted to Sergt. Major Oct. 1, 1864.
William B. Myers	do.	25	Sept. 10, 1864	1 year.	Appointed Sept. 23, 1864; mustered out with company June 29, 1865.
Earl A. Sheffield	do.	27	Sept. 8, 1864	1 year.	Appointed Sept. 23, 1864; mustered out with company June 29, 1865.
Lucius. O. Edson	do.	23	Sept. 16, 1864	1 year.	Appointed from Corporal Feb. 14, 1865; mustered out with company June 29, 1865.
George M. Jones	do.	42	Aug. 25, 1864	1 year.	Appointed from Corporal Feb. 14, 1865; mustered out with company June 29, 1865.
George W. Oldfield	Corporal.	23	Aug. 22, 1864	1 year.	Mustered out May 25, 1865, at Columbus, O., by order of War Department.
George F. Leonard	do.	23	Aug. 30, 1864	1 year.	Appointed Sept 23, 1864; mustered out June 17, 1865, at Columbus, O., by order of War Department.
John Hunter	do.	22	Sept. 1, 1864	1 year.	Appointed Sept. 23, 1864; mustered out with company June 29, 1865.
Peter Kipler	do.	24	Sept. 8, 1864	1 year.	Appointed Sept. 23, 1864; mustered out with company June 29, 1865.
Thomas N. Madden	do.	21	Aug. 20, 1864	1 year.	Appointed Sept. 23, 1864; mustered out with company June 29, 1865.
Josiah Stump	do.	20	Aug. 20, 1864	1 year.	Appointed Feb. 14, 1865; mustered out with company June 29, 1865.
Israel K. Moody	do.	18	Sept. 14, 1864	1 year.	Appointed Feb. 14, 1865; mustered out with company June 29, 1865.
Simeon M. Trump	do.	23	Aug. 29, 1861	1 year.	Appointed Sept. 23, 1864; mustered out July 6, 1865, at Ward U. S. General Hospital, Newark, N. J., by order of War Department.
Samuel M. Ramsey	Musician	19	Sept. 5, 1864	1 year.	Mustered out June 2, 1865, at Camp Dennison, O., by order of War Department.
Aukney, David	Private.	42	Sept. 21, 1864	1 year.	Mustered out May 26, 1865, at Madison, Ind., by order of War Department.
Atkins, John S	do.	27	Aug. 22, 1864	1 year.	Mustered out July 4, 1865, at Murfreesboro, Tenn., by order of War Department.
Beach, Charles	do.	18	Sept. 17, 1864	1 year.	Mustered out May 24, 1865, at Philadelphia, Pa., by order of War Department.
Bender, Simon	do.	44	Sept. 4, 1864	1 year.	Transferred to Co. K, 17th Regiment, Veteran Reserve Corps, March 24, 1865; discharged May 23, 1865, at Indianapolis, Ind., by order of War Department.
Blackman, George	do.	20	Sept. 2, 1864	1 year.	
Blessing, Lewis	do.	28	Sept. 10, 1864	1 year.	
Brooks, George W	do.	29	Sept. 5, 1864	1 year.	Mustered out June 20, 1865, at Columbus, O., by order of War Department.
[illegible], Jeremiah	do.	32	Sept. 9, 1864	1 year.	Mustered out with company June 29, 1865.
Burkhead, James F	do.	33	Aug. 30, 1864	1 year.	Mustered out June 20, 1865, at Philadelphia, Pa., by order of War Department.
Burger, Charles W	do.	24	Sept 27, 1864	1 year.	Mustered out July 1, 1865, at David's Island, New York Harbor, by order of War Department.
Bush, Thomas G	do.	20	Sept. 3, 1864	1 year.	Mustered out with company June 29, 1865.
[illegible], George	do.	30	Sept. 2, 1864	1 year.	Died March 26, 1865, on board hospital transport Northern Light.
[illegible], John	do.	27	Sept. 8, 1864	1 year.	
Chase, David	do.	28	Aug. 24, 1864	1 year.	Mustered out June 2, 1865, at Washington, D. C., by order of War Department.
Clade, Jefferson M	do.	..	....	1 year.	Mustered out July 20, 1865, at Camp Dennison, O., by order of War Department.
Clark, Harvey M.	do.	35	Aug. 22, 1864	1 year.	Died Feb. 25, 1865, at Washington, D. C.
[illegible], John	do.	26	Aug. 12, 1864	1 year.	Mustered out with company June 29, 1865.
[illegible], Isaac V.	do.	27	Aug. 27, 1864	1 year.	Mustered out with company June 29, 1865.
[illegible], Wilson	do.	18	Sept. 17, 1864	1 year.	Mustered out with company June 29, 1865.
[illegible], Thomas	do.	20	Sept. 17, 1864	1 year.	Mustered out with company June 29, 1865.
[illegible], Lorenzo R.	do.	42	Aug. 29, 1864	1 year.	
[illegible], Charles	do.	34	Sept. 5, 1864	1 year.	Mustered out with company June 29, 1865.
[illegible]	do.	18	Sept. 3, 1864	1 year.	Mustered out May 31, 1865, at Cleveland, O., by order of War Department.
Eagle, William	do.	44	Sept. 5, 1864	1 year.	Mustered out with company June 29, 1865.

Names.	Rank.	Age.	Date of Entering the Service.	Period of Service.	Remarks.
Harrop, Stephen	Private..	18	Aug. 23, 1864	1 year.	Mustered out with company June 29, 1865.
Hensley, Ashford L.	....do....	23	Sept. 14, 1864	1 year.	
Jacobs, William T.	....do....	22	Sept. 3, 1864	1 year.	May 25, 1865, at Chester, Pa., by order of War Department.
Jones, John	....do....	22	Sept. 3, 1864	1 year.	Mustered out with company June 29, 1865.
Keyes, Thomas H	....do....	19	Aug. 20, 1864	1 year.	Mustered out with company June 29, 1865.
Launder, Henry C	....do....	16	Sept. 3, 1864	1 year.	Mustered out to date June 29, 1865, by order of War
Lemmon, James H	....do....	22	Sept. 9, 1864	1 year.	June 29, 1865.
Linn, John W	....do....	21	Sept. 16, 1864	1 year.	Mustered out with company June 29, 1865.
McCall, Moses A	....do....	17	Sept. 13, 1864	1 year.	Mustered out with company June 29, 1865.
McCleary, James A	....do....	19	Sept. 5, 1864	1 year.	Mustered out with company June 29, 1865.
McMillan, George	....do....	21	Aug. 30, 1864	1 year.	
Miles, Joseph	....do....	18	Aug. 13, 1864	1 year.	Mustered out with company June 29, 1865.
Miller, Howard	....do....	29	Oct. 20, 1864	1 year.	Transferred to Co. E, 181st O. V. I., June 15, 1865.
Miller, Jeremiah	....do....	38	Sept. 21, 1864	1 year.	Mustered out May 31, 1865, at Camp Dennison, O., by order of War Department.
Miller, Harvey	....do....	28	Sept. 21, 1864	1 year.	Mustered out with company June 29, 1865.
Mitchell, Stephen A	....do....	23	Aug. 23, 1864	1 year.	Mustered out with company June 29, 1865.
Mohler, John W.	....do....	17	Sept. 19, 1864	1 year.	Mustered out with company June 29, 1865.
Moore, Zadok J	....do....	23	Sept. 15, 1864	1 year.	Died March 7, 1865, at Alexandria, Va.
Moore, James	....do....	31	Sept. 21, 1864	1 year.	Mustered out May 8, 1865, at St. Louis, Mo., by order of War Department.
Nesline, Joshua	....do....	19	Sept. 8, 1864	1 year.	Mustered out with company June 29, 1865.
Nesline, John	....do....	21	Aug. 29, 1864	1 year.	Mustered out with company June 29, 1865.
Overs, George W	....do....	30	Sept. 15, 1864	1 year.	Mustered out June 7, 1865, at Columbus, O., by order of War Department.
Pickenpaugh, Jonathan R.	....do....	18	Sept. 17, 1864	1 year.	Died March 11, 1865, at Louisville, Ky.
Price, William L.	....do....	21	Sept. 15, 1864	1 year.	Mustered out June 20, 1865, at Columbus, O., by order of War Department.
Quigley, Lewis F.	....do....	31	Sept. 15, 1864	1 year.	Mustered out May 22, 1865, at Columbus, O., by order of War Department.
Reed, Thomas B	....do....	42	Aug. 15, 1864	1 year.	Transferred to Co. E, 181st O. V. I., June 15, 1865.
Reese, Francis D. Y.	....do....	31	Sept. 23, 1864	1 year.	Mustered out with company June 29, 1865.
Reardon, Dennis	....do....	22	Aug. 29, 1864	1 year.	Captured Dec. 14, 1864, in action near Murfreesboro, Tenn.; mustered out June 2, 1865, at Camp Chase, O., by order of War Department.
Reimensnyder, John	....do....	22	Sept. 20, 1864	1 year.	
Richards, Aaron S.	....do....	22	Aug. 23, 1864	1 year.	Mustered out with company June 29, 1865.
Robinson, Charles D.	....do....	43	Sept. 5, 1864	1 year.	
Sanford, Thomas	....do....	39	Sept. 23, 1864	1 year.	Mustered out with company June 29, 1865.
Seright, James G.	....do....	27	Aug. 27, 1864	1 year.	Mustered out June 19, 1865, at Beaufort, N. C., by order of War Department.
Shrigley, John O.	....do....	20	Aug. 31, 1864	1 year.	Mustered out with company June 29, 1865.
Smith, David	....do....	19	Sept. 11, 1864	1 year.	Mustered out with company June 29, 1865.
Smith, Henry T.	....do....	20	Aug. 20, 1864	1 year.	Mustered out with company June 29, 1865.
Snyder, Gilbert	....do....	21	Aug. 23, 1864	1 year.	Mustered out with company June 29, 1865.
Soliday, Henry	....do....	22	Sept. 15, 1864	1 year.	
Sprague, Andrew	....do....	18	Sept. 13, 1864	1 year.	Mustered out June 19, 1865, at Columbus, O., by order of War Department.
Sprague, Frank M.	....do....	22	Sept. 2, 1864	1 year.	Reduced from Corporal Jan. 1, 1865; mustered out May 25, 1865, at Columbus, O., by order of War Department.
Stires, John	....do....	17	Sept. 19, 1864	1 year.	Died Jan. 11, 1865, at Murfreesboro, Tenn.
Staubus, James A	....do....	32	Sept. 9, 1864	1 year.	Mustered out with company June 29, 1865.
Toland, Gillespie	....do..	16	Sept. 14, 1864	1 year.	Mustered out May 20, 1865, by order of War Department.
Wells, Newton	....do....	19	Aug. 30, 1864	1 year.	Died Sept. 17, 1864, at Putnam, O.
White, George W	....do....	18	Sept. 21, 1864	1 year.	Captured Dec. 14, 1864, in action near Murfreesboro, Tenn.; returned to company June 3, 1865; mustered out with company June 29, 1865.
Wilson, William L.	....do....	20	Sept. 2, 1864	1 year.	Mustered out with company June 29, 1865.
Wilson, William P.	....do....	44	Sept. 20, 1864	1 year.	Mustered out with company June 29, 1865.
Wilson, Edward	....do....	22	Sept. 13, 1864	1 year.	Mustered out May 25, 1865, at Columbus, O., by order of War Department.
Wilson, Thomas D.	....do....	17	Sept. 22, 1864	1 year.	Mustered out with company June 29, 1865.
Williams, James	....do....	25	Oct. 2, 1864	1 year.	Mustered out July 15, 1865, at Hicks' Hospital, Baltimore, Md., by order of War Department.
Winn, Isaac S.	....do....	22	Sept. 19, 1864	1 year.	Transferred to Co. E, 181st O. V. I., June 15, 1865.
Wires, John	....do....	18	Aug. 11, 1864	1 year.	Mustered out with company June 29, 1865.
Young, Henry	....do....	30	Sept. 15, 1864	1 year.	Mustered out with company June 29, 1865.
Zimmer, George V	....do....	20	Sept. 19, 1864	1 year.	

COMPANY G.

Mustered in September 23, 1864, at Camp Chase, O., by W. P. Richardson, Colonel 25th O. V. I. Mustered out June 29, 1865, at Charlotte, N. C., by E. A. Folsom, Captain and A. C. M., Department of North Carolina.

Names.	Rank.	Age.	Date of Entering the Service.	Period of Service.	Remarks.
Mungo D. Miller	Captain	37	Aug. 12, 1864	1 year.	Appointed Sept. 24, 1864; mustered out with company June 29, 1865.
William D. Matthews	1st Lieut.	21	July 27, 1864	1 year.	Appointed Sept. 24, 1864; mustered out with company June 29, 1865.
William H. Weagley	2d Lieut.	36	Aug. 16, 1864	1 year.	Appointed Sept. 24, 1864; mustered out with company June 29, 1865.
Jacob C. Hasen	1st Sergt.	36	Aug. 25, 1864	1 year.	Appointed Sept. 23, 1864; mustered out with company June 29, 1865.
John Boly	Sergeant.	22	Aug. 25, 1864	1 year.	Promoted to Sergt. Major Oct. 1, 1864.
William B. Myers	do.	25	Sept. 10, 1864	1 year.	Appointed Sept. 23, 1864; mustered out with company June 29, 1865.
Earl A. Sheffield	do.	27	Sept. 3, 1864	1 year.	Appointed Sept. 23, 1864; mustered out with company June 29, 1865.
Lucius, O. Edson	do.	23	Sept. 16, 1864	1 year.	Appointed from Corporal Feb. 14, 1865; mustered out with company June 29, 1865.
George M. Jones	do.	43	Aug. 25, 1864	1 year.	Appointed from Corporal Feb. 14, 1865; mustered out with company June 29, 1865.
George W. Oldfield	Corporal.	22	Aug. 22, 1864	1 year.	Mustered out May 25, 1865, at Columbus, O., by order of War Department.
George F. Leonard	do.	28	Aug. 30, 1864	1 year.	Appointed Sept 23, 1864; mustered out June 17, 1865, at Columbus, O., by order of War Department.
John Hunter	do.	22	Sept. 1, 1864	1 year.	Appointed Sept. 23, 1864; mustered out with company June 29, 1865.
Peter Kipfer	do.	24	Sept. 8, 1864	1 year.	Appointed Sept. 23, 1864; mustered out with company June 29, 1865.
Thomas N. Madden	do.	21	Aug. 20, 1864	1 year.	Appointed Sept. 23, 1864; mustered out with company June 29, 1865.
Josiah Stump	do.	20	Aug. 20, 1864	1 year.	Appointed Feb. 14, 1865; mustered out with company June 29, 1865.
Israel K. Moody	do.	18	Sept. 14, 1864	1 year.	Appointed Feb. 14, 1865; mustered out with company June 29, 1865.
Simeon H. Trump	do.	23	Aug. 29, 1864	1 year.	Appointed Sept. 23, 1864; mustered out July 6, 1865, at Ward U. S. General Hospital, Newark, N. J., by order of War Department.
Samuel M. Ramsey	Musician	19	Sept. 5, 1864	1 year.	Mustered out June 2, 1865, at Camp Dennison, O., by order of War Department.
Ankney, David	Private	42	Sept. 21, 1864	1 year.	Mustered out May 26, 1865, at Madison, Ind., by order of War Department.
Atkins, John S.	do.	27	Aug. 22, 1864	1 year.	Mustered out July 4, 1865, at Murfreesboro, Tenn., by order of War Department.
Beach, Charles	do.	18	Sept. 17, 1864	1 year.	Mustered out May 24, 1865, at Philadelphia, Pa., by order of War Department.
Bender, Simon	do.	44	Sept. 4, 1864	1 year.	Transferred to Co. K, 17th Regiment, Veteran Reserve Corps, March 24, 1865; discharged May 28, 1865, at Indianapolis, Ind., by order of War Department.
Blackman, George	do.	20	Sept. 2, 1864	1 year.	
Blessing, Lewis	do.	28	Sept. 10, 1864	1 year.	
Brooks, George W.	do.	39	Sept. 5, 1864	1 year.	Mustered out June 20, 1865, at Columbus, O., by order of War Department.
[illegible], Jeremiah	do.	32	Sept. 9, 1864	1 year.	Mustered out with company June 29, 1865.
Burkhead, James F.	do.	33	Aug. 30, 1864	1 year.	Mustered out June 20, 1865, at Philadelphia, Pa., by order of War Department.
Burger, Charles W.	do.	24	Sept 27, 1864	1 year.	Mustered out July 1, 1865, at David's Island, New York Harbor, by order of War Department.
Bush, Thomas G.	do.	20	Sept. 3, 1864	1 year.	Mustered out with company June 29, 1865.
Callin, George	do.	39	Sept. 2, 1864	1 year.	Died March 26, 1865, on board hospital transport Northern Light.
[illegible], John	do.	27	Sept. 8, 1864	1 year.	
Chase, David	do.	23	Aug. 24, 1864	1 year.	Mustered out June 2, 1865, at Washington, D. C., by order of War Department.
Clade, Jefferson M.	do.	..	....	1 year.	Mustered out July 20, 1865, at Camp Dennison, O., by order of War Department.
Clark, Harvey M.	do.	25	Aug. 23, 1864	1 year.	Died Feb. 25, 1865, at Washington, D. C.
Collins, John	do.	26	Aug. 12, 1864	1 year.	Mustered out with company June 29, 1865.
Conine, [illegible] V.	do.	27	Aug. 27, 1864	1 year.	Mustered out with company June 29, 1865.
Copley, [illegible]	do.	18	Sept. 17, 1864	1 year.	Mustered out with company June 29, 1865.
Crozier, [illegible]	do.	20	Sept. 17, 1864	1 year.	Mustered out with company June 29, 1865.
Cummins, [illegible] R.	do.	42	Aug. 29, 1864	1 year.	
Deatsman, [illegible]	do.	34	Sept. 5, 1864	1 year.	Mustered out with company June 29, 1865.
Dwyer, John	do.	18	Sept. 3, 1864	1 year.	Mustered out May 31, 1865, at Cleveland, O., by order of War Department.
Eagle, William	do.	44	Sept. 5, 1864	1 year.	Mustered out with company June 29, 1865.

Names.	Rank.	Age.	Date of Entering the Service.	
Ewing, Arthur	Private	19	Aug. 20, 1864	1
Floyd, James	...do...	21	Sept. 3, 1864	1
Foster, Amos	...do...	18	Sept. 3, 1864	1
Fout, George W	...do...	28	Aug. 28, 1864	1 year.
Francisco, George	...do...	19	Aug. 24, 1864	1 year.
Gansman, Jacob	...do...	41	Aug. 27, 1864	1 year.
Geary, Thomas J	...do...	25	Aug. 19, 1864	1 year.
Graybill, Charles	...do...	20	Sept. 2, 1864	1 year.
Hasen, John S	...do...	18	Aug. 30, 1864	1 year.
Hamilton, Wyley W	...do...	21	Aug. 31, 1864	1 year.
Hay, John	...do...	20	Sept. 17, 1864	1 year.
Henderson, Wilson D	...do...	19	Sept. 5, 1864	1 year.
Henning, William	...do...	37	Sept. 8, 1864	1 year.
Hissong, John	...do...	19	Aug. 29, 1864	1 year.
Hobbs, Franklin	...do...	38	Sept. 2, 1864	1 year.
Hook, Benjamin	...do...	18	Aug. 29, 1864	1 year.
Jenkins, David A	...do...	28	Sept. 6, 1864	1 year.
Karr, John	...do...	36	Sept. 17, 1864	1 year.
Kiser, Lorenzo D	...do...	18	Sept. 10, 1864	1 year.
Kasenbaker, David	...do...	20	Sept. 9, 1864	1 year.
Leiter, Montervills J	...do...	18	Sept. 17, 1864	1 year.
Lundy, Willits	...do...	18	Sept. 3, 1864	1 year.
McCaffel, James	...do...	27	Aug. 23, 1864	1 year.
McCarty, Charles	...do...	20	Aug. 28, 1864	1 year.
McLain, Alexander	...do...	41	Sept. 4, 1864	1 year.
Major, Proctor H	...do...	26	Aug. 31, 1864	1 year.
Mawhirter, William	...do...	18	Aug. 31, 1864	1 year.
Miller, Joseph	...do...	49	Sept. 2, 1864	1 year.
Moore, Thomas	...do...	38	Aug. 22, 1864	1 year.
Myers, Henry	...do...	18	Sept. 17, 1864	1 year.
Neff, John	...do...	18	Sept. 5, 1864	1 year.
Northrop, Rosswell	...do...	39	Sept. 2, 1864	1 year.
Parker, Benjamin G	...do...	23	Sept. 13, 1864	1 year.
Peters, Ambrose C	...do...	18	Sept. 17, 1864	1 year.
Poulson, Jonathan L	...do...	18	Aug. 26, 1864	1 year.
Pressler, George W	...do...	18	Aug. 26, 1864	1 year.
Rankin, David	...do...	34	Aug. 22, 1864	1 year.
Rathburn, William	...do...	33	Sept. 14, 1864	1 year.
Richenbach, Joel	...do...	20	Sept. 12, 1864	1 year.
Shafer, John S	...do...	18	Aug. 22, 1864	1 year.
Shafer, Nooman	...do...	19	Aug. 22, 1864	1 year.
Sharp, Solomon	...do...	22	Aug. 23, 1864	1 year.
Smith, Daniel B	...do...	18	Sept. 14, 1864	1 year.
Smith, James C	...do...	24	Sept. 2, 1864	1 year.
Smith, Jacob W	...do...	20	Sept. 1, 1864	1 year.
Smith, William H	...do...	18	Aug. 19, 1864	1 year.
Stall, Jonathan	...do...	19	Sept. 3, 1864	1 year.
Stall, Michael	...do...	24	Sept. 5, 1864	1 year.
Swaim, John D	...do...	24	Sept. 17, 1864	1 year.
Thomas, William C	...do...	19	Sept. 5, 1864	1 year.
Travis, John C	...do...	24	Sept. 17, 1864	1 year.
Trump, James M	...do...	18	Sept. 19, 1864	1 year.
Walker, Daniel	...do...	27	Aug. 26, 1864	1 year.
Ward, Alonzo J	...do...	20	Sept. 12, 1864	1 year.
Wasser, Charles A	...do...	40	Sept. 2, 1864	1 year.
Watson, Henry	...do...	45	Sept. 17, 1864	1 year.
Weiger, Conrad	...do...	25	Sept. 17, 1864	1 year.
Welty, Henry	...do...	35	Sept. 16, 1864	1 year.
Will, Richard B	...do...	42	Sept. 1, 1864	1 year.
White, Joseph	...do...	28	Sept. 17, 1864	1 year.
Wilcox, Sampson R	...do...	18	Aug. 17, 1864	1 year.
Wolford, John	...do...	37	Sept. 5, 1864	1 year.

COMPANY H.

ered in September 24, 1864, at Camp Chase, O., by W. P. Richardson, Colonel 25th O. V. I. Mustered out June 29, 1865, at Charlotte, N. C., by E. A. Folsom, Captain and A. C. M., Department of North Carolina.

Names.	Rank.	Age.	Date of Entering the Service.	Period of Service.	Remarks.
ew Davis	Captain.	26	Sept. 24, 1864	1 year.	Detailed as Provost Marshal, 1st Division, 23d Army Corps, Dec. 30, 1864; returned to company March 22, 1865; mustered out with company June 29, 1865.
T. Bedwell	1st Lieut.	22	Sept. 24, 1864	1 year.	Mustered out with company June 29, 1865.
s L. Scott	2d Lieut.	19	Sept. 18, 1864	1 year.	Promoted from private Sept. 24, 1864; mustered out with company June 29, 1865.
am Douglass	1st Sergt.	23	Aug. 22, 1864	1 year.	Appointed from Sergeant March 29, 1865; mustered out with company June 29, 1865.
und C. Christy	Sergeant.	37	Sept. 3, 1864	1 year.	Appointed Sept. 24, 1864; mustered out with company June 29, 1865.
e R. Crooks	...do...	24	Aug. 29, 1864	1 year.	Appointed Sept. 24, 1864; mustered out May 16, 1865, at Washington, D. C., by order of War Department.
ott Bassett	...do...	37	Sept. 1, 1864	1 year.	Appointed Sept. 24, 1864; mustered out with company June 29, 1865.
l L. Mills	...do...	21	Sept. 18, 1864	1 year.	Appointed from Corporal March 29, 1865; mustered out with company June 29, 1865.
h Jones	...do...	21	Aug. 12, 1864	1 year.	Appointed from Corporal May 18, 1865; mustered out with company June 29, 1865.
s Fessenden	Corporal.	23	Aug. 26, 1864	1 year.	Appointed Sept. 24, 1864; mustered out with company June 29, 1865.
on Thompson	...do...	44	Sept. 2, 1864	1 year.	Appointed Sept. 24, 1864; died July 1, 1865, in hospital at City Point, Va.
r P. Trumbull	...do...	36	Sept. 23, 1864	1 year.	Appointed Sept. 24, 1864; mustered out with company June 29, 1865.
mis L. Hoagland	...do...	21	Aug. 18, 1864	1 year.	Appointed Sept. 24, 1864; mustered out with company June 29, 1865.
hart Biehl	...do...	27	Sept. 17, 1864	1 year.	Appointed Sept. 24, 1864; mustered out with company June 29, 1865.
n Gardner	...do...	24	Sept. 1, 1864	1 year.	Appointed Sept. 24, 1864; mustered out with company June 29, 1865.
dore F. Crater	...do...	18	Sept. 13, 1864	1 year.	Appointed March 29, 1865; mustered out with company June 29, 1865.
klin Bowman	...do...	34	Sept. 3, 1864	1 year.	Appointed May 16, 1865; mustered out with company June 29, 1865.
ey Hoagland	Musician	18	Sept. 22, 1864	1 year.	Mustered out to date June 29, 1865, by order of War Department.
C. Jones	...do...	18	Sept. 1, 1864	1 year.	Mustered out with company June 29, 1865.
el, Jacob	Private..	18	Sept. 5, 1864	1 year.	Mustered out with company June 29, 1865.
l, Henry H	...do...	18	Sept. 21, 1864	1 year.	Mustered out with company June 29, 1865.
r, Alexander	...do...	25	Aug. 28, 1864	1 year.	
r, John	...do...	18	Sept. 4, 1864	1 year.	Mustered out with company June 29, 1865.
on, Thomas	...do...	18	Sept. 21, 1864	1 year.	Mustered out with company June 29, 1865.
nold, David	...do...	30	Sept. 9, 1864	1 year.	Mustered out with company June 29, 1865.
shire, Anson	...do...	42	Aug. 31, 1864	1 year.	Mustered out June 12, 1865, at Beaufort, N. C., by order of War Department.
, Washington	...do...	31	Sept. 1, 1864	1 year.	Mustered out with company June 29, 1865.
wick, George	...do...	24	Aug. 22, 1864	1 year.	Mustered out with company June 29, 1865.
, William E	...do...	22	Aug. 29, 1864	1 year.	Mustered out with company June 29, 1865.
n, George	...do...	20	Sept. 22, 1864	1 year.	
ll, Hiram	...do...	19	Aug. 29, 1864	1 year.	Mustered out May 29, 1865, at Newbern, N. C., by order of War Department.
pbell, DeBold	...do...	44	Sept. 21, 1864	1 year.	Mustered out with company June 29, 1865.
r, Ephraim T	...do...	18	Sept. 5, 1864	1 year.	Mustered out with company June 29, 1865.
nah, Nicholas	...do...	18	Sept. 7, 1864	1 year.	Mustered out with company June 29, 1865.
, Joseph	...do...	19	Sept. 9, 1864	1 year.	Mustered out with company June 29, 1865.
mann, David M	...do...	19	Sept. 21, 1864	1 year.	
er, James N	...do...	18	Aug. 20, 1864	1 year.	Mustered out with company June 29, 1865.
er, Thomas J	...do...	28	Sept. 18, 1864	1 year.	Mustered out with company June 29, 1865.
ingham, John	...do...	22	Sept. 23, 1864	1 year.	
ng, Peter	...do...	31	Aug. 22, 1864	1 year.	Mustered out with company June 29, 1865.
, Joseph	...do...	21	Sept. 15, 1864	1 year.	Mustered out with company June 29, 1865.
r, Stephen H	...do...	30	Aug. 22, 1864	1 year.	Mustered out June 2, 1865, at Camp Dennison, O., by order of War Department.
, William L	...do...	24	Sept. 18, 1864	1 year.	Mustered out with company June 29, 1865.
er, John C	...do...	19	Sept. 3, 1864	1 year.	Mustered out with company June 29, 1865.
, Zachary T	...do...	18	Sept. 7, 1864	1 year.	Mustered out with company June 29, 1865.
r, George F	...do...	18	Aug. 20, 1864	1 year.	Mustered out with company June 29, 1865.
r, Thomas	...do...	31	Sept. 21, 1864	1 year.	
ner, Jacob	...do...	31	Sept. 1, 1864	1 year.	Mustered out May 16, 1865, at Washington, D. C., by order of War Department.
ner, William	...do...	20	Aug. 18, 1864	1 year.	Mustered out with company June 29, 1865.
l, James M	...do...	23	Sept. 20, 1864	1 year.	

Names.	Rank.	Age.	Date of Entering the Service.	Period of Service.	Remarks.
Gray, Disbury	Private.	29	Sept. 12, 1864	1 year.	Mustered out with company June 29, 1865.
Graham, John E	...do...	18	Sept. 3, 1864	1 year.	Mustered out with company June 29, 1865.
Green, John L	...do...	19	Aug. 27, 1864	1 year.	Mustered out with company June 29, 1865.
Hager, James W	...do...	18	Sept. 6, 1864	1 year.	Mustered out with company June 29, 1865.
Haley, Samuel H	...do...	26	Sept. 3, 1864	1 year.	Mustered out with company June 29, 1865.
Haughy, Arthur C	...do...	18	Sept. 22, 1864	1 year.	Mustered out with company June 29, 1865.
Hedge, Anderson	...do...	22	Sept. 13, 1864	1 year.	Mustered out with company June 29, 1865.
Herron, Joseph	...do...	30	Sept. 18, 1864	1 year.	Mustered out June 17, 1865, at Columbus, O., by order of War Department.
Heston, Joseph	...do...	24	Sept. 17, 1864	1 year.	Mustered out with company June 29, 1865.
Jennings, Elijah	...do...	22	Sept. 2, 1864	1 year.	Mustered out with company June 29, 1865.
Jones, John	...do...	24	Aug. 22, 1864	1 year.	Mustered out with company June 29, 1865.
Kalix, Christian	...do...	18	Sept. 22, 1864	1 year.	Mustered out with company June 29, 1865.
Keller, Daniel	...do...	18	Sept. 1, 1864	1 year.	Died June 31, 1865, at Louisville, Ky.
Kreiter, James	...do...	18	Sept. 18, 1864	1 year.	Mustered out with company June 29, 1865.
Lacy, John W	...do...	37	Sept. 5, 1864	1 year.	Mustered out with company June 29, 1865.
Long, Samuel	...do...	26	Sept. 3, 1864	1 year.	Mustered out with company June 29, 1865.
Long, Martin	...do...	23	Sept. 1, 1864	1 year.	Mustered out with company June 29, 1865.
McCormick, Nicholas	...do...	19	Sept. 21, 1864	1 year.	
McDivitt, William E	...do...	28	Sept. 18, 1864	1 year.	Promoted to Hospital Steward Oct. 3, 1864.
McGwire, Patrick	...do...	22	Sept. 22, 1864	1 year.	
McNabb, George W	...do...	25	Sept. 4, 1864	1 year.	Mustered out with company June 29, 1865.
Meek, Sylvester C	...do...	28	Sept. 12, 1864	1 year.	Died May 17, 1865, at Charlotte, N. C.
Merrett, Josiah	...do...	18	Aug. 18, 1864	1 year.	Mustered out June 17, 1865, at Charlotte, N. C., by order of War Department.
Miller, David	...do...	31	Sept. 12, 1864	1 year.	Mustered out with company June 29, 1865.
Miller, Josiah	...do...	19	Sept. 12, 1864	1 year.	Mustered out with company June 29, 1865.
Minnis, Wilson	...do...	19	Aug. 29, 1864	1 year.	Mustered out with company June 29, 1865.
Oldham, Joseph B	...do...	33	Sept. 9, 1864	1 year.	Mustered out June 20, 1865, at David's Island, New York Harbor, by order of War Department.
Pearch, Luther	...do...	18	Sept. 1, 1864	1 year.	Mustered out with company June 29, 1865.
Petty, Edward F	...do...	24	Sept. 1[illegible], 1864	1 year.	Mustered out with company June 29, 1865.
Pickard, Joseph	...do...	34	Sept. 19, 1864	1 year.	
Pringle, David M	...do...	30	Sept. 20, 1864	1 year.	Mustered out to date June 29, 1865, by order of War Department.
Price, Jacob	...do...	24	Sept. 23, 1864	1 year.	Mustered out with company June 29, 1865.
Ray, James	...do...	21	Sept. 1, 1864	1 year.	Mustered out with company June 29, 1865.
Richardson, Abram	...do...	30	Sept. 23, 1864	1 year.	Mustered out with company June 29, 1865.
Sanders, [illegible]orge	...do...	25	Aug. 29, 1864	1 year.	Mustered out with company June 29, 1865.
Schoonover, William F	...do...	23	Sept. 1, 1864	1 year.	Mustered out to date June 29, 1865, by order of War Department.
Schwyhart, Jacob	...do...	38	Sept. 13, 1864	1 year.	Mustered out June 6, 1865, at Beaufort, N. C., by order of War Department.
Shafer, Samuel	...do...	21	Aug. 22, 1864	1 year.	Mustered out with company June 29, 1865.
Sherretts, [illegible]mes M	...do...	19	Aug. 30, 1864	1 year.	Mustered out with company June 29, 1865.
Shull, Henry E	...do...	18	Sept. 9, 1864	1 year.	Mustered out with company June 29, 1865.
Sills, Joseph	...do...	24	Aug. 25, 1864	1 year.	Mustered out with company June 29, 1865.
Sills, William H	...do...	25	Aug. 25, 1864	1 year.	Mustered out with company June 29, 1865.
Smith, Jacob	...do...	19	Aug. 27, 1864	1 year.	Mustered out with company June 29, 1865.
Smithyman, James	...do...	18	Sept. 2, 1864	1 year.	Mustered out with company June 29, 1865.
Smothers, Alexander	...do...	18	Sept. 23, 1864	1 year.	
Steel, Marshall P	...do...	18	Sept. 5, 1864	1 year.	Mustered out with company June 29, 1865.
Stubbins, Leonard	...do...	18	Sept. 20, 1864	1 year.	Mustered out with company June 29, 1865.
Taylor, Jacob M	...do...	21	Sept. 15, 1864	1 year.	Mustered out May 17, 1865, at Washington, D. C., by order of War Department.
Todd, John M	...do...	36	Sept. 10, 1864	1 year.	Promoted to Com. Sergeant Oct. 4, 1864.
Tolbert, Sampson A	...do...	19	Sept. 12, 1864	1 year.	Mustered out to date June 29, 1865, by order of War Department.
Vail, Isaac	...do...	39	Sept. 18, 1864	1 year.	Died Feb. 9, 1865, at Jefferson[illegible]ille, Ind.
Waers, Samuel B	...do...	13	Sept. 1, 1864	1 year.	Mustered out w[illegible]h compan[illegible] June 29, 1865.
Williams, Harrison	...do...	42	Aug. 22, 1864	1 year.	Died Feb. 28, 1865, at Morehead City, N. C.
Wilson, William W	...do...	18	Aug. 20, 1864	1 year.	Mustered out with company June 29, 1865.
Wingate, Albert M	...do...	20	Sept. 3, 1864	1 year.	Mustered out with company June 29, 1865.
Wolfe, Henry F	...do...	26	Sept. 1, 1864	1 year.	Reduced from 1st Sergeant March 9, 1865; mustered out with company June 29, 1865.
Yarnal, Samuel	...do...	20	Sept. 12, 1864	1 year.	Mustered out with company June 29, 1865.

COMPANY I.

Mustered in September 26, 1864, at Camp Chase, O., by W. P. Richardson, Colonel 25th O. V. I. Mustered out June 29, 1865, at Charlotte, N. C., by E. A. Folsom, Captain and A. C. M., Department of North Carolina.

Names.	Rank.	Age.	Date of Entering the Service.	Period of Service.	Remarks.
William A. Miller	Captain.	21	Sept. 24, 1864	1 year.	Mustered out with company June 29, 1865.
George L. Emmons	1st Lieut.	28	Sept. 24, 1864	1 year.	Mustered out with company June 29, 1865.
Theodore Crowl	2d Lieut.	21	Sept. 24, 1864	1 year.	Mustered out with company June 29, 1865.
John M. Foulks	1st Sergt.	24	Sept. 5, 1864	1 year.	Appointed from private Dec. 31, 1864; mustered out with company June 29, 1865
Augustus Balmat	Sergeant.	28	Sept. 1, 1864	1 year.	Appointed Sept. 26, 1864; transferred to Co. B, 2d Battalion, Veteran Reserve Corps —, from which mustered out July 6, 1865, at Detroit, Mich., by order of War Department.
Charles S. Burr	....do....	44	Aug. 31, 1864	1 year.	Appointed Sept. 26, 1864; mustered out with company June 29, 1865.
Peter Young	....do....	31	Sept. 9, 1864	1 year.	Appointed from private Dec. 31, 1864; mustered out with company June 29, 1865.
Joseph Hay	....do....	25	Sept. 14, 1864	1 year.	Appointed Corporal Dec. 31, 1864; Sergeant Jan. 7, 1865; mustered out with company June 29, 1865.
George Sherman	....do....	21	Sept. 12, 1864	1 year.	
Zephaniah A. Weldin	Corporal.	24	Sept. 3, 1864	1 year.	Appointed Dec. 31, 1864; mustered out with company June 29, 1865.
John C. Hildenbeitle	....do....	18	Aug. 31, 1864	1 year.	Appointed Sept. 26, 1864; mustered out with company June 29, 1865.
Oliver Davis	....do....	42	Sept. 6, 1864	1 year	Appointed Sept. 26, 1864; mustered out with company June 29, 1865.
William B. Shinn	....do....	27	Sept. 7, 1864	1 year.	Appointed Sept. 26, 1864; mustered out with company June 29, 1865.
Albin Frey	....do....	21	Sept. 3, 1864	1 year.	Appointed Sept. 26, 1864; mustered out with company June 29, 1865.
Thomas Baker	....do....	44	Sept. 6, 1864	1 year.	Appointed May 1, 1865; mustered out with company June 29, 1865.
Michael Miller	....do....	44	Aug. 31, 1864	1 year.	Mustered out May 19, 1865, at Philadelphia, Pa., by order of War Department.
Elishmer D. Gould	Musician	18	Sept. 6, 1864	1 year.	Mustered out with company June 29, 1865.
Christian M. Barnard	....do....	17	Sept. 6, 1864	1 year.	Mustered out with company June 29, 1865.
Ephriam Sonedecker	....do....	34	Aug. 30, 1864	1 year.	Mustered out with company June 29, 1865.
Allensworth, John	Private.	18	Aug. 18, 1864	1 year.	Mustered out with company June 29, 1865.
Andrist, Jacob	....do....	18	Aug. 26, 1864	1 year.	Wounded March 10, 1865, in action in North Carolina; mustered out June 6, 1865, at Beaufort, N. C., by order of War Department.
Barr, Benjamin F.	....do....	26	Sept. 6, 1864	1 year.	Mustered out May 30, 1865, at Cleveland, O., by order of War Department.
Beck, Christian	....do....	44	Sept. 22, 1864	1 year.	Mustered out June 17, 1865, at Columbus, O., by order of War Department.
Burger, John	....do....	18	Aug. 20, 1864	1 year.	Mustered out June 6, 1865, at Beaufort, N. C., by order of War Department.
Carter, Albert	....do....	18	Sept. 12, 1864	1 year.	Died June 22, 1865, at Charlotte, N. C.
Cattrell, John	....do....	43	Sept. 14, 1864	1 year.	Mustered out with company June 29, 1865.
Connell, Philip	....do....	22	Sept. 7, 1864	1 year.	
Connell, Alfred	....do....	28	Sept. 5, 1864	1 year.	Reduced from Corporal June 10, 1865; mustered out with company June 29, 1865.
Courtright, Finly R.	....do....	34	Aug. 31, 1864	1 year.	Mustered out with company June 29, 1865.
Cram, Martin	....do....	24	Sept. 7, 1864	1 year.	Mustered out with company June 29, 1865.
Croft, John	....do....	43	Sept. 2, 1864	1 year.	Mustered out July 1, 1865, at Camp Dennison O., by order of War Department.
Dunn, William	....do....	21	Sept. 20, 1864	1 year.	
Donahue, Francis	....do....	18	Sept. 22, 1864	1 year.	Died Dec. 22, 1864, at Murfreesboro, Tenn.
Donahue, William	....do....	44	Sept. 22, 1864	1 year.	Died Dec. 19, 1864, at Nashville, Tenn.
Duff, Joseph	....do....	26	Sept. 5, 1864	1 year.	Mustered out with company June 27, 1865.
Ewing, Joseph	....do....	41	Sept. 5, 1864	1 year.	Mustered out with company June 29, 1865.
Fanning, Joseph A.	....do....	22	Sept. 5, 1864	1 year.	Discharged Sept. 22, 1864, at Camp Chase, O., by order of War Department.
Folk, Joseph	....do....	18	Sept. 5, 1864	1 year.	Mustered out with company June 29, 1865.
Fried, Henry C.	....do....	22	Sept. 3, 1864	1 year.	Mustered out June 20, 1865, at Wheeling, W. Va., by order of War Department.
[illegible], William	....do....	18	Aug. 30, 1864	1 year.	Mustered out with company June 29, 1865.
[illegible], David H.	....do....	39	Sept. 5, 1864	1 year.	Mustered out June 19, 1865, at Chester, Pa., by order of War Department.
[illegible]	....do....	26	Sept. 5, 1864	1 year.	Mustered out with company June 29, 1865.
[illegible], William	....do....	41	Sept. 6, 1864	1 year.	Mustered out June 6, 1865, at Beaufort, N. C., by order of War Department.
Grimes, Henry	....do....	18	Aug. 16, 1864	1 year.	Mustered out with company June 29, 1865.
Gross, Daniel	....do....	39	Sept. 3, 1864	1 year.	Mustered out with company June 29, 1865.
Hannay, John	....do....	39	Sept. 1, 1864	1 year.	Mustered out with company June 29, 1865.
Heiserman, Gideon	....do....	42	Sept. 3, 1864	1 year.	Mustered out with company June 29, 1865.
Hiner, John	....do....	18	Sept. 2, 1864	1 year.	Mustered out with company June 29, 1865.
Johnson, James R. B.	....do....	[illegible]	Sept. [illegible], 1864	1 year.	
John, Austin	....do....	[illegible]	Aug. [illegible], 1864	1 year.	Died Feb. 12, 1865, at Camp Dennison, O.

Names.	Rank.	Age.	Date of Entering the Service.		
Jones, John K	Private.	35	Sept. 8, 1864		Mustered
Kelly, Ephraim B	do	18	Sept. 19, 1864		Mustered
Kleinman, Dennis	do	38	Sept. 5, 1864		Mustered
Klingaman, Zephaniah	do	18	Aug. 15, 1864		Mustered
Kimes, Asher J	do	20	Sept. 2, 1864		Mustered
Kimes, Milton G	do	18	Sept. 7, 1864		Mustered
King, Fletcher	do	41	Sept. 2, 1864		Mustered
Knoll, Henry	do	24	Sept. 1, 1864		Mustered
Lambright, John	do	18	Sept. 10, 1864		Mustered
Lash, John	do	18	Aug. 31, 1864		Died Feb. 24,
Lenox, John	do	20	Sept. 26, 1864		
McConner, Jacob B	do	18	Sept. 19, 1864		Mustered out
McCoy, Patrick	do	21	Sept. 7, 1864		
McGaffick, Robert S	do	20	Sept. 3, 1864		Mustered out
McGee, John	do	37	Sept. 1, 1864		Mustered out C., by order
Martin, John W	do	30	Sept. 3, 1864		Mustered out pital, New Department
Mason, Thomas	do	23	Sept. 21, 1864		
Milner, Isaac	do	43	Sept. 5, 1864		Mustered out C., by order
Miller, George	do	21	Sept. 20, 1864	1 year.	
Miller, Vanamering	do	18	Aug. 31, 1864	1 year.	Mustered out C., by order
Minard, Eddy	do	22	Sept. 9, 1864	1	Mustered out
Monk, Joseph A	do	18	Aug. 7, 1864	1	Mustered out
Pepple, Sylvanus G	do	19	Aug. 22, 1864	1	Mustered out
Ramsey, John A	do	18	Sept. 5, 1864	1	Mustered out
Riblett, Lewis	do	31	Sept. 5, 1864	1	Mustered out
Riehle, Daniel W	do	21	Aug. 24, 1864	1	Mustered out
Richison, John	do	36	Sept. 6, 1864	1	Mustered out
Rylee, Richard	do	28	Sept. 21, 1864	1	
Saner, Adam	do	37	Sept. 1, 1864		Died Jan. 14,
Settle, John H	do	18	Aug. 18, 1864		Mustered out J by order of
Sherry, Chaney	do	38	Sept. 6, 1864		Mustered out
Sherwood, Preston	do	19	Aug. 30, 1864		Captured Dec son's Pike. out June 2 order of Wa
Smith, Samuel E	do	18	Sept. 1, 1864		Died Feb. 20,
Smith, William E	do	18	Sept. 5, 1864		Mustered out
Snider, John	do	23	Sept. 7, 1864		Mustered out Pa., by orde
Snider, Jehu	do	29	Sept. 7, 1864	1	Died Jan. 19,
Swearingen, George	do	23	Aug. 31, 1864	1	Mustered out
Walker, William	do	28	Sept. 5, 1864	1	Mustered out
Weimer, Jesse	do	23	Sept. 3, 1864	1	Transferred fr 28, 1864; mu 29, 1865.
Welch, Thomas	do	19	Aug. 16, 1864	1	
Wertz, Leander	do	17	Sept. 10, 1864	1	Mustered out
Wertz, Conrad	do	44	Sept. 10, 1864	1	Mustered out
Wickersham, Bayard	do	24	Sept. 3, 1864	1	Mustered out
Wilson, William A	do	18	Sept. 3, 1864	1	
Williams, Charles	do	20	Sept. 20, 1864	1	
Wise, Tobias S	do	21	Sept. 9, 1864	1	Mustered out
Wood, William T	do	18	Aug. 26, 1864	1	Mustered out
Young, Watson	do	23	Sept. 5, 1864	1	

COMPANY K.

Mustered in September 26, 1864, at Camp Chase, O., by W. P. Richardson, Col
June 29, 1865, at Charlotte, N. C., by E. A. Folsom, Captain
Department of North Carolina.

Bela DeL. Dudley	Captain.	21	Sept. 26, 1864	1 year.	Mustered out
Henry H. Dudley	1st Lieut.	26	Sept. 26, 1864	1 year.	Mustered out
Samuel S. Yoder	2d Lieut.	28	Sept. 26, 1864	1 year.	Wounded Nov River, Tenn. 1865, by orde
John W. Shumaker	1st Sergt.	26	Aug. 28, 1864	1 year.	Appointed Se company Ju
David B. Lee	Sergeant.	33	Aug. 26, 1864	1 year.	Appointed Se company Ju
Luther N. Lane	do	21	Aug. 26, 1864	1 year.	Appointed Se company Ju
James Wrigley	do	22	Aug. 15, 1864	1 year.	Appointed Se company Ju

Names.	Rank.	Age.	Date of Entering the Service.	Period of Service.	Remarks.
McGuire	[illegible]	[illegible]	Sept. 17, 1864	1 year.	Appointed Sept. 28, 1864; mustered out June 17, 1865, at Columbus, O., by order of War Department.
n F. Weeks	Corporal.	28	Sept. 1, 1864	1 year.	Appointed Sept. 28, 1864; mustered out with company June 29, 1865.
A. Baker	...do...	20	Aug. 26, 1864	1 year.	Appointed Sept. 28, 1864; mustered out with company June 29, 1865.
d S. Moore	...do...	18	Aug. 22, 1864	1 year.	Appointed Sept. 28, 1864; mustered out with company June 29, 1865.
Sadler	...do...	23	Sept. 5, 1864	1 year.	Appointed Sept. 28, 1864; died Feb. 8, 1865, at Camp Dennison, O.
Utz	...do...	20	Aug. 31, 1864	1 year.	Appointed Sept. 28, 1864; mustered out with company June 29, 1865.
M. McConnell	...do...	18	Aug. 26, 1864	1 year.	Appointed Sept. 28, 1864; died Feb. 19, 1865, at Wheeling, W. Va.
Miller	...do...	40	Aug. 22, 1864	1 year.	Appointed March 1, 1865; mustered out with company June 29, 1865.
anoedall	...do...	29	Sept. 28, 1864	1 year.	Appointed March 1, 1865; mustered out with company June 29, 1865.
Holmes	Musician	27	Sept. 2, 1864	1 year.	Mustered out with company June 29, 1865.
Hartman	...do...	18	Sept. 20, 1864	1 year.	Mustered out with company June 29, 1865.
re, George W	Private.	19	Sept. 5, 1864	1 year.	Mustered out with company June 29, 1865.
David	...do...	18	Aug. 24, 1864	1 year.	Mustered out with company June 29, 1865.
Lewis	...do...	18	Aug. 13, 1864	1 year.	Died Jan. 15, 1865, at Murfreesboro, Tenn.
ac	...do...	24	Sept. 17, 1864	1 year.	
John J	...do...	26	Aug. 26, 1864	1 year.	Absent, sick since Dec. 24, 1864, at Murfreesboro, Tenn. No further record found.
, John E	...do...	26	Aug. 26, 1864	1 year.	Mustered out with company June 29, 1865.
al, James A	...do...	41	Aug. 29, 1864	1 year.	Mustered out May 18, 1865, at Nashville, Tenn., by order of War Department.
William	...do...	18	Aug. 13, 1864	1 year.	Mustered out with company June 29, 1865.
William	...do...	20	Aug. 29, 1864	1 year.	Mustered out with company June 29, 1865.
Levi J	...do...	19	Sept. 5, 1864	1 year.	Mustered out with company June 29, 1865.
d, Cyrus S	...do...	18	Sept. 23, 1864	1 year.	Mustered out with company June 29, 1865.
Nathaniel	...do...	18	Aug. 24, 1864	1 year.	Mustered out with company June 29, 1865.
, Israel	...do...	33	Sept. 19, 1864	1 year.	Mustered out with company June 29, 1865.
ohn Q. A	...do...	23	Aug. 29, 1864	1 year.	Mustered out with company June 29, 1865.
Asa	...do...	23	Aug. 13, 1864	1 year.	Mustered out with company June 29, 1865.
, Richard	...do...	23	Aug. 24, 1864	1 year.	Mustered out with company June 29, 1865.
onrad	...do...	28	Sept. 2, 1864	1 year.	Mustered out with company June 29, 1865.
illiam I	...do...	22	Sept. 20, 1864	1 year.	Mustered out with company June 29, 1865.
, Frederick	...do...	40	Sept. 28, 1864	1 year.	Mustered out with company June 29, 1865.
Theodore	...do...	18	Aug. 31, 1864	1 year.	Mustered out with company June 29, 1865.
, William H	...do...	21	Sept. 29, 1864	1 year.	
Benjamin	...do...	18	Sept. 8, 1864	1 year.	Mustered out with company June 29, 1865.
, Emanuel	...do...	26	Sept. 3, 1864	1 year.	Mustered out with company June 29, 1865.
g, James L	...do...	35	Sept. 20, 1864	1 year.	
or, Christopher	...do...	21	Aug. 25, 1864	1 year.	Mustered out with company June 29, 1865.
cob	...do...	19	Sept. 2, 1864	1 year.	Mustered out June 12, 1865, at Wheeling, W. Va., by order of War Department.
hn	...do...	25	Sept. 20, 1864	1 year.	Mustered out with company June 29, 1865.
ohn	...do...	48	Sept. 22, 1864	1 year.	Mustered out with company June 29, 1865.
, William H	...do...	28	Sept. 20, 1864	1 year.	Mustered out with company June 29, 1865.
d, Abraham	...do...	35	Aug. 31, 1864	1 year.	
, Michael L	...do...	18	Aug. 16, 1864	1 year.	Mustered out with company June 29, 1865.
, David	...do...	19	Sept. 21, 1864	1 year.	Mustered out with company June 29, 1865.
rosvenor D	...do...	42	Sept. 22, 1864	1 year.	Mustered out July 18, 1865, at Columbus, O., by order of War Department.
John J	...do...	26	Aug. 22, 1864	1 year.	Mustered out with company June 29, 1865.
ay L	...do...	20	Feb. 8, 1865	1 year.	Transferred to Co. E, 181st O. V. I., June 15, 1865.
Charles H	...do...	18	Aug. 12, 1864	1 year.	Mustered out with company June 29, 1865.
ad, Isaiah	...do...	21	Sept. 17, 1864	1 year.	Mustered out with company June 29, 1865.
y, John	...do...	22	Aug. 30, 1864	1 year.	
, Peter	...do...	29	Sept. 6, 1864	1 year.	Mustered out with company June 29, 1865.
, George W	...do...	19	Aug. 26, 1864	1 year.	
, Samuel	...do...	42	Sept. 2, 1864	1 year.	
, John H	...do...	23	Sept. 16, 1864	1 year.	Reduced from Corporal April 28, 1865; mustered out with company June 29, 1865.
oseph	...do...	21	Sept. 1, 1864	1 year.	Mustered out with company June 29, 1865.
efferson	...do...	19	Sept. 24, 1864	1 year.	
y, James A	...do...	17	Sept. 29, 1864	1 year.	Mustered out with company June 29, 1865.
ohn	...do...	18	Aug. 29, 1864	1 year.	Mustered out May 29, 1865, at New York City, by order of War Department; also borne on rolls as John Moore.
l, Thomas	...do...	28	Sept. 20, 1864	1 year.	Mustered out with company June 29, 1865.
Jacob	...do...	21	Sept. 21, 1864	1 year.	Mustered out with company June 29, 1865.
Edwin M	...do...	41	Aug. 24, 1864	1 year.	Died April 25, 1865, at Lansingburg, N. Y.
Thomas	...do...	21	Sept. 2, 1864	1 year.	Mustered out July 7, 1865, at Camp Dennison, O., by order of War Department.
Amariah	...do...	40	Sept. 21, 1864	1 year.	Mustered out with company June 29, 1865.
, Lucius B	...do...	29	Aug. 30, 1864	1 year.	Died Oct. 14, 1864, at Spencer, Medina County, Ohio.
h, Henry	...do...	21	Sept. 1, 1864	1 year.	Mustered out with company June 29, 1865.
lonzo	...do...	26	Sept. 22, 1864	1 year.	Mustered out with company June 29, 1865.
, Ephraim	...do...	19	Aug. 24, 1864	1 year.	Mustered out with company June 29, 1865.

Names.	Rank.	Age.	Date of Entering the Service.	Period of Service.	Remarks.
Ramer, Henry	Private	23	Sept. 20, 1864	1 year.	Mustered out with company June 29, 1865.
Sadler, Chancy	....do....	18	Aug. 16, 1864	1 year.	Mustered out with company June 29, 1865.
Saunders, Marion	....do....	18	Aug. 13, 1864	1 year.	Mustered out June 9, 1865, at David's Island, New York Harbor, by order of War Department.
Schroll, William H	....do....	26	Aug. 23, 1864	1 year.	Reduced from Corporal March 1, 1865; mustered out June 6, 1865, at Beaufort, N. C., by order of War Department.
Scott, Matthew B	....do....	24	Sept. 19, 1864	1 year.	Mustered out Jan. 23, 1865, by order of War Department.
Schurr, Godfrey	....do....	18	Aug. 23, 1864	1 year.	Mustered out with company June 29, 1865.
Simmons, Francis	....do....	18	Aug. 23, 1864	1 year.	Died March 18, 1865, at Nashville, Tenn.
Smith, Eugene H	....do....	18	Feb. 8, 1865	1 year.	Transferred to Co. E, 181st O. V. I., June 15, 1865.
Switzer, Henry C	....do....	28	Sept. 23, 1864	1 year.	Mustered out with company June 29, 1865.
Snowberger, John	....do....	21	Sept. 2, 1864	1 year.	Mustered out with company June 29, 1865.
Spencer, John W	....do....	18	Sept. 17, 1864	1 year.	Mustered out with company June 29, 1865.
Stocking, Elmus B	....do....	21	Feb. 8, 1865	1 year.	Mustered out June 26, 1865, at Camp Dennison, O., by order of War Department.
Stover, John	....do....	32	Sept. 6, 1864	1 year.	Discharged May 20, 1865, at Madison, Ind., on Surgeon's certificate of disability.
Stroud, Thomas	....do....	36	Sept. 13, 1864	1 year.	Died March 21, 1865, at Newbern, N. C.
Stump, Morgan M	....do....	18	Aug. 31, 1864	1 year.	Mustered out July 24, 1865, at Camp Dennison, O., by order of War Department.
Thompson, Alfred B	....do....	18	Aug. 31, 1864	1 year.	Mustered out with company June 29, 1865.
Vananda, Jacob A	....do....	44	Aug. 23, 1864	1 year.	Mustered out June 2, 1865, at Camp Dennison, O., by order of War Department.
Wack, Leander	....do....	19	Aug. 16, 1864	1 year.	Mustered out with company June 29, 1865.
Walgamott, Adolphus	....do....	19	Sept. 14, 1864	1 year.	Mustered out with company June 29, 1865.
Willtrout, Jacob	....do....	16	Sept. 3, 1864	1 year.	Mustered out with company June 29, 1865.
Whisler, Samuel	....do....	20	Sept. 2, 1864	1 year.	Mustered out with company June 29, 1865.
White, John B	....do....	25	Sept. 19, 1864	1 year.	Mustered out with company June 29, 1865.
Williams, Joseph	....do....	24	Aug. 17, 1864	1 year.	Mustered out with company June 29, 1865.
Williams, Henry	....do....	22	Aug. 17, 1864	1 year.	Mustered out with company June 29, 1865.
Wrigley, Joseph	....do....	18	Aug. 15, 1864	1 year.	Mustered out Aug. 12, 1865, at New York City, by order of War Department.
Wolf, Alamander	....do....	20	Aug. 17, 1864	1 year.	Mustered out with company June 29, 1865.
Wood, Amos A	....do....	17	Aug. 27, 1864	1 year.	Mustered out with company June 29, 1865.
Young, John	....do....	40	Sept. 19, 1864	1 year.	Mustered out May 24, 1865, at Louisville, Ky., by order of War Department.

UNASSIGNED RECRUITS.

NOTE.—The following list of recruits is found on muster and descriptive rolls for this organization, but not borne on any of the company rolls of the Regiment:

Names.	Rank.	Age.	Date of Entering the Service.	Period of Service.	Remarks.
Bedwell, Samuel W	Private	19	Oct. 12, 1864	1 year.	
Birkhiler, Isaac	....do....	19	Oct. 5, 1864	1 year.	
Brown, George	....do....	23	Oct. 15, 1864	1 year.	
Dibble, Horace M	....do....	19	Sept. 28, 1864	1 year.	
Greiner, Edward	....do....	19	Oct. 10, 1864	1 year.	
Henley, John A	....do....	18	Aug. 30, 1864	1 year.	
Huffman, John C	....do....	40	Oct. 12, 1864	1 year.	
Mohana, Jerry	....do....	25	Sept. 7, 1864	1 year.	
Parker, Clayton G	....do....	29	Jan. 18, 1865	1 year.	
Petit, Alva	....do....	29	Oct. 18, 1864	1 year.	
Scott, James	....do....	41	Oct. 4, 1864	1 year.	
Sparks, George B	....do....	21	Oct. 8, 1864	1 year.	
Thorp, William	....do....	21	Oct. 1, 1864	1 year.	
Wagner, James	....do....	19	Oct. 13, 1864	1 year.	
White, Charles H	....do....	23	Sept. 30, 1864	1 year.	
Wile, William	....do....	18	Oct. 10, 1864	1 year.	

179th Regiment Ohio Volunteer Infantry.

ONE YEAR'S SERVICE.

This Regiment was organized at Camp Chase, O., in September, 1864, to serve one year. It moved to Nashville, Tenn., arriving on the 8th of October, and was placed on duty at that post. It was assigned to the Second Brigade, Fourth Division, Twentieth Army Corps, and was present at the battle of Nashville, December 15 and 16, 1864. The One Hundred and Seventy-ninth remained on duty at Nashville until the 17th of June, 1865, when it was mustered out in accordance with orders from the War Department.

	Rank.	Age.	Date of Entering the Service.	Period of Service.	Remarks.
....	Private.	22	Sept. 12, 1864	1 year.	Mustered out with company June 17, 1865.
....	....do...	23	Aug. 20, 1864	1 year.	Mustered out with company June 17, 1865.
....	... .	23	Sept. 7, 1864	1 year.	
....	... .	16	Sept. 10, 1864	1 year.	Mustered out with company June 17, 1865.
....	... .	18	Sept. 19, 1864	1 year.	Mustered out with company June 17, 1865.
....	... .	21	Aug. 29, 1864	1 year.	Mustered out with company June 17, 1865.
....	... .	18	Sept. 15, 1864	1 year.	Mustered out with company June 17, 1865.
	... .	28	Sept. 15, 1864	1 year.	Mustered out with company June 17, 1865.
....	... .	25	Sept. 12, 1864	1 year.	Mustered out with company June 17, 1865.
....	... .	36	Sept. 17, 1864	1 year.	Mustered out June 13, 1865, at Columbus, O., by order of War Department.
....	....do..	21	Sept. 6, 1864	1 year.	Mustered out with company June 17, 1865.
....	....do..	19	Aug. 20, 1864	1 year.	Mustered out with company June 17, 1865.
....	....do..	18	Sept. 6, 1864	1 year.	Mustered out with company June 17, 1865.
	....do..	41	Sept. 6, 1864	1 year.	
	....do..	21	Aug. 29, 1864	1 year.	Mustered out with company June 17, 1865.
	....do..	18	Aug. 17, 1864	1 year.	Mustered out with company June 17, 1865.
	....do..	19	Sept. 9, 1864	1 year.	Mustered out with company June 17, 1865.
	....do..	32	Sept. 12, 1864	1 year.	Mustered out with company June 17, 1865.
	....do..	25	Sept. 12, 1864	1 year.	Mustered out with company June 17, 1865.
	....do..	18	Sept. 10, 1864	1 year.	Mustered out with company June 17, 1865.

COMPANY C.

tered in September —, 1864, at Camp Chase, O., by W. P. Richardson, Colonel 25th O. V. I. Mustered out June 17, 1865, at Nashville, Tenn., by W. S. Wilson, Captain 71st O. V. I., and A. C. M. 1st Division D. C.

ld J. Jenkins........	Captain.	32	Aug. 20, 1864	1 year.	Appointed Sept. 26, 1864; resigned Feb. 11, 1865.
ıan G. Mills..........	....do....	29	Aug. 16, 1864	1 year.	Promoted from 1st Lieutenant Co. A March 14, 1865; mustered out with company June 17, 1865.
nezer Jones..........	1st Lieut.	30	Sept. 16, 1864	1 year.	Appointed Sept. 26, 1864; mustered out with company June 17, 1865.
n E. Edwards........	2d Lieut.	21	Sept. 1, 1864	1 year.	Appointed Sept. 26, 1864; mustered out with company June 17, 1865.
ld T. Davis..........	1st Sergt.	36	Sept. 1, 1864	1 year.	Appointed Sept. 27, 1864; mustered out with company June 17, 1865.
ld D. Williams......	Sergeant.	30	Sept. 1, 1864	1 year.	Appointed Sept. 27, 1864; mustered out with company June 17, 1865.
ard D. Davis........	....do....	28	Sept. 1, 1864	1 year.	Appointed Sept. 27, 1864; mustered out with company June 17, 1865.
a W. Leonard	....do....	28	Sept. 1, 1864	1 year.	Appointed Sept. 27, 1864; mustered out with company June 27, 1865.
liam H. Williams....	....do....	23	Aug. 30, 1862	1 year.	Appointed Dec. 22, 1864; mustered out with company June 17, 1865.
mas J. Hughes......	Corporal.	23	Sept. 1, 1864	1 year.	Appointed Sept. 27, 1864; mustered out with company June 17, 1865.
es J. B. Davis	....do....	23	Sept. 1, 1864	1 year.	Appointed Sept. 27, 1864; mustered out with company June 17, 1865.
ard Jones...........	....do....	21	Sept. 1, 1864	1 year.	Appointed Sept. 27, 1864; mustered out with company June 17, 1865.
fith Evans...........	....do....	21	Sept. 1, 1864	1 year.	Appointed Sept. 27, 1864; mustered out with company June 17, 1865.
d T. Jenkins........	....do....	21	Sept. 1, 1864	1 year.	Appointed Sept. 27, 1864; mustered out June 8, 1865, at Nashville, Tenn., by order of War Department.
W. Jones	....do....	20	Sept. 1, 1864	1 year.	Appointed Sept. 27, 1864; died Dec. 8, 1864, at Nashville, Tenn.
ophilus D. Davis	....do....	18	Sept. 1, 1864	1 year.	Appointed Sept. 27, 1864; mustered out with company June 17, 1865.
rh R. Morgan........	....do....	24	Sept. 1, 1864	1 year.	Appointed ——; died Nov. 16, 1864, at Nashville, Tenn.
ge Butcher...........	....do....	20	Sept. 17, 1864	1 year.	Appointed Dec. 22, 1864; mustered out with company June 17, 1865.
Daniels........ ...	Musician	16	Sept. 1, 1864	1 year.	Mustered out with company June 17, 1865.
W. Marsh..........	....do....	17	Sept. 1, 1864	1 year.	Mustered out with company June 17, 1865.
ael S. Murphy.......	Wagoner.	28	Sept. 1, 1864	1 year.	Mustered out with company June 17, 1865.
s, George W.........	Private.	21	Sept. 17, 1864	1 year.	Mustered out with company June 17, 1865.
ning, James.........	....do....	28	Sept. 1, 1864	1 year.	Mustered out with company June 17, 1865.
her, James	....do....	22	Sept. 17, 1864	1 year.	Mustered out with company June 17, 1865.
er, Robert E.........	....do....	18	Sept. 1, 1864	1 year.	Discharged April 10, 1865, for wounds received in action.
r, Jacob..............	....do....	19	Sept. 1, 1864	1 year.	Mustered out with company June 17, 1865.
mins, William........	....do....	18	Sept. 12, 1864	1 year.	Mustered out with company June 17, 1865.
, Daniel J...........	....do....	20	Sept. 1, 1864	1 year.	Mustered out June 8, 1865, at Nashville, Tenn., by order of War Department.
, David J............	....do....	20	Sept. 1, 1864	1 year.	Mustered out with company June 17, 1865.

Names.	Rank.	Age.	Date of Entering the Service.	Period of Service.	Remarks.
Milton Sherman	Corporal.	18	Aug. 15, 1864	1 year.	Appointed Sept. 22, 1864; mustered out with company June 17, 1865.
Oliver C. Blanchard	...do...	19	Aug. 18, 1864	1 year.	Appointed Sept. 22, 1864; mustered out with company June 17, 1865.
William W. Lysle	...do...	20	Aug. 23, 1864	1 year.	Appointed Sept. 22, 1864; mustered out with company June 17, 1865.
Enos Barber	...do...	26	Aug. 1, 1864	1 year.	Appointed Sept. 22, 1864; mustered out with company June 17, 1865.
Byron J. Hodgman	...do...	23	Aug. 29, 1864	1 year.	Appointed Sept. 22, 1864; mustered out with company June 17, 1865.
Matthew Lynch	...do...	24	Sept. 28, 1864	1 year.	Appointed Jan. 1, 1865; mustered out with company
Ira D. Harr	...do...	24	Mch. 7, 1865	1 year.	Appointed April 4, 1865; 14, 1865, at Post Hospital, Nashville, Tenn., by order of War Department.
Allbaugh, Jerome	Private..	19	Aug. 21, 1864	1 year.	Mustered out with company June 17, 1865.
Aton, Thomas	...do...	18	Aug. 12, 1864	1 year.	Mustered out with company June 17, 1865; also borne on rolls as Thomas H. Axtell.
Avery, Elbert	...do...	18	Sept. 20, 1864	1 year.	Mustered out with company June 17, 1865.
Barber, George W	...do...	23	Aug. 23, 1864	1 year.	Mustered out with company June 17, 1865.
Bates, Edwin W	...do...	31	Aug. 23, 1864	1 year.	Died June 2, 1865, at Nashville, Tenn.
Bennett, Samuel	...do...	21	Aug. 22, 1864	1 year.	Mustered out with company June 17, 1865.
Brunner, William C	...do...	44	April 4, 1865	1 year.	Mustered out June 7, 1865, at Post Hospital, Nashville, Tenn., by order of War Department.
Butts, Robert	...do...	20	Aug. 15, 1864	1 year.	Mustered out with company June 17, 1865.
Calkins, Cornelius	...do...	18	July 27, 1864	1 year.	Died Dec. 31, 1864, at Nashville, Tenn.
Camp, Newton L	...do...	19	Aug. 23, 1864	1 year.	Died Jan. 16, 1865, at Nashville, Tenn.
Caine, James	...do...	18	Sept. 12, 1864	1 year.	Mustered out with company June 17, 1865.
Cook, Edward	...do...	18	Sept. 17, 1864	1 year.	Mustered out May 17, 1865, at Nashville, Tenn., by order of War Department.
Coomer, Leander	...do...	18	Aug. 2, 1864	1 year.	Mustered out with company June 17, 1865.
Combs, Samuel	...do...	18	Sept. 26, 1864	1 year.	Mustered out with company June 17, 1865.
Corey, Emor N	...do...	18	Sept. 16, 1864	1 year.	Mustered out with company June 17, 1865.
Costine, Michael	...do...	18	Sept. 17, 1864	1 year.	Mustered out with company June 17, 1865.
Corcoran, Robert	...do...	26	Sept. 10, 1864	1 year.	
Craig, Frederick	...do...	36	Sept. 13, 1864	1 year.	Mustered out with company June 17, 1865.
Cromer, Jacob	...do...	38	Sept. 8, 1864	1 year.	
Davis, Joseph	...do...	42	Aug. 3, 1864	1 year.	Mustered out with company June 17, 1865.
Dennison, Leroy	...do...	18	Sept. 7, 1864	1 year.	Transferred to Co. I, 17th Regiment, Veteran Reserve Corps, March 24, 1865; mustered out June 30, 1865, at Indianapolis, Ind., by order of War Department.
Edwards, John	...do...	39	Aug. 22, 1864	1 year.	Mustered out with company June 17, 1865.
Feeny, John	...do...	22	Sept. 10, 1864	1 year.	
Floid, William J	...do...	18	Sept. 14, 1864	1 year.	Mustered out with company June 17, 1865.
Ford, Albert S	...do...	18	Mch. 10, 1865	1 year.	Mustered out June 7, 1865, at Nashville, Tenn., by order of War Department.
Frost, Albert	...do...	24	Aug. 23, 1864	1 year	Mustered out with company June 17, 1865.
Furgison, Slanton A	...do...	18	Aug. 19, 1864	1 year.	Mustered out with company June 17, 1865.
Gidley, Hazen	...do...	18	Aug. 1, 1864	1 year.	Mustered out with company June 17, 1865.
Gilbert, Louis S	...do...	20	Sept. 7, 1864	1 year.	Mustered out with company June 17, 1865.
Hall, John W	...do...	26	Sept. 10, 1864	1 year.	
Hammel, George H	...do...	21	Mch. 7, 1865	1 year.	Mustered out June 14, 1865, at Post Hospital, Nashville, Tenn., by order of War Department.
Hartman, John	...do...	34	Aug. 22, 1864	1 year.	Mustered out with company June 17, 1865.
Herbst, Charles	...do...	18	Aug. 5, 1864	1 year.	Mustered out with company June 17, 1865.
Hinson, Marvin	...do...	18	Sept. 9, 1864	1 year.	Mustered out with company June 17, 1865.
Hobbs, Larkin	...do...	38	Sept. 2, 1864	1 year.	Reduced from Sergeant Jan. 1, 1865; mustered out with company June 17, 1865.
Hobbs, Luther M	...do...	32	Sept. 2, 1864	1 year.	Mustered out with company June 17, 1865.
Houram, Daniel	...do...	18	Sept. 7, 1864	1 year.	
Hueston, George	...do...	18	Sept. 5, 1864	1 year.	Died Jan. 12, 1865, at Nashville, Tenn.
Hulin, Charles	...do...	18	Sept. 28, 1864	1 year.	Mustered out with company June 17, 1865.
Hunt, Charles	...do...	18	Sept. 9, 1864	1 year.	Mustered out with company June 17, 1865.
Hunt, Henry	...do...	20	Sept. 9, 1864	1 year.	
Hunt, William E	...do...	19	Aug. 28, 1864	1 year.	Mustered out with company June 17, 1865.
Ingraham, Asa E	...do...	28	Sept. 5, 1864	1 year.	Promoted to Q. M. Sergeant Oct. 1, 1864.
Jones, Edward	...do...	28	Aug. 22, 1864	1 year.	Mustered out with company June 17, 1865.
Laborn, James S	...do...	21	Sept. 20, 1864	1 year.	Mustered out with company June 17, 1865.
Lay, John	...do...	43	Sept. 23, 1864	1 year	Discharged Feb. 24, 1865, at Camp Dennison, O., by order of War Department.
Layburn, John	...do...	33	Sept. 30, 1864	1 year.	
Lee, Corwin T	...do...	18	Aug. 25, 1864	1 year.	Mustered out with company June 17, 1865.
Lemert, Domini	...do...	33	Sept. 20, 1864	1 year.	Mustered out with company June 17, 1865.
Lepper, Henry I	...do...	18	Aug. 26, 1864	1 year.	Mustered out with company June 17, 1865.
Long, William	...do...	20	Aug. 21, 1864	1 year.	Mustered out with company June 17, 1865.
McCoy, William	...do...	26	Aug. 29, 1864	1 year.	Mustered out June 5, 1865, at Louisville, Ky., by order of War Department.
McEloon, John	...do...	37	Sept. 19, 1864	1 year.	
McWelch, William	...do...	26	Aug. 13, 1864	1 year.	Died March 14, 1865, at Nashville, Tenn.
Miller, Anthony	...do...	20	Sept. 13, 1864	1 year.	Mustered out with company June 17, 1865.
Morehouse, Alonzo	...do...	18	Aug. 2, 1864	1 year.	Mustered out with company June 17, 1865.
Moore, Sylvester	...do...	27	Sept. 2, 1864	1 year.	Mustered out with company June 17, 1865.

COMPANY D.

ered in September 26, 1864, at Camp Chase, O., by W. P. Richardson, Colonel 25th O. V. I. Mustered out June 17, 1865, at Nashville, Tenn., by W. S. Wilson, Captain 71st O. V. I., and A. C. M. 1st Division D. C.

	Rank.	Age.	Date of Entering the Service.	Period of Service.	Remarks.
s Grafton	Captain.	28	Sept. 26, 1864	1 year.	Mustered out with company June 17, 1865.
on Evans	1st Lieut.	23	Sept. 26, 1864	1 year.	Mustered out with company June 17, 1865.
ander H. Armstrong	2d Lieut.	21	Sept. 26, 1864	1 year.	Discharged April 14, 1865, by order of War Department.
than Soule	....do....	33	Aug. 30, 1864	1 year.	Promoted from 1st Sergeant Co. B May 11, 1865; mustered out with company June 17, 1865.
pson Hinds	1st Sergt.	30	Aug. 3, 1864	1 year.	Appointed Sept. 26, 1864; mustered out with company June 17, 1865.
n Russell	Sergeant.	29	Aug. 27, 1864	1 year.	Appointed Sept. 27, 1864; mustered out with company June 17, 1865.
than D. Lloyd	....do....	18	Sept. 5, 1864	1 year.	Appointed Sept. 27, 1864; mustered out with company June 17, 1865.
ge W. Graves	....do....	25	Sept. 5, 1864	1 year.	Appointed Sept. 27, 1864; mustered out with company June 17, 1865.
Musgrove	....do....	22	Sept. 5, 1864	1 year.	Appointed Sept. 27, 1864; mustered out with company June 17, 1865.
n E. Sprague	Corporal.	26	Sept. 13, 1864	1 year.	Appointed Sept. 27, 1864; mustered out with company June 17, 1865.
nois M. Fee	....do....	21	Aug. 26, 1864	1 year.	Appointed Sept. 27, 1864; mustered out with company June 17, 1865.
ert W. Glenn	....do....	37	Sept. 14, 1864	1 year.	Appointed Sept. 27, 1864; mustered out with company June 17, 1865.
n W. Lloyd	....do....	18	Sept. 13, 1864	1 year.	Appointed Sept. 27, 1864; mustered out with company June 17, 1865.
b W. Moore	....do....	20	Aug. 22, 1864	1 year.	Appointed Sept. 27, 1864; mustered out with company June 17, 1865.
iel J. Davis	....do....	21	Aug. 29, 1864	1 year.	Appointed Sept. 27, 1864; mustered out with company June 17, 1865.
a H. Bennett	....do....	26	Aug. 23, 1864	1 year.	Appointed Sept. 27, 1864; mustered out with company June 17, 1865.
ph Callaghan	....do....	18	Aug. 26, 1864	1 year.	Appointed April 1, 1865; mustered out with company 17, 1865.
rew Hammond	Musician	18	Aug. 20, 1864	1 year.	Died Jan. 6, 1865, in Post Hospital, Nashville, Tennessee.
n J. Mannering	....do....	18	Aug. 27, 1864	1 year.	Mustered out with company June 17, 1865.
ins, Parker	Private.	22	Aug. 16, 1864	1 year.	Mustered out with company June 17, 1865.
er, Frederick	....do....	41	Sept. 15, 1864	1 year.	Died March 4, 1865, in Hospital No. 11, Nashville, Tenn.
n, Thomas R	....do....	18	Sept. 3, 1864	1 year.	Died Oct. 20, 1864, in Hospital No. 8, Nashville, Tenn.
kman, Francis M	....do....	18	Aug. 10, 1864	1 year.	Discharged April 26, 1865, at Nashville, Tenn., on Surgeon's certificate of disability.
on, Lenn H	....do....	44	Aug. 30, 1864	1 year.	Mustered out with company June 17, 1865.
pbell, William G	....do....	41	Aug. 20, 1864	1 year.	Mustered out with company June 17, 1865.
tham, James W	....do....	39	Aug. 25, 1864	1 year.	Mustered out with company June 17, 1865.
tham, William A	....do....	33	Sept. 5, 1864	1 year.	Died Jan. 12, 1865, in Hospital No. 2, Nashville, Tenn.
ell, Peter	....do....	44	Sept. 3, 1864	1 year.	Mustered out with company June 17, 1865.
den, James V	....do....	20	Aug. 13, 1864	1 year.	Mustered out with company June 17, 1865.
ps, Joseph S	....do....	18	Aug. 16, 1864	1 year.	Mustered out with company June 17, 1865.
iels, Silas	....do....	34	Sept. 4, 1864	1 year.	Mustered out with company June 17, 1865.
ner, Bartholomew A	....do....	23	Aug. 27, 1864	1 year.	Mustered out with company June 17, 1865.
s, Benjamin F	....do....	18	Aug. 29, 1864	1 year.	Mustered out with company June 17, 1865.
s, David H	....do....	22	Aug. 29, 1864	1 year.	Mustered out with company June 17, 1865.
is, Evan	....do....	18	Aug. 30, 1864	1 year.	Mustered out with company June 17, 1865.
is, John J	....do....	37	Aug. 22, 1864	1 year.	Mustered out with company June 17, 1865.
is, John L	....do....	18	Sept. 13, 1864	1 year.	Mustered out with company June 17, 1865.
is, Stephen	....do....	18	Aug. 5, 1864	1 year.	Mustered out with company June 17, 1865.
is, William J	....do....	18	Aug. 14, 1864	1 year.	Mustered out with company June 17, 1865.
is, William W	....do....	40	Aug. 15, 1864	1 year.	Mustered out with company June 17, 1865.
ney, James W	....do....	18	Aug. 18, 1864	1 year.	Mustered out May 20, 1865, at Nashville, Tenn., by order of War Department.
	....do....	18	Aug. 6, 1864	1 year.	Died Dec. 14, 1864, in camp near Nashville, Tennessee.
	....do....	32	Aug. 31, 1864	1 year.	Mustered out with company June 17, 1865.
	....do....	18	Aug. 6, 1864	1 year.	Mustered out with company June 17, 1865.
	....do....	37	Aug. 22, 1864	1 year.	Mustered out with company June 17, 1865.
	....do....	19	Sept. 5, 1864	1 year.	Died Jan. 8, 1865, in Post Hospital, Nashville, Tennessee.
	....do....	19	Aug. 29, 1864	1 year.	Mustered out with company June 17, 1865.
	....do....	21	Aug. 29, 1864	1 year.	Mustered out with company June 17, 1865.
	....do....	15	Sept. 16, 1864	1 year.	Mustered out June 5, 1865, at Nashville, Tenn., by order of War Department.
	....do....	24	Aug. 5, 1864	1 year.	Mustered out with company June 17, 1865.

Names.	Rank.	Age.	Date of Entering the Service.	Period of Service.	Remarks.
Israel Heath	Corporal.	42	Sept. 6, 1864	1 year.	Appointed Sept. 23, 1864; died Dec. 2, [illegible] Nashville, Tenn.
Abraham B. McCray	....do....	26	Sept. 12, 1864	1 year.	Appointed Dec. 1, 1864; mustered out with company June 17, 1865.
James Snyder	....do....	18	Aug. 20, 1864	1 year.	Appointed Dec. 12, 1864; mustered out with company June 17, 1865.
John P. Bell	....do....	18	Sept. 5, 1864	1 year.	Appointed Jan. 21, 1865; mustered out with company June 17, 1865.
Peter Shaffer	....do....	21	Sept. 7, 1864	1 year.	Appointed May 19, 1865; mustered out with company June 17, 1865.
Benjamin F. Smith	Musician	19	Sept. 10, 1864	1 year.	Mustered out with company June 17, [illegible]
Albright, Emanuel N.	Private..	29	Sept. 10, 1864	1 year.	Mustered out with company June 17, [illegible]
Aldrich, Samuel	....do....	34	Sept. 19, 1864	1 year.	Mustered out with company June 17, [illegible]
Anderson, John B.	....do....	18	Sept. 17, 1864	1 year.	Mustered out with company June 17, [illegible]
Bailey, James	....do....	34	Sept. 19, 1864	1 year.	Mustered out with company June 17, [illegible]
Bailey, Silas	....do....	40	Sept. 19, 1864	1 year.	Mustered out with company June 17, [illegible]
Bailey, William A.	....do....	27	Sept. 19, 1864	1 year.	Mustered out with company June 17, [illegible]
Bair, George A.	....do....	34	Sept. 10, 1864	1 year.	
Barber, George I.	....do....	20	Sept. 13, 1864	1 year.	Mustered out with company June 17, [illegible]
Barrett, Andrew	....do....	24	Sept. 10, 1864	1 year.	
Beistle, William	....do....	18	Sept. 12, 1864	1 year.	Mustered out with company June 17, [illegible]
Blythe, David A.	....do....	19	Sept. 11, 1864	1 year.	Transferred to Co. C, 22d Regiment, Ve[illegible] Reserve Corps, ——; mustered out J[illegible] 1865, at Camp Cleveland, O., by order o[illegible] Department.
Boor, William H.	....do....	41	Sept. 5, 1864	1 year.	Mustered out with company June 17, [illegible]
Brinsley, George C.	....do....	38	Sept. 16, 1864	1 year.	Mustered out with company June 17, [illegible]
Burt, John	....do....	36	Sept. 2, 1864	1 year.	Mustered out with company June 17, [illegible]
Brundege, Nehemiah	....do....	23	Sept. 19, 1864	1 year.	Mustered out with company June 17, [illegible]
Cassidy, William	....do....	20	Sept. 13, 1864	1 year.	Mustered out with company June 17, [illegible]
Chambers, Aaron I.	....do....	26	Sept. 17, 1864	1 year.	Mustered out with company June 17, [illegible]
Clark, Orrin S.	....do....	44	Sept. 13, 1864	1 year.	Mustered out with company June 17, [illegible]
Clewell, William C.	....do....	20	Sept. 13, 1864	1 year.	Mustered out with company
Combs, George W. R.	....do....	28	Sept. 13, 1864	1 year.	Appointed Sergeant Sept. 23, 1864; re[illegible] Jan. 13, 1865; mustered out to date J[illegible] Department.
Counts, Jacob	....do....	22	Sept. 13, 1864	1 year.	Mustered out with company June 17, [illegible]
DeJane, Corwin	....do....	18	Sept. 17, 1864	1 year.	Mustered out with company June 1[illegible] also borne on rolls as Corwin Dejea[illegible]
Dixon, Mordecai P.	....do....	43	Sept. 12, 1864	1 year.	June 17, [illegible]
Durk, John	....do....	19	Sept. 19, 1864	1 year.	June 17, [illegible]
Feighner, Solomon	....do....	27	Sept. 3, 1864	1 year.	Mustered out with company June 17, [illegible]
Frisbie Augustus B.	....do....	24	Oct. 1, 1864	1 year.	Mustered out with company June 1[illegible]
Fryer, Lafayette	....do....	25	Sept. 12, 1864	1 year.	Mustered out with company June [illegible]
Gotlier, Ulrich	....do....	41	Sept. 17, 1864	1 year.	Mustered out with company June [illegible]
Gowing, William O.	....do....	18	Sept. 10, 1864	1 year.	Mustered out with company June [illegible]
Gregg, George W.	....do....	18	Sept. 7, 1864	1 year.	Mustered out with company June [illegible]
Groty, John F.	....do....	18	Sept. 19, 1864	1 year.	Mustered out June 7, 1865, at Tr[illegible] Columbus, O., by order of War De[illegible]
Haganbook, Nathan D. B.	....do....	25	Sept. 12, 1864	1 year.	Mustered out with company June [illegible]
Hill, George	....do....	18	Sept. 18, 1864	1 year.	Transferred to Co. I, 17th Regim[illegible] Reserve Corps, March 24, 186[illegible] June 30, 1865, at Indianapolis [illegible] of War Department.
Hinkle, Henry	....do....	18	Sept. 19, 1864	1 year.	Mustered out with company June [illegible]
Holland, Austin	....do....	18	Sept. 8, 1864	1 year.	Mustered out with company June [illegible]
Howard, Permanyon	....do....	21	Sept. 17, 1864	1 year.	Mustered out with company June [illegible]
Hunter, James D.	....do....	19	Sept. 13, 1864	1 year.	
Keller, Solomon	....do....	40	Sept. 17, 1864	1 year.	Mustered out with company June [illegible]
Kelker, Henry	....do....	38	Sept. 14, 1864	1 year.	Mustered out with company June [illegible]
Keller, George W.	....do....	18	Sept. 8, 1864	1 year.	Died Dec. 30, 1864, at Nashville, T[illegible]
Keller, John	....do....	21	Sept. 12, 1864	1 year.	Mustered out with company June [illegible]
Kime, David	....do....	32	Sept. 17, 1864	1 year.	Mustered out with company June [illegible]
Kinder, John	....do....	23	Sept. 8, 1864	1 year.	
Klingler, Daniel	....do....	23	Sept. 17, 1864	1 year.	Mustered out with company June [illegible]
Lehr, Aaron	....do....	39	Sept. 17, 1864	1 year.	Mustered out with company June [illegible]
Linn, Louis F.	....do....	22	Sept. 17, 1864	1 year.	Mustered out with company June [illegible]
Lumbordson, William	....do....	18	Aug. 17, 1864	1 year.	Mustered out with company June [illegible]
McCullough, John B.	....do....	28	Sept. 2, 1864	1 year.	Mustered out May 16, 1865, at L[illegible] by order of War Department.
McLaughlin, Cornelius	....do....	29	Sept. 8, 1864	1 year.	Mustered out with company June [illegible]
Melrose, Charles H.	....do....	33	Sept. 3, 1864	1 year.	Mustered out June 8, 1865, at Nash[illegible] by order of War Department.
Mitch, Christian	....do....	23	Sept. 13, 1864	1 year.	Mustered out with company June [illegible]
Moses, Hector	....do....	35	Sept. 17, 1864	1 year.	Mustered out with company June [illegible]
N[illegible]rman, [illegible]nry	....do....	33	Sept. 19, 1864	1 year.	Mustered out with company June [illegible]
[illegible], [illegible]oseph M.	....do....	43	Sept. 17, 1864	1 year.	Mustered out with company [illegible]
Peppard, William	....do....	19	Sept. 5, 1864	1 year.	Mustered out with company [illegible]
Pore, Levi	....do....	26	Sept. 17, 1864	1 year.	Mustered out with company June [illegible]
Preitling, George F.	....do....	33	Sept. 8, 1864	1 year.	Died Jan. 14, 1865, at Nashville, Tenn.
Ralston, Joseph	....do....	37	Sept. 10, 1864	1 year.	Died Jan. 7, 1865, at Nashville, Tenn.
Rish, Daniel	....do....	26	Aug. 13, 1864	1 year.	Mustered out with company June [illegible]
Rish, Ira	....do....	18	Sept. 17, 1864	1 year.	Mustered out with company June [illegible]
Sanderlin, Enoch W.	....do....	25	Sept. 3, 1864	1 year.	Mustered out June 7, 1865, at [illegible] Hospital, Columbus, O., by order of [illegible] Department.

Rank.	Age.	Date of Entering the Service.	Period of Service.	Remarks.
orporal.	25	Aug. 25, 1864	1 year.	Appointed Sept. 27, 1864; mustered out with company June 17, 1865.
..do....	18	Aug. 11, 1864	1 year.	Appointed Sept. 27, 1864; mustered out with company June 17, 1865.
..do....	23	Sept. 1, 1864	1 year.	Appointed Sept. 27, 1864; mustered out with company June 17, 1865.
..do....	32	Sept. 1, 1864	1 year.	Appointed Sept. 27, 1864; mustered out May 29, 1865, at Columbus, O., by order of War Department.
..do....	19	Sept. 26, 1864	1 year.	Appointed Sept. 27, 1864; mustered out with company June 17, 1865.
..do....	34	Aug. 29, 1864	1 year.	Appointed Sept. 27, 1864; mustered out May 19, 1865, at Nashville, Tenn., by order of War Department.
..do....	22	Aug. 6, 1864	1 year.	Appointed Jan. 1, 1865; mustered out with company June 17, 1865.
..do....	25	Sept. 2, 1864	1 year.	Appointed Jan. 7, 1865; mustered out with company June 17, 1865.
..do....	21	Aug. 18, 1864	1 year.	Appointed April 1, 1865; mustered out with company June 17, 1865.
usician	32	Sept. 17, 1864	1 year.	Promoted to Principal Musician Oct. 12, 1864.
..do....	17	Aug. 6, 1864	1 year.	Mustered out with company June 17, 1865.
rivate..	20	Aug. 31, 1864	1 year.	Mustered out May 16, 1865, at Nashville, Tenn., by order of War Department.
..do....	18	Aug. 8, 1864	1 year.	Mustered out with company June 17, 1865.
..do....	23	Aug. 14, 1864	1 year.	Mustered out with company June 17, 1865.
..do....	25	Aug. 1, 1864	1 year.	Mustered out with company June 17, 1865.
..do....	18	Aug. 21, 1864	1 year.	Mustered out with company June 17, 1865.
..do....	20	Aug. 1, 1864	1 year.	Mustered out with company June 17, 1865.
..do....	19	Aug. 11, 1864	1 year.	Mustered out with company June 17, 1865.
..do....	32	Sept. 1, 1864	1 year.	Mustered out with company June 17, 1865.
..do....	19	Sept. 5, 1864	1 year.	Mustered out with company June 17, 1865.
..do....	21	Sept. 5, 1864	1 year.	Mustered out with company June 17, 1865.
..do....	44	Sept. 1, 1864	1 year.	Mustered out with company June 17, 1865.
..do....	18	Aug. 4, 1864	1 year.	Mustered out with company June 17, 1865.
..do....	17	Aug. 8, 1864	1 year.	Mustered out with company June 17, 1865.
..do....	18	Sept. 3, 1864	1 year.	Mustered out May 30, 1865, at Nashville, Tenn., by order of War Department.
..do....	20	Sept. 5, 1864	1 year.	Died Dec. 20, 1864, in Post Hospital at Nashville, Tenn.
..do....	36	Sept. 2, 1864	1 year.	Appointed Sergeant Sept. 27, 1864; reduced April 1, 1865; mustered out with company June 17, 1865.
..do....	34	Aug. 31, 1864	1 year.	Mustered out with company June 17, 1865.
..do....	40	Sept. 1, 1864	1 year.	
..do....	35	Sept. 1, 1864	1 year.	Mustered as Wagoner; died Jan. 24, 1865, in Post Hospital at Nashville, Tenn.
..do....	19	Sept. 10, 1864	1 year.	Died Jan. 1, 1865, in Post Hospital at Nashville, Tenn.
..do....	18	Aug. 10, 1864	1 year.	Died Dec. 12, 1864, in Post Hospital at Nashville, Tenn.
..do....	19	Sept. 1, 1864	1 year.	Mustered out with company June 17, 1865
..do....	21	Aug. 9, 1864	1 year.	Mustered out with company June 17, 1865.
..do....	18	Sept. 10, 1864	1 year.	Mustered out with company June 17, 1865.
..do....	21	Sept. 3, 1864	1 year.	Mustered out with company June 17, 1865.
..do....	20	Aug. 23, 1864	1 year.	Died Dec. 10, 1864, in Post Hospital at Nashville, Tenn.
..do....	36	Sept. 1, 1864	1 year.	Died Feb. 2, 1865, in Post Hospital at Nashville, Tenn.
..do....	44	Sept. 15, 1864	1 year.	Mustered out with company June 17, 1865.
..do....	38	Sept. 1, 1864	1 year.	Mustered out June 27, 1865, at Columbus, O., by order of War Department.
..do....	33	Sept. 12, 1864	1 year.	Mustered out with company June 17, 1865.
..do....	18	Sept. 15, 1864	1 year.	Mustered out with company June 17, 1865.
..do....	25	Sept. 13, 1864	1 year.	Died Dec. 18, 1864, in Post Hospital at Nashville, Tenn.
..do....	18	Sept. 12, 1864	1 year.	Mustered out with company June 17, 1865.
..do....	18	Aug. 2, 1864	1 year.	Mustered out to date June 17, 1865, by order of War Department.
..do....	18	Sept. 3, 1864	1 year.	Mustered out with company June 17, 1865.
..do....	20	Sept. 1, 1864	1 year.	Mustered out with company June 17, 1865.
..do....	19	Sept. 1, 1864	1 year.	Mustered out with company June 17, 1865.
..do....	33	Aug. 2, 1864	1 year.	Mustered out with company June 17, 1865.
..do....	18	Aug. 26, 1864	1 year.	Mustered out with company June 17, 1865.
..do....	18	Sept. 3, 1864	1 year.	Mustered out with company June 17, 1865.
..do....	18	Sept. 10, 1864	1 year.	Mustered out with company June 17, 1865.
..do....	20	Sept. 15, 1864	1 year.	Mustered out with company June 17, 1865.
..do....	31	Sept. 2, 1864	1 year.	Mustered out with company June 17, 1865.
..do....	21	Sept. 1, 1864	1 year.	Mustered out with company June 17, 1865.
..do....	19	Sept. 3, 1864	1 year.	Mustered out with company June 17, 1865.
..do....	21	Aug. 6, 1864	1 year.	Mustered out with company June 17, 1865.
..do....	30	Sept. 3, 1864	1 year.	Mustered out with company June 17, 1865.
..do....	41	Sept. 15, 1864	1 year.	Mustered out with company June 17, 1865.
..do....	19	Sept. 2, 1864	1 year.	Mustered out with company June 17, 1865.
..do....	21	Sept. 2, 1864	1 year.	Mustered out with company June 17, 1865.
..do....	22	Aug. 23, 1864	1 year.	Mustered out with company June 17, 1865.

Names.	Rank.	Age.	Date of Entering the Service.	Period of Service.	Remarks.
Davis, Enoch	Private	36	Sept. 1, 1864	1 year.	Mustered out with company June [illegible]
Davis, Evan T.	do	22	Sept. 1, 1864	1 year.	Mustered out with company June [illegible]
Davis, John D.	do	20	Sept. 1, 1864	1 year.	Mustered out with company June [illegible]
Davis, John E.	do	17	Sept. 1, 1864	1 year.	Mustered out with company June [illegible]
Davis, John J.	do	18	Sept. 21, 1864	1 year.	Mustered out with company June [illegible]
Davis, Owen D.	do	18	Sept. 1, 1864	1 year.	Mustered out with company June [illegible]
Davis, Thomas E.	do	25	Sept. 17, 1864	1 year.	Mustered out with company June [illegible]
Davis, Thomas E. T.	do	25	Sept. 1, 1864	1 year.	Died Dec. 3, 1864, at Nashville, Tenn.
Davis, Thomas P.	do	30	Sept. 1, 1864	1 year.	Mustered out June 7, 1865, at Nashville, [illegible] by order of War Department.
Edwards, David N.	do	21	Sept. 17, 1864	1 year.	Mustered out with company June [illegible]
Edwards, David R.	do	19	Sept. 1, 1864	1 year.	Mustered out with company June [illegible]
Edwards, Edward E.	do	31	Sept. 1, 1864	1 year.	Mustered out with company June [illegible]
Evans, David N.	do	18	Sept. 10, 1864	1 year.	Mustered out with company June [illegible]
Evans, Evan J.	do	30	Sept. 1, 1864	1 year.	Mustered out with company June [illegible]
Evans, John D.	do	22	Sept. 1, 1864	1 year.	Mustered out with company June [illegible]
Evans, William W.	do	21	Sept. 17, 1864	1 year.	Mustered out May 17, 1865, at [illegible] by order of War Department.
Gates, Joseph	do	18	Sept. 17, 1864	1 year.	
Graham, Samuel	do	28	Sept. 1, 1864	1 year.	Mustered out with company June [illegible]
Havens, James	do	24	Sept. 1, 1864	1 year.	Mustered out June 7, 1865, at Na[illegible] Tenn., by order of War Department.
Howells, Robert D.	do	25	Sept. 1, 1864	1 year.	Mustered out with company June [illegible]
Hughes, Evan E.	do	18	Sept. 1, 1864	1 year.	Mustered out with company June [illegible]
Hughes, Martin	do	30	Sept. 1, 1864	1 year.	Mustered out with company June [illegible]
Humphrey, Allen	do	38	Sept. 1, 1864	1 year.	Mustered out with company June [illegible]
Jenkins, Andrew	do	18	Sept. 17, 1864	1 year.	Mustered out with company June [illegible]
Jenkins, Francis	do	18	Sept. 23, 1864	1 year.	Died Dec. 15, 1864.
Jenkins, William	do	19	Sept. 10, 1864	1 year.	Mustered out with company June [illegible]
Jones, Daniel D.	do	30	Sept. 1, 1864	1 year.	Mustered out with company June [illegible]
Jones, Edward R.	do	22	Sept. 1, 1864	1 year.	Mustered out with company June [illegible]
Jones, John D. P.	do	24	Sept. 1, 1864	1 year.	Died Sept. 28, 1864; borne as Corpora[illegible] ter-in roll.
Jones, John E.	do	18	Sept. 8, 1864	1 year.	Mustered out with company June [illegible]
Jones, John M.	do	18	Sept. 17, 1864	1 year.	Died Dec. 20, 1864, at Nashville, Tenn.
Jones, Thomas D.	do	20	Sept. 1, 1864	1 year.	Died Dec. 31, 1864, at Nashville, Tenn.
Jones, Thomas L.	do	24	Sept. 12, 1864	1 year.	Discharged April 8, 1865, on Surgeon's [illegible] cate of disability.
Jones, Thomas W.	do	22	Sept. 1, 1864	1 year.	Mustered out with company June [illegible]
Jones, William N.	do	18	Sept. 1, 1864	1 year.	Mustered out with company June [illegible]
Kelly, Jacob	do	19	Sept. 12, 1864	1 year.	Mustered out with company June [illegible]
Kelly, Robinson B.	do	18	Sept. 1, 1864	1 year.	Mustered out with company June [illegible]
King, John J.	do	18	Sept. 17, 1864	1 year.	Mustered out with company June [illegible]
Lewis, Daniel H.	do	17	Sept. 1, 1864	1 year.	Mustered out with company June [illegible]
Lewis, John D.	do	35	Sept. 1, 1864	1 year.	Mustered out with company June [illegible]
McIntire, Joseph	do	37	Sept. 1, 1864	1 year.	Mustered out with company June [illegible]
McManaway, Absalom	do	25	Sept. 1, 1864	1 year.	Mustered out with company June [illegible]
Mays, William	do	18	Sept. 1, 1864	1 year.	Mustered out with company June [illegible]
Morgan, David L.	do	32	Sept. 1, 1864	1 year.	Mustered out with company June [illegible]
Morgan, Enoch	do	21	Sept. 1, 1864	1 year.	Died April 25, 1865.
Morgan, John H.	do	25	Sept. 23, 1864	1 year.	Mustered out with company June [illegible]
Morgan, William E.	do	21	Sept. 1, 1864	1 year.	Appointed Sergeant Sept. 27, 1864; [illegible] Dec. 22, 1864; mustered out [illegible] June 17, 1865.
O'Reiley, Patrick	do	18	Sept. 17, 1864	1 year.	Mustered out with company June [illegible]
Powell, William G.	do	18	Sept. 23, 1864	1 year.	Died Dec. 31, 1864, at Nashville, Tenn.
Seay, Joseph	do	18	Sept. 10, 1864	1 year.	Mustered out with company June [illegible]
Stutler, John	do	44	Sept. 1, 1864	1 year.	Mustered out with company June [illegible]
Thomas, Daniel	do	23	Sept. 1, 1864	1 year.	Mustered out with company June [illegible]
Thomas, David	do	20	Sept. 1, 1864	1 year.	Mustered out with company June [illegible]
Thomas, John	do	22	Sept. 1, 1864	1 year.	Mustered out with company June [illegible]
Thomas, John J.	do	19	Sept. 1, 1864	1 year.	Mustered out with company June [illegible]
Thomas, William H.	do	19	Sept. 1, 1864	1 year.	Mustered out with company June [illegible]
Walters, John	do	30	Sept. 1, 1864	1 year.	Mustered out with company June [illegible]
Warren, John	do	18	Sept. 23, 1864	1 year.	Mustered out with company June [illegible]
Williams, David E. D.	do	21	Sept. 1, 1864	1 year.	Mustered out with company June [illegible]
Williams, David W.	do	31	Sept. 1, 1864	1 year.	Mustered out with company June [illegible]
Williams, Evan	do	18	Sept. 1, 1864	1 year.	Mustered out with company June [illegible]
Williams, James	do	18	Sept. 1, 1864	1 year.	Mustered out with company June [illegible]
Woodruff, Wilson T.	do	18	Sept. 17, 1864	1 year.	Mustered out with company June [illegible]
Yeager, Hiram D.	do	18	Sept. 10, 1864	1 year.	Mustered out with company June [illegible]
Yeager, James A.	do	18	Sept. 17, 1864	1 year.	Died Dec. 31, 1864, at Nashville, Tenn.

Names.	Rank.	Age.	Date of Entering the Service.	Period of Service.	Remarks.
Blackston, John W. C.	Private	29	Sept. 8, 1864	1 year.	Mustered out with company June 17, 1865.
Booth, John R.	do	30	Aug. 31, 1864	1 year.	Mustered out with company June 17, 1865.
Brenneman, Ira	do	28	Sept. 5, 1864	1 year.	Mustered out with company June 17, 1865.
Brown, Alexander	do	34	Sept. 5, 1864	1 year.	Mustered out with company June 17, 1865.
Brown, Washington	do	22	Aug. 30, 1864	1 year.	Mustered out June 8, 1865, at Camp Dennison, O., by order of War Department.
Carr, David J.	do	33	Sept. 20, 1864	1 year.	Mustered out with company June 17, 1865.
Congleton, Thomas	do	31	Sept. 1, 1864	1 year.	Mustered out with company June 17, 1865.
Conklin, Hiram	do	32	Sept. 28, 1864	1 year.	Mustered out with company June 17, 1865.
Conklin, Samuel	do	27	Sept. 23, 1864	1 year.	Mustered out with company June 17, 1865.
Crawley, Peter	do	36	Sept. 8, 1864	1 year.	Mustered out with company June 17, 1865.
Crum, David	do	25	Sept. 29, 1864	1 year.	
Dice, Charles	do	26	Sept. 5, 1864	1 year.	Mustered out with company June 17, 1865.
Dillon, Abraham H.	do	22	Sept. 21, 1864	1 year.	Mustered out with company June 17, 1865.
Dixon, Charles	do	23	Sept. 23, 1864	1 year.	
Donaldson, John B.	do	33	Sept. 9, 1864	1 year.	Mustered out with company June 17, 1865.
Draper, Ariel J.	do	18	Sept. 17, 1864	1 year.	Mustered out with company June 17, 1865.
Ely, Thomas	do	32	Sept. 10, 1864	1 year.	Mustered out with company June 17, 1865.
Farren, Albert	do	21	Sept. 20, 1864	1 year.	Mustered out with company June 17, 1865.
Freeland, John	do	26	Aug. 30, 1864	1 year.	Appointed Corporal Oct. 1, 1864; reduced, at his own request, Jan. 1, 1865; mustered out with company June 17, 1865.
Gatchell, John B.	do	37	Sept. 7, 1864	1 year.	Mustered out with company June 17, 1865.
Gert, William	do	44	Sept. 5, 1864	1 year.	Mustered out with company June 17, 1865.
Gold, John	do	18	Sept. 5, 1864	1 year.	
Gregory, John	do	29	Sept. 3, 1864	1 year.	Mustered out with company June 17, 1865.
Gregory, William	do	21	Sept. 8, 1864	1 year.	Mustered out with company June 17, 1865.
Hall, David	do	19	Aug. 8, 1864	1 year.	Mustered out with company June 17, 1865.
Hildebrand, John F.	do	19	Sept. 1, 1864	1 year.	Mustered out with company June 17, 1865.
Hosler, Levi	do	23	Aug. 29, 1864	1 year.	Mustered out with company June 17, 1865.
Hutchinson, Salathiel K.	do	18	Sept. 5, 1864	1 year.	Mustered out with company June 17, 1865.
Johnston, Andrew C.	do	25	Sept. 5, 1864	1 year.	Mustered out with company June 17, 1865.
Johnson, John H.	do	30	Sept. 5, 1864	1 year.	Mustered out with company June 17, 1865.
Kelly, Calvin	do	18	Sept. 3, 1864	1 year.	Mustered out with company June 17, 1865.
Koon, William	do	22	Sept. 3, 1864	1 year.	Mustered out with company June 17, 1865.
Lamb, William B.	do	29	Sept. 5, 1864	1 year.	Mustered out June 28, 1865, at Columbus, O., by order of War Department.
Logan, Henry	do	27	Sept. 5, 1864	1 year.	Died Feb. 25, 1865, in hospital at Nashville, Tennessee.
McAfee, Joseph F.	do	18	Sept. 16, 1864	1 year.	Mustered out with company June 17, 1865.
McAfee, Thomas H.	do	41	Mch. 2, 1865	1 year.	Mustered out July 25, 1865, at Nashville, Tenn., by order of War Department.
McClead, John W.	do	18	Mch. 13, 1865	1 year.	Mustered out May 30, 1865, at Nashville Tenn., by order of War Department.
McClead, Elias	do	38	Sept. 1, 1864	1 year.	Mustered out June 8, 1865, at Camp Dennison, O., by order of War Department.
McNeale, Thomas J.	do	18	Sept. 5, 1864	1 year.	Mustered out with company June 17, 1865.
Marsh, Benjamin	do	24	Sept. 3, 1864	1 year.	Mustered out with company June 17, 1865.
Marsh, Stanton	do	21	Sept. 3, 1864	1 year.	Mustered out with company June 17, 1865.
Masters, Thomas H.	do	34	Mch. 2, 1865	1 year.	Mustered out to date June 17, 1865.
Megahey, John, Sr.	do	44	Sept. 5, 1864	1 year.	Mustered out with company June 17, 1865.
Megahey, John, Jr.	do	18	Sept. 20, 1864	1 year.	Mustered out with company June 17, 1865.
Momburg, William A.	do	18	Aug. 11, 1864	1 year.	Mustered out with company June 17, 1865.
Murdock, James	do	27	Sept. 5, 1864	1 year.	Mustered out with company June 17, 1865.
Newhouse, George S.	do	20	Aug. 29, 1864	1 year.	Mustered out with company June 17, 1865.
Oller, Benjamin	do	41	Sept. 3, 1864	1 year.	Mustered out with company June 17, 1865.
Poling, Nathan	do	33	Sept. 2, 1864	1 year.	Mustered out with company June 17, 1865.
Porter, John T.	do	30	Sept. 5, 1864	1 year.	Transferred to Co. K, 17th Regiment, Veteran Reserve Corps, April 29, 1865.
Porter, Thomas	do	40	Feb. 24, 1865	1 year.	Mustered out Sept. 6, 1865, at Camp Dennison, O., by order of War Department.
Proser, Kinsey	do	36	Sept. 6, 1864	1 year.	Mustered out with company June 17, 1865.
Purdy, Levi	do	26	Sept. 5, 1864	1 year.	Mustered out with company June 17, 1865.
Redd, Solomon A.	do	20	Sept. 6, 1864	1 year.	Mustered out with company June 17, 1865.
Roberts, Horace M.	do	38	Sept. 24, 1864	1 year.	Mustered out with company June 17, 1865.
Selken, Henry	do	24	Sept. 6, 1864	1 year.	Died Jan. 26, 1865, in hospital at Nashville, Tennessee.
Sorrick, Adam	do	26	Sept. 1, 1864	1 year.	Died April 9, 1865, in hospital at Nashville, Tennessee.
Southwick, Arnold	do	32	Sept. 23, 1864	1 year.	Died April 19, 1865, in hospital at Nashville, Tennessee.
Spencer, William	do	27	Sept. 28, 1864	1 year.	Mustered out with company June 17, 1865.
Stewart, John	do	45	Aug. 26, 1864	1 year.	Mustered out with company June 17, 1865.
Stillings, Lewis	do	19	Sept. 3, 1864	1 year.	Absent ——, sick in hospital. No further record found.
Sutton, John O.	do	25	Sept. 5, 1864	1 year.	Died Feb. 18, 1865, in hospital at Nashville, Tennessee.
Stubbs, Thomas H.	do	35	Sept. 13, 1864	1 year.	Mustered out with company June 17, 1865.
Taylor, David	do	22	Sept. 3, 1864	1 year.	Mustered out July 5, 1865, at Columbus, O., by order of War Department.
Teple, Alexander G.	do	29	Sept. 9, 1864	1 year.	Mustered out with company June 17, 1865.
Travis, John B.	do	19	Sept. 24, 1864	1 year.	Mustered out with company June 17, 1865.
Tyler, Hiram	do	39	Sept. 24, 1864	1 year.	Mustered out with company June 17, 1865.
Vannattor, Washington	do	41	Aug. 29, 1864	1 year.	Mustered out with company June 17, 1865.
Wagner, Jacob	do	18	Sept. 1, 1864	1 year.	Mustered out with company June 17, 1865.
Walker, Curtis H.	do	35	Sept. 20, 1864	1 year.	Mustered out with company June 17, 1865.

Names.	Rank.	Age.	Date of Entering the Service.	Period of Service	Remarks.
Farris, James H	Private	18	Aug. 20, 1864	1 year.	Mustered out June 7, 1865, at Post [illegible] Nashville, Tenn., by order of War [illegible]ment.
Gillespie, Mathias	...do...	18	Aug. 30, 1864	1 year.	Mustered out with company June 17 [illegible]
Glenn, George W	...do...	20	Sept. 20, 1864	1 year.	Mustered out with company June 17 [illegible]
Graves, Thomas	...do...	38	Sept. 12, 1864	1 year.	Mustered out with company June 17 [illegible]
Griffith, Joseph	...do...	21	Aug. 31, 1864	1 year.	Mustered out with company June 17 [illegible]
Griffiths, William	...do...	18	Aug. 8, 1864	1 year.	Mustered out with company June 17 [illegible]
Hammond, Paul	...do...	44	Aug. 8, 1864	1 year.	Mustered out with company June 17 [illegible]
James, David	...do...	21	Aug. 14, 1864	1 year.	Mustered out with company June 17 [illegible]
Jones, David T	...do...	18	Aug. 20, 1864	1 year.	Mustered out with company June 17 [illegible]
Jones, Evan E	...do...	18	Aug. 19, 1864	1 year.	Died Jan. 21, 1865, in Post Hospital, N[illegible] Tennessee.
Jones, John S	...do...	18	Aug. 29, 1864	1 year.	Mustered out with company June 17 [illegible]
Jones, Richard D	...do...	24	Aug. 11, 1864	1 year.	Mustered out with company June 17 [illegible]
Jones, William L	...do...	18	Aug. 31, 1864	1 year.	Mustered out with company June 17 [illegible]
Kinley, James	...do...	21	Aug. 29, 1864	1 year.	Appointed Corporal Sept. 27, 1864 [illegible] March 23, 1865; mustered out with [illegible] June 17, 1865.
Law, John	...do...	28	Sept. 13, 1864	1 year.	Mustered out with company June [illegible] also borne on rolls as John Lowe.
Lloyd, Edward	...do...	44	Aug. 25, 1864	1 year.	Mustered out with company June 17 [illegible]
Lloyd, Enon	...do...	35	Sept. 5, 1864	1 year.	Mustered out with company June 17 [illegible]
Lloyd, James H	...do...	18	Aug. 31, 1864	1 year.	Mustered out with company June 17 [illegible]
Lloyd, John D	...do...	18	Aug. 21, 1864	1 year.	Mustered out with company June 17 [illegible]
McCarley, Robert J	...do...	20	Sept. 18, 1864	1 year.	Mustered out with company June 17 [illegible]
McColla, Thomas	...do...	31	Sept. 23, 1864	1 year.	Mustered out with company June 17 [illegible]
McKinney, Wesley	...do...	33	Aug. 27, 1864	1 year.	Mustered out with company June 17 [illegible]
Markham, Lewis J	...do...	18	Aug. 20, 1864	1 year.	Mustered out with company June 17 [illegible]
Marsteller, David B	...do...	24	Aug. 29, 1864	1 year.	Mustered out with company June 17 [illegible]
Melton, Joseph	...do...	36	Aug. 2, 1864	1 year.	Died Oct. 20, 1864, in Hospital No. [illegible] Tennessee.
Morgan, Thomas J	...do...	18	Aug. 25, 1864	1 year.	Mustered out with company June 17 [illegible]
Mossman, Andrew J	...do...	22	Sept. 13, 1864	1 year.	Mustered out with company June 17 [illegible]
Noel, James P	...do...	19	Aug. 27, 1864	1 year.	Mustered out with company June 17 [illegible]
Noel, John W	...do...	20	Aug. 8, 1864	1 year.	Mustered out with company June 17 [illegible]
Pope, Little A	...do...	19	Aug. 16, 1864	1 year.	Mustered out with company June 17 [illegible]
Pummel, Jacob	...do...	44	Aug. 22, 1864	1 year.	Mustered out with company June 17 [illegible]
Pummel, Joseph	...do...	18	Sept. 23, 1864	1 year.	Mustered out with company June 17 [illegible]
Pummel, William	...do...	18	Sept. 23, 1864	1 year.	Mustered out with company June 17 [illegible]
Reed, Willis	...do...	44	Aug. 19, 1864	1 year.	Mustered out with company June 17 [illegible]
Rees, George	...do...	34	Sept. 13, 1864	1 year.	Mustered out with company June 17 [illegible]
Richards, David	...do...	43	Sept. 5, 1864	1 year.	Mustered out with company June 17 [illegible]
Russell, Charles	...do...	32	Sept. 12, 1864	1 year.	Mustered out with company June 17 [illegible]
Russell, James N	...do...	34	Sept. 13, 1864	1 year.	Mustered out with company June 17 [illegible]
Russell, William	...do...	34	Sept. 12, 1864	1 year	Mustered out with company June 17 [illegible]
Scott, John	...do...	22	Sept. 1, 1864	1 year.	Mustered out with company June 17 [illegible]
Staley, Marquis D L	...do...	18	Aug. 5, 1864	1 year.	Mustered out with company June 17 [illegible]
Stringfellow, William	...do...	18	Sept. 5, 1864	1 year	Mustered out with company June 17 [illegible]
Vaughn, John F	...do...	18	Aug. 24, 1864	1 year	Mustered out with company June 17 [illegible]
White, Wesley B	...do...	18	Sept. 15, 1864	1 year.	Mustered out with company June 17 [illegible]

COMPANY E.

Mustered in September 26, 1864, at Camp Chase, O., by W. P. Richardson, Colonel 25th O. V. I. Mustered [illegible] June 17, 1865, at Nashville, Tenn., by W. S. Wilson, Captain 71st O. V. I., and A. C. M. 1st Division D. C.

Names.	Rank.	Age.	Date of Entering the Service.	Period of Service	Remarks.
Stephen Morgan	Captain	21	July 27, 1864	1 year.	Appointed Sept. 26, 1864; mustered [illegible] company June 17, 1865.
Jacob F. Wickerham	1st Lieut.	20	Aug. 23, 1864	1 year.	Appointed Sept. 26, 1864; mustered [illegible] company June 17, 1865.
John Atwater	2d Lieut.	25	Aug. 3, 1864	1 year.	Appointed Sept. 26, 1864; mustered [illegible] company June 17, 1865.
John T. Leach	1st Sergt.	23	Sept. 10, 1864	1 year.	Appointed Sept. 27, 1864; mustered [illegible] company June 17, 1865.
Joseph Thomas	Sergeant.	19	Sept. 12, 1864	1 year.	Appointed Sept. 27, 1864; mustered [illegible] company June 17, 1865.
John S. Jones	...do...	22	Aug. 4, 1864	1 year.	Appointed Sept. 27, 1864; mustered [illegible] company June 17, 1865.
Henry Ritz	...do...	21	Sept. 1, 1864	1 year.	Appointed Sept. 27, 1864; died March [illegible] in Hospital No. 2, at Nashville, Tenn.
James M. Scott	...do...	26	Sept. 3, 1864	1 year.	Appointed Corporal Sept. 27, 1864 [illegible] April 1, 1865; mustered out with [illegible] June 17, 1865.
John J. Williams	...do...	20	Aug. 29, 1864	1 year.	Appointed April 1, 1865; mustered [illegible] company June 17, 1865.
Morgan D. Morgan	Corporal.	22	Aug. 31, 1864	1 year.	Appointed Sept. 27, 1864; died Jan. [illegible] Post Hospital at Nashville, Tenn.

Names.	Rank.	Age.	Date of Entering the Service.	Period of Service.	Remarks.
Coulson, Job V.	Private.	24	Sept. 1, 1864	1 year.	Died Nov. 22, 1864, in Post Hospital, Nashville, Tenn.
Curan, James	do.	21	Mch. 7, 1865	1 year.	Mustered out Aug. 28, 1865, at Nashville, Tenn., by order of War Department.
Davis, John C.	do.	18	Sept. 23, 1864	1 year.	Mustered out with company June 17, 1865.
Davlin, John	do.	27	Aug. 31, 1864	1 year.	
Decater, James	do.	26	Sept. 12, 1864	1 year.	
Devore, James L	do.	25	Sept. 1, 1864	1 year.	Mustered out with company June 17, 1865.
Devore, John	do.	18	Sept. 7, 1864	1 year.	Mustered out with company June 17, 1865.
Donelly, John	do.	20	Sept. 22, 1864	1 year.	
Dunn, James H.	do.	18	Sept. 13, 1864	1 year.	Mustered out with company June 17, 1865.
Dunn, Philip	do.	19	Aug. 20, 1864	1 year.	Mustered out with company June 17, 1865.
Ferrul, James	do.	19	Sept. 1, 1864	1 year.	Also borne on rolls as James Ferrel.
Forbes, Thomas	do.	20	Sept. 10, 1864	1 year.	Mustered out June 17, 1865, at Nashville, Tenn., by order of War Department.
Gardner, Edward R.	do.	20	Aug. 24, 1864	1 year.	Promoted to Sergt. Major March 24, 1865.
Hartsoe, Samuel	do.	37	Sept. 20, 1864	1 year.	Mustered out with company June 17, 1865.
Hayna, Francis	do.	42	Sept. 12, 1864	1 year.	Mustered out with company June 17, 1865.
Hoobuck, James	do.	20	Aug. 15, 1864	1 year.	Mustered out with company June 17, 1865.
Horner, Clark M	do.	18	Sept. 19, 1864	1 year.	Mustered out with company June 17, 1865.
Jen ins, Charles	do.	22	Sept. 20, 1864	1 year.	
ones, James	do.	18	Sept. 19, 1864	1 year.	
Kessler ohn	do.	22	Aug. 15, 1864	1 year.	Mustered out with company June 17, 1865.
Kidd, James S. M.	do.	33	Sept. 5, 1864	1 year.	
Lawson, James	do.	25	Sept. 20, 1864	1 year.	Also borne on rolls as James Larason.
Lee, Anias	do.	17	Feb. 21, 1865	1 year.	Mustered out June 7, 1865, at Post Hospital, Nashville, Tenn., by order of War Department.
Leisure, Franklin	do.	37	Sept. 7, 1864	1 year.	Mustered out with company June 17, 1865.
Leonard, Jesse	do.	33	Sept. 22, 1864	1 year.	Mustered out with company June 17, 1865.
Leslie, William	do.	20	Aug. 29, 1864	1 year.	
Mc arty, John	do.	21	Sept. 20, 1864	1 year	
McCarty, John	do.	24	Sept. 19, 1864	1 year.	
McCoy, John	do.	30	Sept. 17, 1864	1 year.	
McDrew James	do.	20	Aug. 25, 1864	1 year.	Mustered out with company June 17, 1865.
McGuire, Martin	do.	26	Sept. 8, 1864	1 year.	
McWilliams, Josiah	do.	21	Sept. 20, 1864	1 year.	
Maddis, George	do.	25	Aug. 30, 1864	1 year.	
Martin, Thomas	do.	21	Aug. 20, 1864	1 year.	Mustered out May 27, 1865, at Nashville, Tenn., by order of War Department.
Meade, harles	do.	21	Sept. 30, 1864	1 year.	
Meek John	do.	18	Aug. 31, 1864	1 year.	Died Dec. 6, 1864, in camp at Nashville, Tenn.
Mershon, Daniel	do.	23	Sept. 19, 1864	1 year.	
Michaels, John D.	do.	20	Sept. 19, 1864	1 year.	Mustered out June 3, 1865, at Nashville, Tenn., by order of War Department.
Moody, Thomas P.	do.	18	Sept. 7, 1864	1 year.	Mustered out with company June 17, 1865.
Morris, Mordecai		17	Sept. 23, 1864	1 year.	Mustered out with company June 17, 1865.
Morthland, Abraham	do.	21	Sept. 6, 1864	1 year.	Mustered out with company June 17, 1865.
Neff, Henry	do.	22	Sept. 10, 1864	1 year.	
Nicholson, William	do.	16	Feb. 27, 1865	1 year.	Transferred to Co. G, 18th O. V. I., June 28, 1865.
O'Neal, William	do.	21	Sept. 20, 1864	1 year.	
Price, George W	do.	33	Sept. 5, 1864	1 year.	Mustered out with company June 17, 1865.
Risher, ames M	do.	17	Sept. 6, 1864	1 year.	Mustered out with company June 17, 1865.
Robinson, Washington P	do.	22	Sept. 17, 1864	1 year.	Appointed Corporal Sept. 27, 1864; reduced Dec. 8, 1864; mustered out with company June 17, 1865.
Rose, Lewis P.	do.	26	Aug. 24, 1864	1 year.	Mustered out with company June 17, 1865.
Ruhl, Lewis	do.	30	Aug. 26, 1864	1 year	Mustered out with company June 17, 1865.
Shidler, Eli	do.	21	Aug. 29, 1864	1 year.	Mustered out with company June 17, 1865.
Smith, George	do.	21	Sept. 13, 1864	1 year.	
Smith, Jabez F.	do.	18	Sept. 6, 1864	1 year.	Mustered out with company June 17, 1865.
Smith, Samuel	do.	20	Sept. 7, 1864	1 year.	
Smith, William	do.	28	Sept. 19, 1864	1 year.	
Stephens, Daniel F	do.	16	Sept. 1, 1864	1 year.	Mustered out with company June 17, 1865.
Sulli an, John	do.	18	Feb. 27, 1865	1 year	Transferred to Co. G, 18th O. V. I., June 28, 1865.
Taylor, James	do.	20	Aug. 25, 1864	1 year.	Mustered out with company June 17, 1865.
Taylor, William	do.	25	Sept. 20, 1864	1 year.	
Thomas, Jesse	do.	21	Sept. 1, 1864	1 year.	Mustered out with company June 17, 1865.
Townsend, Joseph B.	do.	18	Aug. 29, 1864	1 year.	
Wallace, John W	do.	18	Aug. 31, 1864	1 year.	Mustered out with company June 17, 1865.
Winters, Thomas P.	do.	23	Mch. 3, 1865	1 year.	Transferred to Co. F, 18th O. V. I., June 28, 1865.
Wood, Isaac	do.	18	Sept. 10, 1864	1 year.	Mustered out with company June 17, 1865.
Yager, Charles L.	do.	25	Sept. 7, 1864	1 year.	Mustered out with company June 17, 1865.

COMPANY [illegible].

Mustered in September 28, 1864, at Camp Chase, O., by W. P. Richardson, Col
June 17, 1865, at Nashville, Tenn., by W. S. Wilson, Captai
and A. C. M. 1st Division D. C.

Names.	Rank.	Age.	Date of Entering the Service.	Period of Service.	
Claud B. Gibson	Captain.	32	Aug. 22, 1864		Appointed S company Ju
Joseph L. Dickelman	1st Lieut.	25	Sept. 7, 1864	1 year.	Appointed Se company Ju
Joseph McMillen	2d Lieut.	40	Sept. 23, 1864	1 year.	Appointed Se 1865.
William H. Saxton	...do...	24	Aug. 29, 1864	1 year.	Promoted fro 1865; muste 1865.
William H. Grafton	1st Sergt.	21	Sept. 12, 1864	1 year.	Appointed O company Ju
James M. Green	Sergeant.	26	Sept. 28, 1864	1 year.	Appointed O company Ju
David W. Rogers	...do...	38	Sept. 23, 1864	1 year.	Appointed O company Ju
John W. Flinn	...do...	41	Sept. 21, 1864	1 year.	Appointed O company Ju
John H. Canaan	...do...	22	Sept. 22, 1864	1 year.	Appointed C Dec. 8, 1864 June 17, 186
John C. Moyer	Corporal.	28	Sept. 23, 1864	1 year.	Appointed O company Ju
John H. Blough	...do...	27	Sept. 21, 1864	1 year.	Appointed O company Ju
Robert H. Johnson	...do...	23	Sept. 23, 1864	1 year.	Appointed O company Ju
John A. Cutting	...do...	26	Sept. 22, 1864	1 year.	Appointed O company Ju
Smith Povenmyer	...do...	27	Sept. 23, 1864	1 year.	Appointed O company Ju
Joseph Belt	...do...	24	Sept. 7, 1864	1 year.	Appointed O company Ju
Andy Miller	...do...	37	Sept. 16, 1864	1 year.	Appointed D company Ju
Christian D. Stemen	...do...	21	Sept. 23, 1864	1 year.	Appointed D company Ju
Samuel F. Hanna	Musician	26	Sept. 29, 1864	1 year.	Mustered out
Archer, Nicholas	Private.	37	Sept. 10, 1864	1 year.	Mustered out
Askins, Jacob L.	...do...	23	Sept. 23, 1864	1 year.	Mustered out
Baker, William C	...do...	29	Sept. 24, 1864	1 year.	Mustered out
Burkhalter, John	...do...	23	Sept. 5, 1864	1 year.	Mustered out
Beery, Jacob G	...do...	31	Sept. 23, 1864	1 year.	Appointed Se 8, 1864; mus 17, 1865.
Botkins, George	...do...	34	Mch. 15, 1865	1 year.	Mustered out by order of
Briggs, Matthew	...do...	28	Oct. 2, 1864	1 year.	Mustered out by order of
Calvin, Jesse G	...do...	32	Sept. 21, 1864	1 year.	Mustered out
Cerfuss, Josiah	...do...	31	Sept. 23, 1864	1 year.	Mustered out
Clauson, William B	...do...	21	Sept. 28, 1864	1 year.	Died April 8,
Cook, Henry	...do...	34	Mch. 20, 1865	1 year.	Absent, sick record foun
Cremean, William J	...do...	34	Sept. 23, 1864	1 year.	Mustered out
Dixon, William	...do...	18	Sept. 17, 1864	1 year.	Mustered out
Doner, Abraham	...do...	42	Sept. 24, 1864	1 year.	Mustered out
Eaton, William H	...do...	22	Mch. 20, 1865	1 year.	Transferred t 1865.
Furry, Franklin	...do...	44	Sept. 24, 1864	1 year.	Mustered out
Gahman, Samuel	...do...	31	Sept. 23, 1864	1 year.	Mustered out
Green, Andrew J	...do...	29	Sept. 28, 1864	1 year.	Mustered out
Hanger, Jesse	...do...	37	Sept. 21, 1864	1 year.	Mustered out
Harbison, James H	...do...	27	Sept. 2, 1864	1 year.	Died Jan. 12, Tennessee.
Heartley, Henry A	...do...	34	Sept. 24, 1864	1 year.	Discharged D on Surgeon'
Heisler, John W	...do...	24	Sept. 24, 1864	1 year.	Mustered out
Houdenchield, Jacob	...do...	32	Sept. 5, 1864	1 year.	Mustered out
Houdenchield, John	...do...	40	Sept. 5, 1864	1 year.	Mustered out
Huber, William	...do...	36	Dec. 31, 1864	1 year.	Mustered out by order of
Hudson, Richard	...do...	26	Mch. 20, 1865	1 year.	Mustered out by order of
Huhn, Joseph S	...do...	44	Sept. 15, 1864	1 year.	Mustered out Tenn., by o
Irvin, John A	...do...	23	Sept. 21, 1864	1 year.	Mustered out by order of

Names.	Rank.	Age.	Date of Entering the Service.	Period of Service.	Remarks.
Johnson, Abram D	Private.	25	Sept. 10, 1864	1 year.	Mustered out with company June 17, 1865.
Johnston, George W	....do....	26	Sept. 10, 1864	1 year.	Mustered out May 18, 1865, at Davenport, Iowa, by order of War Department.
Judkins, Franklin D	....do....	28	Sept. 23, 1864	1 year.	Died Dec. 2, 1864, in Post Hospital, Nashville, Tennessee.
Kesler, George	....do....	25	Sept. 23, 1864	1 year.	Mustered out with company June 17, 1865.
Kesler, Josiah	....do....	29	Sept. 24, 1864	1 year.	Died Jan. 26, 1865, in Post Hospital, Nashville, Tennessee.
Lame, Peter W	....do....	37	Sept. 16, 1864	1 year.	Mustered out June 7, 1865, at Nashville, Tenn., by order of War Department.
Lautzenheiser, Adam	....do....	26	Sept. 22, 1864	1 year.	Mustered out June 17, 1865, at Nashville, Tenn., by order of War Department.
Leatherman, Daniel	....do....	41	Sept. 23, 1864	1 year.	Mustered out with company June 17, 1865.
Leise, Jacob	....do....	37	Sept. 16, 1864	1 year.	Mustered out with company June 17, 1865.
Looker, Joel	....do....	23	Sept. 16, 1864	1 year.	Died Jan. 8, 1865, in Post Hospital, Nashville, Tennessee.
Lenthan, George W	....do....	20	Sept. 21, 1864	1 year.	Mustered out with company June 17, 1865.
McConnell, Alphens	....do....	21	Sept. 17, 1864	1 year.	Mustered out with company June 17, 1865.
McLain, William	....do....	33	Mch. 15, 1865	1 year.	Mustered out June 2, 1865, at Nashville, Tenn., by order of War Department.
McVain, Thomas	....do....	22	Sept. 23, 1864	1 year.	
Marty, Jacob	....do....	29	Sept. 5, 1864	1 year.	Mustered out with company June 17, 1865.
Maus, William A	....do....	31	Sept. 24, 1864	1 year.	See Co. E, 180th O. V. I.
Miller, Absalom	....do....	35	Sept. 23, 1864	1 year.	Mustered out with company June 17, 1865.
Miller, Andrew	....do....	44	Sept. 12, 1864	1 year.	Mustered out with company June 17, 1865.
Miller, Jesse D	....do....	25	Sept. 24, 1864	1 year.	Mustered out with company June 17, 1865.
Miller, Peter	....do....	34	Sept. 5, 1864	1 year.	Died Jan. 21, 1865, in general hospital, Nashville, Tenn.
Miller, Uriah	....do....	36	Sept. 23, 1864	1 year.	Mustered out with company June 17, 1865.
Miller, Ura	....do....	38	Sept. 12, 1864	1 year.	Mustered out with company June 17, 1865.
Miller, William	....do....	35	Sept. 24, 1864	1 year.	Mustered out with company June 17, 1865.
Moore, Thomas	....do....	32	April 4, 1865	1 year.	Mustered out July 15, 1865, at Nashville, Tenn., by order of War Department.
Mulhern, Joseph	....do....	20	April 5, 1865	1 year.	Mustered out June 14, 1865, at Nashville, Tenn., by order of War Department.
Myers, Aaron J	....do....	28	Sept. 23, 1864	1 year.	Mustered out with company June 17, 1865.
Newcom, Frederick	....do....	24	Sept. 3, 1864	1 year.	Mustered out with company June 17, 1865; also borne on rolls as Frederick Newton.
Ogle, Henry	....do....	29	Sept. 5, 1864	1 year.	Mustered out with company June 17, 1865.
Pursell, Peter	....do....	36	Sept. 24, 1864	1 year.	Died Jan. 7, 1865, in general hospital, Nashville, Tenn.
Patch, Sanford	....do....	23	Sept. 12, 1864	1 year.	Mustered out June 7, 1865, at Nashville, Tenn., by order of War Department.
Post, Baker	....do....	21	Sept. 24, 1864	1 year.	Mustered out with company June 17, 1865.
Pevenmyer, Abram	....do....	34	Sept. 23, 1864	1 year.	Mustered out with company June 17, 1865.
Raber, Samuel	....do....	38	Sept. 3, 1864	1 year.	Mustered out with company June 17, 1865.
Rinker, Joseph	....do....	30	Sept. 7, 1864	1 year.	Mustered out with company June 17, 1865.
Ridenour, Isaac	....do....	33	Sept. 23, 1864	1 year.	Died Jan 16, 1865, in Post Hospital, Nashville, Tennessee.
Rien, David C	....do....	18	Sept. 17, 1864	1 year.	Died April 1, 1865, in Post Hospital, Nashville, Tennessee.
Scott, James B	....do....	27	Sept. 21, 1864	1 year.	Mustered out with company June 17, 1865.
Scott, Matthew	....do....	27	Sept. 24, 1864	1 year.	Mustered out with company June 17, 1865.
Scott, Thomas B	....do....	24	Sept. 24, 1864	1 year.	Mustered out with company June 17, 1865.
Sloan, Wilson S	....do....	22	Sept. 23, 1864	1 year.	Mustered out with company June 17, 1865.
Smith, George W	....do....	27	Sept. 12, 1864	1 year.	Appointed Corporal Oct. 1, 1864; reduced Dec. 8, 1864; mustered out June 17, 1865, at Louisville, Ky., by order of War Department.
Snyder, John W	....do....	38	Sept. 21, 1864	1 year.	Mustered out with company June 17, 1865.
Snyder, William	....do....	40	Sept. 20, 1864	1 year.	Mustered out with company June 17, 1865.
Stemen, John B	....do....	34	Sept. 23, 1864	1 year.	Died Jan. 10, 1865, in Regimental Hospital, Nashville, Tenn.
Stephenson, Charles	....do....	20	Sept. 5, 1864	1 year.	Mustered out with company June 17, 1865.
Sprayer, Nicholas	....do....	27	Sept. 23, 1864	1 year.	Mustered out with company June 17, 1865.
Thomas, Frank	....do....	22	Mch. 29, 1865	1 year.	Mustered out July 15, 1865, at Nashville, Tenn., by order of War Department.
Walter, John U	....do....	35	Sept. 5, 1864	1 year.	Mustered out with company June 17, 1865; also borne on rolls as John W. Walter.
Walter, Christopher	....do....	39	Sept. 19, 1864	1 year.	Mustered out with company June 17, 1865.
Ward, George	....do....	31	Sept. 23, 1864	1 year.	Mustered out with company June 17, 1865.
Whirl, William H	....do....	41	Sept. 23, 1864	1 year.	Mustered out with company June 17, 1865.
Wilson, William F	....do....	32	Sept. 23, 1864	1 year.	Discharged Sept. 30, 1864, at Columbus, O., to accept promotion.
Williams, John	....do....	27	Mch. 27, 1865	1 year.	Mustered out June 14, 1865, at Nashville, Tenn., by order of War Department.
Wigginton, Thomas	....do....	20	Sept. 12, 1864	1 year.	Mustered out June 2, 1865, at Nashville, Tenn., by order of War Department.
Wright, John	....do....	33	Sept. 20, 1864	1 year.	Mustered out with company June 17, 1865.

Names.	Rank.	Age.	Date of Entering the Service.	Period of Service.	Remarks.
Walters, James	Private..	17	Aug. 8, 1864	1 year.	Mustered out with company June 17, 1865.
Wells, Richard	....do....	44	Sept. 1, 1864	1 year.	Mustered out with company June 17, 1865.
Wilson, Owen D	....do....	38	Sept. 5, 1864	1 year.	Mustered out with company June 17, 1865.
Winget, William M	....do....	35	Sept. 2, 1864	1 year.	Promoted to Com. Sergeant Oct. 1, 1864.
Wynn, Isaac	....do....	31	Sept. 5, 1864	1 year.	Mustered out June 14, 1865, at Columbus, O., by order of War Department.
Young, Casper	....do....	31	Sept. 5, 1864	1 year.	Mustered out with company June 17, 1865.

COMPANY G.

Mustered in September 27, 1864, at Camp Chase, O., by W. P. Richardson, Colonel 24th O. V. I. Mustered out June 17, 1865, at Nashville, Tenn., by W. S. Wilson, Captain 71st O. V. I., and A. C. M. 1st Division D. C.

Names.	Rank.	Age.	Date of Entering the Service.	Period of Service.	Remarks.
James W. Glasener	Captain..	30	Aug. 3, 1864	1 year.	Appointed Sept. 27, 1864; mustered out with company June 17, 1865.
James L. Hunter	1st Lieut.	27	Aug. 11, 1864	1 year.	Appointed Sept. 27, 1864; mustered out with company June 17, 1865.
George R. Gyger	2d Lieut.	19	Aug. 20, 1864	1 year.	Appointed Sept. 27, 1864; mustered out with company June 17, 1865.
William H. Woodward	1st Sergt.	23	Sept. 23, 1864	1 year.	Appointed Sept. 27, 1864; mustered out May 27, 1865, at Nashville, Tenn., by order of War Department.
Daniel Potter	....do....	22	Sept. 17, 1864	1 year.	Appointed Sergeant Sept. 27, 1864; 1st Sergeant May 27, 1865; mustered out with company June 17, 1865.
Harvey Alten	Sergeant.	42	Sept. 1, 1864	1 year.	Appointed Sept. 27, 1864; mustered out with company June 17, 1865.
Lafayette Coy	....do....	22	Sept. 22, 1864	1 year.	Appointed Sept. 27, 1864; mustered out with company June 17, 1865.
David Stallman	....do....	21	Sept. 23, 1864	1 year.	Appointed Sept. 27, 1864; mustered out with company June 17, 1865.
Daniel J. Powell	....do....	27	Aug. 23, 1864	1 year.	Appointed Corporal Sept. 27, 1864; Sergeant May 27, 1865; mustered out with company June 17, 1865.
Milton H. Thayer	Corporal.	20	Sept. 12, 1864	1 year.	Appointed Sept. 27, 1864; mustered out with company June 17, 1865.
George Bills	....do....	33	Sept. 17, 1864	1 year.	Appointed Sept. 27, 1864; mustered out June 7, 1865, at Nashville, Tenn., by order of War Department.
John H. Allen	....do....	26	Aug. 16, 1864	1 year.	Appointed Sept. 27, 1864; mustered out with company June 17, 1865.
James Everhart	....do....	25	Sept. 19, 1864	1 year.	Appointed Sept. 27, 1864; mustered out with company June 17, 1865.
James W. Wiggington	....do....	33	Aug. 20, 1864	1 year.	Appointed ——; mustered out May 27, 1865, at Nashville, Tenn., by order of War Department.
Wesley D. Lawson	....do....	25	Sept. 8, 1864	1 year.	Appointed ——; died Feb. 14, 1865, in [illegible] Hospital, Nashville, Tenn.
William McCord	....do....	19	Aug. 22, 1864	1 year.	Appointed May 27, 1865; mustered out with company June 17, 1865.
John W. Randels	....do....	21	Sept. 1, 1864	1 year.	Appointed May 27, 1865; mustered out with company June 17, 1865.
Joseph H. Krebs	Musician	18	Aug. 21, 1864	1 year.	Mustered out with company June 17, 1865.
Adams, Thomas	Private..	27	Sept. 19, 1864	1 year.	
Adolph, Edward	....do....	18	Sept. 5, 1864	1 year.	Mustered out with company June 17, 1865.
Arnold, Jesse	....do....	43	Sept. 9, 1864	1 year.	
Atchison, Edward	....do....	21	Sept. 5, 1864	1 year.	Mustered out with company June 17, 1865.
Baird, Henry	....do....	18	Sept. 19, 1864	1 year.	
Baxter, William H	....do....	18	Sept. 12, 1864	1 year.	Mustered out with company June 17, 1865.
Black, Stephen C	....do....	27	Sept. 25, 1864	1 year.	
Bolen, Benjamin F	....do....	23	Sept. 9, 1864	1 year.	Mustered out with company June 17, 1865.
Boyles, John W	....do....	29	Aug. 9, 1864	1 year.	Promoted to Hospital Steward Oct. [illegible] 1864.
Briley, Robert	....do....	23	Sept. 8, 1864	1 year.	
Brown, George	....do....	22	Aug. 27, 1864	1 year.	
Brown, Robert W	....do....	21	Mch. 3, 1865	1 year.	Transferred to Co. F, 18th O. V. I., June [illegible], 1865.
Burns, William	....do....	23	Sept. 22, 1864	1 year.	
Campbell, Robert	....do....	20	Sept. 3, 1864	1 year.	Mustered out with company June 17, 1865.
Carlisle, Jacob	....do....	40	Sept. 12, 1864	1 year.	Mustered out June 7, 1865, at Post Hospital, Nashville, Tenn., by order of War Department.
Carney, James	....do....	23	Sept. 20, 1864	1 year.	
Carr, Thomas	....do....	18	Sept. 22, 1864	1 year.	
Chipman, John	....do....	24	Sept. 20, 1864	1 year.	
Clark, Matthew	....do....	18	Sept. 23, 1864	1 year.	Mustered out with company June 17, 1865.
Coleman, Alexander	....do....	17	Sept. 1, 1864	1 year.	Mustered out with company June 17, 1865.
Coleman, William J	....do....	19	Feb. 27, 1865	1 year.	Transferred to Co. G, 18th O. V. I., June [illegible], 1865.
Conner, John	....do....	35	Aug. 20, 1864	1 year.	Mustered out with company June 17, 1865.

Names.	Rank.	Age.	Date of Entering the Service.	Period of Service.	Remarks.
Huffman, Henry	Private	18	Sept. 20, 1864	1 year.	Mustered out with company June 17, 1865.
Huffman, Lafayette	...do...	23	Feb. 8, 1865	1 year.	Transferred to Co. F, 18th O. V. I., June 28, 1865
Hunt, George P	...do...	20	Sept. 17, 1864	1 year.	Mustered out with company June 17, 1865.
Jarrett, Cyrus	...do...	21	Sept. 16, 1864	1 year.	Mustered out with company June 17, 1865.
Jarrett, James	...do...	28	Sept. 16, 1864	1 year.	Died Nov. 28, 1864, at Post Hospital, Nashville, Tennessee.
Jones, Levi W	...do...	18	Aug. 29, 1864	1 year.	Mustered out June 7, 1865, at Nashville, Tenn., by order of War Department.
Jordan, James W	...do...	21	Aug. 29, 1864	1 year.	Mustered out with company June 17, 1865.
Justice, James B	...do...	18	Aug. 29, 1864	1 year.	Died Nov. 4, 1864, in Regimental Hospital, Nashville, Tenn.
Justice, John W	...do...	20	Aug. 29, 1864	1 year.	Died Jan 31, 1865, in hospital at Nashville, Tennessee.
Kirkbride, James M	...do...	26	Sept. 1, 1864	1 year.	Mustered out with company June 17, 1865.
Kooken, John	...do...	18	Sept. 16, 1864	1 year.	Mustered out with company June 17, 1865.
Leach, Benjamin F	...do...	32	Sept. 18, 1864	1 year.	Mustered out with company June 17, 1865.
Long, Elihu	...do...	18	Aug. 8, 1864	1 year.	
Loy, Jacob	...do...	19	Aug. 17, 1864	1 year.	Mustered out with company June 17, 1865.
Lucas, Charles H	...do...	29	Sept. 20, 1864	1 year.	Mustered out May 30, 1865, at Nashville, Tenn., by order of War Department.
Lucas, Garnet	...do...	40	Sept. 20, 1864	1 year.	Mustered out June 17, 1865, at Nashville, Tenn., by order of War Department.
McFarland, Robert L	...do...	21	Sept. 15, 1864	1 year.	Died Jan. 27, 1865, at general hospital, Nashville, Tenn.
Mantle, Hiram	...do...	18	Sept. 20, 1864	1 year.	Mustered out with company June 17, 1865
Martin, James E	...do...	28	Sept. 1, 1864	1 year.	Appointed Corporal Sept. 30, 1864; reduced April 25, 1865; mustered out with company June 17, 1865.
Martin, James	...do...	32	Sept. 1, 1864	1 year.	Mustered out with company June 17, 1865.
Martin, Joseph A	...do...	22	Sept. 26, 1864	1 year.	Mustered out with company June 17, 1865.
Martin, William	...do...	18	Aug. 8, 1864	1 year.	Mustered out with company June 17, 1865.
Molden, Theodore	...do...	18	Sept. 20, 1864	1 year.	Mustered out with company June 17, 1865.
Monroe, John R	...do...	18	Sept. 8, 1864	1 year.	Mustered out with company June 17, 1865.
Moore, Richard	...do...	20	Sept. 1, 1864	1 year.	Mustered out with company June 17, 1865.
Morris, William	...do...	20	Aug. 20, 1864	1 year.	
Mosburg, James M	...do...	18	Sept. 3, 1864	1 year.	Mustered out with company June 17, 1865.
Nicholson, Valentine	...do...	18	Sept. 5, 1864	1 year.	Mustered out with company June 17, 1865.
Parmer, Alexander	...do...	30	Sept. 5, 1864	1 year.	Mustered out with company June 17, 1865.
Purdew, Horace A	...do...	19	Sept. 15, 1864	1 year.	Mustered out with company June 17, 1865.
Powell, David	...do...	18	Aug. 12, 1864	1 year.	Mustered out with company June 17, 1865.
Reichman, Benjamin F	...do...	18	Sept. 16, 1864	1 year.	Died Nov. 29, 1864, in Post Hospital, Nashville, Tennessee.
Riley, Jesse	...do...	30	Oct. 1, 1864	1 year.	Mustered out with company June 17, 1865.
Rush, John	...do...	18	Aug. 6, 1864	1 year.	Mustered out with company June 17, 1865.
Saffell, Charles	...do...	19	Sept. 6, 1864	1 year.	Mustered out with company June 17, 1865.
Sheppard, Isaac	...do...	..	....	1 year.	
Sbettle, Frederick	...do...	18	Sept. 16, 1864	1 year.	Mustered out with company June 17, 1865.
Sovall, Charles	...do...	20	Sept. 8, 1864	1 year.	Mustered out with company June 17, 1865.
Stansel, Alexis B	...do...	31	Sept. 19, 1864	1 year.	Mustered out with company June 17, 1865.
Thomas, George W	...do...	18	Aug. 12, 1864	1 year.	Mustered out with company June 17, 1865.
Ward, John L	...do...	19	Sept. 14, 1864	1 year.	Mustered out with company June 17, 1865.
Ward, Seth	...do...	20	Sept. 6, 1864	1 year.	Mustered out with company June 17, 1865.
Wheeler, Isaac	...do...	21	Sept. 1, 1864	1 year.	Mustered out with company June 17, 1865.
Wheeler, William B	...do...	18	Sept. 22, 1864	1 year.	Mustered out with company June 17, 1865.
Wheeler, William H	...do...	18	Aug. 12, 1864	1 year.	Mustered out with company June 17, 1865.
Williams, John	...do...	19	Aug. 20, 1864	1 year.	Mustered out with company June 17, 1865.
Willison, Amos	...do...	20	Sept. 4, 1864	1 year.	Mustered out with company June 17, 1865.
Willison, Elias	...do...	18	Sept. 4, 1864	1 year.	Mustered out May 23, 1865, at Nashville, Tenn., by order of War Department.
Willison, James	...do...	24	Sept. 20, 1864	1 year.	Mustered out May 27, 1865, at Nashville, Tenn., by order of War Department
Wise, Asa B	...do...	18	Aug. 19, 1864	1 year.	Died Nov. 30, 1864, in Post Hospital, Nashville, Tennessee.
Wright, Isaac	...do...	34	Sept. 19, 1864	1 year.	Died Nov. 21, 1864, in Post Hospital, Nashville, Tennessee.
Yocum, Lindley	...do...	18	Aug. 13, 1864	1 year.	Mustered out with company June 17, 1865.
Yoho, Samuel	...do...	18	Sept. 16, 1864	1 year.	Mustered out with company June 17, 1865.
Zimmerman, Oliver	...do...	27	Sept. 15, 1864	1 year.	Mustered out with company June 17, 1865.

COMPANY H.

Mustered in September 28, 1864, at Camp Chase, O., by W. P. Richardson, Colonel 25th O. V. I. Mustered out June 17, 1865, at Nashville, Tenn., by W. S. Wilson, Captain 71st O. V. I., and A. C. M. 1st Division D. C.

Names.	Rank.	Age.	Date of Entering the Service.	Period of Service.	Remarks.
Claud B. Gibson	Captain.	32	Aug. 22, 1864	1 year.	Appointed Sept. 29, 1864; mustered out with company June 17, 1865.
Joseph L. Dickelman	1st Lieut.	25	Sept. 7, 1864	1 year.	Appointed Sept. 29, 1864; mustered out with company June 17, 1865.
Joseph McMillen	2d Lieut.	40	Sept. 23, 1864	1 year.	Appointed Sept. 29, 1864; discharged Jan. 1865.
William H. Saxton	....do....	24	Aug. 29, 1864	1 year.	Promoted from 1st Sergeant Co. A March 1865; mustered out with company June 1865.
William H. Grafton	1st Sergt.	21	Sept. 12, 1864	1 year.	Appointed Oct. 1, 1864; mustered out with company June 17, 1865.
James M. Green	Sergeant.	26	Sept. 28, 1864	1 year.	Appointed Oct. 1, 1864; mustered out with company June 17, 1865.
David W. Rogers	....do....	38	Sept. 23, 1864	1 year.	Appointed Oct. 1, 1864; mustered out with company June 17, 1865.
John W. Flinn	....do....	41	Sept. 21, 1864	1 year.	Appointed Oct. 1, 1864; mustered out with company June 17, 1865.
John H. Canaan	....do....	22	Sept. 22, 1864	1 year.	Appointed Corporal Oct. 1, 1864; Sergeant Dec. 8, 1864; mustered out with company June 17, 1865.
John C. Moyer	Corporal.	28	Sept. 23, 1864	1 year.	Appointed Oct. 1, 1864; mustered out with company June 17, 1865.
John H. Blough	....do....	27	Sept. 21, 1864	1 year.	Appointed Oct. 1, 1864; mustered out with company June 17, 1865.
Robert H. Johnson	....do....	23	Sept. 23, 1864	1 year.	Appointed Oct. 1, 1864; mustered out with company June 17, 1865.
John A Cutting	....do....	26	Sept. 22, 1864	1 year.	Appointed Oct. 1, 1864; mustered out with company June 17, 1865.
Smith Povenmyer	....do....	27	Sept. 23, 1864	1 year.	Appointed Oct. 1, 1864; mustered out with company June 17, 1865.
Joseph Belt	....do....	24	Sept. 7, 1864	1 year.	Appointed Oct. 1, 1864; mustered out with company June 17, 1865.
Andy Miller	....do....	37	Sept. 16, 1864	1 year.	Appointed Dec. 8, 1864; mustered out with company June 17, 1865.
Christian D. Stemen	....do....	21	Sept. 23, 1864	1 year	Appointed Dec. 8, 1864; mustered out with company June 17, 1865.
Samuel F. Hanna	Musician	26	Sept. 29, 1864	1 year	Mustered out with company June 17, 1865.
Archer, Nicholas	Private..	57	Sept. 10, 1864	1 year.	Mustered out with company June 17, 1865.
Askins, Jacob L	....do....	23	Sept. 23, 1864	1 year.	Mustered out with company June 17, 1865.
Baker, William C	....do....	29	Sept. 24, 1864	1 year.	Mustered out with company June 17, 1865.
Burkhalter, John	....do....	23	Sept. 5, 1864	1 year.	Mustered out with company June 17, 1865.
Beery, Jacob G	....do....	31	Sept. 23, 1864	1 year	Appointed Sergeant Oct 1, 1864, reduced Dec. 8, 1864; mustered out with company June 17, 1865.
Botkins, George	....do....	34	Mch. 15, 1865	1 year.	Mustered out July 15, 1865, at Nashville, Tenn., by order of War Department.
Briggs, Matthew	....do..	23	Oct. 2, 1864	1 year.	Mustered out June 7, 1865, at Nashville, Tenn., by order of War Department.
Calvin, Jesse G	....do....	32	Sept. 21, 1864	1 year.	Mustered out with company June 17, 1865.
Cerfuss, Josiah	....do....	31	Sept. 23, 1864	1 year.	Mustered out with company June 17, 1865.
Clauson, William B	....do....	21	Sept. 28, 1864	1 year.	Died April 8, 1865, at Elida, O.
Cook, Henry	....do....	34	Mch. 20, 1865	1 year.	Absent, sick ——, in hospital. No further record found.
Cremean, William J	....do....	34	Sept. 23, 1864	1 year.	Mustered out with company June 17, 1865.
Dixon, William	....do....	18	Sept. 17, 1864	1 year.	Mustered out with company June 17, 1865.
Doner, Abraham	....do..	42	Sept. 21, 1864	1 year.	Mustered out with company June 17, 1865.
Eaton, William H	....do..	22	Mch. 20, 1865	1 year.	Transferred to Co. E, 18th O. V. I. June 1865.
Furry, Franklin	....do....	44	Sept. 21, 1864	1 year.	Mustered out with company June 17, 1865.
Gahman, Samuel	....do....	31	Sept. 23, 1864	1 year.	Mustered out with company June 17, 1865.
Green, Andrew J	....do....	29	Sept. 28, 1864	1 year.	Mustered out with company June 17, 1865.
Hanger, Jesse	....do....	37	Sept. 21, 1864	1 year.	Mustered out with company June 17, 1865.
Harbison, James H	....do....	27	Sept. 2, 1864	1 year.	Died Jan. 12, 1865, in Post Hospital, Nashville, Tennessee.
Heartley, Henry A	....do....	34	Sept. 21, 1864	1 year.	Discharged Dec. 16, 1864, at Camp Chase, O., on Surgeon's certificate of disability.
Heisler, John W	....do....	24	Sept. 24, 1864	1 year.	Mustered out with company June 17, 1865.
Houdenchield, Jacob	....do....	32	Sept. 5, 1864	1 year.	Mustered out with company June 17, 1865.
Houdenchield, John	....do....	40	Sept. 5, 1864	1 year.	Mustered out with company June 17, 1865.
Huber, William	....do....	36	Dec. 31, 1864	1 year.	Mustered out July 25, 1865, at Nashville, Tenn., by order of War Department.
Hudson, Richard	....do....	26	Mch. 20, 1865	1 year.	Mustered out June 14, 1865, at Nashville, Tenn., by order of War Department.
Huhn, Joseph S	....do....	41	Sept. 15, 1864	1 year.	Mustered out July 4, 1865, at Murfreesboro, Tenn., by order of War Department.
Irvin, John A	....do....	23	Sept. 21, 1864	1 year.	Mustered out May 27, 1865, at Nashville, Tenn., by order of War Department.

Names.	Rank.	Age.	Date of Entering the Service.	Period of Service.	Remarks.
Good, Joseph	Private	21	Sept. 20, 1864	1 year.	Mustered out with company June 17, 1865.
Hamilton, Cyrus	...do...	32	Sept. 9, 1864	1 year.	Mustered out with company June 17, 1865.
Hartoon, George W	...do...	82	Sept. 23, 1864	1 year.	
Hawley, William E	...do...	18	Sept. 5, 1864	1 year.	Mustered out with company June 17, 1865.
Hennemire, Daniel	...do...	41	Aug. 28, 1864	1 year.	Mustered out with company June 17, 1865.
Henry, James	...do...	19	Sept. 23, 1864	1 year.	Mustered out with company June 17, 1865.
Henry, Moses	...do...	18	Sept. 23, 1864	1 year.	Mustered out with company June 17, 1865.
Hill, Alfred	...do...	20	Aug. 16, 1864	1 year.	Mustered out with company June 17, 1865.
Hoover Benjamin B	...do...	19	Sept. 9, 1864	1 year.	Died Dec. 8, 1864, in Post Hospital, Nashville, Tennessee.
Kirby, Smith V	...do...	27	Sept. 17, 1864	1 year.	Died Dec. 11, 1864, in Post Hospital, Nashville, Tennessee.
Kirby, William	...do...	20	Sept. 16, 1864	1 year.	Mustered out with company June 17, 1865.
Kleppinger, Harvey	...do...	22	Sept. 9, 1864	1 year.	Mustered out with company June 17, 1865.
Landis, Emanuel	...do...	37	Sept. 22, 1864	1 year.	Mustered out with company June 17, 1865.
Lincoln, Will A	...do...	18	Sept. 9, 1864	1 year.	Mustered out with company June 17, 1865.
Logan, Daniel M	...do...	17	Sept. 15, 1864	1 year.	Mustered out with company June 17, 1865.
Losier, John	...do...	21	Sept. 2, 1864	1 year.	Mustered out with company June 17, 1865.
Louis, Charles E	...do...	29	Sept. 20, 1864	1 year.	Promoted to Sergt. Major Oct. 1, 1864.
Loy, Jacob G	...do...	18	Jan. 23, 1865	1 year.	Transferred to Co. F, 18th O. V. I., June 28, 1865.
Lucas, John	...do...	37	Sept. 10, 1864	1 year.	Mustered out with company June 17, 1865.
McGrady Marion	...do...	26	Aug. 13, 1864	1 year.	
McGrew, John	...do...	18	Sept. 23, 1864	1 year.	
McGuire, Patrick	...do...	44	Sept. 17, 1864	1 year.	Mustered out May 25, 1865, at Hospital No. 2, Nashville, Tenn., by order of War Department.
McLain, McNutt	...do...	22	Sept. 9, 1864	1 year.	Mustered out with company June 17, 1865.
McNally, Patrick	...do...	36	Sept. 9, 1864	1 year.	Mustered out with company June 17, 1865.
McNutt, Hiram S	...do...	18	Sept. 26, 1864	1 year.	Mustered out with company June 17, 1865.
Mawzy, James L	...do...	31	Sept. 3, 1864	1 year.	Drowned Oct. 3, 1864, in Ohio River, near Cincinnati, O.
Moffett, Moses F	...do...	28	Sept. 14, 1864	1 year.	Mustered out with company June 17, 1865.
Moody, Thomas J	...do...	26	Sept. 19, 1864	1 year.	Appointed Corporal Sept. 29, 1864; reduced April 29, 1865 mustered out with company June 17, 1865.
Myers, John P	...do...	18	Sept. 13, 1864	1 year.	Mustered out with company June 17, 1865.
Parks, Franklin	...do...	19	Sept. 19, 1864	1 year.	Died April 1, 1865, in Hospital No. 2, Nashville, Tenn.
Peeling, Robert	...do...	18	Sept. 9, 1864	1 year.	Died March 14, 1865, while home on sick furlough.
Peter, Adolph	...do...	42	Sept. 12, 1864	1 year.	Mustered out with company June 17, 1865.
Popenoe, Presley C	...do...	18	Feb. 8, 1865	1 year.	Transferred to Co. F, 18th O. V. I., June 28, 1865.
Popenoe, Thomas C	...do...	19	Sept. 24, 1864	1 year.	Mustered out May 27, 1865, at Hospital No. 2, Nashville, Tenn., by order of War Department.
Randall, Franklin T	...do...	19	Sept. 2, 1864	1 year.	Mustered out with company June 17, 1865.
Rea, John	...do...	22	Sept. 21, 1864	1 year	Appointed Sergeant Sept. 29, 1864; reduced Jan. 1, 1865; mustered out with company June 17, 1865.
Renner, Charles A	...do...	17	Sept. 2, 1864	1 year.	Mustered out with company June 17, 1865.
Rike, David V	...do...	17	Sept. 7, 1864	1 year.	Mustered out with company June 17, 1865.
Rike, Eugene	...do...	17	Sept. 10, 1864	1 year.	Died Dec. 10, 1864, in Hospital No. 3, Nashville, Tennessee.
Saylor, Jacob	...do...	27	Sept. 20, 1864	1 year.	Mustered out May 20, 1865, at Louisville, Ky., by order of War Department.
Seibert, August	...do...	30	Sept. 21, 1864	1 year.	Mustered out with company June 17, 1865.
Simison, Jacob	...do...	18	Sept. 2, 1864	1 year.	Mustered out with company June 17, 1865.
Smith, Cornelius	...do...	21	Sept. 9, 1864	1 year.	Mustered out with company June 17, 1865.
Smith, William W	...do...	48	Sept. 20, 1864	1 year.	Drowned Oct. 3, 1864, in Ohio River, near Cincinnati, O.
Sontag, Thaddeus	...do...	39	Sept. 19, 1864	1 year.	Mustered out with company June 17, 1865.
Stephens, Sergant K	...do...	21	Sept. 9, 1864	1 year.	Mustered out June 7, 1865, at Post Hospital, Nashville, Tenn., by order of War Department.
Stevens, John	...do...	22	Sept. 9, 1864	1 year.	Mustered out with company June 17, 1865.
Stouffer, Josiah	...do...	19	Sept. 2[illegible], 1864	1 year.	Mustered out with company June 17, 1865.
Stouffer, Oliver	...do...	18	Sept. 12, 1864	1 year.	Mustered out with company June 17, 1865.
Waggoner, Alfred	...do...	18	Sept. 1[illegible], 1864	1 year	Mustered out with company June 17, 1865.
Walker, John	...do...	24	Aug. 15, 1864	1 year.	
Walton, Frederick C	...do...	34	Sept. 12, 1864	1 year.	Mustered out June 3, 1865, at Post Hospital, Nashville, Tenn., by order of War Department.
Waters, William	...do...	18	April 6, 1865	1 year.	Transferred to Co. F, 18th O. V. I., June 28, 1865.
Weller, John W	...do...	18	Jan. 25, 1865	1 year.	Transferred to Co. F, 18th O. V. I., June 28, 1865.
Werts, Henry	...do...	18	Sept. 25, 1864	1 year.	Mustered out with company June 17, 1865.
West, Nathaniel S	...do...	18	Sept. 9, 1864	1 year.	Mustered out with company June 17, 1865.
Wharton, Jason	...do...	31	Sept. 12, 1864	1 year.	Mustered out June 8, 1865, at Post Hospital, Nashville, Tenn., by order of War Department.
Wherley, Jonathan	...do...	18	Sept. 1, 1864	1 year.	Mustered out with company June 17, 1865; also borne on rolls as Jonathan Wearley.

COMPANY I.

Mustered in September 28, 1864, at Camp Chase, O., by W. P. Richardson, Colonel 25th O. V. I. Mustered out June 17, 1865, at Nashville, Tenn., by W. S. Wilson, Captain 71st O. V. I., and A. C. M. 1st Division D. C.

Names.	Rank.	Age.	Date of Entering the Service.	Period of Service.	Remarks.
George M. Kemp........	Captain.	25	July 28, 1864	1 year.	Appointed Sept. 29, 1864; mustered out with company June 17, 1865.
Chauncey F. Keller.....	1st Lieut.	39	Sept. 24, 1864	1 year.	Appointed Sept. 29, 1864; mustered out with company June 17, 1865.
Joseph M. Phillips......	2d Lieut.	25	Sept. 29, 1864	1 year.	Resigned Feb. 11, 1865.
William H. Schoch......	....do....	26	Jan. 18, 1865	1 year.	Appointed to date Jan. 18, 1865; mustered out May 15, 1865, at Nashville, Tenn., by order of War Department.
Mark L. Carleton.......	1st Sergt.	21	Sept. 18, 1864	1 year.	Appointed Sept. 30, 1864; mustered out with company June 17, 1865.
Nathaniel A. Worley...	Sergeant.	43	Sept. 23, 1864	1 year.	Appointed Sept. 30, 1864; mustered out with company June 17, 1865.
Henry Kinney..........	....do....	21	Sept. 19, 1864	1 year.	Appointed Sept. 30, 1864; mustered out with company June 17, 1865.
Uriah L. Bechtell.......	....do....	27	Sept. 16, 1864	1 year.	Appointed Sept. 30, 1864; mustered out with company June 17, 1865.
Christopher Dawson....	....do...	19	Aug. 12, 1864	1 year.	Appointed Corporal Sept. 30, 1864; Sergeant April 25, 1865; mustered out with company June 17, 1865.
Joseph K. Mitchell......	Corporal.	18	Aug. 8, 1864	1 year.	Appointed Sept. 30, 1864; mustered out with company June 17, 1865.
Adam Moore............	....do....	28	Sept. 20, 1864	1 year.	Appointed Sept. 30, 1864; mustered out with company June 17, 1865.
Thomas Elrod...........	....do....	19	Aug. 8, 1864	1 year.	Appointed Sept. 30, 1864; mustered out with company June 17, 1865.
Isaac Hinkle............	....do....	18	Sept. 15, 1864	1 year.	Appointed Sept. 30, 1864; mustered out with company June 17, 1865.
John R. Trigg.....	....do....	24	Sept. 14, 1864	1 year.	Appointed Sept. 30, 1864; mustered out with company June 17, 1865.
John W. Brown.........	....do....	24	Sept. 16, 1864	1 year.	Appointed Sept. 30, 1864; died Nov. 9, in Post Hospital, Nashville, Tenn.
Thomas G. Henderson..	....do....	34	Sept. 16, 1864	1 year.	Appointed Dec. 6, 1864; mustered out with company June 17, 1865.
Ephraim Meltchelknaus	....do...	33	Sept. 16, 1864	1 year.	Appointed April 25, 1865; mustered out with company June 17, 1865.
Thomas B. Gillespie ...	....do....	25	Sept. 13, 1864	1 year.	Appointed April 25, 1865; mustered out with company June 17, 1865.
William McCullough...	Musician.	26	Sept. 16, 1864	1 year.	Mustered out with company June 17, 1865.
Thomas F Penn	....do. ..	15	Sept. 20, 1864	1 year.	Mustered out with company June 17, 1865.
Allen, John W..........	Private.	17	Sept. 21, 1864	1 year.	Mustered out with company June 17, 1865.
Andrews, John	....do. ..	18	Aug. 8, 1864	1 year.	Mustered out with company June 17, 1865.
Baker, Benjamin F.....	....do ...	19	Aug. 30, 1864	1 year.	Mustered out with company June 17, 1865.
Barker, James [illegible]......	....do....	18	Aug. 26, 1864	1 year	Mustered out with company June 17, 1865.
Barnes, Lewis C..........	....do....	18	Sept. 20, 1864	1 year	Died Dec. 10, 1864, in hospital at Nashville, Tennessee.
Beach, Samuel....	....do	21	Sept. 20, 1864	1 year	Mustered out with company June 17, 1865.
Bender, Christian	....do....	18	Aug. 20, 1864	1 year.	Mustered out with company June 17, 1865.
Bonnell, George W......	....do....	18	Sept. 20, 1864	1 year.	Mustered out with company June 17, 1865.
Bramhall, Edward R ...	....do....	26	Aug 19, 1864	1 year.	Appointed Sergeant Sept. 30, 1864; reduced Dec. 31, 1864; mustered out with company June 17, 1865.
Brooks, Stephen.........	....do. ..	24	Sept. 1, 1864	1 year.	Mustered out with company June 17, 1865.
Bruce, Nathaniel D.....	....do....	18	Sept. 2, 1864	1 year.	Mustered out June 10, 1865, at [illegible] by order of War Department.
Brunne, John B.........	....do ..	43	Sept. 16, 1864	1 year.	Died Jan 1, 1865, in Post Hospital, Nashville, Tennessee.
Byers, Andrew.....	....do. ..	21	Aug. 28, 1864	1 year	Mustered out with company June 17, 1865.
Caldwell, Fremont......	....do....	18	Sept 23, 1864	1 year.	Mustered out with company June 17, 1865.
Cisney, John............	....do....	28	Sept. 16, 1864	1 year.	Mustered out with company June 17, 1865.
Dowell, Adam S.	....do....	21	Aug. 21, 1864	1 year.	Died Dec. 22, 1864, in Post Hospital, Nashville, Tennessee.
Doyle, Henry............	....do....	30	Aug. 28, 1864	1 year.	
Dunter, Oliver.........	....do....	..	Sept. 20, 1864	1 year.	Mustered out with company June 17, 1865.
Dye, Mathias	....do....	26	Sept. 20, 1864	1 year	Mustered out with company June 17, 1865.
Fisher, Isaac............	....do....	18	Aug. 19, 1864	1 year.	Mustered out with company June 17, 1865.
Gattan, William H......	....do....	18	Aug. 29, 1864	1 year.	Mustered out with company June 17, 1865.
Givens, Jasper N	....do....	24	Sept. 15, 1864	1 year.	Mustered out with company June 17, 1865.
Gregg, William K.. . .	....do....	18	Sept. 23, 1864	1 year.	Died Feb 21, 1865, in Post Hospital, Nashville, Tennessee.
Hammontree, Samuel A.	....do....	18	Sept. 17, 1864	1 year.	Mustered out with company June 17, 1865.
Harbin, Darling	....do....	41	Sept. 26, 1864	1 year	Mustered out with company June 17, 1865.
Harper, James L........	....do....	18	Aug. 27, 1864	1 year.	Discharged May 11, 1865, at [illegible] on Surgeon's certificate of disability.
Harris, William R.......	....do....	18	Aug 29, 1864	1 year.	Mustered out with company June 17, 1865.
Heller, William.........	....do....	28	Sept. 15, 1864	1 year.	Mustered out with company June 17, 1865.
Huffman, Edward....	....do....	19	Aug 30, 1864	1 year.	Mustered out with company June 17, 1865.

		Age.	Date of Entering the Service.	Period of Service.	Remarks.
...man, Henry		18	Sept. 20, 1864	1 year.	Mustered out with company June 17, 1865.
...man, Lafayette	...do...	23	Feb. 8, 1865	1 year.	Transferred to Co. F, 18th O. V. I., June 28, 1865.
...t, George P.	...do...	20	Sept. 17, 1864	1 year.	Mustered out with company June 17, 1865.
...ett, Cyrus	...do...	21	Sept. 16, 1864	1 year.	Mustered out with company June 17, 1865.
...rett, James	...do...	23	Sept. 16, 1864	1 year.	Died Nov. 28, 1864, at Post Hospital, Nashville, Tennessee.
...es, Levi W.	...do...	18	Aug. 30, 1864	1 year.	Mustered out June 7, 1865, at Nashville, Tenn., by order of War Department.
...lan, James W.		21	Aug. 29, 1864	1 year.	Mustered out with company June 17, 1865.
...tice, James S.		18	Aug. 29, 1864	1 year.	Died Nov. 4, 1864, in Regimental Hospital, Nashville, Tenn.
...ine, John W.		20	Aug. 29, 1864	1 year.	Died Jan 31, 1865, in hospital at Nashville, Tennessee.
...kbride, James M.	...	20	Sept. 1, 1864	1 year.	Mustered out with company June 17, 1865.
...ken, John	...	18	Sept. 16, 1864	1 year.	Mustered out with company June 17, 1865.
...ch, Benjamin F.	...	32	Sept. 16, 1864	1 year.	Mustered out with company June 17, 1865.
...g, Elihu	...	18	Aug. 8, 1864	1 year.	
..., Jacob	...	19	Aug. 17, 1864	1 year.	Mustered out with company June 17, 1865.
...s, Charles H.	...	23	Sept. 20, 1864	1 year.	Mustered out May 30, 1865, at Nashville, Tenn., by order of War Department.
...ms, Garnet		40	Sept. 20, 1864	1 year.	Mustered out June 17, 1865, at Nashville, Tenn., by order of War Department.
...farland, Robert L.	...do...	21	Sept. 15, 1864	1 year.	Died Jan. 27, 1865, at general hospital, Nashville, Tenn.
...tle, Hiram	...do...	18	Sept. 20, 1864	1 year.	Mustered out with company June 17, 1865
...tin, James E.	...do...	26	Sept. 1, 1864	1 year.	Appointed Corporal Sept. 30, 1864; reduced April 25, 1865; mustered out with company June 17, 1865.
...tin, James	...do...	32	Sept. 1, 1864	1 year.	Mustered out with company June 17, 1865.
...in, Joseph A.	...do...	22	Sept. 26, 1864	1 year.	Mustered out with company June 17, 1865.
...tin, William	...do...	18	Aug. 8, 1864	1 year.	Mustered out with company June 17, 1865.
...den, Theodore	...do...	18	Sept. 20, 1864	1 year.	Mustered out with company June 17, 1865.
...roe, John R.	...do...	18	Sept. 8, 1864	1 year.	Mustered out with company June 17, 1865.
...re, Richard	...do...	30	Sept. 1, 1864	1 year.	Mustered out with company June 17, 1865.
...ris, William	...do...	20	Aug. 20, 1864	1 year.	
...burg, James M.	...do...	18	Sept. 3, 1864	1 year.	Mustered out with company June 17, 1865.
...olson, Valentine	...do...	18	Sept. 5, 1864	1 year.	Mustered out with company June 17, 1865.
...ner, Alexander	...do...	30	Sept. 5, 1864	1 year.	Mustered out with company June 17, 1865.
...lew, Horace A.	...do...	19	Sept. 15, 1864	1 year.	Mustered out with company June 17, 1865.
...ell, David	...do...	18	Aug. 12, 1864	1 year.	Mustered out with company June 17, 1865.
...hman, Benjamin F.	...do...	18	Sept. 16, 1864	1 year.	Died Nov. 29, 1864, in Post Hospital, Nashville, Tennessee.
...y, Jesse	...do...	30	Oct. 1, 1864	1 year.	Mustered out with company June 17, 1865.
...h, John	...do...	18	Aug. 6, 1864	1 year.	Mustered out with company June 17, 1865.
...ell, Charles	...do...	19	Sept. 6, 1864	1 year.	Mustered out with company June 17, 1865.
...ppard, Isaac	...do...	..	....	1 year.	
...ttle, Frederick	...do...	18	Sept. 16, 1864	1 year.	Mustered out with company June 17, 1865.
...ll, Charles	...do...	20	Sept. 8, 1864	1 year.	Mustered out with company June 17, 1865.
...sel, Alexis B.	...do...	41	Sept. 19, 1864	1 year.	Mustered out with company June 17, 1865.
...mas, George W.	...do...	18	Aug. 12, 1864	1 year.	Mustered out with company June 17, 1865.
...l, John L.	...do...	19	Sept. 14, 1864	1 year.	Mustered out with company June 17, 1865.
...l, Seth	...do...	30	Sept. 6, 1864	1 year	Mustered out with company June 17, 1865.
...eler, Isaac	...do...	21	Sept. 1, 1864	1 year.	Mustered out with company June 17, 1865.
...eler, William B.	...do...	18	Sept. 22, 1864	1 year.	Mustered out with company June 17, 1865.
...eler, William H.	...do...	18	Aug. 12, 1864	1 year.	Mustered out with company June 17, 1865.
...liams, John	...do...	19	Aug. 30, 1864	1 year.	Mustered out with company June 17, 1865.
...ilson, Amos	...do...	20	Sept. 4, 1864	1 year.	Mustered out with company June 17, 1865.
...lison, Elias	...do...	18	Sept. 4, 1864	1 year.	Mustered out May 23, 1865, at Nashville, Tenn., by order of War Department.
...son, James	...do...	24	Sept. 20, 1864	1 year.	Mustered out May 27, 1865, at Nashville, Tenn., by order of War Department
..., Asa B.	...do...	18	Aug. 19, 1864	1 year.	Died Nov. 30, 1864, in Post Hospital, Nashville, Tennessee.
...ght, Isaac	...do...	34	Sept. 19, 1864	1 year.	Died Nov. 21, 1864, in Post Hospital, Nashville, Tennessee.
...nn, Lindley	...do...	18	Aug. 13, 1864	1 year.	Mustered out with company June 17, 1865.
...o, Samuel	...do...	18	Sept. 16, 1864	1 year.	Mustered out with company June 17, 1865.
...merman, Oliver	...do...	27	Sept. 15, 1864	1 year.	Mustered out with company June 17, 1865.

COMPANY K.

Mustered in September 29, 1864, at Camp Chase, O., by W. P. Richardson, Colonel 25th O. V. I. Mustered [illegible] June 17, 1865, at Nashville, Tenn., by W. S. Wilson, Captain 71st O. V. I., and A. C. M. 1st Division D. C.

Names.	Rank.	Age.	Date of Entering the Service.	Period of Service.	Remarks.
Henry P. Shaffer	Captain.	38	Sept. 1, 1864	1 year.	Appointed Sept. 30, 1864; mustered out [illegible] company June 17, 1865.
Ephraim Pippinger	1st Lieut.	20	July 25, 1864	1 year.	Appointed Sept. 30, 1864; mustered out [illegible] company June 17, 1865.
Joshua W. Brelsford	2d Lieut.	20	Sept. 9, 1864	1 year.	Appointed Sept. 30, 1864; mustered out [illegible] company June 17, 1865.
John J. McPherson	1st Sergt.	25	Sept. 5, 1864	1 year.	Appointed Sept. 29, 1864; mustered out [illegible] company June 17, 1865.
James Karnes	Sergeant.	25	Aug. 25, 1864	1 year.	Appointed Sept. 29, 1864; mustered out [illegible] company June 17, 1865.
Edward Krider	....do....	41	Sept. 5, 1864	1 year.	Appointed Sept. 29, 1864; mustered out [illegible] company June 17, 1865.
Joseph R. Imboden	....do....	23	Sept. 21, 1864	1 year.	Appointed Sept. 29, 1864; mustered out [illegible] company June 17, 1865.
Fortunatus S. Lilley	....do....	43	Sept. 26, 1864	1 year.	Appointed Jan. 1, 1865; mustered out [illegible] company June 17, 1865.
Frederick S. Rudy	Corporal.	20	Sept. 16, 1864	1 year.	Appointed Sept. 29, 1864; mustered out [illegible] 29, 1865, at Hospital No. 2, Nashville, Tenn., by order of War Department.
Isaac H. Davis	....do....	23	Sept. 13, 1864	1 year.	Appointed Sept. 29, 1864; mustered out [illegible] company June 17, 1865.
John C. Deitrich	....do....	28	Sept. 5, 1864	1 year.	Appointed Sept. 29, 1864; mustered out [illegible] company June 17, 1865.
Michael Rief	....do....	31	Sept. 22, 1864	1 year.	Appointed Nov. 3, 1864; mustered out [illegible] company June 17, 1865.
Charles A. Palmer	....do....	22	Sept. 22, 1864	1 year.	Appointed Jan. 1, 1865; mustered out [illegible] company June 17, 1865.
Jonas E. Beachley	....do....	23	Sept. 9, 1864	1 year.	Appointed Jan. 1, 1865; mustered out [illegible] company June 17, 1865.
Charles Arbogast	....do....	22	Sept. 5, 1864	1 year.	Appointed May 1, 1865; mustered out [illegible] company June 17, 1865.
William Whittaker	....do....	24	Sept. 9, 1864	1 year.	Appointed May 1, 1865; mustered out [illegible] company June 17, 1865.
Charles M. Kissinger	....do....	26	Sept. 16, 1864	1 year.	Appointed ——; discharged May [illegible] Camp Dennison, O., on Surgeon's [illegible] of disability.
Allen, Franklin P.	Private..	21	Sept. 25, 1864	1 year.	Died May 11, 1865, in Regimental [illegible] near Nashville, Tenn.
Archer, Joseph	....do....	18	Sept. 10, 1864	1 year.	Mustered out with company June [illegible]
Banker, John P	....do....	18	Sept. 26, 1864	1 year	Mustered out with company June [illegible]
Bartenbacher, John	....do....	37	Sept. 13, 1864	1 year.	Mustered out with company June [illegible]
Bickle, Henry	....do....	19	Sept. 13, 1864	1 year.	Mustered out with company June [illegible]
Brelsford, William H.	....do....	21	Feb. 6, 1865	1 year	Transferred to Co. F, 18th O. V. [illegible] 1865.
Burns, Jasper	....do....	18	Sept. 10, 1864	1 year	Died Jan. 5, 1865, in Post Hospital, [illegible] Tennessee.
Burns, John	....do....	20	Sept. 21, 1864	1 year.	Mustered out May 27, 1865, at Hospital [illegible] Nashville, Tenn., by order of War Department.
Butz, Henry J.	....do....	18	Sept. 13, 1864	1 year.	Mustered out July 3, 1865, at [illegible] by order of War Department.
Carter, Henry	....do....	26	Sept. 22, 1864	1 year.	No record subsequent to enlistment.
Carter, John	....do....	38	Sept. 13, 1864	1 year.	Mustered out with company June 17, [illegible]
Carter, William C.	....do....	18	Sept. 13, 1864	1 year.	Mustered out with company June [illegible]
Caswell, George	....do....	25	Sept. 9, 1864	1 year.	Appointed Corporal Sept. 29, 1864; [illegible] April 29, 1865; mustered out with company June [illegible] 1865.
Clutch, John A.	....do....	19	Sept. 13, 1864	1 year.	Mustered out with company June [illegible]
Coler, Anton	....do....	22	Sept. 21, 1864	1 year.	Mustered out with company June [illegible]
Crossland, Allen	....do....	20	Jan. 15, 1865	1 year.	Mustered out June 7, 1865, at Nashville, [illegible] by order of War Department.
Davis, Levi	....do....	18	Sept. 10, 1864	1 year.	Mustered out with company June 17, [illegible]
Dennis, Henry T.	....do....	18	Sept. 13, 1864	1 year.	Mustered out to date June 17, 1865.
Detwiler, Abraham	....do....	44	Sept. 9, 1864	1 year.	Mustered out with company June 17, [illegible]
Dillberry, Michael	....do....	25	Sept. 23, 1864	1 year.	
Dodds, William G.	....do....	25	Feb. 6, 1865	1 year.	Mustered out May 22, 1865, at Hospital [illegible] Nashville, Tenn., by order of War Department.
Eis, William	....do....	18	Sept. 13, 1864	1 year.	Mustered out with company June 17, [illegible]
Fager, Conard	....do....	35	Sept. 9, 1864	1 year.	Mustered out with company June 17, [illegible]
Falvey, Patrick H.	....do....	32	Sept. 8, 1864	3 yrs.	
Geiger, Ferdinand	....do....	32	Sept. 14, 1864	1 year.	Mustered out with company June [illegible]
Gimbel, Conrad	....do....	22	Sept. 13, 1864	1 year.	Mustered out with company June [illegible]
Gleason, John	....do....	33	Aug. 26, 1864	1 year.	Mustered out May 27, 1865, at Hospital [illegible] Nashville, Tenn., by order of War Department.

180TH REGIMENT OHIO VOLUNTEER INFANTRY.

FIELD AND STAFF.

Mustered in October 18, 1864, at Camp Chase, O. Mustered out July 12, 1865, at Charlotte, N. C., by T. M. Ward, 1st Lieutenant M. V. I. and A. C. M., 1st Division, 23d Army Corps.

Names.	Rank.	Age.	Date of Entering the Service.	Period of Service.	Remarks
Willard Warner	Colonel.	35	Dec. 28, 1861	3 yrs.	Promoted from Lieut. Colonel 76th Regiment O. V. I., Oct. 12, 1864; Brevet Brig. General March 13, 1865; mustered out with regiment July 12, 1865.
Hiram McKay	Lt. Col.	30	Oct. 7, 1864	1 year.	Died March 13, 1865, at Newbern, N. C., of wounds received March 8, 1865, in battle of Wise's Fork, N. C.
John T. Wood	....do....	22	Oct. 8, 1864	1 year.	Promoted from Major March 29, 1865; mustered out with regiment July 12, 1865.
Frank E. Powers	Surgeon.	35	Oct. 3, 1864	1 year.	Mustered out with regiment July 12, 1865.
Calvin D. Case	Asst. Sur.	39	Oct. 6, 1864	1 year.	Discharged to date Jan. 24, 1865, by order of War Department.
James N. Bolard	....do....	26	Oct. 8, 1864	1 year.	Mustered out with regiment July 12, 1865.
Horace R. Abbott	Adjutant	22	Oct. 4, 1864	1 year.	Mustered out with regiment July 12, 1865.
Harlan F. Walker	R. Q. M.	24	Oct. 6, 1864	1 year.	Mustered out with regiment July 12, 1865.
John W. Messick	Sergt. Maj	19	Sept. 29, 1864	1 year.	Promoted from private Co. I Oct. 20, 1864; reduced to private Co. I March 28, 1865.
John McAfee	....do....	34	Sept. 18, 1864	1 year.	Promoted from Sergeant Co. E March 28, 1865; mustered out with regiment July 12, 1865.
William W. Hunt	Q. M. S.	24	Oct. 11, 1864	1 year.	Promoted from private Co. A Oct. 20, 1864; mustered out with regiment July 12, 1865.
Benjamin F. Denniston	Com. Ser.	35	Sept. 20, 1864	1 year.	Promoted from Sergeant Co. D Oct. 20, 1864; to 2d Lieutenant July 4, 1865, but not mustered; mustered out with regiment July 12, 1865.
William H. Brown	Hos. St'd.	39	Sept. 17, 1864	1 year.	Promoted from private Co. C Oct. 20, 1864; to Asst. Sergeant July 10, 1864, but not mustered; mustered out with regiment July 12, 1865.
Thomas D. Phillips	Prin. Mus	41	Sept. 1, 1864	1 year.	Promoted from private Co. B Oct. 20, 1864; mustered out with regiment July 12, 1865.

COMPANY A.

Mustered in September 26, 1864, at Camp Chase, O., by W. P. Richardson, Colonel 25th O. V. I. Mustered out July 12, 1865, at Charlotte, N. C., by T. M. Ward, 1st Lieutenant 25th M. V. I. and A. C. M., 1st Division, 23d Army Corps.

Names.	Rank.	Age.	Date of Entering the Service.	Period of Service.	Remarks
Barton A. Holland	Captain.	42	Sept. 28, 1864	3 yrs.	Promoted to Major March 20, 1865, but not mustered; mustered out with company July 12, 1865.
Mathias Ridenour	1st Lieut.	40	Sept. 26, 1864	1 year.	Promoted to Captain Co. H Feb. 10, 1865; mustered out with company July 12, 1865.
John Chapman	....do....	20	Sept. 29, 1864	1 year.	Promoted from 2d Lieutenant Co. B Feb. 10, 1865; mustered out with company July 12, 1865.
Thomas H. Holland	2d Lieut.	18	Nov. 8, 1862	1 year.	Promoted from Corporal Co. K, 118th O. V. I., to date Sept. 27, 1864.
Samuel O. Ridenour	1st Sergt.	30	Sept. 23, 1864	1 year.	Promoted to 2d Lieutenant Co. K Jan. 18, 1865.
Francis G. Davis	....do....	27	Sept. 22, 1864	1 year.	Appointed from Corporal April 8, 1865; mustered out with company July 12, 1865.
Isaac Garwood	Sergeant.	22	Aug. 25, 1864	1 year.	Mustered out with company July 12, 1865.
George Snider	....do....	28	Sept. 20, 1864	1 year.	Mustered out with company July 12, 1865.
William C. Hankins	....do....	37	Sept. 21, 1864	1 year.	Mustered out May 25, 1865, at New York City, N.Y., by order of War Department.
Jacob H. White	....do....	25	Sept. 23, 1864	1 year.	Appointed Corporal Feb. 4, 1865; Sergeant May 8, 1865; mustered out with company July 12, 1865.
Samuel T. Mahon	....do....	41	Sept. 21, 1864	1 year.	Appointed from Corporal June 26, 1865; mustered out with company July 12, 1865.

COMPANY K.

Mustered in September 29, 1864, at Camp Chase, O., by W. P. Richardson, Colonel 25th O. V. I. [illegible] June 17, 1865, at Nashville, Tenn., by W. S. Wilson, Captain 71st O. V. I., and A. C. M. 1st Division D. C

Names.	Rank.	Age.	Date of Entering the Service.	Period of Service.	Remarks.
Henry P. Shaffer	Captain.	38	Sept. 1, 1864	1 year.	Appointed Sept. 30, 1864; [illegible] company June 17, 1865.
Ephraim Pippinger	1st Lieut.	20	July 25, 1864	1 year.	Appointed Sept 30, 1864; [illegible] company June 17, 1865.
Joshua W. Brelsford	2d Lieut.	20	Sept. 9, 1864	1 year.	Appointed Sept. 30, 1864; [illegible] company June 17, 1865.
John J. McPherson	1st Sergt.	25	Sept. 5, 1864	1 year.	Appointed Sept. 29, 1864; [illegible] company June 17, 1865.
James Karnes	Sergeant.	26	Aug. 25, 1864	1 year.	Appointed Sept. 29, 1864; [illegible] company June 17, 1865.
Edward Krider	....do....	41	Sept. 5, 1864	1 year.	Appointed Sept. 29, 1864; [illegible] company June 17, 1865.
Joseph R. Imboden	....do....	23	Sept. 21, 1864	1 year.	Appointed Sept. 29, 1864; [illegible] company June 17, 1865.
Fortunatus S. Lilley	....do....	43	Sept. 26, 1864	1 year.	Appointed Jan. 1, 1865; [illegible] company June 17, 1865.
Frederick S. Rudy	Corporal.	20	Sept. 16, 1864	1 year.	[illegible]ppointed Sept. 29, 1864; [illegible] 29, 1865, at Hospital No. [illegible] by order of War Department.
Isaac H. Davis	....do....	23	Sept. 13, 1864	1 year.	[illegible]ppointed Sept. 29, 1864; [illegible] June 17, 1865.
John C. Deitrich	....do....	28	Sept. 5, 1864	1 year.	[illegible] Sept. 29, 1864; [illegible] company June 17, 1865.
Michael Rief	....do....	31	Sept. 22, 1864	1 year.	Appointed Nov. 3, 1864; [illegible] company June 17, 1865.
Charles A. Palmer	....do....	22	Sept. 22, 1864	1 year.	Appointed Jan. 1, 1865; [illegible] company June 17, 1865.
Jonas E. Beachley	....do....	23	Sept. 9, 1864	1 year.	Appointed Jan. 1, 1865; [illegible] company June 17, 1865.
Charles Arbogast	....do....	22	Sept. 5, 1864	1 year.	Appointed May 1, 1865; [illegible] company June 17, 1865.
William Whittaker	....do....	24	Sept. 9, 1864	1 year.	Appointed May 1, 1865; [illegible] company June 17, 1865.
Charles M. Kissinger	....do....	26	Sept. 16, 1864	1 year.	Appointed ——; discharged [illegible] Camp Dennison, O., on Surgeon's [illegible] of disability.
Allen, Franklin P.	Private..	21	Sept. 25, 1864	1 year.	Died May 11, 1865, in Regimental [illegible] near Nashville, Tenn.
Archer, Joseph	....do....	18	Sept. 10, 1864	1 year.	Mustered out with company June [illegible]
Banker, John P	....do....	18	Sept. 26, 1864	1 year.	Mustered out with company June [illegible]
Bartenbacher, John	....do....	37	Sept. 13, 1864	1 year.	Mustered out with company June [illegible]
Bickle, Henry	....do...	19	Sept. 13, 1864	1 year.	Mustered out with company June [illegible]
Brelsford, William H	....do....	21	Feb. 6, 1865	1 year.	Transferred to Co. F, 18th O. V. I. [illegible] 1865.
Burns, Jasper	....do....	18	Sept. 10, 1864	1 year	Died Jan. 5, 1865, in Post Hospital, [illegible] Tennessee.
Burns, John	....do....	20	Sept. 21, 1864	1 year.	Mustered out May 27, 1865, at [illegible] Nashville, Tenn., by order of [illegible] ment.
Butz, Henry J	....do....	18	Sept. 13, 1864	1 year.	Mustered out July 3, 1865, at C[illegible] by order of War Department.
Carter, Henry	....do....	26	Sept. 22, 1864	1 year.	No record subsequent to enlistment.
Carter, John	....do....	38	Sept. 13, 1864	1 year.	Mustered out with company June [illegible]
Carter, William C	....do....	18	Sept. 13, 1864	1 year.	Mustered out with company June [illegible]
Caswell, George	....do....	25	Sept. 9, 1864	1 year.	Appointed Corporal Sept. 2[illegible] April 29, 1865; mustered out [illegible] pany June 17, 1865.
Clutch, John A	....do....	19	Sept. 13, 1864	1 year.	Mustered out with company June [illegible]
Coler, Anton	....do....	22	Sept. 21, 1864	1 year.	Mustered out with company June [illegible]
Crussland, Allen	....do....	20	Jan. 15, 1865	1 year.	Mustered out June 7, 1865, at [illegible] by order of War Department.
Davis, Levi	....do....	18	Sept. 10, 1864	1 year.	Mustered out with company June [illegible]
Dennis, Henry T.	....do....	18	Sept. 13, 1864	1 year.	Mustered out to date June 17, 1865.
Detwiler, Abraham	....do....	44	Sept. 9, 1864	1 year.	Mustered out with company June [illegible]
Dillberry, Michael	....do....	25	Sept. 23, 1864	1 year.	
Dodds, William G	....do....	25	Feb. 6, 1865	1 year.	Mustered out May 22, 1865, at [illegible] Nashville, Tenn., by order of [illegible] ment.
Eis, William	....do....	18	Sept. 13, 1864	1 year.	Mustered out with company Ju[illegible]
Fager, Conard	....do....	35	Sept. 9, 1864	1 year.	Mustered out with company Ju[illegible]
Falvey, Patrick H	....do....	32	Sept. 8, 1864	3 yrs.	
Geiger, Ferdinand	....do....	32	Sept. 14, 1864	1 year.	Mustered out with company J[illegible]
Gimbel, Conrad	....do....	22	Sept. 13, 1864	1 year.	Mustered out with company J[illegible]
Gleason, John	....do....	33	Aug. 26, 1864	1 year.	Mustered out May 27, 1865, at [illegible] Nashville, Tenn., by order [illegible] ment.

Names.	Rank.	Age.	Date of Entering the Service.	Period of Service.	Remarks.
Marshal, William H.	Private.	26	Sept. 23, 1864	1 year.	Mustered out July 7, 1865, at Columbus, O., by order of War Department.
Martin, Isaac L.	do.	24	Sept. 19, 1864	1 year.	Mustered out with company July 12, 1865.
Myers, William A.	do.	20	Aug. 15, 1864	1 year.	Mustered out with company July 12, 1865.
Neal, William	do.	25	Aug. 27, 1864	1 year.	Mustered out with company July 12, 1865.
Nealy, William	do.	23	Sept. 21, 1864	1 year.	Mustered out with company July 12, 1865.
Newland, William	do.	23	Aug. 16, 1864	1 year.	Mustered out June 14, 1865, at Washington, D. C., by order of War Department.
Patterson, Samuel	do.	26	Sept. 21, 1864	1 year.	Mustered out with company July 12, 1865.
Preston, Jacob	do.	38	Aug. 25, 1864	1 year.	Mustered out with company July 12, 1865.
Schultz, Gephart	do.	44	Sept. 16, 1864	1 year.	Died Nov. 29, 1864, at Decherd, Tenn.
Severs, Jacob	do.	22	Aug. 15, 1864	1 year.	Mustered out June 10, 1865, at Newbern, N. C., by order of War Department.
Shadley, Washington	do.	18	Aug. 26, 1864	1 year.	Mustered out with company July 12, 1865.
Shamberger, Jacob	do.	18	Sept. 24, 1864	1 year.	Mustered out June 10, 1865, at David's Island, New York Harbor, by order of War Department.
Shoube, Isaac	do.	24	Aug. 23, 1864	1 year.	
Slough, Peter	do.	18	Aug. 17, 1864	1 year.	Mustered out with company July 12, 1865.
Smith, Jacob L.	do.	30	Sept. 21, 1864	1 year.	Mustered out with company July 12, 1865.
Smith, James F.	do.	40	Aug. 17, 1864	1 year.	Mustered out with company July 12, 1865.
Snider, Henry	do.	18	Sept. 13, 1864	1 year.	Mustered out with company July 12, 1865.
Staley, Reuben	do.	29	Aug. 26, 1864	1 year.	Mustered out to date Jan. 25, 1865, by order of War Department.
Stafford, Elijah H.	do.	26	Aug. 25, 1864	1 year.	Mustered out with company July 12, 1865.
Stapleton, Anthony J.	do.	18	Aug. 26, 1864	1 year.	Mustered out with company July 12, 1865.
Sutton, Isaiah	do.	41	Sept. 21, 1864	1 year.	Mustered out with company July 12, 1865.
Seifert, Henry O.	do.	33	Sept. 20, 1864	1 year.	Mustered out with company July 12, 1865.
Tipple, Moses B.	do.	34	Sept. 12, 1864	1 year.	Mustered out May 25, 1865, at Louisville, Ky., by order of War Department.
Walters, Robert	do.	26	Sept. 20, 1864	1 year.	Killed March 8, 1865, in battle of Wise's Fork, North Carolina.
Wetherill, William P.	do.	26	Aug. 23, 1864	1 year.	Mustered out with company July 12, 1865.
Williams, Benjamin	do.	29	Sept. 5, 1864	1 year.	Mustered out with company July 12, 1865.
Williams, Michael	do.	28	Sept. 5, 1864	1 year.	Died Feb. 26, 1865, at Washington, D. C.
Wilson, William R.	do.	27	Aug. 27, 1864	1 year.	Returned to duty from Carver Hospital, Washington, D. C., April 22, 1865. No further record found.
Wolley, James	do.	28	Sept. 3, 1864	1 year.	Died Feb. 26, 1865, at Washington, D. C.
Wolley, Stephen	do.	32	Sept. 3, 1864	1 year.	Mustered out with company July 12, 1865.
Yant, Abraham	do.	28	Sept. 21, 1864	1 year.	Mustered out with company July 12, 1865.
Yant, William	do.	20	Sept. 21, 1864	1 year.	Died March 11, 1865, at Newbern, N. C.

COMPANY B.

Mustered in September 29, 1864, at Camp Chase, O., by W. P. Richardson, Colonel 25th O. V. I. Mustered out July 12, 1865, at Charlotte, N. C., by T. M. Ward, 1st Lieutenant 25th M. V. I. and A. C. M., 1st Division, 23d Army Corps.

Names.	Rank.	Age.	Date of Entering the Service.	Period of Service.	Remarks.
Eli S. Anderson	Captain.	21	Sept. 29, 1864	1 year.	Mustered out with company July 12, 1865.
Andrew Smith	1st Lieut.	24	Sept. 29, 1864	1 year.	Promoted to Captain Co. G May 28, 1865.
John Chapman	2d Lieut.	20	Sept. 29, 1864	1 year.	Promoted to 1st Lieutenant Co. A Feb. 18, 1865.
William H. Nichols	do.	28	Sept. 17, 1864	1 year.	Promoted from 1st Sergeant Co. C Feb. 18, 1865; mustered out with company July 12, 1865.
Harrison Frizzell	1st Sergt.	25	Sept. 21, 1864	1 year.	Promoted to 2d Lieutenant Co. F to date Feb. 10, 1865.
Reuben Kelley	do.	19	Sept. 12, 1864	1 year.	Appointed Sergeant Sept. 30, 1864; 1st Sergeant April 29, 1865; mustered out with company July 12, 1865.
Aquilla C. McComas	Sergeant.	24	Sept. 5, 1864	1 year.	Appointed Sept. 30, 1864; mustered out with company July 12, 1865.
Arthur R. White	do.	21	Aug. 31, 1864	1 year.	Appointed from private Nov. 12, 1864; mustered out with company July 12, 1865.
Joseph J. Brown	do.	18	Sept. 2, 1864	1 year.	Appointed Corporal Sept. 30, 1864; Sergeant Feb. 1, 1865; mustered out June 10, 1865, at Newbern, N. C., by order of War Department.
Benjamin F. Jones	do.	18	Sept. 2, 1864	1 year.	Appointed Corporal Sept. 30, 1864; Sergeant April 29, 1865; mustered out with company July 12, 1865.
James W. McCoy	do.	23	Aug. 13, 1864	1 year.	Appointed Corporal Sept. 30, 1864; Sergeant June 10, 1865; mustered out with company July 12, 1865.
Albert S. [illegible]	Corporal.	19	Aug. 29, 1864	1 year.	Appointed Sept. 30, 1864; mustered out with company July 12, 1865.
Jackson Cooper	do.	[illegible]	Sept. 5, 1864	1 year.	Appointed Sept. 30, 1864; mustered out with company July 12, 1865.
Luther F. Conrad	do.	[illegible]	Aug. 31, 1864	1 year.	Appointed Nov. 27, 1864; mustered out with company July 12, 1865.

Names.	Rank.	Age.	Date of Entering the Service.	Period of Service.	Remarks.
Marshal, William H.	Private.	28	Sept. 23, 1864	1 year.	Mustered out July 7, 1865, at Columbus, O., by order of War Department.
Martin, Isaac L.	...do...	34	Sept. 19, 1864	1 year.	Mustered out with company July 12, 1865.
Myers, William A.	...do...	20	Aug. 15, 1864	1 year.	Mustered out with company July 12, 1865.
Neal, William	...do...	25	Aug. 27, 1864	1 year.	Mustered out with company July 12, 1865.
Nealy, William	...do...	23	Sept. 21, 1864	1 year.	Mustered out with company July 12, 1865.
Newland, William	...do...	25	Aug. 16, 1864	1 year.	Mustered out June 14, 1865, at Washington, D. C., by order of War Department.
Patterson, Samuel	...do...	26	Sept. 21, 1864	1 year.	Mustered out with company July 12, 1865.
Preston, Jacob	...do...	35	Aug. 26, 1864	1 year.	Mustered out with company July 12, 1865.
Schultz, Gephart	...do...	44	Sept. 16, 1864	1 year.	Died Nov. 29, 1864, at Decherd, Tenn.
Severs, Jacob	...do...	21	Aug. 18, 1864	1 year.	Mustered out June 10, 1865, at Newbern, N. C., by order of War Department.
Shadley, Washington	...do...	18	Aug. 26, 1864	1 year.	Mustered out with company July 12, 1865.
Shamberger, Jacob	...do...	18	Sept. 24, 1864	1 year.	Mustered out June 10, 1865, at David's Island, New York Harbor, by order of War Department.
Shultz, Isaac	...do...	34	Aug. 23, 1864	1 year.	
Slough, Peter	...do...	18	Aug. 17, 1864	1 year.	Mustered out with company July 12, 1865.
Smith, Jacob L.	...do...	39	Sept. 21, 1864	1 year	Mustered out with company July 12, 1865.
Smith, James F.	...do...	40	Aug. 17, 1864	1 year.	Mustered out with company July 12, 1865.
Snider, Henry	...do...	18	Sept. 13, 1864	1 year.	Mustered out with company July 12, 1865.
Staley, Reuben	...do...	29	Aug. 26, 1864	1 year.	Mustered out to date Jan. 25, 1865, by order of War Department.
Standiford, Elijah H.	...do...	25	Aug. 26, 1864	1 year.	Mustered out with company July 12, 1865.
Stapleton, Anthony J.	...do...	18	Aug. 26, 1864	1 year.	Mustered out with company July 12, 1866.
Sutton, Isaiah	...do...	41	Sept. 21, 1864	1 year.	Mustered out with company July 12, 1865.
Syfert, Henry O.	...do...	35	Sept. 20, 1864	1 year.	Mustered out with company July 12, 1865.
Tipple, Moses B.	...do...	34	Sept. 12, 1864	1 year.	Mustered out May 25, 1865, at Louisville, Ky., by order of War Department.
Walters, Robert	...do...	26	Sept. 20, 1864	1 year.	Killed March 8, 1865, in battle of Wise's Fork, North Carolina.
Wetherill, William F.	...do...	26	Aug. 23, 1864	1 year.	Mustered out with company July 12, 1865.
Williams, Benjamin	...do...	25	Sept. 5, 1864	1 year.	Mustered out with company July 12, 1865.
Williams, Michael	...do...	28	Sept. 5, 1864	1 year.	Died Feb. 26, 1865, at Washington, D. C.
Wilson, William R.	...do...	27	Aug. 27, 1864	1 year.	Returned to duty from Carver Hospital, Washington, D. C., April 22, 1865. No further record found.
Wolley, James	...do...	28	Sept. 3, 1864	1 year.	Died Feb. 26, 1865, at Washington, D. C.
Wolley, Stephen	...do...	22	Sept. 3, 1864	1 year.	Mustered out with company July 12, 1865.
Yant, Abraham	...do...	28	Sept. 21, 1864	1 year.	Mustered out with company July 12, 1865.
Yant, William	...do...	30	Sept. 21, 1864	1 year.	Died March 11, 1865, at Newbern, N. C.

COMPANY B.

Mustered in September 29, 1864, at Camp Chase, O., by W. P. Richardson, Colonel 25th O. V. I. Mustered out July 12, 1865, at Charlotte, N. C., by T. M. Ward, 1st Lieutenant 25th M. V. I. and A. C. M., 1st Division, 23d Army Corps.

Names.	Rank.	Age.	Date of Entering the Service.	Period of Service.	Remarks.
Eli B. Anderson	Captain.	21	Sept. 29, 1864	1 year.	Mustered out with company July 12, 1865.
Andrew Smith	1st Lieut.	24	Sept. 29, 1864	1 year.	Promoted to Captain Co. G May 28, 1865.
John Chapman	2d Lieut.	20	Sept. 29, 1864	1 year.	Promoted to 1st Lieutenant Co. A Feb. 18, 1865.
William H. Nichols	...do...	23	Sept. 17, 1864	1 year.	Promoted from 1st Sergeant Co. C Feb. 18, 1865; mustered out with company July 12, 1865.
Harrison Frizzell	1st Sergt.	25	Sept. 21, 1864	1 year.	Promoted to 2d Lieutenant Co. F to date Feb. 10, 1865.
Reuben Kelley	...do...	19	Sept. 12, 1864	1 year.	Appointed Sergeant Sept. 30, 1864; 1st Sergeant April 29, 1865; mustered out with company July 12, 1865.
Aquilla C. McComas	Sergeant.	24	Sept. 5, 1864	1 year.	Appointed Sept. 30, 1864; mustered out with company July 12, 1865.
Arthur B. White	...do...	21	Aug. 31, 1864	1 year.	Appointed from private Nov. 12, 1864; mustered out with company July 12, 1865.
Joseph J. Brown	...do...	18	Sept. 2, 1864	1 year.	Appointed Corporal Sept. 30, 1864; Sergeant Feb. 1, 1865; mustered out June 10, 1865, at Newbern, N. C., by order of War Department.
Benjamin F. Jones	...do...	18	Sept. 2, 1864	1 year.	Appointed Corporal Sept. 30, 1864; Sergeant April 29, 1865; mustered out with company July 12, 1865.
James W. McCoy	...do...	23	Aug. 13, 1864	1 year.	Appointed Corporal Sept. 30, 1864; Sergeant June 10, 1865; mustered out with company July 12, 1865.
Albert S. [illegible]	Corporal.	18	Aug. 29, 1864	1 year.	Appointed Sept. 30, 1864; mustered out with company July 12, 1865.
Jackson Cooper	...do...	26	Sept. 5, 1864	1 year.	Appointed Sept. 30, 1864; mustered out with company July 12, 1865.
Luther F. Conrad	...do...	[illegible]	Aug. 31, 1864	1 year.	Appointed Nov. 27, 1864; mustered out with company July 12, 1865.

Names.	Rank.	Age.	Date of Entering the Service.	Period of Service.	Remarks.
George Slocum	Corporal.	25	Aug. 15, 1864	1 year.	Mustered out with company July 12, 1865.
Thomas P. Johnson	...do....	23	Sept. 8, 1864	1 year.	Mustered out with company July 12, 1865.
Levi McMillen	...do....	24	Sept. 22, 1864	1 year.	Mustered out with company July 12, 1865.
James W. Clark	...do....	20	Sept. 23, 1864	1 year.	Mustered out May 29, 1865, at Camp Dennison, O., by order of Wa Department.
Wesley L. Ramsdell	...do....	25	Sept. 21, 1864	1 year.	Appointed [illegible] 1865; mustered out with company [illegible]
Samuel Beemer	...do....	33	Sept. 21, 1864	1 year.	Appointed May 8, 1865; mustered out with company July 12, 1865.
Nathaniel McClure	...do....	18	Aug. 6, 1864	1 year.	Appointed May 18, 1865; mustered out with company July 12, 1865.
John R. Bennett	...do....	19	Aug. 19, 1864	1 year.	Appointed June 28, 1865; mustered out with company July 12, 1865.
George Carey	...do....	20	Sept. 13, 1864	1 year.	Appointed June 28, 1864; mustered out with company July 12, 1865.
Baker, David M. D	Private..	20	Sept. 24, 1864	1 year.	Mustered out June 14, 1865, at Washington, D. C., by order of War Department.
Beatty, Wilson S	...do....	22	Sept. 23, 1864	1 year.	Mustered out with company July 12, 1865.
Bennett, Hiram S	...do....	25	Aug. 11, 1864	1 year.	Mustered out June 30, 1865, at Washington, D. C., by order of War Department.
Bishop, John	...do....	18	Aug. 17, 1864	1 year.	Mustered out May 31, 1865, at David's Island, New York Harbor, by order of War Department.
Bolen, James	...do....	37	Sept. 20, 1864	1 year.	Mustered out with company July 12, 1865.
Bougher, Daniel	...do....	26	Sept. 21, 1864	1 year.	Died Oct. 2, 1864, at ——.
Clark, Lloyd H	...do....	19	Aug. 21, 1864	1 year.	Mustered out with company July 12, 1865.
Clark, Oliver	...do....	18	Aug. 21, 1864	1 year.	Mustered out May 29, 1865, at David's Island, New York Harbor, by order of War Department.
Close, Thomas	...do....	38	Sept. 21, 1864	1 year.	Mustered out with company July 12, 1865.
Conner, Elijah J	...do....	38	Sept. 21, 1864	1 year.	Mustered out with company July 12, 1865.
Conner, Josiah	...do....	43	Sept. 7, 1864	1 year.	Mustered out with company July 12, 1865.
Counsellor, Levi J	...do....	18	Aug. 17, 1864	1 year.	Mustered out with company July 12, 1865.
Crawford, Charles C	...do....	29	Aug. 26, 1864	1 year.	Mustered out with company July 12, 1865.
Cremean, Daniel	...do....	18	Aug. 19, 1864	1 year.	Mustered out with company July 12, 1865.
Crosley, Runnels W	...do....	17	Sept. 5, 1864	1 year.	Mustered out July 5, 1865, at Philadelphia, Pa., by order of War Department.
Deborous, William H	...do....	22	Aug. 17, 1864	1 year.	Mustered out with company July 12, 1865.
Evans, Thomas J	...do....	19	Sept. 13, 1864	1 year.	Mustered out with company July 12, 1865.
Fleming, Alexander	...do....	18	Aug. 27, 1864	1 year.	Mustered out with company July 12, 1865.
Fleming, John W	...do....	19	Sept. 19, 1864	1 year.	Mustered out June 13, 1865, at Philadelphia, Pa., by order of War Department.
Ford, Levi R	...do....	18	Aug. 17, 1864	1 year.	Mustered out with company July 12, 1865.
Freeman, Joseph G	...do....	28	Sept. 21, 1864	1 year.	Mustered out with company July 12, 1865.
Garwood, Jehu	...do....	23	Sept. 26, 1864	1 year.	Mustered out with company July 12, 1865.
Gephart, John	...do....	23	Sept. 19, 1864	1 year.	Mustered out with company July 12, 1865.
Giberson, Christopher	...do....	18	Sept. 15, 1864	1 year.	Mustered out with company July 12, 1865.
Gier, Theodore	...do....	18	Aug. 11, 1864	1 year.	Mustered as Musician; wounded March [illegible] 1865, in battle of Wise's Fork, N. C.; discharged June 16, 1865, at Ward [illegible], Newark, N. J., on Surgeon's certificate of disability.
Gill, Thomas H	...do....	23	Sept. 19, 1864	1 year.	Mustered out with company July 12, 1865.
Gould, Kinsey	...do....	23	Aug. 11, 1864	1 year.	Reduced from Sergeant May 8, 1865; mustered out July 10, 1865, at Washington, [illegible] order of War Department.
Gould, Thomas	...do....	18	Aug. 11, 1864	1 year.	Mustered as Musician; mustered out [illegible] 10, 1865, at Washington, D. C., by order of War Department.
Griffith, Isaac M	...do....	29	Aug. 21, 1864	1 year.	Died April 21, 1865, at Raleigh, N. C.
Hawkey, Charles W	...do....	22	Aug. 19, 1864	1 year.	Mustered out with company July 12, 1865.
Howard, William F	...do....	22	Aug. 17, 1864	1 year.	Mustered out with company July 12, 1865.
Howell, Henry	...do....	18	Sept. 13, 1864	1 year.	Mustered out with company July 12, 1865.
Hunt, William W	...do....	23	Oct. 11, 1864	1 year.	Promoted to Q. M. Sergeant [illegible]
Isham, Martin	...do....	27	Sept. 3, 1864	1 year.	Wounded March 8, 1865, in battle of Wise's Fork, N. C.; mustered out July [illegible], at Portsmouth Grove, R. I., by order of War Department.
Johnson, William	...do....	31	Sept. 21, 1864	1 year.	Mustered out with company July 12, 1865.
Keeler, Amos R	...do....	41	Aug. 15, 1864	1 year.	Mustered out with company July 12, 1865.
King, Marinus	...do....	18	Sept. 17, 1864	1 year.	Mustered out with company July 12, 1865.
Kingsbury, William J	...do....	23	Aug. 23, 1864	1 year.	Reduced from Corporal May 18, 1865; mustered out with company July 12, 1865.
Lhamon, Michael	...do....	27	Aug. 19, 1864	1 year.	Mustered out with company July 12, 1865.
Lhamon, John	...do....	21	Aug. 17, 1864	1 year.	Mustered out with company July 12, 1865.
Lowery, James M	...do....	20	Sept. 5, 1864	1 year.	Mustered out July 14, 1865, at [illegible], by order of War Department.
Lyon, Arigon	...do....	18	Aug. 26, 1864	1 year.	Mustered out with company July 12, 1865.
McElhany, John	...do....	20	Aug. 26, 1864	1 year.	Mustered out with company July 12, 1865.
McGinnis, Moses	...do....	36	Sept. 21, 1864	1 year.	Mustered out May 27, 1865, at New York City, N.Y., by order of War Department.
McGinnis, William	...do....	27	Sept. 21, 1864	1 year.	Mustered out with company July 12, 1865.
Marshall, Joseph R	...do....	24	Sept. 23, 1864	1 year.	Reduced from Corporal Feb. 4, 1865; mustered out to date July 12, 1865, by order of War Department.

Names.	Rank.	Age.	Date of Entering the Service.	Period of Service.	Remarks.
Prater, Job S	Private	21	Aug. 20, 1864	1 year.	Mustered out with company July 12, 1865.
Randall, Charles T	...do...	29	Aug. 16, 1864	1 year.	Mustered out with company July 12, 1865.
Retallick, William J	...do...	18	Aug. 16, 1864	1 year.	Mustered out with company July 12, 1865.
Richards, Daniel A	...do...	18	Aug. 25, 1864	1 year.	Died Feb. 9, 1865, at Washington, D. C.
Rittenhouse, Albert P	...do...	20	Sept. 13, 1864	1 year.	Mustered out with company July 12, 1865.
Ross, George W	...do...	18	Feb. 14, 1865	1 year.	Died June 8, 1865, at Charlotte, N. C.
Schlabach, Benjamin F	...do...	20	Aug. 16, 1864	1 year.	Mustered out with company July 12, 1865.
Seigfreid, Henry	...do...	26	Sept. 8, 1864	1 year.	Mustered out with company July 12, 1865.
Slade, Joshua W	...do...	18	Aug. 22, 1864	1 year.	Mustered out with company July 12, 1865.
Smith, Harvey M	...do...	18	Sept. 9, 1864	1 year.	Appointed Corporal Sept. 30, 1864; reduced Feb. 1, 1865; mustered out with company July 12, 1865.
Smith, Joel E	...do...	37	Aug. 16, 1864	1 year.	Mustered out with company July 12, 1865.
Stansbury, John	...do...	33	Sept. 5, 1864	1 year.	Mustered out with company July 12, 1865.
Thompson, John M	...do...	44	Aug. 22, 1864	1 year.	Mustered out June 2, 1865, at Cumberland, Md., by order of War Department.
Waffle, Clinton D	...do...	19	Sept. 1, 1864	1 year.	Mustered out with company July 12, 1865.
Waffle, John	...do...	41	Sept. 1, 1864	1 year.	Mustered out with company July 12, 1865.
Williams, Henry B	...do...	24	Aug. 27, 1864	1 year.	Wounded March 8, 1865, in battle of Wise's Fork, N. C.; discharged Jun. 6, 1865, at Newark, N. J., on Surgeon's certificate of disability.
Williamson, Richard	...do...	18	Aug. 20, 1864	1 year.	Mustered out with company July 12, 1865.
Wollard, Aaron	...do...	19	Sept. 7, 1864	1 year.	Mustered out with company July 12, 1865.

COMPANY C.

Mustered in September 28, 1864, at Camp Chase, O., by W. P. Richardson, Colonel 25th O. V. I. Mustered out July 12, 1865, at Charlotte, N. C., by T. M. Ward, 1st Lieutenant 25th M. V. I. and A. C. M., 1st Division, 23d Army Corps.

Names.	Rank.	Age.	Date of Entering the Service.	Period of Service.	Remarks.
Moses Abbott	Captain.	27	Sept. 28, 1864	1 year.	Mustered out with company July 12, 1865.
Joshua Lemert	1st Lieut.	35	Sept. 28, 1864	1 year.	Promoted to Captain July 4, 1865, but not mustered; mustered out with company July 12, 1865
Oscar L. R. French	2d Lieut.	..	Sept. 29, 1864	1 year.	Promoted to 1st Lieutenant March 29, 1865, but not mustered; mustered out with company July 12, 1865
William H. Nichols	1st Sergt.	28	Sept. 17, 1864	1 year.	Appointed Sept. 28, 1864; promoted to 2d Lieutenant Co. B Feb. 18, 1865.
David H. Hamlin	...do...	21	Sept. 22, 1864	1 year.	Appointed Corporal Sept. 28, 1864; Sergeant April 3, 1865; 1st Sergeant April 8, 1865; mustered out with company July 12, 1865.
Alva French	Sergeant.	25	Sept. 16, 1864	1 year.	Appointed Sept. 28, 1864; mustered out June 7, 1865, at Newbern, N. C., by order of War Department.
Charles W. Brooks	...do...	19	Sept. 6, 1864	1 year.	Appointed Sept. 28, 1864.
John McConnell	...do...	25	Sept. 24, 1864	1 year.	Appointed Sept. 28, 1864; mustered out May 31, 1865, at David's Island, New York Harbor, by order of War Department.
William J. Kuder	...do...	25	Sept. 5, 1864	1 year.	Appointed Sept. 28, 1864; mustered out with company July 12, 1865.
Franklin Rhinehart	...do...	23	Sept. 16, 1864	1 year.	Appointed Corporal Sept. 28, 1864; Sergeant April 8, 1865; mustered out with company July 12, 1865.
Henry M. Ludwig	...do...	18	Sept. 14, 1864	1 year.	Appointed Corporal Sept. 28, 1864; Sergeant June 18, 1865; mustered out with company July 12, 1865.
Joseph B. Moore	...do...	23	Sept. 6, 1864	1 year.	Appointed Corporal Sept. 28, 1864; Sergeant July 5, 1865; mustered out with company July 12, 1865.
David Sherman	Corporal.	21	Sept. 17, 1861	1 year.	Appointed Sept. 28, 1864; mustered out with company July 12, 1865.
Alfred Stephens	...do...	21	Sept. 16, 1864	1 year.	Appointed April 3, 1865; mustered out with company July 12, 1865.
Michael Scammel	...do...	18	Sept. 12, 1864	1 year.	Appointed April 3, 1865; mustered out with company July 12, 1865.
Jacob Nighswander	...do...	20	Sept. 16, 1864	1 year.	Appointed April 3, 1865; mustered out with company July 12, 1865.
Joseph Jordan	...do...	36	Sept. 16, 1864	1 year.	Appointed April 3, 1865; mustered out with company July 12, 1865.
William Gibson	...do...	21	Sept. 23, 1864	1 year.	Appointed April 8, 1865; mustered out with company July 12, 1865.
Isaac H. Green	...do...	18	Sept. 17, 1864	1 year.	Appointed June 18, 1865; mustered out with company July 12, 1865.
Elias M. Wyant	...do...	30	Sept. 15, 1864	1 year.	Appointed July 5, 1865; mustered out with company July 12, 1865.
Orson McIntire	Musician	24	Sept. 17, 1864	1 year.	Mustered out with company July 12, 1865.
Theodore Machold	...do...	18	Sept. 28, 1864	1 year.	Mustered out with company July 12, 1865.

Names.	Rank.	Age.	Date of Entering the Service.		
Aldrich, Thomas	Private	36	Sept. 28, 1864	1 year.	
Baechner, John	....do....	25	Sept. 15, 1864	1	
Baker, Jacob F	....do....	30	Sept. 16, 1864	1 year.	
Bastian, Hiram	....do....	19	Sept. 17, 1864	1	
Bealer, George	....do....	21	Sept. 5, 1864	1	Muste
Beck, Philip	....do....	23	Sept. 16, 1864	1	Muste
Bell, Samuel	....do....	32	Sept. 28, 1864	1	Muste
Brewer, Daniel	....do....	34	Sept. 16, 1864	1	Died [illegible] ston
Brown, William H	....do....	39	Sept. 17, 1864		Promc
Candler, John	....do....	29	Sept. 23, 1864		Muste
Chambers, John A	....do....	19	Sept. 19, 1864		
Clark, Henry	....do....	34	Sept. 2, 1864	1	
Cole, Thomas J	....do....	18	Sept. 7, 1864	1 year.	
Doran, James	....do....	19	Sept. 16, 1864	1 year.	
Doran, John V	....do....	37	Aug. 29, 1864	1 year.	
Dunlap, James	....do....	31	Sept. 19, 1864	1 year.	
Dunn, Michael	....do....	40	Sept. 23, 1864	1 year.	
Edwards, Montgomery	....do....	20	Sept. 23, 1864	1 year.	
Epler, John W	....do....	37	Aug. 30, 1864	1 year.	
Fitzmorris, Thomas J	....do....	18	Sept. 16, 1864	1 year.	
Foglesong, Myron	....do....	17	Mch. 2, 1864	1 year.	
Foglesong, Simon	....do....	26	Sept. 2, 1864	1 year.	
Frick, Jeremiah	....do....	18	Sept. 1, 1864	1 year.	
Green, William R.	....do....	27	Sept. 27, 1864	1 year.	
Hammond, David M	....do....	29	Sept. 16, 1864	1 year.	
Harshburger, Elias F. D.	....do....	18	Sept. 16, 1864	1 year.	
Hathaway, Joseph	....do....	28	Sept. 16, 1864	1 year.	
Hatten, David	....do....	18	Sept. 24, 1864	1 year.	
Healy, John	....do....	34	Sept. 26, 1864	1 year.	
Heilman, John	....do....	22	Sept. 12, 1864	1 year.	
Heimerich, John	....do....	18	Sept. 12, 1864	1 year.	
Henry, Lawrence	....do....	18	Sept. 5, 1864	1 year.	
Hershey, Tobias M	....do....	23	Sept. 11, 1864	1 year.	
Holtz, John J	....do....	18	Sept. 16, 1864	1 year.	
Hoppel, John	....do....	31	Sept. 10, 1864	1 year.	
Inman, Martin	....do....	21	Sept. 15, 1864	1 year.	
Inman, Reuben	....do....	24	Sept. 15, 1864	1 year.	
Kuder, James S	....do....	24	Sept. 5, 1864	1 year.	
Los, Asa B	....do....	33	Sept. 27, 1864	1 year.	
Leffler, Jacob E	....do....	21	Jan. 30, 1865	1 year.	
Luman, Auson	....do....	18	Aug. 3, 1864	1 year.	
McManigal, Thomas R	....do....	18	Sept. 12, 1864	1 year.	
Mandeville, Truman H.	....do....	19	Sept. 16, 1864	1 year.	
Marks, Nicholas	....do....	18	Sept. 5, 1864	1 year.	
Myers, Lambert	....do....	28	Sept. 22, 1864	1 year.	
Needham, Azariah	....do....	36	Sept. 17, 1864	1 year.	
Newbert, Robert	....do....	38	Sept. 23, 1864	1 year.	
Noel, David H	....do....	22	Sept. 17, 1864	1 year.	orde
Pockmire, John W	....do....	23	Sept. 17, 1864	1 year.	Muste
Price, Jonathan	....do....	23	Sept. 6, 1864	1 year.	Muste O., t
Reed, George E	....do....	18	Sept. 24, 1864	1 year.	Muste
Reynolds, Erastus	....do....	44	Sept. 19, 1864	1 year.	Muste by o
Rickert, Benjamin	....do....	40	Sept. 5, 1864	1 year.	Muste
Ringle, John	....do....	19	Sept. 17, 1864	1 year.	Muste
Robertson, John H	....do....	21	Sept. 3, 1864	1 year.	
Robison, Hunter	....do....	24	Sept. 27, 1864	1 year.	
Robison, John	....do....	18	Sept. 23, 1864	1 year.	
Romig, John H	....do....	42	Sept. 12, 1864	1 year.	
Schonebart, Benjamin	....do....	18	Sept. 12, 1864	1 year.	
Seiner, Peter	....do....	37	Sept. 6, 1864	1 year.	
Shuman, Eli	....do....	19	Sept. 17, 1864	1 year.	
Simonis, Michael	....do....	18	Sept. 5, 1864	1 year.	
Slough, Daniel	....do....	21	Jan. 30, 1865	1 year.	Muste N. Y
Sower, William	....do....	35	Sept. 16, 1864	1 year.	Muste
Stockman, Emery	....do....	29	Sept. 8, 1864	1 year.	Dischi by o
Steiner, Samuel D	....do....	27	Sept. 17, 1864	1 year.	Muste
Stoner, Jacob	....do....	18	Sept. 12, 1864	1 year.	Muste
Strouse, Henry	....do....	36	Sept. 12, 1864	1 year.	Muste

Names.	Rank.	Age.	Date of Entering the Service.	Period of Service.	Remarks.
Stoll, Solomon R.	Private.	31	Sept. 17, 1864	1 year.	Mustered out May 29, 1865, at Camp Dennison, O., by order of War Department.
Thompson, John L.	...do...	18	Sept. 28, 1864	1 year.	Mustered out with company July 12, 1865.
Tressel, Christian	...do...	28	Sept. 13, 1864	1 year.	Mustered out with company July 12, 1865.
Van Buskirk, Solon	...do...	24	Sept. 16, 1864	1 year.	Appointed Corporal Sept. 28, 1864; reduced April 8, 1864; mustered out with company July 12, 1865.
Walker, Joseph G.	...do...	28	Sept. 17, 1864	1 year.	Mustered out with company July 12, 1865.
Warner, Samuel	...do...	19	Sept. 16, 1864	1 year.	Mustered out with company July 12, 1865.
Widener, James R.	...do...	18	Sept. 24, 1864	1 year.	Mustered out with company July 12, 1865.
Wise, Jacob F.	...do...	19	Sept. 15, 1864	1 year.	Mustered out with company July 12, 1865.
Wolf, Daniel W.	...do...	27	Sept. 16, 1864	1 year.	Mustered out June 8, 1865, at Camp Dennison, O., by order of War Department.
Yager, Hiram W.	...do...	18	Sept. 17, 1864	1 year.	Mustered out with company July 12, 1865.
Yates, Thomas E.	...do...	28	Sept. 17, 1864	1 year.	Mustered out with company July 12, 1865.
Zerby, David	...do...	44	Sept. 17, 1864	1 year.	Mustered out with company July 12, 1865.

COMPANY D.

Mustered in September 30, 1864, at Camp Chase, O., by W. P. Richardson, Colonel 25th O. V. I. Mustered out July 12, 1865, at Charlotte, N. C., by T. M. Ward, 1st Lieutenant 25th M. V. I. and A. C. M., 1st Division, 23d Army Corps.

Names.	Rank.	Age.	Date of Entering the Service.	Period of Service.	Remarks.
Daniel W. Mills	Captain.	27	Sept. 30, 1864	1 year.	Mustered out with company July 12, 1865.
Thomas C. Hirst	1st Lieut.	24	Dec. 26, 1863	3 yrs.	Promoted from Sergeant Co. I, 128th Regiment, Sept. 30, 1864; discharged May 16, 1865, for wounds received March 8, 1865, in battle of Wise's Fork, N. C.
William H. Blakeley	2d Lieut.	29	Sept. 30, 1864	1 year.	Promoted to 1st Lieutenant July 4, 1865, but not mustered; mustered out with company July 12, 1865.
Joseph W. Stout	1st Sergt.	31	Sept. 22, 1864	1 year.	Appointed Sergeant Oct. 1, 1864; 1st Sergeant Dec. 2, 1864; mustered out May 26, 1865, at Washington, D. C., by order of War Department.
James F. Siebert	...do...	30	Sept. 10, 1864	1 year.	Appointed Sergeant Oct. 1, 1864; 1st Sergeant June 1, 1865; mustered out with company July 12, 1865.
Benjamin F. Denniston	Sergeant.	35	Sept. 20, 1864	1 year.	Promoted to Com. Sergeant Oct. 20, 1864.
William R. Daugherty	...do...	37	Sept. 22, 1864	1 year.	Appointed Oct. 1, 1864; mustered out with company July 12, 1865.
John W. Kemp	...do...	36	Sept. 22, 1864	1 year.	Appointed Corporal Oct. 1, 1864; Sergeant Dec. 2, 1864; mustered out with company July 12, 1865.
George W. Nicholson	...do...	26	Aug. 27, 1864	1 year.	Appointed Corporal Oct. 1, 1864; Sergeant Dec. 2, 1864; mustered out with company July 12, 1865.
David Bigelow	...do...	27	Sept. 22, 1864	1 year.	Appointed Corporal Oct. 1, 1864; Sergeant June 1, 1865; mustered out with company July 12, 1865.
William Winters	Corporal.	23	Sept. 22, 1864	1 year.	Appointed Oct. 1, 1864; mustered out with company July 12, 1865.
Jesse Day	...do...	34	Sept. 20, 1864	1 year.	Appointed Oct. 1, 1864; mustered out with company July 12, 1865.
Francis J. McFarland	...do...	21	Sept. 13, 1864	1 year.	Appointed Oct. 1, 1864; mustered out with company July 12, 1865.
James H. McCoy	...do...	28	Sept. 26, 1864	1 year.	Appointed Oct. 1, 1864; died May 24, 1865, in McDougall Hospital, New York Harbor, of wounds received March 8, 1865, in battle of Wise's Fork, N. C.
Lorenzo D. Elliott	...do...	25	Sept. 24, 1864	1 year.	Appointed Oct. 1, 1864; mustered out May 12, 1865, at Columbus, O., by order of War Department.
Henry C. Kutz	...do...	22	Sept. 29, 1864	1 year.	Appointed Dec. 2, 1864; mustered out with company July 12, 1865.
David R. Maple	...do...	27	Sept. 23, 1864	1 year.	Appointed April 8, 1865; mustered out with company July 12, 1865.
William M. Coil	...do...	26	Sept. 17, 1864	1 year.	Appointed June 1, 1865; mustered out with company July 12, 1865.
Benjamin F. Morris	...do...	28	Sept. 6, 1864	1 year.	Appointed June 1, 1865; mustered out with company July 12, 1865.
Babcock, Lyman	Private.	35	Sept. 22, 1864	1 year.	Mustered out with company July 12, 1865.
Baughman, Henry B.	...do...	19	Sept. 21, 1864	1 year.	Mustered out with company July 12, 1865.
Bier, Jacob	...do...	21	Aug. 27, 1864	1 year.	Mustered out with company July 12, 1865.
Bigelow, Martin	...do...	20	Sept. 22, 1864	1 year.	Mustered out with company July 12, 1865.
Blake, Francis S.	...do...	27	Sept. [illegible], 1864	1 year.	Mustered out with company July 12, 1865.
Bodkin, James	...do...	37	Sept. [illegible], 1864	1 year.	Mustered out with company July 12, 1865.
Bryan, Lorenzo D.	...do...	18	Sept. [illegible], 1864	1 year.	Mustered out with company July 12, 1865.
Bryan, William O.	...do...	24	Aug. [illegible], 1864	1 year.	
Burden, Eli	...do...	33	Sept. [illegible], 1864	1 year.	Died May 12, 1865, at Raleigh, N. C.

Names.	Rank.	Age.	Date of Entering the Service.	Period of Service.	Remarks.
Aldrich, Thomas	Private	36	Sept. 23, 1864	1 year.	Mustered out with company July 12
Baechner, John	do	26	Sept. 15, 1864	1 year.	Mustered out June 9, 1865, at Tren... by order of War Department.
Baker, Jacob F	do	30	Sept. 16, 1864	1 year.	Mustered out with company July 12
Bastian, Hiram	do	19	Sept. 17, 1864	1 year.	Mustered out with company July 12
Bealer, George	do	31	Sept. 5, 1864	1 year.	Mustered out with company July 12
Beck, Philip	do	23	Sept. 16, 1864	1 year.	Mustered out with company July 12
Bell, Samuel	do	32	Sept. 23, 1864	1 year.	Mustered out with company July 12
Brewer, Daniel	do	34	Sept. 16, 1864	1 year.	Died March 26, 1865, at Lewis Hosp... ston, N. C.
Brown, William H	do	39	Sept. 17, 1864	1 year.	Promoted to Hospital Steward Oct. 2
Candler, John	do	29	Sept. 23, 1864	1 year.	Mustered out June 6, 1865, at Beauf... by order of War Department.
Chambers, John A	do	19	Sept. 19, 1864	1 year.	Mustered out July 18, 1865, at Camp ... O., by order of War Department.
Clark, Henry	do	34	Sept. 2, 1864	1 year.	Mustered out with company July 12
Cole, Thomas J	do	18	Sept. 7, 1864	1 year.	Mustered out with company July 12
Doran, James	do	19	Sept. 16, 1864	1 year.	Mustered out with company July 12
Doran, John V	do	37	Aug. 29, 1864	1 year.	Appointed Corporal Sept. 28, 186...; April 3, 1865; mustered out May ..., Newbern, N. C., by order of War ... ment.
Dunlap, James	do	33	Sept. 19, 1864	1 year.	Mustered out with company July 12
Dunn, Michael	do	40	Sept. 23, 1864	1 year.	
Edwards, Montgomery	do	20	Sept. 23, 1864	1 year.	Mustered out with company July 12
Epler, John W	do	37	Aug. 30, 1864	1 year.	Mustered out with company July 12
Fitzmorris, Thomas J	do	18	Sept. 16, 1864	1 year.	Mustered out with company July 12
Foglesong, Myron	do	17	Mch. 2, 1864	1 year.	Mustered out with company July 12
Foglesong, Simon	do	26	Sept. 2, 1864	1 year.	Died March 28, 1865, at —.
Frick, Jeremiah	do	18	Sept. 1, 1864	1 year.	Mustered out with company July 12
Green, William R	do	27	Sept. 27, 1864	1 year.	Died Feb. 10, 1865, at Camp Stoneman, Washington, D. C.
Hammond, David M	do	29	Sept. 16, 1864	1 year.	
Harshburger, Elias F. D.	do	18	Sept. 16, 1864	1 year.	
Hathaway, Joseph	do	28	Sept. 16, 1864	1 year.	Mustered out with company July 12
Hatten, David	do	18	Sept. 24, 1864	1 year.	Mustered out with company July 12
Healy, John	do	34	Sept. 26, 1864	1 year.	Mustered out with company July 12
Hellman, John	do	22	Sept. 12, 1864	1 year.	Mustered out with company July 12
Heimerich, John	do	18	Sept. 12, 1864	1 year.	Mustered out with company July 12
Henry, Lawrence	do	18	Sept. 5, 1864	1 year.	Mustered out with company July 12
Hershey, Tobias M	do	25	Sept. 11, 1864	1 year.	Died March 9, 1865, of wounds received ... 8, 1865, in battle of Wise's Fork, N. C.
Holtz, John J	do	18	Sept. 16, 1864	1 year.	Mustered out with company July 12
Hoppel, John	do	31	Sept. 10, 1864	1 year.	Mustered out with company July 12
Inman, Martin	do	21	Sept. 15, 1864	1 year.	Mustered out with company July 12
Inman, Reuben	do	24	Sept. 15, 1864	1 year.	Died Feb. 9, 1865, at Louisville, Ky.
Kuder, James S	do	21	Sept. 5, 1864	1 year.	Mustered out with company July 12
Lee, Asa B	do	33	Sept. 27, 1864	1 year.	Mustered out Aug. 1, 1865, at Philadelphia ... by order of War Department.
Leffler, Jacob E	do	21	Jan. 30, 1865	1 year.	Mustered out with company July 12
Lutman, Anson	do	18	Aug. 3, 1864	1 year.	Mustered out with company July 12
McManigal, Thomas R	do	18	Sept. 12, 1864	1 year.	Mustered out with company July 12
Mandeville, Truman H	do	19	Sept. 16, 1864	1 year.	Mustered out with company July 12
Marks, Nicholas	do	18	Sept. 5, 1864	1 year.	Discharged Nov. 3, 1864 at Camp ... by order of War Department.
Myers, Lambert	do	28	Sept. 22, 1864	1 year.	Mustered out with company July 12
Needham, Azariah	do	36	Sept. 17, 1864	1 year.	Mustered out with company July 12
Newbert, Robert	do	38	Sept. 23, 1864	1 year.	Mustered out with company July 12
Noel, David H	do	22	Sept. 17, 1864	1 year.	Mustered out May 30, 1865, at ... order of War Department.
Pockmire, John W	do	23	Sept. 17, 1864	1 year.	Mustered out with company July 12
Price, Jonathan	do	23	Sept. 6, 1864	1 year.	Mustered ou une 1865, at Camp ... O., by orde of War Department.
Reed, George E	do	18	Sept. 21, 1864	1 year.	Mustered o t with c mpany July 12
Reynolds, Erastus	do	44	Sept. 10, 1864	1 year.	Mustered ou une 27, 1865, at Columbus ... by order of War Department.
Rickert, Benjamin	do	40	Sept. 5, 1864	1 year.	Mustered out with company July 12
Ringle, John	do	19	Sept. 17, 1864	1 year.	Mustered out with company July 12
Robertson, John H	do	21	Sept. 3, 1864	1 year.	
Robison, Hunter	do	24	Sept. 27, 1864	1 year.	Mustered out with company July 12
Robison, John	do	18	Sept. 23, 1864	1 year.	Mustered out with company July 12
Romig, John H	do	42	Sept. 12, 1864	1 year.	Appointed Corporal Sept. 28, 1864; ... April 3, 1865; mustered out June ... by order of War Department.
Schonehart, Benjamin	do	18	Sept. 12, 1864	1 year.	Mustered out with company July 12
Selner, Peter	do	37	Sept. 6, 1864	1 year.	Mustered out with company July 12
Shuman, Eli	do	19	Sept. 17, 1864	1 year.	Mustered out with company July 12
Simonis, Michael	do	18	Sept. 5, 1864	1 year.	
Slough, Daniel	do	21	Jan. 30, 1865	1 year.	Mustered out Aug. 9, 1865, at New York, N. Y., by order of War Department.
Sower, William	do	35	Sept. 16, 1864	1 year.	Mustered out with company July 12
Stockman, Emery	do	29	Sept. 8, 1864	1 year.	Discharged March 14, 1865, at ... by order of War Department.
Steiner, Samuel D	do	27	Sept. 17, 1864	1 year.	Mustered out with company July 12
Stoner, Jacob	do	18	Sept. 12, 1864	1 year.	Mustered out with company July 12
Strouse, Henry	do	36	Sept. 12, 1864	1 year.	Mustered out with company July 12

Names.	Rank.	Age.	Date of Entering the Service.	Period of Service.	Remarks.
Reese, Frederick	Private	44	Sept. 23, 1864	1 year.	Mustered out with company July 12, 1865.
Rexstrew, Elwood	....do....	24	Sept. 24, 1864	1 year.	Mustered out June 10, 1865, at Newbern, N. C., by order of War Department.
Rexstrew, Job B	....do....	18	Aug. 26, 1864	1 year.	Mustered out with company July 12, 1865.
Rush, Harrison	....do....	18	Aug. 24, 1864	1 year.	Mustered out to date July 12, 1865, by order of War Department.
Schlictig, John	....do....	25	Sept. 5, 1864	1 year.	Mustered out with company July 12, 1865.
Shanks, Michael L	....do....	36	Sept. 20, 1864	1 year.	Mustered out June 13, 1865, at Philadelphia, Pennsylvania.
Sommers, George	....do....	34	Sept. 5, 1864	1 year.	Mustered out with company July 12, 1865.
Tutors, James	....do....	39	Aug. 22, 1864	1 year.	Mustered out with company July 12, 1865.
Walck, Andrew R	....do....	27	Sept. 9, 1864	1 year.	Mustered out May 17, 1865, at Washington, D. C., by order of War Department.
Westbey, Matthias	....do....	44	Sept. 20, 1864	1 year.	Mustered out with company July 12, 1865.
West, Perry	....do....	19	Sept. 10, 1864	1 year.	Mustered out with company July 12, 1865.
Webenmeyer, George	....do....	34	Sept. 22, 1864	1 year.	Mustered out with company July 12, 1865.
Williams, Perry	....do....	36	Aug. 17, 1864	1 year.	Mustered out with company July 12, 1865.
Woolery, John A	....do....	18	Sept. 23, 1864	1 year.	Mustered out with company July 12, 1865.

COMPANY E.

Mustered in October 1, 1864, at Camp Chase, O., by W. P. Richardson, Colonel 25th O. V. I. Mustered out July 12, 1865, at Charlotte, N. C., by T. M. Ward, 1st Lieutenant 25th M. V. I. and A. C. M., 1st Division, 23d Army Corps.

Names.	Rank.	Age.	Date of Entering the Service.	Period of Service.	Remarks.
Calvin S. Brice	Captain.	20	Oct. 1, 1864	1 year.	Mustered out with company July 12, 1865.
James L. Smith	1st Lieut.	38	Oct. 3, 1864	1 year.	Mustered out with company July 12, 1865.
John S. Mott	2d Lieut.	20	Oct. 6, 1864	1 year.	Promoted to 1st Lieutenant July 1, 1865, but not mustered; mustered out with company July 12, 1865.
Alexander J. McBride	1st Sergt.	28	Sept. 21, 1864	1 year.	Appointed Oct. 1, 1864; promoted to 2d Lieutenant May 11, 1865, but not mustered; mustered out with company July 12, 1865.
Hugh N. Boyd	Sergeant.	43	Sept. 24, 1864	1 year.	Appointed Oct. 1, 1864; mustered out with company July 12, 1865.
Benton Hogue	....do....	22	Sept. 24, 1864	1 year.	Appointed Oct. 1, 1864; mustered out with company July 12, 1865.
Sylvester J. Brand	....do....	32	Sept. 24, 1864	1 year.	Appointed Oct. 1, 1864; mustered out with company July 12, 1865.
John McAfee	....do....	33	Sept. 24, 1864	1 year.	Appointed Oct. 1, 1864; promoted to Sergt. Major March 28, 1865.
Henry Hanes	....do....	28	Sept. 27, 1864	1 year.	Appointed Corporal Oct. 1, '64; Sergeant March 28, 1865; mustered out with company July 12, 1865.
Jacob Breneman	Corporal.	21	Sept. 24, 1864	1 year.	Appointed Oct. 1, 1864; mustered out with company July 12, 1865.
Lewis McBride	....do....	30	Sept. 24, 1864	1 year.	Appointed Oct. 1, 1864; mustered out with company July 12, 1865.
Benjamin Hughes	....do....	21	Sept. 23, 1864	1 year.	Appointed Oct. 1, 1864; died March 7, 1865, at Washington, D. C.
Harvey Rumbaugh	....do....	28	Sept. 24, 1864	1 year.	Appointed Oct. 1, 1864; mustered out June 7, 1865, at Washington, D. C., by order of War Department.
William H. Russell	....do....	28	Sept. 22, 1864	1 year.	Appointed Oct. 1, 1864; mustered out with company July 12, 1865.
Cornelius H. Stuckey	....do....	29	Sept. 21, 1864	1 year.	Appointed Dec. 19, 1864; mustered out with company July 12, 1865.
Edward M. Brown	....do....	19	Sept. 21, 1864	1 year.	Appointed March 28, 1865; mustered out with company July 12, 1865.
Elijah Ferguson	....do....	21	Sept. 26, 1864	1 year.	Appointed March 28, 1865; mustered out with company July 12, 1865.
Isaac Briggs	....do....	42	Sept. 27, 1864	1 year.	Appointed March 28, 186 ; mustered out with company July 12, 1865.
Abbott, David	Private	28	Sept. 24, 1864	1 year	Mustered out with company July 12, 1865.
Anderson, David L	....do....	19	Sept. 24, 1864	1 year.	Appointed Corporal Oct. 1, 1864; reduced Dec. 19, 1864; mustered out July 3, 1865, at Chester, Pa., by order of War Department.
Ashing, James R	....do....	37	Sept. 24, 1864	1 year.	Mustered out with company July 12, 1865.
Bacon, Jeremiah	....do....	44	Sept. 26, 1864	1 year.	Mustered out with company July 12, 1865.
Baker, Conrad	....do....	38	Sept. 24, 1864	1 year	Mustered out with company July 12, 1865.
Baker, Henry	....do....	18	Sept. 21, 1864	1 year.	Mustered out with company July 12, 1865.
Bandy, John	....do....	18	Sept. 26, 1864	1 year.	Mustered out with company July 12, 1865.
Bare, Samuel	....do....	27	Sept. 21, 1864	1 year.	Mustered out June 20, 1865, at Washington, D. C., by order of War Department.
Basil, James W	....do....	21	Sept. 19, 1864	1 year.	Died Feb. 9, 1865, at Washington, D. C.
Blair, Alexander	....do....	36	Sept. 26, 1864	1 year.	Mustered out with company July 12, 1865.
Branstitter, Charles M	....do....	32	Sept 24, 1864	1 year.	Died March 5, 1865, at Washington, D. C.
Bromser, August	....do....	22	Sept. 16, 1864	1 year.	
Brower, George	....do....	18	Sept. 22, 1864	1 year	Mustered out with company July 12, 1865.
Bryan, Reason	....do....	21	Sept. 14, 1864	1 year.	Mustered out with company July 12, 1865.

Names.	Rank.	Age.	Date of Entering the Service.	Period of Service.	Remarks.
Burget, Bartholomew F.	Private..	26	Sept. 26, 1864	1 year.	Drowned April 23, 1865, in Potomac River, sinking of steamer Massachusetts.
Carmean, Daniel	....do...	31	Sept. 23, 1864	1 year.	Mustered out June 6, 1865, at David's Island, New York Harbor, by order of War Department.
Coleman, Arnold S.	....do....	44	Sept. 3, 1864	1 year.	Mustered out May 22, 1865, at Covington, Ky., by order of War Department.
Coleman, Osmer C.	....do....	21	Sept. 26, 1864	1 year.	Mustered out with company July 12, 1865.
Conner, Ludlow	....do....	18	Sept. 19, 1864	1 year.	Mustered out with company July 12, 1865.
Coon, George W	....do....	44	Sept. 16, 1864	1 year.	Mustered out May 17, 1865, at Washington, D. C., by order of War Department.
Coon, Isaac A.	....do....	18	Sept. 24, 1864	year.	Mustered out with company July 12, 1865.
Coon, Samuel	....do....	37	Sept. 16, 1864	year.	Died Feb. 25, 1865, at Washington, D. C.
Copeland, Moses A.	....do....	41	Sept. 22, 1864	year.	Mustered out with company July 12, 1865.
Copsey, Franklin	....do....	27	Sept. 10, 1864	year.	Died March 12, 1865, at Washington, D. C.
Copsey, Thomas J.	....do....	25	Sept. 16, 1864	year.	Mustered out with company July 12, 1865.
Copsey, Richard	....do....	38	Sept. 7, 1864	year	Mustered out with company July 12, 1865.
Cox, James E.	....do....	42	Sept. 26, 1864	year.	Mustered out with company July 12, 1865.
Decker, Henry	....do....	30	Sept. 22, 1864	year.	Mustered out June 21, 1865, at Washington, D. C., by order of War Department.
Decker, Peter C.	....do....	39	Sept. 22, 1864	1 year.	Killed March 8, 1865, in battle of [illegible], North Carolina.
Denniston, Isaac N.	....do....	28	Sept. 23, 1864	1 year.	Mustered out with company July 12, 1865.
Douglas, William	....do....	18	Sept. 26, 1864	1 year.	Transferred to 44th Co., 2d Battalion [illegible] Reserve Corps, April 14, 1865 [illegible]; mustered out Sept. 25, 1865, at Washington, D. C., on expiration of term of service.
Dershem, John R.	....do....	23	Sept. 23, 1864	1 year.	Mustered out May 26, 1865, at Washington, D. C., by order of War Department.
Engelbreth, Charles	....do....	35	Sept. 6, 1864	1 year.	Mustered out with company July 12, 1865.
Epperson, Daniel T.	....do....	32	Sept. 7, 1864	1 year.	Mustered out with company July 12, 1865.
Fist, Jacob	....do....	27	Sept. 6, 1864	1 year.	Mustered out with company July 12, 1865.
Fox, Hiram	....do....	33	Sept. 19, 1864	1 year.	Mustered out with company July 12, 1865.
Fry, Jacob	....do....	37	Sept. 24, 1864	1 year.	Mustered out with company July 12, 1865.
Galaway, John H. D.	....do....	26	Sept. 20, 1864	1 year.	Mustered out with company July 12, 1865.
Golden, William H.	....do....	21	Sept. 23, 1864	1 year.	Died March 23, 1865, in hospital at Washington, D. C.
Grubb, Joseph H.	....do....	18	Sept. 24, 1864	1 year.	Mustered out with company July 12, 1865.
Harper, William	....do....	34	Sept 6, 1864	1 year.	Mustered out with company July 12, 1865.
Harshbarger, Henry J.	....do....	32	Sept. 23, 1864	1 year.	Mustered out May 29, 1865, at Camp Dennison, O., by order of War Department.
Harshbarger, John F.	....do....	23	Sept. 23, 1864	1 year.	Wounded March 8, 1865, in battle of [illegible] Fork, N. C.; mustered out with company July 12, 1865.
Heffner, George A.	....do....	30	Sept. 23, 1864	1 year.	Mustered out with company July 12, 1865.
Helms, Abram	....do....	18	Sept. 21, 1864	1 year.	Mustered out July 20, 1865, at [illegible], by order of War Department.
Helms, Daniel	....do....	30	Sept. 26, 1864	1 year.	Mustered out June 5, 1865, at David's Island, New York Harbor, by order of War Department.
Hier, Martin	....do....	39	Sept. 23, 1864	1 year.	Mustered out with company July 12, 1865.
Hiller, Andrew J.	....do....	17	Sept. 12, 1864	1 year.	Mustered out June 15, 1865, at [illegible], by order of War Department.
Hoffman, Benjamin F.	....do....	30	Aug. 29, 1864	1 year.	Mustered out with company July 12, 1865.
Holland, Philip C.	....do....	36	Sept. 3, 1864	1 year.	Mustered out with company July 12, 1865.
Howell, William	....do...	18	Sept. 6, 1864	1 year.	
Imler, Amos	....do....	31	Sept. 22, 1864	1 year	Died June 12, 1865, at McDougal General Hospital, New York Harbor.
Imler, William	....do....	33	Sept. 24, 1864	1 year.	Died March 23, 1865, at Morehead City, [illegible]
Johnston, John P.	....do....	29	Sept. 23, 1864	1 year.	Mustered out with company July 12, 1865.
Johnston, Samuel	....do....	38	Sept. 22, 1864	1 year.	Mustered out with company July 12, 1865.
Jolley, Edward	....do....	26	Sept. 12, 1864	1 year.	Wounded March 8, 1865, in battle of [illegible] Fork, N. C.; mustered out June [illegible], Camp Dennison, O., by order of War Department.
Kates, William H.	....do....	37	Sept. 22, 1864	1 year.	Discharged July 22, 1865, at David's Island, New York Harbor, on surgeon's certificate of disability.
Kelley John	....do....	19	Sept. 5, 1864	1 year.	Mustered out with company July 12, 1865.
Lambert, Nahum	....do....	42	Sept. 23, 1864	1 year.	Mustered out with company July 12, 1865.
Longworth, Jackson	....do....	34	Sept. 13, 1864	1 year.	Died April 21, 1865, at David's Island, New York Harbor.
McMillen, James H.	....do....	28	Sept. 5, 1864	1 year.	Mustered out with company July 12, 1865.
Mack, Christian F.	....do....	36	Sept. 5, 1864	1 year.	Mustered out with company July 12, 1865.
Miller, John W.	....do....	34	Sept. 23, 1864	1 year.	Mustered out with company July 12, 1865.
Perkins, Elias	....do....	41	Sept. 26, 1864	1 year.	Mustered out with company July 12, 1865.
Pillars, Joseph H.	....do....	18	Sept. 6, 1864	1 year.	Mustered out May 29, 1865, at Camp Dennison, O., by order of War Department.
Place, Kelsey	....do....	18	Sept. 19, 1864	1 year.	Mustered out with company July 12, 1865.
Porter, James W.	....do....	37	Sept. 5, 1864	1 year.	Appointed 1st Sergeant Oct. 1, 1864; [illegible] Dec. 2, 1864; mustered out with company July 12, 1865.
Powell, Henry T	....do....	36	Sept. 13, 1864	1 year.	Mustered out with company July 12, 1865.
Powell, John	....do....	22	Sept. 10, 1864	1 year.	Appointed Corporal Oct. 1, 1864; [illegible] April 7, 1865; mustered out with company July 12, 1865.

COMPANY F.

Mustered in October 2, 1864, at Camp Chase, O., by W. P. Richardson, Colonel 25th O. V. I. Mustered out July 12, 1865, at Charlotte, N. C., by T. M. Ward, 1st Lieutenant 25th M. V. I. and A. C. M., 1st Division, 23d Army Corps.

Names.	Rank.	Age.	Date of Entering the Service.	Period of Service.	Remarks.
Harvey Anderson	Captain.	37	Sept. 1, 1864	1 year.	Appointed Oct. 1, 1864; mustered out with company July 12, 1865.
Francis A. Barnes	1st Lieut.	21	Aug. 19, 1864	1 year.	Appointed Oct. 1, 1864; mustered out with company July 12, 1865.
Sid. Newton	2d Lieut.	29	Aug. 12, 1864	1 year.	Appointed Oct. 1, 1864.
Harrison Frizzell	....do....	25	Sept. 21, 1864	1 year.	Promoted from 1st Sergeant Co. B to date Feb. 10, 1865; mustered out with company July 12, 1865.
George W. Lee	1st Sergt.	20	Sept. 27, 1864	1 year.	Appointed Oct. 2, 1864.
James Trigg	....do....	30	Oct. 4, 1864	1 year.	Appointed Sergeant Oct. 11, 1864; 1st Sergeant Dec. 10, 1864; mustered out with company July 12, 1865.
Lewis H. McWilliams	Sergeant.	21	Aug. 22, 1864	1 year.	Appointed Oct. 2, 1864; died Oct. 11, 1864, at Camp Chase, O.
Richard A. Corbin	....do....	35	Sept. 6, 1864	1 year.	Appointed Oct. 2, 1864; mustered out with company July 12, 1865.
Salathiel Rush	....do....	21	Sept. 12, 1864	1 year.	Appointed Oct. 2, 1864; mustered out with company July 12, 1865.
Francis M. Cain	....do....	31	Sept. 16, 1864	1 year.	Appointed Oct. 2, 1864; mustered out with company July 12, 1865.
Isaac Scott	....do....	28	Sept. 27, 1864	1 year.	Appointed Corporal Oct. 19, 1864; Sergeant Dec. 10, 1864; mustered out with company July 12, 1865.
William M. Edwards	Corporal.	22	Sept. 15, 1864	1 year.	Appointed Oct. 2, 1864.
John L. Sindledecker	....do....	44	Sept. 9, 1864	1 year.	Appointed Oct. 2, 1864; mustered out with company July 12, 1865, also borne on rolls as Singledecker.
John A. Brown	....do....	18	Sept. 7, 1864	1 year.	Appointed Oct. 2, 1864; mustered out with company July 12, 1865.
Ezekiel C. Wetzel	....do....	44	Sept. 22, 1864	1 year.	Appointed Oct. 2, 1864; mustered out with company July 12, 1865.
Fleming Harrison	....do....	34	Oct. 4, 1864	1 year.	Appointed April 5, 1865; mustered out with company July 12, 1865.
Reuben Sturgeon	....do....	17	Sept. 13, 1864	1 year.	Appointed Dec. 15, 1864; mustered out with company July 12, 1865.
George Bole	....do....	23	Aug. 20, 1864	1 year.	Appointed Dec. 10, 1864; mustered out with company July 12, 1865.
David A. Pugh	....do....	22	Oct. 4, 1864	1 year.	Appointed April 5, 1865; mustered out with company July 12, 1865.
George H. Stetson	....do....	38	Oct. 4, 1864	1 year.	Appointed May 21, 1865; mustered out with company July 12, 1865.
Stacy H. Stephens	Musician	22	Aug. 29, 1864	1 year.	Mustered out with company July 12, 1865.
Jackson Springer	....do....	18	Aug. 25, 1864	1 year.	Mustered out May 29, 1865, by order of War Department.
Andrew Cornell	Wagoner.	44	Sept. 13, 1864	1 year.	Mustered out with company July 12, 1865.
Armstrong, Richard	Private.	18	Sept. 23, 1864	1 year.	Mustered out with company July 12, 1865.
Baccus, John	....do....	24	Sept. 24, 1864	1 year.	Mustered out with company July 12, 1865.
Barnes, Robert A	....do....	17	Oct. 18, 1864	1 year.	Died March 6, 1865, at Washington, D. C.
Bishop, Reuben	....do....	18	Sept. 10, 1864	1 year.	Mustered out with company July 12, 1865.
Bishop, Thomas W	....do....	24	Sept. 5, 1864	1 year.	Mustered out with company July 12, 1865.
Boarden, William H	....do....	40	Sept. 20, 1864	1 year.	
Bowry, George	....do....	18	Sept. 15, 1864	1 year.	Mustered out with company July 12, 1865.
Brown, James S	....do....	16	Sept. 27, 1864	1 year.	Mustered out with company July 12, 1865.
Bruny, Christian	....do....	18	Oct. 4, 1864	1 year.	Mustered out with company July 12, 1865.
Burditt, William J	....do....	18	Sept. 9, 1864	1 year.	Mustered out May 15, 1865, at Fort Columbus, New York Harbor.
Cameron, Andrew	....do....	18	Sept. 17, 1864	1 year.	See Co. C, 182d O. V. I.
Craig, Robert	....do....	19	Sept. 9, 1864	1 year.	Died Feb. 26, 1865, at Washington, D. C.
Cutshaw, Shannon	....do....	18	Sept. 14, 1864	1 year.	See Co. C, 182d O. V. I.
Dacon, Xenophon	....do....	20	Aug. 30, 1864	1 year.	Died March 11, 1865, at Beaufort, N. C.
Daniels, Alfred	....do....	21	Sept. 21, 1864	1 year	See Co. C, 182d O. V. I.
Davis, George W	....do....	18	Sept. 14, 1864	1 year.	Mustered out with company July 12, 1865.
Davis, Samuel	....do....	18	Oct. 5, 1864	1 year.	Mustered out with company July 12, 1865.
Dennis, Adam	....do....	18	Sept. 24, 1864	1 year.	Mustered out with company July 12, 1865.
Dennis, Henry	....do....	44	Sept. 21, 1864	1 year.	Mustered out with company July 12, 1865.
Geddes, James	....do....	21	Aug. 20, 1864	1 year.	Mustered out with company July 12, 1865.
Gibbons, Homer W	....do....	18	Sept. 24, 1864	1 year.	Mustered out with company July 12, 1865.
Gibson, Robert	....do....	26	Aug. 28, 1864	1 year.	Mustered out June 6, 1865, at David's Island, New York Harbor, by order of War Department.
Gillette, Britton S	....do....	18	Aug. 20, 1864	1 year.	Mustered out with company July 12, 1865.
Harter, James	....do....	22	Sept. 29, 1864	1 year.	Appointed Corporal Dec. 10, 1864; reduced May 21, 1865; mustered out with company July 12, 1865.
Hendershot, Amos	....do....	18	Sept. 17, 1864	1 year.	Mustered out June 7, 1865, at David's Island, New York Harbor, by order of War Department.

Names.	Rank.	Age.	Date of Entering the Service.	Period of Service.	Remarks.
Carmean, Jacob D	Private	34	Sept. 24, 1864	1 year.	Discharged April 13, 1865, at Washington, D. C., on Surgeon's certificate of disability.
Carr, Solomon	...do...	28	Sept. 24, 1864	1 year.	Mustered out with company July 12, 1865.
Clawson, Harrison	...do...	43	Sept. 24, 1864	1 year.	Mustered out with company July 12, 1865.
Clinks, Jacob	...do...	22	Sept. 10, 1864	1 year.	
Conwell, John	...do...	33	Sept. 23, 1864	1 year.	Mustered out with company July 12, 1865.
Coon, John	...do...	37	Sept. 28, 1864	1 year.	Died March 5, 1865, at Washington, D. C.
Corpstein, Joseph	...do...	33	Sept. 27, 1864	1 year.	Died Dec. 11, 1864, at Decherd, Tenn.
Cummons, James	...do...	25	Sept. 23, 1864	1 year.	Mustered out June 10, 1865, at David's Island, New York Harbor, by order of War Department.
Davis, Francis M	...do...	27	Sept. 22, 1864	1 year.	Mustered out June 5, 1865, at Beaufort, N. C., by order of War Department.
Dennings, Robert	...do...	36	Sept. 24, 1864	1 year.	Mustered out with company July 12, 1865.
Dobbins, Thomas W	...do...	30	Sept. 27, 1864	1 year.	Mustered out with company July 12, 1865.
Fettig, William	...do...	38	Sept. 24, 1864	1 year.	Mustered out with company July 12, 1865.
Ford, Jacob	...do...	31	Sept. 24, 1864	1 year.	Mustered out with company July 12, 1865.
Forney, David	...do...	29	Sept. 23, 1864	1 year.	Mustered out with company July 12, 1865.
Goslee, James	...do...	21	Sept. 28, 1864	1 year.	Drafted; mustered out with company July 12, 1865.
Grubbs, James	...do...	18	Sept. 23, 1864	1 year.	Mustered out with company July 12, 1865.
Hawes, Ensign	...do...	18	Sept. 24, 1864	1 year.	Mustered out with company July 12, 1865.
Harvey, Merritt	...do...	40	Sept. 22, 1864	1 year.	Mustered out June 10, 1865, at David's Island, New York Harbor, by order of War Department.
Heindel, Adam F	...do...	21	Sept. 24, 1864	1 year.	Mustered out with company July 12, 1865.
Hiles, Isaac	...do...	27	Sept. 10, 1864	1 year.	
Hoak, Cyrus C	...do...	43	Sept. 28, 1864	1 year.	Mustered out with company July 12, 1865.
Horner, Elijah	...do...	22	Sept. 28, 1864	1 year.	Drafted; died Feb. 20, 1865, at Washington, District of Columbia.
Hughes, John W	...do...	23	Sept. 28, 1864	1 year.	Mustered out June 3, 1865, at Washington, D. C., by order of War Department.
Imler, James	...do...	19	Sept. 23, 1864	1 year.	Mustered out July 12, 1865, at Camp Dennison, O., by order of War Department.
Jinks, William	...do...	31	Sept. 26, 1864	1 year.	
John, Ethan	...do...	39	Sept. 24, 1864	1 year.	Mustered out with company July 12, 1865.
Lusk, Jonathan	...do...	18	Sept. 19, 1864	1 year.	Mustered out with company July 12, 1865.
McBride, Levi	...do...	33	Sept. 24, 1864	1 year.	Mustered out with company July 12, 1865.
Mallett, Daniel	...do...	20	Sept. 17, 1864	1 year.	Transferred to Co. C, 2d Regiment Veteran Reserve Corps, May 17, 1865; mustered out Aug. 3, 1865, at Jackson, Mich., by order of War Department.
Manahan, Erasmus	...do...	19	Sept. 24, 1864	1 year.	Mustered out with company July 12, 1865.
Martin, Absalom	...do...	33	Sept. 24, 1864	1 year.	Mustered out with company July 12, 1865.
Maus, William A	...do...	29	Sept. 24, 1864	1 year.	Mustered out with company July 12, 1865.
Miller, Curtis	...do...	35	Sept. 24, 1864	1 year.	Mustered out with company July 12, 1865.
Miller, Ferdinand	...do...	18	Sept. 23, 1864	1 year.	Died Feb. 2?, 1865, at Washington, D. C.
Miller, Jesse P	...do...	31	Sept. 24, 1864	1 year.	Mustered out with company July 12, 1865.
Morris, Thomas	...do...	18	Sept. 19, 1864	1 year.	Mustered out with company July 12, 1865.
Neely, Joseph	...do...	22	Sept. 22, 1864	1 year.	Appointed Corporal Oct. 1, 1864; [illegible] March 28, 1865; mustered out June [illegible], 1865, at Columbus, O., by order of War Department.
Parker, William	...do...	24	Sept. 28, 1864	1 year.	Drafted.
Read, Thomas L	...do...	21	Sept. 17, 1864	1 year.	
Riggle, Henry	...do...	31	Sept. 24, 1864	1 year.	Left sick Dec. 20, 1864, in hospital at [illegible], Tenn. No further record found.
Roland, Charles	...do...	25	Sept. 16, 1864	1 year.	
Rothgeber, Jacob	...do...	31	Sept. 24, 1864	1 year.	Mustered out May 29, 1865, at Camp Dennison, O., by order of War Department.
Rupert, John W	...do...	36	Sept. 24, 1864	1 year.	Mustered out with company July 12, 1865.
Rupert, Samuel	...do...	25	Sept. 24, 1864	1 year.	Mustered out with company July 12, 1865.
Seldomridge, George	...do...	35	Sept. 2?, 1864	1 year.	Died Feb. 9, 1865, at Washington, D. C.
Shafer, Joseph	...do...	35	Sept. 24, 1864	1 year.	Mustered out with company July 12, 1865.
Shearer, Abraham W	...do...	20	Sept. 26, 1864	1 year.	Mustered out with company July 12, 1865.
Shobe, Smith	...do...	28	Sept. 28, 1864	1 year.	Mustered out with company July 12, 1865.
Shriver, Robert	...do...	30	Oct. 10, 1864	1 year.	Mustered out with company July 12, 1865.
Sloan, William M	...do...	19	Sept. 11, 1864	1 year.	Mustered out with company July 12, 1865.
Smith, Howell G	...do...	42	Sept. 24, 1864	1 year.	Appointed Sergeant Oct. [illegible], 1864; [illegible] Dec. 19, 1864; mustered out June [illegible], 1865, at Camp Dennison, O., by order of War Department.
Smith, James P	...do...	41	Sept. 24, 1864	1 year.	Mustered out with company July 12, 1865.
Stemen, Noah W	...do...	26	Sept. 24, 1864	1 year.	Mustered out May 12, 1865, at Columbus, O., by order of War Department.
Stuckey, Irenius	...do...	22	Sept. 24, 1864	1 year.	Mustered out with company July 12, 1865.
Tressler, Jeremiah	...do...	18	Sept. 9, 1864	1 year.	
Vanosdall, John	...do...	29	Sept. 23, 1864	1 year.	See Co. K, 178th O. V. I.
Warden, James M	...do...	19	Sept. 26, 1864	1 year.	Mustered out with company July 12, 1865.
Wein, Amos K	...do...	27	Sept. 23, 1864	1 year.	Mustered out with company July 12, 1865.
Werr, Wesley	...do...	21	Sept. 17, 1864	1 year.	
Wertz, Jesse	...do...	28	Sept. 24, 1864	1 year.	Mustered out with company July 12, 1865.
Whitehurst, Hugh C	...do...	30	Sept. 24, 1864	1 year.	Mustered out with company July 12, 1865.
Woodruff, Cornelius J	...do...	18	Sept. 14, 1864	1 year.	Died Feb. 25, 1865, at Washington, D. C.
Zerby, William	...do...	25	Oct. 10, 1864	1 year.	Mustered out with company July 12, 1865.
Zurmekley, John	...do...	18	Sept. 24, 1864	1 year.	Mustered out with company July 12, 1865.

COMPANY G.

Mustered in October 3, 1864, at Camp Chase, O., by W. P. Richardson, Colonel 25th O. V. I. Mustered out July 12, 1865, at Charlotte, N. C., by T. M. Ward, 1st Lieutenant 25th M. V. I. and A. C. M., 1st Division, 23d Army Corps.

Names.	Rank.	Age.	Date of Entering the Service.	Period of Service.	Remarks.
John H. Busby	Captain.	..	Oct. 3, 1864	1 year.	
Andrew Smith	....do....	24	Sept. 29, 1864	1 year.	Promoted from 1st Lieutenant Co. B May 23, 1865; mustered out with company July 12, 1865.
Elisha P. Allen	1st Lieut.	30	July 4, 1863	3 yrs.	Promoted from Sergeant Co. I, 88th O. V. I., Oct. 8, 1864; mustered out with company July 12, 1865.
Morris T. Gossett	2d Lieut.	..	Oct. 3, 1864	1 year.	Discharged May 23, 1865, by order of War Department.
John Keys	1st Sergt.	24	Sept. 13, 1864	1 year.	Appointed Oct. 4, 1864; promoted to 2d Lieutenant July 4, 1865, but not mustered; mustered out with company July 12, 1865.
William McCarroll	Sergeant.	40	Sept. 23, 1864	1 year.	Appointed Oct. 4, 1864; mustered out with company July 12, 1865.
William H. Patton	....do....	26	Sept. 30, 1864	1 year.	Appointed Oct. 4, 1864; mustered out with company July 12, 1865.
Francis M. Ingalls	....do....	24	Sept. 27, 1864	1 year.	Mustered out May 29, 1865, at Camp Dennison, O., by order of War Department.
George Hey	....do....	27	Sept. 28, 1864	1 year.	Appointed Corporal Jan. 4, 1865; Sergeant May 29, 1865; mustered out with company July 12, 1865.
Henry Slough	....do....	32	Oct. 5, 1864	1 year.	Appointed Corporal Oct. 5, 1864; Sergeant June 7, 1865; mustered out with company July 12, 1865.
Marshal O'Neal	Corporal.	31	Sept. 23, 1864	1 year.	Appointed Oct. 4, 1864; mustered out with company July 12, 1865.
John W. Elliott	....do....	19	Sept. 28, 1864	1 year.	Appointed Oct. 4, 1864; mustered out with company July 12, 1865.
William A. Harris	....do....	22	Oct. 1, 1864	1 year.	Appointed Oct. 4, 1864; mustered out with company July 12, 1865.
James J. VanSant	....do....	18	Sept. 28, 1864	1 year.	Died March 2, 1865, at Alexandria, Va.
David Dunnavin	....do....	23	Sept. 26, 1864	1 year.	Appointed April 6, 1865; mustered out with company July 12, 1865.
Ira Claflin	....do....	22	Sept. 13, 1864	1 year.	Appointed April 20, 1865; mustered out with company July 12, 1865.
John Blosser	....do....	20	Sept. 28, 1864	1 year.	Appointed May 29, 1865; mustered out with company July 12, 1865.
Jacob Stevens	....do....	39	Sept. 28, 1864	1 year.	Appointed June 2, 1865; mustered out with company July 12, 1865; also borne on rolls as Severns.
Frederick Shifler	....do....	37	Sept. 13, 1864	1 year.	Appointed June 7, 1865; mustered out with company July 12, 1865.
Abbott, James M	Private..	18	Sept. 22, 1864	1 year.	
Allen, John	....do....	28	Sept. 24, 1864	1 year.	
Allwine, Jerome	....do....	22	Sept. 22, 1864	1 year.	
Blackstone, William H.	....do....	22	Sept. 22, 1864	1 year.	See Co. F 179th O. V. I.
Bozman, John R	....do....	21	Sept. 22, 1864	1 year.	
Bray, Samuel P	....do....	19	Sept. 30, 1864	1 year.	Mustered out with company July 12, 1865.
Bremen, Henry	....do....	22	Sept. 27, 1864	1 year.	Mustered out with company July 12, 1865.
Butler, Thomas	....do....	26	Sept. 27, 1864	1 year.	
Callahan, William	....do....	37	Sept. 29, 1864	1 year.	
Campbell, Thomas B	....do....	22	Sept. 28, 1864	1 year.	
Carroll, William	....do....	23	Sept. 23, 1864	1 year.	
Carter, George W	....do....	18	Sept. 29, 1864	1 year.	Mustered out with company July 12, 1865.
Chamberlain, William	....do....	24	Sept. 27, 1864	1 year.	Mustered out with company July 12, 1865.
Clark, Daniel	....do....	37	Sept. 5, 1864	1 year.	
Clark, Joseph	....do....	18	Aug. 16, 1864	1 year.	Mustered out May 26, 1865, by order of War Department.
Coffey, Richard	....do....	40	Aug. 13, 1864	1 year.	Mustered out May 26, 1865, by order of War Department.
Cotton, Mortimer L.	....do....	20	Sept. 29, 1864	1 year.	
Daugherty, Thomas	....do....	21	Sept. 13, 1864	1 year.	
Davis, John	....do....	19	Sept. 25, 1864	1 year.	
Devine, Martin	....do. ..	31	Sept. 24, 1864	1 year.	
Dood, Philip	....do....	22	Sept. 23, 1864	1 year.	
Ellis, David	....do....	38	Sept. 26, 1864	1 year.	Mustered out with company July 12, 1865.
Essick, William	....do....	22	Sept. 23, 1864	1 year.	
Fagan, Patrick	....do....	44	Sept. 30, 1864	1 year.	Mustered out May 29, 1865, at Camp Dennison, O., by order of War Department.
Findley, James	....do....	22	Sept. 28, 1864	1 year.	
Fink, Gottfried	....do....	18	Sept. 28, 1864	1 year.	Mustered out with company July 12, 1865.
Fitch, Edward	....do....	25	Sept. 26, 1864	1 year.	Appointed Corporal Oct. 4, 1864; reduced April 1865 mustered out with company July 12, 1865.
Frickle, George S	....do....	28	Sept. 27, 1864	1 year.	Mustered out with company July 12, 1865.
Gow, Alexander N	....do....	24	Sept. 29, 1864	1 year.	See Field and Staff, 172d O. V. I.

Names.	Rank.	Age.	Date of Entering the Service.	Period of Service	Remarks.
Harding, Charles W.	Private..	18	Sept. 28, 1864	1 year.	
Harkins, Allen	...do....	18	Sept. 5, 1864	1 year.	Mustered out with company July 12, 1865.
Hayden, Robert D.	...do....	28	Sept. 27, 1864	1 year.	
Herriman, Ransom W.	...do....	34	Sept. 22, 1864	1 year.	Appointed Corporal Oct. 4, 1864; reduced Jan. 4, 1865; mustered out with company July 12, 1865.
Inscho, Barnard	...do....	23	Sept. 27, 1864	1 year.	Mustered out with company July 12, 1865.
Jordon, George W.	...do....	31	Sept. 30, 1864	1 year.	Mustered out June 10, 1865, at David's Island, New York Harbor, by order of War Department.
Kaufman, John H.	...do....	18	Sept. 30, 1864	1 year.	Mustered out with company July 12, 1865.
Kinder, James	...do....	33	Sept. 28, 1864	1 year.	Mustered out with company July 12, 1865.
Kinmore, William	...do....	25	Sept. 24, 1864	1 year.	Mustered out with company July 12, 1865.
Konkle, Abraham	...do....	30	Sept. 27, 1864	1 year.	Mustered out June 20, 1865, at Washington, D. C., by order of War Department.
Landis, Emanuel	...do....	37	Sept. 21, 1864	1 year.	
Lanes, Dennis	...do....	30	Sept. 29, 1864	1 year.	
Lanson, John	...do....	19	Sept. 24, 1864	1 year.	
Leonard, John	...do....	24	Sept. 26, 1864	1 year.	
Lewis, William J.	...do....	24	Sept. 26, 1864	1 year.	Mustered out with company July 12, 1865.
Lucas, Charles H.	...do....	29	Sept. 20, 1864	1 year.	
McCauley, Ezra W.	...do....	18	Sept. 30, 1864	1 year.	Mustered out with company July 12, 1865.
McGee, George A.	...do....	16	Sept. 26, 1864	1 year.	Died June 19, 1865, at Charlotte, N. C.
Mattes, Alfred	...do....	18	Sept. 28, 1864	1 year.	Died March 31, 1865, at Lenoir Hospital, Kinston, N. C.
Melson, Michael	...do....	44	Sept. 27, 1864	1 year.	Died Feb. 14, 1865, at Douglas Hospital, Washington, D. C.
Miller, John B.	...do....	20	Sept. 13, 1864	1 year.	Mustered out with company July 12, 1865.
Miller, Orville K.	...do....	31	Sept. 17, 1864	1 year.	Mustered out with company July 12, 1865.
Miller, William H.	...do....	19	Sept. 9, 1864	1 year.	Mustered out with company July 12, 1865.
Millikin, John W.	...do....	21	Sept. 13, 1864	1 year.	Mustered out with company July 12, 1865.
Miskinnin, George W.	...do....	18	Sept. 28, 1864	1 year.	Mustered out with company July 12, 1865.
Morrison, Dallas G.	...do....	21	Sept. 17, 1864	1 year.	
Myers, Charles	...do....	20	Sept. 29, 1864	1 year.	
Myers, George	...do....	18	Sept. 30, 1864	1 year.	Mustered out June 13, 1865, at Philadelphia, Pa., by order of War Department.
Myers, John	...do....	18	Sept. 30, 1864	1 year.	
Nickle, Aaron	...do....	28	Sept. 27, 1864	1 year.	Mustered out with company July 12, 1865.
Nixon, John W.	...do....	26	Aug. 5, 1864	1 year.	Mustered out with company July 12, 1865.
Norris, Thomas S.	...do....	37	Oct. 1, 1864	1 year.	
Pelton, Eugene	...do....	18	Sept. 19, 1864	1 year.	
Price, John	...do....	43	Sept. 27, 1864	1 year.	
Price, Thomas D.	...do....	50	Oct. 3, 1864	1 year.	Mustered out with company July 12, 1865.
Proctor, Ethelbert	...do....	18	Sept. 21, 1864	1 year.	See Co. A, 178th O. V. I.
Purcell, Theodore	...do....	18	Sept. 28, 1864	1 year.	Mustered out with company July 12, 1865.
Scott, Martin B.	...do....	24	Sept. 19, 1864	1 year.	
Shea, John	...do....	57	Sept. 22, 1864	1 year.	
Sherwood, Aaron	...do....	18	Sept. 28, 1864	1 year.	Died Jan. 29, 1865, at Camp Chase, O.
Shipman, James	...do....	39	Sept. 28, 1864	1 year.	
Shuler, Andrew J.	...do....	28	Sept. 30, 1864	1 year.	Died May 27, 1865, at Grant Hospital, Willet's Point, N. Y.
Stephens, Eliphalet H.	...do....	27	Sept. 30, 1864	1 year.	Mustered out June 19, 1865, at Columbus, O., by order of War Department.
Stephens, James	...do....	18	Sept. 3, 1864	1 year.	Mustered out May 29, 1865, at Camp Dennison, by order of War Department.
Stottlemyer, Martin	...do....	21	Sept. 27, 1864	1 year.	Discharged Nov. 3, 1864, at Camp Chase, O., on Surgeon's certificate of disability.
Swiger, William S.	...do....	44	Oct. 1, 1864	1 year.	Mustered out March 6, 1866, at Columbus, O., by order of War Department.
Taylor, Samuel W.	...do....	18	Sept. 30, 1864	1 year.	Mustered out with company July 12, 1865.
Peters, John W.	...do....	23	Aug. 16, 1864	1 year.	Mustered out with company July 12, 1865.
Thomas, Edward	...do....	23	Sept. 27, 1864	1 year.	
Thompson, William	...do....	25	Sept. 28, 1864	1 year.	
Walton, William G.	...do....	25	Sept. 23, 1864	1 year.	
Weakley, George	...do....	22	Sept. 20, 1864	1 year.	
Wheeler, John W.	...do....	38	Sept. 20, 1864	1 year.	Mustered out with company July 12, 1865.
Whittmore, Newman	...do....	26	Sept. 30, 1864	1 year.	Mustered out with company July 12, 1865.
White, Robert	...do....	21	Sept. 28, 1864	1 year.	Appointed Corporal Oct. 4, 1864; reduced April 20, 1865; mustered out with company July 12, 1865.
Williams, John	...do....	27	Oct. 1, 1864	1 year.	
Wilkins, Wesley	...do....	32	Aug. 5, 1864	1 year.	Mustered out June 10, 1865, at Washington, D. C., by order of War Department.

COMPANY H.

Mustered in October 4, 1864, at Camp Chase, O., by W. P. Richardson, Colonel 25th O. V. I. Mustered out July 12, 1865, at Charlotte, N. C., by T. M. Ward, 1st Lieutenant 25th M. V. I. and A. C. M., 1st Division, 23d Army Corps.

Names.	Rank.	Age.	Date of Entering the Service.	Period of Service.	Remarks.
Philip Bauer	Captain.	37	Oct. 4, 1864	1 year.	
Matthias Ridenour	....do....	40	Sept. 28, 1864	1 year.	Promoted from 1st Lieutenant Co. A Feb. 10, 1865; mustered out with company July 12, 1865.
Mahlon C. Moore	1st Lieut.	27	Oct. 4, 1864	1 year.	Mustered out with company July 12, 1865.
George Querner	2d Lieut.	45	Oct. 6, 1864	1 year.	Discharged Feb. 6, 1865, by order of War Department.
Ephraim B. Weirrick	1st Sergt.	22	Aug. 31, 1864	1 year.	Appointed Oct. 4, 1864; promoted to 2d Lieutenant July 4, 1865, but not mustered; mustered out with company July 12, 1865.
Miner A. Rarey	Sergeant.	20	Sept. 20, 1864	1 year.	Appointed Oct. 4, 1864; mustered out with company July 12, 1865.
John Bierley	....do....	26	Sept. 1, 1864	1 year.	Appointed Oct. 4, 1864; mustered out with company July 12, 1865.
Levi Roseberry	....do....	24	Sept. 17, 1864	1 year.	Drafted; appointed Sergeant Oct. 4, 1864; mustered out with company July 12, 1865.
Richard H. Brannon	....do....	35	Sept. 17, 1864	1 year.	Drafted; appointed Sergeant Oct. 4, 1864; mustered out with company July 12, 1865.
John Hartman	Corporal.	29	Aug. 31, 1864	1 year.	Appointed Oct. 4, 1864; mustered out with company July 12, 1865.
Peter Pfeifer	....do....	29	Aug. 30, 1864	1 year.	Appointed Oct. 4, 1864; mustered out with company July 12, 1865.
Francis M. Stone	....do....	22	Sept. 26, 1864	1 year.	Appointed Oct. 4, 1864; mustered out with company July 12, 1865.
William Kauffman	....do....	26	Sept. 12, 1864	1 year.	Appointed Oct. 4, 1864; mustered out with company July 12, 1865.
Andrew D. Kraner	....do....	30	Sept. 20, 1864	1 year.	Appointed Oct. 4, 1864; mustered out with company July 12, 1865.
William Kile	....do....	21	Sept. 13, 1864	1 year.	Appointed Oct. 4, 1864; mustered out with company July 12, 1865.
George Hopkins	....do....	28	Sept. 17, 1864	1 year.	Drafted; appointed Corporal May 15, 1865; mustered out with company July 12, 1865.
Noah C. Barnhart	....do....	37	Sept. 19, 1864	1 year.	Drafted; appointed Corporal May 23, 1865; mustered out with company July 12, 1865.
Abbott, Herman	Private.	19	Sept. 18, 1864	1 year.	
Bailey, William C	....do....	23	Sept. 19, 1864	1 year.	Drafted.
Barnes, John	....do....	43	Aug. 12, 1864	1 year.	
Barnhart, Orange	....do....	41	Sept. 15, 1864	1 year.	Mustered out with company July 12, 1865.
Baughman, John	....do....	25	Sept. 15, 1864	1 year.	Mustered out with company July 12, 1865.
Bergwitz, John	....do....	38	Sept. 1, 1864	1 year.	Appointed Corporal Oct. 6, 1864; reduced May 23, 1865; mustered out with company July 12, 1865.
Berkley, Martin	....do....	41	Sept. 1, 1864	1 year.	Mustered out May 26, 1865, at Louisville, Ky., by order of War Department.
Berry, James C	....do....	42	Sept. 19, 1864	1 year.	Drafted; mustered out with company July 12, 1865.
Blumlin, Lewis	....do....	24	Aug. 24, 1864	1 year.	
Bonnin, Charles H	....do....	33	Sept. 6, 1864	1 year.	
Boxwell, William W	....do....	28	Sept. 18, 1864	1 year.	Mustered out with company July 12, 1865.
Brain, John	....do....	20	Sept. 8, 1864	1 year.	
Brennaiser, Frederick	....do....	26	Aug. 31, 1864	1 year.	Mustered out with company July 12, 1865.
Brooks, Darius W	....do....	40	Sept. 18, 1864	1 year.	Drafted; mustered out with company July 12, 1865.
Brown, Philip	....do....	38	Sept. 1, 1864	1 year.	Mustered out June 5, 1865, at Columbus, O., by order of War Department.
Butler, William	....do....	19	Sept. 10, 1864	1 year.	
Bryson, Charles	....do....	20	Sept. 1, 1864	1 year.	Mustered out with company July 12, 1865.
Cockrell, Gilbert H	....do....	18	Sept. 28, 1864	1 year.	
Cole, Leonard	....do....	41	Sept. 18, 1864	1 year.	Drafted; mustered out June 2, 1865, at Beaufort, N. C., by order of War Department.
Corbett, John	....do....	44	Oct. 3, 1864	1 year.	Discharged March 18, 1865, by order of War Department.
Daring, Emil	....do....	40	Sept. 27, 1864	1 year.	Died Oct. 27, 1864, at Nashville, Tenn.
Dewitt, Wesley	....do....	28	Sept. 1, 1864	1 year.	Mustered out with company July 12, 1865.
Dossen, John	....do....	20	Sept. 10, 1864	1 year.	
Elliott, James	....do....	40	Sept. 1, 1864	1 year.	Mustered out with company July 12, 1865.
Fisher, Garrison	....do....	18	Sept. 26, 1864	1 year.	
Funk, David	....do....	44	Sept. 20, 1864	1 year.	Mustered out with company July 12, 1865.
Green, Andrew	....do....	20	Aug. 26, 1864	1 year.	
Green, Henry F	....do....	18	Sept. 28, 1864	1 year.	Mustered out with company July 12, 1865.
Heinmiller, John	....do....	18	Sept. 28, 1864	1 year.	Mustered out with company July 12, 1865.
Hodgden, Charles	....do....	28	Sept. 19, 1864	1 year.	Drafted; mustered out with company July 12, 1865.
Holzer, Jacob	....do....	40	Sept. 3, 1864	1 year.	Mustered out with company July 12, 1865.
Hoffrichter, George A	....do....	19	Sept. 1, 1864	1 year.	Mustered out with company July 12, 1865.
Huff, James M	....do....	26	Sept. 6, 1864	1 year.	Mustered out with company July 12, 1865.

Names.	Rank.	Age.	Date of Entering the Service.	Period of Service	Remarks.
Harding, Charles W.	Private..	18	Sept. 28, 1864	1 year.	
Harkins, Allen	...do....	18	Sept. 5, 1864	1 year.	Mustered out with company July 12, 1865.
Hayden, Robert D.	...do....	25	Sept. 27, 1864	1 year.	
Herriman, Ransom W.	...do....	34	Sept. 22, 1864	1 year.	Appointed Corporal Oct. 4, 1864; reduced J[illegible] 4, 1865; mustered out with company J[illegible] 12, 1865.
Inscho, Barnard	...do....	23	Sept. 27, 1864	1 year.	Mustered out with company July 12, 1865.
Jordon, George W.	...do....	31	Sept. 30, 1864	1 year.	Mustered out June 10, 1865, at David's Isla[illegible] New York Harbor, by order of War Dep[illegible] ment.
Kaufman, John H.	...do....	18	Sept. 30, 1864	1 year.	Mustered out with company July 12, 1865.
Kinder, James	...do....	33	Sept. 28, 1864	1 year.	Mustered out with company July 12, 1865.
		25	Sept. 24, 1864	1 year.	Mustered out with company July 12, 1865.
		30	Sept. 27, 1864	1 year.	Mustered out June 20, 1865, at Washing[illegible] D. C., by order of War Department.
Landis, Emanuel	...do....	37	Sept. 21, 1864	1 year.	
Lanes, Dennis	...do....	30	Sept. 29, 1864	1 year.	
Lanson, John	...do....	19	Sept. 24, 1864	1 year.	
Leonard, John	...do....	24	Sept. 26, 1864	1 year.	
Lewis, William J.	...do....	24	Sept. 26, 1864	1 year.	Mustered out with company July 12, 1865.
Lucas, Charles H.	...do....	29	Sept. 20, 1864	1 year.	
McCauley, Ezra W.	...do....	18	Sept. 30, 1864	1 year.	Mustered out with company July 12, 1865.
McGee, George A.	...do....	16	Sept. 26, 1864	1 year.	Died June 19, 1865, at Charlotte, N. C.
Mattes, Alfred	...do....	18	Sept. 28, 1864	1 year.	Died March 31, 1865, at Lenoir Hospital [illegible] ston, N. C.
Melson, Michael	...do....	44	Sept. 27, 1864	1 year.	Died Feb. 14, 1865, at Douglas Hospital, Wa[illegible] ington, D. C.
Miller, John B.	...do....	20	Sept. 13, 1864	1 year.	Mustered out with company July 12, 1865.
Miller, Orville K.	...do....	31	Sept. 17, 1864	1 year.	Mustered out with company July 12, 1865.
Miller, William H.	...do....	19	Sept. 9, 1864	1 year.	Mustered out with company July 12, 1865.
Millikin, John W.	...do....	21	Sept. 13, 1864	1 year.	Mustered out with company July 12, 1865.
Miskinnin, George W.	...do....	18	Sept. 28, 1864	1 year.	Mustered out with company July 12, 1865.
Morrison, Dallas G.	...do....	21	Sept. 17, 1864	1 year.	
Myers, Charles	...do....	20	Sept. 29, 1864	1 year.	
Myers, George	...do....	18	Sept. 30, 1864	1 year.	Mustered out June 13, 1865, at Philadelph[illegible] Pa., by order of War Department.
Myers, John	...do....	18	Sept. 30, 1864	1 year.	
Nickle, Aaron	...do....	28	Sept. 27, 1864	1 year.	Mustered out with company July 12, 1865.
Nixon, John W.	...do....	26	Aug. 5, 1864	1 year.	Mustered out with company July 12, 1865.
Norris, Thomas S.	...do....	37	Oct. 1, 1864	1 year.	
Pelton, Eugene	...do....	18	Sept. 19, 1864	1 year.	
Price, John	...do....	43	Sept. 27, 1864	1 year.	
Price, Thomas D.	...do....	30	Oct. 3, 1864	1 year.	Mustered out with company July 12, 1865.
Proctor, Ethelbert	...do....	18	Sept. 21, 1864	1 year.	See Co. A, 178th O. V. I.
Purcell, Theodore	...do....	18	Sept. 28, 1864	1 year.	Mustered out with company July 12, 1865.
Scott, Martin B.	...do....	24	Sept. 19, 1864	1 year.	
Shea, John	...do....	37	Sept. 22, 1864	1 year.	
Sherwood, Aaron	...do....	18	Sept. 28, 1864	1 year.	Died Jan. 29, 1865, at Camp Chase, O.
Shipman, James	...do....	19	Sept. 28, 1864	1 year.	
Shuler, Andrew	...do....	28	Sept. 30, 1864	1 year.	Died May 27, 1865, at Grant Hospital, [illegible] Point, N. Y.
Stephens, Eliphalet H.	...do....	27	Sept. 30, 1864	1 year.	Mustered out June 10, 1865, at Columbu[illegible] by order of War Department.
Stephens, James	...do....	18	Sept. 3, 1864	1 year.	Mustered out May 29, 1865, at Camp Den[illegible] by order of War Department.
Stottlemyer, Martin	...do....	24	Sept. 27, 1864	1 year.	Discharged Nov. 3, 1864, at Camp Chase on Surgeon's certificate of disabil[illegible]
Swiger, William S.	...do..	44	Oct. 1, 1864	1 year.	Mustered out March 6, 1866, at Columbus, by order of War Department.
Taylor, Samuel W.	...do....	18	Sept. 30, 1864	1 year.	Mustered out with company July 12, 1865.
Teters, John W.	...do....	23	Aug. 16, 1864	1 year.	Mustered out with company July 12, 1865.
Thomas, Edward	...do....	23	Sept. 27, 1864	1 year.	
Thompson, William	...do....	25	Sept. 28, 1864	1 year.	
Walton, William G.	...do....	25	Sept. 23, 1864	1 year.	
Weakley, George	...do....	22	Sept. 20, 1864	1 year.	
Wheeler, John W.	...do....	18	Sept. 20, 1864	1 year.	Mustered out with company July 12, 1865.
Whittacre, Newman	...do....	26	Sept. 30, 1864	1 year.	Mustered out with company July 12, 1865.
White, Robert	...do....	21	Sept. 28, 1864	1 year.	Appointed Corporal Oct. 4, 1864; red[illegible] April 20, 1865; mustered out with com[illegible] July 12, 1865.
Williams, John	...do....	27	Oct. 1, 1864	1 year.	
Wilkins, Wesley	...do....	32	Aug. 5, 1864	1 year.	Mustered out June 10, 1865, at Washing[illegible] D. C., by order of War Department.

COMPANY I.

Mustered in October 5, 1864, at Camp Chase, O., by W. P. Richardson, Colonel 25th O. V. I. Mustered out July 12, 1865, at Charlotte, N. C., by T. M. Ward, 1st Lieutenant 25th M. V. I. and A. C. M., 1st Division, 23d Army Corps.

Names.	Rank.	Age.	Date of Entering the Service.	Period of Service.	Remarks.
Henry Williams	Captain.	22	Oct. 5, 1864	1 year.	Mustered out with company July 12, 1865.
Van Buren Pritchet	1st Lieut.	25	Oct. 5, 1864	1 year.	Mustered out with company July 12, 1865.
Hiram C. Reed	2d Lieut.	24	Oct. 5, 1864	1 year.	Mustered out with company July 12, 1865.
John W. Gregg	1st Sergt.	29	Sept. 28, 1864	1 year.	Appointed Oct. 5, 1864; promoted to 2d Lieutenant July 4, 1865, but not mustered; mustered out with company July 12, 1865.
William S. Carson	Sergeant.	27	Sept. 3, 1864	1 year.	Appointed Oct. 5, 1864; mustered out with company July 12, 1865.
Hubbard H. Benschoter	....do....	33	Sept. 19, 1864	1 year.	Appointed Oct. 5, 1864; mustered out May 29, 1865, at Camp Dennison, O., by order of War Department.
George C. Gardner	....do....	32	Sept. 30, 1864	1 year.	Appointed Oct. 5, 1864; mustered out with company July 12, 1865.
Laban Rogers	....do....	38	Oct. 10, 1864	1 year.	Appointed Oct. 10, 1864; mustered out with company July 12, 1865.
Martin V. Headington	....do....	33	Oct. 3, 1864	1 year.	Appointed from private June 27, 1865; mustered out with company July 12, 1865.
John W. Smith	Corporal.	23	Sept. 27, 1864	1 year.	Appointed Oct. 5, 1864; mustered out with company July 12, 1865.
Francis M. McKisson	....do....	21	Sept. 19, 1864	1 year.	Appointed Oct. 5, 1864; mustered out July 6, 1865, at Philadelphia, Pa., by order of War Department.
Francis M. Woolington	....do....	22	Sept. 24, 1864	1 year.	Appointed Oct. 5, 1864; mustered out with company July 12, 1865.
James D. Lea	....do....	21	Sept. 13, 1864	1 year.	Appointed Oct. 5, 1864; mustered out with company July 12, 1865.
Thomas J. Williams	....do....	28	Sept. 3, 1864	1 year.	Appointed Oct. 5, 1864; died Feb. 21, 1865, at Harewood Hospital, Washington, D. C.
William Elzy	....do....	22	Sept. 15, 1864	1 year.	Appointed Oct. 5, 1864; mustered out May 25, 1865, at Columbus, O., by order of War Department.
Henry B. Johnson	....do....	26	Sept. 3, 1864	1 year.	Appointed Oct. 5, 1864, mustered out June 8, 1865, at Newbern, N. C., by order of War Department.
Barnet B. Rowley	....do....	33	Sept. 15, 1864	1 year.	Appointed May 1, 1865; mustered out with company July 12, 1865.
Benjamin F. Weirick	....do....	30	Sept. 3, 1864	1 year.	Appointed June 6, 1865; mustered out with company July 12, 1865.
Matthias Narance	Musician	21	Sept. 29, 1864	1 year.	Mustered out with company July 12, 1865.
Adams, Samuel	Private..	28	Sept. 21, 1864	1 year.	Mustered out Jul 7, 1865, at Columbus, O., by order of War Department.
Bales, Jenkins B	....do....	34	Sept. 3, 1864	1 year.	Mustered out with company July 12, 1865.
Benner, John	....do....	32	Sept. 25, 1864	1 year.	Mustered out with company July 12, 1865.
Borland, Theodore	....do....	16	Sept. 24, 1864	1 year.	Mustered out with company July 12, 1865.
Branton, Augustus	....do....	19	Sept. 19, 1864	1 year.	Mustered out with company July 12, 1865.
Brown, Franklin	....do....	19	Sept. 22, 1864	1 year.	Died March 26, 1865, in Armory Square Hospital, Washington, D. C.
Buchanan, Andrew J	....do....	22	Sept. 26, 1864	1 year.	Mustered out with company July 12, 1865.
Burris, Francis	....do....	31	Sept. 3, 1864	1 year.	Died May 31, 1865, at Charlotte, N. C.
Burton, Abraham	....do....	18	Sept. 28, 1864	1 year.	Died Feb. 21, 1865, at Carver Hospital, Washington, D. C.
Chamberlain, William	....do....	24	Sept. 27, 1864	1 year.	
Cline, David D	....do....	30	Sept. 23, 1864	1 year.	Discharged June 5, 1865, at Columbus, O., on Surgeon's certificate of disability.
Collins, Benair	....do....	22	Sept. 3, 1864	1 year.	Mustered out July 6, 1865, at Philadelphia, Pa., by order of War Department.
Collins, Daniel	....do....	26	Sept. 3, 1864	1 year.	Mustered out with company July 12, 1865.
Collins, James	....do....	32	Sept. 3, 1864	1 year.	Mustered out May 29, 1865, at Camp Dennison, O., by order of War Department.
Collins, Samuel	....do....	22	Sept. 3, 1864	1 year.	Mustered out June 12, 1865, at McDougall Hospital, New York Harbor, by order of War Department.
Curps, John T	....do....	18	Sept. 26, 1864	1 year.	Died May 28, 1865, at Charlotte, N. C.
Davis, William	....do....	27	Sept. 24, 1864	1 year.	Mustered out with company July 12, 1865.
Dewitt, Henry C	....do....	30	Sept. 29, 1864	1 year.	
Dolby, Thomas	....do....	23	Sept. 24, 1864	1 year.	Mustered out May 26, 1865, at Washington, D. C., by order of War Department.
Feasel, Andrew J	....do....	25	Sept. 22, 1864	1 year.	Mustered out to date July 12, 1865, by order of War Department.
Glass, George W	....do....	27	Sept. 28, 1864	1 year.	Died Feb. 12, 1865, at Douglas Hospital, Wash-
Grooms, Benjamin	....do....	43	Sept. 27, 1864	1 year.	
Hiatt, Irwin	....do....	18	Aug. 31, 1864	1 year.	
Hughes, James D	....do....	19	Sept. 24, 1864	1 year.	

Names.	Rank.	Age.	Date of Entering the Service.	Period of Service.	Remarks.
Jones, Thomas	Private	25	Sept. 8, 1864	1 year.	
Kappas, Paul	...do...	31	Sept. 3, 1864	1 year.	Mustered out with company July 12, 18
Kaufman, Edward	...do...	21	Oct. 3, 1864	1 year.	Mustered out with company July 12, 18
Keller, Charles F	...do...	20	Sept. 20, 1864	1 year.	Drafted; mustered out June 8, 1865, at N[illegible] bern, N. C., by order of War Department
Kibler, John	...do...	26	Sept. 19, 1864	1 year.	Drafted; mustered out with company July [illegible] 1865.
King, Francis J	...do...	27	Sept. 14, 1864	1 year.	Mustered out with company July 12, 18
Long, Conrad H	...do...	31	Sept. 18, 1864	1 year.	
Lo[illegible]z, George	...do...	24	Aug. 31, 1864	1 year.	Mustered out with company July 12, 18
McClay, James	...do...	21	Sept. 16, 1864	1 year.	
McKinsey, Joseph	...do...	26	Sept. 15, 1864	1 year.	
Mancraft, Henry	...do...	36	Aug. 31, 1864	1 year.	Mustered out with company July 12, 18
Marsley, William	...do...	24	Sept. 19, 1864	1 year.	Mustered out with company July 12, 18
Milliser, Jacob	...do...	18	Sept. 12, 1864	1 year.	Mustered out with company July 12, 18
Mills, Thompson	...do...	20	Sept. 22, 1864	1 year.	Mustered out June 27, 1865, at Columbus, by order of War Department.
Moffitt, John	...do...	18	Sept. 2, 1864	1 year.	Mustered out with company July 12, 18
O'Donnell, Michael	...do...	33	Sept. 3, 1864	1 year.	Mustered out with company July 12, 18
Oldham, Cumberland	...do...	39	Sept. 27, 1864	1 year.	
Ossot, Daniel	...do...	18	Sept. 10, 1864	1 year.	Mustered out with company July 12, 18
Owens, Gabriel	...do...	44	Oct. 1, 1864	1 year.	Drowned Nov. 14, 1864, in Ohio River, [illegible] en route from Cincinnati, O., to Lou[illegible], Kentucky.
Pfeifer, Matthias	...do...	41	Sept. 22, 1864	1 year.	Mustered out May 23, 1865, at Columbus, by order of War Department.
Phillips, Thomas	...do...	26	Sept. 18, 1864	1 year.	Drafted; mustered out with company [illegible] 1865.
Porter, James	...do...	24	Sept. 9, 1864	1 year.	
Post, Henry	...do...	30	Sept. 3, 1864	1 year.	Mustered out with company July 12, 18
Price, Levins	...do...	25	Sept. 17, 1864	1 year.	Drafted; mustered out with company July 1865.
Rader, John	...do...	19	Sept. 9, 1864	1 year.	
Randal, Joseph	...do...	20	Sept. 20, 1864	1 year.	
Reese, George	...do...	32	Sept. 10, 1864	1 year.	Mustered out with company July 12, 18
Richter, Caspar	...do...	37	Aug. 25, 1864	1 year.	Mustered out with company July 12, 18
Ritter, Henry	...do...	35	Sept. 27, 1864	1 year.	Mustered out with company July 12, 18
Savignay, Albert	...do...	22	Sept. 9, 1864	1 year.	
Sells, John	...do...	32	Sept. 17, 1864	1 year.	Drafted; mustered out with company July 1865.
Shafer, Hiram	...do...	18	Sept. 24, 1864	1 year.	Mustered out with company July 12, 18
Sheaf, Augustus	...do...	18	Oct. 6, 1864	1 year.	Mustered out with company July 12, 18
Sherk, John	...do...	25	Sept. 5, 1864	1 year.	Mustered out May 22, 1865, at Washington, [illegible] C., by order of War Department.
Smith, Albert	...do...	26	Sept. 9, 1864	1 year	
Stiner, Samuel	...do...	18	Oct. 4, 1864	1 year.	Mustered out with company July 12, 18
Troutman, Henry	...do...	19	Sept. 7, 1864	1 year	Mustered out with company July 12, 18
Van Horn, Simon	...do...	25	Sept. 12, 1864	1 year	Mustered out with company July 12, 18
Vestal, David	...do...	22	Sept. 26, 1864	1 year.	Mustered out with company July [illegible]
Vestal, James	...do...	26	Sept. 26, 1864	1 year.	Died Nov. 11, 1864, at Elk River Br[illegible]
Wagner, Frederick	...do...	28	Sept. 21, 1864	1 year.	Mustered out with company July 12, 18
Waltemiers, Martin	...do...	24	Sept. 24, 1864	1 year.	Appointed Corporal Oct. [illegible]; [illegible] May 15, 1865; mustered out with [illegible] July 12, 1865.
Wible, Charles	...do...	18	Sept. 14, 1864	1 year.	Mustered out May 29, 1865, at Camp [illegible] O., by order of War Department.
Wilkening, Henry	...do...	37	Sept. 3, 1864	1 year.	Mustered out with company July 12, 18
Williams, Martin	...do...	18	Sept. 10, 1864	1 year	
Williams, James	...do...	25	Sept. 9, 1864	1 year	
Wilson, Charles	...do...	22	Aug. 31, 1864	1 year	
Wolfert, Henry	...do...	43	Aug. 26, 1864	1 year.	Mustered out May 26, 1865, at Co[illegible] by order of War Department.
Worley, Andrew	...do...	33	Aug. 23, 1864	1 year	Mustered out with company July 12, 18
Wynn, Edward	...do...	20	Sept. 20, 1864	1 year	Drafted; mustered out with company J[illegible] 1865.

Names.	Rank.	Age.	Date of Entering the Service.	Period of Service.	Remarks.
John D. Wheeler	Sergeant.	31	Oct. 1, 1864	1 year.	...pointed Oct. 6, 1864; died March 15, 1865, at
John Downes	...do...	35	Aug. 21, 1864	1 year.	Appointed Corporal Oct. 6, 1864; Sergeant April 5, 1865; mustered out with company July 12, 1865.
Thomas A. Clark	...do...	33	Sept. 26, 1864	1 year.	Appointed Corporal Oct. 6, 1864; Sergeant July 1, 1865; mustered out with company July 12, 1865.
Russell J. F. Gwin	Corporal.	36	Oct. 1, 1864	1 year.	Appointed Oct. 6, 1864; mustered out with company July 12, 1865.
William F. Hoffman	...do...	26	Oct. 1, 1864	1 year.	Appointed Oct. 6, 1864; mustered out with company July 12, 1865.
Levi M. Stump	...do...	25	Sept. 5, 1864	1 year.	Appointed Oct. 6, 1864; mustered out with company July 12, 1865.
Charles M. Bassett	...do...	44	Aug. 25, 1864	1 year.	Appointed Oct. 6, 1864; mustered out July 7, 1865, at Columbus, O., by order of War Department.
Sebra J. Inlay	...do...	29	Oct. 1, 1864	1 year.	Appointed Oct. 6, 1864; mustered out June 9, 1865, at Washington, D. C., by order of War Department.
George W. Smalley	...do...	27	Sept. 17, 1864	1 year.	Appointed April 16, 1865; mustered out with company July 12, 1865.
Enos Terry	...do...	19	Sept. 28, 1864	1 year.	Appointed April 16, 1865; mustered out with company July 12, 1865.
James M. Nelson	...do...	26	Sept. 26, 1864	1 year.	Appointed July 1, 1865; mustered out with company July 12, 1865.
John M. Brown	...do...	18	Sept. 27, 1864	1 year.	Appointed July 1, 1865; mustered out with company July 12, 1865.
Almy, Benjamin	Private..	23	Aug. 18, 1864	1 year.	Mustered out with company July 12, 1865.
Armstrong, Henry	...do...	28	Sept. 16, 1864	1 year.	Mustered out with company July 12, 1865.
Bare, Benjamin	...do...	19	Sept. 29, 1864	1 year.	Mustered out July 7, 1865, at Columbus, O., by order of War Department.
Berlin, Peter Z	...do...	20	Sept. 26, 1864	1 year.	Mustered out with company July 12, 1865.
Birt, John	...do...	33	Sept. 29, 1864	1 year.	Died May 3, 1865, in Judiciary Square Hospital, Washington, D. C.
Bish, William	...do...	26	Sept. 29, 1864	1 year.	Mustered out with company July 12, 1865.
Blue, Samuel D	...do...	38	Sept. 26, 1864	1 year.	Mustered out with company July 12, 1865.
Bogart, James C	...do...	23	Sept. 30, 1864	1 year.	Mustered out with company July 12, 1865.
Brambie, Alfred	...do...	33	Sept. 27, 1864	1 year.	Mustered out with company July 12, 1865.
Brown, James H	...do...	20	Sept. 27, 1864	1 year.	Mustered out with company July 12, 1865.
Burris, James	...do...	25	Sept. 27, 1864	1 year.	
Butt, Simeon	...do...	34	Sept. 26, 1864	1 year.	
Clark, William	...do...	30	Sept. 30, 1864	1 year.	Mustered out June 7, 1865, at Washington, D. C., by order of War Department.
Corbin, Elisha	...do...	44	Sept. 29, 1864	1 year.	
Courtright, Richard	...do...	36	Sept. 28, 1864	1 year	Mustered out with company July 12, 1865.
Cox, Samuel S	...do...	34	Sept. 17, 1864	1 year.	Mustered out with company July 12, 1865.
Cummings, Alexander D	...do...	24	Aug. 21, 1864	1 year.	
Cunningham, Andrew J.	...do...	27	Sept. 16, 1864	1 year.	Mustered out with company July 12, 1865.
Davis, Isaac H	...do...	19	Sept. 29, 1864	1 year.	Mustered out with company July 12, 1865.
Davis, Thomas P	...do...	19	Sept. 29, 1864	1 year.	Mustered out with company July 12, 1865.
Didine, William	...do...	35	Sept. 17, 1864	1 year.	Mustered out with company July 12, 1865.
Dorland, Joseph	...do...	24	Sept. 2, 1864	1 year.	Mustered out with company July 12, 1865.
Drushel, Martin	...do...	28	Sept. 27, 1864	1 year.	Mustered out with company July 12, 1865.
Eshelman, Francis	...do...	25	Oct. 3, 1864	1 year.	Died March 29, 1865, at Kinston, N. C.
Fox, George W	...do...	19	Sept. 27, 1864	1 year.	Mustered out with company July 12, 1865.
France, John C	...do...	18	Sept. 27, 1864	1 year.	Mustered out with company July 12, 1865.
Gordon, John O	...do...	25	Sept. 28, 1864	1 year.	Mustered out with company July 12, 1865.
Green, George	...do...	24	Sept. 6, 1864	1 year.	
Hall, Joseph	...do...	36	Sept. 27, 1864	1 year.	Mustered out July 1, 1865, at David's Island, New York Harbor, by order of War Department.
Hanna, Alexander	...do...	37	Aug. 14, 1864	1 year.	Mustered out with company July 12, 1865.
Harris, John D	...do...	31	Sept. 28, 1864	1 year.	
Heistand, Michael	...do...	29	Oct. 1, 1864	1 year.	Mustered out June 10, 1865, at David's Island, New York Harbor, by order of War Department.
Henbarger, Jacob	...do...	28	Oct. 1, 1864	1 year.	Mustered out with company July 12, 1865.
Hendon, Abraham	...do...	24	Sept. 28, 1864	1 year.	
Hine, George W	...do...	37	Aug. 19, 1864	1 year.	Mustered out with company July 12, 1865.
Hine, James P	...do...	19	Sept. 3, 1864	1 year.	
Hunt, Hiram	...do...	38	Sept. 27, 1864	1 year	Mustered out with company July 12, 1865.
Jackson, Heston	...do...	38	Sept. 29, 1864	1 year.	Mustered out with company July 12, 1865.
Jacobs, Jacob	...do...	25	Sept. 30, 1864	1 year.	Mustered out with company July 12, 1865.
Jones, Timothy P	...do...	43	Sept. 28, 1864	1 year	Appointed Corporal Oct. 6, 1864; reduced April 6, 1865; mustered out with company July 12, 1865.
Kachely, Simeon	...do...	38	Sept. 26, 1864	1 year.	Mustered out with company July 12, 1865.
Kidney, John	...do...	19	Oct. 1, 1864	1 year.	Died March 5, 1865, at Washington, D. C.
Liles, Plimpton J	...do...	18	Oct. 3, 1864	1 year.	Mustered out with company July 12, 1865.
Longwith, James H	...do...	40	Jan. 28, 1865	1 year.	Mustered out with company July 12, 1865.
McClain, Jonathan	...do...	45	Sept. 27, 1864	1 year.	Died Feb. 12, 1865, at Washington, D. C.
McDowell, Oliver	...do...	18	Sept. 30, 1864	1 year.	Discharged June 6, 1865, at Washington, D. C., on Surgeon's certificate of disability.
McKinzie, William	...do...	22	Sept. 29, 1864	1 year.	Mustered out with company July 12, 1865.
Miller, German	...do...	30	Oct. 1, 1864	1 year.	Mustered out with company July 12, 1865.

Names.	Rank.	Age.	Date of Entering the Service.	Period of Service.	Remarks.
Jacobus, Josiah G	Private	18	Sept. 29, 1864	1 year.	Mustered out with company July 12, 1865.
Keck, Isaac	...do...	38	Sept. 15, 1864	1 year.	Mustered out with company July 12, 1865.
Keller, Charles F	...do...	26	Sept. 22, 1864	1 year.	Mustered out with company July 12, 1865.
Kelley, Waldo	...do...	31	Sept. 22, 1864	1 year.	Mustered out with company July 12, 1865.
Kidwell, Thomas	...do...	18	Oct. 3, 1864	1 year.	Mustered out June 27, 1865, at Columbus, O., by order of War Department.
Kile, Adam	...do...	43	Sept. 13, 1864	1 year.	Mustered out with company July 12, 1865.
Lamb, Patrick	...do...	29	Sept. 13, 1864	1 year.	Transferred to Veteran Reserve Corps March 14, 1865.
Lattimore, Lewis	...do...	23	Sept. 3, 1864	1 year.	Mustered out with company July 12, 1865.
Lay, John	...do...	21	Sept. 21, 1864	1 year.	Died March 24, 1865, at Newbern, N. C.
Leamons, John	...do...	37	Sept. 26, 1864	1 year.	Mustered out with company July 12, 1865.
Limes, John	...do...	18	Sept. 11, 1864	1 year.	Mustered out May 28, 1865, at Washington, D. C., by order of War Department.
Link, Conrad	...do...	20	Sept. 16, 1864	1 year.	Mustered out with company July 12, 1865.
Lowery, John	...do...	28	Sept. 24, 1864	1 year.	Mustered out with company July 12, 1865.
Lowery, Laban D	...do...	26	Sept. 16, 1864	1 year.	Mustered out with company July 12, 1865.
Lunceford, John J	...do...	25	Sept. 30, 1864	1 year.	Mustered out with company July 12, 1865.
Maupin, James N	...do...	20	Sept. 26, 1864	1 year.	Mustered out with company July 12, 1865.
Messick, John W	...do...	19	Sept. 29, 1864	1 year.	Promoted to Sergt. Major Oct. 20, 1864; reduced March 24, 1865; mustered out with company July 12, 1865.
Milks, Jay	...do...	21	Sept. 13, 1864	1 year.	
Moles, Charles	...do...	19	Sept. 22, 1864	1 year.	Mustered out with company July 12, 1865.
Morris, Amos	...do...	25	Sept. 24, 1864	1 year.	Mustered out May 10, 1865, at Columbus, O., by order of War Department.
Morris, William H	...do...	36	Sept. 26, 1864	1 year.	
Morse, Jerome B	...do...	18	Sept. 19, 1864	1 year.	Died June 22, 1865, at Charlotte, N. C.
Neeb, Jacob	...do...	34	Sept. 9, 1864	1 year.	Mustered out with company July 12, 1865.
Newbold, Peter	...do...	33	Sept. 3, 1864	1 year.	Mustered out July 1, 1865, at Columbus, O., by order of War Department.
Nice, Jacob	...do...	32	Sept. 22, 1864	1 year.	Mustered out with company July 12, 1865.
Nice, Michael	...do...	34	Sept. 20, 1864	1 year.	Mustered out with company July 12, 1865.
Nuchols, Andrew M	...do...	19	Sept. 26, 1864	1 year.	Mustered out June 10, 1865, at David's Island, New York Harbor, by order of War Department.
O'Harra, William H	...do...	18	Sept. 29, 1864	1 year.	Mustered out with company July 12, 1865.
Place, William H	...do...	22	Sept. 28, 1864	1 year.	Mustered out with company July 12, 1865.
Raths, Henry C	...do...	29	Sept. 21, 1864	1 year.	Mustered out with company July 12, 1865.
Roach, George	...do...	19	Sept. 12, 1864	1 year.	Mustered out with company July 12, 1865.
Shaw, Henry H	...do...	39	Oct. 1, 1864	1 year.	Promoted to Asst. Surgeon 184th O. V. I. Feb. 21, 1865.
Spousler, Winfield	...do...	23	Sept. 17, 1864	1 year.	Mustered out with company July 12, 1865.
Stephenson, John W	...do...	32	Sept. 21, 1864	1 year.	Mustered out with company July 12, 1865.
Stewart, James B	...do...	29	Sept. 17, 1864	1 year.	Mustered out with company July 12, 1865.
Ulen, Hamilton	...do...	17	Sept. 26, 1864	1 year.	Mustered out with company July 12, 1865.
Wallace, Joseph	...do...	18	Aug. 15, 1864	1 year.	Mustered out with company July 12, 1865.
Weddle, Winfield S	...do...	18	Sept. 3, 1864	1 year.	Mustered out June 8, 1865, at Newbern, N. C., by order of War Department.
Widdefield, Henry	...do...	44	Sept. 17, 1864	1 year.	Mustered out with company July 12, 1865.
Williams, John	...do...	18	Aug. 20, 1864	1 year.	Mustered out with company July 12, 1865.
Williams, Manuel L	...do...	18	Aug. 25, 1864	1 year.	Mustered out June 20, 1865, at Washington D. C., by order of War Department.
Wright, Nathaniel	...do...	29	Sept. 23, 1864	1 year.	Absent since Sept. 24, 1864, at Tod Barracks, Columbus, O. No further record found.
Zeilenger, John	...do...	35	Sept. 24, 1864	1 year.	Mustered out with company July 12, 1865.

COMPANY K.

Mustered in October 6, 1864, at Camp Chase, O., by W. P. Richardson, Colonel 25th O. V. I. Mustered out July 12, 1865, at Charlotte, N. C., by T. M. Ward, 1st Lieutenant 25th M. V. I. and A. C. M., 1st Division, 23d Army Corps.

Names.	Rank.	Age.	Date of Entering the Service.	Period of Service.	Remarks.
John N. Cunningham	Captain.	28	Oct. 6, 1864	1 year.	Mustered out with company July 12, 1865.
William A. Potter	1st Lieut.	22	Oct. 29, 1861	3 yrs.	Promoted from private Co. A, 82d O. V. I., Oct. 6, 1864; mustered out with company July 12, 1865.
William M. Cook	2d Lieut.	21	Oct. 6, 1864	1 year.	Died Jan. 7, 1865, at Murfreesboro, Tenn.
Samuel O. Ridenour	...do...	30	Sept. 23, 1864	1 year.	Promoted from 1st Sergeant Co. A Jan. 18, 1865; discharged June 6, 1865, on Surgeon's certificate of disability.
Samuel G. Liles	1st Sergt.	21	Sept. 26, 1864	1 year.	Appointed Oct. 6, 1864; promoted to 2d Lieutenant July 1, 1865, but not mustered; mustered out with company July 12, 1865.
James A. Simpson	Sergeant.	31	Oct. 1, 1864	1 year.	Appointed Oct. 6, 1864; mustered out June 19, 1865, at Beaufort, N. C.
James E. Hueston	...do...	20	Sept. 26, 1864	1 year.	Appointed Oct. 6, 1864; mustered out with company July 12, 1865.
Adam McClurg	...do...	27	Sept. 23, 1864	1 year.	Appointed Oct. 6, 1864; died June 16, 1865, a Charlotte, N. C.

Period of Service.	Remarks.
1 year.	Appointed Oct. 6, 1864; died March 15, 1865, at Newbern, N. C.
1 year.	Appointed Corporal Oct 6, 1864; Sergeant April 5, 1865; mustered out with company July 12, 1865.
1 year.	Appointed Corporal Oct. 6, 1864; Sergeant July 1, 1865; mustered out with company July 12, 1865.
1 year.	Appointed Oct. 6, 1864; mustered out with company July 12, 1865.
1 year.	Appointed Oct. 6, 1864; mustered out with company July 12, 1865.
1 year.	Appointed Oct. 6, 1864; mustered out with company July 12, 1865.
1 year.	Appointed Oct. 6, 1864; mustered out July 7, 1865, at Columbus, O., by order of War Department.
1 year.	Appointed Oct. 6, 1864; mustered out June 9, 1865, at Washington, D. C., by order of War Department.
1 year.	Appointed April 16, 1865; mustered out with company July 12, 1865.
1 year.	Appointed April 16, 1865; mustered out with company July 12, 1865.
1 year.	Appointed July 1, 1865; mustered out with company July 12, 1865.
1 year.	Appointed July 1, 1865; mustered out with company July 12, 1865.
1 year.	Mustered out with company July 12, 1865.
1 year.	Mustered out with company July 12, 1865.
1 year.	Mustered out July 7, 1865, at Columbus, O., by order of War Department.
1 year.	Mustered out with company July 12, 1865.
1 year.	Died May 3, 1865, in Judiciary Square Hospital, Washington, D. C.
1 year.	Mustered out with company July 12, 1865.
1 year.	Mustered out with company July 12, 1865.
1 year.	Mustered out with company July 12, 1865.
1 year.	Mustered out with company July 12, 1865.
1 year.	Mustered out with company July 12, 1865.
1 year.	
1 year.	
1 year.	Mustered out June 7, 1865, at Washington, D. C., by order of War Department.
1 year.	
1 year.	Mustered out with company July 12, 1865.
1 year.	Mustered out with company July 12, 1865.
1 year.	
1 year.	Mustered out with company July 12, 1865.
1 year.	Mustered out with company July 12, 1865.
1 year.	Mustered out with company July 12, 1865.
1 year.	Mustered out with company July 12, 1865.
1 year.	Mustered out with company July 12, 1865.
1 year.	Mustered out with company July 12, 1865.
1 year.	Died March 20, 1865, at Kinston, N. C.
1 year.	Mustered out with company July 12, 1865.
1 year.	Mustered out with company July 12, 1865.
1 year.	Mustered out with company July 12, 1865.
1 year.	
1 year.	Mustered out July 1, 1865, at David's Island, New York Harbor, by order of War Department.
1 year.	Mustered out with company July 12, 1865.
1 year.	
1 year.	Mustered out June 10, 1865, at David's Island, New York Harbor, by order of War Department.
1 year.	Mustered out with company July 12, 1865.
1 year.	
1 year.	Mustered out with company July 12, 1865.
1 year.	
1 year.	Mustered out with company July 12, 1865.
1 year.	Mustered out with company July 12, 1865.
1 year.	Mustered out with company July 12, 1865.
1 year.	Appointed Corporal Oct. 6, 1864; reduced April 6, 1865; mustered out with company July 12, 1865.
1 year.	Mustered out with company July 12, 1865.
1 year.	Died March 5, 1865, at Washington, D. C.
1 year.	Mustered out with company July 12, 1865.
1 year.	Mustered out with company July 12, 1865.
1 year.	Died Feb. 12, 1865, at Washington, D. C.
1 year.	Discharged June 6, 1865, at Washington, D. C., on Surgeon's certificate of disability.
1 year.	Mustered out with company July 12, 1865.
1 year.	Mustered out with company July 12, 1865.

Names.	Rank.	Age.	Date of Entering the Service.	Period of Service.	Remarks.
Miller, John	Private	30	Sept. 6, 1864	year.	Mustered out with company July 12, 1865.
Miller, John H	...do...	20	Aug. 10, 1864	year.	Mustered out with company July 12, 1865.
Moore, Samuel E	...do...	18	Sept. 26, 1864	year.	Mustered out with company July 12, 1865.
Moore, William H	...do...	34	Sept. 28, 1864	year.	Mustered out with company July 12, 1865.
Morris, Thomas F	...do...	36	Sept. 26, 1864	year.	Died Nov. 20, 1864, at Decherd, Tenn.
Mullencoph, Isaac	...do...	38	Oct. 3, 1864	year.	
Nickason, George W	...do...	19	Sept. 30, 1864	year.	Mustered out with company July 12, 1865.
Norris, Nathaniel	...do...	29	Sept. 29, 1864	year.	Mustered out with company July 12, 1865.
Nowlan, Elihu T	...do...	19	Sept. 29, 1864	year.	Mustered out with company July 12, 1865.
Oglesbee, David	...do...	33	Sept. 28, 1864	year.	See Co. K, 183d O. V. I.
Opp, Jacob	...do...	30	Sept. 26, 1864	1 year.	Mustered out with company July 12, 1865.
Park, Charles A	...do...	29	Aug. 21, 1864	1 year.	Mustered out with company July 12, 1865.
Peterson, John G	...do...	38	Sept. 30, 1864	1 year.	Mustered out with company July 12, 1865.
Pierce, Rinaldo	...do...	33	Sept. 28, 1864	1 year.	
Powell, Elijah	...do...	18	Sept. 30, 1864	1 year.	Died Feb. 14, 1865, at Washington, D. C.
Rauch, George	...do...	37	Sept. 26, 1864	1 year.	Mustered out with company July 12, 1865.
Robinson, John	...do...	44	Sept. 5, 1864	1 year.	Mustered out with company July 12, 1865.
Roby, William J	...do...	21	Aug. 10, 1864	1 year.	Mustered out with company July 12, 1865.
Sear, Josiah W	...do...	26	Sept. 27, 1864	1 year.	Mustered out May 29, 1865, at New York, N. Y., by order of War Department.
Shewell, Benjamin F	...do...	39	Sept. 4, 1864	1 year.	Mustered out June 7, 1865, at Washington, D. C., by order of War Department.
Shirkey, Michael	...do...	32	Sept. 28, 1864	1 year.	Mustered out with company July 12, 1865.
Shortell, Richard	...do...	40	Sept. 24, 1864	1 year.	Mustered out with company July 12, 1865.
Simons, John C	...do...	26	Sept. 30, 1864	1 year.	Mustered out June 1, 1865, at David's Island, New York Harbor, by order of War Department.
Spear, James W	...do...	27	Sept. 26, 1864	1 year.	Mustered out with company July 12, 1865.
Terry, Lukens	...do...	18	Sept. 17, 1864	1 year.	Mustered out with company July 12, 1865.
Truitt, Isaac	...do...	39	Sept. 30, 1864	1 year.	Mustered out to date July 12, 1865, by order of War Department.
Warden, James M	...do...	29	Sept. 26, 1864	1 year.	
Warner, Calvin E	...do...	27	Aug. 11, 1864	1 year.	Mustered out with company July 12, 1865.
Watson, John M	...do...	18	Sept. 27, 1864	1 year.	Mustered out with company July 12, 1865.
White, Thomas M	...do...	28	Sept. 26, 1864	1 year.	Mustered out June 19, 1865, at Columbus, O., by order of War Department.
Wright, Jonathan	...do...	21	Sept. 24, 1864	1 year.	

UNASSIGNED RECRUITS.

NOTE.—The following list of recruits is found on muster and descriptive rolls for this organization, but not borne on any of the company rolls of the Regiment:

Names.	Rank.	Age.	Date of Entering the Service.	Period of Service.	Remarks.
Albert, Jacob	Private.	18	Oct. 26, 1864	1 year.	
Burgess, Joseph E	...do...	22	Sept. 28, 1864	1 year.	
Chamberlain, Abraham	...do...	19	Oct. 7, 1864	1 year.	
Clark, Henry S	...do...	..	Oct. 10, 1864	1 year.	
Ford, Jackson	...do...	18	Oct. 10, 1864	1 year.	
Hager, John R	...do...	28	Oct. 4, 1864	1 year.	
Hedrick, Charles E	...do...	19	Sept. 16, 1864	1 year.	
Hutchison, John R	...do...	30	Oct. 12, 1864	1 year.	
Kennedy, Adam	...do...	18	Oct. 1, 1864	1 year.	
Nolan, George	...do...	24	Sept. 16, 1864	1 year.	
Perry, George	...do...	22	Sept. 15, 1864	1 year.	
Rider, Charles	...do...	18	Oct. 10, 1864	1 year.	
Robichaud, Joseph	...do...	22	Aug. 18, 1864	1 year.	
Smith, Frederick L	...do...	27	April 5, 1865	1 year.	Mustered out May 15, 1865, at Hart's Island, New York Harbor, by order of War Department.
Swagger, Taylor	...do...	20	Oct. 8, 1864	1 year.	
Taylor, Thomas	...do...	18	April 5, 1865	1 year.	Mustered out May 15, 1865, at Hart's Island, New York Harbor, by order of War Department.
Wilcox, Benjamin F	...do...	30	Sept. 13, 1864	1 year.	

181st Regiment Ohio Volunteer Infantry.

ONE YEAR'S SERVICE.

THIS Regiment was organized at Camp Dennison, O., from September 29 to October 10, 1864, to serve one year. On the 24th of October the Regiment was ordered to Huntsville, Ala., where it arrived on the 29th. In November the Regiment operated around Decatur, Ala. Evacuating Decatur, the Regiment went by rail to Murfreesboro, Tenn. In December the Regiment took part with other troops in repelling an attack on Murfreesboro by the Rebel General Forest, in which several men were wounded. The greater part of December was spent in foraging around Murfreesboro. In these expeditions the Regiment was frequently engaged with the enemy. On the 24th of December the Regiment was assigned to the Third Brigade, Second Division, Twenty-Third Army Corps, and joined its command at Columbia, Tenn., on the 29th of December. On the 2d of January it was taken to Goldsboro, N. C., where it joined Sherman's Army. In April the One Hundred and Eighty-first joined in the advance on Raleigh, N. C. The Regiment was mustered out July 14, 1865, in accordance with orders from the War Department.

181st REGIMENT OHIO VOLUNTEER INFANTRY.

FIELD AND STAFF.

Mustered in October 10, 1864, at Camp Dennison, O., by Lieutenant Warren and others. Mustered out July 14, 1865, at Salisbury, N. C., by Frederick Anderson, Lieutenant and A. C. M.

Names.	Rank.	Age.	Date of Entering the Service.	Period of Service.	Remarks.
John O'Dowd	Colonel.	35	Oct. 6, 1864	1 year.	Promoted from Captain Co. D Oct. 15, 1864; resigned May 27, 1865.
John E. Hudson	....do....	27	Oct. 4, 1864	1 year.	Promoted to Lieut. Colonel from Captain Co. C Oct. 15, 1864; Colonel June 16, 1865; mustered out with regiment July 14, 1865.
James T. Hickey	Lt. Col.	26	Oct. 13, 1864	1 year.	Promoted to Major from Captain Co. K Oct. 18, 1864; Lieut. Colonel June 16, 1865; mustered out with regiment July 14, 1865.
Solomon B. Wolff	Surgeon.	22	Oct. 14, 1864	1 year.	Mustered out with regiment July 14, 1865.
Alfred Force	Ast. Surg.	42	Oct. 14, 1864	1 year.	Mustered out with regiment July 14, 1865.
Oliver C. McCarty	....do....	50	Oct. 27, 1864	1 year.	Mustered out with regiment July 14, 1865.
Frederick Anderson	Adjutant	..	Oct. 15, 1864	1 year.	Brevet Captain July 31, 1865; mustered out Aug. 1, 1865, by Special Order No. 418.
Herman Rempel	R. Q. M.	47	Sept. 29, 1864	1 year.	Appointed from 1st Lieutenant Co. B Sept. 30, 1864; discharged May 8, 1865.
Frederick Hoeller	....do....	21	Oct. 7, 1864	1 year.	Appointed from 1st Lieutenant Co. H to date May 1, 1865; mustered out with regiment July 14, 1865.
James M. Brown	Chaplain	40	Sept. 26, 1864	1 year.	Promoted from Sergeant Co. A April 11, 1865; resigned July 18, 1865.
John Leonard	Ser. Maj.	41	Sept. 19, 1864	1 year.	Promoted from Sergeant Co. G Oct. 18, 1864; returned to Co. Nov. 30, 1864.
Benjamin F. Heath	....do....	21	Sept. 14, 1864	1 year.	Promoted from Sergeant Co. E Nov. 30, 1864; to 1st Lieutenant July 10, 1865, but not mustered; mustered out with regiment July 14, 1865.
Thomas W. Wright	Q. M. S.	39	Sept. 21, 1864	1 year.	Promoted from private Co. B Oct. 18, 1864; returned to company Feb. 7, 1865.
David R. McCracken	....do....	31	Sept. 6, 1864	1 year.	Promoted from private Co. K Feb. 7, 1865; returned to company May 13, 1865.
Richard Norton	....do....	19	Sept. 19, 1864	1 year.	Promoted from Sergeant Co. C May 13, 1865; mustered out with regiment July 14, 1865.
David T. Snellbaker	Com. Ser.	22	Sept. 21, 1864	1 year.	Promoted from Corporal Co. B Oct. 18, 1864; returned to company Jan. 6, 1865.
John Sheridan	....do....	21	Sept. 19, 1864	1 year.	Promoted from Sergeant Co. D Jan. 6, 1865; returned to company Feb. 1, 1865.
Lucian W. McKee	....do....	18	Sept. 6, 1864	1 year.	Promoted from Sergeant Co. E Feb. 1, 1865; to 2d Lieutenant July 10, 1865, but not mustered; mustered out with regiment July 14, 1865.
John W. Toskay	Hos. St'd.	22	Sept. 7, 1864	1 year.	Promoted from private Co. E Oct. 18, 1864; returned to company Dec. 3, 1864.
James W. Criswell	....do....	34	Sept. 29, 1864	1 year.	Promoted from private Co. G Dec. 3, 1864; mustered out June 1, 1865, at David's Island, New York Harbor, by order of War Department.
Charles Fahr	....do....	30	Sept. 21, 1864	1 year.	Promoted from private Co. B to date June 1, 1865; mustered out with regiment July 14, 1865.
George Anchor	Prin. Mus	26	Aug. 23, 1864	1 year.	Promoted from Corporal Co. A Oct. 18, 1864; mustered out with regiment July 14, 1865.
John Macklen	....do....	26	Sept. 8, 1864	1 year.	Promoted from private Co. C Oct. 18, 1864; discharged Jan. 17, 1865, at Madison, Ind., on Surgeon's certificate of disability.
[illegible]	....do....	18	Sept. 16, 1864	1 year.	Promoted from Musician Co. B Jan. 5, 1865; returned to company Feb. 1, 1865.
William H. Webber	....do....	21	Sept. 29, 1864	1 year.	Promoted from Musician Co. D Feb. 1, 1865; mustered out with regiment July 14, 1865.

COMPANY A.

Mustered in September 29, 1864, at Camp Dennison, O., by Wm. Von Doehn, Captain and A. A. G. [illegible] out July 14, 1865, at Salisbury, N. C., by Frederick Anderson, Lieutenant and A. C. M.

Names.	Rank.	Age.	Date of Entering the Service.	Period of Service.	Remarks.
Ferdinand McDonough	Captain.	26	Sept. 29, 1864	1 year.	Resigned March 24, 1865.
Leonidas H. Pummill	....do...	21	Sept. 29, 1864	1 year.	Promoted from 1st Lieutenant April [illegible]; in command of company since March [illegible]; mustered out with company July 14, [illegible]
Charles H. Weaver	1st Lieut.	20	Sept. 29, 1864	1 year.	Promoted from 2d Lieutenant April [illegible]; Acting Adjutant since March 24, 1865; mustered out with company July 14, 1865.
John T. Cramer	2d Lieut.	26	Sept. 17, 1864	1 year.	Transferred from Co. C, 177th O. V. I., June [illegible], 1865; on detached duty as A. A. D. C. [illegible] Brigade, 2d Division, 23d Army Corps, June 28, 1865; mustered out with company July 14, 1865.
Nathan F. M. Wheeler	1st Sergt.	24	Sept. 22, 1864	1 year.	Mustered as private; appointed 1st Sergeant May 10, 1865; mustered out with company July 14, 1865.
John W. Durbin	Sergeant.	31	Aug. 30, 1864	1 year.	Appointed Sept. 29, 1864; promoted to [illegible] Lieutenant Co. B, 183d O. V. I., Oct. [illegible]
Eden B. Reeder	....do....	26	Sept. 24, 1864	1 year.	Appointed Sept. 29, 1864; promoted to [illegible] Lieutenant Co. F, 183d O. V. I., Oct. [illegible]
Joe P. Smith	....do....	23	Sept. 7, 1864	1 year.	Appointed 1st Sergeant Sept. 27, 1864; reduced to Sergeant March 1, 1865; mustered out June 27, 1865, at Columbus, O., by order of War Department.
August Wrede	... do....	34	Aug. 29, 1864	3 yrs.	Appointed Sept. 29, 1864; mustered out [illegible] 31, 1865, at Beaufort, N. C., by order of War Department.
James M. Brown	....do....	40	Sept. 26, 1864	1 year.	Appointed Corporal Sept. 29, 1864; Sergeant — ; promoted to Chaplain April 11, [illegible]
Samuel S. Stratton	....do....	34	Mch. 22, 1865	1 year.	Appointed June 1, 1865; mustered out with company July 14, 1865.
George W. McLarty	....do....	19	Aug. 31, 1864	3 yrs.	Appointed June 1, 1865; mustered out with company July 14, 1865.
John G. Brown	....do....	33	Aug. 18, 1864	3 yrs.	Appointed Corporal Sept. 29, 1864; Sergeant June 1, 1865; mustered out with company July 14, 1865.
James K. Campbell	Corporal.	18	Sept. 15, 1864	1 year.	Appointed Sept. 29, 1864, mustered out [illegible] 30, 1865, at Columbus, O., by order of War Department
George Anchor	....do....	26	Aug. 23, 1864	1 year.	Appointed Sept. 29, 1864; promoted to Principal Musician Oct. 18, 1864.
Samuel Yoxon	....do....	19	Sept. 15, 1864	1 year.	Appointed Sept. 29, 1864; killed Nov. [illegible] in railroad accident at Stevens Gap [illegible]
Robert W. Minton	....do....	19	Sept. 15, 1864	1 year	Appointed Jan. 1, 1865; died March [illegible] at Newbern, N. C.
George N. Gale	....do....	20	Sept. 16, 1864	1 year.	Appointed Sept. 29, 1864; mustered out with company July 14, 1865.
William T. McCoy	....do....	18	Sept. 5, 1864	1 year.	Appointed Jan. 1, 1865; mustered out with company July 14, 1865.
John T. Sharp	....do....	30	Sept. 26, 1864	1 year.	Appointed Jan. 1, 1865; mustered out with company July 14, 1865.
John Scherer	....do....	21	Oct. 10, 1864	1 year	Appointed June 1, 1865; mustered out with company July 14, 1865.
John Wagner	....do....	20	Mch. 9, 1865	1 year.	Appointed June 1, 1865; mustered out with company July 14, 1865.
Luther Morton	....do....	38	Oct. 3, 1864	1 year.	Transferred from Co. I, 177th O. V. I., June [illegible] 1865; mustered out with company July [illegible] 1865.
Emil Schaerges	Musician	17	Sept. 5, 1864	1 year.	Mustered out with company July 14, 1865.
Horace Upson	....do....	18	Aug. 12, 1864	2 yrs.	Substitute; transferred from Co. B, [illegible] O. V. I., June 15, 1865; mustered out with company July 14, 1865.
William Sholand	Wagoner.	28	Sept. 24, 1864	1 year.	Mustered out with company July 14, 1865.
Anschler, Frank	Private..	18	Sept. 8, 1864	1 year.	Mustered out with company July 14, 1865.
Bailey, Joseph	....do....	20	Sept. 27, 1864	1 year.	Mustered out June 22, 1865, at Cleveland, by order of War Department.
Baker, John R.	....do....	31	Aug. 25, 1864	1 year.	See Co. I, 177th O. V. I.
Baldock, John	....do....	18	Sept. 26, 1864	1 year.	Mustered out with company July 14, 1865.
Barron, Thomas	....do....	34	Aug. 14, 1864	1 year.	Mustered out with company July 14, 1865.
Bingham, John	....do....	31	Oct. 4, 1864	1 year.	Transferred from Co. A, 177th O. V. I., June [illegible] 1865; mustered out with company July [illegible] 1865.
Bowman, Charles	....do....	21	Sept. 24, 1864	1 year.	
Brecken, Thomas P.	....do....	21	Aug. 21, 1864	1 year.	Mustered out with company July 14, 1865.
Brindley, Reynolds	....do....	19	Oct. 3, 1864	1 year.	Transferred from Co. H, 177th O. V. I., June [illegible] 1865; mustered out with company July [illegible] 1865.

Names.	Rank.	Age.	Date of Entering the Service.	Period of Service.	Remarks.
Brunson, Richard A	Private	18	Sept. 2, 1864	1 year.	Mustered out with company July 14, 1865.
Caiar, Andrew	do	22	Sept. 24, 1864	1 year.	Mustered out with company July 14, 1865.
Carson, Albert	do	20	Sept. 9, 1864	1 year.	
Case, Thomas	do	34	Feb. 24, 1865	1 year.	Transferred from Co. D, 177th O. V. I., June 15, 1865; mustered out with company July 14, 1865.
Chahill, Patrick	do	18	Sept. 23, 1864	1 year.	Mustered out with company July 14, 1865.
Chain, Samuel	do	38	Sept. 26, 1864	1 year.	Mustered out June 19, 1865, at Chester, Pa., by order of War Department.
Cluchom, John	do	24	Aug. 31, 1864	1 year.	Mustered out with company July 14, 1865.
Clewers, Robert E. G	do	36	Sept. 26, 1864	1 year.	Mustered out with company July 14, 1865.
Collier, William	do	22	Sept. 22, 1864	1 year.	
Colvin, John W	do	22	Sept. 22, 1864	1 year.	Mustered out with company July 14, 1865.
Cooley, George W	do	22	Feb. 11, 1865	1 year.	Transferred from Co. A, 177th O. V. I., June 15, 1865; mustered out with company July 14, 1865.
Cotton, Lewis	do	29	Sept. 26, 1864	1 year.	Mustered out with company July 14, 1865.
Criddle, Robert F	do	29	Aug. 11, 1864	1 year.	Transferred from Co. C, 177th O. V. I., June 15, 1865; mustered out with company July 14, 1865.
Cropper, Thomas B	do	34	Sept. 26, 1864	1 year.	Mustered out June 5, 1865, at David's Island, New York Harbor, by order of War Department.
Dalton, James	do	22	Sept. 26, 1864	1 year.	
Daugherty, James	do	19	Sept. 27, 1864	1 year.	Mustered as Corporal; mustered out with company July 14, 1865.
Dixon, Henfy	do	22	Sept. 21, 1864	1 year.	Mustered out May 29, 1865, at David's Island, New York Harbor, by order of War Department.
Edmonds, John	do	29	Sept. 23, 1864	1 year	
Eikbush, Frederick H	do	41	Sept. 22, 1864	1 year.	Discharged April 17, 1865, at Camp Dennison, O., on Surgeon's certificate of disability.
Elble, Charles W	do	26	Sept. 22, 1864	1 year.	
Elble, Frank	do	18	Sept. 8, 1864	1 year.	Mustered out to date July 14, 1865, by order of War Department.
Faux, Martin V	do	32	Oct. 4, 1864	1 year	Transferred from Co. I, 177th O. V. I., June 15, 1865; mustered out with company July 14, 1865.
Fisher, Robert M	do	18	Sept. 27, 1864	1 year.	Mustered out with company July 14, 1865.
Frazier, Charles W	do	23	Sept. 22, 1864	1 year.	
Freeborn, George	do	19	Sept. 26, 1864	1 year.	
Gerdes, Altman W	do	26	Sept. 24, 1864	1 year.	Mustered out with company July 14, 1865.
Goodrich, Rollin C	do	18	Sept. 27, 1864	1 year.	Died March 21, 1865, at Jeffersonville, Ind.
Grant, Charles W	do	18	Oct. 12, 1864	1 year.	Transferred from Co. E, 177th O. V. I., June 15, 1865; mustered out with company July 14, 1865.
Harris, Daniel	do	34	Sept. 22, 1864	1 year.	Discharged Dec. 3, 1864, on Surgeon's certificate of disability.
Higgins, Elisha	do	20	Feb. 15, 1865	1 year	Transferred from Co. B, 177th O. V. I., June 15, 1865; mustered out with company July 14, 1865.
Holland, George	do	19	Sept. 21, 1864	1 year	Mustered out with company July 14, 1865.
Hudnall, Russell K	do	18	Sept. 16, 1864	1 year.	Mustered out with company July 14, 1865.
Huff, Henry	do	29	Sept. 23, 1864	1 year.	
Jacobs, Henry	do	24	Sept. 14, 1864	1 year.	
Jenkins, William	do	44	Oct. [illegible], 1864	1 year.	Transferred from Co. B, 177th O. V. I., June 15, 1865; mustered out with company July 14, 1865.
Johnson, Charles	do	19	Sept. 26, 1864	1 year.	
Johnston, Clay	do	22	Aug. 31, 1864	1 year.	Appointed Corporal Jan. 1, 1865; reduced June 1, 1865; mustered out with company July 14, 1865.
Jones, Edgar	do	26	Sept. 13, 1864	1 year.	Mustered out May 31, 1865, at Cleveland, O., by order of War Department.
Karshner, Loammi	do	34	Sept. 24, 1864	1 year.	Mustere[illegible] out with company July 14, 1865.
Kelly, Amos	do	37	Sept. 26, 1864	1 year.	Mustered out May 26, 1865, at Wilmington, N. C., by order of War Department.
Kelly, Thomas	do	20	Sept. 21, 1864	1 year.	
Kernes, Zephaniah	do	18	Sept. 16, 1864	1 year.	Mustered out with company July 14, 1865.
Kirby, George	do	21	Sept. 22, 1864	1 year.	
Knox, Alanson	do	25	Aug. 25, 1864	1 year.	Transferred from Co. I, 177th O. V. I., June 15, 1865; mustered out with company July 14, 1865.
Koch, Eli	do	38	Sept. 21, 1864	1 year.	Mustered out with company July 14, 1865.
Lafner, Henry	do	18	Sept. 15, 1864	1 year.	Mustered out with company July 14, 1865.
Larkby, James	do	41	Sept. 26, 1864	1 year.	Mustered out with company July 14, 1865.
Lee, Patrick	do	19	Sept. 8, 1864	1 year.	Appointed Corporal Jan. 1, 1865; reduced June 1, 1865; mustered out with company July 14, 1865.
McCarty, John	do	18	Aug. 29, 1864	1 year.	Mustered out with company July 14, 1865.
McMillen, Enos W	do	18	Sept. 15, 1864	1 year.	Mustered out with company July 14, 1865.
Melcher, Henry	do	28	Sept. 3, 1864	1 year.	Mustered out with company July 14, 1865.
Miller, James H	do	18	Jan. 31, 1865	1 year.	Transferred from Co. H, 177th O. V. I., June 15, 1865; mustered out with company July 14, 1865.

Names.	Rank.	Age.	Date of Entering the Service.	Period of Service.	Remarks.
Morris, John C.	Private.	30	Sept. 26, 1864	1 year.	Appointed Sergeant Sept. 29, 1864; reduced to ranks March 1, 1865; reappointed Sergeant April 21, 1865; reduced June 1, 1865; mustered out with company July 14, 1865.
Murray, Alvin R.	do.	19	Aug. 26, 1864	1 year.	Appointed Corporal Sept. 29, 1864; Sergeant Nov. 3, 1864; reduced June 1, 1865; mustered out with company July 14, 1865.
Myers, Martin V.	do.	21	Sept. 28, 1864	1 year.	
O'Connor, Daniel	do.	20	Oct. 12, 1864	1 year.	Transferred from Co. F, 177th O. V. I., Ja[illegible] 1865; mustered out to date July 14, 1865, by order of War Department.
Orth, Jacob	do.	17	Oct. 5, 1864	1 year.	Transferred from Co. B, 177th O. V. I., Ja[illegible] 1865; mustered out with company Ju[illegible] 1865.
Palmer, Emmer A.	do.	19	Jan. 31, 1865	1 year.	Transferred from Co. H, 177th O. V. I., Ja[illegible] 1865; mustered out with company Ju[illegible] 1865.
Patterson, Isaac W.	do.	35	Sept. 20, 1864	1 year.	Mustered out with company July 14, 1865.
Plumu, Piers	do.	22	Aug. 30, 1864	1 year.	Mustered out June 2, 1865, at Washington, D. C., by order of War Department.
Powhattan, Henry W.	do.	34	Sept. 21, 1864	1 year.	Mustered out with company July 14, 1865.
Quigley, Thomas R.	do.	18	Sept. 15, 1864	1 year.	Died Jan. 19, 1865, on steamer on Tennessee River.
Ratlif, John	do.	25	Sept. 26, 1864	1 year.	Mustered out with company July 14, 1865.
Reddert, George F.	do.	24	Sept. 24, 1864	1 year.	Mustered out with company July 14, 1865.
Reynolds, Edward C.	do.	18	Sept. 22, 1864	1 year.	
Richards, Simeon	do.	31	Oct. 3, 1864	1 year.	Transferred from Co. A, 177th O. V. I., Ja[illegible] 1865; mustered out with company Ju[illegible] 1865.
Roberts, Chapman	do.	26	Sept. 27, 1864	1 year.	Mustered out June 2, 1865, at Washington, D. C., by order of War Department.
Rogers, Adolphus	do.	43	Oct. 4, 1864	1 year.	Transferred from Co. D, 177th O. V. I., Ja[illegible] 1865; mustered out with company Ju[illegible] 1865.
Ross, Alva C.	do.	43	Oct. 4, 1864	1 year.	Transferred from Co. D, 177th O. V. I., Ja[illegible] 1865; mustered out with company Ju[illegible] 1865.
Rowland, Matthew	do.	19	Oct. 4, 1864	1 year.	Transferred from Co. D, 177th O. V. I., Ja[illegible] 1865; mustered out with company Ju[illegible] 1865.
Ryan, William	do.	28	Sept. 26, 1864	1 year.	
Ruhl, Henry	do.	17	Sept. 3, 1864	1 year.	Mustered out with company July 14, 1865.
Saxton, Daniel	do.	18	Sept. 2, 1864	1 year.	Transferred from Co. B, 177th O. V. I., Ja[illegible] 1865, as Daniel Sackson; mustered out with company July 14, 1865.
Seymour, William	do.	26	Sept. 19, 1864	1 year.	Mustered out with company July 14, 1865.
Seward, Frederick H.	do.	20	Sept. 20, 1864	1 year.	Appointed Sergeant Nov. 4, 1864; reduced to ranks Nov. 23, 1864; appointed [illegible] March 1, 1865; reduced May [illegible]; mustered out with company July 14, 1865.
Smith, Valentine V.	do.	41	Aug. 9, 1864	1 year.	Mustered out with company July 14, 1865.
Sowers, Frederick	do.	18	Sept. 13, 1864	1 year.	Mustered as Musician; mustered out with company July 14, 1865.
Spitznagle, Martin	do.	39	Sept. 16, 1864	1 year.	Mustered out with company July 14, 1865.
Swerne, Alphonso	do.	25	Sept. 24, 1864	1 year.	Mustered out with company July 14, 1865.
Treap, Albert	do.	21	Sept. 17, 1864	1 year.	Transferred from Co. F, 177th O. V. I., Ja[illegible] 1865; mustered out with company Ju[illegible] 1865.
Turner, Cornelius M.	do.	33	Oct. 4, 1864	1 year.	See Musician Co. D, 177th O. V. I.
Weigers, Theodore	do.	22	Sept. [illegible], 1864	1 year.	Mustered out with company July 14, 1865.
Welch, John	do.	26	Sept. 19, 1864	1 year.	
Whetzel, Henry	do.	26	Sept. 26, 1864	1 year.	Mustered out with company July 14, 1865.
Whitesides, John L.	do.	21	Sept. 26, 1864	1 year.	
Whiting, Henry G.	do.	18	Sept. [illegible], 1864	1 year.	
Whortman, Henry	do.	[illegible]	Sept. 26, 1864	1 year.	Mustered out with company July 14, 1865.
Williams, Barney	do.	[illegible]	Sept. 14, 1864	1 year.	
Williams, Charles H.	do.	26	Sept. 26, 1864	1 year.	
Wisematle, Michael	do.	18	Sept. 21, 1864	1 year.	Mustered out with company July 14, 1865.
Wood, William T.	do.	26	Nov. 11, 1864	1 year.	Transferred from Co. I, 177th O. V. I., Ja[illegible] 1865; mustered out with company Ju[illegible] 1865.
Young, Joseph	do.	20	Sept. 26, 1864	1 year.	Mustered out with company July 14, 1865.

COMPANY B.

Mustered in September 29, 1864, at Camp Dennison, O., by Wm. Von Doehn, Captain and A. A. G. Mustered out July 14, 1865, at Salisbury, N. C., by Frederick Anderson, Lieutenant and A. C. M.

Names.	Rank.	Age.	Date of Entering the Service.	Period of Service.	Remarks.
William Ketteler	Captain.	32	Sept. 29, 1864	1 year.	Promoted to Major June 17, 1865, but not mustered; mustered out with company July 14, 1865.
Herman Rampel	1st Lieut.	47	Sept. 29, 1864	1 year.	Appointed Regt. Quartermaster Sept. 30, 1864.
David B. Worley	...do....	24	Sept. 15, 1864	1 year.	Promoted from Sergeant Oct. 19, 1864; mustered out with company July 14, 1865.
John Lang	2d Lieut.	24	Sept. 29, 1864	1 year.	Promoted to Captain Co. C, 183d O. V. I., Oct. 18, 1864.
Joseph C. Roberts	1st Sergt.	26	Sept. 28, 1864	1 year.	Appointed from private Oct. 26, 1864; promoted to 2d Lieutenant July 10, 1865, but not mustered; mustered out with company July 14, 1865.
George Foerster	Sergeant.	37	Aug. 29, 1864	1 year.	Promoted to 1st Lieutenant Co. C, 183d O.V.I., Oct. 18, 1864.
Henry Koenig	....do ...	30	Sept. 24, 1864	1 year.	Appointed Sept. 29, 1864; mustered out with company July 14, 1865.
Henry L. Baker	....do....	25	Sept. 5, 1864	1 year.	Appointed from private Oct. 25, 1864; mustered out with company July 14, 1865.
Zachariah J. Wicker	....do....	38	Sept. 7, 1864	1 year.	Appointed from private Oct. 25, 1864; mustered out with company July 14, 1865.
Charles C. Martin	....do....	29	Sept. 19, 1864	1 year.	Appointed Corporal ——; Sergeant April 1 1865; mustered out June 13, 1865, at Columbus, O., by order of War Department.
Frederick Lutz	Corporal.	32	Sept. 10, 1864	1 year.	Appointed Sept. 29, 1864; promoted to 2d Lieutenant Co. C, 183d O. V. I., Oct. 18, 1864
John Poth	....do....	20	Sept. 13, 1864	1 year.	Appointed Sept. 29, 1864; mustered out with company July 14, 1865.
Conrad Grenig	....do....	18	Aug. 22, 1864	1 year.	Appointed Sept. 29, 1864; mustered out with company July 14, 1865.
Christian Reuter	....do....	43	Aug. 24, 1864	1 year.	Appointed Sept. 29, 1864; mustered out with company July 14, 1865.
William Robinson	....do....	21	Sept. 16, 1864	1 year.	Appointed Sept. 29, 1864; mustered out with company July 14, 1865.
Sheridan Williamson	....do....	39	Sept. 19, 1864	1 year.	Appointed Oct. 25, 1864; mustered out with company July 14, 1865.
James Downey	....do....	20	Sept. 16, 1864	1 year.	Appointed Oct. 25, 1864; mustered out with company July 14, 1865.
Bernhard Stehele	....do...	29	Sept. 16, 1864	1 year.	Appointed March 22, 1865; mustered out with company July 14, 1865.
Joseph Finn	....do....	23	Sept. 21, 1864	1 year.	Appointed April 1, 1865; mustered out with company July 14, 1865
Henry Rohrkasse	Musician	18	Sept. 16, 1864	1 year.	Appointed Sept. 29, 1864; promoted to Principal Musician Jan. 5, 1865; returned to company Feb. 1, 1865; mustered out with company July 14, 1865.
John Phelps	Wagoner	29	Aug. 27, 1864	1 year.	Appointed Oct. 25, 1864; mustered out with company July 14, 1865.
Ahlensdorf, Herman	Private.	18	Sept. 26, 1864	1 year.	Appointed Musician Sept. 29, 1864; mustered out with company July 14, 1865, as private.
Arnold, William	....do....	19	Sept. 12, 1864	1 year.	Mustered out with company July 14, 1865.
Babcock, Isaac N.	....do....	22	Sept. 3, 1864	1 year.	Mustered out with company July 14, 1865.
Babcock, John H. H.	....do....	23	Sept. 19, 1864	1 year.	Mustered out with company July 14, 1865.
Baumgartner, Christian	....do....	38	Sept. 21, 1864	1 year.	Mustered out with company July 14, 1865.
Baxter, John G.	....do....	37	Sept. 19, 1864	1 year.	Mustered out with company July 14, 1865.
Becker, John F.	....do....	42	Aug. 13, 1864	1 year.	Mustered out June 23, 1865, at David's Island, New York Harbor, by order of War Department.
Bouchan, Armond	....do....	25	Sept. 15, 1864	1 year.	Mustered out with company July 14, 1865.
Braunfels, Robert	....do....	21	Sept. 5, 1864	1 year.	Mustered out with company July 14, 1865.
Cody, Patrick	....do....	23	Sept. 16, 1864	1 year.	Mustered out with company July 14, 1865.
Conley, Thomas	....do....	20	Sept. 16, 1864	1 year.	Mustered out with company July 14, 1865.
Dearing, Harrison	....do....	20	Sept. 16, 1864	1 year.	Mustered out with company July 14, 1865.
Deveny, Edward	....do....	18	Sept. 26, 1864	1 year.	Mustered out with company July 14, 1865.
Duval, James L.	....do....	19	Sept. 7, 1864	1 year.	Mustered out with company July 14, 1865.
Enyart, John	....do....	19	Sept. 16, 1864	1 year.	Mustered out with company July 14, 1865.
Ewan, Andrew	....do....	18	Sept. 29, 1864	1 year.	Mustered out with company July 14, 1865.
Fehr, Charles	....do....	30	Sept. 21, 1864	1 year.	Promoted to Hospital Steward to date June 1, 1865.
Fein, George H.	....do....	28	Aug. 27, 1864	1 year.	Mustered as Wagoner; mustered out with company July 14, 1865.
Fouquet, Louis	....do....	21	Sept. 10, 1864	1 year.	Mustered out with company July 14, 1865.
Gaertlein, John A.	....do....	37	Sept. 19, 1864	1 year.	Mustered out with company July 14, 1865.
German, Lorenz	....do....	48	Sept. 29, 1864	1 year.	Mustered out with company July 14, 1865.
Habening, Philip B.	....do....	20	Sept. 9, 1864	1 year.	Mustered out with company July 14, 1865.
Haff, Henry	....do....	30	Sept. 4, 1864	1 year.	Mustered out with company July 14, 1865.
Hamilton, Alexander	....do....	25	Sept. 16, 1864	1 year.	Mustered out with company July 14, 1865.

Names.	Rank.	Age.	Date of Entering the Service.	Period of Service.	Remarks.
Harvey, John	Private	25	Sept. 2, 1864	1 year.	Mustered out with company July 14, 1865.
Hauck, Joseph	do	18	Sept. 4, 1864	1 year.	Mustered out with company July 14, 1865.
Hauck, John G	do	45	Sept. 2, 1864	1 year.	Mustered out with company July 14, 1865.
Hirsh, Henry	do	43	Sept. 1, 1864	1 year.	Mustered out with company July 14, 1865.
Horrocks, Edward G	do	24	Sept. 16, 1864	1 year.	Appointed Corporal Sept. 29, 1864, Sergeant —; reduced March 31, 1865; mustered out with company July 14, 1865.
Hoying, August	do	30	Sept. 12, 1864	1 year.	Mustered out with company July 14, 1865.
Huber, Ludwig	do	18	Sept. 10, 1864	1 year.	Mustered out with company July 14, 1865.
Huey, John	do	19	Sept. 7, 1864	1 year.	Mustered out with company July 14, 1865.
Huff, John D	do	20	Aug. 29, 1864	1 year.	Mustered out May 30, 1865, at Camp Dennison, O., by order of War Department.
Kasper, William G	do	18	Sept. 19, 1864	1 year.	Mustered out June 6, 1865, at Beaufort, [illegible]
Kaufman, Ferdinand	do	27	Sept. 2, 1864	1 year.	
Kelley, Michael	do	20	Aug. 22, 1864	1 year.	
Knapka, Christopher	do	19	Sept. 19, 1864	1 year.	Died Dec. 31, 1864, at Clifton, Tenn.
Kretzberg, John	do	19	Sept. 19, 1864	1 year.	Mustered out with company July 14, 1865.
Kutzer, Jacob	do	31	Sept. 19, 1864	1 year.	Mustered out with company July 14, 1865.
Lang, John	do	24	Sept. 5, 1864	1 year.	Discharged Sept. 29, 1864, at Camp Dennison, Ohio.
McQuigg, George W	do	27	Sept. 20, 1864	1 year.	Mustered out with company July 14, 1865.
Mannias, Matthias	do	35	Sept. 2, 1864	1 year.	Mustered out with company July 14, 1865.
Mellan, Michael	do	40	Sept. 8, 1864	1 year.	
Messenus, Henry	do	39	Sept. 10, 1864	1 year.	Mustered out May 30, 1865, at Camp Dennison, O., by order of War Department.
Meyling, Henry	do	23	Aug. 16, 1864	1 year.	Appointed 1st Sergeant Sept 29, 1864; reduced Oct. 24, 1864; mustered out with company July 14, 1865.
Mohrman, Henry	do	41	Sept. 12, 1864	1 year.	Mustered out with company July 14, 1865.
Moore, Joseph	do	20	Aug. 29, 1864	1 year.	Mustered out with company July 14, 1865.
Moss, Samuel	do	22	Aug. 31, 1864	1 year.	Mustered out July 12, 1865, at David's Island, New York Harbor, by order of War Department.
Nipkin, Louis	do	19	Sept. 18, 1864	1 year.	Mustered out with company July 14, 1865.
Nunger, John	do	18	Aug. 23, 1864	1 year.	Mustered out with company July 14, 1865.
Page, John W	do	34	Sept. 8, 1864	1 year.	Mustered out May 30, 1865, at Camp Dennison, O., by order of War Department.
Pauley, Michael	do	29	Sept. 21, 1864	1 year.	
Raphold, Peter	do	44	Sept. 20, 1864	1 year.	Died April 20, 1865, at Raleigh, N. C.
Rechtein, Joseph	do	18	Sept. 24, 1864	1 year.	Mustered out with company July 14, 1865.
Ritter, Louis	do	44	Sept. 14, 1864	1 year.	Died Dec. 9, 1864, of wounds received Dec. 7, 1864, in battle of Murfreesboro, Tenn.
Rothfuss, Paul	do	22	Sept. 17, 1864	1 year.	Mustered out with company July 14, 1865.
Schaff, Herman	do	27	Sept. 9, 1864	1 year.	Mustered out with company July 14, 1865.
Scheib, Theobald	do	52	Aug. 23, 1864	1 year.	Mustered out with company July 14, 1865.
Schmidt, Charles	do	40	Sept. 17, 1864	1 year.	
Schmidt, John	do	18	Sept. 2, 1864	1 year.	Mustered out with company July 14, 1865.
Schultz, William F	do	30	Sept. 19, 1864	1 year.	
Sharpless, Benjamin	do	22	Sept. 15, 1864	1 year.	Appointed Corporal Sept. 29, 1864; reduced March 22, 1865; mustered out with company July 14, 1865.
Sicking, Bernhard	do	24	Sept. 12, 1864	1 year.	Mustered out with company July 14, 1865.
Sicking, George L	do	29	Aug. 23, 1864	1 year.	Appointed Sergeant Sept. 29, 1864; [illegible] Oct. 18, 1864; promoted to 2d Lieutenant Oct. 19, 1864, but not mustered; mustered out with company July 14, 1865.
Sliven, Michael	do				Borne on detached muster-out roll as mustered out May 30, 1865, at Camp Dennison, O., by order of War Department.
Snelbaker, David T	do	22	Sept. 21, 1864	1 year.	Appointed Corporal Sept. [illegible] 1864; promoted to Sergeant Oct. 18, 1864; [illegible] company Jan 6, 1865; mustered out with company July 14, 1865.
Sohn, Henry	do	18	Sept. 15, 1864	1 year.	Wounded Dec. 7, 1864, in battle of Murfreesboro, Tenn.; mustered out to date [illegible] 1865, by order of War Department.
Speath, Joseph	do	19	Sept. 5, 1864	1 year.	Mustered out with company July 14, 1865.
Stoudre, William	do	31	Sept. 6, 1864	1 year.	Mustered out with company July 14, 1865.
Stuzenbach, George	do	21	Aug. 26, 1864	1 year.	Mustered out with company July 14, 1865.
Tressler, Benjamin F	do	29	Sept. 17, 1864	1 year	Mustered out with company July 14, 1865.
Uhl, August	do	43	Sept. 17, 1864	1 year.	Wounded Dec. 7, 1864, in battle of Murfreesboro, Tenn.; mustered out June [illegible], at Columbus, O., by order of War Department.
Veith, Christian	do	24	Aug. 18, 1864	1 year.	Mustered out with company July 14, 1865.
Vogel, Albert	do	43	Sept. 8, 1864	1 year.	Wounded Dec. 7, 1864, in battle of Murfreesboro, Tenn.; mustered out June [illegible] at Columbus, O., by order of War Department.
Volmer, Valentine	do	40	Sept. 16, 1864	1 year.	Mustered out with company July 14, 1865.
Walcott, Thomas	do	38	Sept. 5, 1864	1 year.	
Weimer, John	do	24	Sept. 20, 1864	1 year.	Died Jan. 20, 1865, on board hospital boat, Ohio River.
Weiss, Martin	do	19	Sept. 5, 1864	1 year.	Mustered out with company July 14, 1865.

Names.	Rank.	Age.	Date of Entering the Service.	Period of Service.	Remarks.
Wetter, Charles	Private	26	Sept. 20, 1864	1 year.	Mustered out with company July 14, 1865.
Wilson, James	....do....	31	Sept. 21, 1864	1 year.	Mustered out with company July 14, 1865.
Wright, Thomas W	....do....	39	Sept. 21, 1864	1 year.	Promoted to Q. M. Sergeant Oct. 18, 1864; reduced Feb. 7, 1865; mustered out with company July 14, 1865.
Zacharitz, Louis	....do....	29	Sept. 21, 1864	1 year.	Mustered out with company July 14, 1865.

COMPANY C.

Mustered in October 5, 1864, at Camp Dennison, O., by Wm. Von Doehn, Captain and A. A. G. Mustered out July 14, 1865, at Salisbury, N. C., by Frederick Anderson, Lieutenant and A. C. M.

Names.	Rank.	Age.	Date of Entering the Service.	Period of Service.	Remarks.
John E. Hudson	Captain.	27	Oct. 4, 1864	1 year.	Promoted to Lieut. Colonel Oct 15, 1864.
Charles Allen	....do....	21	Oct. 4, 1864	1 year.	Promoted from 1st Lieutenant to date Oct. 14, 1864; mustered out with company July 14, 1865.
Patrick Merrick	1st Lieut.	23	Oct. 4, 1864	1 year.	Promoted from 2d Lieutenant Oct. 18, 1864; to Captain July 10, 1865, but not mustered; mustered out with company July 14, 1865.
William F. Gibson	2d Lieut.	24	Sept. 7, 1864	1 year.	Promoted from 1st Sergeant Oct. 18, 1864; to 1st Lieutenant July 10, 1865, but not mustered: mustered out with company July 14, 1865.
John S. Pierce	1st Sergt.	21	Aug. 30, 1864	1 year.	Appointed Sergeant Oct. 5, 1864; 1st Sergeant Oct. 22, 1864; promoted to 2d Lieutenant July 10, 1865, but not mustered: mustered out with company July 14, 1865.
Samuel S. Matthews	Sergeant.	27	Aug. 30, 1864	1 year.	Appointed Oct. 5, 1864; promoted to 2d Lieutenant July 10, 1865, but not mustered; mustered out with company July 14, 1865.
Richard Norton	....do....	19	Sept. 19, 1864	1 year.	Appointed Corporal Oct. 5, 1864: Sergeant Feb. 2, 1865, promoted to Q. M. Sergeant May 13, 1865.
William I. Flannery	....do....	23	Aug. 30, 1864	1 year.	Appointed Oct. 5, 1864; mustered out with company July 14, 1865.
Robert Nichelson	....do....	20	Sept. 17, 1864	1 year.	Appointed Corporal Feb. 1, 1865; Sergeant May 14, 1865; mustered out with company July 14, 1865.
George Sandbrink	....do....	21	Oct. 12, 1864	1 year.	Appointed from private June 10, 1865; mustered out with company July 14, 1865.
Michael Doyle	Corporal.	43	Aug. 21, 1864	1 year.	Mustered out to date July 14, 1865, by order of War Department.
Frank Smith	....do....	24	Oct. 3, 1864	1 year.	Appointed Feb. 1, 1865, mustered out May 29, 1865, at Albany, N. Y., by order of War Department.
Thomas Granger	....do....	19	Sept. 27, 1864	1 year.	
Thomas Maken	....do....	23	Sept. 12, 1864	1 year.	Appointed Oct. 5, 1864; mustered out with company July 14, 1865.
William Butler	....do....	26	Sept. 26, 1864	1 year.	Appointed Oct. 5, 1864; mustered out with company July 14, 1865.
George Yadarah	....do....	34	Sept. 21, 1864	1 year.	Appointed Feb. 2, 1865; mustered out with company July 14, 1865.
Antony Kunk	....do....	32	Oct. 4, 1864	1 year.	Appointed Feb. 2, 1865; mustered out with company July 14, 1865.
John Connelly, Jr	....do....	22	Sept. 15, 1864	1 year.	Appointed Feb. 2, 1865; mustered out with company July 14, 1865.
William E. Cobb	....do....	17	Sept. 15, 1864	1 year.	Appointed May 15, 1865; mustered out with company July 14, 1865.
John McKeaver	Wagoner.	22	Sept. 7, 1864	1 year.	Mustered out with company July 14, 1865.
Ambrose, John W	Private	18	Sept. 1, 1864	1 year.	
Andrews, William	....do....	25	Sept. 28, 1864	1 year.	Mustered out June 14, 1865, at Columbus, O., by order of War Department.
Beach, George W	....do....	19	Sept. 14, 1864	1 year.	
Beckman, George H	....do....	39	Sept. 22, 1864	1 year	Mustered out May 30, 1865, at Camp Dennison, O., by order of War Department.
Boles, William	....do....	20	Sept. 18, 1864	1 year.	Mustered out with company July 14, 1865.
Bonn, Matthias	....do....	25	Sept. 7, 1864	1 year.	Mustered out with company July 14, 1865.
Bowers, Thomas	....do....	32	Sept. 29, 1864	1 year.	Mustered out with company July 14, 1865.
Burden, Wesley	....do....	32	Sept. 12, 1864	1 year.	Mustered out with company July 14, 1865.
Burns, Paul	....do....	23	Sept. 28, 1864	1 year.	
Butler, Michael	....do....	21	Sept. 12, 1864	1 year.	Mustered out with company July 14, 1865.
Collins, Thomas	....do....	21	Sept. 27, 1864	1 year.	Mustered as Corporal.
Connelly, Michael	....do....	27	Sept. 29, 1864	1 year.	Also borne on rolls as Michael Carley.
Cooper, David R	....do....	37	Sept. 8, 1864	1 year.	Mustered out June 2, 1865, at Camp Dennison, O., by order of War Department.
Daugherty, Michael	....do....	43	Aug. 26, 1864	1 year.	Mustered out with company July 14, 1865.
Daugherty, William	....do....	29	Aug. 22, 1864	1 year.	
Davis, John	....do....	48	Sept. 19, 1864	1 year.	Mustered out with company July 14, 1865.
Dearing, August	....do....	34	Sept. 10, 1864	1 year.	Mustered out with company July 14, 1865.
Devine, Joseph	....do....	19	Aug. 26, 1864	1 year.	Mustered out with company July 14, 1865.

Names.	Rank.	Age.	Date of Entering the Service.	Period of Service.	Remarks.
Dickhite, Martin	Private	38	Sept. 10, 1864	1 year.	Mustered out with company July 14, 1865.
Difley, James	...do...	29	Sept. 12, 1864	1 year	Mustered out May 30, 1865, at Camp Dennison, O., by order of War Department.
Donnelly, Martin	...do...	24	Sept. 30, 1864	1 year.	
Early, Moses P.	...do...	26	Sept. 23, 1864	1 year	Mustered out with company July 14, 1865.
Fanning, Dennis	...do...	40	Sept 12, 1864	1 year.	Mustered out with company July 14, 1865.
Farmer, Patrick	...do...	23	Sept. 26, 1864	1 year.	Mustered as Corporal; mustered out with company July 14, 1865.
Farrell, Terrence	...do...	28	Sept. 26, 1864	1 year.	
Fice, Leopold	...do...	26	Sept. 29, 1864	1 year.	Mustered out with company July 14, 1865.
Galentin, Jasper	...do...	26	Sept. 7, 1864	1 year.	Appointed Sergeant ——; reduced Feb. [illegible], 1865; mustered out with company July 14, 1865.
Gillmarten, Patrick	...do...	39	Sept. 12, 1864	1 year.	
Gross, Abraham	...do...	21	Sept. 5, 1864	1 year.	Mustered out with company July 14, 1865.
Handerhan, Edward	...do...	21	Sept. 22, 1864	1 year.	Mustered out with company July 14, 1865.
Harnold, Anthony	...do...	25	Sept. 28, 1864	1 year.	Mustered out with company July 14, 1865.
Hayes, William	...do...	48	Sept. 26, 1864	1 year.	Mustered out with company July 14, 1865.
Henderson, James, Sr.	...do...	43	Sept. 10, 1864	1 year.	Mustered out to date July 14, 1865, by order of War Department.
Henderson, James	...do...	20	Sept. 10, 1864	1 year.	Mustered out with company July 14, 1865.
Hiatt, Clark	...do...	22	Sept. 7, 1864	1 year.	
Hiatt, Marion	...do...	27	Sept. 22, 1864	1 year.	Mustered out with company July 14, 1865.
Holland, Simon	...do...	25	Sept. 21, 1864	1 year.	Mustered as private; appointed Corporal —; Sergeant Feb. 2, 1865; reduced June [illegible]; mustered out with company July 14, 1865.
Johnson, Isaac	...do...	22	Aug. 28, 1864	1 year.	Mustered out with company July 14, 1865.
Kales, John W.	...do...	24	Sept. 7, 1864	1 year.	Mustered out with company July 14, 1865.
Keating, James	...do...	18	Aug. 30, 1864	1 year.	Mustered out with company July 14, 1865.
Kelley, Harrison	...do...	18	Sept. 28, 1864	1 year.	
Kemper, Henry	...do...	21	Sept. 2, 1864	1 year.	Mustered as Sergeant; mustered out with company July 14, 1865.
Kritty, Bernhard	...do...	23	Sept. 13, 1864	1 year.	Mustered out with company July 14, 1865.
Laney, Owen	...do...	21	Sept. 13, 1864	1 year.	Mustered out July 4, 1865, at Murfreesboro, Tenn., by order of War Department; also borne on rolls as Owen Laning.
Land, William	...do...	21	Sept. 2, 1864	1 year.	Mustered as Corporal; mustered out with company July 14, 1865; also borne on rolls as William Lamb.
Lawrence, Michael	...do...	23	Aug. 26, 1864	1 year.	Mustered out with company July 14, 1865.
Lee, George W.	...do...	31	Aug. 26, 1864	1 year.	Discharged Feb 12, 1865, by order of War Department.
Linderman, John	...do...	18	Sept. 22, 1864	1 year.	Mustered out with company July 14, 1865.
Lovie, Moses P.	...do...	26	Sept. 3, 1864	1 year.	Mustered out with company July 14, 1865.
McCaulit, Dennis	...do...	45	Sept. 12, 1864	1 year.	Appointed Corporal ——; reduced Feb. [illegible], 1865; mustered out with company July 14, 1865.
McDonnell, John	...do...	19	Oct. 4, 1864	1 year.	
McLear, John C.	...do...	20	Sept. 28, 1864	1 year.	Mustered out with company July 14, 1865.
McWilliams, James C.	...do...	32	Sept 19, 1864	1 year.	Mustered out June 29, 1865, at David's Island, New York Harbor, by order of War Department.
Macklen, John	...do...	26	Sept. 8, 1864	1 year	Promoted to Principal Musician Oct. [illegible], '64.
Mahoney, Jerry	...do...	20	Sept. 21, 1864	1 year	
Marshall, Benjamin	...do...	20	Sept. 29, 1864	1 year.	
Mills, David I.	...do...	44	Sept. 28, 1864	1 year	Mustered out with company July 14, 1865.
Mohan, Michael	...do...	35	Sept. 8, 1864	1 year	Mustered out with company July 14, 1865; also borne on rolls as Michael [illegible].
Morran, William	...do...	18	Sept. 12, 1864	1 year.	
Mulligan, Thomas	...do...	24	Sept. 29, 1864	1 year.	Mustered out May 30, 1865, at McDougal Hospital, New York Harbor, by order of War Department.
Murphy, William	...do...	37	Sept 20, 1864	1 year	Mustered out with company July 14, 1865.
Murrey, Patrick	...do...	25	Sept. 7, 1864	1 year.	Mustered out with company July 14, 1865.
Newell, Samuel	...do...	30	Sept. 21, 1864	1 year	Mustered out with company July 14, 1865.
O'Brine, Michael	...do...	19	Sept. 19, 1864	1 year	Mustered out with company July 14, 1865.
O'Donnell, Edward C.	...do...	24	Sept. 13, 1864	1 year.	Mustered out with company July 14, 1865.
Oliver, John W.	...do...	21	Sept. 13, 1864	1 year.	Mustered out with company July 14, 1865.
Orr, John	...do...	34	Sept. 10, 1864	1 year.	Mustered out with company July 14, 1865.
Parlen, Patrick	...do...	25	Aug. 26, 1864	1 year.	Mustered out with company July 14, 1865.
Pelcher, George	...do...	40	Sept. 21, 1864	1 year.	Mustered out with company July 14, 1865.
Piesche, Joseph	...do...	35	Sept. 2, 1864	1 year.	Mustered out with company July 14, 1865.
Rowe, William	...do...	19	Sept. 22, 1864	1 year.	
Roush, Joseph	...do...	25	Sept. 29, 1864	1 year.	Mustered out June 2, 1865, at Camp Dennison, O., by order of War Department.
Russell, Marion	...do...	22	Sept. 29, 1864	1 year.	
Schear, Christ.	...do...	30	Sept. 3, 1864	1 year.	Mustered out with company July 14, 1865.
Shanagman, Henry	...do...	30	Sept. 2, 1864	1 year.	Mustered out with company July 14, 1865.
Spisinger, Valentine	...do...	44	Sept. 14, 1864	1 year.	
Teeholz, Marion	...do...	44	Sept. 10, 1864	1 year.	
Thomas, John	...do...	22	Aug. 25, 1864	1 year.	
Troy, John	...do...	30	Sept. 16, 1864	1 year.	Mustered out with company July 14, 1865.
Wance, George	...do...	28	Sept. 20, 1864	1 year	
Walton, Asa	...do...	30	Sept. 18, 1864	1 year.	
Watts, Thomas	...do...	40	Aug. 20, 1864	1 year	
Weber, George	...do...	35	Aug. 29, 1864	1 year.	

Names.	Rank.	Age.	Date of Entering the Service.	Period of Service.	Remarks.
Welsh, Edward	Private.	32	Sept. 30, 1864	1 year.	Mustered out with company July 14, 1865.
West, William B.	...do...	40	Sept. 23, 1864	1 year.	
Wills, Richard	...do...	30	Sept. 23, 1864	1 year.	Mustered out with company July 14, 1865.
Wilson, Thomas	...do...	37	Sept. 3, 1864	1 year.	Absent, sick Jan. 5, 1865, at Columbia, Tenn.; ordered to Nashville, and from there to Cincinnati, Feb. 15, 1865. No further record found.
Wilson, William	...do...	38	Sept. 20, 1864	1 year.	
Woods, George W.	...do...	43	Sept. 21, 1864	1 year.	Mustered out with company July 14, 1865.

COMPANY D.

Mustered in October 6, 1864, at Camp Dennison, O., by Wm. Von Doehn, Captain and A. A. G. Mustered out July 14, 1865, at Salisbury, N. C., by Frederick Anderson, Lieutenant and A. C. M.

Names.	Rank.	Age.	Date of Entering the Service.	Period of Service.	Remarks.
John O'Dowd	Captain.	35	Oct. 6, 1864	1 year.	Promoted to Colonel Oct. 15, 1864.
James Foley	...do...	26	Oct. 6, 1864	1 year.	Promoted from 1st Lieutenant Oct. 18, 1864; mustered out with company July 14, 1865.
Samuel W. McCaslin	1st Lieut.	35	Oct. 6, 1864	1 year.	Promoted from 2d Lieutenant Oct. 18, 1864; discharged May 15, 1865.
John B. Sexton	2d Lieut.	27	Sept. 26, 1864	1 year.	Appointed Sergeant Oct. 6, 1864; 1st Sergeant Oct. 14, 1864; promoted to 2d Lieutenant Oct. 18, 1864; 1st Lieutenant July 10, 1865, but not mustered; mustered out with company July 14, 1865.
Edward Cannon	1st Sergt.	22	Jan. 23, 1865	1 year.	Appointed 1st Sergeant Feb. 6, 1865; promoted to 2d Lieutenant July 10, 1865, but not mustered; mustered out with company July 14, 1865.
Samuel Schroder	Sergeant.	31	Oct. 1, 1864	1 year.	Appointed from private Oct. 30, 1864; mustered out with company July 14, 1865.
Walcott R. Witherby	...do...	27	Oct. 4, 1864	1 year.	Appointed Corporal Dec. 28, 1864; Sergeant Feb. 6, 1865; mustered out with company July 14, 1865.
Edward Donavan	...do...	27	Dec. 8, 1864	1 year.	Appointed Corporal May 1, 1865; Sergeant June 1, 1865; mustered out with company July 14, 1865.
Thomas Noonan	...do...	19	Oct. 4, 1864	1 year.	Appointed Corporal Jan. 6, 1865; Sergeant June 1, 1865; mustered out with company July 14, 1865.
Edward Williams	Corporal.	21	Sept. 3, 1864	1 year.	Appointed Oct. 6, 1864; mustered out June 2, 1865, at Troy, N. Y., by order of War Department.
Thomas M Edgely	...do...	38	Sept. 1, 1864	1 year.	Appointed Oct. 6, 1864; mustered out with company July 14, 1865.
Jacob Mattern	...do...	34	Sept. 1, 1864	1 year.	Appointed Dec. 18, 1864; mustered out with company July 14, 1865.
Kyhran Horan	...do...	27	Oct. 4, 1864	1 year.	Appointed June 1, 1865; mustered out with company July 14, 1865.
Patrick McGarry	...do...	24	Jan. 23, 1865	1 year.	Appointed June 1, 1865; mustered out with company July 14, 1865.
James Murray	...do...	19	Oct. 4, 1864	1 year.	Appointed June 1, 1865; mustered out with company July 14, 1865.
Marion Hargrave	...do...	23	Oct. 4, 1864	1 year.	Appointed 1st Sergeant Nov. 18, 1864; reduced Feb 6, 1865; appointed Corporal June 1, 1865; mustered out with company July 14, 1865.
George A. Reider	...do...	26	Oct. 3, 1864	1 year.	Appointed June 1, 1865; mustered out with company July 14, 1865.
William H. Webber	Musician	21	Sept. 29, 1864	1 year.	Promoted to Principal Musician Feb. 1, 1865.
Nicholas E. Dressel	...do...	18	Oct. 4, 1864	1 year.	Appointed Dec. 1, 1864; mustered out with company July 14, 1865.
Allen, Thomas	Private.	23	Sept. 15, 1864	1 year.	
Bailey, Isaac S.	...do...	32	Sept. 24, 1864	1 year.	Appointed Sergeant Oct. 14, 1864; reduced June 1, 1865; mustered out with company July 14, 1865.
Barbour, John	...do...	34	Sept. 26, 1864	1 year.	
Battell, John	...do...	25	Aug. 31, 1864	1 year.	
Beltcher, Jesse	...do...	18	Sept. 26, 1864	1 year.	Transferred to 22d Battalion, Veteran Reserve Corps, ——; mustered out Sept. 27, 1865, at Washington, D. C., on expiration of term of service.
Bishop, Richard M.	...do...	18	Sept. 18, 1864	1 year.	
Blair, John M.	...do...	19	Sept. 30, 1864	1 year.	Mustered out with company July 14, 1865.
Bogart, George W.	...do...	25	Sept. 2, 1864	1 year.	Mustered as Sergeant.
Boyd, Charles.	...do...	20	Sept. 14, 1864	1 year.	
Boyle, Lawrence	...do...	18	Sept. 13, 1864	1 year.	
Boylston, James	...do...	20	Sept. 12, 1864	1 year.	
Brewer, Wesley	...do...	26	Sept. 20, 1864	1 year.	Mustered out with company July 14, 1865.

Names.	Rank.	Age.	Date of Entering the Service.	Period of Service.	Remarks.
Brown, James	Private	28	Sept. 14, 1864	1 year.	Appointed Sergeant Oct. 6, 1864; reduced Oct. 30, 1864; mustered out with company July 14, 1865.
Burnett, Richard	...do...	29	Sept. 8, 1864	1 year.	
Carney, James B	...do...	19	Sept. 20, 1864	1 year.	Mustered out with company July 14, 1865.
Carroll, James	...do...	27	Sept. 26, 1864	1 year.	
Clegg, Jeremiah	...do...	18	Aug. 26, 1864	1 year.	Mustered out July 12, 1865, at Columbus, O., by order of War Department.
Cleveland, Thomas M	...do...	28	Sept. 14, 1864	1 year.	Appointed Corporal Oct. 6, 1864; reduced Oct. 20, 1864; mustered out with company July 14, 1865.
Clyde, Edwin G	...do...	30	Sept. 29, 1864	1 year.	Appointed Corporal Oct. 30, 1864; Sergeant Dec. 25, 1864; reduced Feb. 6, 1865; mustered out with company July 14, 1865.
Conkling, John	...do...	19	Sept. 7, 1864	1 year.	
Conway, Cornelius	...do...	34	Sept. 3, 1864	1 year.	Died Dec. 8, 1864, of wounds received Dec. 7, 1864, in battle of Murfreesboro, Tenn.
Davis, Thomas	...do...	26	Sept. 11, 1864	1 year.	
Dempsey, James	...do...	23	Sept. 21, 1864	1 year.	Mustered as Corporal.
Dennis, James	...do...	18	Sept. 28, 1864	1 year.	
Donehoe, Patrick R	...do...	25	Sept. 21, 1864	1 year.	
Doran, Richard	...do...	24	Oct. 7, 1864	1 year.	Mustered out with company July 14, 1865.
Drais, Lawson	...do...	23	Sept. 30, 1864	1 year.	Wounded Dec. 7, 1864, in battle of Murfreesboro, Tenn.; mustered out June 2, 1865, at Camp Dennison, O., by order of War Department.
Dressel, Frederick	...do...	44	Oct. 4, 1864	1 year.	Mustered out with company July 14, 1865.
Duffey, Bernard	...do...	27	Sept. 2, 1864	1 year.	
Fagan, Charles	...do...	38	Sept. 12, 1864	1 year.	Mustered out with company July 14, 1865.
Faulk, Engleberg	...do...	21	Sept. 3, 1864	1 year.	Mustered out with company July 14, 1865.
Fay, James	...do...	29	Sept. 19, 1864	1 year.	
Fox, Patrick	...do...	24	Sept. 19, 1864	1 year.	Mustered out with company July 14, 1865.
Fox, Thomas B	...do...	38	Sept. 14, 1864	1 year.	Mustered out with company July 14, 1865
Gaines, Wilson K	...do...	33	Sept. 12, 1864	1 year.	Mustered out June 1, 1865, at David's Island, New York Harbor, by order of War Department.
Gill, George F	...do...	27	Sept. 12, 1864	1 year.	Appointed Corporal Oct. 6, 1864; reduced Oct. 20, 1864; reappointed Corporal May 1, 1865; reduced [illegible] 1865 mustered out with company July 14, 1865
Gould, Robert	...do...	21	Sept. 11, 1864	1 year.	Died March 31, 1865, in 2d Division Hospital, 23d Army Corps.
Griffin, Patrick	...do...	21	Sept. 3, 1864	1 year.	Mustered as Sergeant; mustered out with company July 14, 1865.
Hart, Patrick	...do...	39	Sept. 3, 1864	1 year.	Mustered out with company July 14, 1865.
Hennessy, John	...do...	21	Dec. 8, 1864	1 year.	Mustered out with company July 14, 1865.
Heron, John	...do...	24	Sept. 6, 1864	1 year.	
Hickman, James M	...do...	27	Sept. 20, 1864	1 year.	Appointed Corporal Oct. 6, 1864; reduced Oct. 10, 1864; mustered out to date July 14, 1865, by order of War Department.
Howard, Francis	...do...	18	Sept. 26, 1864	1 year.	Mustered out with company July 14, 1865.
Hubbell, John	...do...	26	Sept. 30, 1864	1 year.	Wounded Dec. 7, 1864, in battle of Murfreesboro, Tenn., mustered out May 30, 1865, at Camp Dennison, O., by order of War Department.
Hudson, Joseph	...do...	41	Sept. 19, 1864	1 year.	Wounded Nov. 25, 1864, in action at Decatur, Ala.; mustered out June 2, 1865, at Camp Dennison, O., by order of War Department.
Joyce, Austin	...do...	18	Sept. 9, 1864	1 year.	Mustered out with company July 14, 1865.
Kehoe, Lawrence	...do...	[illegible]	Sept. 3, 1864	1 year.	
King, Joseph E	...do...	18	Sept. 29, 1864	1 year.	Died March 12, 1865, at Smithville, N. C.
Klein, Peter	...do...	20	Sept. 20, 1864	1 year.	Mustered out with company July 14, 1865.
Klick, James A	...do...	30	Oct. 4, 1864	1 year.	Mustered out with company July 14, 1865.
Kline, John S	...do...	19	Sept. 13, 1864	1 year.	Appointed Corporal May 1, 1865; reduced June 1, 1865; mustered out with company July 14, 1865.
Kratzbutt, George	...do...	19	Sept. 26, 1864	1 year.	Mustered out with company July 14, 1865.
Lautte, John	...do...	1[illegible]	Sept. 9, 1864	1 year.	Mustered out with company July 14, 1865.
Lewis, Joseph F	...do...	25	Sept. 26, 1864	1 year.	Mustered out July 28, 1865, at Washington, D. C., by order of War Department.
Lewis, William A	...do...	42	Oct. 7, 1864	1 year.	Mustered out with company July 14, 1865.
McBride, Thomas	...do...	22	Sept. 11, 1864	1 year.	Mustered out with company July 14, 1865.
McCarty, Patrick	...do...	22	Sept. 22, 1864	1 year.	Mustered out with company July 14, 1865.
McCarty, Patrick	...do...	25	Jan. 24, 1865	1 year.	Mustered out with company July 14, 1865.
McHenry, William	...do...	22	Oct. 1, 1864	1 year.	
McGauley, James	...do...	28	Sept. 22, 1864	1 year.	
Mc[illegible] Thomas	...do...	31	Sept. 17, 1864	1 year.	
Masters, John	...do...	35	Sept. 3, 1864	1 year.	Died March 15, 1865, at Wilmington, N. C.
Mayle, John	...do...	25	Oct. 4, 1864	1 year.	Mustered out with company July 14, 1865.
Metcalf, Moses H	...do...	21	Sept. 3, 1864	1 year.	Appointed Corporal Oct. 6, 1864; Sergeant Jan. 6, 1865; reduced June 1, 1865; mustered out with company July 14, 1865.
Miker, Christopher H	...do...	21	Oct. 4, 1864	1 year.	Mustered out with company July 14, 1865.
Moesch, William	...do...	21	Sept. 13, 1864	1 year.	Mustered out to date July 14, 1865, by order of War Department.
Mongan, Patrick	...do...	32	Sept. 1, 1864	1 year.	Mustered out with company July 14, 1865.

Names.	Rank.	Age.	Date of Entering the Service.	Period of Service.	Remarks.
[illegible], Levi S.	Private .	24	Sept. 16, 1864	1 year.	
[illegible], Joseph	....do....	30	Sept. 16, 1864	1 year	Mustered out June 22, 1865, at Columbus, O., by order of War Department.
Nadand, James W.	....do....	29	Sept. 24, 1864	1 year.	Discharged Dec. 3, 1864, to accept promotion as Hospital Steward in U. S. A.
[illegible]wcomb, Thomas	....do....	29	Oct. 1, 1864	1 year.	
[illegible]ton, Chambers	....do....	21	Sept. 16, 1864	1 year.	Mustered out with company July 14, 1865.
[illegible]d, John	....do....	35	Sept. 20, 1864	1 year.	Mustered out with company July 14, 1865.
[illegible]dgers, Thomas C.	....do....	25	Dec. 2, 1864	1 year.	Mustered out July 3, 1865, at David's Island, New York Harbor, by order of War Department.
[illegible]oney, James	....do....	28	Jan. 25, 1865	1 year.	Mustered out with company July 14, 1865.
[illegible], Richard	....do....	35	Sept. 16, 1864	1 year.	Mustered out with company July 14, 1865.
[illegible]k, Albert F	....do....	18	Sept. 26, 1864	1 year.	Mustered out with company July 14, 1865.
[illegible], James	....do....	29	Sept. 29, 1864	1 year.	Mustered out with company July 14, 1865.
[illegible]an, Thomas	....do....	26	Sept. 3, 1864	1 year.	Mustered out with company July 14, 1865.
[illegible]ese, Ephraim	....do....	30	Sept. 5, 1864	1 year.	Discharged Feb. 10, 1865, at Camp Dennison, O., by order of War Department.
[illegible]atto, Nicholas A.	....do....	30	Oct. 1, 1864	1 year.	Mustered out with company July 14, 1865.
[illegible]eridan, John	....do....	21	Sept. 19, 1864	1 year.	Appointed Sergeant Oct. 20, 1864; promoted to Com. Sergeant Jan. 6, 1865; reduced Feb. 1, 1865; absent, sick, since June 28, 1865; enlisted in this regiment in violation of 50th Article of War; was member of Co. A, 29th Massachusetts Regiment; not recognized as member of this organization.
Smith, James	....do....	25	Sept. 12, 1864	1 year.	Appointed Corporal Feb. 6, 1865; reduced June 1, 1865; mustered out with company July 14, 1865.
Smith, James	....do....	24	Sept. 14, 1864	1 year.	
Smith, Thomas	....do....	38	Sept. 12, 1864	1 year.	Mustered out with company July 14, 1865.
Smith, William H	....do....	28	Sept. 6, 1864	1 year.	Appointed Corporal Oct. 6, 1864; Sergeant Oct. 30, 1864; reduced Dec. 28, 1864; mustered out with company July 14, 1865.
[illegible]fford, Henry	....do....	37	Sept. 29, 1864	1 year.	Died Feb. 28, 1865, at Nashville, Tenn.
[illegible]iner, Theodore	....do....	22	Sept. 17, 1864	1 year.	Mustered out with company July 14, 1865.
[illegible]wart, William	....do....	18	Sept. 9, 1864	1 year.	
[illegible]lman, James	....do....	39	Sept. 24, 1864	1 year.	
[illegible]owell, John M.	....do....	28	Sept. 5, 1864	1 year.	Mustered out with company July 14, 1865.
Sullivan, Daniel	....do....	23	Sept. 28, 1864	1 year.	Mustered out with company July 14, 1865.
Thomas, John	....do....	38	Sept. 8, 1864	1 year.	
[illegible]yman, William H	....do....	23	Oct. 4, 1864	1 year.	Mustered out with company July 14, 1865.
Turner, Howard A.	....do....	42	Sept. 30, 1864	1 year.	Mustered out May 29, 1865, at David's Island, New York Harbor, by order of War Department.
Van Bergen, Harry	....do....	27	Sept. 10, 1864	1 year.	Promoted to 2d Lieutenant Co. D, 183d O. V. I., Oct. 26, 1864.
Wait, William	....do....	28	Sept. 7, 1864	1 year.	Mustered out with company July 14, 1865.
Weldon, Thomas	....do....	35	Sept. 12, 1864	1 year.	Mustered out with company July 14, 1865.
Wilson, Samuel	....do....	20	Sept. 23, 1864	1 year.	Mustered out with company July 14, 1865.
Wilson, William H.	....do....	24	Sept. 26, 1864	1 year.	
Wise, Joseph A.	....do....	25	Oct. 3, 1864	1 year.	Mustered as 1st Sergeant; died June 6, 1865, at Cincinnati, O.
Witherby, Joseph A.	....do....	22	Sept. 30, 1864	1 year.	Mustered out with company July 14, 1865.
Witherby, Wallace W.	....do....	24	Oct. 1, 1864	1 year.	Mustered out with company July 14, 1865.

COMPANY E.

Mustered in October 6, 1864, at Camp Dennison, O., by Wm. Von Doehn, Captain and A. A. G. Mustered out July 14, 1865, at Salisbury N. C., by Frederick Anderson, Lieutenant and A. C. M.

Names.	Rank.	Age.	Date of Entering the Service.	Period of Service.	Remarks.
David Gordon	Captain.	37	Oct. 6, 1864	1 year.	Resigned March 4, 1865.
William Very	....do....	21	Sept. 27, 1864	1 year.	Transferred from Co. G, 177th O.V.I., June 22, 1865; mustered out with company July 14, 1865.
Daniel K. Gordon	1st Lieut.	..	Oct. 6, 1864	1 year.	Borne only on muster-in roll of company. No further record found.
Robert S. Logan	....do....	29	Sept. 5, 1864	1 year.	Appointed 2d Lieutenant from private Oct. 6, 1864; promoted to 1st Lieutenant Oct. 21, 1864; Captain July 10, 1865, but not mustered; mustered out with company July 14, 1865.
John Alexander	2d Lieut.	19	Sept. 26, 1864	1 year.	Appointed Sergeant Oct. 6, 1864; promoted to 2d Lieutenant Oct. 21, 1864; 1st Lieutenant July 10, 1865, but not mustered; mustered out with company July 14, 1865.
Jacob G. [illegible]	1st Sergt.	18	Sept. 30, 1864	1 year.	Appointed Corporal Oct. 6, 1864; Sergeant Oct. 24, 1864; 1st Sergeant Jan. 1, 1865; mustered out with company July 14, 1865.

Names.	Rank.	Age.	Date of Entering the Service.	Period of Service.	Remarks.
Benjamin F. Drury	Sergeant.	21	Sept. 27, 1864	1 year.	Appointed Oct. 6, 1864; promoted to 2d Lieutenant Co. F, 183d O. V. I., Oct. 18, 1864.
Benjamin F. Heath	....do....	21	Sept. 14, 1864	1 year.	Appointed Oct. 6, 1864; promoted to Sergeant Major Nov. 20, 1864.
Oliver R. Frazier	....do....	22	Aug. 31, 1864	1 year.	Appointed Oct. 6, 1864; died Dec. 14, 1864, Murfreesboro, Tenn., of wounds received Dec. 7, 1864, in battle at same place.
Lucian W. McKee	....do....	18	Sept. 6, 1864	1 year.	Appointed 1st Sergeant Oct. 6, 1864; reduced to Sergeant Jan. 1, 1865; promoted to Co. Sergeant Feb. 1, 1865.
Thomas F. Gleason	....do....	19	Sept. 15, 1864	1 year.	Appointed Corporal Oct. 6, 1864; Sergeant Oct. 24, 1864; mustered out with company July 14, 1865.
Frederick Yeager	....do....	20	Oct. 5, 1864	1 year.	Appointed Corporal Oct. 24, 1864; Sergeant Dec. 1, 1864; mustered out with company July 14, 1865.
Martin W. O'Connor	....do....	18	Sept. 14, 1864	1 year.	Appointed Corporal Oct. 6, 1864; Sergeant Dec. 15, 1864; mustered out June 14, 1865, at Louisville, Ky., by order of War Department.
Samuel J. Loomis	....do....	22	Sept. 22, 1864	1 year.	Appointed Corporal Oct. 24, 1864; Sergeant Feb. 1, 1865; mustered out with company July 14, 1865.
John Weaver	Corporal.	32	Sept. 30, 1864	1 year.	Appointed Oct. 6, 1864; mustered out May 2, 1865, at Philadelphia, Pa., by order of War Department.
Alfred B. Nowis	....do....	25	Sept. 3, 1864	1 year.	Appointed Oct. 6, 1864; mustered out with company July 14, 1865.
Abraham Diffenderfer	....do....	19	Sept. 6, 1864	1 year.	Appointed Oct. 6, 1864; mustered out with company July 14, 1865.
Frederick Walter	....do....	19	Aug. 31, 1864	1 year.	Appointed Oct. 6, 1864; mustered out with company July 14, 1865.
John Forsythe	....do....	39	Sept. 16, 1864	1 year.	Appointed Oct. 24, 1864; mustered out with company July 14, 1865.
William Porter	....do....	24	Aug. 3, 1864	1 year.	Appointed Dec. 1, 1864; mustered out with company July 14, 1865.
Reinhart Schindledicker	....do....	30	Sept. 30, 1864	1 year.	Appointed Feb. 1, 1865; mustered out with company July 14, 1865.
William Barlow	....do....	23	Sept. 21, 1864	1 year.	Appointed Feb. 1, 1865; mustered out with company July 14, 1865.
John Dair	....do....	26	Oct. 3, 1864	1 year.	Appointed Dec. 16, 1864; reduced Feb. 1, 1865; reappointed June 1, 1865; mustered out with company July 14, 1865.
James Davis	Wagoner	38	Sept. 14, 1864	1 year.	Mustered out with company July 14, 1865.
Adams, Wilson W	Private..	20	Sept. 30, 1864	1 year.	Wounded Dec. 7, 1864, in battle of Murfreesboro, Tenn.; discharged April 29, 1865, at Camp Dennison, O., by order of War Department.
Aire, Michael	....do....	26	Sept. 28, 1864	1 year.	Mustered out with company July 14, 1865.
Aldrich, Edward	....do....	20	Aug. 2, 1864	1 year.	Transferred from Co. D, 178th O. V. I., June 15, 1865; mustered out with company July 14, 1865.
Ayers, William R	....do....	22	Sept. 3, 1864	1 year.	Transferred from Co. E, 178th O. V. I., June 15, 1865, as William R. Aris; mustered out with company July 14, 1865.
Barcuff, Christopher	....do....	28	Oct. 1, 1864	1 year.	Mustered out with company July 14, 1865.
Bartch, Simon	....do....	28	Sept. 31, 1864	1 year.	Mustered out July 14, 1865, at Columbus, O., by order of War Department.
Bartlett, George	....do....	20	Oct. 3, 1864	1 year.	
Bentel, Louis	....do....	19	Sept. 15, 1864	1 year.	Mustered out to date July 14, 1865, by order of War Department.
Binsley, Eli	....do....	30	Sept. 30, 1864	1 year.	See Co. G, 71st O. V. I.
Blair, Mitchell	....do....	17	Sept. 19, 1864	1 year.	Transferred from Co. F, 178th O. V. I., June 15, 1865; mustered out with company July 14, 1865.
[illegible], William	....do....	19	Sept. 26, 1864	1 year.	Mustered out with company July 14, 1865.
[illegible], John P	....do....	36	Sept. 20, 1864	1 year.	
[illegible], Aaron C	....do....	23	Sept. 30, 1864	1 year.	Mustered out with company July 14, 1865.
[illegible], Lemuel	....do....	22	Oct. 4, 1864	1 year.	Mustered out with company July 14, 1865.
[illegible], Frederick	....do....	40	Aug. 23, 1864	1 year.	Mustered out with company July 14, 1865.
[illegible], Saffron	....do....	21	Sept. 12, 1864	1 year.	Mustered out with company July 14, 1865.
Bradford, James M	....do....	21	Sept. 27, 1864	1 year.	Mustered out with company July 14, 1865.
[illegible], Allen	....do....	20	Oct. 4, 1864	1 year.	Mustered out with company July 14, 1865.
[illegible], Absalom	....do....	44	Oct. 3, 1864	1 year.	See Co. G, 29th O. V. I.
[illegible], Vincent C	....do....	36	Oct. 3, 1864	1 year.	See Co. G, 29th O. V. I.
[illegible], Thomas	....do....	34	Aug. 17, 1864	1 year.	See Thomas Barron, Co. A, 181st O. V. I.
[illegible], Joseph	....do....	18	Mch. 16, 1865	1 year.	Mustered out with company July 14, 1865.
[illegible], William	....do....	31	Sept. 26, 1864	1 year.	Mustered out May 30, 1865, at Camp Dennison, O., by order of War Department.
Campbell, Thomas	....do....	33	Sept. 17, 1864	1 year.	Mustered out June 14, 1865, at Columbus, O., by order of War Department.
[illegible], Isaiah P	....do....	28	Aug. 25, 1864	3 yrs.	Mustered out with company July 14, 1865.
Constantine, Michael	....do....	34	Sept. 6, 1864	1 year.	Mustered out with company July 14, 1865; also borne on rolls as Michael Const[illegible].
Craig, Charles H	....do....	22	Sept. 16, 1864	1 year.	Transferred from Co. F, 178th O. V. I., June 15, 1865; mustered out with company July 14, 1865.

Rank.	Age.	Date of Entering the Service.	Period of Service.	Remarks.
Private..	23	Oct. 1, 1864	1 year.	Transferred from Co. F, 178th O. V. I., June 15, 1865; mustered out with company July 14, 1865.
..do....	18	Sept. 30, 1864	1 year.	
..do....	19	Mch. 22, 1865	1 year.	Mustered out with company July 14, 1865.
..do....	22	Sept. 30, 1864	1 year.	Mustered out with company July 14, 1865.
..do....	27	Oct. 3, 1864	1 year.	See Co. G, 78th O. V. I.
..do....	18	Sept. 28, 1864	1 year.	Mustered out with company July 14, 1865.
..do....	19	Sept. 9, 1864	1 year.	Mustered out with company July 14, 1865.
..do....	19	Sept. 9, 1864	1 year.	Mustered out with company July 14, 1865.
..do....	18	Feb. 6, 1865	1 year.	Mustered out with company July 14, 1865.
..do....	18	Oct. 3, 1864	1 year.	Mustered out with company July 14, 1865; also borne on rolls as Joseph Goell.
..do....	42	Sept. 3, 1864	1 year.	Mustered out to date July 14, 1865, by order of War Department.
..do....	19	Oct. 5, 1864	1 year.	
..do....	32	Oct. 4, 1864	1 year.	Mustered out with company July 14, 1865.
..do....	22	Sept. 8, 1864	1 year.	
..do....	23	Sept. 28, 1864	1 year.	Mustered out with company July 14, 1865.
..do....	17	Sept. 11, 1864	1 year.	Mustered out with company July 14, 1865.
..do....	20	Sept. 30, 1864	1 year.	Mustered out with company July 14, 1865.
..do....	35	Sept. 6, 1864	1 year.	Transferred from Co. E, 178th O.V. I., June 15, 1865; mustered out with company July 14, 1865.
..do....	20	Sept. 27, 1864	1 year.	Mustered out with company July 14, 1865.
..do....	18	Sept. 3, 1864	1 year.	Mustered out with company July 14, 1865.
..do....	30	Sept. 1, 1864	1 year.	Mustered out June 15, 1865, at Philadelphia, Pa., by order of War Department.
..do....	20	Feb. 8, 1865	1 year.	Transferred from Co. K, 178th O. V. I., June 15, 1865; mustered out with company July 14, 1865.
..do....	22	Sept. 8, 1864	1 year.	Mustered out with company July 14, 1865.
..do....	40	Sept. 1, 1864	1 year.	Mustered out June 24, 1865, at David's Island, New York Harbor, by order of War Department.
..do....	28	Sept. 15, 1864	1 year.	Transferred from Co. C, 178th O.V. I., June 15, 1865.
..do....	18	Sept. 2, 1864	1 year.	Mustered out with company July 14, 1865.
..do....	28	Oct. 5, 1864	1 year.	Mustered out with company July 14, 1865.
..do....	29	Oct. 1, 1864	1 year.	See Co. E, 71st O. V. I.
..do....	25	Sept. 14, 1864	1 year.	Transferred from Co. C, 178th O.V. I., June 15, 1865.
..do....	32	Oct. 1, 1864	1 year.	
..do....	18	Sept. 19, 1864	1 year.	Transferred from Co. E, 178th O.V. I., June 15, 1865; mustered out with company July 14, 1865.
..do....	18	Oct. 3, 1864	1 year.	Mustered out June 19, 1865, at Camp Chase, O., by order of War Department.
..do....	44	Sept. 29, 1864	1 year.	Mustered out with company July 14, 1865.
..do....	20	Oct. 4, 1864	1 year.	Mustered out with company July 14, 1865.
..do....	28	Sept. 7, 1864	1 year.	Mustered out with company July 14, 1865.
..do....	22	Sept. 3, 1864	1 year.	Mustered out with company July 14, 1865.
..do....	29	Oct. 20, 1864	1 year.	Transferred from Co. F, 178th O.V. I., June 15, 1865; mustered out with company July 14, 1865.
..do....	18	Sept. 28, 1864	1 year.	Mustered out with company July 14, 1865.
..do....	34	Sept. 5, 1864	1 year.	Mustered out with company July 14, 1865.
..do....	42	Sept. 14, 1864	1 year.	Mustered out with company July 14, 1865.
..do....	21	Sept. 1, 1864	1 year.	See Co. A, 178th O. V. I.
..do....	20	Sept. 27, 1864	1 year.	Mustered out May 16, 1865, at Nashville, Tenn., by order of War Department.
..do....	21	Aug. 22, 1864	1 year.	Transferred from Co. A, 178th O.V. I., June 15, 1865; mustered out to date July 14, 1865, at Columbus, O., by order of War Department.
..do....	21	Oct. 4, 1864	1 year.	
..do....	41	Oct. 4, 1864	1 year.	Died May 16, 1865.
..do....	43	Sept. 16, 1864	1 year.	Mustered out May 17, 1865, at Cincinnati, O., by order of War Department.
..do....	18	Sept. 13, 1864	1 year.	Mustered out with company July 14, 1865.
..do....	42	Sept. 3, 1864	1 year.	Mustered out June 20, 1865, at Camp Chase, O., by order of War Department.
..do....	18	Sept. 8, 1864	1 year.	Transferred from Co. A, 178th O.V. I., June 15, 1865; mustered out with company July 14, 1866.
..do....	42	Aug. 15, 1864	1 year.	Transferred from Co. F, 178th O.V. I., June 15, 1866; mustered out with company July 14, 1865.
..do....	30	Mch. 3, 1865	1 year.	Mustered out with company July 14, 1865.
..do....	18	Sept. 30, 1864	1 year.	Mustered out with company July 14, 1865.
..do....	38	Oct. 3, 1864	1 year.	See Co. G, 29th O. V. I.
..do....	27	Aug. 29, 1864	1 year.	Mustered out with company July 14, 1865.
..do....	20	Aug. 22, 1864	1 year.	Mustered out with company July 14, 1865.
..do....	19	Sept. 5, 1864	1 year.	Transferred from Co. E, 178th O.V. I., June 15, 1865; mustered out with company July 14, 1865.

Names.	Rank.	Age.	Date of Entering the Service.	Period of Service.	Remarks.
Shafer, Isaac	Private..	25	Oct. 4, 1864	1 year.	
Shirtliff, Marcellus	....do....	18	Sept. 30, 1864	1 year.	
Slyh, Frank M	....do....	23	Sept. 6, 1864	1 year.	Appointed Corporal Oct. 6, 1864; reduc[illegible] 7, 1864; mustered out June 19, 1865, at D[illegible] Island, New York Harbor, by order [illegible] Department.
Smith, Eugene H	....do....	18	Feb. 8, 1865	1 year.	Transferred from Co. K, 178th O.V.I., J[illegible] 1865; mustered out with company J[illegible] 1865.
Snyder, Edward	....do....	29	Sept. 27, 1864	1 year.	Mustered out with company July 14, 18[illegible]
Stahl, Louis	....do....	38	Sept. 28, 1864	1 year.	Mustered out with company July 14, 18[illegible]
Stansbury, John	....do....	18	Aug. 29, 1864	1 year.	Mustered out with company July 14, 18[illegible]
Stivers, William	....do....	18	Aug. 29, 1864	1 year.	Mustered out with company July 14, 18[illegible]
Thomas, Charles	....do....	18	Sept. 22, 1864	1 year.	
Thompson, Samuel	....do....	20	Sept. 1, 1864	1 year.	Transferred from Co. D, 178th O.V.I., J[illegible] 1865; mustered out with company J[illegible] 1865.
Toskay, John W	....do....	22	Sept. 7, 1864	1 year.	Promoted to Hospital Steward Oct. 18, [illegible] returned to company Dec. 3, 1864; mu[illegible] out with company July 14, 1865.
Ulam, Ross	....do....	18	Sept. 9, 1864	1 year.	Mustered out with company July 14, 18[illegible]
Vandermark, William	....do....	24	Sept. 6, 1864	1 year.	Mustered out with company July 14, 18[illegible]
Vogel, John	....do....	18	Sept. 27, 1864	1 year.	
Willerding, Clement	....do....	37	Sept. 21, 1864	1 year.	Mustered out with company July 14, 18[illegible]
Willey, James	....do....	21	Oct. 4, 1864	1 year.	
Williams, John	....do....	21	Sept. 27, 1864	1 year.	
Winn, Isaac S	....do....	22	Sept. 19, 1861	1 year.	Transferred from Co. F, 178th O.V.I., J[illegible] 1865; mustered out with company J[illegible] 1865.
Wosstell, Jacob	....do....	23	Sept. 18, 1864	1 year.	Mustered out with company July 14, 18[illegible]

COMPANY F.

Mustered in October 7, 1864, at Camp Dennison, O., by Wm. Von Doehn, Captain and A. A. G. Mus[illegible] out July 14, 1865, at Salisbury N. C., by Frederick Anderson, Lieutenant and A. C. M.

Names.	Rank.	Age.	Date of Entering the Service.	Period of Service.	Remarks.
Gustav A. Gruis	Captain.	31	Oct. 7, 1864	1 year.	
Louis Kuster	1st Lieut.	35	Oct. 7, 1864	1 year.	Promoted to Captain May 11, 1865, but [illegible] mustered; mustered out with company J[illegible] 14, 1865.
Fred. Hoeller	2d Lieut.	21	Oct. 7, 1864	1 year.	Appointed Act. Regt. Quartermaster Ja[illegible] 1865; promoted to 1st Lieutenant [illegible] April 8, 1865.
Henry Elver	1st Sergt.	21	Sept. 20, 1864	1 year.	Appointed Oct. 7, 1864; promoted to 2d Lie[illegible] tenant July 10, 1864, but not mustered; mu[illegible] tered out with company July 14, 1865
John Steffel	Sergeant.	23	Sept. 8, 1864	1 year.	Appointed Oct. 7, 1864; mustered out wi[illegible] company July 14, 1865.
Henry Asbach	....do....	30	Sept. 22, 1864	1 year.	Appointed Oct. 7, 1864; mustered out [illegible] company July 14, 1865.
John Wamsler	....do....	33	Sept. 15, 1864	1 year.	Appointed Oct. 7, 1864; mustered out [illegible] company July 14, 1865.
John Siefert	....do....	28	Sept. 16, 1864	1 year.	Appointed Oct. 7, 1864; mustered out [illegible] company July 14, 1865.
Henry Oliver	Corporal.	38	Sept. 21, 1864	1 year.	Appointed Oct. 7, 1864; mustered out Ju[illegible] 3, 1865, at Camp Dennison, O., by order [illegible] War Department.
Peter Lichtfers	....do....	37	Sept. 17, 1864	1 year.	Appointed Oct 7, 1864; mustered out Ju[illegible] 1865, at David's Island, New York Har[illegible] by order of War Department.
John Reiner	....do....	24	Sept. 14, 1864	1 year.	Appointed Oct. 7, 1864; mustered out [illegible] company July 14, 1865.
Jacob Schweitzer	....do....	27	Sept. 19, 1864	1 year.	Appointed Oct. 7, 1864; mustered out [illegible] company July 14, 1865.
Henry Bauer	....do....	26	Sept. 20, 1864	1 year.	Appointed Oct. 7, 1864; mustered out [illegible] company July 14, 1865.
Constantine Geschwind.	....do....	28	Sept. 26, 1864	1 year.	Appointed Oct. 7, 1864; mustered out [illegible] company July 14, 1865.
Theodore Koehn	....do....	25	Oct. 3, 1864	1 year.	Appointed Oct. 7, 1864; mustered out [illegible] company July 14, 1865.
Gottlieb Knabe	....do....	38	Sept. 20, 1864	1 year.	Appointed Oct. 7, 1864; mustered out [illegible] company July 14, 1865.
Frank Mueller	Musician	19	Sept. 12, 1864	1 year.	Appointed Oct. 7, 1864; mustered out [illegible] company July 14, 1865.
Clemens Oldendick	....do....	18	Sept. 19, 1864	1 year.	Appointed Oct. 7, 1864; mustered out [illegible] company July 14, 1865.
William Ehrhardt	Wagoner	23	Sept. 21, 1864	1 year.	Appointed Oct. 7, 1864; mustered out [illegible] company July 14, 1865.
Amlingmeyer, William.	Private..	26	Sept. 24, 1864	1 year.	Mustered out with company July 14, [illegible]
Barkan, Henry	....do....	39	Sept. 20, 1864	1 year.	Mustered out with company July 14, [illegible]

	Rank.	Age.	Date of Entering the Service.	Period of Service.	Remarks.
	Private.	39	Sept. 19, 1864	1 year.	Mustered out with company July 14, 1865.
	...do...	38	Sept. 20, 1864	1 year.	Mustered out with company July 14, 1865.
	...do...	41	Sept. 29, 1864	1 year.	See Co. C, 183d O. V. I.
	...do...	37	Sept. 30, 1864	1 year.	Mustered out with company July 14, 1865.
	...do...	41	Sept. 19, 1864	1 year.	Mustered out with company July 14, 1865.
	...do...	19	Sept. 29, 1864	1 year.	Mustered out with company July 14, 1865.
	...do...	19	Sept. 27, 1864	1 year.	Mustered out with company July 14, 1865.
	...do...	25	Sept. 21, 1864	1 year.	Died July 9, 1865, at Salisbury, N. C.
	...do...	20	Sept. 21, 1864	1 year.	Mustered out with company July 14, 1865.
m.	...do...	26	Sept. 16, 1864	1 year.	Mustered out with company July 14, 1865.
r.	...do...	34	Sept. 22, 1864	1 year.	Mustered out with company July 14, 1865.
	...do...	36	Oct. 3, 1864	1 year.	Mustered out with company July 14, 1865.
ick.	...do...	37	Sept. 19, 1864	1 year.	Mustered out with company July 14, 1865.
	...do...	24	Sept. 24, 1864	1 year.	Mustered out with company July 14, 1865.
	...do...	20	Sept. 19, 1864	1 year.	Mustered out with company July 14, 1865.
	...do...	38	Sept. 28, 1864	1 year.	Mustered out with company July 14, 1865.
	...do...	34	Sept. 20, 1864	1 year.	Mustered out with company July 14, 1865.
	...do...	40	Sept. 21, 1864	1 year.	Mustered out with company July 14, 1865.
	...do...	35	Sept. 19, 1864	1 year.	Mustered out with company July 14, 1865.
	...do...	36	Sept. 20, 1864	1 year.	Mustered out with company July 14, 1865.
	...do...	42	Sept. 24, 1864	1 year.	Mustered out June 29, 1865, at Columbus, O., by order of War Department.
	...do...	40	Sept. 22, 1864	1 year.	Mustered out June 22, 1865, at Columbus O., by order of War Department.
	...do...	38	Sept. 20, 1864	1 year.	Mustered out with company July 14, 1865.
	...do...	26	Oct. 4, 1864	1 year.	Mustered out with company July 14, 1865.
	...do...	30	Sept. 22, 1864	1 year.	Mustered out with company July 14, 1865.
	...do...	29	Sept. 16, 1864	1 year.	Mustered out with company July 14, 1865.
tian.	...do...	31	Sept. 16, 1864	1 year.	Mustered out with company July 14, 1865.
	...do...	25	Oct. 3, 1864	1 year.	Mustered out with company July 14, 1865.
	...do...	26	Oct. 3, 1864	1 year.	Mustered out with company July 14, 1865.
	...do...	37	Sept. 30, 1864	1 year.	Mustered out with company July 14, 1865.
	...do...	35	Sept. 27, 1864	1 year.	Mustered out with company July 14, 1865.
	...do...	28	Sept. 21, 1864	1 year.	Mustered out May 26, 1865, at Albany, N. Y., by order of War Department.
	...do...	33	Sept. 28, 1864	1 year.	Mustered out with company July 14, 1865.
	...do...	42	Sept. 20, 1864	1 year.	Mustered out with company July 14, 1865.
	...do...	44	Sept. 28, 1864	1 year.	Died Jan. 21, 1865, at Nashville, Tenn.
ioud.	...do...	21	Sept. 27, 1864	1 year.	Mustered out with company July 14, 1865.
	...do...	33	Oct. 4, 1864	1 year.	Mustered out with company July 14, 1865.
	...do...	48	Sept. 28, 1864	1 year.	Mustered out with company July 14, 1865.
	...do...	34	Sept. 19, 1864	1 year.	Mustered out with company July 14, 1865.
	...do...	24	Sept. 26, 1864	1 year.	Mustered out with company July 14, 1865.
	...do...	36	Sept. 22, 1864	1 year.	Mustered out with company July 14, 1865.
	...do...	39	Sept. 19, 1864	1 year.	Mustered out with company July 14, 1865.
	...do...	26	Sept. 17, 1864	1 year.	Mustered out with company July 14, 1865.
	...do...	24	Sept. 20, 1864	1 year.	Mustered out with company July 14, 1865.
	...do...	42	Sept. 17, 1864	1 year.	Mustered out with company July 14, 1865.
	...do...	37	Sept. 28, 1864	1 year.	Mustered out with company July 14, 1865.
	...do...	29	Sept. 19, 1864	1 year.	Mustered out with company July 14, 1865.
us.	...do...	20	Sept. 19, 1864	1 year.	Mustered out with company July 14, 1865.
	...do...	20	Oct. 1, 1864	1 year.	Mustered out with company July 14, 1865.
	...do...	35	Sept. 19, 1864	1 year.	Mustered out with company July 14, 1865.
	...do...	35	Sept. 20, 1864	1 year.	Mustered out May 13, 1865, at Cincinnati, O., by order of War Department.
	...do...	29	Sept. 27, 1864	1 year.	Mustered out with company July 14, 1865.
	...do...	38	Sept. 15, 1864	1 year.	Mustered out with company July 14, 1865.
	...do...	29	Sept. 24, 1864	1 year.	Mustered out with company July 14, 1865.
	...do...	30	Sept. 16, 1864	1 year.	Mustered out with company July 14, 1865.
	...do...	27	Sept. 29, 1864	1 year.	Mustered out with company July 14, 1865.
	...do...	35	Sept. 14, 1864	1 year.	Mustered out with company July 14, 1865.
	...do...	27	Sept. 3, 1864	1 year.	Died Dec. 31, 1864, at Murfreesboro, Tenn.
	...do...	30	Sept. 20, 1864	1 year.	Mustered out with company July 14, 1865.
	...do...	25	Oct. 1, 1864	1 year.	Mustered out with company July 14, 1865.
W.	...do...	27	Sept. 21, 1864	1 year.	Mustered out with company July 14, 1865.
	...do...	33	Oct. 3, 1864	1 year.	Mustered out with company July 14, 1865.
	...do...	24	Sept. 26, 1864	1 year.	Mustered out with company July 14, 1865.
	...do...	24	Sept. 21, 1864	1 year.	Mustered out with company July 14, 1865.
	...do...	19	Sept. 24, 1864	1 year.	Mustered out with company July 14, 1865.
	...do...	30	Sept. 27, 1864	1 year.	Mustered out with company July 14, 1865.
	...do...	19	Sept. 19, 1864	1 year.	Mustered out with company July 14, 1865.
	...do...	20	Oct. 5, 1864	1 year.	Mustered out with company July 14, 1865.
	...do...	26	Sept. 22, 1864	1 year.	Mustered out with company July 14, 1865.
	...do...	23	Sept. 22, 1864	1 year.	Mustered out with company July 14, 1865.
	...do...	28	Sept. 24, 1864	1 year.	Mustered out with company July 14, 1865.
	...do...	48	Sept. 26, 1864	1 year.	Mustered out with company July 14, 1865.
n.	...do...	33	Sept. 24, 1864	1 year.	Mustered out July 19, 1865, at Washington, D. C., by order of War Department.
	...do...	28	Sept. 28, 1864	1 year.	Mustered out with company July 14, 1865.
	...do...	39	Sept. 20, 1864	1 year.	Mustered out with company July 14, 1865.
	...do...	36	Sept. 21, 1864	1 year.	Mustered out with company July 14, 1865.
	...do...	21	Sept. 17, 1864	1 year.	Mustered out with company July 14, 1865.
	...do...	25	Sept. 19, 1864	1 year.	Mustered out with company July 14, 1865.
	...do...	38	Oct. 3, 1864	1 year.	Mustered out with company July 14, 1865.
	...do...	22	Sept. 27, 1864	1 year.	Mustered out with company July 14, 1865.

COMPANY G.

Mustered in October 7, 1864, at Camp Dennison, O., by Wm. Von Doehn, Captain and A. A. G. Mustered out July 14, 1865, at Salisbury, N. C., by Frederick Anderson, Lieutenant and A. C. M.

Names.	Rank.	Age.	Date of Entering the Service.	Period of Service.	Remarks.
George Kounz	Captain.	22	Oct. 7, 1864	1 year.	Mustered out with company July 14, 1865.
Lawrence C. Carpenter.	1st Lieut.	27	Oct. 7, 1864	1 year.	Mustered out May 15, 1865, by order of War Department.
George W. Poling	2d Lieut.	24	Oct. 7, 1864	1 year.	Promoted to 1st Lieutenant April 8, 1865, but not mustered; mustered out with company July 14, 1865.
John Leonard	1st Sergt.	41	Sept. 19, 1864	1 year.	Appointed Sergeant Oct 7, 1864; promoted to Sergt. Major Oct. 18, 1864; reduced to ranks Nov. 30, 1864; appointed 1st Sergeant Dec. 7, 1864; promoted to 2d Lieutenant July 10, 1865, but not mustered; mustered out with company July 14, 1865.
Columbus Thornton	Sergeant.	25	Sept. 22, 1864	1 year.	Promoted to Captain Co. F, 183d O. V. I., Oct. 19, 1864.
Silas F. Hill	....do....	33	Sept. 3, 1864	1 year.	Appointed Oct. 7, 1864; mustered out with company July 14, 1865.
Thomas G. Duncan	....do....	20	Sept. 2, 1864	1 year.	Appointed Oct. 7, 1864; mustered out with company July 14, 1865.
James Fitzgerald	....do....	24	Sept. 19, 1864	1 year.	Appointed Corporal Oct. 7, 1864; Sergeant Oct. 18, 1864; mustered out with company June 14, 1865.
Barnett W. Blakeslee	....do....	31	Oct. 4, 1864	1 year.	Appointed Oct. 23, 1864; mustered out with company July 14, 1865.
John G. Moore	Corporal.	19	Sept. 20, 1864	1 year.	Appointed Oct. 7, 1864; mustered out June 5, 1865, at Columbus, O., by order of War Department.
John C. Owens	....do....	35	Sept. 14, 1864	1 year.	Appointed Oct. 7, 1864; mustered out June 5, 1865, at Columbus, O., by order of War Department.
Heman F. Menough	....do....	20	Sept. 2, 1864	1 year.	Appointed Oct. 7, 1864; mustered out with company July 14, 1865.
George S. Moore	....do....	33	Aug. 29, 1864	1 year.	Appointed Oct. 7, 1864; mustered out with company July 14, 1865.
Vincent Winings	....do....	20	Aug. 29, 1864	1 year.	Appointed Oct. 7, 1864; mustered out with company July 14, 1865.
Thomas Cooper	....do....	23	Oct. 4, 1864	1 year.	Appointed Oct. 18, 1864; mustered out with company July 14, 1865.
Benjamin Dean	....do....	37	Sept. 23, 1864	1 year.	Appointed Dec. 31, 1864; mustered out with company July 14, 1865.
Enoch D. Lamb	....do....	31	Sept. 19, 1864	1 year.	Appointed Jan. 1, 1865; mustered out with company July 14, 1865.
William Hazlebaker	....do....	33	Oct. 3, 1864	1 year.	Appointed June 7, 1865; mustered out with company July 14, 1865.
William H. Wilson	Musician	22	Sept. 20, 1864	1 year.	Appointed Oct. 7, 1864; mustered out with company July 14, 1865.
Aaron Rudy	....do....	28	Sept. 28, 1864	1 year.	Appointed Oct. 7, 1864; mustered out with company July 14, 1865.
James H. Dufley	Wagoner.	23	Aug. 26, 1864	1 year.	Appointed Oct. 7, 1864; mustered out with company July 14, 1865.
Abbott, George W	Private.	18	Sept. 13, 1864	1 year.	Wounded Dec. 7, 1864, in battle of Murfreesboro, Tenn.; mustered out June 9, 1865, at Camp Dennison, O., by order of War Department.
Arnold, Anderson	....do....	27	Sept. 28, 1864	1 year.	Mustered out with company July 14, 1865.
Atwell, Francis M	....do....	43	Sept. 29, 1864	1 year.	
Augenstein, Matthew	....do....	20	Feb. 21, 1865	1 year.	Transferred from Co. D, 178th O. V. I., June 15, 1865; mustered out with company July 14, 1865.
Beach, George W	....do....	26	Sept. 8, 1864	1 year.	Mustered out with company July 14, 1865.
Beach, Solomon	....do....	22	Sept. 8, 1864	1 year.	Mustered out with company July 14, 1865.
Blake, William H	....do....	18	Oct. 13, 1864	1 year.	Transferred from Co. K, 174th O. V. I., June 15, 1865; mustered out with company July 14, 1865.
Boswell, George	....do....	18	Sept. 4, 1864	1 year.	Mustered out with company July 14, 1865.
Bowers, William H	....do....	23	Oct. 1, 1864	1 year.	Mustered out with company July 14, 1865.
Bowman, Henry	....do....	40	Sept. 28, 1864	1 year.	Mustered out with company July 14, 1865.
Bradford, Charles L	....do....	22	Sept. 7, 1864	1 year.	
Breen, Hugh	....do....	36	Sept. 14, 1864	1 year.	See 173d O. V. I. unassigned.
Brown, Vincent	....do....	46	Aug. 30, 1864	1 year.	Transferred from Co. B, 174th O. V. I., June 15, 1865; mustered out with company July 14, 1865.
Bruce, Robert	....do....	18	Sept. 20, 1864	1 year.	Mustered out with company July 14, 1865.
Buck, Wesley	....do....	21	Feb. 28, 1865	1 year.	Transferred from Co. A, 174th O. V. I., June 15, 1865; mustered out with company July 14, 1865.

Rank.	Age.	Date of Entering the Service.	Period of Service.	Remarks.
Private..	22	Aug. 29, 1864	1 year.	Appointed 1st Sergeant Oct. 7, 1864; reduced to ranks Dec. 7, 1864; mustered out with company July 14, 1865.
....do....	20	Aug. 29, 1864	1 year.	Mustered out with company July 14, 1865.
....do....	21	Oct. 3, 1864	1 year.	Discharged June 2, 1865, for wounds received Dec. 7, 1864, in battle of Murfreesboro, Tenn.; also borne on rolls as James Caplinger.
....do....	23	Aug. 27, 1864	1 year.	
....do....	22	Aug. 19, 1864	3 yrs.	Mustered out with company July 14, 1865.
....do....	25	July 27, 1864	1 year.	Transferred from Co. G, 174th O.V.I., June 15, 1865.
....do....	42	Sept. 9, 1864	1 year.	Mustered out June 2, 1865, at Covington, Ky., by order of War Department.
....do....	19	Oct. 25, 1864	1 year.	Mustered out with company July 14, 1865.
....do....	18	Sept. 6, 1864	1 year.	Mustered out with company July 14, 1865.
....do....	44	Oct. 1, 1864	1 year.	Mustered out with company July 14, 1865.
....do....	27	Oct. 6, 1864	1 year.	Transferred from Co. K, 174th O.V.I., June 15, 1865; mustered out with company July 14, 1865.
....do....	18	Aug. 30, 1864	1 year.	Mustered out with company July 14, 1865.
....do....	19	Oct. 4, 1864	1 year.	Mustered out with company July 14, 1865.
....do....	23	Sept. 29, 1864	1 year.	
....do....	18	Aug. 29, 1864	1 year.	Mustered out with company July 14, 1865.
....do....	34	Sept. 29, 1864	1 year.	Promoted to Hospital Steward Dec. 8, 1864.
....do....	28	Sept. 23, 1864	1 year.	Mustered out June 16, 1865, at Columbus, O., by order of War Department.
....do....	25	Sept. 2, 1864	1 year.	Mustered out June 2, 1865, at Camp Dennison, O., by order of War Department.
....do....	18	Aug. 23, 1864	1 year.	Mustered out with company July 14, 1865.
....do....	21	Sept. 20, 1864	1 year.	Mustered out with company July 14, 1865.
....do....	25	Feb. 21, 1865	1 year.	Transferred from Co. D, 174th O.V.I., June 15, 1865; mustered out with company July 14, 1865.
....do....	30	Feb. 21, 1865	1 year.	Transferred from Co. D, 174th O.V.I., June 15, 1865; mustered out with company July 14, 1865.
....do....	18	Aug. 26, 1864	1 year.	Mustered out with company July 14, 1865.
....do....	19	Aug. 24, 1864	1 year.	Mustered out with company July 14, 1865.
....do....	38	Sept. 2, 1864	1 year.	Mustered out June 9, 1865, at Louisville, Ky., by order of War Department.
....do....	21	Sept. 6, 1864	1 year.	Appointed Corporal Oct. 7, 1864; reduced Dec. 31, 1864; mustered out with company July 14, 1865.
....do....	18	Oct. 18, 1864	1 year.	Transferred from Co. E, 174th O.V.I., June 15, 1865, as Corporal; mustered out with company July 14, 1865.
....do....	44	Oct. 4, 1864	1 year.	
....do....	28	Oct. 3, 1864	1 year.	Discharged June 6, 1865, at Camp Dennison, O., for wounds received Dec. 7, 1864, in battle of Murfreesboro, Tenn.; right leg amputated.
....do....	31	Oct. 3, 1864	1 year.	Mustered out with company July 14, 1865.
....do....	28	Sept. 27, 1864	1 year.	Mustered out with company July 14, 1865.
....do....	40	Sept. 2, 1864	1 year.	Mustered out with company July 14, 1865.
....do....	20	Oct. 3, 1864	1 year.	Mustered out with company July 14, 1865.
....do....	27	Oct. 1, 1864	1 year.	Mustered out with company July 14, 1865.
....do....	20	Aug. 4, 1864	3 yrs.	Transferred from Co. A, 174th O.V.I., June 15, 1865; mustered out with company July 14, 1865.
....do....	33	Sept. 19, 1864	1 year.	Mustered out with company July 14, 1865.
....do....	24	Sept. 6, 1864	1 year.	Transferred from Co. G, 174th O.V.I., June 15, 1865.
....do....	18	Sept. 9, 1864	1 year.	Mustered out with company July 14, 1865.
....do....	40	Sept. 21, 1864	1 year.	Mustered out with company July 14, 1865.
....do....	20	Sept. 1, 1864	1 year.	
....do....	19	Aug. 1, 1864	1 year.	Transferred from Co. D, 174th O.V.I., June 15, 1865; mustered out with company July 14, 1865.
....do....	39	Sept. 29, 1864	1 year.	Killed Dec. 7, 1864, in battle of Murfreesboro, Tennessee.
....do....	19	Sept. 26, 1864	1 year.	
....do....	18	Dec. 25, 1864	1 year.	Transferred from Co. A, 174th O.V.I., June 15, 1865; mustered out with company July 14, 1865.
....do....	26	Sept. 27, 1864	1 year.	Mustered out with company July 14, 1865.
....do....	31	Oct. 1, 1864	1 year.	Mustered out with company July 14, 1865.
....do....	22	Sept. 10, 1864	1 year.	Mustered out with company July 14, 1865.
....do....	18	Sept. 14, 1864	1 year.	Mustered out with company July 14, 1865.
....do....	27	Sept. 14, 1864	1 year.	Mustered out with company July 14, 1865.
....do....	45	Aug. 16, 1864	3 yrs.	Mustered out with company July 14, 1865.
....do....	18	Sept. 28, 1864	1 year.	
....do....	19	Sept. 19, 1864	1 year.	Mustered out with company July 14, 1865.
....do....	19	Sept. 28, 1864	1 year.	
....do....	28	Oct. 8, 1864	1 year.	Transferred from Co. H, 174th O.V.I., June 15, 1865, as Corporal; mustered out with company July 14, 1865.

Names.	Rank.	Age.	Date of Entering the Service.	[illegible]	
Moore, George W.	Private.	19	Sept 27, 1864	1 year.	Mustered with
Moore, Isaac L.	....do....	20	Aug. 24, 1864	1 year.	Mustered with
Morrison, Daniel	....do....	21	Sept. 27, 1864	1 year.	Mustered with
Nisch, Jacob	....do....	25	Sept. 10, 1864	1 year.	Died Nov. 28, 1864.
Olmstead, Van R.	....do....	18	Jan. 23, 1865	1 year.	Transferred from 1865.
Perl, John	....do....	34	Aug. 24, 1864	3 yrs.	See Co. G, 174th O.
Pickman, Charles	....do....	21	Aug. 27, 1864	1 year.	Mustered out with
Ratcliff, Thomas	....do....	42	Sept. 1, 1864	1 year.	Mustered out with
Reedel, Joseph	....do....	42	Sept. 1, 1864	1 year.	Discharged March on Surgeon's cer
Reinach, Julius	....do....	24	Oct. 3, 1864	1 year.	Mustered out with
Reynolds, William C.	....do....	44	Oct. 4, 1864	1 year.	Discharged April for gun-shot wou
Robertson, Samuel	....do....	19	Sept. 1, 1864	1 year.	Mustered out with
Robinson, William	....do....	28	Sept. 7, 1864	3 yrs.	
Rohlfing, William	....do....	20	Aug. 29, 1864	1 year.	
Rose, John W.	....do....	21	Aug. 4, 1864	1 year.	
Rudy, Sheppard	....do....	41	Sept. 28, 1864	1 year.	
Ryan, John	....do....	18	Sept. 28, 1864	1 year.	ment. Mustered out with
Shackleford, Henry	....do....	27	Aug. 30, 1864	1 year.	Appointed Corpo Dec. 24, 1864; m July 14, 1865.
Stratton, Enoch B.	....do....	18	Sept. 19, 1864	1 year.	Mustered out Jun C., by order of W
Thompson, John	....do....	22	Sept. 28, 1864	1 year.	
Walker, James	....do....	20	Aug. 27, 1864	1 year.	Mustered out July by order of War
Warner, Peter	....do....	36	Sept. 29, 1864	1 year.	Mustered out with
Weeks, John	....do....	19	Sept. 28, 1864	1 year.	Mustered out with
Weyman, William H.	....do....	23	Aug. 27, 1864	1 year.	
Williams, John	....do....	40	Sept. 9, 1864	1 year.	
Williams, Joseph	....do....	28	Sept. 1, 1864	1 year.	Died May 10, 1865,
Winn, Richard	....do....	26	Sept. 21, 1864	1 year.	

COMPANY H.

Mustered in October 7, 1864, at Camp Dennison, O., by Wm. Von Doehn, Capt[illegible] out July 14, 1865, at Salisbury, N. C., by Frederick Ande[illegible] Lieutenant and A. C. M.

Names.	Rank.	Age.	Date of Entering the Service.	[illegible]	
George A. Boss	Captain.	46	Oct. 7, 1864		Never mustered.
Louis Stuebing	....do....	38	Oct. 7, 1864		Promoted from 1 mustered out wi
August Buddenbrook	1st Lieut.	32	Oct. 7, 1864	1 year.	Promoted from 2d
Fred. Hoeller	....do....	21	Oct. 7, 1864	1 year.	Promoted from 2 1865; appointed to date May 1, 1
Frank D. Russell	2d Lieut.	22	Oct. 3, 1864		ppointed 1st Serg to 2d Lieutenan ant July 10, 186 tered out with c
William Ostendorff	1st Sergt.	40	Sept. 30, 1864		Appointed from moted to 2d Li not mustered; July 14, 1865.
Rudolph Oberding	Sergeant.	30	Aug. 31, 1864		Appointed Oct. 7, 1865, at Columb partment.
John Hess	....do....	28	Sept. 28, 1864	1 year.	Appointed Oct. 7 company July 1
Frank Kork	....do....	28	Sept. 26, 1864		Appointed —; July 14, 1865.
Henry Reiter	....do....	24	Sept. 20, 1864		Appointed —; tle of Murfrees with company J
John Schneider	....do....	46	Sept. 3, 1864		Appointed Corp June 18, 1865; July 14, 1865.
Frederick Ertz	Corporal.	26	Aug. 22, 1864		Appointed Oct. 7 company July 1
August Loeser	....do....	27	Sept. 30, 1864		Appointed Oct. 7 company July 1
Louis Chrisman	....do....	18	Oct. 5, 1864	year.	Appointed Oct. 7 company July 1
Michael Lebean	....do....	38	Oct. 1, 1864	1 year.	Appointed —; July 14, 1865.

Names.	Rank.	Age.	Date of Entering the Service.	Period of Service.	Remarks.
Linne	Corporal.	30	Sept. 20, 1864	1 year.	Appointed ——; mustered out May 13, 1865, at Cincinnati, O., by order of War Department.
..d Hoffman	...do...	26	Aug. 27, 1864	1 year.	Appointed ——; mustered out with company July 14, 1865.
..a Botter	...do...	22	Aug. 12, 1864	1 year.	Appointed Sergeant Oct. 7, 1864; reduced to Corporal May 1, 1865; mustered out with company July 14, 1865.
..n Abbe	...do...	21	Sept. 21, 1864	1 year.	Appointed June 18, 1865; mustered out with company July 14, 1865.
..l Herbolsheimer	Musician	17	Sept. 5, 1864	1 year.	Appointed Oct. 7, 1864; mustered out with company July 14, 1865.
..a Hennesee	...do...	19	Aug. 25, 1864	1 year.	Appointed Oct. 7, 1864; mustered out with company July 14, 1865.
Leerer	Wagoner.	45	Aug. 16, 1864	1 year.	Appointed Oct. 7, 1864; mustered out June 1, 1865, at Albany, N. Y., by order of War Department.
..t, Fred	Private.	19	Sept. 29, 1864	1 year.	Mustered out with company July 14, 1865.
..onrad	...do...	34	Oct. 4, 1864	1 year.	Mustered out with company July 14, 1865.
..r, Jacob	...do...	27	Sept. 26, 1864	1 year.	Mustered out June 17, 1865, at Columbus, O., by order of War Department.
..n, Thomas	...do...	25	Sept. 26, 1864	1 year.	Mustered out June 17, 1865, at Columbus, O., by order of War Department.
.., Louis	...do...	20	Sept. 20, 1864	1 year.	Mustered out with company July 14, 1865.
..er, William	...do...	39	Sept. 16, 1864	1 year.	Mustered as Corporal; mustered out with company July 14, 1865.
..n, John	...do...	30	Aug. 22, 1864	1 year.	Mustered out with company July 14, 1865.
William	...do...	18	Aug. 31, 1864	1 year.	Mustered out July 27, 1865, at Washington, D. C., by order of War Department.
.., Charles	...do...	19	Sept. 24, 1864	1 year.	Mustered out with company July 14, 1865.
..g, Thomas	...do...	28	Sept. 19, 1864	1 year.	Mustered out with company July 14, 1865.
..r, Peter	...do...	36	Oct. 1, 1864	1 year.	Mustered out with company July 14, 1865.
..r, Valentine	...do...	..	....	......	
..rger, Jacob	...do...	18	Oct. 4, 1864	1 year.	Mustered out June 4, 1865, at Nashville, Tenn., by order of War Department.
..mel, John	...do...	19	Sept. 24, 1864	1 year.	Discharged Dec. 30, 1864, on Surgeon's certificate of disability.
..am, Samuel S.	...do...	28	Aug. 15, 1864	1 year.	
..an, John	...do...	19	Sept. 7, 1864	1 year.	Mustered out May 30, 1865, at Camp Dennison, O., by order of War Department.
..trick, James	...do...	31	Sept. 21, 1864	1 year.	Mustered out June 27, 1865, at Columbus, O., by order of War Department.
..r, Henry	...do...	19	Sept. 27, 1864	1 year.	Mustered out with company July 14, 1865.
..l, Henry	...do...	18	Sept. 26, 1864	1 year.	Mustered out with company July 14, 1865.
.., Andrew	...do...	31	Oct. 1, 1864	1 year.	Mustered out with company July 14, 1865.
.., David	...do...	18	Oct. 2, 1864	1 year.	Mustered out with company July 14, 1865.
..r, Julius	...do...	34	Sept. 30, 1864	1 year.	Mustered out with company July 14, 1865.
..ng, Frederick	...do...	37	Aug. 25, 1864	1 year.	Mustered out with company July 14, 1865.
..au, John B.	...do...	22	Sept. 20, 1864	1 year.	Mustered out Aug. 9, 1865, at Washington, D. C., by order of War Department.
..ich, Henry	...do...	19	Sept. 26, 1864	1 year.	Mustered out with company July 14, 1865.
..nghaus, Henry	...do...	27	Sept. 19, 1864	1 year.	Mustered as Corporal; mustered out with company July 14, 1865.
..an, Jacob	...do...	38	Sept. 28, 1864	1 year.	Mustered out with company July 14, 1865.
..an, John	...do...	30	Sept. 16, 1864	1 year.	Mustered out with company July 14, 1865.
..r, Anselm	...do...	30	Oct. 5, 1864	1 year.	Mustered out with company July 14, 1865.
.., Thomas	...do...	45	Mch. 2, 1865	1 year.	Mustered out with company July 14, 1865.
.., William	...do...	19	Oct. 4, 1864	1 year	Mustered out with company July 14, 1865.
.., Louis	...do...	43	Sept. 30, 1864	1 year.	Mustered out with company July 14, 1865.
..an, Charles	...do...	23	Aug. 22, 1864	1 year.	Mustered out with company July 14, 1865.
..an, Thomas	...do...	18	Sept. 21, 1864	1 year.	Mustered out with company July 14, 1865.
.., James	...do...	20	Sept. 7, 1864	1 year.	
..n, John	...do...	45	Sept. 23, 1864	1 year.	Mustered out with company July 14, 1865.
.. Otto	...do...	24	Oct. 3, 1864	1 year.	Mustered out with company July 14, 1865.
..rking, Frederick	...do...	22	Sept. 28, 1864	1 year.	Mustered out with company July 14, 1865.
.. Ehrhardt	...do...	30	Sept. 27, 1864	1 year.	Discharged Dec. 30, 1864, on Surgeon's certificate of disability.
..erson, Alexander	...do...	18	Aug. 26, 1864	1 year.	Mustered out with company July 14, 1865.
..ding, Thomas	...do...	23	Sept. 21, 1864	1 year.	Mustered out with company July 14, 1865.
..all, Charles	...do...	19	Sept. 28, 1864	1 year.	Mustered out July 8, 1865, at Columbus, O., by order of War Department.
..rn, Peter	...do...	22	Sept. 5, 1864	1 year.	Appointed Corporal Oct. 7, 1864; reduced May 1, 1865; mustered out with company July 14, 1865.
..r, Tobias	...do...	24	Aug. 27, 1864	1 year.	Mustered out with company July 14, 1865.
..ing, William	...do...	24	Aug. 31, 1864	1 year.	Mustered out with company July 14, 1865.
.., John	...do...	25	Sept. 28, 1864	1 year.	Mustered out with company July 14, 1865.
..er, George	...do...	40	Oct. 3, 1864	1 year.	Mustered out with company July 14, 1865.
.., David	...do...	19	Oct. 2, 1864	1 year.	
..d, Frank	...do...	[illegible]	Oct. 3, 1864	1 year.	Discharged March 15, 1865, on Surgeon's certificate of disability.
.. John	...do...	[illegible]	Sept. 24, 1864	1 year.	Mustered out with company July 14, 1865.
.., Charles	...do...	21	Sept. 21, 1864	1 year.	Mustered out with company July 14, 1865.
.., Bernard	...do...	17	Sept. 12, 1864	1 year.	Mustered out with company July 14, 1865.
.. Henry	...do...	26	Sept. 20, 1864	1 year.	Mustered out with company July 14, 1865.
..macher, George	...do...	[illegible]	Sept. 22, 1864	1 year.	Mustered out with company July 14, 1865.

Names.	Rank.	Age.	Date of Entering the Service.	Period of Service.	Remarks.
Ross, John	Private..	44	Sept. 18, 1864	1 year.	Mustered out with company July 14, 1865; also borne on rolls as John Roos.
Scheuben, William	....do....	31	Aug. 31, 1864	1 year.	Mustered out with company July 14, 1865.
Schneider, Louis	....do....	32	Oct. 4, 1864	1 year.	Mustered out with company July 14, 1865.
Schwartz, George	....do....	41	Oct. 3, 1864	1 year.	Mustered out with company July 14, 1865.
Seichler, Jacob	....do....	34	Oct. 6, 1864	1 year.	Discharged May 30, 1865, on Surgeon's certificate of disability; also borne on rolls as John Siekler.
Shoewalter, James	....do....	30	Sept. 20, 1864	1 year.	Mustered out with company July 14, 1865.
Steinbrecher, John	....do....	38	Sept. 20, 1864	1 year.	Mustered out with company July 14, 1865.
Stevens, John	....do....	24	Sept. 6, 1864	1 year.	
Tech, William	....do....	38	Sept. 15, 1864	1 year.	
Teschler, Valentine	....do....	28	Sept. 19, 1864	1 year.	Mustered out with company July 14, 1865.
Thole, John	....do....	20	Sept. 20, 1864	1 year.	Drowned May 11, 1865, in the Yadkin River, N. C., while on duty.
Ulmer, Frederick	....do....	30	Sept. 26, 1864	1 year.	Mustered out with company July 14, 1865.
Ulmer, Martin	....do....	24	Sept. 22, 1864	1 year.	Mustered out with company July 14, 1865.
Verwold, Henry	....do....	17	Sept. 19, 1864	1 year.	Mustered out with company July 14, 1865.
Vetter, George	....do....	38	Sept. 29, 1864	1 year.	Mustered out with company July 14, 1865.
Vierheilig, Michael	....do....	25	Sept. 19, 1864	1 year.	Mustered out with company July 14, 1865.
Wahl, John	....do....	32	Sept. 22, 1864	1 year.	Mustered out with company July 14, 1865.
Walker, Edward	....do....	26	Sept. 3, 1864	1 year.	Discharged Dec. 30, 1864, on Surgeon's certificate of disability.
Wehman, Ferdinand	....do....	18	Sept. 7, 1864	1 year.	Mustered out with company July 14, 1865.
Weiss, Leborius	....do....	31	Sept. 22, 1864	1 year.	Mustered out with company July 14, 1865.
Wentzel, Charles	....do....	19	Sept. 26, 1864	1 year.	Mustered out with company July 14, 1865.
Wickenhauser, Charles	....do....	36	Sept. 20, 1864	1 year.	
Wolff, August	....do....	23	Aug. 16, 1864	1 year.	Mustered out with company July 14, 1865.
Wolff, Frank	....do....	20	Sept. 16, 1864	1 year.	Mustered out with company July 14, 1865.
Worst, August	....do....	33	Sept. 21, 1864	1 year.	Mustered out with company July 14, 1865.
Zimmerman, William	....do....	27	Oct. 3, 1864	1 year.	Mustered out with company July 14, 1865.

COMPANY I.

Mustered in September 29, 1864, at Camp Dennison, O., by Wm. Von Doehn, Captain and A. A. G. Mustered out July 14, 1865, at Salisbury, N. C., by Frederick Anderson, Lieutenant and A. C. M.

Names.	Rank.	Age.	Date of Entering the Service.	Period of Service.	Remarks.
John Becker	Captain.	..	Sept. 29, 1864	1 year.	Resigned Oct. 19, 1864.
Rudolph M Gutenstein	....do....	29	Sept. 29, 1864	1 year.	Promoted from 1st Lieutenant Oct. [illegible]; discharged May 15, 1865.
Peter Rath	1st Lieut.	33	Sept. 17, 1864	1 year.	Appointed 1st Sergeant Sept. [illegible]; promoted to 1st Lieutenant Oct. [illegible]; to Captain July 10, 1865, but not mustered; [illegible] command of company since Feb. [illegible]; mustered out with company July 14, 1865.
John C. Stahl	2d Lieut.	19	Sept. 29, 1864	1 year.	Died Jan. 15, 1865, at Clifton, Tenn.
Adolph Kuehn	....do....	21	Sept. 19, 1864	1 year	Appointed Sergeant Sept. 29, 1864; promoted to 2d Lieutenant Jan. 18, 1865; [illegible] and July 10, 1865, but not mustered; mustered out with company July 14, 1865.
Philip Weihrich	1st Sergt.	23	Sept. 5, 1864	1 year	Appointed Sergeant Sept. 29, 1864; [illegible] Jan. 17, 1865; mustered out with company July 14, 1865.
Peter. Krausen	Sergeant.	22	Sept. 16, 1864	1 year	Appointed Sept. 29, 1864; mustered out with company July 14, 1865.
Jacob Kuhn	....do....	37	Sept. 6, 1864	1 year.	Appointed Corporal Sept. 29, 1864; [illegible] Oct. 25, 1864; mustered out with [illegible] July 14, 1865.
Henry Werner	....do....	23	Aug. 16, 1864	1 year.	Appointed Corporal Sept. 29, 1864; [illegible] Jan. 17, 1865; mustered out with [illegible] July 14, 1865.
Conrad Guthard	....do....	35	Sept. 21, 1864	1 year.	Appointed Corporal Oct. 25, 1864; [illegible] June 11, 1865; mustered out with [illegible] July 14, 1865.
Philip Loeffel	Corporal.	27	Sept. 6, 1864	1 year.	Appointed Sept. 29, 1864; mustered out with company July 14, 1865.
John Haeffner	....do....	41	Sept. 16, 1864	1 year.	Appointed Nov. 1, 1864; mustered out with company July 14, 1865.
Henry Weibel	....do....	44	Sept. 6, 1864	1 year.	Appointed Nov. 1, 1864; mustered out with company July 14, 1865.
John Hatzig	....do....	33	Sept. 17, 1864	1 year.	Appointed Nov. 1, 1864; mustered out with company July 14, 1865; also borne on rolls as John Harzig.
Frank Sutter	....do....	38	Sept. 10, 1864	1 year.	Appointed Sept. 29, 1864; reduced [illegible] 1864; reappointed Jan. 17, 1865; mustered out with company July 14, 1865.
Adam Rechel	....do....	24	Sept. 15, 1864	1 year.	Appointed March 1, 1865; mustered out with company July 14, 1865.

Names.	Rank.	Age.	Date of Entering the Service.	Period of Service.	Remarks.
John Roedkle	Corporal.	33	Sept. 4, 1864	1 year.	Appointed June 20, 1865; mustered out with company July 14, 1865.
August Goepper	....do....	18	Sept. 17, 1864	1 year.	Appointed June 20, 1865; mustered out with company July 14, 1865.
Joseph Imhof	Musician	40	Sept. 4, 1864	1 year.	Appointed Sept. 29, 1864; mustered out with company July 14, 1865.
Adams, Joseph	Private..	21	Sept. 16, 1864	1 year.	Mustered out with company July 14, 1865.
Alzheimer, George	....do....	22	Sept. 7, 1864	1 year.	Mustered out with company July 14, 1865.
Appelius, Frederick	....do....	37	Sept. 19, 1864	1 year.	Mustered out with company July 14, 1865.
Arens, Charles	....do....	24	Sept. 19, 1864	1 year.	Mustered out June 30, 1865, at Louisville, Ky., by order of War Department.
Bayer, John	....do....	26	Sept. 17, 1864	1 year.	Appointed Corporal Nov. 1, 1864; reduced Jan. 31, 1865; mustered out with company July 14, 1865.
Becker, Emil	....do....	29	Aug. 23, 1864	1 year.	Mustered out with company July 14, 1865.
Becker, Philip Jacob	....do....	23	Aug. 22, 1864	1 year.	Mustered out with company July 14, 1865.
Beinhard, David	....do....	18	Sept. 15, 1864	1 year.	Mustered out with company July 14, 1865.
Blank, Joseph	....do....	21	Sept. 14, 1864	1 year.	Mustered out with company July 14, 1865.
Bohl, Louis	....do....	23	Sept. 7, 1864	1 year.	Mustered out with company July 14, 1865.
Bosh, Emil	....do....	17	Sept. 6, 1864	1 year.	Mustered out with company July 14, 1865.
Broscutter, Joseph	....do....	20	Sept. 8, 1864	1 year.	Mustered out with company July 14, 1865.
Dalker, Frederick	....do....	33	Sept. 18, 1864	1 year.	Mustered out with company July 14, 1865.
Dahne, Frederick	....do....	19	Aug. 12, 1864	1 year.	Mustered out with company July 14, 1865.
Dewein, George N	....do....	44	Aug. 18, 1864	1 year.	Appointed Corporal Sept. 29, 1864; Sergeant Oct. 22, 1864; reduced June 10, 1865; mustered out with company July 14, 1865.
Dhonan, Jacob	....do....	31	Sept. 10, 1864	1 year.	Mustered out with company July 14, 1865; also borne on rolls as Jacob Dohnan.
Dietz, Jacob	....do....	19	Sept. 19, 1864	1 year.	Mustered out with company July 14, 1865.
Dornberger, Philip	....do....	23	Sept. 13, 1864	1 year.	Mustered out with company July 14, 1865.
Eiselein, Casper	....do....	19	Sept. 22, 1864	1 year.	Mustered out with company July 14, 1865.
Emminger, Joseph	....do....	20	Sept. 22, 1864	1 year.	Mustered out with company July 14, 1865.
Endres, George	....do....	20	Sept. 2, 1864	1 year.	Mustered out with company July 14, 1865.
Falk, John	....do....	32	Sept. 23, 1864	1 year.	Mustered out with company July 14, 1865.
Ficke, Frank	....do....	38	Sept. 9, 1864	1 year.	Mustered out with company July 14, 1865.
Fiedler, Martin	....do....	42	Aug. 10, 1864	1 year.	Mustered out with company July 14, 1865; also borne on rolls as Martin Fredler.
Fox, John	....do....	20	Sept. 13, 1864	1 year.	Mustered out with company July 14, 1865.
Franer, Gustav	....do....	20	Sept. 17, 1864	1 year.	Mustered out with company July 14, 1865.
Geiger, Jacob	....do....	19	Sept. 20, 1864	1 year.	Mustered out with company July 14, 1865.
Goeseman, August	....do....	30	Aug. 26, 1864	1 year.	Mustered out June 8, 1865, at Philadelphia, Pa., by order of War Department.
Haab, Adam	....do....	19	Sept. 20, 1864	1 year.	Mustered out with company July 14, 1865.
Hauk, John	....do....	23	Sept. 14, 1864	1 year.	Died April 18, 1865, at Morehead City, N. C.
Harteth, Bernhard	....do....	26	Sept. 20, 1864	1 year.	Mustered out with company July 14, 1865.
Havencut, August	....do....	40	Aug. 29, 1864	1 year.	Mustered out May 25, 1865, at Albany, N. Y.
Hefter, Joseph	....do....	30	Sept. 17, 1864	1 year.	
Helt, John	....do....	19	Aug. 31, 1864	1 year.	Mustered out with company July 14, 1865.
Hellman, John	....do....	20	Sept. 10, 1864	1 year.	Mustered out with company July 14, 1865.
Herrman, Lorenz	....do....	44	Sept. 15, 1864	1 year.	Mustered out with company July 14, 1865.
Hoffman, George	....do....	20	Sept. 19, 1864	1 year.	Mustered out with company July 14, 1865.
Kauffman, Joseph	....do....	18	Aug. 20, 1864	1 year.	Mustered out with company July 14, 1865.
Kemmerer, Valentine	....do....	48	Sept. 6, 1864	1 year.	Died May 22, 1865, at Cincinnati, O.
Klein, John	....do....	26	Sept. 13, 1864	1 year.	Mustered out with company July 14, 1865.
Kreil, Valentine	....do....	24	Sept. 16, 1864	1 year.	Mustered out with company July 14, 1865.
Kronzburg, William	....do....	19	Sept. 5, 1864	1 year.	Mustered out with company July 14, 1865.
Kuhn, John	....do....	45	Sept. 9, 1864	1 year.	Mustered out with company July 14, 1865.
Leibrand, Christian	....do....	40	Aug. 15, 1864	1 year.	Mustered as Corporal; mustered out with company July 14, 1865.
Le Saint, Peter	....do....	22	Sept. 14, 1864	1 year.	Mustered as Sergeant; mustered out with company July 14, 1865.
Lorentz, Christoph	....do....	31	Sept. 14, 1864	1 year.	Mustered out with company July 14, 1865; also borne on rolls as Lorenz.
Mallet, George	....do....	25	Sept. 19, 1864	1 year.	Mustered out with company July 14, 1865.
Martin, Henry	....do....	18	Sept. 22, 1864	1 year.	Mustered out with company July 14, 1865.
[illegible], Charles	....do....	40	Sept. 8, 1864	1 year.	Mustered as Corporal; mustered out with company July 14, 1865; also borne on rolls as Charles Marschwitz.
Meisterman, John	....do....	32	Sept. 8, 1864	1 year.	Mustered out May 25, 1865, at Albany, N. Y., by order of War Department.
Meyer, Joseph	....do....	20	Sept. 21, 1864	1 year.	Mustered out with company July 14, 1865.
Meyer, Leopold	....do....	30	Sept. 6, 1864	1 year.	
Mueller, Philip	....do....	40	Sept. 12, 1864	1 year.	Mustered out with company July 14, 1865.
Muenner, Frank	....do....	19	Sept. 5, 1864	1 year.	
Ney, Adam	....do....	29	Sept. 12, 1864	1 year.	Mustered out with company July 14, 1865.
Obergfeld, Philip	....do....	21	Sept. 17, 1864	1 year.	Mustered out with company July 14, 1865; also borne on rolls as Obergfield.
Oburg, Frank	....do....	20	Aug. 31, 1864	1 year.	Mustered out with company July 14, 1865.
Opiez, John K	....do....	22	Sept. 16, 1864	1 year.	Mustered out with company July 14, 1865.
Pfaff, Edward	....do....	44	Sept. 10, 1864	1 year.	Mustered out with company July 14, 1865.
Richards, George	....do....	18	Sept. 18, 1864	1 year.	Transferred to 22d Co., 2d Battalion, Veteran Reserve Corps, March 21, 1865; mustered out Sept. 12, 1865, at Washington, D. C., by order of War Department.
Ritter, Charles	....do....	26	Sept. 1, 1864	1 year.	Mustered out with company July 14, 1865.
Rolling, William	....do....	39	Sept. 6, 1864	1 year.	Mustered out with company July 14, 1865.

Names.	Rank.	Age.	Date of Entering the Service.	Period of Service.	
Salzmann, George	Private	25	Sept. 21, 1864		
Schlesinger, John	...do...	22	Sept. 20, 1864		
Schmidberger, Christoph	...do...	25	Sept. 6, 1864		
Schott, Leo	...do...	20	Sept. 20, 1864		
Schwarz, Jacob	...do...	20	Sept. 20, 1864		
Schwier, Anton	...do...	26	Sept. 20, 1864	1	
Schwier, Frederick	...do...	18	Sept. 21, 1864	1	
Sommer, Jacob	...do...	21	Sept. 5, 1864	1	Mustered out w
Stoffel, David	...do...	18	Sept. 22, 1864	1	Mustered out w
Stoffel, Peter	...do...	27	Sept. 6, 1864	1	Mustered out by order of \
Strohmann, William	...do...	32	Sept. 20, 1864	1	Mustered out w
Sturow, Louis	...do...	21	Sept. 20, 1864	1	Mustered out w
Suter, Julius	...do...	19	Sept. 20, 1864	1	Mustered out w
Thormann, Frederick	...do...	26	Sept. 22, 1864	1	Mustered out w
Wegborn, George	...do...	24	Sept. 5, 1864	1	Mustered out w
Weimer, Frederick	...do...	28	Sept. 19, 1864	1	Died Dec. 14, 18 1864, in battl borne on roll
Welther, Joseph	...do...	29	Sept. 19, 1864		Mustered out w
Wild, Andrew	...do...	21	Sept. 20, 1864		Mustered out w
Wild, George	...do...	23	Sept. 6, 1864		Mustered out w
Ziegler, Conrad	...do...	35	Sept. 20, 1864		Mustered out w

COMPANY K.

Mustered in October 10, 1864, at Camp Dennison, O., by Wm. Von Doehn, Ca out July 14, 1865, at Salisbury, N. C., by Frederick And Lieutenant and A. C. M.

James T. Hickey	Captain.	26	Oct. 13, 1864	1 year.	Promoted to M
Charles Le Blanc	...do...	27	Oct. 10, 1864	1 year.	Promoted from mustered out
Timothy Cannon	1st Lieut.	26	Oct. 10, 1864	1 year.	Promoted from mustered out
Francis M. Enyart	2d Lieut.	25	Sept. 23, 1864	1 year.	Appointed 1st S to 2d Lieuten with compan
John B. Lamb	1st Sergt.	26	Sept. 23, 1864	1 year.	Appointed Ser ——; muster 1865.
John Williams	Sergeant.	21	Oct. 12, 1864	1 year.	Appointed Ju company Jul
William Haarer	...do...	36	Oct. 13, 1864	1 year.	Appointed Co 1865; muster 1865.
Thomas Marmion	...do...	20	Oct. 8, 1864	1 year.	Appointed Jun company Jul
James Anderson	...do...	22	Oct. 12, 1864	1 year.	Appointed Ju company Jul
Charles A. Nadand	Corporal.	18	Sept. 28, 1864	1 year.	Appointed Oct. 1865, at Camp Department.
James Creedon	...do...	19	Oct. 6, 1864	1 year.	Appointed Ju company Jul
Josiah C. Newland	...do...	27	Oct. 7, 1864	1 year.	Appointed Jun company Jul
John T. Peterson	...do...	25	Oct. 7, 1864	1 year.	Appointed Ju company Jul
Cornelius Ryan	...do...	22	Oct. 5, 1864	1 year.	Appointed Ju company Jul
Michael Mooney	...do...	22	Mch. 1, 1865	1 year.	Appointed Ju company Jul
Albert Molloy	Musician	17	Sept. 6, 1864	1 year.	Mustered out w
John McCarty	Wagoner.	21	Sept. 21, 1864	1 year.	Mustered out also borne on
Adams, Henry	Private	25	Sept. 7, 1864	1 year.	
Baxter, Philip	...do...	20	Sept. 12, 1864	1 year.	Appointed Cor ——; reduced with compan
Brannon, John	...do...	19	Sept. 17, 1864	1 year.	
Brooks, Frank	...do...	19	Sept. 10, 1864	1 year.	
Brown, Joseph H	...do...	42	Oct. 5, 1864	1 year.	
Cannon, Francis J	...do...	20	Sept. 12, 1864	1 year.	

Age.	Date of Entering the Service.	Period of Service.	Remarks.
	Oct. 5, 1864	1 year.	Mustered out with company July 14, 1865.
	Sept. 7, 1864	1 year.	
	Oct. 5, 1864	1 year.	
	Aug. 26, 1864	1 year.	Appointed Corporal Oct. 10, 1864; Sergeant ——; reduced Feb. 1, 1865; mustered out with company July 14, 1865.
	Oct. 8, 1864	1 year.	
	Sept. 19, 1864	1 year.	
	Sept. 21, 1864	1 year.	
	Oct. 7, 1864	1 year.	Mustered out with company July 14, 1865.
	Oct. 10, 1864	1 year.	Mustered out with company July 14, 1865.
	Sept. 25, 1864	1 year.	
	Sept. 12, 1864	1 year.	Mustered out with company July 14, 1865.
	Sept. 16, 1864	1 year.	Mustered out with company July 14, 1865.
	Oct. 4, 1864	1 year.	
	Sept. 30, 1864	1 year.	
	Sept. 7, 1864	1 year.	
	Sept. 26, 1864	1 year.	Mustered out with company July 14, 1865.
	Mch. 4, 1865	1 year.	Mustered out with company July 14, 1865.
	Oct. 4, 1864	1 year.	
	Aug. 31, 1864	1 year.	Mustered out with company July 14, 1865.
	Sept. 20, 1864	1 year.	
	Oct. 7, 1864	1 year.	Mustered out with company July 14, 1865.
	Oct. 13, 1864	1 year.	
	Oct. 3, 1864	1 year.	Mustered out with company July 14, 1865.
	Sept. 16, 1864	1 year.	Mustered out with company July 14, 1865.
	Oct. 8, 1864	1 year.	
	Sept. 21, 1864	1 year.	Mustered out with company July 14, 1865.
	Oct. 6, 1864	1 year.	Mustered out with company July 14, 1865.
	Sept. 15, 1864	1 year.	Mustered out with company July 14, 1865.
	Oct. 8, 1864	1 year.	Mustered out with company July 14, 1865.
	Oct. 19, 1864	1 year.	Mustered out with company July 14, 1865.
	Sept. 29, 1864	1 year.	Drowned Oct. 25, 1864, in Ohio River, near Louisville, Ky.
	Sept. 20, 1864	1 year.	
	Oct. 4, 1864	1 year.	
	Sept. 14, 1864	1 year.	
	Sept. 7, 1864	1 year.	Mustered out with company July 14, 1865.
	Sept. 24, 1864	1 year.	
	Oct. 12, 1864	1 year.	Mustered out May 30, 1865, at McDougall Hospital, New York Harbor, by order of War Department.
	Oct. 8, 1862	1 year.	Mustered as Sergeant.
	Aug. 24, 1864	1 year.	
	Sept. 20, 1864	1 year.	
	Sept. 19, 1864	1 year.	
	Sept. 22, 1864	1 year.	Mustered out with company July 14, 1865.
	Sept. 20, 1864	1 year.	Mustered out with company July 14, 1865; also borne on rolls as Jno. McRilise
	Oct. 3, 1864	1 year.	Also borne on rolls as Patrick McVaraney.
	Oct. 10, 1864	1 year.	Absent since May 1, 1865. No further record found.
	Sept. 19, 1864	1 year.	Appointed Sergeant Feb. 16, 1865; reduced June 1, 1865; mustered out with company July 14, 1865.
	Sept. 6, 1864	1 year.	Promoted to Q. M. Sergeant Feb. 7, 1865; returned to company May 13, 1865; mustered out with company July 14, 1865.
	Aug. 31, 1864	1 year.	Mustered out with company July 14, 1865.
	Oct. 8, 1864	1 year.	Mustered out with company July 14, 1865.
19	Sept. 3, 1864	1 year.	
18	Mch. 20, 1865	1 year.	Mustered out with company July 14, 1865.
20	Sept. 19, 1864	1 year.	Appointed Corporal March 17, 1865; reduced June 1, 1865; mustered out with company July 14, 1865.
19	Sept. 19, 1864	1 year.	Appointed Corporal ——; reduced June 1, 1865; mustered out with company July 14, 1865
27	Sept. 24, 1864	1 year.	Mustered as Sergeant; mustered out with company July 14, 1865.
22	Sept. 29, 1864	1 year.	Absent, sick Dec. 24, 1864, at Murfreesboro, Tenn. No further record found.
18	Sept. 12, 1864	1 year.	Mustered out with company July 14, 1865.
31	Sept. 29, 1864	1 year.	Mustered as Corporal; mustered out with company July 14, 1865.
21	Sept. 22, 1864	1 year.	Mustered as Sergeant; reduced June 1, 1865; mustered out with company July 14, 1865.
20	Sept. 16, 1864	1 year.	Mustered out with company July 14, 1865.
37	Oct. 7, 1864	1 year.	Died March 16, 1865, at Locust Grove, Adams County, O., while on furlough.
25	Sept. 7, 1864	1 year.	
23	Sept. 18, 1864	1 year.	Mustered out with company July 14, 1865.
24	Sept. 28, 1864	1 year.	Appointed Corporal Oct. 10, 1864; reduced June 1, 1865; mustered out with company July 14, 1865.
26	Oct. 2, 1864	1 year.	

Names.	Rank.	Age.	Date of Entering the Service.	Period of Service.	Remarks.
Nicholson, Robert	Private	20	Sept. 21, 1864	1 year.	
Nowall, John	do	28	Sept. 20, 1864	1 year.	
O'Connole, Patrick	do	22	Sept. 30, 1864	1 year.	Mustered out with company July
O'Donnell, Bartholomew	do	20	Sept. 19, 1864	1 year.	Mustered out with company July
Parks, James	do	25	Oct 4, 1864	1 year.	
Quinn, Robert	do	20	Sept. 21, 1864	1 year.	
Quinn, William	do	27	Oct. 7, 1864	1 year.	
Regan, Patrick	do	25	Sept. 17, 1864	1 year.	Mustered as Corporal.
Reynolds, John	do	21	Sept. 19, 1864	1 year.	
Reynolds, William	do	18	Sept. 13, 1864	1 year.	Mustered out with company July
Rigney, Bernard	do	23	Oct. 8, 1864	1 year.	Absent since May 1, 1865. No fur found.
Rogers, John	do	18	Jan. 28, 1865	1 year.	Mustered out with company July
Rucker, Henry	do	18	Sept. 13, 1864	1 year.	
Russell, Peter	do	18	Sept. 22, 1864	1 year.	Mustered out with company July
Ryan, Dennis	do	29	Sept. 30, 1864	1 year.	
Ryan, John	do	19	Sept. 17, 1864	1 year.	Appointed Corporal ——; reduced 1865; mustered out with compa 1865.
Schweger, August	do	23	Aug. 23, 1864	1 year.	Mustered out with company July
Shannon, Charles L.	do	24	Sept. 26, 1864	1 year.	Mustered out June 9, 1865, at Colu by order of War Department.
Sherdon, Martin	do	40	Sept. 20, 1864	1 year.	Mustered out with company July also borne on rolls as Martin Sher
Sloan, John D.	do	19	Oct. 3, 1864	1 year.	
Smith, John	do	20	Oct. 7, 1864	1 year.	
Spaulding, James	do	35	Sept. 14, 1864	1 year	
Splain, Daniel J.	do	21	Oct. 12, 1864	1 year.	Mustered out with company July 14.
Taylor, Thomas	do	35	Oct. 4, 1864	1 year.	
Tighe, James	do	28	Sept. 27, 1864	1 year.	Mustered as Corporal.
Trimble, Nichols	do	43	Sept. 28, 1864	1 year.	Discharged March 18, 1865, at Washi C., on Surgeon's certificate of disa
Tydings, Michael	do	32	Sept. 20, 1864	1 year.	Mustered out June 13, 1865, at Colum by order of War Department.
Warner, William	do	20	Sept. 16, 1864	1 year.	
Whitrock, John J. R.	do	18	Sept. 2, 1864	1 year.	Mustered out June 25, 1865, at Colum by order of War Department.
Wilson, James	do	24	Sept. 22, 1864	1 year.	

UNASSIGNED RECRUITS.

NOTE.—The following list of recruits is found on muster and descriptive rolls for this organizatio not borne on any of the company rolls of the Regiment:

Names.	Rank.	Age.	Date of Entering the Service.	Period of Service.	Remarks.
Brown, William	Private	23	Nov. 22, 1864	1 year.	
Buckner, James	do	19	Nov. 22, 1864	1 year.	
Fischer, Michael	do	18	Nov. 10, 1864	1 year.	
Gilmore, Newton	do	25	Oct 11, 1864	1 year.	
Haney, Thomas	do	30	Oct. 11, 1864	1 year.	
Hennessey, John	do	21	Dec. 8, 1864	1 year.	
Kelley, John	do	28	Oct. 11, 1864	1 year.	
Larkins, John	do	22	Aug. 13, 1864	1 year.	
Linn, William	do	24	Oct. 12, 1864	1 year.	
Malen, John T.	do	19	Nov. 10, 1864	1 year.	
Martin, John	do	40	Nov. 2, 1864	1 year.	
Means, Jacob	do	28	Oct. 12, 1864	1 year.	
Mercer, David	do	20	Nov. 10, 1864	1 year.	
Mooney, Michael	do	22	Mch. 1, 1865	1 year.	
Morgan, George M.	do	21	Oct. 5, 1864	1 year	
Nelson, Harvey	do	22	Oct. 12, 1864	1 year.	
Rooney, James	do	28	Jan. 25, 1865	1 year.	
Spain, Patrick	do	34	Oct. 12, 1864	1 year.	
Thompson, John L.	do	18	Sept. 23, 1864	1 year.	
Tracy, Robert	do	26	Nov. 10, 1864	1 year.	
Zibsa, Osmun	do	26	Sept. 2, 1864	1 year.	

182nd Regiment Ohio Volunteer Infantry.

ONE YEAR'S SERVICE.

THIS Regiment was organized in the State of Ohio at large from August › October 27, 1864, to serve one year. On the 1st of November the Regi- t was ordered to move to Nashville, Tenn., and on the 6th of November ed General Sherman's forces at that place. The One Hundred and Eighty- d took part in the battle of Nashville, where it remained performing d and provost duty until July 7, 1865, when it was mustered out in lance with orders from the War Department.

COMPANY A.

Mustered in October 1, 1864, at Toledo, O., by Colonel Jesse S. Norton. Mustered out July 7, 18[illegible] [illegible]ville, Tenn., by J. W. Chickering, Captain 88th Illinois Infantry, and A. C. M., 2d Division, 4th Army Corps.

Names.	Rank.	Age.	Date of Entering the Service.	Period of Service.	
Jesse Burke	Captain	25	Aug. 1, 1864	1 year.	Appointed Oct. 1, 1864; resigned [illegible] 1865.
John W. Barkhurst	do	23	Aug. 5, 1864	1 year.	Promoted from 1st Lieutenant [illegible] 1865; mustered out with company [illegible] 1865.
Irving A. Noble	1st Lieut.	25	July 28, 1864	1 year.	Appointed Oct. 1, 1864; promoted to [illegible] Co. C Feb. 23, 1865.
Joseph L. Deputy	do	36	Aug. 8, 1864	1 year.	Promoted from 2d Lieutenant [illegible] 1865; transferred to Co. E June [illegible]
Ernest F. Lepez	2d Lieut.	35	Aug. 9, 1864	1 year.	Appointed Oct. 1, 1864; promoted [illegible] tenant Co. I Feb. 8, 1865.
Samuel D. Morse	do	20	Aug. 18, 1864	1 year.	Promoted from private Co. [illegible] mustered out with company [illegible]
Joseph B. Jennings	1st Sergt.	42	Sept. 12, 1864	1 year.	Appointed Sergeant Oct. 27 1864; [illegible] Jan. 21, 1865; mustered out [illegible] July 7, 1865.
John Fearnside	Sergeant.	32	Aug. 17, 1864	1 year.	Appointed 1st Sergeant Oct. 27 [illegible] to Sergeant Jan. 21, 1865; mustered [illegible] company July 7, 1865.
Charles Bradley	do	21	Aug. 1, 1864	1 year.	Appointed Oct. 27, 1864; mustered [illegible] company July 7, 1865.
John Wallace	do	20	Aug. 11, 1864	1 year.	Appointed Oct. 27, 1864; mustered [illegible] company July 7, 1865.
Thomas Corbit	do	23	Sept. 28, 1864	1 year.	Appointed Oct. 27, 1864; mustered [illegible] company July 7, 1865.
Harrison John	Corporal.	21	Aug. 23, 1864	1 year.	Appointed Oct. 27, 1864; mustered [illegible] 8, 1865, at Cumberland Hospital [illegible] Tenn., by order of War Department.
Kearn Carroll	do	26	Aug. 23, 1864	1 year.	Appointed Oct. 27, 1864; mustered [illegible] company July 7, 1865.
George Fiklor	do	18	Aug. 18, 1864	1 year.	Appointed Oct. 27, 1864; mustered [illegible] company July 7, 1865.
Loyal M. Richardson	do	28	Aug. 25, 1864	1 year.	Appointed Oct. 27, 1864; mustered [illegible] company July 7, 1865.
Harvey Shade	do	37	Sept. 2, 1864	1 year.	Appointed Oct. 27, 1864; mustered [illegible] company July 7, 1865.
John W[illegible]	do	23	Sept. 5, 1864	1 year.	Appointed Oct. 27, 1864; mustered [illegible] company July 7, 1865.
Isaac [illegible]	do	[illegible]	Aug. [illegible], 1864	1 year.	Appointed ——, mustered [illegible] hospital No. [illegible], Nashville [illegible] of War Department.
[illegible]	[illegible]	[illegible]	[illegible], 1864	1 year.	Appointed ——, mustered [illegible] Nashville, Te[illegible] ment.
[illegible]	[illegible]	[illegible]	Sept. [illegible], 1864	1 year.	Appointed June [illegible] company July 7, 1865.
[illegible] Parker	[illegible]	[illegible]	Aug. 17, 1864	1 year.	Mustered out with company [illegible]
[illegible]	[illegible]	[illegible]	[illegible] 2, 1864	1 year.	Mustered out July 7, [illegible] by order of War Department.
[illegible] W[illegible]	[illegible]	[illegible]	Sept. [illegible], 1864	1 year.	Mustered as Corporal; [illegible] company July 7, 1865.
[illegible]	[illegible]	[illegible]	[illegible], 1864	1 year.	Mustered out July 7, 186[illegible] at N[illegible] by order of War Department.
[illegible] W[illegible]	[illegible]	[illegible]	[illegible], 1864	1 year.	Died Nov. [illegible], 1864, in [illegible] Kentucky.
[illegible]	[illegible]	[illegible]	Aug. [illegible], 1864	1 year.	Mustered out with company [illegible]
[illegible]	[illegible]	[illegible]	[illegible], 1864	1 year.	Died Jan. 20, 1865, in hospital [illegible] Indiana.
[illegible]	[illegible]	[illegible]	Aug. 4, 1864	1 year.	
[illegible]	[illegible]	[illegible]	[illegible], 1864	1 year.	Mustered out July [illegible], 1865, at [illegible] Hospital, Nashville, [illegible] Department.
[illegible]	[illegible]	[illegible]	Aug. [illegible], 1864	1 year.	Mustered out with company [illegible]
[illegible]	[illegible]	[illegible]	[illegible], 1864	1 year.	Mustered out with company [illegible]
[illegible]	[illegible]	[illegible]	[illegible], 1864	1 year.	Mustered out July 7, 18[illegible] by order of War Department.
[illegible] W[illegible]	[illegible]	[illegible]	Aug. [illegible], 1864	1 year.	
[illegible]	[illegible]	[illegible]	[illegible], 1864	1 year.	
[illegible] M[illegible]	[illegible]	[illegible]	[illegible], 1864	1 year.	Mustered out with company [illegible]
[illegible]	[illegible]	[illegible]	Aug. [illegible], 1864	1 year.	Mustered out with company [illegible]
[illegible]	[illegible]	[illegible]	Aug. [illegible]4, 1864	1 year.	Mustered out with company [illegible]
[illegible]	[illegible]	[illegible]	Aug. [illegible], 1864	1 year.	Mustered out with company [illegible]
[illegible]	[illegible]	[illegible]	[illegible], 1864	1 year.	Mustered out with company [illegible]
[illegible]	[illegible]	[illegible]	Aug. [illegible], 1864	1 year.	
Carrol[illegible] John	[illegible]	[illegible]	Aug. 4, 1864	1 year.	Mustered as Corporal; mustered [illegible] company July 7, 1865.

Names.	Rank.	Age.	Date of Entering the Service.	Period of Service.	Remarks.
Riley, Patrick	Private	28	Aug. 27, 1864	1 year.	
Roe, Edward	...do...	27	Aug. 25, 1864	1 year.	Mustered out with company July 7, 1865.
Romer, Matthias	...do...	27	Aug. 30, 1864	1 year.	Mustered out with company July 7, 1865.
Rood, Chauncey L	...do...	37	Sept. 3, 1864	1 year.	Mustered out with company July 7, 1865.
Rowe, Daniel	...do...	19	Oct. 18, 1864	1 year.	Mustered out July 7, 1865, at Nashville, by order of War Department.
Rue, Thomas	...do...	30	Aug. 31, 1864	1 year.	Mustered out with company July 7, 1865.
Russell, Josephus	...do...	18	Aug. 25, 1864	1 year.	Mustered out with company July 7, 1865.
Ryan, Charles	...do...	18	Sept. 1, 1864	1 year.	Mustered out with company July 7, 1865.
Schmidlin, John M	...do...	42	Sept. 15, 1864	1 year.	
Schmidt, George	...do...	24	Aug. 24, 1864	1 year.	
Scott, William H	...do...	18	Sept. 30, 1864	1 year.	Mustered out with company July 7, 1865.
Segur, George	...do...	18	Sept. 10, 1864	1 year.	Mustered out with company July 7, 1865.
Segur, Joseph	...do...	44	Sept. 15, 1864	1 year.	Corporal; mustered out with company July 7, 1865.
Sinck, Jacob	...do...	25	Sept. 8, 1864	1 year.	Mustered out with company July 7, 1865.
Sly, Alester D	...do...	18	Oct. 21, 1864	1 year.	Mustered out July 7, 1865, at Nashville, by order of War Department.
Smith, Charles	...do...	28	Aug. 2, 1864	1 year.	Discharged May 27, 1865, at hospital, M[illegible] Ind., on Surgeon's certificate o[illegible]
Smith, Francis	...do...	25	Aug. 19, 1864	1 year.	
Smith, Harrison	...do...	23	Sept. 3, 1864	1 year.	
Smith, James	...do...	28	Sept. 26, 1864	1 year.	
Smith, William	...do...	19	Aug. 25, 1864	1 year.	Mustered out with company July 7, 1865.
Smithland, John	...do...	42	Sept. 15, 1864	1 year.	Mustered out with company July 7, 1865.
Snider, Myron	...do...	25	Aug. 31, 1864	1 year.	
Squires, John	...do...	21	Sept. 21, 1864	1 year.	
Stuman, Charles	...do...	23	Aug. 21, 1864	1 year.	Mustered out with company July 7, 1865.
Sullivan, Amos	...do...	26	Sept. 26, 1864	1 year.	
Sweet, John	...do...	21	Aug. 24, 1864	1 year.	Mustered out with company July 7, 1865.
Taylor, George W	...do...	19	Sept. 21, 1865	1 year.	Mustered out with company July 7, 1865.
Trotter, Peter	...do...	19	Aug. 12, 1864	1 year.	Mustered as Corporal; mustered out with company July 7, 1865.
Tugo, Nelson	...do...	23	Aug. 29, 1864	1 year.	Mustered out with company July 7, 1865.
Wallace, Richard	...do...	18	Aug. 17, 1864	1 year.	Mustered out with company July 7, 1865.
Ward, Ira J	...do...	18	Aug. 27, 1864	1 year.	Mustered out with company July 7, 1865.
Wellington, Charles	...do...	24	Sept. 22, 1864	1 year.	

COMPANY B.

Mustered in October 1, 1864, at Toledo, O., by Colonel Jesse S. Norton. Mustered out July 7, 1865, at [illegible]ville, Tenn., by J. W. Chickering, Captain 88th Illinois Infantry, and A. C. M., 2d Division, 4th Army Corps.

Names.	Rank.	Age.	Date of Entering the Service.	Period of Service.	Remarks.
Henry C. Roemer	Captain.	21	Aug. 1, 1864	1 year.	Appointed Oct. 1, 1864; resigned M[illegible]
John S. Laver	1st Lieut.	30	Aug. 17, 1864	1 year.	Appointed Oct. 1, 1864; promoted to [illegible] Co. K May 2, 1865.
Harvey B. O'Harra	...do...	37	Oct. 8, 1864	1 year.	Promoted from 2d Lieutenant Co. E [illegible] 1865; transferred to Co. C May 30, 1865.
George M. Young	...do...	28	Aug. 10, 1864	1 year.	Transferred from Co. D May 30, 1865; re[illegible] June 5, 1865.
Isaac G. Stall	...do...	30	Oct. 10, 1864	1 year.	Transferred from Co. E June 6, 1865; m[illegible] out with company July 7, 1865.
James S. Merritt	2d Lieut.	19	Aug. 15, 1864	1 year.	Appointed Oct. 1, 1864; resigned Jan. [illegible]
Lawrence Wamsley	...do...	35	Aug. 29, 1864	1 year.	Promoted from [illegible]m. Sergeant March [illegible]; mustered out with company July 7, 1865.
Alfred L. Sargeant	1st Sergt.	20	Aug. 12, 1864	1 year.	Appointed Oct. 27, 1864; promoted to 2d Lieutenant Co. K May 2, 1865.
George D. Newcomer	...do...	20	Aug. 12, 1864	1 year.	Appointed Sergeant Oct. 27, 1864; 1st Se[illegible] May 4, 1865; mustered out with co[illegible] July 1865.
Edward W. Blizzard	Sergeant.	20	Sept. 12, 1864	1 year.	Appointed Oct. 27, 1864; mustered out with company July 7, 1865.
William H. Hamilton	...do...	32	Aug. 27, 1864	1 year.	Mustered as Corporal; appointed Se[illegible] Oct. 27, 1864; mustered out with co[illegible] July 7, 1865.
John W. McQuillen	...do...	28	Sept. 1, 1864	1 year.	Appointed Corporal Oct. 27, 1864; Se[illegible] ——; promoted to Com. Sergeant Marc[illegible] 1865.
Andrew Bardoff	...do...	19	Aug. 22, 1864	1 year.	Appointed Corporal Oct. 27, 1864; Se[illegible] March 27, 1865; mustered out with co[illegible] July 7, 1865.
Adoniram J. Burch	...do...	22	Aug. 31, 1864	1 year.	Appointed Corporal Oct. 27, 1864; Se[illegible] May 4, 1865; mustered out with co[illegible] July 7, 1865.
Lyman R. Jones	Corporal.	20	Sept. 2, 1864	1 year.	Appointed Oct. 27, 1864; mustered out [illegible] company July 7, 1865.
Frank Linfoot	...do...	18	Aug. 12, 1864	1 year.	Appointed Oct. 27, 1864; mustered out [illegible] company July 7, 1865.

182ND REGIMENT OHIO VOLUNTEER INFANTRY.

FIELD AND STAFF.

Mustered in October 27, 1864, at Columbus, O. Mustered out July 7, 1865, at Nashville, Tenn., by J. W. Chickering, Captain 88th Illinois Infantry, and A. C. M., 2d Division, 4th Army Corps.

Names.	Rank.	Age.	Date of Entering the Service.	Period of Service.	Remarks.
Lewis Butler	Colonel.	38	Oct. 10, 1864	1 year.	Promoted from Major 67th O. V. I. ——; mustered out with regiment July 7, 1865.
John A. Chase	Lt. Col.	35	Oct. 8, 1864	1 year.	Mustered out with regiment July 7, 1865.
William W. West	Major.	41	Oct. 27, 1864	1 year.	Resigned Jan. 24, 1865. See Co. F, 70th O.V.I.
Amos S. Whissen	....do....	27	Aug. 27, 1864	1 year.	Promoted from Captain Co. C Feb. 23, 1865; mustered out with regiment July 7, 1865.
Milton Valentine	Surgeon.	35	Oct. 29, 1864	1 year.	Resigned March 18, 1865.
George Cassady	....do....	42	April 1, 1865	1 year.	Promoted from Asst. Surgeon 83d O. V. I. ——; mustered out with regiment July 7, 1865.
Abraham H. Iler	Ast.Surg.	43	Oct. 19, 1864	1 year.	Mustered out with regiment July 7, 1865.
Peter Willett	....do....	29	Oct. 19, 1864	1 year.	Resigned March 20, 1865.
Thomas J. Thompson	....do....	31	Sept. 30, 1864	1 year.	Promoted to Hospital Steward from private Co. D Oct. 26, 1864; to Asst. Surgeon April 10, 1865; mustered out with regiment July 7, 1865.
James Douglass	Adjutant	40	Oct. 25, 1864	1 year.	
Elijah D. Leedom	....do....	32	Sept. 20, 1864	1 year.	Appointed from 1st Lieutenant Co. I Nov. 29, 1864; mustered out with regiment July 7, 1865.
Owen J. Hopkins	R. Q. M.	20	Oct. 25, 1864	1 year.	Honorably discharged March 2, 1865, by order of War Department; recommissioned June 30, 1865, but not mustered previous to muster-out of regiment. See Co. K, 42d O.V.I.
William H. Brooker	Sergt.Maj	30	Oct. 21, 1864	1 year.	Promoted from private Co. B Oct. 26, 1864; to 2d Lieutenant Co. C March 18, 1865.
William H. Cooley	....do....	23	Sept. 16, 1864	1 year.	Promoted from 1st Sergeant Co. G April 1, 1865; mustered out with regiment July 7, 1865.
Samuel D. Morse	Q. M. S.	20	Aug. 18, 1864	1 year.	Promoted from private Co. F Nov. 10, 1864; reduced to ranks and transferred to Co. C March 15, 1865.
Thomas A. Williamson	....do....	25	Sept. 2, 1864	1 year.	Promoted from Sergeant Co. K March 15, 1865; mustered out with regiment July 7, 1865.
Lawrence Wamsley	Com. Ser.	35	Aug. 29, 1864	1 year.	Promoted from private Co. D Oct. 26, 1864; to 2d Lieutenant Co. B March 18, 1865.
John W. McQuillin	....do....	28	Sept. 1, 1864	1 year.	Promoted from Sergeant Co. B March 27, 1865; mustered out with regiment July 7, 1865.
James W. Bunn	Hos. St'd.	22	Sept. 15, 1864	1 year.	Promoted from private Co. G May 1, 1865; mustered out with regiment July 7, 1865.
Michael Butler	Prin.Mus	18	Oct. 3, 1864	1 year.	Promoted from private Co. E Oct. 26, 1864; returned to company March 1, 1865.
William A. Chappel	....do....	25	Aug. 30, 1864	1 year.	Promoted from private Co. B March 1, 1865; mustered out with regiment July 7, 1865.
James Bellinger	....do....	35	Sept. 27, 1864	1 year.	Promoted from private Co. E Dec. 30, 1864; mustered out with regiment July 7, 1865.

Names.	Rank.	Age.	Date of Entering the Service.	Period of Service.	Remarks.
Dunaway, John M	Private	25	Sept. 5, 1864	1 year.	Mustered out June 11, 1865, at Nashville, Tenn., by order of War Department.
Faust, George A. W	...do...	18	Sept. 10, 1864	1 year.	Mustered out May 18, 1865, at Hospital No. 3, Nashville, Tenn., by order of War Department.
Fitch, Robert	...do...	40	Aug. 25, 1864	1 year.	Mustered out with company July 7, 1865.
Flanary, William	...do...	18	Sept. 19, 1864	1 year.	Mustered out with company July 7, 1865.
Furgeson, James A	...do...	22	Sept. 24, 1864	1 year.	Mustered out with company July 7, 1865.
Gettings, Henry C	...do...	21	Aug. 9, 1864	1 year.	Mustered out with company July 7, 1865.
Grandstaff, Lemuel N	...do...	17	Sept. 30, 1864	1 year.	Mustered out with company July 7, 1865.
Green, Obed	...do...	18	Aug. 12, 1864	1 year.	Mustered out with company July 7, 1865.
Hagerman, John B	...do...	43	Sept. 2, 1864	1 year.	Died Feb. 8, 1865, in hospital at Nashville, Tennessee.
Hart, Thomas C	...do...	19	Sept. 14, 1864	1 year.	Mustered out with company July 7, 1865.
Harvey, William	...do...	18	Jan. 24, 1865	1 year.	Mustered out June 16, 1865, at Louisville, Ky., by order of War Department.
Hawk, Isaac B	...do...	19	Aug. 20, 1864	1 year.	Mustered out with company July 7, 1865.
Hedges, Joseph	...do...	28	Sept. 24, 1864	1 year.	Mustered out July 6, 1865, at Columbus, O., by order of War Department.
Holmes, Henry	...do...	26	Oct. 8, 1864	1 year.	
Hoyt, Tillman K	...do...	42	Sept. 17, 1864	1 year.	Mustered out June 25, 1865, at Nashville, Tenn., by order of War Department.
Hull, Rolander	...do...	18	Oct. 19, 1864	1 year.	Mustered out July 7, 1865, at Nashville, Tenn., by order of War Department.
Hulbert, Benoni W	...do...	19	Aug. 10, 1864	1 year.	Mustered out June 25, 1865, at Nashville, Tenn., by order of War Department.
Johnson, Joseph	...do...	18	Oct. 1, 1864	1 year.	Died June 26, 1865, in hospital at Nashville, Tennessee.
Keever, Francis M	...do...	19	Aug. 29, 1864	1 year.	Mustered out with company July 7, 1865.
Kenzig, Christopher	...do...	45	Oct. 7, 1864	1 year.	
Kirkpatrick, Ralph	...do...	37	Sept. 5, 1864	1 year.	Mustered out with company July 7, 1865.
Knox, Benjamin	...do...	20	Jan. 24, 1865	1 year.	Mustered out July 7, 1865, at Nashville, Tenn., by order of War Department.
Knox, Clement	...do...	36	Sept. 17, 1864	1 year.	Mustered out July 4, 1865, at Cumberland Hospital, Nashville, Tenn., by order of War Department.
Lee, James	...do...	44	Sept. 22, 1864	1 year.	Corporal on muster-in roll; mustered out July 7, 1865, at Nashville, Tenn., by order of War Department.
Lewis, William C	...do...	19	Sept. 21, 1864	1 year.	Mustered out with company July 7, 1865.
Long, Theodore	...do...	18	Sept. 6, 1864	1 year.	
McCoy, Thomas	...do...	19	Oct. 14, 1864	1 year.	
Morse, Samuel D	...do...	20	Aug. 18, 1864	1 year.	Reduced from Q. M. Sergeant March 5, 1865; promoted to 2d Lieutenant Co. A March 8, 1865.
Parsons, Silas D	...do...	17	Aug. 18, 1864	1 year.	Mustered out with company July 7, 1865.
Patterson, Isaac	...do...	21	Sept. 28, 1864	1 year.	Mustered out with company July 7, 1865.
Percival, William	...do...	20	Feb. 25, 1865	1 year.	Mustered out July 7, 1865, at Nashville, Tenn., by order of War Department.
Phillis, Andrew	...do...	20	Aug. 27, 1864	1 year.	Mustered out June 11, 1865, at Nashville, Tenn., by order of War Department.
Phillis, Elias	...do...	20	Aug. 15, 1864	1 year.	Mustered out with company July 7, 1865.
Pickering, William F	...do...	19	Oct. 1, 1864	1 year.	Mustered out with company July 7, 1865.
Pierson, Henry	...do...	31	Sept. 2, 1864	1 year.	Died April 11, 1865, in hospital at Nashville, Tennessee.
Rapp, Charles	...do...	33	Sept. 23, 1864	1 year.	Mustered out June 29, 1865, at Columbus, O., by order of War Department.
Rollison, Isaac	...do...	28	Sept. 3, 1864	1 year.	Mustered out July 7, 1865, at Nashville, Tenn., by order of War Department.
Sanders, Stillman	...do...	21	Oct. 6, 1864	1 year.	Mustered out June 6, 1865, at Camp Dennison, O., by order of War Department.
Sanders, Hezekiah	...do...	43	Sept. 10, 1864	1 year.	Mustered out with company July 7, 1865.
Sealock, Benjamin F	...do...	36	Sept. 1, 1864	1 year.	Died Feb. 12, 1865, in hospital at Louisville, Kentucky.
Selanders, Samuel A	...do...	41	Sept. 22, 1864	1 year.	Mustered out with company July 7, 1865.
Sherman, James M	...do...	18	Aug. 29, 1864	1 year.	Mustered out with company July 7, 1865.
Sherman, John B	...do...	18	Mch. 2, 1865	1 year.	Mustered out July 7, 1865, at Nashville, Tenn., by order of War Department.
Skidmore, Francis M	...do...	18	Oct. 20, 1864	1 year.	Mustered out July 7, 1865, at Nashville, Tenn., by order of War Department.
Skidmore, James	...do...	20	Oct. 20, 1864	1 year.	Mustered out July 7, 1865, at Nashville, Tenn., by order of War Department.
Skillington, William O	...do...	22	Aug. 10, 1864	1 year.	Mustered out with company July 7, 1865.
Smith, Eli	...do...	21	Aug. 22, 1864	1 year.	
Smith, James B	...do...	44	Sept. 29, 1864	1 year.	Mustered out with company July 7, 1865.
Stokes, James L	...do...	17	Sept. 1, 1864	1 year.	Mustered out with company July 7, 1865.
Swiger, Leonard	...do...	44	Sept. 29, 1864	1 year.	Mustered out with company July 7, 1865.
Taylor, Theodore C	...do...	18	Aug. 10, 1864	1 year.	Died March 23, 1865, in hospital at Nashville, Tennessee.
Tice, Noah	...do...	19	Sept. 17, 1864	1 year.	Mustered out with company July 7, 1865.
Topel, Oscar	...do...	18	Oct. 5, 1864	1 year.	Mustered out July 7, 1865, at Nashville, Tenn., by order of War Department.
Turner, John F	...do...	42	Sept. 2, 1864	1 year.	Mustered out with company July 7, 1865.
Tyson, Charles	...do...	21	Aug. 10, 1864	1 year.	Mustered out with company July 7, 1865.
Tyson, Ira	...do...	32	Aug. 9, 1864	1 year.	Corporal on muster-in roll; mustered out with company July 7, 1865.

Names.	Rank.	Age.	Date of Entering the Service.	Period of Service.	Remarks.
..n, Franklin A.	Private.	26	Oct. 8, 1864	1 year.	
..., Benjamin	...do...	18	Sept. 22, 1864	1 year.	Mustered out with company July 7, 1865.
..., Silas D.	...do...	18	Sept. 2, 1864	1 year.	Mustered out with company July 7, 1865.
..n, James	...do...	18	Sept. 13, 1864	1 year.	Mustered out with company July 7, 1865.
..n, Robert	...do...	29	Sept. 22, 1864	1 year.	Mustered out with company July 7, 1865.

COMPANY D.

...tered in October 8, 1864, at Camp Chase, O., by W. P. Richardson, Colonel 25th O. V. I. Mustered out July 7, 1865, at Nashville, Tenn., by J. W. Chickering, Captain 88th Illinois Infantry, and A. C. M., 2d Division, 4th Army Corps.

Names.	Rank.	Age.	Date of Entering the Service.	Period of Service.	Remarks.
...en W. Cooke	Captain.	28	Aug. 10, 1864	1 year.	Appointed Oct. 1, 1864; mustered out with company July 7, 1865.
...ge M. Young	1st Lieut.	28	Aug. 10, 1864	1 year.	Appointed Oct. 8, 1864; transferred to Co. B May 30, 1865.
...ah N. Smith	...do...	25	Sept. 5, 1864	1 year.	Promoted to 2d Lieutenant from private Oct. 8, 1864; to 1st Lieutenant June 16, 1865; mustered out with company July 7, 1865.
...rin L. Tenny	1st Sergt.	37	Aug. 25, 1864	1 year.	Appointed from private Oct. 27, 1864; mustered out with company July 7, 1865.
...liam C. Hopkins	Sergeant.	29	Aug. 22, 1864	1 year.	Appointed from private Oct. 27, 1864; mustered out with company July 7, 1865.
...n Furman	...do...	34	Aug. 15, 1864	1 year.	Discharged May 6, 1865, on Surgeon's certificate of disability.
...rew P. Phillips	...do...	22	Oct. 8, 1864	1 year.	Appointed from Corporal —; mustered out July 7, 1865, at Nashville, Tenn., by order of War Department.
...field Saddoris	...do...	21	Sept. 20, 1864	1 year.	Appointed Corporal Oct. 27, 1864; Sergeant May 7, 1865; mustered out with company July 7, 1865.
...s Long	...do...	31	Sept. 5, 1861	1 year.	Appointed Corporal Oct. 27, 1864; Sergeant May 7, 1865; mustered out with company July 7, 1865.
...n Walker	Corporal.	20	Aug. 17, 1864	1 year.	Appointed Oct. 27, 1864; mustered out with company July 7, 1865.
...ge F. Case	...do...	28	Sept. 16, 1864	1 year.	Discharged June 20, 1865, on Surgeon's certificate of disability.
...ben Gager	...do...	28	Aug. 31, 1864	1 year.	Appointed —; mustered out with company July 7, 1865.
...ge Masterman	...do...	20	Sept. 26, 1864	1 year.	Appointed —; mustered out with company July 7, 1865.
...h Bender	...do...	18	Aug. 29, 1864	1 year.	Appointed May 7, 1865; mustered out with company July 7, 1865.
...es Connor	...do...	26	Sept. 26, 1864	1 year.	Appointed May 7, 1865; mustered out with company July 7, 1865.
...ph W. Hackett	...do...	28	Oct. 6, 1864	1 year.	Appointed —; mustered out July 7, 1865, at Nashville, Tenn., by order of War Department.
...W. Wolf	...do...	24	Oct. 7, 1864	1 year.	Appointed —; mustered out July 7, 1865, at Nashville, Tenn., by order of War Department.
...rles W. Segur	Musician	44	Aug. 27, 1864	1 year.	Appointed —; mustered out with company July 7, 1865.
..., Farley	Private.	18	Aug. 27, 1864	1 year.	Mustered out with company July 7, 1865.
...tte, Stephen	...do...	41	Oct. 7, 1864	1 year.	Mustered out July 7, 1865, at Nashville, Tenn., by order of War Department.
...m, Joseph	...do...	41	Aug. 27, 1864	1 year.	Mustered out with company July 7, 1865.
...r, Mahlon	...do...	34	Aug. 18, 1864	1 year.	
...tt, William	...do...	18	Sept. 28, 1864	1 year.	Mustered out with company July 7, 1865.
...saw, Meadows	...do...	31	Oct. 1, 1864	1 year.	
...v, Albert W	...do...	17	Sept. 2, 1864	1 year.	Died Oct. 2, 1864, at his home, Fulton, O.
...nt, Michael	...do...	19	Sept. 26, 1864	1 year.	Mustered out with company July 7, 1865.
...mer, Anthony M	...do...	34	Sept. 1, 1864	1 year.	Mustered out with company July 7, 1865.
...kholder, Jacob K	...do...	37	Sept. 28, 1864	1 year.	Mustered out with company July 7, 1865.
...roll, Virgil S	...do...	39	Aug. 17, 1864	1 year.	Mustered out with company July 7, 1865.
...ney, Michael	...do...	21	Sept. 10, 1864	1 year.	
...over, Joseph	...do...	18	Oct. 12, 1864	1 year.	Mustered out July 7, 1865, at Nashville, Tenn., by order of War Department.
...stman, James	...do...	18	Sept. 14, 1864	1 year.	
...k, Joseph W	...do...	19	Aug. 17, 1864	1 year.	Mustered out with company July 7, 1865.
..., Emery	...do...	23	Aug. 10, 1864	1 year.	Mustered out with company July 7, 1865.
..., Frederick	...do...	21	Mch. 18, 1865	1 year.	Mustered out July 7, 1865, at Nashville, Tenn., by order of War Department.
...er, Clifton H	...do...	19	Sept. 23, 1864	1 year.	Mustered out with company July 7, 1865.
...ze, Frederick	...do...	18	Sept. 14, 1864	1 year.	Mustered out June 19, 1865, at Nashville, Tenn., by order of War Department.
...ney, John	...do...	25	Sept. 26, 1864	1 year.	
...hiz, Augustus	...do...	[illegible]	Sept. 29, 1864	1 year.	Mustered out July 7, 1865, at Nashville, Tenn., by order of War Department.

Names.	Rank.	Age.	Date of Entering the Service.		
Riley, Patrick	Private	28	Aug. 27, 1864	1	
Roe, Edward	...do...	27	Aug. [illegible], 1864	1	Mustered out wi
Romer, Matthias	...do...	27	Aug. 30, 1864	1	Mustered
Snod, Chauncey L.	...do...	37	Sept. [illegible], 1864	1	
Rowe, Daniel	...do...	19	Oct. 13, 1864	1	Mustered out Ju by order of W
Rue, Thomas	...do...	30	Aug. 31, 1864		ustered out wi
Russell, Josephus	...do...	18	Aug. 26, 1864	1	Mustered out wi
Ryan, Charles	...do...	18	Sept. 1, 1864	1	Mustered out wi
Schmidlin, John M	...do...	42	Sept. 15, 1864	1	
Schmidt, George	...do...	24	Aug. 24, 1864	1	
Scott, William H	...do...	18	Sept. 30, 1864		wi
Segur, George	...do...	18	Sept. 10, 1864		M wi
Segur, Joseph	...do...	44	Sept. 15, 1864		Mustered as C company July
Sinck, Jacob	...do...	26	Sept. 8, 1864		Mustered out wi
Sly, Alester D	...do...	18	Oct. 21, 1864		Mustered out Ju by order of W
Smith, Charles	...do...	28	Aug. 2, 1864		Discharged May Ind., on Surg
Smith, Francis	...do...	25	Aug. 19, 1864		
Smith, Harrison	...do...	23	Sept. 3, 1864	1	
Smith, James	...do...	[illegible]	Sept. 26, 1864	1	
Smith, William	...do...	19	Aug. 25, 1864	1	Mustered out wi
Smithland, John	...do...	42	Sept. 15, 1864	1	Mustered out wi
Snider, Myron	...do...	25	Aug. 31, 1864		
Squires, John	...do...	21	Sept. 21, 1864		
Staman, Charles	...do...	23	Aug. 21, 1864		Mustered out wi
Sullivan, Amos	...do...	26	Sept. 28, 1864		
Sweet, John	...do...	21	Aug. 24, 1864		Mustered out wi
Taylor, George W	...do...	19	Sept. 21, 1865	1 year.	Mustered out wi
Trotter, Peter	...do...	19	Aug. 12, 1864	1 year.	Mustered as C company July
Tugo, Nelson	...do...	23	Aug. 29, 1864	1	Mustered out wi
Wallace, Richard	...do...	18	Aug. 17, 1864	1	Mustered out wi
Ward, Ira J	...do...	18	Aug. 27, 1864	1	Mustered out wi
Wellington, Charles	...do...	24	Sept. 22, 1864	1	

COMPANY B.

Mustered in October 1, 1864, at Toledo, O., by Colonel Jesse S. Norton. Muste ville, Tenn., by J. W. Chickering, Captain 88th Illinois Infa A. C. M., 2d Division, 4th Army Corps.

Henry C. Roemer	Captain.	21	Aug. 1, 1864		Appointed Oct.
John S. Laver	1st Lieut.	30	Aug. 17, 1864		Appointed Oct. Co. K May 2, 1
Harvey B. O'Harra	...do...	37	Oct. 8, 1864		Promoted from 1865; transfer
George M. Young	...do...	28	Aug. 10, 1864		Transferred fro June 5, 1865.
Isaac G. Stall	...do...	30	Oct. 10, 1864		Transferred fron out with com
James S. Merritt	2d Lieut.	19	Aug. 15, 1864		Appointed Oct.
Lawrence Wamsley	...do...	25	Aug. 29, 1864		Promoted from mustered out
Alfred L. Sargeant	1st Sergt.	20	Aug. 12, 1864		Appointed Oct. tenant Co. K
George D. Newcomer	...do...	20	Aug. 12, 1864		Appointed Serg May 4, 1865; July 7, 1865.
Edward W. Blizzard	Sergeant.	20	Sept. 12, 1864		Appointed Oct. company July
William H. Hamilton	...do...	32	Aug. 27, 1864		Mustered as C Oct. 27, 1864; July 7, 1865.
John W. McQuillen	...do...	28	Sept. 1, 1864		Appointed Cor ——; promote 1865.
Andrew Bardoff	...do...	19	Aug. 22, 1864		Appointed Cor March 27, 1865 July 7, 1865.
Adoniram J. Burch	...do...	22	Aug. 31, 1864		Appointed Cor May 4, 1865; July 7, 1865.
Lyman R. Jones	Corporal.	20	Sept. 2, 1864	year.	Appointed Oct. company July
Frank Linfoot	...do...	18	Aug. 12, 1864	year.	Appointed Oct. company July

	Rank.	Age.	Date of Entering the Service.	Period of Service.	Remarks.
th, Samuel	Private	19	Sept. 27, 1864	1 year.	
ler, William	...do...	18	Jan. 4, 1865	1 year.	Died July 2, 1865, at Nashville, Tenn.
ohn, John	...do...	22	Sept. 2, 1864	1 year.	Discharged July 1, 1865, on Surgeon's certificate of disability.
sey, Alfred T.	...	30	Sept. 3, 1864	1 year.	Mustered out with company July 7, 1865.
mas, William H.	...	23	Oct. 6, 1864	1 year.	
mpson, George	...	39	Aug. 26, 1864	1 year.	Mustered out July 7, 1865, at Nashville, Tenn., by order of War Department.
mpson, Stephen	...do...	23	Oct. 6, 1864	1 year.	Mustered out July 7, 1865, at Nashville, Tenn., by order of War Department.
mpson, Thomas J.	...do...	31	Sept. 20, 1864	1 year.	Promoted to Hospital Steward Oct. 26, 1864.
ch, Charles	...do...	22	Sept. 18, 1864	1 year.	Mustered out on detached roll Aug. 30, 1865, at Washington, D. C., by order of War Department.
deroff, William K.	...do...	25	Oct. 4, 1864	1 year.	Mustered out July 7, 1865, at Nashville, Tenn., by order of War Department.
ner, John	...do...	38	Oct. 26, 1864	1 year.	Died June 6, 1865, in hospital at Nashville, Tennessee.
ker, William	...do...	26	Oct. 27, 1864	1 year.	Mustered out July 7, 1865, at Nashville, Tenn., by order of War Department.
tmer, John W.	...do...	19	Oct. 3, 1864	1 year.	Mustered out July 7, 1865, at Nashville, Tenn., by order of War Department.
nsley, Lawrence	...do...	35	Aug. 29, 1864	1 year.	Promoted to Com. Sergeant Oct. 26, 1864.
l, James	...do...	24	Sept. 26, 1864	1 year.	
ron, Alfred H.	...do...	18	Sept. 30, 1864	1 year.	Died June 4, 1865, in hospital at Nashville, Tennessee.
ters, David H.	...do...	18	Sept. 25, 1864	1 year.	Mustered out with company July 7, 1865.
h, John H.	...do...	22	Aug. 23, 1864	1 year.	
linson, Thomas A.	...do...	18	Sept. 30, 1864	1 year.	Mustered out with company July 7, 1865.
liams, Charles H.	...do...	17	Sept. 2, 1864	1 year.	On muster in roll as Corporal; mustered out with company July 7, 1865.
liams, John	...do...	22	Sept. 19, 1864	1 year.	
inger, Philip	...do...	30	Sept. 12, 1864	1 year.	Mustered out June 14, 1865, at Louisville, Ky., by order of War Department.
ke, John H. G.	...do...	42	Aug. 31, 1864	1 year.	Mustered out with company July 7, 1865.

COMPANY E.

tered in October 8, 1864, at Toledo, O., by Colonel Jesse S. Norton. Mustered out July 7, 1865, at Nashville, Tenn., by J. W. Chickering, Captain 88th Illinois Infantry, and A. C. M., 2d Division, 4th Army Corps.

	Rank.	Age.	Date of Entering the Service.	Period of Service.	Remarks.
el A. Terry	Captain.	32	Oct. 8, 1864	1 year.	Mustered out with company July 7, 1865.
G. Stall	1st Lieut.	30	Oct. 8, 1864	1 year.	Transferred to Co. B June 6, 1865.
ph L. Deputy	...do...	37	Oct. 8, 1864	1 year.	Transferred from Co. A June 6, 1865; mustered out with company July 7, 1865.
ey B. O'Harra	2d Lieut.	37	Oct. 8, 1864	1 year.	Promoted to 1st Lieutenant Co. B May 2, 1865.
ry G. Patterson	...do...	23	Aug. 15, 1864	1 year.	Promoted from 1st Sergeant Co. C May 2, 1865; mustered out with company July 7, 1865.
ge Clark	1st Sergt.	24	Oct. 5, 1864	1 year.	Appointed from private Oct. 27, 1864; mustered out July 7, 1865, at Nashville, Tenn., by order of War Department.
les H. Davidson	Sergeant.	30	Oct. 10, 1864	1 year.	Appointed from private Oct. 27, 1864; mustered out May 31, 1865, at Columbus, O., by order of War Department.
d Ivy	...do...	26	Aug. 27, 1864	1 year.	Appointed from private Oct. 27, 1864; mustered out with company July 7, 1865.
rt W. Munson	...do...	22	Sept. 20, 1864	1 year.	Appointed from private Oct. 27, 1864; mustered out with company July 7, 1865.
M. Hunter	...do...	23	Aug. 20, 1864	1 year.	Appointed from private Oct. 27, 1864; mustered out with company July 7, 1865.
Ford	Corporal.	37	Sept. 9, 1864	1 year.	Appointed Oct. 27, 1864; mustered out with company July 7, 1865.
ge W. Orders	...do...	29	Sept. 10, 1864	1 year.	Appointed Oct. 27, 1864; mustered out with company July 7, 1865.
Rust	...do...	19	Aug. 31, 1864	1 year.	Appointed Oct. 27, 1864; mustered out with company July 7, 1865.
E. Connell	...do...	31	Sept. 2, 1864	1 year.	Appointed Oct. 27, 1864; mustered out with company July 7, 1865.
Scott	...do...	41	Oct. 4, 1864	1 year.	Appointed Oct. 27, 1864; mustered out July 7, 1865, at Nashville, Tenn., by order of War Department.
M. Cordray	...do...	23	Oct. 3, 1864	1 year.	Appointed Oct. 27, 1864; mustered out July 7, 1865, at Nashville, Tenn., by order of War Department.
ander H. Dall	...do...	21	Oct. 5, 1864	1 year.	Appointed Oct. 27, 1864; mustered out July 7, 1865, at Nashville, Tenn., by order of War Department.
el Scott	...do...	18	Oct. 4, 1864	1 year.	Appointed Oct. 27, 1864; mustered out July 7, 1865, at Nashville, Tenn., by order of War Department.

COMPANY C.

Mustered in October 7, 1864, at Camp Chase, O., by W. P. Richardson, Colonel 25th O. V. I. Mustered out July 7, 1865, at Nashville, Tenn., by J. W. Chickering, Captain 88th Illinois Infantry, and A. C. M., 2d Division, 4th Army Corps.

Names.	Rank.	Age.	Date of Entering the Service.	Period of Service.	Remarks.
Amos A. Whissen	Captain.	27	Aug. 27, 1864	1 year.	Appointed Oct. 8, 1864; promoted to Major Feb. 23, 1865.
Irving A. Noble	....do....	25	July 28, 1864	1 year.	Promoted from 1st Lieutenant Co. A Feb. 23, 1865; mustered out with company July 7, 1865.
John W. Harkhurst	1st Lieut.	23	Aug. 5, 1864	1 year.	Appointed Oct. 8, 1864; promoted to Captain Co. A June 6, 1865.
Harvey B. O'Harra	....do....	37	Oct. 8, 1864	1 year.	Transferred from Co. B to date May 30, 1865; mustered out with company July 7, 1865.
Joseph L. Deputy	2d Lieut.	26	Aug. 8, 1864	1 year.	Appointed Oct. 8, 1864; promoted to 1st Lieutenant Co. A Feb. 23, 1865.
William H. Brooker	....do....	25	Oct. 21, 1864	1 year.	Promoted from Sergt. Major March 18, 1865; mustered out with company July 7, 1865.
Henry G. Patterson	1st Sergt.	22	Aug. 15, 1864	1 year.	Promoted to 2d Lieutenant Co. K May 2, 1865.
John D. Palmer	....do....	21	Aug. 31, 1864	1 year.	Appointed Sergeant Oct. 27, 1864; 1st Sergeant May 11, 1865; mustered out with company July 7, 1865.
Thomas P. McCain	Sergeant.	22	Sept. 7, 1864	1 year.	Appointed Oct. 27, 1864; mustered out with company July 7, 1865.
Christopher C. Andrews	....do....	27	Sept. 16, 1864	1 year.	Appointed Oct. 27, 1864; mustered out with company July 7, 1865.
Martin Hoaglin	....do....	44	Aug. 22, 1864	1 year.	Appointed Oct. 27, 1864; mustered out June 25, 1865, at Nashville, Tenn., by order of War Department.
John W. Cross	....do....	23	Oct. 3, 1864	1 year.	Appointed Corporal Oct. 27, 1864; Sergeant May 11, 1865; died June 19, 1865, in hospital at Nashville, Tenn.
Thomas G. Phillips	....do....	32	Aug. 19, 1864	1 year.	Appointed Corporal Oct. 27, 1864; Sergeant June 26, 1865; mustered out with company July 7, 1865.
John W. Brown	....do....	18	Aug. 10, 1864	1 year.	Appointed Corporal Oct. 27, 1864; Sergeant June 26, 1865; mustered out with company July 7, 1865.
Isaac Clark	Corporal.	22	Sept. 19, 1864	1 year.	Appointed Oct. 27, 1864; mustered out with company July 7, 1865.
Benjamin S. Lukens	....do....	29	Oct. 3, 1864	1 year.	Appointed Oct. 27, 1864; mustered out July [illegible], 1865, at Nashville, Tenn., by order of War Department.
John Scroggan	....do....	19	Aug. 11, 1864	1 year.	Appointed Oct. 27, 1864; mustered out with company July 7, 1865.
Charles W. Vincent	....do....	19	Aug. 11, 1864	1 year.	Appointed Oct. 27, 1864; mustered out with company July 7, 1865.
David M. Brooks	....do....	27	Sept. 4, 1864	1 year.	Appointed Feb. 1, 1865; mustered out June 25, 1865, at Nashville, Tenn., by order of War Department.
James C. Preston	....do....	20	Sept. 1, 1864	1 year.	Appointed May 11, 1865; mustered out with company July 7, 1865.
James Winstanley	....do....	30	Aug. 9, 1864	1 year.	Appointed June 26, 1865; mustered out with company July 7, 1865.
Levi Spicer	....do....	19	Sept. 2, 1864	1 year.	Appointed June 26, 1865; mustered out with company July 7, 1865.
Samuel M. Burrows	....do....	17	Aug. 23, 1864	1 year.	Appointed June 26, 1865; mustered out with company July 7, 1865.
Bacon C. Irwin	Musician	19	Sept. 28, 1864	1 year.	Mustered out with company July 7, 1865.
Allen, Cornelius B.	Private.	19	Aug. 10, 1864	1 year.	Mustered out with company July 7, 1865.
Baker, William H.	....do....	36	Sept. 17, 1864	1 year.	Mustered out with company July 7, 1865.
Camron, Andrew	....do....	18	Sept. 14, 1864	1 year.	
Carey, Andrew J.	....do....	19	Sept. 12, 1864	1 year.	Mustered out with company July 7, 1865.
Carter, Henry	....do....	44	Sept. 16, 1864	1 year.	
Clark, George W.	....do....	16	Aug. 10, 1864	1 year.	Mustered out with company July 7, 1865.
Clark, James H.	....do....	19	Aug. 9, 1864	1 year.	Mustered out with company July 7, 1865.
Comstock, James	....do....	20	Sept. 2, 1864	1 year.	Mustered out with company July 7, 1865.
Conger, Benoni G.	....do....	23	Aug. 9, 1864	1 year.	Mustered out May 16, 1865, at Hospital No. 14, Nashville, Tenn., by order of War Department.
Cutshaw, Shannon	....do....	18	Sept. 14, 1864	1 year.	
Daniels, Alfred	....do....	21	Sept. 24, 1864	1 year.	
Daniels, John	....do....	44	Sept. 24, 1864	1 year.	Mustered out with company July 7, 1865.
Daniels, John, Jr.	....do....	24	Sept. 22, 1864	1 year.	Mustered out with company July 7, 1865.
Daniels, Joseph	....do....	42	Sept. 22, 1864	1 year.	Mustered out with company July 7, 1865.
Deputy, Leonidas O.	....do....	18	Oct. 11, 1864	1 year.	Appointed Corporal Oct. 27, 1864; reduced Jan. 19, 1865; mustered out July 7, 1865, at Nashville, Tenn., by order of War Department.
Dunaway, Jacob E.	....do....	23	Sept. 12, 1864	1 year.	Died April 27, 1865, in hospital at Nashville, Tennessee.

Names.	Rank.	Age.	Date of Entering the Service.	Period of Service.	Remarks.
Betts, Luther	Private	18	Sept. 26, 1864	1 year.	Mustered out with company July 7, 1865.
Bowers, Jacob	...do...	20	Aug. 27, 1864	1 year.	Mustered out with company July 7, 1865.
Brace, George W	...do...	18	Sept. 14, 1864	1 year.	Mustered out with company July 7, 1865.
Bratton, Orlando D	...do...	18	Sept. 17, 1864	1 year.	Mustered out with company July 7, 1865.
Bushong, Andrew	...do...	36	Sept. 3, 1864	1 year.	Mustered out with company July 7, 1865.
Cadwell, John P	...do...	19	Sept. 17, 1864	1 year.	On muster-in roll as Corporal; mustered out with company July 7, 1865.
Carr, Enoch	...do...	27	Sept. 16, 1864	1 year.	Mustered out with company July 7, 1865.
Cassell, Curtis	...do...	33	Sept. 5, 1864	1 year.	Mustered out with company July 7, 1865.
Chappell, James N	...do...	21	Sept. 30, 1864	1 year.	Mustered out with company July 7, 1865.
Clark, Joseph	...do...	20	Aug. 23, 1864	1 year.	Died Dec. 5, 1864, at Nashville, Tenn.
Collins, Abram	...do...	25	Sept. 10, 1864	1 year.	Mustered out July 4, 1865, at Nashville, Tenn., by order of War Department.
Combs, Elias B	...do...	18	Oct. 3, 1864	1 year.	Mustered out July 7, 1865, at Nashville, Tenn., by order of War Department.
Crum, Silas	...do...	41	Sept. 17, 1864	1 year.	Mustered out with company July 7, 1865.
Culver, Thomas	...do...	18	Sept. 25, 1864	1 year.	Mustered out with company July 7, 1865.
Deakins, John	...do...	18	Sept. 23, 1864	1 year.	Mustered out with company July 7, 1865.
Densmore, Amos	...do...	19	Oct. 1, 1864	1 year.	Mustered out with company July 7, 1865.
De Witt, Edward K	...do...	42	Sept. 1, 1864	1 year.	Mustered out with company July 7, 1865.
Doughton, John H	...do...	37	Sept. 20, 1864	1 year.	Mustered out with company July 7, 1865.
Durbin, Charles	...do...	18	Sept. 27, 1864	1 year.	
Ely, Francis D	...do...	19	Sept. 13, 1864	1 year.	Mustered out with company July 7, 1865.
Ely, George W	...do...	18	Oct. 5, 1864	1 year.	Mustered out July 7, 1865, at Nashville, Tenn., by order of War Department.
Ervin, William	...do...	20	Sept. 3, 1864	1 year.	Mustered out with company July 7, 1865.
Esterline, Reuben	...do...	41	Sept. 1, 1864	1 year.	Mustered out with company July 7, 1865.
Ferris, Aaron	...do...	18	Sept. 5, 1864	1 year.	Mustered out with company July 7, 1865.
Fisher, John M	...do...	24	Sept. 10, 1864	1 year.	Reduced from 1st Sergeant ——; mustered out May 12, 1865, at Nashville, Tenn., by order of War Department.
Ford, Francis M	...do...	30	Sept. 30, 1864	1 year.	Mustered out with company July 7, 1865.
Frager, Leander	...do...	19	Sept. 19, 1864	1 year.	Mustered out June 1, 1865, at Nashville, Tenn., by order of War Department.
Freed, George E	...do...	21	Oct. 3, 1864	1 year.	Mustered out July 7, 1865, at Nashville, Tenn., by order of War Department.
Fritz, Frederick	...do...	34	Oct. 4, 1864	1 year.	Mustered out with company July 7, 1865.
Funson, [illegible]	...do...	17	Sept. 21, 1864	1 year.	
Gardner, Chauncey D	...do...	21	Sept. 17, 1864	1 year.	Mustered out with company July 7, 1865.
Haddix, Aaron	...do...	18	Sept. 17, 1864	1 year.	Mustered out with company July 7, 1865.
Hammet, George W	...do...	18	Sept. 5, 1864	1 year.	Mustered out with company July 7, 1865.
Harger, Jesse	...do...	22	Sept. 26, 1864	1 year.	Mustered out with company July 7, 1865.
Hart, John A	...do...	25	Sept. 17, 1864	1 year.	Mustered out with company July 7, 1865.
Heeden, Daniel	...do...	28	Sept. 13, 1864	1 year.	Mustered out Sept. 18, 1865, at Columbus, [illegible] on expiration of term of service.
Hendricks, Henry O	...do...	22	Sept. 19, 1864	1 year.	Mustered out with company July 7, 1865.
Hendricks, Salathiel	...do...	20	Sept. 13, 1864	1 year.	Mustered out with company July 7, 1865.
Hester, Henry H	...do...	23	Sept. 3, 1864	1 year.	Mustered out with company July 7, 1865.
Hicks, James H	...do...	19	Sept. 21, 1864	1 year.	Mustered out with company July 7, 1865.
Hissong, Jonas	...do...	20	Sept. 3, 1864	1 year.	Mustered out with company July 7, 1865.
Holler, William K	...do...	23	Sept. 5, 1864	1 year.	Appointed Corporal ——; reduced [illegible] 1865; mustered out with company July 7, 1865.
Hood, Ezra	...do...	18	Sept. 5, 1864	1 year.	Mustered out May 24, 1865, at Nashville, Tenn., by order of War Department.
Hutchinson, John	...do...	22	Sept. 5, 1864	1 year.	Mustered out with company July 7, 1865.
Kauaur, Adam	...do...	24	Sept. 5, 1864	1 year.	Mustered out with company July 7, 1865.
Kauaur, Franklin	...do...	30	Sept. 5, 1864	1 year.	Mustered out with company July 7, 1865.
Lucas, William C	...do...	18	Oct. 4, 1864	1 year.	Mustered out July 7, 1865, at Nashville, Tenn., by order of War Department.
Lyons, John	...do...	20	Aug. 25, 1864	1 year.	Mustered out with company July 7, 1865.
Martin, James E	...do...	18	Sept. 5, 1864	1 year.	Mustered out with company July 7, 1865.
Mavis, George R	...do...	18	Sept. 21, 1864	1 year.	Mustered out June 1, 1865, at Nashville, Tenn., by order of War Department.
Merryman, Orson	...do...	18	Oct. 4, 1864	1 year.	Mustered out July 7, 1865, at Nashville, Tenn., by order of War Department.
Moody, James W	...do...	21	Aug. 30, 1864	1 year.	Mustered out June 2, 1865, at Philadelphia, Pa., by order of War Department.
Morse, Samuel D	...do...	20	Aug. 18, 1864	1 year.	Promoted to Q. M. Sergeant Nov. 1, 1864.
Newcomer, William D	...do...	21	Sept. 9, 1864	1 year.	Mustered out with company July 7, 1865.
Oberlin, Hiram B	...do...	26	Sept. 22, 1864	1 year.	Mustered out with company July 7, 1865.
Osman, George D	...do...	20	Sept. 5, 1864	1 year.	Mustered out with company July 7, 1865.
Packard, Yocumb D	...do...	24	Sept. 20, 1864	1 year.	
Peach, William	...do...	18	Sept. 3, 1864	1 year.	Mustered out with company July 7, 1865.
Rardin, Lorenzo	...do...	16	Sept. 21, 1864	1 year.	Mustered out with company July 7, 1865.
Reader, Henry	...do...	21	Sept. 4, 1864	1 year.	Mustered out with company July 7, 1865.
Rhoades, Lewis W	...do...	17	Sept. 13, 1864	1 year.	Mustered out with company July 7, 1865.
Richards, John	...do...	18	Sept. 26, 1864	1 year.	Mustered out with company July 7, 1865.
Rose, George W	...do...	18	Sept. 14, 1864	1 year.	Mustered out with company July 7, 1865.
Rutledge, Solomon	...do...	28	Sept. 3, 1864	1 year.	Mustered out with company July 7, 1865.
Scott, Peter	...do...	18	Oct. 3, 1864	1 year.	Mustered out July 7, 1865, at Nashville, Tenn., by order of War Department.
Sheppard, James W	...do...	18	Sept. 1, 1864	1 year.	Mustered out with company July 7, 1865.
Shuller, Eli	...do...	25	Sept. 21, 1864	1 year.	Mustered out with company July 7, 1865.
Shultz, George	...do...	18	Sept. 5, 1864	1 year.	Mustered out with company July 7, 1865.
Smith, John D	...do...	18	Sept. 30, 1864	1 year.	Mustered out with company July 7, 1865.

	Rank.	Age.	Date of Entering the Service.	Period of Service.	Remarks.
., John W.	Private.	23	Sept. 5, 1864	1 year.	Mustered out with company July 7, 1865.
ley, William G.	....do....	19	Sept. 8, 1864	1 year.	Died Nov. 2, 1864, at his home, Williams County, O.
er, Henry	....do....	20	Sept. 6, 1864	1 year.	Mustered out with company July 7, 1865.
ner, John	....do....	37	Sept. 10, 1864	1 year.	Mustered out with company July 7, 1865.
bach, Adam	....do....	23	Sept. 5, 1864	1 year.	Mustered out with company July 7, 1865.
. Horace S.	....do....	18	Sept. 22, 1864	1 year.	Mustered out with company July 7, 1865.
art, George	....do....	28	Oct. 3, 1864	1 year.	Mustered out July 7, 1865, at Nashville, Tenn., by order of War Department.
y, Hiram	....do....	18	Sept. 26, 1864	1 year.	Mustered out with company July 7, 1865.
en, Augustus	....do....	18	Oct. 3, 1864	1 year.	Mustered out July 7, 1865, at Nashville, Tenn., by order of War Department.
on, Thomas	....do....	41	Sept. 15, 1864	1 year.	Discharged June 19, 1865, at Nashville, Tenn., on Surgeon's certificate of disability.
s, John M.	....do....	41	Sept. 24, 1864	1 year.	Mustered out with company July 7, 1865.
., Martin L.	....do....	18	Sept. 19, 1864	1 year.	Mustered out with company July 7, 1865.

COMPANY G.

ered in October 10, 1864, at Camp Chase, O., by W. P. Richardson, Colonel 25th O. V. I. Mustered out July 7, 1865, at Nashville, Tenn., by J. W. Chickering, Captain 88th Illinois Infantry, and A. C. M., 2d Division, 4th Army Corps.

	Rank.	Age.	Date of Entering the Service.	Period of Service.	Remarks.
ander M. Lang	Captain.	..	Oct. 10, 1864	1 year.	Mustered out with company July 7, 1865.
nas Mitchell	1st Lieut.	41	Sept. 3, 1864	1 year.	Resigned June 20, 1865.
L. Conner	2d Lieut.	42	Sept. 3, 1864	1 year.	Mustered out with company July 7, 1865.
am H. Cooley	1st Sergt.	28	Sept. 16, 1864	1 year.	Appointed from private Oct. 27, 1864; promoted to Sergt. Major April 1, 1865.
am J. Ellison	....do....	25	Sept. 25, 1864	1 year.	Appointed Sergeant from private Oct. 27, 1864; 1st Sergeant April 1, 1865; mustered out with company July 7, 1865.
M. Morgan	Sergeant.	39	Sept. 21, 1864	1 year.	Appointed from private Oct. 27, 1864; mustered out with company July 7, 1865.
Dunn	....do....	26	Sept. 15, 1864	1 year.	Appointed from private Oct. 27, 1864; mustered out with company July 7, 1865.
ah B. Freeman	....do....	34	Sept. 28, 1864	1 year.	Appointed Corporal Oct. 27, 1864; Sergeant June 1, 1865; mustered out with company July 7, 1865.
am J. McKinley	....do....	32	Sept. 20, 1864	1 year.	Appointed Corporal Oct. 27, 1864; Sergeant April 1, 1865; mustered out with company July 7, 1865.
h H. Evans	Corporal.	40	Sept. 23, 1864	1 year.	Appointed Oct. 27, 1864; mustered out with company July 7, 1865.
lson Warner	....do....	44	Sept. 19, 1864	1 year.	Appointed Oct. 27, 1864; mustered out with company July 7, 1865.
y Bradford	....do....	41	Sept. 14, 1864	1 year.	Appointed Oct. 27, 1864; mustered out with company July 7, 1865.
Bradford	....do....	26	Sept. 19, 1864	1 year.	Appointed Oct. 27, 1864; mustered out with company July 7, 1865.
Flanagan	....do....	42	Sept. 18, 1864	1 year.	Appointed Oct. 27, 1864; mustered out with company July 7, 1865.
am W. Killen	....do....	28	Sept. 8, 1864	1 year.	Appointed Jan. 1, 1865; mustered out with company July 7, 1865.
d, Peter C.	Private.	37	Sept. 21, 1864	1 year.	Mustered out June 6, 1865, at Camp Dennison, O., by order of War Department.
rson, Daniel	....do....	37	Sept. 2, 1864	1 year.	Mustered out with company July 7, 1865.
pach, Jacob	....do....	18	Sept. 16, 1864	1 year.	Mustered out July 20, 1865, at Louisville, Ky., by order of War Department.
., Adam	....do....	30	Sept. 21, 1864	1 year.	Mustered out with company July 7, 1865.
e, James	....do....	43	Sept. 28, 1864	1 year.	Mustered out with company July 7, 1865.
e, Titus M.	....do....	18	Sept. 28, 1864	1 year.	Mustered out with company July 7, 1865.
nfield, Allen S.	....do....	41	Sept. 7, 1864	1 year.	Mustered out with company July 7, 1865.
., James W.	....do....	22	Sept. 15, 1864	1 year.	Promoted to Hospital Steward May 1, 1865.
., Joseph	....do....	27	Sept. 21, 1864	1 year.	Mustered out with company July 7, 1865.
gan, John	....do....	28	Sept. 30, 1864	1 year.	Mustered out with company July 7, 1865.
es, James	....do....	26	Sept. 13, 1864	1 year.	Mustered out with company July 7, 1865.
er, George A.	....do....	25	Sept. 7, 1864	1 year.	Mustered out with company July 7, 1865.
ton, Greenbury J.	....do....	42	Sept. 19, 1864	1 year.	Mustered out with company July 7, 1865.
er, Granville	....do....	20	Sept. 14, 1864	1 year.	Mustered out with company July 7, 1865.
er, Oliver K.	....do....	18	Sept. 16, 1864	1 year.	Mustered out May 19, 1865, at Nashville, Tenn., by order of War Department.
, Joseph C.	....do....	28	Sept. 28, 1864	1 year.	Mustered out with company July 7, 1865.
son, George W.	....do....	38	Sept. 20, 1864	1 year.	Mustered out with company July 7, 1865.
ey, Moses	....do....	45	Sept. 17, 1864	1 year.	Mustered out May 18, 1865, at Nashville, Tenn., by order of War Department.
ngton, William	....do....	44	Sept. 20, 1864	1 year.	Appointed Sergeant from private Oct. 27, 1864; reduced to ranks Jan. 8, 1865; mustered out with company July 7, 1865.
dge, Samuel	....do....	44	Sept. 20, 1864	1 year.	Mustered out with company July 7, 1865.
s, Anthony	....do....	41	Sept. 28, 1864	1 year.	Mustered out with company July 7, 1865.

Names.	Rank.	Age.	Date of Entering the Service.	Period of Service.	Remarks.
Evans, David	Private..	36	Sept. 24, 1864	1 year.	Discharged June 1, 1865, at Nashville, Tenn., on Surgeon's certificate of disability.
Evans, James	...do....	26	Sept. 23, 1864	1 year.	Mustered out with company July 7, 1865.
Fear, Francis	...do....	41	Sept. 15, 1864	1 year.	Mustered out with company July 7, 1865.
Franklin, John A.	...do....	44	Sept. 7, 1864	1 year.	Mustered out Aug. 12, 1865, at Cincinnati, O., by order of War Department.
Freeman, William S.	...do....	23	Sept. 28, 1864	1 year.	Mustered out with company July 7, 1865.
Graham, Thomas	...do....	44	Sept. 19, 1864	1 year.	Mustered out with company July 7, 1865.
Hall, Franklin	...do....	18	Sept. 16, 1864	1 year.	Mustered out with company July 7, 1865.
Hall, George B.	...do....	18	Sept. 20, 1864	1 year.	Mustered out with company July 7, 1865.
Hall, William	...do....	44	Sept. 16, 1864	1 year.	Mustered out with company July 7, 1865.
Hampton, James A.	...do....	18	Sept. 17, 1864	1 year.	Mustered out with company July 7, 1865.
Herdman, Robert	...do....	26	Sept. 23, 1864	1 year.	Mustered out with company July 7, 1865.
Hicks, John G.	...do....	35	Sept. 7, 1864	1 year.	
Hines, Henry	...do....	17	Sept. 15, 1864	1 year.	Mustered out with company July 7, 1865.
Hines, Jonathan A.	...do....	18	Sept. 15, 1864	1 year.	Discharged June 7, 1865, at Nashville, Tenn., on Surgeon's certificate of disability.
Hines, Josephus	...do....	18	Sept. 17, 1864	1 year.	Mustered out with company July 7, 1865.
Holt, Nathan	...do....	41	Sept. 23, 1864	1 year.	Died Feb. 12, 1865, at Nashville, Tenn.
Hoop, William	...do....	38	Sept. 3, 1864	1 year.	Mustered out with company July 7, 1865.
Howell, William E.	...do....	34	Sept. 17, 1864	1 year.	Mustered out with company July 7, 1865.
Jacobs, Samuel	...do....	33	Sept. 14, 1864	1 year.	Mustered out with company July 7, 1865.
Jobe, Sylvester	...do....	21	Sept. 3, 1864	1 year.	Mustered out with company July 7, 1865.
Kerr, James	...do....	29	Sept. 21, 1864	1 year.	Mustered out May 17, 1865, at Nashville, Tenn., by order of War Department.
Kelly, Samuel	...do....	39	Sept. 21, 1864	1 year.	Mustered out with company July 7, 1865.
Kelly, William G.	...do....	16	Sept. 7, 1864	1 year.	Mustered out with company July 7, 1865.
Lang, James M.	...do....	26	Sept. 21, 1864	1 year.	Died March 7, 1865, at Nashville, Tenn.
McManis, Francis J.	...do....	21	Sept. 20, 1864	1 year.	Mustered out with company July 7, 1865.
Martin, Benjamin F.	...do....	22	Sept. 21, 1864	1 year.	Mustered out with company July 7, 1865.
Miller, Lewis	...do....	38	Oct. 28, 1864	1 year.	
Moore, Isaac F.	...do....	27	Aug. 1, 1864	1 year.	Mustered out with company July 7, 1865.
Mytinger, Charles W.	...do....	35	Sept. 11, 1864	1 year.	Transferred to 22d O. V. I. [illegible] 8, 1864.
Naylor, Clayton	...do....	18	Sept. 20, 1864	1 year.	Mustered out with company July 7, 1865.
Neill, John	...do....	21	Sept. 13, 1864	1 year.	Mustered out with company July 7, 1865.
Nevill, William	...do....	35	Sept. 15, 1864	1 year.	Mustered out with company July 7, 1865.
Newman, David B.	...do....	38	Sept. 21, 1864	1 year.	Mustered out with company July 7, 1865.
Newman, Henry A.	...do....	21	Sept. 28, 1864	1 year.	Mustered out June 27, 1865, at Columbus, O., by order of War Department.
Newman, James K. P.	...do....	19	Sept. 20, 1864	1 year.	Mustered out with company July 7, 1865.
Newman, John R.	...do....	44	Sept. 25, 1864	1 year.	Mustered out with company July 7, 1865.
Newman, Richard	...do....	35	Sept. 20, 1864	1 year.	Mustered out June 6, 1865, at Camp Dennison, O., by order of War Department.
Newman, William G.	...do....	28	Sept. 23, 1864	1 year.	Mustered out with company July 7, 1865.
Nichols, Daniel	...do....	27	Sept. 23, 1864	1 year.	Mustered out with company July 7, 1865.
Oliver, T[illegible] J.	...do....	22	Sept. 20, 1864	1 year.	Mustered out with company July 7, 1865.
Palmer, James C.	...do....	35	Sept. 17, 1864	1 year.	Mustered out with company July 7, 1865.
Parker, William	...do....	28	Sept. 21, 1864	1 year.	Mustered out with company July 7, 1865.
Parks, James	...do....	39	Sept. 3, 1864	1 year.	Mustered out with company July 7, 1865.
Paul, Gilbert M.	...do....	17	Sept. 3, 1864	1 year.	Mustered out with company July 7, 1865.
Phillips, Thomas	...do....	20	Sept. 19, 1864	1 year.	Mustered out with company July 7, 1865.
Platt, John	...do....	30	Sept. 23, 1864	1 year.	Mustered out with company July 7, 1865.
Powers, James	...do....	44	Sept. 3, 1864	1 year.	Mustered out July 12, 1865, at Camp Dennison, O., by order of War Department.
Powers, William H.	...do....	16	Sept. 3, 1864	1 year.	Mustered out with company July 7, 1865.
River, Adam	...do....	30	Sept. 23, 1864	1 year.	Discharged June 1, 1865, at Nashville, Tenn., on Surgeon's certificate of disability.
Ruggles, William	...do....	43	Sept. 16, 1864	1 year.	Mustered out July 3, 1865, at Columbus, O., by order of War Department.
Scott, Benjamin	...do....	23	Sept. 19, 1864	1 year.	Mustered out with company July 7, 1865.
Scott, John A.	...do....	27	Sept. 19, 1864	1 year.	Mustered out with company July 7, 1865.
Stewart, Alexander	...do....	39	Sept. 19, 1864	1 year.	Discharged May 15, 1865, at Nashville, Tenn., on Surgeon's certificate of disability.
Stewart, John M.	...do....	41	Sept. 19, 1864	1 year.	Mustered out with company July 7, 1865.
Thompson, George W.	...do....	21	Sept. 7, 1864	1 year.	Mustered out June 6, 1865, at Camp Dennison, O., by order of War Department.
Thompson, William	...do....	22	Sept. 17, 1864	1 year.	
Thoroman, Uriel S.	...do....	31	Sept. 3, 1864	1 year.	Mustered out with company July 7, 1865.
Thoroman, William F.	...do....	20	Sept. 28, 1864	1 year.	Mustered out with company July 7, 1865.
Wallace, Samuel	...do....	41	Sept. 23, 1864	1 year.	Mustered out with company July 7, 1865.
Warren, Christopher	...do....	29	Sept. 23, 1864	1 year.	Mustered out with company July 7, 1865.
Warren, George	...do....	26	Sept. 17, 1864	1 year.	
Warren, James C.	...do....	24	Sept. 23, 1864	1 year.	Died Feb. 19, 1865, in hospital at Nashville, Tennessee.
Washburn, Thomas	...do....	25	Sept. 20, 1864	1 year.	Mustered out with company July 7, 1865.
Williams, John C.	...do....	29	Sept. 23, 1864	1 year.	Mustered out with company July 7, 1865.

Names.	Rank.	Age.	Date of Entering the Service.	Period of Service.	Remarks.
Smith, Samuel	Private.	19	Sept. 27, 1864	1 year.	
Snyder, William	....do....	18	Jan. 4, 1865	1 year.	Died July 2, 1865, at Nashville, Tenn.
St. John, John	....do....	22	Sept. 2, 1864	1 year.	Discharged July 1, 1865, on Surgeon's certificate of disability.
Sweasey, Alfred T.	....do....	30	Sept. 3, 1864	1 year.	Mustered out with company July 7, 1865.
Thomas, William H.	....do....	23	Oct. 6, 1864	1 year.	
Thompson, George	....do....	39	Aug. 26, 1864	1 year.	Mustered out July 7, 1865, at Nashville, Tenn., by order of War Department.
Thompson, Stephen	....do....	23	Oct. 6, 1864	1 year.	Mustered out July 7, 1865, at Nashville, Tenn., by order of War Department.
Thompson, Thomas J.	....do....	31	Sept. 30, 1864	1 year.	Promoted to Hospital Steward Oct. 26, 1864.
Ulrich, Charles	....do....	22	Sept. 18, 1864	1 year.	Mustered out on detached roll Aug. 30, 1865, at Washington, D. C., by order of War Department.
Vanderoff, William E.	....do....	25	Oct. 4, 1864	1 year.	Mustered out July 7, 1865, at Nashville, Tenn., by order of War Department.
Wagner, John	....do....	38	Oct. 26, 1864	1 year.	Died June 6, 1865, in hospital at Nashville, Tennessee.
Walker, William	....do....	26	Oct. 27, 1864	1 year.	Mustered out July 7, 1865, at Nashville, Tenn., by order of War Department.
Waltner, John W.	....do....	19	Oct. 3, 1864	1 year.	Mustered out July 7, 1865, at Nashville, Tenn., by order of War Department.
Wamsley, Lawrence	....do....	35	Aug. 29, 1864	1 year.	Promoted to Com. Sergeant Oct. 26, 1864.
Ward, James	....do....	24	Sept. 26, 1864	1 year.	
Warren, Alfred H.	....do....	18	Sept. 30, 1864	1 year.	Died June 4, 1865, in hospital at Nashville, Tennessee.
Watters, David H.	....do....	18	Sept. 25, 1864	1 year.	Mustered out with company July 7, 1865.
Welch, John H.	....do....	22	Aug. 23, 1864	1 year.	
Wilkinson, Thomas A.	....do....	18	Sept. 30, 1864	1 year.	Mustered out with company July 7, 1865.
Williams, Charles H.	....do....	17	Sept. 2, 1864	1 year.	On muster in roll as Corporal; mustered out with company July 7, 1865
Williams, John	....do....	22	Sept. 19, 1864	1 year.	
Wininger, Philip	....do....	30	Sept. 12, 1864	1 year.	Mustered out June 14, 1865, at Louisville, Ky., by order of War Department.
Wolke, John H. G.	....do....	42	Aug. 31, 1864	1 year.	Mustered out with company July 7, 1865.

COMPANY E.

Mustered in October 8, 1864, at Toledo, O., by Colonel Jesse S. Norton. Mustered out July 7, 1865, at Nashville, Tenn., by J. W. Chickering, Captain 88th Illinois Infantry, and A. C. M., 2d Division, 4th Army Corps.

Names.	Rank.	Age.	Date of Entering the Service.	Period of Service.	Remarks.
Daniel A. Terry	Captain.	32	Oct. 8, 1864	1 year.	Mustered out with company July 7, 1865.
Isaac G. Stall	1st Lieut.	30	Oct. 8, 1864	1 year.	Transferred to Co. B June 6, 1865.
Joseph L. Deputy	....do....	57	Oct. 8, 1864	1 year.	Transferred from Co. A June 6, 1865; mustered out with company July 7, 1865.
Harvey B. O'Harra	2d Lieut.	27	Oct. 8, 1864	1 year.	Promoted to 1st Lieutenant Co. B May 2, 1865.
Henry G. Patterson	....do....	23	Aug. 15, 1864	1 year.	Promoted from 1st Sergeant Co. C May 2, 1865; mustered out with company July 7, 1865.
George Clark	1st Sergt.	24	Oct. 5, 1864	1 year.	Appointed from private Oct. 27, 1864; mustered out July 7, 1865, at Nashville, Tenn., by order of War Department.
Charles H. Davidson	Sergeant.	30	Oct. 10, 1864	1 year.	Appointed from private Oct. 27, 1864; mustered out May 31, 1865, at Columbus, O., by order of War Department.
Alfred Ivy	....do....	26	Aug. 27, 1864	1 year.	Appointed from private Oct. 27, 1864; mustered out with company July 7, 1865.
Albert W. Munson	....do....	22	Sept. 20, 1864	1 year.	Appointed from private Oct. 27, 1864; mustered out with company July 7, 1865.
John M. Hunter	....do....	23	Aug. 20, 1864	1 year.	Appointed from private Oct. 27, 1864; mustered out with company July 7, 1865.
Cory Ford	Corporal.	37	Sept. 9, 1864	1 year.	Appointed Oct. 27, 1864, mustered out with company July 7, 1865.
George W. Orders	....do....	29	Sept. 10, 1864	1 year.	Appointed Oct. 27, 1864; mustered out with company July 7, 1865.
Ernest Rust	....do....	19	Aug. 31, 1864	1 year.	Appointed Oct. 27, 1864; mustered out with company July 7, 1865.
John E. Connell	....do....	31	Sept. 2, 1864	1 year.	Appointed Oct. 27, 1864; mustered out with company July 7, 1865.
James Scott	....do....	41	Oct. 4, 1864	1 year.	Appointed Oct. 27, 1864; mustered out July 7, 1865, at Nashville, Tenn., by order of War Department.
Isaac M. Cordray	....do....	23	Oct. 3, 1864	1 year.	Appointed Oct. 27, 1864; mustered out July 7, 1865, at Nashville, Tenn., by order of War Department.
Alexander H. Doll	....do....	21	Oct. 5, 1864	1 year.	Appointed Oct. 27, 1864; mustered out July 7, 1865, at Nashville, Tenn., by order of War Department.
Samuel Scott	....do....	18	Oct. 4, 1864	1 year.	Appointed Oct. 27, 1864; mustered out July 7, 1865, at Nashville, Tenn., by order of War Department.

Names.	Rank.	Age.	Date of Entering the Service.	Period of Service.	Remarks.
Albright, Jacob	Private	18	Oct. 7, 1864	1 year.	Mustered out July 7, 1865, at Nashville, Tenn., by order of War Department.
Albright, Thomas	do	27	Aug. 23, 1864	1 year.	Mustered out July 7, 1865, at Nashville, Tenn., by order of War Department.
Baret, Patrick	do	36	Sept. 29, 1864	1 year.	Mustered out with company July 7, 1865.
Barnett, Noah	do	18	Oct. 27, 1864	1 year.	Mustered out July 7, 1865, at Nashville, Tenn., by order of War Department.
Bean, William E.	do	31	Sept. 26, 1864	1 year.	Mustered out June 6, 1865, at Camp Dennison, O., by order of War Department.
Bellinger, James	do	35	Sept. 27, 1864	1 year.	Promoted to Principal Musician Dec. 30, 1864.
Bethel, William	do	42	Sept. 30, 1864	1 year.	
Bevis, Joseph	do	19	Oct. 6, 1864	1 year.	Mustered out July 1865, at Nashville, Tenn., by order of War Department.
Bibby, James	do	18	Oct. 1, 1864	1 year	Mustered out July 7, 1865, at Nashville, Tenn., by order of War Department.
Birkhead, George	do	18	Sept. 25, 1864	1 year.	Mustered out with company July 1865.
Birkhead, Juliette	do	18	Sept. 28, 1864	1 year.	Mustered out May 19, 1865, at Louisville, Ky., by order of War Department.
Burke, John	do	20	Oct. 4, 1864	1 year.	
Burns, Frank	do	25	Oct. 4, 1864	1 year.	
Butler, Michael	do	18	Oct. 3, 1864	1 year.	Promoted to Principal Musician to date Oct. 26, 1864; reduced to the ranks and returned to company March 1, 1865; mustered out July 7, 1865, at Nashville, Tenn., by order of War Department.
Buzick, Francis M.	do	20	Sept. 20, 1864	1 year.	Died Oct. 31, 1864, in hospital at Camp Chase, Ohio.
Canon, James	do	21	Oct. 3, 1864	1 year.	
Ceigenspock, Harmon	do	20	Sept. 5, 1864	1 year.	Mustered out with company July 7, 1865.
Corder, John	do	18	Sept. 30, 1864	1 year.	Mustered out with company July 7, 1865.
Daly, John	do	18	Oct. 3, 1864	1 year.	Mustered out July 7, 1865, at Nashville, Tenn., by order of War Department.
Davy, William	do	23	Sept. 5, 1864	1 year.	Died Feb. 28, 1865, in hospital at Nashville, Tennessee.
Demorest, Amos	do	18	Aug. 30, 1864	1 year	Mustered out with company July 7, 1865.
Dickerson, Silas	do	18	Oct. 6, 1864	1 year.	
Dixon, John	do	34	Sept. 30, 1864	1 year.	Mustered out with company July 7, 1865.
Douglass, Samuel	do	18	Aug. 30, 1864	1 year.	Mustered out with company July 7, 1865.
Edwards, Richard	do	23	Oct. 21, 1864	1 year.	Mustered out July 7, 1865, at Nashville, Tenn., by order of War Department.
Elbert, William H.	do	18	Oct. 5, 1864	1 year.	Mustered out July 7, 1865, at Nashville, Tenn., by order of War Department.
Ellis, William	do	18	Oct. 3, 1864	1 year	
Fair, Amos	do	18	Oct. 1, 1864	1 year	Died June 2, 1865, in hospital at Nashville, Tennessee.
Fair, Chauncey	do	20	Oct. 1, 1864	1 year.	Mustered out July 7, 1865, at Nashville, Tenn., by order of War Department.
Fair, William	do	20	Oct. 3, 1864	1 year	Mustered out July 7, 1865, at Nashville, Tenn., by order of War Department.
Fearign, Aaron	do	21	Aug. 30, 1864	1 year.	
Fearign, Irwin	do	43	Sept. 5, 1864	1 year	Mustered out with company July 7, 1865.
Fearing, Francis	do	18	Sept. 22, 1864	1 year	Mustered out with company July 7, 1865.
Ferguson, Lawrence	do	25	Sept. 28, 1864	1 year	Mustered out with company July 7, 1865.
French, John	do	37	Sept. 3, 1864	1 year.	
Glenn, William	do	18	Oct. 1, 1864	1 year.	Mustered out July 7, 1865, at Nashville, Tenn., by order of War Department.
Gochenouer, George	do	18	Sept. 25, 1864	1 year	Mustered out with company July 7, 1865.
Graham, Samuel	do	18	Oct. 18, 1864	1 year.	Mustered out July 7, 1865, at Nashville, Tenn., by order of War Department.
Grant, Robert	do	18	Aug. 31, 1864	1 year	Mustered out with company July 7, 1865.
Gray, John	do	18	Sept. 6, 1864	1 year.	Mustered out with company July 7, 1865.
Inman, Miram	do	44	Oct. 1, 1864	1 year.	Mustered out June 6, 1865, at Camp Dennison, O., by order of War Department.
Jaynes, John	do	26	Oct. 6, 1864	1 year.	
Jester, Samuel	do	19	Sept. 12, 1864	1 year.	Mustered out with company July 7, 1865.
Johnson, Silas	do	28	Sept. 23, 1864	1 year.	Mustered out with company July 7, 1865.
Kious, Adam	do	18	Sept. 6, 1864	1 year	Mustered out with company July 7, 1865.
Kuhns, Andrew	do	42	Oct. 3, 1864	1 year	Mustered out July 7, 1865, at Nashville, Tenn., by order of War Department.
Lewis, Lewis	do	43	Sept. 27, 1864	1 year	Discharged April 25, 1865, at Nashville, Tenn., on Surgeon's certificate of disability.
McCandless, James	do	18	Aug. 29, 1864	1 year.	Died Feb. 12, 1865, in hospital at Nashville, Tennessee.
McKitrick, Israel	do	20	Oct. 5, 1864	1 year	Mustered out June 6, 1865, at Camp Dennison, O., by order of War Department.
McQueety, Andrew J.	do	19	Sept. 30, 1864	1 year.	Mustered out with company July 7, 1865.
Miller, Samuel J.	do	24	Oct. 5, 1864	1 year.	Mustered out July 7, 1865, at Nashville, Tenn., by order of War Department.
Mohler, Wellington	do	18	Sept. 26, 1864	1 year.	Mustered out with company July 7, 1865.
Mohler, William H. H.	do	21	Sept. 26, 1864	1 year	Mustered out with company July 7, 1865.
Montgomery, Edward	do	18	Oct. 4, 1864	1 year.	Mustered out July 7, 1865, at Nashville, Tenn., by order of War Department.
Murphy, Peter	do	18	Sept. 23, 1864	1 year.	Mustered out with company July 7, 1865.
Murray, William	do	22	Sept. 30, 1864	1 year.	
Neely, John H.	do	44	Oct. 4, 1864	1 year	Mustered out July 7, 1865, at Nashville, Tenn., by order of War Department.

Names.	Rank.	Age.	Date of Entering the Service.	Period of Service.	Remarks.
Newburgh, Aaron B.	Private..	45	Oct. 15, 1864	1 year.	Mustered out May 22, 1865, at Columbus, O., by order of War Department.
Nolan, Edward	...do....	26	Oct. 4, 1864	1 year.	
Norris, John B.	...do....	27	Sept. 25, 1864	1 year.	
Norton, Thomas	...do....	36	Sept. 13, 1864	1 year.	Mustered out with company July 7, 1865.
Oglesbee, Aaron L.	...do....	18	Sept. 6, 1864	1 year.	Mustered out July 7, 1865, at Nashville, Tenn., by order of War Department.
Quinn, William	...do....	43	Sept. 3, 1864	1 year.	Mustered out with company July 7, 1865.
Raber, John	...do....	41	Aug. 30, 1864	1 year.	Mustered out with company July 7, 1865.
Rayrodin, Patrick	...do....	38	Aug. 17, 1864	1 year.	Mustered out with company July 7, 1865.
Reed, Richard	...do....	39	Aug. 15, 1864	1 year.	Mustered out with company July 7, 1865.
Rees, John L.	...do....	19	Aug. 24, 1864	1 year.	Mustered out with company July 7, 1865.
Roberts, Benjamin F.	...do....	25	Oct. 5, 1864	1 year.	Mustered out July 7, 1865, at Nashville, Tenn., by order of War Department.
Rorick, William	...do....	18	Oct. 6, 1864	1 year.	
Shackleford, John W.	...do....	18	Aug. 23, 1864	1 year.	Mustered out with company July 7, 1865.
Shaw, Edmund	...do....	36	Sept. 26, 1864	1 year	
Sipsey, Charles F.	...do....	27	Oct. 5, 1864	1 year.	Mustered out July 7, 1865, at Nashville, Tenn., by order of War Department.
Smith, Joseph	...do....	15	Sept. 23, 1864	1 year.	Mustered out with company July 7, 1865.
Smith, William R.	...do....	18	Oct. 1, 1864	1 year	Died Jan. 15, 1865, in hospital at Nashville, Tennessee.
Strain, Harvey	...do....	28	Aug. 27, 1864	1 year	Mustered out with company July 7, 1865.
Switzer, DeWitt C.	...do....	18	Sept. 7, 1864	1 year.	Mustered out with company July 7, 1865.
Taylor, Abraham	...do....	19	Aug. 26, 1864	1 year.	Mustered out with company July 7, 1865.
Taylor, Charles	...do....	20	Oct. 4, 1864	1 year.	Mustered out July 7, 1865, at Nashville, Tenn., by order of War Department.
Taylor, Ira	...do....	21	Oct. 12, 1864	1 year.	Discharged June 26, 1865, at Nashville, Tenn., on Surgeon's certificate of disability.
Taylor, Joseph	...do....	22	Oct. 10, 1864	1 year.	Mustered out July 7, 1865, at Nashville, Tenn., by order of War Department.
Van Horn, John J.	...do....	40	Sept. 23, 1864	1 year.	Mustered out with company July 7, 1865.
Vittum, James H.	...do....	18	Sept. 28, 1864	1 year.	Died March 28, 1865, in hospital at Nashville, Tenn.
Walsh, Robert	...do....	28	Sept. 29, 1864	1 year.	Mustered out with company July 7, 1865.
Weston, John T.	...do....	26	Sept. 6, 1864	1 year.	Mustered out with company July 7, 1865.
White, Frank M.	...do....	19	Aug. 9, 1864	1 year.	Mustered out with company July 7, 1865.
White, George H.	...do....	18	Oct. 7, 1864	1 year.	Mustered out July 7, 1865, at Nashville, Tenn., by order of War Department.

COMPANY F.

Mustered in October 8, 1864, at Toledo, O., by Colonel Jesse S. Norton. Mustered out July 7, 1865, at Nashville, Tenn., by J. W. Chickering, Captain 88th Illinois Infantry, and A. C. M., 2d Division, 4th Army Corps.

Names.	Rank.	Age.	Date of Entering the Service.	Period of Service.	Remarks.
William C. Coslet	Captain.	30	Oct. 8, 1864	1 year.	Mustered out with company July 7, 1865.
Alfred F. Stoner	1st Lieut.	31	Oct. 8, 1864	1 year.	Mustered out with company July 7, 1865.
Robert R. Turrilton	2d Lieut.	22	Oct. 8, 1864	1 year.	Mustered out with company July 7, 1865.
Salathiel Cowgill	Sergeant.	31	Aug. 27, 1864	1 year.	Mustered out with company July 7, 1865.
David Kosler	...do....	24	Sept. 3, 1864	1 year.	Mustered out with company July 7, 1865.
Lorenzo DeGroff	...do....	22	Sept. 3, 1864	1 year.	Mustered out with company July 7, 1865.
William H. Gump	...do....	28	Aug. 22, 1864	1 year.	Mustered out with company July 7, 1865.
Simon G. Ward	...do....	25	Oct. 5, 1864	1 year.	Appointed from Corporal March 1, 1865; mustered out July 7, 1865, at Nashville, Tenn., by order of War Department
Henry W. Crum	Corporal.	40	Sept. 5, 1864	1 year.	Mustered out with company July 7, 1865.
Jonathan Kosler	...do....	31	Sept. 5, 1864	1 year.	Mustered out with company July 7, 1865.
William H. Spencer	...do....	25	Sept. 12, 1864	1 year.	Mustered out with company July 7, 1865.
John G. Shifller	...do....	32	Sept. 16, 1864	1 year.	Mustered out with company July 7, 1865.
Oscar S. Webb	...do....	18	Sept. 12, 1864	1 year.	Mustered out with company July 7, 1865.
George A. Ely	...do....	19	Sept. 3, 1864	1 year.	Mustered out June 19, 1865, at Nashville, Tenn., by order of War Department.
David Mincer	...do....	22	Sept. 5, 1864	1 year.	Appointed ——; discharged June 16, 1865, at Nashville, Tenn., on Surgeon's certificate of disability
Aaron Shifller	...do....	30	Sept. 16, 1864	1 year.	Appointed March 1, 1865; mustered out with company July 7, 1865.
Winfield S. Bradley	Musician	16	Oct. 4, 1864	1 year.	Mustered out July 7, 1865, at Nashville, Tenn., by order of War Department.
George E. Whetmore	...do....	22	Oct. 3, 1864	1 year.	Mustered out July 7, 1865, at Nashville, Tenn., by order of War Department.
Anspaugh, George	Private..	42	Oct. 21, 1864	1 year.	Discharged June 6, 1865, at Nashville, Tenn., on Surgeon's certificate of disability.
Bailey, Charles A.	...do....	22	Sept. 24, 1864	1 year.	Mustered out with company July 7, 1865.
Barone, Elias	...do....	44	Aug. 22, 1864	1 year.	Discharged Jan. 27, 1865, at Madison, Ind., on Surgeon's certificate of disability.
Bash, Jacob	...do....	38	Oct. 3, 1864	1 year.	Mustered out July 7, 1865, at Nashville, Tenn., by order of War Department.
Bennett, James	...do....	21	Sept. 21, 1864	1 year.	Mustered out with company July 7, 1865.

Names.	Rank.	Age.	Date of Entering the Service.	Period of Service.	Remarks.
Hughs, David S.	Private.	44	Sept. 28, 1864	1 year.	Discharged June 30, 1865, on Surgeon's certificate of disability.
Hunt, Amour	do.	22	Oct. 8, 1864	1 year.	Mustered out June 6, 1865, at Camp Dennison, O., by order of War Department.
Irwin, James	do.	40	Sept. 28, 1864	1 year.	Mustered out with company July 7, 1865.
Jackman, Samuel	do.	29	Sept. 28, 1864	1 year.	Mustered out with company July 7, 1865.
Johnson, Benjamin F.	do.	25	Sept. 30, 1864	1 year.	Mustered out with company July 7, 1865.
Klein, Herman	do.	18	Mch. 14, 1865	1 year.	Mustered out July 7, 1865, at Nashville, Tenn., by order of War Department.
Lewis, James	do.	31	Sept. 28, 1864	1 year.	Mustered out with company July 7, 1865.
Love, Charles	do.	18	Sept. 10, 1864	1 year.	Mustered out with company July 7, 1865.
Love, John	do.	41	Sept. 10, 1864	1 year.	Mustered out with company July 7, 1865.
McCune, Edward R.	do.	34	Sept. 30, 1864	1 year.	Discharged June 30, 1865, on Surgeon's certificate of disability.
McCune, James W.	do.	21	Aug. 24, 1864	1 year.	Mustered out June 19, 1865, in hospital at Nashville, Tenn., by order of War Department.
McDaniel, James S.	do.	37	Sept. 15, 1864	1 year.	Mustered out with company July 7, 1865.
McNeil, John S.	do.	23	Sept. 30, 1864	1 year.	Mustered out with company July 7, 1865.
Magoon, George	do.	22	Sept. 28, 1864	1 year.	Mustered out with company July 7, 1865.
Mosier, Samuel	do.	38	Aug. 25, 1864	1 year.	Mustered out with company July 7, 1865.
Naylor, John	do.	35	Sept. 20, 1864	1 year.	Mustered out with company July 7, 1865.
Nichols, James A.	do.	20	Sept. 30, 1864	1 year.	Mustered out with company July 7, 1865.
Peggs, Samuel S.	do.	21	Sept. 1, 1864	1 year.	Died Nov. 11, 1864, in hospital at Nashville, Tennessee.
Robuck, William	do.	18	Aug. 21, 1864	1 year.	Mustered out with company July 7, 1865.
Shell, Benjamin	do.	23	Sept. 28, 1864	1 year.	Mustered out with company July 7, 1865.
Stone, Edward	do.	23	Oct. 3, 1864	1 year.	Mustered out July 7, 1865, at Nashville, Tenn., by order of War Department.
Stone, Samuel	do.	32	Oct. 3, 1864	1 year.	Discharged July 1, 1865, on Surgeon's certificate of disability.
Tolle, Milton R.	do.	21	Oct. 3, 1864	1 year.	Mustered out July 7, 1865, at Nashville, Tenn., by order of War Department.
Thomas, George A.	do.	31	Sept. 28, 1864	1 year.	Mustered out with company July 7, 1865.
Thomas, George W.	do.	43	Sept. 28, 1864	1 year.	Mustered out with company July 7, 1865.
Thomas, James	do.	23	Sept. 28, 1864	1 year.	Mustered out with company July 7, 1865.
Thomas, John H. W.	do.	18	Sept. 1, 1864	1 year.	Mustered out with company July 7, 1865.
Thomas, Samuel	do.	20	Oct. 3, 1864	1 year.	Mustered out July 7, 1865, at Nashville, Tenn., by order of War Department.
Thompson, Legrand	do.	18	Sept. 23, 1864	1 year.	Mustered out with company July 7, 1865.
Tucker, Hugh M.	do.	40	Sept. 21, 1864	1 year.	Mustered out with company July 7, 1865.
Turner, Peter B.	do.	38	Sept. 28, 1864	1 year.	Mustered out with company July 7, 1865.
Waldron, Henry	do.	43	Sept. 28, 1864	1 year.	Mustered out with company July 7, 1865.
Walters, John W.	do.	37	Sept. 20, 1864	1 year.	
Wilmoth, John M.	do.	41	Oct. 3, 1864	1 year.	Mustered out July 7, 1865, at Nashville, Tenn., by order of War Department.
Willman, Jesse	do.	33	Sept. 28, 1864	1 year.	Mustered out with company July 7, 1865.
Willman, William	do.	31	Sept. 28, 1864	1 year.	Mustered out with company July 7, 1865.

COMPANY K.

Mustered in October —, 1864, at Toledo, O., by Colonel Jesse S. Norton. Mustered out July 7, 1865, at Nashville, Tenn., by J. W. Chickering, Captain 88th Illinois Infantry, and A. C. M., 2d Division, 4th Army Corps.

Names.	Rank.	Age.	Date of Entering the Service.	Period of Service.	Remarks.
Charles A. Wright	Captain.	43	Sept. 12, 1864	1 year.	Appointed Oct. 25, 1864; resigned Apr. [illegible] 1865.
John S. Laver	do.	30	Aug. 17, 1864	1 year.	Promoted from 1st Lieutenant Co. B [illegible] 1865; mustered out with company July 7, 1865.
William H. Wood	1st Lieut.	23	Oct. 19, 1864	1 year.	Appointed Oct. 25, 1864; resigned Jan. [illegible] 1865.
William H. McGrew	2d Lieut.	24	Aug. 27, 1864	1 year.	Appointed Oct. 25, 1864; resigned March [illegible] 1865.
Alfred L. Sargeant	do.	20	Aug. 12, 1864	1 year.	Promoted from 1st Sergeant Co. B May [illegible]; mustered out with company July 7, 1865.
Francis M. Blakeman	1st Sergt.	28	Sept. 3, 1864	1 year.	Appointed Oct. 27, 1864; mustered out with company July 7, 1865.
Robert W. L. Ely	Sergeant.	20	Sept. 3, 1864	1 year.	Appointed Oct. 27, 1864; mustered out with company July 7, 1865.
Samuel L. Richards	do.	24	Oct. 15, 1864	1 year.	Appointed Oct. 27, 1864; mustered out [illegible] 1865, at Nashville, Tenn., by order of War Department.
Thomas A. Williamson	do.	25	Sept. 2, 1864	1 year.	Appointed Oct. 27, 1864; promoted to Q. M. Sergeant March 16, 1865.
Simeon E. Richards	do.	19	Oct. 6, 1864	1 year.	Appointed Corporal Oct. 27, 1864; Sergeant —; mustered out July 7, 1865, at Nashville, Tenn., by order of War Department.
Daniel C. Whistler	do.	44	Oct. 6, 1864	1 year.	Appointed Corporal Oct. 27, 1864; Sergeant March 16, 1865; mustered out July [illegible] at Nashville, Tenn., by order of War Department.

Names.	Rank.	Age.	Date of Entering the Service.	Period of Service.	Remarks.
Smith, John W.	Private.	23	Sept. 5, 1864	1 year.	Mustered out with company July 7, 1865.
Smitley, William G.	...do...	19	Sept. 3, 1864	1 year.	Died Nov. 2, 1864, at his home, Williams County, O.
Snyder, Henry	...do...	20	Sept. 5, 1864	1 year.	Mustered out with company July 7, 1865.
Sommer, John	...do...	37	Sept. 10, 1864	1 year.	Mustered out with company July 7, 1865.
Strasbach, Adam	...do...	33	Sept. 5, 1864	1 year.	Mustered out with company July 7, 1865.
Swift, Horace S.	...do...	18	Sept. 22, 1864	1 year.	Mustered out with company July 7, 1865.
Swihart, George	...do...	23	Oct. 5, 1864	1 year.	Mustered out July 7, 1865, at Nashville, Tenn., by order of War Department.
Talley, Hiram	...do...	18	Sept. 26, 1864	1 year.	Mustered out with company July 7, 1865.
Warren, Augustus	...do...	18	Oct. 5, 1864	1 year.	Mustered out July 7, 1865, at Nashville, Tenn., by order of War Department.
Weston, Thomas	...do...	41	Sept. 15, 1864	1 year.	Discharged June 19, 1865, at Nashville, Tenn., on Surgeon's certificate of disability.
Wines, John M.	...do...	41	Sept. 24, 1864	1 year.	Mustered out with company July 7, 1865.
Wines, Martin L.	...do...	18	Sept. 19, 1864	1 year.	Mustered out with company July 7, 1865.

COMPANY G.

Mustered in October 10, 1864, at Camp Chase, O., by W. P. Richardson, Colonel 25th O. V. I. Mustered out July 7, 1865, at Nashville, Tenn., by J. W. Chickering, Captain 88th Illinois Infantry, and A. C. M., 2d Division, 4th Army Corps.

Names.	Rank.	Age.	Date of Entering the Service.	Period of Service.	Remarks.
Alexander M. Lang	Captain.	..	Oct. 10, 1864	1 year.	Mustered out with company July 7, 1865.
Thomas Mitchell	1st Lieut.	41	Sept. 3, 1864	1 year.	Resigned June 20, 1865.
Levi L. Conner	2d Lieut.	42	Sept. 3, 1864	1 year.	Mustered out with company July 7, 1865.
William H. Cooley	1st Sergt.	23	Sept. 16, 1864	1 year.	Appointed from private Oct. 27, 1864; promoted to Sergt. Major April 1, 1865.
William J. Ellison	...do...	35	Sept. 25, 1864	1 year.	Appointed Sergeant from private Oct. 27, 1864; 1st Sergeant April 1, 1865; mustered out with company July 7, 1865.
John M. Morgan	Sergeant.	39	Sept. 21, 1864	1 year.	Appointed from private Oct. 27, 1864; mustered out with company July 7, 1865.
John Bunn	...do...	26	Sept. 15, 1864	1 year.	Appointed from private Oct. 27, 1864; mustered out with company July 7, 1865
Joseph B. Freeman	...do...	31	Sept. 28, 1864	1 year.	Appointed Corporal Oct. 27, 1864; Sergeant June 1, 1865; mustered out with company July 7, 1865
William J. McKinley	...do...	32	Sept. 20, 1864	1 year.	Appointed Corporal Oct. 27, 1864; Sergeant April 1, 1865, mustered out with company July 7, 1865.
Elijah H. Evans	Corporal.	40	Sept. 25, 1864	1 year.	Appointed Oct. 27, 1864; mustered out with company July 7, 1865.
Harrison Warner	...do...	44	Sept. 19, 1864	1 year.	Appointed Oct. 27, 1864; mustered out with company July 7, 1865.
Henry Bradford	...do...	41	Sept. 14, 1864	1 year.	Appointed Oct. 27, 1864; mustered out with company July 7, 1865.
Jacob Bradford	...do...	35	Sept. 19, 1864	1 year.	Appointed Oct. 27, 1864; mustered out with company July 7, 1865.
Caleb Flanagan	...do...	42	Sept. 13, 1864	1 year.	Appointed Oct. 27, 1864; mustered out with company July 7, 1865.
William W. Killen	...do...	38	Sept. 3, 1864	1 year.	Appointed Jan. 1, 1865; mustered out with company July 7, 1865.
Aldred, Peter C.	Private.	37	Sept. 21, 1864	1 year.	Mustered out June 6, 1865, at Camp Dennison, O., by order of War Department.
Anderson, Daniel	...do...	37	Sept. 2, 1864	1 year.	Mustered out with company July 7, 1865.
Aschpach, Jacob	...do...	18	Sept. 16, 1864	1 year.	Mustered out July 20, 1865, at Louisville, Ky., by order of War Department.
Boen, Adam	...do...	39	Sept. 23, 1864	1 year.	Mustered out with company July 7, 1865.
Bowie, James	...do...	43	Sept. 28, 1864	1 year.	Mustered out with company July 7, 1865.
Bowie, Titus M.	...do...	18	Sept. 28, 1864	1 year.	Mustered out with company July 7, 1865.
Brownfield, Allen S.	...do...	41	Sept. 7, 1864	1 year.	Mustered out with company July 7, 1865.
Bunn, James W.	...do...	22	Sept. 15, 1864	1 year.	Promoted to Hospital Steward May 1, 1865.
Bunn, Joseph	...do...	27	Sept. 21, 1864	1 year.	Mustered out with company July 7, 1865.
Carrigan, John	...do...	28	Sept. 30, 1864	1 year.	Mustered out with company July 7, 1865.
Charles, James	...do...	26	Sept. 15, 1864	1 year.	Mustered out with company July 7, 1865.
Clinger, George A.	...do...	25	Sept. 7, 1864	1 year.	Mustered out with company July 7, 1865.
Cluxton, Greenbury J.	...do...	42	Sept. 19, 1864	1 year.	Mustered out with company July 7, 1865.
Cooper, Granville	...do...	26	Sept. 14, 1864	1 year.	Mustered out with company July 7, 1865.
Conner, Oliver E.	...do...	18	Sept. 15, 1864	1 year.	Mustered out May 19, 1865, at Nashville, Tenn., by order of War Department
Cross, Joseph C.	...do...	33	Sept. 28, 1864	1 year.	Mustered out with company July 7, 1865.
Davidson, George W.	...do...	38	Sept. 20, 1864	1 year.	Mustered out with company July 7, 1865.
Dooley, Moses	...do...	45	Sept. 17, 1864	1 year.	Mustered out May 18, 1865, at Nashville, Tenn., by order of War Department
Edgington, William	...do...	44	Sept. 20, 1864	1 year.	Appointed Sergeant from private Oct. 27, 1864; reduced to ranks Jan. 8, 1865; mustered out with company July 7, 1865.
Eldridge, Samuel	...do...	44	Sept. 20, 1864	1 year.	Mustered out with company July 7, 1865.
Evans, Anthony	...do...	41	Sept. 28, 1864	1 year.	Mustered out with company July 7, 1865.

Names.	Rank.	Age.	Date of Entering the Service.	Period of Service.	Remarks.
Evans, David	Private..	36	Sept. 21, 1864	1 year.	Discharged June 1, 1865, at Nashville, Tenn. on Surgeon's certificate of disability.
Evans, James	...do....	26	Sept. 23, 1864	1 year.	Mustered out with company July 7, 1865.
Fear, Francis	...do....	41	Sept. 15, 1864	1 year.	Mustered out with company July 7, 1865.
Franklin, John A	...do....	41	Sept. 7, 1864	1 year.	Mustered out Aug 12, 1865, at Cincinnati, O. by order of War Department.
Freeman, William S	...do....	23	Sept. 28, 1864	1 year.	Mustered out with company July 7, 1865.
Graham, Thomas	...do....	44	Sept. 19, 1864	1 year.	Mustered out with company July 7, 1865.
Hall, Franklin	...do....	18	Sept. 16, 1864	1 year.	Mustered out with company July 7, 1865.
Hall, George B	...do....	18	Sept. 20, 1864	1 year.	Mustered out with company July 7, 1865.
Hall, William	...do....	41	Sept. 16, 1864	1 year.	Mustered out with company July 7, 1865.
Hampton, James A	...do....	18	Sept. 17, 1864	1 year.	Mustered out with company July 7, 1865.
Herdman, Robert	...do....	26	Sept. 23, 1864	1 year.	Mustered out with company July 7, 1865.
Hicks, John G	...do....	35	Sept. 7, 1864	1 year.	
Hines, Henry	...do....	17	Sept. 15, 1864	1 year.	Mustered out with company July 7, 1865.
Hines, Jonathan A	...do....	18	Sept. 15, 1864	1 year.	Discharged June 7, 1865, at Nashville, Tenn. on Surgeon's certificate of disability.
Hines, Josephus	...do....	18	Sept 17, 1864	1 year.	Mustered out with company July 7, 1865.
Holt, Nathan	...do....	41	Sept. 23, 1864	1 year.	Died Feb. 12, 1865, at Nashville, Tenn.
Hoop, William	...do....	38	Sept. 3, 1864	1 year.	Mustered out with company July 7, 1865.
Howell, William E	...do....	34	Sept. 17, 1864	1 year.	Mustered out with company July 7, 1865.
Jacobs, Samuel	...do....	33	Sept. 14, 1864	1 year.	Mustered out with company July 7, 1865.
Jobe, Sylvester	...do....	23	Sept. 3, 1864	1 year.	Mustered out with company July 7, 1865.
Kerr, James	...do....	20	Sept. 21, 1864	1 year.	Mustered out May 17, 1865, at Nashville, Tenn., by order of War Department.
Kelly, Samuel	...do....	39	Sept. 21, 1864	1 year	Mustered out with company July 7, 1865.
Kelly, William G	...do....	16	Sept. 7, 1864	1 year.	Mustered out with company July 7, 1865.
Lang, James M	...do....	26	Sept. 21, 1864	1 year.	Died March 7, 1865, at Nashville, Tenn.
McManis Francis J	...do....	21	Sept. 20, 1864	1 year.	Mustered out with company July 7, 1865.
Martin, Benjamin F	...do....	22	Sept. 21, 1864	1 year.	Mustered out with company July 7, 1865.
Miller, Lewis	...do....	38	Oct. 28, 1864	1 year.	
Moore, Isaac F	...do....	27	Aug. 1, 1864	1 year.	Mustered out with company July 7, 1865.
Mytinger, Charles W	...do....	35	Sept. 14, 1864	1 year.	Transferred to 22d O. V. I. (unassigned) Oct. 8, 1864.
Naylor, Clayton	...do....	18	Sept. 20, 1864	1 year.	Mustered out with company July 7, 1865.
Neill, John	...do....	21	Sept. 13, 1864	1 year.	Mustered out with company July 7, 1865.
Nevill William	...do....	35	Sept. 15, 1864	1 year.	Mustered out with company July 7, 1865.
Newman, David B	...do....	38	Sept. 24, 1864	1 year.	Mustered out with company July 7, 1865
Newman, Henry A	...do....	21	Sept. 23, 1864	1 year.	Mustered out June 27, 1865, at Columbus, O., by order of War Department
Newman, James K. P	...do....	19	Sept. 20, 1864	1 year.	Mustered out with company July 7, 1865.
Newman, John R	...do....	41	Sept. 25, 1864	1 year.	Mustered out with company July 7, 1865
Newman, Richard	...do..	35	Sept. 20, 1864	1 year.	Mustered out June 6, 1865, at Camp Dennison, O., by order of War Department.
Newman, William G	...do....	28	Sept. 23, 1864	1 year.	Mustered out with company July 7, 1865.
Nichols, Daniel	...do....	27	Sept. 2?, 1864	1 year.	Mustered out with company July 7, 1865.
Olive Thomas J	...do....	22	Sept. 20 1864	1 year	Mustered out with company July 7, 1865
Palmer, James C	...do....	35	Sept. 17, 1864	1 year	Mustered out with company July 7, 1865
Parker, William	...do....	28	Sept. 21, 1864	1 year.	Mustered out with company July 7, 1865.
Parks, James	...do....	39	Sept. 3, 1864	1 year	Mustered out with company July 7, 1865.
Paul, Gilbert M	...do....	17	Sept. 3, 1864	1 year	Mustered out with company July 7, 1865
Phillips, Thomas	...do....	20	Sept. 19, 1864	1 year	Mustered out with company July 7, 1865.
Piatt, John	...do..	30	Sept. 23, 1864	1 year.	Mustered out with company July 7, 1865.
Powers, James	...do....	44	Sept. 3, 1864	1 year.	Mustered out July 12, 1865, at Camp Dennison, O., by order of War Department
Powers, William H	...do....	16	Sept. 3, 1864	1 year	Mustered out with company July 7, 1865
River, Adam	...do....	30	Sept. 2?, 1864	1 year.	Discharged June 1, 1865, at Nashville Tenn on Surgeon's certificate of disability.
Ruggles, William	...do.	43	Sept. 16, 1864	1 year.	Mustered out July 3, 1865, at Columbus O. by order of War Department.
Scott, Benjamin	...do....	23	Sept. 19, 1864	1 year	Mustered out with company July 7, 1865.
Scott, John A	...do....	27	Sept. 19, 1864	1 year	Mustered out with company July 7, 1865
Stewart, Alexander	...do....	39	Sept 19, 1864	1 year	Discharged May 15, 1865, at Nashville, Tenn. on Surgeon's certificate of disability.
Stewart, John M	...do....	41	Sept. 19, 1864	1 year	Mustered out with company July 7, 1865.
Thompson, George W	...do....	21	Sept. 7, 1864	1 year	Mustered out June 6, 1865, at Camp Dennison O., by order of War Department.
Thompson, William	...do....	22	Sept 17, 1864	1 year.	
Thoroman Uriel S	...do....	31	Sept 3, 1864	1 year	Mustered out with company July 7, 1865.
Thoroman, William T	...do....	20	Sept. 28, 1864	1 year	Mustered out with company July 7, 1865.
Wallace, Samuel	...do....	41	Sept. 23, 1864	1 year.	Mustered out with company July 7, 1865.
Warren, Christopher	...do....	29	Sept. 23 1864	1 year	Mustered out with company July 7, 1865
Warren George	...do....	26	Sept. 17, 1864	1 year	
Warren, James C	...do....	21	Sept. 23, 1864	1 year	Died Feb. 19, 1865, in hospital at Nashville Tennessee
Washburn, Thomas	...do....	25	Sept. 20, 1864	1 year	Mustered out with company July 7, 1865.
Williams, John C	...do....	29	Sept. 23, 1864	1 year.	Mustered out with company July 7, 1865.

Names.	Rank.	Age.	Date of Entering the Service.	Period of Service.	Remarks.
Wells, Richard	Private..	28	Oct. 18, 1864	1 year.	
Wheeler, John	....do....	27	Sept. 1, 1864	1 year.	Mustered out with company July 7, 1865.
Whitney, George	....do....	22	Oct. 5, 1864	1 year.	Mustered out July 7, 1865, at Nashville, Tenn., by order of War Department.
Williams, George H....	....do....	22	Aug. 20, 1864	1 year.	Mustered out July 7, 1865, at Nashville, Tenn., by order of War Department.
Wines, George	....do....	18	Oct. 3, 1864	1 year.	Died Jan. 1, 1865, at Nashville, Tenn.

UNASSIGNED RECRUITS.

NOTE.—The following list of recruits is found on muster and descriptive rolls for this organization, but not borne on any of the company rolls of the Regiment

Names.	Rank.	Age.	Date of Entering the Service.	Period of Service.	Remarks.
Blackburn, Wesley K...	Private..	25	Sept. 18, 1864	1 year.	
Boyle, John	....do....	19	Oct. 27, 1864	1 year.	
Bray, Samuel P.	....do....	19	Sept. 30, 1864	1 year.	
Brennon, John	....do....	19	April 7, 1865	1 year.	Mustered out May 15, 1865, at Hart Island, New York Harbor, by order of War Department.
Brooke, Peter	....do....	18	Oct. 23, 1864	1 year.	
Burns, Robert	....do....	19	Oct. 22, 1864	1 year.	
Callahan, James	....do....	22	Oct. 27, 1864	1 year.	
Carson, Robert E.	....do....	30	Oct. 14, 1864	1 year.	
Carter, George W	....do....	18	Sept. 29, 1864	1 year.	
Clutter, Thomas	....do....	22	Aug. 5, 1864	1 year.	
Coleman, Robert	....do....	23	Jan. 5, 1865	1 year.	
Collins, John	....do....	24	Oct. 15, 1864	1 year.	
Compton, John W.	....do....	19	Oct. 5, 1864	1 year.	
Compton, William	....do....	18	Oct. 5, 1864	1 year.	
Cook, Henry	....do....	22	Jan. 5, 1865	1 year.	
Davenport, Richard	....do....	22	Oct. 7, 1864	1 year.	
Davidson, Azariah	....do....	38	Sept. 3, 1864	1 year.	
Dodd, William	....do....	25	Oct. 26, 1864	1 year.	
Ellis, David	....do....	38	Sept. 26, 1864	1 year.	
Fickel, George S.	....do....	28	Sept. 27, 1864	1 year.	
Fox, William	....do....	23	Sept. 28, 1864	1 year.	
Fryman, John	....do....	20	Oct. 12, 1864	1 year.	
Gibbs, Andrew J.	....do....	24	Oct. 6, 1864	1 year.	
Gilbert, Charles	....do....	22	Sept. 28, 1864	1 year.	
Hanawalt, Henry L.	....do....	18	Oct. 17, 1864	1 year.	
Howell, John	....do....	25	Sept. 9, 1864	1 year.	
Ingalls, Francis M.	....do....	24	Sept. 27, 1864	1 year.	
Jackson, Thomas C.	....do....	28	Oct. 7, 1864	1 year.	
Johnson, Madison W.	....do....	24	Sept. 3, 1864	1 year.	
Kane, John	....do....	22	Jan. 5, 1865	1 year.	
Keatings, Thomas	....do....	22	April 12, 1865	1 year.	Mustered out May 15, 1865, at Hart Island, New York Harbor, by order of War Department.
Langue, Charles	....do....	20	Oct. 26, 1864	1 year.	
Lewis, Wm. J.	....do....	24	Sept. 26, 1864	1 year.	
Liggot, John	....do....	20	Oct. 27, 1864	1 year.	
McCarty, William	....do....	22	Sept. 29, 1864	1 year.	
McConley, Ezra	....do....	18	Sept. 30, 1864	1 year.	
McDonald, George	....do....	23	Aug. 21, 1864	1 year.	
McDonald, John	....do....	20	Oct. 22, 1864	1 year.	
Martin, Albert	....do....	23	Sept. 15, 1864	1 year.	
Matthias, Daniel W.	....do....	20	Oct. 5, 1864	1 year.	
Miller, Samuel	....do....	20	Oct. 26, 1864	1 year.	
Milliken, John W.	....do....	21	Sept. 30, 1864	1 year.	
Moor, John	....do....	24	Oct. 18, 1864	1 year.	
Patton, Wm. H.	....do....	26	Sept. 30, 1864	1 year.	
Porter, Henry	....do....	30	Aug. 6, 1864	1 year.	
Rinehart, Cyrus	....do....	19	April 7, 1865	1 year.	Mustered out May 15, 1865, at Hart Island, New York Harbor, by order of War Department.
Robbins, John	....do....	36	Sept. 5, 1864	1 year.	
Robinson, John S.	....do....	31	Oct. 18, 1864	1 year.	
Rogers, Charles	....do....	23	Oct. 8, 1864	1 year.	
Romine, Richard F.	....do....	23	Oct. 3, 1864	1 year.	
Rowland, John	....do....	35	Oct. 4, 1864	1 year.	
Sage, Nathaniel S.	....do....	29	Aug. 27, 1864	1 year.	
Sederstrom, Eugene	....do....	27	Aug. 13, 1864	1 year.	
Smith, John W.	....do....	30	Oct. 25, 1864	1 year.	
Stephens, James	....do....	18	Oct. 3, 1864	1 year.	
Swaney, James	....do....	24	Oct. 26, 1864	1 year.	
Whitacar, Newman	....do....	26	Sept. 30, 1864	1 year.	
Wilber, John	....do....	26	Oct. 18, 1864	1 year.	
Williams, Elias J.	....do....	23	Nov. 10, 1864	1 year.	
Wood, Wm. H.	....do....	23	Oct. 19, 1864	1 year.	
Wright, Charles A.	....do....	41	Sept. 12, 1864	1 year.	
Young, John	....do....	24	Aug. 16, 1864	1 year.	

Names.	Rank.	Age.	Date of Entering the Service.	Period of Service.	Remarks.
Howard, Cyrus	Private	26	Sept. 26, 1864	1 year.	Mustered out with company July 7, 1865.
Howland, Smith	...do...	38	Sept. 30, 1864	1 year.	Mustered out May 23, 1865, at Nashville, Tenn., by order of War Department.
Johnson, George W	...do...	35	Sept. 8, 1864	1 year.	Mustered out with company July 7, 1865.
Johnson, Thomas	...do...	20	Sept. 8, 1864	1 year.	Mustered out with company July 7, 1865.
Kimble, Henry J	...do...	39	Sept. 1, 1864	1 year.	Mustered out June 14, 1865, at Nashville, Tenn., by order of War Department.
Kimble, Jesse	...do...	30	Aug. 27, 1864	1 year.	Mustered out with company July 7, 1865.
Kimble, Uriah	...do...	21	Aug. 27, 1864	1 year.	Mustered out with company July 7, 1865.
Lawwill, Barton B	...do...	38	Sept. 17, 1864	1 year.	Mustered out with company July 7, 1865.
Little, Alexander	...do...	27	Aug. 25, 1864	1 year.	Mustered out with company July 7, 1865.
Little, Robert S	...do...	21	Aug. 27, 1864	1 year.	Died April 14, 1865, in hospital at Nashville, Tennessee.
Low, Elijah	...do...	18	Aug. 27, 1864	1 year.	Mustered out with company July 7, 1865.
Low, James W	...do...	37	Sept. 10, 1864	1 year.	Mustered out with company July 7, 1865.
Low, Thomas	...do...	39	Sept. 17, 1864	1 year.	Discharged April 8, 1865, at Nashville, Tenn., on Surgeon's certificate of disability.
McCally, Charles M	...do...	42	Sept. 5, 1864	1 year.	Mustered out with company July 7, 1865.
McClanahan, William	...do...	35	Sept. 8, 1864	1 year.	Mustered out June 6, 1865, at Camp Dennison, O., by order of War Department.
McDaniel, Isaiah	...do...	38	Aug. 29, 1864	1 year.	Mustered out with company July 7, 1865.
Matthews, Samuel	...do...	27	Aug. 25, 1864	1 year.	Mustered out May 23, 1865, at Nashville, Tenn., by order of War Department.
Miller, James	...do...	35	Sept. 8, 1864	1 year.	Mustered out with company July 7, 1865.
Mitchell, House	...do...	42	Aug. 24, 1864	1 year.	Mustered out with company July 7, 1865.
Mitchell, Joseph	...do...	38	Sept. 1, 1864	1 year.	Mustered out with company July 7, 1865.
Montford, Hugh	...do...	18	Aug. 27, 1864	1 year.	Mustered out with company July 7, 1865.
Morgan, Willis	...do...	42	Sept. 25, 1864	1 year.	Mustered out with company July 7, 1865.
Oberschleake, Lewis	...do...	29	Aug. 26, 1864	1 year.	Mustered out with company July 7, 1865.
Palmer, Harrison	...do...	29	Sept. 5, 1864	1 year.	Mustered out June 23, 1865, at Louisville, Ky., by order of War Department.
Palmer, Newton J	...do...	17	Sept. 19, 1864	1 year.	Mustered out May 23, 1865, at Nashville, Tenn., by order of War Department.
Payne, William H	...do...	40	Sept. 7, 1864	1 year.	Mustered out with company July 7, 1865.
Pence, Edward	...do...	23	Aug. 26, 1864	1 year.	Mustered out June 3, 1865, at Nashville, Tenn., by order of War Department.
Pence, Philip	...do...	20	Sept. 23, 1864	1 year.	Mustered out with company July 7, 1865.
Phillips, Samuel H	...do...	38	Sept. 9, 1864	1 year.	Mustered out with company July 7, 1865.
Pownall, Aaron P	...do...	21	Sept. 1, 1864	1 year.	Mustered out June 21, 1865, at Nashville, Tenn., by order of War Department.
Purdy, Robert W	...do...	30	Aug. 21, 1864	1 year.	Mustered out with company July 7, 1865.
Rice, John R	...do...	24	Sept. 15, 1864	1 year.	
Rinehart, George	...do...	28	Sept. 23, 1864	1 year.	Mustered out with company July 7, 1865.
Rogers, John W	...do...	33	Sept. 26, 1864	1 year.	Mustered out with company July 7, 1865.
Scott, Joseph W	...do...	29	Sept. 14, 1864	1 year.	Mustered out May 23, 1865, at Nashville, Tenn., by order of War Department.
Shelton, Anthony W	...do...	23	Aug. 27, 1864	1 year.	Mustered out with company July 7, 1865.
Shelton, Noah	...do...	27	Sept. 14, 1864	1 year.	Mustered out June 3, 1865, at Nashville, Tenn., by order of War Department.
Smith, Samuel W	...do...	41	Aug. 25, 1864	1 year.	Mustered out with company July 7, 1865.
Starrett, George	...do...	20	Aug. 27, 1864	1 year.	Mustered out with company July 7, 1865.
Taylor, Samuel W	...do...	18	Sept. 30, 1864	1 year.	
Thoroman, William Z	...do...	37	Sept. 8, 1864	1 year.	Mustered out June 3, 1865, at Nashville, Tenn., by order of War Department.
Tomlin, Jeremiah	...do...	21	Sept. 9, 1864	1 year.	Died Nov. 9, 1864, at his home, Adams County, Ohio.
Tomlin, William T	...do...	25	Sept. 10, 1864	1 year.	Mustered out with company July 7, 1865.
Vice, Aaron	...do...	23	Aug. 29, 1864	1 year.	Mustered out with company July 7, 1865.
Walden, Samuel C	...do...	28	Aug. 31, 1864	1 year.	Mustered out with company July 7, 1865.
Walker, Peyton	...do...	32	Sept. 23, 1864	1 year.	Mustered out with company July 7, 1865.
Warden, Albert	...do...	21	Sept. 8, 1864	1 year.	Mustered out with company July 7, 1865.
West, George	...do...	18	Sept. 30, 1864	1 year.	Mustered out with company July 7, 1865.
Wilson, James	...do...	29	Sept. 15, 1864	1 year.	Mustered out with company July 7, 1865.

COMPANY I.

ered in October 13, 1864, at Camp Chase, O., by W. P. Richardson, Colonel 25th O. V. I. Mustered out June 7, 1865, at Nashville, Tenn., by J. W. Chickering, Captain 88th Illinois Infantry, and A. C. M., 2d Division, 4th Army Corps.

	Rank.	Age.	Date of Entering the Service.	eriod Service.	Remarks.
am H. Shriver	Captain.	26	Sept. 3, 1864	1 year.	Appointed Oct. 13, 1864; mustered out with company July 7, 1865.
D. Leedom	1st Lieut.	22	Sept. 20, 1864	1 year.	Appointed Oct. 13, 1864; Adjutant Nov. 29, 1864.
t F. Lopez	...do...	35	Aug. 9, 1864	1 year.	Promoted from 2d Lieutenant Co. A Feb. 8, 1865; mustered out with company July 7, 1865.
K. Pollard	2d Lieut.	21	Aug. 24, 1864	1 year.	Appointed Oct. 13, 1864; mustered out with company July 7, 1865.
J. Thomas	1st Sergt.	22	Sept. 23, 1864	1 year.	Appointed Oct. 27, 1864; mustered out with company July 7, 1865.
McKinney	Sergeant.	33	Sept. 28, 1864	1 year.	Appointed Oct. 27, 1864; mustered out with company July 7, 1865.
y D. Shepherd	...do...	35	Aug. 26, 1864	1 year.	Appointed Oct. 27, 1864; mustered out with company July 7, 1865.
rd Shelton	...do...	34	Sept. 24, 1864	1 year.	Appointed Oct. 27, 1864; mustered out with company July 7, 1865.
T. Wilson	...do...	38	Sept. 15, 1864	1 year.	Appointed Oct. 27, 1864; mustered out with company July 7, 1865.
W. Hayslip	Corporal.	28	Aug. 24, 1864	1 year.	Appointed Oct. 27, 1864; mustered out with company July 7, 1865.
W. Games	...do...	22	Sept. 3, 1864	1 year.	Appointed Oct. 27, 1864; mustered out with company July 7, 1865.
rwell	...do...	31	Sept. 15, 1864	1 year.	Appointed Oct. 27, 1864; mustered out with company July 7, 1865.
s M. Connor	...do...	22	Aug. 29, 1864	1 year.	Appointed Oct. 27, 1864; mustered out with company July 7, 1865.
O. Phillips	...do...	30	Sept. 28, 1864	1 year.	Appointed Oct. 27, 1864; mustered out with company July 7, 1865.
as Haynes	...do...	44	Sept. 28, 1864	1 year.	Appointed Oct. 27, 1864; mustered out with company July 7, 1865.
s Lindsey	...do...	43	Sept. 15, 1864	1 year.	Transferred to 48th Co., 2d Battalion, Veteran Reserve Corps, ——; mustered out June 26, 1865, at Washington, D. C., by order of War Department.
ew S. Lang	...do...	19	Aug. 24, 1864	1 year.	Appointed Oct. 27, 1864; mustered out with company July 7, 1865.
Willman	Musician	25	Sept. 28, 1864	1 year.	Mustered out with company July 7, 1865.
M. Harding	...do...	18	Sept. 30, 1864	1 year.	Mustered out with company July 7, 1865.
t, Amos	Private.	36	Oct. 8, 1864	1 year.	Mustered out July 7, 1865, at Nashville, Tenn., by order of War Department.
ckman, William	...do...	30	Sept. 28, 1864	1 year.	Mustered out with company July 7, 1865.
, Empire M	...do...	32	Sept. 20, 1864	1 year.	Mustered out with company July 7, 1865.
ey, John G	...do...	28	Sept. 20, 1864	1 year.	Mustered out with company July 7, 1865.
n, Lewis	...do...	19	Sept. 28, 1864	1 year.	Mustered out with company July 7, 1865.
nfield, Joseph	...do...	18	Sept. 30, 1864	1 year.	Mustered out with company July 7, 1865.
ules, Robert	...do...	30	Sept. 28, 1864	1 year.	Mustered out with company July 7, 1865.
y, Nelson H	...do...	18	Oct. 8, 1864	1 year.	Mustered out July 7, 1865, at Nashville, Tenn., by order of War Department.
ett, Enos	...do...	19	Sept. 28, 1864	1 year.	Mustered out with company July 7, 1865.
ton, Joseph S	...do...	21	Sept. 30, 1864	1 year.	Mustered out with company July 7, 1865.
ton, Stephen	...do...	18	Oct. 8, 1864	1 year.	Mustered out July 7, 1865, at Nashville, Tenn., by order of War Department.
y, James F	...do...	18	Sept. 28, 1864	1 year.	Mustered out with company July 7, 1865.
ling, Adam M	...do...	25	Sept. 30, 1864	1 year.	Mustered out with company July 7, 1865.
gton, Richard	...do...	21	Sept. 28, 1864	1 year.	Mustered out with company July 7, 1865.
gton, Robbin	...do...	31	Sept. 23, 1864	1 year.	Mustered out with company July 7, 1865.
gton, [illegible]	...do...	20	Sept. 23, 1864	1 year.	Mustered out with company July 7, 1865.
, John R	...do...	30	Sept. 26, 1864	1 year.	Mustered out with company July 7, 1865.
, Thomas J	...do...	31	Sept. 28, 1864	1 year.	Mustered out with company July 7, 1865.
the, William	...do...	22	Sept. 28, 1864	1 year.	Mustered out with company July 7, 1865.
George L	...do...	44	Sept. 28, 1864	1 year.	Mustered out with company July 7, 1865.
ns, Aaron	...do...	20	Sept. 30, 1864	1 year.	Mustered out with company July 7, 1865.
ns, Monroe	...do...	18	Sept. 30, 1864	1 year.	Mustered out with company July 7, 1865.
on, William	...do...	18	Sept. 9, 1864	1 year.	Mustered out with company July 7, 1865.
lge, John	...do...	44	Sept. 30, 1864	1 year.	Mustered out with company July 7, 1865.
rd, William	...do...	18	Sept. 28, 1864	1 year.	Mustered out with company July 7, 1865.
s, Ebenezer	...do...	21	Sept. 28, 1864	1 year.	Mustered out with company July 7, 1865.
man, John	...do...	20	Sept. 28, 1864	1 year.	
rt, Samuel J	...do...	[illegible]	Sept. 28, 1864	1 year.	Mustered out with company July 7, 1865.
old, William	...do...	21	Sept. 20, 1864	1 year.	Mustered out with company July 7, 1865.
Daniel C	...do...	22	Sept. 21, 1864	1 year.	Mustered out with company July 7, 1865.
James	...do...	[illegible]	Sept. 21, 1864	1 year.	Discharged June 30, 1865, on Surgeon's certificate of disability.
an, Alfred	...do...	[illegible]	Oct. 8, 1864	1 year.	Mustered out July 7, 1865, at Nashville, Tenn., by order of War Department.

Names.	Rank.	Age.	Date of Entering the Service.	Period of Service.	Remarks.
Hughs, David S.	Private.	41	Sept. 28, 1864	1 year.	Discharged June 30, 1865, on Surgeon's certificate of disability.
Hunt, Amour	...do...	22	Oct. 8, 1864	1 year	Mustered out June 6, 1865, at Camp Dennison, O., by order of War Department.
Irwin, James	...do...	40	Sept. 28, 1864	1 year.	Mustered out with company July 7, 1865.
Jackman, Samuel	...do...	29	Sept. 28, 1864	1 year.	Mustered out with company July 7, 1865.
Johnson, Benjamin F.	...do...	25	Sept. 30, 1864	1 year.	Mustered out with company July 7, 1865.
Klein, Herman	...do...	18	Mch. 14, 1865	1 year.	Mustered out July 7, 1865, at Nashville, Tenn., by order of War Department.
Lewis, James	...do...	31	Sept. 28, 1864	1 year.	Mustered out with company July 7, 1865.
Love, Charles	...do...	18	Sept. 10, 1864	1 year.	Mustered out with company July 7, 1865.
Love, John	...do...	41	Sept. 10, 1864	1 year.	Mustered out with company July 7, 1865.
McCune, Edward R.	...do...	34	Sept. 30, 1864	1 year.	Discharged June 30, 1865, on Surgeon's certificate of disability.
McCune, James W.	...do...	21	Aug. 24, 1864	1 year.	Mustered out June 19, 1865, in hospital at Nashville, Tenn., by order of War Department.
McDaniel, James S.	...do...	37	Sept. 15, 1864	1 year.	Mustered out with company July 7, 1865.
McNeil, John S.	...do...	23	Sept. 30, 1864	1 year.	Mustered out with company July 7, 1865.
Magoon, George	...do...	22	Sept. 28, 1864	1 year.	Mustered out with company July 7, 1865.
Mosier, Samuel	...do...	38	Aug. 25, 1864	1 year.	Mustered out with company July 7, 1865.
Naylor, John	...do...	35	Sept. 20, 1864	1 year.	Mustered out with company July 7, 1865.
Nichols, James A.	...do...	20	Sept. 30, 1864	1 year.	Mustered out with company July 7, 1865.
Peggs, Samuel S.	...do...	21	Sept. 1, 1864	1 year.	Died Nov. 11, 1864, in hospital at Nashville, Tennessee.
Robuck, William	...do...	18	Aug. 24, 1864	1 year.	Mustered out with company July 7, 1865.
Shell, Benjamin	...do...	23	Sept. 28, 1864	1 year.	Mustered out with company July 7, 1865.
Stone, Edward	...do...	23	Oct. 3, 1864	1 year.	Mustered out July 7, 1865, at Nashville, Tenn., by order of War Department.
Stone, Samuel	...do...	32	Oct. 3, 1864	1 year.	Discharged July 1, 1865, on Surgeon's certificate of disability.
Tolle, Milton R.	...do...	21	Oct. 3, 1864	1 year.	Mustered out July 7, 1865, at Nashville, Tenn., by order of War Department.
Thomas, George A.	...do...	31	Sept. 28, 1864	1 year.	Mustered out with company July 7, 1865.
Thomas, George W.	...do...	43	Sept. 28, 1864	1 year.	Mustered out with company July 7, 1865.
Thomas, James	...do...	23	Sept. 28, 1864	1 year.	Mustered out with company July 7, 1865.
Thomas, John H. W.	...do...	18	Sept. 1, 1864	1 year.	Mustered out with company July 7, 1865.
Thomas, Samuel	...do...	20	Oct. 3, 1864	1 year.	Mustered out July 7, 1865, at Nashville, Tenn., by order of War Department.
Thompson, Legrand	...do...	18	Sept. 23, 1864	1 year.	Mustered out with company July 7, 1865.
Tucker, Hugh M.	...do...	40	Sept. 21, 1864	1 year.	Mustered out with company July 7, 1865.
Turner, Peter B.	...do...	38	Sept. 28, 1864	1 year.	Mustered out with company July 7, 1865.
Waldron, Henry	...do...	43	Sept. 28, 1864	1 year.	Mustered out with company July 7, 1865.
Walters, John W.	...do...	37	Sept. 20, 1864	1 year	
Wilmoth, John M.	...do...	[illegible]	Oct. 3, 1864	1 year.	Mustered out July 7, 1865, at Nashville, Tenn., by order of War Department.
Willman, Jesse	...do...	[illegible]	Sept. 28, 1864	1 year	Mustered out with company July 7, 1865.
Willman, William	...do...	31	Sept. 28, 1864	1 year.	Mustered out with company July 7, 1865.

COMPANY K.

Mustered in October -- 1864, at Toledo, O., by Colonel Jesse S. Norton. Mustered out July 7, 1865, at Nashville, Tenn., by J. W. Chickering, Captain 88th Illinois Infantry, and A. C. M., 2d Division, 4th Army Corps.

Names.	Rank.	Age.	Date of Entering the Service.	Period of Service.	Remarks.
Charles A. Wright	Captain.	[illegible]	Sept. 12, 1864	1 year	Appointed Oct. 25, 1864; resigned April 2[illegible] 1865.
John S. Lavet	...do...	30	Aug. 17, 1864	1 year.	Promoted from 1st Lieutenant Co. B May [illegible] 1865; mustered out with company July 7 1865.
William H. Wood	1st Lieut.	23	Oct. 19, 1864	1 year.	Appointed Oct. 25, 1864; resigned June [illegible] 1865.
William H. McGrew	2d Lieut.	24	Aug. 27, 1864	1 year	Appointed Oct. 25, 1864; resigned March 12, 1865.
Alfred L. Sargeant	...do...	20	Aug. 12, 1864	1 year.	Promoted from 1st Sergeant Co. B May 2, 1865; mustered out with company July 7, 1865.
Francis M. Blakeman	1st Sergt.	28	Sept. 3, 1864	1 year.	Appointed Oct. 27, 1864; mustered out with company July 7, 1865.
Robert W. L. Ely	Sergeant.	20	Sept. 3, 1864	1 year.	Appointed Oct. 27, 1864; mustered out with company July 7, 1865.
Samuel L. Richards	...do...	21	Oct. 15, 1864	1 year.	Appointed Oct. 27, 1864; mustered out July 7, 1865, at Nashville, Tenn., by order of War Department.
Thomas A. Williamson	...do...	25	Sept. 2, 1864	1 year.	Appointed Oct. 27, 1864; promoted to Q. M. Sergeant March 16, 1865.
Simeon E. Richards	...do...	19	Oct. 6, 1864	1 year.	Appointed Corporal Oct. 27, 1864; Sergeant ——; mustered out July 7, 1865, at Nashville, Tenn., by order of War Department.
Daniel C. Whistler	...do...	44	Oct. 6, 1864	1 year.	Appointed Corporal Oct. 27, 1864; Sergeant March 16, 1865; mustered out July 7, 1865, at Nashville, Tenn., by order of War Department.

Names.	Rank.	Age.	Date of Entering the Service.	Period of Service.	Remarks.
Franklin S.	Private.	18	Oct. 10, 1864	1 year.	Mustered out with company July 17, 1865.
, James	do.	18	Oct. 10, 1864	1 year.	Missing Nov. 30, 1864, at battle of Franklin, Tenn. No further record found.
, James	do.	26	Sept. 20, 1864	1 year.	
William	do.	22	Sept. 21, 1864	1 year.	Mustered out with company July 17, 1865.
Jonathan	do.	21	Oct. 1, 1864	1 year.	Died Jan. 28, 1865, at Louisville, Ky.
r, Eli	do.	20	Sept. 22, 1864	1 year.	Mustered out June 6, 1865, at David's Island, New York Harbor, by order of War Department.
r, Andrew J.	do.	37	Aug. 30, 1864	1 year.	Mustered out with company July 17, 1865.
Peter	do.	19	Dec. 5, 1863	3 yrs.	Transferred from Co. D, 100th O. V. I., June 15, 1865; mustered out with company July 17, 1865.
James C.	do.	44	Oct. 6, 1864	1 year.	Died Jan. 22, 1865, at Camp Dennison, O.
son, Albert L.	do.	35	Sept. 29, 1864	1 year.	Mustered out June 2, 1865, at Covington, Ky., by order of War Department.
, James	do.	25	Sept. 20, 1864	1 year.	
Charles R.	do.	39	Sept. 19, 1864	1 year.	Was last seen and supposed to have been killed Nov. 30, 1864, in battle of Franklin, Tennessee.
David	do.	27	Sept. 2, 1864	1 year.	Wounded Dec. 15, 1864, in battle of Nashville, Tenn.; in hospital at Nashville, Tenn., since Dec. 15, 1864. No further record found.
r, George	do.	19	Jan. 5, 1864	3 yrs.	Transferred from Co. K, 100th O. V. I., June 15, 1865; mustered out with company July 17, 1865
Jacob	do.	30	Sept. 19, 1864	1 year.	Mustered out with company July 17, 1865.
le, Newton	do.	18	Dec. 12, 1863	3 yrs.	Transferred from Co. H, 100th O. V. I., June 15, 1865; mustered out with company July 17, 1865.
d, Francis J.	do.	26	Sept. 17, 1864	1 year.	Killed Nov. 30, 1864, in battle of Franklin, Tennessee.
d, James	do.	39	Sept. 19, 1864	1 year.	Mustered out May 25, 1865, at Albany, N. Y., by order of War Department.
d, Philip	do.	41	Sept. 17, 1864	1 year.	Killed Nov. 30, 1864, in battle of Franklin, Tennessee.
d, William H.	do.	27	Sept. 22, 1864	1 year.	Mustered out May 20, 1865, at McDougall General Hospital, New York Harbor, by order of War Department.
, William	do.	26	Dec. 17, 1863	3 yrs.	Transferred from Co. H, 100th O. V. I., June 15, 1865; mustered out with company July 17, 1865.
, James H.	do.	22	Nov. 20, 1863	3 yrs.	Transferred from Co. H, 100th O. V. I., June 15, 1865; mustered out with company July 17, 1865.
ld, Martin V.	do.	18	Nov. 26, 1863	3 yrs.	Transferred from Co. H, 100th O. V. I., June 15, 1865; mustered out with company July 17, 1865.
hill, John A.	do.	37	Sept. 27, 1864	1 year.	Mustered out with company July 17, 1865.
hill, Matthew A.	do.	38	Aug. 20, 1864	1 year.	Mustered out to date July 17, 1865, by order of War Department.
James	do.	36	Sept. 21, 1864	1 year.	Captured Nov. 30, 1864, at battle of Franklin, Tenn.; mustered out June 15, 1865, at Camp Chase, O., by order of War Department.
er, Peter	do.	22	Feb. 14, 1865	1 year.	Transferred from Co. G, 100th O. V. I., June 15, 1865; mustered out with company July 17, 1865.
Benjamin M.	do.	22	Sept. 6, 1864	1 year.	Mustered out with company July 17, 1865.
, Willis	do.	25	Sept. 20, 1864	1 year.	
Isaac	do.	26	Sept. 17, 1864	1 year.	Died Jan. 29, 1865, at Camp Dennison, O.
, Charles	do.	21	Jan. 4, 1864	3 yrs.	Transferred from Co. G, 100th O. V. I., June 15, 1865; mustered out with company July 17, 1865.
Thomas	do.	21	Sept. 30, 1864	1 year.	Died Feb. 25, 1865, at Washington, D. C.
, William N.	do.	18	June 20, 1863	3 yrs.	Transferred from Co. I, 100th O. V. I., June 15, 1865; mustered out with company July 17, 1865.
Samuel M.	do.	21	Aug. 30, 1864	1 year.	Died Jan. —, 1865, at Columbia, Tenn.
George W.	do.	32	Sept. 30, 1864	1 year.	Mustered out July 8, 1865, at Columbus, O., by order of War Department.
ly, Albert	do.	18	Jan. 4, 1864	3 yrs.	Transferred from Co. G, 100th O. V. I., June 15, 1865; mustered out with company July 17, 1865.
William	do.	18	Jan. 4, 1864	3 yrs.	Transferred from Co. G, 100th O. V. I., June 15, 1865; mustered out with company July 17, 1865.
e, John	do.	23	Dec. 21, 1863	3 yrs.	Transferred from Co. A, 100th O. V. I., June 15, 1865; mustered out with company July 17, 1865.
, Mark	do.	18	Sept. 20, 1864	1 year.	Mustered out with company July 17, 1865.
George W.	do.	22	Sept. 3, 1864	1 year.	Died Jan. 29, 1865, at Camp Dennison, O.
William H.	do.	27	Sept. 17, 1864	1 year.	Wounded Nov. 30, 1864, in battle of Franklin, Tenn.; mustered out July 6, 1865, at Louisville, Ky., by order of War Department.
Joseph S.	do.	26	Sept. 20, 1864	1 year.	Died Jan. 14, 1865, at Nashville, Tenn.

Names.	Rank.		Date.	Perio Servi
Heinsohn, William A...	Private..		Oct. 13, 1864	
Henderson, Charles.....	....do....		Oct. 14, 1864	
Heston, John R.........	....do....		Oct. 15, 1864	
Hipkins, Thomas C......	....do....	18	Oct. 4, 1864	
Holten, William L......	....do....	22	Oct. 18, 1864	
Humphrey, David	....do....	18	Oct. 8, 1864	1 year.
Hurlburt, Orrin S.......	....do....	21	Oct. 22, 1864	1 year.
Huston, Alfred..........	....do....	39	Oct. 13, 1864	
Jacobs, Frederick	....do....	28	Oct. 10, 1864	
Jones, William H........	....do....	19	Sept. 21, 1864	
Kent, Daniel M..........	....do....	18	Oct. 12, 1864	
Kimpton, Thomas	....do....	20	Oct. 11, 1864	1
Kinney, John R..........	....do....	26	Oct. 14, 1864	1
Law, George.............	....do....	19	Oct. 15, 1864	1
Leichty, Jacob	....do....	22	Oct. 8, 1864	1
Lentsy, William L.......	....do....	18	Oct. 7, 1864	
Lewis, William...........	....do....	28	Oct. 12, 1864	
Limengrover, Matthias..	....do....	44	Sept. 30, 1864	
McClure, Moses F.......	....do....	18	Oct. 8, 1864	
McCoy, Lucius	....do....	18	Oct. 18, 1864	
McGowen, Wickliffe C...	....do....	18	Oct. 18, 1864	
McGurk, William	....do....	21	Sept. 30, 1864	
Mahan, John K..........	....do....	18	Oct. 4, 1864	
Marriott, Isaiah R......	....do....	38	Oct. 8, 1864	
Martin, Jason B.........	....do....	28	Oct. 11, 1864	
Mason, Charles H.......	....do....	22	Oct. 11, 1864	
Miller, Lawrence........	....do....	22	Oct. 17, 1864	
Murphy, Martin L.......	....do....	20	Oct. 24, 1864	
Nutter, John.............	....do....	18	Sept. 21, 1864	1 year.
Osborne, Peter	....do....	18	Sept. 12, 1864	1 year.
Palmer, James U........	....do....	43	Oct. 13, 1864	1 year.
Parish, Orrin.............	....do....	41	Sept. 1, 1864	1 year.
Pike, Lewis J............	....do....	16	Oct. 1, 1864	1 year.
Pleman, Julius..........	....do....	19	Oct. 7, 1864	1 year.
Porter, John L...........	....do....	26	Oct. 10, 1864	1 year.
Pugh, Joseph C..........	....do....	22	Sept. 16, 1864	1 year.
Quinn, Peter	....do....	19	Oct. 13, 1864	1 year.
Ridenour, Thomas......	....do....	19	Aug. 31, 1864	1 year.
Riker, Perry.............	....do....	18	Sept. 30, 1864	1 year.
Robinson, Coe G.........	....do....	18	Sept. 19, 1864	1 year.
Rowles, William T......	....do....	19	Sept. 2, 1864	1 year.
Ryan, Simon...........	....do....	19	Oct. 13, 1864	1 year.
Sampson, John C........	....do....	30	Sept. 3, 1864	1 year.
Saunders, John	....do....	37	Sept. 21, 1864	1 year.
Simpson, Charles........	....do....	18	Oct. 6, 1864	1 year.
Skidmore, James B......	....do....	38	Oct. 21, 1864	1 year.
Slater, Wilson...........	....do....	18	Oct. 14, 1864	1 year.
Smead, Adelbert	....do....	19	Oct. 4, 1864	1 year.
Smith, George H........	....do....	27	Oct. 10, 1864	1 year.
Snyder, Samuel	....do....	17	Oct. 10, 1864	1 year.
Sole, Lawrence K.......	....do....	21	Oct. 21, 1864	1 year.
Tools, John	....do....	26	Oct. 18, 1864	1 year.
Vetter, Jacob............	....do....	44	Oct. 21, 1864	1 year.
Warren, Solomon S......	....do....	18	Oct. 3, 1864	1 year.
Weldy, David W.........	....do....	27	Oct. 22, 1864	1 year.

Names.	Rank.	Age.	Date of Entering the Service.	Period of Service.	Remarks.
Wells, Richard	Private..	28	Oct. 18, 1864	1 year.	
Wheeler, John	....do....	27	Sept. 1, 1864	1 year.	Mustered out with company July 7, 1865.
Whitney, George	....do....	22	Oct. 5, 1864	1 year.	Mustered out July 7, 1865, at Nashville, Tenn., by order of War Department.
Williams, George H	....do....	22	Aug. 20, 1864	1 year.	Mustered out July 7, 1865, at Nashville, Tenn., by order of War Department.
Wines, George	....do....	18	Oct. 3, 1864	1 year.	Died Jan. 1, 1865, at Nashville, Tenn.

UNASSIGNED RECRUITS.

NOTE.—The following list of recruits is found on muster and descriptive rolls for this organization, but not borne on any of the company rolls of the Regiment:

Names.	Rank.	Age.	Date of Entering the Service.	Period of Service.	Remarks.
Blackburn, Wesley K	Private..	25	Sept. 13, 1864	1 year.	
Boyle, John	....do....	19	Oct. 27, 1864	1 year.	
Bray, Samuel P	....do....	19	Sept. 30, 1864	1 year.	
Brennon, John	....do....	19	April 7, 1865	1 year.	Mustered out May 15, 1865, at Hart Island, New York Harbor, by order of War Department.
Brooke, Peter	....do....	18	Oct. 23, 1864	1 year.	
Burns, Robert	....do....	19	Oct. 22, 1864	1 year.	
Callahan, James	....do....	22	Oct. 27, 1864	1 year.	
Carson, Robert E	....do....	30	Oct. 14, 1864	1 year.	
Carter, George W	....do....	18	Sept. 29, 1864	1 year.	
Clutter, Thomas	....do....	22	Aug. 5, 1864	1 year.	
Coleman, Robert	....do....	23	Jan. 5, 1865	1 year.	
Collins, John	....do....	24	Oct. 15, 1864	1 year.	
Compton, John W	....do....	19	Oct. 5, 1864	1 year.	
Compton, William	....do....	18	Oct. 5, 1864	1 year.	
Cook, Henry	....do....	22	Jan. 5, 1865	1 year.	
Davenport, Richard	....do....	22	Oct. 7, 1864	1 year.	
Davidson, Azariah	....do....	38	Sept. 3, 1864	1 year.	
Dodd William	....do....	25	Oct. 26, 1864	1 year.	
Ellis, David	....do....	38	Sept. 26, 1864	1 year.	
Ficke George S	....do....	28	Sept. 27, 1864	1 year.	
Fox William	....do....	23	Sept. 28, 1864	1 year.	
Fryman, John	....do....	20	Oct. 12, 1864	1 year.	
Gibbs, Andrew	....do....	21	Oct. 6, 1864	1 year.	
Gilbert Charles	....do....	22	Sept. 28, 1864	1 year.	
Hanawalt, Henry L	....do....	18	Oct. 17, 1864	1 year.	
Howell, John	....do....	25	Sept. 9, 1864	1 year.	
Ingalls, Francis M	....do....	21	Sept. 27, 1864	1 year.	
Jackson, Thomas C	....do....	28	Oct. 7, 1864	1 year.	
Johnson Madison W	....do....	21	Sept. 3, 1864	1 year.	
Kane, John	....do....	22	Jan. 5, 1865	1 year.	
Keatings, Thomas	....do....	22	April 12, 1865	1 year.	Mustered out May 15, 1865, at Hart Island, New York Harbor, by order of War Department.
Langue, Charles	....do....	20	Oct. 25, 1864	1 year.	
Lewis, Wm. J	....do....	24	Sept. 26, 1864	1 year.	
Liggot, John	....do....	20	Oct. 27, 1864	1 year.	
McCarty, William	....do....	22	Sept. 2[illegible], 1864	1 year.	
McConley, Ezra	....do....	18	Sept. 30, 1864	1 year.	
McDonald, George	....do....	2[illegible]	Aug. 24, 1864	1 year.	
McDonald, John	....do....	20	Oct. 2[illegible], 1864	1 year.	
Martin, Albert	....do....	2[illegible]	Sept. [illegible], 1864	1 year.	
Matthias, Israel W	....do....	20	Oct. [illegible], 1864	1 year.	
Miller, Samuel	....do....	20	Oct. [illegible], 1864	1 year.	
Milliken, John W	....do....	21	Sept. [illegible], 1864	1 year.	
Moor, John	....do....	24	Oct. [illegible], 1864	1 year.	
Patton, Wm. H	....do....	[illegible]	Sept. [illegible], 1864	1 year.	
Porter, Henry	....do....	[illegible]	Aug. [illegible], 1864	1 year.	
Rinehart, Cyrus	....do....	[illegible]	April 7, 1865	1 year.	Mustered out May 15, 1865, at Hart Island, New York Harbor, by order of War Department.
Robbins, John	....do....	[illegible]	Sept. [illegible], 1864	1 year.	
Robinson John S	....do....	[illegible]	Oct. [illegible], 1864	1 year.	
Rogers, Charles	....do....	2[illegible]	Oct. [illegible], 1864	1 year.	
Romine, Richard F	....do....	[illegible]	Oct. [illegible], 1864	1 year.	
Rowland John	....do....	[illegible]	Oct. 4, 1864	1 year.	
Sage, Nathaniel S	....do....	[illegible]	Aug. [illegible], 1864	1 year.	
Sederstrom, Eugene	....do....	[illegible]	Aug. 1[illegible], 1864	1 year.	
Smith, John W	....do....	[illegible]	[illegible] [illegible], 1864	1 year.	
Stephens, James	....do....	[illegible]	Oct. [illegible], 1864	1 year.	
Sweeney, James	....do....	24	Oct. [illegible], 1864	1 year.	
Whitacar, Newman	....do....	[illegible]	Sept. [illegible], 1864	1 year.	
Wilber, John	....do....	[illegible]	Oct. [illegible], 1864	1 year.	
Williams, Elias J	....do....	22	Nov. [illegible], 1864	1 year.	
Wood, Wm. H	....do....	22	Oct. [illegible], 1864	1 year.	
Wright, Charles A	....do....	[illegible]	Sept. [illegible], 1864	1 year.	
Young, John	....do....	24	Aug. [illegible], 1864	1 year.	

183rd Regiment Ohio Volunteer Infantry.

ONE YEAR'S SERVICE.

THIS Regiment was organized at Cincinnati and Sandusky, O., in September and October, 1864, to serve one year. On the 19th of November the Regiment left Camp Dennison, and arrived at Columbia, Tenn., on the 28th. It was assigned to the Third Brigade, Second Division, Twenty-third Army Corps with which it remained during its entire term of service. The Regiment was engaged with the enemy at Spring Hill, Tenn., on the 29th of November, and at Franklin on the 30th. It was also engaged at Nashville on the 15th and 16th of December.

The Regiment afterward moved with the Corps to Clifton, on the Tennessee River, and thence via Cincinnati, Washington City, and Fort Fisher to Wilmington, N. C. Proceeding via Kinston it joined General Sherman's Army at Goldsboro. After the surrender of Johnston's Army the Regiment moved to Salisbury, and was mustered out July 17, 1865, in accordance with orders from the War Department.

183RD REGIMENT OHIO VOLUNTEER INFANTRY.

FIELD AND STAFF.

Mustered in November 18, 1864, at Camp Dennison, O., by ——— , ———. Mustered out July 17, 1865, at Salisbury, N. C., by Frederick Anderson, — Lieutenant and A. C. M., Department of North Carolina.

Names.	Rank.	Age.	Date of Entering the Service.	Period of Service.	Remarks.
George W. Hoge.........	Colonel.	32	Aug. 7, 1862	3 yrs.	Promoted from Captain Co. B, 126th O. V. I., Nov. 16, 1864: Brevet Brig. General March 13, 1865; mustered out with regiment July 17, 1865
Mervin Clark............	Lt. Col.	21	Nov. 12, 1864	1 year.	Killed Nov. 30, 1864, in battle of Franklin, Tennessee.
August G. Hatry	....do....	..	Nov. 10, 1864	1 year.	Promoted from Major Dec. 21, 1864; discharged April 1, 1865.
John Lang..............	....do....	24	Sept. 29, 1864	1 year.	Promoted from Captain Co. C to date July 10, 1865; mustered out July 17, 1865, by order of War Department.
William F. Scott	Major.	43	Oct. 10, 1864	1 year.	Promoted from Captain Co. A Dec. 21, 1864; discharged June 5, 1865.
Columbus Thornton	....do....	25	Sept. 25, 1864	1 year.	Promoted from Captain Co. F to date July 10, 1865; mustered out July 17, 1865, by order of War Department.
Cyrus Hosack	Surgeon.	32	Nov. 12, 1864	1 year.	Mustered out with regiment July 17, 1865.
Francis C. Plunkett......	Asst. Sur.	22	Nov. 11, 1864	1 year.	Mustered out with regiment July 17, 1865.
Edward F. Baker.. . ..	....do....	21	Nov 12, 1864	1 year.	Mustered out with regiment July 17, 1865.
Robert S. M. Bennett....	Adjutant.	23	Sept. 14, 1864	1 year.	Promoted from private Co. G Dec. 9, 1864; mustered out with regiment July 17, 1865.
William Henigst	R. Q. M	39	Nov. 9, 1864	1 year.	Mustered out with regiment July 17, 1865.
John J. Geer.............	Chaplain	..	Nov. 10, 1864	1 year.	Mustered out with regiment July 17, 1865.
Charles H. Skinner......	Sergt. Maj.	19	Oct. 10, 1864	1 year.	Promoted from Sergeant Co D Nov. 19, 1864; returned to Co. D Feb. 14, 1865.
Absalom Martin.........	....do....	20	Sept. 21, 1864	1 year.	Promoted from private Co. E March 1, 1865; to 2d Lieutenant July 10, 1865, but not mustered; mustered out with regiment July 17, 1865.
Charles W. Schmidt.....	Q. M. S.	34	Nov. 17, 1864	1 year.	Reduced to private Co. B Feb. 14, 1865.
Warren F. Jones.........	....do....	34	Aug 29, 1864	1 year.	Promoted from private Co. E March 1, 1865; mustered out with regiment July 17, 1865.
Thomas Norris..........	Com. Ser.	33	Oct. 1, 1864	1 year.	Promoted from private Co. A Nov. 19, 1864; to 2d Lieutenant July 10, 1865, but not mustered; mustered out with regiment July 17, 1865.
Andrew Leyman........	Hos. St'd.	36	Oct. 13, 1864	1 year.	Promoted from private Co. G Nov. 19, 1864; died March 29, 1865, in hospital at Kinston, North Carolina.
Adolph Hill.............	....do....	27	Nov. 7, 1864	1 year.	Promoted from private Co. I April 14, 1865; mustered out with regiment July 17, 1865.

1.

Names.	Rank.	Age.	Date of Entering the Service.	Period of Service.	Remarks.
Saeger, Joseph	Private..	19	Oct. 7, 1864	1 year.	Mustered out May 27, 1865, at Albany, N. Y., by order of War Department.
Sahm, George	...do....	40	Oct. 8, 1864	1 year.	Mustered out with company July 17, 1865.
Schaeffer, George	...do....	37	Sept. 23, 1864	1 year.	Mustered out with company July 17, 1865.
Schaeffer, Lewis	...do....	18	Oct. 12, 1864	1 year.	Mustered out with company July 17, 1865.
Schmidt, Charles W	...do....	34	Nov. 17, 1864	1 year.	Reduced from Q. M. Sergeant Feb. 14, 1865; mustered out with company July 17, 1865.
Schnepp, Adam	...do....	24	Feb. 1, 1864	3 yrs.	Transferred from Co. G, 58th O. V. I., June [illegible], 1865; mustered out with company July 17, 1865.
Schriefer, Frederick	...do....	19	Oct. 10, 1864	1 year.	
Schwarz, Charles	...do....	38	Sept. 27, 1864	1 year.	
Schwermberger, Charles	...do....	20	Oct. 7, 1864	1 year.	Mustered out with company July 17, 1865.
Seulke, Henry	...do....	37	Sept. 26, 1864	1 year.	Mustered out with company July 17, 1865.
Silvur, Samuel	...do....	25	Jan. 27, 1865	1 year.	Transferred from Co. B, 58th O. V. I., June [illegible], 1865; mustered out with company July 17, 1865.
Sokup, Frank	...do....	24	Oct. 1, 1864	1 year.	Wounded and captured Nov. 30, 1864, at battle of Franklin, Tenn.; mustered out July 3, 1865, at Camp Chase, O., by order of War Department.
Stoeser, Ignaz	...do....	26	Oct. 10, 1864	1 year.	Died April 27, 1865, at McDougall General Hospital, New York Harbor.
Terrill, William A	...do....	22	Aug. 11, 1862	3 yrs.	See Co. C, 58th O. V. I.
Todd, William	...do....	35	Oct. 6, 1864	1 year.	
Utz, Joseph	...do....	26	Oct. 5, 1864	1 year.	Mustered out with company July 17, 1865.
Vogel, William	...do....	40	Sept. 23, 1864	1 year.	Captured Nov. 30, 1864, at battle of Franklin, Tenn.; mustered out June 14, 1865, at Camp Chase, O., by order of War Department.
Von Rohr, Joseph	...do....	39	Sept. 30, 1864	1 year.	Mustered out with company July 17, 1865.
Wagner, Joseph	...do....	18	Oct. 5, 1864	1 year.	Transferred to Co. C, 2d Regiment Veteran Reserve Corps, May 2, 1865; mustered out Aug. 3, 1865, at Jackson, Mich., by order of War Department.
Walker, Julius	...do....	18	Sept. 14, 1864	1 year.	Mustered out with company July 17, 1865.
Walter, Charles	...do....	31	Sept. 27, 1864	1 year.	
Weber, John	...do....	28	Oct. 1, 1864	1 year.	
Wenger, August	...do....	22	Oct. 12, 1864	1 year.	Mustered out with company July 17, 1865.
Weyer, Lewis	...do....	18	Feb. 23, 1864	3 yrs.	Transferred from Co. I, 58th O. V. I., June [illegible], 1865; mustered out with company July 17, 1865.
Wolcott, Minor J	...do....	18	Feb. 22, 1864	1 year	Transferred from Co. I, 58th O. V. I., [illegible] 1865; mustered out with company July 17, 1865.
Wolf, Christian	...do....	42	Oct. [illegible], 1864	1 year.	Killed Nov. 30, 1864, in battle of Franklin, Tennessee.
Wolf, William E	...do....	[illegible]	Oct. 1, 1864	1 year.	Mustered out with company July 17, 1865.
Yates, William	...do....	18	Nov. [illegible], 1863	3 yrs.	Transferred from Co. D, 58th O. V. I., June [illegible], 1865; in hospital at Chattanooga, Tenn. No further record found.
Yockey, Edwin	...do....	[illegible]	Aug. 9, 1862	3 yrs.	Transferred from Co. F, 58th O. V. I., June [illegible], 1865; mustered out with company July 17, 1865.
Young, Andrew	...do....	21	Oct. [illegible], 1864	1 year.	Mustered out with company July 17, 1865.
Young, Charles W	...do....	[illegible]	Nov. [illegible], 1863	3 yrs.	Transferred from Co. G, 58th O. V. I., June [illegible], 1865; mustered out with company July 17, 1865.
Young, John	...do....	[illegible]	July 18, 1862	3 yrs.	In hospital at Chattanooga, Tenn. No further record found.

COMPANY C.

Mustered in October 17, 1864, at Camp Dennison, O., by W. Von Doehn, Captain and A. A. G. Mustered out July 17, 1865, at Salisbury, N. C., by Frederick Anderson, Lieutenant and A. C. M., Department of North Carolina.

Names.	Rank.	Age.	Date of Entering the Service.	Period of Service.	Remarks.
John Lang	Captain	24	Sept. 29, 1864	1 year.	Promoted from 2d Lieutenant Co. [illegible] O. V. I., Oct. 18, 1864; to Lieut. Colonel [illegible] July 10, 1865.
George Foerster	1st Lieut.	37	Aug. 29, 1864	1 year	Promoted from Sergeant Co. B, 181st O. V. I., Oct. 18, 1864; to Captain Co. K [illegible]
Frederic Lutz	...do....	32	Sept. 10, 1864	1 year.	Promoted to 2d Lieutenant from [illegible] Co. B, 181st O. V. I., Oct. 18, 1864; 1st Lieutenant Jan. 21, 1865; mustered out with company July 17, 1865.
James H. Linton	2d Lieut.	32	Sept. [illegible], 1864	1 year.	Promoted from 1st Sergeant Co. A Jan. [illegible], 1865; mustered out with company July 17, 1865.
Michael Walluch	1st Sergt.	[illegible]	Sept. 26, 1864	1 year	Appointed from Sergeant Feb. [illegible], 1865; promoted to 2d Lieutenant July [illegible], 1865, but not mustered; mustered out with company July 17, 1865.

Names.	Rank.	Age.	Date of Entering the Service.	Period of Service.	Remarks.
Saeger, Joseph	Private..	19	Oct. 7, 1864	1 year.	Mustered out May 27, 1865, at Albany, N. Y., by order of War Department.
Sahm, George	...do....	40	Oct. 8, 1864	1 year.	Mustered out with company July 17, 1865.
Schaeffer, George	...do....	37	Sept. 23, 1864	1 year.	Mustered out with company July 17, 1865.
Schaeffer, Lewis	...do....	18	Oct. 12, 1864	1 year.	Mustered out with company July 17, 1865.
Schmidt, Charles W	...do....	34	Nov. 17, 1864	1 year.	Reduced from Q. M. Sergeant Feb. 14, 1865; mustered out with company July 17, 1865.
Schnepp, Adam	...do....	24	Feb. 1, 1864	3 yrs.	Transferred from Co. G, 50th O. V. I., June 26, 1865; mustered out with company July 17, 1865.
Schriefer, Frederick	...do....	19	Oct. 10, 1864	1 year.	
Schwarz, Charles	...do....	38	Sept. 27, 1864	1 year.	
Schwermberger, Charles	...do....	20	Oct. 7, 1864	1 year.	Mustered out with company July 17, 1865.
Seulke, Henry	...do....	37	Sept. 26, 1864	1 year.	Mustered out with company July 17, 1865.
Silvur, Samuel	...do....	25	Jan. 27, 1865	1 year.	Transferred from Co. B, 50th O. V. I., June 26, 1865; mustered out with company July 17, 1865.
Sokup, Frank	...do....	24	Oct. 1, 1864	1 year.	Wounded and captured Nov. 30, 1864, at battle of Franklin, Tenn.; mustered out July 13, 1865, at Camp Chase, O., by order of War Department.
Stoeser, Ignaz	...do....	26	Oct. 10, 1864	1 year.	Died April 27, 1865, at McDougall General Hospital, New York Harbor.
Terrill, William A	...do....	22	Aug. 11, 1862	3 yrs.	See Co. C, 50th O. V. I.
Todd, William	...do....	35	Oct. 6, 1864	1 year.	
Utz, Joseph	...do....	26	Oct. 5, 1864	1 year.	Mustered out with company July 17, 1865.
Vogel, William	...do....	40	Sept. 23, 1864	1 year.	Captured Nov. 30, 1864, at battle of Franklin, Tenn.; mustered out June 14, 1865, at Camp Chase, O., by order of War Department.
Von Rohr, Joseph	...do....	39	Sept. 30, 1864	1 year.	Mustered out with company July 17, 1865.
Wagner, Joseph	...do....	18	Oct. 5, 1864	1 year.	Transferred to Co. C, 2d Regiment, Veteran Reserve Corps, May 2, 1865; mustered out Aug. 3, 1865, at Jackson, Mich., by order of War Department.
Walker, Julius	...do....	18	Sept. 14, 1864	1 year.	Mustered out with company July 17, 1865.
Walter, Charles	...do....	31	Sept. 27, 1864	1 year.	
Weber, John	...do....	28	Oct. 4, 1864	1 year.	
Wenger, August	...do....	22	Oct. 12, 1864	1 year.	Mustered out with company July 17, 1865.
Weyer, Lewis	...do....	18	Feb. 23, 1864	3 yrs.	Transferred from Co. I, 50th O. V. I., June 26, 1865; mustered out with company July 17, 1865.
Wolcott, Minor J	...do....	18	Feb. 22, 1864	1 year.	Transferred from Co. I, 50th O. V. I., June 26, 1865; mustered out with company July 17, 1865.
Wolf, Christian	...do....	42	Oct. 21, 1864	1 year.	Killed Nov. 30, 1864, in battle of Franklin, Tennessee.
Wolf, William E	...do....	21	Oct. 1, 1864	1 year.	Mustered out with company July 17, 1865.
Yates, William	...do....	18	Nov. 15, 1863	3 yrs.	Transferred from Co. D, 50th O. V. I., June 26, 1865; in hospital at Chattanooga, Tenn. No further record found.
Yockey, Edwin	...do....	19	Aug. 9, 1862	3 yrs.	Transferred from Co. F, 50th O. V. I., June 26, 1865; mustered out with company July 17, 1865.
Young, Andrew	...do....	21	Oct. [illegible], 1864	1 year.	Mustered out with company July 17, 1865.
Young, Charles W	...do....	[illegible]	Nov. 15, 1863	3 yrs.	Transferred from Co. G, 50th O. V. I., June 26, 1865; mustered out with company July 17, 1865.
Young, John	...do....	32	July 18, 1862	3 yrs.	In hospital at Chattanooga, Tenn. No further record found.

COMPANY C.

Mustered in October 17, 1864, at Camp Dennison, O., by W. Von Doehn, Captain and A. A. G. Mustered out July 17, 1865, at Salisbury, N. C., by Frederick Anderson, — Lieutenant and A. C. M., Department of North Carolina.

Names.	Rank.	Age.	Date of Entering the Service.	Period of Service.	Remarks.
John Lang	Captain	24	Sept. 29, 1864	1 year.	Promoted from 2d Lieutenant Co. B, 181st O. V. I., Oct. 18, 1864, to Lieut. Colonel to date July 10, 1865.
George Foerster	1st Lieut.	37	Aug. 29, 1864	1 year.	Promoted from Sergeant Co. B, 181st O. V. I., Oct. 18, 1864; to Captain Co. K Jan. 24, 1865.
Frederic Lutz	...do....	32	Sept. 10, 1864	1 year.	Promoted to 2d Lieutenant from Corporal Co. B, 181st O. V. I., Oct. 18, 1864; 1st Lieutenant Jan. 24, 1865; mustered out with company July 17, 1865.
James H. Linton	2d Lieut.	32	Sept. 3, 1864	1 year.	Promoted from 1st Sergeant Co. A, Jan. 24, 1865; mustered out with company July 17, 1865.
Michael Walluch	1st Sergt.	32	Sept. 26, 1864	1 year.	Appointed from Sergeant Feb. 28, 1865; promoted to 2d Lieutenant July 10, 1865, but not mustered; mustered out with company July 17, 1865.

	Rank.	Age.	Date of Entering the Service.	Period of Service.	Remarks.
ammell, George F	Private..	23	Sept. 22, 1864	1 year.	Mustered out with company July 17, 1865.
all, Hiram	....do....	29	April 14, 1864	3 yrs.	Transferred from Co. K, 100th O. V. I., June 15, 1865; mustered out with company July 17, 1865.
therland, Alexander..	....do....	42	Oct. 26, 1864	1 year.	Died Jan. 8, 1865, in Rebel Prison at Andersonville, Ga.
tton, Robert..........	....do....	28	Oct. 11, 1864	1 year.	
ylor, John W	....do....	18	Dec. 1, 1863	3 yrs.	Transferred from Co. C, 100th O. V. I., June 15, 1865; mustered out with company July 17, 1865.
dd, Alexander G......	....do....	26	Sept. 30, 1864	1 year.	Mustered out with company July 17, 1865.
dd, Samuel P	....do....	24	Sept. 6, 1864	1 year.	Mustered out with company July 17, 1865.
omas, Peter A........	....do....	26	Sept. 6, 1864	1 year.	Mustered out with company July 17, 1865.
mmons, John W.....	....do....	31	Aug. 16, 1864	1 year.	
nderwood, Benjamin S	....do....	37	Sept. 8, 1864	1 year.	Mustored out with company July 17, 1865.
rias, Sela............	....do....	19	July 10, 1863	3 yrs.	Transferred from Co. H, 103d O. V. I., June 12, 1865, as Seeley Urias; mustered out with company July 17, 1865.
ahl, Frederick	....do....	19	Dec. 5, 1864	1 year.	Transferred from Co. B, 100th O. V. I., June 15, 1865; mustered out with company July 17, 1865.
alters, James.........	....do....	35	Sept. 6, 1864	1 year.	Died June 8, 1865, at David's Island, New York Harbor.
atkins, John..........	....do....	36	Aug. 30, 1864	1 year.	Mustered out May 29, 1865, at Camp Dennison, O., by order of War Department.
elch, Michael	....do....	40	Dec. 30, 1863	3 yrs.	Transferred from Co. G, 100th O. V. I., June 15, 1865; mustered out with company July 17, 1865.
heeler, John	....do....	42	Jan. 28, 1864	3 yrs.	Transferred from Co. A, 100th O. V. I., June 15, 1865; mustered out with company July 17, 1865.
illholt, Church........	....do....	42	Oct. 1, 1864	1 year.	Mustered out with company July 17, 1865.
illiams, George W.....	....do....	33	Sept. 6, 1864	1 year.	Wounded Nov. 30, 1864, in battle of Franklin, Tenn.; mustered out June 26, 1865, at Camp Dennison, O., by order of War Department.
illiams, Jesse A......	....do....	18	Sept. 6, 1864	1 year.	Mustered out to date July 17, 1865, by order of War Department.
illiams, John F.......	....do....	28	Sept. 7, 1864	1 year.	Mustered out with company July 17, 1865.
illiams, Joseph H.....	....do....	18	Sept. 6, 1864	1 year.	Mustered out with company July 17, 1865.
ilson, Alexander Mc..	....do....	19	Mch. 10, 1864	3 yrs.	Transferred from Co. H, 103d O. V. I., June 12, 1865; mustered out with company July 17, 1865.
ilson, Dewitt C........	....do....	18	Oct. 19, 1864	1 year.	Mustered out with company July 17, 1865.
ilson, Philip H.........	....do..	37	Sept. 8, 1864	1 year.	Mustered out June 19, 1865, at Columbus, O., by order of War Department.
pp, Philip	....do....	38	Sept. 15, 1864	1 year.	Mustered out June ·, 1865, at McDougall General Hospital, New York Harbor.

COMPANY B.

ustered in October 17, 1864, at Camp Dennison, O., by W. Von Doehn, Captain and A. A. G. Mustered out July 17, 1865, at Salisbury, N. C., by Frederick Anderson, — Lieutenant and A. C. M., Department of North Carolina.

aniel Risser............	Captain.	36	Oct. 17, 1864	1 year.	Killed Nov. 30, 1864, in battle of Franklin, Tennessee.
lbert Seibert............	....do....	21	Oct. 17, 1864	1 year.	Promoted from 1st Lieutenant Dec. 21, 1864; mustered out with company July 17, 1865.
hn W. Durbin	1st Lieut.	31	Oct. 17, 1864	1 year.	Wounded Nov. 30, 1864, in battle of Franklin, Tenn.; promoted from 2d Lieutenant Dec. 21, 1864; mustered out with company July 17, 1865.
derick Saeger.........	1st Sergt.	29	Oct. 7, 1864	1 year.	Promoted to 2d Lieutenant Co. I Nov. 15, 1864.
ristopher Reichel.....	....do....	22	Sept. 29, 1864	1 year.	Appointed from Sergeant —; promoted to 2d Lieutenant July 10, 1865, but not mustered; mustered out with company July 17, 1865.
hn Kindel	Sergeant.	29	Sept. 26, 1864	1 year.	Mustered out with company July 17, 1865.
seph Eichelberger....	....do....	32	Sept. 24, 1864	1 year.	Mustered out with company July 17, 1865.
ustav Metzinger.......	....do....	24	Sept. 30, 1864	1 year	
hn M. Harman.........	....do....	28	Sept. 23, 1864	1 year.	Appointed from Corporal Nov. 19, 1864; wounded and captured Nov. 30, 1864, at battle of Franklin, Tenn.; mustered out June 14, 1865, at Camp Chase, O., by order of War Department.
lthasar Buscha.........	....do....	21	Oct. 7, 1864	1 year.	Appointed from Corporal Feb. 6, 1865; mustered out with company July 17, 1865.
illiam Schweitzer.....	Corporal.	36	Sept. 27, 1864	1 year.	Appointed Oct. 17, 1864; wounded Nov. 30, 1864, in battle of Franklin, Tenn.; mustered out with company July 17, 1865.

Names.	Rank.	Age.	Date of Entering the Service.	Period of Service	Remarks.
Junkert, Christian	Private..	19	Sept. 17, 1864	1 year.	Died March 28, 1865, in general hospital, Wilmington, N. C.
Kammerling, Frederick	....do....	35	Oct. 11, 1864	1 year.	Mustered out with company July 17, 1865.
Katterer, Joseph	....do....	39	Sept. 22, 1864	1 year.	Mustered out with company July 17, 1865.
Keefer, Andrew	....do....	24	Sept. 21, 1864	1 year.	
Kern, Henry	....do....	35	Oct. 10, 1864	1 year.	Mustered out with company July 17, 1865.
Klaus, William	....do....	35	Oct. 12, 1864	1 year.	Mustered out with company July 17, 1865.
Knecht, John	....do....	30	Oct. 6, 1864	1 year.	Mustered out with company July 17, 1865.
Kreckel, George	....do....	33	Oct. 14, 1864	1 year.	Mustered out with company July 17, 1865.
Krueger, Clemens	....do....	23	Sept. 27, 1864	1 year.	
Kruse, Fritz	....do....	28	Oct. 5, 1864	1 year.	Mustered out with company July 17, 1865.
Kull, Henry	....do....	26	Sept. 19, 1864	1 year.	Mustered out with company July 17, 1865.
Lautenschlaeger, John	....do....	32	Oct. 12, 1864	1 year.	Mustered out with company July 17, 1865.
Lenzer, William	....do....	23	Oct. 7, 1864	1 year.	Mustered out with company July 17, 1865.
Letterle, John	....do....	23	Sept. 15, 1864	1 year.	
Lippert, Frederick	....do....	33	Oct. 15, 1864	1 year.	Mustered out with company July 17, 1865.
Lohre, Franz	....do....	30	Oct. 15, 1864	1 year.	
Mayer, George	....do....	31	Oct. 10, 1864	1 year.	Mustered out with company July 17, 1865.
Miller, William	....do....	18	Sept. 17, 1864	1 year.	Mustered out with company July 17, 1865.
Muggenbury, Joseph	....do....	39	Sept. 20, 1864	1 year.	Mustered out with company July 17, 1865.
Opetz, Ferdinand	....do....	31	Oct. 7, 1864	1 year.	Mustered out with company July 17, 1865.
Pillman, William	....do....	19	Oct. 13, 1864	1 year.	
Rebholtz, George	....do....	36	Sept. 20, 1864	1 year.	Mustered out with company July 17, 1865.
Rohland, Peter	....do....	40	Sept. 16, 1864	1 year.	Mustered out May 20, 1865, at Camp Chase, O., by order of War Department.
Rost, August	....do....	21	Oct. 12, 1864	1 year.	Mustered out with company July 17, 1865.
Sauker, August	....do....	23	Sept. 19, 1864	1 year.	Mustered out May 20, 1865, at Camp Dennison, O., by order of War Department.
Sauer, Peter	....do....	39	Oct. 12, 1864	1 year.	Mustered out with company July 17, 1865.
Scharenhaus, Henry	....do....	28	Oct. 12, 1864	1 year.	Mustered out with company July 17, 1865.
Schawb, Frederick	....do....	20	Sept. 30, 1864	1 year.	Mustered out with company July 17, 1865.
Schimpf, Michael	....do....	31	Oct. 14, 1864	1 year.	Mustered out with company July 17, 1865.
Schleich, August	....do....	22	Oct. 12, 1864	1 year.	Mustered out with company July 17, 1865.
Schmidt, Max	....do....	23	Oct. 11, 1864	1 year.	Mustered out with company July 17, 1865.
Schneider, Adam	....do....	41	Sept. 21, 1864	1 year.	Perished by explosion of steamer Sultana, on Mississippi River, near Memphis, Tenn., April 27, 1865.
Schwecke, Ferdinand	....do....	35	Oct. 5, 1864	1 year.	Reduced from Sergeant Feb. 14, 1865; mustered out with company July 17, 1865.
Smith, John	....do....	18	Sept. 20, 1864	1 year.	Mustered out with company July 17, 1865.
Smith, John	....do....	18	Oct. 20, 1864	1 year.	Mustered out with company July 17, 1865.
Smith, William	....do....	20	Oct. 4, 1864	1 year.	Mustered out with company July 17, 1865.
Stockman, John	....do....	[illegible]	Sept. 29, 1864	1 year.	Mustered out with company July 17, 1865.
Stoltz, John	....do....	27	Oct. 4, 1864	1 year.	Mustered out with company July 17, 1865.
Thom, George	....do....	33	Oct. 11, 1864	1 year.	Mustered out with company July 17, 1865.
Vogt, Henry	....do....	30	Oct. 11, 1864	1 year.	
Walter, George	....do....	26	Sept. 21, 1864	1 year.	
Watson, John	....do....	23	Oct. 15, 1864	1 year.	
Weber, Frank	....do....	22	Sept. 19, 1864	1 year.	
Weber, William	....do....	25	Oct. 12, 1864	1 year.	Mustered out with company July 17, 1865.
Wegelin, Christian	....do....	21	Oct. 12, 1864	1 year.	Reduced from Corporal May 15, 1865; mustered out with company July 17, 1865.
Werth, Carl	....do....	30	Oct. 11, 1864	1 year.	Mustered out with company July 17, 1865.
Westerman, William	....do....	31	Sept. 7, 1864	1 year.	Mustered out with company July 17, 1865.
White, Jacob	....do....	41	Oct. 15, 1864	1 year.	Captured Nov. 30, 1864, at battle of Franklin, Tenn.; mustered out June 23, 1865, at Camp Chase, O., by order of War Department.
Wieman, Christ	....do....	43	Sept. 19, 1864	1 year.	Mustered out to date July 17, 1865, by order of War Department.
Wisser, John	....do....	30	Oct. 3, 1864	1 year.	Mustered out with company July 17, 1865.
Wonderlich, John	....do....	33	Oct. 10, 1864	1 year.	Killed Nov. 30, 1864, in battle of Franklin, Tennessee.
Zeigler, Adam	....do....	26	Sept. 28, 1864	1 year.	

	Rank.	Age.	Date of Entering the Service.	Period of Service.	Remarks.
...	Private..	25	Sept. 26, 1864	1 year.	Mustered out with company July 17, 1865.
...	....do....	18	Sept. 12, 1864	1 year.	Mustered out with company July 17, 1865.
...	....do....	24	Dec. 28, 1863	3 yrs.	Transferred from Co. C, 50th O. V. I., June 26, 1865; mustered out with company July 17, 1865.
...	....do....	19	Aug. 5, 1862	3 yrs.	Transferred from Co. I, 50th O. V. I., June 26, 1865; mustered out with company July 17, 1865.
...	....do....	40	Sept. 26, 1864	1 year.	Mustered out with company July 17, 1865.
...	....do....	..	May 2, 1865	3 yrs.	Transferred from ——; mustered out with company July 17, 1865.
...	....do....	25	Aug. 11, 1864	1 year.	
...	....do....	28	Sept. 26, 1864	1 year.	Wounded Nov. 30, 1864, in battle of Franklin, Tenn.; mustered out with company July 17, 1865.
...	....do....	24	Sept. 30, 1864	1 year.	Mustered out with company July 17, 1865.
...	....do....	44	Sept. 28, 1864	1 year.	Wounded and captured Nov. 30, 1864, at battle of Franklin, Tenn.; died March 20, 1865, in Rebel Prison at Andersonville, Ga.
...	....do....	28	Aug. 1, 1862	3 yrs.	Transferred from Co. I, 50th O. V. I., June 26, 1865; mustered out with company July 17, 1865.
...	....do....	36	Sept. 30, 1864	1 year.	
...	....do....	25	Oct. 10, 1864	1 year.	
...	....do....	41	Sept. 27, 1864	1 year.	Mustered out May 29, 1865, at Camp Dennison, O., by order of War Department.
...	....do....	26	Oct. 6, 1864	1 year.	Mustered out with company July 17, 1865.
...	....do....	20	Mch. 31, 1865	1 year.	Mustered out with company July 17, 1865.
...	....do....	20	Sept. 24, 1864	1 year.	Mustered out with company July 17, 1865.
...	....do....	30	Sept. 30, 1864	1 year.	Captured Nov. 30, 1864, at battle of Franklin, Tenn.; mustered out June 14, 1865, at Camp Chase, O., by order of War Department.
...	....do....	20	Oct. 3, 1864	1 year.	Mustered out with company July 17, 1865.
...	....do....	34	Oct. 1, 1864	1 year.	
...	....do....	20	Sept. 22, 1863	3 yrs.	Transferred from Co. G, 50th O. V. I., June 26, 1865; mustered out with company July 17, 1865.
...	....do....	41	Sept. 12, 1864	1 year.	Died July 12, 1865, at Salisbury, N. C.
...	....do....	21	Sept. 9, 1863	3 yrs.	Transferred from Co. E, 50th O. V. I., June 26, 1865; mustered out with company July 17, 1865.
...	....do....	26	Oct. 1, 1864	1 year.	
...	....do....	22	Oct. 7, 1864	1 year.	Mustered out with company July 17, 1865.
...	....do....	23	Oct. 7, 1864	1 year.	Died Dec. 6, 1864, at Jeffersonville, Ind., of wounds received Nov. 30, 1864, in battle of Franklin, Tenn.
...	....do....	25	Oct. 5, 1864	1 year.	Mustered out with company July 17, 1865.
...	....do....	24	Oct. 3, 1864	1 year.	Wounded and captured Nov. 30, 1864, at battle of Franklin, Tenn.; died March 2, 1865, in Rebel Prison at Andersonville, Ga.
...	....do....	29	Oct. 3, 1864	1 year	
...	....do....	33	Sept. 29, 1864	1 year.	Mustered out with company July 17, 1865.
...	....do....	27	Oct. 7, 1864	1 year.	
...	....do....	18	Aug. 21, 1862	3 yrs.	Transferred from Co. I, 50th O. V. I., June 26, 1865.
...	....do....	41	Sept. 28, 1863	3 yrs.	See Co. I, 50th O. V. I.
...	....do....	28	Oct. 11, 1864	1 year.	Wounded and missing Nov. 30, 1864, at battle of Franklin, Tenn. No further record found.
...	....do....	19	Nov. 11, 1863	3 yrs.	Transferred from Co. D, 50th O. V. I., June 26, 1865; mustered out with company July 17, 1865.
...	....do....	18	Jan. 2, 1864	3 yrs.	Transferred from Co. I, 50th O. V. I., June 26, 1865; mustered out with company July 17, 1865.
...	....do....	25	Sept. 27, 1864	1 year.	Mustered out with company July 17, 1865.
...	....do....	22	Oct. 7, 1864	1 year.	
...	....do....	18	Dec. 22, 1863	3 yrs.	Transferred from Co. I, 50th O. V. I., June 26, 1865; mustered out with company July 17, 1865.
...	....do....	16	Feb. 18, 1864	3 yrs.	Transferred from Co. B, 50th O. V. I., June 26, 1865; mustered out with company July 17, 1865.
...	....do....	19	Sept. 1, 1863	3 yrs.	Transferred from Co. C, 50th O. V. I., June 26, 1865; mustered out with company July 17, 1865.
...	....do....	27	Sept. 1, 1863	3 yrs.	Mustered out July 18, 1865, at Columbus, O., as of Co. D, 50th O. V. I., by order of War Department.
...	....do....	20	Oct. 12, 1864	1 year.	
...	....do....	22	Sept. 24, 1864	1 year.	Mustered out with company July 17, 1865.
...	....do....	24	Sept. 28, 1864	1 year.	Discharged to date Jan. 23, 1865, at Detroit, Mich., on Surgeon's certificate of disability.
...	....do....	30	Sept. 12, 1864	1 year.	Mustered out with company July 17, 1865.
...	....do....	36	Oct. 10, 1864	1 year.	Reduced from Corporal ——; mustered out with company July 17, 1865.

Names.	Rank.	Age.	Date of Entering the Service.	Period of Service.	Remarks.
Buchanan, Charles	Private..	24	Sept. 15, 1864	1 year.	
Burlew, Daniel	....do....	47	Jan. 24, 1864	3 yrs.	Transferred from Co. C, 111th O. V. I., June 27, 1865; mustered out with company July 17, 1865.
Burt, Edward	....do....	27	Sept. 26, 1864	1 year.	
Bygroph, John	....do....	39	Sept. 27, 1864	1 year.	
Calahan, John	....do....	22	Sept. 19, 1864	1 year.	Missing Nov. 30, 1864, at battle of Franklin, Tenn. No further record found.
Campbell, William	....do....	21	Nov. 4, 1864	1 year.	Transferred from Co. H, 111th O. V. I., June 27, 1865; captured Nov. 29, 1864. No further record found.
Canaway, Charles I	....do....	18	June 29, 1863	3 yrs.	See Co. B, 118th O. V. I.
Carney, Francis	....do....	18	Sept. 10, 1864	1 year.	
Carney, John	....do....	25	Oct. 3, 1864	1 year.	
Carney, Thomas	....do....	18	Sept. 19, 1864	1 year.	Mustered out with company July 17, 1865.
Carr, James	....do....	18	Oct. 12, 1864	1 year.	
Clancy, Thomas	....do....	18	Sept. 19, 1864	1 year.	Mustered out with company July 17, 1865.
Clark, Abner M	....do....	18	Dec. 22, 1863	3 yrs.	Transferred from Co. A, 111th O. V. I., June 27, 1865; mustered out with company July 17, 1865.
Clark, John	....do....	42	Sept. 19, 1864	1 year.	Mustered out to date July 17, 1865, by order of War Department.
Conner, John	....do....	22	Oct. 3, 1864	1 year.	
Coyle, Edward	....do....	25	Oct. 3, 1864	1 year.	
Cristle, Alexander	....do....	27	Oct. 3, 1864	1 year.	Reduced from Corporal ——; mustered out with company July 17, 1865.
Crossland, Charles R	....do....	28	Feb. 15, 1865	1 year.	Transferred from Co. F, 111th O. V. I., June 27, 1865; mustered out with company July 17, 1865.
Davis, George	....do....	22	Sept. 29, 1864	1 year.	
Donohoe, Thomas	....do....	20	Sept. 12, 1864	1 year.	Mustered out with company July 17, 1865.
Dunken, John	....do....	18	Oct. 3, 1864	1 year.	Mustered as Musician.
Dwyer, James	....do....	22	Oct. 10, 1864	1 year.	Mustered out with company July 17, 1865.
Essel, John L	....do....	40	Sept. 14, 1864	1 year.	
Farrar, Henry C	....do....	30	Oct. 8, 1864	1 year.	Appointed Corporal ——; Sergeant March 1, 1865; reduced March 30, 1865; mustered out with company July 17, 1865.
Fitzgerald, Lawrence	....do....	43	Oct. 10, 1864	1 year.	Missing Nov. 30, 1864, at battle of Franklin, Tenn. No further record found.
Folts, Marion	....do....	43	Oct. 17, 1864	1 year.	Died March 16, 1865, in Rebel Prison at Andersonville, Ga.; also borne on rolls as Martin Foltz.
Graham, Joseph	....do....	30	Feb. 20, 1865	1 year.	Transferred from Co. F, 111th O. V. I., June 27, 1865; mustered out with company July 17, 1865.
Grant, Edward	....do....	28	Sept. 13, 1864	1 year.	
Gray, John	....do....	36	Oct. 10, 1864	1 year.	
Hadaker, William	....do....	35	Oct. 17, 1864	1 year.	Mustered out with company July 17, 1865.
Hanna, Cassius B	....do....	19	Mch. 4, 1864	3 yrs.	See Co. H, 103d O. V. I.
Harford, John Q	....do....	27	Sept. 27, 1863	3 yrs.	Transferred from Co. B, 118th O. V. I., June 24, 1865; mustered out with company July 17, 1865.
Haughey, Jacob	....do....	36	Feb. 26, 1864	3 yrs.	Transferred from Co. C, 111th O. V. I., June 27, 1865; mustered out with company July 17, 1865.
Hawn, Almon	....do....	18	Feb. 25, 1864	3 yrs.	Transferred from Co. H, 103d O. V. I., June 22, 1865; mustered out with company July 17, 1865.
Hiett, George W	....do....	25	Aug. 9, 1862	3 yrs.	Transferred from Co. B, 118th O. V. I., June 24, 1865; mustered out with company July 17, 1865.
Hoffer, Jacob	....do....	33	Dec. 21, 1863	3 yrs.	Transferred from Co. I, 111th O. V. I., June 27, 1865; mustered out with company July 17, 1865.
Hogen, E. M	....do....	22	Sept. 6, 1864	1 year.	
Honert, Henry	....do....	29	Oct. 17, 1864	1 year.	Mustered out with company July 17, 1865.
Ikard, John	....do....	35	Oct. 1, 1864	1 year.	
Johnson, William	....do....	40	Sept. 16, 1864	1 year.	
Kanady, Patrick	....do....	36	Oct. 12, 1864	1 year.	Captured Nov. —, 1864, at Franklin, Tenn.; mustered out June 27, 1865, at Camp Chase, O., by order of War Department.
Kief, John	....do....	20	Oct. 10, 1864	1 year.	
King, John	....do....	33	Oct. 12, 1864	1 year.	
King, Lewis	....do....	20	Oct. 10, 1864	1 year.	
Kintigh, James F	....do....	18	May 25, 1863	3 yrs.	Transferred from Co. E, 111th O. V. I., June 27, 1865; mustered out with company July 17, 1865.
Klaymier, Frederick	....do....	35	Oct. 17, 1864	1 year.	Wounded Nov. 30, 1864, in battle of Franklin, Tenn.; mustered out with company July 17, 1865.
Knapp, David P	....do....	32	Dec. 22, 1863	3 yrs.	Transferred from Co. A, 111th O. V. I., June 27, 1865; mustered out with company July 17, 1865.
Krantz, Emanuel	....do....	29	Oct. 30, 1863	3 yrs.	See Co. G, 111th O. V. I.
Labolt, Aaron	....do....	26	Sept. 17, 1864	1 year.	

Date of Entering the Service.	Period of Service.	Remarks.
Oct. 17, 1864		Killed Nov. 30, 1864, in battle of Franklin, Tennessee.
Aug. 8, 1862		Transferred from Co. B, 118th O. V. I., June 24, 1865; mustered out with company July 17, 1865.
Feb. 15, 1865		Transferred from Co. F, 111th O. V. I., June 27, 1865; mustered out with company July 17, 1865.
Feb. 20, 1865		Transferred from Co. F, 111th O. V. I., June 27, 1865; mustered out with company July 17, 1865.
Mch. 12, 1864		Transferred from Co. H, 103d O. V. I., June 12, 1865; mustered out with company July 17, 1865.
Sept. 29, 1864		Mustered out June 16, 1865, at Wilmington, N. C., by order of War Department.
Sept. 8, 1864		Mustered out with company July 17, 1865.
Oct. 16, 1864		Mustered out with company July 17, 1865; also borne on rolls as Christian Lutterman.
Oct. 3, 1864	1	
Oct. 12, 1864	1	
Oct. 12, 1864	1	Mustered out with company July 17, 1865.
Sept. 2, 1864	1	
Oct. 6, 1864	1	
July 24, 1862	3	Transferred from Co. B, 118th O. V. I., June 24, 1865; mustered out with company July 17, 1865.
Sept. 20, 1864		
Oct. 15, 1864		
Aug. 29, 1864		Reduced from Sergeant ——; mustered out with company July 17, 1865.
Dec. 22, 1863		Transferred from Co. G, 111th O. V. I., June 27, 1865; mustered out with company July 17, 1865.
Mch. 28, 1864		Transferred from Co. H, 103d O. V. I., June 12, 1865; mustered out with company July 17, 1865.
Feb. 13, 1865		Transferred from Co. C, 111th O. V. I., June 27, 1865; mustered out with company July 17, 1865.
Sept. 29, 1864	1	
Oct. 10, 1864	1	Reduced from Corporal ——.
Mch. 6, 1864	1	See Co. E, 111th O. V. I.
Sept. 27, 1864	1	Mustered out May 24, 1865, at Madison, Ind., by order of War Department.
Feb. 27, 1864		Transferred from Co. I, 111th O. V. I., June 27, 1865; mustered out with company July 17, 1865.
Jan. 3, 1864		Transferred from Co. C, 111th O. V. I., June 27, 1865; mustered out with company July 17, 1865.
Mch. 8, 1864		Transferred from Co. I, 111th O. V. I., June 27, 1865; mustered out with company July 17, 1865.
Oct. 6, 1864		Mustered out June 7, 1865, at Newbern, N. C., by order of War Department.
Oct. 12, 1864	1	Mustered out with company July 17, 1865.
Sept. 28, 1864	1	
Oct. 17, 1864	1 year.	Mustered out with company July 17, 1865.
Oct. 17, 1864	1	Mustered out with company July 17, 1865.
Aug. 9, 1862	3	Transferred from Co. A, 111th O. V. I., June 27, 1865; mustered out with company July 17, 1865.
Sept. 20, 1864	1	
Sept. 29, 1864	1	Mustered out with company July 17, 1865.
Oct. 4, 1864	1	
Oct. 12, 1864	1	
Sept. 27, 1864	1	Mustered out with company July 17, 1865.
Oct. 17, 1864	1	Mustered out with company July 17, 1865.
Jan. 1, 1864		Transferred from Co. B, 111th O. V. I., June 27, 1865; mustered out with company July 17, 1865.
Sept. 14, 1864		
Oct. 12, 1864		
Aug. 13, 1862		Transferred from Co. K, 111th O. V. I., June 27, 1865; mustered out with company July 17, 1865.
Sept. 27, 1864		Mustered out with company July 17, 1865.
Oct. 8, 1864		Mustered out with company July 17, 1865.
Oct. 15, 1864		Mustered out with company July 17, 1865.
Sept. 9, 1864		
Oct. 17, 1864		Mustered out with company July 17, 1865.
Oct. 17, 1864		Reduced from Corporal ——; mustered out with company July 17, 1865.
Sept. 29, 1864		Reduced from Corporal ——; mustered out with company July 17, 1865.

Names.	Rank.	Age.	Date of Entering the Service.	Period of Service.	Remarks.
Show, Jacob	Private	32	Oct. 1, 1864	1 year.	Mustered out with company July 17, 1865.
Smith, James P	....do....	19	Oct. 13, 1864	1 year.	Mustered out with company July 17, 1865.
Snider, John	....do....	18	Oct. 6, 1864	1 year.	See Co. F, 111th O. V. I.
Snyder, Richard	....do....	19	Feb. 20, 1865	1 year.	Transferred from Co. F, 111th O. V. I., June 27, 1865; mustered out with company July 17, 1865.
Spalding, James	....do....	35	Sept. 20, 1864	1 year.	Mustered out with company July 17, 1865.
Stanton, James	....do....	23	Oct. 13, 1864	1 year.	
Starliper, Parker L	....do....	21	Feb. 15, 1865	1 year.	Transferred from Co. F, 111th O. V. I., June 27, 1865; mustered out with company July 17, 1865.
Stine, John P	....do....	19	Dec. 22, 1863	3 yrs.	Transferred from Co. A, 111th O. V. I., June 27, 1865; mustered out with company July 17, 1865.
Stonsipher, Absalom	....do....	18	Oct. 1, 1863	3 yrs.	Transferred from Co. G, 111th O. V. I., June 27, 1865; mustered out with company July 17, 1865.
Sullivan, John	....do....	25	Sept. 30, 1864	1 year.	
Tacke, Henry	....do....	38	Oct. 17, 1864	1 year.	Mustered as Wagoner; mustered out with company July 17, 1865.
Thrall, Augustus B	....do....	39	Jan. 31, 1865	1 year.	Transferred from Co. F, 111th O. V. I., June 27, 1865; mustered out with company July 17, 1865.
Tracey, Francis	....do....	21	Sept. 14, 1864	1 year.	
Trickler, Lewis	....do....	19	Sept. 21, 1864	1 year.	Died Nov. 27, 1864, at Cincinnati, O.
Vannimins, Frank	....do....	18	April 3, 1864	3 yrs.	See Co. C, 111th O. V. I.
Vaughn, Hiram	....do....	18	May 15, 1864	1 year.	See Co. B, 118th O. V. I.
Wagoner, Henry	....do....	17	Feb. 15, 1864	3 yrs.	Transferred from Co. K, 111th O. V. I., June 27, 1865; mustered out with company July 17, 1865.
White, Washington	....do....	31	Sept. 27, 1864	1 year.	Mustered out with company July 17, 1865.
Wilson, Almon	....do....	23	Dec. 22, 1863	3 yrs.	Transferred from Co. A, 111th O. V. I., June 27, 1865; mustered out with company July 17, 1865

COMPANY E.

Mustered in October 17, 1864, at Camp Dennison, O., by W. Von Doehn, Captain and A. A. G. Mustered out July 17, 1865, at Salisbury, N. C., by Frederick Andetson, — Lieutenant and A. C. M., Department of North Carolina.

Names.	Rank.	Age.	Date of Entering the Service.	Period of Service.	Remarks.
Christian Antus	Captain.	40	Oct. 19, 1864	1 year	Wounded Nov. 30, 1864, in battle of Franklin, Tenn.; mustered out with company July 17, 1865.
Valentine Rapp	1st Lieut	39	Oct. 19, 1864	1 year	Promoted to Captain July 10, 1865, but not mustered; mustered out with company July 17, 1865
Henry Lakel	2d Lieut.	32	Oct. 19, 1864	1 year.	Promoted to 1st Lieutenant July 10, 1865, but not mustered; mustered out with company July 17, 1865.
Anton Geiger	1st Sergt.	28	Oct. 1, 1864	? year.	Appointed from Sergeant ——; promoted to 2d Lieutenant July 10, 1865, but not mustered, mustered out with company July 17, 1865.
Conrad Roth	Sergeant.	30	Oct. 8, 1864	1 year	Mustered out with company July 17, 1865.
George Schuck	....do....	37	Sept. 19, 1864	1 year.	Reduced from 1st Sergeant ——, mustered out with company July 17, 1865
William Arnold	....do....	21	Sept. 2, 1864	1 year	Mustered out with company July 17, 1865.
Conrad Fossler	....do....	19	Oct. 5, 1864	1 year	Mustered out with company July 17, 1865.
John N. Gebhardt	Corporal.	32	Oct. 8, 1864	1 year.	Mustered out with company July 17, 1865.
George W. Taylor	....do....	29	Oct. 5, 1864	1 year	Died Dec. 18, 1864, at Franklin, Tenn., of wounds.
Jacob Halbaur	....do....	45	Oct. 7, 1864	1 year	Mustered out with company July 17, 1865.
Charles Miller	....do....	21	Oct. 11, 1864	1 year.	Appointed ——; mustered out with company July 17, 1865.
Oregon Case	....do....	21	Aug. 16, 1864	1 year.	Mustered out with company July 17, 1865
John Forsbach	....do....	28	Oct. 5, 1864	1 year.	Mustered out with company July 17, 1865.
John Rentschler	....do....	27	Oct. 7, 1864	1 year.	Mustered out with company July 17, 1865.
Charles Hess	....do....	28	Oct. 12, 1864	1 year.	Appointed March 1, 1865; mustered out with company July 17, 1865.
John B. Kronz	....do....	33	Oct. 5, 1864	1 year.	Mustered out May 30, 1865, at Nashville, Tenn., by order of War Department
John Gunther	Musician	18	Oct. 7, 1864	1 year.	Captured Nov. 30, 1864, at battle of Franklin, Tenn.; paroled at Vicksburg, Miss., about April 21, 1864, and perished by explosion of steamer Sultana, on Mississippi River, near Memphis, Tenn., April 27, 1865.
William Houck	....do....	36	Oct. 6, 1864	1 year.	Mustered out with company July 17, 1865.
Christian Kuhlman	....do....	21	Oct. 7, 1864	1 year.	Mustered out with company July 17, 1865.

Names.	Rank.	Age.	Date of Entering the Service.	Period of Service.	Remarks.
Herman Gottberg	Wagoner.	33	Oct. 6, 1864	1 year.	Reduced from Corporal ; mustered out with company July 17, 1865.
Arnold, William	Private..	24	Sept. 12, 1864	1 year.	
Barbett, Joseph	....do....	24	Feb. 22, 1864	3 yrs.	Transferred from Co. K, 50th O. V. I., June 26, 1865; mustered out with company July 17, 1865.
Barnes, Romulus	....do....	39	Mch. 2, 1864	1 year.	Transferred from Co. I, 103d O. V. I., June 12, 1865; mustered out with company July 17, 1865.
Bauer, John	....do....	33	Oct. 13, 1864	1 year.	Mustered out with company July 17, 1865.
Bauman, Conrad H.	....do....	18	Oct. 10, 1864	1 year.	Mustered out with company July 17, 1865.
Boehringer, Wolfgang A.	....do....	35	Sept. 22, 1864	1 year.	Mustered out May 29, 1865, at Albany, N. Y., by order of War Department.
Bohl, Henry	....do....	30	Oct. 5, 1864	1 year.	
Breede, Henry A.	....do....	20	Oct. 10, 1864	1 year.	Mustered out with company July 17, 1865.
Brown, Charles E.	....do....	30	Mch. 25, 1865	1 year.	Transferred from Co. I, 103d O. V. I., June 12, 1865; mustered out with company July 17, 1865.
Brown, John	....do....	22	Sept. 21, 1864	1 year.	Died April 1, 1865, on steamer R. C. Wood.
Burges, James W.	....do....	22	Feb. 22, 1864	1 year.	Transferred from Co. K, 50th O. V. I., June 26, 1865; mustered out with company July 17, 1865.
Caddy, Charles	....do....	19	Aug. 27, 1864	1 year.	Captured Nov. 30, 1864, at battle of Franklin, Tenn.; mustered out June 14, 1865, at Camp Chase, O., by order of War Department.
Cammerer, Ludwig	....do....	30	Sept. 21, 1864	1 year.	Mustered out with company July 17, 1865.
Crum, Wilbur F.	....do....	17	Feb. 29, 1864	3 yrs.	See Co. I, 29th O. V. I.
Daman, Levi	....do....	24	Mch. 22, 1865	1 year.	Transferred from Co. I, 103d O. V. I., June 12, 1865; died July 15, 1865, at Hinckley, Medina County, O.
Daubenbis, Jacob	....do....	20	Oct. 5, 1864	1 year.	Mustered out with company July 17, 1865.
Davenport, John D.	....do....	32	Sept. 21, 1864	1 year.	Mustered out June 9, 1865, at Louisville, Ky., by order of War Department.
Doegen, Charles	....do....	17	Sept. 12, 1864	1 year.	Appointed Musician Co. H, [illegible]
Durek, Charles	....do....	38	Oct. 1, 1864	1 year.	Died May 26, 1865, at Jefferson Barracks, Mo.
Franzreb, Jacob	....do....	33	Sept. 21, 1864	1 year.	Mustered out with company July 17, 1865.
Fries, Frederick	....do....	[illegible]	Sept. [illegible], 1864	1 year.	Died July 11, 1865, at [illegible]
Froehlich, Karl	....do....	[illegible]	Oct. 6, 1864	1 year.	Mustered out with company July 17, 1865.
Goeltz, Jacob	....do....	27	Oct. 6, 1864	1 year.	Mustered out with company July 17, 1865.
[illegible]	....do....	[illegible]	Oct. 5, 1864	1 year.	Mustered out with company July 17, 1865.
[illegible]	....do....	20	Oct. [illegible], 1864	1 year.	
Haas, John	....do....	[illegible]	Oct. [illegible], 1864	1 year.	Mustered out with company July 17, 1865.
Haas, Louis	....do....	[illegible]	Oct. [illegible], 1864	1 year.	Mustered out with company July 17, 1865.
Hagen, John	....do....	[illegible]	Oct. [illegible], 1864	1 year.	Mustered out with company July 17, 1865.
[illegible]	....do....	[illegible]	Oct. [illegible], 1864	1 year.	Mustered out with company July 17, 1865.
[illegible]	....do....	[illegible]	Oct. [illegible], 1864	1 year.	Mustered out with company July 17, 1865.
Harris, Sylvester A.	....do....	[illegible]	[illegible]	[illegible]	[illegible]
Harris, Thomas M.	....do....	[illegible]	[illegible]	[illegible]	[illegible]
[illegible]	....do....	[illegible]	[illegible]	[illegible]	[illegible]
[illegible]	....do....	[illegible]	[illegible]	[illegible]	[illegible]
[illegible]	....do....	[illegible]	[illegible]	[illegible]	[illegible]
[illegible]	[illegible]	[illegible]	[illegible]	[illegible]	[illegible]
[illegible]	[illegible]	[illegible]	[illegible]	[illegible]	[illegible]
[illegible]	[illegible]	[illegible]	[illegible]	[illegible]	[illegible]
[illegible]	[illegible]	[illegible]	[illegible]	[illegible]	[illegible]
[illegible]	[illegible]	[illegible]	[illegible]	[illegible]	[illegible]
[illegible]	[illegible]	[illegible]	[illegible]	[illegible]	[illegible]
[illegible]	[illegible]	[illegible]	[illegible]	[illegible]	[illegible]
[illegible]	[illegible]	[illegible]	[illegible]	[illegible]	[illegible]
[illegible]	[illegible]	[illegible]	[illegible]	[illegible]	[illegible]
[illegible]	[illegible]	[illegible]	[illegible]	[illegible]	[illegible]
[illegible]	[illegible]	[illegible]	[illegible]	[illegible]	[illegible]
[illegible]	[illegible]	[illegible]	[illegible]	[illegible]	[illegible]
[illegible]	[illegible]	[illegible]	[illegible]	[illegible]	[illegible]
[illegible]	[illegible]	[illegible]	[illegible]	[illegible]	[illegible]
[illegible]	[illegible]	[illegible]	[illegible]	[illegible]	[illegible]
[illegible]	[illegible]	[illegible]	[illegible]	[illegible]	[illegible]
[illegible]	[illegible]	[illegible]	[illegible]	[illegible]	[illegible]
Marz, [illegible]	[illegible]	[illegible]	[illegible]	[illegible]	[illegible]
Maurer, Anthony	..do..	22	[illegible]	[illegible]	Mustered out with company July 17, 1865.

Messmer, Christ	Private	31	Sept. 28, 1864	
Meyer, Frederick	....do....	28	Sept. 7, 1864	1
Meyer, William	....do....	36	Oct. 14, 1864	1
Miller, Blasius	....do....	21	Sept. 22, 1864	1
Miller, Franz	....do....	48	Sept. 14, 1864	1
Miller, John	....do....	32	Oct. 10, 1864	1
Nash, Henry	....do....	19	Dec. 27, 1864	1
Parker, John	....do....	31	Oct. 12, 1864	
Pfanzer, Joseph	....do....	33	Sept. 20, 1864	
Porter, Henry T.	....do....	22	Mch. 22, 1865	
Porter, Robert S.	....do....	20	Mch. 22, 1865	1 year.
Rahm, George	....do....	19	Sept. 22, 1864	1 year.
Rapp, George W.	....do....	44	Oct. 8, 1864	1 year.
Rappold, William	....do....	19	Oct. 4, 1864	1 year.
Renner, John	....do....	33	Oct. 12, 1864	1
Ridiman, John	....do....	21	Sept. 22, 1864	1
Rodgers, Amandus P.	....do....	18	Jan. 4, 1864	3 yrs.
Roeder, Ludwig	....do....	29	Oct. 13, 1864	1 year.
Roth, August	....do....	21	Oct. 10, 1864	1 year.
Roth, Ernst	....do....	35	Oct. 5, 1864	1 year.
Sangston, George	....do....	22	Feb. 28, 1864	3 yrs.
Schatz, John	....do....	33	Oct. 13, 1864	1 year.
Schenerlein, Conrad	....do....	40	Oct. 7, 1864	1
Schenerwerk, Charles	....do....	27	Oct. 4, 1864	1
Schepherd, Henry C.	....do....	20	Mch. 28, 1864	3 yrs.
Schloss, Joseph	....do....	18	Oct. 10, 1864	1 year.
Schmalzigang, Fred'ck	....do....	34	Sept. 23, 1864	1 year.
Schneider, John G.	....do....	18	Oct. 10, 1864	1 year.
Schwartz, Andrew	....do....	18	Oct. 6, 1864	1 year.
Schwiman, Jacob	....do....	22	Oct. 4, 1864	1 year.
Seiberling, Charles	....do....	18	Jan. 4, 1864	3 yrs.
Seiberling, Lloyd	....do....	18	Dec. 23, 1863	3 yrs.
Smith, Charles	....do....	40	Sept. 17, 1864	
Spaeth, John	....do....	33	Oct. 8, 1864	
Spahn, Frank	....do....	37	Oct. 10, 1864	
Spanhauer, Christian	....do....	32	Oct. 10, 1864	
Steigle, Leo	....do....	19	Oct. 14, 1864	
Stein, William	....do....	21	Oct. 5, 1864	
Stubert, Cassius	....do....	19	Oct. 8, 1864	
Vorwark, John	....do....	18	Oct. 10, 1864	
Walcher, Michael	....do....	18	Aug. 26, 1864	
Waldo, Justus F.	....do....	17	Mch. 22, 1865	
Waltz, George	....do....	18	Feb. 25, 1864	3 yrs.
Walz, Ernst	....do....	41	Oct. 10, 1864	1 year.
Warner, John	....do....	19	Sept. 26, 1864	1 year.
Watkins, Ephraim	....do....	25	Aug. 12, 1862	3 yrs.
Weldinger, John	....do....	43	Sept. 20, 1864	1
Welde, Matthew	....do....	30	Sept. 20, 1864	1
Whistler, Stephen	....do....	19	Sept. 22, 1864	1
Wirz, Christopher	....do....	22	Feb. 15, 1864	3
Zachel, Charles	....do....	41	Sept. 28, 1864	1
Zeh, Alexander	....do....	40	Oct. 5, 1864	1

Casey, Patrick	....do....	30	Oct. 5, 1864	
Cassady, Edward F	....do....	18	Oct. 12, 1864	
Clark, Charles W	....do....	25	Sept. 24, 1864	
Colcher, Noah	....do....	32	Sept. 2, 1864	
Conner, Thomas	....do....	21	Oct. 5, 1864	1 year
Crawford, Jesse	....do....	25	Nov. 4, 1862	3 yrs.
Daley, William	....do....	19	Oct. 12, 1864	1 year
Davis, James	....do....	28	Nov. 6, 1862	3 yrs.
De Leon, Charles	....do....	28	Sept. 30, 1864	1 year
Dooksoy, James	....do....	18	Sept. 27, 1864	3
Doll, Philip	....do....	35	Feb. 20, 1865	1
Dott, John	....do....	23	Oct. 12, 1864	1
Doss, William	....do....	21	Oct. 12, 1864	1
Duffield, Josiah	....do....	29	Oct. 8, 1864	1
Dunlap, George	....do....	41	Oct. 5, 1864	1
Duppe, Jacob	....do....	18	Sept. 12, 1864	1 year
Edwards, Elisha	....do....	32	Oct. 30, 1862	3 yrs.
Edwards, Jacob	....do....	34	Nov. 4, 1862	3 yrs.
Erfman, Heman	....do....	44	Oct. 4, 1864	1 year
Eversole, John W	....do....	20	Feb. 25, 1864	1 year
Farling, John	....do....	21	Nov. 4, 1862	3 yrs.
Finch, Morton	....do....	35	Oct. 11, 1864	1 year
Fitzgibin, Michael	....do....	22	Oct. 1, 1864	1 year
Forsythe, Robert	....do....	23	Aug. 22, 1862	3 yrs.
Franks, Jasper	....do....	28	Oct. 14, 1862	3 yrs.
Getterman, John	....do....	19	Oct. 3, 1864	1 year
Gilbert, William	....do....	28	Nov. 7, 1862	3 yrs.
Gruis, Edward	....do....	19	Oct. 4, 1864	1
Hall, William D	....do....	26	Oct. 1, 1864	1
Hampton, George N	....do....	44	Sept. 30, 1864	1 year
Hart, Isaac B	....do....	37	Sept. 30, 1864	1 year
Hawk, Hiram B	....do....	18	Oct. 5, 1864	1 year
Heistand, Noah	....do....	30	Oct. 21, 1862	3
Henk, Jacob	....do....	32	Oct. 4, 1864	1 year
Hertzel, Henry	....do....	48	Oct. 10, 1864	1 year
Hilbrandt, Henry	....do....	23	Oct. 7, 1864	
Johnson, John W	....do....	21	Oct. 8, 1864	year
Jones, Abraham	....do....	34	Nov. 7, 1862	yrs.
Jones, John W	....do....	45	Oct. 12, 1864	
Kaney, Joseph	....do....	20	Sept. 26, 1864	
Kesler, Frank	....do....	18	Oct. 1, 1864	1
Ketter, John	....do....	29	Oct. 7, 1864	1 year
King, Ferdinand J	....do....	32	Nov. 7, 1862	3 yrs.
Ladd, James F	....do....	32	Nov. 5, 1862	3 yrs.
Linn, John S	....do....	37	Oct. 5, 1864	
Long, Charles	....do....	18	Oct. 10, 1864	

Names.	Rank.	Age.	Date of Entering the Service.	Period of Service.	Remarks.
rman Gottberg	Wagoner.	25	Oct. 6, 1864	1 year.	Reduced from Corporal —; mustered out with company July 17, 1865.
nold, William	Private.	21	Sept. 12, 1864	1 year.	
rbett, Joseph	...do...	24	Feb. 22, 1864	3 yrs.	Transferred from Co. K, 50th O. V. I., June 26, 1865; mustered out with company July 17, 1865.
rnes, Romulus	...do...	30	Mch. 2, 1865	1 year.	Transferred from Co. I, 103d O. V. I., June 12, 1865; mustered out with company July 17, 1865.
ner, John	...do...	38	Oct. 12, 1864	1 year.	Mustered out with company July 17, 1865.
mann, Conrad H	...do...	18	Oct. 10, 1864	1 year.	Mustered out with company July 17, 1865.
hsinger, Wolfgang A	...do...	35	Sept. 22, 1864	1 year.	Mustered out May 29, 1865, at Albany, N. Y., by order of War Department.
hl, Henry	...do...	20	Oct. 5, 1864	1 year.	
ede, Henry A	...do...	20	Oct. 10, 1864	1 year.	Mustered out with company July 17, 1865.
own, Charles K	...do...	30	Mch. 25, 1865	1 year.	Transferred from Co. I, 103d O. V. I., June 12, 1865; mustered out with company July 17, 1865.
own, John	...do...	22	Sept. 24, 1864	1 year.	Died April 1, 1865, on steamer R. C. Wood.
rges, James W	...do...	22	Feb. 22, 1864	1 year.	Transferred from Co. K, 50th O. V. I., June 26, 1865; mustered out with company July 17, 1865.
ddy, Charles	...do...	19	Aug. 27, 1864	1 year.	Captured Nov. 30, 1864, at battle of Franklin, Tenn.; mustered out June 14, 1865, at Camp Chase, O., by order of War Department.
mmerer, Ludwig	...do...	30	Sept. 21, 1864	1 year.	Mustered out with company July 17, 1865.
m, Wilbur F	...do...	17	Feb. 29, 1864	3 yrs.	See Co. I, 99th O. V. I.
man, Levi	...do...	24	Mch. 22, 1865	1 year.	Transferred from Co. I, 103d O. V. I., June 12, 1865; died July 15, 1865, at Hinckley, Madison County, O.
ubenbis, Jacob	...do...	20	Oct. 5, 1864	1 year.	Mustered out with company July 17, 1865.
venport, John D	...do...	32	Sept. 21, 1864	1 year.	Mustered out June 9, 1865, at Louisville, Ky., by order of War Department.
gan, Charles	...do...	17	Sept. 12, 1864	1 year.	Appointed Musician Co. H, —.
rck, Charles	...do...	28	Oct. 1, 1864	1 year.	Died May 25, 1865, at Jefferson Barracks, Mo.
nzeb, Jacob	...do...	38	Sept. 21, 1864	1 year.	Mustered out with company July 17, 1865.
e, Frederick	...do...	39	Sept. 23, 1864	1 year.	Died July 11, 1865, at Salisbury, N. C.
elich, Karl	...do...	38	Oct. 6, 1864	1 year.	Mustered out with company July 17, 1865.
litz, Jacob	...do...	27	Oct. 6, 1864	1 year.	Mustered out with company July 17, 1865.
sch, Louis	...do...	24	Oct. 5, 1864	1 year.	Mustered out with company July 17, 1865.
ffrey, John	...do...	20	Oct. 12, 1864	1 year.	
s, John	...do...	25	Oct. 10, 1864	1 year.	Mustered out with company July 17, 1865.
s, Louis	...do...	33	Oct. 5, 1864	1 year.	Mustered out with company July 17, 1865.
gen, John	...do...	35	Oct. 10, 1864	1 year.	Mustered out with company July 17, 1865.
ll, Philip	...do...	28	Oct. 12, 1864	1 year.	Mustered out with company July 17, 1865.
pp, Julius	...do...	45	Oct. 12, 1864	1 year.	Mustered out with company July 17, 1865.
rris, Sylvester A	...do...	18	Feb. 27, 1864	3 yrs.	Transferred from Co. K, 50th O. V. I., June 26, 1865; discharged Sept. 12, 1864, at Dennison U. S. General Hospital, O., as of Co. I, 99th O. V. I.
feis, Thomas M	...do...	19	Feb. 24, 1864	3 yrs.	See Co. I, 99th O. V. I.
berts, Peter	...do...	45	Oct. 10, 1864	1 year.	
benleitner, Ignatz	...do...	18	Oct. 8, 1864	1 year.	Mustered out with company July 17, 1865.
pkins, Winfield S	...do...	18	Feb. 22, 1864	3 yrs.	Transferred from Co. K, 50th O. V. I., June 26, 1865; mustered out with company July 17, 1865.
pper, William M. A	...do...	26	Feb. 22, 1864	3 yrs.	Transferred from Co. K, 50th O. V. I., June 26, 1865; mustered out with company July 17, 1865.
bbard, Edward C	...do...	18	Feb. 29, 1864	3 yrs.	Transferred from Co. K, 50th O. V. I., June 26, 1865; mustered out with company July 17, 1865.
ber, Jacob	...do...	29	Oct. 6, 1864	1 year.	Mustered out with company July 17, 1865.
ber, Joseph	...do...	27	Oct. 3, 1864	1 year.	Mustered out with company July 17, 1865.
ber, Leopold	...do...	24	Oct. 12, 1864	1 year.	Mustered out with company July 17, 1865.
laway, Joseph M	...do...	23	Oct. 10, 1864	1 year.	Appointed 1st Sergeant Co. H, —.
nston, Sherman	...do...	22	Mch. 22, 1865	1 year.	See Co. I, 103d O. V. I.
es, Warren F	...do...	34	Aug. 29, 1864	1 year.	Promoted to Q. M. Sergeant March 1, 1865.
[illegible], Henry	...do...	29	Oct. 14, 1864	1 year.	
ler, Samuel L	...do...	19	Feb. 6, 1864	1 year.	Transferred from Co. K, 50th O. V. I., June 26, 1865; mustered out with company July 17, 1865.
sch, Joseph	...do...	28	Oct. 6, 1864	1 year.	Mustered out with company July 17, 1865.
ne, Bernhardt	...do...	36	Oct. 10, 1864	1 year.	Mustered out with company July 17, 1865.
hner, Christian	...do...	30	Sept. 20, 1864	1 year.	Sick, Nov. 17, 1864, at Camp Dennison, O. No further record found.
[illegible], August	...do...	36	Sept. 21, 1864	1 year.	
[illegible], John	...do...	18	Aug. 23, 1864	1 year.	Died Dec. 8, 1864, at Nashville, Tenn., of wounds received Nov. 30, 1864, in battle of Franklin, Tenn.
le, Gottlieb	...do...	36	Sept. 22, 1864	1 year.	Mustered out with company July 17, 1865.
e, Michael	...do...	20	Sept. 20, 1864	1 year.	Mustered out with company July 17, 1865.
rtin, Absalom	...do...	20	Sept. 21, 1864	1 year.	Promoted to Sergt. Major March 1, 1865.
z, John	...do...	30	Sept. 19, 1864	1 year.	Mustered out with company July 17, 1865.
rer, Anthony	...do...	22	Oct. 10, 1864	1 year.	Mustered out with company July 17, 1865.

Names.	Rank.	Age.	Date of Entering the Service.	Period of Service.	Remarks.
Messmer, Christ	Private	31	Sept. 28, 1864	1 year.	Claimed by H. B. Hill, Provost Marshal 4th District of Indiana, Nov. 12, 1864.
Meyer, Frederick	...do...	26	Sept. 7, 1864	1 year.	
Meyer, William	...do...	35	Oct. 14, 1864	1 year.	
Miller, Blasius	...do...	21	Sept. 22, 1864	1 year.	Mustered out with company July 17, 1865.
Miller, Franz	...do...	43	Sept. 14, 1864	1 year.	Mustered out with company July 17, 1865.
Miller, John	...do...	32	Oct. 10, 1864	1 year.	Mustered out with company July 17, 1865.
Nash, Henry	...do...	19	Dec. 27, 1864	1 year.	Transferred from Co. I, 103d O. V. I., June 12, 1865; mustered out with company July 17, 1865.
Parker, John	...do...	31	Oct. 12, 1864	1 year.	
Pfanzer, Joseph	...do...	33	Sept. 20, 1864	1 year.	Wounded Nov. 30, 1864, in battle of Franklin, Tenn.; mustered out with company July 17, 1865.
Porter, Henry T	...do...	22	Mch. 22, 1865	1 year.	Transferred from Co. I, 103d O. V. I., June 12, 1865; mustered out with company July 17, 1865.
Porter, Robert S	...do...	20	Mch. 22, 1865	1 year.	Transferred from Co. I, 103d O. V. I., June 12, 1865; mustered out July 6, 1865, at Mower General Hospital, Philadelphia, Pa., as of Co. I, 103d O. V. I.
Rahm, George	...do...	19	Sept. 22, 1864	1 year.	Captured Nov. 30, 1864, at battle of Franklin, Tenn.; mustered out July 1, 1865, at Camp Chase, O., by order of War Department.
Rapp, George W	...do...	44	Oct. 8, 1864	1 year.	
Rappold, William	...do...	19	Oct. 4, 1864	1 year.	Mustered out with company July 17, 1865.
Renner, John	...do...	33	Oct. 12, 1864	1 year.	Mustered out with company July 17, 1865.
Ridiman, John	...do...	21	Sept. 22, 1864	1 year.	Wounded Dec. 15, 1864, in battle of Nashville, Tenn.; mustered out with company July 17, 1865.
Rodgers, Amandus P	...do...	18	Jan. 4, 1864	3 yrs.	Transferred from Co. I, 103d O. V. I., June 12, 1865; mustered out with company July 17, 1865.
Roeder, Ludwig	...do...	29	Oct. 13, 1864	1 year.	Mustered as Wagoner; mustered out with company July 17, 1865.
Roth, August	...do...	21	Oct. 10, 1864	1 year.	Mustered out with company July 17, 1865.
Roth, Ernst	...do...	36	Oct. 5, 1864	1 year.	Mustered out with company July 17, 1865.
Sangston, George	...do...	22	Feb. 28, 1864	3 yrs.	Wounded Aug. 6, 1864, at siege of Atlanta, Ga.; transferred from Co. F, 10th O. V. I., June 15, 1865; mustered out with company July 17, 1865.
Schatz, John	...do...	33	Oct. 13, 1864	1 year.	Mustered out with company July 17, 1865.
Schenerlein, Conrad	...do...	40	Oct. 7, 1864	1 year.	Mustered out with company July 17, 1865.
Schenerwerk, Charles	...do...	27	Oct. 4, 1864	1 year	Mustered out with company July 17, 1865.
Schepherd, Henry C	...do...	20	Mch. 26, 1864	3 yrs.	See Co. K, 50th O. V. I.
Schloss, Joseph	...do...	18	Oct. 10, 1864	1 year	Mustered out with company July 17, 1865.
Schmalzigang, Fred'ck	...do...	34	Sept. 23, 1864	1 year	Mustered out with company July 17, 1865.
Schneider, John G	...do...	18	Oct. 10, 1864	1 year.	Mustered out with company July 17, 1865.
Schwartz, Andrew	...do...	18	Oct. 6, 1864	1 year	Mustered out with company July 17, 1865.
Schwiman, Jacob	...do...	22	Oct. 4, 1864	1 year.	Mustered out with company July 17, 1865.
Seiberling, Charles	...do...	18	Jan. 4, 1864	3 yrs.	Transferred from Co. I, 103d O. V. I., June 12, 1865; mustered out with company July 17, 1865.
Seiberling, Lloyd	...do...	18	Dec. 22, 1863	3 yrs.	Transferred from Co. I, 103d O. V. I., June 12, 1865, mustered out with company July 17, 1865.
Smith, Charles	...do...	40	Sept. 17, 1864	1 year.	
Spaeth, John	...do...	38	Oct. 8, 1864	1 year.	Reduced from Corporal ——.
Spahn, Frank	...do...	37	Oct. 10, 1864	1 year.	Mustered out with company July 17, 1865.
Spanhauer, Christian	...do...	32	Oct. 10, 1864	1 year	Mustered out with company July 17, 1865.
Steigle, Leo	...do...	19	Oct. 14, 1864	1 year.	Mustered out with company July 17, 1865.
Stein, William	...do...	21	Oct. 5, 1864	1 year.	Sick, Nov. 19, 1864, at Camp Dennison, O. No further record found.
Stubert, Cassius	...do...	19	Oct. 8, 1864	1 year.	Mustered out with company July 17, 1865.
Vorwark, John	...do...	18	Oct. 10, 1864	1 year.	Mustered out with company July 17, 1865.
Walcher, Michael	...do...	18	Aug. 26, 1864	1 year.	Discharged Feb. 21, 1865, at Cincinnati, O., on surgeon's certificate of disability.
Waldo, Justus F	...do...	17	Mch. 22, 1865	1 year.	Transferred from Co. I, 103d O. V. I., June 12, 1865; mustered out July 6, 1865, at Mower General Hospital, Philadelphia, Pa., as of Co. I, 103d O. V. I.
Waltz, George	...do...	18	Feb. 25, 1864	3 yrs.	Transferred from Co. K, 50th O. V. I., June 12, 1865; mustered out with company July 17, 1865.
Walz, Ernst	...do...	41	Oct. 10, 1864	1 year.	Mustered out with company July 17, 1865.
Warner, John	...do...	19	Sept. 26, 1864	1 year.	
Watkins, Ephraim	...do...	25	Aug. 12, 1862	3 yrs.	Transferred from Co. I, 103d O. V. I., June 12, 1865; mustered out with company July 17, 1865.
Weidinger, John	...do...	43	Sept. 20, 1864	1 year.	Mustered out with company July 17, 1865.
Welde, Matthew	...do...	30	Sept. 20, 1864	1 year.	Mustered out with company July 17, 1865.
Whistler, Stephen	...do...	19	Sept. 22, 1864	1 year.	Mustered out with company July 17, 1865.
Wirz, Christopher	...do...	22	Feb. 15, 1864	3 yrs.	See Christopher Ury, Co. F, 108th O. V. I.
Zachel, Charles	...do...	41	Sept. 28, 1864	1 year.	
Zeh, Alexander	...do...	40	Oct. 5, 1864	1 year.	Mustered out with company July 17, 1865.

COMPANY F.

Mustered in October 19, 1864, at Camp Dennison, O., by W. Von Doehn, Captain and A. A. G. Mustered out July 17, 1865, at Salisbury, N. C., by Frederick Anderson, — Lieutenant and A. C. M., Department of North Carolina.

Names.	Rank.	Age.	Date of Entering the Service.	Period of Service.	Remarks.
Columbus Thornton	Captain.	25	Sept. 22, 1864	1 year.	Promoted from Sergeant Co. G, 181st O. V. I., Oct. 19, 1864; to Major to date July 10, 1865.
Eden B. Reeder	1st Lieut.	26	Sept. 24, 1864	1 year.	Promoted from Sergeant Co. A, 181st O. V. I., Oct. 19, 1864; to Captain July 10, 1865, but not mustered; mustered out with company July 17, 1865.
Benjamin F. Drury	2d Lieut.	21	Sept. 27, 1864	1 year.	Promoted from Sergeant Co. E, 181st O. V. I., Oct. 19, 1864; detailed as Acting Regt. Quartermaster June 21, 1865; promoted to 1st Lieutenant July 10, 1865, but not mustered; mustered out with company July 17, 1865.
Edward Cook	1st Sergt.	23	Oct. 8, 1864	1 year.	Appointed Sergeant from Corporal Nov. 30, 1864; 1st Sergeant Feb. 14, 1865; promoted to 2d Lieutenant July 10, 1865, but not mustered; mustered out with company July 17, 1865.
James W. Driskill	Sergeant.	28	Oct. 10, 1864	1 year.	Reduced from 1st Sergeant Dec. 4, 1864; mustered out with company July 17, 1865.
Joseph Turner	....do..	25	Oct. 5, 1864	1 year.	Mustered out with company July 17, 1865.
Thomas Plumb	....do....	43	Sept. 3, 1864	1 year.	Mustered out with company July 17, 1865.
John S. Megrue	....do....	19	Oct. 12, 1864	1 year.	Appointed from Corporal Feb. 28, 1865; mustered out with company July 17, 1865.
William M. Avery	Corporal.	19	Sept. 26, 1864	1 year.	Mustered out with company July 17, 1865.
Silas Brandenburg	....do....	36	Oct. 10, 1864	1 year.	Appointed Dec. 31, 1864; mustered out with company July 17, 1865.
Milton Tilt	....do....	22	Oct. 3, 1864	1 year.	Appointed Dec. 31, 1864; mustered out with company July 17, 1865.
Germanius Fecker	....do....	19	Oct. 5, 1864	1 year.	Appointed Dec. 31, 1864; mustered out with company July 17, 1865.
Anthony Heet	....do....	20	Oct. 4, 1864	1 year.	Appointed Feb. 28, 1865; mustered out with company July 17, 1865.
David W. Miller	....do....	20	Oct. 5, 1864	1 year.	Wounded Nov. 30, 1864, in battle of Franklin, Tenn.; appointed April 8, 1865; mustered out with company July 17, 1865.
Michael Mularky	....do....	29	Oct. 12, 1864	1 year.	Appointed April 8, 1865; mustered out with company July 17, 1865.
William E. Wallace	....do....	40	Oct. 4, 1864	1 year.	Appointed June 30, 1865; mustered out with company July 17, 1865.
Benjamin F. Gilpin	Musician	40	Sept. 22, 1864	1 year.	Appointed Corporal Dec. 31, 1864; reduced Feb. 14, 1865; appointed Musician April 29, 1865; mustered out June 22, 1865, at Columbus, O., as private, by order of War Department.
David Briddenbaugh	Wagoner.	29	Oct. 6, 1862	3 yrs.	Transferred from Co. K, 118th O. V. I., June 24, 1865; mustered out with company July 17, 1865.
Alexander, John M	Private..	36	Sept. 30, 1864	1 year.	Appointed Corporal Dec. 31, 1864; reduced April 8, 1865; mustered out with company July 17, 1865.
Altman, Samuel	....do....	19	Oct. 21, 1862	3 yrs.	Transferred from Co. K, 118th O. V. I., June 24, 1865; mustered out with company July 17, 1865.
Anderson, John	....do....	30	Sept. 14, 1864	1 year.	Mustered out with company July 17, 1865.
Ashley, William B	....do....	31	Oct. 8, 1864	1 year.	
Baker, Ephraim	....do....	37	Oct. 16, 1862	3 yrs.	Transferred from Co. K, 118th O. V. I., June 24, 1865; mustered out with company July 17, 1865.
Bargerding, Henry	....do..	39	Oct. 9, 1862	3 yrs.	Transferred from Co. K, 118th O. V. I., June 24, 1865, as Henry Bargainding; mustered out with company July 17, 1865.
Barrack, William	....do....	43	Nov. 10, 1862	3 yrs.	Transferred from Co. K, 118th O. V. I., June 24, 1865; mustered out with company July 17, 1865.
Beach, Henry	....do....	34	Mch. 30, 1864	3 yrs.	Transferred from Co. K, 118th O. V. I., June 24, 1865; mustered out with company July 17, 1865.
Beatty, John G	....do....	18	Oct. 6, 1864	1 year.	Mustered out June 7, 1865, at David's Island, New York Harbor, by order of War Department.
Beavis, Richard	....do....	21	Oct. 16, 1862	3 yrs.	Transferred from Co. K, 118th O. V. I., June 24, 1865, as Richard A. Beavers; mustered out with company July 17, 1865.
Boswell, Lewis A	....do....	28	Sept. 26, 1864	1 year.	Mustered out with company July 17, 1865.
Brier, Byron	....do....	18	Sept. 30, 1864	1 year.	
Brinkman, Henry	....do....	36	Oct. 11, 1864	1 year.	Mustered out with company July 17, 1865.

Names.	Rank.	Age.	Date of Entering the Service.	Period of Service.	Remarks.
McCabe, Samuel V.	Private.	26	Sept. 29, 1864	1 year.	Mustered out with company July 17, 1865.
Marlatt, James H.	...do...	21	Oct. 14, 1864	1 year.	Mustered out with company July 17, 1865.
Marshall, Thomas	...do...	44	Oct. 17, 1864	1 year.	Mustered out May 29, 1865, at Camp Dennison, O., by order of War Department.
Merchant, James D.	...do...	18	Sept. 27, 1864	1 year.	Mustered out with company July 17, 1865.
Minier, Darius	...do...	26	Oct. 13, 1864	1 year.	Prisoner of war; mustered out May 20, 1865, at Camp Chase, O., by order of War Department.
Moore, James	...do...	34	Feb. 20, 1864	1 year.	Transferred from Co. K, 104th O. V. I., June 15, 1865; mustered out with company July 17, 1865.
Morehart, Jesse	...do...	19	Oct. 18, 1864	1 year.	Mustered out May 15, 1865, at Philadelphia, Pa., by order of War Department.
Morse, Edwin	...do...	18	Oct. 12, 1864	1 year.	Mustered out with company July 17, 1865.
Mullencup, Isaac	...do...	30	Sept. 8, 1864	1 year.	Missing Nov. 30, 1864, at battle of Franklin, Tenn. No further record found.
Myers, Amos	...do...	20	Oct. 19, 1864	1 year.	Mustered out with company July 17, 1865.
Myers, Joshua	...do...	39	Oct. 13, 1864	1 year.	Reduced from Sergeant April 1, 1865; mustered out July 14, 1865, at Columbus, O., by order of War Department.
Nicholson, George W.	...do...	17	Sept. 20, 1864	1 year.	Mustered out with company July 17, 1865
O'Brien, Michael	...do...	42	Sept. 27, 1864	1 year.	Captured Nov. 30, 1864, at battle of Franklin, Tenn.; died Jan. 12, 1865, at Tupelo, Miss., while a prisoner of war
Orwig, Samuel	...do...	32	Oct. 17, 1864	1 year.	Appointed Corporal Dec. 23, 1864; reduced April 1, 1865; mustered out with company July 17, 1865.
Parker, William H.	...do...	18	Sept. 19, 1864	1 year.	Mustered out with company July 17, 1865.
Prehl, John	...do...	39	Feb. 14, 1865	1 year.	Mustered out May 24, 1865, at Louisville, Ky., by order of War Department.
Punches, David	...do...	28	Oct. 18, 1864	1 year.	Mustered out with company July 17, 1865.
Rauch, John	...do...	42	Oct. 17, 1864	1 year.	Reduced from Sergeant Feb. 1, 1865; mustered out July 22, 1865, at Fortress Monroe, Va., by order of War Department.
Ray, Joseph B.	...do...	20	Dec. 22, 1863	3 yrs.	Transferred from Co. G, 104th O. V. I., June 15, 1865; discharged June 30, 1865, at Cleveland, O., as of Co. G, 104th O. V. I., on Surgeon's certificate of disability.
Rhinehart, Adam	...do...	25	Feb. 5, 1864	3 yrs.	See Co. H, 104th O. V. I.
Rogers, Hugh	...do...	18	Sept. 24, 1864	1 year.	Captured Nov. 30, 1864, at battle of Franklin, Tenn.; mustered out June 14, 1865, at Camp Chase, O., by order of War Department
Ross, John	...do...	39	Sept. 26, 1864	1 year	Mustered out with company July 17, 1865.
Rowles, George	...do...	18	Oct. 13, 1864	1 year.	Mustered out June 1, 1865, at David's Island, New York Harbor.
Seaman James	...do...	19	Oct. 4, 1864	1 year	Mustered out June 19, 1865, at Louisville, Ky., by order of War Department.
Sellars, Joshua	...do...	19	Feb. 7, 1864	3 yrs.	See Co. H, 104th O. V. I.
Stokesberry, Joshua	...do...	30	Oct. 11, 1864	1 year.	Mustered out with company July 17, 1865.
Stout, John	...do...	19	Oct. 14, 1864	1 year.	
Thompson, Joseph	...do...	43	Oct. 13, 1864	1 year.	Wounded Nov. 30, 1864, in battle of Franklin, Tenn.; mustered out with company July 17, 1865.
Tipton, William	...do...	42	Oct. 3, 1864	1 year.	Mustered out with company July 17, 1865.
Trimble, Joseph M.	...do...	17	Oct. 3, 1864	1 year.	Mustered out with company July 17, 1865.
Tunstall, William	...do...	18	Sept. 26, 1864	1 year.	Mustered out with company July 17, 1865.
Viers, Daniel M.	...do...	17	Nov. 10, 1863	3 yrs.	Transferred from Co. H, 104th O. V. I., June 15, 1865, mustered out with company July 17, 1865.
Weisbrod, John	...do...	30	Oct. 13, 1864	1 year.	
Willenburg, Frank	...do...	21	Sept 24, 1864	1 year.	
Williams, Benjamin	...do...	28	Oct. 11, 1864	1 year.	Mustered out with company July 17, 1865
Williams, Thomas	...do...	18	Oct. 12, 1864	1 year.	Wounded Nov. 30 1864, in battle of Franklin, Tenn.; mustered out with company July 17, 1865.
Winner, Charles	...do...	43	Sept. 20 1864	1 year.	Mustered out May 29, 1865, at Camp Dennison, O., by order of War Department.
Wise, Michael	...do...	23	Oct. 1, 1864	1 year.	
Wright, Jonathan	...do...	21	Sept. 30, 1864	1 year.	Mustered out with company July 17, 1865.

Names.	Rank.	Age.	Date of Entering the Service.	Period of Service.	Remarks.
...ons, Lewis S.	Private.	22	Oct. 6, 1862	3 yrs.	Transferred from Co. K, 118th O. V. I., June 24, 1865; mustered out with company July 17, 1865.
...Call, John	...do...	18	Oct. 4, 1864	1 year.	Mustered out June 19, 1865, at Camp Chase, O., by order of War Department.
...Cain, Benjamin	...do...	39	Oct. 4, 1864	1 year.	Mustered out with company July 17, 1865.
...Carty, John A.	...do...	23	Sept. 20, 1864	1 year.	Mustered out with company July 17, 1865.
...Cormick, Alfred J.	...do...	24	Sept. 22, 1864	1 year.	Reduced from Sergeant ——; mustered out May 16, 1865, at Camp Dennison, O., by order of War Department.
...Cue, John	...do...	18	Feb. 22, 1865	1 year.	Mustered out with company July 17, 1865.
...Daniel, Hiram G.	...do...	19	Sept. 20, 1864	1 year.	Mustered out June 21, 1865, at Washington, D. C., by order of War Department.
...Farland, John	...do...	27	May 1, 1862	3 yrs.	Transferred from Co. K, 118th O. V. I., June 24, 1865; mustered out with company July 17, 1865.
...mey, Uriah	...do...	21	Oct. 1, 1864	1 year.	Mustered out May 19, 1865, at McDougall General Hospital, New York Harbor, by order of War Department.
...ndenhall, Americus	...do...	18	Aug. 22, 1864	1 year.	Mustered out May 29, 1865, at Camp Dennison, O., by order of War Department.
...lenburger, Charles	...do...	40	Mch. 6, 1865	1 year.	Mustered out with company July 17, 1865.
...ler, Jacob	...do...	20	Nov. 14, 1862	3 yrs.	Transferred from Co. K, 118th O. V. I., June 24, 1865; mustered out with company July 17, 1865.
...ler, James J.	...do...	28	Nov. 6, 1862	3 yrs.	See Co. K, 118th O. V. I.
...ore, Urias	...do...	22	Oct. 16, 1862	3 yrs.	Transferred from Co. K, 118th O. V. I., June 24, 1865; mustered out with company July 17, 1865.
...rris, Francis	...do...	18	Oct. 5, 1864	1 year.	Wounded Nov. 30, 1864, in battle of Franklin, Tenn.; mustered out May 29, 1865, at Camp Dennison, O., by order of War Department.
...rphy, Leander A.	...do...	25	Nov. 2, 1864	1 year.	Mustered out July 25, 1865, at Louisville, Ky., by order of War Department.
...rin, John	...do...	20	Oct. 5, 1864	1 year.	
...ris, Henry	...do...	19	Oct. 10, 1864	1 year.	
...rien, Patrick	...do...	25	Oct. 5, 1864	1 year.	
...onald, Patrick	...do...	24	Sept. 30, 1864	1 year.	Mustered out with company July 17, 1865.
...len, Aaron L.	...do...	30	Oct. 2, 1864	1 year.	Mustered out with company July 17, 1865.
...ott, David F.	...do...	28	Oct. 6, 1862	3 yrs.	See Co. K, 118th O. V. I.
...terson, James	...do...	22	Oct. 3, 1864	1 year.	Reduced from Corporal ——; absent ——. No further record found.
...dleton, Joseph	...do...	29	Sept. 26, 1862	3 yrs.	Transferred from Co. K, 118th O. V. I., June 24, 1865; mustered out with company July 17, 1865.
...kleton, John	...do...	18	Sept. 20, 1864	1 year.	Mustered out June 10, 1865, at Washington, D. C., by order of War Department.
...stian, John	...do...	43	Oct. 5, 1864	1 year.	Prisoner of war; died June 19, 1865, at Andersonville, Ga.
...rk, Michael	...do...	31	Oct. 1, 1864	1 year.	Mustered out with company July 17, 1865.
...p, Peter	...do...	19	Sept. 26, 1864	1 year.	Mustered out with company July 17, 1865.
...ford, Andrew J.	...do...	24	Sept. 26, 1864	1 year.	Mustered out with company July 17, 1865.
...afer, Christian	...do...	19	Oct. 6, 1864	1 year.	Mustered out with company July 17, 1865.
...w, Henry	...do...	25	Sept. 27, 1864	1 year.	Mustered out with company July 17, 1865.
...pson, Thaddeus	...do...	18	Oct. 6, 1864	1 year.	Mustered as Musician; mustered out with company July 17, 1865.
...le, Joseph	...do...	18	Sept. 12, 1864	1 year.	Reduced from Corporal ——; mustered out with company July 17, 1865.
...terly, Thomas	...do...	28	Oct. 11, 1864	1 year.	
...sh, John T.	...do...	21	Oct. 1, 1864	1 year.	
...der, Henry	...do...	19	Oct. 11, 1864	1 year.	
...therland, Thomas	...do...	30	Sept. 26, 1864	1 year.	
...ms, Freeman	...do...	17	Sept. 29, 1864	1 year.	Killed Nov. 30, 1864, in battle of Franklin, Tennessee.
...ng, Ebenezer B.	...do...	43	Oct. 6, 1864	1 year.	Mustered out July 28, 1865, at Cincinnati, O., by order of War Department.
...van, Dennis	...do...	25	Oct. 6, 1864	1 year.	Mustered out May 18, 1865, at Washington, D. C., by order of War Department.
...son, Samuel	...do...	24	Oct. 2, 1864	1 year.	Mustered out May 29, 1865, at Camp Dennison, O., by order of War Department.
...mpson, William	...do...	27	Sept. 26, 1864	1 year.	Wounded Nov. 30, 1864, in battle of Franklin, Tenn.; transferred to Co. B, 22d Regiment, Veteran Reserve Corps, ——; mustered out July 3, 1865, at Camp Cleveland, O., by order of War Department.
..., Simon	...do...	28	Sept. 22, 1864	1 year.	Mustered out with company July 17, 1865.
...r, John	...do...	36	Sept. 15, 1864	1 year.	
...y, Sidney E.	...do...	22	Oct. 10, 1864	1 year.	
...ren, Andrew	...do...	22	Oct. 15, 1864	1 year.	Mustered out with company July 17, 1865.
..., Peter	...do...	36	Oct. 6, 1864	1 year.	Mustered out May 29, 1865, at Camp Dennison, O., by order of War Department.
...ew, John	...do...	38	Oct. 4, 1864	1 year.	Reduced from Sergeant ——; returned to 70th Ill. V. I. Nov. 28, 1864, where he had previously enlisted.
...lerkin, August	...do...	30	Oct. 3, 1864	1 year.	Mustered out with company July 17, 1865.

Names.	Rank.		Date of Entering the Service.	Period of Service
Brown, John	Private	17	Mch. 14, 1865	
Bruening, Christian	do	28	Oct. 6, 1864	
Bullard, Benjamin L	do	38	Sept. 5, 1862	
Burr, Edward	do	26	Aug. 22, 1862	
Burt, James	do	23	Aug. 4, 1862	
Buscroff, John	do	41	Oct. 6, 1864	
Bussert, Adam	do	21	Oct. 17, 1864	
Byron, William	do	31	Aug. 14, 1862	
Calahan, Daniel	do	25	Sept. 8, 1864	1
Carpenter, Thomas	do	18	Oct. 19, 1864	1 year.
Christman, Peter	do	43	Oct. 24, 1864	1 year.
Clifford, Joseph	do	25	Aug. 2, 1862	3 yrs.
Cunningham, James	do	18	Aug. 19, 1862	3 yrs.
Davis, Absalom C	do	27	Sept. 13, 1863	3 yrs.
Dean, Henry J	do	30	Jan. 1, 1865	1 year.
Dobaly, Abraham	do	23	July 30, 1862	3 yrs.
Doyle, John W	do	19	Aug. 27, 1864	1 year
Eder, Henry	do	28	Sept. 28, 1864	1 year.
Eschbach, John	do	18	Sept. 17, 1864	1 year.
Faulkner, Thomas	do	33	Aug. 13, 1862	3 yrs.
Fleig, Gustave	do	..	....	1 year.
Flick, George	do	31	Sept. 10, 1864	1 year.
Franklin, George	do	20	Oct. 25, 1864	1 year.
Freitag, John	do	40	Oct. 13, 1864	1 year.
Fritz, Herman	do	35	Oct. 19, 1864	1 year.
Frommer, Jacob	do	28	Oct. 17, 1864	1 year.
Frommer, Martin	do	21	Oct. 17, 1864	1 year.
Goeppert, Louis	do	..	Oct. 12, 1864	1 year.
Gore, Nathan	do	46	Aug. 22, 1862	3 yrs.
Grenig, Conrad	do	18	Aug. 22, 1864	1 year.
Griffin, Michael	do	33	Sept. 20, 1864	1 year.
Grimmer, Charles A	do	18	Sept. 9, 1864	1 year.
Gross, John	do	41	Mch. 28, 1865	1 year.
Haetty, Joseph	do	38	Aug. 30, 1864	1 year.
Hahn, Henry	do	29	Oct. 8, 1864	1 year.
Hammer, Ernst	do	22	Oct. 20, 1864	1 year.
Hays, Charles	do		Oct. 13, 1864	1 year.
Heintz, Jacob	do	38	Oct. 21, 1864	1 year.
Heller, John	do	20	Oct. 17, 1864	1 year.
Helwig, Louis	do	..	Sept. 16, 1864	1 year.
Hess, Philip	do	23	Sept. 21, 1864	1 year.
Heschong, Michael	do	27	Oct. 12, 1864	1 year.
Hoewiller, George	do	34	Oct. 19, 1864	1 year.
Hoffman, Frederick	do	27	Aug. 22, 1864	1 year.
Huenemeier, Henry	do	30	Oct. 18, 1864	1 year.
Jackson, William	do	18	Oct. 24, 1864	1 year.
Jacobs, Samuel D	do	29	Oct. 18, 1864	1 year.
Kaufman, Adam	do	23	Oct. 31, 1864	1 year.

Names.	Rank.	Age.	Date of Entering the Service.	Period of Service.	Remarks.
[illegible]	Private.	37	Sept. 19, 1864	1 year.	Reduced from Corporal ——.
...d	....do....	18	Jan. 5, 1864	3 yrs.	Transferred from Co. H, 104th O. V. I., June 15, 1865; mustered out July 5, 1865, at Columbus, O., as of Co. H, 104th O. V. I.
...eph F.	....do....	20	Sept. 24, 1864	1 year.	Wounded Nov. 30, 1864, in battle of Franklin, Tenn.; mustered out with company July 17, 1865.
...rank	....do....	29	Jan. 5, 1864	3 yrs.	Transferred from Co. G, 104th O. V. I., June 15, 1865; mustered out with company July 17, 1865.
...an	....do....	18	Mch. 18, 1865	1 year.	Transferred from Co. G, 104th O. V. I., June 15, 1865; mustered out with company July 17, 1865.
...iam R.	....do....	40	Sept. 15, 1864	1 year.	Reduced from Sergeant Dec. 28, 1864; mustered out with company July 17, 1865.
...ld	....do....	19	Sept. 21, 1864	1 year.	Mustered out May 27, 1865, at Albany N. Y., by order of War Department.
...n	....do....	21	Sept. 19, 1864	1 year.	Mustered out with company July 17, 1865.
...e Z.	....do....	18	Oct. 12, 1864	1 year.	Mustered out with company July 17, 1865.
...n	....do....	22	Aug. 5, 1862	3 yrs.	Transferred from Co. H, 104th O. V. I., June 15, 1865; mustered out with company July 17, 1865.
...chariah	....do....	24	Oct. 12, 1864	1 year.	Mustered out with company July 17, 1865.
[illegible]	....do....	28	Oct. 13, 1864	1 year.	Wounded Nov. 30, 1864, in battle of Franklin, Tenn.; mustered out with company July 17, 1865.
...r	....do....	18	Oct. 18, 1864	1 year.	Mustered out with company July 17, 1865.
...rcellus	....do....	26	Sept. 16, 1864	1 year.	Mustered out with company July 17, 1865.
...ace A.	....do....	18	Mch. 7, 1865	1 year.	Transferred from Co. G, 104th O. V. I., June 15, 1865; mustered out with company July 17, 1865.
...e W.	....do....	18	Sept. 16, 1864	1 year.	Mustered out June 27, 1865, at Camp Chase, O., by order of War Department.
...ron T.	....do....	18	Oct. 12, 1864	1 year.	Mustered out July 1, 1865, at David's Island, New York Harbor, by order of War Department.
...rt	....do..	18	Sept. 14, 1864	1 year.	Mustered out with company July 17, 1865.
...S.	....do....	20	Feb. 17, 1864	3 yrs.	Transferred from Co. K, 104th O. V. I., June 15, 1865; mustered out with company July 17, 1865.
...k	....do....	29	Sept. 16, 1864	1 year.	Reduced from Sergeant ——; mustered out with company July 17, 1865.
...mas J.	....do....	19	Oct. 4, 1864	1 year.	Mustered out with company July 17, 1865.
...n D.	....do....	18	Mch. 7, 1865	1 year.	See Co. G, 104th O. V. I.
...n H.	....do....	20	Oct. 12, 1864	1 year.	
[illegible]	....do....	18	Mch. 11, 1865	1 year.	Transferred from Co. G, 104th O. V. I., June 15, 1865; mustered out with company July 17, 1865.
...m	....do....	28	Oct. 12, 1864	1 year.	Mustered out with company July 17, 1865.
...rge W.	....do....	18	Oct. 8, 1864	1 year.	Mustered out with company July 17, 1865.
...S.	....do....	18	Sept. 17, 1864	1 year.	Mustered out with company July 17, 1865.
...is C.	....do....	20	Oct. 8, 1864	1 year.	Wounded Nov. 30, 1864, in battle of Franklin, Tenn.; mustered out June 8, 1865, at De Camp General Hospital, New York Harbor, by order of War Department.
...asey W.	....do....	23	Oct. 3, 1864	1 year.	Mustered out with company July 17, 1865.
...F.	....do....	43	Oct. 14, 1864	1 year.	Mustered out July 7, 1865, at Columbus, O., by order of War Department.
...rus	....do....	34	Oct. 12, 1864	1 year.	Mustered out July 11, 1865, at Columbus, O., by order of War Department.
...L.	....do....	16	Jan. 5, 1864	3 yrs.	See Co. H, 104th O. V. I.
...vid C.	....do....	32	Feb. 24, 1865	1 year.	Transferred from Co. K, 104th O. V. I., June June 15, 1865; mustered out with company July 17, 1865.
...iah	....do....	18	Oct. 12, 1864	1 year.	Died July 7, 1865, at Nashville, Tenn.
...s.	....do....	18	Feb. 29, 1864	3 yrs.	Transferred from Co. H, 104th O. V. I., June 15, 1865; mustered out with company July 17, 1865.
...homas B.	....do....	22	Oct. 3, 1864	1 year.	Mustered out May 29, 1865, at Camp Dennison, O., by order of War Department.
[illegible]	....do....	27	Sept. 17, 1864	1 year.	Captured Nov. 30, 1864, at battle of Franklin, Tenn.; died Jan. 8, 1865, while en route from Corinth, Miss., to Rebel Prison at Andersonville, Ga.
...el	....do....	21	Sept. 28, 1864	1 year.	Mustered out May 29, 1865, at Camp Dennison, O., by order of War Department.
...as	....do....	27	Oct. 8, 1864	1 year.	Mustered out with company July 17, 1865.
[illegible]	....do..	36	Oct. 17, 1864	1 year.	Mustered out with company July 17, 1865.
...D.	....do....	22	Oct. 17, 1864	1 year.	Mustered out with company July 17, 1865.
...rew	....do....	36	Oct. 13, 1864	1 year.	Promoted to Hospital Steward Nov. 19, 1864.
...l	....do....	18	Sept. 19, 1864	1 year.	Mustered out May 27, 1865, at Albany, N. Y., by order of War Department.
...el	....do....	39	Sept. 27, 1864	1 year.	Mustered out May 16, 1865, at Fort Schuyler Hospital, N. Y., by order of War Department.
...on W.	....do....	18	Oct. 7, 1864	1 year.	Mustered out with company July 17, 1865.

Names.	Rank.	Age.	Date of Entering the Service.	Period of Service.	Remarks.
Welch, George	Private..	30	Sept. 1, 1864	1 year.	Prisoner of war; died April 5, 1865, at McPherson Hospital, Vicksburg, Miss.
Weigel, Karl Frederick..	....do...	29	Oct. 22, 1864	1 year.	Mustered out with company July 17, 1865.
Weimar, Michael	....do....	41	Oct. 19, 1864	1 year.	Mustered out with company July 17, 1865.
Wieseford, Matthias	....do....	19	Oct. 19, 1864	1 year.	Mustered out with company July 17, 1865.
Witz, Henry	....do....	34	Aug. 24, 1864	1 year.	Mustered out with company July 17, 1865.

COMPANY I.

Mustered in November 12, 1864, at Camp Dennison, O., by W. Von Doehn, Captain and A. A. G. Mustered out July 17, 1865, at Salisbury, N. C., by Frederick Anderson, — Lieutenant and A. C. M., Department of North Carolina.

Names.	Rank.	Age.	Date of Entering the Service.	Period of Service.	Remarks.
Joseph M. Jackaway	Captain.	33	Oct. 10, 1864	1 year.	Promoted from 1st Sergeant Co. H Nov. 12, 1864; mustered out with company July 17, 1865.
Jacob Jacobs	1st Lieut.	44	Oct. 17, 1864	1 year.	Promoted from Sergeant Co. H, Nov. 12, 1864; mustered out with company July 17, 1865.
Frederic Saeger	2d Lieut.	29	Oct. 7, 1864	1 year.	Promoted from 1st Sergeant Co. B Nov. 15, 1864; to 1st Lieutenant July 10, 1865, but not mustered; mustered out with company July 17, 1865.
John T. Miller	1st Sergt.	31	Oct. 13, 1864	1 year.	Appointed from Sergeant May 16, 1865; mustered out with company July 17, 1865.
Frederick Flatt	Sergeant.	22	Oct. 13, 1864	1 year.	Reduced from 1st Sergeant, at his own request May 14, 1865; mustered out with company July 17, 1865.
Gustave Greeny	....do....	21	Oct. 12, 1864	1 year.	
Ferdinand Herencourt	....do....	22	Nov. 1, 1864	1 year.	Appointed Color Sergeant ——; died Jan. 4, 1865, at Cincinnati, O., of wounds received Nov. 30, 1864, while carrying colors in battle of Franklin, Tenn.
Joseph C. Wagoner	....do....	23	Nov. 4, 1864	1 year.	Appointed from private Dec. 24, 1864; mustered out with company July 17, 1865.
John O. Myers	....do....	24	Mch. 1, 1865	1 year.	Transferred from Co. B, 104th O. V. I., June 15, 1865; mustered out with company July 17, 1865.
John H. McMahon	....do....	32	Oct. 6, 1862	3 yrs.	Transferred from Co. K, 118th O. V. I., June 24, 1865; mustered out with company July 17, 1865.
Warren M. Jones	Corporal.	19	Oct. 4, 1864	1 year.	Mustered out with company July 17, 1865.
Rudolph Keutman	....do....	28	Sept. 5, 1864	1 year.	
Herman Dietrich	....do....	27	Aug. 3, 1864	1 year.	
Charles Miller	....do....	28	Sept. 1, 1864	1 year.	
Henry Mosser	....do....	19	Nov. 1, 1864	1 year.	Appointed Dec. 24, 1864; mustered out with company July 17, 1865.
William Voight	....do....	23	Oct. 4, 1864	1 year.	Appointed April 28, 1865; mustered out with company July 17, 1865.
George W. Coy	....do....	25	Dec. 23, 1863	3 yrs.	Transferred from Co. B, 104th O. V. I., June 15, 1865; appointed Corporal July 3, 1865; mustered out with company July 17, 1865.
William O. Myers	....do....	22	Mch. 1, 1865	1 year.	Transferred from Co. B, 104th O. V. I., June 15, 1865; appointed Corporal July 3, 1865; mustered out with company July 17, 1865.
William Hamilton	....do....	38	Oct. 17, 1862	3 yrs.	Transferred from Co. K, 118th O. V. I., June 24, 1865; mustered out with company July 17, 1865.
John H. Neely	....do....	29	Nov. 7, 1862	3 yrs.	Transferred from Co. K, 118th O. V. I., June 24, 1865; mustered out with company July 17, 1865.
Joseph L. Benn	....do....	19	May 20, 1863	3 yrs.	Transferred from Co. I, 50th O. V. I., June 2?, 1865; mustered out June 13, 1865, at Camp Dennison, O., as of Co. I, 50th O. V. I., by order of War Department.
Abraham B. Gusweller	Musician	16	Oct. 14, 1864	1 year.	Mustered out with company July 17, 1865.
Edward Griner	....do....	19	Oct. 10, 1864	1 year.	Appointed Dec. 14, 1864; mustered out with company July 17, 1865.
Benjamin Impton	Wagoner.	24	Oct. 29, 1864	1 year.	Mustered out with company July 17, 1865.
Albers, Matthew	Private..	22	Sept. 17, 1864	1 year.	Mustered out June 2, 1865, at Louisville, Ky., by order of War Department.
Allen, Edwin H	....do....	22	Sept. 20, 1864	1 year.	
Allen, John	....do....	21	Oct. 12, 1864	1 year.	
Backer, August	....do....	27	Nov. 7, 1864	1 year.	Mustered out May 24, 1865, at Philadelphia, Pa., by order of War Department.
Baker, Philip	....do....	22	Oct. 3, 1864	1 year.	Mustered out with company July 17, 1865.
Banz, Peter	....do....	19	Dec. 28, 1863	3 yrs.	Transferred from Co. E, 104th O. V. I., June 15, 1865; mustered out with company July 17, 1865.
Bauer, George	....do....	29	Sept. 12, 1864	1 year.	
Bedgood, Felix C	....do....	38	Sept. 20, 1864	1 year.	

Names.	Rank.	Age.	Date of Entering the Service.	Period of Service.	Remarks.
Bender, Hiram	Private..	20	Feb. 15, 1864	3 yrs.	Transferred from Co. A, 104th O. V. I., June 15, 1865; mustered out with company July 17, 1865.
Bender, Thomas F.	....do....	18	Jan. 20, 1864	3 yrs.	Transferred from Co. B, 104th O. V. I., June 15, 1865; mustered out with company July 17, 1865.
Bitzenhouser, Wesley	....do....	18	Jan. 28, 1864	3 yrs.	Transferred from Co. B, 104th O. V. I., June 15, 1865; mustered out May 24, 1865, at Philadelphia, Pa., by order of War Department.
Brenninger, William	....do....	43	Oct. 18, 1864	1 year.	Wounded Nov. 30, 1864, in battle of Franklin, Tenn.; discharged July 24, 1865, at West Philadelphia, Pa., on Surgeon's certificate of disability.
Bone, Robert W.	....do....	21	Jan. 29, 1864	3 yrs.	Transferred from Co. F, 104th O. V. I., June 15, 1865; mustered out with company July 17, 1865.
Borgagrein, Peter J.	....do....	19	Dec. 28, 1863	3 yrs.	Transferred from Co. E, 104th O. V. I., June 15, 1865; mustered out with company July 17, 1865.
Bousher, William	....do....	27	Dec. 28, 1863	3 yrs.	Transferred from Co. E, 104th O. V. I., June 15, 1865; mustered out with company July 17, 1865.
Broffman, George	....do....	37	Nov. 10, 1864	1 year.	Drowned Nov. 17, 1864, in Miami River, near Camp Dennison, O.
Brook, John B.	....do....	18	Feb. 3, 1864	1 year.	Transferred from Co. F, 104th O. V. I., June 15, 1865; mustered out with company July 17, 1865.
Brown, Cassius M.	....do....	18	Feb. 2, 1864	3 yrs.	Transferred from Co. E, 104th O. V. I., June 15, 1865; mustered out June 28, 1865, at Louisville, Ky., as of Co. E, 104th O. V. I., by order of War Department.
Chaffee, Nelson	....do....	23	Mch. 21, 1863	3 yrs.	Transferred from Co. D, 104th O. V. I., June 15, 1865; mustered out with company July 17, 1865.
Cooley, Finley	....do....	18	Aug. 25, 1863	3 yrs.	Transferred from Co. C, 104th O. V. I., June 15, 1865; mustered out with company July 17, 1865.
Crider, Joseph	....do....	23	Oct. 18, 1864	1 year.	Mustered out with company July 17, 1865.
Dagy, Calvin	....do....	19	Feb. 29, 1864	3 yrs.	See Co. A, 104th O. V. I.
Davenport, Eugene	....do....	18	Nov. 18, 1863	3 yrs.	Transferred from Co. E, 104th O. V. I., June 15, 1865; mustered out with company July 17, 1865.
Deller, Francis	....do....	21	Oct. 4, 1864	1 year.	Mustered out with company July 17, 1865.
Derbin, John P.	....do....	19	Feb. 9, 1864	3 yrs.	Transferred from Co. F, 104th O. V. I., June 15, 1865; mustered out with company July 17, 1865.
Diehl, Henry	....do....	20	Oct. 13, 1864	1 year.	Reduced from Corporal ——; mustered out with company July 17, 1865.
Dunne, Christopher	....do....	21	Sept. 17, 1864	1 year.	
Early, James	....do....	18	Sept. 19, 1864	1 year.	
Fisher, Christian	....do....	25	Nov. 3, 1864	1 year.	
Fitzgerald, John	....do....	40	Sept. 16, 1864	1 year.	
Flowers, David	....do....	19	Feb. 19, 1864	3 yrs.	Transferred from Co. C, 104th O. V. I., June 15, 1865; mustered out with company July 17, 1865.
Ford, John	....do....	23	Oct. 8, 1864	1 year.	
Fording, Miller	....do....	23	Feb. 18, 1864	3 yrs.	Transferred from Co. A, 104th O. V. I., June 15, 1865; mustered out with company July 17, 1865.
Frase, Jacob	....do....	20	Feb. 29, 1864	3 yrs.	Transferred from Co. A, 104th O. V. I., June 15, 1865; mustered out with company July 17, 1865.
Frazer, James G.	....do....	18	Feb. 24, 1864	3 yrs.	Transferred from Co. C, 104th O. V. I., June 15, 1865; mustered out with company July 17, 1865.
Fritzer, Peter	....do....	19	Sept. 23, 1863	3 yrs.	Transferred from Co. E, 104th O. V. I., June 15, 1865; mustered out with company July 17, 1865.
Gall, August	....do....	21	Nov. 9, 1864	1 year.	
Gardner, Raymond	....do....	22	Oct. 19, 1864	1 year.	Mustered out with company July 17, 1865.
Gesner, Michael	....do....	21	Sept. 2, 1864	1 year	Mustered out with company July 17, 1865.
Gfell, Anthony	....do....	24	Nov. 2, 1864	1 year.	
Gill, James W.	....do....	18	Feb. 9, 1864	3 yrs.	See Co. E, 104th O. V. I.
Haines, John C.	....do....	21	Mch. 25, 1864	3 yrs.	Transferred from Co. I, 104th O. V. I., June 15, 1865; mustered out with company July 17, 1865.
Hatcher, Andrew	....do....	23	Oct. 11, 1864	1 year.	
Hayes, Frank	....do....	19	Oct. 19, 1864	1 year.	
Heiger, John	....do....	23	Oct. 13, 1864	1 year.	Reduced from Sergeant Dec. 23, 1864; mustered out with company July 17, 1865.
Henry, John	....do....	19	Aug. 26, 1864	3 yrs.	See Co. C, 104th O. V. I.
Henry, John	....do....	19	Oct. 4, 1864	1 year.	Transferred from Co. A, 104th O. V. I., June 15, 1865, mustered out with company July 17, 1865.
Hill, Adolph	....do....	27	Nov. 7, 1864	1 year.	Pomoted to Hospital Steward April 14, 1865.

Hill, George	Private..		Nov. 11, [illegible]
Moeller, Frederick	....do....	20	Sept. 2, 1864
Hurtes, Christopher	....do....	28	Oct. 21, 1864
Isaac, John	....do....	40	Sept. 18, 1864
Jeneke, William	....do....	21	Oct. 6, 1864
Jones, Benjamin G	....do....	19	Feb. 5, 1864
Jones, William	....do....	..	....
Kabisius, Herman	....do....	40	Oct. 24, 1864
Kade, John	....do....	19	Aug. 22, 1864
Kalb, Ferdinand	....do....	19	Oct. 27, 1864
Kauhn, George	....do....	19	Sept. 20, 1864
Kelley, Thomas	....do....	24	Sept. 7, 1864
Kinsley, Patrick	....do....	40	Oct. 14, 1864
Klein, Charles	....do....	26	Nov. 6, 1864
Knurr, John	....do....	24	Nov. 7, 1864
Kreiger, Charles	....do....	40	Nov. 7, 1864
Kuva, George	....do....	23	Oct. 29, 1864
Lambert, Louis	....do....	22	Sept. 26, 1864
Leonard, Charles	....do....	18	Feb. 2, 1864
Liebich, Jacob	....do....	27	Aug. 18, 1864
Loser, Joseph	....do....	35	Nov. 17, 1864
Louthan, James N	....do....	22	Aug. 25, 1863
McCartey, Edwin	....do....	20	Sept. 1, 1864
McClellan, James B.	....do....	20	Nov. 7, 1864
McGee, James H	....do....	18	Feb. 2, 1864
McGinness, Charles	....do....	25	Sept. 9, 1864
McGuire, Patrick	....do....	19	Sept. 19, 1864
McMaster, Albert F	....do....	18	Feb. 2, 1864
Maus, Joseph	....do....	39	Nov. 10, 1864
May, Robert	....do....	27	Sept. 5, 1864
Merrick, Gustav	....do....	27	Oct. 14, 1864
Metzner, Joseph	....do....	34	Aug. 27, 1864
Miller, Andrew	....do....	19	Nov. 8, 1864
Miller, Henry	....do....	24	....
Miller, Nicholas	....do....	28	Sept. 12, 1864
Moeller, John	....do....	29	Sept. 17, 1864
Moore, Thomas	....do....	21	Nov. 4, 1864
Morgan, Jameson	....do....	37	Jan. 6, 1864
Monk, Henry	....do....	30	Mch. 8, 1865
Morris, Solon S	....do....	22	Mch. 21, 1864
Muller, Frank	....do....	19	Sept. 12, 1864
Muller, Frederick	....do....	33	Sept. 1, 1864
Murphy, James	....do....	27	Sept. 8, 1864
Nelson, George B	....do....	20	Feb. 23, 1864
Nelson, Thomas	....do....	30	Sept. 9, 1864
Newman, Herman	....do....	30	Oct. 27, 1864
Oakley, William	....do....	22	Aug. 30, 1864
O'Brian, Patrick	....do....	20	Oct. 8, 1864
Packer, Henry	....do....	18	Jan. 28, 1864
Parker, Perry Peter	....do....	39	Sept. 24, 1864
Payne, James	....do....	43	April 26, 1863
Pauli, Michael	....do....	29	Sept. 21, 1864
Purdue, Charles	....do....	19	Oct. 13, 1864
Race, Joseph	....do....	19	Nov. 7, 1862
Raff, Benton	....do....	18	Oct. 8, 1864
Raff, Edwin L.	....do....	21	Oct. 8, 1864

Names.	Rank.	Age.	Date of Entering the Service.	Period of Service.	Remarks.
[illegible], Robert	Private	23	Sept. 12, 1864	1 year.	
[illegible], William D.	....do....	25	Feb. 29, 1864	3 yrs.	See Co. B, 104th O. V. I.
[illegible], William A.	....do....	21	Sept. 16, 1864	1 year.	
[illegible], William	....do....	25	Oct. 19, 1864	1 year.	Mustered out May 18, 1865, at Nashville, Tenn., by order of War Department.
Schmeltzer, Jacob	....do....	43	Nov. 10, 1864	1 year.	Mustered out May 29, 1865, at Camp Dennison, O., by order of War Department.
Schruppe, August	....do....	25	Aug. 23, 1864	1 year.	
[illegible], Henry	....do....	26	Oct. 4, 1864	1 year.	
[illegible], John	....do....	18	Oct. 4, 1864	1 year.	Transferred from Co. A, 104th O. V. I., June 15, 1865; mustered out with company July 17, 1865.
Smith, Charles	....do....	22	Sept. 17, 1864	1 year	Mustered out with company July 17, 1865.
Smith, Thomas	....do....	22	Sept. 19, 1864	1 year.	
Smith, William	....do....	20	Oct. 4, 1864	1 year.	
Staley, Martin	....do....	19	Nov. 7, 1864	1 year.	Captured Nov. 30, 1864, at battle of Franklin, Tenn.; mustered out July 1, 1865, at Camp Chase, O., by order of War Department.
Stitt, Elias	....do....	20	Mch. 4, 1864	3 yrs.	Transferred from Co. F, 104th O. V. I., June 15, 1865; mustered out with company July 17, 1865.
Stitt, Thomas	....do....	18	Mch. 4, 1864	3 yrs.	Transferred from Co. F, 104th O. V. I., June 15, 1865; mustered out with company July 17, 1865.
[illegible], T. M.	....do....	23	Nov. 7, 1864	1 year.	
Sullivan, Thomas	....do....	27	Oct. 12, 1864	1 year.	
[illegible], John	....do....	19	Sept. 20, 1864	1 year.	
[illegible], John	....do....	19	Nov. 2, 1864	1 year.	
Thomas, Uriah	....do....	49	Oct. 28, 1862	3 yrs.	Transferred from Co. C, 104th O. V. I., June 15, 1865; mustered out with company July 17, 1865.
Thompson, Andrew J.	....do....	18	Nov. 11, 1863	3 yrs.	Transferred from Co. I, 104th O. V. I., June 15, 1865; mustered out with company July 17, 1865.
Turner, Edward F.	....do....	30	Sept. 17, 1864	1 year.	
Tweedy, William	....do....	22	Feb. 2, 1864	3 yrs.	Transferred from Co. E, 104th O. V. I., June 15, 1865; mustered out with company July 17, 1865.
Underwood, Jesse	....do....	29	Feb. 19, 1864	3 yrs.	Transferred from Co. C, 104th O. V. I., June 15, 1865; mustered out with company July 17, 1865.
Vennes, Robert	....do....	24	Nov. 8, 1864	1 year.	Mustered out June 25, 1865, at Louisville, Ky., by order of War Department.
Warden, John	....do....	25	Feb. 24, 1864	3 yrs.	Transferred from Co. F, 104th O. V. I., June 15, 1865; mustered out with company July 17, 1865.
Wurts, Frederick	....do....	26	Oct. 28, 1864	1 year.	Mustered out with company July 17, 1865.
Yant, James	....do....	22	Oct. 3, 1864	1 year.	Transferred from Co. A, 104th O. V. I., June 15, 1865; mustered out with company July 17, 1865.

COMPANY K.

Mustered in November 18, 1864, at Camp Dennison, O., by W. Von Doehn, Captain and A. A. G. Mustered out July 17, 1865, at Salisbury, N. C., by Frederick Anderson, — Lieutenant and A. C. M., Department of North Carolina.

Names.	Rank.	Age.	Date of Entering the Service.	Period of Service.	Remarks.
Charles Nichols	Captain.	41	Nov. 15, 1864	1 year.	Died Jan. 15, 1865, at Clifton, Tenn.
George Forester	....do....	37	Aug. 29, 1864	1 year.	Promoted from 1st Lieutenant Co. C Jan. 24, 1865; mustered out with company July 17, 1865.
Elijah S. Hill	1st	61	Nov. 21, 1864	1 year.	Resigned Feb. 28, 1865.
Edgar J. Wells	...	21	July 4, 1862	3 yrs.	Transferred from Co. A, 80th O. V. I., June 26, 1865; mustered out with company July 17, 1865.
Adam Wampool	2d Lieut.	36	Nov. 15, 1864	1 year.	Promoted to 1st Lieutenant July 10, 1865, but not mustered; mustered out with company July 17, 1865.
Festus C. Hays	1st Sergt.	27	Oct. 14, 1864	1 year.	Mustered out June 6, 1865, at David's Island, New York Harbor, by order of War Department.
Abraham Sullivan	Sergeant.	30	Oct. 3, 1864	1 year.	Mustered out with company July 17, 1865.
Francis M. Bradford	....do....	24	Oct. 16, 1864	1 year.	Appointed from private Feb. 16, 1865; mustered out with company July 17, 1865.
Alvin Gear	....do....	18	Oct. 21, 1864	1 year.	Appointed Corporal Dec. 26, 1864; Sergeant March 12, 1865; mustered out with company July 17, 1865.
...	....do....	34	Oct. 10, 1864	1 year.	Appointed from Corporal Jan. 1, 1865; mustered out with company July 17, 1865.

Names.	Rank.	Age.	Date of Entering the Service.	Period of Service.	Remarks.
Samuel Bidwell	Corporal.	19	Oct. 12, 1864	1 year.	Wounded Nov. 30, 1864, in battle of Franklin, Tenn.; mustered out June 9, 1865, at Camp Dennison, O., by order of War Department.
Abraham Beal	....do....	22	....	......	
Richard T. Boyce	....do....	17	Sept. 24, 1864	1 year.	Mustered out June 2, 1865, at Cincinnati, O., by order of War Department.
William Donely	....do....	22	Oct. 3, 1864	1 year.	Missing Nov. 30, 1864, at battle of Franklin, Tenn. No further record found.
William G. Nash	....do....	23	Oct. 3, 1864	1 year.	Mustered out with company July 17, 1865.
Revilow Spohn	....do....	18	Oct. 17, 1864	1 year.	Appointed Feb. 16, 1865; mustered out with company July 17, 1865.
Adrian Muttock	....do....	22	Nov. 14, 1864	1 year.	Appointed March 12, 1865; mustered out with company July 17, 1865.
William B. Zercher	....do....	18	Oct. 17, 1864	1 year.	Appointed June 1, 1865; mustered out with company July 17, 1865.
James M. Rigby	....do. ..	19	Feb. 24, 1864	3 yrs.	Transferred from Co. K, 118th O. V. I., June 24, 1865; mustered out with company July 17, 1865.
Naaman T. Moore	....do....	22	July 1, 1863	3 yrs.	See Co. H, 118th O. V. I.
George W. Burns	Musician	18	Sept. 20, 1864	1 year.	Mustered out with company July 17, 1865.
David McKee	....do....	16	Sept. 16, 1864	1 year.	Mustered out with company July 17, 1865.
Thomas Hise	Wagoner.	44	Oct. 17, 1864	1 year.	Mustered out with company July 17, 1865.
Allen, Isaac	Private..	17	Feb. 29, 1864	1 year.	See Co. I, 118th O. V. I.
Anderson, Henry	....do....	24	Sept. 19, 1864	1 year.	
Antony, Richard	....do....	21	Sept. 3, 1864	1 year.	
Arnett, James	....do....	18	Oct. 7, 1864	1 year.	Transferred to 22d Regiment, Veteran Reserve Corps, April 1, 1865; mustered out July 28, 1865, at Camp Chase, O., by order of War Department.
Ash, Jacob	....do....	18	Oct. 22, 1864	1 year.	Mustered out with company July 17, 1865.
Baker, Elias	....do. ..	19	Nov. 4, 1862	3 yrs.	Transferred from Co. I, 118th O. V. I., June 24, 1865; mustered out with company July 17, 1865.
Baumgardner, W. J	....do....	30	Sept. 27, 1864	1 year.	Prisoner of war; perished by explosion of steamer Sultana, on Mississippi River, near Memphis, Tenn., April 27, 1865.
Beltz, Henry	....do....	37	Aug. 15, 1862	3 yrs.	Transferred from Co. E, 118th O. V. I., June 24, 1865; mustered out with company July 17, 1865.
Bisbing, William	....do....	23	Nov. 12, 1864	1 year.	
Boyle, Richard	....do....	28	Oct. 6, 1864	1 year.	
Brown, John	....do....	22	Aug. 20, 1864	1 year	Mustered out with company July 17, 1865.
Brown, Joshua	....do....	18	Oct. 21, 1864	1 year	Died May 22, 18—, at Troy, N. Y.
Buckner, William I	....do....	25	Oct. 3, 1864	1 year.	
Bull, William	....do....	23	Feb. 26, 1864	3 yrs.	Transferred from Co. I, 118th O. V. I., June 24, 1865; mustered out with company July 17, 1865.
Burton, Basil C.	....do....	22	Feb. 26, 1864	3 yrs.	Transferred from Co. I, 118th O. V. I., June 24, 1865; mustered out with company July 17, 1865.
Byrum, James	....do....	31	Aug. 15, 1862	3 yrs.	Transferred from Co. E, 118th O. V. I., June 24, 1865; mustered out to date July 17, 1865, by order of War Department.
Cadle, William	....do....	28	Sept. 13, 1864	1 year.	
Calopy, John J.	....do....	30	Sept. 19, 1864	1 year.	
Campbell, Theodore	....do....	19	Feb. 22, 1864	3 yrs.	Transferred from Co. I, 118th O. V. I., June 24, 1865; mustered out with company July 17, 1865.
Casperson, Adam M.	....do....	28	Feb. 2, 1864	3 yrs.	See Co. E, 118th O. V. I.
Clark, Charles	....do....	22	Sept. 19, 1864	1 year	
Closby, William	....do....	27	Nov. 12, 1864	1 year	
Closson, Robert	....do....	45	Aug. 13, 1862	3 yrs.	See Co. E, 118th O. V. I.
Coburn, Michael	....do....	22	Sept. 23, 1864	1 year.	
Conley, Patrick	....do....	19	Sept. 18, 1864	1 year.	
Conlon, James	....do. ..	21	Oct. 12, 1864	1 year.	
Corban, Elisha	....do. ..	44	Sept. 29, 1864	1 year.	Mustered out to date July 17, 1865, by order of War Department.
Conghenour, Rudolph	....do....	40	Sept. 23, 1864	1 year.	Reduced from Corporal ——.
Coulter, Americus	....do....	39	Nov. 11, 1864	1 year.	Mustered out with company July 17, 1865.
Crisp, Evanoe	....do....	18	April 11, 1864	3 yrs.	Transferred from Co. A, 118th O. V. I., June 24, 1865; mustered out with company July 17, 1865.
Culp, Samuel	....do....	24	Oct. 21, 1864	1 year.	Captured Nov. 30, 1864, at battle of Franklin, Tenn.; died Feb. 28, 1865, in Rebel Prison at Columbia, Ala.
Curl, William B.	....do....	25	Oct. 18, 1864	1 year.	Mustered out June 30, 1865, at St. Louis, Mo., by order of War Department
Curtis, Lucien B	....do....	20	June 21, 1863	3 yrs.	Transferred from Co. F, 118th O. V. I., June 24, 1865; mustered out with company July 17, 1865.
Davidson, Matthias	....do....	29	Aug. 13, 1862	3 yrs.	Transferred from Co. E, 118th O. V. I., June 24, 1865; mustered out with company July 17, 1865.
Deed, James K	....do....	20	Dec. 26, 1863	3 yrs.	Transferred from Co. G, 118th O. V. I., June 24, 1865; mustered out with company July 17, 1865.

...k.	Age.	Date of Entering the Service.	Period of Service.	Remarks.
....	18	Dec. 28, 1863	3 yrs.	Transferred from Co. G, 118th O.V. I., June 24, 1865; mustered out with company July 17, 1865.
....	19	Sept. 13, 1864	1 year.	
....	20	Sept. 29, 1864	1 year.	Reduced from Sergeant Dec. 25, 1864; mustered out July 6, 1865, at Columbus, O., by order of War Department.
....	16	Feb. 29, 1864	3 yrs.	Transferred from Co. I, 118th O. V. I., June 24, 1865; mustered out with company July 17, 1865.
....	20	Oct. 4, 1864	1 year.	Mustered out with company July 17, 1865.
....	18	Nov. 1, 1864	1 year.	Missing Nov. 30, 1864, at battle of Franklin, Tenn. No further record found.
....	21	Nov. 2, 1864	1 year.	
....	16	Oct. 8, 1864	1 year.	Mustered out with company July 17, 1865.
....	18	Oct. 10, 1864	1 year.	Mustered out with company July 17, 1865.
....	23	Feb. 22, 1864	3 yrs.	Transferred from Co. I, 118th O. V. I., June 24, 1865; mustered out with company July 17, 1865.
....	26	Oct. 3, 1864	1 year.	Reduced from Sergeant March 12, 1865; mustered out with company July 17, 1865.
....	21	Nov. 8, 1864	1 year.	Mustered out with company July 17, 1865.
....	33	Oct. 8, 1864	1 year.	Mustered out with company July 17, 1865.
....	18	Oct. 24, 1864	1 year.	Mustered out with company July 17, 1865.
....	17	Sept. 4, 1864	1 year.	Mustered out with company July 17, 1865.
....	24	Nov. 12, 1864	1 year.	
....	21	Nov. 12, 1864	1 year.	
....	29	Feb. 26, 1864	1 year.	Transferred from Co. I, 118th O. V. I., June 24, 1865; mustered out with company July 17, 1865.
....	26	Feb. 26, 1864	1 year.	Transferred from Co. I, 118th O. V. I., June 24, 1865; mustered out with company July 17, 1865.
....	21	Oct. 7, 1864	1 year.	Reduced from Sergeant March 1, 1865; mustered out with company July 17, 1865.
....	35	Oct. 25, 1864	1 year.	
....	21	Oct. 17, 1864	1 year.	Reduced from Corporal ——.
....	28	Oct. 8, 1864	1 year.	Mustered out June 8, 1865, at Albany, N. Y., by order of War Department.
....	31	Sept. 22, 1864	1 year.	Wounded Dec. 15, 1864, in battle of Nashville, Tenn.; mustered out June 15, 1865, at Washington, D. C., by order of War Department.
....	36	Oct. 10, 1864	1 year.	Died April 3, 1865, in hospital at Lexington, Kentucky.
....	24	June 1, 1863	3 yrs.	Transferred from Co. I, 118th O. V. I., June 24, 1865; sick ——, at Charleston, Tenn. No further record found.
....	34	Oct. 26, 1864	1 year.	
....	18	Oct. 3, 1864	1 year.	Mustered out with company July 17, 1865.
....	22	Dec. 24, 1863	3 yrs.	Transferred from Co. K, 118th O. V. I., June 24, 1865; mustered out with company July 17, 1865.
....	19	Oct. 3, 1864	1 year.	Mustered out with company July 17, 1865.
....	20	Sept. 24, 1864	1 year.	Mustered out with company July 17, 1865.
....	40	Feb. 26, 1864	1 year.	Transferred from Co. E, 118th O. V. I., June 24, 1865; mustered out with company July 17, 1865.
....	23	Oct. 24, 1864	1 year.	Mustered out with company July 17, 1865.
....	44	Oct. 10, 1864	1 year.	Died Jan 29, 1865, at Camp Dennison, O.
....	22	Oct. 1, 1864	1 year.	Mustered out with company July 17, 1865.
....	21	Mch. 5, 1864	3 yrs.	Transferred from Co. A, 118th O.V. I., June 24, 1865; mustered out with company July 17, 1865.
....	41	Oct. 8, 1864	1 year.	Mustered out June 5, 1865, at Washington, D.C.
....	44	Oct. 11, 1864	1 year.	Mustered out with company July 17, 1865.
....	21	Oct. 3, 1864	1 year.	Died Feb. 14, 1865, in hospital at Washington, District of Columbia.
....	18	Oct. 13, 1864	1 year.	Wounded Nov. 30, 1864, in battle of Franklin, Tenn.; mustered out July 7, 1865, at Washington, D. C., by order of War Department.
....	28	Nov. 17, 1864	1 year.	Mustered out with company July 17, 1865.
....	16	....	....	Missing Nov. 30, 1864, at battle of Franklin, Tenn. No further record found.
....	22	Sept. 22, 1864	1 year.	Mustered out with company July 17, 1865.
....	18	Nov. 3, 1864	1 year.	Mustered out with company July 17, 1865.
....	25	Nov. 11, 1864	1 year.	Mustered out June 9, 1865, at Washington, D. C., by order of War Department.
....	28	Oct. 4, 1864	1 year.	Missing Nov. 30, 1864, at battle of Franklin, Tenn. No further record found.
....	24	Nov. 1, 1864	1 year.	
....	18	Feb. 22, 1864	3 yrs.	Transferred from Co. I, 118th O. V. I., June 24, 1865; mustered out with company July 17, 1865.
....	25	Nov. 12, 1864	1 year.	
....	30	Nov. 10, 1863	3 yrs.	Transferred from Co. D, 118th O.V. I., June 24, 1865; mustered out with company July 17, 1865.

Names.	Rank.	Age.	Date of Entering the Service.	Period of Service.	Remarks.
Oglesby, David	Private	37	Sept. 29, 1864	1 year.	Mustered out with company July 17, 1865.
Oliver, Thomas	....do....	18	Oct. 18, 1864	1 year.	Captured Nov. 30, 1864, at battle of Franklin, Tenn.; perished by explosion of steamer Sultana, on Mississippi River, near Memphis, Tenn., April 27, 1865.
Panabaker, Washington	....do....	26	Sept. 27, 1862	3 yrs.	Transferred from Co. K, 118th O.V. I., June 24, 1865; mustered out with company July 17, 1865.
Perkins, James	....do....	19	April 21, 1864	3 yrs.	Transferred from Co. A, 118th O. V. I., June 24, 1865; mustered out with company July 17, 1865.
Purcell, Burr P	....do....	27	Nov. 8, 1864	1 year.	Mustered out with company July 17, 1865.
Rhodes, George	....do....	28	Nov. 17, 1864	1 year.	Mustered out with company July 17, 1865.
Rittles, James	....do....	19	Feb. 26, 1864	3 yrs.	See Co. E, 118th O. V. I.
Ritz, Samuel D	....do....	32	Oct. 26, 1864	1 year.	Mustered out with company July 17, 1865.
Rogers, Morris	....do....	19	Nov. 11, 1864	1 year.	Mustered out June 19, 1865, at Camp Chase, O., by order of War Department.
Rupert, Jacob	....do....	27	Mch. 5, 1864	3 yrs.	Transferred from Co. E, 118th O.V. I., June 24, 1865; mustered out with company July 17, 1865.
Smith, John H	....do....	22	Oct. 17, 1864	1 year.	
Strawbridge, Samuel	....do....	25	Sept. 22, 1864	1 year.	Wounded Nov. 30, 1864, in battle of Franklin, Tenn.; died March 11, 1865, in Rebel Prison at Cahaba, Ala.
Sulcer, Lucian B	....do....	18	Oct. 22, 1864	1 year.	Mustered out with company July 17, 1865.
Sullivan, Thomas	....do....	18	Feb. 26, 1864	3 yrs.	Transferred from Co. E, 118th O.V. I., June 24, 1865; mustered out with company July 17, 1865.
Summers, William	....do....	26	Oct. 18, 1864	1 year	Mustered out with company July 17, 1865.
Titus, Lewis	....do....	18	Feb. 26, 1864	3 yrs.	See Co. E, 118th O. V. I.
Trentham, John	....do....	27	Nov. 12, 1864	1 year.	
Truesdell, Joseph	....do....	44	Oct. 10, 1864	1 year.	Mustered out with company July 17, 1865.
Walker, Abraham	....do....	33	Oct. 2, 1864	1 year.	Killed Nov. 30, 1864, in battle of Franklin, Tennessee.
Walters, Henry	....do....	18	Sept. 30, 1864	1 year.	Transferred from Co. H, 118th O.V. I., June 24, 1865; died July 16, 1865, at Greensboro, N.C.
Watson, William	....do....	20	Nov. 16, 1864	1 year.	
Weaver, John H	....do....	18	Feb. 27, 1864	1 year.	Transferred from Co. I, 118th O. V. I., June 24, 1865; mustered out with company July 24, 1865.
Wiles, William	....do....	18	Oct. 10, 1864	1 year.	Mustered out with company July 17, 1865.
Wright, Thomas J	....do....	22	Nov. 11, 1864	1 year.	
Wymar, Joseph	....do....	22	Oct 24, 1864	1 year.	Mustered out with company July 17, 1865.
Zimmerman, John	....do....	18	Feb. 26, 1864	3 yrs.	Transferred from Co. E, 118th O. V. I., June 24, 1865; mustered out with company July 17, 1865.

UNASSIGNED RECRUITS.

NOTE.—The following list of recruits is found on muster and descriptive rolls of this organization but not borne on any of the company rolls of this Regiment.

Names.	Rank.	Age.	Date of Entering the Service.	Period of Service.	Remarks.
Adkins, Harrison	Private	35	Aug. 9, 1864	1 year.	
Allen, David	....do....	18	Aug. 24, 1864	1 year	
Burnett, William	....do....	41	Aug. 26, 1864	1 year	
Canter, William	....do....	30	Aug. 30, 1864	1 year.	Mustered out Sept. 16, 1865, at Columbus, O., by order of War Department.
Carey, Andrew J	....do....	18	Sept 12, 1864	1 year.	
Fincke, August	....do....	30	April 5, 1865	1 year.	Mustered out May 15, 1865, at Hart Island, New York Harbor, by order of War Department.
Gates, Alexander	....do....	21	Aug. 31, 1864	1 year.	
Gilruth, Henry C	....do....	19	Aug. 25, 1864	1 year.	
Hethington, Henry H	....do....	23	July 30, 1864	1 year.	
Halley, William R	....do....	42	Aug. 15, 1864	1 year.	
Hall, Bickman	....do....	38	Nov. 15, 1864	1 year.	
Kuth, Emanuel	....do....	21	Aug. 31, 1864	1 year.	
Liday, Daniel	....do....	30	Sept. 6, 1864	1 year.	
McKinley, William	....do....	25	Aug. 26, 1864	1 year.	
Murvin, James H	....do....	23	Sept. 10, 1864	1 year.	
Park, Rufus H	....do....	31	Oct. 10, 1864	1 year.	
Pool, William	....do....	27	Aug. 11, 1864	1 year.	
Rose, Thomas M	....do....	21	Nov. 15, 1864	1 year.	
Sheppard, Daniel W	....do....	33	Aug. 26, 1864	1 year.	
Smith, Jefferson	....do....	18	Aug. 26, 1864	1 year.	
Watts, Franklin A	....do....	25	Oct. 3, 1864	1 year.	
Williams, William H	....do....	23	Sept. 19, 1864	1 year.	
Wilson, Robert	....do....	29	Sept. 24, 1864	1 year.	

184th Regiment Ohio Volunteer Infantry.

ONE YEAR'S SERVICE.

This Regiment was organized at Camp Chase, O., in February, 1865, to serve one year. Immediately after muster-in the Regiment was ordered to Nashville, Tenn., where it remained for a short time doing garrison duty. From Nashville it proceeded to Chattanooga, thence to Bridgeport, Alabama, which place it reached about the 21st of March, and was engaged in protecting an important railroad bridge over the Tennessee River. It also guarded the track of the railroad between Bridgeport and Chattanooga, a distance of about thirty miles. On the 25th of July the One Hundred and Eighty-fourth. was ordered to Edgefield, for garrison duty, and remained at that place until it was mustered out of service, September 20, 1865, at Nashville, Tenn.

Names.	Rank.	Age.	Date of Entering the Service.	Period of Service.	Remarks.
Hill, George	Private	20	Nov. 11, 1864	1 year.	Wounded Nov. 30, 1864, in battle of Franklin Tenn.; died ——, in Rebel Prison at Andersonville, Ga.
Hoeller, Frederick	do	20	Sept. 2, 1864	1 year.	
Huries, Christopher	do	28	Oct. 21, 1864	1 year.	
Isaac, John	do	40	Sept. 13, 1864	1 year.	
Jeneke, William	do	21	Oct. 8, 1864	1 year.	
Jones, Benjamin G	do	19	Feb. 5, 1864	3 yrs.	See Co. F, 104th O. V. I.
Jones, William	do	..	....	1 year.	
Kabisius, Herman	do	40	Oct. 24, 1864	1 year.	Drowned Nov. 19, 1864, in Ohio River, by falling overboard from steamer Prima Donna.
Kade, John	do	19	Aug. 22, 1864	1 year.	
Kalb, Ferdinand	do	19	Oct. 27, 1864	1 year.	Mustered out with company July 17, 1865.
Kauhn, George	do	19	Sept. 20, 1864	1 year.	
Kelley, Thomas	do	24	Sept. 7, 1864	1 year.	
Kinsley, Patrick	do	40	Oct. 14, 1864	1 year.	Transferred from Co. B, 104th O. V. I., June 15, 1865; mustered out with company July 17, 1865.
Klein, Charles	do	26	Nov. 6, 1864	1 year.	
Knurr, John	do	24	Nov. 7, 1864	1 year.	Mustered out with company July 17, 1865.
Kreiger, Charles	do	40	Nov. 7, 1864	1 year.	Mustered out with company July 17, 1865; also borne on rolls as Charles Krueger.
Kuva, George	do	23	Oct. 29, 1864	1 year.	Reduced from Corporal April 28, 1865; mustered out with company July 17, 1865.
Lambert, Louis	do	22	Sept. 26, 1864	1 year.	
Leonard, Charles	do	18	Feb. 2, 1864	3 yrs.	Transferred from Co. F, 104th O. V. I., June 15, 1865; mustered out with company July 17, 1865.
Liebich, Jacob	do	27	Aug. 13, 1864	1 year.	Mustered as Musician.
Loeser, Joseph	do	35	Nov. 17, 1864	1 year.	Mustered out with company July 17, 1865.
Louthan, James N	do	22	Aug. 25, 1863	3 yrs.	Transferred from Co. C, 104th O. V. I., June 15, 1865; mustered out with company July 17, 1865.
McCartey, Edwin	do	20	Sept. 1, 1864	1 year.	
McClellan, James B.	do	30	Nov. 7, 1864	1 year.	
McGee, James H	do	18	Feb. 2, 1864	3 yrs.	Transferred from Co. F, 104th O. V. I., June 15, 1865; mustered out with company July 17, 1865.
McGinness, Charles	do	25	Sept. 9, 1861	1 year.	Mustered out with company July 17, 1865.
McGuire, Patrick	do	19	Sept. 19, 1864	1 year.	
McMaster, Albert F.	do	18	Feb. 2, 1864	3 yrs.	See Co. F, 104th O. V. I.
Maus, Joseph	do	39	Nov. 10, 1864	1 year.	Mustered out with company July 17, 1865.
May, Robert	do	27	Sept. 5, 1864	1 year.	
Merrick, Gustav	do	27	Oct. 14, 1864	1 year.	
Metzner, Joseph	do	34	Aug. 27, 1864	1 year.	
Miller, Andrew	do	19	Nov. 8, 1864	1 year.	Mustered out with company July 17, 1865.
Miller, Henry	do	24	....	1 year.	
Miller, Nicholas	do	28	Sept. 12, 1864	1 year.	
Moeller, John	do	29	Sept. 17, 1864	1 year.	
Moore, Thomas	do	21	Nov. 4, 1864	1 year.	
Morgan, Jameson	do	37	Jan. 6, 1864	3 yrs.	Transferred from Co. E, 104th O. V. I., June 15, 1865; mustered out with company July 17, 1865.
Monk, Henry	do	30	Mch. 3, 1865	1 year.	Transferred from Co. B, 104th O. V. I., June 15, 1865; mustered out with company July 17, 1865.
Morris, Solon S	do	22	Mch. 21, 1864	3 yrs.	Transferred from Co. C, 104th O. V. I., June 15, 1865; mustered out with company July 17, 1865.
Muller, Frank	do	19	Sept. 12, 1861	1 year.	
Muller, Frederick	do	33	Sept. 1, 1864	1 year.	
Murphy, James	do	27	Sept. 8, 1864	1 year.	
Nelson, George B	do	20	Feb. 23, 1864	3 yrs.	Transferred from Co. B, 104th O. V. I., June 15, 1865; mustered out with company July 17, 1865.
Nelson, Thomas	do	30	Sept. 9, 1864	1 year.	
Newman, Herman	do	30	Oct. 27, 1864	1 year.	
Oakley, William	do	22	Aug. 30, 1864	1 year	
O'Brian, Patrick	do	20	Oct. 3, 1864	1 year.	
Packer, Henry	do	18	Jan. 28, 1864	3 yrs.	Transferred from Co. B, 104th O. V. I., June 15, 1865; mustered out with company July 17, 1865.
Parker, Perry Peter	do	39	Sept. 21, 1864	1 year.	
Payne, James	do	43	April 26, 1863	3 yrs.	Transferred from Co. D, 104th O. V. I., June 15, 1865; mustered out with company July 17, 1865.
Pauli, Michael	do	29	Sept. 21, 1864	1 year.	
Purdue, Charles	do	19	Oct. 13, 1864	1 year.	
Race, Joseph	do	19	Nov. 7, 1862	3 yrs.	Transferred from Co. E, 104th O. V. I., June 15, 1865; mustered out with company July 17, 1865.
Raff, Benton	do	18	Oct. 3, 1864	1 year.	Transferred from Co. A, 104th O. V. I., June 15, 1865; mustered out with company July 17, 1865.
Raff, Edwin L	do	21	Oct. 3, 1864	1 year.	Transferred from Co. A, 104th O. V. I., June 15, 1865; mustered out with company July 17, 1865.

	Rank.	Age.	Date of Entering the Service.	Period of Service.	Remarks.
...gton, Robert		22	Sept. 12, 1864	1 year.	
...chneider, William D		25	Feb. 29, 1864	3 yrs.	See Co. B, 104th O. V. I.
...son, William		21	Sept. 16, 1864	1 year.	
..., William		25	Oct. 19, 1864	1 year.	Mustered out May 18, 1865, at Nashville, Tenn., by order of War Department.
...eltzer, Jacob		43	Nov. 10, 1864	1 year.	Mustered out May 29, 1865, at Camp Dennison O., by order of War Department.
...ppe, August		23	Aug. 23, 1864	1 year.	
...idt, Henry		25	Oct. 4, 1864	1 year.	
...ley, John		18	Oct. 4, 1864	1 year.	Transferred from Co. A, 104th O. V. I., June 15, 1865; mustered out with company July 17, 1865.
..., Charles		22	Sept. 17, 1864	1 year	Mustered out with company July 17, 1865.
..., Thomas		22	Sept. 19, 1864	1 year.	
..., William		20	Oct. 4, 1864	1 year.	
..., Martin		19	Nov. 7, 1864	1 year.	Captured Nov. 30, 1864, at battle of Franklin, Tenn.; mustered out July 1, 1865, at Camp Chase, O., by order of War Department.
Elias		20	Mch. 4, 1864	3 yrs.	Transferred from Co. F, 104th O. V. I., June 15, 1865; mustered out with company July 17, 1865.
Thomas	do	18	Mch. 4, 1864	3 yrs.	Transferred from Co. F, 104th O. V. I., June 15, 1865; mustered out with company July 17, 1865.
..., T. M.		23	Nov. 7, 1864	1 year.	
...an, Thomas		27	Oct. 12, 1864	1 year.	
..., John		19	Sept. 20, 1864	1 year.	
...as, John		19	Nov. 2, 1864	1 year.	
...as, Uriah		40	Oct. 28, 1862	3 yrs.	Transferred from Co. C, 104th O. V. I., June 15, 1865; mustered out with company July 17, 1865.
...pson, Andrew J.	do	18	Nov. 11, 1863	3 yrs.	Transferred from Co. I, 104th O. V. I., June 15, 1865; mustered out with company July 17, 1865.
...er, Edward F.	do	20	Sept. 17, 1864	1 year.	
...dy, William	do	22	Feb. 2, 1864	3 yrs.	Transferred from Co. E, 104th O. V. I., June 15, 1865; mustered out with company July 17, 1865.
...rwood, Jesse	do	29	Feb. 19, 1864	3 yrs.	Transferred from Co. C, 104th O. V. I., June 15, 1865; mustered out with company July 17, 1865.
...es, Robert	do	24	Nov. 8, 1864	1 year.	Mustered out June 28, 1865, at Louisville, Ky., by order of War Department.
...en, John	do	25	Feb. 24, 1864	3 yrs.	Transferred from Co. F, 104th O. V. I., June 15, 1865; mustered out with company July 17, 1865.
..., Frederick	do	26	Oct. 28, 1864	1 year.	Mustered out with company July 17, 1865.
..., James	do	22	Oct. 3, 1864	1 year.	Transferred from Co. A, 104th O. V. I., June 15, 1865; mustered out with company July 17, 1865.

COMPANY K.

...ered in November 18, 1864, at Camp Dennison, O., by W. Von Doehn, Captain and A. A. G. Mustered out July 17, 1865, at Salisbury, N. C., by Frederick Anderson, — Lieutenant and A. C. M., Department of North Carolina.

...es Nichols	Captain.	41	Nov. 15, 1864	1 year.	Died Jan. 15, 1865, at Clifton, Tenn.
... Foerster	do	37	Aug. 29, 1864	1 year.	Promoted from 1st Lieutenant Co. C Jan. 24, 1865; mustered out with company July 17, 1865.
...h B. Hill	1st Lieut.	61	Nov. 21, 1864	1 year.	Resigned Feb. 28, 1865.
...r J. Wells	do	21	July 4, 1862	3 yrs.	Transferred from Co. A, 80th O. V. I., June 26, 1865; mustered out with company July 17, 1865.
...n Wampool	2d Lieut.	36	Nov. 15, 1864	1 year.	Promoted to 1st Lieutenant July 10, 1865, but not mustered; mustered out with company July 17, 1865.
...n C. Hays	1st Sergt.	27	Oct. 14, 1864	1 year.	Mustered out June 6, 1865, at David's Island, New York Harbor, by order of War Department.
...ham Sullivan	Sergeant.	30	Oct. 3, 1864	1 year.	Mustered out with company July 17, 1865.
...cis M. Sandford	do	24	Oct. 16, 1864	1 year.	Appointed from private Feb. 16, 1865; mustered out with company July 17, 1865.
Gear	do	18	Oct. 21, 1864	1 year.	Appointed Corporal Dec. 25, 1864; Sergeant March 12, 1865; mustered out with company July 17, 1865.
...icus Hise	do	24	Oct. 10, 1864	1 year.	Appointed from Corporal Jan. 1, 1865; mustered out with company July 17, 1865.

Names.	Rank.	Age.	Date of Entering the Service.	Period of Service.
William Caswell	Musician	17	Jan. 21, 1865	1 year.
Aydelott, Benjamin L	Private	19	Jan. 17, 1865	1
Beach, Richard F. H	do	18	Jan. 25, 1865	1
Beardshear, William M	do	18	Jan. 24, 1865	1
Benham, James	do	20	Jan. 16, 1865	1 year.
Benham, John M	do	26	Jan. 16, 1865	1 year.
Bennett, Wallace	do	24	Feb. 11, 1865	1 year.
Bloom, Peter	do	28	Jan. 11, 1865	1 year.
Blum, John F.	do	29	Jan. 21, 1865	1 year.
Bredbenner, Hiram	do	20	Jan. 23, 1865	1 year.
Brentz, Dwight	do	24	Jan. 21, 1865	1 year.
Brownfield, Samuel A	do	18	Jan. 21, 1865	1 year.
Campbell, Francis M	do	18	Jan. 23, 1865	1 year.
Cisle, Thomas J	do	42	Feb. 2, 1865	1 year.
Cranvell, Charles	do	19	Jan. 16, 1865	1 year.
Dillman, Milton	do	18	Feb. 2, 1865	1 year.
Dye, Abbott	do	27	Jan. 13, 1865	1 year.
Emrick, Peter	do	24	Jan. 31, 1865	1 year.
Falk, Jacob	do	31	Feb. 2, 1865	1 year.
Foreman, George	do	40	Jan. 17, 1865	1 year.
Fugate, Marion	do	30	Jan. 26, 1865	1 year.
Funk, James	do	20	Jan. 24, 1865	1 year.
Funk, Samuel J	do	24	Jan. 24, 1865	1 year.
Gephart, Sidney B	do	22	Jan. 24, 1865	1 year.
Gorton, Tyler W	do	39	Jan. 10, 1865	1 year.
Hagar, Nicholas	do	43	Jan. 27, 1865	1 year.
Harris, Charles	do	18	Jan. 28, 1865	1 year.
Hearn, Samuel	do	20	Jan. 18, 1865	1 year.
Heffner, Israel	do	18	Jan. 28, 1865	1 year.
Hiltman, John	do	42	Jan. 16, 1865	1 year.
Hinkle, Francis	do	18	Jan. 30, 1865	1 year.
Howe, Joseph P.	do	40	Jan. 20, 1865	1 year.
Hunter, Henry	do	19	Jan. 7, 1865	1 year.
Karhammer, Maxwell	do	20	Jan. 17, 1865	1 year.
Karnes, William	do	25	Feb. 11, 1865	1 year.
Kaufman, David	do	18	Jan. 20, 1865	1 year.
Kelley, William	do	38	Jan. 20, 1865	1 year.
Kimball, Francis	do	19	Jan. 11, 1865	1 year.
Kylboyle, Michael	do	18	Jan. 20, 1865	1 year.
Lenharr, Abraham	do	29	Jan. 14, 1865	1 year.
Lock, William M	do	19	Jan. 14, 1865	1 year.
Long, Otto	do	25	Jan. 27, 1865	1 year.
McClain, Fergus	do	18	Jan. 23, 1865	1 year.
McClain, Stephen	do	19	Jan. 27, 1865	1 year.
McCray, Thomas	do	19	Jan. 19, 1865	1 year.
McGlaughlin, John	do	43	Jan. 9, 1865	1 year.
McGrevy, William	do	18	Jan. 20, 1865	1 year.
McMillan, Simon L. B.	do	25	Feb. 11, 1865	1 year.
Manning, Charles E.	do	18	Jan. 17, 1865	1 year.
Martin, Henry	do	33	Jan. 6, 1865	1 year.
Marts, Abraham	do	28	Jan. 28, 1865	1 year.
Marts, Silas	do	19	Jan. 16, 1865	1 year.
Miller, Samuel W	do	18	Jan. 21, 1865	1 year.
Molitor, Peter	do	18	Jan. 11, 1865	1 year.
Morford, Taylor	do	18	Jan. 16, 1865	1 year.
Murphy, Joseph	do	19	Jan. 14, 1865	1 year.
Ogden, Jonathan G	do	30	Jan. 10, 1865	1 year.
Overholser, William	do	18	Jan. 21, 1865	1 year.
Parker, Lewis	do	18	Jan. 31, 1865	1 year.
Pattee, Frank	do	18	Jan. 10, 1865	1 year.
Pearson, Robert M	do	18	Jan. 28, 1865	1 year.
Peterman, Sylvester A	do	20	Jan. 9, 1865	1 year.
Pipplinger, John J	do	18	Jan. 2[illegible], 1865	1 year.
Reed, Joseph B.	do	18	Jan. 9, 1865	1 year.
Rice, Alfred	do	19	Feb. 2, 1865	1 year.
Rickard, William	do	23	Jan. 24, 1865	1 year.
Robinson, Charles	do	24	Jan. 18, 1865	1 year.
Rookstool, Michael P	do	20	Jan. 18, 1865	1 year.
Russell, Samuel	do	21	Jan. 28, 1865	1 year.
Schenk, David P.	do	27	Jan. 23, 1865	1 year.
Schroton, George	do	20	Jan. 17, 1865	1 year.
Schurman, Henry	do	22	Jan. 16, 1865	1 year.

Names.	Rank.	Age.	Date of Entering the Service.	Period of Service.	Remarks.
Deed, William	Private.	18	Dec. 26, 1863	3 yrs.	Transferred from Co. G, 118th O.V.I., June 24, 1865; mustered out with company July 17, 1865.
Dix, Charles	...do...	19	Sept. 13, 1864	1 year.	
Duke, George	...do...	29	Sept. 29, 1864	1 year.	Reduced from Sergeant Dec. 25, 1864; mustered out July 6, 1865, at Columbus, O., by order of War Department.
Dunnoven, Squire	...do...	16	Feb. 29, 1864	3 yrs.	Transferred from Co. I, 118th O. V. I., June 24, 1865; mustered out with company July 17, 1865.
Evans, John	...do...	20	Oct. 4, 1864	1 year.	Mustered out with company July 17, 1865.
*Fairman, Erastus	...do...	18	Nov. 1, 1864	1 year.	Missing Nov. 30, 1864, at battle of Franklin, Tenn. No further record found.
Frazer, John W	...do...	21	Nov. 2, 1864	1 year.	
Fristoe, Richard H	...do...	18	Oct. 3, 1864	1 year.	Mustered out with company July 17, 1865.
Fry, Walter	...do...	18	Oct. 10, 1864	1 year.	Mustered out with company July 17, 1865.
Fulton, Isaac	...do...	23	Feb. 22, 1864	3 yrs.	Transferred from Co. I, 118th O. V. I., June 24, 1865; mustered out with company July 17, 1865.
Garrett, James H	...do...	26	Oct. 3, 1864	1 year.	Reduced from Sergeant March 12, 1865; mustered out with company July 17, 1865.
German, William	...do...	21	Nov. 8, 1864	1 year.	Mustered out with company July 17, 1865.
Glasscock, John P	...do...	33	Oct. 3, 1864	1 year	Mustered out with company July 17, 1865.
Gordon, James	...do...	18	Oct. 24, 1864	1 year.	Mustered out with company July 17, 1865.
Green, Lewis J	...do...	17	Sept. 4, 1864	1 year.	Mustered out with company July 17, 1865.
Grover, John W	...do...	24	Nov. 12, 1864	1 year.	
Hands, William	...do...	21	Nov. 12, 1864	1 year.	
Hann, Elhanan	...do...	29	Feb. 26, 1864	1 year.	Transferred from Co. I, 118th O. V. I., June 24, 1865; mustered out with company July 17, 1865.
Hann, George	...do...	26	Feb. 26, 1864	1 year.	Transferred from Co. I, 118th O. V. I., June 24, 1865; mustered out with company July 17, 1865.
Harding, Anson C	...do...	21	Oct. 7, 1864	1 year.	Reduced from Sergeant March 1, 1865; mustered out with company July 17, 1865.
Hare, William	...do...	35	Oct. 25, 1864	1 year.	
Henderson, James B	...do...	21	Oct. 17, 1864	1 year.	Reduced from Corporal —.
Hill, James	...do...	28	Oct. 8, 1864	1 year.	Mustered out June 8, 1865, at Albany, N. Y., by order of War Department.
Hill, William	...do...	31	Sept. 22, 1864	1 year.	Wounded Dec. 15, 1864, in battle of Nashville, Tenn.; mustered out June 15, 1865, at Washington, D. C., by order of War Department.
Himes, George W	...do...	36	Oct. 10, 1864	1 year.	Died April 3, 1865, in hospital at Lexington, Kentucky.
Hockenbery, John	...do...	24	June 1, 1863	3 yrs.	Transferred from Co. I, 118th O. V. I., June 24, 1865; sick —, at Charleston, Tenn. No further record found.
Hueston, Thomas	...do...	34	Oct. 26, 1864	1 year.	
Hughes, Philip C	...do...	18	Oct. 3, 1864	1 year.	Mustered out with company July 17, 1865.
Hussey, Harry W	...do...	22	Dec. 24, 1863	3 yrs.	Transferred from Co. E, 118th O. V. I., June 24, 1865; mustered out with company July 17, 1865.
Irwin, John C	...do...	19	Oct. 3, 1864	1 year.	Mustered out with company July 17, 1865.
Jenkins, David	...do...	20	Sept. 24, 1864	1 year.	Mustered out with company July 17, 1865.
Keis, John	...do...	40	Feb. 26, 1864	1 year.	Transferred from Co. E, 118th O. V. I., June 24, 1865; mustered out with company July 17, 1865.
Keiser, Franklin	...do...	23	Oct. 24, 1864	1 year.	Mustered out with company July 17, 1865.
Kennard, Elbridge	...do...	44	Oct. 10, 1864	1 year.	Died Jan 29, 1865, at Camp Dennison, O.
Klinehans, August	...do...	22	Oct. 1, 1864	1 year.	Mustered out with company July 17, 1865.
Knetle, George	...do...	21	Mch. 5, 1864	3 yrs.	Transferred from Co. A, 118th O.V. I., June 24, 1865; mustered out with company July 17, 1865.
Lawwell, William	...do...	41	Oct. 3, 1864	1 year.	Mustered out June 5, 1865, at Washington, D.C.
List, George W	...do...	44	Oct. 11, 1864	1 year.	Mustered out with company July 17, 1865.
List, Robert C	...do...	21	Oct. 3, 1864	1 year.	Died Feb. 14, 1865, in hospital at Washington, District of Columbia.
Loyd, John	...do...	18	Oct. 13, 1864	1 year.	Wounded Nov. 30, 1864, in battle of Franklin, Tenn.; mustered out July 7, 1865, at Washington, D. C., by order of War Department.
Lutz, Joseph S	...do...	28	Nov. 17, 1864	1 year.	Mustered out with company July 17, 1865.
McFarland, Isaac	...do...	16	....	......	Missing Nov. 30, 1864, at battle of Franklin, Tenn. No further record found.
McMillen, John	...do...	22	Sept. 22, 1864	1 year.	Mustered out with company July 17, 1865.
Madden, Dennis	...do...	18	Nov. 3, 1864	1 year.	Mustered out with company July 17, 1865
Marlatt, James	...do...	25	Nov. 11, 1864	1 year.	Mustered out June 9, 1865, at Washington, D. C., by order of War Department.
Meade, John H	...do...	23	Oct. 4, 1864	1 year.	Missing Nov. 30, 1864, at battle of Franklin, Tenn. No further record found.
Miller, Henry	...do...	24	Nov. 1, 1864	1 year.	
Mitchell, William M	...do...	18	Feb. 22, 1864	3 yrs.	Transferred from Co. I, 118th O. V. I., June 24, 1865; mustered out with company July 17, 1865.
Moore, Charles	...do...	25	Nov. 12, 1864	1 year.	
Myers, Jacob	...do...	30	Nov. 10, 1863	3 yrs.	Transferred from Co. D, 118th O.V. I., June 24, 1865; mustered out with company July 17, 1865.

COMPANY C.

Mustered in February 14, 1865, at Camp Chase, O., by W. P. Richardson, Colonel 25th O. V. I. Mustered out September 20, 1865, at Nashville, Tenn., by J. W. Chickering, Captain and A. C. M., 2d Division, 4th Army Corps.

Names.	Rank.	Age.	Date of Entering the Service.	Period of Service.	Remarks.
Joseph Allen	Captain.	25	Jan. 17, 1865	1 year.	Appointed Feb. 14, 1865; mustered out with company Sept. 20, 1865.
Alexander M. Duck	1st Lieut.	26	Jan. 17, 1865	1 year.	Appointed Feb. 14, 1865; mustered out with company Sept. 20, 1865.
Hiram Reed	2d Lieut.	24	Feb. 14, 1865	1 year.	Mustered out with company Sept. 20, 1865.
Joseph L. Shunk	1st Sergt.	20	Jan. 19, 1865	1 year.	Mustered out with company Sept. 20, 1865.
Samuel Hobbs	Sergeant.	19	Jan. 19, 1865	1 year.	Mustered out Sept. 11, 1865, at Camp Dennison, O., by order of War Department.
Thomas Hanna	...do...	25	Jan. 28, 1865	1 year.	Mustered out with company Sept. 20, 1865.
John Ellis	...do...	18	Jan. 20, 1865	1 year.	Mustered out with company Sept. 20, 1865.
Charles E. Strauss	...do...	18	Jan. 30, 1865	1 year.	Mustered out with company Sept. 20, 1865.
Josiah Gregor	Corporal.	21	Jan. 30, 1865	1 year.	Mustered out with company Sept. 20, 1865.
Franklin Reed	...do...	18	Jan. 31, 1865	1 year.	Mustered out with company Sept. 20, 1865.
William R. Black	...do...	18	Jan. 30, 1865	1 year.	Mustered out with company Sept. 20, 1865.
George W. Duck	...do...	21	Jan. 25, 1865	1 year.	Mustered out with company Sept. 20, 1865.
George W. Wilhelm	...do...	18	Jan. 30, 1865	1 year.	Mustered out with company Sept. 20, 1865.
Albert Hurrow	...do...	19	Jan. 20, 1865	1 year.	Mustered out with company Sept. 20, 1865.
George W. Shires	...do...	28	Jan. 28, 1865	1 year.	Mustered out with company Sept. 20, 1865.
John Crow	...do...	21	Jan. 28, 1865	1 year.	Mustered out with company Sept. 20, 1865.
Josiah Shunk	Musician	18	Feb. 5, 1865	1 year.	Mustered out with company Sept. 20, 1865.
Edward Studer	...do...	18	Jan. 24, 1865	1 year.	Mustered out with company Sept. 20, 1865.
Nathaniel Oaks	Wagoner.	23	Feb. 5, 1865	1 year.	Mustered out with company Sept. 20, 1865.
Adams, George	Private.	28	Jan. 28, 1865	1 year.	Mustered out with company Sept. 20, 1865.
Adams, Henry	...do...	19	Jan. 23, 1865	1 year.	Mustered out with company Sept. 20, 1865.
Amsbaugh, John I	...do...	18	Feb. 2, 1865	1 year.	Discharged July 12, 1865, at Camp Dennison, O., on Surgeon's certificate of disability.
Ashton, George W	...do...	18	Feb. 2, 1865	1 year.	Mustered out with company Sept. 20, 1865.
Baker, John	...do...	18	Jan. 28, 1865	1 year.	Mustered out with company Sept. 20, 1865.
Barnes, Arthur G	...do...	18	Jan. 30, 1865	1 year.	Mustered out with company Sept. 20, 1865.
Barnet, Levi	...do...	18	Jan. 28, 1865	1 year.	Mustered out with company Sept. 20, 1865.
Bash, Philip	...do...	18	Jan. 30, 1865	1 year.	Mustered out with company Sept. 20, 1865.
Belchler, Lewis	...do...	35	Feb. 1, 1865	1 year.	Mustered out with company Sept. 20, 1865.
Bourquin, Joseph	...do...	19	Feb. 16, 1865	1 year.	Mustered out with company Sept. 20, 1865.
Bowers, John	...do...	19	Jan. 28, 1865	1 year.	Mustered out with company Sept. 20, 1865.
Cooper, Francis	...do...	18	Jan. 25, 1865	1 year.	Mustered out with company Sept. 20, 1865.
Corwin, Calvin H	...do...	..	....	1 year.	Mustered out Sept. 19, 1865, at Camp Dennison, O., by order of War Department.
Cramer, William A	...do...	18	Jan. 28, 1865	1 year.	Mustered out with company Sept. 20, 1865.
Cross, Joseph	...do...	18	Jan. 28, 1865	1 year.	Mustered out with company Sept. 20, 1865.
Deeds, William B	...do...	19	Feb. 5, 1865	1 year.	Mustered out with company Sept. 20, 1865.
Doney, Daniel	...do...	18	Jan. 28, 1865	1 year.	Mustered out with company Sept. 20, 1865.
Drabot, John	...do...	18	Feb. 3, 1865	1 year.	Discharged July 12, 1865, at Camp Dennison, O., on Surgeon's certificate of disability.
Duncan, James E	...do...	18	Jan. 28, 1865	1 year.	Mustered out with company Sept. 20, 1865.
Ebert, Michael	...do...	18	Jan. 28, 1865	1 year.	Mustered out with company Sept. 20, 1865.
Erner, Martin C	...do...	18	Jan. 28, 1865	1 year.	Mustered out with company Sept. 20, 1865.
Fink, Isaac	...do...	18	Jan. 28, 1865	1 year.	
Firestone, Eugene T	...do...	18	Jan. 28, 1865	1 year.	Mustered out with company Sept. 20, 1865.
Gamebat, Lewis	...do...	28	Jan. 28, 1865	1 year.	Mustered out with company Sept. 20, 1865.
Gleitsman, Julius	...do...	19	Jan. 28, 1865	1 year.	Mustered out with company Sept. 20, 1865.
Gleitsman, William	...do...	18	Jan. 28, 1865	1 year.	Mustered out with company Sept. 20, 1865.
Hall, William H	...do...	22	Feb. 1, 1865	1 year.	Mustered out with company Sept. 20, 1865.
Harry, Albert J	...do...	20	Jan. 28, 1865	1 year.	Mustered out with company Sept. 20, 1865.
Heider, Leonard	...do...	36	Feb. 1, 1865	1 year.	Discharged May 18, 1865, at Bridgeport, Ala., on Surgeon's certificate of disability.
Hile, George W	...do...	28	Jan. 31, 1865	1 year.	Mustered out with company Sept. 20, 1865.
Hines, George W	...do...	18	Jan. 30, 1865	1 year.	Mustered out with company Sept. 20, 1865.
Hoover, Abraham	...do...	22	Feb. 6, 1865	1 year.	Mustered out with company Sept. 20, 1865.
Hoover, John	...do...	21	Feb. 5, 1865	1 year.	Mustered out with company Sept. 20, 1865.
Hulbert, William	...do...	19	Feb. 1, 1865	1 year.	Mustered out with company Sept. 20, 1865.
Hutchison, James B	...do...	18	Jan. 28, 1865	1 year.	Mustered out with company Sept. 20, 1865.
Irelan, Henry	...do...	18	Jan. 30, 1865	1 year.	Mustered out with company Sept. 20, 1865.
Kib, Frederick	...do...	18	Feb. 1, 1865	1 year.	Mustered out with company Sept. 20, 1865.
Kolmer, Samuel	...do...	18	Feb. 2, 1865	1 year.	Mustered out with company Sept. 20, 1865.
Kern, John	...do...	20	Feb. 5, 1865	1 year.	Mustered out with company Sept. 20, 1865.
Kyle, John B	...do...	18	Jan. 28, 1865	1 year.	Mustered out with company Sept. 20, 1865.
Longbaugh, Peter	...do...	22	Jan. 28, 1865	1 year.	Mustered out Sept. 26, 1865, at Camp Dennison, O., by order of War Department.
Menuez, Adolphus	...do...	18	Jan. 30, 1865	1 year.	Mustered out with company Sept. 20, 1865.
Miller, William	...do...	19	Jan. 28, 1865	1 year.	Mustered out with company Sept. 20, 1865.
Milligan, Benjamin	...do...	19	Jan. 27, 1865	1 year	Mustered out with company Sept. 20, 1865.
Moltz, John H	...do...	21	Feb. 6, 1865	1 year	
Mums, John H	...do...	19	Feb. 10, 1865	1 year.	Mustered out with company Sept. 20, 1865.
Patrick, Samuel	...do...	18	Feb. 2, 1865	1 year.	Mustered out with company Sept. 20, 1865.
Pfeister, John A	...do...	20	Jan. 30, 1865	1 year.	Mustered out with company Sept. 20, 1865.

Names.	Rank.	Age.	Date of Entering the Service.	Period of Service.	
Pherson, Albert	Private..	18	Jan. 30, 1865		
Porter, Francis W	....do....	16	Feb. 8, 1865		
Porter, William S	....do....	18	Jan. 24, 1785		
Priser, Henry K	....do....	18	Jan 28, 1865		
Ralston, George	....do....	19	Jan. 28, 1865		
Reese, James M	....do....	18	Jan. 30, 1865	1 year.	
Reichenbaugh, Christian	....do....	19	Jan. 28, 1865		
Robinson, John M	....do....	18	Jan. 28, 1865	1	
Rogers, Jimsey H	....do....	18	Feb. 1, 1865	1	
Rohn, Haman	....do....	20	Jan. 30, 1865	1	
Rohn, Levi	....do....	18	Jan. 30, 1865	1	ustered
Sear, William H	....do....	18	Feb. 5, 1865	1	ustered
Shank, Matthew	....do....	19	Feb. 1, 1865	1	Mustered out
Shultz, Harman	....do....	26	Jan. 21, 1865	1	Mustered out wi
Smith, Godfrey	....do....	21	Feb. 7, 1865	1	Mustered out wi
Spidle, Clark	....do....	18	Feb. 8, 1865	1	
Sprankle, George W	....do....	18	Jan. 30, 1865	1 year.	
Spring, Solomon	....do....	18	Feb. 2, 1865	1 year	Mustered out wi
Stanbarger, Adam	....do....	18	Feb. 5, 1865	1 year.	
Swank, Jacob	....do....	20	Feb. 4, 1865	1 year.	
Sweringen, George B	....do....	18	Jan. 28, 1865	1	
Teaters, Marion	....do....	18	Feb. 2, 1865	1	Mustered out wi
Teeple, Ephraim	....do....	18	Feb. 5, 1865	1	ustered wi
Thompson, William	....do....	27	Feb. 4, 1865	1	ustered wi
Tom, Isaac	....do....	18	Jan. 24, 1865	1	Mustered out wi
Tracy, John W	....do....	18	Jan. 28, 1865	1	Mustered out wi
Voltz, Ernest	....do....	18	Jan. 28, 1865		Mustered out
Voorhes, Samuel B	....do....	18	Feb. 1, 1865		Mustered out
Weaver, John	....do....	18	Jan. 28, 1865		Mustered out
Weimer, Uriah	....do....	18	Jan. 30, 1865		Mustered out
Wilkison, George W	....do....	48	Jan. 24, 1865		Mustered out t of War Depart
Wilkison, Levi	....do....	39	Feb. 4, 1865	1 year.	Mustered out wi
Walgamot, Joseph	....do....	18	Feb. 2, 1865	1 year.	Mustered out wi
Wright, William	....do....	20	Feb. 3, 1865		Mustered out wi
Zutervan, William	....do....	18	Feb. 5, 1865		Mustered out wi

COMPANY D.

Mustered in February 18, 1865, at Camp Chase, O., by W. P. Richardson, Colon
September 20, 1865, at Nashville, Tenn., by J. W. Chickering,
A. C. M., 2d Division, 4th Army Corps.

Names.	Rank.	Age.	Date of Entering the Service.	Period of Service.	
Josephus W. Wise	Captain.	38	Feb. 18, 1865	1 year.	On detached d and June, 18 Sept. 20, 1865.
John Giller	1st Lieut.	30	Feb. 18, 1865	1 year.	Mustered out w
Alonzo Langdon	2d Lieut.	25	Feb. 18, 1865	1 year.	Discharged May partment.
William S. Eby	1st Sergt.	25	Feb. 8, 1865	1 year.	Mustered out w
John Snyder	Sergeant.	24	Feb. 1, 1865	1 year.	Mustered out w
Samuel Boyer	....do....	23	Feb. 4, 1865	1 year.	Mustered out w
Edward Nills	....do....	37	Jan. 19, 1865	1 year.	Mustered out w
Abraham Crepple	....do....	33	Feb. 11, 1865	1 year	Mustered out w
William Gerard	Corporal.	38	Feb. 3, 1865	1 year.	Mustered out w
Oliver P. Hoffman	....do....	23	Feb. 8, 1865	1 year.	Mustered out w
Hiram Gross	....do....	22	Feb. 3, 1865	1 year.	Mustered out w
John Webb	....do....	26	Jan. 18, 1865	1 year	Mustered out w
George W. Miller	....do....	22	Feb. 2, 1865	1 year.	Mustered out w
Joshua T. Derr	....do....	32	Feb. 11, 1865	1 year.	Mustered out w
Benton Daring	....do....	21	Feb. 3, 1865	1 year.	Mustered out w
Isaac Staley	....do....	18	Feb. 14, 1865	1 year.	Mustered out O O., by order o
Edward Shaffer	Musician	16	Feb. 6, 1865	1 year.	Mustered out w
Anderson, Samuel	Private.	30	Feb. 15, 1865	1 year.	Mustered out w
Baker, Charles	....do....	32	Feb. 7, 1865	1 year.	Mustered out w
Beam, Wesley	....do....	19	Feb. 6, 1865	1 year.	Mustered out w
Blake, John H	....do....	27	Jan. 19, 1865	1 year.	Mustered out w
Boda, Daniel	....do..	18	Feb. 9, 1865	1 year.	Mustered out w
Boyer, David	....do....	22	Feb. 15, 1865	1 year.	Mustered out w
Britton, Abraham	....do....	40	Feb. 8, 1865	1 year.	Mustered out w
Britton, Isaac	....do....	25	Feb. 8, 1865	1 year.	Mustered out w
Christ, Benjamin	....do....	24	Feb. 15, 1865	1 year.	Mustered out w
Clensey, Frederick	....do....	21	Feb. 5, 1865	1 year.	Mustered out w
Coleman, Alfred	....do....	28	Jan. 18, 1865	1 year.	Mustered out w
Coleman, John H	....do....	18	Jan. 18, 1865	1 5ear.	Mustered out w
Conover, Leonidas	....do....	17	Feb. 15, 1865	1 year.	Mustered out w

Names.	Rank.	Age.	Date of Entering the Service.	Period of Service.	Remarks.
Crowley, Lucas	Private	17	Jan. 19, 1865	1 year.	Mustered out with company Sept. 20, 1865.
Daniels, Charles E.	...do...	[illegible]	Feb. 9, 1865	1 year.	Mustered out with company Sept. 20, 1865.
Davidson, James	...do...	19	Feb. 8, 1865	1 year.	Discharged July 7, 1865, at Chattanooga, Tenn., on Surgeon's certificate of disability.
Duckwall, George W	...do...	17	Feb. 12, 1865	1 year.	Mustered out with company Sept. 20, 1865.
Emrick, Franklin	...do...	22	Feb. 9, 1865	1 year.	Mustered out with company Sept. 20, 1865.
Emrick, William H.	...do...	19	Feb. 2, 1865	1 year.	Discharged June 18, 1865, at Bridgeport, Ala., on Surgeon's certificate of disability.
Ealinger, Henry R.	...do...	28	Feb. 7, 1865	1 year.	Mustered out with company Sept. 20, 1865.
Eslam, Joseph G.	...do...	17	Jan. 24, 1865	1 year.	Mustered out with company Sept. 20, 1865.
Gatz, Joseph	...do...	[illegible]	Jan. 19, 1865	1 year.	Mustered out with company Sept. 20, 1865.
Gephart, Henry	...do...	18	Feb. 4, 1865	1 year.	Mustered out with company Sept. 20, 1865.
Gephart, Lewis	...do...	[illegible]	Feb. 2, 1865	1 year.	Mustered out with company Sept. 20, 1865.
Gephart, William H.	...do...	19	Feb. 1, 1865	1 year.	Mustered out with company Sept. 20, 1865.
Gravenstine, William	...do...	[illegible]	Feb. 1, 1865	1 year.	Returned to 58th N. Y. V. June 16, 1865, where he had previously enlisted.
Gregg, William A	...do...	18	Jan. 18, 1865	1 year.	Mustered out with company Sept. 20, 1865.
Gunckel, Michael N	...do...	[illegible]	Feb. 10, 1865	1 year.	Mustered out with company Sept. 20, 1865.
Hamburger, Frank	...do...	29	Feb. 10, 1865	1 year.	Mustered out with company Sept. 20, 1865.
Heckerman, Henry C.	...do...	19	Feb. 8, 1865	1 year.	Mustered out with company Sept. 20, 1865.
Hime, David	...do...	18	Feb. 2, 1865	1 year.	Mustered out with company Sept. 20, 1865.
Hoffman, John H.	...do...	21	Feb. 4, 1865	1 year.	Died Aug. 31, 1865, in hospital at Nashville, Tennessee.
Hopkins, Jacob S.	...do...	41	Jan. 31, 1865	1 year.	Mustered out with company Sept. 20, 1865.
Huber, Benjamin	...do...	31	Feb. 1, 1865	1 year.	Mustered out with company Sept. 20, 1865.
Huber, Daniel W	...do...	16	Feb. 6, 1865	1 year.	Promoted to Prin. Musician May 1, 1865.
Jordan, Lewis	...do...	23	Feb. 3, 1865	1 year.	Mustered out to date Sept. 20, 1865, by order of War Department.
Kemp, Henry L.	...do...	19	Feb. 11, 1865	1 year.	Discharged July 7, 1865, at Bridgeport, Ala., on Surgeon's certificate of disability.
Knouse, George W	...do...	20	Feb. 10, 1865	1 year.	Mustered out with company Sept. 20, 1865.
Kubule, Gottlieb F.	...do...	23	Feb. 15, 1865	1 year.	Mustered out with company Sept. 20, 1865.
Kubale, Tobias	...do...	25	Feb. 10, 1865	1 year.	Mustered out with company Sept. 20, 1865.
Langdon, Cassius C	...do...	20	Jan. 18, 1865	1 year.	Mustered out with company Sept. 20, 1865.
Laughlin, Philip H	...do...	18	Feb. 7, 1865	1 year.	Mustered out with company Sept. 20, 1865.
Lightcap, Wilson	...do...	18	Feb. 9, 1865	1 year.	Mustered out with company Sept. 20, 1865.
Liter, David	...do...	23	Feb. 9, 1865	1 year.	Mustered out with company Sept. 20, 1865.
Lukins, Alfred T.	...do...	19	Jan. 18, 1865	1 year.	Mustered out with company Sept. 20, 1865.
McAneney, William	...do...	33	Feb. 6, 1865	1 year	Mustered out to date Sept. 20, 1865, by order of War Department.
McCranor, James H	...do...	29	Jan. 31, 1865	1 year.	Mustered out with company Sept. 20, 1865.
Maul, Andrew	...do...	31	Feb. 3, 1865	1 year.	Mustered out with company Sept. 20, 1865.
Miller, Henry	...do...	25	Jan. 30, 1865	1 year.	Mustered out with company Sept. 20, 1865.
Miller, Noah H.	...do...	29	Jan. 20, 1865	1 year.	Mustered out with company Sept. 20, 1865.
Miller, William E.	...do...	18	Feb. 6, 1865	1 year.	Mustered out with company Sept. 20, 1865.
Murry, William P.	...do...	18	Jan. 22, 1865	1 year.	Died Sept. 8, 1865, in hospital at Nashville, Tennessee.
Myers, Samuel	...do...	43	Feb. 12, 1865	1 year.	Mustered out with company Sept. 20, 1865.
Newman, Robert A.	...do...	20	Feb. 11, 1865	1 year.	Mustered out with company Sept. 20, 1865.
Osborn, Jesse H.	...do...	23	Feb. 6, 1865	1 year.	Mustered out with company Sept. 20, 1865.
Polegrove, Michael	...do...	28	Feb. 2, 1865	1 year.	Mustered out with company Sept. 20, 1865.
Premier, Aaron	...do...	20	Feb. 4, 1865	1 year.	Mustered out with company Sept. 20, 1865.
Reed, William	...do...	[illegible]	Jan. 18, 1865	1 year.	Mustered out with company Sept. 20, 1865.
Roberts, William	...do...	[illegible]	Jan. 21, 1865	1 year.	Discharged Aug. 7, 1865, at Nashville, Tenn., on Surgeon's certificate of disability.
Root, Jacob A	...do...	22	Feb. 18, 1865	1 year.	Mustered out with company Sept. 20, 1865.
Rowe, Moses B.	...do...	18	Feb. 3, 1865	1 year.	Mustered out Oct. 28, 1865, at Camp Dennison O., by order of War Department.
Sandall, Martin	...do...	22	Feb. 1, 1865	1 year.	Mustered out with company Sept. 20, 1865.
Shaffer, William	...do...	22	Feb. 10, 1865	1 year.	Mustered out with company Sept. 20, 1865.
Shank, Ezra A.	...do...	24	Feb. 11, 1865	1 year.	Mustered out with company Sept. 20, 1865.
Sherley, Henry W.	...do...	20	Feb. 6, 1865	1 year.	Mustered out with company Sept. 20, 1865.
Shell, John	...do...	30	Feb. 1, 1865	1 year.	Mustered out with company Sept. 20, 1865.
Shelley, David	...do...	24	Feb. 5, 1865	1 year.	Mustered out with company Sept. 20, 1865.
Slagman, Andrew	...do...	18	Jan. 31, 1865	1 year.	Mustered out with company Sept. 20, 1865.
Smalley, Isaac N	...do...	20	Jan. 16, 1865	1 year.	Discharged Aug. 4, 1865, at Bridgeport, Ala., on Surgeon's certificate of disability.
Smith, Samuel	...do...	20	Feb. 4, 1865	1 year.	Mustered out with company Sept. 20, 1865.
Spahn, George	...do...	18	Feb. 8, 1865	1 year.	Mustered out with company Sept. 20, 1865.
Spotswood, Martin L.	...do...	20	Jan. 18, 1865	1 year.	Mustered out with company Sept. 20, 1865.
[illegible], George	...do...	19	Feb. 9, 1865	1 year.	Died Sept. 11, 1865, in hospital at Nashville, Tennessee.
Stamm, John H.	...do...	24	Feb. 9, 1865	1 year.	Mustered out with company Sept. 20, 1865.
Stine, Adolphus	...do...	18	Feb. 2, 1865	1 year.	Mustered out with company Sept. 20, 1865.
Strouse, Josiah M.	...do...	17	Jan. 18, 1865	1 year.	Mustered out with company Sept. 20, 1865.
Stump, Daniel	...do...	43	Feb. 6, 1865	1 year.	Mustered out with company Sept. 20, 1865.
Thomas, George W	...do...	19	Feb. 3, 1865	1 year.	
Wagoner, Louis	...do...	23	Feb. 9, 1865	1 year.	Mustered out with company Sept. 20, 1865.
Walter, Oliver P.	...do...	18	Jan. 18, 1865	1 year.	Mustered out with company Sept. 20, 1865.
Weidle, David	...do...	38	Feb. 13, 1865	1 year.	Mustered out with company Sept. 20, 1865.
Whitaker, Orlando L.	...do...	20	Feb. 9, 1865	1 year.	Mustered out with company Sept. 20, 1865.
Willis, George W.	...do...	18	Feb. 1, 1865	1 year.	Died Sept. 10, 1865, in hospital at Nashville, Tennessee.
Wilson, Francis M.	...do...	25	Feb. 1, 1865	1 year.	Mustered out with company Sept. 20, 1865.

Mustered in February 19, 1865, at Camp Chase, O., by W. P. Rich[illegible]
September 20, 1865, at Nashville, Tenn., by [illegible]
A. C. M., 2d Division, [illegible]

Names.	Rank.	Age.	Date of Entering the Service.	Period of Service.	
J. Douglass Moler	Captain.	28	Feb. 20, 1865	1 year.	M
Joseph A. Blair	1st Lieut.	22	Feb. 20, 1865	1 year.	M
Charles E. Warren	2d Lieut.	21	Feb. 20, 1865	1 year.	M
Oscar N. Wheeler	1st Sergt.	20	Jan. 27, 1865	1 year.	M
Nathan K. Taylor	Sergeant.	21	Jan. 21, 1865	1 year.	M
John Coho	...do...	26	Jan. 30, 1865	1 year.	M
James M. Gregg	...do...	22	Feb. 7, 1865	1 year.	M
John Hamlin	...do...	25	Jan. 16, 1865	1 year.	A
William H. Green	Corporal.	26	Jan. 11, 1865	1 year.	A
Edward H. Wheeler	...do...	30	Feb. 8, 1865	1 year.	M
Solon Stratton	...do...	20	Feb. 6, 1865	1 year.	M
John Huff	...do...	28	Jan. 16, 1865	1 year.	M
Jacob J. Betsold	...do...	22	Jan. 28, 1865	1 year.	M
Wallace Elder	...do...	20	Feb. 11, 1865	1 year.	M
John Wildasin	...do...	19	Jan. 24, 1865	1 year.	M
William M. Wilson	...do...	20	Feb. 6, 1865	1 year.	A
Allen, Albert H	Private.	28	Feb. 11, 1865	1 year.	M
Allen, William	...do...	18	Jan. 10, 1865	1 year.	M
Bare, John W	...do...	19	Feb. 17, 1865	1 year.	M
Bare, William H	...do...	20	Jan. 27, 1865	1 year.	M
Barnard, Henry A	...do...	28	Jan. 19, 1865	1 year.	M
Bell, James D	...do...	19	Jan. 17, 1865	1 year.	
Blagg, John R	...do...	18	Jan. 20, 1865	1 year.	M
Bowman, Joseph	...do...	19	Feb. 10, 1865	1 year.	M
Bruden, George	...do...	29	Feb. 7, 1865	1 year.	
Bryan, George	...do...	21	Feb. 6, 1865	1 year.	A
Buck, Samuel D	...do...	20	Jan. 30, 1865	1 year.	M
Burns, William	...do...	24	Jan. 11, 1865	1 year.	
Caine, William	...do...	39	Feb. 4, 1865	1 year.	M
Chapman, Nathaniel C	...do...	20	Feb. 14, 1865	1 year.	M
Clark, James	...do...	34	Feb. 14, 1865	1 year.	M
Clark, Oscar H	...do...	18	Jan. 18, 1865	1 year.	T
Clark, Thomas	...do...	19	Jan. 20, 1865	1 year.	M
Collins, James	...do...	48	Feb. 11, 1865	1 year.	M
Combs, Culbertson	...do...	42	Jan. 12, 1865	1 year.	D
Culver, Henry F	...do...	27	Feb. 3, 1865	1 year.	T
Davis, Hiram	...do...	27	Feb. 8, 1865	1 year.	M
Davis, Wesley	...do...	21	Feb. 2, 1865	1 year.	D
Dunbar, James S	...do...	37	Jan. 25, 1865	1 year.	M
Dunn, James	...do...	23	Jan. 31, 1865	1 year.	M
Elmore, James	...do...	22	Feb. 6, 1865	1 year.	M
Evans, William	...do...	18	Feb. 7, 1865	1 year.	M
Frantz, John	...do...	23	Feb. 18, 1865	1 year.	M
Garrett, Solomon M. T	...do...	18	Jan. 11, 1865	1 year.	M
Geddes, Jackson	...do...	35	Feb. 14, 1865	1 year.	M
Godfrey, Warren P	...do...	20	Feb. 14, 1865	1 year.	M
Grubill, Elias	...do...	34	Jan. 14, 1865	1 year.	M
Greenwood, Thomas S	...do...	18	Jan. 25, 1865	1 year.	M
Haley, George	...do...	19	Feb. 14, 1865	1 year.	D
Haley, Samuel J	...do...	18	Feb. 7, 1865	1 year.	M
Hammel, Jonathan	...do...	18	Jan. 6, 1865	1 year.	M
Hanson, Jehu	...do...	21	Feb. 14, 1865	1 year.	M
Hays, Almon H	...do...	19	Feb. 8, 1865	1 year.	M
Hensel, Frederick	...do...	18	Jan. 31, 1865	1 year.	
Hill, John	...do...	20	Jan. 20, 1865	1 year.	M
Howard, Joseph	...do...	18	Jan. 28, 1865	1 year.	M
Hughes, William	...do...	21	Jan. 30, 1865	1 year.	M
Jamison, Oscar H	...do...	21	Jan. 26, 1865	1 year.	M
Kerns, George	...do...	32	Jan. 14, 1865	1 year.	M
Kills, James M	...do...	18	Feb. 11, 1865	1 year.	M
Kirkpatrick, Samuel	...do...	21	Jan. 19, 1865	1 year.	M
Laney, Cephas	...do...	21	Jan. 23, 1865	1 year.	M
Lantz, Isaac	...do...	24	Jan. 31, 1865	1 year.	M
Lent, Reuben	...do...	20	Jan. 27, 1865	1 year.	
Lochary, Edward	...do...	41	Feb. 14, 1865	1 year.	M

Names.	Rank.	Age.	Date of Entering the Service.	Period of Service.	Remarks.
Loner, Robert	Private	18	Jan. 28, 1865	1 year.	
Long, Samuel	....do....	23	Feb. 7, 1865	1 year.	
McCormick, Amos G.	....do....	23	Feb. 11, 1865	1 year.	Mustered out with company Sept. 20, 1865.
McCoy, James	....do....	20	Feb. 8, 1865	1 year.	Mustered out to date Sept. 20, 1865, by order of War Department.
McDonald, John H.	....do....	27	Feb. 6, 1865	1 year.	Mustered out June 24, 1865, at Camp Chase, O., by order of War Department.
McDonald, J. Wheeler	....do....	26	Feb. 8, 1865	1 year.	Died July 27, 1865, in hospital at Nashville, Tennessee.
McDonald, William	....do....	20	Feb. 6, 1865	1 year.	Mustered out with company Sept. 20, 1865.
McGuire, Andrew	....do....	18	Feb. 6, 1865	1 year.	
Marion, Thomas	....do....	24	Jan. 22, 1865	1 year.	
Mead, William O.	....do....	21	Feb. 6, 1865	1 year.	Mustered out with company Sept. 20, 1865.
Merrill, William C.	....do....	19	Feb. 10, 1865	1 year.	Mustered out with company Sept. 20, 1865.
Messer, William	....do....	18	Jan. 25, 1865	1 year.	Mustered out with company Sept. 20, 1865.
Miller, Louis	....do....	18	Feb. 7, 1865	1 year.	Mustered out with company Sept. 20, 1865.
Morris, John M.	....do....	18	Feb. 6, 1865	1 year.	Mustered out with company Sept. 20, 1865.
Mumma, John H.	....do....	19	Feb. 9, 1865	1 year.	
Nave, Enoch K.	....do....	20	Feb. 9, 1865	1 year.	Mustered out with company Sept. 20, 1865.
Needles, William	....do....	20	Feb. 7, 1865	1 year.	Mustered out with company Sept. 20, 1865.
Neiman, Henry	....do....	29	Feb. 6, 1865	1 year.	Mustered out with company Sept. 20, 1865.
Newton, David	....do....	26	Feb. 8, 1865	1 year.	Mustered out with company Sept. 20, 1865.
Nichols, Erasmus C.	....do....	21	Feb. 8, 1865	1 year.	Mustered out with company Sept. 20, 1865.
O'Brine, Richard	....do....	23	Jan. 25, 1865	1 year.	Mustered out with company Sept. 20, 1865.
O'Harra, Nathan	....do....	18	Feb. 9, 1865	1 year.	Mustered out with company Sept. 20, 1865.
O'Roark, George M.	....do....	20	Feb. 10, 1865	1 year.	Mustered out with company Sept. 20, 1865.
Owens, Richard	....do....	29	Jan. 28, 1865	1 year.	Mustered out with company Sept. 20, 1865.
Palmer, William	....do....	18	Feb. 9, 1865	1 year.	Mustered out with company Sept. 20, 1865.
Patterson, John	....do....	35	Jan. 18, 1865	1 year.	Transferred to Veteran Reserve Corps May 20, 1865.
Peters, Daniel M.	....do....	18	Jan. 21, 1865	1 year.	Transferred to Veteran Reserve Corps May 29, 1865.
Plummer, William	....do....	15	Feb. 9, 1865	1 year	Mustered out Sept. 11, 1865, at Camp Dennison, O., by order of War Department.
Ramsey, Benjamin S.	....do....	36	Feb. 8, 1865	1 year.	Mustered out with company Sept. 20, 1865.
Richcreek, John W.	....do....	20	Feb. 6, 1865	1 year.	
Riley, Vincent	....do....	35	Jan. 26, 1865	1 year.	Mustered out with company Sept. 20, 1865.
Roames, James	....do....	33	Jan. 14, 1865	1 year.	Mustered out with company Sept. 20, 1865.
Shotts, Henry M.	....do....	21	Jan. 30, 1865	1 year.	Mustered out with company Sept. 20, 1865.
Smith, David	....do....	36	Jan. 29, 1865	1 year.	
Smith, John	....do....	42	Jan. 26, 1865	1 year.	Discharged June 16, 1865, at Chattanooga, Tenn., on Surgeon's certificate of disability.
Smidt, William	....do....	24	Jan. 27, 1865	1 year.	
Smith, William C.	....do....	20	Feb. 9, 1865	1 year.	Mustered out with company Sept. 20, 1865.
South, Eli	....do....	18	Jan. 27, 1865	1 year.	Mustered out with company Sept. 20, 1865.
Stuart, R. Berkley	....do....	21	Jan. 28, 1865	1 year.	Discharged Nov. 20, 1865, at Baltimore, Md., on Surgeon's certificate of disability.
Stuart, William	....do....	21	Jan. 26, 1865	1 year.	Mustered out Sept. 29, 1865, at Camp Dennison, O., by order of War Department.
Tench, David	....do....	18	Feb. 11, 1865	1 year.	Mustered out with company Sept. 20, 1865.
Thomas, David C.	....do....	18	Jan. 28, 1865	1 year.	Mustered out with company Sept. 20, 1865.
Warren, John F.	....do....	23	Feb. 16, 1865	1 year.	Mustered out with company Sept. 20, 1865.
Weatherabine, Samuel	....do....	19	Jan. 24, 1865	1 year.	Mustered out with company Sept. 20, 1865.
Weigel, Henry	....do....	30	Feb. 7, 1865	1 year.	Discharged July 7, 1865, at Chattanooga, Tenn., on Surgeon's certificate of disability.
Weigel, Washington	....do....	18	Feb. 8, 1865	1 year.	Mustered out with company Sept. 20, 1865.

COMPANY F.

Mustered in February 19, 1865, at Camp Chase, O., by W. P. Richardson, Colonel 25th O. V. I. Mustered out September 20, 1865, at Nashville, Tenn., by J. W. Chickering, Captain and A. C. M., 2d Division, 4th Army Corps.

Names.	Rank.	Age.	Date of Entering the Service.	Period of Service.	Remarks.
George P. Davis	Captain.	22	Feb. 20, 1865	1 year.	Mustered out with company Sept. 20, 1865.
Charles W. Gerwig	1st Lieut.	23	Feb. 20, 1865	1 year.	Mustered out with company Sept. 20, 1865.
Harrison F. Taylor	2d Lieut.	24	Feb. 20, 1865	1 year.	Mustered out with company Sept. 20, 1865.
Obadiah Morrow	1st Sergt.	22	Jan. 30, 1865	1 year.	Mustered out with company Sept. 20, 1865.
John L. Wier	Sergeant.	20	Feb. 1, 1865	1 year.	Mustered out with company Sept. 20, 1865.
John Findley	....do....	25	Jan. 31, 1865	1 year.	Mustered out with company Sept. 20, 1865.
John Murray	....do....	19	Feb. 7, 1865	1 year.	Appointed from Corporal June 3, 1865; mustered out with company Sept. 20, 1865.
Albert Emmons	....do....	19	Feb. 7, 1865	1 year.	Appointed from Corporal Sept. 1, 1865; mustered out with company Sept. 20, 1865.
Eli Secrest	....do....	24	Jan. 27, 1865	1 year.	Mustered out to date Aug. 22, 1865, by order of War Department.
James P. Comley	....do....	23	Feb. 6, 1865	1 year.	Promoted to Com. Sergeant June 3, 1865.
Isaac Burlingame	Corporal.	23	Jan. 30, 1865	1 year	Mustered out with company Sept. 20, 1865.
Edward Hawley	....do....	21	Jan. 14, 1865	1 year.	Mustered out with company Sept. 20, 1865.
Jonathan Maple	....do....	20	Feb. 8, 1865	1 year.	Mustered out with company Sept. 20, 1865.
Eli M. Edwards	....do....	23	Feb. 7, 1865	1 year.	Mustered out with company Sept. 20, 1865.

Names.	Rank.	Age.	Date of Entering the Service.	[illegible]
John Rice	Corporal.	20	Jan. 12, 1865	1 year.
John M. Hart	...do...	18	Feb. 9, 1865	1 year.
John Whitacre	...do...	20	Feb. 7, 1865	1 year.
Albert Welsh	...do...	18	Feb. 8, 1865	1 year.
Albertus A. Kitsmiller	Musician	18	Feb. 8, 1865	1 year.
William L. Waun	...do...	19	Jan. 30, 1865	1 year.
Barnhart, Zenis	Private	19	Jan. 18, 1865	1 year.
Beaumont, James D	...do...	19	Feb. 10, 1865	1 year.
Behner, Milton	...do...	20	Feb. 13, 1865	1 year.
Best, Henry M	...do...	18	Feb. 1, 1865	1 year.
Betz, Hiram	...do...	19	Feb. 6, 1865	1 year.
Bolinger, Martin	...do...	25	Feb. 7, 1865	1 year.
Brown, Henry H	...do...	34	Feb. 10, 1865	1 year.
Campbell, William H	...do...	19	Feb. 18, 1865	1 year.
Clemmus, Monroe	...do...	18	Feb. 10, 1865	1 year.
Clinton, Daniel M	...do...	19	Feb. 9, 1865	1 year.
Clinton, James M	...do...	18	Feb. 7, 1865	1 year.
Creighton, Aaron B	...do...	27	Feb. 11, 1865	1 year.
Crites, William	...do...	18	Feb. 2, 1865	1 year.
Daniels, James	...do...	18	Feb. 9, 1865	1 year.
Denney, Henry	...do...	18	Feb. 8, 1865	1 year.
Doyle, Eli	...do...	29	Jan. 27, 1865	1 year.
Drake, Thomas F	...do...	18	Feb. 7, 1865	1 year.
Elliott, Daniel	...do...	22	Jan. 27, 1865	1 year.
Elliott, Embrey	...do...	18	Jan. 27, 1865	1 year.
Fligle, Jacob	...do...	27	Feb. 4, 1865	1 year.
Fureacre, Dee J	...do...	18	Feb. 11, 1865	1 year.
Foanight, John H	...do...		Feb. 8, 1865	1 year.
Fryberger, Franklin H	...do...	18	Feb. 8, 1865	1 year.
Grund, Conrad	...do...	36	Feb. 4, 1865	1 year.
Grund, James F	...do...	17	Feb. 4, 1865	1 year.
Haines, Abraham	...do...	22	Feb. 6, 1865	1 year.
Hanaline, John	...do...	18	Feb. 8, 1865	1 year.
Hannay, Robert	...do...	19	Feb. 10, 1865	1 year.
Hawley, Charles	...do...	19	Jan. 16, 1865	1 year.
Hawley, Tine	...do...	18	Feb. 3, 1865	1 year.
Haynam, Emanuel	...do...	19	Feb. 13, 1865	1 year.
Hinman, John	...do...	25	Jan. 17, 1865	1 year.
Hinman, Mack W	...do...	18	Feb. 8, 1865	1 year.
Irvin, John S	...do...	18	Jan. 30, 1865	1 year.
Jerome, John F	...do...	18	Feb. 8, 1865	1 year.
Johnson, Jesse	...do...	21	Feb. 1, 1865	1 year.
Johnson, John	...do...	23	Feb. 1, 1865	1 year.
Keifer, Cyrus W	...do...	18	Jan. 17, 1865	1 year.
Kellogg, William	...do...	19	Jan. 30, 1865	1 year.
Louthan, Benjamin F	...do...	18	Jan. 2, 1865	1 year.
McConnell, Samuel	...do...	18	Jan. 20, 1865	1 year.
McHenry, Samuel M	...do...	18	Feb. 8, 1865	1 year.
McKinney, Franklin	...do...	18	Jan. 31, 1865	1 year.
Manfull, Mortimer	...do...	19	Feb. 9, 1865	1 year.
Mariman, Samuel	...do...	29	Feb. 8, 1865	1 year.
Martin, Thomas	...do...	20	Jan. 26, 1865	1 year.
Masters, David M	...do...	18	Feb. 11, 1865	1 year.
Mead, John	...do...	25	Jan. 26, 1865	1 year.
Menough, John	...do...	17	Feb. 8, 1865	1 year.
Miller, Moses	...do...	18	Jan. 27, 1863	1 year.
Mitchell, David	...do...	18	Feb. 10, 1865	1 year.
Moore, Joseph	...do...	20	Feb. 8, 1865	1 year.
Morlan, Harvey	...do...	18	Feb. 16, 1865	1 year.
Newhouse, Leonard	...do...	17	Feb. 2, 1865	1 year.
Newhouse, Samuel	...do...	17	Feb. 2, 1865	1 year.
Persons, Joseph	...do...	34	Jan. 21, 1865	1 year.
Prince, Edwin	...do...	18	Jan. 27, 1865	1 year.
Roach, Thomas J	...do...	28	Jan. 30, 1865	1 year.
Ryan, Samuel	...do...	18	Feb. 8, 1865	1 year.
Sandon, Charles H	...do...	21	Jan. 26, 1865	1 year.
Sayner, Henry	...do...	21	Feb. 9, 1865	1 year.
Schuyler, William L	...do...	31	Jan. 27, 1865	1 year.
Sheckler, John M	...do...	19	Feb. 6, 1865	1 year.
Shriver, Adam	...do...	39	Jan. 26, 1865	1 year.
Spain, William	...do...	33	Jan. 31, 1863	1 year.
Sprowl, George D	...do...	18	Jan. 30, 1865	1 year.
Stoner, Urias F	...do...	18	Feb. 8, 1865	1 year.
Stratton, Simon C	...do...	21	Feb. 11, 1865	1 year.

Names.	Rank.	Age.	Date of Entering the Service.	Period of Service.	Remarks.
Taylor, George	Private.	18	Feb. 13, 1865	1 year.	Died June 26, 1865, at Bridgeport, Ala.
Taylor, Jeremiah	....do....	26	Feb. 4, 1865	1 year	Died April 1, 1865, at Nashville, Tenn.
Taylor, John L.	....do....	20	Feb. 11, 1865	1 year.	Mustered out with company Sept. 20, 1865.
Tomlinson, George W.	....do....	18	Jan. 27, 1865	1 year.	Mustered out with company Sept. 20, 1865.
Ulman, Adam	....do....	18	Feb. 6, 1865	1 year.	Died March 31, 1865, at Bridgeport, Ala.
Viall, Albert A.	....do....	18	Jan. 26, 1865	1 year.	Mustered out with company Sept. 20, 1865.
Walker, Lewis	....do....	19	Feb. 13, 1865	1 year.	Mustered out with company Sept. 20, 1865.
Welsh, William J.	....do....	19	Feb. 3, 1865	1 year.	Mustered out with company Sept. 20, 1865.
Whitacre, Jonathan	....do....	20	Feb. 7, 1865	1 year.	Mustered out with company Sept. 20, 1865.
Wilson, Harper W.	....do....	18	Feb. 8, 1865	1 year	Mustered out with company Sept. 20, 1865.
Witherspoon, John	....do....	29	Feb. 8, 1865	1 year.	Mustered out with company Sept. 20, 1865.
Yarger, Paul	....do....	43	Feb. 3, 1865	1 year.	Mustered out to date Sept. 20, 1865, by order of War Department.
Yarger, William C.	....do....	18	Feb. 3, 1865	1 year.	Mustered out with company Sept. 20, 1865.
Young, Alfred	....do....	19	Feb. 3, 1865	1 year.	Mustered out with company Sept. 20, 1865.
Young, Jacob	....do....	37	Jan. 27, 1865	1 year.	Mustered out May 18, 1865, at Chattanooga, Tenn., by order of War Department.

COMPANY G.

Mustered in February 20, 1865, at Camp Chase, O., by W. P. Richardson, Colonel 25th O. V. I. Mustered out September 20, 1865, at Nashville, Tenn., by J. W. Chickering, Captain and A. C. M., 2d Division, 4th Army Corps.

Names.	Rank.	Age.	Date of Entering the Service.	Period of Service.	Remarks.
William J. Widener	Captain.	22	Feb. 20, 1865	1 year.	Mustered out with company Sept. 20, 1865.
Robert Detwiler	1st Lieut.	33	Feb. 20, 1865	1 year.	Resigned June 1, 1865.
Michael Stuck	2d Lieut.	28	Feb. 20, 1865	1 year.	Mustered out with company Sept. 20, 1865.
John L. Knight	1st Sergt.	18	Feb. 3, 1865	1 year.	Appointed from Sergeant July 29, 1865; mustered out with company Sept. 20, 1865.
Salathiel Lemon	Sergeant.	22	Feb. 3, 1865	1 year.	Reduced from 1st Sergeant July 29, 1865, at his own request; mustered out with company Sept. 20, 1865.
Henry O. Maaro	....do....	19	Jan. 20, 1865	1 year.	Mustered out with company Sept. 20, 1865.
Joseph Martin	....do....	16	Feb. 3, 1865	1 year.	Mustered out with company Sept. 20, 1865.
John Barclay	....do....	21	Jan. 6, 1865	1 year.	Mustered out with company Sept. 20, 1865.
Miles M. McCowen	Corporal.	23	Jan. 13, 1865	1 year.	Absent, since Aug. 26, 1865, at Chattanooga, Tenn. No further record found.
William A. Hawkins	....do....	19	Feb. 4, 1865	1 year.	Mustered out with company Sept. 20, 1865.
James N. Hawkins	....do....	19	Jan. 13, 1865	1 year.	Mustered out with company Sept. 20, 1865.
John Blair	....do....	30	Jan. 24, 1865	1 year.	Mustered out July 22, 1865, at Cincinnati, O., by order of War Department.
Jacob Rush	....do....	22	Jan. 20, 1865	1 year.	Mustered out with company Sept. 20, 1865.
Henry C. Thompson	....do....	24	Feb. 3, 1865	1 year.	Appointed July 1, 1865; mustered out with company Sept. 20, 1865.
George W. Poole	....do....	24	Feb. 3, 1865	1 year.	Died April 11, 1865, in hospital at Nashville, Tennessee.
John Poland	....do....	36	Feb. 15, 1865	1 year.	
Doctor F. Huffman	....do....	19	Jan. 13, 1865	1 year.	Mustered out to date Aug. 21, 1865, by order of War Department.
Ackley, Armstrong	Private.	18	Feb. 5, 1865	1 year.	Mustered out with company Sept. 20, 1865.
Bates, Isaac	....do....	18	Feb. 6, 1865	1 year.	Mustered out with company Sept. 20, 1865.
Bates, Thomas	....do....	18	Jan. 31, 1865	1 year.	Died March 5, 1865, in hospital at Nashville, Tennessee.
Belford, Joshua	....do....	18	Feb. 5, 1865	1 year.	Died March 17, 1865, in hospital at Nashville, Tennessee.
Blackburn, Samuel	....do....	23	Feb. 10, 1865	1 year.	Mustered out May 18, 1865, at Bridgeport, Ala., by order of War Department.
Bletcher, Jacob		19	Feb. 7, 1865	1 year.	Mustered out with company Sept. 20, 1865.
Bottenfield, Franklin		17	Feb. 6, 1865	1 year.	Mustered out with company Sept. 20, 1865.
Bowersmith, John		18	Jan. 23, 1865	1 year.	Mustered out with company Sept. 20, 1865.
Brennerstahl, Gottlieb		34	Feb. 15, 1865	1 year.	Mustered out with company Sept. 20, 1865.
Brooker, Lewis	....do....	18	Feb. 16, 1865	1 year.	Mustered out with company Sept. 20, 1865.
Brown, Benjamin F.	....do....	30	Feb. 10, 1865	1 year.	Mustered out with company Sept. 20, 1865.
Brown, Wesley	....do....	28	Feb. 4, 1865	1 year.	Mustered out with company Sept. 20, 1865.
Carrell, William	....do....	20	Jan. 9, 1865	1 year.	Mustered out with company Sept. 20, 1865.
Colvin, Charles	....do....	27	Feb. 6, 1865	1 year.	Mustered out with company Sept. 20, 1865.
Colvin, Rosberry	....do....	20	Feb. 6, 1865	1 year.	Mustered out May 18, 1865, at Bridgeport, Ala., by order of War Department.
Conklin, John H.	....do....	21	Feb. 7, 1865	1 year.	Mustered out with company Sept. 20, 1865.
Courtney, Joseph F.	....do....	19	Jan. 31, 1865	1 year.	Died April 5, 1865, in hospital at Bridgeport, Alabama.
Courtney, Lanty L.	....do....	23	Feb. 7, 1865	1 year.	Mustered out with company Sept. 20, 1865.
Covert, Samuel N.	....do....	19	Jan. 30, 1865	1 year.	Mustered out with company Sept. 20, 1865.
Davis, Charles S.	....do....	24	Jan. 31, 1865	1 year.	Died March 14, 1865, in hospital at Nashville, Tennessee.
Dearth, George	....do....	28	Feb. 4, 1865	1 year.	Mustered out with company Sept. 20, 1865.
Deffenbaugh, Loring P.	....do....	23	Jan. 28, 1865	1 year.	Mustered out with company Sept. 20, 1865.
Dickerson, Thomas	....do....	18	Feb. 13, 1865	1 year.	Mustered out with company Sept. 20, 1865.
Dille, Charles H.	....do....	18	Feb. 7, 1865	1 year.	Mustered out with company Sept. 20, 1865.
Dillinger, John W.	....do....	18	Feb. 7, 1865	1 year.	Mustered out with company Sept. 20, 1865.

Names	Rank.	Age.	Date of Entering the Service.	Period of Service.	Remarks.
Duncan, Lee	Private..	38	Jan. 23, 1865	1 year.	Mustered out with company Sept. 20, 1865.
Duosackel, Rudolph	....do....	33	Feb. 15, 1865	1 year.	Mustered out with company Sept. 20, 1865.
Ellis, Benjamin A.	....do....	18	Feb. 8, 1865	1 year.	Mustered out with company Sept. 20, 1865.
Ellis, James F.	....do....	16	Feb. 8, 1865	1 year.	Mustered out with company Sept. 20, 1865.
Elmer, Casper	....do....	18	Jan. 25, 1865	1 year.	Mustered out July 7, 1865, at Chattanooga, Tenn., by order of War De
Elrod, David	....do....	17	Feb. 6, 1865	1 year.	Mustered out with company
Enlow, Joseph	....do....	18	Jan. 31, 1865	1 year.	Mustered out with company
Fartig, Freeman R.	....do....	27	Feb. 17, 1865	1 year.	Mustered ou with company Sept. 20, 1865; on muster-in roll as Reuben R. Fartig.
Fisher, William H.	....do....	25	Feb. 17, 1865	1 year.	Mustered out with company Sept. 20, 1865.
Francis, Frederick	....do....	31	Feb. 13, 1865	1 year.	Mustered out with company Sept. 20, 1865.
Gardner, Lewis R.	....do....	18	Feb. 10, 1865	1 year.	Mustered out Aug 22, 1865, at Camp Dennison, O., by order of War Department.
Geer, Augustus	....do....	18	Feb. 7, 1865	1 year.	Mustered out with company Sept. 20, 1865.
Gibbons, Thomas H.	....do....	18	Jan. 10, 1865	1 year.	Mustered out with company Sept. 20, 1865.
Harsh, Martin L.	....do....	24	Feb. 13, 1865	1 year.	Mustered out with company Sept. 20, 1865.
Hawkins, John M.	....do....	18	Feb. 10, 1865	1 year.	Mustered out with company Sept. 20, 1865.
Hayes, William T.	....do....	18	Jan. 31, 1865	1 year.	Mustered out with company Sept. 20, 1865.
Herrington, David	....do....	18	Jan. 20, 1865	1 year.	Mustered out with company Sept. 20, 1865.
Horton, O'Neil	....do....	18	Feb. 7, 1865	1 year.	Mustered out with company Sept. 20, 1865.
Hysell, Perry	....do....	19	Feb. 10, 1865	1 year.	Mustered out with company Sept. 20, 1865.
Johnson, Russell	....do....	19	Feb. 4, 1865	1 year.	Mustered out with company Sept. 20, 1865.
Jones, Henry	....do....	21	Jan. 16, 1865	1 year.	Mustered out with company Sept. 20, 1865.
Alfred	....do....	19	Jan. 31, 1865	1 year.	Mustered out Sept 26, 1865, at Camp Dennison, O., by order of War Department.
Knight, John H.	....do....	18	Feb. 1, 1865	1 year	Mustered out with company Sept. 20, 1865.
Lee, Horace	....do....	41	Feb. 15, 1865	1 year.	Mustered out July 7, 1865, at Chattanooga, Tenn., by order of War Department.
Lehman, Samuel	....do....	18	Feb. 8, 1865	1 year.	Mustered out with company Sept. 20, 1865.
McCann, William	....do....	25	Jan. 28, 1865	1 year.	
McCowen, Joseph	....do....	18	Feb. 7, 1865	1 year.	Mustered out with company Sept. 20, 1865
McCowen, Taylor J.	....do....	18	Jan. 13, 1865	1 year.	Mustered out with company Sept. 20, 1865.
McLaughlin, James	....do....	26	Jan. 23, 1865	1 year	Mustered out with company Sept. 20, 1865.
McMahon, Alfred D.	....do....	19	Feb. 4, 1865	1 year	Mustered out June 16, 1865, at Chattanooga, Tenn., by order of War Department.
McMahon, William H.	....do....	21	Feb. 3, 1865	1 year.	Mustered out with company Sept. 20, 1865.
McVay, Jacob	....do....	18	Feb. 17, 1865	1 year.	Mustered out with company Sept. 20, 1865.
Marsh, Cornelius	....do....	21	Jan. 13, 1865	1 year.	Mustered out Sept. 26, 1865, at Camp Dennison, O., by order of War Department.
Martindale, James W.	....do....	34	Feb. 10, 1865	1 year.	Mustered out May 25, 1865, at Louisville, Ky., by order of War Department.
Miller, Joshua	....do....	18	Feb. 11, 1865	1 year	
Miller, Samuel	....do....	22	Feb. [illegible], 1865	1 year.	Mustered out with company Sept. 20, 1865.
Molden, Franklin	....do....	35	Feb. 10, 1865	1 year	Mustered out with company Sept. 20, 1865.
Moore, Corwin W.	....do....	23	Feb. 8, 1865	1 year	Mustered out with company Sept. 20, 1865.
Noble, Simeon J.	....do....	19	Jan. 26, 1865	1 year.	Mustered out with company Sept. 20, 1865.
Pain, Joseph	....do....	19	Jan. 20, 1865	1 year.	Mustered out with company Sept. 20, 1865.
Pairtress, Jacob	....do..	35	Jan. [illegible], 1865	1 year.	Mustered out Aug. 4, 1865, at Chattanooga, Tenn., by order of War Department.
Palmer, Robert	....do....	21	Jan. 30, 1865	1 year	Mustered out with company Sept. 20, 1865.
Patton, William W.	....do....	19	Feb. 4, 1865	1 year	Mustered out with company Sept. 20, 1865.
Peck, Oscar M.	....do....	20	Feb. 10, 1865	1 year	Mustered out with company Sept. 20, 1865.
Piatt, James	....do....	18	Feb. 6, 1865	1 year.	Mustered out June 16, 1865, at Chattanooga, by order of War Department.
Poole, Harry	....do...	18	Feb. 17, 1865	1 year	Mustered out with company Sept. 20, 1865.
Romine, George	....do....	18	Feb. 10, 1865	1 year	Died May 7, 1865, in hospital at Nashville, Tennessee.
Schleich, George	....do....	27	Feb. 15, 1865	1 year	Mustered out with company Sept. 20, 1865.
Smith, Andrew	....do....	44	Feb. 13, 1865	1 year	Mustered out with company Sept. 20, 1865.
Snead, John	....do....	35	Jan. [illegible], 1865	1 year	Mustered out with company Sept. 20, 1865.
Snyder, John D.	....do....	29	Feb. 17, 1865	1 year.	Mustered out with company Sept. 20, 1865.
Stockwell, Brutus E.	....do....	19	Feb. 7, 1865	1 year	Mustered out May [illegible], 1865, at Nashville, Tenn., by order of War Department.
Stricklin, Benjamin F.	....do...	18	Jan. 31, 1865	1 year	Mustered out with company Sept. 20, 1865.
Templin, John C.	....do....	18	Jan. 21, 1865	1 year.	Mustered out with company Sept. 20, 1865.
Turner, Garrett	....do....	22	Jan. 28, 1865	1 year	
Watson, Joseph L.	....do....	25	Jan. 21, 1865	1 year.	Mustered out with company Sept. 20, 1865.
Williams, George S.	....do....	18	Jan. 24, 1865	1 year.	Died April 6, 1865, in hospital at Nashville, Tennessee.
Willison, Jacob	....do...	23	Feb. 13, 1865	1 year	Mustered out with company Sept. 20, 1865.
Wilson, Walter	....do ...	18	Jan. 24, 1865	1 year.	Absent, sick since March 15, 1865, in hospital at Nashville, Tenn. No further record found.
Wolshire, John	....do....	21	Feb. 17, 1865	1 year.	Mustered out to date Sept. 20, 1865, by order of War Department.

	Rank.	Age.	Date of Entering the Service.	Period of Service.	Remarks.
r, Robert	Private.	18	Jan. 28, 1865	1 year.	
, Samuel	....do....	23	Feb. 7, 1865	1 year.	
rmick, Amos G	....do....	20	Feb. 11, 1865	1 year.	Mustered out with company Sept. 20, 1865.
y, James	....do....	36	Feb. 8, 1865	1 year.	Mustered out to date Sept. 20, 1865, by order of War Department
onald, John H	....do....	27	Feb. 6, 1865	1 year.	Mustered out June 24, 1865, at Camp Chase, O., by order of War Department.
onald, J. Wheeler	....do....	36	Feb. 8, 1865	1 year.	Died July 27, 1865, in hospital at Nashville, Tennessee.
onald, William	....do....	20	Feb. 6, 1865	1 year.	Mustered out with company Sept. 20, 1865.
uire, Andrew	....do....	18	Feb. 6, 1865	1 year.	
on, Thomas	....do....	24	Jan. 28, 1865	1 year.	
l, William O	....do....	21	Feb. 6, 1865	1 year.	Mustered out with company Sept. 20, 1865.
ill, William C	....do....	19	Feb. 10, 1865	1 year.	Mustered out with company Sept. 20, 1865.
er, William	....do....	18	Jan. 28, 1865	1 year.	Mustered out with company Sept. 20, 1865.
r, Louis	....do....	18	Feb. 7, 1865	1 year.	Mustered out with company Sept. 20, 1865.
is, John M	....do....	18	Feb. 6, 1865	1 year.	Mustered out with company Sept. 20, 1865.
a, John H	....do....	19	Feb. 9, 1865	1 year.	
, Enoch K	....do....	20	Feb. 9, 1865	1 year.	Mustered out with company Sept. 20, 1865.
les, William	....do....	20	Feb. 7, 1865	1 year	Mustered out with company Sept. 20, 1865.
an, Henry	....do....	29	Feb. 6, 1865	1 year.	Mustered out with company Sept. 20, 1865.
on, David	....do....	36	Feb. 8, 1865	1 year.	Mustered out with company Sept. 20, 1865.
ols, Erasmus C	....do....	21	Feb. 6, 1865	1 year.	Mustered out with company Sept. 20, 1865.
ne, Richard	....do....	28	Jan. 28, 1865	1 year.	Mustered out with company Sept. 20, 1865.
rra, Nathan	....do....	18	Feb. 9, 1865	1 year.	Mustered out with company Sept. 20, 1865.
ark, George M	....do....	20	Feb. 10, 1865	1 year.	Mustered out with company Sept. 20, 1865.
s, Richard	....do....	29	Jan. 28, 1865	1 year.	Mustered out with company Sept. 20, 1865.
er, William	....do....	18	Feb. 9, 1865	1 year.	Mustered out with company Sept. 20, 1865.
rson, John	....do....	35	Jan. 18, 1865	1 year.	Transferred to Veteran Reserve Corps May 29, 1865.
s, Daniel M	....do....	18	Jan. 21, 1865	1 year.	Transferred to Veteran Reserve Corps May 29, 1865.
amer, William	....do....	18	Feb. 9, 1865	1 year.	Mustered out Sept. 11, 1865, at Camp Dennison, O., by order of War Department.
cy, Benjamin S	....do....	36	Feb. 8, 1865	1 year.	Mustered out with company Sept. 20, 1865.
rreck, John W	....do....	20	Feb. 6, 1865	1 year.	
, Vincent	....do....	35	Jan. 25, 1865	1 year.	Mustered out with company Sept. 20, 1865.
ies, James	....do....	34	Jan. 11, 1865	1 year.	Mustered out with company Sept. 20, 1865.
Henry M	....do....	21	Jan. 30, 1865	1 year.	Mustered out with company Sept. 20, 1865.
David	....do....	36	Jan. 28, 1865	1 year.	
John	....do....	42	Jan. 23, 1865	1 year.	Discharged June 16, 1865, at Chattanooga, Tenn., on Surgeon's certificate of disability.
William	....do....	24	Jan. 27, 1865	1 year.	
William C	....do....	20	Feb. 9, 1865	1 year.	Mustered out with company Sept. 20, 1865.
Eli	....do....	18	Jan. 27, 1865	1 year.	Mustered out with company Sept. 20, 1865.
E. Berkley	....do....	21	Jan. 28, 1865	1 year.	Discharged Nov. 20, 1865, at Baltimore, Md., on Surgeon's certificate of disability.
t, William	....do....	21	Jan. 26, 1865	1 year.	Mustered out Sept. 29, 1865, at Camp Dennison, O., by order of War Department.
, David	....do....	18	Feb. 11, 1865	1 year.	Mustered out with company Sept. 20, 1865.
nas, David C	....do....	18	Jan. 28, 1865	1 year.	Mustered out with company Sept. 20, 1865.
en, John F	....do....	28	Feb. 16, 1865	1 year.	Mustered out with company Sept. 20, 1865.
ierebine, Samuel	....do....	19	Jan. 24, 1865	1 year.	Mustered out with company Sept. 20, 1865.
el, Henry	....do....	35	Feb. 7, 1865	1 year.	Discharged July 7, 1865, at Chattanooga, Tenn., on Surgeon's certificate of disability.
el, Washington	....do....	18	Feb. 8, 1865	1 year.	Mustered out with company Sept. 20, 1865.

COMPANY F.

ered in February 10, 1865, at Camp Chase, O., by W. P. Richardson, Colonel 25th O. V. I. Mustered out September 20, 1865, at Nashville, Tenn., by J. W. Chickering, Captain and A. C. M., 2d Division, 4th Army Corps.

	Rank.	Age.	Date of Entering the Service.	Period of Service.	Remarks.
e P. Davis	Captain.	22	Feb. 20, 1865	1 year.	Mustered out with company Sept. 20, 1865.
ies W. Gerwig	1st Lieut	23	Feb. 20, 1865	1 year.	Mustered out with company Sept. 20, 1865.
son P. Taylor	2d Lieut.	24	Feb. 20, 1865	1 year.	Mustered out with company Sept. 20, 1865.
iah Morrow	1st Sergt.	32	Jan. 30, 1865	1 year.	Mustered out with company Sept. 20, 1865.
l. Wier	Sergeant.	30	Feb. 1, 1865	1 year.	Mustered out with company Sept. 20, 1865.
Frailey	....do....	26	Jan. 31, 1866	1 year.	Mustered out with company Sept. 20, 1865.
Murray	....do....	19	Feb. 7, 1865	1 year.	Appointed from Corporal June 8, 1865; mustered out with company Sept. 20, 1865
rt Emmons	....do....	19	Feb. 7, 1865	1 year.	Appointed from Corporal Sept. 1, 1865; mustered out with company Sept. 20, 1865.
ecrest	....do....	24	Jan. 27, 1865	1 year.	Mustered out to date Aug. 23, 1865, by order of War Department.
s P. Conley	....do....	23	Feb. 6, 1866	1 year.	Promoted to Com. Sergeant June 8, 1866.
Burlingame	Corporal.	22	Jan. 30, 1865	1 year	Mustered out with company Sept. 20, 1865.
rd Hawley	....do....	21	Jan. 14, 1865	1 year.	Mustered out with company Sept. 20, 1865.
than Maple	....do....	20	Feb. 8, 1865	1 year.	Mustered out with company Sept. 20, 1865.
. Edwards	....do....	23	Feb. 7, 1865	1 year.	Mustered out with company Sept. 20, 1865.

Names.	Rank.	Age.	Date of Entering the Service	Period of Service.	Remarks.
John Rice	Corporal.	30	Jan. 13, 1865	1 year.	Mustered out with company Sept. 20, 1865.
John M. Hart	...do...	18	Feb. 9, 1865	1 year.	Mustered out with company Sept. 20, 1865.
John Whitacre	...do...	20	Feb. 7, 1865	1 year.	Appointed June 3, 1865; mustered out with company Sept. 20, 1865.
Albert Welsh	...do...	18	Feb. 3, 1865	1 year.	Appointed Sept. 1, 1865; mustered out with company Sept. 20, 1865.
Albertus A. Kitzmiller	Musician.	18	Feb. 8, 1865	1 year.	Mustered out with company Sept. 20, 1865.
William L. Waun	...do...	19	Jan. 30, 1865	1 year.	Promoted to Principal Musician March 1, 1865.
Barnhart, Zenis	Private.	19	Jan. 13, 1865	1 year.	Died March 8, 1865, at Camp Chase, O.
Beaumont, James D	...do...	19	Feb. 10, 1865	1 year.	Mustered out July 10, 1865, at Columbus, O., by order of War Department.
Behner, Milton	...do...	20	Feb. 13, 1865	1 year.	Mustered out with company Sept. 20, 1865.
Best, Henry M	...do...	18	Feb. 1, 1865	1 year.	Mustered out with company Sept. 20, 1865.
Betz, Hiram	...do...	19	Feb. 6, 1865	1 year	Mustered out July 7, 1865, at Chattanooga, Tenn., by order of War Department.
Bolinger, Martin	...do...	25	Feb. 7, 1865		out with company Sept. 20, 1865.
Brown, Henry H	...do...	31	Feb. 10, 1865		out with company Sept. 20, 1865.
Campbell, William H	...do...	19	Feb. 13, 1865	1 year.	Mustered out with company Sept. 20, 1865.
Clemns, Monroe	...do...	18	Feb. 10, 1865	1 year.	Mustered out with company Sept. 20, 1865.
Clinton, Daniel M	...do...	19	Feb. 9, 1865	1 year.	Mustered out to date Sept. 20, 1865, by order of War Department.
Clinton, James M	...do...	18	Feb. 7, 1865	1 year.	Mustered out with company Sept. 20, 1865.
Creighton, Aaron B	...do...	27	Feb. 11, 1865	1 year.	
Crites, William	...do...	18	Feb. 2, 1865	1 year.	Mustered out with company Sept. 20, 1865.
Daniels, James	...do...	18	Feb. 9, 1865	1 year.	Mustered out with company Sept. 20, 1865.
Denney, Henry	...do...	18	Feb. 8, 1865	1 year.	Mustered out with company Sept. 20, 1865.
Doyle, Eli	...do...	38	Jan. 27, 1865	1 year.	Mustered out with company Sept. 20, 1865.
Drake, Thomas F	...do...	18	Feb. 7, 1865	1 year.	Mustered out with company Sept. 20, 1865.
Elliott, Daniel	...do...	22	Jan. 27, 1865	1 year.	Mustered out to date Aug. 22, 1865, by order of War Department.
Elliott, Embrey	...do...	18	Jan. 27, 1865	1 year.	Died March 4, 1865, at Nashville, Tenn.
Figle, Jacob	...do...	27	Feb. 4, 1865	1 year.	Mustered out with company Sept. 20, 1865.
Foreacre, Dee J	...do...	18	Feb. 11, 1865	1 year.	Mustered out with company Sept. 20, 1865.
Fosnight, John H	...do...	18	Feb. 8, 1865	1 year.	Died April 10, 1865, at Nashville, Tenn.
Fryberger, Franklin H	...do...	18	Feb. 8, 1865	1 year.	Mustered out with company Sept. 20, 1865.
Grund, Conrad	...do...	36	Feb. 4, 1865	1 year.	Mustered out to date Sept. 20, 1865, by order of War Department.
Grund, James F.	...do...	17	Feb. 4, 1865	1 year.	Mustered out with company Sept. 20, 1865.
Haines, Abraham	...do...	22	Feb. 6, 1865	1 year.	Mustered out with company Sept. 20, 1865.
Hanaline, John	...do...	18	Feb. 3, 1865	1 year.	Mustered out with company Sept. 20, 1865.
Hannay, Robert	...do...	19	Feb. 10, 1865	1 year.	Mustered out with company Sept. 20, 1865.
Hawley, Charles	...do...	19	Jan. 16, 1866	1 year.	Mustered out with company Sept. 20, 1865.
Hawley, Tine	...do...	18	Feb. 3, 1865	1 year.	Mustered out with company Sept. 20, 1865.
Haynam, Emanuel	...do...	19	Feb. 13, 1865	1 year.	Mustered out with company Sept. 20, 1865.
Hinman, John	...do...	26	Jan. 17, 1865	1 year.	Mustered out with company Sept. 20, 1865.
Hinman, Mack W	...do...	18	Feb. 8, 1865	1 year	Mustered out Sept. 19, 1865, at Camp Dennison, O., by order of War Department.
Irvin, John S	...do...	18	Jan. 30, 1865	1 year.	Mustered out with company Sept. 20, 1865.
Jerome, John F	...do...	16	Feb. 8, 1865	1 year.	Mustered out with company Sept. 20, 1865.
Johnson, Jesse	...do...	21	Feb. 1, 1865	1 year.	Died July 20, 1865, at Decherd, Tenn.
Johnson, John	...do...	23	Feb. 1, 1865	1 year.	
Keifer, Cyrus W	...do...	18	Jan. 17, 1865	1 year.	Mustered out with company Sept. 20, 1865.
Kellogg, William	...do...	19	Jan. 30, 1865	1 year.	Mustered out Oct. 9, 1865, at Camp Dennison, O., by order of War Department.
Louthan, Benjamin F	...do...	18	Jan. 2, 1865	1 year	Mustered out May 22, 1865, by order of War Department.
McConnell, Samuel	...do...	18	Jan. 20, 1865	1 year.	Mustered out with company Sept. 20, 1865.
McHenry, Samuel M	...do...	18	Feb. 3, 1865	1 year.	Mustered out with company Sept. 20, 1865.
McKinney, Franklin	...do...	18	Jan. 31, 1865	1 year.	Mustered out with company Sept. 20, 1865.
Mantull, Mortimer	...do...	19	Feb. 9, 1865	1 year.	Mustered out with company Sept. 20, 1865.
Mariman, Samuel	...do...	29	Feb. 8, 1865	1 year.	Mustered out with company Sept. 20, 1865.
Martin, Thomas	...do...	20	Jan. 26, 1865	1 year.	Mustered out with company Sept. 20, 1865.
Masters, David M	...do...	18	Feb. 11, 1865	1 year.	Mustered out with company Sept. 20, 1865.
Mead, John	...do...	26	Jan. 26, 1865	1 year.	Mustered out with company Sept. 20, 1865.
Menough, John	...do...	17	Feb. 8, 1865	1 year.	Mustered out June 16, 1865, at Chattanooga, Tenn., by order of War Department.
Miller, Moses	...do...	18	Jan. 27, 1865	1 year.	Mustered out with company Sept. 20, 1865.
Mitchell, David	...do...	18	Feb. 10, 1865	1 year.	Mustered out with company Sept. 20, 1865.
Moore, Joseph	...do...	20	Feb. 8, 1865	1 year.	Mustered out with company Sept. 20, 1865.
Morlan, Harvey	...do...	18	Feb. 16, 1865	1 year.	Mustered out with company Sept. 20, 1865.
N[illegible]se, [illegible]onard	...do...	17	Feb. 2, 1865	1 year.	Mustered out with company Sept. 20, 1865.
Newhouse, Samuel	...do...	17	Feb. 2, 1865	1 year.	Mustered out with company Sept. 20, 1865.
Pet[illegible]s, [illegible]	...do...	31	Jan. 21, 1865	1 year.	Mustered out with company Sept. 20, 1865.
Prince, Edwin	...do...	18	Jan. 27, 1865	1 year.	Mustered out with company Sept. 20, 1865.
Roach, Thomas J	...do...	28	Jan. 30, 1865	1 year.	Mustered out with company Sept. 20, 1865.
Ryan, Samuel	...do...	18	Feb. 8, 1865	1 year.	Mustered out with company Sept. 20, 1865.
Sandon, Charles H	...do...	21	Jan. 26, 1865	1 year.	
Sayner, Henry	...do...	21	Feb. 9, 1865	1 year.	Mustered out with company Sept. 20, 1865.
Selby, William L	...do...	31	Jan. 27, 1865	1 year.	Mustered out with company Sept. 20, 1865.
Sheckler, John M	...do...	19	Feb. 6, 1865	1 year.	Mustered out with company Sept. 20, 1865.
Shriver, Adam	...do...	39	Jan. 26, 1865	1 year.	Mustered out with company Sept. 20, 1865.
Spain, William	...do...	33	Jan. 31, 1865	1 year	Mustered out with company Sept. 20, 1865.
Sprowl, George D	...do...	18	Jan. 30, 1865	1 year.	Mustered out with company Sept. 20, 1865.
Stoner, Urias F	...do...	18	Feb. 8, 1865	1 year.	Mustered out with company Sept. 20, 1865.
Stratton, Simon C	...do...	21	Feb. 11, 1865	1 year.	Mustered out with company Sept. 20, 1865.

Names.	Rank.	Age.	Date of Entering the Service.	Period of Service.	Remarks.
Taylor, George	Private.	18	Feb. 13, 1865	1 year.	Died June 28, 1865, at Bridgeport, Ala.
Taylor, Jeremiah	....do....	26	Feb. 4, 1865	1 year	Died April 1, 1865, at Nashville, Tenn.
Taylor, John L.	....do....	20	Feb. 11, 1865	1 year.	Mustered out with company Sept 20, 1865.
Tomlinson, George W.	....do....	18	Jan. 27, 1865	1 year.	Mustered out with company Sept. 20, 1865.
Ullman, Adam	....do....	18	Feb. 6, 1865	1 year.	Died March 31, 1865, at Bridgeport, Ala.
Veil, Albert A.	....do....	18	Jan. 26, 1865	1 year.	Mustered out with company Sept. 20, 1865.
Walker, Lewis	....do....	19	Feb. 13, 1865	1 year.	Mustered out with company Sept. 20, 1865.
Welsh, William J.	....do....	19	Feb. 8, 1865	1 year.	Mustered out with company Sept. 20, 1865.
Whitmore, Jonathan	....do....	20	Feb. 7, 1865	1 year.	Mustered out with company Sept. 20, 1865.
Wilson, Harper W.	....do....	18	Feb. 8, 1865	1 year	Mustered out with company Sept. 20, 1865.
Witherspoon, John	....do....	29	Feb. 8, 1865	1 year.	Mustered out with company Sept. 20, 1865.
Yeager, Paul	....do....	48	Feb. 8, 1865	1 year.	Mustered out to date Sept. 20, 1865, by order of War Department.
Yeager, William C	....do....	18	Feb. 3, 1865	1 year.	Mustered out with company Sept. 20, 1865.
Young, Alfred	....do....	19	Feb. 3, 1865	1 year	Mustered out with company Sept. 20, 1865.
Young, Jacob	....do....	37	Jan. 27, 1865	1 year.	Mustered out May 18, 1865, at Chattanooga, Tenn., by order of War Department.

COMPANY G.

Mustered in February 20, 1865, at Camp Chase, O., by W. P. Richardson, Colonel 25th O. V. I. Mustered out September 20, 1865, at Nashville, Tenn., by J. W. Chickering, Captain and A. C. M., 2d Division, 4th Army Corps.

Names.	Rank.	Age.	Date of Entering the Service.	Period of Service.	Remarks.
William J. Widener	Captain.	22	Feb. 20, 1865	1 year.	Mustered out with company Sept. 20, 1865.
Robert Detwiler	1st Lieut.	33	Feb. 20, 1865	1 year.	Resigned June 1, 1865.
Michael Stack	2d Lieut.	28	Feb. 20, 1865	1 year.	Mustered out with company Sept. 20, 1865.
John L. Knight	1st Sergt.	18	Feb. 3, 1865	1 year.	Appointed from Sergeant July 29, 1865; mustered out with company Sept. 20, 1865.
Salathiel Lemon	Sergeant.	22	Feb. 3, 1865	1 year.	Reduced from 1st Sergeant July 29, 1865, at his own request; mustered out with company Sept. 20, 1865.
Henry O. Maare	....do....	19	Jan. 20, 1865	1 year.	Mustered out with company Sept. 20, 1865.
Joseph Martin	....do....	16	Feb. 3, 1865	1 year.	Mustered out with company Sept. 20, 1865.
John Barclay	....do....	21	Jan. 6, 1865	1 year.	Mustered out with company Sept. 20, 1865.
Miles M. McCowen	Corporal.	23	Jan. 13, 1865	1 year.	Absent, since Aug. 26, 1865, at Chattanooga, Tenn. No further record found.
William A. Hawkins	....do....	19	Feb. 4, 1865	1 year.	Mustered out with company Sept. 20, 1865.
James N. Hawkins	....do....	19	Jan. 13, 1865	1 year.	Mustered out with company Sept. 20, 1865.
John Blair	....do....	30	Jan. 24, 1865	1 year.	Mustered out July 22, 1865, at Cincinnati, O., by order of War Department.
Jacob Rush	....do....	22	Jan. 20, 1865	1 year.	Mustered out with company Sept. 20, 1865.
Henry C. Thompson	....do....	24	Feb. 3, 1865	1 year.	Appointed July 1, 1865; mustered out with company Sept. 20, 1865.
George W. Poole	....do....	24	Feb. 3, 1865	1 year.	Died April 11, 1865, in hospital at Nashville, Tennessee.
John Poland	....do....	36	Feb. 15, 1865	1 year.	
Hector F. Huffman	....do....	19	Jan. 18, 1865	1 year.	Mustered out to date Aug. 21, 1865, by order of War Department.
Ashley, Armstrong	Private.	18	Feb. 5, 1865	1 year.	Mustered out with company Sept. 20, 1865.
Bass, Isaac	....do....	18	Feb. 6, 1865	1 year.	Mustered out with company Sept. 20, 1865.
Bass, Thomas	....do....	18	Jan. 31, 1865	1 year.	Died March 5, 1865, in hospital at Nashville, Tennessee.
Bullard, Joshua	....do....	18	Feb. 5, 1865	1 year.	Died March 17, 1865, in hospital at Nashville, Tennessee.
Blackburn, Samuel	....do....	23	Feb. 10, 1865	1 year.	Mustered out May 18, 1865, at Bridgeport, Ala., by order of War Department.
Bletcher, Jacob	....do....	19	Feb. 7, 1865	1 year.	Mustered out with company Sept. 20, 1865.
Bottenfield, Franklin	....do....	17	Feb. 6, 1865	1 year.	Mustered out with company Sept. 20, 1865.
Bowersmith, John	....do....	18	Jan. 23, 1865	1 year.	Mustered out with company Sept. 20, 1865.
Brennenstahl, Gottleib	....do....	34	Feb. 15, 1865	1 year.	Mustered out with company Sept. 20, 1865.
Brooker, Lewis	....do....	18	Feb. 16, 1865	1 year.	Mustered out with company Sept. 20, 1865.
Brown, Benjamin F.	....do....	30	Feb. 10, 1865	1 year.	Mustered out with company Sept. 20, 1865.
Brown, Wesley	....do....	28	Feb. 4, 1865	1 year.	Mustered out with company Sept. 20, 1865.
Carrell, William	....do....	20	Jan. 9, 1865	1 year.	Mustered out with company Sept. 20, 1865.
Colvin, Charles	....do....	27	Feb. 6, 1865	1 year.	Mustered out with company Sept. 20, 1865.
Colvin, Rosberry	....do....	20	Feb. 6, 1865	1 year.	Mustered out May 18, 1865, at Bridgeport, Ala., by order of War Department.
Conklin, John H.	....do....	21	Feb. 7, 1865	1 year.	Mustered out with company Sept. 20, 1865.
Courtney, Joseph F.	....do....	19	Jan. 31, 1865	1 year.	Died April 5, 1865, in hospital at Bridgeport, Alabama.
Courtney, Lanty L.	....do....	28	Feb. 7, 1865	1 year.	Mustered out with company Sept. 20, 1865.
Covert, Samuel N.	....do....	19	Jan. 30, 1865	1 year.	Mustered out with company Sept. 20, 1865.
Davis, Charles S.	....do....	24	Jan. 31, 1865	1 year.	Died March 14, 1865, in hospital at Nashville, Tennessee.
Dearth, George	....do....	28	Feb. 4, 1865	1 year.	Mustered out with company Sept. 20, 1865.
Delfenbaugh, Loring P.	....do....	23	Jan. 23, 1865	1 year.	Mustered out with company Sept. 20, 1865.
Dickerson, Thomas	....do....	18	Feb. 13, 1865	1 year.	Mustered out with company Sept. 20, 1865.
Dille, Charles H.	....do....	16	Feb. 7, 1865	1 year.	Mustered out with company Sept. 20, 1865.
Dillinger, John W.	....do....	18	Feb. 7, 1865	1 year.	Mustered out with company Sept. 20, 1865.

Names	Rank.	Age.	Date of Entering the Service.	Period of Service.	Remarks.
Duncan, Lee	Private..	38	Jan. 23, 1865	1 year.	Mustered out with company Sept. 20, 1865.
Duosackel, Rudolph	...do...	33	Feb. 15, 1865	1 year.	Mustered out with company Sept. 20, 1865.
Ellis, Benjamin A.	...do...	18	Feb. 8, 1865	1 year.	Mustered out with company Sept. 20, 1865.
Ellis, James F.	...do...	16	Feb. 8, 1865	1 year.	Mustered out with company Sept. 20, 1865.
Elmer, Casper	...do...	18	Jan. 25, 1865	1 year.	Mustered out July 7, 1865, at Chattanooga, Tenn., by order of War Department.
Elrod, David	...do...	17	Feb. 6, 1865	1 year.	Mustered out with company Sept. 20, 1865.
Eulow, Joseph	...do...	18	Jan. 31, 1865	1 year.	Mustered out with company Sept. 20, 1865.
Fartig, Freeman R.	...do...	27	Feb. 17, 1865	1 year.	Mustered out with company Sept. 20, 1865; on muster-in roll as Reuben R. Fartig.
Fisher, William H.	...do...	25	Feb. 17, 1865	1 year.	Mustered out with company Sept. 20, 1865.
Francis, Frederick	...do...	31	Feb. 13, 1865	1 year.	Mustered out with company Sept. 20, 1865.
Gardner, Lewis R.	...do...	18	Feb. 10, 1865	1 year.	Mustered out Aug. 22, 1865, at Camp Dennison, O., by order of War Department.
Geer, Augustus	...do...	18	Feb. 7, 1865	1 year.	Mustered out with company Sept. 20, 1865.
Gibbons, Thomas H.	...do...	18	Jan. 10, 1865	1 year.	Mustered out with company Sept. 20, 1865.
Harsh, Martin L.	...do...	24	Feb. 13, 1865	1 year.	Mustered out with company Sept. 20, 1865.
Haw[illegible], [illegible]oh M.	...do...	18	Feb. 10, 1865	1 year.	Mustered out with company Sept. 20, 1865.
Hayes, William T.	...do...	18	Jan. 31, 1865	1 year.	Mustered out with company Sept. 20, 1865.
Herrington, David	...do...	18	Jan. 20, 1865	1 year.	Mustered out with company Sept. 20, 1865.
Horton, O'Neil	...do...	18	Feb. 7, 1865	1 year.	Mustered out with company Sept. 20, 1865.
Hysell, Perry	...do...	19	Feb. 10, 1865	1 year.	Mustered out with company Sept. 20, 1865.
Johnson, Russell	...do...	19	Feb. 4, 1865	1 year.	Mustered out with company Sept. 20, 1865.
Jones, Henry	...do...	21	Jan. 16, 1865	1 year.	Mustered out with company Sept. 20, 1865.
Kenney, Alfred	...do...	19	Jan. 31, 1865	1 year.	Mustered out Sept. 26, 1865, at Camp Dennison, O., by order of War Department.
Knight, John H.	...do...	18	Feb. 1, 1865	1 year	Mustered out with company Sept. 20, 1865.
Lee, Horace	...do...	41	Feb. 15, 1865	1 year.	Mustered out July 7, 1865, at Chattanooga, Tenn., by order of War Department.
Lehman, Samuel	...do...	18	Feb. 8, 1865	1 year	Mustered out with company Sept. 20, 1865.
McCann, William	...do...	25	Jan. 28, 1865	1 year.	
McCowen, Joseph	...do...	18	Feb. 7, 1865	1 year.	Mustered out with company Sept. 20, 1865.
McCowen, Taylor J.	...do...	18	Jan. 13, 1865	1 year.	Mustered out with company Sept. 20, 1865.
McLaughlin, James	...do...	26	Jan. 23, 1865	1 year.	Mustered out with company Sept. 20, 1865.
McMahon, Alfred D.	...do...	19	Feb. 4, 1865	1 year	Mustered out June 16, 1865, at Chattanooga, Tenn., by order of War Department.
McMahon, William H.	...do...	24	Feb. 3, 1865	1 year.	Mustered out with company Sept. 20, 1865.
McVay, Jacob	...do...	18	Feb. 17, 1865	1 year.	Mustered out with company Sept. 20, 1865.
Marsh, Cornelius	...do...	21	Jan. 13, 1865	1 year.	Mustered out Sept. 26, 1865, at Camp Dennison, O., by order of War Department.
Martindale, James W.	...do...	31	Feb. 10, 1865	1 year.	Mustered out May 25, 1865, at Louisville, Ky., by order of War Department.
Miller, Joshua	...do...	43	Feb. 11, 1865	1 year	
Miller, Samuel	...do...	22	Feb. 15, 1865	1 year.	Mustered out with company Sept. 20, 1865.
Moldon, Franklin	...do...	35	Feb. 10, 1865	1 year.	Mustered out with company Sept. 20, 1865.
M[illegible], [illegible]rew W.	...do...	23	Feb. 8, 1865	1 year.	Mustered out with company Sept. 20, 1865.
Noble, Simeon J.	...do...	19	Jan. 26, 1865	1 year.	Mustered out with company Sept. 20, 1865.
Pain, Joseph	...do...	19	Jan. [illegible], 1865	1 year	Mustered out with company Sept. 20, 1865.
Pantress, Jacob	...do...	[illegible]	Jan. [illegible], 1865	1 year.	Mustered out Aug. 4, 1865, at Chattanooga, Tenn., by order of War Department.
Palmer, Robert	...do...	21	Jan. 30, 1865	1 year	Mustered out with company Sept. 20, 1865.
Patton, William W.	...do...	19	Feb. 4, 1865	1 year.	Mustered out with company Sept. 20, 1865.
Peck, Oscar M.	...do...	[illegible]	Feb. 16, 1865	1 year.	Mustered out with company Sept. 20, 1865.
Piatt, James	...do...	18	Feb. 6, 1865	1 year.	Mustered out June 16, 1865, at Chattanooga, Tenn., by order of War Department.
Poole, Harry	...do...	18	Feb. 17, 1865	1 year.	Mustered out with company Sept. 20, 1865.
Romine, George	...do...	18	Feb. 10, 1865	1 year.	Died May 7, 1865, in hospital at Nashville, Tennessee.
Schleich, George	...do...	27	Feb. 15, 1865	1 year.	Mustered out with company Sept. 20, 1865.
Smith, Andrew	...do...	44	Feb. 13, 1865	1 year.	Mustered out with company Sept. 20, 1865.
Snead, John	...do...	[illegible]	Jan. [illegible], 1865	1 year.	Mustered out with company Sept. 20, 1865.
Snyder, John D.	...do...	29	Feb. 17, 1865	1 year.	Mustered out with company Sept. 20, 1865.
Stockwell, Brutus E.	...do...	19	Feb. 7, 1865	1 year.	Mustered out May [illegible], 1865, at Nashville, Tenn., by order of War Department.
Stricklin, Benjamin F.	...do...	18	Jan. 31, 1865	1 year.	Mustered out with company Sept. 20, 1865.
Templin, John C.	...do...	18	Jan. 21, 1865	1 year.	Mustered out with company Sept. 20, 1865.
Turner, Garrett	...do...	22	Jan. 28, 1865	1 year.	
Watson, Joseph L.	...do...	25	Jan. 21, 1865	1 year.	Mustered out with company Sept. 20, 1865.
Williams, George S.	...do...	18	Jan. 24, 1865	1 year.	Died April 6, 1865, in hospital at Nashville, Tennessee.
Willson, Jacob	...do...	23	Feb. 13, 1865	1 year.	Mustered out with company Sept. 20, 1865.
Wilson, Walter	...do...	18	Jan. 24, 1865	1 year.	Absent, sick since March 15, 1865, in hospital at Nashville, Tenn. No further record found.
Wolshire, John	...do...	21	Feb. 17, 1865	1 year.	Mustered out to date Sept. 20, 1865, by order of War Department.

COMPANY H.

ustered in February 20, 1865, at Camp Chase, O., by W. P. Richardson, Colonel 25th O. V. I. Mustered out September 20, 1865, at Nashville, Tenn., by J. W. Chickering, Captain and A. C. M., 2d Division, 4th Army Corps.

	Rank.	Age.	Date of Entering the Service.	Period of Service.	Remarks.
non Perkins	Captain.	30	Jan. 12, 1865	1 year.	Appointed Feb. 21, 1865; mustered out with company Sept. 20, 1865.
illiam H. Bowen	1st Lieut.	40	Jan. 26, 1865	1 year.	Appointed March 3, 1865; mustered out with company Sept. 20, 1865.
vid H. Commager	2d Lieut.	20	Mch. 15, 1865	1 year.	Mustered out with company Sept. 20 1865.
illiam H. Franco	1st Sergt.	20	Jan. 20, 1865	1 year.	Appointed from Sergeant May 4, 1865; mustered out with company Sept. 20, 1865.
llus Knoff	Sergeant.	24	Jan. 28, 1865	1 year.	Mustered out with company Sept. 20, 1865.
hn M. Biddleson	...do...	33	Feb. 3, 1865	1 year.	Appointed from Corporal May 4, 1865; mustered out with company Sept. 20, 1865.
hn Ulm	...do...	26	Jan. 20, 1865	1 year.	Mustered out with company Sept. 20, 1865.
man N. Elliott	...do...	28	Jan. 23, 1865	1 year.	Appointed from private May 4, 1865; mustered out with company Sept. 20, 1865.
yron Collins	...do...	21	Jan. 28, 1865	1 year.	Died April 26, 1865, in hospital at Nashville, Tennessee.
mmett W. Price	...do...	21	Jan. 28, 1865	1 year.	Promoted to Asst. Surgeon April 24, 1865
orge Miller	Corporal.	30	Feb. 2, 1865	1 year.	Mustered out with company Sept. 20, 1865.
in Webber	...do...	18	Jan. 31, 1865	1 year.	Mustered out with company Sept. 20, 1865.
seph Kohl	...do...	36	Jan. 24, 1865	1 year.	Mustered out with company Sept. 20, 1865.
ax M. Carter	...do...	21	Feb. 3, 1865	1 year.	Transferred from Co. D, 188th O. V. I., ——; mustered out with company Sept. 20, 1865.
orge Eck	...do...	30	Jan. 20, 1865	1 year.	Mustered out with company Sept. 20, 1865.
illiam Miller	...do...	21	Feb. 6, 1865	1 year.	Mustered out with company Sept. 20, 1865.
Jab S. Halleck	...do...	19	Feb. 4, 1865	1 year.	Appointed May 20, 1865; mustered out with company Sept. 20, 1865.
illiam R. Bosus	...do...	21	Jan. 26, 1865	1 year.	Appointed June 5, 1865; mustered out with company Sept. 20, 1865.
lmund Gorby	...do...	18	Jan. 30, 1865	1 year.	Mustered out May 16, 1865, at Chattanooga, Tenn., by order of War Department.
tus R. Taylor	...do...	19	Feb. 2, 1865	1 year.	Mustered out May 18, 1865, at Bridgeport, Ala., by order of War Department.
lolph, Adam	Private.	20	Jan. 24, 1865	1 year.	Mustered out Sept. 26, 1865, at Camp Dennison, O., by order of War Department.
lolph, Balsler	...do...	22	Jan. 28, 1865	1 year.	Died Sept. 29, 1865, in hospital at Nashville, Tennessee.
sel, Joseph	...do...	21	Jan. 20, 1865	1 year.	Mustered out with company Sept. 20, 1865.
ans, Henry	...do...	36	Jan. 26, 1865	1 year.	Died April 24, 1865, in hospital at Nashville, Tennessee.
ans, Levi	...do...	23	Jan. 28, 1865	1 year.	Mustered out with company Sept. 20, 1865.
lding, William P.	...do...	17	Feb. 2, 1865	1 year.	Mustered out with company Sept. 20, 1865.
wernox, Jonathan	...do...	18	Feb. 10, 1865	1 year.	Mustered out with company Sept. 20, 1865.
ocretts, Lucius	...do...	24	Feb. 4, 1865	1 year.	Mustered out with company Sept. 20, 1865.
ers, Philonas S.	...do...	34	Feb. 9, 1865	1 year.	Mustered out with company Sept. 20, 1865.
rl, Reuben W.	...do...	18	Feb. 3, 1865	1 year.	Transferred from Co. D, 188th O. V. I., ——; mustered out Aug. 4, 1865, at Bridgeport, Ala., by order of War Department.
urchill, Marvin	...do...	20	Jan. 28, 1865	1 year.	Mustered out with company Sept. 20, 1865.
ark, Oscar H.	...do...	18	Jan. 18, 1865	1 year.	Transferred from Co. E March 20, 1865; died Feb. 9, 1866, in hospital at Nashville, Tenn.
lver, Henry F.	...do...	27	Feb. 3, 1865	1 year.	Transferred from Co. E March 20, 1865; mustered out with company Sept. 20, 1865.
vis, Cavalus	...do...	18	Feb. 2, 1865	1 year.	Mustered out with company Sept. 20, 1865.
llenbarger, John H.	...do...	20	Feb. 11, 1865	1 year.	Mustered out with company Sept. 20, 1865.
sel, Peter	...do...	17	Feb. 9, 1865	1 year.	Mustered out with company Sept. 20, 1865.
merick, William	...do...	20	Jan. 23, 1865	1 year.	Mustered out with company Sept. 20, 1865.
glehart, Peter	...do...	28	Jan. 27, 1865	1 year.	Mustered out with company Sept. 20, 1865.
ylor, Levi	...do...	18	Jan. 24, 1865	1 year.	Mustered out Aug. 30, 1865, at Camp Dennison, O., by order of War Department.
ller, Samuel	...do...	18	Jan. 30, 1865	1 year.	Mustered out with company Sept. 20, 1865.
uch, Isaac	...do...	18	Feb. 4, 1865	1 year.	Mustered out with company Sept. 20, 1865.
ass, Edward	...do...	21	Jan. 30, 1865	1 year.	Mustered out with company Sept. 20, 1865.
ass, John	...do...	32	Feb. 10, 1865	1 year.	Mustered out with company Sept. 20, 1865.
othler, George	...do...	20	Jan. 20, 1865	1 year.	Mustered out with company Sept. 20, 1865.
othler, Michael	...do...	20	Jan. 20, 1865	1 year.	Mustered out with company Sept. 20, 1865.
ohe, George	...do...	18	Jan. 28, 1865	1 year.	Mustered out with company Sept. 20, 1865.
ughton, Lester J.	...do...	19	Feb. 7, 1865	1 year.	Mustered out with company Sept. 20, 1865.
nsch, Peter	...do...	19	Feb. 22, 1865	1 year.	Promoted to Hospital Steward Feb. 22, 1865.
riff, Ira L.	...do...	18	Jan. 27, 1865	1 year.	Mustered out with company Sept. 20, 1865.
usel, William M.	...do...	18	Feb. 10, 1865	1 year.	Mustered out with company Sept. 20, 1865.
bler, Daniel	...do...	32	Feb. 4, 1865	1 year.	Mustered out with company Sept. 20, 1865.
sel, John	...do...	22	Jan. 23, 1865	1 year.	Mustered out with company Sept. 20, 1865.
ubert, Jacob	...do...	19	Jan. 24, 1865	1 year.	Mustered out with company Sept. 20, 1865.
wis, William W.	...do...	20	Feb. 3, 1865	1 year.	Transferred from Co. D, 188th O. V. I., ——; mustered out May 21, 1865, at Nashville, Tenn., by order of War Department.
lly, Austin	...do...	18	[illegible]	1 year.	Mustered out with company Sept. 20, 1865.

Names.	Rank.	Age.	Date of Entering the Service.	Period of Service.	Remarks.
Luley, Michael	Private	19	Jan. 30, 1865	1 year.	Mustered out with company Sept. 20, 1865.
Lynn, Almerin S	...do...	18	Feb. 6, 1865	1 year.	Transferred from Co. D, 196th O. V. I. — mustered out with company Sept. 20, 1865.
Meyer, Philip	...do...	21	Jan. 30, 1865	1 year.	Mustered out with company Sept. 20, 1865.
Moyer, John W	...do...	18	Feb. 10, 1865	1 year.	Mustered out with company Sept. 20, 1865.
Nischwitz, Henry	...do...	20	Jan. 20, 1865	1 year.	Mustered out with company Sept. 20, 1865.
Obey, Eugene	...do...	17	Jan. 30, 1865	1 year.	Mustered out with company Sept. 20, 1865.
Ott, Adam	...do...	21	Jan. 20, 1865	1 year.	Mustered out with company Sept. 20, 1865.
Owens, William	...do...	23	Jan. 30, 1865	1 year.	Mustered out June 16, 1865, at Bridgeport, Ala., by order of War Department.
Parsons, John S	...do...	25	Jan. 26, 1865	1 year.	Died March 21, 1865, in hospital at Nashville, Tennessee.
Paulus, Urias	...do...	18	Jan. 30, 1865	1 year	Died June 29, 1865, in hospital at Nashville, Tennessee
Pontious, Daniel	...do...	33	Feb. 10, 1865	1 year.	Mustered out with company Sept. 20, 1865.
Pontious, Nicholas	...do...	20	Feb. 10, 1865	1 year.	Mustered out with company Sept. 20, 1865.
Potter, Rufus	...do...	27	Feb. 2, 1865	1 year.	Mustered out with company Sept. 20, 1865.
Purrington, Ellsworth C	...do...	19	Jan. 27, 1865	1 year.	Mustered out with company Sept. 20, 1865.
Rhodes, John	...do...	21	Feb. 2, 1865	1 year.	Mustered out with company Sept. 20, 1865
Rhodes, Lawrence	...do...	24	Feb. 4, 1865	1 year.	Mustered out with company Sept. 20, 1865.
Rhoad, John D.	...do...	33	Feb. 10, 1865	1 year	Mustered out with company Sept 20, 1865
Segar, Ruel	...do...	18	Feb. 7, 1865	1 year.	Mustered out with company Sept. 20, 1865.
Sell, John T.	...do...	23	Feb. 11, 1865	1 year.	Mustered out June 16, 1865, at Bridgeport, Ala., by order of War Department.
Sell, William	...do...	28	Feb. 13, 1865	1 year.	Mustered out with company Sept. 20, 1865.
Shaffer, Virgil	...do...	19	Jan. 28, 1865	1 year	
Shoemaker, James F	...do...	18	Feb. 7, 1865	1 year.	Mustered out May 18, 1865, at Bridgeport, Ala. by order of War Department.
Shoemaker, Joshua	...do...	17	Feb. 7, 1865	1 year.	Died May 12, 1865, in hospital at Jeffersonville, Indiana.
Shultz, Peter	...do...	17	Jan. 23, 1865	1 year.	Died March 29, 1865, in hospital at Nashville, Tennessee.
Sigel, William	...do...	35	Feb. 9, 1865	1 year.	Mustered out with company Sept. 20, 1865.
Slabaugh, John	...do...	37	Jan. 30, 1865	1 year.	Mustered out with company Sept 20, 1865
Smith, Joseph	...do...	39	Jan. 30, 1865	1 year.	Died May 15, 1865, in hospital at Nashville, Tennessee.
Southworth, Dallas	...do...	18	Jan. 28, 1865	1 year.	Mustered out with company Sept. 20, 1865.
Spangler, Henry	...do...	20	Jan. 23, 1865	1 year.	Mustered out with company Sept. 20, 1865.
Thompson, George	...do...	21	Jan. 30, 1865	1 year.	Mustered out with company Sept. 20, 1865.
Thorp, Thomas W.	...do...	30	Feb. 3, 1865	1 year.	Mustered out with company Sept. 20, 1865.
Tickner, Sanford	...do...	21	Jan. 30, 1865	1 year.	Mustered out with company Sept. 20, 1865.
Todd, Samuel	...do...	19	Feb. 4, 1865	1 year.	
Waters, Sylvanus	...do...	35	Jan. 30, 1865	1 year.	Mustered out with company Sept. 20, 1865.
Waters, William	...do...	31	Jan. 21, 1865	1 year.	Mustered out with company Sept. 20, 1865.
White, Charles	...do...	19	Feb. 15, 1865	1 year.	Died Feb. 25, 1865, at Camp Chase, O.
White, Riley	...do...	21	Feb. 7, 1865	1 year.	Mustered out with company Sept. 20, 1865.
Wilson, Peter	...do...	21	Jan. 30, 1865	1 year.	Mustered out with company Sept. 20, 1865.
Wolf, Samuel	...do...	18	Jan. 30, 1865	1 year	Mustered out July 20, 1865, at Louisville, Ky., by order of War Department.

COMPANY I.

Mustered in February 20, 1865, at Camp Chase, O., by W. P. Richardson, Colonel 25th O. V. I. Mustered out September 20, 1865, at Nashville, Tenn., by J. W. Chickering, Captain and A. C. M., 2d Division, 4th Army Corps.

Names.	Rank.	Age.	Date of Entering the Service.	Period of Service.	Remarks.
John McNeill	Captain.	34	Feb. 21, 1865	1 year.	Mustered out with company Sept. 20, 1865.
Archibald McNair, Jr.	1st Lieut.	35	Jan. 31, 1865	1 year.	Appointed Feb. 21, 1865; died March [illegible], 1865, at Nashville, Tenn.
William F. Landen	2d Lieut	25	Jan. 18, 1865	1 year.	Appointed Feb. 20, 1865; mustered out with company Sept. 20, 1865.
Robert B. Simpson	1st Sergt	26	Jan. 17, 1865	1 year.	Mustered out with company Sept. 20, 1865.
William H. H. Scott	Sergeant.	44	Jan. 19, 1865	1 year.	Mustered out with company Sept. 20, 1865.
James B. McClain	...do...	34	Jan. 26, 1865	1 year.	Mustered out with company Sept. 20, 1865.
James Boulware	...do...	33	Jan. 19, 1865	1 year.	Mustered out with company Sept. 20, 1865.
John T. Kennedy	Corporal.	19	Jan. 27, 1865	1 year	Mustered out with company Sept. 20, 1865; also borne on rolls as John T. Kasic
William W Ford	...do...	34	Jan. 19, 1865	1 year.	Mustered out with company Sept. 20, 1865.
Silas D. Winans	...do...	42	Jan. 30, 1865	1 year.	Mustered out with company Sept. 20, 1865.
John W. Stewart	...do...	20	Feb. 3, 1865	1 year.	Appointed June 10, 1865; mustered out with company Sept. 20, 1865
William Reese	...do...	39	Feb. 2, 1865	1 year.	Mustered out with company Sept. 20, 1865.
James A. Whiteman	...do...	38	Jan. 18, 1865	1 year.	Mustered out with company Sept. 20, 1865.
Wilber C. McClain	...do...	19	Jan. 23, 1865	1 year.	Mustered out with company Sept. 20, 1865.
Thomas J. Nichols	...do...	24	Feb. 2, 1865	1 year.	Mustered out with company Sept. 20, 1865.
Aaron S. Gray	...do...	32	Jan. 18, 1865	1 year.	Died March 24, 1865, in hospital at Nashville, Tennessee.
Abbott, Elijah B.	Private	30	Jan. 19, 1865	1 year.	Mustered out with company Sept. 20, 1865.
Altman, William A.	...do...	18	Jan. 19, 1865	1 year.	Mustered out with company Sept. 20, 1865.
Anderson, George W.	...do...	19	Jan. 19, 1865	1 year.	Mustered out with company Sept. 20, 1865.

Names.	Rank.	Age.	Date of Entering the Service.	Period of Service.	Remarks.
on, William B...	Private..	22	Jan. 24, 1865	1 year.	Reduced from Sergeant Sept. 5, 1865; mustered out with company Sept. 20, 1865.
William..........	...do....	18	Feb. 11, 1865	1 year.	Mustered out to date Aug. 7, 1865, by order of War Department.
ohn H..........	...do....	20	Feb. 2, 1865	1 year.	Mustered out with company Sept. 20, 1865.
evi L..........	...do....	20	Jan. 28, 1865	1 year.	Mustered out with company Sept. 20, 1865.
er, Jackson........	...do....	23	Feb. 9, 1865	1 year.	Mustered out with company Sept. 20, 1865.
ie..........	...do....	28	Feb. 18, 1865	1 year.	Mustered out with company Sept. 20, 1865.
seph..........	...do....	22	Feb. 10, 1865	1 year.	Died Sept. 2, 1865, in hospital at Camp Dennison, O.
, Samuel M......	...do....	29	Jan. 24, 1865	1 year.	Mustered out with company Sept. 20, 1865.
Charles C.......	...do..	18	Jan. 31, 1865	1 year.	Mustered out with company Sept. 20, 1865.
Sylvester J......	...do...	17	Feb. 1, 1865	1 year.	Mustered out with company Sept. 20, 1865.
son, John R.....	...do....	18	Feb. 1, 1865	1 year.	Died March 20, 1865, in hospital at Nashville, Tennessee.
amuel..........	...do....	30	Jan. 25, 1865	1 year.	Mustered out with company Sept. 20, 1865.
William S.......	...do....	29	Feb. 8, 1865	1 year.	Mustered out with company Sept. 20, 1865.
, William W.....	...do....	18	Feb. 3, 1865	1 year.	Died March 20, 1865, in hospital at Nashville, Tennessee.
James L.........	...do....	18	Feb. 6, 1865	1 year.	Mustered out to date Sept. 20, 1865, by order of War Department.
er, Isaac L.......	...do....	18	Feb. 2, 1865	1 year.	Mustered out to date Sept. 20, 1865, by order of War Department.
n, John A.......	...do....	18	Jan. 31, 1865	1 year.	Mustered out with company Sept. 20, 1865.
ichael H.......	...do....	17	Feb. 10, 1865	1 year.	Mustered out with company Sept. 20, 1865.
Salathiel M......	...do....	27	Jan. 31, 1865	1 year.	
John U.........	...do....	21	Jan. 25, 1865	1 year.	Mustered out with company Sept. 20, 1865.
eorge E........	...do...	18	Feb. 14, 1865	1 year.	Mustered out with company Sept. 20, 1865.
Melanchthon D.	...do....	19	Feb. 8, 1865	1 year.	Mustered out with company Sept. 20, 1865.
Solomon D......	...do....	29	Feb. 3, 1865	1 year.	Mustered out with company Sept. 20, 1865.
George W.......	...do....	21	Jan. 31, 1865	1 year.	Mustered out with company Sept. 20, 1865.
Andrew J......	...do. .	22	Jan. 18, 1865	1 year.	Mustered out May 18, 1865, at Bridgeport, Ala., by order of War Department.
s, Samuel........	...do....	26	Jan. 28, 1865	1 year	Mustered out to date Aug. 6, 1865, by order of War Department.
William........	...do....	22	Feb. 1, 1865	1 year	
ohn..........	...do....	40	Jan. 14, 1865	1 year.	Mustered out with company Sept. 20, 1865.
seph F........	...do....	27	Jan. 27, 1865	1 year.	Mustered out with company Sept. 20, 1865.
William........	...do....	28	Feb. 3, 1865	1 year.	Mustered out with company Sept. 20, 1865.
d, George.......	...do....	18	Jan. 24, 1865	1 year.	Mustered out with company Sept. 20, 1865.
y, Stanford......	...do....	20	Jan. 16, 1865	1 year.	Mustered out with company Sept. 20, 1865.
n, George H.....	...do....	19	Feb. 17, 1865	1 year.	Mustered out with company Sept. 20, 1865.
, John W.......	...do....	31	Feb. 8, 1865	1 year.	Mustered out with company Sept. 20, 1865.
orge L.....	...do....	38	Jan. 26, 1865	1 year.	Mustered out with company Sept. 20, 1865.
Christopher... ..	...do....	34	Feb. 1, 1865	1 year.	Mustered out with company Sept. 20, 1865.
s, John..	...do....	20	Feb. 3, 1865	1 year.	Mustered out with company Sept. 20, 1865.
James A.....	...do....	19	Feb. 1, 1865	1 year.	Mustered out with company Sept. 20, 1865.
William P.......	...do....	19	Jan. 31, 1865	1 year.	Mustered out Oct. 2, 1865, at Cincinnati, O., by order of War Department.
r, Edward.......	...do....	44	Feb. 3, 1865	1 year	Mustered out with company Sept. 20, 1865.
ler, August......	...do....	18	Feb. 11, 1865	1 year.	Mustered out with company Sept. 20, 1865.
naughey, Wm. H.	...do....	34	Jan. 31, 1865	1 year.	Mustered out with company Sept. 20, 1865.
eb, James.......	...do....	21	Jan. 24, 1865	1 year.	Mustered out May 24, 1865, at Bridgeport, Ala., by order of War Department.
ben, David H....	...do....	26	Feb. 8, 1865	1 year.	Mustered out with company Sept. 20, 1865.
, Robert	...do....	24	Jan. 19, 1865	1 year.	Mustered out with company Sept. 20, 1865.
, James P.......	...do....	18	Jan. 20, 1865	1 year.	Mustered out July 7, 1865, at Chattanooga, Tenn., by order of War Department.
, Edward.........	...do....	24	Jan. 21, 1865	1 year.	Mustered out with company Sept. 20, 1865.
l, John..........	...do....	31	Jan. 20, 1865	1 year.	Mustered out with company Sept. 20, 1865.
, William N.....	...do....	22	Feb. 6, 1865	1 year.	Mustered out with company Sept. 20, 1865.
amuel..........	...do....	20	Feb. 11, 1865	1 year.	Mustered out with company Sept. 20, 1865.
, Jacob A........	...do....	32	Jan. 19, 1865	1 year.	Mustered out with company Sept. 20, 1865.
, Thomas J	...do....	24	Feb. 3, 1865	1 year.	Died March 22, 1865, in hospital at Nashville, Tennessee.
John............	...do....	16	Feb. 8, 1865	1 year.	Mustered out with company Sept. 20, 1865.
, Oliver P.......	...do....	18	Feb. 10, 1865	1 year.	Mustered out with company Sept. 20, 1865.
, Milton.........	...do....	18	Feb. 18, 1865	1 year.	Mustered out May 18, 1865, at Bridgeport, Ala., by order of War Department.
dson, Francis M.	...do....	33	Jan. 21, 1865	1 year.	Mustered out Sept. 19, 1865, at Camp Dennison, O., by order of War Department.
John...........	...do....	29	Jan. 30, 1865	1 year.	Mustered out with company Sept. 20, 1865.
s, George W......	...do....	32	Jan. 31, 1865	1 year.	Mustered out with company Sept. 20, 1865.
s, Joseph M......	...do....	24	Jan. 19, 1865	1 year.	Mustered out with company Sept. 20, 1865.
Charles M.......	...do....	25	Jan. 23, 1865	1 year.	Mustered out with company Sept. 20, 1865.
ford, William D .	...do....	27	Jan. 18, 1865	1 year.	Mustered out with company Sept. 20, 1865.
Emanuel.........	...do....	26	Feb. 13, 1865	1 year.	Died Aug. 16, 1865, in hospital at Nashville, Tennessee.
wuck, Anthony..	...do....	19	Feb. 11, 1865	1 year.	Mustered out with company Sept. 20, 1865.
liver P.	...do....	37	Jan. 19, 1865	1 year	Mustered out with company Sept. 20, 1865.
Andrew A........	...do....	18	Feb. 8, 1865	1 year.	Mustered out with company Sept. 20, 1865
Francis M.......	...do....	25	Feb. 7, 1865	1 year.	Died March 14, 1865, in hospital at Nashville, Tennessee.
, Francis M. H..	...do....	25	Jan. 24, 1865	1 year.	Mustered out Oct. 24, 1865, at Camp Dennison, O., by order of War Department.

Names.	Rank.	Age.	Date of Entering the Service.	Period of Service.	Remarks.
Terwilliger, Augustus P.	Private..	19	Jan. 31, 1865	1 year.	Mustered out Oct. 16, 1865, at Louisville, Ky., by order of War Department.
Ulery, John R.	....do....	18	Feb. 9, 1865	1 year.	Mustered out with company Sept. 20, 1865.
Walcut, Lewis	....do....	20	Feb. 13, 1865	1 year.	Mustered out with company Sept. 20, 1865.
Walker, John W.	....do....	25	Jan. 28, 1865	1 year.	Mustered out Oct. 31, 1865, at Camp Dennison, O., by order of War Department.
Ward, Evan M.	....do....	37	Jan. 27, 1865	1 year.	Mustered out with company Sept. 20, 1865.
West, Theodore M.	....do....	29	Jan. 18, 1865	1 year.	Mustered out Sept. 19, 1865, at Camp Dennison, O., by order of War Department.
White, William N.	....do....	18	Feb. 3, 1865	1 year.	Mustered out with company Sept. 20, 1865.
Wilks, Blair	....do....	18	Feb. 4, 1865	1 year.	Mustered out with company Sept. 20, 1865.
Wilson, Nathan C.	....do....	18	Feb. 9, 1865	1 year.	Mustered out with company Sept. 20, 1865.
Wilson, Stephen	....do....	20	Jan. 26, 1865	1 year.	Mustered out with company Sept. 20, 1865.

COMPANY K.

Mustered in February 20, 1865, at Camp Chase, O., by W. P. Richardson, Colonel 25th O. V. I. Mustered out September 20, 1865, at Nashville, Tenn., by J. W. Chickering, Captain and A. C. M., 2d Division, 4th Army Corps.

Names.	Rank.	Age.	Date of Entering the Service.	Period of Service.	Remarks.
Luman A. P. Folkerth	Captain.	22	Feb. 20, 1865	1 year.	Mustered out with company Sept. 20, 1865.
Joseph McCreary	1st Lieut.	23	Feb. 20, 1865	1 year.	Mustered out with company Sept 20, 1865.
Harry Davis	2d Lieut.	24	Feb. 10, 1865	1 year.	Discharged Feb. 10, 1865, by order of War Department.
Elmer B. Hopkins	1st Sergt.	19	Feb. 7, 1865	1 year.	Mustered out with company Sept. 20, 1865.
John Hume	Sergeant.	25	Feb. 6, 1865	1 year.	Mustered out with company Sept. 20, 1865.
Albert Kelley	....do....	20	Jan. 30, 1865	1 year.	Mustered out with company Sept. 20, 1865.
William M. King	....do....	33	Feb. 9, 1865	1 year.	Mustered out with company Sept. 20, 1865.
Jonathan H. Kline	....do....	24	Feb. 9, 1865	1 year.	Appointed from Corporal Aug. 5, 1865; mustered out with company Sept. 20, 1865.
James P. Poland	....do....	20	Feb. 6, 1865	1 year.	Died July 25, 1865, in hospital at Bridgeport, Ala., of wounds.
William Baker	Corporal.	28	Feb. 6, 1865	1 year.	Mustered out with company Sept. 20, 1865.
John Scellen	....do....	21	Jan. 10, 1865	1 year.	Mustered out with company Sept. 20, 1865.
Elias Halteman	....do....	29	Jan. 27, 1865	1 year.	Mustered out with company Sept. 20, 1865.
Joseph M. C. Wilson	....do....	32	Feb. 13, 1865	1 year.	Mustered out with company Sept. 20, 1865.
George A. Carlisle	....do....	24	Feb. 18, 1865	1 year.	Mustered out with company Sept. 20, 1865.
James J. Bailey	....do....	28	Jan. 6, 1865	1 year.	Mustered out with company Sept. 20, 1865.
Samuel W. Cox	....do....	31	Feb. 9, 1865	1 year.	Appointed Aug. 5, 1865; mustered out with company Sept. 20, 1865.
Joel B. Records	....do....	41	Feb. 14, 1865	1 year.	Appointed Aug. 5, 1865; mustered out with company Sept. 20, 1865.
Israel Palmer	....do....	31	Feb. 13, 1865	1 year.	Mustered out July 7, 1865, at Bridgeport, Ala., by order of War Department.
Abby, Patrick	Private..	30	Feb. 7, 1865	1 year.	Mustered out with company Sept. 20, 1865.
Armstrong, Andrew	....do....	32	Feb. 15, 1865	1 year.	Mustered out with company Sept. 20, 1865.
Armstrong, Robert	....do....	22	Feb. 10, 1865	1 year.	Mustered out with company Sept. 20, 1865.
Bagford, John	....do....	28	Feb. 13, 1865	1 year.	Discharged May 18, 1865, at Bridgeport, Ala., for wound in left arm.
Baker, George	....do....	33	Feb. 13, 1865	1 year.	Mustered out with company Sept. 20, 1865.
Baker, Simon E.	....do....	29	Feb. 14, 1865	1 year.	Mustered out with company Sept. 20, 1865.
Barn, Richard	....do....	34	Feb. 6, 1865	1 year.	
Barnes, William H.	....do....	24	Jan. 7, 1865	1 year.	
Bill, James T.	....do....	26	Feb. 11, 1865	1 year.	Mustered out with company Sept. 20, 1865.
Bolen, John	....do....	18	Feb. 13, 1865	1 year.	Died April 27, 1865, at Smithland, Ky.
Boyce, Robert	....do....	19	Feb. 6, 1865	1 year.	Mustered out with company Sept. 20, 1865.
Bozarth, Richard	....do....	30	Feb. 10, 1865	1 year.	Discharged May 18, 1865, at Bridgeport, Ala., on Surgeon's certificate of disability.
Brewer, David R.	....do....	19	Feb. 18, 1865	1 year.	Mustered out with company Sept. 20, 1865.
Bradley, Mitchell	....do....	21	Feb. 18, 1865	1 year.	Mustered out with company Sept. 20, 1865.
Byrd, Francis M.	....do....	19	Jan. 30, 1865	1 year.	Mustered out with company Sept. 20, 1865.
Byrd, Mounce	....do....	18	Jan. 23, 1865	1 year.	Mustered out with company Sept. 20, 1865.
Caldwell, James E.	....do....	23	Feb. 10, 1865	1 year.	Mustered out with company Sept. 20, 1865.
Campbell, Richard	....do....	20	Feb. 14, 1865	1 year.	Mustered out with company Sept. 20, 1865.
Cannon, William W.	....do....	19	Feb. 14, 1865	1 year.	Discharged May 18, 1865, at Bridgeport, Ala., for wound in left arm.
Clark, James L.	....do....	19	Feb. 13, 1865	1 year.	Discharged May 12, 1865, at Nashville, Tenn., on Surgeon's certificate of disability.
Clark, Samuel	....do....	21	Feb. 11, 1865	1 year.	Discharged May 18, 1865, at Bridgeport, Ala., for wound in left arm.
Clifton, Peter	....do....	36	Feb. 9, 1865	1 year.	
Collier, Isaac T.	....do....	23	Jan. 21, 1865	1 year.	Mustered out with company Sept. 20, 1865.
Collins, Nathaniel	....do....	18	Feb. 13, 1865	1 year.	Mustered out with company Sept. 20, 1865.
Compton, William E.	....do....	25	Jan. 10, 1865	1 year.	Mustered out with company Sept. 20, 1865.
Confer, Ike T.	....do....	20	Feb. 13, 1865	1 year.	Mustered out with company Sept. 20, 1865.
Conner, David	....do....	28	Feb. 8, 1865	1 year.	Discharged May 18, 1865, at Bridgeport, Ala., on Surgeon's certificate of disability.
Conner, William	....do....	24	Feb. 8, 1865	1 year.	Died April 8, 1865, in hospital at Nashville, Tennessee.
Craney, John	....do....	44	Feb. 13, 1865	1 year.	Mustered out with company Sept. 20, 1865.

	Rank.	Age.	Date of Entering the Service.	eriod Service.	Remarks.
..s, Albert	.	19	Jan. 25, 1865	1 year.	Mustered out with company Sept. 20, 1865.
..oy, Michael	.	35	Feb. 14, 1865	1 year.	Mustered out with company Sept. 20, 1865.
..gan, William	.	33	Feb. 16, 1865	1 year.	Mustered out with company Sept. 20, 1865.
..lligher, Richard	.	38	Feb. 13, 1865	1 year.	Mustered out with company Sept. 20, 1865.
..lloway, John	.	18	Jan. 30, 1865	1 year.	Mustered out with company Sept. 20, 1865.
..n, John A	.	18	Jan. 20, 1865	1 year.	Mustered out with company Sept. 20, 1865.
..ff, Edward B	.	22	Feb. 13, 1865	1 year.	Mustered out with company Sept. 20, 1865.
..yton, John	.	18	Feb. 14, 1865	1 year.	Mustered out to date Sept. 20, 1865, by order of War Department.
..rrington, George	...do. .	19	Feb. 16, 1865	1 year.	Mustered out with company Sept. 20, 1865.
..pkins, Wilson A	...do. .	20	Feb. 13, 1865	1 year.	Mustered out with company Sept. 20, 1865.
..ward, David	...do. .	32	Feb. 16, 1865	1 year.	Mustered out with company Sept. 20, 1865.
..rah, Cyrus	...do. .	24	Feb. 8, 1865	1 year.	Mustered out with company Sept. 20, 1865.
..ston, John F	...do. .	18	Feb. 10, 1865	1 year.	Mustered out with company Sept. 20, 1865.
..rshner, James W	...do. .	18	Feb. 10, 1865	1 year.	Mustered out with company Sept. 20, 1865.
..ler, George W	.. .	18	Feb. 13, 1865	1 year.	Mustered out with company Sept. 20, 1865.
..ler, William	.. .	18	Feb. 13, 1865	1 year.	Mustered out with company Sept. 20, 1865.
..lleen, James	.. .	34	Feb. 13, 1865	1 year.	Mustered out with company Sept. 20, 1865.
..ng, Nathaniel J	.. .	21	Feb. 4, 1865	1 year.	Died March 20, 1865, in hospital at Nashville, Tennessee.
..ngaberry, Robert		42	Feb. 11, 1865	1 year.	Mustered out with company Sept. 20, 1865.
..ine, Beneval		18	Feb. 14, 1865	1 year.	Mustered out with company Sept. 20, 1865.
..ine, Emanuel		19	Feb. 6, 1865	1 year.	Mustered out with company Sept. 20, 1865.
..wrence, Snow R		20	Jan. 21, 1865	1 year.	Mustered out with company Sept. 20, 1865.
..ness, James		27	Feb. 14, 1865	1 year.	Mustered out with company Sept. 20, 1865.
..tle, Francis B		31	Feb. 11, 1865	1 year.	Mustered out May 18, 1865, at Bridgeport, Ala., by order of War Department.
..Cann, James		27	Feb. 7, 1865	1 year.	Mustered out May 18, 1865, at Bridgeport, Ala., by order of War Department.
..Creary, Francis		30	Feb. 11, 1865	1 year.	Mustered out with company Sept. 20, 1865.
..Gaughey, George		42	Feb. 6, 1865	1 year.	Mustered out Aug. 4, 1865, at Bridgeport, Ala., by order of War Department
..Ginty, James		18	Jan. 30, 1865	1 year.	Mustered out with company Sept. 20, 1865.
..Grew, Matthew		28	Feb. 2, 1865	1 year.	Mustered out with company Sept. 20, 1865.
..coubrie, George M		20	Feb. 6, 1865	1 year.	Mustered out with company Sept. 20, 1865.
..her, Patrick		24	Feb. 13, 1865	1 year.	Mustered out with company Sept. 20, 1865.
..nick, John	....do....	29	Feb. 14, 1865	1 year.	Mustered out with company Sept. 20, 1865.
..es, Zachariah	....do....	33	Feb. 11, 1865	1 year.	Mustered out June 16, 1865, at Bridgeport, Ala., by order of War Department.
..nell, Christopher	....do....	26	Feb. 14, 1865	1 year.	Mustered out with company Sept. 20, 1865.
..ords, Chesteen F	....do....	18	Feb. 10, 1865	1 year.	Mustered out with company Sept. 20, 1865.
..l, Abner	....do....	19	Feb. 8, 1865	1 year.	Mustered out with company Sept. 20, 1865.
..erts, Daniel H.	....do....	19	Feb. 16, 1865	1 year.	Mustered out with company Sept. 20, 1865.
..erts, Jeremiah	....do....	25	Feb. 9, 1865	1 year.	Mustered out with company Sept. 20, 1865.
.., James H	....do....	24	Feb. 13, 1865	1 year.	Mustered out with company Sept. 20, 1865.
..lembridge, Joseph	....do....	21	Jan. 30, 1865	1 year.	Mustered out May 18, 1865, at Bridgeport, Ala., by order of War Department.
..ffer, Daniel	....do....	32	Feb. 10, 1865	1 year.	Mustered out with company Sept. 20, 1865.
..ffer, Jeremiah	....do....	26	Feb. 10, 1865	1 year.	Mustered out with company Sept. 20, 1865.
..ll, Gilead M	....do....	20	Feb. 14, 1865	1 year.	Mustered out with company Sept. 20, 1865.
..ith, Martin	....do....	29	Feb. 3, 1865	1 year.	Mustered out with company Sept. 20, 1865.
..ife, Frank W	....do....	37	Feb. 18, 1865	1 year.	Mustered out with company Sept. 20, 1865.
..tton, Isaac	....do....	28	Feb. 27, 1865	1 year.	Mustered out with company Sept. 20, 1865.
..tton, James M	....do....	30	Feb. 14, 1865	1 year.	Mustered out with company Sept. 20, 1865.
..dner, Albert	....do....	19	Feb. 10, 1865	1 year.	Mustered out with company Sept. 20, 1865.
..nk, Absalom	....do....	25	Jan. 27, 1865	1 year.	Mustered out with company Sept. 20, 1865.
..l.., Thomas O	....do....	33	Jan. 28, 1865	1 year.	Mustered out with company Sept. 20, 1865.
..ll, Francis M	....do....	18	Feb. 8, 1865	1 year.	Mustered out with company Sept. 20, 1865.
..kley, Johnson	....do....	21	Feb. 6, 1865	1 year.	Mustered out with company Sept. 20, 1865.
..alen, William	....do....	19	Feb. 13, 1865	1 year.	Mustered out with company Sept. 20, 1865.
..lson, Joseph S	....do....	34	Feb. 15, 1865	1 year.	Mustered out with company Sept. 20, 1865.
..lson, William L	....do....	28	Feb. 13, 1865	1 year.	Mustered out with company Sept. 20, 1865.
..ight, Theodore	....do....	20	Feb. 13, 1865	1 year.	Mustered out with company Sept. 20, 1865.

UNASSIGNED RECRUITS.

NOTE.—The following list of recruits is found on muster and descriptive rolls for this organization, but borne on any of the company rolls of the Regiment:

.., William S	Private..	43	Sept. 20, 1864	1 year.	
..er, George E	....do....	23	Feb. 14, 1865	1 year.	
..ty, Joseph	....do....	25	Feb. 2, 1865	1 year.	
..ck, William W	....do....	22	Jan. 24, 1865	1 year.	
..ke, John	....do....	20	Jan. 20, 1865	1 year.	
..ford, Samuel	....do....	18	Jan. 28, 1865	1 year.	
..ham, William T	....do....	18	Mch. 7, 1865	1 year.	
..worth, A. Watson	....do....	19	Jan. 28, 1865	1 year.	
..dy, James W	....do....	21	Feb. 8, 1865	1 year.	
..ton, William	....do....	25	Feb. 8, 1865	1 year.	
..gs, Andrew J	....do....	26	Jan. 31, 1865	1 year.	
..rs, Johnson	....do....	18	Feb. 16, 1865	1 year.	

Names.	Rank.	Age.	Date of Entering the Service.	Period of Service.	Remarks.
Briggs, William H.	Private	30	Feb. 20, 1865	1 year.	
Britton, Charles	do	23	Jan. 21, 1865	1 year.	
Brooks, James	do	21	Jan. 27, 1865	1 year.	
Browning, Arch	do	22	Feb. 1, 1865	1 year.	
Burns, Con	do	25	Feb. 6, 1865	1 year.	
Carns, William M	do	28	Feb. 9, 1865	1 year.	
Carroll, Thomas R	do	24	Feb. 7, 1865	1 year.	
Casey, Patrick	do	23	Feb. 8, 1865	1 year.	
Cassidy, Patrick	do	21	Feb. 10, 1865	1 year.	
Celman, Jesse	do	28	Feb. 7, 1865	1 year.	
Chambers, Henry	do	26	Oct. 21, 1864	1 year.	
Cheever, George	do	21	Oct. 21, 1864	1 year.	
Churchill, Henry	do	18	Feb. 4, 1865	1 year.	
Clark, George	do	22	Jan. 25, 1865	1 year.	
Clark, George L	do	19	Feb. 15, 1865	1 year.	
Clark, John	do	39	Mch. 7, 1865	1 year.	
Clayton, Charles	do	28	Jan. 17, 1865	1 year.	
Clifford, Charles	do	21	Feb. 2, 1865	1 year.	
Coat, John	do	24	Feb. 6, 1865	1 year.	
Collier, Henry	do	20	Jan. 24, 1865	1 year.	
Combs, William	do	43	Feb. 17, 1865	1 year.	
Cope, Samuel	do	18	Feb. 20, 1865	1 year.	
Costello, John	do	18	Feb. 1, 1865	1 year.	
Cottrill, William G	do	22	Feb. 15, 1865	1 year.	
Crane, John	do	23	Feb. 24, 1865	1 year.	
Creviston, John	do	30	Feb. 9, 1865	1 year.	
Cubbage, James H.	do	18	Jan. 19, 1865	1 year.	
Cupp, Lewis	do	22	Feb. 2, 1865	1 year.	
Dagg, William	do	22	Feb. 8, 1865	1 year.	
Dean, Sanborn A	do	31	Feb. 28, 1865	1 year.	
Delaney, William	do	30	Feb. 1, 1865	1 year.	
Devlin, William	do	27	Jan. 26, 1865	1 year.	
Doles, Silas	do	18	Feb. 15, 1865	1 year.	
Douglass, Charles	do	41	Jan. 20, 1865	1 year.	
Drummond, Benjamin	do	44	Sept. 2, 1864	1 year.	
Dunn, Thomas	do	22	Jan. 24, 1865	1 year.	
Durrett, Thomas H	do	18	Sept. 21, 1864	1 year.	
Dwyer, James	do	33	Jan. 5, 1865	1 year.	
Elder, Franklin F	do	22	Feb. 27, 1865	1 year.	
Elliott, George	do	21	Jan. 9, 1865	1 year.	
Farley, John	do	18	Jan. 4, 1865	1 year.	
Fields, Theodore	do	28	Feb. 7, 1865	1 year.	
Finley, Peter	do	25	Jan. 10, 1865	1 year.	
Fry, Frank	do	21	Jan. 14, 1865	1 year.	
Gatchel, Charles	do	18	Jan. 23, 1865	1 year.	
Genkins, George	do	23	Feb. 7, 1865	1 year.	
Gilbert, Henry	do	18	Jan. 31, 1865	1 year.	
Gorman, Richard	do	22	Jan. 19, 1865	1 year.	
Gorrell Joseph W	do	25	Sept. 16, 1864	1 year.	
Gram, Henry	do	23	Jan. 16, 1865	1 year.	
Graves, Benton	do	21	Feb. 7, 1865	1 year.	
Gruver, John	do	32	Feb. 17, 1865	1 year.	
Hadden, John	do	21	Feb. 7, 1865	1 year.	
Hanlon, James O	do	25	Feb. 22, 1865	1 year.	
Hart, Nelson	do	21	Sept. 21, 1864	1 year.	
Heatch, John	do	18	Jan. 20, 1865	1 year.	
Henderson, Henry	do	21	Jan. 26, 1865	1 year.	
Hendly, John R	do	20	Jan. 12, 1865	1 year.	
Henry, Charles S	do	27	Feb. 21, 1865	1 year.	
Higgins, Joshua	do	18	Feb. 15, 1865	1 year.	
Hobbs, John W	do	20	Mch. 8, 1865	1 year.	
Hogan, John	do	30	Jan. 7, 1865	1 year.	
Hullback, John R	do	21	Jan. 20, 1865	1 year.	
Hyde, George A	do	22	Feb. 7, 1865	1 year.	
Johnson, [illegible] B	do	25	Feb. 1, 1865	1 year.	
Johnson, George	do	23	Jan. 13, 1865	1 year.	
Jones, William	do	24	Jan. 14, 1865	1 year.	
Kenedy, Daniel	do	21	Jan. 30, 1865	1 year.	
Kling, Jacob B	do	30	Mch. 1, 1865	1 year.	
Kurt, George	do	21	Jan. 18, 1865	1 year.	
Landers, Henry	do	20	Jan. 30, 1865	1 year.	
Lerch, Peter S	do	18	Sept. 21, 1864	1 year.	
Lewis, Henry	do	27	Feb. 10, 1865	1 year.	
Lewis, John W	do	29	Feb. 28, 1865	1 year.	
Long, Robert	do	21	Feb. 7, 1865	1 year.	
McGarry, Findley	do	18	Feb. 25, 1865	1 year.	
McGrath, Daniel	do	20	Jan. 6, 1865	1 year.	
Malone, Thomas	do	21	Mch. 8, 1865	1 year.	
Maloy, Patrick	do	28	Jan. 6, 1866	1 year.	
Marks, David	do	28	Feb. 6, 1865	1 year.	
Martin, Henry M	do	24	Jan. 30, 1865	1 year.	
Martin, Joshua R	do	21	Feb. 2, 1865	1 year.	
Martin, Oren S	do	18	Sept. 21, 1864	1 year.	
Means, William H	do	18	Feb. 6, 1865	1 year.	
Measure, John	do	18	Jan. 13, 1865	1 year.	
Mitchell, John C	do	30	Feb. 28, 1865	1 year.	

ROLL OF HONOR

OF OHIO SOLDIERS.

141ST-184TH REGIMENTS—INFANTRY.

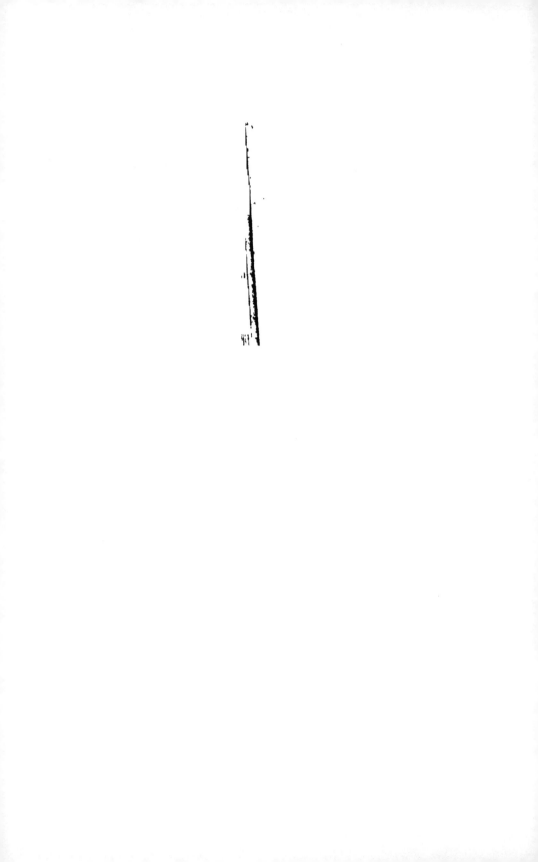

ROLL OF HONOR OF OHIO SOLDIERS.

COMPILED FROM PUBLICATIONS OF THE U. S. WAR DEPARTMENT AND OTHER OFFICIAL SOURCES.

141st REGIMENT OHIO VOLUNTEER INFANTRY.

Names.	Co.	Rank.	Died.	Buried.	Remarks.
Blackburn, Stephen H..	D	Private.	July 5, 1864	Gallipolis, O..........	Died at Barboursville, W. Va.
Bobo, Benson...........	H	Private.	July 26, 1864	....	Died at home, Athens County, Ohio.
Eastman, Samuel.......	A	Private.	July 11, 1864	Gallipolis, O.........	Died at Barboursville, W. Va.
Washburn, William W..	B	Private.	May 25, 1864	Gallipolis, O..........	

142nd REGIMENT OHIO VOLUNTEER INFANTRY.

Names.	Co.	Rank.	Died.	Buried.	Remarks.
Babbs, John W..........	C	Private.	Aug. 27, 1864	Hampton, Va.........	Died at Fortress Monroe, Va. Interred in section E, row 7, grave 50.
Babbs, Thomas..........	C	Private.	Aug. 1, 1864	Hampton, Va.........	Died at Portsmouth, Va. Interred in section C, row 20, grave 12.
Baxter, Porter...........	H	Private.	Aug. 2, 1864	Hampton, Va.........	Interred in section E, row 24, grave 10.
Beabout, William.......	C	Private.	July 25, 1864	City Point, Va........	Died on board hospital boat. Interred in section D, row 4, grave 31.
Best, Alexander.........	D	Private.	Sept. 5, 1864	Arlington, Va........	
Brown, James...........	A	Private.	Aug. 10, 1864	Hampton, Va.........	Died at Fortress Monroe, Va. Interred in section E, row 14, grave 47.
Buchanan, Smith.......	F	Musician	Aug. 9, 1864	City Point, Va........	Died near Point of Rocks, Md. Interred in section F, row 1, grave 2.
Clark, John W..........	G	Private.	June 30, 1864	Hampton, Va.........	
Cogswell, John..........	D	Private.	June 11, 1864	Arlington, Va........	Died at Alexandria, Va.
Dadley, John W.........	I*	Private.	Aug. 26, 1864	Hampton, Va.........	Died at Fortress Monroe, Va. Interred in section E, row 8, grave 39.
Dehuff, Charles..........	G	Private.	Aug. 27, 1864	Arlington, Va........	Died at Washington, D. C.
Dennis John	D	Private.	Aug. 11, 1864	Hampton, Va.........	Died at Portsmouth, Va. Interred in section C, row 22, grave 1.
Elliott, Edwin...........	H	Private.	July 14, 1864	City Point, Va........	Died near Point of Rocks, Md.
Errett, Campbell........	K	Corporal	Aug. 9, 1864	City Point, Va........	Died near Point of Rocks, Md.
Estile, Edwin H.........	H	Private.	Aug. 5, 1864	Hampton, Va.........	Died at Portsmouth, Va.
Evans, Wesley J.........	B	Private.	July 24, 1864	Long Island, N. Y....	Died at Willett's Point, N. Y. Interred in Cypress Hill Cemetery.
Ewers, James E.........	H	Corporal	Aug. 8, 1864	City Point, Va........	Died near Point of Rocks, Md. Interred in section F, row 1, grave 12.

Names.	Co.	Rank.	Died.	Buried.	Remarks.
Hay, Addison C.	E	Private.	July 4, 1864	Hampton, Va.	Interred in section E, row 18, grave 50. Reinterred in Oak Ridge Cemetery, Coshocton, Ohio.
Hill, Leonidas	I	Private.	July 10, 1864	Glendale, Va.	Died at Wilson's Landing, Va.
Huffman, Joseph	G	Private.	Aug. 15, 1864	Hampton, Va.	Died at Fortress Monroe, Va. Interred in section E, row 8, grave 17.
Jennings, Reuben	E	Sergeant	June 27, 1864	Glendale, Va.	Died at Wilson's Landing, Va. Interred in section C, grave 119.
Keen, Frank	D	Private.	Aug. 18, 1864	Hampton, Va.	
Leavet, Sylvester	H	Private.	July 14, 1864	Long Island, N. Y.	Died at David's Island, New York Harbor. Interred in Cypress Hill Cemetery.
McDonald, James M.	B	Private.	Aug. 19, 1864	Hampton, Va.	Died at Fortress Monroe, Va.
McKay, John	B	Private.	July 18, 1864	Hampton, Va.	Died at Norfolk, Va.
McMichael, Edward	E	Private.	Aug. 19, 1864	Hampton, Va.	Reinterred in Oak Ridge Cemetery, Coshocton, O.
Nagle, Frederick	I	Private.	Aug. 2, 1864	Glendale, Va.	Died at Wilson's Landing, Va. Interred in section C, grave 92.
Noble, Alexander	B	Private.	July 18, 1864	Hampton, Va.	Died at Fortress Monroe, Va.
Overholt, Daniel	H	Corporal	July 23, 1864	Hampton, Va.	Died at Portsmouth, Va. Interred in section A, row 10, grave 1.
Reeder, Evan C.	C	Private.	Aug. 10, 1864	Hampton, Va.	Interred in section A, row 5, grave 12.
Rowdybush, James H.	C	Private.	July 23, 1864	Glendale, Va.	Died at Wilson's Landing, Va.
Sayers, Thomas C.	H	Private.	June 22, 1864	Hampton, Va.	Died at Fortress Monroe, Va. Interred in section A, row 7, grave 2.
Scott, Thomas C.	E	Private.	July 1, 1864	Coshocton, O.	Died at Wilson's Landing, Va. Interred in Oak Ridge Cemetery.
Seward, Eli	H	Sergeant	June 25, 1864	Glendale, Va.	Died at Wilson's Landing, Va. Interred in section C, grave 125.
Stevens, Jacob	I	Private.	Aug. 18, 1864	Hampton, Va.	Interred in section E, row 10, grave 21.
Stewart, William	H	Private.	Aug. 13, 1864	Glendale, Va.	Died at Wilson's Landing, Va. Interred in section C, grave 115.
Waters, John	H	Corporal	Aug. 5, 1864	Hampton, Va.	Died at Portsmouth, Va. Interred in section B, row 19, grave 1.
West, Elias	E	Private.	June 18, 1864	City Point, Va.	Died at Point of Rocks, Md. Interred in section F, row 1, grave 93.
Wright, George W.	G	Private.	Aug. 11, 1864	Hampton, Va.	Interred in section E, row 8, grave 22.

144TH REGIMENT OHIO VOLUNTEER INFANTRY.

Names.	Co.	Rank.	Died.	Buried.	Remarks.
Alkire, Mahlon	G	Private.	Nov. 2, 1864	Annapolis, Md.	
Baldwin, Andrew	G	Private.	Sept. 22, 1864	Danville, Va.	Died in Rebel Prison.
Baldwin, Jacob	G	Private.	Sept. 8, 1864	Danville, Va.	Died in Rebel Prison.
Barton, Findlay	I	Musician	Nov. 13, 1864	Salisbury, N. C.	Died in Rebel Prison.
Basset, Austin D.	I	Private.	June 26, 1864	Annapolis, Md.	
Beistle, Joseph R.	A	Private.	Aug. 9, 1864	Antietam, Md.	Died at Frederick, Md.
Bovis, Adam	K	Private.	Dec. 16, 1864	Salisbury, N. C.	Died in Rebel Prison.
Bowsher, Miller	K	Private.	Oct. 14, 1864	Annapolis, Md.	
Brown, William	I	Private.	Dec. 7, 1864	Salisbury, N. C.	Died in Rebel Prison.
Brown, Wilson	I	Private.	Nov. 10, 1864	Salisbury, N. C.	Died in Rebel Prison.
Bryant, Charles A.	K	Corporal	Nov. 14, 1864	Salisbury, N. C.	Died in Rebel Prison.
Burns, Israel	K	Private.	Nov. 12, 1864	Salisbury, N. C.	Died in Rebel Prison.
Carnes, Arthur A.	A	Private.	Jan. 6, 1865	Salisbury, N. C.	Died in Rebel Prison.
Coen, Ebenezer	B	Private.	July 9, 1864	Antietam, Md.	Killed in battle of Monocacy, Maryland.
Coon, Adam	H	Private.	July 28, 1864	Baltimore, Md.	Died at Relay House, Md. Interred in Louden Park Cemetery.
Cozier, Marshall	G	Sergeant	Aug. 13, 1864	Winchester, Va.	Killed in action near Berryville, Va.

Names.	Co.	Rank.	Died.	Buried.	Remarks.
Follett, Jerome	D	Corporal	June 25, 1864	Arlington, Va	Died at Alexandria, Va.
Fowler, William H	E	Private.	July 8, 1864	Hampton, Va	Died on board steamer Monitor. Interred in section E, row 19, grave 47.
Hadley, George	K	Private.	Aug. 26, 1864	Arlington, Va	Died at Washington, D. C.
Hodges, Henry	C	Private.	July 25, 1864	City Point, Va	Died near Point of Rocks, Md. Interred in section A, row 1, grave 114.
Hunt, Philip	F	Private.	Aug. 4, 1864	City Point, Va	Died near Point of Rocks, Md. Interred in section A, row 1, grave 111.
Hunter, Aquilla	D	Private.	Aug. 5, 1864	City Point, Va	Died near Point of Rocks, Md.
Hyatt, Morris	A	Private.	July 3, 1864	Arlington, Va	Died at Washington, D. C.
Hyatt, Washington	A	Private.	Aug. 6, 1864	City Point, Va	Died near Point of Rocks, Md. Interred in section A, row 2, grave 113.
Jones, George W	I	Private.	Aug. 14, 1864	Hampton, Va	Died at Fortress Monroe, Va. Interred in section E, row 9, grave 19.
Knight, Fred W	H	Private.	Aug. 23, 1864	Arlington, Va	Died at Washington, D. C.
Leighninger, George	E	Corporal	June 19, 1864	Philadelphia, Pa	
Lybarger, Harmon	F	Sergeant	Aug. 13, 1864	Hampton, Va	Died at Portsmouth, Va. Interred in section C, row 19, grave 1.
McGuire, Francis	E	Private.	Aug. 21, 1864	Arlington, Va	Died on board steamer Andrew Harder.
McWilliams, Charles	I	Private.	July 15, 1864	City Point, Va	Died near Point of Rocks, Md. Interred in section F row 1, grave 121.
Magness, Walter S	E	Private.	July 15, 1864		Died at Camp Hatcher's, Va.
Ogan, Levi	G	Private.	Aug. 4, 1864	City Point, Va	Died near Point of Rocks, Md. Interred in section A, row 2, grave 135.
Pealer, Ira	F	2d Lieut.	Aug. 11, 1864	Hampton, Va	Died at Fortress Monroe, Va.
Reed, James H	F	Private.	Aug. 13, 1864	City Point, Va	Died near Point of Rocks, Md.
Runnels, Stephen	B	Private.	Aug. 1, 1864	City Point, Va	Died near Point of Rocks, Md.
Schooler, John	I	Private.	July 25, 1864	Hampton, Va	Died on board hospital boat. Interred in section A, row 2, grave 19.
Shepard, Jeremiah	F	Private.	Aug. 15, 1864	City Point, Va	Died near Poin of Rocks, Md. Interred n section F row [illegible] grave 3.
Sturges, Alfred	A	Private.	July 17, 1864	Hampton, Va	Died at Fortress Monroe, Va. Interred in section C, row 1, grave 7.
West, Harrison	E	Private.	Aug. 4, 1864		Died near Hatcher's Run, Va.
Whitney, Gueldon	F	Private.	Aug. 3, 1864	Hampton, Va	Died at Portsmouth, Va. Interred in section C, row 2, grave 3
Williams, William M	E	Private.	Aug. 16, 1864	Hampton, Va	Died at Fortress Monroe, Va.

143RD REGIMENT OHIO VOLUNTEER INFANTRY.

Names.	Co.	Rank.	Died.	Buried.	Remarks.
Amon, William	C	Private.	July 4, 1864	Glendale, Va	Died at Wilson's Landing, Va. Interred in section C, grave 106.
Bates, Henry	A	Private.	Aug. 31, 1864	Baltimore, Md	Interred in Louden Park cemetery.
Bechtel, Samuel E	H	Private.	July 17, 1864	Hampton, Va	Died at Fortress Monroe, Va. Interred in section C, row 2, grave 7.
Butler, William E	E	Private.	June 21, 1864	Hampton, Va	Reinterred at his home, New York State.
Cameron, Allen	B	Private.	July 19, 1864	Glendale, Va	Died at Wilson's Landing, Va.
Carpenter, Thomas W	A	Private.	Aug. 2[illegible], 1864	Hampton, Va	
Clempson, Joseph P	C	Private.	Aug. 28, 1864	Glendale, Va	Died at Wilson's Landing, Va.
Dennis, John	E	Private.	June 25, 1864	Glendale, Va	Died at Wilson's Landing, Va. Interred in section C, grave 123.
Dodd, William	G	Private.	July 31, 1864	Coshocton, O.	Died at Wilson's Landing, Va.
Glover, Joel C	E	Private.	Aug. 28, 1864	Glendale, Va	Died at Fort Pocahontas, Va.
Goddard, John	A	Private.	July 21, 1864	Glendale, Va	Died at Fort Pocahontas, Va. Interred in section C, grave 107.

Names.	Co.	Rank.	Died.	Buried.	Remarks.
Hay, Addison C.	E	Private.	July 4, 1864	Hampton, Va.	Interred in section E, row 18, grave 50. Reinterred in Oak Ridge Cemetery, Coshocton, Ohio.
Hill, Leonidas	I	Private.	July 10, 1864	Glendale, Va.	Died at Wilson's Landing, Va.
Huffman, Joseph	G	Private.	Aug. 15, 1864	Hampton, Va.	Died at Fortress Monroe, Va. Interred in section E, row 8, grave 17.
Jennings, Reuben	E	Sergeant	June 27, 1864	Glendale, Va.	Died at Wilson's Landing, Va. Interred in section C, grave 119.
Keen, Frank	D	Private.	Aug. 18, 1864	Hampton, Va.	
Leavet, Sylvester	H	Private.	July 14, 1864	Long Island, N. Y.	Died at David's Island, New York Harbor. Interred in Cypress Hill Cemetery.
McDonald, James M.	B	Private.	Aug. 19, 1864	Hampton, Va.	Died at Fortress Monroe, Va.
McKay, John	B	Private.	July 18, 1864	Hampton, Va.	Died at Norfolk, Va.
McMichael, Edward	E	Private.	Aug. 19, 1864	Hampton, Va.	Reinterred in Oak Ridge Cemetery, Coshocton, O.
Nagle, Frederick	I	Private.	Aug. 2, 1864	Glendale, Va.	Died at Wilson's Landing, Va. Interred in section C, grave 92.
Noble, Alexander	B	Private.	July 18, 1864	Hampton, Va.	Died at Fortress Monroe, Va.
Overholt, Daniel	H	Corporal	July 23, 1864	Hampton, Va.	Died at Portsmouth, Va. Interred in section A, row 10, grave 1.
Reeder, Evan C.	C	Private.	Aug. 10, 1864	Hampton, Va.	Interred in section A, row 5, grave 12.
Rowdybush, James H.	C	Private.	July 23, 1864	Glendale, Va.	Died at Wilson's Landing, Va.
Sayers, Thomas C.	H	Private.	June 22, 1864	Hampton, Va.	Died at Fortress Monroe, Va. Interred in section A, row 7, grave 2.
Scott, Thomas C.	E	Private.	July 1, 1864	Coshocton, O.	Died at Wilson's Landing, Va. Interred in Oak Ridge Cemetery.
Seward, Eli	H	Sergeant	June 25, 1864	Glendale, Va.	Died at Wilson's Landing, Va. Interred in section C, grave 125.
Stevens, Jacob	I	Private.	Aug. 18, 1864	Hampton, Va.	Interred in section E, row 10, grave 21.
Stewart, William	H	Private.	Aug. 13, 1864	Glendale, Va.	Died at Wilson's Landing, Va. Interred in section C, grave 115.
Waters, John	H	Corporal	Aug. 5, 1864	Hampton, Va.	Died at Portsmouth, Va. Interred in section B, row 19, grave 1.
West, Elias	E	Private.	June 18, 1864	City Point, Va.	Died at Point of Rocks, Md. Interred in section F, row 1, grave 93.
Wright, George W.	G	Private.	Aug. 14, 1864	Hampton, Va.	Interred in section E, row 8, grave 22.

144TH REGIMENT OHIO VOLUNTEER INFANTRY.

Names.	Co.	Rank.	Died.	Buried.	Remarks.
Alkire, Mahlon	G	Private.	Nov. 2, 1864	Annapolis, Md.	
Baldwin, Andrew	G	Private.	Sept. 22, 1864	Danville, Va.	Died in Rebel Prison.
Baldwin, Jacob	G	Private.	Sept. 8, 1864	Danville, Va.	Died in Rebel Prison.
Barton, Findlay	I	Musician	Nov. 13, 1864	Salisbury, N. C.	Died in Rebel Prison.
Basset, Austin D.	I	Private.	June 26, 1864	Annapolis, Md.	
Beistle, Joseph R.	A	Private.	Aug. 9, 1864	Antietam, Md.	Died at Frederick, Md.
Bovis, Adam	K	Private.	Dec. 16, 1864	Salisbury, N. C.	Died in Rebel Prison.
Bowsher, Miller	K	Private.	Oct. 11, 1864	Annapolis, Md.	
Brown, William	I	Private.	Dec. 7, 1864	Salisbury, N. C.	Died in Rebel Prison.
Brown, Wilson	I	Private.	Nov. 10, 1864	Salisbury, N. C.	Died in Rebel Prison.
Bryant, Charles A.	K	Corporal	Nov. 14, 1864	Salisbury, N. C.	Died in Rebel Prison.
Burns, Israel	K	Private.	Nov. 12, 1864	Salisbury, N. C.	Died in Rebel Prison.
Carnes, Arthur A.	A	Private.	Jan. 6, 1865	Salisbury, N. C.	Died in Rebel Prison.
Coen, Ebenezer	B	Private.	July 9, 1864	Antietam, Md.	Killed in battle of Monocacy, Maryland.
Coon, Adam	H	Private.	July 28, 1864	Baltimore, Md.	Died at Relay House, Md. Interred in Louden Park Cemetery.
Cozier, Marshall	G	Sergeant	Aug. 13, 1864	Winchester, Va.	Killed in action near Berryville, Va.

Names.	Co.	Rank.	Died.	Buried.	Remarks.
Dewese, Chauncey H...	I	Private.	Nov. 6, 1864	Danville, Va..........	Died in Rebel Prison.
Edmonds, Simon...... ..	K	Corporal	Oct. 23, 1864	Annapolis, Md........	
Edmonds, Sylvatus L...	K	Private.	Mch. 25, 1865	Wheeling, W. Va......	
Ensminger, Bramwell..	K	Private.	Nov. 12, 1864	Salisbury, N. C........	Died in Rebel Prison.
Eyestone, William H...	H	Private.	Aug. 2, 1864	Washington, D. C....	
Fortney, Henry.........	I	Private.	Mch. 24, 1865	Baltimore, Md	Interred in Louden Park [illegible] etery.
Frisbie, Theodorus H. C.	K	Sergeant	Oct. 22, 1864	Salisbury, N. C........	Died in Rebel Prison.
Fulmer, Lyman..........	K	Private.	Nov. 27, 1864	Salisbury, N. C........	Died in Rebel Prison.
Geiss, Antone...........	B	Private.	Nov. 1, 1864	Salisbury, N. C........	Died in Rebel Prison.
Gingery, Jacob..........	I	Private.	July 9, 1864	Antietam, Md.........	Killed in battle of Mon[illegible] Maryland.
Groves, James...........	B	Private.	Oct. 28, 1864	Salisbury, N. C........	Died in Rebel Prison.
Henry, Cephas E.........	H	Private.	Nov. 21, 1864	Salisbury, N. C........	Died in Rebel Prison.
Hoisington, Albert......	D	Private.	Nov. 19, 1864	Danville, Va	Died in Rebel Prison.
Hurd, William B.........	D	Private.	Nov. 29, 1864	Danville, Va	Died in Rebel Prison. In[illegible] in section B, row 4, gra[illegible]
Jackson, Thomas J......	K	Private.	Dec, 21, 1864	Salisbury, N. C........	Died in Rebel Prison.
Jolly, Abel..............	I	Private.	Jan. 4, 1865	Danville, Va	Died in Rebel Prison.
Kelly, Isaac N...........	I	Private.	Feb. 16, 1865	Danville, Va	Died in Rebel Prison.
Keyzer, Samuel..........	K	Private.	Oct. 20, 1864	Annapolis, Md........	
Lincoln, James S.......	K	Sergeant	Aug. 13, 1864	Winchester, Va........	Killed in action near [illegible] ville, Va.
Lindsey, David..........	G	Corporal	July 10, 1864	Antietam, Md........	Died at Frederick, M[illegible] wounds received July [illegible] in battle of Monocacy. [illegible]
Long, John W...........	K	Private.	Aug. 13, 1864	Winchester, Va........	Killed in action near [illegible] ville, Va.
McCombs, John.........	B	Private.	Nov. 22, 1864	Salisbury, N. C........	Died in Rebel Prison.
McLain, Samuel	I	Musician	Dec. 19, 1864	Salisbury, N. C......	Died in Rebel Prison.
Macklin, Isaiah	I	Private.	April 8, 1865	....	Died at Gilead, Wood Co[illegible] Ohio.
Mars, John..............	K	Private.	Oct. 20, 1864	Salisbury, N. C........	Died in Rebel Prison.
Martin, James	K	Corporal	Jan. 27, 1865	Salisbury, N. C........	Died in Rebel Prison.
Morgan, John...........	K	Private.	Oct. 24, 1864	Salisbury, N. C........	Died in Rebel Prison.
Myers, Charles..........	K	Private.	Jan. 10, 1865	Salisbury, N. C........	Died in Rebel Prison.
Osborn, Warner.........	A	Private.	Aug. 13, 1864	Winchester, Va........	Killed in action near Be[illegible] ville, Va.
Palmer, Randolph......	K	Private.	July 14, 1864	Baltimore, Md	Died at Relay Barracks [illegible] Interred in Louden Pa[illegible] Cemetery.
Poe, John J.............	C	Sergeant	Dec. 18, 1864	Salisbury, N. C........	Died in Rebel Prison.
Price, Aaron R..........	H	Private.	Sept. 19, 1864	Annapolis, Md........	
Price, Isaac.............	B	Private.	Nov. 28, 1864	Salisbury, N. C........	Died in Rebel Prison.
Puffenberger, John.....	A	Private.	Aug. 13, 1864	Winchester, Va........	Killed in action near [illegible] ville, Va. Interred in [illegible] tion 20.
Rainbow, Thomas......	K	Private.	Oct. 4, 1864	Richmond, Va	Died in Rebel Prison
Ralston, Joseph.........	H	Corporal	Oct. 9, 1864	Annapolis, Md........	
Ruble, John.............	K	Private.	Dec. 6, 1864	Salisbury, N. C........	Died in Rebel Prison
Sage, Orrin W...........	K	Private.	Dec 1, 1864	Salisbury, N. C........	Died in Rebel Prison.
Saulter, Andrew........	I	Private.	Jan. 1, 1865	Salisbury, N. C........	Died in Rebel Prison
Sherman, Elkanah......	D	Private.	June 27, 1864	Baltimore, Md........	Died at Relay House Md [illegible] terred in Louden Park Cem etery.
Shutt, William	K	Private.	Oct. 4, 1864	Richmond, Va	Died in Rebel Prison.
Smith, Hiram S.........	K	Private.	Mch. 31, 1865	At Sea.................	Perished by burning of steamer General Lyon, off coast of Cape Hatteras, N C.
Snyder, Leonard........	F	Private.	June 11, 1864	Annapolis, Md	Died at Annapolis Junction Maryland.
Sprague, Thomas	G	Private.	Dec. 14, 1864	Danville, Va	Died in Rebel Prison.
Straw, Irvine............	G	Private.	May 13, 1864	....	Accidentally killed near Pitts burgh, Pa.
Stephens, William L....	K	Private.	Nov. 13, 1864	Annapolis, Md.......	
Walters, Jonathan......	I	Private.	July 19, 1864	Antietam, Md........	Died of wounds received July 9, 1864, in battle of Mon[illegible] Md. Interred in section [illegible] row C, grave 125.
Wood, Walter...........	B	Private.	Nov. 18, 1864	Salisbury, N. C.......	Died in Rebel Prison.

145th REGIMENT OHIO VOLUNTEER INFANTRY.

Names.	Co.	Rank.	Died.	Buried.	Remarks.
Bell, Joseph C.	G	Private.	Aug. 18, 1864	Arlington, Va.	Died at Washington, D. C.
Cole, John M.	C	Corporal	Aug. 12, 1864		Died near Fort Woodbury, Va.
Dunham, John B.	E	Private.	Aug. 7, 1864		Died near Fort Woodbury, Va.
Eddy, William	F	Private.	Aug. 11, 1864		Died at Fort Whipple, Va.
Felkey, Jacob	C	Private.	June 30, 1864		Died near Fort Woodbury, Va.
Jones, Solomon	H	Private.	June 11, 1864		Died in Regimental Hospital.
Lewis, John W.	H	Private.	Aug. 20, 1864	Arlington, Va.	Died at Washington, D. C.
Spear, George T.	H	Private.	Aug. 8, 1864		Died in Regimental Hospital.

146th REGIMENT OHIO VOLUNTEER INFANTRY.

Names.	Co.	Rank.	Died.	Buried.	Remarks.
Earhart, Edgar C.	E	Private.	July 12, 1864		Died at Fayetteville, W. Va.
Fling, William S.	C	Private.	July 12, 1864		Died at Fayetteville, W. Va.
Freise, John F.	G	Private.	May 15, 1864		Drowned, near Charleston, West Virginia.
Gregg, George	H	Private.	July 10, 1864		Died at Fayetteville, W. Va.
Keever, George M.	A	Private.	Sept. 5, 1864		Died at Lebanon, O.
Sellars, George W.	C	Private.	May 12, 1864		Drowned in Ohio River.
Sharp, Charles T.	I	Private.	May 21, 1864		Died at Fayetteville, W. Va.
Todd, James J.	D	Private.	June 1, 1864		Died at Fayetteville, W. Va.
Yarnall, Samuel H.	F	Private.	Aug. 7, 1864		Died at Fayetteville, W. Va.

147th REGIMENT OHIO VOLUNTEER INFANTRY.

Names.	Co.	Rank.	Died.	Buried.	Remarks.
Arnold, Edward	D	Private.	Aug. 23, 1864	Washington, D. C.	
Bundy, William	E	Private.	July 25, 1864	Arlington, Va.	Died at Fort Ethan Allen, Va.
Cress, Isaac	D	Private.	July 17, 1864	Arlington, Va.	Died at Fort Ethan Allen, Va.
De Long, Isaac	B	Private.	Aug. 4, 1864	Arlington, Va.	Died at Fort Ethan Allen, Va.
Demmitt, Thomas	A	Private.	Aug. 1, 1864	Arlington, Va.	Died at Fort Ethan Allen, Va.
Gearhart, William R.	K	Private.	July 11, 1864	Arlington, Va.	Died at Fort Ethan Allen, Va.
Grafton, Sampson	F	Private.	June 30, 1864	Arlington, Va.	Died at Fort Ethan Allen, Va.
Hale, John L.	D	Private.	July 23, 1864	Arlington, Va.	Died at Fort Ethan Allen, Va.
Houser, Bartholomew	E	Private.	July 28, 1864	Arlington, Va.	Died at Fort Ethan Allen, Va.
Lefever, Harrison	I	Private.	July 3, 1864	Arlington, Va.	Died at Fort Ethan Allen, Va.
Lyon, James R.	E	Private.	June 19, 1864	Arlington, Va.	Died at Fort Ethan Allen, Va.
McGowen, John	G	Private.	July 27, 1864	Arlington, Va.	Died at Fort Ethan Allen, Va.
Mayall, George W.	B	Private.	July 9, 1864	Arlington, Va.	Died at Fort Ethan Allen, Va.
Moran, Thomas	A	Private.	Aug. 29, 1864	Arlington, Va.	Died at Washington, D. C.
Patterson, Hamilton	E	Corporal	Aug. 25, 1864	Arlington, Va.	Died at Washington, D. C.
Quagie, John	C	Private.	July 28, 1864	Arlington, Va.	Died at Fort Ethan Allen, Va.
Reiber, Jacob	G	Private.	July 3, 1864		Died at Fort Haney, Va.
Schoeps, Andrew	C	Private.	July 2, 1864	Arlington, Va.	Died at Fort Ethan Allen, Va.
Shaffer, Henry C.	B	Private.	July 9, 1864	Arlington, Va.	Died at Fort Ethan Allen, Va.
Spencer, Daniel B.	K	Private.	July 31, 1864	Arlington, Va.	Died at Fort Ethan Allen, Va.
Warfell, Philip	B	Private.	June 9, 1864	Arlington, Va.	Died at Fort Ethan Allen, Va.

148th REGIMENT OHIO VOLUNTEER INFANTRY.

Names.	Co.	Rank.	Died.	Buried.	Remarks.
Atkinson, William T....	G	Private.	July 23, 1864	City Point, Va........	Died at Bermuda Hundred, Va. Interred in section A, grave 68.
Baker, Henry W.........	E	Private.	Sept. 10, 1864	....	Died at home.
Blough, Rufus.	H	Private.	July 6, 1864	Hampton, Va...	Interred in section E, row 17, grave 48.
Clark, Joseph D..........	A	Private.	Aug. 9, 1864	City Point, Va........	Killed by explosion of ordnance boat.
Coler, Felix W...........	D	Private.	Aug. 30, 1864	....	Died on steamer John A. Warner, on Potomac River.
Coler, George M.........	D	Private.	Aug. 20, 1864	City Point, Va........	
Colerick, Nathaniel......	I	Private.	Aug. 14, 1864	Petersburg, Va........	Died at Clark's Station, Va. Interred in Poplar Grove Cemetery.
Danley, Joseph W.......	I	Private.	June 28, 1864	City Point, Va.	Died at Bermuda Hundred, Va.
Gates, Charles B.........	A	1st Lieut.	May 31, 1864	Winchester, Va.......	Died at Harper's Ferry, W. Va.
Gooden, Stephen........	K	Private.	June 2, 1864	Arlington, Va........	Died at Washington, D. C.
Gorham, Samuel E.......	H	Corporal	Aug. 9, 1864	City Point, Va........	Killed by explosion of ordnance boat.
Haines, Nathaniel.......	D	Private.	May 21, 1864	....	Died near Marietta, O.
Hall, Eli W..............	G	Private.	July 9, 1864	City Point, Va........	Died at Bermuda Hundred, Va. Interred in section 1, row A, grave 34.
Hall, James....	H	Private.	June 26, 1864	City Point, Va........	Died at Point of Rocks, Md. Interred in section F, row [illegible], grave 1[illegible]9.
Hall, John..............	H	Private.	July 26, 1864	Hampton, Va.........	Died at Fortress Monroe, Va. Interred in section D, row [illegible], grave 10.
Hall, Justice W..........	F	Private.	Aug. 24, 1864	Hampton, Va.........	Died at Fortress Monroe, Va.
Hayward, Orloff.	I	Private.	July 2, 1864	Hampton, Va.........	Died at Fortress Monroe, Va. Interred in section E, row [illegible], grave 35.
Henderson, Warren.....	H	Private.	Aug. 27, 1864	Hampton, Va.........	Died at Fortress Monroe, Va. Interred in section E, row [illegible], grave 17.
Heskett, Thomas C......	E	Private.	July 7, 1864	City Point, Va........	Died at Point of Rocks, Md.
Hill, Cornelius	B	Sergeant	July 19, 1864	City Point, Va.... ...	Died at Bermuda Hundred, Va. Interred in section A, row [illegible], grave 142.
Hoffman, William W....	F	Sergeant	Aug. 11, 1864	Hampton, Va.........	Died at Portsmouth, Va. Interred in section C, row [illegible], grave 1
Holland, John S........	C	Private.	June 26, 1864	Arlington, Va........	Died at Washington, D. C.
Huhn, John M	C	Private.	Aug. 3, 1864	City Point, Va........	
Humiston, Charles	I	Private.	June 28, 1864	City Point, Va.......	Died at Point of Rocks, Md.
Hunter, George...... ...	H	Private.	July 2, 1864	....	Died in hospital.
Jobes, John	K	Private.	July 12, 1864	City Point, Va.......	Died at Bermuda Hundred, Va. Interred in section A, row [illegible], grave 78.
Jolly, John..............	C	Corporal	Aug. 13, 1864	City Point, Va	
Lamb, William F..	F	Private.	July 31, 1864	City Point, Va........	Died at Bermuda Hundred, Va.
Long, William H........	C	Private.	Aug. 27, 1864	City Point, Va........	
McNichols, Benjamin...	E	Private.	Aug. 14, 1864	Hampton, Va.........	Died at Portsmouth, Va.
Morlan, Joshua	D	Private.	Sept. 12, 1864	....	Died at home, Welsh Township, Washington County
Nichol, Robert E........	B	Private.	Oct. 3, 1864	Arlington, Va........	Died at Washington, D. C.
Randerson, John W.....	C	Private.	July 5, 1864	City Point, Va........	Died at Bermuda Hundred, Va.
Scott, Samuel G.	E	2d Lieut.	July 12, 1864	City Point, Va..	Died at Bermuda Hundred, Va. Interred in section F, row [illegible], grave 125.
Smith, James H..........	D	Private	Aug. 9, 1864	City Point, Va........	Killed by explosion of ordnance boat.
Stewart, William........	F	Private.	Sept. 11, 1864	....	Died at home.
Stone, Simon B....	H	Private.	July 17, 1864	City Point, Va........	Died at Bermuda Hundred, Va.
Stowell, Benjamin F....	C	Private.	Aug. 2, 1864	City Point, Va........	
Stuckey, Jeremiah......	A	Private.	May 23, 1864	....	Killed by railroad accident near Marietta, O.
Truman, Haze...........	H	Private.	Oct. 22, 1864	Arlington, Va........	Died at Washington, D. C.
Waterman, Charles......	I	Private.	July 24, 1864	Hampton, Va.........	Died on steamer Tilly.

149th REGIMENT OHIO VOLUNTEER INFANTRY.

Names.	Co.	Rank.	Died.	Buried.	Remarks.
Acton, Lot	E	Private.	Aug. 14, 1864	Baltimore, Md	Interred in Louden Park Cemetery.
Armstrong, Edward F	A	Private.	Jan. 9, 1865	Salisbury, N. C	Died in Rebel Prison.
Beath, Granville	I	Private.	Aug. 21, 1864	Antietam, Md	Died at Frederick, Md. Interred in section 1, row 6, grave 98.
Benner, Henry	A	Private.	Nov. 1, 1864	Salisbury, N. C	Died in Rebel Prison.
Bishop, David	F	Private.	June 15, 1864	Baltimore, Md	Interred in Louden Park Cemetery.
Boyer, Richard H	F	Private.	Aug. 31, 1864	Columbus, O	Interred in grave 189, Green Lawn Cemetery.
Brodess, Thomas W	I	Private.	Oct. 20, 1864	Annapolis, Md	
Burnes, Robert	G	Private.	Nov. 28, 1864	Danville, Va	Died in Rebel Prison.
Craig, Franklin	K	Private.	July 9, 1864	Antietam, Md	Killed in battle of Monocacy, Md. Interred in section 1, row C, grave 122.
Cutright, John L	D	Private.	Aug. 12, 1864	Annapolis, Md	
Eachus, Squire	K	Private.	July 14, 1865		Died at Wilmington, O.
Fix, Andrew	H	Private.	Feb. 13, 1865	Salisbury, N. C	Died in Rebel Prison.
Frank, Philip	I	Private.	Oct. 2, 1864	Danville, Va	Died in Rebel Prison.
Ghormley, James	A	Private.	Dec. 21, 1864	Salisbury, N. C	Died in Rebel Prison.
Harrison, James H	I	Corporal	Sept. 13, 1864	Annapolis, Md	
Harrison William H	I	Corporal	Sept. 25, 1864	Annapolis, Md	
Henry, Samuel	B	Private.	July 9, 1864	Antietam, Md	Killed in battle of Monocacy, Maryland.
Hodson, Cyrus	G	Private.	June 8, 1864	Baltimore, Md	Interred in Louden Park Cemetery
Hodson, Isaac	G	Private.	Jan. 23, 1864	Danville, Va	Died in Rebel Prison.
Howser, William	I	Private.	Jan. 27, 1865	Danville, Va	Died in Rebel Prison.
Hubbard, Edward	K	Private.	Mch. 10, 1865	Annapolis, Md	
Hunt, Harvey	K	Private.	June 4, 1864		Died at Easton, Md.
Hussey, Elijah	G	Private.	Feb. 24, 1865	Annapolis, Md	
Junck, Milton P	C	Private.	May 16, 1864	Pittsburgh, Pa	
Kinnamon, Jeremiah	E	Private.	Sept. 25, 1864	Danville, Va	Died in Rebel Prison.
Miller, Smith	E	Private.	Mch. 24, 1865	Annapolis, Md	
Mills, Richard H	B	Private.	Sept. 19, 1864	Danville, Va	Died in Rebel Prison.
Moon, Alvin	G	Private.	July 13, 1864	Baltimore, Md	Interred in Louden Park Cemetery.
Park, William	F	Private.	June 26, 1864	Baltimore, Md	Interred in Louden Park Cemetery.
Parker, John K	B	Private.	Feb. 17, 1865	Danville, Va	Died in Rebel Prison.
Ray, James H	D	Private.	Nov. 15, 1864	Danville, Va	Died in Rebel Prison.
Robinson, Erskine	A	Sergeant	July 7, 1864	Baltimore, Md	Interred in Louden Park Cemetery.
Rowe, John	B	Private.	Aug. 17, 1864	Baltimore, Md	Interred in Louden Park Cemetery.
Ryan, James	G	Private.	Nov. 20, 1864	Danville, Va	Died in Rebel Prison.
Sands, James	D	Private.	Mch. 5, 1865	Richmond, Va	Died in Rebel Prison.
Sayre, Preston H	F	Private.	Dec. 2, 1864	Salisbury, N. C	Died in Rebel Prison.
Stadler, John	F	Private.	July 1, 1864	Baltimore, Md	Interred in Louden Park Cemetery.
Stitt, William G	E	Sergeant	Aug. 15, 1864	Washington, D. C	
Sutton, Moses L	D	Corporal	July 9, 1864	Antietam, Md	Killed in battle of Monocacy, Maryland.
Trochler, George	F	Private.	Aug. 6, 1864	Antietam, Md	Died at Sandy Hook, Md. Interred in section E, row 2, grave 28.
Wall, Clarence	B	Private.	July 9, 1864	Antietam, Md	Killed in battle of Monocacy, Maryland.
West, George W	G	Private.	Oct. 20, 1864	Danville, Va	Died in Rebel Prison.
Whipple, Eldridge G	A	Private.	Oct. 28, 1864	Annapolis, Md	
Woodmansee, Amos	B	Private.	Jan. 15, 1865	Danville, Va	Died in Rebel Prison.

150th REGIMENT OHIO VOLUNTEER INFANTRY.

Names.	Co.	Rank.	Died.	Buried.	Remarks.
Beech, Edgar L.	K	Private.	Aug. 1, 1864	Arlington, Va.	Died at Washington, D. C.
Cowles, Henry A.	K	Private.	July 15, 1864	Arlington, Va.	Died at Washington, D. C.
Eils, Edward A.	K	Corporal	Aug. 4, 1864	Arlington, Va.	Died at Washington, D. C.
Krum, Henry	D	Private.	June 10, 1864	.. .. ..	Died at Bedford, O.
Leach, William E.	K	Private.	July 13, 1864	Arlington, Va.	Died at Washington, D. C., of wounds received in action.
Monroe, John	K	Private.	Aug. 3, 1864	Arlington, Va.	Died at Washington, D. C.
Parker, Albert M.	H	Private.	Aug. 7, 1864	Arlington, Va.	Died at Washington, D. C.
Perkins, Charles	C	Private.	Aug. 18, 1864	Cleveland, O.	
Wright, Arthur	G	Private.	Aug. 29, 1864	Arlington, Va.	Died at Washington, D. C.
Wyman, William H.	C	Corporal	July 4, 1864	Arlington, Va.	Accidentally killed near Washington, D. C.

151st REGIMENT OHIO VOLUNTEER INFANTRY.

Names.	Co.	Rank.	Died.	Buried.	Remarks.
Binkley, Richard	A	Private.	May 18, 1864	Antietam, Md.	Died at New Creek, W. Va.
Collins, William	K	Private.	Aug. 4, 1864	Arlington, Va.	Died at Washington, D. C.
Crawford, William	H	Private.	Aug. 17, 1864	Arlington, Va.	Died at Fort Reno, D. C.
Devol, Luther	G	Private.	Aug. 19, 1864	Arlington, Va.	Died at Fort Simmons, D. C.
Hood, F. K.	I	Private.	July 7, 1864	Arlington, Va.	Died at Fort De Russey, D. C.
Lippercott, William	D	Private.	Aug. 7, 1864	Arlington, Va.	Died at Fort Reno, D. C.
Rhodes, George W.	A	Sergeant	July 31, 1864	Arlington, Va.	Died at Fort Reno, D. C.
Walters, Josiah	A	Corporal	Aug. 21, 1864	Arlington, Va.	Died at Fort Reno, D. C.
Whitcraft, Isaac	I	Private.	Aug. 15, 1864	Arlington, Va.	Died at Fort De Russey, D. C.

152nd REGIMENT OHIO VOLUNTEER INFANTRY.

Names.	Co.	Rank.	Died.	Buried.	Remarks.
Anderson, Joseph	H	Private.	Aug. 28, 1864	Camp Dennison, O.	
Bolton, Ashley	I	Private.	Aug. 30, 1864	Camp Dennison, O.	
Bookwalter, Franklin	C	Private.	July 26, 1864	Antietam, Md.	Died at Cumberland, Md.
Brandon, James	C	Private.	July 28, 1864	Antietam, Md.	Died at Cumberland, Md.
Brandon, John T.	C	Private.	Aug. 22, 1864	Camp Dennison, O.	Died at Cumberland, Md. Interred in grave 27.
Copstick, John	H	Corporal	Aug. 1, 1864	Antietam, Md.	Died at Cumberland, Md.
Cole, David	G	Private.	July 17, 1864	Antietam, Md.	Died at Cumberland, Md.
Davidson, Robert	F	Private.	July 20, 1864	Antietam, Md.	Died at Cumberland, Md.
Dunham, Henry	I	Private.	June 6, 1864	Winchester, Va.	Died at Martinsburg, W. Va.
Fitzpatrick, John	E	Private.	July 10, 1864	Antietam, Md.	Died at Clarysville, Md.
Graman, Adam	A	Private.	May 29, 1864	Antietam, Md.	Died at New Creek, W. Va.
Haynes, George	C	Private.	May 28, 1864	Antietam, Md.	Died at New Creek, W. Va.
Hartzell, James C.	C	1st Sergt.	Aug. 16, 1864	Camp Dennison, O.	
Kimball, William H.	K	Private.	Aug. 21, 1864	Camp Dennison, O.	
Patty, Clark	C	Private.	June 5, 1864	Antietam, Md.	Died at New Creek, W. Va.
Pearson, William	I	Private.	Aug. 2, 1864	Antietam, Md.	Died at Cumberland, Md. Interred in section [illegible], grave 80.
Ross, Josiah	H	Private.	Aug. 21, 1864	Camp Dennison, O.	
Ryan, William H.	B	Private.	May 23, 1864	Antietam, Md.	Died at New Creek, W. Va.
Swisher, Henry	F	Private.	Aug. 19, 1864	Camp Dennison, O.	Died at Cumberland, Md. Interred in grave 26.
Thomas, Daniel	H	Private.	June 21, 1864	.. .. ..	Killed in action at Greenbriar Gap, W. Va.
Weaver, John	C	Private.	Sept. 2, 1864	Camp Dennison, O.	Interred in grave 28.
Williams, Louis C.	G	Corporal	May 29, 1864	Antietam, Md.	Died at New Creek, W. Va.

153rd REGIMENT OHIO VOLUNTEER INFANTRY.

Names.	Co.	Rank.	Died.	Buried.	Remarks.
BeHymer, Clarington...	A	Private.	Nov. 6, 1864	Andersonville, Ga....	Died in Rebel Prison.
BeHymer, Levi..........	A	Private.	Oct. 17, 1864	Andersonville, Ga....	Died in Rebel Prison. Interred in grave 11,072.
BeHymer, Nathaniel ...	A	Private.	Feb. 10, 1865	Florence, S. C.......	Died in Rebel Prison.
Coffield, Arthur.........	F	Private.	Aug. 2, 1864	Antietam, Md........	Killed in battle of Green Springs Depot, W. Va.
Curtis, John, Jr.	G	Private.	May 17, 1864	Parkersburg, W. Va..	
Dean, Joseph S..........	E	Private.	Dec. 10, 1864	Annapolis, Md.......	
Fisher, Gilbert..........	H	Private.	Mch. 12, 1865	Winchester, Va.......	Died at Martinsburg, W. Va.
Frazier, Leonidas W....	C	1st Lieut.	July 3, 1864	Antietam, Md..... ..	Killed in battle of Hammack's Mills, W. Va.
Harry, Edwin...........	H	Private.	Dec. 9, 1864	Andersonville, Ga....	Died in Rebel Prison.
Huddleston, James......	H	Private.	June 5, 1864	Antietam, Md........	Died at Paw Paw, W. Va.
Hutchins, George W. ...	A	Private.	Oct. 28, 1864	Andersonville, Ga....	Died in Rebel Prison.
Hutchins, John W.......	A	Private.	Oct. 31, 1864	Andersonville, Ga....	Died in Rebel Prison. Interred in grave 11,696.
Jones, Albert............	H	Private.	Nov. 28, 1864	Florence, S. C........	Died in Rebel Prison.
Knott, Isaac.............	H	Private.	Oct. 15, 1864	Andersonville, Ga....	Died in Rebel Prison. Interred in grave 11,012.
Rybolt, Charles R.......	H	Private.	May 11, 1865	Jacksonville, Fla.....	
Scorce, William.........	E	Private.	Dec. 8, 1864	Annapolis, Md.	
Shade, William L........	G	Private.	July 11, 1864	....	Died at Batavia, O.
Shaw, William B........	H	Sergeant	Jan. 15, 1865	Florence, S. C........	Died in Rebel Prison.
Simmons, Almetus F....	D	Private.	May 30, 1864	Antietam, Md........	Died at Paw Paw, W. Va.
Smith, Lewis W.........	H	Private.	Sept. 20, 1864	Andersonville, Ga....	Died in Rebel Prison. Interred in grave 9386.
Smith, P. W.............	C	Private.	Oct. 10, 1864	Florence, S. C........	Died in Rebel Prison.
Taylor, Watson..........	F	Private.	Aug. 5, 1864	Antietam, Md........	Died at Cumberland, Md., of wounds received in action. Interred in section 1, row B, grave 38.
Tatman, B. F............	C	Private.	Oct. 7, 1864	Andersonville, Ga....	Died in Rebel Prison. Interred in grave 10,171.
Test, Josephus	C	Private.	April 27, 1865	....	Perished by explosion of steamer Sultana, on Mississippi River, near Memphis, Tennessee.

154th REGIMENT OHIO VOLUNTEER INFANTRY.

Names.	Co.	Rank.	Died.	Buried.	Remarks.
Baldwin, Joseph........	A	Private.	Aug. 8, 1864	Antietam, Md........	Died of wounds received Aug. 4, 1864, in battle of New Creek, W. Va.
Cheney, Benjamin F....	K	Private.	July 31, 1864	Antietam, Md........	Died at New Creek, W. Va.
Gerlaugh, William......	D	Private.	Feb. 5, 1865	Salisbury, N. C.......	Died in Rebel Prison.
Stutsman, David........	K	Corporal	Feb. 14, 1865	Salisbury, N. C.......	Died in Rebel Prison.

155th REGIMENT OHIO VOLUNTEER INFANTRY.

Names.	Co.	Rank.	Died.	Buried.	Remarks.
Baker, Lawrence	D	Private.	Aug. 5, 1864	Hampton, Va	Died at Portsmouth, Va.
Brothers, John W	D	1st Sergt.	Aug. 18, 1864	Hampton, Va	Died at Portsmouth, Va [illegible] terred in section C, ro[illegible] grave 4.
Calvin, Wilson T	D	Sergeant	July 13, 1864	Hampton, Va	Died at Norfolk, Va.
Cunningham, Benj. C	B	Private.	Aug. 27, 1864	Pittsburgh, Pa	
Floor, Hiram	G	Private.	Aug. 14, 1864	Hampton, Va	Died at Portsmouth, Va.
Haggard, Thomas C	I	Private.	Aug. 21, 1864	Hampton, Va	Died at Portsmouth, Va
Holliday, Lewis	E	Private.	July 15, 1864	Hampton, Va	Died at Norfolk, Va.
Howard, Cowden	G	Private.	July 14, 1864	Hampton, Va	Died at Norfolk, Va.
Hunter, William H	C	Private.	July 19, 1864	City Point, Va	
Jacobs, Thomas	B	Private.	Sept. 8, 1864	Arlington, Va	Died at Washington, D. C[illegible]
Justice, G. A	F	Private.	July 17, 1864	City Point, Va	
Kennedy, Henderson G.	D	Private.	Aug. 25, 1864	Arlington, Va	Died at Washington, D. C[illegible]
Leopard, Manuel	D	Private.	Aug. 4, 1864	Hampton, Va	Died at Portsmouth, V[illegible] terred in section B, r[illegible] grave 27.
McClain, John	H	Private.	Aug. 15, 1864	Hampton, Va	Died at Portsmouth, V[illegible] terred in section B, r[illegible] grave 5.
McCollum, Joel	D	Private.	July 20, 1864	Long Island, N. Y	Died on transport Atlant[illegible] terred in Cypress Hil[illegible] tery.
McKinlay, William	E	Private.	July 18, 1864	Arlington, Va	Died at Washington, D. [illegible]
Martz, Solomon	G	Private.	Aug. 1, 1864	Hampton, Va	Died at Portsmouth, Va.
Miller, James C	D	Private.	July 31, 1864	Hampton, Va	Died at Portsmouth, Va.
Shafer, David	G	Private.	Aug. 16, 1864	Hampton, Va	Died at Norfolk, Va. In[illegible] in section A, row 3, gra[illegible]
Warner, A. O	E	Private.	July 21, 1864	Hampton, Va	Died at Portsmouth, Va.

156th REGIMENT OHIO VOLUNTEER INFANTRY.

Names.	Co.	Rank.	Died.	Buried.	Remarks.
Auckey, Theodore C	E	Private.	Aug. 12, 1864		Died at Camden, Pr[illegible] ty, O.
Brown, David L	C	Private.	June 27, 1864	Cincinnati, O	Interred in Spring [illegible] tery
Buxton, Greenbury	I	Private.	Aug. 5, 1864	Lexington, Ky	Interred in sec[illegible] 581.
Buxton, Greenbury S	I	Private.	June 15, 1864	Camp Dennison, O	
Corman, Henry	D	Private.	July 9, 1864	Cincinnati, O	Interred in Spring [illegible] tery.
Crock, William	K	Private.	Aug. 10, 1864	Antietam, Md	Died at Cumberland [illegible] terred in section [illegible] grave 18.
Daniels, Hiram	G	Private.	July 11, 1864	Lexington, Ky	Died at Falmouth, Ky
Drury, Horace M	K	Captain.	June 12, 1864	Lexington, Ky	Died at Falmouth, Ky.
Hapner, Nathan	C	Private.	July 10, 1864	Cincinnati, O	Interred in Spring Gr[illegible] tery.
Horn, Levi F	C	Private.	June 25, 1864	Cincinnati, O	Interred in Spring Gr[illegible] tery.
Jones, Richard	G	Private.	June 30, 1864	Lexington, Ky	Died at Falmouth, Ky
McWhinney, Benj. T	H	Private.	Aug. 19, 1864		
Montreith, John	A	Private.	June 22, 1864	Cincinnati, O	Interred in Spring Gr[illegible] tery.
Patterson, John C	H	Private.	Aug. 10, 1864		
Price, Frederick	B	Private.	June 20, 1864		Died at his home [illegible] County, O.
Rudebaugh, Benj. F	K	Private.	Aug. 7, 1864	Cincinnati, O	Interred in grave [illegible] Grove Cemetery.
Swain, James M.	H	Private.	June 29, 1864		
Taylor, Israel B.	H	Private.	July 30, 1864		
Tennis, James	G	Private.	Aug. 18, 1864	Antietam, Md	Died at Cumberland [illegible] terred in section [illegible] grave 11.
Thompson, James	H	Private.	June 30, 1864		
Wagant, Jonathan	I	Private.	July 24, 1864		Died at his home [illegible] County, O
Young, Thomas	I	Private.	June 25, 1864	Covington, Ky	Interred in Linden Cemetery.

157th REGIMENT OHIO VOLUNTEER INFANTRY.

Names.	Co.	Rank.	Died.	Buried.	Remarks.
Bushong, John	K	Private.	....	....	Died at his home, Carroll County, O.
Crawford, John M.	G	Private.	July 31, 1864	....	Died at Fort Delaware, Del.
Hamilton, Edward C.	B	Private.	July 14, 1864	....	Died at Fort Delaware, Del.
Hastings, Stephen B.	G	Private.	Aug. 28, 1864	....	Died at his home, Jefferson County, O.
McCullough, John A.	E	Private.	Aug. 28, 1864	....	Died at Steubenville, O.
Megrail, Thomas	G	Private.	Aug. 10, 1864	....	Died at his home, Jefferson County, O.
Negus, William	F	Private.	Aug. 1, 1864	....	Died at Fort Delaware, Del.
Speedy, John	K	Private.	July 2, 1864	....	Died at Fort Delaware, Del.
Thompson, George W.	I	Private.	May 27, 1864	Baltimore, Md.	Died at Relay House, Md. Interred in Louden Park Cemetery.
Walters, James	D	Private.	July 24, 1864	....	Died at Fort Delaware, Del.

159th REGIMENT OHIO VOLUNTEER INFANTRY.

Names.	Co.	Rank.	Died.	Buried.	Remarks.
Dunn, George W.	G	Sergeant	July 22, 1864	Baltimore, Md.	Interred in Louden Park Cemetery.
Faisall, Harvey D.	H	Private.	Aug. 7, 1864	Baltimore, Md.	Interred in Louden Park Cemetery.
Fleming, Albert G.	H	Private.	July 25, 1864	Baltimore, Md.	Interred in Louden Park Cemetery.
Goble, Peter	E	Private.	Aug. 16, 1864	Baltimore, Md.	Interred in Louden Park Cemetery.
Hauptman, Charles	B	Private.	Aug. 7, 1864	Baltimore, Md.	Interred in Louden Park Cemetery.
Koos, Louis	D	Private.	July 20, 1864	Baltimore, Md.	Interred in Louden Park Cemetery.
Moore, Joseph G.	..	Chaplain	Aug. 18, 1864	Baltimore, Md.	Interred in Louden Park Cemetery.
Parks, James	H	Private.	July 18, 1864	Baltimore, Md.	Interred in Louden Park Cemetery.
Patterson, Bushrod	K	Private.	Aug. 15, 1864	Roseville, O.	Accidentally killed on railroad, near York, Pa.
Walcott, James	H	Private.	July 31, 1864	Baltimore, Md.	Interred in Louden Park Cemetery.

160th REGIMENT OHIO VOLUNTEER INFANTRY.

Names.	Co.	Rank.	Died.	Buried.	Remarks.
Anderson, Samuel	C	Private.	Aug. 28, 1864	....	Died at Crestline, O.
Beth, Peter	H	Private.	Aug. 13, 1864	Antietam, Md.	Killed in action at Maryland Heights, Md. Interred in section 1, row E, grave 278.
Cramer, Isaac F.	K	2d Lieut.	Sept. 5, 1864	....	Died at Zanesville, O.
Dutro, Francis M.	I	Private.	June 21, 1864	Winchester, Va.	Died at Martinsburg, W. Va.
Fry, Thomas	K	Private.	June 30, 1864	Winchester, Va.	Died at Martinsburg, W. Va. Interred in section 27.
Garrett, Andrew	D	Private.	Aug. 19, 1864	Antietam, Md.	Died at Maryland Heights, Md. Interred in section 1, row E, grave 280.
Kelly, Isaac	H	Private.	Aug. 13, 1864	Antietam, Md.	Killed in action at Maryland Heights, Md. Interred in section 1, row E, grave 279.
Kelly, Nathan S.	F & S	Com.Ser.	Aug. 17, 1864	Baltimore, Md.	Interred in Louden Park Cemetery.

Names.	Co.	Rank.	Died.	Buried.	Remarks.
Lamb, Lyman C.	B	Corporal	Aug. 16, 1864	Annapolis, Md.	
McLees, Josiah	I	Private.	July 20, 1864	Antietam, Md.	Died at Frederick, Md.
Marlow, James W.	F	Sergeant	Feb. 1, 1865	Richmond, Va.	Died in Rebel Prison.
Prall, John	K	Private.	Aug. 31, 1864	Columbus, O.	Interred in grave 188, Green Lawn Cemetery.
Smith, Charles W.	I	Private.	July 16, 1864	Antietam, Md.	Died at Frederick, Md.
State, George	H	Private.	Aug. 13, 1864	Antietam, Md.	Killed in action at Maryland Heights, Md.
Steers, Isaac N.	E	Private.	July 31, 1864	Antietam, Md.	Died at Frederick, Md. Interred in section 1, row C, grave 100.
Stewart, John J.	E	Private.	July 4, 1864	....	Accidentally killed between Sharpsburg and Sandy Hook, Maryland.
White, Isaiah M.	I	Corporal	July 7, 1864	Antietam, Md.	Died at Frederick, Md. Interred in section 1, row C, grave 123.
Wright Andrew J.	F	Sergeant	Aug. 18, 1864	Antietam, Md.	Died at Maryland Heights, Md.

161st REGIMENT OHIO VOLUNTEER INFANTRY.

Names.	Co.	Rank.	Died.	Buried.	Remarks.
Barnes, Carolus J.	C	1st Lieut.	July 28, 1864	....	Drowned at Frederick Junction, Md.
Bingman, Elias	G	Private.	July 21, 1864	Antietam, Md.	Died at Cumberland, Md. Interred in section 1, row A, grave 2.
Bishop, John	C	Private.	....	Antietam, Md.	Died at Cumberland, Md.
Brainard, Oliver	F	Private.	May 28, 1864	Antietam, Md.	Died at Cumberland, Md. Interred in section 1, row B, grave 35.
Briggs, John J.	B	Private	July 19, 1864	Annapolis, Md.	
Daugherty, Harrison	K	Private.	Aug. 14, 1864	....	Died at Camp Distribution, Va.
Flenner, Levi G.	I	Private.	Aug. 9, 1864	Antietam, Md.	Died at Frederick, Md. Interred in section 1, row C, grave 104.
Goodbarn, Alfred	D	Private.	July 6, 1864	Antietam, Md.	Died at Frederick, Md. Interred in section 1, row C, grave 131.
Lippett, Elihu	H	Corporal	June 22, 1864	Winchester, Va.	Died at Martinsburg, W. Va.
Narney, Jacob W.	F	Private.	Oct. 4, 1864	Baltimore, Md.	Interred in Louden Park Cemetery.
Phillips, Frank W.	C	Private.	May —, 1864	Columbus, O.	Died at Camp Chase, O. Interred in Green Lawn Cemetery.
Schwitzer, Samuel	A	Private.	July 7, 1864	Antietam, Md.	Died of wounds received in action at Maryland Heights, Md. Interred in section 1, row C, grave 21.
Trimmer, James	H	Private.	June 9, 1864	Antietam, Md.	Died at Clarysville, Md.
Walker, Joel	B	Corporal	Sept. 3, 1864	....	
Williams, Elijah	K	Corporal	July 5, 1864	Antietam, Md.	Died at Cumberland, Md. Interred in section 1, row A, grave 29.

162nd REGIMENT OHIO VOLUNTEER INFANTRY.

Names.	Co.	Rank.	Died.	Buried.	Remarks.
Breckenridge, Annias	E	Private.	July 31, 1864	Covington, Ky.	Interred in Linden Grove Cemetery.
Gribler, George	I	Private.	Aug. 26, 1864	Covington, Ky.	Interred in Linden Grove Cemetery.
Karns, Michael	C	Private.	July 27, 1864	....	Died at Columbus, O., and sent home for burial.
Keifer, Michael	F	Private.	Aug. 15, 1864	....	Died at Columbus, O., and sent home for burial.

Names.	Co.	Rank.	Died.	Buried.	Remarks.
Killinger, Henry E.	A	Private.	Aug. 19, 1864		Died at Columbus, O., and sent home for burial.
Madder, John, Jr.	A	Private.	Aug. 19, 1864	Covington, Ky	Interred in Linden Grove Cemetery.
Mauger, Samuel	A	Private.	Aug. 25, 1864		Died at Columbus, O., and sent home for burial.
Muckley, John	I	Private.	Aug. 24, 1864		Died at his home, Ohio.
Reiswanger, John	H	Private.	Aug. 9, 1864		Died at Marlboro, Stark County, O.
Oberlin, Isaac	C	Private.	July 30, 1864		Died at Columbus, O., and sent home for burial.
Reed, Edward	I	Private.	July 26, 1864	Covington, Ky	Died at Fort McLean, Ky. Interred in Linden Grove Cemetery.
Rouche, Daniel F.	G	Private.	Sept. 4, 1864	Covington, Ky	Interred in section B, grave 12, Linden Grove Cemetery.
Schrantz, Ephraim	E	Private.	Aug. 21, 1864		Died at his home, Ohio.
Seekins, Frederick B.	B	Private.	Aug. 11, 1864	Covington, Ky	Interred in Linden Grove Cemetery.
Seipe, Jacob	K	Private.	June 21, 1864		Died at Columbus, O., and sent home for burial.
Slanker, John J.	B	Private.	July 2, 1864		Died at Columbus, O., of accidental wounds, and sent home for burial.
Taggart, William	K	Private.	Aug. 21, 1864		Died at Columbus, O., and sent home for burial.
Willaman, John B.	E	Private.	July 31, 1864	Covington, Ky	Interred in Linden Grove Cemetery.
Wise, Franklin	G	Private.	July 19, 1864	Covington, Ky	Interred in Linden Grove Cemetery.

163rd REGIMENT OHIO VOLUNTEER INFANTRY.

Names.	Co.	Rank.	Died.	Buried.	Remarks.
Atkinson, John M	A	Corporal	July 18, 1864	Glendale, Va	Died at Fort Pocahontas, Va. Interred in section C, grave 78.
Avery, James C	A	Private.	July 22, 1864	Glendale, Va	Died at Fort Pocahontas, Va. Interred in section C, grave 90.
Avery, Rufus L.*	A	Captain.	Aug. 2, 1864	City Point, Va	Died at Bermuda Hundreds, Virginia.
Baldwin, George S.	F	Private.	July 20, 1864	Hampton, Va	Died at Fortress Monroe, Va. Interred in section E, row 16, grave 25.
Berry, Philip	C	Private.	Sept. 10, 1864		Died while en route home.
Beverstock, Barney A.	B	Private.	Aug. 18, 1864	Hampton, Va	
Brown, Wesley	E	Private.	Aug. 6, 1864	Glendale, Va	Died at Fort Pocahontas, Va.
Buckingham, Sylvester M	F	Private.	July 27, 1864	Hampton, Va	Died at Fortress Monroe, Va. Interred in section E, row 17, grave 23.
Courtney, Elroy	B	Private.	Sept. 2, 1864		Died at Lexington, O.
Dille, Milton	B	Corporal	July 18, 1864	Glendale, Va	Died at Wilson's Landing, Va. Interred in section C, grave 88.
Eagle, George B.	I	Private.	June 28, 1864	Glendale, Va	Died at Wilson's Landing, Va. Interred in section C, grave 118.
Ewers, William O.	D	Private.	July 31, 1864	Glendale, Va	Died at Wilson's Landing, Va. Interred in section C, grave 68.
Finney, Robert L	B	Private.	Aug. 18, 1864	Hampton, Va	Interred in section E, row 8, grave 33.
Flixer, Eli B.	K	Sergeant	Aug. 18, 1864	Glendale, Va	Accidentally killed. Interred in section C, grave 79.
Friedline, Harrison	I	Private.	Sept. 8, 1864	Baltimore, Md	Interred in Louden Park Cemetery.
Gunn, Cyrus	G	Corporal	Aug. 14, 1864	Hampton, Va	Died on board steamer Wyoming.
Harris, Bradford D.	I	Private.	Sept. 9, 1864	Baltimore, Md	Interred in Louden Park Cemetery.
Hughes, Thomas	E	Private.	Aug. 27, 1864	Hampton, Va	
Leedy, Jacob B.	D	Corporal	Aug. 26, 1864	Hampton, Va	
McGuire, James A.	I	Private.	Sept. 2, 1864	Bristol, Pa	
Melick, J. Benson	H	Private.	Sept. 3, 1864	Baltimore, Md	Interred in Louden Park Cemetery.

Names.	Co.	Rank.	Died.	Buried.	Remarks.
Painter, John	D	Private.	Aug. 31, 1864	....	Died on board steamer City of Albany, en route from Fort Pocahontas, Va., to Washington, D. C.
Palm, James	B	Private.	Aug. 3, 1864	Glendale, Va	Died at Wilson's Landing, Va
Plummer, James L	A	Private.	Aug. 6, 1864	Glendale, Va	Died at Fort Pocahontas, Va. Interred in section C, grave 69.
Ringer, George W	A	Private.	Aug. 6, 1864	Glendale, Va	Died at Fort Pocahontas, Va.
Rohrer, Henry	E	Private.	Aug. 20, 1864	Hampton, Va	Interred in section E, row [illegible] grave 39.
Russell, William	E	Private.	Aug. 27, 1864	Hampton, Va	Interred in section E, row [illegible] grave 24.
Smith, Ebenezer	C	Private.	Aug. 13, 1864	Hampton, Va	Interred in section E, row [illegible] grave 40.
Ward, Jacob	C	Private.	July 30, 1864	Hampton, Va	Interred in section E, row [illegible] grave 51.
Wilson, Mark L	I	Sergeant	Aug. 16, 1864	Hampton, Va	Died at Fortress Monroe, Va.
Wyand, Daniel F	K	Private.	Aug. 1, 1864	Hampton, Va	Interred in section E, row [illegible] grave 1.

164th REGIMENT OHIO VOLUNTEER INFANTRY.

Names.	Co.	Rank.	Died.	Buried.	Remarks.
Berger, William H	E	Private.	Aug. 13, 1864	Arlington, Va	Died at Washington, D.C.
Brown, William T	K	Private.	June 18, 1864	Arlington, Va	Died at Fort Strong, Va.
Calaghan, Christopher	D	Private.	June 6, 1864	Arlington, Va	Died at Fort Cochran, Va.
Cooper, Frederick	K	Private.	July 30, 1864	Arlington, Va	Died at Fort Strong, Va.
Dimmick, Melvin	G	Private.	June 2, 1864	Arlington, Va	Died at Fort Strong, Va.
Frederick, Daniel	E	Private.	July 17, 1864	Arlington, Va	Died at Fort Strong, Va.
Grimes, William	C	Private.	July 31, 1864	Arlington, Va	Died at Fort Strong, Va.
Guingrich, Joseph	D	Private.	Aug. 4, 1864	Arlington, Va	Died at Fort Strong, Va.
Hart, Henry L	D	Private.	May 25, 1864	Arlington, Va	Died at Fort Strong, Va.
Holtz, Jacob S	H	Private.	July 1, 1864	Arlington, Va	Died at Fort Strong, Va.
King, Henry C	F	Private.	Aug. 11, 1864	Arlington, Va	Died at Fort Strong, Va.
Mickey, William E	I	Private.	July 22, 1864	Arlington, Va	Died at Fort Strong, Va.
Miller, Cheselden	I	Private.	Aug. 7, 1864	Arlington, Va	Died at Fort Strong, Va.
Miller, Daniel F	I	Private.	Aug. 19, 1864	Arlington, Va	Died at Washington, D. C.
Patterson, William H	G	Private.	May 20, 1864	Arlington, Va	Drowned in Potomac River near Georgetown, D. C.
Sell, Enos	A	Private.	June 1, 1864	Arlington, Va	Died at Fort Strong, Va.
Smith, Hiram B.	H	Private.	July 24, 1864	Arlington, Va	Died at Fort Strong, Va.
Thomas, Cyrus M	I	Corporal	July 24, 1864	Arlington, Va	Died at Fort Strong, Va.
Thorn, George S	G	Private.	Aug. 7, 1864	Arlington, Va	Died at Fort Strong, Va.
Wilson, William	G	Private.	June 19, 1864	Arlington, Va	Died at Fort Strong, Va.

165th BATTALION OHIO VOLUNTEER INFANTRY.

Names.	Co.	Rank.	Died.	Buried.	Remarks.
Butz, Christ	D	Private.	Aug. 2, 1864	Cincinnati, O	Interred in Spring Grove Cemetery.
Fossler, George	F	Private.	July 20, 1864	Cincinnati, O	Interred in Spring Grove Cemetery.

166th REGIMENT OHIO VOLUNTEER INFANTRY.

Names.	Co.	Rank.	Died.	Buried.	Remarks.
Blair, Lewis H...........	D	Private.	June 2, 1864	....	Died in hospital.
Brown, Edmund C.......	D	Private.	Aug. 20, 1864	....	Died in hospital.
Burr, Charles E.........	B	Private.	Aug. 15, 1864	Arlington, Va........	Died at Fairfax, Va.
Carlton, Eri J	D	Corporal	July 5, 1864	....	Died in hospital.
Close, Jacob.............	I	Private.	Aug. 8, 1864	Columbus, O.........	Died at Camp Chase, O. Interred in Green Lawn Cemetery.
Crittenden, Immer.....	C	Private.	July 12, 1864	....	Died in hospital.
Daniels, Lee............	D	Private.	Aug. 8, 1864	....	Died in hospital.
Fay, Norris D............	B	Corporal	July 14, 1864	....	Died at Fort Ward, Va.
Fitch, Joseph H..........	E	Private.	Aug. 13, 1864	....	Died at Fort Richardson, Va.
Freidt, David B..........	E	Private.	July 4, 1864	....	Drowned in Potomac River.
Green, Sperry...........	B	Private.	July 31, 1864	....	Died at Fort Ward, Va.
Hammond, Isaac........	C	Private	July 24, 1864	....	Died in hospital.
Hammond, Livingston..	I	Private.	Aug. 9, 1864	Columbus, O.........	Died at Camp Chase, O. Interred in Green Lawn Cemetery.
Heckart, Daniel.........	D	Sergeant	July 31, 1864	....	Died in hospital.
Heffner, Benjamin F....	H	Private.	Aug. 2, 1864	....	Died at Fort Richardson, Va.
Hester, Charles T	H	Private.	Aug. 17, 1864	Arlington, Va........	Died at Fairfax, Va.
Hoyman, Jacob E........	I	Sergeant	Aug. 2, 1864	....	Died at Fort Ward, Va.
Hoyt, Frederick.........	H	Corporal	Aug. 7, 1864	....	Died at Fort Richardson, Va.
Knapp, David...........	H	Private.	Aug. 21, 1864	....	Died at Fort Richardson, Va.
Lee, Stephen............	K	Private.	Aug. 22, 1864	Arlington, Va........	Died at Fairfax, Va.
McCleland, Thomas L...	A	Private.	Sept. 5, 1864	Cleveland, O.........	
McClure, Nathan H.....	E	Private.	July 7, 1864	....	Died at Fort Ward, Va.
Martin, William.........	A	Private.	Aug. 15, 1864	Arlington, Va........	Died at Fairfax, Va.
Miller, Jacob............	D	Private.	July 10, 1864	....	Died in hospital.
Miller, Levi.............	D	Private.	July 20, 1864	....	Died in hospital.
Palmer, John A..........	I	Private.	July 24, 1864	Columbus, O.........	Died at Camp Chase, O. Interred in Green Lawn Cemetery.
Pinney, John............	B	Private.	Aug. 19, 1864	Arlington, Va........	Died at Fairfax, Va.
Pine, Cornelius S........	B	Private.	Sept. 2, 1864	....	
Pond, Henry.............	D	Private.	Aug. 11, 1864	....	Died in hospital.
Powers, William........	F	Private.	Sept. 2, 1864	Cleveland, O.........	
Randall, Austin.........	D	Private.	Aug. 19, 1864	....	Died in hospital.
Rayburn, Willis A.......	C	Private.	Aug. 11, 1864	....	Died at Fort Ward, Va.
Reynolds, Hiram	C	Private.	Aug. 1, 1864	....	Died in hospital.
Ruggles, Dwight........	B	Corporal	Aug. 3, 1864	....	Died at Fort Ward, Va.
Shane, Henry...........	E	Sergeant	July 8, 1864	....	Died at Fort Ward, Va.
Shepard, Blair	D	Private.	Aug. 18, 1864	Alexandria Va......	Interred in grave 2571.
Shrimplin, James.	A	Private.	Aug. 18, 1864	Arlington, Va........	Died at Fairfax, Va.
Stokes, J. K..............	F	Private.	Sept. 1, 1864	....	Died at his home.
Walters, James A	I	Private.	Sept. 5, 1864	Cleveland, O.........	
Welch, Benjamin........	I	Private.	Aug. 12, 1864	Columbus, O.........	Died at Camp Chase, O. Interred in Green Lawn Cemetery.

167th REGIMENT OHIO VOLUNTEER INFANTRY.

Names.	Co.	Rank.	Died.	Buried.	Remarks.
Biehlman, John..........	C	Private.	June 25, 1864	....	Accidentally killed by a scouting party.
Ross, Edwin	K	Corporal	Aug. 7, 1864	....	
Smith, George T	A	Private.	Aug. 14, 1864	....	Died at Brownstown, W. Va.
Sterrett, William........	K	Private.	Aug. 15, 1864	....	
Williams, William J	K	Private.	Aug. 14, 1864	....	

168th REGIMENT OHIO VOLUNTEER INFANTRY.

Names.	Co.	Rank.	Died.	Buried.	Remarks.
Bergan, Timothy	D	Private.	June 11, 1864	Lexington, Ky	Killed in battle of Cynthiana, Kentucky.
Brady, J. R.	D	Private.	June 11, 1864	Lexington, Ky	Killed in battle of Cynthiana, Kentucky.
Chaney, W. B.	D	Private.	June 13, 1864	Lexington, Ky	Died of wounds received June 11, 1864, in battle of Cynthiana, Ky. Interred in section 11, grave 128.
Doyle, William H.	I	Private.	June 11, 1864	Lexington, Ky	Killed in battle of Cynthiana, Kentucky.
Edgington, John	A	Private.	July 22, 1864	Cincinnati, O.	Interred in Spring Grove Cemetery.
Fry, Henry	K	Private.	Aug. 3, 1864	Cincinnati, O.	Interred in Spring Grove Cemetery.
Henkle, Simeon W.	F	Private.	Aug. 13, 1864	Cincinnati, O.	Interred in Spring Grove Cemetery.
Hidy, Henry	K	Private.	July 15, 1864	Covington, Ky	Interred in Linden Grove Cemetery.
Irons, William P.	I	Sergeant	July 4, 1864	....	Died of wounds received June 11, 1864, in battle of Cynthiana, Ky.
Lee, James P.	B	Private.	Aug. 22, 1864	....	Died at Hillsboro, O.
McCoy, G. M.	A	Wagoner.	Aug. 16, 1864	Cincinnati, O.	Interred in Spring Grove Cemetery.
Rogers, Alexander	D	Private.	June 11, 1864	Lexington, Ky	Killed in battle of Cynthiana, Kentucky.
Smith, I. J.	E	Sergeant	July 31, 1864	....	Died at home, Highland County, O.
Smith, Levi	I	Private.	June 11, 1864	Lexington, Ky	Killed in battle of Cynthiana, Kentucky.
Smith, S. M.	E	Corporal	Sept. 5, 1864	....	Died at home, Highland County, O.
Sollars, Samuel	I	Private.	Sept. 27, 1864	Covington, Ky	Interred in Linden Grove Cemetery.
Stout, W. D.	A	Private.	June 11, 1864	Marietta, Ga	Killed in battle of Cynthiana, Ky. Interred in section G, grave 1700.
Strode, J. S.	A	Private.	June 23, 1864	....	Died at home, near Hillsboro, Ohio.
Weimer, William G.	D	Corporal	July 21, 1864	Covington, Ky	Died of wounds received June 11, 1864, in battle of Cynthiana, Ky. Interred in Linden Grove Cemetery.
Wood, Samuel	A	Private.	June 11, 1864	Lexington, Ky	Killed in battle of Cynthiana, Kentucky.

169th REGIMENT OHIO VOLUNTEER INFANTRY.

Names.	Co.	Rank.	Died.	Buried.	Remarks.
Beistle, Edson	C	Private.	July 21, 1864	Arlington, Va	Died at Fort Ethan Allen, Va.
Bowlus, Silas	K	Private.	July 3, 1864	Arlington, Va	Died at Fort Ethan Allen, Va.
Bricker, Isaac N.	D	Sergeant	Aug. 7, 1864	Arlington, Va	Died at Fort Ethan Allen, Va.
Cook, William	G	Private.	July 12, 1864	Arlington, Va	Died at Fort Ethan Allen, Va.
Downing, John	K	Private.	Sept. 6, 1864	Arlington, Va	Died at Washington, D. C.
Eberly, Peter	A	Private.	July 17, 1864	Arlington, Va	Died at Fort Ethan Allen, Va.
Fields, James	B	Private.	July 9, 1864	Arlington, Va	Died at Fort Ethan Allen, Va.
Haiter, David	F	Private.	July 24, 1864	Arlington, Va	Died at Fort Ethan Allen, Va.
Hausberger, Jacob	K	Private.	July 21, 1864	Arlington, Va	Died at Fort Ethan Allen, Va.
Hocum, Charles	K	Private.	Aug. 23, 1864	Arlington, Va	Died at Washington, D. C.
Holcomb, Edwin	F	Private.	July 21, 1864	Arlington, Va	Died at Fort Ethan Allen, Va.
Holcomb, Grant	G	Private.	May 30, 1864	Arlington, Va	Died at Fort Ethan Allen, Va.
Hollingshead, Samuel W	I	Private.	Aug. 12, 1864	Arlington, Va	Died at Fort Ethan Allen, Va.
Joyce, Samuel	E	Private.	July 12, 1865	Arlington, Va	Died at Fort Ethan Allen, Va.
Karbler, George	G	Private.	July 6, 1864	Arlington, Va	Died at Fort Ethan Allen, Va.
Karns, John	K	Private.	Aug. 12, 1864	....	Died at Defiance, O.
Lance, Henry	H	Sergeant	July 23, 1864	Arlington, Va	Died at Fort Ethan Allen, Va.
Lichty, David	D	Private.	Aug. 9, 1864	Arlington, Va	Died at Fort Ethan Allen, Va.
Marion, David	I	Sergeant	July 5, 1864	Arlington, Va	Died at Fort Ethan Allen, Va.
Marion, Elias D.	E	Private.	July 12, 1864	Arlington, Va	Died at Fort Ethan Allen, Va.
Mowery, Harrison	K	Private.	Aug. 23, 1864	Arlington, Va	Died at Washington, D. C.

Names.	Co.	Rank.	Died.	Buried.	Remarks.
Mowry, Henry	H	Private.	July 31, 1864	Arlington, Va	Died at Fort Ethan Allen, Va.
Myers, Ross	A	Private.	July 27, 1864	Arlington, Va	Died at Fort Ethan Allen, Va.
Myers, Walter M	A	Corporal	July 30, 1864	Arlington, Va	Died at Fort Ethan Allen, Va.
Orr, James T	D	Corporal	Aug. 9, 1864	Arlington, Va	Died at Fort Ethan Allen, Va.
Parker, William	G	Sergeant	July 26, 1864	Arlington, Va	Died at Fort Ethan Allen, Va.
Peters, Israel G	A	Corporal	Sept. 5, 1864	......	
Rice, Daniel	F	Private.	July 14, 1864	Arlington, Va	Died at Fort Ethan Allen, Va.
Rideout, Lafayette	K	Musician	July 25, 1864	Arlington, Va	Died at Fort Ethan Allen, Va.
Rikerd, William	K	Private.	Aug. 1, 1864	Arlington, Va	Died at Fort Ethan Allen, Va.
Risley, Charles	G	Private.	July 4, 1864	Arlington, Va	Died at Fort Ethan Allen, Va.
Rohrer, Allen K	E	Private.	Aug. 7, 1864	Arlington, Va	Died at Fort Ethan Allen, Va.
Seibert, Jerome	K	Private.	July 17, 1864	Arlington, Va	Died at Fort Ethan Allen, Va.
Shasteen, Beriah	H	Private.	Aug. 19, 1864	Arlington, Va	Died at Fort Ethan Allen, Va.
Shooster, Jacob	H	Private.	June 23, 1864	Arlington, Va	Died at Fort Ethan Allen, Va.
Smith, John	C	Private.	Aug. 1, 1864	Arlington, Va	Died at Fort Ethan Allen, Va.
Snyder, George H	D	Private.	July 29, 1864	Arlington, Va	Died at Fort Ethan Allen, Va.
Snyder, Israel	C	Private.	Aug. 28, 1864	Cleveland, O	
Sparks, Joseph	B	Private.	Aug. 20, 1864	Arlington, Va	Died at Fort Ethan Allen, Va.
Stahl, John M	H	Private.	July 20, 1864	Arlington, Va	Died at Fort Ethan Allen, Va.
West, Elijah	B	Private.	Aug. 31, 1864	......	Died at Clyde, O
Whitehead, William	B	Private.	July 18, 1864	Arlington, Va	Died at Fort Ethan Allen, Va.
Williams, Gilbert	F	Corporal	Aug. 6, 1864	Arlington, Va	Died at Fort Ethan Allen, Va.
Willson, Ferdinand	K	Corporal	Aug. 5, 1864	Arlington, Va	Died at Fort Ethan Allen, Va.

170th REGIMENT OHIO VOLUNTEER INFANTRY.

Names.	Co.	Rank.	Died.	Buried.	Remarks.
Calderhead, John	H	Private.	Aug. 3, 1864	Annapolis, Md	Died at Camp Parole, Md.
Carpenter, George	C	Private.	Aug. 19, 1864	Antietam, Md	Died at Sandy Hook, Md. Interred in section 1, row F, grave 304.
Clark, Robert	I	Private.	July 27, 1864	Antietam, Md	Died at Sandy Hook, Md.
Cox, Thomas	D	Private.	Dec. 21, 1864	Danville, Va	Died in Rebel Prison.
Crumrine, John	B	Private.	Aug. 10, 1864	Annapolis, Md	
Cunningham, John W	I	Private.	Sept. 8, 1864	Baltimore, Md	Interred in Louden Park Cemetery.
Dunlap, William	B	Private.	July 28, 1864	Antietam, Md	Died at Frederick, Md.
Eslick, James	D	Corporal	July 25, 1864	Antietam, Md	Died at Sandy Hook, Md.
Gamble, William T	B	Sergeant	Nov. 23, 1864	Danville, Va	Died in Rebel Prison.
Graham, James H	F	1st Lieut.	Aug. 11, 1864	Antietam, Md	Died at Sandy Hook, Md.
Harper, George	B	Private.	July 18, 1864	Winchester, Va	Killed in battle of Snicker's Ferry, Va.
Haverfield, James H	K	Corporal	July 18, 1864	Winchester, Va	Killed in battle of Snicker's Ferry, Va.
Heatherington, Joseph H	I	Corporal	Mch. 21, 1865	Annapolis, Md	
Hurless, John H	D	Private.	Aug. 15, 1864	Annapolis, Md	
Johnson, Thomas	K	Private.	Aug. 11, 1864	Antietam, Md	Died at Sandy Hook, Md. Interred in section 1, row F, grave 298.
Lanning, George	H	Sergeant	Sept. 1, 1864	Antietam, Md	Died at Sandy Hook, Md.
Leeper, Archibald	K	Private.	Aug. 12, 1864	Antietam, Md	Died at Sandy Hook, Md. Interred in section 1, row F, grave 294.
Mercer, William H. H	F	Private.	Aug. 24, 1864	Antietam, Md	Died at Sandy Hook, Md.
Moore, James	E	Private.	Aug. 9, 1864	Annapolis, Md	Died at Annapolis Junction, Maryland.
Parsons, Israel L	B	Private.	June 27, 1864	Arlington, Va	Died at Fort Simmons, Va.
Perry, Thomas H	G	Private.	June 3, 1864	......	
Rankin, William	I	1st Sergt.	Aug. 11, 1864	Baltimore, Md	Interred in Louden Park Cemetery.
Warner, Daniel	B	Private.	Aug. 26, 1864	Antietam, Md.*	Died at Sandy Hook, Md., of wounds received July 18, 1864, in battle of Snicker's Ferry, Va. Interred in section 1, row F, grave 287.
Wood, John D	D	Private.	Aug. 27, 1864	......	Died near Pittsburgh, Pa.

171st REGIMENT OHIO VOLUNTEER INFANTRY.

Names.	Co.	Rank.	Died.	Buried.	Remarks.
Belden, Hamlet B.	H	Private.	June 27, 1864	Covington, Ky.	Died of wounds received June 11, 1864, in action at Keller's Bridge, Ky. Interred in Linden Grove Cemetery.
Bow, Charles J.	I	Private.	July 8, 1864	Covington, Ky.	Interred in Linden Grove Cemetery.
Chapman, Sanford	F	Private.	July 1, 1864		Died at Johnson's Island, O.
Dilley, Jonathan	C	Private.	June 26, 1864	Camp Dennison, O.	Interred in grave 275.
Dunlap, Orsemus	A	Private.	July 2, 1864	Covington, Ky.	Died of gunshot wound. Interred in Linden Grove Cemetery.
Earl, Edwin D.	I	Corporal	June 11, 1864	Lexington, Ky.	Killed in action at Keller's Bridge, Ky.
Flick, Clark	H	Private.	May 16, 1864		Died at Johnson's Island, O.
Fobes, Joseph	G	Private.	June 23, 1864	Camp Dennison, O.	
Ford, Hezekiah M.	A	1st Sergt.	Aug. 1, 1864		Died at Warren, Trumbull County, O.
Goist, Hiram K.	D	Private.	June 2, 1864		Died at Johnson's Island, O.
Goldie, George G.	I	Private.	June 26, 1864	Camp Dennison, O.	
Granger, James S.	K	Private.	Aug. 9, 1864		Died at Mantua, Portage County, O.
Hood, Scott	B	Private.	July 30, 1864		Died at Ohl's Town, Trumbull County, O.
Kennedy, Samuel	C	Corporal	July 20, 1864		Died at Hubbard, Trumbull County, O.
Lampson, Byron	K	Private.	July 31, 1864		Died at Johnson's Island, O.
Lew, Almon L.	H	Private.	June 11, 1864	Lexington, Ky.	Killed in action at Keller's Bridge, Ky.
Maffitt, George W.	H	Private.	June 11, 1864	Lexington, Ky.	Killed in action at Keller's Bridge, Ky.
Matthews, Thomas, Jr.	C	Private.	June 18, 1864	Lexington, Ky.	Died of wounds received June 11, 1864, in action at Keller's Bridge, Ky.
Millikan, Henry A.	I	Private.	June 11, 1864	Lexington, Ky.	Killed in action at Keller's Bridge, Ky.
Monnasmith, Levi	F	Private.	June 11, 1864	Lexington, Ky.	Killed in action at Keller's Bridge, Ky.
Osborn, Joseph A.	D	Corporal	June 11, 1864	Lexington, Ky.	Killed in action at Keller's Bridge, Ky.
Pike, Daniel H.	I	Private.	July 15, 1864		Died at Windham, Portage County, O.
Porter, Colwell, T.	F	Private.	July 2, 1864	Cleveland, O.	
Reed, Walson	F	Private.	June 11, 1864	Lexington, Ky.	Killed in action at Keller's Bridge, Ky.
Reed, William W.	I	Private.	June 11, 1864	Lexington, Ky.	Killed in action at Keller's Bridge, Ky.
Ripley, Elias S.	G	Private.	June 20, 1864	Camp Denaison, O.	
Risk, William H.	G	Corporal	Aug. 6, 1864		Died at Briarfield, Portage County, O.
Russell, Stephen	F	Private.	June 11, 1864	Lexington, Ky.	Killed in action at Keller's Bridge, Ky.
Stephenson, Jacob	B	Private.	June 11, 1864	Lexington, Ky.	Killed in action at Keller's Bridge, Ky. Interred in section 10, grave 12.
Stoner, John	G	Private.	June 11, 1864	Lexington, Ky.	Killed in action at Keller's Bridge, Ky.
Strickland, Wilbur	H	Private.	Aug. 16, 1864		Died at Johnson's Island, O.
Strong, Horatio N.	I	Private.	Aug. 18, 1864		Died at Ravenna, Portage County, O.
Thompson, Mortimer C.	B	Private.	June 11, 1864	Lexington, Ky.	Killed in action at Keller's Bridge, Ky.
Williams, David	D	Private.	Aug. 7, 1864		Died at Johnson's Island, O.
Wolcott, Leander H.	H	Private.	June 11, 1864	Lexington, Ky.	Killed in action at Kellers Bridge, Ky.

172nd REGIMENT OHIO VOLUNTEER INFANTRY.

Names.	Co.	Rank.	Died.	Buried.	Remarks.
Blackburn, John	D	Private.	Aug. 12, 1864	Gallipolis, O.	
Burt, John P.	E	Private.	May 29, 1864	Gallipolis, O.	
Carr, Cassius	A	Private.	June 7, 1864	Gallipolis, O.	
Elliott, James H.	G	Private.	July 12, 1864	Gallipolis, O.	
Hickle, Elias	E	Private.	June 30, 1864	Gallipolis, O.	
Hill, Nathan	K	Private.	July 30, 1864	Gallipolis, O.	
Lucas, Andrew	F	Private.	July 27, 1864	Gallipolis, O.	
Miller, Asbury J.	K	Corporal	June 11, 1864	Gallipolis, O.	
Rainey, David W.	E	Private.	May 23, 1864	Gallipolis, O.	
Smith, William S.	G	Private.	Aug. 25, 1864	Gallipolis, O.	

173rd REGIMENT OHIO VOLUNTEER INFANTRY.

Names.	Co.	Rank.	Died.	Buried.	Remarks.
Abbott, James W.	B	Private.	April 8, 1865	Nashville, Tenn.	Died at Johnsonville, Tenn. Interred in section M, grave 216.
Addis, Barton D.	I	Private.	Mch. 7, 1865	Nashville, Tenn.	Interred in section M, grave 207.
Altop, Ephraim	K	Private.	Dec. 4, 1864	Nashville, Tenn.	
Balsiger, Christopher	G	Private.	April 29, 1865	Murfreesboro, Tenn.	Interred in section B, grave 200, Stone River Cemetery.
Bogue, Elias	H	Private.	Mch. 3, 1865	Nashville, Tenn.	Died at Johnsonville, Tenn. Interred in section M, grave 214.
Breen, Hugh	*	Private.	Nov. 7, 1864	Camp Dennison, O.	Interred in grave 208.
Calvert, Eli	H	Private.	Feb. 10, 1865	Nashville, Tenn.	
Cameron, William H.	H	Private.	Jan. 15, 1865	Nashville, Tenn.	
Chamberlin, Lucas	D	Private.	April 8, 1865	Nashville, Tenn.	Interred in section J, grave 1496.
Clary, Joseph J.	K	Private.	Mch. 6, 1865	Nashville, Tenn.	Interred in section H, grave 106.
Collings, James L.	H	Private.	Feb. 14, 1865	Nashville, Tenn.	
Corn, George W.	I	Private.	Feb. 5, 1865	Nashville, Tenn.	
Cornell, Harrison	B	Private.	Jan. 7, 1865	Nashville, Tenn.	Interred in section H, grave 428.
Dalton, John	K	Private.	Nov. 28, 1864	Nashville, Tenn.	Interred in section E, grave 2624.
Danner, James H.	C	Private.	Dec. 23, 1864	Nashville, Tenn.	Interred in section G, grave 764.
Davis, Samuel T. S.	H	Private.	Feb. 2, 1865	Nashville, Tenn.	
Davis, William	A	Private.	Feb. 8, 1865	Nashville, Tenn.	Interred in section H, grave 240.
Deckard, Campbell	I	Private.	Jan. 21, 1865	Nashville, Tenn.	Interred in section R, grave 99.
Dillon, Welcome	E	Private.	Dec. 30, 1864	Nashville, Tenn.	
Dixson, William W.	H	Private.	Feb. 14, 1865	Nashville, Tenn.	Interred in section H, grave 383.
Doan, Nicholas	C	Private.	Jan. 25, 1865	Nashville, Tenn.	
Elkins, William	B	Private.	Jan. 2, 1865	Nashville, Tenn.	
Estes, James H.	F	Private.	Dec. 12, 1864	Nashville, Tenn.	Interred in section G, grave 308.
Ewing, George B.	I	Private.	Jan. 12, 1865	Nashville, Tenn.	Interred in section H, grave 450.
Foster, Francis M.	C	Private.	May 6, 1865	Nashville, Tenn.	Died at Johnsonville, Tenn.
Foster, John	E	Private.	Jan. 27, 1865	Nashville, Tenn.	Interred in section H, grave 25.
Fowler, Andy L.	B	Corporal	Jan. 29, 1865	Nashville, Tenn.	
Fox, Jacob	C	Private.	Mch. 4, 1865	Nashville, Tenn.	Died at Johnsonville, Tenn.
[illegible], Henry C.	D	Sergeant	Jan. 28, 1865	Nashville, Tenn.	
[illegible], Hiram	I	Private.	Dec. 7, 1864	Nashville, Tenn.	Interred in section G, grave 321.
[illegible], George A.	C	Private.	Dec. 28, 1864	Nashville, Tenn.	
[illegible], Samuel B.	K	Private.	Feb. 14, 1865	Nashville, Tenn.	
[illegible], George W.	K	Private.	April 4, 1865	Nashville, Tenn.	Died at Johnsonville, Tenn. Interred in section M, grave 182.
Harrison, [illegible]	K	Private.	Dec. 4, 1864	Nashville, Tenn.	Interred in section F, grave 139.
Hively, J[illegible]	[illegible]	Private.	Jan. 21, 1865	Nashville, Tenn.	

Names.	Co.	Rank.	Died.	Buried.	Remarks.
Huggins, Thomas	B	Private.	April 26, 1865	Nashville, Tenn	Died at Johnsonville, Tenn. Interred in section M, grave 195.
Hughes, John W	H	Private.	Feb. 8, 1865	Nashville, Tenn	
Hughes, Joseph C	A	Private.	April 4, 1865	Nashville, Tenn	Died at Johnsonville, Tenn.
Kessinger, Ward W	C	Private.	Mch. 12, 1865	Nashville, Tenn	
Kyre, Joseph N	C	Private.	Mch. 13, 1865	Nashville, Tenn	Died at Johnsonville, Tenn. Interred in section M, grave 204.
Lee, George	G	Private.	Mch. 13, 1865	Nashville, Tenn	Died at Johnsonville, Tenn. Interred in section M, grave 198.
McCarley, John D	C	Private.	Feb. 19, 1865	Nashville, Tenn	
McKean, Hiram F	C	Private.	Feb. 18, 1865	Nashville, Tenn	
McLean, Samuel W. E.	H	Private.	Mch. 28, 1865		Died at Winchester, O.
Mahan, Andrew B	B	Private.	Jan. 4, 1865	Nashville, Tenn	Interred in section H, grave 7.
Mall, George	F	Private.	June 3, 1865	Nashville, Tenn	Mustered out May 2[illegible], 1865, by order of War Department. Interred in section J, grave 1309.
Martt, Isaac M	B	Private.	Dec. 8, 1864	Nashville, Tenn	
Massie, George	B	Private.	Feb. 13, 1865	Nashville, Tenn	Interred in section H, grave 179.
Morehouse, John	G	Private.	Feb. 16, 1865	Nashville, Tenn	Interred in section H, grave 143.
Mount, William G	E	Corporal	Dec. 6, 1864	Nashville, Tenn	Interred in section G, grave 37.
Murdock, Elijah	F	Private.	Dec. 24, 1864	Nashville, Tenn	
Neighborgall, John L	I	Private.	Dec. 18, 1864	Nashville, Tenn	Interred in section G, grave 3[illegible].
Noble, James	A	Private.	Mch. 21, 1865	Nashville, Tenn	Died at Johnsonville, Tenn. Interred in section M, grave 208.
Null, William W	B	Private.	Aug. 3, 1865	Louisville, Ky	Interred in section D, row 4, grave 7, Cave Hill Cemetery.
Partlow, Andrew J	A	Wagoner	Feb. 8, 1865	Nashville, Tenn	Interred in section H, grave 2.
Paul, Joshua	E	Private.	July 5, 1865	Camp Dennison, O	Mustered out with company June 26, 1865.
Peck, Alfred	E	Private.	Feb. 15, 1865	Nashville, Tenn	Interred in section H, grave 141.
Pemberton, Elisha	E	Private.	Feb. 11, 1865	Nashville, Tenn	
Petry, Jacob	E	Private.	May 6, 1865	Nashville, Tenn	Died at Johnsonville, Tenn.
Petty Marion	E	Private.	June 16, 1865	Nashville, Tenn	Died at Johnsonville, Tenn.
Price, George P.	C	Private.	Jan. 17, 1865	Nashville, Tenn	
Ramsey, William E	K	Private.	Mch. 21, 1865	Nashville, Tenn	Died at Johnsonville, Tenn. Interred in section M, grave 191.
Rockwell, John	B	Private.	Jan. 14, 1865	Nashville, Tenn	Interred in section H, grave 161.
Roush, Richard M	B	Private.	Dec. 8, 1864	Nashville, Tenn	
Russell, Audley	I	Private.	Mch. 19, 1865	Nashville, Tenn	
Russell, John M.	H	Private.	Feb. 15, 1865	Nashville, Tenn	
Sayre, Israel S	F	Corporal	Mch. 7, 1865	Nashville, Tenn	Died at Johnsonville, Tenn. Interred in section M, grave 221.
Selman, Denton G	H	Private.	July 1, 1865	Nashville, Tenn	Interred in section J, grave [illegible]
Shaw, John	H	Private.	May 20, 1865		Died at Ash Ridge, O.
Shepard, Joseph	D	Private.	Dec. 14, 1864	Nashville, Tenn	
Shuff, James	K	Private.	Jan. 17, 1865	Nashville, Tenn	Interred in section H, grave 160.
Shteran, Joshua	D	Private.	April 8, 1865	Nashville, Tenn	Died at Johnsonville, Tenn. Interred in section M, grave 187.
Simpson, John	F	Private.	April 13, 1865	Nashville, Tenn	Died at Johnsonville, Tenn. Interred in section M, grave 2[illegible].
Sims, John M	C	Corporal	Feb. 22, 1865	Nashville, Tenn	Died at Johnsonville, Tenn.
Sipher, James W	K	Private.	Jan. 18, 1865	Nashville, Tenn	Interred in section H, grave [illegible]
Sowards, Henry J	F	Private.	April 28, 1865	Louisville, Ky	Interred in section [illegible], grave 128, Cave Hill Cemetery.
Spencer, Thomas	K	Private.	Mch. 27, 1865	Nashville, Tenn	Died at Johnsonville, Tenn. Interred in section M, grave 186.
Suthers, James	E	Private.	Jan. 6, 1865	Nashville, Tenn	Interred in section H, grave 410.
Swick, John	I	Private.	Jan. 30, 1865	Nashville, Tenn	
Swick, Martin	I	1st sergt	Feb. 4, 1865	Nashville, Tenn	
Sydenstricker, Sam. H.	B	Corporal	Jan. 3, 1865	Louisville, Ky	Interred in section [illegible], grave 67, Cave Hill Cemetery.
Taylor, Andrew J	C	Private.	April 26, 1865	Nashville, Tenn	Died at Johnsonville, Tenn. Interred in section M, grave 170.
Taylor, Nathaniel	E	Private.	Feb. 9, 1865	Nashville, Tenn	Interred in section H, grave 117.
Thomas, Morgan	C	Private.	April 13, 1865	Nashville, Tenn	Interred in section J, grave 1328.
Triggs, Eli	D	Private.	June 16, 1865	Nashville, Tenn	Died at Johnsonville, Tenn. Interred in section M, grave 183.

Names.	Co.	Rank.	Died.	Buried.	Remarks.
Galligher, Elza	G	Private.	April 4, 1865	Murfreesboro, Tenn.	Died of wounds received Dec. 7, 1864, in battle of the Cedars, Tenn. Interred in section A, grave 79, Stone River Cemetery.
Hamler, Isaac	C	Private.	Dec. 23, 1864	Murfreesboro, Tenn.	Interred in section E, grave 403, Stone River Cemetery.
Hamler, John	C	Private.	May 27, 1865	Newbern, N.C.	Interred in section 17, grave 115.
Hartman, John	B	Private.	Feb. 1, 1865	Arlington, Va.	Died at Washington, D. C.
Hecker, Frederick	I	Private.	Dec. 24, 1864	Murfreesboro, Tenn.	Died of wounds received Dec. 7, 1864, in battle of the Cedars, Tenn. Interred in section E, grave 402, Stone River Cemetery.
Henry, William A.	A	Private.	June 28, 1865	Salisbury, N. C.	Died at Charlotte, N. C., of wounds.
Hilderman, Riley	H	Private.	Sept. 28, 1864	Columbus, O.	Interred in Green Lawn Cemetery.
Johnson, Joseph	B	Private.	Jan. 1, 1865	Murfreesboro, Tenn.	Interred in Stone River Cemetery.
Jones, Thomas	H	Private.	Dec. 4, 1864	Nashville, Tenn.	Interred in section E, grave 2725.
Kempton, Benjamin	H	Private.	Jan. 20, 1865	Murfreesboro, Tenn.	Interred in section N, grave 279, Stone River Cemetery.
Lawrence, John W.	E	Corporal	Mch. 15, 1865	Newbern, N. C.	Died of wounds received March 10, 1865, in battle of Wise's Fork, N. C. Interred in section 17, grave 81.
Ludwick, Henry	D	Private.	Feb. 12, 1865	Murfreesboro, Tenn.	Died at Nashville, Tenn. Interred in section N, grave 451, Stone River Cemetery.
McAllister, Nelson	C	Private.	April 10, 1865		Died at Moseby Hall, N. C.
McCutcheon, Peter	H	Private.	Feb. 19, 1865	Arlington, Va.	Died at Washington, D. C.
McVay, Marcus L.	D	Private.	Feb. 9, 1865	Arlington, Va.	Died at Washington, D. C.
Mallory, Mortimer G.	C	Private.	Dec. 25, 1864	Murfreesboro, Tenn.	Interred in Stone River Cemetery.
Matheny, William M.	E	Private.	Mch. 29, 1865	Murfreesboro, Tenn.	Interred in section I, grave 2, Stone River Cemetery.
Matthews, Albert	A	Private.	Feb. 27, 1865	Antietam, Md	Died at Cumberland, Md. Interred in section 1, row B, grave 82.
Miller, Silas H.	I	Private.	Mch. 9, 1865	Newbern, N. C.	Interred in section 17, grave 145.
Milligan, Samuel L.	A	Corporal	May 7, 1865	Raleigh, N. C.	Interred in section 4, grave [illegible]
Mitchell, Albert	B	Private.	Dec. 4, 1864	Murfreesboro, Tenn.	Killed in battle of Overall's Creek, Tenn. Interred in section N, grave 475, Stone River Cemetery.
Mobley, John	B	Private.	Jan. 28, 1865	Nashville, Tenn.	Interred in section H, grave 147.
Monahan, Robert M.	E	Private.	Oct. 6, 1864	Columbus, O.	Interred in grave 1[illegible]8 Green Lawn Cemetery.
Moody, Robert	B	Private.	Dec. 7, 1864	Murfreesboro, Tenn.	Killed in battle of the Cedars Tenn. Interred in section N, grave 405, Stone River Cemetery.
More, Alonzo	F	Private.	Dec. 8, 1864	Murfreesboro, Tenn.	Died of wounds received Dec. 7, 1864, in battle of the Cedars, Tenn. Interred in section E, grave 212, Stone River Cemetery
Morton, Caleb A.	D	Private.	Feb. 10, 1865	Louisville, Ky.	Interred in section C, row 8, grave 97, Cave Hill Cemetery
Mowry, Cyrus	A	Private.	Jan. 22, 1865	Nashville, Tenn.	Interred in section H, grave 180.
Mulvane, Daniel	B	Private.	Mch. 10, 1865	Newbern, N. C.	Killed in battle of Wise's Fork, N. C. Interred in section 17, grave 15.
Murphy, Joseph P.	F	Private.	Feb. 11, 1865	Murfreesboro, Tenn.	Interred in section E grave 326, Stone River Cemetery.
Nettleton, Judson	H	Sergeant	Dec. 11, 1864	Murfreesboro, Tenn.	Died of wounds received Dec. 4, 1864, in battle of Overall's Creek, Tenn. Interred in section E, grave 169, Stone River Cemetery.
Nichols, Melville W.	A	Private.	Feb. 19, 1865	Nashville, Tenn.	Interred in section G, grave 782.
Norris, Bradford D.	E	Private.	Dec. 27, 1864	New Albany, Ind.	Died at Jeffersonville, Ind. Interred in section B, grave [illegible]
Osborn, William H.	E	Private.	June 8, 1865	Newark, N. J.	
Parker, William M.	K	Private.	Mch. 30, 1865	Nashville, Tenn.	Interred in section J, grave 1081.
Parks, Alexander M.	K	Private.	Mch. 7, 1865	Arlington, Va.	
Parks, Clarkson C.	K	Private.	Jan. 14, 1865		
Parrish, John S.	D	Private.	Dec. 4, 1864	Murfreesboro, Tenn.	Killed in battle of Overall's Creek, Tenn. Interred in Stone River Cemetery.

Names.	Co.	Rank.	Died.	Buried.	Remarks.
[illegible], Asa [illegible]	[illegible]	Private.	Feb. [illegible], [illegible]	Arlington, Va.	Died at Washington, D. C.
[illegible], David J.	[illegible]	Private.	Dec. 7, 1864	Murfreesboro, Tenn.	Killed in battle of the Cedars, Tenn. Interred in section N, grave [illegible], Stone River Cemetery.
Wesley [illegible]	A	Private.	April [illegible], 1865	Raleigh, N. C.	Interred in section 4, grave 40.
[illegible], Joseph	H	Private.	Nov. 4, 1864	Murfreesboro, Tenn.	Interred in Stone River Cemetery.
[illegible], Wesley	B	Private.	April [illegible], 1865	Nashville, Tenn.	Interred in section J, grave [illegible].
[illegible], Isaac	A	Private.	Feb. [illegible], 1865	Louisville, Ky.	Interred in section C, row 4, grave 94, Cave Hill Cemetery.
[illegible], Jerome B.	F	Private.	Sept. 22, 1864	Columbus, O.	Died at Camp Chase, O. Interred in Green Lawn Cemetery.
[illegible], William	B	Private.	Jan. [illegible], 1865	Nashville, Tenn.	Interred in section H, grave [illegible].
[illegible], Isaac	I	Private.	Feb. 10, 1865	Arlington, Va.	Died at Camp Stoneman, D. C.
[illegible], Benjamin C. G.	..	Major.	Dec. 7, 1864	Murfreesboro, Tenn.	Killed in battle of the Cedars, Tenn. Interred in Stone River Cemetery.
[illegible], Joseph	A	Private.	Jan. 12, 1865	Murfreesboro, Tenn.	Died at Columbia, Tenn. Interred in Stone River Cemetery.
[illegible]son, Henry	G	Private.	April 30, 1865	Long Island, N. Y.	Interred in grave [illegible], Cypress Hill Cemetery.
[illegible]son, William	G	Private.	Oct. 4, 1864	Columbus, O.	Died at Camp Chase, O. Interred in grave 200, Green Lawn Cemetery.
[illegible], William A.	F	Private.	Mch. 20, 1865	Wilmington, N. C.	
[illegible], Gardner	A	Private.	Jan. 9, 1865	New Albany, Ind.	Died on board steamer R. C. Wood. Interred in section B, grave 1271.
[illegible], Franklin	E	Private.	Mch. 2, 1865	Grafton, W. Va.	
[illegible], Israel	K	Private.	Mch. 29, 1865	Newbern, N. C.	Interred in section 17, grave 108.
[illegible]son, Solomon	B	Private.	Jan. 28, 1865	Louisville, Ky.	Interred in section C, row 2, grave 92, Cave Hill Cemetery.
[illegible], William M.	D	Private.	Feb. 16, 1865	Arlington, Va.	Died at Washington, D. C.
[illegible], Franklin T.	A	Private.	Jan. 7, 1865	Murfreesboro, Tenn.	Died of wounds received Dec. 7, 1864, in battle of the Cedars, Tenn. Interred in section D, grave 285, Stone River Cemetery.
[illegible], Nathan J.	D	Corporal	Dec. 7, 1864	Murfreesboro, Tenn.	Killed in battle of the Cedars, Tenn. Interred in section D, grave 139, Stone River Cemetery.
[illegible]wick, Corydon C.	I	Private.	Jan. 22, 1865	Murfreesboro, Tenn.	Interred in section E, grave 211, Stone River Cemetery.
[illegible], Joseph	B	Private.	Jan. 12, 1865	Murfreesboro, Tenn.	Interred in section D, grave 298, Stone River Cemetery.
[illegible], William	D	Private.	Mch. 8, 1865	Nashville, Tenn.	Interred in section G, grave 613.
[illegible]ens, Levi A.	C	Private.	Mch. 10, 1865	Newbern, N. C.	Killed in battle of Wise's Fork, N. C. Interred in section 17, grave 17.
[illegible], William	I	Private.	Mch. 2, 1865	Newbern, N. C.	Interred in section 17, grave 11.
[illegible]p, Abraham B.	G	Corporal	Feb. 16, 1865	Nashville, Tenn.	
[illegible]r, James M.	D	Private.	Dec. 7, 1864	Murfreesboro, Tenn.	Killed in battle of the Cedars, Tenn. Interred in section D, grave 290, Stone River Cemetery.
[illegible], Andrew J.	G	Private.	Oct. 24, 1864	Murfreesboro, Tenn.	Accidentally killed at Duck River Bridge, Tenn. Interred in section N, grave 240, Stone River Cemetery.
[illegible]er, Masham	D	Private.	Feb. 1, 1865	Murfreesboro, Tenn.	Interred in section D, grave 179, Stone River Cemetery.
[illegible], Alfred	G	Private.	Oct. 12, 1864	Louisville, Ky.	Interred in section C, row 7, grave 28, Cave Hill Cemetery.
[illegible], Franklin	B	Private.	Mch. 10, 1865	Newbern, N. C.	Killed in battle of Wise's Fork, N. C. Interred in section 17, grave 19.
[illegible], Josiah	D	Private.	Dec. 4, 1864	Murfreesboro, Tenn.	Killed in battle of Overall's Creek, Tenn. Interred in section E, grave [illegible], Stone River Cemetery.
[illegible], Wilbur	H	Private.	May 7, 1865	Long Island, N. Y.	Died at David's Island, New York Harbor. Interred in Cypress Cemetery.
[illegible], Ephraim R. J.	F	Private.	Dec. 25, 1864	Murfreesboro, Tenn.	Died while on the march. Interred in Stone River Cemetery.
[illegible]rd, William	C	Private.	Dec. 6, 1864	Murfreesboro, Tenn.	Interred in section E, grave [illegible], Stone River Cemetery.

Names.	Co.	Rank.	Died.	Buried.	Remarks.
Woodford, Julius M.....	K	Private.	Dec. 8, 1864	Murfreesboro, Tenn.	Died of wounds received Dec. 7, 1864, in battle of the Cedars, Tenn. Interred in section E, grave 176, Stone River Cemetery.
Woodruff, George C.....	C	Corporal	Mch. 10, 1865	Newbern, N C.......	Killed in battle of Wise's Fork, N. C.
Wyatt, David H.........	I	Private.	Oct. 11, 1864	Murfreesboro, Tenn..	Interred in Stone River Cemetery.
Yanger, James H.......	F	Private.	Dec. 23, 1864	Murfreesboro, Tenn.	Interred in section E, grave 109, Stone River Cemetery.

175th REGIMENT OHIO VOLUNTEER INFANTRY.

Names.	Co.	Rank.	Died.	Buried.	Remarks.
Allison, Samuel.........	K	Private.	Mch. 14, 1865	Murfreesboro, Tenn..	Died at Columbia, Tenn. Interred in section M, grave 528, Stone River Cemetery.
Argo, James.............	B	Private.	Mch. 4, 1865	....	Died at Sinking Springs, O.
Badgly, Benton..........	G	Private.	April 27, 1865	....	Perished by explosion of steamer Sultana, on Mississippi River, near Memphis, Tennessee.
Baird, Smith H..........	D	Private.	Feb. 21, 1865	Marietta, Ga..........	Died in Rebel Prison at Cahaba, Ala.
Barnes, Edward.........	F	Musician	April 27, 1865	....	Perished by explosion of steamer Sultana, on Mississippi River, near Memphis, Tennessee.
Barnett, Alvertus.......	K	Private.	Mch. 21, 1865	Nashville, Tenn	Interred in section G, grave 696.
Barrere, William........	G	2d Lieut.	April 27, 1865	....	Perished by explosion of steamer Sultana, on Mississippi River, near Memphis, Tennessee.
Bayne, James...........	D	Private.	April 27, 1865	....	Perished by explosion of steamer Sultana, on Mississippi River, near Memphis, Tennessee.
Beekman, Allen H......	H	Private.	Nov. 30, 1864	Murfreesboro, Tenn.	Killed in battle of Franklin, Tenn. Interred in Stone River Cemetery.
Beekman, Rhuny.......	H	Private.	Dec. 24, 1864	New Albany, Ind....	Died at Jeffersonville, Ind.
Beekman, William D....	B	Corporal	Feb. 15, 1865	Corinth, Miss........	Died in Rebel Prison at Okalona, Miss.
Bercaw, Norman........	G	Private.	April 27, 1865	....	Perished by explosion of steamer Sultana, on Mississippi River, near Memphis, Tennessee.
Bobb, Isaac.............	B	Private.	May 18, 1865	Chalmette, La........	Died at New Orleans, La. Interred in Monument Cemetery.
Bogan, William.........	A	Private.	Nov. 30, 1864	Murfreesboro, Tenn..	Killed in battle of Franklin, Tenn. Interred in Stone River Cemetery.
Boroughs, James........	G	Private.	April 14, 1865	Vicksburg, Miss......	Interred in section L, grave 335.
Boyd, George W........	G	Private.	April 27, 1865	....	Perished by explosion of steamer Sultana, on Mississippi River, near Memphis, Tennessee.
Brace, William..........	F	Private.	Mch. 4, 1865	Murfreesboro, Tenn..	Died at Columbia, Tenn. Interred in Stone River Cemetery.
Carr, William...........	K	Private.	Feb. 6, 1865	Murfreesboro, Tenn..	Died at Columbia, Tenn. Interred in Stone River Cemetery.
Carroll, William.........	D	Private.	April 27, 1865	....	Perished by explosion of steamer Sultana, on Mississippi River, near Memphis, Tennessee.
Chaney, Henry O........	B	Private.	Oct. 8, 1864	Camp Dennison, O...	
Coker, David...........	K	Private.	Jan. 25, 1865	New Albany, Ind.....	Died at Jeffersonville, Ind. Interred in section B, grave 216.
Cole, Warren E..........	E	Private.	Mch. 13, 1865	Murfreesboro, Tenn..	Interred in section M, grave 520, Stone River Cemetery.

Names.	Co.	Rank.	Died.	Buried.	Remarks.
Congleton, William	K	Private.	April 28, 1865	Murfreesboro, Tenn.	Died at Columbia, Tenn. Interred in Stone River Cemetery.
Conover, James	F	Sergeant	Feb. 17, 1865	....	Died in Rebel Prison at Medina, Ala.
Conover, Sommers	B	Private.	Jan. 19, 1865	Andersonville, Ga.	Died in Rebel Prison. Interred in grave 12,798
Cordery, William H.	A	Private.	Mch. 23, 1865	Nashville, Tenn	Interred in section G, grave 540.
Covey, Morgan	K	Private.	May 21, 1865	Murfreesboro, Tenn.	Died at Columbia, Tenn. Interred in Stone Cemetery.
Cowman, Henry W.	C	Private.	Jan. 24, 1865	New Albany, Ind.	Died at Jeffersonville, Ind., of wounds received Nov. 30, 1864, in battle of Franklin, Tennessee.
Crabtree, William	D	Private.	Nov. 30, 1864	Murfreesboro, Tenn.	Killed in battle of Franklin, Tenn. Interred in Stone River Cemetery.
Crosson, Edward	G	Private.	May 1, 1865	St. Louis, Mo.	Interred in Jefferson Barracks Cemetery.
Cuthbert, Ralph W.	K	Corporal	May 11, 1865	Murfreesboro, Tenn.	Died at Columbia, Tenn. Interred in section M, grave 377, Stone River Cemetery.
Cutshaw, Shannon	K	Private.	Mch. 28, 1865	Nashville, Tenn	
Deniston, John D.	G	1st Sergt.	Oct. 15, 1864	Cincinnati, O.	Died of injuries received Oct. 13, 1864. Interred in Spring Grove Cemetery.
Dennis, William H.	I	Private.	Dec. 17, 1864	New Albany, Ind.	Died at Jeffersonville, Ind.
Dillinger, Thomas	D	Private.	Jan. 19, 1865	New Albany, Ind.	Died at Jeffersonville, Ind.
Dixon, Thomas J.	D	Private.	April 18, 1865	St. Louis, Mo.	Interred in section 45, grave 150, Jefferson Barracks Cemetery.
Dumford, Daniel	H	Private.	Dec. 20, 1864	Nashville, Tenn	Interred in section F, grave 160.
Earhart, William D.	B	Private.	Mch. 31, 1865	Vicksburg, Miss.	Interred in section L, grave 211.
Easter, Carey	G	Private.	Mch. 20, 1865	Marietta, Ga.	Died in Rebel Prison at Cahaba, Ala.
Easton, George O.	C	Musician	Dec. 31, 1864	Covington, Ky.	Died of wounds received Nov. 30, 1864, in battle of Franklin, Tenn. Interred in Linden Grove Cemetery.
Elliott, Thomas	A	1st Sergt.	Nov. 30, 1864	Murfreesboro, Tenn.	Killed in battle of Franklin, Tenn. Interred in Stone River Cemetery.
Erskine, Enoch P.	B	Musician	Feb. 16, 1865	....	Died while prisoner of war.
Farmer, Eli	E	Private.	Jan. 21, 1865	Camp Dennison, O.	
Fite, Samuel W.	B	Private.	April 6, 1865	Mound City, Ill	
Foulk, Jacob	B	Private.	Nov. 30, 1864	Murfreesboro, Tenn.	Killed in battle of Franklin, Tenn. Interred in Stone River Cemetery.
Frump, Joel	B	Private.	Mch. 30, 1865	....	Died at Big Black River Bridge, Mississippi.
Gibson, Hugh A.	A	Sergeant	Jan. 7, 1865	St. Louis, Mo.	Interred in Jefferson Barracks Cemetery.
Gillespie, Cornelius	K	Private.	Jan. 24, 1865	Nashville, Tenn	Interred in section H, grave 15.
Girton, William	C	Private.	Dec. 6, 1864	Nashville, Tenn	Interred in section F, grave 256.
Gray, Thomas J.	E	Private.	April 27, 1865	....	Perished by explosion of steamer Sultana, on Mississippi River, near Memphis, Tennessee
Greely, Morris	G	Private.	Feb. .., 1865	Marietta, Ga.	Died in Rebel Prison at Cahaba, Ala.
Guthridge, Martin	G	Corporal	Feb. 6, 1865	Murfreesboro, Tenn.	Died at Columbia, Tenn. Interred in Stone River Cemetery.
Hahn, Philip	C	Private.	Dec. 14, 1864	Camp Dennison, O.	Died of wounds received Nov. 30, 1864, in battle of Franklin, Tennessee.
Hall, John B.	A	Private.	Mch. 7, 1865	New Albany, Ind.	Died at Jeffersonville, Ind.
Hanson, Samuel	D	Private.	April 18, 1865	St. Louis, Mo.	Interred in section 45, grave 198, Jefferson Barracks Cemetery.
Hare, Daniel	D	Private.	Oct. 20, 1864	Nashville, Tenn	
Hatch, Hiram	E	Private.	Mch. 31, 1865	Vicksburg, Miss.	Interred in section L, grave 218.
Hayes, Bailey P.	D	Private.	Nov. 30, 1864	Murfreesboro, Tenn.	Killed in battle of Franklin, Tenn. Interred in Stone River Cemetery.
Hemmings, Thomas	E	Private.	Jan. 1, 1865	....	Died in Rebel Prison at Meridian, Miss.
Hendrixon, George W.	E	Private.	April 27, 1865	....	Perished by explosion of steamer Sultana, on Mississippi River, near Memphis, Tennessee.
Hensel, Josiah	H	Private.	Mch. 11, 1865	Murfreesboro, Tenn.	Died at Columbia, Tenn. Interred in section M, grave [illegible], Stone River Cemetery.

Names.	Co.	Rank.	Died.	Buried.	Remarks
Hiser, Daniel F.	A	Private.	April 7, 1865	Vicksburg, Miss.	
Holmes, Samuel A.	D	Private.	April 27, 1865	....	Perished by explosion of steamer Sultana, on Mississippi River, near Memphis, Tennessee.
Hopkins, John	F	Private.	Nov. 30, 1864	Murfreesboro, Tenn.	Killed in battle of Franklin, Tenn. Interred in Stone River Cemetery.
Howland, Samuel.	G	Corporal	Feb. 22, 1865	Murfreesboro, Tenn.	Died at Columbia, Tenn. Interred in Stone River Cemetery.
Howland, William O.	G	Private.	April 1, 1865	Murfreesboro, Tenn.	Died at Columbia, Tenn. Interred in section M, grave 525, Stone River Cemetery.
Hudson, James	G	Private.	April 27, 1865	....	Perished by explosion of steamer Sultana, on Mississippi River, near Memphis, Tennessee.
Jennings, Israel F.	D	Private.	Jan. 25, 1865	Nashville, Tenn	Died of wounds received in action. Interred in section H, grave 3[illegible]4.
Keplinger, Isaac W.	H	Private.	Mch. 26, 1865	Murfreesboro, Tenn.	Died at Columbia, Tenn. Interred in section M, grave 521, Stone River Cemetery.
Kibler, Isaac	F	Private.	Nov. 9, 1864	Murfreesboro, Tenn.	Died at Columbia, Tenn. Interred in section M, grave 380, Stone River Cemetery.
Kimmell, David	I	Private.	April 5, 1865	Murfreesboro, Tenn.	Died at Columbia, Tenn. Interred in section M, grave 522, Stone River Cemetery.
Kimmell, William	I	Private.	Mch. 7, 1865	Murfreesboro, Tenn.	Died at Columbia, Tenn. Interred in section M, grave 519, Stone River Cemetery.
Kridler, Andrew J.	I	Corporal	Dec. 31, 1864	Nashville, Tenn.	Interred in section G, grave 578.
Little, William	D	Private.	April 7, 1865	Andersonville, Ga.	Died in Rebel Prison. Interred in grave 12,826.
Logan, Wilson B.	D	Captain.	Nov. 30, 1864	Murfreesboro, Tenn.	Killed in battle of Franklin, Tenn. Interred in Stone River Cemetery.
Loper, George W.	I	Private.	Nov. 20, 1864	Murfreesboro, Tenn.	Died at Columbia, Tenn. Interred in section M, grave 515, Stone River Cemetery.
McBerney, James	K	Sergeant	Feb. 9, 1865	Murfreesboro, Tenn.	Died at Columbia, Tenn. Interred in Stone River Cemetery.
McCandless, Samuel D.	K	Private.	Feb. 1, 1865	New Albany, Ind.	Died at Jeffersonville, Ind. Interred in section [illegible], grave 286.
McCollum, Joseph B.	A	Corporal	Feb. 11, 1865	Murfreesboro, Tenn.	Died at Columbia, Tenn. Interred in Stone River Cemetery.
McCoy, William A.	A	Private.	Nov. 30, 1864	Murfreesboro, Tenn.	Killed in battle of Franklin, Tenn. Interred in Stone River Cemetery.
McCoy, William H.	F	Private.	April 27, 1865	....	Perished by explosion of steamer Sultana, on Mississippi River, near Memphis, Tennessee.
Mackinson, Thomas H.	K	Private.	Dec. 31, 1864	New Albany, Ind.	Died at Jeffersonville, Ind.
Madigan, James	D	Private.	Mch. 1, 1865	Nashville, Tenn.	
Matthews, James H.	F	Corporal	Mch. 11, 1865	Murfreesboro, Tenn.	Died at Columbia, Tenn. Interred in Stone River Cemetery.
Meeker, Timothy	E	Private.	April 27, 1865	....	Perished by explosion of steamer Sultana, on Mississippi River, near Memphis, Tennessee.
Meredith, Charles H.	B	Private.	Oct. 19, 1864	....	Died in Highland County, O.
Miller, Daniel M.	F	Private.	May 3, 1865	Murfreesboro, Tenn.	Died at Columbia, Tenn. Interred in Stone River Cemetery.
Moore, John	D	Private.	April 11, 1865	Nashville, Tenn.	Interred in section J, grave 754.
Moore, John	E	Private.	Mch. 3, 1865	Marietta, Ga.	Interred in section [illegible], grave 169.
Morris, Stacy	G	Private.	April 27, 1865	....	Perished by explosion of steamer Sultana, on Mississippi River, near Memphis, Tennessee.
Morrow, William	G	Private.	Jan. 31, 1865	Murfreesboro, Tenn.	Died at Columbia, Tenn. Interred in Stone River Cemetery.
Myers, William H.	K	Private.	Dec. 31, 1864	Nashville, Tenn.	Interred in section F, grave [illegible]
Myers, William O.	D	Private.	April 27, 1865	....	Perished by explosion of steamer Sultana, on Mississippi River, near Memphis, Tennessee.

Names.	Co.	Rank.	Died.	Buried.	Remarks.
Osborn, John M.	F	Private.	Dec. 30, 1864	Nashville, Tenn.	Interred in section F, grave 181.
Pancoast, Timothy	D	Corporal	Jan. 3, 1865		Died in Rebel Prison at Meridian, Miss.
Paul, William W.	D	Private.	Oct. 20, 1864	Camp Dennison, O.	
Peabody, John J.	B	Private.	Jan. 13, 1865	Nashville, Tenn.	Interred in section G, grave 533.
Quigley, Wesley	D	Corporal	Jan. 17, 1865	Camp Dennison, O.	Died of wounds received in action.
Raines, Joab	A	Private.	Nov. 24, 1864	Murfreesboro, Tenn.	Died at Columbia, Tenn. Interred in section M, grave 514, Stone River Cemetery.
Reed, Francis M.	B	Sergeant	Oct. 24, 1864	Nashville, Tenn.	
Reed, James	D	Private.	April 18, 1865	Vicksburg, Miss.	Interred in section I, grave 323.
Rice, Asher	I	Sergeant	Nov. 30, 1864	Murfreesboro, Tenn.	Killed in battle of Franklin, Tenn. Interred in Stone River Cemetery.
Rice, Martin L.	A	Private.	April 27, 1865		Perished by explosion of steamer Sultana, on Mississippi River, near Memphis, Tennessee.
Richmond, William	D	Private.	April 27, 1865		Perished by explosion of steamer Sultana, on Mississippi River, near Memphis, Tennessee.
Rosenberry, John H.	K	Private.	Mch. 2, 1865	Murfreesboro, Tenn.	Died at Columbia, Tenn. Interred in Stone River Cemetery.
Rumney, John B.	A	Private.	Nov. 11, 1864	Murfreesboro, Tenn.	Died at Columbia, Tenn. Interred in section M, grave 518, Stone River Cemetery.
Seaton, Henry	F	Private.	Dec. 18, 1864	Nashville, Tenn.	Interred in section F, grave 260.
Settles, Bennett	A	Private.	Nov. 30, 1864	Murfreesboro, Tenn.	Killed in battle of Franklin, Tenn. Interred in Stone River Cemetery.
Shank, James H.	G	Private.	Jan. 21, 1865	Marietta, Ga.	Died in Rebel Prison at Cahaba, Ala. Interred in section L, grave 484.
Shelton, William	D	Private.	April 27, 1865		Perished by explosion of steamer Sultana, on Mississippi River, near Memphis, Tennessee.
Sidles, Israel	G	Private.	Mch. 3, 1865	Marietta, Ga.	Died in Rebel Prison at Cahaba, Ala.
Sigling, Michael	H	Private.	April 6, 1865	Nashville, Tenn.	Interred in section J, grave 1556.
Slagle, Jacob R.	B	Private.	Mch. 4, 1865	Marietta, Ga.	Died in Rebel Prison at Cahaba, Ala.
Smith, Henry	I	Private.	April 27, 1865		Perished by explosion of steamer Sultana, on Mississippi River, near Memphis, Tennessee.
Smith, Sylvester	F	Private.	June 17, 1865	New Albany, Ind.	Died at Jeffersonville, Ind. Interred in section B, grave 878.
Smith, William	D	Private.	Mch. 30, 1865	Marietta, Ga.	Died in Rebel Prison at Cahaba, Ala.
Sroufe, Joseph C.	D	Private.	July 27, 1865	St. Louis, Mo.	Interred in section 45, grave 376, Jefferson Barracks Cemetery.
Staton, George W.	E	Private.	April 27, 1865		Perished by explosion of steamer Sultana, on Mississippi River, near Memphis, Tennessee.
Taylor, Richard	K	Private.	May 29, 1865	Camp Dennison, O.	
Tener, Joseph	B	Sergeant	Jan. .., 1865	Marietta, Ga.	Died in Rebel Prison at Cahaba, Ala.
Timmons, Othello	D	Private.	May 4, 1865	St. Louis, Mo.	Interred in Jefferson Barracks Cemetery.
Trovillo, Paul J.	C	Corporal	Jan. 23, 1865	Camp Dennison, O.	
Van Eman, Matthew T.	G	Sergeant	April 27, 1865		Perished by explosion of steamer Sultana, on Mississippi River, near Memphis, Tennessee.
Vigor, John H.	D	Private.	Oct. 16, 1864	Cincinnati, O.	Died of injuries received in railroad accident. Interred in section B, grave 317, Spring Grove Cemetery.
Wallace, James H.	D	Private.	Nov. 30, 1864	Murfreesboro, Tenn.	Killed in battle of Franklin, Tenn. Interred in Stone River Cemetery.
Washburn, Elisha P.	B	Private.	Jan. 1, 1865	Corinth, Miss.	Died in Rebel Prison.
Williams, John A.	G	Private.	June 25, 1865	Murfreesboro, Tenn.	Died at Columbia, Tenn. Interred in Stone River Cemetery.

Names.	Co.	Rank.	Died.	Buried.	Remarks.
Wrestler, John	E	Private.	April 2, 1865	Vicksburg, Miss	Interred in section L, grave 223.
Wright, Samuel W	G	Sergeant	Dec. 4, 1864	Nashville, Tenn	Died of wounds received Nov. 30, 1864, in battle of Franklin, Tenn.

176th REGIMENT OHIO VOLUNTEER INFANTRY.

Names.	Co.	Rank.	Died.	Buried.	Remarks.
Albright, Daniel	F	Private.	Jan. 25, 1865	Nashville, Tenn	Interred in section H, grave 61.
Ash, Elias	D	Private.	Sept. 24, 1864	Columbus, O	Died at Camp Chase, O. Interred in grave 196, Green Lawn Cemetery.
Barber, Alexander C	E	Private.	Jan. 17, 1865	Nashville, Tenn	Interred in section G, grave 768.
Bennett, Ephraim	A	Private.	Mch. 7, 1865	Nashville, Tenn	Interred in section H, grave 48.
Bennett, Levi B	H	Private.	Mch. 25, 1865	Nashville, Tenn	
Berns, Anthony	B	Private.	Feb. 13, 1865	Nashville, Tenn	Interred in section H, grave 86.
Bivens, Reason	K	Private.	Oct. 19, 1864	Nashville, Tenn	Interred in section F, grave 91.
Brayton, William	B	Private	Dec. 29, 1864	Nashville, Tenn	
Brooks, Ira H	B	Private.	Mch. 29, 1865	Nashville, Tenn	
Brown, Hugh S	H	Private.	April 22, 1865	Nashville, Tenn	
Brown, Luther S	C	Private.	Dec. 16, 1864	Nashville, Tenn	
Burkett, Stephen	B	Private.	Jan. 9, 1865	Nashville, Tenn	
Bushshawn, Eli	B	Private.	Jan. 12, 1865	Nashville, Tenn	Interred in section H, grave 421.
Chambers, Eugene H	K	Private.	Mch. 19, 1865	Nashville, Tenn	
Chester, John	K	Private.	Dec. 20, 1864	Nashville, Tenn	Interred in section G, grave 495.
Cook, James	H	Private.	Feb. 1, 1865	Nashville, Tenn	Interred in section H, grave 386.
Coon, Simpson	I	Private.	May 9, 1865	Nashville, Tenn	
Corder, James	K	Private.	Jan. 14, 1865	Nashville, Tenn	Interred in section H, grave 123.
Cottrall, Benjamin J	H	Private.	Jan. 25, 1865	Nashville, Tenn	Interred in section E, grave 2228.
Culbertson, Martin	D	Private.	April 21, 1865	Nashville, Tenn	Interred in section J, grave 1093.
Doleson, Frederick M	B	Private.	Oct. 11, 1864	Columbus, O	Interred in grave 203, Green Lawn Cemetery.
Downard, George W	D	Private.	June 30, 1865	Columbus, O	Mustered out with company June 11, 1865. Interred in grave 374, Green Lawn Cemetery.
Drake, William A	H	Private.	May 11 1865	Nashville, Tenn	Interred in section G, grave 763.
Dyke, John W	D	Private.	Nov. 26, 1864	Nashville, Tenn	Interred in section G, grave 405.
Enochs, James	G	Private.	Jan. 22, 1865	Nashville, Tenn	Interred in section H, grave 209.
Fishburn, Jacob	F	Private.	Feb. 19, 1865	Nashville, Tenn	Accidentally shot. Interred in section C, grave 234.
Fisher, Daniel	H	Private.	June 2, 1865	Nashville, Tenn	
Fleming, Sylvester B	B	Private.	Feb. 5, 1865	Nashville, Tenn	
Foote, James	C	Private.	May 2, 1865	Nashville, Tenn	
Forbes, Albert	C	Private.	Dec. 5, 1864	Nashville, Tenn	
Fouracre, William H	F	Private.	April 4, 1865	Nashville, Tenn	Interred in section J, grave 1380.
Freshour, Nathan T	H	Private.	Jan. 29, 1865	Nashville, Tenn	
Fritter, Ransom	A	Corporal	April 21, 1865	Nashville, Tenn	
Gall, Jacob A	H	Private.	April 6, 1865	Nashville, Tenn	Interred in section J, grave 1246.
Gilkison, John	E	Private.	Feb. 18, 1865	Nashville, Tenn	Interred in section H, grave 52.
Gorby, Pierce	D	Private.	Jan. 5, 1865	Nashville, Tenn	Interred in section H, grave 380.
Gracier, Godfred	F	Private.	Sept. 25, 1864	Louisville, Ky	Interred in section C, row 5, grave 47, Cave Hill Cemetery.
Greenland, John H	F	Private.	Jan. 3, 1865	Louisville, Ky	Interred in Cave Hill Cemetery.
Grey, Nathan	C	Private.	Nov. 2, 1864	Nashville, Tenn	Interred in section F, grave 182.
Hall, Charles	B	Private.	Feb. 11, 1865	Nashville, Tenn	Interred in section G, grave 688.
Hatfield, Henry	K	Private.	Mch. 11, 1865	Nashville, Tenn	
Hatton, Ezekiel	C	Private.	Mch. 6, 1865	Nashville, Tenn	
Heath, Charles A	B	Private.	Oct. 2, 1864	Nashville, Tenn	Interred in section E, grave 2867.

Names.	Co.	Rank.	Died.	Buried.	Remarks.
James A........	I	Private.	Jan. 14, 18[illegible]	Nashville, Tenn......	Interred in section H, grave 14.
[illegible], Robert......	B	Private.	Mch. [illegible], 18[illegible]	Nashville, Tenn......	
[illegible]ton, Henry W	C	1st Sergt.	Mch. 2, 18[illegible]	Nashville, Tenn......	
[illegible], Alfred W....	B	1st Sergt.	Dec. 19, 18[illegible]	Nashville, Tenn......	
[illegible]leson, William	A	Corporal	April [illegible], 18[illegible]	....	Died at home.
[illegible]ley, William...	F	Private.	April 13, 18[illegible]	Nashville, Tenn......	Interred in section J, grave 1540.
[illegible]on, Elijah........	G	Private.	Jan. 20, 1865	Nashville, Tenn......	Interred in section E, grave 2998.
[illegible]on, Thomas.......	D	Private.	Dec. 6, 1864	Nashville, Tenn......	Interred in section F, grave 260.
[illegible]ton, Thomas	D	Private.	Nov. 6, 1864	Nashville, Tenn......	Interred in section E, grave 2784.
[illegible], Benjamin F.......	E	Corporal	Jan. 4, 1865	Nashville, Tenn......	
[illegible], George W.......	G	Private.	Dec. 17, 1864	New Albany, Ind......	Died at Jeffersonville, Ind.
[illegible], John.....	K	Private.	Jan. 4, 1865	Nashville, Tenn......	Interred in section G, grave 496.
[illegible], William.........	K	Private.	May 18, 1865	Nashville, Tenn......	Interred in section J, grave 1471.
[illegible]r, Jacob..........	H	Private.	Mch. 15, 1865	Nashville, Tenn......	
[illegible] George..........	B	Private.	Jan. 4, 1865	Nashville, Tenn......	Interred in section F, grave 263.
[illegible]s, William	F	Private.	Feb. 27, 1865	Nashville, Tenn......	Interred in section H, grave 67.
[illegible]r, Samuel......	H	Private.	Mch. 10, 1865	Nashville, Tenn......	Interred in section G, grave 600.
[illegible]er, Frederick......	A	Private.	Oct. 19, 1864	Nashville, Tenn......	
[illegible] Peter..............	B	Private.	Jan. 6, 1865	Nashville, Tenn......	Interred in section G, grave 776.
[illegible]ls, Loren K.......	B	Private.	Dec. 5, 1864	Nashville, Tenn.....	
[illegible]well, Luke	I	Private.	Jan. 13, 1865	Nashville, Tenn......	Interred in section H, grave 148.
[illegible]k, George.........	I	Private.	Feb. 15, 1865	Nashville, Tenn......	
[illegible]all, Thomas W....	D	Private.	Jan. 11, 1865	Nashville, Tenn......	
[illegible] James W..........	H	Private.	Mch. 8, 1865	Nashville, Tenn......	
[illegible], Abram..........	D	Private.	June 26, 1865	Nashville, Tenn......	Interred in section J, grave 790.
[illegible], Michael T.......	H	Private.	April 5, 1865	Nashville, Tenn......	
[illegible] Alexander.......	D	Private.	Oct. 22, 1865	Nashville, Tenn......	Died at Clarksville, Tenn. Interred in section V, grave 188.
[illegible]ell, Jacob J........	D	Private.	April 16, 1865	Nashville, Tenn......	
[illegible]ell, John L..	D	Private.	Dec. 22, 1864	Nashville, Tenn......	
[illegible], Allen	K	Private.	April 29, 1865	Nashville, Tenn.....	Interred in section J, grave 1398.
[illegible]mb, Rudolph.....	A	Private.	Feb. 4, 1865	Nashville, Tenn......	Interred in section H, grave 91.
[illegible] Christopher.......	E	Private.	Feb. 19, 1865	Nashville, Tenn......	
[illegible]r, Jacob...........	G	Private.	Feb. 22, 1865	Nashville, Tenn......	
[illegible] Morris W.........	C	Private.	April 14, 1865	Nashville, Tenn......	
[illegible]ide, Albert S......	C	Private.	Dec. 24, 1864	Nashville, Tenn......	
[illegible]son, Sylvanus L...	G	Private.	Feb. 6, 1865	Nashville, Tenn......	Interred in section H, grave 402.
[illegible]ll, John S..........	H	Private.	Jan. 23, 1865	Nashville, Tenn......	Interred in section H, grave 449.
[illegible], Jesse.............	H	Private.	Jan. 16, 1865	Nashville, Tenn......	Interred in section G, grave 406.
[illegible]ider, George.......	B	Musician	Jan. 2, 1865	New Albany, Ind.....	Interred in section B, grave 279.
[illegible]rd, Henry W......	E	Private.	Jan. 12, 1865	Nashville, Tenn......	Interred in section H, grave 367.
[illegible], Panal S..........	B	Private.	Jan. 18, 1865	Nashville, Tenn......	
[illegible], William H.....	B	Private.	Jan. 6, 1865	Cleveland, O.........	
[illegible], William N.......	C	Private.	June 8, 1865	Nashville, Tenn......	Interred in section J, grave 1219.
[illegible]r, Philander C.....	I	Private.	Jan. 5, 1865	Louisville, Ky........	Interred in Cave Hill Cemetery.
[illegible]s, George.........	K	Private.	Jan. 24, 1865	New Albany, Ind.....	Died at Jeffersonville, Ind. Interred in section B, grave 1033.
[illegible]son, Zephaniah P	A	Sergeant	Jan. 10, 1865	Louisville, Ky........	Interred in Cave Hill Cemetery.
[illegible], Isaac A..........	I	Private.	Dec. 8, 1864	St. Louis, Mo.........	Interred in section [illegible], grave 199, Jefferson Barracks Cemetery.
[illegible]r, Abraham	E	Private.	Mch. ..., 1865	Columbus, O.........	Interred in grave 98, Green Lawn Cemetery.
[illegible], Jackson.......	B	Private.	Feb. 10, 1865	Nashville, Tenn......	
[illegible], Samuel.........	H	Private.	Jan. 17, 1865	Nashville, Tenn......	Interred in section H, grave 281.
[illegible], Samuel	E	Private.	May 5, 1865	Nashville, Tenn......	Interred in section J, grave 1720.
[illegible], Edward..... ...	F	Corporal	Jan. 5, 1865	Nashville, Tenn......	
[illegible] David K.........	B	Private.	Jan. 26, 1865	Nashville, Tenn......	
[illegible], Joel............	H	Private.	June 4, 1865	Nashville, Tenn......	Interred in section J, grave 771.
[illegible], Thomas..........	B	Private.	Feb. 8, 1865	Nashville, Tenn......	Interred in section H, grave 568.
[illegible]am, Nathan	G	Private.	Jan. 7, 1865	Nashville, Tenn......	

Names.	Co.	Rank.	Died.	Buried.	Remarks.
Wilson, David...........	I	Corporal	Dec. 29, 1864	Cincinnati, O.........	Interred in section B, 286, Spring Grove Cem
Wolf, John..............	I	Private.	June 8, 1865	Nashville, Tenn......	Interred in section J, 1307.
Woodruff, Henry.........	H	Private.	Jan. 28, 1865	Nashville, Tenn......	Interred in section H, 268.
Young, Theodore J.......	B	Corporal	Dec. 14, 1864	Nashville, Tenn	

177th REGIMENT OHIO VOLUNTEER INFANTRY.

Names.	Co.	Rank.	Died.	Buried.	Remarks.
Ackley, James H........	E	Private.	Feb. 25, 1865	Wilmington, N. C....	Died at Smithville, N. C.
Alderman, Demetrius F.	C	Musician	Feb. 12, 1865	Louisville, Ky........	Interred in section C, grave 99, Cave Hill tery.
Baker, Newell...........	K	Private.	June 17, 1865	Raleigh, N. C.........	Died at Greensboro, N. C.
Barr, James E...........	H	Private.	May 16, 1865	Jacksonville, Fla.....	
Barrett, George W.......	H	Private.	Mch. 22, 1865	Wilmington, N. C....	
Beldin, Charles T.......	G	Private.	Feb. 3, 1865	Nashville, Tenn......	Interred in section G, 524.
Bonesteel, David........	H	Private.	April 19, 1865	Long Island, N. Y....	Died on hospital transport Deford, en route from head City, N. C., to York City. Interred in 2576, Cypress Hill Ceme
Brazee, Peter, Jr........	K	Private.	Mch. 23, 1865	Wilmington, N. C....	
Buck, Orson H..........	H	Corporal	April 29, 1865	....	Died in hospital.
Carter, John E..........	H	Private.	Mch. 15, 1865	Wilmington, N. C....	Interred in grave 718.
Chamberlin, Walter C...	H	Private.	Feb. 15, 1865	....	Died at Federal Point, N. C.
Champlain, Lewis	I	Private.	April 4, 1865	Long Island, N. Y....	Died at Willett's Point, N. Y. Interred in grave 2[illegible] press Hill Cemetery.
Clark, Russell R.........	C	Private.	Mch. 7, 1865	Long Island, N. Y....	Died at New York City. Interred in grave 2310, Cypress Hill Cemetery.
Cochran, Leonard H....	A	Corporal	Jan. 23, 1865	....	Killed by cars.
Cogswell, Marion........	B	Private.	Jan. 27, 1865	Camp Dennison, O...	
Coleman, Latham N.....	K	Sergeant	Dec. 1, 1864	Nashville, Tenn......	Interred in section E, 2648.
Dart, William H........	K	Private.	June 20, 1865	Long Island, N. Y....	Died at David's Island, York Harbor. Interred Cypress Hill Cemetery
Demo, George W........	D	Private.	Jan. 17, 1865	Nashville, Tenn......	Died of wounds received line of duty. Interred section G, grave 7[illegible].
Ernst, Daniel G.........	K	Private.	Dec. 13, 1864	Murfreesboro, Tenn	Interred in Stone River tery.
Evans, Daniel	C	Private.	May 17, 1865	Newbern, N. C.......	
Eversole, Simeon........	D	Private.	May 3, 1865	Arlington, Va.........	Died at Washington, D. C.
Fails, John..............	K	Private.	April 21, 1865	Wilmington, N. C....	
Fay, Romanzo...........	F	Private.	Mch. 4, 1865	Nashville, Tenn......	Interred in section E, 574.
Fisher, Herbert B.......	K	Sergeant	April 23, 1865	Louisville, Ky........	Interred in Cave Hill tery.
Flick, Daniel	A	Private.	May 9, 1865	Wilmington, N. C....	Died at Smithville, N. C.
Foote, Curtis............	D	Private.	Feb. 27, 1865	Nashville, Tenn......	
Foster, James A	C	Private.	Sept. 19, 1864	Cleveland, O..........	
Gardner, David N.......	C	Private.	Feb. 11, 1865	Wilmington, N. C....	Died at Fort Fisher, N. C.
Gaskill, Benjamin.......	G	Private.	May 22, 1865	Raleigh, N. C.........	Died at Greensboro, N. C.
Gasser, John	A	Private.	Feb. 16, 1865	Wilmington, N. C....	Died at Fort Fisher, N. C.
Gillmore, Joseph	K	Private.	Mch. 7, 1865	Wilmington, N. C....	Interred in grave 1[illegible]
Grover, Justin L........	I	Private.	Mch. 31, 1865	Newbern, N. C.......	Died at Kinston, N. C. Interred in section [illegible] 150.
Grover, Leonard	C	Private.	July 3, 1865	....	Died at home.
Hadlock, Aaron.	B	Private.	Feb. 6, 1865	Arlington, Va.........	Died at Washington, D. C.
Hall, Aaron G...........	D	Private.	Mch. 20, 1865	Wilmington, N. C....	
Hall, Andrew J..........	H	Private.	Jan. 22, 1865	Louisville, Ky........	Interred in section C, grave 74, Cave Hill Cemetery.
Hall, Nathan............	K	Private.	Dec. 31, 1864	Nashville, Tenn......	Interred in section E, 360.
Hartson, Alfred C.......	K	Private.	Jan. 31, 1865	Nashville, Tenn.....	
Harvey, George W.......	I	Private.	Mch. 20, 1865	Wilmington, N. C....	
Hatch, Americus A.....	G	Private.	Feb. 25, 1865	Wilmington, N. C....	Died at Smithville, N. C.
Hatch, Augustus J......	G	Private.	Feb. 22, 1865	Wilmington, N. C....	Died at Smithville, N. C.
Henry, James M.........	D	Corporal	Mch. 10, 1865	....	
Higley, George G........	I	Private.	Mch. 19, 1865	Wilmington, N. C....	Interred in grave 2[illegible]

Names.	Co.	Rank.	Died.	Buried.	Remarks.
Hooge, Willis F.	D	Private.	Feb. 7, 1865	Wilmington, N. C.	Died at Fort Fisher, N. C.
Hosmer, Newell A.	E	Private.	May 1, 1865	Long Island, N. Y.	Died at David's Island, New York Harbor. Interred in Cypress Hill Cemetery.
Hubbard, Selah B.	C	Private.	April 28, 1865	Wilmington, N. C.	Interred in grave 1907.
Jenkins, Chauncey	C	Private.	Mch. 1, 1865	Wilmington, N. C.	Interred in grave 1900.
Johnson, John W.	H	Private.	Feb. 25, 1865	....	Died in hospital.
Johnston, Samuel G.	G	Private.	Feb. 3, 1865	Annapolis, Md.	
Kihr, August	F	Private.	Dec. 12, 1864	Murfreesboro, Tenn.	Interred in section D, grave 853, Stone River Cemetery.
Knowles, John O.	C	Wagoner.	April 6, 1865	Wilmington, N. C.	Interred in grave 1818.
Lamont, David	D	Private.	April 30, 1865	Newbern, N. C.	Died at Beaufort, N. C. Interred in section 17, grave 2972.
Leggett, Newton	E	Corporal	Feb. 22, 1865	Wilmington, N. C.	Died at Smithville, N. C.
Long, Samuel W.	E	Private.	Jan. 18, 1865	Nashville, Tenn.	Interred in section G, grave 614.
Longworthy, Irving J.	C	Private.	Dec. 22, 1864	Murfreesboro, Tenn.	Died of wounds received Dec. 14, 1864, in action. Interred in section E, grave 127, Stone River Cemetery.
Matthews, Lewis	I	Private.	Oct. 1, 1864	Louisville, Ky.	Interred in Cave Hill Cemetery
Morse, George R.	D	Private.	Jan. 20, 1865	Louisville, Ky.	Interred in section C, row 6, grave 72, Cave Hill Cemetery.
Mountain, Sylvester	G	Private.	Mch. 1, 1865	Murfreesboro, Tenn.	Interred in Stone River Cemetery.
Muller, John E.	F	Private.	July 7, 1865	Raleigh, N. C.	Died at Greensboro, N. C.
Napp, Augustus	H	Private.	April 7, 1865	Long Island, N. Y.	Interred in Cypress Hill Cemetery.
Nash, James M.	E	Private.	Feb. 25, 1865	Louisville, Ky.	Interred in Cave Hill Cemetery.
Norris, Monroe J.	C	Private.	Jan. 28, 1865	Murfreesboro, Tenn.	Died at Tullahoma, Tenn. Interred in Stone River Cemetery.
Northrop, George W.	I	Private.	Dec. 31, 1864	Nashville, Tenn.	Interred in section G, grave 526.
Olcott, George H.	F	Private.	April 19, 1865	Long Island, N. Y.	Died at David's Island, New York Harbor. Interred in Cypress Hill Cemetery.
Orr, John J.	C	Private.	Feb. 18, 1865	Arlington, Va.	Died at Washington, D. C.
Palmiter, Allen	A	Private.	April 11, 1865	....	Died on hospital transport J. K. Barnes.
Partridge, Milo L.	C	Private.	Feb. 22, 1865	Wilmington, N. C.	Died at Smithville, N. C.
Pelton, William S.	G	Private.	Sept. 19, 1864	....	Died at Greensburg, Trumbull County, O.
Perkins, Zethan	K	Private.	Jan. 15, 1865	Shiloh, Tenn.	Died at Clifton, Tenn.
Piper, Edwin C.	C	Corporal	Feb. 16, 1865	Louisville, Ky.	Interred in Cave Hill Cemetery.
Pugsley, Samuel	K	Private.	Mch. 18, 1865	Wilmington, N. C.	
Reames, Jonathan	H	Private.	Feb. 23, 1865	Arlington, Va.	Died at Washington, D. C.
Reber, Jacob G.	F	Private.	Feb. 15, 1865	....	Died in hospital at Cape Fear River, N. C.
Rentler, William H.	K	Private.	April 29, 1865	Camp Dennison, O.	
Roath, Milton	K	Private.	Mch. 9, 1865	Wilmington, N. C.	
Root, James D.	D	Private.	Jan. 29, 1865	Nashville, Tenn.	Interred in section H, grave 845.
Sell, Michael	K	Private.	Mch. 18, 1865	Wilmington, N. C.	
Shears, Minard C.	K	Private.	Jan. 6, 1865	Murfreesboro, Tenn.	Interred in section N, grave 162, Stone River Cemetery.
Shinn, Samuel A.	G	Private.	Feb. 20, 1865	Wilmington, N. C.	Died at Smithville, N. C.
Sours, John	K	Private.	Feb. 27, 1865	Wilmington, N. C.	Died at Smithville, N. C.
Staley, William H.	E	Private.	Feb. 7, 1865	Louisville, Ky.	Interred in section C, row 6, grave 87, Cave Hill Cemetery.
Stearnes, Charles W.	F	Private.	Feb. 7, 1865	Louisville, Ky.	Interred in section C, row 6, grave 89, Cave Hill Cemetery.
Stevens, James	E	Private.	Mch. 10, 1865	Wilmington, N. C.	
Tatro, George	I	Private.	Jan. 10, 1865	Murfreesboro, Tenn.	Interred in section N, grave 58, Stone River Cemetery.
Way, Erastus J.	C	Private.	Feb. 16, 1865	....	Died at home, New Lyme, O.
Wilder, Leonard	C	Private.	June 1, 1865	Long Island, N. Y.	Died at David's Island, New York Harbor. Interred in Cypress Hill Cemetery.
Williams, Thomas	K	Private.	Feb. 4, 1865	Wheeling, W. Va.	
Woodworth, Marcus M.	F	Private.	Mch. 4, 1865	Louisville, Ky.	Interred in section C, row 1, grave 115, Cave Hill Cemetery.

178th REGIMENT OHIO VOLUNTEER INFANTRY.

Names.	Co.	Rank.	Died.	Buried.	Remarks.
Allen, Cineas	D	Private.	Feb. 20, 1865	Arlington, Va	Died at Washington, D. C.
Andrews, Robert	D	Private.	Dec. 16, 1864	Louisville, Ky	Interred in section C, row 7, grave 39, Cave Hill Cemetery.
Ankrom, Joseph	C	Private.	Mch. 7, 1865	Newbern, N. C	Interred in section 17, grave 12.
Arthur, Lewis	K	Private.	Jan. 15, 1865	Murfreesboro, Tenn	Interred in section E, grave 210
Bellows, Nathaniel	D	Private.	May 12, 1865	Newbern, N. C	Interred in section 17, grave 144.
Bolen, John H	B	Private.	Jan. 30, 1865		Died at Lockbourne, O.
Callin, George	G	Private.	Mch. 26, 1865	Long Island, N. Y	Died on hospital transport Northern Light. Interred in Cypress Hill Cemetery.
Carter, Albert	I	Private.	June 22, 1865	Charlotte, N. C	
Clark, Harvey M	G	Private.	Feb. 25, 1865	Arlington, Va	Died at Washington, D. C.
Decker, Frederick	D	Private.	Jan. 11, 1865	St. Louis, Mo	Interred in Jefferson Barracks Cemetery.
Detchon, Francis	I	Private.	Dec. 22, 1864	Murfreesboro, Tenn	Interred in section E, grave 427, Stone River Cemetery.
Detchon, William	I	Private.	Dec. 19, 1864	Nashville, Tenn	Interred in section G, grave 69.
Emmons, Harley	D	Private.	Jan. 31, 1865	Murfreesboro, Tenn	Interred in Stone River Cemetery.
Flanegan, Archibald	E	Private.	Dec. 6, 1864	Chattanooga, Tenn	Interred in section G, grave 272.
Flower, William	F	Corporal	Feb. 1, 1865	Cincinnati, O	Interred in section B, grave 278, Spring Grove Cemetery.
Foltz, Ervin	B	Private.	Dec. 10, 1864	Nashville, Tenn	Interred in section F, grave 243.
Gregg, Henry	C	Private.	Mch. 10, 1865	Nashville, Tenn	
Gregg, Lewis	C	Private.	April 8, 1865	Newbern, N. C	Interred in section 17, grave 57.
Griffith, Thomas W	B	Sergeant	Jan. 23, 1865	Louisville, Ky	Interred in Cave Hill Cemetery.
Groff, Zachariah A	E	Private.	Jan. 22, 1865	Louisville, Ky	Interred in Cave Hill Cemetery.
Harding, Charles	A	Private.	Jan. 13, 1865	Murfreesboro, Tenn	Died at Columbia, Tenn. Interred in Stone River Cemetery.
Hedges, Thomas W	B	1st Sergt.	Feb. 1, 1865	Camp Dennison, O	
Heinberger, Daniel	E	Private.	May 16, 1865	Columbus, O	Interred in Green Lawn Cemetery.
Hollar, David R	A	Private.	Dec. 15, 1864	Murfreesboro, Tenn.	Interred in Stone River Cemetery.
Huggett, Robert	B	Private.	Mch. 30, 1865	Arlington, Va	Died at Washington, D. C.
Jenkins, David A	G	Private.	Dec. 6, 1864	Murfreesboro, Tenn	Killed while on picket duty Interred in Stone River Cemetery.
John, Austin	I	Private.	Feb. 12, 1865	Camp Dennison, O	
Keller, Daniel	E	Private.	Oct. 10, 1864	Columbus, O	Interred in Green Lawn Cemetery.
Keller, Daniel	H	Private.	June 30, 1865	Louisville, Ky	Interred in section C, row 6, grave 82, Cave Hill Cemetery.
Lawrence, Joseph P	F	Corporal	Jan 7, 1865	Murfreesboro, Tenn	Interred in section E grave 435, Stone River Cemeters.
Lesh, John	I	Private.	Feb. 24, 1865	Louisville, Ky	Interred in Cave Hill Cemetery.
Lindzly, James E	E	Private.	Jan. 14, 1865	Murfreesboro, Tenn	Interred in section N, grave 454, Stone River Cemetery.
Lower, John	C	Private.	Mch. 25, 1865	Arlington, Va	Died at Washington, D. C.
McConnell, Thomas M.	K	Corporal	Feb. 19, 1865	Wheeling, W. Va	
Meek, Sylvester C	H	Private.	May 17, 1865	Charlotte, N. C	
Mills, Edwin M	K	Private.	April 25, 1865	Lansingburg, N. Y	
Moakler, Edward	A	Private.	May 1, 1865	Raleigh, N. C	Killed by musket shot.
Moore, Zadok J	F	Private.	Mch. 7, 1865	Alexandria, Va.	
Morris, New Year B	D	Private.	Feb. 16, 1865	Columbus, O	Died at Camp Chase, O. Interred in Green Lawn Cemetery.
Munson, Lucius B	K	Private.	Oct. 14, 1864		Died at Spencer, Medina County, O.
Paugburn, Charles E	B	Private.	Mch. 21, 1865	Columbus, O	Died at Camp Chase, O. Interred in grave 302, Green Lawn Cemetery.
Pickenpaugh, Jonathan R	F	Private.	Mch. 11, 1865	Louisville, Ky	Interred in section C, row 4, grave 102, Cave Hill Cemetery.
Powell, George	B	Private.	Oct. 15, 1864	Columbus, O	Died at Camp Chase, O. Interred in Green Lawn Cemetery.
Ramsey, William W	B	Private.	Jan. 16, 1865	Murfreesboro, Tenn	Died at Columbia, Tenn. Interred in Stone River Cemetery.

Names.	Co.	Rank.	Died.	Buried.	Remarks.
Rawson, Andrew	D	Private.	Feb. 2, 1865	St. Louis, Mo.	Interred in Jefferson Barracks Cemetery.
Ringer, Jacob	C	Private.	Jan. 15, 1865	Pittsburgh, Pa	Interred in Allegheny Cemetery.
Ross, Milo	D	Private.	Dec 7, 1864	Murfreesboro, Tenn.	Killed in action at Wilkerson's Pike, Tenn.
Sadler, John L.	K	Corporal	Feb. 3, 1865	Camp Dennison, O.	
Saner, Adam	I	Private.	Jan. 14, 1865	Murfreesboro, Tenn.	Died at Columbia, Tenn. Interred in Stone River Cemetery.
Scott, Alexander	A	Private.	Jan. 31, 1865	Camp Dennison, O.	Interred in grave 327.
Shafer, John S.	G	Private.	Jan. 20, 1865	Louisville, Ky.	Interred in Cave Hill Cemetery.
Shafer, Nooman	G	Private.	Jan. 24, 1865	Nashville, Tenn.	Interred in section E, grave 2262.
Simmons, Francis	K	Private.	Mch. 18, 1865	Nashville, Tenn.	Interred in section J, grave 1543.
Smith, Samuel E.	I	Private.	Feb. 20, 1865	New Albany, Ind.	Interred in section B, grave 1040.
Snider, John	I	Private.	Jan. 19, 1865	Nashville, Tenn.	
Stires, John	F	Private.	Jan. 14, 1865	Murfreesboro, Tenn.	Interred in section E, grave 331, Stone River Cemetery.
Stroud, Thomas	K	Private.	Mch. 21, 1865	Newbern, N. C.	Interred in section 17, grave 105.
Taylor, Lewis P.	D	Private.	May 8, 1865		Died in New York and sent home for burial.
Thompson, Mahlon	H	Corporal	July 1, 1865	City Point, Va.	
Udall, Luther	D	Private.	Feb. 8, 1865	Murfreesboro, Tenn.	Interred in section N, grave 517, Stone River Cemetery.
Vail, Isaac	H	Private.	Feb. 9, 1865	New Albany, Ind.	Died at Jeffersonville, Ind. Interred in section B, grave 412.
Wells, Newton	F	Private.	Sept. 17, 1864		Died at Putnam, O.
White, James H.	C	Private.	Mch. 25, 1865	Newbern, N. C.	Interred in section 17, grave 107.
Williams, Harrison	H	Private.	Feb. 28, 1865	Newbern, N. C.	Died at Morehead City, N. C. Interred in section 17, grave 49.
Williamson, Henry C.	D	Private.	May 22, 1865	Long Island, N. Y.	Interred in Cypress Hill Cemetery.

179th REGIMENT OHIO VOLUNTEER INFANTRY.

Names.	Co.	Rank.	Died.	Buried.	Remarks.
Allen, Franklin P.	K	Private.	May 11, 1865	Nashville, Tenn.	
Baker, Frederick	D	Private.	Mch. 4, 1865	Nashville, Tenn.	
Barnes, Lewis C.	I	Private.	Dec. 10, 1864	Nashville, Tenn.	Interred in section E, grave 2794.
Bates, Edwin W.	A	Private.	June 2, 1865	Nashville, Tenn.	
Beven, Thomas R.	D	Private.	Oct. 20, 1864	Nashville, Tenn.	
Brown, John W.	I	Corporal	Nov. 30, 1864	Nashville, Tenn.	Interred in section G, grave 136.
Brunne, John B.	I	Private.	Jan. 1, 1865	Nashville, Tenn.	Interred in section G, grave 604.
Burns, Jasper	K	Private.	Jan. 5, 1865	Nashville, Tenn.	
Calkins, Cornelius	A	Private.	Dec. 31, 1864	Nashville, Tenn.	Interred in section G, grave 751.
Camp, Newton L.	A	Private.	Jan. 16, 1865	Nashville, Tenn.	
Cheatham, William A.	D	Private.	Jan. 12, 1865	Nashville, Tenn.	Interred in section G, grave 577.
Clawson, William B.	H	Private.	April 8, 1865		Died at Elida, Allen County, O.
Coulson, Job V.	G	Private.	Nov. 22, 1864	Nashville, Tenn.	
Davis, Thomas E. T.	C	Private.	Dec. 3, 1864	Nashville, Tenn.	
Dinsmore, Samuel	E	Private.	Dec. 20, 1864	Nashville, Tenn.	Interred in section G, grave 561.
Donnelly, Charles W.	D	Private.	Dec. 14, 1864	Nashville, Tenn.	
Dowell, Adam S.	I	Private.	Dec. 24, 1864	Nashville, Tenn.	Interred in section G, grave 97.
Drake, Jacob	E	Private.	Jan. 24, 1865	Nashville, Tenn.	Interred in section H, grave 870.
[illegible], Thomas	E	Private.	Jan. 1, 1865	Nashville, Tenn.	
[illegible], James D.	E	Private.	Dec. 12, 1864	Nashville, Tenn.	Interred in section G, grave 205.
[illegible]	D	Private.	Jan. 8, 1865	Nashville, Tenn.	
[illegible], Henry C.	E	Private.	Dec. 10, 1864	Nashville, Tenn.	Interred in section E, grave 2906.
Gregg, William K.	I	Private.	Feb. 21, 1865	Nashville, Tenn.	

Names.	Co.	Rank.	Died.	Buried.	Remarks.
Hagen, Alois	E	Private.	Feb. 2, 1865	Nashville, Tenn	Interred in section 451.
Hammond, Andrew	D	Musician	Jan. 6, 1865	Nashville, Tenn	
Harbison, James H	H	Private.	Jan. 12, 1865	Nashville, Tenn	Interred in section 652.
Heath, Israel	B	Corporal	Dec. 2, 1864	Nashville, Tenn	Interred in section 2843.
Holland, William B	E	Private.	Dec. 18, 1864	Nashville, Tenn	Interred in section 135.
Hoover, Benjamin B	K	Private.	Dec. 8, 1864	Nashville, Tenn	Interred in section 177.
Hueston, George	A	Private.	Jan. 12, 1865	Nashville, Tenn	Interred in section 480.
Jarrett, James	I	Private.	Nov. 28, 1864	Nashville, Tenn	Interred in section 193.
Jenkins, Francis	C	Private.	Dec. 15, 1864		
Jones, Evan E	D	Private.	Jan. 21, 1865	Nashville, Tenn	
Jones, John D. P	C	Private.	Sept. 28, 1864		
Jones, John M	C	Private.	Dec. 20, 1864	Nashville, Tenn	
Jones, John W	C	Corporal	Dec. 8, 1864	Nashville, Tenn	
Jones, Thomas D	C	Private.	Dec. 31, 1864	Nashville, Tenn	
Judkins, Franklin D	H	Private.	Dec. 2, 1864	Nashville, Tenn	
Justice, James B	I	Private.	Nov. 4, 1864	Nashville, Tenn	
Justice, John W	I	Private.	Jan. 31, 1865	Nashville, Tenn	Interred in section 456.
Keller, George W	B	Private.	Dec. 30, 1864	Nashville, Tenn	
Kesler, Josiah	H	Private.	Jan. 26, 1865	Nashville, Tenn	
Kirby, Smith V	K	Private.	Dec 11, 1864	Nashville, Tenn	Interred in section 2789.
Lawson, Wesley D	G	Corporal	Feb. 14, 1865	Nashville, Tenn	
Logan, Henry	F	Private.	Feb. 25, 1865	Nashville, Tenn	
Looker, Joel	H	Private.	Jan. 3, 1865	Nashville, Tenn	Interred in section 678.
McFarland, Robert L	I	Private.	Jan. 27, 1865	Nashville, Tenn	
McWelch, William	A	Private.	Mch. 14, 1865	Nashville, Tenn	
Mawzy, James L	K	Private.	Oct. 3, 1864		Drowned in Ohio Cincinnati, O.
Meek, John	G	Private.	Dec. 6, 1864	Nashville, Tenn	Interred in section 247.
Melton, Joseph	D	Private.	Oct. 20, 1864	Nashville, Tenn	
Miller, Peter	H	Private.	Jan. 21, 1865	Nashville, Tenn	Interred in section 385.
Morgan, D. Morgan	E	Corporal	Jan. 1, 1865	Nashville, Tenn	
Morgan, Enoch	C	Private.	April 25, 1865		
Morgan, Enoch E	C	Corporal	Nov. 16, 1864	Nashville, Tenn	
Parks, Franklin	K	Private.	April 1, 1865	Nashville, Tenn	
Passell, Peter	H	Private.	Jan. 7, 1865	Nashville, Tenn	Interred in section
Peeling, Robert	K	Private.	Mch. 14, 1865		Died at home.
Powell, William G	C	Private.	Dec. 31, 1864	Nashville, Tenn	Interred in section 673.
Preitling, George F	B	Private.	Jan. 11, 1865	Nashville, Tenn	Interred in section 481.
Preston, Hezekiah	A	Private.	Feb. 15, 1865	Nashville, Tenn	Interred in section 164.
Quayle, Ashley	E	Private.	April 2, 1865	Nashville, Tenn	Interred in section 1311.
Ralston, Joseph	B	Private.	Jan. 7, 1865	Nashville, Tenn	
Reed, William	E	Private.	Feb. 15, 1865	Nashville, Tenn	
Reichman, Benj. F	I	Private.	Nov. 29, 1864	Nashville, Tenn	Interred in section
Rhoads, Eli	A	Private.	Oct. 2, 1864	Columbus, O	Died at Camp Chase
Richards, James	E	Private.	Mch. 19, 1865	Nashville, Tenn	
Ridenour, Isaac	H	Private.	Jan. 16, 1865	Nashville, Tenn	
Rien, David C	H	Private.	April 1, 1865	Nashville, Tenn	Interred in section 843.
Rike, Eugene	K	Private.	Dec. 10, 1864	Nashville, Tenn	
Ritz, Henry	E	Sergeant	Mch. 18, 1865	Nashville, Tenn	
Russ, James A	A	Private.	Nov. 30, 1864	Nashville, Tenn	
Selke, Henry	F	Private.	Jan. 26, 1865	Nashville, Tenn	
Senters, John R	E	Private.	Feb. 8, 1865	Nashville, Tenn	
Smith, William W	K	Private.	Oct. 3, 1864		Drowned in Ohio R Cincinnati, O
Sorrick, Adam	F	Private.	April 9, 1865	Nashville, Tenn	Interred in section 253.
Southwick, Arnold	F	Private.	April 19, 1865	Nashville, Tenn	
Sprague, Philander M	A	Private.	Jan. 9, 1865	Nashville, Tenn	
Squires, Orrin	A	Private.	Jan. 9, 1865	Nashville, Tenn	Interred in section 1250.
Stemen, John B	H	Private.	Jan. 10, 1865	Nashville, Tenn	
Stotler, John O	F	Private.	Feb. 18, 1865	Nashville, Tenn	Interred in section 1442.
Stout, Elias	A	Private.	Jan. 10, 1865	New Albany, Ind	Died on board steam Wood. Interred in B, grave 172.
Strong, Abner	A	Private.	June 24, 1865	Nashville, Tenn	Mustered out Jr order of War D terred in section
Terrell, Samuel E	A	Private.	Nov. 26, 1864	Nashville, Tenn	Interred in se 274.

Names.	Co.	Rank.	Died.	Buried.	Remarks.
Wilson, Martin	E	Private.	Dec. 18, 1864	Nashville, Tenn.	Interred in section G, grave 361.
Wise, Asa B	I	Private.	Nov. 20, 1864	Nashville, Tenn.	Interred in section F, grave 272.
Wright, Isaac	I	Private.	Nov. 21, 1864	Nashville, Tenn.	Interred in section E, grave 2563.
Yeager, James A	C	Private.	Dec. 31, 1864	Nashville, Tenn.	

180th REGIMENT OHIO VOLUNTEER INFANTRY.

Names.	Co.	Rank.	Died.	Buried.	Remarks.
Barnes, Robert A	F	Private.	Mch. 6, 1865	Arlington, Va.	Died at Washington, D. C.
Basil, James W	E	Private.	Feb. 9, 1865	Arlington, Va.	Died at Washington, D. C.
Birt, John	K	Private.	May 8, 1865	Arlington, Va.	Died at Washington, D. C.
Blackford, Henry	B	Private.	Feb. 10, 1865	Arlington, Va.	Died at Washington, D. C.
Bougher, Daniel	A	Private.	Oct. 2, 1864		
Bowman, Abraham	B	Private.	Feb. 3, 1865	Louisville, Ky	Interred in Cave Hill Cemetery.
Branstitter, Charles M	E	Private.	Mch. 5, 1865	Arlington, Va.	Died at Washington, D. C.
Brewer, Daniel	C	Private.	Mch. 26, 1865	Newbern, N. C.	Died at Kinston, N. C.
Brown, Franklin	I	Private.	Mch. 26, 1865	Arlington, Va.	Died at Washington, D. C.
Burden, Eli	D	Private.	May 12, 1865	Raleigh, N. C.	Interred in section 4, grave 58.
Burget, Bartholomew F.	D	Private.	April 23, 1865		Drowned in Potomac River.
Burris, Francis	I	Private.	May 31, 1865	Charlotte, N. C.	
Burton, Abraham	I	Private.	Feb. 21, 1865	Arlington, Va.	Died at Washington, D. C.
Cook, William M	K	2d Lieut.	Jan. 7, 1865	Murfreesboro, Tenn.	Interred in Stone River Cemetery.
Coon, John	K	Private.	Mch. 5, 1865	Arlington, Va.	Died at Washington, D. C.
Coon, Samuel	D	Private.	Feb. 25, 1865	Arlington, Va.	Died at Washington, D. C.
Copsey, Franklin	D	Private.	Mch. 12, 1865	Arlington, Va.	Died at Washington, D. C.
Corpstein, Joseph	E	Private.	Dec. 11, 1864	Vicksburg, Miss.	Died at Decherd, Tenn. Interred in section H, grave 628.
Cosart, John	B	Private.	Mch. 28, 1865	Arlington, Va.	Died at Washington, D. C.
Crais, Robert	F	Private.	Feb. 20, 1865	Arlington, Va.	Died at Washington, D. C.
Curps, John T	I	Private.	May 28, 1865	Charlotte, N. C.	
Dacon, Xenophon	F	Private.	Mch. 11, 1865	Beaufort, N. C.	
Daring, Emil	H	Private.	Oct. 27, 1864	Nashville, Tenn.	Interred in section F, grave 56.
Davis, John F	B	Private.	Mch. 9, 1865	Newbern, N. C.	Interred in section 17, grave 118.
Decker, Peter C	D	Private.	Mch. 8, 1865	Newbern, N. C	Killed in battle of Wise's Fork, N. C. Interred in section 17, grave 85.
Ebelman, Francis	K	Private.	Mch. 20, 1865	Newbern, N. C	Died at Kinston, N. C. Interred in section 17, grave 87.
Foglesong, Simon	C	Private.	Mch. 28, 1865		
Giddings, Jesse H	B	Private.	Feb. 19, 1865		Died at Waynesville, O.
Glass, George W	I	Private.	Feb. 12, 1865	Arlington, Va.	Died at Washington, D. C.
Golden, William H	D	Private.	Mch. 23, 1865	Arlington, Va.	Died at Washington, D. C.
Green, William R	C	Private.	Feb. 10, 1865	Arlington, Va.	Died at Camp Stoneman, D. C.
Griffith, Isaac M	A	Private.	April 21, 1865	Raleigh, N. C.	Interred in section 4, grave 51.
Hembey, Tobias M	C	Private.	Mch. 9, 1865	Newbern, N. C.	Died of wounds received March 8, 1865, in battle of Wise's Fork, N. C. Interred in section 17, grave 151.
Hiatt, Irwin	I	Private.	April 5, 1865	Arlington, Va.	Died at Washington, D. C.
Horner, Elijah	E	Private.	Feb. 20, 1865	Arlington, Va.	Died at Washington, D. C.
Howell, Freeman	F	Private.	Feb. 13, 1865	Louisville, Ky.	Interred in section C, row 5, grave 28, Cave Hill Cemetery.
Huff, George	F	Private.	Feb. 11, 1865	Arlington, Va.	Died at Washington, D. C.
Hughes, Benjamin	E	Corporal	Mch. 7, 1865	Arlington, Va.	Died at Washington, D. C.
Hughes, James D	I	Private.	May 24, 1865	Long Island, N. Y.	Interred in grave 2181, Cypress Hill Cemetery.
Imler, Amos	D	Private.	June 12, 1865	Long Island, N. Y.	Interred in Cypress Hill Cemetery.
Imler, William	D	Private.	Mch. 28, 1865	Newbern, N. C.	Died at Morehead City, N. C.
Inman, Reuben	C	Private.	Feb. 9, 1865	Louisville, Ky.	Interred in Cave Hill Cemetery.
Kidney, John	K	Private.	Mch. 5, 1865	Arlington, Va.	Died at Washington, D. C.
Lay, John	I	Private.	Mch. 24, 1865	Newbern, N. C.	Interred in section 17, grave 137.
Legg, William M	B	Private.	Feb. 14, 1865	Arlington, Va.	Died at Washington, D. C.
Longworth, Jackson	D	Private.	April 21, 1865	Long Island, N. Y.	Died at David's Island, New York Harbor. Interred in Cypress Hill Cemetery.
McClain, Jonathan	K	Private.	Feb. 12, 1865	Arlington, Va.	Died at Washington, D. C.

Names.	Rank.		
McClurg, Adam.........		June 15, 1865	Charlotte, N. C.......
McCoy, Jonas H.........		May 24, 1865	Long Island, N. Y....
McGee, George A........		June 19, 1865	Charlotte, N. C.......
McKay, Hiram		Mch. 18, 1865	Newbern, N. C.......
McWilliams, Lewis H...		Oct. 11, 1864	Columbus, O.........
Malling, Lewis..........		Feb. 4, 1865	Arlington, Va........
Mattes, Alfred.		Mch. 31, 1865	Newbern, N. C.......
Melson, Michael.........		Feb. 14, 1865	Arlington, Va........
Miller, Ferdinand.......	Private.	Feb. 28, 1865	Arlington, Va........
Mobley, John N.........	Private.	Feb. 7, 1865	Arlington, Va........
Morse, Jerome B........		June 22, 1865	Charlotte, N. C.......
Morris, Thomas F.......		Nov. 20, 1864	Murfreesboro, Tenn..
Oblinger, Frederick.....	Private.	Jan. 12, 1865	Nashville, Tenn.....
Owens, Gabriel..........		Nov. 14, 1864	....
Powell, Elijah...........		Feb. 14, 1865	Arlington, Va........
Richards, Daniel A......		Feb. 9, 1865	Arlington, Va........
Ross, George W..........	Private.	June 8, 1865	Charlotte, N. C.......
Schulte, Gephart........	Private.	Nov. 29, 1864	Murfreesboro, Tenn..
Seldomridge, George....		Feb. 9, 1865	Arlington, Va........
Sheppard, William J....	Private.	Feb. 28, 1865	Arlington, Va........
Sherwood, Aaron.......	Private.	Jan. 29, 1865	Columbus, O.........
Shuler, Andrew J.......	Private.	May 27, 1865	Long Island, N. Y....
Smith, Emanuel.........	Private.	Feb. 26, 1865	Wheeling, W. Va.....
Still, Thomas...........	Private.	Feb. 25, 1865	Arlington, Va........
Van Sant, James J......	Corporal	Mch. 2, 1865	Alexandria, Va.......
Vestal, James..........	Private.	Nov. 14, 1864	Murfreesboro, Tenn..
Walters, Robert.........	Private.	Mch. 8, 1865	Newbern, N. C.......
Wheeler, John D........	Sergeant	Mch. 15, 1865	Newbern, N. C.......
Williams, Michael.......	Private.	Feb. 25, 1865	Arlington, Va........
Williams, Thomas J.....	Corporal	Feb. 21, 1865	Arlington, Va........
Wolley, James..........	Private.	Feb 26, 1865	Arlington, Va........
Woodruff, Cornelius J...	Private.	Feb. 23, 1865	Arlington, Va........
Yant, William...........	Private.	Mch. 11, 1865	Newbern, N. C.......

181st REGIMENT OHIO VOLUNTEER

Names.	Co.	Rank.	Died.	
Braun, Peter............	F	Private.	July 9, 1865	Salisbury, N. C.......
Conway, Cornelius.....	D	Private.	Dec. 8, 1864	Murfreesboro, Tenn..
Frazier, Oliver R........	E	Sergeant	Dec. 14, 1864	Murfreesboro, Tenn..
Goodrich, Rollin C......	A	Private.	Mch. 24, 1865	New Albany, Ind.....
Gould, Robert...........	D	Private.	Mch. 31, 1865	....
Hauk, John.............	I	Private.	April 18, 1865	Newbern, N. C.......
Hopkins, Thomas.......	K	Private.	Oct. 25, 1864	....
Jones, Laton............	F	Private.	Jan. 21, 1865	Nashville, Tenn......
Kelley, Michael.........	B	Private.	Mch. 27, 1865	Newbern, N. C.......

Names.	Co.	Rank.	Died.	Buried.	Remarks.
Kemmerer, Valentine...	I	Private.	May 22, 1865	Cincinnati, O.........	Interred in Spring Grove Cemetery.
[illegible], Joseph E.........	D	Private.	Mch. 18, 1865	Wilmington, N. C....	Died at Smithville, N. C. Interred in grave 1998.
[illegible], Christopher....	B	Private.	Dec. 31, 1864	Shiloh, Tenn.........	Died at Clifton, Tenn.
L[illegible], Timothy.........	G	Private.	Dec. 7, 1864	Murfreesboro, Tenn..	Killed in battle. Interred in Stone River Cemetery.
[illegible], John...........	D	Private.	Mch. 14, 1865	Wilmington, N. C....	Interred in grave 1978.
[illegible], Robert W.......	A	Corporal	Mch. 29, 1865	Newbern, N. C.......	Interred in section 17, grave 134.
[illegible]son, James........	K	Private.	Mch. 16, 1865	....	Died at Locust Grove, Adams County, O.
[illegible], Jacob...........	G	Private.	Nov. 28, 1864	Nashville, Tenn.....	Interred in section G, grave 171.
Peterson, Ralph.........	E	Private.	May 16, 1865	Newbern, N. C.......	Interred in section 17, grave 142.
Quigley, Thomas E......	A	Private.	Jan. 19, 1865	Louisville, Ky........	Died on board steamer, on Tennessee River. Interred in section C, row 4, grave 82, Cave Hill Cemetery.
[illegible], Peter..........	B	Private.	April 20, 1865	Raleigh, N. C........	
Ritter, Louis...........	B	Private.	Dec. 9, 1864	Murfreesboro, Tenn..	Died of wounds received Dec. 7, 1864, in battle. Interred in section E, grave 288, Stone River Cemetery.
[illegible], David..........	F	Private.	Dec. 31, 1864	Murfreesboro, Tenn..	Interred in section D, grave 255, Stone River Cemetery.
Stafford, Henry..........	D	Private.	Feb. 28, 1865	Nashville, Tenn......	Interred in section G, grave 552.
Stahl, John C............	I	2d Lieut.	Jan. 15, 1865	Shiloh, Tenn.........	Died at Clifton, Tenn. Interred in section O G, grave 6.
[illegible], John............	H	Private.	May 11, 1865	....	Drowned in Yadkin River, N.C.
[illegible], Frederick......	I	Private.	Dec. 14, 1864	Chattanooga, Tenn...	Died of wounds received Dec. 7, 1864, in battle of Murfreesboro, Tenn. Interred in section G, grave 180.
[illegible], John...........	B	Private.	Jan. 20, 1865	....	Died on hospital boat, on Ohio River.
Williams, Joseph........	G	Private.	May 10, 1865	Lansingburg, N. Y...	Died near Troy, N. Y.
[illegible], Joseph A.........	D	Private.	June 6, 1865	Cincinnati, O.........	Interred in Spring Grove Cemetery.
Yoxon, Samuel..........	A	Corporal	Nov. 25, 1864	....	Killed in railroad accident, at Stephens' Gap, Ala.

182nd REGIMENT OHIO VOLUNTEER INFANTRY.

Names.	Co.	Rank.	Died.	Buried.	Remarks.
Anderson, William O...	A	Private.	Nov. 5, 1864	Louisville, Ky........	Interred in Cave Hill Cemetery.
Armstrong, Milton......	B	Private.	June 25, 1865	Nashville, Tenn......	
Ashley, Nelson..........	A	Private.	Jan. 20, 1865	New Albany, Ind.....	Died at Jeffersonville, Ind. Interred in section B, grave 234.
Avery, John............	K	Private.	April 28, 1865	Nashville, Tenn......	Interred in section J, grave 1431.
Ayres, John R..........	K	Corporal	Feb. 9, 1865	Nashville, Tenn......	
Beam, Nelson..........	H	Private.	June 21, 1865	Nashville, Tenn....	
Berge, Henry...........	B	Private.	Mch. 22, 1865	Nashville, Tenn......	Interred in section J, grave 990.
Betts, Albert W.........	C	Private.	Oct. 2, 1864	....	Died at home, Fulton County, Ohio.
Brookover, William.....	H	Private.	June 5, 1865	Nashville, Tenn......	
Brownlee, Robert.......	I	Private.	July 13, 1865	Nashville, Tenn......	Mustered out with company July 7, 1865. Interred in section J, grave 1112.
Buzick, Francis M.......	E	Private.	Oct. 31, 1864	Columbus, O.........	Died at Camp Chase, O. Interred in Green Lawn Cemetery.
Cadwalader, Silas.......	H	Private.	Oct. 20, 1864	Nashville, Tenn......	
Cannon, Robert.........	K	Private.	June 25, 1865	Nashville, Tenn......	
Carter, Joseph..........	B	Private.	Oct. 15, 1864	....	Died in Fulton County, O.
Clark, James H.........	C	Private.	July 10, 1865	Nashville, Tenn......	Mustered out with company July 7, 1865. Interred in section J, grave 822.
Clark, Joseph...........	F	Private.	Dec. 6, 1864	Nashville, Tenn......	
Cook, John G...........	A	Private.	Feb. 1, 1865	Nashville, Tenn......	

Cross, John W.	C	Sergeant	June 19, 1865	Nashville, Tenn.
Davy, William	E	Private.	Feb. 28, 1865	Nashville, Tenn.
Dunaway, Jacob E.	C	Private.	April 27, 1865	Nashville, Tenn.
Eagle, John H.	K	Private.	Feb. 2, 1865	Nashville, Tenn.
Eddy, Charles C.	A	Private.	Nov. 2, 1864	Lexington, Ky.
Fair, Amos	E	Private.	June 2, 1865	Nashville, Tenn.
Fornash, George	A	Private.	Dec. 17, 1864	Nashville, Tenn.
Freck, Jonas	A	Private.	Oct. 21, 1864	
Gaul, John	A	Private.	Oct. 27, 1864	
Hagerman, John B.	C	Private.	Feb. 8, 1865	Nashville, Tenn.
Harger, John	K	Private.	Mch. 20, 1865	Nashville, Tenn.
Holly, Stephen C.	D	Private.	Nov. 8, 1864	Louisville, Ky.
Holt, Nathan	G	Private.	Feb. 12, 1865	Nashville, Tenn.
Humphrey, David	K	Private.	Mch. 27, 1865	Nashville, Tenn.
Johnson, Joseph	C	Private.	June 26, 1865	Nashville, Tenn.
Keppler, Franklin	D	Private.	Dec. 1, 1864	Nashville, Tenn.
Kirkpatrick, Ralph	C	Private.	July 14, 1865	Columbus, O.
Lang, James M.	G	Private.	Mch. 7, 1865	Nashville, Tenn.
Little, Robert S.	H	Private.	April 14, 1865	Nashville, Tenn.
McCandless, James	E	Private.	Feb. 12, 1865	Nashville, Tenn.
Marsh, Squire	D	Private.	June 5, 1865	Nashville, Tenn.
Morgan, Charles W.	A	Private.	Mch. 28, 1865	Nashville, Tenn.
Parish, Orrin	K	Private.	Feb. 4, 1865	New Albany, Ind.
Peggs, Samuel S.	I	Private.	Nov. 11, 1864	Nashville, Tenn.
Pierson, Henry	C	Private.	April 11, 1865	Nashville, Tenn.
Schoonover, Charles	B	Private.	Feb. 4, 1865	Nashville, Tenn.
Sealock, Benjamin F.	C	Private.	Feb. 12, 1865	Louisville, Ky.
Simpson, Charles	K	Private.	May 8, 1865	Nashville, Tenn.
Smith, William R.	E	Private.	Jan. 15, 1865	Nashville, Tenn.
Smitley, William G.	F	Private.	Nov. 2, 1864	
Snyder, Samuel	K	Private.	Jan. 31, 1865	Nashville, Tenn.
Snyder, William	D	Private.	July 2, 1865	Nashville, Tenn.
Stahl, Nicholas	B	Private.	April 11, 1865	Nashville, Tenn.
Taylor, Theodore C.	C	Private.	Mch. 22, 1865	Nashville, Tenn.
Tomlin, Jeremiah	H	Private.	Nov. 9, 1864	
Vittum, James H.	E	Private.	Mch. 28, 1865	Nashville, Tenn.
Wagner, John	D	Private.	June 6, 1865	Nashville, Tenn.
Walker, Jonas B.	B	Private.	April 20, 1865	Nashville, Tenn.
Warren, Alfred H.	D	Private.	June 4, 1865	Nashville, Tenn.
Warren, James C.	G	Private.	Feb. 19, 1865	Nashville, Tenn.
Williams, George H.	B	Private.	Jan. 22, 1865	Nashville, Tenn.
Wines, George	K	Private.	Jan. 1, 1865	Nashville, Tenn.

183rd REGIMENT OHIO VOLUNTEER INFANTRY.

Names.	Co.	Rank.	Died.	Buried.	Remarks.
Bahn, John	H	Private.	April 27, 1865	....	Perished by explosion of steamer Sultana, on Mississippi River, near Memphis, Tennessee.
Baker, Ephraim O.	G	Private.	May 4, 1865	Wilmington, N. C.	Died at Smithville, N. C.
Baumgardner, W. J.	K	Private.	April 27, 1865	....	Perished by explosion of steamer Sultana, on Mississippi River, near Memphis, Tennessee.
Becker, Charles	C	Private.	Jan. 15, 1865	Shiloh, Tenn.	Accidentally killed at Clifton, Tennessee.
Belch, Josiah A.	A	Private.	Feb. 6, 1865	Nashville, Tenn.	Interred in section H, grave 245.
Binkley, Henry	B	Private.	June 20, 1865	Hampton, Va.	Died at Fortress Monroe, Va.
Briggs, Isaac	A	Private.	Nov. 30, 1864	Murfreesboro, Tenn.	Died at Franklin, Tenn., of wounds received same day in battle. Interred in Stone River Cemetery.
Broffman, George	I	Private.	Nov. 17, 1864	Camp Dennison, O.	Drowned in Miami River. Interred in grave 806.
Brown, John	K	Private.	April 1, 1865	Vicksburg, Miss.	Died on board steamer R. C. Wood. Interred in section L, grave 216.
Brown, Joshua	K	Private.	May 22, 1865	....	Died at Troy, N. Y., and sent home for burial.
Burnett, George	F	Private.	Nov. 30, 1864	Murfreesboro, Tenn.	Killed in battle of Franklin, Tenn. Interred in Franklin section, Stone River Cemetery.
Buscroff, John	M	Private.	July 7, 1865	Salisbury, N. C.	
Clark, Mervin	..	Lt. Col.	Nov. 30, 1864	Murfreesboro, Tenn.	Killed in battle of Franklin, Tenn. Interred in Franklin section, Stone River Cemetery.
Colcher, Noah	F	Private.	Nov. 30, 1864	Murfreesboro, Tenn.	Killed in battle of Franklin, Tenn. Interred in Franklin section, Stone River Cemetery.
Culp, Samuel	K	Private.	Feb. 28, 1865	Marietta, Ga.	Died in Rebel Prison at Columbia, Ala. Interred in section L, grave 154.
Daman, Levi	E	Private.	July 15, 1865	....	Died at Hinckley, Madison County, O.
Davis, Jonathan	A	Private.	Jan. 28, 1865	Louisville, Ky.	Interred in Cave Hill Cemetery.
Doble, James C.	A	Private.	Jan. 22, 1865	Camp Dennison, O.	Interred in grave 828.
Dockroy, James	F	Private.	June 2, 1865	Cincinnati, O.	Interred in Spring Grove Cemetery.
Durck, Charles	E	Private.	May 26, 1865	St. Louis, Mo.	Interred in section 45, grave 175, Jefferson Barracks Cemetery.
Finn, John A.	B	Private.	Nov. 20, 1864	....	Accidentally drowned in Ohio River.
Folts, Marion	D	Private.	Mch. 16, 1865	Andersonville, Ga.	Died in Rebel Prison. Interred in grave 12,781.
Freitag, John	H	Private.	April 5, 1865	St. Louis, Mo.	Died on board hospital steamer R. C. Wood. Interred in section 45, grave 106, Jefferson Barracks Cemetery.
Friedeking, August	B	Private.	Jan. 14, 1865	Murfreesboro, Tenn.	Died at Columbia, Tenn., of wounds received Nov. 30, 1864, in battle of Franklin, Tenn. Interred in Stone River Cemetery.
Fries, Frederick	E	Private.	July 11, 1865	Salisbury, N. C.	
Getterman, John	F	Private.	April 27, 1865	....	Perished by explosion of steamer Sultana, on Mississippi River, near Memphis, Tennessee.
Gossard, Francis J.	A	Private.	Nov. 30, 1864	Murfreesboro, Tenn.	Killed in battle of Franklin, Tenn. Interred in Franklin section, Stone River Cemetery.
Gossard, Philip	A	Private.	Nov. 30, 1864	Murfreesboro, Tenn.	Killed in battle of Franklin, Tenn. Interred in Franklin section, Stone River Cemetery.
Gunther, John	E	Musician	April 27, 1865	....	Perished by explosion of steamer Sultana, on Mississippi River, near Memphis, Tennessee.

Name	Co.	Rank	Date	Place
Haner, William		Private.	Jan. 22, 1865	[illegible]
Herencourt, Ferdinand.	I	Sergeant	Jan. 6, 1865	Cincinnati, O..
Herchong, Michael......	H	Private.	Jan. 15, 1865	....
Hill, George............	I	Private.	....	Andersonville,
Himes, George W.........	K	Private.	April 8, 1865	Lexington, Ky
Holt, Isaac	A	Private.	Jan. 29, 1865	Camp Denniso
Houser, Jeremiah.......	G	Private.	July 7, 1865	Nashville, Ten
Hunt, Joseph	G	Private.	Jan. 5, 1865	....
Irwin, Thomas...........	A	Private.	Feb. 25, 1865	Arlington, Va.
Jenkins, James M.......	A	Corporal	June 3, 1865	Salisbury, N. C
Jones, Samuel M........	A	Private.	Jan. —, 1865	Murfreesboro,
Junkert, Christian......	C	Private.	Mch. 28, 1865	Wilmington, N
Kablaius, Herman	I	Private.	Nov. 19, 1864	....
Karch, Joseph...........	B	Private.	Mch. 20, 1865	Andersonville,
Kennard, Elbridge......	K	Private.	Jan. 27, 1865	Camp Dennison
Koogle, Henry C........	G	2d Lieut.	June 27, 1865	Salisbury, N. C
Korn, Jacob.............	H	sergeant	Dec. 15, 1864	Nashville, Ten
Lambert, Henry	D	Private.	Nov. 30, 1864	Murfreesboro,
Lambur, John	E	Private.	Dec. 8, 1864	Nashville, Ten
Lease, George W.........	A	Private.	Jan. 29, 1865	Camp Denniso
Lee, Joseph S............	A	Private.	Jan. 16, 1865	Nashville, Ten
Layman, Andrew	..	Hos. St'd.	Mch. 29, 1865	Newbern, N. C
List, Robert C...........	K	Private.	Feb. 14, 1865	Arlington, Va.
Loewe, Christ. Jacob....	B	Private.	July 12, 1865	Salisbury, N. C
Meyer, Joseph...........	B	Private.	Dec. 6, 1864	New Albany, I
Morehart, Jackson	A	Private.	May 16, 1865	Salisbury, N. C
Mulholland, Robert.....	B	Private.	Mch. 2, 1865	Andersonville,
O'Brien, Michael........	G	Private.	Jan. 12, 1865	Corinth, Miss..
O'Neil, Edward..........	D	Private.	July 22, 1865	Raleigh, N. C..
Poustian, John..........	F	Private.	June 19, 1865	Andersonville,
Prather, Benjamin D....	D	Corporal	Dec. 28, 1864	Nashville, Ten
Reed, Joseph...........	A	Private.	Feb. 10, 1865	Camp Denniso
Reeder, Allen S.........	G	Sergeant	July 18, 1865	Louisville, Ky.
Risser, Daniel...........	B	Captain.	Nov. 30, 1864	Murfreesboro,
Schneider, Adam	C	Private.	April 27, 1865	....
Sessler, Thomas F.......	A	Private.	Feb. 5, 1865	Camp Denniso
Sheldon, William........	A	Private.	Dec. 17, 1864	Nashville, Ten
Stoeser, Ignaz...........	B	Private.	April 27, 1865	Long Island, N
Stokes, Freeman	F	Private.	Nov. 30, 1864	Murfreesboro,
Stork, Lorance	H	Private.	Jan. 7, 1865	Nashville, Ten